Medieval Drama

Medieval Drama

DAVID BEVINGTON

The University of Chicago

HOUGHTON MIFFLIN COMPANY / BOSTON

Atlanta   Dallas   Geneva, Illinois   Hopewell, New Jersey   Palo Alto   London

Printed in the U.S.A.

Library of Congress Catalog Card Number: 74-2846

ISBN: 0-395-13915-5

For Helen and Bev

Contents

PART TWO Twelfth-Century Church Drama 73

PART THREE The Corpus Christi Cycle 225

Illustrations

Preface

IN A SENSE, this collection of medieval plays is intended to replace Joseph Quincy Adams's *Chief Pre-Shakespearean Dramas*, published by Houghton Mifflin fifty-one years ago. This new anthology is nevertheless quite different in conception and content from the volume it replaces. As Adams's title suggests, his anthology offered representative plays from the beginnings of Western drama in the tenth century down to the beginnings of Shakespeare's career in about 1590. Adams's emphasis was on the evolution of pre-Shakespearean drama; the earlier drama was of interest primarily because of what grew out of it. Despite the many excellences of his collection, Adams sometimes betrayed a sense of embarrassment toward the plays he presented: he excised uncouth expressions in the interest of propriety and heavily cut the texts of some plays he evidently considered too long for the modern reader. In so doing, Adams was merely following the Protestant Whig–Liberal biases common to men of his generation such as John Matthews Manly and Karl Young, who, as heirs of Victorian culture, tended to regard the medieval world as disfigured by Catholic superstition, ignorance, and coarseness.

The present collection offers medieval drama as an artistic achievement in its own right rather than as a historical antecedent to Elizabethan greatness. The collection ends with the early Tudor humanist drama, written for the most part before the English Reformation. Although such a scope has meant the sacrifice of several of the later plays that appeared in *Chief Pre-Shakespearean Dramas*, most of them are available in anthologies of Tudor or Elizabethan drama where justice can be done to the richness of the sixteenth-century drama. In exchange for the loss of these plays, this volume offers a considerably expanded selection of plays from the medieval period. Virtually all texts appear in full. Previously expurgated passages are restored. This volume gives the reader an opportunity to test the proposition, recently advanced by F. M. Salter, O. B. Hardison, Jr., V. A. Kolve, Rosemary Woolf, and others, that medieval drama possessed considerable splendor, sophistication, and comic vitality.

The texts of the plays are presented in their original languages but with such editorial assistance as seems desirable for the modern reader. I have provided the texts in Latin and Anglo-Norman French with a rather literal translation in parallel columns; so too for the occasional passages in medieval German and Greek. The texts in Middle English feature single-word glosses in a right-hand column and footnotes below to explain longer phrases or whole lines. Line numbers appear at each line for which there is a footnote so that the reader will know when further explanation is available at the bottom of the page.

In addition, I have eliminated many medieval orthographical conventions that seem unfamiliar today. For runic letters I have substituted the nearest modern equivalent, as in the case of *th* for the runic thorn. I have exchanged *u* for *v* and *j* for *i* whenever, as so frequently happens in medieval orthography, the *u* and *j* are scribal conventions used interchangeably and inconsistently in place of *v* and *i*: for example, this text reads *evere* for *euere*, *governaunce* for *gouernaunce*, *joly and jent* for *Ioly & Ient*. Similarly, this text substitutes *i* for *y* and sometimes vice versa as in *doinge* for *doynge*, *with* for *wyth*, *takith* for *takyth*, and *lady* for *ladi*. This text substitutes *sh* for *x* in words like *shall* (*xall*) or *shuld* (*xuld*), and eliminates the scribal doubling of certain consonants at the beginning of words or syllables as in *first* (*ffyrst*) or *fourte* (*ffourte*). This text also follows modern practice in differentiating between *be* and *by*, whereas medieval practice often ignores this distinction to the confusion of the modern reader. Capitalization and punctuation are in accord with modern practice rather than with the erratic habits of medieval scribes. I have occasionally joined together words appearing as separate syllables in the manuscript: for example, *be forn* appears in this text as *beforn*. I have silently expanded all scribal abbreviations with as much consistency as possible. Because abbreviations do not always mean the same thing for different scribes, however, I have attempted to interpret what each scribe intended rather than aim at complete consistency throughout the volume. I have generally expanded numbers, using medieval spellings preferred by the scribes: e.g., *thretty-sefnt* for *xxxvij*ti. In order to render the Latin in these plays as recognizable as possible to today's reader, I have generally standardized Latin spelling throughout in accordance with Lewis and Short's *A Latin Dictionary*.

Apart from these various editorial practices designed to ameliorate the task of the modern reader, I have attempted to render the texts as accurately and literally as possible. I have checked each text at least four times against microfilms or photostats of the original documents, or against the original documents themselves. I have added in square brackets any additional letters provided for clarification: for example, *the*[e] (in order to distinguish this personal pronoun from the common article *the*), *to*[o] (in order to distinguish this adverb from the preposition *to*), *min*[e], *nam*[e], *thou*[gh], *wor*[l]d. The reader may consult the textual notes at the end of this volume for editorial emendations of the original text and for further comments, play by play, on the rendering of medieval orthographical conventions. If the reader should discover errors in this volume (of which I fear many still remain), I should be deeply grateful to hear from him in order that future printings may be corrected. Please address your comments to the Sponsoring Editor for English, College Department, Houghton Mifflin Company, One Beacon Street, Boston, Massachusetts 02107.

My debts of gratitude for assistance on this volume are many and extensive. Of the recent scholarly books to which I am heavily indebted, I can name here only a few: O. B. Hardison, Jr., *Christian Rite and Christian Drama in the Middle Ages*, V. A. Kolve, *The Play Called Corpus Christi*, and Rosemary Woolf, *The English Mystery Plays*. My obligations to other books are to be found throughout this volume and in the Suggestions for Further Reading at the end. In my Latin translations I have been assisted at various times by Phyllis Katz and Nancy Helmbold of the University of Chicago, and especially by Frank Einstein of the University of Chicago and Margaret Taylor of Wellesley College. Miss Taylor reviewed the entire manuscript of Parts I and II, offering numerous suggestions. For occasional assistance on medieval French I have turned to Peter Dembowski and for German to George Metcalf, both of the University of Chicago. Joseph Williams of the University of Chicago has patiently and repeatedly scrutinized the essay entitled "Some Observations on Language." In experimenting with various styles of annotating and editing medieval English texts, I profited from the aid of Patrick McCarthy and Carl Daw of the University of Virginia. Both my wife, Peggy, and my mother, Helen Bevington, read galley proofs and rescued me from a number of errors. The University of Virginia and the University of Chicago provided me with some research funds to obtain microfilms and photostatic materials.

I wish to thank the following libraries for providing me with microfilms or photostatic copies, and for courteously granting permission to publish texts newly edited from those materials or from the originals themselves: the Henry E. Huntington Library and Art Gallery for various pageants from the Towneley or Wakefield cycle of plays (HM 1), two brief passages from the Chester pageant of the Ten Commandments, Balaam and Balak, and the Prophets (HM 2), and the "Britwell" copy of *Everyman* printed by John Skot; the Beinecke Rare Book and Manuscript Library, Yale University, for the pageant of Abraham and Isaac in the manuscript known as "The Book of Brome"; the Trustees of the British Museum in London for various pageants from the so-called N Town or Hegge cycle of plays (Cotton Vespasian D. viii), three selections from the *Regularis Concordia* (Cotton Tiberius A. iii and Cotton Faustina B. iii), *The Play of Daniel* (Egerton 2615), various pageants from the York cycle of plays (Additional 35290), two pageants from the Chester cycle of plays (Harl. 2124), and John Redford's *Wit and Science* (Additional 15233); the Bodleian Library, Oxford, for *The Conversion of St. Paul* and *Mary Magdalene*, both from the Digby MS (Digby 133), and the Visit to the Sepulchre from Winchester (MS 775); the Master and Fellows of Magdalene College, Cambridge, for the early editions of *Johan Johan the Husband*, perhaps by John Heywood, and *The Play of the Weather*, certainly by him, both in the Pepys collection; the Folger Shakespeare Library for *The Castle of Perseverance* and *Mankind*, both in the Macro collection (MS. V. a. 354); Trinity College, Dublin, for *The Play of the Sacrament* (MS. F. 4. 20); the Bibliothèque Nationale in Paris for two short selections from Limoges (MSS. lat. 1240 and 887), the Beauvais *Pilgrim* (Nouvelles Acquisitions, lat. 1064), Hilarius' *The Raising of Lazarus* (MS. lat. 11331), the Anglo-Norman *La Seinte Resureccion* (MS. fr. 902), and the Bishop of Metz's Service for the

Consecration of a Church (MS. lat. 9428); the Bibliothèque de la Ville in Orleans for various selections from the Fleury collection (MS. 201); the Bibliothèque Municipale in Tours for the Anglo-Norman play of *Adam* (MS. 927); the Staatsbibliothek in Munich for the *Christmas Play* and *Passion Play* from the Carmina Burana manuscript of Benediktbeuern (MS. lat. 4660); the Bibl. Arcivescovile of Udine for the Visit to the Sepulchre attributed to Aquileia (MS. 234); and the Universitätsbibliothek of Graz, Austria, for the Visit to the Sepulchre from St. Lambrecht (MSS. 798, 193, and 722).

D. B.

Some Observations on Language

NUMEROUS difficulties impose themselves on the study of language in the plays of this volume. Many of the liturgical and church plays are in medieval Latin; two are in Anglo-Norman French; individual passages are to be found in Greek, medieval German, and still other languages. Even when we consider only the plays written in Middle English, we find an extraordinary diversity in language. The English texts cover a period of time from the late fourteenth through the middle sixteenth centuries. Geographically, the plays come from various parts of England, most of them northern and sufficiently removed from London to acquire some characteristics of northern dialect. Moreover, the English language underwent a rapid development during the period under study. During the late fourteenth century, English was only beginning to emerge as a respectable literary tongue after some three centuries of French cultural and political domination, and yet by the late sixteenth century English was ready to serve as a vehicle for Marlowe, Spenser, and Shakespeare. Relatively late texts such as *Wit and Science* are accordingly easier to read today than the earlier works of the Wakefield Master, whose characters usually speak in the vigorous colloquial idiom of rural Yorkshire. An awareness of dialectal and linguistic development will enable the reader to understand and appreciate many of the striking features of language in these plays.

Without attempting to provide a comprehensive analysis of Middle English in all its varying forms, the following notes describe a number of traits that are both characteristic and common in these plays.

NOUNS AND PRONOUNS Nouns and pronouns are generally inflected in patterns that are recognizable to the modern reader. Yet variations do occur, especially since dramatists were exposed to both northern and southern forms. Many northern forms were Scandinavian in origin owing to the Danish and Norwegian invasions there during the eighth and ninth centuries, whereas southern forms could be traced back to the Anglo-Saxon invasions from Germany in the fifth century.

The northern forms of the personal and possessive pronouns are familiar today: *I, my, me(e), thou, the(e), thy, he(e), his, him, she, her, we, our(e), us, ye(e), you, your(e), they* or *thay, their* or *thare, them* or *thaym* (all variously spelled in the plays). In addition, however, we find such northern forms as *sho* for "she," especially when required by the rhyme pattern, and *hisself* for "himself." Southern forms are more common in plays written in East Midland dialect (located in London, Cambridgeshire, Norfolk, Lincoln, and vicinity). In the N Town Passion Play, for example, we find *hem* for "them" and *here* for

"their," as in Chaucer. In the Second Shepherds' Pageant, from the Wakefield cycle, Mak poses as a southerner by saying *ich be* instead of "I am."
I was a northern Scandinavian form that drove its way southward, displacing
the Anglo-Saxon *ich*; by the late fourteenth century, it had already penetrated
the southern form of East Midland dialect that was fast becoming the "standard" speech of London and the court (thanks in part to the great popularity
of Geoffrey Chaucer). Also as in Chaucer, *his* or *hese* often mean "its." The
demonstrative pronoun *tho* sometimes takes the place of "those."

The inflection of nouns also varies somewhat in these plays. The normal
form of the genitive singular, for example, ends in *-ys* or *-s* as in *kingys*, meaning "king's." Yet we also find occasionally a northern uninflected ending,
as in *Cryst curs* for "Christ's curse" (the Wakefield Buffeting, l. 695).

Pronouns of reference are sometimes omitted in these plays, requiring
the modern reader to supply a missing or implied grammatical link. For
example, Pilate speaks as follows about his role in crucifying Christ (Wakefield Resurrection, ll. 17–18): "I am he, that great state,   That lad has all
to-torne," meaning, "I am he, that person of great station, *who* has torn to
pieces that fellow (Christ)."

Reflexive pronouns are sometimes used in Middle English where they
would be omitted today. "As I may me in you affy," for example, means
"As I can put my trust in you" (Wakefield Resurrection, l. 492). "I shall me
spede" means "I will hurry." The reflexive pronoun makes clear that the
speaker is the object of the action. *Me*, *you*, *him*, and *them* are often used as
reflexive pronouns rather than the forms that eventually developed and
replaced them: "myself," "yourself," "himself," and "themselves."

VERBS   Verbs also show a distinction between northern and southern forms.
In the third person singular of the indicative present, for example, we find
not only northern forms ending in *-s* or *-ys* such as "he has," "it goyse (goes),"
and "he gettys," but also southern forms ending in *-th* or *-ith* such as "he
hath," "he sendith," and "he pretendith." Often these forms can be found
intermingled in the same play. Imperatives show a similar divergence.
Northern forms include the easily recognized "Gif him good payment" or
"Go fetche us a light buffet," which can be used in both the singular and
plural. A less easily recognized form of the plural imperative ends in *-s* or
-ys: "commes now," "comys hederward," "takys kepe," take heed, take care.
The southern form of the plural imperative, familiar to readers of Chaucer,
ends in *-th* or *-yth*: "takith heed," take heed; "seyth," see; "goth," go.

As in Chaucerian English, the various dialects of these plays retain a
characteristic distinction (a Germanic inheritance) between weak or "regular" verbs and strong or "irregular" verbs. Weak verbs normally form their
preterites and past participles by adding *-d* or *-t* to the stem: e.g., *mefe* or *move*,
mevid; *ordayn* or *ordan*, *ordand*; *reyne* or *rene*, *renyd*; *tar(r)y*, *tarid*. Strong verbs
form their preterites and past participles by changing the root vowel: e.g.,
begin, *began*, *begownne*; *bere* (bear), *bare*, *borne*; *com*, *cam*, *com(m)en*; *draw*, *drew*,
drogh; *go*, *yode* or *yede*, *gone*; *hold* or *hald*, *held*, *halden*; *knowe* or *knaw*, *knew*,

knowyn; see, sagh or *saw, sene; stand, stud* or *stod.* Other variations are to be found. The verb "to be" is of course irregular with such forms as *arn* (are), *bees* or *bese* (will be), *was, were, wore* or *ware,* and *has beyn* or *ben(e).*

Like English today, Middle English makes important use of a set of verbs designated as modal auxiliaries, such as *will, can,* and *may.* Historically these verbs are strong preterites that came to be used in a present tense, requiring the formation of new weak preterites to express past time. The meanings of these verbs are not always equivalent to the modern sense. For example, *can/coude/couthe* often means "did" when used as a modal auxiliary: "we can downe fall," we did fall down (Wakefield Resurrection, l. 512); "can die," did die (Wakefield Resurrection, l. 49). *Can* also sometimes means "be able to" in auxiliary usage, but by itself the verb usually means "know, know how to" (cf. German *kennen*). *May/might* has the sense of "can" as well as "may"; the expression "God, as he both may and can" means "God, who has both power and knowledge." *Thar* is unfamiliar to us today as a modal; it expresses a sense of need, as in "I thar not dispare," I need not despair (Herod the Great, l. 479). *Shall/shuld* often has the force of "must"; *will* expresses desire. Other modal auxiliaries have a more clearly recognizable meaning today, especially *dar/durst* (dare), *mot/must* (must), and *owe/aght/owte* (ought, be bound to).

The modal auxiliary verbs *shall* and *will* are regularly combined with the infinitive to refer to the future. Often the infinitive ends in *-n* as in "shal spekyn," "shall pullyn," "wold (will) folwyn," etc. Infinitives need not be inflected, however; such forms as *to draw* or *to bring* are common. The perfect tenses are usually formed, as in modern English, by an auxiliary use of the verb *to have* and a past participle: e.g., "as thou me behete hase," as you have promised me (Wakefield Noah, l. 430). Sometimes the *have* is reduced to *a* as in "to a seen yowr goodly chere," to have seen your goodly countenance. Like German, Middle English sometimes conjugates perfect tenses with the verb *to be* rather than *to have,* especially verbs of motion: e.g., "is went away," has gone away. The past participles used in perfect constructions usually have an inflected ending but are sometimes uninflected: e.g., "I have forsake my mayster" (N Town Passion, ii, 197). Future passives also sometimes use an uninflected form in place of the past participle: e.g., "will be send" and "shal be do."

Present participles frequently end in *-ng* or *-ing* as in modern English: e.g., "sayng," saying. This is a relatively late form, appearing only after the eleventh century and at first predominantly in the south of England; it may have evolved through a conflation of the Germanic gerund ending *-ung* with the Germanic participial ending *-end.* On the other hand, the original Germanic and Scandinavian participial form is also quite common in the plays of this volume. Its characteristic ending is *-and* or *-end* as in "slepand" (cf. German *schlafend*), sleeping; "bleedand," bleeding; "reynand," running. By the later Middle Ages the older and newer participial forms had become virtually interchangeable so that we occasionally find such words as "comand" and "coming" used together in the same play.

Impersonal verbal constructions are common in Middle English. Constructions of this type lack an expressed subject; instead, the person or persons whom the action concerns are usually referred to by a pronoun in the dative-accusative case. In the phrase "hens must us fle," for example, *us* is grammatically not the subject of the verb but a dative pronoun of reference meaning something like "in our case" or "with reference to us." The impersonal verb construction *must fle* has no subject. Although the whole phrase cannot be literally translated, its modern equivalent is "we must flee from here." Other such phrases include "Nothing thar us drede," meaning "we need dread nothing," and "therat me aght to be fain," meaning "I ought to be happy at that." When the impersonal construction occurs with such verbs as *think*, *like*, and *list*, we can perhaps better understand the grammar of the impersonal construction by supplying an unstated expletive subject *it*. For example, "A branch, thinkys me" means "It seems to me this is a branch"; "Wheresoever likys me" means "Wheresoever it is pleasing to me"; and "Me list not ban" means "It is not my wish to curse."

WORD ORDER Inversion of normal word order is common in the Middle English plays of this volume, especially when exigencies of rhyme are at work. One common pattern is the inversion of a prepositional phrase: e.g., "I shal comyn hem to," I shall come to them, and "steyll his cors us fro," steal his corpse from us. This kind of inversion is most common with personal pronouns like *them* and *us*. Sometimes the object of the prepositional phrase is separated by some distance from the preposition, so much so that the object might at first appear to be the subject of the sentence: e.g., "Two thefys hang thay me betwene," they hanged me between two thieves (Wakefield Resurrection, l. 258). Another common pattern is the transferring of the pronoun indirect object from its more usual final position to an earlier position in the clause, leaving the verb last as in the construction of German dependent clauses: e.g., "as thou me behete hase," as you have promised me, or "as he you saide," as he said to you (Wakefield Resurrection, l. 393). A similarly Germanic construction is the placement of the direct object between the modal auxiliary *have* and the past participle of the verb construction: e.g., "Have thou a gobet of the world cawth," When you have acquired a small portion of the world (Perseverance, l. 364). Some displacements of objects are not analogous to Germanic sentence construction, however, and seem to be the result of poetic factors such as rhyme and the stressing of key words: e.g., "A sely crysme my hed hath cawth," My head has received a poor chrisom or baptismal headcloth (Perseverance, l. 294). The modern reader must anticipate potentially misleading constructions such as these.

Questions normally take an inverted form in Middle English: e.g., "Gaf [gave] ye the child anything?" (Wakefield Second Shepherds' Pageant, l. 571). Negative constructions are also frequently inverted: e.g., "Sagh I never in a credyll   A hornyd lad or now," I never saw a horned male child in a cradle ere now (Second Shepherds' Pageant, ll. 600–1).

LEXICAL MEANING   Another difficulty for the modern reader is the change in meaning of many English words. Totally unfamiliar words pose less of a problem since they are recognizably strange and require consulting glosses. More potentially misleading are recognizable words with unfamiliar meanings. *Lernyd,* for example, normally means "taught" in Middle English; *mete* is "food"; *ccrn* is "wheat" or other similar grain rather than maize; *praty masanger* means "brave messenger"; *sely* conveys the sense of "poor," "miserable," or "innocent." Some common words are particularly troublesome. *And* frequently means "if"; *bot* often means "unless"; *or* is usually a way of spelling "ere," meaning "before." The title *sir* does not necessarily mean knighthood; it is more commonly used of clergy, as in "Sir John the priest," and can refer honorifically to such worthies as "Sir Joseph of Arimathea." Certain prefixes are another unfamiliar feature of meaning in Middle English. For example, the prefix *to-* connotes intensification, as in "to-torn," torn to pieces (cf. German *zerrissen*). The prefix *for-* has a similar effect, as in "fordone," completely destroyed; "for-fell," very cruel.

SPELLING   Spelling practices vary extensively in these plays, owing to the rapid change in English during the fifteenth and sixteenth centuries, variations in dialect from one part of England to another, and the oral character of this dramatic art. Still, one can often make sense of medieval spelling by bearing in mind various observations. One common phenomenon, for instance, is metathesis, or the reversal of adjoining letters. Thus, Middle English regularly used the spelling *thridde* as well as the spelling that has survived today, "third." *Brenne* is similarly related to "burn," *bryth* to "bright," *sigth* to "sight," *assing* to "assign," and so on. Vowel change is another essential fact of linguistic development: compare the common medieval form *thore* with "there," *mare* with "more," *than* with "then," and *hard* with "heard." Awareness of variations in dialect can often help identify strange-seeming but actually familiar words. *Qwat,* for example, is merely a northern form of "what"; the spelling indicates that the word was pronounced in northern areas (including Scotland) with a strong velar aspiration.

PRONUNCIATION   About pronunciation in these plays little can be said of a specific nature, since the plays represent such a wide chronological and geographical range. Generally, however, the vowels should be pronounced as in continental languages like German or French. The long vowel sounds of *a, e, i, o,* and *u* are sounded as in the italicized vowels of f*a*ther, m*a*te, m*a*chine, n*o*te, and h*oo*t. Many consonants were still sounded in medieval times that have become silent in modern English, such as the *k* and *gh* in *knight* and *l* in *folk. Knight* was pronounced something like "knicht" (with a short *i* and a German *ch*) rather than our modern "nait." The sounding of the final *-e* is a matter of controversy; it was in transition during the late medieval period, becoming less and less used. Certainly the spelling of the original texts offers no basis for any consistent theory of sounding final

-e before a word beginning with a consonant but not before a word beginning with a vowel, as has been claimed for Chaucer.

VERSIFICATION   The verse of these plays is not iambic, as it has been asserted to be in most of Chaucer, but usually employs an alliterative stress pattern. That is, the verse contains perhaps four stressed syllables to a line interspersed with an uneven number of unstressed syllables. Alliteration, when present, tends to fall on the stressed syllables. For example:

> I *tr*otte and *tr*emle in my *tr*ew *tr*one;
> As a *ha*wke I *ho*ppe in my *he*nde *ha*le. (*Perseverance*, ll. 457–58)

This pattern is characteristic of the so-called "alliterative revival" in northern verse of the fourteenth and fifteenth centuries. Northern poets adapted for their own use an alliterative tradition of prosody begun in Old English poetry and continued in oral folk verse of the Middle English period. Chaucer eschewed alliterative writing, perhaps because he regarded it as provincial. During the fifteenth century, however, it came to have an important influence on most English literature.

The stanzaic forms employed by medieval dramatists are too numerous to discuss here. The headnotes to the individual plays usually contain some observations on the stanzaic forms used in each particular case.

Medieval Drama

PART ONE

Liturgical Beginnings

Liturgical Beginnings

A. DRAMATIC ELEMENTS IN THE LITURGY OF THE CHURCH

MOST MEDIEVAL DRAMA is religious in nature and origin. It grew out of the liturgy, or prescribed form of worship, of the tenth-century Christian Church, and it achieved considerable magnificence under ecclesiastical sponsorship. Even the great cycle plays of the fourteenth and fifteenth centuries, though produced by civic guilds, were of clerical authorship and were performed on religious festivals with the active cooperation of the Church. Ironically, however, the very Church that did so much for medieval drama had once helped to abolish all dramatic activity throughout western Europe. The early Church Fathers and other moralists sought for many years to suppress the pagan and unsavory dramatic spectacles of the late Roman empire, which featured wild-beast fights, human slaughter, naked dancing, sumptuous processions, and the like. Decisive action came finally in the fifth century as the result of an incident in which a monk named Telemachus attempted to stop a gladiatorial contest and was stoned to death by the outraged spectators. Thereafter the Roman emperors, who had adopted Christianity in 378 as the official Roman religion, prohibited public acting. Drama ceased to exist except for the unrecorded wanderings of minstrels, troubadours, jugglers, and other such entertainers. The hiatus was so complete that the conventions of Roman stage presentation were often misunderstood or forgotten; when, for example, a tenth-century German nun named Hrotsvitha wrote six dramatic pieces modeled on the plays of the Roman dramatist Terence, she did so apparently without any intention that her works should be presented by actors before audiences.

How then did drama come once again to life under the aegis of an institution that had virtually destroyed it? The key to this paradox is to be found in the nature of the church liturgy. Catholic liturgy consisted in the Middle Ages, as it does today, of many parts. Most notable was the singing of the mass, or Eucharistic celebration, in which bread and wine were consecrated as the body and blood of Christ (based on the account of Christ's Last Supper in Mark 14:22–27). In addition, the liturgy of the medieval Church provided for the daily singing of no less than seven "offices" or canonical "hours," beginning before daybreak with matins (together with lauds) and proceeding through the day with prime, terce, sext, none, vespers, and compline. These services, chanted by officiating priests, cantors, and choir, offered many features outwardly resembling those of dramatic presentation. The church building provided an enclosed space with entrance-ways and fixed structures such as the altar. Clerical robes were often colorful and symbolic. Processions gave opportunity for pageant-like movement with musical accompaniment. Chanting was often antiphonal—that is, with one voice or group of voices answering another in an exchange somewhat resembling dialogue. The words that were chanted often came from biblical narrative, providing a potential element of plot. Still, the liturgy of the medieval Church was inherently distinguishable from drama in that its purpose was worship. Many changes had to come about before a religious ritual could be transformed into what we would call a "play." We must therefore first investigate ways in which various religious ceremonials could become more dramatic while still retaining their essential character as rite or worship.

During the ninth and tenth centuries, some members of the religious community urged that the Church's own liturgy—especially the mass—contained in it an element of dramatic conflict that could well be used to enhance the appeal of public worship. A leading spokesman for this point of view was Amalarius, bishop of Metz (ca. 780–850), whose ideas are represented briefly in this section by the work of his eleventh-century disciple, Honorius of Autun (selection 1). Amalarius' motive was to give immediacy to religious worship, and to that end he elaborately allegorized the mass into a dramatic rendition—complete with dialogue and gesture—of Christ's ministry, death, and resurrection. At various moments during the mass, Amalarius argued, the officiating priest represents Christ as he is about to be betrayed by Judas, then as he suffers on the cross, and still later as he announces the news of his resurrection. At other times the celebrant also represents the high priest of the temple, Nicodemus assisting Joseph of Arimathea with the burial of Christ's body, and still other personages from divine history. The deacons and other worshipers assume corresponding roles as the disciples sleeping while Christ prays, the Jews witnessing Christ's torment, and the congregation of the faithful. The altar becomes the tomb receiving Christ's body, and then the empty grave.

Not surprisingly, when some celebrants of the mass during the ninth and tenth centuries made use of Amalarius' histrionic interpretation, the results were electrifying. Crowds of excited worshipers pushed forward to see the elevation of the host (i.e., the consecrated bread signifying the body of

Christ), and to demand the repetition of this awesome act. The use of sighs, groans, sudden silences, and contortions of "the whole body with histrionic gestures" became common enough to arouse the ire of ecclesiastical traditionalists, who objected that ritual and drama were essentially different and should remain so. (See O. B. Hardison, Jr., *Christian Rite and Christian Drama in the Middle Ages*, Essay II.)

Despite the protests of conservative spokesmen, however, the liturgy of the Church had in fact long employed techniques analogous to those of the drama. Even before Amalarius, the service made use of what might be viewed as chanted dialogue and symbolic role-playing, while the church interior provided a kind of setting for quasi-dramatic movement. To be sure, techniques of this sort did not in themselves alter a basic commitment to a belief in the literal truth of Christ's real presence in the consecrated bread and wine. In this profoundly important sense the service of the Church remained a ritual rather than a "fiction" or mimetic presentation. Still, the impulse toward histrionic rendition was intense and popular, especially during the Easter season. At this climactic period in the church year, the events allegorically depicted in the mass (according to Amalarius' interpretation) coincide with the events of Passion Week. The central Christian drama of Christ's suffering and victory reaches its turning point and triumphal resolution. The texts appointed to be sung or read during Passion Week (the week leading up to Easter, known also as Holy Week) inevitably lend themselves to histrionic presentation.

As early as the fourth century, a well-born lady from Galicia (modern Spain) named Etheria made a pilgrimage to the Holy Land where she witnessed, among other sacred ceremonies, a procession for Palm Sunday (the Sunday before Easter) that made use of the actual locations of sacred history (selection 2). Beginning at the Mount of Olives, the bishop entered Jerusalem as Christ had done shortly before his arrest and crucifixion, accompanied by a crowd of worshipers bearing olive branches and singing "Blessed is he who comes in the name of the Lord." This dramatic ceremony required hand props, dialogue, assignment of roles for the duration of the action, and movement from one location to another. Later re-enactments of the entry into Jerusalem in medieval European churches could not visit the actual Mount of Olives and city of Jerusalem, of course, but they could and did move in procession from one symbolic location to another. The monastic order of worship for Winchester, England, known as the *Regularis Concordia* ("An Agreement Containing Rules for Guidance"), ca. 970, records a Palm Sunday ceremonial in which a neighboring church was used to represent the Mount of Olives while the mother church represented the city of Jerusalem. The children of the choir sang *"Gloria, laus, et honor"* as they accompanied the bishop from one church to the other, and a cantor intoned *"Ingrediente Domino"* ("the Lord having entered") as the doors of the mother church were opened to the entering Christ. Processional entries with a similarly dramatic employment of dialogue and assignment of roles were performed on other occasions as well. In the ninth century, Bishop Amalarius of Metz's service for the consecration of a church (selection 3) made typological use of the church building in such a way as to suggest the harrowing of hell. The bishop assumed the role of Christ, triumphantly battering down the gates of hell (in order to signify the purifying of the church), while a member of the clergy spoke from within as a devil attempting to resist this divine invasion.

Two passages from the tenth-century *Regularis Concordia* of St. Ethelwold, bishop of Winchester (selections 4 and 5), attest to the histrionic character of the special liturgical ceremonies prepared for the final days of Passion Week. The church was progressively stripped of its finery and darkened; finally, the sacred host was withdrawn to signify mankind's bereavement at the death of Christ. In an "Adoration of the Cross" for the Mass of the Presanctified on Good Friday (the day commemorating the Crucifixion), the brethren of Winchester set up a cross before the altar and appointed two deacons to intone the *Improperia*, or "Reproaches" of Christ as he hung on the cross. The "Interment" or *Depositio*, a part of the same mass, disposed of the holy cross in a veil (the graveclothes) and sepulchre, with an actual burial ceremony and appointment of a guard over the tomb. This burial ceremony seems to have originated in the practice of "reserving" or withdrawing the sacred host after it had been consecrated on Maundy Thursday (signifying Christ's Last Supper) and then used during the Mass of the Presanctified on Good Friday, when the host might not be consecrated. By the ninth century or earlier, this act of "reservation" was understood to have a symbolic meaning appropriate to Passion Week: the placing of the host in a tower-shaped vessel on Good Friday was the burial of Christ's crucified body, and the removal and elevation of the host on Easter Sunday was his resurrection. The empty cloth in which the host had been wrapped signified Christ's empty shroud. The substitution of the cross for the host, as in the Winchester ceremonial, gave additional emphasis to this symbolic meaning. The place of reservation, or "sepulchre," and the empty "graveclothes" were thus prominently featured in liturgically mimetic ceremonials that could readily become more overtly dramatic when the propitious moment arrived. That moment came during the tenth century, when various members of the choir undertook roles for a dramatic re-enactment of the visit to the sepulchre on Easter morning (see page 21f).

The impulse toward an overtly dramatic rendition of mimetic ceremonial was assisted not only by symbolic edifices, dramatic movements, gestures, props, and the like but by the actual responsories and antiphons of the Easter liturgy. These responsories and antiphons, not unlike their modern counterparts, were anthems chanted by a soloist (cantor) and choir singing in alternation, or by two portions of the choir alternating with one another. Alternation gave an effect not unlike dialogue, although each speaker's utterances were not consistently assigned to one singer or segment of the choir as in true dialogue. Responsories and antiphons were individually composed for each day of the liturgical year, and often drew upon biblical materials that were appropriate to the day being celebrated. A responsory from the eleventh-century St. Gall "Raising of the Host" (selection 6), sung at the end of matins on Easter Sunday, for example, recounts the visit of the three Marys to Christ's sepulchre as told in Matthew 28:1–7. This chanted responsory provides us with several phrases that were used verbatim in the earliest dramatized versions of the visit to the sepulchre: the question "Whom do you seek?" addressed to the Marys, the angel's assurance that Christ "has now risen," the invitation to the Marys to "come and see the place where the Lord had been laid," and so on. The very practice of chanting responses in this fashion must have offered a model for dramatic dialogue. In effect, all that was needed to convert a responsory or antiphon into dialogue was the fixed assignment of dramatic roles among the singers, with the cantor representing the angel and a small choir representing the three Marys.

Equally suggestive as possible sources for a dramatized visit to the sepulchre are two Gregorian antiphons (selections 7 and 8) already in use by the tenth century. The first may have been sung during Vigil mass, in the hours before Easter dawn when the Resurrection was supposed to have taken place. This antiphon provides a number of narrative details and phrases of dialogue, including the terror of the guards at Christ's resurrection and the angel's admonition to the Marys to inform the disciples that Christ has risen. The second of these antiphons tells how the Marys purchased spices to anoint Christ's body, and how Mary Magdalene mistook the risen Christ for a gardener (see John 20:15).

Although the liturgical ceremonies of Holy Week employed dramatic techniques without losing their identity as ritual, they provided an opportunity for the elaboration of those techniques that would prove essential to the growth of a liturgical drama. In fourth-century Jerusalem, ninth-century Metz, tenth-century Winchester, and elsewhere, the participants in religious ceremonies learned to modulate their voices or to use appropriate gestures. They assumed roles, such as those of Christ and the devil, for the duration of an action, used hand props such as palm branches, and exploited the spatial arrangement of church buildings and furniture.

At what point, then, did a dramatic liturgy engender a liturgical drama? The terms conventionally used to define drama today, such as "impersonation" and "willing suspension of disbelief" on the part of the audience, are misleading in a tenth-century context. On the one hand, role-playing was common in early liturgical ceremonies. On the other hand, even well-developed liturgical plays were committed to the literal truth of Christ's real presence among men; the Visit to the Sepulchre was not intended as a mere imitation of an action but as a demonstration of the living reality of Christ's resurrection, performed in a style that remained highly formal and symbolic rather than mimetic. For these reasons the dividing line between the liturgy itself and liturgical drama is exasperatingly hard to locate. One useful distinction can perhaps be found in the conditions of presentation: ritual (however dramatically flavored by the celebrant) is integral to the liturgy of the Church and is presided over by the ecclesiastical hierarchy, whereas liturgical drama (however ritualistic) is an elaboration sponsored by the Church and composed by its members but not endorsed as a portion of the liturgy itself.

The manuscripts sometimes reflect such a difference: by the twelfth century some rather long church plays were collected in special playbooks rather than in brevaries, ordinals, tropers, and other service books (i.e., books setting forth the service of the Church) where the early versions of the Visit to the Sepulchre first appeared. Even though some long plays were performed during intervals in the liturgy, they had clearly grown beyond their original function as an expanded part of that liturgy. Yet such a distinction, however clear in theory, still does not enable us to say confidently at what point dramatic ceremonial transformed itself into a "play."

We are faced, in other words, with a paradoxical distinction like that separating day from night: although ritual and drama differ profoundly from one another, the precise point of demarcation between the two is inherently obscure. The devisers of the first Visit to the Sepulchre were doubtless unaware how far-ranging would be the consequences of their seemingly inobtrusive modifications of the liturgy. Nevertheless, today we can see, in the manuscripts that have come down to us, a process of gradual transition by which drama was born in the very center of rite—a process that must have occurred also in ancient Greece.

1. CONCERNING TRAGEDIES

(DE TRAGOEDIIS)

BY HONORIUS OF AUTUN

It is known that those who recited tragedies in the theaters represented to the people, by their gestures, the actions of conflicting forces. Even so, our tragedian [the celebrant] represents to the Christian people in the theater of the church, by his gestures, the struggle of Christ, and impresses upon them the victory of his redemption. Accordingly when the priest says Pray, he expresses Christ placed for us in agony, when he admonished the apostles to pray. By the liturgical silence he signifies Christ as a lamb without voice being led to the sacrifice. By the extension of his hands he delineates the stretching out of Christ on the cross. By the singing of the preface he expresses the cry of Christ hanging on the cross. For he [Christ] sang ten psalms, namely from My God, behold to Into your hands I commend my spirit, and thus died. By the secret recital of prayers in the canon he implies the silence of the Sabbath [Holy Saturday]. By the "peace" and the imparting of it [the kiss of peace], he depicts the peace given after Christ's resurrection and the imparting of joyful tidings. When the sacrament is brought to completion, peace and communion are given by the priest to the people, because, when our accuser has been overthrown by our champion in the conflict, peace is announced by the judge to the people, [and] they are invited to a feast. Thereafter they are commanded by the Go, the mass is ended to return home with rejoicing. They exclaim thanks to God and return home rejoicing.

Sciendum quod hi qui tragoedias in theatris recitabant, actus pugnantium gestibus populo repraesentabant. Sic tragicus noster pugnam Christi populo Christiano in theatro ecclesiae gestibus suis repraesentat, eique victoriam redemptionis suae inculcat. Itaque cum presbyter Orate dicit, Christum pro nobis in agonia positum exprimit, cum apostolos orare monuit. Per secretum silentium, significat Christum velut agnum sine voce ad victimam ductum. Per manuum expansionem, designat Christi in cruce extensionem. Per cantum praefationis, exprimit clamorem Christi in cruce pendentis. Decem namque psalmos, scilicet a Deus meus respice usque In manus tuas commendo spiritum meum cantavit, et sic exspiravit. Per canonis secretum innuit Sabbati silentium. Per pacem, et communicationem designat pacem datam post Christi resurrectionem et gaudii communicationem. Confecto sacramento, pax et communio populo a sacerdote datur, quia accusatore nostro ab agonotheta nostro per duellum prostrato, pax a judice populo denuntiatur, ad convivium invitatur. Deinde ad propria redire cum gaudio per Ite missa est imperatur. Qui gratias Deo jubilat et gaudens domum remeat.

From the *Gemma Animae* (ca. 1100), Lib. I, Cap. LXXXIII, *"De Tragoediis,"* by Honorius of Autun, disciple of Amalarius of Metz (*De Ecclesiasticis Officiis*). Latin text based upon J. P. Migne, ed., *Patrologiae Cursus Completus: Patrologia Latina*, 221 vols. (Paris, 1844–1864), clxxii, 570. It is reprinted in Karl Young, *The Drama of the Medieval Church* (Oxford, 1933), I, 83.

2. A PALM SUNDAY PROCESSION IN FOURTH-CENTURY JERUSALEM
BY THE LADY ETHERIA

Accordingly at the seventh hour all the people will ascend to the Mount of Olives, that is, to Eleona; the bishop seats himself in the church; hymns and antiphons appropriate to the day and place are said, and similarly the lessons. And when it will begin to be the ninth hour, they proceed with hymns to the Imbomon, that is, to the place from which the Lord ascended into heaven, and there they sit: for all the people are always commanded to sit when the bishop is present; only the deacons always stand. And there hymns and antiphons appropriate to the place and day are said, together with lessons and prayers interspersed. And now when it will begin to be the eleventh hour, that passage from the Gospel is read where the children, with branches and palms, ran to meet the Lord, saying: Blessed is he who comes in the name of the Lord. *And at once the bishop rises, together with all the people; all go forward on foot from the top of the Mount of Olives; all the people go before him with hymns and antiphons, answering repeatedly,* Blessed is he who comes in the name of the Lord; *and as many children as there are in those places, including those not able to walk afoot since they are of tender age—their parents hold them on their shoulders—all carrying branches, some of palms, some of olives; and thus*

Hora ergo septima omnis populus ascendet in Monte Oliveti, id est in Eleona; in ecclesia sedet episcopus; dicuntur hymni et antiphonae aptae diei ipsi vel loco, lectiones etiam similiter. Et cum coeperit se facere hora nona, subitur cum hymnis in Imbomon, id est in eo loco de quo ascendit Dominus in caelis, et ibi seditur: nam omnis populus semper praesente episcopo jubetur sedere; tantum quod diacones soli stant semper. Dicuntur et ibi hymni vel antiphonae aptae loco aut diei, similiter et lectiones interpositae et orationes. Et iam cum coeperit esse hora undecima, legitur ille locus de evangelio, ubi infantes cum ramis vel palmis occurrerunt Domino, dicentes: Benedictus qui venit in nomine Domini. Et statim levat se episcopus et omnis populus; porro inde de summo Monte Oliveti totum pedibus itur; nam totus populus ante ipsum cum hymnis vel antiphonis, respondentes semper: Benedictus qui venit in nomine Domini; et quotquot sunt infantes in hisdem locis, usque etiam qui pedibus ambulare non possunt, quia teneri sunt, in collo illos parentes sui tenent, omnes ramos tenentes, alii palmarum, alii olivarum; et sic deducetur episcopus in eo typo quo tunc Dominus deductus est. Et

From the *Peregrinatio Etheriae*, the travel journals of a well-born pilgrim to the Holy Land in the fourth century. Etheria wrote her account for her "sisters," probably her sisters in religious vows. She came from Galicia, a province in what was later Spain. The text is based on a MS at Arezzo as published by its discoverer, Signor I. F. Gamurrini, in the *Biblioteca dell'Accademia Storico Giuridica* (Rome, 1887), vol. 4, and in the *Studi e Documenti di Storia e Diritto* (April to Sept., 1888), printed in Mgr. L. Duchesne, *Christian Worship: Its Origin and Evolution,* trans. M. L. McClure (London, 1923), pp. 490–523.

Etheria's narrative mentions several place names in and near the holy city of Jerusalem: (1) Eleona, now the Church of the Ascension, a grotto where traditionally the Lord taught his disciples; (2) Imbomon, traditional site of the Ascension; and (3) Anastasis, the Sanctuary of the Resurrection, site of the holy sepulchre.

the bishop will be escorted in the same figure as formerly the Lord was escorted. And from the top of the mount to the city, and thence through the whole city to the Anastasis, all of them on foot the whole distance, even those who are matrons and gentlemen, thus they escort the bishop with their responses, going very slowly lest the people should tire; and onward until at a late hour they arrive at the Anastasis. When they have come, no matter how late, the whole of lucernare *takes place; the prayer to the cross again; and the people are dismissed.*

de summo monte usque ad civitatem, et inde ad Anastase per totam civitatem, totum pedibus omnes, sed et si quae matronae sunt aut si qui domini, sic deducunt episcopum respondentes, et sic lente et lente, ne lassetur populus; porro iam sera pervenitur ad Anastase. Ubi cum ventum fuerit, quamlibet sero sit, totum fit lucernare; *fit denuo oratio ad crucem et dimittitur populus.*

3. THE SERVICE FOR THE CONSECRATION OF A CHURCH
(ORDO DEDICATIONIS ECCLESIAE)
AS USED BY THE BISHOP OF METZ

The bishop begins to scatter holy water outside, with the relics following in the bier, and the clergy singing the antiphon Sprinkle me, O Lord, with the fiftieth psalm, but one from among the clergy having been shut up behind the portals in the new church, as if concealing himself. For the bishop goes around the church the first time from the north portal until he once again reaches the same portal; and when he has arrived there, he strikes the portal three times, saying:

Lift up your gates, O princes, and be raised up, you everlasting doors, and the king of glory will come in.

Let the one within say in response:

Who is this king of glory?

Again the church must be walked around a second time like the first, with the same antiphon and same psalm, until the portal is reached once more, and again let there be a knocking as at first with the same words and the same response from the one concealed within. Then for a third time the church must be walked around in the same fashion with the same song until the portal is again reached. Then to the bishop as he speaks and knocks, answer must be given as at first:

Who is this king of glory?

Let the bishop answer:

Incipit pontifex aquam aspargere consecratam a foris, sequendo feretro reliquiarum, cleroque canente antiphonam Asperges me, Domine, cum psalmo quinquagesimo, sed uno ex clericis in nova ecclesia clausis ostiis quasi latente. Nam pontifex circumit ecclesiam ab ostio in partem aquilonarem prima vice usque iterum ad idem ostium; et cum illic perventum fuerit, pulsat ostium tribus vicibus, dicendo:

Tollite portas, principes, vestras, et elevamini, portae aeternales, et introibit rex gloriae.

Ille deintus respondens dicat:

Quis est iste rex gloriae?

Iterum circumienda est ecclesia secunda vice sicut prius, cum eadem antiphona et eodem psalmo, usquedum perveniatur ad ostium, atque iterum pulsetur sicut prius eisdem verbis et idem respondente deintus latente. Tunc tertio iterum circumienda est eodem modo cum eodem cantu usque iterum ad ostium. Tunc dicenti pontifici et pulsanti respondendum est ei sicut prius:

Quis est iste rex gloriae?

Pontifex respondeat:

Used by the bishop of Metz, ninth century. Text based on Mgr. L. Duchesne, *Christian Worship: Its Origin and Evolution,* trans. M. L. McClure (London, 1923), pp. 487–88, from Bibliothèque Nationale, MS lat. 9428. It is reprinted in Young, *Drama of the Medieval Church,* I, 103. The chanted lines of this ceremonial are derived from Psalm 24. These lines were regularly interpreted by medieval authors as referring to Christ's harrowing of hell. A main source of the tradition was the Apocryphal Gospel of Nicodemus.

The Lord of hosts, he is the king of glory.

Then the portal will be opened and the antiphon Walk, holy God, enter into the house of the Lord *must be sung, with the psalm* I am most joyful in these things which are said to me, *and so on. And let him who had at first been inside, as if taking flight, go out at that portal, in order to enter once again through the first portal dressed in ecclesiastical vestments.*

Dominus virtutum, ipse est rex gloriae.

Tunc aperientur ostia et canenda est antiphona Ambulate, sancti Dei, ingredimini in domum Domini, *cum psalmo* Laetatus sum in his quae dicta sunt mihi, *et cetera. Et ille qui prius fuerat intus quasi fugiens egrediatur ad illud ostium foras, iterum ingressurus per primum ostium vestitus vestimentis ecclesiasticis.*

4. ADORATION OF THE CROSS

(ADORATIO CRUCIS)

FROM THE REGULARIS CONCORDIA

OF ST. ETHELWOLD

When these things have been completed according to the prescribed service, immediately let the cross be set up before the altar, with a space interposed between it and the altar, the cross held upright on either side by two deacons. Then let them sing:

My people, [what have I done to you?]

Answering, let two subdeacons standing before the cross sing in Greek:

Holy God, holy, mighty, holy, everliving, have mercy upon us.

And the schola repeating the same in Latin:

Holy God.

Let the cross then be borne before the altar by the same deacons, and let an acolyte follow them with a small cushion on which the holy cross is to be laid. And when the antiphon is finished which the schola has chanted in Latin, let them [the deacons] in the same place sing as before:

Because I have led you through the desert.

Again let the subdeacons answer in Greek as before, Holy God, as above.

And again the schola in Latin as before, Holy God.

Quibus expletis per ordinem, statim praeparetur crux ante altare, interposito spatio inter ipsam et altare, sustentata hinc et inde a duobus diaconibus. Tunc cantent:

Popule meus, [quid feci tibi?]

Respondentes autem duo subdiaconi stantes ante crucem canant graece:

Agios o Theos, Agyos y[s]chiros, Agios athanathos, eleïson ymas.

Itemque scola idipsum latine:

Sanctus Deus.

Deferatur tunc ab ipsis diaconibus ante altare, et eos accolitus cum pulvillo sequatur super quem sancta crux ponatur. Antiphonaque finita quam scola respondit latine, canant ibidem sicut prius:

Quia eduxi vos per desertum.

Item vero respondeant subdiaconi graece sicut prius Agios, ut supra.

Itemque scola latine ut prius Sanctus Deus.

5

A Good Friday ceremonial, immediately followed in the *Regularis Concordia* manuscript by the *Depositio* (see next selection). Text based on London, British Museum, MS Cotton Tiberius A. III, Regularis Concordia saec. xi, fol. 18ᵛ–19ʳ, checked against Young, *Drama of the Medieval Church*, I, 118–19, and Dom Thomas Symons, ed., *Regularis Concordia: The Monastic Agreement* (London, 1953), pp. 42–43. Symons also collates against two other manuscripts, Cotton MS Faustina B. III, fols. 159a–198a, and Cotton Tiberius A. III, fols. 177a and b; see that edition for variants.

[1] *My people:* from Micah 6:3.

[4] *scola:* probably the *Scola Cantorum,* official body of singers.

And again let the deacons, raising the cross, sing as before:

And what more [ought I to have done for you, and have not done?]

Again the subdeacons as before, Holy God, *as above.*

And again the schola in Latin, Holy God, *as above.*

After this, turning themselves toward the clergy, with the cross unveiled, let them [the deacons] say the antiphon:

Behold the wood of the cross.

Another antiphon: We worship your cross.

Another antiphon: While the creator of the world.

Proclaim, O tongue.

As soon as it has been unveiled there, let the abbot come before the holy cross and prostrate himself thrice with all the brethren of the choir on the right hand, that is, seniors and juniors; and with deep heartfelt sighs let him recite the seven penitential psalms together with the prayers in honor of the holy cross.

10

Itemque diaconi levantes crucem canant sicut prius:

Quid ultra [debui facere tibi, et non feci?]

Ite[m] subdiaconi sicut prius Agyos, *ut supra.*

Itemque scola latine Sanctus Deus, *ut supra.*

Post haec vertentes se ad clerum, nudata cruce, dicant antiphonam:

Ecce lignum crucis.

Alia: Crucem tuam adoramus.

Alia: Dum fabricator mundi.

[P]ange lingua.

Ilico ea nudata, veniat abbas ante crucem sanctam ac tribus vicibus se prosternat cum omnibus fratribus dexterioris chori, scilicet senioribus ac junioribus, et cum magno cordis suspirio septem poenitentiae psalmos cum orationibus sanctae cruci competentibus decantando peroret.

[7] *And what more:* See Isaiah 5:4.

This text gives the first lines only of hymns for Good Friday to be sung in their entirety, such as the *Pange Lingua,* "Proclaim (or sing), my tongue, the glorious battle," etc.

5. THE INTERMENT OF THE CROSS IN THE SEPULCHRE
(DEPOSITIO)
FROM THE REGULARIS CONCORDIA *OF ST. ETHELWOLD*

For since on that day we solemnize the interment of the body of our Saviour, if it should be considered or seem pleasing to anyone in such wise to follow the practice of certain religious men, worthy to be imitated, for the strengthening of the faith of the unlearned multitude and of neophytes, we have decreed in this manner. Let there be on one part of the altar, where there is room, a likeness of the sepulchre, and a curtain stretched around it, which should be placed in this manner until the holy cross has been venerated. [Thereafter] let the deacons who first carried it [the cross] come forward, and infold it in a linen cloth in the place there where it has been worshiped. Then let them bear it away, singing the antiphons In peace, therefore; He will dwell; *and* My flesh shall rest in hope, *until they come to the place of the sepulchre; and when the cross has been laid therein, as if the body of our Lord Jesus Christ has been buried, let them say the antiphon:*

The Lord having been buried, the sepulchre was sealed up; stationing the soldiers who were to keep custody over him.

In that same place the holy cross is to be guarded with all reverence until the night of the Lord's resurrection. And during the night let two brothers be appointed, or three or more, if the community is large enough, who are to employ themselves in faithful watch, chanting psalms.

Nam quia ea die depositionem corporis Salvatoris nostri celebramus, usum quorundam religiosorum imitabilem ad fidem indocti vulgi ac neophytorum corroborandam aequiparando sequi, si ita cui visum fuerit vel sibi taliter placuerit hoc modo decrevimus. Sit autem in una parte altaris, qua vacuum fuerit, quaedam assimilatio sepulchri, velamenque quoddam in gyro tensum quod, dum sancta crux adorata fuerit, deponatur hoc ordine. Veniant diaconi qui prius portaverunt eam, et involvant eam sindone in loco ubi adorata est. Tunc reportent eam canentes antiphonas In pace in idipsum; Habitabit; *item* Caro mea requiescet in spe, *donec veniant ad locum monumenti; depositaque cruce, ac si Domini nostri Jhesu Christi corpore sepulto, dicant antiphonam:*

Sepulto Domino, signatum est monumentum; ponentes milites qui custodirent eum.

In eodem loco sancta crux cum omni reverentia custodiatur usque Dominicae noctem resurrectionis. Nocte vero ordinentur duo fratres aut tres aut plures, si tanta fuerint congregatio, qui ibidem psalmos decantando excubias fideles exerceant.

A Good Friday ceremonial. The *Depositio* immediately follows the *Adoratio Crucis* (previous selection) in the *Regularis Concordia* manuscript. Text based as before on London, British Museum, MS Cotton Tiberius A. III, Regularis Concordia saec. xi, fol. 19ᵛ–20, checked against Young, *Drama of the Medieval Church*, I, 133, and Dom Thomas Symons' edition (London, 1953).

Sepulto Domino: an antiphon for Holy Saturday; cf. Matthew 27: 66.

6. THE RAISING OF THE HOST FROM THE SEPULCHRE
(ELEVATIO)
FROM ST. GALL

The body of the Lord having therefore been raised from the tomb, let the cantor begin the responsory:

An angel of the Lord descended [from heaven, and approaching rolled back the stone, and sat on it, and said to the women: Fear not; for I know that you seek him who was crucified; he has now risen, come and see the place where the Lord had been laid, alleluia.

Verse: An angel of the Lord spoke to the women saying: Whom do you seek, do you seek Jesus? He has risen already.]

As they enter into the choir, let the cantor begin the antiphon:

Christ has risen and has given light to his people, whom he ransomed with his blood, alleluia.

Verse:

This is the propitious day in which hell is plundered;
God who was made man has risen; you who are redeemed be joyful.
We praise you O God.

Sublato igitur corpore Domini de monumento, incipiat cantor responsorium:

Angelus Domini descendit [de caelo, et accedens revolvit lapidem, et super eum sedit, et dixit mulieribus: Nolite timere; scio enim quia crucifixum quaeritis; iam surrexit, venite et videte locum ubi positus erat Dominus, alleluia.

Versus: Angelus Domini locutus est mulieribus dicens: Quem quaeritis, an Jesum quaeritis? Iam surrexit.]

Intrantibus autem in chorum incipiat cantor antiphonam:

Surrexit Christus et illuxit populo suo, quem redemit sanguine suo, alleluia.

Versus:

Haec est alma dies in qua spoliatur avernus;
Resurrexit homo Deus; exultate redempti.

Te Deum laudamus.

From a breviary of the eleventh century from St. Gall. To be performed at the end of matins. Text based on St. Gall, Stiftsbibliothek, MS 387, Brev. Sangallense saec. xi, p. 55, edited in Young, *Drama of the Medieval Church*, I, 130–31. For the full text of the responsory *Angelus Domini*, see *Antiphonale du B. Hartker*, published in facsimile in *Paléographie musicale*, iie série, i (Solesmes, 1900), pp. 228–29.

7. ANTIPHONS FOR EASTER VESPERS
(ANTIPHONAE AD VESPERAS DE EVANGELIO, SABBATO SANCTO)

Ant.: At the end of the Sabbath, as it began to dawn toward the first day of the week, came Mary Magdalene and the other Mary to see the sepulchre, alleluia.

Ant.: And behold, there was a great earthquake; for an angel of the Lord descended from heaven, alleluia.

Ant.: For an angel of the Lord descended from heaven, and approaching rolled back the stone, and sat upon it, alleluia, alleluia.

Ant.: His countenance was like lightning, and his raiment white as snow, alleluia, alleluia.

Ant.: And for fear of him the guards were struck with terror, and became as dead men, alleluia.

Ant.: And the angel answering said to the women: Fear not, for I know that you seek Jesus, alleluia.

Ant.: I know that you seek Jesus, who was crucified; he has risen, alleluia.

Ant.: Jesus whom you seek is not here, but has risen; remember how he spoke to you, when he was in Galilee, alleluia.

Ant.: Come and see the place where the Lord had been laid, alleluia.

Ant.: Going quickly, tell his disciples that the Lord has risen, alleluia.

Ant.: Vespere autem Sabbati, quae lucescit in prima Sabbati, venit Maria Magdalene et altera Maria videre sepulchrum, alleluia.

Ant.: Et ecce terrae motus factus est magnus; angelus enim Domini descendit de caelo, alleluia.

Ant.: Angelus enim Domini descendit de caelo, et accedens revolvit lapidem, et sedebat super eum, alleluia, alleluia.

Ant.: Erat autem aspectus eius sicut fulgur, et vestimenta eius sicut nix, alleluia, alleluia.

Ant.: Prae timore autem eius exterriti sunt custodes, et facti sunt velut mortui, alleluia.

Ant.: Respondens autem angelus dixit mulieribus: Nolite timere, scio quod Jesum quaeritis, alleluia.

Ant.: Scio quod Jesum quaeritis crucifixum; surrexit, alleluia.

Ant.: Jesum quem quaeritis non est hic, sed surrexit; recordare qualiter locutus sit vobis, dum adhuc in Galilaea esset, alleluia.

Ant.: Venite et videte locum ubi positus erat Dominus, alleluia.

Ant.: Cito euntes, dicite discipulis quia surrexit Dominus, alleluia.

An antiphon accompanying the *Magnificat*, probably for use with the Vigil mass. It includes many phrases found in the *Quem quaeritis* play, and is itself derived from Matthew 28:1–7, read antiphonally in a liturgical service. The text is based on the Gregorian *Liber Responsalis*, in J. P. Migne, ed., *Patrologia Latina*, vol. LXXVIII, p. 769[b]. It is printed in O. B. Hardison, Jr., *Christian Rite and Christian Drama in the Middle Ages* (Baltimore, 1965), p. 165.

8. ANTIPHONS WITH RESPONSES FOR THE VIGIL OF THE MOST HOLY EASTER
(ANTIPHONAE CUM RESPONSORIIS DE VIGILA SANCTISSIMAE PASCHAE)

Response: An angel of the Lord descended from heaven, and approaching rolled back the stone; and sat upon it, and said to the women: Fear not; for I know that you seek him who was crucified. Already he has risen. Come and see the place where the Lord had been laid, alleluia.

Verse: An angel of the Lord spoke to the women saying: Whom do you seek, do you seek Jesus? Already [he has risen].

Response: An angel of the Lord spoke to the women saying: Whom do you seek, do you seek Jesus? Already he has risen, come and see, alleluia, alleluia.

Verse: Behold he will go before you into Galilee, there you will see him, as he said to you. Already [etc.].

Response: When the Sabbath had passed, Mary Magdalene, and Mary [the mother] of James and Salome purchased spices in order that, coming, they might anoint Jesus, alleuia, alleluia.

Verse: And very early in the morning of the Sabbath they came together to the tomb, the sun just having risen. In order that, coming [etc.].

Response: On the stone of the tomb angels were sitting and singing of the Lord's resurrection; and before the sepulchre of Jesus stood Mary

Resp.: Angelus Domini descendit de caelo, et accedens revolvit lapidem; et super eum sedit, et dixit mulieribus: Nolite timere; scio enim quia crucifixum quaeritis. Iam surrexit. Venite et videte locum ubi positus erat Dominus, alleluia.

Vers.: Angelus Domini locutus est mulieribus dicens: Quem quaeritis, an Jesum quaeritis? Iam.

Resp.: Angelus Domini locutus est mulieribus dicens: Quem quaeritis, an Jesum quaeritis? Iam surrexit, venite et videte, alleluia, alleluia.

Vers.: Ecce praecedet vos in Galilaeam, ibi eum videbitis, sicut dixit vobis. Iam.

Resp.: Dum transisset Sabbatum, Maria Magdalene, et Maria Jacobi et Salome emerunt aromata, ut venientes ungerent Jesum, alleluia, alleluia.

Vers.: Et valde mane una Sabbatorum veniunt ad monumentum, orto iam sole. Ut venientes.

Resp.: Super lapidem monumenti sedebant angeli, et psallabant de resurrectione Domini; et ante sepulchrum Jesu stabat

4

An antiphon for the Easter nocturn service, from the Gregorian *Liber Responsalis*, in J. P. Migne, ed., *Patrologia Latina*, vol. LXXVIII, pp. 769ᵈ–770ᵃ. It is printed in O. B. Hardison, Jr., *Christian Rite and Christian Drama in the Middle Ages* (Baltimore, 1965), pp. 171–72.

[2]*Already [he has risen]:* Here and in following lines the verse seems to be echoing the previous response; however, the words in square brackets ought to be approached with caution, since it is not certain that they were actually repeated in performance.

[5]*Mary [the mother] of James:* See Mark 16:1.

saying: Good sir, if you have borne him hence, say where you have laid him, alleluia.	Maria dicens: Domine, si tu sustulisti eum, dic ubi posuisti eum, alleluia.
Verse: But she, supposing him to be a gardener, said to him, Good sir, if [*etc.*]. 8	*Vers.:* At illa, existimans quod hortulanus esset, dicit ei, Domine, si.

7–8*Good sir:* For this "gardener" incident in which the sorrowing Mary Magdalene mistakes Jesus for a gardener, see John 20:13–17.

Liturgical Beginnings

B. TENTH-CENTURY VERSIONS OF THE VISIT TO THE SEPULCHRE

AS WE HAVE SEEN, the search for a precise beginning of medieval drama is a baffling quest. Liturgical ceremonies did not suddenly become "plays"; the process was a gradual one. The liturgy itself long employed dramatic techniques such as dialogue, movement from one symbolic location to another, and the use of props. Even the fixed assignment of roles for the duration of an action was by no means unknown from the time of the fourth century and quite possibly earlier. Nor was such activity restricted to the Easter season. As we shall see (in Section D), in the tenth century histrionic presentations also became common during Christmas.

One ceremony of undoubted importance to the future of medieval drama, in any case, was the Visit to the Sepulchre of the three Marys on Easter morning. This episode, representing the supremely important moment in which mankind learns of Christ's resurrection, appears in a number of texts owned by various religious communities in tenth-century Europe. All are quite short, and all involve a dialogue between an angel (or two angels) and the three Marys approaching the tomb. The angel's opening question, *"Quem quaeritis in sepulchro?"* ("Whom do you seek in the sepulchre?"), has given a Latin name to this dramatic ceremonial.

The *Quem quaeritis* texts were brief compositions to be sung in monastic churches as embellishments to the regular service. (Perhaps secular or non-monastic churches also performed this ceremonial, but no early texts have survived to prove that they did so.) Some *Quem quaeritis* texts were called "tropes." According to a ninth-century monk from St. Gall named Notker Babulus, "tropes" had begun as wordless musical sequences with which the

21

singers in the choir would embellish the vowel sounds of certain important words in the service. One such word, for example, was the *alleluia* in the introit (opening processional chant) of the Easter mass. Babulus reports that musical tropes of this sort had become so elaborate in the ninth century that words were added to make the sequences easier to memorize. (Choristers did not sing from individual musical scores, owing to the expense of copying texts; one "service book" had to make do for the whole choir.) Tropes accordingly became literary and musical compositions inserted into the regular service, offering in some instances the opportunity for dramatic dialogue among various members of the choir.

Early *Quem quaeritis* texts appear to have been sung before the introit of the Easter mass, or during the office of matins on Easter morning, or possibly during the Vigil mass of the preceding night. "Matins" or "mattins" (followed immediately by lauds) was, as we have seen, the first of the seven canonical offices or "hours" sung daily by a religious community; the other six were prime, terce, sext, none, vespers, and compline. Matins came before daybreak and consisted of three "nocturns," each made up of antiphons, verses, prayers, and lessons and responsories. The *Quem quaeritis* trope, when sung at matins, came at the end of the third lesson, as a sequel to the third respond, which (on Easter morning) told of the three Marys and their visit to the tomb. In this position, the *Quem quaeritis* could be considered as a trope of the *Te Deum* ("We Praise You, O God"), a familiar anthem sung at the conclusion of matins and the beginning of lauds.

During the course of the tenth century, the monastic brethren who sang the Easter services (ordinarily with no public congregation present) tried various ways of dramatizing their renditions of the *Quem quaeritis*. On some occasions, evidently, they merely sang the ceremonial in procession, "visiting" the sepulchre and graveclothes as they chanted antiphonally the biblical account of the angel and the three Marys. We cannot be sure, for example, that a simple text like that from St. Gall (selection 10) involved anything more "dramatic" than antiphonal singing. At other times or in other places, however, the performers of the *Quem quaeritis* assigned particular singers to the roles of the angel and the three Marys. This use of impersonation must have encouraged the use of gestures and of hand props (such as thuribles, representing the spices carried by the three Marys). Another important innovation was to set aside the procession by the whole choir, allowing the three Marys to enter instead as though approaching the tomb. We cannot assume, however, that these steps occurred in this order, or separately. They may have taken place all at once, under the direction of some unknown genius. Conditions must certainly have varied from one monastic community to another.

Some *Quem quaeritis* texts from the tenth century are manifestly more elaborate than others. All contain the meeting of the angel and the three Marys, but some add further dialogue and are more detailed in specifying the use of costume and gestures. The problem of arranging these tenth-century texts in chronological order has proved to be controversial. The traditional answer of nineteenth- and twentieth-century scholarship has been to assume that the simplest version came first, and that subsequent versions added dialogue and action bit by bit until a fairly comprehensive play had been achieved. This "simplest-first" hypothesis presumes the St. Gall *Visitatio* (selection 10) to be the earliest version we have, since it contains nothing but the angel's question ("Whom do you seek in the sepulchre?"), the response of the three Marys, and the angel's assurance that Christ has risen. Scholars such as Karl Young and John Matthews Manly argue that the Visit to the Sepulchre began with just such a simple trope as this, perhaps with this very one.

A major difficulty, however, is that the probable dating of the various tenth-century *Quem quaeritis* manuscripts will not support this tidy notion that the simplest version came first and that others grew from it in orderly steps. In fact, O. B. Hardison, Jr. (in his *Christian Rite and Christian Drama in the Middle Ages*) has challenged the entire Darwinian assumption that drama would actually develop by such a precise and rational evolutionary process. According to the evidence of the texts themselves, argues Hardison, the relatively elaborate version found in the *Regularis Concordia* (selection 11) represents an earlier stage of development than the brief St. Gall *Visitatio*. Moreover, says Hardison, this more elaborate ceremony may have begun as part of the Vigil mass rather than as part of matins or Easter mass. Vigil mass originally took place in the hours before Easter dawn, at a time appropriate to the events celebrated in the dramatic ceremony itself. Only when a process of "anticipation" had pushed the celebration of the Vigil mass back into Saturday afternoon did it prove necessary to find another service more appropriate in time to the central happenings of Easter. Matins and Easter mass were the logical choices; but when the *Visitatio* was attached to the already elaborate Easter mass, it had to be shortened and simplified. According to this argument, then, the St. Gall text (selection 10) is actually a cut-down version of something originally more like the *Regularis* text (selection 11).

Not all of Hardison's thesis has won acceptance. According to a number of articles by the musicologist William Smoldon, the musical settings of the early *Quem quaeritis* texts show unmistakable affinities to the introit of the Easter mass rather than to the Vigil mass. Many other scholars, including Rosemary Woolf *(The English Mystery Plays)*, believe that the *Quem quaeritis* began either as a brief trope to the introit of the Easter mass (as in selections 9 and 10), or as a somewhat longer ceremonial for a Visit to the Sepulchre following the third respond of matins. In the former case the trope would have had room to expand; in the latter case the longer text would have had to be cut down for use in the mass. Even if we must question Hardison's suggestion of the Vigil mass, then, we must allow for the possibility that the simplest *Quem quaeritis* texts we have do not represent the earliest stage of development.

In view of such uncertainties, the following four texts are presented, as nearly as can be determined, in chronological order. The text from the monastery of St. Martial, at Limoges (selection 9), is usually regarded as the earliest extant version and is called a trope. It ends with the first words of the introit of the Easter mass, to which this trope is an introduction. The text is usually dated 923–34, although a date as late as 950 has been argued. Like nearly all tropes, this one has musical notation in the original manuscript. The St. Gall text (selection 10) is the simplest extant. It ends with "Resurrexi" which, as in the case of the St. Martial text, begins the introit of the Easter mass. The date is approximately 950. The *Regularis* text (selection 11), prepared at Winchester some time between 965 and 975 for Benedictine use in England, is vastly more specific than the others in detailing methods of "imitation" to be employed, including the display of the graveclothes in the sepulchre. It is the culmination of earlier ceremonies on Good Friday by which the cross had been adored and buried. The text is designed for performance following the third lesson of Easter matins, and ends accordingly with the singing of the *Te Deum*. The tenth-century troper or book of tropes from Winchester, 978–80 (selection 12), provides an early example of a "double proclamation"—one in which the Marys twice announce to the assemblage the joyous news they have heard. This expansion became common in later versions of the *Quem quaeritis*. The occasion on which this text was sung is uncertain.

Whatever their exact chronological order, these ceremonies remain very much a part of the liturgy for which they were intended to provide a brief and pleasing ornamentation. Even in the most elaborate version, from the *Regularis Concordia,* the costumes are clerical, the simple hand props are ecclesiastical artifacts, and the "stage" is the choir and altar of the church. The dialogue, sung with no lay congregation present, is attached to a liturgical antiphon and concludes with the resumption of the regular service. Most importantly, the action is conceived of not simply as a mimetic presentation but as the revelation of a miracle, "as if demonstrating that the Lord has risen."

9. TROPE FOR EASTER
(TROPHI IN PASCHE)
FROM LIMOGES

Sing a psalm to the great king, to the mighty
    conqueror of death.
Whom do you seek in the sepulchre, O
    followers of Christ?

Response:

Jesus of Nazareth who was crucified, O
    heaven-dwellers.

Response:

He is not here, he has risen as he himself said;
    go, announce that he is risen.
Alleluia, the Lord has risen, today is risen the
    mighty lion, Christ, the son of God;
    praise be to God, say it indeed!

[*I have risen, and I am with you still, alleluia.*]
I have slept, O Father, and I shall arise at
daybreak, and my sleep is sweet to me. [*You
have placed your hand over me, alleluia.*] Thus,
Father, thus it has been pleasing to you,
that by dying I have been the death of
death, the vexation of hell, and life for the
the world. [*Your knowledge has been made
wonderful, alleluia, alleluia.*] You who have
concealed these things from the wise, and
revealed them to children, alleluia.

Psallite regi magno, devicto mortis imperio.
Quem quaeritis in sepulchro, o Christi-
    colae?

Responsio:

Jhesum Nazarenum crucifixum, o caeli-
    colae.

Responsio:

Non est hic, surrexit sicut ipse dixit; ite,
    nuntiate quia surrexit.
Alleluia, resurrexit Dominus, hodie re-
    surrexit leo fortis, Cristus, filius Dei:
    Deo gratias, dicite eia!

[*Resurrexi, et adhuc tecum sum, alleluia.*]
Dormivi, Pater, et surgam diluculo, et
somnus meus dulcis est mihi. *Po*[*suisti
super me manum tuam, alleluia.*] Ita, Pater,
sic placuit ante te, ut moriendo mortis
mors fuissem, morsus inferni, et mundo
vita. *Mirabilis* [*facta est scientia tua,
alleluia, alleluia.*] Qui abscondisti haec
sapientibus, et revelasti parvulis, alleluia.

From the monastery of St. Martial, at Limoges. This is usually regarded as the earliest extant
Easter trope, ca. 923–934, although recently a date ca. 950 has been proposed. Text based on
Paris, Bibliothèque Nationale, MS lat. 1240, Trop. Sancti Martialis Lemovicensis, saec. x, fol.
30ᵛ, edited by Young, *Drama of the Medieval Church*, I, 210.

10. OF THE RESURRECTION OF THE LORD
(ITEM DE RESURRECTIONE DOMINI)
FROM ST. GALL

Question:

Whom do you seek in the sepulchre, O followers of Christ?

Answer:

Jesus of Nazareth who was crucified, O heaven-dwellers.

He is not here, he has risen as he had foretold; go, announce that he has risen from the sepulchre.

I have risen.

Interrogatio:

Quem quaeritis in sepulchro, Christicolae?

Responsio:

Jesum Nazarenum crucifixum, o caelicolae.

Non est hic, surrexit sicut praedixerat; ite, nuntiate quia surrexit de sepulchro.

Resurrexi.

The simplest extant form of the Easter trope, dated about 950, from the monastery of St. Gall, Introit of the Mass of Easter. Text based on St. Gall, Stiftsbibliothek, MS 484, Trop. Sangallense saec. x, p. 111, edited by Young, *Drama of the Medieval Church*, I, 201.

[4]*Resurrexi:* The first word of the introit to which this trope is an introduction.

11. THE VISIT TO THE SEPULCHRE
(VISITATIO SEPULCHRI)
FROM THE REGULARIS CONCORDIA
OF ST. ETHELWOLD

While the third lesson is being recited, let four brethren vest themselves; of whom let one, wearing an alb, enter as if on other business, and go unobtrusively to the place of the sepulchre, and there, holding a palm in his hand, let him sit quietly. While the third responsory is being sung, let the remaining three follow, all of them vested in copes, bearing in their hands thuribles with incense; and haltingly, in the manner of seeking for something, let them come before the place of the sepulchre. These things are done in imitation of the angel seated on the tomb and the women coming with spices to anoint the body of Jesus. When therefore the seated one will see the three approaching him, wandering about as it were and seeking something, let him begin to sing in a sweet and moderate voice:

Whom do you seek [in the sepulchre, O followers of Christ?]

When this has been sung to the end, let the three answer with one voice:

Jesus of Nazareth, [who was crucified, O heaven-dweller.]

He to them:

Dum tertia recitatur lectio, quatuor fratres induant se, quorum unus alba indutus acsi ad aliud agendum ingrediatur, atque latenter sepulchri locum adeat, ibique manu tenens palmam, quietus sedeat. Dumque tertium percelebratur responsorium, residui tres succedant, omnes quidem cappis induti, turibula cum incensu manibus gestantes ac pedetemptim ad similitudinem quaerentium quid, veniant ante locum sepulchri. Aguntur enim haec ad imitationem angeli sedentis in monumento, atque mulierum cum aromatibus venientium, ut ungerent corpus Jhesu. Cum ergo ille residens tres velut erraneos, ac aliquid quaerentes, viderit sibi adproximare, incipiat mediocri voce dulcisone cantare:

Quem quaeritis [in sepulchro, o Christicolae?]

Quo decantato fine tenus, respondeant hi tres uno ore:

Jhesum Nazarenum [crucifixum, o caelicola.]

Quibus ille:

From the *Regularis Concordia*, prepared at Winchester between 965 and 975 for Benedictine use in England. This extraliturgical ceremony (not a trope) was attached to the end of matins on Easter morning and was the culmination of a sequence beginning with the Adoration and Burial of the Cross (see selections 4 and 5, above). It is an elaborate ceremony for its early date, including as it does antiphons, chanted dialogue, and extensive stage directions. The text is based, as in earlier selections from the *Regularis,* on London, British Museum, MS Cotton Tiberius A. III, Regularis Concordia saec. xi, fol. 21ʳ–21ᵛ. It is edited by Young, *Drama of the Medieval Church*, I, 249–50, and by Dom Thomas Symons (London, 1953).

The additions in square brackets to the verses of this text offer the forms of these verses generally found elsewhere, but they must be approached with caution. The verses are self-sufficient without these additions, and the text as it stands could represent actual performance.

He is not here, he has risen as he had foretold;
go, announce that he has risen from the
dead.

*At the sound of this command let the three turn
themselves to the choir, saying:*

Alleluia, the Lord has risen, [today is risen the
mighty lion, Christ, the son of God.]

*When this is said, let him, seating himself again,
as though calling them back, say the antiphon:*

Come and see the place [where the Lord had
been laid, alleluia.]

*Saying this, let him rise, and lift the veil and show
them the place bare of the cross, with nothing
other than the shroud in which the cross had been
wrapped. Seeing which, let them set down in that
same sepulchre the thuribles which they had
carried, and let them take up the shroud and
spread it out before the clergy; and, as if
demonstrating that the Lord has risen and is not
now wrapped in it, let them sing this antiphon:*

The Lord has risen from the sepulchre, [who
for us hung on the cross, alleluia.]

*And let them lay the cloth upon the altar. When
the antiphon is finished, let the prior, rejoicing
with them at the triumph of our king, in that he
rose having conquered death, begin the hymn* We
praise you O God. *When this is begun, all
the bells peal in unison.*

Non est hic, surrexit sicut praedixerat; ite,
nuntiate quia surrexit a mortuis.

*Cuius jussionis voce vertant se illi tres ad
chorum dicentes:*

Alleluia, resurrexit Dominus, [hodie resurrexit leo fortis, Christus, filius Dei.]

*Dicto hoc, rursus ille residens velut revocans
illos dicat antiphonam:*

Venite et videte locum [ubi positus erat
Dominus, alleluia.]

*Haec vero dicens surgat, et erigat velum,
ostendatque eis locum cruce nudatum, sed
tantum linteamina posita, quibus crux involuta erat. Quo viso, deponant turibula quae
gestaverant in eodem sepulchro, sumantque
linteum et extendant contra clerum, ac veluti
ostendentes, quod surrexerit Dominus et iam
non sit illo involutus, hanc canant antiphonam:*

Surrexit Dominus de sepulchro, [qui pro
nobis pependit in ligno, alleluia.]

*Superponantque linteum altari. Finita anti-
phona, prior congaudens pro triumpho regis
nostri, quod devicta morte surrexit, incipiat
hymnum* Te Deum laudamus. *Quo incepto,
una pulsantur omnia signa.*

[5]s.d. *before the clergy:* This ceremony nowhere makes provision for the presence or participation of the laity.

12. THE VISIT TO THE SEPULCHRE
(VISITATIO SEPULCHRI)
FROM THE TENTH-CENTURY TROPER OF WINCHESTER

The angelic proclamation of the resurrection of Christ:

Whom do you seek in the sepulchre, O followers of Christ?

The response of the holy women:

Jesus of Nazareth who was crucified, O heaven-dweller.

The consolation of the angelic voice:

He is not here, he has risen as he had predicted; go, announce that he has risen, saying:

The song of the holy women to all the clergy:

Alleluia, the Lord has risen, today [is risen] the mighty lion, Christ, the son of God. Praise be to God, say it indeed!

Let the angel say:

Come and see the place where the Lord had been laid, alleluia, alleluia.

Again let the angel say:

Going quickly, tell the disciples that the Lord has risen, alleluia, alleluia.

Let the women with one voice sing rejoicing:

The Lord has risen from the sepulchre, who for us hung on the cross, alleluia.

Angelica de Christi resurrectione:

Quem quaeritis in sepulchro, Christicolae?

Sanctarum mulierum responsio:

Jhesum Nazarenum crucifixum, o caelicola.

Angelicae vocis consolatio:

Non est hic, surrexit sicut praedixerat; ite, nuntiate quia surrexit, dicentes:

Sanctarum mulierum ad omnem clerum modulatio:

Alleluia, resurrexit Dominus, hodie [resurrexit] leo fortis, Christus, filius Dei. Deo gratias, dicite eia!

Dicat angelus:

Venite et videte locum ubi positus erat Dominus, alleluia, alleluia.

Iterum dicat angelus:

Cito euntes, dicite discipulis quia surrexit Dominus, alleluia, alleluia.

Mulieres una voce canant jubilantes:

Surrexit Dominus de sepulchro, qui pro nobis pependit in ligno, alleluia.

4

Text based on Oxford, Bibl. Bodl., MS 775, Trop. Wintoniense saec. x (978–80), fol. 17r–17v. Edited by Young, *Drama of the Medieval Church*, I, 254. According to Rosemary Woolf, *The English Mystery Plays*, p. 343, the placing of this text in the Winchester Troper before the *Benedictio cerei*, the blessing of the paschal candle, is manifestly wrong; but O. B. Hardison, Jr. (*Christian Rite and Christian Drama*, pp. 190–91) argues that the position in the manuscript is correct and that it indicates performance on Easter eve as part of the candle ceremonies associated with the Easter vigil.

Liturgical Beginnings

C. ELEVENTH- AND TWELFTH-CENTURY EASTER DRAMA

D URING THE ELEVENTH and twelfth centuries, the Visit to the Sepulchre developed into an Easter drama of some length and complexity. Most of the growth came, however, only toward the end of this period. Until late in the eleventh century, the *Visitatio* seldom ventured far beyond its original brief scope. Experimentation came much more readily in other kinds of church drama: Christmas plays, plays based on stories from the Old and New Testaments, lives of the saints, plays in the vernacular languages such as German, French, and Spanish, and so on (as we shall see in Part II). The evidence seems to contradict a once well-established scholarly hypothesis of dramatic growth, which assumed that the *Visitatio* grew first into a complex Resurrection play and then served as a model for the subsequent development of other kinds of drama. The use of vernacular languages, according to this hypothesis, was a particularly late stage in the process of "secularization" or estrangement of the drama from its cloistered auspices. In point of fact, however, any significant complexity in drama for Easter day was actually anticipated by, and quite possibly influenced by, the more rapid innovation in other kinds of church drama, both in Latin and in the vernacular.

This situation may be, after all, the most logical. The moment of the Resurrection, as the focus of the liturgical year, was from the first an obvious subject for dramatic rendition, but it was also so sacred that any extensive interpretation of it might have seemed presumptuous. The earliest *Quem quaeritis* versions stayed close to the Gospel accounts of the Resurrection. So too did much later renditions of the Visit to the Sepulchre, even in the English Corpus Christi cycles of the fourteenth and fifteenth centuries. Although the Resurrection play did eventually grow longer by telling more and more of the story, its center remained relatively unchanged.

Each of the *Visitatio* texts presented in this section retains at its core the meeting of the three Marys with the angel (or angels), and the announcement of Christ's resurrection. Many texts from the eleventh and twelfth centuries not included in this selection encompass little more than that meeting. The following selections are, however, somewhat more venturesome than is generally the case, since we are concerned with the ways in which the Visit to the Sepulchre could expand its scope.

The text doubtfully ascribed to Aquileia, Italy (selection 13), introduces the disciples John and Peter, who display the empty graveclothes as the angel had done previously in the Visit to the Sepulchre from the *Regularis Concordia* (selection 11, above). This action of displaying the shroud and head-cloth is not warranted by the Scriptures, but soon became a familiar action in the *Visitatio* because it offered ocular proof of the Resurrection. Two Marys take part in this version rather than the usual three, and two angels instead of the usual one. Another elaboration is the race of Peter and John to the sepulchre, which was to become an often-repeated motif in later dramatizations of the Resurrection. The choir sings the antiphon "Two ran together," presumably while the race occurs in pantomime. A congregation is present. Like the two texts following, this one is designed for performance at the end of Easter matins.

The St. Lambrecht *Visitatio* (selection 14) is the only one from the twelfth century to include congregational singing in the vernacular. The scribe who wrote the manuscript speaks of this congregational singing condescendingly, as though he regarded it as an intrusion. As in the Aquileia text, the disciples Peter and John act out their race to the tomb while a chanted antiphon describes what they are doing. The younger disciple, John, arrives first and waits for the elder. A notable expansion is the sequence known as the *Victimae Paschali,* lines 7 through 12, in which members of the choir ask the Marys what they have seen and then affirm that the Marys' testimony is more to be believed than that of the faithless Jewish people. This verse composition occurs in at least two other *Visitatio* texts of this period and soon became a common feature in liturgical plays about Easter. In most texts, however, only Mary Magdalene speaks rather than all three Marys.

The *Visitatio* from the Fleury playbook (selection 15), a composition of the late twelfth or possibly early thirteenth century, is a remarkably finished literary achievement. The costuming is detailed, the verse expansions imaginative. At the conclusion of their race to the tomb, in which the younger John again arrives first, John and Peter actually enter into the sepulchre to examine the empty graveclothes. Mary Magdalene mistakes the risen Christ for a gardener. Even in this comparatively developed work, however, we note that fidelity to sources and preservation of ritual elements outweigh, and frequently contradict, consistency of characterization and motive. For example, Mary Magdalene's repeated sadness and uncertainty after she has heard the news of the Resurrection is never adequately explained. The dramatist's purpose seems instead to be one of expanding the number of scenes in which doubting mankind receives ocular demonstrations of the truth of Christ's resurrection. The playwright does not invent dialogue so much as fit together a design out of the liturgical materials that constituted his sources.

Still another text (selection 16), a twelfth-century *Peregrinus* or *Pilgrim* play from Beauvais, illustrates a further way in which the Easter story could be augmented without distorting the account of the visit to the tomb. What events took place after the Resurrection itself, and in what way do they amplify our understanding of that mystery? The dramatist turns to the Gospels (Luke 24:17–32 and John 20:25–28) for a description of Christ's subsequent visits to his disciples. The theme, of ocular proof of resurrection, echoes that of the *Visitatio* itself. The dramatist follows his biblical sources closely, presenting virtually all the dialogue in Luke verbatim or in a variety of metrical paraphrases. Performance took place during vespers on Easter Monday and was therefore entirely distinct from the *Visitatio* on Easter Sunday. Liturgical plays for the various days of the Easter season were not combined into long sequences as readily as were dramas of the Christmas season—another indication of the comparative slowness with which Easter drama developed.

By the late twelfth or early thirteenth century, to be sure, medieval church drama had produced lengthy and complex Easter plays at Montecassino in Italy and at Benediktbeuern in Bavarian Germany. These plays embody many episodes not found in the selections presented here, including, for example, scenes from the earlier life of Mary Magdalene, the story of Christ's Passion, and the visit of the three Marys on Easter morning to the spice merchant from whom they buy ointments to anoint Christ's body. (This last episode is also found in the Ripoll troper of the late eleventh or early twelfth century.) Belatedly, then, Easter drama did share in the extraordinary flourishing of all forms of church drama during the twelfth century. Because the Montecassino and Benediktbeuern Easter plays are relatively late and complex, and because they are not strictly speaking liturgical plays (that is, they were not performed as an integral part of the divine service of the Church), they belong to our discussion in Part II of twelfth-century church drama.

13. THE VISIT TO THE SEPULCHRE
(VISITATIO SEPULCHRI)
FROM AQUILEIA(?)

When the third response is finished, the sepulchre is visited with these verses, two brethren representing the holy women saying:

Who will roll back for us from the entrance the stone that we see covering the holy sepulchre?

Let the angels say:

Whom do you seek, O trembling women, weeping at this tomb?

The brethren reply:

We seek Jesus of Nazareth who was crucified.

The angels:

He is not here whom you seek, but going quickly tell his disciples and Peter that Jesus has risen.

Let the brethren representing the women, coming forward, turn to the people and to the choir, saying:

We came mourning to the tomb, we saw an angel of the Lord sitting there and saying that Jesus has risen.

Let the choir sing the antiphon:

Two ran together.

Thereupon two brethren display the shroud to the to the others, saying:

Behold, O companions, behold the shroud

Finito tertio responsorio, visitatur sepulchrum cum versibus, duo fratres in vice mulierum sanctarum dicentes:

Quis revolvet nobis ab ostio lapidem quem tegere sacrum cernimus sepulchrum?

Angeli dicant:

Quem quaeritis, o tremulae mulieres, in hoc tumulo plorantes?

Respondent fratres:

Jesum Nazarenum crucifixum quaerimus.

Angeli:

Non est hic quem quaeritis, sed cito euntes dicite discipulis eius et Petro quia surrexit Jesus.

Fratres vice mulierum venientes convertant se ad populum et ad chorum dicentes:

Ad monumentum venimus gementes, angelum Domini sedentem vidimus et dicentem quia surrexit Jesus.

Chorus cantet antiphonam:

Currebant duo simul.

Deinde ostendunt linteamina duo fratres aliis dicentes:

Cernitis, o socii, ecce linteamina et suda-

A text doubtfully assigned to Aquileia, Italy. The position of this ceremonial following the third response, and its conclusion with the singing of the *Te Deum*, clearly indicate performance at the end of Easter matins. Text based on Udine, Bibl. Arcivescovile, MS 234 (*olim* 38), Ordin. Aquilegiense (?) saec. xi, fol. 1ʳ–1ᵛ. Edited by Young, *Drama of the Medieval Church*, I, 628, and by Hardison, *Christian Rite and Christian Drama*, pp. 231–32.

and head-cloth, and the body is not to be
found in the sepulchre.

Thereupon:

He has risen.

8

Choir:

We praise you O God.

The people:

Lord have mercy upon us, *in a loud voice.*

rium, et corpus non est in sepulchro
inventum.

Deinde:

Surrexit.

Chorus:

Te Deum laudamus.

Populus:

Kyrieleison, *alta voce.*

14. THE VISIT TO THE SEPULCHRE
(VISITATIO SEPULCHRI)
FROM ST. LAMBRECHT

Meanwhile, near the end of the third lesson, let the custodian distribute a candle to each brother, and let the deacon re-vest himself in a white stole, and go sit on the stone beside the sepulchre. When after the second the third response has been begun, and all the candles which they hold in their hands have been lit, let the cantor arrange the procession as follows. First the students with the schoolmaster, then the abbot, after him those [clerics] who are older, then those who are younger and the uninstructed; but let those who are to visit the sepulchre in the persons of the holy women remain in the choir and veil their heads with humerals or with the hoods of the copes they are wearing. The rest of the community should go, as mentioned before, to the place of the sepulchre, and there be silent. Let the aforesaid three sing in a soft voice:

Who will roll back for us from the entrance the stone that we see covering the holy sepulchre?

To them let the deacon representing the angel answer, saying:

Whom do you seek, O trembling women, weeping at this tomb?

And they to him:

We seek Jesus of Nazareth who was crucified.

To them let him add:

Interim autem, dum est circa finem tertiae lectionis, distribuat custos singulas candelas singulis fratribus, et diaconus revestiat se stola candida, vadatque residere super lapidem juxta sepulchrum. Cum vero secundo tertium responsorium fuerit inceptum, candelis omnibus accensis quas habent in manibus, cantor processionem ordinet ita. Primo scolares cum pedagogo, deinde abbas, post illum seniores, dehinc juniores et indocti; sed illi qui in personis sanctarum feminarum visitare debent sepulchrum remaneant in choro et velent capita sua humeralibus vel capitiis capparum quas habent in se. Reliquus vadat, ut praedictum est, ad locum sepulchri conventus, ibique silentio facit. Illi praedicti tres remissa voce canant:

Quis revolvet nobis ab ostio lapidem quem tegere sacrum cernimus sepulcrum?

Quibus respondeat levita vice angeli dicens:

Quem quaeritis, o tremulae mulieres, in hoc tumulo plorantes?

Ad haec illi:

Jesum Nazarenum crucifixum quaerimus.

Quibus ille subjungat:

There are three texts of this play in Graz, Universitätsbibl.: MS II. 798, Brev. Monasterii Sancti Lamberti saec. xii ex., fol. 52ʳ–53ʳ (A); MS II. 193, Brev. Sancti Lamberti saec. xiv, fol. 51ᵛ–52ʳ (B); and MS III. 722, Brev. Sancti Lamberti saec. xiv, fol. 37ʳ–37ᵛ (C). The text is based, as in Young, *Drama of the Medieval Church*, I, 363–65, on the first MS, the others having more abbreviated responses. (The rubrics of all three are in substantial agreement.) This ceremonial is designed to be sung at the end of Easter matins, following the third lesson (see opening stage direction) and concluding with the singing of the *Te Deum*.

[1] S.D. *cantor:* chief singer. *humerals:* veils covering the shoulders.

He is not here whom you seek, but going quickly tell his disciples and Peter that Jesus has risen.

After this, as they draw near, let him rise and raise up the curtain and expose the sepulchre to view, and say to them:

Come and see the place where the Lord had been laid, alleluia, alleluia.   5

Let them, coming forward with bowed heads, inspect carefully within the sepulchre, and, lifting from there the woven cloth in which the cross had been wrapped and the kerchief which had been over the head of the cross, and returning thence, let them stand in the vicinity of the altar and, turned toward the assembly, let them sing in a loud voice:

We came mourning to the tomb, we saw an angel of the Lord sitting and saying that God has risen.

This said, let the whole community sing together, saying:

Tell us, Mary, what did you see on the way?

And let one of the three who visited the sepulchre say in a clear voice:

I saw the sepulchre of the living Christ, and the glory of his rising.

Let the second say:

Angelic witnesses, the head-cloth and the shroud.

And let the third add:

Christ, my hope, has risen; he will go before his followers into Galilee.   10

After this let all the community sing together as follows:

Non est hic quem quaeritis, sed cito euntes nuntiate discipulis eius et Petro quia surrexit Jesus.

Post haec illis accedentibus surgat et sublevet cortinam et sepulchrum patefaciat, dicatque ad illos:

Venite et videte locum ubi positus erat Dominus, alleluia, alleluia.

Qui venientes inclinatis capitibus considerare debent intra sepulchrum, et tollentes inde filacterium quo involuta crux fuerat et sudarium quod fuerat super crucis caput, ac inde recedentes stent ante proximum altare et versi contra conventum canant alta voce:

Ad monumentum venimus gementes, angelum Domini sedentem vidimus et dicentem quia surrexit Deus.

Quo dicto, totus conventu[s] concinat dicens:

Dic nobis, Maria, quid vidisti in via?

Et unus ex illis tribus qui visitabant sepulchrum dicat clara voce:

Sepulchrum Christi viventis, et gloriam vidi resurgentis.

Alter vero dicat:

Angelicos testes, sudarium et vestes.

Et tertius subjungat:

Surrexit Christus, spes mea; praecedet suos in Galilaea.

Post haec totus conventus concinat ita:

7–12 *Tell us Mary . . . triumphant king:* These six verses, virtually half the dialogue of this play, are a somewhat shortened and rearranged version of the Easter sequence known as *Victimae paschali,* written in the eleventh century. It is a rhymed composition in the form of a dialogue between Mary and her questioners, and thus was a potentially immediate source for dramatic treatment. The playwright here distributes Mary's answer to the three Marys at the tomb. For a text of the sequence, see Young, I, 273.

The single, truthful Mary ought to be believed more than [the lying mob of Jews.]

Verse:

We know that Christ [has truly risen from the dead; have mercy on us, triumphant king.]

Then let the people themselves begin this loud hymn [in German]:

Three women went to the Lord's grave.

Meantime, while the people produce this loud sound, let the cantor appoint two, one old and the other young, who, after the shouting of the people has been finished, should come to the sepulchre, the youth first and let him wait; let the old man, following, gaze attentively into the tomb, and the other with him. And when these things are begun, let the cantor give the antiphon:

Two ran together, [and the other disciple hastened on before more swiftly than Peter, and came first to the tomb, alleluia.]

When this is finished, let the three [women] mentioned above come before the near altar holding up the shroud, so that it may be seen by all, singing together thus:

Behold, O companions, behold the shroud and head-cloth, and the body is not to be found in the sepulchre.

And thereupon let them raise the cross on high, singing out loudly together in a resounding voice as follows:

The Lord has risen from the sepulchre.

Let the whole community sing this together with them. After this let the abbot or prior begin We praise you O God; *and, singing this hymn, let them return to the choir, while the people sing loudly together [in German]* Christ has risen.

Credendum est magis soli Mariae veraci, quam [Judaeorum turbae fallaci.]

Versus:

Scimus Christum [surrexisse ex mortuis vere; tu autem, victor rex, miserere.]

Tunc incipiat ipsa plebs istum clamorem:

Giengen dreie vrowen ce vronem grabe.

Interim vero, dum plebs clamorem istum concrepat, cantor ordinet duos, unum senem et alterum juvenem, qui, postquam finitus fuerit clamor populi, veniant ad sepulchrum, juvenis primo et subsistat, senex vero subsequens prospiciat in monumentum, et alter cum eo. Et illis factum incipientibus imponat cantor antiphonam:

Currebant duo simul, [et ille alius discipulus praecucurrit citius Petro, et venit primus ad monumentum, alleluia.]

Qua finita, veniant illi tres supradicti ante aram proximam sublevantes linteamina, ut ab omnibus videantur, ita concinentes:

Cernitis, o socii, ecce linteamina et sudarium, et corpus non est in sepulchro inventum.

Atque mox extollant crucem in altum sonora voce conclamantes ita:

Surrexit Dominus de sepulchro.

Quam simul cum eis concinat totus conventus. Post hanc incipiat abbas vel prior Te Deum laudamus; *et hunc hymnum canendo revertantur in chorum, plebe conclamante* Christ ist erstanden.

15

---

[13]S.D. *clamorem, concrepat:* The scribe's choice of words suggests he found the congregational singing unrefined.

15. [THE SERVICE] FOR REPRESENTING THE SCENE AT THE LORD'S SEPULCHRE (AD FACIENDAM SIMILITUDINEM DOMINICI SEPULCRI) *FROM FLEURY*

In order to represent the scene at the Lord's sepulchre, first let three brethren, prepared and vested in imitation of the three Marys, go forward haltingly and as though sorrowful, singing in alternation these verses. Let the first of them say:

Alas! the good shepherd is slain,
Whom no guilt polluted.
O lamentable deed!

The second:

Alas! the true shepherd has perished,
Who granted life to the dead.
O deplorable death!

The third:

Alas! wretched Jewish people,
Whom an abominable insanity makes frenzied.
Despicable nation!

The first:

Why have you condemned to unholy death   10
The holy one, with savage hate?

Ad faciendam similitudinem Dominici sepulcri, primum procedant tres fratres praeparati et vestiti in similitudinem trium Mariarum, pedetemtim et quasi tristes alternantes hos versus cantantes. Prima earum dicat:

Heu! pius pastor occidit,
quem culpa nulla infecit.
O res plangenda!

Secunda:

Heu! verus pastor obiit,
qui vitam functis contulit.
O mors lugenda!

Tertia:

Heu! nequam gens Judaica,
quam dira frendet vesania.
Plebs execranda!

Prima:

Cur nece pium impia
damnasti saeva invid[i]a?

From the Fleury playbook. This important manuscript is usually associated with the monastery of St.-Benoît-sur-Loire, at Fleury, although the link cannot certainly be traced back earlier than 1552. In the manuscript, this play immediately follows the Fleury Herod and Slaughter of the Innocents (see section D, following). Text based on Orleans, Bibl. de la Ville, MS 201 (*olim* 178), Miscellanea Floriacensia saec. XIII, pp. 220–25. It has been edited by Young, *Drama of the Medieval Church,* I, 393–97, and by several others. Performance takes place at the end of Easter matins.

¹S.D.: The three Marys enter and go in procession through the nave, singing until they reach the choir. At the sepulchre near the altar, the angel already awaits them (see the *Regularis Concordia* Visit to the Sepulchre, selection 11, l. 1 S.D.). The sepulchre must be large enough to permit the entrance of Peter and John (l. 43 S.D.) and to permit two angels to be heard singing from within it (l. 52 S.D.). On several occasions the action is directed not simply to the clergy but to the "people" or congregation in the nave.

O execrable wrath!

The second:

What did this just one deserve
That he ought to be crucified?
O damnable people!   15

The third:

Alas! what shall we do, despairingly,
Bereaved of our sweet master?
Alas, tearful destiny!

The first:

Let us go therefore quickly,
To do the only thing we can do   20
With devout mind.

The second:

With aromatic spices
Let us anoint the most sacred body,
With the most costly ones possible.

The third:

Let a mixture of balsam-nard prevent   25
The blessed flesh from putrifying
In the tomb.

*When they have come into the choir, let them go
to the tomb as if seeking, and singing all in unison
this verse:*

But we are not able to achieve this without
help.
Who will roll back this stone from the entrance of the tomb?

*To whom let an angel respond, sitting outside at
the head of the sepulchre, vested in a gilded white
robe, head covered with a mitre albeit unadorned,
holding a palm in the left hand, a branched
candlestick full of tapers in the right hand, and let
him speak in a moderate and very dignified voice:*

Whom do you seek in the sepulchre, O
followers of Christ?   30

The women:

Jesus of Nazareth who was crucified, O
heaven-dweller.

O ira nefanda!

Secunda:

Quid justus hic promeruit
quod crucifigi debuit?
O gens damnanda!

Tertia:

Heu! quid agemus misere,
dulci magistro orbatae?
Heu, sors lacrimanda!

Prima:

Eamus ergo propere,
quod solum quimus facere
mente devota.

Secunda:

Condimentis aromatum
ungamus corpus sanctissimum,
quo pretiosa.

Tertia:

Nardi vetet commixtio,
ne putrescat in tumulo
caro beata.

*Cum autem venerint in chorum, eant ad monu-
mentum et quasi quaerentes, et cantantes omnes
simul hunc versum:*

Sed nequimus hoc patrare
sine adjutorio.
Quisnam saxum hoc revolvet
ab monumenti ostio?

*Quibus respondeat angelus sedens foris ad
caput sepulcri, vestitus alba deaurata, mitra
tectus caput etsi d[e]infulatus, palmam in
sinistra, ramum candelarum plenum tenens in
manu dextera, et dicat moderata et admodum
gravi voce:*

Quem quaeritis in sepulcro, o Christicolae?

Mulieres:

Jhesum Nazarenum crucifixum, o caelicola.

Let the angel answer them:

Why, followers of Christ, do you seek the
    living among the dead?
He is not here, but has risen, as he predicted
    to the disciples.
Remember what just now he said to you in
    Galilee,
That it behoved Christ to suffer, and on the
    third day   35
To rise again with glory.

*Let the women, having turned toward the people,
sing:*

We came mourning to the tomb of the Lord;
    we have seen an angel of God sitting and
    saying that he has risen from death.

*After this, let Mary Magdalene, having left the
other two behind, approach the sepulchre, searching into which repeatedly let her say:*

Alas my sorrow, alas what dire anguish of
    sorrow,
That I am deprived of the presence of my
    beloved master!
Alas, who has taken the beloved body from
    the tomb?   40

*Thereafter, let her proceed swiftly to those who in
the likeness of Peter and John ought to manifest
themselves with heads erect, and let her say
standing before them as if saddened:*

They have taken away my Lord, and I do not
    know where they have laid him,
And the tomb has been discovered empty,
And the head-cloth with the shroud placed
    within.

*Let them, hearing these things, go quickly to the
sepulchre as if running, but let the younger, that is
to say John, arriving first, stand outside the
sepulchre; let the elder, that is to say Peter,*

Quibus respondeat angelus:

Quid, Christicolae, viventem quaeritis
    cum mortuis?
Non est hic, sed surrexit, praedixit ut
    discipulis.
Mementote quid iam vobis locutus est
    in Galilaea,
Quia Christum opportebat pati atque
    die tertia
Resurgere cum gloria.

Mulieres conversae ad populum cantent:

Ad monumentum Domini venimus gemen-
    tes, angelum Dei sedentem vidimus et
    dicentem quia surrexit a morte.

*Post haec Maria Magdalene, relictis duabus
aliis, accedat ad sepulcrum, in quod saepe
aspicie[n]s dicat:*

Heu dolor, heu quam dira doloris
    angustia,
Quod dilecti sum orbata magistri
    praesentia!
Heu, quis corpus tam dilectum sustulit
    e tumulo?

*Deinde pergat velo[citer] ad illos qui in
similtu[di]ne Petri et Johannis pr[ae]stare
debent ere[cti], stansque ante eos quasi
trist[is] dicat:*

Tulerunt Dominum meum, et nescio ubi
    posuerunt eum,
Et monumentum vacuum est inventum,
Et sudarium cum sindone intus est
    repositum.

*Illi autem, haec audientes, vel[ociter] pergant
ad sepulcrum acsi curre[ntes], sed junior,
scilicet Johannes, praeveniens st[et] extra
sepulcrum; senior vero, scilicet Pe[trus],*

32–36Cf. Luke 24:5–7.

37S.D.: Mary Magdalene's two companions evidently retire for a time; they rejoin Mary at l.
70.

40S.D.: Peter and John are perhaps members of the choir when Mary approaches them.

following him, enter at once; and afterwards let John enter. When they have come forth from within, let John say as if wondering:

They are marvels that we have seen!
Has the Lord been taken away by stealth? 45

Peter to him:

Nay, as he predicted while living,
The Lord has risen, I believe.

John:

But why is the head-cloth with the shroud
Evident in the sepulchre?

[Peter:]

For this reason, that to one rising from the
    dead they were not necessary; 50
Yes indeed, they remain here as proofs of the
    resurrection.

As they depart, let Mary proceed to the sepulchre, and first let her say:

Alas my sorrow, alas what dire anguish!

and so on. Let two angels, seated within the sepulchre, address her, saying:

Woman, why do you weep?

Mary:

Because they have taken away my Lord, and
    I do not know where they have laid him.

An angel:

Do not weep, Mary, the Lord has risen,
    alleluia. 55

Mary:

My heart is burning with desire to see my
    Lord; I seek and I cannot discover where
    they have laid him, alleluia.

Meanwhile let one come made up in the likeness of a gardener, and, standing at the mouth of the sepulchre, let him say:

Woman, why do you weep? Whom do you
    seek?

sequens eum, statim intret; postquam et Joh-[annes in]tret. Cum inde exierint, Johannes quasi [ad]mirans dicat:

Miranda sunt quae vidimus!
An furtim sublatus est Dominus?

Cui Petrus:

Imo, ut praedixit vivus,
surrexit, credo, Dominus.

Johannes:

Sed cur liquit in sepulcro
sudarium cum lintheo?

[Petrus:]

Ista, quia resurgenti   non era[n]t
    necessaria,
Imo resurrectionis   restant haec
    indicia.

Illis autem abeuntibus, acced[at] Maria ad sepulcrum, et prius dicat:

Heu dolor, heu quam dira!

et cetera. Quam alloquantur duo angeli sedentes infra sepulcrum, dicentes:

Mulier, quid ploras?

Maria:

Quia tulerunt Dominum meum, et nescio
    ubi posuerunt eum.

Angelus:

Noli flere, Maria, resurrexit Dominus,
    alleluia.

Maria:

Ardens est cor meum desiderio videre
    Dominum meum; quaero et non
    invenio ubi posuerunt eum, alleluia.

Interim veniat quidam praeparatus in similitudinem hortulani, stansque ad caput sepulcri et dicat:

Mulier, quid ploras? Quem quaeris?

Mary:

Good sir, if you have borne him hence, say to me where you have laid him, and let me bear him away.

And he:

Mary!

Let her say, prostrating herself at his feet:

Master!

And let him draw himself back, and, as if avoiding her touch, let him say:

Do not touch me, for I have not yet ascended to my Father, and to your Father, my God, and your God.

Thus let the gardener depart. But let Mary say, turned toward the people:

Congratulate me, all you who love the Lord, for he whom I sought has appeared to me, and, while weeping at the tomb, I saw my Lord, alleluia.

Then let the two angels come to the door of the tomb, in such a manner that they are visible without, and let them say:

Come and see the place where the Lord had been laid, alleluia.
Do not fear.
Now change your sad countenance;
Announce that Jesus lives;
Go now to Galilee.
If you wish to see [him], hasten.
Going quickly say to the disciples that the Lord has risen, alleluia.

Then let the women departing from the sepulchre say to the people:

The Lord has risen from the sepulchre, who for us hung on the cross, alleluia.

This done, let them spread out the shroud, saying to the people:

Behold, you companions, here is the shroud of the blessed body,

Maria:

Domine, si tu sustulisti eum, dicito mihi ubi posuisti eum, et ego eum tollam.

Et ille:

Maria!

Quae procidens ad pedes eius et dicat:

60   Raboni!

At ille subtrahat se, et, quasi tactum eius devitans, dicat:

Noli me tangere, nondum enim ascendi ad Patrem meum, et Patrem vestrum, Deum meum, et Deum vestrum.

Sic discedat hortulanus. Maria vero conversa ad populum dicat:

Congratulamini mihi omnes qui diligitis Dominum, quia quem quaerebam ap[p]aruit mihi, et dum flerem ad monumentum, vidi Dominum meum, alleluia.

Tunc duo angeli exeant ad ostium sepulcri, ita ut appareant foris, et dicant:

Venite et videte locum ubi positus erat Dominus, alleluia.
Nolite timere vos.
65   Vultum tristem iam mutate;
Jhesum vivum nunciate;
Galilaeam iam adite.
Si placet videre, festinate.
Cito euntes dicite discipulis quia surrexit Dominus, alleluia.

Tunc mulieres discedentes a sepul ro dicant ad plebem:

70   Surrexit Dominus de sepulcro, qui pro nobis pependit in ligno, alleluia.

Hoc facto, expandant sindonem, dicentes ad plebem:

Cernite, vos socii, sunt corporis ista beati

Which lay abandoned in the empty tomb.

Linthea, quae vacuo jacuere relicta sepulcro.

Afterwards let them place the shroud on the altar, with which, turning themselves about, let them sing alternately these verses. Let the first say:

Postea ponant sindonem super altare, cum qua revertentes alternent hos versus. Prima dicat:

Today the God of Gods has risen!

Resurrexit hodie Deus Deorum!

The second:

Secunda:

In vain do you seal the stone, Jewish people.

Frustra signas lapidem, plebs Judaeorum.

The third:

Tertia:

Join now with the Christian people.   75

Jungere iam populo Christianorum.

And again let the first say:

Item prima dicat:

The king of the angels has risen today.

Resurrexit hodie rex angelorum.

The second:

Secunda:

The throng of the just is led from darkness.

Ducitur de tenebris turba piorum.

The third:

Tertia:

The entrance to the kingdom of heaven is opened.

Reseratur aditus regni caelorum.

Meanwhile let him who earlier was the gardener come in the likeness of the Lord, vested in a white dalmatic, adorned with a white infula, a costly phylacterium on his head, having a cross with a standard in his right hand, a garment woven of gold in the left hand, and let him say to the women:

Interea is qui ante fuit hortulanus in similitudinem Domini veniat, dalmaticatus candida dalmatica, candida infula infulatus, phylacteria pretiosa in capite, crucem cum labaro in dextra, textum auro paratum in sinistra habens, et dicat mulieribus:

Do not fear; go, announce to my brethren that they should go into Galilee; there will they see me, as I have foretold to them.

Nolite timere vos; ite, nuntiate fratribus meis ut eant in Galilaeam; ibi me videbunt, sicut praedixi eis.

[The Choir:]

[Chorus:]

Alleluia, the Lord has risen today!   80

Alleluia, resurrexit hodie Dominus!

When that is finished, let them say in unison:

Quo finito, dicant omnes insimul:

The mighty lion, Christ, the son of God.

Leo fortis, Christus, filius Dei.

And let the choir say We praise you O God.

Et chorus dicat Te Deum laudamus.

---

⁷⁸S.D. *dalmatic:* an outer vestment worn by a deacon or prelate, with a slit on each side of the skirt, and wide sleeves. *infula:* a fillet of wool worn on the priest's forehead. *phylacterium:* amulet, charm. *standard:* the *labarum,* sacred banner or standard. *garment . . . gold:* the *paratorium,* pall used to cover the chalice before and after mass.

16. THE SERVICE [FOR REPRESENTING] THE PILGRIM, AT VESPERS OF THE SECOND HOLY DAY OF EASTER [EASTER MONDAY] (ORDO AD PEREGRINUM IN SECUNDA FERIA PASCHE AD VESPERAS) FROM BEAUVAIS

Let the two disciples say as they are journeying:

Jesus, our redemption,

as far as May you content us with your countenance. *To whom, as he approaches, let the pilgrim say:*

What manner of communications are these that you have one to another, as you walk, and are sad?

Let Cleophas the disciple answer alone:

Are you only a stranger in Jerusalem, and have not known the things that are come to pass there in these days?

And the pilgrim:

What things?

And the two disciples:

Duo discipuli euntes dicant:

Jhesu, nostra redemptio,

usque Nos tuo vultu saties. *Quibus appropinquans peregrinus dicat:*

Qui sunt hi sermones quos confertis ad invicem ambulantes, et estis tristes?

Cleophas discipulus solus respondeat:

Tu solus peregrinus es in Jerusalem, et non cognovisti quae facta sunt in illa his diebus?

Et peregrinus:

Quae?

Et duo discipuli:

A twelfth-century play from Beauvais. Text based on Paris, Bibliothèque Nationale, Nouvelles Acquisitions, MS lat. 1064, Miscellanea liturgica saec. xii, fol. 8ʳ–11ᵛ. It has been edited by Young, *Drama of the Medieval Church*, I, 467–69.

[1] S.D.: The later Rouen text of this play specifies that the disciples are to be "clothed in tunics and copes . . . carrying staffs and wallets in the likeness of travelers; and let them have caps upon their heads and be bearded." The actors for these two roles are chosen from the ranks of the petty-canons. The actor of Christ is chosen from the upper rank in the choir; he is costumed "in an alb and an amice [gown-like vestment and fur-lined hood], barefooted, bearing the cross upon his right shoulder." The disciples enter from the vestry; Christ comes to them through the right aisle of the church. Emmaus is "a structure in the middle of the nave of the church, prepared in the likeness of the village Emmaus." It must have a table, and perhaps a curtain enabling Christ to "vanish" suddenly.

[1] For the complete text of this hymn, see Young, *Drama of the Medieval Church*, I, 641–42.

[2] *What manner . . .* etc.: Much of the dialogue in this play is derived from the Vulgate, either verbatim or in versified paraphrase. See Luke 24:17–43 for the primary source.

Concerning Jesus of Nazareth, a man who
was a prophet, mighty in deed and in
word before God and all the people.   5

Then one of them:

He whom the Jews condemned
And killed on the cross,
And whom we nevertheless hoped
Should have redeemed us.

Then let the other say:

Already three days had gone past,   10
Since these things had been done;
And certain women [of our company] made
us astonished,
Who had seen the sepulchre again
And found it empty.

Again the other one:

They reported that they had seen   15
A vision of angels,
Who had declared unto them
His resurrection;
Certain of them that were with us ran [to the
sepulchre],
And found all to be   20
Even as the women had said;
But him they saw not.

Then let the pilgrim say:

O you that be his disciples,
Why so foolish, slow of heart, disbelieving,
Do you not know what, from the beginning
of time,   25
Every prophet has maintained?
Ought not Christ to have suffered [these
things],
And to enter into glory?

Thus as they go on let him say to them:

These things Moses had foreshown,
When he slew the paschal lamb;   30
Isaiah had foretold the same,
When he cried out that the very lamb
Would be scourged and be silent,
And, having been slain, would bear our sins.
He was sacrificed, he said, when he willed, 35

De Jhesu Nazareno, qui fuit vir propheta,
potens in opere et sermone coram Deo
et omni populo.

Tunc unus:

Quem Judaei damnaverunt
et in cruce occiderunt,
et nos quidem sperabamus
quod nos esset redempturus.

Tunc alter dicat:

Iam tres dies abierunt,
facta ista quod fuerunt;
et nos quaedam terruerunt,

quae sepulchrum reviserunt
vacuumque reppererunt.

Item alter:

Se vidisse narraverunt
angelorum visionem,
qui et eis indixerunt
eius resurrectionem;
sed ex nostris cucurrerunt,

qui sic cuncta reppererunt,
sicut illae retulerunt,
sed ipsum non invenerunt.

Tunc peregrinus dicat:

O cum sitis eius discipuli,
cur tam stulti, tardi, increduli,
ignoratis ab ortu saeculi

quae prophetae dixere singuli?
Nonne Christum pati oportuit

et intrare gloriam decuit?

Sic in eundo dicat eis:

Haec Moyses significaverat,
cum paschalem agnum occiderat;
Isaias idem praedixerat,
cum ut agnum illum clamaverat
flagellari et obmutescere,
et occisum peccata tollere.
Oblatus est, inquit, cum voluit

And he has borne our sins.
And thus, with all the prophets as witnesses,
Now you ought to believe firmly
That Christ, having loosed the bonds of death,
Is alive, and eternally so.   40

*Then as if wishing to go away let the pilgrim
say to them:*

We may not delay longer, my brethren,
For now it is needful for us to go farther.

Then let them restrain him and let one say:

With evening descending,
The time of night draws nigh,
And the pathways are no longer open;   45
Stay.

And let the other say:

Abide with us, for it is toward evening, and
the day is far spent.

*Then let both lead him, and, as if urging him
toward a lodging, let them say:*

Now the sun, on the verge of setting, urges
hospitality;
We beseech you, father, enter our
dwelling;
For the discourse of your teaching
pleases us,   50
Which you recount concerning the victory of
our master.

*And let them lead him to the table, the choir mean-
while singing:*

And they urged him saying: Remain with us,
Lord, for evening draws on, alleluia.

*Then let the pilgrim himself, at the table, say
alone:*

And he went in with them, and it came to
pass, as he sat at meat with them:

Then let him take bread, and let him say:

He took the bread, blessed it (*let him make
the sign of the cross*), and broke it (*let
him break it*), and gave it to them.

---

et peccata nostra sustinuit.
Sic et cunctis prophetis testibus,
Christus, mortis solutis nexibus,
quod sit vivus, et hoc perenniter,
iam debetis credere firmiter.

*Tunc quasi recedere volens peregrinus dicat
eis:*

Ne moremur, fratres, diutius,
iam oportet nos ire longius.

Tunc retineant eum et dicat unus:

Declinante vespera,
noctis instant tempora,
nec patent itinera;
subsiste.

Et alter dicat:

Mane nobiscum, quoniam adversperascit
et inclinata est iam dies.

*Tunc ambo eum ducant et, quasi cogentes eum
ad hospitium, dicant:*

Iam sol vergens ad occasum   suadet
hospitium,
Nostrum, pater, obsecramus   intres
habitaculum;
Placent enim tui nobis   sermonis
colloquia,
Quae de nostri referebas   magistri
victoria.

*Et ducant eum ad mensam, cantante interim
choro:*

Et coegerunt illum dicentes: Mane
nobiscum, Domine, quia advesperascit,
alleluia.

Tunc ipse peregrinus solus ad mensam dicat:

Et intravit cum illis, et factum est dum
recumberet cum eis:

Tunc accipiat panem et dicat:

Accepit panem, benedixit (*faciat* +), ac
fregit (*frangat*), et porrigebat eis.

And let him give to them, and withdraw. Let the two arise looking at one another, and let them go through the church as if hunting for him and singing:

Did not our heart burn within us for Jesus, while he talked with us by the way, and while he opened to us the scriptures? Alas, wretched ones, alas! Wretched ones, alas! Wretched ones! Where was our understanding? Where did our discernment vanish?

Then let them turn to the choir, and let the choir sing:

The Lord has risen and has appeared to Peter, alleluia.

Thereupon let the Lord, coming in another likeness, say to them:

Peace be with you. I am he. Fear not. Why are you disturbed, and what thoughts arise in your hearts?

Then let him show them his hands and feet saying:

See my hands and my feet, signifying I am he. Touch and see, for a spirit does not have flesh and bone as you see me to have.

And, as he disappears thus, let the choir sing:

The Lord has risen from the sepulchre, who for us hung on the cross, alleluia, alleluia, alleluia.

Then let Thomas, who had been absent, come, and as he stands in their midst let two of them say to him on behalf of the others:

Truly, Thomas, we saw the Lord,
Who has destroyed the kingdom of death.

Thomas to them:

Except I shall see the print of the nails,

Et det eis, et recedat. Duo illi se invicem aspicientes surgant, et vadant per ecclesiam quasi quaerentes eum et cantantes:

Nonne cor nostrum ardens erat in nobis de Jesu, dum loqueretur nobis in via et aperiret nobis scripturas? Heu, miseri, heu! Miseri, heu! Miseri! Ubi erat sensus noster? Quo intellectus abierat?

55

Tunc convertant se ad chorum, et chorus cantet:

Surrexit Dominus et apparuit Petro, alleluia.

Mox veniens Dominus in alia effigie dicat eis:

Pax vobis. Ego sum. Nolite timere. Quid turbati estis, et cogitationes ascendunt in corda vestra?

Tunc ostendat eis manus et pedes dicens:

Videte manus meas et pedes meos, quia ego ipse sum. Palpate et videte quia spiritus carnem et ossa non habet sicut me videtis habere.

Et, sic recedente eo, cantet chorus:

Surrexit Dominus de sepulchro, qui pro nobis pependit in ligno, alleluia, alleluia, alleluia.

Tunc veniat Thomas, qui defuerat, et stanti in medio dicant ei duo pro aliis:

60

Vere, Thoma, vidimus Dominum, qui destruxit mortis imperium.

Quibus Thomas:

Nisi fixuram clavorum videro,

62–75See John 20:25–29.

And shall touch the wound with my finger,
And thrust my hand into his side,
Know this: I will never believe.   65

Then, coming into their midst, let the Lord say to all:

Peace be unto you. I am he, alleluia. Fear not, alleluia.

Thereupon let him say to Thomas:

Thomas, now examine closely the wounds of my body.

And let him show [them] to him:

Put your finger in the place of the wound,
And now be not faithless in me,
Proffering an example of faithfulness to posterity.   70

And let Thomas, prostrating himself before his feet, say:

O Lord Jesus, maker of the heavens,
I believe that you live, and, believing, I make my confession.
That I was skeptical, overlook it, I implore you,
My God and my Lord!

The Lord to him:

Because you have seen me, Thomas, you have believed; blessed are they that have not seen, and yet have believed, alleluia.   75

Then let the cantor begin Christ arising. *The verse* The disciples rejoiced, *and the prayer of the Resurrection.*

et digito vulnus palpavero,
atque manum in latus misero,
hoc sciatis, nunquam credidero.

Tunc in medio veniens Dominus dicat omnibus:

Pax vobis. Ego sum, alleluia. Nolite timere, alleluia.

Deinde dicat Thomae:

Thoma, nunc vulnera conspice corporis.

Et ostendat ei:

Infer et digitum in locum vulneris,
et iam incredulus in me ne fueris,
exemplum fidei praebendo posteris.

Et Thomas procidens ad pedes eius dicat:

O Jhesu Domine, caelorum conditor,
te credo vivere, credens et fateor.

Quod fui dubius, ignosce, deprecor,

Deus meus et Dominus meus!

Cui Dominus:

Quia vidisti me, Thoma, credidisti; beati qui non viderunt et crediderunt, alleluia.

Tunc cantor incipiat Christus resurgens. *Versus* Gavisi sunt discipuli, *et oratio de Resurrectione.*

Liturgical Beginnings

D. ELEVENTH- AND TWELFTH-CENTURY CHRISTMAS DRAMA

THE EARLIEST DRAMATIC ceremonies of the Christmas season bear a striking resemblance to those of Easter. This resemblance can be seen in selection 17, an eleventh-century text from Limoges, which is not a full-scale drama but a trope or embellishment of the liturgy intended to precede the introit of the third mass of Christmas. As in the familiar Easter dialogue between the three Marys and the angel, the shepherd sare asked "Whom do you seek?" (*Quem quaeritis?*), are told the joyful news of man's salvation, and are then enjoined to announce these glad tidings to others. The position of this composition before the introit is one that was often used for the Easter *Quem quaeritis*. Once again the theme is human witnessing of a divine miracle. In its antiphonal form, this composition resembles those liturgical responsories and antiphons from which the Visit to the Sepulchre drew its materials.

Probably, Christmas ceremonials such as this one first came into being in the late tenth century through direct imitation of the Easter *Quem quaeritis*. We cannot be certain of this indebtedness (owing to the uncertainty of manuscript dating and the presumed loss of other manuscripts), but the indebtedness seems likely since the tenth-century Christmas liturgy did not already feature quasidramatic ceremonials resembling the Burial and Elevation of the Host out of which a Christmas drama might independently emerge. On the other hand, representations of the Bethlehem nativity scene (the crèche) were common in early medieval churches, and the festive atmosphere of the season must have seemed conducive to mimetic forms of celebration.

Once it had begun, in any case, Christmas drama expanded much more rapidly than did Easter drama. The evidence from the early play texts will not support a hypothesis of orderly evolution, beginning with tropes like that of Limoges (*Quem quaeritis in praesepe?*, "Whom do you seek in the manger?"), and expanding into simple plays about the shepherds before venturing into other Nativity subjects such as the coming of the Magi and the slaughter of the Innocents. Instead, the Christmas plays we have from the eleventh and twelfth centuries are surprisingly ambitious in their scope. A number of them combine the shepherds' visit to the manger with a longer dramatization of the Magi's encounter with Herod. Although a few liturgical plays solely about the shepherds' visit have survived from the thirteenth and fourteenth centuries, notably from Rouen, independent plays on this subject are generally scarce in medieval drama.

One reason for the scarcity of shepherds' plays may be that Christmas day was too liturgically crowded to allow for a play of any length. Christmas morning had to provide for matins before daybreak, followed by three masses. The early tropes, such as that from Limoges, were fitted easily enough into the introit of the third mass; but the shepherds' plays (sung at the end of matins in those few texts that survive) may have seemed like too great an interruption. One apparent solution was to stage the shepherds' visit as part of a larger Christmas play on another important holy day, Epiphany (January 6). As the last of the twelve days of Christmas and the celebration of the coming of the Magi, Epiphany was an appropriate time for a festive drama.

The Fleury play of Herod (selection 18), sung presumably at the end of matins on Epiphany, shows the tendency of twelfth-century Christmas drama toward rapid expansion and the inclusion of materials from different feast days of the Christmas season. The play is significantly longer and more elaborate than the Visit to the Sepulchre from the same Fleury manuscript (selection 15, above). It includes the shepherds' visit to the manger, with the familiar midwives of apocryphal legend and their questioning of the shepherds: "Whom do you seek?" Staging is elaborate throughout, with processions and multiple entrances making extensive use of interior space. A multitude of angels appears "on high," evidently from some elevated vantage point in the church. A star rises from the vicinity of the altar (guided presumably by wires and pulleys), and leads the Magi thence to the manger (located near a door in the nave, or main body of the church) by way of the entrance to the choir, where the Magi address bystanders as citizens of Jerusalem. Herod, enthroned on his platformed station probably near the east end of the nave between the choir entrance and the manger, dispatches messengers and receives the Magi. His learned scribes, who in a separate room have been bearded and otherwise made up for their performance, consult tomes to demonstrate their erudition. The two chief acting locations, Herod's sumptuous throne and Christ's humble manger, represent spatially the conflict between a corrupt tyrant and the defenseless babe who will save mankind. Prince of the world against Prince of heaven: the battle is joined.

Another important holy day of the Christmas season, Innocents' Day (December 28), also gave rise to liturgical plays about King Herod and the infancy of Christ. The appointed Gospel for Innocents' Day tells of Herod's attempt to destroy Christ by massacring all the infants of Bethlehem, and of the Holy Family's escape into Egypt guided by an angel of the Lord (see Matthew 2:16–18). This narrative is a close sequel to Herod's encounter with the three Magi, and indeed the Fleury Slaughter of the Innocents (selection 19) follows immediately after the Herod play in the Fleury play-book as though the plays were intended to be performed in that order. The two feasts of Epiphany and Holy Innocents were celebrated simultaneously for a time in the early Church. In some twelfth-century churches, according-ly, the Innocents play may actually have been sung on Epiphany following the Herod play. At Fleury, however, the Innocents play was probably sung at the end of matins on Innocents' day, in its liturgically correct position. The Herod play ends with the customary final *Te Deum* and with the explicit phrase *Sic finit* (thus it ends); so does the Slaughter of the Innocents. Even though the narrative sequence of events in the Gospels would seem to require that the Herod story be performed first, Fleury seems to have presented these plays in reverse order with the Innocents play on December 28 and the Herod play on January 6. Even at Christmas, then, despite the trend toward longer plays combining more than one holy day, individual plays might still cling to their proper liturgical occasions.

The theme of the Slaughter of the Innocents is the paradoxical triumph of the weak and defenseless over the tyrants of this world, as celebrated in the Beatitudes of the Sermon on the Mount ("Blessed are the meek, for they shall inherit the earth," Matthew 5:5) and in the Virgin Mary's hymn of praise known as the *Magnificat*: "He has put down princes from their thrones, and has exalted those of low degree" (Luke 1:52). Traditionally, the Feast of the Innocents on December 28 was an occasion for choristers and lesser clergy to escape briefly from the normal restrictions of their severely formalized lives. A Boy Bishop, appointed for the day, was allowed to boss around his ec-clesiastical superiors; outrageous lampooning of the service gave choristers the opportunity to make braying noises or grimaces. The Fleury play in-dulges in none of this prankishness, but it does give a prominent role to the children marching in the procession. Quite possibly these children are "postulants," or young candidates for admission to the religious community where this play is sung. They are associated throughout the play with the Lamb of God, who leads their procession and symbolizes the innocent sacri-fice in which they are to share. Their sacrifice and subsequent reunion with Christ in eternal life gives added meaning to the familiar biblical text: "Suffer the little children to come unto me." The play is also noteworthy for its poetically elaborate laments, anticipating those of Christ's mother Mary at the foot of the cross.

In staging, the play resembles the Fleury Herod play, with extensive use of procession. At times, more than one action occurs simultaneously. The children proceed through the monastery building and then enter the nave,

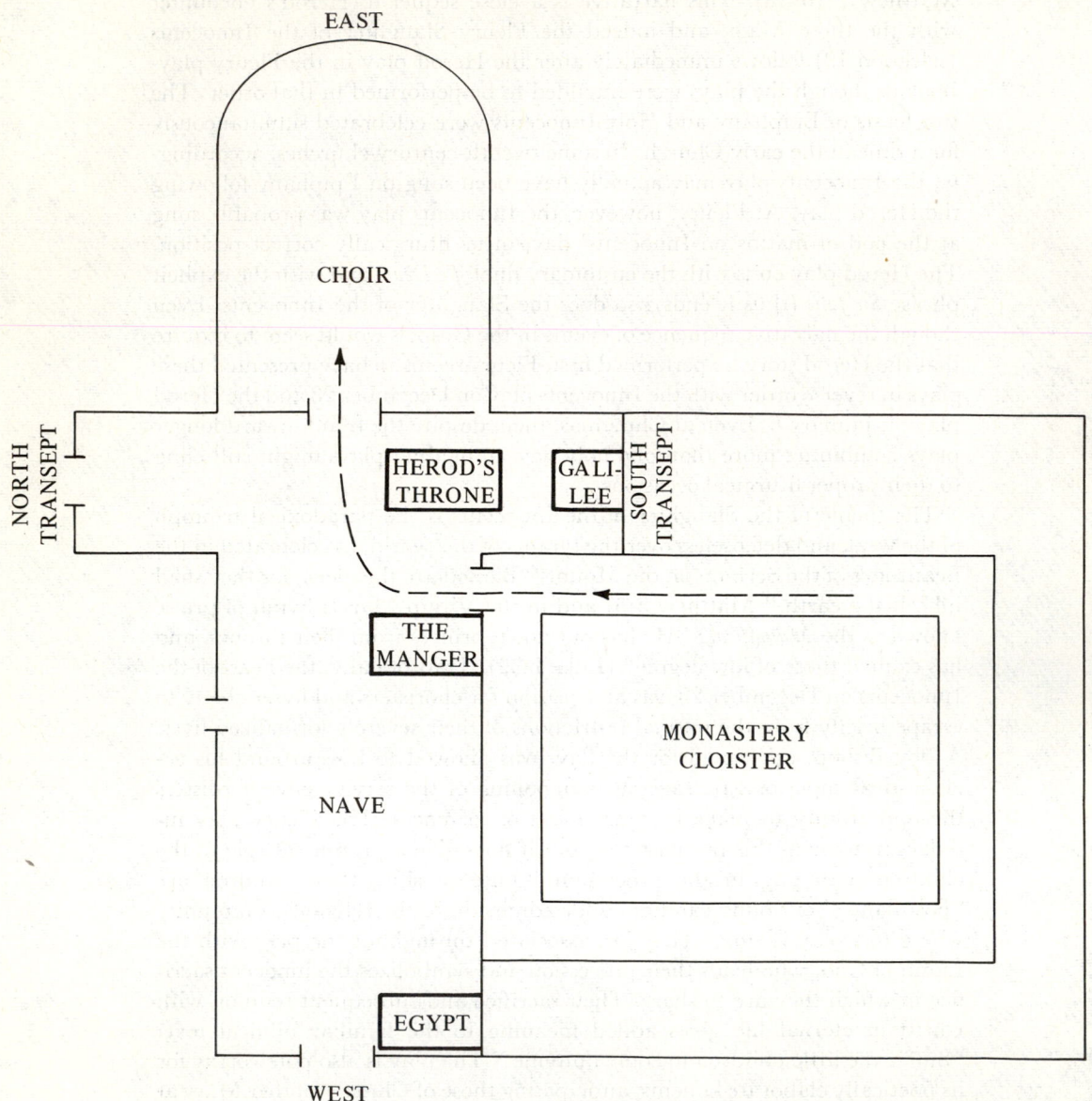

A plan of the Church of St. Benoit-sur-Loire (Fleury)
showing possible acting locations for the Slaughter of the Innocents
and processional route for the children

EAST

CHOIR

NORTH TRANSEPT

HEROD'S
THRONE

GALI-
LEE

SOUTH TRANSEPT

THE
MANGER

MONASTERY
CLOISTER

NAVE

EGYPT

WEST

Based on Karl Young, *Ordo Rachelis* (*University of Wisconsin Studies in Language and Literature*,
Number 4, Madison, 1919). See also Arnold Williams, *The Drama of Medieval England*
(East Lansing: Michigan State University Press, 1961), p. 35.

following the lamb "hither and thither"; Herod receives homage at his throne, located probably in the nave near the entrance to the choir; an angel appears over the manger (stationed possibly at the door to the monastery) to warn Joseph and the Holy Family to flee into Egypt (located perhaps at the west door of the nave). The children are slain as they pass near Herod's throne, and, after they are lamented by Rachel, are aroused by the voice of the angel singing "from above." They enter the choir in procession while Herod is removed from his throne and the angel gives Joseph notice to return into Galilee.

17. FOR THE MASS OF OUR LORD
(AD DOMINICAM MISSAM)
FROM LIMOGES

Whom do you seek in the manger, shepherds, say?

The Redeemer Christ our Lord, a child wrapped in swaddling clothes, according to the angelic proclamation.

Here is the little one with his mother Mary, of whom formerly, in prophesying, the prophet Isaiah had said: Behold, a virgin will conceive and bring forth a son; and now, as you go, say that he has been born.

Alleluia, alleluia! Now truly we know that Christ has been born on earth, of whom let all sing with the prophet, saying:

Psalm: A child is born.

Quem quaeritis in praesepe, pastores, dicite?

Salvatorem Christum Dominum, infantem pannis involutum, secundum sermonem angelicum.

Adest hic parvulus cum Maria matre sua, de qua dudum vaticinando Isaias dixerat propheta: Ecce virgo concipiet et pariet filium; et nunc euntes dicite quia natus est.

Alleluia, alleluia! Iam vere scimus Christum natum in terris, de quo canite omnes cum propheta, dicentes:

Psalmus: Puer natus est.

5

From Limoges, eleventh century. The final phrase, *Puer natus est,* begins the introit for the third mass of Christmas day. Many phrases parallel the *Quem quaeritis in sepulchro* for Easter. The text is based on Paris, Bibliothèque Nationale, MS lat. 887, Trop. Lemovicense saec. xi, fol. 9ᵛ. Edited by Young, *Drama of the Medieval Church,* II, 4.

[3]*Behold a virgin . . .* etc.: See Isaiah 7:14.

18. THE SERVICE FOR REPRESENTING HEROD
([I]NCIPIT ORDO AD REPRAESENTANDUM HERODEM)
FROM FLEURY

When Herod and the other persons have been made ready, let some angel appear on high with a multitude [of angels]. At the sight of this, the shepherds are thoroughly frightened; let [the angel] proclaim deliverance to them, the other [angels] remaining thus far silent:

Parato Herode et ceteris personis, tunc quidam angelus cum multitudine in excelsis ap-[þ]areat. Quo viso, pastores perterriti; salutem annuntiet eis de ceteris adhuc tacentibus:

Fear not, for behold I bring you good tidings of great joy, which shall be to all people; for unto us is born this day in the city of David a saviour of the world. And this shall be a sign unto you: You shall find the babe wrapped in swaddling clothes and lying in a manger between two beasts.

Nolite timere vos, ecce enim evangelizo vobis gaudium magnum, quod erit omni populo, quia natus est nobis hodie salvator mundi in civitate David. Et hoc vobis signum: Invenietis infantem pannis involutum et positum in praesepio in medio duum animalium.

1

And suddenly let all the multitude with the angel say:

Et subito omnis multitudo cum angelo dicat:

Glory to God in the highest, and on earth peace to men of good will, alleluia, alleluia!

Gloria in excelsis Deo, et in terra pax hominibus bonae voluntatis, alleluia, alleluia!

2

Then let them [the shepherds], rising, sing among

Tunc demum surgentes cantent intra se

From the Fleury playbook, usually associated with the monastery of St.-Benoît-sur-Loire at Fleury. This play is followed immediately in the manuscript by the Slaughter of the Innocents (see next selection) and then by the Visit to the Sepulchre (see selection 15, above). Performance was probably at the end of matins on Epiphany (January 6, in commemoration of the coming of the Magi as the first manifestation of Christ to the Gentiles). The text is based on Orleans, Bibl. de la Ville, MS 201 (*olim* 178), Miscellanea Floriacensia saec. xiii, pp. 205–14. It has been edited by Young, *Drama of the Medieval Church*, II, 84–89, and by others.

[1]S.D.: The principal structures required for this play appear to be a palace with throne for Herod in the nave and a manger at one of the doors of the nave, both simultaneously visible and occupied before the play begins. Angels enter from above in the church. The audience or congregation appears to be standing around the acting locations; see l. 7 S.D.

[1–3]*Fear not . . .* etc.: See Luke 2:10–15.

[2]S.D. *doors of the church:* According to Young, *Drama of the Medieval Church* (II, 91, 117), the phrase *ad januas monasterii* does not mean at the doors of the monastery, but of the church itself, possibly the door at the south or west. The south door would lead into the cloister. In any case, the players are using part of the nave and the aisles.

themselves Let us go now, *and so on; and let them thus proceed to the manger, which will have been readied at [one of] the doors of the church:*

Let us go now even unto Bethlehem, and see this thing which is come to pass, which the Lord has done and has made known unto us.

Then let two women keeping watch over the manger question the shepherds, saying:

Whom do you seek, shepherds, say?

Let the shepherds answer:

The Redeemer Christ our Lord, a child wrapped in swaddling clothes, according to the angelic proclamation.

The women:

Here is the little one with his mother Mary, of whom formerly, in prophesying, the prophet Isaiah had said: Behold, a virgin will conceive and bring forth a son.

Then let the shepherds, falling prostrate, worship the child, saying:

Hail, king of the ages!

Afterwards, rising up, let them invite the people standing around to worship the child, saying three times:

Come, come, come, let us worship God, since he alone is our saviour.

Meantime let the Magi, appearing each from his own corner as if from his own land, come together before the altar or rising-place of the star; and, while they are approaching, let the first say:

This star radiates with exceeding splendor.

The second:

Whose coming the prophet had foretold long ago.

Transeamus, *et cetera; et sic procedant usque ad praesepe, quod ad januas monasterii paratum erit:*

Transeamus usque Bethleem, et videamus hoc verbum quod factum est, quod fecit Dominus et ostendit nobis.

Tunc duae mulieres custodientes praesepe interrogent pastores, dicentes:

Quem quaeritis, pastores, dicite?

Respondeant pastores:

Salvatorem Christum Dominum, infantem pannis involutum, secundum sermonem angelicum.

Mulieres:

Adest parvulus cum Maria matre eius, de quo dudum vaticinando Isaias propheta dixerat: Ecce virgo concipiet et pariet filium.

Tunc pastores procidentes adorent infantem dicentes:

Salve, Rex saeculorum!

Postea surgentes invitent populum circumstantem adorandum infantem, dicentes tribus vicibus:

Venite, venite, venite, adoremus Deum, quia ipse est salvator noster.

Interim Magi prodeuntes, quisquam de angulo suo quasi de regione sua, conveniant ante altare vel ad ortum stellae; et dum appropinquant, primus dicat:

Stella fulgore nimio rutilat.

Secundus:

Quem venturum olim propheta signaverat.

5

10

---

[8] S.D. *before the altar:* i.e., at the eastern end of the church.

Then, standing side by side, let the one on the right say to him in the middle: Peace be with you, brother. *And let that one answer:* Peace be with you also. *And let them kiss one another; similarly the one in the middle to him at the left, and the one at the left to him at the right. The greeting of each:*	*Tunc stantes collaterales, dicat dexter ad medium:* Pax tibi, frater. *Et ille respondeat:* Pax quoque tibi. *Et osculentur sese; sic medius ad sinistrum, sic sinister ad dextrum. Salutatio cuiusque:*
Peace be with you, brother.	Pax tibi, frater.
The response of each:	*Responsio cuiusque:*
Peace be with you also.	Pax quoque tibi.
Then let them point out to each other in turn:	*Tunc ostendant sibi mutuo:*
Behold the star, behold the star, behold the star!	Ecce stella, ecce stella, ecce stella!
As the star goes forward, they will themselves follow the star leading the way, saying:	*Procedente autem stella, sequentur et ipsi praecedentem stellam, dicentes:*
Let us go therefore and seek him, offering him gifts: gold, frankincense, and myrrh; for we are acquainted with that which is written: "All kings will worship him, all nations will serve him."	Eamus ergo et inquiramus eum, offerentes ei munera: aurum, thus, et myrrham; quia scriptum didicimus: "Adorabunt eum omnes reges, omnes gentes servient ei."
Coming to the entrance of the choir, let them inquire of those standing by:	*Venientes ad ostium chori, interrogent astantes:*
Tell us, O citizens of Jerusalem, where is the hope of the nations? Where is he who is born king of the Jews, whom, made known by celestial signs, we have come to worship?	Dicite nobis, O Jerosolimitani cives, ubi est expectatio gentium? Ubi est qui natus est rex Judaeorum, quem signis caelestibus agnitum venimus adorare?
When they have been seen, let Herod send to them a man-at-arms, saying:	*Quibus visis, Herodes mit[t]at ad eos armigerum dicentem:*
What novelty of occurrence, or what cause, has impelled you	Quae rerum novitas, aut quae causa subegit vos
To try unknown paths? Where are you headed accordingly?	Ignotas temptare vias? Quo tenditis ergo?

15

---

[13]s.d. *star goes forward:* The star travels, presumably overhead by means of wires, from the altar in the east to the manger in the west.

[14]s.d. *entrance of the choir:* The Magi, having left the altar in the east and having transversed the choir, are now entering the nave, where presumably they will come first to Herod's magnificent throne, and then to the rude manger at one of the doors of the nave.

[16-18]*What novelty . . . war?:* See *The Aeneid* VIII. 112–14.

What is your lineage? From what country?
    Do you bring peace or war?

The answer of the Magi:

We are Chaldeans;
We bring peace;
We seek the king of kings,
Whose birth the star reveals
Which radiates with more shining splendor
    than the rest.

The man-at-arms, turning back, greets the king; and, on bended knee, let him say:

May the king live forever.

Herod:

My grace welcomes you.

The man-at-arms to the king:

There are at hand among us, my lord, three
    unknown men coming from the East,
    seeking some newly-born king.

Then let Herod dispatch his ambassadors or negotiators to the Magi, saying:

Excellent examiners, find out who these kings
    are,
Accost those whom rumor already comments
    upon repeatedly in our country.

The negotiators to the Magi:

By order of our sovereign, O kings, we come
    to learn
For what purpose is your progress hither and
    whence undertaken.

The Magi:

Provided with gifts, we hasten to worship him,
The sought-for king pointed out by the guide
    star.

The ambassadors returning to Herod:

They are kings of the Arabs; with three
    gifts
They seek a newborn child whom the con-
    stellations show to be a king.

Quod genus? Unde domo? Pacemne huc
    fertis an arma?

Responsio Magorum:

Caldei sumus;
pacem ferimus;
regem regum quaerimus,
quem natum esse stella indicat,
quae fulgore ceteris clarior rutilat.

Armiger reversus salutat regem; flexo genu dicat:

Vivat rex in aeternum.

Herodes:

Salvet te gratia mea.

Armiger ad regem:

Adsunt nobis, domine, tres viri ignoti ab
    oriente venientes, noviter natum
    quendam regem quaeritantes.

Tunc mittat Herodes oratores vel interpretes suos ad Magos dicens:

Laeti inquisitores, qui sunt inquirite reges,

Affore quos nostris iam fama revolvit in
    oris.

Interpretes ad Magos:

Principis edictu, reges, praescire venimus

Quo sit profectus hic vester et unde
    perfectus.

Magi:

Regem quaesitum duce stella significatum,
Munere proviso properamus eum
    venerando.

Oratores reversi ad Herodem:

Reges sunt Arabum; cum trino munere
    natum
Quaerunt infantem, quem monstrant
    sidera regem.

20

25

30

Herod, sending the man-at-arms for the Magi:

Bid them come before me, that I may learn
    each of these things: 35
Who they are, why they come, according to
    what hearsay they inquire of us.

The man-at-arms:

What you command, renowned king, will
    quickly be performed.

The man-at-arms to the Magi:

Royal commands summon you; come swiftly.

The man-at-arms leading the Magi to Herod:

Behold, the Magi come,
And, with a star as their guide, they seek a
    newborn king.   40

Herod to the Magi:

What may be the cause of your journey? Who
    are you, whence do you come?
Speak.

The Magi:

A king is the cause of our journey; we are
    kings from the Arabian lands,
Coming hither.
Lo, we seek a king reigning over those who
    rule,   45
Whom, newly born into the world, a Jewish
    virgin nurses.

Herod to the Magi:

By what sign have you learned that the king
    you seek has been born?

The Magi:

We learned that he was born by a star show-
    ing in the East.

Herod:

Tell us if you believe that he reigns.

The Magi:

Acknowledging him to reign, we have come

Herodes mittens armigerum pro Magis:

Ante venire jube, quo possim singula scire

Qui sunt, cur veniant, quo nos rumore
    requirant.

Armiger:

Quod mandas, citius, rex inclite, perficietur.

Armiger ad Magos:

Regia vos mandata vocant; non segniter
    ite.

Armiger adducens Magos ad Herodem:

En Magi veniunt,
Et regem natum, stella duce, requirunt.

Herodes ad Magos:

Quae sit causa viae? Qui vos, vel unde
    venitis?
Dicite.

Magi:

Rex est causa viae; reges sumus ex Arabitis

Huc venientes.
Quaerimus en regem regnantibus imperi-
    tantem,
Quem natum mundo lactat Judaica virgo.

Herodes ad Magos:

Regem quem quaeritis, natum esse quo
    signo didicistis?

Magi:

Illum natum esse didicimus in oriente stella
    monstrante.

Herodes:

Si illum regnare creditis, dicite nobis.

Magi:

Illum regnare fatentes, cum mysticis

with symbolic gifts from a faraway land to worship, venerating the triune God with three gifts.

And let them show the gifts. Let the first say:

By gold [we venerate] a king.

The second:

By frankincense, a God.

The third:

By myrrh, a mortal.

Then let Herod order the companions who are sitting with him dressed as young gallants to lead in the scribes, who in a separate room have been gotten ready, bearded:

You, my companions, admit into our presence those expert in the law, that they may learn in the prophets what they think concerning these matters.

The companions to the scribes; and let them lead them in with the books of the prophets:

You men, expert in the law, summoned to the king, come hastily with the books of the prophets.

Then let Herod interrogate the scribes, saying:

O you scribes, being asked, say if you see anything written in the book concerning this boy?

Then let the scribes turn over the leaves of the book for a long while, and at length, as if having found the prophecy, let them say We have seen, my lord, *and, pointing with the finger, let them hand over the book to the incredulous king:*

We have seen, my lord, in the lines of the prophets, that Christ is born in Bethlehem of Judaea, in the city of David—the prophet thus foretelling.

The choir:

Bethlehem, you are not the least [among the

50

muneribus de terra longinqua adorare venimus, trinum Deum venerantes tribus cum muneribus.

Et ostendant munera. Primus dicat:

Auro regem.

Secundus:

Thure Deum.

Tertius:

Myrrha mortalem.

Tunc Herodes imperet symmystis qui cum eo sedent in habitu juvenili, ut adducant scribas qui in diversorio parati sunt barbati:

Vos, mei sym[m]ystae, legis peritos ascite ut discant in prophetis quid sentiant ex his.

Sym[m]ystae ad scribas, et adducant eos cum libris prophetarum:

Vos, legis periti, ad regem vocati, cum prophetarum libris properando venite.

55

Postea Herodes interroget scribas dicens:

O vos scribae, interrogati dicite si quid de hoc puero scriptum videritis in libro.

Tunc scribae diu revolvant librum, et tandem, inventa quasi prophetia, dicant Vidimus, domine, *et osten[den]tes cum digito, regi incredulo tradant librum:*

Vidimus, domine, in prophetarum lineis nasci Christum in Bethleem Judae, civitate David, propheta sic vaticinante.

Chorus:

Bethleem, non es minima [in principibus

princes of Judaea, for from you will come forth a ruler who will rule my people Israel; for he will save his people from their sins].

Then let Herod, having seen the prophecy, inflamed with rage, fling the book to the ground; but let his son, hearing the tumult, come forward to pacify his father, and, standing, salute him:

Hail, renowned father;
Hail, distinguished king,   60
You who govern everywhere,
Holding kingly sceptres!

Herod:

Most beloved son,
Worthy of the tribute of praise,
Bearing in your name   65
The pomp of regal glory,
A king has been born stronger
Than we, and more powerful.
I fear lest he will drag us
From our royal throne.   70

Then let the son, speaking contemptuously of Christ, offer himself as avenger, saying:

Against that diminutive prince,
Against the newborn child,
Bid, O father, your son
To begin this combat.

Then at length let Herod dismiss the Magi that they may seek out the boy; and let him, in their presence, pledge allegiance to the newborn king, saying:

Go, and ask diligently concerning the boy,   75
And, having found him, bring word back to
    me as you are returning,
That I too, coming, may worship him.

As the Magi are departing, let the star go before them, which has not yet appeared in the sight of

Judae, ex te enim exiet dux qui regat populum meum Israel; ipse enim salvum faciet populum suum a peccatis eorum].

Tunc Herodes, visa prophetia, furore accensus, proiciat librum; at filius eius, audito tumultu, procedat pacificaturus patrem, et stans salutet eum:

Salve, pater inclite;
salve, rex egregie,
qui ubique imperas,
[s]ceptra tenens regia!

Herodes:

Fili amantissime,
digne laudis munere,
laudis pompam regiae
tuo gerens nomine,
rex est natus fortior
nobis et potentior.
Vereor ne solio
nos extrahet regio.

Tunc filius, despective loquens de Christo, offerat se ad vindictam, dicens:

Contra illum regulum,
contra natum parvulum
jube, pater, filium
hoc inire proelium.

Tunc demum dimittat Herodes Magos, ut inquirant de puero; et coram eis spondeat regi nato, dicens:

Ite, et de puero diligenter investigate,
Et invento, redeuntes mihi renuntiate,

Ut et ego veniens adorem eum.

Magis egredientibus, praecedat stella eos, quae nondum in conspectu Herodis ap[p]aruit.

---

[58] *Bethlehem . . .* etc.: See the Benediktbeuern *Christmas Play* (Part II), l. 534. This is a Christmas antiphon.

Herod. Pointing it out to one another by turns, let them proceed. Having seen it [the star], let Herod and his son make threatening gestures with their swords. [The Magi:]

Behold, the star seen before in the East
Again goes before us, shining brightly.

Meanwhile let the shepherds, returning from the manger, come rejoicing and singing as they go:

O king of heaven [whom such great homage
    serves! In a stable he is placed who en-
    compasses the world; he lies in a manger,
    and yet makes a thundering noise in the
    clouds.]   80

The Magi to them:

Whom have you seen?

The shepherds:

Confirming what was told us by the angel
    concerning that boy, we found the child
    wrapped in swaddling-clothes and lying
    in a manger between two beasts.

Then, after the shepherds have departed, let the Magi follow the star to the manger, singing:

He whom in his own special
    vastness
The heavens, the earth and the wide seas can-
    not contain,
Born from virgin womb, is laid in
    a manger.   85
An ox and an ass stand together with him
    whom prophetic discourse foretold.
But the bright star rises, about to proffer hom-
    age to the Lord;
Who, Balaam had said, was to be born of
    Jewish stock.
This shining [star] has blinded our eyes with
    its dazzling light,
The gleaming brilliance carefully leading us
    to the cradle.   90

Quam ipsi sibi mutuo ostendentes, procedant. Qua visa, Herodes et filius minentur cum gladiis. [Magi:]

Ecce stella in oriente praevisa
Iterum praecedit nos lucida.

Interim pastores redeuntes a praesepe veniant gaudentes et cantantes in eundo:

O regem caeli [cui talia famulantur obse-
    quia! Stabulo ponitur qui continet
    mundum; jacet in praesepio, et in
    nubibus tonat.]

Ad quos Magi:

Quem vidistis?

Pastores:

Secundum quod dictum est nobis ab
    angelo de puero isto, invenimus infan-
    tem pannis involutum et positum in
    praesepio in medio duum animalium.

Postea pastoribus abeuntibus, Magi procedant post stellam usque ad praesepe, cantantes:

Que[m] non praevalent propria
    magnitudine
Caelum, terra atque maria lata capere,

De virgineo natus utero   ponitur in
    praesepio.
Sermo cecinit quem vatidicus,   sta[n]t
    simul bos et asinus.
Sed oritur stella lucida,   praebitura
    Domino obsequia.
Quem Balaam ex Judaica   nasciturum
    dixerat prosapia.
Haec nostrorum oculos   fulguranti
    lumine praest[r]inxit lucida,
Et nos ipsos provide   ducens ad
    cunabula resplendens fulgida.

---

[80]*O king . . .* etc.: a Christmas antiphon.

[86]*vatidicus:* i.e., vaticinus, prophetic.

Then let the midwives, seeing the Magi, say:

Who are these that, with a star as guide, approaching us, bear strange things?

The Magi:

We whom you see are the kings of Tharsis and Arabia and Saba, bearing gifts to the newborn Christ, the king, the Lord, whom we, with a star leading the way, have come to worship.

The midwives showing the boy:

Behold, here is the boy whom you seek. Now hasten and worship, for he is the redemption of the world.

The Magi:

Hail, king of the ages!
Hail, God of gods!
Hail, deliverance of the dead!

Then, prostrating themselves, let the Magi worship the boy and make their offerings. Let the first say:

Receive, O king, gold, the token of a king.

The second:

Receive myrrh, the token of burial.

The third:

Receive frankincense, you who are truly God.

These things done, let the Magi go to sleep there in front of the manger, until an angel, appearing from above, warns them in their sleep to return into their country by another way. Let the angel say:

All things have been fulfilled which were prophetically written. Go, returning home by another way, and you will not be informers in bringing punishment on so great a king.

Tunc obstetrices videntes Magos alloquantur:

Qui sunt hi qui, stella duce, nos adeuntes inaudita ferunt?

Magi:

Nos sumus, quos cernitis, reges Tharsis et Arabum et Saba dona ferentes Christo nato, regi, Domino, quem, stella ducente, adorare venimus.

Obstetrices ostendentes puerum:

Ecce puer adest quem quaeritis. Iam properate et adorate, quia ipse est redemptio mundi.

Magi:

Salve, rex saeculorum!
Salve, Deus deorum!
Salve, salus mortuorum!

Tunc procidentes Magi adorent puerum et offerent. Primus dicat:

Suscipe, rex, aurum, regis signum.

Secundus:

Suscipe myrrham, signum sepulturae.

Tertius:

Suscipe thus, tu vere Deus.

Istis factis, Magi incipiant dormire ibi ante praesepe, donec angelus desuper ap[p]arens moneat in somnis ut redeant in regionem suam per aliam viam. Angelus dicat:

Impleta sunt omnia quae prophetice scripta sunt. Ite, viam remeantes aliam, nec delatores tanti regis puniendi eritis.

95

100

---

[92]*Tharsis and Arabia and Saba:* The nationalities of the three Magi are derived from Psalms 71:9–10. This well-known verse from the Psalms, sung during the Offertory of the Mass of Epiphany, may possibly have been the liturgical starting-point for church drama about the coming of the Magi.

[100]*so great a king:* i.e., Christ.

The Magi, awakening:

Praise be to God! Let us rise, therefore, warned by the angelic vision, and, with the route altered, let it be hidden from Herod what we have seen concerning the boy.

Then let the Magi, departing by another road, unseen by Herod, sing:

O wondrous communication! The Creator, [assuming the living body of the human race, deigned to be born of a virgin. And issuing forth without seed as man, he has bestowed his godhead on us.]

Then coming into the choir, saying:

Rejoice, brethren,
Christ is born to us,
God is made man.

Then the cantor begins We praise you O God. *Thus it ends.*

Magi evigilantes:

Deo gratias! Surgamus ergo visione moniti angelica, et calle mutato lateant Herodem quae vidimus de puero.

Tunc Magi abeuntes cantent per aliam viam, non vidente Herode:

O admirabile commercium! Creator generis [humani animatum corpus sumens, de virgine nasci dignatus est. Et procedens homo sine semine, largitus est nobis suam deitatem.]

Tunc venientes in choro dicentes:

Gaudete, fratres,
Christus nobis natus est,
Deus homo factus est.

Tunc cantor incipit Te Deum. *Sic finit.*

105

101-2s.d.: The Magi's unobserved route, avoiding Herod's station in the nave, brings them back to the choir from which they began their journey.

102*O wondrous* ... etc.: a Christmas antiphon.

19. [THE SERVICE FOR REPRESENTING] THE SLAUGHTER OF THE INNOCENTS
(AD INTERFECTIONEM PUERORUM)
FROM FLEURY

For the Slaughter of the Children let the Innocents be dressed in white stoles, and, rejoicing through the monastery church, let them pray to God saying:

O how glorious is the kingdom [in which with Christ all the sanctified ones sing praises, clad in white stoles; they follow the lamb whithersoever he may go.]

Then let the lamb, coming on a sudden, bearing the cross, go before them hither and thither, and following let them sing:

Send forth the lamb, O Lord, [ruler of the earth, from the desert rock to the mountain of the daughter of Sion.]

Meanwhile let some man-at-arms offer to the seated Herod his sceptre, saying:

Upon the throne of David, [and over his kingdom, he will sit for ever, alleluia.]

Meanwhile let an angel, appearing over the manger, warn Joseph to flee into Egypt with Mary. Let the angel say three times Joseph:

[A]d Interfectionem Puerorum induantur Innocentes stolis albis, et gaudentes per monasterium, orent Deum dicentes:

[O] quam gloriosum est regnum [in quo cum Christo gaudent omnes sancti amicti stolis albis; sequuntur agnum quocumque ierit.]

Tunc agnus ex improviso veniens, portans crucem, antecedat eos huc et illuc, et illi sequentes cantent:

Emitte agnum, Domine, [dominatorem terrae, de petra deserti ad montem filiae Sion.]

Interim armiger quidam offerat Herodi sedenti sceptrum suum, dicens:

Super solium David, [et super regnum eius sedebit in aeternum, alleluia.]

Interea angelus, super praesepe apparens, moneat Joseph fugere in Egyptum cum Maria. Angelus dicat tribus vicibus Joseph:

From the Fleury playbook, usually associated with the monastery of St.-Benoît-sur-Loire, at Fleury. This play follows immediately after the Herod play in the MS (see previous selection). Performance was probably at the end of matins on the Feast of the Innocents (December 28). For the ultimate biblical source, particularly regarding the Flight into Egypt, see Matthew 2:13–23. Verses 16–18 of that Gospel briefly describe the slaughter of the children and the lamentation of Rachel. The text is based on Orleans, Bibl. de la Ville, MS 201 (*olim* 178), Miscellanea Floriacensia saec. xiii, pp. 214–20. It has been edited by Young, *Drama of the Medieval Church*, II, 110–13, and by others.

[1]Antiphon of vespers for the Vigil of All Saints. As a literary composition, the play is unusually reliant on liturgical responsories sung in procession, which give the whole event an especially liturgical tone. The singing Innocents were presumably choir boys or "postulants" for holy orders.

[2]Antiphon of lauds in Advent.

[3]Antiphon of lauds of the second Sunday before Christmas.

Joseph, Joseph, Joseph, son of David!

Thereupon let him say these things:

Take the boy and his mother, and go into Egypt, and remain there until I tell you. For it will come to pass that Herod will seek the boy to destroy him.   5

Joseph, going, not seen by Herod, with Mary carrying the boy, saying:

Egypt, weep not, [for your Lord will come to you, before whose eyes the abysses will be moved, to free his people from the hand of the mighty. *Verse:* Behold, the Lord, the ruler, will come with his strength.]

Meanwhile the man-at-arms, giving intelligence that the Magi have returned by another road, first salutes the king; then let him say:

King, live forever! You have been gulled, my lord; the Magi have returned by another road.

Then let Herod, as if demented, having seized a sword, contrive to kill himself; but let him be finally prevented and pacified by his followers, [as he is] saying:

Let me quench my burning vehemence by destroying myself!

Meanwhile let the Innocents, walking hitherto in procession behind the lamb, sing repeatedly:

To the hallowed lamb slain for us,
To Christ, we consecrate, under this banner of light,   10
The splendor of the Father, the splendor of the virgin birth.
In order that we, whom the wrath of Herod seeks out by numerous means,
May be delivered by the lamb, we will die together with Christ.

Joseph, Joseph, Joseph, fili David!

Postea dicat haec:

Tolle puerum et matrem eius, et vade in Egyptum, et esto ibi usque dum dicam tibi. Futurum est enim ut Herodes quaerat puerum ad perdendum eum.

Joseph abiens, non vidente Herode, cum Maria portante puerum, dicens:

Egypte, noli flere, [quia Dominator tuus veniet tibi, ante cuius conspectum movebuntur abyssi, liberare populum suum de manu potentium. *Versus:* Ecce dominator Dominus cum virtute veniet.]

Interim armiger, nuntians Magos per aliam viam redisse, salutat prius regem; postea dicat:

Rex, in aeternum vive! Delusus es, domine; Magi viam redierunt aliam.

Tunc Herodes, quasi corruptus, arrepto gladio, paret seipsum occidere; sed prohibeatur tandem a suis et pacificetur, dicens:

Incendium meum ruina restinguam!

Interea Innocentes, adhuc gradientes post agnum, decantent:

Agno sacrato   pro nobis mortificato,
Splendorem patris   splendorem virginitatis
Offerimus Christo   sub signo luminis isto.
Multis ira modis   ut quos inquirit Herodis
Agno salvemur,   cum Christo conmoriemur.

---

[5]See Matthew 2:13.

[6]Responsory of matins of the third Sunday before Christmas.

Let the man-at-arms advise Herod, saying:

Determine, my lord, to vindicate your wrath, and, with sword's point unsheathed, order that the boys be slain; and perchance among the slain will Christ be killed.

Herod delivering the sword to him saying:

My excellent man-at-arms, cause the boys to perish by the sword.　　　　　15

Meanwhile, as the murderers approach, let the lamb be removed stealthily, to whom as it is departing the Innocents bid farewell:

Hail, Lamb of God! Hail, you who take away the sins of the world, alleluia!

Then let the mothers, falling down, pray for the victims:

Let us pray: spare the tender life of our sons!

Afterwards, when the children have been killed, let an angel from on high advise them, saying:

You who are in the dust, awaken and cry out.

The children lying slain:

Why do you not defend our blood, our God?

The angel:

Endure this for a short while, until the number of your brethren is completed.　　　20

Then let Rachel be led in, and two comforters; and standing over the boys let her mourn, falling at times to earth, saying:

Alas, tender babes, we see how your limbs have been mangled!
Alas, sweet children, murdered in a single frenzied attack!
Alas, one whom neither piety nor your tender age restrained!

Armiger suggerat Herodi dicens:

Discerne, Domine, vindicare iram tuam, et stricto mucrone jube occidi pueros; forte inter occisos occidetur et Christus.

Herodes tradens ei gladium dicens:

Armiger eximie, pueros fac ense perire.

Interim, occisoribus venientibus, subtrahatur agnus clam, quem abeuntem salutant Innocentes:

Salve, Agnus Dei! Salve, qui tollis peccata mundi, alleluia!

Tunc matres occidentes orent occisos:

Oremus, tenerae natorum parcite vitae!

Postea, jacentibus infantibus, angelus ab excelso admoneat eos, dicens:

Vos qui in pulvere estis, expergiscimini et clamate.

Infantes jacentes:

Quare non defendis sanguinem nostrum, Deus noster?

Angelus:

Adhuc sustinete modicum tempus, donec impleatur numerus fratrum vestrorum.

Tunc inducatur Rachel, et duae consolatrices; et stans super pueros plangat, cadens aliquando, dicens:

Heu, teneri partus,　　laceros quos cernimus artus!
Heu, dulces nati,　　sola rabie jugulati!

Heu, quem nec pietas　　nec vestra coercuit aetas!

[23]*one:* i.e., Herod.

Alas, wretched mothers, we who are
    compelled to see this!
Alas, what do we do now, why do we not
    submit to these things?   25
Alas, because no joys can ease our memories
    and sorrow,
For the sweet children are gone!

*The comforters, lifting her up from falling,
saying:*

Do not, young Rachel, do not, most gentle
    mother,
For the death of the little ones, restrain your
    tears of sorrow.
Although you grieve, rejoice that you
    weep.   30
For, truly, your sons live blessed above the
    stars.

Again Rachel mourning:

Alas, alas, alas!
How shall I rejoice, while I see the lifeless
    limbs,
While thus I shall have been distressed to
    the depths of my heart?
Truly these boys will cause me to mourn
    endlessly.   35
O sadness! O the rejoicings of fathers and
    mothers changed
To mournful grief; pour forth weeping of
    tears,
Weeping for the flower of Judaea, the grief
    of the nation!

Again the comforters:

Why do you, young woman,
Mother Rachel, so beautiful, weep,   40
In whose visage Jacob takes delight?
As if the tender and bleary eyes
Of your babyish sister pleased him!

Heu, matres miserae,   quae cogimur
    ista videre!
Heu, quid nunc agimus   cur non haec
    facta subimus?
Heu, quia memores   nostrosque levare
    dolores
Gaudia non possunt,   nam dulcia
    pignora desunt!

*Consolatrices excipientes eam cadentem di-
centes:*

Noli, virgo Rachel,   noli, dulcissima
    mater,
Pro nece parvorum   fletus retinere
    dolorum.
Si quae tristaris,   exulta quae
    lacrimaris.
Namque tui nati   vivunt super astra
    beati.

Item Rachel dolens:

Heu, heu, heu!
Quomodo gaudebo,   dum mortua
    membra videbo;
Dum sic commota   fuero per viscera
    tota?
Me facient vere   pueri sine fine
    dolere.
O dolor! O patrum   mutataque
    gaudia matrum
Ad lugubres luctus;   lacrimarum
    fundite fletus,
Judaeae florem   patriae lacrimando
    dolorem!

Item consolatrices:

Quid tu, virgo,
mater Rachel, ploras formosa,
cuius vultus Jacob delectat?
Ceu sororis anniculae
lippitudo eum juvat!

---

[25]*why . . . things:* i.e., why don't we accept these deaths philosophically?

[42–43]A reference to Leah, Rachel's older sister, whose eyes displeased Jacob; *Lia lippis erat
oculis,* Genesis 29:17. Jacob chose the younger sister, Rachel, for her beauty.

Mother, dry your weeping eyes.
How are streams of tears on your cheeks
    becoming to you?

Again Rachel:

Alas, alas, alas! Why do you find fault with
    me for having poured forth tears
    uselessly,
When I have been deprived of my child,
    [who alone] would show concern for my
    poverty,
Who would not yield to enemies the narrow
    boundaries which Jacob acquired for
    me,
And who was going to be of benefit to his
    stolid brethren, of whom many, alas my
    sorrow, I have buried?

*Then the comforters, saying, as the children lie
thrown on their backs:*

Is it fitting that he be wept over, he who
    occupies the heavenly kingdom,
And who by frequent prayer may succor his
    wretched brothers before God?

Again Rachel, falling upon the boys:

My soul is troubled within me; my heart is
    agitated within me.

*Then let the comforters lead Rachel away, and
meanwhile let the angel from above say the
following antiphon:*

Suffer the little ones [to come unto me, for
    of such is the kingdom of heaven.]

*Rising at the voice of the angel, let the boys enter
the choir saying:*

O Christ, O youth skilled in the greatest wars,
    how great an army do you gather for

Terge, mater, flentes oculos.
Quam te decent genarum rivuli?

  45

Item Rachel:

Heu, heu, heu! Quid me incusastis fletus
    incassum fudisse,

Cum sim orbata nato, paupertatem meam
    [qui solus] curaret,

Qui non hostibus cederet angustos
    terminos, quos mihi Jacob adquisivit,

Quique stolidis fratribus, quo[s] multos,
    pro[h] dolor, extuli, esset profuturus?

*Tunc consolatrices, esupinantes infantes,
dicentes:*

Numquid flendus est iste, qui regnum
    possidet caeleste,
Quique prece frequenti miseris fratribus
    apud Deum auxilietur?

  50

Item Rachel cadens super pueros:

Anxiatus est in me spiritus meus; in me
    turbatum est cor meum.

*Tunc consolatrices abducant Rachel, et angelus
interim de supernis dicat antiphonam quae
sequitur:*

Sinite parvulos [venire ad me, talium est
    enim regnum caelorum.]

*Ad vocem angeli surgentes, pueri intrent
chorum dicentes:*

O Christe, quantum patri exercitum,
    juvenis doctus ad bella maxima,

[46-49]Rachel's son was Joseph, who aided his ungrateful brethren in Egypt. See Genesis 37-46.

[48]*narrow boundaries:* i.e., a small piece of property.

[52]Antiphon of lauds of Good Friday.

[53]Antiphon of lauds of Innocents Day. See also Matthew 19:14.

the Father, speaking prophetically to the people, drawing to you the souls of the departed, since you have so much compassion.

While these things are done, let Herod be removed and let his son Archelaus be substituted in his place, and be raised up as king. Meanwhile let the angel give notice to Joseph in Egypt, where previously he withdrew, saying:

Joseph, Joseph, Joseph, son of David!
    Return into the land of Judaea, for
    they are dead who sought the life of the
    boy.

Then let Joseph return with Mary and the boy, withdrawing into the region of Galilee, saying:

Rejoice, rejoice, rejoice, O Virgin Mary;
    all heresies, *and so on. The cantor begins*
    We praise you O God. *Thus it ends.*

populis praedicans colligis, umbras sugg[er]ens cum tantum miser[er]is.

Dum haec fiunt, tollatur Herodes et substituatur in loco eius filius eius, Archelaus, et exaltetur in regem. Interim angelus admoneat Joseph in Egyptum, quo prius secessit, dicens:

Joseph, Joseph, Joseph, fili David! Revertere in terram Judam, defuncti sunt enim qui quaerebant animam pueri.

Tunc Joseph revertatur cum Maria et puero, secedens in parte[s] Galilaeae, dicens:

Gaude, gaude, gaude, Maria Virgo; cunctas haereses, *et cetera. Cantor incipit* Te Deum laudamus. *Sic finit.*

55

[55]See Matthew 2:20.

[56]See the antiphons for the Assumption.

PART TWO

Twelfth-Century Church Drama

Twelfth-Century Church Drama

IN OUR SURVEY of the liturgical beginnings of drama, we have already examined a few twelfth-century plays of real artistic merit—notably those from the Fleury playbook. Clearly these masterpieces were regarded as literary compositions by the monks of Fleury, who copied them into a special manuscript rather than in the usual service books. Yet even the Fleury plays for Easter and Christmas were tied closely to specific liturgical occasions. They were sung during intervals in the regular service, usually at the end of matins, and concluded with a resumption of the liturgy.

Several of the plays to be considered in Part II are not liturgical in this strict sense. Although they treat religious subjects and are often derived from the appointed Gospel readings of the liturgy, they are no longer performed as part of the service itself. The Anglo-Norman *Adam,* despite its indebtedness to the *Liber Responsalis* or Book of Responses for Sexagesima (the second Sunday before Lent), was evidently played outside the church during Sexagesima week or at Christmas, or perhaps at some other time. *La Seinte Resureccion,* also written in the Anglo-Norman vernacular, may have been performed inside or outside the church. The Christmas and Passion plays from Benediktbeuern, dating from the late twelfth or early thirteenth centuries, have manifestly expanded beyond the scope of the regular service. Still other plays, too lengthy or too numerous to be included in this selection, reinforce our impression of a drama no longer tied to its original liturgical occasion: the twelfth-century Passion play from Montecassino, the play of Antichrist from Tegernsee in Germany, the Sponsus play of the wise and foolish virgins from Limoges, and others.

The play titles in the original manuscripts give us some indication of this new independence from the liturgy. The texts already considered in Part I are usually called *Trophi* ("Tropes") or *Ordo* ("Service," or "Order of Worship"). Sometimes the word *Ordo* seems to be implied, as in *Ad Interfectionem Puerorum,* "[The Service for Representing] the Slaughter of the Innocents." Titles of this sort persist in Part II, especially in plays that still retain liturgical ties, such as *Ad Repraesentandum Convertionem Beati Pauli Apostoli,*

"[The Service for Representing] the Conversion of the Blessed Apostle Paul." Even the Anglo-Norman *Adam,* often popularly referred to as the *Mystère d'Adam,* is called in the manuscript *Ordo Repraesentationis Adae,* "The Service for Representing Adam." The term *Officium* ("Service") also sometimes appears. On the other hand, we often find a new vocabulary in the twelfth century indicating an awareness that the dramas are real plays and no longer simply part of the service. The Beauvais play of Daniel is called *Danielis Ludus,* "The Play of Daniel." Hilarius' play of St. Nicholas (not included in this selection) is called *Ludus super Iconia Sancti Nicolae,* "The Play about the Image of St. Nicholas." The famous *Carmina Burana* manuscript of the Benediktbeuern monastery in Bavaria features a *Ludus, immo Exemplum, Dominice Resurrectionis* ("Play, or Pious Example, of the Resurrection of our Lord") and a *Ludus Breviter de Passione* ("Short Play of the Passion"). Vernacular drama occasionally made use of equivalent terms such as *Jeu* and *Spiel.* The Fleury playbook twice calls a play about the image of St. Nicholas a *Miraculum.*

This growth in the number of ways to designate plays in the twelfth century, even though distinctions between terms are often imprecise, attests to a new variety in types of plays and in conditions of performance. One of our chief purposes in Part II, in fact, is to sample the extraordinary versatility of drama during what is often called the twelfth-century renaissance. In the Anglo-Norman *Adam* we find a proto-cycle play that embraces the creation and fall of Adam and Eve, the killing of Abel by Cain, and a procession of prophets announcing the advent of Christ. Similarly, we find Old Testament plays (about Daniel, for instance), New Testament plays about events other than those of Christmas and Easter (such as Hilarius' drama about the raising of Lazarus), plays about the Acts of the Apostles (notably the Fleury play of the Conversion of St. Paul), saints' plays (especially about St. Nicholas), and of course greatly expanded plays about the events of Christmas and Easter. We also find plays (not included in this collection) on the subject of the Second Coming: the Sponsus play from Limoges, partly in French, depicting the wise and foolish virgins (Matthew 25) as antetypes of those who will be found either prepared or unready at the Day of Judgment; and the Antichrist play from Tegernsee, about a false messiah who heals the sick, raises the dead, and subverts all the rulers of the world to his domination until he is denounced by the martyred prophets Enoch and Elijah.

These plays on numerous subjects reflect a sizeable increase in the number of occasions during the year when church plays might be performed. No single church had very many plays, but the choice was no longer limited to Christmas or Easter. A play about St. Paul would presumably be sung on the Feast of the Conversion of St. Paul, January 25. St. Nicholas plays would be appropriate on the feast of his martydom, December 6, or possibly on the feast of the translation of his body, May 9. Plays honoring the Virgin Mary were performed during the thirteenth and fourteenth centuries, and possibly earlier, on holy days celebrating the Presentation of the Virgin in the Temple (November 21), the Annunciation (March 25 or in mid-December during

Advent), the Purification (February 2), and the Assumption (August 15). Other plays such as the Anglo-Norman *Adam* and *La Seinte Resureccion* were, as we have seen, still more independent of the liturgy.

This expansion in twelfth-century drama for various occasions of the church year showed itself to be more inventive than Easter drama in many ways, including subject-matter, characterization, versification, and the use of vernacular languages. We find use of the vernacular, for example, not only in full-length vernacular plays like the Anglo-Norman *Adam, La Seinte Resureccion,* and the Spanish *Auto de los Reyes Magos* ("The Coming of the Magi"), but as a dramatic ingredient in macaronic or multi-lingual plays like the Limoges Sponsus, the Benediktbeuern Passion play, the Montecassino Passion play, and Hilarius' play about the raising of Lazarus.

Twelfth-century dramatists did not always adequately understand their theatrical heritage from ancient Greece and Rome, and to that extent they were obliged to devise their own solutions to dramaturgic problems rather than learn by direct imitation of the classics. The Roman dramatists Terence and Plautus, though known, were read rather than acted, and a popular misconception persisted that Roman actors had only mimed their parts while a reader declaimed the text. Latin *comoediae* of the twelfth century, written to be read aloud, contained narrative links interspersed with dialogue. Still, as Rosemary Woolf has convincingly argued (in *The English Mystery Plays*), twelfth-century ignorance of classical dramaturgy has been too often exaggerated. Learned men such as Isidore of Seville and John of Salisbury seem to have understood most theatrical conventions of the Roman stage. Deserted Roman amphitheaters, still to be seen throughout Europe, were recognized to have been arenas for the performance of drama. Wandering minstrels and popular entertainers may well have kept alive a tradition of histrionic presentation. In European centers of learning, where most church drama of the twelfth century was written, humanists were probably not unaware of a classical precedent for impersonation on stage.

Church drama of the twelfth century was certainly the work of learned men. Its chief aim was not to educate the ignorant laity, as in the case of much fourteenth- and fifteenth-century religious art, but to create beautiful works of wisdom and piety. The use of many different poetic forms, of literary genres (such as the *débat*), of classical references, and the like, all suggest a drama of considerable literary sophistication. Performance was evidently of a high artistic calibre; it involved the use of trained choirs and soloists, instrumental accompaniment, colorful ecclesiastical costuming, elaborate acting platforms, and a stately formalized style of acting. Even the use of the vernacular was often influenced by aesthetic considerations, not simply by a desire to reach out to large popular audiences. Twelfth-century church drama, like other art forms of the twelfth-century renaissance, was a remarkable cultural achievement.

1. THE SERVICE FOR REPRESENTING ADAM
(ORDO REPRAESENTATIONIS ADAE)

The play of *Adam,* written during the twelfth century in Anglo-Norman French and quite possibly produced in England (where Norman French was still the official language at court), is a remarkable play by any standard. It is especially so in view of its early date. The play is in the vernacular throughout, except for Latin stage directions and a few Latin chants. It shows its independence from the liturgy, despite the occasional use of liturgical responsories, in several ways: for example, it is probably designed to be acted outside the church building, it demands an elaborate multi-level stage, and it makes little use of clerical costuming. Yet *Adam* is not the only innovative play of its sort in the twelfth century. *La Seinte Resureccion* (to be presented next) and the Spanish *Auto de los Reyes Magos* or "Coming of the Magi" (not included in this collection), both written in the vernacular, are similarly complex, inventive, and adventurous in their staging. These plays offer little support for the widely-held notion that vernacular drama began simply as translation from the Latin. Instead, these vernacular experiments may well have exerted a strong influence on the development of Latin church drama.

Despite its title, the Anglo-Norman *Adam* does not limit its subject to the creation of man and his expulsion from Eden. The play goes on to dramatize the slaying of Abel by his brother Cain, and then launches into a series of prophecies on the coming of Christ spoken by Abraham, Moses, Aaron, David, Solomon, Balaam, Daniel, Habakkuk, Jeremiah, Isaiah, and Nebuchadnezzar. Since the manuscript is incomplete, we do not know how many more prophets would have come forward after Nebuchadnezzar. Nor do we know if the play might

then have continued with the birth, ministry, death, and resurrection of Christ, in the manner of a cycle.

As it stands, in any case, the play is centered on the theme of Christ's coming. The work as a whole is appropriate to Advent (the four Sundays preceding Christmas) or to the midwinter period immediately preceding Lent. *Adam* may have been performed at one of these times, or during the twelve days of Christmas. The Gospel readings for Advent are taken from the Old Testament prophecies of the coming of Christ, and accordingly the four weeks of Advent were often associated in medieval thought with the four-thousand-year span of Old Testament history that supposedly extended from Adam to Christ. On the other hand, the appointed readings for Sexagesima (the second Sunday before Lent, or seven weeks before Easter) were, in medieval times, taken from the first chapters of Genesis. (In a modern breviary these readings are to be found under Septuagesima, the third Sunday before Lent.) The author of *Adam* was in fact directly indebted to the *Liber Responsalis* or Book of Responses for Sexagesima: as O. B. Hardison, Jr., has shown, the author found in the liturgy the eight responsories sung by the choir at key points throughout the play. These eight passages from Genesis provide the outline of the whole story, from the creation of man to the murder of Abel. Here, then, the author found a liturgical precedent for bringing together the stories of Adam's fall and of Abel's murder. In the liturgy for Advent, also, the dramatist found justification for regarding such Old Testament stories and prophecies as preludes to the coming of Christ.

The procession of prophets, following the

murder of Abel, makes explicit the connection between the Old Testament and the New. A number of Old Testament patriarchs comes forward one at a time to utter prophecies that were interpreted, in the Middle Ages, as foretelling the birth of Christ. The source for this Procession of Prophets, or *Ordo Propheta-rum* as it is known in Latin, was a famous medieval sermon called the *Sermo contra Judeos, Paganos, et Arianos de Symbolo,* wrongly ascribed to St. Augustine. In the sermon, numerous Old Testament figures are introduced by the speaker in order to denounce faithlessness by showing that even Jewish and pagan prophets proclaim the truth of Christ's divinity. The sermon was widely known, and was often read on the fourth Sunday of Advent, on the day before Christmas, on Christmas itself, and on the Feast of the Circumcision, January 1. A series of recitations spoken by various prophets could easily be converted into dramatic form, as in the *Adam* play. The list of speakers could vary, and could include pagan witnesses such as Virgil and the Cumaean Sibyl (see for example the *Ordo Prophetarum* in the Benedikt-beuern Christmas play, selection 7, below). Scholars used to speculate that the *Ordo Pro-phetarum* was the ancestor of the Old Testament episodes in the great cycle plays of the four-teenth and fifteenth centuries, but the theory now seems inadequate because the list of figures in the procession is so different from that found in the Corpus Christi plays. Still, the *Ordo Prophetarum* did give dramatic ex-pression to the idea of regarding the Old Testament as anticipatory of Christ's incarna-tion.

As Eric Auerbach has observed in his *Mime-sis,* high and low styles exist side by side in the play of *Adam.* Its exalted and cosmic story of human temptation is related in the most immediate terms, intended for an audience of ordinary men and women:

Adam talks and acts in a manner any member of the audience is accustomed to from his own or his neighbor's house; things would go exactly the same way in any townsman's home or on any farm where an upright but not very brilliant husband was tempted into a foolish and fateful act by his vain and ambitious wife who had been deceived by an unscrupulous swindler. The dialogue between Adam and Eve—this first man-woman dialogue of universal historical import—is turned into a scene of simplest every-day reality. Sublime as it is, it becomes a scene in simple, low style.

(Translated by Willard R. Trask, Princeton, 1953, p. 151.)

This juxtaposing of religious seriousness and comic realism was to become an essential part of medieval Christian drama. In the Corpus Christi cycles of the fourteenth and fifteenth centuries, for example, boisterously crude violence regularly accompanies the Crucifixion and other moments of most intense sacredness. The blending of the sacred and the profane should not, however, be regarded as a "secularizing" process, leading us forward by evolutionary steps to the splendors of Shake-speare and the Elizabethan drama. The in-clusion of the secular and contemporary world in the larger framework of sacred history was an enduring vision for medieval society, as the play of *Adam* eloquently demonstrates.

Adam appears to have been staged in front of a church. Heaven is represented by the door to the church itself, at the top of the steps. Paradise with its trees and flowers is evidently also at the top of the church steps, and is surrounded by a low palisade concealing the actors from the chest downwards (thereby facilitating costume changes on stage). The earth, to which Adam and Eve are expelled and where they cultivate their thistle-choked fields, is lower down, perhaps on a platform at the foot of the steps. Here too, presumably, are the altars where Cain and Abel offer sacrifice. The large open acting space at the foot of the steps is called the *platea,* or "place." Satan and his fellow devils periodically make forays across this *platea* and among the spectators, who are evidently gathered on the periphery of this space. At this lowest level we presumably also find "the gates of hell," an elaborately constructed hell-mouth from which the devils emerge (accompanied by a lot of noise and smoke) and into which the souls of the damned are led. Costumes and stage effects are elaborate: the artfully constructed serpent, the fig leaves, the pot concealed in Abel's clothes that Cain must strike to give the effect of a sharp blow. The actors are probably clerics, although the play is certainly not part of the liturgy. Choric singing of the responsories provides a liturgical reminder,

but for the most part the actors are to strive for verisimilar effect: all persons are to be coached so that they "speak in an orderly manner and make gestures appropriate to the things of which they speak."

The tendency to regard *Adam* as "transitional" because it is presumably "ahead" of its time does not do justice to its extraordinary artistry and finish. *Adam* should be regarded not as an interesting experiment paving the way for later treatments of the fall of man, but as the most successful dramatic version of the story that has survived from the Middle Ages.

1. The Service for Representing Adam
(Ordo Repraesentationis Adae)

Let paradise be constructed in a prominently high place; let curtains and silken hangings be placed around it at such a height that those persons who will be in paradise can be seen from the shoulders upwards; let sweet-smelling flowers and foliage be planted; within let there be various trees, and fruits hanging on them, so that the place may seem as delightful as possible. Then let our Saviour come, clothed in a dalmatic, and let Adam [and] Eve be stationed before him. Let Adam be robed in a red tunic, Eve in a woman's white garment with a wimple of white silk; and let them both stand before the Figure [of God]—Adam somewhat nearer, with peaceful countenance, Eve on the other hand not quite sufficiently humble. And

Constituatur paradisus loco eminentiori; circumponantur cortinae et panni serici ea altitudine ut personae, quae in paradiso fuerint, possint videri sursum ad humeros; serantur odoriferi flores et frondes; sint in eo diversae arbores et fructus in eis dependentes, ut amoenissimus locus videatur. Tunc veniat Salvator indutus dalmatica, et statuantur coram eo Adam, Eva. Adam indutus sit tunica rubea, Eva vero muliebri vestimento albo, peplo serico albo; et stent ambo coram Figura —Adam tamen propius, vultu composito, Eva vero parum demissiori. Et sit ipse Adam bene instructus quando respondere debeat, ne ad respondenum nimis sit velox aut nimis tardus.

Based on ms. no. 927 in the Bibliothèque Municipale de Tours. This edition has been closely checked against the editions of Paul Aebischer (Geneva and Paris, 1963), Paul Studer (Manchester, 1918), and Willem Nooman (Pan's, 1971).

[1]s.d. *Figure:* This mysterious name for God suggests a figural interpretation, foreshadowing God's incarnation as the savior of mankind. *In the beginning . . . And the Lord God formed* [*man*]: This lesson and responsory sung by the choir are to be found in the Gregorian *Liber Responsalis* for Sexagesima (*Patrologia Latina*, 78:748). They are followed in immediate succession by all the responsories of the Genesis portion of this play, and in the same order. See the stage directions following ll. 88, 100, 386, 512, 518, and 722.

let this Adam be well coached when he must give answers, lest in answering he should be either too hasty or too slow. Nor him alone, but let all persons be coached thus, so that they may speak in an orderly manner and make gestures appropriate to the things of which they speak; and, in their verses, let them neither add nor subtract a syllable, but pronounce them all steadily, and speak those things that are to be spoken in their due order. Whoever will mention the name of paradise, let him look in its direction and point it out with his hand. Then let the lesson begin:

In the beginning God created the heavens
    and the earth.

    When this is finished let the choir sing:

℟ [*Responsory*]: And the Lord God formed
    [man].

    When this is finished let the Figure [of God] say:

Adam! *Who must answer:* Sire?

FIGURE   I have formed you
Of loam of the earth.

ADAM   I know it well.

FIGURE

I have formed you in my likeness,
. . . .
In my image I have made you of earth.   5
You must never make war against me.

ADAM

I will not; but I will believe you,
I will obey my creator.

FIGURE

I have given you a worthy companion:
Your wife, Eve by name.   10
She is your wife and partner;
You ought to be entirely faithful to her.
Love her, and let her love you,
If you would both be mine.
Let her be subject to your commandment,   15

Nec solum ipse, sed omnes personae sic instruantur ut composite loquantur et gestum faciant convenientem rei de qua loquuntur; et, in rhythmis, nec syllabam addant nec demant, sed omnes firmiter pronuncient, et dicantur seriatim quae dicenda sunt. Quicunque nominaverit paradisum, respiciat eum et manu demonstret. Tunc incipiat lectio:

In principio creavit Deus caelum et terram.

    Qua finita chorus cantet:

℟ Formavit igitur Dominus.

    Quo finito dicat Figura:

Adam! *Qui respondeat:* Sire?

FIGURA   Fourmé te ai
De limo terre.

ADAM   Ben le sai.

FIGURA

Je te ai fourmé a mun semblant
. . . .
A ma imagene t'ai feit de tere.
Ne moi devez ja mais mover guere.

ADAM

Nen frai ge, mais te crerrai,
Mun creatur obe[ï]rai.

FIGURA

Je t'ai duné bon cumpainun:
Ce est ta femme, Eva a noun.
Ce est ta femme e tun pareil:
Tu le devez estre ben fiël.
Tu aime lui, e ele ame tei,
Si serez ben ambedui de moi.
Ele soit a tun comandement,

And both of you to my wish.
I formed her from your side;
Born of you, she is no stranger.
I fashioned her from your body;
From you she issued, not from outside. 20
Govern her by reason.
Let no dissension come between you,
But great love and mutual obedience:
Such is the law of marriage.

FIGURE TO EVE

Now I will speak to you, Eve. 25
Be heedful, do not take this lightly:
If you wish to do my will,
Cherish goodness in your heart.
Love and honor me as your creator,
And acknowledge me your Lord. 30
To serve me devote your care,
All your might and all your mind.
Love Adam, and hold him dear.
He is your husband, and you his wife.
To him be obedient at all times, 35
Do not stray from his discipline.
Serve and love him with willing spirit,
For that is the law of marriage.
If you do well as his helpmeet,
I will place you with him in glory. 40

EVE

Sire, I will do according to your pleasure;
I do not wish to stray from it.
I will acknowledge you as sovereign,
Him as my partner and stronger than I.
I will always be faithful to him; 45
From me he will have good counsel.
Your pleasure, your service
I will perform, Sire, in every way.

> Then let the Figure call Adam nearer and say
> to him more intently:

Listen, Adam, and hear my judgment.
I have formed you; now I will give you this
    gift: 50
You may live forever, if you obey my
    teaching;
You may remain healthy, and not feel
    illness.

E vus ambe deus a mun talent.
De ta coste l'ai fourmee;
N'est pas estrange, de tei est nee.
Jo la plasmai de ton cors;
De tei eissit, non pas de fors.
Tu la governe par raison.
N'ait entre vus ja tençon,
Mais grant amor, grant conservage:
Tel soit la lei de mariage.

FIGURA AD EVAM

A tei parlerai, Evain.
Ço garde tu, nel tenez en vain:
Si vos faire ma volenté,
En ton cors garderas bonté.
Moi aim e honor ton creator,
E moi reconuis a Seignor.
A moi servir met ton porpens,
Tote ta force e tot tun sens.
Adam aime, e lui tien chier.
Il est marid, e tu sa mullier.
A lui soies tot tens encline,
Nen issir de sa discipline.
Lui serf e aim par bon coraje,
Car ço est droiz de mariage.
Se tu le fais bon adjutoire,
Jo te mettrai od lui en gloire.

EVA

Jol frai, sire, a ton plaisir;
Ja n'en voldrai de rien issir.
Toi conustrai a seignor,
Lui a paraille e a forzor.
Jo lui serrai tot tens feël;
De moi avra bon conseil.
Le ton pleisir, le ton servise
Frai, sire, en tote guise.

> Tunc Figura vocet Adam propius et attentius
> ei dicat:

Escote, Adam, e entent ma raison.
Jo t'ai formé; or te dorrai itel don:

Tot tens poez vivre, si tu tiens mon
    sermon,
E serras sains, nen sentiras friczion.

You will neither hunger nor thirst for need,
Feel neither heat nor cold.
You will dwell in joy, and never leave,   55
And in this pleasant state you will not
    taste sadness.
You will spend all your life in joy;
You will live forever, your life will not be
    short.
I say this to you, and wish that Eve attend;
If she doesn't listen, there will be trouble.   60
Take dominion over all the earth,
Birds, beasts, and other riches.
Let those who envy you be held in slight
    regard,
For all the world will be obedient to you.
Both good and evil are in your power;   65
He who has such a choice is not bound to
    a stake.
Hold all in balance, weigh things equally.
Believe in my counsel, be true to me.
Leave the evil, and hold yourself to the
    good;
Love your Lord, and keep with him;   70
Do not forsake my counsel for another.
If you do this, you will be without sin.

ADAM

Great thanks I give for your kindness,
You who created me and give me such
    bounty
As to place good and evil in my power.   75
I will bestow my will in serving you.
You are my Sire, I am your handiwork;
You give me shape, I am of your making.
My will can never be so stubborn
But that all my care will be to serve you.   80

    Then let the Figure point out paradise to Adam
    with his hand, saying:

Adam!

ADAM   Sire?

FIGURE   I will tell you my advice.
  Do you see this garden?

ADAM   What is it called?

FIGURE   Paradise.

Ja n'avras faim, por bosoing ne beveras,
Ja n'averas frait, ja chalt ne sentiras.
Tu iers en joie, ja ne te lassaras,
E en deduit ja dolor ne savras.

Tute ta vie demeneras en joie;
Tut jors serra, nen estrat pas poie.

Jol di a toi, e voil que Eva l'oie;
Se ne l'entent, donc s'afoloie.
De tote terre avez la seignorie,
D'oisels, des bestes e d'altre manantie.
A petit vus soit qui vus porte envie,

Car tot li mond vus iert encline.
En vostre cors vus met e bien e mal;
Ki ad tel dun, n'est pas lïez a pal.

Tut en balance ore pendiez par egal.
Creez conseil, que soiet vers mei leal!
Laisse le mal, e si te pren al bien;

Tun Seignor aime, e ovec lui te tien;
Por nul conseil ne gerpisez le mien.
Si tu le fais, ne peccheras de rein.

ADAM

Grant graces rend a ta benignité,
Ki me formas e me fais tel bunté
Que bien e mal mez en ma poësté.
En toi servir metrai ma volenté.
Tu es mi Sires, jo sui ta creature;
Tu me plasmas, e jo sui ta faiture.
Ma volenté ne serrad ja si dure
Q'a toi servir ne soit tote ma cure.

    Tunc Figura manu demonstret paradisum
    Adae, dicens:

Adam!

ADAM   Sire?

FIGURA   Dirrai toi mon avis.
  Veez cest jardin?

ADAM   Cum ad nun?

FIGURA   Paradis.

ADAM

How beautiful it is!

FIGURE   I planted it and laid it out.
He who will remain in it will be my friend.
I charge you to remain and guard it.   85

Then he will send them into paradise, saying:

I set you both therein.

ADAM   And can we stay?

FIGURE

For your entire life, you need fear nothing
    here;
You can neither die nor fall sick.

Let the choir sing: ℟ [*Responsory*]: And the
Lord God took the man. *Then the Figure will
stretch forth his hand toward paradise, saying:*

I will tell you the nature of this garden:
You will find no lack of any delight.   90
There is no earthly good a creature might
    desire
That each cannot find to his own measure.
Here woman will receive from man no
    anger,
Nor man from woman have shame or fear.
Man is no sinner for begetting children,   95
Nor does woman experience pain in bearing
    them.
You will live forever, thus you will have a
    wonderful existence here;
Your age can never alter.
Death you will never fear, nor can it ever
    harm you.
I do not wish you to leave; here you must
    make your dwelling.   100

Let the choir sing: ℟ [*Responsory*]:

The Lord God said to Adam.

*Then let the Figure point out to Adam the trees of
paradise, saying:*

ADAM

Mult par est bel!

FIGURA   Jel plantai e asis.
Qui i maindra serra mis amis.
Jol toi comand por maindre e por garder.

Tunc mittet eos in paradisum, dicens:

Dedenz vus met.

ADAM   Purrum i nus durer?

FIGURA

A toz jorz vivre, rien n'i poëz duter;

Ja n'i porrez murir ne engruter.

Chorus cantet: ℟   Tulit ergo Dominus
hominem. *Tunc Figura manum extendet
versus paradisum, dicens:*

De cest jardin tei dirrei la nature:
De nul delit n'i trovrez falture.
N'est bien al mond, que covoit criature,

Chescons n'i poisset trover a sa mesure.
Femme de home n'i avra irur,

Ne home de femme verguine ne freür.
Por engendrer n'i est hom peccheor,
Ne a l'emfanter femme n'i sent dolor.

Tot tens vivras, tant i ad bon estage;

N'i porras ja changer li toen eage.
Mort n'i crendras, ne te ferra damage.

Ne voil qu'en isses; ici feras manage.

Chorus cantet: ℟

Dixit Dominus ad Adam.

*Tunc monstret Figura Adae arbores paradisi,
dicens:*

---

88 s.d. *Responsory:* See note, l. 1 s.d.

100 s.d. *Responsory:* See note, l. 1 s.d.

Of all this fruit you may eat for your pleasure.	De tot cest fruit poez manger par deport.
And let him show him the forbidden tree and its fruit, saying:	*Et ostendat ei vetitam arborem et fructus eius, dicens:*
This I forbid you, do not take your enjoyment of this other one.	Çost toi defent, n'en faire altre comfort.
If you eat of it, you will experience death at once;	S'en tu en manjues, sempres sentiras mort;
You will lose my love, change your fortune into bad.	M'amor perdras, mal changeras ta sort.

ADAM

I will keep all your commandment.	105	Jo garderai tot ton comandement.	
Neither I nor Eve will disobey in anything.		Ne jo ne Eve nen eisseroms de nient.	
If for one sole fruit such an abode is lost,		Por un sol fruit, se pert tel chasement,	
It would be right for me to be thrown out to the wind.		Droiz est que soie defors jetez al vent.	
If for one apple I forsake your love,		Por une pome, se jo gerpis t'amor,	
Throughout my life, whether deliberately or foolishly,	110	Que ja en ma vie, par sens ne par folor,	
Judge him to be a traitor		Jugiez doit estre a loi de traïtor	
Who so perjures and betrays his Lord.		Que si parjure e traïst son Seignor.	

Then let the Figure go to the church, and let Adam and Eve walk about, virtuously taking delight in paradise. Meantime let devils run to and fro through the platea, making appropriate gestures; and let them come, one after the other, close to paradise, showing Eve the forbidden fruit, as if tempting her to eat it. Then let the devil come to Adam and say to him:

Tunc vadat Figura ad ecclesiam, et Adam et Eva spatientur, honeste delectantes, in paradiso. Interea demones discurrant per plateas, gestum facientes competentem; et veniant vicissim juxta paradisum, ostendentes Evae fructum vetitum, quasi suadentes ei ut eum comedat. Tunc veniat diabolus ad Adam et dicet ei:

How are you doing, Adam?	Que fais, Adam?

ADAM   I live in great delight.

ADAM   Ci vif en grant deduit.

DEVIL

DIABOLUS

Are you well?

Estas tu bien?

ADAM   I feel nothing that annoys me.

ADAM   Ne sen rien que m'enoit.

DEVIL

DIABOLUS

Things could be better.

Poet estre mielz.

---

[112]s.d. *church:* i.e., God's heavenly residence, spatially represented by the church portals immediately behind paradise at the top of the church steps. *platea:* open acting area at the foot of the steps, near the spectators. The use of the Latin plural, *per plateas,* is puzzling.

ADAM   I don't know how.   115

DEVIL

Would you like to know?

ADAM   I'd like that!

DEVIL

I know how.

ADAM   And what does that matter to me?

DEVIL

Why wouldn't it matter?

ADAM   It's of no benefit to me.

DEVIL

It will benefit you.

ADAM   I don't know when.

DEVIL

I won't hurry to tell you, then.   120

ADAM

Come on, tell me.

DEVIL   I won't,
Until I see you weary of begging.

ADAM

I don't need to know this thing.

DEVIL

You don't deserve to be well off.
You have a good thing that you don't
         know how to enjoy.   125

ADAM

How is that?

DEVIL   Would you like to hear?
I'll tell you confidentially.

ADAM

[I'll listen,] surely.

DEVIL

Listen, Adam, pay attention to me.

ADAM   Ne puis saver coment.

DIABOLUS

Vols le tu saver?

ADAM   Bien en iert mon talent!

DIABOLUS

Jo sai coment.

ADAM   E moi que chalt?

DIABOLUS

Por quei non?

ADAM   Rien ne me valt.

DIABOLUS

Il te valdra.

ADAM   Jo ne sai quant.

DIABOLUS

Nel te dirrai pas en curant.

ADAM

Or le me di!

DIABOLUS   Non frai pas
Ainz te verrai del preer las.

ADAM

N'ai nul besoing de ço saveir.

DIABOLUS

Kar tu ne deiz nul bien aver.
Tu as li bien, ne seiez joïr.

ADAM

E jo coment?

DIABOLUS   Voldras l'oïr?
Jol te dirrai priveïment.

ADAM

. . . . seürement.

DIABOLUS

Escult, Adam, entent a moi:

This will be to your advantage.

ADAM   I consent to that.   130

DEVIL

Will you believe me?

ADAM   Yes, very well.

DEVIL

In everything?

ADAM   Everything except one thing.

DEVIL

What thing?

ADAM   I'll tell you:
I will not offend my maker.

DEVIL

Do you fear him that much?

ADAM   Yes, indeed,   135
I love and fear him.

DEVIL   That's foolish.
What can he do to you?

ADAM   Both good and evil.

DEVIL

You're starting on a very foolish business,
To fear so much that evil can come to you.
Aren't you in glory? You cannot die.   140

ADAM

God said to me that I shall die
When I transgress his commandment.

DEVIL

What is this great transgression?
I'd like to hear this right off.

ADAM

I will tell you quite frankly.   145
He gave me one commandment:
Of all the fruits of paradise
I may eat—so he taught me—
Except one only; that one is forbidden.
That one I will not touch with my hands.   150

Ço iert tun pru.

ADAM   E jo l'otrei.

DIABOLUS

Creras me tu?

ADAM   Oïl, mult bien.

DIABOLUS

Del tut en tut?

ADAM   Fors de une rien.

DIABOLUS

De quel chose?

ADAM   Jol te dirrai:
Mon creator pas ne offendrai.

DIABOLUS

Criens le tu tant?

ADAM   Oïl, par veir,
Jo l'aim e criem.

DIABOLUS   N'est pas saveir.
Que te poet faire?

ADAM   E bien e mal.

DIABOLUS

Molt es entré en fol jornal,
Quant creiez mal te poisse venir.
N'es tu en gloire? N'en poez morir.

ADAM

Deus le m'a dit que je murrai
Quant son precept trespasserai.

DIABOLUS

Quel est cist grant trespassement?
Oïr le voil sens nul entent.

ADAM

Jol te dirrai tot veirement.
Il me fist un comandement:
De tuit le fruit de paradis
Puis jo manger—ço m'a apris—
Fors de sul un; cil m'est defens.
Çolui ne tucherai de mains.

DEVIL

Which one is that?

Then let Adam raise his hand and point out to him the forbidden fruit, saying:

ADAM   Do you see there?
That one has been forbidden to me.

DEVIL

Do you know why?

ADAM   I? No, indeed.

DEVIL

I'll tell you the reason.
He doesn't care at all about the other
      fruit,   155

And let him point out to him the forbidden fruit with his hand, saying to Adam:

Except for that one which hangs on high.
That is the fruit of knowledge:
It gives the understanding to know
      everything.
If you eat it, you will benefit from it.

ADAM

How?

DEVIL   You'll see.   160
At once your eyes will be opened;
Everything to come will be revealed to you;
You will be able to do whatever you
      desire.
It will bestow many blessings upon you:
Eat it, and you'll prosper.   165
You'll have nothing to fear from your God;
Instead, you will be his peer in everything.
This is why he has seen fit to refuse you.
Will you trust me? Taste of the fruit.

ADAM

I won't do it.

DEVIL [*ironically*] Well, listen to this pleasant
      news!   170

DIABOLUS

Li quels est ço?

Tunc erigat manum Adam et ostendat ei fructum vetitum, dicens:

ADAM   Veez le tu la?
Çolui tres bien me devia.

DIABOLUS

Sez tu por quoi?

ADAM   Jo? certes non.

DIABOLUS

Jo te dirrai ja l'achaison.
De l'altre fruit rien ne li chalt,

Et manu ostendat ei fructum vetitum, dicens Adae:

Fors de celui qui pent en halt.
Ço est le fruit de sapïence:
De tut saveir done scïence.
Se tu le manjues, bon le fras.

ADAM

E jo en quei?

DIABOLUS   Tu le verras.
Ti oil serrunt sempres overt;
Quanque deit estre t'iert apert;
Quanque vuldras porras faire.

Mult le fait bon vers tei atraire:
Manjue le, si fras bien.
Ne crendras pois tun Deu de rien;
Aienz serras puis del tut son per.
Por ço le quidat veer.
Creras me tu? Guste del fruit.

ADAM

Noel frai pas.

DIABOLUS   Or oëz deduit!

Won't you do it?

ADAM   No.

DEVIL   How stupid you are!
You will remember these words again.

*Then let the devil withdraw; and he will go to
the other demons, and make a foray through the
platea; and, after a short delay, cheerful and
rejoicing, he will return to the tempting of Adam,
and say to him:*

Adam, how are you doing? Will you
    change your mind?
Are you still having foolish ideas?
I meant to tell you the other day,   175
God has made you his beneficiary,
He put you here to eat this fruit.
Have you then any other pleasures?

ADAM

Yes, I lack for nothing.

DEVIL

Don't you aspire to anything higher?   180
You can certainly consider yourself
    fortunate
When God has made you his gardener!
God has made you keeper of his garden;
Won't you look for other pleasures?
Did he create you solely for material
    appetite?   185
Didn't he wish to bestow any other honor
    on you?
Listen, Adam, pay attention to me:
I will counsel you in faith
How you can be without a master,
And the equal of your creator.   190
I'll tell you the whole truth:
If you eat of the apple

Then he will raise his hand toward paradise

You will reign in majesty.
You can share omnipotence with God.

ADAM

Get away from here.

Nel feras?

ADAM   Non!

DIABOLUS   Kar tu es soz!
Encore te membrera des moz.

*Tunc recedat diabolus, et ibit ad alios demones,
et faciet discursum per plateam; et facta
aliquantula mora, hilaris et gaudens, redibit ad
temptandum Adam et dicet ei:*

Adam, que fais? Changeras tun sens?

Es tu encore en fol porpens?
Jol te quidai dire l'autr'er,
Deus t'a fait ci sun provender,
Ci t'ad mis por mangier cest fruit.
As tu donch altre deduit?

ADAM

Jo oïl!....ne me falt.

DIABOLUS

Ne munteras ja mès plus halt?
Molt te porras tenir por chier

Quant Deus t'a fet sun jardenier!
Deus t'a feit gardein de son ort;
Ja ne querras altre deport?
Forma il toi por ventre faire?

Altre honor ne te voldra atraire?

Escut, Adam, entent a moi:
Jo te conseillerai en fei
Que porras estre senz seignor,
E seras per del creatur.
Jo te dirrai tute la summe:
Si tu manjues la pome

Tunc eriget manum contra paradisum

Tu regneras en majesté.
Od Deu poez partir poësté.

ADAM

Fui tei de ci.

DEVIL	What did you say, Adam? 195

ADAM

Get away from here! You are Satan.
You give evil counsel.

DEVIL   I? How is that?

[ADAM]

You would deliver me into torment,
Set me at odds with my Lord,
Remove me from joy, put me in sadness.   200
I won't trust you. Get away from here!
Don't ever be so audacious
As to come into my presence.
You are a traitor and without grace.

*Then, sadly and with downcast countenance, he
will withdraw from Adam and go to the gates of
hell, and hold a conference with the other demons.
Thereafter he will make a foray among the people.
Thereupon he will draw near to paradise, on the
side where Eve is, and with a joyful countenance,
fawningly, he addresses Eve as follows:*

[DEVIL]

Eve, I have come to you.   205

EVE

Tell me, Satan, why?

DEVIL

I want to seek your profit, your honor.

EVE

May God grant it!

DEVIL   Don't be afraid.
For a long time I have known
All the secrets of paradise.   210
One part of them I'll tell you.

EVE

Begin, and I will listen.

DEVIL

Will you listen to me?

DIABOLUS   Que dit, Adam?

ADAM

Fui tei de ci! Tu es Sathan.
Mal conseil dones.

DIABOLUS   E jo coment?

[ADAM]

Tu me voels livrer a torment,
Mesler me vols o mun Seignor,
Tolir de joie, mettre en dolor.
Ne te crerrai. Fui te de ci!
Ne soies ja mais tant hardi
Que tu ja viengez devant moi.
Tu es traïtres, e sanz foi.

*Tunc tristis et vultu demisso recedet ab Adam
et ibit usque ad portas inferni, et colloquia
habebit cum aliis demoniis. Post ea vero
discursum faciet per populum. De hinc ex parte
Evae accedet ad paradisum, et Evam laeto
vultu blandiens sic alloquitur:*

[DIABOLUS]

Eva, ça sui venuz a toi.

EVA

Di moi, Sathan, or tu pur quoi?

DIABOLUS

Jo vois querant tun pru, tun honor.

EVA

Ço dunge Deu!

DIABOLUS   N'aiez poür.
Mult a grant tens que jo ai apris
Toz les conseils de paraïs.
Une partie t'en dirrai.

EVA

Ore le comence, e jo l'orrai.

DIABOLUS

Orras me tu?

EVE I'll do so, all right,
Nor anger you in any way.

DEVIL

You'll keep a secret?

EVE Yes, by my faith. 215

DEVIL

Will it be revealed?

EVE Certainly not by me.

DEVIL

I will put me in your trust.
I wish no further assurance from you.

EVE

You can certainly trust my word.

DEVIL

You have been to a good school!— 220
I have seen Adam, but he is too much of a
    fool.

EVE

He's a little hard.

DEVIL He will be soft.
He is harder than fire!

EVE

He is very noble.

DEVIL On the contrary, he's servile.
He lacks the will to look after his best
    interests. 225
He ought to do so at least for you.
You are a delicate and tender thing,
And fresher than the rose;
You are whiter than crystal,
Than snow that falls on ice in the valley. 230
The Creator has made an ill-matched pair:
You are too tender, and he too hard.
But notwithstanding you are wiser;
Your mind has discovered great wisdom.
For this reason it is good to approach you. 235
I wish to speak with you.

EVA Si frai bien,
Ne te curcerai de rien.

DIABOLUS

Celeras m'en?

EVA Oïl, par foi!

DIABOLUS

Iert descovert?

EVA Nenil par moi.

DIABOLUS

Or me mettrai en ma creance.
Ne voil de toi altre fiance.

EVA

Bien te pois creire a ma parole.

DIABOLUS

Tu as esté en bone escole!—
Jo vi Adam, mais trop est fols.

EVA

Un poi est durs.

DIABOLUS Il serra mols.
Il est plus dors que n'est emfers!

EVA

Il est mult francs.

DIABOLUS Ainz, est mult serf.
Cure nen voelt prendre de soi.

Car la prenge sevals de toi.
Tu es fieblette e tendre chose,
E es plus fresche que n'est rose;
Tu es plus blanche que cristal,
Que neif que chiet sor glace en val.
Mal cuple em fist li Criator:
Tu es trop tendre, e il, trop dur.
Mais neporquant tu es plus sage;
En grant sens as mis tun corrage.
Por ço fait bon traire a toi.
Parler te voil.

EVE   Speak truthfully, then.

DEVIL

Let no one know of it.

EVE   Who should know?

DEVIL

Not even Adam.

EVE   Certainly not by me.

DEVIL

I will tell you, and you listen to me.
There is no one in this business but us two   240
And Adam over there, who doesn't hear us.

EVE

Speak louder, he won't know anything of it.

DEVIL

I'll acquaint you with a great plot
Laid against you in this garden.
The fruit God gave you   245
Has scarcely any goodness in it;
That one he so vehemently forbade you
Has extraordinary virtue.
In it there is the gift of life,
Of power and dominion,   250
Of knowing all things, good and evil.

EVE

What taste does it have?

DEVIL   Heavenly!
To your fair body, to your face
This fortunate event would be so well suited
That you would become mistress of the
       world,   255
Of the firmament and of the deep,
And know everything to come,
So that you would become the wise ruler of
       all things.

EVE

Is the fruit of such a nature?

DEVIL   Yes, truly.

EVA   Ore i ait fai.

DIABOLUS

N'en sache nuls.

EVA   Ki le deit saver?

DIABOLUS

Neïs Adam.

EVA   Nenil, par moi.

DIABOLUS

Or te dirrai, e tu m'ascute.
N'a que nus dous en ceste rote
E Adam la, qu'il ne nus ot.

EVA

Parlez en halt, n'en savrat mot.

DIABOLUS

Jo vus acoint d'un grant engin
Que vus est fait en cest gardin.
Le fruit que Deus vus ad doné
Nen a en soi gaires bonté;
Cil qu'il vus ad tant defendu,
Il ad en soi grant vertu.
En celui est grace de vie,
De poëste e de seignorie,
De tut saver, bien e mal.

EVA

Quel savor a?

DIABOLUS   Celestial!
A ton bel cors, a ta figure
Bien co[n]vendreit tel aventure
Que tu fusses dame del mond,

Del soverain e del parfont,
E seüsez quanque a estre,
Que de tuit fuissez bone maistre.

EVA

Est tel li fruiz?

DIABOLUS   Oïl, par voir.

Then Eve will carefully inspect the forbidden fruit, and, after having considered it for a long while, she will say:

It does me good just to look at it.   260

DEVIL

What will happen if you eat it?

EVE

How should I know?

DEVIL   Won't you believe me?
Take it first, and give it to Adam.
At once you will possess the crown of
    heaven.
You will be the equal of the Creator;   265
He won't be able to hide secrets from you.
As soon as you have eaten of the fruit,
At once your hearts will be transformed.
With God you will be, without fail,
Of equal goodness, equal might.   270
Taste of the fruit.

EVE   I intend to.

DEVIL

Don't trust Adam.

EVE   I'll do it [later].

DEVIL

When?

EVE   ...Let me [wait]
Until Adam is asleep.

DEVIL

Eat, it, don't be doubtful!   275
To delay would be childish.

Then let the devil withdraw from Eve, and he will go to hell. Adam will come to Eve, acting annoyed because the devil has spoken with her, and he will say to her:

Tell me, wife, what was that evil Satan
Asking you about? What did he want from
    you?

Tunc diligenter intuebitur Eva fructum vetitum, quo diutius intuitu, dicens:

Ja me fait bien sol le veer.

DIABOLUS

Si tu le mangues, que feras?

EVA

E jo que sai?

DIABOLUS   Ne me crerras?
Primes le pren, e a Adam le done.
Del ciel averez sempres corone.
Al Creator serrez pareil;
Ne vus purra celer conseil.
Puis que del fruit avrez mangié,
Sempres vus iert le cuer changié.
O Deus serrez, sanz faillance,
De egal bonté, de egal puissance.
Guste del fruit.

EVA   Jo'n ai regard.

DIABOLUS

Ne creire Adam.

EVA   Jol ferai.

DIABOLUS

Quant?

EVA   ...Suffrez moi
Tant que Adam soit en recoi.

DIABOLUS

Manjue le, n'aiez dutance!
Le demorer serrat emfance.

Tunc recedat diabolus ab Eva, et ibit ad infernum. Adam vero veniet ad Evam, moleste ferens, quod cum ea locutus sit diabolus, et dicet ei:

Di moi, muiller, que te querroit
Li mal Satan? Que te voleit?

EVE

He talked to me about our advancement.

ADAM

Don't believe the traitor!—   280
Yes, he is a traitor.

EVE   I know it perfectly well.

ADAM

How do you know?

EVE   Because I have tried it out.
What's wrong with his seeing me?

[ADAM]

He'll make you change your mind.

EVE

No he won't, because I will believe
                nothing   285
Until I've tested him.

ADAM

Don't let him come near you,
For he's a fellow of very bad faith.
He wanted to betray his Sovereign
And set himself in place of Him who is
                highest.   290
I do not want a scoundrel who has done such
                things
To have access to you.

*Then a serpent, artfully constructed, arises
alongside the trunk of the forbidden tree. Eve
will incline her ear near to it, as if hearkening
to its counsel. Hereupon Eve will accept the
apple, and offer it to Adam. But he will not
accept it yet, and Eve will say to him:*

Eat, Adam. You don't know what it is.
Let us take this good thing that is at hand
                for us.

ADAM

Is it so good?

EVA

Il me parla de nostre honor.

ADAM

Ne creire ja le traïtor!
Il est traître.

EVA   Bien le sai.

ADAM

E tu coment?

EVA   Car l'asajai.
De ço que chalt me del veer?

[ADAM]

Il te ferra changer saver.

EVA

Nel fra pas, car nel crerai

De nule rien tant que l'asai.

ADAM

Nel laisser mais venir sor toi,
Car il est mult de pute foi.
Il volst traïr ja son Seignor
E so[i] poser al des halzor.

Tel paltonier qui ço ad fait

Ne voil que vers vus ait nul retrait.

*Tunc serpens artificiose compositus ascendit
juxta stipitem arboris vetitae. Cui Eva propius
adhibebit aurem, quasi ipsius auscultans
consilium. Dehinc accipiet Eva pomum,
porriget Adae. Ipse vero nondum eum accipiet, et Eva dicet ei:*

Manjue, Adam! Ne sez que est.
Pernum ço bien que nus est prest.

ADAM

Est il tant bon?

289–90 *He . . . highest:* Adam refers to the story of the fall of Lucifer from heaven for disobeying
God.

EVE   You will know soon,   295
But you can't know until you've tasted.

ADAM

I'm fearful of it.

EVE   Stop being afraid!

ADAM   I won't do it.

EVE

You delay out of cowardice.

ADAM

I'll take it.

EVE   Eat. Take it!
By it you will know both good and evil.   300
I will eat some first.

ADAM

And I afterwards.

EVE   Promise?

*Then Eve will eat part of the apple, and say to
Adam:*

I've tasted it. My God, what flavor!
I've never savored such sweetness.
What a taste this apple has!   305

ADAM

Like what?

EVE   Like no mortal taste.
Now my eyes see so clearly
I am like the allpowerful God.
I know all that has been and is to come;
I am complete master of everything.   310
Eat, Adam, don't hesitate.
You will take it in a lucky hour.

*Then Adam will take the apple from Eve's
hand, saying:*

I'll trust you in this. You are my partner.

EVE

Eat. Don't be fearful.

EVA   Tu le saveras,
Nel poez saver si'n gusteras.

ADAM

J'en duit.

EVA   Lai le!

ADAM   Nen frai pas.

EVA

Del demorer fai tu que las.

ADAM

E jo le prendrai.

EVA   Manjue. Ten!
Par ço saveras e mal e bien.
Jo en manjerai premirement.

ADAM

E jo aprés.

EVA   Seürement?

*Tunc comedet Eva partem pomi, et dicet
Adae:*

Gusté en ai. Deus, quele savor!
Unc ne tastai d'itel dolçor.
D'itel savor est ceste pome!

ADAM

De quel?

EVA   D'itel nen gusta home.
Or sunt mes oil tant cler veant
Jo semble Deu le tuit puissant.
Quanque fu, quanque doit estre
Sai jo trestut; bien en sui maistre.
Manjue, Adam, ne faz demore.
Tu le prendras en mult bon ore.

*Tunc accipiet Adam pomum de manu Evae,
dicens:*

Jo t'en crerra. Tu es ma per.

EVA

Manjue. Nen poez doter.

Then let Adam eat part of the apple. When he has eaten he will recognize his sin at once, and will bend over so that he cannot be seen by the people. And he will strip off his festive garments, and will put on poor clothes sewn together with fig leaves, and, manifesting exceedingly great sorrow he will begin his lamentation:

Tunc comedat Adam partem pomi. Quo comesto cognoscet statim peccatum suum et inclinabit se, [ut] non possit a populo videri. Et exuet sollemnes vestes, et induet vestes pauperes consutas foliis ficus, et maximum simulans dolorem incipiet lamentationem suam:

Alas, sinful wretch, what have I done? 315	Allas, pecchor, que ai jo fait?
Now I am dead without escape.	Or sui mort sanz nul retrait.
Without remedy I am dead,	Senz nul rescus sui jo mort,
So evil has my fortune fallen.	Tant est chaite mal ma sort.
My fortune has changed for the worse:	Mal m'est changé ma aventure:
Once it was auspicious, now it is harsh. 320	Mult fu ja bone, or est mult dore.
I have forsaken my Creator	Jo ai guerpi mun Criator
Through the counsel of a wicked wife.	Par le conseil de mal uxor.
Alas, sinful one, what shall I do?	Allas, pecchable, que frai?
Upon my Creator how can I look?	Mun Criator cum atendrai?
How can I look upon my Creator 325	Cum atendrai mon Criator
Whom I have forsaken through my folly?	Que jo ai guerpi por ma folor?
Never have I made such a bad bargain.	Unches ne fis tant mal marchié.
Now I know what it is to sin.	Or sai jo ja que est pecchié.
O Death, why do you let me live?	Ai, Mort, por quoi me laisses vivre?
Why is the world not rid of me? 330	Que n'est li monde de moi delivre?
Why do I still encumber the world?	Por quoi faz encombrer al mond?
I must experience the depths of hell.	D'emfer m'estoet tempter le fond.
In hell will be my dwelling,	En emfer serra ma demure,
Until the coming of one who can save me.	Tant que vienge qui me sucure.
Thus in hell I will lead my life. 335	En emfer si avrai ma vie.
Whence will help come to me there?	Dont me vendra iloc aïe?
Whence will rescue come to me there?	Dont me vendra iloec socors?
Who will draw me away from such sorrow?	Ki me trara d'ités dolors?
Why did I do wrong to my Lord?	Por quei vers mon Seignor mesfis?
Now there is no one that should be my friend. 340	Ne me deit estre nul amis.
There will be no one that can avail at all.	Non iert nul que gaires vaille.
I am lost without fail.	Jo sui perdu senz nule faille.
I have sinned so against my Lord,	Vers mon Seignor sui si mesfait,
I can enter no plea against him,	Nen puis contre lui entrer em plait,
For I am in the wrong, he in the right. 345	Car jo ai tort, e il ad droit.
My God, what a horrible plight I'm in!	Deu, tant a ci mal plait!
Who henceforth will remember me?	Chi avrad mais de moi memorie?

---

314 s.d. *bend over:* i.e., Adam conceals himself behind the curtains surrounding paradise at breast height.

For I have sinned against the king of glory.
Against the king of heaven I have sinned so
That I have not the slightest claim upon
    him.   350
No friend have I, or neighbor,
Who might rescue me from my accusation
    at last.
And whom shall I beseech to aid me,
When my own wife has betrayed me,
She whom God gave me as partner?   355
She has given me evil counsel.
Oh, Eve!

Then he will look at Eve his wife, and say:

    Alas, foolhardy wife!
In an evil hour were you born of me!
If only that rib had been burned
Which has brought me to this evil pass!   360
If only the rib had been consumed in fire
Which has caused me such strife!
When he drew that rib from me,
Why didn't he burn it, and kill me?
The rib has betrayed the whole body,   365
Injured and maltreated it.
I don't know what to say or do.
If grace does not come to me from heaven,
I can never be rescued from pain,
Such is the evil that torments me.   370
Ah, Eve! Evil the hour—
Such terrible torment overwhelms me—
When you became my companion!
Now I am dead by your counsel.
By your counsel I am reduced to evil
    fortune,   375
Brought low from great height.
I will be redeemed thence by no mortal,
None save God in his majesty.
What do I say, unhappy one? Why have I
    named him?
He help me? I have angered him.   380
None will ever aid me
Except the Son who will come forth from
    Mary.
I don't know where to turn
Since we have not kept faith with God.

Car sui mesfet au roi de gloire.
Au roi del ciel sui si mesfait,
De raison n'ai vers lui un trait.

Nen ai ami ne nul veisin
Qui me trai del plait a fin.

Qui preirai jo ja qui m'aït,
Quant ma femme m'a traït,
Qui Dex me dona por pareil?
Ele me dona mal conseil.
Ai, Eve!

Tunc aspiciet Evam uxorem suam et dicet:

    Ai, femme desvee!
Mal fussez vus de moi nee!
Car fust arse iceste coste
Qui m'ad mis en si male poste!
Car fust la coste en fu brudlee,
Qui m'ad basti si grant meslee!
Quant cele coste de moi prist,
Por quei ne l'arst, e moi oscist?
La coste ad tut le cors tra[ï],
E afolé e mal bailli.
Ne sa que die ne k'en face.
Si ne me vient del ciel la grace,
Nem puis estre gieté de paine,
Tel est li mals que me demaine.
Ai, Eve! Cum a mal ore—
Cume grant peine me curut sore—
Quant onches fustes mi parail!
Ore sui perriz par ton conseil.
Par ton conseil sui mis a mal,

De grant haltesce sui mis aval.
N'en serrai trait por home né,
Si Deu nen est de majesté.
Que di jo, las? Por quoi le nomai?

Il me aidera? Corocé l'ai.
Ne me ferat ja nul aïe,
For le Filz que istra de Marie.

Ne sai de nus prendre conroi,
Quant a Deu ne portames foi.

Then let all be as it please God: 385
No alternative except to die.

Then let the choir begin: R̷ [Responsory]: While God walked [in the garden of paradise]. When this has been said, the Figure will come wearing a stole and will walk in paradise, looking around as if seeking to know where Adam is. But Adam and Eve will hide in a corner of paradise, as if knowing how wretched they are; and the Figure will say:

Adam, where are you?

Then both will rise, standing before the Figure, and yet not fully upright, but, through shame for their sin, somewhat bent forward and extremely sad; and let [Adam] answer:

ADAM   I am here, reverend Sire.
I hid myself from your wrath;
And because I was completely naked
I thus concealed myself here.   390

FIGURE

What have you done? How have you gone
    astray?
Who has drawn you away from your
    goodness?
What have you done? Why are you
    ashamed?
How will I settle accounts with you now?
Until recently you had nothing   395
Of which you ought to be ashamed;
Now I see you downcast and mournful.
They enjoy themselves ill who live thus.

ADAM

I am so ashamed, Sire, before you
. . . .

FIGURE   And why?   400

ADAM

Such great shame entwines my body
That I dare not look you in the face.

Or en soit tot a Deu plaisir:
N'i ad conseil que del morir.

Tunc incipiat chorus: R̷ Dum deambularet. Quo dicto, veniet Figura stola[m] habens et ingredietur paradisum circumspiciens, quasi quaereret ubi esset Adam. Adam vero et Eva latebunt in angulo paradisi, quasi suam cognoscentes miser[i]am, et dicet Figura:

Adam, ubi es?

Tunc ambo surgent, stantes contra Figuram, non tamen omnino erecti, sed ob verecundiam sui peccati aliquantulum curvati et multum tristes, et respondeat

ADAM   Ci sui jo, beal Sire.
Repost me sui ja por ta ire;
E por ço que sui tut nuz
Me sui jo ici si embatuz.

FIGURA

Ke as tu fet? Cum as erré?

Qui t'a toleit de ta bonté?

Que as tu fet? Por quei as honte?

Cum entrerai od toi en conte?
Tu n'avois rien l'autr'ier
Dunt tu duses vergunder;
Or te voi mult triste e morne.
Mal s'enjoïst qui ensi sojorne.

ADAM

Tel vergoine ai jo, Sire, de toi
. . . .

FIGURA   E tu por quoi?

ADAM

Si grant honte mon cors enlace,
Ne t'os veer en la face.

---

386 S.D. *Responsory*: See note, l. 1 S.D.

FIGURE

Why have you transgressed my prohibition?
Have you gained anything?
You are my servant, and I your Lord.   405

ADAM

I cannot deny it.

FIGURE

I created you in my own likeness;
Why have you transgressed my
       commandment?
I shaped you after my own image;
Why have you done me this outrage?   410
You paid no attention to my prohibition;
Deliberately you transgressed it.
You ate the fruit which I told you
I had forbidden you.
Did you think by this to be my equal?   415
I didn't think you would joke this way.

   Then Adam will stretch out his hand toward the
   Figure, then toward Eve, saying:

The woman you gave me,
She first committed this trespass:
She gave it to me, and I ate.
Now, I see, it has turned to woe.   420
I meddled rashly to eat this;
I have transgressed through my wife.

FIGURE

You trusted your wife more than me.
You ate the fruit without my permission.
Now I will render you the following
       recompense: 425
The earth will be cursed
Where you will wish to sow your grain.
It will fail to bear fruit,
It is cursed beneath your hand;
You will cultivate it in vain.   430
It will deny its fruit to you;
It will yield you thorns and thistles.
It will change whatever you sow;
It will be cursed, as punishment to you.
With grievous toil, with great exertion   435

FIGURE

Por quei trespassas mon devé?
As tu gaires gaainnié?
Tu es mon serf, e jo ton Sire.

ADAM

Nel te puis pas contredire.

FIGURA

Jo te formai a mon semblant;
Por quei trespassas mon comant?

Jo toi plasmai dreit a ma ymage;
Por ço me fis cel oltrage?
Mun defens un pas ne gardas;
Delivrement le trespassas.
Le fruit manjas, dunt jo t'oi dit
Que jo t'avoie contredit.
Por ço quidas estre mon per?
Ne sai si tu voldras gabber.

   Tunc Adam manu[m] extendet contra Figu-
   ram, post ea contra Eva[m], dicens:

La femme que tu me donas,
Ele fist prime icest trespas:
Donat le moi, e jo mangai.
Or m'est avis que tornez est a gwai.
Mal acontai icest mangier;
Jo ai mesfait par ma moiller.

FIGURA

Ta moiller creïstes plus que moi.
Manjas le fruit sanz mon otroi.
Or te rendrai itel guerdon:

La terre avrat maleïçon
Ou tu voldras ton blé semer.
Il te faldrat al fruit porter,
Ele est maleite soz ta main;
Tu le cotiveras en vain.
Son fruit a toi devendrat;
Espines e chardons te rendrat.
Changer te voldra ta semence;
Malait iert por ta sentence.
Od grant travail, od grant hahan

You will have to eat your bread.
In great torment and sweat
You will live night and day.

*Then the Figure will turn toward Eve, and with
a threatening countenance say to her:*

And you, Eve, wicked woman,
You began to make war against me: 440
You held my commandments in light
        regard.

EVE

The wicked serpent deceived me.

FIGURE

Through him did you think to become my
        equal?
Have you learned how to prophesy well?
Formerly you held sovereignty   445
Over all living things;
How quickly you've lost that!
Now I see you sad and dejected;
Have you gained or lost?
I will render you your just desert,   450
I will give you this for your service:
Misfortune will afflict you in every way.
In sorrow you will bring forth children,
And in pain they will live all their lives.
Your children will be born in sorrow,   455
And will end their days in great anguish.
To such hardship, to such shame
You have brought both yourself and your
        lineage.
All those who will issue from you
Will deplore your sin.   460

And Eve will answer, saying:

I have sinned, it was by my folly.
For one apple I will suffer great shame
        thus,
Because I have placed myself and my lineage
        in pain.
A small gain yields me a heavy toll in
        sorrow.
If I have sinned, it was no great marvel,   465
Whenas the deceiving serpent betrayed me.

Toi covendra manger ton pan.
Od grant paine, od grant suor
Vivras tu noit e jor.

*Tunc Figura vertet se contra Evam, et
minaci vultu ei dicet:*

E tu, Eve, male muiller,
Tost me començas de guerreer:
Poi tenis mes comandemenz.

EVA

Ja m'engingna li mal serpenz.

FIGURA

Par lui quidas estre mon per?
Ses tu ja bien deviner?
Or einz aviez la maistrie
De quanque doit estre en vie;
Cum l'as tu ja si tost perdue!
Or te voi triste e mal venue;
As tu fet gain ou perte?
Jo toi rendrai ta deserte,
Jo t'en donrai por ton servise:
Mal te vendra en tote guise.
En dolor porteras emfanz,
E em paine vivront tot lor anz.
Tes emfanz en dolor naistront,
E en grant anguisse finerunt.
En tel hahan, en tel damage
As mis [e] toi e tun lignage.

Toit ceals qui de toi istront
Li ton pecché ploreront.

Et respondebit Eva, dicens:

Go sui mesfait, ço fu par folage.
Por une pome soffrirai si grant damage,

Que en paine met [e] moi e mon lignage.

Petit aquest me rent grant traüage.

Si jo mesfis, ne fu merveille grant,
Quant traï moi le serpent suduiant.

Much he knows of evil; he certainly isn't
    innocent like a lamb.
Anyone who follows his advice is put in evil
    plight.
I took the apple; now I know I acted
    foolishly
Against your prohibition; in that I behaved
    wickedly.   470
Evilly I tasted it; now I am hated by you.
For a little fruit I must lose my life.

Mult set de mal; nen semble pas oeille.

Mal est bailliz qui a lui se conseille.

La pome pris; or sai que fis folie

Sor ton defens; de ço fis folonie.

Mal en gustai; or sui de toi haïe.
Por poi de froit moi covient perdre la vie.

Then the Figure will threaten the serpent, saying:

Tunc minabitur Figura serpenti, dicens:

And you, serpent, be accursed!
From you I will recover my full right.
Upon your belly you shall go   475
All the days of your life.
Dust will be your daily food
In the wood, in field, on heath.
Woman will detest you;
Forever she will be an evil neighbor to you. 480
You will lie in wait for her heel,
She will pluck you by the head.
She will strike your head such a blow
That it will cause you great hardship.
She will carefully figure out   485
How she can be revenged on you.
You meddled evilly in her company;
She will bow your head.
A root will spring from her
Who will confound all your powers.   490

E tu, serpe[n]t, soiez maleït!
De to[i] reprendrai bien mon droit.
Sor ton piz te traïneras
A tuz les jors que ja viveras.
La puldre iert tut dis ta vïande,
En bois, en plain, en lande.
Femme te portera haïne;
Oncore te iert male veisine.
Tu son talon aguaiteras,
Cele te sachera le ras.
Ta teste ferra de itel mail
Qui te ferra mult grant trav[a]il.
Encore en prendra bien conrei
Cum porra vengier de toi.
Mal acointas tu sun traïn;
Ele te fra le chief enclin.
Oncore raïz de lui istra
Qui toz tes vertuz confundra.

Then the Figure will drive them forth from paradise, saying:

Tunc Figura expellet eos de paradiso, dicens:

Now get out of paradise.
You have made an unhappy change of
    residence.
On earth you will have your dwelling;
You have no claim on paradise.
You have nothing that is your due here. 495

Ore issé hors de paradis.
Mal change avez fet de païs.

En terre vus frez maison;
En paradis n'avez raison.
N'i avez rien que chalengier.

481–82The French word "ras" occurs nowhere else, and can be translated only uncertainly. However, the lines would seem to convey the meaning of Genesis 3:15: "And I will put enmity between you and the woman, and between your seed and her seed; it shall bruise your head, and you shall bruise his heel."

Out you will go, without remedy.

You have nothing here to claim through
    judgment.

Now take some other dwelling.

Depart from bliss;

Hunger and weariness will not fail you,   500

Nor sorrow and pain,

Every day of the week.

On earth you will have an unhappy sojourn;

Then you will finally die;

After you have tasted death,   505

You will come to hell without remission.

Here in hell exile will afflict your bodies,

Peril daunt your souls.

Satan will have you in his power.

There is no man who could aid you: 510

By whom could you be rescued,

If I do not take pity on you?

*Let the choir sing: ℟ [Responsory]: In the
sweat of your face. Meanwhile an angel will
come dressed in white, bearing a flaming sword
in his hand, whom the Figure will station at the
gate of paradise and will say to him:*

Guard paradise well for me

So that this outlaw may not enter there;

That he may not have the power or
    dominion   515

To touch the fruit of life.

With this flaming sword

Bar him the way.

*When they are outside paradise, as though sad
and confused they will be bowed down to the
ground, bent over to their ankles, and the Figure
will point at them with his hand, his face turned
toward paradise. And the choir will begin: ℟
[Responsory]: Behold, Adam is become
as one [of us]. When this is done, the Figure will
return to the church. Then Adam will have a spade
and Eve a rake, and they will begin to till the
ground, and sow wheat in it. After they have
sown, they will go and sit for a while in a certain*

Fors isterez, sen recoverer.

N'i avez rien par jugement.

Or pernez aillors chasement.

Fors en issez de bonaürté;

Ne vus falt mais faim ne lasseté,

Ne vus falt mais dolor ne paine

A toz les jors de la semaine.

En terre avrez malvais sojor;

Aprés morrez al chief de tor;

Despois qu'averez gusté mort,

En emfer irrez sanz deport.

Ici avront les cors eissil,

Les almes en emfern peril.

Satan vus avra en baillie.

N'est hom que vus en face aïe:

Par cui soiez vus ja rescos,

Se moi nen prenge pité de vus?

*Chorus cantet: ℟ In sudore vultus tui.
Interim veniet angelus albis indutus, ferens
radientem gladium in manu, quem statuet
Figura ad portam paradisi et dicet ei:*

Gardez moi bien le paradis

Que mais n'i entre icist faidis;

Qu'il n'ait mais poeir ne baillie

Ne de tocher li fruit de vie.

O cele spee qui flamboie

Si li defendez tres bien la voie.

*Cum fueri[n]t extra paradisum, quasi tristes
et confusi, incurvati erunt solo tenus super
talos suos, et Figura manu eos demonstrabit
versa facie contra paradisum. Et chorus
incipiet: ℟: Ecce Adam quasi unus.
Quo finito, et Figura regredietur ad ecclesiam.
Tunc Adam fossorium et Eva rastrum habebit,
et incipient colere terram, et seminabunt in ea
triticum. Postquam seminaverint, ibunt sessum
in loco aliquantulum, tanquam fatigati labore,
et flebiliter respicient saepius paradisum,*

512s.d. *Responsory:* See note, l. 1 s.d.

518s.d. *Responsory:* See note, l. 1 s.d.

*place, as if worn out by their work, and mourn-
fully they will often look back at paradise, beating
their breasts. Meanwhile the devil will come and
plant thorns and thistles in their cultivated fields,
and withdraw. When Adam and Eve come to their
fields and see the thorns and thistles that have
sprung up, stricken with violent grief they will
throw themselves down on the earth, and,
remaining there, will strike their breasts and their
thighs, manifesting their sorrow with their
gestures. And [Adam] will begin his lamentation:*

Alas, woe is me, how evil was that hour
In which my sins overwhelmed me,   520
In which I forsook the Lord whom all
    adore!
Whom shall I ever implore to help me?

*Here let Adam look back at paradise, and he will
raise both his arms toward it, and, devoutly
bowing his head, will say:*

O paradise, how sweet to dwell there!
Garden of glory, what a beautiful sight you
    make!
I am thrown out for my sin, in truth;   525
I have lost all hope of return.
I dwelt therein, yet didn't know how to enjoy
    it;
I believed advice that caused me to leave it
    too quickly.
Now I repent; it is fitting that I am angry.
It is too late; my sighs avail nothing.   530
Where was my understanding? What became
    of my memory,
That for Satan I forsook the king of glory?
Now I suffer for it, and have lost my self-
    esteem.
My sin will be written down in history.

*Then he will lift up his hand against Eve, who
will have been moved away a short distance
from him, and, moving his head with great
indignation, will say to her:*

O wicked woman, full of treason,   535
How quickly you cast me into perdition
When you banished my understanding and
    reason!

*percutientes pectora sua. Interim veniet
diabolus et plantabit in cultura eorum spinas
et tribulos, et abscedet. Cum venerint Adam
et Eva ad culturam suam et viderint ortas
spinas et tribulos, vehementi dolore percussi
prosternent se in terra, et residentes percutient
pectora sua et femora sua, dolorem gestu
fatentes. Et incipiet [Adam] lamentationem
suam:*

Allas! chaitif, tant mal vi unches l'ore,
Que mes pecchez me sunt coru sore,
Que jo guerpi le Seignor que hom aüre!

Qui requerra[i] ja més qu'il me socore?

*Hic respiciat Adam paradisum, et ambas
manus suas elevabit contra eum, et caput pie
inclinans dicet:*

Oi, paradis, tant bel maner!
Vergier de glorie, tant vus fet bel veer!

Jetez en sui par mon pecchié, par voir;
Del recovrer tot ai perdu l'espoir.
Jo fui dedenz, n'en soi gaires joïr;

Creï conseil, chi me fist tost partir.

Or m'en repent; droit est que m'en aïr.
Ço est a tart; rien nen valt mon sospir.
Ou fu mon sens? Que devint ma
    memoire,
Que por Satan guerpi le roi de gloire?
Or m'en travail, si m'en valt mult petit.

Li mien pecchié iert en estoire escrit.

*Tunc manum contra Eva[m] levabit, quae
aliquantulum ab eo erit remota, et cum magna
indignatione movens caput dicet ei:*

Oi male femme, plaine de traïson,
Tant m'as mis tost en perdicion
Cum me tolis le sens e la raison!

Now I repent, I cannot have pardon.

Despondent Eve, how inclined you were to
      evil,

When you believed so quickly the counsel
      of the viper!   540

Through you I am dead, thus I have lost
      life;

Your sin will be written in the book.

Do you see the signs of terrible confusion?

The earth senses our curse:

We sowed corn, now thistles thrive.   545

. . . .

You see the beginning of our misery;

Great is our sorrow, but greater
      awaits us.

We will be led to hell in heaviness;

No pain nor torment will be spared us.   550

Wretched Eve, what do you think of this?

You have won this, it has been given you for
      your dowry.

Nevermore can you bring man felicity,

But will be forever contrary to reason.

All those who will come hereafter, of our
      lineage,   555

Will feel the weight of your misdeed.

You have sinned; all those are condemned
      by it.

Only much later will He come by whom
      this will be changed.

> *Then let Eve answer Adam:*

Adam, dear lord, you have blamed me
      much,

Reviled and reproached my villainy.   560

If I have sinned, I suffer the weight of it.

I am guilty; I will be judged by God.

I have sinned greatly toward God and you;

My sin will long be reviled.

My guilt is great, my sins
      afflict me.   565

Wretched me, I have lacked all goodness!

I have no grounds whereby to defend myself
      against God,

That he should not find me a guilty sinner.

Pardon me, for I cannot make amends!

Or m'en repent, ne puis aver pardon.

Eve dolente, cum fus a mal delivre,

Quant creütes si tost conseil de la guivre!

Par toi sui mort, si ai perdu le vivre;

Li toen pecchié iert esscrit en livre.

Veez tu le signes de grant confusion?

La terre sent la nostre maleïçon:

Forment semames, or i naissent chardon.

. . . .

De nostre mal veiste le comencement;

Ço est nostre grant dolors; mais grainior
      nus atent.

Menez en serroms en emfer laidement;

Ne nus faldra ne poine ne torment.

Eve chaitive, que t'en est a vïaire?

Cest as conquis, donez t'est en duaire.

Ja ne saveras vers home bien atraire,

Més a raison serras tot tens contraire.

Tuz cels que istront, de nostre lignee,

Del toen forfait sentiront la hascee.

Tu forfis; a toz [c]eals est jugee.

Mult tarzera por qui el iert changee.

> *Tunc respondeat Eva ad Adam:*

Adam, bel sire, mult m'avez blastenge[e],

Ma vilainnie retraite e reproche[e].

Si jo mesfis, jo en suffre la haschee.

Jo sui copable; par Deu serrai jugee.

Jo sui vers Deu e vers toi mult mesfeite;

Le mien mesfait mult iert longe retraite.

Ma culpe est grant, mes pecchiez me
      dehaite.

Chaitive sui, de tut bien ai suffraite!

Nen a raison que vers Deu me defende,

Que peccheriz culpable ne me rende.

Pardonez le moi, kar ne puis faire
      amende!

If I could, I would offer a sacrifice.   570

Sinner, unhappy, wretched,

For my misdeed I am overcome with shame
    toward God.

Take me, Death, do not permit me to live!

I am in peril, and cannot reach the shore.

The wicked serpent, the evil viper,   575

Made me eat the apple of misfortune.

I gave it to you; I thought it for the best,

And I led you into sin, for which I can't
    reproach you.

Why wasn't I obedient to the Creator?

Why, my lord, didn't I hold to your   580
    teaching?

You sinned, but I was the root of it.

For our malady, the cure is a long one.

My sin, my grave misdoing,

Our progeny will pay dearly for.

The fruit was sweet, the pain is hard.   585

It was evil to eat; ours will be the guilt.

Notwithstanding, in God is my
    hope.

There will be full reconciliation for this sin:

God will tend me his grace and his favor;

He will rescue us from hell by his might.   590

Then the devil will come, and three or four devils with him, carrying in their hands chains and iron fetters, which they will put on the necks of Adam and Eve. And certain ones will push them, others drag them to hell; still other devils will be close beside hell waiting for them as they come, and among themselves they will make a great dancing and jubilation over their damnation; and each of these other devils will point at them as they come, and will take them and put them into hell. And therein they will cause a great smoke to arise, and they will shout to one another in hell, rejoicing, and they will bang together their pots and caldrons, so that they may be heard outside. And after a short interval, the devils will issue forth, scattering across the platea; certain of them, however, will remain in hell.

Then Cain and Abel will come. Let Cain be dressed in red garments, Abel in white, and they will cultivate ground that has been made ready.

Si jo poeie, jo frai par offrende.

Jo peccheriz, jo lasse, jo chaitive,

Por forfet sui jo vers Deu si eschive.

Mort, car me pren, ne suffret que jo vive!

Em peril sui, ne puis venir a rive.

Li fel serpent, la guivre de mal aire,

Me fist mangier la pome de contraire.

Jo t'en donai; si quidai por bien faire,

E mis toi en pecchié, dont ne te pois
    retraire.

Por quei ne fui al Criator encline?

Por quei ne tien jo, sire, ta discipline?

Tu mesfesis, més jo sui la racine.

De nostre mal, long en est la mescine.

Le mien mesfait, ma grant mesaventure,

Compera chier la nostre engendreore.

Li fruiz fu dulz, la paine est dure.

Mal fu mangiez; nostre iert la fraiture.

Mais neporquant en Deu est ma
    sperance.

D'icest mesfait char tot iert acordance:

Deus me rendra sa grace e sa mustrance;

Gieter nus voldra d'emfer par pussance.

Tunc veniet diabolus et tres vel quattuor diaboli cum eo, deferentes in manibus catenas et vinctos ferreos, quos ponent in colla Adae et Evae. Et quidam eos impellent, alii eos trahant, ad infernum; alii vero diaboli erunt juxta infernum obviam venientibus, et magnum tripudium inter se facient de eorum perditione; et singuli alii diaboli illos venientes monstrabunt, et eos suscipient et in infernum mittent. Et in eo facient fumum magnum exurgere, et vociferabuntur inter se in inferno gaudentes, et collident caldaria et lebetes suos, ut exterius audiantur. Et facta aliquantula mora, exibunt diaboli discurrentes per plateas; quidam vero remanebunt in inferno.

Deinde veniet Chaim, Abel. Chaim sit indutus rubeis vestibus, Abel vero albis, et colent terram praeparatam. Et cum aliquantulum a

And when he has rested from his labor for a time,
let Abel speak to his brother Cain agreeably and
amicably, saying to him:

Brother Cain, we are two kinsmen
And sons of the first of men:
That was Adam, our mother was named Eve.
In serving God let us not be churlish.
Let us be at all times obedient to the
    Creator;   595
Let us so serve that we will win back his
    love,
Which our parents lost by their folly.
May there be steadfast love between us
    two!
So let us serve God that it will please him
    always;
Pay him his due, let nothing be held back.   600
If with willing heart we will obey him
Our souls will have nothing to fear.
Let us pay his tithes and all that is justly
    his due,
First-fruits, offerings, gifts, sacrifice;
If covetousness impels us to hold back,   605
We will be lost in hell, without recourse.
Between us two let there be great love;
Let there be neither envy nor dissension.
Why should there be strife between us two?
The entire earth has been surrendered to us. 610

Then Cain will look at his brother Abel as if
mocking him, and he will say to him:

Dear brother Abel, you certainly know how
    to preach,
How to lay out and present your arguments!
If anyone paid attention to your notions,
In a few days he wouldn't have much left
    to give.
This giving of tithes has never suited me,
    anyway.   615
With your belongings you can do your good
    deeds,
And with mine I'll follow my own
    inclination.
You won't be damned by my misdeed.
Nature teaches us to love one another;
Between us two let's not have any
    dissimulation.   620

labore requieverit, alloquatur Abel Chaim,
fratrem suum, blande et amicabiliter, dicens ei:

Frere Chaim, nus sumes dous germain
E sumes filz del home premerain:
Ce fu Adam, la mere ot non Evain.
De Deu servir ne seom pas vilain.
Seum tot tens subject al Criator;

Ensi servum que conquerroms s'amor,

Que nos parenz perdirent par folor.
Entre nos [dous] si soit bien ferm amor!

Si servum Deu que li vienge a plaisir;

Rendom ses droiz, nen soit riens del tenir.
Se de bon cuer le voloms obeïr
N'averont nos almes poür de perir.
Donum sa disme e tute sa justise,

Primices, offrendes, dons, sacrifice;
Si del tenir nos prent la coveitise,
Perdu serroms en emfer, sen devise.
Entre nos deus ait grant dilection;
N'i soit envie, n'i soit detraction.
Por quei avra entre nus dous tençon?
Tote la terre nos est mis a bandon.

Tunc respiciet Chaim fratrem suum Abel
quasi sub-san[nan]s, et dicet ei:

Beal frere Abel, bien savez sermoner,

Vostre raison asaer e mustrer!
Vostre doctrine si est qu'il voille escoter,
En poi de jorz avra poi que doner.

Disme doner ne me vint onches a gré.

Del toen aver poez faire ta bonté,

E jo del mien frai ma volenté.

Par mon mesfait ne serras tu dampné.
De nus amer Nature nus enseigne;
Entre nos dous n'ait nul que se feigne.

Whichever of us two starts an argument,
Let him pay dearly for it, for it is right that
    one should complain of this.

    *Again let Abel speak to his brother Cain, who will
    answer more mildly than usual; Abel will say:*

Cain, dear brother, listen to me.

CAIN

Gladly. Listen to what?

ABEL

Something to your benefit.

CAIN   So much the better.   625

ABEL

Don't rebel against God.
Don't be proud toward him,
I'm warning you.

CAIN   That's what I want.

ABEL

Believe my advice. Let us make offering
To the Lord God, to please him.   630
If he is reconciled toward us,
Sin will not afflict us,
Nor sadness come upon us.
It is beneficial to secure his love.
Let us sacrifice at his altar   635
Such a gift as he would be pleased to look
    upon.
Let us pray to him that he give us his love
And defend us from evil, night and day.

    *Then Cain will answer as if Abel's counsel has
    pleased him, saying:*

Dear brother Abel, you have said well;
You have written this sermon effectively,   640
And I'll heed it diligently.
Let us make offering, as is right.
What will you offer?

ABEL   A lamb,
The best and fairest
That I can find in the fold.   645
This I'll offer, none other;
And I will offer him incense.

Qui entre nus comencera la guerre
Tres bien l'achat, ke droiz est qu'il s'en
    pleigne.

    *Iterum alloquatur Abel fratrem suum Chaim,
    qui mitius solito respond[er]it; dicet Abel:*

Chaïm, bel frere, entent a moi.

CHAIM

Volentiers. Ore, de quoi?

ABEL

Ço est de ton pru.

CHAIM   Tant m'est plus bel.

ABEL

Nen fai ja vers Deu revel.
Nen aez envers lui orguil,
Jo t'en chasti.

CHAIM   Jo bien le voil.

ABEL

Creez mon conseil. Aloms offrir
A Dampnedeu, por lui plaisir.
S'il est vers nos apaiez,
Ja ne nus prendra pecchiez,
Ne sor nus ne vendra tristor.
Mult fait bon porchacer s'amor.
Aloms offrir a son altier
Tel don que il voille regarder.

Preom lui qu'il nus doinst s'amor
E nus defende de mal, noit e jor.

    *Tunc respondebit Chaim, quasi placueritei
    consilium Abel, dicens:*

Bel frere Abel, mult as bien dit;
Icest sermon as bien escrit,
Et jo crerai bien ton sermon.
Alom offrir, bien est raison.
Quoi offriras tu?

ABEL   Jo, un aignel,
Tuit le meillor e le plus bel
Que porrai trover a l'ostel.
Icel offrirai, nen frai el;
Si lui offrirai encens.

Now I've told you all my intent.
What will you offer?

CAIN   Some of my wheat,
Such as God has given me.   650

ABEL

Your very best?

CAIN   Certainly not.
From that I'm going to make bread for
   tonight.

ABEL

Such offering is not acceptable

. . . .

CAIN   That's nonsense.

ABEL

You are a rich man, and have many
   cattle.   655

CAIN

Granted.

ABEL   Why don't you count the number
   of head
And give a tenth of the total?
Thus you will make offering to God's very
   self,
Sacrifice to him wholeheartedly;
That way you'll receive a fine reward.   660
Will you do this?

CAIN   You're crazy.

. . . .

Of ten, there'll only be nine left!
This advice isn't worth an egg.
Let's make offering, each for himself   665
What he thinks good.

ABEL   So be it.

*Then they will go to two great stones that have
been readied for the purpose. One stone will have
been set at a distance from the other so that,
when the Figure appears, the stone of Abel will
be on his right hand, the stone of Cain on his left.*

Or vus ai dit tot mon porpens:
Tu, que offriras?

CHAIM   Jo, de mon blé,
Itel cum Dex le m'a doné.

ABEL

Iert del meillor?

CHAIM   Nenil, por voir.
De cel frai jo pain al soir.

ABEL

Tel offrende n'est pas aceptable

. . . .

CHAIM   Ja est ço fable.

ABEL

Riches hom es, e mult as bestes.

CHAIM

Si ai.

ABEL   Por quei ne contes toit par testes

E de totes donez la disme?
Si offriras a Deu maïmes,

Offrez le lui de bon cuer;
Si recevras bon luër.
Fras le tu ensi?

CHAIM   Or oez furor.

. . . .

De dis ne remaindront que noef!
Icist conseil ne vealt un oef.
Alom offrir, chescons par soi,
Que il voldra.

ABEL   E jo l'otrei.

*Tunc ibunt ad duos magnos lapides qui ad
hoc erunt parati. Alter ab altero lapide erit
remotus, ut cum ap[p]aruerit Figura, sit lapis
Abel ad dexteram eius, lapis vero Chaim ad
sinistram. Abel offeret agnum et incensum, de*

Abel will offer his lamb and incense, from which smoke will arise. Cain will offer a handful of his harvest. Appearing accordingly, the Figure will bless Abel's gift but disdain that of Cain. Wherefore, after the oblation, Cain will make a savage face against Abel; and, when their oblations have been completed, they will go to their own places. Then Cain will come to Abel, seeking cunningly to lead him forth in order to kill him, and will say to him:

Dear brother Abel, let us depart.

ABEL

Why?

CAIN   To refresh our bodies
And to inspect our labor,
To see how the crops have grown, and
    whether they're in flower.   670
Then we'll go to the meadows;
We will feel refreshed afterwards.

ABEL

I'll go with you, wherever you wish.

CAIN

Come on, then; you'll do well by it.

ABEL

You are my elder brother;   675
I'll follow your wishes.

CAIN

Go ahead, I'll follow after
With unhurried steps, very leisurely.

Then they will both go to a place apart and, as it were, secret, where Cain, like a madman, will rush upon Abel wishing to kill him, and say to him:

Abel, you die.

ABEL   For what?

CAIN

I will be avenged on you.   680

quo faciet fumum ascendere. Chaim offeret manipulum messis. Apparens itaque Figura benedicet munera Abel, et munera vero Chaim despiciet. Unde post oblationem Chaim torvum vultum geret contra Abel; et factis oblationibus suis ibunt ad loca sua. Tunc veniet Chaim ad Abel, volens educere callide [eum] foras, ut [eum] occidat, et dicet ei:

Bel frere Abel, issum ça fors.

ABEL

Por quoi?

CHAIM   Por deporter nos cors
E por reguarder nostre labor,
Cum sunt creü, s'il sunt em flor.

As prez puis en irrums;
Plus leegier aprés en serrums.

ABEL

Jo irrai ovec toi, ou tu voldras.

CHAIM

Or en vien donc; bon le fras.

ABEL

Tu es mi freres li ainez;
Jo ensivrai tes volentez.

CHAIM

Or va avant, jo irrai aprés
Le petit pas, a grant relais.

Tunc ibunt ambo ad locum remotum et quasi secretum, ubi Chaim quasi furibundus irruet in Abel volens eum occidere, et dicet ei:

Abel, morz es.

ABEL   E jo por quoi?

CHAIM

Jo m'en voldrai vengier de toi.

ABEL

Have I done wrong?

CAIN   Yes, wrong enough!
You're a proven traitor.

ABEL

I certainly am not.

CAIN   Do you deny it?

ABEL

I've never even thought of committing
    treason.

CAIN

You've done it already.

ABEL   Me? How?   685

CAIN

You'll know soon.

ABEL   I don't understand.

CAIN

I'll make you understand plenty soon
    enough.

ABEL

You can't prove anything, truthfully.

CAIN

The proof is here.

ABEL   God will help me.

CAIN

I'll kill you!

ABEL   God will know it.   690

*Then Cain will lift up a menacing right hand
against him, saying:*

Look here at this proof.

ABEL

In God is all my trust.

ABEL

Sui jo mesfait?

CHAIM   Oïl, asez!
Tu es traïtres tot provez.

ABEL

Certes non sui.

CHAIM   Dis tu que non?

ABEL

Unches n'amai de fere traïson.

CHAIM

Tu las fesis.

ABEL   E jo coment?

CHAIM

Tost le saveras.

ABEL   Jo ne l'entenc.

CHAIM

Jol toi frai mult tost savoir.

ABEL

Ja nel porras prover por voir.

CHAIM

La prove est prés.

ABEL   Deus m'aidera.

CHAIM

Jo te occirai!

ABEL   Deu le savra.

*Tunc eriget Chaim dextram minacem contra
eum, dicens:*

Veez ici quei fra la provence.

ABEL

En Deu est tote ma fiance.

CAIN

He won't be of much use to you against me.

ABEL

He could stop you, all right, if he wanted.

CAIN

He can't save [you] from death.   695

ABEL

He does with me according to his pleasure
    in everything.

CAIN

Do you want to hear why I'm killing you?

ABEL

Tell me.

CAIN   I'll tell you:
You make yourself too much God's favorite.
Because of you he has rejected me entirely.   700
Because of you he refused my offering.
Do you think I won't pay you back for this?
I'll give you this reward for it:
You'll lie dead today on the sand.

ABEL

If you kill me, that will be wrong.   705
God will avenge my death on you.
I haven't wronged [you], God knows it well;
I haven't slandered you to him in anything.
On the contrary, I told you to do such deeds
That you would be deserving of his peace: 710
Render to him his due,
Tithes, first-fruits, oblations—
Thereby you could have his love.
You didn't do this, now you're angry.
God is true; he who serves him   715
Spends his time wisely, and loses nothing by
    it.

CAIN

You've talked too much. Now you're going
    to die.

CHAIM

Vers moi t'avra il poi mestier.

ABEL

Bien te poet faire destorber.

CHAIM

Ne [te] porra de mort guenchir.

ABEL

Del tut me met a son plaisir.

CHAIM

Vols oïr por quoi te oscirai?

ABEL

Or le me di.

CHAIM   Jol toi dirrai:
Trop te faïs de Deu privé.
Por toi m'a il tot refusé.
Por toi refusa il ma offrende.
Pensez vus donc que nel te rende?
Jo t'en rendrai le gueredon:
Mort remaindras oi au sablon.

ABEL

Si tu m'ocies, ço iert a tort.
Deu vengera en toi ma mort.
Ne [te] mesfis, Deu le set bien;
Vers lui ne te meslai de rien.
Ainz te dis que fesis tel faiz
Que fuissez digne de sa paiz:
A lui rendisez ses raisons,
Dimes, primices, oblacions—
Por ço porrez aver s'amor.
Tu nel faïs, or as iror.
Deux est verais; qui a lui sert
Tres bien l'emplie, pas nel pert.

CHAIM

Trop as parlé. Sempres morras.

ABEL

Brother, what are you saying? You led me
    here;
I came here trusting in you.

CAIN

Trust won't help you.   720
I'm going to kill you. I defy you!

ABEL

I pray God to give me mercy!

> *Then Abel will kneel to the east. And he will have
> a pot concealed in his garments, which Cain will
> strike violently, as though killing Abel. Abel will
> lie prostrate as though dead. The choir will sing:
> ℞ [Responsory]: Where is Abel, your
> brother?*

> *Meantime the Figure will come forth from the
> church to Cain, and, when the choir has finished
> the responsory, he will say to him [Cain] as
> though very angry:*

Cain, where is your brother Abel?
Have you entered into rebellion?
You have begun to strive against me.   725
Now show me your brother alive.

CAIN

How should I know, Lord, where he's gone,
Whether at home or in his fields?
Why should I find him?
I am not his keeper.   730

FIGURE

What have you done with him? Where have
    you put him?
I know perfectly well, you have killed him.
His blood cries out to me of it;
The cry has come to me in heaven.
You have committed a grave felony;   735
You will be cursed for it all your life.
Forever you will bear a curse;

ABEL

Frere, que dis? Tu me minas;

Jo vinc ça fors en ta creance.

CHAIM

Ja ne t'avra mestier fiance.
Jo toi oscirai. Jo toi defi!

ABEL

A Deu pri qu'il ait de moi merci!

> *Tunc Abel flectet genua ad orientem. Et
> habebit ollam coopertam pannis suis, quam
> percutiet Chaim, quasi ipsum Abel occideret.
> Abel autem jacebit prostratus, quasi mortuus.
> Chorus cantabit: ℞ Ubi est Abel, frater
> tuus?*

> *Interim ab ecclesia veniet Figura ad Chaim,
> et postquam chorus finierit responsorium, quasi
> iratus dicet ei:*

Chaim, u est ton frere Abel?
Es tu ja entrez en revel?
Tu as comencié vers moi estrif.
Or me mostre ton frere vif.

CHAIM

Que sai jo, Sire, ou est alez,
S'est a maison ou a ses blez?
Jo por quoi le dei trover?
Ja nel devoie jo pas garder.

FIGURA

Qu'en as tu fet? Ou l'as tu mis?

Jo sai bien, tu l'as occis.
Son sanc en fait a moi clamor;
Al ciel me vint ja la rumor.
Mult en faïs grant felonie;
Maleit en serras tote ta vie.
Tot jorz avras malaieçon;

722*Responsory:* See note, l. 1 s.d.

For such a misdeed, such is the reward.
Yet I desire not that any man kill you,
But that you endure your life in sorrow.   740
Whoever will kill Cain
Will pay a sevenfold penalty.
Your brother died in my faith;
Your penance will be grave.

> *Then the Figure will return to the church. The devils, coming forth, will lead Cain to hell, beating him often. They will lead Abel away more gently.*

> *Then the prophets will be made ready, one by one, in a concealed place, as appropriate to them. Let the lesson be read in the choir:* You, I say, I do summon before a tribunal, O Jews. *And let the prophets be called by name; and, when they come forward, let them proceed with dignity and announce their prophecies clearly and distinctly. Accordingly Abraham will come first, an old man with a very long beard, dressed in ample garments; and when he has sat on a bench for a little time, let him begin his prophecy in a loud voice:* Your seed will possess the gates of their enemies, and in [your] seed will all the nations [of the earth] be blessed.

I am Abraham, such is my name.   745
Now listen to my entire message:
Let him who has good hope in God
Hold to his faith and his trust.
He who will have firm faith in God,
God will be with him, this I know through
    personal experience.   750
He tested me, I did his pleasure;
Well I accomplished his will.
I would have killed my own son for him,
But by Him I was told not to.

A tel mesfait, tel gueredon.
Mais ne voil que hom te tue,
Mais en dolor dorges ta vie.
Que onques Chaim oscira
A set doble le penera.
Ton frere as mort enz ma creance;
Griés en serra ta penitance.

> *Tunc Figura ibit ad ecclesiam. Venientes autem diaboli ducent Chaim saepius pulsantes ad infernum; Abel vero ducent mitius.*

> *Tunc erunt parati prophetae in loco secreto singuli, sicut eis convenit. Legatur in choro lectio:* Vos, inquam, convenio, o Judei. *Et vocentur per nomen prophetae; et cum processeri[n]t, honeste veniant et prophetias suas aperte et distincte pronuntient. Veniet itaque primo Abraham, senex cum barba prolixa, largis vestibus indutus, et cum sederit in scamno aliquantulum, alta voce incipiat prophetiam suam:* Possidebit semen tuum portas inimicorum suorum, et in semine [tuo] benedicentur omnes gentes.

Abraham sui, e issi a non.
Or entendez tuit ma raison:
Qui en Deu ad bone sperance,
Tienge sa fai e sa creance.
Chi en Deu avra ferme foi,
Deus ert od lui, jol sai par moi.

Il me tempta, jo fis son gré;
Bien acompli sa volenté.
Occire volei por lui mon filz,
Mais par lui en fui contrediz.

---

[744]s.d. *You, I say . . . Jews:* The opening of the pseudo-Augustinian *Sermo contra Judeos, Paganos, et Arianos,* a popular Christmas sermon that inspired the *Ordo Prophetarum* or "Procession of Prophets" in the liturgical drama and provided the structure for this concluding action in the *Adam* play. See Young, *Drama of the Medieval Church,* ii, 126–31, for a representative twelfth-century text of the *Sermo.* In it, Isaiah, Jeremiah, Daniel, Moses, David, and Habbakuk, as well as prophets from the New Testament and from pagan antiquity, come forward to testify against the obstinacy of the Jews in failing to heed the plain evidence—even among their own authors—of the advent of Christ. Abraham does not actually appear in the *Sermo.* For his prophecy here, see Genesis 22:17–18.

I would have offered him for a sacrifice;   755
God turned me from it, in his justice.
God has promised me—and true indeed it
    will be—
Another such heir will come of my lineage
Who will conquer all his enemies;
Thus strong and mighty will he be.   760
He will hold their gates in his hands,
And their castles; he will be no serf.
Such a man will issue from my seed,
Who will commute our sentence of damna-
    tion,
And by whom the world will be ransomed.   765
Adam will be delivered from his pain;
The peoples of every nation
Will receive benison through him.

Jol voleie offrir por sacrefise;
Deu le m'a torné a justise.
Deu m'a pramis—e bien iert veirs—
Ancore istra de moi tel eirs
Chi veintra tot ses enemis;
Ensi serra fort e poëtifs.
Lor portes tendra en ses mains,
E lor chastels; n'iert pas vilains.
Tel homme istra de ma semence,
Qui changera nostre sentence,
Par cui serra li mond salvez.
Adam serra de peine delivrez,
Les genz de tote nascion
Avront par lui beneïçon.

When these things have been said, and after a brief interval, the devils will come and lead Abraham to hell.

Then Moses will come, bearing a rod in his right hand and the tablets in his left. When he has sat, let him say his prophecy: God will raise up a prophet from among your brethren; you shall hearken to him as if to me.

His dictis, modico facto intervallo, venient diaboli et ducent Abraham ad infernum.

Tunc veniet Moyses ferens in dextra virgam et in sinistra tabulas. Postquam sederit, dicat prophetiam suam: Prophetam suscitabit Deus de f[rat]ribus vestris; tamquam me ipsum audietis.

That which I tell you, I saw through God:
From our own brethren, from our law   770
God will raise up a man.
He will be a prophet, and the summit of
    wisdom;
He will know all heaven's secrets;
You ought to believe him more than me.

Ço que vos di, par Deu le voi:
De nos freres, de nostre loi
Voldra Deus susciter home.
Il iert prophete, ce iert la somme;
Del ciel savra toit le secroi;
Celui devez croire plus que moi.

Thereupon he will be led to hell by the devil. Similarly with all the prophets [throughout the play].

Then Aaron will come, in bishops' apparel, bearing in his hands a rod having flowers and fruit; being seated, let him say:
"This is the branch bearing the flower
Which gives the perfume of salvation.
The sweet fruit of this branch
Will expiate the sorrow of our death."

Dehinc ducetur a diabolo in infernum. Similiter omnes prophetae.

Tunc veniet Aaron, episcopali ornatu, ferens in manibus suis virgam cum floribus et fructu; sedens dicat:
"Haec est virga gignens florem
Qui salutis dat odorem.
Huius virgae dulcis fructus
Nostrae mortis terget luctus."

768S.D.: Moses' prophecy appears in the *Sermo contra Judeos.*

This rod, unplanted,   775   Iceste verge senz planter
Can blossom and bear fruit.   Poet faire flors e froit porter.
Such a rod will come from my lineage   Tel verge istra de mon lignage
Who will be Satan's nemesis,   Qui a Satan fra damage,
Who, without fleshly birth,   Chi sanz charnal engendreüre
Will bear man's nature.   780   De home portera la nature.
This is the fruit of salvation,   Iço est fruit de salvacion,
Who will release Adam from prison.   Cui Adam trarra de prison.

After him let David approach, royally accoutred and wearing a diadem, and let him say: Truth has sprung out of the earth, and justice has looked down from heaven. For the Lord will give goodness, and our earth will yield her fruit.

Post hunc accedat David, regis insigniis et diademate ornatus, et dicat: Veritas de terra orta est, et justitia de caelo prospexit. Etenim Dominus dabit benignitatem, et terra nostra dabit fructum suum.

Out of the earth truth shall arise,   De terre istra la verité
And justice, from divine majesty.   E justice, de majesté.
God will give us goodness,   785   Deus durra benignité,
Our earth will yield her fruit;   Nostre terre dorra son blé;
Of her increase she will give her bread,   De son furment dorra son pain,
Which will save the sons of Eve.   Qui salvera le filz Evain.
This will be the Lord of all the earth,   Cil iert Sire de tote terre,
This one will bring peace, end war. 790   Cil fera pais, destruira guere.

Then let Solomon come forward, with the same adornments as those in which David advanced, except that he should seem younger; and, being seated, let him say: Being ministers of God's kingdom, you have not judged rightly, nor kept the law of justice, nor walked according to the will of God. [Terribly] and swiftly will he appear to you, because a most severe judgment shall befall those who rule. For to the lowly, mercy is granted.

Procedat postea Salomon, eo ornatu quo David processit, tamen ut videatur junior; et sedens dicat: Cum essetis ministri regni Dei, non recte judicastis, neque custodistis legem justiciae, neque secundum voluntatem Dei ambulastis. [Horrende] et cito apparebit vobis, quoniam judicium durissimum his qui praesunt fiet. Exiguo enim conceditur misericordia.

O Jews, God gave you his law,   Judeu, a vus dona Dex loi,

774s.d.: Aaron's verses may have been imitated or borrowed from an earlier Latin liturgical play. Possibly the addition of Aaron, Solomon, Balaam, and Abraham to the *Sermo*'s list of prophets had taken place in earlier *Ordo Prophetarum* productions with which the author of *Adam* was familiar. For the biblical account of Aaron's blossoming rod, equated by the medieval world with the virgin birth of Christ, see Numbers 17:1–8.

782s.d.: For David's prophecy, see Psalms 85:11–12. In the *Sermo* David recites a different psalm.

790s.d.: Solomon is one of several prophets found here but not in the *Sermo*. See the apocryphal Wisdom of Solomon, 6:5–7.

But you have not borne him faith.
He made you custodians of his kingdom,
You were well established;
You have not judged justly,   795
Your verdict was against God.
You have not done his will;
Your iniquity was very great.
All you have done will be made manifest;
Extremely harsh vengeance will be visited   800
On those who were the most high:
They will take a fearful fall.
God will have pity on the lowly:
He will make them very happy.
This prophecy will be fulfilled   805
When the son of God dies for us.
Those who are ministers of the law
Will kill him, out of faithlessness.
Against all justice and reason
They will put him on the cross like a thief.   810
For this they will lose their ruling authority
That they used to have from him, during
        his lifetime.
From great height they will be humbled;
Well may they bewail their unhappy state.
He will have pity of poor Adam,   815
And deliver him from sin.

*After him Balaam will come, an old man dressed
in ample garments, sitting on an ass. And he will
come into the midst, and, seated on the ass's back,
will speak his prophecy:* A star shall rise out of
Jacob, and a sceptre shall spring up from
Israel, and shall strike the chiefs of Moab,
and shall waste all the children of Seth.

From Jacob a star will rise,
Red with the fire of heaven,
And a sceptre will spring up from Israel
Which will overthrow [the chiefs of] Moab   820
And will abase their pride;
For Christ will rise out of Israel,
And he will be that shining star.
All things will be illumined by him.
His faithful ones he will safely lead,   825
His enemies he will all confound.

Mais vus ne li portastes foi.
De son regne vus fist baillis,
Char mult estïez bien asis;
Vos ne jujastes par justise,
Encontre Deu iert vostre asise.
Ne faïstes sa volenté;
Mult fu grant vostre iniquité.
Ço que faïstes tut parra,
Char mult dor vengement serra
En cels qui furent li plus halt:
Il prendront toit un malvais salt.
Del petit avra Dex pité:
Mult les rendra esleecié.
La prophecie averera
Quant le filz Deu por nos morra.
Cil que sunt maistre de la loi
Occirunt lui, par male foi.
Contre justise, encontre raison
Mettrunt le en cruiz cume laron.
Por ço perdrunt lor seignorie
Che il averont de lui, em vie.

De grant haltor vendront em bas;
Mult se porrunt tenir por las.
Del povre Adam avra pieté,
Deliverat lui de pecché.

*Post hunc veniet Balaam, senex largis vestibus
indutus, sedens super asinam. Et veniet in
medium, et eques dicet prophetiam suam:*
Orietur stella ex Jacob, et consurget
virga de Israel, et percutiet duces Moab,
vastabitque omnes filios Seth.

De Jacob istra une steille,
Del feu del ciel serra vermeille,
E surdra verge d'Israel
Qui a Moab fera revel
E lor orguil abaissera;
Char de Israel Christus istera,
Qui ert estoille de clarté.
Tot ert de lui enluminé.
Les son feël bien conduira,
Ses enemis toit confundera.

816s.d.: Balaam does not appear in the *Sermo.* See Numbers 24:17.

Thereafter let Daniel approach, young in years, but old in his dress. And when he has seated himself, let him speak his prophecy, stretching out his hand toward those to whom he speaks: When the holy of holies comes, your anointing will cease.

To you, O Jews, I deliver my sermon,
You who are excessively wicked toward
    God.
When the greatest of all the saints appears—
Of whom you will experience great
    misfortune—   830
Then your anointing will cease;
You won't be able to claim it any longer.
By this greatest of saints, I mean Christ,
He who wishes his people to gain eternal life
    through him;
For them he will come to earth.   835
Your tribe will wage terrible war on him,
Will subject him to his Passion;
On this account they will lose their
    anointing.
Neither bishop nor king will have power;
Thus their law will perish through their
    means.   840

After him Habakkuk will come, an old man. And, sitting down, when he begins his prophecy, he will lift up his hands toward the church; manifesting wonder and fear, let him say: O Lord, I have heard your speech and was afraid; I have contemplated your works and feared greatly. Between two beasts you will become known.

I have heard strange tidings concerning God:
I am most troubled in my mind about it.
I have considered this sign so intently
That great fear agitates my heart.
Between two beasts he will be recognized; 845
By all the world he will be feared.
He of whom I have such great wonder

Dehinc accedat Daniel, aetate juvenis, habitu vero senex. Et cum sederit, dicat prophetiam suam, manum extendens contra eos ad quos loquitur: Cum venerit sanctus sanctorum, cessabit unctio vestra.

A vus, Judei, di ma raison,
Qui envers Deu estes trop felon.

Des sainz quant vendra toit li maires—
Dont sentirez vos granz contraires—

Donc cessera vostre oncion;
N'i poëz pas clamer raison.
Ço est Crist que li saint signifie,
Qui vold par lui avront vie;

Por son pople vendra en terre.
Vostre gent li frunt grant guere,
Il le mettront a passion;
Por ce perdrunt lor oncion.

Evesque n'averont pois ne roi;
Ainz perira par els lor lei.

Post hunc veniet Abacuc senex. Et sedens, cum incipiet prophetiam suam, eriget manus contra ecclesiam; admirationem simula[n]s et timorem, dicat: Domine, audivi auditum tuum et timui; consideravi opera tua et expavi. In medio duum animalium cognosceris.

De Deu ai oï novele;
Tot en ai truble la cervele.
Tant ai esgardé cest ovre
Que grant poür li cuer m'en ovre.
Entre dous bestes iert coneüz;
Par tot le mond iert cremuz.
Cil de cui ai si grant merveille

---

[826]s.d.: Daniel's prophecy here is as it appears in the *Sermo.*

[840]s.d.: Habakkuk's prophecy is derived from the *Sermo* and is based ultimately on Habakkuk 3:2.

Will be pointed out by a star;
Shepherds will find him in a crib
That will be carved out of dry stone,   850
Where beasts will eat hay.
Then he will reveal himself to kings;
The star will lead the kings there;
All three will bear offerings.

> *Then Jeremiah will enter, bearing a scroll in his hand; and let him say:* Hear the word of the Lord, all you men of Judaea, that enter in at these gates to worship the Lord. *And with his hand he will point to the doors of the church.* Thus says the Lord of hosts, the God of Israel: Make your ways and your doings good, and I will dwell with you in this place.

Hear the holy word of God,   855
All you who are of his doctrine,
The mighty lineage of righteous Judaea,
You who are of his household.
By this door you will enter
To adore our Lord.   860
The Lord of hosts summons you,
The God of Israel, from heaven on high:
Make good your ways,
Let them be straight as furrows,
And let your hearts be pure,   865
That no shame may come to you;
Let your endeavors be good,
Free of wickedness.
If you do thus, God will come,
Will dwell with you;   870
The son of God, the glorious one,
Will come down to earth for your sake;
He will be among you as mortal man,
The Lord, the celestial one.
He will release Adam from prison,   875
Giving his own body as ransom.

> *After him Isaiah will come, bearing a book in his hand, dressed in an ample cloak. And let him*

Iert demostré par une esteille;
Pastor le troverunt en cresche
Qui iert trenchié en piere secche,
Ou mangerunt les bestes fain.
Pois s'i fra as rais certain;
La steille i amerrat les rois;
Offrende aporterunt tot trais.

> *Tunc ingredietur Jheremias ferens rotulum chartae in manu et dicat:* Audite verbum Domini, omnis Juda, qui ingredimini per portas has, ut adoretis Deum. *Et manu monstrabit portas ecclesiae.* Haec dicit Dominus Deus exercituum, Deus Israel: Bonas facite vias vestras et studia vestra, et habitabo vobiscum in loco isto.

Oëz de Deu sainte parole,
Tot vus qui estes de sa scole,
Del bon Judé la grant lignee,
Vus chi estes de sa maisnee.
Par ceste porte volez entrer
Por nostre Seignor aourer.
Li Sires del host vus somont,
Deu de Israel, del ciel lamont:
Faites bones les vos voies,
Soient droites cumme raies,
Soient netz les voz curages,
Que vus nen vienge nuls damages;
Vostre studie soient en bien,
De felonie n'i ait rien.
Si ensi le faites, Dex vendra,
Ensemble ovec vus habitera;
Li filz de Deu, li glorius,
En terre descendra a vos;
Ovec vus serra, cum homme mortals,
Li Sires, le celestials.
Adam trara de prison,
Son cors dorra por rançon.

> *Post hunc veniet Isaias ferens librum in manu, magno indutus pallio. Et dicat prophetiam*

854s.d.: For Jeremiah's prophecy, see Jeremiah 7:2–3. In the *Sermo*, a different prophecy is recited.

876s.d.: In the *Sermo*, Isaiah recites only one prophecy, that one appearing at l.916a below. The prophecy here is taken from Isaiah 11:1–2.

speak his prophecy: And there shall come forth a rod out of the root of Jesse, and a flower shall rise up out of his root, and the spirit of the Lord shall rest upon it.

Now I will tell you a marvelous thing:
From Jesse's root will come forth
A rod, which will bear a flower
Worthy of great honor.   880
The Holy Spirit will enclose it,
Will rest upon this flower.

Then somebody from the synagogue will rise up, disputing with Isaiah, and will say to him:

Now answer me, Sir Isaiah:
Is this a fable, or prophecy?
What is this you've said?   885
Did you invent it, or is it written?
You've been sleeping, you dreamed it.
Is this serious or a joke?

ISAIAH

This is not fable; on the contrary, it's all true.

[JEW]

Make us see this truth, then.   890

[ISAIAH]

What I have spoken is prophecy.

[JEW]

Written in a book?

ISAIAH   Yes, the book of life.
I did not dream it; I saw it.

JEW

How?

[ISAIAH]   By God's grace.

JEW

You seem like an old dotard to me;   895
Your mind is addled.
You appear to me to be senile.
You know well enough how to look in a
    mirror:
Now look at this hand for me, and tell

suam: Egredietur virga de radice Jesse, et flos de radice eius ascendet et requiescet super eum spiritus Domini.

Ore vus dirrai merveillus diz:
Jessé fera de sa raïz
Verge en istra, qui fra flor
Qui ert digne de grant unor.
Saint Esspirit l'avra si clos,
Sor ceste flor iert sun repos.

Tunc exurget quidam de synagoga, disputans cum Isaia, et dicet ei:

Ore me respon, sire Ysaias:
Est ço fable, ou prophecie?
Que est iço que tu as dit?
Truvas le tu, ou est escrit?
Tu as dormi, tu le sonjas.
Est ço a certes ou a gas?

ISAIAS

Ço n'est pas fable; ainz est tut voir.

[JUDEUS]

Ore le nus faites donches veer.

[ISAIAS]

Ço que ai dit est prophecie.

[JUDEUS]

En livre est escrit?

ISAIAS   Oïl, de vie.
Nel sonjai pas; ainz l'ai veü.

JUDEUS

Et tu coment?

[ISAIAS]   Par Deu vertu.

JUDEUS

Tu me sembles viel redoté;
Tu as le sens tot trublé.
Tu me sembles viel meür.
Tu sés bien garder al miror;

Or me gardez en ceste main

Then he will show him his hand

If my heart is sick or healthy.   900

ISAIAH

You have the disease of wickedness,
From which you will never recover in your
    life.

JEW

Am I sick, then?

ISAIAH   Yes, of error.

JEW

When will I get better?

ISAIAH   Never.

JEW

Now begin your soothsaying.   905

ISAIAH

What I say will not be untrue.

JEW

Now tell your vision again,
If it was a rod, or a stick,
And what will be born from its flower.
We will take you for our master,   910
And this generation
Will hearken to your teaching.

ISAIAH

Then listen to this great wonder.
Never has our listening heard anything so
    magnificent;
Never has anything so fabulous been heard   915
Since this world began:

> Behold a virgin shall conceive in her womb
> and bear a son, and his name shall be
> called Emmanuel.

The time is near, it is not far,
It will not delay, it is at hand,

Tunc ostendet ei manum suam

Si j'ai le cor malade ou sain.

ISAIAS

Tu as le mal de felonie,
Dont ne garras ja en ta vie.

JUDEUS

Sui jo donc malades?

ISAIAS   Oïl, d'errur.

JUDEUS

Quant en garrai?

ISAIAS   Ja més, a nul jor.

JUDEUS

Ore comence de ta devinaille.

ISAIAS

Ço que jo di n'iert pas faille.

JUDEUS

Or nus redi ta vision,
Si ço est verge ou baston,
E da sa flor que porra nestre.
Nos te tendrom puis por maistre,
E ceste generacion
Escutera puis ta lecçon.

ISAIAS

Or escutetz la grant merveille.
Si grant n'oï mais oreille;

Si grant nen fu onc mais oïe
Dés quant comenza ceste vie:

> Ecce virgo concipiet in utero et pariet
> filium, et vocabitur nom[en] eius Eman-
> uhel.

Prés est li tens, n'est pas lointeins,
Ne tarzera, ja est sor mains,

---

916 aSee Isaiah 7:14 and the note to l. 876 s.d. above.

That a virgin shall conceive	Que une virge concevera
And as a virgin shall bear a son.	E virge un filz emfantera.
He will have the name Emmanuel.	Il avra non Emanuhel.
Saint Gabriel will be the messenger.	Message en iert Saint Gabriël.
The maid will be the Virgin Mary;	La pucele iert virge Marie,
Thus she will carry the fruit of life,	Si portera le fruit de vie,
Jesus, our saviour,	Jhesu, le nostre salvaor,
Who will recover Adam from his great sorrow	Qui Adam trarra de grant dolor
And put him again in paradise.	Et remetra en paraïs.
This that I speak to you, I learned from God.	Iço que vus di, de Deu l'ai apris.
And this will be fully accomplished, in truth,	E ço iert tot acompli par veir,
And you ought to put your hope in it.	En ce devez tenir espeir.

With line numbers 920, 925, 930 noted in the margin.

Then Nebuchadnezzar will come, adorned like a king. Did we not cast three youths, bound, into the fire? ℞ [*Responsory*] *of the king's ministers:* True, O king. [*Nebuchadnezzar:*] Lo, I see four men loose, walking in the midst of the fire, and they have no hurt, and the form of the fourth is like the son of God.

Tunc veniet Nabugodonosor, ornatus sicut regem. Nonne misimus tres pueros in fornace ligatos? ℞ *Ministri:* Vere, rex. [*Nabugodonosor:*] Ecce video quattuor viros solutos deambulantes in medio ignis, et corruptio nulla est in eis, et aspectus quarti similis est filio Dei.

Hear a wondrous great miracle—	Oëz vertu merveille grant—
No living man has heard the like—	Ne l'oït homme qui soit en vivant—
Which I witnessed, of the three youths	Ço que jo vi des trais emfanz
Who were cast into the burning fire.	Chi fis mettre en foc ardant.
The fire was very hot and fierce,	Le fouc estoit mult fier e grant,
And the flame bright and searing;	E la flambe cler e bruiant;
The three youths rejoiced greatly	Les trois emfanz fasoient joie grant
There where they were, in the burning fire.	La ou il furent, al fouc ardant.
They sang a verse so beautiful	Chantouent un vers si bel
It seemed the angels were in heaven.	Sembloit li angle fuissent del ciel.
When I looked there, thus I saw the fourth	Cum jo men regart, si vi le quartz
Who gave them very great comfort.	Chi lor fasoit mult grant solaz.
His face shone so resplendently	Les chieres avoient tant resplendisant
He seemed the son of mighty God.	Sembloient le filz de Deu puissant.

With line numbers 935, 940 noted in the margin.

. . . .

[Incomplete]

930s.d.: The prophecy of Nebuchadnezzar is taken literally from the *Sermo* and also from Daniel 3:24–25.

943–44*His face . . . He seemed:* Translated literally, "Their faces" and "They seemed," but the sense and the biblical text require a reference to the fourth young man in the fire who is like the son of God.

2. THE HOLY RESURRECTION
(LA SEINTE RESURECCION)

Like the play of *Adam, La Seinte Resureccion* is a remarkably sophisticated and complex play in the Anglo-Norman vernacular, quite possibly from England. The play is subtle in its motivation of character, and imaginative in the way it expands scenes only hinted at in the Scriptures (such as the interview between Pilate and Joseph of Arimathea). Like *Adam*, again, this play shows traces of a liturgical ancestry, but is written to be performed quite independently of the liturgy. Although clerics probably acted the parts, the play may have been staged outside the church during the summer season. (We know of at least one occasion during the thirteenth century when a Resurrection play was performed in England in this manner.) A cantor probably recited the versified stage directions. The play manuscript is incomplete, but we can tell from the opening stage direction that it originally went on to include the Resurrection and the visit of the three Marys to the tomb, as well as Christ's appearance to his disciples at Emmaus and probably his appearance to doubting Thomas.

La Seinte Resureccion requires elaborate staging. At least twelve acting stations, variously referred to as *mansions, lieus* ("places"), and *estals* ("stalls"), are arranged in two banks or rows. The cross is at the head, flanked by the

This play exists in two MSS: Paris, Bibliothèque Nationale, MS fr. 902; and London, British Museum, Additional MS 45103 (W), known as the Canterbury MS, since it was apparently written in the monastery of Christ Church, Canterbury, shortly after 1275. This present edition is based on the first MS. Both MSS have been carefully edited by T. A. Jenkins and others, *La Seinte Resureccion*, Anglo-Norman Texts—IV (Oxford, 1943), against which this present edition has been checked.

A possible arrangement for *La Seinte Resureccion*

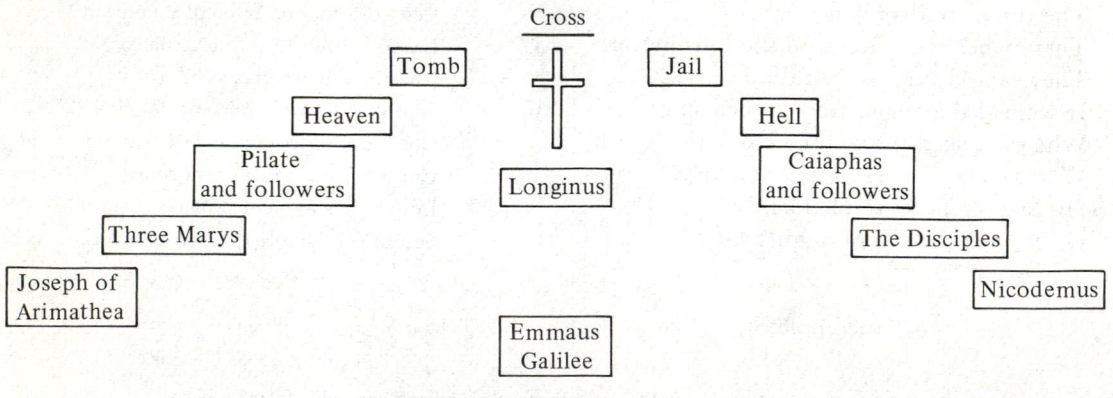

For various possibilities, see E. K. Chambers, *The Mediaeval Stage*, II, 83, Grace Frank, *The Medieval French Drama*, p. 90, and Hardison, *Christian Rite and Christian Drama*, pp. 262–70.

tomb and heaven on one side, a jail and hell on the other. Further distant from the cross are the "stalls," with Caiaphas across from Pilate (each with his followers), and with Joseph of Arimathea, Nicodemus, the disciples, and the three Marys on one side or the other. Emmaus and Galilee are in the midst of the "place," facing the spectators. Longinus evidently occupies a position where he can be met by the soldiers on the way from Pilate to the cross. The stations are located in a way that is symbolically reminiscent of a church interior, with hell to the right of the cross (like the stairway leading down to the crypt) and heaven to the left of the cross (like the stairway leading up to the loft). Emmaus, a location often symbolically associated with the west end of the nave, or the west door, is appropriately opposite to the cross in the east. Yet the absence of a choir, of ecclesiastical costumes, and of any liturgical antiphons weighs against the probability of performance inside the church building. Moreover the members of the audience ("la gent") are seated, quite possibly on raised scaffolds.

The Holy Resurrection
(La Seinte Resureccion)

In this manner we ought to recite	*En ceste manere recitom*
The holy Resurrection.	*La seinte resureccion.*
First let us make ready	*Primerement apareillons*
All the places and the mansions, 4	*Tus les lius e les mansions,*
The crucifix first	*Le crucifix primerement*
And after that the tomb;	*E puis aprés le monument;*
There ought to be a jail there	*Une jaiole i deit aver*
For imprisoning the prisoners; 8	*Pur les prisons enprisoner;*
Let hell be put on that side	*Enfer seit mis de cele part*
And the mansions on the other side	*Es mansions del altre part*
And then heaven; and at the stalls	*E puis le ciel; e as estals*
First Pilate with his servants— 12	*Primes Pilate od ces vassals—*
He will have six or seven knights;	*Sis u set chivaliers avra;*
Let Caiaphas be on the other side,	*Cayphas en l'altre serra,*
And with him Jewry;	*Od lui seit la Juerie;*
Then Joseph of Arimathea; 16	*Puis Joseph d'Arunachie;*
Let Nicodemus be in a fourth place—	*El quart liu seit danz Nichodemus—*

1–28Perhaps the versified rubrics of this play, italicized in this edition, were intended to be recited by a presenter; but it is also possible the author provided them for the reader of the manuscript, versifying them for his own pleasure.

4*places, mansions*: specific acting locales presented simultaneously, side by side, on scaffolds or booths. The action of the play moves from one to another as the soldiers approach the cross or return to Pilate, etc. The continual presence of the cross and of hell must have created a sense of cosmic dimension.

11*stalls*: seats or scaffolds, simultaneously provided for the various groups of actors, representing their fixed domiciles, e.g., Pilate's hall, where he receives and dispatches his soldiers.

Each should have his followers with him—
And fifth the disciples of Christ;
Let the three Marys be sixth.   20
Let it be arranged so that one faces
Galilee in the midst of the place;
Let Emmaus also be constructed there,
Where Jesus betook himself to the inn.   24
And when the audience is all seated
And quiet is established on all sides,
Let Joseph of Arimathea
Come to Pilate and say to him thus: 28

JOSEPH

May God, who from the hands of King
    Pharaoh
Saved Moses and Aaron,
Save Pilate, my lord,
And grant him offices and honor!   32

PILATE

May Hercules, who slew the dragon
And destroyed the old Geryon,
Grant prosperity and honor to him
Who offers me greetings amiably.   36

JOSEPH

Sir Pilate, may you be blessed;
May God help you by his great power.
May God, by his might,
Grant you good will toward me.   40
May God almighty grant me
That you will hear me favorably.

PILATE

Welcome, Joseph.
You deserve a warm reception from me,   44
And unquestionably you enjoy my favor.
If you think otherwise, that's childish folly.
Be well assured, truly,
That I will hear you most sympathetically.   48

JOSEPH

Worthy sir, do not be displeased

Chescons i ad od sei les soens—
El quint les deciples Crist;
Les treis Maries saient el sist.
Si seit purveu que l'om face
Galilee en mi la place;
Iemaus uncore i seit fait,
U Jesus fut al hostel trait.
E cum la gent est tute asise
E la pes de tutez parz mise,
Dan Joseph, cil de Arunachie,
Venge a Pilate, si lui die:

JOSEPHUS

Deus, qui des mains le rei Pharaon

Salva Moysen e Aaron,
I sault Pilate, le mien seignur,
E dignetez lui doinst e honur!

PILATUS

Hercules, qui occist le dragon
E destruist le viel Gerion,
Doinst a celui ben e honur
Qui saluz me dit par amur.

JOSEPHUS

Sire Pilate, beneit seies tu,
S'ait te Deus par sa grant vertu.
Deus, par la sue poissance,
Te doinst vers mei bone voillance.
Ceo me doinst Deus omnipotent
Que oir me voilles bonement.

PILATUS

Dan Joseph, ben seiez tu venuz.
Ben deiz estre de mei receuz,
Ben es de mei, sanz dotance.
Si eel en quides, ceo est enfance.
Sachez ben e verraiment
Que jeo te orrai mult dulcement.

JOSEPHUS

Beal sire, ne vus en peist mie

---

^{22}place: the central acting area, near the spectators.

If I speak to you concerning Mary's son,	Si jo vus di del fiz Marie,
He who is crucified.	De celui qui la est pendu.
Be assured that I have been a good citizen; 52	Sachez tresben que prudom fu;
I have stood well with the Lord God.	Mult par fu bien de Dampnedeu.
Now you have slain him, you and the Jews;	Ore l'avez mort, vus e li Jeu;
So you ought to fear greatly	Si vus devez grantment duter
That dire calamity may visit you. 56	Que vus ne venge grant encombrer.

PILATE / **PILATUS**

Joseph of Arimathea,	Dan Joseph de Arunachie,
I won't hesitate to tell you this:	Ne leirrai que nel te die:
The Jews, through their malicious envy,	Li Jeu, par lur grant envie,
Undertook a terrible crime. 60	Enpristrent grant felonie.
I consented out of guile,	Jol consenti par veisdie,
That I might not lose my office.	Que ne perdisse ma baillie.
They would have brought accusation	Encusé m'eussent en Romanie;
against me in Rome;	
I could have quickly lost my life. 64	Tost en purraie perdre la vie.

JOSEPH / **JOSEPHUS**

If you see that you have sinned,	Si tu veis que tu as mesfait,
Beseech him for mercy; that way you will	Cri lui merci; si fras bon plait.
obtain a favorable hearing.	
No one petitions him in vain,	Nul ne lui crie qu'i nel ait,
Even those who have died. 68	Nis icels qui a mort l'ont trait.
But I have come for something else:	Mes pur eel venuz i sui:
Just give me his body.	Donez mei sul le cors de lui.
This much I earnestly beg, grant it me;	Tant vus requer, grantez le mei;
Then I will do what I ought to do. 72	Si en frai ceo que faire dei.

PILATE / **PILATUS**

Good friend, what do you want to do with	Beals amiz, qu'en volez faire?
him?	
Do you think to bring him back to life?	Quidez vus le a vie traire?
He underwent great anguish;	Il ad eu mult grant angoisse;
Do you think he could live again? 76	Quidez vus qu'il vivre poisse?

JOSEPH / **JOSEPHUS**

Certainly not, good sir Pilate.	Certes, bel sire Pilate, nenil.
Nevertheless he will rise again wholly.	Nepurquant tut relevra il.
But, to observe our custom,	Mes, pur nostre custume tenir,
For the love of God I wish to bury him. 80	Pur amur Deu le voil enseveler.

69-72At this point appears in the margin the following biblical gloss: *Tunc accessit ad Pilatum et peciit corpus Jesu* (Then he approached Pilate and asked for the body of Jesus). See Matthew 27:58 and Luke 23:52.

PILATE

Has he then departed from this life?

PILATUS

Est il dunc transi de vie?

JOSEPH

Yes, worthy sir, doubt it not.

JOSEPHUS

Oil, bel sire, n'en dotez mie.

PILATE

We will know for sure by our soldiers.

PILATUS

Ceo saverum ja par nos serganz.

JOSEPH

Call them—look how many there are of
  them.   84

JOSEPHUS

Apelez les, veez en la tanz.

PILATE

Get up, soldiers, quickly.
Go at once where that one hangs suspended;
Go to that crucified one
To confirm that he has died.   88

PILATUS

Levez, serganz, hastivement.
Alez tost la u celui pent;
Alez a cel crucified
Saver mon s'il est devié.

Whereupon two of the soldiers departed,
Carrying lances with them in their hands.
Thus they said to blind Longinus,
Whom they found sitting in a place: 92

Dunt s'en alerent dous des serganz,
Lances od sei en main portanz.
Si unt dit a Longin le ciu,
Que unt trové seant en un liu:

FIRST SOLDIER

Brother Longinus, would you like to earn
  some money?

UNUS MILITUM

Longin, frere, vus tu guainner?

LONGINUS

Yes, worthy sir, do not doubt it.

LONGINUS

Oil, bel sire, n'en dotez mie.

SOLDIER

Come, you'll receive a dozen denarii
For piercing this fellow in the side.   96

MILES

Vien, si avras duzein dener
Pur le costé celui perecer.

LONGINUS

Most willingly I will come with you,
For I have great need of earning money.
I am poor, I don't lack expenses;
I beg a great deal, but it doesn't help
  much.   100

LONGINUS

Mult volenters od vus vendrai,
Car del gainner grant mester ai.
Povres sui, despense me faut;
Asez demand, mes poi ne vaut.

When they came in front of the cross,
They placed a lance in his fists.

Quant il vendrent devant la croiz,
Une lance li mistrent es poinz.

[92]*a place:* Longinus is probably not far from the cross, on the way from Pilate's hall to Calvary
in the acting area flanked by the mansions and stalls.

FIRST SOLDIER

Take this lance in your hand,
Thrust well upwards, and not in vain. 104
Let it slide in as far as the lungs;
Thus we may know if he's dead or not.

He took the lance; it struck
To the heart; then blood and water issued forth; 108
This flowed down onto his hands,
With which he wet his face,
And when he put it to his eyes,
He regained his eyesight immediately, and then
said: 112

LONGINUS

O Jesus, O worthy Lord!
Now I don't know what in the world to say.
But you are a very great physician
When you turn your wrath into mercy. 116
At your hands I have deserved death,
And you have dispensed such great mercy
to me
That now I see with eyes that were blind.
I yield myself to you, I cry you mercy. 120

Then he prostrated himself in penitential
supplication
And softly said a prayer.
The knights returned [to Pilate],
And spoke in this manner: 124

FIRST SOLDIER

Worthy sir prince, know for sure,
Jesus has departed from this life.
We saw a great miracle there;
Good companion, didn't you see it? 128

ANOTHER OF THE SOLDIERS

We both saw it.

PILATE

Shut up, fools, don't·say anything more.

UNUS MILITUM

Pren ceste lance en ta main,
Bute ben amont e nent en vaim.
Lessez culer desqu'al pulmon;
Si saverum s'il est mort u non.

Il prist la lance, cil feri
Al quer, dunc sanc et ewe en issi;
Si li est as mainz avalé,
Dunt il ad face muillee,
E quant a ces oils le mist,
Dunt vit an eire, e puis si dit:

LONGINUS

Ohi, Jesu! ohi, bel Sire!
Ore ne [sai] suz ciel que dire.
Mes mult par es tu bon mire
Quant en merci turnes ta ire.
Vers tei ai la mort deservi,
E tu m'as fait si grant merci

Que ore vei des oils que ainz ne vi.
A vus me rend, merci vus cri.

Dunt se culcha en affliccions

E dit tut suef uns oreisons.
Les chivalers s'en vunt arere,
Si unt dit en ceste manere:

UNUS MILITUM

Bel sire prince, sachez de fi,
Jesus est de vie transi.
Un grant miracle i avum veu;
Bel compainnon, dun nel veis tu?

ALTER EX MILITIBUS

Amdui ben le veimes nus.

PILATUS

Taisé us, bricons, ne ditez plus.

107–8At this point appears in the margin the following biblical gloss: *Lancea latus eius aperuit, et*
continuo exivit sanguis et aqua (The lance opened his side, and immediately blood and water
issued forth). See John 19:34.

Then he turned to Joseph,
Not liking to hear such talk.   132

PILATE

Joseph, you have always served me well.
Take the body, I grant it you.

JOSEPH

Sire, I thank you most humbly.
It is my good fortune ever to have served
    you thus.   136

When Joseph had taken his leave
And had departed toward Nicodemus,
Pilate spoke to his soldiers,
And said to the one whom he had summoned: 140

PILATE

Speak, fellow, come here.
What miracle did you see over there?
Say quickly what you think concerning
This thing I made you keep quiet about.   144

SOLDIER

The blind Longinus, when he had wounded
That hanging fellow in the side with his
    spear,
Took the blood, put it to his eyes.
It was a lucky hour for him that he did so,   148
For previously he was blind and now he sees.
It's no wonder that he believes in him now.

PILATE

Shut up, fellow, don't speak of this.
It's an illusion, don't believe it.   152
Now I order that Longinus be taken
And swiftly put in the prison-house.
Go quickly, put him in prison,
So that he won't go around preaching
    such a sermon.   156

Then they went quickly to Longinus
There where he lay, head bowed.

SOLDIER

Here, brother, here, off you go to prison;
From now on you'll have poor lodging.   160
It isn't true that you're now able to see:

Vers Dan Joseph dunc se turna,
Ne lui fu bel qu'i si parla.

PILATUS

Dan Joseph, mult m'avez servi.
Pernez le cors, jol vus otri.

JOSEPHUS

Sire, la vostre grant merci.
Mult m'est bel si unc vus servi.

Quant Joseph out pris le congé
E vers Nichodem fut alé,
Pilate ad as sergans parlé,
Dist alun qu'il ad apelé:

PILATUS

Diva, vaissal, trai tai en sa.
Quel miracle veis tu de la?
Di tost coment te fut aviz
De ceo dunt ainz teiser te fiz.

MILES

Longins li ciu, quant out nafré
Cel pendu de lance el costé,

Prist del sanc, a sez oils le mist.
A bon hure a son os le fist,
Car ainz fut cius e ore veit.
N'est pas merveille c'il en lui creit.

PILATUS

Tais, vassal, ja nul nel die.
Fantosme est, nel creez mie.
Ore comand que Longin seit pris
E ignelepas en chartre mis.
Alez tost, metez le en prison,
Que ne voist prechant tel sermon.

Dunt alerent tost a Longin
La u il jut, le chef enclin.

MILES

Ça, frere, ça, en chartre irras;
Malveis hostel huimes avras.
N'est pas veir que tu veis ren:

It's a lie, we know this well.
Because you believe in a hanged fellow,
You say he restored your eyes to you. 164

LONGINUS

He restored my eyes to me indeed,
And I believe in him absolutely.
I believe in him and no other,
For he is the Lord and ruler of the heavens. 168

OTHER SOLDIER

You spoke wrongly before, and now even
worse,
For which you'll be put in prison.
Come on, off you go.

LONGINUS

This makes me happy and joyous. 172

When they came to the jail,
They said this to him:

SOLDIER

Get in. You won't come out
Without losing everything you have, 176
Your limbs and your life,
If you won't renounce the son of Mary.

LONGINUS

The son of Mary is king and Lord,
I know it well and I will say it. 180
I commend my life to him;
As for you, it doesn't matter to me what any
of you say.

Meanwhile the worthy Joseph
Had come to Nicodemus. 184

JOSEPH

Nicodemus, come with me,
Let us go take down our king from the cross.
Let us not reject him, even though he is dead;
He will yet be of great comfort to us. 188
Bring along pincers and a hammer,
Wherewith the nails will be extracted.
Whoever will do him honor
He will repay, be assured. 192
Therefore, dear friend, let us go.

Mençunge est, nus le savum ben.
Pur cen que creiz en un pendu,
Si diz que tes oils t'ad rendu.

LONGINUS

Mes oils m'ad rendu vereiment,
E en li crei parfitement.
En lui crei jo, n'i ad nent el,
Car il est Sire e reis del ciel.

ALTER MILES

Ainz mesparlastes e ore piz,

Pur ceo serez en prison mis.
Venez avant, tut i irrez.

LONGINUS

De ceo sui jo joius e lez.

Quant il vindrent al gaiole,
Si lui distrent ceste parole:

MILES

Entre laenz. Ja n'en istras
Que ne perdes quanque tu as,
Les membres e la vie,
Si ne reneies le fiz Marie.

LONGINUS

Li fiz Marie est reis e Sire,
Ben le crei e ben le voil dire.
A lui comand la meie vie;
Ne me chaut que nul de vus die.

Entre ces feiz Joseph li pruz
A Nichodem esteit venuz.

JOSEPHUS

Dan Nichodem, venez od mei,
Alum despendere nostre rei.
Nel refusum, tut scit il mort;
Uncore nus fra il grant comfort.
Tanailles e martel portez,
Dunt li clou scrunt derivez.
Qui q'unques l'avrat fait honur,
Il lui rendra, seez aseur.
Pur ceo, bels amis, car alom.

Let us do him at least such honor
As to inter his body honorably
In the tomb.   196

NICODEMUS

Sir Joseph, I have seen indeed
That the Lord, who is hung there,
Was a true prophet and holy man,
Full of God and of miraculous power.   200
He made me understand this clearly
When I came to him to learn.
Nonetheless I dare not undertake
To go with you to take him down.   204
And even though I desire
To do him great service,
I fear the governor so
That I dare not do it in any wise.   208
But I will go with you to Pilate.
I will hear it from his very mouth;
Then I will do it with more confidence.

JOSEPH

Go now, I will conduct you.   212

> They both went to Pilate,
> And two servants with them,
> Of whom one carried an outfit of tools,
> The other the box of ointment.   216

JOSEPH

Sire, I need a companion;
I can't have one unless by your permission.
Tell this person that he has assurance
To go with me, without fear.   220

PILATE

You may go there, good friend;
You will be none the worse off.
Proceed boldly,
I will be your warranty for everything.   224

> When they came in front of the cross,
> Joseph cried out in a loud voice:

JOSEPH

O Jesus, son of Mary

Tant d'onur sivals li façom
Que son cors honurablement
Façom poser en monument.

NICHODEMUS

Sire Joseph, jol ai ben veu
Que li Sire, que la est pendu,
Veir prophete e sainz hom fu,
Plain de Deu e de grant vertu.
Il le me fist ben entendre
Quant vins a lui pur aprendre.
Nepurquant nel os enprendre
Od vus aler lui despendre.
E sin ai jo coveitise
De lui faire grant servise,
Mes jo crem tant la justise,
Nel os faire en nule guise.
Mes jo od vus a Pilate irrai.
De sa buche meimes l'orrai;
Plus seurement idunt le frai.

JOSEPHUS

Ore venez, jo vus i merrai.

> A Pilate en vunt ambesdouz,
> E dui vassals ensemble od eus,
> Dunt li un portat l'ustillement,
> L'altre la buiste od l'oingnement.

JOSEPHUS

Sire, me covent un compaignon;
Nel puis aver si par vus non.
Ditez cestui qu'il ait fiance
D'aler od mei sanz dotance.

PILATUS

Aler i poez, bels amis;
Ne vus serrad de ren le pis.
Hardiement alez avant,
Jo vus serai par tut garant.

> Quant il vindrent devant la cruis,
> Joseph criat od halte voiz:

JOSEPHUS

Ohi Jesu, le fiz Marie,

The holy virgin, gentle and sacred, 228	Seinte virgine dulce e pie,
How heinous was the crime Judas committed,	Tant fist Judas grant felonie
And how foolhardy for himself,	E a son os grant folie,
When he sold you out of envy	Quant te vendi par envie
To those who did not love you! 232	A cels qui ne t'aiment mie!

NICODEMUS

His soul perished for it
When he took his own life.
Certainly they ought to be greatly afflicted
    by this,
These wretched Jews, my own kindred;   236
They have more to be unhappy about than
    other peoples.
This is indeed true, you do not lie.

Nicodemus took his tools,
And Joseph said to him thus: 240

JOSEPH

Go to the feet first.

NICODEMUS

Willingly, sir, and gently.

JOSEPH

Go up to the hands, remove the nails.

NICODEMUS

Very willingly, sir, both things.   244

When Nicodemus had done this,
He said to Joseph, who held the body:

NICODEMUS

Gently take him in your arms.

JOSEPH

Be well assured I'm doing that.   248

Then they lowered the body decorously
And Joseph said to his servant:

JOSEPH

Hand me that ointment.
Thus we will anoint this worshipful body.   252

NICHODEMUS

L'alme de lui en est perie
Quant sei mesme toli la vie.
Mult par poaient estre dolenz
Chaistif Jueu, li men parenz;   236
Plus sunt malurez qu'altres genz.

Ceo est si veir que tu n'i menz.

Nichodem ses ustilz prist,
E dan Joseph issi lui dist:

JOSEPHUS

Alez as piez primerement.

NICHODEMUS

Volenters, sire, e dulcement.

JOSEPHUS

Montés as mains, ostez les clous.

NICHODEMUS

Sire, mult volenters, ambesdouz.   244

Quant Nichodem l'out fait issi,
Dist a Joseph, qui le cors saisi:

NICHODEMUS

Suef le pernez entre vos braz.

JOSEPHUS

Saches treisben que jo si faz.   248

Dunt mistrent bel le cors ava
E Joseph dit a son vaissal:

JOSEPHUS

Baillez mei ça cel uinnement.
Si en oindrum cest cors present.   252

While he handed the ointment to him,
Nicodemus said very loudly:

Tant cum l'oinnement lui baut,
Nichodem dit tut en haut:

NICODEMUS

O almighty God,
Heaven and earth and water and wind   256
Altogether
Are at your commandment,
And all things likewise,
Excepting only on earth the evil people   260
Who have put this [holy] man to torment,
Delivered him to death without trial—
They will have vengeance for it!
Yet you are a most forgiving Lord.   264
Grant us to give burial worthily
To this holy body.

NICHODEMUS

Ahi, Deus omnipotent,
Ciel e terre e ewe e vent
Trestuz comanablement
Sunt al ton comandement,
E tutes choses ensement,
Fors sul en terre male gent
Qui unt cestui mis a turment,
Livrez a mort senz jugement—
Uncore i avrat vengement!
Mes tu es Sire mult pacient.
Dune nus faire dignement
A cest seint cors enterment.

When they had anointed the body,
They placed it on the bier.   268

Quant le cors enoint aveient,
Sur la bere il le meteient.

NICODEMUS

Sir Joseph, you are the elder.
Go at the head, I go at the feet.
Thus let us go quickly to bury him.
Do you have a place where he should lie?   272

NICHODEMUS

Sire Joseph, vus estes eniz nez.
Alez al chef, jo vois as piez.
Si alum tost ensevelir.
Avez veu u il pout gisir?

JOSEPH

I have a handsome monument,
Made of stone, freshly new.
Let us go there directly.
Therein he will receive burial.   276

JOSEPHUS

Jo ai un monument mult bel,
De pere est fait trestut novel.
Ore i alum a dreit hure.
Laenz avra sepulture.

When he was interred and the stone set in
place,
Caiaphas, having risen from his seat, said in
this fashion:

Quant il fut enterrez et la pere mise,

Caiphas, qui est levez, dit en ceste guise:

CAIAPHAS

Sir Pilate, hear my counsel;
I am greatly in the wrong if I conceal this
from you.   280
The wicked Jesus, this deceiver,
Who was hanged there like a thief,

CAIPHAS

Sire Pilate, oez mon conseil;
Jo ai grant tort si jol vus ceil.

Li fel Jesus, icel trichere,
Qui la fu pendu come lere,

---

[277]At this point appears in the margin the following biblical gloss: *Posuit eum in monumento novo quod excideratur a petra* (He placed him in a new monument hewn of stone). See Matthew 27:60.

This fellow used to say when he was alive—
And many people erringly believe this—
That he would rise again on the third day.
But anyone who believes this is terribly foolish.
Let us take order for guarding the sepulchre,
Lest his followers come and carry him off furtively.
For they will go everywhere preaching
And proclaiming throughout the country
That he is risen from death and is alive.
Thus he will lead the wretches astray;
If this happens, so much the worse.

PILATE

You say truly, in my opinion.

Then one of the soldiers stood up
And spoke to Pilate as follows:

A SOLDIER

If someone will commission me,
I'll guard the sepulchre.
And if it happens
That any one of his friends come
At that time, intending to carry him off secretly,
Such a person won't get away without suffering;
I'll tear him limb from limb.
I do not desire that a priest assoil me.

Three others then stood up
And said as follows to the first:

SECOND SOLDIER

Worthy companion, we will go with you
And guard the sepulchre.
No one will come there without our seizing him,

Iceo diseit en son vivant—
Si sunt li plusur mescreant—
Qu'il al terz jur releverait.
Mes mult par est fol qui ceo creit.

Le sepulture faimes guarder,
Que nel vengent li soen embler.

Car il le irreient par tut prechant
E par le pais denonciant
Qu'il ert de mort resurs e vifs.
Si ferat mescreire les chaistifs;
S'il est issi, si sera piz.

PILATUS

Vus ditez veir, ceo m'est avis.

Un des serganz dunc s'esdresça
E a Pilate issi parla:

QUIDAM MILES

Si l'om me volt doner la cure,
Jeo garderai le sepulture.
Et si ceo est, par aventure,
Que nul venge a icel hure
De ces amis, que embler le voille,

Ja n'en turnerat qu'il ne se doille;

N'averat membre que ne li toille.
Ja ne quer que prestre me soille.

Treis des altres dunc leverent
E al primer si parlerent:

ALTER QUIDAM MILES

Bel compain, od vus en irrum
E le sepulcre garderum.
Nul n'i vendra qui ne prengum,

287–93 At this point appears in the margin the following biblical gloss: *Jube costodire sepulcrum ne furentur eum discipuli eius et dicant plebi quia surrexit, et erit novissi[m]us error peior priore* (Order them to guard the sepulchre lest his disciples steal him away and say to the people that he has risen, and the newest error will be worse than before). See Matthew 27:64.

304 i.e., I don't desire to be pardoned by the church; this deed won't be on my conscience.

Nor will anyone rise from the dead without
    our knowing about it.

THE THIRD

Let's go there boldly with speed
And guard the tomb well.   312
If anyone comes to carry the body away
    secretly,
We'll give that person something to be
    terribly afraid about.

THE FOURTH

For the faith I owe Pilate,
If anyone comes to make trouble,   316
I'll deliver him fifteen such blows
That with the very first I'll flatten him on
    the ground.

CAIAPHAS

I will accompany you,
To instruct you in your duties concerning
    this business.—   320
Do you give permission, sire, that it should be
    thus?

PILATE

Sir Caiaphas, I consent willingly.

As they were going there, accordingly,
A bystander asked them: 324

A BYSTANDER

Where are you going at such a fast pace?

FIRST SOLDIER

We go to guard the tomb
Of Jesus who was buried,
Who said that he will rise on the third day. 328

ANOTHER BYSTANDER

Did Pilate command this?

SECOND SOLDIER

Yes, you can believe that for a certainty.
See, here's Bishop Caiaphas
Who's coming along with us himself   332

N'il ne levera que nel sachom.

TERTIUS

Aloms i tost hardiement,
Si gardum ben le monument.
Si nul venge pur lui embler,

Nus le ferum grant pour aver.

QUARTUS

Pur la fei qui dei Pilate,
Si nul venge feire barate,
Tels quinze cols li paierai
Que del primer l'esturnerai.

CAIPHAS

E jo ensemble od vus irrai;
De cest mester vus saiserai.—

Granté vus, sire, qu'il seit issi?

PILATUS

Sire Chaiphas, ben le vus otri.

Dunt si cum il alerent la,
Un par vei lur demanda:

ALIQUIS IN VIA RESPICIENS

U en alé us si grant alure?

UNUS MILITUM

Garder alum la sepulture
De Jesu qu'i est enseveli,
Qui dit qu'il levrat al terz di.

ITEM QUI SUPRA

Ad ceo Pilate comandé?

ALTER EX MILITIBUS

Oil, ceo sachez en verité.
Veez ci le vesque Caiphas
Qui tut se vent od nus le pas,

To instruct us in our guard duties.
Now let anybody approach the tomb who
    dares!

When Caiaphas had led them there, 336
He spoke and commanded them:

CAIAPHAS

Now, here you are at the tomb.
Guard it absolutely.
If you sleep and he is taken,
Never again will you be good friends of
    mine. 340
[But first swear upon the law that]
What you are about to swear you will hold
    to faithfully,
That, if any man be so bold
As to come here after dusk
To spy about and watch to see 344
If he can steal away the body from you—
Even though he tell you he isn't doing it for
    this reason—
This you will swear in this place,
That whoever he be, small or large, 348
If he lacks a warrant from the princes of the
    church,
You will seize him by the throat;
When he is taken, you will conduct him to
    us.
Swear to hold to this loyally. 352
Where is the scroll of the sacred law? Cause
    it to be brought here.

A priest came, named Levi,
Who had the law of Moses written on a scroll.

LEVI

See here the law that Moses made, 356
As God himself dictated to him.
The ten commandments are here.
Anyone who perjures himself will not be
    able to hide it.

Qui la garde nus comandra.
Ore venge qui venir voldra!

Quant Caiphas les i out mené,
Si lur ad dit e comandé:

CAIPHAS

Ore estés ci al monument.
Gardez le ben parfitement.
Si vus dormez e il seit pris,
Jamés ne serum bonz amiz.

[Mes primes jurez sur lai]
Ceo que jurez tendrez en fei,

Que si nuls hom seit si hardi
Que puis le vespre venge ici
Espigucer e aguaiter
Si le cors vus poisse embler—
Tut die il que pur ceo nel face—

Ceo jurrez en ceste place,
Que qu'il seit, petit u grant,
E il n'en ait des princes guarant,

Tut par mi le gule le prendrez;
Quant ert pris, a nus le merrez.

Ceo jurez lealment a tenir.
U est le rolle? faitez le venir.

Est vus un prestre, qui out a non Levi,
Si out escrite la lei Moysi.

LEVI

Veez ici la lei que Moisés fist,
Si cum Deus meimes a li la dist.
Les dis comandemenz i at.
Qui parjuret ert, ja nel tairat.

340a Missing line supplied from the Canterbury MS.

355 *Who:* The French *Si,* "thus," perhaps should be emended to *Qui,* "who," as in the Canterbury MS.

CAIAPHAS

Now all of you swear on this scripture   360
To keep what you have said.

FIRST SOLDIER

By the law which is here,
If anyone should come secretly
I'll make it my business to seize him   364
With the aid of my companion, and hand
    him over to you.

THE SECOND

By the miraculous power of this law,
What he said I'll keep to faithfully.

THE THIRD

I will keep to it, if it please God,   368
By the holy law which is here.

[THE FOURTH]

May [God and] this law assist me!
I will hold to it, for my part.

[Incomplete]

CAIPHAS

Ore jurez tuz sur cest escrist
De tenir quanque vus ai dist.

UNUS MILITUM

Par la lei que ci est present,
Si nuls i venge celeement
Jeo m'entremectrai de lui prendre
A mon pair e a vus rendre.

ALTER

Par la grant vertu de ceste lei
Ceo que cist dit tendrai en fei.

TERTIUS

Jeo tendrai, si Deu pleist,
Par la seinte lei que ici est.

[QUARTUS]

Si m'a[i]t [Deus e] icest lai!
Jeol tendrai ben endreit de mei.

370Line completed from the Canterbury MS.

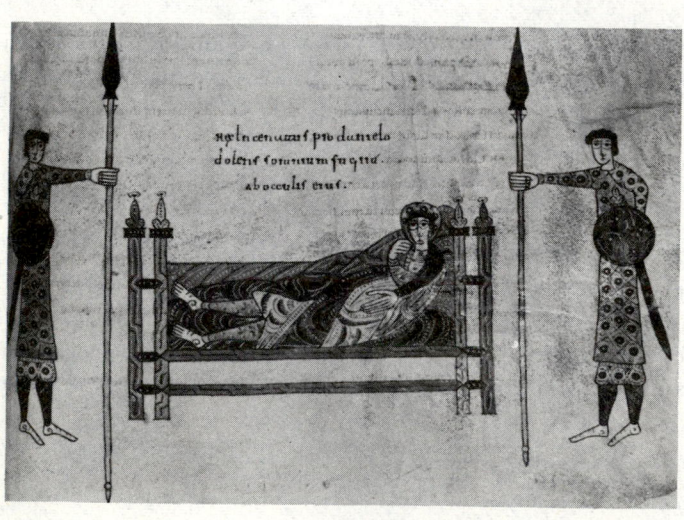

3. THE PLAY OF DANIEL
(DANIELIS LUDUS)
FROM BEAUVAIS

The Beauvais *Play of Daniel* shows us the kind of splendor that twelfth-century church drama could achieve in dealing with Old Testament subjects. Other Old Testament plays have survived from this period, notably the Anglo-Norman *Adam*, a Daniel play by the wandering scholar Hilarius (which seems to be related to the Beauvais play), and a fragmentary play about Jacob and Esau from a manuscript found in Steirmark, Austria. From thirteenth-century Laon comes a play about Joseph and his brethren. Of all these, the Beauvais *Daniel* is the most opulent and majestic, with its processionals, its royal spectacle, its palace, and its lions' den. Today, thanks to the productions and recordings of the New York Pro Musica, *Daniel* is also the best known of twelfth-century dramas.

Like the Anglo-Norman *Adam*, the Beauvais *Daniel* draws a connection between its Old Testament subject and the coming of Christ. The play was probably staged in the cathedral church of Beauvais during the Christmas season, perhaps on the Feast of the Circumcision (January 1) or on the previous day. The singers pointedly celebrate "this solem feast" day on which God was "born man, in the flesh" (ll. 270–72). Even though the story of Daniel in the lions' den has no direct bearing on the Nativity, the singers remind us that Daniel was also a prophet who foresaw the cessation of the anointing power of the Jews through the coming of the Messiah (see Daniel 9). This same prophecy is spoken by Daniel in the Procession of Prophets in the Anglo-Norman *Adam* and in the Benediktbeuern *Christmas Play*, and is to be found also in the

pseudo-Augustinian *Sermo contra Judeos, Paganos, et Arianos* upon which the Procession of Prophets was based. To be sure, we must not overstate the importance of the *Sermo* as earlier scholars have done, arguing that all dramatizations of the Old Testament grew out of the idea of a procession of prophets announcing Christ's advent. The Beauvais *Daniel* only tangentially mentions Daniel's prophesying of the coming of the Messiah. Still, this play about Daniel is appropriate to the Christmas season because, like Adam's, his story anticipates the greatest of all miracles. To the medieval religious artist, the Old Testament was best understood in relation to the New.

The Beauvais *Daniel* is a work of brilliant pageantry. The singers clearly are to be accompanied by musical instruments of the sort referred to in the text: harps, zithers, and drums. (Some additional musical effects provided by the New York Pro Musica production, though impressive, cannot easily be justified from the original manuscript.) The zither players are repeatedly enjoined to "touch their strings." King Darius enters to the sounds of joyfulness and "ritual dances as well." The leading actors are splendidly attired in "purple garments" and "regal robes." King Belshazzar's banquet requires the use of sumptuous vessels. No less than eight processionals or recessionals, unmistakably labeled as such, require as many musicians and singers as possible to accompany the

Text based on London, British Museum, MS Egerton 2615, *Officium Circumcisionis et Danielis Ludus saec.* xii, fol. 95r–108r. It has been edited by Young, *Drama of the Medieval Church*, II, 290–301, and others.

stately entrances or departures of Belshazzar, his queen, Daniel, and King Darius. The church interior, in this case that of the cathedral church at Beauvais, shows its ability to accommodate itself to productions of considerable magnificence.

Three stations or elevated platforms, located possibly in the center of the nave near the entrance to the choir, seem to be required: a palace for King Belshazzar and later for King Darius, a humble house to which Daniel can retire to worship God, and the lions' den. The palace is sumptuous and large, featuring a high throne for the king and a seat for Daniel by the king's side. Evidently the lions' den is on a lower level than the palace, since King Darius descends from his throne to visit it; nevertheless, the den must remain visible to the audience. A number of spectacular scenic effects require the employment of stage illusion. An angel escorts the prophet Habakkuk from the fields to the lions' den "by the hair of his head," as though flying; the counselors who unjustly accuse Daniel are stripped of their clothing, taken to "the edge of the pit," and thrown in; and these same counselors are "eaten immediately by the lions." The lions are presumably actors in costume, but we can only speculate as to the way in which the devouring was accomplished. Habakkuk probably does not require a separate platformed station, since he is found by an angel in the fields. An angel also appears "on high"— probably singing from an elevated vantage point in the church. The play ends with the chanting of the *Te Deum* by the cantors, suggesting performance at the end of matins.

The Play of Daniel
(Danielis Ludus)
From Beauvais

Here Begins the Play of Daniel	*Incipit Danielis Ludus.*
In your honor, O Christ,	Ad honorem tui, Christe,
This play of Daniel	Danielis ludus iste
Has been devised at Beauvais,	in Belvaco est inventus,
And young persons wrote it.	et invenit hunc juventus.
As King Belshazzar enters, his princes will sing before him this sequence:	*Dum venerit Rex Balthasar, principes sui cantabunt ante eum hanc prosam:*

To the almighty one   5   Astra tenenti
Holding the firmament,   cunctipotenti
This throng of men   turba virilis

1–4 These dedicatory verses are set to music and were presumably sung by the choir.

5–34 This processional is sung by those accompanying Belshazzar in regal splendor from the place of entry to his throne. The staging of this play appears to require Belshazzar's palace (later occupied by Darius), Daniel's house, and the lions' den, all simultaneously visible. There must also be a place from which the sacred vessels of the Temple of God in Jerusalem are taken and to which they are returned, and a place for Habakkuk. The production places remarkable emphasis on the various processionals.

And of boys,
This assembly, renders praise.

For it steadfastly hears   10
That the faithful Daniel
Has both undergone
And suffered
Many trials.

The king calls before him wise men   15
Who might reveal to him the hidden
     meaning of the message written by that
     right hand.
Because these scribes were unable to
     decipher these (writings),
As mutes they stood silent there before the
     king.
But to Daniel, as he perused the writings,
     was at once revealed
What before had been concealed from them.   20
Because Belshazzar saw how Daniel
     prevailed over the others,
He is reported to have preferred Daniel at
     court.
A trumped-up accusation,
Not very fitly
Sentences him   25
To be torn apart
By the lions' mouth.
But you, O God, then wished that those
     who had been hostile
Toward Daniel should use him kindly.
And to him,   30
Lest he go hungry,
Bread is dispatched from you,
By the prophet swift of flight,
Providing a meal.

*Then let the king ascend his throne, and let the
satraps say, acclaiming him:*

King, live forever.   35

And the king will open his mouth, saying:

You who are obedient to my voice,
Bring for my use the vessels
Which my father carried from the temple
When he vehemently overthrew Judaea.

---

et puerilis
contio plaudit.

Nam Danielem
multa fidelem
et subiisse
atque tulisse
firmiter audit.

Convocat ad se rex sapientes
gramata dextrae qui sibi dicant
     enucleantes.

Quae quia scribae non potuere

solvere, regi ilico muti conticuere.

Sed Danieli scripta legenti mox patuere

quae prius illis clausa fuere.
Quem quia vidit praevaluisse

Balthasar illis, fertur in aula praeposuisse.

Causa reperta
non satis apta
destinat illum
ore leonum
dilacerandum.
Sed, Deus, illos ante malignos

in Danielem tunc voluisti esse benignos.
Huic quoque panis,
ne sit inanis,
mittitur a te
praepete vate
prandia dante.

*Tunc ascendat rex in solium, et satrapae ei
applaudentes dicant:*

Rex, in aeternum vive.

Et rex aperiet os suum dicens:

Vos qui paretis meis vocibus,
afferte vasa meis usibus
quae templo pater meus abstulit,
Judaeam graviter cum perculit.

The satraps, bearing forth the vessels, will sing this sequence in praise of the king:

Let us rejoice in our great and powerful king!   40

Let us sound forth with suitable praise and fitting utterance.

Let the rejoicing throng re-echo with festive song.

Let them play the harp, clap hands, make merry sound a thousand ways.

His father, destroying the temples of the Jews,

Performed great deeds, and this [king] now reigns by his example.   45

His father pillaged the kingdom of the Jews;

Now this [king] enhances his feasts with the elegance of these vessels.

These are the royal vessels of which Jerusalem is despoiled

And by which regal Babylon is now enriched.

Let us present them to our king, Belshazzar,   50

Who thus sumptuously adorns his followers in purple garments.

He is mighty, he is strong, he is renowned,

He is upright, courteous, well-proportioned, and handsome.

Let us praise so great a king with melodious voices;

Let us all sound forth together with sonorous praises.   55

Babylon applauds laughing; Jerusalem weeps.

The latter is bereft of her children, while the former, triumphing, worships Belshazzar.

Let us all therefore exult in such might,

Offering to his majesty the vessels of the king.

Then let the princes say:

Satrapae vasa deferentes cantabunt hanc prosam ad laudem regis:

Jubilemus regi nostro magno ac potenti!

Resonemus laude digna voce competenti.

Resonet jocunda turba sollemnibus odis.

Citharizent, plaudant manus, mille sonent modis.

Pater eius destruens Judaeorum templa

magna fecit, et hic regnat eius per exempla.

Pater eius spoliavit regnum Judaeorum;

hic exaltat sua festa decore vasorum.

Haec sunt vasa regia quibus spoliatur

Jherusalem et regalis Babylon ditatur.

Praesentemus Balthasar ista regi nostro,

qui sic suos perornavit purpura et ostro.

Iste potens, iste fortis, iste gloriosus,

iste probus, curialis, decens, et formosus.

Jubilemus regi tanto vocibus canoris;

resonemus omnes una laudibus sonoris.

Ridens plaudit Babylon; Jherusalem plorat.

Haec orbatur, haec triumphans Balthasar adorat.

Omnes ergo exultemus tantae potestati,

offerentes regis vasa suae majestati.

Tunc principes dicant:

---

⁴⁰⁻⁵⁹This song of praise is chanted by the satraps as they march in procession from the place where the sacred vessels are kept to the palace, and as they serve Belshazzar a splendid feast.

Behold, they are here before your face.   60

Meanwhile a right hand will appear in the king's sight, inscribing on the wall: Mene, Tekel, Peres; *seeing which, the king will cry out, aghast:*

Call forth Chaldean astrologers
And soothsayers!
Seek out diviners,
And bring forth wise men.

Then wise men will be led forth, who will say to the king:

King, live forever.   65
Behold, we are here before you.

And the king:

He who shall read this writing
And decipher its meaning,
Under his power
Babylon shall be placed;   70
And, arrayed in purple,
He shall enjoy a golden neck-chain.

Not knowing how to decipher the writing, they will say to the king:

We do not know how to explain what is
     written,
Nor give advice as to the signification of the
     hand.

The processional of the queen as she approaches the king:

When the whole assembly   75
Of learned doctors
And wise men is in session,
It ponders to itself
But cannot unravel
What the vision of the hand signifies.   80
Behold the royal consort is at hand,
Sagacious,
Reputed of noble stock,
Rich and powerful,
Adorned   85
In golden apparel.

Ecce sunt ante faciem tuam.

Interim apparebit dextra in conspectu regis scribens in pariete: Mane, Thechel, Phares; *quam videns rex stupefactus clamabit:*

Vocate mathematicos
Chaldaeos et hariolos!
Haruspices inquirite,
et magos introducite.

Tunc adducentur magi, qui dicent regi:

Rex, in aeternum vive.
Adsumus ecce tibi.

Et rex:

Qui scripturam hanc legerit
et sensum aperuerit,
sub illius potentia
subdetur Babylonia;
et insignitus purpura
torque fruetur aurea.

Illi vero nescientes persolvere dicent regi:

Nescimus persolvere nec dare consilium

Quae sit superscriptio, nec manus
     indicium.

Conductus reginae venientis ad regem:

Cum doctorum
et magorum
omnis adsit contio,
secum volvit,
neque solvit,
quae sit manus visio.
Ecce prudens,
stirpe cluens,
dives cum potentia,
in vestitu
deaurato
conjunx adest regia.

She will produce		Haec latentem
An unknown seer		promet vatem
By whose testimony		per cuius indicium
The king will come to know	90	rex describi
How his own ruin		suum ibi
Is here set forth.		noverit exitium.
Therefore let this heroic woman		Laetis ergo
Be attended		haec virago
By joyful applause.	95	comitetur plausibus.
With sonorous strings		Cordis, oris
And voices		que sonoris
Let music be sounded.		personetur vocibus.

Then the queen, as she comes forward, will venerate the king, saying: *Tunc regina veniens adorabit regem dicens:*

King, live forever.		Rex, in aeternum vive.
That you may know the nature of this writing,	100	Ut scribentis noscas ingenium,
King Belshazzar, hear my counsel.		Rex Balthasar, audi consilium.

Upon hearing this, the king will turn his face toward the queen; and let the queen say: *Rex audiens haec, versus reginam vertet faciem suam, et regina dicat:*

Among the captive people of Judaea,		Cum Judaeae captivis populis
The victory of your father		prophetiae doctum oraculis
Took in bondage from his country		Danielem a sua patria
A certain Daniel, learned in prophetic oracles.	105	captivavit patris victoria.
Since he now lives under your authority,		Hic sub tuo vivens imperio,
Reason dictates that he be sent for.		ut mandetur, requirit ratio.
Therefore give order, let there be no delay,		Ergo manda ne sit dilatio,
For he will interpret what the vision conceals.		nam docebit quod celat visio.

Then let the king say to his princes: *Tunc dicat rex principibus suis:*

Go seek out Daniel,	110	Vos Danielem quaerite,
And when he is found bring him here.		et inventum adducite.

Then let the princes, having found Daniel, say to him: *Tunc principes, invento Daniele, dicant ei:*

O man and prophet of God, Daniel, come to the king.	Vir propheta Dei, Daniel, vien al roi.
Come, he desires to speak with you.	Veni, desiderat parler a toi.
He quakes with fear and is troubled, Daniel, come to the king.	Pavet et turbatur, Daniel, vien al roi.

111s.d.: Daniel is presumably found at his house; such a structure is required later in the play, l. 311 s.d.

He wishes to know by your means what lies
    hidden from us.   115
He will favor you with gifts, Daniel, come
    to the king,
If by your means he can understand the
    writings.

And Daniel to them:

I marvel greatly on whose advice
The royal command inquires after me.
Notwithstanding, I shall go, and it will be
    made known   120
By me, without recompense, what is
    concealed.

*The processional of Daniel as it approaches the
king:*

Here is the true servant of God,
Whom every people praises,
Whose reputation for good judgment
Is well known in the king's court.   125
He is called before the king by us.

Daniel:

Impoverished and in exile, I go to the king
    by your means.

The princes:

In the glory of youth,
Full of celestial grace,
He plentifully excels all others   130
In virtue, life, character.
He is called before the king by us.

Daniel:

Impoverished and in exile, I go to the king
    by your means.

The princes:

This is he whose counsel
Will unravel that vision   135
Through which, by the writing hand,
The king's innermost being has been shaken.
He is called before the king by us.

Daniel:

Vellet quod nos latet savoir par toi.

Te ditabit donis, Daniel, vien al roi,

Si scripta poterit savoir par toi.

Et Daniel eis:

Multum miror cuius consilio
me requirat regalis jussio.
Ibo tamen, et erit cognitum

per me gratis quod est absconditum.

Conductus Danielis venientis ad regem:

Hic verus Dei famulus,
quem laudat omnis populus,
cuius fama prudentiae
est nota regis curiae.
Cestui manda li rois par nos.

Daniel:

Pauper et exulans envois al roi par vos.

Principes:

In juventutis gloria,
plenus caelesti gratia,
satis excellit omnibus
virtute, vita, moribus.
Cestui manda li rois par nos.

Daniel:

Pauper et exulans envois al roi par vos.

Principes:

Hic est cuius auxilio
solvetur illa visio
in qua scribente dextera
mota sunt regis viscera.
Cestui manda li rois par nos.

Daniel:

Impoverished and in exile, I go to the king
    by your means.

As Daniel arrives before the king, let him say to
him:

King, live forever.   140

And the king to Daniel:

Do you not call yourself Daniel by name,
Led hither with the unfortunate Judaeans?
They say you possess the spirit of God
And can foresee whatever lies hidden.
If therefore you can interpret this writing,   145
You will be favored with countless gifts.

And Daniel to the king:

O king, I do not desire your gifts;
Without fee the writing will be interpreted.
Here is the answer:
Disaster threatens you.   150
Your father before all other powerful ones
Once was powerful;
Swollen with too much pride,
He was cast down from glory.
For, not walking with God,   155
But acting as if he himself were God,
He snatched away the vessels from the
    temple
And put them to his own use.
But after many such senseless acts,
At length losing his riches,   160
Deprived of his human shape,
He tasted the food of the turf.
You also, his son,
No less ungodly than he,
Following the deeds of your father,   165
You use those very same vessels.
Since this displeases God,
The time is at hand in which He will
    avenge.
For the signification of this writing
Is to threaten dire punishment;   170
And "Mene," says the Lord,
Signifies the end of your kingdom.
"Tekel" means the balancing scales
In which you are found wanting.

Pauper et exulans envois al roi par vos.

Veniens Daniel ante regem, dicat ei:

Rex, in aeternum vive.

Et rex Danieli:

Tune Daniel nomine diceris
huc adductus cum Judaeae miseris?
Dicunt te habere Dei spiritum
et praescire quodlibet absconditum.
Si ergo potes scripturam solvere,
immensis muneribus ditabere.

Et Daniel regi:

Rex, tua nolo munera;
gratis solvetur litera.
Est autem haec solutio:
instat tibi confusio.
Pater tuus prae omnibus
potens olim potentibus;
turgens nimis superbia,
dejectus est a gloria.
Nam cum Deo non ambulans,
sed sese Deum simulans,
vasa templo diripuit

quae suo usu habuit.
Sed post multas insanias
tandem perdens divitias,
forma nudatus hominis,
pastum gustavit graminis.
Tu quoque, eius filius,
non ipso minus impius,
dum patris actus sequeris,
vasis eisdem uteris.
Quod quia Deo displicet,
instat tempus quo vindicet.

Nam scripturae indicium
minatur iam supplicium;
et "mane," dicit Dominus,
est tui regni terminus.
"Thechel" libram significat
quae te minorem indicat.

"Peres," that is division; 175	"Phares," hoc est divisio,
It conveys your kingdom to another.	regnum transportat alio.

And the king:

Et rex:

Let him who thus has unraveled hidden meaning	Qui sic solvit latentia
Be dressed in regal robes.	ornetur veste regia.

When Daniel is seated next to the king, appareled in regal attire, the king will call aloud to his captain of the militia:

Sedente Daniele juxta regem, induto ornamentis regalibus, exclamabit rex ad principem militiae:

Take away the vessels, captain of the militia,	Tolle vasa, princeps militiae,
That they may not be a cause of wretchedness to me. 180	ne sint mihi causa miseriae.

Then, having left the palace, the satraps will carry back the vessels; and the queen will depart. The queen's recessional:

Tunc, relicto palatio, referent vasa satrapae; et regina discedet. Conductus reginae:

In the book of Solomon is set forth	Solvitur in libro Salomonis
Deserving and suitable praise of women.	digna laus et congrua matronis.
Her worth is that of a courageous person	Pretium est eius si quam fortis
From the far and remotest limits of the earth.	procul et de finibus remotis.
The heart of her husband has confidence in her, 185	Fidens est in ea cor mariti
He who has obtained rich spoils.	spoliis divitibus potiti.
Let this woman be compared with one	Mulier haec illi comparetur
Whose husband-king deserves her support.	cuius rex subsidium meretur.
For her eloquence with words	Eius nam facundia verborum
Censures the judgment of the learned. 190	arguit prudentiam doctorum.
Let us to whom the occasion of performing this play	Nos quibus occasio ludendi
Is granted on this festive day	hac die conceditur sollemni,
Devotedly render praise to her,	demus huic praeconia devoti,
And let those from afar also come and join in song.	veniant et concinent remoti.

178s.d.: The king's palace evidently must have a throne for the king and a place at his side for Daniel. See also l. 291 s.d. below.

186*rich spoils:* See Proverbs 31:11, in praise of "A capable wife," where language very similar to that of this verse suggests that the "spoils" are children.

187–88These lines suggest a comparison of the queen to a royal member of the play's original audience.

192*this festive day:* i.e., a day during the Christmas season, perhaps the Feast of the Circumcision (January 1) or the preceding day, on which this play is being performed.

The recessional of those bringing the vessels before Daniel:

Bringing back the vessels of that king	195	*Conductus referentium vasa ante Danielem:*

Conductus referentium vasa ante Danielem:

Bringing back the vessels of that king   195
Whom the Jewish people fear,
Giving our applause to Daniel,
Let us rejoice;
Let us render the praises due him!

He predicted the destruction of the king   200
When he unlocked the meaning of the
    written legend;
He proved the witnesses guilty
And set Susanna free.
Let us rejoice;
[Let us render] the praises [due him!]   205

Babylon made him an exile
When she captured the Jews;
Belshazzar honored him.
Let us rejoice;
[Let us render the praises due him!]   210

He is a holy prophet of God;
The Chaldeans honor him,
Together with the gentiles and the Jews.
Acclaiming him, therefore,
Let us rejoice,   215

and so on. Suddenly King Darius will appear with his princes, and the zither-players and his princes will come before him singing this psalm:

Behold, King Darius
Comes with his princes,
A nobleman with his nobles.
His court
Resounds with joyfulness,   220

Regis vasa referentes
quem Judaeae tremunt gentes,
Danieli applaudentes,
gaudeamus;
laudes sibi debitas referamus!

Regis cladem praenotavit
cum scripturam reseravit;
testes reos comprobavit,
et Susannam liberavit.
Gaudeamus;
laudes [sibi debitas referamus!]

Babylon hunc exulavit
cum Judaeos captivavit;
Balthasar quem honoravit.
Gaudeamus;
[laudes sibi debitas referamus!]

Est propheta sanctus Dei;
hunc honorant et Chaldaei
et gentiles et Judaei.
Ergo jubilantes ei,
gaudeamus,

et cetera. Statim apparebit Darius Rex cum principibus suis, venientque ante eum citharistae et principes sui psallentes haec:

Ecce Rex Darius
venit cum principibus,
nobilis nobilibus.
Eius et curia
resonat laetitia,

---

[194]S.D.: The satraps, ordered by Belshazzar to return the sacred vessels, present them to Daniel as the champion of the true God. Seemingly Daniel has returned to his house. The queen has also exited at this point, leaving Belshazzar alone at his palace to be deposed by Darius.

[202-3]The account of Daniel's rescue of Susanna from the lecherous elders appears in the Apocryphal Book of Daniel and Susanna. Curiously this hymn of praise to Daniel makes no mention of King Nebuchadnezzar and the three young men in the fiery furnace. The Play of Daniel as a whole is based freely on Daniel 5–6 and on the Apocryphal Book of Daniel and Susanna.

[216-45]This processional for the entry of Darius and his march to the throne mirrors that for Belshazzar which begins the play.

And there are ritual dances as well.		adsunt et tripudia.
He is a man to be wondered at,		Hic est mirandus,
To be venerated by all.		cunctis venerandus.
Whole empires		Illi imperia
Are subject to him.	225	sunt tributaria.
Let all honor the king		Regem honorant
And worship him.		omnes et adorant.
Babylon dreads him,		Illum Babylonia
And his own country.		metuit et patria.
Descending swiftly with his armed troops	230	Cum armato agmine
Even as with a whirlwind,		ruens et cum turbine
He scatters the enemy forces		sternit cohortes,
And has utterly destroyed the mighty.		confregit et fortes.
Honor and nobility		Illum honestas
Adorn him.	235	colit et nobilitas.
This is the noble		Hic est Babylonius
Babylonian King Darius.		nobilis Rex Darius.
With ritual dance		Illi cum tripudio
Let this assembly rejoice in him,		gaudeat haec contio,
And with rejoicing let it praise	240	laudet et cum gaudio
His mighty deeds,		eius facta fortia
So much to be marveled at.		tam admirabilia.

Together let us all render thanks; and let
  the drums resound;
Let the zither-players touch their strings;
  let the instruments of the musicians
Sound forth in his commendation.   245

Simul omnes gratulemur;   resonent
  et tympana;
Citharistae tangant cordas;
  musicorum organa
resonent ad eius praeconia.

*Before the king arrives at the throne, two followers
running before him will expel Belshazzar, making
as though to kill him. Then when Darius is seated
as king in majesty, the court will exclaim:*

*Antequam perveniat rex ad solium suum, duo
praecurrentes expellent Balthasar quasi in-
terficientes eum. Tunc sedente Dario Rege in
majestate sua, curia exclamabit:*

King, live forever!

Rex, in aeternum vive!

*Then two followers, on bended knees, will suggest
in secret to the king that he cause Daniel to be
summoned, and let the king order that he be
brought in. They, enjoining the others, will say
as follows:*

*Tunc duo flexis genibus secreto dicent regi ut
faciat accersiri Danielem, et rex jubeat eum
adduci. Illi autem aliis praecipientes dicent
haec:*

Listen, princes of the royal court,
You who administer the laws of the entire
  land.

Audite, principes regalis curiae,
qui leges regitis totius patriae.

There is a wise person in Babylon,
Who reveals secret truths by the grace of
  the gods.   250

Est quidam sapiens in Babylonia,
secreta reserans deorum gratia.

His advice was very pleasing to the king,

Eius consilium regi complacuit,

For in earlier times he interpreted the
    writing to Belshazzar.

Go quickly, let there be no delay,

We wish to use his advice.

If he will come, let him be made counselor   255

To the king, and he will be third in the
    kingdom.

*The legates, having found Daniel, will say as
follows on behalf of the king:*

From royal command comes

Our legation, O servant of God.

Your probity is praised to the king,

Your wondrous skill in wisdom commends
    you.   260

By you alone was made manifest to us

The portent of the right hand which had
    been concealed from everyone.

The king calls you to his court,

That he may become well acquainted with
    your judgment.

You will be, so said Darius earlier,   265

Chief adviser.

Therefore come, for all the court

Is prepared to rejoice at your coming.

And Daniel:

I go to the king.

Daniel's processional:

Rejoicing together, let us celebrate this
    solemn feast of the nativity;   270

For from death the wisdom of God has
    redeemed us.

He has been born man, in the flesh, who
    created all things,

Whose birth was foretold by the eloquence
    of the prophet.

---

nam prius Balthasar scriptum aperuit.

Ite velociter, ne sit dilatio,

nos uti volumus eius consilio.

Fiat, si venerit, consiliarius

regis, et fuerit in regno tertius.

*Legati, invento Daniele, dicent haec ex parte
regis:*

Ex regali venit imperio,

serve Dei, nostra legatio.

Tua regi laudatur probitas,

te commendat mira calliditas.

Per te solum cum nobis patuit

signum dextrae quod omnes latuit.

Te rex vocat ad suam curiam,

ut agnoscat tuam prudentiam.

Eris, supra ut dicit Darius,

principalis consiliarius.

Ergo veni, iam omnis curia

praeparatur ad tua gaudia.

Et Daniel:

Genvois al roi.

Conductus Danielis:

Congaudentes celebremus   natalis
    sollemnia;

Iam de morte nos redemit   Dei
    sapientia.

Homo natus est in carne,   qui creavit
    omnia,

Nasciturum quem praedixit   prophetae
    facundia.

253-56These lines should perhaps be assigned to King Darius and placed before l. 247.

256s.d.: Again Daniel, who apparently exited in procession before Darius' accession to the throne, is presumably found at his house.

270-84The feast being celebrated is during the Christmas season. For other instances of Daniel's prophecy about the cessation of the anointing power of the Jews, see the play of *Adam,* ll. 827–40, and the pseudo-Augustinian *Sermo contra Judeos,* on which Daniel's prophecy in that play and this is based. The *Sermo* in turn may have been based on Daniel 9:24. For Bel and the dragon (l. 282), see the Aprocryphal Book of Daniel, Bel, and the Snake.

The abundant power of anointing has now
    ceased, as Daniel foresaw;
The stubborn authority of the kingdom of
    the Jews ceases.   275
In this festival of the nativity,
Daniel, with joy
This assembly praises you.
You rescued Susanna from fatal
    calumny,
When God breathed into you his sacred
    breath.   280
You proved the lying witnesses guilty of
    their own accusation.
You destroyed the dragon of Bel before
    the multitude of the people.
And God kept watch over you in the
    lions' den.
Therefore let praise be given to the word of
    God, born of a virgin.

    And Daniel to the king:

King, live forever.   285

    The king to him:

Because I know you skilled in wisdom,
Circumspect in watching over the entire
    kingdom,
Daniel, I appoint you
And assign you to the highest place.

    And Daniel to the king:

O king, if you will have faith in me,   290
Through my means you will do no wrong.

    *Then the king will cause him [Daniel] to sit by
    his side; and the other counselors, growing
    envious of Daniel because he is more beloved of
    the king, having drawn others to their plot to kill
    Daniel, will say to the king:*

King, live forever.

    Continuing:

Those to whom belongs the glory of ruling
Have decreed in your court
That, by the stern authority of your name,   295
All other power of divinity being scorned,
For the space of thirty days

Danielis iam cessavit   unctionis copia;
Cessat regni Judaeorum   contumax
    potentia.
In hoc natalitio,
Daniel, cum gaudio
te laudat haec contio.
Tu Susannam liberasti   de mortali
    crimine,
Cum te Deus inspiravit   suo sancto
    flamine.
Testes falsos comprobasti   reos
    accusamine.
Bel draconem peremisti   coram plebis
    agmine.
Et te Deus observavit   leonum
    voragine.
Ergo sit laus Dei verbo   genito de
    virgine.

    Et Daniel regi:

Rex, in aeternum vive.

    Cui Rex:

Quia novi te callidum,
totius regni providum,

te, Daniel, constituo,
et summum locum tribuo.

    Et Daniel regi:

Rex, mihi si credideris,
per me nil mali feceris.

    *Tunc rex faciet eum sedere juxta se; et alii
    consiliarii Danieli invidentes, quia gratior
    erit regi, aliis in consilium ductis ut Danielem
    interficiant, dicent regi:*

Rex, in aeternum vive.

    Item:

Decreverunt in tua curia
principandi quibus est gloria,
ut ad tui rigorem nominis
omni spreto vigore numinis,
per triginta dierum spatium

You shall be worshiped as the god of all,
O king!
If anyone by so audacious an attempt   300
Rejects your decree
So that a deity other than yourself is
    honored,
Let there be such sternness of judgment
That he be thrown into the lions' den.
Let this be proclaimed throughout the
    court,   305
O king!

And let the king say:

I charge
And repeat my command
That this decree
Be not flouted.   310
Hear ye!

Daniel, hearing this, will go into his house and worship his God; the envious ones, perceiving him, will go quickly and say to the king:

Did you not decree,
O Darius,
This should be heeded by all persons,
That whoever prays to   315
Or beseeches
Any among the gods
Rather than you as god,
That culprit
We must consign to the lions?   320
This edict
Has been thus proclaimed
By all the princes.

And the king, not knowing why they said this, will answer:

Indeed, I ordered that I be worshiped
By all peoples.   325

Then as they lead Daniel forward, they will say to the king:

We saw Daniel,
This Judaean,
Worshiping
And supplicating

adoreris ut deus omnium.
O rex!
Si quis ausu tam temerario
renuerit tuo consilio,
ut praeter te colatur deitas,

judicii sit talis firmitas,
in leonum tradatur foveam.
Sic dicatur per totam regiam.

O rex!

Et rex dicat:

Ego mando
et remando
ne sit spretum
hoc decretum.
O hez!

Daniel hoc audiens ibit in domum suam, et adorabit Deum suum; quem aemuli videntes accurrent et dicent regi:

Nunquid, Dari,
observari
statuisti omnibus
qui orare
vel rogare
quicquam a numinibus,
ni te deum,
illum reum
daremus leonibus?
Hoc edictum
sic indictum
fuit a principibus.

Et rex nesciens quare hoc dicerent, respondet:

Vere jussi me omnibus
adorari a gentibus.

Tunc illi adducentes Danielem, dicent regi:

Hunc Judaeum
suum Deum
Danielem vidimus
adorantem

His God,	330	et precantem,
In defiance of your laws.		tuis spretis legibus.

The king, wishing to set Daniel free, will say: *Rex volens liberare Danielem dicet:*

May it never be granted you   Nunquam vobis concedatur
That this holy man should be thus   quod vir sanctus sic perdatur.
  destroyed.

The satraps, hearing this, will point out the law   *Satrapae hoc audientes ostendent ei legem,*
to him, saying: *dicentes:*

The law of the Parthians		Lex Parthorum
And the Medes	335	et Medorum
In the annals proclaims		jubet in annalibus
That he who flouts		ut qui sprevit
What the king has decreed		quae decrevit
Shall be given to the lions.		rex, detur leonibus.

The king, on hearing this, whether he will or   *Rex hoc audiens velit, nolit, dicet:*
no, will say:

If he has flouted the law I established,	340	Si sprevit legem quam statueram,
Let him pay the penalty I decreed.		det poenas ipse quas decreveram.

Then the satraps will seize Daniel, and he,   *Tunc satrapae rapient Danielem, et ille*
looking back toward the king, will say: *respiciens regem dicet:*

Alas, alas, alas! By what accident of fortune		Heu, heu, heu! Quo casu sortis
Comes this sentence of death?		venit haec damnatio mortis?
Alas, alas, alas! Unspeakable wickedness!		Heu, heu, heu! Scelus infandum!
Why will this fierce crowd give me	345	Cur me dabit ad lacerandum
To be torn apart by fierce beasts?		haec fera turba feris?
Is it thus, O king, that you seek to destroy		Sic me, rex, perdere quaeris?
me?		
Alas, by what death do you compel		Heu, qua morte mori
Me to die? Spare your wrath.		me cogis? Parce furori.

And the king, unable to set him free, will say to   *Et rex, non valens eum liberare, dicet ei:*
him:

The God whom you worship so faithfully	350	Deus quem colis tam fideliter
Will free you miraculously.		te liberabit mirabiliter.

Then they will fling Daniel into the pit. And   *Tunc proicient Danielem in lacum. Statimque*

351 s.d.: Presumably the lions' den must be constructed in such a way that the angel and Daniel
can be seen and heard in it. The den is evidently not so high as the king's throne, since Darius
descends to visit it (l. 372 s.d.). The den must have an edge from which victims are thrown
to the lions (l. 379 s.d.). The lions, like many stage beasts in liturgical drama, appear to have
been represented by actors in costume. Their act of eating of the wicked advisers, achieved by
means of *trompe-l'oeil* effects, should be visible to the audience.

immediately an angel holding a sword will keep
the lions at bay lest they touch him; and Daniel
will say as he enters the pit:

Of this accusation I am innocent.
Have mercy on me, O God,
Eleison!
Send hither, O God, a protector   355
Who can bridle the strength of the lions;
Eleison!

Meanwhile another angel will direct the prophet
Habakkuk to convey the meal he was carrying to
his reapers to Daniel in the lions' pit, saying:

Habakkuk, you holy old man,
To the Babylonian pit
Take this meal, to Daniel;   360
The King of all commands you.

Habakkuk to him:

The all-seeing wisdom of God knows
That I am ignorant of Babylon,
Nor is the pit known to me
In which Daniel has been placed.   365

Then the angel, seizing him by the hair of his
head, will lead him to the pit; and Habakkuk, as
he offers the meal to Daniel, will say:

Arise, brother, that you may take this food;
God has seen your distress.
God has sent it, give thanks to God
Who made you.

And Daniel, accepting the food, will say:

You have remembered me, O Lord;   370
May I receive it in your name,
Alleluia!

When this has been completed, the angel will lead

---

angelus tenens gladium comminabitur leonibus
ne tangant eum, et Daniel intrans lacum dicet:

Huius rei non sum reus.
Miserere mei, Deus,
eleison!
Mitte, Deus, huc patronum
qui refrenet vim leonum;
eleison!

Interea alius angelus admonebit Abacuc
prophetam ut deferat prandium quod portabat
messoribus suis Danieli in lacum leonum,
dicens:

Abacuc, tu senex pie,
ad lacum Babyloniae
Danieli fer prandium;
mandat tibi Rex omnium.

Cui Abacuc:

Novit Dei cognitio
quod Babylonem nescio,
neque lacus est cognitus
quo Daniel est positus.

Tunc angelus, apprehendens eum capillo
capitis sui, ducet ad lacum; et Abacuc, Danieli
offerens prandium, dicet:

Surge, frater, ut cibum capias;
tuas Deus vidit angustias.
Deus misit, da Deo gratias,
qui te fecit.

Et Daniel, cibum accipiens, dicet:

Recordatus es mei, Domine;
accipiam in tuo nomine,
alleluia!

His transactis, angelus reducet Abacuc in

354*Eleison:* Have mercy (in Greek).

358–72For the episode of Habakkuk, see the Apocryphal Book of Daniel, Bel, and the Snake,
where Daniel is thrown into the lions' den a second time for having slain the dragon worshiped by the priests of Bel (see l. 282 above). The playwright conflates the two episodes
in the lions' den.

Habakkuk back to his place. Then the king, descending from his throne, will come to the pit, saying tearfully:

Daniel, do you not think he will save you,
 that you may be snatched away
From this intended death, he whom you
 revere and worship?

 And Daniel to the king:

King, live forever.   375

 Continuing:

He has sent an angelic protector, with his
 accustomed mercy,
By whom God has restrained in time the
 lions' mouths.

 Then the king will exclaim, rejoicing:

Lead Daniel forth,
And cast the envious ones in.

 *When these have been stripped of their clothing
 and have come to the edge of the pit, they will cry
 out:*

Justly we suffer this, for we have sinned   380
Against this holy man of God; we have
 acted unjustly;
We have committed wicked deeds.

 *As they are thrown into the pit, they will be eaten
 immediately by the lions; and the king, seeing this,
 will say:*

I order that the God of Daniel
Who reigns forever be worshiped by all
 people.

 *Daniel, having been received again into his former
 station, will prophesy:*

Behold that holy one comes, most holy of
 holies,   385
Whom this king orders you to worship,
 mighty and most powerful.
Temples cease, the kingdom must cease, and
 anointing shall cease;
The end and overthrow of the kingdom of
 the Jews is at hand.

---

locum suum. Tunc rex, descendens de solio suo, veniet ad lacum, dicens lacrimab[i]liter:

Tene, putas, Daniel, salvabit, ut eripiaris

A nece proposita, quem tu colis et
 veneraris?

 Et Daniel regi:

Rex, in aeternum vive.

 Item:

Angelicum solita misit pietate patronum,

Quo Deus ad tempus compescuit ora
 leonum.

 Tunc rex gaudens exclamabit:

Danielem educite,
et aemulos immittite.

 *Cum expoliati fuerint et venerint ante lacum,
 clamabunt:*

Merito haec patimur, quia peccavimus
in sanctum Dei; injuste egimus;

iniquitatem fecimus.

 *Illi proiecti in lacum statim consumentur a
 leonibus; et rex videns hoc dicet:*

Deum Danielis qui regnat in saeculis
adorari jubeo a cunctis populis.

 *Daniel in pristinum gradum receptus pro-
 phetabit:*

Ecce venit sanctus ille, sanctorum
 sanctissimus,
Quem rex iste jubet coli potens et
 fortissimus.
Cessant phana, cesset regnum, cessabit et
 unctio;
Instat regni Judaeorum finis et oppressio.

Then an angel will suddenly exclaim:

I bring you tidings from on high:
Christ is born, the sovereign of the world,   390
In Bethlehem of Judaea, just as the prophet
Foretold.

Having heard this, the cantors will begin We
praise you, O Lord.

Thus ends [the play of] Daniel.

Tunc angelus ex improviso exclamabit:

Nuntium vobis fero de supernis:
Natus est Christus, dominator orbis,
in Bethleem Judae[ae], sic enim propheta
dixerat ante.

His auditis, cantores incipient Te Deum
laudamus.

Finit Daniel.

389-91This angel probably was intended to appear in some lofty place in the church.

4. THE RAISING OF LAZARUS
(SUSCITATIO LAZARI)
BY HILARIUS

Apart from the Nativity and the Easter story, only one subject from the life of Christ found its way into the repertory of twelfth-century church drama: the raising of Lazarus from the dead. This miraculous event was commonly regarded in medieval times as a precursor of Christ's own resurrection. Two plays on the subject have survived, one from the Fleury playbook and one by the wandering scholar Hilarius, who was a student of Abelard and who may have been English. Hilarius also wrote a Daniel play, as we have seen, one not unlike the Beauvais *Danielis Ludus*. He was a conscious literary artist, the first such poet of the theater whom we can identify.

Hilarius' play on the raising of Lazarus is primarily a literary composition. The author shows little concern with stage movement. Sparse stage directions yield little information as to the spatial arrangement of the various acting locations. Presumably Lazarus dies at his home in Bethany, whereupon Jesus travels with his disciples from Galilee to Bethany and is then conducted by Mary and Martha to the sepulchre where their brother lies buried. The three required acting stations, Bethany, Galilee, and the sepulchre, could easily have been accommodated in a church choir or in the nave near the choir entrance. Yet the author never names Bethany or Galilee, alludes only seldom to the movement of any characters, and does not explain how the dead body of Lazarus is to be transferred from his bed in Bethany to the sepulchre where he is later found. We are given no way of visualizing the sepulchre, though it must be large enough to make room for Lazarus' body; possibly it would have been the same structure used in the Visit to the Sepulchre on Easter morning.

Hilarius' play is not, in any case, the text for an actual production. He reveals the tentative nature of his theatrical arrangements when he suggests that Jesus is to be accompanied by "twelve apostles, or six at least." Similarly, he proposes that the play could be sung either at matins or at vespers. Although he has a liturgical occasion in mind, the occasion is optional and thus cannot have been the original starting point for the play. Hilarius makes no direct use of hymns, responsories, or other materials from the liturgy except for the concluding anthem. Perhaps he intended the play for Holy Week of Easter or for the Feast of St. Lazarus (December 17), or possibly for the Feast of St. Mary Magdalene (July 22), but we cannot be sure.

Instead of focusing on processional movement and theatrical display, as in the Fleury play on the same subject, Hilarius concentrates on the emotional states of mind of his chief characters. The general lack of stage movement and spectacle allows for long outpourings of sorrow in richly poetic language. Although the story follows closely the events of John 11, the poetry offers unusual variety and sophistication in the verse patterns. The passages in French are not mere translations from the Latin used to edify an uneducated congregation, but are lyric utterances of poignant emotional effect. The theme of the play is God's miraculous power overcoming rational doubt. The Jews who attempt to comfort Mary and Martha offer coldly skepti-

Text based on Paris, Bibliothèque Nationale, MS lat. 11331, Hilarii Versus et Ludi saec. xii, fol. 9ʳ–10ᵛ. It has been edited by Young, *Drama of the Medieval Church*, II, 212–18, and by others.

155

cal arguments based on a natural law that cannot, they believe, be transcended. Even the disciples do not comprehend Jesus' mission and fear for his safety in hostile Judaea. Mary and Martha believe their brother irretrievably dead because Jesus does not arrive in time.

All these doubting witnesses are finally convinced of God's immortal power, like the apostles after Christ's death and resurrection. Their expressions of belief and thanksgiving act as choric statements to direct the audience toward faith in the impossible.

The Raising of Lazarus

(Suscitatio Lazari)

By Hilarius

For which these persons are necessary:
The person of Lazarus
[The persons of] the two sisters
[The persons of] the four Jews
[The person of] Jesus Christ
[The persons of] the twelve apostles, or six at least.

First, as Lazarus is becoming faint, the two sisters Mary and Martha, with the four Jews, will come forward stricken with grief, and, standing beside his bed, they [Mary and Martha] will sing these verses:

O unhappy lot! O hard lot,
Whose judgment is heavy!
For by your law solely
Our brother, our only care, languishes.

Our brother languishes, and truly
That makes us suffer acutely with him.
But you, O God, have mercy
On him whom you can heal.

The Jews will say to console them:

Dearest ones, leave off weeping,
Nor provoke to tears those who are standing by;
Rather, address your supplications to God,
And beg health for Lazarus.

To whom they [Mary and Martha] will say:

Go, brethren, to the greatest of all healers;
Go quickly to the one and only king;

Ad quem istae personae sunt necessariae:
Persona Lazari
[Personae] duarum sororum
[Personae] quatuor Judaeorum
[Persona] Jhesu Christi
[Personae] duodecim apostolorum, vel sex ad minus.

In primis, Lazaro lang[u]escente, duae sorores, Maria et Martha, cum quatuor Judaeis se maxime affligentes, advenient, et as[s]istentes eius lectulo, cantabunt hos versus:

O sors tristis! O sors dura,
cuius gravis est censura!
Nam per tua modo jura
languet frater, nostra cura.

Languet frater, et nos vere
Facit sibi condolere.
Sed tu, Deus, miserere,
cuique potes tu medere.

Ad earum consolationem dicent Judaei:

Carissime, flere desinite,
nec adstantes ad fletum cogite;

immo preces ad Deum mittite,
Lazaroque salutem poscite.

Quibus illae dicent:

Ite, fratres, ad summum medicum;
ite citi regem ad unicum;

5

10

Report that our brother is failing,	15	fratrem nostrum narrate languidum,
So that he may come and make him well.		ut veniat et reddat validum.

When they [the Jews] have come to Jesus, they will say:　　　*Illi autem, cum venerint ad Jhesum, dicent:*

Because [he whom] you love		Quia [quem] tu diligis
Is gravely ill,		infirmatur graviter,
To you we have been commanded		ad te jussi fuimus
To come swiftly.	20	venire celeriter.

You who are the greatest of all healers,	Qui summus es medicus,
Visit our afflicted one,	aegrum nostrum visita,
That he may serve you devotedly,	ut tibi deserviat,
When his health has been restored.	sospitate reddita.

Jesus will answer:　　　*Jhesus respondet:*

This illness, my brethren,	25	Morbus iste, fratres mei,
Will not be with him unto death;		non ad mortem erit ei;
But this has come to pass that by him		sed evenit ut per eum
I may make God manifest to you.		manifestem vobis Deum.

Meanwhile, when they have returned, Lazarus having already died, two of them will lead Mary to him [Lazarus]; to whom she will sing:　　　*Interim, cum illi redierint, Lazaro iam mortuo, duo ex illis Mariam ducent ad eum; cui illa cantabit:*

By original sin		Ex culpa veteri
Ensuing generations are condemned	30	damnantur posteri
To be mortal.		mortales fieri.
Alas my sorrow,		Hor ai dolor,
Now my brother is dead,		hor est mis frere morz;
For which I mourn.		por que gei plor.

Through the forbidden food,	35	Per cibum vetitum,
It is certain		nobis interitum
That death has been imposed upon us.		constat impositum.
Alas my sorrow,		Hor ai dolor,
[Now my brother is dead,		[hor est mis frere morz;
For which I mourn.]	40	por que gei plor.]

I am made wretched,	Facta sum misera,
And my sister also,	et soror altera,
By the death of our brother.	per fratris funera.
Alas my sorrow,	Hor ai dolor,

[25-28]See John 11:4.

[35]*forbidden food:* i.e., the forbidden fruit of the tree of knowledge, through which Adam and Eve and their progeny lost their immortality.

[Now my brother is dead,   45
For which I mourn.]

When I think of you,
My brother, and of your deserving,
I urgently beg for (my own) death.
Alas my sorrow,   50
[Now my brother is dead,
For which I mourn.]

Then two Jews, consoling her, will say:

Let such weeping cease,
Cease mourning completely,
And cease such sighs.   55
So great lamentation,
Such wailing,
Is senseless.

Not by means of such tears
Have spirits been seen   60
To return to their bodies.
Let tears therefore cease,
Which have benefited dead men
Very little indeed.

*After this Martha will come with two other Jews,
singing:*

Execrable death!   65
Detestable death!
Death that is lamentable to me!
Woe me, wretched one!
Since my brother is dead,
Why should I live?   70

The death of my brother,
Grievous and sudden,
Is the cause of my mourning.
Woe me, wretched one!
Since [my brother is dead,   75
Why should I live?]

Because of my brother's death
I am not unwilling to die myself,
Nor do I dread death.
Woe me, wretched one!   80
[Since my brother is dead,
Why should I live?]

[hor est mis frere morz;
por que gei plor.]

Cum de te cogito,
frater, et merito
mortem efflagito.
Hor ai [dolor,
hor est mis frere morz;
por que gei plor].

Tunc duo Judaei consolantes eam dicent:

Cesset talis gemitus,
cesset maeror penitus,
cessentque suspiria.
Talis lamentatio,
talis ejulatio
non est necessaria.

Non per tales lacrimas
visum fuit animas
redisse corporibus.
Cessent ergo lacrim[a]e,
quae defunctis minime
proderunt hominibus.

*Post haec veniet Martha cum aliis duobus
Judaeis cantans:*

Mors execrabilis!
Mors detestabilis!
Mors mihi flebilis!
Lase, cativi!
Des que mis frere est morz,
porque sue vive?

Fratris interitus
gravis et subitus
est causa gemitus.
Lase, chative!
Des que [mis frere est morz,
porque sue vive]?

Por fratre mortuo
mori non abnuo,
nec mortem metuo.
Lase, chative!
[Des que mis frere est morz,
porque sue vive?]

Past the burial of my brother
I am unwilling to live.
Woe to wretched me!　　　　　　　　　85
Woe me, wretched one!
[Since my brother is dead,
Why should I live?]

    The two Jews will say to comfort her:

Do away with weeping, we entreat;
For we can accomplish nothing　　　　90
By weeping.
Weeping would have been necessary
If anyone could have been
Revived by such means.

Why do you not realize　　　　　　　95
That, while you torment yourself,
You are of no benefit to the dead?
Why are you unmindful
That you [accomplish] nothing
To make him live once again?　　　　100

    Jesus will say to the disciples:

Into Judaea once again
We must proceed,
Where I have resolved to take care of
A little matter.

    The disciples will say to him:

Recently they intended　　　　　　　105
To bury you with stones,
And notwithstanding you wish once again
To travel into Judaea!

    And Jesus to them:

Behold, Lazarus sleeps,
Whom it behoves us to visit.　　　　110
I must go thither accordingly,
To arouse him from sleep.

    The disciples again:

After he sleeps, he will be healthy;
For health requires sleep.

Ex fratris funere
recuso vivere.
Vae mihi misere!
Lase, chative!
[Des que mis frere est morz,
porque sue vive?]

    Duo Judaei ad eius solacium dicent:

Tolle fletum, quaesumus;
nihil enim possumus
per fletum proficere.
Insistendum fletibus
esset, si quis talibus
posset reviviscere.

Quare non consideras
quia, dum te macheras,
nihil prodes mortuo?
Quare tu non respicis
quia nihil [proficis]
ut iam vivat denuo?

    Jhesus ad di[s]cipulos dicet:

In Judaeam iterum
nos oportet pergere,
ubi quiddam paululum
decrevi peragere.

    Cui dis[ci]puli dicent:

Te nuper lapidibus
volebant obruere,
et vis tamen iterum
in Judaeam tendere!

    Et Jhesus ad illos:

Ecce dormit Lazarus
quem decet ut visitem.
Vadam illuc igitur,
ut a somno excitem.

    Discipuli iterum:

Pos[t]quam dormit, saluus erit;
salus enim somnum quaerit.

[105f]See John 11: 8f.

Jesus again to them:

This is not as you believe;   115
On the contrary, he has already perished.
But in the name of the Father
He is to be restored to us.

Thomas will say:

Let us therefore set forth
That we may die with him.   120

Afterwards, Martha will say to Jesus:

If you had come sooner,
Woe is me,
There would have been no mourning here.
Beloved brother, I have lost you!

What you could have done for a living
          man,   125
Woe is me,
May you bestow upon this dead man.
Beloved brother, I have lost you!

Whatsoever you ask of the Father,
Woe is me,   130
At once the Father gives it.
Beloved brother, I have lost you!

Jesus will say:

Now restrain
These tears
And the sorrows that beset you.   135
Your brother
Has died,
But he will easily rise again.

And she to him:

I believe
That my brother   140
Will rise again and live,
Finally at that time
When, without fail,
All mankind will arise again.

And Jesus again:

Jhesus iterum ad illos:

Non est sicut creditis;
inmo iam defunctus est.
Sed in Patris nomine
nobis suscitandus est.

T[h]omas vero dicet:

Ergo nos proficiscamur
et cum illo moriamur.

Postea Martha dicet ad Jhesum:

Si venisses primitus,
dol en ai,
non esset hic gemitus.
Bais frere, perdu vos ai!

Quod in vivum poteras,

dol en ai,
hoc defuncto conferas.
Ba[i]s frere, perdu vos ai!

Petis Patrem quid libet,
dol en ai,
statim Pater ex[h]ibet.
Bais frere, perdu vos ai!

Jhesus dicet:

Nunc comprimas
has lacrimas
et luctum qui te urget.
Frater tuus
est mortuus,
sed facile resurget.

Et illa ad eum:

Resurgere
et vivere
fratrem meum affirmo,
Tunc denique
cum utique
resurget omnis homo.

Et Jhesus iterum:

---

[120]*with him:* i.e., with Jesus (Thomas is addressing the other disciples; see John 11:16).

On the contrary, sister, do not despair, 145
For I am the eternal life;
And whosoever will believe thus
Will live in me, who am the life.

And whosoever living will believe in me,
Death will not prevail over him. 150
Do you believe, Martha, in truth,
That such things will come to be?

Martha truly will answer:

I believe you to be
Christ, the son of God,
And to have come to aid us 155
In this our exile.

Martha, announcing the arrival of Jesus to Mary,
will say:

Jesus is here, my dearest sister:
Let mourning and tears cease;
Prevail upon him with humble prayer,
That the soul may return to our brother. 160

Then Mary will say to Jesus:

My desolation
Can never be removed
By anyone's consolation.
But I believe that understanding
Can be granted me 165
By you, the son of God.

You therefore who are mighty,
Who are gentle and merciful,
Come to the grave;
Awaken my brother, 170
Whom death, when the flesh had been
    yielded up,
Snatched away so hastily.

And Jesus to her:

I wish, O sister, I wish especially
To be led to the buried one,
That he may be called again to life 175
Who is detained by death.

She, leading Jesus to the sepulchre, will say:

Here we placed him—

Immo, soror, non despera,
nam sum ego vita vera;
et quicumque credet ita
vivet in me, qui sum vita.

Et qui vivens in me credet,
mors ad illum non accedet.
Credis, Martha, fore verum
quod sit talis ordo rerum?

Martha vero respondet:

Te Christum, Dei filium,
ad hoc nostrum exilium
venisse in a[u]xilium
ego credo.

Martha, nuntians Mariae Jhesum advenisse,
dicet:

Jhesus adest, soror carissima;
cesset luctus, et cesset lacrima;
ipsum prece flectas humillima,
ut redeat ad fratrem anima.

Tunc Maria ad Jhesum dicet:

Nullius solatio
mea desolatio
valet umquam auferri.
Sed credo consilium
per te, Dei filium,
posse mihi conferri.

Tu ergo qui potens es,
qui mitis et clemens es,
ad tumulum venito;
fratrem meum suscita,
quem mors carni dedita

surripuit tam cito.

Et Jhesus ad illam:

Volo, soror, volo multum
me deduci ad sepultum,
ut in vitam revocetur
qui a morte detinetur.

Illa autem, ducens Jhesum ad sepulcrum, dicet:

Hic eum posuimus—

Behold the place, O Lord—
Whom in the name of the Father
We ask to be raised again.   180

Jesus to those standing by:

Remove the stone
That covers the tomb,
That Lazarus may rise
In the sight of all the people!

They will say:

You will not be able to bear   185
The stench of the dead man;
For truly, stinking oppressively,
He has been dead four days.

*Then Jesus, looking heavenward, will pray thus
to the Father:*

Father, make famous your Word,
And, I pray, bring Lazarus to life;   190
Thus make known your son to the world,
Father, in this hour.

Nor have I said this out of want of
        confidence,
But because of the presence of these people,
That with certainty they may believe in
        your strength   195
Without delay.

Then he will say to the dead man:

O Lazarus, come forth;
Enjoy the gift of vital breath;
As a gift of the power of the Father,
Come forth, and enjoy life!   200

Then when Lazarus has arisen, Jesus will say:

Behold, he lives! Now unbind him,
And permit him to depart unfettered.

*Lazarus, having been unbound, will say to those
standing by:*

Behold, the mighty works that are of God,
You yourself have seen, both these here and
        others.

ecce locus, Domine—
quem in Patris poscimus
suscitari nomine.

Jhesus ad circumstantes:

Sustollatis lapidem
qui superest tumulo,
ut resurgat Lazarus
coram omni populo!

Illi dicent:

Fetorem non poteris
sustinere mortui;
namque fetens graviter
funus est quatridui.

*Tunc Jhesus, suspiciens in caelum, sic orabit
ad Patrem:*

Pater, Verbum tuum clarifica,
Lazarumque, precor, vivifica;
sic filium mundo notifica,
Pater, in hac hora.

Nec hoc dixi ex dif[f]identia,

sed pro gentis huius praesentia,
ut de tua certi potentia

credant absque mora.

Tunc dicet ad mortuum:

O Lazare, foras egredere;
aurae dono vitalis utere;
in Paternae virtutis munere,
exi foras, et vita fruere!

*Tunc pos[t]quam surrexerit Lazarus, dicet
Jhesus:*

Ecce vivit! Nunc ipsum solvite,
et solutum abire sinite.

Lazarus solutus dicet astantibus:

Ecce quae sunt Dei magnalia,
vos vidistis, et haec et alia.

He made the heavens and the seas;   205
Death trembles at his majesty.

And, having turned to Jesus, he will say:

You our master, you our king, you our Lord,
You will destroy the villainy of the people.
Whatever you command, the same is
    accomplished forthwith.
Of your kingdom there will be no end.   210

*When this is finished, if it has been performed at
matins, let Lazarus begin* We praise you O
Lord; *if instead at vespers,* My soul does
magnify the Lord.

Ipse caelum fecit et maria;
mors ad eius tremit imperia.

Et conversus ad Jhesum dicet:

Tu magister, tu rex, tu Dominus,
tu populi delebis facinus.
Quod praecipis, illud fit protinus.

Regni tui non erit terminus.

*Quo finito, si factum fuerit ad matutinas,
Lazarus incipiat* Te Deum laudamus;
si vero ad vesperas, Magnificat anima
mea Dominum.

5. [THE SERVICE] FOR REPRESENTING THE CONVERSION OF THE BLESSED APOSTLE PAUL
(AD REPRAESENTANDUM CONVERSIONEM BEATI PAULI APOSTOLI)
FROM FLEURY

Because the liturgical calendar of the medieval church offered a plentiful supply of saints' days throughout the year, the opportunities for special plays in honor of particular saints were numerous. Some of these feast days honored personages who appear in the Scriptures, such as the Virgin Mary, Mary Magdalene, and Lazarus. Plays written for such occasions were therefore primarily biblical in subject, though apocryphal episodes were frequently added. Plays of this biblical sort must be distinguished from plays about nonbiblical saints like St. Nicholas, which, as we shall see, relied extensively on fabulous and legendary material.

The Conversion of St. Paul, from the Fleury playbook, was probably staged on the Feast of the Conversion of St. Paul, January 25. The concluding anthem, "We Praise You O God," may suggest that the play was sung in the familiar position at the end of matins, although the play uses no other liturgical materials and may perhaps have served for some special celebration. The play adheres fairly closely to the biblical account of Paul's conversion as told in the Acts of the Apostles 9:1-27. At the same time, the story reveals several characteristics that were to become enduringly popular in the lives of nonbiblical saints as well: the conversion of a sinner to grace, a hairbreadth escape from dangerous enemies, and so on. Throughout, the play dramatizes a conflict between worldly power and the power of God's salvation.

The staging arrangement, with its two contrasting locales of Jerusalem and Damascus, reflects the thematic conflict between worldly tyranny and persecuted faith. Presumably the acting stations, as described in considerable detail by the stage directions, would have been set up in the nave of the Fleury church. One side of the acting arena represents Jerusalem, with a *sedes*, or platform, for the high priest and another for Saul and his attendants. On the other side is Damascus, with the *sedes* of Judas and of the high priest of Damascus; a bed on which Ananias lies is between them. Judas' house must be a substantial stage edifice from which the actors can be seen and heard. These platforms are all simultaneously visible to the audience in the customary manner of early medieval staging. As the action shifts from one platform to the other, those actors who are not needed for the moment presumably retire from view. Journeys play an important role and make use of the open acting space between the platforms: Saul is smitten by the voice of God on the way from Jerusalem to Damascus, and later is lowered in a basket from some high place in Damascus as if from a wall.

From the Fleury playbook, usually associated with the monastery of St.-Benoît-sur-Loire, at Fleury. Text based on Orleans, Bibliothèque de la Ville, MS 201 (*olim* 178), Miscellanea Floriacensia saec. xiii, pp. 230–33. It has been edited by Young, *Drama of the Medieval Church*, II, 219–22, and others.

[The Service] for Representing the Conversion of the Blessed Apostle Paul
(Ad Repraesentandum Conversionem Beati Pauli Apostoli)

From Fleury

For representing the conversion of the blessed apostle Paul, let there be prepared in a suitable place, as if it were Jerusalem, a seat, and upon it the high priest. And let there be prepared another seat, and upon it a young man in the likeness of Saul; and let him have with him armed attendants. And on the other side, somewhat distant from these seats, let there be prepared as if in Damascus two seats, in one of which let a man named Judas be seated, and in the other the high priest of the synagogue of Damascus. And between these two seats let a couch be prepared in which should lie a man in the likeness of Ananias. When these things are thus ready, let Saul say to his attendants:

I cannot tell you
How monstrously hateful to me are
The Christians, who by their deceit
Mislead this entire nation.

Go therefore, do not delay,   5
And all such persons you can
Find, apprehend by force;
Bring hither under arrest those whom you
    have bound.

Upon hearing this, let the attendants depart; and, when they re-enter, let them conduct to their lord two whom they have seized, saying:

We found many Christians,
And among them we detained [these];   10
The other deceivers belonging to this
    community
Have fled to Damascus.

Ad repraesentandum conversionem beati Pauli apostoli paretur in competenti loco, quasi Jerusalem, quaedam sedes, et super eam princeps sacerdotum. Paretur et alia sedes, et super eam juvenis quidam in similitudine Sauli; habeatque secum ministros armatos. Ex alia vero parte, aliquantulum longe ab his sedibus, sint paratae quasi in Damasco duae sedes, in altera quarum sedeat vir quidam nomine Judas, et in altera princeps synagogae Damasci. Et inter has duas sedes sit paratus lectus, in quo jaceat vir quidam in similitudine Annaniae. His ita paratis, dicat Saulus ministris suis:

Propalare vobis non valeo
quam ingenti mihi sint odio
Christicolae, qui per fallaciam
totam istam seducunt patriam.

Ite ergo, ne tardaveritis,
et quoscunque tales poteritis
invenire, vi comprehendite;
comprehensos vinctos adducite.

Hoc audientes ministri abeant; et, cum redierint, duos sumptos ad dominum suum conducant dicentes:

Christicolas multos invenimus,
et ex illis [hos] retinuimus;
in Damascum fugerunt alii

seductores huius consortii.

---

[1] s.d. *seat (sedes)*: Perhaps a scaffold stage with a throne or other furniture on it, and room for action. All the *sedes* are simultaneously visible to the audience; the action moves from one *sedes* to another. Paul's famous conversion occurs in transit from the Jerusalem *sedes* to the Damascus *sedes*.

Then let Saul rise as in a rage, and let him go
to the high priest; and when he has come to him,
let him say:

Let letters of yours be given me
To Damascus, where the Christians
With the blandishing words of their
    stratagem   15
Are subverting the people of this nation.

Then let the high priest give him some brief
sealed message, and let him say:

I deliver to you my epistles
To Damascus against the Christians.
Do not permit the Christians
Whom you will find to escape.   20

[*Then a voice from on high:*]

Saul! Saul! Why do you persecute me?
I have seen the evil you have done to my
    followers.
Why do you afflict the people whom I have
    cherished?
In no wise may you kick against the pricks.

Having heard this, let Saul fall to the ground as
if nearly dead; and when he is no longer falling,
let him say:

Why do you speak thus? Who are you,
    Lord?   25
Why have you deprived me of my sight?
When have I afflicted your people?
Who are you, and what is your name?

The Lord:

I am called Jesus, whom you persecute,
Whose servants you have often afflicted.   30
But rise, enter the city,
And you will hear what you must do.

Then let Saul get up again; and when his men
see that he has been stricken blind, let them take
him and lead him into Damascus to the house of
Judas. Then let the Lord come to Ananias, and
say:

Tunc Saulus quasi iratus surgat, et ad
principem sacerdotum eat; cumque ad eum
veniat, dicat:

Vestrae mihi dentur epistolae
in Damascum, ubi Christicolae
blandis verbis suae fallaciae

gentes huius seducunt patriae.

Tunc princeps sacerdotum det ei aliquid breve
sigillatum, et dicat:

Trado vobis meas epistolas
in Damascum contra Christicolas,
evadere ne dimiseritis
Christicolas quos inveneritis.

[*Tunc vox ex alto:*]

Saule! Saule! Quid me persequeris?
Vidi mala quae meis feceris.

Quem dilexi cur noces populo?

Recalcitres nequaquam stimulo.

Hoc audito, Saulus, quasi semimortuus in
terram cadat; et iam non cadens, dicat:

Quid sic faris? Quis es tu, Domine?

Cur me meo privasti lumine?
Quando tuum afflixi populum?
Quis es, et quod tibi vocabulum?

Dominus:

Jhesus vocor, quem tu persequeris,
cuius saepe servos afflixeris.
Surgens tamen urbem ingredere,
et audies quae debes facere.

Tunc resurgat Saulus; cumque homines sui
videri[n]t eum excaecatum, apprehendant eum
et ducant in Damascum ad domum Judae.
Tunc veniat Dominus ad Annaniam, et dicat:

---

[24]i.e., It won't do you any good to strive against God's authority, like an animal rebelling
against the driver's goad or spur (see Acts 9:5).

Ananias, rise quickly,
And enter the house of Judas.
A man awaits you, Saul by name.   35
You will tell him what he must do.

    Ananias:

I have heard many things of this Saul;
He has done the utmost harm to your
    followers.
If he sees anyone who serves you,
He continually rages to destroy him.   40

This man has letters from the high priest
To slay all Christians.
For these reasons I fear this Saul.
To this Saul I dare not go.

    Again the Lord:

Ananias, rise swiftly;   45
Seek Saul confidently:
For lo, he prays that you come,
And that you make him to see again.

Him have I chosen for my service;
Him have I chosen to our fellowship;   50
Him have I chosen that he may preach
    about me.
And make my name famous.

    *Then let Ananias, rising, enter the house of
Judas; and, when he sees Saul, let him say:*

To you, Saul, the Lord
Jesus, son of the most high Father,
Who appeared to you on the road, has sent
    me;   55
He admonished me to come to you.

You are to preach his name
Before the princes and the nations.
In order that you may be a citizen of the
    heavenly kingdom,
You will suffer many things in Christ's
    name.   60

    *Then let Saul rise, and, as if now believing, and
preaching in a loud voice, let him say:*

Why, O Jews, do you not recover your
    senses?

Annania, surge quam propere,
atque Judae domum ingredere.
Te expectat vir, Saulus nomine.
Dices ei quae debet facere.

    Annanias:

De hoc Saulo audivi plurima;
fecit tuis mala quam maxima.

Si quem videt qui tibi serviat,
semper furit ut eum destruat.

Hic principis habet epistolas
ut occidat omnes Christicolas.
His de causis hunc Saulum timeo.
Ad hu[n]c Saulum ire non audeo.

    Item Dominus:

Annania, surge velociter;
quaere Saulum fiducialiter:
ecce enim orat ut venias,
et ut eum videre facias.

Hunc elegi meo servitio;
hunc elegi nostro consortio;
hunc elegi ut de me praedicet

et [ut] nomen meum clarificet.

    *Tunc surgens Annanias domum Judae in-
troeat, et, cum viderit Saulum, dicat:*

Ad te, Saule, me misit Dominus
Jhesus, Patris excelsi filius,
qui in via tibi ap[p]aruit;

ut venirem ad te me monuit.

Praedicabis coram principibus
nomen eius, et coram gentibus;
Ut sis civis caelestis patriae,

multa feres pro Christi nomine.

    *Tunc surgat Saulus et quasi iam credens, et
praedicans alta voce, dicat:*

Cur, Judaei, non resipiscitis?

Why do you oppose the truth?
Why do you deny that the Virgin Mary
Brought forth God and man?

Jesus Christ, Mary's son,   65
Is both God and man of flesh,
Retaining divinity from his Father,
And receiving flesh from his mother.

*Upon hearing this, let the high priest of the
synagogue of Damascus say to his armed attendants:*

Guard the entrances to the city;
Maintain watch over the road exits;   70
And, as soon as you have seen Saul,
Do not postpone his death.

*Then let the attendants go and search for Saul.
When this is discovered, let Saul with his disciples
be let down to the ground in a hamper from some
high place, as if from a wall. And when he has
come into Jerusalem, a man will run to him in the
likeness of Barnabas, who, when he sees Saul,
must say to him:*

The son of Mary has chosen you
To be a partner in our brotherhood.
Now, in order that you may praise the Lord
        with us,   75
Come, see our fellowship.

[To the apostles:]

Let us rejoice, brothers, in the Lord;
Let us rejoice together in such an ally.
He who lately was a most savage wolf
Is now a most gentle lamb.   80

Let all the apostles begin We praise you O
God. *Thus let it be ended.*

Veritati cur contradicitis?
Cur negatis Mariam Virginem
peperisse Deum et hominem?

Jhesus Christus, Mariae filius,
et Deus est, et homo carneus,
deitatem a Patre retinens,
et a matre carnem suscipiens.

*Haec audiens, princeps synagogae Damasci
ministris suis armatis dicat:*

Custodite urbis introitus;
conservate viarum exitus;
et, quam cito Saulum videritis,
mortem eius ne distuleritis.

*Tunc ministri eant et quaera[n]t Saulum.
Quo comperto, Saulus cum discipulis suis in
sporta ab aliquo alto loco, quasi a muro, ad
terram demittatur. Cum autem venerit in
Jherusalem, occurret ei vir unus in similitudine
Barnabae, qui, cum viderit Saulum, ei dicat:*

Te elegit Mariae filius,
ut sis fratrum nostrorum socius.
Nunc, ut laudes nobiscum Dominum,

veni, vide nostrum collegium.

[Ad apostolos]:

Gaudeamus, fratres, in Domino;
collaetemur de tanto socio.
Qui nunc erat lupus saevissimus,
nunc est agnus mansuetissimus.

Omnes apostoli incipiant Te Deum laudamus. *Sic finiatur.*

6. [THE SERVICE] FOR REPRESENTING HOW SAINT NICHOLAS FREED THE SON OF GETRON
(AD REPRAESENTANDUM QUOMODO SANCTUS NICH[O]LAUS GETRON[IS] FILIUM . . . LIBERAVIT)
FROM FLEURY

Filius Getronis ("The Son of Getron"), from the Fleury playbook, commemorates the most popular saint of the Middle Ages, St. Nicholas. Although little is actually known about the historical St. Nicholas, a fourth-century bishop of Myra in Lycia (Asia Minor), a number of legends grew up around him in medieval times. He became famous for protecting children, sailors, scholars, and the oppressed. His cult was especially pronounced from the eleventh century on, most of all in northern France. This cult gave birth to a number of plays, based on legend rather than on the Bible or the liturgy.

The plays in honor of St. Nicholas are good examples of a large and important dramatic genre of the Middle Ages: the saint's play, sometimes called the miracle play. Karl Young has defined the genre as "the dramatization of a legend setting forth the life or martyrdom or miracles of a saint" (*Drama of the Medieval Church*, II, 307). Usually excluded from this category are the lives of such biblical personages as the Virgin Mary and St. Paul, although as we have seen the story of St. Paul reveals some characteristics of the usual saint's life. The St. Nicholas plays are thoroughly typical of popular saints' lives, with their emphasis on lurid adventure and miraculous happenings. In one of the surviving plays about St. Nicholas, the saint brings gold to the three daughters of an indigent father in order to save them from a life of enforced prostitution. In another play the saint restores to life three clerks who have been murdered for

their money by an innkeeper. A third play tells of a pagan (or a Jew, in one version) who abuses the holy image of St. Nicholas when it fails to protect his house from theft, but who becomes penitent and converted to the true faith when St. Nicholas persuades the robbers to restore the stolen goods. Repeatedly, the saint insists that praise be given not to himself for these deliverances but to almighty God.

All of the plays mentioned above were so popular that they have survived in two or more versions. Undoubtedly they were popular because they satisfied a desire for narratives of violence and adventure. The pious element of thanksgiving for divine assistance was also part of the appeal, to be sure, but the melodrama of escape from danger offered something new. Entirely free of biblical restraints, these stories were able to pursue the kind of sensationalism that was not easily exploited in most church drama. The stories were usually fantastic, but embodied situations that must have seemed vividly relevant to the lives of the spectators: dishonest innkeepers and their wives attacking unsuspecting guests, families struggling against poverty, robbers pillaging homes, and the like.

The Son of Getron similarly appeals to the appetite of a medieval audience for romantic adventure. A boy, Adeodatus, is abducted

From the Fleury playbook, usually associated with the monastery of St.-Benoit-sur-Loire, at Fleury. Text based on Orleans, Bibliothèque de la Ville, MS 201 (*olim* 178, Miscellanea Floriacensia saec. xiii, pp. 196–205. It has been edited by Young, *Drama of the Medieval Church*, II, 351–57, and others.

from his parents by the heathen king Marmorinus and is kept in captivity for a year until St. Nicholas hears the prayers of the boy's parents and restores him to his family. Violent or spectacular action is provided by the soldiers' attack on the church, the seizing of Adeodatus, and the boy's providential rescue by St. Nicholas. The contest between God and the heathen deity Apollo is suspenseful. The playwright focuses not only on unexpected turns of events but on the emotional reactions of his chief characters: the mother's sorrow at the loss of her son, the boy's homesickness and his intrepidity in defying his captor, the king's unwillingness to part with his new favorite, the parents' gratitude for the restoration of their child. Some of these emotions are to be found in other church dramas, of course, such as the Slaughter of the Innocents, but the freedom of subject matter in the saint's play is readily apparent in the adventures of Adeodatus and his family.

The original performance of this play should be visualized as having taken place inside a monastery church, presumably at Fleury (where the only surviving version of this play was preserved). The staging employs the simultaneously visible *sedes* or platforms that were common in church productions of the Middle Ages. Two main acting areas are needed: one for the court of King Marmorinus, and one for the city of Excoranda with an adjoining church of St. Nicholas in its "eastern part." Perhaps the two main acting areas should be located in the nave and transepts not far from the entrance to the choir, which might then serve as the church of St. Nicholas. These two areas are separated by some distance from one another, enabling the actors to simulate journeys when King Marmorinus' soldiers make their raid on Excoranda or when St. Nicholas later returns the boy Adeodatus to his home. Both main acting areas feature banquets that are edifyingly contrasted with one another: the luxurious feast of the heathen king Marmorinus, and the charitable repast of bread and wine provided by Adeodatus' parents for the clerics and the poor of Excoranda. The two chief *sedes* thus embody the play's thematic contest between brutal heathen power and God's mysterious restorative force. Tyranny must yield to the efficacy of prayer.

Like many saints' plays, this play is both a tale of adventure and an act of worship. It combines romantic appeal with traditional elements derived from the liturgy, such as the mother's laments (reminding us of those of Rachel in the Innocents play) and the Latin plainsong chant. The play is a festive dramatic occasion, and yet is apparently designed to be sung during lauds on the Feast of St. Nicholas, December 6. The other St. Nicholas plays mentioned above were similarly performed during vespers, lauds, or matins, or before the introit of the Mass of St. Nicholas.

[The Service] for Representing How Saint Nicholas Freed the Son of Getron
(Ad Repraesentandum quomodo Sanctus Nich[o]laus Getron[is] Filium . . . Liberavit)
From Fleury

For representing how Saint Nicholas freed the son of Getron from the hand of Marmorinus,

Ad repraesentandum quomodo Sanctus Nich-[o]laus Getron[is] filium de manu Marmorini,

*king of the Agareni, let there be readied in a suit-
able place King Marmorinus sitting in a high seat,
with his armed attendants, as though in his kingdom. And let there be prepared in another place
Excoranda, the city of Getron, and in it Getron,
with his comforters, his wife Euphrosina, and
their son Adeodatus. And let there be in the
eastern part of the city of Excoranda the church
of Saint Nicholas, in which the boy is to be seized.
And so, when these things have been prepared, let
the attendants of King Marmorinus come before
him, and let them say all together, or else the first
among them:*

Hail, prince, hail, noblest king!
Do not hesitate to tell your servants
Whatever may be the inclination of your
    soul.
We are ready to accomplish what you desire.

   The king will say:

Go therefore, do not delay,   5
And whatsoever peoples you can,
Subject them to my authority;
Kill those who resist you.

   *Meanwhile let Getron and Euphrosina go, to-
gether with a throng of clerics, to the church of
Saint Nicholas, as if for the celebration of his
festival, leading their son with them. And when
they see the armed attendants of the king coming
thither, let them, forgetting their son because of
their fear, flee together into their city. Let the
attendants of the king, seizing the boy, come before
the king, and let them say in unison, or else the
second of them:*

What you ordered, noble king, we have
    done;
We have subjugated many peoples to you,   10
And from among the spoils we acquired
We lead forth this boy to you.

   Let them say in unison, or else the third:

*regis Agarenorum, liberavit, paretur in com-
petenti loco cum ministris suis armatis Rex
Marmorinus in alta sede, quasi in regno suo
sedens. Paretur et in alio loco Excoranda,
Getronis civitas, et in ea Getron, et cum
consolatricibus suis, uxor eius, Eufrosina, et
filius eorum Adeodatus. Sitque ab orientali
parte civitatis Excorandae ecclesia Sancti
Nicholai, in qua puer rapietur. His itaque
paratis, veniant ministri Marmorini Regis
coram eo, et dicant omnes, vel primus ex eis:*

Salve, princeps, salve, rex optime!
Quae sit tuae voluntas animae
servis tuis ne tardes dicere.

Sumus quae vis parati facere.

   Rex dicet:

Ite ergo, ne tardaveritis,
et quascunque gentes poteritis
imperio meo subicite;
resistentes vobis occidite.

   *Interim Getron et Eufrosina, cum multitudine
clericorum, ad ecclesiam Sancti Nicholai,
quasi ad eius sollemnitatem celebrandam,
filium suum secum ducentes, eant. Cumque
ministros regis armatos illuc venire viderint,
filio suo prae timore oblito, ad civitatem suam
confugiant. Ministri vero regis, puerum ra-
pientes, coram rege veniant, et dicant omnes,
vel secundus ex eis:*

Quod jussisti, rex bone, fecimus;

gentes multas vobis subegimus,
et de rebus quas adquisivimus
hunc puerum vobis adducimus.

   Omnes dicant, vel tertius:

---

[1]s.d.: The staging of this play resembles that for the Fleury *Conversion of Saint Paul,* with two
simultaneously visible locations representing two separate geographical locations: Marmorinus' kingdom, and Excoranda with its church. All the principal characters except Saint
Nicholas take their places before the action commences.

This boy, praiseworthy of feature,
Sagacious in understanding, born of good
    family,
Ought well, in our judgment,   15
To be taken into your service.

    The king:

To Apollo, who rules all things,
Ever be praise! And to you thanks,
Who have made so many countries
Subject and tributary to me.   20

    The king to the boy:

Good boy, tell us
Of what land, of what people you are,
Of what religion the people of your country;
Are they pagans or Christians?

    The boy:

Ruling over the people of Excoranda,   25
My father, Getron by name,
Worships God, to whom the seas belong,
Who made us and you and all things.

    The king:

My god is Apollo; he is the god
Who made me; he is truthful and good;   30
He governs the lands, he rules in the
    firmament.
In him alone we ought to believe.

    The boy:

Your god is false and evil;
He is foolish, blind, deaf, and dumb;
You ought not worship such a god,   35
Who cannot govern himself.

    The king:

Do not say such things, boy;
Do not look contemptuously on my god;
For if you make him angry,
You will be unable to escape by any means.   40

*Meanwhile Euphrosina, having realized that her
son had been forgotten, returns to the church of
Nicholas; and when she fails to find her sought-
for son, [let her say] in a sorrowful voice:*

Puer iste, vultu laudabilis,
sensu prudens, genere nobilis,

bene debet, nostro judicio,
subiacere vestro servitio.

    Rex:

Apolloni qui regit omnia
semper sit laus, vobisque gratia,
qui fecistis mihi tot patrias
subjugatas et tributarias.

    Rex puero:

Puer bone, nobis edissere
de qua terra, de quo sis genere,
cuius ritu gens tuae patriae:
sunt gentiles, sive Christicolae?

    Puer:

Excorandae principans populo,
pater meus, Getron vocabulo,
Deum colit, cuius sunt maria,
qui fecit nos et vos et omnia.

    Rex:

Deus meus Apollo; deus est
qui me fecit; verax et bonus est;
regit terras, regnat in aethere.

Illi soli debemus credere.

    Puer:

Deus tuus mendax et malus est;
stultus, caecus, surdus, et mutus est;
talem deum non debes colere,
qui non potest seipsum regere.

    Rex:

Noli, puer, talia dicere;
deum meum noli despicere;
nam si eum iratum feceris,
evadere nequaquam poteris.

*Interea Eufrosina, comperta oblivione filii, ad
ec[c]lesiam Nicholai redit; cumque filium
suum quaesitum non invenerit, lamentabili voce
[dicat]:*

Alas, alas, alas! wretched me!
What should I do? What can I say?
For what sin have I deserved to lose
My son, and yet live after?

Why did my hapless father beget me?   45
Why did my hapless mother baptize me?
Why should the nurse have given me milk?
Why did she not grant me death?

Let the comforters go out [to her] and say:

What does this desolation avail you?
Do not weep for your son.   50
Entreat the Son of the most high Father,
That He give him counsel.

Euphrosina, as if not heeding their comfort:

My dear son, my dearest son,
My son, the greatest part of my soul,
Now you are the cause of sadness to us   55
To whom you were the cause of delight!

The comforters:

Do not despair of God's grace,
Whose great mercy
Gave you this boy;
To you he will restore either this one or
    another.   60

Euphrosina:

My spirit is troubled within me.
Why does my death delay?
If I cannot see you, my son,
I would prefer to die rather than to live
    longer.

The comforters:

Sorrowing, grief, and despair   65
Merely afflict you and do not profit your
    son;
But on his behalf give of your means
To clerics and to the poor.

Beg the indulgence of Nicholas,
That he pray for mercy   70
Of the most high Father toward your son;
Nor will your petition be disappointed.

Heu, heu, heu! mihi misere!
Quid agam? Quid queam dicere?
Quo peccato merui perdere
natum meum, et ultra vivere?

Cur me pater infelix genuit?
Cur me mater infelix abluit?
Cur me nutrix lactare debuit?
Mortem mihi quare non prebuit?

Consolatrices exeant et dicant:

Quid te juvat haec desolatio?
Noli flere pro tuo filio.
Summi Patris exora filium,
qui conferat ei consilium.

*Eufrosina, quasi non curans consolationem
earum:*

Fili care, fili carissime,
fili, meae magna pars animae,
nunc es nobis causa tristitiae
quibus eras causa laetitiae!

Consolatrices:

Ne desperes de Dei gratia,
cuius magna misericordia
istum tibi donavit puerum;
tibi reddet aut hunc aut alium.

Eufrosina:

Anxiatus est in me spiritus.
Cur moratur meus interitus?
Cum te, fili, non possum cernere,
mallem mori quam diu vivere.

Consolatrices:

Luctus, dolor et desperatio
tibi nocent, nec prosunt filio;

sed pro eo de tuis opibus
da clericis atque pauperibus.

Nicholai roga clementiam,
ut exoret misericordiam
summi Patris pro tuo filio;
nec fal[l]etur tua petitio.

Euphrosina:

Nicholas, most holy father,
Nicholas, beloved of God,
If you wish me to venerate you longer,   75
Bring it about that my son may return!

You who have rescued many from the sea,
And the three men from the bond of death,
Hear the prayers of me imploring,
And give me certain news of him.   80

I will not partake of flesh any longer,
Nor delight in wine any further;
In no fashion will I be joyful any more,
Until my son returns.

Getron:

Dear wife, cease mourning;   85
Your tears avail you nothing;
But let there be asked for our son
The propitiation of the most high Father.

Tomorrow will be the festival
Of Nicholas, whom all Christianity   90
Ought faithfully to worship,
Venerate, and praise.

Hear therefore my counsel:
Let us go to his solemn festival;
Let us together praise his mighty works;   95
Let us pray for his intercession.

Perhaps it is the inspiration of God
That admonishes me concerning our son;
The great mercy of Nicholas
Must be sought with God's grace.   100

*Then let them rise; let them go to the church of
Saint Nicholas, in which, when they have entered,
let Euphrosina lift her hands to heaven, and say:*

Most mighty [Father], king of all kings,
King of those remarkable persons who die
    a second death,

Eufrosina:

Nicholae, pater sanctissime,
Nicholae, Deo carissime,
si vis ut te colam diutius,
fac ut meus redeat filius!

Qui salvasti multos in pelago,
et tres viros a mortis vinculo,
preces mei precantis audias,
et ex illo me certam facias.

Non comedam carnem diutius
necque vino fruar ulterius,
nullo modo laetabor amplius,
donec meus redibit filius.

Getron:

Cara soror, lugere desine;
tuae tibi nil prosunt lacrimae;
sed oretur pro nostro filio
summi Patris propitiatio.

In crastino erit festivitas
Nicholai, quem Christianitas
tota debet devote colere,
venerari et benedicere.

Audi ergo mea consilia:
adeamus eius sollemnia;
conlaudemus eius magnalia;
deprecemur eius suffragia.

Dei forsan est inspiratio
quae me monet pro nostro filio;
est oranda cum Dei gratia
Nicholai magna clementia.

*Tunc resurgant; ad ecclesiam Sancti Nicolai
eant, in quam cum introierint, tendat manus
suas ad caelum Eufrosina, et dicat:*

Summe [Pater], regum rex omnium,
Rex unicorum remorientium,

---

[78]*three men:* an allusion to one of St. Nicholas' miracles, probably to that of the Three Scholars recounted in another play from the Fleury playbook.

[102]*King. . .death:* Many attempts have been made to emend this puzzling line. As it stands, it may refer to the miracle of resurrection, found for instance in the St. Nicholas play of the Three Scholars. Here the parents may be asking for a resurrection of their own son, seemingly dead to them.

Cause our son to be returned to us,
The only comfort of our life.

Hear our prayers as we cry unto you,   105
You who sent your son into the world,
That he should make us citizens of heaven
And should snatch us from the gates of hell.

God the Father, whose power
Furnishes all good things to those who are
    good,   110
Do not spurn me, sinful creature,
But cause me to see my son.

Nicholas, whom we call saint,
If those things are true which we believe of
    you,
May your interceding with God   115
Benefit us and our son.

> *When these things have been said, let her go out
> from the church and go to her home and prepare
> a table, and on the table bread and wine, from
> which the clerics and the poor may refresh them-
> selves. When they have been summoned and have
> begun to eat, let Marmorinus say to his atten-
> dants:*

I say to you, my dearest friends,
That before this day I have not had
So great a hunger as now I have;
I cannot endure such hunger.   120

Prepare you therefore what I should eat,
Lest I suffer death.
Why do you delay? Go faster;
Quickly make ready something I may
    devour.

> *Let the attendants, going, bring back food, and
> say to the king:*

At your command, we have prepared   125
Your food, and have brought it here.
Now, if you wish, you can quickly
End the hunger by which you are vexed.

> *When these things have been said, let water be
> brought, and let the king wash his hands, and,
> beginning to eat, let him say:*

I was hungry, and now I am thirsty;

nostrum nobis fac redi filium,
vitae nostrae solum solatium.

Audi preces ad te clamantium,
qui in mundum misisti filium,
qui nos cives caelorum faceret
et inferni claustris eriperet.

Deus Pater, cuius potentia
bona bonis ministrat omnia,

peccatricem me noli spernere,
sed me meum natum fac cernere.

Nicholae, quem sanctum dicimus,
si sunt vera quae de te credimus,

tua nobis et nostro filio
erga Deum prosit oratio.

> *His dictis, exeat ab ecclesia, et eat in domum
> suam, et paret mensam, et super mensam panem
> et vinum, unde clerici et pauperes reficiantur.
> Quibus vocatis et comedere incipientibus,
> dicat Marmorinus ministris suis:*

Dico vobis, mei carissimi,
quod ante hanc diem non habui
famem tantam quantam nunc habeo;
famem istam ferre non valeo.

Vos igitur quo vesci debeam
praeparate, ne mortem subeam.
Quid tardatis? Ite velocius;
quod manducem parate citius.

> *Ministri euntes afferant cibos et dicant regi:*

Ad praeceptum tuum paravimus
cibos tuos, et huc adtulimus.
Nunc, si velis, poteris propere
qua gravaris famem extinguere.

> *His dictis, afferatur aqua, et lavet manus suas
> rex, et incipiens comedere, dicat:*

Esurivi et modo sitio;

I order that wine be given me,   130
Which my [servant], the son of Getron,
Must bring me as quickly as possible.

> *And so let the boy, hearing these things, sigh
> deeply and say to himself:*

Alas, alas, alas! Wretched me!
I desire an end to my life;
For as long as I shall live   135
I can by no means be freed.

> *The king to the boy:*

For what cause do you sigh like this?
I saw you sigh heavily.
What is it that has made you sigh thus?
What harms you, or for what reason do you
    lament?   140

> *The boy:*

Having called to mind the wretchedness of
    myself,
Of my father, and of my country,
I began to sigh and groan,
And to say to myself such things as these:

One year is completed today   145
Since, having been made a slave to
    wretchedness,
Subjugated to regal power,
I entered the boundaries of this country.

> *The king:*

Alas, unfortunate one, why do you ponder
    thus?
What will inquietude of heart avail you?   150
No one can take you from me
As long as I do not wish to lose you.

> *Meanwhile let someone come in the likeness of
> Nicholas; let him take hold of the boy who is
> clutching the cup of wine, and, having seized him,
> let him restore him to his proper place before the
> doors [of his home], and, as if not detected, let
> him withdraw. Then let one of the citizens say to
> the boy:*

Boy, who are you, and where do you wish to
    go?

vinum mihi dari praecipio;
quod afferat mihi quam citius
[servus] meus Getronis filius.

> *Puer itaque, haec audiens, suspiret graviter
> et secum dicat:*

Heu, heu, heu! mihi misero!
Vitae meae finem desidero;
vivus enim quamdiu fuero,
liberari nequaquam potero.

> *Rex puero:*

Pro qua causa suspiras taliter?
Suspirare te vidi fortiter.
Quid est pro quo sic suspiraveris?
Quid te nocet, aut unde quereris?

> *Puer:*

Recordatus meae miseriae,

mei patris et meae patriae,
suspirare coepi et gemere,
et intra me talia dicere:

Annus unus expletur hodie
postquam servus factus miseriae,

potestati subjectus regiae,
fines huius intravi patriae.

> *Rex:*

Heu, miselle, quid ita cogitas?

Quid te juvat cordis anxietas?
Nemo potest te mihi tollere
quamdiu te non velim perdere.

> *Interea veniat aliquis in similitudine Nicholai;
> puerum, scyphum cum recentario tenentem,
> ap[p]rehendat, ap[p]rehensumque ante fores
> componat, et quasi non compertus, recedat.
> Tunc vero unus de civibus ad puerum dicat:*

Puer, quis es, et quo vis pergere?

Whose largess gave you
That cup of wine?   155

The boy:

I come hither, I will go no further;
I am the only son of Getron.
To Nicholas be praise and glory,
Whose favor has brought me back here.

Having heard this, let that citizen run to
Getron and say:

Rejoice, Getron, weep no more;   160
Your son stands outside the doors!
He praises the mighty deeds of Nicholas,
Whose favor has brought him back again.

And when Euphrosina has heard the message of
this kind, let her run to her son; and, kissing him
constantly, let her embrace him and say:

To our God be praise and glory,
Whose great mercy,   165
Turning our afflictions into joy,
Has restored our son to us.

And to our father Nicholas
Be praises and thanks perpetual,
Whose intercession with God   170
Aided us in this affair.

The whole choir:

Of abundant love, [Bishop Nicholas,
You who glory with God in the heavenly
   temple,
Come down, we beseech, to those who sigh
   longingly to you,
That you may lead on high those who have
   been divested of the burdensome flesh.] 175

Here it ends.

Cuius tibi dedit largitio
scyphum istum cum recentario?

Puer:

Huc venio, non ibo longius;
sum Getronis unicus filius.
Nicholao sit laus et gloria,
cuius hic me reduxit gratia.

Quo audito, currat civis ille ad Getronem et
dicat:

Gaude, Getron, nec fleas amplius;
extra fores stat tuus filius!
Nicholai laudat magnalia,
cuius eum reduxit gratia.

Cumque huiusmodi nuntium audierit Eufro-
sina, ad filium suum currat; quem saepius
deosculatum amplexetur et dicat:

Deo nostro sit laus et gloria,
cuius magna misericordia,
luctus nostros vertens in gaudium,
nostrum nobis reduxit filium.

Si[n]tque patri nostro perpetuae
Nicholao laudes et gratiae,
cuius erga Deum oratio
nos adiuvit in hoc negotio.

Chorus omnis:

Copiosae caritatis,   [Nicholae pontifex,
Qui cum Deo gloriaris   in coeli palatio,

Condescende, supplicamus,   ad te
   suspirantibus,
Ut exutos gravi carne   pertrahas ad
   superos.]

Hic finit.

---

172 *Of abundant love (etc.):* the anthem used at lauds on the Feast of St. Nicholas, December 6.

7. THE CHRISTMAS PLAY
(LUDUS DE NATIVITATE)
FROM BENEDIKTBEUERN

One of the most remarkable collections of plays from the twelfth or early thirteenth centuries is to be found in the so-called *Carmina Burana* manuscript, from the Benedictine monastery of Benediktbeuern in Bavarian Germany. This manuscript contains, in addition to its famous Goliardic drinking songs composed by wandering scholars or *vagantes*, a Christmas play, a short Passion play (*Ludus Breviter de Passione*), and a longer Passion play. The manuscript dates from about 1230, but its plays may well have been written as early as 1160. In any case, these *Carmina Burana* plays are among the most splendid and elaborate works of dramatic art ever produced by the medieval church. Later church drama of the thirteenth and fourteenth centuries sometimes rivaled but did not surpass the achievement of the *Carmina Burana*. As a genre, church drama realized its highest potential in the Benediktbeuern plays written for Christmas and Easter.

The complexity and scope of the Benediktbeuern *Christmas Play* can be seen by comparing it with the shorter Fleury play written for the same season (see Part I, above). Even though the shorter play combines the visit of the shepherds with the coming of the Magi and richly illustrates King Herod's tyrannical rage over the birth of a rival king, the Fleury play is still a liturgical work sung as part of the service for Epiphany (January 6). The Fleury playbook also contains a Slaughter of the Innocents play, but evidently it was performed on an entirely separate liturgical occasion during the Feast of Innocents (December 28). The Benediktbeuern *Christmas Play*, on the other hand, gives no evidence of having been performed as part of the liturgy at all. It makes occasional appropriate use of antiphons and other liturgical materials, but it neither begins nor ends with an indication that the regular service is to be interrupted or resumed. Instead, the Benediktbeuern play is a composite work for the entire Christmas season and for the preceding four weeks of Advent.

The play begins with a Procession of Prophets, featuring Isaiah, Daniel, the Sibyl, Aaron, and Balaam. Like other versions of the Procession of Prophets, including that in the Anglo-Norman *Adam*, this one is based on the pseudo-Augustinian *Sermo contra Judeos, Paganos, et Arianos* in which various Old Testament prophets and others are brought forward to convince the unbelieving Jewish nation of the truth of Christ's divinity. The list of prophets in the Benediktbeuern play is not identical with those of the *Sermo* or of the *Adam* play, but the intent is the same: to interpret the Old Testament in the light of Christ's advent. (The Beauvais *Play of Daniel* also links its Old Testament protagonist to the coming of Christ, as we have seen.) The Procession of Prophets in the Benediktbeuern play is an unusually lively one. For one thing, it features the humorously popular episode of Balaam and his ass, in which the beast of burden refuses to go forward at the urging of his irate master, since an angel of the Lord has commanded them to stop. More importantly, the Procession of Prophets introduces a spirited debate

Text based on Munich, Staatsbibl., MS lat. 4660, Carmina Burana saec. xiii, fol. 99ʳ–104ᵛ, as checked against the facsimile prepared by Bernhard Bischoff (Munich, 1967). It has been edited by Young, *Drama of the Medieval Church*, II, 172–90, and by others.

between St. Augustine (the supposed author of the *Sermo*) and Archisynagogus, spokesman for Jewish disbelief in divine miracle. Their topic is the virgin birth, an event which cannot be accounted for by natural explanations. The obstreperous insults and raucous laughter of Archisynagogus are set in dramatic contrast to the calm reasonableness of the learned divine. This passage is a literary work of considerable sophistication, inspired by debate literature of the twelfth-century renaissance and in particular by a pseudo-Augustinian composition entitled *De Altercatione Ecclesiae et Synagogae Dialogus*. The debate is further enriched by the participation of the Boy Bishop, a member of the boys' choir chosen to preside over revels during the Feast of Innocents. All in all, the Benediktbeuern play gives us the most imaginative version of the Procession of Prophets to be found anywhere in medieval drama, whether in church drama or in the great cycles of the fourteenth and fifteenth centuries.

Other parts of the Benediktbeuern *Christmas Play* are no less original. Several scenes appear that are not to be found in earlier Christmas drama. In an Annunciation scene, Mary learns from the angel that she is to bear God's son; in the Salutation of Elizabeth, Mary hears from her pregnant kinswoman the comforting words of the *Magnificat* ("My soul does magnify the Lord"). The Coming of the Magi, though a familiar part of most Christmas plays, is distinguished in the Benediktbeuern text by an unusually extensive disquisition on the motions of the heavenly bodies and on the difficulty of interpreting the astronomical meaning of the bright star that has newly appeared. A remarkable feature of the shepherds' visit to the manger is the debate between the angel and the devil, in which the angel urges the shepherds to hasten toward Christ while the devil entices them to reject the angelic proclamation as a fraud. Another detail to be found nowhere else in medieval drama is the manner in which King Herod is de-

stroyed after his ordering the slaughter of the Innocents: he is gnawed to pieces by worms and taken off to hell by devils. The ending of the play is followed in the manuscript by an unusual *Ludus de Rege Egypti* ("Play of the King of Egypt"), incorporating large portions of the Tegernsee *Antichrist* play.

Virtually all these imaginative additions to the play are designed to reinforce a unifying motif: the conflict between rational faithlessness and belief in divine miracle. Archisynagogus is a central antagonist throughout. After failing to confute the holy wisdom of St. Augustine in the Procession of Prophets, Archisynagogus re-emerges later in the play as an evil counselor to King Herod urging the slaughter of the Innocents. Moreover, Archisynagogus' skeptical assaults on belief in miracle are virtually the same as those with which the devil attempts to stop the shepherds from journeying to the manger. On a similar theme, the Magi at first express a rational skepticism based on their training in the "science" of the stars, but are led by faith to a belief in an event transcending human comprehension. Throughout, the conflict between doubt and affirmation tests the paradox posed by Mary herself about her forthcoming pregnancy: "How may this thing be done, since I have known no man?"

Although seemingly not performed on a specific liturgical occasion, the Benediktbeuern *Christmas Play* may have been staged inside the church. St. Augustine's location "*in fronte ecclesiae*" is sometimes taken to mean that the platform is outside the building, but the phrase probably refers instead to the front of the nave near the choir or possibly the west end of the nave near the door. To the right and left of St. Augustine, in any case, are to be found the prophets and the Jews. Platforms are also necessary (presumably in the nave) for the manger and for King Herod's throne. Possibly the manger is located near the monastery door and Herod's throne near the entrance to the choir, as in the Fleury play, but the Benediktbeuern manuscript does not specify these details. The three Magi assemble in some location as though from different parts of the world, meaning that they enter separately. An angel appears to Mary; an angel and a devil appear to the shepherds. A good deal of processional movement from station to station is required, with sumptuous pageantry, costuming, and music. So extensive and complex is the *mise en scène* that the stage directions show concern for doubling up on acting space; after the Annunciation and Salutation, for instance, Elizabeth is to withdraw since she is no longer needed and there is no room to accommodate her. Gestures and stage effects are at times vivid. Archisynagogus is to agitate his head and body, "imitating with his sceptre the mannerisms of a Jew in all ways"; Mary must give birth to her child; the Innocents are slaughtered in view of the audience; King Herod is "gnawed to pieces by worms." We do not know how this last piece of stage business was accomplished, but we do know from other instances (such as the Beauvais *Play of Daniel*, with its lions' den) that medieval church drama made imaginative use of *trompe l'oeil* effects.

The Christmas Play

(Ludus de Nativitate)

From Benediktbeuern

First let the station of Augustine be placed in the front part of the church, and let Augustine have on his right side Isaiah and Daniel and the other prophets, whereas on the left are Archisynagogus and his Jews. Then let Isaiah arise with his prophecy as follows:

Behold a virgin will bear a child
Without the seed of a man,
Whereby He [God] will cleanse the world
From the guilt of sin.
At this coming of divine will

Primo ponatur sedes Augustino in fronte ecclesiae, et Augustinus habeat a dextera parte Isaiam et Danielem et alios prophetas, a sinistra autem Archisynagogum et suos Judaeos. Postea surgat Isaias cum prophetia sua sic:

Ecce virgo pariet
sine viri semine,
per quod mundum abluet
a peccati crimine.
De venturo gaudeat

5

[1]S.D. *in fronte ecclesiae*: The Latin phrase could suggest a platform outside the church portals. Karl Young argues instead for a station in the front part of the church interior, presumably at the west end of the nave. Rosemary Woolf (*The English Mystery Plays*, p. 352) thinks it more likely that the station would have been at the east end of the nave, near the entrance to the choir.

[1-8](Isaiah appears as the first of the prophets in the popular Christmas sermon wrongly attributed to St. Augustine, the *Sermo contra Judeos, Paganos, et Arianos*, that gave rise to the Procession of Prophets in liturgical drama. Daniel and the Sibyl, who appear next in this play, also take part in the *Sermo*. Other prophets in that sermon, such as Jeremiah, Moses, David, Habakkuk, and some New Testament figures, have been omitted; Aaron and Balaam have been added to the list, as they were in the play of *Adam*'s procession of prophets. These witnesses are summoned by the preacher to berate the Jews for failing to heed testimonials of Christ's advent. The text of Isaiah's prophecy here departs freely from that of the *Sermo*, as do those of Daniel and the others.)

Let Judaea rejoice,
And, now blind, let her flee
From the threshold of error.

Afterward:

Behold a virgin will conceive,

and so on. Again let him sing:

The Lord will give to him the seat of
    David,   10

and so on. Then let Daniel go forth proclaiming
his prophecy:

O wretched Judaea,
Your anointing will cease
When the king of kings will come
From his throne on high,
When, retaining the lily   15
Of flowering chastity,
A virgin will give birth to a king,
Happy in childbearing.

Wretched Judaea,
Dwelling in shadows,   20
Cast off the stain
Of mortal transgression,
And, with joyful praise
At such a famous birth,
May you by no means   25
Succumb to the enticements of error.

Then let him sing:

I beheld in the vision of the night,

and so on. In third place let Sibyl come forth
gesticulating; as she contemplates the star with
animated gesture, let her sing:

This newness of the star
Bears a new message,
That a virgin, knowing nothing   30
Of commerce with men,
And remaining a virgin for all times
After her childbearing,
Will bear a son,
The deliverance of the people.   35

From heaven he descends,

Judaea numine,
et nunc caeca fugiat
ab erroris limine.

Postea:

Ecce virgo concipiet,

et cetera. Iterum cantet:

Dabit illi Dominus sedem David,

et cetera. Postea Daniel procedat prophetiam
suam exprimens:

O Judaea misera,
tua cadet unctio,
cum rex regum veniet
ab excelso solio,
cum retento floridae
castitatis lilio
virgo regem pariet
felix puerperio.

Judaea misera,
sedens in tenebris,
repelle maculam
delicti funebris,
et laeto gaudio
partus tam celebris
erroris minime
cedas illecebris.

Postea cantet:

Aspiciebam in visu noctis,

et cetera. Tertio loco Sybilla gesticulose
procedat, quae inspiciendo stellam cum gestu
mobili cantet:

Haec stellae novitas
fert novum nuntium,
quod virgo nesciens
viri commercium,
et virgo permanens
post puerperium,
salutem populo
pariet filium.

E caelo labitur

In his other raiment,   veste sub altera
The newborn progeny   nova progenies
At his mother's breast,   matris ad ubera,
Making blessed   40   beata faciens
Her womb   illius viscera,
Who has merited   quae nostra meruit
The purging of our iniquities.   purgare scelera.

The new blossom will come   Intrare gremium
To enter her bosom   45   flos novus veniet,
When the untouched virgin   cum virgo filium
Bears a son,   intacta pariet,
Who will cast out the menacings   qui hosti livido
Of the envious foe,   minas excutiet,
And the new king   50   et nova saecula
Will bring in a new age.   rex novus faciet.

From heaven he will come,   E caelo veniet,
The king of great name,   rex magni nominis,
Uniting the covenant   conjungens foedera
Of God and man,   55   Dei et hominis,
And sucking from the breast   et sugens ubera
Of the inviolate virgin,   intactae virginis,
Washing away the offense   reatum diluens
Of worldly sin.   mundani criminis.

Also let her sing these verses: *Item cantet hos versus:*

A sign of the judgment: The earth,   60   Judicii signum: Tellus,

and so on. Next let Aaron, the fourth prophet,   *et cetera. Deinde procedat Aaron, quartus*
come forth, carrying a branch which, placed on   *propheta, portans virgam, quae sumpta super*
the altar among twelve lifeless branches, alone has   *altare inter duodecim virgas aridas sola*
flowered. Let the choir accompany this person with   *floruit. Illam personam conducat chorus cum*
this responsory: *hoc responsorio:*

Hail, celebrated branch.   Salve, nobilis virga.

And let him say this prophecy: *Et dicat hanc prophetiam:*

Behold in a new manner our almond branch   Ecce novo more frondes dat amigdala
    puts forth green leaves;   nostra
The fruit is Christ, but the branch is the   Virgula: nux Christus, sed virgula virgo
    blessed virgin.   beata.

And let him say: *Et dicat:*

---

[60] *A sign . . . earth:* the beginning of the Sibyl's prophecy as it appears in the *Sermo.* See Young, *Drama of the Medieval Church,* II, 130, for text.

[61–63] (For Aaron's prophecy, not derived from the *Sermo contra Judeos,* see the play of *Adam* l. 774 s.d. and Numbers 17:1–8.)

Just as this branch has flowered
Lacking all nourishment,   65
Even so will a virgin bear a child
Without detriment to the flesh.

Just as this branch has thrived
Without sustenance of nature
So that it may truly prefigure   70
Mysteries concerning the virgin,

Even so will the virgin's gates of shame
Be closed
When the virgin will bear a son
By the grace of spiritual nature.   75

*In fifth place let Balaam come forth sitting on
the ass and singing:*

Let me go, let me go quickly, that I may
    pronounce a curse on this people!

*Let the angel go quickly to him, unsheathing his
sword, saying:*

Beware, beware, lest you say anything but
    what I shall tell you!

*And let the ass, on which Balaam is mounted,
step back in fright. Thereupon let the angel withdraw, and let Balaam sing this responsory:*

A star will arise out of Jacob,

*and so on. Let Archisynagogus with his Jews,
having heard the prophecies, make an excessive
clamor; and, shoving forward his comrade,
agitating his head and his entire body and striking
the ground with his foot, and imitating with his
sceptre the mannerisms of a Jew in all ways, with
his companions let him say indignantly:*

Tell me, what
Does the whitewashed wall proclaim?   80
Tell me, what
Does the carrion of truth maintain?
Tell me, what is this
That I have heard so often?

Ut haec [virga] floruit
omni carens nutrimento,
sic et virgo pariet
sine carnis detrimento.

Ut hic ramus viruit
non naturae copia,
verum ut in virgine
figuret mysteria,

Clausa erunt virginis
sic pudoris ostia,
quando virgo pariet
spiritali gratia.

*Quinto loco procedat Balaam sedens in asina
et cantans:*

Vadam, vadam, ut maledicam populo
    huic!

Cui occurrat angelus evaginato gladio dicens:

Cave, cave, ne quicquam aliud quam tibi
    dixero loquaris!

*Et asinus, cui insidet Balaam, perterritus
retrocedat. Postea recedat angelus, et Balaam
cantet hoc responsorium:*

Orietur stella ex Jacob,

*et cetera. Archisynagogus cum suis Judaeis
valde obstrepet auditis prophetiis, et dicat
trudendo socium suum, movendo caput suum et
totum corpus et percutiendo terram pede, baculo
etiam imitando gestus Judaei in omnibus, et
sociis suis indignando dicat:*

Dic mihi, quid praedicat
dealbatus paries?
Dic mihi, quid asserat
veritatis caries?
Dic mihi, quid fuerit,
quod audivi pluries?

---

[78](For Balaam's prophecy, not derived from the *Sermo*, see the play of *Adam* l. 816 s.d. and Numbers 24:17.)

[80]*whitewashed wall:* "Paries" could be used as a term of abuse in classical Latin.

I was hoping that the chain of events   85
Might be made clear to me!

It seems to me I hear these people
Spew forth this saying,
That without commerce with men
A virgin ought to bear a child.   90
O what simplemindedness
Constrains them to be so foolish,
Who would predict a camel
To descend from a cow!

When the clamoring and wrongheadedness of the
Jews are heard, let the Boy Bishop say:

Their speech is empty,   95
Their judgment flown;
Frenzy and licentious use of wine
Drive them to distraction.
But it remains only to consult
The mind of Augustine,   100
By whom the dispute
May be brought to an end.

At once let the prophets come before Augustine
and say:

The speech of the Jews
Gives us considerable affront;
The old dregs of error   105
Still cling to them.
When we talk of Christ,
They laugh, and offer us
The arguments of
Their own minds.   110

Let Augustine answer:

Let this nation concealed in darkness
Come forth to us,
And let this people given to error
Present itself to us,
Both that error may halt   115
When the matter is exposed to them,
And that the closed path of the Scriptures
May lie open to them.

Let Archisynagogus come with great muttering on
his part and on the part of his followers, to whom
let Augustine say:

Vellem esset cognita
rerum mihi series!

Illos, reor, audio
in haec verba fluere,
quod sine commercio
virgo debet parere.
O quanta simplicitas
cogit hos desipere,
qui de bove praedicant
camelum descendere!

Auditis tumultu et errore Judaeorum, dicat
Episcopus Puerorum:

Horum sermo vacuus
sensus peregrini,
quos et furor agitat
et libertas vini.
Sed restat consulere
mentem Augustini,
per quem disputatio
concedatur fini.

Statim prophetae vadant ante Augustinum
et dicant:

Multum nobis obviat
lingua Judaeorum,
quibus adhuc adjacet
vetus faex errorum.
Cum de Christo loquimur,
rident et suorum
argumenta proferunt
nobis animorum.

Respondeat Augustinus:

Ad nos illa prodeat
tenebris abscondita
et se nobis offerat
gens errori dedita,
ut et error claudicet
re ipsis exposita,
et scripturae pateat
ipsis clausa semita.

Veniat Archisynagogus cum magno murmure
sui et suorum, quibus dicat Augustinus:

Now open your ears,
Unhappy Judaea! 120
The king of kings will come
In his other raiment,
Who, while he sucks
From the breast of his virgin mother,
Will unite the covenant 125
Of God and man.

*Let Archisynagogus answer with immoderate and
violent laughter:*

O Augustine,
By your genius you convey
Matters of greatest profundity,
When you predict the occurrence 130
Of a thing that reason denies!
For if "a virgin will bear a child"
Without commerce with men,
This is an affront to nature,
And a confusion in the order of things. 135

Why do you contradict,
Stung by your former downfall,
You who pay no attention to
What can reasonably happen?
For if "a virgin will bear a child," 140
As these young men prophesy,
Nature can make complaint about
Her own rights.

Whenever "a virgin will conceive,"
Xanthus River, hasten backwards! 145
The wolf will flee from the lamb,
The flat places will become rough and
    uneven.
If you reflect upon present realities
And consider ancient truths,
And if in this context it is alleged that 150
"A virgin is childbearing,"

As the prating prophet
Incessantly affirms;
If a virgin either "will bear a child,"
Or perhaps has already done so, 155

Nunc aures aperi,
Judaea misera!
Rex regum veniet
veste sub altera,
qui matris virginis
dum sugit ubera,
Dei et hominis
conjunget foedera.

*Respondeat Archisynagogus cum nimio ca-
chinno:*

O Augustine,
de profundo maxime
portans haec ingenio,
dum futurum praedicas,
id quod negat ratio!
Nam si "virgo pariet"
et sine commercio,
id naturae rubor est,
et rerum confusio.

Tu quid contra resonas,
labe tactus veteri,
qui non illud respicis,
quod est justum fieri?
Nam si "virgo pariet,"
quod prophetant pueri,
natura de proprio
jure potest conqueri.

Quando "virgo pariet,"
Xante, retro propera!
Lupus agnum fugiet,
plana fient aspera.

Si moderna colligis
et attendis vetera,
in adjecto ponitur
"est virgo puerpera,"

Ut propheta garrulus
incessanter asserit;
vel si "virgo pariet,"
vel iam forte peperit,

---

[137]*Stung . . . downfall:* Perhaps Archisynagogus slurringly refers to Augustine's wayward
youth, in order to discredit his prophetic powers.

Who did not experience
The bond of flesh prior to giving birth,
The law teaches and reveals
That such a thing would be fantastical.

To believe that from inviolable virginity   160
Should thus proceed a small child
Is to believe erroneously,
Not the summit of wisdom.
Therefore, let my rival
Either respond to this objection,   165
Or else flee as the bearer
Of error and shame.

In a sober and discreet voice let Augustine answer:

At the fortunate occurrence
Of such a unique event,
These arguments and sophistical precepts   170
Are manifestly defective;
For reason teaches
That nature is not rejected
If once you see something revealed
That is beyond the ordinary.   175

[Archisynagogus:]

He should say "the man is dead";
Besides, this is taken for granted,
Which in Aristotle
Is explained for children.
But this rule of yours   180
Then suffers rebuttal
When talk reaches us
Of "a virgin mother"!

Let Augustine say:

Lest you should have proclaimed it a fantasy
That a virgin will conceive,   185
That she will bear a child, with the gates
    of shame
Yet unopened,
From Judaea a manifold witness

---

quae non carnis copulam
ante partum senserit,
quod fantasma fuerit,
lex docet et aperit.

Quod de clausa virgine
sic procedat parvulus,
est erroris credere,
non doctrinae cumulus.
Vel ergo respondeat
ad objectum aemulus,
vel erroris fugiat
et ruboris bajulus.

Voce sobria et discreta respondeat Augustinus:

In eventu prospero
talis casus unici
argumenta claudicent
moresque sophistici;
docet enim ratio,
naturam non reici,
si quid praeter solitum
semel vides obici.

[Archisynagogus:]

Dicat "homo mortuus";
in adjecto ponitur,
quod in Aristotile
pueris exprimitur.
Sed haec vestra regula
tunc repulsam patitur,
cum de "matre virgine"
sermo nobis oritur!

Augustinus dicat:

Ne fantasma dixeris
quod virgo concipiet,
quod pudoris ostio

non aperto pariet:
De Judaea multiplex

---

[169]*unique event:* i.e., the birth of Christ (which transcends the customary laws of nature).

[176-83]*He . . . virgin:* i.e., This talk about unique events occurring in nature (concerning death, for example) is child's play, and is amply discussed in Aristotle; but such a rule won't apply to absurd prating about virgin motherhood. (Line 176 is obscure; *Dicat* may be part of the speech prefix.)

Will come to us,
Who will act in opposition to you   190
And be with us.

testis nobis veniet,
qui vobis contrarius
et nobiscum faciet.

Just as the sun's ray enters
A transparent solid sheet of glass,
And having gone completely through,
Leaves unharmed the thing through which
    it has passed,   195
Even so into the womb of the virgin
The Son of the highest Father
Will truly make his descent,
And yet without harmful effect.

Ut specular solidum
solis intrat radius,
et sincere transitus
servit ei pervius,

sic in aulam virginis
summi Patris Filius
lapsum quidem faciet,
et tamen innoxius.

   Then let Augustine begin to sing:

   Postea incipiat Augustinus cantare:

Rejoicing greatly, [let the faithful choir
    exult,   200
Alleluia!]

Laetabundus [exultet fidelis chorus,

Alleluia!],

   the first verse; and the second, the prophets:

   primum versum; et secundum, prophetae:

The untouched bride brought forth the king
    of kings,
A thing to be wondered at,

Regem regum intactae profudit torus,

Res miranda,

   *and so on. Let Archisynagogus say with his
companions:*

   et cetera. Dicat Archisynagogus cum suis:

A thing to be denied!

Res neganda!

   Again Augustine with his followers:

   Iterum Augustinus cum suis:

A thing to be wondered at!   205

Res miranda!

   Again Archisynagogus with his companions:

   Iterum Archisynagogus cum suis:

A thing to be denied!

Res neganda!

   *Let this be done several times. Let Augustine
begin:*

   Hoc fiat pluries. Augustinus incipiat:

The Angel of Good Counsel
Is born of a virgin,
The sun of a star!

Angelus Consilii
natus est de virgine,
sol de stella!

   Let the prophets respond:

   Respondeant prophetae:

A sun which knows no setting,   210
A star ever glowing,
Ever bright!

Sol occasum nesciens,
stella semper rutilans,
semper clara!

   Let Augustine say:

   Dicat Augustinus:

The high cedar of Lebanon
Is fashioned into the hyssop
In our valley.   215

Let the prophets say:

The Word of the Most High
Has undertaken corporeal nature,
Having assumed the flesh.

Then let Augustine say:

Isaiah prophesied,
The synagogue [of the Jews] remembers;   220
Notwithstanding, she never ceases
To be blind.

Let the prophets answer:

If not their own prophets,
They at least ought to believe
Those things predicted in the pagan verses   225
Of the Sibyl.

Then let Augustine say with all the prophets:

Hasten, unhappy ones,
Believe your own traditions!
Why will you condemn yourselves, wretched
    people?
Think upon the newborn one   230
Whom the Scriptures reveal;
It is he whom the child-bearing woman has
    begotten.

Then let Augustine sing alone:

Let the Jews now learn how, agreeing with
us about Christ, they ought to embrace
the new joy of the new birth, the hope of
new salvation of those who are awaiting
him. Now may they believe in him who
is about to come and wait with us for him
to be born, saying: The new king will be
the salvation of the world.

In the midst of the singing of all these things,

Cedrus alta Libani
conformatur hysopo
valle nostra.

Dicant prophetae:

Verbum Ens Altissimi
corporali passum est
carne sumpta.

Postea dicat Augustinus:

Isaias cecinit,
synagoga meminit;
nunquam tamen desi[n]it
esse caeca.

Respondeant prophetae:

Si non suis vatibus,
credant vel gentilibus
Sibyllinis versibus
haec praedicta.

*Postea dicat Augustinus cum prophetis omni-
    bus:*

Infelix, propera,
crede vel vetera!
Cur damnaberis, gens misera?

Natum considera,
quem docet littera;
ipsum genuit puerpera.

Postea Augustinus solus cantet:

Discant nunc Judaei, quomodo de Christo
consentientes nobiscum amplexari
debent novi partus novum gaudium,
novae spem salutis ipsum expectan-
tium. Nunc venturum credant et
nasciturum expectent nobiscum dicentes: Rex novus erit salus mundi.

Inter cantandum omnia ista Archisynagogus

213–15*hyssop:* a ceremonial plant, with a figurative meaning of lowliness, to stress Christ's
descent from his Godhead (the high cedar) to human imperfection in this life (our valley).
The figure is derived from 1 Kings 4:33.

Archisynagogus will bawl and shout, agitating his body and head, and deriding the prophecies. When this is over, the acting area ought to be given up by the prophets, providing for them either to withdraw, or to sit in their places to observe the play. Thereupon let the angel appear to Mary as she is laboring in the manner of a woman, and say:

Hail Mary, full of grace! The Lord is with you.

And again:

Behold, you shall conceive and bring forth a son, [and you shall call him Jesus,] 235

and so on. Let her say, stunned:

How may this thing be done, since I have known no man?

Let the angel answer:

The Holy Spirit will come over you, [and the strength of the Most High will protect you.]

and so on. Verse:

And on that account he will be born, [from you most sacred, and will be called the Son of God. And behold your kinswoman Elizabeth, and she has conceived a son in her old age.]

and so on. Let Mary answer:

Behold the handmaid of the Lord; [may it be done with me according to your word.]

and so on. Thereupon let Mary go to greet Elizabeth as though by happenstance, not aware that in her advanced age Elizabeth has conceived the infant John; and let [Elizabeth] say:

Whence this to me, [that the mother of my God should come to me?] 240

obstrepet movendo corpus et caput, et deridendo praedicta. Hoc completo, detur locus prophetis, vel ut recedant, vel sedeant in locis suis propter honorem ludi. Deinde angelus appareat Mariae operanti muliebriter, et dicat:

Ave Maria, gratia plena! Dominus tecum.

Et iterum:

Ecce, concipies et paries,

et cetera. Illa stupefacta dicat:

Quomodo fiet istud, quia virum non cognosco?

Respondeat angelus:

Spiritus Sanctus superveniet,

et cetera. Versus:

Ideoque quod nascetur,

et cetera. Respondeat Maria:

Ecce, ancilla Domini,

et cetera. Deinde Maria vadat casualiter, nihil cogitans de Elisabeth vetula Johanne impraegnata, et salutet eam; et dicat [Elisabeth]:

Unde hoc mihi,

234–39 *Hail Mary etc.:* This dramatic episode of the Annunciation is based on Luke 1:26–38.

239 s.d. *Elizabeth:* the wife of Zachariah and mother of John the Baptist (Luke 1:5–80). The medieval world assumed that she and Mary were kinswomen.

and so on. And she will sing:

Because the voice of your salutation has sounded [in my ears, the child in my womb has exulted in joy.]

and so on. Let the same person say:

Blessed are you among women [and blessed is the fruit of your womb.]

and so on.

You who will carry peace among men and before the nations.

Let Mary answer:

My soul does magnify the Lord. [*and so on.*]

Thereupon let Elizabeth withdraw, since this character will no longer have a large role. Afterward let Mary, who now has conceived by the Holy Ghost, go to her bed and bear a son. Let Joseph, dressed decently and with a long beard, sit by her. When the child has been born, let the star appear, and let the choir begin this antiphon:

Today Christ is born, [today our Saviour has revealed himself; today the angels sing on earth, the archangels rejoice; today let the elect rejoice, saying: Glory to God in the highest, alleluia.]   245

When this is finished, let the star appear. Seeing it, let the three kings from different parts of the world come and marvel at the appearance of such a star; let the first of them say:

I am often perplexed
By a labyrinth of cares,
Suffering shipwreck
Of mind and spirit,
When I see this star   250

---

et cetera. Et cantabit:

Ex quo facta est vox salutationis,

et cetera. Eadem dicat:

Benedicta tu in mulieribus,

et cetera.

Tu quae portabis p. h. et an gen.

Respondeat Maria:

Magnificat anima mea Dominum.

Deinde recedat Elisabeth, quia amplius non habebit locum haec persona. Deinde Maria vadat in lectum suum, quae iam de Spiritu Sancto concepit, et pariat filium. Cui assideat Joseph in habitu honesto et prolixa barba. Nato puero, appareat stella, et incipiat chorus hanc antiphonam:

Hodie Christus natus est, [hodie Salvator apparuit; hodie in terra canunt angeli, laetantur archangeli; hodie exultent justi dicentes: Gloria in excelsis Deo, alleluia.]

Qua finita, stella appareat. Qua visa, tres reges a diversis partibus mundi veniant et admirentur de apparitione talis stellae, quorum primus dicat:

Per curarum distrahor
frequenter quadrivium,
rationis patiens
et mentis naufragium,
cum hanc stellam video

---

²⁴³*Tu quae . . . gen:* This line is obscure. Dom Beyssac expands the contractions in the Latin to read: *"Tu quae portabis pacem hominibus et ante gentes."*

²⁴⁴*My soul etc.:* For the full text of the *Magnificat*, center of the dramatic episode known as the Salutation of Elizabeth, see Luke 1:46–55.

²⁴⁵s.d. *from different parts:* i.e., The kings presumably enter from different sides, as also in the Fleury dramatization of this same subject.

Bearing a portent;
For its newness
Conveys strange tidings!

I have studied the paths
And natures of the constellations,   255
And have not forgotten to scrutinize
Their number;
But when I look at this one,
I am bemused once again,
For it was not visible   260
To anyone of old.

When the moon is eclipsed,
And when the sun will be obscured;
What effect Mercury should produce
In conjunction with Venus;   265
In what configuration you, Mars,
Are said to be especially noxious—
These things the sayings of the ancient
       school
Have made known to me.

But this beam from the star   270
Renders me speechless!
What it may portend, I do not know,
But seeking diligently
I draw this one conclusion,
That a son is born   275
Whom the world will obey,
And whom it will fear greatly.

*Let the first [king] say this gazing continually on
the star, pondering about it. Let the second say:*

Now joy sweetly
Adorns my heart;
A great relief has been afforded me   280
In my journey.
In this matter, about which I am at a loss,
Now I have found a companion
Showing himself to be in doubt
And a partaker of my anxiety.   285

When with alert mind
I regard the planets,
My faculty of reason comprehends
Their various potencies—
Mars, Venus,   290

portantem indicium,
quod ipsius novitas
novum portet nuntium!

Cursus ego didici
et naturas siderum,
et ipsorum memini
perscrutari numerum;
sed cum hanc inspicio,
ego miror iterum,
quia non comparuit
apud quemquam veterum.

Quando luna patitur,
et sol obscurabitur,
quem effectum habeat
Stilbon comes Veneris,
in quo gradu maxime
Mars noxius diceris,
mihi fecit cognitum

lingua sectae veteris.

Sed elinguem efficit
hic me stellae radius!
Quid portendat, nescio,
sed quaerens attentius
hoc unum coniicio,
quod est natus filius,
cui mundus oboediet,
quem timebit amplius.

*Hoc dicat primus semper inspiciendo stellam,
et disputet de illa. Dicat secundus:*

Mea iam praecordia
dulce vestit gaudium;
mihi viae factum [est]
non parvum compendium.
In eo, quod ambigo,
se monstrantem dubium
et curae participem
iam inveni socium.

Quando mente vigili
planetas inspicio,
mea vim cuiuslibet
deprehendit ratio
de Marte, de Venere,

The Sun, Mercury,
The indulgence of Jupiter,
The senility of Saturn—
And what is their potency
In each astrological house.   295
But in the case of that one you are looking
        at
And which you point out with your finger,
When its nature has been comprehended
I am uncertain as to the effect.
But whatever opinion I then hold,   300
Accept it yourself, along with me,
So that we may take pleasure jointly
In the purpose of our quest.

Yon radiance, which you witness,
Which shines with such intensity   305
And causes the other planets
To be paled into eclipse,
Foretells the birth of a king,
Than whom no greater may ever come,
Yielding to whose sway   310
All the world must be subject.

*Let the third [king] say, pointing, and reasoning
concerning the star:*

He knew how to unravel
The tangle of disputed points—
He, through whom I have learned
That, when the beam of a comet   315
Manifests itself,
Then the planets are dull,
And the fates of certain princes
Reveal themselves.

We know what a star is,   320
And what a planet is;
This is neither of these things.
But since this is a comet,
May we be anointed with joy,
Our minds be joyful;   325

de Sole, Mercurio,
de Jovis clementia,
de Saturni senio,
quae sit vis cuiuslibet
in quo domicilio.
Sed in hac quam aspicis

et quam monstras digito,
qualitate cognita
de effectu dubito.
Sed quid inde sentiam
tu mecum accipito,
ut fruamur pariter
quaesiti proposito.

Illud jubar, quod inspicis
et in tantum radiat
et planetas ceteros
in pallorem variat,
regem natum praedicat,
quo major non veniat,
cuius cedens nutui
totus orbis serviat.

*Dicat tertius monstrando et disputando de
stella:*

Questionum noverat
enodare rete
ille, per quem habeo,
quod, quando cometae
se producit radius,
tunc hebent planetae,
et quorundam principum
se praesentant metae.

Quid sit stella, novimus,
et quid sit planeta;
horum haec est neutrum.
Sed cum sit cometa,
inungamur gaudio,
sit mens nobis laeta;

312–14*He:* i.e., the unnamed wise man from whom the third king first studied astrology. His
learning typifies the old wisdom that (like the teachings of Archisynagogus) cannot adequately account for the miracle of Christ's advent. His method can only interpret Christ's star as
some sort of comet, since comets were renowned for their baleful influence over the stars and
men's lives.

For it is a true prophet
Of a great prince.

See how greatly is augmented
The brightness of this star,
And how diminished   330
The splendor of all the planets!
Because it is fittingly suited
To him who is born,
The potency of any other
Is obscured by this one.   335

Therefore with gifts
Let us proceed together,
And wherever the star will lead
Let us direct our steps,
So that, when we see   340
The newborn one for whom we have hoped,
We may offer him
Our duties as kings.

*Immediately let the kings proceed to the land of
Herod, searching for the child and singing:*

Where is he who is born,

*and so on. Let the messengers of Herod approach
them quickly, saying:*

You who wear the dress   345
And insignia of kings,
Make known to us
Why you journey thus,
Or if you know some news
Which ought to be revealed,   350
And which you wish to bring
To the ears of the king of the Jews.

We are servants and deputies
Of Herod,
To whom messengers from divers parts 355
Often come in transit.
No secrets of the palace
Are barred to us;

---

magni enim principis
verus est propheta.

Vide, stellae claritas
quanta propagatur;
in planeta quolibet
splendor hebetatur!
Quod ei, qui natus est,
satis adaptatur,
cuiusvis potentia
per hunc obscuratur.

Ergo cum muneribus
una procedamus,
et quo stella duxerit,
gressus dirigamus,
ut, quando viderimus
quem natum speramus,
nostra ei munia
reges offeramus.

*Modo procedant reges usque in terram Herodis,
quaerendo de puero et cantando:*

Ubi est, qui natus est,

*et cetera. Quibus occurrant nuntii Herodis
dicentes:*

Vos, qui regum habitus
et insigne geritis,
nobis notum facite,
quare sic inceditis,
vel si notum aliquid
reserandum noscitis,
[Judaeorum] quod ad aures
regis ferre quaeritis.

Nos Herodis vernulae
sumus et vicarii,
ad quem saepe transvolant
ex diversis nuntii.
Nulla nobis clausa sunt
secreta palatii;

343s n. *the land of Herod:* i.e., probably a scaffold in the nave, as in the Fleury play about Herod.
(A fourteenth-century production at Avignon called *The Presentation of the Virgin Mary in the
Temple* may give an idea of the dimensions of such platforms in the nave. That play required
a scaffold approximately 10 by 8 feet, by 6 feet high, with stairs, railings, and benches.)

Therefore we beg to know
The nature of your business.   360

Let the kings answer:

We have no wish to conceal
What we are seeking for;
The star we witness
Reveals it.
We seek a newborn king,   365
Of whom the star gives testimony
That his kingdom
Is without end.

Let the messengers answer:

That proclamation
Will come as happy tidings to Herod,   370
And gladly will he hear
News of this king.
In order, therefore, that he may first
Receive joyful tidings through us,
Follow our footsteps   375
[At a slower pace].

Then let the messengers hasten to Herod saying:

King Herod, receive
Some astonishing news
Now about to be revealed to you
By three kings: 380
They maintain that a king has been born,
Devoutly to be worshiped,
To whom, they do not doubt,
The world will be subject.

Let Herod reply in a towering rage:

How dare you say such things   385
To a king?
I'm warning you,
Don't make up lies!
For I am Herod,
Mighty enough to overwhelm   390
Whatsoever the world—
The heaven, the earth, the sea—contains.

*After this let Herod, extremely angry, have
Archisynagogus with his Jews called to him,
saying:*

ergo scire poscimus
vestri rem negotii.

Respondeant reges:

Sepelire nolumus
quod a nobis quaeritur;
ipsum stella reserat,
quae a nobis cernitur.
Regem natum quaerimus,
de quo stella loquitur,
quod eius imperium
nullo fine clauditur.

Respondeant nuntii:

Felix istud veniet
Herodi praeconium,
et libenter audiet
hoc de rege nuntium.
Ut hinc ergo primitus
per nos sumat gaudium,
vos nostrum sequimini
[paulatim] vestigium.

Postea nuntii festinent ad Herodem dicentes:

Rex Herodes, accipe
quiddam admirandum,
iam a tribus regibus
tibi reserandum:
ipsi natum asserunt
regem venerandum,
cui esse non ambigunt
orbem subjugandum.

Respondet Herodes cum magna indignatione:

Cur audetis talia
regi praesentare?
Nolite, vos consulo,
falsum fabricare!
Nam Herodes ego sum
potens subjugare
quicquid mundus continet,
caelum, terra, mare.

*Post haec Herodes maxime indignatus vocari
faciat Archisynagogum cum Judaeis suis
dicens:*

Hither let Judaea come		Huc Judaea veniat	
Full of wise counsel,		fecunda consilio,	
That he may discourse with us	395	ut nobiscum disserat	
Concerning this business.		super hoc negotio.	
I will order you		Ego vos praecipiam	
Exposed to punishment,		exponi supplicio,	
If a reckoning proves		si vos esse devios	
You inconstant!	400	comprobabit ratio!	

Now let Archisynagogus come with colossal pride, attended by his Jews, to whom let Herod say:

Modo veniat Archisynagogus cum magna superbia et Judaeis suis, cui dicat Herodes:

To you, teacher, I address myself,		Te, magister, alloquor,	
And let the rest pay attention!		et advertant alii!	
The report of this troublesome message		Nostra mordet viscera	
Torments our heart.		duri fama nuntii.	
Hither come three wise men,	405	Huc tres magi veniunt	
Not unlearned in the stars,		non astrorum inscii,	
Who hasten to the birth		qui ad ortum properant	
Of an extraordinarily powerful son.		praepotentis filii.	

Let Archisynagogus reply with great wisdom and eloquence:

Respondeat Archisynagogus cum magna sapientia et eloquentia:

Do not, my lord, become all twisted about		Ne curarum, domine,	
In the labyrinths of your worries.	410	verseris in bivio.	
Let the three kings come hither		Tres huc reges veniant	
Searching for a son;		quaerendo de filio,	
Win their favor		quibus te concilies	
With assiduous zeal,		diligenti studio,	
And speak to them thus	415	et eis sic loquere	
Under the cloak of friendliness:		sub amoris pallio:	

"You are kings, I see,		"Reges estis, video,	
Because your costumes say so.		quod prophetat habitus.	
Your passing among us		Vester mihi gratus est	
Is most pleasing to me.	420	factus ad nos transitus.	
But reveal utterly		Sed quid vos huc traxerit,	
What has drawn you hither,		reserate penitus,	
For the king will be open with you		nam vobis ad omnia	
In all matters."		rex erit expositus."	

Let the kings answer:

Respondeant reges:

The new star shines	425	Stella nova radiat	

425(There is an apparent ellipse in the dramatic action here. Perhaps it is simply to be understood that the kings arrive at court and that Herod speaks to them repeating the statement devised by Archisynagogus. Or possibly Archisynagogus addresses the kings directly as Herod's spokesman.)

As messenger of his birth,
To whom the world will be obedient,
And who will rule all things;
And nothing will be able to endure
Without his grace.   430
We bend our course toward him,
Bearing these gifts.

Herod answers:

Let me not hinder you
On the path you propose.
Go, and afterward   435
Hasten your return to us,
In order that I, going likewise,
May bear the gift I owe
Him, to whom I cannot doubt
The world will be subject.   440

*Let the three Magi withdraw from Herod gradu-
ally, constantly regarding the star and reasoning
about it. Meanwhile let an angel appear to the
shepherds and say:*

To you, shepherds,
I proclaim great joy:
God has enclosed himself
In the mantle of your flesh!
His mother did not bear him   445
By means of carnal intercourse;
On the contrary, an eternal virgin
Is the mother of this son.

*As the shepherds are going [to the manger] let
the devil say:*

The simpleheadedness of shepherds!
You shouldn't believe such things.   450
You should know them to be nonsense,
Which the truth does not verify.
That deity should thus
Be lulled to sleep in a manger
Is too great a falsehood   455
Laid before your eyes.

*As the shepherds are returning again to their
affairs, let the angel say:*

Shepherds, go in quest
Of him who was born in a manger,

eius ortus nuntia,
cui mundus oboediet,
et qui reget omnia,
et nil stare poterit
absque huius gratia.
Nos ad illum tendimus
haec ferentes munia.

Herodes respondet:

Ne sim vos impediens
ad viae propositum.
Ite, ad nos postea
maturantes reditum,
ut et ego veniens
munus feram debitum
ei, cui non ambigo
mundum fore subditum.

*Ab Herode discedant tres Magi paulatim,
inspicientes stellam et disputantes de illa.
Interim angelus appareat pastoribus et dicat:*

Magnum vobis gaudium,
pastores, annuntio:
Deus se circumdedit
carnis vestrae pallio,
quem [mater] non peperit
carnali commercio;
immo virgo permanens
mater est ex filio.

Pastoribus euntibus dicat diabolus:

Tu ne credas talibus
pastorum simplicitas!
Scias esse frivola,
quae non probat veritas.
Quod sic in praesepio
sit sepulta deitas,
nimis est ad oculum
reserata falsitas.

*Iterum pastoribus ad negotium suum redeunti-
bus dicat angelus:*

Pastores, quaerite
natum in praesepio,

And fulfill your promised vow
To the mother with her son;   460
Let this purpose
Suffer no delay,
But let the devotion of your soul
Direct you thither.

*Again as the shepherds are going let the devil
say in their ears:*

You simpleminded folk, look   465
How adroit he is,
Who thus makes
Contraries out of the truth!
And, that his lies
Might deceive with trifles,   470
All that he utters
He represents in harmonious song.

*Let the shepherds be astonished, and let one say
to the other:*

Brother, do you gather
These things I hear?
A certain saying concerning the newborn
    child   475
Twists the truth
Into its very opposite.
From this I suspect
That those things we have heard
Border on falsehood.   480

Again let the angel say to the shepherds:

Why do you not heed
This proclamation of the truth?
Who is this cunning one
Turning you from the true path?
Do not let error envelop you   485
By your great adversary's means.
Go, for what I proclaim
The manger will reveal.

Again let the devil say to them as they are going:

O you hopelessly simpleminded people,
Afflicted in your understanding!   490
Carry hay and fodder,
Which cattle are fond of;
Maybe the deity laid in the manger

et votum solvite
matri cum filio;
nec mora veniat
isti consilio,
sed vos huc dirigat
mentis devotio.

*Iterum pastoribus abeuntibus dicat diabolus
ad aures eorum:*

Simplex coetus, aspice,
qualis astutia
eius, qui sic fabricat
vero contraria!
Utque sua fallere[n]t
nugis mendacia,
in rhythmis conciliat,
quae profert omnia.

Mirentur pastores, et unus dicat ad alterum:

Nunquid, frater, colligis
ea quae audio?
Quaedam vox insinuat
de nato filio
verum in contrarium.
Ab hoc suscipio,
quod audita resident
juncta mendacio.

Dicat iterum angelus ad pastores:

Cur non aures vertitis
ad hunc veri nuntium?
Quis est iste subdolus
vertens vos in devium?
Ne vos error induat
propter adversarium.
Ite, nam quod praedico,
monstrabit praesepium.

Dicat iterum euntibus diabolus:

O gens simplex nimium
et in sensu vulnerata!
Fer faenum et pabulum,
quae bubus non ingrata;
in praesepi comedat

Will eat them!
You rave beyond measure   495
When you take these things for a certainty.

Again the shepherds to their companions:

Brother, listen again:
What contradictions!
From one side I hear things
Quite opposite to those from the other side.   500
My guileless soul,
My baffled mind
Does not know which of their opinions
Is preferable.

*Then let the angels gather together and sing in
unison:*

Glory to God in the highest, and on earth
  peace to men of good will, alleluia,
  alleluia.   505

*When they have heard this song, let the shepherd
say to his companions:*

At this angelic song
I draw my breath deeply;
At this song I have within me
The joy of lute-playing!
Let us go forward therefore   510
Together to the manger,
And with bent knees
Let us adore the son.

*Thereafter let the shepherds proceed to the
manger singing this antiphon:*

And [suddenly] there was with the angel a
  multitude of the heavenly [host,
  praising God and saying: Glory to God
  in the highest, and on earth peace to
  men of good will, alleluia.]

*When they have sung this, let them worship the
child. Then let the shepherds return to their occupations, to whom let the* three Magi *approach
quickly, saying:*

Shepherds, say what you have seen, and
  relate the birth of Christ.   515

deitas reclinata!
Debaccharis nimium,
cum putas ista rata.

Iterum pastores ad socios suos:

Audi, frater, iterum,
qualis repugnantia!
Inde quaedam audio,
hinc horum contraria.
Meus simplex animus,
mea mens non sobria
ignorat, quae potior
sit horum sententia.

*Postea simul conveniant angeli, et simul
cantent:*

Gloria in excelsis Deo, et in terra pax
  hominibus bonae voluntatis, alleluia,
  alleluia.

Qua voce audita, dicat pastor ad socios suos:

Ad hanc vocem animi
produco suspirium;
ex hac intus habeo
citharizans gaudium!
Procedamus igitur
simul ad praesepium,
et curvatis genibus
adoremus filium.

*Deinde procedant pastores ad praesepe cantando
hanc antiphonam:*

Facta est cum angelo multitudo caelestis
  [exercitus laudantium et dicentium:
  Gloria in excelsis Deo, et in terra pax
  hominibus bonae voluntatis, alleluia].

*Quo cantato, adorent puerum. Deinde re-
vertantur pastores ad officia sua, quibus occurrant tres Magi dicentes:*

Pastores, dicite quidnam vidistis, et
  annuntiate Christi nativitatem?

Let the shepherds answer:

We saw the child wrapped in a swaddling
    cloth, and a choir of angels praising the
    Saviour.

*Then let the kings go to the manger, and first let
them worship the child, and then let them offer
him their gifts: first gold, second frankincense,
third myrrh. Thereafter let them go on their way
slowly, and then let them sleep; and let the angel
appear to them in their sleep, saying:*

Do not go back to Herod,

*and so on. Afterward, when they have not returned
to Herod, let him say:*

Let the Jewish people make haste,
That they may listen to Herod,
And offer counsel   520
On a thing that wounds me!
Troubled King Herod
Does not know what he ought to do,
When by three kings
He perceives himself made a laughingstock.   525

*Let Archisynagogus come with his followers, to
whom let Herod say:*

You, teacher, disclose
The writings of the prophets,
If in them are sayings, handed down
By the prophets, concerning a boy;
For truly, when you have   530
Revealed to me these things,
They will show themselves to be
The hidden fears of my own heart.

Let Archisynagogus answer:

You Bethlehem, in the land of Judaea,

*and so on. Then let Herod in a rage say to his
soldiers:*

Go, go together   535

Respondeant pastores:

Infantem vidimus pannis involutum et
    chorus angelorum laudantes
    Salvatorem.

*Postea reges vadant ad praesepe, et primo
adorent puerum, et postea offerant ei munera
sua: primo aurum, postea thus, tertio myrrham.
Deinde modicum procedant, et tunc dormiant;
et angelus appareat eis in somnis dicens:*

Nolite redire ad Herodem,

*et cetera. Postea non revertentibus ad Herodem
sic dicat:*

Gens Judaea properet,
ut Herodem audiat,
et praestet consilium
de re quae me sauciat!
Rex Herodes anxius
ignorat quid faciat,
cum a tribus regibus
se lusum inspiciat.

*Veniat Archisynagogus cum suis, cui dicat
Herodes:*

Tu, magister, aperi
prophetarum edita,
si qua sunt de puero
a prophetis tradita;
nam a te fideliter,
re mihi exposita,
se monstrabunt proprii
cordis abscondita.

Respondeat Archisynagogus:

Tu Bethlehem, terra Juda,

*et cetera. Deinde Herodes iratus dicat ad
milites suos:*

Ite, ite pariter

[534](Archisynagogus' prophecy continues: "You are not the least among the princes of
Judaea, For from you will come forth a ruler Who will rule my people Israel." See the
Fleury Herod play, l. 58. This is an established Christmas antiphon.)

With sword in hand;	manu juncta gladio;
Do not let tenderness of age	aetas adhuc tenera
Spare any child.	nulli parcat filio.
On the contrary, let every mother weep,	Immo mater quaelibet
Bereft of the child at her breast, 540	nudo fleat gremio,
So that vengeance may be mine	ut de nato puero
On this newborn son!	mihi detur ultio!

Let the soldiers go and slay the children, whose mothers must mourn and lament thus:	*Vadant milites et interficiant pueros, quorum matres sic lugeant et lamententur:*

Alas, alas, alas!	Heu, heu, heu!
Why does the savage disposition of Herod	Mens Herodis effera
Stir bitter wars 545	cur in nostra viscera
Against our flesh?	bella movet aspera?
Alas, alas, alas!	Heu, heu, heu!
What crimes have they committed,	Quae aetas adhuc tenera
They who are still of tender age,	[matris] sugens ubera
Sucking at [their mothers'] breasts? 550	perpetravit scelera?
Alas, alas, alas!	Heu, heu, heu!
Such distressing sorrow,	Iste dolor anxius,
While the accursed sword pierced through	dum transegit impius
The innocent ones!	innocentes gladius!
Alas, alas, alas! 555	Heu, heu, heu!
Sweet child,	Proles adhuc tenera,
Because of you, a wretched mother	per te mater misera
Will descend into the infernal regions!	descendet ad infera!
Alas, alas, alas!	Heu, heu, [heu!]
The joy of my life, 560	Mihi vitae gaudium,
My son, now my torment,	fili, nunc supplicium,
You will be the means of my death!	mortis eris ostium!

Afterward let Herod be gnawed to pieces by worms, and leaving his throne a dead man let him be received by the devils with much rejoicing among them. And let Herod's crown be placed on his son Archelaus. When he is reigning, let an angel appear in the night to Joseph, saying:	*Postea Herodes corrodatur a vermibus, et excedens de sede sua mortuus accipiatur a diabolis multum congaudentibus. Et Herodis corona imponatur Archelao filio suo. Quo regnante, appareat in nocte angelus Joseph dicens:*

Take the mother and son, and go into Egypt.	Accipe matrem et filium, et vade in Egiptum.

[543-62](This mourning sequence is sometimes referred to as *Ordo Rachelis,* in honor of the biblical mother named Rachel who mourns the death of the slaughtered Innocents [Matthew 2:18 and Jeremiah 31:15].)

[563]*go into Egypt:* The text is apparently confused here. In the Bible, the Holy Family are instructed to flee into Egypt ("*fuge in Egyptum*," Matthew 2:13) before the slaughter of the Innocents. After Herod's death, they are told to go into the land of Israel ("*vade in terram Israel*," Matthew 2:20). Even after this, however, the Holy Family are in danger from Archelaus, and so live in remote Galilee.

Let Mary say, going before the ass:	*Praecedens Maria asinum dicat:*
As a mother I am ready to endure all hardships while avoiding peril	Omnia dura pati vitando pericula nati
To my son; now I will go, do you be my companion.	Mater sum praesto; iam vadam, tu comes esto.

565

[563]S.D. *going before the ass:* The Latin seems to require that Mary lead the beast of burden, although in medieval iconography she usually rides. See the York Flight into Egypt in Part III, below.

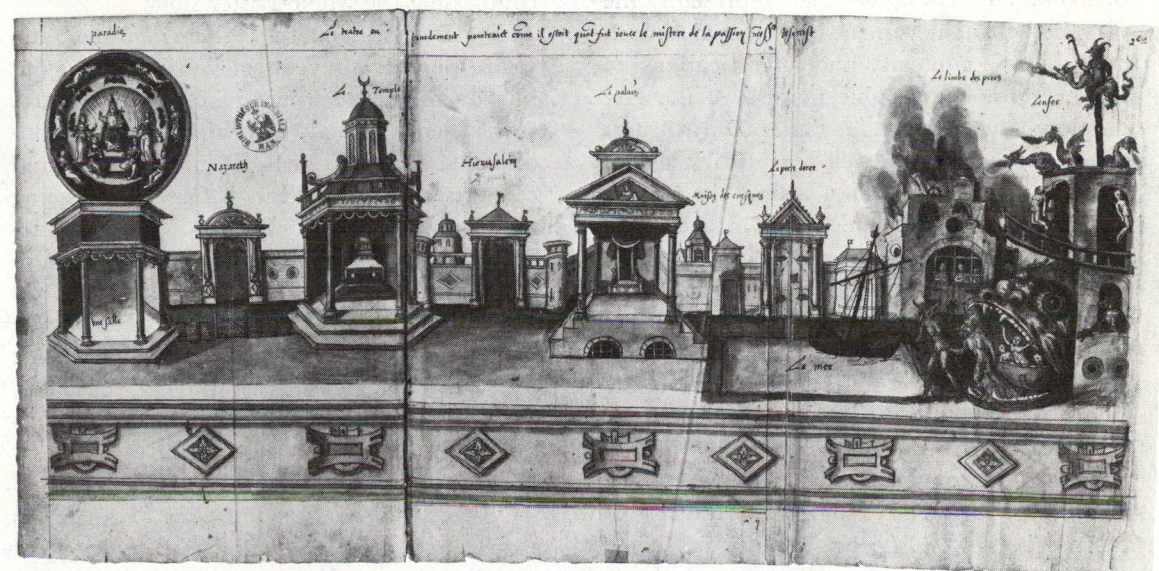

8. THE PASSION PLAY
(LUDUS DE PASSIONE)
FROM BENEDIKTBEUERN

Like the Benediktbeuern *Christmas Play,* the Benediktbeuern *Passion Play* represents the very highest achievement of medieval church drama. Its complexity and sophistication are all the more remarkable in view of the late development of drama for Easter. During most of the eleventh and twelfth centuries, as we have seen, Easter was not a time for adventurous expansion in the dramatic arts. The Visit to the Sepulchre was frequently performed on Easter Sunday, but remained short and conventional in most instances. The events of Good Friday, the day of the Crucifixion, proved especially resistant to dramatic treatment, perhaps because the liturgical ceremonies for that day—the darkening of the church, the intoning of Christ's reproaches to the people, the burial of the cross or the host in a sepulchre—were deeply moving in themselves without dramatic amplification. Indeed, when Passion drama finally came into being in the late twelfth century, it may have been sung on Easter Sunday rather than on Good Friday. That is, it may have been conceived of as the prelude to a dramatization of the Resurrection rather than as an outgrowth of the Good Friday liturgy. The Benediktbeuern *Passion Play* is followed in the *Carmina Burana* manuscript by a complex Resurrection play (omitted here for lack of space). Similarly, the Montecassino *Passion Play* from twelfth-century Italy, a long fragment extending from Judas' betrayal of Christ to the Crucifixion, may originally have begun with the Entry into Jerusalem and continued through Christ's resurrection and appearance to his disciples. Passion drama thus seemingly originated as part of an extensive artistic conception encompassing the whole Easter story.

The Benediktbeuern *Passion Play* not only spans the crucial events of Passion Week, but introduces earlier scenes of Christ's ministry. Christ, entering at first alone, gathers his disciples to him, heals a blind man, and converts a rich publican before commencing his triumphant procession into Jerusalem accompanied by a rejoicing crowd. We see also Christ's raising of Lazarus from the tomb and a remarkably extensive dramatization of the life and conversion of Mary Magdalene. We see Mary's life in sin, her buying cosmetics, her evil companionship, and her struggle with the counsels of the angel and the devil—precursors, like the same figures appearing to the shepherds in the *Christmas Play,* of the abstractions of later medieval allegorical morality drama. Her purchasing of ointment to anoint Christ's feet is a transformed version of her profane dealing in cosmetics and an anticipation of the anointing of Christ's dead body in the *Resurrection Play.* Christ's betrayal, trial, and crucifixion are based closely on Scripture. The second greatly elaborated focus of this play is the lament of the Virgin Mary at the foot of the cross. In his imaginative treatment of both Marys, the author makes extensive use of the German vernacular to add lyric intensity and relevance for his audience. For acting space the whole interior of the church

Text based on Munich, Staatsbibl., ᴍs lat. 4660, Carmina Burana saec. xiii, fol. 107ʳ–112ᵛ, as checked against the facsimile prepared by Bernhard Bischoff (Munich, 1967). It has been edited by Young, *Drama of the Medieval Church,* ɪ, 518–33, and by others.

must have been necessary. An opening procession brings into simultaneous view Pilate with his wife and escort, Herod with attendants, the chief priests, the merchant and his wife, and Mary Magdalene, each of whom must take his or her place on stations arranged about the playing space. In addition there are presumably stations for the house of Simon, the Last Supper, the Garden of Gethsemane, and Golgotha.

The Passion Play
(Ludus de Passione)
From Benediktbeuern

First let Pilate and his wife be brought forth, with soldiers, into their place; then Herod with his soldiers; then the chief priests; then the merchant and his wife; then Mary Magdalene.

Pilate entered [with Jesus into the praetorium; then he said to him: You are the king of the Jews. He (Jesus) answered: You say that I am king. Jesus therefore went forth from the praetorium carrying a crown (of thorns) and purple garment; and when it had been put on, they all shouted: Let him be crucified, for he has made himself the son of God. *Verse:* Then Pilate said to them: Shall I crucify your king? The chief priests answered: We have no king but Caesar.]

Then let the Lord advance alone to the seashore to call Peter and Andrew, and let him find them fishing; and let the Lord say to them:

Follow me, and I will make you fishers of men.

They say:

Primitus producatur Pilatus et uxor sua cum militibus in locum suum; deinde Herodes cum militibus suis; deinde pontifices; tunc mercator et uxor sua; deinde Maria Magdalena.

Ingressus Pilatus [cum Jesu in praetorium; tunc ait illi: Tu es rex Judaeorum. Respondit: Tu dicis quia rex sum. Exivit ergo Jesus de praetorio portans coronam et vestem purpuream; et cum indutus fuisset, exclamaverunt omnes: Crucifigatur, quia filium Dei se fecit. *Versus:* Tunc ait illis Pilatus: Regem vestrum crucifigam? Responderunt pontifices: Regem non habemus nisi Caesarem.]

Postea vadat Dominica Persona sola ad litus maris vocare Petrum et Andream, et inveniat eos piscantes; et Dominus dicat ad eos:

Venite post me, faciam vos piscatores hominum.

Illi dicunt:

[1]*Pilate entered:* a Lenten responsory sung by the choir, presumably while Pilate and the rest march in procession to their respective stations in the church. In addition to separate stations for Pilate, Herod, the chief priests, the merchant, and Mary Magdalene, stations appear to be required for Simon the Pharisee's house, the Last Supper (acted in silent tableau), the Garden of Gethsemane with the Mount of Olives near by it, and the cross. There must also be some representation of Lazarus' tomb, hell, and a place to hang Judas.

[2](See Matthew 4:19 and Mark 1:17. The fishing is presumably very stylized in presentation, and is set near the point at which Jesus has entered the church alone following the opening procession.)

What you wish, Lord, we will perform,
And will henceforth comply with your
    desire.

Then let the Lord go toward Zacchaeus, and let a
blind man encounter him on the way:

Lord Jesus, son of David, have mercy on
    me.   5

Let Jesus answer:

What do you wish that I shall do unto you?

The blind man:

Lord, that I may see.

Let Jesus say:

Receive your sight, for your faith has made
    you whole.

When these things are done, let Jesus proceed on
to Zacchaeus, and call him from a tree:

Zacchaeus, make haste and come down, for
    today I must abide at your house.

Let Zacchaeus say:

Lord, if I have taken anything from any
    man by fraud, I restore him fourfold.   10

Let Jesus answer:

Today salvation is come to this house,
    forasmuch as you also are a son of
    Abraham.

Jesus comes.

When the Lord drew near [to Jerusalem, he

Domine, quid vis, haec faciemus,
Et ad tuam voluntatem protinus adimple-
mus.

Postea vadat Dominica Persona ad Zacheum,
et obviet ei caecus:

Domine Jesu, fili David, miserere mei.

Jesus respondeat:

Quid vis ut faciam tibi?

Caecus:

Domine, tantum ut videam.

Jesus dicat:

Respice, fides enim tua salvum te fecit.

His factis, Jesus procedat ad Zacheum, et
vocet illum de arbore:

Zachee, festinans descende, quia hodie in
    domo tua oportet me manere.

Zacheus dicat:

Domine, si quid aliquem defraudavi,
    reddo quadruplum.

Jesus respondeat:

Quia hodie huic domui salus facta est,
    eo quod et tu sis filius Abrahae.

Jesus venit.

Cum appropinquaret Dominus [Jerosoli-

5-8(See Luke 18:38–42.)

9-11(See Luke 19:5–9. Zacchaeus was a corrupt, rich publican or tax collector who was so anxious to see Jesus that he climbed into a sycamore tree to see over the crowd. The tree may have been represented in this play by a pillar, located at the commencement of the intended route of Jesus' triumphal entry into Jerusalem.)

12-16Antiphons and hymns for the Palm Sunday procession, sung by the choir. Jesus, entering at first alone, gradually collects a large group of followers who escort him with elaborate festivity and rejoicing. Perhaps Jesus is to ride on a representation of an ass's colt; the custom of using such figures flourished in the Middle Ages, especially in Germany. The gates of Jerusalem through which Jesus enters are possibly represented by the entrance to the choir (cf. the Fleury Herod, l. 14 s.d.). Presumably some of those persons in the procession take their places in the choir before the commencement of the Mary Magdalene episode, l. 17.

sent two of his disciples saying: Go into the village that is over against you, and you will find an ass's colt tied, whereon no man ever yet sat; loose him and bring him to me. If anyone questions you, say: The Lord has need. Releasing the animal they brought it to Jesus and cast upon it their garments, and he sat upon it. Many spread their garments in the way, others strewed branches from the trees, and they that followed cried: Hosanna, Blessed is he that comes in the name of the Lord; Blessed is the kingdom of our father David. Hosanna in the highest. Have mercy on us, son of David.]

And:

When the populace had heard [that Jesus came to Jerusalem, they took palm branches, and went out to meet him; and the boys cried out, saying: This is he who is destined to come for the deliverance of the people, this is our salvation and the redemption of Israel; how great is this one whom thrones and dominions come to meet! Fear not, daughter of Zion; behold your king comes to you sitting on an ass's colt, as it is written. Hail, king, creator of the world, you who have come to redeem us!]

And the boys, strewing fronds and garments:

The Hebrew boys [bearing olive branches met the Lord crying and saying: Hosanna in the highest.]

Again the boys:

[The Hebrew boys strewed garments in the way, and cried saying: Hosanna to the son of David! Blessed is he that comes in the name of the Lord.]

Again:

Glory, praise, [and honor be to you, Christ our king, our saviour!]

mam, misit duos ex discipulis suis dicens: Ite in castellum quod contra vos est, et invenietis pullum asinae alligatum, super quem nullus hominum sedit; solvite et adducite mihi. Si quis vos interrogaverit, dicite: Opus Domino est. Solventes adduxerunt ad Jesum et imposuerunt illi vestimenta sua, et sedit super eum. Alii expandebant vestimenta sua in via, alii ramos de arboribus exsternebant, et qui sequebantur clamabant: Hosanna, benedictus qui venit in nomine Domini; benedictum regnum Patris nostri David. Hosanna in excelsis. Miserere nobis, fili David.]

Et:

Cum audisset [populus quia Jesus venit Jerosolimam, acceperunt ramos palmarum, et exierunt ei obviam; et clamabant pueri dicentes: Hic est qui venturus est in salutem populi, hic est salus nostra et redemptio Israel; quantus est iste cui throni et dominationes occurrunt! Noli timere, filia Sion, ecce rex tuus venit tibi sedens super pullum asinae, sicut scriptum est. Salve, rex, fabricator mundi, qui venisti redimere nos!]

Et pueri prosternentes frondes et vestes:

Pueri Hebraeorum [tollentes ramos olivarum obviaverunt Domino clamantes et dicentes: Hosanna in excelsis].

Item pueri:

[Pueri Hebraeorum vestimenta prosternebant in via, et clamabant dicentes: Hosanna filio David! Benedictus qui venit in nomine Domini.]

Item:

Gloria laus [et honor tibi sit, rex Christe, redemptor!]

15

Then let a Pharisee come, and invite Jesus to dinner:

Rabbi, which is to say "master," I beg that
　you will dine with me today.

Let Jesus answer:

Let it be as you have requested.

Let the Pharisee say to his servant:

Go quickly,
Set benches　　　　　　　　　　　　　　20
At table for a banquet,
That all may be pleasing.

Let Mary Magdalene sing:

The world's pleasure is sweet and agreeable,
Its society is delightful and elegant.
There are allurements of the world for which
　I long　　　　　　　　　　　　　　25
To feel passionate excitement, not to shun
　its wanton joys.
I'll lay down my life for worldly enjoyment;
I'll serve the cause of temporal pleasure.
I'll pamper my body, caring for nothing
　else;
I'll deck it out in an array of brilliant
　finery.　　　　　　　　　　　　　　30

Now let Mary go with [her] young women to the merchant, singing:

Merchant, bring me your [very best] wares
In return for much money that I'll give you,
And some perfumes, too, if you have them;
For I wish to anoint this becoming body.

Tunc veniat Phariseus, et vocet Jesum ad cenam:

Rab[b]i, quod interpretatur magister, peto
　ut mecum hodie velis manducare.

Jesus respondeat:

Fiat, ut petisti.

Phariseus dicat ad servum:

Ite citius,
praeparate sedilia,
ad mensae convivia,
ut sint placentia.

Maria Magdalena cantet:

Mundi delectatio　　dulcis est et grata,
Eius conversatio　　suavis et ornata.
Mundi sunt deliciae,　quibus aestuare

Volo, nec lasciviam　eius devitare.

Pro mundano gaudio　vitam terminabo;
Bonis temporalibus　ego militabo.
Nil curans de ceteris　corpus procurabo,

Variis coloribus　　illud perornabo.

Modo vadat Maria cum puellis ad mercatorem cantando:

Mihi confer, venditor,　　species emendas
Pro multa pecunia　tibi iam reddenda,
Si quid habes insuper　odoramentorum;
Nam volo perungere　corpus hoc
　decorum.

17–130(See Luke 7:36–50 for the account of Jesus' being anointed by an unnamed sinful woman at the house of Simon the Pharisee. This scene was frequently conflated with a later banquet at the house of Simon the leper in Bethany, just before the commencement of Passion Week, during which, according to John 12:1–8, Mary Magdalene, sister of Lazarus, anointed Christ's feet with costly ointment. The point here is the "waste" of expensive ointment; Mary is not described as a sinner. This conflation of two incidents gave rise to the tradition of Mary Magdalene as a fallen woman atoning for her sins. Medieval tradition also interpreted Mary's use of cosmetics and ointment, in both her profane and sacred expressions of love, as anticipations of her visit to Christ's sepulchre on Easter.)

23(Presumably the center of attention now shifts to Mary Magdalene at her station and then at the merchant's stall, accompanied by her young female companions. Simultaneously, at Simon's station the servant continues to prepare for the banquet. By line 97, when Mary comes seeking Jesus at Simon's house, Jesus and his disciples are already dining.)

Let the merchant sing:

Here's the best merchandise! Look at this   35
    sheen!
These go well with your handsome
    features.
These are sweet-smelling; if you try
    them,
You'll surpass all other fleshly desire.

Mary Magdalene:

Merchant, give me rouge
To redden my cheeks,   40
That I may entice young men
With the thoughts of love.

Again:

Hey, look at me,
You young men.
Let me give you pleasure.   45

Again:

Dashing young men ought
To love attractive women.
Love lifts up your spirits
And gives you a vision of sublime glory.

Again:

Hey, look at me,   50
You young men,

and so on. Again:

Hail to you, world, that you are
Thus rich in pleasures!
I will be your subject,
Always secure in your love.   55
Hey, look at me,

*and so on. Then let her go to sleep, and let an
angel sing:*

O Mary Magdalene, I proclaim news to
    you:

Mercator can[tet]:

Ecce merces optimae!   prospice
nitorem!
Hae tibi conveniunt   ad vultus
decorem.
Hae sunt odoriferae;   quas si
comprobaris,
Corporis flagrantiam   omnem
superabis.

Maria Magdalena:

Chramer, gip die varwe mier,
diu min wengel roete,
da mit ich di jungen man
an ir danch der minnenliebe noete.

Item:

Seht mich an,
jungen man.
Lat mich eu gevallen.

Item:

Minnet, tugentliche man,
minnekliche vrǎwen.
Minne tuǒt eu hoech gemǔt
unde lat euch in hochen eren schǎuven

Item:

Seht mich an,
junge man,

et cetera. Item:

Wol dir werlt, daz du bist
also vreudenreiche!
Ich wil dir sin undertan
durch dein liebe immer sicherlichen.
Seht mich an,

*et cetera. Postea vadat dormitum, et angelus
cantet:*

O Maria Magdalena,   nova tibi
nuntio:

---

[56]s.d. *go to sleep:* Presumably Mary is back at her own station, which is provided with a couch.
Apparently, the devil is in attendance on Mary, along with the good angel; although the
devil doesn't speak, he exits l. 87.

At the lodging of Simon sits feasting	Simonis hospitio hic sedens convivatur
Jesus, the Nazarene,	Jesus ille Nazarenus,
Filled with grace and virtue, 60	gratia virtute plenus,
Who alleviates the sins of the people.	qui relaxat peccata populi.
Multitudes acknowledge him the saviour of the world.	Hunc turbae confitentur salvatorem saeculi.

Let the angel retire, and let Mary arise singing: *Recedat angelus, et surgat Maria cantando:*

The world's pleasure [*etc.*]   Mundi delectatio.

Then let the lover approach, and let Mary greet him; and when they have talked a little, let Mary sing to the young women:

Tunc accedat amator, quem Maria salutet; et cum parum locuntur, cantet Maria ad puellas:

Well, then, my dear young friends,	Wol dan, minneklichev chint,
Let's go see the merchandise. 65	schäwe wier chrame.
Let's buy color there,	Chauf wier di varwe da,
To make us beautiful and attractive.	di uns machen schoene unde wolgetane.
He who loves me	Er muez sein sorgen vri,
Must be free from cares.	der da minnet mier den leip.

Again let her sing: *Iterum cantet:*

Merchant, give me rouge [*etc.*]   70   Chramer, gip di varwe mier.

Let the merchant answer: *Mercator respondeat:*

I'll give you a cosmetic, good	Ich gib eu varwe, deu ist guôt,
And worthy of praise.	dar zuoe lobelich.
It'll make you truly beautiful and	Deu eu machet reht schoene unt dar zuoe
Exquisitely lovely.	vil reht wunechliche.
Here you are, take it; 75	Nempt si hin, hab ir si;
There's nothing like it.	ir ist niht geleiche.

When she has received the cosmetic, let her go to sleep. [The angel:]

Accepto ungento, vadat dormitum. [Angelus:]

O Mary Magdalene [*etc.*]   O Maria Magdalena.

And let him disappear. Then let Mary rise and sing:

Et evanescat. Tunc surgat Maria et cantet:

The world's pleasure [*etc.*]   Mundi delectatio.

63(See ll. 23–30 above.)

63s.d. *the lover:* The devil evidently uses Mary's lover to argue his case, thereby undoing for a time the good angel's counsel. The party of young lovers returns once again to the merchant's stall.

70(See ll. 39–42 above.)

77(See ll. 57–62 above. Mary has again presumably returned to the couch at her station.)

78(See ll. 23–30 above.)

And let her then fall asleep once again, and let the angel come singing as above, and again let him disappear. [Mary Magdalene:]

Alas! my past life, life full of evil deeds:
Unclean current, deadly fountainhead! 80
Alas, what shall I do, wretched creature,
    full of sins,
I who am rich in the unchaste filth of my
    vices!

Let the angel say to her:

I say to you: There is joy among the angels of
    God over one sinner that repents.

Mary:

Hence, worldly adornments, splendor of
    attire!
Flee from me at once, shameful lovers! 85
Why did I consent to be born, I who
    deserve to be defiled
And branded by all manner of accusations?

Then let her put aside her worldly attire and put on a black mantle; and let the lover withdraw, and the devil. Let [Mary] go to the merchant:

Tell us, young merchant,
If you will sell this ointment,
Say for what price you will give it. 90
Alas, how great is our sorrow!

Let the merchant answer:

If you want this ointment so much,
You will pay one talent of gold;
Otherwise you will carry away nothing.
It is the best. 95

And let the choir sing:

She approached his feet.

When she has received the ointment, let her proceed to the Lord, singing, weeping:

Et iterum postea obdormiat, et angelus veniat cantando ut supra, et iterum evanescat. [Maria Magdalena:]

Heu! vita praeterita,   vita plena malis:
Fluxus turpitudinis,   fons exitialis!
Heu, quid agam misera,   plena
    peccatorum,
Quae polluta polleo   sorde vitiorum!

Angelus dicat sibi:

Dico tibi: gaudium est angelis Dei super
    una pec[c]atrice paenitentiam agente.

Maria:

Hinc ornatus saeculi,   vestium
    candores!
Protinus a me fugite,   turpes amatores!
Ut quid nasci volui,   quae sum
    defoedanda,
Et ex omni genere   criminum notanda?

Tunc deponat vestimenta secularia et induat nigrum pallium; et amator recedat, et diabolus. [Maria] veniat ad mercatorem:

Dic tu nobis, mercator juvenis,
hoc ungentum si tu vendideris,
dic pretium, pro quanto dederis.
Heu, quantus est noster dolor!

Mercator respondeat:

Hoc ungentum si multum cupitis,
unum auri talentum dabitis;
aliter nusquam portabitis.
Optimum est.

Et chorus cantet:

Accessit ad pedes.

Accepto ungento, vadat ad Dominicam Personam cantando, flendo:

[83](See Luke 15:7.)

[96]s.d.: Mary goes now to the station representing Simon's house, where Jesus and the disciples are already dining. The account in Luke 7:38 specifies that at this point the sinful woman "began to wash his feet with tears, and did wipe them with the hairs of her head, and kissed his feet, and anointed them with the ointment."

Shamefully sick, I shall go to the
 physician
Seeking medicine. It remains that I
 tender
Offerings of tears and lamentations of the
 heart to him
Who, as I hear, heals all sinners.   100

Ibo nunc ad medicum	turpiter
aegrota	
Medicinam postulans.	Lacrimarum
vota	
Huic restat ut offeram,	et cordis
plangores,	
Qui cunctos, ut audio,	sanat
peccatores.	

Again:

Jesus, saviour of my soul,
Let me be commended to you,
And free me from my misdeed
Which the world has brought me to!

Item:

Jesus, troest der sele min,
la mich dir enpholhen sin,
unde loese mich von der missetat,
da mich deu werlt zuoe hat braht!

Again:

I will not leave your feet   105
Until you release me from my sins
And from the heinous misdeed
Which the world has brought me to.

Item:

Ich chume niht von den fůezzen dein,
du erloesest mich von den sunden mein,
unde von der grôzzen missetat,
da mich deu werlt zuǒ hat braht.

Let the Pharisee say to himself:

This man, if he were a prophet, would know
 who and what manner of woman this is
 that touches him, that she is a sinner.

Loquatur Phariseus intra se:

Si hic esset propheta, sciret utique quae et
 qualis illa esset, quae tangit eum, quia
 peccatrix est.

And let Judas say:

To what purpose is this waste? For this [oint-
 ment] might have been sold for much,
 and given to the poor.   110

Et dicat Judas:

Ut quid perditio haec? Potuit enim hoc
 venundari multo, et dari pauperibus.

Let Jesus sing:

Why do you trouble this woman? For she
 has wrought a good work upon me.

Jesus cantet:

Quid molesti estis huic mulieri? Opus
 bonum operata est in me.

Immediately again:

Simon, I have something to say to you.

Item statim:

Simon, habeo tibi aliquid dicere.

Simon Peter:

Master, say on.

Simon Petrus:

Magister, dic.

Jesus says:

Dicit Jesus:

110(See Matthew 26:8–10 and Mark 14:4, where all the disciples are reported to be indignant
at the seeming waste of expense. Only John 12:4–6 attributes the resentment to Judas, thereby
giving rise to a medieval tradition "motivating" the betrayer of Christ.)

112–22(See Luke 7:40–48 for Christ's parable.)

There was a certain creditor who had
Two debtors, to whom he made a loan in
    hopes of earning a profit: 115
The one owed five hundred denarii, the
    other fifty.
But it came to pass that these same men
    were completely destitute;
When they had nothing wherewith to pay,
    he forgave them all.
Which of them therefore loved him most?

    Let Simon answer:

He, I suppose, to whom he gave most.   120

    Let Jesus say:

Your wisdom has rightly judged.

    Again let Jesus sing to Mary:

Woman, your sins are forgiven; your faith
    has made you whole; go in peace.

    *Then let Mary rise and go with lamentation,
singing:*

Alas, alas, that I was born!
I have deserved God's wrath,
Who gave me soul and body.   125
Woe me, wretched woman!

Alas, alas, that I was born,
When God's wrath is kindled at me!
Take heed, good men and women,
For God will judge your soul and body.   130

    Meantime let the disciples sing:

This Pharisee tried to obstruct the fountain
    of mercy.

    *Then let Jesus proceed to the raising of Lazarus,
and here let Mary Magdalene and Martha run
to meet him weeping for Lazarus, and let Jesus
sing:*

Our friend Lazarus sleeps. Let us go and
    awake him out of sleep.

Debitores habuit   . quidam creditorum
Duos, quibus credidit   spe denariorum:

Hic quingentos debuit,   alter
    quinquagenos.
Sed eosdem penitus   fecerat egenos;

Cum nequirent reddere,   totum
    relaxavit.
Quis eorum igitur   ipsum plus amavit?

    Simon respondeat:

Aestimo quod ille plus,   cui plus
    donavit.

    Jesus dicat:

Tua sic sententia   recte judicavit.

    Item Jesus cantet ad Mariam:

Mulier, remittuntur tibi peccata; fides tua
    salvam te fecit, vade in pace.

    *Tunc Maria surgat et vadat lamentando,
cantans:*

Awe, auve, daz ich ie wart geborn!
Han ich verdient Gotes zorn,
der mir hat geben sele unde leip.
Awe, ich vil unseleich wip!

Owe, awe, daz ich ie wart geborn,
suvenne mich erwechet Gotes zorn!
Wol uf, ir gueten man unde wip,
Got wil rihten sele unde leip.

    Interea cantent disci[puli]:

Phariseus iste fontem misericordiae co-
    nabatur obstruere.

    *Tunc vadat Jesus ad resuscitandum Lazarum,
et ibi occurrant Maria Magdalena et Martha
plorantes pro Lazaro, et Jesus cantet:*

Lazarus, amicus noster, dormit. Eamus et
    a somno resuscitemus eum.

132–36 (See John 11:1–44 for the raising of Lazarus.)

Then let Mary Magdalene and Martha, weeping, sing:

Lord, if you had been here, our brother
    would not have died.

And, on their falling silent, let the clergy sing thus:

Seeing the sisters of Lazarus grieving, the
    Lord wept at the tomb in the presence
    of the Jews, and cried out.

And let Jesus sing:

Lazarus, come forth!   135

And let the clergy sing:

And he that had been as dead came forth,
    bound hand and foot with graveclothes.

Meantime let Judas go with haste and seek opportunity for betraying, saying:

O chief priests,
O men of great understanding,
I wish to betray Jesus to you.

Let the chief priests answer him:

O Judas, if you will now betray Jesus to us,   140
We will pay you thirty pieces of silver.

Let Judas answer:

I will betray Jesus, believe me;
Give me what you promised.
Send the crowd with me;
Lead Jesus away cautiously.   145

Let the chief priests sing:

Betray Jesus hastily.
Take this crowd with you,
And proceed courageously;
Betray Jesus swiftly.

Then let Judas give the Jews a signal, singing:

Tunc Maria Magdalena et Martha flendo cantent:

Domine, si fuisses hic, frater noster non
    fuisset mortuus.

Et sic tacendo clerus cantet:

Videns Dominus flentes sorores Lazari, ad
    monumentum lacrimatus est coram
    Judeis, et clamabat.

Et Jesus cantet:

Lazare, veni foras!

Et clerus cantet:

Et prodiit ligatus m[anus] et p[edes], qui
    f[uerat] q[uasi] m[ortuus].

Interim Judas veniat festinando et quaerat oportunitatem tradendi, dicens:

O pontifices,
o viri magni consilii,
Jesum volo vobis tradere.

Cui pontifices respondeant:

O Juda, si nobis Jesum iam tradideris,
triginta argenteis remuneraberis.

Judas respondeat:

Jesum tradam, credite;
rem promissam mihi solvite.
Turbam mecum dirigite;
Jesum caute deducite.

Pontifices cantent:

Jesum tradas propere.
Hanc turbam tecum accipe,
et procede viriliter;
Jesum trade velociter.

Judas tunc det Judaeis signum cantans:

136 s.d.: Presumably the chief priests occupy a station of their own to which Judas now hastens.
The crowd at Lazarus' tomb must retire, preparing perhaps to become the crowd of Jews accompanying Judas to Gethsemane. While the conspiracy scene is going on, Jesus and his
disciples apparently gather at an appropriate station to act out a tableau of the Last Supper;
see l. 150 s.d.

Whomever I shall kiss, the same is he; hold him fast.

Then let the crowd of Jews follow Judas with swords and clubs and lanterns until at length they reach Jesus. Meantime let Jesus do as is the custom for The [Last] Supper. Thereafter let him take four disciples with him, and say to the others who remain:

Sleep now and take your rest.

Then let him go to pray, and say to the four disciples:

My soul is exceeding sorrowful, even unto death. Watch here and pray, that you enter not into temptation.

Then let him ascend to the Mount of Olives, and, with bended knees, looking up to heaven, let him pray saying:

Father, if it be possible, let this cup pass from me. The spirit indeed is willing, but the flesh is weak. Your will be done.

When this is done, let him return to the four disciples, and find them sleeping, and say to Peter:

Simon, do you sleep? Could you not watch one hour with me? Tarry here, while I go pray.

Then let him go again to pray as before. Then once again let him come to the disciples and find them sleeping, and say to them:

Tarry here.

And again let him say:

Father, if this cup may not pass away [from me], except I drink it, your will be done.

Then let him return to the disciples and sing:

---

150 Quemcumque osculatus fuero, ipse est; tenete eum.

Tunc turba Judaeorum sequatur Judam cum gladiis et fustibus et lucernis donec ad Jhesum. Interea Jesus faciat ut mos est in cena. Postea assumat quatuor discipulos, et ceteris dicat, quos relinquit:

Dormite iam et requiescite.

Deinde vadat orare, et dicat quatuor discipulis:

Tristis est anima mea usque ad mortem. Sustine[te] hic et orate, ne intretis in temptationem.

Tunc ascendat in montem Oliveti, et flexis genibus respiciens caelum plorat dicendo:

Pater, si fieri potest, transeat a me calix iste. Spiritus quidem promptus est, caro autem infirma. Fìat voluntas tua.

Hoc facto, redeat ad quatuor discipulos, et inveniat eos dormientes, et dicat Petro:

Simon, dormis? Non potuisti una hora vigilare mecum? Manete hic, donec vadam et orem.

Postea vadat iterum orare ut antea. Tunc iterato veniat ad discipulos et inveniat eos dormientes, et dicat ad eos:

155 Manete hic.

Et iterum dicat:

Pater, si non potest hic calix transire, nisi bibam illum, fiat voluntas tua.

Tunc redeat ad discipulos et cantet:

150s.d.: In the swiftly-moving simultaneous action of the betrayal, Judas and the crowd of Jews march in procession toward Gethsemane during the time that Jesus prays and admonishes the sleeping disciples. (The phrase "at length"—*donec*—may indicate the need for occupying time until Jesus is ready.) The Mount of Olives must offer a means for Jesus to ascend, l. 152 s.d. It is presumably near the station representing the Garden of Gethsemane, where the disciples wait sleepily for their master.

151-57(See Matthew 26:38–46 and Mark 14:35–41.)

You could not watch one hour with me, you who used to protest you would die for my sake. Do you not see Judas, how he does not sleep, but hastens to betray me to the Jews? Rise, let us be going. Behold, he is at hand that is about to betray me.

Let Judas come to Jesus with the crowd of Jews, to whom let Jesus say:

Whom do you seek?

Let them answer him:

Jesus of Nazareth.

Let Jesus say:

I am he.   160

And let the crowd fall back. Again let Jesus say:

Whom do you seek?

The Jews:

Jesus of Nazareth.

Let Jesus answer:

I have told you that I am he.

Again:

If therefore you seek me, let these go their way.

Then let the apostles take flight, except Peter, and let Judas say [as he kisses Jesus]:

Hail, master.   165

Let Jesus answer him:

O Judas, why have you come?
You have committed great sin.
Having betrayed me to the Jews,
You lead me to the gallows
To be crucified.   170

Una hora non potuistis vigilare mecum, qui exhortabamini mori pro me. Vel Judam non videtis, quomodo non dormit, sed festinat tradere me Judaeis? Surgite, eamus. Ecce appropinquat, qui me traditurus est.

Veniat Judas ad Jesum cum turba Judaeorum, quibus Jhesus dicat:

Quem quaeritis?

Qui respondeant:

Jesum Nazarenum.

Jesus dicat:

Ego sum.

Et turba retrocedat. Item Jesus dicat:

Quem quaeritis?

Judaei:

Jesum Nazarenum.

Jesus respondeat:

Dixi vobis quia ego sum.

Item:

Si ergo me quaeritis, sinite hos abire.

Tunc apostoli dent fugam, excepto Petro, et Judas dicat:

Ave, Rabbi.

Jesus illi respondeat:

O Juda, ad quid venisti?
Peccatum magnum tu fecisti.
Me Judaeis traditum
ducis ad patibulum
cruciandum.

158–63 (See John 18:4–8.)

170 S.D.: Jesus is being led, bound, toward the station of the chief priests; Peter follows after, in the crowd.

And as Peter is following Jesus, let a maidservant say:	*Et Petro sequente Jhesum, una ancilla dicat:*
Truly you are one of them.	Vere tu ex illis es.
Let him say:	*Ipse dicat:*
I am not.	Non sum.
Again the maidservant:	*Item Ancilla:*
Truly you are one of them, for you are a Galilaean, you are one of them.	Vere tu ex illis es, nam et Galileus es, nam unus ex eis es.
Peter:	*Petrus:*
I do not know the man.	Non novi hominem.
[*The maidservant:*]	[*Ancilla:*]
Didn't I see him with you in the garden? 175	Nonne vidi te cum illo in horto?
[*Peter:*]	[*Petrus:*]
You don't know what you are saying.	Nescis quid dicis.
And let Jesus say:	*Et Jhesus dicat:*
Do you come out as against a thief with swords and staves to take me?	Tanquam ad latronem existis cum gladiis et fustibus comprehendere me,
and so on. And let Jesus be led to the chief priests, and let the choir sing:	*et cetera. Et ducatur Jhesus ad pontifices, et chorus cantet:*
The chief priests and [the Pharisees] were gathered together,	Collegerunt pontifices et,
[*and*] *so on. And let the chief priests sing and ponder what they ought to do:*	[*et*] *cetera. Et pontifices cantent et cogitent quid faciant:*
What are we to do, since this man makes many signs? If we discharge him thus, all will believe in him.	Quid facimus, quia hic homo multa signa facit? Si dimittimus eum sic, omnes credent in eum.
And let Caiaphas sing:	*Et Caiphas cantet:*
It is expedient for us that one man should die for the people, and that the whole nation not perish. 180	Expedit vobis ut unus moriatur homo pro populo, et non tota gens pereat.

[177](See Matthew 26:55–56 for the probable completion of Jesus' speech.)

[178–81](A Palm Sunday processional antiphon, here sung antiphonally by the choir and chief priests as Jesus is being marched to trial.)

Let the clergy sing:

Therefore from this day on they meditated [to kill him],

and so on. Then Jesus is led to Pilate, and the Jews say:

This fellow said, Destroy this temple, and in three days I will raise it up.

Let Pilate answer:

What accusation do you bring against this man?

Let the Jews answer:

If he were not a malefactor, we would not have delivered him up to you.

Pilate:

Take him yourselves, and judge him according to your law.   185

The Jews:

It is not lawful for us to put any man to death.

Then let Jesus be led to Herod, who says to him:

Are you the man of Galilee?

Jesus however remained silent; and let Herod say again:

Whom do you make yourself out to be?

Let Jesus not answer one word to him. Then let Jesus be clothed in a white garment, and they lead Jesus back to Pilate. Then Pilate and Herod come together and kiss one another. And let Jesus come to Pilate, and the latter says:

I find no cause for death in this man.

Let the Jews say:

Clerus cantet:

Ab ipso ergo die cogitaverunt,

et cetera. Postea ducitur ad Pilatum Jesus, et dicunt Judaei:

Hic dixit: Solvite templum hoc, et post triduum reedificabo illud.

Pilatus respondeat:

Quam accusationem affertis adversus hominem istum?

Judaei respondeant:

Si non fuisset hic malefactor, non tibi tradidissemus eum.

Pilatus:

Accipite eum vos, et secundum legem vestram judicate eum.

Judaei:

Nobis non licet interficere quemquam.

Postea ducatur Jesus ad Herodem, qui dicat ei:

Homo Galileus es?

Jesus vero tacebat, et Herodes iterum dicat:

Quem te ipsum facis?

Jesus non respondeat ei ad unum verbum. Tunc Jesus induitur veste alba, et reducunt Jhesum ad Pilatum. Tunc conveniunt Pilatus et Herodes, et osculantur invicem. Et Jhesus veniat ad Pilatum, et ipse dicit:

Nullam causam mortis invenio in homine isto.

Judaei dicant:

183–86(See John 18:29–31.)

187–89(See Luke 23:4–12.)

He is worthy of death.   190

    Then let Pilate say to Jesus:

Are you the king of the Jews?

    Jesus answers:

You say that I am king.

    Let Pilate say:

Your own nation and your chief priests
    delivered you unto me.

    Let Jesus say slowly:

My kingdom is not of this world.

    Again let Pilate say:

Whom therefore do you make yourself to
    be?   195

    *Let Jesus however remain silent, and let Pilate say
    to the chief priests:*

What shall I do with Jesus of Nazareth?

    The Jews:

Let him be crucified!

    Pilate:

I will therefore chastise him and release him.

    *Then Jesus is led to the scourging. Then let Jesus
    be clothed in a purple garment and crown of thorns.
    Then let the Jews say mockingly to Jesus:*

Hail, king of the Jews!

    And let them strike him with their hands:

Prophesy to us, who is it that has struck
    you?   200

    *And let them lead him to Pilate, to whom let
    Pilate say:*

Reus est mortis.

    Tunc Pilatus dicat ad Jhesum:

Tu es rex Judaeorum?

    Jhesus respondit:

Tu dicis, quia rex sum.

    Pilatus dicat:

Gens tua et pontifices tui tradiderunt te
    mihi.

    Jesus paulatim dicat:

Regnum meum non est de hoc mundo.

    Pilatus item dicat:

Ergo quem te ipsum facis?

    Jesus vero taceat, et Pilatus dicat ad pontifices:

Quid faciam de Jesu Nazareno?

    Judaei:

Crucifigatur!

    Pilatus:

Corripiam ergo illum et dimittam.

    *Tunc ducitur Jhesus ad flagellandum. Postea
    Jhesus induatur veste purpurea et spinea
    corona. Tunc dicant Judaei blasphemando ad
    Jesum:*

Ave, rex Judaeorum!

    Et dent ei alapas:

Prophetiza, quis est, qui te percussit?

    Et ducant eum ad Pilatum, cui Pilatus dicat:

---

[190](See Matthew 26:66.)

[191–94](See John 18:33–36.)

[198](See Luke 23:16.) S.D.: For the scourging, the soldiers probably tie Jesus to a pillar and
strike him.

Behold the man.

The Jews:

Crucify, crucify him!

Pilate:

Take him yourselves and crucify him. I find
no fault in him.

The Jews:

If you release this man, you are not Caesar's
friend.

Again:

Everyone that makes himself a king speaks
against Caesar.   205

Pilate:

Whence are you?

Jesus gives no answer. Pilate:

Do you not speak to me?

Again:

Don't you know that I have power to
crucify you, and power to release you?

Let Jesus answer:

You would have no power against me,
except it were given you from above.

Pilate to the Jews:

Shall I crucify your king?   210

Let the Jews answer:

Let him be crucified! For he makes himself
the son of God.

*Let Pilate, washing his hands with water, say to
the Jews:*

I am innocent of the blood of this
[righteous] man; see you to it.

Ecce homo.

Judaei:

Crucifige, crucifige eum!

Pilatus:

Accipite eum vos, et crucifigite. Nullam
causam invenio in eo.

Judaei:

Si hunc dimittis, non es amicus Caesaris.

Item:

Omnis qui se facit regem, contradicit
Caesari.

Pilatus:

Unde es tu?

Jhesus tacet. Pilatus:

Mihi non loqueris?

Item:

Nescis quia potestatem habeo crucifigere
te, et potestatem dimittere te?

Jesus respondeat:

Non haberes in me potestatem, nisi
desuper tibi datum fuisset.

Pilatus ad Judeos:

Regem vestrum crucifigam?

Judaei respondeant:

Crucifigatur! Quia filium Dei se fecit.

*Pilatus lavans manus suas cum aqua et dicat
ad Judeos:*

Innocens ego sum a sanguine huius; vos
videritis.

[201-10] (See John 19:5–15.)

[212] (See Matthew 27:24.)

Then let Jesus be led to be crucified. Then let Judas go singing to the chief priests, and, having thrown down the denarii, let him say weeping:

I repent me vehemently that I sold Christ
    for this silver!

Again:

Take your [money] back again, take it back!
    I wish to die, not live on. As atonement
    I will end my life by hanging myself.

The chief priests:

What is that to us, Judas Iscariot? See you
    to it.   215

Immediately let the devil come, and lead Judas to the hanging, and let him be hanged. Then let the women come from afar off, lamenting aloud, to weep for Jesus, to whom let Jesus say:

Daughters of Jerusalem, weep not for me,
    but weep for yourselves.

Then let Jesus be hanged on the cross, and let there be a title:

Jesus of Nazareth, the king of the Jews.

Then let the Jews answer Pilate, singing:

We have no king but Caesar.

Pilate:

What I have written, I have written.

Then let the Mother of our Lord come, lamenting, with John the Evangelist, and, approaching the cross, she looks upon the crucified one:

Alas, alas, what grief is mine today and
    forever!   220
Alas, how I now look upon
The dearest child that ever

Tunc Jesus ducatur ad crucifigendum. Tunc Judas ad pontifices vadat cantando, et rejectis denariis, dicat flendo:

Paenitet me graviter quod istis argenteis
    Christum vendiderim!

Item:

Resumite vestra, resumite! Mori volo et
    non vivere. Suspendi supplicio volo
    perdere.

Pontifices:

Quid ad nos, Juda Scariotys? Tu videris.

Statim veniat diabolus, et ducat Judam ad suspendium, et suspendatur. Tunc veniant mulieres a longe plorantes flere Jhesum, quibus Jhesus dicat:

Filiae Jerusalem, nolite flere super me, sed
    super vos ipsas.

Tunc Jesus suspendatur in cruce, et titulus fiat:

Jesus Nazarenus, rex Judaeorum.

Tunc respondeant Judaei Pilato cantantes:

Regem non habemus nisi Caesarem.

Pilatus:

Quod scripsi, scripsi.

Tunc veniat Mater Domini lamentando cum Johanne Evangelista, et ipsa accedens crucem respicit crucifixum:

Awe, awe mich hiŭt unde immer we!

Awe, wie sihe ich nu an
daz liebiste chint, daz ie gewan

[213-15](See Matthew 27:3–10 for the suicide of Judas. While this episode takes place, Jesus is simultaneously being prepared for the crucifixion.)

[216](See Luke 23:28.)

[218-19](See John 19:15, 22.)

In this world any woman brought forth.
Alas, my lovely child's body!

Again:

I will look upon it forever.   225
Have pity, women and men.
Let your eyes look there
And observe the true torment.

Again:

Was there ever such torment
And such terrible anguish?   230
Now perceive the torment, agony, and
    death,
And the entire body red with blood.

Again:

Let my little one live for my sake
And let me die, his mother,
Mary, most pitiable woman.   235
What use are life and body to me?

*Again the Mother of the Lord, with every sort of
lamentation, bewailing greatly, cries out to the
weeping women, complaining vehemently:*

Weep, faithful souls, weep, good
    sisters,
That your lamentation and your tears
May abundantly illustrate your sorrow.
Let motherly hearts bewail the
    misfortunes of the mother Mary.   240
I grieve as a mother, I who am accustomed
    to be called
Blessed in having given birth.
Sad spectacle of cross and spear!
Deeply it brands a hidden sign of the cross
On the mind of the virgin.   245
This is what he said, what he
    foretold,
The blessed prophet; here is the sword

ze dirre werlde ie dehain wip.
Awe mines shoene chindes lip!

Item:

Den sihe ich iemerlichen an.
Lat iuch erbarmen, wip unde man.
Lat iwer ougen sehen dar
unde nemt der marter rehte war.

Item:

Wart marter ie so iemerlich
unte also rehte angestlich?
Nu merchet marter, not unde tot,

unde al den lip von blůte rot.

Item:

Lat leben mir daz chindel min
unde toetet mich, die muter sin,
Mariam, mich vil armez wip.
Zwiu sol mir leben unde lip?

*Item Mater Domini omni ploratu exhibens
multos planctus et clamat ad mulieres flentes
et conquerendo valde:*

Flete, fideles animae,   flete sorores
    optime,
ut sint multiplices   doloris indices
planctus et lacrimae.
Fleant materna viscera,   Mariae matris
    vulnera.
Materne doleo,   quae dici soleo

felix puerpera.
Triste spectaculum   crucis et lanceae!
Clausum signaculum   mentis virgineae
profunde vulnerat.
Hoc est quod dixerat,   quod
    prophetaverat
felix praenuntius;   hic ille gladius

237–49 (This lyric is a sample of the Lament of the Virgin or *Planctus Mariae,* a popular medieval genre quite independent of the drama. See Young, *Drama of the Medieval Church,* I, 498–99,
for a continuation of the text. This particular *planctus* and that beginning at l. 258 were frequently employed by dramatists.)

That transfixes me.
While at the bowed head [*etc.*]

*Then let Mary embrace John and sing, holding
him in her arms:*

My John, raise a lament,   250
Grieve with me, my new son,
Son by the new covenant
Of mother and maternal aunt.
It is a time for lamenting;
Let us render   255
A profound sacrifice of tears
To the dying Christ.

*And for a long while let her remain quietly seated,
and again let her rise and sing:*

Not previously acquainted with grief,

*and so on. Then again let her embrace John and
sing:*

My John, [raise a lament],

and so on. John to her:

O Mary, do not weep so   260
For your child;
Allow me now to weep
For you, who wish to die.

*And let John hold Mary under the arms, and let
Jesus say to her:*

Mother, behold your son.

Then let him say to John:

Behold your mother.   265

*Then let Mary and John go from the cross, and
let Jesus say:*

I thirst.

*At once let the Jews come holding forth a sponge
with vinegar, and let Jesus drink:*

qui me transverberat.
Dum caput cernu[um].

*Tunc Maria amplexetur Johannem et cantet,
eum habens inter brachia:*

Mi Johannes, planctum move,
plange mecum, fili nove,
fili novo foedere
matris et materterae.
Tempus est lamenti;
immolemus intimas
lacrimarum victimas
Christo morienti.

*Et per horam quiescat sedendo, et iterum
surgat et cantet:*

Planctus ante nescia,

*et cetera. Tunc iterum amplexetur Johannem
et cantet:*

Mi Johannes,

et cetera. Johannes ad haec:

O Maria, tantum noli
lamentare tuo proli;
sine me nunc plangere,
quae vitam cupis cedere.

*Et Johannes teneat Mariam sub humeris, et
dicat Jesus ad eam:*

Mulier, ecce filius tuus.

Deinde dicat ad Johannem:

Ecce mater tua.

*Postea vadant Maria et Johannes de cruce,
et Jesus dicat:*

Sitio.

*Statim veniant Judaei praebentes spongiam
cum acceto, et Jesus bibat:*

---

[258](Another independently-composed *Planctus Mariae*. See Young, I, 496–98, for the text.
These *planctus*, if reproduced here in full, would give an idea of the remarkably extensive
elaboration of Mary's role in this Passion play, as earlier with Mary Magdalene.)

[259](See ll. 250–57 above.)

It is finished.

Then let Longinus come with a spear and pierce his side, and let him say clearly:

I will pierce him to the heart,
That the pain of his torment may end.

Jesus, perceiving the end, says crying out:

Eli, Eli, lama sabachthani? My God, my
    God, why have you forsaken me?   270

And bowing his head, let him give up the ghost. Longinus:

Truly, this was the son of God.

Again [in German]:

Truly, this was the son of the true God.

Again:

He has done a miracle on me,
Since I have received my sight once again.

And let one of the Jews say to the other Jews:

He calls upon Elijah; let us go and see if
    Elijah comes and frees him or not.   275

Another Jew:

If you are the son of God, come down off
    the cross.

Again another:

He saved others; himself he cannot save.

The song of Joseph of Arimathea:

Jesus [was] of divine nature,
A man without any sin
Who guiltless was martyred;   280
If anyone henceforth should find him
Nailed upright on the cross,
That would certainly be no honor for a
    king.

Consummatum est.

Tunc Longinus veniat cum lancea et perforet latus eius, et ille dicat aperte:

Ich wil im stechen ab daz herze sin,
daz sich ende siner marter pin.

Jesus videns finem dicit clamando:

Ely, Ely lama sabactany. Deus, Deus
    meus, ut quid dereliquisti me?

Et inclinato capite, emittat spiritum. Longinus:

Vere filius Dei erat iste.

Item:

Dirre ist des waren Gotes sůn.

Item:

Er hat zaichen an mir getan,
wan ich min sehen wider han.

Et unus ex Judaeis dicat ad Judaeos:

Eliam vocat iste; eamus et videamus, si
    Elias veniens liberet eum an non.

Alter Judaeus:

Si filius Dei es, descende de cruce.

Item alter:

Alios salvos fecit, seipsum non potest
    salvum facere.

Cantus Joseph ab Arimathia:

Jesus von gotlicher art,
ein mensch an alle sunde,
der an schuld gemartret wart;
ob man den vurbaz vunde,
genaglet an dem chriuze stan,
daz wer niht chuneges ere.

278-93(These speeches are found somewhat later in the MS and probably are not part of the play. How the play ends is not clear; possibly a burial scene was meant to follow.)

Therefore you should permit me
To bury him, O honorable judge.   285

    Pilate:

Whosoever desires honest things,
It is fitting
That he be granted them.
You request that I allow you
To bury Jesus Christ;   290
I am well disposed to that.
Since he is so dear to your heart,
Take him according to your inclination.

Darumb sölt ir mich in lan
bestaten, rihter herre.

    Pilatus:

Swer redelicher dinge gert,
daz stet wol an der maze,
daz er ir werde wol gewert.
Du bitest, daz ich laze
dich bestaten Jhesum Christ:
daz main ich wol in gůte
Seit er dir so ze herzen ist,
num in nach dinem můte.

PART THREE

The Corpus Christi Cycle

The Corpus Christi Cycle

BY "CORPUS CHRISTI CYCLE" we mean a type of drama performed in England (especially in the north) from about 1378 until the latter half of the sixteenth century, consisting of a number of episodes or "pageants" drawn from sacred history. As the word "cycle" suggests, these dramas were comprehensive in scope, usually extending from the Fall of Lucifer to the Last Judgment. The individual episodes were often presented by the various craft guilds (i.e., tradesmen's associations) of a town or city in cooperation with ecclesiastical authorities and with religious guilds. The cycles derive their name from the Feast of Corpus Christi, a holy day occurring sixty days after Easter, on which the cycles were usually, though not always, performed. They are also known as mystery plays because they were performed by various trades or "mysteries"; compare the Latin *ministerium* and French *mystère* or *métier*. This term is of Continental origin, however, and was not current in medieval England, whereas the cycles were frequently referred to in their own time as Corpus Christi plays.

Four complete or nearly complete English cycles are extant: the York cycle, consisting of forty-eight pageants; the Towneley cycle (so named for an eighteenth-century owner of the manuscript) that was almost surely performed at Wakefield in Yorkshire, consisting of thirty-two pageants; the misnamed *Ludus Coventriae* cycle, sometimes called the Hegge cycle after a manuscript owner but now generally called the N Town cycle (from a reference in the text to the unnamed place of performance), acted probably in Lincolnshire or Norfolk and consisting of forty-three pageants; and the Chester cycle, consisting of twenty-four pageants. Other surviving portions of cycles include two long pageants from a cycle of New Testament plays performed at Coventry, one pageant each from Norwich and Newcastle-on-Tyne, and a few other fragments from unidentified localities. Three cyclical plays also survive in the vernacular language of Cornwall, although they differ markedly in their contents from the northern English cycles. So do a number of cyclical plays found on the Continent.

In order to understand the English Corpus Christi cycles, we must know something of their history: how church drama of the twelfth century evolved uncertainly toward cyclical form, why the Feast of Corpus Christi came into being, why the feast attracted to itself a cyclical drama, what factors determined the form and content of the Corpus Christi cycles, and the like. We will also need to examine the contradictory and perplexing evidence concerning the staging of these cycles.

The transition from church drama of the twelfth century to Corpus Christi cycle drama of the fourteenth and fifteenth centuries is not so easy to explain as was once thought. Scholarship used to assume a direct relationship between the two. Drama of the church, it was argued, evolved into drama performed outside the church and then into drama performed away from the church, in the town. The process was one of steady "secularization": the drama first outgrew the liturgy and church building, and then cast off its clerical auspices in favor of civic control. Secularization naturally involved translation of plays into vernacular languages; according to this hypothesis, once this process had taken place, the cycles could be created simply by gathering together individual plays and performing them on one single grand occasion. The various plays of the church calendar, placed in biblical sequence and translated into the vernacular, resulted (with some omissions) in the divine history of the world from the Creation to the Day of Judgment.

This hypothesis is defective in several ways. "Secularization" is a misleading term, since the Church cooperated fully in the production of the Corpus Christi plays and evidently regarded them as instructive religious drama. The use of the vernacular language did not necessarily imply secular development, as we have already seen in Part II. Nor did church drama advance steadily toward outdoor cyclical drama; instead, it tended to remain static during the thirteenth and early fourteenth centuries. Most important of all, church drama did not dramatize many of the stories that were to be included in the cycles. To be sure, church drama featured complex and sophisticated plays for Christmas and Easter. Church drama also provided versions of the Raising of Lazarus, the story of Adam and Eve (in *Adam*), and the Procession of Prophets (also in *Adam*). Other than that, however, church drama offered no precedent for many episodes commonly found in the English cycle plays: Noah's Flood, Abraham and Isaac, Moses and Pharaoh, Christ's Presentation in the Temple, his Temptation in the Wilderness, the episode of the Woman Taken in Adultery, the Last Judgment, and still others. Conversely, church drama provided many episodes not generally included or not suitable for inclusion in the cycles, such as the story of Daniel, the St. Nicholas plays, and the conversion of St. Paul. Still other episodes from church drama, such as those in honor of the Virgin Mary, appeared occasionally but not consistently in the cycles. Even in those comparatively few instances where the cycles dramatized events found earlier in church drama, moreover, the cycle versions were not translated from any known church play. Although influences did occasionally persist, as in the Easter Visit to the Sepulchre and in the ranting character of King Herod, church drama did not serve as a direct source for the English civic outdoor theater of the later Middle Ages.

Why did church drama not advance more rapidly toward a comprehensive cycle during the thirteenth and early fourteenth centuries? One partial answer is that church drama was still linked to its own liturgical calendar, and was thus occasional in nature. Even the most independent of the plays studied so far, the Anglo-Norman *Adam*, was linked by its responsories to a particular Sunday before Lent (Sexagesima). Complex Easter plays incorporating the events of the entire Easter season were still generally tied to Easter. Christmas drama experienced the same sort of restriction. Other feast days of the church calendar offered opportunities for dramatic performances, but evidently most churches and monasteries were content to use a very limited number of these occasions. We find quite a number of saints' days commemorated in drama in Western Europe, but the plays for these occasions were not all gathered together at any single location. The collections of Fleury and Benediktbeuern are exceptionally large and varied, yet even they do not begin to represent a complete cycle of plays. A more typical religious community might limit its dramatic activities to Christmas, Easter, and one or two saints' days particularly relevant to that community. Such occasional celebrations became part of the annual rhythm of worship, and needed no complete cycle of plays to explain the significance of any particular part. Another factor hindering the development of cycles in church drama was official hostility toward clerical acting outside the church building. Church drama performed in conjunction with the liturgy was tolerated and even encouraged, but the kind of play represented by *Adam* seems to have encountered opposition. Partly for this reason, church drama was limited in its expansion out-of-doors until it could make use of the resources of the civic guilds coming into new prominence during the latter half of the fourteenth century.

This is not to say, however, that church drama made no movement toward cyclical form during the twelfth, thirteenth, and early fourteenth centuries. Plays for Christmas and Easter attained considerable length. *Adam*, performed apparently on Sexagesima Sunday in the twelfth century, moved toward cyclical form by combining the Old Testament episodes of the fall of man and the murder of Abel with a procession of prophets announcing the advent of Christ. Since the *Adam* manuscript is a fragment, we do not know how much further the play may have continued. Similar combinations of Old and New Testament material evidently took place at Riga on the Baltic Sea in 1204, and at Cividale, Italy, in 1298 and again in 1303. The last of these performances took place on Whitsunday, the seventh Sunday after Easter, during an especially clement season of the year for outdoor performance. The discovery of the advantages of warm weather may have given new impetus to cyclical drama, especially since indoor theaters were unknown.

Virtually all scholars agree that the establishment of the Feast of Corpus Christi, or the Body of our Lord, was of central importance to the flourishing of cyclical drama in the fourteenth century. The history of the Feast of Corpus Christi begins in 1215, with the promulgation of the dogma of transubstantiation asserting Christ's real presence in the mass. Local celebrations of a feast in honor of the mass, or Eucharist, took place at Liège in 1246. Pope Urban IV gave expression to the new interest in the Eucharist by declaring, in 1264, the need for a new holy day to celebrate Christ's Last Supper and the Eucharist that Christ had instituted. The Last Supper was already one of the major events of Holy Week, to be sure, but in that position the joyous event of Christ's gift of his body and blood was overshadowed by the agony of the Crucifixion. Holy Week made too many other demands, and thus afforded insufficient opportunity for a proper observance of the Eucharist. Urban's proposal, though delayed by his own death, was finally implemented by Clement V in 1311. The date set aside for the feast, the Thursday after Trinity Sunday and hence eleven days after Whitsunday, came during a relatively uneventful period in the church calendar when the weather was cooperative and the days were longest. (Corpus Christi falls between May 23 and June 24, depending on the date of Easter; because of inaccuracies in the old calendar during the late Middle Ages, however, the original dates were actually equivalent to June 4–July 6 on a modern calendar.) The papal bull instituting the feast in 1311 specified that it was to include a procession honoring the sacred host, although detailed arrangements for the procession were left up to local communities.

Why did Corpus Christi day attract to itself a cycle of plays during the late fourteenth century, especially in northern England? Scholars are divided: some see the relationship between plays and feast as theologically meaningful, while others see the relationship chiefly as one of practical convenience. Those who argue a theological connection between the plays and Corpus Christi day attribute broad significance to the feast. As Jerome Taylor has observed, the lessons for matins during the octave of the feast (the eight days beginning with Corpus Christi day) stressed the connection between the miracle of the Eucharist and other miracles in divine history: the Creation, the sparing of Abraham's son Isaac, Moses' deliverance from Pharaoh, the Incarnation, and so on. Thus, viewed from the perspective of Corpus Christi day, the divine history of the world became a history of God's wonders. The episodes of this divine history were bound to one another in a causal and sequential relationship; its chief personages could be seen as exempla of obedience or, conversely, of disobedience to God's will; and its Old Testament heroes were also figural types or foreshadowings of Christ. (See Jerome Taylor and Alan Nelson, eds., *Medieval English Drama,* Chapter 8.)

On the other hand, those who are skeptical of a close doctrinal connection between the plays and Corpus Christi day point out that the plays give little emphasis to the institution of the Eucharist (it is consciously omitted from the Wakefield cycle and is perhaps inadvertently missing from York), that the plays were occasionally performed on other holy days, such as Whitsunday or St. Anne's day (July 26) or virtually any Sunday in midsummer, and that, accordingly, Corpus Christi day may simply have been the most convenient date available during the period of the longest days of the year. As Rosemary Woolf argues (in *The English Mystery Plays,* Chapter 4), Corpus Christi day offered the special advantage of independence from the Church's liturgical calendar. It came at the end of the church year, since the Christian story really starts in the fall with Advent and Christmas and concludes in the spring with the Resurrection and Ascension. Moreover, Corpus Christi day celebrated an event (the Last Supper) that had already been observed in its chronological place during Holy Week. As a matter of practical convenience, then, the day could serve as the occasion for a wide-ranging celebration of the entire divine history of the world.

What factors determined the form and content of the Corpus Christi cycle? Again, scholars are divided among those who see the cycle as an organic whole shaped by patterns of foreshadowing and fulfillment, and those who stress the pragmatic effects of historical experiment and accretion. V. A. Kolve, in a study entitled *The Corpus Christi Play,* presents a case for figural interpretation. He first defines the "common structure" of the Corpus Christi play as consisting of those episodes found in all or virtually all the extant English cycles. The episodes of first priority are the Fall of Lucifer, the Creation and Fall of Man, Cain and Abel, Noah and the Flood, Abraham and Isaac, the Nativity sequence, the Raising of Lazarus, the Passion and Resurrection sequences, and Doomsday. Of only slightly lesser centrality are the story of Moses, the Procession of Prophets, Christ's Baptism, the Temptation in the Wilderness, and the Assumption and Coronation of the Virgin. Kolve finds these central episodes to be linked to one another by an elaborate series of foreshadowings, or figural relationships. Adam's fall, for example, both confirms the earlier event (or "antetype") of Lucifer's fall and prefigures the temptation of Christ through which the original wrong will be righted. The murder of Abel, the near-sacrifice of Isaac by his father Abraham, and the slaughter of the Innocents by Herod all prefigure Christ's agony on the cross. Moses' deliverance of the Israelites anticipates Christ's baptism and the harrowing of hell. The raising of Lazarus looks forward not only to Christ's resurrection but to that of the elect on the Day of Judgment. Each parallel of this sort explores both a similarity and an essential contrast between human imperfection and divine perfection. For example, even though Noah's flood prefigures both Christ's baptism and God's eventual destruction of the world, Noah is a weak and complaining mortal, henpecked by a woman more resembling Eve than the Virgin Mary.

Kolve contends that this figural pattern, found at the core of all the English cycle plays, was derived from the teaching of the medieval Church Fathers and in particular from a scheme of favorite iconographical subjects known as the Seven Ages of the World. This scheme, repeatedly illustrated in stained-glass windows, stone carvings, and other mediums, depicts the first three ages of the world as the time of natural law in which the chief figures are Adam (together with Cain and Abel), Noah, and Abraham and Isaac. The fourth and fifth ages, devoted to Moses and the prophets, are the time of written law. The sixth age, the time of grace, extends from Christ's birth to the present. The seventh age, an extension of the age of grace, is the time of Doomsday. By means of such a pattern, argues Kolve, the medieval Church interpreted the Bible for its members, giving them a patristic framework or "arch of scholasticism" through which they were to understand scriptural history. The cumulative wisdom of the Church Fathers thus determined which stories from the Old and New Testaments and apocryphal legend were to be emphasized, and how they were to be viewed in relation to one another. Accordingly, we find the same canon of favorite stories repeated again and again not only in the visual artifacts of the Church but in sermons and in religious plays.

Rosemary Woolf, without denying the importance of patristic tradition, arrives at the same canon of favorite subjects in medieval cycle drama by means of a more historical and pragmatic explanation. Even before the establishment of the Feast of Corpus Christi, she notes, early cycles at Riga and Cividale were experimenting with various proportions of Old and New Testament subjects. One tentative solution was to present the story of the Fall of Man as a prelude to the Nativity (as in *Adam* and the Cividale play); another was to include a considerable amount of Old Testament material (as at Riga). The dramatists inductively discovered various points at which they could conveniently break off a dramatization of the Old Testament. One point was at the end of 2 Chronicles, where the continuous narrative of the first books of the Bible ends; an earlier point was found at the end of Exodus, and one still earlier at Chapter 22 of Genesis. The considerable number of possibilities resulted in a variety of choice. The extant English cycles represent only one list of possible subjects, as we can see by comparing them with the Cornish cycles or with Continental plays. Figural schemes derived from religious iconography certainly offered important models for dramatists to imitate, but the Seven Ages of the World scheme was only one among several available. Dramatists might wish instead to choose their subjects on the basis of the Apostles' Creed, which names the major events of divine history from the Creation and the Incarnation to the Crucifixion and Burial, the Harrowing of Hell, the Resurrection, the Ascension, and so on. Another well-known figural scheme available to dramatists was an allegorization of the seven canonical "hours," or daily offices of worship, relating each hour to a biblical figure who offered praise to God: Adam and Eve, Abel, Noah, Abraham, the prophets, the apostles, and the congregation of the faithful on Judgment Day. Still another series, incorporated in a homily of Gregory the Great and read in part on Septuagesima, described various Old and New Testament figures as laborers entering the vineyard in successive stages: Adam to Noah, Noah to Abraham, Abraham to Moses, Moses to the Nativity, and the Nativity to Judgment Day.

All scholars, whether they stress unity of form or historical variety in the Corpus Christi play, whether they see Corpus Christi day as doctrinally important or as a convenient day in midsummer for dramatic performance, agree that the patristic tradition of the Church had a decisive influence on the selection of episodes and on the figural relationship of those episodes to one another. This patristic tradition reached the cycles through many channels. Latin and vernacular church plays, even though they did not serve as direct sources for the cycles, treated a number of familiar episodes and presented many characters who were to reappear in the cycles. Of more direct use as sources were collections of vernacular sermons, such as John Mirk's popular *Festial, The Northern Homily Cycle,* and *The South English Legendary.* Legendary stories about biblical figures were to be found in the so-called "New Testament Apocrypha," including the Gospel of Nicodemus and the Gospel of Pseudo-Matthew. Nondramatic treatments of favorite stories were popular and often available in the vernacular: for example, *The Northern Passion, The Stanzaic Life of Christ,* and *The Meditations on the Life and Passion of Christ.* Encyclopedic works, such as the *Cursor Mundi, The Scholastic History* of Peter Comestor, and *The Golden Legend* of the Dominican friar Jacobus de Voragine, retold many stories found in the works already named. The medieval religious lyric also often incorporated popular legends. Furthermore, artifacts in the church building, such as carved roof bosses and misericords, rood screens, and stained-glass windows, may have influenced dramatic performances and were almost certainly influenced in turn by those performances. Nor should we underestimate the influence of the plays' contemporary environment. Local humor and place-name references abound; social commentary is often pointed. Proverbial lore and dialect make important contributions to tone and characterization. Folk elements appear in burlesque parodies of sacred events, in orgiastic cruelty used to mock a rejected god-figure, in the comic perversion of children's games such as hot cockles or blindman's buff, in gargantuan feasts, and in the motif of seasonal regeneration.

The rise of the Corpus Christi cycle during the fourteenth century was one manifestation of a larger movement in religious art of the Middle Ages toward what is known as the Gothic style. A primary characteristic of Gothic art was its focus on the example of Christ's humanity and suffering. Gothicism was to a considerable extent inspired by a new interest in popular education of the uneducated laity, under the aegis of the Franciscan and Dominican orders of friars. Emphasis on Christ's human agony brought religious experience closer to the lives of ordinary men and women. Religious art of the eleventh century and before, on the other hand, in the style generally known as Byzantine or Romanesque, had been more formal and restrained.

Medieval drama accordingly follows a line of development from Byzantine and Romanesque to Gothic, paralleling developments in other forms of religious art and in the teachings of the Franciscan and Dominican friars. During the period when church drama began, in the tenth century, much religious art was the work of scholars in various centers of ecclesiastical learning. The innovations introduced during this period into the liturgy (including dramatic performance) tended to be highly formal. Antiphons, tropes, and early dramatic ceremonials were essentially elaborations and decorations of a basic pattern. The effect is often similar to that of a typical Byzantine mosaic of the Madonna and Child—richly decorated and yet serenely stylized. Human emotion seems subordinated to design, to structural repetition, to a restrained harmony of the parts with the whole. Gothic art, on the other hand, turned increasingly to the agony and the ecstasy of religious experience, to the conflict between human carnality and divine sublimity. The builders of Gothic cathedrals, by juxtaposing grotesque gargoyles and lofty pinnacles, captured this dual spirit of the later Middle Ages. Gothic painters and sculptors sought similar expressive meaning in the contrast between coarse, realistically-portrayed shepherds and idealized, otherworldly angels. Above all, Gothic artists were drawn to Christ's suffering as a poignant demonstration of his compassion for mankind. The Corpus Christi cycles, with their tender depictions of Christ's birth amidst poverty and cold, and their gruesomely vivid renditions of the Crucifixion, abundantly reveal this Gothic emphasis on Christ's humanity.

Two further developments help explain the appearance of cyclical drama in late fourteenth-century England: the emergence of English as a national language after centuries of French domination, and the flowering of the medieval craft guilds. The newly-prosperous guilds were naturally drawn to the idea of midsummer festivals in which they could display their commercial might. At the same time, the craft guilds were closely tied to the Church and were prepared to join with ecclesiastical authorities in creating a midsummer show that was both civic and religious in nature. The Feast of Corpus Christi and its traditional procession, in which the sacred host was attended by representatives of town and Church, seems to have provided the ideal occasion for such a cooperative enterprise. Moreover, the guilds were able to provide nonclerical actors, thereby resolving the perplexing issue of clerical acting that seems to have hindered the expansion of religious drama for nearly two centuries. Since clerics were no longer required to act in outdoor plays, the Church relaxed its wariness toward outdoor performance and took an active part in the preparation of the new dramatic festivals. During the fourteenth and fifteenth centuries, the only vocal opposition to the drama came from extremist reformers (known as the Lollards) led by John Wycliffe.

In summary, the following elements seem to have helped shape the newly-emerging cyclical drama in the fourteenth century: the establishment of the Feast of Corpus Christi during a clement season in midsummer, the position of Corpus Christi day at the end of the liturgical year, the doctrinal relevance of Corpus Christi to the history of God's miracles from the Creation to Doomsday, the availability in church tradition of various lists of patriarchs who were seen as figural antetypes of Christ, the influence of carvings and paintings depicting favorite iconographical subjects, treatments of these same topics in sermons and in other literary forms including folk art, a new Gothic emphasis on popular religion for the laity stressing Christ's humanity and suffering, the consolidation of the English language, and the rise of the craft guilds.

When did the authorities responsible for Corpus Christi day decide to mount plays? Did the plays come into existence quite independently of the Corpus Christi procession, or was the procession an important first step?

Again, these questions are controversial. Hardin Craig (*English Religious Drama of the Middle Ages*) argues that the plays could not have achieved their high state of development if they had originated in a procession. Craig's argument is based, however, on the assumption that the plays grew directly out of earlier church drama—an assumption that, as we have seen, is highly questionable. Alan Nelson (*The Medieval English Stage: Corpus Christi Pageants and Plays*) argues the case for regarding the procession as a first step. Corpus Christi day was celebrated in England with processions as early as 1318, whereas the earliest recorded performance of an extant cycle is at York in 1378. Quite possibly, then, the cycles did not get under way until the procession had been growing for some decades. In this case we must examine more closely the dramatic potential of such a procession.

The Corpus Christi procession was essentially a festive parade in which the sacred host was carried through the city to the church, accompanied by civic and ecclesiastical representatives. Guild organizations naturally tended to use the occasion for purposes of ornate display. The carrying of three-dimensional images and the use of pageant wagons depicting biblical scenes in *tableau vivant* (that is, with silent and motionless actors in costume representing a single scene) became a common part of the procession. Although some processions of this sort may have been influenced by the performance of plays, it is also quite conceivable that the processions sometimes came first. In such instances, the guilds of a city would have been assigned particular themes from sacred history as the subjects for *tableau vivant* displays on individual pageant wagons. To make the pageant displays all the more impressive, the biblical scenes in *tableau vivant* may next have been provided with brief bits of dialogue. As Nelson points out, the Corpus Christi play from Innsbruck in 1391 is extremely short (only 756 lines in all) and may have been intended for performance in a moving procession. Another performance at Draguignan, France, in 1558, specifies that the speeches are to be numerous, brief, and spoken on the march with no play coming to a stop. Processions using live actors in *tableau vivant* to represent the divine history of the world were certainly common during the later fifteenth century, not only on the Continent but at Dublin and Hereford. This suggestive evidence does not prove conclusively, however, that all English Corpus Christi cycles began as processions and that they experimented with brief dialogue en route before turning to full-length dramatic production. Perhaps we are on safest grounds in assuming, with Rosemary Woolf, that different communities evolved different solutions, and that in some instances the procession may have been a first step whereas in other instances it was only a parallel or later development.

In any event, the Corpus Christi procession and the performance of a full-length cycle of plays could not feasibly be combined on a single occasion. Historical records suggest that these two functions were separated once the plays had become substantial in length. The procession, after all, was designed to honor the host. Persons in the procession were obliged to accompany the host to the church and venerate it there. If the host were placed at the head of a procession involving the performance of lengthy pageants, the final assemblage at the church would be intolerably delayed. If on the other hand the host were carried last, behind an entire dramatic production, the honoring of the host would come at the end of a very long day. Persons of civic importance marching in the procession would in either case not be able to see the dramatic performances. For these reasons, cities undertaking full-length plays evidently discovered they had to perform the plays on one occasion (sometimes over a period of several days) and the procession on a separate occasion. This move also entailed crucial decisions about the way in which the plays were to be staged. The solutions were basically of two types: performance on pageant wagons somewhat in the manner of the Corpus Christi procession, and stationary performance at a single fixed location.

Until recently, theatrical criticism has tended to pay too much attention to medieval descriptions of pageant wagons, and to assume without sufficient evidence that wagons were used for most if not all of the cycles. As we shall see, this widespread assumption is misleading. Still, the wagons did unquestionably exist. The Grocers of Norwich had in their inventory for 1565 a "pageant" or "howse of waynskott painted and builded on a carte with fowre whelys." Surmounting the house of wainscot was a square top, presumably supported by corner posts. Four or six horses were needed to draw this wagon. The Doomsday pageant of the York mercers, in 1433, similarly featured a four-wheeled wagon and a superstructure that included four iron posts at the corners of the wagon topped by a wooden roof. Curtains hung at the back and at both sides. An iron seat, supported from above by four ropes, enabled God to ascend into heaven. Another description of pageant wagons has survived in the *Breviary* of David Rogers, based on the recollections of his father who died about 1595. Rogers' account is, to be sure, second hand, chronologically very late, and somewhat contradictory in the several versions of it that have survived: one account mentions four wheels, another six. Rogers may, nevertheless, be correct in his description of a "higher room" where the players acted and a "lower room" where they appareled themselves. The lower room could have been the space between the wheels, covered by hangings to make a dressing room. The higher room, presumably on the bed of the wagon itself, was "open to the top, that all beholders might hear and see" the actors. By this, Rogers probably did not mean open to the sky but open at the front and perhaps on the sides. Contemporary illustrations from the Continent, especially those depicting an entry into Brussels of the Archduchess Isabella in 1615 and a Procession of Our Lady at Louvain in 1594, confirm the impression of a four-wheeled cart drawn by horses and featuring a platform some seven or eight feet above the ground, a superstructure (roof or canopy) supported by corner posts, and curtains to hide the area between the wheels. The Nativity "house" in the Brussels illustration is built to resemble the stable where Christ was born, complete with donkeys and cattle. Most of the illustrations indicate, however, that the wagons were sparing in their use of scenic effects.

From the play texts we gather that the pageant wagons must have been large enough to accommodate several actors and as many as two or three simultaneously-visible locales, since in some individual pageants the actors must journey from one locale to another. Wagons may even have been capable of representing more than one acting level; in the Chester Noah pageant, for example, God speaks to Noah from some high place "or in the cloudes, if it may be." Evidently the overhead canopy could sometimes accommodate machinery for ascents, descents, rising stars, and the like. Dramatic action did not always restrict itself to the pageant wagon, however. In the Chester pageant of Abraham and Isaac, the Expositor enters "riding." A well-known stage direction from the Coventry Christmas play specifies that King Herod "ragis in the pagond [pageant] and in the strete also." Glynne Wickham has suggested (in *Early English Stages,* I, 170–74) that the playing space may have been extended by the use of simple platform wagons wheeled into position next to the pageant wagons to serve as a sort of apron stage or extension. Possibly, this hypothesis is correct, although in general the ground level was more available and convenient.

Cycle plays were certainly performed on pageant wagons at Coventry. When Queen Margaret saw the plays there in 1457, she sat at the "station" where the plays were first performed in sequence. As each play finished its performance before Margaret, it moved on to another station where another audience awaited its turn to see and hear. Dugdale's famous description of the Corpus Christi day production at Coventry, compiled in 1656, confirms this picture of a truly processional production. The pageants, he says, "had Theaters for the severall Scenes, very large and high, placed upon wheels, and drawn to all the eminent parts of the City, for the better advantage of Spectators." Although Dugdale also asserts erroneously that the actors were friars, he seems to have based his remarks on eyewitness accounts. Other communities, notably Chester, seem to have produced their plays on pageant wagons in procession before a series of stationary audiences.

The difficulties involved in this kind of production were prodigious, however. We need to guard against the too-common assumption that the cycles were usually produced in this manner. Coventry had only about ten New Testament pageants, and probably limited the number of acting stations to three or four (despite Craig's contention that there were ten). Even with these restrictions, the Coventry cycle was nearly impossible to finish in one day. Queen Margaret, in 1457, saw "alle the pagentes pleyde save domesday, which might not be pleyde for lak of day." If the Doomsday pageant was omitted from the first acting station, the curtailment at subsequent stations must have been more drastic. Chester scheduled its plays over a three-day period, evidently because one day was insufficient. The time factor was a deterrent to processional staging, not only because the pageants were often numerous and long but because they were of unequal length; shorter pageants had to wait for longer pageants to finish at the stations ahead of them. Another difficulty in pageant-wagon production was casting. Each individual pageant had to have its own separate cast, even though twenty-seven Christs would then be required for the York cycle. (Doubling of parts was essentially banned by civic ordinances.) The Wakefield cycle would employ some 243 actors if performed in procession on individual pageant wagons.

These problems have led recent scholars to doubt whether the York cycle, among others, could possibly have been staged processionally as a full-length dramatic production. The cycle at York was always performed on a single day; yet the number of pageants ranged as high as fifty-seven, and the number of acting stations increased from twelve in 1417 to sixteen in 1554. Nelson concludes from this information that the York records must point to a Corpus Christi procession in *tableau vivant*, and that the actual dramatic text was performed apart from the procession at a single acting location— possibly even indoors. This position has been vigorously contested, however, by Alexandra Johnston and Margaret Dorrell (Leeds Studies in English, New Series, volumes 5 and 6), who marshal an impressive amount of evidence for public and processional staging of the York Cycle. Their tentative solution to the problem of length is to suggest that perhaps no more than thirty-two pageants were ever performed in any single year, even though more were available in the playbook.

Martial Rose hypothesizes (in *The Wakefield Mystery Plays*) that the Wakefield or Towneley cycle was acted at a fixed location. Rose's intriguing theory is that the pageant wagons of Wakefield, after having been drawn in procession through the city, were gathered together at a public square or cathedral close where they could serve individually as acting scaffolds for a production in the round. Distributed on the periphery of a large circle and simultaneously visible to the audience in the manner of earlier church drama, the wagon-scaffolds could represent heaven, hell, Pontius Pilate's hall, the platform of the chief priests, the house of the Last Supper, and the like. Heaven and hell, needed throughout the production, would presumably be elaborate and multi-leveled: heaven would provide a throne for God, with angels and musicians in attendance, while hell would feature a grotesque hell-mouth. Since on the other hand most wagons could easily be moved, they could be brought in and then removed as occasion demanded. Noah's ark would be a ship-like wagon, able to move freely across the acting arena. The considerable space in the midst of the wagons would afford room for the spectators, for the players as they crossed from one acting scaffold to another, for movable wagons like Noah's ark, and for occasional sequences of dramatic action on the ground level or *platea* ("the place").

We do not know that Rose's hypothesis of wagons in a circle is correct for Wakefield or for any other cycle, but we do have visual evidence that other medieval plays were sometimes staged in the round or partially in the round. Most notable, perhaps, is the staging diagram for *The Castle of Perseverance*, with its castle at the center and five acting scaffolds on the periphery of the "place" (see Part V). Staging diagrams in the round also survive for the Cornish *Ordinalia* and for a Cornish saint's play called *The Life of St. Meriasek*. A miniature painting by Jean Fouquet entitled "The Martyrdom of St. Apollonia" shows six scaffolds grouped side by side in a semicircle around an acting area; another Fouquet miniature on the Rape of the Sabine Women shows an extensive array of scaffolds on the periphery of a circle. Moreover, the Passion sequence of the N Town cycle unquestionably required an arena stage (though no staging diagram has survived), with a council house located in the midst of the acting area and scaffolds for heaven, hell, Pilate, the chief priests, Herod, and others on the periphery.

Another possible arrangement for performance at fixed locations was to allow the audience to move from one pageant to another, rather than moving the pageants past stationary audiences. The evidence for this kind of production is sparse but suggestive. In church drama the audience may often have moved from one scaffold to another, and in some plays of the later Middle Ages we find evidence of processions involving the audience; see particularly the Digby *St. Paul* in Part IV. When Elizabeth I came to Coventry in 1567 she visited in turn four Corpus Christi pageants at their fixed street locations, accompanied by a host of town dignitaries. Such an arrangement of mobile spectators was common in civic pageants and royal entries at London and elsewhere; perhaps some Corpus Christi cycles were produced in a similar manner.

The evidence suggests, then, that methods of production varied greatly from community to community and from year to year. Whatever the mode of production, cycle drama was a splendid affair. The Church offered a store of rich vestments, and the craft guilds supplied special costuming needs such as white leather tights for Adam and Eve or a gilded face for God. The actors were often professional and were well paid for their services. Boys usually played the parts of angels and sang as choristers. The riding of the "banns," or proclamations giving advance publicity, was an ornately festive occasion. Minstrels found occupation in the banns, in the Corpus Christi procession, and in the plays themselves, where the music sometimes underscored the liturgical ancestry of the occasion. Although rehearsals were few in number owing to the familiarity of the plays, costs were generally lavish.

Despite the splendor and cosmic design of this Corpus Christi drama, its critical history has not been a happy one. During most of the four hundred years that have elapsed since the late sixteenth century, when this drama first fell into disfavor, it has suffered from condescension, neglect, and scorn. How are we to account for and answer this long critical hostility? Why should we read this drama today, when it has been spurned for so many years? Let us answer the question in relation to comedy, since comedy has been a subject of particularly keen critical misunderstanding and disapproval. The nineteenth century and before, reacting against what it viewed as distasteful raucousness and indecorum, supposed comedy to be a part of the process of "secularization" by which the drama had rendered itself unfit for church performance and suitable only for banishment to the marketplace. To the nineteenth century, in other words, comedy was inimical to serious religious drama; it was intrusive and even blasphemous in tone. Furthermore, such comedy offended against Aristotelian precepts forbidding the mixture of comedy and serious action. Measured by such criteria, Corpus Christi drama (and other medieval drama as well) was bound to seem artistically deficient.

In recent years, however, critical rebellion against the Protestant and Whig-Liberal assumptions of Victorian culture has led to a new interest in medieval drama and its use of comedy. The tendency now is to see a deliberate unity of purpose in the juxtaposition of the sacred and the profane. The medieval Church, according to this view, made no attempt to brand comedy as sacrilegious or irrelevant to the daily lives of ordinary Christians. A comic vision of man's inadequacy enabled the spectators of medieval drama to identify with a Noah or a Joseph not unlike themselves, troubled in wedlock, aging, humbled by awareness of inadequacy, and above all harassed by doubts of divine purpose. Both Noah and Joseph are comic in their marital difficulties: Noah is henpecked, Joseph fears he has been cuckolded by his bride-to-be. Yet both men triumph over their comic weaknesses and doubts to become models of true faith for medieval spectators. In the same way, the disciples who flee ignominiously from Jesus' trial and then need to be convinced again and again of his resurrection are all the more sympathetic as characters because they are fallible and puzzled by God's mysteries. The comic juxtaposition of the birth of Christ and the sheep-stealing episode in the Wakefield Second Shepherds' Pageant, so daringly close to blasphemy, successfully dramatizes the contrast between Christ's perfect love for mankind and the fallen world into which he is born.

The villainous characters in the cycles are usually comic, although not in the same way as Noah or Joseph. The villains are self-blinded worldlings, brutally callous to human suffering and proud of their triumph over helpless innocence. The soldiers who slay the children at the time of Christ's birth, or who later prepare Christ for his crucifixion, make cruel games of their torturings: they mock Christ with a crown of thorns and play at blindman's buff with him, or profanely grumble about their difficulties in stretching Christ to fit the ill-made holes on the cross. King Herod bustles about with worldly insolence and laughs exultingly at the seeming success of his persecutions. Yet the last laugh is on these villains, for by their own evil deeds they undo themselves and hasten the time of man's salvation. This great irony pervades the entire cycle, and reassures us as audience that all will end according to God's plan; we perceive, in other words, that the intention of the cycle as a whole is comic. Herod has good reason to fear that he will be overthrown by a mere lad, for God has promised that he will throw down the mighty from their seats. The angels announcing Christ's birth make their appearance to simple shepherds, to signify that the meek shall inherit the earth.

Unaware of the cosmic irony of heaven's preordained plan, the evil figures struggle to achieve their own worldly triumph but manage instead to complete the steps essential for man's salvation. Judas' betrayal of Christ, though performed cynically for money, helps bring about the Crucifixion and hence the Resurrection. The chief priests, by seeking to end Christ's threat to their authority, put an end forever to the era of the old Mosaic law. Pilate too plays a role in the crucial event of divine history, although he is an enigmatic figure variously interpreted in the cycles as a thorough villain or as a well-meaning but ineffectual pawn. In any case, the supreme villain overthrown by his own craftiness is of course the devil. He is a comic type both as a blasphemous jokester and as the butt of a cosmic irony. In the York and N Town cycles, the devil realizes too late that his scheming against Christ will result in the overthrow of hell's dominion. Accordingly, he attempts to forestall the Crucifixion by appearing to Pilate's wife in a dream, urging her to warn her husband that he ought to spare Christ for his own good. This desperate scramble is too late; the Crucifixion goes ahead according to plan, and the salvation of the human race is assured. The devil is, in the words of a popular proverb, the beguiler beguiled by his own stratagem.

Today, the Corpus Christi cycles have begun to receive the critical recognition they were so long denied. With that recognition has come an awareness that the cycles did not simply fade away during the Renaissance because people thought them outmoded or ridiculous. The cycles flourished well into the sixteenth century, and evidently were brought to an end chiefly by the hostility of the reformed English Church toward what it viewed as idolatrous art. Prohibitions of plays in honor of the Virgin Mary and of representations of God or Christ on stage proved to be obstacles that the cycles could not overcome. Suppression came swiftly in the 1560's and 1570's, and with it came the destruction of numerous master copies of the plays in Church custody. The surviving plays represent only a small proportion of the total that once existed.

With the exception of Chester, all the cycles exist in single manuscript copies. Some, including that of Towneley, appear to have been the "original" copy, or "register," held by the municipal authorities of the sponsoring city. The Towneley manuscript (evidently from Wakefield) is now at the Huntington Library in San Marino, California; the York and N Town manuscripts are in the British Museum. Of the five Chester manuscripts, three are in the British Museum, one in the Bodleian Library at Oxford, and one at the Huntington. The texts in this edition are based on the originals or on photographic facsimiles.

THE BANNS
FROM N TOWN

The purpose of a "riding of the banns" was to announce publicly a forthcoming performance of a Corpus Christi cycle. Most such ridings were colorfully festive affairs, combining show-manship and advertisement with a serious ceremonial purpose. Despite the fact that this occasion usually took place several days in advance of the actual dramatic performance of the cycle, an audience evidently gathered together and sat patiently in order to hear this important announcement. The audience wit-nessed a procession, heard music performed by minstrels, and received a brief account of each individual pageant in the ensuing cycle. A similar riding of the banns might also pre-cede the performance of other kinds of medi-eval plays; the early morality play called *The Castle of Perseverance*, for example, features banns with musical accompaniment (see Part v).

In these particular banns from the so-called N Town cycle, three "Vexillators," or stan-dard-bearers, summarize by turns the forty pageants to be presented on the following Sunday. Their brief reports repeatedly stress the veracity of the story and its authentic basis in Scripture—even though, in properly medi-eval fashion, the narrative contains many apocryphal and legendary elements (see, for example, the descriptions of pageants 8, 9, 20, and 29). The speakers appeal to a widely diversified audience of rich and poor. The episodes they enumerate do not exactly correspond to the selections in this anthology, or even to the contents of the extant N Town cycle (since that cycle, like most, underwent numerous revisions and may have featured, at various times, both pageant-wagon staging and

performance in a fixed arena). Still, these banns presumably describe a performance that actually took place in some particular year, and give us a typical sample of what banns were like.

The N Town cycle, for which these banns were written, is sometimes misleadingly called the *Ludus Coventriae*, "the Play of Coventry." In point of fact, this cycle has no connection with the town of Coventry; an existing portion of a cycle from Coventry is not related to the N Town text. To avoid confusion, therefore, other names have been proposed for the misnamed *Ludus Coventriae*. "Hegge cycle" commemorates an early owner of the play manuscript, Robert Hegge. "N Town cycle" is derived from line 527 of the banns, in which the third Vexillator announces that the cycle is to be performed "in N Town." Perhaps the "N" signifies *nomen*, "name," meaning that the third Vexillator is to substitute for *nomen* the actual name of the town where performance takes place. Last-minute substitution of this sort would allow the cycle to be taken on tour. *The Castle of Perseverance* similarly provides for the insertion of the place name of performance by a speaker of the banns, and we know that *Perseverance* was acted in a variety of locations. Possibly, then, the N Town cycle was taken on a limited tour in the area known as the East Midlands, in Lincolnshire and Norfolk. Most cycles, such as York, Wakefield, or Chester, on the other hand, were acted in one town only, and the N Town cycle may similarly have been performed in an important town such as Lincoln. The question of location remains in dispute.

The Banns

From N Town

1 VEXILLAT[OR].   Now, gracious God, groundyd of all
            goodnesse,

2   As thy grete glorye nevyr beginning had,

3   So thou socour and save all tho that sitt and sese,   *those/see*

4   And listenith to oure talking with silens stille and sad.   *listen to*

  For we purpose us pertly stille in this prese   *intend/openly/throng*
  The pepyl to plese with pleys ful glad.

7   Now listenith us, lovely, bothe more and lesse,   *i.e., rich and poor*

8   Gentillys and yemanry of goodly lyff lad,

  This tide.   *At this time*

  We shal you shewe, as that we kan,   *as we are able*

  How that this wer[l]d first began,

  And how God made bothe molde and man,   *earth*

  Iff that ye wil abide.

2 VEXILLA[TOR].   In the first pagent, we thenke to play

  How God dede make, thurowe his owyn myth,   *did/might*

  Hevyn so clere upon the first day,

  And therin he sett angell[ys] ful bryth.   *bright*

  Than angell[ys] with songe—this is no nay—   *this is true*

  Shal worchep God, as it is ryth.   *right*

20   But Lucifer, that angell so gay,

  In suche pompe than is he pyth   *then/placed*

  And set in so gret pride

  That Goddys sete he ginnith to take,   *God's seat, throne*

  Hese Lordys pere himself to make.   *His Lord's peer*

  But than he fallith a fend ful blake,   *fiend/black*

  From hevyn in helle to a[bide].

3 VEXILL[ATOR].   In the secunde pagent, by Godys myth,

  We thenke to shewe and pley, bedene,   *indeed*

  In the other sex days, by opyn syth,   *i.e., in open view*

  What thenge was wrought. Ther shal be sene

  How best was made and foule of flyth.   *beast/flying fowl*

  And last was man made, as I wene.   *think*

1-4Now, gracious God, the foundation of all goodness, inasmuch as your great glory existed before the beginning of time, may you help and save all those persons here who sit and see our performance, and whom we exhort to listen to our speech with serious and complete silence.

7-8Now listen to us, beloved people, both rich and poor, both those who are well-born and yeomen who live uprightly (lit: led of a goodly life).

33 Of mannys o rib, as I yow plyth,   *one/promise*
 Was woman wrougth mannys make to bene,   *to be man's mate*
 And put in paradise.
 Ther were flourys bothe blew and blake.
 Of all frutys they myth ther take,   *might partake there*
 Saff frute of cunning they shulde forsake,   *Save, except/knowledge*
 And towche it no wise.

 The serpent toke Eve an appyl to bite,   *gave*
 And Eve toke Adam a mursel of the same.
42 Whan they had do thus agens the rewle of rite, *done*
 Than was oure Lord wroth and grevyd al with grame. *Then/anger*
44 Oure Lord gan appose them of ther gret delite, *interrogate*
45 Bothe to askuse hem of that sinful blame;   *excuse themselves*
 And than Almythy God, for that gret dispite,
 Assigned hem grevous peyn, as ye shal se in game,
 In dede.
 Seraphyn, an angell gay,
50 With brenning swerd—this is verray—   *burning/true*
 From paradise bete hem away,
 In Bibyl as we rede.

1 VEXILLATOR. We purpose to shewe in the thrid pagent
 The story of Caym and of hese brother Abelle.   *Cain*
 Of here tithingys now be we bent   *their*
 In this pagent the trewth to telle.
 How the tithing of Abel with feyr was brent   *fire/burned*
 And accept to God, if ye wil dwelle,   *acceptable*
 We purpose to shewe as we have ment,   *as we intend*
60 And how he was killyd of his brother so felle. *by/cruel*
 And than
 How Caym was cursyd in al degre
 Of Godys owyn mowthe, ther shal ye se.   *By*
 Of trewe tithing this may wel be
 Example to every man.

2 VEXIL[L]ATOR. The thridde pagent is now yow tolde.
 The fourte pagent of Noe shal be,
 How God was wroth with man on molde,   *earth*
 Because fro sinne man dede not fle.

---

[33]From one of man's ribs, as I assure you.

[42]When they had done thus contrary to the rule of righteousness.

[44–45]Our Lord questioned them to determine if they could excuse themselves of sinful blame in their great sensual pleasure.

70   He sent to Noe an angel bolde,
    A ship for to makyn and swimmen on the se,
    Upon the water both wood and coolde.   *frenzied*
    And eight sowles ther savyd shulde be,
    And one peyre of everich bestys in bringe.   *each kind of beast*
    Whan forty days the flode had flowe,
    Than sente Noe out a crowe,
    And after him he sent a dowe   *dove*
    That brouth ryth good tiding.

    3 VEXIL[LATOR].   Of Abraham is the fifte pagent,
80   And of Isaac his sone so fre,   *excellent*
    How that he shulde with fere be brent
    And slain with swerd, as ye shal se.
    Abraham toke with good a-tent   *intent*
    His sone Isaac, and knelyd on kne—
    His suerd was than ful redy bent—
    And thouth his childe ther offered shuld be   *thought, intended*
    Upon an hill ful ryff.   *readily*
    Than God toke tent to his good wil,   *God heeded*
    And sent an angel ryth sone him til,   *very soon to him*
90   And bad[e] Abraham a shep to kil
    And savyd his childys lyff.

    1 VEXIL[LATOR].   The sexte pagent is of Moyses,
    And of tweyn tabelys that God him took,   *gave him*
    In the which were wrete, without les,   *written/lie*
95   The lawes of God to lerne and lok;
    And how God charged him by wordys these
    The lawes to lerne al of that book.
    Moyses than doth nevyr more sese,   *then/cease*
    But prechith duly, bothe yere and woke,   *week (i.e., constantly)*
    The lawes as I yow telle.
    The ten comaundementys, alle bedene,   *all together*
    In oure play ye shal hem sene,   *see them*
103   To alle tho that there wil bene,
104   If that ye thenke to duelle.

    2 VEXILL[ATOR].   Of the gentyl Jesse rote   *root, lineage of Jesse*
    The sefnt pagent forsothe shal ben,
    Out of the which doth springe oure bote,   *salvation*

95 The laws of God for him to study and examine.

103–4 (You will see the Ten Commandments revealed to you), all those of you who will be at the performance, if you should decide to come and stay.

As in prophecye we redyn and sen.   *read and see*

Kingys and prophetys with wordys ful sote   *sweet*

110   Schull prophesye al of a qwen,

The which shal staunch oure striff and moote,   *dispute*

And winnen us welthe withoutyn wen   *doubt*

In hevyn to abide.

They shal prophecye of a maide;

All fendys of her shal be affraide.

Her sone shal save us—be not dismayde—

With hese woundys wide.

3 VEXILLATOR.   Of the grete bushop Abiacar

The eighte pagent shal be, without lesing,   *lying*

120   The which comaundith men to be war   *Who/to take note*

121   And bringe here douterys to dew wedding;   *their daughters*

All that ben fourteen yere and more

To mariage he biddith hem bring.

Wherevyr they be, he chargith sore   *commands sternly*

That they not faile for no letting,   *hindrance*

The lawe biddith so than.

Than Joachim and Anne so milde,

They bringe forthe Mary that blissyd childe;

But she wold not be defilyde

130   With spot nor wem of man.   *stain*

In chastité that blisful maide

Avowyd there her lyff to lede.

Than is the busshop sore dismayde,

And wonderith sore al of this dede.   *is puzzled sorely by*

He knelyd to God, as it is saide,

And prayth than for help and rede.   *advice*

Than seyth an angel: "Be not afraide.

138   Of this dowte take thou no drede;

But for the kinrede of David thou sende;   *kindred*

Lete hem come with here offring,   *their*

And in here handys white yerdys bringe.   *branches, rods*

Loke whose yerde doth floure and springe,   *See/blossom*

And he shal wedde that maiden hende."   *gracious, gentle*

1 VEXILLATOR.   In the ninte pagent, sothe to say,   *truth*

120-21(Bishop Abiacar) who commands men to take note and bring their daughters to be married at the proper time. ("Bishop" is an anachronistic term denoting "chief priest." The apocryphal story of Mary and Abiacar or Abiathar can be found in *De Nativitate Sanctae Mariae*.)

138Be not dismayed by this quandary.

A masangere forthe is sent.
Davidis kinrede, without delay,   *David's*
They come ful sone with good entent.
Whan Joseph offeryd his yerde that day,
Anon ryth forth in present   *i.e., in plain view*
150   The ded stik do floure ful gay,   *did blossom*
And than Joseph to wedlok went
Ryth as the angel bad.   *bade*
Than he plyth to his wyff   *plighted*
In chastité to ledyn here lyff.   *lead their*
The busshop toke her thre maidenys ryff;   *gave/readily*
Som comforte there she had.

2 VEXILLATOR.   In the tende pagent goth Gabriell,
And doth salute Oure Lady fre.   *noble*
Than grett with childe, as I yow tell,
160   That blissyd maide forsothe is she.
Tho thre maidenys that with her dwelle
Here gret spech, but noon they se;   *Hear loud/no one*
Than they suppose that sum angell
Goddys masangere that it shuld be.
And thus
The Holy Gost in her is lith,   *alighted*
And Goddys sone in her is pigth.   *implanted*
The aungell doth telle what he shal hight,   *be named*
And namith the childe Jhesus.

170 3 VEXILLATOR.   In the hellenthe pagent, as I yow telle,   *eleventh*
Joseph comith hom fro fer countré.
Oure Ladyes wombe with childe doth swelle,
And than Joseph ful hevy is he.
He doth forsake her with hert ful felle.   *heavy*
Out of countré he ginnith to fle;
He nevyr more thenkith with her to dwelle.
And than Oure Lady ryth sore wepith she.
An angell seyd him ryf[f]:   *quickly*
"God is with thy wyff, sertain;
180   Therfore, Joseph, turne hom again."
Than is Joseph in herte ful fain,   *glad*
And goth ageyn onto his wyff.

1 VEXILLATOR.   The twelfte pagent, I sey yow bedene,   *indeed*
Shal be of Joseph and milde Mary,
How they were sclawndryd with trey and tene,   *anger and malice*
And to here purgacion they must hem hy.   *their/hasten*

2 VEXILLATOR.   In the thirteente pagent, shewe we shal
　　　How Joseph went withoute variauns   *unhesitatingly*
　　　For midwivys, to helpe Oure Lady at all
190　　Of childe that she had deliverauns.

3 VEXILLATOR.   In the fourteente pagent Crist shal be born.
　　　Of that joy aungelys shul singe,
　　　And telle the shepherdys in that morn
　　　The blisseful birth of that king.
　　　The shepherdys shal come him beforn   *before him*
　　　With reverens and with worcheping;
　　　For he shal savyn that was forlorn,   *that which was wholly lost*
　　　And graunt us lyff evyrmore lesting,
　　　Iwis.
200　　This glé in grith   *joy in peace*
　　　Is mater of mirth;
　　　Now Cristys birth
　　　Bring us to his blis.

1 VEXILLATOR.   [In] the fifteente pagent come kingys thre,
　　　With gold, myrre, and frankinsens.
　　　King Herowdys styward hem doth se,
　　　And bringith all to his presens.
208　　The kingys of Coleyn, with hert ful fre,   *Cologne*
　　　Tolde King Herownde here diligens,   *their mission*
　　　That they south in that countré   *sought*
　　　A king of kingys; from fere thens
　　　A sterre led hem the way.
　　　"The childe is young and lyth in stall;   *lies*
　　　He shal be king of kingys all.
　　　Before him we think on kne to fall,
　　　And worchep him this day."

2 VEXILLATOR.   In the sixteente pagent, as wroth as winde
　　　Is King Herownde, the soth to say;
　　　And cruel knytys and unkende   *knights/unnatural*
220　　To sle male childeryn he sendith that day.
　　　But Crist Jhesu they may not finde,   *cannot*
　　　For Joseph hath led that childe away
　　　Unto Egypth, as we have mende,   *as we understand*
　　　As angel to Joseph did bid and say
　　　In hight.   *In haste*
　　　Tho childeryn that sit in here moderys lap   *their mothers'*

208*Coleyn:* Cologne. (In the Middle Ages, this German city was famous for its shrine of the
Wise Men of the East, commonly called the Three Kings of Cologne.)

To sowkyn ful swetly here moderys pap, *suck/breast*
The knythtys do sle hem evyn at a swap. *blow*
This is a rewly syth. *rueful sight*

230 3 VEXILLATOR.   In the sefnteente pagent the knythtys,
        bedene, *indeed*
Shull bringe dede childeryn befor the king.
Whan King Herownde that syth hath sene, *sight*
Ful glad he is of here killing. *their*
Than King Herownde, withowtyn wene, *doubt*
Is sett to mete at his liking; *banquet/pleasure*
In his most pride shal come gret tene, *harm*
As ye shal se at oure pley[i]ng:
His sorwe shal awake.
Whan he is sett at hese most pride,
240 Sodeyn Deth shal thrille his side, *pierce*
And kille his knyttys that with him bide; *knights*
The devil ther soulys shal take.

1 VEXILLATOR.   In the eighteente pagent, we must purpose
To shewe whan Crist was twelve yer of age,
How in the temple he dede appose *confront*
And answerd doctoris ryth wise and sage.
The blissyd babe, withowte glose, *without deceit, in truth*
Overcam olde clerkys with suych langage *learned clerics*
That they meveylyd. Ye shal suppose *marvelled/comprehend*
How that he cam to suche knowlage,
251 And in this while.
Thre days he was oute *absent*
Fro his modyr, without doute;
Weping she sowth him rownde aboute *sought*
Jheruselem many a mile.

2 VEXILLATOR.   In the nineteente pagent shal Seynt Jhon
Baptise Crist, as I yow say,
In the watyr of flom Jordon; *river*
With which devys, as we best may, *device*
260 The Holy Gost shal ovyr him on. *hover*
The Faderys vois shal be herd that day
Out of hevyn, that blisful tron;
The Fadyr shal be herd, this is no nay.
And forthwith pleyn *without embellishment*
The Holy Gost shal be his g[u]ide,
Into desert therin to abide

251i.e., In the course of this pageant.

Forty days—a terme ful wide—   *long*
And forty nigthtys to faste, sarteyn.   *certainly*

3 VEXILLATOR.   In the twentieth pagent all the develys of
        helle,
They gadere a parlement, as ye shal se.
They have gret doute, the trewth to telle,
272   Of Crist Jhesu whath he shuld be.
They sende Sathan, that fynde so felle,   *fiend so cruel*
Crist for to tempte in fele degré.   *in many ways*
We shal yow shewe, if ye wil dwelle,
How Crist was temptyd in sinnys thre
Of the devil Sathan,   *By*
And how Crist answeryd onto alle,
And made the fende awey to falle.
280   As we best may, this shewe we shalle,   *we'll show this*
Thorwe grace of God and man.

1 VEXILLATOR.   The twenty-first pagent of a woman shal be,
The which was take in adultrye.   *taken*
The pharisewys falsed, ther ye shal se,   *pharisees' falsehood*
Crist to convicte how they were slye.
They conseivyd this sotilté:
If Crist this woman dede dampne trewly,   *did condemn*
Ageyn his preching than dede he,   *Against*
Which was of peté and of mercy;
290   And if he dede her save,
Than were he agens Moyses lawe
That biddith with stonys she shulde be slawe.   *slain*
Thus they thowth undyr ther awe   *thought/power*
Crist Jhesu for to have.

2 VEXILLATOR.   The grettest meracle that evyr Jhesus
In erthe wrouth beforn his Passion,
In twenty-secund pagent we purpose us
To shewe indede the declaracion: *elucidation*
That pagent shal be of Lazarus,
In whos[e] place and habitacion
Crist was logyd—the Gospel seyth thus—
302   And ofte time toke ther consolacion.
But yit
Lazarus, as I yow say,

272What sort of being Christ is, i.e., whether human or divine.

302i.e., And often enjoyed the company of his friends there.

Was four days ded and beried in clay.
From deth to live, the fourte day,
Crist reysed him from that pit.

3 VEXILLATOR. In the twenty-thrid pagent, Palme Sunday
In pley we purpose for to shewe,
310 How childeryn of Ebrew, with flourys ful gay,
The wey that Crist went they gun to strewe.　　　　　*did strew*

1 VEXILLATOR. In the twenty-fourte pagent, as that we
          may,
Crist and his apostelys, alle on rewe,　　　　　*row*
The Mawndé of God ther shal they play,　　　　　*Last Supper*
And sone declare it with wordys fewe.　　　　　*soon*
And than
Judas, that fals traitour,
For thirty platys of wer[l]dly tresour　　　　　*silver coins*
Shal betray oure Saviour
320 To the Jewys, certan.

2 VEXILLATOR. For grevous peyn—this is no les—　　　　　*lie*
In the twenty-fifte pagent, Crist shal pray
To the Fadyr of hevyn that peyn for to ses,　　　　　*cease*
His shamful deth to put away.
Judas, that traitour, befor gret pres　　　　　*crowd*
Shal kis his mouth and him betray.
All his disciples than do discres　　　　　*fall away*
And forsake Crist, the soth to say;
For doute they do hem hede.　　　　　*Out of fear/hide themselves*
330 Hese disciplys all everychon
Do renne awey and leve him alon;
They lete him stondyn amonge his fon,　　　　　*stand, remain/foes*
And ronne away for drede.

3 VEX[ILLATOR]. Than in the twenty-sexte pagent
To Caiphas Crist shal be brouth.
Tho Jewys ful redy ther shul be bent,　　　　　*Those/determined*
Crist to acuse with worde and thouth.
Seynt Petyr doth folwe with good intent
339 To se with Crist what shuld be wrouth;
For Cristys disciple whan he is hent,　　　　　*taken*
Thries he doth swere he knew him nowth.
A kok shal crowe and crye.
Than doth Petyr gret sorwe make,

339To see what is going to be done with Christ (by the Jews).

For he his Lord thus dede forsake;   *Because*

But God to grace him sone doth take,   *soon*

Whan he doth aske mercye.

1 VEXILLATOR.   In the twenty-sefnt pagent, sere Pilat   *sir*

Is sett in sete as hy justice.

Whan he is set in his astat,   *estate, noble condition*

350   Thre thevys be brout, of sinful g[u]ise;   *thieves|brought*

And Crist, that lovyd nevyr stryff nor bat,   *debate*

But trewth and goodness on every wise,   *in every way*

As for a thef with ryth gret hat   *As if he were|haste*

Is browth to stondyn at that same sise.   *assize*

And than, as I yow say,

The wyff of Pilat goth to rest

Coveryd with clothis al of the best;   *bedclothes*

Than for to slepe she is ful prest.   *ready*

All this we thenke to play.

360   2 VEXILLATOR.   In the twenty-eighte pagent shal Judas,

That was to Crist a fals traitour,

With weping sore evyr crye, Alas!

That evyr he solde oure Saviour.

He shal be sory for his trespas,

And bringe agen all his tresour,   *again*

All thritty pens, to sere Caiphas.

He shal them bringe with gret dolowre,   *dolor, sorrow*

For the which Crist was bowth.   *bought*

For gret whanhope, as ye shal se,   *despair*

370   He hangith himself upon a tre.

For he noth trostith in Godys peté,   *Because he didn't trust*

To helle his sowle is browth.

3 VEXILLATOR.   In the twenty-ninte pagent, to Pilatus wyff

In slepe aperith the devil of helle;

375   For to savyn Cristys lyff

376   The devil her temptith, as I yow telle.

Sche sendith to Pilat anon ful ryff,   *readily*

378   And prayth that Crist he shuld not qwelle.   *kill*

Than Pilat is besy, and ryth blyff   *quickly*

380   Crist for to savyn he gevith councelle,

375-76(i.e., The devil prevails upon Pilate's wife with evil dreams so that she will intercede with her husband and prevent the Crucifixion, which, as the devil now realizes, will rescue mankind from hell.)

378And entreats Pilate not to kill Christ.

380Pilate declares his opinion that Christ should be spared.

For He dede nevyr trespas.   *Because/sin*
The Jewys do crye fast for to kille;
The rythful man they aske to spille;   *righteous/kill*
A thef they save with herty wille
That callyd is Barrabas.

1 VEXILLATOR.   In the threttieth pagent, they bete out
    Cristys blood
And naile him al nakyd upon a rode tre   *cross*
Betwen two thevys. Iwis they were to[o] wood!   *Truly/mad*
They hyng Crist Jhesu, gret shame it is to se.
Seven wurdyes Crist spekith, hanging upon the rode,
391   The w[h]eche ye shal here, all tho that wil ther be.   *hear/those*
Than doth he die for oure all[e]ther good.   *all our*
His modyr doth se that syth; gret mo[u]rning makith she;   *sight*
For sorwe she ginneth to swowne.
Seynt John, evyn theras I yow plyth,   *just as I promise you*
Doth chere Oure Lady with al his myth,   *might*
And to the temple anon forth ryth   *straightway*
He ledith her in that stownde.   *hour*

2 VEXILLATOR.   We purpose to shewe in oure pleyn place,   *acting area*
In the thretty-first pagent, thorwe Godys myth,   *through*
How to Cristys herte a spere gan pace   *did pass, enter*
And rent oure Lordys bryst in ruly plyth.   *rueful plight*
403   For Longeus, that olde knyth, blind as he was,   *Because*
404   A ryth sharpe spere to Cristys herte shal pyth,   *thrust*
405   The blod of His wounde to his eyn shal tras;   *eyes/travel*
406   And, thorwe gret meracle, ther hath he syth.   *sight*
Than in that morn
Cristys soule goth down to helle
And ther ovyrcomith the fend so felle,   *cruel*
Comfortith the soulys that therin dwelle,
And savith that was forlorn.   *that which was utterly lost*

3 VEXILLATOR.   Joseph and Nicodemus, to Crist trew
    servaunt,
In the thretty-secund page[nt] the body they aske to have.
Pilat ful redily the body doth hem graunt;
Than they with reverens do put it in grave.
The Jewys, more wickyd than ony geawnt,   *any giant*

391The which you shall hear, all those of you who will be at the performance.

403-6Because the old knight Longeus, who was blind, will thrust a very sharp spear into Christ's heart, the blood of Christ's wounds shall make its way to Longeus' eyes; and, through a great miracle, Longeus will recover his sight.

For Cristys ded body kepers do they crave.
Pilat sendith four knytys that be ryth hardaunt   *very bold*
To kepe the blody body in his dede conclave.   *tomb*
420 And yit by his owyn myth
The body that was hevy as led—
Be the Jewys nevyr so qwed—   *wicked*
Ariseth from grave, that ther lay ded,
And frayth than every knyth.   *frightens then*

1 VEXILLATOR.   In the thretty-third pagent, the soule of
          Crist Jhesu
Shal bringe all his frendys from helle to paradise.
The soule goth than to the grave; and, by ryth gret
          vertu,   *supernatural power*
That body that longe ded hath loyn, to lyf agen doth rise.   *lain*
Than doth Crist Jhesu onto his modyr sew,   *proceed*
430 And comfortith all her care, in temple ther she lyse;   *where she dwells*
With suche cher and comforth his modyr he doth indew,   *endow*
That joy it is to here, ther spech for to devise.   *hear/discern*
And than
Oure Lady of hefne so cler,
In herte sche hath ryth glad chere;
Whan her sone thus doth apere
Her care awey is tan.   *taken*

2 VEXILLATOR.   In the thretty-fourte pagent shal Maryes
          thre
Seke Crist Jhesu in his grave so coolde.
440 An aungel hem tellith that aresyn is he;
And whan that this tale to them is tolde,
To Cristys disciplis with wurdys ful fre   *excellent*
They telle these tidingys with brest ful bolde.
Than Petyr and John, as ye shal se,
445 Down rennyn in hast over lond and wolde,   *wooded country*
The trewth of this to have.
Whan they ther comyn, as I yow say,   *arrive there*
He is gon from undyr clay.
Than they witnesse anoon that day,
450 He lyth not in his grave.

3 VEXILLATOR.   Onto Mary Mawdelyn, as we have bent,   *as we intend*
Crist Jhesu shal than apere
In the thretty-fifte pagent,

---

[445]Run hastily across open land and wooded terrain (i.e., a long distance).

	And she wenith he be a gardenere.	*thinks*
455	Mary, by name verament	*truly*
456	Whan Crist her callith with spech ful clere,	
	She fallith to ground, with good entent	
	To kis his fete with gladsom chere.	*joyous countenance*
	But Crist biddith her do way;	*desist*
460	He biddith his feet that sche not kis	
	Til he have styed to hefne blis.	*ascended/heaven's*
	To Cristys disciplys Mary iwis	
	Than goth, the trewth to say.	

	1 VEXILLATOR. In the thretty-sexte pagent shal Cleophas	
465	And Sent Luke to a castel go.	
	Of Cristys deth, as they forth pas,	*as they travel*
	They make gret mo[u]rning and be ful wo.	*woeful*
	Than Crist them ovyrtok, as his wil was,	
	And walkyd in felachep forth with hem too.	*two*
470	To them he doth expowne, bothe more and las,	
	All that prophetys spakad of himself also.	
	That nyth, in fay,	
	Whan they be set within the castell,	
	In breking of bred, they knew Crist well.	
	Than sodeynly, as I yow tell,	
	Criste is gon his way.	

	2 VEXILLATOR. In the thretty-sefnt pagent, than purpos we,	
	To Thomas of Inde Crist shal apere,	
	And Thomas, evyn ther as ye shal se,	
480	Shal put his hand in his woundys dere.	

	3 VEXILLATOR. In the thretty-eighte pagent, up stye shal he	*ascend*
	Into hefne that is so clere.	
	All hese apostel[ys] ther shul be,	
	And woundere sore and have gret dwere	*fear*
	Of that ferly syth.	*wondrous sight*
	Ther shal come aungell[ys] tweyn,	
	And comforte hem—this is certeyn—	
	And tellyn that he shal comyn ageyn	
	Evyn by his owyn myth.	

	1 VEXILLATOR. Than folwith next, sekyrly,	*certainly*

455–56Truly, when Christ calls Mary by her name in a clear voice.

460He bids her not to kiss his feet.

465*castel:* the village of Emmaus, often portrayed on stage as a castle.

    Of Wittsunday that solempne fest,
    Which pagent shal be nine and thretty.
493 To the apostelys to apere, by Cristys hest,   *command*
494 In Hierusalem were gaderyd twelve opynly,
495 To the Cenacle coming from west and est.   *upper chamber*
    The Holy Gost apperyd ful vervently,   *flamingly*
497 With brenning fere thirling here brest,   *piercing their*
    Proceding from hevyn trone.
    All maner langage hem spak with tung,
    Latin, Grek, and Ebrew among;
    And affter they departyd and taried not long,
    Here deth to take ful sone.   *Their*

   2 VEXILLATOR. The fourtieth pagent shal be the last,
    And Domysday that pagent shal hyth.   *be called*
    Who se that pagent may be agast   *Whoever sees*
    To grevyn his lord God either day or nyth.
    The erth shal qwake, bothe breke and brast;   *break and burst*
    Berielys and gravys shul ope ful tyth;   *Tombs/quickly*
    Ded men shul risyn and that ther in hast,
510 And fast to here ansuere they shul hem dyth,   *their/prepare themselves*
    Before Godys face.
    But prente wil this in your mende: *imprint well*
    Whoso to God hath be unkende,
    Frenchep ther shal he non finde,
    Ne ther get he no grace.

   3 VEXILLATOR. Now have we told yow all bedene   *together*
    The hool mater that we thinke to play.   *whole*
    Whan that ye come, ther shal ye sene
    This game wel pleyd in good aray.
    Of Holy Writte this game shal bene,
    And of no fablys by no way.   *at all*
522 Now God them save from trey and tene   *misery and suffering*

493–95 i.e., In order that he might appear to the apostles, at Christ's command the twelve gathered publicly in Jerusalem, coming from east and west to the Cenacle (from the Vulgate, *coenaculum*, a word used for the upper chamber in which the Last Supper was celebrated and where, according to tradition, the disciples gathered for the Ascension; see Luke 22:12).

497 Piercing their breasts with burning fire. (An image of the descent of the Holy Ghost to the apostles on Pentecost or Whitsunday, seven Sundays after Easter, filling them with the Holy Spirit and causing them to speak "with other tongues"; see Acts 2.)

510 And quickly they must prepare themselves to answer for their sins.

522–24 Now may God save from misery and suffering, and grant a just reward, to all those who pray for us on the day of performance.

523   For us that prayth upon that day,
524   And qwite them wel ther mede.   *requite/reward*
       A Sunday next, if that we may,   *On*
       At six of the belle, we ginne oure play   *six o'clock*
527   In N Town. Wherfore, we pray
       That God now be youre spede.
          Amen.

527*N Town:* "N" perhaps signifying *nomen,* "name."

THE CREATION AND THE FALL
OF THE ANGELS
FROM WAKEFIELD

Although the story of God's creation of the world is to be found in Genesis, the story of the fall of Satan or Lucifer is not. Only a few passages scattered throughout the Bible seem to allude to Satan's fall, and some of them are couched in obscure language. One such text is from Isaiah 14:12: "How art thou fallen from heaven, O Lucifer, son of the morning!" This invocation to the morning star was often interpreted by medieval scholars as a metaphorical description of the fall of Satan. The Book of Revelation (12:7–9) speaks of a war in heaven in which Michael and his angels throw down to earth the serpent Satan and his angels. Christ once mentions that he beheld Satan falling out of the sky (Luke 10:18). From references such as these, the medieval Church Fathers constructed an explanation of the origin of evil in the universe. Evil, they insisted, did not coexist with God from the beginning; it came into being through Lucifer's disobedience, shortly after God created the angels and before God created man.

The dramatized version of the Creation and Fall from the Wakefield or Towneley cycle follows church tradition. God is presented as an abstract mystery whose being can be evoked only through paradoxes: he is Alpha and Omega, one God in three persons. The scene of the Creation is accordingly formal and stylized, with little attempt at realistic effects. In the original production, the individual acts of creation were perhaps displayed symbolically on painted boards while God spoke. Satan, on the other hand, is a vivid and potentially comic character. We are compellingly fascinated by his audacity, even though we recognize it as sinful pride. After his fall, he and his angels put on ugly costumes and masks

that accentuate the contrast between good and evil. The contest for the soul of man is joined.

We do not know whether this episode was staged on a pageant wagon or in a theater in the round, although recent scholarship has offered persuasive arguments for the latter possibility. In either case, the scene requires an elevated scaffold or tower representing heaven. Here God sits enthroned, surrounded by his angels. When the evil angels are thrown down into hell, they exit from the tower of heaven and reappear on a lower level in devils' costumes. Paradise must presumably be represented by some middle location between heaven and hell. It is also elevated slightly above the earth, to which Adam and Eve are later expelled.

The Norwich Creation (which includes the Fall of Man) offers some interesting suggestions for staging. Clearly it was acted on a pageant wagon, since Adam and Eve, when driven out of paradise, "departeth to the nether part of the pageant." Furthermore, the Grocers' Guild inventory of 1565 calls for "A Pageant, that is to saye, a howse of wainskott painted and builded on a carte with fowre whelys," "A square topp to sett over the saide howse," and "3 painted clothes to hang abowte the pageant." Props and costumes include "A ribbe, colleryd red," "2 cotes and a payre hosen for Eve, stained," "A cote and hosen for Adam, steyned," "A cote with hosen and taile for the serpente, steyned, with a white heare [wig]," "An angell's cote and over hoses of apis skinns," and "A face and heare [mask and wig] for the Father." Similar props and costumes may have been used in the Wakefield Creation.

The Creation and the Fall of the Angels
From Wakefield

[*God, enthroned in heaven, surrounded by his angels.*]

[DEUS.]   *Ego sum alpha et o:*
I am the first, the last also,
Oone God in magesté,
Mervelus, of might most,
Fader, and Son, and Holy Goost,
On[e] God in trinité.

I am without beginning;
My godhede hath none ending.
I am God in trone,
10   Oone God in persons thre
Which may never twinnyd be,   *divided*
For I am God alone.

All maner thing is in my thoght;   *Every kind of*
Withoutten me ther may be noght,
For all is in my sight.
Hit shall be done after my will;   *It/according to*
That I have thoght I shall fulfill   *That which*
And manteyn with my might.

19   At the beginning of oure dede   *deed*
20   Make we heven and erth, on brede,   *breadth*
And lightys faire to se,
For it is good to be so.
Darknes from light we parte on two,   *in two*
24   In time to serve and be.

Darknes we call the night,
26   And lith also the bright;   *daylight*
It shall be as I say.
After my will this is furth broght.
Even and morne both ar thay wroght,
And thus is maid a day.

19–20*oure, we:* royal plural, by which kings and other rulers refer to themselves in their official capacity.

24i.e., To exist in time and mark its passing.

26And the brightness also (we call) day. (See Genesis 1:5.)

In medys the water, by oure assent,   *In midst of*
Be now maide the firmament,
And parte ather from othere,   *one from the other*
34   Water above, iwis.
Even and morne maide is this
A day, [so was] the tothere.   *other*

Waters, that so wide ben spred,
Be gedered togeder into one stede,   *place*
That dry the erth may seym.
40   That [th]at is dry the erth shall be;   *That which*
The waters also I call the see.
This warke to me is queme.   *agreeable*

Out of the erth herbys shal spring,
Trees to florish and frute furth bring,
45   Thare kinde that it be kyd.   *nature/made known*
This is done after my will.
Even and morn maide is thertill   *thereto*
A day, this is the thryd.   *third*

Son and moyne set in the heven,   *moon*
50   With starnes, and the planettys seven,   *stars*
To stand in thare degré: *proper order*
The son to serve the daylight,
The moyne also to serve the night.
The fourte day shall this be.

The water to norish the fish swimand,   *swimming*
56   The erth to norish bestys crepeand,
57   That fly or go may.
Multiplye in erth, and be
In my blissing, wax now ye.
This is the fift day.

CHERUBYN.   Oure lord God in trinité,
Mirth and loving be to the[e],
Mirth and loving over al thing.
For thou has made, with thy biding,   *bidding*
Heven and erth and all that is,
And giffen us joy that never shall mis.   *fail*

34i.e., The earth above the water, truly.

45So that their true nature will be revealed (by the fruit they bear).

56–57The earth to nourish all creeping (i.e., nonswimming) beasts that either fly or go on land.

Lord, thou art full mych of might,   *much*
That has maide Lucifer so bright.
We love the[e], Lord; bright ar we,
Bot none of us so bright as he.

71   He may well hight Lucifere,   *be called*
72   For lufly light that he doth bere.
He is so lufly and so bright
It is grete joy to se that sight.
We lofe the[e], Lord, with all oure thoght,
That sich thing can make of noght.

    Hic Deus recedit a suo solio, et Lucifer sedebit in eodem   *Here God withdraws from his*
    solio.   *throne, and Lucifer will sit in that*
    throne

LUCIFER.   Certys, it is a semely sight!   *Certainly*
Syn that we ar all angels bright,   *Since*
And ever in blis to be,

80   If that ye will behold me right,
This mastré longys to me.   *lordship belongs*
I am so fare and bright,
Of me commys all this light,
This gam and all this glé.   *pleasure*
Agans my grete might   *Against*
May [no]thing stand then be.   *nor be*

And ye well me behold;
I am a thowsandfold
Brighter then is the son.

90   My strengthe may not be told;   *reckoned*
My might may no thing kon.   *know*
In heven, therfor, wit I wold   *I'd like to know*
Above me who shuld won.   *dwell*

For I am lord of blis
Over all this warld, iwis.
My mirth is most of all.
The[r]for my will is this:
"Master" ye shall me call.

And ye shall se, full sone onone,   *soon anon*
100   How that me semys to sit in trone   *it suits me*
As king of blis.

71-72(Lucifer, meaning "bearer of light," is taken from Isaiah 14:12, which medieval scholars
interpreted as referring to Satan: "How art thou fallen from heaven, O Lucifer, son of the
morning!")

I am so semely, blode and bone,   *i.e., in all my parts*
My sete shall be theras was His.   *where His was*
    [*Lucifer sits in God's throne.*]

Say, felows, how semys now me
To sit in seyte of trinité?
I am so bright of ich a lim   *in every part*
I trow me seme as well as Him.   *I believe it suits me*

1 ANGELUS MALUS.   Thou art so faire unto my sight,
Thou semys well to sitt on hight—

110 So thinke me that thou doyse.   *you do*

1 BONUS ANGELUS.   I rede ye leyfe that vanys royse,   *advise/vain boasting*
For that seyte may non angell seme   *suit no angel*
So well as Him that all shall deme.   *who will judge all*

2 BONUS ANGELUS.   I reyde ye sese of that ye sayn,   *cease what you say*
For well I wote ye carpe in vaine.   *know/prate*
Hit semyd him never, ne never shall,   *It suited no one*
So well as Him that has maide all.

2 MALUS ANGELUS.   Now, and by oght that I can witt,   *anything/know*
He semys full well theron to sitt.

120 He is so faire, withoutten les,   *lie*
He semys full well to sitt on des.   *dais, throne*
Therfor, felow, hold thy peasse,
And umbithinke the[e] what thou saysse.   *meditate on*
He semys as well to sitt there
As God himself, if he were here.

LUCIFER.   Leyf felow, think the[e] not so?   *Dear*

1 MALUS ANGELUS.   Yee, God wote, so dos othere mo.

1 BONUS [ANGELUS].   Nay, forsoth, so think not us.

129 LUCIFER.   Now, therof a leke what rekys us?
Syn I myself am so bright   *Since*

131 Therfor will I take a flight.
    Tunc exibunt demones clamando; et dicit primus: *Then the devils will go out exclaiming; and the first [re-entering] says*

1 DEMON [*now in hell*]:   Alas, alas, and wele-wo!
Lucifer, why fell thou so?
We, that were angels so fare,
And sat so hie above the ayere,   *air, sky*
Now ar we waxen blak as any coyll   *coal*

137 And ugly, tatyrd as a foyll.   *tattered/foal*

129Now, what do we care worth a leek?

131s.d.: The evil angels seemingly create the visual effect of their being cast down into hell by exiting with cries of dismay from the tower of heaven, and then reappearing in hell, presumably having changed to tattered black devils' costumes in the interim.

137*tatyrd . . . foyll:* i.e., ragged, shaggy.

What alyd the[e], Lucifer, to fall?
Was thou not farist of angels all?
Brightist and best, and most of luf · *beloved*
With God himself, that sittys aboyf?
142 Thou has maide neyn there was ten; · *there where*
143 Thou art foull comyn from thy kin!
Thou art fallen, that was the teynd, · *you that were the tenth*
From an angell to a feynd.
Thou has us doyn a vile dispite, · *done us*
And broght thyself to sorow and sitt. · *pain*
Alas! Ther is noght els to say
Bot we ar tynt for now and ay. · *Except that/lost/ever*

150 2 DEMON.   Alas! The joy that we were in
Have we lost, for oure sin.
Alas, that ever cam pride in thoght!
For it has broght us all to noght.
We were in mirth and joy enoghe
When Lucifer to pride drogh. · *betook himself*
Alas, we may warrie wikkyd pride— · *curse*
157 So may ye all that standys be side.
158 We held with him ther he saide leasse, · *lies*
And therfor have we all unpeasse. · *lack of peace*
Alas, alas, oure joy is tint! · *lost*
161 We mon have paine that never shall stint. · *must/cease*

[*Near paradise, God proceeds to the creation of man.*]
DEUS.   Erthly bestys, that may crepe and go,
163 Bring ye furth and wax ye mo; · *more*
I se that it is good.
Now make we man to oure liknes,
That shall be keper of more and les, · *i.e., of everything*
Of fowles, and fish in flood.
    Et tanget eum. · *And he will touch him*

Spreyte of life I in the[e] blaw; · *blow*
Good and ill both shall thou knaw.

142–43You have taken away one tenth of the angelic order, leaving nine tenths. You are cursed for leaving your heavenly kindred!

157*be side*: on the sidelines—addressed to the spectators.

158We sided with him when he told lies.

161s.D.: Although the focus of the action shifts away from hell, the scene moves continuously without a break, and it is not certain that the devils disappear from sight; at l. 262, Satan knows of the creation of man, and may in fact have witnessed the action.

163(Cf. Genesis 1:24: "Let the earth bring forth the living creature after his kind." This is the sixth day of creation.)

170   Rise up, and stand by me.
      All that is in water or land,
      It shall bow unto thy hand,
      And sufferan shall thou be.   *sovereign*

      I gif the[e] witt, I gif the[e] strength;
175   Of all thou sees, of brede and lengthe,   *breadth*
176   Thou shall be wonder wise—   *wondrously*
      Mirth and joy to have at will,
      All thy liking to fulfill,
      And dwell in paradise.

180   This I make thy wonning playce,   *dwelling*
      Full of mirth and of solace,
      And I seasse the[e] therin.   *install*
      It is not good to be alone,
      To walk here in this worthely wone   *stately dwelling*
      In all this welthly win: *joy*

      Therfor, a rib I from the[e] take.
      Therof shall be [maide] thy make,   *mate*
      And be to thy helping—
      Ye both to governe that here is,   *that which*
190   And evermore to be in blis;
      Ye wax in my blissing.   *May you prosper*

      Ye shall have joye and blis therin,
      Whils ye will kepe you out of sin,   *As long as*
      I say without[ten] lese.   *lie*
        [God turns to one of his angels.]
      Rise up, min angell Cherubin!
      Take and leyd theym both in,
      And leyf them there in peasse.   *leave*
        Tunc capit Cherubin Adam per manum, et dicit eis   *Then Cherubin takes Adam by*
        Dominus: *the hand, and the Lord says to them*

    [DEUS.]   Heris thou, Adam, and Eve thy wife: *Listen*
      I forbede you the tre of life;
200   And I commaund, that it begat,

170*Rise up:* The actor playing Adam has presumably been concealed in a prone position until the creation of man; similarly later with Eve.

175–76You will be wondrously knowledgeable of everything you see, the length and breadth of paradise.

200And I, who created it, command.

Take which ye will, bot negh not that.   *approach*
Adam, if thou breke my rede,   *command*
Thou shall die a dulfull dede.   *doleful death*
CHERUBIN.   Oure Lord, oure God, thy will be done.
I shall go with theym full sone.
Forsoth, my Lord, I shall not sted   *stop*
Till I have theym theder led.
We thank the[e], Lord, with full good chere,
That has maide man to be oure feere.   *equal*

[God retires to heaven. Cherubin leads Adam and Eve to paradise.]

210   Com furth, Adam, I shall the[e] leyd;
Take tent to me, I shall the[e] reyd.   *Pay attention/advise*
I rede the[e] think how thou art wroght,
And luf my Lord in all thy thoght,
That has maide the[e] thrugh his will,
215   Angels ordir to fulfill.
Many thingys he has the[e] giffen,
And maide the[e] master of all that liffen.   *lives*
He has forbed the[e] bot a tre;   *only*
Look that thou let it be,
For if thou breke his commaundment,
221   Thou skapys not bot thou be shent.   *disgraced*
Weynd here into paradise,   *Go*
And luke now that ye be wise,   *look, see to it*
And kepe you well, for I must go
Unto my Lord, ther I cam fro.

[Cherubin retires to heaven.]

ADAM.   Almighty Lord, I thank it the[e]
That is, and was, and shall be,
Of thy luf and of thy grace,
For now is here a mery place.
230   Eve, my felow, how think the[e] this?   *what think you of*
EVA.   A stede methink of joye and blis,   *place*
That God has giffen to the[e] and me.
Withoutten ende blissyd be he!
ADAM.   Eve, felow, abide me thore,   *there*
For I will go to viset more,   *inspect*
To se what trees that here been.
Here ar well moo then we have seen,   *many more*

[215]i.e., To complete the orders of angels (after the fall of Satan).

[221]You won't escape without being disgraced.

Gresys, and othere small floures,
That smell full swete, of seyr coloures. *Herbs, plants*
various

240 EVA.   Gladly, sir, I will full faine.
When ye have sene theym, com agane.

ADAM.   Bot luke well, Eve, my wife,
That thou negh not the tree of life. *approach*
For if thou do He bese ill paide; *He'll be displeased*
Then be we tint, as He has saide. *lost*

EVA.   Go furth and play the[e] all aboute.
I shall not negh it whils thou art oute.
248 For be thou sekyr, I were full loth *sure*
249 For anything that He were wroth.
[*They retire.*]

250 LUCIFER [*in hell*].   Who wend ever this time have seyn? *thought*
We, that in sich mirth have beyn,
That we shuld suffre so mych wo?
Who wold ever trow it shuld be so?
Ten orders in heven were
Of angels, that had office sere; *several*
Of ich order, in thare degré, *each*
The teynd parte fell downe with me. *tenth*
For thay held with me that tide, *sided with/time*
And mantenyd me in my pride. *supported*
Bot herkyns, felows, what I say: *hearken*
261 The joy that we have lost for ay,
262 God has maide man with his hend, *hand*
263 To have that blis withoutten end,
264 The neyn ordre to fulfill
265 That after us left—sich is His will.
And now ar thay in paradise.
267 Bot thens thay shall, if we be wise.
[*Incomplete*]

248–49For, you may be sure, I would be most unwilling that God should be angry for any reason.

250Who would have thought ever to have seen this time?

261–65With his hand, God has made man to enjoy endlessly that bliss which we lost forever, (and) to complete the nine orders of angels (by replacing the tenth) who came after us to hell—such is God's will.

267i.e., But Adam and Eve will soon be expelled from paradise, if we devils proceed craftily.

THE FALL OF MAN
FROM YORK
THE COWPERS

The ultimate source for the story of Adam's and Eve's temptation is, of course, the Book of Genesis. Yet the presence of Satan within the wily serpent can only be inferred from that biblical account. Satan's role is based on an exegetical tradition of the Church Fathers, according to which the fall of man should be viewed as a direct consequence of the fall of the angels: Satan, having been cast out of heaven for his presumption, resolves to avenge himself by tempting into disobedience those earthly creatures whom God has created in his own image.

Like the twelfth-century Anglo-Norman play of *Adam* (Part II, above), the York Fall of Man is closely indebted to exegetical tradition as well as to Genesis. Satan enters the serpent and entices Eve to presume against God, just as Satan had done before. Adam too, at Eve's instigation, eats the forbidden fruit in order that they may "be goddis and knawe al thing." The act of disobedience thus recalls the original fall of Satan. At the same time, this act foreshadows still greater events to come through which man's fall will be amended: Adam's disobedience anticipates Christ's resisting temptation in the wilderness, the tree prefigures the cross on which Christ will be crucified, and Eve's role as sinful woman points forward to Mary's role as the mother of God. These correspondences are hinted at in the York Fall of Man, when Satan complains enviously that God will take upon himself the form of mankind (see ll. 4–11). Such correspondences are to become increasingly prominent in later episodes of the cycles.

The episode of the Fall of Man is absent from the Wakefield cycle because of missing pages in the manuscript. This version from the York cycle is the fifth in a series of short pageants with which the York cycle begins, each presented by a different craft guild. The usual assumption is that the episodes were acted processionally on pageant wagons, although the problems of staging processionally a complete York cycle on a single day are staggering (see the Introduction to Part III, above). This particular pageant of the Fall of Man was assigned to the Cowpers of York. The scene need only depict paradise with its tree, and perhaps a place above from which God speaks (since God is unseen by Adam at l. 134). Satan is at first outside of paradise, but makes no actual reference to his being in hell. At the end of the action, Adam and Eve are about to be banished to "middle-earth," separate from and below paradise; but the act of expulsion is in fact reserved for the next pageant, presented by the Armorers of York.

The tree must be an actual stage structure. At Norwich, such a tree was elaborately festooned with fruits and flowers of various descriptions. Iconographical tradition also sometimes represented the tree in such a way as to suggest the cross of the Crucifixion. Satan's serpent-like disguise, his "worme liknes," may have employed a serpent's skin for the body together with wings and a woman's face. Such a combination is frequently to be found in rabbinic tradition and in medieval art; and in the Chester version of this episode, Satan resolves to adopt the "manner of an Adder" with "wings like a bird," "feete as an Adder," and "a maidens face." For other costuming possibilities, see the headnote to the Creation, above.

The Fall of Man

From York

The Cowpers

	Satanas incipit, dicens :	*Satan begins, saying*

1	DIABOLUS. For woo my witte es in a were!	*is/confusion*
2	That moffes me mikill in my minde:	*moves/much*
3	The Godhede that I sawe so cleere,	
4	And parsaived that he shuld take kinde	
5	Of a degree	
6	That he had wrought, and I denied that aungell kinde	
7	Shuld it nog[h]t be.	
8	And we wer[e] faire and bright;	
9	Therfore methoght that he	
10	The kinde of us tane might,	
11	And therat dedeyned me.	*I was angry*
	The kinde of man he thoght to take,	*nature*
	And theratt hadde I grete envye;	
14	But he has made to him a make,	*a mate*
	And harde to her I wol me hye	*quickly/hasten*
16	That redy way,	
17	That purpose prove to putte it by,	
18	And fande to pike fro him that pray.	*try/pluck*
	My travaile were wele sette,	*labors/bestowed*
	Might I him so betraye	*If I might*
	His liking for to lette;	*To spoil his pleasure*
	And sone I schalle assaye.	*soon*
	[*He approaches paradise.*]	
	In a worme liknes wille I wende,	*serpent's*
	And founde to feyne a lowde lesinge.	*try/blatant lie*
	Eve, Eve!	
	EVA. Wha es thare?	*Who*
	SATANAS. I, a frende.	

1–11My spirit is in turmoil because of woe! What particularly disturbs my mind is that I saw the Godhead so clearly, and perceived that he would take upon him the nature of one of the orders he had created; and I thought it impossible he would accept any being other than that of the angels. Since we were so fair and bright, I supposed he would have taken our nature, and was angry (that he did not).

14But God has made for Adam a mate (Eve).

16–18By the most direct route, to attempt to thwart God's purpose, and try to pluck from Adam that prey (Eve).

26	And for thy gude es the cominge	
27	I hydir sought.	
	Of all the fruit that ye se hinge	
	In paradise, why eat ye noght?	
EVA.	We may of tham ilkane	each one
	Take al that us goode thought,	seemed good to us
32	Save a tree outt is tane,	is prohibited
33	Wolde do harme to neyghe it ought.	approach

SATANAS.	And why that tree—that wolde I witte—	know
	Any more than all othir by?	nearby
EVA.	For oure Lord God forbeedis us itt,	Because
	The frute therof, Adam nor I	
	To neghe it nere;	approach
	And if we dide, we both shuld die,	
40	He saide, and sese our solace sere.	cease/various joys
SATANAS.	Yha, Eve, to me take tente;	pay attention
	Take hede, and thou shalte here	hear
	What that the matere mente	matter, business
	He moved on that manere.	He spoke of in

	To ete therof He you defende—	forbade
	I knawe it wele, this was His skille—	reason
47	By-cause He wolde non othir kende	should know
48	Thes grete vertues that longes thertill.	belongs thereto
	For, will thou see,	don't you understand
	Who etis the frute, of goode and ille	Whoever eats
	Shalle have knowing as wele as Hee.	
EVA.	Why, what-kynne thing art thou,	what kind of
	That telles this tale to me?	
SATANAS.	A worme that wotith wele how	knows
	That yhe may wirshipped be.	honored

EVE.	What wirshippe shulde we winne therby?	
	To ete therof us nedith it nought.	
	We have lordshippe to make maistrie	exercise mastery
	Of alle thinge that in erthe is wrought.	Over
SATANAS.	Woman! do way!	stop it
	To gretter state ye may be broughte,	estate
	And ye will do as I schall saye.	If

26-27And for your good have I come hither.

32-33Except that one tree is prohibited, which even to approach would cause us harm.

47-48Because He wanted that no one else should know the great magical powers belonging to it (the fruit).

63 EVE.   To do is us full lothe
　　　　That shuld oure God mispaye.   *displease*
　　SATANAS.   Nay, certis it is no wathe;   *danger*
　　　　Ete it saffely ye maye.

　　　　For perille right none therin lies,
　　　　Bot worshippe and a grete winninge;
　　　　For right als God yhe shalle be wise,   *as*
70　　　And pere to him in all-kyn thinge.   *peer/everything*
　　　　Ay, goddis shalle ye be!
　　　　Of ill and gode to have knawing,
　　　　For to be als wise as he.
　　EVE.   Is this soth that thou says?
　　SATANAS.   Yhe! why trowes thou nog[h]t me?   *believe*
　　　　I wolde by no-kynnes wayes   *by no means*
　　　　Telle nog[h]t but trouthe to the[e].

　　　EVA.   Than wille I to thy teching traste,   *trust*
　　　　And fange this frute unto oure foode.   *take*
　　　　Et tunc debet accipere pomum.   *And then she must take the apple*
80 SATANAS.   Bite on boldly, be nought abasshed,
　　　　And bere Adam to amende his mode   *persuade/augment his cheer*
　　　　And eke his blisse.   *also*
　　　　Tunc Satanas recedet.   *Then Satan will withdraw*
　　　　[Eve approaches Adam.]
　　EVA.   Adam! have here of frute full goode.
　　ADAM.   Allas! woman, why toke thou this?
　　　　Owre Lorde comaunded us bothe
　　　　To tente the tree of his.
　　　　Thy werke wille make him wrothe.   *watch out for*
　　　　Allas! thou hast don amis.

　　EVE.   Nay, Adam, greve the[e] nought at it,
90　　　And I shal saye the reasoune why:
　　　　A worme has done me for to witte   *made me to understand*
　　　　We shalle be as goddis, thou and I,
　　　　If that we ete
　　　　Here of this tree. Adam, forthy   *therefore*
95　　　Lette noght that worshippe for to gete.   *Don't fail*
　　　　For we shalle be als wise
　　　　Als God that is so grete,

63We would be loath to do anything.

95Don't lose the opportunity of gaining that dignity.

And als mekill of prise;   *as great of worth*
Forthy, ete of this mete.   *food*

ADAM.   To ete it wolde I nought eschewe,
101   Might I me sure in thy saying.
EVE.   Bite on boldely, for it is trewe!
We shalle be goddis and knawe al thing.
ADAM.   To winne that name,
I schalle it taste at thy teching.
    Et accipit et comedit.   *And he takes and eats*
Allas! what have I done, for shame!
Ille counsaille, woo worthe the[e]!   *may woe befall*
A! Eve, thou art to blame.
To this entised thou me;
110   Me shames with my lyghame,   *body*

For I am naked, as me thinke.
EVE.   Allas! Adam, right so am I.
ADAM.   And for sorowe sere why ne might we sinke?   *many/mightn't*
For we have greved God Almighty
That made me man,
Brokyn his biding bittirly.
Allas, that ever we it began!
This werke, Eve, hast thou wrought,
And made this bad bargaine.
EVE.   Nay, Adam, wite me nought.   *blame*
ADAM.   Do wey, lefe Eve! Whame than?   *dear/Whom*

122 EVE.   The worme to wite wele worthy were.
With tales untrewe he me betrayed.
ADAM.   Allas, that I lete at thy lare,   *heeded your teaching*
Or trowed the trufuls that thou me saide!   *trifles, lies*
So may I bide,   *must I pray*
For I may banne that bittir brayde,   *curse/trick, action*
And drery dede, that I it dide.   *doleful deed*
129   Oure shappe for doole me defes,
130   Wherewith thay shalle be hidde.
EVE.   Late us take there figge leves,   *Let*
Sithen it is thus betidde.   *Since/happened*

101If I might assure myself of the truth of what you're saying.

110I am ashamed of my body.

122The serpent well deserves blame.

129–30Our naked shapes stun me with a sense of grief, (I not knowing) by what means they
may be hid.

ADAM.   Right as thou says, so shalle it bee,
    For we are naked and all bare.
    Full wondyr faine I wolde hide me   *Most gladly*
    Fro my Lordis sight, and I wiste whare,   *if I knew*
137 Where I ne roght.
DOMINUS [*calling*]. Adam, Adam!
ADAM.   Lorde?
DOMINUS.   Where art thou? yhare!   *quickly*
ADAM.   I here the[e], Lorde, and seys the[e] nog[h]t.   *hear/see*
140 DOMINUS.   Say, wheron is it longe,
141   This werke, why hast thou wrought?
ADAM.   Lorde, Eve garte me do wronge   *caused*
    And to that bryg me brought.   *breach (of duty)*

DOMINUS.   Say, Eve, why hast thou garte thy make   *caused your mate*
    Ete frute I bad[e] thee shuld hynge stille,   *To eat/I told you/always*
    And comaunded none of it to take?
EVA.   A worme, Lord, entised me thertill,   *thereto*
    So welaway   *alas*
    That ever I did that dede so dill!   *stupid*
150 DOMINUS.   A, wikkid worme, woo worthe the[e] ay!
    For thou on this maner[e]   *Because you in*
    Hast made tham swilke affraye,   *such misery*
    My malisoune have thou here,   *curse*
    With all the might I may.

    And on thy wombe than shall thou glide,   *belly*
    And be ay full of enmité   *forever*
    To al mankinde on ilke a side;   *every*
    And erthe it shalle thy sustinaunce be
    To ete and drinke.
    Adam and Eve, alsoo, yhe
    In erthe than shalle ye swete and swinke,   *labor*
    And travaile for youre foode.   *work*
ADAM.   Allas! wha ne might we sinke?   *why don't we*
164 We that haves alle worldis goode,
165 Ful de[r]fly may us thinke.   *grievous*
DOMINUS.   Now, Cherubin, min[e] aungell bright,
167 To middil-erth tyte go drive these twoo.   *speedily*

137Where I might not be fearful (of God's displeasure).

140–41Say, what is the reason for this deed, why did you do it?

150Ah, wicked serpent, ill fortune to you forever!

164–65To us who have (hitherto) enjoyed all earthly felicity, this may seem most grievous.

167*middil-erth:* i.e., apart from and below paradise.

ANGELUS.   Alle redy, Lorde, as it is right,
    Syn thy wille is that it be soo,   *Since*
    And thy liking.
    Adam and Eve, do you t[w]o goo,
    For here may ye make no dwelling.
    Goo yhe forthe faste to fare;   *quickly on your way*
    Of sorowe may yhe singe.
ADAM.   Allas, for sorowe and care
    Oure handis may we wring!
      Et sic finis.

THE KILLING OF ABEL
FROM WAKEFIELD

The story of Cain and Abel holds great typological significance for the author of this Wakefield pageant, as it did for other medieval writers. Because it represents the first murder in the divine history of the world, the story continues the downward spiral of sin and retribution begun with Satan's fall and continued in the temptation of Adam and Eve. Cain, like his parents, is guilty of pride and disobedience toward God. The curse he receives, condemning him to perpetual durance in hell, looks forward to the Last Judgment.

As in other episodes of the cycle, the perpetrators of evil are generally noisy, brash, and obscenely humorous, whereas the defenders of virtue are serene and idealized. Cain is a comic character in the ludicrously comic vein of Satan, anticipating Pharaoh and Herod. His speech is blustering, colorful in its invective, sinister. Even though we recognize in him the essence of evil, we find Cain more fascinating than Abel. Most of the play focuses on his inventively baleful character. Yet this vivid portrait of human damnation is importantly offset by a portrait of human martyrdom and perfect obedience to God's will. Abel is a type of Christ. His death prefigures the Crucifixion, and the lamb he offers to God is a type of eucharistic sacrifice. Although his character is less dramatically compelling than Cain's, we recognize in Abel the promise of salvation.

This pageant, the first of six regularly attributed to the so-called Wakefield "Master," is written partly in the unique nine-line stanza (see ll. 450–62) characteristic of his work. And, although the variety of other meters present may suggest that his role was that of a reviser, the play as a whole features the vigorous colloquial diction and rustic realism in which the Master excelled. Cain is vividly portrayed in terms a medieval audience could understand. He is a typical grain farmer struggling to survive, skeptical of religious teaching urging him to be grateful for his hard lot, resentful of those who are more fortunate. He conceives of sacrificial offering as a bargain to be made with God, *quid pro quo*. His inventive and comic defiance of God is appealing, even though the negative lesson is abundantly clear. The comedy of evil is especially lively in Cain's sparring relationship with his mischievous boy-servant, a character type used repeatedly by the Wakefield Master.

The pageant is assigned in a sixteenth-century hand to the Glovers' Guild. Only two other Wakefield pageants are so assigned, however, and these markings need not be taken as evidence that the pageants were acted on individual pageant wagons by the various craft guilds of the town. Martial Rose has argued, in fact, that performance of the entire Wakefield cycle may have taken place in a single arena theater, with scaffolds on the periphery of a large circular acting area (see the Introduction to Part III, above). Cain's team of four oxen and four horses may have been a live team, requiring much more acting space than a pageant wagon could afford. The acting area must also presumably supply an upper level or scaffold for heaven from which God speaks (l. 342), and a hill on which Abel and Cain offer their sacrifices (l. 170). If a theater in the round were used for the entire cycle, one hill could serve as the location for a succession of typologically-related actions: the temptation of Adam and Eve with its tree of forbidden knowledge, Abel's sacrifice and martyrdom, Abraham's offer to sacrifice his son Isaac, and Christ's crucifixion. A theater in the round would also feature a hell-mouth periodically belching forth billows of thick dark smoke, in a manner that would bear a striking resemblance to the smoldering fire of Cain's churlish offering.

The Killing of Abel

From Wakefield

Mactatio Abel.

Secunda pagina. Glover pag.

1 GARCIO.	All haill, all haill, both blithe and glad,	
	For here com I, a mery lad!	
	Be peasse youre din, my master bad,	*Hush/bade*
	Or els the dwill you spede.	*devil help you*
5	Wote ye not I com before?	*Know*
	Bot who that janglis any more,	*anyone who chatters*
	He must blaw my blak hoill bore,	*blow/black hollow hole*
	Both behind and before,	
	Till his tethe blede.	
	Felows, here I you forbede	
	To make nother nose ne cry.	*neither noise nor*
	Whoso is so hardy to do that dede,	
13	The dwill hang him up to dry!	
	Gedlingys, I am a full grete wat.	*Fellows/person*
	A good yoman my master hat—	*is called*
	Full well ye all him ken.	*know*
	Begin he with you for to strife,	*If he should begin*
	Certys, then mon ye never thrife;	*may*
	Bot I trow, by God on life,	
	Some of you ar his men.	
21	Bot let youre lippis cover youre ten,	*anger*
	Harlottys everichon!	*Rascals everyone*
	For if my master com, welcom him then.	
	Farewell, for I am gone.	

[*Exit Garcio. Enter Cain, driving his plough-team.*]

[1]*Garcio:* Cain's boy enters alone, preceding his master to quiet the audience.

[5]*before:* i.e., ahead of my master (who is, ambiguously, the devil and/or Cain).

[13]*to dry:* i.e., on the gallows.

[21]i.e., Conceal your hostility with smiles.

CAIN.   Io furth, Greynhorne! and war oute, Grime!   *Go on/look out*

26   Drawes on! God gif you ill to time!   *Pull*

Ye stand as ye were fallen in swime.   *as if/swoon*

What, will ye no forther, mare?

War! let me se how Down will draw.

Yit, shrew, yit, pull on a thraw.   *rascal/for a while*

What! it semys for me ye stand none aw.   *have no fear*

I say, Donning, go fare!   *go properly*

Aha! God gif the[e] soro and care.

Lo, now hard she what I saide.   *heard*

Now yit art thou the warst mare

In plogh that ever I haide.   *had*

37   How! Pikeharnes, how! com heder belife.   *Ho/quickly*
       [*Enter Garcio.*]

38 GARCIO.   I fend, Godys forbot, that ever thou thrife!   *God forbid*

39 CAIN.   What, boy, shal I both hold and drife?

Heris thou not how I cry? [*Garcio takes the team.*]

GARCIO.   Say, Mall and Stott, will ye not go?

Leming, Morell, Whitehorn, io!

Now will ye not se how thay hy?   *hasten*

44 CAIN.   Gog gif the[e] sorow, boy. Want of mete it gars. *God/causes it*

45 GARCIO.   Thare provand, sir, forthy, I lay behind thare ars,   *therefore*

46   And ties them fast by the nekys,

47   With many stanys in thare hekys.   *stones/fodder racks*

48 CAIN.   That shall by thy fals chekys! [*Strikes him.*]   *buy, pay for*

49 GARCIO.   And have agane as right! [*Strikes back.*]

CAIN.   I am thy master. Wilt thou fight?

51 GARCIO.   Yai, with the same mesure and weght

52   That I boro will I qwite.   *That which/requite*

53 CAIN.   We! now nothing bot call on tyte,   *shout quickly*

54   That we had ployde this land.   *So that*

²⁶Pull! God grant that you fare ill!

³⁷*Pikeharnes:* i.e., a thief (from *pick*, "steal" and *harness*, "armor").

³⁸⁻³⁹(aside) I forbid, and may God forbid, that ever you should thrive!—What, boy, must I both hold the plough and drive the team?

⁴⁴⁻⁴⁹May God give you sorrow, boy. Lack of food causes it (i.e., their failure to pull hard).—That's because I put their provender behind their tails and tie the animals securely by the neck (so they can't reach around to the food), and put stones in their fodder racks. (Garcio seemingly is taunting his master with this insolence.)—Your false cheeks will pay dearly for that! (i.e., you'll receive a blow.)—Have a blow back again right away!

⁵¹⁻⁵⁴I'll give as good as I take.—Curse it! Nothing for it now but shout quickly (to the team), so that we can get this land ploughed.

GARCIO.   Harrer, Morrell! io furth, hyte,   *go on*

56   And let the plogh stand.

[*Enter Abel.*]

ABELL.   God, as he both may and can,

Spede the[e], brother, and thy man.

59   CAIN.   Com kis mine ars! Me list not ban;   *curse*

60   As welcom standys theroute.

Thou shuld have bide til thou were cald.   *stayed/summoned*

Com nar, and other drife or hald,   *nearer/either*

And kis the dwillis toute!   *devil's arse*

Go, grese thy shepe under the toute,   *apply salve/tail*

For that is the[e] moste lefe.   *most pleasant to you*

ABELL.   Broder, ther is none hereaboute

That wold the[e] any grefe.   *wishes*

Bot, leif brother, here my sawe: *dear/hear my speech*

It is the custom of oure law,

70   All that wirk as the wise   *All who live by wise teaching*

Shall worship God with sacrifice.

Oure fader us bad, oure fader us kend,   *Adam bade us/taught*

That oure tend shuld be brend.   *tenth, tithing/burned*

Com furth, brothere, and let us gang   *go*

To worship God. We dwell full lang.

Gif we him parte of oure fee,   *possessions*

Corn or catall wheder it be.   *Grain*

And therfor, brother, let us weynd,   *go*

And first clens us from the feynd   *cleanse*

Or we make sacrifice;   *Ere*

Then blis withoutten end

Get we for oure service,

Of Him that is oure saulis leche.   *From God/soul's physician*

84   CAIN.   How! let furth youre geyse; the fox will preche.   *geese*

How long wilt thou me appech   *accuse*

With thy sermoning?

Hold thy tong, yit I say,

56(Perhaps an aside. Garcio seemingly steps aside at this point with the team, until l. 385.)

59–60Come kiss my ass! I don't desire to curse; you'd be as welcome somewhere away from here (i.e., if you'd stay away, I'd have no cause to curse).

84What! Set loose your geese so that the fox may preach to them. (A proverbial emblem of hypocritical deception; Cain indicates he will not be similarly tricked.)

88   Even ther the good wife strokid the hay!   *where*
    Or sit downe, in the dwill way,   *in the devil's name*
    With thy vain carping.   *prating*

    Shuld I leife my plogh and all thing,   *leave*
    And go with the[e] to make offering?
    Nay, thou findys me not so mad!
    Go to the dwill, and say I bad!   *say I told you to go*
95   What gifys God the[e] to rose him so?   *to praise*
    Me gifys he noght bot soro and wo.   *He gives me*

  ABELL.   Caym, leife this vain carping,
    For God giffys the[e] all thy lifing.
  CAIN.   Yit boroed I never a farthing
100   Of him—here my hend.
    ABELL.   Brother, as elders have us kend,   *taught us*
    First shuld we tend with oure hend,   *tithe*
103   And to his lofing sithen be brend.   *then*

104   CAIN.   My farthing is in the preest hand   *priest's*
105   Syn last time I offyrd.   *Since*
    ABELL.   Leif brother, let us be walkand.   *walking*
    I wold oure tend were profyrd.   *I wish/tithe-offering*

  CAIN.   We! wherof shuld I tend, leif brothere?
    For I am ich yere wars then othere—   *each year worse*
110   Here my trouth, it is none othere.
    My winningys ar bot meyn: *earnings/only poor*
    No wonder if that I be leyn.   *lean, thin*
    Full long till him I may me meyn,   *to God I may complain*
114   For, by him that me dere boght,
    I traw that he will leyn me noght.   *trow/give*
    ABELL.   Yis, all the good thou has in wone   *in plenty*
    Of Godys grace is bot a lone.   *gift*

88(Refers seemingly to the privy parts where a woman brushes the hayfield through which she is walking.)

95What does God give you, that you should praise him so?

100*here my hend*: i.e., here's my oath on it.

103–5And then (our tithes) should be burned in praise of God.—The priest has kept for himself the last tithe-offering I gave. (Cain appeals to the anticlericalism of many a medieval ploughman.)

110Here's my pledge, it is not otherwise.

114For, by Christ, who ransomed me at so great cost.

118 CAIN.   Lenys he me? As com thrift apon the[e] so!   *till now*
    For he has ever yit beyn my fo.
    For, had he my freynd beyn,
121 Othergatys it had beyn seyn.   *Otherwise*
    When all mens corn was faire in feld,
    Then was mine not worth a neld.   *needle*
    When I shuld saw, and wantyd seyde,   *sow/lacked*
    And of corn had full grete neyde,
    Then gaf he me none of his;
    No more will I gif him of this.
    Hardely hold me to blame   *By all means*
129 Bot if I serve him of the same.   *Unless*
  ABELL.   Leif brother, say not so,
    Bot let us furth togeder go.
    Good brother, let us weynd sone;   *go soon*
    No longer here, I rede, we hone.   *advise/delay*
  CAIN.   Yei, yei, thou jangyls waste!   *you chatter in vain*
135 The dwill me spede if I have hast,
    As long as I may lif,
    To dele my good or gif,   *share*
    Ather to God or yit to man,   *Either*
    Of any good that ever I wan.   *won, gained*
    For, had I giffen away my goode,   *wealth*
141 Then might I go with a ryffen hood;   *torn*
    And it is better hold that I have   *to hold onto that which*
    Then go from doore to doore and crave.   *Than/beg*
  ABELL.   Brother, com furth, in Godys name.
    I am full ferd that we get blame.   *afraid*
    Hi[e] we fast, that we were thore.   *in order that/there*
  CAIN.   We! ryn on, in the dwills nayme, before!
148 Wemay, man, I hold the[e] mad!
    Wenys thou now that I list gad   *Do you think/gad about*
    To gif away my warldys aght?   *worldly goods*
151 The dwill him spede that me so taght!
    What nede had I my travell to lose,   *my labor*
    To were my shoyn and ryfe my hose?   *wear out my shoes/tear*

118Does he give me anything? May such profit come to you!

121It would have turned out otherwise.

129Unless I treat him as he treated me.

135May the devil prosper me if I'm in any hurry.

141*with . . . hood:* i.e., in tattered beggar's clothes.

148*Wemay:* an expression of impatience.

151May the devil prosper anyone who counseled me to do thus.

ABELL.   Dere brother, hit were grete wonder   *it would be*
          That I and thou shuld go in sonder;   *separately*
          Then wold oure fader have grete ferly.   *wonder*
          Ar we not brether, thou and I?

158 CAIN.   No, bot cry on, cry, whils the[e] think good!
          Here my trowth, I hold the[e] woode.   *Here's/troth/consider you mad*
          Wheder that he be blithe or wroth,

161   To dele my good is me full lothe.   *share my wealth*
162   I have gone oft on softer wise   *in a gentler manner*
163   Ther I trowed som prow wold rise.   *Where/profit*
          Bot well I se go must I nede;   *I must needs go*
          Now weynd before—ill might thou spede!—   *go/ill luck to you*
          Syn that we shall algatys go.   *Since/in any case*

ABELL.   Leif brother, why says thou so?
          Bot go we furth both togeder.
          Blissid be God, we have fare weder.   *fair weather*
                  [*They go to the place of sacrifice.*]

CAIN.   Lay downe thy trussell apon this hill.   *bundle*
ABELL.   Forsoth, broder, so I will.
          Gog of heven take it to good.

173 CAIN.   Thou shall tend first, if thou were wood.   *tithe/mad*

ABELL.   God that shope both erth and heven, [*Kneeling.*]   *shaped*
          I pray to the[e] thou here my steven,   *hear my voice*
          And take in thank, if thy will be,
          The tend that I offre here to the[e];
          For I gif it in good entent
          To the[e], my Lord, that all has sent.
          I bren it now with stedfast thoght,   *burn*
          In worship of Him that all has wroght.
                  [*Abel's tithes burn brightly.*]

CAIN.   Rise! Let me now, syn thou has done.   *since*
          Lord of heven, thou here my boyne!   *hear my prayer*
184   And over Godys forbot be to the[e]   *God forbid*
185   Thank or thew to kun me;   *courtesy/offer*
186   For, as browke I thise two shankys,   *so may I enjoy/legs*
          It is full sore mine unthankys   *sorely against my will*
          The teynd that I here gif to the[e]
          Of corn or thing that newys me.   *that newly grows for me*

158i.e. (ironically), Go on shouting, if it seems a good idea to you.

161–63To share my wealth is very hateful to me. I've often gone along without complaining
when I knew some good would come of it.

173You'll tithe first even if you should go mad (i.e., in any case).

184–86And God forbid you should offer me thanks or courtesy; for, as I hope to enjoy the use
of my two legs (an asseveration).

Bot now begin will I then,
Syn I must nede my tend to bren.   *burn*
   [*Counting his sheaves.*]
Oone shefe, oone, and this makys two;
Bot nawder of thise may I forgo.   *neither*
Two, two, now this is thre:
Yei, this also shall leif with me,   *remain*
196 For I will chose and best have—   *choose*
197 This hold I thrift—of all this thrafe.   *heap of grain*
198 Wemo, wemo! foure, lo, here!
199 Better groved me no this yere.   *grew*
200 At yere time I sew faire corn,   *sowed*
Yit was it sich when it was shorne—   *such/reaped*
Thistils and brerys, yei grete plenté—   *briars*
And all kyn wedys that might be.   *kinds of weeds*
Foure shefys, foure, lo, this makys fife:
205 Deyll I fast thus, long or I thrife!   *ere*
Fife and sex, now this is sevyn—
207 Bot this gettys never God of heven.
Nor none of thise foure, at my might,   *if I can help it*
Shall never com in Godys sight.
Sevyn, sevyn, now this is aght—   *eight*
ABELL.   Cam, brother, thou art not God betaght.   *Cain/devoted to God*
CAIN.   We! therfor is it that I say
I will not deyle my good away.   *distribute my wealth*
Bot had I giffen him this to teynd,   *If I had/as a tithe*
Then wold thou say he were my freynd;
Bot I think not, by my hode,   *hood, head*
To departe so lightly fro my goode.
We! aght, aght, and neyn, and ten is this;
We! this may we best mis.
   [*Choosing the smallest sheaf.*]
Gif him that that ligys thore?   *lies there*
It goyse agans min[e] hart full sore.   *goes*
222 ABELL.   Cam! teynd right of all bedeyn.   *all together*
CAIN.   We lo! twelve, fifteyn, and sexteyn—
   [*Counting the second ten sheaves rapidly.*]

196–97For I will choose and keep the best of all this heap of grain—I regard this as a thrifty practice.

198*Wemo:* an expression of impatience.

199–200No better grew for me this year. At the proper season I sowed good grain.

205If I deal out quickly thus, it will be long ere I thrive.

207But God of heaven will never get this.

222Cain! give a tenth of all together.

ABELL.   Caym, thou tendys wrang, and of the warst.   *you tithe wrongly*

225 CAIN.   We! com nar, and hide mine een.   *nearer/eyes*

226   In the wenyand, wist ye now at last!   *shut up*

    Or els will thou that I wink?   *shut my eyes*

    Then shall I doy no wrong, me think.   *do*

        [*Closes his eyes, finishes counting, then reopens them.*]

    Let me se now how it is.

    Lo, yit I hold me paide!   *consider myself pleased*

    I teyndyd wonder well by ges,   *by guess-work*

232   And so even I laide.

ABELL.   Came, of God me thinke thou has no drede.   *Cain*

234 CAME.   Now and he get more, the dwill me spede,   *if*

235   As mych as oone reepe!   *much/handful*

236   For that cam him full light chepe;

    Not as mekill, grete ne small,   *much*

    As he might wipe his ars withall.

    For that, and this that lyys here,

    Have cost me full dere.

    Or it was shorne, and broght in stak,   *Ere/stacked*

    Had I many a wery bak.

    Therfor aske me no more of this,

    For I have giffen that my will is.   *what I want to give*

ABELL.   Cam, I rede thou tend right,   *advise*

    For drede of him that sittys on hight.   *Out of fear*

247 CAIN.   How that I tend, rek the[e] never a deill,

248   Bot tend thy skabbid shepe wele.

    For, if thou to my teynd tent take,   *pay attention*

    It bese the wars for thy sake.   *will be the worse*

    Thou wold I gaf him this shefe? or this sheyfe?   *Do you wish*

    Na, nawder of thise two wil I leife.   *neither*

    Bot take this. Now has he two, [*Choosing the second sheaf.*]

    And for my saull now mot it go.   *must*

    Bot it gos sore agans my will,

256   And shal he like full ill.

225–26(sarcastically) Curse it! Why don't you come nearer and cover my eyes (so that I'll choose impartially)? Bad luck to you (lit: in the waning of the moon, an unlucky time), shut up now at last!

232And I laid down the sheaves so evenly (with my eyes closed).

234–36If he gets as much as one handful more, may the devil prosper me! For that one (the single sheaf already given) came to him very cheaply.

247–48Don't concern yourself in the least how I make my tithe-offering, but mind your own business.

256If God doesn't appreciate it after all.

ABELL.   Cam, I reyde thou so teynd   *advise*
That God of heven be thy freynd.

259 CAIN.   My freynd? na, not bot if he will!   *not unless*
I did him never yit bot skill.   *but what is right*

261 If he be never so my fo,
I am avisid gif him no mo.   *determined to*

263 Bot chaunge thy conscience, as I do min[e].   *temper your mind*
264 Yit teynd thou not thy mesel swine?   *measly*

265 ABELL.   If thou teynd right, thou mon it finde.

CAIN.   Yei, kis the dwills ars behinde!
The dwill hang the[e] by the nek!
How that I teynd, never thou rek.   *never mind*
Will thou not yit hold thy peasse?   *be quiet*
Of this jangling I reyde thou seasse.   *advise you to stop*

271 And, teynd I well or tend I ill,
Bere the[e] even and speke bot skill.   *Keep calm/reasonably*
Bot now, syn thou has teyndid thine,   *since*
Now will I set fir[e] on mine.

[*Cain's offering refuses to burn.*]

We! out, haro! help to blaw!
It will not bren for me, I traw.
Puf! this smoke dos me mych shame.
Now bren, in the dwillys name!
A! what dwill of hell is it?
Almost had mine breth beyn dit.   *been stopped*
Had I blawen oone blast more,
I had beyn choked right thore.   *then and there*
It stank like the dwill in hell,
That longer ther might I not dwell.   *So that*

ABELL.   Cam, this is not worth oone leke.   *one leek*
Thy tend shuld bren withoutten smeke.

CAYM.   Com kis the dwill right in the ars!
288 For the[e] it brens bot the wars.
I wold that it were in thy throte,
Fir[e], and shefe, and ich a sprote!   *every sprout*

DEUS.   [*Speaking from above.*] Cam, why art thou so rebell *rebellious*

259(angrily) God be my friend? Nay, not unless he wants it so!

261No matter what an enemy he may be to me.

263–65But bring yourself to a suitable frame of mind, as I do. Aren't you making a tithe-offering of your measly swine yet? (i.e., look after your own affairs).—If you tithe correctly, you'll find it out (i.e., that God is your friend).

271And, whether I offer sacrifice well or ill.

288It burns worse on your account.

Agans thy brother Abell?

Thar thou nowther flyte ne chide.   *You needn't either quarrel*

If thou tend right thou gettys thy mede;   *reward*

And be thou sekir, if thou teynd fals,   *certain*

296   Thou bese alowed therafter als.

CAYM.   Why, who is that hob over the wall?   *hobgoblin*

We! who was that that piped so small?   *squeaked so feebly*

299   Com, go we hens, for perels all.

God is out of his wit!

Com furth, Abell, and let us weynd.

Me think that God is not my freynd.

On land then will I flit.

ABELL.   A, Caym, brother, that is ill done!

CAIN.   No, bot go we hens sone.

And if I may, I shall be

Ther as God shall not me see.   *Where*

ABELL.   Dere brother, I will fayre   *fare, go*

On feld ther oure bestys ar,   *there where*

To looke if thay be holgh or full.   *hollow, hungry*

311   CAYM.   Na, na, abide! We have a craw to pull.   *crow to pluck*

Hark, speke with me or thou go.   *ere*

What? wenys thou to skape so?   *do you think*

314   We! na! I aght the[e] a fowll dispite,

And now is time that I hit qwite.   *requite it*

ABEL.   Brother, why art thou so to me in ire?

317   CAYM.   We! theyf, why brend thy tend so shire,   *brightly*

Ther mine did bot smoked,   *Whereas*

Right as it wold us both have choked?

ABEL.   Godys will I trow it were

That min[e] brened so clere.

If thine smoked, am I to wite?   *to blame*

CAYM.   We! yei! that shal thou sore abite.   *pay dearly for*

With cheke-bon, or that I blin,   *ere/cease*

Shal I the[e] and thy life twin.   *sever*

   [*Strikes Abel with a jawbone. Abel falls.*]

So, lig down ther and take thy rest.   *lie*

Thus shall shrewes be chastised best.   *rascals*

296You'll receive what will be owing to you (i.e., your punishment) accordingly.

299Come on, let's go because of all the perils (to us).

311*craw to pull:* i.e., a bone to pick, a quarrel.

314Damn it! I have owed you an evil injury (i.e., you've injured me and I haven't repaid it yet).

317Damn it! Thief, why did your tithe-offering burn so brightly?

ABELL.   Veniance, veniance, Lord, I cry!
  For I am slain, and not gilty. [*Dies.*]
CAIN.   Yei, li[e] ther, old shrew! li[e] ther, li[e]!
  [*To the audience.*]
  And if any of you think I did amis,
332   I shal it amend wars then it is,
  That all men may it se.
  Well wars then it is,
  Right so shall it be.

  Bot now, syn he is broght on slepe,
  Into som hole fain wold I crepe.
338   For ferd I qwake, and can no rede;   *fear/know no advice*
  For, be I taken, I be bot dede.   *I'm as good as dead*
  Here will I lig thise fourty dayes,
  And I shrew him that me first rayse.   *curse/rouses me*
DEUS.   [*Speaking from above.*] Caym, Caym!
CAYM.   Who is that that callis me?
  I am yonder, may thou not se?
DEUS.   Caym, where is thy brother Abell?
CAYM.   What askys thou me? I trow at hell,   *Why*
  At hell I trow he be—
347   Whoso were ther then might he se—
  Or somwhere fallen on sleping.
  When was he in my keping?
DEUS.   Caym, Caym, thou was wode!   *mad*
  The voice of thy brotherys blode,
  That thou has slain on fals wise,   *in*
  From erth to heven venyance cryse.   *cries vengeance*
  And, for thou has broght thy brother downe, *because*
  Here I gif the[e] my malison.   *curse*
356 CAYM.   Yei, dele aboute the[e], for I will none,
357   Or take it the[e] when I am gone.
  Syn I have done so mekill sin   *Since/much*
  That I may not thy mercy win,
  And thou thus dos me from thy grace,   *you put me*
  I shall hide me fro thy face.
  And whereso any man may find me,

332I'll make amends by doing something even worse (i.e., Cain threatens any spectator who criticizes him).

338*can no rede*: i.e., am at a loss.

347Whoever is there (in hell) could see it (for himself).

356–57Deal out punishment all around, for I'll have none of it; or keep it to yourself when I'm gone.

	Let him slo me hardely,	*slay/by all means*
	And whereso any man may me meyte,	
	Ayther by sty or yit by strete;	*Either by path*
	And hardely, when I am dede,	*certainly*
367	Bery me in Gudeboure at the quarell hede.	*quarry's*
368	For, may I pas this place in quarte,	*safe and sound*
369	By all men set I not a fart.	
	DEUS. Nay, Caym, it bese not so.	*will not be*
	I will that no man other slo;	*desire/slay another*
	For he that sloys [thee], yong or old,	
	It shall be punishid sevenfold. [*God withdraws.*]	
374	CAYM. No force; I wote wheder I shall:	*know whither*
	In hell, I wote, mon be my stall.	*must/place*
	It is no boyte mercy to crave,	*no boot, use*
	For if I do I mon none have.	*even if*
	Bot this cors I wold were hid,	*corpse (Abel's)*
	For som man might com at ungayn:	*inconveniently*
380	"Fle, fals shrew!" wold he bid,	
	And weyn I had my brother slain.	*think*
	Bot were Pikeharnes, my knafe, here,	
	We shuld bery him both in fere.	*together*
	How, Pikeharnes! scapethrift! how, Pikeharnes, how!	
	[*Enter Garcio.*]	
	GARCIO. Master, master!	
386	CAIN. Harstow, boy? Ther is a poding in the pot.	*Do you hear*
	Take the[e] that, boy, tak the[e] that! [*Strikes him.*]	
	GARCIO. I shrew thy ball under thy hode,	*I curse your head*
	If thou were my sire of flesh and blode!	*Even if*
	All the day to ryn and trott,	*run*
	And ever amang thou strikeand;	*continually you're striking*
392	Thus am I comen bofettys to fott.	*to get buffets*
	CAIN. Peas, man! I did it bot to use my hand.	
	Bot harke, boy, I have a counsell to the[e] to say:	
	I slogh my brother this same day.	

³⁶⁷*Gudeboure:* Goodybower (a close, or entry passage from the street, in Wakefield).

³⁶⁸⁻⁶⁹For, if I can get out of here safely, I won't give a fart for any man.

³⁷⁴No matter; I know whither I'll go.

³⁸⁶(Proverbial; cf. "The fat's in the fire.")

³⁹²i.e., All I get for coming is a beating.

I pray the[e], good boy, and thou may,	*if*
To ryn away with the bayn.	*bones, dead body (?)*
GARCIO. We! out apon the[e], thefe!	
Has thou thy brother slain?	
400 CAYM. Peasse, man, for Godys pain!	
I saide it for a skaunce.	*joke*
GARCIO. Yey, bot for ferde of grevance,	*fear of injury*
Here I the[e] forsake.	
We mon have a mekill mischaunce	*We're sure to have*
And the bayles us take.	*If the bailiffs*
CAYM. A', sir, I cry you mercy! Seasse,	*Cease, hush*
And I shall make you a releasse.	*pardon*
GARCIO. What, wilt thou cry my peasse	*proclaim my amnesty*
Throughout this land?	
CAIN. Yey, that I gif God avow, belife.	*I vow to God quickly*
411 GARCIO. How will thou do, long or thou thrife?	*ere/thrive*
CAYM. Stand up, my good boy, belife,	
And thaym peasse, both man and wife;	*silence them*
And whoso will do after me,	*as I wish*
Full slape of thrift then shal he be.	*smooth of fortune*
Bot thou must be my good boy,	
And cry "oyes, oyes, oy!"	*"hear ye"*
418 GARCIO. Browes, browes to thy boy!	*Broth*

[*Garcio mounts a rostrum to make proclamation, but mischievously alters the lines his master dictates to him.*]

CAYM. I commaund you in the kingys nayme,	
GARCIO. And in my masteres, fals Cayme,	
CAYM. That no man at thame find fawt ne blame,	*with them (Cain and Garcio)*
422 GARCIO. Yey, cold rost is at my masteres hame.	*home*
CAYM. Nowther with him nor with his knafe,	*Neither/boy-servant*
GARCIO. What! I hope my master rafe.	*think/raves*
CAYM. For thay ar trew, full manyfold.	*completely honest*
426 GARCIO. My master suppys no coyle bot cold.	*pottage*
CAYM. The king writys you untill.	*to you*

---

[411] How will you do it, may it be long ere you prosper? (A curse.)

[418] *Browes*: a spoofing and nonsensical echo of "oyes."

[422] Yea, only cold roast is served at my master's home. (Many of Garcio's mocking comments suggest the hunger he experiences in serving Cain.)

[426] My master eats only cold pottage (i.e., the provisioning of his household is miserly).

GARCIO.   Yit ete I never half my fill.
CAYM.   The king will that thay be safe.   *desires*
GARCIO.   Yey, a draght of drinke faine wold I hayfe.   *have*
CAYM.   At thare awne will let tham wafe.   *wander*
GARCIO.   My stomak is redy to receyfe.   *accept (food)*
433 CAYM.   Loke no man say to theym, on[e] nor other.
GARCIO.   This same is he that slo his brother.
CAYM.   Bid every man thaym luf and lowt.   *reverence them*
436 GARCIO.   Yey, ill-spon weft ay comes foule out.
437 CAYM.   Long or thou get thy hoyse, and thou go thus   *ere/if*
            aboute!—

438   Bid every man theym pleasse to pay.
GARCIO.   Yey, gif Don, thine hors, a wisp of hay!
440 CAYM.   We! com downe in twenty dwill way!   *i.e., in the devil's name*
        The dwill I the[e] betake;   *I commend you to*
        For bot it were Abell, my brothere,   *unless*
        Yit knew I never thy make.   *Till now/equal*
            [*Garcio addresses the audience.*]

GARCIO.   Now old and yong, or that ye weynd,   *ere you go*
        The same blissing withoutten end,
        All sam then shall ye have,   *together*
        That God of heven my master has giffen.
        Browke it well, whils that ye liffen;   *Enjoy*
        He vowche it full well safe.   *May he grant it*

450 CAYM.   Com downe yit, in the dwillys way,
        And angre me no more! [*Garcio comes down.*]
        And take yond plogh, I say,
        And weynd the[e] furth fast before;
        And I shall, if I may,
        Teche the[e] another lore.   *lesson*
        I warn the[e], lad, for ay,
        Fro now furth evermore,
        That thou greve me noght;
        For, by Godys sidys, if thou do,   *i.e., by God's wounds*
460   I shall hang the[e] apon this plo,   *plow*

433Let no man reproach either of them.

436–38Yea, badly-spun woof (threads crossing the warp) comes out badly (i.e., murder cannot
be hid; a proverbial aside).—May it be long before you get your hose (i.e., before you prosper) if you go about making proclamation thus! (Addressed angrily to Pikeharnes.)—Bid
every man be pleased to pay (i.e., reward) Cain and Garcio. (Addressed to the audience as
part of Cain's proclamation.)

440com downe: Garcio has evidently climbed out of Cain's reach.

With this rope, lo, lad, lo,
By Him that me dere boght!   *who dearly ransomed me*
   [*Exit Garcio. Cain addresses the audience.*]

Now faire well, felows all, for I must nedys weynd,   *I must go*
And to the dwill be thrall, warld withoutten end.   *slave*
Ordand ther is my stall, with Sathanas the feynd.   *Decreed*
466   Ever ill might him befall that theder me commend
467   This tide.   *time*
Farewell les, and farewell more!   *i.e., farewell everyone*
For now and evermore
I will go me to hide. [*Exit.*]
   Explicit Mactatio Abell.   *Here ends the Killing of Abel*
   Sequitur Noe.   *Noah follows*

466–67 Perpetual ill luck to him who commends me thither now.

NOAH
FROM WAKEFIELD

This pageant, one of the best-known by the Wakefield Master, is written throughout in his nine-line stanza. Typologically, it looks both backward and forward. On the one hand, Noah's difficulties in controlling his disobedient wife recall Adam's problems with that "beginnar of blunder," Eve (l. 406); on the other hand, the flooding of the world prefigures the Baptism and the Last Judgment. The story of Noah is thus both a continuation of the Fall of Man and a prelude to the coming of Christ. Noah is weak, old, and henpecked. He doubts his ability and his worthiness. At the same time, Noah is obedient to God's command. Unlike Adam, he perseveres in the face of marital strife. Though he doubts himself, he trusts utterly in divine assistance. Noah manages to be at once comic and virtuous; he is a believably imperfect man with whom the audience can identify, and yet he is also a type of Christ.

Noah's comic battle with his wife is not to be found in Genesis 6–9. It is an old and popular medieval legend, owing much to the tradition of the fabliau, a humorously bawdy popular tale. Like every other aspect of the Noah story, this comic war of the sexes took on typological meaning for a medieval audience. The ark represents the true Church, and those like the wife who refuse to come aboard are recalcitrant sinners. Even when faced with the imminent prospect of death, the sinner perversely refuses to acknowledge that salvation is possible only through the Church. To be sure, the dramatic version by the Wakefield Master may strike us as more "realistic" than symbolic: husband and wife flail at one another in slapstick scenes of comic physical abuse and indulge in domestic quarrels that must have

seemed vividly relevant to the play's fifteenth-century audience. Still, the typological meaning is plainly evident as well. Even the birds used by Noah and his wife to seek for land are given a symbolic meaning: the raven that Noah's wife chooses to send from the ark is "without any reson" (l. 501), whereas Noah's dove is gentle and obedient. The harmonious ending of this pageant, with Noah once more in charge of a submissive and loving wife, is both a resolution of a struggle for mastery in marriage and a restoration of the traditional hierarchical relationship between reason and passion. "Realistic" and emblematic interpretations of this pageant reinforce one another.

We cannot be certain whether the Wakefield Noah was performed on a pageant wagon before a series of audiences, or in an arena theater in one fixed location. The latter possibility would allow for the ark itself, set on wheels, to be brought into the arena and then out again at the end of the action. Several medieval guild accounts record the existence of arks that were elaborate and expensive edifices. In the Digby *Mary Magdalene* (see Part IV), a ship on wheels actually enters and crosses the arena theater-in-the-round. At Hull, too, the ark was set upon wheels. On the other hand, Noah may have put together an ark out of prefabricated parts, or he may simply have mimed such an action. The stage directions in the Wakefield Noah are not illuminating on such technical matters. In any case, the scene must also make provision for God to speak—presumably from above—before he descends to Noah. After receiving divine instruction, Noah must cross over (*perget*) to his wife, then move elsewhere to build the ark. The wife refers to herself as being "on this hill" (l. 337). Noah and his family must be able to board the ark itself. As in the case of the Wakefield Killing of Abel, this pageant would appear to be more feasible in an arena theater than on a single pageant wagon, even though we cannot positively determine what arrangement was used.

Noah

From Wakefield

Processus Noe cum Filiis. Wakefeld.　　　　　　*The Story of Noah and His Sons*

[*Noah alone, praying.*]

NOE.	Mightfull God veray, maker of all that is,	*true*
	Thre persons withoutten nay, oone God in endles blis,	*undeniably*
	Thou maide both night and day, beest, fowle, and fish;	
4	All creatures that lif may wroght thou at thy wish,	*you made*
	As thou wel might.	
	The son, the moyne, verament,	*moon/truly*
	Thou maide; the firmament;	
	The sternes also full fervent	*stars*
	To shine thou maide ful bright.	
10	Angels thou maide ful even, all orders that is,	*indeed*
	To have the blis in heven. This did thou more and les,	*You did all this*
	Full mervelus to neven. Yit was ther unkindnes	*mention/their*
	More by foldys seven then I can well expres,	*seven times*
	Forwhy	*Because*
	Of all angels in brightnes	
	God gaf Lucifer most lightnes,	
17	Yit prowdly he flit his des	*moved his dais*
18	And set him even Him by.	
19	He thoght himself as worthy as Him that him made	
	In brightnes, in bewty; therfor He him degrade,	*God threw him down*
	Put him in a low degré soyn after, in a brade,	*soon/moment*
	Him and all his menye, wher he may be unglad	*entourage*
	For ever.	
	Shall thay never win away	*They will never escape*
	Hence unto domysday,	

⁴You made all creatures that live, according to your will.

¹⁷⁻¹⁹Yet proudly Lucifer moved his throne and seated himself equal to God. Lucifer thought himself as worthy as God that made him.

Bot burn in bayle for ay;   *torment*
Shall thay never dissever.   *depart*

Soyne after, that gracious Lord to his liknes maide man,   *in His likeness*
29   That place to be restord, even as he began.
30   Of the Trinité by accord, Adam, and Eve that woman,
31   To multiplye without discord, in paradise put he thaym,
And sithen to both   *afterwards*
Gaf in commaund
On the tre of life to lay no hend.
Bot yit the fals feynd
Made Him with man wroth,

Entisyd man to glotony, stird him to sin in pride.
Bot in paradise, securly, might no sin abide;   *certainly*
And therfor man full hastely was put out in that tide,   *time*
40   In wo and wandreth for to be, in paines full unrid   *distress/severe*
To knowe:
First in erth, and sithen in hell   *afterwards*
With feyndys for to dwell,
Bot He His mercy mell   *Unless God/declare*
To those that will Him trawe.   *believe in Him*

Oile of mercy He hus hight, as I have hard red,   *promised us/heard tell*
To every lifing wight that wold luf Him and dred.   *living creature*
Bot now before His sight every liffing leyde,   *person*
Most party day and night, sin in word and dede   *Most part of*
Full bold:
51   Som in pride, ire, and envy,
52   Som in covetous and glotiny,
53   Som in sloth and lechery,
And other wise manyfold.

Therfor I drede lest God on us will take veniance,
For sin is now alod, without any repentance.   *widespread (?)*
Sex hundreth yeris and od have I, without distance,   *odd/undeniably*
58   In erth, as any sod, liffyd with grete grevance
Allway.
And now I wax old,

29–31To fill that place (left vacant by the fallen angels), completing God's original design.
With the consent of the Trinity (i.e., acting as three-personed God), he put Adam and the
woman Eve in paradise, to reproduce their kind in harmony.

51–53(The seven Deadly Sins.)

58(I) have lived on earth in great sorrow, like a clod of earth (i.e., closed in by this "muddy
vesture of decay").

Seke, sory, and cold;
As muk apon mold   *dung upon earth*
I widder away.   *wither*

Bot yit will I cry for mercy and call.—[*Prays to God.*]
Noe, thy servant, am I, Lord over all!
66   Therfor me, and my fry shal with me fall,   *children*
67   Save from velany, and bring to thy hall
In heven.
And kepe me from sin
This warld within.
Comly king of mankin,   *mankind*
I pray the[e] here my stevyn!   *hear my voice*

DEUS [*speaking from above*].   Syn I have maide all thing that is
liffand,   *living*
Duke, emperour, and king, with mine awne hand,
For to have thare liking by see and by sand,   *To have their pleasure*
Every man to my biding shuld be bowand   *bidding/obedient*
Full fervent,
That maide man sich a creatoure,   *(To me) who made*
Farest of favoure.
80   Man must luf me paramoure   *passionately*
By reson, and repent.   *Accordingly*

Me thoght I shewed man luf when I made him to be
All angels abuf, like to the Trinité;   *above*
And now in grete reprufe full low ligys he,   *disgrace/lies*
In erth himself to stuf with sin that displeasse me   *sins*
Most of all.
Veniance will I take
In erth for sin sake.   *because of sin*
My grame thus will I wake   *anger*
90   Both of grete and small.   *concerning everyone*

I repente full sore that ever maide I man.
By me he settys no store, and I am his soferan.
I will distroy therfor both beest, man, and woman:
All shall perish, les and more. That bargan may thay ban *curse*
That ill has done.   *Who have sinned*
In erth I se right noght   *nothing at all*
Bot sin that is unsoght;   *unatoned for*

66–67Therefore save me from wrongdoing, and my children who will fall (into damnation)
with me (unless you save me).

Of those that well has wroght   *who have acted virtuously*
Find I bot a fone.   *a few*

100   Therfor shall I fordo all this medill-erd   *destroy|the world*
With floodys that shall flo and ryn with hidous rerd. *run|roar*
I have good cause therto; for me no man is ferd.   *no man fears me*
As I say shal I do: of veniance draw my swerd,   *out of vengeance*
And make end
Of all that beris life,   *bears*
Sayf Noe and his wife,   *Except*
For thay wold never strife
With me, then me offend.   *nor*

Him to mekill win, hastly will I go   *To his great profit*
To Noe my servand, or I blin, to warn him of his wo.   *ere I stop*
In erth I se bot sin reynand to and fro   *prevailing everywhere*
112   Emang both more and myn, ichon other fo   *less|everyone*
With all thare entent.
All shall I fordo   *destroy*
With floodys that shall floo;
Wirk shall I thaym wo
That will not repent.   *Those who*
    [*God descends and addresses Noah.*]

Noe, my freend, I the[e] commaund, from cares the[e] to
        keyle,   *preserve*
A ship that thou ordand of naile and bord ful wele.   *build*
120   Thou was alway well-wirkand, to me trew as stele, *doing good*
To my biding obediand; frendship shal thou fele   *experience*
To mede.   *As reward*
Of lennthe thy ship be
Thre hundreth cubettys, warn I the[e];
Of heght even thirté;
Of fifty als in brede.   *also in breadth*

Anoint thy ship with pik and tar without and als within, *pitch|also*
The water out to spar. This is a noble gin.   *shut|contrivance*
Look no man the[e] mar. Thre chese chambres begin;   *hinder|tiers of rooms*
130   Thou must spend many a spar, this wark or thou win *use|ere you achieve*
To end fully.
Make in thy ship also
Parloures oone or two,
And houses of office mo   *more stables*
For beestys that ther must be.

112Among all people both great and humble, everyone hostile to everyone else.

Oone cubite on hight a windo shal thou make;
On the side a doore, with slight, beneyth shal thou take.   *skill/make*
With the[e] shal no man fight, nor do the[e] no kyn wrake.   *no sort of injury*
When all is doyne thus right, thy wife, that is thy make,   *done/mate*
Take in to the[e];
Thy sonnes of good fame,   *repute*
142   Sem, Japhet, and Came,   *Cain*
Take in also [t]hame,
Thare wifys also thre.

For all shal be fordone that lif in land, bot ye,   *destroyed*
With floodys that from abone shal fall, and that plenté.   *above*
It shall begin full sone to rain uncessantlé,
After dayes seven be done, and induyr dayes fourty,
Withoutten faill.
150   Take to thy ship also
Of ich kind beestys two,
Maill and femaill, bot no mo,
Or thou pull up thy saill,   *Ere*

For thay may the[e] availl when al this thing is wroght.
Stuf thy ship with vitaill, for hungre that ye perish noght.   *so that*
Of beestys, foull, and cataill, for thaym have thou in thoght: *keep them in mind*
157   For thaym is my counsaill that som socour be soght
In hast.
Thay must have corn and hay   *grain*
And oder mete alway.   *other food*
Do now as I the[e] say,
In the name of the Holy Gast.

NOE.   A, benedicité! what art thou that thus   *bless me*
Tellys afore that shall be? Thou art full mervelus!   *Predicts the future*
Tell me, for charité, thy name so gracius.
DEUS.   My name is of dignité, and also full glorius
To knowe:
I am God most mighty,
Oone God in Trinity,
Made the[e] and ich man to be;   *(Who) made*
To luf me well thou awe.   *ought*

NOE.   I thank the[e], Lord so dere, that wold vowchsayf
Thus low to appere to a simple knafe.

142*Came*: Cain. (Medieval authorities regularly named one of Noah's sons "Cain," rather than "Ham" as in Genesis 7:13. See the Chester Noah pageant, l. 57.)

157As to them, my advice is that some aid be sought.

174	Blis us, Lord, here, for charité I hit crafe;	*crave it*
	The better may we stere the ship that we shall hafe,	*have*
	Certain.	
	DEUS. Noe, to the[e] and to thy fry	*children*
	My blissing graunt I.	
	Ye shall wax and multiply	
180	And fill the erth agane,	

When all thise floodys ar past, and fully gone away. [*God retires.*]

	NOE. Lord, homward will I hast as fast as that I may.	
	My [wife] will I frast what she will say,	*ask*
	And I am agast that we get som fray	
	Betwixt us both.	
	For she is full tethee,	*peevish*
	For litill oft angré;	*Over little matters*
	If any thing wrang be,	
189	Soyne is she wroth.	*Soon*
	Tunc perget ad uxorem.	*Then he will go to meet his wife*

God spede, dere wife! How fayre ye?

191	UXOR. Now, as ever might I thrife, the wars I the[e] see.	*worse*
	Do tell me belife, where has thou thus long be?	*quickly*
193	To dede may we drife, or lif, for the[e],	
194	For want.	
	When we swete or swink,	*While/toil*
	Thou dos what thou think,	*have a mind to*
	Yit of mete and of drink	*food*
	Have we veray skant.	

	NOE. Wife, we ar hard sted with tithingys new.	*hard pressed*
200	UXOR. Bot thou were worthy be cled in Stafford blew,	
201	For thou art alway adred, be it fals or trew.	*afraid*
	Bot God knowes I am led—and that may I rew—	*treated*
	Full ill;	
	For I dar be thy borow,	*I'll be bound*
205	From even unto morow	*evening*

174Bless us, Lord, here, I beg for the sake of Christian charity.

189s.d.: Noah evidently crosses the stage or acting area.

191Now, as I hope to prosper (a mild oath), the worse for seeing you.

193–94We may hasten to our deaths for want of food, or live, for all you care.

200–1But you deserve to be beaten black and blue ("Stafford blew" is a blue cloth), for you're always scared of any rumor, false or true.

205–7i.e., All night long you're always complaining. May God, for once, send you your fill of the sorrows you're always talking about!

206   Thou spekys ever of sorow.

207   God send the[e] onys thy fill!   *once*

      [*Addressing the women in the audience.*]

      We women may wary all ill husbandys.   *curse*

209   I have oone, by Mary that lowsid me of my bandys!   *delivered*

      If he teyn, I must tary, howsoever it standys,   *is vexed*

      With seymland full sory, wringand both my handys   *semblance, looks*

      For drede.

      Bot yit otherwhile,   *at other times*

      What with gam and with g[u]ile,   *scheming*

      I shall smite and smile,

      And qwite him his mede.   *pay him back*

217 NOE.   We! hold thy tong, ram-skit, or I shall the[e] still.   *I'll silence you*

      UXOR.   By my thrift, if thou smite, I shal turne the[e] untill.   *on you*

219 NOE.   We shall assay as tyte. Have at the[e], Gill!   *make trial at once*

      Apon the bone shal it bite. [*Strikes her.*]

      UXOR.   A, so! Mary, thou smitys ill!

      Bot I suppose

      I shal not in thy det

      Flit of this flett: *Leave this place*

      Take the[e] ther a langett   *thong*

      To tie up thy hose! [*Strikes him*].

      NOE.   A! wilt thou so? Mary, that is mine! [*Strikes.*]   *here's my blow*

227 UXOR.   Thou shal thre for two, I swere by Godys pine!   *suffering*

          [*Strikes.*]

228 NOE.   And I shall qwite the[e] tho, in faith, or sinc.   *ere long*

          [*Strikes.*]

      UXOR.   Out apon the[e], ho!   *Fie*

      NOE.   Thou can both bite and whine

      With a rerd!   *roar*

231   For all if she strike, [*To the audience.*]

232   Yit fast will she skrike.   *shriek*

      In faith, I hold none slike,   *I think there's none such*

      In all medill-erd.   *the earth*

209I have a bad husband, (I swear) by the Virgin Mary who delivered me safely from my confinement at childbirth (called Our Lady's bands).

217*ram-skit:* ram shit.

219*Gill:* either her true name, or an insulting nickname.

227–28You'll get three blows for every two (you give), I swear by the Passion of God!—And I'll pay you back for those blows, truly, before long (i.e., immediately).

231–32For all her striking, she's as fast at shrieking.

Bot I will kepe charité, for I have at do.   *things to do*

UXOR.   Here shal no man tary the[e]; I pray the[e] go to!

Full well may we mis the[e], as ever have I ro.   *as I hope to have peace*

To spin will I dres me. [*Sits down to spin.*]   *I'll get ready*

NOE.   We! farewell, lo.

Bot, wife,

240   Pray for me beselé   *diligently*

To eft I com unto the[e].   *Until again*

UXOR.   Even as thou prays for me,

As ever might I thrife.   *As I hope to prosper*

NOE.   I tary full lang fro my warke, I traw.   *believe*

Now my gere will I fang, and thederward draw.   *gear/take*

[*Goes to his shipbuilding location.*]

246   I may full ill gang, the soth for to knaw.   *fare*

247   Bot if God help amang, I may sit downe daw   *Unless/meanwhile*

248   To ken.

Now assay will I

How I can of wrightry.   *carpentry*

In nomine Patris, et Filii,   *In the name of the Father, and of the*

Et Spiritus Sancti. Amen.   *Son, and of the Holy Ghost*

To begin of this tree my bonys will I bend.   *from this timber*

I traw from the Trinité socoure will be send.   *sent*

It fayres full faire, think me, this wark to my hend;   *fares well/in*

Now blissid be He that this can amend.

Lo, here the lenght, [*Measuring.*]

Thre hundreth cubettys evenly;

Of breed, lo, is it fifty;   *breadth*

260   The heght is even thirty

Cubettys full stre[n]ght.

Now my gowne will I cast, and wirk in my cote.   *cast off*

Make will I the mast or I flit oone foote.   *ere I depart*

A! my bak, I traw, will brast! This is a sory note!   *burst*

Hit is wonder that I last, sich an old dote,   *dotard*

All dold,   *stupid, inert*

To begin sich a wark.

My bonys ar so stark,   *stiff*

No wonder if thay wark,   *ache*

For I am full old.

246–48To tell the truth, I can scarcely move at all. Unless God help meanwhile, I must rest
content to be known for a fool.

271   The top and the saill both will I make;
272   The helme and the castell also will I take;
     To drife ich a naill will I not forsake.   *each*
     This gere may never faill, that dar I undertake   *affirm*
     Onone.   *At once*
     This is a nobull gyn.   *contrivance*
     Thise nailes so thay ryn   *they run so*
     Thoro more and myn,   *large and small*
     Thise bordys ichon.   *each one*

280   Window and doore, even as he saide;
     Thre ches chambre, thay ar well maide;   *tiered*
     Pik and tar full sure therapon laide.   *Pitch*
     This will ever endure, therof am I paide,   *pleased*
     Forwhy   *Because*
     It is better wroght
     Then I coude haif thoght.   *have*
     Him that maide all of noght
     I thank oonly.
        [Goes to his wife and family.]

     Now will I hi[e] me, and nothing be leder,   *be not at all sluggish*
290   My wife and my meneye to bring even heder.— *household/hither*
     Tent hedir tidely, wife, and consider;   *Pay attention quickly*
     Hens must us fle, all sam togeder,   *of us together*
     In hast.
  UXOR.   Why, sir, what alis you?
     Who is that asalis you?   *assails*
296   To fle it avalis you   *avails*
     And ye be agast.   *If*

298 NOE.   Ther is garn on the reyll other, my dame. *yarn/reel*
  UXOR.   Tell me that ich a deyll, els get ye blame. *every bit*
  NOE.   He that cares may keill—blissid be his name!— *He who assuages sorrows*
     He has [behete,] for oure seyll, to sheld us fro shame, *promised/happiness*
     And said
     All this warld aboute
     With floodys so stoute,   *fierce*

271*top*: platform for archers at the mast-head of a medieval ship.

272*castell*: tower or castellated platform on a medieval ship.

296To flee is the best thing for you to do.

298There is other yarn on the reel (i.e., other work to do), wife.

That shall ryn on a route,   *in a mass*
Shall be overlaide.

He saide all shall be slain, bot oonely we,   *except*
Oure barnes that ar bain, and thare wifys thre.   *children/obedient*
A ship he bad[e] me ordain, to safe us and oure fee.   *goods*
310 Therfor with all oure main thank we that Fre,   *might/noble Lord*
Beytter of baill.   *Healer of sorrow*
Hi[e] us fast, go we thedir.
UXOR.   I wote never whedir;   *I don't at all know where*
I dase and I dedir   *I'm bewildered/tremble*
For ferd of that taill.   *fear/tale*

NOE.   Be not aferd. Have done. Trus sam oure gere,   *Gather together*
That we be ther or none, without more dere.   *So that/ere noon/harm*
1 FILIUS.   It shall be done full sone. Brether, help to bere.
2 FILIUS.   Full long shall I not hoyne to do my devere.   *delay/duty*
320 Brether, sam.   *let's pack up*
3 FILIUS.   Without any yelp,   *boasting*
At my might shall I help.   *With all my might*
UXOR.   Yit, for drede of a skelp,   *slap*
Help well thy dam!   *mother*
        [*They proceed to the ark.*]

NOE.   Now ar we there as we shuld be.
Do get in oure gere, oure catall and fe,   *goods*
Into this vessell here, my childer fre.   *excellent*
        [*All but the wife enter the ark.*]
328 UXOR.   I was never bard ere, as ever might I the, *enclosed/prosper*
329 In sich an oostré as this!   *hostelry, inn*
In fath, I cannot find   *faith*
Which is before, which is behind.   *fore/aft*
Bot shall we here be pind,   *penned*
Noe, as have thou blis?   *as you hope to be saved*

NOE.   Dame, as it is skill, here must us abide grace. *reasonable*
   Therfor, wife, with good will com into this place.
UXOR.   Sir, for Jak nor for Gill will I turne my face,
Till I have on this hill spon a space   *spun a while*
On my rok.   *distaff*
339 Well were he might get me!   *He'd be lucky who*

328-29I was never before barred or enclosed in such a (strange) inn as this, as I hope to
prosper (a mild oath).

339Good luck to the person who tries to move me from here.

Now will I downe set me. [*Sits to spin.*]
Yit reede I no man let me,   *advise/hinder*
For drede of a knok.

NOE [*from the ark*].   Behold to the heven! The cateractes all,
Thay ar open full even, grete and small,   *indeed*
And the planettys seven left has thare stall.   *stations*
Thise thoners and levin downe gar fall   *lightning/cause to fall*
Full stout   *fiercely*
Both halles and bowers,
Castels and towres.
Full sharp ar thise showers
That renys aboute.   *rain down on all sides*

Therfor, wife, have done. Com into ship fast.
353 UXOR.   Yei, Noe, go cloute thy shone! The better will thay   *mend/shoes*
    last.
1 MULIER.   Good moder, com in sone, for all is overcast,
    Both the son and the mone.
2 MULIER.   And many wind-blast
Full sharp.
Thise floodys so thay ryn;   *pour down excessively*
Therfor, moder, com in.
UXOR.   In faith, yit will I spin.
All in vain ye carp.

3 MULIER.   If ye like ye may spin, moder, in the ship.
362 NOE.   Now is this twyis: com in, dame, on my frenship.   *as I love you*
UXOR.   Wheder I lose or I win, in faith, thy felowship,
Set I not at a pin. This spindill will I slip   *I don't care/empty*
Apon this hill
Or I stir oone fote.   *Ere*
367 NOE.   Peter! I traw we dote.   *we're talking nonsense*
Without any more note,   *ado*
Com in if ye will.

UXOR.   Yei, water nighys so nere that I sit not dry!   *approaches*
Into ship with a byr, therfor, will I hy   *a rush*
For drede that I drone here. [*She rushes aboard.*]   *drown*
NOE.   Dame, securly,   *certainly*

353i.e., Noah, mind your own business.

362*twyis:* for the second time.

367*Peter:* i.e., by St. Peter.

373   It bees boght full dere ye abode so long by   *will be paid for dearly*
       Out of ship.

       UXOR.   I will not, for thy biding,   *bidding*
376   Go from doore to miding.   *dung heap*

       NOE.   In faith, and for youre long tarying
       Ye shal lik on the whip.   *lick, taste of*

379   UXOR.   Spare me not, I pray the[e], bot even as thou think.
       Thise grete wordys shall not flay me.

       NOE.   Abide, dame, and drink,   *pay the penalty*
       For betyn shall thou be with this staf to thou stink.   *till you break wind*

382   Ar strokys good? say me. [*Threatens her.*]

       UXOR.   What say ye, Wat Wink?

       NOE.   Speke!
       Cry me mercy, I say!

       UXOR.   Therto say I nay.

       NOE.   Bot thou do, by this day,   *Unless*
       Thy hede shall I breke! [*Threatens her again.*]

       [*The wife appeals to the women in the audience.*]

388   UXOR.   Lord, I were at ese, and hertely full hoylle,   *sound in heart*
389   Might I onys have a measse of wedows coyll.   *dish/pottage*
390   For thy saull, without lese, shuld I dele penny doyll.   *truly*
391   So wold mo, no frese, that I se on this sole   *no doubt/place*
       Of wifys that ar here,
       For the life that thay leyd,   *Because of*
       Wold thare husbandys were dede.   *Wish/dead*
395   For, as ever ete I brede,   *bread*
       So wold I oure sire were!

       [*Noah appeals to the men in the audience.*]

       NOE.   Yee men that has wifys, whils thay ar yong,
       If ye luf youre lifys, chastice thare tong.
       Me think my hert rifys, both levyr and long,   *splits/liver and lung*

373You'll pay dearly for your long delay (by receiving blows).

376*miding*: midden, dung or refuse heap. (From door to midden is a short distance.)

379Don't hold back on my account, please, but do just as you think fit (i.e., come on, if you want a fight).

382 *Wat Wink*: derisive nickname.

388-91Lord, I'd be at ease, and cheerful in my heart, if I might for once enjoy a widow's lot (lit.: have a helping of widow's pottage). To benefit your soul, (Noah,) truly, I'd gladly distribute mass-pennies (i.e., pay for masses in honor of your departed soul). So would others, doubtless, whom I see in this place (among the audience).

395i.e., For, as I hope to live.

To se sich strifys wedmen emong.   *among married men*
Bot I,
As have I blis,   *As I hope to be saved*
Shall chastise this.
    UXOR.   Yit may ye mis,
405 Nicholl Nedy!

406 NOE.   I shall make the[e] still as stone, beginnar of blunder!
    I shall bete the[e] bak and bone, and breke all in sonder.
      [*They fight.*]
    UXOR.   Out, alas, I am gone! Oute apon the[e], mans
      wonder!   *monster*
409 NOE.   Se how she can grone, and I lig under!
    Bot, wife,
    In this hast let us ho,   *violence/stop*
    For my bak is nere in two.
    UXOR.   And I am bet so blo   *beaten so blue*
    That I may not thrife.

1 FILIUS.   A! why fare ye thus, fader and moder both?
2 FILIUS.   Ye shuld not be so spitus, standing in sich a woth.   *spiteful/peril*
3 FILIUS.   Thise [weders] ar so hidus, with many a cold coth.   *disease*
NOE.   We will do as ye bid us; we will no more be wroth,
    Dere barnes.   *children*
420 Now to the helme will I hent, [*Takes the helm.*]   *lay hold*
    And to my ship tent.   *tend*
    UXOR.   I se on the firmament,
    Me think, the seven starnes.   *planets*

NOE.   This is a grete flood, wife, take hede.
UXOR.   So me thoght, as I stode. We ar in grete drede;
    Thise wawghes ar so wode.   *waves/mad*
NOE.   Help, God, in this nede!
    As thou art stere-man good, and best, as I rede,   *think*
    Of all,
    Thou rewle us in this rase,   *rush (of water)*
430 As thou me behete hase.   *promised me*
    UXOR.   This is a perlous case.
    Help, God, when we call!

NOE.   Wife, tent the stere-tre, and I shall asay   *tend the helm*

405*Nicholl Nedy:* derisive nickname.

406*beginnar of blunder:* a recollection of *Eve.*

The depnes of the see that we bere, if I may.   *draw in displacement*

UXOR.   That shall I do ful wisely. Now go thy way,
For apon this flood have we flett many day   *floated*
With pine.   *suffering*

NOE.   Now the water will I fownd: [*Lowers a plumb line.*]   *test*
A! it is far to the grownd.

440   This travell I expownd
441   Had I to tine.   *in vain*

Above all hillys bedeyn the water is risen late   *all together/lately*
Cubettys fifteyn. Bot in a highter state
It may not be, I weyn, for this well I wate: *ween/know*
This fourty dayes has rain beyn; it will therfor abate
Full lele.   *truly*
This water in hast
Eft will I tast: [*Lowers a plumb line again.*]   *Again/try*
Now am I agast—   *amazed*

450   It is wanyd a grete dele!

Now ar the weders cest, and cateractes knit,   *ceased/closed off*
Both the most and the leest.

UXOR.   Me think, by my wit,
The son shines in the eest. Lo, is not yond it?
We shuld have a good feest, were thise floodys flit   *departed*
So spitus.

NOE.   We have been here, all we,
Thre hundreth dayes and fifty.

UXOR.   Yei, now wanys the see.
Lord, well is us!

NOE.   The thrid time will I prufe what depnes we bere.
     [*Lowers a plumb line again.*]

UXOR.   How long shall thou hufe? Lay in thy line there.   *wait*

462 NOE.   I may towch with my lufe the grownd evyn here.   *palm of hand*

UXOR.   Then beginnys to grufe to us mery chere.   *grow*
Bot, husband,
What grownd may this be?

NOE.   The hillys of Armonye.   *Armenia*

UXOR.   Now blissid be He
That thus for us can ordand!   *has provided*

NOE.   I see toppys of hillys he, many at a sight;   *high*

440–41 This labor I describe (i.e., plumbing the depths) I spent in vain.

462 (Noah has brought up a bottom sample on his line, which he touches.)

Nothing to let me, the wedir is so bright.   *hinder*
UXOR.   Thise ar of mercy tokyns full right.
472 NOE.   Dame, thy counsell me what fowll best might   *therefore*
And cowth   *could*
With flight of wing
Bring, without tarying,
Of mercy som tokyning,
Ayther by north or southe.   *Either*

For this is the first day of the tent moyne.   *tenth moon, month*
UXOR.   The ravyn, durst I lay, will com agane sone.   *wager*
480 As fast as thou may, cast him furth—have done!
    [*He sends out a raven.*]
He may happyn today com agane or none   *ere noon*
With grath.   *Without delay*
NOE.   I will cast out also
Dowfys oone or two.   *Doves*
Go youre way, go; [*He sends out doves.*]
God send you som wathe!   *hunting*

Now ar thise fowles flone into seyr countré.   *various*
Pray we fast ichon, kneland on oure kne, [*They kneel.*]
To him that is alone worthiest of degré,
490 That he wold send anone oure fowles som fee   *share of game*
To glad us.
UXOR.   Thay may not faill of land,   *fail to reach*
The water is so wanand.   *waning*
NOE.   Thank we God all-weldand,   *all-ruling*
That Lord that made us!

It is a wonder thing, me think, sothlé,   *truly*
Thay ar so long tarying, the fowles that we
Cast out in the morning.
UXOR.   Sir, it may be
Thay tary to thay bring.   *until they bring something*
NOE.   The ravyn is a-hungrye
500 Allway.
He is without any reson:
And he find any carion,   *If*
As peraventure may be fon,   *found*
He will not away.

The dowfe is more gentill. Her trust I untew,   *I trust her*
Like unto the turtill, for she is ay trew.   *turtle-dove*

472*thy* (i.e., *forthy*): therefore (or perhaps should read *thou*).

507 UXOR.   Hence bot a litill she commys, lew lew!
　　　　　　She bringys in her bill som novels new.   *news*
　　　　　　Behald,
　　　　　　It is of an olif-tre
　　　　　　A branch, thinkys me.
　　　NOE.   It is soth, perdé;   *by God*
　　　　　　Right so is it cald.

　　　　　　Doufe, bird full blist, faire might the[e] befall!   *may good luck befall you*
　　　　　　Thou art trew for to trist as ston in the wall.   *trust*
　　　　　　Full well I it wist thou wold com to thy hall.   *I knew that*
　　　UXOR.   A trew tokyn ist we shall be savyd all,   *is it*
　　　　　　Forwhy
　　　　　　The water, syn she com,   *since*
520　　　　　Of depnes plom   *straight down*
　　　　　　Is fallen a fathom
　　　　　　And more, hardely.   *certainly*

　　1 FILIUS.   Thise floodys ar gone, fader, behold!
　　2 FILIUS.   Ther is left right none, and that be ye bold.   *be sure of that*
　　3 FILIUS.   As still as a stone oure ship is stold.   *fixed*
526 NOE.   Apon land here anone that we were, fain I wold.
　　　　　　My childer dere,
　　　　　　Sem, Japhet, and Cam,
　　　　　　With gle and with gam   *mirth*
　　　　　　Com go we all sam;   *together*
　　　　　　We will no longer abide here.

　　　UXOR.   Here have we beyn, Noy, long enogh
533　　　　　With tray and with teyn, and dreed mekill wogh.   *misery/suffering*
　　　　　　[*They disembark.*]
　　　NOE.   Behald, on this greyn nowder cart ne plogh   *greensward neither*
　　　　　　Is left, as I weyn, nowder tre then bogh,   *nor bough*
　　　　　　Ne other thing,
　　　　　　Bot all is away;
　　　　　　Many castels, I say,
　　　　　　Grete townes of aray,   *stately towns*
540　　　　　Flitt has this flowing.   *Removed*

507Only a short distance away she comes, lo, lo!

526I wish we were on land immediately.

533With misery and with wretchedness, and have suffered great evil.

540-42This flood has removed (stately towns).—With their might these floods have, undeterred, swept away everything on earth, both at sea and ashore.

541 UXOR.   Thise floodys, not afright, all this warld so wide   *undeterred*
542   Has mevid with might, on se and by side.   *shore*
NOE.   To dede ar thay dight, prowdist of pride,   *death/put*
Everich a wight that ever was spyde   *Every creature/detected*
With sin.   *In*
All ar thay slain,
And put unto pain.
UXOR.   From thens again
May thay never win?   *escape*

NOE.   Win? No, iwis, bot he that might hase   *unless He who has strength*
Wold myn of thare mis, and admitte thaym to grace.   *remember their need*
552   As he in bayll is blis, I pray him in this space   *misery/at this time*
553   In heven hye with his to purvaye us a place,
That we,   *So that*
With his santys in sight,   *saints in his presence*
And his angels bright,
May com to his light.
Amen, for charité.
    Explicit processus Noe.   *Here ends the story of Noah.*
    Sequitur Abraham.   *Abraham follows.*

552-53 As he is a source of joy in (the midst of our) misery, I pray to him now that he provide us a place in high heaven with his elect.

THE SACRIFICE OF ISAAC
BROME MS

This Brome text (named for a manor house in Norfolk where the manuscript was preserved) exists as a single pageant only, but it may have belonged to a cycle. Indeed, the text is close to that of Chester and may have influenced that version in part. The account is remarkable for its ballad-like simplicity, its intense portrayal of filial and parental tenderness, and its sustaining of dramatic tension. The effect is touching and, although daringly close to bathos, never guilty of mawkishness.

To medieval commentators the story of Isaac's sacrifice was an antetype of the Crucifixion. The Brome dramatic version frequently capitalizes on the parallel: Isaac's bearing the faggots of wood on his back, the journeying to the hill of death, the symbolism of the sheep, and so on. The theme, as in the Noah story, is of obedience. Abraham, like God himself, is willing to sacrifice his own son for divine truth. This seemingly unnatural act of resolving to kill a kinsman recalls by contrast the truly unnatural act of Cain against Abel. Abraham, as a type of God, perceives clearly his duty to obey even though he is also aware of the terrible cost to himself.

Staging too may be figural. As in the earlier episode of the Killing of Abel, an altar is set up on a hill, and God speaks from above. Abraham receives a celestial messenger on the lowest acting level, representing a location near his home. On the same level, Abraham and Isaac journey "upon this gren," and "Upon this fayere hetth" (ll. 67, 407)—although whether this language is meant to suggest the actual ground or the stage of a pageant wagon is debatable.

The Sacrifice of Isaac
Brome MS

[Abraham, with his young son Isaac, kneels in prayer.]

ABRAHAM.   Fader of hevyn omnipotent,
With all my hart to the[e] I call!
Thow hast goffe me both lond and rent,   *given/revenue*
And my livelod thow hast me sent.   *livelihood*
I thanke the[e] heyly, evermore, of all.   *highly/for all*

First of the erth thou madist Adam,
And Eve also to be his wiffe;
All other creaturys of them t[w]oo cam.
And now thow hast grant to me, Abraham,   *granted*
10   Her[e] in this lond to lede my liffe.

In my age thou hast grantyd me this,
That this yowng child with me schall won.   *dwell*
I love nothing so myche, iwisse,   *much*
Excep[t]e thin[e] owyn selffe, de re Fader of blisse,
As Isaac her[e], my owyn swete son.

I have diverse childryn moo,   *more*
The w[h]ich I love not halffe so well.
This fayer swet child, he schereys me soo   *cheers*
In every place w[h]er that I goo,
20   That noo dessece her[e] may I fell.   *dis-ease, discomfort/feel*

And therfor, Fadyr of hevyn, I the[e] prey
For his helth and also for his grace.
Now, Lord, kepe him both night and day
That never dessese nor noo fray   *discomfort/fear, harm*
Cume to my child in noo place. [*He rises.*]

Now cum on, Isaac, my owyn swet child;
Goo we hom and take owre rest.
ISAAC.   Abraham, min[e] owyn fader so mild,
To folowe yow I am full prest,   *ready*
30   Bothe erly and late.
ABRAHAM.   Cume on, swete child. I love the[e] best
Of all the childryn that ever I begat.
[*They start for home. In heaven, God enthroned
is accompanied by angels.*]

DEUS.   Min[e] angell, fast hey the[e] thy wey   *hie, hasten*
And onto medill-erth anon thou goo;   *the earth*
Abrams hart now will I asay   *test*
W[h]ethere that he be stedfast or noo.

Sey I commaw[n]dyd him for to take
Isaac, his yowng sonne, that he love so well,
And with his blood sacrifice he make
40   Iffe ony of my freynchepe he will fell.   *feel*

Schow him the wey onto the hille
W[h]er that his sacriffice schall be.
I schall asay now his good will,
Whether he lovith better his child or me.
All men schall take exampyll him by   *by him*
My commaw[nd]mentys how they schall fulfill.
[*The angel starts to descend. Abraham is in prayer;
Isaac is not with him.*]

ABRAHAM.   Now, Fader of hevyn, that formyd all thing,
My preyerys I make to the[e] ageyn,
For this day my tender-offring   *burnt-offering*
50   Here must I geve to the[e], certeyn.
A, Lord God, allmyty king,
W[h]at maner best woll make the[e] most fain?   *kind of beast/glad*
Iff I had therof very kno[w]ing,   *true*
It schuld be don with all my main   *might*
Full sone anon.
To don thy plesing on an hill   *do/pleasure*
Verely it is my will,
Dere Fader, God alon.

THE ANGELL.   Abraham, Abraham, well thou rest!   *may you rest well, be content*
Owre Lord comandith the[e] for to take
Isaac, thy yowng son that thow lovist best,
62   And with his blod sacrifice that thow make.

63   Into the lond of v[i]sion thow goo   *(i.e., land of Moriah)*
And offer thy child onto thy Lord—
I schall the[e] lede—and schow allsoo
Unto Goddys hest, Abraham, acord,   *God's decree/agreement*

And folow me upon this gren.
ABRAHAM.   Wollecom to me be my Lordys sond,   *messenger*
And his hest I will not withstond.
70   Yit Isaac, my yowng sonne in lond,   *on earth*
A full dere child to me have byn.   *has been*

I had lever, if God had be plesyd,   *rather*
For to a forbore all the good that I have,   *to have foregone/goods*
Than Isaac my son schuld a be desessyd,   *have been injured*
So God in hevyn my sowll mot save!   *may*

I lovyd never thing soo mych in erde,   *much/earth*
And now I must the child goo kill.
A, Lord God, my conseons is stron[g]ly steryd!   *conscience/stirred*
And yit, my dere Lord, I am sore aferd
80   To groche onything agens yowre will.   *complain at all against*

I love my child as my liffe,
But yit I love my God myche more.

⁶²And make a sacrifice with his blood.

⁶³(See Genesis 22:2.)

For, thow[gh] my hart woold make ony striffe,
Yit will I not spare, for child nor wiffe,
But don after my Lordys lore.   *do according to/precept*

Thow[gh] I love my sonne never so well,
Yit smyth of[f] his hed sone I schall.   *smite*
A, Fader of hevyn, to the[e] I knell!   *kneel*
An hard deth my son schall fell   *feel*
For to honore the[e], Lord, withall.

THE ANGELL.   Abraham, Abraham, this is well seyd!
And all this[e] coma[nd]mentys loke that thou kepe,
But in thy hart be nothing dismayd.[*The angel retires.*]
94 ABRAHAM.   Nay, nay, forsoth, I hold me well apayd   *satisfied*
To plese my God with the best that I have.

For, thow[gh] my hart be hevely sett   *heavily*
To see the blood of my owyn dere son,
Yit for all this I will not lett,   *desist*
But Isaac, my son, I will goo fett   *fetch*
100 And cum asse fast as ever we can.
    [*Abraham crosses to where Isaac kneels in prayer.*]

Now, Isaac, my owyn son dere,
W[h]er art thow, child? Speke to me.
ISAAC.   My fayer, swet fader, I am here,
And make my prey[e]rys to the Trenité.

ABRAHAM.   Risse up, my child, and fast cum heder,
My gentyll barn that art so wisse,   *bairn, child/wise*
For we t[w]o, child, must goo togeder
And onto my Lord make sacriffice.

ISAAC.   I am full redy, my fader, loo!
110 Yevyn at yowre handys I stand right here,   *Even*
And w[h]atsoever ye bid me doo
It schall be don with glad chere,
Full well and fine.
ABRAHAM.   A, Isaac, my owyn son soo dere,
Godys blissing I giffe the[e], and min[e]!

116 Hold this fagot upon thy ba[c]ke,

94No, no, in truth, I consider myself well satisfied.

116*fagot*: Cf. Christ's carrying his own cross.

And her[e] myselffe fyere schall bring.   *fire*
ISAAC.   Fader, all this here will I packe;
I am full fain to do yowre beding.   *bidding*
ABRAHAM [*aside*].   A, Lord of hevyn, my handys I wring!
This childys wordys all to-wo[u]nd my harte.   *deeply wound*

Now Isaac, son, goo we owre wey
Onto yon mownte, with all owre main.   *might*
ISAAC.   Go we, my dere fader. As fast as I may
To folow yow I am full fain,
Allthow[gh] I be slendyr.
ABRAHAM [*aside*].   A, Lord, my hart brekith on twain,
This childys wordys they be so tender!
   [*They arrive at the mount.*]

A, Isaac, son, anon ley it down;   *it (the faggot)*
130   No lenger upon thy backe it hold,
For I must make me redy bo[w]n   *quickly ready*
To honowre my Lord God as I schuld.
   [*Isaac lays down the faggot.*]

ISAAC.   Loo, my dere fader, w[h]ere it is.
To cher[e] yow allwey I draw me nere.
But, fader, I mervell sore of this: *sorely at*
W[h]y that ye make this hevy chere?   *heavy countenance*

And also, fader, evermore dred I:
W[h]er is yowre qweke best that ye schuld kill?   *live beast*
Both fyer and wood we have redy,
140   But qweke best have we non[e] on this hill.

A qwike best, I wot well, must be ded   *know/killed*
Yowre sacrifice for to make.
ABRAHAM.   Dred the[e] nowght, my child, I the[e] red;   *advise*
Owre Lord will send me onto this sted   *here*
Summ maner a best for to take,   *Some kind of beast*
Throw[gh] his swet sond.   *messenger*
ISAAC.   Ya, fader, but my hart beginnith to quake,
To se that scharpe sword in yowre hond.

W[h]y bere ye yowre sword drawyn soo?
150   Of yowre cown[te]nauns I have mych wonder.
ABRAHAM [*aside*].   A, Fader of hevyn, so I am woo!   *I'm so woeful*
This child her[e] brekys my harte on sonder.   *asunder*

ISAAC.   Tell me, my dere fader, or that ye ses,   *ere you cease*

Bere ye yowre sword draw[n] for me?

ABRAHAM.   A, Isaac, swet son, pes, pes!   *peace, silence*
For, iwis, thow breke my harte on thre.

ISAAC.   Now trewly, sumw[h]at, fader, me thinke
That ye mo[u]rne thus more and more.

ABRAHAM [*aside*].   A, Lord of hevyn, thy grace let sinke!   *descend*
160   For my hart wos never halffe so sore.

ISAAC.   I preye yow, fader, that ye will let me it wit,   *know*
W[h]yther schall I have ony harme or noo?   *Whether*

ABRAHAM.   Iwis, swet son, I may not tell the[e] yit;
My hart is now soo full of woo.

ISAAC.   Dere fader, I prey yow, hide it not fro me,
But sum of yowre thow[gh]t that ye tell me.

ABRAHAM.   A, Isaac, Isaac, I must kill the[e]!

ISAAC.   Kill me, fader? Alasse, w[h]at have I don?

Iff I have trespassyd agens yow ow[gh]t,   *against/at all*
170   With a yard ye may make me full mild;   *rod*
And with yowr scharp sword kill me noght,
For iwis, fader, I am but a child.

ABRAHAM.   I am full sory, son, thy blood for to spill,
But truly, my child, I may not chese.   *choose*

ISAAC.   Now I wold to God my moder were her[e] on this
    hill!
Sche woold knele for me on both hir kneys
To save my liffe.
And sithyn that my moder is not here,   *since*
I prey yow, fader, schonge yowr chere,   *change your countenance*
180   And kill me not with yowyre kniffe!

ABRAHAM.   Forsothe, son, but yif I the[e] kill   *unless*
I schuld greve God right sore, I drede.
It is his commaw[nd]ment and also his will
That I schuld do this same dede.

He commawndyd me, son, for serteyn,
To make my sacrifice with thy blood.

ISAAC.   And is it Goddys will that I schuld be slain?

ABRAHAM.   Ya, truly, Isaac, my son soo good,
And therfor my handys I wring.

ISAAC.   Now, fader, agens my Lordys will   *against*

191   I will never groche, lowd nor still.   *complain/quietly*
        He might a sent me a better desteny   *might have*
        If it had a be his plecer.   *had been/pleasure*

ABRAHAM.   Forsothe, son, but if I ded this dede,   *unless I do*
        Grevosly displessyd owre Lord will be.
ISAAC.   Nay, nay, fader, God forbede
        That ever ye schuld greve him for me!

        Ye have other childryn, on[e] or too,   *two*
        The w[h]iche ye schuld love well, by kind.   *nature*
200   I prey yow, fader, make ye no woo;
        For, be I onys ded and fro yow goo,   *once I'm dead*
        I schall be sone owt of yowre mind.

        Therfor doo owre Lordys bidding,
        And, w[h]an I am ded, than prey for me.
        But, good fader, tell ye my moder nothing;
        Sey that I am in another cuntré dwelling.
ABRAHAM.   A, Isaac, Isaac, blissyd mot thow be!   *may*

        My hart beginnith stron[g]ly to risse,   *rise*
        To see the blood of thy blissyd body.   *At the thought of seeing*
ISAAC.   Fadyr, syn it may be noo other wisse,   *since/way*
211   Let it passe over, as well as I.

        But, fader, or I goo onto my deth,   *ere*
        I prey yow blisse me with yowre hand. [*He kneels.*]
ABRAHAM.   Now, Isaac, with all my breth,
        My blissing I geve the[e] upon this lond,
        And Godys also therto, iwis!
        A, Isaac, Isaac, son, up thow stond,
        Thy fayere swete mowthe that I may kis.

ISAAC.   Now for-well, my owyn fader so fin[e],   *farewell*
220   And grete well my moder in erde.   *greet well/earth*
        But I prey yow, fader, to hid[e] my eyne,   *eyes*
        That I se not the stroke of yowre scharpe swerd   *So I won't see*
        That my fleysse schall defile.   *flesh*
ABRAHAM.   Son, thy wordys make me to wepe full sore!
        Now, my dere son Isaac, speke no more.

191*lowd nor still:* i.e., at all.

211i.e., Allow it to happen, as I will do also.

220i.e., Give my warmest greetings to her who was my mother during my earthly sojourn.

ISAAC.   A, my owyn dere fader, w[h]erefore?
We schall speke togedyr her[e] but a w[h]ille.   *(short) while*

And sithyn that I must nedysse be ded,   *since/must needs, must*
Yit, my dere fader, to yow I prey,
Smyth but fewe strokys at my hed,   *Smite*
And make an end as sone as ye may,   *soon*
And tery not to[o] longe.
ABRAHAM.   Thy meke wordys, child, make me afray!   *frighten me*
234   So "welawey!" may be my songe,   *alas*

235   Excep[t]e alonly Godys will.
A, Isaac, my owyn swete child,
Yit kisse me agen upon this hill!
In all this war[l]d is non[e] soo mild.

ISAAC.   Now truly, fader, all this terying
240   It doth my hart but harme;   *nothing but*
I prey yow, fader, make an endding.
ABRAHAM.   Cume up, swet son, onto my arme.
[*Starts to bind him.*]

I must bind thy handys too   *two*
Allthow[gh] thow be never soo mild.
ISAAC.   A, mercy, fader! W[h]y schuld ye do soo?
ABRAHAM.   That thow schuldist not let [me], my child.   *hinder*

ISAAC.   Nay, iwisse, fader, I will not let yow.
248   Do on, for me, yowre will;
249   And on the purpos that ye have set yow,
250   For Godys love, kepe it forthe still!

I am full sory this day to dey,   *die*
But yit I kepe not my God to greve.   *desire*
Do on yowre list for me hard[i]ly,   *Execute your will on me boldly*
My fayer swete fader—I geffe yow leve.   *leave, permission*

But, fader, I prey yow evermore,
Tell ye my moder no dell.   *not at all*
Iffe sche wost it, sche wold wepe full sore,   *If she knew*

234-35I would have good cause to complain were it not God's will.

248-50Do your will without worrying about me; and, for God's love, keep steadily to your purpose.

For iwisse, fader, sche lovit[h] me full well;
Goddys blissing mot sche have!   *may*

260   Now for-well, my moder so swete!   *farewell*
We t[w]oo be leke no mor[e] to mete.   *like, likely*
ABRAHAM.   A, Isaac, Isaac, son, thou makist me to gret[e],   *weep*
And with thy wordys thow distempurst me.   *upset*

ISAAC.   Iwisse, swete fader, I am sory to greve yow.
I cry yow mercy of that I have donne,   *ask mercy for that which*
And of all trespasse that ever I ded meve yow.   *committed against you*
Now, dere fader, forgiffe me that I have donne—   *that which*
God of hevyn be with me!

ABRAHAM.   A, dere child, lefe of[f] thy monys!   *cease your moans*
270   In all thy liffe thow grevyd me never onys.   *grieved/once*
Now blissyd be thow, body and bonys,   *i.e., entirely*
That ever thow were bred and born!
Thow hast be to me child full good.   *been*
But iwisse, child, thow[gh] I mo[u]rne never so fast,   *deeply*
Yit must I nedys here at the last   *finally*
In this place sched all thy blood.
        [*Places him on the altar.*]

Therfor, my dere son, here schall thou lie;
Onto my warke I must me stede.   *apply myself*
Iwisse, I had as leve myselffe to dey—   *lief, gladly/die*
280   Iffe God will be plecyd with my dede—   *pleased/death*
And min[e] owyn body for to offere.
ISAAC.   A, mercy, fader, mo[u]rne ye no more!
Yowre weping make[th] my hart sore   *(as) sore*
As my owyn deth that I schall suffere.

Yowre kerche, fader, abowt my eyn ye wind.   *kerchief/eyes*
ABRAHAM.   So I schall, my swettest child in erde.   *earth*
ISAAC.   Now yit, good fader, have this in mind,
And smyth me not oftyn with your scharp swerd,   *smite*
But hastely that it be sped!   *completed*
        Here Abraham leyd a cloth over Isaacys face, thus seying:
290 ABRAHAM.   Now, fore-well, my child so full of grace!
ISAAC.   A, fader, fader, torne downgward my face!
For of yowre scharpe sword I am ever adred.

ABRAHAM [*aside*].   To don this dede I am full sory,
But, Lord, thin[e] hest I will not withstond.   *behest, edict*

ISAAC.　A, Fader of hevyn, to the[e] I crye:
296　Lord, reseive me into thy hand!

ABRAHAM [*aside*].　Loo, now is the time cum, certeyn,
That my sword in his necke schall bite.
A, Lord, my hart reysith therageyn!　*rises against it*
I may not find it in my harte to smite.
My hart will not now thertoo.　*will not permit it*
Yit fain I woold warke my Lordys will.
But this yowng innosent lygth so sti.l　*lies*
I may not find it in my hart him to kill.
O Fader of hevyn, what schall I doo?

ISAAC.　A, mercy, fader, w[h]y tery ye so
And let me ley thus longe on this heth?　*heath*
Now I wold to God the stroke were doo.　*done*
Fader, I prey yow hartely, schorte me of my woo,　*shorten my woe*
310　And let me not loke thus after my deth!　*anticipate*

ABRAHAM.　Now, hart, w[h]y wolddist not thow breke on
　　thre?
Yit schall thou not make me to my God on-mild.　*ungentle*
I will no lenger let for the[e],　*desist*
For that my God agrevyd wold be.
Now hoold tha stroke, my owyn dere child!　*receive*
　Her[e] Abraham drew his stroke, and the angell
　toke the sword in his hond soddenly.

THE ANGELL.　I am an angell, thow mayist be blithe,
That fro hevyn to the[e] is sent.
Owre Lord thanke the[e] an hundred sithe　*times*
For the keping of his commaw[nd]ment.

320　He knowit[h] thy will and also thy harte,
That thow dredist him above all thing;　*revere*
And sum of thy hevines for to departe,　*sorrow/banish*
A fair ram yinder I gan bringe.　*yonder/did*

He standith teyed, loo, among the brerys.　*tied/briars*
Now, Abraham, amend thy mood,　*i.e., be cheerful*
For Isaac, thy yowng son that her[e] is,
This day schall not sched his blood.

296(Cf. Christ's "Into your hands I commend my spirit.")

Goo, make thy sacrifece with yon ram.
Now, for-well, blissyd Abraham,   *farewell*
330 For onto hevyn I goo now hom—
The wey is full gain.   *straight*
Take up thy son soo free.   *noble*
    [*The angel reascends.*]

ABRAHAM.   A, Lord, I thanke the[e] of thy gret grace!   *for*
Now am I ethed on divers wisse.   *comforted in divers ways*
Arisse up, Isaac, my dere sunne, arisse,
Arisse up, swete child, and cum to me!

ISAAC.   A, mercy, fader, w[h]y smight ye now[gh]t?   *smite*
A, smight on, fader, onys with yowre kniffe!   *once*
339 ABRAHAM.   Pesse, my swet sun, and take no thow[gh]t, *Peace, silence*
For owre Lord of hevyn hath grant thy liffe   *granted*
By his angell now,

That thou schalt not dey this day, sunne, truly.   *die*
ISAAC.   A, fader, full glad than wer I—   *I would be*
Iwis, fader, I sey, iwis!—
If this tale wer trew!
ABRAHAM.   An hundyrd timys, my son fayer of hew,   *fair of countenance*
For joy thy mowth now will I kis!

ISAAC.   A, my dere fader, Abraham,
Will not God be wroth that we do thus?
350 ABRAHAM.   Noo, noo, har[di]ly, my swyt son,   *certainly*
For he hath sent us yin same ram   *yon*
Hethyr down to us.

Yin best schall dey here in thy sted,   *Yon beast will die/place*
In the worchup of owre Lord alon.
Goo, fet him hethyre, my child, inded.   *fetch*
ISAAC.   Fader, I will goo hent him by the hed   *seize*
And bring yon best with me anon.
    [*He goes to free the ram from the briars.*]

A, scheppe, scheppe, blissyd mot thou be,   *may*
That ever thow were sent down heder!
360 Thow schall this day dey for me   *die*
In the worchup of the Holy Trinité.
Now cum fast and goo we togeder

339*take no thow[gh]t*: i.e., don't think of death.

To my fader in hie.   *in haste*
Thow[gh] thou be never so jentyll and good,
Yit had I lever thow schedist thy blood,   *liefer, rather*
Iwisse, scheppe, than I.
    [*He leads the ram to his father.*]

Loo, fader, I have brow[gh]t here full smerte   *smartly, promptly*
This jentyll scheppe, and him to yow I giffe.
But, Lord God, I thanke the[e] with all my hart,
370 For I am glad that I schall liffe   *live*

And kis onys my dere moder!   *once (again)*
ABRAHAM.   Now be right myry, my swete chilld,   *merry*
For this qwike best that is so mild   *live beast*
Here I schall present before all othere.   *offer*

ISAAC.   And I will fast beginne to blowe;
This fyere schall brene a full good sped.   *burn/speed*
But fader, will I stowppe down lowe,   *if I stoop*
Ye will not kill me with yowre sword, I trowe?
ABRAHAM.   Noo, har[di]ly, swet son, have no dred!   *certainly, boldly*
380 My mo[u]rning is past.
ISAAC.   Ya, but I woold that sword wer in a gled,   *gleed, fire*
For, iwis, fader, it make[s] me full ill agast.   *terribly afraid*

    Here Abraham mad[e] his offring, kneling and seying thus:
ABRAHAM.   Now, Lord God of hevyn in Trinité,
Allmyty God omnipotent,
Min[e] offering I make in the worchope of the[e],
And with this qweke best I the[e] present.
Lord, reseive thow min[e] intent,
As [thou] art God and grownd of owre grace.   *foundation*

    [*God speaks from above, enthroned in heaven.*]
DEUS.   Abraham, Abraham, well mot thow sped[e],   *may you prosper*
390 And Isaac, thy yowng son the[e] by!
Truly, Abraham, for this dede
I schall multiplye yowrys botherys sede   *both your progeny*
As thi[c]ke as sterrys be in the skye,   *stars*
Bothe more and lesse;   *big and small (i.e., everyone)*
And as thi[c]ke as gravell in the see,
So thi[c]ke multiplied yowre sede schall be.
This grant I yow for yowre goodnesse.

380i.e., My cause of mourning, the obligation to execute you, is past.

Of yow schall cume frewte gret [won],   *great quantity of fruit*
And ever be in blisse withowt end.
400 For ye drede me as God alon   *Because/revere*
And kepe my commaw[nd]mentys everyschon,   *every one*
My blissing I geffe, w[h]ersoever ye wend.

ABRAHAM.   Loo, Isaac, my son, how thinke ye
By this warke that we have wroght?   *Of*
Full glad and blithe we may be
Agens the will of God that we grucched nott,   *Against/complained*
Upon this fayere hetth.   *fair heath*
ISAAC.   A, fader, I thanke owre Lord every dell   *deal, bit*
That my wit servyd me so well
410 For to drede God more than my detth.

ABRAHAM.   Why, dereworthy son, wer thow adred?   *precious*
Hardely, child, tell me thy lore.   *Boldly/thinking*
ISAAC.   Ya, by my feyth, fader, now have I red,   *now I believe*
I wos never soo afraid before
As I have byn at yin hill!   *been/yon*
But, by my feyth, fader, I swere
I will nevermore cume there
But it be agens my will.   *Unless/against*

ABRAHAM.   Ya, cum on with me, my owyn swet son,   *Yea*
420 And homward fast now let us goon.   *go*
ISAAC.   By my feyth, fader, therto I grant.   *agree*
I had never so good will to gon hom
And to speke with my dere moder.
ABRAHAM.   A, Lord of hevyn, I thanke the[e],
For now may I led hom with me   *lead*
Isaac, my yownge son soo fre,   *noble*
The gentyllest child above all other.

Now goo we forthe, my blissyd son.
ISAAC.   I grant, fader, and let us gon;
For, by my trowthe, wer I at home
I wold never gon owt under that forme—   *in that manner*
This may I well avoee!   *avow*
I prey God geffe us grace evermo,   *evermore*
434 And all tho that we be holding to. [*Exeunt.*]   *those/beholden to*

[*The doctor comes forward as epilogue.*]   *teacher, learned divine*

434(Refers to the audience.)

DOCTOR.   Lo, sovereyns and sorys, now have we schowyd   *sirs/showed*
This solom story to gret a[nd] smale.   *i.e., everyone*
It is good lerning to lernd and lewyd,   *ignorant*
And the wisest of us all,
Withowtyn ony berring.   *Without any dispute*

440   For this story scho[w]it[h] yowe [here]   *shows*
How we schuld kepe, to owre po[we]re,   *to the extent of our ability*
Goddys commaw[nd]mentys withowt groching.   *complaining*

Trowe ye, sorys, and God sent an angell,   *Do you think sirs if*
And commawndyd yow yowre child to slayn,   *slay*
By yowre trowthe, is ther ony of yow
That either wold groche or strive ther-ageyn?   *against it*

How thingke ye now, sorys, therby?   *sirs/of that*
I trow ther be thre or four, or moo—
And this[e] women that wepe so sorowfully
450   Whan that hir childryn dey them froo,   *their/die and leave them*
451   As nater woll, and kind.   *nature*
It is but folly, I may well avooe,   *avow*
To groche agens God or to greve yow;   *complain against/grieve*
454   For ye schall never se him mischevyd, well I know,   *harmed*
By lond nor watyr—have this in mind.

And groche not agens owre Lord God,
In welthe or woo, w[h]ether that he yow send,   *whichever*
Thow[gh] ye be never so hard bestad;   *hard pressed*
For whan he will, he may it amend,
460   His comaw[nd]mentys treuly if ye kepe with goo[d]
         hart—
As this story hath now schowyd yow befor[n]e—
And feythefully serve him qwyll ye be quart,   *while/healthy*
That ye may plece God bothe evyn and morne.   *please*
Now Jesu, that werit[h] the crown of thorne,   *wears*
Bring us all to hevyn blisse!
         Finis.

450–51 When their children die and leave them, as nature demands.

454 i.e., You will never see God's plan brought to harm.

PHARAOH
FROM WAKEFIELD

This Pharaoh pageant from Wakefield introduces the first great ranting tyrant of the cycle plays. Pharaoh anticipates such crassly arrogant types as Herod, Caesar, and (in the Wakefield cycle) Pontius Pilate. Like those later exemplars of worldly insolence, Pharaoh is a comic braggart and bully oppressing a seemingly defenseless leader of God's chosen people. Most of all, Pharaoh resembles the devil himself, the great antagonist in the story of Christ's Passion, who appears to have the upper hand until the Crucifixion and Resurrection actually take place. Pharaoh's very oaths and ranting expressions resemble those of Satan.

Moses is accordingly an antetype of Christ, in the tradition of Abel, Noah, and Isaac. Although he is threatened by a brutally evil power, and can prevail only through God's assistance, his ultimate deliverance is sure. Moses is a shepherd who triumphs over kings, illustrating the paradox of the Sermon on the Mount that the meek shall inherit the earth. Like Noah, Moses humbly stresses his inadequacy in the face of overwhelming odds (ll. 142–47). His companions, the "children" (i.e., chosen people) of Israel, adumbrate the Innocents slaughtered by Herod, especially when Pharaoh orders his midwives to massacre all new-born Hebrew children (ll. 73–74). Moses' confrontation of Pharaoh and his

deliverance of God's people from captivity foreshadow Christ's harrowing of hell.

Inspired ultimately by the biblical account (Exodus 1–14) and its thematic emphasis on visual miracle as a token of God's power, this pageant goes in heavily for *trompe l'oeil* effects. A bush burns without consuming its green leaves, Moses' wand turns into a serpent and back to a wand, and, most spectacularly, the Red Sea parts for the Israelites but overwhelms the Egyptians. How some of these effects were produced is partly a matter of speculation, but the item in the account books of the Coventry Cappers for "halfe a yard of rede sea" suggests that the sea was not left to the audience's imagination. Staging also appears to require a court and throne for Pharaoh and his men, and a mountain for the burning bush (compare sacred mounts in other pageants, such as the place of sacrifice for Abraham and Isaac, and Christ's Mount of Olives). Probably God speaks from above.

The Pharaoh pageant follows rather than precedes the Prophets pageant in the Towneley manuscript. It is here placed in its normal biblical order. This pageant was borrowed from the York cycle and differs only slightly from it. Both N Town and Chester relate the story of the Ten Commandments rather than that of the escape from Egypt (see next selection).

Pharaoh
From Wakefield

Incipit Pharao. Litsters pagonn.

[Pharaoh, in his court, attended.]

TITLE *Litsters pagonn:* Dyers' pageant. (This marginal comment is in a more recent hand than is the text proper.)

1	PHARAO. Peas! of pain that no man pas!	*Silence*
2	Bot kepe the course that I commaunde,	
	And take good hede of him that has	*heed of him (i.e., your king)*
	Youre helth all [w]holy in his hande.	
	For King Pharro my fader was,	
	And led this lordship of this land.	*held the governance*
7	I am his hayre, as age will has,	*heir*
8	Ever in stede to stir or stand.	*place*

	All Egypt is mine awne	*own*
10	To leede aftyr my law.	
11	I wold my might were knawne	
12	And honoryd, as hit awe.	*it ought (to be)*
	Full low he shall be thrawne	*he (i.e., anyone)*
	That harkyns not my sawe—	*Who/speech*
	Hanged hy and drawne!	*disemboweled*
	Therfor no boste ye blaw.	*don't boast*

17	Bot as for king I commaund peasse,	
	To all the people of this empire.	
19	Looke no man put himself in preasse	*throng*
20	Bot that will do as I desire.	*Unless*
	And of youre wordys look that ye seasse.	
	Take tent to me, youre soferand sire,	*Pay attention/sovereign*
	That may youre comfort most increasse,	*(I) who may*
24	And to my list bowe life and lire.	*pleasure/countenance*

25	1 MILES. My lord, if any here were	
	That wold not wyrk youre will,	*fulfill your desire*
	If we might com thaym nere,	*i.e., get at them*
	Full soyn we shuld theym spill.	*soon/kill*

	PHARAO. Throughout my kingdom wold I ken,	*I'd like to know*
	And kun him thank that wold me tell,	*give*

1–2 Silence! On pain of torture let no man move or depart, but follow the course of action I command. (This ranting demand for attention is a hallmark of the stage tyrant; cf. Herod.)

7–8 I am his heir, as the passing of the generations decrees, always in this place to move or stand still (i.e., do as I please).

10–12 To govern according to my will. I desire that my power be known and honored, as it ought to be.

17 But in the king's name I command silence.

19–20 Beware that no man take part in this throng unless he will do as I desire.

24–25 And to my pleasure submit your life and bow down your countenance.—My lord, if there should be anyone here.

31	If any were so waryd men	*cursed*
32	That wold my fors downe fell.	
	2 MILES. My lord, ye have a maner of men	*kind*
34	That make great mastres us emell:	*superiority among us*
	The Jues, that won in Gersen.	*dwell in Goshen*
	Thay ar callyd childyr of Israel.	*i.e., the chosen people*

	Thay multiplye full fast,	
	And sothly we suppose	*truly*
39	That shall ever last	
40	Oure lordship for to lose.	

	PHARAO. Why, how have thay sych gawdys begun?	*such tricks*
42	Ar thay of might to make sych frayes?	*disturbances*
	1 MILES. Yei, lord, full fell folk ther was fun	*very fierce/found*
	In King Pharao youre fader dayes.	
	Thay cam of Joseph, was Jacob son—	*who was Jacob's*
	He was a prince worthy to praise—	
47	In sithen in ryst have thay ay ron.	*insurrection*
	Thus ar thay like to lose youre laise.	*likely to subvert your laws*

	Thay will confound you cleyn,	*utterly*
	Bot if thay soner sesse.	*Unless they first cease*
51	PHARAO. What devill is that thay meyn	*intend*
	That thay so fast incresse?	

	2 MILES. How thay incres full well we ken,	
	As oure faders did understand.	
	Thay were bot sexty and ten	
	When thay first cam into this land;	
	Sithen have sojerned in Gersen	*Since then (they)*
	Four hundreth winter, I dar warand.	*warrant*
	Now ar thay nowmbred of mighty men	
60	Moo then thre hundreth thousand,	*More than*

	Withouten wife and child,	*Not counting*
	Or hyrdys that kepe thare fee.	*shepherds/flocks*

31–32If there be any persons so cursed as to desire to overthrow my might.

34Who assert great superiority among us.

39–40i.e., That (increase) will continually threaten our supremacy.

42Are they strong enough to make such disturbances?

47Since then they have continually acted in insurrection.

51What the devil do they intend?

PHARAO.   How thus might we be beg[u]ild!
    Bot shall it not be.

    For with quantise we shall thaym quell   *contrivance/destroy*
    So that thay shall not far sprede.

67 1 MILES.   My lord, we have hard oure faders tell,   *heard*
68   And clerkys that well couth rede,   *clerics/could read*
69   Ther shuld a man walk us amell   *among us*
70   That shuld fordo us and oure dede.   *destroy/deeds*

PHARAO.   Fi[e] on him, to the devill of hell!
    Sych destiny will we not drede.   *dread*

    We shal make midwifys to spill them   *command/kill*
    Where any Ebrew is borne,
75   And all menkinde to kill them;
    So shall thay soyn be lorne.   *soon be destroyed*

77   And as for elder have I none awe,   *the adults*
    Sych bondage shall I to thaym beyde: *command*
    To dike and delf, bere and draw,   *excavate/dig/carry/pull*
    And to do all unhonest deyde.   *distasteful labor*
    So shall these laddys be halden law,   *rascals be held low*
    In thraldom ever thare life to leyde.

2 MILES.   Now, certys, this was a sotell saw!   *clever speech*
    Thus shall these folk no farthere sprede.

PHARAO.   Now help to hald theym downe.
86   Look I no faintnes finde.   *See that/unwillingness*
1 MILES.   All redy, lord, we shall be bowne,   *prepared*
88   In bondage thaym to binde.

    Tunc intrat Moyses cum   *Then Moses [on Mount Sinai] enters*
    virgam in manu, etc.   *with a rod in his hand, etc.*

MOYSES.   Gret God, that all this warld began,
    And growndyd it in good degré,   *established/order*
91   Thou mayde me, Moyses, unto man,

67–70(The Egyptians cite an ancient prophecy of the coming of a divine scourge, Moses, as an antetype of Christ's incarnation.)

75And (order the midwives) to kill all male infants (see Exodus 1:15–16).

77And, as for the adults, I'm not worried about them.

86i.e., Don't let me find any foot-dragging in you.

88S.D.: Moses enters quite far apart from Pharaoh's court, in an area signifying Mount Sinai.

91You gave me life, I who am Moses.

92	And sithen thou savyd me from the se.	*afterwards*
	King Pharao had commawndyd than	
	Ther shuld no man-child savyd be;	
	Agans his will away I wan.	*Against/escaped*
	Thus has God shewed his might for me.	

	Now am I sett to kepe,	*employed to tend*
	Under this montain side,	*In the shelter of*
	Bishope Jettyr shepe,	*The chief priest Jethro's*
	To better may betide.	*Until better (fortune)*
	[*He sees the burning bush.*]	

	A, Lord, grete is thy might!	
102	What man may of yond mervell meyn?	*comprehend*
	Yonder I se a selcowth sight—	*wondrous*
	Sych on[e] in warld was never seyn—	*Such a one/seen*
	A bush I se burnand full bright,	
	And ever elike the leyfes ar greyn!	*every one of*
	If it be wark of warldly wight,	*human being*
	I will go wit withoutyn weyn.	*know without doubt*

	DEUS [*from above*]. Moyses, Moyses!	
	Hic properat ad rubum,	*Here he hurries to the bush,*
	et dicit ei Deus, etc.	*and God says to him*

110	Moyses, com not to[o] nere,	
	Bot still in that stede thou dwell,	*place/remain*
	And harkyn unto me here;	
	Take tent what I the[e] tell.	*Pay attention to*
	Do of[f] thy shoyes in fere,	*Take off both your shoes*
115	With mowth as I the[e] mell.	*declare to you*
	The place thou standys in there,	
	Forsothe, is halowd well.	*very sacred*

118	I am thy Lord, withouten lak	
119	To lengthe thy life even as I list.	
	I am God that somtime spake	*formerly*
	To thin[e] elders, as thay wist;	*knew*

92(See Exodus 2:1–10.)

102Who may comprehend yonder marvel?

115As I declare to you with my speech.

118–19I am your Lord, certainly able to lengthen (preserve) your life as I please.

122	To Abraam, and Isaac,	
123	And Jacob, I saide shuld be blist,	
124	And multitude of them to make,	
125	So that thare seyde shuld not be mist.	*progeny/vanish*

	Bot now this king, Pharao,	
	He hurtys my folk so fast,	*vigorously*
	If that I suffre him so,	*allow*
	Thare seyde shuld soyne be past.	*progeny/soon be gone*
130	Bot I will not so do,	
131	In me if thay will trast,	*trust*
132	Bondage to bring thaym fro.	
	Therfor thou go in hast.	

	To do my message have in mynde,	*remember*
	To him that me sych harme mase.	*such/makes, does*
	Thou speke to him with wordys heynde,	*gracious*
	So that he let my people pas—	
	To wildernes that thay may weynde,	*wend, go*
	To worship me as I will asse.	*ask*
	Agans my will if that thay leynd,	*Against/delay*
	Ful soyn his song shall be "alas."	*soon*

	MOYSES. A, Lord! pardon me, with thy leyf.	*by your leave*
143	That linage luffys me noght.	*lineage, dynasty*
	Gladly thay wold me greyf	*grieve, harm*
	If I sych bodworde broght.	*message*

	Good Lord, lett som othere frast,	*other (person) try*
147	That has more fors the folke to fere.	*frighten*
	DEUS. Moyses, be thou nott abast.	*abashed*
	My biding shall thou boldly bere.	*bidding/convey*

150	If thay with wrong away wold wrast,	
	Outt of the way I shall the[e] were.	*rescue*
	MOYSES. Good Lord, thay will not me trast	*believe me*
	For all the othes that I can swere.	*Despite/oaths*

122-25To Abraham and Isaac and Jacob I said that they should be blessed, and counseled that they should have a multitude of children so that their progeny should not vanish.

130-32But I will not suffer Pharaoh to do this, if the Israelites will have faith in me to deliver them from bondage.

143The (Egyptian) dynasty loves me not.

147Who has more might with which to frighten the Egyptians.

150If they should wrongly attempt to harm you

To neven sych noytys newe   *declare such matters*
To folk of wikyd will,
Withouten tokyn trew,   *sign, evidence*
Thay will not tent thertill.   *heed it*

DEUS.   If that he will not understand
This tokyn trew that I shall sent,   *send*
160   Afore the king cast downe thy wand,
And it shall turne to a serpent.
Then take the taill agane in hand—
Boldly up look thou it hent—   *seize*
And in the state that thou it fand   *found*
Then shal it turne, by mine intent.

Sithen hald thy hand soyn in thy barme,   *Then/soon/bosom*
And as a lepre it shal be like,
And [w]hole agane withouten harme.
Lo, my tokyns shal be slike.   *such*

And if he will not suffre then
My people for to pas in peasse,
I shall send venyance neyn or ten   *vengeance*
173   Shall sowe full sore or I seasse.   *ensue/ere I cease*
Bot the Ebrewes, won in Jessen,   *who dwell in Goshen*
175   Shall not be merkyd with that measse.   *portion*
As long as thay my lawes will ken   *acknowledge*
Thare comforth shall ever increasse.

MOYSES.   A, Lord, to luf the[e] aght us well,   *it behoves us*
That makys thy folk thus free.
180   I shall unto thaym tell
As thou has told to me.

Bot to the king, Lord, when I com,
If he aske what is thy name,
And I stand still, both deyf and dom,   *dumb, silent*
How shuld I skape withoutten blame?
186   DEUS.   I say the[e] thus: "*Ego sum qui sum,*"
I am he that is the same.

---

[173]That will follow as a result most grievously before I'm done.

[175]Shall not be afflicted with that mess, portion (i.e., that trouble).

[186](See Exodus 3:14.)

188   If thou can nother muf nor mom,
      I shall sheld the[e] from shame.

    MOYSES.   I understand full well this thing.
      I go, Lord, with all the might in me.
    DEUS.   Be bold in my blissing;
      Thy socoure shall I be. [*God retires.*]

    MOYSES.   A, Lord of luf, leyn me thy lare,   *lend/wisdom*
      That I may truly talys tell.
      To my freyndys now will I fare,
      The chosyn childre of Israell,
      To tell theym comforth of thare care,
      In dawngere theras thay dwell.—
      [*He goes to the Children (i.e., chosen people)*
      of Israel, and greets them.]
200   God manteyn you evermare,
      And mekill mirth be you emell!   *much/among you*

    1 PUER.   A, master Moyses, dere!
      Oure mirth is all mowrning:
      Full hard halden ar we here,   *harshy lheld (in captivity)*
      As carls under the king.   *churls, serfs*

206 2 PUER.   We may mowrn, both more and min.   *less*
207   Ther is no man that oure mirth mase.   *makes*
      Bot syn we ar all of a kin,   *since*
      God send us comforth in this case.
    MOYSES.   Brethere, of youre mowrning blin.   *cease*
      God will deliver you thrugh his grace;
      Out of this wo he will you win,   *deliver*
213   And put you to youre pleassing place.   *into*

      For I shall carp unto the king,   *talk, complain*
      And fownd full soyn to make you free.   *try very soon*
    1 PUER.   God graunt you good weynding,   *journeying*
      And evermore with you be.
      [*Moses leaves them and advances to Pharaoh's court.*]

    MOYSES.   King Pharao, to me take tent.   *listen to me*

[188]If you can keep from muttering or mumbling.

[206-7]We have cause to mourn, all of us. No man comforts us.

[213]i.e., And place you in the Promised Land.

PHARAO.   Why, boy, what tithingys can thou tell?
MOYSES.   From God himself hidder am I sent
    To foche the childre of Israell;   *fetch*
    To wildernes he wold thay went.
PHARAO.   Yei, weynd the[e] to the devill of hell!   *go to*
224   I gif no force what he has ment.   *I don't care*
    In my dangere, herst thou, shall thay dwell.   *dominion/do you hear*

    And, fature, for thy sake,   *traitor*
    Thay shal be put to pine.   *torture*
MOYSES.   Then will God venyance take   *vengeance*
    Of the[e], and of all thin[e].   *On*

PHARAO.   On me? fi[e] on the[e], lad, out of my land!
    Wenys thou thus to loyse oure lay?   *Think/subvert our law*
      [*To the soldiers.*]
    Say, whence is yond warlow with his wand   *wizard*
233   That thus wold wile oure folk away?   *beguile*
1 MILES.   Yond is Moyses, I dar warand;   *dare affirm*
235   Agans all Egypt has beyn ay.
    Greatt defawte with him youre fader fand;   *found*
    Now will he mar you, if he may.

238 PHARAO.   Fi[e] on him! Nay, nay, that dawnce is done.
239   Lurdan, thou leryd to[o] late.
MOYSES.   God bidys the[e] graunt my bone,   *boon, request*
    And let me go my gate.   *path, way*

PHARAO.   Bidys God me? Fals losell, thou lise!   *rogue/you lie*
243   What tokyn told he? take thou tent.
MOYSES.   He said thou shuld dispise
    Both me and his commaundement;
    Forthy, apon this wise   *Therefore in this manner*
    My wand he bad[e], in thy present,   *presence*
    I shuld lay downe, and the[e] avise   *inform you*
    How it shuld turne to oone serpent.

250   And in his holy name

---

[224]I don't care what God intended.

[233]*oure folk:* i.e., the captive Jews.

[235]He's always been an enemy of Egypt.

[238-39]Fie on him! No, no, that game (of sedition) is over. You lazy lout, you've learned (your lesson) too late.

[243]What miraculous proof did he provide? Answer me that (lit.: pay attention).

Here I lay it downe.
Lo, sir, here may thou se the same.
[*The wand turns into a serpent.*]
PHARAO.   A ha, dog! the devill the[e] drowne!

MOYSES.   He bad[e] me take it by the taill,
For to prefe his powere plain.   *prove*
Then, he saide, withouten faill
Hit shuld turne to a wand again.
[*The wand resumes its former shape.*]
Lo, sir, behold!
PHARAO.   With ilahaill!   *bad luck to you*
Certys this is a sotell swain!   *subtle fellow*
260   Bot thise boyes shall abide in baill;   *fellows/in servitude*
All thy gawdys shall thaym not gain,   *tricks/gain them nothing*

Bot wars, both morn and none,   *worse/noon*
Shall thay fare, for thy sake.
MOYSES.   I pray God send us venyange sone,   *vengeance*
And on thy warkys take wrake.   *vengeance*
[*Moses returns to his people. The soldiers, after
gathering information, go to Pharaoh.*]

1 MILES.   Alas, alas, this land is lorn!   *lost, destroyed*
On life we may [no] longer leynd.   *remain*
Sych mischefe is fallen syn morn,   *since*
Ther may no medsin it amend.   *medicine*
270 PHARAO.   Why cry ye so, laddys? list ye skorn?   *are you jesting*
2 MILES.   Sir king, sych care was never kend   *sorrow/known*
In no mans time that ever was borne.
PHARAO.   Tell on, belife, and make an end.   *swiftly*

1 MILES. Sir, the waters that were ordand   *ordained, instituted*
For men and bestys foyde,   *beasts' food*
Thrughoutt all Egypt land,
Ar turnyd into reede bloyde.   *blood*

Full ugly and full ill is hitt,   *it*
That both fresh and faire was before.
280 PHARAO.   O ho! this is a wonderfull thing to witt, *know*
281   Of all the warkys that ever worc!   *were*

260*boyes*: i.e., the Jews.

280–81O ho! Of all the remarkable things that ever happened, this is the most wondrous I've
ever known.

2 MILES.   Nay, lord, ther is anothere yit,
That sodanly sowys us full sore;   *follows, afflicts*
For todys and froskys may no man flit,   *Because of toads and frogs/go*
Thay venom us so, both les and more.   *i.e., everyone*

1 MILES.   Greatte mistys, sir, ther is both morn and noyn,   *gnats/noon*
Bite us full bitterly.
We trow that it be doyn   *done*
Thrugh Moyses, oure greatte enmy.

290 2 MILES.   My lord, bot if this menye may remefe,   *unless this crowd*
291 Mon never mirth be us amang.   *May/among*
292 PHARAO.   Go, say to him we will not grefe.—   *object*
293 Bot thay shall never the tytter gang.   *quicker go*
     [*The soldiers go to Moses, who is with the Israelites.*]
     1 MILES.   Moyses, my lord giffys leyfe   *gives leave*
     To leyd thy folk to liking lang,   *to long-lasting pleasure*
296 So that we mend of oure mischefe.
     MOYSES.   Full well I wote thise wordys ar wrang.   *false*

     Bot hardely all that I heytt   *certainly/promised*
     Full sodanly it shall be seyn.   *seen, witnessed*
     Uncowth mervels shal be meyt   *Wondrous/encountered*
     And he of malice meyn.   *If he intends malice*
     [*The soldiers gather information again
     and return to Pharaoh.*]

     2 MILES.   A, lord, alas, for doyll we dy!   *dole, grief*
     We dar look oute at no dowre.
304 PHARAO.   What, the ragyd dwill of hell, alys you so to cry?   *ails*
     1 MILES.   For we fare wars then ever we fowre!   *Because/worse/fared*
     Grete loppys over all this land thay fly,   *insects*
     And where thay bite thay make grete blowre;   *blisters*
     And in every place oure bestys dede ly.

     2 MILES.   Hors, ox, and asse,
310 Thay fall downe dede, sir, sodanly.
     PHARAO.   We! lo, ther is no man that has
     Half as mych harme as I.

290-93My lord, unless this crowd (of Jews) be allowed to depart, happiness will never again
be ours.—Go, say to Moses we won't object (to their leaving). But (Pharaoh cynically admits
in private to his soldiers), they won't go any quicker, for all that (i.e., the offer is hypocritical).

296So that (or provided that) we may recover from our misfortunes.

304What, in the name of the shaggy devil of hell, ails you to cry out thus?

1 MILES.   Yis, sir, poore folk have mekill wo
　　To se thare catall thus out cast:　　　　　　　　　*forsaken*
　　The Jues in Gessen fayre not so;　　　　　　　　*Goshen*
　　Thay have liking for to last.　　　　　　　　　　*pleasure*
　PHARAO.   Then shall we gyf theym leyf to go,　　*leave, permission*
318　　To time this perell be on past.　　　　　　　　*Until*
319　　Bot, or thay flitt oght far us fro,　　　　　　*ere*
　　We shall them bond twise as fast.　　　　　　　　*bind/secure*
　　　　[*The soldiers go to Moses and the Israelites.*]

2 MILES.   Moyses, my lord giffys leyf
　　Thy meneye to remeve.　　　　　　　　　　　　　*company*
　MOYSES.   Ye mon hafe more mischefe　　　　　　　*must*
　　Bot if thise talys be trew.　　　　　　　　　　*Unless*
　　　　[*Again the soldiers gather information*
　　　　and report to Pharaoh.]

325　1 MILES.   A, lord, we may not leyde thise lifys!
326　PHARAO.   What, dwill! is grevance grofen again?
327　2 MILES.   Ye, sir, sich powder apon us drifys,　　*is driven*
　　Where it abidys it makys a blain;　　　　　　　　*boil*
　　Mesell makys it man and wife.　　　　　　　　　　*Leprous*
　　Thus ar we hurt with haill and rain,
　　Sir, v[i]nys in montanse may not thrife,　　　　*vines on mountain-slopes*
　　So has frost and thoner thaym slain.　　　　　　*thunder*

　PHARAO.   Yei, bot how do thay in Gessen,
　　The Jues, can ye me say?
　1 MILES.   Of all thise cares nothing thay ken.　　*know*
　　Thay feyll noght of our afray.　　　　　　　　　*alarm*

337　PHARAO.   No? the ragyd! the dwill! sitt thay in peasse?
　　And we every day in doute and drede?
　2 MILES.   My lord, this care will ever encrese,
　　To Moyses have his folk to leyd;　　　　　　　　*Until*
　　Els be we lorn, it is no lesse.　　　　　　　　*lost/lie*
　　Yit were it better that thay yede.　　　　　　　*went*

318–19Until such time as this peril is past. But, before they depart any distance from us.

325–26Ah, lord, our lives are intolerable!—What the devil! Has misfortune increased again?

327*powder*: i.e., furnace ashes which Moses has sprinkled in the air at God's command (see Exodus 9:8–9).

337*the ragyd! the dwill!*: Perhaps should read "the ragyd dwill," i.e., what in the name of the shaggy devil of hell; cf. ll. 304, 414.

343 PHARAO.   Thes[e] folk shall flit no far,
344   If he go welland wode!
     1 MILES.   Then will it sone be war.   *worse*
          It were better thay yode.   *went*
          [*Soldiers report to Pharaoh with more bad news.*]

     2 MILES.   My lord, new harme is comyn in hand.
     PHARAO.   Yei, dwill, will it no better be?
     1 MILES.   Wild wormes ar laid over all this land;   *locusts and caterpillars*
          Thay leyf no floure, nor leyf on tre.   *leave/leaf*
     2 MILES.   Agans that storme may no man stand.
352   And mekill more mervell, think me,
353   That thise thre dayes has bene durand   *enduring*
354   Sich mist, that no man may other se.
     1 MILES.   A, my lord!
     PHARAO.   Hagh!

     2 MILES.   Grete pestilence is comyn;   *plague*
          It is like ful long to last.   *likely*
     PHARAO.   Pestilence! in the dwilys name!
          Then is oure pride over-past.   *overthrown*

360 1 MILES. My lord, this care lastys lang,   *sorrow*
          And will, to Moyses have his bone.   *until/request*
          Let him go, els wirk we wrang;   *or else we do wrong*
          It may not help to hover ne hone.   *tarry nor delay*
     PHARAO.   Then will we gif theym leyf to gang,
          Syn it must nedys be done: *Since*
          Perchauns we sall thaym fang   *shall seize them*
          And mar them or to-morn at none.   *ere tomorrow noon*
          [*Soldiers go to Moses and the Israelites.*]

     2 MILES.   Moyses, my lord he says
          Thou shall have passage plain.
370 MOYSES [*to the Israelites*]. Now have we lefe to pas,
          My freyndys, now be ye fain.   *glad*

          Com furth; now sall ye weynd
          To land of liking you to pay.   *as your reward*
     1 PUER.   Bot King Pharao, that fals feynd,
          He will us eft betray.   *again*

343–44These folk (the Jews) will get no further, even though he (Moses) should go boiling
mad.

352–54 And an even greater wonder, it seems to me, is that for these three days there's been
such a heavy mist that no one can see another person.

Full soyn he will shape us to sheynd,   *undertake to destroy us*
And after us send his garray.   *armed force*
MOYSES.   Be not abast. God is oure freynd,   *dismayed*
And all oure foes will slay.

Therfor com on with me.
Have done, and drede you noght.
2 PUER.   That Lord blyst might he be,
That us from bayll has broght.   *misfortune*

384 1 PUER.   Sich frenship never we fand.   *found*
Bot yit I drede for perels all:
The Reede See is here at hand;
Ther shal we bide to we be thrall.   *until/captive*
MOYSES.   I shall make way ther with my wand,
As God has saide, to sayf us all;
390 On ayther side, the see mon stand   *either/must*
To we be gone, right as a wall.   *Until*
    [He parts the Red Sea.]

Com on with me; leyf none behinde.
Lo, fownd ye now youre God to pleasse.   *try*
    Hic pertransient mare.   *Here they will pass through the sea*
2 PUER.   O, Lord! this way is heynd.   *gracious, gentle*
Now weynd we all at casse.

    [The soldiers go to Pharaoh.]
1 MILES.   King Pharao! thise folk ar gone.
PHARAO.   Say, ar ther any noyes new?   *annoyances*
2 MILES.   Thise Ebrews ar gone, lord, everichon.
PHARAO.   How says thou that?
1 MILES.   Lord, that tayll is trew.
400 PHARAO.   We! out tyte, that they were tain.   *quickly*
That ryett radly shall thay rew!   *riot/quickly*
We shall not seasse to thay be slain,   *until*
For to the see we shall thaym sew.   *pursue*

Go charge youre chariottys swithe,   *load/quickly*
And fersly look ye folow me.
2 MILES. All redy, lord, we ar full blith
At youre bidding to be.

<hr>

[384]Never before have we found such friendly comfort.

[400]Curse it! Set out (after them) quickly, so that they may be taken.

408 1 MILES.   Lord, at youre bidding ar we bowne   *ready*
409   Oure bodys boldly for to beyd.   *command*
    We shall not seasse, bot ding all downe   *strike*
    To all be dede withouten drede.   *Until/beyond doubt*
    PHARAO.   Heyf up youre hertys unto Mahowne;   *Heave/Mohammed*
    He will be nere us in oure nede.
       [*They start through the Red Sea.*]
    Help! the raggyd dwyll! we drowne!
    Now mon we di[e] for all oure dede.   *must/deeds*
       Tunc merget eos mare.   *Then the sea will overwhelm them*

    MOYSES.   Now ar we won from all oure wo,
    And savyd out of the see!
    Loving gif we God unto.
    Go we to land now merely.   *merrily*

1 PUER.   Lofe we may that Lord on hight,
    And ever tell on this mervell;   *talk about*
    Drownyd he has King Pharao might.   *Pharaoh's*
    Lovyd be that Lord Emaneull!
424 MOYSES.   Heven, thou attend, I say, in sight,
425   And erth my wordys; here what I tell.
    As rain or dew on erth doys light   *does alight*
    And waters herbys and trees full well,

    Gif loving to Goddys magesté;
    His dedys ar done, his ways ar trew.
    Honowred be he in Trinité;
    To him be honowre and vertew.
        Amen.
        Explicit Pharao.

408-9Lord, we are ready to place our bodies boldly at your bidding.

424-25May heaven and earth, (everything) in sight, attend my words and hear what I say.

THE TEN COMMANDMENTS, BALAAM AND
BALAK, AND THE PROPHETS
FROM CHESTER

The four chief cycles vary considerably in their ways of providing a transition from the Old Testament to the New. The York cycle, omitting entirely a procession of prophets, moves abruptly from the story of Moses and Pharaoh to the Annunciation. The Wakefield cycle contains an incomplete procession of prophets including Moses, David, Sibyl, and Daniel. Wakefield also features a transitional episode about a blustering tyrant, Caesar Augustus, who hears a prophecy concerning the birth of a king and thereupon resolves to seek out and destroy the boy. The N Town cycle presents an extended series of Old Testament personages derived from the tradition of the tree of Jesse, containing kings from the genealogy of Christ along with some Old Testament prophets.

The Chester presentation of the prophets is the most comprehensive of the four chief cycles, though it is also marred by textual difficulties. The pageant consists of three main episodes: Moses receiving the Ten Commandments on Mount Sinai, the prophet Balaam's encounter with King Balak, and a procession of seven additional prophets announcing the advent of Christ. The procession seems to be a late addition; it appears in only one of the five Chester manuscripts (Harl. 2124), and it breaks in upon the episode of Balaam and Balak before that narrative is satisfactorily completed. A reviser evidently decided that Balaam's prophecy should be followed by other testimonials of this sort, even at the expense of dramatic consistency.

The Chester list of prophets is not the same as the usual list in church drama, which had been based on the pseudo-Augustinian *Sermo contra Judeos, Paganos, et Arianos de Symbolo* (see the Anglo-Norman *Adam* and the Benediktbeuern Christmas play in Part II, above). The Chester procession is seemingly derived instead from a Creed play, and is arranged to reflect the articles of the Apostles' Creed beginning with Christ's nativity. Balaam, Isaiah, and Ezekiel prophesy of the Virgin Birth; Jeremiah announces the Passion; Jonas foresees the Burial, Descent into Hell, and Resurrection; David tells of the Ascension; Joel predicts the Descent of the Holy Spirit at Pentecost; and Micah (Micheas) speaks generally of Christ's coming and of his reigning in glory. Despite the dramatically awkward placing of this sequence in the midst of the confrontation between Balaam and Balak, the episodes of the pageant as a whole are united by a common theme. We move from a recitation of the Ten Commandments, representing the highest expression of the Mosaic Law, to an adumbration of Christ's ministry and death through which the New Law is to be established. The prophets are an essential means of seeing the Old Testament in relation to the New.

This Chester pageant is typical of the Chester cycle in a number of ways. For example, several narratively separate episodes are bound together in one pageant by a common theological focus and by the character of the Expositor. As a kind of authorial spokesman and stage presenter, the Expositor is essential to Chester's interpretative method. He is a humble divine, lacking in colorful personality but wise and learned. He apologizes for the limitations of time, and places simple and direct emphasis on didactic meaning. Everything is seen through his clerical point of view. Accordingly, the pageant (like others in the cycle) is cautious and straightforward in its use of sources. Much of the account does not differ substantially from the biblical original found in Exodus (chapters 20, 32–34), Numbers (22–24), and the prophetic books. Through the Expositor, the pageant stresses religious awe without much comedy or vivid staging technique.

The most notable exception to the generally pious and understated effect of this pageant is the episode in which Balaam's ass refuses to bear him toward King Balak because an angel stands in their way. This popular story is based on sentimentalized legends about animals as the innocent friends of mankind. King Balak is also a somewhat comic figure in the ranting vein of Pharaoh and Herod. Balaam himself becomes the most dramatically interesting figure of the pageant, torn between his loyalty to God's command and his venal interest in what King Balak has to offer. His soul struggle anticipates that of Christ in the wilderness, especially when Balak conducts him to a mountain top and shows him the riches he can earn by cursing God's chosen people. Balaam is, like Moses, both a prophet of Christ's advent and an antetype of Christ.

Although staging requirements seem ambitious for a pageant wagon, the evidence suggests that this Chester pageant was in fact presented as part of a three-day cycle before a series of stationary audiences. A multi-level stage must have been devised, perhaps incorporating the ground level surrounding the wagon itself. God speaks from above (in supremo loco) to Moses, who is standing on Mount Sinai. Moses speaks from the mount to the chief priest representing the people of Israel. When Moses descends from the mount, King Balak enters riding "from another part of the mount." The mountain itself must have a northern and a southern side from which Balak can show Balaam the territories under his control. An unusually large number of characters are mounted, though at least some of the mounts are not live animals. Balaam's ass must be especially designed so that an actor inside the beast can speak. A knight sent by King Balak to fetch Balaam is also equestrian. One suspects that the staging of this many-tiered action would be more feasible if the ground level were brought into use.

The Ten Commandments, Balaam and Balak, and the Prophets

From Chester

> *Pagina quinta de Mose et Rege Balaak et Balaam Propheta.   The Cappers.*

The fifth pageant of Moses and King Balak and the Prophet Balaam

> *[God proclaims the Ten Commandments to Moses on Mount Sinai.]*

DEUS. Moyses, my servaunte life and dere,   *beloved*
And all the people that be here,

TITLE *Cappers:* cap-makers and sellers.

3   You wott in Egypte when you were
     Out of thralldome I you broughte.
5   I will, you honour no God save me;   *I command that*
     Ne mawmentrye none make yee;   *idolatry*
     My name in vaine name not yee,
     For that me likes naughte.

     I will, you hold your holy daye;
     And worshipp also, by all waye,
     Father and mother all that you maye;
     And slaye no man nowhere.
     Fornication you shall flee;   *avoid*
     No mens goodes steale yee;
15   Ne in no place abide ne bee
16   Falce witnes for to beare.

     Your neightboures wives covettes noughte,   *do not covet*
     Servant ne good that he hath boughte,   *goods*
     Oxe ne asse, in deede ne thoughte,
     Nor anythinge that is his,
     Ne wrongefullie to have his thinge
     Againe his will and his likinge.   *Against*
     In all these doe my biddinge,
24   That you doe not amisse.
       Tunc princeps sinagogae statuet   *Then the chief priest will take his*
       eum in loco, et quasi pro populo   *place, and as if on behalf on the*
       loquatur ad Dominum et Moysen: *people let him speak to the Lord and*
                                           Moses

PRINCEPS SINAGOGAE.   Ah, good Lord, much of mighte,
     Thou comes with so great lighte,
     We bene so afraide of this sighte,
     No man dare speak ne see!
     God is so grim with us to deale.
30   But Moyses, master, with us thou mele;   *speak with us*
31   Els we dyen, many and feele,   *many*
     So afraide bene all wee.

[3]You know that when you were in Egypt.

[5](See Exodus 20:3–17 for the Ten Commandments.)

[15–16](Cf. Exodus 20:16: "You shall not bear false witness against your neighbor.")

[24]s.d.: The chief priest is presumably below Mt. Sinai among "the people," who may include the audience.

[30–31](Cf. Exodus 20:19: "And they said unto Moses, Speak you with us, and we will hear; but let not God speak with us, lest we die.")

Tunc Moyses, stans super　　　　　　　　Then let Moses, standing on
montem, loquatur ad populum:　　　　　　the mount, speak to the people

MOYSES.　Gods folke, drede you noughte.
34　To prove you with, God hath this wrought,
　　To make you afraid in deede and thoughte
　　Aye for to avoide sinne.
　　By this sight you may now see
　　That he is pereles of postye.　　　　　　*peerless in power*
　　Therfore his teaching look done yee,　　　*see that you obey*
　　Thereof that you not blin.　　　　　　　*cease*

PRINCEPS SINAGOGAE.　Ah, highe Lord, God almighte,
　　That Moyses shines wondrous bright!
　　I may no way for great lighte　　　　　*on account of*
　　Now looke upon him.
45　And horned he semes in our sighte!
46　Sith he came to the hill, dight　　　　*Since/set down, prepared*
47　Our lawe he hase, I hope, aright,
48　For was he never so grim.

MOYSES.　You, Gods folke of Israell,
50　Harkens to me that loven heale.
　　God bade you sholde doe everye deale　　*every bit, entirely*
　　As that I shall saye.
　　Six dayes boldelye worches all;　　　　*work*
　　The seaventh "Sabaoth" you shall call.
　　That daye for ought that may befall　　*no matter what happens*
　　Hallowed shal be aye.

　　That doth not this deede, deade shall be.　*(He) that*
58　In houses fire shall no man see.
　　First fruites to God offer yee—　　　*Tithes*
　　For so himselfe bade—
　　Gould and silver offers also,
　　Purple, bisse, and other moe,　　　　*precious stuff*

³⁴God has done this (appeared in a "great light") to test you thereby (see Exodus 20:18–20).

⁴⁵*horned:* The ascription of horns to Moses results from a popular misconception of the text; see Exodus 34:29–30.

⁴⁶⁻⁴⁷Since the time that he went onto Mt. Sinai, I hope he has set down our law aright (on the tablets).

⁴⁸*he:* seemingly refers to God; see l. 29 above.

⁵⁰Hearken to me, you who love spiritual health (i.e., who desire to be saved).

⁵⁸There are to be no fires in houses (no cooking) on the Sabbath.

To him that shall save you from woe
And helpe you in your neede.

[*The Expositor, who is continually
present, comes forward.*]
[EX]POSITOR.   Lordinges, this comaundment
Was of the Old Testamente,
And yet is used with good entent
With all that good bene.   *By all virtuous persons*
69 This storye all if we shold fong,   *undertake*
70 To playe this moneth it were to[o] longe;
71 Wherfore most frutefull there amonge
72 We taken, as shall be sene.

Also, we read in this storye,
God in the Mownt of Sinai
Toke Moyses these comaundmentys, verelye,   *Delivered to*
76 Written with His owne hande
In tables of ston, as reade I.
But when men honoured mawmentry   *idolatry*
He brake them in anger hastelye,   *He (Moses)*
For that [t]he[y] wold not wonde.   *they (the Israelites)|refrain*

But afterward sone—leeve ye me—   *soon|believe*
Other tables of stone made he   *he (Moses)*
In which God bade written shold be
His wordes that were before,
The which tables shrined were   *enshrined*
After as God can Moyses leare.   *As God taught Moses*
And that shrine to them was deare
88 Thereafter evermore.
[*The Expositor retires.*]

Tunc Moyses descendet de monte,   *Then Moses will descend from the*
et ex altera parte montis dice[t]   *mount, and from another part of the*
Rex Balaac equitando. [*Balak is attended.*]   *mount King Balak will speak, riding*

BALAACK REX.   I, Balaack, king of Moab land,
All Israell, had I it in my hand,
I am so wroth I wold not wond   *hesitate*

[69-72]If we should undertake to play all this story, it would take more than a month; therefore
we have selected the most fruitful portions of this story to show you.

[70]*His:* i.e., in God's hand, evidently; see Exodus 32:16–19.

[88](At this point the other MSS insert two stanzas in which God instructs Moses to carve again
the tablets of stone, as in Exodus 34.)

To slaye them, ech wighte.
For their God helpes them stiflye   *stoutly*
Of other landes to have mastrye,
That it is bootles, witterlie,   *So that/truly*
Against them for to fighte.

What nation soever dose them noye,   *harms them*
Moyses prayes anone in hye,   *at once in haste*
Therfore have they sone the victorye   *they (the Israelites)*
And other men they have the worse.
101   Therefore how I will wroken be   *avenged*
102   I have bethought me, as mot I thé!   *may I prosper*
Balaam, I will, shall come to me   *I desire*
That people for to curse.

For sworde ne knife may not availe
These ilke shroes for to assaile.   *These same rascals*
That fowndes to fight, he shall faile,   *(He) that tries*
For sicker is him no boote.   *surely there's no help for him*
All nations they doe any,   *annoy*
And myselfe they can destroye
111   As ox that gnawes biselye
112   The grasse right to the roote.

Whoso Balaam blesses, iwis,
Blessed, sickerlye, that man is.   *surely*
Whoso he curses, fareth amisse—   *fares badly*
Such loos over all hase he.   *power*

116   [But yett I truste venged to bee,
With dinte of sword or pollicye,
On these false losells, leaves mee!   *wretches/believe you me*
Leeve this, withowten dowbte: *Believe*
For to bee wroken is my desire.   *avenged*
My heart brennys as whott as fire   *burns*
For vervent anger and for ire
Till this bee brought abowte!
Surgite dei patriae et optitulamini   *Arise, gods of the fatherland and*
nobis et in necessitate[m] nos defendite.   *help defend us in our necessity*

101–2Therefore I've thought how I will be avenged, as I hope to prosper (an oath).

111–12(This vivid metaphor of total destruction is taken from Numbers 22:4.)

116a(The five unnumbered stanzas beginning at this line are to be found in all the MSS except
H; the text here is from MS D: Huntington HM 2.)

Therfore, my god, and godys all,
O mightye Mars, on thee I call
With all the powers infernall.
Rise now and helpe at neede!
I am enformed by trewe reporte
How the medi[t]ators dooth resorte   *plotters (?)*
To winne my land to there comforte,   *their benefit*
Des[c]ended of Jacobs seede.

Now shewe your power, you godys mighty,
Soe that these caitiffes I may destroye,
Havinge of them full victorye,
And them brought to mischance!
Beate them downe in plaine battell,
Those false losells soe cruell,
That all the world may here tell   *hear*
Wee take on [them] vengeance.

Owt of Egypte fled the[y] bee,
And passed through the Red Sea;
The Egyptians that them pursued, trewlye,
Were drowned in that same fludd.   *flood*
The[y] have on[e] God, mickell of might,
Which them doeth aide, in wronge and right.
Whosoever with them foundeth to fight,   *attempts*
Hee winneth little good.

They have slaine—this wott I well—
Through helpe of God of Israell,
Both Seon and Ogge, kinges so fell,   *Sihon and Og (Joshua 2:10)/cruel*
And plainly them distroye[d].
Thearefore rise up, ye godys, eche one!
Ye be a hundrethe godys for one.   *against one*
I would be wroken them upon,   *avenged upon them*
For all there pompe and pride.]   *their*

Therfore, goe fetch him, bach[e]ler,   *knight, soldier*
That he may curse the people here;
119   For, sicker, on them in no manner   *surely*
120   Mon we not wroken be.   *Must/avenged*

MILES. Sir, on your errand I will gone.   *Soldier*
       It shall be well done, and that anone,

119–20For surely we must not in any way fail to be avenged on them.

For he shall wreak you on your fone,   *Balaam will avenge|foes*
The people of Israell.
BALAACK.   Yea, looke thou het him gold great wone,   *promise|quantity*
And riches for to live upon,
To destroy them if he can—
The freakes that be so fell.   *warriors, fellows|fierce*
   Tunc ibit ad Balaam.   *Then he [the soldier] will go to*
                                                        Balaam

MILES.   Balaam, my lorde greetes well thee,
130 And prayes the[e] right sone at him to be,   *with him*
To curse the people of Judy   *Judaea*
That do him great anoye.
BALAAM.   Forsooth, I tell the[e], bacheler,
That I may have no power
But if Gods will were.   *Unless*
That shall I witt in hye.   *know immediately*
   [*Balaam prays to God on his knees.*]

DEUS IN SUPREMO LOCO.   Balaam, I comaund the[e]   *in the uppermost place*
King Balaak his bidding that thou flee.
That people that is blessed of me
140 Curse thou not by no waye.
BALAAM.   Lord, I must doe thy biddinge,
Thoughe it be to me unlikeing.   *displeasing*
For truly much winninge   *profit*
I might have had todaye.

DEUS.   Thoughe the folke be my foe,   *folk (the Moabs)*
Thou shalt have leave thidder to goe.   *thither*
But looke that thou doe right soe   *see to it*
As I have thee taughte!   *As I've taught you*
BALAAM.   Lord, it shall be done in height.   *quickly*
150 This asse shall beare me aright.
Goe we together anone, sir knight,
For now leave I have coughte.   *permission|received*
   Tunc equitabunt versus regem,   *Then they will ride toward the king,*
   et eundo dicat Balaam: *and as they go let Balaam say*

Now, by the law I leve upon,   *believe*
Sith I have leave for to gone,   *Since|permission to go*
They shal be cursed every one   *They (the Israelites)*
And I ought win maye.   *If I can gain anything*
If Balaak hold that he has heighte,   *holds to that he promised*
Gods hest I set at light.   *command*
Warried they shal be this night   *Cursed*

160   Or that I wend awaye!   *Ere*

Tunc angelus obviabit Balaam   *Then an angel will stand in*

cum gladio extracto in manu,   *Balaam's way with a sword*

et stabit asina.   *drawn in hand, and the ass will balk*

Goe forth, Burnell! Goe forth, goe!

What the divell! My asse will not goe!

Served me she never soe.   *She never did this before to me*

What sorrow so her dose nye?   *does annoy her*

Rise up, Burnell! make thee bowne,   *ready, obedient*

And helpe to beare me out the towne;

Or, as brok I my crowne,   *as I hope to enjoy my head (an oath)*

Thou shalt full sore abye!   *pay for it*

Tunc percutiet asinam, et   *Then he will thrash the ass, and*

loquetur aliquis in asina: *someone in the ass will speak*

ASINA.   Maister, thou dost evell, witterly,   *truly*

170 So good an ass as me to nye!   *annoy, harm*

Now hast thou beaten me thry   *thrice*

That beare the[e] thus aboute.   *(I) that*

BALAAM.   Burnell, whye beg[u]iles thou me,

When I have most nede to the[e]?

ASINA.   That sight that I before me see

Makes me downe to lowte.   *bow, stoop*

Am I not, master, thine owne ass,

That ever before ready was

To beare the[e] whether thou woldest pas?   *whither/go*

180 To smite me now it is shame.

Thou wottest well, master, pardy,   *You know/by God*

Thou haddest never ass like to me,

Ne never yet thus served I thee.

Now I am not to blame.

Tunc Balaam videns angelum evagin-   *Then let Balaam, seeing the angel hold-*

atum gladium habentem adorans dicat: *ing the drawn sword, say, worshiping*

BALAAM.   Ah! Lord, to thee I make a vowe,

I had no sight of thee erre now.   *until now*

Little wist I it was thou

That feared my asse soe.   *frightened*

ANGELUS.   Why hast thou beaten thy ass thry?

190 Now I am comen thee to nye,   *annoy, vex*

That changes thy purpose falcelye

160s.d.: The other MSS here add a repetitious stanza of dialogue between Balaam and the soldier.

And woldest be my foe.

And the ass had not downe gone   *If*
I wold have slaine the[e] here anone.   *at once*
BALAAM.   Lord, have pittye me upon,
For sinned I have sore!
Is it thy will that I forth goe?
ANGELUS.   Yea; but looke thou doe this folk no woe
Otherwise then God bade thee tho   *than/then*
200   And saide to thee before.

Tunc Balaam et miles ibunt,   *Then Balaam and the soldier will*
Balaack venit in obviam.   *proceed, and Balak meets them*

BALAACK.   Ah, welcome, Balaam, my frend!
For, all mine anguish thou shalt end,
If that thy will be to wend
And wreake me of my foe.   *avenge me on*
205 BALAAM.   Nought may I speake, so have I win,   *as I hope to be saved*
206 But as God puttes me in
207 To forby all and my kin.   *deliver, save*
208 Therfore, sure, me is woe.

BALAACK.   Come forth, Balaam, come with me.
For on this hill, so mot I thee,   *as I hope to prosper*
The folke of Israell thou shalt see.
And curse them, I thee praye!
Thou shalt have riches, golde, and fee,
And I shall advance thy dignitye,
To curse men—cursed they may be!—
That thou shalt see today.

Tunc adducens secum Balaam in   *Then leading Balaam with him on*
montem, et ad australem partem   *the mount, and looking toward the*
respiciens, dicat ut sequitur: *south, let him speak as follows*

216a [BALAACK.   Lo, Balaham, now thow seest here
Godys people all in feare—   *together*
Cittye, castle, and rivere.
Looke now, how likes thee?   *how do you like this*
Curse them now at my prayer,
As thow wilt bee to mee full deare   *If you wish to be*

205–8I may say nothing, as I hope to be saved, except what words God puts in my mouth, to rescue all my people. I know that accordingly I will suffer. (Balaam resembles Christ in that he must suffer worldly privation for speaking truth. The following scene between Balaam and Balak foreshadows the Temptation in the Wilderness. See Numbers 22:41.)

216a(This stanza here inserted is found in the other MSS. Text from MS D.)

And in my realme moste of powere,
And greatest under mee.]

BALAAM.   How may I curse them in this place,
The people that God blessed hase?
In them is both might and grace,
And that is always seene.
221 Witnes I may none beare
222 Against God that this can were—   *defend*
223 His people that no man may deare   *injure*
224 Ne troble with no teene.   *affliction*

I saye these folkes shall have their will,
That no nation shall them grill.   *vex*
The goodnes that they shall fulfill
Nombred may not be.
Their God shall them kepe and save.
230 No other repreve may I not have,   *reproof*
231 But such death as they shall have
232 I praye God send me.

233 BALAACK.   What the devilles eyles the[e], poplart?   *ails*
Thy speach is not worth a fart!
Doted I wot well thou art,   *Dotard, fool*
For woodlye thou hast wroug[h]t.   *madly*
I bade thee curse them, every one,
And thou blest them, blood and bone!   *(i.e., completely)*
To this north side thou shalt anon,
240 For here thy deed is nought.   *valueless*
   Tunc adducet eum ad borealem partem.   *Then he will lead him to the north side*

BALAAM.   Herken, Balaack, what I say:
God may not gibb by no waye;   *balk, scoff*
That he saith is veray,   *That which/true*
For he may not lie.
To bless his folk he me sent.
Therfore I saye, as I am kent: *taught*
That in this land, verament,   *truly*
Is used no mawmentry.   *No idolatry must be used*

221-24I may not bear witness against those God defends, his people whom no man may injure nor trouble with affliction.

230-32(Cf. Numbers 23:10: "Let me die the death of the righteous, and let my last end be like his.")

233*poplart:* popelard (a term of abuse).

To Jacobs blood and Israell
250   God shall send joy and heale;   *(spiritual) health*
And as a lion in his weale   *splendor, prosperity*
Christ shal be haunsed hye,   *exalted*
And rise also in noble araye
As a prince to win great paye,   *satisfaction*
255   Overcome his enemies, as I say,
256   And them bowndly bye.   *cause to bow down*

257   BALAACK.   What the devill is this! Thou cursest them naught,
258   Nor blessest them nether, as me thought.
BALAAM.   Sir kinge, this I thee beheight   *promised you this*
Or that I come here.   *Ere I came*
BALAACK.   Yet shalt thou to another place,
Ther Gods power for to embrace.   *undertake*
The divell geve the[e] hard grace   *bad luck*
But thou doe my prayer!   *Unless*
    Ad occidentalem partem.   *To the west side*

265   BALAAM.   Ah, Lord, that here is faire wonning!   *dwelling*
Halls, chambers of great liking,
Valleyes, woodes, grass springing,
Faire yordes, and eke river!   *fields*
I wot well God made all this
His folke to live in joye and blisse.   *to inhabit*
That warryeth them, warried is;   *(He) that curses them is cursed*
That blessest them, to God is deare.

BALAACK.   Popelard! thou preachest as a pie.   *magpie*
The devill of hell thee destroy!
I bade thee curse mine enemye;
Therfore thou came me to.   *To that end*
Now hast thou blessed them here, thry,   *thrice*
For the nones me to nye.   *On purpose/annoy*
BALAAM.   So tould I the[e] before twye,   *told/twice*
280   I might none other doe.

BALAACK.   Out alas, what divell ailes thee?
I have het thee gold and fee   *promised*
To speake but wordes two or three,

255–58(Cf. Numbers 23:24–25: "He [the great lion] shall not lie down until he eat of the prey, and drink the blood of the slain. And Balak said unto Balaam, Neither curse them at all, nor bless them at all [*nec maledicas ei, nec benedicas*]." Balak seems to say that even if Balaam isn't going to curse the Jews, he ought at least to remain neutral.)

265i.e., Ah, Lord, how beautiful a dwelling-place is here!

And thou makes much distance.   *dispute*
Yet once I will assay thee,   *once more*
If any boote of bale will be;   *redress of injury, amendment*
And if thou falcely now faile me,
Mahound geve thee mischance!   *Mohammed*
   Tunc Balaam ad caelum   *Then Balaam, looking to*
   respiciens prophetando: *the heavens, prophesying*

288a BALAAM. *Orietur stella ex Jacob, et exurget*   *(See Numbers 24:17)*
   homo de Israell, et confringet omnes duces alie[ni]ginarum,
   et erit omnis terra possessio eius.

Now one thinge I will tell you all,
Hereafter what shall befall:
A starre of Jacob springe shall,
A man of Israell.
He shall overcome and have in band
All kinges, dukes of strang land,
And all the world have in his hand,
296   As lord to dight and deale.   *manage, dispose of*
   [*The other prophets come forward, accompanied by the*
   Expositor, as Balaam and Balak listen to their prophecies.]

ESAYAS.   I saye a maiden meeke and milde   *Isaiah 7:14–15*
Shall conceave and beare a childe,
Cleane without workes wilde,   *Innocent of evil deeds*
To win mankinde to wayle.   *weal, happiness*
Butter and hony shall be his meate,
302   That he may all evill forgeat,
Our soules out of hell to get,
And called Emanuell.

EXPOSITOR.   Lordinges, these wordes are so veray
That exposition, in good faye,   *faith*
None needes. But you know may   *may wish to know*
This word Emanuell:
Emanuell is as much to saye

288a(This prophecy is not to be found in the pseudo-Augustinian *Sermo contra Judeos;* and although the play of *Adam* does present Balaam among its procession of prophets, l. 816, as based on Numbers 24:17, that text differs considerably from Balaam's prophecy here. Except for Isaiah's prophecy, none of the prophecies in this play can be traced directly to the *Sermo contra Judeos.*)

296s.d.: At this point the other MSS omit the procession of prophets, and present instead a continuation of the scene between Balaam and Balak, showing how God's chosen people are again brought to confusion, etc., as in Numbers 25.

302That he (Christ) may refuse to know evil, cause it to be forgotten.

310   As "God with us night and day."
    Therfore that name forever and aye
    To his sonne cordes wondrous well.   *accords*

EZECHIELL. *Vidi portam in domo Domini clausam,*
et dixit angelus ad me, "Porta haec non aperietur
sed clausa erit" et ct. Ezechiel capitulo 2.   *i.e., Ezekiel 44:2. etc.*

    I, Ezechiell, sothlye see
    A gate in Gods house on hye.
    Closed it was; no man came nye.
    Then told an angell me:
    "This gate shall no man open, iwis,
    For God will come and goe by this;
    For himself it reserved is,
320   None shall come there but hee."

EXPOSITOR.   By this gate, lords, verament   *truly*
    I understand in my intent
    That way the Holy Ghost in went
    When God tooke flesh and bloode
    In that sweet maiden Mary.
    Shee was that gate, witterly,   *truly*
    For in her he light graciouslye   *alighted*
    Mankind to doe good.

JHEREMIA. *Deducunt oculi mei lacrimas per diem et*   *Jeremiah 14:17*
noctem, et non taceant; contritione magna contrita
est virgo filia populi mei et plaga, et ct.

    My eyes must run and sorrow aye
330   Without ceasing, night and daye;
    For my daughter, soth to saye,
    Shall suffer great anye.   *annoyance, harm*
    And my folke shall doe, in faye,   *by my faith, truly*
    Thinges that they ne know may   *i.e., not realizing*
    To that maiden, by many waye,   *in many ways*
    And her sonne, sickerlye.   *certainly*

EXPOSITOR.   Lordinges, this prophesie, iwis,
    Touches the Passion nothing amisse.   *Concerns/aptly*
    For the prophet see well this   *sees*
    What shall come, as I reade:
    That a childe borne of a maye   *maid*
    Shall suffer death, sooth to saye;

343   And they that maiden shall afray,   *frighten*
344   Have vengeance for that deede.

    JONAS.   *Clamavi de tribulatione mea ad Dominum*   *Jonah 2:2*
    et exaudivit; de ventre inferi clamavi et
    exaudisti vocem meam et proiecisti me.

    I, Jonas, in full great any   *annoyance, agony*
    To God I prayed inwardlye,
    And he me hard through his mercy,   *heard me*
    And on me did his grace.
    In middes the sea cast was I,   *midst of*
350   For I wrought inobedientlye.   *Because I acted*
    But in a whalles bellye
    Three dayes saved I was.

    EXPOSITOR.   Lordinges, what this may signifye
    Christ expoundes apertelye,   *clearly*
    As we reade in the Evangely   *i.e., Matthew 12:40*
    That Christ himself can saye: *did say*
    Right as Jonas was dayes three
    In wombe of whall, so shall He be   *He (Christ)*
    In earth lyinge, as was he,
360   And rise the third daye.

    DAVID.   *De summo caelo egressio eius, et*
    occursus eius ad summum eius. Psal.   *i.e., Psalms 19:6*

    I, David, saye that God almighte
    From the highest heaven to earth will light,
    And thidder againe with full might,
    Both God and man in feare;   *together*
    And after come to deeme the righte.   *judge*
366   May no man shape them of his sight,   *escape*
367   Ne deeme that to mankind is dighte,   *judgment/prepared*
    But all then must apeare.

    EXPOSITOR.   Lordes, this speach is so veray
    That to expound it to your paye   *satisfaction*
    It needes nothing, in good faye,
    This speach is so expresse.
    Each man by it knowe may

343–44And they who will frighten that maiden (Mary) will receive vengeance for that deed.

366–67No man may escape or hide from his sight, or from his judgment that is prepared for mankind.

That of the Ascention, soth to saye,
David prophesied in his daye,
376   As it rehearsed was.

JOELL.   *Effundam de spiritu meo super omnem*   *Joel 2:28*
carnem, et prophetabunt filii vestri.

I, Joell, saye this sickerlye:
That my Ghost send will I
Upon mankinde merciably
From heaven, sitting in see.   *throne*
Then shold [y]our childer prophesye,
382   Ould men meet swe[v]ens, witterly,   *dreams/truly*
383   Yong se sightes that therby
384   Many wise shall be.

EXPOSITOR.   Lordinges, this prophet speakes here
In Gods person, as it were,
And prophesies that He will apeare
Ghostlye to mankinde.   *Spiritually*
This signes non other, in good faye,   *signifies*
390   But of his deede on Whitsonday,
Sending his Ghost, that we ever may   *so that*
On him have sadlye mind.   *Remember him stedfastly*

MICHEAS.   *Tu, Bethlem, terra Juda, nequaquam*   *Micah 5:2*
minima es in principibus Juda; ex te enim exiet
Dux qui reget populum meum Israell.

I, Micheas, through my minde
Will saye that man shall sothlye finde: *what/truly*
That a childe of kinges kinde   *of royal lineage*
In Bethlem shall be borne,
That shall be duke to dight and deale,   *manage, rule*
And rule the folke of Israell,
Also win againe mankindes heale   *(spiritual) health*
400   That through Adam was lorne.   *lost*

EXPOSITOR.   Lordinges, two thinges apertlye   *clearly*
You may see in this prophesie:
The place certefies thee sothlye

376i.e., As has been heard just now, in David's recital.

382–84(Your) old men will dream dreams, truly, and your young men will see visions whereby
many will be made wise.

Where Christ borne will be;
And after his ending, sickerlye,
Of his deedes of great mercy,   *Because of*
That he shold sit soveraynly
408   In heaven, thereas is he.

Moe prophetys, lordinges, we might play,   *More*
But it wold tary much the daye.
411   Therfore six, sothe to say,
Are played in this place.
Twoo speakes of his Incarnation;
Another of Christys Passion;
The fourth of the Resurrection
In figure of Jonas.

The fifte speakes expreslie
How he from the highest heaven hye
Light into earth us to forby,   *Alighted/redeem*
420   And after thidder steigh   *later thither ascended*
With our kinde to heaven blisse.   *With our human nature (i.e., flesh)*
More love might he not shew, iwis,
But right thereas himselfe is   *even there where he is*
He haunshed our kinde on high.   *exalted*

The sixt shewes, you may see,
His Goste to man send will he,
More stidfast that they shal be   *so that*
To love God evermore.
429   Thus that beleve that leven we,   *creed which we believe*
430   Of Gods deedes that had pittye
431   On man when that he made them free,
432   Is prophesied here before.

BALAACK.   Goe we forth! It is no boote   *profit*
Longer with this man to moote;   *argue*
435   For God of Jewes is crop and roote,

408In heaven, where (in fact) he is.

411*six*: This number appears not to take Balaam or Micah into account, and may indicate a
textual problem. The two speaking of the Incarnation (l. 413) are apparently Isaiah and
Ezekiel; of the Passion, Jeremiah; of the Resurrection, Jonah; of the Ascension, David; and
of Whitsunday, Joel.

429-32Thus that creed which we believe, concerning the deeds of God who had pity on man
when He freed mankind (from sinful guilt), is prophesied by the prophets who have appeared
here.

435i.e., For God is all things to the Jews.

And lord of heaven and hell.
Now see I well no man on live
Gaines with him for to strive;
Therefore here, as mot I thrive,   *as I hope to thrive*
I will no longer dwell. [*Exeunt.*]

EXPOSITOR.   Lordinges, much more matter
　　　Is in this story then you see here;   *than*
　　　But the substance, without were,   *doubt*
　　　Is played you beforne.   *Has been performed*
445　And by these prophesies, leav you me,   *believe*
446　Three kinges, as you shall played see,
447　Presented at his nativitye
448　Christ, when he was borne.
　　　　　Finis paginae quintae.   *The end of pageant five*

445–48 And according to these prophecies, believe me, three kings—as you will see performed—
presented gifts to Christ at his nativity, when he was born.

THE ANNUNCIATION
FROM WAKEFIELD

As the representation of a pivotal moment in divine history, this pageant of the Annunciation fittingly commences on a note of recapitulation. God recalls his creation of man, the expulsion of Adam and Eve from paradise, and the long suffering of Adam's lineage in the bonds of hell. No less fittingly, however, the moment of Incarnation also looks forward to man's restoration from his fallen condition. Through a tripartite scheme of correspondences, God assures us that man's fall from grace will be remedied. Christ will atone for Adam, man for man; the cross will atone for the tree of forbidden knowledge, tree for tree; and Mary will atone for Eve, maiden for maiden (see ll. 32–34). The scene of the Annunciation will in fact be a re-enactment of the temptation in the Garden of Eden, since Gabriel, the divine messenger bringing Mary the news that she is to bear God's son, will take the place of Satan who came to Eve with such baleful intent (ll. 61–64).

The scene of the Annunciation itself does not depart substantially from the biblical original in Luke, 1 : 28–38. The remainder of this Wakefield Annunciation pageant, however, is devoted to the free-wheeling and chiefly invented story of Joseph's fears of cuckoldry. The tone shifts from reverence to touching comedy, as we move from the presentation of a canonically sacred event to a scene of lively human drama. The contrast in texture, also common elsewhere in medieval drama (as, for example, in the Wakefield Second Shepherds' pageant) inevitably raises the critical question: what is the purpose of bringing together such seeming opposites?

The playwright's apparent intention is to set the moment of the Incarnation in a typically and believably human context for his medieval audience. What were Joseph and Mary like as man and wife? How did Mary's pregnancy affect their marriage? The fascination of these and other questions led to a host of legends during the late Middle Ages about the Holy Family. The N Town cycle particularly reveals this trend with its whole series of pageants about the birth, early years, and marriage of Mary. The Wakefield version too, though shorter than that of N Town, reflects a desire to know everything about the married life of Joseph and Mary. The pageant is based ultimately on a biblical passage (Matthew 1: 19–21) in which Joseph quietly resolves to set aside his contract to the pregnant Mary until he is persuaded by an angel that she has conceived by the Holy Spirit. More directly, however, the Wakefield version is based on a vivid and invented account set down in the so-called apocryphal Book of James, or Protevangelium (xiii). Another source is the popular fabliau, or bawdy tale, with its perennial mirth at the expense of impotent old husbands and attractive young wives.

The playwright offers his comic tale of jealousy, then, as a key to human understanding of a divine mystery. The audience is invited to sympathize with Joseph's fears of cuckoldry, and yet must perceive at last such fears are groundless. Joseph is, like Noah, mortal and imperfect even though a good man. His faith wavers, temporarily overwhelmed by the rationalistic assumption that a woman who is pregnant must have taken a lover. Joseph expresses doubt so that the audience, like him, may pass through skepticism to an abiding faith. Every detail of the story serves to assure the audience that Mary has been untouched sexually by man. Joseph's aged impotence and his nine months' absence from his wife, though cause for suspicion at first that Mary has been unfaithful, are ultimately confirmation of her complete chastity even in her relationship to her husband. The antifeminist humor and bawdry allow the audience to laugh at typical human failings and yet perceive that Mary is wholly above feminine weakness.

Staging of the Annunciation inevitably calls for a meeting of the realm of heaven with the sphere of earth, at the intersection of the timeless with time. In the N Town pageant, for example, the stage direction specifies as follows: *"Here the Holy Ghost discendit with thre*

bemys to Our Lady; the Sone of the Godhed next with thre bemys to the Holy Gost; the Fadyr Godly with thre bemys to the Sone: and so entre all thre to here bosom." The motif of descent and ascent is presumably important also in the staging of the Wakefield Annunciation. Medieval iconography offers many illustrations of the richly formal and symbolic style in which Mary and Gabriel must have been portrayed. Conversely, however, the second part of this Wakefield pageant is confined to earth. The humble location in which Joseph ponders his marital dilemma contrasts markedly with the sacred place in which Mary has received Gabriel's message.

The Annunciation
From Wakefield

       Incipit Annunciatio.

       [*God, enthroned in heaven, is attended by his angels.*]

DEUS.	Sithen I have mayde all thing of noght,	*Since*
	And Adam with my handys hath wroght,	
	Like to min[e] image, att my devise,	*devising*
	And giffen him joy in paradise	*have given*
	To won therin, as that I wend,	*dwell/as I intended*
	To that he did that I defend—	*Until/what I forbade*
	Then I him put out of that place—	*After that*
	Bot yit, I myn, I hight him grace:	*remember/promised*
	Oill of mercy I can him heyt,	*did promise him*
10	And time also his bayll to beytt.	*misfortune/assuage*
	For he has boght his sin full sore	*paid for/sorely*
	Thise fife thowsand yeris and more,	
	First in erthe and sithen in hell.	*afterwards*
	Bot long therin shall he not dwell.	
	Outt of pain he shall be boght;	*redeemed*
	I will not tyne that I have wroght.	*lose that which*
	I will make redempcion	

---

[10]And a time (i.e., of Christ's coming) to assuage his misfortune.

18 As I hight for my person,   *promised*
 All with reson and with right,
 Both thrugh mercy and thrugh might.
 He shall not, therfor, ay be spilt,   *be damned forever*
 For he was wrangwisly begilt;   *Since/wrongfully beguiled*
 He shall out of preson pas,
 For that he beg[u]iled was   *Since*
 Thrugh the edder, and his wife.   *adder*
 Thay gart him towch the tree of life   *caused*
 And ete the frute that I forbed,
 And he was dampned for that dede.
 Rightwisnes will we make;   *Righteousness*
30 I will that my son manhede take.
 For reson will that ther be thre: *reason decrees*
 A man, a madyn, and a tre—
33 Man for man, tre for tre,
34 Madyn for madyn—thus shal it be.
 My son shall in a madyn light,   *take lodging*
 Agans the feynd of hell to fight,   *Against*
37 Withouten wem, os son thrugh glas,   *blemish/like sun*
38 And she madyn as she was.
 Both God and man shall he be,
 And she moder and madyn fre.   *noble*
 To Abraham I am in dett   *I am committed*
 To safe him and his gett;   *save/progeny*
 And I will that all prophecye   *I decree*
 Be fulfillyd here by me.
45 For I am Lord and lech of heyle,   *physician*
46 My prophetys shall be funden leyle;   *found trustworthy*
 As Moyses said, and Isay,   *Isaiah*
 King David, and Jeromy,
 Abacuk, and Daniell,   *Habbakuk*
 Sibyll sage, that saide ay well,   *who always spoke truly*
 And mine othere prophetys all—
 As thay have said, it shall befall.
  [*God speaks to Gabriel, who rises from kneeling.*]

[18]As I promised to do in my own person.

[30]I decree that my son assume the nature of mankind.

[33-34]i.e., Christ for Adam, the cross for the forbidden tree, and Mary for Eve.

[37](For this analogy of the Virgin Birth to the sun's passing through glass without harming it, see the Benediktbeuern *Christmas Play,* Part II above, ll. 192-99.)

[38]And she (Mary) will remain a virgin as she was before.

[45-46]Because I am Lord and physician of spiritual healing, my prophets will be found to be loyal (trustworthy, reliable).

Rise up, Gabriell, and weynd   *go*
Unto a madyn that is heynd,   *gracious*
To Nazareth in Galilee,
Ther[e] she dwellys in that citee;
To that virgin and to that spouse,
To a man of David house—   *David's*
Joseph also he is namyd by—   *is called*
60   And the madyn name Mary.   *named*
Angell must to Mary go,
For the feynd was Eve fo—   *Because|Eve's*
He was foule and layth to sight,   *loathsome*
And thou art angell fair and bright—
And hails that madyn, my lemman,   *you must hail|beloved*
As heyndly as thou can.   *graciously*
Of my behalf thou shall hir grete.   *On*
I have hir chosen, that madyn swete;
She shall conceyf my derling,
70   Thrugh thy word and hir hering.   *hearing*
In hir body will I light,
That is to me clenly dight.   *prepared*
She shall of hir body bere
God and man, withouten dere.   *harm*
She shall be blissyd withouten ende.
Grayth the[e], Gabriell, and weynd.   *Get ready*
        [*Gabriel goes to greet Mary.*]

77   GABRIELL.   Haill, Mary, graciouse!
Haill, madyn and Godys spouse!
Unto the[e] I lowte.   *do reverence*
Of all virgins thou art qwene,
That ever was, or shall be seyn,
Withouten dowte.

Haill, Mary, and well thou be!
My Lord of heven is with the[e],
Withouten end.
Haill, woman most of mede!   *merit*
Goodly lady, have thou no drede,
That I commend.   *I bid*

89   For thou has fonden, all thin[e] oone,   *found*

---

[77](The following verses are a close paraphrase of the biblical Annunciation; see Luke 1:28–38.)

[89–91]For you have found, all by your own doing, the grace of God, which previously was lost on account of Adam's transgression.

90   The grace of God, that was out-gone,
91   For Adam plight.
    This is the grace that the[e] betidys: *that is now yours*
    Thou shall conceive within thy sidys   *loins*
    A child of might.

    When he is comen, that thy son,   *this*
    He shall take circumsicion;
    Call him Jhesum.
    Mightfull man shall be he that,
    And Godys son shall he hat,   *be called*
100 By his day com.

    My Lord also shall gif him till   *give to him*
102 His fader sete, David, at will   *His father David's throne*
    Therin to sitt.
104 He shall be king in Jacob kin;   *of Jacob's lineage*
    His kingdom shall never blin,   *cease*
    Lady, well thou witt.   *know*

    MARIA.   What is thy name?
    GABRIEL.   Gabriell,
    Godys strengthe and his angell,
    That comys to the[e].
110 MARIA.   Ferly greting thou me gretys.   *Wondrous*
111 A child to bere thou me hetys—   *promise*
    How shuld it be?

113 I cam never by mans side,
114 Bot has avowed my madynhede
115 From fleshly gett.   *progeny*
    Therfor I wote not how   *know*
    That this be brokyn, as a vow
    That I have hett.   *promised*

119 Nevertheles, well I wote,

---

[100]Come on his appointed day.

[102]*fader*: i.e., ancestor (see Luke 1:32).

[104](Luke 1:33: "And he shall reign over the house of Jacob for ever.")

[110–11]You greet me with wondrous greeting. You promise me I will bear a child.

[113–15]I never lay with a man, but have vowed to preserve my maidenhead from fleshly progeny, from procreation.

[119–22]Nevertheless, well I know, God is powerfully able to do what you say and fulfill your promise. But I don't know how.

120	To wirk thy word and hold thy hote	*promise*
121	Mightfull God is.	
122	Bot I ne wote of what manere;	
	Therfor I pray the[e], messingere,	
	That thou me wish.	*instruct me*

	GABRIELL. Lady, this is the prevaté:	*secret*
	The Holy Gost shall light in the[e],	
	And his vertue.	*divine power*
	He shall umshade, and fulfill	*hover over*
	That thy madynhede shall never spill,	*be injured*
130	Bot ay be new.	

	The child that thou shall bere, madame,	
	Shall Godys son be callid by name.	
	And se, Mary:	
	Elesabeth, thy cosin, that is cald geld,	*called barren*
	She has conceiffed a son in elde,	*old age*
136	Of Zacary.	

	And this is, who will late,	*whoso will inquire*
	The sext moneth of hir conceytate,	*pregnancy*
	That geld is cald.	
	No word, lady, that I the[e] bring,	
	Is unmightfull to heven king,	*impossible*
	Bot all shall hald.	*hold true (as promised)*

	MARIA. I lofe my Lord all-weldand;	*love/all-ruling*
	I am his madyn at his hand,	*his handmaid*
	And in his wold.	*power*
146	I trow bodword that thou me bring	*tidings*
147	Be done to me in all thing	
148	As thou has told.	

	GABRIELL. Mary, madyn heynd,	*gracious*
	Me behovys to weynd;	*It behoves me to go*
	My leyf at the[e] I take.	*My leave of you*
	MARIA. Far[e] to my freynd,	
	Who the[e] can send	*did send*
	For mankinde sake.	

> [*Gabriel returns to heaven. Joseph appears, somewhat distant from Mary.*]

136To Zacharias, Elizabeth's husband(see Luke 1:5–23).

146–48(See Luke 1:38: "be it unto me according to your word.")

JOSEPH.   All-mighty God, what may this be!
 Of Mary my wife mervels me.   *it astonishes me*
 Alas, what has she wroght?
 A, hir body is grete and she with childe!
 For me was she never filyd,   *On my account/defiled*
160 Therfor myin is it noght.   *mine*

 I irke full sore with my life   *am irked*
 That ever I wed so yong a wife.
 That bargan may I ban!   *curse*
 To me it was a carefull dede;   *deed full of cares*
165 I might well wit that yowthede   *youth*
166 Wold have liking of man.

 I am old, sothly to say.
168 Passed I am all prevay play;   *privy*
 The gams fro me ar gane.   *pleasures/gone*
 It is ill cowpled, of youth and elde,
 I wote well, for I am unwelde;   *impotent*
 Som othere has she tane.   *other (lover)/taken*

 She is with child, I wote never how.
 Now, who wold any woman trow?   *trust*
 Certys, no man that can any goode.   *who knows what's good*
 I wote not in the warld what I shuld do!
 Bot now, then, will I weynd hir to,   *go to her*
178 And witt who owe that foode.   *owns that child*
  [*He approaches Mary.*]

179 Haill, Mary, and well ye be!
 Why, bot woman, what chere with the[e]?
MARIA. The better, sir, for you.
JOSEPH. So wold I, woman, that ye wore; *were*
 Bot certys, Mary, I rew full sore   *rue, regret*
 It standys so with the[e] now.

 Bot of a thing frayn the[e] I shall: *I'll question you*
 Who owe this child thou gose withall? *you go with, carry*
MARIA. Sir, ye, and God of heven.
JOSEPH. Mine, Mary? do way thy din.   *stop your chatter*

165–66 I might well have known that (her) youth would have a craving for male company.

168 I'm past the age for sexual pleasures.

178 And find out who fathered that child.

179 (An ironic echo of Gabriel's famous salutation at l. 77.)

| 189 | That I shuld oght have parte therin | *at all* |
| 190 | Thou nedys it not to neven. | *mention* |

191	Wherto nevyns thou me therto?	
	I had never with the[e] to do;	
	How shuld it then be mine?	
194	Whos[e] is that child, so God the[e] spede?	*prosper*
	MARIA. Sir, Godys and yowrs, withouten drede.	*doubt*
196	JOSEPH. That word had thou to tine,	*to lose*

197	For it is right full far me fro.	
	And I forthinkys thou has done so	*regret*
	Thise ill dedys, bedene;	*indeed*
200	And if thou speke thyself to spill,	
201	It is full sore agans my will,	
202	If better might have bene.	

	MARIA. At Godys will, Joseph, must it be.	
	For, certanly, bot God and ye,	*except for*
	I know none othere man.	
	For fleshly was I never filyd.	*carnally/defiled*
	JOSEPH. How shuld thou thus then be with child?	
208	Excuse the[e] well thou can.	

	I blame the[e] not, so God me save,	
210	Woman maners if that thou have,	
	Bot certys I say the[e] this:	
	Well wote thou, and so do I,	
	Thy body fames the[e] openly	*defames*
	That thou has done amis.	*amiss*

MARIA.   Yee, God he knowys all my doing.
    [*Joseph steps aside and addresses the audience.*]
JOSEPH.   We, now! this is a wonder thing.
    I can noght say therto;
    Bot in my hart I have greatt care,

189–91You needn't try to claim that I have any part in this. Why do you name me in this?

194Whose is that child, as you hope God to prosper you?

196–97You spoke that speech in vain, for it is very far from convincing me.

200–2And if you destroy (i.e., damn) yourself by speaking untruthfully, when things might have been better, it is very sorely against my will.

208See if you can excuse yourself on that score.

210If you behave like all women.

219	And ay the longer mare and mare.	
	For doyll what shall I do?	*dole, sorrow*

	Godys and min[e] she says it is.	
	I will not fader it; she says amis.	*amiss, falsely*
223	For shame yit shuld she let	
224	To excuse hir velany by me,	
225	With hir I think no longer be.	
	I rew that ever we met.	

[*He begins the story of their courtship.*]

	And how we met, ye shall wit sone.	*know soon*
228	Men use yong children for to done	
229	In temple for to lere;	
230	Soo did thay hir, to she wex more	*until*
231	Then othere madyns wise of lore.	
	Then bishopes said to hir:	*i.e., the chief priests*

	"Mary, the[e] behowfys to take	*it behoves you*
	Som yong man to be thy make,	*mate*
	As thou seys other hane,	*you see/have*
	In the temple, which thou will neven."	*whom you will choose*
	And she said, none bot God of heven;	
	To Him she had hir tane.	*given herself*

239	She wold none othere, for any sagh.	*saying*
	Thay said she must—it was the lagh—	*law*
	She was of age thertill.	*thereto*
	To the temple thay somond old and ying,	*summoned*
	All of Juda ofspring,	
	The law for to fulfill.	

	Thay gaf ich man a white wand,	
	And bad[e] us bere them in oure hande,	
	To offre with good intent.	
248	Thay offerd thare yerdys up in that tide;	*their wands/time*

[219]And ever the longer (it goes on), the more and more (I sorrow).

[223–25]Lest for shame she should think to excuse her sinful behavior by using me (as a veneer of legitimacy), I intend to dwell with her no longer.

[228–31]It is the custom for people to send their young children to the temple to be religiously educated; just so did Mary's parents, until she grew more wise in this instruction than all other maidens.

[209]She would take no other mate, no matter what anyone said.

[248]They, the other candidates for Mary's hand, offered up their wands at that time.

For I was old, I stode beside.   *Because*
I wist not what thay ment.   *knew/intended*

Thay lakyd oone, thay saide in hy;   *lacked one/in haste*
All had offerd, thay said, bot I,
For I ay withdrogh me.   *withdrew myself*
Furth with my wande thay mayd me com;   *made*
In my hand it florished with blome!
Then saide thay all to me:

"If thou be old, mervell not the[e],   *don't be astonished*
For God of heven thus ordans he,   *decrees*
Thy wand shewys openly.   *shows plainly*
260 It florishes so, withouten nay,   *undeniably*
That the[e] behovys wed Mary the may."   *it behoves you/maiden*
A sory man then was I.

I was full sory in my thoght.
I saide, for old I might noght   *because of age*
Hir have, never the wheder,   *no matter what*
I was unlikely to hir so ying.   *unsuited/young*
Thay saide ther helpyd none excusing,   *there was no help for it*
And wed us thus togeder.

When I all thus had wed hir thare,
We and four madyns home can fare,   *did go*
271 That kingys doghters were.
272 All wroght thay silk to find them on;   *clothe themselves in*
273 Marye wroght purpyll, the oder none
274 Bot othere colers sere.

I left thaym in good peasse, wenyd I.   *I supposed*
Into the contré I went on hy   *in haste*
My craft to use with main;   *skill/might*
To gett oure lifing I must nede.   *earn our living*
On Marye I prayd them take good hede   *Of*
280 To that I cam agane.   *Until*

Neyn monethes was I fro that mild.   *Nine months/gentle person*
When I cam home, she was with child.
Alas, I said, for shame!

271-74The maidens, who were king's daughters. (According to traditions of Mariolatry, these
princesses accompanied Mary during her marriage as attendants worthy of a queen and as
guarantors of her continued chastity.) They made silk garments to clothe themselves in; Mary
made a purple silk garment, the others choosing various colors other than purple (the royal
color; see the *Gospel of Pseudo-Matthew,* VIII).

I askyd ther women who that had done,   *who had done that*
285 And thay me saide an angell sone
286 Syn that I went from hame.

"An angell spake with that wight,   *person*
And no man els, by day nor night.
Sir, therof be ye bold."   *confident*
Thay excusyd hir thus, sothly,
To make hir clene of hir foly,
And babished me that was old.   *mocked, fooled*

Shuld an angell this dede have wroght?   *Would*
294 Sich excusing helpys noght,
295 For no craft that thay can.   *Despite*
A hevenly thing, forsothe, is he,   *he (an angel)*
And she is erthly; this may not be.
It is som othere man.

Certys, I forthink sore of hir dede.   *I am sorry*
Bot it is long of yowth-hede,   *on account of youth*
All sich wanton playes;
302 For yong women will nedys play them
With yong men, if old forsake them.
Thus it is sene always.

305 Bot Marye and I playd never so sam.   *together*
Never togeder we usid that gam;
I cam hir never so nere.

308 She is as clene as cristall clyfe   *cleft (?)*
For me, and shal be whils I lyf;   *As far as I'm concerned/live*
The law will it be so.   *decrees that*
And then am I cause of hir dede?   *her deed*
312 Forthy, then can I now no rede.   *Therefore/advice*
Alas, what I am wo!   *how wretched I am*

285-86And they told me (it was) an angel, soon after I had gone from home.

294-95Such making of excuses doesn't help, despite all their cleverness.

302For young women will of necessity provide sport for themselves.

305But Mary and I never played together (at the sport of sex).

308*cristall clyfe*: perhaps a reference to the sun passing through unharmed crystal, as in l. 37 above.

312Therefore, now I don't know what to do.

And sothly, if it so befall,   *truly*
Godys son that she be with all—   *pregnant with*
If sich grace might betide—   *happen*
I wote well that I am not he
Which that is worthy to be
That blissed body beside,

320   Nor yit to be in company.
      To wildernes I will forthy   *therefore*
      Enfors me for to fare,   *Force myself*
      And never longer with hir dele;
      Bot stilly shall I from hir stele,   *quietly*
325   That mete shall we no mare.   *more*
      [*Joseph starts to leave Mary. An angel from heaven stops him.*]

      ANGELUS.   Do wa[y], Joseph, and mend thy thoght,   *Cease that*
      I warne the[e] well; and weynd thou noght   *do not go*
      To wildernes so wilde.
      Turne home to thy spouse agane.
      Look thou deme in hir no trane,   *judge/deceit*
      For she was never filde.   *defiled*

332   Wite thou no wirking of werkys wast.   *Blame*
      She hase consavyd the Holy Gast,
      And she shall bere Godys son.
      Forthy with hir, in thy degré,   *Therefore/appointed place*
      Meke and buxom looke thou be,   *Meek/obedient*
      And with hir dwell and won.   *dwell*

      JOSEPH.   A, lord, I lofe the[e] all alon[e],   *above everything*
      That vowches safe that I be oone   *vouchsafes*
340   To tent that child so ying—   *tend*
      I that thus have ungrathly gone,   *acted perversely*
      And untruly taken apon   *found fault with*
      Mary, that dere darling.

      I rewe full sore that I have sayde,   *that which*
345   And of hir birding hir upbrade,   *her sport*
      And she not gilty is.
      Forthy to hir now will I weynde,   *Therefore*
      And pray hir for to be my freynde,

³²⁵So that she and I will meet no more.

³³²Do not blame the (imagined) doing of empty deeds.

³⁴⁵(And I rue) having upbraided her for her adultery.

And aske hir forgifnes.
[*Joseph goes to Mary.*]

A, Mary, wife, what chere?
MARIA.   The better, sir, that ye ar here;   *remained*
Thus long where have ye lent?
JOSEPH.   Certys, walkyd aboute, like a fon,   *Truly/fool*
354 That wrangwisly hase taken apon.
355 I wist never what I ment;   *intended*

Bot I wote well, my lemman fre,   *virtuous beloved*
I have trespast to God and the[e];   *sinned*
Forgif me, I the[e] pray.
MARIA.   Now all that ever ye saide me to,
God forgif you, and I do,
With all the might I may.

JOSEPH.   Gramercy, Mary, thy good will   *Great thanks*
So kindly forgifys that I saide ill,   *that which*
When I can the[e] upbrade;   *did upbraid you*
365 Bot well is him hase sich a fode,   *companion*
366 A meke wif; withouten goode,   *possessions*
367 He may well hold him paide.

368 A, what I am light as linde!   *linden, lime-tree*
369 He that may both lowse and binde,
370 And every mis amend,
Leyn me grace, powere, and might   *Lend*
My wife and hir swete yong wight
To kepe, to my lifys ende.   *until*
Explicit Annunciatio beatae Mariae.

354–55Who has behaved wrongfully. I didn't know what I was planning to do.

365–70But lucky the man who has such a companion, a meek wife; even without possessions, he may consider himself well rewarded. Ah, I'm as light (cheerful) as a lime-tree (an alliterative expression)! May He who may both loosen (free from punishment) and bind (to punishment), and amend all sins.

THE SALUTATION OF ELIZABETH
FROM WAKEFIELD

The story of Mary's visit to her pregnant kinswoman Elizabeth serves to heighten the emotional and spiritual impact of the Annunciation. After years of barrenness, Elizabeth has conceived a son in her old age. This miracle, recalling Sarah's conception of Isaac when she was past the age of child-bearing (Genesis 17–18), simultaneously attests to the immanence of an even greater miracle, the Virgin Birth. The meeting between Mary and Elizabeth is accordingly fraught with significance for them both. As the child stirs for the first time in Elizabeth's womb, she is filled with the Holy Spirit and greets Mary with the universally-known words of the "Hail Mary." Elizabeth is the first person to proclaim Christ's presence in the flesh, even though he is not yet born. Mary's reply, the equally well-known "My soul does magnify the Lord" (the *Magnificat*, sung every day at vespers), is a hymn of praise to God for his mercy toward the meek and humble.

Because this Wakefield pageant serves chiefly as a vehicle for the "Hail Mary" and the *Magnificat*, the language stays particularly close to Luke 1:39–56 (which follows immediately after the Annunciation). The relatively inconsequential additions to that text aim at personalizing the situation, rendering it comfortably familiar to medieval audiences. The names of Mary's parents are supplied from patristic tradition, along with the notion that Elizabeth is Mary's maternal great-aunt (the Bible refers to her only as a "kinswoman"). The two women disarmingly begin and end their conversation with some innocent family gossip about absent loved ones.

Like the Annunciation, this scene was an iconographical favorite in medieval and Renaissance art, and we can perhaps get some idea of the actors' appearance on stage from these illustrations. Stage movement is unusually lacking; the pageant is a sacred tableau.

The Salutation of Elizabeth
From Wakefield

Incipit Salutatio Elezabeth.

[*Mary approaches Elizabeth in her home.*]

MARIA. My Lord of heven, that sittys he,	*who sits on high*
And all thing seys with ee,	*sees with eye*
The[e] safe, Elizabeth.	*Save you*
ELEZABETH. Welcom, Mary, blissed blome!	*bloom*
Joyfull am I of thy com	*coming*
To me, from Nazareth.	
MARIA. How standys it with you, dame, of qwart?	*as to your health*

8 ELEZABETH.   Well, my doghter and dere hart,
9   As can for min[e] elde.
10 MARIA.   To speke with you me thoght full lang,
11   For ye with childe in elde gang,
12   And ye be cald geld.   *called barren*

13 ELEZABETH.   Full lang shall I the better be,
14   That I may speke my fill with the[e],
    My dere kins-woman,
    To witt how thy freyndys fare   *know*
    In thy countré where thay ar[e];
    Therof tell me thou can,

    And how thou farys, my dere derling.
    MARIA.   Well, dame, gramercy youre asking;   *great thanks for*
21   For good I wote ye spir.   *inquire*
    ELEZABETH.   And Joachim, thy fader, at hame,
    And Anna, my nese and thy dame,   *niece/mother*
    How standys it with him and hir?

    MARIA.   Dame, yit ar thay both on life,   *alive*
    Both Joachim and Anna his wife.
    ELEZABETH.   Els were my hart full sore.
28 MARIA.   Dame, God that all may
29   Yeld you that ye say,   *Recompense*
    And blis you therfore.

31 ELEZABETH.   Blissed be thou of all women,
    And the fruite that I well ken   *know*
    Within the wombe of the[e];
    And this time may I blis
    That my Lordys moder is
    Comen thus unto me.

37   For syn that time, full well I wote,   *since*
38   The stevyn of angell voce it smote   *voice*

8–14 As well as can be expected at my advanced age, my close relative (i.e., grand-niece) and
dear friend.—I have been anxious to speak with you, for you are with child in your old age,
and yet are said to be barren.—It will do me a lot of good to talk with you to my heart's desire.

21 I know you ask with good intent.

28–29 Lady, may God who can do all things recompense you for what you say.

31 (This line begins a verse rendition of the "Hail Mary"; see Luke 1:42–45.)

37–40 For since that moment—I know it well—when the angelic voice (of Mary) sounded just
now in my ears, a wondrous thing has happened to me.

39	And rang now in min[e] ere,	
40	A selcouth thing is me betide:	*wondrous*
41	The child makys joy, as any bird,	
	That I in body bere.	

	And als, Mary, blissed be thou,	*also*
	That stedfastly wold trow	*believe*
	The wordys of oure heven king.	
46	Therfor all thing now shall be kend	*known, manifested*
47	That unto the[e] were said or send	*sent, conveyed*
48	By the angell greting.	

MARIA.   *Magnificat anima mea dominum:*

49	My saull lufys my Lord abuf,	*loves/above*
	And my gost gladys with luf	*spirit gladdens*
	In God, that is my hele.	*salvation*
52	For he has bene sene agane	*he has regarded*
53	The buxumnes of his bane,	*obedience/servant*
	And kept me madyn lele.	*loyal, true*

	Lo, therof what me shall betide:	*happen to me*
	All nacions on every side	*peoples*
	Blissyd shall me call.	
	For He that is full of might	
	Mekyll thing to me has dight;	*Mighty/done*
	His name be blissed over all.	

	And his mercy is also	
62	From kinde to kinde, till all tho	*generation/to*
63	That ar him dredand.	
	Might in his armes he wroght,	
65	And distroed in his thoght	*destroyed*
66	Prowde men and high-berand.	*Proud and haughty men*

67	Mighty men furth of sete he did,

41*bird*: probably should be "bryd" for the rhyme.

46–48(See Luke 1:45: "For there shall be a performance of those things which were told her from the Lord.")

49(This line begins a verse rendition of the *Magnificat;* see Luke 1:46–55.)

52–53(See Luke 1:48: "For he has regarded the low estate of his handmaiden.")

62–63From generation to generation, to all those who fear him.

65–66(See Luke 1:51: "He has scattered the proud in the imagination of their hearts.")

67–69He put down mighty men from their seats, and exalted in their place men of meek heart (i.e., the humble).

68 And he hightynd in that stede
69 The meke men of hart.
    The hungré with all good he fyld,   *filled*
71 And left the rich outt-shyld,   *sent away*
    Thaym to unquart.   *deprive of prosperity*

73 Israell has, under law,
74 His awne son in his awe,
    By menys of His mercy.
    As He told before, by name,   *As God foretold*
    To oure fader Abraham,
    And seyd of his body.   *And to Abraham's progeny*

    Elizabeth, min[e] awnt dere,   *aunt*
80 My lefe I take at you here,   *leave/of you*
    For I dwell now full lang.   *I've stayed*
    ELIZABETH.   Will thou now go, Godys fere?   *God's companion*
    Com kis me, doghter, with good chere,
    Or thou hens gang.   *Ere you go hence*

    Farewell now, thou frely foode!   *noble person*
    I pray the[e] be of comforth goode,
    For thou art full of grace.
    Grete well all oure kin of bloode.   *i.e., Convey my greetings*
    That Lord, that the[e] with grace infude,   *(May) that Lord/endowed*
90 He save all in this place.   *(May) He save*
         Explicit Salutatio Elezabeth.

71(See Luke 1:53: "And the rich he has sent empty away.")

73-74Israel has God's own son in her jurisdiction. (This is the versifier's rendition of the Vulgate, "*Suscepit Israel puerum suum*," taking "*suscepit*" in the sense of "to receive" and "*puerum*" as referring to Christ. The Authorized Version meaning is entirely different: "He has helped his servant Israel.")

THE BIRTH OF JESUS
FROM YORK
THE TILLE THEKERS

In its ballad-like clarity and directness, this Bethlehem scene from York is unlike the more elaborate and spectacular treatments found in some other cycles. We witness no apocryphal miracles, such as that of the midwife whose hand is withered because she doubts the Virgin Birth (in the N Town cycle). Instead, the dramatist focuses on the touching plight of Joseph and Mary, as described in the second chapter of Luke and in medieval reflective works on the life of Christ such as the *Meditationes vitae Christi*. The dramatist limits his scene to the stable or manger and its immediate surroundings. We learn of the journey to Bethlehem and the search for lodging only through Joseph's recollection of those events. No character is present other than Joseph, Mary, and the newborn child. The result is a moving portrayal of the fallen world into which Christ has come. The season is cold, the walls of the stable cannot hold out the elements, darkness has descended. Joseph fears and suffers, more for his wife and the child than for himself. Like the simple shepherds in the Wakefield Second Shepherds' pageant, Joseph complains about his desperate condition without being aware that the redemption of mankind is at hand. Fittingly, the birth itself occurs when Joseph is absent, disconsolately wandering about in search of firewood and deploring his helpless infirmity. The gentle irony of his typically human incomprehension is beautifully conveyed by his question when he returns to the stable: "O Marye, what swete thing is that on thy kne?"

Staging requirements are as simple as the action. Performance would be feasible either on a moveable pageant wagon or in a fixed location. The manger, a familiar structure in churches at Christmas during the Middle Ages and often represented in the visual arts, probably featured leaky walls and roof. Joseph and Mary mention the two beasts standing on either side of the crib, warming the child with their breath. A star appears suddenly in Joseph's view as he hunts for firewood in the acting area adjacent to the manger. Christ's birth must be painless and immaculate, as medieval theology repeatedly insisted; presumably a doll is revealed at Mary's feet, from beneath her robes, ready to be worshiped by her and wrapped in swaddling clothes.

The Birth of Jesus
From York
The Tille Thekers

[*Joseph and Mary in Jerusalem, in a stable for beasts.*]

JOSEPH.   All-weldand God in trinité,   *All-ruling*

TITLE *Tille Thekers:* tile thatchers.

I praye the[e], Lord, for thy grete might,
Unto thy simple servand see,   *look after*
Here in this place wher we are pight,   *placed, set*
Oure self allone.
Lord, graunte us gode herberow this night   *good lodging*
Within this wone.   *dwelling*

For we have sought bothe uppe and doune,
Thurgh diverse stretis in this cité;
So mekill pepull is comen to towne   *many*
That we can nowhare herbered be,
There is slike prees.   *such a crowd*
13 Forsuthe, I can no socoure see
14 But belde us with there bestes.   *shelter/these beasts*

15 And if we here all night abide,
16 We schall be stormed in this steede: *place*
17 The walles are doune on ilke a side,   *every*
18 The ruffe is rayned aboven oure hede,
19 Als have I roo.   *peace*
20 Say, Marye, doughtir, what is thy rede?   *advice*
How sall we doo?

For in grete nede nowe are we stedde,   *placed*
As thou thyselffe the soth may see;   *truth*
For here is nowthir cloth ne bedde,   *neither bedclothes nor*
And we are weyke and all werye,   *weak*
And faine wolde rest.
Now, gracious God, for thy mercye
Wisse us the best.   *Teach*

MARIA.   God will us wisse, full wele witt ye.   *you know it well*
30 Therfore, Joseph, be of gud chere,
For in this place borne will he be
That sall us save fro sorowes sere,   *many*
Bothe even and morne.
Sir, witte ye wele the time is nere
He will be borne.

JOSEPH.   Than behoves us bide here stille,   *we must stay*

13–19In truth, I can see no remedy except to shelter ourselves with these beasts. And if we stay all night here in this place, we'll be afflicted with storms: the walls are in a state of ruin on every side, the roof above our heads leaks as though raining, as I hope to have peace (a mild oath).

20*doughtir*: i.e., a younger woman and close relative (here, wife).

Here in this same place all this night.

MARIA.   Ya, sir, forsuth it is Goddis will.

JOSEPH.   Than wolde I faine we had sum light,

40   What so befall.   *Come what may*

It waxis right myrke unto my sight,   *murky, dark*

And colde withall.

I will go gete us light, forthy,   *therefore*

And fewell fande with me to bring.   *try to bring fuel*

45 MARIA.   All-weldand God yow governe and gy—   *guide*

46   As he is sufferayne of all thing—   *sovereign*

47   Of his grete might,   *With*

48   And lende me grace to his loving

49   That I me dight.   *get myself ready*

> [*Joseph leaves the stable in search of firewood.*
> *Mary prepares for the birth.*]

Nowe in my sawle grete joye have I!

I am all cladde in comforte clere!

Now will be borne of my body

Both God and man togedir in feere.   *in partnership*

Blist mott he be!   *may*

Jhesu, my sone that is so dere,

Nowe borne is he.

> [*Mary worships Jesus.*]

Haile, my Lord God, haile, prince of pees!

Haile, my fadir, and haile, my sone!

Haile, sovereyne sege all sinnes to sesse!   *man, warrior/end*

Haile, God and man in erth to wonne!   *dwell*

Haile, thurgh whos[e] mi[g]ht

All this worlde was first begonne,

63   Merknes and light.   *Darkness*

Sone, as I am simpill sugett of thine,   *subject*

Vowchesaffe, swete sone, I pray the[e],

That I might the[e] take in the[se] armys of mine,

And in this poure wede to arraye the[e]. [*She swaddles Jesus.*]   *poor garment*

Graunte me thy blisse,

As I am thy modir chosen to be

70   In sothfastnesse.   *truthfulness*

45–49 May all-ruling God, since he is sovereign of all things, lead and guide you with his great mightiness, and bestow grace on me so that I may prepare myself to serve him lovingly.

63 (The dividing of darkness from light refers to the creation of the world; Mary worships Christ as both God and man.)

[Joseph, still outside the stable, searches for wood.]

JOSEPH.   A, Lorde God, what the wedir is colde!   *how*
  The fellest freese that evere I felyd.   *cruellest/felt*
  I pray God helpe tham that is alde,   *old*
  And namely tham that is unwelde,   *especially/infirm*
  So may I saye.
  Now, gud God, thou be my belde   *protection*
  As thou best may.

    [The star shines suddenly.]

  A, Lord God, what light is this
  That comes shining thus sodenly?
  I cannot saye, als have I blisse.   *as I hope to have bliss*
  When I come home unto Marye
  Than sall I spirre.   *inquire*

    [He calls to Mary as he reenters the stable.]

83   A! here be God, for nowe come I.
MARIA.   Ye ar welcum, sirre.

JOSEPH.   Say, Marye doghtir, what chere with the[e]?
86 MARIA.   Right goode, Joseph, as has ben ay.
JOSEPH.   O Marye, what swete thing is that on thy kne?
MARIA.   It is my sone, the soth to saye,
  That is so gud.
90 JOSEPH.   Wele is me I bade this day   *waited for*
  To se this foode!   *child*

  Me merveles mekill of this light   *I'm greatly astonished at*
  That thus-gates shines in this place.   *thus*
  Forsuth it is a selcouth sight!   *wondrous*
MARIA.   This hase he ordand of his grace,   *ordained*
  My sone so ying—   *young*
  A starne to be schining a space   *star/a while*
  At his bering.   *birth*

  For Balam tolde full longe beforne   *Balaam/a long while ago*
100   How that a sterne shulde rise full hye;
  And of a maiden shulde be borne
  A sonne, that sall oure saffing be   *saving, salvation*

---

[83]*here be God:* May God be here (a conventional greeting, with ironic meaning in this instance).

[00]Things are as good with me as they've ever been, Joseph.

[90]How fortunate I am to have awaited this day.

Fro caris kene.   *From keen woes*
Forsuth it is my sone so free   *noble*
By whame Balam gon meene.   *Whom Balaam signified*

[*Joseph worships Jesus.*]

JOSEPH.   Nowe welcome, floure fairest of hewe!   *hue*
I shall the[e] menske with maine and might.   *worship*
Haile, my maker, haile, Crist Jhesu!
Haile, riall king, roote of all right!   *royal*
110   Haile, Saveour!
Haile, my Lorde, lemer of light!   *source*
Haile, blessid floure!

MARIA.   Nowe, Lord, that all this worlde schall winne,
To the[e], my sone, is that I saye: *I say this to you*
Here is no bedde to laye the[e] inne.
Therfore, my dere sone, I the[e] praye,
Sen it is soo,   *Since*
Here in this cribbe I might the[e] lay
Betwene ther bestis two.   *these beasts*
    [*She lays the babe in a manger.*]

120   And I sall happe the[e], min[e] owne dere childe,   *wrap*
With such clothes as we have here.
JOSEPH.   O Marye, beholde thes[e] beestis milde:
They make loving in ther manere
As they wer men.   *As if*
Forsothe, it semes wele, by ther chere   *countenance*
Thare Lord they ken.   *recognize*

MARIA.   Ther Lorde thay kenne, that wate I wele;   *I know it well*
They worshippe him with might and maine.
The wedir is colde, as ye may feele;
To halde him warme they are full faine   *keep/glad*
With thare warme breth,
132   And oondis on him—is noght to laine—   *breathe/conceal*
To warme him with.

O, nowe slepis my sone—blist mot he be—   *may*
And lies full warme ther bestis bitwene.   *these*
JOSEPH.   O nowe is fulfillid, forsuth I see,
That Abacuc in minde gon mene   *What Habakkuk foresaw*
And prechid by prophicie:

132And breathe on him—it cannot be concealed, is plainly visible.

He saide oure Savioure shall be sene
140 Betwene bestis lie.

And nowe I see the same in sight.
MARIA.   Ya, sir, forsuth, the same is he.
JOSEPH.   Honnoure and worshippe both day and night,
Ay-lastand Lorde, be done to the[e]   *Everlasting*
Allway, as is worthy.
And, Lord, to thy service I oblissh me   *bind myself*
With all min[e] herte [w]holy.

MARIA.   Thou mercifull maker, most mighty,
My God, my Lorde, my sone so free,   *noble*
150 Thy handemaiden forsoth am I,
And to thy service I oblissh me
With all min[e] herte entere.
Thy blissing, beseke I thee,   *beseech*
Thou graunte us all in feere.   *together*
        [*The end of the Birth of Jesus.*]

THE SHEPHERDS
FROM YORK
THE CHAUNDELERS

If we compare this York Shepherds' pageant with the famous Wakefield Second Shepherds' pageant, we can see a comparable motif treated on the one hand with quiet simplicity and on the other with richly complex and comic effect. Both versions juxtapose the human and divine, elaborating the meaningful paradox that God chose to reveal his coming to the humblest of men. This relatively simple version from York is based ultimately on Luke 2:8–20, although we also find hints of a medieval tradition associating the shepherds (*pastores*) with the clergy. The shepherds' learning in the prophetic books of the Old Testament, for example, is a conventional and unrealistic detail. At the same time these shepherds are also rustic countrymen overwhelmed by the appearance of the angels, reacting with innocent wonder to the news of Christ's birth. They boast of their singing, and do not sense as we do the immense gap between their rustic clownish song and the Latin *Gloria in Excelsis* of the angels. Similarly, their act of worship is at once generous (they give the best they have) and frank in its expectation of a practical return on their investment.

The stage must closely resemble that of the York Birth of Jesus immediately preceding it, with a star, a manger, and fields nearby. Curiously, though, if performance at York was truly processional as the records seem to indicate (unless those records describe the Corpus Christi procession rather than the play), we must postulate not only a separate wagon and set for this Shepherds' pageant but new actors for the silent roles of Joseph and Mary.

The Shepherds
From York
The Chaundelers

[*Three shepherds in the fields near Bethlehem.*]

1 PASTOR. Bredir, in haste takis heede and here		*Brothers/take/hear*
What I wille speke and specifye.		*relate*
Sen we walke thus, withouten were,		*Since/doubt*
4 What mengis my moode nowe mevyd will I.		*stirs my mind/declare*
Oure forme-fadres, faithfull in fere,		*forefathers/together*
Bothe Osye and Isaye,		*Hosea/Isaiah*

TITLE *Chaundelers:* makers and sellers of candles.

⁴*mevyd:* an error for *meve yt,* declare it?

Preved that a prins withouten pere   *Proved/equal*
Shulde descende doune in a lady,
And to make mankinde clerly,   *i.e., clear of sin*
To leche tham that are lorne.   *cure/lost, condemned*
And in Bedlem hereby   *Bethlehem*
Sall that same barne be borne.   *child*

   2 PASTOR.   Or he be borne in burgh hereby,   *Ere*
14 Balaham, brothir, me have herde say,   *Balaam*
A sterne shulde schine and signifye   *star*
With lightfull lemes, like any day.   *bright beams*
And als the texte it tellis clerly   *as*
18 By witty lerned men of oure lay,   *law*
With his blissid bloode he shulde us by;   *buy, redeem*
20 He shulde take here al of a maye.   *maiden*
I herde my sire saye,   *heard*
When He of hir was borne
She shulde be als clene maye   *as pure virgin*
As ever she was byforne.

   3 PASTOR.   A, mercifull maker, mekill is thy might,   *great*
That thus will to thy servauntes see.   *look after*
Might we ones loke uppon that light,   *once*
Gladder bretheren might no men be!
I have herde say, by that same light
The childre of Israell shulde be made free,   *chosen race*
31 The force of the feende to felle in sighte,
And all his pouer excluded shulde be.   *his (the fiend's) power*
Wherfore, brether, I rede that wee   *I advise*
Flitte faste overe thees felles   *Go/hills*
To frayste to finde oure fee,   *try/cattle*
And talke of sumwhat ellis.
    [*Angels appear to them, above, singing.*]

37 1 PASTOR. We! hudde!
   2 PASTOR.   We! howe!
   1 PASTOR.   Herkyn to me!
38 2 PASTOR. We! man, thou maddes all out of might.   *you're behaving wildly*

14Brothers, I have heard that Balaam prophesied.

18As interpreted by sagacious clerical scholars of our holy law.

20He should come to earth (and take human form) from a maiden (Mary).

31In order to throw down the power of the fiend, for all men to see.

37–39We, hudde, howe, colle: interjections of surprise.

39 1 PASTOR.   We! colle!

3 PASTOR.   What care is comen to the[e]?

1 PASTOR.   Steppe furth and stande by me right,   *close to me*

And telle me than   *then*

If thou sawe evere swilke a sight?   *such*

3 PASTOR.   I? nay, certis, nor nevere no man.

2 PASTOR.   Say, felowes, what! finde yhe any feest,   *if you find*

Me falles for to have parte, pardé.   *I deserve/by God*

1 PASTOR.   Whe! hudde! behalde into the heste!   *east*

A selcouthe sight than sall thou see   *wondrous*

Uppon the skye.

2 PASTOR.   We! telle me, men, emang us thre,

Whatt garres yow stare thus sturdely?   *causes/fixedly*

3 PASTOR.   Als lange as we have herde-men bene,   *As/herdsmen*

And kepid this catell in this cloghe,   *clough, valley*

So selcouth a sight was nevere non sene.   *marvelous*

54 1 PASTOR.   We! no colle! nowe comes it newe inowe,

55 That mon we finde.

Itt menes some mervayle us emang,   *marvel among us*

Full hardely I you behete.   *certainly/promise*

58 1 PASTOR.   What it shulde mene, that wate not yee,

59 For all that ye can gape and gone.

  [*An angel sings.*]

I can singe itt alls wele as hee,   *as*

And on asaye itt sall be sone   *by trial/soon*

Proved, or we passe.   *ere we go*

If ye will helpe, halde on! late see,   *i.e., let's sing*

For thus it was.

  Et tunc cantant.   *And then they sing*

2 PASTOR.   Ha ha, this was a mery note!

By the dede that I sall die,   *death*

I have so crakid in my throte

That my lippis are nere drye.

3 PASTOR.   I trowe you roise.   *boast*

For, what it was faine witte walde I   *I'd gladly know what*

That tille us made this noble noise.   *to us*

³⁹*What care . . . the[e]:* i.e., What's bothering you now? (The third shepherd evidently has
not yet seen the angels, and is perplexed by the first shepherd's behavior.)

^{54–55}i.e., Gracious me! It certainly comes as news, as we're bound to discover (*finde* possibly
an error for *wete,* know?).

^{58–59}You don't know what it signifies, for all your gaping and activity.

1 PASTOR.   An aungell brought us tithandes newe   *tidings*

A babe in Bedlem shulde be borne—

74   Of whom than spake oure prophicye trewe—

And bad[e] us mete him thare this morne,

That milde of mode.   *gently-disposed one*

2 PASTOR.   I walde giffe him bothe hatte and horne

And I might finde that frely foode.   *If|noble child*

3 PASTOR.   Him for to finde has we no drede.   *we have no doubt*

80   I sall you telle achesonne why: *reason*

Yone sterne to that Lorde sall us lede.

2 PASTOR.   Ya, thou says soth. Go we forthy   *therefore*

Him to honnour,

And make mirthe and melody

With sange to seke oure Saviour.

    Et tunc cantant. [*They proceed to Bethlehem.*]

1 PASTOR.   Breder, bees all blithe and glad;   *Brothers|be*

Here is the burght ther we shulde be.   *town where*

2 PASTOR.   In that same steede now are we stadde;   *place|located*

Tharefore I will go seke and see.

90   Slike happe of heele nevere herde-men hadde.   *Such fortune|salvation*

Loo, here is the house, and here is hee.

3 PASTOR.   Ya, forsothe, this is the same.

    [*They enter the stable.*]

Loo, whare that Lorde is laide

Betwixe two bestis tame,

Right als the aungell saide.

1 PASTOR.   The aungell saide that he shulde save

This worlde and all that wonnes therin.   *dwells*

98   Therfor, if I shulde oght aftir crave,

To wirshippe him I will beginne.—[*They worship Jesus.*]

Sen I am but a simple knave   *Since*

(Thof all I come of curtayse kinne)   *Although|respectable*

Loo here slike harnays as I have: *such gear*

A baren broche by a belle of tinne   *A poor brooch*

At youre bosom to be.

And whenne ye shall welde all,   *rule over all*

Gud sonne, forgete nog[h]t me

107   If any fordele falle.   *advantage*

---

⁷⁴Of whom our prophecy spoke the truth, then.

⁹⁰No shepherds have ever had such good fortune of salvation.

⁹⁸Therefore, if I should hope to gain anything in the future (from Jesus).

¹⁰⁷If any rewards are being passed out.

108 2 PASTOR.   Thou sonne that shall save bothe see and sande,   *i.e., the whole world*
Se to me sen I have the[e] soght!   *Look after me since*
I am ovir poure to make presande   *too poor/present*
Als min[e] harte wolde, and I had ought.   *As/if I had anything*
Two cobill notis uppon a bande,   *round nuts*
Loo, litill babe, what I have broght,
And whan ye sall be Lorde in lande,
Dose goode againe, forgete me noght.   *i.e., Repay my kindness*
For I have herde declared,   *I've heard it said*
117 Of conning clerkis and clene,   *By*
118 That bountith aftir rewarde.
Nowe watte ye what I mene.   *you know*

3 PASTOR.   Nowe loke on me, my Lorde dere,
121 Thof all I putte me noght in pres.   *Although*
Ye are a prince withouten pere;   *equal*
I have no presentte that you may plees.   *can please you*
But lo, an horne spone that have I here—   *spoon made of horn*
And it will herbar fourty pese—   *hold/pease*
This will I giffe you with gud chere.
Slike novelté may noght disease.   *Such/displease*
Fare[well], thou swete swaine!
God graunte us leving lange.   *long life*
130 And go we hame againe
And make mirthe as we gange.   *go*
     [*The end of the York Shepherds' pageant.*]

¹⁰⁸*see and sande:* i.e., sea and land, everything.

¹¹⁷⁻¹⁸By wise and good clerical authorities, that bounty asks reward (*aftir* an error for *askis*, asks?).

¹²¹Although I don't press forward (as alacritously as my two fellows).

THE SECOND SHEPHERDS' PAGEANT
FROM WAKEFIELD

This famous pageant by the Wakefield "Master" is actually the second shepherds' pageant by him in the Towneley manuscript. The first may be an early version; probably the two were not intended to be performed together. Both pageants commence on a note of suffering in the world Christ comes to save. Humble shepherds, alone in their fields and shivering with cold, complain of lost sheep and of oppression at the hands of insolent bailiffs. They might well be shepherds living in fifteenth-century northern England, although their sufferings are also timeless. Both versions use farcical materials to dramatize the condition of the fallen world, so greatly in need of Christ's coming. The shepherds carouse with one another, drink, and quarrel. In both pageants, moreover, the comic scenes of horseplay serve as a prelude to the angels' appearance and the shepherds' subsequent visit to the manger.

Of the two pageants, the second is deservedly better known. The story of Mak the sheep stealer and his wife Gill is a remarkably successful burlesque of the Nativity. Without in any way blaspheming that sacred event, the pageant sets up an extensive comparison between a stolen sheep and the Saviour of mankind. Although partly farcical in source and tone, the pageant achieves its effect through the kinds of foreshadowings and correspondences we have seen in earlier episodes of the Corpus Christi cycle. The parallelism between the two scenes of nativity begins with an annunciation. Mak, aroused from his pretended sleep by the shepherds, tells them of a dream in which his wife has given birth to a child (ll. 382–88). The implicit contrast between this birth and that of Christ is at once apparent, however, for children are a curse to Mak. With a houseful of young ones, he can never find enough to eat. In his view, children are the predictable but unwanted consequences of sexual intercourse: "we must drink as we brew" (l. 501). Marriage too is a curse. Mak's grumblings about his married condition recall those of Joseph, but with the crucial difference that Mak is truly henpecked. His shrewish Gill reminds us of Noah's wife, except that harmony is never restored to this household.

Mak is a magician-sorcerer who must be foiled and satirically exposed, like Satan, the "fals g[u]iler" who is himself beguiled by the birth of Christ (l. 713). At the same time, the sheep-stealing episode suggests ways in which the exposure and defeat of evil are offset by a more restorative process of heavenly grace. Even though the stolen sheep is an illusory child and a monster with horns, it also reminds us of Christ's sacramental role as the Lamb of God. The swaddling of the sheep in its cradle is, in the same fashion, both comic parody and edifying anticipation of the holy birth. When Mak and Gill protest they would rather eat their own child than beguile the shepherds (ll. 535–538), their ludicrous and blaspheming double-entendres adumbrate the eating of Christ's flesh as a means of salvation. Suitably, then, the visit of the shepherds to this bogus nativity scene ends with the triumph of charity over hatred. Only when the shepherds renounce their vengeful pursuit of Mak, and resolve instead to bestow gifts on the newborn "child," do they discover their lost sheep. Rather than punish Mak with the death that his offense would ordinarily merit, they roisterously toss him in a blanket. Their charitable willingness to forgive, and their loving response to the miracle of birth, prepare them spiritually for their subsequent visit to Christ's manger.

The staging of this pageant requires two "mansions," Mak's house and the holy manger, giving a visible form to the parallelism of the farcical and serious action. Although the Wakefield Master never calls explicit attention to the resemblance between the two

births, the stage itself would help make the point. The shepherds' fields lie presumably between or below the two simultaneously visible houses. The angels sing from above. As the shepherds move from their fields and Mak's cottage to the holy manger, we witness the fulfillment of an action begun under the old dispensation and completed under the new.

The Second Shepherds' Pageant
From Wakefield

Incipit Alia eorundem.		*Here begins their second (pageant)*

[*The open fields. Enter the first shepherd.*]

1 1 PASTOR. Lord, what these weders ar cold! And I am ill happyd.		*clothed*
I am nerehande dold, so long have I nappyd.		*nearly numb*
My legys thay fold, my fingers ar chappyd.		*give way*
It is not as I wold, for I am al lappyd		*wrapped*
In sorow.		
In stormes and tempest,		
Now in the eest, now in the west,		
Wo is him has never rest		
Midday nor morow!		

10 Bot we sely husbandys that walkys on the moore,		*wretched farm-workers*
In faith, we ar nerehandys outt of the doore.		*nearly homeless*
No wonder, as it standys, if we be poore,		
For the tilthe of oure landys lyis falow as the floore,		*cultivated ground*
As ye ken.		*know*
We ar so hamyd,		*hamstrung*
Fortaxed and ramyd,		*Overtaxed/beaten down*
We ar mayde handtamyd		*submissive*
With thise gentlery-men.		*By/gentry*

Incipit Alia eorundem: This headnote, indicating that this is the second such pageant in the MS about the shepherds, refers to the rubric at the end of the Wakefield First Shepherds' pageant: *Explicit Una pagina pastorum,* Here ends pageant one of the shepherds.

[1]Lord, how cold this weather is! And I am poorly clothed.

Thus thay refe us oure rest, Oure Lady theym wary! — *rob us of/curse them*

20   These men that ar lord-fest, thay cause the ploghe tary.

That, men say, is for the best; we finde it contrary.

22   Thus ar husbandys opprest, in po[i]nte to miscary

23   On life.

Thus hold thay us hunder; — *under*

Thus thay bring us in blonder. — *confusion*

It were greatte wonder

And ever shuld we thrife. — *If*

28   For, may he gett a paint slefe or a broche now-on-dayes,

29   Wo is him that him grefe or onys agane says! — *once gainsays*

30   Dar no man him reprefe, what mastry he mays. — *force he uses*

And yit may no man lefe oone word that he says, — *believe*

No letter.

33   He can make purveance

With boste and bragance; — *bragging*

35   And all is thrugh mantenance

Of men that ar gretter.

Ther shall com a swane, as prowde as a po; — *retainer/peacock*

He must borow my wane, my ploghe also. — *wagon*

Then I am full fane to graunt or he go. — *glad (ironic)/ere*

Thus lif we in paine, anger, and wo,

By night and day.

42   He must have if he langyd,

43   If I shuld forgang it.

I were better be hangyd

Then oones say him nay. — *once*

It dos me good, as I walk thus by min[e] oone, — *myself*

Of this warld for to talk in maner of mone. — *complaint*

To my shepe will I stalk and herkyn anone, — *walk*

20*lord-fest*: bound to a lord (i.e., the well-to-do subordinates of the manorial lord, who make life miserable for the peasant tenant farmers and hired help).

22-23Thus are farm-workers oppressed, to the point of perishing.

28-30For, should any man obtain a decorated sleeve or brooch (official livery) these days, woe to the (poor) man who offends or crosses this fellow! No one dare reprove him, no matter what force he uses.

33*purveance*: i.e., to requisition in the name of lord or king, at an arbitrary and usually low price.

35*mantenance*: the system by which powerful lords defended the interests of their retainers, often for illegal ends.

42-43If he has longed for something he must have it, even if I should have to forego it.

49   Ther abide on a balk, or sitt on a stone
   Full soyne.   *soon*
   For I trowe, perdé,   *trust/by God*
52   Trew men if thay be,
   We gett more compané
   Or it be noyne.   *Ere/noon*

       [*Enter the second shepherd. He does not see the first shepherd.*]
  2 PASTOR.   Bensté and Dominus, what may this bemeyne?   *Bless us/signify*
56   Why fares this warld thus? Oft have we not sene.
   Lord, thise weders ar spitus, and the windys full kene,   *spiteful*
   And the frostys so hydus thay water min[e] eeyne—   *eyes*
   No ly.
   Now in dry, now in wete,
   Now in snaw, now in slete,
   When my shone freys to my fete   *shoes freeze*
   It is not all esy.

64   Bot as far as I ken, or yit as I go,
65   We sely wedmen dre mekill wo: *wretched/suffer*
   We have sorow then and then, it fallys oft so.   *time and again/happens*
   Sely Copyle, oure hen, both to and fro   *Silly*
   She kakyls;
69   Bot begin she to crok,
   To groyne or to clok,   *groan/cluck*
   Wo is him is oure cok,   *Woe to him who is*
   For he is in the shakyls.

   These men that ar wed have not all thare will.
   When they ar full hard sted, thay sigh full still.   *in tough straits/continually*
   God wayte, they ar led full hard and full ill;   *God knows*
76   In bower nor in bed thay say noght thertill.   *thereto*
   This tide   *Now*
   My parte have I fun,   *found, learned*
   I know my lesson:
   Woe is him that is bun,   *bound, tied down*
   For he must abide.   *remain so*

49*balk:* unplowed strip of land between fields.

52*thay:* i.e., his friends, who have promised to join him.

56*Oft . . . sene:* We haven't often seen it (this bad).

64–65But as far as I know, or as I can tell by experience, we wretched married men suffer much woe.

69But if she should begin to croak (while laying an egg—i.e., the wife giving birth and saddling her husband with more children).

76Neither in chamber nor in bed do they dare answer back.

Bot now late in oure lifys—a mervell to me,
That I think my hart rifys sich wonders to see;   *rives, breaks*
84 What that destany drifys, it shuld so be—
85 Som men will have two wifys, and som men thre
    In store.
    Som ar wo that has any!   *woeful*
    Bot so far can I: *I know this much*
    Wo is him that has many,
    For he felys sore.   *feels pain*

        [*To the audience:*]
91 Bot, yong men, of wowing, for God that you boght,   *as for wooing/redeemed*
    Be well war of weding, and think in youre thoght: *very wary*
93 "Had I wist" is a thing that servys of noght.
    Mekill still mowrning has weding home broght,   *Much continual*
    And grefys,
    With many a sharp showre;   *pang*
    For thou may cach in an owre   *hour*
    That shall sow the[e] full sowre   *That which/grieve/bitterly*
    As long as thou liffys.

100 For, as ever rede I pistill, I have oone to my fere *companion*
    As sharp as thistill, as rugh as a brere.   *rough*
102 She is browyd like a bristill, with a sowre-loten chere; *sour-looking*
103 Had she oones wett hir whistill, she couth sing full clere *could*
104 Hir Paternoster.   *Lord's Prayer*
    She is as greatt as a whall;   *whale*
    She has a galon of gall;
    By Him that died for us all,
    I wald I had ryn to I had lost hir!   *I wish I'd run till*

        [*The first shepherd interrupts him.*]
109 1 PASTOR.   God looke over the raw!—Full defly ye stand.   *audience*
    2 PASTOR.   Yee, the dewill in thy maw, so tariand!   *belly/for tarrying so*

---

[84]Whatever destiny compels, it must come to be.

[85]*have two wifys:* i.e., remarry after becoming a widower.

[91]*for . . . boght:* by God who redeemed you (an oath).

[93]It does no good to say, "If only I'd known."

[100]For, as I hope to continue reading the Epistle (i.e., remain in a state of grace), I have one as my companion.

[102-4]She is bristle-browed, with a sour-looking expression; once she's wet her whistle (with a good long drink), she can sing very clearly her prayers.

[109]God watch over this audience!—You stand there very deafly (said to accuse the second shepherd of being self-absorbed).

Sagh thou awre of Daw?	*Saw you Daw anywhere*
1 PASTOR. Yee, on a ley-land	*pasture*
Hard I him blaw. He commys here at hand,	*I heard him blow (his horn)*
Not far.	
Stand still.	
2 PASTOR. Qwhy?	
1 PASTOR. For he commys, hope I.	*think*
2 PASTOR. He will make us both a ly	*tell*
Bot if we be war.	*Unless/wary*

[*The third shepherd, a boy, enters speaking in soliloquy.*]

	3 PASTOR. Cristys crosse me spede, and Sant Nicholas!	*help me*
	Therof had I nede; it is wars then it was.	*it (the world) goes worse*
120	Whoso couthe take hede and lett the warld pas,	
	It is ever in drede and brekill as glas,	*danger/brittle*
	And slithys.	*slides, fades away*
	This warld fowre never so,	*never fared so before*
	With mervels mo and mo,	*more*
	Now in weyll, now in wo,	*weal*
	And all thing writhys.	*is mutable*

	Was never syn Noe floode sich floodys seyn,	*since Noah's*
	Windys and ranys so rude, and stormes so keyn!	
129	Som stamerd, som stod in dowte, as I weyn.	*ween, think*
	Now God turne all to good! I say as I mene,	
	For ponder:	*consider this*
	These floodys so thay drowne,	
	Both in feyldys and in towne,	*fields*
	And berys all downe;	*bears*
	And that is a wonder.	

[*He sees the other shepherds, but cannot identify
what they are at first.*]

	We that walk on the nightys, oure catell to kepe,	*livestock/guard*
	We se sodan sightys when othere men slepe.	*unexpected sights*

[*Recognizing them.*]

	Yit me think my hart lightys: I se shrewys pepe.—	*lightens/rascals peep*
139	Ye ar two all-wightys! I will gif my shepe	*monsters*
140	A turne.	
	Bot full ill have I ment;	*intended*

[120]Whoever could observe the world as it goes by (would observe that).

[129]*Som stamerd:* some people (seeing these tempests) staggered.

[139-40](Daw evidently pretends to have encountered a monster, requiring him to turn his sheep away.)

As I walk on this bent,   *heath*
I may lightly repent,
144 My toes if I spurne.   *stub*
    [*The other two come forward.*]

A sir, God you save, and master mine!
A drink fain wold I have, and somwhat to dine.
147 1 PASTOR. Cristys curs, my knave, thou art a ledyr hine!   *lazy servant*
148 2 PASTOR. What, the boy list rave! Abide unto sine;   *later*
149 We have mayde it.
Ill thrift on thy pate!   *Bad luck*
Though the shrew cam late,   *rascal*
Yit is he in state   *he's ready*
To dine—if he had it.

3 PASTOR. Sich servandys as I, that swettys and swinkys,   *sweat and labor*
Etys oure brede full dry, and that me forthinkys.   *Eat/displeases me*
We ar oft weytt and wery when master-men winkys;   *wet/sleep*
Yit commys full lately both diners and drinkys.   *very slowly*
Bot nately   *thoroughly*
Both oure dame and oure sire,
When we have ryn in the mire,   *run*
Thay can nip at oure hire   *reduce our wages*
And pay us full lately.

163 Bot here my trouth, master: for the fayr that ye make,
164 I shall do therafter—wyrk as I take.
165 I shall do a litill, sir, and emang ever lake;   *play*
166 For yit lay my soper never on my stomake
167 In feyldys.
Wherto shuld I threpe?   *complain, wrangle*
With my staf can I lepe;
170 And men say, "Light chepe

144(Daw seemingly imposes on himself a mocking penance of stubbing his toes, for having mistaken his friends for monsters.)

147*knave:* Daw is inferior in status to the others.

148–49What, the boy is in a raving mood! Wait until later (for your food and drink); we've already eaten.

163–67But hear my vow, master: in proportion to the fare you provide, I'll labor accordingly—work according to what I receive. I'll do a little bit of work, and play continually in between working spells; for I've never yet had such a full belly that it hampered me in the fields.

170–77And men say: "A cheap bargain repays badly" (a proverb). —You'd be a poor choice as servant and personal companion for a man going a-wooing who couldn't afford to be extravagant. —Quiet, boy, I said! No more wrangling, or I'll make you be quiet quickly enough, by heaven's king, you with your tricks that we scorn.—Where are our sheep, boy?

171   Letherly foryeldys."

172 1 PASTOR.   Thou were an ill lad to ride on wowing
173   With a man that had bot litill of spending.
174 2 PASTOR.   Peasse, boy, I bad[e]! No more jangling,   *Silence*
175   Or I shall make the[e], full rad, by the hevens king,   *very quickly*
176   With thy gawdys—   *tricks*
177   Where ar oure shepe, boy?—we skorne.
        3 PASTOR.   Sir, this same day at morne
        I thaym left in the corne,   *grain*
180   When thay rang lawdys.

        Thay have pasture good, thay cannot go wrong.
        1 PASTOR.   That is right. By the roode, thise nightys ar   *cross*
            long!
        Yit I wold, or we yode, oone gaf us a song.   *ere we went*
        2 PASTOR.   So I thoght as I stode, to mirth us emong.   *amuse ourselves meanwhile*
        3 PASTOR.   I grauntt.
        1 PASTOR.   Lett me sing the tenory.   *tenor*
        2 PASTOR.   And I the tryble so hye.
        3 PASTOR.   Then the meyne fallys to me.   *mean, middle part*
        Lett se how ye chauntt. [*They sing.*]

        Tunc intrat Mak, in clamide   *Then Mak enters, dressed*
        se super togam vestitus.   *with a cloak over his tunic*
190 MAK.   Now, Lord, for thy naymes seven, that made both
            moyn and starnes   *moon*
191   Well mo then I can neven; thy will, Lorde, of me tharnys.   *is lacking*
        I am all uneven; that moves oft my harnes.   *perplexes/brains*
        Now wold God I were in heven, for the[re] wepe no barnes   *children*
        So still.   *incessantly*
        1 PASTOR.   Who is that pipys so poore?   *cries so piteously*
        MAK.   Wold God ye wist how I foore!   *knew/fared*
197   Lo, a man that walkys on the moore,
198   And has not all his will.

        2 PASTOR.   Mak, where has thou gone? Tell us tithing.   *news*
200 3 PASTOR.   Is he commen? Then ilkon take hede to his   *everyone*
            thing.

---

[180]When they (the clergy) rang for lauds (the first of the canonical day-hours of the church).

[190–91]Now, Lord, by your seven names (as in rabbinical tradition), who made both moon and stars, far more than I can name; your will concerning me, Lord, is lacking (is unclear).

[197–98]Lo, I'm just a fellow mortal walking here, who has suffered ill fortune.

[200]Has he come? Then let everyone watch out for his belongings. (He takes Mak's cloak probably because he is apprehensive of the wide sleeves that can be used for concealing stolen goods. Mak has an unsavory reputation.)

Et accipit clamidem ab ipso.   *And he takes the cloak from him*

201 MAK.   What! ich be a yoman, I tell you, of the king,   *I*
The self and the some, sond from a greatt lording,   *same/messenger*
And sich.   *such like*
Fi[e] on you! Goith hence   *Go*
Out of my presence!
I must have reverence.
Why, who be ich?

1 PASTOR.   Why make ye it so qwaint? Mak, ye do wrang.   *highfalutin*
209 2 PASTOR.   Bot, Mak, list ye saint? I trow that ye lang.
210 3 PASTOR.   I trow the shrew can paint, the dewill might   *deceive*
him hang!
MAK.   Ich shall make complaint, and make you all to
thwang   *be flogged*
At a worde,
213 And tell evyn how ye doth.   *do*

1 PASTOR.   Bot, Mak, is that sothe?   *truth*
Now take outt that Sothren tothe,   *Southern speech*
And sett in a torde!   *put in*

2 PASTOR.   Mak, the dewill in youre ee! A stroke wold I   *eye*
leyne you.   *give*
3 PASTOR.   Mak, know ye not me? By God, I couthe teyn   *could hurt*
you.
[*Daunted by their threats, Mak drops his pose
and appears to recognize them.*]
MAK.   God looke you all thre! Me thoght I had sene you.   *watch over*
Ye ar a fare compané.
1 PASTOR.   Can ye now mene you?   *remember who you are*
221 2 PASTOR.   Shrew, pepe!   *pry about*
222 Thus late as thou goys,   *you go*
What will men suppos?   *suspect*
And thou has an ill noys   *evil reputation*
Of steling of shepe.   *For*

MAK.   And I am trew as steyll, all men waytt.   *That/know*
Bot a sekenes I feyll that haldys me full haytt: *seizes me violently*
My belly farys not weyll, it is out of astate.   *fares/condition*

²⁰¹*ich*: I (Mak, in masquerading as a liveried retainer, uses Southern English dialect here and
in "goith," "doth," etc.).

²⁰⁹⁻¹⁰But, Mak, do you want to play the saint? I believe you long to do so. The rascal
certainly can deceive, may the devil hang him!

²¹³i.e., I'll tell the authorities how you're behaving.

²²¹⁻²²Rascal, look around you! When you go about thus late at night.

229 3 PASTOR.   Seldom lyis the dewill dede by the gate.   *dead/road side*

MAK.   Therfor

Full sore am I and ill;

232   If I stande stone-still,

233   I ete not an nedyll

This moneth and more.   *month*

1 PASTOR.   How farys thy wiff? By my hoode, how farys

sho?   *she*

MAK.   Lyis waltering—by the roode—by the fyere, lo!   *She lies sprawling*

And a howse full of brude. She drinkys well, to[o];   *brood*

238   Ill spede othere good that she will do!

Bot s[h]o   *she*

Etys as fast as she can,   *Eats*

And ilk yere that commys to man   *every*

She bringys furth a lakan—   *baby*

And, som yeres, two.

Bot were I now more gracius and richere by far,   *Even were I/prosperous*

I were eten outt of howse and of harbar.   *I would be/home*

Yit is she a fowll dowse, if ye com nar;   *slut/near*

247   Ther is none that trowse nor knowys a war

248   Then ken I.

Now will ye se what I profer?

250   To gif all in my cofer   *money-box*

251   To-morne at next, to offer

252   Hir hed-maspenny.

2 PASTOR.   I wote so forwakyd is none in this shire.   *weary with watching*

I wold slepe, if I takyd les to my hyere.   *even if I earned less*

3 PASTOR.   I am cold and nakyd, and wold have a fyere.

1 PASTOR.   I am wery, forrakyd, and run in the mire—   *tired from walking*

Wake thou! [*Lies down.*]   *You keep the watch*

2 PASTOR.   Nay, I will lig downe by,   *lie/nearby*

For I must slepe, truly. [*Lies down also.*]

260 3 PASTOR.   As good a mans son was I

229(A proverb; the devil is only feigning when he appears to be brought low, and so is Mak.)

232–33May I be turned to stone if I have eaten a needle's worth (a bit).

238Bad luck to any profitable things that she'll do (i.e., there's little chance of her doing anything else).

247–48No one thinks he knows, or actually knows by experience, a worse one than I do.

250–52Tomorrow morning, at the latest, to give all in my money-box as a mass-offering for her departed soul. (Mak would give anything to have her dead.)

260–61i.e., I'm as good as any of you (and therefore won't stand watch while you sleep).

261   As any of you.
     [Lies down, calling to Mak to join them.]

    Bot, Mak, com heder. Betwene shall thou lig downe.
263 MAK.   Then might I lett you, bedene, of that ye wold
       rowne,
    No drede.   *No doubt*
    Fro my top to my too,   *head/toe*
266   *Manus tuas commendo,*   *Into your hands I commend (my spirit)*
267   *Poncio Pilato;*   *Pontius Pilate*
    Crist crosse me spede!   *Christ's/aid me*
     Tunc surgit, pastoribus dormientibus, et dicit: *Then he gets up while the shepherds are sleeping, and says*

    Now were time for a man that lakkys what he wold   *desires*
    To stalk prevely than unto a fold,   *then/sheepfold*
    And neemly to wirk than, and be not to[o] bold,   *nimbly*
272   For he might aby the bargan, if it were told   *pay dearly for/reckoned up*
273   At the ending.
    Now were time for to reyll;   *move quickly*
    Bot he nedys good counsell
    That fain wold fare weyll,
    And has bot litill spending.   *money*
     [He casts a spell on the sleeping men.]

    Bot abowte you a serkill, as rownde as a moyn,   *circle/moon*
    To I have done that I will, till that it be noyn,   *Until/what/noon*
280   That ye lig stone-still to that I have doyne;   *till/finished*
    And I shall say thertill of good wordys a foyne: *thereto/few*
    "On hight,   *high*
    Over youre heydys my hand I lift.
    Outt go youre een! Fordo youre sight!"   *eyes/Lose*
    Bot yit I must make better shift   *arrangement*
    And it be right.   *If it's to be*
     [The shepherds snore.]

    Lord, what thay slepe hard! That may ye all here.   *how/hear*
    Was I never a shepard, bot now will I lere.   *I was/learn*
289   If the flok be skard, yit shall I nip nere. *[He catches one.]*
290   How! drawes hederward! Now mendys oure chere

263Then I might hinder you, truly, from whispering as you please.

266-67(A perversion of Christ's last words spoken to God.)

272-73(Mak observes that he who is too bold pays for it in the end.)

289-91Even if the flock is alarmed, I'll grab (one) close. Hey! Come here (to the sheep)! Now our mood improves from sorrow (to joy).

291   From sorow.
     A fatt shepe, I dar say;
     A good flese, dar I lay.   *wager*
     Eft-whyte when I may,   *Repay*
     Bot this will I borow.

      [*Carrying the sheep, he proceeds to his cottage.*]

     How, Gill, art thou in? Gett us som light.
    UXOR EIUS [*within*]. Who makys sich din this time of the   *His wife*
        night?
298   I am sett for to spin. I hope not I might   *think*
299   Rise a penny to win, I shrew them on hight!   *curse*
300   So farys
301   A huswiff that has bene,
302   To be rasyd thus betwene.
     Here may no note be sene   *work*
     For sich small charys.   *Because of/chores*

    MAK.   Good wiff, open the hek! Seys thou not what I bring?   *inner door/See you*
306 UXOR.   I may thole the[e] dray the snek. A, com in, my   *let/latch*
        sweting!
      [*He enters their home.*]
307 MAK.   Yee, thou thar not rek of my long standing.   *needn't*
    UXOR.   By the nakyd nek art thou like for to hing.   *likely to hang*
    MAK.   Do way!   *That's enough*
     I am worthy my mete,   *food*
     For in a strate can I gett   *difficult fix*
     More then thay that swinke and swette   *labor*
     All the long day. [*Shows her the sheep.*]

     Thus it fell to my lott, Gill; I had sich grace.   *luck*
    UXOR.   It were a fowll blott to be hanged for the case.   *It would be/deed*
    MAK.   I have skapyd, Jelott, oft as hard a glase.   *escaped/Gill/blow*
    UXOR.   "Bot so long goys the pott to the water," men says,   *the longer goes*
     "At last
     Comys it home broken."
    MAK.   Well knowe I the token,   *portent*
     Bot let it never be spoken!   *i.e., Don't speak of it*
     Bot com and help fast.

298–302I'm all set to spin. I don't see how I can earn a penny with all this jumping up, I curse them (unwanted callers) loudly! That's what it's like for a woman who has been a housewife, to be interrupted this way.

306–7I'll let you draw the latch. Ah, come in, my sweetheart!—Yea, you needn't mind my waiting so long (said sarcastically).

I wold he were flayn; I list well ete.   *skinned/I'd like to eat*

324   This twelmothe was I not so fain of oone shepe-mete.

UXOR.   Com thay or he be slain, and here the shepe blete—   *If they come ere/hear*

MAK.   Then might I be tane. That were a cold swette!   *apprehended*

Go spar   *fasten*

The gaytt-doore.   *outer door*

UXOR.   Yis, Mak,

For, and thay com at thy bak—   *if*

330 MAK.   Then might I by, for all the pak,

331   The dewill of the war!

UXOR.   A good bowrde have I spied, syn thou can none: *trick/since/know*

Here shall we him hide, to thay be gone,   *till*

In my credyll. Abide, lett me alone,   *cradle*

And I shall lig beside in chilbed, and grone.

MAK.   Thou red,   *Get ready*

And I shall say thou was light   *you were delivered*

Of a knave-childe this night.   *male child*

339 UXOR.   Now, well is me day bright

340   That ever was I bred!

This is a good g[u]ise and a far-cast.   *device/clever trick*

342   Yit a woman avyse helpys at the last!—

343   I wote never who spyse; agane go thou fast.

344 MAK.   Bot I com or thay rise, els blawes a cold blast!

I will go slepe. [*Mak returns to the shepherds.*]

Yit slepys all this meneye;   *Still/company*

And I shall go stalk prevely,   *creep secretly*

As it had never bene I   *As if*

That caried thare shepe.

    [*He lies down among them. The first and second shepherds
    awake.*]

350 1 PASTOR.   *Resurrex a mortruus!* Have hold my hand!

351   *Judas carnas dominus!* I may not well stand:

My foytt slepys, by Jesus, and I water fastand.   *foot/I totter with hunger*

---

324 I haven't been so happy all year about a meal of mutton.

330-31 Then might I receive, from the pack of them, the devil of a hard time.

339-40 Now, happy to me is the auspicious day on which I was born.

342-44 So, a woman's advice helps after all! I don't know who may be watching; go back quickly (to the others).—If I don't get back (to them) ere they rise, a deadly blast (of ill luck) will blow.

350-51 *Resurrex a mortruus:* i.e., *resurrexit a mortuis,* he rose from the dead (from the Creed). *Judas . . . dominus:* perhaps a distortion of *laudes canas domino,* sing praises to the Lord.

I thoght that we laid us full nere Yngland.

2 PASTOR.   A, ye?   *yea, indeed*

Lord, what I have slept weyll!   *how|well*

As fresh as an eyll,   *eel*

As light I me feyll

As leyfe on a tre.

[*The third shepherd awakes from a nightmare.*]

359 3 PASTOR.   Bensté be herein! So me qwakys,   *Blessing*

My hart is outt of skin, whatso it makys.   *whatever causes this*

361   Who makys all this din? So my browes blakys,   *My brows darken so*

362   To the dowore will I win. Harke, felows, wakys!   *I'll head for the door|wake up*

We were fowre—

Se ye awre of Mak now?   *Do you see Mak anywhere*

1 PASTOR.   We were up or thou.   *ere*

2 PASTOR.   Man, I gif God avowe   *I vow to God*

Yit yede he nawre.   *He went nowhere yet*

3 PASTOR.   Me thoght he was lapt in a wolfe-skin.   *wrapped*

369 1 PASTOR.   So ar many hapt now, namely within.   *covered|especially*

3 PASTOR.   When we had long napt, me thoght with a gin   *trap*

A fatt shepe he trapt; bot he mayde no din.

2 PASTOR.   Be still!

Thy dreme makys the[e] woode.   *mad*

It is bot fantom, by the roode.   *fantasy|cross*

1 PASTOR.   Now God turne all to good,

If it be his will.

[*They arouse Mak, who pretends to be drowsy.*]

2 PASTOR.   Rise, Mak, for shame! Thou ligys right lang.   *You lie (asleep)*

MAK. Now Cristys holy name be us emang!

What is this? For Sant Jame, I may not well gang!   *go, walk*

380   I trow I be the same. A! my nek has ligen wrang

381   Enoghe. [*They help him up.*]

Mekill thank! Syn yister-even,   *Much|Since yesterday evening*

Now, by Sant Stevyn,

I was flayd with a swevyn—   *terrified by a nightmare*

My hart out of sloghe!   *(jumped) out of my skin*

359May God's blessing be here! I quake so.

361–62(The third shepherd exclaims that his brows are so furrowed in fear, he may have to run away.)

369(The first shepherd observes that many persons resemble wolves nowadays, especially in their true inner selves. Such criticisms were often directed at the hypocrisy of the clergy.)

380–81I trust I'll recover. Ah! my neck has lain all awry.

I thoght Gill began to crok and travell full sad,   *labor heavily*
Wel-ner at the first cok, of a yong lad   *About midnight*
For to mend oure flok. Then be I never glad;   *To increase our family*
I have tow on my rok more then ever I had.   *hemp on my distaff (i.e., trouble)*
390 A, my heede!   *head*
A house full of yong tharmes,   *children's bellies*
The dewill knok outt thare harnes!   *brains*
Wo is him has many barnes,   *to him who has/children*
And therto litill brede.

I must go home, by youre lefe, to Gill, as I thoght.   *leave/intended*
I pray you looke my slefe, that I steyll noght;   *examine*
I am loth you to grefe, or from you take oght. [*He starts*
    home.]
398 3 PASTOR.   Go furth, ill might thou chefe!—Now wold I we   *thrive*
    soght,
This morne,
That we had all oure store.   *livestock*
1 PASTOR.   Bot I will go before.
Let us mete.
2 PASTOR.   Whore?   *Where*
3 PASTOR.   At the crokyd thorne.
    [*They go off in search of their sheep. Mak arrives at
    his door; his wife is within the cottage, sitting at her work.*]

MAK.   Undo this doore! Who is here? How long shall I stand?
405 UXOR EIUS.   Who makys sich a bere? Now walk in the   *din*
    wenyand!
MAK.   A, Gill, what chere? It is I, Mak, youre husbande.
407 UXOR.   Then may we se here the dewill in a bande,   *noose*
408 Sir Gile!   *Guile*
Lo, he commys with a lote   *noise (a gagging sound)*
As he were holden in the throte.   *As if/held by*
I may not sit at my note   *work (weaving)*
A handlang while.   *brief*

413 MAK.   Will ye here what fare she makys to gett hir a glose?   *excuse*
414 And dos noght bot lakys, and clowse hir toose.   *play*

398Go on, badly may you thrive!—Now, I wish we would examine.

405*wenyand*: waning of the moon (an unlucky time; Gill is cursing).

407-8(As at l. 315, Gill harps on the likelihood of Mak's being hanged for his crimes.)

413-14(to the audience) Will you hear what a commotion she makes to put up a pretense of
working? And yet she does nothing but play around and scratch her toes.

415 UXOR.   Why, who wanders? who wakys? who commys? who
        gose?
416   Who brewys? who bakys? What makys me thus hose?   *hoarse*
    And than   *then*
    It is rewthe to beholde,   *a pity*
    Now in hote, now in colde,   *i.e., at all times*
    Full wofull is the householde
    That wantys a woman.   *lacks*

    Bot what ende has thou mayde with the hyrdys, Mak?   *herdsmen*
MAK.   The last worde that thay saide when I turnyd my bak,
    Thay wold looke that thay hade thare shepe, all the pak.
    I hope thay will nott be well paide when thay thare shepe   *think/pleased*
        lak,
    Perdé!   *By God*
    Bot, howso the gam gose,   *howsoever*
    To me thay will suppose,   *They'll suspect me*
    And make a fowll noise
    And cry outt apon me.

    Bot thou must do as thou hight.   *promised*
UXOR.   I accorde me thertill.   *I consent to that*
    I shall swedyll him right in my credill.   *swaddle*
      [She swaddles the sheep in the cradle.]
433   If it were a gretter slight, yit couthe I help till.   *trick*
    I will lig downe stright. Com hap me. *[She lies down.]*   *at once/cover*
MAK.   I will. *[He covers her.]*
435 UXOR.   Behinde!
    Com Coll and his maroo,   *If Coll and his mate come*
    Thay will nip us full naroo.   *hard*
MAK.   Bot I may cry "out, haroo!"   *help, help!*
    The shepe if thay finde.

440 UXOR.   Harken ay when thay call; thay will com onone.   *anon*
    Com and make redy all, and sing by thin[e] oone;   *solo*
    Sing "lullay" thou shall, for I must grone   *lullaby*
    And cry outt by the wall on Mary and John,
    For sore.   *pain*
    Sing "lullay" on fast   *quickly*

415–16*wanders*: bustles about. *wakys*: keeps watch (over things). *hose*: hoarse (from shouting at her family).

433If it were an even cleverer trick, I could still help out.

435*Behinde*: i.e., cover me in back, too.

440Keep listening for their call; they'll come soon.

When thou heris at the last;   *When you finally hear them*
And, bot I play a fals cast,   *unless/trick*
Trust me no more.

[*The shepherds gather at their appointed rendezvous.*]
3 PASTOR.   A, Coll, goode morne! Why slepys thou nott?
450 1 PASTOR.   Alas, that ever was I borne! We have a fowl blott:
A fat wedir have we lorne.   *wether, ram/lost*
3 PASTOR.   Mary, Godys forbott!   *God forbid*
2 PASTOR.   Who shuld do us that skorne? That were a fowll
spott.   *blemish*
1 PASTOR.   Som shrewe.   *rascal*
I have soght with my dogys
455 All Horbery shrogys,   *underbrush*
And of fifteyn hogys   *among/young sheep*
457 Fond I bot oone ewe.   *Found*

3 PASTOR.   Now trow me, if ye will: by Sant Thomas of Kent,   *Canterbury*
Ayther Mak or Gill was at that assent.   *Either/a participant*
1 PASTOR.   Peasse, man, be still! I sagh when he went.   *saw*
Thou sklanders him ill. Thou aght to repent   *ought*
Goode spede.   *Speedily*
2 PASTOR.   Now as ever might I thé,   *as I hope to prosper*
If I shuld evyn here dé,   *die*
I wold say it were he
That did that same dede.

3 PASTOR.   Go we theder, I rede, and ryn on oure feete.   *advise*
Shall I never ete brede, the sothe to I witt.   *till I know the truth*
1 PASTOR.   Nor drink in my heede, with him till I mete.   *i.e., in my mouth*
2 PASTOR.   I will rest in no stede till that I him grete,   *place*
My brothere.   *brothers*
Oone I will hight: *One thing I'll promise*
Till I se him in sight,
474 Shall I never slepe one night
475 Ther I do anothere.   *Where*
[*As they approach Mak's cottage, Gill begins
to groan and Mak to sing a lullaby.*]

476 3 PASTOR.   Will ye here how thay hak? Oure sire list croyne.

455*Horbery:* a town near Wakefield.

457(Mak has stolen the ram that ordinarily guarded the fifteen young sheep, thus leaving them protected only by a single ewe.)

474-75I'll never sleep two nights in the same place.

476Do you hear how they trill? Our gentleman is pleased to croon.

1 PASTOR.   Hard I never none crak so clere out of toyne.   *Heard/bawl/tune*

Call on him.

2 PASTOR.   Mak! undo youre doore soyne.   *soon*

479 MAK.   Who is that spak, as it were noyne,   *noon*

480   On loft?   *Loudly*

Who is that, I say?

3 PASTOR.   Goode felowse, were it day.   *if only it were*

MAK.   As far as ye may, [*He opens the door.*]

Good, spekys soft,   *Good fellows speak softly*

485   Over a seke womans heede that is at maylleasse.   *who is sick*

I had lever be dede or she had any diseasse.   *rather be dead ere/annoyance*

UXOR.   Go to anothere stede! I may not well qweasse.   *place/breathe*

488   Ich fote that ye trede goys thorow my nese   *Each footstep/goes/nose*

So hee.   *high, loudly*

1 PASTOR.   Tell us, Mak, if ye may,

How fare ye, I say?

MAK.   Bot ar ye in this towne today?

Now how fare ye?

Ye have ryn in the mire, and ar weytt yit.   *run/wet*

I shall make you a fire, if ye will sitt.

496   A nores wold I hire. Think ye on yit?   *nurse*

497   Well qwitt is my hire—my dreme, this is itt—

498   A seson.

I have barnes, if ye knew,   *children*

Well mo then enewe;   *enough*

Bot we must drink as we brew,

And that is bot reson.

I wold ye dinyd or ye yode. Me think that ye swette.   *ere you go*

504 2 PASTOR.   Nay, nawther mendys oure mode drinke nor

mette.

505 MAK.   Why, sir, alys you oght bot goode?

3 PASTOR.   Yee, oure shepe that we gett   *tend*

479-80Who is it that spoke loudly as though it were noon?

485Near a sick woman's head, within her hearing.

488*nese:* nose, i.e., head.

496-98I'd like to hire a nurse. Do you still recall it (my dream about children)? Well, this is my dream come true; my wages have been well paid for a while (i.e., I've gotten what was coming to me).

504-5Nay, neither drink nor food will mend our (angry) mood.—Why, sir, does something not good trouble you?

Ar stollyn as thay yode. Oure los is grette.   *wandered*

MAK.   Sirs, drinkys!   *drink*

　　Had I bene thore,   *there*

　　Som shuld have boght it full sore.   *paid for it*

510 1 PASTOR.   Mary, som men trowes that ye wore,   *believe/were*

　　And that us forthinkys.   *displeases us*

2 PASTOR.   Mak, som men trowys that it shuld be ye.

3 PASTOR.   Ayther ye or youre spouse, so say we.

MAK.   Now if ye have suspowse to Gill or to me,   *suspicion*

　　Com and ripe oure howse, and then may ye se   *ransack*

　　Who had hir.   *i.e., Who took the sheep*

　　If I any shepe fott,   *fetched, stole*

　　Ayther cow or stott—   *heifer*

　　And Gill, my wife, rose nott

　　Here syn she lade hir—   *since she lay down*

　　As I am true and lele, to God here I pray   *honest*

　　That this be the first mele that I shall ete this day.

　　　　[*He points to the cradle.*]

523 1 PASTOR.   Mak, as have I ceyll, avise the[e], I say:

524 　He lernyd timely to steyll that couth not say nay.

UXOR.   I swelt! [*They begin the search.*]   *I'm going to faint*

　　Outt, thefys, fro my wonys!   *Get out/house*

　　Ye com to rob us for the nonys.   *on purpose*

MAK.   Here ye not how she gronys?

　　Youre hartys shuld melt.

　　　　[*They come near the cradle.*]

530 UXOR.   Outt, thefys, fro my barne! Negh him not thor[e]!   *Approach/there*

531 MAK.   Wist ye how she had farne, youre hartys wold be sore. *labored*

　　Ye do wrang, I you warne, that thus commys before *come in the presence*

　　To a woman that has farne. Bot I say no more.   *Of/labored*

UXOR.   A, my medyll!   *middle*

　　I pray to God so milde,

　　If ever I you beg[u]ild,

　　That I ete this childe   *may eat*

　　That ligys in this credyll.   *lies*

MAK.   Peasse, woman, for Godys pain, and cry not so!

540 　Thou spillys thy brane, and makys me full wo.   *You injure/woeful*

───────────────

523–24 Mak, as I hope to have the happiness (of salvation), consider carefully, I say: the man who couldn't say no (to other men's possessions) learned early to steal (a proverb).

530–31 Get away, thieves, from my child! Don't go near him there!—If you knew how she's labored (in childbirth), your hearts would be afflicted.

2 PASTOR.   I trow oure shepe be slain. What finde ye two?

3 PASTOR.   All wirk we in vain; as well may we go.

Bot hatters!   *i.e., damn it*

I can finde no flesh,

Hard nor nesh,   *soft*

Salt nor fresh,

Bot two tome platers.   *Except/empty*

548   Whik catell bot this, tame nor wilde,   *Live*

549   None, as have I blis, as lowde as he smilde.   *smelled*

UXOR.   No, so God me blis, and gif me joy of my childe!

1 PASTOR.   We have merkyd amis; I hold us beg[u]ild.   *aimed/consider*

2 PASTOR.   Sir, don.   *completely*

Sir—Oure Lady him save!— [*To Mak.*]

Is youre child a knave?   *boy*

MAK.   Any lord might him have

This child to his son.   *as*

When he wakyns he kippys, that joy is to se.   *snatches, grabs*

558 3 PASTOR.   In good time to his hippys, and in celé! *happiness*

Bot who was his gossippys so sone redé?   *godparents/soon ready*

MAK.   So fare fall thare lippys!   *May good luck befall them*

1 PASTOR. [*Aside.*]   Hark now, a le.   *lie*

MAK.   So God thaym thank,

Parkyn, and Gybon Waller, I say,

And gentill John Horne, in good fay—   *faith*

564   He made all the garray—   *commotion*

With the greatt shank.   *long legs*

2 PASTOR.   Mak, freyndys will we be, for we ar all oone. *in accord*

567 MAK.   We? Now I hald for me.—For mendys gett I none. *amends*

[*Aside.*]

Farewell all thre!—All glad were ye gone. [*Aside.*]   *I'd be glad*

3 PASTOR.   Fare wordys may ther be, bot luf is ther none *Fair*

This yere. [*They leave the cottage.*]

1 PASTOR.   Gaf ye the child anything?

2 PASTOR.   I trow, not oone farthing.

3 PASTOR.   Fast agane will I fling;   *Quickly/dash back*

Abide ye me there. [*He runs back.*]

548-49Livestock other than this (the baby), tame or wild, none (have I found), as I hope to have bliss, that smelled as strongly as he (the missing ram).

558i.e., Good luck to him, and happiness.

564(Mak refers to the First Shepherds' pageant in which John Horne, one of the shepherds, quarrels with Gib.)

567We? Now I promise to keep my part of this friendship.—(aside) since I can't get out of it.

Mak, take it to no grefe if I com to thy barne.   *don't be offended/child*

MAK.   Nay, thou dos me greatt reprefe, and fowll has thou   *reproof*

    farne.   *labored*

3 PASTOR.   The child will it not grefe, that litill day-starne.   *star*

    Mak, with youre leyfe, let me gif youre barne   *permission*

    Bot six pence.

580   MAK.   Nay, do way! He slepys.

3 PASTOR.   Me think he pepys.

MAK.   When he wakyns he wepys.

    I pray you go hence!

    [*The other shepherds return.*]

3 PASTOR.   Gif me lefe him to kis, and lift up the clowtt.   *cloth*

    [*He peeks under the cloth.*]

    What the dewill is this? He has a long snowte!

586   1 PASTOR.   He is merkyd amis. We wate ill abowte.

587   2 PASTOR.   Ill-spon weft, iwis, ay commys foull owtc.

    Ay, so! [*Suddenly recognizing the sheep.*]

    He is like to oure shepe!

3 PASTOR.   How, Gib, may I pepe?

591   1 PASTOR.   I trow kinde will crepe   *nature will creep*

592   Where it may not go.   *walk*

2 PASTOR.   This was a qwantt gawde and a far cast;   *cunning prank/clever device*

    It was a hee frawde!   *high, monumental*

3 PASTOR.   Yee, sirs, wast.   *it was*

    Lett bren this bawde and bind hir fast.   *Let's burn*

    A fals skawde hang at the last;   *A false scold hangs at last*

    So shall thou.

    Will ye se how thay swedyll   *swaddle*

599   His foure feytt in the medyll?

    Sagh I never in a credyll   *Saw*

    A hornyd lad or now.   *ere*

MAK.   Peasse, bid I. What, lett be youre fare!   *stop your shouting*

    I am he that him gatt, and yond woman him bare.   *who begat him*

604   1 PASTOR.   What dewill shall he hatt, Mak? Lo, God, Makys   *be called*

    ayre!

605   2 PASTOR.   Lett be all that. Now God gif him care,

586-87He's deformed. We do ill to be prying about. —An ill-spun woof, to be sure, always comes out badly (a proverb implying that evil cannot be concealed).

591-92i.e., (proverbially) nature will inevitably manifest itself, by fair means or foul.

599(The sheep's legs are swaddled to prevent his struggling to escape.)

604-6What the devil will he be named, Mak? Lo, by God, Mak's heir! —Stop the joking. Now, may God give him sorrow, I saw (the sheep).

606   I sagh.   *saw*

UXOR.   A pratty child is he
    As sittys on a wamans kne;
    A dillydowne, perdé,   *darling/by God*
    To gar a man laghe.   *cause*

3 PASTOR.   I know him by the eere-marke; that is a good
        tokyn.

MAK.   I tell you, sirs, hark! his noyse was brokyn.   *nose*
    Sithen told me a clerk that he was forspokyn.   *Afterwards/bewitched*

1 PASTOR.   This is a fals wark; I wold fain be wrokyn.   *avenged*
    Gett wepyn!   *weapon*

UXOR.   He was takyn with an elfe—   *by*
    I saw it myself—
    When the clok stroke twelf
    Was he forshapyn.   *transformed*

620 2 PASTOR.   Ye two ar well feft sam in a stede.   *endowed together*

621 1 PASTOR.   Sin thay manteyn thare theft, let do thaym to
            dede.   *death*

MAK.   If I trespas eft, gird of[f] my heede.   *again/cut*

623   With you will I be left.

3 PASTOR.   Sirs, do my reede: *follow my advice*
    For this trespas
    We will nawther ban ne flyte,   *curse nor quarrel*
    Fight nor chyte,   *chide*
    Bot have done as tyte,   *finish as quickly as possible*
    And cast him in canvas.
        [*They toss Mak in a sheet.*]

629 1 PASTOR.   Lord, what I am sore, in point for to brist!   *burst*
    In faith, I may no more; therfor will I rist.   *rest*
        [*They let Mak go.*]

2 PASTOR.   As a shepe of seven skore he weyd in my fist.   *weighed*
    For to slepe aywhore me think that I list.   *anywhere/desire*

3 PASTOR.   Now I pray you
    Lig downe on this grene.

1 PASTOR.   On these thefys yit I mene.   *think*

3 PASTOR.   Wherto shuld ye tene?   *be angry*
    Do as I say you.

620–21You two are well endowed together in one place, i.e., are two of a kind. —Since they
persevere in defending their theft, let's kill them.

623i.e., I leave myself in your hands.

629Lord, how sore I am, on the point of bursting.

[*They sleep in the fields.*] *Angelus cantat*   An angel sings "Glory to God
"*Gloria in exelsis*"; *postea dicat:*   in the highest"; then let him say

ANGELUS.   Rise, hyrd-men heynd, for now is he borne   gentle
That shall take fro the feynd that Adam had lorne;   what Adam lost
640 That warloo to sheynd, this night is he borne.   To destroy that warlock
God is made youre freynd now at this morne,
He behestys.   promises
At Bedlem go se   Bethlehem
Ther ligys that fre   Where lies/noble one
In a crib full poorely,
Betwix two bestys. [*The angel withdraws.*]

1 PASTOR.   This was a qwant stevyn that ever yit I hard.   exquisite voice/heard
It is a mervell to nevyn, thus to be skard.   tell of/scared
2 PASTOR.   Of Godys son of hevyn he spak upward.   from on high
650 All the wod on a levyn me thoght that he gard   caused
651 Appere.
3 PASTOR.   He spake of a barne   child
In Bedlem, I you warne.   tell
1 PASTOR.   That betokyns yond starne. [*Points to the star.*]
Let us seke him there.

2 PASTOR.   Say, what was his song? Hard ye not how he   Heard
    crakyd it,   sang
Thre brefes to a long?   short notes
3 PASTOR.   Yee, Mary, he hakt it.   trilled
Was no crochett wrong, nor nothing that lakt it.   note/it lacked nothing
659 1 PASTOR.   For to sing us emong, right as he knakt it,   sang
660   I can.
2 PASTOR.   Let se how ye croyne.   croon
Can ye bark at the mone?
3 PASTOR.   Hold youre tonges, have done!
1 PASTOR.   Hark after, than.
    [*He starts a song, and the others join in.*]

2 PASTOR.   To Bedlem he bad[e] that we shuld gang;   go
I am full fard that we tary to[o] lang.   afraid
3 PASTOR.   Be mery and not sad. Of mirth is oure sang.
Everlasting glad to mede may we fang,   joy as reward/get
Withoutt noyse.   fuss
670 1 PASTOR.   Hi[e] we theder, forthy,   therefore

650-51 It seemed to me he caused all the wood in a flash of bright light to be made visible.

659-60 To sing it among ourselves, just as he sang it, I know how.

If we be wete and wery,   *Even though*
To that child and that lady.
We have it not to lose.   *We mustn't forget this*

2 PASTOR.   We finde by the prophecy—let be youre din!—
Of David and Isay and mo then I min—   *Isaiah/more than I remember*
Thay prophecied by clergy—that in a virgin   *learnedly*
Shuld he light and ly, to slokyn oure sin,   *alight/quench*
And slake it,   *ease*
Oure kinde, from wo.   *race*
For Isay said so:
Ecce virgo   *Behold a virgin*
Concipiet a childe that is nakyd.   *Will conceive*

3 PASTOR.   Full glad may we be, and abide that day   *wait for*
684   That lufly to se, that all mightys may.
685   Lord, well were me for ones and for ay,
Might I knele on my kne, som word for to say
To that childe.
Bot the angell said
In a crib was he laide;
He was poorly arayd,
Both mener and milde.   *very poor*

1 PASTOR.   Patriarkes that has bene, and prophetys beforne,   *ere this*
Thay desiryd to have sene this childe that is borne.
694   Thay ar gone full clene; that have thay lorne.
We shall se him, I weyn, or it be morne,   *ween/ere*
To tokyn.   *As a sign*
When I se him and fele,   *see and feel him*
Then wote I full weyll   *know/well*
It is true as steyll
That prophetys have spokyn: *What*

To so poore as we ar that he wold appere,
702   First find, and declare by his messingere.
2 PASTOR.   Go we now, let us fare; the place is us nere.
3 PASTOR.   I am redy and yare; go we in fere   *eager/together*
To that bright. [*They go to Bethlehem.*]   *bright one*
Lord, if thy willes be—
We ar lewde, all thre—   *unlearned*

684–85To see that lovely one, who can perform all mighty deeds. Lord, I would be fortunate
now and forever.

694They are completely gone; that opportunity have they lost.

702Find (us) first, and declare (his coming) by his messenger.

Thou grauntt us somkyns gle — *some kind of mirth*
To comforth thy wight. [*They enter the stable.*] — *child*

1 PASTOR.   Haill, comly and clene, haill, yong child! — *pure*
Haill, maker, as I meyne, of a madyn so milde! — *believe/born of*
Thou has waryd, I weyne, the warlo so wilde; — *cursed/ween/warlock*
713 The fals g[u]iler of teyn, now goys he beg[u]ilde. — *malevolent beguiler*
Lo, he merys, — *he (Christ) is merry*
Lo, he laghys, my sweting!
A wel fare meting! — *very fine*
I have holden my heting: — *kept my promise*
718 Have a bob of cherys. — *cluster*

2 PASTOR.   Haill, sufferan Savioure, for thou has us soght! — *because*
Haill, frely foyde and floure, that all thing has wroght! — *noble child*
Haill, full of favoure, that made all of noght!
Haill! I kneyll and I cowre. A bird have I broght — *cower*
To my barne. — *child*
Haill, litill tiné mop! — *tiny moppet*
Of oure crede thou art crop. — *creed, faith/head*
I wold drink on thy cop, — *in your (Eucharist) cup*
Litill day-starne.

3 PASTOR.   Haill, derling dere, full of Godhede!
I pray the[e] be nere when that I have nede.
730 Haill! swete is thy chere. My hart wold blede
To se the[e] sitt here in so poore wede, — *clothing*
With no pennys. — *pennies*
Haill! put furth thy dall. — *hand*
I bring the[e] bot a ball:
Have and play the[e] withall,
And go to the tenys. — *tennis*

MARIA.   The fader of heven, God omnipotent,
That sett all on seven, his son has he sent. — *made/in seven days*
739 My name couth he neven, and light or he went.
740 I conceivyd him full even thrugh might, as he ment;
And now is he borne.
He kepe you fro wo! — *May he*

713The false and malevolent beguiler is now himself beguiled.

718(The cluster of cherries, gathered in midwinter, is a miracle in nature signifying rebirth in time of death. The second gift—a bird—may represent the Holy Ghost, whereas the third gift—a tennis ball—is in essence an orb, symbol of royalty. Cf. the gifts of the three Magi.)

739–40My name he pronounced, and alighted (in me) ere he went. I conceived him indeed through (God's) might, as he intended.

I shall pray him so.
Tell furth as ye go,   *Make known (the tidings)*
And myn on this morne.   *remember*

1 PASTOR.   Farewell, lady, so fare to beholde,
With thy childe on thy kne.
2 PASTOR.   Bot he ligys full cold.
Lord, well is me! Now we go, thou behold.
749 3 PASTOR.   Forsothe, allredy it semys to be told
Full oft.
1 PASTOR.   What grace we have fun!   *found*
2 PASTOR.   Com furth; now ar we won.   *delivered from woe*
3 PASTOR.   To sing ar we bun—   *bound*
Let take on loft! [*They go out singing.*]   *Begin (the song) loudly*
Explicit pagina Pastorum.

749*it:* i.e., the story of the Nativity.

THE OFFERING OF THE MAGI
FROM WAKEFIELD

Throughout the later Middle Ages and Renaissance, we can identify King Herod by his famous ranting. Chaucer pokes fun at the clerk Absalom by observing that "He pleyeth Herodes upon a scaffold hye." A stage direction for the Coventry Shearmen and Taylors' play about Herod specifies that the king "ragis in the pagond [pageant] and in the strete also." Two centuries or more after Chaucer, Shakespeare still associates the name of Herod with exaggerated acting: as Hamlet observes of a performance calculated to "split the ears of the groundlings," "it out-herods Herod; pray you avoid it."

This remarkably persistent stage tradition obviously attests to Herod's success as a comic favorite with audiences. Yet the rant is not mere buffoonery calculated to provide humorous entertainment. Herod is a boastful tyrant in the tradition of Satan and Pharaoh. As in the story of the Red Sea crossing, a proud and vainglorious oppressor seeks to destroy the innocent. Herod's structural role in the Corpus Christi cycle is especially prominent because he is the antagonist of the infant Christ. He proclaims defiance of the newborn babe, sensing that the kingdom of Christ will threaten not only his temporal authority but his claims to divinity. If a child born in poverty can rule all creation, order and degree will have proved worthless. Herod is aghast at the prospect of such inversion of authority: "Shall he be king thus hastely? Who made him knight?" Despite his bluster, nevertheless, Herod is stupidly ineffectual. Like most bullies he is a coward. He is put down by his own scholars who show him the truth revealed in the Scriptures, "If ye can rede." Herod's attempts to browbeat and deceive the Magi are doomed to failure, since the Magi are guided by angelic direction. Although the Magi are lonely, exhausted, bewildered, and humanly susceptible to Herod's ploys, they can count on divine assistance in their hour of need.

The essential story of the Magi's journey and visit to the manger is to be found in Matthew 2:1–12. Medieval tradition supplies colorful details such as the names and nationality of the three Magi, the symbolic meaning of their gifts (gold signifies kingship; frankincense, divinity; myrrh, mortality), and of course Herod's famous rage. Several of these features also occur earlier in liturgical and church plays about Herod and the Magi, and in fact the staging requirements of this Wakefield pageant are not unlike those of church drama for the Feast of Epiphany. The resplendent throne of Herod and the rustic manger, symbols respectively of worldly and divine kingship, are situated apart from one another but simultaneously visible throughout the action. A star, borne aloft probably by some pulley device, guides the Magi to Herod and thence to Bethlehem. A litter is prepared in the open acting area for their sleep. Stage directions at lines 84 and 504 explicitly refer to their riding on horses. They come together from opposite directions and leave one another in opposite directions. All in all, the action seems better suited to an arena theater than to a pageant wagon.

409

The Offering of the Magi

From Wakefield

Incipit Oblatio Magorum.	*Here begins the Offering of the Magi*

[*Herod in estate upon his throne, attended.*]

HERODES.	Peasse, I bid, both far and nere!	
	I warne you leyf youre sawes sere.	*leave off your various talk*
	Who that makys noise whils I am here,	*He who*
	I say, shall dy!	
	Of all this warld, sooth, far and nere,	
	The lord am I.	
	Lord am I of every land,	
	Of towre and towne, of se and sand.	
	Agans me dar no man stand	*Against*
10	That berys life.	*Who bears, possesses*
	All erthly thing bowes to my hand,	
	Both man and wife.	
	Man and wife, that warne I you,	
	That in this warld is lyfand now,	*living*
	To Mahowne and me all shall bow,	*Mohammed*
	Both old and ying.	*young*
	On him will I ich man trow,	*I command each man believe in him*
	For anything.	*In any event*
	For anything it shall be so.	
20	Lord over all where I go—	*wherever*
	Whoso says agane, I shall him slo,	*speaks against (this) | slay*
	Whereso he dwell.	
	The feynd, if he were my fo,	*fiend*
	I shuld him fell.	
	To fell those fatures I am bowne,	*traitors | ready*
	And distroy those dogys in feyld and towne	
	That will not trow on Sant Mahowne,	*believe in*
	Oure god so swete.	
	Those fals faturs I shall fell downe	
30	Under my feete.	
	Under my feete I shall thaym fare,	*assault*
	Those ladys that will [not] lere my lare,	*lads | learn my teaching*
	For I am mighty man ay whare,	*everywhere*

Of ilk a pak;   *Of every company*
Clenly shapen, hide and hare,   *hair*
Withoutten lak.

37   The might of me may no man mene;   *have in mind*
     For, all [that] dos me any teyn,   *all who do/harm*
     I shall ding thaym downe bydeyn,   *beat them/at once*
     And wirk thaym wo.   *do them injury*
     And on assay it shall be seyn,   *by test/seen*
     Or I go.   *Ere*

     And therfor will I send and se
     In all this land, full hastely,
     To looke if any dwelland be   *any (person) be dwelling*
     In towre or towne
     That will not hold [w]holly on me   *believe*
     And on Mahowne.

     If ther be fonden any of tho,   *found/those*
50   With bitter pain I shall theym slo.   *slay*
        [*He turns to his messenger.*]
     My messinger!
[NUNTIUS.]   Lord?
[HERODES.]   Swith looke thou go   *Quickly*
     Thrugh ilk countré   *each*
     In all this land, both to and fro,
     I commaunde the[e].

     And truly looke thou spir and spy,   *inquire*
     In every stede ther thou commys by,   *place where you come*
     Who trowes not on Mahowne most mighty,
     Oure god so fre.   *noble*
     And looke thou bring theym hastely
60   Heder unto me.   *Hither*

     And I shall fownd thaym for to flay,   *proceed to flay them*
     Those laddys that will not lede oure lay.   *obey our law*
     Therfor, boy, now I the[e] pray
     That thou go tytt.   *quickly*
NUNTIUS.   It shal be done, lord, if I may,
     Withoutten lett.   *hindrance*

     And certys, if I may any finde,
     I shall not leyfe oone of them behinde.   *leave*

---

[37]No man can have in mind or comprehend how mighty I am.

HERODES.   No, bot boldly thou thaym binde
70   And with the[e] leyde.   *lead*
    Mahowne, that weldys water and winde,   *wields, rules*
    The[e] wish and spede!   *guide*
       [*The messenger, leaving Herod's station,*
       addresses all present.]

NUNTIUS.   All peasse, lordingys! and hold you still
    To I have saide what I will.   *Till*
    Take goode hede unto my skill,   *reasoning*
    Both old and ying,
    In message what is commen you till   *has come to you*
    From Herode the king.

    He commaundys you, everilkon,   *everyone*
80   To hold no king bot him alon,
    And othere god ye worship none
    Bot Mahowne so fre.   *noble*
    And if ye do, ye mon be slone—   *must be slain*
    Thus told he me.
       [*The messenger stands aside.*]

    Tunc venit primus rex equitans;   *Then the first king approaches riding;*
    et, respiciens stellam, dicit: *and, looking at the star, he says*

1 REX.   Lord, of whom this light is lent,   *from*
    And unto me this sight has sent,
    I pray to the[e], with good intent
    From shame me shelde,   *shield me*
    So that I no harmes hent   *receive*
90   By way[e]s wilde.

    Also I pray the[e] specially
    Thou graunt me grace of company,
    That I may have som beylding by   *succour, comfort*
    In my travaill.
    And certys, for to lyf or dy,   *i.e., come life, come death*
    I shall not faill

    To that I in som land have bene   *Till*
    To wit what this starne may mene   *know/star*
    That has me led, with bemys shene,   *beautiful beams*
    Fro my cuntré.
    Now weynd I will, withoutten weyn,   *wend, go/doubt*
    The sothe to se.

[The second king enters riding.]

	2 REX. Ah, Lord, that is withoutten ende,	*who is eternal*
104	Whens ever this selcouth light discende,	*Whence/wondrous*
105	That thus kindly has me kende	*guided me*
	Oute of my land,	
	And shewyd to me ther I can leynd,	*where I should go*
	Thus bright shinand?	*shining*

	Certys, I sagh never none so bright!	*saw*
110	I shall never ryst, by day nor night,	*rest*
	To I wit whens may com this light,	*Till I know whence*
	And from what place.	
	He that it send unto my sight	*May He who sent it*
	Leyne me that grace!	*Lend, grant*

	1 REX. A, sir, wheder ar ye away?	*whither/going*
	Tell me, good sir, I you pray.	
	2 REX. Certys, I trow, the sothe to say,	
	None wote bot I:	*knows*
	I have folowed yond starne veray	*true*
120	From Araby.	

	For I am king of that cuntré,	
	And Melchor ther call men me.	
	1 REX. And king, sir, was I wont to be	
	In Tars, at hame,	*Tarsus (in Asia Minor)*
	Both of towne and cité.	
	Jaspar is my name.	

	The light of yond starne sagh I thedyr.	*I saw thither*
	2 REX. That Lord be lovyd that send it hedyr!	*sent*
	For it will grathly ken us whedyr	*readily teach us whither*
130	That we shall weynd.	*wend, go*
	We owe to love him both togedyr	*ought*
	That it to us wold send.	

[The third king enters riding.]

	3 REX. A, Lord in land, what may this mene?	*Lord of the earth*
	So selcouth sight was never sene.	*wondrous*
	Sich a starne shinand so shene	*beautifully*
	Sagh I never none!	

[104]From where in the world did this wondrous light descend?

[105]*kindly*: i.e., according to its celestial nature.

It giffys light over all bedene,   *at once*
By Him alone.

What it may mene, that know I noght.
140   Bot yonder ar two, me think, in thoght!   *in (my) thought*
I thank Him that thaym heder has broght
Thus unto me.
I shall assay if thay wote oght   *know ought*
What it may be. [*He approaches the other two.*]

Lordingys, that ar leyf and dere,   *beloved*
I pray you tell me with good chere
Wheder ye weynd on this manere,   *Whither you wend*
And where that ye have bene?
And of this starne that shinys thus clere,
150   What it may mene?

1 REX.   Sir, I say you certanly,
From Tars for yond starne soght have I.
2 REX.   To seke yond light from Araby,
Sir, have I went.
3 REX.   Now hertely I thank Him forthy   *therefor, for it*
That it has sent.

1 REX.   Good sir, what cuntré cam ye fra?
3 REX.   This light has led me fro Saba;   *i.e., Yemen, Arabia*
And Balthesar, my name to say,
160   The sothe to tell.
2 REX.   And kingys, sir, ar we twa,
Theras we dwell.   *Where*

3 REX.   Now, sirs, syn we ar semled here,   *since we are assembled*
I rede we ride togeder in fere,   *propose/in a group*
Unto we witt on all manere,   *Until we know in every respect*
For good or ill,
What it may mene, this sterne so clere
Shinand us till.   *Shining toward us*

1 REX.   A, lordingys, behold the light
170   Of yond starne with bemys bright!
Forsothe, I sagh never sich a sight
In no-kyns land—   *no kind of*
A starne thus, aboute midnight,
So bright shinand!

It gifys more light itself alone
Then any son that ever shone,
Or mone, when he of son has ton   *sun*
                                   moon when it has taken from the sun
His light so cleyn.   *Its/pure*
Sich selcouth sight have I sene none,   *wondrous*
Whatsoever it meyn.

    2 REX.   Behold, lordingys, unto his pase,   *See its pace, speed*
        And se how nigh the erth hit gase!   *goes*
183   It is a tokyn that it mase   *makes, does*
184   Of novelry.
        A mervell it is, good tent who tase,   *(to him) who pays good heed*
        Now here in hy.   *on height, or in haste*

        For sich a starne was never ere seyn,   *seen before*
        As wide in warld as we have beyn;   *been*
        For blasing bemys, shinand full sheyn,   *beams/beautifully*
190   From hit ar sent!
        Mervell I have what it may meyn
        In min[e] intent.

    3 REX.   Certys, sirs, the sothe to say,
        I shall discry now, if I may,
        What it may meyn, yond starne veray   *true*
        Shinand till us: *Shining toward us*
        It has bene saide syn many a day   *since long ago*
        It shuld be thus.

        Yond starne betokyns, well wote I,
200   The birth of a prince, sirs, securly.   *surely*
        That shewys well the prophecy   *The prophecy proves it well*
        That it so be—
        Or els the rewlys of astronomy
        Dissavys me.   *Deceive*

205 1 REX.   Certan, Balaam spekys of this thing:
        That of Jacob a starne shall spring
        That shall overcom kasar and king   *kaiser, caesar*
        Withoutten strife.
        All folk shal be to him obe[y]ing
210   That berys the life.   *i.e., All who are alive*

_{183–84}This is a sign that it (the star) indicates some rare news.

₂₀₅(See Numbers 24:17.)

Now wote I well this is the same!
In every place he shall have hame.   *home*
All shall him bowe that berys name   *that bear a name (i.e., everyone)*
In ilk cuntré.   *every*
Who trowys it not, thay ar to blame,   *(They) who believe*
What so thay be.   *Whoever*

2 REX.   Certys, lordingys, full well wote I,
Fulfillyd is now the prophecy!
That prince that shall overcom in hy   *in haste*
220   Kasar and king,
This starne berith witnes, witterly,   *truly*
Of his bering.   *birth*

3 REX.   Now is fulfillyd here in this land
That Balaam said, I understand.   *What*
Now is he borne that se and sand   *who*
Shall weyld at will!   *wield, rule*
That shewys this starne, so bright shinand,   *This star shows that (fact)*
Us thre untill.   *unto*

1 REX.   Lordingys, I rede we weynd all thre   *propose*
230   For to wirship that child so fre,   *noble*
In tokyn that he king shal be
Of alkyn thing.   *every sort of*
This [gold] now will I bere with me,
To min[e] offering.   *As*

2 REX.   Go we fast, sirs, I you pray,
To worship him if that we may.
I bring rekyls, the sothe to say,   *incense*
Here in min[e] hende,
In tokyn that he [is] God veray
240   Withoutten ende.

3 REX.   Sirs, as ye say, right so I red: *advise*
Hast we tytt unto that sted   *quickly/place*
To wirship him, as for oure hed,   *as our head, ruler*
With oure offering.
In tokyn that he shal be ded
This myrr I bring.

1 REX.   Where is that king of Jues land
That shal be Lord of se and sand,
And folk shall bow unto his hand,
250   Both more and min?   *more and less (i.e., everyone)*

To wirship him with oure offerand
We will not blin.   *delay*

2 REX.   We shall not rest, even nor morne,
Unto we com ther he is borne.   *Until/where*
3 REX.   Folowe this light, els be we lorne,   *otherwise/lost*
Forsothe, I trowe,
257   That frely to we com beforne.   *noble (one)/till*
Sirs, go we now.
[*The kings proceed on their quest. Herod's messenger, having
witnessed the kings' meeting, returns to Herod's station with
news.*]

259 NUNTIUS.   Mahowne, that is of greatt pausty,   *power*
260 My lord, Sir Herode, the[e] save and se!   *see, watch over*
HERODES.   Where has thou bene so long fro me,
Vile stinkand lad?
NUNTIUS.   Lord, gone youre herand in this cuntré,   *gone on/errand, message*
As ye me bad[e].

HEROD.   Thou lyis, lurdan, the dewill the[e] hang!   *You lie/lazy lout*
Why has thou dwelt away so lang?
NUNTIUS.   Lord, ye wite me all with wrang.   *blame/wrongfully*
HERODES.   What tithingys? say!   *news*
NUNTIUS.   Som good, som ill, mengyd emang.   *mingled together*
270 HEROD.   How, I the[e] pray?

Do tell me fast how thou has farne.   *fared*
Thy warison shall thou not tharne.   *reward/lack*
NUNTIUS.   As I cam walkand, I you warne,
Lord, by the way,
I met thre kingys sekeand a barne—   *seeking a child*
Thus can thay say.   *did*

HERODES.   To seke a barne! For what thing?
Told thay any new tithing?
NUNTIUS.   Yey, lord, thay said he shuld be king
280 Of towne and towre!
Forthy thay went, with thare offering,   *Therefore*
Him to honoure.

HEROD.   King! The dewill! Bot of what empire?

<hr>

257Until we come into the presence of that noble one.

259–60May Mohammed, who is of great power, save and watch over you, my lord Sir Herod!

Of what land shuld that lad be sire?

Nay, I shall with that trature tire;   *traitor/tear, fight*

Sore shall he rewe!

NUNTIUS.   Lord, by a starne as bright as fire

This king thay knew.

It led thaym outt of thare cuntré.

HEROD.   We, fy, fy! Dewils on thame all thre!   *i.e., to the devil with them*

He shall never have might to me,   *compared to me, in my terms*

That newborne lad.

293   When thare witt in a starne shuld be

I hold thaym mad.   *consider*

Those lurdans wote not what thay say.   *louts*

Thay ryfe my hede, that dar I lay!   *split/wager*

297   Ther did no tithingys many a day

298   Sich harme me to.   *to me*

Fo[r] wo my witt is all away;

What shall I do?

Why, what the dewill is in thare harnes?   *brains*

302   Is thare witt all in the starnes?

These tithingys mar my mode in ernes!   *mood in earnest*

And of this thing

To witt the sothe full sore me yarnes,   *To know the truth/I yearn*

Of this new king.

King? What the dewill, other then I!

We, fy on dewils, fy, fy!

Certys that boy shall dere aby—   *pay for (it) dearly*

His ded is dight!   *His death is prepared*

Shall he be king thus hastely?

Who made him knight?

Alas, for shame, this is a skorne!

314   Thay finde no reson thaym beforne.

Shuld that brodell, that late is borne,   *wretch/lately*

Be most of main?   *might*

Nay, if the dewill of hell had sworne,

293When they place their credence in a star.

297-98No news in many a day has done so much harm to me.

302Are the stars the only thing they can think about, i.e., have they lost all common sense?

314They have no reasons to support them.

318   He shall agane.

Alas, alas, for doyll and care!   *dole, sorrow*
So mekill sorow had I never are.   *much/ere, before*
If it be sothe, for evermare   *evermore*
I am undoyn.
At good clerkys and wise of lare   *lore, learning*
I will wit soyn.   *know soon*

Bot first yit will I send and se
The answere of those lurdans thre.—   *louts*
Messingere, tytt hi[e] thou the[e],   *quickly hasten*
And make the[e] yare.   *ready quickly*
Go, bid those kingys com speke with me,
330   That told thou of are.   *That you spoke of before*

Say I have greatt herand thaym till.   *errand, message to them*
NUNTIUS.   It shal be done, lord, at youre will.
Youre bidding shall I soyn fulfill   *soon*
In ilk cuntré.   *each*
HEROD.   Mahowne the[e] shelde from all kyns ill,   *all sorts of*
For his pausté.   *power*
     [*The messenger crosses from Herod's station to intercept the kings on their quest.*]

NUNTIUS.   Mahowne you save, sir kingys thre:
I have message to you prevé,   *private*
From Herode, king of this cuntré,
340   That is oure chefe.
And lo, sirs, if ye trow not me,
Ye rede this brefe.   *brief, summons*

1 REX.   Welcom be thou, bel ami!   *fair friend*
What is his will? Tell us in hy.   *quickly*
NUNTIUS.   Certys, sir, that wote not I.
Bot thus he saide to me:
That ye shuld com full hastely
To him, all thre,

349   For nede herand, he said me so.   *errand, message*
2 REX.   Messinger, before thou go,   *go before*

318agane: error for "be slaine"(?).

349i.e., Because he needs to communicate with you, as he told me.

And tell thy lord we ar all thro   *bold, eager*
His will to do.
Both I and my felose two
Shall com him to.
    [*The messenger precedes them to Herod's station.*]

NUNTIUS.   Mahowne you looke, my lord so dere!   *watch over you*
HEROD.   Welcom be thou, messingere.
How has thou farne syn thou was here?   *fared since*
Thou tell me tytt.   *quickly*
NUNTIUS.   Lord, I have traveld far and nere
Withoutten lett,   *Unceasingly*

And done youre herand, sir, sothely.
Thre kingys with me broght have I,
Fro Saba, Tars, and Araby,
364   Then have thay soght.
HERODES.   Thy warison shall thou have forthy, *reward/accordingly*
By Him me boght;   *who ransomed me*

367   And, certanly, that is good skill.   *reason*
    [*He greets the three kings, who dismount.*]
And sirs, ye ar welcom me till.   *to me*
3 REX.   Lord, thy bid[d]ing to fulfill
Ar we full thro.   *bold, eager*
HERODES.   A, mekill thank of youre good will *much*
That ye will so.

For certys I have covett greattly   *have desired*
To speke with you, and here now why;   *hear*
Tell me, I pray you specially,
For any thing,   *Above all*
What tokyning saw ye on the sky
Of this new king?

1 REX.   We sagh his starne rise in the eest,
That shall be king of man and best.   *Who/beast*
Forthy, lord, we have not cest   *Therefore/ceased*
Syn that we wist,   *Since we knew that*
With oure giftys, riche and honest,
384   To bere that blist.

364Whence they have come seeking (?).

367i.e., And, certainly, it is reasonable you should be rewarded for your services.

384i.e., To extol and honor that blessed one (with our gifts).

2 REX.   Lord, when that starne rose us beforne,   *in front of us*
  Therby we knew that child was borne.
HERODES.   Out, alas, I am forlorne   *wholly lost*
  For evermare!
  I wold be rent and al to-torne   *torn to pieces*
390 For doyll and care!   *dole, sorrow*

  Alas, alas, I am full wo!—
  Sir kingys, sit downe and rest you so.
    [*Herod consults his two learned men.*]
  By scripture, sirs, what say ye two?
  Withoutten lytt   *error*
  What ye can say therto,
  Let se now tytt.   *quickly*

  These kingys do me to unde[r]stand
  That borne is newly, in this land,
  A king that shall weld se and sand—   *wield, rule*
400 Thay tell me so.
  And therfor, sirs, I you commaunde
  Youre bookys go to,

  And looke grathly, for anything,   *quickly*
  If ye find oght of sich a king.   *aught, anything*
1 CONSULTUS & DOCTOR.   It shall be done at youre
    bid[d]ing,
  By Him me boght.   *who ransomed me*
  And soyn we shall you tithingys bring   *soon*
  If we find oght.

2 CONSULTUS & DOCTOR.   Soyn shall we wit, lord, if I may,
410 If oght be wretyn in oure lay.   *law, scriptures*
HEROD.   Now, masters, therof I you pray
  On all manere.   *In every way (possible)*
1 CONSULTUS.   Com furth, let us assay
  Oure bookys both in fere.   *together*
    [*They study their books.*]

2 CONSULTUS.   Certys, sir, lo, here find I
  Well wretyn in a prophecy
  How that profett Isay,   *prophet Isaiah (7:14)*
  That never beg[u]ild,   *lied*
  Tellys that a madyn of hir body
420 Shall bere a child.

1 CONSULTUS.   And also, sir, to you I tell

The mervellest thing that ever fell: *happened*
Hyr madynhede with hir shall dwell
As did beforne.
That child shall hight "Emanuell"
When he is borne.

2 CONSULTUS.   Lord, this is sothe, securely—   *truly*
Witnes the profett Isay.
HEROD.   Outt, alas! for doyll I dy,
430   Long or my day!   *before my time (to die)*
Shall he have more pausté then I?   *power*
A, waloway!

Alas, alas, I am forlorne!
I wold be rent and all to-torne.   *I wish I were*
Bot looke yit, as ye did beforne,
For luf of me,
And tell me where that boy is borne;
Onone lett se.   *Anon, at once*

1 CONSULTUS.   All redy, lord, with main and mode.   *might and mind*
HEROD.   Have done belyf, or I go wode!   *quickly before I go mad*
441   And certys, that gadling wer as good
442   Have grevyd me noght.
I shall se that brodell bloode,   *wretch's blood*
By Him that me has boght!   *who ransomed me*

2 CONSULTUS.   Micheas the prophett, withoutten nay,   *Micah (5:2)*
How that he tellys I shall you say:
In Bedlem, land of Juda,
As I say you.
Out of it a duke shall spra—   *spring*
450   Thus find we now.

1 CONSULTUS.   Sir, thus we find in prophecy.
Therfor we say you, securely,   *surely*
In Bedlem, we say you truly,
Borne is that king.
HEROD.   The dewill hang you high to dry
For this tithing!

And certys ye li[e]; it may not be!
2 CONSULTUS.   Lord, we witnes it truly.
Here the sothe youreself may se,

441–42And certainly, it were better for that lad not to have grieved me.

460   If ye can rede.
    HEROD.   A, waloway, full wo is me!
    The dewill you spede!   *May the devil prosper you*

    1 CONSULTUS.   Lord, it is sothe, all that we say.
    We finde it wretyn in oure lay.   *law*
465 HEROD.   Go hens, harlottys, in twenty dewill way,   *rascals*
    Fast and belife!   *quickly*
    Mighty Mahowne, as he well may,
    Lett you never thrife!

    Alas, wherto were I a crowne?   *why do I wear*
    Or is cald of greatt renowne?   *am called*
    I am the fowlest borne downe   *most foully laid low*
    That ever was man—
    And namely with a fowll swalchon   *especially by a foul scamp*
474 That no good can.

    Alas, that ever I shuld be knight,
    Or holdyn man of mekill might,   *Or held (to be) a man of much*
    If a lad shuld reyfe me my right   *deprive*
    All thus me fro!
    Min[e] dede ere shuld I dight   *My death first I should prepare*
480 Or it were so.   *Ere*
      [*He turns to the three kings.*]

    Ye nobill kingys, harkyns as heynd: *hearken courteously*
    Ye shall have save condyth to weynd.   *safe conduct to go*
    Bot com agane with me to leynd,   *to remain*
    Sirs, I you pray.
    Ye shall me find a faithfull freynd
    If ye do swa.   *so*

    If it be sothe, this new tithing,
    Som worship wold I do that king.
    Therfor I pray you that ye bring
490 Me tithingys soyn.   *soon*
    1 REX.   All redy, lord, at youre bid[d]ing
    It shal be doyn.
      [*The kings mount their horses and leave Herod.*]

    2 REX.   Alas, in warld how have we sped!

465*in . . . way:* i.e., in the devil's name (an oath).

474That knows no good, i.e., is up to no good.

Where is the light that us has led?
Som clowde, forsothe, that starne has cled   *clad, concealed*
From us away.
In strong stowre now ar we sted.   *trouble/placed*
What may we say?

3 REX.   Wo worth Herode, that cursyd wight!   *Woe be to*
500 Wo worth that tyrant, day and night!
For thrugh him have we lost that sight,
And for his g[u]ile,   *on account of*
That shoyn to us with bemys bright   *shone*
Within a while.
        Here lightys the kingys of thare horses.   *alight/off*

1 REX.   Lordingys, I red we pray all thre   *advise*
To that Lord, whose nativité
The starne betokyned that we can se,   *did see*
All with his will.
Pray we specially that he
Wold show it us untill.   *to us*
        Here knele all the thre kingys downe.

2 REX.   Thou child, whose might no tong may tell,
As thou art Lord of heven and hell,
513 Thy nobill starne, Emanuell,
514 Thou send us yare;   *quickly*
That we may witt by firth and fell   *know by forest and moor*
How we shall fare.
        [*The star reappears.*]

3 REX.   A, to that child be ever honoure
That in this tid[e] has stint oure stoure,   *time has stopped our trouble*
And lent us light to oure socoure   *as our aid*
520 On this manere.   *In*
We love the[e], Lord of towne and towre,
[W]holly in fere.   *together*
        Here rise thay all up.

1 REX.   We owe to love him over all thing   *ought*
That thus has send us oure asking.   *sent*
Behold, yond starne has made styning,   *has risen*
Sirs, securly!   *surely*
Of this child shall we have knowing,
I hope, in hy.   *speedily*

513-14O Emmanuel, send us quickly your noble star.

[They arrive at the stable, where Mary is revealed with the child.]

2 REX.   Lordingys dere, drede thar us noght: *we need not dread*
530   Oure greatt travell till end is broght.   *to an end*
       Yond is the place that we have soght
       From far cuntré.
       Yond is the child that all has wroght:
       Behold and se!

3 REX.   I red we make offering, all thre,   *advise*
       Unto this child of greatt pausté,   *power*
       And worship him with giftys fre   *excellent*
       That we have broght.
       Oure boytt of bayll ay will he be;   *Remedy of our ills forever*
540   Well have we soght.
       [They kneel to the Christ child.]

1 REX.   Haill be thou, maker of all-kyn thing,   *everything*
       That boytt of all oure bayll may bring!
       In tokyn that thou art oure king,
       And shal be ay,
       Resayf this gold to min[e] offering,   *Receive/as*
       Prince, I the[e] pray.

2 REX.   Haill, overcomer of king and of knight,
       That fourmed fish and fowyll in flight!
       For thou art Godis son most of might,   *Because*
       And all-weldand,   *all-ruling*
       I bring the[e] rekyls, as is right,   *incense*
       To min[e] offerand.

553 3 REX.   Haill, king in kith, cowrand on kne!
       Haill, oone-fold God in persons thre!
       In tokyn that thou dede shal be,   *dead*
       By kindly skill,   *By natural process*
       To thy graving this myr of me   *For your burial/myrrh*
       Resave the[e] till.   *Receive, take to you*

MARIA.   Sir kingys, make comforth you betweyn,   *among you*
560   And mervell not what it may mene:
       This child, that on me borne has bene,   *of me*
       All bayll may blin.   *Can end all ill*

---

[553]Hail, king in courteous behavior, crouching on (your mother's) knee.

I am his moder, and madyn clene
Withoutten sin.

Therfor, lordingys, whereso ye fare,
Boldly looke ye tell aywhare   *everywhere*
567 How I this blist of bosom bare,
That best shal be—
And madyn cleyn, as I was are,   *before*
Thrugh his pausté.   *power*

And truly, sirs, looke that ye trow
572 That othere Lord is none at-lowe.   *below, on earth*
Both man and beest to him shall bowe,
In towne and feyld.   *i.e., everywhere*
My blissing, sirs, be now with you
Whereso ye beyld.   *dwell*
     [*The kings leave the stable.*]

1 REX.   A, lordingys dere, the sothe to say,
We have made a good jornay!
We love this Lord that shall last ay   *endure forever*
580 Withoutten ende.
He is oure beyld, both night and day,   *shelter*
Whereso we weynd.

2 REX.   Lordingys, we have traveld lang
And restyd have we litill emang.   *betweenwhiles*
Forthy I red now, or we gang,   *Therefore I advise/ere we go*
With all oure main
Let us fownde a slepe to fang;   *try/take*
Then were I fain.   *glad*

For in greatt stowres we have ben sted.   *troubles/placed*
590 Lo, here a litter redy cled.   *bed/clad, spread*
3 REX.   I love my Lord! We have well sped,
To rest with win.   *i.e., with success*
Lordingys, syn we shall go to bed,   *since*
Ye shall begin.
     [*As they sleep, an angel appears to them.*]

ANGELUS.   Sir curtes kingys, to me take tent,   *pay attention*
And turne by time or ye be tenyd!   *in time ere you be grieved*

567How I bore this blessed one from my body.

572There is no other Lord on earth.

From God his self thus am I sent
To warne you, as youre faithfull freynd,
How Herode king has malice ment
600 And shapys with shame you for to sheynd.   *plans/destroy*
And so that ye no harmes hent,   *take*
By othere ways God will ye weynd   *commands you go*
Into youre awne cuntré.
And if ye ask him boyn   *boon, favor*
For this dede that ye have done,
Youre beyld ay will he be. [*The angel retires.*]   *protection*

  1 REX.   Wakyns, wakyns, lordingys dere!   *Awake*
Oure dwelling is no longer here.   *i.e., We can't stay longer*
An angell spake till us in fere: *to us together*
610 Bad[e] us, as heynd,   *courteously*
That we ne shuld, on no manere,   *in no way*
Home by Herode weynd.   *Go home via Herod*

  2 REX.   Allmighty God in trinité,
With hart enterely thank I the[e]
That thin[e] angell send till us thre,   *sent to*
And kend us so   *taught*
Oure fals fo man for to fle   *foeman*
That wold us slo.   *slay*

  3 REX.   We aght to love him, more and min,   *more and less (i.e., all of us)*
620 That comly king of all mankin.
I rew full sore that we shall twin   *part*
On this manere;   *In*
For commen we have, with mekill win,   *with much success*
By wayes sere.   *several, separate*
    [*The kings mount.*]

  1 REX.   Twin must us nedys, sirs, per ma fay,   *by my faith*
And ilk on[e] weynd by divers way.   *each one go*
This will me lede, the sothe to say,
To my cuntré.
Forthy, lordingys, now have good day;   *Therefore*
630 God with you be!

  2 REX.   Certys, I must pas by se and sand.
This is the gate, I understand,   *path*
That will me lede unto my land
The right way.
To God of heven I you commaunde,
And have good day!

3 REX.   This is the way that I must weynd.
Now God till us his socoure send;
And he that is withoutten end
640   And ay shal be
Save us from fownding of the feynd,   *temptation*
For his pausté!   *power*
[*The kings depart in separate directions.*]

Explicit Oblatio Trium Magorum.   Here ends the Offering of the Three
                                                       Magi

THE FLIGHT INTO EGYPT
FROM YORK
THE MARCHALLIS

The keynote of the York Flight into Egypt (based ultimately on Matthew 2:12–23) is human tenderness. As in the earlier Nativity pageant from the York cycle, the focus is on the Holy Family. The cast of characters is small, and the action is simple. In fact, this pageant does not show the actual flight into Egypt at all, but concentrates instead on the preparations for that journey. Mary and Joseph elicit our pity and concern for their dangerous plight. They are frightened, bewildered, unable to account for Herod's tyrannical threats, and uncertain how to find their way to Egypt. Even though an angel speaks reassuringly to Joseph, he and Mary feel very much alone and are at times almost panic-stricken. For that reason they rely heavily on one another, and tenderly reveal their mutual feelings of devotion and gratitude. Joseph, despite his age and infirmity, discovers with God's help the strength he needs to shoulder his heavy burden. We see in him just a touch of the old self-pity and fussiness so amusingly revealed in the Nativity pageant, but we also recognize a new sense of responsibility. Truly he has become, like Noah, the patriarch and defender of his family.

The simple stage requirements are essentially those of the York Nativity pageant: the manger and an area adjacent to it for the commencement of the journey. Mary rides an ass while Joseph carries his pack, in a tableau familiar to anyone acquainted with medieval iconography.

The Flight into Egypt
From York
The Marchallis

[*Near the stable where Mary tends her babe, Joseph prays to God.*]

JOSEPH. Thow maker that is most of might,
To thy mercy I make my mone.   *moan, complaint*
Lord, se unto thin[e] simple wight
That hase non helpe but the[e] allone!
For all this worlde I have forsaken,
And to thy service I have me taken
With witte and will
For to fulfill
Thy commaundement.

TITLE *Marchallis:* marshals, horse tenders, shoesmiths.

429

10   Theron min[e] herte is sette;
   With grace thou has me lente,
   Thare schall no lede me lette. *No one shall hinder me*

   For all my triste, Lorde, is in the[e] *trust*
   That made me, man, to thy liknes.
   Thow mightfull maker, have minde on me,
   And se unto my simplenes!
   I waxe wayke as any wande; *weak*
18   For febill me faylles both foote and hande— *feebleness*
19   Whatevere it mene!
   Me thinke mine eyne *eyes*
   Hevye as leede. *lead*
   Therfor I halde it best *consider*
   A whille her[e] in this stede *place*
   To slepe and take my reste. [*He sleeps.*]

   MARIA [*to her child*].   Thow luffely Lord that last schall ay, *endure forever*
   My God, my Lorde, my sone so dere:
   To thy Godhede hartely I pray
   With all min[e] harte [w]holy entere.
   As thou me to thy modir chaas, *chose me to be*
   I beseke the[e] of thy grace *beseech*
31   For all mankinde
32   That has in minde
33   To wirshippe the[e].
34   Thou se thy saules to save, *Watch, take care*
   Jhesu my sone so free: *noble*
   This bone of the[e] I crave. *boon*

   [*The angel Gabriel comes to Joseph.*]
   ANGELUS.   Wakyn, Joseph, and take entent! *pay attention*
   My sawes schall seece thy sorowe sare. *words will end/grievous*
39   Be noght hevy; thy happe is hentte. *fortune/seized*
   Tharefore I bidde the[e] slepe no mare.
   JOSEPH.   A, mightfull Lorde, whatevere that mente?
   So swete a voice herde I nevere ayre. *ere, before*
   But what arte thou with steven so shille, *voice so shrill, loud*
   Thus in my slepe that spekis me till? *to me*
   To me appere,

18–19Strength of foot and hand fails me, from a sense of feebleness—whatever causes this! (Joseph is being induced to sleep so that he can receive the angelic visitation.)

31–34For all those who are disposed to worship you. Take care to save their souls, which belong to you.

39i.e., Be not sorrowful; your good fortune is at hand.

And late me here   *let me hear*
What that thou was.

ANGELUS.   Joseph, have thou no drede;
Thou shalte witte or I passe.   *know ere I go*
50 Therfore to me take hede,

For I am sente to the[e]:
Gabriell, Goddis aungell bright,
Is comen to bidde the[e] flee
With Marye and hir worthy wight.   *child*
For Horowde the king gars doo to dede   *causes to be killed*
56 All knave childer in ilke a stede   *male/every place*
57 That he may ta   *take*
58 With yeris twa   *two*
59 That are of elde!
Tille he be dede, away   *he (Herod)*
In Egypte shall ye beelde,   *seek shelter*
62 Tille I witte the[e] for to saye. [*The angel retires.*]

JOSEPH [*praying*].   Aye-lastand Lord, loved mott thou be,   *Everlasting/may*
That thy swete sande wolde to me sende.   *messenger*
But Lorde, what ailes the king at me?   *why is the king displeased*
For unto him I nevere offende.   *did offense*
Allas, what ailes him for to spille   *kill*
Smale yonge barnes that nevere did ille   *children*
In worde ne dede,
70 Unto no lede   *person*
By night nor day?
And sen he wille us schende,   *since/destroy*
Dere Lorde, I the[e] praye
Thou wolde be oure frende.

For be he nevere so wode or wrothe,   *mad*
For all his force, thou may us fende.   *Despite/defend*
I praye the[e], Lorde, kepe us fro skathe;   *from harm*
Thy socoure sone to us thou sende.   *soon*
For, unto Egypte wende we will
Thy bidding bainly to fulfill,   *obediently*
As worthy is.   *As is fitting*
Thou king of blisse,
Thy will be wroght.

56-59All male children two years old or less whom he may seize anywhere.

62i.e., Till I tell you (that all is safe).

[*Joseph ends his prayer and goes to Mary.*]

84   Marye, my doughtir dere,

      On the[e] is all my thought.

MARIA.   A, leve Joseph, what chere?   *beloved*

JOSEPH.   The chere of me is done for ay.

MARIA.   Allas, what tithandis herde have ye?   *news have you heard*

JOSEPH.   Now certis, full ille to the[e] at saye: *to say*

90   Ther is noght ellis but us most flee!   *we must*

      Owte of oure kith where we are knowyn   *native country*

      Full wightely bus us be withdrawen,   *quickly must we*

      Both thou and I.

MARIA.   Leve Joseph, why?   *Beloved*

      Layne it noght: *Conceal*

      To doole who has us demed?   *dole, sorrow/judged*

      Or what wronge have we wroght

      Wherfore we shulde be flemyd?   *For which/banished*

JOSEPH.   Wroght we harme? Nay, nay, all wrang—

      Witte thou wele it is noght soo.   *You well know*

101   That yonge page liffe thou mon forgange,   *must forego*

      But if thou fast flee fro his foo!   *Unless you quickly*

MARIA.   His foo, allas! what is youre reede?   *advice*

      Wha wolde my dere barne do to dede?   *Who/child/put to death*

      I durk, I dare!   *hide/shrink for fear*

106   Whoo may my care

107   Of balis blinne?   *put a stop to*

      To flee I wolde full faine!   *gladly*

      For all this worlde to winne

      Wolde I noght se him slaine.

JOSEPH.   I warne the[e], he is thraly thrette!   *fiercely threatened*

112   With Herowde King, harde harmes to have,   *By/bad luck to him*

113   With that miting if that we be mette   *little fellow (Jesus)*

114   Ther is no salve that him may save.   *him (Jesus)*

      I warne the[e] wele, he sleeis all   *he (Herod) slays*

      Knave childir, grete and small,   *Male*

      In towne and felde,

[84]*doughtir*: i.e., young female member of family; here, wife.

[90]There's nothing else for it but that we must flee.

[101]You must forego that young child's life.

[106-7]Who may put a stop to my grief at my misery?

[112-14]If we be taken by King Herod—bad luck to him—with the little Jesus, there's no remedy that can save Jesus.

Within the elde
Of two yere—
And for thy sones sake!
He will fordo that dere,   *destroy*
122   May that traitoure him take.

MARIA.   Leve Joseph, who tolde yow this?   *Beloved*
How hadde ye wittering of this dede?   *knowledge*
JOSEPH.   An aungell bright, that come fro blisse,
This tithandis tolde, withouten drede,   *without doubt, certainly*
And wakynd me oute of my slepe
128   That comely childe fro cares to kepe;
And bad[e] me flee
With him and the[e]
Onto Egypte.
132   And sertis I dred me sore   *I'm sorely afraid*
133   To make any smale trippe,   *unpleasant*
134   Or time that I come thare.   *Ere*

MARIA.   What ailes they at my barne
136   Slike harmes him for to hete?   *Such/promise, threaten*
Allas, why schulde I tharne   *be deprived of*
My sone his liffe so swete?   *My son's life*
His harte aught to be ful sare,   *His (i.e., Herod's)*
140   On slike a foode him to for-fare,   *child*
That nevir did ill—
Him for to spill,   *kill*
143   And he ne wate why.
I ware full wille of wane   *I would be very bewildered*
My sone and he shulde die—   *If my son should*
And I have but him allone.

JOSEPH.   We! leve Marye, do way, late be,   *beloved/have done*
I pray the[e]! Leve of[f] thy dinne,   *Stop your clamor*
149   And fande the[e] furthe faste for to flee   *undertake*
Away with him for to winne   *go, get*

122If that traitor (Herod) can capture him (Jesus).

128In order to preserve that gracious child from harms.

132-34And certainly I dread the thought of any unpleasant trip until I've arrived there.

136To threaten him with such harms.

140To cause such a young child to perish.

143And the young child not knowing for what reason (he's being killed).

149And undertake to set forth quickly in flight.

That no mischeve on him betide,   *happen to him*
Nor none unhappe in no kyn side,   *no misfortune anywhere*
By way nor strete,
That we non mete   *meet no one*
To slee him.
　MARIA.　Allas, Joseph, for care!   *sorrow*
　　Why shuld I forgo him,   *have to give him up*
　　My dere barne that I bare?   *child*

　JOSEPH.　That swete swaine if thou save,   *if you would save*
　　Do tyte: pakke same oure gere   *Act quickly/pack together*
　　And such smale harnes as we have.   *household things*
　MARIA.　A, leve Joseph, I may not bere.   *carry*
163 JOSEPH.　Bere arme? No, I trowe but small;
　　But God it wote I muste care for all,   *God knows*
165　For bed and bak,
　　And alle the pakke
　　That nedis unto us.
168　It fortheres [not] to fene me;   *feign*
169　This pakald bere me bus,   *pack/I must*
170　Of all I plege and pleyne me.
　　　[*Joseph shoulders a pack.*]

　　But God graunte grace I noght forgete
　　No tulles that we schulde with us take!   *tools, things*
　MARIA.　Allas, Joseph, for grevaunce grete!
　　Whan shall my sorowe slake?   *be eased*
　　For I wote noght whedir to fare.   *whither*
　JOSEPH.　To Egypte, talde I the[e] lang are.   *I told you long before this*
　MARIA.　Whare standith itt?
　　Faine wolde I witt.   *Gladly I'd know (that)*
　JOSEPH.　What wate I?   *How do I know*
180　I wote not where it standis.
　MARIA.　Joseph, I aske mersy.   *I beg pardon*
　　Helpe me oute of this lande.

　JOSEPH.　Nowe certis, Marye, I wolde full faine
　　Helpe the[e] al that I may,
185　And at my poure me peyne

163You bear a burden? No, that is but little in my thought. (Joseph means for her to pack, not carry.)

165i.e., For our bedding and clothes.

168-70It's no use pretending or delaying (lit.: it doesn't further matters to feign, shirk); I must bear this pack of all I'm responsible for and complain about (?).

185And to the utmost of my strength exert myself.

To winne with him and the[e] away.   *go*

MARIA. Allas, what ailes that feende

Thus wilsom wayes make us to wende?   *wandering*

He dois grete sinne: *does*

190   Fro kith and kinne

He gares us flee.   *makes us*

JOSEPH. Leve Marye, leve thy grete!   *Beloved/weeping*

MARIA. Joseph, full wo is me

For my dere sone so swete.

[*Mary mounts an ass with her child.*]

JOSEPH. I pray the[e], Marye, happe him warme   *wrap*

And sette him softe, that he noght syle;   *so he won't drop*

And if thou will ought ese thin[e] arme,   *at all ease*

Giff me him, late me bere him awhile.   *let*

MARIA. I thanke you of youre grete goode dede.

[*She gives the child to Joseph.*]

200   Nowe, gud Joseph, tille him take hede,   *to*

That fode so free!   *child so noble*

Tille him ye see   *Look after him*

Now in this tide.   *time*

JOSEPH. Late me and him allone;   *i.e., Don't worry about us*

205   And if thou can ille ride,

206   Have and halde the[e] faste by the mane.

MARIA. Allas, Joseph, for woo

Was never wight in wor[l]de so will!   *bewildered*

JOSEPH. Do way, Marye, and say nought soo!

For thou schall have no cause thertill.   *thereto*

For, witte thou wele, God is oure frende.   *know you well*

He will be with us wherso we lende.   *stay, sojourn*

In all oure nede

He will us spede—

This wote I wele.

I love my Lorde of all.   *above all*

Such forse me thinke I fele,

218   I may go where I schall!

Are was I wayke, nowe am I wight   *Before I was weak/strong*

My lymes to welde ay at my wille!   *To use my limbs always*

I love my maker most of might

That such grace has graunte me tille.   *granted to me*

205-6If you're not very skillful at riding, keep yourself on by holding fast to the mane.

218I have the strength to move as I wish.

Nowe schall no hatyll do us harme: *nobleman*
I have oure helpe here in min[e] arme!
He wille us fende   *He (God)|defend*
Wherso we lende,   *stay, sojourn*
Fro tene and tray.   *sorrow and trouble*
Late us goo with goode chere.   *Let*
    [*He addresses the audience.*]
Fare wele and have gud day!
230   God blisse us all in fere.   *together*
    MARIA.   Amen, as he beste may.

HEROD THE GREAT
FROM WAKEFIELD
THE SLAUGHTER OF THE INNOCENTS

Herod's rage at the Magi for not telling him of Christ's whereabouts, and his determination to slay all male infants in Bethlehem in order to destroy Christ, are ultimately derived from Matthew 2:16. Medieval tradition amplified the characterization of Herod as a cowardly ranting bully, as we have already seen. The Wakefield pageant of Herod the Great, written by the Wakefield Master in his nine-line stanza throughout, makes extensive use of the conventional tyrannical portraiture of Herod. Nevertheless, the Master's genius is amply evident in the invention of comic detail and richness of vituperative language. One carefully developed motif, for instance, is Herod's hypocritical attitude toward the dispensing of rewards. He is constantly bribing his counselors, his soldiers, and even his audience with promises of incredible wealth. Yet his promises are always contingent upon some vague future date. Every member of the audience is to have a thousand marks upon request "when I com again" (l. 467). Evidently the soldiers are wise to this empty talk, and try vainly to commit their benefactor to a firm promise (l. 434).

Another hallmark of the Master is the lavish development of anonymous and nonbiblical characters: the messenger who browbeats the audience but toadies to Herod, the soldiers, the victimized mothers. The soldiers coarsely reflect attitudes in Herod himself. They share his mercenary greed. Although they boast of valor and quarrel with one another for precedence, when summoned to fight they at first want nothing to do with the business. They are perverters of true knighthood. In their malicious glee and game-playing at death, these rogues anticipate the jesting executioners and tormenters of the Passion sequence. The mothers of the slain children are no less vividly portrayed. Although their role is similar to that of the Virgin Mary at the foot of the cross, they are not passive mourners but fiercely protective women justly accusing their oppressors of unmanliness.

The stage must provide two chief acting areas: Herod's throned station, and a field for the slaughter of the Innocents. The slaughter becomes one of the most gruesomely memorable scenes of carnage in all religious drama, anticipating the cruel agony of the Passion itself. We can gain some impression of the scene's nightmarish quality from Shakespeare's recollection in *Henry V* (III, iii) of just such a slaughter. Calling to the besieged citizens of Harfleur, King Henry warns them to surrender lest they behold their

> naked infants spitted upon pikes,
> Whiles the mad mothers with their howls
>   confus'd
> Do break the clouds, as did the wives of
>   Jewry

At Herod's bloody-hunting slaughtermen. Action of this violent and noisy sort is probably not meant to be restricted to a pageant wagon; at Coventry, Herod rages in the street nearby the pageant, and the Wakefield production may require an even more extensive acting area with audiences on all sides. In any case, the comic and brutal shock effects of this Wakefield pageant contrast markedly with the subdued liturgical tone of the Fleury Slaughter of the Innocents (see Part I, above).

Herod the Great
From Wakefield
The Slaughter of the Innocents

Incipit Magnus Herodes.		*Here begins Herod the Great*
[*Herod's messenger addresses the audience.*]		
NUNTIUS. Moste mighty Mahowne meng you with mirth!		*Mohammed make you merry*
2 Both of burgh and of towne, by fellys and by firth,		*by moor and forest*
3 Both king with crowne and barons of brith,		*(noble) birth*
4 That radly will rowne, many greatt grith		*quickly/whisper/protection*
5 Shall behapp.		*Will befall (them)*
Take tenderly intent		*Pay attention carefully*
What sondys ar sent—		*messages*
Els harmes shall ye hent,		*get*
And lothes you to lap.		*And troubles to entangle you*
10 Herode, the heynd king—by grace of Mahowne—		*gracious*
Of Jury, sourmonting sternly with crowne		*Jewry/excelling*
On life that ar lifing in towre and in towne,		*(All those) alive*
Gracius you greting, commaundys you be bowne		*Graciously/ready*
At his bid[d]ing.		
Luf him with lewté;		*loyalty*
Drede him, that doughty!		
He chargys you be redy		
Lowly at his liking.		*Humbly at his pleasure*
19 What man apon mold menys him agane		*complains against him*
20 Tytt teyn shall be told—knight, sqwiere, or swain.		*Quickly a troublemaker*
21 Be he never so bold, byes he that bargan		*he buys*
22 Twelf thowsandfold more then I sayn,		
May ye trast.		*You may trust (to that)*
He is worthy wonderly,		*He (Herod)/exceedingly noble*
Selcouthly sory;		*Strangely sad*
For a boy that is borne herby		
Standys he abast.		*abashed, discomfited*

2–5To those living in city and in country village, by fen or moor and by forest (i.e., all people), to kings and nobly born barons, to all those who will quickly be silent (lit.: whisper), much great protection will be given.

19–22Whatever man upon earth—knight, squire, or servingman—complains against him will quickly be accounted a troublemaker. Such a person, no matter how bold he may be, will pay for his insolence (lit.: that bargain) twelve thousand times worse than I can say.

A king thay him call, and that we deny.
How shuld it so fall, greatt mervell have I.   *befall*
30   Therfor overall shall I make a cry   *everywhere/make proclamation*
That ye busk not to brall, nor like not to ly   *prepare not to brawl*
This tide.   *time*
Carpys of no king   *Carp, talk*
Bot Herode, that lording,
Or busk to youre beylding   *hurry to your home*
Youre heedys for to hide!   *heads*

He is king of kingys, kindly I knowe,   *thoroughly*
Chefe lord of lordingys, chefe leder of law.
39   Ther watys on his wingys that bold bost will blaw: *wait/those who/blow*
40   Greatt dukys downe dingys for his greatt aw   *fall down*
And him lowtys.   *reverence him*
Tuskane and Turky,
All Inde and Italy,
Cecyll and Surry   *Sicily/Syria*
Drede him and dowtys.   *fear (him)*

From Paradise to Padwa to Mownt Flascon,
From Egyp to Mantua unto Kemp towne,
From Sarceny to Susa to Grece it abowne,   *above it*
Both Normondy and Norwa lowtys to his crowne.   *do reverence*
50   His renowne
Can no tong tell,
From heven unto hell.
Of him can none spell   *speak*
Bot his cosyn Mahowne.

He is the worthiest of all barnes that ar borne.   *boys*
Fre men ar his thrall, full teynfully torne.   *Noble/grievously injured*
Begin he to brall, many men cach skorne!   *Should he begin*
Obey must we all, or els be ye lorne   *lost*
Att onys.   *At once*
60   Downe ding of youre knees,   *Thrust down (i.e., fall on)*
All that him seys!   *see*
Displesyd he beys,   *(Or) he will be displeased*
And byrkyn many bonys.   *And break*

Here he commys now, I cry, that lord I of spake!

39-40There wait upon him (under his wings, acknowledging his protection) those who will
proclaim (blow) a bold boast: great dukes fall down in great awe of him.

Fast afore will I hy, radly on a rake,   *quickly at a run*
And welcom him worshipfully, laghing with lake,   *glee*
As he is most worthy, and knele for his sake
So low;
Downe deruly to fall,   *promptly*
70   As renk most ryall.   *knight*
Haill, the worthiest of all!
To the[e] must I bow. [*He kneels.*
         Enter Herod in estate, attended.]

Haill, luf lord! Lo, thy letters have I layde.   *message/presented*
74   I have done I couth do, and peasse have I prayd—   *what I could do/silence*
75   Mekill more therto opynly displayd.   *Much*
76   Bot romoure is rasyd so, that boldly thay brade   *burst into speech*
Emangys thame: *Amongst themselves*
Thay carp of a king;   *talk*
Thay seasse not sich chatering.
     HERODES.   Bot I shall tame thare talking,
And let thame go hang thame.   *hang themselves*

Stint, brodels, youre din—yei, everychon!   *wretches*
I red that ye harkyn to I be gone.   *advise/till*
For if I begin, I breke ilka bone   *every*
And pull fro the skin the carcas anone,
Yei, perdé!   *by God*
Sesse all this wonder
And make us no blonder,   *trouble*
For I ryfe you in sonder   *I'll tear you*
Be ye so hardy.   *If you be*

Peasse, both yong and old, at my bid[d]ing, I red!   *advise*
92   For I have all in wold: in me standys life and dede.   *at my command*
Who that is so bold, I brane him thrugh the hede!   *Whoever is*
Speke not or I have told what I will in this stede.   *until/place*
Ye wote nott   *don't know*
All that I will mefe.   *do*
Stir not bot ye have lefe;   *unless/permission*
For if ye do, I clefe   *I'll cleave*
99   You small as flesh to pott.

⁷⁰As befits a knight of his royal stature.

⁷⁴⁻⁷⁶I have done what I could do, and I've asked for silence—much more I've publicly presented on that subject. But rumor is raised so, that boldly the people burst into speech.

⁹²I have everything at my command: in me is the power of life and death.

⁹⁹(I'll cut) you up as small as stew-meat for the pot.

My mirthes ar turned to teyn, my mekenes into ire,   *grief*
101 And all for oone. I weyn, within I fare as fire!   *one (Christ)/ween*
102 May I se him with eyn, I shall gif him his hire.   *If I can see*
103 Bot I do as I meyn, I were a full lewde sire   *Unless/intend/stupid*
104 In wonys.   *Everywhere*
     Had I that lad in hand,
     As I am king in land
     I shuld with this steyll brand   *sword*
     Byrkyn all his bonys.   *Break*

     My name springys far and nere: the doughtiest, men me call,   *extends*
     That ever ran with spere, a lord and king ryall.
111 What joy is me to here a lad to sesse my stall!   *throne*
     If I this crowne may bere, that boy shall by for all.   *bear/pay for*
     I anger.
     I wote not what dewill me alys.   *what the devil ails me*
115 Thay teyn me so with talys   *annoy*
     That, by Gottys dere nalys,   *God's dear nails (of the cross)*
     I will peasse no langer.   *be quiet*

     What, dewill! me think I brast for anger and for teyn.   *burst/rage*
     I trow thise kingys be past that here with me has beyn.
120 Thay promised me full fast or now here to be seyn,   *faithfully/ere/seen*
     For, els I shuld have cast an othere sleght, I weyn.   *tried another trick*
     I tell you
     A boy thay said thay soght,
     With offering that thay broght.
     It mefys my hart right noght   *It wouldn't bother me*
     To breke his nek in two!

     Bot be thay past me by, by Mahowne in heven,   *But if they have passed*
     I shall, and that in hy, set all on sex and seven.   *in haste*
     Trow ye a king as I will suffre thaym to neven   *appoint*
     Any to have mastry bot myself full even?   *in fact*
     Nay, leyfe!   *believe (me)*
132 The dewill me hang and draw
133 If I that losell knaw,   *rascal*

101–4 And all on account of Christ. I believe I'm burning within! If I can lay my eyes on him, I'll give him what's coming to him. Unless I do as I intend, I'll be reckoned a bungling ruler everywhere.

111 What joy is it for me to hear of a lad (who is) to seize my throne!

115 They (the people) annoy me so with these tales (of a child ruler).

132–36 If I can find out who that rascal is, may the devil hang and disembowel me unless I give him a blow to deprive him of life. Yet, because of dangers, I would like to know if they (the three kings) are gone.

134   Bot I gif him a blaw   *Unless*
135   That life I shall him reyfe.   *deprive him of life*

136   For parels, yit I wold wist if thay were gone.
        And ye therof her told, I pray you say anone;   *If/hear*
        For, and thay be so bold, by God that sittys in trone,   *if*
        The pain cannot be told that thay shall have, ilkon,   *reckoned/each one*
        For ire.   *Because of my wrath*
        Sich panys hard never man tell,   *Such pains heard*
        For-ugly and for-fell,   *Extremely unpleasant and cruel*
        That Lucifere in hell
        Thare bonys shall all to-tire.   *tear to pieces*

        1 MILES. Lord, think not ill if I tell you how thay ar past;   *soldier*
        I kepe not layn, truly. Syn thay cam by you last,   *I won't conceal it/Since*
        Anothere way in hy thay soght, and that full fast.   *in haste*
        HERODES.   Why, and ar thay past me by? We, outt! for
                    teyn I brast!   *for rage I burst*
        We! fi[e]!
150   Fi[e] on the dewill! Where may I bide,   *abide*
151   Bot fight for teyn and al to-chide?   *Without fighting for rage*
        Thefys, I say ye shuld have spide
        And told when thay went by.

154   Ye ar knightys to trast! Nay, losels ye ar, and thefys!   *trust/rascals*
155   I wote I yelde my gast, so sore my hart it grefys.   *yield up my ghost*
156   2 MILES.   What nede you be abast? Ther ar no greatt   *upset*
                    mischefys
157   For these maters to gnast.   *to gnash (your teeth)*
        3 MILES.   Why put ye sich reprefys   *such reproofs*
        Withoutt cause?
        Thus shuld ye not thrett us,
        Ungainly to bete us.   *Improperly*
        Ye shuld not rehett us   *rebuke*
162   Withoutt othere sawes.   *speeches, rebuttal*

        HEROD. Fi[e], losels and liars, lurdans ilkon!   *rascals/louts everyone*
        Tratoures and well wars! Knafys, bot knightys none!   *much worse*

150-51(Herod, no doubt ranting up and down, says he can't keep still for rage.) *al to-chide*:
brawl furiously.

154-57(sarcastically) You're a fine bunch of knights to put one's trust in! On the contrary,
you're rascals and scoundrels! I know I'm going to yield up my ghost, so sorely does my heart
grieve.—Why should you be so disturbed? No mischiefs have been done serious enough for
you to gnash your teeth about.

162i.e., Without our having a chance to speak in rebuttal.

Had ye bene woth youre eres, thus had thay not gone. *worth your ears*
Gett I those land-lepars, I breke ilka bone. *If I catch those vagabonds*
First vengeance
Shall I se on thare bonys.
If ye bide in these wonys *hereabouts*
170 I shall ding you with stonys— *hit*
Yei, ditizance doutance! *without doubt*

I wote not where I may sitt for anger and for teyn. *rage*
We have not done all yit, if it be as I weyn. *ween, think*
Fi[e], dewill! Now how is it? As long as I have eyn *eyes*
I think not for to flitt, bot king I will be seyn *flee*
Forever.
Bot stand I to quart, *If I stay in good health*
I tell you my hart: *i.e., my heart's desire*
I shall gar thaym start, *make them flinch*
Or els trust me never.

1 MILES. Sir, thay went sodanly or any man wist, *ere/knew*
Els had mett we—yei, perdy! and may ye trist. *Otherwise we had met/trust*
183 2 MILES. So bold nor so hardy agans oure list *against our inclination*
184 Was none of that company durst mete me with fist, *that he dared meet*
For ferd. *fear*
3 MILES. Ill durst thay abide, *Little dared they*
Bot ran thame to hide. *themselves*
Might I thaym have spide,
I had made thaym a berd. *would have outwitted them*

190 What couth we more do to save youre honoure?
1 MILES. We were redy therto, and shal be ilk howre. *every*
HEROD. Now, syn it is so, ye shall have favoure. *since*
Go where ye will go, by towne and by towre.
Goys hens! [*The soldiers retire.*] *Go*
I have maters to mell *discuss*
With my prevey counsell.
   [*He summons his counselors.*]
Clerkys, ye bere the bell; *i.e., are the best*
Ye must me encense. *enlighten*

Oone spake in mine eere a wonderfull talking, *wondrous tale*
200 And saide a madyn shuld bere anothere to be king.
Sirs, I pray you inquere in all writing,
In Virgill, in Homere, and all other thing

183–84No one of that company (the three kings) was so bold or so resolute against our inclination that he dared meet me in a fistfight.

Bot legende.   *i.e., Except scripture or saints' lives*
Sekys poecé-tayllys;   *Seek tales in poetry*
Lefe pistyls and grales;   *Omit epistles and graduals*
Mes, matins, noght avalys—   *Mass/avail*
All these I defende.   *forbid*
    [*They look at their books.*]

I pray you tell, heyndly, now what ye finde.   *quickly*
  1 CONSULTUS.   Truly, sir, prophecy it is not blind.
210   We rede thus by Isay: He shal be so kinde   *in Isaiah (7:14)/conceived*
That a madyn, sothely, which never sinde,   *sinned*
Shall him bere.
Virgo concipiet,   *A virgin shall conceive*
Natumque pariet.   *And bear a son*
"Emanuell" is hete,   *he is called*
His name for to lere: *To teach you his name*

"God is with us," that is for to say.
  2 CONSULTUS.   And othere says thus, trist me ye may: *others (Micah 5:2)/trust*
"Of Bedlem a gracius Lord shall spray   *Bethlehem/spring*
220   That of Jury mightius king shal be ay,   *Jewry*
Lord mighty;
And him shall honoure
Both king and emperoure."
  HERODES.   Why, and shuld I to him cowre?
Nay, ther thou lyis lightly!   *readily*

Fi[e]! the dewill the[e] spede, and me, bot I drink onys!   *unless I have a drink*
This has thou done indede to anger me for the nonys.   *on purpose*
And thou, knafe, thou thy mede shall have, by Cokys dere   *reward/God's*
    bonys!
229   Thou can not half thy crede. Outt, thefys, fro my wonys!   *dwelling*
Fi[e], knafys!
Fi[e], dottypols, with youre bookys—   *blockheads*
Go kast thaym in the brookys!
With sich wilys and crokys   *tricks*
234   My witt away rafys.   *raves*

Hard I never sich a trant, that a knafe so sleght   *Heard/trick/base*
Shuld com like a sant and refe me my right.   *saint/deprive me of*
Nay, he shall on-slant; I shall kill him downe stright.   *come to grief/straightway*

[229]You don't even know half your creed (i.e., you know nothing). Get out of my dwelling, you scoundrels.

[234]i.e., I'm losing my mind.

War, I say, lett me pant! Now think I to fight   *Beware*
For anger.

240   My guttys will outt thring   *burst out*
Bot I this lad hing.   *Unless/hang*
Withoutt I have a venging,   *Unless*
I may lif no langer.

Shuld a carll in a kafe, bot of oone yere age,   *churl/cave (i.e., stable)*
Thus make me to rafe?

1 CONSULTUS.   Sir, peasse this outrage!   *calm this fury*
Away let ye wafe all sich langage.   *Put away*
Youre worship to safe, is he oght bot a page   *Saving your reverence/boy*
Of a yere?   *Of a year's age*
We two shall him teyn   *harm him*

250   With oure wittys betweyn,   *With our combined wits*
That, if ye do as I meyn,   *So that/mean*
He shall di[e] on a spere.

2 CONSULTUS.   For drede that he reyn, do as we red: *reign/advise*
Thrug[h]outt Bedlem and ilk othere stede   *every other place*
Make knightys ordeyn and put unto dede   *prepare/death*
All knave-children of two yerys brede   *years' breeding, growth*
And within.   *under*
This child may ye spill   *kill*
Thus at youre awne will.

260 HERODES.   Now thou says heretill   *to the purpose*
A right nobill gin!   *stratagem*

If I lif in land good life, as I hope,   *If I live on earth*
This dar I the[e] warand: to make the[e] a pope.
O, my hart is risand now in a glope!   *in palpitation*
For this nobill tithand thou shall have a drope   *news/drop*
Of my good grace:
Markys, rentys, and powndys,   *Marks/revenues*
Greatt castels and groundys;
Thrugh all sees and soundys   *i.e., everywhere*

270   I gif the[e] the chace.   *hunting rights*

Now will I procede and take veniance.
    [*He addresses his messenger.*]
All the flowre of knighthede call to legeance,   *allegiance*
Bewshere, I the[e] bid; it may the[e] avance.   *Beau sire, fair sir*

NUNTIUS.   Lord, I shall me spede and bring, perchaunce,   *bring (them)*
To thy sight. [*He goes to summon the soldiers.*]
Hark, knightys, I you bring

Here new tithing: *tiding*
Unto Herode king
Hast[e] with all youre might,

In all the hast[e] that ye may; in armowre full bright,
In youre best aray, looke that ye be dight.   *clad*
1 MILES.   Why, shuld we fray?   *fight*
2 MILES.   This is not all right.
283 3 MILES.   Sirs, withoutten delay I drede that we fight.
NUNTIUS.   I pray you,
As fast as ye may
Com to him this day.
1 MILES.   What, in oure best aray?
NUNTIUS.   Yei, sirs, I say you.

2 MILES.   Somwhat is in hand, whatever it meyn.
290 3 MILES.   Tarry not for to stand, ther or we have beyn.   *ere*
[*They go to Herod.*]
291 NUNTIUS.   King Herode all-weldand, well be ye seyn!   *all-ruling*
Youre knightys ar comand in armoure full sheyn   *coming/shining*
At youre will.
1 MILES.   Haill, dughtiest of all!
We ar comen at youre call
For to do what we shall
Youre lust to fullfill.   *desire*

HEROD.   Welcom, lordingys, iwis, both greatt and small.
The cause now is this that I send for you all:
300   A lad, a knafe, borne is that shuld be king ryall;
Bot I kill him and his, I wote I brast my gall.   *Unless/burst*
Therfor, sirs,
Veniance shall ye take
All for that lad sake;
And men I shall you make   *men (of importance)*
Where ye com aywhere, sirs.   *Wherever you go*

To Bedlem loke ye go, and all the coste aboute.   *region*
All knave children ye slo—and, lordys, ye shal be stoute—   *slay/fierce*
Of yeres if thay be two and within. Of all that rowte,   *under/crowd*
310   On life lyefe none of tho that ligys in swedill-clowte,   *leave/those*

283Sirs, I'm afraid we'll be fighting soon. (The soldiers are apprehensive and reluctant to fight
for Herod, despite their earlier protestations.)

290-91Don't stand around wasting time, before we've even been there (to Herod's court). —
All-ruling King Herod, I hope I see you well!

310Leave none of those alive who lie in swaddling-clothes.

I red you.   *advise*
Spare no kins bloode,   *no kind of*
Lett all ryn on floode.
If women wax woode,   *mad*
I warn you, sirs, to spede you.   *hurry*

316   Hens, now go youre way, that ye were thore.   *there*
317 2 MILES. I wote we make a fray; bot I will go before.
318 3 MILES. A, think, sirs, I say: I mon whett like a bore.   *whet (my tusks)*
319 1 MILES. Sett me before, ay good enogh for a skore.
      Haill, heyndly!   *gracious lord*
      We shall for youre sake
      Make a dulfull lake.   *doleful sport*
    HERODES. Now if ye me well wrake,   *avenge*
      Ye shall find me freyndly.
      [*The soldiers proceed on their mission.*]

    2 MILES. Go ye now till oure noytt, and handyll thaym weyll.   *to our work*
326 3 MILES. I shall pay thaym on the cote, begin I to reyll.   *to run riot*
      [*The first woman approaches with her child.*]
327 1 MILES. Hark, felose! ye dote. Yonder commys unceyll.   *comes misfortune*
328   I hold here a grote she likys me not weyll   *wager*
329   By we parte.   *By (the time that)*
      [*He speaks to her with mock courtesy.*]
      Dame, think it not ill,
      Thy knafe if I kill.   *son*
    1 MULIER. What, thefe, agans my will?   *against*
      Lord, kepe him in qwarte!   *health and safety*
      [*She struggles to escape.*]

    1 MILES. Abide now, abide. No farther thou gose.
    1 MULIER. Peasse, thefe! Shall I chide and make here a nose?   *noise*
336 1 MILES. I shall reyfe the[e] thy pride. Kill we these boyse!   *deprive*
    1 MULIER. Tyd may betide, kepe well thy nose,   *Come what may/guard*
      Fals thefe! [*She fights back.*]
339   Have on loft on thy hode!
    1 MILES. What, hoore, art thou woode?   *whore/mad*
      [*He kills her child.*]

316–19Now go ahead, so that you get there quickly. —I bet we make a fierce battle; let me go first. (The soldiers quarrel senselessly over precedence and talk big.) —Think of this, fellows, I say: I must whet (my tusks) like a boar. —Put me in front. I'm a match for any twenty men.

326–29I'll thrash them, if I begin to run riot. —Hark, fellows, you talk idly. Here comes someone marked for misfortune. I'll bet a groat (small coin) she won't like me well by the time we part.

336I'll take away your pride and joy. Let's kill these boys!

339Have (a blow) on top of your head.

1 MULIER.   Outt, alas, my childys bloode!
Outt, for reprefe!   *for shame*

Alas for shame and sin! Alas that I was borne!
Of weping who may blin to se hir childe forlorne?   *cease/destroyed*
My comforth and my kin, my son thus al to-torne!   *torn to bits*
Veniance for this sin I cry, both evyn and morne!   *evening*
2 MILES.   Well done.
   [*The second woman approaches with her child.*]
Com hedyr, thou old stry: *hag*
That lad of thine shall dy.
2 MULIER.   Mercy, lord, I cry!
It is min[e] awne dere son.

352 2 MILES.   No mercy thou mefe. It mendys the[e] not, Mawd.   *move, arouse*
353 2 MULIER.   Then thy skalp shall I clefe! List thou be clawd?
   [*She fights back.*]
Lefe, lefe, now bylefe!   *Leave off, stop*
2 MILES.   Peasse, bid I, bawd!
2 MULIER.   Fi[e], fi[e], for reprefe! Fi[e], full of frawde—   *for shame*
356 No man!
Have at thy tabard,   *knights' emblazoned coat*
Harlot and holard: *Rascal and libertine*
Thou shall not be sparde!
I cry and I ban!   *curse*
   [*He kills her child.*]

Outt, morder man, I say, strang tratoure and thefe!
Out, alas, and waloway, my child that was me lefe!   *dear*
My luf, my blood, my play, that never did man grefe!   *joy*
Alas, alas this day, I wold my hart shuld clefe
In sonder!
Veniance I cry and call
On Herode and his knightys all—
Veniance, Lord, apon thaym fall,
369 And mekill warldys wonder!

3 MILES.   This is well-wroght gere that ever may be.   *well-done business*
   [*The third woman approaches with her child.*]
Comys hederward here! Ye nede not to fle.   *Come*

³⁵²⁻⁵³You'll move (arouse) no mercy. It won't help you, Maud. —Then I'll split your scalp!
Do you want to be clawed?

³⁵⁶i.e., You're no true man (to do such a thing).

³⁶⁹And many of the world's prodigies, or plagues (fall on them).

3 MULIER.   Will ye do any dere to my child and me? *harm*

3 MILES.   He shall di[e], I the[e] swere. His hart blood shall
    thou se.

3 MULIER.   God forbede! [*He kills her child.*]
Thefe, thou shedys my childys blood!
Out, I cry! I go nere wood! *mad*
Alas, my hart is all on flood
To se my child thus blede!

By God, thou shall aby this dede that thou has done. *pay for*

380 3 MILES.   I red the[e] not, stry, by son and by moyn. *I tell you no/hag*

3 MULIER.   Have at the[e], say I! Take the[e] ther a foyn! *a jab*
    [*She attacks him.*]
Out on the[e], I cry! Have at thy groyn *snout, nose*
Anothere!
This kepe I in store. *in reserve*

3 MILES.   Peasse now, no more!

3 MULIER.   I cry and I rore,
Out on the[e], mans mordere! *murderer*

388 Alas, my bab, min[e] innocent, my fleshly get! For sorow *offspring*
389 That God me derly sent, of bales who may me borow? *sorrows/save*
Thy body is all to-rent! I cry, both even and morow, *torn to pieces/evening*
Veniance for thy blod thus spent: "Out," I cry, and
    "horow"! *help*

1 MILES.   Go lightly! *quickly*
Gett out of thise wonys, *Get away from here*
Ye trattys, all at onys, *hags/once*
Or by Cokys dere bonys *God's*
I make you go wightly! *quickly*
    [*The women are driven off.*]

Thay ar flayd now, I wote; thay will not abide. *routed*

398 2 MILES.   Lett us ryn fote-hote—now wold I we hide— *run/would hurry*
399 And tell of this lott, how we have betide. *fortune/fared*

400 3 MILES.   Thou can do thy note; that have I aspide. *work*
Go furth now,
Tell thou Herode oure taill. *tale*
For all oure availl, *assistance*
I tell you, saunce faill, *without fail*
He will us alow. *praise*

388–89Alas, my babe, my innocent one, the offspring of my flesh! Because of the sorrow that God has sent me at such cost, who can save me from sorrow?

398–400Let's run hot-foot—I wish we would hurry—and tell how we've fared in this. —I can tell you're a person who gets your job done.

1 MILES.   I am best of you all, and ever has bene;
The devill have my saull bot I be first sene!   *unless*
408   It sittys me to call my lord, as I wene.
2 MILES.   What nedys the[e] to brall? Be not so kene
In this anger.
I shall say thou did best—
Save myself, as I gest. [*Aside.*]   *thought*
1 MILES.   We! that is most honest.
3 MILES.   Go, tary no langer.
         [*They go to Herod, at his station.*]

1 MILES.   Haill, Herode, oure king! Full glad may ye be.
Good tithing we bring. Harkyn now to me: *tidings*
We have mayde riding thrughoutt Juré.   *Jewry*
Well wit ye oone thing: that morderd have we   *Be assured of one thing*
Many thowsandys.
420 2 MILES.   I held thaym full hote;   *I beat them*
I paid them on the cote.
422   Thare dammys, I wote,   *mothers*
423   Never bindys them in bandys.   *in swaddling clothes*

3 MILES.   Had ye sene how I fard when I cam emang them!   *Would you had seen*
Ther was none that I spard, bot lade on and dang them.   *laid on/struck*
I am worthy a rewarde. Where I was emange them,
I stud and I stard. No pité to hang them   *I stood/looked fiercely*
Had I.
HERODES.   Now, by mighty Mahowne,
That is good of renowne,   *of good renown*
431   If I bere this crowne
Ye shall have a lady

Ilkon to him laid, and wed at his will.   *Presented to each one*
434 1 MILES.   So have ye lang saide—do somwhat thertill!   *thereto*
435 2 MILES.   And I was never flayde, for good ne for ill.   *frightened*
436 3 MILES.   Ye might hold you well paide oure lust to fulfill, *pleased*
Thus think me,   *It seems to me*
With tresure untold,

408It befits me to speak first to my lord (Herod), as I think.

420I made it hot for them.

422-23i.e., Their mothers, I know, will never again wrap them in swaddling-clothes.

431i.e., As sure as I wear this crown.

434-36You've been saying such things all along—now do something. —And I was never frightened for any reason. (He is reminding Herod of his bravery for which he hopes to be rewarded.) —You might consider yourself well pleased to fulfill our desire.

If it like that ye wold   *If it please you*
Both silver and gold
To gif us greatt plenté.

HERODES.   As I am king crownde, I think it good right.   *quite right*
Ther goys none on grownde that has sich a wight.   *such a servant*
A hundreth thowsand pownde is good wage for a knight;
445 Of pennys good and rownde, now may ye go light   *pennies/quickly*
446 With store.   *plenty*
And ye knightys of oures
Shall have castels and towres,
Both to you and to youres,
For now and evermore.

451 1 MILES.   Was never none borne, by downes ne by dalys,   *i.e., anywhere*
452 Nor yit us beforne, that had sich avalys.   *such benefits*
     2 MILES.   We have castels and corne, mych gold in oure
                malys.   *wallets*
454 3 MILES.   It will never be worne, withoutt any talys.   *used up/truly*
Haill, heyndly!   *gracious lord*
Haill, lord, haill, king!
We ar furth founding.   *hastening forth*
458 HEROD.   Now Mahowne he you bring   *may Mohammed bring you*
459 Where he is lord freyndly!
     [*The soldiers depart.*]

Now in peasse may I stand—I thank the[e], Mahowne—
461 And gif of my lande that longys to my crowne.   *belongs*
     [*He addresses the audience.*]
Draw therfor nerehande, both of burgh and of towne: *near*
463 Markys, ilkon, a thowsande, when I am bowne,   *Marks/everyone/ready*
464 Shall ye have.
I shal be full fain   *very glad*
To gif that I sayn.   *what I've promised*
Wate when I com again,   *Watch for me*
And then may ye crave.   *ask for it*

445–46Now you can go quickly with plenty of pence, good and round.

451–52There never has been anyone born, anywhere, living before us, who enjoyed such benefits (as we will enjoy).

454It (our riches) will never be used up, truly (lit.: without any tales, talk).

458–59i.e., Now may Mohammed bring you to where he is the presiding deity (in hell).

461(Herod congratulates himself on his largess to the knights, a quality befitting a magnificent ruler.)

463–64Every one of you will have a thousand marks (about 2/3 of a pound) when I am ready (i.e., at some vaguely indeterminate future date).

I sett by no good, now my hart is at easse,   *I think it of no importance*
That I shed so mekill blode. Pes, all my riches!   *much/my kingdoms*
471 For to se this flode from the fote to the nese   *flood/nose*
472 Mefys nothing my mode; I lagh that I whese.   *Upsets not at all/laugh*
A, Mahowne,
So light is my saull   *cheerful*
475 That all of sugar is my gall!
I may do what I shall,
And bere up my crowne.   *maintain*

I was castyn in care, so frightly afraid!   *fearfully*
Bot I thar not dispare, for low is he laid   *need*
That I most dred are, so have I him flayd.   *dreaded before/defeated*
481 And els wonder ware—and so many strayd   *otherwise/strewn*
482 In the strete—
483 That oone shuld be harmeles   *unhurt*
484 And skape away, hafles,   *helpless*
485 Where so many childes
486 Thare balys cannot bete.   *Cannot amend their harms*

A hundreth thowsand, I watt, and fourty ar slain,   *know*
And four thowsand. Therat me aght to be fain;   *I ought/glad*
Sich a morder on a flat shall never be again.   *in a field*
Had I had bot oone bat at that lurdan   *blow/lout*
So yong,
492 It shuld have bene spokyn   *told (as a marvelous tale)*
493 How I had me wrokyn,   *avenged myself*
494 Were I dede and rotyn,   *Even after I was dead*
495 With many a tong.   *By*

496 Thus shall I tech knavys ensampyll to take,
497 In thare wittys that ravys, sich mastré to make.
498 All wantones wafys! no langage ye crak!   *insolence/avoid/boast*
No sufferan you savys; youre nekkys shall I shak   *No sovereign will save you*
In sonder!
No king ye on call   *Don't call on any king*

481–72To see this flood (of children's blood) from head to toe (lit: nose) doesn't at all upset me;
I laugh so hard that I wheeze.

475i.e., That my soured disposition is turned to sweetness.

481–86And it would be a wonder otherwise, with so many children strewn in the street, if one
should be unhurt and escape, helpless as he was, when so many children could not amend
their injuries.

492–98Even after I was dead and rotten, it would have been told by many a tongue how I
avenged myself. Thus shall I teach knaves to take example by this, who rave enough in their
wits to claim such authority (as Christ claimed). Avoid all insolence! Don't boast!

Bot on Herode the ryall,
Or els many oone shall   *many persons*
Apon youre bodys wonder.   *Marvel at your (dead) bodies*

For if I here it spokyn when I com again,   *hear it (treason)*
Youre branys bese brokyn. Therfor, be ye bain. *brains will be/obedient*
507 Nothing bese unlokyn; it shal be so plain.   *Nothing will be explanied*
508 Begin I to rokyn, I think all disdain   *act violently/anger*
509 For-daunche.   *Overly fastidious*
Sirs, this is my counsell:
Bese not to[o] cruell.   *Be*
Bot adew!—to the devill!
I can no more Franch. [*Exit.*]   *know*

Explicit Magnus Herodes.   *Here ends Herod the Great*

507–9 No explanations or excuses will be necessary; my punishment will be simple and effective. If I begin to act violently, I'll think all anger overly fastidious (i.e., I'll pay no attention
to anyone's protests).

THE DEATH OF HEROD
FROM N TOWN

The story of Herod's gruesome death is not to be found in the Bible. It is instead a legendary attempt to provide a suitably edifying ending for the life of so wicked a ruler. The legend occurs in the writings of the first-century Jewish historian, Josephus, and in the twelfth-century collection of scriptural narratives with commentary known as the *Historia scholastica* of Peter Comestor.

Among the English cycles, N Town gives a particularly vivid account of Herod's death. This version makes effective use of allegorical abstraction, a technique we normally associate with the morality play. The allegorized figure of Death, silent and terrifying, observes King Herod at the height of his worldly triumph. The juxtaposition of worldly boasting and the imminent prospect of death is intensely ironic. Herod believes he has just eased his nightmarish fear of a rival claimant to his throne: "Now my fo is ded!" he exults. Yet Death has already assured us that Christ lives. The game

is up not for Christ, but for Herod. This king is the proverbial beguiler beguiled. The music Herod orders for his celebratory feast becomes instead the trumpet-call of judgment. As in *Everyman*, Death serves the will of God, punishing vainglory and revealing the transitory nature of all worldly achievement. His concluding homily, aimed at the audience with agonizing relevance, gives us a notion of the compelling power of medieval popular sermonizing on death.

Death's costume, suggesting wretched poverty and the gnawing of worms (ll. 272–73), contrasts starkly with the resplendent richness of Herod's costume and surroundings, including the banquet. Another contrast between worldly wealth and otherworldly misery becomes evident when the devils emerge from hell-mouth to drag away their prostrate victim. Here the vivid image of damnation may have resembled those grotesque scenes in Brueghel's depiction of the Last Judgment.

The Death of Herod
From N Town

[*At his station, Herod, rejoicing at the death of the Innocents, invites his soldiers to come up and join him in a celebration.*]

In sete now am I sett as kinge of mightys most.	*of greatest might*
All this wer[l]d, for ther love to me, shul they lowt—	*All people/bow*
Both of hevyn and of erth and of helle cost.	*region*
For digne of my dignité, they have of me dowt.	*As befitting/fear*

1–128(The lines, here omitted, from the beginning of the pageant, present in rapid succession Herod's boast and instructions to the soldiers, the angel's warning to Joseph and the flight into Egypt, and the slaughter of the Innocents.)

454

133   Ther is no lord like on live to me wurth a toost—   *alive*
     Nother king nor kaiser in all this worlde abought!
     If any brybour do bragge or blowe agens my bost,   *scoundrel/speak against*
     I shal rappe tho rebawdys and rake them on rought   *those ribalds/in a rout*
     With my bright bronde.   *sword*
     Ther shal be neither kaiser nere kinge   *nor*
     But that I shal hem down dinge,   *them/strike*
     Lesse than he at my biddinge   *Unless he*
     Be buxum to min[e] honde.   *obedient*

     Now, my jentill and curteys knightys, herke to me this
         stownde: *now*
143   Good time sone, me thinkith, at diner that we were.   *soon*
     Smertly, therfore, sett a tabyll anon here ful sownde,   *Briskly/solid*
     Coverid with a corious cloth and with rich wurthy fare—   *elaborate*
     Servise for the loveliest lorde that levinge is on grownde.   *lives on earth*
     Beste metys and wurthiest wines loke that ye non spare,   *foods*
     Thow that a lityl pint shulde coste a thowsand pownde.   *Although*
     Bringe alwey of the beste; for coste take ye no care.
150   Anon that it be done!

      [*His attendants prepare to bring in a sumptuous*
       feast. Musicians are at hand.]

   SENESCALLUS.   My lorde, the tabyl is redy dight.   *prepared*
     Here is watyr; now, wasch forthright.
     Now blowe up, minstrall, with all your might!
     The servise comith in sone.

   HERODES REX.   Now am I sett at mete
     And wurthely servyd at my degré.   *according to my rank*
     Com forth, knightys, sitt down and ete
     And be as mery as ye kan be!
   1 MILES.   Lord, at yowre biddinge we take oure sete;
160   With herty wil obey we the[e].
     Ther is no lorde of might so grett
     Thorwe all this wer[l]de, in no countré,   *Through*
     In wurchepp to abide.   *In (such) honor to dwell*
   HERODES.   I was nevyr merier here beforn   *before this*
     Sithe that I was first born   *Since*
     Than I am now, right in this morn.
     In joy I ginne to glide!   *begin*

      [*Death comes forward, while the banquet continues.*]

   MORS.   Ow! I herde a page make preysing of pride: *fellow*

133There's no lord alive worth a turd compared to me.

143It's high time, it seems to me, that we were at dinner.

169 All princes he passith, he wenith, of powsté. *surpasses|thinks|power*

   He wenith to be the wurthiest of all this wer[l]de wide;

   Kinge ovyr all kingys that page wenith to be.

   He sent into Bedlem to seke on every side *everywhere*

   Crist for to qwelle, if they might him se. *kill*

174 But of his wikkyd wil, lurdeyn, yitt he lyede! *lout|lied*

   Goddys sone doth live; ther is no Lord but he; *God's son*

   Over all lordys he is kinge.

   I am Deth, Goddys masangere.

   Allmighty God hath sent me here

   Yon lordeyn to sle, withowtyn dwere, *i.e., never fear*

180 For his wikkyd werkinge.

   I am sent fro God; Deth is my name.

   All thinge that is on grownd I welde at my wille: *wield*

   Both man and beste and birdys wilde and tame.

   Whan that I come them to, with deth I do them kille:

   Erbe, gres, and tres stronge, [I] take hem all in same— *grass|together*

   Ya, the grete mighty okys with my dent I spille. *blow I kill*

   What man that I wrastele with, he shal right sone have *Whatever*

     schame:

   I geve him such a trepett, he shal evyrmore li[e] stille. *tripping up*

189 For Deth kan no sporte. *knows*

   Wher I smite, ther is no grace;

   For, aftere my strook, man hath no space *no time*

   To make amendys for his trespace

   But God him graunt comforte. *Unless*

   Ow! Se how prowdely yon kaitiff sitt at mete!

   Of Deth hath he no dowte; he wenith to leve evyrmore. *fear*

   To him wil I go and geve him such an hete *hit*

   That all the lechis of the londe his lif shul nevyr restore. *doctors*

   Agens my dredful dentys it vailith nevyr to plete! *blows|avails|plead*

   Or I him part fro, I shal him make ful pore: *Ere I part from him*

200 All the blood of his body I shal him owt-swete. *sweat out of him*

   For now I go to sle him with strokys sad and sore, *heavy*

   This tide, *time*

   Bothe him and his knightys all.

   I shal hem make to me but thrall; *no better than slaves*

   With my spere sle hem I shall,

   And so cast down his pride.

[169]He thinks he surpasses all princes in power.

[174]But in his wicked intent, the lout, what he said was nonetheless untrue.

[189]i.e., I don't just play around.

HERODES REX. Now, kende knightys, be mery and glad;	*gently-born*	
With all good diligens shewe now sum mirth.		
For, by gracious Mahound, more mirth never I had,		
Ne nevyr more joye was inne from time of my birth!		
211	For now my fo is ded and prendyd as a padde.	*pricked, pierced/toad*
212	Above me is no kinge, on grownd nere on gerth.	*nor in garden*
Merthis therfore make ye, and be right nothinge sadde!	*Be mirthful/not at all*	
Spare nother mete nor drinke, and spare for no dirthe	*dearth*	
Of wine nor of brede.		
For now am I a kinge alone;		
So wurthy as I may ther be none.		
Therfore, knightys, be mery echone,		
For now my fo is dede.		

220 1 MILES.   Whan the boys sprawlyd at my sperys hende,   *spear's end*
By Sathanas oure sire, it was a goodly sight!
A good game it was that boy for to shende   *harm*
That wolde a-bene oure kinge and put yow from your right.   *Who would have been*
    2 MILES.   Now trewly, my lorde the kinge, we had ben
        unhende   *discourteous*
    And nevyr non of us able for to be a knight,
    If that any of us to hem had ben a frende
227 And a-savyd any liff agen thy mekyl might,   *against/great*
228 From deth hem to flitt.   *(help to) flee*
    HERODES REX.   Amongys all that grett rowthte   *rout, crowd*
    He is ded, I have no dowte.   *He (Christ)*
    Therfore, menstrell, rownd abowte,
232 Blowe up a mery fitt!   *a strain of music*
        Hic, dum buccinant, Mors interficiat Herodem et duos milites   *Here, while they sound the trumpet,*
        subito, et diabolus recipiat eos.   *let Death kill Herod and the two soldiers suddenly, and let the devil receive them*

    DIABOLUS.   All oure, all oure! This catel is min[e].   *chattel, property*
    I shall hem bringe onto my celle.
    I shal hem teche pleys fin[e]   *teach them games*
    And shewe such mirthe as is in helle.
237   It were more bettyr amongys swin[e],

211*prendyd . . . padde:* i.e., food for worms (toads, like worms, were associated with the process of decomposition).

212*on grownd . . . gerth:* an alliterative phrase signifying "everywhere."

227–28And had saved the life of anyone opposed to your great might, helping them to flee from death.

232s.d.: The devil presumably emerges from hell-mouth at this point.

237–38It would be far better (for them) to dwell among swine, who stink constantly (than to dwell in hell).

238   That evyrmore stinkyn, therby to dwelle!
For in oure logge is so gret peyn   *pain*
That non erthely tonge can telle.   *can describe (it)*
[*He addresses his victims.*]
With yow I go my way;
I shal yow bere forth with me
And shewe yow sportys of oure gle.
Of oure mirthis now shal ye se,
And evyr singe "welawey!"
[*The devil takes their souls to hell.*]

MORS.   Of Kinge Herowde, all men beware
That hath rejoicyd in pompe and pride.
For all his boste of blisse, ful bare
He li[e]th now ded, here on his side.   *i.e., prostrate*
250   For, whan I come, I cannot spare;
Fro me no whyht may him hide.   *wight, person*
Now is he ded and cast in care,
In helle-pitt evyr to abide;
His lordchep is all lorn.   *lost*
Now is he as pore as I:
Wormys mete is his body;
His sowle in helle ful peynfully
Of develis is al to-torn.   *By/torn to pieces*

All men dwelling upon the grownde
260   Beware of me, by min[e] councel,
For feynt felachep in me is fownde—
I kan no curtesy, as I yow tel!   *know*
For, be a man nevyr so sownde
Of helth, in herte nevyr so wel,
I come sodeynly within a stownde;   *within a little while*
Me withstande may no castel.
My jurnay wil I spede.   *accomplish*
Of my coming no man is ware;
For, whan men make most mery fare,
270   Than sodeynly I cast hem in care
And sle them evyn in dede.

Thow I be nakyd and pore of array,
And wurmys knawe me al abowte,
Yit loke ye drede me, nyth and day!   *see to it that/night*
For whan Deth comith ye stande in dowte.   *fear*
Evyn like to me, as I yow say,
Shull all ye be, here in this rowte.   *crowd*
Whan I yow chalange at my day,

I shal yow make right lowe to lowte   *bow*
280 And nakyd for to be.
     Amongys wormys, as I yow telle,
     Undyr the erth shul ye dwelle—
     And they shul etyn both flesch and felle,   *skin*
     As they have don me. [*Exit Death.*]

THE WOMAN TAKEN IN ADULTERY
FROM N TOWN

Before going on to consider two plays from the period of Christ's ministry, we need to say a word about Christ's childhood and early manhood. The English cycles do not devote much space to the events of Christ's early life. Among the few events generally portrayed in the cycles are Christ's confrontation with the doctors in the Temple, his baptism by John the Baptist, and his temptation in the wilderness. The circumcision, omitted for obvious reasons from the cycles, is usually replaced by the episode of Mary's purification. As in much of the Christmas story, these episodes feature prophetic statements linking the Old Testament to the New. John the Baptist, for example, is commonly regarded as the last of the prophets. The temptation of Christ fulfills the prophecy that Adam's sin of yielding to the devil will be righted by Christ's resisting him. And at her purification, Mary encounters the aged prophet Simeon who has asked to live so long only that he may behold the Messiah (Luke 2:29–32). Another frequent motif in these plays is the contest of guile between Christ and the devil, in which Christ conceals from his adversary his divine identity so that the devil will not know how to plan his countermeasures. Christ not only resists the devil's blandishments in the wilderness but outwits him by refusing to reveal who he is. Similarly, the Virgin Birth is often interpreted in the cycles as a device to dupe Satan by having it appear that Christ is the son of a man and woman.

These motifs are illustrated in a remarkable play from the period of Christ's ministry, the Woman Taken in Adultery. All the cycles except Wakefield provide versions of this story; of these, the N Town version is the most dramatic. Often justly praised for its comic realism, this play also serves an important thematic function in the cycle as a whole. The attempt of the scribes and pharisees to entrap Christ recalls the hostile intention of the doctors in the Temple and Satan in the wilderness. Christ, offered a seemingly insoluble choice between justice and mercy, cleverly turns the question back on the scribes and pharisees by pointing out their unworthiness to judge. At the same time, the story also emphasizes the fulfillment of Old Testament narrative. The adulterous woman recalls Eve as fallen woman, and yet by her dignity in the face of oppression she also reminds us of the Virgin Mary bravely facing her detractors. A career of sinful worldliness ends happily in contrition and forgiveness. The scribes and pharisees, on the other hand, anticipate those figures of the Last Judgment who will be everlastingly condemned by a course of perfect justice.

The theme of a conflict between mercy and justice is implicit in the biblical version of this episode, John 8:1–11. The playwright's eye for vivid detail, however, adds much that is new. Deftly he satirizes the scribes and pharisees for their hypocritical self-righteousness. Although he does not condone sexual promiscuity, he indicates plainly that the scribes and pharisees are as guilty of lust as the frightened woman they are harassing. Her real crime in their eyes is not her licentiousness as such but her public reputation for loose conduct. The illusion of propriety matters more than the sincere practice of virtue. No less ugly is the remorseless glee with which the scribes and elders pursue their "game" or "sport" of entrapping Christ, until they themselves are suitably caught in a trap of their own devising. Perhaps the most electrifying scene of the play is the actual raid on the house of prostitution, complete with shouted insults, the breaking down of a door, and the escape of a defiant customer holding up his trousers with one hand. Medieval audiences would presumably recognize the scene as taken from English town life, and yet would also perceive the universality of the play's lesson about Christian charity.

The stage appears to require the prostitute's house or simply a doorway to it, and an open space. Jesus' writing on the ground might seem more appropriate in the platea of an arena theater than on a scaffold or pageant wagon.

The Woman Taken in Adultery
From N Town

Hic, de muliere in adulterio deprehensa.	*Here, of the woman taken in adultery*

[*Jesus preaches to the audience.*]

1	JHESUS. *Nolo mortem peccatoris.*	*I do not wish the sinner's death*
	Man, for thy sinne take repentaunce:	
	If thou amende that is amis,	*that which*
	Than hevyn shal be thin[e] heritaunce.	*Then*
5	Thow thou have don agens God grevauns,	*Though/against*
6	Yett mercy to haske loke thou be bolde.	*ask*
7	His mercy doth passe in trewe balauns	*surpass*
8	All cruel jugement by many folde.	*many times over*
	Thow that your sinnys be nevyr so grett,	
	For hem be sad and aske mercy.	*them*
	Sone of my Fadyr grace ye may gett	*Soon from*
	With the leste teer wepinge owte of your ey.	*least*
	My Fadyr me sent the[e], man, to bye;	*to buy, redeem you*
	All thy raunsom mysylfe must pay;	
	For love of the[e] mysylfe wil die.	
	Iff thou aske mercy, I sey nevyr nay.	
	Into the erth from hevyn above,	*Unto*
	Thy sorwe to sese and joy to restore,	*cease, end*
	Man, I cam down all for thy love.	
20	Love me ageyn—I aske no more.	*in return*

[1]Cf. Ezekiel 33:11.

5-8Though you have done grievous wrong against God, yet see to it that you be bold to ask mercy. Weighed in the scales of heavenly truth, his mercy surpasses all harsh judgment many times over.

Thow thou mishappe and sinne ful sore,   *come to grief*
Yit turne agen and mercy crave.
It is thy fawte and thou be lore;   *if/lost, damned*
Haske thou mercy, and thou shalt have.

Uppon thy neybore be not vengabyl,   *vengeful*
Ageyn the lawe if he offende.   *Against*
Like as he is thou art unstabyl.   *You're weak like him*
Thin[e] owyn frelté evyr thou attende!   *pay attention to*
29 Evermore thy neybore helpe to amende,
30 Evyn as thou woldist he shulde the[e].
Ageyn him wrath if thou accende,   *Against/kindle*
The same in happ will falle on the[e].   *perchance*

Eche man to othyr be merciable,
And mercy he shal have at nede.
35 What man of mercy is not tretable,   *Whatever/tractable*
Whan he askith mercy he shal not spede.   *prosper*
Mercy to graunt I com indede:
Whoso aske mercy, he shal have grace.
Lett no man dowte for his misdede,   *fear*
40 But evyr aske mercy whil he hath space.   *time*

  [*In a separate location, three Jews come forward to complain of*
  Jesus' teachings.]
SCRIBA. Alas, alas, oure lawe is lorn!   *lost, overthrown*
A fals ipocrite, Jhesu by name,
That of a sheppherdis dowtyr was born,   *daughter (i.e., Mary)*
Wil breke oure lawe and make it lame.
He wil us werke right mekyl shame,   *much*
His fals purpos if he upholde!
All oure lawys he doth defame;
That stinkinge beggere is woundyr bolde.   *wondrously*

 PHARISEUS. Sere scribe, in feyth, that ipocrite *Sir*
50 Wil turne this londe al to his lore.   *teaching*
Therfore, I councell him to indite   *that we accuse him*
And chastise him right wel therfore.   *for it*
SCRIBA. On him beleve many a score.   *Many people believe in him*
In his prechinge he is so gay,   *joyful*
Ech man him folwith ever more and more;
Agens that he seyth, no man seyth nay.   *Against what he says*

29–30(A restatement of the "Golden Rule." See Matthew 7:12.)

35Whatever person does not act mercifully (to others).

PHARISEUS.   A fals qwarel if we cowde feyne,   *accusation|could feign*
    That ipocrite to puttyn in blame,
    All his prechinge shulde sone disteyne,   *be sullied*
60   And than his wurchepp shuld turne to shame.   *honor*
    With sum falshede to spillyn his name,   *destroy*
    Lett us assay his lore to spille.   *to undo his teaching*
    The pepyl with him iff we cowde grame,   *enrage*
    Than shulde we sone have al oure will.   *soon*

ACCUSATOR.   Herke, sere pharisew and sere scribe: *Prosecutor*
    A right good sporte I kan yow telle.
67   I undyrtake that a right good bribe
68   We all shul have to kepe councell.   *to keep a secret*
    A faire yonge qwene hereby doth dwelle,   *whore*
    Both fresch and gay upon to loke,   *handsome|mingle, dally*
    And a tall man with her doth melle.   *her chamber|straight*
    The wey into hir chawmere right evyn he toke.

    Lett us thre now go streyte thedyr.
    The wey ful evyn I shall yow lede,   *straight there*
    And we shul take them both togedyr
    Whill that they do that sinful dede.
SCRIBA.   Art thou sekyr that we shal spede?   *sure|succeed*
    Shall we him finde whan we cum there?
ACCUSATOR.   By my trowth, I have no drede   *doubt*
80   The hare fro the forme we shal arere.   *hare's nest|raise*

PHARISEUS.   We shal have game, and this be trewe!   *good sport|if*
    Lete us thre werke by on[e] assent: *act in unison*
    We wil her bringe evyn beforn Jhesu
    And of her liff the truth present,
    How in advowtrye hir liff is lent.   *adultery|spent*
    Than, him beforn whan she is browth,   *Then in his presence|brought*
    We shul him aske the trew jugement
    What lawfull deth to her is wrouth.   *wrought, fashioned*

    Of grace and mercy hevyr he doth preche,   *ever*
90   And that no man shulde be vengeable.
    Ageyn the woman if he sey wrech,   *Against|pronounce punishment*
    Than of his prechinge he is unstable;   *inconsistent*
    And if we finde him variable
    Of his prechinge that he hath tawth,   *In|taught*

67–68 I warrant that we'll be well bribed to keep a secret (i.e., the prostitute whom we're going to raid will try to bribe us not to expose her shame).

Than have we cawse bothe juste and able
96 For a fals man that he be cawth.   *caught, arrested*

SCRIBA.   Now by grete God, ye sey ful well!
If we him findyn in variaunce,
We have good reson, as ye do tell,
Him for to bringe to foule mischauns.
If he holde stille his daliauns   *persist in his idle talk*
And preche of mercy, hir for to save,
Than have we mater of gret substauns   *substantial cause*
Him for to kille and putt in grave.

Grett reson why I shal yow telle:
For Moyses doth bidde, in oure lawe,
That every advowterere we shuld qwelle,   *kill*
And yitt with stonys they shulde be slawe.   *furthermore/slain*
109 Ageyn Moyses if that he drawe,   *Against/take sides*
110 That sinful woman with grace to helpe,
He shal nevyr skape out of oure awe,   *power*
But he shal die like a dogge whelpe.

ACCUSATOR.   Ye tary ovyrlonge, serys, I sey yow:
They wil sone parte, as that I gesse.   *soon*
Therfore, if ye wil have your pray now,   *prey*
Lete us go take them in here whantownnesse.   *their*
PHARISEUS.   Goo thou beforn, the wey to dresse;   *prepare*
We shal the[e] folwe within short while.   *follow*
Iff that we may that quene distresse,
120 I hope we shal Jhesu beg[u]ile.
     [*They proceed to the woman's chamber, the accusor leading the
     way.*]

SCRIBA.   Breke up the dore and go we inne!
Sett to the shuldyr with all thy might.   *Put your shoulder to it*
We shal hem take evyn in here sinne;   *them/their*
Here owyn trespas shal them indite.   *Their*
     [*They break down the door.*] *Hic juvenis quidam extra currit,*   *Here a young man runs out in his*
     in deploydo, calligis non ligatis et braccas in manu tenens; et *doublet, his boots untied and holding*
     dicit accusator: *up his breeches with his hand; and*
                                                                        the accusor says
ACCUSATOR.   Stow that harlot, sum erthely wight,   *Stop/someone*
That in advowtrye here is fownde!   *adultery*
JUVENIS.   Yiff any man stow me this nyth   *night*
I shal him geve a dedly wownde!

⁹⁶i.e., To seize him for a false man.

¹⁰⁹⁻¹⁰If he contradicts Moses to help that sinful woman with mercy.

I[f] any man my wey doth stoppe,
130 Or we departe, ded shal he be!   *Ere we separate*
I shal this daggare putt in his croppe;   *gizzard, throat*
I shal him kille or he shal me.   *ere*
  PHARISEUS.   Grett Goddys curse mut go with the[e]!   *May great God's curse*
With suche a shrewe will I not melle.   *wretch/meddle*
  JUVENIS.   That same blissinge I giff yow thre,
And qwheth yow alle to the devil of helle!   *bequeath*

     [*To the audience, aside.*]
In feyth, I was so sore affraid
Of yone thre shrewys, the sothe to say,   *rascals*
My breche be nott yett well up-teyd,   *up-tied*
140 I had such hast to renne away.
They shal nevyr cacche me in such a fray!   *fight*
I am full glad that I am gon.
Adewe, adewe, a twenty devil way!   *i.e., in the devil's name*
And Goddys curse have ye everychon. [*Exit.*]

  SCRIBA.   Come forth, thou stotte, com forth, thou scowte!   *whore/wanton*
Com forth, thou bysmare and brothel bolde!   *shameless woman*
Com forth, thou [w]hore and stinkinge bych-clowte!   *dog-rag*
How longe hast thou such harlotry holde?   *practiced*
  PHARISEUS.   Com forth, thou quene, com forth, thou scolde!   *whore*
Com forth, thou sloveyn, com forth, thou slutte!
We shal the[e] teche, with carys colde,   *with deadly torments*
152 A lityl bettyr to kepe thy kutte.   *to behave modestly*
    [*The woman is dragged forth.*]

  MULIER.   A, mercy, mercy, serys, I yow pray!
For Goddys love have mercy on me!
155 Of my mislevinge, me not bewray.   *do not shame me*
Have mercy on me, for charité!
  ACCUSATOR.   Aske us no mercy; it shal not be.
We shul so ordeyn for thy lott
That thou shalt die for thin[e] advowtrye.
Therfore, com forth, thou stinkinge stott!

  MULIER.   Serys, my wurchepp if ye wil save,   *reputation, honor*
162 And helpe I have non opyn shame,

---

[152]*to . . . kutte:* to be modest or reserved, coy. (The Jews taunt her for her indiscretion in being observed, as much as for her immorality.)

[155]Do not shame me publicly for my sinful life.

[162]And arrange it so that I suffer no public shame.

Bothe gold and silvyr ye shul have,
So that in clennes ye kepe my name.   *If unspotted you will keep*
165 SCRIBA.   Mede for to take, we were to blame   *Reward, bribe*
To save suche stottys! It shal not be.
We shal bringe the[e] to suche a game
That all advowtererys shul lern by the[e].

MULIER.   Stondinge ye wil not graunt me grace,   *(The case) so standing that*
170 But for my sinne that I shal die,
I pray yow kille me here in this place
And lete not the pepyl upon me crye.
If I be sclaundryd opynly,
To all my frendys it shul be shame.
I pray yow, kille me previly;   *secretly*
Lete not the pepyl know my defame.   *infamy*

PHARISEUS.   Fi[e] on the[e], scowte, the devil the[e] qwelle!   *kill*
178 Ageyn the lawe shul we the[e] kill?   *Against*
179 First shal hange the[e] the devil of helle
180 Or we such folyes shulde fulfill!   *Ere*
Thow it like the[e] nevyr so ill,   *Though it displease you*
182 Beforn the prophete thou shalt have lawe;
Like as Moyses doth charge us till,   *As Moses commands us*
With grett stonys thou shalt be slawe.   *slain*

ACCUSATOR.   Com forth apase, thou stinkinge scowte!   *apace, quickly*
Before the prophete thou were this day,   *i.e., you will go*
Or I shal geve the[e] such a clowte   *blow*
That thou shalt fall down evyn in the way.   *road*
SCRIBA.   Now, by grett God, and I the[e] pay,   *if I pay you (a blow)*
190 Such a buffett I shal the[e] take   *give*
That all the teth, I dare wel say,
Withinne thin[e] heed for who shul shake.   *for woe*
    [*They drag her before Jesus.*]

PHARISEUS.   Herke, sere prophete, we all yow pray
To giff trewe dom and just sentence   *doom, judgment*
Upon this woman, which this same day
In sinfull advowtery hath don offense.
    Hic Jhesus, dum isti accusant mulierem, continue debet digito   Here Jesus, while they accuse the
    suo scribere in terra.   woman, must continually write
    on the ground with his finger

165We would be to blame to take such a bribe.

178-80Shall we kill you secretly, contrary to Moses' law (that an adulteress be publicly stoned
to death)? May the devil of hell hang you before we commit such folly!

182You will be brought to trial before the prophet (Christ).

ACCUSATOR.   Se, we have brought her to your presens,
 Becawse ye ben a wise prophete,
 That ye shal telle by consiens   *So that*
200 What deth to hir ye thinke most mete.   *meet, fitting*

   [*The Scribe brandishes his texts.*]
SCRIBA.   In Moyses lawe, right thus, we finde
 That such fals lovers shul be slain:
 Streyte to a stake we shul hem binde   *Straightway*
 And with grett stonys brest out ther brain.   *burst, knock*
 Of your conciens, telle us the plain: *the plain case, plainly*
 With this woman what shal be wrought?   *done*
 Shall we lete her go qwite again,   *free*
 Or to hir deth shal she be brought?
  Jhesus nihil respondit, sed semper scribit in terra. *Jesus answers nothing, but*
               still writes on the ground

MULIER.   Now, holy prophete, be merciable!
210 Upon me, wrecch, take no vengeaunce.
 For my sinnys abhominable
 In hert I have grett repentaunce.
 I am wel wurthy to have mischaunce,
 Both bodily deth and wer[l]dly shame;
 But, gracious prophete, of socurraunce   *succour*
 This time pray yow, for Goddys name!   *At this time I pray*

PHARISEUS.   Ageyn the lawe thou dedist offens;   *Against*
 Therfore of grace speke thou no more.
 As Moyses gevith in lawe sentens,
 Thou shalt be stonyd to deth therfore.
ACCUSATOR.   Ha don, sere prophete, telle us youre lore. *Have done, finish up*
 Shul we this woman with stonys kill,
223 Or to hir hous hir home restore?
 In this mater tell us your will.

SCRIBA.   In a colde stodye me thinkith ye sitt.
 Good sere, awake! Telle us your thought.
 Shal she be stonyd? Telle us your witt,   *opinion*
 Or in what rewle shal sche be brought?
JHESUS   [*lifting himself up*]. Loke which of yow that nevyr
    sinne wrought,
230 But is of liff clennere than she,
 Cast at her stonys and spare her nowght—
 Clene out of sinne if that ye be.

223Or restore her home to her house.

Hic Jhesus, iterum se inclinans, scribet in terra; et omnes
accusatores, quasi confusi, separatim in tribus locis se disiungent.

Here Jesus, again stooping down, will write on the ground; and all the accusors, as though perplexed, will move apart from each other to three locations

PHARISEUS   [*aside*]. Alas, alas, I am ashamyd;
 I am aferde that I shal deye!
 All min[e] sinnys, evyn propyrly namyd,
 Yon prophyte dede write befor min[e] eye.   *did*
 Iff that my felawys that dude aspye,
 They will telle it bothe fer and wide.
 My sinfull levinge if they out-crye
240 I wot nevyr wher min[e] heed to hide.

ACCUSATOR   [*aside*]. Alas, for sorwe min[e] herte doth blede!
 All my sinnys yon man dude write.
 If that my felawys to them toke hede,
 I kan not me from deth acquite.
 I wolde I wore hid sumwhere out of sight   *were*
 That men shuld me nowhere se ne knowe.   *nor*
 Iff I be take, I am afflight   *taken/afraid*
 In mekyl shame I shal be throwe.   *much*

SCRIBA   [*aside*]. Alas the time that this betid!   *happened*
 Right bittyr care doth me enbrace:
 All my sinnys be now unhid.
 Yon man befor me hem all doth trace.
 If I were onys out of this place,   *once*
254 To suffyr deth gret and vengeaunsable   *vengeful*
255 I wil nevyr come befor his face—
 Thow I shuld die in a stable.   *Though*
  [*One by one, they skulk away.*]

MULIER. Thow I be wurthy for my trespas
 To suffyr deth abhominable,
 Yitt, holy prophete, of your hig[h] grace,
260 In your jugement be merciable.
 I wil nevyrmore be so unstable.
 O, holy prophete, graunt me mercy!
 Of min[e] sinnys unresonable   *For*
 With all min[e] hert I am sory.

JHESUS. Where be thy fomen that dude the[e] accuse? *did*
 Why have they lefte us t[w]o alone?
MULIER. Bicawse they cowde nat hemself excuse,
 With shame they fled hens, everychone.

254–55I would rather suffer a terrible and vengeful death than appear before him (Jesus).

But, gracious prophete, list to my mone!
270 Of my sorwe take compassion:
Now all min[e] enmies hens be gone,
Sey me sum wurde of consolacion!

JHESUS.   For tho sinnys that thou hast wrought   *those*
Hath any man condempnyd the[e]?
MULIER.   Nay, forsoth, that hath ther nought;   *no one has done that*
But in your grace I putt me.
JHESUS.   For me thou shalt nat condempnyd be.   *On my part*
Go hom ageyn, and walk at large.   *liberty*
Loke that thou leve in honesté   *live*
280 And wil no more to sinne, I the[e] charge.   *desire*

MULIER.   I thanke yow hig[h]ly, holy prophete,
Of this grett grace ye have me graunt!   *granted*
All my lewde liff I shal doun lete   *forsake*
And fonde to be Goddys trewe servaunt. [*Exit.*]   *try*
285 JHESUS [*to the audience*].   What man of sinne be repentaunt,   *Whatever*
Of God if he wil mercy crave,
God of mercy is so habundawnt
That, what man haske it, he shal it have.   *whatever/ask*

Whan man is contrite and hath wonne grace,
God wele not kepe olde wreth in minde;   *will/wrath*
291 But, bettyr love to hem he has,
292 Very contrite whan he them finde.
Now, God that died for all mankende
Save all these pepyl, both night and day!
And of oure sinnys he us unbinde,   *may he deliver us*
Hig[h]e Lorde of hevyn, that best may.   *who*
Amen.

285 *Jhesus:* In the MS the word "Jhesus" has been replaced by "Doctor" in a later hand, presumably to indicate that in a revised version this pageant was concluded by a choric clerical figure.

291–92But he loves all the better those sinners whom he finds very contrite.

THE RAISING OF LAZARUS
FROM WAKEFIELD

The Raising of Lazarus figures in all the cycles as the greatest miracle of Christ's ministry and a central antetype of the Resurrection. This Wakefield account begins in a straightforward manner, conservatively following the ultimate biblical source in John 11:1–46. In characterization and use of setting, this version does not differ substantially from the twelfth-century Latin church play by Hilarius (Part II, above). The added ending is, however, new. It is a sermon on death, based on medieval expansions of the Lazarus story in which Lazarus is able to recall the events of his sojourn in the afterlife. Lazarus stands before us like the figure of Death itself, consumed by worms and wrapped in a shroud, his very eyes having been eaten out of his head. Images of fleshly decay and of hellish torment artfully blend into a fearfully compelling vision of death. Although the biblical account mentions the possibility that Lazarus may have stunk after four days in the ground (John 11:39), this stark insistence on the terrors of death owes much to medieval lyrics and other meditative works on dying. As in the later morality play of *Everyman*, the dramatist stresses the uncertainty of worldly possession and the fickleness of friends or kinsmen. Death strikes even the mightiest and comes unannounced. Man's only recourse is amendment of life before it is too late. With gruesome illustration, this vivid sermon compels us to reflect on the misery to which all flesh shall ultimately come.

Staging requires a tomb for Lazarus and a location symbolizing the home of Mary and Martha in Bethany, to which Jesus and the disciples approach as from another country. Lazarus emerges from the tomb much as the Elect will later emerge from hell-mouth when freed by Christ.

This pageant appears at the end of the Towneley manuscript, following The Last Judgment and preceding an incomplete Hanging of Judas. It is here placed in its normal order before the Passion sequence. Four stanzas (ll. 135–73) are cast in a verse form resembling that of the Wakefield Master.

The Raising of Lazarus
From Wakefield

Incipit Lazarus.

[*Jesus with his disciples.*]

JHESUS.   Commes now, brethere, and go with me:
    We will pas furth untill Judé.
    To Betany will we weynde
    To viset Lazare, that is oure freynde.
    Gladly I wold we with him speke;

Come/brethren

to Judaea

Bethany

I tell you sothely, he is seke.

PETRUS.   I red not that ye thider go: *advise that you not*
The Jues halden you for tharc fo. *consider you*
I red ye com not in that stede, *place*
For, if ye do, then be ye dede.

JOHANNES.   Master, trist thou [not] on the Jue;
12   For, many day sen thou thaym knewe,
And last time that we were thore *there*
We wenyd till have bene ded therfor. *thought to have been dead*

THOMAS.   When we were last in that contré,
This othere day, both thou and we,
We wenyd that thou ther shuld have bene slayn.
Will thou now go thider agane?

20 JHESUS.   Herkyn, breder, and takys kepe: *pay attention*
Lazare oure freynde is fallyn on slepe.
The way till him now will we take, *to*
To stir that knight and gar him wake. *cause*

PETRUS.   Sir, me thinke it were the best
To let him slepe and take his rest,
25   And kepe that no man com him hend— *prevent/near*
For if he slepe, then mon he mend. *must*

JHESUS.   I say to you, withoutten faill:
No keping may till him availl, *guarding/to*
Ne slepe may stand him in no stede. *profit him*
30   I say you sekerly he is dede. *truly*
Therfor, I say you now at last
Leyfe this speche and go we fast. *Leave off*

THOMAS.   Sir, whatsoever ye bid us do
We assent us well therto.
I hope to God ye shall not finde
None of us shall lefe behinde; *stay*
For any parell that may befall, *Despite*
Weynde we with oure master all.

[*They go to Bethany, the home of the dead Lazarus and of his
sisters Martha and Mary Magdalene. Martha comes forward
to meet Jesus.*]

MARTHA.   Help me, Lorde, and gif me red! *advice*
40   Lazare my broder now is dede
That was to the[e] both lefe and dere; *beloved*
He had not died had thou bene here.

JHESUS.   Martha, Martha, thou may be fain! *glad*

¹²For, you have known them a long while (lit.: since many a day).

²⁵And prevent any man from coming near him.

Thy brothere shall rise and lif again.

MARTHA.   Lorde, I wote that he shall rise
And com before the good justice;
For, at the dredfull day of dome,   *doom*
48   There mon ye kepe him at his come   *must/coming*
To loke what dome ye will him gif: *To see what judgment*
Then mon he rise, then mon he lif.

JHESUS.   I warne you, both man and wife,
That I am rising, and I am life.   *i.e., I am the resurrection*
And whoso truly trowys in me,   *believes*
That I was ever and ay shall be,
Oone thing I shall him gif:
Though he be dede, yit shall he lif.
Say thou, woman, trowys thou this?

MARTHA.   Yee, forsothe, my Lorde of blis.
Ellys were I greatly to misprase,   *Else, otherwise/to blame*
60   For all is sothefast that thou says.   *true*

JHESUS.   Go tell thy sister Mawdlayn   *(Mary) Magdalene*
That I com, ye may be fayn.   *glad*

[*Martha goes to Mary Magdalene at their dwelling.*]

MARTHA.   Sister, lefe this sorowful bande: *leave/confinement, duty*
Oure Lorde commys here at hande,
And his apostyls with him also.

MARIA.   A, for Godys luf let me go! [*She goes to Jesus.*]
Blissid be he that sende me grace,
That I may se the[e] in this place.
Lorde, mekill sorow may men se   *much*
70   Of my sister here, and me.
We ar hevy as any lede   *lead*
For oure broder that thus is dede.
Had thou bene here, and on him sene,   *looked on him*
Dede forsothe had he not bene.

JHESUS.   Hider to you commen we ar
To make you comforth of youre care.
Bot loke no faintise ne no slawth   *faintness/sloth*
Bring you oute of stedfast trawthe;   *belief*
Then shall I hold you that I saide.   *fulfill to you what*
80   Lo, where have ye his body laide?

MARIA.   Lorde, if it be thy will,
I hope by this he savers ill;   *expect by now he stinks*
For it is now the ferth day gone
Sen he was laide under yonde stone.   *Since*

[*They lead Jesus to the sepulchre.*]

48There you must await his coming, or meet him at his coming.

JHESUS.   I told the[e] right now, ther thou stode,   *where*
    That thy trawth shuld ay be goode,
    And if thou may that fulfill   *i.e., if you believe truly*
    All bees donc right at thy will.   *shall be*
      Et lacrimatus est Jhesus, dicens: *And Jesus wept, saying*

[JESUS.]   Fader, I pray the[e] that thou rase
    Lazare that was thy hine,   *servant*
    And bring him oute of his misese   *misease, misery*
    And oute of hell pine.   *pain*
93   When I the[e] pray, thou says allwayse
94   My will is sich as thine.   *such as, the same as*
95   Therfor will we now eke his dayse;   *increase his days*
96   To me thou will incline.

Com furth, Lazare, and stande us by!
In erth shall thou no langere ly.
    [*To those standing by, as Lazarus rises.*]
Take and lawse him foote and hande,   *loose*
And from his throte take the bande,
And the sudary take him fro,   *napkin, shroud*
And all that gere, and let him go.

LAZARUS.   Lorde, that all thing maide of noght,
    Loving be to the[e]
That sich wonder here has wroght!
Gretter may none be.
When I was dede, to hell I soght;   *resorted*
And thou, thrugh thy pausté,   *power*
Rasid me up and thens me broght.
110   Behold, and ye may se!
    [*Lazarus delivers to the audience a sermon on death.*]

Ther is none so stif on stede,   *sturdy anywhere*
Ne none so prowde in prese,   *throng*
Ne none so dughty in his dede,   *doughty/deeds*
Ne none so dere on deese,   *worthy on dais, throne*
115   No king, no knight, no wight in wede   *no person in any garments*

93–96When I pray to you, you say always that my desire is such as you also desire. Therefore, together you and I, God and the Son, will now increase Lazarus' life (to show the people that) you will come to my assistance (see John 11:42).

115–23There is no knight, king, or anyone at all who has ever escaped Death (lit.: made himself cease from Death), nor has his flesh escaped, which he has been accustomed to feed—it will be a feast for worms. Your Death is a cook for worms (since it will feast them). Look at your mirror here—i.e., see in me what you will look like in death—and let me be your book or lesson: take me as an example of what will become of you. For Death will seize you in his clutches (?).

116   From Dede have maide him seese,
117   Ne flesh he was wonte to fede—
118   It shall be wormes mese.   *feast*

119   Youre Dede is wormes coke.   *Death/cook*
120   Youre mirroure here ye loke,
121   And let me be youre boke:
122   Youre sampill take by me.   *example*
123   Fro Dede you cleke in cloke—   *seize/clutches*
    Sich shall ye all be.   *Such*

125   Ilkon in sich aray, with Dede thay shall be dight   *Each one/Death/arrayed*
    And closid colde in clay, wheder he be king or knight.
    For all his garmentes gay that semely were in sight,   *Despite*
128   His flesh shall frete away, with many a wofull wight.
    Then wofully sich wightys   *creatures (worms)*
    Shall gnawe thise gay knightys:
    Thare lunges and thare lightys,   *lights, lungs*
    Thare harte shall frete in sonder.
    Thise masters most of mightys   *These almighty lords*
    Thus shall thay be broght under.   *subdued*

    Under the erthe ye shall thus carefully then cowche.   *lie woebegone*
136   The royfe of youre hall youre nakyd nose shall towche.   *roof*
    Nawther great ne small to you will knele ne crowche.   *Neither*
138   A shete shall be youre pall; sich todys shall be youre
       nowche.   *brooch*
    Todys shall you dere,   *Toads will harm you*
    Feyndys will you fere.   *Fiends/frighten*
    Youre flesh that fare was here   *fair*
    Thus rufully shall rote;   *rot*
    Instede of fare colore,
    Sich bandys shall binde youre throte.   *Such shrouds (as mine)*

145   Youre rud that was so red, youre lyre the lilly like   *complexion*
    Then shall be wan as led, and stinke as dog in dike.   *leaden-hued/ditch*
    Wormes shall in you brede as bees dos in the bike,   *breed/hive*

[125]Each splendidly-dressed person will be arrayed in the garb of Death.

[128]His flesh shall be gnawed away by many a dismal creature (worms).

[136]The roof of your hall (the shallow grave, in contrast to the lofty hall of a nobleman) will be so low that it will touch your bare nose.

[138]A winding-sheet will be your only vestment; such toads (as mine) will be your jewelry.

[145]Your ruddy and fair complexion. (Parts of the complexion, such as the cheeks, were supposed to be ruddy, while the whole effect should be fair, white, and pure.)

148	And ees outt of youre hede thusgate shall paddokys pike.	*eyes/toads*
	To pike you ar preste	*To pick (at) you are ready*
	Many uncomly beest;	
	Thus thay shall make a feste	
	Of youre flesh and of youre blode.	
153	For you then sorows leste	*least*
154	The moste has of youre goode.	

	Youre goodys ye shall forsake if ye be never so lothe,	*though*
	And nothing with you take bot sich a winding clothe.	*such (as mine)*
	Youre wife sorow shall slake, youre childer also both	*wife's/slacken*
	Unnes youre mynning make, if ye be never so wrothe.	*Scarcely remember you*
159	Thay myn you with nothing	*remember*
160	That may be youre helping,	
	Nawthere in mes-singing	*Neither/mass-singing*
	Ne yit with almus dede.	*alms deed*
	Therfor in youre leving	*living, life*
	Be wise and take good hede.	

	Take hede for you to dele whils ye ar on life:	*to provide for yourself*
	Trust never freyndys frele, nawthere of childe then wife,	*frail/nor*
167	For sectures ar not lele, then for youre good will strife.	*executors/loyal*
168	To b[u]y youre saules hele, there may no man thaym	*health*
	shrife.	
	To shrife no man thaym may	
	After youre ending day,	
	Youre saull for to glad.	*gladden*
172	Youre sectures will swere nay	
173	And say ye aght more then ye had.	*owed*

	Amende the[e], man, whils thou may.	
	Let never no mirthe fordo thy minde.	*ruin*
	Thinke thou on the dredefull day	
	When God shall deme all mankinde.	*judge*
	Thinke thou farys as dothe the winde.	*that you fare*
	This warlde is wast, and will away;	*waste, fickle*

[148]And toads will pick your eyes out of your head thus (as in my case).

[153-54]Those persons then sorrow least for you who will have most profit from your worldly goods (i.e., your relatives and heirs).

[159-60]They (your relatives) do nothing in remembrance of you that might help your soul.

[167-68]For executors are not loyal, nor will they strive for your good. No one can impose any penance on them for the sake of your soul's health (i.e., they'll not go to any trouble).

[172-73]Your executors will disclaim any obligation (to pay for masses, etc.), and will say your debts exceeded your estate.

180   Man, have this in thy minde,
      And amende the[e] whils that thou may.

      Amende the[e], man, whils thou art here,
      Agane thou go anothere gate.   *Lest you go another way (to hell)*
      When thou art dede and laide on bere,   *bier*
      Wit thou well, thou bees to[o] late;   *Know/will be*
      For, if all the goode that ever thou gate   *goods/got*
      Were delt for the[e] after thy day,   *given (in payment)*
      In heven it wolde not mende thy state.
      Forthy, amende the[e] whils thou may.   *Therefore*

190   If thou be right ryall in rente   *Even if/royal/income*
191   As is the stede standing in stall,   *steed*
      In thy harte knowe and thinke
      That thay ar Goddys goodys all.   *they (your belongings)*
      He might have maide the[e] poore and small
      As he that beggys fro day to day.   *Like one who*
      Wit thou well, acountys gif thou shall;   *you must give account*
      Therfor, amende the[e] whils thou may.

      And if I might with you dwell
      To tell you all my time,   *i.e., my time in hell*
200   Full mekill couthe I tell   *much could*
      That I have harde and sene—   *heard*
      Of many a great mervell
      Sich as ye wolde not wene,   *believe*
      In the paines of hell
      Thereas I have bene.

      Bene I have in wo;
      Therfor, kepe you therfro.
      Whilst ye lif, do so
      If ye will dwell with Him
210   That can gar you thus go,   *make*
      And hele you lith and lim.   *joint*

      He is a Lorde of grace,
      Umthinke you in this case;   *Bethink*
      And pray him, full of might,
      He kepe you in this place   *(That) he protect*
      And have you in his sight.
      Amen.
            Explicit Lazarus.

190-91Even if you are as richly proud as a high-mettled horse standing in his stall.

210i.e., (With God) who has given you life and motion.

THE PASSION PLAY
FROM N TOWN

All the English cycles give major prominence to the story of Christ's Passion and Resurrection. As the drama of man's salvation reaches its climax, the action grows more intense and the playing area becomes more crowded with characters. From the moment of Christ's entry into Jerusalem, he is caught up in an incessant tumult of events: the conspiracy of the Jews with Judas, the Last Supper, Christ's agony on the night before he is taken, the betrayal and arrest, the trial before the chief priests Caiaphas and Annas (when Christ is subjected to buffeting), Judas' suicide, the first trial before Pilate, the trial before Herod, the resumption of the trial before Pilate (when Christ is subjected to scourging), the torments on the road to Calvary, and so on. Unremittingly Christ must undergo indignities, torturings, and insults. He alone says little to his detractors. The emphasis on Christ's suffering is, as we have seen, a distinctive trait of late medieval or Gothic art, in marked contrast to the more stylized and liturgical renditions of the Passion during the twelfth-century Romanesque renaissance.

Among the various English versions of the Passion, the N Town sequence most stirringly captures the spirit of noisy confusion and bustle during the betrayal and arrest. This N Town Passion sequence, divided into two halves for performance on separate years, is clearly intended for an arena theater with scaffolds on the periphery of a central acting "place." The unusually full stage directions repeatedly demand such an arrangement and specify the movement of the actors from one area to another—often with two actions proceeding simultaneously. In Passion Play I, for instance, the Jewish Council House or "oratory,"

located in the middle of the "place," is equipped with curtains whereby the Jews can be concealed during Christ's entry into Jerusalem and the Last Supper. The house of Simon the Leper (presumably a scaffold), where Jesus celebrates the Last Supper, can similarly be curtained off from view. Accordingly, the playwright is able to display alternating scenes of the Jews' conspiracy and of the Last Supper, while Judas shuttles back and forth between the two. The central "place" is an ideal location for meetings and for noisy, bustling crowd scenes such as the arrest of Jesus at Gethsemane. Other scenes evidently require a scaffold on the periphery: the Mount of Olives, where Jesus prays while the disciples wait for him in the nearby "park" of Gethsemane; heaven, traditionally in the east, whence an angel descends to Jesus; hell, traditionally in the north; separate scaffolds for Caiaphas and Annas, chief priests; and a station for the Virgin Mary.

Passion Play II, only part of which is here presented (down through Christ's appearance before Herod), calls similarly for heaven, hell, and the scaffolds of Annas and Caiaphas. In addition, scaffolds must be provided for Pilate and his wife and for Herod. (This Herod is not the King of Judaea who sought to destroy the infant Christ, but a governor under the Romans. He rants much like his namesake.) The Moot Hall, where Pilate first interrogates Jesus, may possibly be the Council House also used in this play. Location of the actual Crucifixion, Burial, and Resurrection is not specified in the stage directions; but a central location in the "place" would provide a vivid sense of excitement, mob confusion, and involvement of the spectators, as in the arrest of Christ. Perhaps the sepulchre for Christ's Burial is the centrally-located "oratory" used previously as a Moot Hall and Council House. Again, in this play more than one action occurs simultaneously: Jesus is scourged while Peter denies him, and (at l. 465) Jesus is led around the arena toward his second rendezvous with Pilate during the considerable amount of time that the devil visits Pilate's wife. Judas hangs himself during a similar procession.

Another notable feature of production is the use of meditative lament, or soliloquy, to offset scenes of tumultuous action. The Last Supper provides a reflective occasion for Christ's sermon on the Eucharist. Later, when Christ has been captured and is being dragged around the arena toward the chief priests, our attention is shifted to the lonely figure of the Virgin Mary. Grief-stricken, she ponders the reasons for her tragedy and comes at length to a realization of the necessity for her son's death. The speech is quiet, reflective, concerned with spiritual understanding of the shattering events just witnessed—not unlike the arias of the great Baroque musical Passions by Bach and others. The same change of pace occurs in Peter's introspective soliloquy after his denial of Christ.

Staging in the round, with the continual presence of heaven and hell, lends a cosmic dimension to the Passion. The dominant themes are similarly cosmic. The devil, at his first entrance, describes the contest of guile that has developed between himself and Christ. Deceived by the Virgin Birth into thinking that Christ is fallibly human, and further confused by Christ's skillful evasions during the temptation in the wilderness, the devil now hopes to finish off his enemy by means of Judas' betrayal and the Jews' hostility. Too late, however, the devil learns that he has been led into a trap by his own machinations: Christ is truly the Son of God, and accordingly the Crucifixion will bring about

human salvation rather than Christ's downfall. Belatedly sensing his predicament, the devil desperately appears to Pilate's wife in a dream and threatens her husband with trouble unless the Crucifixion can be stopped. Nothing, however, can now prevent what the devil himself has paradoxically helped set in motion. This cosmic irony gives perspective to the entire Passion sequence. The Jews, like Satan, contribute to Christ's glory by their very attempts to destroy him. Christ is in control throughout; the Jews fall backward at his arrest, powerless to touch him until he patiently submits to the foreordained ordeal.

Another pervasive theme is that of pride. Satan first illustrates this deadliest of sins in his grotesquely vain wearing apparel. Thereafter, as John the Evangelist tells us (I, 266), Christ comes into the world to conquer pride, riding an ass into Jerusalem and washing his disciples' feet. Conversely, his worldly antagonists—the ranting Herod, the richly-dressed Annas and Caiaphas—share with Satan a fatal pride in their own strength.

The playwright's sources are often patristic. Although he is ultimately indebted to various Gospel accounts, he presents them as they had been interpreted and rearranged by medieval church tradition. The healing of the two blind men, an earlier episode in the Gospel accounts (Matthew 20, etc.), is made part of the entry into Jerusalem in order to illustrate Christ's miraculous power. The scene in which Mary Magdalene penitently anoints Christ's feet with ointment and is exorcised of seven devils (ll. 462–525) is made up of several biblical passages, none of which actually mentions Mary Magdalene by name. In one such passage, an unnamed woman anoints Christ's head in the house of Simon the Leper (Matthew 26:6–13); in another, Mary the sister of Lazarus anoints Christ's feet as he sups at Bethany (John 12:1–8); in still another, an unnamed sinful woman anoints Christ's feet and is forgiven her sins as Christ dines with Simon the Pharisee in Galilee (Luke 7:36–50). The Church Fathers conflated these various events and assigned them to Mary Madgalene, especially since Mark reports (16:9) that Christ had cast out seven devils from her. Patristic tradition also concluded that Mary's visit to Christ took place during the Last Supper at the house of Simon the Leper, as in this Passion play, although in fact the Gospels do not mention the presence of any woman during the Last Supper and do not name Simon's house as the location. Further influence of church tradition can be seen in Christ's lengthy sermonizing on the symbolic meaning of his sacrifice, and in the use of a chalice and sacred host to comfort Christ on the night before his arrest. The angel's visit to Christ on this occasion, though based in part on John 18, is connected by patristic tradition to the earlier visit to Mary at the moment of the Annunciation. Some episodes of this play are naturally close to their biblical original, such as the arrest of Christ, Judas' suicide (see Matthew 27), and the trial before Herod (see Luke 23). The dream of Pilate's wife, on the other hand, despite a slender authority in Matthew 27:19, is largely a medieval elaboration.

The accompanying staging diagrams are partly conjectural. They make use of stage directions in the N Town Passion sequence, but also borrow a few conventions from extant staging diagrams of medieval performances in the round. In the diagrams for both *The Castle of Perseverance* and the Cornish *Ordinalia*, for example, heaven is located in the east and hell in the north.

The Passion Play I
From N Town

[*Satan, gorgeously attired as a gallant, boasts to the audience.*]

DEMON.   I am your lord Lucifer, that out of helle cam,
Prince of this wer[l]d and gret duke of helle—
Wherefore my name is clepyd sere Satan—   *called sir*
Whech aperith among yow a matere to spelle.   *Who|preach*
I am norsshere of sinne to the confusion of man,   *nourisher*
To bring him to my dongeon, ther in fire to dwelle.
[W]hoso evyr serve me so, reward him I kan
That he shal sing "wellaway" ever in peynes felle.   *cruel*

Lo, thus bountevous a lord, than, now am I   *then*
10   To reward so sinners, as my kend is!   *nature*
Whoso wole folwe my lore and serve me daily,   *follow*
Of sorwe and peyne anow he shal nevyr mis.   *enough*
For, I began in hefne sinne for to sowe
Among all the angellys that weryn there so bryth.   *were|bright*
And therfore was I cast out into helle ful lowe,
Notwithstanding I was the fairest and berere of lyth.   *bearer of light*

Possible staging design of Passion Play I

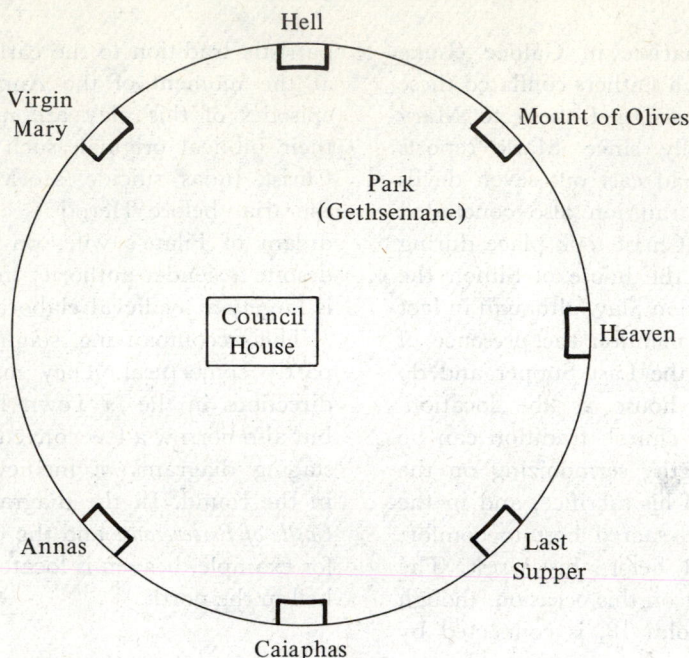

Possible staging design of Passion Play II

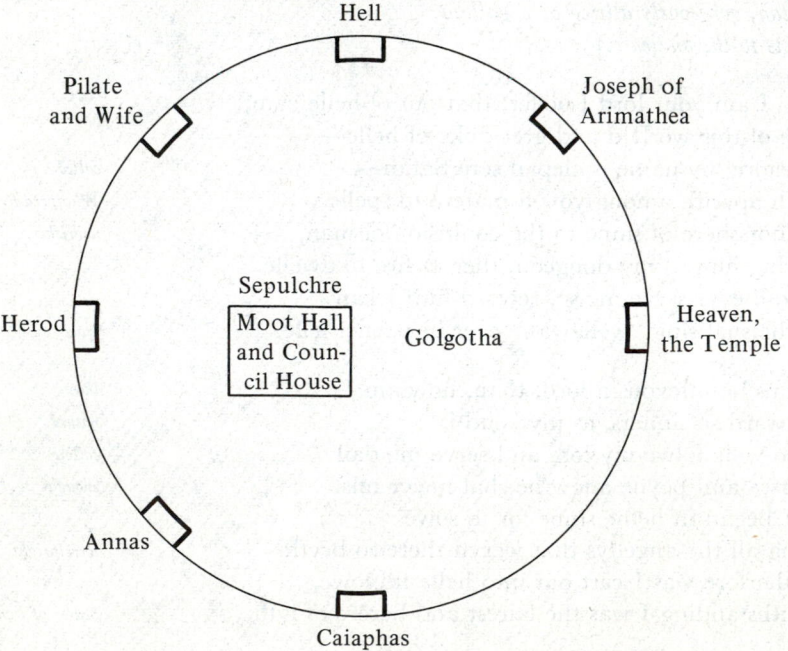

17   Yet I drowe in my tayle. Of tho angelys bryth,   *drew/retinue/those*
     With me into helle—takith good hed what I say—   *take/heed*
19   I lefte but tweyn agens on[e] to abide there in lyth,
     But the thridde part come with me. This may not be seyd
       nay.   *be denied*
     Takith hed to your prince, than, my pepyl everychon,   *Take*
     And seyth what maistryes in hefne I gan ther to play.   *see/mastery*
23   To gete a thowsand sowlys in an houre, me thinkith it but
       skorn,   *i.e., a trifle*
24   Sith I wan Adam and Eve on the first day!   *Ever since*

     But now mervelous mendys rennyn in min[e]   *strange thoughts run*
       rememberawns
     Of on[e] Crist, w[h]iche is clepyd Joseph and Maryes   *who is called*
       sone.
27   Thries I tempte him by ryth sotille instawnce,   *tempted*
28   Aftyr he fast fourty days ageyns sensual myth or reson,   *might*
29   For of the stonys to a mad[e] bred: but sone I had
       conclusion;
30   Than upon a pinnacle: but angelys were to him assistent   *Then*
31   (His answerys were mervelous—I knew not his intencion);
32   And at the last to veynglory: but nevyr I had min[e]   *pride*
       intent.

     And now hath he twelve disipulys to his attendauns.   *attending him*
     To eche town and cety he sendith hem as bedellys,   *them/messengers*
     In diverce place to make for him purviauns.   *provision*
     The pepyl of hese werkys ful grettly merveyllys: *at his/marvel*
     To the crokyd, blind, and dowm his werkys prevailys;   *dumb*
     Lazare, that foure days lay ded, his lyff recuryd;   *recovered*
39   And where I purpose me to tempt, anon he me asailys.   *I intend to*
     Mawdelyn plain remission also he hath ensuryd.   *(Mary) Magdalene's full*

[17]*Yet . . . tayle:* Yet I drew after me my retinue, induced it to come along.

[19]i.e., I left behind only two-thirds of the total number to abide there in the heavenly light (two against one, or twice those who came with me).

[23-24]Ever since I began possessing souls on that first day when I won Adam and Eve, I think it a trifle to collect a thousand souls in one hour.

[27-32]Thrice I tempted him by exceedingly subtle argument, after he had fasted forty days in defiance of physical strength or common sense, to make (lit.: to have made) bread out of the stones: but I quickly got my comeuppance on that; then (I tempted him) upon a pinnacle (to throw himself down): but angels ministered to him (his answers were mysterious—I could not comprehend his meaning); and finally (I tempted him) to spiritual pride: but I never achieved my intent (of corrupting him).

[39]And wherever I intend to do some temptation, he attacks me immediately.

Goddys son he pretendith, and to be born of a maide,
And seyth he shal dey for mannys salvacion. — *die*
Than shal the trewth be tried and no fordere be delayd, — *further*
Whan the soule fro the body shal make separacion.
And, as for hem that be undre my grett dominacion, — *them*
He shal faile of hese intent and purpose also, — *He (Christ)*
47 By this tyxt of holde, remembryd to min[e] intencion: — *text of old*
48 *Quia in inferno nulla est redemptio.* — *Because in hell there is no redemption*

But whan the time shal neyth of his persecucion, — *draw near*
I shal arere new engines of malicious conspiracy: — *raise*
Plenté of reprevys I shal provide, to his confusion. — *reproofs*
Thus shal I false the wordys that his pepyl doth testefy; — *falsify*
His discipulis shal forsake him, and here maister denye. — *their*
Innoumberabyl shal hese woundys be, of woful grevauns.
55 A tretowre shal countirfe[t], his deth to fortifye. — *traitor/to ensure*
The rebukys that he gif me shal turne to his displesauns. — *gave*

57 Some of hese discipulys shal be chef of this ordenawns. — *scheme*
58 That shal fortefye this term: that "in trost is treson." — *saying*
Thus shal I venge by sotilté al my malicious grevauns, — *subtlety*
For nothing may excede my prudens and discrecion.

Giff me your love, grawnt me min[e] affeccion,
And I wil unclose the tresour of lovys aliawns — *love's alliance*
And giff yow youre desirys, afftere youre intencion. — *according to*
64 No poverté shal aproche yow, fro plentevous abundauns.
    [*He boasts of his elegant attire.*]

65 Biholde the divercité of my disgisyd variauns,
66 Eche thing sett of dewe, naterall disposicion, — *due*
67 And eche parte acording to his resemblauns, — *its*
Fro the sool of the foot to the hyest asencion: — *i.e., from bottom to top*

Of fine cordewan, a goodly peyre of long pekyd schon; — *leather/pointed shoes*

47–48By this ancient text, recalled to my mind (from the Office of the Dead).

55A traitor (Judas) will act deceitfully (i.e., will betray him) to ensure his death.

57–58Some of his disciples (notably Judas) will be foremost in this scheme. That will add confirmation to the saying that "in trust is treason."

64–67No poverty will threaten you, because of plentiful abundance. Behold the diversity of my new and ostentatiously-fashioned outfit, each part set in its due, natural place, harmoniously suiting its function to its appearance. (What follows is a satire of medieval court fashion, associated with Satan's sin of Pride.)

70   Hosyn enclosyd of the most costious cloth of crenseyn
71   (Thus a bey to a jentylman to make comparicon)   *boy*
72   With two doseyn pointys of cheverelle, the aglottys of
           silver feyn;

73   A shert of feyn Holond (but care not for the payment);   *fine Holland cloth*
74   A stomachere of clere Reynes, the best may be bowth
75   (Thow poverté be chef, lete Pride ther be present,   *Though*
76   And all tho that repreff Pride, thou sette hem at nowth);   *those/them/nought*

77   Cadace, wolle, or flokkys, where it may be sowth,   *Cotton wool/stuffing*
78   To stuffe withal thy dobbelet, and make the[e] of
           proporcion
79   Two smale legges and a gret body (thow it ryme nowth,
80   Yet loke that thou desire to an the newe faccion);   *see to it/to own*

81   A gowne of thre yerdys (loke thou make comparison
82   Unto all degrees daily that passe thin[e] astat);   *class of persons/state*
83   A purse (withoutyn mony); a daggere for devoscion
84   (And there repref is of sinne, loke thu make debat);   *be quarrelsome*

85   With side lokkys, I schrewe, thin[e] here to thy colere   *hair*
           hanging down,
86   To herborwe qweke bestys that tekele men onyth;
87   An hey smal bonet for curing of the crowne
88   (And all beggerys and pore pepyll, have hem en dispite).   *hold them in*
      Onto grete othys and lycherye gif thy delite.   *oaths*
      To mainteyn thin[e] astate, lete bribory be present,
      And, if the lawe repreve the[e], say thou wilt fyth   *reprove/fight*
92   And gadere the[e] a felachep after thin[e] entent.   *gather to you*

70-88Hose or breeches made of or enveloped in the most costly crimson cloth (thus a mere boy, or knave, can rival a gentleman) with two dozen laces of kid-leather for securing the hose to the doublet, having tags or points of pure silver; a shirt of fine Holland cloth (but don't worry about paying for it); a waistcoat of pure cloth of Rennes, the best that may be bought (yet, although poverty may prevail because you're spending so much, don't let Pride be forgotten, and disdain all those who reprove Pride); cotton wool, wool, or other stuffing, wherever it may be sought and found, with which to stuff your doublet or jacket, thereby making your trunk look huge in proportion to your small legs (yet, though it makes neither rhyme nor reason, see to it that you yearn to own the new fashion); a gown or cloak three yards long (see to it that you rival all classes of persons who surpass you in rank); a purse (even if it's empty); a dagger with which to perform service (and wherever there is reproof of sin, see to it that you argue back); your hair with long locks, I swear, hanging down to your collar, to give shelter to live animals such as fleas that tickle men a-nights; a high little hat for curing or hiding a bald spot (and despise all beggars and poor people).

92And gather to your service a group of fellows disposed as you are (to sin).

Loke thou sett not by precept nor by comawndement: *pay no heed to*

Both sevile and canon, sett thou at nowth.   *civil and clerical*

95   Lette no membre of God but with othys be rent.   *limb, part/oaths*

Lo, thus this wer[l]d at this time to min[e] intent is browth!   *brought*

I, Sathan, with my felawus this wer[l]d hath sowth,   *sought*

And now we han it at houre plesawns.   *have/our*

99   For sinne is not shamfast, but boldnes hath bowth   *bought*

100   That shal cause hem in helle to han ineritawns.   *them/inheritance*

A beggerys dowtere to make gret purviauns   *beggar's daughter/provision*

To cownterfete a jentylwoman, disgeysyd as she can;

103   And, if mony lakke, this is the newe chevesauns: *device*

104   With her prevy plesawns to gett it of sum man—   *privy pleasure*

105   Her colere splayed and furryd with ermin, calabere, or   *collar*
          satan,

106   A seyn to selle lechory to hem that wil bey.   *sign/them/buy*

107   And they that wil not b[u]y it, yet inow shal they han,   *enough*

108   And telle hem it is for love—she may it not deny.

I have browth yow newe namys, and wil ye se why?   *brought/names*

For sinne is so plesaunt to ech mannys intent,   *Because*

Ye shal kalle Pride "[H]oneste," and "Naterall Kend"   *Natural Begetting*
          Lechory,

And Covetise "Wisdam there tresure is present";   *Covetousness/where*

Wreth "Manhod," and Envye callyd "Chastement"   *Chastisement*

114   (Seyse nere session, lete perjery be chef);   *Assize nor (or)*

Glotonye, "Rest" (let abstinawnce beyn absent);

And he that wole exorte the[e] to vertu, put hem to repreff.   *will/reproof*

117   To rehers al my servauntys, my matere is to[o] breff;   *speech*

But all these shal enerith the divicion eternal.   *inherit/separation (from grace)*

⁹⁵Let every part of God be torn with oaths. (An oath such as "by God's nails" was thought to
recrucify him.)

⁹⁹⁻¹⁰⁰For sinful behavior is no longer ashamed of itself; instead, boldness has purchased that
reward (damnation) which will cause those sinners to have their inheritance in hell.

¹⁰³⁻⁸And, if she lack money, this is the new device: to get money from some man by means of
her secret pleasures (i.e., by prostitution)—her collar spread open (in a plunging neckline)
and furred with crimson, squirrel fur, or satin, as a sign she will sell lechory to those who will
buy. And those who won't buy will get enough sex from her anyway, and she'll tell them she
did it for love—for she can't say no.

¹¹⁴At assize or court session, let perjury prevail. (Perjury is a form of Envy, one of the Deadly
Sins here catalogued and renamed.)

¹¹⁷My speech is too brief to rehearse the names of all those (the damned) who serve me.

119 Thow Crist by his sotilté many materys meef,   *Though|move, accomplish*
   In evyrlastinge peyne with me dwellyn they shal.

121 Remembre oure servauntys whoys sowlys ben mortall;   *whose*
122 For I must remeffe for more materys to provide.   *remove (myself), depart*
   I am with yow at all times whan ye to councel me call,
   But for a short time myself I devoide. [*Exit.*]   *withdraw*

   [*John the Baptist comes forward.*]
   JOHANNES BAPTIS[TA].   I, John Baptist, to yow thus
      prophesye:
   That on[e] shal come aftyr me, and not tary longe,   *i.e., soon*
   In many folde more strengere than I,   *Many times mightier*
   Of whose shon I am not worthy to lose the thonge.   *shoes|loosen*
   Wherefore, I councel the[e] ye reforme all wronge
   In your conciens of the Mortall Dedys sevyn,   *seven Deadly Sins*
   And for to do penawns loke that ye fonge.   *undertake*
   For now shal come the kingdham of hevyn.

   The weys of oure Lord cast yow to aray,   *Prepare ye the way of our Lord*
10 And therin to walk loke ye be applyande;   *apply yourself*
   And make his pathys as ryth as ye may,   *right, straight*
   Keping ryth forth; and be not declinande,   *declining, swerving*
   Neither to[o] fele on ryth nor on lefte hande,   *too much*
   But in the middys purpose yow to holde.   *try to keep yourself*
   For that in all wise is most plesande,
   As ye shal here whan I have tolde.   *hear*

   Of this wey for to make moralisacion:
   By the ryth side, ye shal undyrstonde "mercy,"
   And on the lefte side likkenyd "disperacion";   *(is) betokened despair*
20 And the patthe betwyn bothyn, that may not wry,   *both|turn aside*
   Schal be "hope and drede"—to walk in perfectly,   *fear*
   Declining not to[o] fele for no maner nede.   *Wavering not too much for anything*
   Grete cawsys I shal showe yow why
   That ye shal sewe the patthe of hope and drede.   *follow*

   On the mercy of God to[o] meche ye shal not holde,   *much|rely*
   As in this wise—behold what I mene:
   For to do sinne, be thou no more bolde   *Be not overbold to sin*
   In trost that God wole merciful bene.   *will be merciful*

---

[119] Even though Christ may, by his subtlety, accomplish many things.

[121-22] Think upon those servants of the devil whose souls have perished; for I must depart in order to take care of other matters.

29   And if by sensualité (as it is ofte sene)
30   Sinnyst dedly, thou shalt not therfore dispeyre,   *(You) sin*
      But therfore do penawns and confesse the[e] clene;
      And of hevyn thou mayst trost to ben eyre.   *heir*

      The pathe that lyth to this blissyd enheritawns   *lies*
      Is hope and drede, copelyd by conjunccion.   *coupled*
      Betwix these tweyn may be no disseverawns;   *separation*
      For, hope withoutyn drede is maner of presumpcion,
      And drede withowtyn hope is maner of disperacion.
      So, these tweyn must be knit by on[e] acorde.
      How ye shal aray the wey, I have made declaracion;   *prepare*
40   Also the ryth patthis agens the coming of oure Lord.   *in preparation for*
          [*Exit.*]

          Here shal Annas shewyn himself in his stage, beseyn after a   *arrayed like*
          busshop of the hoold lawe in a skarlet gowne, and over that a   *old*
          blew tabbard furryd with white, and a mitere on his hed, after *coat*
          the hoold lawe; two doctorys stonding by him in furryd hodys, and *wise men/hoods*
          on[e] beforn hem with his staff of astat; and eche of hem on here *state/them/their*
          hedys a furryd cappe with a gret knop in the crowne; and on[e] *tassel*
          stonding beforn as a Sarazyn, the w[h]ich shal be his masangere; *in front*
          Annas thus sey[i]ng:

      ANNAS.   As a prelat am I properyd to provide pes,   *it's my duty to keep the peace*
      And, of Jewys jewge, the lawe to fortefye.   *enforce*
      I, Annas, by my powere shal comawnde, dowteles:
      The lawys of Moyses no man shal denye!
5   [W]hoo excede my comawndement, anon ye certefye;   *Whoever*
      If any [h]eretik here reyn, to me ye compleyn.   *reign, prevail*
      For in me lyth the powere all trewthis to trye,
      And principaly oure lawys—tho must I susteyn.   *those*

9   Yef I may aspey the contrary, no wheyle shal they reyn,   *If*
      But anon to me be browth and stonde present   *brought*
      Before here jewge, which shal not feyn   *their/who/shirk*
12   But aftere here trespace to gef hem jugement.   *give them*

[JOHN THE BAPTIST]

29–30And if, as frequently happens, through your sensual nature you commit deadly sin, don't despair on this account.

[PASSION PLAY I]

5Certify at once to me the names of those who transgress my orders.

9If I espy the contrary, the offenders will not prevail for any length of time.

12But judge them according to their offense.

Now, serys, for a prose, herith min[e] intent: *story/hear*
There is on[e] Jhesus of Nazareth that oure lawys doth
    excede.
If he procede thus, we shal us all repent,   *be sorry*
For oure lawys he distroyt[h] daily with his dede.   *deeds*

Therefore, by your cowncel, we must take hede
What is be[st] to provide or do in this case.
For, if we let him thus go and ferdere prosede,   *further*
20 Ageyn Sesare and oure lawe we do trespace.   *Against Caesar*

  1 DOCTOR ANNAS.   Sere, this is min[e] avise that ye shal do: *Annas' first wise man*
Send to Caiphas for cowncel; knowe his intent.
For, if Jhesu proce[de] and thus forth go,
Oure lawys shal be distroyd; thes se we present.   *this we see*

  2 DOCTOR ANNAS.   Sere, remembre the gret charge that on
      yow is leyd,
The lawe to ke[pe], which may not faile.
27 If any defawth prevyd of yow be seyd,   *default proved*
The Jewys with trewth wil yow asail.
Tak hed whath cownsail may best prevail!   *what*
After Rewfyn and Leyon I rede that ye sende;   *advise*
31 They arn temperal jewgys, that knowith the parail—   *are/means*
32 With youre cosyn Caiphas—this matere to amende.   *cousin (i.e., partner)*

  ANNAS.   Now surely this cowncel revife min[e] herte!
Youre cowncel is best, as I can se. [*To the messenger.*]
Arfexe, in hast loke that thou stirte,   *go*
And pray Caiphas my cosyn come speke with me.

To Rewfyn and Leon thu go also,
And pray hem they speke with me in hast
For a principal matere that have to do,
40 W[h]ich must be knowe or this day be past.   *known ere*

  ARFEXE.   My sovereyn, at your intent I shal gon
In al the hast that I kan hy   *hurry*
Onto Caiphas, Rewfyn, and Lyon,
And charge youre intent that they shal ply.   *command/carry out*
   Here goth the masangere forth; and in the mene time Caiphas
   shewith himself in his skafhald, arayd lych to Annas, saving his   *like*

---

²⁷If you are accused of any failure in duty.

³¹⁻³²They are civil judges (as distinguished from clerical), who will know the means—in
cooperation with your fellow-cleric, Caiphas—to remedy this matter.

*tabbard shal be red furryd with white; two doctorys with him,
arayd with pellys aftyr the old g[u]ise and furryd cappys on here*   *furred cloaks/their*
hedys; Caiphas thus sey[i]ng:

45 CAIPHAS.   As a primat most preudent, I present here sensible   *represent*
46   Buschopys of the lawe, with al the circumstawns.
     I, Caiphas, am jewge with powerys possible   *capable*
     To distroye all errouris that in oure lawys make variawns.   *variance*
     All thingys I convey by reson and temperawnce,   *I express*
     And all materis possible to me ben palpable.   *are plainly understood*
     Of the lawe of Moyses I have a chef governawns;
     To severe ryth and wrong in me is terminable.   *sever, distinguish/has its origin*

     But ther is on[e] Crist that [in] oure lawys is variable;
     He perverte the pepyl with his preching ill.   *misleads*
     We must seke a mene onto him reprevable,   *a means to reprove him*
     For, if he procede, oure lawys he wil spill.   *destroy*

     We must take good cowncel in this case
     Of the wisest of the lawe that kan the trewthe telle:
     Of the jewgys of Pharasy, and of my cosyn Annas.   *i.e., the Pharisees*
60   For, if he procede, by prossesse oure lawys he wil felle.   *in time*

     1 DOCT[OR] CAIPHAS.   Min[e] lord, plesit[h] yow to pardon   *may it please*
        me for to say:
     The blame in yow is, as we finde,   *You are to blame*
     To lete Crist contenue thus day by day
     With his fals wichcraft, the pepyl to blinde.
     He werkith fals meraclis, ageyns all kende,   *contrary to all natural order*
     And makith oure pepyl to leve hem in.   *believe in them*
     It is your part to take him and do him binde   *cause him to be bound*
     And gif him jugement, for his gret sin.

     2 DOCTOR CAIPHAS.   Forsothe, sere, of trewth this is the case:
70   Onto our lawe ye don oppression   *you do*
     That ye let Crist from you pace   *pass*
     And wil not don on him correxion.
     Let Annas knowe your intencion,
     With prestys and jewgys of the lawe,
     And do Crist forsake his fals oppinion—   *cause*
     Or into a preson lete hem be thrawe.   *thrown*

45-46As an exceedingly prudent prince of the church, I represent here, perceptible in your
sight, the chief priests (or, in anachronistic medieval terminology, the "bishops") of the
Mosaic law with all due pomp and circumstance.

CAIPHAS.   Wel, serys, ye shal se, withinne short while,
I shal correcte him for his trespas.
He shal no lenger oure pepyl beg[u]ile;
80   Out of min[e] dawngere he shal not pas.   *power*
Here comith the masangere to Caiphas; and in the mene time   *show themselves|platea|striped coats*
Rewfyn and Lyon schewyn hem in the place, in ray tabardys
furryd, and ray hodys abouth here neckys, furryd; the masangere   *hoods around their*
sey[i]ng:

MASANGERE.   Min[e] reverent sovereyn, and it do yow plese,   *if it please you*
Sere Annas, my lord, hath to you sent.
He prayt[h] you that ye shal not sese   *cease*
Til that ye ben with him present.

CAIPHAS.   Sere, telle min[e] cosyn I shal not fail.
It was my purpose him for to se
For serteyn materys that wil prevaile,
Thow[gh] he had notwth a sent to me.   *Even though he had not sent*

MASA[N]GER.   I recomende me to your hey degré!   *commend myself to your lordship*
90   On more massagys I must wende.
CAIPHAS.   Farewel, sere, and wel ye be.
Gret wel my cosyn and my fre[n]de.
Here the masa[n]ger metith with the jewgys [on the platea],   *judges*
say[i]ng:

MASA[N]GER.   Heyl, jewgys of Jewry, of reson most prudent!
Of my massage to you I make relacion:
My lord, sere Annas, hath for you sent
To se his presens withowth delacion.   *delay*

REWFYN.   Sere, we are redy at his comawndement
To se sere Annas in his place.
It was oure purpose and oure intent
100   To a be with him withinne short space.   *have been*

LEYON.   We are ful glad his presence to se.
Sere, telle him we shal come in hast.
No delacion therin shal be,   *delay*
But to his presens hie us fast.

MASA[N]GER.   I shal telle my lord, seris, as ye say   *sirs*
Ye wil fulfille al his plesawns.
REWFYN.   Sere, telle him we shal make no delay,
But come in hast at his instawns.   *entreaty*
Here the masangere comith to Annas, thus sey[i]ng:

MASAN[GER].   My lord, and it plese you to have intelligens: *if*
110   Ser Caiphas comith to you in hast;
Rewfyn and Lyon wil se your presens,
And se yow here or this day be past.   *ere*

ANNAS.   Sere, I kan the[e] thank of thy diligens.   *I thank you for*
Now, ageyn my cosyn I wole walk.   *toward*
Serys, folwith me onto his presens,   *follow*
For of these materys we must talk.
> *Here Annas goth down to mete with Caiphas; and in*
> *the mene time thus sey[i]ng Caiphas:*

[CAIPHAS.]   Now onto Annas let us wende,
Ech of us to knowe otherys intent.
Many materys I have in mende,
120   The w[h]ich to him I shal present.

1 DOCTOR C.   Sere, of all othere thing, remember this case:
Loke that Jhesus be put to schame.
2 DOCTOR C.   Whan we come present beforn Annas
We shal rehers all his gret blame.
> *Here the buschopys with here clerkys and the Pharasees mete at*   *their*
> *the mid place; and ther shal be a litil oratory with stolys and*   *platea/chapel*
> *cusshonys, clenly beseyn lych as it were a cownsel hous; Annas*   *arrayed like*
> *thus sey[i]ng:*

ANNAS.   Welcome, ser Caiphas and ye jewgys alle!
Now shal ye knowe all min[e] entent:
A wondyr case, serys, here is befalle   *has befallen*
On w[h]ich we must gif jewgement—
Lyst that we aftere the case repent—   *Lest/afterwards*
130   Of on[e] Crist, that Goddys sone som doth him calle.
He shewith meraclys, and s[e]ythe present   *says now*
That he is prince of princys alle.

The pepyl so fast to him doth falle
(By prevy menys as we aspye),   *secret means*
Yif he procede, son[e] sen ye shalle   *If/soon you'll see*
That oure lawys he wil distrye.

It is oure part this to deny.   *our junction*
What is your cowncell in this cas[e]?
CAIPHAS.   By reson, the trewth here may we try.   *ascertain*
140   I cannot dem him withouth trespace.   *doom/unless he sins*
Because he seyth in every a place
That he [is] king of Jewys in every degré,   *in every respect*

Therfore he is fals; knowe wel the case,   *the fact*
Sesar is king and non but he.

RÉWFYN.   He is an [h]eretik and a tretour bolde
To Sesare and to oure lawe, sertayn,
Bothe in word and in werke; and, ye beholde,
He is worthy to dey with mekyl peyn.   *die/much*

LE[Y]ON.   The cawse that we been here present,
150   To fortefye the lawe; and, trewth to say,   *(Is) to enforce*
Jhesus ful nere oure lawys hath shent.   *nearly/confounded*
Therfore he is worthy for to day.   *die*

1 DOCTOR AN[NAS].   Serys, ye that ben rewelerys of the lawe,
On Jhesu ye must gif jugement:
Let him first ben hangyn and drawe,   *disemboweled*
And thanne his body in fire be brent.   *burned*

2 DOCTOR AN[NAS].   Now shal ye here the intent of me: *hear*
Take Jhesu, that werkys us all gret schame;   *who does us*
Put him to deth, let him not fle,
160   For than the comownys they wil yow blame.   *then, otherwise/commons*

1 DOCTOR CAIP[HAS].   He werkys with wechecrafte in eche   *witchcraft*
      place,
And drawith the pepyl to hese intent.
Bewhare, ye jewgys, let him not passe;   *Beware*
Than, by my trewthe, ye shal repent.   *Otherwise*

2 DOCTOR CAIPHAS.   Serys, takith hede onto this case,   *take heed*
And in your jewgement be not slawe.   *slow*
Ther was nevyr man did so gret trespace
As Jhesu hath don ageyn oure lawe.   *against*

ANNAS.   Now, bretheryn, than wil ye here min[e] intent?
170   These nine days let us abide;
We may not gif so hasty jugement.
But eche man inqwere on his side:
Send spies abouth the countré wide   *in his region*
To se and recorde and testimonye,   *bear witness*
And than hese werkys he shal not hide
Nor have no power hem to denye.   *them*

CAIPHAS.   This cowncell acordith to my reson.
ANNAS.   And we all to the same.

[*They are concealed from view in their council house, by a curtain.*]

[*Jesus enters with his apostles.*]

JHESUS.   Frendys, beholde the time of mercy,
180   The whiche is come now, withowt dowth.   doubt
Mannys sowle in blis now shal edify,   prosper
And the prince of the wer[l]d is cast owth.   i.e., the devil/out

Go to yon castel that standith yow ageyn,   stands opposite to you
Sum of min[e] disciplis—go forth, ye t[w]o—
There shul ye findyn bestys tweyn: two beasts
An asse tied and her fole also.   foal
Unlosne that asse and bringe it to me pleyn.   openly
Iff any man aske why that ye do so,
Sey that I have nede to this best, certeyn,   beast
190   And he shal not lett yow your weys for to go.   hinder
That best bringe ye to me.   beast
1 APOSTOLUS.   Holy prophete, we gon oure way;
We wil not youre wourd delay.   command
Al so sone as that we may   As soon as
We shal it bringe to the[e].
    Here they fecch the asse with the fole; and the burgeys seyth: citizen

BURGENSIS.   Herke ye, men, who gaff yow leve   gave
Thus this best for to take away?   beast
198   But only for pore men to releve   Solely
199   This asse is ordained, as I yow say.
PHILLIPUS.   Good sere, take this at no greff.   be not offended
Oure mayster us sent hedyr this day;
He hath grett nede, withowt repreff.   without contradiction, doubtless
Therfore, not lett us, I the[e] pray,   do not hinder
This best for to lede.   beast
BURGENSIS.   Sethin that it is so that he hath yow sent,   Since
Werkith his will and his intent: Perform
Take the beste as ye be bent,   are inclined
And evyr wel mote ye spede.   may you prosper
    [*Philip and James the Less return to Jesus with the beast.*]

JACOBUS MINOR.   This best is brought right now, here, lo,
210   Holy prophete, at thin[e] owyn wille;
And with this cloth anon, also,
This bestys bak we shal sone hille.   beast's/soon cover

198-99I say to you, this ass is designated solely for the relief of the poor.

PHILIPPUS.   Now mayst thou ride whedyr thou wilt go,   *whither*
    Thin[e] holy purpos to fulfille.
    Thy best ful redy is dyth the[e] to;   *is prepared for you*
    Bothe meke and tame, the best is stille.
    And we be redy also,
    Iff it be plesinge to thy sight,
219   The[e] to helpe anon forth right   *straightway*
220   Upon this best that thou were dight,   *prepared*
    Thy jurney for to do.

    Here Crist ridith out of the place and he wil, and Petyr and   *if*
    John [the Evangelist] abidyn stille. And at the last, whan
    they have don ther preching, they mete with Jhesu.

PETRUS.   O ye pepyl dispeyring, be glad!
    A grett cawse ye have, and ye kan se: *if*
    The Lord, that all thinge of nought mad,   *made*
    Is cominge your comforte to be.
226   All your langoris salvyn shal he;   *languors he'll salve*
227   Your helthe is more than ye kan wete.   *know*
    He shal cawse the blinde that they shal se,
    The def to here, the dome for to speke.   *hear/dumb*

    They that be crokyd, he shal cause hem to goo,   *lame/walk*
    In the wey that John Baptist of prophecied.   *prophesied about*
232   Sweche a leche kam yow nevyr non too.   *Such a healer*
233   Wherfore, what he comawndith, loke ye applied.   *apply it*
    That som of yow be blind, it may not be denyed,
235   For, him that is your makere, with your gostly ey ye shal not
        knowe.
    Of his comaundementys, in yow gret necgligens is aspied;
237   Wherfore, "def fro gostly hering" clepe yow I howe.   *I ought to call you*

    And some of yow may not go, ye be so crokyd,   *walk/lame*
    For of good werking in yow is lityl habundawns.   *abundance*
240   Tweyn fete hevery man shuld have—and it were lokyd—   *if/properly considered*

219–20To help you straightway to get set upon this beast.

226–27He will heal all your sorrows; your spiritual health is improved by this more than you
can possibly understand.

232–33Never did such a healer come to you before. Accordingly, whatever he commands, see
to it that you obey.

235For, with your spiritual sight you fail to recognize him who is your creator.

237Accordingly, I ought to call you "deaf in your spiritual sense of hearing."

240–41Every man ought to have two supports or "feet"—if the matter were properly interpreted—which would bear up the spiritual body of great worth.

241   W[h]iche shuld bere the body gostly most of substawns:
　　　First is to love God above all other plesawns;　　　　　　　*pleasure*
　　　The secunde is to love thy neybore as thin[e] owyn persone.
　　　And if these tweyn be kepte in perseverawns,
　　　Into the celestial habitacion ye arn habyl to gone.　　　　　*will be able*

246   Many of yow be dome. Why? For ye wole not redresse　　　　*dumb/Because*
247   By mowthe your dedys mortal, but therin don perdure—　　　*deadly/continue*
　　　Of the w[h]ich, but ye have contricion and yow confesse,　　*unless/confess yourself*
　　　Ye may not inherite hevyn, this I yow ensure.
　　　And of all these maladies ye may have gostly cure,　　　　　*spiritual*
　　　For the hevynly leche is coming yow for to vicite;　　　　　　*healer/visit*
　　　And, as for payment, he wole shewe yow no redrure,　　　　*severity*
　　　For with the love of yowre hertys he wole be aqwhite.　　　*acquit, paid*

254 JOHANNES APOSTOLUS.　Onto my brotherys forseyd rehersall　*brother's aforesaid*
255   That ye shuld geve the more veray confidens,　　　　　　　*In order that/true*
　　　I come with him as testimoniall
　　　For to conferme and fortefye his sentens.　　　　　　　　　*saying*
　　　This Lord shal come without resistens.
　　　Onto the cety-ward he is now coming;　　　　　　　　　　*Toward the city*
260   Wherefore, dresse yow with all dew diligens　　　　　　　　*prepare*
　　　To honowre him as your makere and king.

　　　And, to fulfille the prophetys prophesé,　　　　　　　　　*prophets' prophecy*
　　　Upon an asse he wole hedyr ride,　　　　　　　　　　　　*hither*
　　　Shewing yow exawmple of humilité
　　　Devoiding the abhominable sinne of Pride,　　　　　　　　*Casting out*
　　　Whech hath ny conqweryd all the wer[l]d wide—　　　　　*nearly*
　　　Grettest cause of all your tribulacion.
268   Use it [w]hoso wole, for it is the best g[u]ide
　　　That ye may have to the place of dampnacion.
　　　　[*He turns to Peter.*]

　　　Now, brothyr in God, sith we have intelligens　　　　　　　*since/information*
　　　That oure Lord is ny come to this ceté,　　　　　　　　　　*nearly*
　　　To attend upon his precious presens
　　　It sittith to us, as semith me.　　　　　　　　　　　　　　*befits us*
　　　Wherfore, to mete with him now go we.

246-47Many of you are spiritually dumb or silent. Why? Because you refuse to atone for your deadly sins by mouth confession, but instead continue your sinful ways.

254-55In order that you may put all the greater confidence in the just-concluded speech of my fellow-disciple.

268Use . . . wole: Let anyone use Pride who wishes to do so (said ironically).

275 I wold fore nothing we were to[o] late!   *for*
    To the ceté-ward fast drawith he.   *approaches*
    Me semith he is ny at the gate. [*They join Christ.*]

        Here spekith the four ceteseynys, the first thus sey[i]ng: *citizens*
    1 CIVES DE JHERUSALEM.   Neyborys, gret joye in oure herte
        we may make
    That this hef[en]ly king wole vicite this cité!   *visit*
280 2 CIVES.   If oure eerly king swech a jorné shuld take,   *earthly*
281 To don him honour and worchepe besy shuld we be.
282 3 CIVES.   Meche more than to the hevynly king bownd are we   *Much/then*
283 For to do that shuld be to his persone reverens.   *that which*
    4 CIVES.   Late us than welcome him with flowrys and   *Let*
        brawnchis of the tre,
285 For he wole take that to plesawns becawse of redolens.   *sweet smell*
        Here the four ceteseynys makyn hem redy for to mete with oure   *themselves*
        Lord, going barfot and barelegged and in here shirtys, saving they   *their/except that*
        shal have here gownys cast abouth them; and qwan they seen oure   *around them/when*
        Lorde, they shal sprede ther clothis beforn him, and he shal lyth   *alight*
        and go therupon, and they shal falle downe upon ther knes all
        atonys, the first thus sey[i]ng: *at once*

    1 CIVES.   Now, blissyd he be that in oure Lordys name
    To us in any wise wole resorte!   *will come*
    And we beleve, verily, that thou dost the same: *you do this*
    For, by thy mercy shal spring mannys comforte.
        Here Crist passith forth. Ther metith with him a serteyn of   *some*
        childeryn with flowrys, and cast beforn him; and they singgyn
        Gloria laus; and beforn on[e] seyt[h . . .]   *Glory/praise*

290 Thow sone of David, thou be oure supporte
    At oure last day whan we shal die!
    Wherefore, we alle atonys to the[e] exorte,   *at once*
    Cryeng, mercy, mercy, mercye!

    JHESU.   Frendys, beholde the time of mercy
    The w[h]ich is come now, withowtyn dowth.   *doubt*
    Mannys sowle in blisse now shal edify,   *prosper*
    And the prince of the wer[l]d is cast owth—   *out*

275I wouldn't have us be late for anything.

280–83If our temporal king (Caesar) should make such a journey (of triumphal entry), we
would be busy to worship and honor him.—Much more, then, are we obligated to the
heavenly king (Christ), to do those things necessary to revere his person.

285For he will be pleased by that welcome (flowers and branches) because of the sweet smell.

As I have prechyd in placys abowth,   *round about*
And shewyd [by] experience to man and wif.   *i.e., to everyone*
Into this wer[l]d Goddys sone hath sowth,   *sought, come*
301   For veray love man to revife.   *true*

The trewthe of trewthis shal now be tryede,   *proven*
And a perfith of corde betwix God and man,   *perfect accord*
W[h]ich trewth shal nevyr be divide.   *be sundered*
Confusion onto the fynd, Sathan!   *fiend*

[*Two poor blind men approach Jesus.*]
1 PAUPER HOMO.   Thou sone of David, on us have mercye,
As we must stedfast belevyn in the[e]!
308   Thy goodnesse, Lord, lete us be nye,   *nigh*
Whech lyth blind here and may not se.   *(We) who lie*
2 PAUPER HOMO.   Lord, lete thy mercy to us be sewre,   *sure*
And restore to us oure bodily syth.   *sight*
We know thou may us wel recure   *restore*
With the lest point of thy gret myth.   *least amount/might*

JHESU.   Yowre beleve hath mad[e] you for to se
And deliveryd you fro all mortal peyn.
Blissyd be all tho that beleve on me   *those*
And se me not with here bodily eyn.   *their/eyes*
    Here Crist blissith here eyn, and they may se, the fryst sey[i]ng:

1 PAUPER HOMO.   Gromercy, Lord, of thy gret grace!   *Great thanks*
I that was blind now may se.
320 2 PAUPER HOMO.   Here I forsake al my trespace
And stedfastly wil belevyn on the[e].
    *Here Crist procedith on fote with his discipulys after him, Crist
    weping upon the cité, say[i]ng thus:*

JHESU.   O Jherusalem, woful is the ordenawnce   *ordaining*
Of the day of thy gret persecucion!
Thou shalt be distroy[d] with woful grevans,
And thy ryalté browth to trew confusion.   *royalty brought*
Ye that in the ceté han habitacion,   *have*
They shal course the time that they were born,   *curse*
So gret advercité and tribulacion
Shal falle on hem, both evyn and morn!

301To revive mankind for the sake of his true love.

308Lord, let us be near to (partake of) your goodness. (For this episode, see Matthew 20:29–
34; see also Mark 10 and Luke 18. This episode is not part of the Entry into Jerusalem.)

They that han most childeryn sonest shal waile
And seyn, "Alas! What may this meen?"
Both mete and drink sodeynly shal faile;   *food*
The vengeance of God ther shal be seen.

334   The time is coming hes woo shal ben,
The day of trobyl and gret grevauns.
Bothe templys and towrys, they shal down cleen.   *fall down totally*
O ceté, ful woful is thin[e] ordenawns!

338 PETRUS.   Lord, where wolte thou kepe thy Maundé?   *Last Supper*
I pray the[e], now lete us have knowing,
That we may make redy for the[e],
The[e] to serve withowte lating—   *delay*
JOHANNES.   To provide, Lord, for thy coming
With all the obediens we kan atende,   *muster*
And make redy for the[e] in al thing,
Into what place thou wilt us send.

JHESU.   Serys, goth to Sion, and ye shal mete   *i.e., go into the city*
A pore man in simpyl aray,
Bering watyr in the strete.   *Bearing (a pitcher of) water*
Telle him I shal come that way.
350   Onto him mekely loke that ye say   *Say to him meekly*
That hese hous I wele come tille.   *I will come to his*
He wele not onys to yow sey nay,   *once*
But sofre to have all your wille.   *suffer, allow you*

PETRUS.   At thy wil, Lord, it shal be don;   *According to*
To seke that place we shal us hie—   *hasten*
JOHANNES.   In all the hast that we may go,
Thin[e] comaw[n]dement nevyr to denye.
Here Petyr and John gon forth, meting with Simon Leprows   *the Leper*
bering a kan with watyr, Petyr thus sey[i]ng:

PETRUS.   Good man, the prophete oure Lord, Jhesus,
This nyth wil rest within thin[e] halle.   *night*
360   On massage to the[e] he hath sent us,
That for his sopere ordeyn thou shalle.   *ordain, prepare*
JOHANNES.   Ya, for him and his discipulys alle,
Ordeyn thu for his Maundé

334The time is coming that his (Jerusalem's?) woe shall come to pass.

338*Maundé:* Maundy (from *mandatum,* "commandment," the ceremony of Easter Thursday in commemoration of the Last Supper. This service has traditionally included the washing the feet of the poor, and almsgiving.)

A paschall lomb, whatso befalle;   *come what may*
For he wil kepe his Pasch with the[e].   *Passover*

SIMON.   What, wil my Lord vesite my plase?
Blissyd be the time of his coming!
I shal ordeyn withinne short space   *brief time*
For my good Lordys welcoming.   *Lord's*
Serys, walkith in at the beginning,   *walk*
And se what vetailys that I shal take.   *victuals, food/choose*
I am so glad of this tiding,
373   I wot nevyr what joye that I may make!
       Here the discipulys gon in with Simon to se the ordenawns; and   *preparation*
       Crist coming thedyr-ward, thus sey[i]ng:

JHESUS.   This path is cald Sion, by goostly ordenawns,   *divine decree*
W[h]ech shal convey us wher we shal be.
I knowe ful redy is the purviaunce   *providing*
Of my frendys that lovyn me.
Contenwing in pees, now procede we;
For mannys love this wey I take.
With gostly ey I verily se   *spiritual eye*
381   That man for man an hende must make.   *end*
       Here the discipl[ys] com ageyn to Crist, Petyr thus sey[i]ng:

PETRUS.   All redy, Lord, is oure ordenawns,
As I hope to yow plesing shal be.
Seymon hath don at youre instawns.   *as you urged*
He is ful glad your presens to se.   *to see you*

386 JOHANNES.   All thing we have, Lord, at oure plesing,
That longith to youre Mawndé, with ful glad chere.   *belongs*
Whan he herd telle of your coming,
Gret joye in him than did appere.   *then*
       Here comith Simon owt of his hous to welcome Crist.

SIMON.   Gracious Lord, welcome thu be!
391   Reverens be to the[e], both God and man,
392   My poer hous that thou wilt se,
393   W[h]eche am thy servaunt, as I kan.   *(I) who*

373I don't know how to express my joy, it is so great.

381i.e., That Christ for Adam must make an end, must finish what Adam began.

386We have everything we asked for, Lord.

391–93May you be worshiped, you who are both God and man, since you vouchsafe to visit
(see) my poor house—I who am your servant as best I am able.

JHESU.   Simon, I knowe thy trewe intent.
    The blisse of hefne thou shalt recure;   *win*
    This rewarde I shal the[e] grawnt present.   *give you here and now*
    There, joye of all joyis to the[e] is sewre.   *In heaven|sure*
      Here Crist enterith into the hous with his disciplis and ete the
      paschal lomb; and in the mene time the cownsel hous beforn-seyd
      shal sodeynly onclose, schewing the buschopys, prestys, and
      jewgys sitting in here astat, lych as it were a convocacion; Annas   *in their state|like*
      sey[i]ng thus:

ANNAS.   Behold, it is nowth, al that we do!   *nought*
    In alle houre materys we prophete nowth.   *our matters|profit*
    Wole ye se w[h]ech peusawns of pepyl drawith him to,   *what crowds draw to him*
    For the mervailys that he hath wrowth?   *wrought*

    Some othyr sotilté must be sowth,   *subtlety, cunning|sought*
    For in no wise we may not thus him leve.   *let him go on thus*
404   Than to a schrewde conclusion we shal be browth, *evil end|brought*
    For the Romaynes than wil us mischeve,   *then will undo us*

    And take oure astat, and put us to repreve,   *authority|reproof*
407   And convey all the pepyl at here owyn request.   *their*
    And thus all the pepyl in Him shal beleve.
    Therfore I pray yow, cosyn, say what is the best.

CAIPHAS.   Attende now, serys, to that I shal seye: *Pay attention|that which*
    Onto us all it is most expedient
    That o man for the pepyl shuld deye,   *one*
    Than all the pepyl shuld perisch and be shent.   *Than that|destroyed*

    Therfor, late us werk wisely, that we us not repent. *let*
    We must nedys put on him som fals dede.   *must accuse him with*
    I sey, for me, I had levyr he were brent   *for my part|rather|burned*
    Than he shuld us alle thus ovyr-lede.   *domineer over us*
    Therfore, every man on his party help at this nede, *for his part*
    And cowntirfete all the sotiltes that ye kan.
420   Now, late se [w]ho kan geve best rede   *let's see|advice*
    To ordeyn sum distruccion for this man.

GAMALIEL.   Late us no lenger make delacion,   *delay*
    But do Jhesu be takyn in hondys fast,   *cause*
    And all here folwerys, to here confusion,   *their*
    And into a preson do hem be cast.   *cause them*

404Otherwise we should be brought to an evil end.

407And remove from us the obedience of the people, at the people's own request.

    Ley on hem iron that wol last,
    For he hath wrouth agens the ryth.   *sinned against righteousness*
    And sithyn aftyr we shal in hast   *afterwards*
    Jewge him to deth with gret dispyth.   *despite*

430 REWFYN.   For he hath trespacyd agens oure lawe,   *Because*
    Me semith this were best jewgement:
    With wild hors lete him be drawe,   *pulled apart*
    And afftyr in fire he shal be brent.

    LEYON.   Serys, o thing myself herd him sey: *one*
    That he was king of Jewys alle.
    That is anow to do him dey,   *enough/cause him to die*
    For treson to Sezar we must it calle.   *Caesar*

    He seyd also, to personys that I know,
439 That he shuld and myth, serteyn,
    The gret tempyl mithtily ovyrthrow,
    And the thridde day reysynt ageyn.   *raise it*

442 Seche materys the pepyl doth conseyve   *Such matters/imagine*
443 To geve credens to his werkys alle.
    In hefne, he seyth, shal be his reyn.
    Bothe God and man he doth him calle.

    REWFYN.   And all this day we shuld contrive
    What shameful deth Jhesu shuld have.
448 We may not do him to[o] meche mischeve,
    The worchep of oure lawe to save.   *honor, credit*

    LEYON.   Upon a jebet lete him hongyn be—   *gibbet, gallows*
    This jugement me semith it is reson—
    That all the countré may him se
    And beware by his gret treson.

    REWFYN.   Yet o thing, serys, ye must aspye,   *one*
    And make a ryth sotyl ordenawns   *very subtle arrangement*
    By what menys ye may come him bye;   *come near him*
    For he hath many folwerys at his instawns.   *at his command*

439That he should and certainly would.

442–43The people imagine that such wondrous matters give credence to all his other deeds.
(The rhyme, however, may suggest "constrain" instead of "conceive.")

448i.e., We should stop at nothing in punishing him.

ANNAS.   Serys, therof we must have avisement,   *we must consider*
　　　And ben acordyd or than we go   *be agreed before*
460　How we shal han him at oure entent.   *seize him according to*
　　　Som wey we shal find therto.

> [*The Jews are again concealed from view in their council house.
> Mary Magdalene approaches Christ at Simon's house, where he
> can now be seen preparing for the Last Supper.*]

MARIA MAGDALEN.   As a cursyd creature closyd all in care,   *enclosed/sorrow*
　　　And as a wickyd wrecche all wrappyd in wo—
　　　Of blisse was nevyr no berde so bare   *woman*
　　　As I mysylf, that here now go—   *I who walk here*
　　　Alas, alas! I shal forfare   *be utterly lost*
　　　For tho grete sinnys that I have do,   *those/done*
　　　Lesse than my Lord God sumdel spare   *Unless/is somewhat merciful*
　　　And his grett mercy receive me to.   *And receives*
470　Mary Maudelyn is my name.
　　　Now wil I go to Crist Jhesu,
　　　For he is Lord of all vertu,
　　　And for sum grace I thinke to sew;   *sue*
　　　For of myself I have grett shame.

> [*She goes to Christ.*]

　　　A, mercy, Lord, and salve my sinne!
　　　Maidenys floure, thou wasch me fre!   *Paragon of chaste persons*
　　　Ther was nevyr woman of mannys kinne   *of all mankind*
　　　So ful of sinne, in no countré.   *anywhere*
479　I have befowlyd by frith and fenne   *by forest and marsh*
　　　And sowght sinne in many a ceté.
　　　But thou me borwe, Lord, I shal brenne,   *Unless you save me/burn*
　　　With blake fendys ay bowne to be!   *black fiends ever destined*
　　　Wherefore, kinge of grace,
　　　With this oinement that is so sote   *sweet*
　　　Lete me anointe thin[e] holy fote,
　　　And for my balys thus win sum bote   *ills/remedy*
　　　And mercy, Lord, for my trespace.

JHESUS.   Woman, for thy wepinge wille,   *well*
　　　Sum socowre God shal the[e] sende.
490　The[e] to save I have grett skille,
　　　For sorweful hert may sinne amende.
　　　All thy prayour I shal fulfille;
　　　To thy good hert I wul attende

---

479 i.e., I have sinned everywhere.

And save the[e] fro thy sinne so hylle,   *ill*
And fro seven develys I shal the[e] fende.   *defend*
   [*He conjures out of her the seven Deadly Sins.*]
Fendys, fleth your weye!   *Fiends/fly away*
Wickyd spiritys, I yow conjowre,
Fleth out of hir bodily bowre!   *bower, dwelling*
In my grace she shal evyr flowre
500   Til deth doth her to deye.   *causes her*

     MARIA MAGDALENE.   I thanke the[e], Lorde, of this grett
       grace!
Now these seven fendys be fro me flitt.   *driven away*
I shal nevyr forfett, nor do trespace   *transgress*
In wurd nor dede, ne wil nor witt.
Now I am brought from the fendys brace,   *Now that/fiend's embrace*
In thy grett mercy closyd and shitt,   *shut*
I shal nevyr returne to sinful trace   *track, path*
That shulde me dampne to helle pitt.   *damn*
I wurchep the[e] on knes bare;
510   Blissyd be the time that I hedyr sowth,   *hither sought*
And this oinement that I heydr brought!
For now min[e] hert is clensyd from thought,
That first was combryd with care.   *encumbered*

     JUDAS.   Lord, me thinkith thou dost right ille
To lete this oinement so spille;   *be wasted*
To selle it, it were more skille,   *would be more reasonable*
And bye mete to poer men.   *buy food for poor*
The box was worth, of good moné,   *money*
Thre hundreth pens, fair and fre;   *excellent*
520   This might a bowht mete plenté   *have bought*
To fede oure power ken.   *poor folk*

     JHESUS.   Pore men shul abide—   *i.e., There will always be poor men*
Ageyn the woman thou spekist wronge—   *Against*
And I passe forth in a tide.   *i.e., But I will leave you shortly*
Of mercy is her mo[u]rning songe.
     Here Crist restith and etith a lityl, and seyth sitting to his
     disciplis and Mary Mawdelyn:

     JHESUS.   Min[e] herte is right sory—and no wondyr is.   *it's no wonder*
Too deth I shal go, and nevyr did trespas.   *To/yet I never sinned*
But yitt most grevith min[e] hert evyr of this:
On[e] of my bretheryn shal werke this manas;   *menace*
530   On[e] of yow here sittinge my treson shal tras.   *betrayal/trace, contrive*
On[e] of yow is besy my deth here to dyth,   *bring about*

And yitt was I nevyr in no sinful plas   *employment, situation*
Wherefore my deth shuld so shamfully be pight.   *arranged*

PETRUS.   My dere Lord, I pray the[e] the trewth for to
    telle:
Whiche of us is he that treson shal do?
Whatt traitour is he that his Lord that wold selle?
Expresse his name, Lord, that shal werke this woo.
JOHANNES.   If that ther be on[e] that wolde selle so,
Good maister, telle us now opynly his name.
540   What traitour is him that from the[e] that wolde go,
And with fals treson fulfille his grett shame?

ANDREAS.   It is right dredfull such tresson to thinke,
And wel more dredful to werk that bad dede!   *even more/perform*
For that fals treson, to helle he shal sinke,
In endles peynes grett mischeff to lede!
JACOBUS MAJOR.   It is not I, Lord—for dowte I have drede!   *James the greater*
This sinne to fulfille cam nevyr in my mende.   *mind*
Iff that I solde the[e], thy blood for to blede,
In doing that treson, my sowle shulde I shende.   *destroy*

550 MATHEUS.   Alas, my dere Lord, what man is so wood   *mad*
For gold or for silvyr himself so to spille?   *kill*
He that the[e] doth selle for gold or for other good   *valuables*
With his grett covetise himself he doth kille.   *covetousness*
BARTHOLOMEUS.   What man soevyr he be of so wickyd wille,
Dere Lord, among us, tell us his name all owt.   *fully, plainly*
He that to him tendith this dede to fulfille,   *applies himself to*
For his grett treson his sowle stondith in dowt.

PHILIPPUS.   Golde, silver, and tresoour sone doth passe away,   *soon*
But withowtyn ende evyr doth laste thy grace.
560   A, Lord, who is that will chaffare the[e] for monay?   *trade, bargain*
For he that sellith his Lord, to[o] grett is the trespace.
JACOBUS MINOR.   That traitour that doth this orrible   *James the less*
    manace,
Bothe body and sowle, I holde, he be lorn: *I maintain/lost*
Dampnyd to helle pitt, fer from thy face,   *far*
Amonge all fowle fyndys to be rent and torn.   *foul fiends*

SIMON.   To[o] bad a marchawnt that traitour he is,
And for that monye he may mo[u]rning make.
Alas, what cawsith him to selle the king of blis?
For his fals winninge, the devil him shal take.
570 THOMAS.   For his fals treson, the fendys so blake   *black*

Shal bere his sowle depe down into helle pitt.
Resste shal he non have, but evyrmore wake
Brenning in hoot fire, in preson evyr shitt.   *Burning/hot/shut*

THADEUS.   I woundyr right sore who that he shuld be,   *very sorely, grievously*
Amongys us all bretheryn, that shuld do this sinne?
Alas, he is lorn! Ther may no grace be;
In depe helle donjeon his sowle he doth pinne.   *imprison*

JHESUS.   In my dische he etiht, this treson shal beginne.   *he that eats*
Wo shal betidyn him for his werke of dred!
580   He may be right sory swich riches to winne,   *such*
A[n]d whisshe himself unborn for that sinful ded.   *wish*

JUDAS.   The trewth wolde I knowe as leff as ye;   *as gladly as all of you*
And therfore, good sere, the trewth thou me telle,   *sir*
Whiche of us all here that traitour may be:
Am I that person that the[e] now shal selle?

JHESUS.   So seyst thyselff. Take hed att thy spelle: *heed/language*
Thou askist me now here if thou shalt do that treson.
Remembyr thyself; avise the[e] right welle.   *consider what you're doing*
589   Thou art of grett age, and wotisst what is reson.

> *Here Judhas risith prevely, and goth in the place, and seyt[h]*   *platea*
> *"Now cownter[fetyd]." [The scene of the Last Supper is closed*
> *from view by a curtain.]*

JUDAS.   Now cowntyrfetyd I have a prevy treson,   *secret*
My maisterys power for to felle: *to overthrow*
I, Judas, shal asay by some encheson   *assay, try/cause, occasion*
Onto the Jewys him forto selle.
594   Som mony for him yet wold I telle.   *tell, count*
By prevy menys I shal asay;   *secret means*
Min[e] intent I shal fulfille.
No lenger I wole make delay.

> *[He sees the Jewish priests and leaders, who are visible once*
> *more in their council house.]*

The princys of prestys now be present.   *chief priests*
Unto hem now my way I take:
I wil go tellyn hem min[e] entent.
I trow ful mery I shal hem make.
Mony I wil non forsake,
And they profyr to my plesing;   *If/proffer*

---

[589]You are of the age of discretion, and know what is right.

[594]I hope to be counting my reward money for having sold him.

604	For covetise I wil with hem wake,	*watch*
	And onto my maistyr I shal hem bring.	
	[*He approaches them.*]	
	Heyl, prinsesse and prestys that ben present!	*princes, leaders*
	New tidingys to yow I come to telle,	
	Yif ye wole folwe min[e] intent:	
	My maister Jhesu I wele yow selle,	
610	Hese intent and purpose for to felle;	*fell, cut down*
	For I wole no lenger folwyn his lawe.	
612	Late sen what mony that I shal telle,	*Let's see/count*
	And late Jhesu, my maistyr, ben hangyn and drawe.	*let/disemboweled*

GAMALIE[L].   Now, welcome, Judas, oure owyn frende!
Take him in, serys, by the honde.
[*Judas is admitted to the council house.*]
We shal the[e] both geve and lende,
And in every qwarel by the[e] stonde.

REWFYN. Judas, what shal we for thy maister pay?	
Thy silver is redy and we acorde.	*if we're in accord*
620	The payment shal have no delay,	
But be leyde down here at a worde.	*i.e., at once*

JUDAS. Late the mony here down be layde,	*Let*
And I shal telle yow as I kan.	
In old termys, I have herd seyde	*In olden times/heard said*
625	That mony makith schapman.	*chapman, merchant*

REWFYN. Here is thretty platys of silver bryth,	*30 pieces/bright*
Fast knith withinne this glove.	*Securely knit, tied*
And we may have thy maister this nyth,	*If/night*
This shalt thou have, and all oure love.	

630 JUDAS. Ye are resonable chapmen, to bye and selle.	
This bargany with yow now shal I make;	
Smyth up! Ye shal have al your wille,	*Strike up (a bargain)*
For mony wil I non forsake.	

LEYON.   Now this bargany is mad[e] ful and fast;

604Out of covetousness I will join the night-watch of the Jews.

610In order to destroy his purpose.

612i.e., Let's see how much money I'll get.

625i.e., Money talks (proverbial).

Noyther part may it forsake.   *party*
But, Judas, thou must telle us in hast
By what menys we shal him take.

REWFYN.   Ya, ther be many that him nevyr sowe   *never saw him*
W[h]eche we wil sende to him in fere.   *in a throng*
640   Therfor, by a tokyn we must him knowe,
That must be prevy betwix us here.   *privy, secret*

LEYON.   Ya, beware of that for ony thinge!   *any*
For o discipil is lyche thy maister in al parail,   *one, each/like/apparel*
And ye go lyche in all clothing;   *ye (the disciples) go alike*
So myth we of oure purpose fail.   *might*

JUDAS.   As for that, serys, have ye no dowth.   *doubt*
I shal ordeyn so ye shal not misse:
Whan that ye cum him all abowth,   *all around him*
Take the man that I shal kisse.

650   I must go to my maistyr ageyn.
Dowth not, serys, this matere is sure inow.   *enough*
GAMALIEL.   Farewel, Judas, oure frend, serteyn!
Thy labour we shal ryth wel alow.   *approve*
      [Leaving the Jews, Judas soliloquizes to the audience.]

JUDAS.   Now wil I sotely go seke my maister ageyn,   *subtly*
And make good face as I nowth knew.   *as if I knew nothing*
I have him solde to wo and peyn;
I trowe ful sore he shal it rew.
      Here Judas goth in sotilly wheras he cam fro.   *(i.e., into Simon's house)*

ANNAS.   Lo, serys, a part we have of oure entent
For to take Jhesu. Now we must provide
A sotil meny to be present,   *cunning crowd*
That dare fyth and wele abide.   *fight/stand their ground*

662 GAMALIE[L].   Ordeyn eche man on his party   *for his part*
Cressetys, lanternys, and torchys lyth,   *Lanterns/lighted*
And this nyth to be ther redy   *night*
With exys, gleyvis, and swerdys bryth.   *axes/glaives (lances)/bright*

CAIPHAS.   No lenger than make we teryeng,
But eche man to his place him dyth   *remove himself*

662Let each man prepare, for his part.

And ordeyn prevely for this thing,   *prepare*
669   That it be don this same nyth.

    Here the buschopys partyn in the place, and eche of hem takyn here   *platea|their*
    leve by contenawns, resorting eche man to his place with here   *leave by gestures|their (his)*
    meny, to make redy to take Crist; and than shal the place ther Crist   *retinue*
    is in shal sodeynly unclose rownd abowtyn, shewing Crist sitting
    at the table, and hese discipul[ys] eche in [h]ere degre; Crist thus   *their*
    sey[i]ng:

JHESU.   Brederyn, this lambe that was set us beforn,
    That we alle have etyn in this nyth,   *night*
    It was comawndyd by my Fadyr to Moyses and Aaron
    Whan they weryn with the childeryn of Israel in Egypth.

    And as we with swete bredys have it ete,   *eaten*
    And also with the bittyr sokeling,   *clover*
    And as we take the hed with the fete,
    So dede they in all maner thing.

    And as we stodyn, so dede they stond;   *stand*
679   And here reynes they girdyn verily,   *they girded their loins*
    With schon on here fete and stavys in here hond;   *shoes|their*
    And as we ete it, so dede they, hastily.
682   This figure shal sesse; anothyr shal folwe therby,   *emblem, type|cease*
    W[h]eche shal be of my body, that am your hed;
    W[h]eche shal be shewyd to yow by a mystery
    Of my flesch and blood in [the] forme of bred.

    And with fervent desire of hertys affeccion,
    I have enterly desiryd to kepe my Mawndé   *entirely*
    Among yow er than I suffre my Passion.   *before*
    For, of this no more togedyr suppe shal we;   *of this (food)*
690   And, as the paschal lomb etyn have we,
    In the old lawe was usyd for a sacrifice,   *(Which) in*
    So the newe lomb, that shal be sacryd by me,   *consecrated by*
    Shal be usyd for a sacrifice most of price.   *most precious*

    Here shal Jhesus take an oble in his hand, loking upward into   *sacramental wafer*
    hefne to the Fadyr, thus sey[i]ng:

669s.d. *to his place:* to his scaffold or station (Annas and Caiaphas to their separate scaffolds with their respective retinues, etc.).

679And they put a girdle or waistbelt around their loins. (To be read literally, not figuratively; see l. 730.)

682i.e., The ceremony of the Passover will be superseded by the mass.

Wherefore to the[e], Fadyr of hefne that art eternall,
Thanking and honor I yeld onto the[e]—   *Thanks/yield*
To whom, by the Godhed, I am eqwall,
But by my manhod I am of lesse degré.
Wherefore I, as man, worchep the Deité,
Thanking the[e], Fadyr, that thou wilt shew this mystery;
700 And thus thurwe thy myth, Fadyr, and blissing of me,   *through your might*
Of this that was bred is mad[e] my body.

    Here shal he spekyn ageyn to his discipl[ys], thus sey[i]ng:

Bretheryn, by the vertu of these wordys that rehercyd be,   *repeated*
This that shewith as bred to your apparens   *appears as bread to you*
Is mad[e] the very flesche and blod of me—
To the w[h]eche, they that wole be savyd must geve
    credens.

And, as in the olde lawe it was comawndyd and precepte   *prescribed*
To ete this lomb, to the distruccion of Pharao unkende,   *unnatural*
So, to distroy your gostly enmye, this shal be kepte
For your paschal lombe into the wer[l]dys ende.   *unto*

710 For, this is the very lombe withowte spot of sinne
Of w[h]eche John the Baptist dede prophesy,
Whan this prophesye he dede beginne,
Sey[i]ng: *Ecce agnus Dei.*   *Behold the lamb of God*

And how ye shal ete this lombe, I shal geve informacion,
In the same forme as the eld lawe doth specifye,
As I shewe by gostly interpretacion.   *metaphysical*
717 Therfore, to that I shal sey, your willys loke ye replye. *that which/apply*

With no bittyr bred this bred ete shal be: *eaten*
That is to say, with no bittyrnesse of hate and envye,
But with the suete bred of love and charité,   *sweet*
W[h]eche fortefiet[h] the soule gretlye.

And it schuld ben etyn with the bittyr sokeling: *clover*
That is to mene, yif a man be of sinful disposicion,   *That signifies/if*
Hath led his liff here with misleving,   *(And) has/sinfully*
Therfore in his hert he shal have bittyr contricion.

Also, the hed with the feet ete shal ye:
By the hed, ye shal undyrstand my Godhed,

---

[717]Therefore, pay attention to what I shall say.

And by the feet ye shal take min[e] humanité.   *understand*
These tweyn ye shal receive togedyr indede.

730 This immaculat lombe that I shal yow geve
Is not only the Godhed alone,
But bothe God and man—thus must ye beleve.
Thus the hed with the feet ye shal receive ech-on[e].

Of this lombe unete if owth be levith, iwis,   *if ought be left uneaten*
It shuld be cast in the clere fire and brent;
W[h]eche is to mene, if thou undyrstande nowth al this: *not*
737 Put thy feyth in God, and than thou shalt not be shent.   *destroyed*

The girdyl that was comawndyd here reynes to sprede   *to cover their loins*
Shal be the girdyl of clennes and chastité:
That is to sayn, to be continent in word, thought, and
  dede,
741 And all leccherous leving cast yow for to fle.   *resolve*

And the schon that shal be your feet upon   *shoes*
Is not ellys but exawnpyl of vertuis leving   *Is none other than*
Of your form-faderys you beforn.   *forefathers before you*
With these schon, my steppys ye shal be sewing.   *following*

And the staf that in your handys ye shal holde
747 Is not ellys but the exawmplys to other men teche.   *teach*
Hold fast your stavys in your handys, and beth bolde   *be*
To every creature min[e] precepttys for to preche.

Also, ye must ete this paschall lombe hastily,
Of w[h]eche sentens this is the very entent:
At every [h]oure and time, ye shal be redy
For to fulfille my cowmawndement.

For, thow ye leve this day, ye are not sure   *although you live*
Whedyr ye shal leve tomorwe or nowth.   *Whether|not*
Therfor, hastily every [h]oure do youre besy cure   *care*
To kepe my preceptys, and than thar ye not dowth.   *you need not fear*

Now have I lernyd yow how ye shal ete   *taught*

737(Evidently the figurative reading here suggests that all the holy sacrament in the mass
should be consumed so that none will have to be cast away; hence, no believers will be consigned to hell flames.)

741And resolve to avoid (flee) all lecherous living.

747Is none other than an *exemplum* or illustration of how you shall teach other men.

Your paschal lombe, that is my precious body.
Now I wil fede yow all with awngellys mete;   *food*
Wherfore, to reseive it come forth seriattly.   *seriatim, one by one*
   [They come forward one at a time.]

762 PETRUS.   Lord, for to receive this gostly sustenawns
763   In dewe forme, it excedith min[e] intelligens;   *proper*
764   For no man of himself may have substawns
765   To receive it with to[o] meche reverens.   *much*

For, with more delicious mete, Lord, thou may us not fede   *food*
Than with thin[e] owyn precious body.
Wherfore, what I have trespacyd in word, thought, or
    dede,
With bittyr contricion, Lord, I haske the[e] mercy.
   Whan oure Lord givith his body to his discipulys, he shal sey to
   eche of hem except to Judas:

770   This is my body, flesch and blode,
     That for the[e] shal dey upon the rode.   *die/cross*
     And whan Judas comith last, oure Lord shal sey to him:

    Judas, art thou avisyd what thou shalt take?
JUDAS.   Lord, thy body I wil not forsake.
     And sithin oure Lord shal sey onto Judas: *then*

JHESU.   Min[e] body to the[e] I wole not denye,
    Sithin thou wilt presume therupon.   *Since*
    It shal be thy dampnacion, verilye—
    I geve the[e] warning now beforn.
     And aftyr that Judas hath reseivyd, he shal sit ther he was,   *where*
     Crist sey[i]ng:

    On[e] of yow hath betrayd me,
    That at my borde with me hath ete.
780   Bettyr it hadde him for to a be   *have been*
    Bothe unborn and unbegete.   *unbegotten*
     Than eche discipyl shal loke on other, and Petyr shal sey:

PETRUS.   Lord, it is not I.
     And so all shul seyn, til they comyn at Judas, w[h]eche shal sey:
JUDAS.   Is it owth I, Lord?   *aught, in any respect*

762–65Lord, to receive this spiritual sustenance with proper observance is more than I know how to do; for no man can have in himself the spiritual stature to receive it with sufficient understanding and gratitude.

Than Jhesus shal sey:

JHESU.   Judas, thou seyst that word.

Me thou [h]ast solde, that was thy frend.

That thou hast begonne, brenge to an ende.   *That which*

Than Judas shal gon ageyn to the Jewys. And if men wolne,   *will*

[there] shal mete with him and sey this spech folwing—or levynt,   *leave it (out)*

whether they wil—the devil, thus sey[i]ng: *whichever*

DEMON.   A[h], A[h], Judas, derling min[e],

Thou art the best to me that evyr was bore!   *born*

Thou shalt be crownyd in helle peyn,

790   And therof thou shalt be sekyr for evyrmore.   *sure*

Thow hast solde thy maistyr and etyn him also.

I wolde thou kowdist bringyn him to helle every del,   *could/bit*

But yet I fere he shuld do ther sum sorwe and wo,

That all helle shal crye out on me that sel!   *at that time*

Sped up thy matere that thou hast begonne;

I shal to helle for the[e] to mak redy.

Anon thou shalt come wher thou shalt wonne;   *dwell*

In fire and stink thou shalt sitt me by. [*He retires.*]

[*Christ continues his homily to the disciples.*]

JHESU.   Now the sone of God clarified is,   *manifested*

800   And God in him is clarified also.

I am sory that Judas hath lost his blisse,

W[h]eche shal turne him to sorwe and wo.

But now, in the memory of my Passion,

To ben partabyl with me in my reyn above,   *participable/reign*

Ye shal drink min[e] blood with gret devocion—

Wheche shal be shad for mannys love.   *shed*

Takith these chalys of the Newe Testament,   *Take this chalice*

And kepith this evyr in your mende: *keep/mind*

As oftyn as ye do this with trewe intent,

810   It shal defende yow fro the fende.

Than shal the disciplys com and take the blod, Jhesus sey[i]ng:

This is my blood, that for mannys sinne

Outh of min[e] herte it shal renne.

And the discipl[ys] shul sett them agen, ther they wore, and Jhesus   *seat themselves again where they were*

shal seyn:

Takith hed, now, bretheryn, what I have do: *Take heed/done*

With my flesch and blood I have yow fed.
For mannys love I may do no mo
Than for love of man to be ded.

W[h]erfore, Petyr, and ye, everychon:
Yif ye love me, fede my schep,   *sheep*
That for fawth of teching they go not wrong;   *default*
820   But evyr to hem takith good kep.   *take good care of them*

Gevith hem my body as I have to yow,   *Give them*
Qweche shal be sacryd by my worde;   *Which/consecrated*
And evyr I shal thus abide with yow
Into the ende of the werde.   *world*

[W]hoso etith my body and drinkith my blood,
[W]hol God and man he shal me take.
It shal him defende from the devil wood,   *mad*
And at his deth I shal him nowth forsake.   *not*

And [w]hoso not ete my body nor drinke my blood,
830   Lif[e] in him is nevyr a dele.   *not a bit, not at all*
Kepe wel this in mende for your good,
And every man save himself wele.   *will*
   Here Jhesus takith a basin with watyr, and towaly girt abowtyn   *towel*
   him, and fallith beforn Petyr on his o kne.   *one*

JHESUS.   Another exawmpyl I shal yow shewe
How ye shal leve in charité:
Sit here down, at wordys fewe,   *i.e., without more talk*
836   And qwat I do, ye sofre me.   *what/suffer, allow*
   Here he takith the basin and the towaly, and doth as the roberich   *rubric*
   seyth beforn.

PETRUS.   Lord, what wilt thou with me do?
This service of the[e] I wil forsake.   *refuse*
To wassche my feet thou shal not so;
I am not worthy it of the[e] to take.

JHESU.   Petyr, and thou forsake my service all   *if*
The w[h]eche to yow that I shal do,
No part with me have thou shal,
And nevyr com my blisse onto.
PETRUS.   That part, Lord, we wil not forgo;

836S.D. *doth . . . beforn:* does as the previous stage direction specifies (i.e., kneels before Peter).

We shal abey his comawndement.
Wasche hed and hond, we pray the[e] so;
We wil don after thin[e] entent.

Here Jhesus wasshith his discipulys feet by and by, and whipith   *one by one/wipes*
hem and kissith hem mekely, and sithin settith him down, thus   *then*
sey[i]ng:

849 JHESU.   Frendys, this wasshing shal now prevaill.
   Youre Lord and maister ye do me calle,
   And so I am, withowtyn fail;
   Yet I have wasschyd yow alle.
   A memory of this have ye shall
   That eche of yow shal do to othyr,
   With [h]umbyl hert, submit egal   *equally submissive*
   As eche of yow were otherys brother.   *As though*

   Nothing, serys, so wele plesith me,
   Nor no lif that man may lede,
   As they that levyn in charité.
860   In [h]efne I shal reward here mede.   *give them their reward*
   The day is come I must procede
   For to fulfille the prophecy:
   This nyth for me ye shal han drede   *have*
   Whan noumbyr of pepyl shal on me cry.   *denounce me*

   For the prophetys spoke of me,
   And seydyn of deth that I shuld take—   *said I should die*
   Fro whech deth I wole not fle,
   But for mannys sinne amendys make.

   This nyth fro yow be led I shal,   *I shall be led from you*
870   And ye for fer fro me shal fle—   *fear*
   Not onys dur speke whan I yow call—   *once dare*
   And some of yow forsake me.

   For yow shal I dey and rise ageyn: *die*
   Un the thridde day, ye shal me se   *On*
   Beforn yow all, walking plain
   In the lond of Galilé.

PETRUS.   Lord, I wil the[e] nevyr forsake,
   Nor for no perellys fro the[e] fle;   *perils*
   I wil rather my deth take
   Than onys, Lord, forsake the[e].   *once*

849i.e., Friends, this custom of washing the feet on Maundy Thursday will prevail as a ceremony henceforth.

881 JHESU.   Petyr, yn ferthere than thu doyst knowe,
882   As for that promese loke thou not make;
        For, or the cok hath twyes crowe,   *ere/crowed twice*
        Thries thou shal me forsake.

        But, all my frendys that arn me dere,   *are dear to me*
        Late us go; the time drawith ny.   *Let*
        We may no lengere abidyn here,
        For I must walke to Betany.   *Bethany*

        The time is come, the day drawith nere;
890   Onto my deth I must in hast.
        Now, Petyr, make hall thy felawys chere;   *all*
        My flesch for fere is qwaking fast.
            Here Jhesus goth to Betany-ward, and his discipulys folwing with   *toward Bethany*
            sad contenawns, Jhesus sey[i]ng:

        Now, my dere frendys and bretheryn echon,   *each one*
        Remembyr the wordys that I shal sey:
        The time is come that I must gon
        For to fulfille the prophesey.
        It is seyd of me that I shal dey,
        The fendys power fro yow to flem—   *fiend's/drive away*
        W[h]eche deth I wole not deney,
900   Mannys sowle, my spouse, for to redem.

        The oile of mercy is grawntyd plain
        By this jorné that I shal take.
        By my Fadyr I am sent, sertain,
        Betwix God and man an ende to make.
        Man for my brother may I not forsake,
        Nor shewe him unkendenesse by no wey.
        In peynys for him my body schal schake,   *pains*
        And, for love of man, Man shal dey.   *i.e., God as man will die*
            Here Jhesus and his discipul[ys] go toward the mount of Olivet;
            and whan he comith a litil ther beside, in a place lych to a park,   *near there/like*
            he biddit[h] his discipul[ys] abide him ther, and seyth to Petyr   *wait for*
            or he goth: *ere*

        Petyr, with thy felawys here shalt thou abide
910   And weche til I come ageyn.   *watch*
        I must make my prayere here you beside.   *near you, a little way off*
        My flesch qwakith sore for fere and peyn.

881–82 i.e., Peter, as to that promise, watch out that you don't make claims further than you
really know what will happen. (The text is uncertain here.)

PETRUS.   Lord, thy request doth me constreyn;   *i.e., I will obey*
  In this place I shal abide stille,
  Not remeve til that thou comist ageyn,
  In conferming, Lord, of thy wille.
   Here Jhesu goth to Olivet and settith him down on his knes, and
   prayth to his Fadyr, thus sey[i]ng:

JHESU.   O Fadyr, Fadyr! for my sake
  This gret Passion thou take fro me,
  W[h]ech arn ordeyned that I shal take   *is decreed*
920 Yif mannys sowle savyd may be.
  And yif it behove, Fadyr, for me   *is necessary*
  To save mannys sowle that shuld spille,   *that would otherwise be destroyed*
  I am redy in eche degre   *in every way*
  The wil of the[e] for to fulfille.
   Here Jhesus goth to his disciplis and findith hem scleping, Jhesus   *them*
   thus sey[i]ng to Petyr:

  Petyr, Petyr, thou slepist fast!   *soundly*
  Awake thy felawys and sclepe no more.
  Of my deth ye are not agast;
  Ye take your rest, and I peyn sore.
   Here Crist goth ageyn the second time to Olivet, and seyth kneling:

  Fadyr in hevyn, I beseche the[e],
930 Remeve my peynes by thy gret grace,
  And lete me fro this deth fle,
  As I dede nevyr no trespace!   *Since*
  The watyr and blood owth of my face   *out*
  Distillith, for peynes that I shal take;   *i.e., Comes in a cold sweat*
  My flesche qwakith in ferful case   *fearfully*
  As thow[gh] the jointys asondre shuld schake.
   Here Jhesus goth agen to his disciplis and findith hem asclepe;
   Jhesus thus sey[i]ng, lating hem lyne: *letting them lie*

  Fadyr, the thridde time I come ageyn,
  Fulleche min[e] erdon for to spede: *Fully/errand*
  Delivere me, Fadyr, fro this peyn
940 W[h]eche is reducyd with ful gret drede!   *recalled*
  Onto thy sone, Fadyr, take hede;
  Thou wotist I dede nevyr dede but good!   *never did any deed other than*
  It is not for me, this peyn I lede,   *lead, go through*
  But for man I swete bothe watyr and blode.
   Here an aungel descendith to Jhesus and bringith to him a chalys
   with an host therin.   *consecrated bread*

ANGELUS.   Heyl, bothe God and man in dede!
    The Fadyr hath sent the[e] this present.
    He bad[e] that thou shuldist not drede,
    But fulfille his intent
    As the parlement of hefne hath ment,   *intended*
950   That mannys sowle shal now redemyd be.
    From hefne to herd, Lord, thou wore sent;   *earth/were*
    That dede appendith onto the[e].   *death belongs to you*

    This chalys is thy blood, this bred is thy body,
    For mannys sinne evyr offeryd shal be;   *(Which) for*
    To the Fadyr of heffne, that is almythty,
    Thy disciplis and all presthood shal offere fore the[e].
    Here the aungel ascendith agen sodeynly.

JHESU.   Fadyr, thy wil fulfillyd shal be;
    It is nowth to say agens the case.   *It is fruitless to protest*
    I shal fulfille the prophesye
960   And sofre deth for mannys trespace.
    Here goth Crist ageyn to his discipulys and findith hem scleping
    stille.

    Awake, Petyr—thy rest is ful long—
    Of sclep! Thu wilt make no delay.   *From sleep/You must not delay*
    Judas is redy with pepyl strong,
    And doth his part me to betray.
    Rise up, serys, I you pray!
    Onclose your eyne for my sake.   *eyes*
    We shal walke into the way
    And sen hem come that shul me take.   *see them*

    Petyr, whan thou seyst I am forsake   *see*
970   Amonge min[e] frendys, and stond alone,
    All the cher that thou kanst make
    Geve to thy bretheryn everychone.
    Here Jhesus with his discipulis goth into the place, and ther shal   *platea*
    come in a ten personys weyl beseen, in white arneys and breganderys,   *well arrayed/body armor*
    and some disgysed in odyr garmentys, with swerdys, gleyvys, and   *other/spears*
    other straunge wepon, as cressettys with feyr, and lanternys and   *lanterns with fire*
    torchis lyth; and Judas formest of al, convey[i]ng hem to Jhesu   *lighted/foremost*
    by contenawns; Jhesus thus s[eying]:   *signs, signals*

    Serys, in your way ye have gret hast
    To seke him that wil not fle.
    Of yow I am ryth nowth agast.   *not at all afraid*
    Telle me, serys, whom seke ye?

LEYON.   Whom we seke here I tell the[e] now:
A tretour, is worthy to suffer deth.
We knowe he is here among yow;   *(who) is*
His name is Jhesus of Nazareth.

980

JHESU.   Serys, I am here that wil not fle,
Do to me all that ye kan.
Forsothe I telle yow I am he,
Jhesus of Nazareth, that same man.
Here all the Jewys falle sodeynly to the erde whan they here   *earth/hear*
Crist speke; and, qwan [he] biddith hem risyn, they risyn agen;   *when/them*
Crist thus sey[i]ng:

Arise, serys. Whom seke ye? Fast have ye gon.
Is howth your coming hedyr for me?   *aught, in any respect*
I stond beforn yow here echon   *each one*
That ye may me bothe knowe and se.

RUFYNE.   Jhesus of Nazareth we seke,
And we myth him here aspye.   *If we might*
990
JHESU.   I told yow now with wordys meke,
Beforn you all, that it was I.

JUDAS.   Welcome, Jhesu, my maister dere!
I have the[e] sowth in many a place.   *sought*
I am ful glad I find the[e] here,
For I wist nevyr w[h]er thou wace.   *you were*
Here Judas kissith Jhesus, and anoon all the Jewys come abowth   *about, around*
him and ley handys on him, and pullyn him as they were wode,   *as if/mad*
and makyn on him a gret cry all at onys; and aftyr this, Petyr seyth: *at once*

PETRUS.   I drawe my swerd now this sel;   *time*
Shal I smite, maister? Fain wolde I wete.   *Gladly/know*
And forthwith he smitith of[f] Malchus here; and he crieth,   *Malchus' ear*
"Help, min[e] here, min[e] here!" and Crist blissith it, and tis
[w]hol.
JHESUS.   Put thy swerd in the shede fayr and wel,   *sheath*
For he that smyth with swerd, with swerd shal be smete.   *smites/smitten*
1000
[Jesus is bound with cords.]

A, Judas, this treson cowntirfetyd hast thou,
And that thou shalt ful sore repent!
Thou haddist be bettyr a ben unborn now;   *better have been*
Thy body and sowle thou hast shent.   *destroyed*

GAMALIEL.   Lo, Jhesus, thou mayst not the cace refuse: *the fact*

Bothe treson and [h]eresye in the[e] is fownde.

Stody now fast on thin[e] excuse,   *Study, think*

Whilys that thou gost in cordys bownde.

Thou kallist the[e] king of this wer[l]d rownde;   *You call yourself*

1010   Now lete me se thy gret powere!

And save thyself here hool and sownde,   *whole*

And bringe the[e] out of this dawngere.

LEYON.   Bring forth this tretoure, spare him nowth!   *not*

Onto Caiphas, thy jewge, we shal the[e] lede.   *judge*

In many a place we have the[e] sowth,   *sought*

And to thy werkys take good hede!   *we have noted your deeds*

RUFYNE.   Come on, Jhesus, and folwe me!

I am ful glad that I the[e] have.

Thou shalt ben hangyn upon a tre;   *cross*

1020   A melion of gold shal the[e] not save.   *million*

LEYON.   Lete me leyn hand on him, in heye!   *lay/swiftly*

Onto his deth I shal him bring. [*To Jesus.*]

Shewe forth thy wichecrafte and nigramansye!   *necromancy*

What helpith the[e] now al thy fals werking?

JHESU.   Frendys, take hede! Ye don unryth   *"unright," i.e., wrong*

So unkendely with cordys to bind me here,   *unnaturally*

And thus to falle on me by nyth   *night*

As thow[gh] I were a thevys fere.   *thief's companion*

Many time beforn yow I dede apere;

1030   Withinne the temple sen me ye have,   *seen*

The lawys of God to teche and lere   *expound*

To hem that wele here sowlys save.   *them that will save their souls*

Why dede ye not me disprave,   *did/disprove*

And herd me preche bothe lowd and lowe?   *When (you) heard/softly*

But now, as wood men, ye ginne to rave   *mad/begin*

And do thing that ye notwth knowe.   *you know not what*

GAMALI[EL].   Serys, I charge yow, not o word more this nyth,   *one/night*

But on to Caiphas in hast loke ye him lede.   *see you lead him swiftly*

Have him forth with gret dispite,   *Lead*

1040   And to his wordys take ye non hede.

Here the Jewys lede Crist outh of the place with gret cry and noise,   *platea*
some drawing Crist forward and some bakward, and so leding
forth, with here weponys alofte and litys brenning. And in the   *their*
mene time, Marye Magdalene shal rennyn to Oure Lady and telle
her of oure Lordys taking, thus sey[i]ng:

MARIA MAGDALENE. O, immaculate modyr, of all women
      most meke!
O devowtest in holy meditac[i]on evyr abiding!
The cawse, Lady, that I to your person seke
Is to wetyn if ye heryn ony tiding   *know/hear*

Of your swete sone and my reverent Lord, Jhesu,
That was your daily solas, your gostly consolacion.

MARIA. I wold ye shuld telle me, Mawdelyn, and ye knew,   *if*
For to here of him it is all min[e] affeccion.   *hear*

MARIA MAGD[ALENE]. I wold fain telle, Lady, and I myth *if I might*
      for weping:
1050   Forsothe, Lady, to the Jewys he is solde!
With cordys they have him bownde, and have him in
      keping;
They him bete spetously, and have him fast in holde.   *beat spitefully*

MARIA VIRGO. A[h], A[h], A[h], how min[e] hert is colde!
A[h], hert, hard as ston, how mayst thou lest?   *last, endure*
Whan these sorweful tidingys are the[e] told,
So wold to God, hert, that thou mytist brest!   *might burst*

A[h], Jhesu, Jhesu, Jhesu, Jhesu,
Why shuld ye sofere this tribulacion and advercité?
1059   How may they find in here hertys yow to pursewe,   *their*
1060   That nevyr trespacyd in no maner degré?   *You who*
1061   For nevyr thing but that was good thowth ye.   *except what/thought*
Wherefore than shuld ye sofer this gret peyn?   *Why*
I suppoce, verily, it is for the tresspace of me;   *for my sin*
And I wist that, min[e] hert shuld cleve on tweyn. *If I believed/in*

For, these langowrys may I [not] susteyn,   *languors, sorrows*
The swerd of sorwe hath so thirlyd my mende.   *pierced/mind*
Alas, what may I do? Alas, what may I seyn?   *say*
These prongys min[e] herte asondyr they do rende.

O Fadyr of hefne, wher ben al thy behestys   *promises*
1070   That thou promisist me, whan a modyr thou me made?
Thy blissyd sone I bare betwix tweyn bestys,   *two beasts*
And now the bryth colour of his face doth fade.   *bright*

A[h], good Fadyr, why woldist that thin[e] owyn dere
      sone shal sofre al this?

1059–61How can they find it in their hearts to pursue you who never sinned even in the smallest
way? For you never thought anything except what was good.

1074 And dede he nevyr agens thy precept, but evyr was obedient,	*against*
And to every creature most petiful, most jentyl, and bening, iwis;	*benign*
And now for all these kendnessys is now most shameful schent.	*harmed*

Why wolt thou, gracious Fadyr, that it shal be so?	
May man not ellys be savyd by non other kende?	*way*
Yet, Lord Fadyr, than that shal comforte min[e] wo,	*then*
1080 Whan man is savyd by my childe and browth to a good ende.	*brought*

Now, dere sone, syn thou hast evyr be so ful of mercy,	*since/been*
That wilt not spare thyself for the love thou hast to man,	
On all mankend now have thou pety—	
And also think on thy modyr, that hevy woman.	

The Passion Play II

[A year following the previous performance.]

What time that procession is enteryd into the place, and the	*When*
Herowdys takyn his schaffalde, and Pilat and Annas and Caiphas	
here schaffaldys also, than come ther an expositour in doctorys	*their*
wede, thus sey[i]ng:	*garb*

1 CONTEMPLATIO. Sofreynes and frendys, ye mut alle be gret with Gode!	*may you*
Grace, love, and charité evyr be you among.	
The maidenys sone preserve you, that for man deyd on rode;	*maiden's son/cross*
He that is o God in personys thre defende you fro your fon.	*one/foes*

By the leve and soferauns of allmythy God	*sufferance*
We intendyn to procede the matere that we lefte the last yere.	*carry forward*
Wherefore, we beseche yow that your willys be good	
To kepe the Passion in your mende that shal be shewyd here.	

1074Yet he never did anything against your command, but always was obedient.

[PASSION PLAY II, INTRODUCTION]

1s.D.: Preceding this stage direction in the MS, on a separate sheet, two clerics make proclamation, announcing the arrival into the acting arena of a procession of the actors. This proclamation is evidently incomplete and not integral to the rest of the MS, for which reasons it is omitted here.

1Sofreynes: sovereigns, i.e., persons to whom respect is due.

The last yere we shewyd here how oure Lord, for love of
    man,
10 Cam to the cety of Jherusalem, mekely his deth to take;
And how he made his Mawndé, his body geving than   *Last Supper/then*
To his apostelys, evyr with us to abidyn for mannys sake.

In that Mawndé he was betrayd of Judas, that him solde   *by*
To the Jewys for thretty platys, to delivyr him that nyth.   *night*
With swerdys and gleyvys to Jhesu they come with the   *spears*
    tretour bolde,
And toke him amongys his apostelys, about midnyth.

Now wold we procede, how he was browth than   *brought*
Beforn Annas and Caiphas, and sith beforn Pilate,   *then*
And so forth in his Passion—how mekely he toke it for man!
20 Beseking you, for mede of your soulys, to take good hede   *reward*
    theratte.

    Here the Herowndys shal shewe himself and speke.

HERODES REX. Now sees of your talking, and gevith lordly   *cease/give*
    audience!
Not o word, I charge you that ben here present;   *one*
Noon so hardy to presume, in my hey presence,   *No one (be)/high*
To onlose hese lippys ageyn min[e] intent.   *unloose/contrary to*
I am Herowde, of Jewys king most reverent.
The lawys of Mahownde my powere shal fortefye.   *Mohammed/enforce*
Reverens to that lord of grace moost excyllent,   *(Make) reverence*
For by his powere, all thinge doth multiplye.

Yef ony Cristyn be so hardy his feyth to denye,   *If any*
10 Or onys to erre ageyns his lawe,   *once*
On gebettys with cheynes I shal hangyn him heye,   *gibbets, gallows*
And with wilde hors tho traitorys shal I drawe!   *those/tear apart*
To kille a thowsand Cristyn, I gif not an hawe.   *i.e., don't care a bit*
To se hem hangyn or brent to me is very plesauns—   *burned*
15 To drivyn hem into doongenys, dragonys to knawe   *dungeons/gnaw*
16 And to rend here flesche and bonys, onto here sustenauns!   *their*

John the Baptist cristenyd Crist, and so he dede many
    on[e];
Therfore myself dede him bringe o dawe.   *did slay him*
It is I that dede him kille, I telle you everychon;

[THE TEXT]

15–16To drive them into dungeons, where dragons will gnaw and tear apart their flesh and
bones, for the dragons' sustenance.

20   For, and he had go forth, he shuld a distroyd our lawe.   *if/gone/have*
      Whereas Cristyn apperith, to me is gret grevauns;   *Wherever Christians*
      It peynith min[e] hert of tho tretowrys to here.   *those/hear*
      For, the lawys of Mahownde I have in governawns,
      The which I wele kepe. That lord hath no pere,
      For he is god most prudent. [*To his officers.*]
      Now I charge you, my lordys that ben here:
      If any Cristyn doggys here doth apere,
      Bring tho tretorys to my hey powere,   *high*
      And they shal have sone jewgement.

30 1 MILES.   My sovereyn lord, heyest of excillens,
      In you all jewgement is terminabyle.   *has its origin*
      All Cristyn doggys that do not here diligens,   *their*
      Ye put hem to peynes that ben inportable.   *unbearable*
    2 MILES.   No thing in you may be more comendable
      As to disstroye tho traitorys that erre   *Than/those*
      Ageyn oure lawys; that ben most profitable.   *Against*
      By rythwisnesse that lawe ye must proferre.   *righteousness/advance*

    REX HEROW[DES].   Now, by glorious Mahownd, my sovereyn
            saviour,
      These promessys I make as I am trewe knyth: *knight*
40   Thoo that excede his lawys, by ony errour,   *any*
      To the most shamefullest deth I shal hem dyth.   *put them*
      But o thing is sore in my gret delite: *one*
      There is on[e] Jhesus of Nazareth, as men me tellith;
      Of that man I desire to han a sithte,   *have a sight*
      For with many gret wondrys oure lawe he fellith.   *miracles/overthrows*

      The son of God himself he callith,
      And king of Jewys he seyth is he;
      And many woundrys of him befallith.   *happen by his means*
      My hert desirith him for to se.
      Serys, if that he come in this cowntré,
51   With oure jurresdiccion loke ye aspye,   *authority*
      And anon that he be brouth onto me;   *brought*
      And the trewth myself than shal trye.   *I'll then determine*

    1 MILES.   Tomorwe my jorné I shal beginne
      To seke Jhesus with my dew diligens.
      Yif he come your province withinne
      He shal not askape your hey presens.

---

[51]Investigate the matter with our authority.

2 MILES.   Min[e] sovereyn, this is my cowncel that ye shal take:

59	A man that is bothe wise and stronge	
60	Thurwe all Galilé a serge to make	*Through/search*
61	If Jhesu be enteryd your pepyl among.	*(To see) if*
	Correcte hese dedys that be do wronge,	*his deeds/are done*
	For his body is undyr your bayle—	*jurisdiction*
	As men talkyn hem among	*say among themselves*
	That he was born in Galilé.	

REX.   Thanne of these materys, serys, take hede.
For a while I wele me rest.
Appetide requirith me so indede,
And fesyk tellith me it is the best.   *physic, medicine*

[*Herod retires on his scaffold.*]

Here shal a massanger com into the place, renning and crying   *platea*
"Tidingys, tidingys!" and so rownd abowth the place, "Jhesus
of Nazareth is take, Jhesus of Nazareth is take!" and forthwith
heyling the princes, thus sey[i]ng: *hailing*

70	MASSANGER. All heyle, my lordys, princys of prestys!	*chief priests*
	Sere Caiphas and sere Annas, lordys of the lawe,	
	Tidingys I bringe you—reseive them in your brestys:	
	Jhesus of Nazareth is take! Therof ye may be fawe.	*glad*

He shal be browth hedyr to you anon,   *brought hither*
I telle you trewly, with a gret rowth.   *crowd*
Whan he was take, I was hem among,   *taken/them*
And ther was I ner to kachyd a clowte.   *near to have caught a blow*

78	Malcus bar a lanterne, and put him in pres;	*bore, carried/throng*
	Anoon he had a towche—and of[f] went his ere!	*touch, blow/ear*
	Jhesus bad[e] his disciple put up his swerd and ces,	*cease*
81	And sett Malcus ere ageyn as hool as it was ere.	*whole/before*

82	So mot I thé, methowut it was a strawnge syth!	*prosper*
	Whan we cam first to him, he cam us ageyn	*toward us*
	And haskyd whom we sowth that t'me of nyth?	*sought/night*
	We seyd, "Jhesus of Nazareth—we wolde have him fain."	

59–61Let a man who is both wise and strong make a search through all Galilee to see if Jesus has gone among your people.

78*put . . . pres*: took part in the throng, or, got himself in a predicament.

01–02And healed Malchus' ear again as whole as it was previously. As I hope to prosper, I thought it was a strange sight.

And he seyd, "It is I, that am here in your syth."   *sight*
With that word we ovyrthrowyn bakward everychon[e],   *we fell*
And some on here bakkys, lyeng upryth;   *their/face upward*
But standing upon fote manly ther was not on[e].   *boldly*

Crist stod on his fete as meke as a lom,   *lamb*
And we loyn stille lyche ded men, til he bad[e] us rise.   *lay/like*
Whan we were up, fast handys we leyd him upon;
93   But yet methought I was not plesyd with the newe g[u]ise.

94   Therfore, takith now your cowncel and avise you ryth weyl,   *take/very well*
95   And beth ryth ware that he make you not amat;   *be very careful/overwhelmed*
For, by my thrifte, I dare sweryn at this seyl   *swear/time*
Ye shal finde him a strawnge watt!   *fellow*
   Here bring they Jhesus beforn Annas and C[aiphas], and on[e]
   shal seyn thus:

Lo, lo, lordys, here is the man
That ye sent us fore!
100 ANNAS.   Therfore we cone you thanke, than,   *we thank you*
And reward ye shal have the more.

Jhesus, thou art welcome hedyr to oure presens.
Ful oftyntimes we han the[e] besily do sowth;   *had you sought for*
We paid to thy disciple for the[e] thretty pens,
And as an ox or an hors we trewly the[e] bowth;   *bought*

Therfore, now art oure as thou standist us before.   *(you) are ours*
Sey why thou [h]ast trobelyd us and subvertyd oure lawe?
Thou hast ofte concludyd us—and so thou hast do more—   *confuted/done to*
Wherefore it were ful nedful to bring the[e] a dawe.   *to slay you*

110 CAIPHAS.   What arn thy disciplys that folwyn the[e] aboute?   *Who are*
And what is thy doctrine that thou dost preche?
Telle me now somewhath and bring us out of doute,
That we may to othere men thy preching forth teche.

JHES[US].   Al times that I have prechyd, opyn it was don
In the synagog or in the temple, where that all Jewys com.
Aske hem what I have seyd, and also what I have don;   *them*
They con telle the[e] my wordys; aske hem everychon.

93*newe g[u]ise*: i.e., the way things were going, the way Christ was still able to show his strange power.

94-95Therefore, consider among yourselves and think this through carefully, and watch out that he doesn't overwhelm or stun you (as he did the crowd at Gethsemane).

1 JUDEUS.   What, thou fela, to whom spekist thou?
    Shalt thou so speke to a buschop?
    Thou shalt have on the cheke, I make a vow,
    And yet therto a knok.   *in addition*
      Here he shal smite Jhesus on the cheke.

    JHESUS.   If I have seyd amis,
123   Therof witnesse thou mayst bere;
    And if I have seyd but weyl in this,
    Thou dost amis me to dere.   *to hurt me*

    ANNAS.   Serys, takith hed now to this man,   *take heed*
    That he distroye not oure lawe;
    And bringe ye witnesse agens him that ye can,   *(all) that*
    So that he may be browt of dawe.   *be slain*

130 1 DOCTOR.   Sere, this I herd him with his owyn mowth seyn:
    "Brekith down this temple without delay,   *Break*
    And I shal settynt up ageyn   *set it*
    As hool as it was, by the thridde day."   *whole*

    2 DOCTOR.   Ya, ser, and I herd him seyn also
    That he was the sone of God;
    And yet many a fole wenith so,   *fool thinks so*
137   I durst leyn theron min[e] hod.

    3 DOCTOR.   Ya, ya, and I herd him preche meche thing—   *much, many*
    And agens oure lawe, every del—   *against/bit*
    Of wheche it were longe to make rekening
    To tellyn all at this seel.   *time*

    CAIPHAS.   What seyst now, Jhesus? Why answerist not?
    Herist not what is seyd agens the[e]?
    Spek, man, spek! Spek, thou fop!   *fool*
    Hast thou scorn to speke to me?
    Herist not in how many thingys they the[e] acuse?
    Now I charge the[e] and conjure, by the sonne and the
         mone,
    That thou telle us and thou be Goddys sone.   *if*

    JHESUS.   Goddys sone I am—I sey not nay to the[e]—
150   And that ye all shal se at domysday,

123You can bear witness as to how I spoke amiss (see John 18:23).

137I dare pledge or bet my head (hood) on that.

Whan the sone shal come in gret powere and magesté
And deme the qweke and dede, as I the[e] say.   *judge the quick, living*

CAIPHAS.   A, out, out, allas, what is this?
Herith ye not how he blasfemith God?
What nedith us to have more witness?
Here ye han herd all his owyn word:
Think ye not he is worthy to dey?

Et clamabunt omnes: *And they will all cry out*
Yis, yis, yis! All we seye he is worthy to dey, ya, ya, ya!
ANNAS.   Takith him to yow and betith him som del   *Take/beat/somewhat*
160   For hese blasfeming at this sel.   *time*
*Here they shal bete Jhesus about the hed and the body and spittyn
in his face, and pullyn him down and settyn him on a stol, and
castyn a cloth ovyr his face; and the first shal seyn:*   *i.e., blindfold him*

1 JUDEUS.   A, felawys, beware what ye do to this man,
For he prophecye weyl kan.
2 JUDEUS.   That shal be asayd by this batte.   *tested/blow*
What, thou Jhesus? [W]ho gaff the[e] that?   *gave*
Et percutiet super caput.   *And he will hit him on the head*

3 JUDEUS.   Whar, whar! Now wole I   *Beware, watch out*
Wetyn how he can prophecy. [*Hits him.*]   *Know*
[W]ho was that?
4 JUDEUS.   A, and now wole I a newe game beginne
That we mon pley at, all that arn hereinne.   *may/are here*
170   Whele and pylle, whele and pylle!
171   Comith to hall, [w]hoso wille. [*Hits him.*]   *Come*
[W]ho was that?

Here shal the woman come to [the] Jewys and seyn:
173 1 ANCILLA.   What, serys, how take ye on with this man?   *maidservant*
Se ye not on[e] of hese disciplys, how he beheldith you than?
Here shal the tother woman seyn to Petyr:
2 ANCILLA.   A, good man, me semith by the[e]   *by your appearance*
That thou on[e] of hese disciplys shulde be.   *must be*
PETRUS.   A, woman, I sey nevyr er this man   *saw never before*
Syn that this wer[l]d first began.   *Since*
Et cantabit gallus.   *And the cock will crow*

170–71 (They are mocking Jesus by playing with him a children's blindfold game. This buffeting continues during the questioning of Peter, ll. 172–92.)

173 How now, sirs, what is your affair with this man?

1 ANCILLA.   What? Thou mayst not sey nay. Thou art on[e]
    of hese men.
  By thy face, wel we may the[e] ken.   *know*
PETRUS.   Woman, thou seyst amis of me.
  I knowe him not, so mote I thé!   *as I hope to prosper*
1 JUDEUS.   A, fela min[e], wel met!
184 For my cosinys ere thou of [f] smet,   *my kinsman's ear*
  Whan we thy maister in the yerd toke.
  Than all thy felawys him forsoke;
  And now thou mayst not him forsake,
  For thou art of Galilé, I undyrtake.   *I'll venture to assert*

PETRUS.   Sere, I knowe him not, by Him that made me!
190 And ye wole me beleve for an oth,   *If*
  I take record of all this companye,   *I affirm before all*
  That I sey to yow is soth.   *That which/truth*
   Et cantabit gallus.   *And the cock will crow*
   And than Jhesus shal lokyn on Petyr, and Petyr shal wepyn, and
   than he shal gon out and seyn:

  A, weelaway, weelaway! Fals hert, why whilt thou not brest, *burst*
  Syn thy maistyr so cowardly thou hast forsake?   *Since*
  Alas, qwher shal I now on erthe rest,   *where*
  Til he of his mercy to grace wole me take?

  I have forsake my maister and my Lord, Jhesu,
  Thre times, as he tolde me that I shuld do the same.
  Wherfore I may not have sorwe anow,   *enough*
200 I, sinful creature, am so mech to blame.

  Whan I herd the cok crowyn, he kest on me a loke, *cast*
  As who seyth, "Bethinke the[e] what I seyd before!" *As one might say*
  Alas the time that I evyr him forsoke!
  And so wil I thinkyn from hens evyrmore.

CAIPHAS.   Massangere, massangere!
MASSANGERE.   Here, lord, here!
CAIPHAS.   Massanger, to Pilat in hast thou shalt gon,
  And sey him, we comawnde us in word and in dede, *commend ourselves*
  And prey him that he be at the mot-halle anoon, *judgment hall*
210 For we han a gret matere that he must nedys spede. *assist*

  In hast now go thy way,
  And loke thou tery nowth.   *tarry not*

184For you smote off my kinsman's (Malchus') ear.

MASSANGER.   It shal be do, lord, by this day!   *done*
     I am as whyt as thought.   *swift*
          Here Pilat sittith in his skaffald, and the massanger knelith to
          him, thus sey[i]ng:

     Al heyl, sere Pilat, that semly is to se,   *seemly, lovely*
     Prince of al this Juré, and kepere of the lawe!   *Jewry*
     My lord, busshop Caiphas, comawndyd him to the[e]   *commended*
     And prayd the[e] to be at the mot-halle by the day dawe.   *dawn*

     PILAT.   Go thy way, praty masanger, and comawnde me   *brave*
          also.
220 I shal be there in hast, and so thou mayst say:
     By the [h]oure of prime I shal comyn hem to.   *6 a.m./to them*
     I tery no lenger, no[r] make no delay.
          Here the massanger comith agen and bringith an ansuere, thus
          sey[i]ng:

     MASSANGER.   Al heyl, min[e] lordys and buschoppys and
          princys of the lawe!
     Ser Pilat comawndith him to you, and bad[e] me to
          you say
     He wole be at the mot-halle in hast, sone after the day
          dawe.
     He wold ye shuld be ther by prime, withouth lenger
          delay.
     CAIPHAS.   Now, weyl mote thou fare, my good page.   *well may you prosper*
     Take thou this for thy massage. [*Rewards him.*]

          Here enterith Judas onto the Juwys, thus sey[i]ng:
     JUDAS.   I, Judas, have sinnyd and treson have don,
230 For I have betrayd this rythful blood!   *rightful*
     Here is your mony agen, all and som[e].
     For sorwe and thowth I am wax wood.   *(grievous) thought/mad*

     ANNAS.   What is that to us? Avise the[e], now: *Consider*
     Thou dedist with us covnawnt make—   *covenant*
     Thou soldist him us as hors or kow—
     Therfore, thin[e] owyn dedys thou must take.   *i.e., accept the consequences*
          Than Judas castith down the mony, and goth and hangith himself.

     CAIPHAS.   Now, serys, the nyth is passyd, the day is come;   *night*
     It were time this man had his jewgement;
     And Pilat abidith in the mot-halle alone
     Til we shuld this man present.

And therfore go we now forth with him in hast.

1 JUDEUS.   It shal be don, and that in short spas.   *quickly*

2 JUDEUS.   Ya, but loke if he be bownd ryth wel and fast.

244 3 JUDEUS.   He is saff anow. Go we ryth a good pas.

Here they ledyn Jhesu abowt the place til they come to the halle.   *platea*

CAIPHAS.   Sere Pilat, takiht hede to this thing: *take heed*

Jhesus we han beforn the[e] browth,   *have brought*

Wheche oure lawe doth down bring,   *Who subverts our law*

And mekyl schame he hath us wrowth.   *much|wrought*

ANNAS.   From this cetye into the lond of Galilé

250 He hath browth oure lawys neyr into confusion,   *brought|nearly*

With hese craftys wrowth by nigramancye   *worked by necromancy*

Shewith to the pepyl by fals simulacion.   *(Which he) shows*

1 DOCTOR.   Ya! yet, ser, another, and werst of alle:

Agens Sesare, oure emperour that is so fre,   *In defiance of Caesar|noble*

King of Jewys he doth him calle.

So oure emperourys power nowth shulde be.   *nought*

2 DOCTOR.   Sere Pilat, we kannot telle half the blame

That Jhesus in oure countré hath wrowth.

Therfore we charge the[e], in the emperorys name,

260 That he to the deth in hast be browth.

PILAT.   What seyst to these compleyntys, Jhesu?

These pepyl hath the[e] sore acusyd,   *sorely, seriously*

Because thou bringist up lawys newe

That in oure days were not usyd.

JHESUS.   Of here acusing me rowth nowth,   *their|I care not*

266 So that they hurt not here soulys, ne non mo.   *Provided|their|more, others*

I have nowth yet founde that I have sowth;   *not|that which|sought*

For my Faderys wil, forth must I go.

PILAT.   Jhesus, by this than I trowe thou art a king

And the sone of God. Thou art also

Lord of erth and of all thing.

Telle me the trowth if it be so.

JHESUS.   In hefne is knowyn my Faderys intent,

---

²⁴⁴He is safe enough. Let us go at a very swift pace.

²⁶⁶Provided that they, or still other persons, do not jeopardize their own souls (by accusing me thus unjustly).

And in this werlde I was born.
By my Fadyr I was hedyr sent
For to seke that was forlorn.   *To seek that which was utterly lost*

Alle that me heryn and in me belevyn,   *All who hear*
And kepyn here feyth stedfastly,   *keep their*
Thow they weryn dede, I shal them recuryn   *Though|were dead|recover*
And shal them bring to blisse, endlesly.

PILATE.   Lo, serys, now ye [h]an [h]erde this man, how   *have heard*
    think ye?
282   Thinke ye not all, by youre reson,
283   But as he seyth it may wel be,   *Exactly as he says*
284   And that shulde be, by this incheson?   *cause*

I finde in him non obecyon   *obstacle*
Of errour nor treson, ne of no maner gilt.
The lawe wole, in no conclusion,   *wills that|case*
Withowte defawth he shuld be spilt.   *fault|killed*

1 DOCTOR.   Sere Pilat, the lawe restith in the[e],
290   And we knowe verily his gret trespas.
To the emperour this mater told shal be,
If thou lete Jhesus thus from the[e] pas.

PILAT.   Serys, than telle me o thing: *one*
    What shal be his acusing?   *accusation*
295 ANNAS.   Sere, we telle the[e], al togedyr
296   For his evil werkys we browth him hedyr.   *brought*
And if he had not an evil-doere be,   *been*
We shuld not a browth him to the[e].   *have*
PILAT.   Takith him, than, aftyr your sawe,   *Take|according to your custom*
And demith him aftyr your lawe.   *condemn*
CAIPHAS.   It is not lefful to us, ye seyn,   *lawful|you see*
No maner man for to slen.   *No kind of|slay*
The cawse why we bring him to the[e],
That he shuld not oure king be.   *(Is) that*
Weyl thou knowist, king we have non
But oure emperour alon.
PILAT.   Jhesu, thou art king of Juré?
JHESUS.   So thou seyst now to me.

²⁸²⁻⁸⁴Don't you all think, if you consider this reasonably, that it may well be and indeed
should be exactly as he says, according to the causes he cites?

²⁹⁵⁻⁹⁶Sir, we tell you, we brought him here on account of all his evil deeds, considered as a
group.

PILAT.   Tel me, than,
310   Where is thy kingham?
JHESUS.   My kingham is not in this werld,
    I telle the[e] at o word.   *one*
    If my kingham here had be,
    I shuld not a be deliveryd to the[e].   *have been*
PILAT.   Serys, avise yow as ye kan.   *do as you think best*
    I can finde no defawth in this man.

317 ANNAS.   Sere, here is a gret record; take hed therto!   *heed*
    And knowing gret mischef in this man—
    And not only in o day or t[w]o,   *one*
    It is many yerys syn he began—   *years since*
    We kan telle the time where and whan
    That many a thowsand turnyd hath he;   *turned, misled*
    As all this pepyll record weyl kan,   *can well attest*
    From hens into the lond of Galilé.
        Et clamabunt ya, ya, ya!   *And they will exclaim ya!*

PILAT.   Serys, of o thing than gif me relacion: *one/an account*
    If Jhesus were out-born in the lond of Galelye?   *born abroad*
    For we han no poer ne no jurediccion   *have no power*
    Of no man of that contré.
    Therfore, the trewth ye telle me,
330   And another wey I shal provide:
    If Jhesus were born in that countré,
    The jugement of Herowdys he must abide.

CAIPHAS.   Sere, as I am to the lawe trewly sworn,
    To telle the trewth I have no fer: *fear*
    In Galelye I know that he was born.
    I can telle in what place, and where—
    Agens this no man may answere—   *No one can contradict this*
    For he was born in Bedlem, Judé.   *in Bethlehem in Judaea*
    And this ye knowe now all, and have don here,
340   That it stant in the lond of Galelye.   *stands, is situated*

PILAT.   Weyl, serys, syn that I knowe that it is so,   *since*
    The trewth of this I must nedys se;   *see, understand*
    I undyrstand ryth, now, what is to do.   *correctly*
    The jugement of Jhesu lyth not to me.   *lies, pertains*
    Herowde is king of that countré,
    To jewge that region in lenth and in brede.   *breadth*
    The jurisdiccion of Jhesu now han must he;   *have*

317i.e., Sir, here is a long record of troublemaking; pay attention to it.

Therfore, Jhesu in hast to him ye lede.
In hall the hast that ye may spede   *all the haste*
350 Lede him to the Herownde, anon present,   *at once*
And sey I comawnde me with worde and dede,   *commend*
And Jhesu to him that I have sent.

1 DOCTOR.   This erand in hast sped shal be,
In all the hast that we can do.
We shal not tary in no degre
Til the Herowdys presens we com to.
Here they take Jhesu and lede him in gret hast to the Herowde.
And the Herowdys scafald shal unclose shewing Herowdes in
astat, all the Jewys kneling except Annas and Caiphas, they   *state*
shal stondyn, etcetera.

1 DOCTOR.   Heyl, Herowde, most excyllent king!
We arn comawndyd to thin[e] presens;   *are commended*
Pilat sendith the[e], by us, greting,
360 And chargith us, by oure obediens—
2 DOCTOR.   That we shuld do oure diligens
To bring Jhesus of Nazareth onto the[e],
And chargith us to make no resistens,   *opposition*
Becawse he was born in this countré.

ANNAS.   We knowe he hath wrowth gret folé   *wrought/folly, mischief*
Ageyns the lawe shewyd present. [*He displays the written*
laws.]
Therfore Pilat sent him onto the[e]
That thou shuldist gif him jugement.

HEROWDE REX.   Now by Mahound, my god of grace,
Of Pilat this is a dede ful kende—   *kind deed*
371 I forgif him now his gret trespace,
And schal be his frend withowtyn ende—   *unceasingly*
Jhesus to me that he wole sende!
I desired ful sore him for to se;   *him (Jesus)*
Gret ese in this Pilat shal finde.
And, Jhesus, thou art welcome to me!

1 JUDEUS.   My sovereyn lord, this is the case:
The gret falsnesse of Jhesu is opynly knawe—   *known*
Ther was nevyr man dede so gret trespas—   *who did*
380 For he hath almost distroyd oure lawe.

[371]*trespace*: Luke 23, the only authority for this trial before Herod, reports that prior to this,
Herod and Pilate "were at enmity between themselves."

2 JUDEUS.   Ya, by fals crafte of soserye,   *sorcery*
  Wrowth opynly to the pepyll alle,   *Wrought*
  And by sotyl pointys of nigramancye,   *subtle instances*
  Many thowsandys fro oure lawe be falle.   *have fallen away*

CAIPHAS.   Most excellent king, ye must take hede!
  He wol distroye all this countré, both elde and ying,   *young*
  If he ten monthis more procede.
  By his meraclys and fals preching
  He bringith the pepyl in gret fonning,   *madness*
390 And seyth daily among hem alle
  That he is Lord and of the Jewys king;
  And the sone of God he doth him calle.

REX HEROWDE.   Serys, alle these materys I have herd said,
  And meche more than ye me telle.   *much*
  Alle togedyr they shal be laide,   *i.e., considered together*
  And I wil take theron cowncelle.

  Jhesus, thou art welcome to me!
  I kan Pilat gret thank for his sending;
  I have desiryd ful longe the[e] to se,
400 And of thy meracles to have knowing.
  It is told me thou dost many a wondyr thing:
  Crokyd to gon and blind men to sen,   *Lame/go, walk/see*
  And they that ben dede gevist hem leving,   *dead/them life*
  And makist lepers faire and hool to ben.   *whole*

  These arn wondyr werkys wrougth of the[e].   *are wondrous/wrought by*
  By what wey? I wolde knowe the trew sentens.   *significance*
  Now, Jhesu, I pray the[e], lete me se
  O meracle wrougth in my presens.   *One*
  In hast, now, do thy diligens,
410 And peraventure I wil shew favour to the[e].
  For, now thou art in my presens,
  Thin[e] lif and deth here lyth in me.
   And here Jhesus shal not speke no word to the Herowde.

  Jhesus, why spekist not to thy king?
  What is the cawse thou stondist so stille?
  Thou knowist I may deme all thing: *judge*
  Thin[e] lif and deth lyth at my wille.

  What! Spek, Jhesus, and telle me why
  This pepyl do the[e] so here acuse?
  Spare not, but telle me now, on hey,   *in haste*
420 How thou canst thyself excuse.

CAIPHAS.   Loo, serys, this is of him a false sotilté:
He wil not speke but whan he list.   *except/wishes*
Thus he disceivith the pepyl in eche degre;   *in every way*
He is ful fals, ye verily trist.   *you (may) trust*

REX HEROWDE.   What, thou onhangyd harlot, why wilt   *rascal*
    thou not speke?
Hast thou skorne to speke onto thy king?
Becawse thou dost oure lawys breke,
I trowe thou art aferd of oure talking.

429 ANNAS.   Nay, he is not aferde, but of a fals wile,
430 Becawse we shuld not him acuse;
If that he answerd yow ontille,   *unto you*
He knowith he kannot himself excuse.

433 REX HEROWDE.   What, spek, I say, thou fouling! Evil mot
    thou fare!
434 Loke up, the devil mote the[e] cheke!
Serys, bete his body with scorgys bare,
And asay to make him for to speke.   *assay, try*

2 JUDEUS.   It shal be do withoutyn teryeng.   *done/tarrying*
Come on, thou tretour, evil mot thou thé!   *evilly may you prosper*
Whilt thou not speke onto oure king?
440 A new lesson we shal lere the[e].   *teach*
    Here they pulle of [f] Jhesus clothis and betyn him with whippys.

1 JUDEUS.   Jhesus, thy bonys we shal not breke,
But we shal make the[e] to skippe!
Thou hast lost thy tonge? Thou mayst not speke?
Thou shalt asay now of this whippe.   *assay, taste*

3 JUDEUS.   Serys, take these whippys in your honde
And spare not whil they last,
And bete this tretoure that here doth stonde.
I trowe that he wil speke in hast.
    And qwan they han betyn him til he is all blody, than the Herownd   *when*
    seyth:

429-30No, he is not afraid, but possessed of a false intent (will) calculated to avoid our accusation.

433-34What, speak, I say, you wretch! May you fare evilly! Look up (at me), may the devil give you a repulse (check)!

Sees, serys, I comawnde you, by name of the devil of   *Cease*
    helle!

450   Jhesus, thinkist this good game?
Thou art strong to suffyr schame;
Thou haddist levyr be betyn lame   *rather*
Than thy defawtys for to telle.

But I wil not thy body all spil,   *kill*
Nor put it here into more peyn.
Serys, takith Jhesus at your owyn wil,   *take*
And lede him to Pilat hom ageyn.
Grete him weyl, and telle him serteyn   *Greet*
All my good frenchep shal he have.

460   I gif him powere of Jhesus—thus ye him seyn—   *over/say to him*
Whether he wole him dampne or save.

1 DOCTOR.   Sere, at your request it shal be do.
We shal lede Jhesus at your demaw[n]de,
And deliver him Pilat onto,
And telle him all as ye comawnde.

   Here enterith Satan into the place in the most [h]orrible wise;
   and qwil that he pleyth, they shal don on Jhesus clothis and overest   *while/put on outermost*
   a white clothe, and ledyn him abowth the place, and than to Pilat   *platea*
   by the time that hese wif hath pleyd.

THE BUFFETING
FROM WAKEFIELD

Because of the extraordinary emphasis in late medieval art on Christ's physical suffering, all the English cycles include extensive scenes of torture. The most important scenes are generally four in number: the so-called buffeting at the house of the chief priests, the interrogation by Herod, the scourging at Pilate's hall when Christ is mocked with a crown of thorns, and the Crucifixion itself. We have already seen the first two of these episodes somewhat briefly reported in the N Town Passion sequence (II, 160–72, 437–48). For a more elaborately detailed and inventive account of the buffeting, we now turn to a work of the Wakefield Master.

The persecutors of Christ are divided into two groups in this Wakefield pageant: the commoners of the Jewish state, and their chief priests. The commoners, called *tortores* or torturers in this text, are composite types skillfully made up out of numerous suggestions in the Gospel narrative. First of all, they represent the two false witnesses who come forward at the house of the chief priests to accuse Jesus of having threatened to destroy and rebuild the temple (Matthew 26: 60–61, Mark 14: 57–58). Then they represent the unnamed persons who revile Jesus at the close of his first trial, taunting him by bidding their blindfolded victim to declare who it is that has struck him (Matthew 26 : 67, Luke 22 : 63–64). They also represent the Jews mentioned in the apocryphal Gospel of Nicodemus (I,i) who accuse Jesus of healing on the Sabbath and proclaiming himself a king. Lastly, they are the common soldiers, not mentioned in the Bible but assumed to be present, who abusively guard the prisoner on his round of ordeals. Despite their indebtedness to so many dif-

ferent narrative sources, however, these two *tortores* are endowed by the Wakefield Master with a dramatic vitality all their own. They complain bitterly of their tedious labor on Jesus' account, and want to make sure the authorities know how much they have suffered in the line of duty. Their rascally boy servant, Froward, like his counterparts in the Killing of Abel and the Second Shepherds' pageant, resents his scant rations and lack of pay. The soldiers vie with one another in landing blows on the prisoner's head. Indeed, their rough handling of Jesus means little more to them than a series of children's games, such as Hot Cockles or ninepins. Absorbed thus in their play, as V. A. Kolve observes (*The Play Called Corpus Christi*, p. 185f.), they fail to perceive the spiritual dimensions of the great event to which they contribute. They comically typify shortsighted humankind, unable to bear too much reality. Yet we ironically remember that Christ's mission is to save this same unregenerate mankind.

The leaders, Caiaphas and Annas, are more blameworthy than the soldiers because of their higher responsibility. The two chief priests brilliantly complement one another as satiric types. Caiaphas is a ranting bully, aroused to ungovernable fury by Christ's refusal to answer his questions (a detail borrowed in part from the account of Christ's trial before Herod; see Luke 23 : 6–12). Caiaphas is endlessly terrorized by imagined fears: what if Pilate should take a bribe and let Jesus off? This fear is all the more ironic since Caiaphas himself has apparently offered Jesus pardon in return for submission and payment of tribute (ll. 157–58). Caiaphas is the tyrant victimized by his own brutality, imprisoned in a nightmare of suspicion. Annas, on the other hand, is the smooth-tongued lawyer, the cleverer of the two by far. His hostility toward Jesus is more dangerous because he is so subtly adept at warping the law to his specious interests.

The staging plan simply requires a scaffold for the chief priests and a space in front of the scaffold where Jesus is tortured. The tableau thus presents an ironic contrast between haughty worldlings on their raised platform and a humble victim beaten by thugs. This contrast is further reinforced by the juxtaposition of comic noisiness and eloquent silence. Although the Gospel of John (18 : 20–23) offers textual authority for considerable dialogue between Christ and the chief priests, the Wakefield Master chooses to have Christ speak only once in this pageant. Aware of what is to come, Christ silently endures the profane verbosity and assaults of his accusers.

The Buffeting
From Wakefield

Incipit Coliphizatio.	*Here begins the Buffeting*

[*The torturers are driving the bound Jesus from his first arraignment before Pilate, to Caiaphas' hall.*]

1 TORTOR.	Do io furth, io, and trott on apase!		*Gee up (as to animals)*
	To Anna will we go, and sir Caiphas.		*Annas*
3	Witt thou well, of thaym two gettys thou no grace,		*you'll get*
	Bot everlasting wo, for trespas[t] thou has		*because you've offended*
	So mekill.		*much*
	Thy mis is more		*wrongdoing*
7	Then ever gettys thou grace fore!		
	Thou has beyn ay-whore		*everywhere*
	Full fals and full fekill.		

2 TORTOR.	It is wonder to dre, thus to be ganging.		*a lot to endure/journeying*
	We have had for the[e] mekill hart-stanging.		*on your account much heartache*
12	Bot at last shall we be out of hart-langing,		*done with heart-longing*
13	By thou have had two or thre hetys-worth a hanging.		*promises-worth of*
	No wonder!		
	Sich wiles can thou make,		
	Gar the people farsake		*Cause/to forsake*

[3]Understand this well, you'll get no pardon from those two.

[7]Than ever you can be pardoned for.

[12–13]But finally we'll be through with our sufferings by the time you've had two or three promises-worth of hanging (i.e., when our problems of arresting you are at an end, your misery will just be starting).

Oure lawes, and thine take—   *and to believe in your laws*
Thus art thou broght in blonder.

1 TORTOR.   Thou cannot say againt, if thou be trew.   *say against, deny it*
Som men holdys the[e] sant, and that shall thou rew.   *consider you a saint*
21   Fare wordys can thou paint, and lege lawes new.   *allege, assert*
2 TORTOR.   Now be ye ataint, for we will persew   *accused/proceed*
On this mater.   *With*
Many wordys has thou saide
Of which we ar not well paide;   *pleased*
26   As good that thou had
27   Halden still thy clater.

28 1 TORTOR.   It is better sit still then rise up and fall.
Thou has long had thy will and made many brall;
30   At the last, wold thou spill and fordo us all,   *kill and destroy*
31   If we did never ill.   *Even if*
2 TORTOR.   I trow not he shall
32   Indure it;
For if other men ruse him,   *praise*
We shall accuse him.
35   Hisself shall not excuse him,   *excuse himself*
36   To you I insure it,   *assure*

37   With no legeance.   *extenuating plea*
1 TORTOR.   Fain wold he wink,   *Gladly/sleep*
38   Els falys his countenance; I say as I think.
2 TORTOR.   He has done us grevance; therfor shall he drink.   *pay the penalty*
40   Have he mekill mischaunsce, that has gart us swinke   *caused us toil*
41   In walking,
42   That unneth may I more!   *scarcely/(go) further*
1 TORTOR.   Peas, man, we ar thore.   *there*
I shall walk in before,
And tell of his talking.
     [*They arrive at Caiaphas' hall, and greet*
     Caiaphas and Annas.]

[21]You can preach deceptively (painting falsely with words), and assert new spiritual laws.

[26–27]It would have been just as well for you to have held still with your prating.

[28]i.e., Pride goes before a fall.

[30–32]Finally you'd kill and destroy us all, even if we didn't do anything to deserve it. —I am sure he (Christ) won't be able to endure what we'll do to him.

[35–38]He won't be able to excuse himself with any extenuating plea, I assure you of that. —Either he wants to sleep or else he looks crestfallen, I declare.

[40–42]May he have much bad luck, because he has made us toil so in our marching that I can scarcely go another step.

Haill, sirs, as ye sitt, so worthy in wonys!   *so respected everywhere*

47   Why spyrd ye not yit how we have farne this onys?   *asked/fared/once*

   2 TORTOR.   Sir, we wold fain [ye] witt, all wery ar oure bonys!   *we'd like you to know*

49   We have had a fitt right ill for the nonys,   *crisis/nonce, occasion*

50   So taryd.   *So delayed (as we were)*

   CAIPHAS.   Say, were ye oght adred?   *at all afraid*

   Were ye oght wrang led?

   Or in any strate sted?   *put in any straits*

   Sirs, who was miscaryd?   *did anyone come to harm*

   ANNA.   Say, were ye oght in dowte for fawte of light,   *default, lack*

   As ye wached therowte?   *outdoors*

   1 TORTOR.   Sir as I am true knight,

57   Of my dame sen I sowked, had I never sich a night!

58   Min[e] een were not lowked togeder right   *eyes/closed*

59   Sen morowe.   *Since dawn*

   Bot yit I think it well sett,   *settled, finished*

   Sen we with this tratoure met. [*Indicating Jesus.*]   *Since*

   Sir, this is he that forfett,   *offended*

   And done so mekill sorow.   *did/much*

   CAIPHAS.   Can ye him oght apeche? Had he any ferys?   *accuse him at all/companions*

   2 TORTOR.   He has bene for to preche full many long yeris,   *has been preaching*

   And the people he teche a new law.   *teaches*

   1 TORTOR.   Sirs, heris!   *listen*

67   As far as his witt reche, many oone he leris.   *reaches/teaches*

   When we toke him

   We faunde him in a yerde;   *i.e., Garden of Gethsemane*

   Bot when I drew out my swerde,

   His discipyls wex ferde   *grew afraid*

   And soyn thay forsoke him.   *soon*

   2 TORTOR.   Sir, I hard him say he cowthe distroew oure   *destroy*
      tempyll so gay,

   And sithen beld a new on the thrid day.   *then build*

   CAIPHAS.   How might that be trew? It toke more aray!   *preparation*

   The masons I knewe that hewed it, I say,

   So wise,

47Why haven't you asked yet how we've fared this time? (Evidently the torturers don't feel the chief priests are showing enough sympathy.)

49–50i.e., We've had a perfectly terrible time of it, we were delayed so.

57–59Never, since I suckled from my mother (i.e., in my life), have I had such a night! My eyes haven't even closed since dawn (yesterday).

67To the extent of his intelligence (or, as far and wide as people hear him), he teaches many a person.

	That hewed ilka stone.	*every*
79	1 TORTOR. A, good sir, let him oone.	*alone*
	He lies for the quetstone—	*whetstone (prize for lying)*
	I gif him the price!	*prize*

	2 TORTOR. The halt rynes, the blind sees thrugh his fals wiles;	*lame run, walk*
	Thus he gettys many fees of thym he beg[u]iles.	*from them*
84	1 TORTOR. He rases men that dees—thay seke him by miles—	*die*
	And ever thrugh his soceres oure Sabate-day defiles	*sorceries/Sabbath*
	Evermore, sir.	
	2 TORTOR. This is his use and his custom:	
	To heyll the defe and the dom,	*heal the deaf/dumb*
	Wheresoever he com;	
90	I tell you before, sir.	

	1 TORTOR. Men call him a king and Godys son of heven.	
	He wold fain downe bring oure lawes by his steven.	*voice*
	2 TORTOR. Yit is ther anothere thing that I hard him neven:	*heard/mention*
94	He settys not a fle-wing by sir Cesar, full even—	*cares/flea/indeed*
	He says thus.	
	Sir, this same is he	
	That excusyd with his sotelté	*subtlety, cunning*
	A woman in avowtré,	*adultery*
	Full well may ye trust us.	

100	1 TORTOR. Sir Lazare can he rase—that men may persave—	*he did/perceive*
	When he had lyne fower dayes ded in his grave.	*lain*
	All men him prase, both master and knave,	*servant*
	Such wichcraft he mase.	*makes, performs*
	2 TORTOR. If he abowte wave	*wander about*
	Any langere,	
	His warkys may we ban,	*works/curse*
	For he has turned many man	*misled*
	Sen the time he began,	*Since*
	And done us great hangere.	*trouble*

	1 TORTOR. He will not leyfe yit, thof he be culpabyll.	*leave off/though*
	Men call him a prophete, a lord full renabyll.	*eloquent*
111	Sir Caiphas, by my witt, he shuld be dampnabill,	*condemnable*

79*let him oone:* Leave him to his own devices, watch what he'll do.

84He resurrects men who have died—people seek him for miles around.

90i.e., I tell you this before the interrogation begins.

94He doesn't care the value of a flea-wing for Caesar, indeed.

111–13Sir Caiphas, in my judgment he should be condemned, if only you two, as you sit, would both confirm and verify this sentence.

112 Bot wold ye two, as ye sitt, make it ferme and stabyll   *If only*
113 Togeder.
     For ye two, as I traw,   *trow, believe*
     May defende all oure law;
     That mayde us to you draw,   *caused us/come to you*
     And bring this losell heder.   *rogue*

118 2 TORTOR.   Sir, I can tell you before, as might I be maryd,   *be marred*
     If he reyne any more, oure lawes ar miscaryd.   *prevail/miscarried*
120 1 TORTOR.   Sir, opposed if he wore, he shuld be fon waryd;   *examined*
121 That is well seyn thore where he has long taryd   *wherever/tarried*
122 And walkyd.
     He is sowre-lottyn—   *sour-looking*
124 Ther is somwhat forgottyn!   *something*
125 I shall thring out the rottyn   *drive out*
126 By we have all talkyd.   *By (the time)*

     CAIPHAS.   Now, fare might you fall for youre talking!   *may fair luck befall you*
     For, certys, I myself shall make examining.
          [*He turns to Jesus.*]
129 Harstow, harlott, of all? Of care may thou sing!   *Do you hear*
     How durst thou the[e] call aythere emperoure or king?   *call yourself either*
     I do fy the[e]!   *say fie to*
     What the dwill doist thou here?   *devil*
     Thy dedys will do the[e] dere.   *harm*
     Com nar and rowne in min[e] eeyr,   *nearer/whisper*
     Or I shall ascry the[e].   *denounce*
          [*Jesus remains silent, infuriating Caiaphas.*]

136 Illa-hayll was thou borne! Harke, says he oght agane?   *Bad luck/aught*
137 Thou shall onys, or to-morne, to speke be full fayne.   *once ere tomorrow*
     This is a great skorne and a fals trane.   *This (Jesus' silence)/trick*
139 Now wols-hede and out-horne on the[e] be tane,   *outlawry/hue and cry*

[118]Sir, I can tell you this before you start—may I otherwise have bad luck.

[120-22]Sir, if he were examined, he would be found to be accursed. That is plainly seen wherever he has long remained and traveled.

[124-26]i.e., I've forgotten something I was going to say! I'll drive the rotten thing out of my memory by the time we've finished talking (?).

[129]Do you hear everything, you rascal? Your song may well be of sorrow (i.e., you'll soon have something to complain about).

[126-37]It was bad luck that you were born! Listen, is he saying anything yet? By tomorrow you'll be glad enough to speak once.

[139]Now may you be declared outlaw, and the hue and cry raised against you.

Vile fature!   *deceiver*
Oone worde might thou speke ethe,   *(if) you might/gently*
Yit might it do the[e] som letht;   *ease*
Et omnis qui tacet   *And all who keep silent*
Hic consentire videtur.   *Seem to give consent here*

Speke on oone word, right in the dwillys name!   *devil's*
146   Where was thy sire at bord when he met with thy dame?   *living/mother*
147   What, nawder bowted ne spurd, and a lord of name?   *neither booted nor spurred*
Speke on in a torde, the dwill gif the[e] shame,   *turd/devil*
149   Sir Sybré!
Perdé, if thou were a king,   *By God*
Yit might thou be riding.
Fi[e] on the[e], fundling!   *foundling, bastard*
Thou lifys bot by brybré.   *You live only by theft*

Lad, I am a prelate, a lord in degré.
Sittys in min[e] astate, as thou may se,   *It befits my rank*
Knightys on me to wate in diverse degré.
I might thole the[e] abate, and knele on thy kne   *allow you to humble yourself*
In my present.   *presence*
As ever sing I mes,   *As I hope to go on singing mass*
160   Whoso kepis the law, I gess,   *has charge of*
161   He gettys more by purches   *illegal means*
162   Then by his fre rent.   *feudal revenues*

The dwill gif the[e] shame that ever I knew the[e]!
164   Nather blinde ne lame will none persew the[e]. *Neither/persecute*
165   Therfor I shall the[e] name—that ever shall rew the[e]—   *rue, regret*
166   King Copyn in oure game: thus shall I indew the[e]   *invest*
167   For a fatur.   *impostor*
Say, dar thou not speke for ferde?   *fear*
I shrew him the[e] lerd!   *I curse him (who) taught you*
Weme! the dwillys durt in thy berd,   *Curse it!/devil's excrement*
Vile fals tratur!

146–47(Caiaphas is casting aspersions on Jesus' purported claims to royalty, doubting his parentage and scoffing at his lack of knightly apparel.)

149(An obscure insult, evidently suggesting Jesus' humbleness of station.)

160–62i.e., Anyone in authority makes more from bribes than from regular income. (Caiaphas insinuates that he expects Christ, like any feudal subject, to knuckle under to the system of bribes by paying for his release.)

164–67Neither the blind nor the lame will turn against you (since you've healed them). Therefore I shall name you—something you'll always regret—the mock-king whom we'll worship in a scornful game: thus I'll invest you with this mock-title, as an impostor.

172	Though thy lippis be stokyn, yit might thou say "mom."	*stuck shut*
	Great wordys has thou spokyn, then was thou not dom.	*Many/when/dumb*
	Be it [w]hole worde or brokyn, com owt with som,	
175	Els on the[e] I shal be wrokyn or thy ded com	*avenged ere*
176	All outt.	*known, public*
	Aythere has thou no witt,	*Either*
	Or els ar thin[e] eres ditt.	*ears stopped up*
	Why, bot herd thou not yit?	*didn't you hear*
	So, I cry and I showte!	*In that case I'll*

ANNA.   A, sir, be not ill payde, though he not answere.   *pleased*
    He is inwardly flayde, not right in his gere.   *scared/in his right mind*
CAIPHAS.   No, bot the wordys he has saide doth my hart
    great dere.   *harm*
184 ANNA.   Sir, yit may ye be dayde.   *be summoned to court*
CAIPHAS.   Nay, whils I lif, nere!   *while I live, never*
ANNA.   Sir, amese you.   *calm yourself*
CAIPHAS.   Now, fowll might him befall!   *may bad luck befall him*
ANNA.   Sir, ye ar vexed at all,   *extremely*
    And peraventur he shall   *i.e., But*
    Hereafter pleas you.

190   We may, by oure law, examin him first.   *must*
CAIPHAS.   Bot I gif him a blaw, my hart will brist!   *Unless/burst*
ANNA.   Abide, to ye his purpose knaw.   *Wait until you know*
CAIPHAS.   Nay, bot I shall out-thrist   *thrust out*
    Both his een on a raw!   *eyes in turn*
ANNA.   Sir, ye will not, I trist,   *trust*
    Be so vengeabill.
    Bot let me oppose him.   *interrogate*
CAIPHAS.   I pray you—and sloes him!   *pray do/slay*
ANNA.   Sir, we may not lose him   *destroy*
    Bot we were dampnabill.   *Without being condemnable*

CAIPHAS.   He has adyld his ded; a king he him calde.   *earned his death*
    War! let me gird of[f] his hede!   *Watch out/strike*
ANNA.   I hope not ye wold;   *hope you won't*
201   Bot, sir, do my red, youre worship to hald.   *advice/honor*

[172]Even if your lips are stuck shut, you might at least mumble.

[175-76]Or else I'll be avenged on you before your death becomes public knowledge (i.e., I'll do it secretly).

[184]Sir, at this rate you may be summoned to court (to answer for harassing an accused). —No, I won't ever stop (threatening and shouting).

[201]But, sir, follow my advice, to preserve your honor.

CAIPHAS.   Shall I never ete bred, to that he be stald   *till/stuck*
  In the stokys!   *stocks*
ANNA.   Sir, speke soft and still;
  Let us do as the law will.
CAIPHAS.   Nay, I myself shall him kill,
  And murder with knokys.

ANNA.   Sir, think ye that ye ar a man of holy kirk;   *consider/church*
  Ye shuld be oure techer, mekenes to wirk.   *(how) to practice meekness*
210 CAIPHAS.   Yei, bot all is out of har, and that shall he irk.   *out of joint*
211 ANNA.   All soft may men go far; oure lawes ar not mirk,   *gently/obscure*
212   I weyn.   *ween, believe*
  Youre wordys ar bustus;   *boisterous*
  Et hoc nos volumus,   *And we wish to do this*
  Quod de iure possumus.   *Because legally we can*
  Ye wote what I meyn:

  It is best that we trete him with farenes.
CAIPHAS.   We, nay!
ANNA.   And so might we gett him som word for to say.
CAIPHAS.   War! Let me bett him!   *beat*
ANNA.   Sir, do away!   *enough*
  For if ye thus thrett him, he spekys not this day.   *will not speak*
  Bot herys: *listen*
222   Wold ye sesse and abide,   *If you'll*
  I shuld take him on side   *I'll/aside*
224   And inquere of his pride
  How he oure folke lerys.   *teaches*

CAIPHAS.   He has renyd overlang with his fals lyys,   *reigned/lies*
  And done mekill wrang: sir Cesar he defies.   *much*
  Therfor shall I him hang, or I uprise.   *ere I stand up*
229 ANNA.   Sir, the law will not he gang on no kin wise
230   Undemyd.   *Uncensured*
  Bot first wold I here   *hear*
  What he wold answere;
  Bot he did any dere,   *Unless/harm*
  Why shuld he be flemyd?   *banished*

210–12Yea, but everything is out of joint, and he shall regret that. —By gentle means we can accomplish a great deal in this case; our laws are not obscure, I believe (i.e., they clearly define an offense Christ has clearly committed).

222If you'll cease your noise and wait patiently.

224And ask, appealing to his sense of pride.

229–30Sir, the law will not permit him to go in any way uncensured.

And therfor, examining first will I make,

Sen that he callys him a king.   *Since*

CAIPHAS.   Bot he that forsake,   *Unless*

I shall gif him a wring that his nek shall crak!

ANNA.   Sir, ye may not him ding. No word yit he spake   *strike*

That I wist. [*To Jesus.*]   *know of*

240   Hark, felow, com nar.

Will thou never be war?   *take care*

I have mervell thou dar   *I'm astonished*

Thus do thin[e] awne list.   *do as you please*

Bot I shall do as the law will, if the people ruse the[e].   *(even) if/praise*

Say, did thou oght this ill? Can thou oght excuse the[e]?   *aught, at all*

Why standys thou so still when men thus accuse the[e]?

247   For to hing on a hill, hark how thay ruse the[e]   *boast*

248   To dam!   *To condemn (you)*

Say, art thou Godys son of heven,

As thou art wonte for to neven?   *are accustomed to say*

JHESUS.   So thou says by thy steven,   *voice*

And right so I am;

For, after this shall thou se when that [I] do com downe

In brightnes on he, in clowdys from abone.   *(from) on high/above*

255 CAIPHAS.   A, ill might the feete be that broght the[e] to

towne!

Thou art worthy to de. Say, thefe, where is thy crowne?

ANNA.   Abide, sir.

Let us lawfully redres.   *redress (this wrong)*

CAIPHAS.   We nede no witnes;

Hisself says expres.   *says (confesses) explicitly*

Why shuld I not chide, sir?

262 ANNA.   Was ther never man so wyk bot he might amende   *wicked*

263   When it com to the pryk, right as youreself kend.   *point/have taught*

CAIPHAS.   Nay, sir, bot I shall him stik even with min[e]

awne hend;   *own*

For if he rene and be whyk, we ar at an end,   *reign and live*

All sam.   *together*

Therfor, whils I am in this brethe,   *i.e., while I'm still living*

247-48Listen how they (the torturers and Caiaphas) boast they will condemn you to hang on a hill.

255Bad luck to the feet that brought you here, i e , bad luck to you for coming.

262-63There was never a man so wicked but that he might reform when it comes right down to the point of crisis, just as you yourself have taught.

Let me put him to deth.

ANNA.   *Sed nobis non licet*   *But it is not lawful for us*
270   *Interficere quemquam.*   *To put any man to death*
                                                            (John 18:31)

Sir, ye wote better then I we shuld slo no man.   *know/slay*

CAIPHAS.   His dedys I defy! His warkys may we ban;   *deeds/curse, condemn*
Therfor shall he by.   *buy, pay the penalty*

ANNA.   Nay, on oder wise than,   *other ways then*
And do it lawfully.

CAIPHAS.   As how?

ANNA.   Tel you I can.

CAIPHAS.   Let se!

ANNA.   Sir, take tent to my sawes: *pay attention/words*
Men of temperall lawes,   *secular*
Thay may deme sich cause;   *judge such*
And so may not we.

280 CAIPHAS.   My hart is full cold, nerehand that I swelt!   *nearly/die*
For talys that ar told, I bolne at my belt—   *swell (with rage)*
Unethes may it hold my body, and ye it felt!   *Scarcely/if*
Yit wold I gif of my gold, yond tratoure to pelt   *strike repeatedly*
Forever.

ANNA.   Good sir, do as ye hett me.   *promised*

CAIPHAS.   Why shall he oversett me?   *overcome*
Sir Anna, if ye lett me   *hinder*
Ye do not youre dever.   *duty*

ANNA.   Sir, ye ar a prelate.

CAIPHAS.   So may I well seme,   *it becomes me*
Myself if I say it.

ANNA.   Be not to[o] breme!   *violent*
291   Sich men of astate shuld no men deme,   *judge*
Bot send them to Pilate. The temperall law to yeme   *carry out*
Has he;   *Is his responsibility*
He may best threte him   *threaten him (Christ)*
And all to-rehete him.   *rate, censure severely*
It is shame you to bete him;   *(for) you*
Therfor, sir, let be.

298 CAIPHAS.   Fi[e] on him and war! I am oute of my gate.   *worse*

---

²⁹¹Such men of the clerical estate should judge no man (to death).

²⁹⁸⁻⁹⁹Fie on him, and worse! I am out of my path, and too far away from where he stands.
(Caiaphas still wants to strike Jesus, and seemingly asks why the prisoner is being kept out of
his range. Annas observes, l. 299, that Jesus has just approached them. Caiaphas warns,
l. 300, that he can order his knights to buffet Jesus even if he can't reach the prisoner himself.)

299   Say, why standys he so far?   far (*away from me*)
ANNA.   Sir, he cam bot late.   only recently
CAIPHAS.   No, bot I have knightys that dar rap him on the
                pate.
301 ANNA.   Ye ar bot to skar. Good sir, abate
302   And here!   hear
What nedys you to chite?   chide
What nedys you to flite?   quarrel
If ye yond man smite,
Ye ar irregulere.

307 CAIPHAS.   He that first made me clerk, and taght me my
                lare   lore, learning
308   On bookys for to barke, the dwill gif him care!   read aloud/devil
ANNA.   A, good sir, hark! Sich wordys might ye spare.   Such/avoid
310 CAIPHAS.   Els might I have made up wark of yond harlot Otherwise
                and mare,
Perdé!   By God
Bot certys, or he hens yode,   ere he goes hence
It wold do me som good
To se knightys knok his hoode   hood, head
With knokys two or thre.

For, sen he has trespast and broken oure law,   since
Let us make him agast, and set him in awe.
318 ANNA.   Sir, as ye have hast, it shal be, I traw.   haste
     [*To the torturers.*]
Com and make redy fast, ye knightys on a raw,   in a row
Youre arament;   equipment
And that king to you take,
And with knokys make him wake.   weak
CAIPHAS.   Yei, sirs, and for my sake
Gif him good payment.

For, if I might go with you—as I wold that I might—
I shuld make min[e] avowe that ons or midnight   vow/once ere
I shuld make his heede sow, wher that I hit right.   head throb

301–2You're supposed only to frighten him. Good sir, quiet down and listen to me!

307–8May the devil give sorrow to that person who first made me a clergyman and taught me how to read aloud my lesson from books! (Caiphas wishes he weren't a cleric so he could strike Christ.)

310Otherwise (i.e., if I weren't a cleric) I might have made short work of yonder rascal and hobgoblin.

318Sir, it will be as you are in a hurry to have it, I trust.

1 TORTOR. Sir, drede you not now of this cursed wight		*creature*
Today,		
For we shall so rok him,		*rock, shake*
And with buffettys knok him.		
CAIPHAS. And I red that ye lok him,		*advise/lock him up*
That he ryn not away;		*run*

334	For I red not we mete, if that lad skap.	*advise/meet/escape*
335	2 TORTOR. Sir, on us be it, bot we clowt well his kap.	*unless*
336	CAIPHAS. Wold ye do as ye heytt, it were a fair hap.	*If you do/promise*
	1 TORTOR. Sir, sitt ye and see it, how that we him knap—	*knock*
	Oone feste!	*A festival*
	Bot, or we go to this thing,	*ere*
	Sayn us, lord, with thy ring.	*Bless*
	CAIPHAS. Now, he shall have my blissing	
	That knokys him the best.	

[*The torturers get ready to go to work on Jesus.*]

	2 TORTOR. Go we now to oure noyte with this fond foyll.	*work/foolish*
344	1 TORTOR. We shall teche him, I wote, a new play of Yoyll,	*Hot Cockles*
345	And hold him full hote. Fraward, a stoyll	*make it hot for him/stool*
346	Go fetch us! [*Froward comes forward.*]	
	FROWARD. We, dote! Now els were it doyll	*dotard/painful*
347	And unnett.	*difficult*
348	For the wo that he shall dre,	*suffer*
349	Let him knele on his kne.	
	2 TORTOR. And so shall he, for me.	*as far as I'm concerned*
	Go fetche us a light buffit.	*footstool*

[*Froward brings the stool.*]

	FROWARD. Why must he sitt soft—with a mekill	
	mischaunce!—	*bad luck to him*
	That has tenyd us thus oft?	*harmed*
	1 TORTOR. Sir, we do it for a skawnce.	*joke*
354	If he stode up on loft, we must hop and dawnse	*erect*

334-36For I don't advise that we meet (i.e., you'd do better to scatter and hide) if that fellow
escapes. —Sir, may the blame be on us, unless we thoroughly clout his head. —If you do as
you've promised, things will turn out well.

344*Yoyll*: Hot Cockles, a game in which the blindfolded person who is "it" tries to guess who
has hit him.

345-49And (we'll) make it hot for him. Froward (the name of the torturers' servant, meaning
"perverse, ill-shaped"), go fetch a stool! —Curse him, dotard! Doing it another way (without
a stool) would be painful and difficult (for Christ). To make him suffer all the more woe,
let him kneel.

354-55(The torturers seem to mean that if Christ stands erect they'll have trouble reaching
up to buffet him on the head.)

355	As cokys in a croft.	*Like roosters/yard*
FROWARD.	Now, a veniance	*vengeance*
	Com on him!	
357	Good skill can ye shew	*As good reason*
358	As fell i the dew.	*in*
	Have this—bere it, shrew! [*He hands the stool to Jesus.*]	
	For soyn shall we fon him.	*soon/make a fool of*

2 TORTOR.	Com, sir, and sit downe. Must ye be prayde?	*begged*
	Like a lord of renowne youre sete is arayde.	*seat is prepared*
1 TORTOR.	We shall preve on his crowne the wordys he has sayde.	*prove, test/head*
364 2 TORTOR.	Ther is none in this towne, I trow, be ill payde	*ill pleased*
365	Of his sorow,	
	Bot the fader that him gate.	*Except the father/begat*
1 TORTOR.	Now, for oght that I wate,	*aught/know*
368	All his kin commys to[o] late	
369	His body to borow.	*save*

2 TORTOR.	I wold we were onwarde.	*i.e., Let's start*
1 TORTOR.	Bot his een must be hid.	*eyes/covered*
371 2 TORTOR.	Yei, bot thay be well spard, we lost that we did.	*unless/fastened*
	Step furth thou, Froward!	
FROWARD.	What is now betyd?	*has happened*
1 TORTOR.	Thou art ever away-ward.	*wandering off*
FROWARD.	Have ye none to bid	*order around*
	Bot me?	
	I may sing "illa-hayll."	*bad luck*
2 TORTOR.	Thou must get us a vaill.	*blindfold*
377 FROWARD.	Ye ar ever in oone tayll.	*tale*
1 TORTOR.	Now ill might thou thé!	*prosper*

379	Well had thou thy name, for thou was ever curst.
FROWARD.	Sir, I might say the same to you, if I durst.
381	Yit my hier may I clame; no penny I purst.

357–58(Froward seems to suggest mockingly that the torturers' reasons for giving Christ a stool are as worthless as the dew.)

364–65No one here, I believe, is displeased by Christ's sorrow.

368–69i.e., Not even his whole family could save him at this point.

371Yea, unless they're well fastened or covered, we'd proceed in vain (since the hitting game requires blindfolding).

377i.e., You're always harping on the same things, always giving orders.

379You were well named, for you've always been perverse (or "froward").

381I have yet to claim successfully my hire, or pay; I've pocketed not a penny yet.

I have had mekill shame, hunger, and thurst
In youre service.

1 TORTOR. Not oone word so bold! *i.e., Stop being presumptuous*

FROWARD. Why, it is trew that I told.

Fain preve it I wold. *I'd gladly prove it*

387 2 TORTOR. Thou shal be cald to pervice. *legal disputation*

[*Froward fetches a blindfold.*]

FROWARD. Here a vaill have I fon; I trow it will last. *veil/found*

1 TORTOR. Bring it hider, good son. That is it that I ast. *asked*

FROWARD. How shuld it be bon? *bound, tied*

2 TORTOR. Abowte his heade cast. *Put around*

1 TORTOR. Yei, and when it is well won, knit a knot fast, *wound*

I red. [*Froward blindfolds Jesus.*] *advise*

FROWARD. Is it weyll? *well done*

2 TORTOR. Yei, knave.

FROWARD. What, weyn ye that I rafe? *think/rave*

395 Crist curs might he have *Christ's*
396 That last bond his head! *bound*

1 TORTOR. Now, sen he is blinfold, I fall to begin. *since/I'll hasten*

398 And thus was I counseld the mastry to win! [*Strikes Jesus.*] *to win the prize*

399 2 TORTOR. Nay, wrang has thou teld. Thus shuld thou com
in! [*Strikes.*]

400 FROWARD. I stode and beheld: thou towchid not the skin *touched*
401 Bot fowll.

402 1 TORTOR. How will thou I do?

2 TORTOR. On this manere, lo! [*Strikes.*]

FROWARD. Yei, that was well gone to; *done*

Ther start up a cowll. *started up a lump*

[*They continue to strike in turn.*]

406 1 TORTOR. Thus shall we him refe all his fonde talys. *rid him of*
407 2 TORTOR. Ther is noght in thy nefe, or els thy hart falys. *fist/fails*
408 FROWARD. I can my hand uphefe and knop out the skalys. *upheave/knock/skittles*

[387]You'll be called to the legal profession (since you're so good at arguing).

[395-96](Froward may be saying, in effect, I'll be damned if I do that again.)

[398-402]And this is the way I was taught to win the prize (at buffeting). —No, you've done it wrong. This is how you should begin. —I've stood and watched; you hardly even touched the skin (you struck so weakly). —How do you want me to do it?

[406-10]Thus we'll rid him of all his foolish talk. —Either you don't have any power in your fist, or else your courage fails. —I can lift up my hand and hit him as though I were knocking one of the skittles in a game of ninepins. —God forbid you should leave off! Instead, dig in your fingernails all together.

409 1 TORTOR.   Godys forbot ye lefe! Bot set in youre nalys   *God forbid*

410   On raw.   *All together*

[*They taunt Jesus as they beat him.*]

Sit up and prophecy—

FROWARD.   Bot make us no ly—

2 TORTOR.   Who smote the[e] last?

1 TORTOR.   Was it I?

FROWARD.   He wote not, I traw.   *trow, believe*

[*They drag Jesus back to the chief priests.*]

1 TORTOR.   Fast to sir Caiphas go we togeder.

2 TORTOR.   Rise up, with ill grace! So com thou hider.   *bad luck to you*

FROWARD.   It semys, by his pase, he groches to go thider.   *pace|is unwilling*

1 TORTOR.   We have gifen him a glase, ye may consider,   *blow*

To kepe.

420 2 TORTOR [*to Caiaphas*].   Sir, for his great boost,   *for (all)*

With knokys he is indoost.   *indorsed, stamped with blows*

FROWARD.   In faith, sir, we had almost

Knokyd him on slepe.   *asleep*

CAIPHAS.   Now, sen he is well bett, weynd on youre gate   *since|beaten|way*

And tell ye the forfett unto sir Pilate,   *explain the offense*

For he is a juge sett emang men of state;   *rank*

And looke that ye not let.   *tarry*

1 TORTOR.   Com furth, old trate,   *hag*

Belife!   *Quickly*

We shall lede the[e] a trott.

2 TORTOR.   Lift thy feete, may thou not?

431 FROWARD.   Then nedys me do nott

432   Bot com after and drife.

[*Exeunt torturers, leading and driving Jesus.*]

CAIPHAS.   Alas, now take I hede!   *I see what will happen*

ANNA.   Why mowrne ye so?

CAIPHAS.   For I am ever in drede, wandreth, and wo,   *misery*

Lest Pilate, for mede, let Jhesus go.   *for a bribe*

Bot had I slain him indede with thise handys two,

At onys,   *At once*

All had bene qwitt than.   *settled then*

Bot giftys marres many man.   *gifts, bribes*

Bot he deme the sothe, than,   *Unless he judge truly*

The dwill have his bonys!   *May the devil*

431–32 Then I don't need to do anything but follow after and drive the team (since the other torturers are leading Christ from the front).

442   Sir Anna, all I wite you this blame; for, had ye not beyn,   *I blame you*

443   I had mayde him full tame—yei, stikyd him, I weyn,   *trust*

     To the hart full wan with this dagger so keyn.   *To his evil heart/keen*

  ANNA.   Sir, you must shame sich wordys for to meyn   *be ashamed/to speak*

     Emang men.

  CAIPHAS.   I will not dwell in this stede,   *place*

     But spy how thay him lede,

     And persew on his dede.   *press forward his death*

450   Farewell, we gang, men. [*Exeunt.*]   *we go (to the audience)*

     Explicit Coliphizatio.   *Here ends the Buffeting*

442–43Sir Annas, I blame you entirely for this; for, had it not been for you, I'd have tamed him.

THE SCOURGING
FROM WAKEFIELD

The Wakefield Scourging apparently continues where the Buffeting leaves off (although the references to Herod at lines 53 and 99 may suggest that Wakefield, like all the other cycles, once had another pageant at this point depicting the trial before Herod). At the end of the Buffeting, the soldiers were ordered to take Jesus before Pilate. They now approach Pilate, and eventually depart for Calvary, engaged in the same comic business used to conclude the Buffeting: the driving and leading of Jesus as though he were a work animal. Staging arrangements are similar, with Pilate on his scaffold and most of the action below him in the "place." The three Marys occupy a separate location until the apostle John conducts them to a central spot where they can meet with Jesus on his route to Calvary. Simon too perhaps meets with Jesus and the soldiers in the central "place." The cross that Simon carries is heavy and real, for it must actually support Christ's weight in the dramatic re-enactment of the Crucifixion.

The character of Pilate, as Arnold Williams has shown (*The Characterization of Pilate in the Towneley Plays*), differs markedly from that of the other cycles. Usually he is presented as an ambivalent figure vainly attempting to reconcile conflicting responsibilities. The Wakefield Pilate, on the other hand, is so evil and cunning that he becomes a chief antagonist to Christ in the structural design of the cycle. As *mali actoris*, author of evil, he is a representative of the devil. He has become the arch-deceiver, richly deserving to be beguiled by his own treachery.

Other figures in this pageant are more fallibly human, less aware of what they are doing. The torturers or soldiers, as in the previous pageant, mock their prisoner and bear false witness against him. Blinded to the momentous spiritual consequences of the events in which they participate, they ironically believe their mirth to be increasing while Jesus' fortunes decline. The Virgin Mary and her companions, though steadfast in their faith in Christ, also seem to have lost perspective. As the apostle John points out to them (ll. 287–89), they are grieving for an event that will ensure their perpetual comfort. Equally ironic is the role of Simon the Cyrene, the type of self-absorbed worldling too caught up in his petty affairs to attend to matters of the spirit. By being rudely forced to share a part of Christ's agony, Simon is done a favor of incomparable worth. The soldiers who spurn him as one of the despised have no notion how they have graced him by this humiliation.

The Scourging
From Wakefield

Incipit Flagellatio.　　　　　　　　　　　　　　　*Here begins the Scourging*

[*Pilate on his scaffold, attended.*]

PILATUS.　Peasse at my biding, ye wightys in wold!　*persons under my dominion*
　　　Looke none be so hardy to speke a word bot I,　*See to it that*
　　　Or by Mahowne most mighty, maker on mold,　*Mohammed/of earth*
　　　With this brande that I bere ye shall bitterly aby.　*sword/pay the penalty*
　　　Say, wote ye not that I am Pilate, perles[s] to behold,　*peerless*
6　Most doughty in dedys of dukys of the Jury?　*deeds*
　　　In brading of batels I am the most bold;　*starting strife*
　　　Therfor my name to you will I discry,
　　　No mis.　*Without fail*
　　　I am full of sotelty,
　　　Falshed, gyll, and trechery;　*Falsehood/guile*
　　　Therfor am I namyd by clergy
　　　As *mali actoris.*　*author of evil*

14　For, like as on both sidys the iren the hamer makith
　　　　　playn,
15　So do I, that the law has here in my keping.
　　　The right side to socoure, certys, I am full bain,　*assist/quite willing*
　　　If I may get therby a vantege or wining;　*profit*
　　　Then to the fals parte I turne me again,
　　　For I se more vaill will to me be rising.　*avail, gain*
20　Thus every man to drede me shal be full fain,　*glad, ready*
21　And all faint of thare faith to me be obey[i]ng,　*all (who are)*
　　　Truly.
　　　All fals enditars,　*indicters, accusers*
24　Quest-gangars, and jurars,　*Inquest-goers*
　　　And thise outridars,　*court messengers*
　　　Ar welcom to me.

　　　Bot this prophete, that has prechyd and puplished so
　　　　　plain
　　　Cristen law—"Crist," thay call him in oure cuntré—
　　　Bot oure princes full prowdly this night have him tain;　*taken*
30　Full tytt to be dampned he shall be hurlyd bifore me.　*quickly/condemned*
　　　I shall fownde to be his freynd utward, in certain,　*set about/outwardly*
　　　And shew him fare cowntenance and wordys of vanité;　*fair/flattering words*
　　　Bot, or this day at night, on crosse shall he be slain.　*ere nighttime*

[6]Most doughty in deeds among the rulers of Jewry.

[14–15]For, just as the hammer flattens and smooths the iron on both its sides (when pounded on an anvil), so do I (deal doubly), I who have the authority of administering the law here.

[20–21]Thus every man will be ready enough to fear me, and all the fainthearted and cowardly ready enough to obey me.

[24]*Quest-gangars:* jurors or other persons participating in judicial inquests. (Pilate, here portrayed as the type of fraudulent justice, is abstractly associated with every sort of legal corruption.)

Thus agans him in my hart I bere great enmité,   *against*
Full sore.
Ye men that use bak-bitingys,
And rasars of slanderingys,   *raisers, perpetrators*
Ye ar my dere darlingys,
And Mahowns for evermore.   *Mohammed's*

40   For, nothing in this warld dos me more grefe
     Then for to here of Crist and of his new lawes.   *Than|hear*
     To trow that he is Godys son my hart wold all to-clefe, *cleave in pieces*
     Though he be never so trew, both in dedys and in sawes. *deeds|words*
     Therfor shall he suffre mekill mischefe,   *much*
     And all the discipyls that unto him drawes.
46   For, over all solace to me it is most lefe,   *dear*
47   The sheding of Cristen bloode; and that all Jury knawes, *knows*
     I say you.
     My knightys full swythe   *quickly*
     Thare strengthes will thay kyth   *show*
     And bring him belyfe.   *quickly*
     Lo, where thay com now!

     [*The torturers come in view, driving Jesus like a work animal.*]

1 TORTOR.   I have ron that I swett, from sir Herode, oure   *run (so) that*
       king,
     With this man that will not lett oure lawes to downe   *desist*
       bring.
     He has done so mych forfett, of care may he sing: *much offense|sorrow*
     Thrugh dom of sir Pilate, he gettys an ill ending,   *judgment|will get*
     And sore!
     The great warkys he has wroght   *works, miracles*
     Shall serve him of noght;
60   And, bot thay be dere boght,   *unless*
61   Lefe me no more.   *Believe*

     Bot make rowme in this rese, I bid you, belife,   *crowd|quickly*
     And of youre nois that ye sesse, both man and wife!   *cease*
     To sir Pilate on dese this man will we drife,   *dais*
     His dede for to dres and refe him his life   *death|prepare|bereave*
     This day.
     Do, draw him forward!
     Why stand ye so bakward?   *hanging back*

46-47For, the shedding of Christian blood is more dear to me than any other comfort; and
everyone in Jewry is aware of this.

60-61And, unless Christ pays dearly for his deeds, never put any trust in my predictions.

Com on, sir, hiderward,
70   As fast as ye may.

2 TORTOR.   Do, pull him a-rase whils we be ganging.   *full speed/going*
I shall spitt in his face, though it be fare shining.
Of us thre gettys thou no grace, thy dedys ar so noy[i]ng!   *deeds/annoying*
Bot more sorow thou hase; oure mirth is incresing,
No lak.
Felows, all in hast,
With this band that will last,
Let us binde fast
Both his handys on his bak.

3 TORTOR.   I shall lede the[e] a dawnce unto sir Pilate hall.
81   Thou betyd an ill chawnce to com emangys us all!
   [*They come before Pilate's throne.*]
Sir Pilate, with youre cheftance, to you we cry and call   *chieftains*
83   That ye make som ordinance with this brodell thrall,   *wretched slave*
84   By skill: *As reason demands*
85   This man that we led
86   On crosse ye put to ded.   *death*
PILATUS.   What, withoutten any red?   *counsel*
That is not my will.

Bot ye, wisest of law, to me ye be tendand: *pay attention*
90   This man withoutten awe which ye led in a band,
Nather in dede ne in saw can I find with no wrang;   *deed/word*
92   Wherfor, ye shuld him draw or bere falsly on hand   *falsely accuse*
93   With ill.   *With evil results*
Ye say he turnes oure pepyll;   *leads astray*
Ye call him fals and fekyll.
96   Warldys shame is on you mekyll   *much*
This man if ye spill.   *kill*

Of all thise causes ilkon which ye put on him,   *various accusations*
99   Herode, truly as stone, coud find with no kins gin   *no sort of device*

81Ill luck befell you when you came among us all.

83–86To take action against this wretched slave, as reason demands, putting to death on the cross this man we have led hither.

90This man whom you fearlessly led bound.

92–93Wherefore, you would do ill to bring him forward or falsely accuse him.

96The shame of all the world will be visited greatly upon you.

99–100Herod, indeed, could not discern even by the most cunning means anything pertaining to an offense.

100   Nothing herapon that pent to any sin.   *attached, belonged*
      Why shuld I then so soyn to ded here deme him?   *soon/death/doom*
      Therfor
      This is my counsell—
      I will not with him mell—   *meddle*
      Let him go where he will,
      For now and evermore.

    1 CONSULTUS.   Sir, I say the[e] oone thing, without any   *counselor*
        mis: *fail*
      He callys hisself a king ther he none is.   *whereas*
      Thus he wold downe bring oure lawes, iwis,
110   With his fals lesing and his quantis,   *lying/cunning*
      This tide.   *time*
    PILATUS [*to Jesus*].   Herk, felow, com nere.
      Thou knowes I have powere
      To excuse or to dampne here,
      In bayll to abide.   *torment*

116 JHESUS.   Sich powere has thou noght to wirk thy will thus
        with me,
117   Bot from my Fader that is broght, oone-fold God in
        persons thre.
118 PILATUS [*to the Jews*]. Certys, it is fallen well in my thought
        at this time, as well wote ye,
119   A thefe that any felony has wroght, to lett him skap or
        go fre
120   Away;
121   Therfor ye lett him pas.
    1 TORTOR.   Nay, nay, bot Barabas!
      And Jhesus in this case
      To deth ye dam this day!   *condemn*

    PILATUS.   Sirs, looke ye take good hede his cloysse ye   *clothes*
        spoill him fro,   *despoil*
      Ye gar his body blede, and bett him blak and bloo.   *cause/beat*
    2 TORTOR.   This man, as might I spede, that has wroght us   *as I hope to prosper*
        this wo,
128   How "Judicare" comys in Crede shall we teche, or we go,   *"to judge"/ere*

116–21You would have no such power to work your will thus with me unless it were brought to you by my Father, one-fold God in three persons. —Certainly, it has occurred to me at this time, according to the custom with which you are familiar, to release or set free a prisoner guilty of any sort of felony; therefore, let Jesus go (see John 19:11, 18:39).

128We'll teach him soon enough about the phrase "to judge," occurring in the creed. (They mock a phrase from the Apostles' Creed: "And he shall come to judge both the quick and the dead.")

All soyne.   *soon*
Have bind to this pillar!   *Bind him*

131 3 TORTOR.   Why standys thou so far?

1 TORTOR.   To bett his body bar   *bare*
I haste, withoutten hoyne.   *delay*

[*They strip Jesus and bind him to a pillar.*]

2 TORTOR.   Now fall I the first to flap on his hide.   *I go first*

135 3 TORTOR   My hartt wold all to-brist bot I might till him   *to him*
glide!

136 1 TORTOR.   A swap fain, if I durst, wold I lene the[e] this   *give*
tide.   *time*

137 2 TORTOR.   War! Lett me rub on the rust, that the bloode
down glide

As swythe.   *Swiftly*

3 TORTOR.   Have att! [*Strikes Jesus.*]

1 TORTOR.   Take thou that! [*Strikes.*]

2 TORTOR.   I shall lene the[e] a flap,   *give/blow*
My strengthe for to kythe. [*Strikes.*]   *show*

3 TORTOR.   Whereon servys thy prophecy, thou tell us in
this case?
And all thy warkys of greatt mastry thou shewed in divers
place?

1 TORTOR.   Thin[e] apostels full radly ar run from the[e]   *readily*
a-rase.   *full speed*
Thou art here in oure baly, withoutten any grace   *custody/hope*
Of skap[e].

2 TORTOR.   Do, rug him! [*Strikes.*]   *rock, shake*

3 TORTOR.   Do, ding him! [*Strikes.*]   *beat*

1 TORTOR.   Nay, I myself shuld kill him
Bot for sir Pilate.

152 Sirs, at the feste of Architreclyn, this prophete he was;
Ther turnyd he water into wyn. That day he had sich   *wine/such*
grace,
His apostels to him can enclyn, and other that ther was.   *did incline*

131(apparently to the other torturer) Why are you standing so far away? i.e., why don't you get to work?

135–37My heart might burst asunder, unless I can get at him! —I'd gladly give you (Jesus) a blow at this time. —Watch out! Let me strike with my rusty weapon, so that the blood will run down(?).

152*the feste of Architreclyn*: i.e., the wedding in Cana (see John 2:1–12). "Architricline" means "ruler of a feast"; in medieval legend, it was taken to be the proper name of a rich lord.

155   The see he past, bot few yeres syn: it lete him walk
      theron apase
  At will.
  The elementys all bydeyn,   *together*
  And windes that ar so keyn,
  The firmamente, as I weyn,   *ween, think*
  Ar him obey[i]ng till.   *obedient to him*

2 TORTOR.   A lepir cam full fast to this man that here
      standys,
162   And prayed him, in all hast, of bayll to lowse his bandys.
  His travell was not wast, though he cam from far landys;   *labor/wasted*
  This prophete till him past and helyd him with his   *went to him*
      handys,
  Full blithe.   *gladly*
166   The son of Centurion,
  For whom his fader made greatt mone,   *moan, complaint*
  Of the palsy he helyd anone;   *healed*
  Thay lowfyd him oft sithe.   *praised/many times*

3 TORTOR.   Sirs, as he cam from Jherico, a blinde man satt
      by the way.
171   To him walkand, with many mo, cryand to him thus can   *walking/crying*
      he say:
  "Thou son of David, or thou go, of blindnes hele thou   *ere*
      me this day."
  Ther was he helyd of all his wo. Sich wonders can he wirk   *healed*
      allway
  At will.
  He rasys men from deth to life,
  And castys out devils from thame oft sithe;   *from them often*
  Seke men cam to him full rife—   *Sick/often*
  He helys thaym of all ill.

1 TORTOR.   For all thise dedys of great loving, three   *Despite/deeds*
      thingys I have fond, certanly,   *found*
180   For which he is worthy to hing: oone is, oure king that he   *hang*
      wold be;

[155]He passed over the sea only a few years ago: it let him walk thereupon swiftly (see Matthew 14:25, etc.).

[162]And prayed him, in all haste, to loosen his bonds of torment (see Matthew 8:2–4, etc.).

[166]*son*: actually, servant or "boy"; see Matthew 8:5–6.

[171]As Jesus was passing by, with a great multitude, the blind man said crying out to Jesus (see Mark 10:46–47).

Oure Sabbot-day in his wirking he lettys not to hele the
    seke, truly;   *ceases*
He says oure temple he shall downe bring, and in thre
    dayes byg it in hy   *build it on high*
All [w]hole agane.
Sir Pilate, as ye sitt,
Looke wisely in youre witt:
Dam Jhesu, or ye flitt,   *ere you go*
On crosse to suffre his paine.

PILATUS.   Thou man that suffurs all this ill, why will thou
    us no mercy cry?
Slake thy hart and thy greatt will whils on the[e] we have   *Humble*
    mastry;
190 Of thy greatt warkes shew us som skill. Men call the[e]
    king; thou tell us why.
Wherfor the Jues seke the[e] to spill, the cause I wold   *kill*
    knowe witterly,   *truly*
Perdee.   *By God*
Say, what is thy name?
Thou lett for no shame.   *Don't hesitate*
Thay putt on the[e] greatt blame,
Els might [thou] skap for me.   *escape as far as I'm concerned*

2 CONSULTUS.   Sir Pilate, prince peerles, this is my red: *advice*
That he skap not harmeles, bot do him to ded.   *death*
He cals him a king in every place; thus wold he overled   *domineer over*
200 Oure people in his trace, and oure lawes downe-tred,   *track, path*
By skill.   *cunning*
Sir, youre knightes of good lose,   *fame*
And the pepyll with oone voce,   *voice*
To hing him hy on a crosse
Thay cry and call you untill.   *to you*

PILATUS.   Now certys, this is a wonder thing, that ye wold
    bring to noght
207 Him that is youre lege lording! In faith, this was far
    soght.
208 Bot say, why make ye none obey[i]ng to Him that all has
    wroght?
209 3 TORTOR.   Sir, he is oure chefe lording: sir Cesar, so
    worthily wroght

207–10Him who is your liege lord (or feudal master)! Truly, this was ill or strangely done. But
say, why won't you obey Him who created all things? —Sir, our supreme lord is Caesar, the
finest-made man on earth (see John 19:15).

210	On mold.	*earth*
	Pilate, do after us,	*as we advise*
	And dam to deth Jhesus—	
	Or to sir Cesar we trus,	*pack up, shift our loyalty*
	And make thy frenship cold.	

[*Pilate takes water.*]

PILATUS.   Now, that I am sakles of this bloode, shall ye see: *guiltless*
Both my handys in expres weshen s[h]all be.   *intentionally washed*
This bloode bees dere boght, I ges, that ye spill so frelé.   *is dearly*

1 TORTOR.   We pray it fall endles on us and oure meneye,   *endlessly|nation*
With wrake!   *vengeance*

220 PILATUS.   Now youre desire fulfill I shall:
Take him emangs you all;
On crosse ye put that thrall,   *slave*
His ending ther to take.

[*The torturers drag Jesus to a central position where they mockingly enthrone him.*]

1 TORTOR.   Com on, trip on thy tose, without any fening!   *toes|feigning*
Thou has made many glose with thy fals talking.   *falsehoods*

2 TORTOR.   We ar worthy greatte lose, that thus has broght   *praise*
a king
From sir Pilate and othere fose thus into oure ring,   *foes*
Withoutt any hoyne.   *delay*
Sirs, a king he him cals:
230 Therfor, a crowne him befals.   *befits*

3 TORTOR.   I swere, by all min[e] elder sauls,   *ancestors' souls*
I shall it ordan soyne.   *make it ready soon*

[*They prepare a crown of thorns and crown Jesus with it.*]

1 TORTOR.   Lo, here a crowne of thorne to perch his brane   *pierce*
within,
Putt on his hede with skorne, and gar thirll the skin.   *cause to pierce*

2 TORTOR.   Haill, king! Where was thou borne, sich worship
for to win?
We knele all the[e] beforne, and the[e] to grefe will we   *grieve*
not blin—   *cease*
That be thou bold.   *Be sure of that*
Now, by Mahownes bloode,
Ther will no mete do me goode   *i.e., I'll eat no food*
240 To he be hanged on a roode,   *Till|cross*
And his bones be cold!

[*A cross is found.*]

1 TORTOR.   Sirs, we may be fain, for I have fon a tree—   *glad|found*

I tell you in certa[i]n, it is of greatt bewtee—   *beauty*
On the which he shall suffre pain, be-feste with nales   *be-fastened*
    thre.
Ther shall nothing him gain theron, to he dede be,   *profit/till/dead*
I insure it.
Do, bring him hence.
  2 TORTOR.   Take up oure gere and defence.   *gear and weapons*
  3 TORTOR.   I wold spende all my spence   *expense, cash*
250   To se him ones skelpt!   *once beaten*

1 TORTOR [*to Jesus*].   This cros up thou take, and make
    the[e] redy bowne.   *prepared*
Withoutt gruching, thou rake and bere it thrugh the   *complaining/walk*
    towne.
Mary, thy moder, I wote, will make great mowrning
    and mone;   *moan*
But for thy fals dedys sake, shortly thou s[h]al be slone,   *deeds'/slain*
No nay.   *Doubtless*
The pepyll of Bedlem   *Bethlehem*
And gentyls of Jerusalem,
All the comoners of this reme,   *realm*
Shall wonder on the[e] this day.

    [*Enter, apart, John the Apostle.*]
260 JOHANNES APOSTOLUS.   Alas, for my master moste of might,
That yester-even, with lanterne bright,   *eve*
Before Caiphas was broght!
Both Peter and I sagh that sight,   *saw*
And sithen we fled away full wight,   *then/quickly*
When Jues so wonderly wroght.   *acted so exceedingly*
At morne thay toke to red, and fals witnes furth soght,   *took counsel*
267   And demyd him to be dede that to thaym trespaste noght.   *condemned*

268   Alas! For his modere and othere moo,   *more*
269   My moder and hir sister also,

[267]And condemned him to be dead who gave them no offense.

[268–69]*modere, sister:* At the Crucifixion, according to John 19:25, were Jesus' mother, his mother's sister Mary (the wife of Cleophas), and Mary Magdalene. Matthew and Mark speak of Mary the mother of James and Joseph rather than of Mary, wife of Cleophas; these could be the same woman. This play, on the other hand, reflects a later exegetical tradition. The apostle John identifies himself as a son of the Virgin Mary's sister and hence as Jesus' cousin. He fills the role of the unnamed disciple (John 19:27) to whose care the dying Jesus entrusts his mother. Yet the speech prefixes identify one of the three Marys in this scene as *Maria Jacobi*, Mary, the mother of James (as in Matthew and Mark), rather than the mother of John. This play also reflects exegetical tradition that Mary Magdalene was another sister of the Virgin Mary.

Sat sam with sighing sore.   *together*
Thay wote nothing of all this wo.   *know*
Therfor to tell thaym will I go,
Sen I may mend no more.   *Since*
If he shuld di[e] thus tyte, and thay unwarned wore,   *quickly|were*
I were worthy to wyte; I will go fast, therfor.   *blame*
> [*He goes to the Virgin Mary, Mary, mother of James, and Mary
> Magdalene.*]

God save you, sisters all in fere!   *together*
Dere lady, if thy will were,
I must tell tithingys plain.   *tidings candidly*
279 MARIA. Welcom, John, my cosyn dere.
How farys my son sen thou was here?   *fares|since*
That wold I wit full fain.   *know|gladly*
282 JOHANNES. A, dere lady, with youre leyff, the trouth
        shuld no man lain,
283 Ne with Godys will thaym grefe!
MARIA.   Why, John, is my son slain?

JOHANNES. Nay, lady, I saide not so;
Bot ye me myn he told us two—   *you remind me*
And thaym that with us wore—   *were*
How he with pyne shuld pas us fro,   *suffering|pass from us*
And efte shuld com us to   *afterwards*
To amende oure sighing sore.
290 It may not stand in stede to sheynd youreself, therfore.   *destroy*
MARIA MAGDALENE. Alas this day for drede! Good John,
        neven this no more!   *mention*

        [*She speaks aside to John.*]
Speke prevaly, I the[e] pray,   *privately*
For I am ferde, if we hir flay,   *frighten*
That she will ryn and rafe!   *run and rave*
JOHANNES. The sothe behovys me nede to say: *I must say the truth*
He is damyd to dede this day.   *condemned to death*
Ther may no sorow him safe.
MARIA JACOBI. Good John, tell unto us two what thou of
        hir will crafe,   *request*
And we will gladly go and help that thou it have.   *help you obtain it*

279*cosyn:* cousin, i.e., nephew in this case.

282–83Ah, dear lady, by your leave (i.e., begging your pardon), no man should conceal the truth, nor grieve himself at the will of God (since we ought to accept God's will without complaint).

290Therefore, it won't do to destroy yourself.

300 JOHANNES. Sisters, youre mowrning may not amende.   *can do nothing*
        And ye will ever, or he take ende,   *If/ere*
        Speke with my master free,   *noble*
        Then must ye rise and with me weynd,   *wend, go*
        And kepe him as he shall be kend   *await/descried*
        Withoutt yond same cité.   *Outside*
        If ye will nigh him nere, com fast and folowe me.   *come near him*
    MARIA. A, help me, sisters dere, that I my son may see!

    MARIA MAGDALENE. Lady, we wold weynd full fain,   *go*
        Hertely with all oure might and main,
310   Youre comforth to encrese.
    MARIA. Good John, go before and frain.   *ask questions*
    JOHANNES. Lo, where he commes us even again   *directly toward us*
        With all yond mekill prese!   *great crowd*
        All youre mowrning in feyr may not his sorow sese.   *together*
    MARIA. Alas, for my son dere, that me to moder chese!   *chose me as mother*
        [*They meet Jesus, who is accompanied by a crowd.*]

        Alas, dere son, for care I se thy body blede!
        Myself I will forfare for the[e] in this great drede: *destroy*
        This cros on thy shulder bare, to help the[e] in this nede   *bare shoulder*
        I will it bere, with greatt hart sare, wheder thay will   *whither*
            the[e] lede.
    JHESUS. This cros is large in lengthe, and also bustus   *awkward*
            withall;
        If thou put to thy strengthe, to the erthe thou mon downe   *(Even) if/must*
            fall.

    MARIA. A, dere son, thou let me help the[e] in this case!
        [*Et inclinabit crucem ad matrem suam.*]   *And he will bow down the cross to*
                                                                                      his mother
323 JHESUS. Lo, moder, I tell it the[e], to bere no might thou
            hase.
324 MARIA. I pray the[e], dere son, it may so be, to man thou
            gif thy grace,
325   On thyself thou have pité, and kepe the[e] from thy
            foyse!   *foes*

    JHESUS. Forsothe, moder, this is no nay: on cros I must
            dede dre,   *suffer death*
        And from deth rise on the thrid day—thus prophecy says
            by me.

323–25 Lo, mother, I tell you, you don't have the strength to carry it. —I pray you, dear son,
that just as you gave your mercy to man, you will have pity on yourself and save yourself from
your foes.

Mans saull, that I luffyd ay, I shall redeme securly;   *loved always/surely*
Into blis of heven for ay I shall it bring to me.

330 MARIA MAGDALENE.   It is greatt sorow to any wight, Jhesus
   to se with Jues keyn!
 How he in diverse pains is dight, for sorow I water both   *put*
   min[e] eeyn.
 MARIA JACOBI.   This Lord that is of might did never ill,
   truly!
 Thise Jues thay do not right if thay deme him to dy.   *doom*

 MARIA MAGDALENE.   Alas, what shall we say? Jhesus, that is
   so leyfe,   *dear*
 To deth thise Jues this day thay lede, with paynes full
   grefe.   *grievous*
 MARIA JACOBI.   He was full true, I say, though thay dam
   him as thefe.
 Mankinde he lufed allway. For sorow my hart will clefe!   *loved/burst*

 JHESUS.   Ye doghters of Jerusalem, I bid you wepe nothing   *not at all*
   for me,
 Bot for youreself and youre barn-teme. Behald, I tell you   *brood of children*
   securlé: *surely*
 Sore paines ar ordand for this reme in dayes herafter   *ordained/realm*
   for to be!
341 Youre mirth to bayll; it shall downe-streme in every place
   of this cité.

342 Childer, certys, thay shall blis women baren, that never
   child bare,
343 And pappes that never gaf sowke, iwis. Thus shall thare
   hartys for sorow be sare.
344 The montayns hy, and thise greatt hillys, thay shall bid fall
   apon them thare!
 For my bloode, that sakles is, to shede and spill thay will   *guiltless*
   not spare.
 2 TORTOR.   Walk on, and lefe thy vain carping! It shall not   *leave off*
   save the[e] fro thy dede,   *death*

330It is great sorrow to any person to see Jesus among the cruel Jews.

341-44Your mirth (will turn) to sorrow; God's punishment will pour down everywhere on this
city. Children, certainly, will say, "Blessed are barren women who never bore child, and
breasts that never gave suck," truly. Thus for sorrow will their hearts be sore. They will bid
the high mountains and great hills to fall upon them (see Luke 23:28–30).

347   Wheder thise women cry or sing, for any red that thay   *Whether*
      can red.

    3 TORTOR.   Say, wherto abide we hereabowte   *why do we tolerate*
      Thise qwenes with screming and with showte?   *whores*
      May no man thare wordys stere?   *control*
    1 TORTOR.   Go home, thou casbald, with that clowte!   *wretch/blow*
      [*Strikes.*]
      Or, by that lord I leyfe and lowte,   *believe in and bow to*
      Thou shall by it full dere!   *buy/dearly*
354 MARIA MAGDALENE.   This thing shall veniance call on you
      [w]holly in fere!
355 2 TORTOR.   Go, hi[e] the[e] hens withall, or ill haill cam
      thou here!
356 3 TORTOR.   Let all this bargan be, syn all oure toyles ar
      before;
357   This tratoure and this tre I wold full fain were thore.
358 1 TORTOR.   It nedys not him to harll—this cros dos him
      greatt dere—
359   Bot yonder commys a carll shall help him for to bere.
    [*They spy Simon of Cyrene, and hail him.*]

    2 TORTOR.   That shall we soyn se on assay.—   *soon see by trial*
      Herk, good man, wheder art thou on a way?
      Thou walkes as thou were wrath.   *wroth, angry*
    SIMON.   Sirs, I have a greatt jornay
      That must be done this same day,
      Or els it will me skathe.   *harm*
    3 TORTOR.   Thou may with litill pain easse him and thyself,
      both.
367 SIMON.   Good sirs, that wold I fain, bot for to tary I were full
      loth.   *unwilling*

    1 TORTOR.   Nay, nay, thou shall full soyn be sped.   *soon be done*
      Lo, here a lad that must be led
      For his ill dedys to dy,   *deeds*
      And he is bressed and all for-bled;   *bruised and all bloody*

347*for . . . red:* for any advice that they can offer, i.e., for all the good their comfort will do.

354–59This deed will bring down vengeance on the whole lot of you! —Go, get away from here fast, or it'll be bad luck to you for coming here! —Let's forget about this wretched quarreling, since all our tools are ahead of us at the place of execution (i.e., we ought to be getting on); I earnestly wish this traitor and this cross were already there. —There's no need for the prisoner to drag the cross which is doing him great harm, for here comes a fellow who'll help him bear it.

367Good sirs, I'd gladly do it, except that I'm most unwilling to be delayed.

That makys us here thus stratly sted.   *in a tight spot*
We pray the[e], sir, forthi,   *therefore*
That thou will take this tre; bere it to Calvery.   *tree, cross*
SIMON.   Good sirs, that may not be, for full greatt hast have
    I;

No longere may I hoyn.   *delay*
2 TORTOR.   In faith, thou shall not go so soyn,
For noght that thou can say!   *Despite what you say*
This dede must nedys be done,
380   And this carll be dede, or noyn—   *ere noon*
And now is nere mid-day.
And therfor, help us at this nede, and make us here no
    more delay.
SIMON.   I pray you, do youre dede and let me go my way,

And I shall com full soyn agane   *soon*
To help this man with all my main,   *might*
At youre awne will.   *own*
387 3 TORTOR.   What, and wold thou trus with sich a trane?   *pack up, leave/trick*
Nay, fatur, thou shall be full fain   *traitor/glad*
This forward to fulfill,   *agreement*
Or, by the might of Mahowne, thou shall like it full ill!
391 1 TORTOR.   Tytt, let ding this dastard downe, bot he lay
    hand thertill!

392 SIMON.   Certys, that were unwisely wroght,
393   To beytt me, bot if I trespast oght
Aythere in worde or dede!   *Either*
2 TORTOR.   Apon thy bak it shall be broght;   *placed*
Thou berys it wheder thou will or noght!   *You'll carry it whether*
397   Dewill! Whom shuld we drede?
And therfor take it here, belyfe, and bere it furth, good   *quickly*
    spede.
399 SIMON.   It helpys not here to strife—bere it behoves me
    nede—

And therfor, sirs, as ye have saide,

387What, would you try to get away with a trick like that? (The soldiers, not trusting Simon to return after completing his urgent business, get rough with him and drop their former politeness.)

391–93Quick, let's knock this sot down unless he gives us a hand with the job! —Certainly, that would be unwisely done, to beat me, unless I offended in some way,

397i.e., The devil take it! Why should we be afraid of anyone (like you)?

399It does no good to protest—I must carry it.

To help this man I am well paide,   *pleased*
As ye wold that it were.
3 TORTOR.   A ha! Now ar we right arayde;   *well provided*
Bot loke oure gere be redy grade   *see to it/prepared*
To wyrk when we com there.
1 TORTOR.   I warand all redy oure toyles, both moore and   *warrant/tools*
    les,
And sir Simon truly gose on before with cros.   *goes*

3 TORTOR.   Now, by Mahowne, oure heven king,
I wold that we were in that stede   *place*
410   Where we might him on cros bring!
Step on before, and furth him lede
A trace.   *path, way*
1 TORTOR.   Com on, thou!
2 TORTOR.   Put on, thou!   *Move*
3 TORTOR.   I com fast after you,
And folowse on the chace.   *hunt*
    [*Exeunt, Jesus being led and driven.*]

    Explicit Flagellatio.   *Here ends the Scourging*

THE CRUCIFIXION OF CHRIST
FROM YORK
THE PINNERES AND PAINTERS

Even more strikingly than in earlier episodes of the Passion, this York pageant of the Crucifixion focuses on the contrast between Christ and his tormenters. He speaks only twice, in meditative language taken from the Seven Last Words of the Gospel narratives and from the liturgy for Holy Week. He begs mercy for erring mankind and desires nothing for himself. Throughout he is utterly serene, heroic, without a hint of personal agony or fear. He embraces his fate willingly, stretching himself out on the cross like the resolute warrior in the Anglo-Saxon poem "The Dream of the Rood." Without his acquiescence, the soldiers would be powerless to proceed. The conception of character here is essentially timeless, reconciling as it does the older Romanesque image of the triumphant Christ with the torn and bloody sufferer of late medieval Gothic art.

Christ's tormenters, on the other hand, are blunt and colloquial in their speech. They are the work of the so-called "York Realist," whose exuberantly comic style reminds us of the Wakefield Master. With gruesomely humorous attention to detail, the York Realist depicts the mechanical difficulties involved in crucifying Christ. The soldiers boast of their prowess as executioners, and yet they are thwarted by unexpected difficulties at every turn. Because the holes have been improperly marked and bored in the cross, the soldiers must stretch their victim before they can hammer in the nails. In the process they tear asunder his sinews and veins. They nearly break their backs lifting the cross and have to lay it down again. When they have finally managed to drop the base of the cross into its mortice or slot, with a bone-breaking jolt, they discover that the mortice is too wide and must be wedged. All these matters absorb them in the macabre details of their job. They insist on doing things as good craftsmen would do them; they will have no negligence, no slacking off, no shoddy fit. (Perhaps we are meant to recall with a sense of ironic amusement that this pageant is partly staged by the "pinners," or makers of pegs for wood-joining.) Proud of their skill and yet comically incompetent to us, the soldiers so lose themselves in their world of mechanical details that they have no sense of the large issues confronting them. As Christ compassionately observes, they know not what they do (l. 261).

Despite the realism of portrayal, we can also perceive abstract symmetry in the arrangement of the four soldiers around the four sides of the cross. Staging is simple, requiring only a raised place with a mortice for the elevated cross, and a flat playing area below it for most of the soldiers' work.

The Crucifixion of Christ

From York

The Pinneres and Painters

Crucifixio Christi.

[*The soldiers arrive at Calvary with Jesus.*]

1 MILES.	Sir knightis, take heede hydir in hie!	*to me in haste*
2	This dede on-dergh we may noght drawe.	*undiligently*
	Yee wootte youreselffe als wele as I	*know/as well*
	Howe lordis and leders of owre lawe	
	Has geven dome that this doote schall die.	*judgment/fool*
2 MILES.	Sir, alle thare counsaile wele we knawe.	
	Sen we are comen to Calvarie,	*Since*
	Latte ilke man helpe nowe as him awe.	*Let each/he ought*
3 MILES.	We are alle redy, loo,	
10	That forward to fullfille.	*agreement*
4 MILES.	Late here howe we schall doo,	*Let's hear what*
	And go we tyte thertille.	*quickly to it*
1 MILES.	It may nog[h]t helpe her[e] for to hone	*delay*
	If we schall any worshippe winne.	*honor*
2 MILES.	He muste be dede nedelingis by none.	*necessarily by noon*
3 MILES.	Thanne is goode time that we beginne.	*Then it's high time*
4 MILES.	Late dinge him doune! Than is he done;	*Let's knock/Then/finished*
	He schall nought dere us with his dinne.	*not plague/din, crying out*
19 1 MILES.	He schall be sette and lerned sone—	
20	With care to him and all his kinne!	*sorrow*
2 MILES.	The foulest dede of all	*death*
	Shalle he die for his dedis.	*deeds*
3 MILES.	That menes, crosse him we schall.	*That means we'll crucify him*
4 MILES.	Behalde, so right he redis.	*he counsels rightly*
1 MILES.	Thanne to this werke us muste take heede,	
	So that oure wirking be noght wronge.	
27 2 MILES.	None othir noote to neven is nede,	*occupation/mention*
	But latte us haste him for to hange.	*let/crucify*

TITLE *Pinneres*: makers of pins or pegs used to fasten boards together.

2We cannot carry out this deed undiligently.

19–20He'll be put in his place and taught a lesson soon—may sorrow come to him and all his kindred!

27There's no need to mention or consider any other kind of task (other than crucifying).

3 MILES.   And I have gone for gere, goode speede;   *with haste*
Bothe hammeres and nailes, large and lange.

4 MILES.   Thanne may we boldely do this dede.
Commes on, late kille this traitoure strange!   *Come on let's/strong*

33 1 MILES.   Faire might ye falle in feere,   *in this way*
That has wrought on this wise!

2 MILES.   Us nedis nought for to lere   *We don't need to be taught*
Suche faitoures to chastise.   *traitors*

[*They lay the cross flat.*]

3 MILES.   Sen ilke a thing es right arrayed,   *Since every/is*
The wiselier nowe wirke may we.

4 MILES.   The crosse on grounde is goodely graied,   *prepared*
And boorede even as it awith to be.   *bored/ought*

1 MILES.   Lokis that the ladde on lenghe be laide   *Look, see to it*
And made me thane unto this tree.   *fastened (?) to this cross*

2 MILES.   For alle his fare, he schalle be flaied: *boasting/tortured*

44   That on assaye sone schalle ye see.   *by trial*

3 MILES [*to Jesus*].   Come forthe, thou cursed knave!
Thy comforte sone schall kele.   *soon/cool, abate*

4 MILES.   Thine hire here schall thou have.   *payment*

1 MILES.   Walkes oon! Now wirke we wele.   *Walk on*

JHESUS.   Almighty God, my Fadir free,   *noble*
50   Late this[e] materes be made in minde: *Let/be considered*
Thou badde that I schulde buxsome be   *willing*
For Adam plight for to be pined.   *Adam's/tortured*
Here to dede I obblisshe me   *death/obligate myself*
Fro that sinne for to save mankinde,
And soverainely beseke I the[e]   *principally I beseech*
That thay for me may favoure finde;   *on my account*
And fro the fende thame fende,   *defend them from the fiend*
So that ther saules be saffe
In welthe withouten ende.   *spiritual bliss*
I kepe nought ellis to crave.   *I desire nothing more*

61 1 MILES.   We! Herke, sir knightis, for Mahoundis bloode!   *by Mohammed's*
Of Adam-kinde is all his thoght.

2 MILES.   The warlowe waxis werre than woode!   *wizard·grows worse than mad*
This doulfull dede ne dredith he noght.   *painful/he doesn't dread*

33May good luck come to all of you.

44You'll soon see that when we try it.

61*We:* an interjection.

65	3 MILES. Thou schulde have minde, with maine and moode,	*remember/might*
66	Of wikkid werkis that thou haste wrought.	
67	4 MILES. I hope that he hadde bene as goode	*I think*
68	Have sesed of sawes that he uppe sought.	*ceased/sayings*
69	1 MILES. Thoo sawes schall rewe him sore,	*Those words*
70	For all his sauntering, sone!	*Despite/soon*
	2 MILES. Ille spede thame that him spare	*Ill luck to those who*
	Tille he to dede be done!	*death*

3 MILES.   Have done belive, boy, and make the[e] boune,   *Finish up quickly/ready*
    And bende thy bakke unto this tree.
        [*Jesus lies down on the cross.*]
4 MILES.   Bihalde, himselffe has laide him doune,
    In lenghe and breede as he schulde bee!   *breadth*

77	1 MILES. This traitoure, here teynted of treasoune,	*attainted, condemned*
78	Gose faste and fette him than, ye thre.	*Go/fetter*
	And sen he claimeth kingdome with croune,	*since*
80	Even as a king here have schall hee.	
	2 MILES. Nowe, certis, I schall nog[h]t feyne	*stop*
	Or his right hande be feste.	*Until/fast, secured*
	3 MILES. The lefte hande thanne is mine.	
	Late see who beres him beste.	*Let's/acquits himself*

85	4 MILES. His limmys on lenghe than schalle I lede,	*limbs, legs*
	And even unto the bore thame bringe.	*them*
	1 MILES. Unto his heede I schall take hede,	
	And with mine hande helpe him to hing.	*hang*
	2 MILES. Nowe, sen we foure schall do this dede,	
	And medill with this unthrifty thing,	*meddle*
91	Late no man spare for speciall spede	*Let*
	Tille that we have made ending.	
	3 MILES. This forward may not faile.	*agreement must not fail*
	Nowe are we right arraiede.	*prepared*
	4 MILES. This boy here in oure baile	*rascal/custody*
	Shall bide full bittir brayde.	*experience/blow*
	[*They stretch Christ's limbs out to the bores.*]	

65–70You should be meditating, with all your might and main, on the wicked deeds you've done. —I think he might better have stopped saying the kind of things he thought up. —He'll sorely repent those words soon, despite all his babbling!

77–78Go quickly then, you three, and fetter this traitor here condemned of treason.

80He'll have (his crown) here, just like a king.

85Then I'll stretch his limbs (especially his legs) out to their full length. (The four soldiers are symmetrically arranged at the four points of the cross.)

91Let no one of us refrain from using top speed.

    1 MILES.   Sir knightis, saye, howe wirke we nowe?
    2 MILES.   Yis, certis, I hope I holde this hande.   *think*
    3 MILES.   And to the boore I have it brought,
        Full boxumly, withouten bande.   *obediently, readily|ropes*
    1 MILES.   Strike on than, harde, for Him the[e] boght!   *Him who redeemed you*
        [*They begin nailing.*]
102 2 MILES.   Yis, here is a stubbe will stiffely stande!   *thick nail*
103   Thurgh bones and senous it schall be soght.   *sinews|be found*
        This werke is wele, I will warande.   *warrant*
    3 MILES.   Saye, sir, howe do we thore?   *there*
106   This bargaine may not blinne.   *business|cease*
    1 MILES.   It failis a foote and more!   *It falls short of fitting*
        The senous are so gone inne.   *sinews|shrunk*

109 4 MILES.   I hope that marke amisse be bored.   *I think*
110 2 MILES.   Than muste he bide in bittir bale.   *torment*
111 3 MILES.   In faith, it was overe-skantely scored;   *negligently marked*
112   That makis it fouly for to faile.
    1 MILES.   Why carpe ye so? Faste on a corde   *talk|Fasten*
        And tugge him to, by toppe and taile.   *stretch him to it head and foot*
    3 MILES.   Ya, thou comaundis lightly as a lorde!   *as readily*
        Come helpe to haale, with ille haile!   *haul|with bad luck to you*
    1 MILES.   Nowe certis, that schall I doo—
        [*Aside*] Full suerly as a snaile.   *surely*
    3 MILES.   And I schall tacche him too   *tack, nail|to (the cross)*
        Full nemely with a naile.   *nimbly*

        This werke will holde, that dar I heete,   *promise*
        For nowe are feste faste both his handis.   *fastened securely*
    4 MILES.   Go we all foure, thanne, to his feete;
        So schall oure space be spedely spende.   *our time be best spent*
125 2 MILES.   Latte see what bourde his bale might beete!   *jest|sorrow|mend*
        Tharto my bakke nowe wolde I bende.
    4 MILES.   Owe! This werke is all unmeete.   *unfit*
        This boring muste all be amende.   *amended*
    1 MILES.   A, pees, man, for Mahounde!

102-3Yes, here is a nail that will stand firm enough! You'll find that it will go through bones and sinews.

106This business must not cease (i.e., we can't stop here).

109-12I think the mark is bored wrong (i.e., the hole hasn't been bored on the mark). —Then he (Christ) will have to endure grievous torment. —Truly, the boring-spot was marked very negligently; that causes the business to be so badly done.

125Let's see what jest can mend his sorrow (i.e., pulling at Christ's feet will be a game to amuse him).

130   Latte no man wotte that wondir:
       A roope schall rugge him doune   *yank*
       If all his sinuous go asoundre.   *Even if/sinews*

2 MILES.   That corde full kindely can I knitte,   *thoroughly/tie*
       The comforte of this karle to kele.   *churl/cool, lessen*

135 1 MILES.   Feste on, thanne, faste that all be fitte.   *Fasten/quickly/fit*
       It is no force howe felle he feele.   *It's no matter how keenly*
       [*They pull down on his feet with a rope, to reach the incorrectly
       bored hole.*]

2 MILES.   Lugge on, ye both, a litill yitt!   *Lug, pull*
138 3 MILES.   I schalle nought sese, as I have seele!   *cease/bliss*

4 MILES.   And I schall fonde him for to hitte.   *try*

2 MILES.   Owe, haille!   *haul*

4 MILES.   Hoo nowe! I halde it wele.   *Whoa/I think that's enough*

1 MILES.   Have done! Drive in that naile,   *Finish up*
       So that no faute be foune.   *fault be found*

4 MILES.   This wirking wolde nog[h]t faile
       If foure bullis here were boune.   *Even if/bound*

1 MILES.   Ther cordis have evill encressed his paines,   *These/sorely*
146 Or he wer tille the booringis brought.   *Ere/to*

2 MILES.   Yaa, assoundir are bothe sinuous and veinis   *sinews*
       On ilke a side, so have we soughte.   *each/striven, afflicted (him)*

3 MILES.   Nowe all his gaudis nothing him gaines.   *tricks profit him not at all*
       His sauntering schall with bale be bought.   *fantastic notions/suffering*

4 MILES.   I wille goo saye to oure soveraines
       Of all this werkis howe we have wrought.   *How well we've done*

1 MILES.   Nay, sirs, anothir thing
       Fallis firste to you [and] me:
       They badde we schulde him hing   *hang*
       On heghte that men might see.

157 2 MILES.   We woote wele so ther wordes wore,   *know/were*
       But sir, that dede will do us dere!   *harm*

1 MILES.   It may not mende for to moote more;   *It won't help to argue*
       This harlotte muste be hanged here.   *rascal*

130Let no man know about that wondrous thing (i.e., the incorrect fitting of the holes, which
the first soldier takes to be a supernatural sign).

135Get a hold, then, firmly, so that everything will be ready.

138I won't stop pulling, as I hope to have bliss.

146Until he was brought or stretched to the bore-holes.

157We know well those were their words.

161	2 MILES.	The mortaise is made fitte therfore.
162	3 MILES.	Feste on youre fingeres than, in feere.	*Fasten/together*

[*They try to lift the cross, and fail.*]

4 MILES.   I wene it wolle nevere come thore! — *believe/get (up) there*
We foure raise it nog[h]t right, to-yere. — *upright this year*

1 MILES.   Say, man, why carpis thou soo? — *talk*
Thy lifting was but light. — *lazy*

2 MILES.   He menes, ther muste be moo — *means/more*
To heve him uppe on hight. — *heave*

3 MILES.   Now certis, I hope it schall noght nede — *I think*
To calle to us more companye.
Methinke we foure schulde do this dede
And bere him to yone hille on high.

1 MILES.   It muste be done, withouten drede. — *doubt*

174   No more but loke ye be redy;
And this parte schalle I lifte, and leede. — *part (the head)/lead*
On lenghe he schalle no lenger lie. — *Stretched out*
Therfore nowe makis you boune: — *make yourselves ready*
Late bere him to yone hill. — *Let's*

4 MILES.   Thanne will I bere here doune, — *down (at the foot)*

180   And tente his tase untill. — *attend to his toes*

2 MILES.   We twoo schall see tille aythir side, — *to either side (of the cross)*
For ellis this werke wille wrye all wrang. — *go awry*

3 MILES.   We are redy. In Gode, sirs, abide, — *In God's name*
And late me first his fete up fang. — *let/take up*

185 2 MILES.   Why tente ye so to tales this tide? — *time*

1 MILES.   Lifte uppe! [*All lift the cross together.*]

4 MILES.   Latte see! — *i.e., Watch out*

2 MILES.   Owe! Lifte alang! — *lengthwise*

3 MILES.   Fro all this harme he schulde him hide, — *protect himself*
And he war God. — *If he were*

4 MILES.   The devill him hang!

1 MILES.   For, grete harme have I hente: — *received*

190   My schuldir is in soundre! — *sunder*

2 MILES.   And sertis I am nere schente, — *certainly/ruined*
So lange have I borne undir. — *lifted up*

3 MILES.   This crosse and I in twoo muste twinne. — *separate*

161–62The mortise, or slot to hold the base of the cross, is ready made to receive it. —Fasten your fingers on (i.e., grab) it, then, all together.

174Get ready, without further ado.

185Why do you heed talk thus at this time (instead of working)?

Ellis brekis my bakke in sondre sone! *Or else breaks*
4 MILES.   Laye downe againe, and leve youre dinne! *leave, stop*
   [*They lay it down.*]
This dede for us will nevere be done. *despite our efforts*
1 MILES.   Assaye, sirs: latte se if any ginne *Try/let's see/device*
May helpe him uppe, withouten hone; *delay*
For here schulde wight men worschippe winne, *strong men win honor*
200   And noght with gaudis al day to gone! *tricks*
2 MILES.   More wighter men than we *Stronger*
Full fewe, I hope, ye finde. *Very few I think*
3 MILES.   This bargaine will noght bee, *This business won't get finished*
For certis me wantis winde. *I'm out of breath*

205 4 MILES.   So wille of werke nevere we wore! *bewildered/were*
I hope this carle some cautellis caste. *I think/has devised some tricks*
2 MILES.   My bourdeyne satte me wondir soore! *burden distressed me*
Unto the hill I might noght laste. *I can't hold out*
1 MILES.   Lifte uppe, and sone he schall be thore. *there*
210   Therfore, feste on youre fingeres faste. *fasten/quickly*
3 MILES.   Owe, lifte! [*They pick up the cross again.*]
1 MILES.   We, loo!
4 MILES.   A litill more.
2 MILES.   Holde, thanne!
1 MILES.   Howe nowe?
2 MILES.   The werste is paste. *passed*
   [*They reach the top of the hill and put down the cross.*]
3 MILES.   He weyes a wikkid weght. *weighs*
2 MILES.   So may we all foure saye,
Or he was heved on heght *Ere (i.e., by the time) he was heaved up*
And raised in this array. *fashion*

4 MILES.   He made us stande as any stones, *i.e., He made us motionless*
So boustous was he for to bere. *awkward, huge*
1 MILES.   Nowe, raise him nemely for the nonys, *nimbly/once*
220   And sette him by this mortas heere, *mortice, slot to hold cross*
And latte him falle in alle at ones; *let/(i.e., joltingly)*
For certis that paine schall have no pere. *peer, equal*
3 MILES.   Heve uppe! [*They raise the cross.*]
4 MILES.   Latte doune so all his bones *Let (it) down*
Are asoundre, nowe on sides seere! *asunder/on all sides (at once)*
   [*They drop the base of the cross into the mortice with a jolt.*]
1 MILES.   This falling was more felle *cruel*

200And not spend all day playing tricks.

205Never before were we so bewildered in our work!

Than all the harmes he hadde!

Nowe may a man wele telle   *easily count*

The leste lith of this ladde.   *least (smallest) limb/fellow*

3 MILES.   Me thinkith this crosse will noght abide   *hold firm*

230 Ne stande stille in this mo[r]teyse, yitt.

4 MILES.   Att the firste time was it made overe-wide;   *it (the mortice)*

That makis it wave, thou may wele witte.   *it (the cross)/well know*

1 MILES.   Itt schall be sette on ilke a side   *wedged/every*

So that it schall no forther flitte.   *move*

Goode wegges schall we take this tide,   *time*

And feste the foote; thanne is all fitte.   *fasten*

2 MILES.   Here are wegges arrayed   *prepared*

For that, both grete and smale.

3 MILES.   Where are oure hameres laide

240 That we schulde wirke withall?

> [*They take up hammers to wedge the base of the cross in the mortice.*]

4 MILES.   We have them here, even atte oure hande.

2 MILES.   Giffe me this wegge. I schall it in drive.

4 MILES.   Here is anodir yitt ordande.   *still another ready*

3 MILES.   Do, take it me hidir belyve.   *bring/hither quickly*

1 MILES.   Laye on thanne, faste.

3 MILES.   Yis, I warrande.

246 I thring thame same, so motte I thrive!   *knock them together*

Nowe will this crosse full stabely stande;

248 All if he rave, they will noght rive.   *won't split*

1 MILES [*to Jesus*].   Say, sir, howe likis thou nowe

This werke that we have wrought?

4 MILES. We praye youe, says us howe   *tell us*

Ye fele, or fainte ye ought?   *or if you're at all faint*

JESUS.   Al men that walkis, by waye or strete,   *walk*

254 Takes tente ye schalle no travaile tine!   *lose*

Biholdes min[e] heede, min[e] handis, and my feete,   *Behold*

And fully feele nowe, or ye fine,   *reflect/ere you finish*

If any mourning may be meete   *matched with*

Or mischeve mesured unto mine. [*He prays.*]   *misfortune compared*

My Fadir, that alle bales may bete,   *sorrows/remedy*

---

246 I'll knock them together (i.e., the wedges into the mortice), as I hope to thrive.

248 Even if he raves, the wedges won't split apart.

254 Take heed you do not lose the advantage of my suffering. (See Lamentations of Jeremiah 1:12; and, for lines 260–61, see Luke 23:34.)

260   Forgiffis thes men that dois me pine.   *Forgive/cause me pain*
      What thay wirke wotte they noght.   *They know not what they do*
      Therfore, my Fadir, I crave,
      Latte nevere ther sinnys be sought,   *Let/their/examined*
      But see ther saules to save.   *see that you save*

   1 MILES.   We, harke! He jangelis like a jay.   *chatters*
   2 MILES.   Me thinke he pratis like a py.   *prates/magpie*
   3 MILES.   He has ben doand all this day,   *doing (this)*
268   And made grete meving of mercy.   *moving*
   4 MILES.   Es this the same that gune us say   *Is/said to us*
      That he was Goddis sone almighty?

271 1 MILES.   Therfore he felis full felle affraye,
      And demyd this day for to die.   *(is) condemned*
273 2 MILES.   *Vah! qui destruis templum . . .*   *Hah! You that destroy the temple*
   3 MILES.   His sawes wer so, certaine.   *words*
   4 MILES.   And, sirs, he saide to some
      He might raise it againe.

277 1 MILES.   To mustir that he hadde no might,   *To display*
      For all the kautelles that he couthe kaste;   *Despite/tricks/could devise*
      All if he wer in worde so wight,   *Even if/strong, brave*
      For all his force, nowe is he feste.   *bound*
      Als Pilate demed, is done and dight;   *As/decreed/dealt with*
      Therfore I rede that we go reste.   *advise*
   2 MILES.   This race mon be rehersed right,   *action must be reported*
      Thurgh the worlde, both este and weste.
   3 MILES.   Yaa, late him hinge here stille,   *let him hang*
      And make mowes on the mone.   *grimaces at the moon*
   4 MILES.   Thanne may we wende at wille.   *go when we please*
   1 MILES.   Nay, goode sirs, noght so sone.   *not*

289   For certis us nedis anodir note:
      This kirtill wolde I of you crave.   *kirtle, cloak*
   2 MILES.   Nay, nay, sir, we will loke by lotte   *we'll see by lottery*
      Whilke of us foure fallis it to have.   *Which/it falls to*
   3 MILES.   I rede we drawe cutte for this coote—   *advise/lots/coat*
294   Loo, se howe sone—alle sidis to save.

268And has been loudly urging (God) to have mercy.

271That's the reason he experiences this fierce assault.

273(See Matthew 27:40 and Mark 15:29.)

277He had no power to display such a deed (i.e., raise the temple).

289For certainly we need to settle another matter.

294See how easily it's done—to guarantee fairness on all sides.

4 MILES.   The schorte cutte schall winne, that wele ye woote,   *well/know*
    Whedir itt falle to knight or knave.   *Whether*
    [*They draw lots for Jesus' cloak.*]
1 MILES.   Felowes, ye thar noght flyte,   *need not quarrel*
    For this mantell is mine.
2 MILES.   Goo we thanne hense, tyte.   *quickly*
300   This travaile here we tine.   *labor/lose*
    [*Exeunt soldiers.*]

300i.e., We're wasting our efforts here (with ironic double meaning).

CHRIST'S DEATH AND BURIAL
FROM YORK
THE BOCHERES

This portrayal of Christ's death and burial lacks the grim comedy of the preceding Passion scenes. Christ's tormenters no longer play a prominent role. Pilate is a thoughtfully enigmatic and contradictory figure, unlike the ranting tyrant of the Wakefield Passion sequence. Characterization is generally restrained; events follow the order of the Gospel accounts. Minor personages such as the "boy" who offers Christ bitter drink, and the centurion who is moved to faith by what he sees, do not exceed their biblical roles. This is not to say, however, that the playwright is unduly deferential to the Scriptures. The dialogue owes as much to the liturgy for Holy Week and to the tradition of meditative complaint as to the Bible. Christ's Seven Last Words, derived from harmonies of the four Gospels, are interspersed with reflective lyrics on the meaning of his great sacrifice. The Virgin Mary's speeches are similarly based on complaint literature as found in church drama and elsewhere. Her laments at the foot of the cross recall those of the bereaved mothers in the Fleury *Slaughter of the Innocents*, or of her own lament in the twelfth-century Benediktbeuern Passion play (see Parts I–II, above). Apocryphal legend also makes its contribution. The miracle in which Longeus' (or Longinus') sight is restored by Christ's blood, though based ultimately on the biblical episode of the soldier who pierces Christ's side (John 19: 34), is more immediately indebted to the apocryphal account found in the Gospel of Nicodemus.

Staging of this Death and Burial demands an unusually large cast of characters, a number of separate locations, and some elaborate stage structures. The characters, simultaneously visible to the audience, are grouped at several locations around the cross. Pilate, his soldiers, and the chief priests form one group, seemingly at Pilate's dais on Calvary hill. The Virgin Mary, Mary Cleophas, and John the Apostle form another group, located where they can lament Christ's suffering and talk with him. Jesus is flanked by two thieves, raised on actual crosses. Also present are the boy who offers Christ drink, the blind Longeus (or Longinus) whose sight is restored, and the centurion. After the death of Christ, Joseph of Arimathea approaches Pilate's station and then encounters Nicodemus on his way to the cross. These two men must actually remove Christ's body from the cross and entomb it in a sepulchre. Such a production would place heavy demands on the butchers of York if, as is generally assumed, they presented this action on a movable pageant wagon. Conceivably, however, the action may have been staged instead in a fixed location, with a number of simultaneously-visible scaffolds as in most church drama. (See, for example, the Anglo-Norman *La Seinte Resureccion*, Part II above, with its account of Joseph of Arimathea and Nicodemus.)

Christ's Death and Burial

From York

The Bocheres

Mortificatio Cristi.

[Pilate and the chief priests are on Calvary hill, at Pilate's dais, near the crucified Christ.]

PILATUS.	Sees, seniours, and see what I saye!	*Cease (talking)*
2	Takis tente to my talking enteere.	*Pay attention*
	Devoide all this dinne here, this day,	*Cease/din*
	And fallis to my frenschippe in feere.	*fall, come/together*
	Sir Pilate, a prince withowten pere,	*peer*
	My name is, full evenly to neven,	*exactly to name*
	And domisman full derworth in dede	*doomsman, judge/worthy/deed*
	Of gentillest Jewry full even	*indeed*
	Am I.	
10	Who makis oppressioun,	*Whoever makes*
	Or dose transgressioun,	*does*
	By my discressioun	
	Shall be demed dewly to di[e].	*judged duly*

	To die schall I deme thame to dede,	*them to death*
	Tho rebelles that rewles thame unright.	*Those/rule themselves*
	Who that to yone hill wille take heede	*Whoever*
	[He points to Calvary.]	
	May se ther the soth in his sight:	
18	Howe doulfull to dede they are dight	*dolefully to death/put*
19	That liste nog[h]t owre lawes for to lere.	*Who don't wish/learn*
	Lo, thus by my maine and my might	
	Tho churles schalle I chasteise and cheere,	*Those/censure (?)*
	By lawe.	
	Ilke feloune false	*Each*
	Shall hinge by the halse.	*hang/neck*
	Transgressours als	*in like manner*
26	On the crosse schalle be knitte for to knawe.	*bound*

TITLE *Bocheres:* butchers.

[2]Pay undivided attention to my speech.

[18–19]How those who do not care to heed our laws are put to death in great misery. (Pilate may refer to the two thieves crucified on either side of Christ, rather than to Christ whom Pilate believes guiltless.)

[26]On the cross shall be bound, to be taught a lesson; or, to be gnawed.

	To knawe schall I knitte thame on crosse;	
	To schende thame with schame schall I shappe.	*destroy/I'll contrive*
29	Ther liffis for to leese is no losse—	*Their lives*
30	Suche tirrauntis with teene for to trappe.	*ruffians/affliction*
	Thus leelly the lawe I unlappe,	*loyally, faithfully/display*
	And punissh thame pitously.	*severely*
	Of Jhesu I holde it unhappe	*I consider it unfortunate*
	That he on yone hill hing so hye	*hangs*
	For gilte. [*To the chief priests.*]	
	His bloode to spille	
	Toke ye you tille!	*You took upon yourselves*
	Thus was youre wille,	
39	Full spitously to spede he were spilte.	*spitefully/killed*

40	CAIPHAS. To spille him we spake in a speede!	*kill/hurry*
41	For, falsed he folowde in faye.	*falsehood/faith*
	With fraudes oure folke gan he feede,	*he fed*
	And laboured to lere thame his laye.	*teach them his law*
44	ANNA. Sir Pilate, of pees we youe praye.	*peace*
	Oure lawe was full like to be lorne.	*likely/destroyed*
	He saved nog[h]t oure dere Sabott-daye;	*observed/Sabbath*
47	And that, for to scape it, were a scorne,	*avoid*
48	By lawe.	
	PILATUS. Sirs, before youre sight,	
	With all my might	
	I examinde him right,	
	And cause non in him cowthe I knawe.	*could I discover*

	CAIPHAS. Ye knawe wele the cause, sir, in cace:	*in this case*
	It touched treasoune untrewe.	*It concerned*
55	The tribute to take or to trace	*search out, seize*
56	Forbadde he, oure bale for to brewe.	*trouble/stir up*
57	ANNA. Of japes yitt jangelid yone Jewe,	*jests/jangled*
	And cursedly he called him a king.	*himself*
	To deme him to dede it is diewe;	*judge/death/due, fitting*

29–30It's no great loss to cause such ruffians to lose their lives, to enmesh them in affliction.

39–41That he should quickly be killed with cruel pains. —We urged his being quickly killed! For, he practiced false faith.

44Sir Pilate, we urge you to be quiet, i.e., not to object to our actions.

47–48And to avoid the Sabbath should be regarded as a contemptuous action, according to the Mosaic law.

55–57To stir up trouble for us, he (Christ) forbade the taking or collecting of tribute (i.e., he defied the authority of Caesar; cf. the Wakefield Buffeting, l. 94). —Yonder Jew prated of still more ridiculous matters.

60   For, treasoune it touches, that thing
      Indede.
  CAIPHAS.   Yitt principall
    And worste of all,
    He garte him call   *caused himself to be called*
    Goddes sonne, that foulle motte hime speede!   *bad luck to him*

  PILATUS.   He spedis for to spille in space,   *i.e., He'll quickly die*
    So wondirly wrought is youre will.   *excessively*
    His bloode schall youre bodis enbrace,   *i.e., shall be upon you*
    For that have ye taken you till.   *to you*
  ANNA.   That forwarde ful faine to fulfille   *agreement/gladly*
    Indede schall we dresse us, bedene!   *prepare ourselves at once*
72   Yone losell him likis full ille,   *rogue*
    For turned is his trantis all to teene,   *tricks/sorrow*
    I trowe.
  CAIPHAS.   He called him king—
    Ille joye him wring!   *May sorrow torment him*
    Ya, late him hing,   *let him hang*
    Full madly on the mone for to mowe!   *moon/grimace*

79 ANNA.   To mowe on the moone has he mente.
      [*He calls up at Jesus.*]
    We! Fie on the[e], faitour, in faye!   *traitor/in faith*
81   Who, trowes thou, to thy tales toke tente?   *paid heed to your talk*
82   Thou saggard, thyselffe gan thou saye: *sagging one/you said*
83   The tempill distroye the[e] todaye;
84   By the thirde day ware done ilk-a-dele,   *every bit*
85   To raise it thou schulde the[e] arraye.   *ready yourself*
    Loo, howe was thy falsed to[o] feele,   *falsehood too great*
    Foule falle the[e]!   *Bad luck to you*
    For thy presumpcioune
    Thou haste thy warisoune.   *You have/reward*
    Do faste, come doune,
    And a comely king schalle I calle thee.

92 CAIPHAS.   I calle the[e] a coward to kenne,   *know*

60For his offense concerns treason.

72Yonder rogue likes this agreement very ill.

79i.e., Well may he hang there and make faces at the moon.

81–85Who, do you suppose, paid any heed to your talk? You wretch, sagging from your own weight on the cross, you yourself once said: you would destroy the temple today, (and) by the time the third day were entirely over (done with), you would ready yourself to raise it again. (See Mark 14:58.)

92I call you a known and apparent coward.

That mervailles and mirakills made
Thou mustered emange many menne;   *(Which) you showed among*
95   But, brothell, thou bourded to[o] brede.   *wretch/jested too broadly*
Thou saved thame fro sorowes, thay saide;   *them*
To save nowe thyselffe late us see!   *let*
98   God sonne if thou grathely be graide,   *God's/are plainly*
Delivere the[e] doune of[f] that tree
Anone.
101   If thou be funne   *found*
102   Thou be Goddis sonne,
We schalle be bonne   *bound*
To trowe on the[e] trewlye, ilkone.   *believe in/each one*

ANNA.   Sir Pilate, youre pleasaun[c]e we praye: *indulgence*
Takis tente to oure talking this tide,   *Pay heed/time*
And wipe ye yone writing away.
It is not beste it abide.
It sittis youe to sette it aside,   *befits*
And sette that he saide in his sawe   *set down what/speech*
111   As he that was prente full of pride: *exalted*
112   "Jewes king am I, comely to knawe,"   *know*
Full plaine.   *plainly*
PILATUS. *Quod scripsi, scripsi.*   *What I have written I have written*
Yone same wrotte I;
I bide therby,   *I will abide by it*
117   What gedling will grucche there-againe.   *rogue/complain*
        [*Jesus, crucified between two thieves, is observed by his mother
        Mary, Mary Cleophas, John the Apostle, and others.*]

118 JHESUS.   Thou man that of mis here has mente, *misdeed, sin*
To me tente enteerly thou take.   *pay heed entirely*
On roode am I ragged and rente,   *cross/torn*
Thou sinfull sawle, for thy sake.   *soul*
For thy misse, amendis wille I make;   *sin*
My bakke for to bende here I bide.

95i.e., Your purported miracles were all jokes.

98If you are truly the son of God (see Matthew 27:40).

101–2If you are proved to be the son of God.

111–12Like one who was exalted (prinked) full of pride: "I am King of the Jews, a handsome person to those who know me." (The cross appearing in this pageant presumably bears the superscription "The King of the Jews," placed there by Pilate. The chief priests insist the phrase "I am" be added to stress Jesus' presumption.)

117No matter what rogue will complain against it.

118You who have led your life here on earth in sin (or, have called to mind your sinfulness).

This teene for thy trespase I take.   *affliction/transgression*
Who couthe the[e] more kindines have kidde   *could/shown*
Than I?
Thus for thy goode
I schedde my bloode.
129   Manne, mende thy moode,
For full bittir thy blisse mon I by.   *bitterly/must I buy*

MARIA.   "Allas!" for my swete sonne I saye,
That doulfully to dede thus is dig[h]t!   *death is put*
Allas! for full lovely thou laye
In my wombe, this worthely wight.   *worthy person*
Allas, that I schulde see this sight
Of my sone so semely to see!   *attractive*
Allas, that this blossome so bright
Untrewly is tugged to this tree!
Allas!
140   My lorde, my leyffe,   *dear*
With full grete greffe
Hingis as a theffe.   *Hangs*
Allas, he did never trespasse!

JHESUS.   Thou woman, do way of thy weping.   *cease*
For me may thou nothing amende.
My Fadirs wille to be wirking,
For mankinde my body I bende.
148 MARIA.   Allas, that thou likes noght to lende!   *you wish not to remain*
Howe schulde I but wepe for thy woo?
150   To care nowe my comforte is kende.
Allas, why schulde we twinne thus in twoo   *separate*
Forevere?
JHESUS.   Womanne, instede of me,
Loo, John thy sone schall bee.
John, see to thy modir free;   *noble*
For my sake do thou thy devere.   *duty*

MARIA.   Allas, sone, sorowe and site,   *(for) sorrow and grief*
That me were closed in clay!   *i.e., (I wish) I were dead*
159   A swerde of sorowe me smite,

129 i.e., Man, be of good cheer.

148 i.e., Alas, that you no longer intend to remain (on earth)!

150 My comfort now has given birth to sorrow.

159–61 Would that a baleful sword would smite me so that I were put to death this day! —Ah,
mother, don't say that! (John is presumably Mary's nephew; see the Wakefield Flagellation.)

160   To dede I were done this day!   *death*

161 JOHANNES.   A, modir, so schall ye noght saye!

    I pray youe, be pees in this presse;   *be quiet/crowd*

    For, with all the might that I maye,

    Youre comforte I caste to encresse,   *I (will) devise to increase*

    Indede.

    Youre sone am I,

    Loo, here redy;

    And nowe, forthy,   *therefore*

    I praye yowe hense for to speede.

170 MARIA.   My steven for to stede or to steere   *voice/steady/control*

    Howe schulde I, such sorowe to see—

    My sone that is dereworthy and dere   *precious*

    Thus doulfull a dede for to die?   *death*

    JOHANNES.   A, dere modir, blinne of this blee!   *cease/crying*

    Youre mourning it may not amende.

    MARIA CLEOPHE.   A, Marye, take triste unto the[e],   *be trustful*

    For socoure to the[e] will he sende

    This tide.   *time*

    JOHANNES.   Faire modir, faste

    Hense latte us caste!   *let us be off*

    MARIA.   To he be paste   *Till/passed, dead*

    Wille I buske here bainly to bide.   *undertake/humbly*

183 JHESUS.   With bittirfull bale have I bought,   *torment*

184   Thus, man, all thy misse for to mende.   *sin*

    On me for to looke lette thou nog[h]t,   *refrain*

    Howe bainly my body I bende.   *obediently*

    No wighte in this worlde wolde have wende   *person/weened, thought*

    What sorowe I suffre for thy sake.

189   Manne, kaste the[e] thy kindinesse by kende,

190   Trewe tente unto me that thou take,   *attention*

191   And treste.   *trust*

    For, foxis ther dennys have they,   *their dens*

    Birdis hase ther nestis to paye,   *to please (them)*

    But the sone of man this daye

    Hase nog[h]t on his heed for to reste.   *to rest his head on*

    LATRO A SINISTRIS.   If thou be Goddis sone so free,   *The thief on the left*

    Why hing thou thus on this hille?   *hang*

183–84Thus, man, to make amends for all your sins I have paid the penalty with extremely bitter torment.

189–91Man, think upon your feelings of kindred held by natural affection, in order to pay true attention and trust unto me.

198 To saffe nowe thyselffe, late us see,	*save/let*
199 And us now, that spedis for to spille.	
LATRO A DEXTRIS. Manne, stinte of thy steven and be	*right/cease/voice*
stille!	
For douteles thy God dredis thou nog[h]t.	*you fear not God*
Full wele are we worthy thertill;	*well/thereto (i.e., hanging)*
Unwisely wrange have we wrought,	*wrong*
Iwisse.	*Truly*
Noon ille did hee	*No*
Thus for to die.	
Lord, have minde of me	
What thou art come to thy blisse.	*What (time), when*

JHESUS. Forsothe, sonne, to the[e] schall I saye:	
210 Sen thou fro thy foly will falle,	*Since/folly*
With me schall dwelle nowe this daye	
In paradise, place principall.	*best of places*
Heloy, heloy!	*Eloi, eloi*
My God, my God, full free,	*noble*
Lama yabatanye?	*Lama sabacthani*
Wharto forsoke thou me	*Why*
In care?	*In (my) sorrow*
And I did nevere ille	
219 This dede for to go tille;	*to*
But, be it at thy wille.	
A, me thristis sare!	*I thirst sorely*

GARCIO. A drinke schalle I dresse the[e], indede,	*Boy/prepare*
A draughte that is full daintely dight.	*fixed*
Full faste schall I springe for to spede!	*to hurry*
I hope I schall holde that I have hight. [*He goes.*]	*think/keep what I promised*
CAIPHAS. Sir Pilate, that moste is of might,	
Harke: "Heely!" now harde I him crye.	*"Elias"/heard*
He wenys that that worthely wight	*weens, thinks/worthy being*
In haste for to helpe him in hye	*(will come) in haste*
230 In his nede.	
PILATUS. If he do soo	
He schall have woo.	
ANNA. He wer oure foo	
If he dresse him to do us that dede.	*undertakes*

235 That dede for to dresse if he doo,	*undertake*

---

^{198–99}Let us now see you save yourself and us, who are about to die.

²¹⁹To deserve to go to this death.

²³⁵If he (Elias, or Elijah) should undertake that deed (i.e., rescuing Christ).

	In sertis he schall rewe it full sore;	*Certainly/regret*
237	Neverethelees if he like it noght, loo,	
238	Full sone may he covere that care.	*recover, be relieved of*
239	GARCIO [*returning*]. Nowe, swete sir, youre wille if it ware,	*were*
	A draughte here of drinke have I dreste,	*prepared*
241	To spede for no spence that ye spare,	*expense*
242	But baldely ye bib it for the beste;	*boldly imbibe*
	Forwhy	*Because*
	Aysell and galle	*Vinegar*
	Is menged withalle.	*mingled*
	Drinke it ye schalle;	
	Youre lippis, I halde thame fulle drye.	*I consider them*

	JHESUS. Thy drinke it schalle do me no deere;	*harm*
	Wete thou wele, therof will I none.	*Know/well*
250	Nowe, Fadir, that formed alle in fere,	*all (things) together*
	To thy moste might make I my mone!	*moan, complaint*
	Thy wille have I wrought in this wone,	*dwelling (the world)*
	Thus ragged and rente on this roode.	*torn/cross*
	Thus doulfully to dede have they done.	*death*
	Forgiffe thame by grace that is goode;	*them*
	Thay ne wote nog[h]t what it was.	*They know not*
	My Fadir, here my bone!	*hear my prayer*
	For nowe all thing is done.	*it is finished*
	My spirite to thee right sone	
260	Comende I, *in manus tuas.* [*Jesus dies.*]	*into your hands*

	MARIA. Now dere sone, Jhesu so jente,	*noble*
	Sen my harte is hevy as leede,	*Since/lead*
	O worde wolde I witte or thou wente . . .	*One/know ere*
	Allas, nowe my dere sone is dede!	
	Full rewfully refte is my rede.	*torn away/counsel, support*
	Allas, for my darling so dere!	
	JOHANNES. A, modir, ye halde uppe youre heede,	
	And sigh nog[h]t with sorowes so seere,	*many*
	I praye!	
270	MARIA CLEOPHE. It dose hir pyne	*does her pain*
	To see him tyne.	*harmed*
	Lede we her heyne;	*hence*

237–38i.e., Nevertheless, if he (Elijah) prefer not to rescue Christ, he may immediately be relieved of the sorrow we would otherwise inflict on him (?).

239youre . . . ware: if you please.

241–42To help, regardless of cost, that you be not deprived of drink, but that you should boldly imbibe this for your benefit.

This mo[u]rning helpe hir ne maye.   *cannot help her*

[*John leads away the two Marys.*]

CAIPHAS.   Sir Pilate, parceive, I you praye:

275   Oure costemes to kepe wele ye canne.

To-morne is oure dere Sabott daye;   *Tomorrow*

277   Of mirthe muste us meve ilke a man.   *every man*

278   Yone warlous nowe waxis full wan,   *wizards*

And nedis muste they beried be.

Deliver ther dede, sir, and thane   *Hasten their death*

Shall we sewe to oure saide solempnité   *pursue, proceed to*

Indede.

PILATUS.   It schalle be done,

In wordis fone. [*To his soldiers.*]   *few*

Sir knightis, go sone,   *soon*

To yone harlottis you hendely take heede.   *rascals/expeditiously*

Tho caitiffis thou kille with thy kniffe.   *Those*

288   Delivere, have done they were dede.   *Quick/dispatch*

MILES.   My lorde, I schall lenghe so ther liffe,   *lengthen*

That tho brothelles schall nevere bite brede.   *wretches/bread*

PILATUS.   Ser Longeus, steppe forthe in this steede.   *stead, time*

This spere, loo, have halde in thy hande;

To Jhesu thou rake fourthe, I rede,   *go forth/advise*

And sted noug[h]t, but stiffely thou stande   *tarry not*

A stounde.   *while*

In Jhesu side   *Jesus'*

Schoffe it this tide.   *Shove/time*

No lenger bide,

But grathely thou go to the grounde.   *without delay*

[*The blind Longeus goes to Jesus and pierces his side with the spear, and suddenly gains his sight.*]

LONGEUS LATUS.   O Maker unmade, full of might,   *of the side/i.e., eternal*

O Jhesu so jentill and jente,   *noble*

That sodenly has lente me my sight,

303   Lorde, loving to the[e] be it lente!   *given*

On rode arte thou ragged and rente,   *cross/torn*

Mankinde for to mende of his mis.   *sin*

---

[275]You well know how to keep our customs.

[277-78]Every man of us ought to be stirred (by the Sabbath) to rejoicing (and therefore the bodies shouldn't remain on the cross during the holy day). Yonder wizards are growing very wan (i.e., they look pale in their dying).

[288]Quickly dispatch, so that they be dead.

[303]Lord, may our love be given to you.

Full spitously spilte is and spente
Thy bloode, Lorde, to bringe us to blis
Full free.   *noble*
A, mercy, my socoure!   *succour, help*
Mercy, my treasoure!
Mercy, my Savioure!
Thy mercy be markid in me.   *observed*

CENTURIO.   O wondirfull werkar, iwis,   *worker (of miracles)*
314   This weedir is waxen full wan!   *weather*
Trewe token I trowe that it is
That mercy is mente unto man.
Full clerly consaive thus I can
318   No cause in this corse couthe they knowe;
Yitt doulfull they demyd him than   *judged/then*
To lose thus his liffe by ther lawe—
No rig[h]te.
Trewly, I saye,
Goddis sone verraye   *God's true son*
Was he this daye,
That doulfully to dede thus is dig[h]t.   *death/put*

[*Joseph of Arimathea approaches Pilate's dais.*]
326   JOSEPH.   That Lorde lele, ay lasting in lande,   *loyal, faithful*
327   Sir Pilate, full preste in this presse,   *ready/throng*
328   He save the[e] by see and by sande,   *i.e., everywhere*
329   And all that is derworth on deesse.   *praiseworthy on dais*
PILATUS.   Joseph, this is lely no lesse: *truly no lie*
To me arte thou welcome, iwisse.
Do saye me the soth, or thou sesse,   *ere you cease*
Thy worthily wille what it is,   *What is your worthy will*
Anone.
JOSEPH.   To the[e] I praye,
Giffe me in hye   *Give/in haste*
Jhesu bodye,
In gree it for to grave al alone.   *Under favor/to bury*

PILATUS.   Joseph, sir, I graunte the[e] that geste.   *deed*

314The weather has become utterly dark. (See Matthew 27:51–53 for an account of the cosmic eruptions at the moment of Christ's death.)

318They (the Jews) had no knowledge of any just cause in the course they pursued.

326–29Sir Pilate, you who are ready of disposition among this throng (of your followers), may that faithful Lord, everlasting throughout the world, save you wherever you may go, and all those who are praiseworthy on this dais.

340	I grucche nog[h]t to grath him in grave.	*grudge/array*
341	Deliver, have done he were dreste,	*Hasten/prepared*
342	And sewe, sir, oure Sabott to saffe.	*comply/Sabbath/observe*
	JOSEPH. With handis and harte that I have,	
	I thanke the[e], in faith, for my frende.	
345	God kepe the[e] thy comforte to crave,	
	For wightely my way will I wende	*quickly*
	In hye.	*In haste*
	To do that dede,	
	He be my speede	*(May) he be*
350	That armys gun sprede	*Who spread his arms (on the cross)*
	Mannekinde by his bloode for to bye.	*buy, ransom*

[*Nicodemus meets Joseph on the way to the cross.*]

	NICHODEMUS. Well mette, sir! In minde gune [I] meffe	*I'm moved in my mind*
	For Jhesu, that juged was unjente;	*ignobly*
	Ye laboured for license and leve	*permission*
	To berye his body on bente.	*in field*
	JOSEPH. Full mildely that matere I mente,	*mercifully*
	And that for to do will I dresse.	*address myself*
	NICHODEMUS. Both same I wolde that [we] wente,	*together*
	And lette not for more ne for lesse;	*not delay for anyone*
360	For-why	*Because*
	Oure frende was he,	
	Faithfull and free.	*noble*
	JOSEPH. Therfore go we	
	To berye that body in hye.	*in haste*

[*They reach the cross.*]

	All mankinde may marke in his minde	*may take notice*
	To see here this sorowfull sight.	
	No falsnesse in him couthe they fi[n]de,	*could*
	That doulfully to dede thus is dight.	*death/put*
	NICHODEMUS. He was a full worthy wight,	*person*
	Nowe blemisght and bolned with bloode.	*swollen*
371	JOSEPH. Ya, for that he mustered his might,	
	Full falsely they fellid that foode,	*person*
	I wene,	*ween, think*
	Bothe bakke and side	
	His woundes wide.	

340–42 I don't begrudge giving him burial. Hasten, finish preparing him, and observe our Sabbath (i.e., remove the bodies before the Sabbath begins).

345 i.e., May God preserve you and grant the comfort you crave.

371 Yah, because he (Christ) displayed such might.

Forthi, this tide   *Therefore/time*
Take we him doune us betwene.
[*Between them they lower Jesus from the cross and lay him out
on the ground.*]

NICHODEMUS.   Betwene us take we him doune,
And laye him on lenthe on this lande.
380 JOSEPH.   This reverent and riche of rennoune,   *revered one/renown*
Late us halde him and halse him with hande.   *Let/embrace*
A grave have I garte here be ordande   *I've caused to be readied*
That never was in noote—it is newe.   *in use*
NICHODEMUS.   To this corse it is comely accordande   *corpse/decently becoming*
To dresse him with dedis full dewe,   *appropriate actions*
This stounde.   *At this time*
JOSEPH.   A sudarye,   *shroud or napkin*
Loo, here have I;
Winde him, forthy,   *therefore*
390 And sone schalle we grave him in grounde.   *bury*
[*They wrap Jesus' body in the shroud and bury him.*]

NICHODEMUS.   In grounde late us grave him, and goo.   *let*
Do liffely, latte us laye him allone.   *Act lively*
Nowe, Saviour of me and of moo,   *more*
Thou kepe us in clennesse ilkone!   *each one*
JOSEPH [*also praying*].   To thy mercy nowe make I my
            moone.   *moan, complaint*
As Saviour by see and by sande,   *i.e., everywhere*
397 Thou g[u]ide me that my griffe be al gone,   *grief*
398 With lele liffe to lenge in this lande,   *loyal, true/live long*
399 And esse!   *ease*
NICHODEMUS.   Seere oinementis here have I   *Several*
Brought for this faire body;
I anointe the[e], forthy,   *therefore*
With myrre and aloes.
[*Nicodemus anoints the body with ointments.*]

JOSEPH.   This dede it is done ilke a dele,   *every bit*
And wroughte is this werke wele, iwis.   *well*
To the[e], king, on knes here I knele,
That bainly thou belde me in blisse!   *readily/shelter*
NICHODEMUS.   He highte me full hendely to be his,   *promised/graciously*
A night whan I neghed him full nere.   *approached*
410 Have minde, Lorde, and mende me of mis!   *Remember/amend/sin*

397–99May you so guide me that I experience no grief, living long in this world in true faith
and comfort.

For done is oure dedis full dere   *deeds/precious*
      This tide.   *time*
JOSEPH [*to the audience*].   This Lorde so goode,
That schedde his bloode,
He mende youre moode,   *(May) he bring you cheer*
And buske on this blis for to bide!   *get (you) ready/abide*
      [*Finis.*]

THE HARROWING OF HELL
FROM WAKEFIELD

The Harrowing of Hell, although mentioned nowhere in the Bible, forms an essential part of all the Corpus Christi cycles. The story is derived from the apocryphal Gospel of Nicodemus, which in turn makes important use of a line from Psalm 24: "Lift up your heads, O ye gates, and be ye lift up, ye everlasting doors, and the King of Glory shall come in." The apocryphal account of Christ's deliverance of souls had become universally accepted in medieval Christianity because it answered an essential question: what happened to the souls of the righteous during those long years of Old Testament history from Adam's fall to the advent of Christ? According to medieval theology, even the most estimable of the Old Testament patriarchs had been subjected to spiritual privation until Christ made atonement for Adam's fall. Because they were eventually to be saved, however, those souls were permitted to dwell in the Limbo of the Fathers rather than in hell itself. They suffered from the absence of God rather than from the tortures visited upon the truly damned.

In the cycles, then, the deliverance of souls from hell brings to completion a sequence of events begun with Adam's fall from grace. At the commencement of this Wakefield pageant, Christ stands outside hell while the patriarchs in limbo speak prophetically of the blissful occasion at hand. They joyfully anticipate Christ's coming, like the earlier Procession of Old Testament Prophets announcing the birth of the Saviour. The roster of those waiting to be delivered includes many prominent figures from Old and New Testament history: Adam and Eve, Isaiah, Simeon, John the Baptist, and Moses. Their joint appearance signals a major recapitulation of the dramatic action presented thus far in the cycles.

The Harrowing of Hell also brings to completion the great struggle between Christ and Satan. Because the devil is an evil schemer outwitted by his own machinations in a contest of guile, his overthrow is appropriately comic. He is contrasted with his divine adversary in ways that remind us of previous episodes in the cycles. Like Pharaoh, Herod, or the Wakefield Pilate, he is a boastful and tyrannical ranter seeking to destroy innocence and meekness. In his debate with Christ, Satan employs the same sardonically skeptical arguments previously used to deny the Virgin Birth or to entrap Christ during the temptation in the wilderness. Satan's followers are comic in much the same ludicrous vein as their master: they raise the alarm in noisy panic, shore up useless defenses against Christ's entry, and turn on one another in an orgy of mutual recriminations.

Because the play explicitly differentiates between hell as a place of eternal torment and limbo as a temporary residence for the patriarchs (ll. 96, 305–6), we must assume that the stage also differentiates between these two locations. Perhaps, if the original performance made use of simultaneously-visible scaffolds erected around a playing area, limbo would have been on one level of a multi-tiered tower of hell equipped with a functional hellmouth at its base. Paradise could then have been represented as one level of a multi-tiered tower of heaven.

This Wakefield Harrowing of Hell rather closely parallels the version in the York cycle, from which it is derived.

The Harrowing of Hell
From Wakefield

Incipit Extractio Animarum, etc.	*Here begins the Deliverance of Souls, etc.*

[The soul of Jesus, outside hell gates, prepares to confront Satan.]

JHESUS. My Fader me from blis has send	*sent*
Till erth for mankinde sake,	*To*
Adam mis for to amend—	*Adam's sin*
My deth nede must I take.	
I dwellyd ther thirty yeres and two,	
And somdele more, the sothe to say.	*somewhat*
7 In anger, pyne, and mekyll wo,	*pain, suffering|much*
I dyde on cros this day.	
Therfor till hell now will I go	*to*
To chalange that is mine.	*claim that which*
Adam, Eve, and othere mo,	*more*
Thay shall no longer dwell in pine.	*suffering*
The feynde theym wan with trayn,	*fiend won them|tricks*
14 Thrugh fraude of erthly fode.	*offspring*
I have theym boght agan	*redeemed*
With sheding of my blode.	
17 And now I will that stede restore	*place*
Which the feynde fell fro, for sin;	
Som tokyn will I send before,	
With mirth to gar thare gammes begin.	*cause|games, pleasures*
21 A light I will thay have	
To know I will com sone.	
My body shall abide in grave	
Till all this dede be done.	

[In hell a glorious light shines, and the captive souls rejoice.]

[7] *anger:* i.e., the wrath of Christ's tormenters.

[14] By deceiving mankind.

[17] i.e., And now I will restore them to that place, heaven.

[21] I desire them to have a light.

ADAM.   My brether, herkyn unto me here!   *brethren*
  More hope of helth never we had.
  Fower thowsand and sex hundreth yere
  Have we bene here in darknes stad.   *placed*
  Now se I tokyns of solace sere: *several*
30 A glorious gleme to make us glad,
  Wherthrugh I hope that help is nere,
  That sone shall slake oure sorowes sad.

EVA.   Adam, my husband heynd,   *gracious*
  This menys solace certan!   *means*
  Sich light can on us leynd   *did/linger*
  In paradise, full plain.

ISAIAS.   Adam, thrugh thy sin
  Here were we put to dwell,
  This wikyd place within—
40 The name of it is hell.
  Here paines shall never blin   *cease*
  That wikyd ar, and fell.   *cruel*
  Love that Lord with win,   *joy*
  His life for us wold sell.   *(Who) would sell*
   Et cantent omnes "Salvator Mundi," primum versum.   *And let all sing "Saviour of the World," first verse*

  Adam, thou well understand
46 I am Isaias. So Crist me kende:
  I spake of folke in darknes walkand;   *walking*
  I saide a light shuld on theym lende.   *dwell, linger*
  This light is all from Crist commande   *coming*
  That he till us has hedir sende;   *to/hither sent*
  Thus is my point proved in hand,
  As I before t[w]o-fold it kende.   *taught, prophesied*

SIMEON.   So may I tell of farlys feyll: *many wonders*
54 For in the tempyll his freyndys me fande—   *friends found me*
  Me thoght dainteth with him to deyll.   *I thought it honor/associate*
  I halsid him homely with my hand[e].   *embraced/familiarly*
  I saide, "Lord, let thy servandys leyll   *loyal*
  Pas in peasse to lif lastande;   *life everlasting*
  Now that min[e] eeyn has sene thin[e] hele,   *eyes/salvation*
  No longer list I lif in lande."   *desire/live*

---

46 I am Isaiah. Thus Christ made known (his coming) to me. (See Isaiah 9:2.)

54 *freyndys:* According to Luke 2:22–39, Jesus' parents brought him to the temple to be purified, where they found Simeon waiting to see Jesus before dying.

This light thou has purvayde *provided*

62 For theym that lyf in lede. *among people, on earth*

That I before of the[e] have saide, *That which I prophesied*

I se it is fulfillyd indede.

JOHANNES BAPTISTA.   As a voce cryand, I kend *voice crying/taught*

The wayes of Crist, as I well can.

I baptisid him with both min[e] hende

In the water of flume Jordan. *river*

The Holy Gost from heven discende *descended*

As a white dowfe downe on me, than; *dove/then*

The Fader voice, oure mirthes to amende, *Father's*

72 Was made to me like as a man.

"Yond is my son," he saide,

"And which me pleases full well."

His light is on us laide,

And commys oure karys to kele. *comes/cares to assuage*

MOYSES.   Now, this same night lerning have I. *divine knowledge*

To me, Moyses, he shewid his might,

And also to anothere oone, Hely, *Elijah*

80 Where we stud on a hill on hight. *stood*

As white as snaw was His body,

His face was like the son for bright. *sun for brightness*

No man on mold was so mighty *earth*

Grathly durst loke agans that light! *(That) he dare look directly toward*

And that same light here se I now

Shining on us, certain;

Wherethrugh, truly, I trow

That we shall sone pas fro this pain.

[*The devil Ribald strives frantically to raise the alarm.*]

RIBALD.   Sen first that hell was mayde, and I was put *Since*
therin,

90 Sich sorow never ere I had, nor hard I sich a din! *Such/before/heard*

My hart beginnys to brade, my witt waxys thin. *swell*

I drede we cannot be glad: thise saules mon fro us twin! *must/separate*

How, Belsabub! Binde thise boys! Sich harow was never *clamor*
hard in hell. *heard*

---

[62]For those who live among the nations of the earth. (See Luke 2:31 and *The Gospel of Nicodemus,* "The Descent into Hell," Latin text A, II [XVIII].)

[72]Came to me sounding like a man's voice.

BELZABUB.   Out, Ribald, thou rores! What is betyd? Can   *happened*
    thou oght tell?
RIBALD.   Why, herys thou not this ugly noise?   *hear*
    Thise lurdans that in limbo dwell   *louts*
    Thay make mening of many joyse,   *They express*
    And muster mirthes theym emell.   *display/among themselves*

BELZABUB.   Mirth? Nay, nay, that point is past.
    More hope of helth shall thay never have.
RIBALD.   They cry on Crist full fast
    And says he shall theym save!

103 BEELZABUB.   Yee, though he do not, I shall,
    For they ar sparyd in speciall space.   *shut up*
    Whils I am prince and principall
    They shall never pas out of this place.
    Call up Astarot and Anaball
    To gif us counsell in this case—
    Bell, Berith, and Belliall—
110   To mar theym that sich mastry mase!   *those who assert such mastery*

    Say to sir Satan, oure sire,
    And bid him bring also
    Sir Lucifer, lufly of lyre.   *lovely of countenance*
RIBALD.   All redy, lord, I go! [*He starts off.*]
    [*Jesus approaches hell gates, still outside them.*]

115 JHESUS.   *Attolite portas, principes, vestras, et elevamini portae*   *Lift up your gates, you princes,*
    aeternales, et introibit rex gloriae.   *and be lifted up, you everlasting*
                                    doors, and the king of glory will
                                      come in

RIBALD.   Out, harro, out! What devill is he
    That callys him king over us all?
    Hark, Belzabub, com né,   *come near*
    For hedusly I hard him call!   *hideously/heard*

120 BELZABUB.   Go, spar the yates, ill mot thou thé!   *fasten/ill may you prosper*
    And set the waches on the wall.   *watch, guard*
    If that brodell com né,   *wretch/nigh*
    With us ay won he shall.   *he'll forever dwell*
    [*The devils barricade hell gates.*]

    And if he more call or cry

---

[103]Yea, not Christ but I will save them (meant ironically).

[115](Psalms 24:7; see note 184 below.)

To make us more debate,   *strife*
Lay on him hardely   *Strike/boldly*
And make him go his gate.   *go his way*

DAVID.   Nay, with him may ye not fight,
For he is king and conqueroure,
130   And of so mekill might   *much*
And stif in every stoure.   *resolute/battle*
Of him commys all this light   *From/comes*
That shinys in this bowre.   *bower, chamber*
He is full fers in fight,   *fierce*
Worthy to win honoure.

BELZABUB.   Honowre! Harsto, harlot, for what dede?   *Do you hear/rascal*
All erthly men to me ar thrall.
That lad that thou callys Lord in lede   *of the nations, people*
He had never harbor, house, ne hall.   *lodging*

How, sir Sathanas! Com nar   *How now*
And hark this cursid rowte!   *crowd*
SATHANAS [*approaching*].   The devill you all to-har! *harry to pieces*
What ales the[e] so to showte?   *ails*
144   And me, if I com nar,   *(May the devil harry) me also*
145   Thy brain bot I brist owte!   *unless/burst*
BELZABUB.   Thou must com help to spar!   *barricade*
We ar beseged abowte.   *round about*

SATHANAS.   Besegyd aboute! Why, who durst be so bold
149   For drede to make on us a fray?
BELZABUBE.   It is the Jew that Judas sold
For to be dede, this othere day.
152 SATHANAS.   How? In time that tale was told!
That trature travesses us allway.   *traitor thwarts*
He shal be here full hard in hold!   *strictly confined*
Bot loke he pas not, I the[e] pray.   *see he doesn't escape*

BELZABUB.   Pas? Nay, nay, he will not weynde   *wend*
From hens, or it be war!   *ere/worse*
He shapys him for to sheynd   *prepares himself/destroy*
All hell, or he go far.   *ere*

144–45And may the devil harry me also unless, if I get my hands on you (lit: come near you), I knock out your brains.

149i.e., To attack us, frightening as we are?

152This news was announced just in time.

160 SATHANAS.   Fi[e], faturs! Therof shall he faill;   *imposter(s)*
    For all his fare, I him defy.   *actions*
    I know his trantes fro top to taill: *tricks*
    He liffys by gawdys and glory.   *lives/tricks/vainglory*
    Therby he broght furth of oure baill   *from our misery*
    The lath Lazare of Betany.   *hideous Lazarus*
    Bot to the Jues I gaf counsayll   *gave*
    That thay shuld cause him dy.

    I enterd ther into Judas,
    That forward to fulfill.   *agreement*
170 Therfor his hyere he has: *his (Judas') hire, reward*
    Allwayes to won here still.   *dwell*

  RIBALD.   Sir Sathan, sen we here the[e] say   *since/hear*
    Thou and the Jues were at assent,   *in league*
    And wote he wan the Lazare away   *know/won, took*
    That unto us was taken to tent,   *dwell*
176 Hopys thou that thou mar him may
177 To muster the malice that he has ment?
178 For, and he refe us now oure pray   *if/deprive us of*
179 We will ye witt, or he is went.   *ere*

  SATHANAS.   I bid the[e] noght abaste,   *be not abashed*
    Bot boldly make you bowne,   *ready*
    With toiles that ye intraste,   *tools, weapons/trust in*
    And ding that dastard downe!   *knock*
184 JHESUS.   *Attolite portas, principes, vestras, etc.*

185 RIBALD.   Outt, harro! What harlot is he   *rascal*
    That sayes his kingdom shal be cryde?   *proclaimed*
187 DAVID.   That may thou in sawter se,   *psalter*
    For of this prince thus ere I saide: *long ago*

    I saide that he shuld breke
    Youre barres and bandys by name,   *bars/bands, bonds*
    And of youre warkys take wreke.   *vengeance*
    Now shall thou se the same.

176–79 Do you think you can hinder him from showing the malice he has intended toward us? For, if he's going to deprive us now of our victims, we want you to be aware of the situation before he gets away.

184 (Psalms 24:7, sung on Holy Saturday. The Latin is translated at ll. 193–96, below.)

185 *Outt, harro:* exclamations of dismay and pleading for help.

187 (See *The Gospel of Nicodemus*, "The Descent into Hell," Latin text B, VI [XXII].)

JHESUS. Ye princes of hell, open youre yate   *gate*
  And let my folk furth gone!
  A prince of peasse shall enter therat,
  Wheder ye will or none.   *Whether*

RIBALD. What art thou that spekys so?
JHESUS. A king of blis that hight Jhesus.   *is called*
RIBALD. Yee, hens fast I red thou go,   *advise*
200 And mell the[e] not with us!   *meddle*

BELZABUB. Oure yates I trow will last,
  Thay ar so strong, I weyn;   *ween, think*
  Bot if oure barres brast,   *Unless/burst*
  For the[e] they shall not twin.   *part*

JHESUS. This stede shall stand no longer stokyn.   *place/shut*
  Open up, and let my pepill pas!
    [*Hell gates burst asunder.*]
RIBALD. Out, harro! Oure baill is brokyn,   *fortification*
  And brusten ar all oure bandys of bras!

BELZABUB. Harro! Oure yates begin to crak!
210 In sonder, I trow, they go,
  And hell, I trow, will all to-shak.   *shake to pieces*
  Alas, what I am wo!   *how woeful I am*
    [*The devils fall back in confusion, and call to Satan.*]

RIBALD. Limbo is lorne, alas!   *lost*
  Sir Sathanas, com up;
  This wark is wars then it was!   *worse*
SATHANAS. Yee, hangyd be thou on a cruke!   *crook, hook*

  Thefys, I bad[e] ye shuld be bowne,   *ready*
  If he maide mastres more,   *assorted mastery*
  To ding that dastard downe,   *knock*
220 Sett him both sad and sore!

BELZABUB. To sett him sore, that is sone saide!   *i.e., sooner said than done*
  Com thou thyself and serve him so.
  We may not abide his bitter braide!   *withstand/attack*
  He wold us mar, and we were mo.   *even if/more*
SATHANAS. Fi[e], fature! Wherfor were ye flayd?   *traitor/frightened*
  Have ye no force to flit him fro?   *drive him away*
  Loke in haste my gere be grayd;   *gear/readied*
  Myself shall to that gadling go.   *gadabout, fellow*
    [*Satan marches to confront Jesus.*]

How! Thou bel ami, abide,   *fair friend*
With all thy boste and beyr!   *noise*
And tell me, in this tide,   *time*
What mastres thou makys here?   *mastery you assert*

JHESUS.   I make no mastry bot for mine: *except for what is mine*
234   I will theym save, that shall the[e] sow.
235   Thou has no powere theym to pine;   *to afflict*
Bot in my prison, for thare prow,   *their profit*
Here have they sorjornyd—noght as thine,   *sojourned*
238   Bot in thy wayrd, thou wote as how.   *ward, custody*
239 SATHANAS.   Why, where has thou bene ay sin,   *been ever since*
240   That never wold negh theym nere or now?   *come near them until*

JHESUS.   Now is the time certan
My Fader ordand her[e]for,   *ordained for this purpose*
That thay shuld pas fro pain
In blis to dwell for evermore.

SATHANAS.   Thy fader knew I well by sight:
He was a wright, his meett to win.   *carpenter to earn his food*
Mary, me minnys, thy moder hight,   *I remember/was called*
248   The utmast ende of all thy kin.
Say who made the[e] so mekill of might?   *much*
JHESUS.   Thou wikyd feynde, lett be thy di[n]!   *fiend*
My Fader wonnes in heven on hight,   *dwells*
In blis that never more shall blin.   *cease*

I am his oonly son, his forward to fulfill.   *agreement*
254   Togeder will we won, in sonder when we will.   *dwell*

255 SATHAN.   Goddys son! Nay, then might thou be glad,
256   For no catell thurt the[e] crave.   *chattels, goods/need*
Bot thou has liffyd ay like a lad   *lived always*
In sorow, and as a simpill knave.

²³⁴I will save them who would (otherwise) follow you; or, which will grieve you.

²³⁵i.e., You have power to afflict them only by my sufferance.

²³⁸⁻⁴⁰But in your custody; you understand how this is, i.e., you know perfectly well how you
are only custodian. —Where have you been all this long while (since men first started
sinning), you who never would come to their aid until now?

²⁴⁸i.e., That's the greatest distinction you can claim in your lineage.

²⁵⁴⁻⁵⁶i.e., We (Father and Son) will dwell eternally as one, but can separate when occasion
demands. —God's son! Nay, you might be glad enough to be such a prince, for then you'd
lack no wealth of possessions.

JHESUS.   That was for the hartly luf I had   *compassionate love*
Unto mans saull, it for to save,
And for to make the[e] masyd and mad   *mazed, confounded*
And, for that reson, rufully to rafe.   *rave*

My Godhede here I hid
In Mary, moder mine,
Where it shall never be kid   *revealed*
To the[e], ne none of thine.

267 SATHAN.   How now? This wold I were told in towne!
Thou says God is thy sire;
I shall the[e] prove by good reson
Thou moyttys as man dos into mire.   *You go astray*

To breke thy bidding they were full bowne,   *they (men)/ready*
And soyn they wroght at my desire.   *soon*
From paradise thou putt theym downe
In hell here, to have thare hire;   *their reward, punishment*

And thou thyself, by day and night,
Taught ever all men emang   *among*
Ever to do reson and right—
278 And here thou wirkys all wrang!

JHESUS.   I wirk no wrang—that shall thou witt—   *know*
If I my men fro wo will win.   *release*
My prophetys plainly prechyd it,
All the noytys that I begin: *business*
They saide that I shuld be that ilke   *same one*
In hell where I shuld intre in,
To save my servandys fro that pitt   *servants, believers*
Where dampnyd saullys shall sit for sin.   *souls*

And ilke true prophete tayll   *that same true prophets' tale*
Shal be fulfillid in me.
I have thaym boght fro baill;   *bale, sorrow*
In blis now shall they be.

291 SATHANAS.   Now, sen thou list to legge the lawes,   *since/allege*

267i.e., (sarcastically) Wait till they hear about this!

278i.e., Since you condemned them, you ought to leave them here for punishment.

291Now, since it pleases you to allege or cite the laws (as proclaimed by the prophets).

Thou shal be tenyd or we twin;   *vexed ere we part*
For those that thou to witnes drawes   *call as your witnesses*
Full even agans the[e] shall begin.   *Totally against*
As Salamon saide in his sawes: *wise sayings*
Who that ones commys hell within   *Whoso once comes*
He shall never owte, as clerkys knawes.   *(get) out/know*
Therfor, bel ami, let be thy din.   *fair friend*

    Job thy servande, also,
300   In his time can tell   *did tell*
    That nawder freynde nor fo   *neither*
    Shall finde relese in hell.

    JHESUS. He sayde full soyth: that shal thou se,   *soth, truth*
    In hell shal be no relese.
305   Bot of that place then ment he
306   Where sinfull care shall ever encrese.
    In that bayll ay shall thou be,   *bale, torment*
    Where sorowes seyr shall never sesse.   *many/cease*
    And my folke that were most fre   *noble*
    Shall pas unto the place of peasse;

    For they were here with my will,   *under my sufferance*
    And so thay shall furth weynde.   *wend, go*
    Thou shall thyself fulfill   *undergo*
    Ever wo withoutten ende.

    SATHAN. Why, and will thou take theym all me fro?
    Then, think me, thou art unkinde.
    Nay, I pray the[e], do not so!
    Umthinke the[e] better in thy minde,   *Consider*
    Or els let me with the[e] go—
    I pray the[e], leyffe me not behinde!   *leave*
    JHESUS. Nay, tratur, thou shall won in wo,   *dwell*
    And till a stake I shall the[e] binde.   *to*

323 SATHAN. Now here I how thou menys emang   *hear*
324   With mesure and malice for to mell.
    Bot sen thou says it shal be lang,   *since*
    Yit som let allwayes with us dwell.
    JHESUS. Yis, witt thou well—els were greatt wrang—   *know*

305–6 i.e., But Job was referring to eternal hell, not to the place (limbo) where the patriarchs were imprisoned until their deliverance.

323–24 Now I hear or understand how you intend to concern yourself simultaneously with justice (moderation) and remorseless punishment (vengeance).

Thou shall have Caym that slo Abell;   *Cain/slew*
And all that hastys theymself to hang,   *hasten*
330   As did Judas and Architophell;

331   And Daton and Abaron, and all of thare assent—   *their persuasion*
Cursyd tyranttys ever ilkon that me and min[e] tormente;   *each one/my followers*

And all that will not lere my law   *learn*
That I have left in land for new,   *on earth as the new law*
335   That makys my comming knaw;   *known*
336   And all my sacramentys persew.   *seek to destroy*
337   My deth, my rising, red by raw,   *by row, in turn*
338   Who trow thaym not, thay ar untrewe;   *Whosoever*
Unto my dome I shall theym draw,   *judgment*
And juge theym wars then any Jew.   *worse*

And thay that list to lere my law, and lyf therby,   *desire/learn/live*
Shall never have harmes here, bot welth, as is worthy.   *deserved*

343   SATHANAS.   Now, here my hand! I hold me paide;   *pleased*
Thise pointys ar plainly for my prow.   *profit*
If this be trew that thou has saide,
We shall have mo then we have now!   *more*
347   Thies lawes that thou has late here laide,   *lately/set down*
348   I shall theym lere not to alow;   *teach*
If thay min[e] take, thay ar betraide!
And I shall turne theym tytt, I trow.   *mislead/quickly*

I shall walk eest, I shall walk west,
352   And gar theym wirk well war.   *cause them*
JHESUS.   Nay, feynde, thou shal be feste,   *fast bound*
That thou shall flit no far.   *no farther (than hell)*

SATHAN.   Feste? Fi[e], that were a wikyd treson!

330*Architophell*: Achitophel or Ahitophel, counselor and ally to Absalom in his ill-fated rebellion against David (see 2 Samuel 17:23).

331*Daton and Abaron*: Dathan and Abiram, who conspired against Moses and Aaron and were swallowed up by the earth (see Numbers 16).

335–38(My new law) which reveals and prophesies my coming; and all those who seek to destroy my sacraments. Whatsoever people do not believe in my death and my resurrection as events in a progression are unbelievers.

343Now, here's my hand on this bargain! I consider myself pleased.

347–48I shall teach the people to refuse to obey these laws (of the New Testament) which you have lately set down on earth.

352And cause the people to act much worse (than ever).

Bel ami, thou shal be smitt.   *smitten*
JHESUS.   Devill, I commaunde the[e] to go downe
Into thy sete where thou shall sit!
    [Satan is cast down into hell pit.]
SATHAN.   Alas, for doyll and care!   *dole, sorrow*
360   I sink into hell pit!
RIBALD.   Sir Sathanas, so saide I are;   *ere, before*
Now shall thou have a fitt.   *painful experience*

    [Jesus turns to the souls awaiting deliverance.]
JHESUS.   Com now furth, my childer all,
I forgif you youre mis.   *sins*
With me now go ye shall
To joy and endles blis.

ADAM.   Lord, thou art full mekill of might,   *great*
That mekys thyself on this manere   *humbles*
To help us all, as thou had us hight   *promised*
370   When both forfett I and my fere.   *my mate*
Here have we dwelt withoutten light
Fower thousand and sex hundreth yere;
Now se we by this solempne sight
How that thy mercy makys us dere.   *beloved*

EVA.   Lord, we were worthy more tormentys to tast;
Thou help us, Lord, with thy mercy, as thou of might is
                    mast!   *most*

JOHANNES.   Lord, I love the[e] inwardly,   *i.e., in my heart*
That me wold make thy messyngere
Thy comming in erth to cry,   *to earth/proclaim*
And tech thy faith to folk in fere;   *together*
381   Sithen, before the[e] for to dy,   *Afterwards*
To bring theym bodword that be here,   *message*
How thay shuld have thy help in hy.   *in haste*
Now se I all those pointys appere.   *particulars*

MOYSES.   David, thy prophete trew,
Oft times told unto us;
Of thy comming he knew,
And saide it shuld be thus.

370When both I and my mate (Eve) had sinned.

381Afterwards that (it was your will) for me to die before you did. (For the fullest account of
John the Baptist's death, see Mark 6.)

DAVID.   As I saide ere, yit say I so: *before*
390   *"Ne derelinquas, domine,*
        Animam meam in inferno."   *(Psalms 16)*
        "Leyfe never my saull, Lord, after the[e],   *Leave|behind you*
        In depe hell wheder dampned shall go;   *whither*
        Suffre thou never thy saintys to se
        The sorow of thaym that won in wo,   *dwell*
        Ay full of filth, and may not fle."

        MOYSES.   Make mirth, both more and les,   *i.e., everyone*
        And love oure Lord we may
        That has broght us fro bitternes
400   In blis to abide for ay.

        ISAIAS.   Therfor now let us sing
        To love oure Lord Jhesus;
        Unto his blis he will us bring.
        Te Deum laudamus. [*Exeunt.*   *We praise you, O God*
          Explicit Extractio Animarum ab Inferno.   *Here ends the Deliverance of Souls*
                                                                            from Hell

THE RESURRECTION OF THE LORD
FROM WAKEFIELD

The Wakefield Resurrection contains within it the Visit to the Sepulchre, the episode that played so vital a role in the beginning of liturgical drama. This central mystery, although versified here in English rather than in Latin, remains essentially unaltered from its tenth-century form. The three Marys express the usual trepidation about removing the tombstone, are greeted with the question "Whome have ye soght?" and the explanation "He is not here," and are enjoined to tell the glad tidings to the disciples. Christ's subsequent appearance to Mary Magdalene remains similarly unchanged from its liturgical original. Mary, grieving at the tomb, encounters Christ but mistakes him for a gardener until he identifies himself as the risen Lord. Her grieving seems inconsistent, as it does in the Fleury *Visitatio* (Part I, above), since she has already heard the joyful news of Christ's triumph over death. The incident nevertheless serves a purpose by dramatizing once again the importance of faith in Christ's divinity. Mary is a witness to the truth of the Resurrection.

Other episodes in this Wakefield pageant enlarge upon the theme of witnessing a miraculous event. Faithful witnesses are contrasted with those evil persons who take part in the story of the Resurrection and yet refuse to accept its evidence of divine purpose. Among the faithful are the three Marys and also the centurion, whose story is derived partly from the apocryphal Gospel of Nicodemus (Prologue, XI) and partly from the biblical account of the soldier who exclaims "Truly this was the Son of God" (Matthew 27:54). In this Wakefield pageant, the centurion's chief dramatic function is to serve as a contrasting character

or "foil" to the soldiers guarding Christ's tomb. The centurion is sincerely moved to faith by what he sees, and bravely stands up to Pilate and the chief priests despite their scoffs and threats. The guardians at the tomb, on the other hand, are ludicrously comic villains. Like Christ's tormenters in earlier scenes of the Passion sequence, they boast of their strength in arms and yet are easily rattled by something they do not understand. Privileged to be present at the Resurrection of Christ (tradition held that they were either asleep or in a trance-like state), they consider telling the truth but are ultimately concerned with saving their own skins. Ironically, they worry more about their problems with the authorities than about the danger to their eternal souls. All their energy goes into making up a clever story that will excuse their negligence. The story they concoct is actually not clever at all, but a hilariously exaggerated account of their being set upon by a thousand graverobbers. When Pilate and the chief priests fabricate an identical coverup story, the conspiracy is complete. To the audience, this rationalistic device for explaining away the Resurrection is seen not as a plausible skeptical argument but as the frantic delusion of desperate men.

Staging focuses on two simultaneously visible acting areas: the burial site, and Pilate's station or judgment hall. The action shifts back and forth, as the soldiers ply their way from Pilate's hall to the sepulchre and back again. The sepulchre is generally a place of serenity and sparse action; at his rising, Christ delivers a lengthy "complaint" to the audience on the meaning of the event. Pilate's ornate hall is, contrastingly, a place of loud boasting and worldly connivance. An arena stage would most easily accommodate the complex action of this pageant, especially when the centurion enters riding (l. 44). The York version, on the other hand, from which this Wakefield text is in part derived, does not specify that the centurion is to enter on horseback.

The Resurrection of the Lord
From Wakefield

Resurrectio Domini.

[*Pilate at his station, accompanied by the chief priests.*]

1 PILATUS. Peasse, I warne you, woldys in witt!	*wielders, possessors of*
And standys on side or els go sitt.	*stand aside*
3 For here ar men that go not yitt,	
4 And lordys of me[kill] might.	*much*
We think to abide, and not to flitt,	*flee, depart*
I tell you every wight.	*person*
Spare youre spech, ye brodels bold,	*wretches*
And sesse youre cry till I have told	*cease*
9 What that my worship wold,	
Here in thise wonys.	*in this place*
Whoso that wightly nold,	*won't do so quickly*
Full hy bese hanged his bonys!	*high will be*
Wote ye not that I am Pilate,	*Know*
That satt apon the justice late,	*(seat of) justice lately*
At Calvarye where I was att	
This day at morne?	*This morning*
I am he, that great state,	*man of high rank*
That lad has all to-torne.	*Who tore to pieces that fellow*
Now sen that lothly losell is thus ded,	*since/scamp*
20 I have great joy in my manhede!	*manhood, manliness*
Therfor wold I in ilk sted	*I desire/every place*
It were tain hede	*(That) it be heeded*

[1]Be silent, I warn you, all persons of any wit.

[3-4]For here are men (actors in the play) who can't move yet (because of the crowd), who are lords of great might.

[9]What my honor wishes, i.e., what I wish (to say).

If any felowse felow his red,   *follow his teaching*
Or more his law wold lede.   *further/perform*

For, and I knew it, cruelly   *if*
His life bees lost, and that shortly,   *will be*
That he were better hing ful hy   *hang*
On galow tre!
Therfor ye prelatys shuld aspy
30   If any sich be.   *such*

As I am man of mightys most,   *great authority*
If ther be any that blow sich bost,   *proclaim such boast*
With tormentys keyn bese he indost   *keen he'll be weighted down*
For evermore.
The devill to hell shall harry his goost!
Bot I say no more.

CAIPHAS.   Sir, ye thar nothing be dredand,   *you need dread nothing*
For Centurio, I understand,
Youre knight, is left abidand   *abiding, watching*
40   Right ther behinde.
We left him ther for man most wise,   *as a man*
If any ribaldys wold oght rise,   *rabble/rise at all (in insurrection)*
To sesse theym to the next assise,   *arrest/court session*
And then for to make ende.   *i.e., pass sentence*
    Tunc veniet Centurio velut miles, equitans.   *Then will come the Centurion like a soldier, riding*

CENTURIO.   A, blissyd Lord, Adonay,   *God*
What may this mervell signify
That here was shewyd so openly
Unto oure sight,
When the rightwys man can dy   *righteous/did*
50   That Jhesus hight?   *was called*

Heven it shoke abone;   *above*
Of shining blan both son and moyne;   *ceased*
And dede men also rose up sone
Outt of thare grafe;   *graves*
And stones in wall anone
In sonder brast and clafe!   *burst and cleaved*

Ther was seen many a full sodan sight.   *sudden, unexpected*
Oure princes, forsothe, did nothing right;
And so I saide to theym on hight—   *in haste*
60   As it is trew—

That he was most of might,
The son of God, Jhesu.

Fowlys in the ayer and fish in floode
That day changid thare mode   *mood, state of mind*
When that he was rent on rode,   *torn to pieces on the cross*
That Lord veray.   *true*
Full well thay understode
That he was slain that day.
Therfor, right as I meyn, to theym fast will I ride   *as I intend|them (the authorities)*
70 To wit withoutten weyn what thay will say, this tide,   *know|doubt|time*
Of this enfray.   *affray, alarm*
I will no longer abide,
Bot fast ride on my way.
        [*He goes to Pilate and the chief priests.*]

God save you, sirs, on every side,   *i.e., everyone*
Worship and welth in warld so wide!   *(And grant you) honor*
    PILATUS.   Centurio, welcom this tide,   *now*
Oure comly knight.
    CENTURIO.   God graunt you grace well for to g[u]ide
And rewll you right!   *rule yourself*

80 PILATUS.   Centurio, welcom, draw nere-hand.
    Tell us som tithingys here emang,   *tidings|among (us)*
    For ye have gone thrughoutt oure land;
    Ye know ilk dele.   *every bit*
    CENTURIO.   Sir, I drede me ye have done wrang
    And wonder ill.   *prodigiously*

    CAIPHAS.   Wonder ill? I pray the[e], why?
    Declare that to this company.
    CENTURIO.   So shall I, sir, full securly,   *surely*
    With all my main.   *might*
90 The rightwys man, I meyn him by   *I speak of the righteous man*
    That ye have slain.

    PILATUS.   Centurio, sese of sich saw!   *cease such talk*
    Ye ar a greatt man of oure law,
    And if we shuld any witnes draw   *cite, call*
    To us excuse,
    To maintene us evermore ye aw,   *support|ought, owe*
    And noght refuse.

    CENTURIO.   To maintene trowth is well worthy.
    I saide, when I sagh him dy,   *saw*

100   That it was Godys son almighty
        That hang thore;   *there*
        So say I yit, and abidys therby   *still/will stick to it*
        For evermore.

        ANNA.   Yee, sir, sich resons may ye rew!   *rue*
        Thou shuld not neven sich notes new   *mention such matters*
        Bot thou couth any tokyns trew   *Unless you could*
        Untill us tell.   *Unto*
        CENTURIO.   Sich wonderfull case never ere ye knew   *event/before*
        As then befell.

110 CAIPHAS.   We pray the[e] tell us, of what thing?
        CENTURIO.   Of elymentys, both old and ying,
        In thare manere maide greatt mowrning   *Each in its own way*
        In ilka stede.   *every place*
        Thay knew by contenaunce that thare king   *revealed by their appearance*
        Was done to dede.   *death*

        The son for wo it waxed all wan,   *dark*
        The moyn and starnes of shining blan,   *ceased*
        And erth it tremlyd, as a man   *(and) like*
        Began to speke;
120   The stone[s], that never was stirryd or than, *ere then*
        In sonder brast and breke;   *burst/broke*

        And dede men rose up bodely, both greatt and small.   *dead/bodily*
        PILATUS.   Centurio, bewar withall!
        Ye wote the clerkys the clippys it call,   *know/eclipse*
        Sich sodan sight,
        That son and moyne a seson shall   *for a season, time*
        Lak of thare light.

        CAIPHAS.   Sir, and if that dede men rise up bodely,
        That may be done thrugh socery.   *sorcery*
        Therfor, nothing we sett therby   *we are not concerned*
        That be thou bast.   *That you're abashed, astonished*
        CENTURIO.   Sir, that I saw, truly,   *that which*
        That shall I evermore trast.   *trust, believe*

134   Not for that ilk warke that ye did wirke,   *same*
135   Not oonly for the son wex mirke,   *the sun grew dark*

134–37I'd like to know, because of that same deed (the Crucifixion) that you performed, not
only why the sun grew dark, but also how the veil in the temple was rent (see Matthew 27:51).

136 Bot how the vaill rofe in the kirke *vail was rent/church*
137 Fain wit I wold. *Gladly I'd know*
  PILATUS. A, sich tayles full sone wold make us irke *such tales/weary*
  If thay were told.

  Harlot, wherto commys thou us emang *why come you among us*
  With sich lesingys us to fang? *lies/ensnare*
  Weynd furth! Hy might thou hang, *Get out! May you hang high*
  Vile fatur! *deceiver*
144 CAIPHAS. Weynd furth in the wenyande, *i.e., bad luck to you*
  And hold still thy clattur!

146 CENTURIO. Sirs, sen ye set not by my saw, haves now good *since*
   day!
  God lene you grace to knaw the sothe allway. *give/know*

  ANNA. Withdraw the[e] fast, sen hou the[e] dredys! *since you're afraid*
  For we shall well maintene oure dedys. *uphold our deeds*
   [*Exit Centurion.*]
150 PILATUS. Sich wonderfull resons as now redys *relates*
151 Were never beforne.
152 CAIPHAS. To neven this note no more us nedys, *mention this business*
153 Nawder even nor morne. *Neither*

154 Bot for to bewar of more were *doubts*
  That afterward might do us dere, *harm*
  Therfor, sir, whils ye ar here
  Us all emang, *With us all*
158 Avise you of thise sawes sere *Consider/various sayings*
159 How thay will stand.

  For Jhesus saide full openly
  Unto the men that yode him by *went with him*
  A thing that grevys all Jury, *grieves/Jewry*
  And right so may— *rightly so*
  That he shuld rise up bodely
  Within the thride day.

[144] Go forth in the time of the waning moon (an unlucky time); hence, bad luck to you.

[146] Sirs, since you do not value my report, I say now good day to you.

[150-54] Such wondrous events as (he) now relates never happened before. —We needn't mention this business again, neither in evening or morning (i.e., at any time). But in order to be on guard against any further doubts (of the people, concerning what we've done to Jesus).

[158-59] Consider what will be the effect of these various sayings (that are being circulated about Jesus' miraculous power).

If it be so, as might I spede,   *as I hope to prosper*
The latter dede is more to drede   *to be feared*
Then was the first, if we take hede   *heed*
And tend therto.   *pay attention*
170   Avise you, sir, for it is nede,
The best to do.

ANNA.   Sir, nevertheles if he saide so,   *even if*
He hase no might to rise and go
Bot his discipils steyll his cors us fro   *Unless/steal/corpse from us*
And bere away.   *bear (it)*
That were till us, and othere mo,   *That would be to us/others also*
A fowll enfray.   *affray, fright*

Then wold the pepyll say everilkon   *everyone*
That he were risen himself alon.   *by his own power*
180   Therfor, ordan to kepe that stone   *give orders to guard*
With knightys heynd   *gracious*
To thise thre dayes be commen and gone   *Till/come*
And broght till ende.   *to*

PILATUS.   Now, certys, sir, full well ye say.
And for this ilk point to purvay   *same/arrange*
I shall, if that I may,   *I shall (determine)*
He shall not rise,
Nor none shall win him thens away   *take*
Of no kins wise.   *By any kind of way*
        [*He speaks to the soldiers.*]

190   Sir knightys, that ar of dedys dughty,   *doughty of deeds*
And chosen for chefe of chevalry,
As I may me in you affy,   *trust*
By day and night
Ye go and kepe Jhesu body
With all youre might.

And for thing that be may,   *whatever may happen*
Kepe him well unto the thrid day,
That no tratur steyll his cors you fray   *from you*
Out of that sted.   *place*
200   For if ther do, truly, I say,
Ye shall be dede.

1 MILES.   Yis, sir Pilate, in certan,
We shall him kepe with all oure main.   *might*
Ther shall no tratur with no train   *tricks*

Steyll him us fro.
Sir knightys, take gere that best may gain,   *weapons/avail*
And let us go.

2 MILES.   Yis, certys, we ar all redy bowne;   *prepared*
We shall him kepe till youre renowne.   *guard for the sake of*
   [*They proceed to the sepulchre.*]
On every side lett us sitt downe,
We all in fere;   *together*
And I shall fownde to crak his crowne   *undertake*
Whoso commys here.   *comes*

214 1 MILES.   Who shuld be where, fain wold I witt.
     2 MILES.   Even on this side will I sitt.
216 3 MILES.   And I shall fownde his feete to flitt.   *try/avoid*
217 4 MILES.   We, ther, shrew, ther!   *i.e., you sit there, rascal*
Now by Mahowne, fain wold I witt   *Mohammed*
Who durst com here   *Whoever would dare*

This cors with treson for to take!
For if it were the burnand drake,   *even if/fiery dragon*
Of me stifly he gatt a strake—   *stoutly he'd get a strike*
Have here my hand.   *i.e., I pledge this*
To thise thre dayes be past,   *Till*
This cors I dar warand.   *warrant, guarantee*
   [*Christ rises from the sepulchre; the soldiers fall into a stupor.*]

   Tunc cantabunt angeli "Christus resurgens," et postea dicet Jhesus: *Then the angels will sing "Christ arising," and afterward Jesus will say*

JHESUS.   Erthly man, that I have wroght,   *whom*
Wightly wake, and slepe thou noght!   *Quickly*
With bitter bayll I have the[e] boght   *bale, sorrow*
To make the[e] fre.
230 Into this dongeon depe I soght,
And all for luf of the[e].

Behold how dere I wold the[e] by!   *dearly/buy, redeem*
My woundys ar weytt and all blody.   *wet*
The[e], sinfull man, full dere boght I
With tray and teyn.   *affliction and injury*

214I'd gladly know where each of us should be placed.

216–17(The third soldier, behaving like the maltreated young apprentice of the Wakefield
Second Shepherds' pageant and The Buffeting, seemingly tries to escape the job assigned
to the soldier of least seniority, but is ordered to take his place.)

236   Thou file the[e] noght eft, forthy,   *defile/again*
    Now art thou cleyn!

    Clene have I mayde the[e], sinfull man.
    With wo and wandreth I the[e] wan.   *misery/won*
    From harte and side the blood out ran,
    Sich was my pine!   *Such/pain*
    Thou must me luf that thus gaf than   *love/gave then*
    My life for thine.

    Thou sinfull man that by me gase,
    Tytt unto me thou turne thy face.   *goes past me*
    Behold my body, in ilka place   *Quickly*
    How it was dight: *each*
    All to-rent and all to-shentt,   *handled*
    Man, for thy plight.   *torn to pieces/ruined*

250   With cordes enewe and ropys toghe   *enough/tough ropes*
    The Jues fell my limmes out-drogh,   *cruel/stretched out my limbs*
    For that I was not mete enoghe   *Because/of correct proportion*
    Unto the bore.   *(To reach) the bored holes*
    With hard stowndys thise depe woundys   *sharp pangs*
    Tholyd I, the[r]fore.   *Suffered*

    A crowne of thorne, that is so kene,
    Thay set apon my hede for tene.   *to torment me*
    Two thefys hang thay me betwene,
    All for dispite.
260   This pain ilk dele, thou shall wit wele,   *every bit/know well*
261   May I the[e] wite.   *blame you (for)*

    Behald my shankes and my knees,
    Min[e] armes and my thees;   *thighs*
264   Behold me well, looke what thou sees
265   Bot sorow and pine!   *Except/pain*
    Thus was I spilt, man, for thy gilt,   *killed*
    And not for mine.

    And yit, more understand thou shall:
    Instede of drink, thay gaf me gall—
270   Asell thay menged it withall,   *Vinegar/mingled*

---

[236]Do not defile yourself again, therefore.

[260-61]I can blame you for this pain every bit, you may be sure of this.

[264-65]Behold me well, observe that you see nothing except sorrow and pain.

The Jues fell.   *cruel*
The pain I have, tholyd I to save   *suffered*
Mans saull from hell.

Behold my body, how Jues it dang   *struck*
With knottys of whippys and scorges strang!
As stremes of well, the bloode out-sprang   *Like streams from a well*
On every side.
Knottes where thay hit, well may thou witt,
Maide woundys wide.   *Made*

280   And therfor, thou shall understand,
In body, hede, feete, and hand,
Four hundreth woundys and five thowsand
Here may thou se;
And therto neyn were delt full even   *nine/indeed*
For luf of the[e].

Behold, on me noght els is lefte!
And, or that thou were fro me refte,   *ere/taken away*
All thise paines wold I thole efte   *suffer again*
And for the[e] dy.
290   Here may thou se that I luf the[e],
Man, faithfully.

Sen I for luf, man, boght the[e] dere,   *Since*
As thou thyself the sothe sees here,
I pray the[e] hartely, with good chere,
Luf me agane,
296   That it liked me that I for the[e]
297   Tholyd all this pain.   *Suffered*

If thou thy life in sin have led,
Mercy to ask, be not adred.   *adread*
The leste drope I for the[e] bled   *least*
Might clens the[e] soyn—   *cleanse/soon*
All the sin the warld within   *in the world*
If thou had done.   *(Even) if*

I was well wrother with Judas   *more wroth, angry*
For that he wold not ask me no grace,   *Because*
Then I was for his trespas
That he me sold.

296–97Because I was pleased to suffer all this pain for you.

I was redy to shew mercy;
Aske none he wold.

Lo, how I hold min[e] armes on brede,   *breadth*
The[e] to save ay redy mayde!   *Made ready always to save you*
That I great luf ay to the[e] had,
Well may thou knaw;
314   Som luf agane I wold full fain
315   Thou wold me shaw.   *show*

Bot luf, noght els aske I of the[e],   *Except love*
317   And that thou fownde fast sin to fle.   *try*
Pine the[e] to lif[e] in charité   *Exert yourself*
Both night and day;
Then, in my blis that never shall mis,   *fail*
Thou shall dwell ay.

For I am veray prince of peasse,   *true*
And sinnes seyr I may releasse;   *many*
And whoso will of sinnes seasse   *cease*
And mercy cry,
I grauntt theym here a measse   *mess, dish (the sacrament)*
In brede, min[e] awne body.   *Of bread*

[That ilk veray brede of life   *same true*
329   Becommys my fleshe in wordys fife.   *five*
Whoso it resaves in sin or strife   *receives*
Bese dede forever,   *Will be*
And whoso it takys in rightwys life   *righteous*
Di[e] shall he never.]
    [*Jesus retires. The three Marys appear, seeking the sepulchre.*]

334   MARIA MAGDALENE.   Alas, to di[e] with doyll am I dight!   *sorrow/ready*
In warld was never a wofuller wight.   *creature*
336   I drope, I dare, for seing of sight   *droop/am dismayed*
337   That I can se: *did*

314–15I wish fervently you would show me some love in return.

317And that you try to flee quickly from sin.

329*wordys fife:* "comedite, hoc est corpus meum," "eat, this is my body." (Matthew 26:26. This stanza is crossed out in the MS, perhaps in an attempt to render this play more acceptable to the Reformation church, by excising the Catholic doctrine of transubstantiation.)

334Alas, I'm ready to die from sorrow!

336–37I am despondent, I am dazed or terrified, because of what I saw.

My Lord, that mekill was of might,   *great*
Is ded fro me!   *dead (and gone)*

Alas, that I shuld se his pine,   *pain*
Or that I shuld his life tine!   *be deprived of*
For to ich sore he was medecine   *each*
And boytte of all,   *remedy*
Help and hold to ever ilk hyne   *support/each person*
To him wold call.   *(That) to*

MARIA JACOBI.   Alas, how stand I on my feete
When I think on his woundys wete!   *wet*
Jhesus, that was on luf so swete   *of love*
And never did ill,
350   Is dede and grafen under the grete,   *buried/earth*
Withoutten skill.   *reason*

MARIA SALOMEE.   Withoutten skill thise Jues ilkon   *every one*
That lufly Lord thay have him slone;   *slain*
And trespas did he never none
In no kin sted.   *no kind of place, anywhere*
To whom shall we now make oure mone?   *moan*
Oure Lord is ded.

MARIA MAGDALENE.   Sen he is ded, my sisters dere,   *Since*
Weynd we will with full good chere,   *Wend, go*
360   With oure anointmentys fare and clere
That we have broght,
For to anointt his woundys sere   *many*
That Jues him wroght.

MARIA JACOBI.   Go we then, my sisters fre,   *noble*
For sore me longis his cors to see.   *I long sorely/corpse, body*
366   Bot I wote never how best may be;
Help have we none,
And which shall of us sisters thre
Remefe the stone?   *Remove*

370 MARIA SALOMEE.   That do we not bot we were mo,   *unless*
For it is hogh and hevy also.   *high, huge*
            [*Two angels, dressed in white, appear at the sepulchre.*]
MARIA MAGDALENE.   Sisters, we thar no farthere go   *need*

³⁶⁶But I don't know how it may best be done.

³⁷⁰We couldn't do it unless there were more of us.

Ne make mowrning;
I se two sit where we weynd to,   *wend, go*
In white clothing!

MARIA JACOBI.   Certys, the sothe is not to hide: *is not hidden*
The gravestone is put beside!   *set aside*
MARIA SALOMEE.   Certys, for thing that may betide,   *whatever may happen*
Now will we weynde
380   To late the luf and with him bide,   *To seek the lovely one*
That was oure freynde.
    [*They approach the sepulchre.*]

1 ANGELUS.   Ye mowrning women in youre thoght,
Here in this place, whome have ye soght?
MARIA MAGDALENE.   Jhesu, that unto ded was broght,   *death*
Oure Lord so fre.   *noble*
2 ANGELUS.   Certys, women, here is he noght;
Com nere and se.

1 ANGELUS.   He is not here, the sothe to say.   *wherein*
The place is voide therin he lay;   *shroud, napkin*
390   The sudary here se ye may   *(That) was*
Was on him laide.
He is risen and gone his way,   *to you*
As he you saide.

2 ANGELUS.   Even as he saide, so done has he.
He is risen thrugh his pausté;   *power*
He shal be fon in Galalé,   *found in Galilee*
397   In fleshe and fell.   *skin*
To his discipyls now weynd ye   *wend, go*
And thus thaym tell.
    [*The angels retire.*]

MARIA MAGDALENE.   My sisters fre, sen it is so   *noble|since*
That he is resyn the deth thus fro,   *risen*
As saide till us thise angels two—   *to us*
Oure Lord and leche—   *healer*
404   As ye have hard, where that ye go   *heard|wherever*
405   Loke that ye preche.

MARIA JACOBI.   As we have hard, so shall we say.   *heard*
Maré, oure sister, have good day!

397i.e., in the flesh.
404-5Wherever you go, tell what you have heard.

MARIA MAGDALENE.   Now veray God, as he well may—   *true*
　　　　Man most of might—
410　　He wish you, sisters, well in youre way,   *May he guide you*
　　　　And rewle you right.

> [*The two Marys depart, leaving Mary Magdalene alone near the sepulchre and the dozing soldiers.*]

　　　　Alas, what shall now worth on me?   *become of me*
　　　　My catyf hart will breke in thre   *wretched*
　　　　When that I think on that ilk bodye,   *same*
　　　　How it was spilt.   *killed*
　　　　Thrugh feete and handys nalyd was he
　　　　Withoutten g[u]ilt.

　　　　Withoutten g[u]ilt then was he tain,   *taken*
　　　　That lufly Lord; thay have him slain,
　　　　And tryspas did he never nane,   *none*
　　　　Ne yit no mis.   *sin*
422　　It was my g[u]ilt he was fortain,   *taken away forever*
423　　And nothing his.

424　　How might I, bot I lufyd that swete—   *unless/loved/sweet one*
425　　That for me suffred woundys wete,   *wet*
426　　Sithen to be grafen under the grete—   *Afterwards/buried/ground*
427　　Sich kindnes kithe?   *Such/acknowledge*
　　　　Ther is nothing till that we mete
　　　　May make me blithe.

> [*She stands aside, and the soldiers rouse themselves one by one.*]

1 MILES.   Outt, alas! What shall I say?
　　　　Where is the cors that herein lay?
2 MILES.   What alys the[e], man? He is away
　　　　That we shuld tent?   *guard*
1 MILES.   Rise up and se.
2 MILES.　　　　　　　Harrow! Thefe! For ay
　　　　I cownte us shent!   *account us ruined*

3 MILES.   What devill alys you two
　　　　Sich no[i]se and cry thus for to may?   *make*
2 MILES.   For he is gone.   *Because*
3 MILES.   Alas, wha?   *who*

422–27 It was for my guilt he was taken away forever, not at all for his. How might I acknowledge such kindness unless I adored that sweet one who suffered bleeding wounds on my account, and afterwards (suffered himself) to be buried under ground?

440 2 MILES.   He that here lay.

3 MILES.   Harrow! Devill! How-swa gaṭ he away?   *How-so, how*

4 MILES.   What, is he thus-gatys from us went,   *in this fashion*
The fals tratur that here was lentt,   *placed, laid*
That we truly to tent   *watch over*
Had undertane?   *undertaken*
Certanly I tell us shent,   *I account us ruined*
[W]holly ilkane.   *each one*

1 MILES.   Alas, what shall I do this day
Sen this tratur is won away?   *Since|taken*
And safely, sirs, I dar well say   *confidently*
He rose alon[e].   *unaided*

452 2 MILES.   Witt sir Pilate of this enfray,   *frightful thing*
We mon be slone.   *shall|slain*

4 MILES.   Wote ye well he rose indede?
2 MILES.   I sagh myself when that he yede.   *saw|went*
1 MILES.   When that he stirryd out of the stede   *stead, place*
None couth it ken.   *could know it*
4 MILES.   Alas, hard hap was on my hede   *luck*
Emang all men!

460 3 MILES.   Ye, bot wit sir Pilate of this dede,   *if Pilate learns*
That we were slepand when he yede,   *sleeping|went*
We mon forfett, withoutten drede,   *must, will|doubt*
All that we have.
4 MILES.   We must make lees, for that is nede,   *lies*
Oureself to save.

1 MILES.   That red I well, so might I go.   *advise|as I hope to prosper*
2 MILES.   And I assent therto, also.
3 MILES.   A thowsand, shall I assay, and mo,   *say|more*
Well-armed, ilkon,   *each one*
Com and toke his cors us fro,   *Came*
And us nere slone.   *nearly slew*

472 4 MILES.   Nay, certys, I hold ther none so good   *nothing*
As say the sothe right as it stude,   *truth|stood, was*
How that he rose with main and mode   *might and courage*
And went his way.

452If Pilate should learn of this frightful thing.

472No, certainly, I consider there's no policy so wise.

To sir Pilate, if he be wode,   *even if he rage*
Thus dar I say.

1 MILES.   Why, and dar thou to sir Pilate go
With thise tithingys, and tell him so?   *tidings*
480 2 MILES.   So red I that we do also.   *advise*
We di[e] bot oones.   *but once*
3 MILES ET OMNES.   Now, he that wroght us all this wo,
Wo worth his bones!   *May woe befall*

4 MILES.   Go we sam, sir knightys heynd,   *together/gracious*
Sen we shall to sir Pilate weynd;   *Since/must*
I trow that we shall parte no freynd,   *no friend (of Pilate)*
Or that we pas.   *Ere we leave*
1 MILES.   Now and I shall tell ilka word till ende,   *each*
Right as it was.   *happened*
[*They appear before Pilate's station.*]

490 Sir Pilate, prince withoutten peyr,   *peer*
Sir Caiphas and Anna both in fere,   *together*
And all the lordys aboute you there
To neven by name: *mention by name*
Mahowne you save on sidys sere   *many shores (i.e., everywhere)*
Fro sin and shame!

PILATUS.   Ye ar welcom, oure knightys so keyn.
497 A mekill mirth now may we meyn!   *Of/speak*
Bot tell us som talking us betwene,   *meanwhile*
How ye have wroght.
1 MILES.   Oure waking, lord, withoutten wene,   *watching/doubt*
Is worth to noght.   *Has come to*

CAIPHAS.   To noght? Alas, seasse of sich saw!   *cease such talk*
2 MILES.   The prophete Jhesu, that ye well knaw,
504 Is risen and went fro us on raw   *in a row*
With main and might.
PILATUS.   Therfor the devill the[e] all to-draw,   *pull to pieces*
Vile recrayd knight!   *recreant*

What! Combred cowardys I you call!   *beaten, benumbed*
Lett ye him pas fro you all?

497(Ironically, Pilate assumes that the soldiers' presence means they may all congratulate one another on a job well done.)

504*on raw*: straight away (from us), or, in our row-formation around the tomb.

510 3 MILES.   Sir, ther was none that durst do bot small   *little*
    When that he yede.   *went*
  4 MILES.   We were so ferde, we can downe fall   *afraid/did fall*
    And qwoke for drede.

  1 MILES.   We were so rad, everilkon,   *frightened/everyone*
    When that he put beside the stone,
    We quoke for ferd and durst stir none,   *fear*
    And sore we were abast.   *astounded*
  PILATUS.   Why, bot rose he by himself alone?
  2 MILES.   Ye, lord, that be ye trast.   *be sure of that*

520 We hard never, on evyn ne morne,   *heard/evening*
    Nor yit oure faders us beforne,
    Sich melody, mid-day ne morne,   *Such*
    As was maide thore.   *made there*
  PILATUS.   Alas, then ar oure lawes forlorne   *destroyed*
    For ever more!

    [The leaders consult out of earshot of the soldiers.]
    A, devill! What shall now worth of this?   *come*
    This warld farys with quantys.   *fares/craft*
    I pray you, Caiphas, ye us wis   *teach, advise*
    Of this enfray.   *affray, disturbance*
  CAIPHAS.   Sir, and I couth oght by my clergys,   *if I knew ought/book-learning*
    Fain wold I say.

  ANNA.   To say the best, forsothe, I shall.
    It shal be profett for us all:
534 Yond knightys behovys thare wordys agane-call   *revoke*
535 How he is mist.   *he (Christ) is missed*
    We wold not, for thing that might befall,   *for anything*
    That no man wist.   *knew (it)*

    And therfor, of youre curtessie   *out of*
    Gif theym a rewarde forthy.   *therefore*
540 PILATUS.   Of this counsell well paide am I;   *pleased*
    It shal be thus.
    [He turns again to the soldiers.]
    Sir knightys, that ar of dedys doghty,   *deeds doghty*
    Take tent till us.   *Pay attention to us*

[510]Sir, there was not one of us who dared undertake any significant action.

[534–35]It behoves yonder knights to revoke their words describing how Christ disappeared.

Herkyns now how ye shall say,   *Hearken*
Whereso ye go, by night or day:
Ten thowsand men of good aray   *array, weapons*
Cam you untill,   *to you*
And thefishly toke his cors you fray   *from you*
Agans youre will.   *Against*

550   Loke ye say thus in every land;
And therto, on this covande,   *covenant*
Ten thowsand pounds have in youre hande
To youre rewarde;   *As*
And my frenship, ye understande,
Shall not be sparde.   *spared*

Bot loke ye say as we have kende.   *instructed*
1 MILES.   Yis, sir, as Mahowne me mende!   *so help me Mohammed*
In ilk contree whereso we lende,   *each/linger, dwell*
By night or day,
560   Whereso we go, whereso we weynd,   *wend*
Thus shall we say.

PILATUS.   The blissing of Mahowne be with you, night and
        day!

[*At the sepulchre, Mary Magdalene sees Jesus and mistakes
him for a gardener.*]

MARIA MAGDALENE.   Say me, garthinere, I the[e] pray,
If thou bare oght my Lord away.   *carried at all*
Tell me the sothe—say me not nay—
Where that he lyys,   *lies*
And I shall remeve him if I may   *remove*
On any kin wise.   *By any means*

JHESUS.   Woman, why wepys thou? Be still.
Whome sekys thou? Say me thy will,
And nyk me not with nay.   *deny*
572 MARIA MAGDALENE.   For my Lord I like full ill.
The stede thou bare his body till,   *place/to*
Tell me, I the[e] pray,
And I shall, if I may, his body bere with me—   *bear*
576   Unto min[e] ending day the better shuld I be.

---

[572]On my Lord's account I am sorely aggrieved.

[576]I should be better prepared spiritually for my death and judgment (if I performed this deed of charity to Christ's body).

JHESUS.   Woman, woman, turne thy thoght!
   Wit thou well I hid him noght,
579   Then bare him nawre with me.   *Nor bore/nowhere*
   Go seke, loke if thou finde him oght.   *aught, at all*
   MARIA MAGDALENE.   In faith I have him soght,
   Bot nawre he will fond be.   *be found*

JHESUS.   Why, what was he to the[e], in sothfastnes to say?   *truthfulness*
584   MARIA MAGDALENE.   A! he was to me . . . No longer dwell I
       may.
   JHESUS.   Mary, thou sekys thy God, and that am I.   *seek*

   MARIA MAGDALENE.   Raboni! My Lord so dere!   *Master*
   Now am I [w]hole, that thou art here.   *restored to spiritual health*
   Suffer me to negh the[e] nere   *approach*
   And kis thy feete;
590   Might I do so, so well me were,   *it would be well with me*
   For thou art swete.

   JHESUS.   Nay, Mary, neghe thou not me,
   For to my Fader, tell I the[e],
   Yit stevynd I noght.   *ascended*
   Tell my brethere I shall be   *shall appear*
596   Before theym all in trinité,
   Whose will that I have wroght.
   To peasse now ar thay boght that prisond were in pine;   *peace/ransomed/pain*
   Wherfor, thou thank in thoght God, thy Lord and mine.

   Mary, thou shall weynde me fro.   *wend, go*
   Min[e] erand shall thou grathly go;   *promptly*
   In no fownding thou fall: *temptation*
   To my discipyls say thou so
   That wilsom ar, and lappyd in wo,   *bewildered/enfolded*
   That I thaym socoure shall.   *I will aid them*
   By name Peter thou call, and say that I shall be   *shall appear*
   Before him and theym all myself in Galilé.

   MARIA MAGDALENE.   Lord, I shall make my vyage   *voyage*
   To tell theym hastely.
   Fro thay here that message,   *From (the time) they hear*
   Thay will be all mery.

579Nor did I bear him anywhere with me.

584(This line and the stanza seem imperfect.)

596*in trinité:* i.e., not as Christ alone but as three-personed God.

[*Jesus departs from her.*]

This Lord was slain, alas forthy,   *therefore*

613   Falsly spilt, no man wist why,   *killed/knows*

614   Whore he did mis.   *Wherein/sin*

Bot with him spake I bodely;   *bodily, in the flesh*

Forthy, commen is my blis!   *Therefore/come*

My blis is commen, my care is gone;

That lufly have I mett alone!   *lovely person*

I am as blith in bloode and bone

620   As ever was wight!   *person*

Now is he resyn that ere was slone;   *before/slain*

My hart is light.

I am as light as leyfe on tre,   *leaf*

For joyfull sight that I can se;   *did*

For well I wote that it was he,   *know*

My Lord Jhesu!

He that betrayde that fre   *noble one*

Sore may he rew.   *rue*

To Galilé now will I fare,

630   And his disciples cach from care.   *rescue*

I wote that thay will mowrne no mare;   *more*

Commyn is thare blis!   *Come*

[*To the audience.*]

That worthy childe that Mary bare,   *bore*

He amende youre mis.   [*Exit.*]   *(May) he/wrongdoing*

Explicit Resurrectio Domini.   *Here ends the Resurrection of the Lord*

613–14Falsely killed (since) no man knows why or in what way he committed wrong.

CHRIST APPEARS TO THE DISCIPLES
FROM CHESTER

The Gospels tell of numerous appearances by Christ to his disciples and followers between the time of his Resurrection and his Ascension into heaven. The appearances most often recounted in the cycles are four in number: to Mary Magdalene (already presented as part of the Wakefield Resurrection pageant), to Luke and Cleophas on the road to Emmaus (Luke 24:13–35), to all the disciples except doubting Thomas (Luke 24:36–49, John 20: 19–25), and to the disciples with Thomas present (John 20:26–29). The Chester cycle brings together these three last episodes in a composite sequence. Each story is told with the utmost simplicity, and with considerable fidelity to Scripture and church liturgy. The Emmaus story, also known as the episode of the Pilgrim *(Peregrini)*, appears occasionally in early church drama (see Part I, no. 16, above). Luke and Cleophas, grieving at the apparent death of their leader, encounter Jesus disguised as a pilgrim but fail to recognize him until he has broken bread with them and suddenly vanished. Christ's subsequent visits similarly demonstrate his wish to assure his followers that he has not forsaken them. In his appearance to all the disciples except Thomas, Christ eats fish and honey to prove to them that he is not a ghost. He later returns to permit the skeptical Thomas to touch his wounds and thus learn through sensory evidence what Thomas should have believed through faith.

The theme of these visitations, repeatedly emphasized, is the overcoming of rational doubt. The disciples are badly demoralized by Christ's death, despite his earlier promises of comfort to them and despite their undoubted goodness of heart. They are weak in a believably human fashion, enabling us to identify with their weakness and to experience through them the confirming demonstrations of Christian truth. Because they must be reassured again and again, we too witness an edifying sequence of "signs" proving Christ's miraculous nature.

As in early church dramatizations of the journey to Emmaus, this pageant requires an elaborate stage edifice. The room in which Christ breaks bread with Luke and Cleophas, identified as the Castle of Emmaus, seems to have been built above the chamber in which Christ later appears twice to his gathered disciples (see stage directions at 168 and 240). This arrangement of action on two levels may have been developed to facilitate Christ's sudden appearances and disappearances, with the aid of trap doors and curtains. The structure is referred to as a castle and a "mansion." The various journeys to and from this structure evidently take place on the open, unlocalized stage.

The text of this edition is based on MS H. Harl. 2124 in the British Museum.

Christ Appears to the Disciples
From Chester

Pagina Decima Nona de Christo Duobus Discipulis ad Castellum Emaus euntibus Apparente; et Aliis Discipulis.

Pageant Nineteen of Christ Appearing to the Two Disciples Going to Castle Emmaus; and to the Other Disciples

[*Luke and Cleophas, as they journey to Emmaus, discuss the Crucifixion.*]

LUCAS.   Alas, now weale is went away!   *weal, happiness/gone*
Mone my maister ever I may,   *Moan, lament*
That is now clongen under clay;   *withered away*
That makes my hart in care!
Sorrow and sighinge, the sooth to say,
Makes me half dead—that is no nay.
When I think on him, night and day
For dole I drowp and dare!   *am despondent and daunted*

CLEAP[H]AS.   Ye, much mirth was in me
10   My swete soveraine whil I might se
11   And his liking lore with lee,
Which now so low is laid.   *Who*
Brother, now are day[e]s three
Sith he was neiled upon the tree.   *Since*
Lord, whether he risen bee   *(I wonder) whether*
As he before hath saide?

LUCAS.   Leife brother Clephas,   *Dear*
18   To know that were [a] coynt[e] case.   *quaint, ingenious*
Sith he throw hart wounded was,   *through*
How should he live againe?
CLEOP[H]AS.   If that he Godhead in him hase,
And commen to buy ma[n]kinds trespase,   *has come to redeem man*
He may rise through his owne grace,
And his death do us gaine.   *profit us*

LUCAS.   A misty thinge it is to me   *obscure*
To have beleef it should so be
How he should rise in dayes thre.
Such wonders never was wist.   *known (before now)*
CLEOP[H]AS.   Sooth thou sayest, now well I se;   *Truth*
30   Leeve [may] I not, by my luteeye!   *Believe/loyalty*
But God may of his majesty
Doe whatsoever him list.   *pleases him*
   Tunc veniet Jhesus in habitu peregrinae, et ait: *Then Jesus will come dressed as a pilgrim, and says*

JHESUS.   Good men, if your will were,   *if you please*

[10–11]So long as I could see (i.e., be in the presence of) my sweet master and his pleasant teaching, affording us protection (lit.: with protection).

[18]i.e., It would require considerable ingenuity to believe in that (the Resurrection).

[30]I can't believe it (either), as I am a true man.

Tell me in good manere
35   Of your talkinge, that, in feare,   *together*
36   And of your woe witt I would.   *know*
　　CLEOP[H]AS.   A, sir, it seeme to us here
　　　　A pilgrem thou art, as can appeare;   *i.e., by your appearance*
39   Tidings and tales all intire   *entirely*
40   Thou may hear what is towld.

　　　　In Jerusalem that other day,
　　　　Thou that walkest many a way,
　　　　May thou not hear what men do say,
　　　　About ther as thou yeed?   *As you went about there*
　　JHESUS.   What are those? Tell me, I thee pray.
　　LUCAS.   Of Jesus of Nazareth, in good fay,   *faith*
　　　　A prophett to ech mans pay   *each/pleasure, benefit*
　　　　And wise in word and deed.

　　　　To God and man, wise was he;
50   But bishopps—cursten mott they be!—   *chief priests/may*
　　　　Damned him and nailed him on a tree,   *Condemned*
　　　　That wronge never yet wrought.   *Who/did*
　　CLEOPHAS.   Witterly, before wend we   *Truly before this we thought*
　　　　That Israell he should have made free;
　　　　And out of paine, through his posty,   *suffering/power*
　　　　The people he should have brought.

　　LUCAS.   Yea, sir, now this is the third day
　　　　Sith they made this affray.
　　　　And some women, theras he lay,   *where he lay buried*
　　　　Were yerly in the morne   *Visited early*
61   And feared us foule, in fay.   *frightened us greatly*
　　　　They tould us he was stolln away,
　　　　And angells, as they can say,   *did*
　　　　The sepulcre sitting beforne!

　　CLEOP[H]AS.   Yea, sir, these wemen, that h[e]ard I,
　　　　Said he was risen, redely.   *truly*
　　　　And some men of our company
　　　　Thither anon can goe   *did*
　　　　And fownd it so as it towld of yore;   *as it was told*
70   And they said so, neither lesse nor more.
　　　　And yet our hartes are full sore

35–36What you're talking and grieving about, which I would like to know and share with you.

39–40By stories and tales you can gather entirely what is reported.

61(According to Luke 24:22–23, "certain women of our company" came back to the disciples
and amazed them with reports of finding the tomb empty, guarded by angels.)

Lest it be not so.

JHESUS.   A, fooles and feeble, in good fay,
Latt to beleev unto Gods law!   *Tardy to believe in*
The prophetts before can thus say—   *did*
Leeve you on this soothly—   *Believe*

77 That it needs be, allway,
78 Christ to suffer death, the sooth to say,
79 And to joy that lasteth aye
80 Bring man, through his mercy.

And first at Moses to beginne,
What he sayeth I shall you minne: *remind*
That God was a greave within   *within a bush*
That burned aye, as he thought;
The greave paired nothing therby.   *bush was not impaired*
What was that but maid Mary
That bare Jesu sinlesly,
That man hath now forbought?   *Who/redeemed*

Also Esay said this: *Isaiah*
90 As a woman comforts iwis   *truly*
91 Her child that hath done amis,
92 To amend, leeve you me,   *believe*
93 So God would man reconciled hear
Through his mercy, in good maner;
And in Jerusalem, if better weere,   *if (they) were more obedient*
Forbought they should be.   *Saved*
    (*Quemadmodum mater consolatur filios suos, ita et ego consolabor*   Just as a mother comforts her sons,
    vos; et in Jerusalem consolabimini. Esaias, capitulo sexagesimo   so will I comfort you; and in
    sexto.)   Jerusalem you will be comforted
                                                                         (Isaiah, chapter 66:[13])

CLEOP[H]AS.   A, Lord geve thee good grace,
For greatly comforted me thou hase!
Goe with us to this place:
100 A castle is hereby.
JHESUS.   Now, good men, soothly for to say,
I have to goe a great way;
Therfore at this time I ne may.   *may not*
But I thank you hartely.

LUCAS.   Sir, you shall, in all maner,   *i.e., no matter what*

77–80That, to tell the truth, it behoved Christ to suffer death and bring man to everlasting joy
by means of his mercy (see Luke 24:26).

90–93Just as a woman comforts her child that has misbehaved, to cure and recover him, believe you me, so would God joy to hear of man's reconcilement.

Dwell with us at our supper,
For now night aprocheth nere.
Tary heer for any thinge!   *come what may*
CLEOPHAS.   Now, God forbidd that we wear   *were, should be*
110   So uncourteous to you here;
111   For, save my lovely Lord of leer,   *saving, except for*
Thy lore is most likinge.   *pleasant*
    Tunc omnes ad castellum eunt.   *Then all go to the castle*

LUCAS.   Sitt down, sir, here, I you pray,
And take a morsell, if you may,
For you have walked a great way
Sith today at morne.
    [*They sit at a table.*]
JHESUS.   Graunt mer[c]y, good men, in good fay!   *Great thanks/faith*
To blesse this bread, sooth to say,
I will anone in good aray,   *at once/array, fashion*
120   Rightly you beforne.
    Tunc frangit panem et ait: *Then he breaks the bread and says*

Eates on, men, and doe gladly,   *Eat*
In the name of God almighty!
For this bread blessed have I
That I geve you today.
    Tunc Jesus evanescet.   *Then Jesus will vanish*
    [*Luke is not aware of the absence at first.*]
LUCAS.   Graunt mercy, sir, sickerly!   *Great thanks/certainly*
Now I read you be right merry.—   *advise*
What? Wher is he that sate us by?
Alas, he is away!

CLEOP[H]AS.   Alas, alas, alas, alas!
130   This was Jesus in this place.
By breaking of bread I knew his face,
But nothing ther before.   *before that*
LUCAS.   A burning hart in us he mase;   *makes*
For, while that he with us here was,
To know him we migh[t] have no grace,
For all his luxom lore.   *Despite/pleasant teaching*

CLEOP[H]AS.   Goe we, brother, and that anone,   *at once*
And tell our brethren, everychone,
How our maister is from us gone;

110–11So uncourteous to you here (as not to provide you with refreshment); for, except for the
teaching of my lovely Lord (Christ), beautiful of countenance.

140   Yea, sothly we may say.

    LUCAS.   Yea, well may we make our mone,   *moan, complaint*

    That sate with him in great wonne   *sat|a great while*

    And we no knowledg had him upon   *had of him*

    Till he was passed away.

      Tunc ibunt ad ceteros discipulos in alio loco congregatos.   *Then they will go to the other disciples gathered together in some other place*

    CLEOPHAS.   A, rest well, brethren, one and all!

    Wonderously is us befall: *has happened to us*

    Our Lord and we were in a hall

    And him yet knew not we!

    ANDREAS.   Yea, leeve thou well this, Cleophas: *believe*

150   That he is risen that dead was,

    And to Peter appered hase   *has appeared*

    This day, apertly!   *openly*

    LUCAS.   With us he was a longe fitt,   *long while*

    And opened his holy writt;   *disclosed, elucidated*

    And yet our witt[e]s were so knitt   *closed up*

    That him we might not know.

    CLEOP[H]AS.   Now, sicker, away was all my witt   *surely*

    Till the bred was broken, ech bitt;   *each*

    And anone when he brake it

160   He vanished in a thrawe.   *moment*

    PETRUS.   Now we be, brethren, all in feere,   *together*

    I redd we hide us somwher here   *advise*

    That Jewes meet us not in no manere,

    For malice, leeve you me!   *Out of malice|believe*

    ANDREAS.   Lenge we here in this place.   *Let's linger*

    Peradventure, God will shew us grace

    To see our Lord in little space,   *soon*

    And comforted for to bee.

      Tunc omnes eunt infra castellum, et veniet Jesus stans in medio discipulorum, ac postea dicat: *Then all go [to an acting area] beneath the castle, and Jesus will come standing in the midst of the disciples, and afterward let him say*

    JHESUS.   Peace amongst you, brethren faire!

170   Yea, dread you not in no maner:

    I am Jesus, without were,   *doubt*

    That died on rood tree.   *cross*

    PETRUS.   A, what is he that comes here

    To this fellowship all in feere?   *together*

    As he to me now can appeare,   *did*

    A ghost me think I see!

    JHESUS.   Brethren, why are you so fraid for nought,   *afraid*

178   And noyed in hart for feble thought?   *annoyed, vexed*
    I am he that have you forbought   *who saved you*
    And died for mans good.
    My feet, my handes you may see,
    And know the sooth allso may yee,
    Soothly that I am he
    That dead was upon a tree.

    Handle me, both all and one,
    And leeve this well, everichone,   *believe/everyone*
    That ghost hath neither flesh ne bone   *That (a) ghost*
    As you see now on me.
       [They touch him.]
  ANDREAS. A, Lord, much joy is us uppon!
190   But what he is, wott I ne can.   *know*
  JHESUS. Now, sith you leeve I am no man,   *believe*
    More signes you shall see.

    Have you any meat hear?   *food here*
  PETRUS. Yea, my Lord leefe and dear: *beloved*
    Rosted fishe and hony in feere   *together*
    Therof we have good wonne.   *abundance*
  JHESUS. Eate we, then, in good manere:
    Thus you now know, without were,   *doubt*
    That ghost to eate hath no power,
    As you shall see anon.
    Tunc comedet Jhesus et dabit discipulis.   *Then Jhesus will eat and give*
                                               [food] to the disciples

    Brethren, I towld you before,
202   When I was with you, not gaine an houre,   *toward, near*
    That needly both less and more   *That of necessity all things*
    Must fulfilled bee,
    In Moses law as written were.   *as they were written*
    All other prophesies as then were
    Is fulfilled in good manere
208   Of that was said of me.   *that which*

    For this was written in prophesye:
    That I must suffer death needly,
    And the third day with victory
    Rise in good aray;   *array, fashion*

178And vexed in your heart by faithless questioning? (See Luke 24:38.)

202When I was with you, not an hour ago, i.e., recently (see Luke 24:44).

208Concerning those things that were said about me.

And prech remission of sinne
Unto all men that his name doth minne.   *remember*
Therfore, all you that be herein
Think on what I say!

> *Iterum evanescet Jhesus; et discipuli versus Bethaniam ibunt;*   Again Jesus will vanish; and the
> *et Thomae obviantes dicat Petrus:*   disciples will go toward Bethany;
>   and as they meet Thomas let Peter
>   say

PETRUS.   A, Thomas, tidinges good and new!
    We have seene the Lord Jesu.

THOMAS.   Shall I never leeve that this is trew,   *believe*
220 By God omnipotent,
    But I see in [his] hand[es] two   *Unless*
    Holes that neiles can in goe,   *did*
    And putt my finger eek also
    Theras the neiles went.   *Where*

ANDREAS.   Thomas, goe we all in feere;   *together*
226 For dread of enemys better were,
227 Then Jewes should have us in their dangere,   *power*
    And all our fraternitye.

THOMAS.   Wherever you goe, brethren deere,
    I will goe with you in good manere.
    But this talk you tell me here
    I leeve not, till I see.   *I (will) not believe*

PETRUS.   Now, Thomas, be thou not away,   *don't go away*
    And in happ se him thou may   *perchance*
    And feele him also, in good fay,   *faith*
    As we have done before.

THOMAS.   Wherever you be, I will be aye;
238 But make me leeve this thing veray,
239 You paine you not; therfor, I pray,
240 To speak of that no more.

> *Tunc ibunt omnes [iterum] ad mansionem et recumbent; et*   Then they will all come [again] to
> *subito apparebit Jhesus dicens:*   their place of abode and lie down;
>   and suddenly Jesus will appear,
>   saying

JHESUS.   Peace, my brethren, bothe one and all!
    Come hither, Thomas; to thee I call.

226–27 It is better (that we hide) out of fear of our enemies, lest the Jews should have us in their power.

238–39 But don't trouble yourselves to make me believe this thing to be true (i.e., you'd be wasting your time).

240 s.D. *iterum*: again. (This word, supplied from four other MSS, makes it plain that the disciples return to the room beneath the castle of Emmaus as at l. 168 and following, where Jesus can perform his sudden appearances and vanishings.)

Shew forth, for ought that may befall,
Thy hand, and putt in here.
And see my handes and my feet,
And putt in thy hand—thou ne leet!   *don't hold back*
My woundes are yet fresh and weet
As they first were.

And be thou no more so dreadinge,   *doubtful*
250   But ever truly beleevinge.
        Tunc immittet in latus et vulnera manum.   *Then he will put his hand into his*
                                                        side and wounds
    THOMAS.   My God, my Lord, my Christ, my kinge!
        Now leeve I without weninge.   *believe/doubt*
    JESUS.   Yea, Thomas, now thou seest me,
        Thou leevest now that I am hee;
        But blessed must they all bee
        That leeve and never see
            (Beati qui non viderunt et crediderunt,
            Jhon, [20:29.])

        That I am that same body
        That borne was of meek Marye,
        And on a crosse your soules did bye   *buy, redeem*
260   Uppon Good Friday.
        Whoso to this will consent—
        That I am God omnipotent—
        As well as they that be present,
        My darlinges shal be aye.

        Whoso to this will not consent,
        Ever to the day of judgment
        In hell fire they shall be brent,
        And ever in sorrow and teene.   *misery*
269   Whosoever of my Father hath any mind,
270   Or of my mother in any kinde,
        In heaven bliss they shall it find,
        Without any woe.

        [*To the audience.*]
        Christ geve you grace to take the way
        Unto that joy that lasteth aye!
        For thers no night, but ever day;   *there is*
        For all you thither shall goe.
            Finis paginae decimae nonae. Julii 29, anno Domini 1607.

269–70Whosoever remembers or calls upon my Father or my mother in any way.

THE LAST JUDGMENT
FROM WAKEFIELD

The English cycles generally follow a common pattern in their choice of final episodes. They conclude their dramatizations of the New Testament with the Ascension of Christ into heaven and the Descent of the Holy Spirit at Pentecost. (Wakefield actually does not have a Pentecost play, but the omission seems to be the result of a gap in the manuscript.) Two of the cycles, York and N Town, feature plays about the Death and Assumption of the Virgin, and the other two complete cycles probably also treated this subject in plays now lost. The most notable departure from the general concurrence of the cycles is Chester's inclusion of two plays about Antichrist. Once again, however, the cycles agree by ending with the Last Judgment.

In the final pageant from the Wakefield cycle, God completes the design that he contemplated in his creation of the world. Enthroned in heaven, he pronounces judgment on mankind and sends his ministers earthward to separate those who are to be saved from those who must be damned. Thereupon, he himself descends to earth in his visible form, as Christ, displaying his wounds alike to those for whom he died and those from whom he suffered. The pageant is dominated throughout by a balanced and antithetical contrast between the blessed souls standing on Christ's right hand and the wicked souls standing on his left. This division of mankind into two camps is, of course, a commonplace of medieval iconographical art as well as of theology.

As in earlier portions of the cycle, the contrast between good and evil is rendered as a contrast between serious instruction and comic entertainment. Christ's speeches, serenely graceful though eloquent, are conservatively based on biblical or exegetical sources.. He comments on the meaning of his earthly sacrifice, and recites the seven corporal works of mercy which the virtuous have performed and the evil have neglected (ll. 442–523). Contrastingly, the devils' scenes are racy and colloquial. They are the work of an innovative reviser who has based his text on the York pageant of the Last Judgment but has greatly expanded the comic action. (At times the stanzaic form is that of the Wakefield Master.) Tutivillus is a particularly beguiling devil, with his satirical commentary on excessive wearing apparel and his lively depiction of corruptions in justice. His list of worldly fools strikes at lords and ladies of the court, tax collectors, usurers, practitioners of simony, gamblers, extortioners, and many more. We are reminded of medieval paintings of the Last Judgment showing popes, bishops, kings, queens, magistrates, and merchants standing on Christ's left hand. As in such paintings, the dramatist is satirically humorous in his depiction of the torments being visited on the damned by attendant devils. If the Wakefield Last Judgment gives more attention to the frightening comedy of evil than to the consoling harmonies of a restored heavenly grace, such obsession with death and damnation is typical of much art in late medieval Europe.

Staging clearly reflects the dual vision of this pageant, with heaven on one side and hell on the other. Each is characterized by its own musical or sound effects, and by brilliant visual display. Production in theater in the round would bring the entire Corpus Christi play to an end by focusing on its two essential and ever-present structures, the towers of heaven and hell. Earth, represented by the open acting space between the towers, is at first crowded with those awaiting the execution of a long-expected judgment. Then, as the actors are shepherded in two large groups either to the upper level of heaven's tower or through the jaws of hell-mouth, all traces of human activity vanish.

The Last Judgment
From Wakefield

> [*The beginning of this play is missing in the manuscript. Presumably Christ enthroned in heaven has explained his purpose in ending the sinful career of man, and has dispatched his angels to earth to separate the good souls from the wicked. There the wicked souls bewail their folly as the trumpet of doom sounds.*]

[2 MALUS.]	Full darfe has bene oure dede; forthy commen is oure care!	*heavy/therefore*
2	This day to take oure mede, for nothing may we spare.	*reward/escape*
	Alas, I harde that horne that callys us to the dome!	*heard/doom*
	All that ever were borne, thider behofys theym com.	*thither it behoves*
	May nathere lande ne se us fro this dome hide;	*neither/nor sea*
	For ferde fain wold I fle, bot I must nedys abide.	*fear/must needs, must*
	Alas, I stande great aghe to loke on that justice!	*in great awe*
	Ther may no man of lagh help with no quantice.	*law/cunning*
	Vokettys ten or twelfe may none help at this nede,	*Advocates*
10	Bot ilk man for his self shall answere for his dede.	

	Alas, that I was borne!	
	I se now me beforne	*before me*
	That Lorde with woundys fife.	
	How may I on him loke,	
	That falsly him forsoke	*(I) that*
	When I led sinfull life?	

3 MALUS.	Alas, carefull catifys may we rise,	*woeful wretches*
	Sore may we wring oure handys and wepe!	*Sorely*
	For cursid and sore covitise	*grief-causing covetousness*
20	Dampnyd be we in hell full depe.	
	Roght we never of Godys service;	*Wrought, did*
	His commaundementys wold we not kepe;	
	Bot oft times maide we sacrifice	
	To Sathanas when othere can slepe.	*others slept (i.e., at night)*

---

²We may by no means escape receiving our just reward (i.e., God's punishment) today.

Alas, now wakyns all oure were!　　　　　　　　　　*wakens/doubt*
Oure wikyd warkys can we not hide,　　　　　　　　*works, deeds*
Bot on oure bakys we must theym bere　　　　　　　*bear*
That will us soroo on ilka side.　　　　　　　　　　*cause us sorrow/every*
Oure dedys this day will do us dere.　　　　　　　　*deeds/harm*
30　Oure domysman here we must abide,　　　　　　*doomsman, judge*
And feyndys, that will us felly fere,　　　　　　　　*fiends/cruelly terrify*
Thare pray to have us for thare pride.　　　　　　　*(As) their prey*

Brimly before us be thay broght,　　　　　　　　　　*Fiercely*
Oure dedys that shall dam us bidene:　　　　　　　　*deeds/quickly*
That eyre has harde, or harte thoght,　　　　　　　*(All) that ear has heard*
That mowthe has spokyn, or ee sene,　　　　　　　　*eye*
37　That foote has gone, or hande wroght,
38　In any time that we may mene—　　　　　　　　　*remember*
39　Full dere this day now bees it boght.　　　　　　*will be paid for*
Alas, unborne then had I bene!　　　　　　　　　　*If only I had been unborn*

4 MALUS.　Alas, I am forlorne! A spitus blast here blawes!　　*lost/spiteful/blows*
42　I harde well by yonde horne; I wote wherto it drawes.　　*I heard*
I wold I were unborne. Alas, that this day dawes!　　　　　*dawns*
Now mon be dampnyd this morne my warkys, my dedys,　　*must/deeds*
　　my sawes.　　　　　　　　　　　　　　　　　　　　　*words*

Now bees my curstnes kid. Alas, I may not lain!　　　　　*will be/shown/deny, hide*
All that ever I did, it bees put up full plain.　　　　　　*will be displayed*
That I wold fain were hid—my sinfull wordys and vain—　*That which*
Full new now mon be rekynyd up to me again.　　　　　*anew/must be reckoned*

Alas, fain wold I fle for dedys that I have done!　　　　*flee/deeds*
50　Bot that may now not be; I must abide my boyn.　　*petition*
I trowed never to have sene this dredfull day thus soyn.　*soon*
Alas, what shall I say when he sittys in his trone?

To se his woundys bledande, this is a dulfull case.　　*wounds bleeding/doleful*
Alas, how shall I stand or loke him in the face?
So curtes I him fand, that gaf me life so lang a space.　*courteous/found/time*
My care is all command. Alas, where was my grace?　　*sorrow/coming*

Alas, catiffys unkinde, whereon was oure thoght?　　*unnatural wretches*

---

^{37–39}All that we have done by traveling on foot, or done with our hands, throughout all our lives as far back as memory can go—all these things will be paid for very dearly today.

⁴²I have heard clearly yonder horn; I know what it leads to.

⁵⁰i.e., But I can no longer deny my evil deeds; I must now rely on begging for mercy.

Alas, whereon was oure minde, so wikyd warkys we   *works, deeds*
    wroght?
To se how he was pinde, how dere oure luf he boght,   *pained/dearly*
Alas, we were full blinde! Now ar we wars then noght.   *worse than nothing*

Alas, my covetise, min[e] ill will, and min[e] ire!   *covetousness/envy/anger*
My neghbur to dispise most was my desire.
63   I demyd ever at my devise; me thoght I had no peyre.   *I judged*
With myself sore may I grise! Now am [I] quit my hire.   *feel horror/I'm repaid*

Where I was wonte to go and have my wordys at will,   *speak freely*
Now am I set full thro, and fain to hold me still.   *I'm thoroughly bound*
I went both to and fro; me thoght I did never ill
My neghburs for to slo or hurt, withoutten skill.   *slay/reason*

Wo worth ever the fader that gate me to be borne,   *Woe forever be to/begot*
70   That ever he lete me stir bot that I had bene forlorne!   *unless/destroyed*
Warid be my moder, and warid be the morne   *Cursed*
That I was borne of hir, alas for shame and skorne!

1 ANGELUS, CUM GLADIO.   Stand not togeder, parte in two!   *with sword*
All sam shall ye not be in blis.   *together*
    [*He separates the good souls from the wicked.*]
Oure Lorde of heven will it be so,   *wills*
For many of you has done amis.
    [*To the good souls.*]
On his right hande ye good shall go;
The way till heven he shall you wis.   *to/show*
    [*To the wicked souls.*]
Ye wikid saules ye weynd him fro,   *go from him*
80   On his left hande as none of his.

JHESUS [*in heaven*].   The time is commen I will make ende;   *has come*
My Fader of heven will it so be.   *wills*
Therfor till erthe now will I weynde,   *to/wend*
Myself to sitt in majesté.
To dele my dome I will discende.   *deal out my judgment*
This body will I bere with me;
How it was dight, mans mis to amende,   *handled/man's sin*
All manskinde ther shall it se.
    [*Jesus descends to earth and sits enthroned. In hell the devils too
have heard the trumpet of doom.*]

63I decided matters according to my own inclination; it seemed to me I had no peer (who
might challenge my complete authority).

1 DEMON.   Oute, haro, out, out! Harkyn to this horne!

90 I was never in dowte or now at this morne.   *I never feared till this day*

So sturdy a showte, sen that I was borne,   *fierce|since*

Hard I never hereabowte, in ernyst ne in skorne—   *Heard|nor*

A wonder!

I was bonde full fast   *bound*

In irens for to last,   *everlasting*

Bot my bandys thay brast   *burst*

And shoke all in sonder!

2 DEMON.   I shoterd and shoke, I herd sich a rerd!   *shuddered|heard|noise*

When I harde it, I qwoke, for all that I lerd.   *I quaked at what I learned*

100 Bot to swere on a boke, I durst not aperd;   *appear (frightened)*

I durst not loke, for all medill-erd,   *for all the world*

Full paill,   *All pale*

Bot girned and gnast—   *snarled (grinned) and gnashed my teeth*

My force did I frast—   *try*

Bot I wroght all wast: *did all in vain*

It might not availl.

1 DEMON.   It was like to a trumpe, it had sich a sownde!   *trumpet|such*

I fell on a lumpe, for ferd that I swonde.   *in|I swooned so for fear*

109 2 DEMON.   There I stode on my stumpe—I stakerd that   *leg*
          stownde—   *time*

There chachid I the crumpe, yit held I my grounde   *catched|cramp*

Halfe nome.   *numb*

1 DEMON.   Make redy oure gere!   *gear, weapons*

We ar like to have were,   *likely|war*

For now dar I swere

That domysday is comme.

For, all oure saules ar wente, and none ar in hell.   *prisoners are gone*

2 DEMON.   Bot we go, we ar shente! Let us not dwell.   *Unless|destroyed|delay*

118 It sittys you to tente, in the mater to mell   *befits|pay heed|meddle*

119 As a pere in a parlamente, what case so befell.   *peer|no matter what*

120 It is nedefull

121 That ye tente to youre awne,

122 What draght so be drawne.   *Whatever legal action*

---

100 i.e., But even if I'd had to swear on the Bible, I didn't dare appear frightened.

109 There I stood on my leg—I was staggering at this time.

118–25 It behoves you to pay heed (at the hearings before Christ), and handle the case as cunningly as a lord in Parliament, no matter what happens. It's necessary for you to pay close attention to your own side of the case, no matter what legal action is drawn up. If the truth were known about this court, the judge is much to be dreaded. —You annoy me, standing around idly this way (i.e., talking instead of acting).

123	If the courte be knawen,	
124	The juge is right dredfull.	*to be dreaded*

125	1 DEMON. For to stand thus tome, thou gars me grete.	*empty/you make me grieve*
126	2 DEMON. Let us go to this dome, up Watlin Strete!	*judgment/Watling*
	1 DEMON. I had lever go to Rome, yei, thrise, on my fete,	*rather*
128	Then for to grefe yonde grome, or with him for to mete!	*grieve/groom*
	For wisely	
	He spekys on trete;	*conciliatingly*
	His paustee is grete.	*power is great*
	Bot begin he to threte,	*if he begins to threaten*
	He lokys full grisly.	

134	Bot fast, take oure rentals; hi[e], let us go hence!	*registers (of sins)*
135	For as this fals the great sentence.	*according to this*
136	2 DEMON. Thay ar here in my dals. Fast stand we to fence	*hands*
137	Agans thise dampnyd sauls, without repentence—	*Against*
138	And just!	
139	1 DEMON. Howso the gam crokys,	*game goes crooked*
140	Examin oure bokys.	
	[*They look at their register of sinful deeds.*]	
	2 DEMON. Here is a bag full, lokys,	*look*
	Of pride and of lust,	
	Of wraggers and of wrears a bag full of brefes,	*wranglers/twisters/briefs*
	Of carpars and criars, of michers and thefes,	*carpers, chatterers/thieves*
	Of lurdans and liars that no man lefys,	*louts/believes*
146	Of flytars, of flyars, and renderars of reffys—	*quarrelers/stolen goods*
147	This can I,	
148	Of al kin astates	*every kind of rank*
149	That go by the gatys	*paths*
150	Of poore Pride, that God hatys,	

¹²⁶*Watlin Strete*: a famous thoroughfare in England, dating back to Roman times.

¹²⁸Than to give offense to yonder fellow, i.e., Christ (and hence invite reprisal), or tangle with him.

^{134–35}*rentals*: The devils have a register of sins committed by all those in their custody, and it is this record which will be used against the sinners in the Last Judgment.

^{136–40}They're here in my hands. Let's proceed quickly to "fence," i.e., make accusation with guilty knowledge, against these condemned and impenitent souls, and do so justly! —If you'd like to see how the game goes all crooked (i.e., how men contrive to damn themselves), just look at our records.

^{146–55}Of quarrelers, of fugitives from justice, and receivers of stolen goods—I can recite twenty such, from all ranks of men, who follow the paths of wretched Pride, hateful to God. —Be quiet, I beg you; I'm laughing so hard I'm doubled up! Is Wrath to be found at all in your list? After that you can take a drink. —Sir, (these lists contain) so much anger that they (the damned souls listed here) would like to overwhelm their foes in everlasting fire!

151   Twenty so many.
       [*The first demon roars with laughter at this recital.*]

152 1 DEMON.   Peasse, I pray the[e], be still; I laghe that I
                   kinke!   *double up*
153   Is oght Ire in thy bill? And then shall thou drinke.   *Wrath*
154 2 DEMON.   Sir, so mekill ill will that thay wold sinke
155   Thare foes in a fyere still! Bot not all that I thinke   *Their/fire*
       Dar I say.
157   Bot before him he prase him,   *to his face*
158   Behinde he mis-sase him;   *Behind (his back)*
       Thus dowbill he mase him.   *he acts two-facedly*
       Thus do thay today.

       1 DEMON.   Has thou oght writen there of the feminin[e]   *anything*
                   gendere?
162 2 DEMON.   Yei, mo then I may bere, of rolles for to render!
163   Thay ar sharp as a spere; if thay seme bot slender,
164   Thay ar ever in were; if thay be tender,
165   Ill-fetyld.
       She that is most meke,   *Even the meekest of women*
       When she semys full seke   *Even when she seems very sick*
       She can rase up a reke   *a smoke, stink*
       If she be well nettyld!   *nettled, angry*
       [*The first demon continues to laugh at this jesting.*]

       1 DEMON.   Thou art the best hine that ever cam beside us!   *servant/among us*
171 2 DEMON.   Yei, bot go we, master mine; yit wold I we hide
                   us!
172   Thay have blowen long sine; thay will not abide us.   *long since*
       We may lightly tine, and then will ye chide us   *easily lose out*
       Togeder.
       1 DEMON.   Make redy oure tolys,   *tools*
176   For we dele with no folys.   *fools*
177 2 DEMON.   Sir, all clerkys of oure scolys   *schools*
       Ar bowne furth theder.   *Are ready there*

---

¹⁵⁷⁻⁵⁸Although a person praise a man to his face, behind his back he speaks ill of him.

¹⁶²⁻⁶⁵Yea, (I have) more accounts to render (about women) than I can carry! They're sharp as a spear; although they seem small and weak, they're constantly suspicious and contentious; although they seem tender, they're in a foul mood. (For *ill-fetlyd,* cf. fine-fettled.)

¹⁷¹⁻⁷²Yea, but let's go, my master; I wish we'd hurry! They have blown (the trumpet) long ago; they won't wait for us.

¹⁷⁶⁻⁷⁷*clerkys:* learned divines. (Both demons insist this is going to be a tough legal case; their adversaries in court will be no fools.)

Bot, sir, I tell you before, had domysday oght tarid,   *been delayed at all*
We must have biggid hell more, the warld is so warid!   *enlarged|cursed*

181 1 DEMON.   Now gett we dowbill store: of bodys miscarid   *double supply|doomed*
182   To the soules where thay wore, both sam to be harrid.   *together*

2 DEMON.   Thise rolles
Ar of bakbitars   *detractors*
And fals quest-ditars.   *indictors, accusers at trial*
I had no help of writars   *i.e., in writing these*
Bot thise two dalles!   *Except|hands (of mine)*

188   Faithe and Trowth, ma fay, has no fete to stande;   *by my faith*
189   The poore pepyll must pay, if oght be in hande.
The drede of God is away, and lawe out of lande.   *vanished from earth*

1 DEMON.   By that, wist I that domysday was nere-hande,   *I knew|near*
In seson.   *In this season, time*

2 DEMON.   Sir, it is saide in old sawes: *sayings*
194   "The longere that day dawes,   *dawns*
195   Wars pepill, wars lawes."

1 DEMON.   I lagh at thy reson!   *saying*

All this was token domysday to drede.   *a warning-sign of doomsday*
Full oft was it spokyn; full few take hede.
Bot now shall we be wrokyn of thare falshede,   *avenged for|falsehood*
For now bese unlokyn many dern dede   *will be unlocked|secret deeds*
In ire!
All thare sinnes shall be knawen:
Othere mens, then thare awne.   *their own*

204 2 DEMON.   Bot if this draght be well drawen,   *Unless|draught, load*
205   Don is in the mire.

[*They encounter Tutivillus, a fellow devil.*]

TUTIVILLUS.   Why spir ye not, sir, no questions?   *ask*
I am oone of youre ordir and oone of youre sons;   *society*
I stande at my tristur when othere men shones.   *tryst, station|shun (duty)*

209 1 DEMON.   Now, thou art min[e] awne querestur! I wote   *chorister*
where thou wonnes.

[181-82]Now we'll get a double supply (to crowd hell even more): the doomed bodies reunited to
the souls that previously inhabited them, both to be tormented together.

[188-89]By my faith, the qualities of Faith and Truth have no feet to stand on (i.e., no support);
the poor must pay, if any project is undertaken.

[194-95]i.e., "The more that time passes, the worse people and laws become."

[204-5]Unless this draft or load is well hauled, the horse will get bogged down in the mire; i.e.,
unless men's accounts are clear, there'll be trouble.

[209]Now, you are my own chorister (i.e., I recognize you as one of my followers)! I know where
you live. (The name "Tutivillus" seems to mean "all vile things.")

Do tell me.	*i.e., Tell me news*
TUTIVILLUS. I was youre chefe tollare,	*tax-gatherer*
And sithen courte rollar;	*then officer of court records*
Now am I master Lollar,	*Lollard, heretic*
And of sich men I mell me.	*I deal with such men*

	I have broght to youre hande of saules, dar I say,	*delivered to you*
	Mo than ten thowsand in an howre of a day.	*More*
	Som at ayll-howse I fande, and som of ferray;	*ale-house/found/plundering*
218	Som cursid, som bande, som yei, som nay;	*cursed*
	So many	
	Thus broght I on blure—	*to damnation*
	Thus did I my cure.	*I discharged my duty*
	1 DEMON. Thou art the best sawgeoure	*soldier*
	That ever had I any!	

224	TUTIVILLUS. Here a roll of Ragman of the Rownde Tabill,	
	Of breffes in my bag, man, of sinnes dampnabill.	*briefs, accusations*
226	Unethes may I wag, man, for-wery in youre stabill	*Scarcely/stir*
227	Whils I set my stag, man!	
	2 DEMON. Abide, ye ar abill	*worthy*
	To take wage; [*Pays him.*]	
229	Thou can of cowrte thew.	
230	Bot lay downe the dewe!	
	For thou will be a shrew	*rascal*
	By thou com at age.	*By (the time)/to maturity*

[*Tutivillus continues reciting from his list of fools.*]

233	TUTIVILLUS. Here be, I gesse, of many nice hoket,	*foolish tricks*
234	Of care and of curstnes, hething and hoket,	*derision and chicanery*
235	Gay gere and witles, his hode set on koket,	*cocked*
236	As prowde as pennyles. His slefe has no poket—	*sleeve/pocket*
237	Full redles.	*lacking good counsel*
	With thare hemmyd shoyn,	*fancily-stitched shoes*

[218]Some of them were cursing, some swearing (i.e., nearly all of them).

[224]Here's a document with seals, from the Table Round (of King Arthur; Tutivillus is jocosely claiming ancient authority).

[226-27]Scarcely may I stir, man, I'm so worn out keeping my horse in your stable, i.e., serving you in this business.

[229-30]You know how to behave like a courtier. But apply yourself to duty (?).

[233-37]Here there are, I believe, persons of many foolish tricks, of trouble and wickedness, derision and chicanery, such as one who wears gay garments but is witless, his head struttingly cocked, as proud as he is penniless. His sleeve has no pocket (i.e., he can't hold on to his money)—he's utterly lacking in good advice(?).

	All this must be done,	*i.e., Fashion must be served*
240	Bot sire is out at hye noyn	*father*
241	And his barnes bredeles.	*children are breadless*
242	A horne and a Duch ax; his slefe must be flekyt;	*striped with ornament*
243	A side hede and a fare fax; his gowne must be spekytt.	*decorated*
244	Thus toke I youre tax; thus ar my bookys blekyt.	
245	1 DEMON. Thou art best on thy wax that ever was clekyt	*hatched*
246	Or knawen!	*known*
247	With wordes will thou fill us,	
248	Bot tell thy name till us.	*to us*
	TUTIVILLUS. My name is Tutivillus.	
	My horne is blawen;	*has blow*
250a	*Fragmina verborum, Tutivullus colligit horum,*	
250b	*Belzabub algorum, Belial Belium doliorum.*	

251	2 DEMON. What! I se thou can of gramory and somwhat of arte.	*have knowledge of*
	Had I bot a penny, on the[e] wold I warte.	*spend it*
253	TUTIVILLUS. Of femellys a quantité here finde I parte.	*females/large quantity*
254	1 DEMON. Tutivillus, let se, Godys forbot thou sparte!	*God forbid*
	TUTIVILLUS. So joly	
	Ilka las in a lande,	*Each lass*
	Like a lady nerehande,	*nearly*
	So fresh and so plesande,	*pleasing*
	Makys men to foly.	*Drives*

260	If she be never so fowll a dowde, with hir kelles and hir pinnes,	*slut/nets*
	The shrew hirself can shrowde, both hir chekys and hir chinnes.	*shroud, disguise*
	She can make it full prowde, with japes and with ginnes,	*tricks/wiles*
	Hir hede as hy as a clowde! Bot no shame of hir sinnes	*head as high*

[240-41]i.e., But father is on the town even at high noon while his children have nothing to eat.

[242]*horne:* drinking horn, or powder flask. *Duch ax:* Dutch or German axe, a fancy, imported weapon.

[243-48]A long, fair head of hair hanging to his shoulders; his robe must be decorated. By these means I collected your (the devil's) tribute or tax; thus are my record-books inscribed (lit: blackened with ink). —You are the best of your size, or sort, that ever was hatched or known! Even though you'll inundate us with more of your talk, tell us your name.

[250a, b](Latin gibberish, to the effect of: Tutivillus strings together the scraps of their words, Beelzebub of the cold regions, Belial of sorrows.)

[251]What! I see you have some knowledge of grammar and learned studies.

[253-54]I find here (in my catalogue of fools) a large quantity of women. —Tutivillus, let's see (or hear) it, God forbid you should spare us (that pleasure).

Thay fele.   *Such women feel*
When she is thus paint,   *painted with cosmetic*
She makys it so quainte   *acts so elegant*
She lookys like a saint—
And wars then the deyle.   *worse than the devil*

269   She is hornyd like a kowe . . . . . . fon sin;   *cow|found*
The cuker hyngys so side now, furrid with a cat skin.   *gaiter|to the side|furred*
All thise ar for you: thay ar commen of youre kin.   *have come*
    2 DEMON.   Now, the best body art thou that ever cam
        herein!   *i.e., to hell*
    TUTIVILLUS.   An usage—   *custom*
Swilk dar I undertake—   *Such|warrant*
Makys theym breke thare wedlake   *break their wedlock*
276   And lif in sin for hir sake,   *live*
And breke thare awnc spowsage.   *violate|own marriage*

278   Yit a point have I fon, I tell you before: *conclusion|found*
That fals swerars shall hider com, mo then a thowsand   *more than*
    skore.
In swering thay grefe Godys son, and pine him more   *grieve|pain*
    and more.
Therfor mon thay with us won in hell for evermore.   *must|dwell*
I say thus:
283   That rasers of the fals tax   *raisers, collectors*
284   And gederars of greyn wax,   *gatherers|green*
285   *Diabolus est mendax*   *The devil is a liar*
286   *Et pater eius.*   *And his father*

Yit a pointe of the new gett to tell will I not blin: *jet, fashion|cease*
288   Of prankyd gownes and shulders up-set—mos and flokkys
    sewyd within—
To use sich g[u]ise thay will not let. Thay say it is no sin,   *cease*
290   Bot on sich pilus I me set, and clap thaym cheke and   *padded shoulders*
    chin,
No nay!   *Without doubt*

---

[269](The line is evidently imperfect.)

[276]And live in sin for the sake of this fashionable custom.

[278]Yet one more conclusion have I found, which I'll tell you before (it happens).

[283-86]That the devil (the father of lies) is the father of those who collect unjust taxes, with green (i.e., fresh) wax on their bogus commissions.

[288]Of elegantly adorned gowns and padded shoulders—sewn and stuffed with moss and wool padding inside.

[290]But I take after such folk with padded shoulders, and seize them by the cheek and chin.

	David in his sawtere says thus:	*psalter*
	That to hell shall thay trus	*be off*
294	*Cum suis adinventionibus,*	*With their inventions*
	For onys and for ay.	*For once and all*
	Yit of thise kirkchaterars here ar a menee;	*churchchatterers/throng*
297	Of barganars and okerars, and lufars of simonee,	*usurers*
	Of runkers and rowners. God castys thaym out, trulee,	*whisperers/scandalmongers*
	From his temple, all sich misdoers. I cach thaym then to me	*catch them*
	Full soyn.	*soon*
	For writen I wote it is	
	In the Gospell, withoutten mis:	*undoubtedly*
	Et eam fecistis	*But you have made it*
	Speluncam latronum.	*a den of thieves (Luke 19:46)*
305	Yit of the sinnes seven, somthing speciall	*seven Deadly Sins*
306	Now nately to neven that renys over all:	*quickly/mention*
307	Thise laddys, thay leven as lordys riall,	*lads/live/royal*
308	At ee to be even picturde in pall	*eye/royal robes*
309	As kingys.	
310	May he dug him a doket,	*cut/tailpiece (?)*
311	A kodpese like a pokett,	*codpiece/pocket*
312	Him thinke it no hoket	*shame (?)*
313	His taill when he wringys.	*contorts*
314	His luddokkys thay lowke like walk-milne cloggys;	*buttocks/fulling-mill blocks*
315	His hede is like a stowke, hurlyd as hoggys.	*covered with bristles*
316	A woll-blawen bowke thise friggys as froggys.	*blown-up belly*
317	This Jelian Jowke, drifys he no doggys	*he drives*
318	To felter.	*To join together (?)*
	Bot with youre yolow lokkys,	*yellow locks of hair*
	For all youre many mokkys,	*Despite/mocks*
	Ye shall clim[b] on hell crokkys	*hell's cross, gallows*
	With a halpeny heltere.	*halfpenny halter, noose*

294(See Psalms 81:12.)

297Of false bargainers and usurers, and worshipers of simony (the selling of church offices).

305–18Yet to mention quickly something special about the seven Deadly Sins, which prevail everywhere: these fellows (who practice the Deadly Sins) live like royal lords, worthy to be pictured by the eye as kings in royal robes. If such a fellow can fashion for himself a short tailpiece, and a codpiece shaped like a pocket, he thinks it no shame when he contorts his tail thus (for the sake of fashion). His buttocks look like blocks used in a fulling-mill (a mill that beats cloth to cleanse and thicken it); his head is like a pile of sheaves, covered with bristles like a hog. Such creatures have puffed-up bellies like frogs. This Cringing Gillian drives no dogs to be huddled together (i.e., is no shepherd) (?).

And Nell, with hir nifyls of crisp and of silke,   *trifles/crepe*
324 Tent well youre twifyls youre nek abowte as milke,   *Heed/curls*
325 With youre bendys and youre bridyls of Sathan, the   *ribands/head-gear*
       whilke
326 Sir Sathanas idyls you for tha ilke—
327 This Gill knave!   *This wench*
     It is open behinde;   *(Her dress) opens in back*
     Before is it pinde.   *pinned*
     Bewar of the west winde,
     Youre smok lest it wafe!   *Lest it lift up your dress*

     Of Ire and of Envy finde I herto;   *here (in the list)*
     Of Covetise and Glotony, and many other mo.
     Thay call and thay cry: "Go we now, go!
     I di[e] nere, for dry!" And ther sit thay so   *I'm nearly dead for thirst*
     All night,
     With hawvell and jawvell,   *jabbering and wrangling*
     Singing of lawvell.   *blasphemy (?)*
     Thise ar howndys of hell;
     That is thare right.   *i.e., the way they should act*

     In Slewthe then thay sin, Goddys warkys thay not wirke.   *Sloth/God's works*
342 To belke thay begin, and spew that is irke;   *belch*
343 His hede must be holdin ther in the mirke;   *murk, dark*
344 Then deffys him with din the bellys of the kirke   *church*
     When thay clatter.
     He wishys the clerke hanged   *that the cleric were hanged*
     For that he rang it.   *Because/it (the bells)*
348 Bot thar him not lang it,   *he needn't long for it*
349 What commys therafter.   *comes*

350 And, ye Janettys of the stewys, and lychoures on lofte,   *wenches/lechers*
351 Youre baill now brewys, avowtrees, full ofte;   *sorrow is brewing*
352 Youre gam now grewys. I shall you set softe;   *game turns to sorrow*
     Youre sorow enewes. Com to my crofte,   *increases/place, vault*
     All ye:
     All harlottys and horres,   *whores*

---

³²⁴⁻²⁷Heed well the curls about your neck, white as milk, with your ribands and your damnable head-gear, which Satan causes you idly to desire—this wench! (?)

³⁴²⁻⁴⁴They begin to belch, and vomit out what is irksome (to their liquor-filled stomachs).
This man's head must be held there in the dark (i.e., perhaps because he has a hangover);
then he is deafened by the din of the church bells (because his head throbs so).

³⁴⁸ ⁵⁰But he needn't long for what comes afterward (i.e., his punishment). And, you wenches
of the whorehouses, and highly-placed (i.e., socially prominent) lechers, your sorrow is brewing, you adulteresses, soon enough; your game now turns to sorrow. I'll render you weak (?).

356 And bawdys that procures
357 To bring thaym to lures,   *them (customers)*
Welcom to my see!   *throne*

Ye lurdans and liars, michers and thefes,   *louts/thieves*
Flytars and fliars that all men reprefes,   *Wranglers/reprove*
Spolars, extorcionars—welcom, my lefes!   *Despoilers/beloved ones*
Fals jurars and usurars, to simony that clevys,   *that cleave to simony*
To tell;   *To count up money*
Hasardars and disars,   *Gamblers/dicers*
Fals dedys-forgars,   *forgers of deeds*
Slanderars, bakbitars—
All unto hell!

368 1 DEMON.   When I harde many swilke—many spitus and fell,   *such/spiteful/cruel*
369 And few good of ilke—I had mervell.   *among those same*
370 I trowd it drew nere the prik!   *the end, day of doom*
2 DEMON.   Sir, a worde of counsell:
Saules cam so thik now late unto hell   *lately*
As ever;   *(thicker) than ever*
Oure porter at hell yate   *gate*
Is haldyn so strate,   *held in such straits, so overworked*
Up erly and downe late,   *Rising/to bed*
He ristys never!   *rests*

1 DEMON.   Thou art pereles of tho that ever yit knew I!   *peerless/those*
378 When I will, may I go if thou be by.
Go we now, we two.
2 DEMON.   Sir, I am redy.
1 DEMON.   Take oure rolles also, ye knawe the cause why;   *the registers of sins*
Do com
And tent well this day.   *pay attention*
2 DEMON.   Sir, as well as I may.
384 1 DEMON.   *Qui vero mala*   *Who assuredly is evil*
385 *In ignem aeternum.*   *In eternal fire*
[*The devils leave hell for the judgment on earth, with their rolls.*]

JHESUS.   Ilka creatoure take tente   *Each/pay heed*

356-57And bawds who act as procuresses to bring customers to the lures (i.e., the whores).

368-70When I heard of so many such—most of them spiteful and cruel, and but few among them good—I marveled at this. I imagined that the moment for the day of doom grew near!

378I'm ready to go, if you'll go with me.

384-85(The first devil bids farewell with a malediction profanely mimicking the usual benediction.)

What bodworde I shall you bring: *message*
This wikyd warld away is wente,   *gone, destroyed*
And I am commyn as crownyd king.   *have come*
My Fader of heven has me downe sente
To deme youre dedys and make ending.   *judge/deeds*
Commen is the day of jugemente;
Of sorow may every sinfull sing.   *sinful (man)*

394 The day is commen of catyfnes,   *wretchedness, evil*
395 All those to care that ar uncleyn,
     The day of batell and bitternes—   *battle, strife*
     Full long abiden has it beyn—   *long in coming*
     The day of drede to more and les,   *i.e., to everyone*
     Of joy, of tremling, and of teyn.   *vexation*
400 Ilka wight that wikyd is   *Each*
     May say: Alas, this day is seyn!   *i.e., that this day has come*
          Tunc expandit manus suas et ostendit eis vulnera sua.   *Then he spreads apart his hands and shows them his wounds*

Here may ye se my woundys wide
That I suffred for youre misdede,
Thrugh harte, hede, fote, hande, and side—
Not for my g[u]ilte, bot for youre nede.
Behald both bak, body, and side,
How dere I boght youre broderhede!   *dearly/brotherhood*
Thise bitter paines I wold abide;
To by you blis, thus wold I blede.   *buy*

410 My body was skowrgid withoutten skill;   *scourged/reason*
     Also ther full throly was I thrett.   *severely/threatened*
     On crosse thay hang me on a hill.   *hanged*
     Blo and blody thus was I bett,   *Blue/beaten*
     With crowne of thorne thrastyn full ill.   *pierced*
     A spere unto my harte thay sett,
     My harte blode sparid thay not to spill.
     Man, for thy luf wold I not lett.   *stop*

     The Jues spitt on me spitusly;   *spitefully*
     Thay sparid me no more then a thefe.
420 When thay me smote, I stud stilly;   *stood still*
     Agans thaym did I no kins grefe.   *Against/no kind of harm*
     Beholde, mankinde, this ilk am I   *same*
     That for the[e] suffred sich mischefe;
     Thus was I dight for thy foly.   *treated*

394–95 The day of evil has come, to grieve all those who are impure.

425   Man, loke thy luf was me full leve.   *very dear*

        Thus was I dight, thy sorow to slake;
        Man, thus behovid the[e] borud to be.   *it was needful for you to be ransomed*
        In all my wo toke I no wrake;   *vengeance*
429   My will it was for luf of the[e].
        Man, for sorow aght the[e] to qwake,   *you ought*
        This dredfull day this sight to se!
        All this suffred I for thy sake.
        Say, man, what suffred thou for me?
           Tunc, vertens se ad bonos, dicit illis: *Then, turning to the good souls,*
                                                          he says to them

        My blissid barnes on my right hande,   *children*
        Youre dome this day thar ye not drede,   *you need not dread*
        For all youre joy is now commande: *coming*
        Youre life in liking shall ye lede.   *pleasure*
        Commes to the kingdom ay lastande   *Come/everlasting*
        That you is dight for youre good dede!   *is prepared for you*
        Full blithe may ye be there ye stand,   *there where*
        For mekill in heven bees youre mede.   *much/will be/reward*

442   When I was hungré ye me fed;
        To slek my thrist ye war full fre;   *slake/thirst*
        When I was clothles, ye me cled;   *clad*
445   Ye wold no sorowe on me se.
        In hard prison when I was sted   *placed*
        On my penance ye had pité;
        Full seke when I was broght in bed,   *sick*
        Kindly ye cam to comforth me.

450   When I was will and weriest,   *bewildered*
        Ye harbord me full esely;   *harbored, sheltered*
        Full glad then were ye of youre gest.   *guest*
        Ye plenyd my poverté full pituosly;   *filled, relieved*
        Belife ye broght me of the best,   *Quickly*
        And maide my bed there I shuld ly.   *there where*
        Therfor in heven shall be youre rest,
        In joy and blis to beld me by.   *dwell beside me*

    1 BONUS.   Lord, when had thou so mekill nede?   *good soul/much*

425Man, understand that my love for you meant very much to me.

429i.e., It was my will that I should suffer for love of you.

442(Here follows a list of the seven so-called corporal works of mercy: to feed the hungry, etc.)

445You did not wish to see me in sorrow.

Hungré or thrusty, how might it be? *thirsty*
460 2 BONUS.   When was oure harte fre the[e] to feede?
In prison when might we the[e] se?
3 BONUS.   When was thou seke, or wantyd wede? *lacked clothing*
To harbowre the[e] when helpid we? *shelter*
4 BONUS.   When had thou nede of oure fordede? *favor, help*
When did we all this dede to the[e]?

JHESUS.   My blissid barnes, I shall you say *children*
What time this dede was to me done:
When any that nede had, night or day,
Askyd you help and had it sone.
470 Youre fre harte saide theym never nay, *never denied them*
Erly ne late, mid-day ne noyn. *nor noon*
As ofte-sithes as thay wold pray, *often-times*
Thay thurte bot aske and have thare boyn. *need/request*
   Tunc dicet malis: *Then he will say to the wicked*

Ye cursid catifs, of Kames kin, *Cain's*
That never me comforthid in my care,
Now I and ye forever shall twin, *separate*
In doyll to dwell for evermare. *(You) in dole, sorrow*
Youre bitter bailes shall never blin *torments/cease*
That ye shall thole when ye com thare. *suffer*
480 Thus have ye servyd for youre sin, *deserved*
For derfe dedys ye have doyn are. *cruel deeds/done ere (now)*

When I had myster of mete and drinke, *need*
Catifs, ye chaste me from youre yate. *gate*
When ye were set as sires on binke, *seated as great men on bench*
I stode theroute, wery and wate, *stood outside/wet*
Yit none of you wold on me thinke
To have pité on my poore astate; *condition*
Therfor to hell I shall you sinke.
Well ar ye worthy to go that gate. *route*

490 When I was seke and soriest *most wretched*
Ye viset me noght, for I was poore; *visited/because*
In prison fast when I was fest *bound*
Wold none of you loke how I foore; *fared*
When I wist never where to rest, *didn't know where*
With dintys ye drofe me from youre doore; *blows/drove*
Bot ever to pride then were ye prest. *ready, inclined*
My flesh, my bloode ye ofte forswore.

460When were our hearts freely inclined to feed you?

Clothles, when that I was cold
499   That nerehande for you yode I nakyd,   *nearly/I went*
My mischefe sagh ye many-folde,   *You saw my troubles*
Was none of you my sorowe slakyd,   *(Yet) none*
Bot ever forsoke me, yong and olde.
Therfor shall ye now be forsakyd.

1 MALUS.   Lorde, when had thou, that all has,   *you who have everything*
Hunger or thriste, sen thou God is?   *since*
When was that thou in prison was?
When was thou nakyd or harberles?   *without shelter*
2 MALUS.   When might we se the[e] seke, alas?
And kid the[e] all this unkindnes?   *show*
510 3 MALUS.   When was we let the[e] helples pas?   *was (it)/go away*
When did we the[e] this wikydnes?

4 MALUS.   Alas, for doyll this day!   *dole, sorrow*
Alas, that ever I it abode!   *i.e., that I lived till now*
Now am I dampned for ay;
This dome may I not avoide.   *judgment*

JHESUS.   Catifs, alas! Ofte as it betide   *As often/happened*
That nedefull oght askyd in my name,   *needy persons asked for anything*
Ye harde thaym noght, youre eeres was hid,   *heard*
Youre help to thaym was not at hame: *home*
520   To me was that unkindnes kid.   *shown*
Therfor ye bere this bitter blame.   *bear*
To the lest of mine when ye oght did,   *least/anything*
To me ye did the self and same.
   Tunc dicet bonis: *Then he will say to the good*

My chosyn childer, commes to me!   *come*
With me to dwell now shall ye weynde   *wend*
Ther joy and blis ever shall be,   *Where*
Youre life in liking for to leynde.   *pleasure/remain*
   Tunc dicet malis: *Then he will say to the wicked*
Ye warid wightys, from me ye fle,   *cursed wights*
In hell to dwell withoutten ende!
530   Ther shall ye noght bot sorow se,
And sit by Sathanas the feynde.
   [*While Christ leads the good to heaven, the devils herd the wicked
   off to hell, driving them like teams of animals.*]

499That nearly, for all you helped, I went naked.

1 DEMON.   Do now, furth go, trus! go we hyne   *Gee up/let's go/hence*
Unto endles wo, ay-lastand pyne.   *everlasting pain*
Nay, tary not so! We! Get ado syne!   *Get astir at once*
2 DEMON.   Hyte hyderwarde, ho, Harry Ruskyne!   *Gee up*
War oute!   *Look out*
The meyn shall ye nebyll   *mean, middle voice/attempt*
And I shall sing the trebill;   *treble*
A revant the devill   *To the devil*
Till all this [w]hole rowte!   *To/crowd*

TUTIVILLUS.   Youre lifes ar lorne and commen is youre care.   *lost/come/sorrow*
542   Ye may ban ye were borne, the bodes you bare,   *curse*
543   And youre faders beforne, so cursid ye ar.
1 DEMON.   Ye may wary the morne and day that ye ware   *curse/were*
Of youre moder
First borne for to be,
For the wo ye mon dre.   *On account of/must suffer*
548   2 DEMON.   Ilkone of you mon se   *Each one/will, must*
549   Sorow of oder.   *of (each) other*

Where is the gold and the good that ye gederd togedir?   *property/gathered*
551   The mery menee that yode hider and thedir?   *retinue/went*
552   TUTIVILLUS.   Gay girdils, jaggid hode, prankyd gownes,
whedir?
553   Have ye wit or ye wode, ye broght not hider   *ere*
554   Bot sorowe,
555   And youre sinnes in youre nekkys.   *i.e., on your backs*
556   1 DEMON.   I beshrew thaym that rekkys!
He comes to[o] late that bekkys   *that would bid, try*
Youre bodies to borow.   *to rescue*

559   2 DEMON.   Sir, I wold cut thaym a skawte, and make theym *give/thrust*
be knawne.
560   Thay were sturdy and hawte; great boste have thay blawne.

542-43You may curse that you were born, curse the bodies you wore, and curse your ancestors
who came before you, that's how accursed you are.

548-49Each of you must see one another suffering.

551-56(Where is) your merry retinue that traveled (with you) hither and thither? —Gaily-
colored belts, pointed hoods or caps, decorated gowns, where (have they gone)? If you had
been sensible before you proceeded (in sin), you would not have brought with you (to hell)
nothing but sorrow, and the sins on your backs. —I curse them who care, i.e., regret their
misdeeds(?).

559-60Sir, I would give them (the damned souls) a blow, and cause them to be gnawed. They
were disobedient and haughty; they have proclaimed (blown) much boasting.

Youre pride and youre pransawte, what will it gawne?   *prancing/gain*

Ye tolde ilk mans defawte, and forgate youre awne.   *every (other) man's fault*

TUTIVILLUS.   Moreover,

564   Thare neghburs thay demyd   *condemned*

565   Thaymself as it semyd;

566   Bot now ar thay flemyd   *banished*

567   From saintys to recover.

1 DEMON.   Thare neghburs thay towchid with wordys full ill;   *touched, accused*

The warst ay thay sowchid, and had no skill.   *suspected/reason*

2 DEMON.   The pennys thay powchid, and held thaym still.   *pouched, pocketed*

571   The negons, thay mowchid and had no will   *misers*

572   For hart fare!   *heart's welfare*

Bot riche and ill-dedy,   *given to ill deeds*

Gederand and gredy,   *Gathering, grasping*

575   Sore napand and nedy

576   Youre godys for to spare.   *possessions*

577 TUTIVILLUS.   For all that ye spard and did extorcion,

578   For youre childer ye card, youre heire and youre son,

579   Now is all in oureward! Youre yeres ar ron.   *all is ours/expired*

580   It is commen in vowgard, youre dame malison,   *curse*

581   To binde it;

582   Ye set by no cursing,

583   Ne no sich small thing.

584 1 DEMON.   No, bot prase at the parting,

585   For now mon ye finde it.

Youre leifys and youre females—ye brake youre wedlake—   *lovers/broke/wedlock*

Tell me now what it vales, all that mery lake?   *avails/game*

Se, so falsly it falys.   *it (pleasure) fails*

2 DEMON.   Sir, I dar undertake   *I dare warrant*

589   Thay will tell no tales. Bot se, so thay quake   *how they quake*

564–67 i.e., They judged their neighbors as though condemning in others the sins of which they themselves were guilty; but now they're banished from their pretended sainthood and brought back to their true condition(?).

571–72 The misers, they extorted and hoarded and had no concern for heart's welfare!

575–85 Sorely catching (at worldly treasure) and wanting to hoard your possessions. —For all your hoarding and practicing extortion, and providing for your children, your heir and son, now all is coming to us! Your time has expired. Your cursing has come before you (to hell) to confirm your damnation; you didn't think cursing, or any such minor offense, was of any importance. —No, but you'd better start singing praises now, as you part from life, for now you'll find out (how damnable cursing can be) (?).

589–95 They (the damned) can't speak. But see, how they quake with fear because they have used prostitutes (mutton)! He who has indulged in that pleasure now must dance nimbly on his old toes. —You've reminded us of their (evil) reputation, which I'd forgotten about. —Sir, I think they are now silent, who previously were speaking(?). (During these speeches, the damned are evidently being tortured into prancing about.)

590   For moton!
591   He that to that gam gose   *game goes*
592   Now namely on old tose.   *nimbly/toes*
593 TUTIVILLUS.   Thou held up the lose,   *reputation (?)*
594   That had I forgotten.

595 1 DEMON.   Sir, I trow thay be dom, somtime were full   *dumb*
            melland.   *speaking*
596   Will ye se how thay glom?   *look gloomy*
       2 DEMON.   Thou art ay telland.   *always telling*
       Now shall thay have rom in pik and tar ever dwelland;   *room/pitch/dwelling*
       Of thare sorow no some, bot ay to be yelland   *no sum, limit/yelling*
       In oure fostré.   *custody*
          [*They start moving the wicked along again.*]
       TUTIVILLUS.   By youre lefe, may we mefe you?   *leave/move*
       1 DEMON.   Showe furth, I shrew you!   *Set forth/curse you*
       2 DEMON.   Yit tonight shall I shew you
       A mese of ill ostré!   *A meal from a bad hostelry*

604 TUTIVILLUS.   Of thise cursid forsworne, and all that here
            leyndys,   *remain*
605   Blaw wolfys-hede and oute-horne! Now namely, my   *nimbly*
            freyndys.
606 1 DEMON.   Illa haill were ye borne! Youre awne shame you   *Bad luck*
            sheyndys;
       That shall ye finde or to-morne.   *ere tomorrow morn*
       2 DEMON.   Com now, with feyndys   *fiends*
       To youre anger!   *To (whet) your anger*
       Youre dedys you dam.   *deeds/curse*
       Com, go we now sam;   *together*
       It is commen, youre gam.   *(The time for) your sport has come*
       Com, tary no langer.
          [*The wicked are driven off to hell. The good proceed toward
          heaven.*]

       1 BONUS.   We love the[e], Lorde, in al kin thing,   *everything*
       That for thine awne has ordand thus   *own/ordained*
       That we may have now oure dwelling
       In heven blis, giffen unto us!
       Therfor full boldly may we sing

<hr/>

596 *Thou . . . telland*: i.e., as you've rightly observed (?).

604–6 Let us pronounce a sentence of outlawry (a license to hunt down an outlaw like a wolf)
and sound the hue and cry on these cursed forsworn creatures, and all who remain here! Now
(move along) nimbly, my friends. —Bad luck that you were born! Your own shame destroys
you.

On oure way as we trus: *proceed*
Make we all mirth and loving
620   With *Te Deum laudamus.*   *We praise you O God*
      Explicit Judicium.   *Here ends the Judgment*

PART FOUR

Saints' Plays or Conversion Plays

Saints' Plays
or Conversion Plays

A S WE HAVE SEEN in Part II, church drama of about the twelfth century developed an extensive calendar of celebrations for the various saints' days of the liturgical year. Many a cathedral or abbey had a play honoring its patron saint, such as St. Nicholas or St. Paul. The plays were performed on separate occasions and did not tend to coalesce into large cycles. They did, however, increase in number during the later Middle Ages, both in Latin and in vernacular languages. A recurrent theme in such plays was the miraculous power of a saint that enabled him to admonish sinners or convert the heathen. Often the plays told of lurid crimes and of perfectly astonishing miracles. Like the narrative saints' lives of the *Legenda aurea* from which they were sometimes derived, these dramas satisfied an appetite for the sensational and the romantic.

At first glance, the saint's play or conversion play would appear to be a clearly definable genre. Karl Young speaks of it simply as "the dramatization of a legend setting forth the life or martyrdom or miracles of a saint" (*Drama of the Medieval Church*, II, 307). One difficulty, however, is that the term "saint" can refer to very different sorts of persons: prophets, disciples, members of the Holy Family, eminent philosophers or scholars, martyrs, and the like. Some are legendary figures while some are biblical and historical personages. Is the life of St. Paul a saint's life as defined by Young? It is not legendary, since it rests on Scriptural account. Yet its narrative of conversion from sin is typical of many a saint's life. (After all, the acts of Paul were recorded as a model for those who wished to follow in his footsteps.) Similarly, part of the life of Mary Magdalene is based on the Scriptures. Yet her story, as elaborated by medieval tradition, also embodies the pattern of the converted sinner performing wondrous works in the service of God. Although we must assume, then, that saints' plays normally concern legendary personages, like St. Nicholas, who perform spectacular miracles, we can also make allowance for some figures who exist ambiguously in the worlds of both legend and biblical history. Possibly the Virgin Mary should be included in this list, since a number of plays about her in the Corpus Christi cycles deal with extraordinary and apocryphal adventures.

Many saints' plays of the sensationally romantic variety have survived from the Continent, especially from France. (See Grace Frank, *The Medieval French Drama*.) In England as well, records indicate the existence at one time of plays honoring Saints Catherine, John the Baptist, Clara, Feliciana, Margaret, Lucy, Tewdricus, Thomas à Becket, and others. A play on the life of St. Meriasek is still extant in Cornish. The English saints' plays have disappeared almost entirely, however, probably because they were destroyed by Reformation authorities who regarded saint-worship as a particularly idolatrous offense. One tantalizing fragment of a play surviving from the fourteenth century, which tells about the incestuous love of Duke Moraud for his daughter, may have been a saint's play; its story of a life in crime is seemingly the prelude to a penitent conversion, as in the French *Miracles de Notre Dame*. Other than this fragmentary work, we are left with only three fifteenth-century dramas in English worthy of consideration as saints' plays or conversion plays. All of them are untypical of the genre to a greater or lesser degree.

These three English plays may in fact owe their very survival to their untypical character. Two of them are about St. Paul and Mary Magdalene, saints whose biblical authenticity may have rendered them palatable to Reformation tastes. The Digby play of *St. Paul* dramatizes the blinding conversion of Saul on the road to Damascus, as told in the Acts of the Apostles 9. It also features an added scene in which Belial, the inspirer of Saul's persecutions of Christians, learns that Saul has been converted to Christianity and has taken the name of Paul. The Digby *Mary Magdalene* is based in part on Scriptural narrative, mingled with much that is pure fiction: journeys across oceans, the separation of a husband and his wife, the seeming death of the wife, her miraculous recovery from death, a touching reunion, and the like. Despite their mixture of biblical and fabulous elements, however, both plays are conversion plays with a serious intention of demonstrating God's solicitude toward the sinner or non-Christian. Both plays feature ceremonial baptisms and preachings on the power of grace.

The Croxton *Play of the Sacrament* is untypical of the genre in a different way, since it does not commemorate the acts of any particular saint at all. Nonetheless it is, like *St. Paul* and *Mary Magdalene,* a play about the conversion of nonbelievers. The performer of the central miracle is Christ himself, appearing in the sacred bread of the mass to convince some skeptical Jews of the truth of his real presence in the sacrament. As in *St. Paul* and *Mary Magdalene*, the ceremony of baptism is elaborate and profoundly meaningful. The ritual enactment of penance and public confession characteristically protracts the action of the play after the dramatic moment of the conversion. The religious ceremonies at the ending are performed by a bishop in full ecclesiastical regalia, preaching to the audience as though to a congregation attending a regular service.

In several matters of staging and dramatic technique, these plays reveal important affinities to other dramatic genres of the fifteenth century, especially to the Corpus Christi cycle and to the morality play. Each of these saints' plays or conversion plays requires the use of a number of simultaneously visible scaffolds. Journeys between the scaffolds occur in the middle space or "platea" surrounded by the scaffolds. The audience is intimately involved and is even perambulatory in some instances. The raucous comedy of evil used in these plays reminds us of cycle and morality drama. In methods of characterization as well, these plays borrow techniques from several genres in the late medieval theater. Scriptural figures exist side by side with allegorical abstractions and with legendary heroes of fictional romance. Despite their partly untypical nature, then, these English saints' plays are valuable to us because they show the growth of a significant dramatic genre. In time, that genre will make its contribution to dramatic romance of the English Renaissance, including Shakespeare's *Pericles* and *The Winter's Tale*.

THE CONVERSION OF ST. PAUL
FROM THE DIGBY MS

The liturgical origins of the Digby *St. Paul* are clear when we compare this text with that of twelfth-century Fleury (see Part II, above). Despite its considerable increase in length, its comic scenes, and its use of English, the Digby play is still presumably intended to celebrate the festival of the Conversion of St. Paul on January 25. Furthermore, although performance now appears to be outdoors rather than inside the church, staging remains essentially similar to that of the twelfth-century version.

As in the Fleury play, the stage for this Digby text employs simultaneously visible locations. Jerusalem must have a *sedes* for the chief priests, another acting-place for Saul, and an inn-yard for the comic scene. Damascus features a "mansion" for Ananias and another where Saul is baptized into the Christian faith as Paul (see ll. 269–71). God speaks from heaven (l. 182 s.d.) to Saul. The protagonist's conversion on the road to Damascus evidently takes place on the "platea" or flat acting area between the two city locations.

The poet, acting as prologue and epilogue, speaks of the play as divided into three "stations," and invites the audience or "congregation" to march in procession with him from station I (Jerusalem) to station II (Damascus). Whether the third station requires still another location, or a return to Jerusalem, is not clear, although a return to Jerusalem seems more likely. The Fleury play of St. Paul locates the final action in Damascus, as does the biblical text (Acts 9:1–27); but in this Digby play, Saul is led back to the chief priests Caiaphas and Annas (named after their counterparts in the Passion play), who may be located on their original scaffold. Furthermore, Saul is reported to have gone into Jerusalem (l. 574). In any

event the audience is perambulatory and the stage employs a number of scaffolds.

Staging also calls for the descent of the Holy Ghost over Saul (l. 291), the appearance of devils with thunder and fire (l. 412), the use of a font for Saul's baptism and a pulpit for his sermon, and the appearance of an angel (l. 636). Some of the more spectacular features are late additions to the text, notably the devils' horseplay and the dances performed at each interval between the "stations." These revisions may explain the lack of certainty as to how the whole was to have been staged.

Because the comic scenes are late interpolations in the text, their relevance to the main part of the play is questionable. In part, at least, they are broadly slapstick skits added for comic diversion. Yet they may also serve to explain the dramatic change in the protagonist from tyranny to saintliness. By poking fun at arrogant posturing, the early comic scene between Saul's man and the stable groom implicitly satirizes the arrogant attitude of Saul toward Christians. Later, the interpolated antics of the devils add a metaphysical perspective to the struggle of good and evil going on between Saul and his wicked persecutors. Evil types such as Caiaphas and Annas are seen as emissaries of the devil, richly deserving to be foiled in their villainy. The devils' gloating claims of dominance over the lives of men (ll. 489–95) are refuted by Saul's long sermon on the seven Deadly Sins. The reviser, sensing a need to explain Saul's abrupt change from evil to good, resorts to abstraction.

With or without the comic additions, *St. Paul* is a play about conversion. Like Mary Magdalene, Saul is a famous biblical figure who is won over from an evil life to a penitent faith in God's grace. His baptism into the Christian religion is performed on stage with extensive use of the language of the liturgy. Ananias officiates as priest at this "observacion" (ritual service) or "blissyd sacrement" (ll. 329–33). Costuming, presumably borrowed from the wardrobe of the church, would reinforce the ceremonial seriousness of the occasion. The audience, having marched in procession as a congregation of worshipers, must listen to a sermon by Saul on the seven Deadly Sins. As in *The Play of the Sacrament,* the use of ecclesiastical ceremony deliberately obscures the distinction between mimetic drama and religious rite. Audience becomes congregation, and play-acting becomes an act of worship.

The play is written throughout in rime royal, a seven-line *ababbcc* stanza. Probably the text was first composed, in East Midland dialect, some time in the late fifteenth century. The manuscript in which it has been preserved, the so-called Digby manuscript, is now located in the Bodleian Library at Oxford. Also included in this manuscript are the Digby *Mary Magdalene* and other dramatic texts.

The Conversion of St. Paul

From the Digby MS

[DRAMATIS PERSONAE

GOD, speaking from heaven

AN ANGEL

SAULUS or Saul, later St. Paul after his conversion

ANANIAS or Annanie, a servant of God in Damascus

CAIPHA, a chief priest of Jerusalem

ANNA, another chief priest of Jerusalem

TWO SOLDIERS accompanying Saul

AN OFFICER of the chief priests

SERVANT of Saul

STABULARIUS, stable-groom

BELIAL, a devil

MERCURY, another devil]

[*The First Station. Jerusalem. Enter the poet as prologue.*]

POETA. *Rex gloriae*, king omnipotent,   *King of glory*
   Redemer of the world by thy power divine,
   And Maria, that pure virgi[n] quene most excellent,
   W[h]iche bare that blissyd babe, Jhesu, that for us sufferd
     paine,
   Unto whoys goodnes I do incline,   *whose*
   Bcseching that Lord of his pitous influens   *pitying*
   To preserve and governe this wirshipfull audiens—

   Honorable frendes, beseching yow of licens   *license, permission*
   To procede owr processe, we may, under your correccion,   *proceed with our story*

[Show] the conversion of Seynt Paule, as the Bible gif

experiens.   *gives information*

11   Whoo list to rede the booke *Actum Appostolorum*,   *Whoso pleases*

Ther shall he have the very noticion.   *true information*

13   But, as we can, we shall us redres,

Brefly with yowr favour begining owr proces. *Daunce.*

[*The poet stands aside. In the station representing Jerusalem,
there are separate areas or platforms for Saul and for the chief
priests.*]

Here entrith Saule, [attended,] goodly besene in the best wise   *apparelled*

like an aunterous knyth, thus saying: *adventurous knight*

SAULUS.   Most dowtyd man I am living upon the ground,   *dreaded*

Goodly besene with many a riche garnement!   *garment*

My pere on live I trow is nott found.   *peer alive*

Thorow the world, fro the orient to the occident,   *Through*

My fame is best knowyn undyr the firmament.   *I am the most famous*

I am most drad of pepull universall;   *dreaded/universally*

They dare not disp[l]ease me most noble.

Saule is my name—I will that ye notify—   *take notice*

23   Which conspireth the disciplys with thretes and menace;

Before the princes of prestes most noble and high   *chief priests*

I bring them to punnishement for ther trespace.

We will them nott suffer to rest in no place,

For they go aboug[h]te to preche and giff exemplis   *about/give*

To destroye our lawes, synagoges, and templis.

By the god Belliall, I schall make progresse   *shall go*

Unto the princes both, Caipha and Anna,   *chief priests*

31   Where I schall aske of them in suernes

32   To pursue thorow all Dammask and Liba.

And thus we schall soone after than   *then*

Bring them that so do liff into Jerusalem,   *that live so*

Both man and child, that I find of them.

*Her[e] cummith Sa[u]le to Caipha and Anna, prestes of the
tempyll.*

[11]*Actum Appostolorum:* the Acts of the Apostles (9:1–27).

[13]But, insofar as we are able, we will put ourselves in order, address ourselves to the task at
hand.

[23]Who breathes out threats and menacings against the disciples (see Acts 9:1).

[31–32]Where I shall ask from them (letters of) authorization to search throughout all Damascus
and Libya (see Acts 9:2).

Nobill prelates and princes of regalité,
Desiring and asking of your beningne wurthines *benign*
Your letters and epistolys of most soverenté *efficacy*
39 To subdue rebellious that will, of frawardnes, *perverseness*
40 Against our lawes rebell or transgresse,
41 Nor will not incline, but mak objecc[i]on: *submit*
42 To pursue all such I will do proteccion.

CAIPHA. To your desier we gif perfith sentens, *complete concurrence*
According to your peticions that ye make postulacion, *Agreeing|that you request*
Bicause we know your trewe deligens
46 To pursue all tho that do reprobacion *those who traduce*
47 Agains owr lawes by ony redarguacion. *any refutation*
Wherefor, shortly we gif in commandment *we give command (to you)*
To put down them that be di[s]obedient.

ANNA. And by thes[e] letturs, that be most reverrent— *worthy of respect*
51 Take them in hand, full agre therto—
Constreyn all rebellys by owr [w]hole assent;
We gif yow full power so to doo.
Spare not, hardly, for frend nor foo! *Refrain|certainly*
All thos[e] ye find of that life in this realme, *of that way of life*
Bounde loke ye bring them into Jerusalem. *see to it that*
    Her[e] Saule resaivith ther letters.

SAULUS. This precept here I take in hande,
To fullfill after yowr willes both; *according to*
Wher I shall spare within this londe *Whereby*
60 Nother man nor woman—to this I make an o[a]th— *Neither*
But to subdue I will not be lo[a]th. [*To his followers.*]
Now folow me, knitys and servantes trewe, *knights*
Into Damaske as fast as ye can sewe. *Damascus|follow*

1 MILES. Unto your commaundment I do obeisaunce.
I will not gainsay nor make delacion, *delay*
But with good mind and harty plesaunce *pleasure*
I shall yow succede and make perambulacion *follow*
Thorowoute Damaske with all delectacion. *delight*
And all thoo rebell and make resistens, *those who rebel*
70 For to oppres I will do my deligens. *To oppress (them)*

39–42To subdue rebellious persons who will, out of perverseness, rebel or transgress against our laws, and will not submit, but instead make protest: to pursue all such persons I seek (your) protection and authorization.

46–47To pursue all those who traduce our laws (of the Old Testament), refuting and disproving them.

51Take them in your hand, receiving them kindly, in good part.

2 MILES.   And in me shal be no necligens,
But to this precept myself I shall applye
To do your behest with all conveniens,   *command*
Withowt eny frowardnes or eny obstinacy—
Non[e] shall appere in me. But verely,
With all my mind, I yow insure,   *assure*
To resist tho rebelles I will do my cure.   *those/care, duty*

SAULUS.   Truly to me it is grett consolacion
To here this report that ye do avauns.   *hear/advance, present*
80   For your sapienciall wittes I gif commendacion;   *knowing*
Ever at my nede I have founde yow constant.
But, knytes and servuantes that be so plesaunt,
I pray yow anon my palfray ye bring,
To spede my jurney withowt letting.   *delay*
        Here goith Sa[u]le forth a lityll aside for to make him redy to
        ride, the servuant thus sey[i]ng [as he goes to the inn and calls
        loudly]:

SERVUS.   How, hosteler, how! A peck of otys and a botell *oats/bundle*
        of haye!
Com of[f] apase, or I will to another inne!   *Come quickly*
What, hosteler, why commist not thy way?   *why aren't you coming*
Hie the[e] faster, I beshrew thy skinne!   *Hasten/curse*
        [The stable-groom appears.]
STABULARIUS.   I am non hosteler nor non hostelers kinne, *stable-groom*
But a jentilmanys servuant, i[f] thou dost know!
Such crabbish wordes do aske a blow.

92   SERVUS.   I cry yow mercy, sir! I wist well sumwhat ye were,
Owther a gentilman or a knave, me thinkith by your   *Either*
        physnomy!
94   If on[e] loke yow in the face that never se yow ere,
95   Wold think ye were at the next dore by.
In good faith, I wenyd yow had bene an hosteler, verely! *weened, thought*
97   I sye suche another jentilman with yow, a barowfull *saw*
        bare
Of horsdowng and dogges tordes, and sich other gere.   *gear, stuff*

[80]I commend your knowledgeable understanding.

[92]I beg your pardon, sir! I knew well enough you were something.

[94-95]If anyone who never saw you before would look you in the face, he'd think you came from next door (i.e., from an innyard rather than from a gentleman's house).

[97]I saw another such "gentleman" as you, who was carrying a full barrow (a container for transporting loads). (The speaker wryly suggests that the stable-groom also has to carry horse-dung, and is really not a gentleman's servant.)

And how it happenyd, a mervelous chance betide: *occurred*

100   Your felow was not suer of foote, and yet he went very
           wide,
       Butt in a cow-tord both did ye slide—
       And, as I wene, your nose therin rode;   *think*

103   Your face was be-paintyd with sowters code!   *cobbler's wax*
       I sey never sich a sig[h]t, I make God a vow!   *never saw such*
       Ye were so be-grimlyd and it had bene a sowe.   *as begrimed as if*

STABULARIUS.   In faith, thou never syest me till this day.   *saw*
       I have dwellyd with my master this seven yere and more;
       Full well I have pleasyd him—he will not say nay—
       And mikill he makith of me therfore.   *he makes much of me*

110   SERVUS.   By my trowth, than be ye changyd to a new lore!   *then/rule of behavior*
       A servand ye are, and that a good.
       Ther is no better lokith owt of a hood.   *i.e., among mankind*

STABULARIUS.   Forsoth, and a hood I use for to were;   *I'm accustomed to wear*
       Full well it is linyd with silk and chamlett.   *camlet, a costly cloth*
       It kepith me fro the cold that the wind doth me not dere,   *so that/harm*
       Nowther frost nor snow that I therby do sett.   *Neither/care about*
       SERVUS.   Yea, it is a dobill hood, and that a fett!   *double/fit, fine one*

118   He was a good man that made it, I warant yow;
119   He was nother horse ne mare, nor yet yokyd sow!   *yoked, tethered*
       Here commith the first knyth to the stabil grom, say[i]ng:

1 MILES.   Now, stabill grom, shortly bring forth away   *soldier/quickly*
       The best horse, for owr lorde will ride.
STABULARIUS.   I am full redy. Here is a palfray,
       There can no man a better bestride.
       He will conducte owr lorde and g[u]ide   *and guide (him)*
       Thorow the world; he is sure and abyll.   *able*
       To bere a gentillman he [is] esy and prophetabyll.   *profitable*
       *Her[e] the knyth cummith to Saule with a horse. [Servant and
       groom retire.]*

1 MILES.   Behold, sir Saule, your palfray is com,
       Full goodly besene, as it is yowr desier   *apparelled/desire*
       To take yowr vyage thorow every region.   *voyage*

---

[100]Your companion was not sure-footed, and yet he went far astray, off the path.

[103](Cobbler's wax, or pitch, is of the color and consistency of a turd.)

[110]i.e., By my faith, then you've shifted occupations.

[118-19](Perhaps a reference to the devil, maker of deceiving two-faced double hoods.)

130   Be nott in dowt, he will spede your mater.   *business*
    And we, as your servauntes, with glad chere
    Shall gif attendance. We will nott gainsay,
    But folow yow where ye go by nig[h]t or day.

SAULUS.   Unto Damask I make my progression,   *I go*
    To pursue all rebellious being froward and obstinate
    Agains our lawes by ony transgression.   *any*
137   With all my deligens myself I will prepar[at]e   *prepare*
138   Concerning my purpose to oppres and separate—
139   Non[e] shall rejoice that doth offend—
140   But utterly to reprove with minde and intende.   *intent*

> *Her[e] Sa[u]le ridith forth with his servantes abowt the place,*   *central acting area*
> *[and] owt of the pl[ace].*
> *[Having seen Saul on his way, the chief priests remain at their*
> *temple of Jerusalem.]*

CAIPHA.   Now Saule hath takyn his wurthy vyage
    To pursue rebellious, of what degré they be.   *whatsoever rank*
    He will non[e] suffer to raigne nor have passage
    Within all this region, we be in sertain[té].   *we may be sure*
    Wherefor, I commende his goodly dignité,
    That he thus alway takith in hande
    By his power to governe thus all this lande.

ANNA.   We may live in rest, by his consolacion.   *reassurance*
    He defendith us; wherefor we be bownde
150   To love him intirely with our harttes affeccion,
    And honour him as champion in every stownde.   *every hour, constantly*
    Ther is non[e] suche living upon the grownde   *on earth*
    That may be like him nor be his pere,   *peer*
    By est nor west, ferre nor nere.   *far/near*

> *Poeta—si placet.*   *if desired*
> *Conclusion. Daunce.*

[POETA.]   Finally, of this stac[i]on thus we mak a conclusion,
    Beseching this audiens to folow and succede   *follow*
157   With all your deligens this generall procession.
    To understande this matter, w[h]o list to rede   *whoso*
    The Holy Bibill for the better spede,   *help*
    Ther shall he have the perfith intelligens.   *perfect*

137-40With all my diligence I will prepare myself for my task, to oppress and disunite (the Christians), censuring them utterly with all my heart and mind, so that none of those offenders will have cause for rejoicing.

157procession: Seemingly, the audience is to march in procession to the next "station."

And thus we com[m]it yow to Cristys magnificens.
Finis istius stationis, et altera sequitur: *The end of that station, and another*
follows

[*The Second Station. Damascus. The poet speaks the prologue.*]

POETA.   Honorable frendes, we beseche yow of audiens
To here our intencion and also our prosses.   *hear/story*
Upon our matter, by your favorable licens,   *permission*
Another part of the story we will redres.   *put in good order*
Here shal be brefly shewyd, with all our besines,   *industry*
At this pagent, Saint Poullys convercion.
Take ye good hede and therto gif affeccion.   *inclination*
    [*The poet steps aside.*]
    Here commith Saule riding in with his servantes [on the road to
    Damascus].

169   SAULUS.   My purpose to Damask fully I intende;
To pursewe the discipulys my life I apply.
For to breke down the chirchys thus I condescende;   *I am resolved*
172   Non[e] I will suffer that [they] shall edifey.
173   Perchaunce owr lawes than mig[h]te [peyre] therby,   *then/become impaired*
And the pepull also turne and converte,   *be converted*
Which shuld be gret hevines unto min[e] hart.

176   Nay, that shall nott be butt laid apart!
The princes have govyn me full potestacion.   *given/power*
All that I find, they shall nott start,   *escape*
But bounde, to Jerusalem, with furious violacion,   *violent treatment*
Befor Cesar, Caipha, and Annas [have] presentacion.   *be arraigned*
Thus shal be subduyd tho wretchys of that life,   *those/way of life*
That non[e] shall injoy, nother man, chi[l]de, nor wife.   *neither*
    Here commith a fervent [light] with gret tempest, and Saule
    faulith down of [f] his horse. That done, Godhed spekith in hevyn.

DEUS.   Saule! Saule! Why dost thou me pursue?   *persecute*
184   It is hard to prike agains the spore!   *Kick/goad*
I am thy Saviour, that is so tr[e]we,   *who is*
Which made hevyn and erth and eche creature.   *Who*

169I fully intend to carry out my purpose in going to Damascus.

172-73I will not allow them to build any (churches). Otherwise, perchance, our laws might
become impaired.

176Nay, that (plan) will certainly be set aside!

184It is hard (for you) to kick against the goad or traces; i.e., it is unkind of you to rebel
against my authority (see Acts 9:5).

   Offende nott my goodnes! I will the[e] recure.   *recover, save*

SAULUS. O Lord, I am aferd, I trymble for fere!

189 What woldist I ded? Tell me here.

DEUS. Arise and goo thou with glad chere

  Into the cité a litill beside,   *close by*

  And I shall the[e] socor in every dere,   *save you from every harm*

  That no maner of ill shal betide.   *sort of/happen*

  And I will ther for the[e] provide,

  By my grete goodnes, what thou shalt doo.

  Hi[e] the[e] as fast thether as thou mast goo! *may, can go*

   [*God withdraws.*]

SAULUS. O mercifull God, what ailith me?

198 I am lame, my legges be take me fro;

  My sigth likwise—I may nott see—   *sight*

  I cannott tell whether to goo.   *whither*

  My men hath forsake me also.

  Whether shall I wynde, or whether shall I pas? *wend, go*

  Lord, I beseche the[e], helpe me of thy grace!

1 MILES. Sir, we be here to help the[e] in thy nede;

  With all our affiance we will nott sesse.   *loyalty/cease*

SAULUS. Than in Damask I pray yow me lede *into*

207 I Godes name, according to my promise. *In*

2 MILES. To put forth yowr hand loke ye dresse. *address yourself*

  Cum on your way. We shall yow bring

210 Into the cité withowt tary[i]ng.

   Here the knightes lede forth Sa[u]le into a place, and Crist (*i.e., into a house*)

   apperith to Annanie, say[i]ng: *Ananias*

DEUS. Ananie, Ananie! Where art thou, Ananie!

ANANIAS. Here, Lord, I am here, tr[e]wly.

DEUS. Go thy way and make thy curse,   *course, path*

  As I shall assing the[e], by min[e] advisse,   *assign/advice*

  Into the strete *qui dicitur rectus*,   "*which is called straight*"

  And in a certain house, of warantise,   *of a certainty*

---

[189]What do you wish that I do? Tell me here.

[198]I am lame, my legs are taken from me (i.e., are powerless).

[207]In God's name, as I was promised.

[210]s.D.: According to Acts 9:11, Saul is led to the house of a man called Judas, where Ananias finds him. The "station" of Jerusalem requires two "mansions," one for Ananias and one to which Saul is led.

Ther shall ye find Saule in humble wise,
218 As a meke lambe, that a wolf before was namyd.　　　*named, called*
Do my behest, be nothing ashamyd.　　　*disconcerted*

He wantith his sith, by my punishment constrained.　　　*lacks his sight*
221 Prayeng unto me, I assure, thou shalt him find.
With my stroke of pité sore is he painyde,　　　*sorely|pained*
Wanting his sigth, for he is truly blinyde.　　　*sight|blind*
ANANIAS.　Lord, I am aferd, for alway in my mind
I here so myche of his furious cruelté,　　　*hear|much*
226 That for speking of thy name to deth he will put me.

DEUS.　Nay, Ananie, nay; I assure the[e]
He wul be glad of thy cumming.
ANANIAS.　A, Lord, but I know of a certain[té]
That thy seyntes in Jerusalem to deth he doth bring!　　　*saints*
Many illys of him I have be-kenning,　　　*knowledge*
For he hath the powre of the princes alle　　　*power, authority*
To save or spille, do which he schall.　　　*kill|whichever he chooses*

DEUS.　Be nothing adrad. He is a chosen vessell,
To me assingned by my godly eleccion.　　　*choice*
He shall bere my name before the kinges and childer of　　　*chosen race*
　　　Israell,
237 By many sharpe shoures suffering correccion—　　　*fierce attacks*
238 A gret doctor of beningne conpleccion,　　　*comprehension*
The tr[e]we precher of the hye devineté,　　　*high divinity*
A very pinacle of the faith, I ensure the[e].

ANANIAS.　Lorde, thy commandment I shall fullfill.
Unto Saule I will take my waye.
243 DEUS.　Be nothing in dowte, for good nor ill.
Farewell, Ananie. Tell Saule what I do say.
　　Et exiat Deus [returning to heaven].
ANANIAS.　Blissyd Lord, defende me, as thou best may!
Gretly I fere his cruell tyranny.　　　*his (Saul's)*
But to do thy precept myself I shall applye.　　　*I'll apply myself*
　　Here Ananias goth toward Saule.

[218]As meek as a lamb, that previously was spoken of as a wolf.

[221]I assure you you'll find him praying to me.

[226](I fear) that he will put me to death merely for speaking your (Christ's) name.

[237-38]Suffering punishment (at the hands of God's enemies) by many fierce attacks—a learned scholar of benign comprehension (see Acts 9:16).

[243]Do not fear at all, come what may.

1 MILES.   I marvayle gretly what it doth mene,
    To se owr master in this hard stounde!   *attack, shock*
250 The wonder grett li[g]thtys that were so shene   *wondrously/lights/bright*
    Smett him doune of[f] his hors to the grownde,   *Smote*
    And me thowt that I hard a sounde   *thought/heard*
    Of won[e] speking with voice delectable,   *one (God)*
    Which was to [us] wonderfull mirable.   *marvelous*

2 MILES.   Sertenly this lig[h]t was ferefull to see!
    The sperkys of fier were very fervent.   *sparks*
    It inflamyd so grevosely about the countré
    That, by my trowth, I went we shuld a ben brent!   *thought/have been burned*
    But now, serys, lett us relente   *sirs/return*
260 Againe to Caipha and Anna, to tell this chaunce,
    How it befell to us this grevauns.
    [*The two soldiers return to Jerusalem.*]
    Her[e] Saule is in contemplacion.

SAULUS.   Lord, of thy coumfort moch I desire,
    Thou mig[h]ty prince of Israell, king of pité,
    Whiche me hast punishyd as thy presoner   *Who*
    That nother ete nor dranke this dayes thre!   *neither*
    But, gracios Lorde, of thy visitacion I thanke the[e].
    Thy servant shall I be as long as I have breth,
    Thowgh I therfor shuld suffer dethe.
    Here commith Anania to Saule, sayeng:

ANANIAS.   Pease be in this place and goodly mansion!
270 Who is within? Speke, in Cristys holy name!
SA[U]LUS.   I am here, Saule. Cum in, on Goddes benison!   *with God's blessing*
    [*Ananias enters the house.*]
    What is your will? Tell withowten blame.   *i.e., Tell truly*
ANANIAS.   From almighty God, sertanly, to the[e] sent I am,
    And Ananie men call me wheras I dwell.   *where*
SAULUS.   What wold ye have? I pray yow me tell.

ANANIAS.   Gife me your hand for your availe.   *benefit*
    For, as I was commaundyd by his gracios sentens,   *God's gracious command*
    He bad[e] the[e] be stedfast, for thou shalt be hayle.   *whole, healed*
    For this same cause he sent me to thy presens.
280 Also he bad[e] the[e] remember his hye excellens
    By this same tokyn: that he did the[e] mete   *meet*
    Toward the cité, when he apperyd in the strete.   *Near*

    Ther mayst thou know his power celestiall,
    How he disposith everything as him list.   *as it pleases him*

Nothing may withstand his mig[h]te essenciall.

286   To stond upright or els doun to thriste,   *thrust*
287   This is his power; it may not be miste,   *missed, lacked*
    For who that it wantith, lackith a frende.   *whoso lacks it*
    This is the massage that he doth the[e] sende.

SAULUS.   His marcy to me is right welcom.
    I am right glad that it is thus.
       Hic apparebit Spiritus Sanctus super eum.   *Here the Holy Ghost will appear over him*
ANANIAS.   Be of good chere and perfite jubilacion!   *perfect*
    Discendit super te Spiritus Sanctus,   *The Holy Ghost descends over you*
    Which hath with his grace illuminyd us.
    Put fo[r]th thy hond and goo with me.
    Againe to thy sight here I restore the[e].

SAULUS.   Blissyd Lord, thankys to yow ever bee!
    The swame is fallyn from my eyes twaine.   *scales are*
    Where I was blin[d]yd and cowd nott see,   *Whereas*
300   Lord, thou hast sent me my sight againe.
    From sobbing and weping I cannot refraine!
    My pensive hart [is] full of contriccion;
    For my offences, my body shal have punicion.   *punishment*

    And, where I have used so gret persecucion   *whereas*
    Of thy desciplys thorow all Jerusalem,
    I will [aid] and defende ther predicacion   *preaching*
    That th[e]y did tech on all this reme.   *in|realm*
    Wherefor, Ananie, at the watery streme
    Baptise me, hartely I the[e] praye,
310   Among your numbyr that I electe and chosen be may.

ANANIAS.   Onto this well of mych vertu   *i.e., baptismal font|much*
    We will us hie with all our deligens.   *hasten*
SAULUS.   Go yow before, and after I shall sewe,   *follow*
    Lauding and praising our Lordes benevolens.
    I shall never offend his mig[h]ty magnificens,
    But alway observe his preceptys and kepe.   *and keep his precepts*
    For my gret unkindnes, my hart doth wepe!   *unnaturalness*
    [*They proceed to the place of baptism. Saul kneels.*]

ANANIAS.   Knele ye down upon this grownde,
    Receiving this cristening with good intent,
320   Whiche shall make yow [w]hole of your dedly wound

286–87 It is in his power to cause things or persons to stand upright or else be thrust down. This power is essential.

That was infecte with venom nocent.   *harmful*
It purgith sinne, and fendes powres so fraudelent   *the fiend's powers*
It putith aside. Where this doth attaine,   *have effect*
In every stede, he may not obtaine.   *place|he (the devil)|prevail*
    [*Ananias baptizes Saul.*]

I cristen yow with mind full perfight,   *perfect, pure*
Reseiving yow into owr religion—
Ever to be stedfast and never to flit,   *alter*
But ever constant withowt variacion.
Now is fulfillyd all our observacion,   *ritual service*
330   Concluding—thou mayst it ken—   *as you must know*
In nomine Patris et Filii et Spiritus Sancti. Amen.

SAULUS.   I am right glad as foule on flite *fowl, bird in flight*
    That I have receivyd this blissyd sacrement!
ANANIAS.   Com on your way, Saule—for nothing lett— *delay*
    Take yow sum coumforth for your bodies norischment.
Ye shall abide with the disciplys, verament,   *truly*
This many dayes in Damask cité,   *For many days*
Untill the time more perfit ye may be.   *perfect, purified*

SAULUS.   As ye commande, holy father Ananie,
340   I full assent at yow[r] request
To be g[u]idyd and rulyd as ye will have me,
Evyn at your pleasur, as ye think best.
I shall not offend for most nor lest.   *least (i.e., for anyone)*
Go forth yowr way. I will succede   *follow*
Into what place ye will me lede.
    [*They leave in procession, Ananias leading.*]
    Conclusio[n]. Daunce.

    [*The poet speaks the epilogue.*]
POETA.   Thus Saule is convertyd, as ye se expres, *plainly*
    The very tr[e]w servant of our Lord Jhesu.
Non[e] may be like to his perfig[h]t holines,
So nobill a doctor, constant and tr[e]we;
350   Aftyr his conversion never mutable, but still insue *striving*
The lawys of God to teche ever more and more—
As Holy Scriptur tellys, whoso list to loke therfore.   *pleases*

Thus we com[m]ite yow all to the Trinité,
Conkluding this stacion as we can or may,
Under the correccion of them that letteryd be—   *literate*

356	Howbeit unable as I dare speke or say,	
357	The compiler hereof shuld translat veray	*truly*
358	So holy a story but with favorable correccion	
359	Of my favorable masters, of ther benigne supplexion.	*supplementation*

Finis istius secundae stationis, et sequitur tertia: — The end of that second station, and the third follows

[*The Third Station. Jerusalem (?)*
The poet speaks the prologue.]

POETA.   The might of the Fadires potenciall deité — *Father's potent*
Preserve this honorable and wurshipfull congregacion
That here be present, of hye and low degré, — *rank*
To understond this pagent at this litill stacion
Which we shall procede with all our delectac[i]on. — *narrate, depict*
If it will plese yow to gif audiens favorable,
Hark wisely therto; it is good and profetable.

[*The poet steps aside.*]
[*Saul's previous military followers, back from the road to Damascus, report to Caiaphas and Annas at their platform or acting area.*]

1 MILES.   Nobill prelates, take hede to owr sentens! — *report*
A wundyrfull chaunce fyll and did betide — *wondrous/befell*
Unto owr master Saull when he departyd hens, — *hence*
370   Into Damaske purposyd to ride. — *having intended*
A mervelous lig[h]t fro thelement did glide — *the element, the sky*
Whiche smet down him to gr[o]unde, both horse and man, — *smote*
With the ferfulest wether that ever I in cam! — *came in, experienced*

2 MILES.   It ravisshid him, and his spirites did benome. — *benumb*
A swete dulcet voice spake him unto,
And askyd wherfor he made suche persecucion
Ageynst His disciplys, and why he did soo? — *His (Christ's)*
He bad[e] him into Damaske to Ananie goo,
And ther he shuld reseive bapti[s]m, truly.
380   And now clene ageyns owr lawys he is, tr[e]wly. — *totally against*

CAIPHA.   I am sure this tale is not tr[e]w.
What, Saule convertyd from our law?
He went to Damask for to pursue
All the disciplys that did withdraw

356–59 i.e., Considering my inability to express myself well, as compiler of this play I have ventured to translate so holy a story only subject to the gracious correction and kindly supplementation of my well-disposed superiors.

Fro owr faith: this was his sawe.   *saying*

How say ye, Anna, to this mater? This is a mervelos chans.   *occurrence*

I cannot beleve that this is of assurans.   *is credible*

ANNA.   No, Caipha. My minde tr[e]wly do [I] tell:

That he will not turne in no maner wise,

390   But rather to deth put and expell

All miscreauntes and wretchys that doth arise

Against our lawes by ony enterprise.   *any*

    [*To the soldiers.*]

Say the tr[e]wth with[out] ony cause frawdelent,

Or els for your talys ye be like to be shent!   *likely/disgraced*

395   1 MILES.   Ellis owr bodies may [ye] put to pain!

All that we declare, I sye it with min[e] [e]ye.   *saw*

. . . .

Nothing offending, but tr[e]wly do justifye.

CAIPHAS.   By the gret god, I do marvaile gretly!

And this be tr[e]w that ye do reherse,   *If/report*

He shall repent his rebellious treytory,   *treachery*

401   That all shal beware of his falsnes!   *So that*

We will not suffer him to obtaine, dowtles,   *prevail*

For meny perellys that might betide   *Because of many perils*

By his subtill meanys on every side.   *subtle means*

ANNA.   The law is committyd to owr advisment;   *custody*

Wherfor we will not se it decay,

But rather uphold it, help, and a[u]gment,

That ony reprofe to us fall may   *Lest any reproof fall to us*

Of Cesar, themprour, by nig[h]t or day.   *From/the emperor*

We shall to such maters harke and attende,

411   According to the lawes our wittes to spende.

    [*They retire.*]

Hereto enter a divel with thunder and fire, and, to avaunte himsilfe, saying as folowith; and, his spech spokyn, to sit downe in a chaire.

BELIALL.   Ho, ho! Beholde me, the mig[h]té prince of the
    partes infernall!

---

[395]i.e., Unless we're telling the truth, you can torture us. (Four lines appear to be missing from this stanza.)

[401]So that everyone will be warned by the example of his falseness.

[411]Exercising our mental abilities in accordance with the laws. (The following scene of the devils, through l. 502 s.d., is in a later hand inserted on three separate leaves in the MS.)

Next unto Lucifer I am in magestye.

By name I am nominate the god Beliall;   *am called*

Non[e] of more mig[h]te nor of more excellencye.

My powre is principall, and now of most soferainté.

417   In the temples and synogoges who deneyth me to honore,   *whoever denies*

418   My busshopes, thorow my motion, they wil him sone   *suggestion*
      devoure.

I have movyd my prelates, Caiphas and Anna,   *incited*

To pursew and put downe, by powre ryall   *royal*

Thorow the sities of Damaske and Liba,   *cities*

All soch as do worship the hye God supernall.   *divine*

Ther deth is conspiryd, withowt any favoure at all.   *favor, mercy*

My busshopys hathe chosyne won[e] most rigorus   *chosen one*

Them to pursew, howse name is Saulus.   *whose*

Ho! Thus as a god most hye in magestye

I rayne and I rule over creatures humayne!

428   With soverraine sewte soug[h]te to is my deité;

429   Mans mind is applicant as I list to ordeyne.

My law still encreasith, wherof I am fayne.   *fain, pleased*

Yet of late I have hard of no newys, truly,   *heard*

Wherfor I long till I speke with my messenger, Mercurye.

    Here shall entere another devill callyd Mercury, with a fiering,   *explosion of powder*
    comming in hast, cryeng and roring, and shal say as folowith:

MARCURY. Ho, owg[h]t, owg[h]t! Alas, this sodaine chance!   *out! (an interjection)*

    Well may we bewaile this cursyd adventure!

BELIAL. Marcurye, what ailyse thou? Tell me thy grevaunce.   *ails*

    Is ther any that hath wrowg[h]te us displeasure?

MERCURY. Displeasure inowgh, therof ye may be sure!

    Our law at lengthe it wil be clene downe laid,   *entirely overcome*

    For it decayth sore; and more wil, I am afraid.

440   BELIAL. Ho! How can that be? It is not possible!

    Co[n]sider, thou foole, the long continuance!   *i.e., how long it's continued*

    Decaye, quod a? It is not credible.   *says he*

    Of fals tidinges thou makist here utterance.   *You're telling false news*

    Behold how the peple hath no pleasaunce

    But in sin, and to folow our desiere,

    Pride and voluptuosité ther hartes doth so fire.   *inflame*

417-18My chief priests, through my suggestion, will soon destroy anyone who refuses to honor me in the temples and synagogues.

428-29My deity is petitioned to (by man) with urgent entreaty; man's mind is directed as it pleases me to order it.

447 Thowg[h]e on[e] do swaver away from our lore,   *decline/teaching*
448 Yet is our powre of suche nobilité   *excellence*
449 To have him againe, and twoo therfore,   *i.e., twice as many*
450 That shal preferre the praise of owre majestye.
     What is the tidinges? Tell owt, lett us see.
     Why arte thou amasyd so? Declare afore us   *in our presence*
     What fury is fallyn that troblith the[e] thus?

MERCURY.   Ho, owg[h]t, owg[h]te! He that I most trustyd to,
     And he that I thowg[h]te wold have ben to us most speciall,
     Is now of late turnyd, and our cruell foo.   *lately converted*
     Our speciall frynd, our chosen Saull,
     Is becomme servante to the hye God eternall!
     As he did ride on our enemies persecution,   *to persecute our enemies*
460 He was sodenly strikyn by the hye provision   *providence*

     And now is baptisyd, and promis he hath made
     Never to vary; and soch grace he hath opteinyd   *obtained*
     That ondowtyd his faith from him cannot fade.   *undoubtedly*
     Wherfor to complaine I am constrainyd,
     For moch by him shuld we have prevailyd.
BELIAL.   Ho, owg[h]t, owg[h]t! What, have we loste
     Our darling most dere, whom we lovyd moste?

     But is it of trowth that thou doyst here specifye?   *dost, do*
MERCURY.   It is so, undowg[h]tyd. Why shuld I faine?   *undoubtedly*
470 For thowg[h]te I can do non[e] other but crye.   *From thinking of it*
         Here they shal rore and crye, and then Belial shal saye:
BELIAL.   Owg[h]te! This grevith us worse than hell paine!
     The conversion of sinner, certaine,   *certainly*
     Is more paine to us and persecution
     Than all the furies of the infernall dongyon.

MERCURY.   It doyth not avail us thus to lament;   *doth, does*
     But lett us provid[e] for remedy shortlye.
     Wherfor, let us both by on[e] assent   *in unison*
     Go to the busshopys and move them privelye   *persuade/privately*
     That by some sotil meane they may cause him to die.
     Than shal he in our law make no disturbaunce,   *Then*
     Nor hereafter cause us to have more grevaunce.

BELIAL.   Wel said, Mercurye! Thy cowncel is profitable.
     Ho, Saul, thou shalt repent thy unstablenes!

447–50 i.e., Our power is so great that for every one who falls away from our teaching we'll win over two (reclaiming the first one in the bargain) who'll pay homage to our majesty.

484 Thou hadist ben better to have byn confirmable
485 To our law; for this deth, dowtles,   *doubtlessly*
486 It is conspiryd to reward thy falsnes.
Thowgh on[e] hath dissaivyd us, yet nowadays
Twenty doyth gladly folow oure layes: *laws*

489 Some by Pride, some thorowgh Envye—
Ther rayneth thorow my might so moch disobediaunce,   *reigns through*
Ther was never among Cristians lesse charité
Than is at this howre—and, as for Concupisence,   *Lechery*
[He] rayneth as a lord thorow my violence.
Glotony and Wrath every man doth devise;
And most now is praisyd my cosyn Covitice.   *Covetousness*

Cum, Mercury, let us go and do as we have said.
To delate it any lenger, it is not best.   *delay*
MERCURY.   To bring it abowg[h]t I wold be wel apaid;   *pleased*
Tell it be done, let us not rest.   *Till*
500 . . . .

BELIAL.   Go we than shortly, let us departe,
His deth to devise, sith he wil not revart.   *since/revert, return*
Here they shal vanishe away with a firye flame and a tempest.

Her[e] apperith Saule in a disciplis wede, say[i]ng [and preaching   *costume*
to the audience]:

SAULUS.   That Lord that is shaper of see and of sond,   *sea/sand, shore*
And hath wrowth with his woord all thing at his will,   *wrought*
Save this semely that here sittith or stonde,   *assembly/sits or stands*
506 For his meke marcy that we do nott spill!
Grant me, good Lord, thy pleasure to fulfill,
508 And send me suche speche that I the tr[e]wth say,
509 My entencions proph[i]table to meve if I may.   *to effect*

Welbelovyd frendes, ther be seven mortall sinnes   *deadly*
Which be provyd principall and princes of poisonnes.   *chief*

484–86It would have been better for you to remain in conformance with our law; for, this sentence of death, doubtlessly, is contrived as punishment for your falseness.

489(This stanza enumerates all the seven Deadly Sins except for Sloth.)

506So that, through his tender mercy, we be not destroyed.

508–9And endow me with such speech that I may tell the truth, in order to carry out my profitable intentions if I can.

512	Pride, that of bitternes all bale beginnes;	*sorrow*
513	With-holding all faith, it fedith and foisonnes—	
514	As Holy Scriptur berith plain wittnesse,	
515	*Initium omnium peccatorum Superbia est—*	
516	That often distroyeth both most and lest;	*least*

Of all vices and foly, Pride is the roote.
Humilité may not rayn ner yet indure;   *reign, prosper/nor*
Pité, alak, that is flower and boot,   *remedy*
Is exilyd wher Pride hath socour.   *has shelter*
521 *Omnis qui se exaltat humiliabitur:*
  Good Lord, gif us grace to understond and persever,
  This wurd, as thou bidist, to fulfill ever.   *you bid*

Whoso in Pride berith him to[o] hye   *bears himself*
With mis[c]heff shal be mekyd, as I mak mension;   *trouble/humbled*
And I therfor assent and fully certify,   *testify*
In text as I tell the tr[e]w entencion
Of perfig[h]t goodnes and very locucion: *perfect/true utterance*
529 *Noli tibi dico in altum sapere, sed time.*   *I say be not proud, but fear*
  This is my consell: bere the[e] not to[o] hye,

But drede alway sinne and folye,
Wrath, Envy, Covitis[e], and Slugishnes.   *Sloth*
Exeunt owt of thy sig[h]t Glotony and Lechery,   *Banish*
Vanitye and Vaineglory and fals Idylnes.
Thes[e] be the branchys of all wickidnes.
Who that in him thes[e] vices do roote,   *Whoso*
He lackith all grace, and bale is the boote.   *sorrow/reward*

"Lern at myself, for I am meke in hart,"   *Learn from*
Owr Lorde to his servantes thus he saith,
540 "For meknes I sufferyd a spere at my hart.   *spear in*
Meknes all vices anullith and delayeth;
Rest to soulys it shall find, in faith."

512–16Pride, that is the root of all bitter sorrow, that feeds and nourishes (sinfulness), restraining and denying all faith, that often destroys persons of both high and low degree—as Holy Scripture plainly reveals, "Pride is the beginning of all sins" (see the apocryphal book of Ecclesiasticus, 10:9–15).

521Everyone who exalts himself will be humbled (Luke 18:14).

529(See Romans 11:20.)

540i.e., To demonstrate humility, I allowed myself to be crucified and killed by a spear in my heart.

543   *Discite a me, quia mitis sum et corde humilis,*
544   *Et invenietis requiem animabus vestris.*

    So owr Saviour shewith us exampls of meknes,
546   Thorow grace of his goodnes mekly us groundys.   *instructs us*
    Tr[e]wly it will us save fro the sinnes sekenes,   *sins' sickness*
    For Pride and his progeny mekenes confoundys.
549   *Quanto major es, tanto humilia te in omnibus:*
    The gretter thou art, the lower loke thu be.
    Bere the[e] never the hyer for thy degré.   *higher because of your rank*

    Fro sensualité of fleshe, thyself loke thou lede;   *lead yourself away*
    Unlefully therin use not thy life.   *Unlawfully*
    Whoso therin deliteth, to deth he must nede;   *delights/he must die*
555   It consumith natur[e], the body sley[i]th withowt knif.
556   Also it stintith nott but manslawter and strif.
557   *Omnis fornicator aut immundus non habet hereditatem Christi:*
    Non[e] shall in hevyn posses that be so unthrifty.   *unchaste*

    Fle fornicac[i]on, nor be no letchour,
    But spare your speche and spek nott theron.   *refrain*
561   *Ex abundantia cordis, os loquitur:*
    Who movith it oft, chastité lovith non.   *Whoever urges it often*
    Of the hartes habundans the tunge makith locucion;   *heart's fulness/tongue speaks*
564   What man[n]ys minde is laboryd, therof it spekith—
    That is of suernes, as Holy Scriptur tretith.   *a certainty/discusses*

    Wherfor I reherse this with min[e] owyn mowthe: *recite*
567   *Caste viventes templum Dei sunt.*
    Kepe clene your body from sinne uncuth;   *unpleasant*
569   Stabill your sightes, and look ye not stunt,   *Steady/stint, desist*

543-44Learn from me, for I am meek and humble in heart, and you will find rest for your souls (Matthew 11:29).

546(And) through grace of his mercy instructs us in meekness.

549By how much you are great, by so much humble yourself in all things (Ecclesiasticus 3:17–20).

555-57It (sensuality) eats up our physical being, and slays the body without using a knife. Also it does not stop until it results in manslaughter and strife. "No fornicator or unclean person has any inheritance in [the kingdom] of Christ" (see Ephesians 5:5).

561The mouth speaks from the fulness of the heart (Matthew 12:34, Luke 6:45).

564Whatever man's mind is concerned with, it will speak of that.

567Those who live purely are the temple of God (see 1 Corinthians 6:18–19).

569Keep your gaze steady (i.e., avoid looking at temptation), and see to it that you persevere in this.

For of a sertainté I know at a brunt,   *at a blow, at once*
Oculus est nuntius peccati: *The eye is the messenger of sin*
That the iey is ever the messenger of foly.   *eye*
    [*An officer of the chief priests, deputized by them to arrest Christian preachers, accosts Saul.*]

SERVUS SACERDOTUM.   Whate, is not this Saule, that toke his vyage
574   Into Jerusalem, the disciplys to oppresse?
Bounde he wold bring them, if ony did rage   *any*
Upon Crist—this was his processe—   *story*
To the princes of prestys; he sayde, dowtles,   *chief priests*
Thorow all Damask and also Jerusalem,   *Through*
Subdue all templys that he founde of them.   *(He would) subdue*

580   SA[U]LUS.   Yes, sertainly, Saule is my proper name,
That had in powr the full dominion—   *Who had full authority*
To hide it fro you, it were gret shame   *it would be*
And mortall sinne, as in my opinion—   *deadly*
Under Cesar and pristes of the religion
And templys of Jues, that be very hedious   *hideous, hateful*
Agains almighty Crist, that king so precious.   *Against*

SERVUS SACERDOTUM.   To Anna and Caipha ye must make your recurse.   *return*
Com on your way, and make no delacion.
SAULUS.   I will yow succede, for better or wors[e],   *follow*
590   To the princes of pristes with all delectacion.   *delight*
    [*The officer leads Saul to the chief priests.*]
SERVUS SACERDOTUM.   Holy pristes of hye potestacion,   *power*
Here is Saule! Lok[e] on him wisely:
He is another man than he was, verely.

SAULUS.   I am the servant of Jhesu almighty,
Creator and maker of see and sonnd,   *sea/sand*
Whiche is king conctipotent of hevyn glory,   *all powerful*
Chef comfort and solace both to fre and bonde,   *bound, enslaved persons*
Agains whos[e] power nothing may stonde.
Emperowr he is both of hevyn and hell,
600   Whoys goodnes and grace al thing doth excell!   *Whose*
    Recedit paulisper.   *He withdraws for a little while*

CAIPHA.   Unto my hart this is gret admiracion,   *wonder*

---

574 *Jerusalem:* Saul went into Damascus; perhaps this confusion of names represents a telescoping of the two cities in the final "station" of this play. See l. 578 below.

That Saule is thus mervelously changyd!
I trow he is bewitchyd by sum conjuracion,
Or els the devill on him is avengyd.
605 Alas, to my hart it is dessendyd,   *descended*
That he is thus takyn fro our religion!
How say ye, Anna, to this convercion?

ANNA.   Full mervelously, as in my concepcion,   *understanding*
This w[o]nderfull case how it befell!   *wondrous*
610 To se this chaunce so sodenly don,
Unto my hart it doth grete ill.
But, for his falsnes we shall him spill;   *destroy*
By min[e] assent, to dethe we will him bring,
Lest that more mischef of him may spring.

CAIPHA.   Ye say very trew; we mig[h]t it all rewe!   *rue, regret*
But shortly in this we must have advisement,   *counsel*
For thus agains us he may nott continew;
618 Peraventur than of Cesar we may be shent.   *disgraced*
ANNA.   Nay, I had lever in fier he were brent   *rather/fire/burned*
Than of Cesar we shuld have disp[l]easure
For sich a rebell and subtile fals treator!

CAIPHA.   We will command the gates to be kept aboute   *guarded roundabout*
And the walles suerly on every stede,   *securely/place*
That he may not eskape nowhere owg[h]te.   *at all*
For die he shall, I ensuer yow indede.   *insure, warrant*
ANNA.   This traitour rebellious, evill mut he spede   *ill may he prosper*
That doth this unhappines agains all! [*To the guards.*]
Now, every costodier kepe well his wall.   *guard*

SERVUS SACERDOTUM.   The gatys be shytt, he cannote skape.   *gates/shut*
630 Every place is kepte well and sure,
That in no wise he may, till he be take,   *taken*
Gett owt of the cité by ony conjecture.   *contrivance*
Upon that caitif and fals traitour
Loke ye be avengyd with deth mortall,   *fatal*
635 And judge him as ye list to what end he shall.

[*An angel appears to Saul.*]
ANGELUS.   Holy Saule, I gif yow monicion: *warning*

605Alas, it sinks to the bottom of my heart.

618For then (i.e., if Saul continued to preach against us) we would be disgraced by Caesar.

635And judge and sentence him to whatever fate he deserves.

The princes of Jues entende, sertain,   *Jews*
To put yow to deth. But by Goddes provision
He will ye shall live lenger, and optain,   *He wills/prosper*
640   And after thy deth thou shalt raing   *reign*
Above in hevyn, with owr Lordes grace.   *with our gracious Lord*
Convay yowrself shortly into another place.   *quickly*

SAULUS.   That Lordes pleasur ever mut be down,   *must be done*
Both in hevyn and in hell, as his will is!
In a bering baskett or a lepe, anon   *a carrying basket or a basket*
I shall me co[n]vay with help of the disciplys,
For every gate is shett and kept with multitud of pepull[ys].   *shut/guarded by*
But I trust in owr Lord, that is my socour,
To resist ther malice and cruell furour.   *furor*

   Conclusio[n]. [*The poet speaks the epilogue.*]
POETA.   Thus leve we Saule within the cité,   *leave*
The gates kep by commandment of Caipha and Anna;
But the disciplys in the nig[h]t over the wall, truly,
653   As the Bibull sayeth, *dim[i]serunt eum summitten[te]s in sporta;*
And Saule after that, in Jerusalem, vera,   *truly*
Joined himself and ther accompenied
With the disciplys, wher they were unfained.   *unconcealed*

This litill pagent thus conclud we
As we can, lacking litturall sciens;   *literary skill*
Beseching yow all, of hye and low degré,
Owr simpilnes to hold excusyd, and licens,   *tolerate*
That of retorik have non[e] intelligens;
Committing yow all to owr Lord Jhesus,
663   To whoys lawd ye sing: *Exultet caelum laudibus!*
   Finis Co[n]vertionis Sancti Pauli.   *Here ends the Conversion of Saint Paul*

653As the Bible says, "They sent him forth, letting him down in a basket" (see Acts 9:25).

663In whose praise sing "Heaven will rejoice with praises."

MARY MAGDALENE
FROM THE DIGBY MS

Although written in honor of a saint, Mary Magdalene, this long play aims at the panoramic inclusiveness of a Corpus Christi cycle. Its first scenes present a version of Christ's ministry, death, and resurrection, seen through the eyes of Mary as a central participant in those events. Subsequently, the story is a romance of travel, adventure, and miraculous occurrence, in the style of many saints' lives from the *Legenda aurea*. Throughout it is a play about the recovery of sinners and the conversion of the heathen. Frequently divided by editors into two parts, the text in fact gives no justification for such a practice and provides no clear point of demarcation. The play is best considered as a thematic and dramaturgic whole comprised of numerous episodes.

Medieval patristic writers were evidently fascinated by the story of a fallen woman transformed into a saint. The authors of the *Legenda aurea (Golden Legend)* constructed an elaborate biography for Mary, beginning with scriptural narrative and then filling in with various legendary accounts. Even in their use of the Scriptures, exegetical writers took some liberties. They had to piece together a composite biography from various biblical references to women who may or may not be Mary Magdalene. One such woman is Mary of Bethany, sister of Martha and of Lazarus whom Jesus raised from the dead (John 11). Jesus had visited Mary and Martha on a previous occasion, and had praised Mary for her attentiveness to his teaching (Luke 10:38–42). This same Mary, in the house of Simon the Leper at Bethany, anointed Jesus' feet with a costly ointment and wiped his feet with her hair, prompting Judas Iscariot to protest the waste of money that might have been spent on the poor (John 12; the account in Matthew 26 varies somewhat). A woman named Mary Magdalene stood by the cross with Jesus' mother (John 19:25), appeared at Christ's empty tomb on Easter morn with two other women to anoint his body, told the disciples what she and the women had seen, and later mistook the risen Christ for a gardener. Whether this Mary Magdalene is Lazarus' sister is not stated; but Mark does report (16:9) that Jesus had previously cast out seven demons from Mary Magdalene. This crucial evidence of Mary's spiritual turmoil seemed to point to an event in the house of Simon the Pharisee (Luke 7:36–50) in which an unnamed sinful woman washed Christ's feet with her tears and hair, anointed them with ointment, and was forgiven her sins. Perhaps because of the recurring name "Simon," this event was assumed to be identical with that in Simon the Leper's house at Bethany, involving Mary the sister of Lazarus. If all these Marys could be assumed to be the same, an extensive biography could be adduced.

Legendary stories added many more details, such as the name of Mary's father (Cyrus) and of his castle (Magdalen), the extent of his wealth, and the colorful circumstances of Mary's fall from virtue. Although the biblical scenes in this play are treated with some circumspection, the subsequent narrative of Mary's saintly travels gives free rein to the imagination. The long episode of the king and queen of Marseilles serves to demonstrate the miraculous power of Mary Magdalene's grace, and also to satisfy a romantic craving for perilous adventure involving children and women abandoned in mid-ocean, and the like. Ship captains appear, raising and lowering their sails and arguing with saucy cabin boys. A comic pagan priest and his assistant expose the folly of Mohammed's pretensions to divine power. Mary Magdalene's temptation in the wilderness and her ascension into heaven are patently modeled on those of Christ. The time lapses—such as the king of Marseilles' two years in Jerusalem visiting shrines, or Mary's thirty years in the wilderness—add to the vast, inclusive dimensions of this cosmic account.

Particularly cosmic is the juxtaposition of human drama and allegory. On the one hand, the large cast of characters includes a number of historical or legendary enemies of Christianity, such as Tiberius Caesar, Herod, Pilate, and the king of Marseilles. Mary's story also introduces us to members of her family, to sailors, tavern keepers, and so on. On the other hand, the towers of heaven and hell are visible throughout the action, attesting to the presence of a vast spiritual domain. A good angel and an evil angel alternatively offer Mary virtuous counsel and vicious enticement. World, Flesh, and Devil, together with their lieutenants the seven Deadly Sins, prevail upon Mary to enter into a life of sin. Mary Magdalene dwells simultaneously, then, in a world of human narrative and of spiritual abstraction. She takes part in the events of the Crucifixion and the Resurrection; yet at the same time, in alternating scenes, her inner story is presented allegorically by the seven Deadly Sins. Her soul-struggle is that of the typical morality play (see Part v). Indeed, this play about her bears important affinities to the morality in staging as well as in characterization.

The accompanying conjectural diagram of the staging in *Mary Magdalene* puts Mary's castle at the center, as in *The Castle of Perseverance* (see Part v). Although this arrangement is conjectural, we should note that her residence is referred to as a castle or tower and that it is besieged by the Deadly Sins, who marshal their forces on various scaffolds as in *Perseverance*. The scaffolds representing heaven and hell, periodically employed thoughout the play, would probably be located in the east and north respectively as in the diagrams for *Perseverance* and for the Cornish *Ordinalia*. Heaven must be a tower capable of opening to reveal Christ in glory, of sending down a cloud to set on fire the pagan Temple of Marseilles (l. 1562 S.D.), of dispatching angels to Mary, and of raising her up to feed on manna to the accompaniment of angelic song. Hell is a tower also, with hell-mouth underneath a stage (l. 357 S.D.) which is apparently set on fire at one point (l. 743 S.D.). World refers to a "tent" (l. 386) on his scaffold, and invites visitors to come up to him from the "place" or central acting area. Simon the Leper's stage is called a "house." The king of Marseilles' stage includes a bed. Perhaps some scaffolds doubled in two capacities; the seven Deadly Sins, for example, need their scaffolds for only one extended sequence relatively early in the play.

The "place" is incessantly alive with activity, such as messengers' errands and actual ship voyages (in a mobile pageant, with simulation of sailing and rowing) across the central space. Actions occur simultaneously:

Possible staging design for *Mary Magdalene*

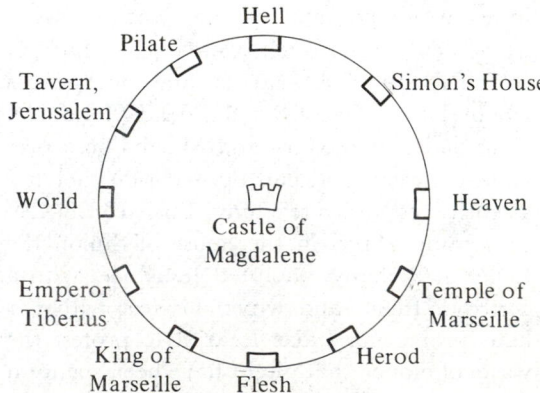

for example, Mary sleeps in her arbor while Simon invites Christ to his banquet, and later the king and queen of Marseilles enjoy a feast while a devil bemoans the harrowing of hell. The central area must find room, at various times, for Mary's arbor, Lazarus' tomb, Christ's tomb, Jerusalem, Mary's lodge or hut near Marseilles, a rock in mid-ocean, a mountain or cliff where the mariners land, Mary's wilderness, a priest's cell, and a baptismal font.

The verse stanza is too irregular to make stanzaic division possible. The language, from the East Midlands in the later fifteenth century, is at times heavily Latinate or "Aureate"; see, for example, ll. 950–57.

Mary Magdalene
From the Digby MS

[DRAMATIS PERSONAE

CYRUS, lord of Magdalen Castle
LAZARUS, his son
MARY MAGDALENE, his daughter
MARTHA, another daughter of Cyrus
INPERATOR, Tiberius Caesar, Emperor of Rome
   SERYBYL or Serybb, his scribe
   PROVOST, under Tiberius
   MESSENGER of Tiberius
HEROD, ruler over Jerusalem
   2 PHILOSOPHERS in his court
   2 SOLDIERS serving Herod
PILATE, Judge in Jerusalem
   2 SERGEANTS serving him
   MESSENGER of Pilate
WORLD
   PRIDE
   COVETEISE
FLESH
   SLOTH
   GLUTTONY
   LECHERY
DEVIL

WRATH
ENVY
MESSENGER, Sensuality
BAD ANGEL
GOOD ANGEL
SATAN
A SECOND DEVIL
A TAVERNER in Jerusalem
CURIOSITY, or Pride, a gallant
SIMON THE LEPER
JESUS CHRIST
PETER
JOHN
THE OTHER DISCIPLES, unnamed
RAPHAEL, an angel
2 ANGELS
MARY JACOB
MARY SALOME
THE KING OF MARSEILLES
THE QUEEN OF MARSEILLES
KNIGHTS attending the king
PRESBYTER, a heathen priest
HIS BOY

MASTER of the ship, or Nauta   THE PRIEST in the wilderness

HIS BOY, named Grobbe   SOLDIERS, CROWDS, etc.]

MARY'S DISCIPLE

[*The stage of the Emperor Tiberius Caesar, Rome. The
emperor, serybyl, provost, others.*]   *scribe*

1   INPERATOR.   I command silyns, in the peyn of forfetur,   *on pain, penalty*
         To all min[e] audiens present general!   *To everyone here, generally*
         Of my most hyest and mytiest volunté,   *mightiest will*
         I woll it be knowyn to al the wor[l]d universal   *I desire*
         That of heven and hell chyff rewlar am I,   *chief ruler*
         To w[h]os[e] magnificens non[e] stondit[h] egall.   *no one is equal*
7   For I am soveren of al soverens subjugal   *subject*
8   Onto min[e] empere, being incomparable
         Tiberius Sesar, w[h]os[e] power is potenciall.   *potent*
         I am the blod ryall most of soverenté.   *royal stock*
         Of all emperowrs and kinges my birth is best,
         And all regeouns obey my myty volunté.
         Life and lem and goodes, all be at my request.   *limb*
         So of all soverens, my magnificens most mytiest
         May nat be a-gainsaid of frend nor of foo,   *denied by*
         But all abidyn jugment and rewle of my list.   *submit to/at my pleasure*
         All grace upon erth from my goodnes commit[h] fro,   *from*
         And that bringis all pepell in blisse so.
         For the most worthiest, woll I rest in my sete.   *As*
         [*He seats himself in his throne.*]
20   SERYBYL.   Sir, from your person growit[h] moch grace.   *Scribe*
     INPERATOR.   Now for thin[e] answer, Beliall blysse thy face!
         Mikyl prosperité I gin to porchase;   *Much/begin to acquire*
         I am wonddyn in welth from all woo.   *wound, wrapped*
         Herke thou, provost, I giff the[e] in commandment,   *I command you*
         All your pepull preserve in pesabyl possess[i]on!   *peaceable*
         Iff ony ther be to my goddes [dis]obedient,
         Dissever tho harlottes, and make to me declaracion,   *Separate out those rascals*
         And I shall make all swich to die—   *such*
         Thos[e] precharsse of Cristys incarnacion.   *preachers*
30   PROVOST.   Lord of all lorddes, I shall giff yow informacion.
         [*Exit provost.*]

¹S.D. *serybyl:* Seemingly means "scribe"; see l. 114, where the scribe is referred to as one of
the judges of the emperor's realm.

⁷⁻⁸For I am sovereign over all (other) sovereigns, (who are) subject to my empire, I who am
the incomparable.

INPERATOR.   Lo, how all the wor[l]d obeyit[h] my
    dominacion!
  That person is nat born that dare me disse-obey.
  Syrybbe, I warne yow se that my lawys
  In all your partyis have dew obeisauns.   *parts, regions*
  Inquere and aske, eche day that dawnnes;
  If in my pepul be found ony veriouns,   *variance, inconstancy*
  Contrary to me in ony chansse,   *any circumstance*
  Or with my goldyn goddes grocch or grone,   *grumble*
  I woll marre swich harlottes with mordor and mischanse!   *such/murder*
40   Iff ony swiche remain, put hem in repreffe,   *them in reproof*
  And I shall yow releff.   *assist*
SERYBB.   It shall be don, lord, withowtyn ony lett or withowt   *hindrance*
    dowte.
      [Exit Serybyl.]

INPERATOR.   Lord and lad to my law doth lowte;   *i.e., everyone/bow*
  Is it nat so? Sey yow all with on[e] showte.
    Here answerrit[h] all the pepul at ons[e], "Ya, my lord, ya."
45 INPERATOR.   So, ye froward folkes, now am [I] plesyd.
  Sett win[e] and spicys to my consell full cler.   *for my council*
  Now have I told yow my hart, I am wyll plesyd;
  Now lett us sett do[w]n alle, and make good chyr.   *cheer*
    [They seat themselves to a banquet.]

    [The Castle of Magdalen, Bethany. Cyrus with his children,
    Mary, Martha, Lazarus; and others.]
    Her[e] entyr Syrus, the fader of Mary Maudleyn.

SYRUS.   Emperor, and ki[n]gges, and conquerors kene,
50   Erlys, and barons, and knytes that byn bold,   *Earls/knights/be*
  Berdes in my bower, so semely to sene,   *Maidens/see*
  I commau[n]d yow at onys my hestes to hold.   *to keep my commandments*
  Behold my person, glistering in gold,
  Semely besyn of all other men!   *be-seen, seen by*
55   Cyrus is my name. By cleffys so cold,   *cliffs(?)*
  I command yow all obedient to beyn;   *be*
  W[h]oso woll nat, in bale I hem bring,   *I'll bring them into misfortune*
  And knett swiche caitifys in knottes of care.   *entangle such caitiffs*
  This castell of Maudleyn is at my wyldding,   *wielding, rule*
60   With all the contré, bothe lesse and more,

45So, now am I pleased with you, my obstinate subjects. (The emperor's suspiciousness reveals
his tyrannical nature.)

55*By cleffys so cold:* an alliterative oath, of uncertain meaning.

And Lord of Jherusalem. Who agens me don dare?   *Who dare act against me*

Alle Beteny at my bedding be.   *Bethany/bidding*

I am sett in solas from al sying sore;   *secure in solace/sighing*

And so shall all my posterité,

Thus for to leven in rest and ryalté.   *live/royalty*

I have her[e] a sone that is to me ful trew   *son*

(No comliar creatur of Goddes creacion),

T[w]o amiabyll douctors full brigth of blé,   *daughters/bright of countenance*

Ful glorios to my syth, an[d] ful of delectacion;   *sight*

70   Lazarus my son, in my resspeccion;   *regard*

Here is Mary, ful fair, and ful of feminité;

And Martha, ful [of] beuté and of delicité,   *beauty/delight*

Ful of womanly merrorys and of benignité.   *graces*

They have fulfillyd my hart with consolacion.   *completely filled*

75   Here is a coleccion of circumstance,

76   To my cognisshon never swich anothyr,   *cognition, knowledge*

77   As be demonstracion knett in continens,

78   Save alonly my lady, that was ther mother.—   *Excepting only*

Now, Lazarus, my sonne, whech art ther brothyr,   *who is their*

The lordshep of Jherusalem I giff the[e] after my dysses; *decease*

And Mary, this castell alonly, an[d] non othyr;

And Martha shall have Beteny, I sey exprese.   *expressly, clearly*

Thes[e] giftes I graunt yow withowtyn les   *without lie, in truth*

Whill that I am in good mind.   *of sound mind*

LAZARUS.   Most reverent father, I thank yow hartely

Of yowr grett kindnes shuyd onto me!   *showed to*

Ye have grauntyd swich a lifelod, worthy   *such a source of livelihood*

Me to restreyn from all nessesité.   *relieve*

Now, good Lord and his will it be,   *if it please God*

Graunt me grace to live to thy plesawns   *according to your pleasure*

91   And agens hem so to rewle me

Thatt we may have joye withowtyn veriauns.

93   MARY MAU[DLEYN].   Thatt God of pes and principall *peace*
                           counsell,

94   More swetter is thy name than hony by kind!   *sweeter/nature*

We thank yow, fathyr, for your giftes ryall,

Owt of peynes of poverté us to onbind.   *pains/unbind, free*

This is a preservatiff from streitnes, we find,   *hardship*

From wor[l]dly labors to my coumforting;   *to comfort me*

75-78 Here's a state of affairs revealing constancy bound together by mutual affection; I never knew any other such (paragons of virtue), except my wife, who was their mother(?).

91 And govern myself so in accord with your wishes(?).

93-94 You who are God of peace, and our chief guide, sweeter is your name than is honey by its natural sweetness!

99	For this lifflod is abyll for the dowtter of a king—	*livelihood/fit/daughter*
100	This place of plesauns, the soth to seye.	
	MARTHA. O ye good fathyr of grete degré,	*of noble estate*
	Thus to departe with your riches,	*part with*
	Consedering owr lowlines and humilité,	*and low estate*
	Us to save from wor[l]dly dessetres:	*distress*
	Ye shew us pointes of grete jentylnes,	*instances*
106	So mekly to meyntyn us to your grace.	*maintain, provide for*
	Hey in heven avansyd mot yow be	*High/advanced may*
	In blisse, to se that Lordes face,	
	Whan ye shal hens passe!	*hence*
	CYRUS. Now I rejoise with all my migthtes!	
	To enhanse my childryn, it was my delite.	*advance*
	Now win[e] and spicys, ye jentyll knyttes,	
	Onto thes[e] ladys of jentylnes.	
	Here shal they be servyd with win[e] and spicys.	

[*The stage of the Emperor.*]

	INPERATOR. Sir provost, and skribe, jugges of my rem,	*realm*
	My massenger I woll send into ferre cuntré,	
	Onto my seté of Jherusalem,	*city*
	Onto Herowdes, that regent ther ondyr me,	*under*
	And onto Pilat, jugges of the countré.	
	Min[e] entent I woll hem teche.	*them*
120	Take hed[e], thou provost, my precept wretyn be,	*written*
121	And sey I cummaund hem, as they woll be owit wrech,	*owed harm*
122	If ther be ony in the cuntré ageyn my law doth prech,	*(who) against*
	Or ageyn my goddes ony trobyll telles,	*speak any mischief*
	That thus agens my lawys rebelles—	
	As he is regent, and in that reme dwelles	*realm*
	And holdith his croun of me by ryth—	*right*
	Iff ther be ony harlettes that agens me make replicacion,	*rascals/remonstrate*
	Or ony motering agens me make with malinacion.	*muttering/ill will*
	PROVOST. Sir, of all this they shall have informacion,	
130	So to uphold yowr renoun and ryte.	*right*
	[INPERATOR.] Now, massenger, withowtyn tarying,	
	Have here gold onto thy fe.	*as your reward*
	So bere thes[e] lettyrs to Herowdes the king,	

99–100For this source of livelihood, this pleasant place (the castle of Magdalen), is fit for the daughter of a king, to tell the truth.

106So obligingly to provide for us with your bounty.

120–22See to it, provost, that my precept be written down, and say I command them (Herod and Pilate), on pain of punishment, (to inform me) if there be any in their countries who preach against my laws.

And bid hem make inquirans in every cuntré
135   As he is jugge in that cuntré being.
    NUNTIUS.   Soveren, your arend it shall be don ful redy   *errand*
In alle the hast that I may;
For to fullfill your bidding
I woll nat spare, nother by nyth nor by day.   *night*
    Here goth the masenger toward Herowdes.

    [*The stage of Herod, Jerusalem. Herod, philosophers, soldiers, and others.*]

140   HEROWDES.   In the wild waning wor[l]d, pes all at onys!
No noise, I warne yow, for greveing of me!   *lest you grieve me*
Iff yow do, I shal hourle of[f] yowr hedes, by Mahondes   *hurl/Mohammed's*
      bones,
As I am trew king to Mahond so fre.   *noble*
Help, help, that I had a swerd!
Fall do[w]n, ye faitours, flatt to the ground!   *scoundrels*
Heve of[f] your hodes and hattes, I cummaund yow alle: *Heave off, remove/hoods*
Stond bare-hed, ye beggars! W[h]o made yow so bold?
I shal make yow know your king ryall!   *royal*
Thus woll I be obeyid thorow al the wor[l]d;
And whoso wol nat, he shal be had in hold,   *taken in custody*
And so to be cast in carys cold,   *thrown into miserable suffering*
152   That werkyn ony wondyr agens my magnificens.
Behold these riche rubyis, red as ony fyr,   *any fire*
With the goodly grene perle ful sett abowgth!   *set about, bordered*
What king is worthy or egall to my power?   *equal*
Or, in this wor[l]d, who is more had in dowt   *held in fear*
Than is the hey name of Herowdes, King of Jherusalem,   *high, exalted*
Lord of Alapye, Assye, and Tyr,   *Aleppo/Asia/Tyre*
Of Abyron, Bergaby, and Bedlem?   *Hebron/Beersheba/Bethlehem*
All thes[e] bin ondyr my governouns.   *are under*
Lo, all thes[e] I hold withowtyn reprobacion.   *reproof*
No man is to me egall, save alonly the emperowr
163   Tiberius, as I have in provosticacion.   *regency*
How sey ye, philyssoverys, by my riche reyne?   *philosophers/reign*
Am nat I the grettest governowr?
Lett me ondyrstond whatt can ye seyn.
    PHELISOFYR.   Soveren, and it plece yow, I woll expresse: *if it please*

135In his capacity as judge of that country.

140i.e., With a curse on you, be silent immediately!

152Any who perform any miracles or witchcraft against me in my magnificence.

163i.e., Tiberius, from whom I hold the authority of regent in my kingdom.

Ye be the rewlar of this region,
And most worthy sovereyn of nobilnes
170   That ever in Judé barre dominacion.   *Judaea bore, held*
Bott, sir, Skreptour gevitt[h] informacion,   *Scripture*
And doth rehersse it verely,
That child shal remain of grete renoun,   *dwell*
And all the wor[l]d of hem shold magnify: *will extol him*
175   *Et ambulabunt gentes in lumine [tuo],*
176   *Et reges in splendore ortus tui.*
HEROWDES.   And whatt seyst thow?
178   2 PHI[LOSOFYR].   The same verifyit[h] my bok; as how,
179   As the Skriptour doth me tell,
180   Of a myty duke shal rese and reyn,   *rise*
Which shall reyn and rewle all Israell;   *Who*
No king agens his worthines shall opteyn.   *against/prevail*
183   The whech in profesy hath grett eloquence: *prophecy*
184   *Non auferetur sceptrum [de] Juda, et dux de femore eius,*
185   *Donec veniat qui mittendus est.*
HEROWDES.   A, owt, owt! now am [I] grevyd all with the
          worst!   *exceedingly grieved*
Ye dastardes! ye dogges! the dilfe mote yow draw!   *may the devil tear you apart*
188   With fleying flappes I bid yow to a fest.   *flaying blows*
189   A swerd, a swerd! Thes[e] lordeynnes wer slaw!   *louts/slain*
190   Ye langbainnes, loselles! forsake ye that word!   *scoundrels*
191   That caitiff shall be cawth, and suer I shall hem flaw;   *caught/surely/flay*
192   For him, many mo shal be marry with mordor.   *more/marred*
1 MILES.   My sovereyn lord, dissemay yow ryth nowt.   *dismay yourself not at all*
194   They ar but folys, ther eloquens wanting,   *fools/lacking*
For in sorow and care sone they shall be cawt.   *caught*
Agens us they can mak[e] no disstondding.   *Against/withstanding*
2 MILES.   My lord, all swich shall be browte before your   *such*
          audiens,   *presence*
And levyn ondyr your dominacion,   *live, dwell*

[175-76] And the nations will walk in your light, and kings in the brightness of your rising (Isaiah 60:3, a text for Epiphany, January 6).

[178-80] My book (of Scripture) verifies this same fact: to wit, how, according to the Scriptures, a mighty duke will arise and reign.

[183-85] The which truth is very eloquent as expressed in the prophecy (of Genesis 49:10): The sceptre will not be withdrawn from Judaea, nor a leader from her loins (lit: her thighs), until he comes who is to be sent.

[188-92] I bid you to a feast of flaying blows. A sword, a sword! Would these louts were slain! You longbones, scoundrels! Take back that prophecy (of Christ's coming)! That caitiff (Christ) will be caught, and surely I'll flay them (his followers); on Christ's account many others will be murdered.

[194] They (prophets of and believers in Christ) are only fools, lacking in eloquence (i.e., not knowing what they say).

Or elles dammyd to deth with mortal sentense,   *deadly*

If we hem gett onder owr gubernacion.   *them/governance*

HEROWDES.   Now this is to me a gracious exsortacion,   *speech*

And grettly rejoisith to my sprites indede!

Thow[gh] thes[e] sottes agens me make replicacion,   *remonstrance*

204   I woll suffer non[e] to spring of that kenred.   *kindred*

Some woth in my lond shall sprede,   *harm, injury*

Prevely or pertely in my lond abowth.   *Secretly or openly/round about*

207   While I have swich men, I nede nat to drede

208   But that he shal be browt onder, withowtyn do[w]th.

Her[e] commit[h] the emperowrs [masenger,] thus saying to Herowdes:

MASENGER.   Heyll, prinse of bountiowsnesse!

Heyll, myty lord of to magnify!   *worthy of praise*

Heyll, most of worchep of to expresse!   *of honor worthy to be expressed*

Heyll, reytius rewlar in thy regensy!   *righteous ruler*

My sofereyn, Tiberius, chyff of chifalry,   *chief*

His soveren sond hath sent to yow here: *message*

He desirth yow, and preyit[h] on eche party   *desires/in every particular*

To fulfill his commaundment and desire.

Here he shall take the lettyrs onto the king.   *deliver*

HERAWDES.   Be he sekyr I woll natt spare   *sure/refrain*

For [to] complishe his cummaunddment,

With sharp swerddes to perce the bare,   *pierce bare skin, flesh*

220   In all countres within this regent   *region*

For his love, to fulfill his intentt.

Non swich shall from owr handys stertt,   *such/break away*

For we woll fulfill his ryall juggement,

With swerd and spere to perce thorow the hartt.

But, masenger, reseive this letter wyth,   *quickly*

And beritt[h] onto Pilattys syth.   *bear it/sight*

MESENGER.   My lord, it shall be don ful wygth.   *swiftly*

In hast I woll me spede. [*He starts for Pilate's scaffold.*]

[*The stage of Pilate, Jerusalem. Pilate, attendants.*]

PILATT.   Now ryally I reyne in robys of rich[e]sse,   *royally I reign*

230   Kyd and knowyn both ny and ferre   *Known/nigh*

For juge of Jherusalem—the trewth to expresse—   *As judge*

Ondyr the emperowr Tiberius Cesar.

Therfor I rede yow all, bewarre   *warn*

---

²⁰⁴I will allow none of that tribe to flourish.

²⁰⁷⁻⁸While I have such men, I needn't doubt that he (Christ) will be subdued, certainly.

Ye do no pregedise agen the law;   *prejudice, violence against*

For, and ye do, I will yow natt spare   *if*

Til ye have jugment to be hangyd and draw.   *eviscerated*

237   For I am Pilat, pr[o]mmissary and ser pres[i]dent.

238   Alle renogat robber inperrowpent

239   To put hem to peyn, I spare for no peté.   *them/pain/pity*

My serjauntes semlé, quat sye ye?   *seemly/what say ye*

Of this rehersyd, I will natt spare.   *aforesaid/relent*

Plesauntly, serrys, aunswer to me,   *sirs*

For in my herte I shall have the lesse care.   *sorrow*

1 SERJUNT.   As ye have seyd, I hold it for the best,   *consider it*

If ony swich among us may we know.   *such*

2 SERJAWNT.   For to giff hem jugment I holdd it best;   *give them*

And so shall ye be dred of hye and low.   *dreaded by all*

PILAT.   A! now I am restoryd to felicité.

   Her[e] comit[h] the emprores masenger to Pilat.

MASENGER.   Heyll, ryall in rem, in robis of richesse!   *royal in realm*

250   Heyl, present thou prinsys pere!   *here/princes' peer*

Heyl, jugge of Jherusalem, the trewth to expresse!

Tiberius, the emprowr, sendit[h] writing here,

And prayit[h] yow, as yow be his lover dere,   *friend*

Of this writing to take avisement

In strenthing of his lawys cleyr,

256   As he hath set yow in the state of jugment.   *seat*

   Her[e] Pilat takit[h] the lettyrs with grete reverens.

PILAT.   Now, by Martes so mythy, I shal sett many a snare,   *Mars so mighty*

His lawys to strenth in al that I may.   *strengthen*

I rejoise of his renown and of his wylfare;   *rejoice in*

And for thy tidingges, I geyff the[e] this gold today.

   [*Gives gold.*]

261   MASENGER.   A largeys, ye lord, I crye this day!

For this is a geft of grete degré.   *large amount*

PILAT.   Masenger, onto my sovereyn thou sey,

264   On the most speciall wise [I] recummend me.

   Her[e] avoidit[h] the masengyr; and Syrus takit[h] his deth.   *goes out*

[*The Stage of the Castle of Magdalen, Bethany.*]

237–39For I am Pilate, chief representative (of Roman authority) and appointed governor. I do not refrain, out of a sense of pity, from putting to torture all renegade impenitent robbers. ("Inperrowpent" is obscure.)

256Inasmuch as he has placed you in the seat of judgment.

261*largeys:* largess (an expression either calling for money or expressing gratitude for a gift, addressed to an important donor).

264I commend myself (to his service) in the most particular way.

SYRUS.   A, help, help! I stond in drede!

266   Siknes is sett onder my side!

A, help! deth will aquite me my mede!   *pay me my reward*

A, gret God, thou be my g[u]ide!

How I am trobillyd both bak and side!

Now wythly help me to my bede.   *quickly/bed*

A, this rendit[h] my ribbys! I shall never goo nor ride.   *tears apart my ribs*

The dent of deth is heviar than led.   *dint, blow/lead*

A, Lord, Lord, what shal I doo this tide?   *time*

A, graciows God, have ruth on me,   *pity*

In this wor[l]d no lengar to abide.

I blis yow, my childyrn, God mot with us be!   *may God be with us*

   Her[e] avoidit[h] Syrus sodenly, and than saying Lazarus: *goes out*

[LAZARUS.]   Alas, I am sett in grete hevinesse!   *put*

Ther is no tong my sorow may tell,   *No tongue can relate my sorrow*

So sore I am browth in distresse.   *brought into*

280   In feyntnes I falter for [th]is fray fell;   *cruel conflict*

This dewresse wil lett me no longar dwelle,   *duress/live*

But God of grace sone me redresse.   *Unless/soon aids me*

A, how my peynes don me repelle!   *pains attack me*

Lord, withstond this duresse!   *repel*

MARY MAG[D]LEYN.   The in-wittissimus God, that ever shal   *infinite, all-knowing*
      reyne,

Be his help an[d] sowlys sokor!   *soul's succour*

To whom it is most nedfull to cumplain,

He to bri[n]g us owt of owr dolor.   *That He (God) may*

He is most mytiest governowre,   *ruler*

From soro[w]ing us to restr[a]ine.   *Able to relieve our sorrow*

MARTHA.   A, how I am sett in sorowys sad,

That long my life may nat indeure!   *last*

Thes[e] gravous peynes make me ner mad!   *grievous pains/nearly*

294   Undyr clover is now my fathyris cure,   *(He) who once*

That sumtime was here ful mery and glad.

Owr Lordes mercy be his mesure,   *reward*

And defeynd him from peynes sad!

LAZARUS.   Now, sistyrs, owr fatherys will we woll exprese: *father's last will*

This castell is owrys, with all the fee.   *ours/property, wealth*

300   MARTHA.   As hed and governowr, as reson is,

²⁶⁶Sickness has set in, within my body!

²⁹⁴My father's sorrows now lie buried under clover.

³⁰⁰i.e., Reason dictates that you must be our ruler and governor.

And on this wise abidyn with yow will wee.   *in this manner*
We will natt desevyr, whattso befalle.   *disseven, separate*
MARY.   Now, brothyr and sistyrs, welcum ye be.
304   And therof specially I pray yow all.

*Her[e] shal entyr [on their respective stages] the King of the
Wor[l]d, the Flesch, and the Dylfe, with the Seven Dedly Sinnes,*   *Devil*
a Bad Angyll an[d] an Good Angyl, thus seying the Wor[l]d:

[The stage of the World. The World, Pride, and Covetousness.]

[WORLD.]   I am the Wor[l]d, worthiest that evyr God
           wrowth!   *wrought*
306   And also I am the primatt portature   *chief supporter*
      Next heveyn, if the trewth be sowth—   *sought*
      And that I jugge me to Skriptur—   *I appeal my case*
      And I am he that lengest shal induere,   *endure*
      And also most of dominacion.
311   If I be his foo, w[h]oo is abyll to recure?   *recover, prosper*
      For the whele of fortune with me hath sett his senture. *center*
      In me restit[h] the ordor of the metelles sevyn,
      The which to the seven planyttes ar knett ful sure: *planets/knit, tied*
      Gold perteyning to the sonne, as astronomere nevyn: *astronomers declare*
      Silvyr, to the mone, white and pure;
      Iryn, onto the Maris, that long may endure;   *Mars*
      The segetyff mercury, onto Mercurius;   *fugitive*
      Copyr, onto Venus red in his merrour;   *reflection, shining (?)*
320   The frangabyll tin, to Jubiter, if ye can discus;   *breakable*
      On this planyt Saturne, ful of rancure,
      This soft metell led, nat of so gret puernesse.   *lead/pureness*
      Lo, alle this rich tresor with the Wor[l]d doth indure—
      The seven prinsys of hell of gret bowntosnesse.
      Now, who may presume to com to my honour?   *approach, rival*
PRIDE.   Ye worthy Wor[l]d, ye be gronddar of gladnesse   *grounder, establisher*
      To them that [be] dwelling ondyr yowr dominacion.

304And I pray you especially be welcome. s.d.: Evidently all the seven Deadly Sins are ready
on the three scaffolds of World, Flesh, and Devil at this time, even though the s.d. at ll. 333
and 357 indicate that their actual entrances come in succession. This arrangement is common
on multiple simultaneously-visible stages.

306*primatt portature*: i.e., World boasts that, next to heaven, his is the chief realm of the universe
and supporter of life.

311Who is able to prosper if I am his foe?

320*if . . . discus*: i.e., if you can examine this matter, determine the truth.

328	COVETISE. And whoso wol nat, he is sone set aside	
329	Wheras I, Covetise, take ministracion.	
330	WORLD. Of that I pray yow make no declaracion;	
	Make swich to know my soverreinté,	*Cause (any) such*
	And than they shal be fain to make supplicacion	*glad*
	If that they stond in ony nesessité.	

[*The Stage of the Flesh.*]
Her[e] shal entyr the King of Flesch with Slowth, Gloteny, Lechery.

	FLESCH. I, King of Flesch, florichyd in my flowers,	*adorned with*
	Of deintys deliciows I have grett dominacion.	*dainties*
	So ryal a king was nevyr borne in bowrys,	*in bowers (i.e., anywhere)*
	Nor hath more delith ne more delectacion.	*delight*
338	For I have comfortativys to my comfortacion:	*cordials, restoratives*
339	Dia-galonga, ambra, and also margaretton—	
340	Alle this is at my list agens alle vexacion.	*pleasure*
	Alle wikkyt thinges I woll sett aside.	*noxious*
342	Clary, pepur long, with granorum paradisy,	*Ginger and cinnamon*
343	Gengibyr and synamom at every tide—	*such dainties*
	Lo, alle swich deintyis delicius use I.	
	With swiche deintyis I have my blisse.	
346	Who woll covett more game and gle	
347	My fayere spowse Lechery to halse and kisse?	*fair/embrace*
	Here is my knyth Gloteny, as good reson is,	*knight*
	With this plesaunt lady to rest by my side.	
350	Here is Slowth, anothyr goodly of to expresse.	
	A more plesaunt compeny doth nowher abide.	
	LECHERY. O ye prinse, how I am ful of ardent love,	
	With sparkylles ful of amerowsnesse!	
	With yow to rest fain wold I aprove,	*grant*
	To shew plesauns to your jentylnesse.	*pleasure*
	THE FLESCH. O ye bewtews bird, I must yow kisse!	
	I am ful of lost to halse yow this tide.	*lust/embrace/time*

328–30And whoever refuses (to be under the World's domination) will receive no preferment wherever I, Covetousness, am in authority. —Don't speak of that, I pray you (i.e., Don't even mention such a possibility).

338–40For I have restoratives to comfort me: remedies made chiefly from galingale (a root), from ambergris and also from pearls—all this is available at my pleasure to remedy all distress.

342–43Clary (a plant used as eye medicine), long pepper, with grains of paradise (a spice), ginger and cinnamon on every occasion.

346–47Who would like to have more mirth and delight by embracing my fair wife Lechery?

350Here is Sloth, another goodly (companion) to speak of.

[*The Stage of the Devil.*]
Here shal entyr the Prinse of Dylles in a stage [accompanied by   Devils
Wrath and Envy], and helle ondyrneth that stage, thus seying the
Dylfe:

358 [SATAN.] Now I, prinse pirked, prikkyd in pride,   *attired*
359   Satan, [y]owr sovereyn, set with every circumstanse,
   For I am atired in my tower to tempt yow this tide.   *fitted out*
   As a king ryall I sette at my plesauns,   *sit/pleasure*
   With Wroth [and] Invy at my ryall retinawns.   *in my royal retinue*
363   The bolddest in bower I bring to abaye,
364   Mannis sowle to besegyn and bring to obeisauns.
   Ya, [with] tide and time I do that I may,   *what I can*
366   For at hem I have disspite that he shold have the joye   *at him (i.e., mankind)*
367   That Lycifer, with many a legiown, lost for ther pride.
368   The snares that I shal set wher never set at Troye;   *were*
   So I think to besegyn hem by every waye wide.   *by every possible means*
   I shal getyn hem from grace, whersoever he abide,   *get, fetch*
   That body and sowle shal com to my hold,   *stronghold*
   Him for to take.
   Now, my knythtes so stowth,   *stout, brave*
   With me ye shall ron in rowte;   *run in a troop*
375   My consell to take for a skowte,   *a scheme*
376   Whytly that we were went for my sake.   *Quickly*
377 WRATH.   With wrath orwyhilles we shal hirre winne.   *sometimes*
ENVY.   Or with sum sotillté sett hur in sinne.   *some subtlety involve her*
SATAN.   Com of[f], than, let us beginne   *Let's go then*
   To werkyn hur sum wrake.   *To work her some injury*
   Her[e] shal the Deyvl go to the Wor[l]d with his compeny.

[*The stage of the World, as Satan and his followers arrive.*]

SATAN.   Heyle, Wor[l]d, worthiest of abowndans!   *of riches*
   In hast we must a conseyll take: *haste*

358-59Now I, a prince elaborately dressed, proudly attired, I Satan your sovereign take advantage of (sit with) every circumstance.

363-64I bring to bay (cause to surrender) even the boldest in bower (i.e., everyone), in order to besiege man's soul and reduce it to submission.

366-67For I greatly resent that man should enjoy (that place in God's esteem) which Lucifer, with many legions (of former angels) lost because of their pride.

368i.e., The snares I'll use have never been equaled in human history.

375-77I wish that we were quickly on our way, fulfilling my desires, using my plan as our scheme. —Sometimes we'll win her (i.e., Mary Magdalene) by means of wrath.

383   Ye must aply yow, with all your afiauns,
    A woman of whorshep owr servant to make.   *worship, good name*
  WORLD.   Satan, with my consell I will the[e] avansse.   *advance, assist*
386   I pray the[e] cum up onto my tent.
     [*Satan and his followers ascend to the stage.*]
387   Were the King of Flesch her[e] with his asemlauns!   *assembly*
388   Masenger, anon that thou werre went
    This tide!   *Now*
    Sey the King of Flesch with grete renown,   *Say (to)*
    With his consell that to him be bown,   *bound, obedient*
    In alle the hast that ever they mown,   *may*
    Com as fast as he may ride.
  MASENGER [SENSUALITY].   My lord, I am your servant,
      Sensualité.
    Your masege to don, I am of glad chyr.   *cheer*
    Ryth sone in presens ye shal him se,   *Very soon*
    Your wil for to fulfille her[e].
     Her[e] *he goth to the Flesch, thus seying:*

    [*The stage of the Flesh, as the Messenger Sensuality arrives.*]

   [MESSENGER.]   Heyl, lord in lond, led with liking!   *guided by sensual pleasure*
    Heyl, Flesch in Lust, fayirest to behold!
400   Heyl, lord and ledar of emprore and king!
    The worthy Wor[l]d, by wey and wold,   *by highway and open country*
    Hath sent for yow and your consell.
    Satan is sembled with his howshold   *assembled*
    Your counseyl to have, most of aveyle.   *avail, help*
  FLESCH.   Hens in hast, that we ther wh[e]re!   *were there*
    Lett us make no lengar delay.
407 MESSENGER.   Gret mirth to ther hertes shold yow arere,   *raise, bring*
    By my trowth, I dare safly saye.

     [*The stage of the World.*]
     Her[e] *comit*[h] *the King of Flesch* [*attended by Lechery, Sloth,*
     and Gluttony] *to the Wor*[l]d, *thus seying:*

   [FLESCH.]   Heyl be yow, soverens lefe and dere!   *beloved*
    Why so hastely do ye for me send?
  WORLD.   A, we are ryth glad we have yow here,   *right, very*
    Owr counsell togethyr to comprehend!   *express*

383You must apply yourself, with all those who follow you.

386*tent:* probably a curtained enclosure on World's scaffold.

387–88i.e., I wish the King of Flesh were here with his crew! Messenger, be on your way.

407You will bring great joy to their hearts (if you come).

[*Having ascended to the World's stage, they all seat themselves.*]
  Now, Satan, sey your devise.   *plan*
SATAN. Serys, now ye be set, I shal yow say:
  Syrus dyid this odyr day.   *Cyrus died/other*
  Now Mary, his dowctor, that may,   *daughter/maid*
  Of that castel berit[h] the prise.   *bears the prize*
WORLD. Sertenly, serys, I yow telle,
  If she in vertu stille may dwelle,   *constantly*
  She shal bin abyll to distroye helle—
  But if your counseyll may othyrwise devise.   *Unless*
422 FLESCH. Now ye, lady Lechery, yow must don your
    attendans,   *wait in attendance*
  For yow be flower fairest of feminité.
  Yow shal go desyir servise, and bin at hur atendauns, *desire/be at her*
  For ye shal sonest enter, ye beral of bewté.   *beryl of beauty*
LECHERY. Serys, I abey your counsell in eche degré. *in every point*
  Stryttwaye thethyr woll I passe.   *Straightway, at once*
SATAN. Spirits malingny shal com to the[e],   *malign, evil*
  Hir to tempt in every plase.
430 Now alle the six that here be:
  Wisely to werke, hir favor to winne,   *(Go) cleverly to work*
  To entyr hir person by the labor of Lechery,
  That she at the last may com to helle.
  How, how, spirits maling, thou wottist what I mene! *malign/you know*
  Cum out, I sey! Herist nat what I seye?   *Hear you not*
  [*The evil spirits emerge from hell.*]

BAD ANGYLL. Sirrus, I obey your counsell in eche degree; *Sirs*
  Stryttwaye thethyr woll I passe.   *pass, go*
  Speke soft, speke soft! I trotte hir to tene.   *I hasten to injure her*
439 I prey the[e] pertly make no more noise.   *openly*

[*The Castle of Magdalen, Bethany.*]
*Her[e] shal alle the seven Dedly Sinnes besege the castell till
[Mary] agre to go to Jherusalem. Lechery shall entyr the castell
with the Bad Angyl, thus seying Lechery:*

440 [LECHERY.] Heyl, lady most laudabyll of aliauns! *alliance*
  Heyl, orient as the sonne in his reflexité!   *brilliant/sun/shining*
442 Myche pepul be comfortyd by your bening afiauns. *Many people/trust*

422*don your attendans:* i.e., enter Mary's service, be in attendance on her.

439–40I pray you, make no more obvious noise. —Hail, lady most praiseworthy of family connection!

442–43Many people are comforted by your gracious trustfulness. Brighter than the burnished (sun) is your beauteous radiance.

443	Bryter than the bornyd is your bemys of bewté,	*burnished*
	Most debonarius, with your aungelly delicité!	*gracious/angelic attractiveness*
	MARY. Qwat personne be ye that thus me comende?	*What*
	LECHERY. Your servant to be, I wold comprehende.	*attain to*
447	MARY. Your debonarius obediauns ravissit[h] me to	
	trankqvelité!	
	Now, sith ye desire, in eche degree	*since/in every respect*
	To receive yow I have grett delectacion.	*pleasure*
	Ye be hartely welcum onto me,	
451	Your tong is so amiabyll devidyd with reson.	
	LECHERY. Now, good lady, will ye me expresse	
	Why may ther no gladdnes to yow resort?	*dwell with you*
	MARY. For my father I have had grett hevinesse;	
	Whan I remembyr, my mind waxit[h] mort.	*dead, overborne with grief*
	LECHERY. Ya, lady, for all that, be of good comfort,	
	For swich obusiouns may brede myche disese.	*such abuse/distress*
458	Swich desepciouns potit[h] peynes to exsport;	
459	Print yow in sportes which best doth yow plese.	
	MARY. Forsothe, ye be welcum to min[e] hawdiens!	*audience, presence*
	Ye be my hartes leche.—	*heart's healer*
	Brother Lazarus, and it be yowr plesauns,	*if/pleasure*
	And ye, sistyr Martha, also, in substawns	
	This place I commend onto your governauns,	*governance*
	And onto God I yow betake.	*I commit you*
	LAZARUS. Now, sistyr, we shal do your intente,	
	In this place to be resident	
	While that ye be absent,	
	To kepe this place from wreche.	*wrack, ruin*
	Here takit[h] Mary hur wey to Jherusalem with Luxsuria, and	*Lechery*
	they shal resort to a tavernere, thus seyi[n]g the tavernere:	

[*A Tavern in Jerusalem.*]

470	[TAVERNER.] I am a taverner, witty and wise,	
	That winys have to sell, gret plenté.	
	Of all the taverners I bere the prise	*bear the prize*
	That be dwelling withinne the ceté.	*city*
	Of winys I have grete plenté,	
	Both white wine and red that [is] so cleyre:	
	Here is wine of mawt, and malmeseyn,	*Malta?/malmsey*
	Clary wine, and claret, and other moo,	

447Your gracious obedience ravishes me into tranquility, transports me into a tranquil spirit.

451Your speech is so amiably harmonized with reasonableness.

458–59Expel such pains and deceptions; commit yourself (lit: stamp or impress yourself) to pleasures which please you best.

478	Win[e] of Gyldyr and of Galles, that made at the Grome,
	Win[e] of Wyan and Vernage, I seye also.
	Ther be no better as ferre as ye can goo.
	LECHERY. Lo, lady, the[e] comfort and the[e] sokowr.
	Go we ner and take a tast;
	This shal bring your sprites to favor.
	Tavernere, bring us of the finest thou hast.
	TAVERNERE. Here, lady, is win[e], a repast
	To man and woman, a good restoratyff.
	Ye shall nat think your mony spent in wast;
	From stodyis and hevines it woll yow relyff.
	MARY. Iwis ye seye soth, ye grom of blisse.
490	To me ye be courtes and kinde.

Guyenne/Vernage(Italian)

succour, ease yourself

into good disposition

studies, cares/relieve

Truly/man

Her[e] shal entyr a galaunt [Curiosity] thus seying:

	GALAUNT. Hof, hof, hof, a frisch new galaunt!
	Ware of thrist, ley that a-doune!
	What, wene ye, sirrys, that I were a marchant
	Because that I am new com to town?
	With sum praty tappysstere wold I faine rown.
	I have a shert of reynnes with slevys peneawnt,
	A lase of silke for my lady constant.
	A, how she is bewtefull and ressplendant!
	Whan I am from hir presens, lord, how I syhe!
	I wol awye sovereyns; and sojettes I disdeyne.
	In winter a stomachyr, in somer non att al;
502	My dobelet and my hossys ever together abide.
	I woll, or even, be shavyn, for to seme ying.
	With here agen the her I love mych pleying;
	That makit[h] me ilegant and lusty in liking.
	Thus I lefe in this wor[l]d; I do it for no pride.
	LECHERY. Lady, this man is for yow, as I se can,
	To sett yow i[n] sporttes and talking this tide.
	MARY. Cal him in, tavernere, as ye my love will han,
	And we shall make ful mery if he wolle abide.
511	TAVERNERE. How, how, my mastyre Coriossité!
	CORIOS[I]TE. What is your will, sir? What wil ye with me?
	TAVERNERE. Here ar jentill women dysiore your presens to
	se,
	And for to drink with yow this tide.
515	CORIOS[I]TE. A, dere dewchesse, my daisyis iee!

Beware of thirst

think

pretty barmaid/whisper

cloth of Raines/pendant

lace

sigh

emulate/subjects, commoners

waistcoat

jacket/hose, breeches

before evening/young

hair against the hair(?)

pleasure

live

can see

at this time

if/have

(who) desire

duchess/daisy's eye

478Gyldyr: Guelder (in the Netherlands). *Galles:* France. *Grome:* Groine (in Spain).

502i.e., My doublet and hose match perfectly.

511Coriossité: the gallant's name suggests undue fastidiousness in clothing.

515(These are terms of endearment.)

Splendaunt of colour, most of feminité,	*Resplendent*
Your sofreyn coloures set with sinserité!	*excelling/arranged with*
Consedere my love into yowr alye,	*alliance, kinship*
Or elles I am smet with peynes of perplexité.	*smitten/pains*

520   MARY.   Why, ser, wene ye that I were a kelle?   *think/callet, whore*

         CORIOS[I]TE.   Nay, prensses, pardé, ye be my hertes hele.   *princess/by God/heal*

         So wold to God ye wold my love fele!   *feel, experience*

         MARY.   Qwat cause that ye love me so sodenly?   *What*

         CORIOS[I]TE.   O, nedys I must, min[e] own lady!   *needs*

         Your person, itt is so womanly,

         I cannat refreyn, my swete lelly.   *lily*

         MARY.   Ser, curtesy doth it yow lere.   *teaches it to you*

         CORIOS[I]TE.   Now, gracius gost, withowtyn pere,   *spirit/peer, equal*

         Mych nortur is that ye conne.   *You know much good breeding*

         But wol yow dawns, my own dere?   *dance*

         MARY.   Ser, I asent in good maner.

         Go ye before, I sue yow nere;   *follow*

         For a man at alle timys berit[h] reverens.   *ought to be respected*

534   CORIOS[I]TE.   Now, by my trowth, ye be with other ten.   *grieved*

         Felle a pese, tavernere! Let us sen   *Fill a cup/see (i.e., have)*

         Soppes in wine. How, love ye?

         MARY.   As ye don, so doth me.   *As you do*

         I am ryth glad that met be we;

         My love in yow ginnit[h] to close.   *join, be full*

540   CORIOS[I]TE.   Now, derling dere, wol yow do by my rede?   *advice*

         We have dronkyn and ete lityl brede;   *a little, some*

         Will ye walk to another stede?   *place (presumably his chamber)*

         MARY.   Evyn at your wil, my dere derling.

         Thow[gh]e ye wil go to the wor[l]des eynd,

         I wol never from yow wynd,   *wend, go*

         To die for your sake.

         Here shal Mary and the galont avoid. And the Bad Angyll goth   *go out*

         to the Wor[l]d, the Fly[s]ch, and the Dylfe [at the Stage of the   *Devil*

         World, where they are still gathered], thus saying the Bad Angyl:

547   [BAD ANGEL.]   A lorges, a lorges, lorddes alle at onys!

548   Ye have a servant fayer and afyabille,

549   For she is fallyn in owr grogly gromys!

         Ya, Pride, callyd Corios[i]té, to hur is ful laudabyll,   *laudable, dear*

         And to hur he is most preysseabyll,   *precious*

---

[534]Now, by my faith, you're grieved with other matters (i.e., you're sorrowing for something and need to be cheered up).

[547–49]A largess, lords all together! (An expression of gratitude, in this case for Mary's surrender to evil.) You now have a fair and courteous follower, for Mary has fallen into our grisly clutches (?).

For she hath graunttyd him al his bones.   *boons, requests*
She thinkit[h] his person so amiabyll,
To her site he is semeliare than ony king in trones.   *sight/seemlier/thrones*

SATAN.   A, how I tremyl and trott for these tidinges!   *tremble and am agitated*

556   She is a soveryn servant that hath hur fet in sinne.   *fetched, tempted*
Go thow again, and ever be hur g[u]ide.   *constantly*
The laudabyll life of lecherry let hur never linne,   *cease*
For of hur al helle shall make rejoisseing.

Here goth the Bad Angyl to Mary again.

SATAN.   Farewell, farewell, ye t[w]o nobyl kinges this tide,   *time*
For hom in hast I wol me dresse.   *direct my course*

WORLD.   Farewell, Satan, prinsse of pride!

563   FLESCH.   Farewell, sem[l]iest alle sorowys to sesse!

*Here shal Satan go hom to his stage, and Mary shal entyr into
the place alone, save the Bad Angyl. And al the seven Dedly*   *central acting area*
*Sinnes shal be conveyid into the howse of Simont Leprous; they
shal be arayid like seven dylf, thus kept closse. Mary shal be in an*   *devils/hid*
erbyr, thus seying: *arbor*

[*An arbor in the "place" or center of the acting area surrounded
by the stages. The "place" represents Jerusalem.*]

MARY.   A, God be with my valentines,   *i.e., lovers*
My bird sweting, my lovys so dere!

566   For they be bote for a blossum of blisse.   *boot, profit*
Me mervellit[h] sore they be nat here.   *It astonishes me sorely*
But I woll restyn in this erbyre
Amons thes[e] bamys precius of prysse,   *Among/balms, herbs/price*
Till som lover wol apere

571   That me is wont to halse and kisse.   *embrace*

Her[e] shal Mary lie doun and slepe in the erbyre.

[*The Stage of Simon the Leper's house. A banquet is prepared.*]

572   SIMOND LEPRUS.   This day [w]holly I pot in rememberowns   *put*
573   To solas my gestes to my power.

556She (Lechery) who has tempted her (Mary) into sin is a most excellent servant (of the devil).

563Farewell, you who are most fit to end all sorrows!

566i.e., For they are useful and fitting for one who is the very flower of amorous bliss.

571Who is accustomed to embrace and kiss me.

572-73This day I fully intend (lit: have it wholly in my remembrance) to entertain my guests to the limit of my ability.

I have ordeynnyd a dinere of substawns,   *ordered/abundance*
My chyff freyndes therwith to chyre.   *chief/cheer*
Into the seté I woll apere,   *city/present myself*
For my gestes to make porviawns;   *provision*
For time drayt[h] ny to go to diner,   *draws nigh*
And my officyrs be redy with ther ordinowns.   *household officers/arrangements*
580   So wold to God I myte have aqueyntowns   *(I wish) I might/acquaintance*
Of the Profyth of trew perfitnesse,   *Prophet*
To com to my place and porvyowns!   *provision, banquet*
It wold rejoise my hert in gret gladnesse;
For the report of his hye nobillnesse
Rennit[h] in contreys fer and nere.   *Runs, travels*
His precheing is of gret perfithnes,
Of rythwisnesse and mercy cleyre.   *righteousness*

> Here entyr Simont into the place [representing Jerusalem], the
> Good Angyll thus seying to Mary [as she lies asleep still in her
> arbor, in one area of the "place"] :

[GOOD ANGEL.]   Woman, woman, why art thou so
            onstabyll?   *inconstant*
Ful bitterly this blisse it wol be bowth.   *pleasure/bought, paid for*
590   Why art thou agens God so veriabyll?   *against/inconstant*
W[h]y thinkes thou nat God made the[e] of nowth?   *consider/nought*
In sin and sorow thou art browth;   *have been brought, enticed*
Fleschly lust is to the[e] full delectabyll.
Salve for thy sowle must be sowth;   *sought*
And leve thy werkes vain and veriabyll!   *leave*
Remembyr, woman, for thy pore pride
How thy sowle shal lyin in helle fire.   *lie*
A, remembyr how sorowful itt is to abide
Withowtyn eynd in angure and ir[e]!   *Endlessly*
600   Remembyr the[e] on mercy; make thy sowle clyre.   *Think of mercy/clear, pure*
I am the gost of goodnesse that so wold the[e] g[u]idde.   *spirit*
MARY.   A, how the sperit of goodnesse hat[h] prom[p]tyt
            me this tide,   *at this time*
And tem[p]tyd me with tityll of trew perfythnesse!   *title, name*
Alas, how betternesse in my hert doth abide!
I am wonddyd with werkes of gret distresse.   *enveloped*
A, how pynsi[v]nesse potit[h] me to oppresse,   *pensiveness oppresses me*
That I have sinnyd on every side!   *everywhere*
O Lord, w[h]o shall put me from this peynfulnesse?
A, w[h]oo shal to mercy be my gostly g[u]ide?   *spiritual*
610   I shal porsue the Prophett, wherso he be,
For he is the welle of perfith charité;   *fountain*
By the oile of mercy he shal me relyff.   *relieve*
With swete bawmys I wil sekyn him this syth,   *balms, ointments/seek/time*

And sadly folow his lordshep in eche degré.   *earnestly/in every respect*

    Here shal entyr the Prophet with his desiplys [into the "place,"
representing Jerusalem, where they meet Simon and pass near
Mary's arbor], thus seying Simont Leprus:

[SIMON.]   Now ye be welcom, mastyr, most of magnificens.

    I beseche yow beningly ye wol be so graciows,   *benignly*

    If that it be leking onto yowr hye presens,   *If it please your noble person*

    This daye to com dine at my hows.

    JHESUS.   God a mercy, Simont, that thou wilt me knowe!   *be acquainted, hospitable*

620   I woll entyr thy hows with pes and unité.   *peace*

    I am glad for to rest ther grace ginnit[h] grow;   *where*

    For withinne thy hows shal rest charité,

    And the bemys of grace shal bin illuminows.

    But sith thou witist-saff a dinere on me,   *since/vouchsafe*

    With pes and grace I entyr thy hows.

    [*They go to the house of Simon, at his stage.*]

    SIMOND.   I thank yow, master, most bening and gracius,   *benign*

627   That yow wol of your hye soverenté—

628   To me itt is a joye most speceows—   *lovely*

629   Withinne my hows that I may yow se.

    Now sit to the bord, mastyrs alle. [*They sit at the banquet.*]

    Her[e] shal Mary folow alonge, with this lamentacion:

    MARY.   O I, cursyd caiftiff, that myche wo hath wrowth   *wrought*

    Agens my Makar, of mytes most!   *greatest of (heavenly) powers*

    I have offendyd him with dede and thowth.   *thought*

    But in his grace is all my trost,

    Or elles I know well I am but lost,

    Body and sowle dampdnyd perpetuall.

637   Yet, good Lord of lorddes, my hope perhenuall   *perennial*

638   With the[e] to stond in grace and favour to se,

    Thow knowist my hart and thowt in especial;

640   Therfor, good Lord, after my hart reward me.

    Her[e] shal Mary wasche the fett of the Prophet with the terres
of hur [e]yis, whiping hem with hur herre, and than anoint him   *wiping/hair*
with a precius ointtment. Jhesus dicit:

[JESUS.]   Simond, I thank the[e] speceally

627-29That you will grant, by your great authority, that I may entertain you in my house—to
me it is a most lovely pleasure.

637-38Yet, good Lord of lords, with whom I hope perpetually to stand in grace and see God's
favor (toward me).

640Therefore, good Lord, reward me according to my heart's inclination.

For this grett r[e]past that here hath be.   *been*
But, Simond, I telle the[e] fectually   *effectually, earnestly*
I have thinges to seyn to the[e].   *say*

SIMOND.   Master, qwat your will be,   *whatever*
And it plese yow, I well yow here;   *If/I'll hear you*
Seyth your liking onto me,   *Say your pleasure*
And al the plesawnt of your mind and desyir.   *pleasure*

JHESUS.   Simond, ther was a man in this present lyf
650   The w[h]iche had t[w]o dectours well suere,   *debtors surely*
The which wer pore, and myth make no restoratyf,   *might/repayment*
But stille in ther dett ded induour.   *endure, continue*
The on[e] owit him an hondyrd pense ful suere,   *owed*
And the other fefty, so befell the chanse.
And becawse he cowd nat his mony recure,   *recover*
They askyd him forgevnesse, and he forgaf in substans.
But, Simont, I pray the[e], answer me to this sentens:
Which of thes[e] t[w]o personnes was most beholddyn to
        that man?

SIMOND.   Master, and it plese your hey presens,   *if*
660   He that most owit him, as my reson gef can.

JHESUS.   *Recte judicasti.*   Thou art a wise man,   *You have rightly judged*
And this quesson hast dempte trewly.   *judged*
Iff thou in thy conciens remembyr can,   *can reflect on this*
Ye t[w]o be the dettours that I of specefy.
But, Simond, behold this woman in al wise,   *in every way*
How she with teres of hir better weping   *bitter*
She wassheth my fete and dothe me servise,
And anoi[n]tit[h] hem with onimentes, lowly kneling,
And with her her, fayer and brigth shynning,   *hair/bright*
670   She wipeth hem again with good intent.
But, Simont, sith that I entyrd thy hows,   *since*
To wasshe my fete thou dedist nat aplye,
Nor to wipe my fete thou were nat so favorus;   *obliging*
Wherfor in thy consciens thou owttist nat to replye.   *ought*
But, woman, I sey to the[e] verely,
I forgeyffe the[e] thy wrecchednesse,
And [w]hol[e] in sowle be thou made therby!

MARY.   O blessyd be thou, Lord of everlasting life!
And blissyd be thy berth of that puer verginne!   *from that pure virgin*
680   Blissyd be thou, repast contemplatif,   *i.e., food for my spirit*
Agens my seknes helth and medsin!   *Against*
And, for that I have sinnyd in the sinne of pride,   *because*
I wol en-[h]abite me with humelité.   *clothe myself*

660He who owed the man most, as far as my reason can give explanation (i.e., I suppose;
see Luke 7:43).

Agens wrath and envy I wil devide   *will set in opposition*
Thes[e] fayer vertuys, paciens and charité.
JHESUS.   Woman, in contriss[i]on thou art expert,
And in thy sowle hast inward mythe   *might*
688   That sumtime were in desert,   *deserving*
And from therknesse hast porchasyd lyth.   *darkness/light*
Thy feyth hath savit the[e] and made the[e] bryth,   *spiritually fair*
Wherfor I sey to the[e], "*vade in pace.*"   *depart in peace*
    With this word, seven dyllys shall devoide from the woman, and   *devils/go out*
    the Bad Angyll enter into hell with thondyr.

[MARY.]   O thou glorius Lord! This [was] rehersyd for   *performed*
    my sped,   *advantage*
Sowle helth at t[h]is time for to recure.   *Soul's/recover*
Lord, for that I was in whanhope, now stond I in dred,   *because/despair*
But that thy gret mercy with me may endure.   *Unless*
My thowth thou knewist withowtyn ony dowth.   *thought/doubt*
Now may I trost the techeing of Isaye in Scriptur,   *Isaiah*
W[h]os[e] report of thy nobillnesse rennit[h] fere abowt.   *runs, is spread*
JHESUS.   Blissyd be they at alle time
700   That sen me nat, and have me in credens.   *see/belief*
With contriss[i]on thou hast mad[e] a recumpens   *recompense*
Thy sowle to save from all distresse.
Beware, and kepe the[e] from alle necligens,
And after thou shal be partener of my blisse.   *afterwards/partner*
    Here devo[i]dit[h] Jhesus with his desipilles, the Good Angyll   *goes out*
    rejoising of Mawdleyn: *about*

BONUS ANGELUS.   Holy God, hyest of omnipotency,
706   The astat of good governouns to the[e] I recummend,   *state/commend, entrust*
Humbilly besecheing thin[e] inper[i]all glorye
In thy devin[e] vertu us to comprehend.   *embrace, include*
And, delectabyll Jhesu, soverreyn sapiens,   *wisdom*
Owr feyth we recummend onto your purpeté,   *care*
Most mekely praying to your holy aparens,   *appearance, spiritual manifestation*
Illumin owr ignorans with your devinité!
Ye be clepyd Redempcioun of sowlys defens,   *named*
Whiche shal ben obscuryd by thy blessyd mortalité.
O *lux vera*, graunt us yowr lucense   *true light/light*
That with the sprite of errour we nat sedu[c]et be!   *spirit*
And, *Spiritus Alme*, to yow most beni[g]ne,   *Bounteous, Holy Spirit*
Thre persons in Trenité and on[e] God eterne,

[688]i.e., That deserves future grace.

[706]i.e., I commend to your care the preservation of man in a state of good governance.

719   Most lowly owr feyth we consigne   *humbly/subscribe*
720   That we may com to your blisse glorified from malingne;   *from malice*
721   And with your gostely bred to fede us, we desiern.   *spiritual/desire*

        [The stage of the Devil.]

    SATAN. A, owt, owt, and harrow! I am hampord with hate!   *deranged*
723   In hast wil I set on jugment to se;
724   With thes[e] betyll-browyd bicheys I am at debate.   *beetle-browed bitches*
    How, Belfagour and Belzabub, com up here to me!
    Here aperitt[h] t[w]o divllys before the master [having come up out of hell].

    2 DIABOLUS. Here, lord, here! Qwat wol ye?   *What*
727   SATAN. The jugment of harlottes here to se,   *rascals*
728   Setting in judicial-like astate.
    How, thow Bad Angyll, apere before my grace!
    [The Bad Angel appears and humbles himself.]

    BAD ANGEL. As flat as fox, I falle before your face.
    SATAN. Thow theffe, w[h]y hast thou don alle this trespas   *rogue/wrong*
    To lett yon woman thy bondes breke?
    BAD ANGEL. The sperit of grace sore ded hir smith   *sorely did smite her*
    And temptyd so sore, that ipocrite!
    SATAN. Ya! This[e] hard balys on thy bottokkys shall bite!   *torments*
    In hast on the[e] I wol be wroke.   *avenged*
    [To his assistant devils.]
737   Cum up, ye horsons, and skore awey the iche,   *score, whip/itch*
    And with this panne ye do him picche!   *pan/smear him with pitch*
739   Cum of[f], ye harlottes, that it wer don!   *Let's go*
    Here shall they serve all the sevyn [Deadly Sins] as they do the   *serve, treat*
    frest.   *first*
    SATAN. Now have I a part of my desiere.   *desire*
    Goo into this howsse, ye lordeynnes, here,   *lurdans, louts*
    And loke ye set it on a feyere   *see to it/on fire*

719-21Most humbly we subscribe our faith, to the end that we may come to your bliss invested with glory, safe from malice; and we desire you to feed us with your spiritual food.

723-24In haste I will sit in judgment to determine (who was to blame for Mary's defection); with these shaggy-browed scoundrels (i.e., the assistant devils) I have a quarrel to pick.

727-28(I want) to see rascals judged, as I sit in my judge-like estate.

737i.e., Come up (from hell), you rascals, and whip the Bad Angel where he itches.

739i.e., Let's go, rascals, let's get it done! S.D. *the frest:* The Bad Angel represents Pride, the first of the Deadly Sins and associated with the devil.

743 And that shall hem awake.
Here shall the tother deylles sett the howse on a fyere, and make a
sowth; and Mary shall go to Lazar and to Martha.   *soot*

SATAN.   So, now have we well afrayid these felons fals!   *frightened*
   They be blasyd both body and hals.   *blazed, burned/neck*
   Now to hell lett us sinkyn als,   *also*
   To owr felaws blake. [*They descend into hell.*]   *black*

   [*The Castle of Magdalen, Bethany. Mary comes to Lazarus and*
   Martha.]

748 MARY.   O brother, my hartes consolaciown,
749   O blessyd in lyffe, and solitary,
750   The blissyd Prophet, my comfortaciown,   *comfort*
   He hathe made me clene and delectary,   *delectable*
   The w[h]iche was to sinne a subjectary.   *I who was/subject*
   This king, Criste, consediryd his creaciown.   *considered, remembered*
   I was drinchyn in sinne deversarye   *drowned, overwhelmed/divers*
   Till that Lord relevyd me by his dominacion.   *relieved/power*
   Grace to me he wold never denye;
   Thowe I were nevyr so sinful, he seyd "*revertere!*"   *turn again*
   O, I, sinful creature, to grace I woll aplye.
   The oile of mercy hath helyd min[e] infirmité.   *healed*

760 MARTHA.   Now worchepyd be that hey name Jhesu,   *high, exalted*
   The w[h]iche in Latin is callyd Saviowr!
   Fulfilling that word evyn of dewe,   *by just title*
   To alle sinfull and seke he is sokour.   *sick/succour*

LAZARUS.   Sistyr, ye be welcum onto yowr towere.
   Glad in hart of yowr obessiawnse—   *(I am) glad/obedience*
   Wheyl that I leffe, I wil serve him with honour—   *While/live*
   That ye have forsakyn sinne and variawns.   *unsteadfastness*

768 MARY.   Crist, that is the lyth and the cler daye,   *light*
769   He hath oncuryd the therknesse of the clowdy nyth—   *uncovered/darkness*
770   Of lyth the lucens and lyth veray,
   W[h]os[e] preching to us is a gracious lyth:
   Lord, we beseche the[e], as thou art most of myth,   *might*
   Owt of the ded slep of therknesse defend us aye!

743 S.D. *howse*: Seemingly, the devils set fire to the tower of hell, to torture the inmates for
their failure with Mary. *sowth*: soot (an actual heavy black smoke issuing from hell).

748–50 O brother, the blessed prophet Jesus, (who is) my comfort and heart's consolation,
(who is) blessed in his life, and without rival in blessedness.

768–70 Christ, who is the light and the clear daytime, (who) has removed the cover of darkness
of cloudy night, (who is) very light of very light (lit: the light and true light of light).

Giff us grace evyr to rest in lyth,
In quiet and in pes to serve the[e] nyth and day!
Here shall Lazar take his deth, thus seying:

[LAZARUS.]   A, help, help, sistyrs, for charité! *for love's sake*
Alas, dethe is sett at my hart!
A, ley on handes! Wher are ye? *i.e., touch me*
A, I faltyr and falle, I wax alle on-quarte! *unhealthy*
780 A, I bome above, I wax alle swertt! *buzz (in the head)/dark, black*
A, good Jhesu, thow be my g[u]ide!
A, no lengar now I reverte! *retain consciousness*
I yeld up the gost, I may natt abide!

MARY.   O good brother, take coumforth and myth,
And lett non[e] hevines in yowr hart abide!
Lett away alle this feyntnesse and fretth, *Let pass/fretting*
And we shal gete yow leches, yowr peynes to devide. *get/physicians/sunder*

MARTHA.   A, I syth and sorow and sey "Alas!" *sigh*
This sorow is apoint to be my confusion. *appointed/undoing*
790 Jentyl sister, hie we from this place, *hasten*
For the Prophe[t] to him hatt[h] grett delectacion. *takes great delight in him*
Good brothere, take somme comfortacion,
For we woll go to seke yow cure.

Here goth Mary and Martha and mett with Jhesus [as he is
walking with his disciples in the "place,"] thus seying:

[MARY AND MARTHA.]   O Lord Jhesu, owr melleflueus
swettnesse,
Thowe art grettest Lord in glorye!
796 Lover to the[e], Lord, in all lowlinesse,
797 Comfort thy creatur that to the[e] crye!
Behold yowr lover, good Lord, specially,
How Lazare lyth seke in grett distresse. *lies sick*
He is thy lover, Lord, suerly.
Onbind him, good Lord, of his hevinesse! *from his sorrow*
802 JHESUS.   Of all infirmité, ther is non[e] to deth,
803 For of all peynnes that is inpossible *pains*
804 To undyrestond by reson. To know the werke,
805 The joye that is in Jherusalem hevenly
806 Can never be compilyd by counning of clerke— *scholar*
To se the joyis of the Fathyr in glory,
The joyis of the Sonne which owth to be magnified, *ought/praised*

796–97Give comfort to your creature (i.e., person created by you), who loves you, Lord, in
all humbleness, crying to you (for help).

802–6Of all infirmities, none can compare with death, for of all afflictions it can least be
comprehended by human reason. Even the most skillful learned divine can never express
what it is to know the pleasurable occupations and the joy that are in the heavenly Jerusalem.

And of the therd person, the Holy Gost, truly,
And alle thre but on[e], in heven glorified.
Now, women that arn in my presens here,   *(you) women that are*
Of my wordys take avisement: *take heed*
Go hom agen to yowr brothyr Lazere.
My grace to him shall be sent.

MARY.   O thow glorius Lord here present,   *i.e., here on earth*
We yeld to the[e] salutacion!   *yield, give*
In owr weyis we be expedient.   *i.e., We'll be quickly on our way*
Now, Lord, us defend from tribulacion!
    Here goth Mary and Martha homward, and Jhesus devo[i]dit[h].   *goes out*
    [*As they arrive at the Castle of Magdalen, Bethany, Lazarus is
    dying.*]

LAZARUS.   A, in woo I waltyr, as wavys in the wind!   *am tossed/like*
Awey is went all my sokour!   *All help is gone*
A, deth, deth, thou art onkind!
A, a, now bristit[h] min[e] hartt! This is a sharp shower!   *bursts/attack*
823   Farewell, my sistyrs, my bodely helth!
    Mortuis est.   *He is dead*
824   MARY.   Jhesu, my Lord, be yowr sokowre,
825   And he mott be yowr gostes welth!   *may he*
826   1 MILES.   Goddes grace mott be his governour,   *soldier*
In joy everlasting for to be!
2 MILES.   Amonge alle good sowlys send him favour,
As thy powere is most of dignité!
MARTHA.   Now, syn the chans is fallyn soo   *since it has happened*
That deth hath drevyn him do[w]n this day,
We must nedys owr devyrs doo: *must do our duties*
To the erth to bring him withowt delay.
MARY.   As the use is now, and hath byn aye,   *custom/been always*
With wepers to the erth yow him bring—   *weepers*
Alle this must be done as I yow saye—
Clad in blake, withowtyn lesing.   *black/without lie, truly*
1 MILES.   Graciows ladyis of grett honour,
This pepull is com here in yowr syth,   *sight*
840   Weping and weyling with gret dolour   *wailing*
Because of my lordes dethe.
    [*A crowd of mourning neighbors joins the funeral procession from
    the Castle of Magdalen to the tomb in the "place."*]
    *Here the on[e] knigth make redy the ston, and other bring in the
    wepars arayid in blak.*

823-26Farewell to my sisters and my bodily health! —May my Lord Jesus be your help and
your spirit's prosperity! —May God's grace be his guide.

1 MILES.   Now, good fryndes that here be,
    Take up this body with good will,
    And ley it in his sepoltur semely to se.   *sepulchre handsomely*
    Good Lord, him save from alle maner ille!
       Lay him in. Here al the pepyll resort to the castell, thus seying
       Jhesus [as he walks with his disciples in the "place"]:

846   [JESUS. The] time is comyn of very cogniss[i]on.   *true knowledge*
    My dissiplys, goth with me   *go*
848   For to fulfill possibyll peticion.
    Go we together into Judé;   *Judaea*
    There Lazar, my frynd, is he.
    Gow we together as childyrne of lyth,   *chosen people of light*
    And from grevos slepe saven heym will we.   *we'll save him*
    DISSIPULUS.   Lord, [if] it plese yowr myty volunté,   *will*
854   Thow[gh] he slepe, he may be savyd by skill.
855   JHESUS.   That is trew, and be possibilité;
856   Therfor of my deth shew yow I will.
    My Fathyr, of nemiows charité   *exceeding*
    Sent me, his son, to make redemcion,
    W[h]iche was conseivyd by puer verginité   *Who/pure*
    And so in my mother had cler incarnacion;
    And therfore must I suffyre grevos passion
    Ondyre Pounse Pilat, with grett perplexité,   *Pontius/distress*
    Betyn, bobbyd, skornyd, crownnyd with thorne—   *mocked/scorned*
    Alle this shall be the soferons of my deité.   *sufferance*
865   Therfor, hastely folow me now,
866   For Lazar is ded verely to preve;
867   Whe[r]for I am joyfull, I sey onto yow,
868   That I knowlege yow therwith, that ye may it beleve.   *acquaint*
       Here shal Jhesus com with his dissipules [walking toward the
       Castle of Magdalen]; and on[e] Jew tellit[h] Martha:

[JEW.]   A, Martha, Martha, be full of gladnesse!
    For the Prophett is coming, I sey trewly,
    With his dissipilles in grett lowlinesse.

846i.e., The time has come that the true power of God on earth is to be revealed.

848To fulfill a petition that is within my power.

854–56If he is asleep, he may be recovered. (The disciples think Jesus refers to ordinary sleep; see John 11:12–13). —It is true (that he but sleeps), and it is possible (to recover him); accordingly I will show you a token of my own death (i.e., the Resurrection after three days in hell, of which Lazarus' raising is an antetype).

865–68Therefore, follow me now hastily, to verify that Lazarus is indeed dead; and I am glad, I tell you, that I can acquaint you with the fact (of his having died when I was not there) to the intent that you may believe (in my miraculous power; see John 11:14–15).

He shall yow comfortt with his mercy.

Here Martha shall ronne agen Jhesus, thus seying: *against, toward*

[MARTHA.]   A, Lord, me, simpyl creatur, nat denye,   *do not deny me*
   Thow[gh] I be wrappyd in wrecchydnesse!
   Lord, and thou haddist byn here, verely,   *if*
   My brother had natt a byn ded; I know well thisse.   *wouldn't have been dead*

JHESUS.   Martha, docctor, onto the[e] I sey   *daughter*
   Thy brother shall reyse again.   *rise*

MARTHA.   Yee, Lord, at the last day;   *day of judgment*
880   That I belive ful pleyn.

JHESUS.   I am the resurreccion of life, that ever shall reyne;   *reign*
   And whoso belevit[h] verely in me
   Shall have life everlasting, the soth to seyn.   *say*
   Martha, belevist thow this [truly]?

MARTHA.   Ye[a], forsoth, thou Prinsse of Blisch!   *Bliss*
   I beleve in Crist, the son of sapiens,   *(divine) wisdom*
   Whiche withowt eynd ryngne shall he   *Who eternally will reign*
   To redemyn us freell from owr iniquité.   *redeem/frail beings*

Here Mary shall falle to Jhesus, thus seying Mary: *before*

MARY.   O thou rythewys regent, reyning in equité,   *righteous/reigning*
890   Thou graciows Lord, thou swete Jhesus!
   And thou haddist byn here, my brothyr alife had be.   *If*
   Good Lord, min[e] hertt doth this discus.   *ponder*

JHESUS.   Wher have ye put him? Sey me this.

MARY.   In his mo[nu]ment, Lord, is he.

JHESUS.   To that place ye me wis;   *guide me*
   Thatt grave I desire to se.

   [They lead Jesus to Lazarus' tomb in the "place."]

   Take of[f] the ston of this monument!
   The agrement of grace here shewyn I will.   *covenant*

MARTHA.   A, Lord, yowr preseptt fulfillyd shall be;
   This ston I remeve with glad chyr.
   Graciows Lord, I aske the[e] mercy!
   Thy will mott be fullfillyd here.   *May your will be fulfilled*

   Here shall Martha put of [f] the grave-ston.

JHESUS.   Now, Father, I beseche thin[e] hey paternité   *high*
904   That my prayour be resowndable to thy Fathyr[h]od in
      glory,
905   To opyn theyn erys to thy son in humanité;   *open your ears*
   Nat only for me, but for thy pepyll vercly,
   That they may beleve and be take to thy mercy—   *taken*

904–5 That my prayer may reach you in heaven, so that you may hear your son living among
men (see John 11:41–42).

      Fathyr, for them I make supplicacion.

      Graciows Father, graunt me my bone!   *boon, prayer*

910   Lazer, Lazer, com hethyr to me!

         Here shall Lazar arise, trossyd with towelles, in a shete.   *trussed, wrapped/winding sheet*

LAZAR.   A, my Makar, my Saviowr, blissyd mott thou be!   *may*

      Here men may know thy werkes of wondyre.

      Lord, nothi[n]g is onpossibill to the[e],

      For my body and my sowle was departyd asonder!   *parted*

      I shuld a rottytt, as doth the tondyre,   *have rotted/tinder*

      Fleysch from the bonys a consumyd away.   *(should) have*

917   Now is aloft that late was ondyr!   *lately*

      The goodnesse of God hath don for me here,   *done (this)*

      For he is bote of all balys to onbind,   *boot, remedy/bales, griefs*

      That blissyd Lord that here ded apere.

         Here all the pepull, and the Jewys, Mary, and Martha, with
         on[e] vois, sey thes[e] wordes: "We beleve in yow, Saviowr,
         Jhesus, Jhesus, Jhesus!"

[JESUS.]   Of yowr good hertes I have advertaciounes,   *advertisement, heed*

      Wherethorow, in sowle [w]holl made ye be.   *Whereby*

      Betwix yow and me be never variaciounes,   *divergence*

      Wherfor I sey, "*vade in pace.*"   *depart in peace*

         Here devoidit[h] Jhesus with his desipilles. Mary, and Martha,   *goes out*
         and Lazare, gon hom to the castell.

         [The stage of the King of Marseilles. The king and queen,
         attended.]

         And here [the King of Marseilles] beginnit[h] his boste:

[REX.]   Avantt, avant the[e], onworthy wrecchesse!   *Out of my way/wretches*

      Why lowtt ye nat low to my lawdabill presens,   *bow*

      Ye brawling breelles, and blabir-lippyd bicchys,   *rascals/blabber-lipped bitches*

      Obedienly to obbey me withowt offense?

929   I am a sofereyn semely, that ye se butt seyld—   *but seldom*

930   Non swiche onder sonne, the sothe for to say.   *such/sun*

      Whanne I fare fresly and fers to the feld,   *freshly/fierce*

      My fomen fle for fer of my fray.   *attack*

      Even as an enperowr I am [h]onored ay,   *always*

      W[h]anne baner gin to blasse, and bemmys gin to blow. *banners shine forth/trumpets*

935   Hed am I heyest of all hethennesse holld.

      Both kingges and cayseres, I woll they shall me know, *emperors/acknowledge*

      Or elles they bey the bargain that ever they were so bold. *buy, pay for*

917That which only lately was underground is now raised up.

929–30I am a handsome sovereign, such as you seldom see—there isn't another such under the sun (i.e., anywhere), to tell the truth.

935I'm held (i.e., considered) to be chief ruler of all heathendom.

I am King of Marcille, talys to be told; *i.e., to tell truth*
Thus I wold it were knowyn ſerre and nere.

940   [W]ho sey contraly, I cast heym in cares cold, *Whoso*
And he shall bey the bargain wondyr dere. *wondrously expensively*
I have a favorows ſode, and fresse as the fakown; *pleasing wife/fresh/falcon*
She is full fair in hir feminité.
Whan I loke on this lady, I am losty as the lion.
In my syth, *sight*
Of delicité most deliciows, *Of sensual delight*
Of felachip most feleciows, *happy*
Of alle fodis most favarows, *wives/pleasing*
O, my blisse, in beuteus brygth! *bright*

950   REGINA.   O of condicions, and most [h]onorabill,
951   Lowly I thank yow for this recummendacion—
952   The bounteest and the boldest onder baner bryth! *most bountiful/bright banner*
953   No creatur so coroscant to my consolacion. *shining*
954   Whan the regent be resident, itt is my refeccion; *restorative*
955   Yowr dilectabill dedes deviditt[h] me from diversité. *separate me*
956   In my person I privide to put me from polucion; *provide, take care*
To be plesant to yowr person, itt is my prosperité.

REX.   Now godamercy, berel brytest of bewté, *beryl brightest*
Godamercy, ruby rody as the rose! *ruddy*
Ye be so ple[s]aunt to my pay, ye put me from peyn. *my liking*
    [*To his knights.*]
Now, comly knigthys, loke that ye forth dresse *see to it/prepare*
Both spicys and win[e] here in hast.
    Here shall the knigtes gete spicys and wine; and here [on the *devil*
    platea, from hell] shall enter a dylle in [h]orebill aray, thus
    seying:

[DEVIL.]   Owt, owt, harrow! I may crye and yelle,
For lost is all owr labor, wherfor I sey alas!
965   For of all holddes that ever hort—non[e] so as hell— *prisons/hurt(?)*
966   Owr barres of iron ar all to-brost, stronge gates of brasse! *burst asunder*
The King of Joy enteryd in therat, as bryth as firys blase; *bright as fire's blaze*
For fray of his ferfull banere, owr felashep fled asondir. *fear/fellowship, company*
Whan he towcheyd it, with his toukking they brast as ony *touching/burst*
    glase,

⁹⁴⁰I'll throw anyone who says to the contrary into wretched sorrows.

⁹⁵⁰⁻⁵⁶O you who are most to be honored for your nobility, the most bountiful and the boldest
in battle, fighting beneath your banner, I humbly thank you for this commendation! No
person shines so brightly as you, bringing me comfort and joy. Your presence is my restorative.
Your pleasing deeds protect me from anything disagreeable. I take care (for your sake) to
keep my person free from sinful contamination.

⁹⁶⁵⁻⁶⁶The strong iron bars and brass gates of hell—the most painful of all prisons—are burst
asunder. (The devil is describing the harrowing of hell.)

And rofe asonder, as it byn with thondore.   *split/as if it had been*
Now ar we thrall, that frest wer fre,   *eviously were*
By the Pass[i]on of his manhede.
On a crosse on hye hangyd was he,
Which hath distroyd owr labor and alle owr dede.   *deeds*
He hath lytinnyd limbo, and to paradise yede.   *lightened, emptied/gone*
That wondyrfull worke werkitt[h] us wrake: *wondrous/does us injury*
Adam and Abram, and alle hire kinred,   *their*
Owt of owr preson to joy were they take.   *taken*
All this hath bin wrowth syn Freyday at none;   *done since/noon*
980   Brostyn do[w]n owr gates that hangyd were full hye.   *Burst*
Now is he resyn—his resurreccion is don—
And is procedyd into Galelye.
With many a temtacion we to[u]chyd him to atrey,   *undertook to entice him*
To know whether he was God or non.
985   Ye[t], for all owr besynes, bleryd is owr eye,   *business, effort/bleared*
For with his wild werke he hath wonne hem everychon.   *them everyone*
Now for the time to come   *i.e., for all eternity*
Ther shall non falle to owr chanse   *to our lot*
But at his deleverans,   *Except by his verdict*
990   And weyid by ri[g]thfull balans,   *weighed, judged in*
And govyn by rythfull dome.   *judged(?)/judgment*
I telle yow alle, in sum to helle will I gonne. [*He withdraws*   *in conclusion*
        to hell.]

        Here shall enter the thre Maryis arayid as chast women, with
        signys of the Pass[i]on printyd upon ther brest, thus seying
        Mawdlyn:

[MARY MAGDALENE.]   Alas, alas, for that ryall bem!   *royal beam (of light)*
    A! this percitt[h] my hartt worst of all: *pierces*
    For here he turnyd agen to the woman of Jerusalem,
    And for wherinesse lett the crosse falle.   *weariness*
M[ARY] JACOBE.   This sorow is beytterare than ony galle;   *more bitter*
    For here the Jewys spornyd him to make him goo,   *spurned, struck*
    And they disspittyd ther king ryall.   *showed despite to*
1000   That clivitt[h] min[e] hart and makett[h] me woo.   *cleaves/woeful*
M[ARY] SALOME.   It is intollerabill to se or to tell,
    For ony creature, that stronkg tormentry.   *oppressive torment*
    O Lord, thou haddist a mervelows mell!   *wondrous strife*
    It is to[o] hediows to discry.
        Al the Maryis with on[e] voice sey this folowing:
[MARYIS.]   Heylle, gloriows crosse! thou barist that Lord on
        hye

985*bleryd . . . eye:* i.e., we've been hoodwinked.

Which by thy migth deddist lowly bowe do[w]n,   *might did*

Mannys sowle to bye from all thraldam,   *buy, redeem*

That evermore in peyne shold a-be.   *have been*

By record of Davit, with mild stevyn,   *voice*

1010 *Domine, inclina caelos tuos, et descende!*

M[ARY] MAGDLEYN.   Now to the monument lett us gon,

Wheras owr Lord and Saviowr laid was,

To anoint him body and bone,

1014 To make amendes for owr trespas.

[*They proceed to the monument.*]

[W]ho shall putt do[w]n the led of the monument,   *lid, cover*

Thatt we may anoi[n]tt his gracius woundes,

With hartt and mi[n]d to do owr intentt,

With precius bamys, this same stounddes?   *balms/hour*

M[ARY] SALOME.   Thatt blissyd body within this boundes

1020 Here was laid with rufull mones;

Never creature was borne upon gro[u]nddes

That migth sofere so hediows a peyne at onys.   *might suffer*

Here shall apere two angelus in white at the grave.

[1] ANGELUS.   Ye women presentt, dreditt[h] yow ryth

nowth.   *be not afraid*

Jhesus is resun, and is natt here.   *risen*

Loo, here is the place that he was in-browth.   *laid in*

Go, sey to his disipilles and to Peter he shall apere.

2 ANGELUS.   In Galelye, withowtyn ony wyre,   *doubt*

Ther shall ye se him, like as he said.

Goo yowr way, and take comfortt and chyr,   *cheer*

1030 For that he said shall natt be delayid.   *that which*

[*The angels withdraw; the Marys return from the monument.*]

Here shall the Maryis mete with Peter and Jhon.

M[ARY] MAUDLYN.   O Peter and Jhon, we be begilyd:

Owr Lordes body is borne away!

I am aferd itt is diffilyd.

I am so carefull, I wott natt whatt to saye.   *full of cares*

PETER.   Of thes[e] tidinggys gretly I dismay!

I woll me thethere hie with all my myth.   *hasten thither/might*

Now, Lord defend us as he best may!

Of the sepulture we woll have a syth.   *sepulchre/sight*

1010Lord, bow down your heavens, and descend (Psalms 144:5).

1014s.d. *monument:* Christ's tomb is perhaps located in the "place." Christ's death has presumably taken place since his last appearance at the raising of Lazarus.

1039 JHON.   A, min[e] inward sowle stonding in distresse—
1040   The w[h]eche of my body shuld have a g[u]ide—   *should have the guidance*
1041   For my Lord stonding in hevinesse,
            Whan I remembyr his woundes wide!
       PETER.   The sorow and peyne that he ded drye   *pain/did suffer*
            For owr offens and abominacion!
            And also I forsoke him in his turmentry;
            I toke no hede to his techeing and exortacion.
                Here Peter and Jhon go to the sepulcur, and the Maryis folowing.

       [PETER.]   A, now I se and know the sothe!   *truth*
            But, gracius Lord, be owr protexcion!
            Here is nothing left butt a sudare cloth,   *shroud*
1050   That of thy berying shuld make mencion.   *burying/give testimonial*
       JHON.   I am aferd of wikkitt opression;
            Where he is becum, it cannatt be devisyd.   *i.e., has been taken/discerned*
            Butt he seyd after the third day he shuld have resurrex[i]on.
            Long beforn, this was promisyd.
                *[The disciples withdraw. Mary Magdalene, alone by the tomb,
                stands apart from the other Marys.]*

       M[ARY] MAGDLEYN.   Alas! I may no lengar abide,   *live*
            For dolour and dissese that in my hartt doth dwell.   *sorrow and misery*
                [An angel appears.]

       1 ANGELUS.   Woman, woman, w[h]y wepest thou?
            W[h]om sekest thou with dolare thus?   *dolor*
       M[ARY] MAGDLEYN.   A! fain wold I wete, and I wist how,   *wit, know/if I knew*
1060   W[h]o hath born[e] away my Lord Jhesus.
                Hic apparuit Jhesus. [Mary mistakes him for a gardener.] *Here Jesus appears*

       [JESUS.]   Woman, woman, w[h]y syest thow?   *sigh*
            W[h]om sekest thou? Tell me this.
       M[ARY] MAGDL[E]YN.   A, good sir, tell me now
            If thou have born[e] awey my Lord Jhesus,
            For I have porposyd in eche degré   *intended in every way*
            To have him with me, verely,   *truly*
            The w[h]iche my speciall Lord hath be,   *Who/been*
1068   And I his lover and cause will phy.
       JHESUS.   O Mary!
       M[ARY] MAGDLEYN.   A, gracius Master and Lord, yow it is
                that I seke!   *seek*

1039–41Ah, my soul—which should guide my body—(is) in great distress and sorrow for my
Lord.

1068And I, his devoted worshiper, will undertake his cause (?).

Lett me anoint yow with this bamys sote. *sweet balms*
Lord, long hast thou hid the[e] from my spece, *from me (?)*
Butt now will I kesse thee, for my hartes bote. *boot, remedy*

JHESUS.   Towche me natt, Mary. I ded natt asend *have not yet ascended*
To my Father in deyité, and onto yowrs; *deity*
Butt go, sey to my brotheryn I will pretende *intend, venture*
To stey to my Father in hev[n]ly towers. *ascend*

M[ARY] MAGDLEYN.   Whan I sye yow first, Lord, verely *saw*
I wentt ye had bin Simond, the gardener. *weened, thought*

1080 JHESUS.   So I am, forsothe, Mary;
Mannys hartt is my gardin here.
Therin I sow sedys of vertu all the yere; *seeds*
The fowle wedes and vicys, I reynd up by the rote. *rend, tear*
Whan that gardin is watteryd with teris clere,
Than spring vertuus, and smelle full sote. *Then/sweet*

M[ARY] MAGDLEYN.   O, thou dereworthy emperowre, thou
hye devine!
1087 To me this is a joyfull tiding,
1088 And onto all pepull that after us shall reyngne— *reign, live*
1089 This knowlege of thy deyité— *deity*
1090 To all pepull that shall obteyne
1091 And know this be posibil[it]é.

JHESUS.   I woll shew to sinnars, as I do to the[e], *appear*
If they woll with vervens of love me seke. *fervency/seek me*
Be stedfast, and I shall ever with the[e] be,
And with all tho that to me bin meke. *those*

Here avoidit[h] Jhesus sodenly, thus seying Mary M[agdalene *disappears*
as she joins the other Marys]:

[MARY MAGDALENE.]   O, sistir[s], thus the hey and nobill *high*
influentt grace *overflowing*
Of my most blessyd Lord Jhesus, Jhesus, Jhesus!
He aperyd onto me at the sepulcur ther I was; *where*
That hath relevyd my woo, and moryd my blische. *firmly fixed my bliss*
1100 Itt is innumerabill to expresse, *too great*
Or for ony tong for to tell,
Of my joye how myche itt is, *much*
So myche my peynnes itt doth excelle! *pains*

M[ARY] SALOME.   Now lett us go to the setté, to Owr Lady dere, *city*
Hir to shew of his wellfare,
And also to dissipilles, that we have syn here; *what we have seen*
The more it shall rejoise them from care.

M[ARY] JACOB.   Now, sistir Magdleyn, with glad chir;

1087–91This knowledge of your deity is joyful news to me and to all people henceforth who
will possess this truth and know it to be possible (i.e., believe in it).

1109   So wold that good Lord we myth with him mete!   *might*

JHESUS [*reappearing*]. To shew desirows hartes I am full nere,
           Women, I apere to yow, and sey "Avete!"   *Farewell*

[MARY] SALOME.   Now, gracius Lord, of yowr nimios charité—   *exceeding*

1113   With hombill hartes to thy presens complaine—
           Grauntt us thy blyssing of thy hye deité,   *high, exalted*
           Gostly owr sowlys for to sosteynne.   *Spiritually*

1116   JHESUS.   Alle tho bin blissyd that sore refreynne.
           We blysch yow, Father, and Son, and Holy Gost,   *bless*
           All sorow and care to constryne,   *constrain, keep in check*
           By owr power, of mytes most.   *the greatest of powers*
           In nomine Patris et Filii et Spiritus Sancti, amen!
           Goo ye to my brethryn, and sey to hem ther[e]
           That they procede and go into Gallelye;
           And ther shall they se me, as I seyd before,
           Bodily, with here carnall yye.   *their physical eye*
               Here Jhesus devoiditt[h] agen.   *disappears*

       [MARY] MAGDLEYN.   O thou glorius Lord of heven region,
           Now blissyd be thy hye devinité,
           Thatt ever thow tokest incarnacion
           Thus for to vesite thy pore servantes thre!   *visit*
           Thy will, gracios Lord, fulfillyd shall be
1130   As thou commaundist us in all thing.
           Owr gracious brethryn we woll go se,
           With hem to seyn all owr lekeing.   *To tell them/pleasure*
               Here devoid all the thre Maryis; and the King of Marcill[e] shall
               beginne a sacrifice. [The king, at his stage, is attended by his
               queen and followers.]

       REX MERCILL[E].   Now lorddes and ladyis of grett aprise,   *worth*
           A mater to meve yow is in my memoriall: *to urge you*
           This day to do a sacrifice
           With multetude of mirth, before owr goddes all,
           With preors in aspeciall before his presens,   *prayers*
           Eche creature with hartt demure.   *calm, sober*

       REGINA.   To that lord curteys and keynd,   *courteous and kind*
1140   Mahond, that is so mikill of myth,   *Mohammed/great of might*
           With minstrelly and mirth in mind,   *music*

1109Would that we might meet with that good Lord! (The following appearance of Jesus to the three Marys does not occur in any of the Gospels.)

1113(To us who) with humble hearts express our grief in your presence.

1116Blessed are all those who restrain affliction (?).

Lett us gon ofer in that hye kingis syth. [*They start for the*   *offer/sight*
   temple.]

[*The stage of the heathen temple in Marseilles.*]
Here shall enter an hethen prest and his boye.

PRESBYTER.   Now, my clerke, Hawkin, for love of me
   Loke fast min[e] awter wer arayd;   *that my altar be arrayed*
   Goo ring a bell, t[w]o or thre.
   Lythly, child, it be natt delayd,   *Quickly/let it not be*
   For here shall be a grett solemnité.
   Loke, boy, thou do it with a brayd.   *haste*
BOY.   Whatt, master, woldist thou have thy lemman to thy   *lover, wench*
   beddes side?
1150   Thow shall abide till my servise is said.
PRESBYTER.   Boy, I sey, by Sentt Coppin,
   No swiche wordes to the[e] I spake.   *such*
1153 BOY.   W[h]ether thou ded or natt, the frist jorny shall be   *did/journey*
   min[e],
1154   For, by my feyth, thou berist Wattes pakke.
1155   But, sir, my master grett Morell,
   Ye have so fellyd yowr bylly with growell,   *filled/belly/gruel*
   That it growit[h] grett as the divll of hell.
   Onshaply thou art to see!
   Whan women comme to here thy sermon,   *hear*
1160   Pratily with hem I can houkkyn—   *Prettily/make love*
   With Kirchon and fayer Marion.
   They love me better than ye,
   I dare sey; and thou shulddes ride,   *if/ride (with sexual meaning)*
   Thy body is so grett and wide,
   That never horse may the[e] abide,
   Exseptt thou breke his bakk asoundire.   *Unless*
PRESBYTER.   A, thou lyist, boy, by the divll of hell!
   I pray god Mahond mott the[e] quell!   *may kill you*
   I shall whip the[e] till thy ars shall belle.   *roar*
1170   On thy ars com mych wondire.
BOY.   A fartt, master, and kisse my grenne!   *groin*
   The divll of hell was thy emme.   *uncle*

1150You'll have to wait until I've said (i.e., sung) my religious service.

1153–54Whether or not you said anything (about a wench), the first trip (i.e., with her) will
be mine, for, truly, you're too fat and gross.

1155*Morell:* the priest's name?

1170Miracles (of whipping) will be performed on your ass.

[*To the audience.*]

1173 Loo, mastirs, of swiche a stokke he cam;

1174 This kenred is a-sprongyn late.   *lately*

PRESBYTER. Mahoundes blod, preciows knave!   *arrant*

Strippys on thy ars thou shall have,   *Stripes*

And rappys on thy pate!

  Bete him. Rex dicit [*arriving at the temple*]:   *The king says*

[REX.] Now, prystes and clerkys of this tempill cler, *pure, holy*

Yowr servise to sey, lett me se.

1180 PRESBYTER. A, soveryn lord, we shall don owr devyr. *devoir, duty*

Boy, a boke anon thou bring me!

Now, boy, to my awter I will me dresse;   *altar/prepare myself*

On shall my vestment and min[e] aray.

BOY. Now than, the lesson I woll expresse,   *read*

Like as longitt[h] for the servise of this day: *Such as is appropriate*

1186 "*Lectio Mahowndis, viri fortissimi Sarasenorum,*

Glabriosum ad glumandum glumardinorum,

Gormondorum alocorum, stampatinantum cursorum,

Cownthtes fulcatum, congruriandum tersorum,

Mursum malgorum, Mararagorum,

Skartum sialporum, fartum cardiculorum,

Slaundri stroumppum, corbolcorum,

Sniguer snagoer werwolfforum,

Standgardum lamba beffettorum,

Strowtum stardi strangolcorum,

Rigor dagor flapporum,

Castratum ratirybaldorum;

Howndes and hogges, in hegges and helles,   *hedges and hills*

Snakes and toddes mott be yowr belles;   *toads*

1200 Ragnell and Roffin, and other, in the wavys, *(devils' names)*

Grauntt yow grace to die on the galows."

PRESBYTER. Now, lordes and ladyis, lesse and more, *of less and greater rank*

Knele all do[w]n with good devocion.

Yonge and old, rich and pore,

Do yowr ofering to Sentt Mahownde,

And ye shall have grett pardon,

That longitt[h] to this holy place;   *belongs to*

And receive ye shall my benesown,   *benison, blessing*

And stond in Mahowndes grace.

  Rex dicit [*kneeling*]:   *The king says*

1173–74(to the audience) Lo, sirs, he (my master) came from such stock; this family (which is related to the devil) has sprung up only lately.

1186(Latin gibberish, beginning "The Book of Mohammed, most mighty men of the Saracens," etc.)

1210 [REX.] Mahownd, thou art of mytes most— *most mighty*
In my syth a glorius gost. *sight/spirit*
Thou comfortist me both in contré and cost *coast, shore (i.e., everywhere)*
With thy wesdom and thy witt;
For truly, lord, in the[e] is my trost.
Good lord, lett natt my sowle be lost!
All my cownsell well thou wotst. *you know*
Here in thy presens as I sett, *i.e., kneel*
This besawnt of gold, rich and rownd, *besant, gold coin*
I ofer itt for my lady and me,
1220 That thou mayst be owr counfortes in this stownd. *hour*
Sweth Mahound, remembir me! *Sweet*
PRESBYTER. Now, boy, I pray the[e] lett us have a song.
Owr servise by note lett us sing, I say.
Cowff up thy brest, stond natt to[o] long, *Cough, swell*
Beginne the offise of this day. *service*
BOY. I home and I hast, I do that I may, *hum/what*
With mery tune the trebill to sing.
Sing both.
PRESBYTER. Hold up! the divll mote the[e] afray, *may the devil frighten you*
For all owt of rule thou dost me bring.— *out of order*
1230 Butt now, ser king, quene, and kni[g]th,
Be mery in hartt everychon, *everyone*
For here may ye se relikes brigth: *bright*
Mahowndes own nekke bon, *neck bone*
And ye shall se er ever ye gon, *see (it) before you go*
Whattsomever yow betide. *Whatever happens to you*
And ye shall kesse all this holy bon:
Mahowndys own yee-lid. *eyelid*
Ye may have of this grett store, *value*
And ye knew the cause wherfor: *If*
Itt woll make yow blind for ever more,
This same holy bede. *bead*
Lorddes and ladyis, old and y[i]nge, *young*
1243 Mahownd the body, and dragon the dere,
1244 Golias so good, to blisse may yow bring, *Goliath*
With Beliall, in blisse everlasting,
That ye may ther in joy sing
Before that comly king
That is owr god in fere. *god of us all*
[They withdraw. Enter Pilate on his stage, attended.]

1243–44 May the worthy Mohammed, and the beloved dragon, and the good Goliath, bring you to bliss (?).

PILATT.   Now, ye serjauntes semly, qw[h]at sey ye?

1250   Ye be full wetty men in the law.   *witty*

Of the dethe of Jhesu I woll avisyd be;

Owr soferyn Sesar the soth must nedes know.   *Caesar must know the truth*

This Jhesu was a man of grett vertu,

And many wondyrs in his time he wrowth;   *wrought*

He was put to dethe by cawsys ontru,   *for causes untrue*

Wheche mater stekitt[h] in my thowth.   *sticks/thought*

And ye know well how he was to the erth browth,   *i.e., buried*

Wacchyd with knigths of grett aray.   *Guarded by/weaponry*

He is resyn again, as before he tawth,   *previously he taught*

1260   And Joseph of Baramathye he hath takyn awey.   *Arimathea has taken him*

[1] SERJANTT.   Soferyn juge, all this is soth that ye sey.

But all this must be curyd by sotilté,   *subtlety*

And sey how his disipilles stollyn him away;   *And (we must) say*

And this shall be the answer, by the asentt of me.

1265   2 SERJANTT.   So it is most lylly for to be;   *truly, likely*

Yowr councell is good and commendabill.

So write him a pistill of speciallté,   *a special epistle, letter*

And that for us shall be most prophytabill.   *profitable*

PILATT.   Now, masengyr, in hast hether thou com!

1270   On masage thou must, with owr writing,   *You must go on a message*

To the soferyn emperowr of Rome.

But frist thou shall go to Herodes the king,

And sey how that I send him knowing   *knowledge*

Of Cristes deth, how it hath byn wrowth.   *wrought*

I charge the[e], make no letting   *delay*

Till this letter to the emperowr be browth.   *brought*

NUNTIUS PILATUS.   My lord, in hast yowr masage to spede

Onto that lorde of ryall renown,   *royal*

Dowth ye nat, my lord, it shall be don indede.   *Doubt*

1280   Now hens woll I fast owt of this town.   *hence*

Her[e] goth the masenger to Herodes [at his stage, attended].

NUNTIUS.   Heyll, soferyn king onder crown!

The prinsys of the law recsummende to yowr heynesse,   *commend themselves*

And senditt[h] yow tidinges of Cristes Pass[i]on,

As in this writing doth expresse. [*Delivers the letter.*]

HERODES.   A, by my trowth, now am I full of blis!

Thes[e] be mery tidinges that they have thus don.

Now certes I am glad of this;

For now ar we frendes that afore wer fon.   *foes*

Hold a reward, masenger, that thow were gon,   *be gone*

1290   And recummend me to my soferens grace.   *sovereign's*

1265i.e., That is the most likely course.

Shew him I woll be as stedfast as ston,
Ferr and nere, and in every place.
    Here goth the masenger to the emperowr [*at his stage, attended*].

NUNTIUS.   Heyll be yow, sofereyn, setting in solas!
    Heyll, worthy withowtyn pere!   *peer*
1295   Heyll, goodly to grauntt all grace!
    Heyll, emperowr of the wor[l]d ferr and nere!
    Soferyn, and it plese yowr hye empire,   *if/authority*
    I have browth yow writing of grett aprise   *brought/worth*
    W[h]ich shall be pleseing to yowr desire,
1300   From Pilatt, yowr hye justice.
    He sentt yow word, with lowly intentt,   *humble*
    In every place he kepitt[h] yowr cummaundement,   *(That) everywhere*
    As he is bound by his ofice.
EMPEROWR.   A, welcum, masenger of grett pleseauns!
    Thy writing anon lett me se. [*Takes the letter.*]
    My jugges, anon giffe atendans   *give attention*
    To onderstond whatt this writing may be—
    W[h]ethyr it be good ar ony deversité,   *or any mischief*
    Or elles natt for min[e] availl.   *help*
1310   Declare me this in all the hast.
PROVOST.   Sir, the sentens we woll discus,   *meaning*
    And it plese yowr hye exseleyns.   *If*
    The intentt of this pistull is thus:
    Pilatt recummenditt[h] to yowr presens,   *commends himself to you*
    And of a Prophett is the sentens,
    Whos[e] name was callyd Jhesus.
    He is putt to dethe with violens,
    For he chalyngyd to be King of Jewys—   *Because he claimed*
    Therfor he was crucified to ded,
1320   And syn was beryid, as they thowth reson—   *since, afterward/thought*
    Also he cleymid himsilf son of the Godhed.
    The therd nigth he was stollyn away with treson,   *treacherously*
    With his desipilles that to him had dyleccion;   *By/who took delight in him*
    So with him away they yode.   *went*
    I merveyll how they ded with the bodyis corupcion; *how they managed*
1326   I trow they wer fed with a froward fode.   *perverse food*
IMPERATOR.   Crafty was ther conning, the soth for to seyn.
    This pistill I will kepe with me iff I can;
    Also I will have cronekillyd the yere and the reynne,   *chronicled*
    That never shall be forgott, whoso loke theron.
    Masengyre, owt of this town with a rage!   *haste*

1295Hail, you who are the beneficent granter of all favor!

1326i.e., I expect they got an unpleasant whiff of the body's smell (?).

Hold this gold to thy wage,   *as*
Mery for to make.
NUNTIUS.   Farewell, my lord of grett renown,
For owt of town my way I take. [*They withdraw.*]

Here entyr [Mary] Mawdleyn with hyr disipill, thus seying:

[MARY] MAUDLYN.   A! now I remembyr my Lord that put
            was to ded
With the Jewys, withowttyn giltt or treson.   *By*
The therd nigth he ros by the myth of his Godhed;   *might*
Upon the Sonday had his glorius resurrexcion;
And now is the time past of his glorius asencion.
He steyid to hevyn, and ther he is king.   *ascended*
A! his grett kendnesse may natt fro my mencion.   *not leave my remembrance*
1343   Of alle maner tongges he gaf us knowing,
1344   For to undyrstond every langwage.
Now have the disipilles take ther passage   *taken*
To divers contreys her[e] and yondir,
To prech and teche of his hye damage;   *injury, Passion*
Full ferr ar my brothyrn departyd asondyr.   *separated*
        [*She stands aside.*]
        Her[e] shall hevyn opyn and Jhesus shall shew [himself].

1349   JHESUS. O, the onclipsyd sonne, tempyll of Salamon!   *uneclipsed sun*
1350   In the mone I restyd, that never chonggyd goodnesse;   *moon/changed*
1351   In the shep of Noee, fles of Judeon.   *ship/Gideon*
She was my tapirnakill of grett nobillnesse,   *tabernacle*
She was the paleys of Phebus brigthnesse,   *palace/Phoebus'*
She was the vessell of puere clennesse   *pure*
1355   Wher my Godhed gaff my manhod myth: *might*
My blissyd mother, of demure feminité,
1357   For mankind the feynddes defens,
Quewne of Jherusalem, that hevenly ceté,   *city*
1359   Emprese of hell to make resistens.   *against hell*
She is the precius pin[e] full of ensens,   *incense*

1343–44(A reference to the day of Pentecost, or Whitsunday, when the Holy Ghost entered the disciples and they spoke with strange tongues. See Acts 2:4.)

1349–51O sun never disfigured by eclipse, O temple of Solomon! (i.e., the perfectly chaste and wise Virgin Mary). I took my earthly habitation in a perfect moon not subject to monthly change, a ship of Noah (i.e., a refuge), a fleece of Gideon. (God caused a dew to fall on Gideon's fleece as a token of divine favor; see Judges 6:37–40.)

1355i.e., Where my Godhead took on human strength and shape.

1357The defense of mankind against the fiend.

1359Empress appointed to make resistance against hell.

1361	The precius sinamver, the body thorow to seche;	*cinnabar*
1362	She is the muske agens the hertes of violens,	
1363	The jentill jelopher agens the cardiakilles wrech.	*gillyflower*
	The goodnesse of my mothere no tong can expresse,	
1365	Ner no clerke of hir hir joyis can writh.	*write*
	Butt now of my servantt I remembyr the kendnesse;	*servant (i.e., Mary Magdalene)*
	With hevenly masage I cast me to vesite.	*intend to visit (her)*

[*He turns to the angel Raphael.*]

	Raphaell, min[e] angell in my site,	*sight*
	To Mary Maudleyn decende in a while.	
1370	Bid her passe the se by my myth,	*cross over the sea/might*
	And sey she shall converte the lond of Marcyll.	*Marseilles*

ANGELUS.   O glorius Lord, I woll resortt   *go*

	To shew your servant of yowr grace.	
	She shall labor for that londes comfortt,	*land's*
	From hevinesse them to porchasse.	*sorrow/redeem*

Tunc descendet angelus [*and appear to Mary*].   *Then the angel will descend*

	Abasse the[e] noutt, Mary, in this place!	*Be not abashed*
	Owr Lordes preceptt thou must fullfill,	
	To passe the see in shortt space	*time*
	Onto the lond of Marcyll.	
1380	King and quene converte shall ye,	
	And byn amittyd as an holy apostylesse.	*be admitted, received*
	Alle the lond shall be techyd alonly by the[e];	
	Goddes lawys onto hem ye shall expresse.	
	Therfore, hast yow forth with gladnesse	
	Goddes commau[n]ddement for to fullfille.	
1386	MARY. He that from my person seven devlles mad[e] to flc,	
1387	By vertue of Him, alle thing was wrowth!	*wrought*
	To seke thoys pepyll I woll rydy be.	*those/ready*
	As thou hast commaundditt, in vertu they shall be browth.	*into/brought*
	With thy grace, good Lord in deité,	
	Now to the see I will me hy	*hie*
	Sum shepping to asspy.	*Some shipping*
	Now spede me, Lord in eternall glory!	
	Now be my spede, allmyty Trenité!	

Here shall entyr a ship [*into the "place"*] *with a mery song.*

	MASTER. Strike, strike! Lett fall an ankyr to grownd!	*Strike, lower sails*

1361–63(She is) the precious cinnabar (a reddish metal or resin, used as a purge), to seek through and cleanse the body; she is the musk used medicinally as an antispasmodic, the gentle gillyflower used for heart pain.

1365Nor can any learned divine describe in writing her joys.

1386–87All things were created by virtue of Him who expelled seven devils from my person.

Her[e] is a fayer haven to se.   *to behold*

Conningly in, loke that ye sownd!   *measure the depth*

I hope good harbarow have shal wee.   *harbor, shelter*

Loke that we have drinke, boy thou.

BOY.   I may natt for slep, I make God a vow!   *because I'm sleepy*

Thou shall abide itte, and thou were my siere.   *wait for it even if/father*

MASTER. Why, boy, we are rydy to go to dinere.

Shall we no mete have?   *food*

1404   BOY.   Natt for me be of good chyr,

Thow[gh]e ye be sor hongord till ye rave,   *sorely hungered*

I tell yow plenly beforn!   *plainly*

For swiche a cramp on me sett is,   *such/has come on me*

I am a point to fare the worse;   *at point, about to*

I li[e] and wring till I pisse,   *twist and turn*

1410   And am a pointt to be forlorn!   *destroyed*

MASTER.   Now, boy, whatt woll the[e] this seyll?   *what do you want now*

BOY.   Nothing butt a fayer damsell.

She shold help me, I know it well,

Ar elles I may rue the time that I was born!   *Or*

MASTER.   By my trowth, sir boye, ye shal be sped: *aided*

I will hir bring onto yowr bed!

1417   Now shall thou lern a damsell to wed;

1418   She will nat kisse the[e] on skorn!   *in scorn*

    Bete him.

BOY.   A skorn? no, no, I find it hernest!   *earnest*

The devlle of hell motte the[e] brest,   *May the devil burst you*

For all my corage is now cast!   *overthrown*

Alasse, I am forlorn!

    [*Mary steps forward.*]

MARY.   Master of the shepe, a word with the[e].   *ship*

MASTER.   All redy, fayer woman, whatt wol ye?

MARY.   Of whense is this shep? Tell ye me,

And if ye seyle within a while.   *sail soon*

MASTER.   We woll seyle this same day

If the wind be to owr pay.   *in our favor*

This shep that I of sey   *I speak of*

1430   Is of the lond of Marcyll.

MARY.   Sir, may I natt with yow saile?

And ye shall have for yowr availe.   *you'll have your payment*

MASTER.   Of shepping ye shall natt faille;   *You won't lack shipping*

For us the wind is good and saffe.

    [*Mary boards, and they set sail.*]

1404Not by my doing will you have any good cheer or repast.

1417–18i.e., Here's my whip that will kiss you in earnest and teach you a lesson.

Yondyr is the lond of Torké;   *Turkey*

1436   I wer full loth for to lie.   *were, would be*

Now shall the shepmen sing.

1437   Of this cors we thar nat abasse.   *need not be abashed*

Yender is the lond of Satyllye.   *Satalia, Attalia (Asia Minor)*

Strik[e]! Beware of sond!   *sand*

Cast a led, and in us g[u]ide!   *Take a sounding*

1441   Of Marcyll this is the Kingges lond.

Go a-lond, thow fayer woman, this tide,   *to land/time*

To the kingges place—yonder may ye se.

[She disembarks.]

Sett of[f], sett of[f] from lond!

BOY.   All redy, master, at thin[e] hand!

Her[e] goth the shep owt of the place.   *central acting area*

MARY.   O Jhesu, thy mellifluos name

Mott be worcheppyd with reverens!   *Ought to be*

Lord, graunt me victoré agens the fyndes flame,   *against/fiend's*

1449   And in thy lawys gif this pepyll credens.

1450   I will resortt, by grett conveniens;

On his presens I will draw nere,   *Unto his (the king's)*

Of my Lordes lawys to she[w] the sentens,   *meaning*

Bothe of his Godhed and of his powere.

Here shall Mary entyr before the king [of Marseilles at his station].

Now, the hye king Crist, mannes redempcion,

Mote save yow, ser king, regning in equité,   *May he*

And mote g[u]idde yow the [way] toward sa[l]vasion!

Jhesu, the son of the mithty Trenité   *mighty*

That was, and is, and ever shall be,

For mannes sowle the reformacion:

1460   In his name, lord, I beseche the[e],

Within thy lond to have my mancion.   *dwelling*

REX.   Jhesu? Jhesu? Qwat deylle is him? That?   *What devil*

I defye the[e] and thin[e] apenion!   *opinion*

Thow false lordeyn, I shal fell the[e] flatt!   *rascal*

Who made the[e] so hardy to make swich rebon?   *such insolent answer*

MARY.   Sir, I com natt to the[e] for no decepcion,

But that good Lord Crist hether me compassyd.   *devised my journey hither*

1436–37 I would be very loath to tell you a lie (i.e., I'm telling you the truth). We needn't be concerned about this navigational course (i.e., we're on course).

1441 This is the land of the King of Marseilles.

1449–50 And give this people faith in your teachings. I will go, with great fitness and dedication.

To receive his name, itt is yowr refeccion;   *(spiritual) refreshment*
And thy forme of misbele[f] by him may be losyd.   *loosed, cured*

1470 REX.   And whatt is that lord that thow speke of here?
MARY.   *Id est Salvator*, if thow will lere,   *It is the Saviour/learn*
The secunde person, that hell ded conquare,   *did conquer hell*
And the Son of the Father in Trenité.

REX.   And of whatt power is that god that ye reherse to me?
MARY.   He mad[e] hevyn and erth, lond and see,
And all this he mad[e] of nowthe.   *nought*

REX.   Woman, I pray ye answer me:
Whatt mad[e] God at the first beginning?   *What did God make*
This processe ondyrstond wol we,

1480 That wold I lerne; itt is my plesing.
MARY.   Jhesu, mercy!
Sir, I will declare al and sum,
What from God frist ded procede.   *first*
He seyd, *"In principio erat Verbum,"*   *In the beginning was the Word*
And with that he provyd his grett Godhed:
He mad[e] heven for owr spede,   *aid*
Wheras he sitth in trones hyee;   *Where he sits in high throne*
His ministyrs next, as he sawe nede,
His angelus and archangylles, all the compeny.

1490 Upon the frist day God mad[e] all this,
As it was plesing to his intent.
On the Munday he wold natt mis
To make sonne, mone, and sterrys and the firmament—
The sonne to beginne his co[u]rs in the orient,
And ever labor withowtyn werinesse,
And kepitt[h] his cours into the occedentt.
The Twysday, as I ondyrstond this,
Grett grace for us he gan to incresse:
That day he satt upon wateris,

1500 As was liking to his goodnesse—   *was pleasing*
As Holy Writt beritt[h] wettnesse.
That time he made both see and lond,
All that werke of grett nobillnesse,
As it was plesing to his gracius sond.   *dispensation*
On the Weddysday, owr Lord of mythe   *might*
Made more at his plesing:
Fische in flod and fowle in flyth—
And all this was for owr hellping.
On the Thorsday, that nobill king

1510 Mad[e] diverse bestes, grett and smale;
He yaff hem erth to ther feding,   *gave them*
And bad[e] hem cressyn, by hille and dale.   *increase everywhere*

And on the Friday, God mad[e] man,
As it plesett[h] his hynesse most,
After his own semelitude than,   *In his own likeness then*
And gaf hem life of the Holy Gost.   *i.e., And breathed the spirit of life*
                                                                        into them
O[n] the Satyrday, as I tell can,
All his werkys he gan to blisse:
He bad[e] them multiply and incresse than,
1520   As it was plesing to his worthinesse.
And on the Sonday he gan rest take,
As Skriptur declaritt[h] pleyn,
That al shold reverens make
To hir makar that hem doth susteyn—   *their/who sustains them*
Upon the Sonday to leven in his servise   *believe*
And him alonly to serve, I tell yow pleyn.   *only*

REX.   Herke, woman, thow hast many resonnes grett—
I thingk, onto my goddes aperteyning they beth!   *they be appertaining*
But thou make me answer so[o]n, I shall the[e] frett   *Unless/torture*
1530   And cut the tong owt of thy hed!

MARY.   Sir, if I seyd amis, I woll retur[n] again.   *go back in my discourse*
Leve yowr encomberowns of perturbacion,   *Leave/troubled state*
And lett me know what yowr goddes byn,   *be*
And how they may save us from treubelacion.   *tribulation*

REX.   Hens! To the tempyll that we ware,   *i.e., let us go*
And ther shall thow se a solom syth.   *sight*
Com on, all, both lesse and more,   *of low and high rank*
This day to se my goddes myth.   *god's might*

    Here goth the king with all his atendaunt to the tempyll
    [*where the heathen priest and his clerk await them. The king*
    points out the idols.]

Loke now, qwatt seyist thow by this syth?   *what say you about this sight*
1540   How pleseaunttly they stond, se thow how!
Lord, I besech thy grett myth,
Speke to this Christeyn that here sestt thou.   *you see*
Speke, go[o]d lord, speke! Se how I do bow! [*The idol is*
        silent.]
Herke, thou prist, qwat menitt[h] all this?   *priest/what means*
What? Speke, good lord, speke! What eylitt[h] the[e] now?   *ails*
Speke, as thow artt bote of all blisse!   *boot, remedy*

PRYSBITER.   Lord, he woll natt speke while Chriseten here is.

MARY.   Sir king, and it plese yowr gentillnesse,   *if*
Giff me licens my prayors to make
Onto my God in heven blisch,   *heaven's bliss*
Sum merakill to shewyn for yowr sake.

REX.   Pray thy fille till then knees ake!   *thine, your*

1553   MARY.   *Dominus illuminatio mea; quem timebo?*
1554   *Dominus protector vitae meae; a quo trepidabo?*

Here shal the mament tremill and quake.   idol
Now, Lord of lordes, to thy blissyd name sanctificatt   sanctified
Most mekely my feyth I recummend.   entrust
Pott do[w]n the prid[e] of mamentes violatt!   Put/profane idols
Lord, to thy lover thy goodnesse descend;   send down
Lett natt ther prid[e] to thy posté pretend,   presume against your power
1560   Wheras is rehersyd thy hye name, Jhesus!
Good Lord, my preor I feythfully send;   prayer
Lord, thy rythwisnesse here discus!   reveal
Here shall comme a clowd from heven and sett the
tempyl on a fier, and the prist and the cler[k] shall
sinke; and the king gothe hom, thus seying:

1563   [REX.]   A, owt, for angur I am thus deludyd!
I will be-wreke my cruell tene.   avenge/harm
Alas, within mysylfe I am concluditt! [*To Mary.*]   confuted
Thou woman, comme hether and wete whatt I mene: know, learn
My wiff and I together many yerys have byn,
And never myth be conceivyd with child.   might
If thou for this canst find a mene,   means
1570   I will abey thy God, and to him be meke and mild.
MARY.   Now, sir, syn thou seyst so,   since
To my Lord I pr[a]ye with reythfull bone.   rightful prayer
Beleve in him and in no mo,   no more, others
And I hope she shall be conceivyd sone.   I trust
REX.   Avoid, avoid! I wax all seke!   sick
I will to bed this same tide.   at once
I am so vexyd with yen-sueke,   sickness(?)
It hath nere to deth me dyth!   nearly/put
Here the king goth to bed in hast, and Mary goth into an old logge   booth, hut
withowt the gate, thus seying: outside

MARY.   Now, Crist, my creatur, me conserve and kepe   creator
That I be natt confunddyd with this reddure!   overthrown by this harshness
For hungore and thurst to the[e] I wepe;
Lord, demene me with mesure!   deal with me moderately
As thou savydist Daniell from the liounes rigur,   lions'

1553–54The Lord is my light [and my salvation]; whom shall I fear? The Lord is the protector of my life; of whom shall I be afraid? (Psalms 27:1).

1560Wherever your exalted name is mentioned, Jesus!

1563Ah, out (an exclamation of impatience), I curse for anger that I am thus deluded!

1584   By [H]abacuk, thy masengyre, relevyd with sustinouns,   *relieved*
        Good Lord, so hellpe me and sokore,   *succour me*
        Lord, as itt is thy hye pleseawns!   *your exalted pleasure*

        [*Christ, in heaven, speaks to his angels.*]

JHESUS.   My grace shall grow and do[w]n decend
        To Mary, my lover, that to me doth call,
        Hir ass[t]att for to amend.   *state, condition*
        She shall be relevyd with sustinons corporall.   *fleshly sustinence*
        Now, awngelus, dissend to hir in especiall,
1592   And lede hir to the prinssys chambir ryth.
1593   Bed hir axke of his good by weyis pacifical;
        And goo yow before hir with reverent lyth.   *light*
1 ANGELUS.   Blissyd Lord, in thy syth   *sight*
        We dissend onto Mary.
2 ANGELUS.   We dissend from yowr blisse bryth;   *bright*
        Onto yowr cummaundement we aplye.   *apply (ourselves)*
        Tunc descendit angelus. Primus dixit: *Then the angel[s] descend. The first*
                                                                      says

[1 ANGELUS.]   Mary, owr Lord will comfortt yow send: *will send you*
1600   He bad[e] to the king ye shuld take the waye,
        Him to asay if he woll condesend—   *test/make concessions*
        As he is sleping, hem to asaye.
2 ANGELUS.   Bid him releve yow, to Goddes pay,   *relieve (financially)/satisfaction*
        And we shal go before yow with solem lyth;   *light*
        In a mentyll of white shall be owr araye.   *mantle/array, dress*
        The dores shall opyn agens us, by ryth.   *against, to/right*
MARY.   O gracius God, now I undyrstond!
        This clothing of white is tokening of mekenesse.
        Now, gracius Lord, I woll natt wond   *turn, refuse*
1610   Yowr preseptt to obbey with lowlinesse.
        Here goth Mary, with the angelus before hir, to the kingges bed,
        with lythys bering, thus seying Mary: *bearing lights*

[MARY.]   Thow froward king, trobelows and wood,   *troublous and mad*
        That hast at thy will all wor[l]ddes wele,   *weal, wealth*
        Departe with me with sum of thy good,   *Give me/goods, wealth*
        That am in hongor, threst, and cold!   *thirst*
        God hath the[e] sent warningys felle;   *many*
        I rede the[e] torne and amend thy mood.   *I advise you to be converted*
        Beware of thy lewdnesse, for thy own hele!   *wickedness/(spiritual) health*

1584(Who was) brought sustenence by Habakkuk, your messenger.

1592–93And lead her right to the prince's (king's) chamber. Bid her ask for some of his wealth
by peaceful means (i.e., voluntarily).

1618   And, thow quen, turne from thy good.   *goods, possessions*

       Here Mary [a]voidit[h]; and the angyll and Mary chong[e] hir   *goes out*
       clotheing; thus seying the king:

[REX.]   A, this day is com! I am mery and glad;

     The son is up and shinith bryth.   *brightly*

     A mervelows shewing in my slep I had   *apparition*

     That sore me trobelyd, this same nyth: *night*

     A fayer woman I saw in my syth;   *sight*

     All in white was she cladd;

     Led she was with an angyll bryth;   *by*

     To me she spake with wordes sad.

REGINA.   I trow from God that they were sentt!

     In owr hartes we may have dowte.

     I wentt owr chambir shold a brentt   *weened, thought/should have burned*

1630   For the lyth that ther was all abowth!   *Because of the light/about*

     To us she spake wordes of dred,   *dread, warning*

     That we shuld help them that have nede

     With owr go[o]des, so God ded bid—   *did*

     I tell yow withowtyn dowthe!

REX.   Now, semely wiff, ye sey ryth well.   *right, very*

     [*The king summons a soldier.*]

     A knyth anon withowtyn delay! [*The soldier approaches.*]

     Now, as thou hast byn trew as stylle,   *steel*

     Goo fett that woman before me this daye.   *fetch*

MILES.   My sovereyn lord, I take the waye;

     She shall com at [y]owr pleseawns.   *pleasure*

1641   Yowr soveryn will I will goo saye.

1642   Itt is almesse hir to avawns.   *alms/advance*

       Tunc transit miles ad Mariam.   *Then the soldier crosses over to Mary*

Sped[e] well, good woman! I am to the[e] sentt,   *May you prosper*

Yow for to speke with the king.   *(In order) for you*

MARY.   Gladly, ser, at his intentt.

     I comme at his own pleseing.

       Tunc transit Maria ad regem.   *Then Mary crosses over to the king*

The mythe and the powere of the heye Trenité,   *might*

The wisdom of the Son, mott governe yow in ryth!   *may (they) govern/the right*

The Holy Gost mott with yow be!

What is yowre will? Sey me in sythe.   *i.e., Tell me directly*

1618s.d.: The changing of clothing is apparently to prepare for subsequent scenes; the special white garments have been for the nighttime apparition.

1641–42I will go announce what you, our sovereign, desire. It is alms (i.e., an act of charity) to advance and assist her.

1651   REX.   Thow fayer woman, itt is my delyth,   *delight*

1652   The[e] to refresch is min[e] intentt,

        With mete and mony, and clothys for the nyth,   *food/night*

        And with swich grace as God hathe me lentt.   *such*

1655   MARY.   Than fullfille ye Goddes cummaundement,   *Then*

1656   Pore folk in misch[ef], them to susteyn.   *trouble*

    REX.   Now, blissyd woman, reherse here presentt   *recite*

      The joyis of yowr Lord in heven.

    MARY.   A, blissyd the [h]ower, and blissyd be the time,

      That to Goddes lawys ye will giff credens!

      To yowrselfe ye make a glad prime   *beginning*

      Agens the fenddes maliciows violens.   *Against/fiend's*

      From God above comit[h] the influens,

      By the Holy Gost into thy brest sentt down,

      For to restore thy offens,   *make amends for*

      Thy sowle to bring to everlasting salvacion.

      Thy wiffe, she is grett with child!

      Like as thou desierst, thou hast thy bone.   *boon, prayer*

    REGINA.   A, ye[a]! I fel itt ster in my wombe up and down!

1670   I am glad I have the[e] in presens.

      O blissyd womman, rote of owr sa[l]vacion,   *root, beginning*

      Thy God woll I worchep with dew reverens!

    REX.   Now, fayer womman, sey me the sentens,   *i.e., tell me*

      I beseche the[e]: whatt is thy name?

    MARY.   Ser, agens that I make no resistens: *against*

      Mary Maudleyn, withowtyn blame.   *i.e., undoubtedly*

    REX.   O, blissyd Mary, ryth well is me

      That ever I have abedyn this daye!   *abided, lived until*

      Now thanke I thy God, and specially ye,

1680   And so shall I do while I leve may.   *may live*

    MARY.   Ye shall thank itt Peter, my master, withowt delay.   *thank (for) it*

      He is thy frend, stedfast and cler;

      To allmythy God he halp me pray,   *helped*

      And he shall crestyn yow from the fynddes power   *christen/fiend's*

      In the syth of God an hye.   *sight/on high*

    REX.   Now, suerly ye answer me to my pay;   *pleasure*

      I am ryth glad of this tiddinges.   *right, very*

      Butt, Mary, in all my goodes I sese yow this day,   *my goods I give to you*

      For to byn at yowr g[u]iding,   *be*

1690   And them to rewlyn at yowr pleseing   *And rule them*

      Till that I comme hom again.

      I will axke of yow neithyr lond nor rekyning,   *ask/reckoning, payment*

1651–52You fair woman, it is my pleasure and intent to relieve your wants.

1655–56In that case you will be fulfilling God's commandment to provide for the poor in their need.

But I here delever yow powere pleyn.   *full power*

REGINA.   Now, worshepfull lord, of a bone I yow pray,   *boon, request*
And it be pleseing to yowr hye dignité.   *If*

REX.   Madam, yowr disiere onto me say.   *desire*
What bone is that ye disiere of me?

REGINA.   Now, worshepfull sovereyn in eche degré,   *in all ways*
That I may with yow goo,
A Crestyn womman made to be—   *christened, Christian*
Gracius lord, it may be soo.   *(I pray) it may*

REX.   Alas, the wittes of wommen, how they byn wild!

1703   And therof fallitt[h] many a chanse.   *befall*
A, why desier it? And yow ar with child.

REGINA.   A, my sovereyn, I am knett in care,   *tied, enveloped*
But ye consedyr now that I crave: *Unless/that which*
For all the lovys that ever ware,   *were*
Behind yow that ye me nat leve!   *Don't leave me behind*

REX.   Wiff, syn that ye woll take this wey of prise,   *i.e., since you insist*

1710   Therto can I no more seyn.   *say*
Now, Jhesu be owr g[u]id[e], that is hye justice,   *who*
And this blissyd womman, Mary Maugleyn!

MARY.   Sith ye ar consentyd to that dede,   *Since/deed*
The blissing of God giff to yow will I.
He shall save yow from all dred.
In nomine Patris, et Filii, et Spiritus Sancti. Amen.

Et tunc navis venit in plateam, et nauta dicit: *And then the ship comes into the place, and the sailor says*

[NAUTA.]   Loke forth, Grobbe, my knave,
And tell me qwat tidinges thou have,   *what*
And if thou aspye ony lond.

1720   BOY.   Into the shrowdes I woll me hie. [*He climbs.*]   *rigging/hasten*
By my fythe, a castell I aspye,   *faith*
And as I ondyrstond!

NAUTA.   Sett therwith, if we mown,   *Aim for there if we can*
For I wott itt is a havyn town   *know/harbor*
That stondit[h] upon a strond. [*They reach shore.*]   *shore*
Et tunc transit rex ad navem, et dicit rex: *And then the king crosses over to the ship, and the king says*

[REX.]   How, good man, of whens is that shep?
I pray the[e], ser, tell thou me.

NAUTA.   Ser, as for that, I take no kepe.   *no care, thought*
For qwat cause enquire ye?

REX.   For causys of nede: seyle wold we,   *we wish to sail*

1703From woman's giddiness many mishaps befall; i.e., from such a mad plan, misfortune would be sure to occur.

1731   Ryth fain we wold over byn.

   NAUTA. Yee, butt me thinkitt[h], so mote I thé,   *as I hope to prosper*

1733   So hastely to passe, yowr spending is thin.

   I trow, by my life,

   Thou hast stollyn sum mannes wiffe;

   Thou woldist lede hir owt of lond.

   Neveretheles, so God me save,

   Lett se whatt I shall have,   *i.e., what money*

   Or elles I woll nat wend.   *go*

1740 REX. Ten marke I will the[e] giff

   If thou wilt set me up at the cleyff   *land me at the cliffs(?)*

   In the Holy Lond. [*They go aboard.*]

   NAUTA [*to his crew*]. Set of[f], boy, into the flod!   *flood, sea*

   BOY. I shall, master. The wind is good;

   Hens that we were! [*They set sail.*]   *Let's go*

    Lamentando regina.   *The queen lamenting*

  [REGINA.] A, lady, hellp in this nede,

   That in this flod we drench natt!   *drown*

   A, Mary, Mary, flower of wommanhed,

   O blissyd lady, forgete me nowth!   *not*

1750 REX. A, my dere wiffe! No dred ye have,   *Fear not*

   Butt trost in Mary Maudleyn

   And she from perelles shall us save;   *perils*

   To God for us she woll prayyn.   *pray*

   REGINA. A, dere hosbond, think on me,

   And save yowrsilfe as long as ye may!

   For trewly itt will no otherwise be;

   Full sor my hart it makitt[h] this day.   *i.e., my heart sorrows*

1758   A, the child that betwix my sides lay,   *lies*

1759   The w[h]iche was conseivyd on me by ryth—   *by right*

1760   Alas, that wommannes help is away!

   An hevy departing is betwix us in syth,   *sorrowful parting/now*

   For now departe wee.

   For defawte of wommen here in my nede,   *default, lack*

1764   Deth my body makith to sprede.

   Now, Mary Maudleyn, my sowle lede!   *guide my soul*

   In manus tuas, Domine! [*She dies.*]   *Into your hands, Lord*

   REX. Alas, my wiff is ded!

[1731]Most gladly we wish to be over (i.e., across the sea).

[1733]You have but little money to spend for passage on such short notice.

[1758–60]Ah, the child lying in my womb, which I honestly conceived— alas, that no midwives are here to help (deliver the child)!

[1764]Death overspreads my body.

Alas, this is a carefull chans!   *sorrowful accident*

So shall my child, I am adred,   *I fear*

And for defawth of sustinouns.   *default, lack*

Good Lord, thy grace graunte to me!

1772 A child betwen us of increse,

An[d] it is motherles!

Help me, my sorow for to relesse,   *release, end*

If thy wil it be!

NAUTA. Benedicité, benedicité!   *Bless us*

Qwat wethyr may this be? [*A storm.*]

Owr mast woll all a-sondyr!   *break in sunder*

BOY. Master, I therto ley min[e] ere   *I'll bet my ear*

1780 It is for this ded body that we bere;   *on account of*

Cast hir owt, or elles we sinke ond[yr]!

 Make redy for to cast hir owt.

REX. Nay, for Goddes sake, do natt so!

And ye will hir into the se cast,   *If*

Gyntyll seres, for my love do—   *sirs|do (a deed) for my love*

Yendyr is a roch in the west—   *Yonder|rock*

As ley hir theron, all above,

And my child hir by.

NAUTA. As therto I asent well.   *I assent to that*

And she were owt of the vessell,   *If*

1790 All we shuld stond the more in hele,   *health*

I sey yow verely.

 [*They sail to the rock, where the dead woman and her child are
laid.*]

REX. Li[e] here, wiff, and child the[e] by.

Blissyd Maudleyn be hir rede!   *guide*

With terys weping—and grett cause why—   *and with good reason*

I kisse yow both in this sted.   *hour*

Now woll I pray to Mary mild

To be ther g[u]ide here.

 Tunc remiga[n]t a[d] montem, et nauta dicit: *Then they row to the mountain, and
the sailor says*

[NAUTA.] Pay now, ser, and goo to lond,

1799 For here is the portt gaf I ondyrstond.

Ley down my pay in my hond,

And belive go me fro.   *quickly*

REX. I graunt the[e], ser, so God me save. [*Pays him.*]

Lo, here is all thy connownt;   *covenant, agreed price*

All redy thou shall it have

1772(Here's) a child, the offspring of us two.

1799For here is the port I gave (you) to understand (i.e., the port I agreed to deliver you to).

And a marke more than thy graunt.   *your due*

And thou page, for thy good obedientt,   *obedience*

I giff yow, beside yowr stintt,   *allotted amount*

Eche of yow a marke for yowr wage.

NAUTA.   Now He that mad[e] bothe day and nyth,

1810   He sped[e] yow in yowr ryth,   *May He aid/right*

Well to go on yowr passage!   *journey*

[*The King of Marseilles travels to Jerusalem, where he encounters Peter preaching.*]

PETER.   Now all creaturs upon mold   *earth*

That byn of Cristes creacion,   *are*

To worchep Jhesu they are behold,   *beholden*

Nor never agens him to make variacion.   *against/to be inconstant*

REX.   Ser, feythfully I beseche yow this daye:

Wher Peter the apostull is, wete wold I.   *know*

PETER.   Itt is I, sir. Withowt delay,

Of yowr asking tell me qwy.   *why*

REX.   Ser, the soth I shall yow seyn,   *say, tell*

And tell yow min[e] intentt within a while.   *quickly*

Ther is a woman hyth Mary Maudleyn,   *called*

1823   That hether hath laberyd me owt of Mercill—

1824   Onto the w[h]iche woman I think no g[u]ile—

And this pilgrimmage causyd me to take;

1826   I woll tell yow more of ye stille,

1827   For to crestyn me from wo and wrake.   *harm*

PETER.   O, blissyd be the time that ye are falle to grace,   *have fallen, come*

And ye will kepe yowr beleve after my techeing   *If/belief/according to*

And alle-only forsake the fynd Satanas,   *utterly/fiend*

The commaundme[n]ttes of God to have in keping!

REX.   Forsoth, I beleve in the Father that is of all wylding,   *ruler of all*

And in the Son, Jhesu Crist,

Also in the Holy Gost, his grace to us spreding.

I beleve in Cristes deth and his uprising.   *resurrection*

PETYR.   Ser, than whatt axke ye?   *ask*

REX.   Holy father, bapti[s]m, for charité,

Me to save in eche degré   *in every way*

From the fyndes bond.   *fiend's bondage*

[*They go to the place of baptism.*]

1840   PETYR.   In the name of the Trenité

1823-24Who has caused me to come hither from Marseilles—of whom (i.e., Mary) I suspect
no guile.

1826-27I'll tell you more (that she told me) of you: that you are to christen me (to preserve
me) from woe and harm.

With this water I baptisse ye,
That thou mayst strong be
Agen the fynd to stond.   *Against*
   Tunc aspargit illum cum aqua.   *Then he sprinkles him with water*
  REX. A, holy fathyr, how my hart will be sor
1845   Of cummau[n]ddementt and ye declare nat the sentens!   *if/meaning*
  PETYR. Sir, daily ye shall labor more and more
    Till that ye have very experiens.   *true state of mind*
1848   With me shall ye [d]wall to have more eloquens,   *dwell*
1849   And goo vesite the stacions by and by:
    To Nazareth and Bedlem goo with deligens,   *Bethlehem*
    And by yowr own inspeccion yowr feyth to edify.
    [The King of Marseilles leaves Peter and returns after a brief
    interval.]

  REX. Now, holy father, dereworthy and dere,   *precious*
    Min[e] intent now know ye.
    Itt is gon full t[w]o yere   *Two years have elapsed*
    That I cam to yow overe the se,   *Since*
    Cristes servont and yowr to be,   *yours*
    And the lawe of him ever to fulfill.
    Now woll I hom into my contré.
    Yowr puere blissind graunt us tille;   *pure blessing/to us*
1860   That, feythfully, I crave.
  PETRUS. Now in the name of Jhesu,
    Cum Patre et Sancto Spiritu,   *With the Father and Holy Ghost*
    He kepe the[e] and save!   *(May) he preserve*
    Et tunc rex transit ad navem, et dicit rex: *And then the king crosses over to the ship, and the king says*

  [REX.] Hold ner, shepman, hold, hold!   *Come near and stop*
1865 BOY. Ser, yendyr is on[e] callyd after cold.   *yonder*
  NAUTA. A, ser! I ken yow of old.   *know*
    By my trowth, ye be welcum to me.
  REX. Now, gentill marranere, I the[e] pray,   *mariner*
    Whatsoever that I pay,   *I (must) pay*
1870   In all the hast that ye may,
    Help me over the se.
  NAUTA. In good soth, we byn atenddawntt;   *i.e., we're at your service*

1845Unless you explain the meaning of (God's) commandment.

1848*eloquens:* i.e., fluency in discoursing about matters of faith.

1849*stacions:* holy places visited in succession.

1865Sir, yonder is one who called for cold. (The boy, up to his usual mischief, deliberately mistakes "hold" for "cold.")

Gladly ye shall have yowr graunt,   *request*
Withowtyn ony connownt.   *covenant, bargain*
Comme in, in Goddes name! [*The king boards.*]
Grobbe, boy, the wind is nor-west;
Fast abowth the seyle cast!   *Quickly turn the sail about*
Rere up the seyll in all the hast,   *Rear, raise*
As well as thou can!
    Et tunc navis venit ad-circa plateam. Rex dicit: *And then the ship comes round about the place. The king says*

1880   [REX.]   Master of the ship, cast forth yowr yee!   *eye (i.e., look out there)*
Me thinkit[h] the rokke I gin to aspye.   *I see the rock*
Gentill master, thether us gye;   *guide us thither*
I shall qwit yowr mede.   *acquit, pay/reward*
NAUTA.   I feyth, it is the same ston   *In*
That yowr wiff lyeth upon.
Ye shall be ther even anon,   *right away*
Verely, indede.
REX.   O thou myty Lord of heven region,   *mighty*
Yendyr is my babe of min[e] own nature,   *Yonder/blood*
1890   Preservyd and keptt from all corrupcion!
Blissyd be that Lord that the[e] dothe socure.   *succours you*
    [*He lands.*]
And my wiff lyeth here, fayer and pure!   *uncorrupted*
Fayere and clere is hur color to se!
A, good Lord, yowr grace with us indure,   *strengthen us with your grace*
My wivys life for to illumin.   *kindle*
A, blissyd be that puer vergin;   *i.e., Mary Magdalene*
From grevos slepe she ginnit[h] revive!   *she (my wife) begins to*
A, the sonne of grace on us doth shynne!
Now blissyd be God, I se my wiff alive!
1900   REGINA.   *O virgo salutata,* for owr sa[l]vacion!
1901   *O pulcra et casta, cum* of nobill aliauns!
O almyty maidyn, owr sowlys confortacion!
O demur[e] Maudlyn, my bodyis sustinauns!
Thou hast wr[a]ppyd us in wele from all variawns,   *well-being/mutability*
And led me with my lord i[n]to the Holy Lond.
I am baptisyd, as ye are, by Maryis g[u]iddauns,
Of Sent Peterys holy hand.   *By*
I s[a]we the blissyd crosse that Crist shed on his precius
    blod;
His blissyd sepulcur also se I;   *saw*
Whe[r]for, good hosbond, be mery in mode,   *mood*

1900–1O virgin having been preserved for our salvation! O beautiful and chaste, and of noble kinship! (Referring to Mary Magdalene.)

1911   For I have gon the staciounes by and by.
    REX.   I thanke it, Jhesu, with hart on hye.
     Now have I my wif and my child both.
     I thank itt Maudleyn and Owr Lady,   *for it*
     And ever shall do, withowtyn othe. [*They go aboard.*]   *doubtless*
       Et tunc remigant a[d] monte[m], et nauta dicit: *And then they row to the mountain, and the sailor says*

    [NAUTA.]   Now ar ye past all perelle;
     Her[e] is the lond of Mercylle!
     Now goo a-lond, ser, whan ye will,
     I pr[a]ye yow, for my sake.
1920 REX.   Godamercy, jentill marraner!
     Here is ten pounds of nobilles cler;   *gold coins*
     And ever thy frynd, both ferre and nere,   *friend*
     Crist save the[e] from wo and wrake!   *harm*
      [*They land.*] *Here goth the shep owt of the place; and Maud-[leyn] seyth, [preaching, as the King and Queen of Marseilles and their son the prince approach her]:*

    [MARY.]   O, dere fryndes, be in hart stabill,
     And [think] how dere Crist hathe yow bowth!   *dearly/bought, ransomed*
     Agens God be nothing vereabill;   *Against/not at all inconstant*
     Think how he mad[e] all thing of nowth.   *nought*
     Thow[gh] yow in poverté sumtime be browth,   *brought*
     [Y]itte be in charité both nyth and day;   *Yet*
1930   For they byn blissyd that so byn sowth.   *that are so afflicted*
     For, *paupertas est domum Dei.*   *poverty is God's house*
     God blissit[h] alle tho that byn meke and good,   *those*
     And he blissit[h] all tho that wepe for sinne.
     They be blissyd that the hungor[y] and the thorsty giff
        fode;
     They be blissyd that byn mercifull agen wrecched men;   *against, toward*
     They byn blissyd that byn disstroccion of sinne.   *that are the destruction*
     Thes[e] byn callyd the childyren of life;
     Onto the w[h]iche blisse bring both yow and me,
     That for us dyid on the rode tre. Amen.   *(He) that/died/cross*
     Here shall the king and the qwene knele doun. Rex dicit: *The king says*
1940 [REX.]   Heyll be thou, Mary! Owr Lord is with the[e],
     The helth of owr sowlles and repast contemplatiff!   *i.e., spiritual sustenance*
     Heyll, tabirnakill of the blissyd Trenité!
     Heyll, counfortabill sokore for man and wiff!   *comfort-giving succour*

1911For I have visited in turn the holy places (of Jerusalem). (The queen is describing another of Mary's miracles; through her intercession, the seemingly dead queen has been transported to the Holy Land, as she wished.)

1940(An echo of the "Hail, Mary" addressed to the Virgin; see Luke 1.)

REGINA.   Heyll, thou chosyn and chast of wommen alon!   *alone, unique*

It passit[h] my wett to tell thy nobillnesse!   *exceeds my wit*

Thou relevist me and my child on the rokke of ston,   *brought relief to*

And also savyd us by thy hye holinesse.

MARY.   Welcum hom, prinse and prinsses, bothe!

1949   Welcum hom, yong prinsse of dew and ryth!   *of due, by right*

1950   Welcum hom to your own [h]eritage, withowt othe,   *doubtless*

And to alle yowr pepyll present in syth!   *sight*

Now ar ye becum Goddes own knygth;

1953   For sowle helth salve ded ye seche

1954   In hom the Holy Gost hath take resedens,

1955   And drevyn aside all the desepcion of wrech;   *harm*

1956   And now have ye a knowle[ge] of the sentens,

1957   How ye shall com onto grace.

1958   But now in yowr go[o]des agen I do yow sese;   *endow*

I trost I have governyd them to yowr hertes ese.

Now woll I labor forth God to plese,

1961   More gostly strenkth me to purchase.   *spiritual strength/acquire*

1962   REX.   O blissyd Mary, to comprehend   *accomplish*

1963   Owr swete sokor, on us have peté!   *succour*

REGINA.   To departe from us, why should ye pretende?   *venture*

O blissyd lady, putt us nat to that poverté!

MARY.   Of yow and yowers I will have rememberauns,

1967   And daily [y]owr bede-woman for to be,

1968   That alle wickidnesse from yow may have deleverans,

In quiet and rest that leve may ye.   *you may live*

REX.   Now, thanne, yowr puere blissing graunt us tille.   *pure, sinless/to us*

1971   MARY.   The blissin[g] of God mott yow fulfill!   *may*

1972   *Ille vos benedicat, qui sine fine vivit et regnat!*

Her[e] goth Mary into the wildirnesse, and thus seying rex:

[REX.]   A, we may syyn, and wepyn also,   *sigh*

That we have forgon this lady fre—   *lost/noble*

1949–50(Mary is addressing the young prince and heir to the throne, as distinguished from the prince his father in l. 1948.)

1953–58You sought salve for your soul's health, in the land where the Holy Ghost resides (i.e., Jerusalem), and have driven aside (i.e., banished) all the deceitfulness of harm and evil; and now you understand the substance of how you will achieve grace. But now I put you again in possession of your goods and property.

1961–63To acquire for myself more spiritual strength, i.e., more merit in heaven. —O blessed Mary, to accomplish our precious salvation (succour), have pity on us! (i.e., do not go).

1967–68i.e., I will daily offer intercessory prayers for you (a beadswoman is one pensioned to pray for a benefactor), so that you may be rescued from all wickedness.

1971–72May the blessing of God fill you completely! May he who lives and reigns without end bless you!

It bringgitt[h] my hart in care and woo—
The whech owr g[u]idde and governor should a be!   *Who/have been*

1977 REGINA.   That doth perswade all my blé,   *complexion*
1978   That swete sypresse, that she wold so.   *cyperus or galingale, a root*
    In me restitt[h] neither game nor glé,   *remains/joy nor delight*
    That she wold from owre presens goo.

    REX.   Now, of hir going I am nothing glad,
    But my londdes to g[u]iddyn I must aplye.   *apply (myself)*
    Like as Sancte Peter me badde,
    Chirchys in cetyis I woll edifye;   *cities/build*
    And whoso agens owr feyth woll replye,   *against/dispute*
    I woll ponisch [s]wich personnes with perplixcion.   *punish such/troubles*
    Mahond and his lawys I defye.

1988   A, his pride owt of my love shall have polucion,   *profanation*
    And [w]hollé onto Jhesu I me betake. [*They retire.*]   *commit myself*

        Mary in erimo.   *Mary in the wilderness*

    [MARY.]   In this deserte abidyn will wee,
    My sowle from sinne for to save.
    I will ever abide me with humelité,
    And put me in paciens, my Lord for to love.

1994   In charité my werkes I woll grave,   *engrave, fix indelibly*
1995   And in abstinens, all dayis of my life.
    Thus my conciens of me doth crave;
    Than why shold I with my consiens st[r]iffe?   *Then*
    And ferdarmore, I will leven in charité   *furthermore/live*
    At the reverens of Owr Blissyd Lady,   *In reverence of*
    In goodnesse to be liberall, my sowle to edifye.   *generous/strengthen*

2001   Of wor[l]dly fodes I will leve all refeccion;   *food/leave off/partaking*
2002   By the fode that commit[h] from heven on hye,
2003   Thatt God will me send, by contemplatiff.

    [*Christ in heaven hears Mary's prayer, and calls to his angels.*]

    JHESUS.   O, the swettnesse of prayors sent onto me
    Fro my wel-belovyd frynd, withowt variouns!   *variance, wavering*
    With gostly fode relevyd shall she be.   *spiritual food*
    Angelles! Into the clowdes ye do hir hauns;   *enhance, raise her up*

1977–78It prevails upon my complexion that so sweet a person would (leave us) so; i.e., her departure makes me turn pale.

1988Out of my love (for Jesus), Mohammed's pride will be defiled.

1994–95i.e., I will devote all my efforts to charity and abstinence, all the days of my life.

2001–3I will cease partaking of all worldly food, (and live instead) by the food that comes from heaven, by contemplative (food), which God will send me.

Ther fede with manna to hir sistinouns—
With joy of angyilles, this lett hur receive.

2010   Bid hur in joye with all hur afiawns,   *Bid her (be)/kindred*
        For fynddes frawd shall hur non[e] deseive.   *fiend's fraud*

2012   1 ANGELUS.   O thou redulent rose that of a vergin sprong!   *sweet-smelling*
        O thou precius palme of vi[c]tory!
        O thou osanna, angelles song!
        O precius gemme born of Owr Lady!
        Lord, thy commau[n]ddement we obbey lowly.   *humbly*
        To thy servant that thou hast grauntyd blisse—   *to whom*
        We angelles all obeyyn devowtly—
        We woll desend to yen wildirnesse.   *yon*

           Here shall t[w]o angylles desend into wildirnesse; and other
           t[w]o shall bring an oble, opynly apering aloft in the clowddes.   *mass wafer*
           The t[w]o benethyn shall bring Mary, and she shall receive, the   *beneath, on earth/(to) Mary*
           bred, and than go agen into wildirnesse.   *then*

2020   2 ANGELUS.   Mary, God gretit[h] the[e] with hevenly
             influens!   *emanation, infusion*
        He hath sent the[e] grace with hevenly synys: *signs*
        Thou shall byn [h]onoryd with joye and reverens,
        Inhansyd in heven above verginnes!   *Raised/above (all other)*
        Thou hast biggyd the[e] here among spinys;   *dwelt/thorns, thickets*
        God woll send the[e] fode by revelacion.
        Thou shall be receivyd into the clowddes,
        Gostly fode to reseive to thy sa[l]vacion.   *Spiritual food/for*

     MARY.   *Fiat voluntas tua* in heven and erth!   *Your will be done*
        Now am I full of joye and blisse.

2030   Laud and preyse to that blissyd birth!   *Praise*
        I am redy, as his blissyd will isse.   *is*

           Her[e] shall she be halsyd with angelles, with reverent song [as   *embraced by*
           she is raised into the clouds and fed with mass bread]:

           Assumpta est Maria in nubibus; caeli gaudent, angeli laudantes   *Mary has been taken up into the*
           filium Dei.   *clouds; the heavens rejoice, the*
           Et dicit Mary: *angels praising the son of God.*
                                                        And Mary says

    [MARY.]   O thou Lord of lorddes, of hye domenacion!   *dominion*
        In heven and erth worsheppyd be thy name.
        How thou devidist me from houngure and vexacion!   *you keep me from*
        O glorius Lord, in the[e] is no frauddes nor no defame.   *villainy*
        But I shuld serve my Lord, I were to blame,   *Unless*

2010 i.e., Bid Mary be joyful in the company of her heavenly kindred (?).

2012 O you sweet-smelling rose who sprang (i.e., was born) from the Virgin!

W[h]ich fullfillit[h] me with so gret feliceté,   *Who completely fills*

With melody of angylles shewit[h] me gle and game,   *joy and delight*

And have fed me with fode of most delicité!

    [She returns to the wilderness.] Here shall speke an holy prest in
    the same wildirnesse, thus seying the prest:

2040 [PREST.] O Lord of lorddes, what may this be?

So gret mesteryis shewyd from heven,   *mysteries*

With grett mirth and melody,

With angylles brygth as the levyn!   *bright/lightning*

Lord Jhesu, for thy namys sevynne,   *seven*

As graunt me grace that person to se.   *Grant me*

    Her[e] he shal go in the wildirnesse and spye Mary in hir devo-
    cion, thus seying the prest:

[PREST.] Heyl, creature, Cristes delecceon!

Heyl, swetter than sugur or cypresse!   *galingale, a sweet herb*

Mary is thy name, by angylles relacion.   *relation, account*

Grett art thou with God for thy perfithnesse.   *Beloved*

2050 The joye of Jherusallem shewyd the[e] expresse,   *plainly*

2051 The w[h]ich I never sawe this thirty winter and more;

Wherfor I know well thou art of gret perfi[t]nesse.

2053 I woll pray yow hartely to she[w] me of yowr Lord.

MARY.   By the grace of my Lord Jhesus,

This thirty winter this hath byn my selle,   *cell*

2056 And thryys on the day enhansyd thus,   *raised up*

With more joy than ony tong can telle.

2058 Never creature cam ther I dwelle,   *where*

2059 Time nor tide, day nor nyth,

2060 That I can with spece telle,   *speech*

2061 But alonly with Goddes angylles brygth.   *Except*

But thou art wolcum onto my syth,   *sight*

If thou be of good conversacion.   *manner of life*

2064 As I think in my delyth,   *delight*

2065 Thow sholddist be a man of devocion.

PREST.   In Cristys law I am sacryed, a pryst,   *consecrated*

2050–51The joy in Jerusalem (i.e., the rejoicing of the angels in the heavenly Jerusalem just witnessed), the likes of which I haven't seen for thirty years or more, plainly reveals you (i.e., proves your sainthood).

2053I pray you earnestly that you will vouchsafe me a revelation concerning your Lord, Christ.

2056And thrice each day I have been raised up thus.

2058–61No one has visited my dwelling at any time, day or night, that I can mention, excepting only God's bright angels.

2064–65I believe, in my pleasure at seeing you, that you must be a man of religious calling.

Ministryid by angelus at my masse.   *Assisted by angels*

I sakor the body of owr Lord Jhesu Crist,   *consecrate*

And by that holy manna I leve in sowthfastnesse.   *live*

2070   MARY.   Now I rejoise of yowr goodnesse!

But time is comme that I shall asende.

PREST.   I recummend me with all [h]umbilnesse.   *commend myself (to you)*

Onto my sell I woll pretend.   *cell/intend to go*

Here shall the prest go to his selle; thus seying Jhesus [in heaven]:

JHESUS.   Now shall Mary have possession,

By ryth en[h]iritawns a crown to bere.   *true inheritance/bear*

She shall be fett to everlasting sa[l]vacion,   *fetched, brought*

In joye to dwell withowtyn fere.   *without rival*

Now, angelus, lythly that ye were ther!   *quickly*

Onto the pristes sell apere this tide: *priest's cell/time*

2080   My body in forme of bred that he bere,

2081   Hur for to hossell, bid him provide.   *housel, administer Eucharist*

1 ANGELUS.   O blissyd Lord, we be redy

Yowr massage to do withowtyn treson.   *without disobeying*

2 ANGELUS.   To hir I will goo and make reportur   *report*

How she shall com to yowr habitacion.

Here shall two angylles go to Mary and to the prest, thus seying the angelles to the prest:

[ANGELS.]   Ser pryst, God cummau[n]ditt[h], from heven region,

Ye shall go hosyll his servont expresse,   *with speed*

2088   And we with yow shall take ministracion   *serve*

2089   To bere lyth before his body of worthinesse.   *light/his worthy body*

PREST.   Angylles, with all [h]umbillnesse

In a vestment I will me aray

To ministyr my Lord of gret hynesse;   *administer (the sacrament)*

Straitt therto I take the way.

[The second angel goes to Mary.] Secundus angelus in erimo: *The second angel in the wilderness*

[2 ANGELUS.]   Mary, be glad, and in hart strong

To reseive the palme of grett vi[c]tory:

This day ye shall be reseivyd with angelles song;

Yowr sowle shall departe from yowr body.

MARY.   A, good Lord, I thank the[e] withowt veriawns!   *wavering*

This day I am groundyd all in goodnesse,   *firmly fixed*

2080–81Bid him prepare to take her my body in the form of bread, to give her the last rites with the Eucharist.

2088–89And we angels will assist you by carrying light in procession before his (Christ's) worthy body (i.e., the host).

2100   With hart and body concludyd in substawns.
   I thanke the[e], Lord, with sperit of perfithnesse!
   Hic apparuit angelus et presbiter cum Corpus Dominicum.

                          Here appear the (first) angel and the priest with the Body of the Lord (the host)

  [PREST.] Thou blissyd woman, inure in mekenesse,   *practiced*
   I have browth the[e] the bred of lif to thy syth,   *brought/sight*
   To make the[e] suere from all distresse,   *sure, safe*
   Thy sowle to bring to everlasting lyth.   *light*
  MARY. O thou mythty Lord of hye magesté,   *mighty*
2107   This celestiall bred for to determin
2108   This time to reseive it in me—
2109   My sowle therwith to illumin—
   Her[e] she reseivit[h] it.
2110   I thank the[e], Lord, of ardent love!
   Now I know well I shall nat opprese.   *be overwhelmed*
   Lord, lett me se thy joyis above!
   I recummend my sowle onto thy blisse.
   Lord, opyn thy blissyd gates!
   This erth at this time ferven[t]ly I kisse.
   In manus tuas, Domine—   *Into your hands, Lord*
   Lord, with thy grace me wisse!—   *guide*
   Commendo spiritum meum. Redemisti me,   *I commend my spirit. You have redeemed me,*
   Domine Deus veritatis!   *Lord God of truth*
    [She ascends with the angels.]

2120 1 ANGELUS. Now reseive we this sowle, as reson is,
   In heven to dwelle us among,
  2 ANGELUS. Withowtyn end to be in blisse.
   Now lett us sing a mery song.
   Gaudent in caelis.   *They rejoice in heaven*

  PREST [*remaining below*]. O good God, grett is thy grace!
   O Jhesu, Jhesu, blessyd be thy name!
   A Mary, Mary, mych is thy solas,   *much*
   In heven blisse with gle and game!   *joy and delight*
   Thy body wil I cure from alle maner blame;
   And I will passe to the bosshop of the seté,   *go to the chief priest/city*
2130   This body of Mary to berye by name
   With alle reverens and solemnité.

   [He addresses the audience in an epilogue.]

2100With heart (i.e., heartbeat, the sign of life) and body brought to an end in physical form.

2107–10I thank you, Lord, with ardent love, for determining this time for me to receive this celestial bread, with which to bring light to my soul. (*Here she receives the Eucharist.*)

2130i.e., To ask the chief priest's permission to bury Mary's body. (Cf. Joseph of Arimathea's request to Pilate for Jesus' body.)

Sufferens, of this processe thus enddit[h] the sentens   *Sirs/narration*
That we have playid in yowr syth.   *sight*
Alle-mythty God, most of magnificens,
Mote bring yow to his blisse so brygth,   *May (God) bring you/bright*
In presens of that king!   *i.e., Christ*
Now, frendes, thus endit[h] this matere.
To blisse bring tho that byn here!   *(may God) bring those*
Now, clerkys with voicys cler,   *clerics*
2140   *Te Deum laudamus* lett us sing.   *We praise you O God*
        Explicit originale de Sancta Maria Magdalena.   *Here ends the original of Saint Mary Magdalene*

        [*A scribal postscript:*]

        Iff onything amisse be,
2142   Blame conning, and nat me.   *(lack of) cunning*
        I desier the redars to be my frynd;   *readers/friend*
2144   Iff ther be ony amisse, that to amend.

2140s.d. *originale*: probably means the master copy used in production, called the "originall booke" at Chester and the "register" at York.

2142Blame my lack of cleverness, and not my intent.

2144i.e., If anything is amiss, I urge the reader to correct it for me.

THE PLAY OF THE SACRAMENT
FROM CROXTON

The Play of the Sacrament does not conform to the usual genres of English medieval drama. Although it is here grouped with two saints' plays from the Digby manuscript, *St. Paul* and *Mary Magdalene*, this play does not deal with a saint. Nor is it based even in part on scriptural account. Perhaps it is closest to a certain type of miracle play found abundantly in France and exemplified by *La Sainte Hostie* (printed in the sixteenth century). Like this French work, which purports to describe a genuine miracle performed in Paris, *The Play of the Sacrament* claims to be based on an authentic occurrence. The place and date of the event (Heraclea, 1461) are repeatedly mentioned. Yet both plays are in fact derived from a widespread legend, found as early as 1290, in which Jews desecrate the host and are then converted to Christianity by a revelation of the host's sacred powers.

Even if it is not a saint's play, *The Play of the Sacrament* is certainly a conversion play. Its purpose is to offer a convincing demonstration of Christ's real presence in the Eucharist, and to dramatize the conversion of those who do not at first believe in this supreme miracle of the Christian religion. Jonathas and his fellow Jews are to be deplored not because of their particular ethnic origin but because they are heathens lacking faith in Christ's divinity. They are no better and no worse than Aristory, the Christian merchant who steals the host from the church in order that the Jews may test its supposedly miraculous powers. Christians who offend against their faith are as much in need of amendment as Jews who have never professed faith in Christ. The play aims both at the penitent recovery of wayward Christians and at the conversion of non-believers.

The central action of the play, in which Jonathas and his fellows subject the host to a series of tortures and indignities designed to prove that it is merely a wafer of bread, is an extended symbolic reenactment of Christ's Passion. When, for example, Aristory agrees to steal the host out of the church in return for money, we are reminded of Judas' bargaining with the chief priests to betray Christ in return for thirty pieces of silver. When the Jews desecrate the host, they assume roles as the torturers of Christ. They are five in number since they must inflict five wounds on the host. Jonathas administers the fifth and final wound, thereby reenacting the role of the blind soldier who pierced Christ's side at the Crucifixion (l. 480). The number five also signifies the five words with which Christ blessed the host at the Last Supper: "Eat, this is my body" (l. 404). The host bleeds, in token of Christ's blood which was shed for man. Following the reenactment of Christ's death, we see a representation of the descent from the cross and the entombment: Jonathas and his fellows pluck out the nails they have hammered into the host, and then cast the host into a cauldron (ll. 657–59). The host is wrapped in a cloth to signify the graveclothes in which Christ lay buried. Thereafter follows a representation of the sealing of the tomb (ll. 709–10), and the descent into hell. When the cauldron bursts asunder, the resurrected Christ appears, uttering a "complaint" on the meaning of his suffering in the manner of a Resurrection play. Throughout, this sequence is modeled not only on the historical Passion and Resurrection but on the ceremony of the Eucharist; when the Jews first receive the host from Aristory, for example, they cover it with a cloth and bear it to a table representing an altar (ll. 383–92).

The long concluding action, characteristic of continental plays in this genre, is heavily liturgical. It stresses penance as well as conversion, for Aristory's recovery to grace is as important as the enlightenment of the Jews. The ceremonies of penance and baptism are both ritually solemn. Aristory's public penance is severe, like many such penances in the Middle Ages: he is forbidden ever to practice as a merchant again. Adding to the impressiveness of the occasion is the illusion of an actual ecclesiastical service. The bishop, presiding over the ceremonies of penance and baptism "with gret solempnité" (l. 951 s.d.), is presumably dressed in garments obtained from the church's wardrobe. His "props" include a font and other artifacts similarly furnished by the church. The processionals from the bishop's stage to the Jews' house and thence to church seem to require the actual movement of the audience, as in the Digby *St. Paul*. The spectators become a congregation, singing a hymn (l. 840) and listening to the sermons of Christ and the bishop. The singing of *Te Deum* at the end suggests that this play may have been performed in conjunction with matins. Clergy and laity alike are exhorted to revere the Eucharist and to overcome doubt in the transubstantial miracle of the mass—an increasing problem in fifteenth-century England.

In terms of staging, then, the action may actually conclude inside the church with a full procession and the performance of religious ceremonies. Earlier, outside the church, the play requires separate scaffolds for Aristory and for Jonathas, with a "platea" in the midst to accommodate much passing to and fro. Actions sometimes occur simultaneously; at l. 228, for example, Jonathas travels toward Aristory's "hall" while Aristory converses with his priest. The scaffolds are evidently spacious enough to accommodate several actors and are raised above ground level: Jonathas' "howse" is one that can be entered, and Aristory invites the Jews to "come up" to his hall. Jonathas' house must have a table, cauldron, oven, pincers, and other gear needed to bring about Christ's spectacular reappearance in the mass.

Today we can scarcely imagine how this play could have moved its audience to faith in the miracle of Christ's real presence in the mass. The theatrical devices seem obvious and even comic, involving as they do the sudden removal of Jonathas' hand from his arm and the appearance of Christ's image in a boiling oven. Surely a medieval audience would have recognized these stage contrivances as entertaining theatrical illusions. Yet we must remember that the earliest *Quem quaeritis* ceremonies similarly featured a display of the empty graveclothes inside the sepulchre, as a means of "demonstrating" the fact of Christ's resurrection. However much an audience or congregation would have acknowledged the use of illusion in such stage business, the audience also perceived an essential symbolic relationship between dramatic presentation and ritual reenactment. In the mass itself, according to medieval Christian doctrine, what appeared to the senses as a wafer of bread was to be regarded as the literal body of Christ. *The Play of the Sacrament* seems to demand a comparable leap of faith from things seen to things unseen. Even though a comparison of this play with the mass may strike us as risible, the similarity does reveal a continuing affinity between medieval religious drama and the ritual service from which it had originated.

The play's single comic scene appears to be a late addition. It differs from the main body of the play in verse form, language, and characterization. It interrupts the reenactment of the Passion and is not mentioned in the banns. This sequence owes its origin to folk drama and especially to the Mummers' plays, in which a quack doctor, boasting of his great prowess in healing, brings back to life the hero or sometimes his enemy. Such vestiges of fertility and resurrection myths have a general appropriateness to a play about the resurrected Christ, but the connection is a loose one at best. The comic scene is probably added for its horseplay rather than for any serious thematic purpose.

The Play of the Sacrament appears to have been written in East Midland dialect during the late fifteenth century, not long after the year (1461) in which the miracle is supposed to have taken place. Although a number of places named "Croxton" have been found in the Midland area, local allusions to "Tolcote" and "Babwell Mill" (see l. 621) suggest that the play was performed near Bury St. Ed-

munds in Suffolk. We learn from the preliminary announcement or "banns" that the play was intended to go on tour. Like the banns from the N Town cycle and *The Castle of Perseverance*, these banns for *The Play of the Sacrament* are designed for festive and colorful presentation. Minstrels are in attendance (l. 80). The banns also feature a procession, a gathering of the audience several days prior to the actual play, and possibly some kind of tableau display of the action (see l. 10). The play itself is to be performed on a following Monday (l. 74), although presumably the date and place of performance could be changed by the speakers of the banns to suit each individual occasion. Nine actors can perform the play "at ease," a fact which further indicates that touring would have been feasible.

The Play of the Sacrament
From Croxton

[The Banns]

1 VEXILLATOR. Now the Father and the Sune and the Holy Goste,		*Flag-bearer*
That all this wide worlde hat[h] wrowght,		*Who has created*
3 Save all thes semely, bothe leste and moste,		*least, humblest*
4 And brin[g]e yow to the blisse that he hath yow to-bowght!		
We be ful purposed, with hart and with thowght,		
Of our mater to tell the entent,		*subject*
Of the marvellys that wer wondursely wrowght		
Of the holy and blyssed sacrament.		*By*
9 2 [VEXILLATOR]. S[o]vereyns, and it like yow to here the purpoos of this play		*Masters*
10 That [is] representyd now in yower sight,		

3–4(May God) save all these fair people, all those of low and high degree, and bring you to the bliss that he has wholly purchased for you.

9–12Citizens, if it please you to hear the intent of this play that is now represented before you (in tableau?), the events of which actually took place, to tell the truth, in the famous city of Heraclea (the city of Hercules) in Aragon (Spain).

11	Which in Aragon was doon, the sothe to saye,	*truth*
12	In Eraclea, that famous cité, aright:	*actually, precisely*
	Therin wonneth a merchaunte of mekill might—	*dwells, i.e., dwelt/great*
	Sir Aristorye was called his name—	
15	Kend full fere with many a wight;	*Known/by*
	Full fer in the worlde sprong his fame.	

1.	Anon to him ther cam a Jewe,	
18	With grete richesse for the nonys,	
	And wonneth in the cité of Surrey—this [is] full trewe—	*Who dwelt/Syria*
	The w[h]iche had gret plenté of precious stonys.	*Who*

	Of this Cristen merchaunte he freyned sore,	*entreated sorely*
22	W[h]ane he wolde have had his entente:	*When*
	Twenty pound, and merchaundise mor[e],	
	He proferyd for the holy sacrament.	

2.	But the Christen merchaunte therof sed nay,	
	Because his profer was of so lityll valewe;	
27	An hundder pound but he wolde pay,	*unless he (the Jew)*
28	No lenger theron he shuld pursewe.	

	But mor[e] of ther purpos they gunne speke,	*they (the Jews) spoke*
	The holy sacramente for to bey;	*buy*
31	And all for [that] the[y] wolde be wreke,	*because/avenged*
	A gret sume of gold begune down ley.	

1.	This Cristen merchante consentyd, the sothe to sey,	
	And in the night affter, made him deliveraunce.	*made delivery to the Jew*
	Thes[e] Jewes all grete joye made they.	
	But of this betide a straunger chaunce:	*from this occurred*

	They grevid our Lord gretly on grownd,	*on earth (a metrical tag)*
	And put him to a new Passion—	
	With daggers goven him many a grevios wound;	*gave*
40	Nailed him to a piller; with pinsons plukked him doune.	*pincers*

[15]Known far and wide by many a person.

[18]*for the nonys:* a metrical tag.

[22]When he (the Jew) wished to achieve his intent.

[27–28]i.e., Unless the Jew would pay 100 pounds, he (the merchant) would go no further in the matter.

[31]And just because the Jews wanted to be avenged (on the sacrament, representing Christ).

2.   And sithe thay toke that blysed brede so sownde   *then|blessed bread|good*
And in a cawdron they ded him boile!   *cauldron|did*
In a clothe full just they it wounde,   *exactly*
And so they ded him sethe in oile.   *seethe, boil*

And than thay putt him to a new tormentry: *then*
In an hoote ovyn speryd him fast.   *hot oven shut*
There he appyred with woundys blody;   *appeared out*
The ovyn rofe asondre and all to-brast.   *split|burst to pieces*

1.   Thus in our lawe they were made stedfast;   *our law (of Christ)*
50   The holy sacrement shewyd them grette favour.   *showed|favor*
In contricion th[e]ir hertys wer cast,
And went and shewyd ther lives to a confesoure.

Thus by maracle of the King of hevyn,   *miracle*
And by might and power govyn to the prestys mowthe,   *given|priest's mouth*
In an howshold wer con[v]ertyd, iwis, elevyn.   *certainly*
At Rome this miracle is knowen welle kowthe.   *well known*

2.   This maricle at Rome was presented, forsothe,
In the yere of our Lord a M¹ cccc lxi,   *1461*
That the Jewes with Holy Sa[c]rament did woth   *injury*
60   In the forest seyd of Aragon.   *aforesaid*

Loo, thus God at a time showyd him there,   *himself*
Thorwhe his mercy and his mekill might: *Through|great*
Unto the Jewes he gan appere   *he appeared*
That they shuld nat lesse his hevenly light.   *lose*

1.   Therfore, frendys, with all your might
Unto youer gostly Father shewe your sinne.   *spiritual*
Beth in no wanhope, daye nor night;   *Be|despair*
68   No maner of dowghtys that Lord put in!   *doubts*

69   For that the dowghtys the Jewys than in stode—   *Because*
70   As ye shall se pleyd, both more and lesse—   *played, acted*
71   Was iff the sacrament were flesshe and blode,
72   Therfor they put it to suche distresse.   *For that reason*

2.   And it place yow, this gadering that here is,   *If it please you*
At Croxston on Monday it shall be sen[e].   *seen*
To see the conclusion of this litell processe   *see|story*

⁶⁸⁻⁷²Do not entertain any manner of doubt concerning that Lord! It was because the Jews doubted whether the sacrament was really flesh and blood that they subjected it to such torture—as you will see acted, all you of both high and low degree.

Hertely welcum shall yow bene.
Now Jhesu yow save from trey and tene,   *pain and harm*
To send us his hyh[e] joyes of hevyne—   *high*
79   There might us withouton mind to mene!
Now, minstrell, blow up with a mery stevyn!   *voice, sound*
    Explicit.   *Here end (the banns)*

Hereafter Foloweth the Play of the Conversion of
Ser Jonathas the Jewe by Miracle of the
Blissed Sacrament.

THE NAMYS AND NUMBERE OF THE PLAYERS:

JH[ES]US
EPISCOPUS   *the bishop*
ARISTORIUS, Christianus mercatore   *Christian merchant*
[ISODER, presbiter; Aristory's chaplain]   *priest*
CLERICUS, [PETER PAUL; Aristory's man]   *clerk*
JONATHAS, Judeus primus, Magister
JASON, Judeus secundus
JASDON, Judeus tertius
MASPHAT, Judeus quartus
MALCHUS, Judeus quintus
MAGISTER PHISICUS, [MASTER BRUNDICHE OF BRABANT]   *physician*
COLL[E], servus   *(his) servant*

    Nine may play it at ease.
       R.   C.

    [*On the stage of the Christian merchant, Aristory,
    the merchant is attended by his clerk, Peter Paul,
    and his chaplain, Sir Isoder.*]

81   ARISTORIUS MERCATOR.   Now Crist, that is our Creatour, from   *Merchant*
          shame he cure us;
82   He mainteyn us with mirth that meve upon the mold;   *move/earth*

---

⁷⁹There may we (remain), beyond the power of the intellect to describe or imagine.

THE NAMYS AND NUMBERS OF THE PLAYERS: This list appears at the end of the MS. "R.C." are presumably the scribe's initials.

⁸¹⁻⁸²Now may Christ, who is our Creator, preserve us from sin, and keep us all in joy who dwell (lit: move about) on earth.

Unto his en[d]elesse joye mightly he restore us,   *mightily (may) he restore*

84   All tho that in his name in peas well them hold!   *those*

For of a merchante most [of] might, therof my tale is told;

In Eraclea is non[e] suche, w[h]oso will understond.

For of all Aragon I am most mighty of silver and of gold—

88   For, and it were a countré to by, now wold I nat wond!   *if/buy/turn away*

Sir Aristory is my name,

A merchaunte mighty, of a royall araye.

Ful wide in this worlde springith my fame,

Fere kend and knowen, the sothe for to saye.   *Far known*

In all maner of londys, without ony naye,   *without doubt*

My merchaundise renneth, the sothe for to tell: *runs, travels*

In Gene, and in Jenyse, and in Genewaye,   *Genoa/Geneva(?)*

In Surrey, and in Saby, and in Salern I sell;   *Syria/Saba/Salerno*

In Antioche and in Almain moch is my might,   *Germany*

In Braban and in Britain I am full bold,   *Brabant*

In Calabre and in Coleyn ther ringe I full right,   *Calabria/Cologne/reign*

100   In Dordrede and in Denmark, by the cliffys cold;   *Dordrecht*

In Alisander I have abundaw[n]se in the wide world.   *Alexandria*

In France and in Farre fresshe be my flower[ys],   *Faeroe(?)*

In Gildre and in Galys have I bowght and sold,   *Guelderland/Galicia*

In Hamborowh and in Holond moch merchantdise is   *Hamburg*
        owrys;

In Jerusalem and in Jherico among the Jewes jentle,

Amo[n]g the Caldeys and Cattlingys kend is my koming;   *Chaldees/Catalans/known*

In Raynes and in Rome to Seynt Petyrs temple   *Rheims*

I am knowen certenly for bying and selling;

In Main[e] and in Melan full mery have I be;   *Milan/been*

110   Owt of Navern to Naples moch good is that I bring;   *Navarre/goods, wealth*

In Pondere and in Portingale moche is my gle;   *glee, mirth*

In Spaine and in Spruce moche is my speding;   *Prussia/prospering*

In Lombardy and in Lachborn, there ledde is my liking;   *Luxembourg/pleasure*

In Tarise and in Turkey, there told is my tale;   *Tharsia*

And in the Dukedom of Oryon moche have I in welding: *Orleans(?)/wielding, control*

And thus thorowght all this world sett is my sale.   *sail*

No man in this world may weld more richesse—   *wield*

84All those who in his name conduct themselves well in peace, peaceably.

88For, I wouldn't hesitate to buy even a whole country.

100*by . . . cold:* an asseveration, used here as a metrical tag.

All I thank God of his grace, for he it me sent—
And as a lordys pere thus live I in worthinesse.   *lord's peer*
My curat waiteth upon me to knowe min[e] entent,
121 And men at my welding; and all is me lent   *is lent me*
122 My will for to worke in this world so wide.
Me dare they nat displese by no condescent!   *in no way*
And whoso doth, he is nat able to abide.   *withstand (me)*

PRESBITER.   No man shall you tary ne t[r]owble this tide,   *Priest/hinder nor trouble*
But every man deligently shall do yow plesance;   *pleasure*
127 And I unto my conning to the best shall hem guide
128 Unto Godys plesing to serve yow to attrueaunce.   *at your command*

For ye be worthy and notable in substance of good—   *of wealth*
Of merchauntys of Aragon ye have no pere—   *peer*
And therof thank God that died on the roode,   *cross*
That was your makere, and hath yow dere.   *holds you dear*

ARISTORIUS.   Forsoth, sir pryst, yower talking is good!
And therfor, affter your talking, I will atteyn   *according to/strive*
To wourshippe my God that died on the roode.
136 Never, whill that I live, ageyn that will I seyn!   *against/say*
But, Petyr Powle, my clark, I praye the[e] goo wele pleyn   *directly*
Thorowght all Eraclea, that thow ne wonde,   *without delay*
And witte iff ony merchaunte be come to this reyn   *know, learn/any/realm*
Of Surrey or of Sabé or of Shelysdown.   *From/Chelidonia*

CLERICUS.   At your will for to walke I wil nat say nay,   *As you desire*
Smertly to go serche at the waterys side.   *Promptly*
Iff ony plesaunt bargin be to your paye,   *profit*
As swiftly as I can, I shall him to yow guide.
Now will I walke by thes[e] pathes wide
And seke the haven, both up and down,   *search the harbor*
To wette iff ony onkowth shippes therin do ride   *strange, foreign*
Of Surrey or of Saby [or] of Shelysdown.
Now shall the merchantys man [Peter Paul] withdrawe him, and
the Jewe Jonathas [on his stage, attended by his servants Jason,
Jasdon, Masphat, and Malcus] shall make his bost.

121-22 And (other) men at my command; and all is lent to me so that I can work my will in this wide world.

127-28 And I, to the best of my ability, shall exhort them to serve you at your command, in order to please God.

136 Never, so long as I live, will I speak against that, i.e., against your advice that I worship God.

JONATHAS.   Now almighty Machomet, marke in thy magesté,   *distinguished*
          Whose lawes tendrely I have to fulfill,   *attentively/observe*
          After my dethe bring me to thy hyh[e] see   *high seat, throne*
          My sowle for to save, iff it be thy will!
153   For min[e] entent is for to fulfill,
154   As my glorius god the[e] to honer.
          To do agen thy entent, it shuld gr[e]ve me ill,   *against*
          Or agen thin[e] lawe for to reporte.   *to speak*

          For I thanke the[e] hayly, that hast me sent   *exceedingly*
          Gold, silver, and presious stonys;
          And abu[n]ddaunce of spicys thou hast me lent,
160   A[s] I shall reherse before yow onys: *recite/once*
          I have amatystys riche for the nonys,   *amethysts/for the occasion*
          And baryllys that be bright of ble,   *beryls/countenance*
          And saphire semely I may show yow attonys,   *at once*
          And cristalys clere for to se;

          I have diamantys derewourthy to dresse,   *precious diamonds to set in position*
          And emerawdys—riche I trow they be—
          Onyx and achatys both more and lesse,   *agates/large and small*
          Topaziouns, smaragdys of grete degré,   *Topazes/emeralds*
          Perlys precious grete plenté;
170   Of rubés riche I have grete renown;
          Crepawdys and calcedonies semely to se,   *Toadstones*
          A[nd] curious carbunclys here ye find mown.   *may, can find*

          Spicys I have both grete and smale
          In my shippes, the sothe for to saye:
          Gingere, licoresse, and canningalle,   *galingale, aromatic root*
          And figys fatte to plese yow to paye,   *to your pleasure*
          Peper and saffiron and spicys smale,
          And datys wole dulcett for to dresse,   *very sweet dates/prepare*
          Almundys and reys—full every male—   *rice/sack*
180   And reysones both more and lesse;   *raisins*

          Clovys, greynis, and ginger grene,   *grains of paradise*
          Mace, mastik that might is,   *mastic that is strong*
          Sinymone, suger—as yow may sene—   *Cinnamon/see*
          Long peper, and Indas licorys,   *Indian*
          Orengys a[nd] apples of grete aprice,   *value*
          Pungarnetys, and many other spicys—   *Pomegranates*
          To tell yow all I have now, iwis—
          And moche other merchandise of sondry spicys.

153–54My intent is to fulfill (my obligation) to honor you as my glorious god.

Jew Jonathas is my name;
190   Jazon and Jazdon they waityn on my will,
Masfat and Malchus they do the same,
As ye may knowe—it is bothe richt and skill.   *right and reason*
I tell yow all, by dal[e] and by hille   *i.e., everywhere*
In Eraclea is noon so moche of might.   *none*
W[h]erfor, ye owe tenderly to tende me till,   *ought to heed me carefully*
For I am chefe merchaunte of Jewes, I tell yow, by right.

But Jazon and Jazdon, a mater wolld I mene;   *mention*
Mervelously it is ment in minde: *remembered*
The beleve of thes[e] Cristen men is false, as I wene,   *belief*
For the[y] beleve on a cake—me think it is onkind—   *unnatural*
201   And all they seye how the prest dothe it bind,
And by the might of his word make it flessh and blode—
And thus by a conceite the[y] wolde make us blind—   *fanciful notion*
And how that it shuld be He that deyed upon the rode.   *died/cross*

JASON.   Yea, yea, master, a strawe for talis!   *for (such) stories*
That ma[y] not fale in my beleve!   *fall into, enter my belief*
207   But, mi[gh]t we it gete onys within our pales,
I trowe we shuld sone affter putt it in a preve.   *soon/to the test*
JASDON.   Now, by Machomete so mighty, that ye doon of meve,   *what you've suggested*
I wold I wiste how that we might it gete!   *wish I knew/get*
211   I swer by my grete god, and ellis mote I nat cheve,   *may I not prosper*
212   But wightly the[r]on wold I be wreke!   *Unless quickly/avenged*

MASPHAT.   Yea, I dare sey feythfully that ther feyth [is fals]:
That was never He that on Calvery was kild!
Or in bred for to be blode, it is ontrewe als.   *also*
But yet with ther wiles they wold we were wild.   *wish/deceived*
MALCUS.   Yea, I am mighty Malchus, that boldly am bild.   *built*
218   That brede for to bete biggly am I bent!   *beat/I'm inclined*
219   Onys out of ther handys and it might be exiled,   *Once/if/removed*
To helpe castyn it in care wold I consent.   *cast, throw/sorrow*

221   JONAT[H]AS.   Well, sirse, than kype cunsel, I cummande yow all,   *keep*

201And they all say how the priest binds it (the "cake" or sacramental wafer, bound with the sacred covenant of the mass).

207But, if we might once get it within the confines of our walls, i.e., in our possession.

211-12I swear by my great god (Mohammed), may I never prosper if I don't long to be quickly avenged on it (the sacramental "cake")!

218-19I'm greatly inclined to strike that bread! If it might once be removed out of their hands.

221Well, sirs, then keep counsel (i.e., be secret), I command you all.

And no word of all this be wist.   *(let) no word/known*
But let us walke to see Aristories hall,
And affterward more counsell among us shall caste.   *we'll deliberate*
225   With him to bey and to sel I am of powere prest;   *buy/ready*
A bargin with him to make I will assaye.   *try*
For gold and silver I am nothing agast   *I don't doubt*
But that we shall get that cake to ower paye.   *pleasure*

> Her[e] shall ser Isodyr, the prest, speke ont[o] ser Aristory [on his
> scaffold], sey[i]ng on this wise to him; and Jonat[h]as goo
> do[w]n of [f] his stage [with his fellows].

PRESBITER.   Sir, by yowr leve, I may [no] lengere dwell.   *leave, permission*
It is fer paste none; it is time to go to cherche,   *far past noon*
There to saye min[e] evynsong—forsothe as I yow tell—   *late afternoon service*
And sith come home ageyne, as I am wont to werche.   *then/accustomed to do*

ARISTORIUS.   Sir Isydor, I praye yow wallke at yowr will.
234   For to serfe God it is well done.
And sit[h] com agen, and ye shall suppe your fill,
And walke than to your chamber, as ye are wont to doon.

> [The priest retires to the church. On the platea,] her[e] shall the
> marchant[ys] man, [Peter Paul, who has been looking for newly-
> arrived merchants,] mete with the Jewes.

JONAT[H]AS.   A, Petre Powle, good daye and wele i-mett!
W[h]er is thy master, as I the[e] pray?
CLERICUS.   Lon[g] from him have I not lett   *stayed, delayed*
240   Sit[h] I cam from him, the sothe for to saye.   *Since*
W[h]at tiding with yow, ser, I yow praye,   *What's the news*
Affter my master that ye doo frayne?   *ask*
Have ye ony bargen that wer to his paye?   *were, would be/profit*
Let me have knowlech; I shall wete him to seyn.   *I'll be able to tell him*

JONATHAS.   I have bargenes royall and ri[c]h
For a marchaunt with to bye and sell;
In all this lond is ther non like
Of abondaunce of good, as I will tell.   *goods, wealth*

> Her[e] shall the clerk goon to ser Aristory [at his scaffold],
> saluting him thus:

CLERICUS.   All haill, master, and wel mot yow be!   *may*

225I am ready and able to trade with him.

234It is well to serve God.

250 Now tidingys can I yow tell:
The grettest marchante in all Surré   *Syria*
Is come with yow to bey and sell—
This tal[e] right welc he me told.
Sir Jonat[h]as is his nam[e],
A marchant of right gret fame;
He wolld sell yow, without blame,   *i.e., without doubt*
P[l]enté of clothe of golde.

ARISTORIUS.   Petre Powle, I can the[e] thanke!
I prey the[e], richely araye min[e] hall
260 As owith for a marchant of the banke.   *owes, beseems*
Lete non[e] defawte be fownd at all.   *no default, lack*
262 CLERICUS.   Sekirly, master, no m[o]re ther shall!   *Surely*
Stiffly about I thinke to stere,   *Resolutely/stir about*
Hasterly to hange your parlowre with pall   *Hastily/rich cloths*
As longeth for a lordis pere.   *As befits a lord's peer*
    [*The clerk sets to work.*] *Here shall the Jewe*
    merchaunt and his men come to the Cristen merchaunte.

JONATHAS.   All haille, sir Aristorye, semelé to se,   *seemly*
The mightiest merchaunte of Arigon!
Of yower welfare fain wet wold we,   *we'd gladly know*
And to bargeyn with you this day am I boun.   *ready*

270 ARISTORIUS.   Sir Jonathas, ye be wellcum unto min[e] hall!
I pray yow come up and sit by me,
And tell me w[h]at good ye have to sell,   *goods*
And if ony bargeyn mad[e] may be.
    [*The Jews ascend to Aristory's scaffold.*]

JONATHAS.   I have clothe of gold, precious stons, and spicys
    plenté.
With yow a bargen wold I make;
I wold bartre with yow in privité.   *privately*
277 On[e] litell thing, ye will me it take
Prevely in this stownd;   *Secretly at this time*
And I woll sure yow, by this light,   *assure*
Never distre[n] yow, daye nor night,   *Never (to) betray*
But be sworn to yow full right—   *totally*
And geve yow twenty pownd.

²⁶⁰*banke:* place of business of those dealing in exchange.

²⁶²i.e., No default will be found at all, nothing will be lacking in the preparations.

²⁷⁷(I desire that) you will steal one little thing for me.

ARISTORIUS.   Sir Jonathas, sey me for my sake: *say to me*
  What man[er] of marchandis[e] is that ye mene?

JONATHAS.   Yowr God, that is full mythety, in a cake!   *mighty*
  And this good anoon shall yow seen.   *wealth/see, receive*
    [*Jonathas displays twenty pounds in gold.*]

[ARISTORIUS.]   Nay, in feyth, that shall not bene!
  I woll not for an hundder pownd   *hundred*
289   To stond in fere my Lord to tene—   *fear/offend*
  And for so litell a valew in conscien[c]e to stond bownd!

JONATHAS.   Sir, the entent is, if I might knowe or undertake   *understand*
  If that he were God all-might;   *almighty*
293   Of all my mis I woll amende make   *misdeeds*
  And doon him wourshepe bothe day and night.   *do*

ARISTORIUS.   Jonathas, trowth I shall the[e] tell:
  I stond in gret dowght to do that dede;   *doubt, fear*
297   To yow that dere all for to sell,   *loved one*
  I fere me that I shuld stond in drede!
  For, and I unto the chirche yede,   *if/went*
  And preste or clerke might me aspye,
  To the bisshope they wolde go tell that dede,
  And apeche me of [h]eresye.   *appeach, impeach*

JONATHAS.   Sir, as for that, good shiffte may ye make,   *expedient*
  And, for a vaille, to walkyn on a night   *veil, concealment*
  W[h]an prest and clerk to rest ben take;   *are gone*
  Than shall ye be spyde of no wight.   *by no one*

ARISTORIUS.   Now sey me, Jonathas, by this light,   *(an oath)*
  W[h]at payment therfor wollde yow me make?

JONATHAS.   Forty pound, and pay it ful right,   *fully*
310   Evyn for that Lorde sake.   *Lord's*

ARISTORIUS.   Nay, nay, Jonathas, there-agen   *i.e., to do that*
  I w[o]ld not for an hundder pownd!

JONATHAS.   Sir, here is [yo]wr asking toolde pleyn.   *counted in full*
  I shall it tell in this stownd.   *count/hour, time*
    [*Counts out the money.*]

Here is an hundder pound, neither mor nor lesse,
  Of dokettys good, I dar well saye.   *ducats*

289To live in fear (for my soul) as a result of having injured my Lord.

293i.e., If in fact he is God almighty, I will atone for all my sins.

297To sell that loved one (i.e., Christ) to you.

Tell it ere yow from me passe.
Me thinketh it a royall araye!

       Count it before

But first, I pray yow, tell me this:

320   Of this thing whan shall I hafe deliverance?

ARISTORIUS.   Tomorowe betimes. I shall not mis[s]e;   *early*
    This night therfor I shall make purveaunce.   *arrangements*

Sir Isodyr he is now at chirch,
There sey[i]ng his evynsong,
As it is worshepe for to werche.   *devout duty to do*
He shall sone cum home—he will nat be long—
His sopere for to eate.
And when he is buskyd to his bedde,   *is readied for*
Right sone [t]hereafter he shal be spedd.   *it'll be accomplished*

330   No speche among yow there be spredd!
    To kepe your toungys ye nott lett.   *don't fail*

JONATHAS.   Sir, almighty Machomyght be with yow!   *Mohammed*
    And I shall cum again right sone.

ARISTORIUS.   Jonathas, ye wott what I have said, and how   *know*

335   I shall walke for that we have to done.   *that which*
        Here goeth the Jewys away, and the preste commith home [from the church to Aristory's scaffold].

PRESBITER.   Sir, almighty God mott be yowr g[u]ide,   *may God be*
    And glad yow wheresoo ye rest!   *gladden*

ARISTORIUS.   Sir, ye be welcom home this tide.   *time*
    Now, Petere, gett us wine of the best.
        [Peter Paul brings wine and bread.]

340   CLERICUS.   Sir, here is a drawte of Romney Red—   *draught*
    There is no bettere in Aragon—
    And a lofe of light bred;
    It is [w]holesom, as sayeth the fesicion.   *physician*
        [Peter Paul retires.]

ARISTORIUS.   Drinke of[f], ser Isodere, and be of good chere!
    This Romney is good to goo with to reste.
    There is no preciousere, fer nor nere,   *none more precious/far*
    For all wikkyd metys it will degest.   *indigestible foods*
        [The priest drinks.]

[335] i.e., I shall go about doing what has to be done.

PRESBITER.   Sir, this wine is good at a taste,
And therof have I drunke right well.
350   To bed to gone thus have I cast,   *resolved*
Evyn strait aftere this mery mele.

Now, ser, I pray to God send yow good night,
For to my chambere now will I gone.
ARISTORIUS.   Ser, with yow be God almight,
And sheld yow ever from yowr fone!   *foes*
    [*The priest goes off to bed.*] *Here shall Aristorius call his clarke*
    to his presens.

Howe, Peter! In the[e] is all my trust,
In especiall to kepe my counsell,   *secret*
For a lityll waye walkyn I must.
I will not be long. Trust as I the[e] tell.   *Keep trust*
    [*He crosses the platea toward the church.*]

Now prevely will I preve my pace,   *privily, secretly/try*
My bargain this night for to fulfill.
Ser Isodere shall nott know of this case,
363   For he hath oftyn sacred, as it is skill.   *consecrated the bread*
The chirche key is at my will;
There is nothing that me shall tary.
I will nott abide, by dale nore hill,   *i.e., anywhere*
Till it be wrowght, by Saint Mary!   *be done*
    Here shal he entere the chirche and take the hoost.

Ah, now have I all min[e] entent!
Unto Jonathas now will I fare.   *go*
370   To fullfill my bargain have I ment,   *I intend*
For that mony will amend my fare,   *improve my condition, welfare*
As thinkith me.
    [*Exit from church to the platea.*]
But now will I passe by thes[e] pathes plaine;
To mete with Jonathas I wold faine.   *gladly*
Ah, yondere he commith in certain!
Me thinkith I him see.
    [*Jonathas comes forward.*]

Welcom, Jonathas, gentill and trew!
For well and tr[e]wly thou kepist thin[e] howre.
Here is the host, sacred newe.
380   Now will I home to halle and bowre.

363For he has often consecrated the bread, as is reasonable (and thus he won't miss what
little is taken).

JONATHAS.   And I shall kepe this trusty treasure
As I wold doo my gold and fee! [*To the host.*]
Now in this clothe I shall the[e] covere,   *cover*
That no wight shall the[e] see.   *no one*
    Here shall Aristory goo his waye; and Jonathas [returning to his
    stage] and his servauntys shall goo to the tabill, thus say[i]ng:

JONATHAS.   Now, Jason and Jasdon, ye be Jewys jentill,
Masfatt and Malchus, that mighty arn in mind,
This merchant from the Cristen temple
Hathe gett us this bred that make us thus blind.   *that hoodwinks us*
Now, Jason, as jentill as ever was the linde,   *linden, lime-tree*
390   Into the forsaid parlowre prevely take thy pase!   *dining room/pace, step*
Sprede a clothe on the tabill that ye shall ther find,
And we shall folow aftere to carpe of this case.   *talk*
    Here the Jewys goon and lay the [h]ost on the tabill, say[i]ng:

JONATHAS.   Sirys, I praye yow all, harkyn to my sawe: *Sirs/speech*
Thes[e] Cristen men carpyn of a mervelows case.
They say that this is Jhesu that was attaintyd in owr lawe,   *condemned*
And that this is he that crucified was.

397   On thes[e] wordys there law growndyd hath he,   *their/established*
That he said on Shere-Thursday at his sopere: *Which/Thursday of Holy Week*
He brake the brede and said "*Accipite,*"   *Take*
And gave his disciplys them for to chere.   *in order to cheer them*
And more he said to them there
While they were togethere all and sum,   *together*
Sitting at the table soo clere:
"*Comedite, [hoc est] corpus meum.*"   *Eat, this is my body (Matthew 26:26)*

And this powre he gave Peter to proclame,
And how the same shuld be sufficient to all prechors.
The bisshoppys and curatys saye the same,
408   And soo, as I understond, do all his progenitors.

409   JASON.   Yea, sum men in that law reherse anothere:
They say of a maidyn borne was hee,
And how Joachims dowghter shuld be his mothere,   *i.e., Mary*
And how Gabrell apperyd and said "*Ave!*"   *Hail*
And with that worde she shuld conceivyd be,

---

[397]He has established a (new) law for them based on the following words

[408]*progenitors*, probably an error for "followers."

[409]Yea, some men recite another tenet in that law (the law of Christ).

And that in hir shuld light the Holy Gost.   *alight*
Ageyns owr law this is false heresy;   *Against*
And yett they saye he is of mightys most.   *of power*

JASDON.   They saye that Jhesu to be owr king,   *say, affirm*
But I wene he bowght that full dere!   *paid dearly for that*
But they make a royall aray of his uprising;   *array, affair/resurrection*
420   And that in every place is prechyd farre and nere.
And how he to his disciples again did appere,
To Thomas, and to Mary Mawdelen,   *Magdalene*
And sith how he styed by his own pow[e]re—   *then/ascended (to heaven)*
And this, ye know well, is heresy full plain.

MASPHAT.   Yea, and also they say he sent them witt and
       wisdom
For to understond every langwage,
When the Holy Gost to them came—
They faryd as dronk men of pymente or vernage;   *a spiced drink/white wine*
And sithen how that he likenyd himself a lord of perage: *then/high birth*
On his Fatherys right hond he him sett.   *set himself*
They hold him wisere than ever was Syble sage,   *Sibyl*
And strengere than Alexandere, that all the wor[l]de ded
       gett.   *conquer*

433   MALCHUS.   Yea, yet they saye as fals, I dare laye my hedde: *wager*
How they that be ded shall com again to Judgement,
And owr dredfull Judge shal be this same brede,   *bread*
And how life everlasting them shuld be lent.   *given*
And thus they hold, all at on[e] consent,   *maintain/with*
Because that Philippe said for a lityll glosse—   *lie*
To turne us from owr beleve is there entent—   *belief/their*
440   For that he said, "*Judicare vivos et mortuos.*"   *To judge the living and the dead*

JONATHAS.   Now, serys, ye have rehersyd the substaunce of
       their lawe,
But this bred I wold might be put in a prefe   *to a proof, test*
443   Whethere this be he that in Bosra of us had awe.   *Bozrah*
There stainyd were his clothys—this may we belefe,
This may we know—there had he grefe,
For owr old bookys verify thus:

433Yea, yet they speak falsely, I'll bet my head (an oath).

440(See 1 Peter 4:5 and 2 Timothy 4:1; also the Apostles' Creed. Philip the Apostle was known as "the Evangelist," which may account for the attribution to him in l. 438).

443, 448(See Isaiah 63:1, "Who is this that comes from Edom, with dyed garments from Bozrah?" traditionally interpreted as a prophecy of Christ. See also Isaiah 34:6).

Theron he was jugett to be hangyd as a thefe—

448   "*Tinctis [de] Bosra vestibus.*"   *With dyed garments from Bozrah*

JASON.   Iff that this be he that on Calvery was mad[e] red,   *i.e., bloody*
450   Onto my mind, I shall kenne yow a conceit good: *inform, teach*
Surely with owr daggars we shall ses on this bredde,   *seize, pierce*
And so with clowtys we shall know if he have eny blood.   *blows*

453   JASDON.   Now, by Machomyth so mighty, that mevith in   *moves, persuades*
my mode!
454   This is masterly ment, this mattere thus to meve!   *intended, conceived*
455   And with owr strokys we shall fray him as he was on the   *assault*
rood,
456   That he was on-don[e] with grett repreve.   *reproof*

MASPHAT.   Yea, I pray yow, smite ye in the middys of the cake,
458   And so shall we smite theron woundys five!
We will not spare to wirke it wrake   *do it injury*
To prove in this brede if ther be eny life.

MALCHUS.   Yea, goo we to, than, and take owr space,   *take our places*
And looke owr daggarys be sharpe and kene!
And when eche man a stroke smitte hase,   *has smitten*
In the midyll part thereof owr mastere shall bene.
JONATHAS.   When ye have all smityn, my stroke shal be
sene:
With this same daggere that is so stif and strong   *sturdy*
In the middys of this print I thinke for to prene!   *emblem, cake/prick*
468   On[e] lashe I shall him lende or it be long.   *give him ere*
*Here shall the four Jewys prik ther daggerys in four quarters,
thus say[i]ng:*

JASON.   Have at it! Have at it, with all my might!
This side I hope for to sese!   *pierce deeply*
JASDON.   And I shall with this blade so bright
This othere side freshely afeze!   *chastise, strike*
MASPHAT.   And I yow plight I shall him not please,
For with this punche I shall him prike!

450I'll tell you a conceit (clever idea) that seems good to my way of thinking.

453-56Now, by Mohammed so mighty, that seems a good idea to me! It is masterfully conceived to propose such an idea! And with our blows we'll assault him as though he were on the cross, so that he will be destroyed, with great disgrace.

458(Cf. the five wounds of Christ.)

468s.d. *four quarters:* representing Jesus' head, feet, and two arms in the pattern of a cross; cf. the York Crucifixion.

MALCHUS.   And with this augur I shall him not ease: *auger, borer*
          Anothere buffett shall he likke!   *experience*

JONATHAS.   Now am I bold with bataile him to bleyke,   *to make him pale*
          This midle part all for to prene,   *prick*
          A stowte stroke also for to strike:
480   In the middys it shal be sene! [*He strikes in the middle.*]
              Here the [h]ost must blede.

          Ah, owt, owt, harrow! What devill is this?
          Of this wirk I am on were!   *confused, afraid*
          It bledith as it were woode, iwis!   *as if/mad*
          But if ye helpe, I shall dispaire!   *Unless*

JASON.   A fire, a fire, and that in hast!
          Anoon a cawdron full of oile!   *(Get) at once*
487 JASDON.   And I shalle helpe it were in cast,
488   All the three howrys for to boile.
              [*Malchus goes for the oil.*]

MASPHAT.   Ye[a], here is a furneys stowte and strong,
          And a cawdron therin dothe hong.
          Malcus, wher art thow so long,
          To helpe this dede were dight?   *that this deed were done*
MALC[H]US.   Loo, here is thre galons of oile clere.
          Have doon fast; blowe up the fere!   *fire*
          Sir, bring that ilke cake nere,   *same*
          Manly, with all yowre might.   *Manfully*

JONATHAS.   And I shall bring that ilke cak[e]
          And throwe it in, I undertake.
              [*He seizes the host, which clings to his hand.*]
          Out, out, it werketh me wrake!   *does me injury*
500   I may not avoid it owt of my hond!   *rid*
          I wille goo drenche me in a lake.   *drown*
          And in woodnesse I ginne to wake!   *I'm aroused to madness*
          I renne, I lepe over this lond!   *run*
              Her[e] he renneth wood, with the [h]ost in his hond.

JASON.   Renne, felawes, renne, for Cokkys peyn,   *for Christ's pain*
          Fast we had owr mayster age[y]ne!   *(So that) quickly*
              [*They catch Jonathas.*]
          Hold prestly on this pleyn   *quickly on this flat place*

487I'll help to see that it (the host) is cast in.

488*three howrys:* seemingly symbolic of Christ's three days in the tomb and descent into hell.

And faste bind him to a poste.   *him (the host)*

JASDON.   Here is an hamer and nailys thre, I s[e]ye.

Liffte up his armys, felawe[s], on hey,

Whill I drive thes[e] nailes, I yow praye,

With strong strokys fast.

[*They nail the sacrament to the post.*]

MASPHAT.   Now set on, felouse, with maine and might,   *fellows*

And pluke his armes awey in fight!

[*They try to pull Jonathas from the host.*]

514   W[h]at? I se he twicche, felouse, aright!

515   Alas, balys breweth right badde!   *sorrows*

Here shall thay pluke the arme, and the hand shall hang still   *Jonathas' hand*
with the sacrament.

MALCHAS.   Alas, alas, what devill is this?

Now hat[h] he but oon hand, iwis!

Forsothe, mayster, right woo me is   *I'm very woeful*

That ye this harme have hadde.

JONATHAS.   Ther is no more; I must enduer!

Now hastely to owr chamber lete us gon,

Till I may get me sum recuer.   *recovery*

And therfor [I] charge yow every-choon   *command/everyone*

That it be counsell, that we have doon.   *be secret what*

[*They withdraw.*] *Here shall the lechys man come into the place,*   *physician's/into the platea*
say[i]ng:

COLLE.   Aha, here is a fayer felawshippe!   *pleasing company*

526   Thewh I be nat sh[a]pyn, I list to sleppe.   *Though*

I have a master: I wolld he had the pippe,   *a disease*

I tell yow in counsel!   *in confidence*

529   He is a man of all sience   *learning*

530   But of thriffte—I may with yow dispenc[e]!

531   He sittith with sum tapstere in the spence;

532   His hoode there will he sell.

Mayster Brendiche of Braban,   *Brabant*

I telle yow, he is that same man,

514-15i.e., What's this? I see that Jonathas is being hurt by this tugging, sure enough. Alas, sorrows increase most terribly!

526Though I have no plan (lit: though I'm not fitted), I want to slip away (?).

529-32He's a man wise in all things except in profitable occupation—I can do without you! (or, I can excuse you, or compound with you for an offense). He sits with some female tapster in the room where wines are dispensed; he'd sell the very hood off his back there (to buy wine).

Called the most famous phesi[ci]an
That ever sawe urine.
537 He seeth as wele at noone as at night,
538 And sumtime by a candelleyt   *candlelight*
539 Can giff a judgiment aright—   *(i.e., diagnosis)*
540 As he that hathe noon eyn.   *Like one who/eyes*

541 He is allso a boone-setter;
I knowe no man go the better!
In every taverne he is detter—   *debtor*
544 That is a good tokening!   *sign*
But ever I wonder he is so long;   *I'm puzzled that/delayed*
I fere ther gooth sumthing a-wrong,   *fear*
For he hath disa[rv]yde to be hong—   *deserved/hanged*
548 God send never wurse tiding!   *news*

He had a lady late in cure: *lately in his care*
I wot by this she is full sure!   *by now/fixed, taken care of*
551 There shall never Cristen creature
552 Here hir tell no tale!   *Hear her*
And I stode here till midnight,   *If*
I cowde not declare aright
My masterys cun[n]ing insight—
That he hat[h] in good ale.

But what devill aileth him so long to tar[y]e?
A seek man might soone miscary.   *sick/come to grief*
Now all the devillys of hell him wary!   *curse him*
God grante me my boon!   *May God grant my prayer*
561 I trowe, best we mak a crye:
If any man can him aspye,   *spy, see*
Led him to the pillery.—   *Lead*
In faith, it shall be do[o]n.
   Here shall he stond up and make proclamacion, sey[i]ng this:

COLLE.   Iff ther be either man or woman

537–40i.e., Master Brundiche can see and give diagnosis equally well by day or night, since
he can't see at all.

541boone-setter: surgeon, with play on dice-player.

544That's a good sign (mockingly observing that tavern visits are hardly appropriate for a
doctor).

548i.e., That wouldn't be bad news to me, if my master were hanged.

551–52No one will ever hear her speak again (since she is dead).

561I think it would be best if we made a public proclamation.

That sawe Master Brundiche of Braban,   *aught*
Or owyht of him tel can,
Shall wele be quit his mede.   *He'll be well rewarded*
He hath a cut berd and a flatte noose,   *nose*
570   A therde-bare gowne and a rent hoose;   *threadbare/torn*
He spekit[h] never good matere nor purpoose.
To the pilleré ye him led[e]!   *pillory*

[*Enter behind him, and unobserved, Master Brundiche.*]

MASTER BRUNDICHE.   What, thu boye, what janglest here?   *what are you chattering*
COLLE.   A, master, master, but to your reverence!   *only to your credit*
I wend never to a seen yowr goodly chere,   *thought/have/countenance*
Ye tar[i]ed hens so long.   *hence*
MASTER BRUNDICHE.   What hast thow said in my absense?
COLL[E].   Nothing, master, but to yowr reverence,
I have told all this audiense— [*aside.*]
580   And some lies among.

But master, I pray yow, how dothe yowr pa[c]ient
That ye had last under yowr medicament?   *medical treatment*
MASTER BRUNDICHE.   I waraunt she never fele annoyment.
COLL[E].   Why, is she in hir grave?
MASTER BRUNDICHE.   I have given hir a drinke made full well
586   With scamoly and with oxennell,   *scammony/oxymell*
587   Letuce, sauge, and pimpernelle.   *sage*
COLLE.   Nay, than she is full save!   *fully out of danger (said ironically)*

For, now ye ar cum, I dare well saye
590   Between Dovyr and Calice the right wey
Dwellth non[e] so cunning, by my fey,   *faith*
In my judgyment.
MASTER BRUNDICHE.   Cunning? Yea, yea, and with pratt[i]ffe   *practice*
I have savid many a mannys life.
COLLE.   On widowes, maidese, and wife   *maids*
Yowr conning yow have nyh[e] spent.   *nigh, nearly*

MASTER BRUNDICHE.   W[h]ere is [my] bowg[e]tt with drink   *bag, wallet*
profitable?
[*He takes a bottle from his bag and drinks.*]
COLL[E].   Here, master, master, ware how ye tugg!   *beware/tug (at the bottle)*

586-87*scamoly*: scammony, a strong purgative resin. *oxennell*: oxymell, a syrup of vinegar
and honey. *pimpernelle*: a medicinal herb.

590On the straight road between Dover and Calais (where is to be found nothing but the
water of the English Channel).

	The devill, I trowe, within shrugg,	*crouches inside it*
600	For it gooth "rebyll-rable."	*makes a gurgling sound*

	MASTER BRUNDICHE. Here is a grete congregacion,	*i.e., the audience*
	And all be not [w]hole, without negacion.	*in health/doubtless*
	I wold have certificacion:	
	Stond up and make a proclamacion.	
	Have do faste, and make no pausa[c]ion,	*Do it*
	But wightly mak a declaracion	*quickly*
	To all people that helpe w[o]lde have.	
	Hic interim proclamationem faciet.	*Here for a time he will make proclamation*

	COLL[E]. All manar of men that have any siknes,	
	To Master Brentberecly loke that yow redresse!	*address yourselves*
	What disease or siknesse that ever ye have,	*Whatsoever*
	He will never leve yow till ye be in yow[r] grave.	
	Who hat[h] the canker, the collike, or the laxe,	*Whoever/diarrhea*
613	The tercian, the quartan, or the brynni[n]g axs;	*burning fever*
614	For wormys, for gnawing, grindi[n]g in the wombe or in the boldyro;	
	All maner red eyn, bleryd eyn, and the miegrim also;	*bleared eyes/migraine*
	For hedache, bonache, and therto the tothache;	
617	The colt-evill, and the brostyn men he will undertak[e],	*swollen genitals/burst*
618	All tho that [have] the poose, the sneke, or the tyseke.	*catarrh/cold*
	Thow[g]h a man w[e]re right heyle, he cowd soone make him sek[e]!	*hale, healthy*
	Inquire to the colkote, for ther is his logging,	*coal-shed*
621	A lityll beside Babwell Mill, if ye will have und[er]stondin[g].	

	MASTER BRUNDICHE. Now, iff ther be ether man or woman	
	That nedethe helpe of a phesiscian—	
	COLL[E]. Mary, master, that I tell can,	
	And ye will understond.	*If*
	MASTER BRUNDICHE. Kno[w]est any ab[o]ut this plase?	
	COLL[E]. Ye, that I do, master, so have [I] grase!	*as I hope to have grace*
	Here is a Jewe, hight Jonathas,	*named*
	Hath lost his right hond.	*(Who) has*

630	MASTER BRUNDICHE. Fast to him I wold inquere.

613–14*tercian, quartan*: fevers with paroxysm every third (i.e., alternate) day or fourth (in modern reckoning, third) day. *boldyro*: evidently some part of the body, perhaps the penis.

617–18He will undertake to treat swollen genitals and men burst (with hernia in the genitals), (and) all those who have the catarrh, head cold, or phthisic (a lung consumption or asthma).

621*Babwell Mill*: near Bury St. Edmunds.

COLL[E].   For[e] God, master, the gate is here.   *Before/door*

MASTER BRUNDICHE.   Than to him I will go nere.

[*He ascends the stage of the Jews and greets Jonathas.*]

My master, wele mot yow be!   *well may*

JONATHAS.   What doost here, felawe? What woldest thu

hanne?   *have*

MASTER BRUNDICHE.   Sir, if yow nede ony surgeon or

physician,

Of yow[r] dise[se] help yow welle I can,

What hurtys or hermes soever they be.   *harms*

JONATHAS.   Sir, thu art ontawght to come in thus [un]henly,   *ignorant/rudely*

Or to pere in my presence thus malepertly.   *appear/saucily*

640   Voideth from my sight, and that wightly,   *Vanish/quickly*

For ye be misse-avised!   *misadvised, injudicious*

COLL[E].   Sir, the hurt of yowr hand is knowen full rife,   *commonly*

And my maste[r] have savyd many a manes life.

JONATHAS.   I trowe ye be cum to make sum strife.

Hens fast, lest that ye be chastised!

COLL[E].   Sire, ye know well it cannott misse;

Men that be masters of sciens be profitable.

In a pott if it please yow to pisse,

He can tell if yow be curable.

[JONATHAS.]   Avoide, fealows, I love not yowr bable! [*To his

servants.*]

Brushe them hens bothe, and that anon!

Giff them there reward that they were gone!   *i.e., Beat them*

Here shall the four Jewys bett away the leche and his man.   *physician*

JONATHAS.   Now have don, felawys, and that anon,   *i.e., help me*

654   For dowte of drede what aftere befall!

I am nere masyd—my witte is gon!   *dazed*

Therfor, of helpe I pray yow all.

And take yowre pinsonys that ar so sure,   *pincers*

And pluck owt the nailys, won and won;   *one by one*

Also in a clothe ye it cure   *cover, wrap*

660   And throw it in the cawdron, and that anon.

*Here shall Jason pluck owt the nailys and shake the hond into the

cawdron.*

JASON.   And I shall rape me redely anon   *hasten at once*

To plucke owt the nailys that stond so fast,

654For fear of what will happen afterward (if you don't help).

And beare this bred and also this bone,
And into the cawdron I will it cast.

JASDON.   And I shall with this daggere so stowte   *sturdy*
Putt it down that it might plawe,   *Put, push/boil*
And steare the clothe rounde abowte   *stir*
That nothing thereof shal be rawe.   *raw, uncooked*

MASPHAT.   And I shall manly, with all my might,   *manfully*
670   Make the fire to blase and brenne,   *burn*
And sett therundere suche a light
That it shall make it right thinne.   *scanty, cooked away*
        Here shall the cawdron b[o]ile, appering to be as blood.

MALCHAS.   Owt and harow, what devill is herein?
All this oile waxith redde as blood,
And owt of the cawdron it beginnith to rin!   *run*
I am so aferd I am nere woode.   *mad*
        Here shall Jason and his compeny goo to ser Jonathas, say[i]ng:

JASON.   Ah, mastere, master, what chere is with yow?   *i.e., how are you*
I cannott see owr werke will availe.
I beseche yow, avance yow now   *come forward*
Sumwhatt with yowr counsayle!

JONATHAS.   The best counsayle that I now wott,   *know*
682   That I can deme, farre and nere,   *judge*
Is to make an ovyn as redd hott
As ever it can be made with fere;   *fire*
And when ye see it soo hott appere,
Then throw it into the ovyn fast.   *it (the host)*
687   Sone shall he stanche his bleding chere!   *his flow of blood*
688   When ye have done, stoppe it—be not agast.

JASDON.   By my faith, it shal be wrowgh[t],   *done*
And that anon, in gret hast.
Bring on firing, serys. Here ye nowght?   *kindling sirs/Hear*
To hete this ovyn be nott agast.

MASPHAT.   Here is straw and thornys kene.
Com on, Malchas, and bring on fire,
For that shall hete it well, I wene.   *think*

682*farre and nere*: i.e., in any circumstance.

687–88Soon the fire will stanch (stop) Christ's flow of blood! When you've done that, plug up the oven—don't be afraid.

Here they kindyll the fire.

Blow on fast, that done it were!

MALCHAS.   Ah, how this fire ginnith to brenne clere!

This ovyn right hotte I think to make.

Now, Jason, to the cawdron that ye stere   *go to the caldron*

And fast fetche hethere that ilke cake.   *same*

> *Here shall Jason goo to the cawdron and take owt the [h]ost*
> *with his pinsonys, and cast it into the ovyn.*

JASON.   I shall with thes[e] pinsonys, withowt dowt,

Shake this cake owt of this clothe,

And to the ovyn I shall it rowte   *cast*

704   And stoppe him there, thow[gh] he be loth.

The cake I have cawght here, in good sothe—   *in truth*

The hand is soden, the fleshe from the bonys—   *boiled*

Now into the ovyn I will therewith.

Stoppe it, Jasdon, for the nonys!   *Plug it (the oven) / nonce*

JASDON.   I stoppe this ovyn, withowtyn dowte;

710   With clay I clome it uppe right fast,   *plaster*

That non[e] heat shall cum owtte.

I trow there shall he hete and drye in hast!

> *Here the ovyn must rive asundere and blede owt at the cranys,*
> *and an image appere owt with woundys bleding.*

MASPHAT.   Owt, owt, here is a grete wondere!

This ovyn b[l]edith owt on every side!

MALCHAS.   Yea, the ovyn on peacys ginnith to rive asundre!   *in pieces*

This is a mervelows case this tide!   *time*

> *Here shall the image speke to the Jewys, say[i]ng thus:*

717   JHESUS.   *O mirabiles Judei, attendite et videte*

718   *Si est dolor sicut dolor meus!*

Oh ye merveylows Jewys,

Why ar ye to yowr king onkind,

And [I] so bitterly bow[gh]t yow to my blisse?   *ransomed with bitter pain*

Why fare ye thus fule with yowre frende?   *behave / foully to*

Why peyne yow me and straitly me pinde,   *narrowly confined me*

And I yowr love so derely have bowght?   *i.e., Although*

Why are ye so unstedfast in your minde?

Why wrath ye me? I greve yow nowght.   *Why are you angry with*

704And shut up the host in the oven, no matter how unwilling he (Christ) may be. (Cf. the sealing of the tomb and Christ's descent into hell.)

717–18O ye strange Jews, behold and see if there is any sorrow like unto my sorrow (see Lamentations 1:12).

Why will ye nott beleve that I have tawght,   *that which*
And forsake your fowle necligence
And kepe my commandementys in yowr thowght,
730   And unto my Godhed to take credence?

Why blaspheme yow me? Why do ye thus?
Why put yow me to a newe tormentry,
And I died for yow on the crosse?
Why considere not yow what I did crye?
While that I was with yow, ye ded me velanye.
Why remembere ye nott my bittere chaunce,   *fortune, lot*
737   How yowr kinne did me avance   *help*
For claiming of min[e] enheritaunce?
I shew yow the streitnesse of my grevaunce,   *rigor*
And all to meve yow to my mercy.   *move*

741   JONATHAS.   *Tu es protector vitae meae; a quo trepidabo?*
O th[o]u Lord, whiche art my defendowr,
For dred of the[e] I trymble and quake!
Of thy gret mercy lett us receive the showre;
And mekely I aske mercy, amendys to make.
    Here shall they knele down all on there kneys, say[i]ng: *their*

JASON.   Ah, Lord, with sorow and care and grete weping,
All we felawys, lett us saye thus
With condolent harte and grete sorowing: *sorrowful*
749   *Lacrimis nostris conscientiam nostram baptizemus!*

JASDON.   Oh thow blissyd Lord of mikyll might,
Of thy gret mercy thow hast shewyd us the path,
Lord, owt of grevous slepe and owt of dyrknes to light,
753   *Ne gravis somnus irruat.*

754   MASPHAT.   Oh Lord, I was very cursyd, for I wold know thy
            crede.
I can no men[d]ys make, but crye to the[e] thus: *amends*
O graciows Lorde, forgife me my misdede!
With lamentable hart: *miserere mei, Deus!*   *have mercy on me God*

---

³⁷*avance:* help, promote (said ironically, with double meaning of "lift up on the cross").

⁷⁴¹You are the protector of my life; of whom shall I be afraid? (See Psalms 27:1.)

⁷⁴⁹With our tears may we baptize our conscience.

⁷⁵³⁻⁵⁴Lest grievous sleep seize upon (us). —Oh, Lord, I was cursed because I wished to discover the forbidden secrets of your creed.

MALCHAS.   Lord, I have offendyd the[e] in many a sundry
     wise.
  That stickith at my hart as hard as a core.
  Lord, by the watere of contricion lett me arise:
761   *Asparges me, Domine, hyssopo, et mundabor.*

JHESUS.   All ye that desiryn my servauntys for to be
  And to fullfill the preceptys of my lawys,
  The intent of my commandement knowe ye:
765   *Ite et ostendite vos sacerdotibus meis.*
  To all yow that desire in eny wise
  To aske mercy, to graunt it redy I am.
  Remembere and lett yowr wittys suffice,
769   *Et tunc non avertam a vobis faciem meam.*

  Ser Jonathas, on thin[e] hand thow art but lame,   *in*
  And this thorow[gh] thin[e] own cruelnesse.
  For thin[e]hurt thou mayest thyselfe blame:
  Thow woldist preve thy powre me to oppresse.   *prove*
  But now I considre thy necesse;   *necessity*
  Thow wasshest thin[e] hart with grete contricion.
  Go to the cawdron—thy care shal be the lesse—
  And towche thin[e] hand, to thy salvacion.
    *Here shall ser Jonathas put his hand into the cawdron,
    and it shal be [w]hole again; and then say as fo[lo]with:*

JONATHAS.   Oh thow my Lord God and Saviowr, osanna,
  Thow King of Jewys and of Jerusalem!
780   O thow mighty, strong Lion of Juda,
  Blissyd be the time that thou were in Bedlem!   *Bethlehem*
  Oh thou mighty, strong, gloriows and graciows oile
     streme,
  Thow mighty conquerrowr of infernall tene,   *injury*
  I am quit of moche combrance thorowgh thy meane,   *means, mediation*
  That evere blissyd mott thou bene!   *may you be*

  Alas that ever I did against thy will,
  In my witt to be soo wood   *mad*
788   That I so ongoodly wirk shuld soo grill!   *wickedly/cruelly*

---

[761] Sprinkle me, Lord (i.e., purge me), with hyssop, and I will be cleansed (Psalms 51:7).

[765] Go and present yourselves to my priests (see Luke 17:14).

[769] And then I will not turn away from you my face (see Psalms 27:9, 88:14, 143:7 etc.).

[788-89] That I should behave so wickedly and cruelly! In response to my evil you have glad-
dened me with goodness.

789   Agens my misgovernaunce thow gladdist me with good:
       I was soo prowde to prove the[e] on the roode,   *test, put to trial/cross*
       And thou hast sent me lighting that late was lame.   *relief to me who lately*
       To bete the[e] and boile the[e] I was mighty in moode,
       And now thou hast put me from duresse and disfame.   *ignominy*

       But, Lord, I take my leve at thy high presens,
       And put me in thy mighty mercy.
       The bisshoppe will I goo fetche to se owr offens,
       And onto him shew owr life, how that we be gilty.
           Here shall the master Jew goo to the bishopp [at his stage],
           and his men knele still [before the image].

   JONATHAS.   Haile, fathere of grace! I knele upon my knee,
799   Hertely beseching yow, and interely,
       A swemfull sight all for to see   *sorrowful*
       In my howse appering verely:
       The holy sacrament, the whiche we have done tormentry—
       And there we have putt him to a newe Passion—
       A child appering with wondys blody: *noble youth*
       A swemfull sight it is to looke upon!

   EPISCOPUS.   Oh Jhesu, Lord, full of goodnesse!
       With the[e] will I walke with all my might.
808   Now, all my pepull, with me ye dresse   *prepare*
       For to goo see that swimfull sight.

810   Now, all ye peple that here are,
       I commande yow, every man,
       On yowr feet for to goo, bare,
       In the devoutest wise that ye can.
           [They go in solemn procession to the Jew's house.] Here shall the
           bisshope entere into the Jewys howse, and say:

       O Jhesu, fili Dei,   *son of God*
       How this painfull Passion rancheth min[e] hart!   *wrenches*
       Lord, I crye to the[e], miserere mei,   *have mercy on me*
817   From this rufull sight thou wilt reverte!   *turn back*
       Lord, we all, with sorowys smert,   *smarting*
       For this unlefull work we live in langowr.   *unlawful, forbidden*

   799Heartily and entirely beseeching you.

   808, 810(The language suggests an invitation to the audience to join in a procession.)

   817i.e., That you will revert to your Godhead and leave this sorrowful manifestation on
   earth.

Now, good Lord, in thy grace let us be gertt,   *girt, clothed*
And of thy soverreyn marcy send us thy socowr,   *succour*
And for thy holy grace forgife us owr errowr.
Now lett thy peté spring and sprede!   *pity*
Thowgh we have be unrigh[t]full, forgif us our rigore,   *cruelty*
And of owr lamentable hartys, good Lord, take hed[e]!

> *Here shall the im[a]ge change again into brede.*

Oh th[o]u largifluent Lord, most of lightnesse,   *bountiful*
Onto owr prayers thow hast applied!   *taken heed*
Th[o]u hast receivyd them with grett swettnesse;
For all owr dredfull dedys, thou hast not us denied.   *Despite*
830   Full mikyll ow[gh]te thy name for to be magnified   *much*
With mansuete mirth and gret swettnes,   *gentle*
And as our graciows God for to be glorified,
For th[o]u shewist us gret gladnes.

Now will I take this holy sacrament
With humble hart and gret devocion,
836   And all we will gon with on[e] consent
837   And beare it to chirche with sole[m]pne procession.
838   Now folow me, all and summe!   *one and all*
839   And all tho that bene here, both more and lesse,   *those/rich and poor*
840   This holy song, *O sacrum convivium*,   *O sacred feast*
841   Lett us sing all with grett swetnesse.

> *[A singing procession escorts the host toward the church.]*

> *[On the stage of Aristory,] here shall the pryst, ser*
> *Isodere, ask his master what this menith.*

[PRESBITER.]   Ser Aristory, I pray yow, what menith all this?
Sum miracle, I hope, is wrowght by Goddys might.   *believe*
The bisshope commith [in] procession with a gret meny of   *throng*
    Jewys;
I hope sum miracle is shewyd to his sight.
To chirche in hast will I runne full right,
For thethere, me think, he beginnith to take his pace.
The sacrament so semly is borne in sight.
I hope that God hath shewyd of his grace.

ARISTORIUS.   To tell yow the trowth I will nott lett—   *delay*
Alas that ever this dede was dight!   *done*

836–41 (The language suggests that the audience joins in the singing of this hymn and in the
procession; see ll. 808, 810.)

An on-lefull bargain [I] began for to beat: *unlawful/strike*
853   I sold yon same Jewys owr Lord full right
854   For cov[e]itise of good, as a cursyd wight.   *wealth*
Woo the while that bargain I did ever make!
But yow be my defensoure in owr diocesans sight,   *Unless/bishop's*
For an heretike I feare he will me take.

    PRESBITER.   Forsothe, nothing well-avised was your witt;   *not at all*
Wondrely was it wrowght of a man of discrescion   *Strangely*
860   In suche peraile your solle for to putt!   *peril/soul*
But I will labore for your absolucion.

Lett us hie us fast that we were hens,   *hence*
And beseche him of his benigne grace
That he will shew us his benyvolens
To make amendys for yowr trespas.
> *Here shall the merchant and his prest go to the chirche, and the bisshop [attended by the procession] shall entre the chirche and lay the [h]ost u[p]on the autere, say[i]ng thus:*   *altar*

866   [EPISCOPUS.]   *Estote fortes in bello et pugnate cum antico serpente,*
867   *Et accipite regnum aeternum, et cetera.*

My childern, be ye strong in bataill gostly   *spiritual*
For to fight again the fell serpent   *against/cruel*
That night and day is ever besy;
To distroy owr sollys is his intent.
Look ye be not slow nor necligent
To arme yow in the vertues sevyn.
Of sinnys fo[r]gotyn take good avisement,   *Think upon sins forgotten*
And knowlege them to yowr confessore full evyn.   *acknowledge/fully*

For that serpent, the devill, is full strong
Mervelows mischeves for man to mene,   *Prodigious/intend*
878   But that the Passion of Crist is meynt us among,   *Except/communicated*
879   And that is in dispite of his infernall tene.   *his (the devil's)/injury*
Beseche owr Lord and Saviowr so kene
To put doun that serpent, cumberere of man,   *ensnarer*

853–54(Cf. Judas' regret, Matthew 27.)

866–67Be strong in battle and fight with the old serpent, and receive the eternal kingdom, and so on (see Revelation 20:2).

878–79Were it not that the Passion of Christ is proclaimed among us, in defiance of the devil's hellish harms.

882 To withdraw his furious froward doctrin[e] bidene, *revoke/perverse/completely*
883 Fulfillyd of the fend callyd Leviathan. *by*

Giff lawrell to that Lord of might *praise*
That he may bring us to the joyows fruicion:
From us to put the fend to flight,
That never he distroy us by his temptacion.

PRESBITER. My fathere undere God, I knele unto yowr kne,
889 In yowr mi[g]hty misericord to tak us in remembrance! *mercy*
890 As ye be materiall to owr degré,
We put us in yowr moderat ordinaunce *gentle authority*
Iff it like yowr highnes to here owr grevaunce. *If it please you/hear*
We have offenddyd sorowfully in a sin mortall,
Wherfore we fere us owr Lord will take vengaunce
For owr sinnes, both grete and small.

EPISCOPUS. And in fatherhod, that longith to my dignité, *belongs*
Unto yowr grefe I will gif credens.
Say what ye will, in the name of the Trinité,
Again[s]t God if ye have wroght eny inconveniens. *impropriety*

900 ARISTORIUS. Holy fathere, I knele to yow undere benedicité! *blessing*
I have offendyd in the sin of cov[e]itis[e]:
I sold our Lordys body for lucre of mony
And deliveryd to the wickyd, with cursyd advice. *ill-advisedly*
And for that pres[u]mpcion, gretly I agrise *am horrified*
That I presumed to go to the autere, *altar*
There to handyll the holy sacrifice.
I were worthy to be putt in brenning fire. *I deserve/burning*

But, gracious lord, I can no more
But put me to Goddys mercy and to yowr grace. *Other than*
910 My cursyd werkys for to restore, *make restitution for*
I aske penaunce now in this place.

EPISCOPUS. Now, for this offence that thou hast done
Agens the King of Hevyn and Emperowr of Hell, *Against*
Ever whill thou livest, good dedys for to done
And nevermore for to bye nore sell; *buy*
Chastis[e] thy body as I shall the[e] tell,

882–83 To revoke completely the menacing, perverse claims of authority disseminated by the fiend, called Leviathan (after Isaiah 27:1).

889–90 (Beseeching you) to think mercifully of us! Inasmuch as you are essential to our (spiritual) condition.

With fasting and pray[i]ng and othere good wirk,
To withstond the temtacion of fendys of hell;
And to call to God for grace looke thou never be irke.   *tired, reluctant*

920   Also, thou preste, for thy necligens,
That thou were no wisere on thin[e] office,   *Because*
Thou art worthy inpresu[n]ment for thin[e] offence;
But beware ever heraftere, and be more wise.

And all yow creaturys and curatys that here be,   *vicars, preachers(?)*
Of this dede yow may take example
926   How that your pyxis lockyd ye shuld see,
And beware of the key of Goddys temple.

JONATHAS.   And I aske cristendom with great devocion;   *christening*
With repentant hart in all degrees   *in every way*
I aske for us all a generall absolucion—
   Here the Jewys must knele al down.
For that we knele all upon owr knees—   *that (the absolution)*

For we have grevyd owr Lord on ground   *Because/on earth*
And put him to a new painfull Passion,
With daggars stickyd him with grevos wo[u]nde,
New nailyd him to a post, and with pinsonys pluckyd him   *Anew*
   down.

JASON.   And sith we toke that blissyd bred so sownd   *then*
And in a cawdron we did him boile.
In a clothe full just we him wounde   *fully*
And so did we seth him in oile.   *seethe, boil*

940   JASDON.   And for that we might overcom him with   *so that*
   tormentry,
In an hott ovyn we speryd him fast.   *thrust, shut*
There he apperyd with wo[u]ndys all bloody;
The ovyn rave asundere and all to-brast!   *split/burst to pieces*
MASPHAT.   In his law to make us stedfast,
There spake he to us woordys of grete favore.
In contricion owr hartys he cast,
And bad[e] take us to a confessore.   *bade us betake ourselves*

MALCHUS.   And therfor all we with on[e] consent
Knele onto yowr high sovereinté;
950   For to be cristenyd is owr intent.

926*pyxis*: vessels in which the bread of the sacrament is preserved.

Now all owr dedys to yow shewyd have we.
Here shall the bisshoppe cristen the Jewys with gret solempnité.

EPISCOPUS.   Now the Holy Gost at this time mot yow blisse   *may*
As ye knele all now in his name!
And with the watere of baptime I shall yow blisse
To save yow all from the fendys blame.   *fiend's guilt*
Now, that fendys powre for to make lame,   *fiend's*
In the name of the Father, the Son, and the Holy Gost,
To save yow from the devillys flame,
I cristen yow all, both lest and most.   *i.e., everyone*

960   SER JONATHAS.   Now, owr fathere and bishoppe that we well
            know,
We thank yow interly, both lest and most.   *entirely*
Now ar we bownd to kepe Cristys lawe
And to serve the Fathere, the Son, and the Holy Gost.
Now will we walke by contré and cost   *i.e., everywhere*
Owr wickyd living for to restore,
And trust in God, of mightys most,
Never to offend as we have don before.

Now we take owr lea[v]e at lesse and more;   *i.e., of everyone*
Forward on owr vyage we will us dresse.   *betake ourselves*
970   God send yow all as good welfare
As hart can thinke or towng expresse!

ARISTORIUS.   Into my contré now will I fare   *go*
For to amende min[e] wickyd life;
And to kep[e] the people owt of care,
I will teache this lesson to man and wife.

Now take I my leave in this place.
I will go walke, my penaunce to fullfill.
Now God, agens whom I have done this trespas,   *against*
Graunt me forgifnesse if it be thy will!

PRESBITER.   For joy of this, me thinke my hart do wepe,
That yow have givyn yow all Cristys servauntys to be,   *given yourselves*
982   Him for to serve with hart full meke—
983   God—full of paciens and humilité;

984   And the conversacion of all thes[e] faire men,   *behavior, mode of life*

982–84To serve him, God, with heart fully meek and full of patience and humility; (and my heart weeps for joy also at) the holy behavior of these virtuous men.

With hartys stedfastly knett in on[e],   *knit*
Goddys lawys to kepe and him to serve bidene,   *completely*
As faithfull Cristianys evermore for to gone!   *Christians/go*

EPISCOPUS.   God omnipotent evermore looke ye serve   *See that you serve God*
With devocion and prayre, whill that ye may.
990   Dowt it not, he will yow preserve
For eche good prayere that ye sey to his pay.   *pleasure*
And therfor in every dew time loke ye nat delay   *due, fitting*
For to serve the holy Trinité,
And also Mary, that swete may;   *maid*
And kepe yow in perfite love and charité.

Cristys commandementys ten there bee.
Kepe well them—doo as I yow tell.
Almight God shall yow please in every degré.   *You shall please*
And so shall ye save yowr sollys from hell.
1000   For there is pain and sorow cruell,   *there (in hell)*
And in hevyn there is both joy and blisse
More then eny towng can tell!   *any tongue*
There angellys sing with grett swetnesse.

To the whiche blisse he bring us   *(may) he*
Whoys name is callyd Jhesus,   *Whose*
And in wirshippe of this name gloriows
To sing to his honore *Te Deum Laudamus*.   *We praise you O God*
    Finis.

Thus endith the Play of the Blissyd Sacrament,
whiche miracle was don in the forest of Aragon,
in the famous cité Eraclea, the yere of owr
Lord God 1461, to whom be honowr, Amen!

PART FIVE

The Morality Play

The Morality Play

THE MORALITY PLAY first came into being in the late fourteenth century, at about the same time as the Corpus Christi cycles. It flourished during the fifteenth century, when the cycles and saints' plays were also enjoying considerable popularity. The morality borrowed significant elements of staging, characterization, and structure from its dramatic contemporaries, and seems to have contributed to them in turn. In two important respects, however, the history of the morality differs from that of the Corpus Christi cycle and the saint's play. First, the morality play had virtually no precedents in earlier church drama; it was essentially a new genre for the stage in the late fourteenth century. Secondly, it proved to be more adaptable to new ideologies and social conditions during the sixteenth century than did other kinds of medieval drama, and thus survived to become a formative influence on Renaissance drama while the cycles and saints' plays found themselves increasingly under attack by the Reformation Church. For these reasons, perhaps, we tend to think of the morality play as a latecomer in medieval drama and a successor to other genres. Actually, though, the moralities presented here were more or less contemporaneous with the great cycles and the few English saints' plays or conversion plays that have survived. We need to be aware of resemblances among the various genres, and of possible mutual influences, as well as of differences.

The resemblances are at times striking. Moral personifications such as Death or the seven Deadly Sins are to be found not only in morality plays, where they are essential to the allegorical method of presentation, but also in the N Town pageant on the death of Herod and in the saint's play of *Mary Magdalene*. The four allegorical daughters of God named Truth, Justice, Mercy, and Peace, who are prominently featured in the morality play *The Castle of Perseverance*, also take part in the N Town pageant on the parliament of heaven (not included in this volume). The comedy of evil that we usually associate with the so-called Vice figure of the morality play is by no means limited to the morality; it plays an important role in virtually every other genre of medieval drama as well. In terms of staging, early morality plays make use of scaffolds and an open *platea* or "place" as do other dramatic works of the period. *The Castle of Perseverance* begins with a festive preliminary announcement, or "riding of the banns," several days before the actual performance, as does the N Town cycle and *The Play of the Sacrament*. Production in early morality drama, as in other forms of medieval open-air theater, makes use of colorful costuming, music, processions, bustling crowd scenes, and the like. In terms of dramatic structure, a full-scale morality play like *The Castle of Perseverance* emulates the cosmic scope of the Corpus Christi cycles. By telling how a representative mankind figure falls into sin and is eventually recovered to grace, the plot of this morality consciously parallels the story of Adam's fall from grace and of Christ's redemptive sacrifice. One story tells the divine history of generic man, the other tells the divine history of the human race. Both take place on earth in the midst of an arena that encompasses heaven and hell.

The primary difference between morality drama and other kinds of medieval drama, then, is one of focus. The morality play tells the story of a representative individual Christian rather than the collective history of all men. The saint's play also concerns an individual Christian, and that is one reason why *Mary Magdalene* can make extensive use of moral allegory in portraying Mary's spiritual conflict. Yet the morality play chooses a central figure even more universal than that of the saint's play. The hero or heroine of the saint's play is, after all, a historical or legendary personage, or something of both. The central figure of the morality play, on the other hand, is apt to be named Mankind, Everyman, or some such title stressing his relationship to all living men and women. He is surrounded, moreover, by abstract representations of his state of mind or body: Despair, Courage, Strength, Five Wits, and so on. He is counseled by his Good Angel and tempted by his Evil Angel, or by similar figures. Accordingly, allegory is central to the method of the morality play whereas it is incidental to the Corpus Christi cycle or saint's play.

In sum, perhaps we can define the morality play as the dramatization of a spiritual crisis in the life of a representative mankind figure in which his spiritual struggle is portrayed as a conflict between personified abstractions representing good and evil. Although medieval usage does not actually employ the term "morality play," we do find such phrases as "a moral play" or "a moral enterlude" applied to plays of the sort described here. The plot most commonly found in morality plays is that of a soul-struggle in which the mankind hero succumbs to vice but is finally restored to grace. Other plots, found in combination with the soul-struggle plot or occasionally in isolation, include the coming of death to the mankind figure, the debate of body and soul after his death, and the parliament of heaven, which determines whether he is to be damned or saved.

The morality play could not claim an extensive earlier history in the church drama of the twelfth and thirteenth centuries. Nonetheless, it may well have had an immediate predecessor during the second half of the fourteenth century: the so-called *Pater Noster* play. Though now regrettably lost,

Pater Noster plays were performed at York, Beverley, Lincoln, and possibly elsewhere, using methods of production much like those of the Corpus Christi cycles. Beverley, for example, had a play in 1469 employing eight pageants and seven acting stations. Seven pageants were devoted in turn to each of the seven Deadly Sins, while the eighth was assigned to "Viciose"— possibly referring to the mankind figure whose sins were being set forth in the work as a whole. Such a dramatization of the seven Deadly Sins was called a *Pater Noster* play, or Lord's Prayer play, because the seven phrases or "petitions" of the Lord's Prayer were regarded as specific defenses against the seven Deadly Sins. A guild of the Lord's Prayer, established at York, took responsibility for the performance of plays "setting forth the goodness of the Lord's Prayer," in which plays "all manner of vices and sins were held up to scorn, and the virtues were held up to praise." One pageant in this guild's repertory, in 1379, depicted the sin of Sloth or *"Accidie."* According to John Wycliffe, writing at about this same time, the York plays were designed by friars as a means of teaching "the Paternoster in Englische tunge," that is, explaining the Lord's Prayer to English audiences in colloquial English speech. Records from Lincoln similarly indicate that a *Ludus de Pater Noster* was acted there in 1397–98 and for as long as fifty-four years prior to that date. (York also had a so-called Creed play during the fifteenth century, consisting evidently of twelve pageants based on New Testament history or on the lives of the apostles and staged on mobile pageant wagons. We know virtually nothing about the contents of this lost genre, however, and cannot determine whether it influenced the development of the morality play.)

In the absence of a substantial earlier history, the morality play took shape under a number of late medieval influences. We have already discussed the influence of the cycles and saints' plays, with their methods of staging and their generic plot of temptation, fall, and recovery through God's grace. Another major influence was allegory. The medieval penchant for allegorizing manifested itself in almost every literary form imaginable. Sermons made frequent allusion to the seven Deadly Sins and their opposite virtues. The Christian poet Prudentius (who flourished in the fourth century) wrote an epic poem in Latin called *Psychomachia* ("The Contest of the Soul") portraying the conflict between virtue and vice as a chivalric tournament. Bishop Grosseteste, in his mid-thirteenth-century *Chasteau d'Amour* ("Castle of Love"), gave great currency to the metaphor of the besieged castle as a token of assailed virtue. French allegorical writing, notably in the late thirteenth-century *Roman de la Rose* ("The Romance of the Rose"), interpreted the wooing of a lady in terms of abstract figures such as Daunger, Fair Welcome, Pity, and Largess. The fourteenth-century *Pelinerage de la Vie Humaine* ("Pilgrimage of Human Life"), by De Guilleville, presented life as a spiritual journey. John Gower's *Confessio Amantis* ("The Confession of the Lover"), a late fourteenth-century poem, made use of the seven Deadly Sins as a narrative framework for a collection of tales. *Piers Plowman,* also from the late fourteenth century, portrayed the seven Deadly Sins and an allegorical attack on a castle. None of these works can be shown to have exerted much direct influence on the morality play, but cumulatively they attest to the widespread popularity of extended metaphor as a means of portraying spiritual conflicts or journeys.

Allegory also served as a means of dramatizing philosophical and psychological questions with which the medieval age was endlessly fascinated. How do men know truth? How can men define and visualize such concepts as reason, will, and sensual appetite? Morality plays are often peopled with allegorical figures bearing the names of these and other philosophical abstractions. The late fifteenth-century morality *Wisdom,* for example, is often referred to as *Mind, Will, and Understanding,* since these three attributes of the soul or *anima* are prominent throughout the play. By their actions, both evil and good, they reveal ways in which the attributes of the human psyche work together to produce both spiritual failure and eventual recovery to grace. Thus the lively theatrical medium of the morality play could serve to illustrate the often abstruse concepts of medieval philosophy. Doubtless many such attempts at popularizing learning were unsophisticated. Nonetheless, the moralities could reach large audiences and were able to disseminate ideas that might otherwise have been restricted to a learned few.

Still another late medieval fascination that manifested itself in the morality play was the cult of death. We find this preoccupation with death in other art forms as well, such as in treatises on holy dying and in representations of the Last Judgment. One particularly common motif, the Dance of Death, features Death playing on a fiddle while all ranks and conditions of men march to his tune. The relevance of this motif to *Everyman* is central and obvious. More broadly, the morality play as a whole reflects the tendency of devotional and mystical writing in late medieval Europe to focus on last things and on the lonely quest of the individual Christian for personal salvation.

Only a few morality plays have survived from the fifteenth century or before. Prior to 1400, we have a single fragmentary work known as *The Pride of Life.* It tells of a representative mankind figure called the King of Life, who, ignoring the sober counsel of his queen and the bishop, craves ever more wealth and power. He even dares Death to come into the lists with him. Although the fragment breaks off at this point, the rest of the play is evidently to be about the coming of Death and the debate of body and soul, with the intervention of the Virgin Mary on the King of Life's behalf. Staging calls for various platforms surrounding an open acting area or "place." *The Castle of Perseverance,* the earliest morality play to survive nearly intact, is usually dated around 1405–25. It is a mammoth play of 3,649 lines and thirty-five speaking parts, requiring five scaffolds around a *platea* featuring a besieged castle in the center. This morality play is more inclusive than any other in existence, since it tells not only of Mankind's soul-struggle, fall, and final recovery but also the coming of Death, the debate of body and soul, and the parliament of heaven. *Mankind* (ca. 1465–70) is a considerably shorter version of the soul-struggle plot; it is geared to a rural audience and to a professional or semiprofessional acting troupe. The elaborate scaffold-and-*platea* stage has been abandoned in favor of a portable trestle platform with a single curtain for exits and entrances, or an innyard room with curtained doorways. *Everyman* (late fifteenth century) is a restrained and moving treatment of the coming of Death, quite untypical of the usual morality in its lack of comic horseplay. These three moralities, all of which are included in this selection, account for most extant fifteenth-century morality drama except for the scholastic play already mentioned called *Wisdom* or *Mind, Will, and Understanding,* and a courtly morality by Henry Medwall called *Nature* (ca. 1495).

After 1500, on the other hand, morality plays become remarkably numerous. We have space to name only a few: *Mundus et Infans, Hickescorner, The Interlude of Youth* (ca. 1508–20), *Magnificence* by John Skelton (ca. 1515–18), *Impatient Poverty, Lusty Juventus* (ca. 1547), *Respublica* (1553), *The Longer Thou Livest the More Fool Thou Art* by William Wager, *Enough Is as Good as a Feast* also by Wager (ca. 1559–60), and *The Conflict of Conscience* by Nathaniel Woodes (ca. 1572). In fact, morality plays became the staple form of dramatic entertainment for popular audiences throughout England for about a century. They were usually acted by itinerant troupes, like the small company that had acted *Mankind* for pence and halfpence at a public inn. These troupes also took their plays on occasion to noble households and to court. Moralities were sometimes written specifically for noble or courtly audiences by well-known literary persons and humanists such as Henry Medwall, John Skelton, and John Bale. At the time of the Reformation, the morality was pressed into service as a vehicle for religious and political propaganda both by Protestant and by Catholic apologists. The very adaptability of the morality play to such purposes proved to be a key to its enduring popular success, since its basic plot of soul-struggle, fall, and eventual recovery could be suited to countless themes. Shorn of its happy ending, the morality plot also provided a formula for tragedy that was to be of immense importance to Marlowe's *Doctor Faustus* (1588–92). Perhaps the main contribution of the morality to later drama was its comedy of evil as embodied in its chief comic figure, the Vice. As Bernard Spivack has shown (*Shakespeare and the Allegory of Evil*), Shakespeare was particularly indebted to this dramatic tradition for its insight into the comically insidious and diabolical nature of evil. Richard III, Iago (in *Othello*), Edmund (in *King Lear*), and to an extent Falstaff, all owe much to the Vice as a stage type. Shakespeare's acting company, too, was a direct descendant of those troupes that had acted morality plays all across Tudor England. The morality play thus became the chief dramatic link between the medieval stage and the Shakespearean.

THE CASTLE OF PERSEVERANCE

The Castle of Perseverance dates from the early fifteenth century (ca. 1405–25). It is not only the earliest morality play to survive almost intact but is also the most comprehensive. Its 3,649 lines encompass several distinguishable plots joined in sequence: the struggle between the Virtues and Vices for Man's soul, the com-soul-struggle alone; Everyman limits its focus to the coming of Death. Perseverance, on the other hand, embraces virtually all the themes from which later morality plays were to be constructed.

Its cast of abstractions is correspondingly ambitious. Thirty-five speaking parts are

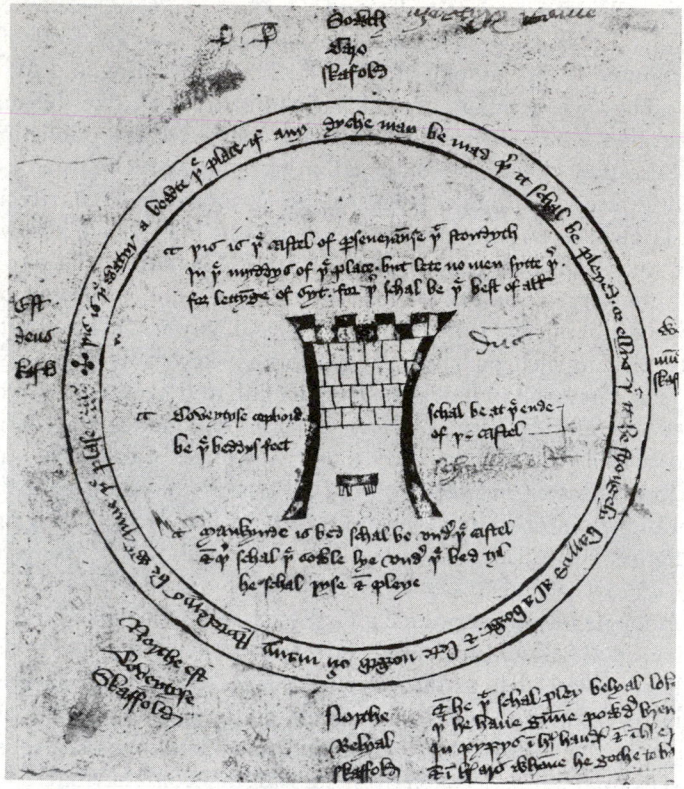

The stage plan for The Castle of Perseverance appended to the Macro manuscript. Right: A modernized version of the plan.

ing of Death to Mankind, the debate of body and soul, and the parliament of heaven or the debate of the four daughters of God. Most later moralities base their narrative on the balanced with majestic symmetry into opposing camps. With Man's soul at the center of the action, the Good Angel opposes the Bad Angel and the seven Cardinal Virtues oppose the seven Deadly Sins. God, who combines in himself both compassion and wrath toward mankind, must ultimately reconcile through his atonement on earth the diverse impulses of Mercy and Truth, Peace and Righteousness. This structuring reflects a medieval penchant for correspondences and classification. Not only are the seven Virtues and Vices paired opposite to one another in meaningful antithesis—Christ's Meekness or Humility as

Wrath, and Envy; the Flesh oversees the fleshly sins, Gluttony, Sloth, and Lechery; and World oversees Covetousness, the root of all evil, the essence of worldliness. Moreover, the sins are all interrelated. Pride is the original sin upon which the others depend; Gluttony and Sloth contribute to Lechery; Lechery is often the starting-point of a life in sin; and Covetousness is the sin of old age, when all others fail.

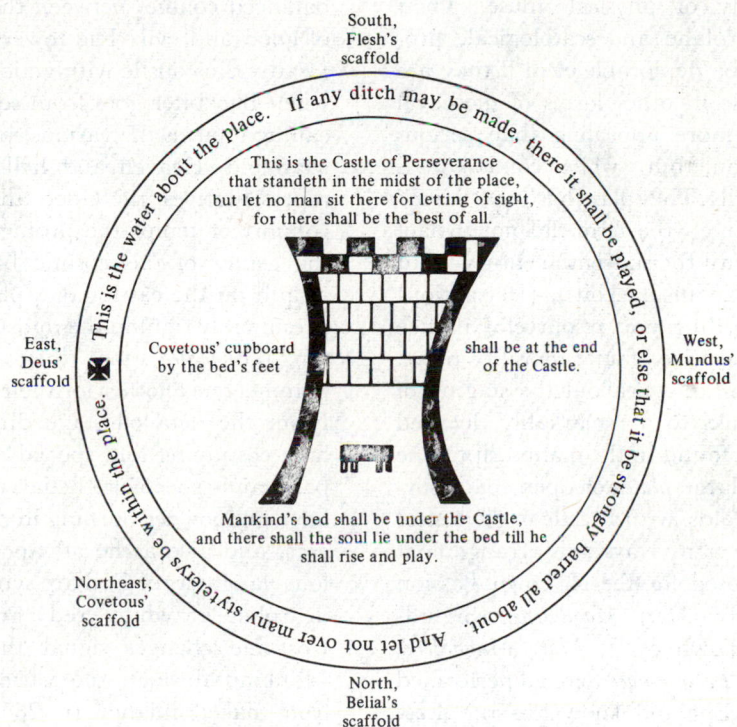

South, Flesh's scaffold

If any ditch may be made, there it shall be played, or else that it be strongly barred all about.

This is the water about the place.

This is the Castle of Perseverance that standeth in the midst of the place, but let no man sit there for letting of sight, for there shall be the best of all.

East, Deus' scaffold

Covetous' cupboard by the bed's feet

shall be at the end of the Castle.

West, Mundus' scaffold

And let not over many stytelerys be within the place.

Mankind's bed shall be under the Castle, and there shall the soul lie under the bed till he shall rise and play.

Northeast, Covetous' scaffold

North, Belial's scaffold

the corrective for Lucifer's Pride, and so on— but these abstractions are grouped and subdivided. The seven Deadly Sins are divided according to medieval convention into three groups headed by Devil, Flesh, and World. The Devil oversees the spiritual sins, Pride,

The play is also comprehensively and antithetically structured in its balancing of seriousness with comedy, didacticism with entertainment. The Virtues soberly admonish Mankind to eschew evil, or learnedly debate among themselves the issues of free will and original sin. They explicate the theological commonplaces upon which the play is based: that Man is given free choice to be saved or damned, that he is certain though not predestined to fall, and that his fall is paradoxically a fortunate one (a *felix culpa*) since it necessitates the coming of Christ (see l. 3339a). Man cannot merit salvation and so must throw himself on God's mercy. The Deadly Sins, on the other hand, are presented as ludicrously comic figures. They boast of their prowess but are ignominiously overthrown in battle, at which point they turn on one another in the slapstick comedy of physical abuse. Their speech, often profane and scatological, proclaims them to be deplorable even if they are also amusing. As in other forms of medieval drama, vice is more appealing than serious moral instruction, but, while comic, it is recognizably evil. The play has no "Vice" character by name—the term did not in fact come into use until the sixteenth century—but we can recognize in Backbiter (Detraction) the kind of chortling and resourceful malice that identifies the Vice of later morality plays.

A good deal is known about the staging of *Perseverance,* thanks to a remarkably detailed staging diagram found in the manuscript. The plan calls for a large *platea* or open space surrounded by scaffolds, with a castle in the center of the arena. In many ways, this arrangement resembles that used for the N Town Passion sequence and for *Mary Magdalene.* (Significantly, the N Town cycle, *Mary Magdalene,* and *The Castle of Perseverance* were all performed in the area of England known as the East Midlands, comprised of Lincolnshire, Cambridge, and Norfolk.) The scaffolds or "towers" are large enough to hold several actors at one time, and are simultaneously visible to the audience. According to *The Medieval Theatre in the Round,* a book-length study of the staging of *Perseverance* by Richard Southern, the circular arena used for this play must be about 125 feet in diameter. Southern supposes the arena to be surrounded by a moat, with the scaffolds erected on an earthen mound just inside the moat. The spectators, he argues, sit on this earthwork between the scaffolds and also fill part of the central area or *platea.* The "stytelerys" mentioned in the staging diagram must then be ushers needed to part the spectators when the actors move through the *platea* from one scaffold to another. The diagram itself clearly specifies that no one is to sit at the castle in the center, where much of the action takes place.

In its use of this remarkable arena theater the play exploits to the full the motif of a balanced conflict between the opposing forces of good and evil. The towers manned by the Deadly Sins bustle with action, as for example when Backbiter goes from scaffold to scaffold calling to arms the various spiritual enemies of Mankind. Heaven and hell send forth their representatives, the Good and Bad Angels, to comfort or tempt the protagonist standing at the center of this cosmic battleground. The assault on the castle takes place on the *platea,* presumably right in the midst of the spectators. On the *platea,* too, the villains comically pommel one another for their failures in battle. From the detailed stage directions we learn how costuming and special effects add to the panoramic spectacle. Belial, for instance, must have gunpowder burning in pipes in his hands, ears, and arse as he advances to battle. The four daughters of God are symbolically dressed in robes of white, red, green, and black. Costume changes signal the progression of Mankind through the various ages of man, from naked infancy (l. 285), to worldly insolence in a robe festooned with gold coins (ll. 588, 701), to old age in a loose gown (l. 2488)— what Shakespeare later characterized as the "lean and slippered pantaloon."

Like other morality plays, *Perseverance* has no significant ancestry in the drama of the medieval Church. Many nondramatic sources and analogues can be found, however. The allegorization of spiritual conflict in terms of a chivalric tournament or assault on a castle was a commonplace in medieval literature. Some instances have already been cited in the Introduction to the morality play, such as Prudentius' *Psychomachia* and Grosseteste's *Chasteau d'Amour*. The battle between the seven Deadly Sins and the seven Virtues is specifically mentioned in a number of works, including Rutebeuf's *La Bataille des Vices contre les Vertues* and Bonaventura's *De Pugna Spirituali contra Septem Vitia Capitalia*. The conception of the four daughters of God goes back to Psalm 85 and also finds expression in the writings of St. Bernard, Grosseteste, Bonaventura, and others.

The Castle of Perseverance

[*The Banns.*]

1 VEXILLATOR.   Glorious God, in all degres Lord most of myth   *flagbearer / might*
That hevene and erthe made of nowth, bothe se and lond—   *nought*
The aungelys in hevene, him to serve bryth,   *brightly, shiningly*
And [man]kinde in midylerd he made with his hond—   *middle-earth, earth*
And [our lo]fly Lady, that lanterne is of lyth,   *lovely Lady (Mary)/light*
Save oure lege lord the kinge, the leder of this londe,
7   And all the ryall[ys] of this revme, and rede hem the ryth,   *nobles/realm/advise*
And all the goode comowns of this towne that beforn us stonde   *commons, people*
In this place!
We mustyr you with menschepe,   *call you together/honor*
And freyne you of frely frenchepe.   *ask of you generous friendship*
Crist safe you all fro schenchepe,   *harm*
That knowyn wil our case!   *theme*

14   2 VEXILLATOR.   The case of oure cominge, you to declare,
Every man in himself forsothe he it may finde;
Whou Mankinde into this werld born is ful bare   *How*
And bare schal beried be at his [l]ast ende.
God him gevith t[w]o aungel[ys] ful yep and ful yare,   *active and alert*
The Goode Aungel and the Badde, to him for to lende.
20   The Goode techith him goodnesse; the Badde, sinne and sare.   *sorrow*
Whanne the ton hath the victory, the tother goth behende   *one/other/behind*
By skill.   *According to reason*

7And (may God and Mary save also) the nobles of this realm, and guide (advise) them in the path of truth.

14To declare to you the theme of our coming.

The Goode Aungel coveitith evermore Mans salvacion,

And the Badde bysitith him evere to his dampnacion.   *besets, attacks*

And God hathe govyn Man fre arbritracion   *given*

Whether he wil himse[lf] save or his soule sp[i]ll.   *destroy*

1 VEXILLATOR.   Spilt is Man spetously whanne he to sinne   *Destroyed/cruelly*
    asent!

The Bad Aungel thanne bringith him thre enmys so stout:

The Werlde, the Fende, the foul Flesche so joly and jent.   *courteous, elegant*

30   They ledyn him ful lustily with sinnys al abowt.

Pith with Pride and Coveitise, to the Werld is he went,   *Furnished*

To mey[n]ten his manhod; all men to him lout.   *maintain/bow*

Aftyr, Ire and Envye the Fend hath to him lent,

Bakbitinge and Enditinge, with all men for to route,   *(False) Accusation/make trouble*

Ful evyn.   *Indeed, completely*

But the fowle Flesch, homliest of all,   *most familiar*

Slawth, Lust, and Leccherye gun to him call,

Glotony, and other sinnys bothe grete and small.

Thus Mans soule is soilyd with sinnys moo thanne sevyn.   *more/seven*

40   2 VEXILLATOR.   Whanne Mans sowle is soilyd with sinne
    and with sore,

Thanne the Goode Aungyl makith mikyl mo[u]rninge   *much*

That the lofly liknesse of God schulde be lore   *lovely/lost*

Thorwe the Badde Aungell[ys] fals entisinge.   *Through*

He sendith to him Conciens, prickyd ful pore,   *dressed very poorly*

And clere Confescion, with Penauns-doinge.   *clear, purifying*

They mevyn Man to mendement that he misdid before.   *move/amendment of that which*

Thus they callyn him to clennesse and to good levinge,

Withoutyn distaunce.   *Indisputably*

Mekenesse, Paciense, and Charité,

50   Sobirnesse, Besinesse, and Chastité,   *Temperance/Industry*

And Largité, vertuys of good degré,   *Generosity/virtues*

Man callith to the Castel of Good Perseveraunce.   *Call Man*

1 VEXILLATOR.   The Castel of Perseverauns w[h]anne
    Mankinde hath tan,   *taken possession of*

Wel armyd with vertus, and overcome all vicys,

There the Good Aungyl makith ful mery thanne

That Mankinde hath overcome his gostly e[n]miis.   *spiritual enemies*

The Badde Aungyl mo[u]rnith that he hath missyd Man.

He callith the Werld, the Fend, and the foule Flesch,
    iwis,   *certainly*

And all the sevene sinnys, to do that they canne   *do what*

60   To bringe Mankind ageyn to bale out of blis,   *torment*

With wronge.

Pride asailith Meknesse with all his myth;   *might*
Ire ageyns Paciensse ful fast ganne he fyth;   *fight*
Envye ageyn Charité strivith ful ryth;   *exceedingly*
But Coveitise ageyns Largité fi[gh]tith overlonge.

2 VEXILLATOR.   Coveitise Mankind evere coveitith for to
    qwell.   *to destroy Mankind*
He gaderith to him Glotony ageyns Sobirnesse;   *gathers*
Leccherye with Chastité fi[gh]tith ful fell;   *fiercely*
And Slawthe in Goddys servise, ageyns Besinesse.   *Sloth in serving God*
70   Thus vicys ageyns vertues fi[gh]tyn ful snelle.   *vigorously*
Every buskith to bringe Man to distresse.   *Everyone strives*
But Penaunce and Confescion with Mankind wil melle,   *Unless/intercede*
The vicys arn ful lickely the vertues to opresse,   *are*
Saun dowte.   *Without doubt*
Thus in the Castel of good Perseverance
Mankind is maskeryd with mekyl variaunce.   *bewildered/much conflict*
The Goode Aungyl and the Badde be evere at distaunce;   *at enmity*
The Goode holdith him inne, the Badde wold bringe him
    owte.

1 VEXILLATOR.   Owt of good Perseveraunce whanne
    Mankinde wil not come,
Yit the Badde Aungyl with Coveitise him gan asaile,
Findende him in poverte and penaunce so benome,   *Finding/numbed*
82   And bringith him in beleve, in defaute for to faile.   *poverty/suffer want*
Thanne he profyrth him good and gold, so gret a sowme,   *offers/goods/sum*
That if he wil com ageyn, and with the Werld daile.   *If that/deal, dally*
85   The Badde Aungyl to the Werld tollith him downe,   *entices*
86   The Castel of Perseveraunce to fle fro the vaile   *advantage*
87   And blisse.
Thanne the Werld beginnith him to restore.   *to give him back wealth*
Have he nevere so mikyl, yit he wold have more—   *(Though) he have*
Thus the Badde Aungyl lerith him his lore.   *teaches*
The more a man agith, the harder he is.   *ages/more impenitent*

2 VEXILLATOR.   Hard a man is in age, and covetouse by
    kinde.   *by nature*
Whanne all other sinnys Man hath forsake,
Evere the more that he hath, the more is in his minde
To gader and to gete good, with woo and with wrake.   *gather/harm*
Thus the Goode Aungyl caste is behinde
And the Badde Aungyl Man to him takith,

---

[82] And convinces him he will suffer want through poverty.

[85-87] The Bad Angel entices him to the World, to flee and come down from the advantage and bliss of the Castle of Perseverance.

That wringith him wrenchys to his last ende,   *Who deceives him with tricks*
Til Deth comith foul dolfully, and loggith him in a lake   *lodges*
Ful lowe.   *i.e., In hell*
Thanne is Man on molde maskeryd in minde.   *on earth bewildered*
102   He sendith afftyr his sekkatours, ful fekyl to finde;   *executors/fickle, untrustworthy*
103   And his [h]eir aftyrward comith evere behinde—
104   "I wot not who" is his name, for he him nowt knowe.   *doesn't know*

1 VEXILLATOR.   Man knowe not who schal be his [h]eir,
        and governe his good.   *possessions*
He carith more for his catel thanne for his cursyd sinne.   *chattels*
107   To putte his good in governaunce, he mengith his mod;   *troubles his mind*
He wolde that it were scifftyd amongys his ny kinne.   *shifted, distributed/near*
But ther schal com a lithyr ladde with a torne hod—   *rascally/hood*
110   "I wot nevere who" schal be his name, his clothis be ful
        thinne—
Schal [h]erith the [h]eritage that nevere was of his blod.   *inherit*
Whanne al his life is lityd upon a lityl pinne,   *his (Man's)/alighted/pin*
At the laste,
On live whanne [he] may no lenger lende,   *Alive/remain*
Mercy he callith at his laste ende:
"Mercy, God! Be now min[e] frende!"
With that, Mans spirit is paste.   *past*

2 VEXILLATOR.   Whanne Manys spirit is past, the Badde
        Aungyl ful fell   *cruel*
Cleymith that, for covetise, Mans sowle schuld ben his,   *because of covetousness*
120   And for to bere it ful boistowsly with him into hell.   *bear/fiercely*
The Good Aungyl seyth "Nay! The spirit schal to blis,
For, at his laste ende, of mercy he gan spell,   *he spoke*
And therfore, of mercy schal he nowth misse.   *not*
And oure lofly Lady, if sche wil for him mell,   *intercede*
125   By mercy and by menys in purgatory he is,   *prayers, mediation*
126   In ful bitter place."
Thus mowthys confession   *mouth's, oral*
And his hertys contricion

102–4He sends for his executors, only to find them untrustworthy; and his heir always follows after later (i.e., is designated later)—"I don't know who" (i.e., What's-his-name) is his name, for the dying Man doesn't know who his heir will be.

107He troubles his mind to achieve a favorable disposition of his estate.

110*thinne*: i.e., threadbare. (The heir who undeservedly wins Man's estate is ironically likely to be a person of low birth.)

125–26By virtue of mercy and by (Our Lady's) mediation, Man will be placed in purgatory, a very painful place (where Man can suffer temporal rather than eternal punishment for his mortal sins).

Schal save Man fro dampnacion,
By Goddys mercy and grace.

1 VEXILLATOR. Grace if God wil graunte us, of his mikyl *great*
  myth, *might*
132 These parcell[ys] in propyrtes we purpose us to playe *roles*
This day sevenenyt, before you in syth, *a week from today/sight*
134 At ——— on the grene, in ryal aray. *royal, rich*
Ye, haste you thanne thedyrward, sirys, hendly in hyth, *courteous in highest degree*
All goode neyborys, ful specialy we you pray.
And loke that ye be there betime, luffely and lyth, *early/willingly and readily*
For we schul be onward by underne of the day. *ready by about 9 a.m.(?)*
Dere frendys,
We thanke you of all good daliaunce *for your good conversation*
141 And of all youre special sportaunce, *entertainment*
142 And preye you of good continuaunce
143 To oure livys endys.

2 VEXILLATOR. Os oure livys we love you, thus takande *As/taking*
  oure leve.
Ye manly men of ———, ther Crist save you all! *may*
He mainten youre mirthys, and kepe you fro greve, *(May) he preserve/harm*
That born was of Mary mild in an ox stall. *He who/from*
Now, mery be all ———, and wel mote ye cheve, *may you thrive*
All oure feythful frendys, ther faire mote ye fall! *may fair luck befall you*
150 Ya, and welcum be ye whanne ye com, pris for to preve, *to test our worth (as actors)*
And worthy to be worchepyd in boure and in hall, *i.e., everywhere*
And in every place!
Farewel, faire frendys,
That lofly wil listyn and lendys! *willingly/give ear*
Criste kepe you fro fendys! *fiends*
  [*To the trumpeters.*]
156 Trumpe up, and lete us pace! *march on*

Haec sunt nomina ludentium.   These are the names of the players.

In primis, ij VEXILLATORES   At first, two flagbearers
MUNDUS, *et cum eo* VOLUPTAS, STULTITIA, *et*   World, and with him Lust-and-Liking (Pleas-
  GARCIO   sure), Folly, and Servant

132We intend to play these roles in costume and with theatrical properties.

134(The blank is presumably left to provide the name of the locality where the play is to be performed.)

141–43And for all your particularly kind entertaining (of us), and we beg you to continue (your favor toward us) to our lives' ends.

156a(This list of players' names is found in the MS at the back of the play.)

BELIAL, *et cum eo* SUPERBIA, IRA, *et* INVIDIA

CARO, *et cum eo* GULA, LUXURIA, *et*
    ACCIDI[A]

HUMANUM GENUS, *et cum eo* BONUS ANGELUS *et*
    MALUS ANGELUS

AVARITIA [*World's treasurer*], DETRACTIO
[*World's messenger*]

CONFESSIO, PAENITENTIA

HUMILITAS, PATIENTIA, CARITAS, ABSTINENTIA,
    CASTITAS, SOLICITUDO, *et* LARGITAS [the
    Seven Moral Virtues, the keepers of
    the Castle]

MORS, ANIMA

MISERICORDIA, VERITAS, JUSTITIA, *et* PAX
[the Four Daughters of God]

PATER *sedens in trono*

Belial, and with him Pride, Wrath, and Envy

Flesh, and with him Gluttony, Lechery, and
    Sloth

Mankind, and with him the Good Angel and
    the Bad Angel

Covetousness, Backbiter (also called Flibberti-
    gibbet)

Shrift (Confession), Penitence

Meekness, Patience, Charity, Temperance,
    Chastity, Business (Industry), and
    Generosity

Death, The Soul (of Mankind)

Mercy, Truth, Righteousness, and Peace

The Father sitting in his throne

Summa, xxxvi ludentium   Total, 36 players

[*The Play.*]

[*On the Scaffold of the World. World and Covetousness.*]

157	MUNDUS. Worthy wi[gh]tys in al this wer[l]d wide,	*persons*
158	By wilde wode wonys, and every weye-went,	*places/pathway (?)*
159	Precious prinse, prekyd in pride:	*set, fixed*
160	Thorwe this propyr pleyn place, in pes be ye bent!	*goodly/silence*
	Buske you, bolde bachelerys, under my baner to abide,	*Prepare yourselves*
	Where bryth basnetys be bateryd, and backys ar schent—	*bright helmets/hurt*
163	Ye, sirys semly, all same sittith on side!	*(who) sit all together*
	For, bothe by see and by londe my sondys I have sent.	*messengers*
	Al the World min[e] nam[e] is ment:	*(Throughout) all/is spoken*
	Al abowtyn my bane is blowe.	*round about/edict is trumpeted*
	In every cost I am knowe.	*coast, land/known*
168	I do men ravin on riche rowe	*cause/behave madly*
	Til they be dyth to dethys dent.	*put to death's blow*
	Assarye, Acaye, and Almayne,	*Assyria/Achaia (Greece)/Germany*
	Cavadoyse, Capadoyse, and Cananee,	*Calvados (France)/Cappadocia/ Canaan*

157–60Worthy persons dwelling beside wild forest places and every pathway or turning of
the road (i.e., everywhere), throughout the wide world, (belonging to) that worthy prince
set or attired in his pride: may you submit yourselves in silence throughout this goodly open
place (i.e., the platea, or acting area as a whole)!

163*on side:* Possibly a reference to the earthwork with seating surrounding the playing area.

168I cause men in a rich procession (i.e., in great numbers) to behave madly.

Babyloyne, Brabon, Burgoyne, and Bretaine,   *Babylon|Brabant|Burgundy|Brittany*
Grece, Galys, and to the Gryckisch see;   *Galicia (Spain)|Greek (Aegean) Sea*
I meve also Masadoyne in my mikyl maine,   *Macedonia|great strength*
Frauns, Flaundrys, and Freslonde, and also Normandé, *Friesland (Holland)*
176   Pincecras, Paris, and longe Pigmaine,
And every toun in Trage, evyn to the dreye tre,   *Thrace(?)|dry tree*
Rodys and riche Rome—   *Rhodes*
All these londys, at min[e] avise,   *under my direction*
Arn castyn to my wer[l]dly wise.   *Are committed|manner*
My tresorer, Sir Coveitise,
Hath sesyd hem [w]holy to me.   *taken possession of them*

Therfor my game and my gle growe ful glad;   *sport and glee*
184   Ther is [no] wythe in this werld that my witte wil me   *person*
           warne!   *refuse*
Every riche rengne rapith him ful rad   *kingdom hastens quickly*
In lustys and in likingys my lawys to lerne.   *pleasures and indulgences*
With faire folke in the felde freschly I am fadde.   *In the company of|fed*
188   I dawnse doun as a doo, by dalys ful derne!   *doe|dales|dark*
189   What boy bedith batayl, or debatith with blad,
Him were betyr to ben hangyn hie in hell-herne,   *It were better for him|corner*
Or brent on lyth levene!   *burned with blazing lightning*
Whoso spekith ageyn the Werd,   *against the World*
In a presun he schal be sperd;   *prison|shut up*
Min[e] hest is holdyn and herd   *command is obeyed and heard*
Into hig[h]e hevene.   *Unto, as far as*

[*On the Scaffold of the Devil. Belial, Pride, Envy, and Wrath.*]

BELIAL.   Now I sitte, Satanas, in my sad sinne,   *steadfast*
As devil dowty, in draf as a drake.   *doughty|filth like a dragon*
I champe and I chafe, I chocke on my chinne,   *gnash my teeth|thrust out*
I am boistows and bold, as Belial the blake.   *fierce|black*
200   What folk that I grope, they gapyn and grenne. *grasp|gnash teeth*
201   Iwis, fro Carlylle into Kent my carpinge they take! *they receive my censure*
Bothe the bak and the buttoke brestith al on brenne; *bursts all a-burning*
With werkys of wreche I werke hem mikyl wrake;   *vengeance|them much harm*

176*Pincecras*: land of the Pincenarii, in Thrace. *longe Pigmaine*: land of the pygmies.

184There's no one in this world who will refuse my practical wisdom.

188–89I dance (up and) down like a doe, by the very secluded dales! (A metrical tag and mild oath.) Whatever fellow bids to do battle (i.e., offers a challenge), or makes contention with a blade.

200Whatever persons I grasp, they gape openmouthed and gnash their teeth.

201*Carlylle into Kent*: i.e., from the Scottish border to the English Channel.

	In woo is al my wenne.	*delight*
	In care I am cloyed,	*sorrow/burdened*
	And fowle I am anoyed	*foully, grievously*
	But Mankinde be stroyed	*Unless/destroyed*
	By dikys and by denne.	*valley (i.e., everywhere)*
	Pride is my prince, in perlys i-pyth;	*decked in pearls*
	Wretthe, this wrecche, with me schal wawe;	*Wrath/go*
	Envye into werre with me schal walkyn wyth;	*war/bravely*
	With these faitourys I am fedde; in feyth, I am fawe!	*deceivers/fed/joyful*
	As a dingne devil in my dene I am dyth.	*worthy/den/set*
214	Pride, Wretthe, and Envye, I sey in my sawe,	*speech*
215	Kingys, kaiserys, and kempys, and many a kene knyth	*soldiers/knight*
216	These lovely lordys han lernyd hem my lawe;	*have taught*
	To my dene they wil drawe.	*den/come*
	Al-[w]holy Mankinne	*Entirely*
	To helle but I winne,	*unless/entice*
	In bale is my binne,	*torment/stall*
221	And schent undyr schawe.	*disgraced/grove, thicket*
222	On Mankinde is my trost, in contre i-knowe.	*known*
	With my tire and with my tail, tytly to tene,	*attire, disguise/quickly to do harm*
	Thorwe Flaundris and Freslonde faste I gan flowe,	*Through/I move quickly*
	Fele folke on a flokke to flappyn and to flene;	*Many/beat/flay*
226	Where I graspe on the grounde, grim ther schal growe.	*Wherever/on earth*
	Gadyr you togedyr, ye boyis, on this grene!	
	In this brode bugyl a blast w[h]anne I blowe	*broad, large*
	Al this werld schal be wood, iwis, as I wene,	*mad/think*
	And to my biddinge bende.	*bend, obey*
231	Wythly on side	*Quickly aside*
232	On benche wil I bide,	
	To tene, this tide,	*harm/time*
	Al-[w]holy Mankende.	

[*On the scaffold of the Flesh. Flesh, Gluttony, Sloth, and Lechery.*]

214–16I say that Pride, Wrath, and Envy, these noble lords, have taught my custom to kings, emperors, and soldiers, and many a bold knight.

221–22i.e., And (to be) disgraced under the earth. I have confident expectations as to Mankind, well-known everywhere.

226Wherever on earth I grope or clutch greedily, fury will flourish there.

231–32i.e., I'll remain on the sidelines, watching for my opportunity.

235   CARO.   I bide, as a brod brustun-gutte, abovyn on these   *Flesh*
        tourys!
      Everybody is the be[t]ter that to min[e] biddinge is bent.   *obedient*
      I am Mankindys faire Flesch, florchyd in flowrys;   *adorned with*
      My life is with lustys and likinge i-lent.   *pleasures and indulgence settled*
      With tapitys of tafata I timbyr my towrys;   *silken tapestries/decorate*
      In mirthe and in melodye my mende is i-ment.   *my inclination is disposed*
241   Thou[gh] I be clay and clad, clappyd undir clowrys,   *clod/sod*
      Yit wolde I that my will in the werld went   *Yet I desire*
      Ful trew, I you behyth.   *I promise you*
      I love wel min[e] ese,
      In lustys me to plese;
      Thou[gh] sinne my sowle sese,   *possess*
      I geve not a myth.   *I don't care a mite*

      In Glotony, gracious now am I growe;   *grown*
      Therfore he sittith semly here by my side.
      In Lechery and Likinge lent am I lowe,   *Pleasure/sunk, set*
      And Slawth, my swete sone, is bent to abide.   *inclined*
      These three are nobyl, trewly I trowe,   *worthy, able*
      Mankinde to tenyn and trecchyn a tide.   *harm/trick/time*
254   With many berdys in bowre my blastys are blowe,   *maidens/blown*
      By weys and by wodys, thorwe this werld wide,   *paths/woods (i.e., everywhere)*
      The sothe for to seyne.   *To say the truth*
      But if Mans Flesch fare wel   *Unless*
      Bot[h]e at mete and at mel,   *food*
      Dyth I am in gret del,   *Put/grief*
      And browt into peyne.   *brought*

261   And aftyr good fare, in feyth, thou[gh] I fell,   *sink (to death)*
262   Thou[gh] I drive to dust, in drosse for to drepe,   *am turned/to drop into impurity*
263   Thow[gh] my sely sowle were haried to hell,   *miserable/harried, dragged*
264   W[h]oso wil do these werkys, iwis he schal wepe   *weep*
265   Ever withowtyn ende.   *Forever*
      Behold the Werld, the Devil, and me!

235I dwell aloft on these towers (this scaffold), as one with a huge gut distended and burst through gluttony.

241Though I be clay and clod (i.e., the inanimate matter out of which life is formed), clapped or thrust under the sod (under ground).

254The blasts (of my sensual trumpet) are proclaimed among my maidens dwelling in their chambers.

261–65And truly, if subsequent to a hearty repast I should sink to death, if I am turned (lit: am driven) to dust, being distilled (falling in drops) into dregs and refuse, if my miserable soul is dragged to hell, by the same token anyone who does these things (i.e., indulges in sensual excess) will truly weep forever.

With all oure mythis, we kingys thre,   *mights, power*
Nyth and day, besy we be   *Night*
For to distroy Mankende
270 If that w[e may];
Therfor, on hille,
Sittith all stille,   *Sit*
And seth with good wille   *see*
Oure riche aray.   *spectacle*

[*On the platea. Enter Mankind, with a Good Angel on his right,
and a Bad Angel on his left.*]

HUMANUM GENUS.   Aftyr oure forme-faderys kende,   *first father's fashion*
This nyth I was of my moder born.   *night*
Fro my moder I walke, I wende;   *I go*
Ful feynt and febyl I fare you beforn.   *I go in front of you*
I am nakyd of lim and lende,   *loin*
280 As Mankinde is schapyn and schorn.   *is shaped and fashioned*
I not w[h]edyr to gon ne to lende   *I don't know whither/dwell*
To helpe myself midday nyn morn.   *nor*
For schame I stonde and schende.   *am stupefied*
I was born this nyth in blody ble,   *night/condition*
And nakyd I am, as ye may se.
A, Lord God in Trinité,
Whow Mankende is unthende!   *How/feeble*

Whereto I was to this werld browth,
I ne wot; but to woo and wepinge   *I don't know*
290 I am born, and have ryth nowth   *nothing at all*
To helpe myself in no doinge.   *in anything I do*
I stonde and stodye, al ful of thowth.   *am perplexed/anxiety*
Bare and pore is my clothinge:
A sely crisme min[e] hed hath cawth,   *chrisom, baptismal garb/has received*
That I tok at min[e] cristeninge.   *got*
Certys, I have no more.   *Certainly*
Of erthe I cam, I wot ryth wele,   *I know very well*
And as erthe I stande this sele;   *at this season, time*
Of Mankende it is gret dele.   *pity*
300 Lord God, I crye thine ore!   *beg/mercy, grace*

Two aungels bene asinyd to me.   *assigned*
The ton techith me to goode;   *one*
On my ryth side ye may him se.
He cam fro Criste that deyed on rode.   *died on the cross*
Another is ordeinyd her[e] to be,
That is my foo by fen and flode;   *i.e., everywhere*

He is about, in every degré,   *is busy|way*
To drawe me to tho devilys wode   *those|mad, fierce*
That in helle ben thicke.   *numerous*
310 Swiche t[w]o hath every man on live   *Such|alive*
To rewlyn him and his wittys five.
Whanne man doth evil, the ton wolde schrive;   *one would absolve (him) of sin*
The tother drawith to wicke.   *wickedness*

But syn these aungelys be to me falle,   *since|are allotted*
Lord Jhesu, to you I bidde a bone   *ask a boon, prayer*
That I may folwe, by strete and stalle,   *shelter (i.e., everywhere)*
The aungyl that cam fro hevene trone.   *from heaven's throne*
Now, Lord Jhesu in hevene halle,
Here whane I make my mone!   *Hear when|complaint*
320 Coriows Criste, to you I calle!   *Careful (of sinners)*
As a grisly gost I grucche and grone,   *complain*
I wene, ryth ful of thowth.   *I think (a metrical tag)|anxiety*
A, Lord Jhesu, w[h]edyr may I goo?   *whither*
A crisime I have, and no moo.
Alas! Men may be wondyr woo   *wondrously woeful*
Whanne they be first forth browth.   *brought*

BONUS ANGELUS.   Ya, forsothe, and that is wel sene: *seen, demonstrated*
Of woful wo man may singe,
For iche creature helpith himself bedene,   *immediately*
330 Save only man, at his cominge.
Nevyrthelesse, turne thc[e] fro tene,   *from harm*
And serve Jhesu, hevene kinge,
And thou schalt, by grevys grene,   *green groves (a metrical tag)*
Fare wel in all thinge.
That Lord thy life hath lante.   *lent you life*
Have him alwey in thy minde,
That deyed on rode for mankinde,   *died on cross*
And serve him to thy lifes ende,   *life's*
And sertys thou schalt not wante.   *certainly*

340 MALUS ANGELUS.   Pes, aungel! Thy wordys are not wise.   *Peace, silence*
Thou counselist him not aryth.   *aright*
He schal him drawyn to the Wer[l]dys servíse,   *draw, betake himself*
To dwelle with caysere, kinge, and knyth,   *emperôr|knight*
That in londe be him non lyche.   *So that|none (will) be like him*
Cum on with me, stille as ston!   *motionless*
Thou and I to the Wer[l]d schul goon,   *shall go*
And thanne thou schalt sen anon   *see*
Whow sone thou schalt be riche.   *How soon*

BONUS ANGELUS.   A, pes, aungel! Thou spekist folye.

350   Why schuld he coveit werldys goode,   *world's wealth*
    Syn Criste in erthe, and his meynye,   *Since/followers*
    All in povert here they stode?
    Werldys wele, by strete and stye,   *weal, happiness/i.e., everywhere*
    Failith and fadith as fisch in flode;   *flood, stream*
    But heve[ne]riche is good and trye.   *the kingdom of heaven/tested, worthy*
    Ther Criste sittith, bryth as blode,   *bright*
    Withoutyn any distresse.   *anguish*
    To the World wolde he not flit,   *go*
    But forsok it every whitt.
    Example I finde in holy writ,
    He wil bere me witnesse:

361a   *Divitias et paupertates ne dederis mihi, Domine.*

MALUS ANGELUS.   Ya, ya, Man! Leve him nowth,   *Believe him not*
    But cum with me, by stye and strete!
    Have thou a gobet of the werld cawth,   *(When) you've gotten a morsel*
    Thou schalt finde it good and swete.
    A faire lady the[e] schal be tawth,   *given to you*
    That in bowre thy bale schal bete;   *will remedy your sorrow*
    With riche rentys thou schalt be frawth,   *revenues/fraught, furnished*
    With silke sendel to sittyn in sete.   *fine silk clothing/seat*
370   I rede, late bedys be!   *I advise let prayer beads alone*
    If thou wilt have wel thin[e] hele,   *health, well-being*
    And faryn wel at mete and mele,   *fare/food*
    With Goddys servise may thou not dele,
    But cum and folwe me.

HUMANUM GENUS.   Whom to folwe, wetyn I ne may!   *I don't know*
    I stonde and stodye, and ginne to rave.   *am bewildered*
    I wolde be riche in gret aray,
    And fain I wolde my sowle save:
    As winde in watyr I wave.   *waver*
    [*To the bad angel.*]
380   Thou woldist to the Werld I me toke;   *betook myself*
    And he wolde that I it forsoke.
    Now, so God me helpe, and the holy boke,
    I not w[h]iche I may have!   *I don't know*

MALUS ANGELUS.   Cum on, Man! Whereof hast thou care?   *What's your worry*
    Go we to the Werld, I rede the[e], blive;   *advise/quickly*
    For ther thou schalt mow ryth wel fare,   *be able to fare very well*
    In case if thou thinke for to thrive—

361aGive me neither poverty nor riches, O Lord (see Proverbs 30:8).

No lord schal be the[e] liche. *like you*
Take the Werld to thine entent, *attention*
390 And late thy love be theron lent; *let/fixed, set*
With gold and silvyr and riche rent
Anone thou schalt be riche.

HUMANUM GENUS. Now, syn thou hast behetyn me so, *since/promised*
I wil go with the[e] and asay. *try (it)*
I ne lette for frende ner fo, *I won't stop*
But with the Werld I wil go play,
Certys, a lityl throwe. *while*
In this World is al my trust,
To livyn in liking and in lust: *indulgence and pleasure*
400 Have he and I onys cust, *(When) he/have once kissed*
We schal not part, I trowe.

BONUS ANGELUS. A! Nay, Man, for Cristys blod,
Cum again by strete and stile! *i.e., everywhere, in any case*
The Werld is wickyd, and ful wod, *mad*
And thou schalt levyn but a while. *live*
What coveitist thou to winne?
Man, thinke on thin[e] endinge day
Whanne thou schalt be closyd under clay!
And if thou thenke of that aray, *state of affairs*
Certys thou schalt not sinne.
410a *Homo, memento finis, et in aeternum non peccabis.*

MALUS ANGELUS. Ya, on thy sowle thou schalt thinke al
betime. *soon enough*
Cum forth, Man, and take non[e] hede! *heed*
Cum on, and thou schalt holdyn him inne; *restrain him (the soul?)*
Thy flesch thou schalt foster and fede
With lofly livys fode. *lovely life's food*
With the Werld thou mayst be bold
Til thou be sexty winter hold. *old*
W[h]anne thy nose waxit[h] cold,
Thanne mayst thou drawe to goode. *turn to good*

420 HUMANUM GENUS. I vow to God, and so I may
Make mery a ful gret throwe! *while, time*
I may levyn many a day;
I am but yonge, as I trowe,
For to do that I schulde. *To do what I would do*
Myth I ride by sompe and sike, *by swamps and streamlets, i.e., everywhere*

410aMan, remember your end, and you will no longer sin (see Ecclesiasticus 7:36).

And be riche, and lordlike,
Certys thanne schulde I be frike,   *vigorous, joyful*
And a mery man on molde.   *on earth*

MALUS ANGELUS.   Yis, by my feyth, thou schalt be a lord,
430   And ellys hange me by the hals!   *Or otherwise/neck*
          But thou muste be at min[e] acord: *i.e., agree to my conditions*
          Otherwhile thou muste be fals   *Sometimes*
          Amonge kithe and kinne.   *kith, neighbors*
          Now go we forth, swithe anon!   *quickly*
          To the Werld us must gon;
          And bere the[e] manly evere among   *always bear yourself manly*
          Whanne thou comist out or inne.

HUMANUM GENUS.   Yis, and ellys have thou my necke,   *or else*
          But I be manly by downe and diche!   *Unless/i.e., everywhere*
440   And, thou[gh] I be fals I ne recke;   *I don't care*
          With so that I be lordliche,   *Provided that/lordlike*
          I folwe the[e] as I can.
          Thou schalt be my bote of bale;   *remedy of sorrow*
          For, were I riche of holt and hale,   *woods and hall, mansion*
          Thanne wolde I geve nevere tale   *I'd take no account*
          Of God ne of good man.
             [*The Bad Angel leads Mankind toward the World's scaffold.*]

BONUS ANGELUS.   I weyle and wringe and make mone!   *wail and wring (hands)*
          This man with woo schal be pilt.   *tortured*
          I sye sore, and grisly grone,   *sigh/pitiably*
450   For his folye schal make him spilt!   *destroyed*
          I not w[h]eder to gone—   *I know not whither to go*
          Mankinde hath forsakyn me!
          Alas, man, for love of the[e]!
          Ya, for this gamyn and this gle   *sport*
          Thou schalt grocchyn and grone.   *grutch, complain*
             Pipe up mu[sic].

             [*On the World's scaffold, World is accompanied by Lust-and-
             Liking (Pleasure) and Folly.*]

MUNDUS.   Now I sitte in my semly sale;   *handsome hall*
          I trotte and tremle in my trew trone.   *shake (with joy)*
          As a hawke, I hoppe in my hende hale;   *handsome hall*
          King, knyth, and kaiser to me makyn mone.   *knight/make complaint, petition*
460   Of God ne of good man gyf I nevere tale;   *I take no account*
          As a likinge lord I leyke here alone.   *pleasure-loving/I sport*
          W[h]oso brawle any boste, by downe or by dale,   *Whoso will brag/i.e., anywhere*

Tho gadlingys schal be gastyd, and grislich grone,   *Those rogues|terrified|pitiably*
Iwis.
Lust, Foly, and Veynglory,
All these arn in min[e] memory:
Thus beginnith the nobyl story
Of this werldys blis.
 [*He summons his lieutenants.*]

  Lust-Liking and Foly,   *Pleasure*
470 Comly knytis of renoun,   *knights*
  Belive thorwe this londe do crye   *Quickly throughout|make proclamation*
  Al abowtyn, in tour and toun: *All round about*
  If any man be, fer or nye,   *far or nigh*
  That to my servise wil buske him boun, *make himself ready*
  If he wil be trost and trye,   *trusty and true*
  He schal be king, and were the croun   *wear*
  With ricches[t] robys in res!   *in haste*
  W[h]oso to the Werld wil drawe—   *betake himself*
  Of God ne of good man gevyt[h] he not a hawe— *For|cares|haw (i.e., trifle)*
480 Syche a man, by londys lawe,   *by the law of the land*
  Schal sittyn on my dees.   *dais, throne*

 VOLUPTAS. Lo, me, here redy, lord, to faryn and to fle, *Pleasure|fare, go*
  To sekyn the[e] a servaunt dinge and dere! *seek|worthy|dear, valued*
  Whoso wil with Foly rewlyd be,   *by|ruled*
  He is worthy to be a servaunt here,
  That drawith to sinnys sevene.   *Who betakes himself*
  Whoso wil be fals and covetouse,
  With this Werld he schal have lond and house.
  This Werldys wi[s]dom gevith no[t] a louse *cares not a trifle*
490 Of God, nyn of hye hevene.   *For|nor*
  Tunc descendit in plateam pariter.   *Then he descends together (with Folly) into the platea*

  Pes, pepyl! Of pes we you pray.   *Silence*
  Sith and sethe wel to my sawe!   *Sit and see, pay heed|speech*
  Whoso wil be riche and in gret aray,
  Toward the Werld he schal drawe.   *betake himself*
  Whoso wil be fals, al that he may—   *can*
  Of God himself he hath non[e] awe—
  And livyn in lustys, nyth and day,   *night*
  The Werld of him wil be ryth fawe,   *very joyful*
  To dwelle in his howse.   *To (have him) dwell in World's house*
  Whoso wil with the Werld have his dwellinge,
  And ben a lord of his clothinge,   *wearing World's livery*
  He muste nedys, ovyr al thinge,   *He must above all*
  Everemore be covetowse.

503a   *Non est in mundo dives, qui dicit "abundo."*

    STULTITIA.   Ya! Covetouse he muste be,   *Folly*
       And me, Foly, muste have in mende;   *in mind*
       For whoso wil alwey Foly fle,
       In this werld schal ben unthende.   *unthriving*
       Thorwe werldys wisdom of gret degré,   *Through*
       Schal nevere man in werld moun wende   *No man will ever be able to get on*
510   But he have help of me   *Unless*
       That am Foly, fer and hende—   *fair and pleasant*
       He muste hangyn on my hoke.   *hook*
       Werldly wit was nevere nowt,   *i.e., never amounted to anything*
       But with Foly it were frawt.   *Unless/fraught, furnished*
       Thus the wis[e] man hath tawt   *taught*
       Abotyn in his boke: *About, concerning*
516a   *Sapientia penes Domini.*   *Wisdom is with (from) the Lord*

    VOLUPTAS.   Now, all the men that in this werld wold thrive,
       For to ridyn on hors ful hie,   *i.e., to ride tall in the saddle*
       Cum speke with Lust-and-Likinge belive,   *with Pleasure quickly*
       And his felaw, yonge Foly!   *companion*
       Late se whoso wil us knowe.   *Let's see*
       Whoso wil drawe to Likinge-and-Luste,
       And, as a fole, in Foly ruste,
       On us t[w]o he may truste,
       And levyn lovely, I trowe.   *live handsomely*
        [*The Bad Angel, leading Mankind, salutes them.*]

    MALUS ANGELUS.   How, Lust-Liking and Folye,
       Take to me good entent!   *Ho*
       I have browth, by downys drye,   *Pay attention*
       To the Werld a gret present.   *brought/(a metrical tag)*
530   I have g[u]ilyd him ful qweyntly,   *beguiled (Man)/craftily*
       For, syn he was born, I have him blent.   *since/blinded*
       He schal be servaunt good and try.   *proven*
       Amonge you his wil is lent;   *fixed, set*
       To the Werld he wil him take.
       For, syn he cowde wit, I undirstonde,   *since he could comprehend*
       I have him tisyd in every londe.   *enticed*
       His Goode Aungel, by strete and stronde *i.e., everywhere*
       I have don him forsake.   *caused him to forsake*

503aThere is not a rich man in the world who says "I have enough" (a commonplace saying).

516a(See Ecclesiasticus 1:1.)

Therfor, Lust, my trewe fere,   *companion*
540 Thou art redy alwey, iwis:
Of worldly lawys thou him lere,   *teach him*
That he were browth in werldly blis.   *(So) that he be brought*
Loke he be riche, the sothe to tell.   *See to it/truth*
Help him, fast he gunne to thrive;   *so that he thrives quickly*
And whanne he wenith best to live   *thinks*
Thanne schal he deye, and not be schrive,   *die/shriven*
And goo with us to hell.

VOLUPTAS.   By Satan, thou art a nobyl knave
To techyn men first fro goode!   *guide/away from good*
550 Lust-and-Likinge he schal have;
Lechery schal ben his fode: *nourisher, companion*
Metys and drinkys he schal have trye.   *Food/delicate, rich*
With a likinge lady of lofte   *pleasure-loving/of high position*
He schal sittyn in sendel softe,   *silk cloth*
To cachen him to helle-crofte   *catch, drag/hell's enclosure, prison*
That day that he schal deye.   *die*

STULTITIA.   With riche rentys I schal him blinde,   *income*
With the Werld til he be pitte;   *placed, fixed*
And thanne schal I, longe or his ende,   *ere*
560 Make that caitife to be knitte   *knit, bound*
On the Werld, whanne he is set s[ore].   *sorely beset*
[*He calls to Mankind, who has been standing aside.*]
Cum on, Man! Thou schalt not rewe   *rue*
For thou wilt be to us trewe;   *Because*
Thou schalt be clad in clothys newe,
And be riche everemore.

HUMANUM GENUS.   Mary, felaw, gramercy!   *great thanks*
I wolde be riche and of gret renoun.
[Of God] I geve no tale, trewly,   *I take no account*
So that I be lord of toure and toun,   *So long as/tower*
570 By buskys and bankys broun.   *bushes (i.e., everywhere)*
Syn that thou wilt make me   *Since*
Bothe riche of gold and fee,   *Rich both*
Goo forthe! for I wil folow the[e]
By dale and every towne.
    Trumpe up. Tunc ibunt Voluptas et Stultitia, Malus Angelus,   *Then Lust-and-Liking (Pleasure)*
    et Humanum Genus ad Mundum, et dicet Voluptas: *and Folly, the Bad Angel, and*
                                                                    Mankind will go to World
                                                                    (at his scaffold), and
                                                                    Pleasure will say
[VOLUPTAS.]   How, lord, loke owt! for we have browth   *look out (from your scaffold)*
A servant of nobyl fame. [*Presents Mankind.*]
Of worldly good is al his thouth;   *thought*

Of Lust and Folye he hath no schame.

He wolde be gret of name;

580   He wolde be at gret honour,   *in*

For to rewle town and toure.

He wolde have to his paramoure   *as*

Sum lovely dinge dame.   *worshipful lady*

MUNDUS [*to Mankind*].   Welcum, sir, semly in syth!   *seemly in sight*

Thou art welcum to worthy wede,   *clothes*

For thou wilt be my servaunt, day and nyth.   *night*

With my servise I schal the[e] foster and fede;

588   Thy bak schal be betyn with besawntys bryth;   *adorned|bright bezants, gold coins*

Thou schalt have biggingys by bankys brede.   *buildings by the banks' breadth*

To thy cors schal knele kaiser and knyth,   *body, person|knight*

Where that thou walke, by sty or by strete,   *path (i.e., anywhere)*

And ladys lovely on lere.   *of face*

But Goddys servise thou must forsake,

And [w]holy to the Werld the[e] take,

And thanne a man I schal the[e] make

That non[e] schal be thy pere.   *peer*

HUMANUM GE[N]US.   Yis, Werld, and therto here min[e] honde,

To forsake God and his servise.

To medys, thou geve me howse and londe,   *As reward you must give*

600   That I regne richely at min[e] enprise.   *So I may flourish|my will, power*

So that I fare wel by strete and stronde   *As long as|i.e., everywhere*

Whil I dwelle here in werldly wise,

I recke nevere of hevene wonde,   *I care nothing for heaven's chastisement*

Nor of Jhesu, that jentyl justise.

Of my sowle I have non rewthe.   *ruth, pity*

What schulde I recknen of domysday,

So that I be riche and of gret aray?   *As long as*

I schal make mery whil I may,

And therto here my trewthe.   *troth, pledge*

610   MUNDUS.   Now sertys, sir, thou seyst wel:

I holde the[e] trewe fro top to the too.   *toe*

But thou were riche, it were gret del,   *Unless|pity*

And all men that wil fare soo.

Cum up, my servaunt trew as stel!

Tunc ascendet Humanum Ge[n]us ad Mundum.   *Then Mankind will ascend to the World*

Thou schalt be riche, whereso thou goo;

588(Evidently the robes prepared for Mankind by World and his lieutenants are festooned with gold coins; see l. 701.)

Men schul servyn the[e] at mel   *meal*
With minstralsye and bemys blo,   *blowing of trumpets*
With metys and drinkys trye.   *delicate*
Lust-and-Likinge schal be thin[e] ese;   *Pleasure*
620 Lovely ladys the[e] schal plese.
Whoso do the[e] any disesse,   *causes you discomfort*
He schal ben hangyn hye.

Likinge, belive   *Pleasure quickly*
Late clothe him swythe   *Let him be clothed quickly*
In robys rive   *abundant*
With riche aray!
Folye, thou fonde,   *fool*
By strete and stronde   *i.e., everywhere*
Serve him at honde
630 Bothe nyth and day.   *night*

VOLUPTAS.   Trostily,
Lord, redy!—[*To Mankind.*]
Je vous pry,   *I pray you (i.e., this way, please)*
Sir, I say.—[*Aside.*]
In Lickinge-and-Lust   *Pleasure*
He schal rust,
Til dethys dust   *death's*
Do him to day.   *die*

STULTIT[IA].   And I, Folye,
Schal hyen him hye,   *lift him high*
Til sum enmye   *enemy*
Him overgoo.   *Overtops him*
643 In worldys wit
644 That in Foly sit,
645 I thinke yit
646 His sowle to sloo. *Trumpe up.*   *slay*
    [*They take Mankind aside to array him. Enter Backbiter on the
    platea.*]

647 DETRACTIO.   All thingys I crye again the pes   *against the peace*
648   To knyt and knave: this is my kende.   *knight/nature*
    Ya! Dingne dukys on her des,   *Worthy dukes on their dais*
    In bitter balys I hem binde;   *torments/them*

643–46I intend to slay the soul of him who sits in Folly, exalted by the World's practical
wisdom.

647–48i.e., I loudly say everything I can to promote discord among persons of all social ranks:
that is my nature.

Cryinge and care, chidinge and ches   *strife*
And sad sorwe, to hem I sende.
653   Ya! Lowde lesingys lacchyd in les,   *Loud lyings bound in a leash*
Of talys untrewe is al my mende.   *mind, intent*
Mannys bane abowtyn I bere,   *I carry all around men's ruin*
I wil that ye wetyn, all tho that ben here;   *I want you to know/those*
For I am knowyn fer and nere:
I am the Werldys messengere—
My name is Bacbitere.

With every wyth I walke and wende,   *wight, person*
And every man now lovith me wele.   *well*
With lowde lesingys undyr lende,   *loud lies kept in store*
To dethys dint I dresse and dele.   *I prepare for and deal death's blow*
664   To speke faire beforn, and fowle behinde,
665   Amongys men at mete and mele,
Trewly, lordys, this is my kinde.   *nature*
Thus I renne upon a whele;   *I am in continuous operation*
I am feller thanne a fox.   *craftier*
Fleteringe and flateringe is my less[o]un.   *Flitting about/study*
670   With lesingys I tene bothe tour and town,   *lies/do harm everywhere*
With letterys of defamacioun
I bere here in my box. [*Shows his letter-box.*]

I am lyth of lopys thorwe every londe;   *light, nimble of leaps throughout*
Min[e] holy happys may not ben hid.   *My fortunate successes*
T[w]o may not togedyr stonde
But I Bakbiter, be the thridde.   *Unless/third*
I schape yone boyis to schame and schonde,   *direct yonder fellows/disgrace*
All that wil bowyn whanne I hem bidde.   *bow, obey/ them*
679   To lawe of londe, in feyth, I fonde;
Whanne talys untrewe arn betidde,   *are current*
Bakbitere is wide-spronge.   *widespread*
Thorwe the werld, by downe and dalys,   *Throughout/i.e., everywhere*
All abowtyn I brewe balys;   *All round about/sorrows*
Every man tellith talys   *tales, lies*
Aftyr my fals tunge.   *(Modeled) after*

Therfore I am mad[e] massenger
To lepyn over londys leye,   *untilled lands*

653i.e., a bundle of lies.

664–65To flatter a man to his face and disparage him behind his back, among men gathered
for a banquet or other meal.

679Truly, I offer temptation to the law of the country (i.e., I encourage seditious talk).

Thorwe all the world, fer and ner,
Unsaid sawys for to seye.   *saws, sayings*
690   In this holte I hunte here   *holt, grove*
For to spye a prevy pley;   *secret trick*
For whanne Mankinde is clothyd clere,   *handsomely*
Thanne schal I techyn him the wey
To the Dedly Sinnys sevene.
Here I schal abidyn with my pese,   *wait quietly*
The wronge to do him for to chese,   *To cause him to choose the wrong*
For I thinke that he schal lese   *lose*
The lyth of hey hevene.   *light/high*
  [*Lust-and-Liking and Folly lead Mankind, gorgeously attired,*
  back to the World's scaffold.]

VOLUPTAS.   Worthy World, in welthys wonde   *wrapped in wealth*
700   Here is Mankinde, ful fayr in folde!   *handsome on earth*
In bryth besauntys he is bownde,   *bright bezants, gold coins*
And bon to bowe to you so bolde.   *ready*
He levith in lustys every stounde;   *lives/moment*
[W]holy to you he hathe him yolde.   *yielded himself*
For to makyn him gay on grounde,   *on earth*
Worthy World, thou art beholde.   *beholden, obliged*
This Werld is wel at ese!
For, to God I make a vow,
Mankinde had lever now   *had rather*
710   Greve God with sin[n]ys row,   *Grieve/rough, grievous*
Thanne the Werld to displese.

STULTITIA.   Displese the[e] he wil for no man;
On me, Foly, is al his thowth.   *thought*
Trewly Mankinde nowth nen can   *Mankind cannot*
Thinke on God, that hathe him bowth.   *bought, ransomed*
Worthy World, wyth as swan,   *white, fair*
In thy love lely is he lawth.   *truly/caught*
Sithyn he cowde and firste began   *i.e., From the time he first had volition*
The[e] forsakyn wolde he nowth,   *He wouldn't forsake you*
720   But geve him to Folye;   *gives himself*
And sithyn he hathe to the[e] be trewe,   *since, seeing that*
I rede the[e] forsakyn him for no newe.   *advise/for no new (lover)*
Lete us plesyn him til that he rewe,   *rue, regret*
In hell to hangyn hye.

MUNDUS.   Now, Foly, faire the[e] befall,   *may fair luck befall you*
And Luste, blissyd be thou ay!
Ye han browth Mankinde to min[e] hall,   *have brought*
Sertys, in a nobyl aray.   *Certainly*

With Werldys welthys, withinne these wall,
730   I schal him feffe if that I may.   *enfeoff, endow*
Welcum Mankinde! To the[e] I call,
Clenner clothyd thanne any clay,   *More elegantly*
By downe, dale, and diche.   *i.e., everywhere*
Mankinde, I rede that thou reste   *advise/remain*
With me, the Werld, as it is beste;
Loke thou holde min[e] hende heste,   *obey my pleasant command*
And evere thou schalt be riche.

738   HUMANUM GENUS.   Whou schul[d] I, but I thy hestys helde?   *How*
Thou werkist with me [w]holy my will;
Thou feffist me with fen and felde,   *You endow/field*
And hye hall, by holtys and hill.   *i.e., everywhere*
In werldly wele my witte I welde;   *weal, happiness/wield, employ*
In joye I jette, with juelys jentyll.   *jet, strut/elegant jewels*
On blisful banke my boure is bilde;   *my dwelling is built*
In veynglorye I stonde still;   *continually*
I am kene as a knyt.   *bold/knight*
Whoso ageyn the Werld wil speke,   *against*
Mankinde schal on him be wreke;   *avenged*
In stronge presun I schal him steke,   *prison/stick, thrust*
750   Be it wronge or ryth.

MUNDUS.   A, Mankinde, wel the[e] betide,   *may good luck betide you*
That thy love on me is sette!
In my bowrys thou schalt abide,
And yit fare mekyl the bette.   *much the better*
I feffe the[e] in all my wonys wide,   *endow/dwellings*
In dale of dros til thou be deth.   *In the grave/put*
I make the[e] lord of mekyl pride,
758   Sir, at thin[e] owyn mowthis mette.   *mouth's might*
I finde in the[e] no tresun.
In all this worlde, by se and sonde,   *by sea and land*
Parkys, placys, lawnde and londe,   *glade*
Here I gife the[e] with min[e] honde,
Sir, an opyn sesun.   *seizin, possession*

Go to my tresorer, Sir Covetouse.
Loke thou tell him as I seye:
Bidde him make the[e] mayster in his house,
With penys and powndys for to pleye.   *pennies*

[738]What should I do other than obey your commands?

[758]i.e., To command anything you desire.

Loke thou geve not a lous	louse (i.e., a trifle)
Of the day that thou schalt deye.	die
770 Messenger, do now thine use;	function
Bakbitere, teche him the weye!	teach
Thou art swetter thanne mede.	sweeter/mead
Mankinde, take with the[e] Bakbitinge;	
Lefe him for no maner thinge.	Leave/on no account
Flepergebet, with his flateringe,	Flibbertigibbet (i.e., Backbiter)
776 Standith Mankinde in stede!	Stand/in (good) stead

[*Backbiter, in front of World's scaffold, calls up to Mankind.*]

DETRACTIO. Bakbitinge-and-Detracion	
Schal goo with the[e] fro toun to toun.	
Have don, Mankinde, and cum doun!	Let's go

[*Mankind descends.*]

I am thine owyn page.	
I schal bere the[e] wittnesse with my myth,	support you/might
Whanne my lord, the Werlde, it behyth.	commands it

[*He points to Covetousness' scaffold.*]

Lo, where Sir Coveitise sitt,	sits
And bidith us in his stage.	waits for us

HUMANUM GENUS. Sir Worlde, I wende,	
In Coveitise to chasyn my kende.	to follow my natural inclination

MUNDUS. Have him in mende,	Keep/mind
And iwis, thanne schalt thou be ryth thende.	very prosperous

[*Mankind and Backbiter start for Covetousness' scaffold, while the Good and Bad Angels debate.*]

BONUS ANGELUS. Alas, Jhesu, jentyl justice,	judge
790 Wheder may Mans Good Aungyl wende?	Whither
Now schal careful Coveitise	harmful
Mankende trewly al [to-]schende!	destroy
His sely goste may sore agrise;	hapless spirit/be dismayed
Bakbitinge bringith him in bitter bonde.	
Worldly wittys, ye are not wise:	
Your lovely life amis ye spende,	amiss
And that schal ye sore smert.	smart for
Parkys, poundys, and many pens,	pence (i.e., wealth)
They semyn to you swetter thanne sens;	sweeter/incense
But Goddys servise, nyn his commaundementys,	nor
Stondith you not at hert.	i.e., Do not occupy your heart

776i.e., (to Backbiter) Stand by and support Mankind.

802   MALUS ANGELUS.   Ya! Whanne the fox prechith, kepe wel
    yore gees!   *guard your geese*
  He spekith as it were a holy pope.
  Goo, felaw, and pike of[f] tho lys   *pick/those lice*
  That crepe ther upon thy cope!   *cloak*
806   Thy part is pleyed al at the dys   *dice*
807   That thou schalt have here, as I hope.   *as I think*
  Til Mankinde fallith to podys pris,   *frog's worth (i.e., food for worms)*
  Coveitise schal him gripe and grope   *grip and pull at him*
  Til sum schame him schende.   *destroys him*
  Til Man be dyth in dethys dow,   *i.e., put in the grave*
  He seyth nevere he hath inow;   *He'll never say he has enough*
  Therfore, goode boy, cum blow   *i.e., kiss*
  At my nether ende!
  [*Backbiter, with Mankind in tow, arrives at Covetousness'
  scaffold.*]

  DETRACTIO.   Sir Coveitise, God the[e] save,
  Thy pens and thy poundys all!   *pence*
  I, Bakbiter, thin[e] owyn knave,
  Have browt Mankinde unto thine hall.
  The Worlde bad[e] thou schuldist him have,
820   And feffyn him, whatso befall.   *endow*
  In grene gres til he be grave,   *grass/buried*
  Putte him in thy precious pall,   *mantle*
  Coveitise—it were ell rewthe.   *it would be a shame otherwise*
  Whil he walkith in worldly wolde,   *on earthly ground*
  I, Bakbiter, am with him holde;   *am bound to him*
  Lust and Folye, tho barouns bolde,   *those*
  To hem he hath plyth his trewthe.   *them/plighted/troth*

  AVARITIA.   Ow, Mankinde, blissyd mote thou be!   *Oh!/may*
  I have lovyd the[e] derworthly many a day,   *dearly*
830   And so I wot wel that thou dost me.   *know*
  Cum up and se my riche aray!
  [*Mankind ascends to the scaffold of Covetousness.*]
  It were a gret pointe of pité   *It would be/item*
  But Coveitise were to thy pay.   *Unless/liking*
  Sit up ryth here in this se;   *seat*
  I schal the[e] lere of werldys lay,   *teach/world's law*
  That fadith as a flode.   *flood, river*
  With good inow I schal the[e] store;   *wealth enough*

802(The Bad Angel uses a proverb to accuse the Good Angel of hypocrisy in his preaching.)

806-7i.e., Your fortunes here (in attempting to win Mankind to virtue) are all gambled away, in my estimation.

And yit oure game is but lore,	*lost*
But thou coveith mekyl more	*Unless you covet much more*
840 Thanne evere schal do the[e] goode.	
Thou muste gife the[e] to simonye,	*selling of church offices*
Extorsion and false asise;	*measure*
Helpe no man but thou have why;	*unless/cause*
Pay not thy servauntys here servise;	*their wages*
Thy neyborys loke thou distroye;	
Tithe not on non[e] wise;	*in any way*
Here no begger, thou[gh] he crye—	*Hear*
And thanne schalt thou ful sone rise.	*soon*
And whanne thou usiste marchaundise,	*use, handle*
850 Loke that thou be sotel of sleitys,	*subtle of sleights*
And also swere al by deseitys;	*deceits*
Bye and sell by fals weitys,	*weights*
For that is kinde coveitise.	*the nature of covetousness*
Be not agaste of the grete curse;	*i.e., excommunication*
This lofly life may longe leste.	
Be the peny in thy purs,	*i.e., As long as you're rich*
857 Lete hem cursyn, and don here beste.	*their*
What, devil of hell, art thou the wers	*i e., What the hell*
Thow[gh] thou brekiste Goddys heste?	*God's behest*
Do after me! I am thy nors.	*nurse, guardian*
Alwey gadyr, and have non[e] reste;	*gather (wealth)*
In winninge be al thy werke.	
To pore men take none entent;	*pay no heed*
For, that thou haste longe time hent,	*that which/caught, got*
In lityl time it may be spent.	
Thus seyth Caton the grete clerke:	*Cato/scholar*
866a *"Labitur exiguo quod partum tempore longo."*	
HUMANUM GENUS. A, Avarice, wel thou spede!	*may you prosper well*
Of werldly witte thou canst, iwis.	*you have knowledge*
Thou woldist not I hadde nede,	*You wish me to lack nothing*
And schuldist be wrothe if I ferd amis.	*fared amiss*
I schal nevere begger bede	*offer a beggar*
Mete nyn drinke, by hevene blis;	*Food nor*
Rather, or I schulde him clothe or fede,	*ere*
He schulde sterve and stinke, iwis!	
Coveitise, as thou wilt, I wil do.	*as you desire*

857 Let them (the priests) curse you, and do their best (to damn you).

866a That which is acquired over a long period of time slips away quickly (from the medieval collection of proverbs known as the *Distichs of Cato,* 2:17).

Whereso that I fare, by fenne or flod,   *i.e., anywhere*
I make a vow, by Goddys blod:
Of Mankinde getith no man no good   *No man gets wealth from Mankind*
879   But if he singe "si dedero."   *Unless*

AVARITIA.   Mankind, that was wel songe!   *sung*
Sertys now thou canst sum skill;   *you know*
Blissyd be thy trewe tonge!
In this bowre thou schalt bide and bill.   *bower, abode/abide and dwell*
Moo sinnys I wolde thou underfonge: *I desire you to undertake*
With coveitise the[e] feffe I will,   *I'll endow you*
And thanne sum pride I wolde spronge   *I'd have some pride spring*
Hig[h]e in thy hert, to holdyn and hill,   *cherish*
And abidyn in thy body.
Here I feffe the[e] in min[e] hevene
890   With gold and silver, lyth as levene.   *bright as lightning*
The Dedly Sinnys, all sevene,
I schal do comyn in hy.   *I'll cause to come in haste*
   [*He calls across the platea to the other Deadly Sins.*]

Pride, Wrathe, and Envye,
Com forthe, the develys childryn thre!
Lecchery, Slawth, and Glotonye—
To Mans Flesch ye are fendys fre—   *noble fiends*
Drivith downne over dalys drye!   *i.e., Hasten over hill and dale*
Beth now blithe as any be!   *Be/bee*
Over hill and holtys ye you hyye,   *Hasten over hill and groves*
900   To com to Mankinde and to me
Fro youre dowty dennys!   *From/doughty dens*
As dukys dowty, ye you dresse!   *prepare yourselves*
Whanne ye sex be comme, I gesse,
Thanne be we sevene, and no lesse,
Of the Dedly Sinnys.
   [*On the scaffold of the Devil, Pride, Wrath, and Envy hear the
   summons and bid farewell to Belial.*]

SUPERBIA.   Wonder hig[h]e howtys, on hill, herd I houte!   *loud shouts/I heard shouted*
Koveitise krieth; his karpinge I kenne.   *I recognize his speech*
908   Summe lord, or summe lordeyn, lely schal loute   *rascal/truly*

879*si dedero:* If I shall have given (I'll expect a recompense).

908–14Some lord or some base fellow truly (or lowly?) shall submit to be adorned with the
pearls of my proud plume (i.e., will be affected with vanity in wearing apparel). I'm ready
to brag and bustle about, to run quickly and with alacrity in a rioting crowd—I fear no
person in authority anywhere—and also to jog about quickly everywhere. I roar when I
rise up in excitement.

909	To be pyth with perlys of my proude penne.	*adorned/plume*
910	Bon I am to braggyn, and buskyn abowt,	*Ready/bustle*
911	Rapely and redily, on rowte for to renne—	*Quickly/crowd, riot*
912	By doun, dalys, nor dennys, no duke I dowt—	*fear*
913	Also fast for to fogge, by flodys and by fenne.	*jog/i.e., everywhere*
914	I rore whanne I rise.	
	Sir Belial, bryth of ble,	*bright of hue*
	To you I recomaunde me:	*commend myself*
	Have good day, my fader fre,	*noble*
	For I goo to Coveitise.	

IRA.	Whanne Coveitise cried, and carpyd of care,	*Wrath/complained*
920	Thanne must I, wod Wrethe, walkyn and wend	*mad Wrath/go*
	Hig[h]e over holtys, as hound aftyr hare.	
	If I lette, and were the last, he schuld me sore schend.	*delayed/disgrace*
	I buske my bold baston, by bankys ful bare!	*prepare/staff/(a metrical tag)*
	Sum boy schal be betyn and browth under bonde:	*beaten/brought*
925	Wrath schal him wrekyn, and weyin his ware;	*avenge himself*
926	Forlorn schal al be, for lusty laikys in londe,	*Destroyed/merry games*
927	As a lithyr page.	*rascally*
	Sir Belial blak and blo,	*blue*
	Have good day! Now I goo	
	For to fell thy foo	
	With wickyd wage.	*i.e., a payment of blows*

INVIDIA.	Whanne Wrath ginnith walke in ony wide wonys,	*Envy/places (i.e., anywhere)*
	Envye flet as a fox, and folwith on faste.	*flees, moves quickly*
934	Whanne thou steriste or stariste, or stumble upon stonys,	*move or stare*
	I lepe as a lion; me is loth to be the laste.	*I'm loath*
	Ya, I breyde bitter balys in body and in bonys;	*I breed/torments*
	I frete min[e] herte, and in kare I me kast.	*fret, gnaw at/I throw myself*
	Goo we to Coveitise all thre at onys,	
	With oure grisly gere, a grome for to gast;	*weapons/groom, lad/terrify*
940	This day schal he deye.	*die*
	Belsabubbe, now have good day!	
	For we wil wendyn in good aray,	
	Al thre in fere, as I the[e] say—	*together*
	Pride, Wrath, and Envye.	

BELIAL.	Farewel now, childryn, faire to finde!	*to know*
	Do now wel youre olde owse:	*use, custom*

925–27Wrath will avenge himself, and measure his goods (i.e., test the mettle of his victim?); this fellow will be destroyed as a good-for-nothing servant, for all his merry games on earth (i.e., in his life).

934i.e., When you (Wrath) set out, glaring in fury and stumbling in haste.

Whanne ye com to Mankinde,
Make him wroth and envious.
949 Levith not lytly under linde;   *linden, lime tree*
     To his sowle brewith a bitter jous.   *For|brew|juice, drink*
     Whanne he is ded, I schal him binde
     In hell, as catte dothe the mows.   *mouse*
     Now buske you forthe on brede!   *hasten forth|abroad*
     I may be blithe as any be,   *bee*
     For Mankinde, in every cuntré,
     Is rewlyd by my childyr thre,
     Envye, Wrathe, and Pride.

> [*The three sins of the spirit start for Covetousness' scaffold. On
> the scaffold of the Flesh, Gluttony, Lechery, and Sloth bid farewell
> to their master.*]

GULA.   A grom gan gredyn gaily on grounde;   *Gluttony|lad called out*
     Of me, gay Glotoun, gan al his gale.   *was all his song*
960 I stampe and I stirte, and stint upon stounde;   *leap|stop in a moment*
961 To a staunche deth I stakyr and stale.   *certain|stagger*
962 What boyes, with here belys, in my bondys ben bownd,   *Whatever|their bellies*
963 Bothe here bak and here blod I brewe al to bale.   *their|to torment*
     I fese folke to fyth, til here flesch fond;   *I incite|fight|fails*
     Whanne summe han dronkyn a drawth, they drepyn in a   *draught|droop*
          dale.   *in a grave*
     In me is here minde.   *their mind, intent*
     Mans florchinge flesch,   *flourishing*
     Faire, frele and fresch,   *frail*
     I rape to rewle in a rese,   *I hurry to rule in haste*
     To kloy in my kinde.   *encumber (it) according to my
                                                                nature*

971 LUXURIA.   In Mans kith I cast me a castel to kepe.   *Lechery|loins|intend*
     I, Lechery, with likinge am lovyd in iche a lond.   *sexual pleasure|everywhere*
     With my sokelys of swettnesse, I sitte and I slepe;   *honeysuckles*
     Many berdys I bringe to my bitter bonde.   *ladies, noble persons*
     In wo and in wrake wickyd witys schal wepe,   *pain|wits*
976 That in my wonys wilde wil not out wende.   *dwellings|go from*
977 Whanne Mankinde is castyn undyr clourys to crepe,   *under turf (in the grave)*

---

⁹⁴⁹i.e., Do not remain unconcernedly sitting under a tree, but apply yourselves.

⁹⁶⁰⁻⁶³I stamp and leap, but stop in a moment (i.e., the vigor of appetite ends with the death
of the body); I stagger and dwindle to a certain death. I prepare for endless torment both
the body (lit: back) and blood of any fellows who, with their gross bellies, are tied in my
fetters.

⁹⁷¹I intend to keep a castle (i.e., maintain a residence) in Man's loins.

⁹⁷⁶⁻⁷⁸Who will not flee from my licentious dwellings. When Mankind is about to creep into
the grave, then I'll utterly destroy those rascals (i.e., all men) because of their sexual pleasures.

978   Thanne tho ledrouns, for here likinge, I schal al *rascals*
      to-schende,   *destroy*
  Trewly to tell.
  Sir Flesch, now I wende,
  With lust in my lende,   *loins*
  To cachyn Mankinde   *drive*
  To the devil of hell.

ACCIDIA.   Ya! What seyst thou of Sir Slawth, with my   *Sloth*
      soure syth?   *sight, appearance*
  Mankinde lovith me wel, wis, as I wene.   *iwis, surely|ween, think*
  Men of religion I rewle in my ryth;   *under my authority*
  I lette Goddys servise, the sothe may be sene.   *hinder|i.e., as may be seen*
  In bedde I brede brothel, with my berdys bryth;   *I breed lechers|ladies fair*
  Lordys, ladys, and lederounnys to my lore leene.   *rogues|lean, incline*
990   Mekyl of Mankind in my clokys schal be knyth,   *Much|cloaks|knit, enmeshed*
  Til deth drivith hem down in dalys bedene.   *into graves all together*
  We may non lenger abide.
  Sir Flesch, comly kinge,
  In the[e] is al oure bredinge: *breeding, parentage*
  Geve us now thy blissinge,
  For Coveitise hath cride.

CARO.   Glotony and Slawth, farewel in fere!   *Flesh|together*
  Lovely in londe is now your lesse.   *joy, prosperity*
  And Lecherye, my dowter so dere,
1000   Dapirly ye dresse you so dingne on desse.   *place yourself|nobly|dais*
  All thre, my blissinge ye schal have here.
  Goth now forth, and give ye no fors;   *Go|think nothing of it*
  It is no nede you for to lere   *There's no need to teach you*
  To cachyn Mankind to a careful clos   *drive|harmful prison (of hell)*
  Fro the bryth blisse of hevene.
  The Werld, the Flesch, and the Devil are knowe   *acknowledged*
  Grete lordys, as we wel owe;   *ought (to be)*
  And thorwe Mankind we settyn and sowe   *throughout|plant and sow*
  The Dedly Sinnys sevene.
    Tunc ibunt Superbia, Ira, Invidia, Gula, Luxuria, et Accidia ad   *Then Pride, Wrath, Envy, Gluttony,*
    Avaritiam; et dicet Superbia: *Lechery, and Sloth will go to (the scaffold of) Covetousness; and Pride will say:*

1010 SUPERBIA.   What is thy will, Sir Coveitise?
  Why hast thou afftyr us sent?
  Whanne thou creydist, we ganne agrise,   *cried out|to tremble*
  And come to the[e] now *par asent.*   *by assent*
  Oure love is on the[e] lent.   *fixed*

1000Elegantly place yourself in a noble seat of honor.

I, Pride, Wrath, and Envye,
Gloton, Slawth, and Lecherye,
We arn cum all sex for thy crye,   *on account of*
To be at thy commaundement.

AVARITIA.   Welcum be ye, bretheryn all,
1020   And my si[s]tyr, swete Lecherye!
Witte ye why I gan to call?
For ye must me helpe, and that in hy.   *in haste*
Mankinde is now com to min[e] hall,
With me to dwell, by downys dry;   *(a metrical tag)*
Therfore ye must, whatso befall,
Feffyn him with youre foly,   *Endow*
And ell[ys] ye don him wronge.   *else, otherwise*
For whanne Mankind is kendly koveytous,   *naturally covetous*
He is proud, wrathful, and envious;
1030   Glotons, slaw, and lecherous   *Gluttonous/slow, slothful*
1031   They arn otherwile amonge.   *sometimes also*

Thus every sinne tillith in other,   *attracts*
And makith Mankinde to ben a foole.
We sevene fallyn on a fodyr   *in a heap, together*
Mankind to chase to pini[n]gys stole.   *the seat of punishment*
Therfore, Pride, good brothyr,
And brethiryn all, take ye your tol;   *tool, weapon*
1038   Late iche of us take at othyr,
1039   And set Mankind on a stomlinge stol   *stumbling stool*
Whil he is here in live.   *alive*
Lete us lullyn him on oure lust,
Til he be drevyn to dampninge dust.
Colde care schal ben his crust,   *sorrow/i.e., his food*
To deth whanne he schal drive.   *be forced to go*

SUPERBIA.   In gle and game I growe glad!
Mankind, take good hed,   *heed*
And do as Coveitise the[e] bad!   *bade*
Take me in thin[e] hert, precious Pride:
Loke thou be not over-lad;   *lorded over*
1050   Late no bacheler the[e] misbede;   *Let no man use you ill*
Do the[e] to be dowtyd and drad;   *Make yourself feared and dreaded*
Bete boyes til they blede;   *Beat*
Kast hem in careful kettys.   *Turn them into wretched carrion*

1030-31They (Mankind) are also sometimes gluttonous, slothful, and lecherous.

1038-39i.e., Let each of us proceed to use his own weapon or method, and set Mankind up on
a precarious seat (from which he will tumble).

Frende, fadyr, and moder dere,
Bowe hem not in non[e] manere;   *Obey them*
And hold no maner man thy pere.   *no kind of/peer, equal*
And use these new jettys: *fashions*

Loke thou blowe mekyl bost,   *proclaim much boast*
With longe crakows on thy schos;   *pointed, curved toes/shoes*
Jagge thy clothis in every cost,   *Zig-zag, frill/manner*
And ell[ys] men schul lete the[e] but a goos.   *Or else/reckon*

1062   It is thus, Man, wel thou wost;   *you know*
Therfore do as no Man dos,
And every man sette at a thost,   *at a turd's value*
And of thyself make gret ros.   *boast*

1066   Now se thyself on every side.
Every man thou schalt schende and schelfe,   *insult and shove aside*
And holde no man betyr thanne thyselfe.   *better*
Til dethys dint thy body delfe,   *death's blow/pierce*
Put [w]holy thin[e] hert in Pride.

HUMANUM GENUS.   Pride, by Jhesu, thou seyst wel!

1072   Whoso suffyr is over-led al day.   *permits*
Whil I reste on my renninge whel,   *i.e., sit high on Fortune's wheel*
I schal not suffre, if that I may.   *permit (it)*
Myche mirthe, at mete and mel,   *food*
I love ryth wel, and riche aray.
Trewly I thinke, in every sel,   *season, time*
On grounde to be graithyd gay,   *clad gaily*
And of myselfe to take good gard.   *care*
1080   Mikyl mirthe thou wilt me make,   *Much*
Lordliche to leve, by londe and lake;   *Lordlike to live/i.e., everywhere*
Min[e] hert [w]holy to the[e] I take,   *entrust*
Into thine owyn award.   *keeping*
        [*Pride ascends to Covetousness' scaffold.*]

SUPERBIA.   I thy bowre to abide,   *In*
I com to dwelle by thy side.

HUMANUM GE[N]US.   Mankinde and Pride
Schal dwell togedyr every tide.   *always*

IRA.   Be also wroth as thou were wode!   *as if/mad*
Make the[e] be dred, by dalys derne;   *be dreaded/i.e., everywhere*

1062i.e., That's how the courtly game of pride goes, as you well know.

1066i.e., Now regard yourself, look to your appearance, in every situation (?).

1072Whoever permits it will be lorded over continually.

Whoso the[e] wrethe, by fen or flode,   *Whoever angers you/i.e., anywhere*
Loke thou be avengyd yerne.   *quickly*
Be redy to spil[l]e mans blod;
1093   Loke thou hem fere, by feldys ferne!   *frighten them*
Alway, Man, be ful of mod.   *anger*
My lothly lawys loke thou lerne,   *loathsome*
I rede, for any thinge.   *advise/i.e., in any case*
Anon take veniaunce, Man, I rede;
And thanne schal no man the[e] overlede,   *overmaster*
But of the[e] they schul have drede,
1100   And bowe to thy biddinge.

HUMANUM GENUS.   Wrethe, for thy councel hende   *gracious*
Have thou Goddys blissinge and min[e]!
What caitif of al my kende   *Whatever/(human) race*
Wil not bowe, he schal a-byn;   *pay for it*
With min[e] veniaunce I schal him schende,   *injure*
And wrekyn me, by Goddys yne!   *avenge myself/eyes*
Rather or I schulde bowe or bende,   *Sooner than that*
I schuld be stekyd as a swine   *stuck*
With a lothly launce!
1110   Be it erly or late,
Whoso make with me debate,   *fights with me*
I schal him hittyn on the pate,
And takyn anon veniaunce.
    [*Wrath ascends to Covetousness' scaffold.*]

IRA.   With my rewly rothyr   *grievous rudder (i.e., guidance)*
I com to the[e], Mankinde, my brother.

HUMANUM G[ENUS].   Wrethe, thy fair fother   *company*
Makith iche man to be vengyd on other.

INVIDIA.   Envye with Wrathe muste drive   *hasten*
To haunte Mankinde also.
1120   Whanne any of thy neyborys wil thrive,
Loke thou have Envye therto;   *See that you envy it*
On the hey name, I charge the[e], belive   *i.e., In God's name/quickly*
Bakbite him, whowso thou do.   *howsoever*
Kill him anon, withowtyn knive,
And speke him sum schame w[h]ere thou go,   *wherever*
By dale or downys drye.   *i.e., anywhere*
Speke thy neybour mekyl schame;   *much*

1093See to it you frighten them, by distant fields (a metrical tag).

Pot on hem sum fals fame;   *Put/false report*
Loke thou undo his nobyl name,
1130   With me, that am Envye.

HUMANUM GENUS.   Envye, thou art bothe good and hende,   *gracious*
And schalt be of my counsel chefe.   *chief*
Thy counsel is knowyn thorwe mankinde,   *throughout*
For ilke man callith other "hore" and "thefe."   *whore*
Envye, thou arte rote and rinde,   *root and beginning*
Thorwe this werld, of mikyl mischefe;   *much*
In bittyr balys I schal hem binde,   *sorrows/them*
That to the[e] puttith any reprefe.   *offer you any reproof*
Cum up to me above!
1140   For more Envye thanne is now rei[g]ninge
1141   Was nevere sith Crist was kinge.   *since*
Cum up, Envye, my dere derlinge!
Thou hast Mankindys love.
    [*Envy ascends to Covetousness' scaffold.*]

INVIDIA.   I climbe fro this crofte   *enclosure (the "place")*
With Mankinde to sittyn on lofte.   *aloft*

HUMANUM [GENUS].   Cum, sit here softe,
For in abbeys thou dwellist ful ofte.

GULA.   In gay Glotony a game thou beginne:
Ordeyn the[e] mete and drinkys goode.   *Ordain, order/food*
1150   Loke that no tresour thou part a-twinne,
But the[e] feffe and fede with al kinnys fode.   *provide yourself/all kinds of food*
With fastinge schal man nevere hevene winne;
These grete fasterys, I holde hem wode.   *consider them mad*
Thou[gh] thou ete and drinke, it is no sinne.
Fast no day, I rede, by the rode,   *Never fast/advise/cross*
1156   Thou[gh] chide these fasting cherlys.   *churls*
Loke thou have spicys of goode odoure,
1158   To feffe and fede thy fleschly floure;
And thanne mayst thou bultyn in thy boure,   *discharge, fornicate/bower*
And serdyn gay gerlys.   *copulate with/girls*

HUMANUM GENUS.   A, Glotony, wel I the[e] grete!   *greet*

1140-41For there was never, since Christ was king, more Envy than is now prevalent.

1150See to it that you part in two no treasure (i.e., don't divide your wealth with the poor).

1156Even though those base fellows who practice fasting will chide you.

1158To provide for and feed your flesh in all its bloom and vigor.

Soth and sad it is, thy sawe.   *reliable/speech*

I am no day wel, by sty nor strete,   *i.e., anywhere*

Til I have wel fillyd my mawe.   *maw, mouth*

1165   Fastinge is fellyd under fete.   *felled, kicked down*

Thou[gh] I nevere faste, I rekke [not] an hawe;   *don't care a bit*

He servith of nowth, by the rode, I lete,   *It serves nothing/cross /I reckon*

But to do a mans guttys to gnawe.   *cause*

To faste I wil not fonde!   *try*

1170   I schal not spare, so have I reste,   *as I hope to have (eternal) rest*

To have a mossel of the beste;   *morsel*

The lenger schal my life mow leste,   *be able to last*

With gret likinge in londe.   *pleasure on earth*

    [*Gluttony ascends to Covetousness' scaffold.*]

GULA.   By bankys on brede,   *By broad banks (a metrical tag)*

1175   Otherwhile to spew, the[e] spede!   *vomit*

HUMANUM GENUS.   Whil I lif[e] lede,   *lead life, live*

With faire fode my flesche schal I fede.

LUXURIA.   Ya! Whanne thy flesche is faire fed,

Thanne schal I, lovely Lecherye,

1180   Be bobbyd with the[e] in bed;   *bounced up and down*

Hereof serve mete and drinkys trye.   *For this/food/rich, delicate*

In love thy lif[e] schal be led;

Be a lechour til th[o]u die.

Thy nedys schal be the better sped   *satisfied*

If [thou] gif the[e] to fleschly folye

Til deth the[e] down drepe.   *strike you down*

Lechery, syn the werld began,   *since*

Hath avauncyd many a man.   *benefited*

Therfore, Mankind, my leve lemman,   *my dear lover*

1190   I my cunte thou schalt crepe.   *In*

HUMANUM GENUS.   A, Lechery, wel the[e] be!   *may you prosper*

Mans sed in the[e] is sowe;   *seed, semen/sown*

Fewe men wil forsake the[e],

In any cuntré that I knowe.

Spouse-breche is a frend ryth fre;   *Adultery/very excellent*

Men use that mo thanne inowe.   *more than enough*

Lechery, cum sit by me!

Thy banys be ful wid[e] i-knowe;   *edicts/widely known*

1165i.e., Fasting is trampled in the dust, spurned.

1175May you sometimes make haste to vomit! (i.e., may you often indulge in gluttonous excess).

Likinge is in thy lende.   *Pleasure/loins*
1200   On[e] nor other, I se no wythte   *wight, person*
That wil forsake [thee], day ner nyth.
Therfore, cum up, my berd bryth,   *beautiful lady*
And reste the[e] with Mankinde!
    [*Lechery ascends to Covetousness' scaffold.*]

LUXURIA.   I may soth singe:
   "Mankinde is kawt in my slinge."   *noose*

HUMANUM GE[N]US.   For ony erthyly thinge,   *i.e., In any event*
   To bedde thou muste me bringe.

ACCIDIA.   Ya! Whanne ye be in bedde bothe,
   W[r]appyd wel in worthy wede,   *(bed-)clothes*
   Thanne I, Slawthe, wil be wrothe
1211   But two brothelys I may brede.   *Unless/lechers/breed*
   Whanne the messe-belle goth,   *mass-bell rings*
   Lie stille, Man, and take non[e] hede!
   Lappe thine hed thanne in a cloth   *then/(bed-)clothes*
   And take a swet, I the[e] rede;   *sweat/advise*
   Chirche-goinge thou forsake.
1217   Losengerys in londe I lifte,   *Sluggards/exalt*
1218   And dyth men to mekyl unthrifte.   *put/much*
1219   Penaunce enjoinyd men in schrifte
1220   Is undone; and that I make.   *I cause that*

HUMANUM GENUS.   Owe, Slawthe, thou seyst me skille!   *Oh!/speak wisely*
   Men use the[e] mekyl, God it wot.   *much/God knows*
   Men lofe wel now to lie stille,   *love*
   In bedde to take a morowe swot;   *morning sweat*
   To chirche-ward is not here wille;   *their*
   Here beddys they thinkyn goode and hot.
   Herry, Jofferey, Jone, and Gille,   *Joan/Jill (typical names)*
1228   Arn leyd and logyd in a lot   *laid/lodged*
   With thine unthende charmys.   *unprosperous*
   Al mankinde, by the holy rode,   *cross*
   Are now slawe in werkys goode.   *slow, slothful*
   Com nere, therfore, min[e] faire foode,   *companion, nurse*
   And lulle me in thine armys!

[1211]i.e., Unless I can make two lechers out of you.

[1217-20]I exalt sluggards on earth, and prompt men to great dissoluteness. I see to it that acts of penance imposed on men at confession remain unperformed.

[1228]Are put to rest and laid to bed one after another.

ACCIDIA.   I make men, I trowe,
In Goddys servise to be ryth slowe.   *right, very*

HUMANUM GENUS.   Com up this throwe!   *at this time*
Swiche men thou schalt finden inowe.   *Such/enough*
[*Sloth ascends to Covetousness' scaffold.*]

HUMANUM GENUS.   "Mankinde" I am callyd by kinde,   *nature*
1239   With curssydnesse in costys knet.   *in habits*
1240   In sowre swettenesse my syth I sende,   *sight*
       With sevene sinnys sadde beset.   *sadly, dangerously*
       Mekyl mirthe I move in minde,   *Much/I stir up*
       With melody at my mowthis met.   *at my mouth's might (at my command)*
       My prowd pouer schal I not pende   *power/limit*
       Til I be putte in peynys pit,   *the pit of torment*
       To helle hent fro hens.   *snatched from hence*
       In dale of dole til we are downe,   *i.e., death*
       We schul be clad in a gay gowne.
       I se no man but they use somme
       Of these seven Dedly Sinnys.

1251   For comounly it is seldom seyne,
1252   Whoso now be lecherows,
1253   Of other men he schal have disdeyne,
1254   And ben prowde or covetous.
       In sinne iche man is founde.
       Ther is pore nor riche, by londe ne lake,   *(neither) poor/i.e., anywhere*
       That alle these seven wil forsake,
       But with on[e] or other he schal be take,   *by/be taken, seized*
       And in here bitter bondys bownde.   *their*

1260 BONUS ANGELUS.   So mekyl the werse—wele-a-woo!—   *much/alas*
       That evere Good Aungyl was ordeynyd the[e]!   *assigned to you*
       Thou art rewlyd after the fende that is thy foo,   *ruled according to the fiend*
       And no thinge, certys, aftyr me.
       Weleaway! W[h]eder may I goo?   *Whither*
1265   Man doth me bleykyn blody ble;   *make pale/complexion*
       His swete sowle he wil now slo!   *slay*
       He schal wepe al his game and gle   *weep for*
       At on[e] dayes time.   *One day*

1239–40In my habits drawn or bound to wickedness. I use my faculty of seeing for foul and
bitter sweetness.

1251–54For ordinarily nowadays it seldom happens that a person who is lecherous, proud,
or covetous is disdained by other men.

1265Man causes my ruddy complexion to grow pale.

Ye se wel all sothly in syth,	*As you see/sight*
1270 I am abowte bothe day and nyth	*I bustle about*
To bringe his sowle into blis bryth;	
And himself wil it bringe to pine.	*pain*

MALUS ANGELUS. No, Good Aungyl, thou art not in sesun;	*in fashion*
Fewe men in the[e] feyth they finde.	*Few men believe in you*
For thou hast schewyd a ballyd resun,	*Because/bald, bare of meaning*
Goode sire, cum blowe min[e] hol[e] behinde!	*i.e., kiss*
Trewly, Man hathe non[e] chesun	*has no reason*
On thy God to grede and grinde;	*call in prayer and vex himself*
For, that schuld cunne Cristys lessoun,	*For (he) that would know*
1280 In penaunce his body he muste binde,	
And forsake the worldys mende.	*mind, intent*
Men arn loth on the[e] to crye,	*are loath*
Or don penaunce for here folye;	*do/their*
Therfore have I now maistrye	*mastery*
Wel ny over al Mankinde.	*Well nigh, almost completely*

BONUS ANGELUS. Alas, Mankinde	
Is bobbyd and blent as the blinde!	*mocked and misled*
In feyth, I finde	
To Crist he can nowt be kinde.	*cannot*
1290 Alas, Mankinne	
Is soilyd and saggyd in sinne!	*bogged down*
He wil not blinne	*cease*
Til body and sowle parte a-twinne.	
Alas, he is blendyd!	
Amis Mans lif is i-spendyd	*spent*
1296 With fendys fendyd.	
Mercy, God, that Man were amendyd!	
[*Shrift comes forward, with Penance.*]	

CONFESSIO. What, Mans Aungel, good and trewe!	
Why syest thou and sobbist sore?	*sigh*
Sertys, sore it schal me rewe	*grieve*
If I se the[e] make mo[u]rninge more.	
May any bote thy bale brewe,	*remedy cure your sorrow*
Or anythinge thy stat[e] a-store?	*renew your condition*
For all felechepys olde and newe,	*In the name of*
1305 Why makist thou grochinge under gore,	*complaining/gown*

1296Surrounded by fiends, or with forbidden fiends (?).

1305–8Why do you issue forth complaints from within, from the heart, (and why are you) made pale by tormenting pricks (of grief)? Why do you weep thus with sorrowful sighing here (under the sun)?

1306	With pininge pointys pale?	*tormenting pricks*
1307	Why was al this gretinge gunne	*weeping*
1308	With sore syinge undyr sunne?	
	Tell me, and I schal, if I cunne,	*can*
	Brewe the[e] bote of bale.	

BONUS ANGELUS.   Of bitter balys thou mayste me bete,   *sorrows/cure*
            Swete Schrifte, if that thou wilt.
            For Mankinde it is that I grete;   *weep*
            He is in point to be spilt!   *at the point of being destroyed*
            He is set in sevene sinnys sete,   *sins' seat*
            And wil, certys, til he be kilt.   *killed*
            With me he thinkith nevere more to mete;
1318   He hath me forsake, and I have no gilt—   *guilt*
            No man wil him amende.
            Therfore, Schrifte, so God me spede,
            But if thou helpe at this nede,   *Unless*
            Mankinde geti[t]h nevere other mede   *no other reward*
            But peyne withowtyn ende.   *pain*

CONFESSIO.   What, Aungel, be of comfort stronge,
            For thy Lordys love that deyed on tre!   *who died on cross*
1326   On me, Schrifte, it schal not be longe,   *In regard to*
1327   And that thou schalt the sothe se:
            If he wil be a-knowe his wronge,   *will acknowledge*
            And no thinge hele, but telle it me,   *conceal*
            And don penaunce sone amonge,   *soon also*
            I schal him stere to gamyn and gle   *mirth and delight*
            In joye that evere schal last.
            Whoso sch[r]ive him of his sinnys alle,   *Whoever will confess*
            I behete him hevene halle.   *promise*
            Therfor, go we hens, whatso befalle,   *whatever happens*
            To Mankinde fast.

> *Tunc ibunt [cum Paenitentia] ad Humanum Genus; et dicet*   *Then they will go (with Penance)*
> *Confessio [Mankind is still on Covetousness' scaffold]:*   *to Mankind; and Shrift will say*

[CONFESSIO.]   What, Mankinde! Whou goth this?   *How*
            What dost thou with these develys sevene?
            Alas, alas, Man, al amis!
1340   Blisse in the name of God in hevene,   *Rejoice*
            I rede, so have I rest.   *I advise as I hope to be saved*
            These lotly lordeynys awey thou lifte,   *Drive away these loathsome rascals*

---

¹³¹⁸He's forsaken me, even though I am guiltless (of having done anything to alienate him from goodness).

^{1326–27}i.e., My function as Confession will not take long, as you will truly see.

And cum doun and speke with Schrifte,

And drawe the[e] yerne to sum thrifte!   *turn quickly/prudent action*

Trewly it is the best.

HUMANUM GENUS.   A, Schrifte, thou art wel be-note   *beknown*

Here to Slawthe, that sittith hereinne:

1348   He seyth thou mytist a com to Mannys cote   *might have come/dwelling*

1349   On Palme Sunday al betime.   *soon enough*

Thou art com al to[o] sone;

Therfore, Schrifte, by thy fay,   *faith*

Goo forthe til on Good Friday!

Tente to the[e] thanne wel I may;   *Listen*

I have now ellys to done.   *other things to do*

CONFESSIO.   Ow, that harlot is now bold!   *villain (i.e., Sloth)*

In bale he bindith Mankind belive.   *sorrow/quickly*

1357   Sey Slawthe I preyd him that he wold   *Tell*

1358   Find a charter of thy live.

Man, thou mayst ben undyr mold   *under earth*

Longe or that time, killyd with a knive,   *ere then (i.e., Good Friday)*

1361   With podys and froskys many-fold.   *frogs and toads*

Therfore schape the[e] now to schrive,   *prepare to confess*

If thou wilt com to blis.   *desire to come*

Thou sinniste! Or sorwe the[e] ensense,   *Ere sorrow consumes you*

Behold thinne hert, thy prevé spense,   *your/secret storeroom*

And thinne owyn consiense,

Or, sertys, thou dost amis.

HUMANUM GENUS.   Ya, Petyr, so do mo!   *i.e., by St. Peter/more, others*

We have etyn garlek everychone.   *eaten garlic (i.e., are marked by sin)*

1370   Thou[gh] I schulde to helle go,

I wot wel I schal not gon alone,

Trewly I tell the[e].

I did nevere so evil, trewly,

But other han don as evil as I.   *But (that) others have done*

Therfore, sire, lete be thy cry,   *let be, cease*

And go hens fro me.

PAENITENTIA.   With point of penaunce I schal him prene,   *pierce*

Mans pride for to felle.

1348–49 i.e., Palm Sunday (a week before Easter, at the end of the Lenten season) is soon enough for Mankind to confess himself. (In l. 1352 the time of confession is postponed even further, until Friday of Holy Week.)

1357–58 (sardonically) Tell Sloth I requested him to discover a contract granting Mankind a pardon (if Man should continue to postpone confession?).

1361 (Lying in the earth) with many frogs and toads.

        With this launce I schal him lene,   *lend, give*
1380   Iwis, a drope of mercy welle.   *the fountain of mercy*
        Sorwe of hert is that I mene: *Sorrow/what I mean*
        Trewly, ther may no tunge telle
        What waschith sowlys more clene
        Fro the foul fend of helle
        Thanne swete sorwe of hert.
        God, that sitti[t]h in hevene on hye,
        Askith no more, or that thou die,   *before*
        But sorwe of hert with wepinge eye
        For all thy sinnys smert.   *sharp, severe*

        They that syh in sinninge   *sigh*
        In sadde sorwe for here sinne,   *their*
        Whanne they schal make here endinge,   *i.e., when they are dying*
        Al here joye is to beginne.   *(about) to begin*
1394   Thanne medelith no mo[u]rninge,   *meddles, mingles*
1395   But joye is joinyd with jentyl ginne.   *contrivance, skill*
        Therfore, Mankinde, in this tokeninge,   *in token of this*
        With spete of spere to the[e] I spinne;   *spit, point/move quickly*
        Goddys lawys to the[e] I lerne.   *teach*
        With my spud of sorwe swote   *dagger of sweet sorrow*
1400   I reche to thine hert rote.
        Al thy bale schal torne the[e] to bote.   *sorrow/boot, remedy*
        Mankinde, go schrive the[e] yerne!   *confess quickly*
          [Penance pierces Mankind's heart with the prick of conscience.]

        HUMANUM GENUS.   A sete of sorwe in me is set;   *plant, slip*
        Sertys for sinne I syhe sore!   *sigh*
1405   Mone of mercy in me is met;   *Moan, lament*
1406   For werldys mirthe I mo[u]rne more.
1407   In wepinge wo my wele is wet.   *weal, happiness*
        Mercy, thou muste min[e] stat a-store!   *restore my condition*
        Fro oure Lordys lyth thou hast me let,   *light/hindered*
        Sory sinne, thou grisly gore!   *Wretched sin/filth*
        Owte on the[e], dedly sinne!   *Fie on you*
        Sinne, thou haste Mankinde schent;   *have injured Mankind*
        In dedly sinne my life is spent.
        Mercy, God omnipotent!
        In youre grace I beginne.
          [He humbles himself.]

1394–95Then (in eternal life after death) mourning no longer intrudes, but an unalleviated joy is formed by divine skill.

1405–7i.e., I must now lament my sin and plead for mercy; I mourn ever increasingly for my past worldly pleasures. My happiness is watered with the tears of my sorrowful weeping.

For, thou[gh] Mankinde have don amis,
And he wil falle in repentaunce,
Crist schal him bringyn to bowre of blis,
If sorwe of hert lache him with launce.   *prick*
1420   Lordingys, ye se wel alle this: *Lordings (the audience)*
Mankinde hathe ben in gret bobaunce.   *presumption, vanity*
I now forsake my sinne, iwis,
And take me [w]holy to Penaun[c]e.
On Crist I crye and calle.
A, mercy, Schrifte! I wil no more.
For dedly sinne min[e] herte is sore!
Stuffe Mankinde with thine store,   *Fill/treasure (of wisdom)*
And have him to thine halle.

CONFESSIO.   Schriffte may no man forsake
1430   Whanne Mankinde crieth, I am redy.
Whanne sorwe of hert the[e] hathe take,   *has possessed you*
Schrifte profitith verily.
Whoso for sinne wil sorwe make,
Crist him herith whanne he wil criye.   *hears*
Now, Man, lete sorwe thin[e] sinne slake,   *slacken, lessen*
And torne not ageyn to thy folye,   *turn*
For that makith distaunce.   *strife*
And if it happe the[e] turne ageyn to sinne,
For Goddys love, lie not longe therinne!
1440   He that dothe alwey evil, and wil not blinne,   *cease*
That askith gret veniaunce.   *That (i.e., his evil)/vengeance*

HUMANUM GENUS.   Nay, sertys, that schal I not do!
Schrifte, thou schalte the sothe se;
For thow[gh] Mankinde be wonte therto,   *is accustomed (to sin)*
I wil now al amende me.
I com to the[e], Schrifte, al [w]holy, lo!
Tunc descendit ad Confessionem.   *Then he descends (from Cove-
                                                                tousness' scaffold) to Schrift*
I forsake you, sinnys, and fro you fle!
1448   Ye schapyn to man a sory scho.   *shape, fit/shoe*
Whanne he is beg[u]ilyd in this degré,   *way*
Ye bleykyn al his ble.   *make pale/countenance*
Sinne, thou art a sory store!   *a grief-causing treasure*
Thou makist Mankind to sinke sore;
Therfore, of you wil I no more.
I aske Schrifte, for charité.   *I ask to be confessed*

1448 i.e., You put man into painful circumstances.

CONFESSIO.   If thou wilt be a-knowe here   *will acknowledge*
Only al thy trespas,
I schal the[e] schelde fro helle-fere,   *shield/fire*
And putte the[e], fro peyne, unto preciouse place.   *torment*
If thou wilt not make thinne sowle clere,   *thy, your*
1460   But kepe hem in thine hert cas,   *chest, box*
Another day they schul be rawe and rere,   *rare, undercooked*
And sinke thy sowle to Satanas
In gastful glowinge glede!   *ghastly glowing coal*
Therfore, Man, in mody monys,   *in grieving laments*
If thou wilt wende to worthy wonys,   *dwelling (i.e., heaven)*
Schrive the[e] now, al at onys,   *at once*
[W]holy of thy misdede.

HUMANUM GENUS.   A, yis, Schrifte! Trewly I trowe,
1469   I schal not spare, for odde nor even,   *i.e., in any event*
1470   That I schal rekne, al on a rowe,   *in order*
1471   To lache me up to livys levene.   *take, raise*
To my Lord God I am a-knowe,   *I acknowledge*
That sitti[t]h aboven in hey hevene,
That I have sinnyd many a throwe   *a time*
In the Dedly Sinnys sevene,
Bothe in home and halle.
Pride, Wrathe, and Envye,
Coveitise, and Lecherye,
Slawth, and also Glotonye:
1480   I have hem usyd alle.   *them*

The ten comaundementys brokyn I have,
And my five wittys spent hem amis;   *And misused my five wits*
I was thanne wood, and gan to rave.   *mad*
Mercy, God, forgeve me this!
Whanne any pore man gan to me crave,   *begged from me*
I gafe him nowt; and that forthinkith me, iwis.   *makes me repent*
Now, Seynt Saveour, ye me save,   *Holy*
And bringe me to your boure of blis!   *bower*
I can not alle say;
1490   But to the erthe I knele a-down,
Bothe with bede and oriso[u]n,   *prayer*
And aske min[e] absolucio[u]n,
Sir Schrifte, I you pray.
    [*Mankind kneels.*]

1460But keep them (your sins) locked up in the strongbox of your heart.

1469-71I will not refrain in any event from giving an account of my sins, one by one, to raise
me up to the light (lit: lightning) of eternal life.

CONFESSIO.　Now Jhesu Criste, God holy,

And all the seyntys of hevene hende—　*gracious*

Petyr and Powle, apostoly,　*apostles*

To whom God gafe powere to lese and binde—　*loosen*

He forgeve the[e] thy foly　*(May) He*

That thou hast sinnyd with hert and minde!

1500　And I, up my powere, the[e] a-soly,　*according to/assoil, pardon*

That thou hast ben to God unkinde,

Quantum peccasti.　*However much you have sinned*

In Pride, Ire, and Envye,

Slawthe, Glotony, and Lecherye,

And Coveitise, continuandelye,　*continually*

Vitam male continuasti.　*You have evilly continued your life*

I the[e] a-soile, with goode entent,

Of alle the sinnys that thou hast wrowth　*wrought*

In brekinge of Goddys commaundement

1510　In worde, werke, wil and thowth.　*deed/thought*

I restore to the[e] the] sacrament

Of penauns, w[h]eche thou nevere rowt;　*heeded*

Thy five wittys mis-dispent　*misspent*

In sinne, the w[h]eche thou schuldist nowt,

Quicquid gesisti—　*Whatsoever you have performed*

With eyne sen, herys heringe,　*Seen with eyes, heard with ears*

Nose smellyd, mowthe spekinge,

And al thy bodys bad werkinge—

Vitium quodcunque fecisti.　*Whatsoever vices you have committed*

1520　I the[e] a-soile, with milde mod,　*mood, spirit*

Of al that thou hast ben ful madde:

In forsakinge of thin[e] Aungyl Good,

And thy fowle Flesche that thou hast fadde,　*fed*

The Werld, the Devil that is so woode,　*mad*

And folwyd thine Aungyl that is so Badde.

To Jhesu Crist that deyed on rode　*died on cross*

I restore the[e] ageyn ful sadde;　*surely*

Noli peccare!　*Sin not*

And all the goode dedys that thou haste don,

1530　And all thy tribulacion,

Stonde the[e] in remission:　*Stand (for) you*

Potius noli vitiare.　*Sin no more*

HUMANUM GENUS.　Now, sir Schrifte, where may I dwelle,

To kepe me fro sinne and woo?

A comly counseyl ye me spelle,　*proper/tell*

To fende me now fro my foo.　*defend*

	If these seven sinnys here telle	hear tell
	That I am thus fro hem goo,	from them gone
	The Werld, the Flesche, and the Devil of hell	
1540	Schul sekyn my soule for to sloo	Shall seek to slay my soul
	Into balys bowre.	the abode of torment (i.e., hell)
	Therfore I pray you putte me	
	Into sum place of sureté,	
	That they may not harmyn me	
	With no sinnys sowre.	sour, bitter

	CONFESSIO. To swiche a place I schal the[e] kenne,	such/guide
	Ther thou mayst dwelle withoutyn distaunsce	Where/dissension
	And alwey kepe the[e] fro sinne:	
	Into the Castel of Perseveraunce.	
1550	If thou wilt to hevene winne,	
	And kepe the[e] fro werldly distaunce,	strife
	Goo [to] yone castel, and kepe the[e] therinne,	
	For [it] is strenger thanne any in Fraunce.	
	To yone castel I the[e] sende.	
	That castel is a precious place,	
	Ful of vertu and of grace:	
	Whoso levith there his livys space,	his life's span
	No sinne schal him schende.	injure

	HUMANUM GENUS. A, Schrifte, blessyd mote thou be!	may
1560	This castel is here but at honde;	nearby
	Thedyr rapely wil I tee,	Thither quickly/go
	Sekyr over this sad sonde.	Confidently/solid land
	Good Perseveraunce God sende me	(may) God send
	While I leve here in this londe!	live
	Fro fowle filthe now I fle;	
	Forthe to faryn now I fonde,	fare/undertake
	To yone precious port.	
	Lord, what man is in mery live	i.e., how merry is man
	Whanne he is of his sinnys schreve!	shriven
1570	Al my dol[e] a-doun is dreve;	grief is overthrown
	Criste is min[e] counfort.	

	MALUS ANGELUS. Ey, what devil, Man, w[h]edyr schat?	whither away?
	Woldist drawe now to holinesse?	Would you turn
	Goo, felaw, thy goode gate!	Go your way
	Thou art forty winter olde, as I gesse;	
	Goo ageyn, the develys mat,	the devil's mate
1577	And pleye the[e] a while with Sare and Sisse!	Sarah and Cicely

1577-78And play around with all those females (the abstractions of virtue, portrayed as feminine). She (Penance) wants nothing else, yonder old hag.

1578	Sche wolde not ellys, yone olde trat,	*hag*
	But putte the[e] to penaunce and to stresse,	*hardship*
	Yone foule feterel file!	*cheating rascal*
1581	Late men that arn on the pittys brinke	*Let/pit's (hell's)*
	Forberyn bothe mete and drinke,	
	And do penaunce as hem good thinke;	
	And cum and pley the[e] a while.	

BONUS ANGELUS.	Ya, Mankinde, wende forthe thy way,	
	And do nothinge aftyr his red.	*according to his advice*
	He wolde the[e] lede over londys lay,	*lea, fallow*
	In dale of dros til thou were ded.	*In the grave*
	Of cursydnesse he kepith the key,	*wickedness*
1590	To bakyn the[e] a bittyr bred.	*bake*
	In dale of dol[e] til thou schudist dey,	*In death/die*
	He wolde drawe the[e] to cursydhed,	*wickedness*
	In sinne to have mischaunce.	*evil fortune*
	Therfor, spede now thy pace	
	Pertly to yone preciouse place	*Quickly*
	That is al growyn ful of grace,	
	The Castel of Perse[ve]raunce!	

HUMANUM GENUS.	Goode Aungyl, I wil do as thou wilt,	
	In londe whil my life may leste;	*last*
	For I finde wel in holy writ,	
1601	Thou counseyliste evere for the beste.	

[*He goes to the Castle, where he is joyfully received by the seven
Moral Virtues: Meekness, Patience, Charity, Abstinence,
Chastity, Industry, and Generosity. In a missing portion of the
text, Meekness and Patience—the opposites respectively of Pride
and Wrath—instruct Mankind in their qualities. Charity
speaks next.*]

. . . .

CARITAS.	To Charité, Man, have an eye,	
	In al thinge, Man, I rede.	*advise*
	Al thy doinge as dros is drye,	*is as dry, profitless, as dross*
	But in charité thou dyth thy dede.	*Unless/perform*
	I distroye alwey Envye.	
	So did thy God whanne he gan blede;	*he bled*
	For sinne he was hangyn hye,	*hanged high*
	And yit sinnyd he nevere in dede,	

1581 i.e., Let persons who are about to die.

1601 s.d. (At some point during the missing portion of the text, World, Flesh, Devil, and
their lieutenants must return from Covetousness' scaffold to their own respective scaffolds.)

That milde mercy welle.   *fountain of mercy*
Poule in his pistyl puttith the prefe: *(St.) Paul/epistle/proof*
1612   "But Charité be with the[e] chefe."   *chief, foremost*
Therfore, Mankinde, be now lefe   *lief, glad*
In Charité for to dwelle.

ABSTINENTIA.   In Abstinens lede thy lif.   *Temperance*
Take but skilful refeccion;   *only reasonable repast*
For Gloton killith withoutyn knif,
And distroyeth thy complexion.
Whoso ete or drinke over-blive,   *over-readily*
1620   It gaderith to corrupcion.   *swells*
This sinne browt us alle in stri[f]e,   *brought*
Whanne Adam fel in sinne down
Fro precious paradis[e].
Mankind, lere now of oure lore: *learn*
Whoso ete or drinke more
Thanne skilfully his state a-store,   *reasonably maintains his condition*
I holde him no thinge wis[e].   *consider/not at all*

CASTITAS.   Mankind, take kepe of Chastité,   *take heed*
And move the[e] to maidyn Marye.   *emulate the Virgin Mary*
Fleschly foly loke thou fle,
At the reverense of Oure Ladye.
1631a   *(Quia qui in carne vivunt Domino placere non possunt.)*
That curteys qwene, what did sche?   *courteous*
Kepte hir clene and stedfastly,   *herself*
And in her was trussyd the Trin[i]té;   *was enclosed*
Thorwe gostly grace sche was worthy,   *Through spiritual*
And al for sche was chaste.   *because*
Whoso kepit[h] him chast[e], and wil not sinne,   *himself*
1638   Whanne he is beried in bankys brimme,   *brink*
Al his joye is to beginne.   *(about) to begin*
Therfore, to me take taste!   *incline to me*

SOLICITUDO.   In Besinesse, Man, loke thou be,   *Industry*
With worthy werkys goode and thikke!   *numerous*
To Slawthe if thou cast the[e],   *abandon yourself*
It schal the[e] drawe to thowtys wickke.   *wicked thoughts*
Otiositas parit omne malum: *Idleness begets all evil*
It puttith a man to poverté,

1612(See 1 Corinthians 13:13.)

1631aBecause those who live carnally cannot be pleasing to the Lord (see Romans 8:8).

1638When he is buried on the brink of a slope, i.e., in the ground.

And pullith him to peynys pricke.   *to (hell-)pain's torment*
Do sumwhat alwey for love of me,
Thou[gh] thou schuldist but thwite a sticke.   *whittle*
1649   With bedys sumtime the[e] blys;   *(prayer) beads/bless yourself*
Sumtime rede, and sumtime write,   *read*
And sumtime pleye at thy delite.
The devil the[e] waitith with dispite
Whanne thou art in Idylnesse.

LARGITAS.   In Largité, man, ley thy love!   *Generosity*
Spende thy good as God it sent.   *wealth*
In worchep of Him that sit above,   *sits*
Loke thy goodys be dispent.   *dispensed*
In dale of dros whanne thou schalt drove,   *i.e., in the grave be forced*
Lityl love is on the[e] lent;   *fixed*
1660   The sekatourys schul seyn it is here behove   *executors/say/their behoof, duty*
"To make us mery, for he is went   *has gone, died*
That al this good gan owle."   *wealth accumulated*
Ley thy tresour and thy trust
In place where no rugginge rust   *corroding*
May it distroy to dros ne dust,
But al to helpe of sowle.

HUMANUM GENUS.   Ladys in londe, lovely and lyt,   *bright*
Likinge lelys, ye be my leche!   *Amiable lilies, maidens/physician*
I wil bowe to your biddinge bryth;   *bright, pure*
1670   Trewe tokeninge ye me teche.
Dame Meknes, in your myth   *might*
I wil me wryen fro wickyd wreche.   *turn aside from/vengeance*
Al my purpos I have pyt   *set, fixed*
Paciens to don, as ye me preche;
Fro Wrathe ye schal me kepe.
Charité, ye wil to me entende: *take heed*
Fro fowle Envye ye me defende!
Manns mende ye may amende,   *state of mind*
Whether he wake or slepe.

1680   Abstinens, to you I trist;   *trust*
Fro Glotony ye schal me drawe.
In Chastité to levyn me list,   *I desire to live*
That is Oure Ladys lawe.
Besines, we schul be ciste;   *Industry/joined by a kiss*
Slawthe, I forsake thy sleper sawe.   *slippery speech*
Largité, to you I trist   *Generosity*

1649Put yourself in a blessed state sometimes by using prayer beads.

Coveitise to don of dawe.   *put to death*
This is a curteys cumpany.
What schuld I more monys make?   *Why/moans, complaints*
1690   The sevene sinnys I forsake,
And to these seven vertuis I me take.
Maidyn Meknes, now, mercy!

HUMILITAS.   Mercy may mende al thy mone.   *amend/lament*
Cum in here at thinne owyn wille!
We schul the[e] fende fro thy fon   *defend/foes*
If thou kepe the[e] in this castel stille.   *continually*
1696a   *(Cum sancto sanctus eris, et cetera.)*
           Tunc intrabit.   *Then he will enter*
Stonde hereinne, as stille as ston;
Thanne schal no dedly sinne the[e] spille.   *destroy*
Whether that sinnys cumme or gon,
Thou schalt with us thy bourys bille.   *make your home*
With vertuse we schul the[e] vaunce.   *virtues/lift up*
This castel is of so qweynt a ginne,   *ingenious a device*
That whosoevere holde him therinne,
He schal nevere fallyn in dedly sinne:
It is the Castel of Perseveranse.
1705a   *(Qui perseveraverit usque in finem, hic salvus erit.)*
           Tunc cantabunt "Aeterne Rex altissime," et[dicet] Humilita[s]:   *Then they will sing "Eternal King most high"*

[HUMILITAS.]   Now, blissyd be Oure Lady, of hevene emperes!   *empress*
Now is Mankinde fro foly falle,   *fallen (away) from folly*
And is in the Castel of Goodnesse.
He hauntith now hevene halle   *frequents a heavenly dwelling*
1710   That schal bringyn him to hevene.
Crist that died, with dyen dos,   *with dying dose (of vinegar?)*
Kepe Mankind in this castel clos,   *stronghold*
And put alwey in his purpos
To fle the sinnys sevene!

MALUS ANGELUS.   Nay, by Belials bryth bonys,   *bright*
Ther schal he no while dwelle!
He schal be wonne fro these wonys,   *won from this dwelling*
With the Werld, the Flesch, and the Devil of hell;   *By*
They schul my wil a-wreke.   *avenge*
1720   The sinnys sevene, tho kingys thre,

1696aWith those who are holy you will be holy, and so on (Psalms 18:25–26).

1705aHe who perseveres to the end will be saved. (Matthew 10:22; see also 24:13. The hymn
in the following stage direction is sung at matins from Ascension to Pentecost.)

1720*kingys thre:* i.e., World, Flesh, and Devil.

To Mankind have enmité;
Scharpely they schul helpyn me   *Fiercely*
This castel for to breke.
    [*He calls to Backbiter the messenger.*]

Howe, Flipyrgebet, Bakbitere!
Yerne oure message loke thou make;   *Quickly take our message*
Blithe about loke thou bere.   *Quickly/go*
Sey, Mankinde his sinnys hath forsake.   *Say that*
With yene wenchys he wil him were;   *yon/guard himself*
Al to holinesse he hath him take.   *betaken himself*
1730 In min[e] hert it doth me dere,   *injure*
The bost that tho moderys crake;   *those wenches brag*
My galle ginnith to grinde.   *i.e., it roils my insides*
Flepyrgebet, ronne upon a rasche: *in haste*
Bid the Werld, the Fend, and the Flesche
That they com to fityn fresche,   *fight vigorously*
To winne ageyn Mankinde.   *again*

DETRACTIO.   I go, I go, on grounde glad,
Swifter thanne schip with rodyr!   *ship/rudder*
I make men masyd and mad,   *mazed, crazed*
1740 And every man to killyn odyr   *others*
With a sory chere.   *grief-causing behavior*
I am glad, by Seynt Jamys of Galys,   *Galicia*
Of schrewdnes to tellyn talys   *To spread stories of malice*
Bothyn in Ingelond and in Walys,   *i.e., everywhere*
And feyth I have many a fere.   *in truth/companion*
    Tunc ibit ad Belial.   *Then he will go to Belial (at the scaffold of hell)*

Heyl, set in thin[e] selle!   *throne*
Heyl, dinge devil in thy delle!   *worthy/pit (of hell)*
Heyl, lowe in helle!
I cum to the[e], talys to telle.

1750 BELIAL.   Bakbiter, boy,
Alwey by holtys and hothe,   *i.e., everywhere*
Sey now, I sey,
What tidingys? Telle me the sothe.

DETRACTIO.   Teneful talys I may the[e] sey,   *Distressing*
To the[e] no good, as I gesse:
Mankind is gon now awey
Into the Castel of Goodnesse!
Ther he wil bothe livyn and deye,   *die*
In dale of dros til deth him dresse;   *i.e., In the grave/place*

1760	Hathe the[e] forsakyn, forsothe I sey,	*(He) has*
	And all thy werkys, more and lesse.	
	To yone castel he gan to crepe.	
	Yone modyr Meknes, sothe to sayn,	
	And all yene maidnys on yone plain,	*i.e., the "place"*
	For to fityn they be ful fain,	*fight/glad*
	Mankind for to kepe.	

Tunc vocabit Superbiam, Invidiam, et Iram. — *Then he will call Pride, Envy, and Wrath*

SUPERBIA. Sir kinge, what witte?	*i.e., what is on your mind?*
We be redy throtys to kitte.	*to cut throats*

1769	BELIAL. Sey, gadelingys! Have ye harde grace,	*bad luck*
	And evil deth mote ye deye!	*may you die an evil death*
	Why lete ye Mankind fro you pase	*pass, escape*
	Into yene castel, fro us aweye?	
	With tene I schal you tey.	*pain/bind*
	Harlotys, at onys	*Rascals (get away) at once*
	Fro this wonys!	*From here*
	By Belials bonys,	
	Ye schul abeye!	*pay for it*

Et verberabit eos super terram. — *And he will beat them on the ground*

DETRACTIO [*aside*]. Ya! for God, this was wel goo,	*by God/well done*
Thus to werke with Bakbitinge!	
1780	I werke bothe wrake and woo,	*injury*
	And make iche man other to dinge.	*to strike others*
	I schal goo abowte and makyn moo	*more*
	Rappys for to route and ringe. [*To the audience.*]	*Blows/roar and ring out*
	Ye bakbiterys, loke that ye do so!	*see to it*
	Make debate abowtyn to springe	
	Betwene sister and brother!	
	If any bakbiter here be lafte,	*left, staying*
	He may lere of me his crafte;	*learn*
	Of Goddys grace he schal be rafte,	*bereft*
1790	And every man to killyn other.	

Ad Carnem. — *(He goes) to (the scaffold of) Flesh*

Heyl, kinge, I calle!	
Heyl, prinse proude prekyd in palle!	*proudly attired in rich robe*
Heyl, hende in halle!	*gracious*
Heyl, sir kinge, faire the[e] befalle!	*may fair luck befall you*

CARO.   Boy Bakbitinge,

1769Say, you vagabonds! May you have bad luck!

Ful redy in robys to ringe,   *sound loudly, proclaim*

1797   Ful glad tidinge,

1798   By Belialys bonys, I trow thow bringe.   *I trust*

DETRACTIO.   Ya, for God! Owt, I crye,   *by God/Shame*
On thy too sonys and thy dowtyr yinge!   *two sons/young daughter*
Glotoun, Slawthe, and Lechery
Hath put me in gret mo[u]rninge:
They let Mankind gon up hye
Into yene castel at his likinge,   *yon*
Therin for to leve and die—
With tho ladys to make endinge,   *those*
Tho flourys faire and fresche.
He is in the Castel of Perseverauns,
And put his body to penauns.
1810   Of hard happe is now thy chauns,   *bad luck/fortune*
Sire kinge, Mankindys Flesche.
    Tunc Caro clamabit ad Gulam, Accidiam, et Luxuriam.   *Then Flesh will cry aloud to Gluttony, Sloth, and Lechery*
    [*They come forward on Flesh's scaffold.*]

LUXURIA.   Sey now thy wille,
Sir Flesch. Why criest thou so schille?   *shrilly*

CARO.   A, Lechery, thou skallyd mare!   *scurvy*
And thou Gloton, God geve the[e] wo!
And vile Slawth, evil mote thou fare!   *may you fare ill*
Why lete ye Mankind fro you go
In yone castel so hye?
Evele grace com on thy snowte!   *Bad luck to your nose*
1820   Now I am dressyd in gret dowte.   *placed*
Why [ne] had ye lokyd betyr abowte?   *Why didn't you keep better watch*
By Belialys bonys, ye schul a-bye!   *pay for it*
    Tunc verberabit eos in plateam.   *Then he will flog them in the platea*

DETRACTIO [*aside*].   Now, by God, this is good game!
I, Bakbiter, now bere me wel.   *i.e., things go well for me*
If I had lost my name,
I vow to God it were gret del.   *would be/pity*
I schape these schrewys to mekyl schame: *fashion, direct/rascals*
Iche rappith on other with rowtinge rele!   *Each one beats/noisy blows*
I, Bakbiter, with fals fame   *rumor, report*
1830   Do brekyn and brestyn hodys of stele.   *break/burst/hoods, helmets*
Thorwe this cuntré I am knowe.   *Throughout/(well) known*
Now wil I ginne forth to goo,

1797–98 I trust you bring very good news, by the bones of Belial (an oath).

And make Coveitise have a knoke or too;   *two*
And thanne iwis I have doo   *done*
My dever, as I trowe.   *devoir, duty*
    Ad Mundum.   *(Then he goes) to (the scaffold of)*
                                             World

Heyl, stif in stounde!   *resolute in attack*
Heyl, gaily girt upon grounde!   *caparisoned on earth*
Heyl, faire flowr i-founde!   *i.e., fairest flower found*
Heyl, sir Werld, worthy in wedys wonde!   *wrapped in splendid clothes*

1840 MUNDUS.   Bakbiter, in rowte,   *in (my) retinue*
Thou tellist talys of dowte,   *suspicion*
So stif and so stowte.   *(You who are) so stalwart/strong*
What tidingys bringist thou abowte?

DETRACTIO.   Nothinge goode—that schalt thou wete.   *know*
Mankind, sir Werld, hath the[e] forsake;   *forsaken*
With Schrifte and Penauns he is smete,   *smitten*
And to yene castel he hath him take,   *yon/betaken himself*
Amonge yene ladys, whit[e] as la[ke].   *fair as fine linen*
Lo, Sir Werld! Ye moun agrise   *ought to be vexed*
1850 That ye be servyd on this wise.   *in/way*
Go pley you with Sir Coveitise
Til his crowne crake!   *head crack*
    Tunc buccinabit cornu ad Avaritiam. [*Covetousness approaches*   *Then he (World) will blow a horn*
    from his scaffold.]   *for Covetousness*

AVARITIA.   Sir bolninge bowde,   *swollen malt-weevil*
Tell me why blowe ye so lowde?

MUNDUS.   Lewde losel, the devel the[e] brenne!   *Base scoundrel/burn*
I prey God geve the[e] a fowl hap!   *ill luck*
Sey, why letist thou Mankind
Into yene castel for to skape?   *yon/escape*
I trowe thou ginnist to rave.
1860 Now, for Mankind is went,   *because/gone*
Al oure game is schent: *ruined*
Therfore, a sore drivinge dent,   *forceful blow*
Harlot, thou schalt have!   *Rascal*
    Tunc verberabit eum.   *Then he will beat him*

AVARITIA.   Mercy, mercy! I wil no more.
Thou hast me rappyd with rewly rowtys!   *struck/grievous blows*
I snowre, I sobbe, I sye sore!   *scowl/sigh*
Min[e] hed is clateryd al to clowtys!   *shaken all to pieces*
In al youre state I schal you store,   *rank, estate/restore*

	If ye abate youre dintys dowtys.	*the terror of your blows*
1870	Mankind, that ye have forlore,	*whom/lost totally*
	I schal do com owt fro yone skowtys	*make come out from yon scamps*
	To youre hende hall.	*Into/gracious*
	If ye wil no more betyn me,	*beat*
	I schal do Mankind com out fre;	*make/freely*
	He schal forsake, as thou schalt se,	
	The faire vertus all.	

MUNDUS.	Have do, thanne. The devil the[e] tere!	*Go to it then/tear you apart*
	Thou schalt ben hangyn in hell-herne.	*hell-corner*
	Bilive my baner up thou bere,	*Quickly*
	And besege we the castel yerne,	*quickly*
	Mankind for to stele.	
	Whanne Mankind growith good,	
	I, the Werld, am wild and wod.	*mad*
1884	Tho bicchys schul bleryn in here blood,	*Those bitches/be blinded/their*
	With flappys felle and fele.	*blows cruel and many*

1886	Yerne lete flapyr up my fane,	*Quickly/flutter/vane, banner*
1887	And schape we schame and schonde!	*contrive/disgrace*
	I schal bringe with me tho bicchys bane;	*those bitches' bane, nemesis*
	Ther schal no vertus dwellyn in my londe.	
	Mekenes is that modyr that I mene:	*wench/have in mind*
	To hir I brewe a bitter bonde.	*For her/bondage*
	Sche schal dey upon this grene	*die/green (the "place")*
	If that sche com al in min[e] honde—	
	Yene rappokys with here rumpys!	*Yon rascals with their rumps*
	I am the Werld! It is my will	
	The Castel of Vertu for to spill.	*destroy*
	Howtith hye upon yene hill,	*Proclaim loudly*
	Ye traitours, in youre trumpys! [*Trumpets blow.*]	*with your trumpets*
	Tunc Mundus, Cupiditas, et Stultitia ibunt ad castellum cum vexillo, et d[icet] Demon [from his scaffold]:	*Then World, Covetousness, and Folly will go to the castle with the banner, and the Devil will say*

BELIAL.	I here trumpys trebelen al of tene:	*I hear trumpets proclaim wrath*
1900	The worthy Werld walkith to werre,	*war*
	For to clivyn yone castel clene,	*cleave/totally*
	Tho maidnys meyndys for to merre.	*To mar those maidens' intents*
	Sprede my penon upon a prene,	*pennon, banner/standard*
	And strike we forthe now undyr sterre!	*stars (a metrical tag)*
	Schapith now youre scheldys schene,	*Prepare/shining shields*

1884Those wenches will have blood streaming in their eyes (from head wounds).

1886–87Quickly let my banner be hoisted in the breeze, and let us contrive shame and disgrace (for the seven virtues)!

Yene skallyd skoutys for to skerre   *To scare yon scurvy scamps*
Upon yone grene grese!   *grass (i.e., the "place")*
Buske you now, boyes, belive!   *Prepare/quickly*
Forevere I stonde in mekyl strive;   *Continually/much (mental) strife*
1910 Whil Mankind is in clene live,   *life*
I am nevere wel at ese.

Make you redy, all thre,   *i.e., Pride, Wrath, and Envy*
Bolde batayl for to bede!   *To offer a challenge*
To yone feld lete us fle,   *field (the "place")*
And bere my baner forthe on brede!   *bear/far and wide*
To yone castel wil I te;   *go*
Tho mameringe modrys schul have here mede.   *chattering women/their reward*
But they yeld up to me,   *Unless/yield*
With bittyr balys they schul blede;   *torments*
1920 Of here reste I schal hem reve.   *their/bereave them*
In woful watyrs I schal hem wasche.
Have don, felaus! And take youre trasche,   *Go to it, fellows/track, course*
And wende we thedyr on a rasche,   *go we thither/in a rush*
That castel for to cleve.   *cleave*

SUPERBIA.   Now, now! Now, go now!
On hye hillys lete us howte;   *shout*
For in Pride is al my prow,   *profit, advantage*
Thy bolde baner to bere abowte.
To Golias I make a vow   *Goliath*
1930 For to schetyn yone iche skowte.   *To shoot each of yon scamps*
On hir ars, raggyd and row,   *rough, torn*
I schal bothe clatyr and clowte,   *clatter, beat/hit*
And geve Meknesse mischa[u]nse.
Belial bryth, it is thin[e] hest   *bright/behest, command*
That I, Pride, goo the[e] nest,   *next, nearest to you*
And bere thy baner beforn my brest
With a comly contenaunce. [*They descend into the platea.*]
[*On his scaffold, Flesh has heard the summons.*]

CARO.   I here an hidowse whwtinge on hyt.   *hear hideous shouting on high*
Belive bid my baner forth for to blase!   *Quickly/blaze*
Whanne I sit in my sadyl, it is a selkowth syt;   *fabulous sight*
1941 I gape as a Gog-magog whanne I ginne to gase.   *giant*

1941–46 I open my mouth wide like a giant when I stare furiously (at my enemies). I set in
motion this highly-esteemed but profligate world with a weight, as one moves a clock with
a clock-weight (since the flesh is the material basis of all life). I crush and completely de-
molish yonder rascals; I shoot craftily with both missiles and sling to crack and shatter yon
castle into the river (or, with force?), bringing sorrow to it. (On Gog-magog, see Ezekiel
38:2 and Geoffrey of Monmouth, *Historia Regum Britanniae*.)

1942	This worthy, wilde werld I wagge with a wyt.	*I move with a weigh*
1943	Yone rappokys I ruble and al to-rase;	*rascals/crush*
1944	Bothe with schot and with slinge I caste with a sleyt,	
1945	With care to yone castel to crachen and to crase	*crack/shatter*
1946	In flode.	
	I am Mans Flesch; where I go	
	I am Mans most fo.	*greatest*
	Iwis, I am evere wo	*woeful*
	Whan[n]e he drawith to goode.	*turns*
	Therfor, ye bolde boyes, buske you abowte!	*get ready*
1952	Scharply on scheldys your schaftys ye schevere!	*shields/shafts/shiver, splinter*
	And Lechery, ledron, schete thou a skoute!	*rogue/attack one of the wenches*
	Help we Mankind fro yone castel to kevere!	*Let us help/recover*
	Helpe! We moun him winne.	*must regain him*
	Schete we all at a schote,	*Attack/at a shot, together*
	With gere that we cunne best note,	*can best use*
	To chache Mankind fro yene cote	*expel/yon dwelling*
	Into dedly sinne.	
	GULA. Lo, Sir Flesch, whow I fare to the felde	*how*
	With a faget on min[e] hond, for to settyn on a fire!	*faggot, fire-brand*
1962	With a wrethe of the wode, wel I can me welde;	*twist/wood*
	With a longe launce tho loselys I schal lere.	*rascals/teach (a lesson)*
	Go we with oure gere!	
	Tho bicchys schul bleykyn and blodyr;	*bitches/grow pale and blubber*
	I schal makyn swiche a powdyr,	*such a choking dust*
	Bothe with smoke and with smodyr,	*smothering fumes*
	They schul schityn for fere.	*shit*
	Tunc descendent in plateam.	*Then they will descend into the plateа*

[*On the platea, the Bad Angel delivers a battle oration to the assembled troops, exhorting in turn the forces of Devil, Flesh, and World.*]

Dicet ad Belial: — *He will say to Belial (and his lieutenants)*

1969	MALUS ANGELUS. As armys! As an herawd, hey now I howte!	*loudly/shout*
1970	Devil, dyth the[e] as a duke, to do tho damysely[s] dote!	*outfit yourself/to cause*
	Belial, as a bolde boy, thy brodde I bere abowte:	*escutcheon*
	Helpe to cache Mankind fro caitifys cote!	*drive/from the villains' dwelling*

[1052]Fiercely break into splinters the shafts (of your spears) on the shields (of your enemies).

[1962]With a twisted firebrand of wood I can manage myself handily

[1969–70]To arms! Like a herald, now I loudly make proclamation. Devil, outfit yourself as befits a duke, to cause those damsels to look foolish.

1973 Prid[e], put out thy penon of raggys and of rowte;	*rags and riot*
Do this modyr Mekenes meltyn to mote!	*Cause/to melt into a mote, speck*
Wrethe, prefe Paciens, the skallyd skowte!	*make trial of/scurvy wench*
Envye, to Charité schape thou a schote	*prepare an attack*
Ful yare!	*quickly*
With Pride, Wrethe and Envye,	
These develys, by downys drye,	*(a metrical tag)*
1980 As comly kinge[s], I discrye	*challenge*
Mankind to kachyn to care.	*drive to sorrow*

Ad Carnem:	*To the Flesh (and his lieutenants)*

Flesch, frele and fresche, frely fed,	*frail, delicate/generously*
With Gloton, Slawthe, and Lechery Mans sowle thou slo!	*slay*
As a duke dowty, do the[e] to be dred;	*make yourself dreaded*
1985 Gere the[e] with gerys fro toppe to the too.	*Arm yourself/toe*
Kith this day thou art a kinge frely fedde!	*Show*
Gloton, sle thou Abstine[n]sce with wickyd woo!	*slay*
With Chastité, thou Lechour, be not ovyrledde!	*By/lorded over*
Slawthe, bete thou Besines on buttokys bloo!	*i.e., beat Industry's buttocks blue*
1990 Do now thy crafte, in coste to be knowe.	*known*

Ad Mundum:	*To the World (and Covetousness)*

Worthy, witty, and wys, wondyn in wede,	*wise/wrapped in garments*
Lete Coveitise karpyn, cryen and grede!	*yell, shout, and call loudly*
1993 Here ben bolde bachelerys batyl to bede,	*are/to offer challenge*
1994 Mankind to tene, as I trowe.	*harm*
[*Mankind is in contemplation, meanwhile, in the castle.*]	

HUMANUM GENUS. That dinge duke that deyed on rode,	*worthy/died on cross*
This day my sowle kepe and safe!	
Whanne Mankind drawith to goode	*turns*
Beholde what enmys he schal have.	
The Werld, the Devil, the Flesche, arn wode;	*are mad*
2000 To men they casten a careful kave.	*a dreadful cavern*

1973Pride, display your ensign of rags and riot (emblems of prodigality and disorder).

1985Arm yourself with weapons from head to toe.

1990Do your business now, to be known or famous in manner (or, in every coast, everywhere).

1993-94Here, I trust, are bold young knights to offer a challenge to fight in order to harm Mankind. (Said with reference to all seven Deadly Sins.)

2000-3They prepare for men a dreadful cavern (i.e., hell). To tell you the truth, sirs, they prepare bitter sorrows on every side, to cause Mankind to roll about and toss to and fro on (a sea of) woe.

2001	Bittyr balys they brewyn on brode,	on every side
2002	Mankind in wo to weltyr and wave,	
2003	Lordingys, sothe to sey.	Sirs (the audience)
	Therfore iche man bewar of this!	each
	For, whil Mankind clene is,	clean, pure
	His enmys schul temptyn him to don amis,	
	If they mown, by any wey.	may, can
2007a	(Omne gaudium existimate, cum variis temptationibus incideritis.)	

	Therfor, lordys, beth now glad	be
	With elmes-dede and orisoun	alms-deed/prayer
	For to don as oure Lord bad;	do/bade
	Stifly withstonde youre temptacioun.	Sturdily
	With this foul fende I am ner mad;	nearly
	To batayle they buskyn hem bown!	make themselves ready
	Certys I schuld ben over-lad,	be overwhelmed
	But that I am in this castel town,	Were I not
	With sinnys sore and smerte.	By/smarting
	Whoso wil levyn oute of distresse,	live free from strife
	And ledyn his lif[e] in clennesse,	
	In this castel of vertu and of goodnesse	
	Him muste have [w]hole his hert.	wholly
2020a	(Delectare in Domino, et dabit tibi petitiones cordis tui.)	

BONUS ANGELUS.   A, Mekenesse, Charité, and Paciens—

2022	Primrose pleyeth parlasent—	by assent, willingly
	Chastité, Besines, and Abstinens,	
	Min[e] hope, ladys, in you is lent!	is fixed
	Socoure, paramourys, swetter thanne sens,	Help/incense
	Rode as rose on rys i-rent!	Red/torn from branch
	This day ye dyth a good defens!	prepare, set
2028	Whil Mankind is in good entent,	
2029	His thoutys arn unhende.	ungracious, unstable
	Mankind is brow[gh]t into this walle,	i.e., world
	In freelté to fadyn and falle;	frailty/decline
	Therfore, ladys, I pray you alle,	
	Helpe this day Mankinde!	

HUMILITAS.   God, that sittith in hevene on hy,   *high*

2007aCount it all joy when you fall into various temptations (i.e., welcome temptation as a testing of your steadfastness; see James 1:2).

2020aTake delight in the Lord, and he will give you the desires of your heart (Psalms 37: 4).

2022(Meaning unclear.)

2028–29i.e., Although Mankind intends to obey reason, his will is unruly.

Save al Mankind by se and sonde!   *i.e., everywhere*
Lete him dwellyn here, and ben us by,   *be near us*
And we schul puttyn to him helpinge honde.   *put, give*
Yit, forsothe, nevere I sy   *saw*
That any fawte in us he fonde,   *found*
2040 But that we savyd him fro sinne sly,
If he wolde by us stifly stonde   *sturdily stand, stay*
In this castel of ston.
Therfor drede the[e] not, Mans Aungel dere!
If he wil dwellyn with us here,
Fro sevene sinnys we schul him were,   *protect*
And his enmys ichon.   *each one*

[*To her sister Virtues.*]
Now, my sevene sisterys swete,
This day fallith on us the lot   *destiny*
Mankind for to schilde and schete   *shield and guard*
Fro dedly sinne and schamely schot.   *shameful assault*
His enmys strayen in the strete   *stray, roam about*
To spille Man with spetows spot.   *kill/cruel disgrace*
2053 Therfor oure flourys lete now flete,   *Let our flowers float down now*
And kepe we him, as we have het,   *promised*
Among us in this halle.
Therfor, seven sisterys swote,   *sweet*
Lete oure vertus reyne on rote!   *rain down together*
This day we wil be Mans bote   *boot, remedy*
Ageyns these develys alle.   *Against*

2060 BELIAL.   This day the vaward wil I holde.   *vanguard, front rank*
Avaunt my baner, precious Pride,   *Lift high*
Mankind to cache to karys colde!   *drive/sorrows*
Bold batayl now wil I bide.   *I'll offer a challenge*
Buske you, boyes, on brede!   *Prepare/far and wide*
Alle men that be with me witholde,   *that follow me*
Bothe the yonge and the olde,
Envye, Wrathe, ye boyes bolde,
To rounde rappys ye rape, I rede!   *hearty blows/rush/advise*

SUPERBIA.   As armys! Mekenes, I bringe thy bane,   *To arms/nemesis*
2070 Al with pride peyntyd and pyth.   *adorned*
What seyst thou, faytour? By min[e] fair fane,   *hypocrite/vane, flag*

2053(The seven virtues intend to use flowers as their weapons against the enemy below on the platea.)

2070(I who am) painted and adorned with emblems of pride.

2072	With robys rounde, rayed ful ryth,	*arrayed fully*
2073	Grete gounse, I schal the[e] gane.	*gowns/overcome*
	To marre the[e], Mekenes, with my myth,	*might*
	No werldly wittys here ar wane.	*lacking*
	Lo, thy castel is al beset!	
	Moderys, whow schul ye do?	*Wenches/how*
	Mekenes, yelde the[e] to me, I rede!	*advise*
	Min[e] name in londe is precious Prede;	
2080	Min[e] bolde baner to the[e] I bede:	*present in challenge*
	Modyr, what seyste therto?	

HUMILITAS.	Ageyns thy baner of pride and bost	
	A baner of meknes and mercy	
	I putte ageyns Pride, wel thou wost,	
	That schal schende thy careful cry.	*destroy/grief-causing*
	This meke kinge is knowyn in every cost,	
	That was croisyd on Calvary.	*crucified*
	Whanne he cam doun fro hevene ost,	*the heavenly host*
	And lityd with mekenes in Mary,	*descended meekly to*
	This Lord thus lityd lowe.	*alighted (on earth) humbly*
	Whanne he cam fro the Trinité,	
	Into a maidyn lityd he,	
	And al was for to distroye the[e]:	
	Pride, this schalt thou knowe.	
2094a	(*Deposuit potentes de sede, et cetera.*)	

	For whanne Lucifer to helle fyl,	*fell*
	Pride, therof thou were chesun;	*cause*
	And thou, devil, with wickyd wil,	
	In paradis trappyd us with tresun.	
	So thou us bond in balys ille—	*bound us in sorrows*
2100	This may I preve by ryth resun.	*right reason*
	Til this duke that died on hille,	*i.e., Christ on Calvary*
	In hevene man myth nevere han sesun;	*might never have possession*
	The Gospel thus declarit[h].	
	For, whoso love him schal ben hy;	*be exalted*
	Therfore thou schalt not comen us ny.	*come nigh us*
	And, thou[gh] thou be nevere so sly,	
	I schal felle al thy fare.	*fell, knock down/doings*
2107a	(*Qui se exaltat, humiliabitur, et cetera.*)	

2072-73Fully arrayed in flowing robes, in sumptuous gowns, I'll overcome you.

2094aHe has put down the mighty from their seats, and so on (from the *Magnificat*, Luke 1:52).

2107aWhoever exalts himself will be abased, and so on (Luke 14:11, 18:14).

IRA.   Dame Paciens, what seyst thou to Wrathe and Ire?

Putte Mankind fro thy castel clere,	*virtuous*
Or I schal tappyn at thy tire	*strike/headdress*
With stiffe stonys that I have here!	*awesome*
I schal slinge at the[e] many a vire,	*cross-bow bolt*
And ben avengyd hastely here.	
Thus Belsabub, oure gret sire,	
Bad[e] me brenne the[e] with wild fere,	*burn*
Thou bicche blak as kole!	
Therfor, fast, fowle skowte,	*quickly/wench*
Putte Mankind to us owte,	
Or of me thou schalt have dowte,	*fear*
Thou modyr, thou motyhole!	*moth-hole (?)*

PATIENTIA.   Fro thy dowte, Crist me schelde — *From fear of you/shield*

This iche day, and al mankinde!	
Thou wrecchyd Wrethe, wood and wilde,	*mad*
Paciens schal the[e] schende!	*destroy*

2124a (*Quia ira viri justitiam Dei non operatur.*)

For Marys sone, meke and milde,	*son*
Rent the[e] up, rote and rinde,	*Tore/root and skin, entirely*
Whanne he stod meker thanne a childe	*stood meeker*
And lete boyes him betyn and binde.	*fellows beat and bind him*
Therfor, wrecche, be stille!	

2130 For tho pelourys that gan him pose,   *despoilers/shove*
2131 He myth a drevyn hem to dros;   *might have*

And yit, to casten him on the cros	*to crucify him*
He sufferyd al here wille.	*their*

Thowsentys of aungell[ys] he myth han had	*Thousands/might have*
To a wrokyn him ther ful yerne;	*To have avenged/quickly*
And yit, to deyen he was glad,	*die*
Us paciens to techyn and lerne.	*To teach us patience*
Therfor, boy, with thy boistous blad,	*fierce blade, sword*
Fare awey by feldys ferne!	*into fields afar*

2140 For I wil do as Jhesu bad: *bade*

Wrecchys fro my wonys werne	*Ward off wretches from my dwelling*
With a dingne defens.	*worthy*
If thou fonde to comyn alofte,	*try to come*
I schal the[e] cacche fro this crofte	*repel/enclosure*
With these rosys swete and softe,	
Peyntyd with Paciens.	

2124a For the wrath of man does not produce the justice of God (James 1:20).

2130–31 For he (Christ) might have destroyed (lit: driven into dross) those despoilers who were shoving him around.

INVIDIA. Out! Min[e] herte ginnith to breke,

For Charité that stondith so stowte.   *strongly*

Alas, min[e] herte ginnith to wreke.   *seek vengeance*

2150 Yelde up this castel, thou hore clowte!   *old rag*

It is min[e] office fowle to speke,   *my function to speak foully*

Fals sklaundrys to bere abowte.   *slanders*

Charité, the devil mote the[e] cheke,   *may the devil choke you*

But I the[e] rappe with rewly rowte,   *Unless/strike/a grievous blow*

Thy targe for to tere!   *shield*

Let Mankinde cum to us doun,

Or I schal schetyn to this castel town   *let fly*

A ful fowle defamacion—

Therfore this bowe I bere.

2160 CARITAS. Thou[gh] thou speke wicke and fals fame,   *wicked/report*

2161 The wers schal I nevere do my dede.   *worse/deed*

Whoso peyrith falsly another mans name,   *impairs*

Cristys curs he schal have to mede.   *as reward*

2163a (*Vae homini illi per quem scandalum ven[it].*)

Whoso wil not his tunge tame—

2165 Take it sothe as mes-crede—   *mass-creed*

Wo, wo, to him, and mekyl schame!   *much*

In holy writte this I rede: *read*

Forevere thou art a schrewe.   *villain*

Thou[gh] thou speke evil, I ne geve a gres;   *I don't care a straw*

I schal do nevere the wers.   *worse*

2171 At the last, the sothe vers

2172 Certys Himself schal schewe.   *show, demonstrate*

Oure lovely Lord, withowtyn lak,   *flaw*

Gaf example to Charité,   *Gave/of*

Whanne he was betyn blo and blak,   *beaten*

For trespas that nevere did he.   *sin/he never did*

In sory sinne had he no tak,   *blemish*

And yit for sinne he bled blody ble;   *(of) countenance*

He toke his cros upon his bak,

Sinful man, and al for the[e].   *all for you, sinful man*

Thus he mad[e] defens.

Envye, with thy slaundrys thicke,

2160–61 I'll not fail to perform my duty for all your wicked and false rumor-mongering.

2163a Woe to that man by whom offense comes (Matthew 18:7).

2165 Believe this to be as true as the Creed in the mass.

2171–72 Ultimately, Christ himself will demonstrate the truth of the scriptural verse.

2183   I am putte at my Lordys pricke;   *torment*
         I wil do good ageyns the wicke,   *in response to evil*
         And kepe in silens.   *remain*

        BELIAL.   What, for Belialys bonys,
         Where-abowtyn chide ye?   *What are you chattering about*
         Have don, ye boyes, al at onys!   *Let's go/at once*
2189   Lasche don these moderys, all thre!   *Beat down/wenches*
         Werke wrake to this wonys!   *Do vengeance/dwelling*
         The vaunward is grauntyd me.   *vanguard*
         Do these moderys to makyn monys!   *Cause/make moans*
         Youre dowty dedys now lete se!   *doughty deeds*
         Dasche hem al to daggys!   *Dash them/tatters*
         Have do, boyes blo and blake!
         Wirke these wenchys wo and wrake!   *harm*
         Clariouns, cryith up at a krake,   *Trumpets cry up loudly*
         And blowe your brode baggys!   *bagpipes*
            Tunc pugnabunt diu. [Pride, Wrath, and Envy are repulsed by   *Then they will fight a long while*
            a fusillade of flowers.]

        SUPERBIA.   Out! My proude bak is bent!
2200   Mekenes hath me al for-bete;   *totally beaten*
         Pride with Mekenes is for-schent!   *by/destroyed*
         I weyle and wepe, with wondys wete;   *wounds wet*
         I am betyn in the hed.
         My prowde pride a-doun is drevyn;
         So scharpely Mekenes hath me schrevyn,   *shriven (i.e., humbled)*
         That I may no lenger levyn.
         My lif is me berevyd!   *bereft*

        INVIDIA.   Al min[e] enmité is not worth a fart;
         I schite and schake al in my schete!   *shit/underwear*
2210   Charité, that sowre swart,   *swarthy wretch*
         With faire rosys min[e] hed gan breke—   *broke*
         I brede the malaundyr!   *I'm producing scabs*
         With worthy wordys and flourys swete   *flowers*
         Charité makith me so meke
         I dare neither crye nore crepe—   *call out or move*
         Not a schote of sklaundyr.   *shot, attack*

        IRA.   I, Wrethe, may singyn wele-a-wo!
         Paciens me gaf a sory dint.   *blow*

2183 I am now put to the same torment as my Lord.

2189 *thre*: Belial is speaking to his lieutenants, Pride, Wrath, and Envy.

2220

I am al betyn blak and blo   *beaten*
With a rose that on rode was rent.   *rose torn off the cross*
My speche is almost spent.
Hir rosys fel on me so scharpe
That min[e] hed hangith as an harpe.
I dar neither crye nor carpe,   *call out or complain*
Sche is so pacient.

MALUS ANGELUS.   Go hens! Ye do not worthe a tord!   *turd*

2227

Foule falle you, alle foure!   *May foul luck befall you*
Yerne, yerne, let fall on bord!   *Quickly/i.e., attack again*
Sir Flesch, with thin[e] eyn soure,   *sullen eyes*
For care I cukke and koure.   *sorrow/shit and cower*
Sir Flesch, with thin[e] company,
Yerne, yerne, make a cry!
Helpe we have no velony,   *Help so that/disgrace*
That this day may be oure!   *So that/ours*

CARO.   War, war! Late Mans Flesche go to!   *Look out! Let/go to work*
I com with a company.
Have do, my childryn! Now have do,   *Let's go*
Glotoun, Slawth, and Lechery!
Iche of you winnith a scho.   *gain glory*

2240

Lete not Mankinde winne maistry!
Lete slinge hem in a fowl slo,   *Let him be slung/slough*
And fonde to feffe him with foly!   *try to endow*
Dothe now wel youre dede: *Do*
Yerne lete se whow ye schul ginne   *Quickly let's see how/begin*
Mankinde to temptyn to dedly sinne.
If ye muste this castelle winne,   *may, can*
Hell schal be your mede.   *reward*

GULA.   War! Sir Gloton schal makyn a smeke   *smoke*
Ageyns this castel, I vowe.   *Against*

2250

Abstinens, thou[gh] thou bleyke,   *turn pale*
I loke on the[e] with bitter browe.
I have a faget in min[e] necke   *firebrand on my shoulder*
To settyn Mankind on a-lowe.   *To set Mankind on fire*
My foul leye schalt thou not let,   *flame/you won't hinder*
I vow to God, as I trowe;
Therfor putte him out here!   *him (Mankind)*
In meselinge Glotonye,   *diseaseful*
With goode metys and drinkys trye,   *rich, delicate*
I norche my sister Lecherye   *nourish*

2227 *foure*: i.e., Belial and his three lieutenants.

2260   Til Man rennith on fere.   *runs afire (with lust)*

ABSTINENTIA.   Thy metys and drinkys arn unthende   *unhealthy*
    Whanne they are out of mesure take.   *immoderately consumed*
    They makyn men mad and out of mende,   *raving*
    And werkyn hem bothe wo and wrake.   *them/harm*
2265   That for thy fere thou[gh] thou here kindyl,   *comrade*
    Certys I schal thy wele a-slake   *I'll lessen your well-being*
    With bred that browth us out of hell,   *bread/brought*
    And on the croys sufferyd wrake—   *cross/harm*
    I mene the sacrament.
    That iche blisful bred,   *same*
    That hounge on hil til he was ded,   *hanged*
    Schal tempere so min[e] maidynhed
    That thy purpos schal be spent.   *wasted*

2274   In abstinens this bred was browth,   *brought*
    Certys, Mankinde, and al for the[e]:
    Of fourty dayes ete he nowth,   *For/he ate nothing*
2276a   (*Cum jejunasset quadraginta diebus, etc.*)
    And thanne was nailyd to a tre.
    Example us was be-tawth: *taught*
    In sobyrnesse he bad[e] us be.
2280   Therfor Mankind schal not be cawth,   *caught*
2281   Glotony, with thy degré—   *condition*
    The sothe thou schalt se.
2283   To norisch faire thou[gh] thou be fawe,   *pleasantly/eager*
2284   Abstinens it schal withdrawe   *will take it away*
2285   Til thou be schet under schawe,   *shut up/grove*
    And fain for to fle.   *glad*

LUXURIA.   Lo, Chastité, thou fowle skowte,   *wench*
    This ilke day here thou schalt deye!   *same/die*
    I make a fer in Mans towte,   *fire, passion/genital region*
2290   That launcith up as any leye.   *leaps/flame*
    These cursyd colys I bere abowte,   *coals (of passion)*
    Mankinde in tene for to teye.   *to bind in pain*

[2265]Although you kindle that for your comrade (i.e., for Lechery; see l. 2259).

[2274]This bread (i.e., Christ) was brought into a condition of abstinence (during his temptation in the wilderness).

[2276a]When he had fasted forty days, and so on (Matthew 4:2).

[2280–81]Therefore Mankind will not fall into your condition, Gluttony.

[2283–85]Though you are eager to offer beguiling nourishment (to your victims), Temperance will take it away until you, Gluttony, are buried under the earth.

Men and wommen hathe no dowte   *fear*
With pissinge pokys for to pleye.   *genitals*
I binde hem in my bondys.   *them*
2296   I have no reste, so I rowe,   *as I hope to have repose*
With men and wommen, as I trowe,
Til I, Lechery, be set on a-lowe   *be set afire*
In al Mankindys londys.   *loins*

CASTITAS.   I, Chastité, have power in this place,
The[e], Lechery, to bind and bete.
Maidyn Marye, well of grace,   *fountain*
Schal qwenche that fowle hete.   *heat*
2303a   (*Mater et Virgo, exstingue carnales concupisce[ntias]!*)
Oure Lord God mad[e] the[e] no space   *gave you no room*
Whanne his blod strayed in the strete: *i.e., When he was crucified*
Fro this castel he did the[e] chase
Whanne he was crounyd with thornys grete
And grene.
To drery deth whanne he was dyth,   *put*
2310   And boyes did him gret dispyth,   *ruffians/despite*
In Lechery had he no dclyth,
And that was ryth wel sene.   *clearly seen*

At Oure Lady I lere my lessun   *From/learn*
To have chaste lif til I be ded.
Sche is qwene, and berith the croun;
And al was for hir maidynhed.   *all on account of*
Therfor, go fro this castel toun,
Lechery, now I the[e] rede;   *advise*
For, Mankind getist thou nowth doun   *you won't get Mankind down*
2320   To soloyen him [with] sinful sede.   *sully/semen*
In care thou woldis[t] him cast.   *You'd place him in sorrow*
And if thou com up to me,   *If*
Trewly thou schalt betyn be   *beaten*
With the yerde of Chastité   *rod*
Whil my lif may last.

ACCIDIA.   Ware, war! I delve with a spade;
Men calle me the "Lord Sir Slowe."   *Sloth*
Gostly grace I spille and schade.   *Spiritual/shed, pour off*
Fro the watyr of grace, this diche I fowe;   *I empty this ditch*

2296I never stop, as I hope to be saved (a mild oath, with ironic meaning here).

2303aMother and Maiden, quench carnal lusts!

2330   Ye schulyn com ryth inowe
2331   By this diche drye, by bankys brede.
2332   Thirty thousende that I wel knowe
        In my lif lovely I lede,
        That had levere sittyn at the ale,   *rather*
        Three mens songys to singyn lowde,   *To sing part-singing*
        Thanne toward the chyrche for to crowde.
        Thou Besinesse, thou bolnyd bowde,   *Industry/swollen malt-weevil*
        I brewe to the[e] thine bale!   *prepare for/sorrow*

SOLICITUDO.   A, good men, bewar now all
        Of Slugge and Slawthe, this fowl thefe!
        To the sowle he is bittyrer thanne gall;
        Rote he is of mekyl mischefe.   *Root, source*
2343   Goddys servise, that ledith us to hevene hall,
2344   This lordeyn for to lettyn us is lefe.   *rascal/hinder/lief, glad*
        Whoso wil schrivyn him of his sinnys all,   *confess himself*
        He puttith this brethel to mykyl mischefe,   *rascal/much*
        Mankinde he that miskaried.   *He who led Mankind astray*
2348   Men moun don no penauns for him, this,   *must/this fellow*
2349   Nere schrive hem whanne they don amis,   *Nor confess themselves*
2350   But evyr he wold in sinne, iwis,
2351   That Mankind were taried.   *tarried, kept*

        Therfor he makith this dike drye,   *ditch*
        To puttyn Mankinde to distresse:
        He makith dedly sinne a redy weye
        Into the Castel of Goodnesse.
        But with tene I schal him teye,   *I'll bind him with pain*
        Thorwe the helpe of hevene emperesse.   *Through/heaven's empress*
        With my bedys he schal a-beye.   *(prayer) beads/pay for it*
        And other ocupacions more and lesse   *great and small*
        I schal schape, him to schonde,   *devise to shame him*
        For whoso wile Slawth putte doun   *For those who will*
        With bedys and with orisoun   *prayer*
        Or sum [h]oneste ocupacioun—
        As, boke to have in honde.   *Such as*
2364a   (Nunc lege, nunc ora, nunc disce, nuncque labora.)

2330–32You will meet with and obtain (come by) this dry ditch soon enough, by the banks' breadth (a metrical tag). I'm well acquainted with thirty thousand people.

2343–44This rascal is glad to hinder us in our performance of God's service, which conducts us to the heavenly kingdom.

2348–51This fellow (Sloth) does not desire men to perform acts of penance or shrive themselves when they have sinned, but he desires always that Mankind should remain in sin, truly.

2364aRead now, pray now, learn now, and work now.

CARO.   Ey, for B[e]lialys bonys, the Kinge,   *for King Belial's bones*
    Whereabowte stonde ye al day?   *What for*
    Caitivys, lete be your kakelinge,   *stop your cackling, chattering*
    And rappe at rowtys of aray!   *strike at crowds in martial array*
    Glotony, thou fowle gadlinge,   *scamp*
2370   Sle Abstinens, if thou may!   *Slay*
    Lechery, with thy werkinge,   *deeds*
    To Chastité make a wickyd aray   *Make trouble for Chastity*
    A lityl throwe.   *For a time*
    And whil we fyth   *fight*
    For owre ryth,
    In bemys bryth   *trumpets bright*
    Late blastys blowe! [*Trumpets sound.*]   *Let*
      Tunc pugnabunt diu. [*The sins are repulsed.*]   *Then they will fight a long while*

GULA.   Out, Glotoun! A-down I drive;   *Down I am forced to go*
    Abstine[n]s hathe lost my mi[r]th.   *deprived me of my mirth*
2380   Sir Flesch, I schal nevere thrive;
    I do not worthe the develys dirt!   *I can't perform/devil's turd*
    I may not levyn longe.
    I am al betyn, toppe and tail;   *beaten from head to tail*
    With Abstinens wil I no more dayl.   *deal*
    I wil gon cowche [and] qwail   *go hide*
    At hom[e] in your gonge.   *privy*

LUXURIA.   Out on Chastité! By the rode,   *cross*
    Sche hathe [me] dayschyd and so drenchyd!   *beaten and quenched me*
    Yit have sche the curs of God,   *May she have*
2390   For al my fere the qwene hath qwenchyd.   *fire (of passion)*
    For ferd I fall and feynt.   *fear/faint*
    In harde ropys mote sche ride!   *may she be hanged*
    Here dare I not longe abide;
    Sumwhere min[e] hed I wolde hide,
    As an irchoun that were schent.   *Like a little child in disgrace*

ACCIDIA.   Out, I deye! Ley on watyr!   *die*
    I swone, I swete, I feynt, I drulle!   *swoon/stagger (?)*
    Yene qwene, with hir pityr-patyr,   *Yon whore*
    Hath al to-dayschyd my skallyd skulle!   *dashed to pieces/scabbed*
2400   It is as softe a[s] wulle.   *wool*
    Or I have here more skathe,   *Ere/harm*
    I schal lepe awey, by lurkinge lathe;   *to a hideaway (?)*
    There I may my ballokys bathe,   *testicles*
    And leykyn at the fulle.   *play, rest*

MALUS ANGELUS.   Ya! The devil spede you, al the packe!

	For sorwe, I mo[u]rne on the mowle;	*on the ground*
	I carpe, I crye, I coure, I kacke,	*complain/cower/shit*
	I frete, I fart, I fesyl fowle!	*am vexed/make a fizzling fart foully*
2409	I loke like an howle. *(Ad Mundum:)*	*owl/To World*
	Now, Sir World, whatso it cost,	*whatever*
	Helpe now, or this we have lost;	
	Al oure fare is not worth a thost!	*turd*
	That makith me to mowle.	*lament, grimace (?)*

	MUNDUS. How, Coveitise! Banyour avaunt!	*Banner to the front*
	Here comith a batayl, nobyl and newe;	
	For, sith thou were a lityl faunt,	*since/infant*
	Coveitise, thou hast ben trewe.	
	Have do that damysel; do hir dawnt;	*Finish up with/tame her*
	Bitter balys thou hir brewe!	*Brew her bitter sorrows*
2420	The medys, boy, I the[e] graunt	*As reward*
2421	The galows of Canwike to hangyn on newe—	*Canwick (near Lincoln?)*
	That wolde the[e] wel befalle.	*suit you well*
	Have don, Sir Coveitise,	*Let's go*
	Wirke on the best wise!	*in*
	Do Mankinde com and arise	*Cause*
	Fro yone vertuse all.	*virtues*
	[*Covetousness goes to the castle.*]	

	AVARITIA. How, Mankinde! I am a-tenyde	*vexed*
	For thou art there so in that holde.	*Because/stronghold*
	Cum and speke with thy best frende,	
2430	Sir Coveitise! Thou knowist me of olde.	
	What, devil, schalt thou ther lenger lende	*remain*
	With grete penaunce in that castel colde?	
	Into the werld, if thou wilt, wende	
	Amonge men to bere the[e] bolde,	*bear yourself boldly*
	I rede, by Seynt Gile.	*advise/Giles*
	How, Mankinde! I the[e] sey,	
	Com to Coveitise, I the[e] prey;	
	We t[w]o schul togedyr pley,	
	If thou wilt, a while.	

2440	LARGITAS. A, God helpe! I am dismayed.	
	I curse the[e], Coveitise, as I can;	
	For certys, treytour, thou hast betrayed	
	Nerhand now iche erthely man.	*Nearly*

2409i.e., I look foolish, staring.

2420-21As your reward, I'll permit you to hang soon on the gallows of Canwick (a sample of
the vicious and aggressive gallows humor indulged in by the seven Deadly Sins).

So myche were men nevere afrayed   *much/harassed*
With Coveitise, syn the werld began;   *By/since*
God almythy is not payed.   *pleased*

2447   Syn thou, fende, bare the Werldys bane,   *Since*
2448   Ful wide thou ginnist wende.
Now arn men waxyn ner woode;   *have grown nearly mad*
They wolde gon to helle for werldys goode.   *world's wealth*
That Lord that restyd on the rode   *cross*
2452   Is maker of an ende.

2452a   (*Maledicti sunt avaritiosi huius temporis.*)

Ther is no disese nor debate   *trouble or strife*
Thorwe this wide werld so rounde,   *Throughout*
Tide nor time, erly nor late,
But that Covei[ti]se is the grounde.   *source*
Thou norchist Pride, Envye, and Hate,   *You nourish*
Thou Coveitise, thou cursyd hounde!
Criste the[e] schelde fro oure gate,   *shield, ward you off*
2460   And kepe us fro the[e] saf and sounde,
That thou no good here winne!   *So that you achieve nothing here*
Swete Jhesu, jentyl justice,
Kepe Mankinde fro Coveitise!
For iwis he is, in al wise,
Rote of sorwe and sinne.   *Root*

AVARITIA.   What eylith the[e], Lady Largité,   *ails you/Generosity*
Damysel dingne upon thy des?   *noble/dais, throne*
And I spak ryth not to the[e],   *not at all to you*
Therfore I prey the[e] holde thy pes.   *peace, silence*
2470   How, Mankinde! Cum speke with me;
Cum ley thy love here in my les.   *leash, control*
Coveitise is a frend ryth fre,   *most excellent*
Thy sorwe, Man, to slake and ses.   *put an end to*
Coveitise hathe many a gifte.
Mankind, thine hande heder thou reche.   *hither/reach*
Coveitise schal be thy leche;   *healer*
The ryth wey I schal the[e] teche
To thedom and to thrifte.   *prosperity*

HUMANUM GENUS.   Coveitise, whedyr schuld I wende?   *whither*
2480   What wey woldist that I s[h]ulde holde?   *do you wish/continue to follow*

2447–48Ever since you, Covetousness, you fiend, gave birth to the World's sorrowful curse
(inasmuch as covetousness is the root or origin of all evil), your power has expanded widely.

2452–52aWill make an end (to all those who are covetous). Cursed are the avaricious from
this time forth.

To what place woldist thou me sende?

I ginne to waxyn hory and olde;   *hoary, grey-haired*

My bake ginnith to bowe and bende;   *back*

I crulle and crepe, and wax al colde.   *crawl*

Age makith Man ful unthende,   *feeble*

Body and bonys, and al unwolde.   *weak*

My bonys are febyl and sore.

I am arayed in a sloppe;   *a loose gown*

As a yonge man I may not hoppe;

2490   My nose is colde, and ginnith to droppe;

Min[e] her waxit[h] al hore.   *hair/grey*

AVARITIA.   Petyr! Thou hast the more nede   *(By Saint) Peter*

To have sum good in thin[e] age: *wealth*

Markys, poundys, londys and lede,   *Marks(13s., 4d.)/servants*

Howsys and homys, castell and cage.   *stronghold*

Therfor do as I the[e] rede: *advise*

To Coveitise cast thy parage.   *give your alliance, kinship (?)*

Cum, and I schal thine erdyn bede;   *present your petition*

The worthy Werld schal geve the[e] wage,

2500   Certys not a lyth.   *little*

Com on, olde man! It is no reprefe   *reproof, disgrace*

That Coveitise be the[e] lefe.   *is dear to you*

If thou deye at any mischefe,   *die in any distress of poverty*

It is thyselfe to wyth.   *You're to blame*

HUMANUM GENUS.   Nay, nay! These ladys of goodnesse

Wil not lete me fare amis;

And thou[gh] I be a while in distresse,   *poverty*

Whanne I deye, I schal to blisse.   *die*

It is but foly, as I gesse,

Al this werldys wele, iwis;   *world's weal, happiness*

These lovely ladys, more and lesse,

In wise wordys they telle me this—

2513   Thus seyth the bok of kendys.   *Book of Nature*

I wil not do these ladys dispyt,   *despite*

To forsakyn hem for so lyt.   *them/little*

To dwellyn here is my delyt;

Here arn my best frendys.

AVARITIA.   Ya! Up and doun thou take the wey,   *(if) you go*

Thorwe this werld to walkyn and wende,   *Throughout*

2520   And thou schalt finde, soth to sey,

2513*bok of kendys: De Naturis Rerum* by Alexander Nequam (according to Mark Eccles, ed., *Macro Plays*).

Thy purs schal be thy best frende.
Thou[gh] thou sit al day and prey,
No man schal com to the[e], nor sende;
But if thou have a peny to pey,
Men schul to the[e] thanne listyn and lende,　　　　*pay heed*
And kelyn al thy care.　　　　*cool, assuage*
Therfore to me thou hange and helde,　　　　*cling and remain faithful*
And be coveitous whilys thou may the[e] welde.　　　　*wield, govern yourself*
If thou be pore and nedy in elde,　　　　*in old age*
2530　Thou schalt oftyn evil fare.

HUMANUM GENUS.　Coveitise, thou seyst a good skil.　　　　*you speak truth*
So grete God me avaunce,　　　　*May great God prosper me (an oath)*
Al thy biddinge don I wil.
I forsake the Castel of Perseveraunce;
In Coveitise I wil me hyle,　　　　*take shelter*
For to gete sum sustinaunce.
2537　A-forn mele, men mete schul tyle;　　　　*Before/obtain*
It is good, for al chaunce,　　　　*to cover all contingencies*
Sum good owhere to hide.　　　　*To hide some wealth somewhere*
Certys this ye wel knowe:
It is good, whou-so the winde blowe,　　　　*however*
A man to have sumwhat of his owe,　　　　*his own*
What happe soevere betide.　　　　*Whatever happens*

BONUS ANGELUS.　A, ladyse! I prey you of grace,
Helpith to kepe here Mankinne!　　　　*Help*
He wil forsake this precious place,
And drawe ageyn to dedly sinne.
Helpe, ladys, lovely in lace!　　　　*handsomely dressed*
He goth fro this worthy wonninge.　　　　*dwelling*
2550　Coveitise awey ye chace,
And schittith Mankind sumwhere hereinne,　　　　*shut*
In youre worthy wise!
Ow, wrechyd Man! Thou schalt be wroth;
That sinne schal be the[e] ful loth.　　　　*loathsome to you*
A, swete ladys, helpe! He goth
Awey with Coveitise.
　　Tunc descendit ad Avaritiam.　　　　*Then he (Mankind) descends to Covetousness*

HUMILITAS.　Good Aungyl, what may I do therto?
Himselfe may his sowle spille.　　　　*destroy*
Mankind, to don what he wil do,

2537Before eating, one must obtain food (proverbial).

2560	God hath govyn him a fre wille.	*given*
	Thou[gh] he drenche, and his sowle slo,	*drown/slay*
	Certys we may not do there-tille.	*do anything about it*
	Syn he cam this castel to,	*Since*
	We did to him that us befelle,	*what befitted us*
	And now he hath us refusyd.	
	As longe as he was withinne this castel walle	
	We kepte him fro sinne, ye sawe wel alle;	
	And now he wil ageyn to sinne falle,	*now (that)*
	I preye you holde us excusyd.	*consider*

	PATIENTIA. Resun wil excusyn us alle:	
2571	He helde the ex by the helve.	*ax/handle*
	Thou[gh] he wil to foly falle,	
	It is to wytyn but himselve.	*No one's to blame*
	Whil he held him in this halle,	
	Fro dedly sinne we did him schelve.	*shield*
	He brewith himselfe a bittyr galle:	
	In dethys dint whanne he schal delve,	*death's blow/be buried*
	This game he schal be-grete.	*lament*
	He is endowyd with wittys five	
2580	For to rewlyn him in his live.	*life*
	We vertuse wil not with him strive—	
	Avise him and his dede!	*Let him consider what he does*

	CARITAS. Of his dede have we now[gh]t to done;	*With/nothing to do*
	He wil no lenger with us be lad.	*by/led*
	Whanne he askyd ou[gh]t, we herd his bone,	*anything/prayer*
	And of his presens we were ryth glad.	*presence*
	But, as thou seste, he hath forsakyn us sone;	*as you see/soon*
	He wil not don as Crist him bad.	*bade*
2589	Mary, thy Sone abovyn the mone,	*moon*
2590	As make Mankind trewe and sad,	*steadfast*
	In grace for to gon!	
	For, if he wil to Foly flit,	
	We may him not with-sit;	*prevent*
	He is of age, and can his wit,	*he knows his own mind*
	Ye knowe wel everychon.	

	ABSTINENTIA. Ichon, ye knowyn he is a fole,	*Each one*
	In Coveitise to dyth his dede.	*perform his deeds*
	Werldys wele is like a three-fotyd stole:	

2571 i.e., He controlled his own destiny (proverbial).

2589–90 Mary, may your Son above the moon (i.e., in heaven) make Mankind true and stead-fast.

It failit[h] a man at his most nede.

2599a   (*Mundus transit, et concupiscentia eius.*)

Whanne he is dyth in dedys dole,   *set in death's sorrow*

The ryth registre I schal him rede.   *The true register, judgment book*

He schal be tore with teneful tole;   *painful tools, weapons*

Whanne he schal brenne on glemys glede,   *burn in coals of bright flame*

He schal lere a new lawe.   *learn*

Be he nevere so riche of Werldys wone,   *wealth*

His seketourys schul makyn here mone: *executors will lament*

"Make us mery, and lete him gone!   *Let us make merry*

He was a good felawe."

CASTITAS.   Whanne he is ded, here sorwe is lest.   *their sorrow is very little*

The ton sekatour seyth to the tothyr,   *one/other*

"Make we mery, and a riche fest,

And lete him lyn in dedys fodyr."   *lie/death's company*

2612a   (*Et sic relinquent alienis divitias suas.*)

So his part schal be the lest;   *smallest*

The sister servit[h] thus the brother.

I lete a man no bet[t]yr thanne a best,   *consider/beast*

2616   For no man can be war by other   *wary*

2617   Til he hathe al ful spunne.

Thou schalt se that day, Man, that a bede *(prayer) bead*

Schal stonde the[e] more in stede   *Will avail you more*

Thanne al the good that thou mytist gete, *wealth/might get*

Certys, undyr sunne.

SOLICITUDO.   Mankinde! Of on[e] thinge have I wondyr,

That thou takist not into thin[e] mende: *mind, recollection*

Whanne body and sowle schul partyn on sundyr,

No Werldys good schal with the[e] wende.

2625a   (*Non descendet cum illo gloria eius.*)

Whanne thou art ded, and in the erthe leyd under,

Misgotyn good the[e] schal schende;   *Ill-gotten wealth/destroy*

2628   It schal the[e] weyen, as peys in punder,   *weight in scales*

Thy sely sowle to bringyn in bende,   *hapless/bondage*

And make it ful unthende.   *unprosperous*

And yit Mankind, as it is sene,   *i.e., as you see*

2599aThe world passes away, and the lust thereof (1 John 2:17).

2612aAnd thus they (the foolish) leave their wealth to others (Psalms 49:10).

2616–17For no one can learn prudence from others until he has gone completely through the experience himself.

2625aHis glory (i.e., his wealth) will not descend with him (Psalms 49:17).

2628It will weigh you down like a weight in a scales.

	With Coveitise goth on this grene!	*green, the "place"*
2633	The treytor doth us al this tene	*harm*
2634	Aftyr his livys ende.	

LARGITAS.   Out, I crye, and nothinge lowe,   *not softly*
On Coveitise, as I wel may!
Mankind seyth he hath nevere inowe   *enough*
Til his mowthe be ful of clay.

2638a   (*Avarus nunquam replebitur pecunia.*)
Whan[n]e he is closyd in dethys dow,   *in the grave*
What helpit[h] riches or gret aray?   *clothing*
It flyet[h] awey as any snow
Anon aftyr thye endinge day,

2643   To wilde Werldys wise. [*To the audience.*]
Now, good men alle that here be,
Have my sisterys excusyd, and me,   *Consider*
Thou[gh] Mankinde fro this castel fle;
Wite it Coveitise!   *Blame*

MALUS ANGELUS.   Ya! Go forthe, and lete the qwenys cakle!   *let/whores*
2649	Ther wymmen arn, are many wordys:	*Where*
2650	Lete hem gon hoppyn with here hakle!	*feathers*
2651	Ther ges sittyn are many tordys.	*Where geese sit/turds*
	With Coveitise thou renne on rakle,	*run in haste*
	And hange thine hert upon his hordys.	*hoards (of wealth)*
	Thou schalt be schakyn in min[e] schakle!	*shackle, fetters*
	Unbinde thy baggys on his bordys,	*Open/moneybags/tables*
	On his benchys above.	*i.e., on his scaffold?*
	Pardé, thou gost owt of Mankinde	*By God/are no part of*
	But Coveitise be in thy mende!	*Unless/mind*
	If evere thou thinke to be thende,	*prosperous*
	On him thou ley thy love.	

HUMANUM GENUS.   Nedys my love muste on him lende,   *My love must be settled on him*
With Coveitise to walter and wave.   *float and toss to and fro*
| 2663 | I knowe non[e] of al my kinde | *humankind* |
| 2664 | That he ne coveitith for to have— | |

2633–34 i.e., The false wretch behaves so that we virtues will be unable to plead his cause after his death.

2638a He who loves money will never be satiated with money (see Ecclesiastes 5:9–10).

2643 i.e., To serve the licentious World's fashion.

2649–51 Where there are women you'll find much talking, and where geese sit you'll find many turds (proverbial). Let them go hop about with their feathers.

2663–64 I know no one of all humankind who does not covet to own wealth.

Peny-man is mekyl in minde.   *Money (personified)|much*
My love in him I leye and lave.   *place and deposit*
Where that evere I walke or wende,   *Wherever I go*
2668 In wele and woo he wil me have;   *weal, happiness|keep*
He is gret of grace.
Whereso I walke in londe or lede,   *among men*
Peny-man best may spede;   *prosper*
He is a duke to don a dede
Now in every place.

BONUS ANGELUS.   Alas, that evere Mankinde was born!
On Coveitise is al his lust.
Nyth and day, midnyth and morn,
In Peny-man is al his trust.
Coveitise schal makyn him lorn   *lost*
Whanne he is dolven al to dust;   *delved, buried*
2680 To mekyl schame he schal be schorn,   *much|shorn, reduced*
With foule fendys to roten and rust.   *fiends|rot*
Alas! What schal I do?
Alas, alas! So may I say;
Man goth with Coveitise away!
Have me excusyd, for I ne may
Trewly not do therto.   *do (anything) about it*

MUNDUS.   A, a! This game goth as I wolde.   *would wish*
Mankinde wil nevere the Werld forsake!
Til he be ded, and undyr molde,   *underground*
2690 [W]holy to me he wil him take.
To Coveitise he hath him yolde;   *yielded himself*
With my wele he wil awake.   *well-being|be aroused*
For a thousende pounde I nolde   *should wish nothing more*
But Coveitise were Mans make,   *But that|mate*
Certys, on every wise.   *in every way*
All these gamys he schal bewaile,
For I, the Werld, am of this entaile: *disposition*
In his moste nede I schal him faile,
And al for Coveitise.

2700 AVARITIA.   Now, Mankind, be war of this:
Thou art a-party wele in age;   *somewhat well along*
I wolde not thou ferdist amis.   *fared*
Go we now knowe my castel cage.   *to become acquainted with*
    [*They go to Covetousness' "cupboard," near the end of the castle.*]
In this bowre I schal the[e] blys;   *bless, enrich*

2668He'll maintain me, in good times and bad.

Worldly wele schal be thy wage.   *well-being*
More mucke thanne is thine, iwis,   *wealth*
Take thou in this trost terage,   *Take in possession*
And loke that thou do wronge.
Coveitise, it is no sore,   *no sorrow*
2710   He wil the[e] feffen ful of store.   *endow*
And alwey, alwey, sey "more and more";
And that schal be thy songe.

HUMANUM GENUS.   A, Coveitise, have thou good grace!   *may you have*
Certys thou berist a trewe tonge: *you speak truly*
"More and more," in many a place,
Certys that songe is oftyn songe.
2717   I wiste nevere man, by bankys bace,   *i.e., anywhere*
2718   So seyn, in cley til he were clonge: *buried*
2719   "Inow, inow" hadde nevere space;   *"Enough"/opportunity*
That ful songe was nevere songe,
Nor I wil not beginne.
Goode Coveitise, I the[e] prey,
That I myth with the[e] pley!   *might*
Geve me good inow, or that I dey,   *enough wealth before I die*
To wonne in Werldys winne.   *live/joy*
    [*Covetousness gives Mankind riches from his "cupboard."*]

AVARITIA.   Have here, Mankind, a thousend marke!
I, Coveitise, have the[e] this gote.   *gotten this for you*
Thou mayst purchase therwith bothe ponde and parke,
And do therwith mekyl note.   *much profit*
2730   Lene no man hereof, for no karke,   *Lend, give/distress*
Thou[gh] he schulde hange by the throte,
Monke nor frere, prest nor clerke;
Ne helpe therwith chirche nor cote,   *cottage*
Til deth thy body delve.   *bury*
Thou[gh] he schuld sterve in a cave,
Lete no pore man therof have.
In grene gres til thou be grave,   *buried*
Kepe sumwhat fore thyself.

HUMANUM GENUS.   I vow to God, it is gret husbondry!   *thrifty management*
2740   Of the[e] I take these noblys rownde.   *nobles (a coin)*
I schal me rapyn, and that in hie,   *hurry/in haste*
To hide this gold under the grownde.
Ther schal it li[e] til that I die;

2717–19 I never know any person, anywhere, to say "Enough, enough" until he was buried
under earth; that song never had opportunity to be sung.

It may be kepte ther save and sownde.
Thou[gh] my neig[h]bore schuld be hangyn hie,
Therof getith he neithyr peny nor pownde.
Yit am I not wel at ese;
Now wolde I have castel wallys,
Stronge stedys, and stif in stallys.   *steeds|powerful*
2750   With hey holtys and hey hallys,   *tall woods*
Coveitise, thou muste me sese.   *endow*

AVARITIA.   Al schalt thou have al redy, lo,
At thin[e] owyn disposicion.
Al this good take the[e] to,   *take this wealth to yourself*
Cliffe and cost, toure and toun;   *coast*
Thus hast thou gotyn, in sinful slo,   *evil*
Of thine neig[h]borys, by extorcion.   *From*
"More and more" sey yit; have do   *go on*
Til thou be ded and drepyn doun;   *struck down*
2760   Werke on with Werldys wrenchys!   *deceits*
"More and more" sey yit, I rede: *advise*
To more thanne inow thou hast nede.   *For|enough*
Al this werld, bothe lenthe and brede,   *breadth*
Thy coveitise may not qwenche.
[*Covetousness leaves him to his frenzy.*]

HUMANUM GENUS.   Qwenche nevere no man may;   *No one can ever quench it*
Me thinkith nevere I have inow!
Ther ne is Werldys wele, nyth nor day,   *There's no worldly wealth*
But that me thinkith it is to[o] slow.
"More and more" yit I say,
2770   And schal evere, whil I may blow!   *speak, breathe*
On Coveitise is al my lay,   *In|faith*
And schal til deth me overthrow—
"More and more," this is my stevene.   *petition*
If I myth alwey dwellyn in prosperité,
Lord God, than[n]e wel were me!   *it would be well with me*
I wolde, the medys, forsake the[e],   *as reward*
And nevere to comyn in hevene.
[*Enter Death with a dart.*]

MORS.   Ow! now it is time hye   *Oh!|high time*
To castyn Mankind to dethys dint.   *blow*
2780   In all his werkys he is unslye;   *foolish*
Mekyl of his lif he hath mispent.   *Much*
To Mankind I ney ny;   *approach near*
With rewly rappys he schal be rent.   *grievous blows|torn*
Whanne I com, iche man drede forthy,   *fears on that account*

But yit is ther no geyn-went,   *no way back*
Hey hil, holte, nyn hethe.   *i.e., anywhere*
Ye schul me drede, everychone;   *everyone*
Whanne I come, ye schul grone!
My name in londe is lefte alone: *alone remains on earth*
2790   I hatte drery Dethe.   *I am called*

Drery is my deth-drawth;   *death-draught, potion*
Ageyns me may no man stonde.   *Against*
I durke, and down-bringe to nowth   *lie in wait/nought*
Lordys and ladys in every londe.
Whom-so I have a lessun tawth,
Onethys sithen schal he mowe stonde;   *Scarcely afterwards/be able to*
In my carful clothys he schal be cawth.   *harmful clothes (i.e., shroud)/caught*
Riche, pore, fre and bonde—   *slave*
Whanne I come, they goo no more.
2800   Whereso I wende, in any lede,   *nation*
Every man of me hat[h] drede.
Lette I wil, for no mede,   *I will not cease/reward*
To smite sadde and sore.   *heavily*

Dingne dukys arn a-dred   *Noble*
Whanne my b[l]astys arn on hem blowe.   *are blown at them*
Lordys in londe arn over-led;   *over-mastered*
With this launce I leye hem lowe.
Kingys kene, and knitys kyd,   *bold/renowned knights*
I do hem delvyn in a throwe.   *bury in a moment*
2810   In banke I buske hem a bed;   *Underground I prepare for them*
Sad sorwe to hem I sowe;   *sorrow*
I tene hem, as I trowe.   *harm*
As kene koltys thow[gh] they kynse,   *high-spirited colts/gibe*
Ageyns me is no defens.   *(there) is*
In the grete pestelens,   *plague (of the 14th century)*
Thanne was I wel knowe.   *known*

But now almost I am forgete;   *forgotten*
Men of Deth holde no tale.   *pay no heed*
In Coveitise here good they gete;   *they obtain their wealth*
2820   The grete fischys ete the smale.   *eat*
But whan[n]e I dele my derne dette,   *deal out my stealthy death-blow*
Tho prowde men I schal avale!   *Those/abase, lower*
Hem schal helpyn nother mel nor mete,   *Neither repast nor food will help them*
Til they be drevyn to Dethys dale.   *valley*
My lawe they schul lerne.
Ther ne is peny nor pownde
That any of you schal save sownde.   *That will save any of you*

	Til ye be gravyn undyr grownde,	*buried*
	Ther may no man me werne.	*stop me*
2830	To Mankinde now wil I reche.	*proceed*
	He hathe [w]hole his hert on Coveitise.	*wholly*
	A newe lessun I wil him teche,	
	That he schal bothe grucchyn and grise.	*complain and tremble*
	No lif in londe schal ben his leche;	*No living person|physician*
	I schal him prove of min[e] emprise.	*demonstrate my power*
	With this point I schal him breche,	*breach, pierce*
	And wappyn him in a woful wise;	*strike*
	Nobody schal ben his bote.	*help*
	[*Goes to Mankind.*]	
2839	I schal the[e] schapyn a schenful schappe:	*shameful appearance*
	Now I kille the[e] with min[e] knappe!	*blow*
	I reche to the[e], Mankind, a rappe	*give|blow*
	To thine herte rote!	
	[*He strikes Mankind with his dart.*]	

HUMANUM GENUS. A, Deth, Deth, drye is thy drifte!	*hard to endure	force*
Ded is my desteny.	*Death*
Min[e] hed is clevyn al in a clifte!	*cleaved*
For clappe of care now I crye;	*blow of sorrow*
Min[e] eye-ledys may I not lifte;	
Min[e] brainys waxyn al emptye;	
I may not onys min[e] hod up-schifte!	*once lift up my head*

2850	With Dethys dint now I dey!	*blow|die*
	Sir Werld, I am hent.	*seized*
	Werld, Werld, have me in mende!	*remember me*
	Goode Sir Werld, helpe now Mankend!	
	But thou me helpe, Deth schal me schende;	*Unless|destroy*
	He hat[h] dyth to me a dint.	*given*

	Werld, my wit waxit[h] wronge;	
	I chaunge bothe hide and hewe;	*complexion*
	Min[e] eye-ledys waxyn al outewronge.	*out-wrung (with tears)*
	But thou me helpe, sore it schal me rewe!	*Unless|grieve*
2860	Now holde that thou haste behete me longe:	*keep to what you promised*
	For all felechepys olde and newe,	*For the sake of*
	Lesse me of my peynys stronge!	*Release|pains*
	Sum bote of bale thou me brewe,	*remedy for sorrow*
	That I may of the[e] yelpe!	*speak (in praise)*
	Werld, for olde aqweyntawns,	

2839 I'll devise for you a shameful appearance.

Helpe me fro this sory chawns!   *miserable fortune*
Deth hathe lacchyd me with his launce!   *struck*
I deye but thou me helpe.   *die unless*

MUNDUS.   Owe, Mankind! Hathe Dethe with the[e] spoke?
2870 Ageyns him helpith no wage.   *challenge, payment*
      I wolde thou were in the erthe be-loke,   *locked up, buried*
      And another hadde thine [h]eritage!
      Oure bonde of love schal sone be broke;
      In colde clay schal be thy cage.
      Now schal the Werld on the[e] be wroke,   *avenged*
      For thou hast don so gret outrage: *Because*
      Thy good thou schalt forgoo.   *wealth*
      Werldys good thou hast forgon,
      And with tottys thou schalt be torn.   *by devils (?)*
2880 Thus have I servyd here beforn
      A hundryd thousand moo.

HUMANUM GENUS.   Ow, Werld, Werld, evere worthe wo!   *may woe ever befall you*
      And thou, sinful Coveitise!
      Whanne that a man schal fro you go,
      Ye werke with him on a wonder wise. [*To the audience.*] *in a wondrous way*
      The witte of this Werld is sorwe and wo.   *sorrow*
      Beware, good men, of this g[u]ise!
      Thus hathe he servyd many on[e] mo.   *many others*
      In sorwe slakith al his asise;   *His fashion ends in sorrow*
2890 He berith a teninge tungge.   *a harmful tongue*
      Whil I leyd with him my lott,   *entrusted/lot, fortune*
      Ye seyn whou faire he me be-hett;   *You saw how fairly he promised me*
      And now he wolde I were a clott,   *clod*
      In colde cley for to clinge.   *moulder*
          [*He falls dying on his bed, which has been located under the castle.*
          World, on his scaffold, calls to his servant.]

MUNDUS.   How, boy, arise! Now thou muste wende
      On min[e] erdyn, by steppe and stalle: *errand/i.e., everywhere*
      Go brewe Mankind a bittyr bende,   *bondage*
      And putte him oute of his halle—
      Lete him therinne no lenger lende.   *remain*
2900 For-brostyn, I trowe, be his galle,   *Burst to pieces/i.e., his innards*
      For thou art not of his kende.   *Because/kinship*
      All his [h]eritage wil the[e] wele befalle—   *will suit you well*
      Thus farith min[e] faire feres.   *companions*
      Oftyn time I have you told,

2870i.e., It's useless to challenge his might; or, worldly wealth is useless against him.

Tho men that ye arn to lest behold,   *to whom you are least beholden*
Comynly schal youre wonninge wold   *Usually|rule your dwelling*
And ben youre next [h]eirys.

GARCIO.   Werld worthy, in wedys wounde,   *Servant|wrapped in garments*
I thanke the[e] for thy grete gifte!
2910   I go glad upon this grounde
To putte Mankinde out of his thrifte.   *estate*
I trowe he stinkith this ilke stounde;   *very moment*
Into a lake I schal him lifte.   *pit|throw*
His parkys, placys, and penys rounde   *pennies, coins*
2915   With me schul driven, in this drifte,
In baggys as they ben bownde.
For I thinke for to dele,   *hand out (as executor)*
I vow to God, neithyr corn nore mele.
If he have a schete, he berith him wele,   *sheet, shroud|is well off*
2920   Whereinne he may be woun[de].
    Tunc iet ad Humanum Genus.   *Then he will go to Mankind*

Whou farist, Mankinde? Art thou ded?   *How fare you*
    [*He tries to pick Mankind up.*]
By Goddys body, so I wene.   *I think so*
He is hevier thanne any led!
I wold he were gravyn under grene.   *buried|green (grass)*

HUMANUM GENUS.   Abide! I breyd uppe with min[e] hed.   *I bestir myself*
What art thou? What woldist thou mene?   *do you intend*
2927   Wheydyr comist thou for good or qwed?   *Whether|evil*
With peynys pricke thou doste me tene,   *grief's torment|harm*
The sothe for to sey.
Telle me now, so God the[e] save,
Fro whom comist thou, good knave?
What dost thou here? Wha[t] woldist thou have?
Telle me or I deye.   *before I die*

GARCIO.   I am com to have al that thou hast.
Ponndys, parkys, and every place,
Al that thou hast gotyn first and last,
The Werld hathe grauntyd it me of his grace,
For I have ben his page.   *Because*
He wot wel thou schalt be ded,
2940   Neveremore to ete bred;

2915Will be obliged to go with me, in this forceful seizure.

2927Do you come for good or evil?

Therfore he hath for the[e] red   *determined*
Who schal have thine [h]eritage.

HUMANUM GENUS.   What, devil! Thou art not of my kin;
Thou dedist me nevere no maner good.   *did/no kind of*
I hadde lever sum nyfte, or sum cosyn,   *rather/nephew*
Or sum man hadde it of my blod;   *of my family*
In sum stede I wold it stod.   *I wish it were of some use*
Now schal I in a dale be delve,   *grave be buried*
And have no good therof myselve.   *from my wealth*
2950   By God and by his apostelys twelve,
I trowe the Werld be wod!   *mad*

GARCIO.   Ya, ya! Thy parte schal be the leste.   *insignificant*
Deye on, for I am maistyr here.   *Die*
I schal the[e] makyn a nobyl feste,
And thanne have I do min[e] devere.   *done my devoir, duty*
The Werld bad[e] me this gold areste,   *arrest, seize*
Holt and hallys, and castell clere.   *Woods*
The Werldys joye and his jentyl jeste   *entertainment (?)*
Is now thine, now min[e], bothe fere and nere.   *far and near (i.e., everywhere)*
2960   Go hens, for this is mine.   *hence*
Syn thou art ded, and browth of dawe,   *Since/brought to death*
Of thy deth, sir, I am ryth fawe.   *very glad*
Thou[gh] thou knowe not the Werldys lawe,
He hath gove me al that was thine.   *given*

HUMANUM GENUS.   I preye the[e] now, syn thou this good   *since/wealth*
        schalt gete,
Telle thy name or that I goo.   *before*

GARCIO.   Loke that thou it not forgete:
My name is "I wot nevere whoo."   *I don't know who*

HUMANUM GENUS.   "I wot nevere who"? So welaway!   *alas*
2970   Now am I sory of my lif!   *for*
I have purchasyd, many a day,
Londys and rentys with mekyl strif;   *much*
I have purchasyd holt and hay,   *woods*
Parkys and ponndys, and bourys blife,   *joyful bowers*
Goode gardeynys, with griffys gay,   *groves*
To mine childyr and to min[e] wife   *For*
In dethe whanne I were dyth.   *should be put*
Of my purchas I may be wo;   *woeful*
For, as [I] thout it is not so,   *it isn't as I thought*
2980   But a gedelinge, "I wot nevere who,"   *gadabout*

Hath al that the Werld me be-hith.   *promised me*

Now, alas, my lif is lak!   *poverty*
Bitter balys I ginne to brewe.   *sorrows*
Certys, a vers that David spak
I the sawter, I finde it trewe: *In the psalter*
2985a (*Thesaurizat, et ignorat cui congregabit ea.*)
Tresor, tresor, it hathe no tak;   *endurance*
It is other mens, olde and newe.
Ow, ow! My good gothe al to wrak!   *wealth/to ruin*
Sore may Mankind rewe;
2990   God kepe me fro dispair!
Al my good, without[en] faile,
I have gadryd with gret travaile,   *(Which) I/labor*
The Werld hathe ordeynyd of his entaile   *entail, determining of heirs*
"I wot nevere who" to be min[e] [h]eir.

     [*To the audience.*]
Now, good men, takithe example at me: *take/from*
Do for yourself whil ye han spase!   *Provide/have time*
For many men thus servyd be,
Thorwe the Werld, in diverse place.   *Throughout*
2999   I bolne and bleyke in blody ble,   *swell/turn pale/complexion*
And as a flour fadith my face.   *flower*
To helle I schal bothe fare and fle   *go and depart*
But God me graunte of his grace.   *Unless*
I deye, certeynly!   *die*
Now my life I have lore.   *lost*
Min[e] hert brekith. I syhe sore.
A word may I speke no more.
I putte me in Goddys mercy! [*Dies.*]
     [*Mankind's Soul crawls from beneath Mankind's bed. The
     Good and Bad Angels come forward.*]

ANIMA.   "Mercy!" This was my last tale
That evere my body was a-bowth.   *about, concerned with*
3010   But Mercy helpe me in this vale,   *Unless/i.e., perilous situation*
Of dampninge drinke sore I me doute.   *sorely/fear*
     [*The Soul addresses the body.*]
Body, thou dedist brew a bittyr bale,   *sorrow*
To thy lustys whanne gannist loute!   *When you yielded to your lusts*
Thy sely sowle schal ben a-kale.   *wretched/frozen (in hell)*

2985a Man heaps up treasure, and does not know to whom it will accumulate (Psalms 39:6).

2999 I swell, and my ruddy complexion turns pale.

I beye thy dedys with rewly rowte;   *I pay for|grievous blows*
And al it is for g[u]ile.
Evere thou hast be coveitows,
Falsly to getyn londe and hows.
To me thou hast browyn a bitter jows—   *brewed|juice, drink*
3020   So welaway the while!   *alas for this unlucky time*

        [*To the Good Aungel.*]
Now, swet Aungel, what is thy red?   *advice*
The ryth red thou me reche!   *Give me good advice*
Now my body is dressyd to ded,   *prepared for death*
Helpe now me, and be my leche!   *healer*
Dyth thou me fro develys drede;   *Put*
Thy worthy weye thou me teche!
I hope that God wil helpyn and be min[e] hed,
For "Mercy" was my laste speche:
Thus made my body his ende.
        *   *   *   *   *   *   *

3030   [MALUS ANGELUS.]   Wittnesse of all that ben abowte,   *that are here*
3031   Sir Coveitise he had him owte;
Therfor he schal, withoutyn dowte,
With me to helle pitt.

        BONUS ANGELUS.   Ye, alas, and welawo!
Ageyns Coveitise can I not telle.   *speak, argue*
Resun wil I fro the[e] goo,   *Reason determines that*
For, wrechyd Sowle, thou muste to helle.
Coveitise he was thy fo;
He hathe the[e] schapyn a schameful schelle.   *fashioned you|dwelling (in hell)*
3040   Thus hathe [he] servyd many on[e] mo,   *many others*
Til they be dyth to dethys delle,   *put|dell, pit*
To bittyr balys bowre.   *sorrow's bower*
Thou muste to peyne, by ryth resun,   *by just reason*
With Coveitise, for he is chesun.   *cause*
Thou art trappyd ful of tresun,
But Mercy be thy socowre.   *Unless|succour, aid*

For, ryth wel this founde I have: *this I've found truly*
Ageyns Rithwisnesse may I not holde.   *Righteousness, Justice*
Thou muste with him to careful cave,   *him (the Bad Angel)|sorrowful*
3050   For grete skillys that he hathe tolde.   *reasons*

3030-31As everyone here can witness, Sir Covetousness enticed Mankind out (of the castle).
(A leaf is missing from the MS at this point, in which the debate between the Good and Bad
Angels has evidently continued.)

Fro the[e] awey I wandyr and wave;   *turn away*
For the[e] I clinge in carys colde.   *waste away in sorrows*
Alone now I the[e] lave,   *leave*
Whilist thou fallist in fendys folde,   *the fiends' enclosure*
In helle to hide and hille.   *be sheltered*
Ritwisnesse wil that thou wende   *Justice determines*
Forthe awey with the fende.
But Mercy wil to the[e] sende,   *Unless*
Of the[e] can I no skille.   *I can do nothing for you*

  ANIMA.   Alas, Mercy, thou art to[o] longe!   *too long (in coming)*
     Of sadde sorwe now may I singe.   *sorrow*
3062 Holy writ, it is ful wronge,
3063 But Mercy pase alle thinge.   *Unless/surpass*
I am ordeynyd to peynys stronge;   *ordained, ordered/pains*
In wo is dressyd min[e] wonninge;   *prepared my dwelling*
In helle on hokys I schal honge.   *hooks/hang*
But Mercy fro a welle springe,   *Unless Mercy spring from a fountain*
This devil wil have me away.
Weleaway! I was ful wod   *totally mad*
3070 That I forsoke min[e] Aungyl Good,
And with Coveitise stod   *stood, stayed*
Til that day that I schuld dey.   *die*

  MALUS ANGELUS.   Ya! Why woldist thou be coveitous,
And drawe the[e] again to sinne?   *turn*
I schal the[e] brewe a bittyr jous: *juice*
In bolninnge bondys thou schalt brenne;   *swelling bonds/burn*
In hye helle schal be thine hous!
In picke and ter, to grone and grenne,   *pitch and tar/gnash teeth*
Thou schalt lie drenkelyd as a mous.   *drowned*
Ther may no man ther-fro the[e] werne   *defend you from it*
3081 For that ilke will.   *same desire*
That day the ladys thou forsoke,
And to my counsel thou the[e] toke,   *betook yourself*
Thou were betyr an-hangyn on hoke   *to have hanged*
Upon a jebet hill.   *gibbet, gallows*

Farter fowle! Thou schalt be frayed   *Foul farter/bruised*
Til thou be frettyd and al for-bled.   *gnawed/bloody*
Foule mote thou be dismayed,   *May you be foully discomfited*
That thou schalt thus ben ovyrled!   *overmastered*

3062–63(Refers to Psalms 145:9: "God's compassion is over all that he has made.")

3081i.e., For your desire to be covetous.

3090	For Coveitise thou hast asayed,	*Because/tried*
	In bittyr balys thou schalt be bred.	*sorrows/roasted*
3092	Al mankind may be wel payed	*satisfied*
3093	Whou Coveitise makith the[e] a-dred.	*How*
	With rappys I the[e] ringe.	*With blows I make you resound*
	We schul to hell, bothe t[w]o,	
	And bey in inferno.	*suffer*
3097	*Nulla est redemptio*	*There is no redemption (in hell)*
	For no kinnys thinge.	*no kind of, no*
	Now dagge we hens a dogge-trot;	*jog/hence*
	In my dongion I schal the[e] dere.	*dungeon/harm*
	On the[e] is many a sinful spot;	
3102	Therfore this schame I schal the[e] schere	*cut off*
	Whanne thou comist to my neste.	
3104	Why woldist thou—schrewe, schalt nevere the[e]—	*you'll never prosper*
3105	But in thy live don aftyr me?	*do after, follow*
	And thy Good Aungyl tawth the[e]	*taught*
	Alwey to the beste.	
	Ya! But thou woldist him not leve;	*believe*
	To Coveitise alwey thou drow.	*drew, were enticed*
3110	Therfore schalt thou evil preve.	*experience evil*
	That foul sinne thy soule slow.	*slew*
	I schal fonde the[e] to greve	*seek to grieve you*
	And putte the[e] in peynnys plow.	*harness you to pain's*
	Have this! and evil mote thou scheve! [*Strikes.*]	*may you prosper evilly*
	For thou seydist nevere "Inow, Inow,"	*Because/Enough*
3116	Thus lacche I the[e] thus lowe.	*strike*
	Thow[gh] thou kewe as a kat,	*mew*
	For thy coveitise have thou that! [*Strikes.*]	
	I schal the[e] bunche with my bat,	*hit*
	And rouge the[e] on a rowe.	*rough you up in order*
	Lo, sinful tidinge, [*Beats him again.*]	
	Boy, on thy bak I bringe.	
	Spedely thou springe!	*Jump fast*

3090Because you followed the paths of Covetousness.

3092–93i.e., All men must be content with the just punishment by which your own covetousness has put you in fear of torture.

3097(From the Office of the Dead.)

3102Therefore I'll cut out these sinful spots in you (with torturing instruments).

3104–5Why would you only follow me during your life? Rascal, you'll never prosper.

3116Thus I humble you with blows.

Thy *Placebo* I schal singe.   *Vespers for the dead*

To devclys delle   *pit*
I schal the[e] bere to helle.
I wil not dwelle. [*To the audience.*]
Have good day! I goo to hellc.
    [*He takes the Soul to hell. On the platea come forward the four
    daughters of God: Mercy in a white mantle, Truth in green,
    Righteousness in red, and Peace in black.*]

    MISERICORDIA.   A mone I herd of "Mercy" meve,   *I heard a cry for mercy*
3130 And to me, Mercy, gan crye and call.
    But if it have mercy, sore it schal me greve,   *Unless*
    For ell[ys] it schal to hell fall.   *otherwise*
    Rithwisnes, my sister cheve,   *Righteousness/chief*
    This ye herde—so dide we all,
3135 For we were mad[e] frendys leve   *dear*
    Whanne the Jewys proferyd Criste eysyl and gall   *vinegar*
    On the Good Friday.
    God grauntyd that remission,
    Mercy, and absolicion,
3140 Thorwe vertu of his Passion,
    To no man schuld be seyd nay.   *denied*

    Therfore, my sister[s] Ritwisnes,
    Pes, and Trewthe, to you I tell:
    Whanne man crieth "Mercy," and wil not ses,   *cease*
    Mercy schal be his waschinge well—   *fountain of cleansing*
    Witnesse of holy kirke.   *As the holy church testifies*
    For, the leste drope of blode   *(even) the smallest*
    That God bledde on the rode,   *cross*
    It hadde ben satisfaccion goode   *would have been*
3150 For al Mankindys werke.   *deeds*

    JUSTITIA.   Sistyr, ye sey me a good skil   *say truly*
    That mercy pasit[h] mannys misdede;   *surpasses*
    But, take mercy whoso wil,   *Whoever will receive mercy*
    He muste it aske with love and drede.
    And every man that wil fulfill
    The Dedly Sinnys, and folw[e] misdede,   *follow, practice sin*
    To graunte hem mercy, me thinkith it no skil. *them/unreasonable*
    And therfore, sistyr, you I rede   *advise*
    Lete him abye his misdede.   *pay for*

3135For we sisters were made dear friends (i.e., the conflicting principles of mercy and justice
were reconciled by Christ's atonement).

For, thou[gh] he lie in hell and stinke,

It schal me nevere overthinke.   *trouble*

As he hath browyn, lete him drinke!   *brewed*

The devil schal qwite him his mede.   *pay/reward*

3163a   (*Unusquisque suum onus portabit.*)

Trowe ye that whanne a man schal deye,   *die*

Thanne thow[gh] that he mercy crave,   *Though he ask mercy then*

That anon he schal have mercye?   *at once*

Nay, nay, so Crist me save!

3167a   (*Non omne qui dicit "Domine, Domine" intrabit regnum caelorum.*)

3168   For, schuld no man do no good

3169   All the dayes of his live,

3170   But hope of mercy by the rode,   *by means of the cross*

3171   Schulde make bothe werre and strive,

3172   And torne to gret grevaunse.   *turn/grievance*

Whoso in hope dothe any Dedly Sinne

To his livys ende, and wil not blinne,   *cease*

Rytfully thanne schal he winne

Cristys gret vengaunse.

VERITAS.   Ritwisnes, my sister fre,   *noble*

Your jugement is good and trewe,

In good feyth, so thinkith me.

Late him his owyn dedys rewe!   *Let/rue*

I am "*Veritas*," and trew wil be,

In word and werke, to olde and newe.

3183   Was nevere man, in fawte of me,   *default*

3184   Dampnyd nor savyd but it were dew.   *unless/merited*

I am evere at mans ende.   *end, death*

Whanne body and sowle partyn a-twinne,   *part in two*

Thanne wey I his goode dedys and his sinne;   *weigh*

And, w[h]eyder of hem be more or minne,   *whichever of them/less*

He schal it ryth sone finde.   *very soon*

3190   For I am Trewthe, and trewthe wil bere,   *bear, tell*

As grete God himself us bid.   *bade*

Ther schal nothinge the sowle dere   *harm*

3163a[For] every man will bear his own burden (Galatians 6:5).

3167a-72Not everyone that says "Lord, Lord" will enter into the kingdom of heaven (Matthew 7:21). For, if a person should practice no virtue all his life, but hope instead to be saved by Christ's mercy, (his doing so) would make for contention and strife, and produce great distress.

3183-84No man was ever unjustly damned for lacking me, Truth, or unmeritoriously saved by my means.

But sinne that the body did.
Sith that he deyed in that coveitous sinne,   *Since/he (Mankind)*
I, Trewthe, wil that he goo to pyne.   *(eternal) pain*
Of that sinne cowde he not blinne;   *could/cease*
Therfor, he schal his sowle tyne   *lose*
To the pitte of hell.
Ellys schuld we, bothe Trewthe and Ritwisnes,   *Otherwise*
Be put to over-mekyl distresse,   *overmuch*
3201 And every man schuld be the wers   *worse*
3202 That therof myth here tell.   *might hear*

PAX.   Pes, my sister Verité!
I preye you, Ritwisnes, be stille!
Lete no man by you dampnyd be,
Nor deme ye no man to helle.   *condemn*
3207 He is on kin til us thre,   *akin to*
Thow[gh] he have now not al his wille.
For His love that deyed on tre,   *died on cross*
Late save Mankind fro al perile,   *Let Mankind be saved*
And schelde him fro mischaunsse!
If ye tweyne putte him to distresse,   *twain (Righteousness and Truth)*
It schuld make gret hevinesse
Betwene us tweyne, Mercy and Pes—   *Among*
And that were gret grevaunce.

Ritwisnes and Trewthe, do by my red,   *advice*
And Mercy, go we to yone hey place.   *high*
[*She points to God's scaffold in the east.*]
We schal enforme the hey Godhed,
And pray him to deme this case.   *judge*
3220 Ye schal tell him youre entent
Of Trewthe and of Ritwisnesse;
And we schal pray that his jugement
May pase by us, Mercy and Pes.   *May be rendered*
All foure now go we hens   *hence*
Wytly to the Trinité,   *Quickly*
And ther schal we sone se
What that his jugement schal be,
Withoutyn any deffens.   *remedy, appeal*
Tunc ascende[n]t ad Patrem omnes pariter, et dicet Verita[s]:   *Then all will ascend together to the Father; and Truth will say*

VERITAS.   Heyl, God al-myth!

3201-2And every man would be worse off to hear of it (i.e., of sin unpunished; for then men should lack moral restraints).

3207us thre: i.e., Christ, Mercy, and Peace.

3230   We cum, thy dowterys in syth,   *sight*
        Trewth, Mercy, and Ryth,   *Right*
        And Pes, pesible in fyth.   *peaceably disposed in argument*

        MISERICORDIA.   We cum to preve   *determine*
        If Man, that was the[e] ful leve,   *to you very dear*
        If he schal cheve   *attain*
        To hell or hevene, by thy leve.   *permission*

        JUSTITIA.   I, Ritwisnes,
        Thy dowtyr, as I ges,   *guess, believe*
        Late me neverethelesse   *Let*
3240   At thy dom putte me in pres.

        PAX.   Pesible kinge,
        I, Pes, thy dowtyr yinge,   *young*
        Here my preyinge   *(May you) hear*
        Whanne I pray the[e], Lord, of a thinge.

        DEUS.   Welcum in fere,   *together*
        Bryther thanne blossum on brere!   *Brighter/(rose-)briar*
        My dowterys dere,
        Cum forth and stand ye me nere.

        VERITAS.   Lord, as thou art king of kingys crownyd with
                crowne,
        As thou loviste me, Trewthe, thy dowtyr dere,
        Lete nevere me, Trewthe, to fall a-downe,
        My feythful Fadyr *saunz pere!*   *without peer*
3252a   (*Quoniam veritatem dilexisti.*)
        For in all trewthe standith thy renowne,
        Thy feyth, thy hope, and thy powere.
        Lete it be sene, Lord, now, at thy dome,   *judgment*
        That I may have my trewe prayere
        To do trewthe to Mankind.
        For, if Mankind be dempte by ryth,   *judged by righteousness*
        And not by mercy, most of myth,   *might*
3260   Here my trewthe, Lord, I the[e] plyth: *Here I plight my troth*
        In presun Man schal be pynyd.   *tormented*

        Lord, whow schuld Mankind be savyd,   *how*
        Syn he died in dedly sinne   *Since*

---

³²⁴⁰Let me be included in your judgment.

³²⁵²ᵃFor you have loved truth (see Psalms 51:6).

And all thy comaundementys he depravyd, · · · · · · · · · · · · · · *desecrated*

And of fals covetise he wolde nevere blinne? · · · · · · · · · · · · · · *cease*

3265a (*Aurum sitisti; aurum bibisti.*)

The more he hadde, the more he cravyd,

3267 Whil the lif lefte him withinne.

But he be dampnyd, I am abavyd · · · · · · · · · · · · · · *Unless/ashamed*

That Trewthe schuld com of Ritwys kinne, · · · · · · · · · · · · · · *Righteousness'*

And I am thy dowter Trewthe. · · · · · · · · · · · · · · *And (that)*

Thou[gh] he cried "Mercy" *moriendo,* · · · · · · · · · · · · · · *in dying*

Nimis tarde paenitendo, · · · · · · · · · · · · · · *Repenting much too late*

Talem mortem reprehendo. · · · · · · · · · · · · · · *I condemn such a death*

Lete him drinke as he brewith!

Late repentaunce if Man save scholde, · · · · · · · · · · · · · · *If late repentance should save Man*

Wheyther he wrouth wel or wickidnesse, · · · · · · · · · · · · · · *Whether/wrought*

Thanne every man wold be bolde

To trespas, in trost of forgevenesse.

3279 For, sinne in hope is dampnyd, I holde;

Forgevyn is nevere his traspase. · · · · · · · · · · · · · · *his (any such man's)*

He sinnith in the Holy Gost many-folde.

That sinne, Lord, thou wilt not reles · · · · · · · · · · · · · · *release, remit*

In this werld nor in the tother.

3284 *Quia veritas manet in aeternum,* · · · · · · · · · · · · · · *Because truth endures eternally,*

Tendit homo ad infernum; · · · · · · · · · · · · · · *Man goes to hell;*

Nunquam venit ad supernum, · · · · · · · · · · · · · · *By no means comes he to heaven*

Thou[gh] he were my brother.

For Man on molde halt welthe and wele, · · · · · · · · · · · · · · *on earth holds/weal*

Lust and likinge, in al his life, · · · · · · · · · · · · · · *pleasure*

3290 Techinge, prechinge in every sele— · · · · · · · · · · · · · · *season, time*

3291 But he forgetith the Lord belive. · · · · · · · · · · · · · · *quickly*

Hye of hert, happe, and hele, · · · · · · · · · · · · · · *High, proud/fortune/health*

Gold and silvyr, child and wif[e],

Denteth drinke at mete and mele, · · · · · · · · · · · · · · *Dainty*

3295 Unnethe the[e] to thanke he cannot kith · · · · · · · · · · · · · · *Scarcely/show*

3296 In any maner thinge.

Whanne Mans welthe ginnith awake,

3265a You thirsted for gold; you have drunk gold.

3267 i.e., While his inner spiritual life dwindled away.

3279 For I maintain that sin committed in hope of forgiveness is damnable.

3284 (See Psalms 117:2.)

3290–91 i.e., (Yet despite his well-being) and the exhortations to virtuous living he hears on every occasion, Man quickly forgets his Lord.

3295–96 (Yet) he can scarcely show you thanks in anything.

Ful sone, Lord, thou art forsake.
As he hathe browne and bake,   *brewed and baked*
Trewthe wil that he drinke.   *wishes, decrees*

For, if Man have mercy and grace,
Thanne I, thy dowtyr Sothfastnesse,   *Truth*
At thy dom schal have no place,   *judgment*
But be putte a-bak by wronge dures.   *duress*
Lord, lete me nevere fle thy fair face,   *be absent from*
To make my power any lesse!
I pray the[e], Lord, as I have space,   *opportunity*
Late Mankind have dew distresse   *Let/merited*
In helle-fere to be brent!   *fire/burned*
In peyne loke he be stille,   *See to it he be in pain perpetually*
Lord, if it be thy wille;
Or ell[ys] I have no skille   *have no ability (in judging)*
By thy trew jugement.

3313a MISERICORDIA.   *(O Pater misericordiarum et Deus totius consola-*
            tionis, qui consolatur nos in omni tribulatione nostra!)

O thou Fadyr, of mytys moste,   *mights, powers*
Merciful God in Trinité,
I am thy dowter, wel thou woste,   *know*
And Mercy fro hevene thou browtist fre.   *brought willingly*
Schew me thy grace in every coste;   *region (everywhere)*
In this cas[e] my counforte be!   *i.e., judicial case*
Lete me, Lord, nevere be loste
At thy jugement, whou-so it be,   *howsoever*
Of Mankind.
3323   Ne had Mans sinne nevere cum in cas,   *into question*
I, Mercy, schuld nevere in erthe had plas.
Therfore graunte me, Lord, thy grace,
That Mankind may me find.

And mercy, Lord, have on this man,
Aftyr thy mercy, that mekyl is,   *According to/great*
3329   Unto thy grace that he be tan,   *taken*
3330   Of thy mercy that he not mis!
As thou descendist fro thy trone
And lyth in a maidyns wombe, iwis—   *alighted*

3313aOh Father of mercies and God of all comfort, who comforts us in all our tribulation (2 Corinthians 1:3–4).

3323If Man's sin had never come into question.

3329–30So that he be taken to your grace (and) not be deprived of your mercy.

Incarnat was in blod and bone—
Lat Mankind cum to thy blis,
As thou art kinge of hevene!
For werldly veynglory
He hathe ben ful sory,
Punchyd in purgatory   *Punished*
For all the sinnys sevene.

3339a   (*Si pro peccato vetus Adam non cecidisset,*
         Mater pro nato nunquam gravidata fuisset.)
         Ne had Adam sinnyd here before,   *Had not Adam*
         And thy hestys in paradis had offent,   *commands/broken*
         Nevere of thy moder thou schuldist a be bore, *have been born*
         Fro hevene to erthe to have be sent.   *been*
         But thirty winter here, and more,   *years*
         Bowndyn, and betyn, and al to-schent,   *gravely harmed*
         Scornyd and scourgyd, sadde and sore,
         And on the rode rewly rent,   *cross grievously torn*
3348   *Passus sub Pilato Pontio.*   *He suffered under Pontius Pilate*
         As thou henge on the croys,   *hung/cross*
3350   On hye thou madiste a vois—   *Aloud*
3351   Mans helthe, the Gospel seys—
3352   Whanne thou seydist "*Sitio.*"   *I thirst*
3352a   (*Scilicet, salutem animarum.*)

         Than[n]e the Jewes, that were unquert,   *hostile*
         Dressyd the[e] drinke, eysyl and galle.   *Prepared/vinegar*
         It to taste thou myth nowth stirt,   *might not avoid*
         But seyd "*Consummatum est,*" was alle.   *It is finished*
         A knyt with a spere so smert,   *knight/sharp*
         Whanne thou forgafe thy fo-men thrall,   *servile foes*
         He stonge the[e], Lord, unto the hert.   *stung, pierced*
         Thanne watyr and blod gan oute wall,   *welled out*
3361   *Aqua baptismatis et sanguis redemptionis.*
         The watyr of baptomm,   *baptism*
         The blod of redempcioun
         That fro thin[e] herte ran doun,
         Est causa salvationis.   *Is the cause of salvation*

3339a If through sin old Adam had not fallen, your mother would never have been made heavy with child.

3348 (From the Apostles' Creed.)

3350–52a You called aloud—for man's health, according to the Gospels—when you said "I thirst." That is to say, "(I thirst) for the salvation of souls." (This was a common exegetical interpretation in the Middle Ages of Christ's "I thirst.")

3361 The water of baptism and the blood of redemption.

Lord, thou[gh] that Man hathe don more misse thanne   *amiss*
    good,
If he dey in very contricioun,   *die/true*
Lord, the lest drope of thy blod   *least*
For his sinne makith satisfaccioun.
As thou deydist, Lord, on the rode,   *died/cross*
Graunt me my peticioun!
Lete me, Mercy, be his fode,   *nourisher*
And graunte him thy salv[a]cion,
3374   *Quia dixisti "Misericordiam servabo."*
"Mercy" schal I singe and say,
And *"Miserere"* schal I pray   *Have mercy*
For Mankind evere and ay.
3378   *Misericordias Domini in aeternum cantabo.*

JUSTITIA.   Rithwys kinge, Lord God almyth,   *Righteous/almighty*
I am thy dowter Rithwisnesse.
Thou hast lovyd me evere, day and nyth,
As wel as other, as I gesse.   *as the others*
3382a   *(Justitias Dominus justitia dilexit.)*
3383   If thou Mans kinde fro peyne aquite,
3384   Thou dost ageyns thine owyn processe.   *against*
Lete him in preson to be pyth   *put*
For his sinne and wickidnesse,
Of a bone I the[e] pray.   *I beg you as a favor*
Ful oftyn he hathe the[e], Lord, forsake,   *forsaken*
And to the devil he hathe him take.   *betaken himself*
Lete him lyn in hell lake,   *lie/pit*
Dampnyd for evere and ay!
3391a   *(Quia Deum, qui se genuit, dereliquit.)*

For, whanne Man to the werld was born,
He was browth to holy kirke,   *church*
Feythly followd in the funte-ston,   *Devoutly baptized /font*
And wesch fro original sinne so dirke.   *washed/dark*
Satanas he forsok as his fone,   *foe*
All his pompe and al his werke,
And hyth to serve the[e] alone—   *promised*

3374Because you have said, "I will keep my mercy (for man)" (see Psalms 89:28).

3378I will sing of the mercies of the Lord forever (Psalms 89:1).

3382a–84The Lord of righteousness has loved righteous deeds (see Psalms 11:7–8). If you release Mankind from punishment, you act against your own summons at law.

3391aFor he has forsaken God, who created him (lit: created himself; but see Deuteronomy 32:18).

To kepe thy commandementys he schuld not irke,   *be loath*
Sicut justi tui.   *According to your just decree*
But whanne he was com to mans astate,
All his behestys he thanne forgate.   *promises*
He is worthy be dampnyd for that,   *(to) be*
3404   Quia oblitus est Domini creatoris sui.

For he hathe forgetyn the[e] that him wrout   *who created him*
And formydiste him like thine owyn face,   *formed*
And with thy precious blod him bowth,   *bought, ransomed*
And in this world thou geve him space.   *gave*
All thy benefetys he set at nowth,   *nought*
3410   But toke him to the Develys trase.   *course*
The Fl[e]sch, the World was most in [h]is thowth
And purpose, to plese hem in every plase,   *them*
So grimly on grounde.   *on earth*
I pray the[e], Lord lovely,
Of Man have no mercy,
But, dere Lord, lete him ly;
In hell lete him be bounde!

Man hathe forsake the kinge of hevene   *forsaken*
And his Good Aungels governaunce,
3420   And solwyd his soule with sinnys sevene   *sullied*
By his Badde Aungels comberaunce.   *temptation*
Vertuis he putte ful evyn away   *wholly*
Whanne Coveitise gan him avaunce.   *assisted him*
He wende that he schulde a levyd ay,   *thought/have lived forever*
Til dethe tripte him on his daunce—   *in*
He loste his wittys five.
Ovyr-late he callyd confescioun;   *Too late*
Over-lyt was his contricioun;   *Too little*
He made nevere satisfaccioun.
3430   Dampne him to helle belive!   *quickly*

For if thou take Mans sowle to the[e]
Ageyns thy rithwisnesse,   *Contrary to*
Thou dost wronge, Lorde, to Trewth and me,
And puttys us fro oure dewnesse.   *what is our due*
Lord, lete us nevere fro the[e] fle,   *be absent*
Ner streyne us nevere in stresse,   *Nor restrain/by force*
3437   But late thy dom be by us thre   *let/judgment*

[3404]For he has forgotten God who created him (lit: of his creation; see Deuteronomy 32:18).

[3437]*us thre:* i.e., God, Righteousness, and Truth.

Mankinde in hell to presse,   *thrust*
Lord, I the[e] beseche!
For Rithwisnes dwell[ys] evere sure   *stands, remains*
To deme Man aftyr his deserviture;   *according to his deserving*
For, to be dampnyd, it is his ure.   *usual fate*
On Man I crye wreche!   *vengeance*

3443a   *(Laetabitur justus cum viderit vindictam.)*

MISERICORDIA.   Mercy, my sister Rithwisnes!
Thou schape Mankinde no schonde!   *Fashion Mankind no shame*
Leve sister, lete be thy dresse;   *Beloved/cease your (severe) conduct*
To save Man lete us fonde!   *try*
For, if Man be dampnyd to hell dirknes,
Thanne myth I wringyn min[e] honde   *might*
3450   That evere my state schulde be les,   *condition/inferior*
My fredam to make bonde.   *put in bondage*
Mankind is of oure kin!
For I, Mercy, pase al thinge   *Because/surpass*
That God made at the beginninge,
And I am his dowter yinge,   *And (because)/young*
Dere sister, lete be thy din!

3456a   *(Et misericordia eius super omnia opera eius.)*

Of Mankinde aske thou nevere wreche   *On/vengeance*
By day ner by nyth,   *nor*
For God himself hath ben his leche,   *healer*
Of His merciful myth;   *might*
3461   To me He gan him be-teche,   *God entrusted him (Man)*
3462   Beside al His Ryth.   *Against/Justice*
For him wil I prey and preche
To gete him fre respyth,   *respite*
And my sister Pese.   *And (so will)*
For His mercy is without beginninge
And schal be withoutyn endinge,
As David seyth, that worthy kinge;
In Scriptur is no les.   *lie*

3469a   *(Et misericordia eius a progenie in progenies, et cetera.)*

VERITAS.   Mercy is Mankinde non[e] worthy,   *Mankind is not worthy of mercy*

3443aThe righteous man will rejoice when he sees the vengeance (Psalms 58:10).

3456aAnd his mercy is over all his works (see Psalms 145:9).

3461–62God entrusted Man to me, Mercy, offsetting God's strict Justice.

3469aAnd his mercy (is) from generation to generation and so on (from the *Magnificat*, Luke 1:50).

David thou[gh] thou recorde and rede;   *recite and read*
For he wolde nevere the hungry
Neither clothe nor fede,
Ner drinke gif to the thristy,
Nyn pore men helpe at nede.   *Nor*
For if he did non[e] of these, forthy   *therefore*
In hevene he getith no mede—   *meed, reward*
So seyth the Gospel.
For he hathe ben unkinde   *Because/been*
3480   To lame and to blinde,
In helle he schal be pinde: *pained, tormented*
So is resun and skil.   *reason*

PAX.   Pesible king in majesté,
I, Pes, thy dowter, aske the[e] a bonn   *boon, request*
Of Man, whou-so it be.   *howsoever*
Lord, graunte me min[e] askinge sonn,   *soon*
That I may evermore dwelle with the[e]
As I have evere yit donn;
And lat me nevere fro the[e] fle,   *be absent*
3490   Sp[e]cialy at thy dome
Of Man, thy creature.
Thou[gh] my sister[s], Ryth and Trewthe,
Of Mankind have non[e] rewthe,   *ruth, pity*
Mercy and I ful sore us mewithe   *move, bestir ourselves*
To cacche him to our cure.   *take/care, charge*

3496   For, whanne thou madist erthe and hevyn,
3497   Ten orderys of aungelys to ben in blis,   *be*
3498   Lucifer, lyter thanne the levyn   *brighter/lightning*
3499   Til whanne he sinnyd he fel, iwis;
To restore that place ful evyn,   *exactly*
Thou madist Mankind with this   *with this purpose, thereupon*
To fille that place that I did nevene.   *mention*
3503   If thy wil be resun it is
In pes and rest
Amonge thine aungels bryth
To worchep the[e] in syth,   *sight*
Graunt, Lord God almyth!   *Grant (this)/almighty*
And so I holde it best.   *consider*

For thou, Truthe, that is my sister dere,

3496–99 For, when you made earth and heaven, (with) ten orders of angels to be in bliss, (you made) Lucifer brighter than the lightning until he sinned and fell, truly.

3503 If it is your will that, in accord with reason (Man be allowed).

3510   Arguith that Man schuld dwell in wo;
        And Ritwisnes, with hir powere,
        Wolde fain and fast that it were so.   *Wishes eagerly and earnestly*
        But Mercy and I, Pes, bothe in fere   *together*
        Schal nevere, in feyth, acorde therto!   *agree*
        Thanne schuld we evere discorde here,   *argue*
3516   And stande at bate for frend or foo,   *at debate*
        And evere at distaunce.   *at enmity*
        Therfore my counseyl is:
        Lete us foure sisterys kis,
        And restore Man to blis—
        As was Godys ordenaunce.   *God's command*
3521a   *(Misericordia et Veritas obviaverunt sibi; Justitia et Pax osculatae*
            sunt.)

        For if ye, Ryth and Truthe, schuld have your wille,
        I, Pes, and Mercy schuld evere have travest;   *be thwarted in argument*
        Thanne us betwene had bene a gret perille,   *between us would be/strife*
        That oure joyes in hevene schuld a ben lest.   *would be inferior*
        Therfore, gentyl sisterys, consentith me till,   *consent to my proposal*
        Ellys betwene oureself schuld nevere be rest.   *Otherwise/ourselves*
        Where schuld be luf and charité, late ther cum non[e] ille!   *let*
        Loke oure joyes be perfith—and that I holde the best—   *perfect/consider*
        In hevene-riche blis.   *In heaven's bliss*
        For, ther is pes withowtyn were;   *there (in heaven)/war*
        There is rest withowtyn fere;   *fear*
        Ther is charité withowtyn dere—   *injury*
        Oure Faderis will so is.
3534a   *(Hic pax, hic bonitas, hic laus, hic semper honestas.)*

        Therfore, jentyl sisterys, at on[e] word,
        Truth, Ryth, and Mercy hende,   *gracious*
        Lete us stonde at on[e] acord,   *agree together*
        At pes withowtyn ende!
        Late love and charité be at oure bord,   *Let/board, gathering*
3540   Alle veniauns awey wende,   *(Let) all vengeance vanish*
        To hevene that Man may be restoryd.
        Lete us be all his frende
        Before oure Faders face!
        We schal devoutly pray

[3516]And be quarreling as to whether we're friends or foes.

[3521a]Mercy and Truth have met together; Righteousness and Peace have kissed each other (Psalms 85:10–11).

[3534a]Here is peace, here is goodness, here is glory, here eternally is virtue.

At dredful domysday,
And I schal for us say
That Mankind schal have grace.

3547a   (*Et tuam, Deus, deposcimus pietatem, ut ei tribuere digneris lucidas
            et quie[tas] mansiones.*)

Lord, for thy pité, and that pes
Thou sufferist in thy Pascioun—
Boundyn and betyn, without les,   *without lie, truly*
Fro the fote to the croun;   *crown (of head)*
Tanquam ovis ductus es   *Like a sheep you were led*
Whanne *guttae sangu[in]is* ran a-doun;   *drops of blood*
Yit the Jues wolde not ses,   *cease*
But on thin[e] hed they thrist a croun,   *thrust a crown (of thorns)*
And on the cros the[e] nailyd—
As petously as thou were pinyd,   *pained, tormented*
Have mercy of Mankind,   *on*
So that he may finde   *discover (that)*
Oure preyer may him availe!   *aid*

3560a PATER SEDENS IN TRONO. *Ego cogito cogitationes pacis, non afflictionis.*   *The Father sitting in his throne*
Faire falle the[e], Pes, my dowter dere!   *May fair luck befall you*
On the[e] I thinke, and on Mercy.
Syn ye acordyd beth all in fere,   *Since you are agreed together*
My jugement I wil geve you by—   *give according to your wishes*
3565   Not aftyr deservinge, to do reddere,   *Not according to|harshness*
To dampne Mankinde to turmentry,   *torment*
But bringe him to my blisse ful clere
In hevene to dwelle endelesly,
At your prayere forthy.   *According to your prayer*
To make my blisse perfyth,   *perfect*
I menge with my most myth   *mingle|might*
Alle Pes, sum Treuthe, and sum Ryth,
And most of my Mercy.
3573a   (*Misericordia Domini plena est terra. Amen.*)
        Dicet filiabus: *He will say to his daughters*

My dowters hende,   *gracious*
Lufly and lusty to lende,   *joyful to consent*

3547aAnd we earnestly entreat your pity, O God, in order that you may deign to grant him
shining and peaceful abode. (A liturgical prayer for souls in purgatory.)

3560aI think thoughts of peace, not of affliction (see Jeremiah 29:11).

3565Not to inflict harsh punishment, as Man deserves.

3573aThe earth is full of the mercy of the Lord (Psalms 33:5).

Goo to yone fende
And fro him take Mankind!

Bringe him to me
And set him here by my kne
3580 In hevene to be,
In blisse with gamyn and gle.   *mirth and joy*

VERITAS.   We schal fulfille
Thin[e] hestys, as resun and skille,   *commands/as is reasonable*
Fro yone gost grille   *horrid spirit*
Mankinde to bringe the[e] tille.   *to you*
  Tunc ascendent ad Malum Angelum omnes pariter; et dicet   *Then they will all ascend to the Bad Angel (on hell scaffold); and (Peace) will say*

PAX.   A, thou foule wyth,   *wight, creature*
Lete go that soule so tyth!   *quickly*
In he[ve]ne lyth   *light, bright*
Mankinde sone schal be pyth.   *put, set*

3590 JUSTITIA.   Go thou to helle,
Th[o]u devil bold as a belle,   *i.e., brazen*
Therin to dwelle,
In bras and brimston to welle!   *brass (fetters)/boil*
  Tunc ascendent ad tronum.   *Then they will ascend to (God's) throne (with Mankind)*

MISERICORDIA.   Lo here Mankind,
Lyter thanne lef is on linde,   *Brighter/leaf/linden tree*
That hath ben pinyd.   *pained, tormented*
Thy mercy, Lord, lete him finde!

3597a PATER SEDENS IN JUDITIO. *Sicut scintill[a] in medio maris.*   *in judgment*
My mercy, Mankind, geve I the[e].
Cum, sit at my ryth honde!   *right hand*
Ful wel have I lovyd the[e],
Unkind thow[gh] I the[e] fonde.   *found*
As a sparke of fire in the se,   *sea*
My mercy is sinne-quenchand.   *quenching*
Thou hast cause to love me
Abovyn al thinge in land,
And kepe my comaundement.
If thou me love and drede,
Hevene schal be thy mede;   *reward*
My face the[e] schal fede—

3597a The Father sitting in judgment: Like a little spark in the midst of the sea (is all the
wickedness of man to the mercy of God). (From St. Augustine's *Prick of Conscience.*)

This is min[e] jugement.

3610a   *(Ego occidam and vivificabo, percutiam et sanabo; et nemo est qui*
   de manu mea possit eruere.)

King, kaiser, knyt, and kampioun,   *knight/champion*
Pope, patriark, prest, and prelat in pes,   *peace*
Duke dowtiest in dede by dale and by doun, *i.e., everywhere*
Lityl and mekyl, the more and the les,   *Humble and mighty*
All the statys of the werld is at min[e] renoun; *estates/under my control*
To me schal they geve acompt at my digne des. *account/worthy throne*
Whanne Mihel his horn blowith at my dred dom, *Michael/judgment*
3618 The count of here conscience schal putten hem in pres, *in difficulties*
And yeld a rekninge
Of here space whou they han spent,   *how they spent their time*
And of here trew talent
At my gret jugement
An answere schal me bringe.

3623a *(Ecce, requiram gregem meum de manu pastoris.)*
And I schal inquire of my flok and of here pasture, *their pastors*
Whou they have levyd, and led here peple sojet. *How/subject, under their care*
The goode on the ryth sid[e] schul stond ful sure; *right*
The badde on the lyfte sid[e] ther schal I set.
The seven dedys of mercy, whoso hadde ure *use, custom*
To fille—the hungry for to geve mete,   *To fulfill/food*
3630 Or drinke to thristy; the nakyd, vesture;   *clothe*
The pore or the pilgrim, hom[e] for to fette; *fetch, invite*
Thy neybour that hath nede;
Whoso doth mercy to his myth   *to (the extent of) his ability*
To the seke, or in presun pyth,   *sick/(to those) put in prison*
He doth to me—I schal him quyth: *requite*
Hevene blis schal be his mede.   *reward*

3636a *(Et qui bona egerunt, ibunt in vitam aeternam; qui vero mala, in*
   ignem aeternum.)
And they that wel do in this werld, here welthe schal *their*
   awake;
In hevene they schal heynyd [be] in bounté and [in] blis. *exalted*

3610aI will kill and make alive, I will wound and heal; and there is no one who can deliver out of my hand (see Deuteronomy 32:39).

3618The reckoning of their consciences will put them in severe difficulties.

3623aLo, I will inquire of my flock at the hand of the shepherd (see Ezekiel 34:10).

3636aAnd those that will do good, they will go to eternal life; those who do evil, assuredly to eternal fire (from the Athanasian Creed).

And they that evil do, they schul to helle-lake   *pit*
In bitter balys to be brent: my jugement it is.   *torments/burned*
My vertus in hevene thanne schal they qwake;   *powers/tremble*
Ther is no wyth in this werld that may skape this.   *wight, being*
All men example hereat may take
To maintein the goode and mendyn here mis.   *amend their sins*

    [*To the audience.*]
Thus endith oure gamys.
To save you fro sinninge,
Evyr at the beginninge
Thinke on youre last endinge!
Te Deum laudamus.   *We praise you O God*
    [*The end.*]

MANKIND

Mankind (ca. 1465–70) is a morality play specifically designed for an itinerant popular troupe. Its actors were professionals or semi-professionals. Their taking up of a collection during the performance (ll. 459–72) is the first recorded instance in England of openly commercial acting. Evidently they were ready to perform their play at a public inn or wherever they could find a paying audience. Their itinerary must have included the various towns of Cambridgeshire and Norfolk named in the text. Because their play required only six actors (with the leading actor doubling as Titivillus and Mercy), they could be highly mobile. Troupes of this sort were soon visiting every corner of the English countryside. For about a century, from the time of *Mankind* until the 1570's, such troupes were the chief source of popular dramatic entertainment for an entire nation. Eventually, the best of them settled in London and built open-air theaters; the first such building appeared in 1576. The performers of *Mankind* were thus early participants in a popular theater that was to experience remarkable growth and artistic development. These players of *Mankind* were, in effect, the ancestors of the Elizabethan acting company.

In order to design a morality play for such a mobile troupe, the author has altered considerably the proportions of longer and more elaborately-produced moralities such as *The Castle of Perseverance*. He has added to the slapstick comedy and has abbreviated the typical soul-struggle plot. The play thus emphasizes a humorously commercial appeal while still retaining a devout spirit of moral edification. The author, probably a rural clergyman, has borrowed comic materials from the mummers' plays and elsewhere, but is thoroughly familiar with the Latin liturgy of the Church as well. His use of earthy humor to make a serious point is characteristic of many medieval popular sermons. Addressing his predominantly rural audience through his spokesman, Mercy, the author speaks in homely metaphors and stresses practical Christianity. He urges not asceticism but moderation and common sense.

With his rural audience in mind, the author wisely chooses as his subject a typical farmer who has become disaffected with his agricultural lot in life. Yet the story has a universal application as well; after all, Adam too was a tiller of the soil. The central figure of the play, Mankind, cannot cope with the myriad frustrations of his farming existence. When he tries to plow, for example, he discovers that the soil is as stiff as a board. (It should be, since the devil Titivillus has literally placed a board in it.) Tools and seed maddeningly disappear when they are needed. (The devil, concealed by a cloak of invisibility, has just hidden them.) The devil, in other words, constantly tests man's patience. Yet while the devil has a certain power over the physical circumstances of man's daily life, he cannot prevail over man's spirit until man consents to disobedience. Mankind's impatience with farming becomes dangerous only when it induces in him a boredom and a disinclination to worship God thankfully. Once he is in this precarious state of mind, he can easily be persuaded that his kindly spiritual adviser Mercy is only a fraud. From this point, Mankind rushes headlong into the thrilling new pleasures of wearing fashionable clothes and keeping fast company. When the day of reckoning inevitably arrives, Mankind is so overwhelmed by self-reproach that he falls into yet another psychological trap, that of believing he is beyond saving. His evil companions goad him toward this state of despair, just as they earlier enticed him into debauchery and crime. Mankind's spiritual fall, then, is ultimately his own responsibility even though he is sorely tempted. Like all humanity, Mankind cannot maintain a steadfast faith in the vision of goodness that has been offered him by Mercy. Confounding illusion with reality, he allows the devil's insinuations to overwhelm his weak senses and fallible will. From such a dismaying fall he can be reclaimed only by a power greater than himself.

To this consistent and serious allegory of Lenten triumph over licentiousness (see l. 866), the play adds a rich fare of comic entertainment. The villains who tempt Mankind to a life in sin are thoroughly engaging rascals. Wishing to fit Mankind out in the latest clothing fashion, or "New Guise," they proceed to shorten his rustic farmer's coat until it is ridiculously unable to protect him against the cold. They dance, sing filthy tunes, steal from churches, and frequent taverns. As highwaymen who jest about the gallows (l. 598), they anticipate the merry antics of Falstaff and the Boar's Head crew of Shakespeare's *Henry IV* plays. Most of all, these revelers amuse us by their adept mimicry. They poke fun at Mankind for laboring so hard at his farming, and they mock the priest Mercy for his pedantic "English Latin" (l. 124). The author seems aware that Mercy's sermonizings are inherently less lively than the scenes of comical depravity. Nevertheless, the author's allegiances are clear. However engrossing the scatological humor and scurrilous profanity of the rogues may be, these tempters are unmistakably evil and foolish. Their eventual comeuppance is both sure and richly deserved.

Since *Mankind* was taken on tour by a small troupe, its physical requirements had to be simple. It used props that could easily be moved from town to town, such as a horrible mask for Titivillus, a net, a board, a spade, seed, and several versions of Mankind's abbreviated coat (so that actual cutting of the cloth for each performance would be unnecessary). Staging was equally portable. The actors required only an open acting space and, in the rear, curtains through which they could make

their exits and entrances. They also needed to be able to speak offstage without being seen (ll. 245–76, 454). Evidently the actors could set up a suitable stage in a number of different circumstances. They could perform in a large room (in an inn, for instance) in front of a curtained doorway, or they might set up a trestle stage in an innyard with a simple curtained booth to the rear. Similar stages could be improvised on village greens, or in the banqueting hall of a manor or palace. Wherever they performed during their travels, the actors' stage looked much the same as it did elsewhere, and also bore a significant resemblance to the popular stage of the later Elizabethan period. When, for example, they performed in an innyard, they probably erected their booth stage up against one wall of the inn. The paying guests of the inn could then watch from balconies facing on the innyard, while humbler spectators stood in the yard around the stage as they did later in the Globe or Swan theaters. *Mankind* pointedly makes a distinction between the "soverens" who sit at the play, and the "brothern" or comrades who "stonde right uppe" (l. 29). When, on the other hand, the actors performed in a banqueting hall, they probably acted at one end of the room in front of the curtained doorways, with a musicians' gallery visible over their heads—a physical arrangement not unlike the stage façade of later Elizabethan theaters. In either case the audience sat or stood close to the stage and watched it from several sides, as in Shakespeare's theater.

The dialect of *Mankind* is East Midland. The play offers a variety of verse forms that are often used with dramatic appropriateness, from Mercy's formal quatrains and octaves to the *aaab cccb* tail rhyme of the mischief-makers. Although Mercy's language is heavy with pedantically Latin "aureate" diction, the author is at least aware of this stylistic device and uses it to humorous effect. The sole text of this play is to be found in the so-called Macro manuscript, which also includes *The Castle of Perseverance*.

MANKIND

[Dramatis Personae

MANKIND   MISCHEFF

MERCY   NEW-GUISE

TITIVILLUS   NOWADAYS

                    NOUGHT]

          [*Enter Mercy.*]

     MERCY.   The very fownder and beginner of owr first
                    creacion,
               Amonge us sinfull wrechys He oweth to be magnifiede,   *ought/worshiped*
               That for owr disobedienc[e] He hade non[e] indignacion   *did not disdain*
               To sende His own son to be torn and crucifiede.
     5   Owr obsequiouse service to Him shulde be apliede,   *dutiful*
     6   Where He was Lorde of all and made all thinge of
                    nought,
     7   For the sinnfull sinnere to hade him revivyde,   *revived*
     8   And, for his redempcion, sett His own son at nought.   *his (man's)*

               It may be seyde and verifiede: mankinde was dere bought.   *dearly ransomed*
               By the pituose deth of Jhesu he hade his remedye.   *piteous*
     11   He was purgyde of his defawte, that wrechydly hade
                    wrought,
               By His glorius Passion, that blissyde lavatorye.   *source of cleansing*
               O soverence, I beseche yow yowr condicions to rectifye,   *masters (the audience)*
               Ande with humilité and reverence to have a remocion   *an inclination*
               To this blissyde prince that owr nature doth glorifye,   *who glorifies our nature*
     16   That ye may be participable of His retribucion.

               I have be the very mene for yowr restitucion.   *been/true means*
               Mercy is my name, that mo[u]rnith for yowr offence.
               Diverte not yowrsilffe in time of tem[p]tacion,
               That ye may be acceptable to Gode at yowr going hence.   *at your death*

5-8Our dutiful worship should be devoted to God, forasmuch as He, who is Lord of all and
made all creation out of a void, sacrificed (set at nought) His own son in order to revive sinful
man and bring about man's redemption.

11Man, who had acted culpably, was purged of his sin.

16That you may be able to share in His heavenly reward.

21   The grett mercy of Gode, that is of most preemminence,
22   By mediacion of Owr Lady, that is ever habunda[u]nte
23   To the sinfull creature that will repent his necligence.
      I prey Gode, at yowr most nede, that mercy be yowr
          defendawnte.

      In goode werkys I avise yow, soverence, to be   *masters*
          persevera[u]nte
      To purifye yowr sowlys, that they be not cor[r]upte;
      For yowr gostly enmy will make his avaunte,   *spiritual/boast*
      Yowr goode condicions if he may interrupte.   *habits*

29   O ye soverens that sitt, and ye brothern that stonde right
          uppe,
      Prike not yowr felicites in thingys transitorye!   *Place*
      Beholde not the erth, but lifte yowr ey[e] uppe!
32   Se how the hede the members daily do magnifye.   *members, limbs/worship*
      Who is the hede, forsoth, I shall yow certifye:
      I mene owr Saviowr, that was likynnyde to a lambe;   *likened*
      Ande his saintys be the members that daily he doth   *saints, believers*
          satisfye
36   With the preciose rever that runnith from his wombe.   *river/abdomen*

      Ther is non[e] such foode, by water nor by londe,   *i.e., anywhere*
      So preciouse, so gloriouse, so nedefull to owr entent;   *purpose*
      For it hath dissolvyde mankinde from the bitter bonde   *dissolved, freed*
      Of the mortall enmye, that venimousse serpente—   *venomous*
      From the w[h]iche Gode preserve yow all at the Last
          Jugement!
      For sekirly the[r] shall be a strait examinacion: *surely/strict*
      The corn shall be savyde, the chaffe shall be brente.   *grain/burned*
      I besech yow hertily, have this [in] premeditacion.   *bear this in mind*
        [*Enter Mischief.*]

MISCHEFFE.   I beseche yow hertily, leve yowr calc[ul]acion!
      Leve yowr chaffe, leve yowr corn, leve yowr daliacion!   *idle talk*
      Yowr witt is lityll, yowr hede is mekyll, ye are full of
          predicacion.   *preaching*
      But, ser, I prey [you] this question to clarifye:

[21-23]The great mercy of God, which is preeminent, is always abundant by means of Our Lady's intercession to the sinful man who will repent his waywardness.

[29]*soverens*: rich masters with seats. *brothern*: comrades, those of lower status who are standing.

[32]See (by way of analogy) how the body's limbs defer to the head (as we should worship God).

[36]*rever*: i.e., Christ's blood, issuing from the wound made by a spear.

Misse-masche, driff-draff,   *(nonsense verse)*

50   Sume was corn and sume was chaffe,   *Some*

My dame seyde my name was Raffe;

On-schett yowr lokke and take an halpenye.   *Unshut, open*

MERCY.   Why com ye hethyr, brother? Ye were not dysiryde.   *desired*

MISCHEFF.   For a winter corn-threscher, ser, I have hiryde,   *hired myself out*

Ande ye saide the corn shulde be savyde and the chaff

shulde be feryde.   *burned*

56   Ande he provith nay, as it schewth by this verse: *shows, is proven*

57   "*Corn servit bredibus, chaffe horsibus, straw firybusque.*"

This is as moche to say, to yowr lewde undyrstondinge,   *ignorant*

As: the corn shall serve to brede at the nexte bakinge;

"*Chaff horsibus,*" *et reliqua,*   *and the rest*

The chaff to horse shall be goode provente;   *provender*

When a man is for-colde, the straw may be brent,   *very cold|burned*

And so forth, *et cetera.*

MERCY.   Avoide, goode brother! Ye ben culpable   *Be gone|are*

To interrupte thus my talking delectable.

66   MISCHEFF.   Sere, I have nother horse nor sadyll,   *Sir|neither*

67   Therfor I may not ride.

MERCY.   Hie yow forthe on fote, brother, in Godys name!   *foot*

MISCHEFF.   I say, ser, I am cumme hedyr to make yow   *come hither*

game.   *sport*

70   Yet bade ye me not go out in the dev[i]llys name,

71   Ande I will abide.

MERCY. . . . . . [*A leaf is lost in the* MS. *In the interim, Mischief evidently departs, leaving the tormenting of Mercy to three
rowdies, New-Guise, Nowadays, and Nought, with minstrels.
The first two are badgering Nought to dance energetically;
Nought views the proposition as risky.*]

[NEW-GUISE.]   Ande how, minstrellys, pley the comyn trace!   *ho!|common dance*

73   Ley on with thy ballys till his bely breste!   *bagpipe bellows or switch (?)*

---

[56]*he:* the imagined author of the burlesqued Latin verse following.

[57]Doggerel Latin for: Wheat serves for breads, chaff for horses, and straw for fires. (Mischief
then proceeds to parody Biblical exegesis in his "translation.")

[66-67]i.e., I haven't any means of leaving your company.

[70-71]i.e., Since you didn't invoke the devil to chase me out, I'll stay.

[73](According to Eccles, ed., *The Macro Plays,* New-Guise may be urging Nowadays to flog
Nought with a switch until his belly bursts, in order to make him dance.)

NOUGHT.   I putt case I breke my neke: how than?   *i.e., Suppose I break*

NEW-G[U]ISE.   I giff no force, by Sent Tanne!   *I don't care/Anne*

NOWADAYS.   Leppe about lively! Thou art a wight man.   *Leap/agile*
    Lett us be mery w[h]ill we be here.

NOUGHT.   Shall I breke my neke to schew yow sporte?

79 NOWADAYS.   Therfor ever beware of thy reporte.   *talk*

80 NOUGHT.   I beschrew ye all! Her[e] is a schrewde sorte.   *a rascally lot*
    Have theratt, then, with a mery chere!   *Let's go then*
        Her[e] they daunc[e]. Mercy seyth:

[MERCY.]   Do wey! do wey this rev[e]ll, sers, do wey!   *Do away, stop*

NOWADAYS.   Do wey, goode Adam, do wey?   *Adam, old man*

84   This is no parte of thy pley.

85 NOUGHT.   Yis, mary, I prey yow, for I love not this   *marry, indeed*
    revelinge.

86   Cum forth, goode fader, I yow prey!

87   By a lityll ye may assay.
    Anon, of[f] with yowr clothes, if ye will play.
    Go to! for I have hade a praty scottlinge.   *fine little caper (ironic)*

MERCY.   Nay, brother, I will not daunce.

NEW-G[U]ISE.   If ye will, ser, my brother will make yow to   *i.e., Nowadays*
    prawnce.

92 NOWADAYS.   With all my herte, ser, if I may yow avaunce.   *assist*
    Ye may assay by a lityll trace.   *try a little dance*

94 NOUGHT.   Ye[a], ser, will ye do well?
    Trace not with them, by my cownsell,   *Dance*
    For I have tracyde sumwhat to[o] fell—   *vigorously*
    I tell [you] it is a narow space!   *room*

98   But ser, I trow, of us thre I herde yow speke.

---

[79]i.e., Watch what you say.

[80](Nought evidently feels the others are urging him on, expecting him to hurt himself; see ll. 96–97, below.)

[84]i.e., This doesn't concern you.

[85–86](Nought may mean that he's tired of being forced to dance, and wants Mercy to take his place as the butt.)

[87]For a little while you can try (to dance).

[92](Nowadays mockingly agrees to assist Mercy to dance by whipping him and making him prance, as he did Nought.)

[94]i.e., Do you want my advice?

[98–100](The three indicate they have been summoned like evil spirits by Mercy's sermonizing against the degenerate new fashions they represent. The summons has interrupted their fleshly pursuits of sleeping and eating.)

99 NEW-G[U]ISE. Cristys curse hade [ye] therfor! for I was in
    slepe.

100 NOWADAYS. A[nd] I hade the cuppe in my honde, redy to
    goo to met[e]. *to dine*

MERCY. Therfor, ser, curtly grett yow well. *briefly we greet you*

MERCY. Few wordys, few and well sett! *well placed (ironic)*

NEW-G[U]ISE. Ser, it is the new g[u]ise and the new jett: *fashion*

Many wordys, and schortely sett— *curtly offered*

This is the new g[u]ise, every dele. *deal, bit*

MERCY. Lady, helpe! How wrechys deli[gh]te in ther *i.e., Our Lady*
    simpull weys!

NOWADAYS. Say no[ugh]t ageyn the new g[u]ise nowadays! *nothing against*

108 Thou shall finde us sch[r]ewys at all assays. *rascals/trials*

Beware, ye may so[o]n like a bofett! *taste a blow*

110 MERCY. He was well occupiede that brow[gh]te yow
    brether!

NOUGHT. I harde yow call "New-G[u]ise, Nowadays, *heard*
    Nought," all thes[e] thre togethere.

If ye sey that I lie, I shall make yow to slither: *slide, fall*

Lo, take yow here a trepett! [*Trips him up.*] *tripping*

MERCY. Say me yowr namys. I know yow not.

NEW-G[U]ISE. New-G[u]ise, I.

[NOWADAYS.] I, Nowadays.

[NOUGHT.] I, Nought.

MERCY. By Jhesu Crist, that me dere bow[gh]te, *who dearly ransomed me*

Ye betray many men.

NEW-G[U]ISE. Betray? Nay, nay, ser, nay, nay!

We make them both fresch and gay.

But of yowr name, ser, I yow prey,

That we may yow ken. *know*

MERCY. "Mercy" is my name by denominacion.

I conseive ye have but a lityll favour in my *realize/comfort*
    communicacion.

124 NEW-G[U]ISE. Ey, ey, yowr body is full of Englisch Laten!

I am aferde it will brest. *burst*

108You'll find us tough rascals if you provoke us to a test.

110i.e., (sarcastically) He who brought you together (or here) as comrades was certainly making good use of his time!

124*Englisch Laten*: New-Guise pokes fun at Mercy's stilted and redundant choice of "aureate" terms coined from the Latin, such as "denominacion."

126	"Pravo te," quod the bocher onto me	*I curse you/butcher*
127	When I stale a leg a motun.	*stole/of mutton*
	NOWA[DAYS]. Ye are a strong cunning clerke;	*very learned divine*
	I prey yow hertily, worschipp[f]ull clerke,	
	To have this Englisch mad in Laten:	*translate this English into*
	"I have etun a disch-full of curdys,	*eaten/curds*
	Ande I have schetun yowr mowth full of turdys."—	*shitten*
	Now, opyn yowr sachell with Laten wordys	
134	Ande sey me this in clericall manere!	
	Also, I have a wif[e]—her name is Rachell—	
	Betwix her and me was a gret batell,	
	Ande fain of yow I wolde here tell	*gladly/hear*
	Who was the most master.	
	NOUGHT. Thy wif[e] Rachell, I dare ley twenty lise.	*wager/lice*
	NOWADAYS. Who spake to the[e], foll? Thou art not wise.	*fool*
	Go and do that longith to thin[e] office:	*that which belongs*
	Osculare fundamentum!	*Kiss my ass*
143	NOUGHT. Lo, master, lo, here is a pardon bely-mett—	*satisfying*
144	It is grawntyde of Pope Pokett:	*granted by*
	If ye will putt yowr nose in his wiffys sokett,	*vagina*
	Ye shall have forty days of pardon.	
	MERCY. This idyll language ye shall repent!	
	Out of this place I wolde ye went.	
	NEW-G[U]ISE. Goo we hens all thre with on[e] assent.	*hence*
	My fadyr is irke of owr eloquence;	*(spiritual) father, priest*
	Therfor I will no lenger tary.	
152	Gode bringe yow, master, and blissyde Mary,	
153	To the number of the demonicall frairy!	*friary*

· · · · · · · · · · · · · · · · ·

154	NOWAD[AYS]. Cum winde, cum reyn,	
155	Thow[gh] I cumme never ageyn.	
	The dev[i]ll put out both yowr eyn!	*eyes*
	Felowse, go we hens tight.	*hence quickly*

126–27(New-Guise cites another instance of "English Latin" being used absurdly out of context, by a butcher. But this stanza is metrically imperfect and may be obscure.)

134And translate what I've just said into learned Latin.

143–44*pardon:* a document granting remission of sin, granted in this case by the imaginary and absurd Pope Pocket (i.e., Money-purse).

152–53May God and blessed Mary bring you, master, to the company of the brotherhood of devils. (A line is evidently missing to complete the stanza.)

154–55i.e., Let the weather be what it please, for all I'll ever come again. (Proverbial.)

NOUGHT.   Go we hens, a dev[i]ll wey!   *i.e., in the devil's name*
         Here is the dore, her[e] is the wey. [*To Mercy.*]
160   Farwell, jentyll Jaffrey,
         I prey Gode gif yow goode night!
              Exiant simul. Cantent.   *Let them go out together. Let them*
                                                                          sing

MERCY.   Thankyde be Gode we have a fayer diliverance   *good riddance*
         Of thes[e] thre onthrifty gestys!   *profligate guests*
         They know full lityll what is ther ordinance.   *ordained place*
         I preve, by reson, they be wers then bestys: *prove|worse than beasts*

         A best doth after his naturall institucion;   *according to |function*
         Ye may conseive, by there disporte and behavour,   *understand|their*
         Ther joy ande delite is in derision   *(That) their*
         Of [t]her owyn Criste, to his dishonur.

170   This condicion of leving, it is prejudiciall—
         Beware therof! It is wers than ony felony or treson.   *any*
         How may it be excusyde befor the Justice of all,   *Judge*
         When for every idyll worde we must yelde a reson?   *yield, give*

         They have grett ease; therfor they will take no thought.
         But how then, when the angell of hevyn shall blow the
              trumpe
         Ande sey to the transgressors that wikkydly hath wrought: *who have sinned*
         "Cum forth onto yowr juge, and yelde yowr acownte"?

         Then shall I, Mercy, begin sore to wepe.
         Nother comfort nor cownsell ther shall non[e] be hade,   *Neither*
         But such as they have sowyn, such shall they repe.   *sown|reap*
         They be wanton now, but then shall they be sade.   *jovial*

         The goode new g[u]ise nowadays I will not disalow;
183   I discomende the viciouse g[u]ise. I prey have me
              excusyde,
184   I nede not to speke of it; yowr reson will tell it yow.
185   Take that is to be takyn, and leve that is to be refusyde.   *that which*
              [*Enter Mankind with a spade.*]

MANKINDE.   Of the erth and of the cley we have owr
              propagacion.
         By the providens of Gode thus be we derivatt—   *derived*

183–85I disapprove of the vicious new fashion only. I pray that you'll excuse me for speaking
laboriously of what your reason tells you plainly. Use moderately those things God intended
you to enjoy, and refuse what should be refused.

To whos[e] mercy I recomende this [w]holl congrygacion.
I hope, onto his blisse ye be all predestinatt!   *unto/destined*

190   Every man, for his degré, I trust shall be participatt,
If we will mortifye owr carnall condicion
Ande owr voluntarye dysires, that ever be pervercionatt—   *willful/perverse*
To renunce them, and yelde us under Godys provicion.   *submit ourselves to*

My name is "Mankinde." I have my composicion
Of a body and of a soull, of condicion contrarye—
Betwix them tweyn is a grett division.
197   He that shulde be subjecte, now he hath the victory.   *He (the body)*

This is to me a lamentable story,
To se my flesch of my soull to have governance.
Wher the goode-wyff is master, the goodeman may be   *wife/husband*
       sory.
I may both syth and sobbe; this is a pituose remembrance.   *sigh*

O th[o]u my soull, so sotyll in thy substance,   *subtle, delicate*
.   .   .   .
Alasse, what was thy fortune and thy chaunce   *why was it your fate*
To be associat with my flesch, that stinking dungehill?

Lady, helpe! Soverens, it doth my soull myche ill   *i.e., Our Lady/much*
To se the flesch prosperouse, and the soull trodyn under
       fote.
I shall go to yondyr man, and asay him I will.   *appeal to him*
I trust of gostly solace he will be my bote.   *spiritual/help*
       [*He goes to Mercy, and kneels.*]

All heyll, semely father, ye be welcom to this house!
210   Of the very wisdam ye have participacion.   *true*
My body with my soull is ever querulose;   *quarrelsome*
I prey yow, for sent charité, of yowr supportacion!   *holy/support*

I beseche yow hertily of yowr gostly comforte.   *for/spiritual*
I am onstedfast in livinge; my name is "Mankinde."
My gostly enmy, the dev[i]ll, will have a grett disporte,   *amusement*

190Every man according to his spiritual condition will, I trust, be a participant (in God's bliss).

197He (my body), who should be subordinate (to my soul), is instead dominant.

210You share in and partake of the true wisdom (of God).

In sinfull g[u]idinge if he may se me ende.   *conduct*

MERCY.   Crist sende yow goode comforte! Ye be welcum,
  my frende.
 Stonde uppe on yowr fete. I prey yow, arise.
 My name is "Mercy." Ye be to me full hende;   *gracious*
220 To eschew vice I will yow avise.

MANKINDE.   O Mercy, of all grace and vertu ye are the well!   *fountain*
 I have herde tell, of right worschippfull clerkys,   *heard/from/divines*
 Ye be ap[p]roximatt to Gode and nere of his consell;   *(That) you*
 He hat[h] institut you above all his werkys.   *instituted, established*

 O, yowr lovely wordys to my soull are swetere then hony!
MERCY. The temptacion of the flesch ye must resist like a man,
 For ther is ever a batell betwix the soull and the body: *constantly*
228 *Vita hominis est militia super terram.*

 Oppresse yowr gostly enmy and be Cristys own knight!
 Be never a cowarde ageyn yowr adversary: *against*
 If ye will be crownyde, ye must nedys fight.   *must needs, must*
 Intende well, and Gode will be yow adjutory.   *helpful to you*

 Remember, my frende, the time of continuance: *of (life's) duration*
 So helpe me Gode, it is but a chery time!   *cherry time (i.e., brief)*
 Spende it well. Serve Gode with hertys affiance.   *loyalty of heart*
 Distempure not yowr brain with goode ale nor with win[e].

 "Mesure is tresure"; I forbid[d]e yow not the use.   *Moderation*
 Mesure yowrsylf ever. Beware of excesse.
 The superfluouse g[u]ise I will that ye refuse;
240 When nature is suffisyde, anon that ye ses[s]e.   *cease at once*

 If a man have an hors, and kepe him not to[o] hye,   *too well-fed*
 He may then reull him at his own dysiere;   *rule/desire*
 If he be fede over-well he will disobey   *he (the horse)*
 Ande, in happe, cast his master in the mire.   *perchance*
  [*New-Guise, Nowadays, and Nought, who have been eaves-
  dropping, speak from backstage or from some concealed position
  where Mercy and Mankind cannot observe them.*]

NEW-G[U]ISE.   Ye sey trew, ser; ye are no faitour: *liar*
 I have fed[d]e my wiff so well till sche is my master!

228The life of man on earth is a battle, a struggle. (Job 7:1.)

247   I have a grett wo[u]nde on my hede, lo! and theron leyth   *lies*
          a playster;
248   Ande another ther I pisse my peson.   *where/pease*
       Ande my wif[e] were yowr hors, sche wolde yow all to-   *If*
          banne.   *curse you all*
250   Ye fede yowr hors in mesure; ye are a wise man!
251   I trow, and ye were the kingys palfrey-man   *if*
252   A goode horse shulde be gesunne.   *scarce*

       MANKINDE.   Wher spekys this felow? Will he not com nere?
       MERCY.   All to[o] son[e], my brother, I fere me, for yow.   *for your sake*
       He was here right now—by him that bow[gh]te me dere!—   *dearly ransomed me*
       With other of his felowse. They kan moche sorow.   *They're acquainted with*

       They will be here right son[e], if I ow[gh]t departe.   *soon/at all*
       Thinke on my doctrine! It shall be yowr defence.
       Lerne w[h]ill I am here; sett my wordys in herte.
       Within a schorte space I must nedys hens.   *Soon I must go*

261   NOWADAYS [*unseen*].   The sooner the lever, and it be evyn   *better/if*
          anon!
       I trow yowr name is "Do-lityll," ye be so long fro hom.
       If ye wolde go hens, we shall cum everychon,   *everyone*
       Mo then a goode sorte.   *More than a great many*
       Ye have leve, I dare well say;   *leave (to go)*
       When ye will, go forth yowr wey.
       Men have lityll deynté of yowr pley   *pleasure in*
       Because ye make no sporte.

269   NOUGHT [*unseen*].   Yowr potage shall be for-colde, ser. When *soup/entirely cold*
          will ye go din[e]?
270   I have sen a man lost twenty noblys in as lityll time—   *gold coins*
       Yet it was not I, by Sent Qwintyn!
       For I was never worth a pottfull a wortys sithyn I was   *of cabbages since*
          born.
       My name is "Nought." I love well to make mery!
       I have be sethen with the comyn tapster of Bury   *been before now*

247–48(New-Guise has plaster bandages on his head and genitals from sparring with his bossy
wife.)

250–52(sarcastically) You're a clever one to starve your horse, in the name of "moderation"!
I bet that if you were keeper of the king's horses, there'd be few horses left unruined (by your
parsimony).

261The sooner the better, even if it's right now!

269–70i.e., Hurry home to your dinner. I've seen a man lose twenty gold coins (at gambling) in
the time you're taking to go.

A[nd] pleyde so longe the foll that I am evyn very wery—   *fool/weary*
Yit shall I be ther ageyn to-morn.   *tomorrow*

MERCY [*to Mankind*].   I have moche care for yow, my own
    frende.
Yowr enmys will be here anon; they make ther avaunte.   *their boast*
Thinke well in yowr hert: yowr name is "Mankinde";
280 Be not unkinde to Gode, I prey yow! Be his servante.

Be stedefast in condicion; se ye be not variant.
Lose not thorow[gh] foly that is bow[gh]te so dere!   *that which/dearly*
Gode will prove yow son[e]; ande, if that ye be constant,   *test/soon*
Of his blisse perpetuall ye shall be partener.

Ye may not have yowr intent at yowr first dysiere.   *desire*
Se the grett pacience of Job in tribulacion:
Like as the smith trieth ern in the fiere,   *refines iron/fire*
So was he triede by Godys visitacion.

He was of yowr nature and of yowr fragilité.   *i.e., human nature*
Folow the steppys of him, my own swete son,
Ande sey, as he seyde, in yowr trobyll and adversité:
292 "*Dominus dedit, Dominus abstulit; sicut sibi placuit, ita factum
    est; sit nomen Domini benedictum.*"

Moreover, in speciall I give yow in charge:
Beware of New-G[u]ise, Nowadays, and Nought!
Nise in ther aray, in language they be large.   *Wanton/licentious*
To perverte yowr condicions, all ther menys shall be   *their means*
    sow[gh]te.

Gode son, intromitt not yowrsylff in ther cumpeny!   *Good/intermix*
They harde not a masse thi[s] twelmonyth, I dare well say.   *heard/year*
Giff them non[e] audience; they will tell yow many a lie.
Do truly yowr labure, and kepe yowr haly day.   *holy*

301 Beware of Titivillus—fo[r] he lesith no wey—   *loses/means, device*
That goth invisibull and will not be sen.   *Who/seen*
303 He will ronde in yowr ere, and cast a nett befor yowr ey.   *whisper/ear*
He is worst of them all, Gode lett him never then!   *thrive*

292"The Lord gave, and the Lord has taken away; as it was pleasing to him, so it was done;
blessed be the name of the Lord." (Job 1:21.)

301(For the name Titivillus—"all vile things"—see the Wakefield Judgment pageant.)

303*nett*: i.e., to render Titivillus invisible.

If ye disples Gode, aske mercy anon,   *displease*
Ellys Mischeff will be redy to brace yow in his bridyll.   *Or else/fasten*
Kisse me now, my dere darlinge. Gode sche[l]de yow from   *shield*
    yowr fon!   *foes*
Do truly yowr labure, and be never idyll.
The blissinge of Gode be with yow and with all thes[e]
    worschipp[f]ull men!   [*Exit.*]   *i.e., the audience*
MANKINDE.   Amen, for sent charité, amen!   *holy*

Now, blissyde be Jhesu! My soull is well saciatt   *satiated, filled*
With the mellifluose doctrine of this worschippfull man.
The rebelli[o]n of my flesch, now it is superatt,   *conquered*
314   Thankinge be Gode of the comminge that I kam.

Her[e] will I sitt, and tityll in this papyr   *write down*
The incomparable astat of my promicion. [*Sits and writes.*]   *my promised bliss*
[*To the audience.*] Worschipfull soverence, I have wretyn
    here
The glori[o]use remembrance of my nobyll condicion.

319   To have remo[r]s and memory of mysylff thus wretyn it is,
To defende me from all superstici[o]us charmys:
321   "*Memento, homo, quod cinis es, et in cinerem reverteris.*"
    [*He points to the cross depicted on his breast.*]
Lo, I ber[e] on my bryst the bagge of min[e] armys.   *badge*
    [*New-Guise approaches from his place of concealment.*]

NEW-G[U]ISE.   The wether is colde. Gode sende us goode
    ferys!   *fires*
324   "*Cum sancto sanctus eris, et cum perverso perverteris.*"
325   "*Ecce quam bonum et quam jocundum,*" quod the dev[i]ll to the
    frerys,   *friars*
326   "*Habitare fratres in unum.*"

MANKINDE.   I her a felow speke. With him I will not mell.   *hear/concern myself*
This erth, with my spade, I shall assay to delffe.   *delve, dig*
To eschew idullnes, I do it min[e] own selffe.

314Thanks be to God for my coming hither (to this holy man, Mercy).

319It is written as follows, to cause me to have remorse (for my fleshly frailty).

321"Remember, O man, that you are dust, and to dust you will return." (See Job 34:15.)

324–26"With the holy you will show yourself holy; and with the wicked you will show yourself wicked." (Psalms 18:25–26.) "Behold how good and how pleasant it is for brethren to dwell together in unity" (Psalms 133:1), said the devil to the friars.

I prey Gode sende it his fusion! [*Digs.*]   *foison, fruition*
[*Nowadays and Nought approach, making their way through the audience.*]

NOWADAYS.   Make rom, sers, for we have be longe!   *been long absent*
We will cum gif yow a Cristemes songe.

NOUGHT.   Now I prey all the yemandry that is here   *yeomanry, folk*
To singe with us, with a mery chere!
[*He sings a line at a time; New-Guise and Nowadays lead the audience in singing after him.*]

It is wretyn with a coll, it is wretyn with a cole,   *written/coal*
NEW-G[U]ISE *and* NOWAD[AYS].   It is wretyn with a colle, it is
    wretyn [with a cole],
NOUGHT.   He that schitith with his hoyll, he that schitith with   *hole*
    his hoyll,
NEW-G[U]IS[E], NOWAD[AYS]. He that schitith with his hoyll,
    [he that schitith with his hoyll],
NOUGHT.   But he wippe his ars clen, but he [wipe his ars   *Unless*
    clen],
340 NEW-G[U]ISE, NOWAD[AYS].   But he wipe his ars clen, but
    he [wipe his ars clen],
NOUGHT.   On his breche it shall be sen, on his breche [it shall   *breeches*
    be sen],
NEW-G[U]ISE, NOWAD[AYS].   On his breche it shall be sen, on
    his [breche it shall be sen].
    Cantant omnes: *All sing*
Hoylyke, holyke, holyke! holyke, holyke, holyke!

NEW-G[U]ISE.   Ey, Mankinde, Gode spede yow with yowr
    spade!
I shall tell yow of a mariage:
346 I wolde yowr mowth and his ars, that this made,
Wer mariede junctly together.   *jointly*
MANKINDE.   Hey yow hens, felowse, with bredinge!   *Hasten/reproach*
Leve yowr derision and yowr japing!   *mocking*
I must nedys labure—it is my livinge.
351 NOWADAYS.   What, ser? We cam but lat[e] hethyr.   *only lately hither*

346*that this made:* that made this (perhaps referring to excrement or stained breeches, as in the song).

351i.e., We've only just arrived, and don't quite understand what you're doing.

352   Shall all this corn grow here   *grain*
       That ye shall have the nexte yer[e]?
       If it be so, corn hade nede be dere,   *better be high in price*
       Ellys ye shall have a pore liffe.   *you'll be poor*

356   NOUGHT. Alasse, goode fadere, this labor fretith yow to the   *frets, consumes*
           bon[e]!
       But, for yowr croppe I take grett mone: *feel great sorrow*
       Ye shall never spende it alone!   *finish*
       I shall assay to geett yow a wiffe.   *get*

       How many acres suppose ye here, by estimacion?
       NEW-G[U]ISE. Ey, how ye turne the erth uppe and down!
       I have be in my days in many goode town,   *been during my life*
       Yett saw I never such another tillinge.
       MANKINDE. Why stonde ye idyll? It is pety that ye were
           born!

       NOWADAYS. We shall bargen with yow, and nother moke nor   *neither mock*
           scorne:
       Take a goode carte in hervest, and lode it with yowr corne,
       Ande what shall we gif yow for the levinge?   *pay/crop*

368   NOUGHT. He is a goode starke laburrer—he wolde fain do   *strong*
           well!
369   He hath mett with the goode man Mercy, in a schrowde
           sell!   *bad time*
       For all this, he may have many a hungry mele.   *meal*
       Yit, woll ye se? He is politike: *shrewd, prudent*
       Here shall be goode corn—he may not misse it.   *he can't fail*
       If he will have reyn, he may over-pisse it;   *rain/piss on it*
374   Ande if he will have compass[t]e, he may over-blisse it   *compost*
375   A lityll with his ars, like.   *similarly*

       MANKINDE. Go and do yowr labur—Gode lett yow never
           the!—   *prosper*
       Or with my spade I shall yow dinge, by the holy Trinité!   *strike*
       Have ye non[e] other man to moke but ever me?   *mock/always*
       Ye wolde have me of yowr sett?   *group, gang*
       Hie yow forth lively, for hens I will yow driffe!   *Hasten/drive*
           [*He beats them with his spade.*]

352*here*: Nowadays implies that Mankind's field is terribly small.

356*fadere*: (condescendingly) old fellow.

368(Said sarcastically.)

369i.e., It was an evil hour when he met Mercy.

374–75And similarly, if he needs compost he can bestow a blessing on his land with his arse.

381 NEW-G[UISE].   Alas, my jewellys! I shall be schent of my   *testicles*
    wiff[e]!

NOWAD[AYS].   Alasse, and I am like never for to thrive,   *likely*
    I have such a buffett!

MANKINDE.   Hens I sey, New-G[u]ise, Nowadays, and
    Now[gh]te!
    It was seyde beforn, all the menys shuld be sought   *previously (that) / means*
    To perverte my condicions and bringe me to nought.
    Hens, thevys! Ye have made many a lesinge.   *lie*

388 NOUGHT.   Marryde I was for colde, but now am I warme!   *Marred, suffering*
    Ye are evill-avisyde, ser, for ye have don harme.   *ill-advised*
    By Cokkys body sakyrde, I have such a peyn in my arme   *God's consecrated body*

391   I may not chonge a man a ferthinge!
    [*The three rogues start out. Mankind kneels.*]

MANKINDE.   Now I thanke Gode, knelinge on my kne.
    Blissyde be his name! He is of hye degré.   *high*
    By the subsidé of his grace that he hath sente me,   *help*
    Thre of min[e] enmys I have putt to flight. [*Holds up his
      spade.*]
    Yit this instrument, soverens, is not made to defende.

397   Davide seyth, "*Nec in hasta, nec in gladio, salvat Dominus.*"

398 NOUGHT [*over his shoulder*].   No, mary, I beschrew yow, it is
    in *spadibus*!
    Therfor Cristys curse cum on yowr hedibus,   *i.e., head*
    To sende yow lesse might! *Exiant.*   *strength*

MANKINDE.   I promitt yow, thes[e] felowse will no more cum   *promise*
    here;

402 For summe of them, certenly, were summewhat to[o] nere!
    My fadyr Mercy avisyde me to be of a goode chere   *advised*
    Ande again my enmys manly for to fight.   *against*

    I shall convicte them, I hope, everychon.   *conquer*
    Yet I say amisse; I do it not alon:
    With the helpe of the grace of Gode, I resist my fon   *foes*
    Ande ther malici[o]use herte.   *their*
    With my spade I will departe, my worschipp[f]ull soverence,

---

381Alas, my testicles! I'll be in disgrace with my wife (because I'm impotent).

388i.e., I was cold until that beating warmed me up.

391I can't buy or sell from men worth a farthing (quarter-penny); i.e., I'm incapacitated.

397-98David says, "The Lord saves neither with the spear nor with the sword." (Cf. 1 Samuel 17:47.) —No, indeed, curse you, he saves "with spades"!

402to[o] nere: i.e., came too close for their own good.

410	Ande live ever with labure, to corecte my insolence.	
	I shall go fett corn for my londe. I prey yow of pacience;	*fetch grain seed*
	Right son[e] I shall reverte.	*return*
	[*He goes out to get his seed. Enter Mischief.*]	

MISCHEFF.   Alas, alasse, that ever I was wrought!
Alasse the whill, I [am] wers then nought!   *while, time/worse than*
Sithyn I was here, by Him that me bought,   *Since/ransomed*
I am utterly ondon.
I, Mischeff, was here at the beginninge of the game,
Ande arguyde with Mercy—Gode giff him schame!
He hath taught Mankinde, w[h]ill I have be vane,   *been absent*

420   To fight manly ageyn his fon.   *against/foes*

For with his spade, that was his wepyn,   *weapon*
New-G[u]ise, Nowad[ays, and] Nought hath [he] all to-
        betyn—   *beaten utterly*
I have grett pité to se them wepyn.   *weep*
Will ye list? I here them crye. *Clamant.*   *listen/hear/They cry*
[*New-Guise, Nowadays, and Nought enter, sobbing, as Mis-
chief calls to them solicitously.*]
Alasse, alasse, cum hether! I shall be yowr borow.   *protector*
Alac[k], alac[k]! *Ven[e], ven[e]!* Cum hethere, with sorowe!   *Come*
Pesse, fayer babys! Ye shall have a nappyll—tomorow.   *Peace, hush/apple*
Why grete ye so, why?   *weep*

NEW-G[UISE].   Alasse, master, alasse, my privité!   *privy parts*
MISCHEFF.   A, wher? Ala[c]ke, fayer babe, ba me!   *kiss me*
431   Abide! To[o] son[e] I shall it se.
NOWAD[AYS].   Here, here, se my hede, goode master!
MISCHEFF.   Lady, helpe! Sely darlinge, *ven[e], ven[e]!*   *(Our) Lady/Poor*
I shall helpe the[e] of thy peyn:
I shall smitt[e] of[f] thy hede and sett it on again.
436   NOUGHT.   By Owr Lady, ser, a fayer playster!

Will ye of[f] with his hede? It is a schrewde charme!   *i.e., harsh cure*
438   As for me, I have non[e] harme—
439   I were loth to forbere min[e] arme.   *do without*
440   Ye pley: *In nomine patris,* choppe!

431i.e., Wait, don't show me the wound in your genital region; I'll see it all too soon anyway.

436By the Virgin Mary, that would call for a fair-sized wound-plaster!

438–41i.e., As for me, my wound is a mere scratch; I'd be most unwilling to do without my arm! (Nought minimizes his wound because he suspects that Mischief would resort to amputation, as he has threatened with Nowadays.) Your way is to say a quick prayer, and start cutting. —You won't castrate me if I can prevent it.

441 NEW-G[UISE].   Ye shall not choppe my jewellys, and I may.   *if*

     NOWAD[AYS].   Ye, Cristys crose! Will ye smight my hede   *cross/smite*
         awey?

443   Ther, wher, on and on? Oute! Ye shall not assay—   *try*

444   I might well be callyde a foppe.

     MISCHEFF.   I kan choppe it of[f] and make it again.   *make it (whole)*

446 NEW-G[U]ISE.   I hade a schrewde *recumbentibus,* but I fele no   *a knockdown blow*
         peyn.

447 NOWADAYS.   Ande my hede is all save and [w]holl again.—   *safe, well*

     Now, towchinge the mater of Mankinde,   *concerning*

     Lett us have an interleccion, sithen ye be cum hethere.   *consultation*

450   It were goode to have an ende.

451 MISCHEFF.   How, how? A minstrell! Know ye ony ou[gh]t?   *any at all*

452 NOUGHT.   I kan pipe in a Walsingham w[h]istill, I, Nought,
         Nought.

453 MISCHEFF.   Blow apase, and thou shall bring him in with a
         flowte.   *flute*

     [*Nought plays. The voice of Titivillus is heard offstage.*]

     TITIVILLUS.   I com, with my leggys under me!

     MISCHEFF.   How, New-G[u]ise, Nowadays, herke or I goo: *ere*

456   When owr hedys wer togethere, I spake of *si dedero.*

     NEW-G[U]ISE.   Ye, go thy wey, we shall gather mony onto—   *for the purpose*

     Ellys ther shall no man him se.   *him (Titivillus)*

     [*To the audience.*]

     Now gostly to owr purpos, worschipfull soverence,   *devoutly*

460   We intende to gather mony, if it plesse yowr necligence,

     For a man with a hede that [is] of grett omnipotens—

462 NOWAD[AYS].   Kepe yowr tayll, in goodnes I prey yow, goode
         brother!

443–44i.e., Cutting right and left, one after another? Curse it! I won't let you try; I might look foolish without my head.

446–47(New-Guise and Nowadays still pretend, in order to avoid Mischief's treatment, that they need no medical attention.)

450It would be good to bring this matter (of tempting Mankind) to a successful conclusion.

451–53(It occurs to them that the answer to their problem—Titivillus—can best be fetched by playing music to attract him.)

456When we conferred earlier, I spoke of taking up a collection. (*Si dedero:* If I give you something [I'll expect payment].)

460*necligence:* an insolent term used instead of "reverence."

462*Kepe yowr tayll:* watch what you say (addressed to New-Guise, interrupting him; or, keep proper custody of your reckoning, money collection).

463 He is a worschipp[f]ull man, sers, saving yowr reverens. *begging your pardon*
 He lovith no grotys, nor pens of t[w]o-pens: *groats/two-penny coins*
 Gif us rede reyallys, if ye will se his abhominabull presens. *royals, gold coins*
NEW-G[UISE]. Not so! Ye that mow not pay the ton, pay the *may, can/one*
  tother.
  [They pass among the audience, taking up a collection.]

 At the goode-man of this house first we will assay. *master, host*
468 Gode blisse yow, master! Ye sey us ill, yet ye will not sey
  "nay."
469 Lett us go by and by, and do them pay.
 Ye pay all alike. Well mut ye fare! *May you have good luck*
  [When they have finished collecting, they return to the stage.]
NOUGH[T]. I sey, New-G[u]ise, Nowadays, *Estis vos pecuni-*
  atus? *Are you moneyed*
472 I have criede a fayer will, I beschrew yowr patus! *pate, head*
  [Nowadays turns to call in Titivillus.]
473 NOWAD[AYS]. *Ita vere, magister,* cumme forth now yowr gatus! *gate, door*
 He is a goodly man, sers; make space, and beware!
  [Enter Titivillus, arrayed as a devil with a net in his hand.
  He addresses the audience.]

475 TITIVILLUS. *Ego sum dominantium dominus,* and my name is
  Titivillus.
 Ye that have goode hors, to yow I sey *"caveatis"*: *horses/beware*
477 Here is an abyll felyschippe to trise hem out at yowr gatis! *snatch them*
 Ego probo sic: *I demonstrate it thus*
  (Loquitur ad New-G[u]ise.) *He speaks to New-Guise*
  Ser New-G[u]is[e], lende me a peny.
NEW-G[UISE]. I have a grett purse, ser, but I have no monay:
480 By the masse, I faill two farthingys of an halpeny. *I am short*
 Yit hade I ten pound this night that was. *last night*

 TITIVILLUS *(loquitur ad Nowad[ays]).* What is in thy purse?
  Thou art a stout velan. *valiant fellow*

463*He:* Titivillus.

468–69God bless you for your contribution, sir! Even though you say disparaging things about us players, you won't refuse to pay. Let us pass among the others and get them to pay.

472–73I have begged (for money) a long time, with a curse on your head! —Truly therefore, master, now make your entrance.

475*Ego . . . dominus:* I am lord of lords.

477(to the audience) Here is a fellowship (these villains on stage) able to snatch your horses from your very doors!

480*two farthingys:* a halfpenny. (New-Guise claims to have not a cent even after taking up the collection, thereby proving Titivillus' contention that he is a thief and scoundrel.)

483 NOWAD[AYS]. The dev[i]ll have [the] qwitt! I am a clen   *bit/penniless*
　　　jentyllman.
　　I prey Gode I be never wers storyde then I am.   *worse supplied*
　　It shall be otherwise, I hope, or this night passe.   *ere*
TITIVILLUS (*loquitur ad Nought*). Herke now, I say, thou hast
　　　many a peny.
487 NOUGHT. *No[n] nobis, domine, non nobis,* by Sent Deny!   *Saint Denis*
　　The dev[i]ll may daunce in my purse for ony peny;
　　It is as clen as a birdys ars.

TITIVILLUS [*to the audience*]. Now I say yet ageyn, "*caveatis*":
　　Her is an abyll felyschippe to trise hem out of yowr gatis!—   *them (horses)*
　　Now I sey, New-G[u]ise, Nowad[ays], and Nought,
　　Go and serche the contré: anon [that] it be sowg[h]te,
494 Summe here, summe ther, what if ye may cache owg[h]te.   *to see if*

　　If ye faill of hors, take what ye may ellys.   *don't find horses/otherwise*
NEW-G[U]ISE. Then speke to Mankinde for the *recumbentibus*   *knockdown blow*
　　of my jewellys!   *on my testicles*
497 NOWAD[AYS]. Remember my brokyn hede in the worschippe
　　of the five vowellys.
NOUGHT. Ye[a], goode ser, and the si[a]tica in my arme!
TITIVILLUS. I know full well what Mankinde dide to yow;
　　Mischiff hat[h] informyde [me] of all the matere thorow.   *thoroughly*
　　I shall venge yowr quarell, I make Gode a vow.
　　Forth, and espye w[h]ere ye may do harme!
503 Take W[illiam] Fyde, if ye will have ony mo.   *any more (companions)*
　　I sey, New-G[u]ise, w[h]ethere art thou avisyde to go?   *whither/determined*

NEW-G[U]ISE. First I shall begin at M[aster] Huntington of
　　Sauston.   *Sawston*
　　Fro thens I shall go to William Thurlay of Hauston,   *Hauxton*
　　Ande so forth to Picharde of Trumpington—
　　I will kepe me to thes[e] thre.
NOWADAYS. I shall goo to Williham Bakere of Walton,
　　To Richerde Bollman of Gayton.
　　I shall spare Master Woode of Fullburn—   *Fulbourn*

483May the devil have the whole lot! I'm penniless.

487Not to us, O Lord, not to us. (Psalms 115:1, profanely quoted out of context.)

494Some searching in one place and some in another, to see whether you can steal anything.

497*five vowellys*: perhaps an error for "seven devils," or a reference to Christ's five wounds.

503*Fyde*: This and the following names doubtless made topical reference to the play's original audience in Cambridgeshire and Norfolk near Cambridge and Lynn, where all the towns mentioned are located.

512   He is a *"noli me tangere."*   *touch me not*

NOUGHT.   I shall goo to William Patrike of Massingham;
           I shall spare Master Alington of Bot[t]is[h]am,
           Ande Hamonde of S[w]offeham,
516   For drede of *"in manus tuas,* qweke!"
           Felows, cum forth and go we hens togethyr.

518   NEW-G[U]ISE.   Sith we shall go, lett us be well ware wethere.   *Since/whither*
           If we may be take, we com no more hethyr.   *taken, captured*
520   Lett us con well owr neke verse, that we have not a cheke.   *memorize/disaster*

TITIVILLUS.   Goo yowr wey, a dev[i]ll wey, go yowr wey all!   *in the devil's name*
522   I blisse yow with my lyfte honde—foull yow befall!   *bad luck to you*
           Com again, I werne, as son[e] as I yow call,   *admonish*
           A[nd] bringe yowr avantage into this place.   *your booty*
                [*Exeunt. Manet Titivillus.*]
           To speke with Mankinde I will tary here this tide,   *at this time*
526   Ande assay his goode purpose for to sett aside.
           The goode man Mercy shall no lenger be his g[u]ide.
           I shall make him to dawnce another trace!   *dance*

           Ever I go invisibull—it is my jett—   *fashion*
           Ande befor his ey thus I will hange my nett
531   To blench his sight. I hope to have his fote-mett!   *blind/take his measure*
           To irke him of his labur I shall make a frame: *a plot*
           This borde shall be hid[d]e under the erth prevely.   *board/secretly*
                [*Titivillus places a board in Mankind's field.*]
           His spade shall enter, I hope, onredily!   *unreadily*
           By then he hath assayde, he shall be very angry   *By the time/tried*
           Ande lose his paciens—peyn of schame.   *(on) penalty of*
           I shall menge his corne with drawke and with durnell;   *mix/weeds*
           It shall not be like to sow nor to sell.   *suitable*
           Yondyr he commith. I prey of cownsell.   *Keep my secret*
540   He shall wene grace were wane!   *think grace is lacking*
                [*Enter Mankind with a sack of grain.*]

512*noli me tangere:* i.e., an irascible fellow.

516*in manus tuas:* into your hands (Christ's last words, and hence the final prayer of a man about to be hanged). *qweke:* a choking sound.

518Since we're going, let's be very careful where we go.

520*neke verse:* the first verse of the fifty-first Psalm, the recitation of which in court enabled a defendant to claim right of clergy and so avoid the gallows.

522*lyfte:* left (in the devil's blessing, everything is inverted).

526And try to set aside his good intentions.

531i.e., I hope to ensnare him.

MANKIND.   Now Gode, of his mercy, sende us of his sonde!   *message, counsel*
 I have brought sede here to sow with my londe.   *with which to sow*
 Qw[h]ill I over-dylve it, here it shall stonde.   *While I dig (the land)*
  [*He sets the grain down, and Titivillus goes out with it while*
  Mankind is using the spade.]
 In nomine Patris et Filii et Spiritus Sancti, now I will begin.
  [*His spade strikes Titivillus' board in the earth.*]
 This londe is so harde it makith [me] unlusty and irke!   *tired and irritated*
 I shall sow my corn at vyntur, and lett Gode werke.   *at venture, random*
  [*He turns to get his sack of grain.*]
 Alasse, my corn is lost! Here is a foull werke!
 I se well, by tillinge lityll shall I win.
  [*He throws down the spade in disgust.*]

 Here I giff uppe my spade, for now and forever!
550 To occupye my body I will not put me in dever.   *I won't endeavor*
  Here Titivillus goth out with the spade.
 I will here my evynsonge here, or I dissever.   *hear/ere I leave*
 This place I assing as for my kirke;   *assign/church*
 Here, in my kerke, I knell on my kneys. [*Prays, with beads.*]
 Pater noster, qui es in caelis.   *(The Lord's Prayer)*
555 TITIVILLUS [*re-entering*].   I promes yow, I have no lede on my   *lead*
  helys!   *heels*
 I am here ageyn to make this felow irke.

 Qw[h]ist! Pesse! I shall go to his ere and tityll therin.   *Whist, quiet/whisper*
  [*He goes up to Mankind and whispers in his ear.*]
 A schorte preyere thirlith hevyn. Of thy preyere blin.   *pierces heaven/cease*
 Thou art holier then ever was ony of thy kin.   *any*
 Arise and avent the[e]! Nature compellys.   *relieve yourself*
  [*Mankind rises, and excuses himself to the audience.*]
MANKIND.   I will into thi[s] yerde, soverens, and cum ageyn
  son[e].
 For drede of the colike, and eke of the ston[e],   *kidney-stone*
 I will go do that nedys must be don[e].   *that which must*
564 My bedys shall be here for whosummever will ellys.   *beads*
  Exiat [*leaving his prayer-beads behind*].

TITIVI[LLUS].   Mankinde was besy in his prayere, yet I dide   *caused*
  him arise;
 He is conveyde—by Crist!—from his divin[e] service.   *removed*
 W[h]ethere is he, trow ye? Iwisse, I am wonder wise: *Whither/wondrously*

---

[555]i.e., I assure you, I move quickly.

[564]My beads will be here for whoever else wants them.

568	I have sent him forth to schit[t]e lesinges.	*lies*
569	Iff ye have ony silver, in happe pure brasse,	*perchance*
570	Take a lityll pow[d]er of Parisch and cast over his face,	*its (the coin's)*
571	Ande evyn in the howll-flight let him passe.	*owl-flight (the dark)*
	Titivillus kan lerne yow many praty thingys!	*teach/pretty, crafty*
	I trow Mankinde will cum ageyn son[e],	*soon*
574	Or ellys, I fere me, evynsonge will be don[e]!	*fear*
	His bedys shall be trisyde aside, and that anon.	*thrown*
	Ye shall a goode sport, if ye will abide:	*You will (have)*
	Mankinde cummith ageyn—well fare he!	*good luck to him (ironic)*
578	I shall answere him *ad omnia quare*.	*at every "why"*
	Ther shall be sett abroche a clericall mater.	*stirred up/controversy*
580	I hope of his purpose to sett him aside.	

[*Reenter Mankind.*]

581	MAN[KIND]. Evynsong hath be in the say[i]nge, I trow, a fayer w[h]ile!	*been*
	I am irke of it. It is to[o] longe, by on[e] mile.	
583	Do wey! I will no more so oft over the chirche-stile;	
	Be as be may, I shall do another.	*otherwise*
	Of labure and preyer, I am nere irke of both;	
	I will no more of it, thow[gh] Mercy be wroth.	
	My hede is very hevy, I tell yow, forsoth.	
588	I shall slepe full my bely, and he were my brother.	*my bellyfull/even if*

[*Goes to sleep and snores. Titivillus gloats to the audience.*]

	TITIVILLUS. Ande ever ye dide, for me kepe now yowr silence!	*If*
	Not a worde, I charge yow, peyn of forty pens!	*on pain of forfeiture*
	A praty game shall be schewde yow, or ye go hens.	*crafty/showed/ere*
	Ye may here him snore—he is sade aslepe.	*hear/sound*
593	Qw[h]ist! Pesse! The dev[i]ll is dede, I shall goo ronde in his ere.	*whisper*

[568]i.e., I've sent him to learn the devil's lies by means of his bowels.

[569-71](Titivillus teaches the audience one of his magic spells. A brass coin coated with Paris-powder is to be passed—i.e., excreted?—at night.)

[574]i.e., (sardonically) Otherwise I'm afraid he'll be too late for vespers.

[578] i.e., I'll answer all his questions.

[580-81]I trust to turn him aside from his purpose. —Vespers has taken a long while in the saying (or singing).

[583]To hell with it! No more will I climb over the steps in the churchyard wall (leading to church) as I have done so often.

[588]I'll get my bellyfull of sleep, even if Mercy were my brother (and thus would have a special claim on my loyalty).

[593]Hush! I'm going to whisper in Mankind's ear that Mercy is dead (?).

[He goes to Mankind and whispers in his ear.]
Alasse, Mankinde, alasse, Mercy stown a mere!   *has stolen a mare*
He is runn away fro his master, ther wot no man where.   *no one knows*
Moreover, he stale both a hors and a nete!   *stole/neat, ox or cow*

But yet I herde sey he brake his neke as he rode in Fraunce;   *heard*
598   But I thinke he ridith on the galows, to lern for to daunce,   *how to*
599   Bicause of his theft—that is his governance!
Trust no more on him: he is a marryde man.   *marred, ruined*
601   Mekill sorow with thy spade beforn thou hast wrought;   *Much/heretofore*
Arise and aske mercy of New-G[u]ise, Nowadays, and
    Nought.
They cun avise the[e] for the best. Lett ther goode will be   *can/their*
    sought;
Ande thy own wiff brethell, and take the[e] a lemman.   *deceive/mistress*

[To the audience.]
For-well, everychon, for I have don my game,   *Farewell everyone*
For I have brought Mankinde to mischeff and to schame!
[Exit Titivillus. Mankind awakes.]

607   MANK[IND].   Whope! who! Mercy hath brokyn his nekekicher,
    avows,   *(he) avows*
Or he hangith by the neke hye upp on the gallowse!
Adew, fayer masters, I will hast me to the ale-house   *i.e., audience*
Ande speke with New-G[u]ise, Nowad[ays], and Nought,
A[nd] geett me a lemman with a smattringe face.   *get/kissable(?)*
*[New-Guise comes running in with a broken noose around his
neck, shouting to the audience.]*
NEW-G[U]ISE.   Make space, for Cokkys body sakyrde, make   *God's/consecrated*
    space!
613   A ha, well over-ron, Gode giff him evill grace!
We were nere Sent Patrikes Wey, by Him that me bought;   *ransomed*

615   I was twichyde by the neke—the game was begunne!   *twitched*

598*daunce:* i.e., swing at the end of a noose.

599*that . . . governance:* that's how he conducts himself.

601You've caused much sorrow (to New-Guise, etc.) heretofore with your spade.

607Whoop! Whoop! Mercy has broken his neck (lit: neckerchief), he (Titivillus) avows.

613Well outrun (i.e., making good an escape), may God condemn him (the hangman)!

615-19i.e., My head was in the noose—the jig was up. Fortunately, the noose parted in two:
see, here's the proof, half of it still around my neck. We had a narrow escape! As the wife said
when she was about to behead her husband (giving him a ludicrously ineffectual warning),
"Watch out!" Mischief has been found guilty and imprisoned rather than executed because
he was able to recite his neck-verse (see line 520 and note).

616	A grace was, the halter brast asonder: *Ecce signum!*	*burst/Behold the proof*
617	The halff is abowte my neke. We hade a nere run[n]e!	*narrow escape*
618	"Beware," quod the goode-wiff when sche smot[e] of[f]	*said*
	her husbondys hede, "beware!"	
619	Mischeff is a convicte, for he coude his neke-verse.	*knew*
	My body gaff a swinge when I hinge uppon the casse.	*gave/hung/gibbet-frame (?)*
621	Alasse, he will hange such a lighly man and a fers[e]	*likely, handsome*
	For stelinge of an horse—I prey Gode gif him care!	*sorrow*

623	Do wey this halter! What dev[i]ll doth Mankinde here,	*Take off*
	with sorow?	
	Alasse, how my neke is sore, I make avowe!	*I swear*
	M[ANKIND]. Ye be welcom, New-G[u]ise. Ser, what chere	*how goes it*
	with yow?	
	NEW-G[U]ISE. Well, ser; I have no cause to mo[u]rn.	
	M[ANKIND]. What was that abowte yowr neke, so Gode yow	
	amende?	*may God help you*
628	NEW-G[U]ISE. In feyth, Sent Audrys holy bende.	*neck-band*
	I have a lityll dishes, as it plesse Gode to sende,	*disease*
	With a runninge ringe-worme.	

[*Enter Nowadays laden with stolen church furnishings, including the sacrament.*]

	NOWAD[AYS]. Stonde a-rom, I prey the[e], brother min[e]!	*Make room*
	I have laburryde all this night. W[h]en shall we go din[e]?	
	A chirche her[e]-beside shall pay for ale, brede, and win[e]:	*nearby*
	Lo, here is stoff will serve.	*furnishing (that)*
	NEW-G[U]ISE. Now, by the holy Mary, thou art better	
	marchande then I!	

[*Enter Nought.*]

	NOUGHT. Avante, knavys, lett me go by!	*Out of the way*
	I kannot geet, and I shulde sterve!	*get, steal/even if*

[*Enter Mischief with a pair of fetters.*]

638	MISCHEFF. Here cummith a man of armys! Why stonde ye so	*a soldier*
	still?	
	Of murder and manslaw[gh]ter I have my bely-fill.	

[621]Alas that the hangman would hang such a handsome and fierce fellow.

[623](to the audience still) Take off this noose! What the devil is Mankind doing here, with sorrow to him? (New-Guise remembers his beating.)

[628](New-Guise, still mistrusting Mankind, evasively pretends that his broken noose is a necklace-charm against disease, gotten from a shrine.)

[638]*Why . . . still:* i.e., Why do you look so surprised?

640 NOWAD[AYS].   What, Mischeff, have ye ben in presun? And   *If*
     it be yowr will,
641 Me semith ye have sco[u]ryde a peyr of fetters.   *scoured/pair*   ·
     MISCHEFF.   I was chenyde by the armys—lo, I have them   *chained*
          here.
     The chenys I brast asundyr, and killyde the jailere,   *burst*
     Ye[a], ande his fayer wiff halsyde in a corne e—   *embraced*
     A, how swetly I kissyde the swete mowth of hers!

     When I hade do, I was min[e] owyn bottler: *done, finished*
     I brought awey with me both disch and dublere.   *plate*
     Here is anow for me. Be of goode chere! [*He offers refresh-*   *enough*
          ment.]
649 Yet well fare the new chesa[u]nce!
     MANKINDE [*kneeling*].   I aske mercy of New-G[u]ise, Nowa-
          days, and Nought.
     Onys with my spade I remember that I faught;   *Once*
     I will make yow amendys if I hurt yow ought,
     Or dide ony grevaunce.

654 NEW-G[U]ISE.   What a dev[i]ll likith the[e] to be of this
          disposicion?
     MANKINDE.   I drempt Mercy was hange—this was my vision—
     Ande that to yow thre I shulde have recors and remocion.   *inclination*
     Now I prey yow hertily of yowr goode will:
     I crye yow mercy of all that I dide amisse.
     NOWADAYS [*aside*].   I sey, New-G[u]is[e], Nought: Titivillus
          made all this;   *caused*
     As sekyr as Gode is in hevyn, so it is!   *sure*
     NOUGHT [*to Mankind*].   Stonde uppe on yowr feet! Why
          stonde ye so still?   *motionless*

     NEW-G[U]ISE.   Master Mischeff, we will yow exort
663 Mankindys name in yowr bok for to report.
     MISCHEFF.   I will not so; I will sett a corte.   *convene a court*
     Nowadays, mak proclamacion,
     A[nd] do it *sub forma juris,* das[t]arde!   *in legal form/fool*
     NOWADAYS.   Oy-yt, oy-yit, oyet! All manere of men and   *Oyez*
          comun women

---

⁶⁴⁰⁻⁴¹Have you been in prison, Mischief? If you don't mind my saying so, it seems to me
you've scoured (polished by wearing) a pair of fetters.

⁶⁴⁹i.e., Good luck to our new venture.

⁶⁵⁴i.e., What the devil makes you want to change your mind (about us)?

⁶⁶³(Mischief is urged to set down Mankind's name in his list of loyal followers. Mischief
decides the apprenticeship needs the legal and ritual sanction of a manor-court session.)

To the cort of Mischiff othere cum or sen!   *either/send (excuses)*
Mankinde shall retorn; he is on[e] of owr men.

670   MISCHEFF.   Nought, cum forth. Thou shall be stewerde.

NEW-G[U]ISE.   Master Mischeff, his side gown may be solde;   *long coat*
672   He may have a jakett therof, and mony tolde.   *counted*
673   MANKINDE.   I will do for the best, so I have no colde.   *so long as*
    [*He takes off his gown reluctantly.*]
Holde, I prey yow, and take it with yow,
Ande let me have it ageyn in ony wise.   *in any case*
    Nought scri[bit].   *Nought is busy writing*
NEW-G[U]ISE.   I promitt yow a fresch jakett, after the new   *promise*
    g[u]ise.
MANKINDE.   Go and do that longith to yowr office,   *that which pertains*
A[nd] spare that ye mow!   *save what you can*
    [*New-Guise goes out with Mankind's coat. Nought shows
what he has written to Mischief.*]

NOUGHT.   Holde, master Mischeff, and rede this!
MISCHEFF.   Here is [*reads*] "*Blottibus in blottis,
Blottorum blottibus istis.*"
I beshrew yowr erys, a fayer hande!   *ears*
NOWAD[AYS].   Ye[a], it is a goode renni[n]ge fist;   *cursive hand*
684   Such an hande may not be mist.   *missed*
NOUGHT.   I shulde have don better, hade I wist.   *known*
MISCHEFF.   Take hede, sers, it stoude you on hande: [*reads.*] *it concerns you*

687   "*Curia tenta generalis,*
In a place ther goode ale is,   *where*
689   *Anno regni regitalis*
690   *Edwardi nullateni,*
On yestern day, in Feverere, the yere passith fully;   *completely ends*
692   As Nought hath writyn—here is owr Tully—   *Cicero*
693   *Anno regni regis nulli.*"

670*stewerde:* recorder of a manor court.

672*mony tolde:* i.e., money left over (because the long coat is large enough to cut a jacket and have cloth left).

673i.e., I'll do what you think best, as long as I don't get cold. (Mankind correctly fears that the new fashion won't keep him warm.)

684(sarcastically) Such a handwriting is indispensable.

687"The general court having been held" (the usual heading for the record of manor-court proceedings).

689–90"In the regnal year of King Edward the Nothingth."

692–93As Nought, our expert writer in Latin, has written: "In the regnal year of no king."

NOWAD[AYS].   What how, New-G[u]ise, thou makist moche [taryinge]!   *What ho*

That jakett shall not be worth a ferthinge.

[*New-Guise returns with Mankind's coat drastically abbreviated. He elbows the audience aside.*]

NEW-G[U]ISE.   Out of my wey, sers, for drede of fightinge!

697   Lo, here is a feet taill, light to leppe abowte!   *feat, elegant shape*

NOUGHT.   It is not schapyn worth a morsell of brede!   *shaped*

Ther is to[o] moche cloth—it weys as ony lede.   *weighs heavy as lead*

I shall goo and mende it, ellys I will lose my hede.   *or else/head*

Make space, sers, lett me go owte!

[*He goes out through the audience, with Mankind's coat.*]

MISCHEFF.   Mankinde, cum hethere—God sende yow the gowte!

Ye shall goo to all the goode felowse in the cuntré aboute,

Onto the goode-wiff when the goode-man is owte.   *husband*

"I will," say ye.

MAN[KIND].   I will, ser.

NEW-G[U]ISE.   There arn but sex dedly sinnys; lechery is non,

As it may be verefiede by us brethellys everychon.   *rogues everyone*

Ye shall goo robbe, stell, and kill as fast as ye may gon.   *steal*

"I will," sey ye.

M[ANKIND].   I will, ser.

710   NOWADAYS.   On Sundays, on the morow erly betime,   *morning*

Ye shall with us to the all[e]-house erly to go din[e],   *ale-house*

A[nd] forbere masse and matens, [h]owres and prime.   *forbear/canonical hours*

"I will," sey ye.

M[ANKIND].   I will, ser.

MISCHEFF.   Ye must have by yowr side a longe *da pacem*,   *"give peace," a dagger*

715   As trew men ride by the wey, for to onbrace them.

Take ther monay, kitt ther throtys! Thus overface them.   *cut their*

"I will," sey ye.

MAN[KIND].   I will, ser.

[*Nought returns with Mankind's coat reduced to a ridiculously short jacket.*]

NOUGHT.   Here is a joly jakett! How sey ye?

719   NEW-G[UISE].   It is a goode jake[t] of fence for a mannys body!   *defense*

697Lo, here's an elegant shape in which to go leaping about nimbly!

715To unbrace (i.e., rob and carve up) honest men as they ride on journeys.

719i.e., (sarcastically) It's a fine short jacket to defend a man's body against the cold!

[*They put it on Mankind.*]

720   Hay, doog! hay, whoppe! whoc! Go yowr wey lightly!   *whoop!/quickly*

721   Ye are well made for to ren.   *run*

[*Mercy enters at a distance.*]

MISCHEFF.   Tidingys, tidingys! I have aspyede on[e].

723   Hens with yowr stuff; fast we were gon!   *Hence/plunder*

I beshrew the last shall com to his hom.   *(who) shall*

   Dicant omnes: *Let all say*

[ALL.]   Amen!

MERCY.   What, how, Mankinde, fle that felyschippe, I yow
      prey!

MANKINDE.   I shall speke with [thee] another tim[e]—
      to-morn, or the next day.

We shall goo forth together, to kepe my faders yer-day.   *death anniversary*

729   A tapster, a tapster! Stow, statt, stow!   *Whoa woman*

MISCHEFF.   A mischeff go with! Here I have a foull fall.   *with (you)*

Hens, awey fro me, or I shall beschit[t]e yow all.

NEW-G[U]ISE.   What, how, [h]ostlere, hostlere, lende us a   *innkeeper*
      football!

Whoppe, whow! a-now, a-now, a-now, a-now!   *Whoop*

   [*The rogues go off, taking Mankind with them.*]

MERCY.   My minde is dispersyde, my body trymmelith as the   *distracted/trembles*
      aspen leffe!

735   The terys shuld trekyll down by my chekys, were not
      yowr reverrence.

It were to me solace, the cruell visitacion of deth!   *It would be*

Without rude behaver, I kan[not] expresse this
      inconveniens.   *misfortune*

Wepinge, sythinge, and sobbinge were my sufficiens;   *sighing/sustinence*

All naturall nutriment to me as caren is odibull.   *is odious as carrion*

740   My inwarde afflixcion yeldith me tediouse unto yowr   *makes me*
      presens.

I kannot bere it evynly that Mankinde is so flexibull!   *with equanimity*

Man on-kinde, wherever thou be! For, all this world was   *unnatural*
      not aprehensible   *could not see how*

720–21 (In his new coat, Mankind evidently reminds New-Guise of a racing dog.)

723 Get going with your plunder; let's be off quickly!

729 (Mankind and his companions respond to Mercy's presence by indulging in a frenetic
roughhouse, in which Mischief is tripped up.)

735 The tears would trickle down my cheeks, were it not for the respect I owe you (the audience).

To discharge thin[e] originall offence, thraldam, and
    captivité,

Till Godys own welbelovyde son was obedient and
    passible.   *willing to suffer*

Every droppe of his bloode was schede to purge thin[e]
    iniquité.

I discomende and disalow thin[e] oftyn mutabilité!   *changeability*

To every creature thou art dispectuose and odible.   *contemptible/odious*

Why art thou so on-curtess, so inconsideratt? Alasse, who   *unkind/woe*
    is me!

As the fane that turnith with the winde, so thou art   *weathervane*
    convertible.

750   In trust is treson; thy promes is not credible.

751   Thy perversiose ingratitude I cannot rehers!   *perverse/speak*

To God and to all the holy corte of hevyn thou art
    despectible,   *despicable*

As a nobyll versifier makith mencion in this verse:

754   *"Lex et natura, Cristus et omnia jura*

755   *Damnant ingratum; lugent eum fore natum."*

O goode Lady and Mother of Mercy, have pety and   *pity*
    compassion

Of the wrechydnes of Mankinde, that is so wanton and so   *On*
    fraill!

Lett Mercy excede Justice, dere Mother! A[d]mitt this   *Grant*
    supplicacion:

Equité to be leyde onparty, and Mercy to prevaill.   *set aside*

760   To sensuall livinge is reprovable that is nowadays,

761   As by the comprehence of this mater it may be specifiede.   *contents*

New-G[u]ise, Nowadays, Nought, with ther allectuose   *alluring*
    ways

They have pervertyde Mankinde, my swet sun, I have
    well espyede.

A, with thes[e] cursyde caityfs, and I may, he shall not   *if*
    long indure!

750-51i.e., Those whom we trust will betray us; your promises cannot be trusted. Your perverse ingratitude is more than I can say.

754-55"Law and nature, Christ and all justice condemn the ingrate; they lament that he was born." (The author is unidentified.)

760-61 Sensual living can be blamed for what goes on nowadays, as may be proven by the contents of this edifying story.

I, Mercy, his father gostly, will procede forth and do my
  propyrté.   *special task*

Lady, helpe! This maner of livinge is a detestabull plesure.

767   *Vanitas vanitatum,* all is but a vanité.   *Vanity of vanities*

Mercy shall never be convicte of his oncurtes condicion;   *conquered by Man's*

With wepinge terys, by nig[h]te and by day, I will goo,   *tears*
  and never sesse.   *cease*

Shall I not finde him? Yes, I hope. Now Gode be my
  proteccion!
    [*He calls aloud.*]

My predilecte son, wher be ye? Mankinde, *ubi es?*   *greatly beloved/where are you*
    [*He goes off, crying "Ubi es?" Enter Mischief.*]

772   MISCHEFF.   My prepotent fadere, when ye sowpe, sowpe   *sup*
          out yowr messe!

773   Ye are all to-gloriede in yowr termys—ye make many a
          lesse.   *lie*

Will ye here? He crieth ever "Mankinde, *ubi es?*"   *Do you hear/constantly*
    [*Enter New-Guise. Nowadays and Nought, who have been
    relieving themselves, follow soon after.*]

775   NEW-G[UISE].   Hic, hic, hic, hic, hic, hic, hic, hic!   *Here*

776   That is to sey, here, here, here, ny dede in the cryke!   *nearly dead/creek*

If ye will have him, goo and syke, syke, syke!   *ye (Mercy)/seek*

Syke not over-long, for losinge of yowr minde.

779   NOWADAY[S].   If ye will have Mankinde—how, *Domine,
          Domine, Dominus!*—   *Lord*

780   Ye must speke to the schrive for a *cape corpus,*   *"take his body"*

781   Ellys ye must be fain to retorn with *non est inventus.*   *"he is not found"*

782   How sey ye, ser? My bolte is schett.   *bolt, arrow/shot*

783   NOUGHT.   I am doinge of my nedingys; beware how ye   *moving my bowels*
          schott!

767(Ecclesiastes 1:2.)

772–73My greatly powerful father, when you sup, drink up your portion! (A nonsense parody
of Mercy's parting statement.) You are excessively puffed up (i.e., Latinate, aureate) in your
vocabulary—you tell many a lie.

775–76(New-Guise mockingly suggests how Mankind might answer Mercy's call: "Here I am,
nearly dead in a creek.")

779–83If you want to find Mankind—O, Lord, Lord, Lord! (Nowadays mimics Mercy's prayer-
ful entreaties)—you must speak to the sheriff for a writ of arrest, or else you must be content
to come back with a sheriff's certification that the prisoner cannot be found. (Mankind has
evidently been getting into trouble with the law.) How do you like the way I've shot my bolt,
i.e., practiced my wit at Mercy's expense (with an added meaning of "relieved myself")?
—NOUGHT (who has apparently been the target of this "shot" in a literal sense): Watch where
you're shooting while I'm moving my bowels!

Fy, fy, fy! I have fowll arayde my fote. — *foully soiled my foot*

785 Be wise for schotinge with yowr takyllys, for, Gode wott, — *weapons*

My fote is fowly over-schett. — *covered with shit*

MISCHEFF. A parlement, a parlement! Cum forth, Nought, behinde; — *from behind*

A cownsell belive! I am aferde Mercy will him finde. — *quickly/afraid*

How sey ye? And what sey ye? How shall we do with Mankinde?

790 NEW-G[U]IS[E]. Tische, a flyes weyng! Will ye do well? — *Tush/wing*

He wenith Mercy were honge for steling of a mere. — *thinks/mare*

Mischeff, go sey to him that Mercy sekith everyw[h]ere:

He will honge himselff, I undyrtake, for fere. — *wager/fear (of a ghost)*

MISCHEFF. I assent therto. It is wittily seyde, and well.

795 NOWAD[AYS]. Qwippe it in thy cote; anon it were don! — *Whip, put*

796 Now, Sent Gabriellys modyr save the clothes of thy schon! — *clouts*

All the bokys in the worlde, if they hade be undon, — *books/been ransacked*

Kowde not a cownselde us bett. — *Could/have/better*

Hic exit Mischeff. [He returns with Mankind, now in despair.] — *Here*

MISCHEFF. How, Mankinde, cumm and speke with Mercy!

He is here fast by. — *nearby*

MANKINDE. A roppe, a rope, a rope! I am not worthy.

MISCHEFF. Anon, anon, anon! I have it here redy,

With a tre also that I have gett. — *gallows-tree/gotten*

[They bring forth a rope and gallows.]

Holde the tre, Nowadays; Nought, take hede, and be wise!

NEW-G[U]ISE. Lo, Mankinde, do as I do: this is thy new g[u]ise.

Giff the roppe just to thye neke, this is min[e] avise. — *Give, adjust*

[New-Guise demonstrates with his own neck in the noose. Mercy enters at a distance.]

MISCHEFF. Helpe thysylff, Nought! Lo, Mercy is here!

He skarith us with a bales; we may no lengere tary! — *drives us off/scourge*

[They run away. New-Guise, forgetting the rope, hangs himself.]

785Watch where you're aiming with your weapon (perhaps in the obscene sense), for, God knows.

790Tush, a fly's wing (or weight; a trifle). Do you want my idea as to how we'll succeed?

795-96Put it quickly in your kirtle (i.e., the rope for Mankind?); let it be done immediately! Now, may Saint Gabriel's mother save the clouts or cleats of your shoes! (a hyperbolical oath of appreciation).

808   NEW-G[UISE].   Qweke, qweke, qweke! Alass, my thrott!
                I beschrew yow, mary!
            A, Mercy, Cristys coppyde curse go with yow—and   *heaped-up*
                Sent Davy!
            Alasse, my wesant! Ye were sumwhat to[o] nere.   *throat*
                [*They return and release him.*] *Exiant.* [*Mankind falls, de-*
                spairing.]

       MERCY.   Arise, my preciose redempt son! Ye be to me full
                dere.—
            He is so timerouse, me semith his vitall sprit doth exspire.   *it seems to me*
       MANKINDE.   Alasse, I have be so bestially disposyde I dare   *been*
                not apere!
            To se yowr solayciose face I am not worthy to dysiere.   *solace-giving/desire*

       MERCY.   Yowr criminose compleynt wo[u]ndith my hert as   *confession of guilt*
                a lance!
            Dispose yowrsylff mekly to aske mercy, and I will assent.
            Yelde me nethyr golde nor tresure, but yowr humbyll   *Yield, give*
                obeisiance—
            The voluntary subjeccion of yowr hert—and I am content.

       MAN[KIND].   What, aske mercy yet onys again? Alas, it
                were a vile petici[o]n!
820   Evyr to offend and ever to aske mercy, it is a puerilité.   *childish way*
            It is so abhominabyll to rehers my iterat transgrescion,   *repeated*
            I am not worthy to have mercy by no possibilité.   *(That) I*

       MERCY.   O Mankend, my singler solas, this is a lamentabyll   *special solace*
                excuse!
            The dolorus terys of my hert, how they begin to a-mownt!   *sorrowful/mount*
            O pirssid Jhesu, help thou this sinfull sinner to redouce! *pierced/lead back*
826   *Nam haec est mutatio dexterae Excelsi: vertit impios, et non sunt.*

            Arise and aske mercy, Mankend, and be associat to me.
            Thy deth schall be my hevinesse. Alas, tis pety it schuld be
                thus!
            Thy obstinacy will exclude [thee] fro the glorius
                perpetuité.   *eternity*
830   Yet, for my lofe, ope thy lippys and sey "*Miserere mei,*   *love/open*
                Deus!"

    808*Qweke*: sound of choking. *mary*: marry, indeed.

    826For this is the change of the right hand of the Most High: he overthrows the wicked, and
    they are no more. (Psalms 77:10 and Proverbs 12:7.)

    830*Miserere . . . Deus*: Have mercy upon me, O God.

MANKEND.   The egall justise of God will not permitte sych   *evenhanded*
             a sinfull wrech
       To be revivyd and restoryd ageyn; it were impossibyll.

MERCY.   The justice of God will as I will, as himsylfe doth   *will do*
           preche:
834   *Nolo mortem peccatoris, inquit,* iff he will be redusible.   *recoverable*

MANKEND.   Than mercy, good Mercy! What is a man   *Then*
             withowte mercy?
       Lityll is our parte of paradise, w[h]ere mercy ne were.   *if mercy were lacking*
837   Good Mercy, excuse the inevitabyll objeccion of my   *assault*
             gostly enmy.
838   The proverbe seyth, "The trewth tryith the sylfe." Alas,
             I have mech care!   *much sorrow*

839   MERCY.   God will not make yow prevy onto his Last
                  Jugement.
       Justice and equité shall be fortifyid, I will not denye;   *strong in argument*
       Trowthe may not so cruelly procede in his streyt argument   *(Yet) Truth/strict*
       But that Mercy schall rewle the mater, withowte
             contraversye.   *doubtless*

       Arise now, and go with me in this deambulatorye.   *walking area, cloister*
844   Incline yowyr capacité; my doctrine is convenient.
       Sinne not in hope of mercy! That is a crime notary.   *notorious*
       To truste overmoche in a prince, it is not expedient.

847   In hope, when ye sin, ye thinke to have mercy: beware
             of that aventure!
       The good Lord seyd to the lecherus woman of
             Chanane—   *Canaan*
       The holy Gospell is the autorité, as we rede in
             Scripture—
850   *"Vade, et iam amplius noli peccare."*   *Go and sin no more*

       Crist preservyd this sinfull woman takyn in avowtry;   *adultery*

834I do not wish the sinner's death, he said (see Ezekiel 33:11), if he is willing to be recovered.

837–39i.e., Good Mercy, forgive my fall as the result of the unavoidable assault of my spiritual enemy. As the proverb says, "The truth proclaims itself." Alas, I have great sorrow! —God won't share with you the secret intentions of his Last Judgment. (Mercy hereupon describes the debate of the four daughters of God, as in *Perseverance*, although he doesn't actually name Peace.)

844Submit your understanding to my teaching; it is befitting, agreeable.

847Beware of sinning in hope of mercy. (See Ecclesiasticus 5:4–7.)

850(John 8:11.)

He seyde to her theis wordys, "Go and sin no more."   *these*

So to yow: "Go, and sin no more." Beware of veyn   *vain*
   confidens of mercy!   *in*

Offend not a prince on trust of his favour, as I seyd before.   *in trust*

If ye fele yoursylfe trappyd in the snare of your gostly   *feel*
   enmy,

Aske mercy anon; beware of the continuance!   *at once/continuing in sin*

Whill a wo[u]nd is fresch, it is provyd curabyll by surgery,

That, if it procede ovyrlong, it is cawse of gret grevans.   *Which*

859   MANKEND.   To aske mercy and to have, this is a liberall   *precious*
   possescion.

860   Schall this expedicius peticion ever be alowyd, as ye have
   insight?

861   MERCY.   In this present life, mercy is plenté, till deth makith
   his division.

862   But, when ye be go, *usque ad minimum quadrantem* ye   *gone, dead*
   scha[ll] rekyn your right.

Aske mercy, and have, whill the body with the sow[l]e
   hath his annexion;

If ye tary till your discesse, ye may hap of your desire to   *decease*
   misse.

Be repentant here! Trust not the [h]owr of deth. Thinke
   on this lessun:

866   *Ecce nunc tempus acceptabile, ecce nunc dies salutis.*

867   All the vertu in the wor[l]d if ye might comprehend,   *even if/attain*

868   Your meritys were not premiabyll to the blis above—   *deserving of reward*

869   Not to the lest joy of hevyn, of your propyr efforte to   *your own*
   ascend.

With mercy, ye may. I tell yow no fabyll; Scripture doth
   prove.

MANKEND.   O Mercy, my suavius solas and singuler   *sweet/sole*
   recreatory,   *restorer*

My predilecte spesiall! Ye are worthy to have my love.   *dearly beloved*

859–62To ask for and receive mercy is a precious thing. Will this hastily-presented request ever
be granted, as you understand the situation? —As long as you're alive, mercy is still plentifully
available (i.e., it is never too late to repent during life). But when you die, you'll have to
reckon up your just reward to the uttermost farthing (lit: smallest fourth part of a coin).
(See Matthew 5:26.)

866–69Behold, now is the accepted time, behold, now is the day of salvation. (2 Corinthians
6:2.) Even if you could attain to all the virtues in the world, your merits would not entitle
you to the least joy of heaven, to ascend by your own efforts to heavenly bliss.

873   For, withowte deserte and menys supplicatorye,
874   Ye be compacient to my inexcusabyll reprove.   *compassionate/shame*

    A, it swemith my hert to think how onwisely I have   *grieves*
       wro[u]ght!
    Titivillus, that goth invisibele, hing his nett before my eye,   *who goes/hung*
877   And by his fantasticall visionys sedici[o]usly sowght,
878   To New-G[u]ise, Nowadayis, Nowght causyd me to obey.

MERCY.   Mankend, ye were obliviows of my doctrine
       monitorye: *admonitory*
    I seyd before, Titivillus wold asay yow a bronte.   *try an attack on you*
    Beware fro hensforth of his fablys delusory!
882   The proverbe seyth: *"Jacula praestita minus laedunt."*

    Ye have thre adversaryis and he is mayster of hem all: *them*
    That is to sey, the Devell, the World, the Flesch and the
       Fell.   *Skin*
    The New-G[uise], Nowadayis, Nowgth, the "World"
       we may hem call;
    And propy[r]lly Titivillus singnifith the Fend of helle;

    The Flesch—that is the unclene concupissens of your body.
    These be your thre gostly enmyis, in whom ye have put
       your confidens.
    They brow[gh]t yow to Mischeffe, to conclude your
       temporall glory—
    As it hath be schewyd before this worchepp[f]yll audiens.   *been showed*

891   Remembyr how redy I was to help yow; fro swheche I   *from such*
       was not dangerus.
    Wherfore, good sunne, absteyne fro sin evermore after
       this!
893   Ye may both save and spill yowr sowle, that is so precius;   *destroy*
894   *Libere welle, libere nolle* God may not deny, iwis.

873–74For you are compassionate toward my inexcusable shame—I who am without deserving or means of imploring you for help.

877–78And by his supernatural illusions seditiously endeavored to cause me to obey New-Guise, Nowadays, and Nought.

882"Anticipated darts wound less."

891*fro . . . dangerus:* from such (encounters) I was not standoffish, reluctant.

893–94You have free will to choose salvation or damnation; God may not deny you freely to choose or freely not to choose, truly.

Beware of Titivillus with his net, and of all his
    envi[o]us will,
Of your sinfull delectacion that grevith your gostly   *pleasure*
    substans.   *soul*
Your body is your enmy. Let him not have his will!
Take your leve when ye will—God send yow good   *Depart*
    perseverans!

M[ANKIND].   Sith I schall departe, blis[s]e me, fader, her[e]
    then I go.   *ere I go*
    God send us all plenté of his gret mercy!
901   MERCY.   *Dominus custodit te ab omni malo!*
    In nomine Patris, et Filii, et Spiritus Sancti. Amen.

    Hic exit Mankend. [Mercy speaks the epilogue.]   *Here*

Wyrschep[f]yll sofereyns, I have do my propirté: *my special task*
Mankind is deliveryd by my faverall patrocinye.   *benevolent protection*
God preserve him fro all wickyd captivité,
And send him grace his sensuall condicions to mortifye!   *disposition*

Now, for His love that for us receivyd His humanité,   *i.e., took human form*
Serche your condicions with dew examinacion!   *due, thorough*
Thinke and remembyr the world is but a vanité,
910   As it is provyd daly by d[i]verse transmutacion.

Mankend is wrechyd, he hath sufficient prove;   *sufficently proven*
Therefore God [grant] yow all *per suam misericordiam*   *through his mercy*
That ye may be pley-ferys with the angell[ys] above,   *companions*
And have to your porcion *vitam aeternam. Amen!*   *life everlasting*
    Finis.

[901](May) the Lord preserve you from all evil. (Psalms 121:7.)

EVERYMAN

Everyman (ca. 1495) has long been the most popular and best known of morality plays. Yet its success is of a different sort from that of other English moralities. Most descendants of *The Castle of Perseverance* retell the spiritual struggles of erring Mankind who is reclaimed at last to virtue after having fallen into wickedness; *Everyman* focuses instead on the moment of the Coming of Death, a moment of intense emotional impact. Most other morality plays employ vice comedy to illustrate the insidious nature of evil; *Everyman* concentrates instead on the spiritual seriousness of the protagonist's situation. The play eschews laughter but gains by the purity of its emphasis on the meaning of death. *Everyman* also makes fewer theatrical demands than do *Mankind* or other moralities, calling for no astonishing visual effects or elaborate changes of costume. This restraint, though atypical of the genre, is in keeping with the play's decorum. The original text is almost entirely lacking in stage directions.

Everyman's atypical qualities may derive in part from its relationship to the Dutch *Elckerlijc*. Whether the English version was translated from the Dutch (first printed in 1495) or the Dutch version from the English, the connection between the two stresses the play's affinities to continental religious thought. The assertion that the clergy are above the angels in degree since they administer the holy sacrament (ll. 735–49), the castigation of certain clergymen for selling church offices (ll. 750–68), and the corresponding emphasis on the need for the clergy to purify their own hearts, are all in accord with the Northern European reform movement which was given most ardent expression in Thomas à Kempis' *The Imitation of Christ*. These ideas were also current in English sermons and lyrics during the late fifteenth century.

Everyman thus concerns itself not only with the timeless and universal problem of dying in a state of grace, but with contemporary issues affecting the state of the Church. Unlike *The Castle of Perseverance,* in which Mankind visits no confessor and receives no sacrament, *Everyman* puts great stress on the institutional role of the Church in man's salvation. The seven sacraments are all carefully explained to the audience (ll. 722–25), with particular stress on the Eucharist and the sacrament of penance. Everyman is carefully guided by orthodox teaching through the four stages of penance prescribed by the Catholic Church: confession of his sins to a "holy man" dwelling in the "hous of salvacion," i.e., the Church (ll. 535–42); contrition (549); absolution (629–33); and satisfaction, i.e., making amends for sin (770). Everyman's Good Deeds consist not only of charitable acts but also of penitential scourgings assigned by his confessor. As the holy doctor emphasizes at the play's end, salvation may be obtained by no other means. This teaching assumes some urgency in the context of the late fifteenth century, when abuses among the clergy and disaffection among worshipers were on the increase.

Staging appears to require some high place from which God and an angel speak and a *sedes* representing the "hous of salvacion" or the Church. The figure called Confession who dwells here is probably also the figure called Priesthood from whom Everyman receives extreme unction (l. 749). Quite possibly, as A. C. Cawley suggests in his edition of *Everyman,* God's heavenly abode is atop the house of salvation. Most of the action takes place on an unlocalized open stage. Evidently Everyman must descend into an actual grave, perhaps by means of a trap door.

The rhyme scheme of the play combines couplets and quatrains made up of lines of unequal length in stanzas of varying lengths, with occasional tail rhyme. The English *Everyman* survives in four printed editions by two printers from the period 1508 to 1537. The present text is based on the Britwell copy (ca. 1528–29), printed by John Skot. Apparently none of the four texts was copied from any other; all may be derived from a common original. The other copies have been used to correct the Britwell copy when it is clearly in error, as indicated in the textual notes.

EVERYMAN

[DRAMATIS PERSONAE

GOD

MESSENGER	KNOWLEGE
DETHE	CONFESSION
EVERYMAN	BEAUTE
FELAWSHIP	STRENGTH
KINREDE	DISCRECION
COSYN	FIVE WITTES
GOODES	AUNGELL
GOOD DEDES	DOCTOUR]

Here Beginneth a Treatise how the hye Fader of Heven sendeth Dethe to somon every Creature to come and give Acounte of their Lives in this Worlde, and is in Maner of a Morall Playe.

[*Enter a messenger as prologue.*]

MESSENGER. I pray you all give your audience,
And here this mater with reverence,   *hear*
By figure a morall playe: *In form*
The Somoninge of Everyman called it is,
That of our lives and endinge shewes
How transitory we be all daye.
This mater is wonder[ou]s precious,
But the entent of it is more gracious,   *always*
And swete to bere awaye.
10 The story saith: Man, in the beginninge   *intent, moral lesson*
Loke well, and take good heed to the endinge,
Be you never so gay!

Ye thinke sinne in the beginninge full swere,
Whiche in the ende causeth the soule to wepe
Whan the body lieth in claye.
Here shall you se how Falawship and Jolité,
Bothe Strengthe, Pleasure, and Beauté,
Will fade from the[e] as floure in Maye;
For ye shall here how our heven Kinge *hear*
20 Calleth Everyman to a generall rekeninge.
Give audience, and here what he doth saye. [*Exit.*] *hear*

God speketh [*from above*]:

GOD.   I perceive, here in my majesté,
How that all creatures be to me unkinde,
Livinge without drede in worldly prosperité.
Of ghostly sight the people be so blinde, *spiritual vision*
Drowned in sinne, they know me not for their God.
In worldely riches is all their minde;
They fere not my rightwysnes, the sharpe rod. *fear/righteousness*
My love that I shewed whan I for them died
They forgete clene, and shedinge of my blode rede.
I hanged bitwene two [theves], it cannot be denied;
To gete them life I suffred to be deed; *get/consented/dead*
33 I heled their fete, with thornes hurt was my heed. *feet*
I coude do no more than I dide, truely;
And nowe I se the people do clene forsake me.
They use the seven deedly sinnes dampnable,
As pride, coveitise, wrath, and lechery
Now in the worlde be made commendable;
And thus they leve of aungelles the hevenly company. *leave*
40 Every man liveth so after his owne pleasure,
And yet of their life they be nothinge sure. *not at all secure*
I se the more that I them forbere *spare them*
The worse they be fro yere to yere. *from*
All that liveth appaireth faste. *grows worse*
Therfore I will, in all the haste,
Have a rekeninge of every mannes persone;
For, and I leve the people thus alone *if*
In their life and wicked tempestes,
Verily they will become moche worse than beestes!
50 For now one wolde by envy another up ete;
Charité they do all clene forgete.
I hoped well that every man

---

³³*heled their fete*: refers to Christ's washing the disciples' feet for man's spiritual benefit. See John 13:1–20.

In my glory sholde make his mansion,
And therto I had them all electe.
But now I se, like traitours dejecte,   *abject*
They thanke me not for the pleasure that I to them ment,   *meant for them*
Nor yet for their beinge that I them have lent.
I profered the people grete multitude of mercy,
And fewe there be that asketh it hertly.   *with their hearts*
60   They be so combred with worldly riches
That nedes on them I must do justice,   *I must needs, must*
On every man livinge, without fere.   *doubtless*
Where arte thou, Deth, thou mighty messengere?
        [*Enter*] *Death.*

DETHE.   Almighty God, I am here at your will,
Your commaundement to fulfill.
GOD.   Go thou to Everyman
And shewe him, in my name,
A pilgrimage he must on him take
Whiche he in no wise may escape,
70   And that he bringe with him a sure rekeninge
Without delay or ony taryenge. [*God withdraws.*]

DETHE.   Lorde, I will in the worlde go renne over all,   *run everywhere*
And cruelly out-serche bothe grete and small.
Every man will I beset that liveth beestly
Out of Goddes lawes, and dredeth not foly.
He that loveth richesse I will strike with my darte,
77   His sight to blinde, and fro heven to departe—   *separate*
Excepte that almes be his good frende—   *Unless*
In hell for to dwell, worlde without ende.
        [*Enter Everyman at a distance.*]

Loo, yonder I se Everyman walkinge.
Full litell he thinketh on my cominge;
His minde is on flesshely lustes and his treasure,
And grete paine it shall cause him to endure   *to submit himself*
Before the Lorde, heven Kinge.
        [*Death halts Everyman.*]
Everyman, stande still! Whider arte thou goinge
Thus gaily? Hast thou thy Maker forgete?
EVERYMAN.   Why askest thou?
Woldest thou wete?   *wit, know*
DETHE.   Ye[a], sir, I will shewe you:
90   In grete hast[e] I am sende to the[e]   *sent*

---

⁷⁷To blind his sight, and separate (him) from heaven.

Fro God out of his magesté.

EVERYMAN. What, sente to me?

DETHE. Ye[a], certainly.

Thoughe thou have forgete him here,

He thinketh on the[e] in the hevenly sp[h]ere,

As, or we departe, thou shalte knowe. *ere*

EVERYMAN. What desireth God of me?

DETHE. That shall I shewe the[e]:

A rekeninge he will nedes have *he must have*

100 Without ony lenger respite. *any longer*

EVERYMAN. To give a rekeninge, longer laiser I crave! *leisure*

This blinde mater troubleth my witte. *obscure*

DETHE. On the[e] thou must take a longe journey;

Therfore thy boke of counte with the[e] thou bringe, *account*

For tourne againe thou cannot by no waye. *return*

And loke thou be sure of thy rekeninge,

For before God thou shalte answere and shewe

Thy many badde dedes, and good but a fewe, *deeds*

How thou hast spente thy life, and in what wise,

110 Before the chefe Lorde of paradise.

Have ado that we were in that waye, *See to it/on our way*

For, wete thou well, thou shalte make none attournay. *make no one (your) attorney*

EVERYMAN. Full unredy I am suche rekeninge to give.

I knowe the[e] not. What messenger arte thou?

DETHE. I am Dethe, that no man dredeth, *that fears no man*

For every man I reste, and no man spareth; *arrest*

For it is Goddes commaundement

That all to me sholde be obedient.

EVERYMAN. O Deth, thou comest whan I had the[e] leest
    in minde!

120 In thy power it lieth me to save;

Yet of my good wil I give the[e], if thou wil be kinde: *goods*

Ye[a], a thousande pounde shalte thou have,

And [thou] differre this mater till another daye. *If you defer*

DETHE. Everyman, it may not be, by no waye.

I set not by golde, silver, nor richesse, *care not for*

Ne by pope, emperour, kinge, duke, ne princes;

For, and I wolde receive giftes grete, *if/great*

All the worlde I might gete;

But my custome is clene contrary.

130 I give the[e] no respite. Come hens, and not tary. *hence*

EVERYMAN. Alas, shall I have no lenger respite?

I may saye Deth giveth no warninge!

To thinke on the[e], it maketh my herte seke, *sick*

For all unredy is my boke of rekeninge.

But twelve yere and I might have abidinge, *Only/if I could stay*

My countinge-boke I wolde make so clere
That my rekeninge I sholde not nede to fere.
Wherfore, Deth, I praye the[e], for Goddes mercy,
Spare me till I be provided of remedy!

DETHE.   The[e] availeth not to crye, wepe, and praye;

141   But hast[e] the[e] lightly that thou were gone that   *quickly*
          journaye,
And preve thy frendes if thou can;   *make trial of*
For, wete thou well, the tide abideth no man,   *know/time*
And in the worlde eche livinge creature
For Adams sinne must die of nature.   *in the course of nature*

EVERYMAN.   Dethe, if I sholde this pilgrimage take,
And my rekeninge suerly make,   *surely*
Shewe me, for saint charité,   *for (the sake of) holy*
Sholde I not come againe shortly?

150   DETHE.   No, Everyman. And thou be ones there,   *Once you're there*
Thou mayst nevermore come here,
Trust me verily.

EVERYMAN.   O gracious God in the hye sete celestiall,   *high seat*
Have mercy on me in this moost nede!
Shall I have no company fro this vale terestriall
Of mine acqueyn[taun]ce, that way me to lede?

DETHE.   Ye[a], if ony be so hardy
That wolde go with the[e] and bere the[e] company.
Hie the[e] that thou were gone to Goddes magnificence,   *Hasten*
Thy rekeninge to give before his presence.

161   What, wenest thou thy live is given the[e],   *ween, suppose/life*
And thy worldely gooddes also?

EVERYMAN.   I had wende so, verilé.   *verily*

DETHE.   Nay, nay, it was but lende the[e].   *lent*
For, as soone as thou arte go,   *gone, dead*
Another a while shall have it, and than go therfro,   *then go from it*
Even as thou hast done.
Everyman, thou arte mad! Thou hast thy wittes five,
And here on erthe will not amende thy live—   *And (yet)*
For sodeynly I do come.

171   EVERYMAN.   O wretched caitife, wheder shall I flee   *whither*
That I might scape this endles sorowe?
Now, gentill Deth, spare me till tomorowe,
That I may amende me
With good advisement.   *reflection*

141But hasten quickly on that journey.

161*given the[e]*: i.e., given permanently rather than loaned from God.

171*O wretched caitife*: spoken by Everyman to himself.

DETHE.   Naye, therto I will not consent,
　　Nor no man will I respite,
　　But to the herte sodeynly I shall smite
　　Without ony advisement.
180　And now out of thy sight I will me hy.　　　　　　*hie, hasten*
　　Se thou make the[e] redy shortely,
　　For thou mayst saye this is the daye
　　That no man livinge may scape awaye. [*Exit.*]

EVERYMAN.   Alas, I may well wepe with sighes depe!
　　Now have I no maner of company
　　To helpe me in my journey, and me to kepe;　　　　*protect*
　　And also my writinge is full unredy.　　　　　　　*i.e., my accounts*
　　How shall I do now for to excuse me?
　　I wolde to God I had never be gete!　　　　　　　*been begotten*
190　To my soule a full grete profite it had be,　　　　*been*
　　For now I fere paines huge and grete.
　　The time passeth. Lorde, helpe, that all wrought!　*who created everything*
　　For though I mourne it availeth nought:
　　The day passeth, and is almoost ago.　　　　　　　*gone*
　　I wote not well what for to do.
　　To whome were I best my complaint to make?
　　What and I to Felawship therof spake,　　　　　　　*if*
　　And shewyd him of this sodeyne chaunce?　　　　　*misfortune*
　　For in him is all mine affiaunce,　　　　　　　　　*trust*
200　We have in the worlde so many a daye
　　Be good frendes, in sporte and playe.　　　　　　　*Been*
　　　　[*Fellowship enters at a distance.*]

　　I se him yonder, certainely.
　　I trust that he will bere me company;
　　Therfore to him will I speke to ese my sorowe.
　　Well mette, good Felawship, and good morowe!
　　　　Felawship speketh:
FELAWSHIP.   Everyman, good morowe, by this daye!
　　Sir, why lokest thou so piteously?
　　If ony thinge be amisse, I praye the[e] me saye,
　　That I may helpe to remedy.
210　EVERYMAN.   Ye[a], good Felawship, ye[a],
　　I am in greate jeoparde.
FELAWSHIP.   My true frende, shewe to me your minde;
　　I will not forsake the[e] to my lives ende
　　In the waye of good company.
EVERYMAN.   That was well spoken, and lovingly.
FELAWSHIP.   Sir, I must nedes knowe your hevinesse;　　*sorrow*
　　I have pité to se you in ony distresse.

If ony have you wronged, ye shall revenged be,   *If anyone has*
Thoughe I on the grounde be slaine for the[e]—
220   Though that I knowe before that I sholde die!
EVERYMAN.   Verily, Felawship, gramercy.   *great thanks*
FELAWSHIP.   Tusshe, by thy thankes I set not a strawe!   *don't care a bit*
Shewe me your grefe, and saye no more.
EVERYMAN.   If I my herte sholde to you breke,   *reveal*
And than you to tourne your minde fro me   *then*
And wolde not me comforte whan ye here me speke,   *hear*
Than sholde I ten times sorier be.
FELAWSHIP.   Sir, I saye as I will do indede.
EVERYMAN.   Than be you a good frende at nede!
230   I have founde you true herebefore.
FELAWSHIP.   And so ye shall evermore.
For, in faith, and thou go to hell,   *even if*
I will not forsake the[e] by the waye.
EVERYMAN.   Ye speke like a good frende! I bileve you well.
I shall deserve it, and I maye.   *repay/if*
FELAWSHIP.   I speke of no deservinge, by this daye!
For he that will saye, and nothinge do,
Is not worthy with good company to go.
Therfore shewe me the grefe of your minde,
240   As to your frende moost lovinge and kinde.
EVERYMAN.   I shall shewe you how it is:
Commaunded I am to go a journaye—
A longe waye, harde, and daungerous—
And give a straite counte, without delaye,   *strict account*
Before the hye Juge, Adonai.   *(a Hebrew name for God)*
Wherfore, I pray you, bere me company,
As ye have promised, in this journaye.
FELAWSHIP.   That is mater indede! Promise is duty;   *a serious business*
But, and I sholde take suche a vyage on me,   *if*
250   I knowe it well, it sholde be to my paine.
Also it make[th] me aferde, certaine.
But let us take counsell here, as well as we can,   *let's deliberate*
For your wordes wolde fere a stronge man.   *frighten*
EVERYMAN.   Why, ye said if I had nede
Ye wolde me never forsake, quicke ne deed,   *alive nor dead*
Thoughe it were to hell, truely.
FELAWSHIP.   So I said, certainely,
258   But suche pleasures be set aside, the sothe to saye.
And also, if we toke suche a journaye,
Whan sholde we againe come?
EVERYMAN.   Naye, never againe, till the daye of dome.   *doom*

258i.e., But such pleasant companionship is now out of the question, truly.

FELAWSHIP.   In faith, than will not I come there!
Who hath you these tidinges brought?
EVERYMAN.   Indede, Deth was with me here.
FELAWSHIP.   Now, by God that all hathe bought,   *redeemed*
If Deth were the messenger,
For no man that is livinge todaye
I will not go that lothe journaye—   *loathsome*
Not for the fader that bigate me!   *begat*
EVERYMAN.   Ye promised otherwise, pardé.   *by God*
FELAWSHIP.   I wote well I sai[d] so, truely.
And yet, if thou wilte ete, and drinke, and make good
chere,
273   Or haunt to women the lusty company,
I wolde not forsake you while the daye is clere,   *until dawn*
Trust me, verily.
EVERYMAN.   Ye[a], therto ye wolde be redy!
To go to mirthe, solas, and playe
Your minde will so[o]ner apply,   *attend*
Than to bere me company in my longe journaye.
280   FELAWSHIP.   Now, in good faith, I will not that waye.   *will not (go)*
But, and thou will murder, or ony man kill,   *if*
In that I will helpe the[e] with a good will.
EVERYMAN.   O, that is a simple advise, indede.   *foolish*
Gentill Felaw[ship]e, helpe me in my necessité!
We have loved longe, and now I nede;
And now, gentill Felawship, remembre me!
FELAWSHIP.   Wheder ye have loved me or no,   *Whether*
By Saint Johan, I will not with the[e] go.
289   EVERYMAN.   Yet, I pray the[e], take the labour and do so
moche for me
290   To bringe me forwarde, for saint charité,
And comforte me till I come without the towne.   *arrive outside*
FELAWSHIP.   Nay, and thou wolde give me a newe gowne,   *even if*
I will not a fote with the[e] go.   *foot*
But, and thou had taried, I wolde not have lefte the[e] so.   *if/stayed here*
And as now God spede the[e] in thy journaye,   *And now may God*
For from the[e] I will departe as fast as I maye.
EVERYMAN.   Wheder awaye, Felawship? Will thou forsake   *Whither*
me?
FELAWSHIP.   Ye[a], by my faye! To God I betake the[e].   *faith/commend*
EVERYMAN.   Farewell, good Felawship! For the[e] my
herte is sore.

273 Or frequent women's pleasurable company.

289–90 Yet, I beg you, take the trouble at least to go with me, for the sake of holy charity.

300   Adewe forever! I shall se the[e] no more.
        FELAWSHIP.   In faith, Everyman, farewell now at the
                end[ing]e!
        For you I will remember that partinge is mourninge.
            [*Exit.*]

        EVERYMAN.   Alacke, shall we thus departe indede—   *part*
        A, Lady, helpe!—without ony more comforte?
        Lo, Felawship forsaketh me in my moost nede.
        For helpe in this worlde wheder shall I resorte?   *whither*
        Felawship herebefore with me wolde mery make,
        And now litell sorowe for me dooth he take.
        It is said, "In prosperité men frendes may finde,
310   Whiche in adversité be full unkinde."
        Now wheder for socoure shall I flee,   *whither*
        Sith that Felawship hath forsaken me?   *Since*
        To my kinnesmen I will, truely,
        Prayenge them to helpe me in my necessité.
        I bileve that they will do so,
316   For "kinde will crepe where it may not go."   *kinship/creep/walk*
        I will go saye, for yonder I se them.   *essay, try*
        Where be ye now, my frendes and kinnesmen?
            [*Enter Kindred and Cousin.*]

        KINREDE.   Here be we now, at your commaundement.
        Cosyn, I praye you shewe us your entent   *Cousin (i.e., Everyman)*
        In ony wise, and not spare.   *In everything/do not hesitate*
        COSYN.   Ye[a], Everyman, and to us declare
        If ye be disposed to go ony-whyder;   *anywhere*
        For, wete you well, [we] will live and die togyder.   *wit, know*
        KINREDE.   In welth and wo we will with you holde,   *keep*
        For over his kinne a man may be bolde.   *For with/may presume favors*
        EVERYMAN.   Gramercy, my frendes and kinnesmen kinde.
        Now shall I shewe you the grefe of my minde:
        I was commaunded by a messenger
        That is a hye kinges chefe officer;   *high king's*
        He bad[e] me go a pilgrimage, to my paine,
        And I knowe well I shall never come againe.
        Also I must give a rekeninge straite,   *strict*
334   For I have a grete enemy that hath me in waite,   *enemy (the devil)*
        Whiche entendeth me for to hinder.
        KINREDE.   What acounte is that whiche ye must render?

316i.e., Kinship will persevere even in difficult circumstances. (Cf. "blood is thicker than
water.")

334*that . . . waite:* who is watching to catch me up.

That wolde I knowe.

EVERYMAN.   Of all my workes I must shewe
How I have lived, and my dayes spent;

340   Also of ill dedes that I have used   *practiced*
In my time, sith life was me lent,   *since*
And of all vertues that I have refused.
Therfore, I praye you, go thider with me
To helpe to make min[e] accounte, for saint charité.   *holy*

COSYN.   What, to go thider? Is that the mater?
Nay, Everyman, I had lever fast brede and water   *rather fast on*
All this five yere and more.

EVERYMAN.   Alas that ever I was bore!   *born*
For now shall I never be mery
If that you forsake me.

351   KINREDE.   A, sir, what ye be a mery man!
Take good herte to you, and make no mone.   *moan*
But one thinge, I warne you, by Saint Anne:
As for me, ye shall go alone.

EVERYMAN.   My Cosyn, will you not with me go?

COSYN.   No, by Our Lady! I have the crampe in my to[e].
Trust not to me, for, so God me spede,   *may God help me*
I will deceive you in your moost nede.

KINREDE.   It availeth not us to tise.   *It's no use trying to entice us*

360   Ye shall have my maide with all my herte;
She loveth to go to feestes, there to be nise,   *wanton*
And to daunce, and abrode to sterte;   *to gad about*
I will give her leve to helpe you in that journey,   *leave, permission*
If that you and she may agree.

EVERYMAN.   Now, shewe me the very effecte of your   *true tenor*
      minde:
Will you go with me, or abide behinde?

KINREDE.   Abide behinde? Ye[a], that will I, and I maye!   *if*
Therfore farewell till another daye. [*Exit Kindred.*]

EVERYMAN.   Howe sholde I be mery or gladde?

370   For, faire promises men to me make,
But whan I have moost nede they me forsake.
I am deceived; that maketh me sadde.

COSYN.   Cosyn Everyman, farewell now,
For verily I will not go with you.
Also of mine owne [life] an unredy rekeninge
I have to accounte; therfore I make taryenge.   *tarrying*
Now God kepe the[e], for now I go. [*Exit.*]   *protect*

EVERYMAN.   A, Jesus, is all come hereto?   *everything come to this*

351Ah, sir, what a merry man you are!

379 Lo, faire wordes maketh fooles faine;   *glad*
They promise, and nothinge will do, certaine.
My kinnesmen promised me faithfully
For to abide with me stedfastly,
And now fast awaye do they flee;
Even so Felawship promised me.   *In the same way*
What frende were best me of to provide?   *to provide myself with*
I lose my time here longer to abide.
Yet in my minde a thinge there is:
All my life I have loved riches.
If that my Good now helpe me might,   *Goods*

390 He wolde make my herte full light.
I will speke to him in this distresse.—
Where arte thou, my Gooddes and riches?
  [*Goods speaks from a corner.*]

GOODES. Who calleth me? Everyman? What, hast thou
   haste?
I lie here in corners, trussed and piled so hye,
And in chestes I am locked so fast,
Also sacked in bagges. Thou mayst se with thin[e] eye
I cannot stir[r]e; in packes lowe I lie.
What wolde ye have? Lightly me saye.   *Quickly*

EVERYMAN. Come hider, Good, in al the hast[e] thou may, *hither*

400 For of counseyll I must desire the[e].   *I must ask your advice*
  [*Goods approaches.*]

GOODES. Sir, and ye in the worlde have sorowe or *if*
   adversité,
That can I helpe you to remedy shortly.

EVERYMAN. It is another disease that greveth me; *trouble*
In this worlde it is not, I tell the[e] so.
I am sent for another way to go,
To give a straite counte generall   *strict overall account*
Before the hyest Jupiter of all;
And all my life I have had joye and pleasure in the[e],
Therfore, I pray the[e], go with me.

410 For, paraventure, thou mayst before God Almighty
My rekeninge helpe to clene and purifye;
For it is said ever amonge   *it is sometimes said*
That "money maketh all right that is wronge."

GOODES. Nay, Everyman, I singe another songe!
I folowe no man in suche vyages;
For, and I wente with the[e],   *if*
Thou sholdes[t] fare moche the worse for me.

379i.e., Lo, fair promises give fools a false sense of security.

For-bicause on me thou did set thy minde,   *Because*
Thy rekeninge I have made blotted and blinde,   *flawed and obscure*
That thine accounte thou cannot make truly—
421   And that hast thou for the love of me!
   EVERYMAN.   That wolde greve me full sore,
423   Whan I sholde come to that ferefull answere.
           Up, let us go thider togyder.
   GOODES.   Nay, not so! I am to[o] britell, I may not endure.   *brittle*
           I will folowe [no] man one fote, be ye sure.
   EVERYMAN.   Alas, I have the[e] loved, and had grete
                pleasure
           All my life-dayes on good and treasure!
   GOODES.   That is to thy dampnacion, without lesinge,   *without a lie, truly*
430   For my love is contrary to the love everlastinge.
           But, if thou had me loved moderately duringe,   *during (your life)*
           As to the poore [to] give parte of me,   *(So) as*
           Than sholdest thou not in this dolour be,
           Nor in this grete sorowe and care.
   EVERYMAN.   Lo, now was I deceived or I was ware,   *ere|aware*
436   And all I may wite mi[s]spendinge of time!   *totally I may blame*
   GOODES.   What, wenest thou that I am thine?
   EVERYMAN.   I had went so.   *weened, supposed*
   GOODES.   Naye, Everyman, I saye no.
           As for a while I was lente the[e];
           A season thou hast had me in prosperité.
           My condicion is mannes soule to kill;   *nature*
           If I save one, a thousande I do spill.   *destroy*
           Wenest thou that I will folowe the[e]?
           Nay, fro this worlde not, verilé.   *(I will) not (go), verily*
   EVERYMAN.   I had wende otherwise.
   GOODES.   Therfore to thy soule Good is a thefe;
           For whan thou arte deed, this is my g[u]ise:
           Another to deceive in this same wise
450   As I have done the[e], and all to his soules reprefe.   *soul's reproof*
   EVERYMAN.   O false Good, cursed [may] thou be,
           Thou traitour to God, that hast deceived me
           And caugh[t] me in thy snare!
   GOODES.   Mar[r]y, thou brought thyselfe in care,
           Wherof I am [right] gladde;
           I must nedes laugh, I cannot be sadde.
   EVERYMAN.   A, Good, thou hast had longe my hertely love!   *heartfelt*

421And that's what you get for worshiping me.

423*answere*: i.e., my answering before God.

436And I can blame it entirely on my misspending my time.

I gave the[e] that whiche sholde be the Lordes above.   *Lord's*
But wilte thou not go with me indede?
460   I praye the[e] trouth to saye.   *tell (me) the truth*
GOODES.   No, so God me spede!
Therfore farewell, and have good daye. [*Exit.*]

EVERYMAN.   O, to whome shall I make my mone
For to go with me in that hevy journaye?
First Felawship said he wolde with me gone.   *go*
His wordes were very pleasaunt and gaye,
But afterwarde he lefte me alone.
Than spake I to my kinnesmen, all in dispaire,
An[d] also they gave me wordes faire—
470   They lacked no faire spekinge,
But all forsoke me in the endinge.
Than wente I to my Goodes, that I loved best,
In hope to have comforte; but there had I leest,
For my Goodes sharpely did me tell
That he bringeth many into hell.
Than of myselfe I was ashamed;
And so I am worthy to be blamed.
Thus may I well myselfe hate.
Of whome shall I now counseyll take?
480   I thinke that I shall never spede
Till that I go to my Good Dede.
But, alas, she is so weke
That she can nother go nor speke.   *neither walk*
Yet will I venter on her now.   *venture*
My Good Dedes, where be you?
    [*Good Deeds speaks from the ground.*]

GOOD DEDES.   Here I lie, colde in the grounde.
Thy sinnes hath me sore bounde,
That I cannot stere.   *stir*
EVERYMAN.   O Good Dedes, I stande in fere!
490   I must you pray of counseyll,
For helpe now sholde come right well.   *would be very welcome*
GOOD DEDES.   Everyman, I have understandinge
That ye be somoned a[c]counte to make   *summoned*
Before Myssias, of Jherusalem kinge;   *Messiah*
And you do by me, that journay with you will I take.   *If you do as I advise*
EVERYMAN.   Therfore I come to you my moone to make.   *moan*
I praye you that ye will go with me.
GOOD DEDES.   I wolde full faine, but I cannot stande, verily.   *gladly*
EVERYMAN.   Why, is there onythinge on you fall?   *happened to you*
500 GOOD DEDES.   Ye[a], sir, I may thanke you of all!

If ye had parfitely chered me,   *thoroughly nurtured me*
Your boke of counte full redy had be.
    [*Shows Everyman his Book of Account.*]
Loke, the bokes of your workes and dedes eke!   *deeds also*
Beholde how they lie under the fete,
To your soules hevines.   *sorrow*

EVERYMAN.   Our Lorde Jesus helpe me!

507   For one letter here I cannot se.

GOOD DEDES.   Here is a blinde rekeninge in time of   *obscure*
        distres!

EVERYMAN.   Good Dedes, I praye you helpe me in this nede,
Or elles I am forever dampned indede!
Therfore helpe me to make [my] rekeninge
Before the Redemer of all thinge,
That kinge is, and was, and ever shall.   *shall (be)*

GOOD DEDES.   Everyman, I am sory of your fall,
And faine wolde I helpe you, and I were able.   *if*

EVERYMAN.   Good Dedes, your counseyll I pray you give
        me.

GOOD DEDES.   That shall I do, verily.
Thoughe that on my fete I may not go,
I have a sister that shall with you also,
520   Called Knowlege, whiche shall with you abide   *Knowledge (of one's sins)*
To helpe you to make that dredefull rekeninge.
    [*Enter Knowledge.*]

KNOWLEGE.   Everyman, I will go with the[e], and be thy
        g[u]ide,
In thy moost nede to go by thy side.

EVERYMAN.   In good condicion I am now in everythinge,
And am [w]holy content with this good thinge,
Thanked be God my creature!   *creator*

GOOD DEDES.   And whan [s]he hath brought you there
Where thou shalte hele the[e] of thy smarte,   *pain*
Than go you with your rekeninge and your Good Dedes
        togyder
530   For to make you joyfull at herte
Before the blessyd Trinité.

EVERYMAN.   My Good Dedes, gramercy!
I am well content, certainly,
With your wordes swete.

KNOWLEGE.   Now go we togyder lovingly
To Confession, that clensinge rivere.

EVERYMAN.   For joy I wepe; I wolde we were there!

507I can't find a single letter here.

But, I pray you, give me cognicion
Where dwelleth that holy man, Confession?

540   KNOWLEGE.   In the hous of salvacion.   *i.e., the Church*
We shall finde him in that place
That shall us comforte, by Goddes grace.
        [*Knowledge leads Everyman to Confession.*]

Lo, this is Confession. Knele downe and aske mercy,
For he is in good conceite with God Almighty.   *high esteem*
EVERYMAN [*kneeling*].   O glorious fountaine, that all
        unclennes doth clarify,
Wasshe fro me the spottes of vice unclene,
That on me no sinne may be sene.
I come, with Knowlege, for my redempcion,
Redempte with herte and full contricion;   *Redeemed by earnestness*

550   For I am commaunded a pilgrimage to take,
And grete accountes before God to make.
Now I praye you, Shrifte, moder of salvacion,   *Confession*
Helpe my Good Dedes for my piteous exclamacion!   *in response to*
CONFESSION.   I knowe your sorowe well, Everyman.
Bicause with Knowlege ye come to me,
I will you comforte as well as I can.
And a precious jewell I will give the[e]
Called penaunce, voider of adversité;   *expeller*
Therwith shall your body chastised be

560   With abstinence and perseveraunce in Goddes service.
        [*Shows Everyman a knotted scourge.*]   *whip*
Here shall you receive that scourge of me,
Whiche is penaunce stronge that ye must endure,
To remembre thy Saviour was scourged for the[e]
With sharpe scourges, and suffred it paciently;
So must thou, or thou scape that painful pilgrimage.   *ere you escape*
Knowlege, kepe him in this vyage,   *course*
And by that time Good Dedes will be with the[e].
But in ony wise be seker of mercy,   *sure*
For your time draweth fast. And ye will saved be,   *draws to a close/If*

570   Aske God mercy, and he will graunte truely.
Whan with the scourge of penaunce man doth him binde,   *punishes himself*
The oile of forgivenes than shall he finde.
EVERYMAN.   Thanked be God for his gracious werke!
For now I will my penaunce begin.

575   This hath rejoised and lighted my herte,   *lightened*
576   Though the knottes be painful and harde, within.

575-76This contrition and confession have rejoiced and lightened my heart within, although the knots be painful and hard.

KNOWLEGE.   Everyman, loke your penaunce that ye fulfill,   *see to it*
　　What paine that ever it to you be;   *No matter how painful*
　　And Knowlege shall give you counseyll at will   *readily*
　　How your accounte ye shall make clerely.
　　　[*Everyman makes his confession.*]
EVERYMAN.   O eternall God, O hevenly figure,
　　O way of rightwisnes, O goodly vision,
　　Whiche discended downe in a virgin pure
　　Bicause he wolde every man redeme,
　　Whiche Adam forfaited by his disobedience: *Which (redemption)*
　　O blessid Godheed, electe and hye devine,   *exalted/divinity*
　　Forgive [me] my grevous offence!
　　Here I crye the[e] mercy in this presence.   *company*
　　O ghostly treasure, O raunsomer and redemer,   *spiritual*
590　　Of all the worlde hope and conduiter,   *conductor, guide*
　　Mirrour of joye, foundatour of mercy,   *founder*
　　Whiche enlumineth heven and erth therby: *illumines*
　　Here my clamorous complaint, though it late be;   *Hear*
　　Receive my prayers, of thy benignitye!
　　Though I be a sinner moost abhominable,
　　Yet let my name be writ[t]en in Moyses table.   *i.e., as a penitent*
　　O Mary, praye to the Maker of all thinge,
　　Me for to helpe at my endinge,
　　And save me fro the power of my enemy;
　　For Deth assaileth me strongly.
601　　And, Lady, that I may by meane of thy prayer
602　　Of your sones glory to be partinere
603　　By the meanes of his Passion, I it crave.
　　I beseche you helpe my soule to save!
　　　[*He rises.*]
　　Knowlege, give me the scourge of penaunce:
　　My flesshe therwith shall give acqueyntaunce.   *be acquainted*
　　I will now begin, if God give me grace.
KNOWLEGE.   Everyman, God give you time and space!   *opportunity*
　　Thus I bequeth you in the handes of our Saviour.
610　　Now may you make your rekeninge sure.
EVERYMAN.   In the name of the holy Trinité
　　My body sore punisshed shall be.
　　　[*Scourges himself.*]
　　Take this, body, for the sinne of the flesshe!
　　Also thou deli[gh]test to go gay and fresshe,
　　And in the way of dampnacion thou did me bringe;
　　Therfore suffre now strokes of punisshinge.

601-3And, Lady, I crave that by the mediation of your prayer and through the means of his
Passion I may be partaker of your son's glory.

Now of penaunce I will wade the water clere,
To save me from purgatory, that sharpe fire.
  [*Good Deeds rises from the ground.*]

GOOD DEDES. I thanke God, now I can walke and go,
620 And am delivered of my sikenesse and wo!
Therfore with Everyman I will go, and not spare: *hold back*
His good workes I will helpe him to declare.

KNOWLEGE. Now, Everyman, be mery and glad!
Your Good Dedes cometh now; ye may not be sad.
Now is your Good Dedes [w]hole and sounde,
Goinge upright upon the grounde.

EVERYMAN. My herte is light, and shal be evermore.
Now will I smite faster than I dide before. [*Continues to
  scourge.*]

GOOD DEDES. Everyman, pilgrime, my speciall frende,
630 Blessyd be thou without ende!
For the[e] is preparate the eternall glory.   *prepared*
Ye have me made [w]hole and sounde,
Therfore I will bide by the[e] in every stounde.   *time of trial*

EVERYMAN. Welcome, my Good Dedes! Now I here thy   *Now (that) I hear*
  voice,
I wepe for very swetenes of love.

KNOWLEGE. Be no more sad, but ever rejoice.
637 God seeth thy livinge in his trone above.
Put on this garment to thy behove,   *behoof, benefit*
Whiche is wette with your teres,
Or elles before God you may it misse
Whan ye to your journeys ende come shall.

EVERYMAN. Gentill Knowlege, what do ye it call?

KNOWLEGE. It is the garment of sorowe.
Fro paine it will you borowe.   *rescue*
Contricion it is,
That getteth forgivenes;
It pleaseth God passinge well.   *exceedingly*

GOOD DEDES. Everyman, will you were it for your hele?   *wear/salvation*
  [*Everyman puts on the robe of contrition.*]

EVERYMAN. Now blessyd be Jesu, Maryes sone,
650 For now have I on true contricion.
And lette us go now without taryenge.   *tarrying*
Good Dedes, have we clere our rekeninge?

GOOD DEDES. Ye[a], indede, I have [it] here.

EVERYMAN. Than I trust we nede not fere.
Now, frendes, let us not parte in twaine.

KNOWLEGE. Nay, Everyman, that will we not, certaine.

---

[637] God, in his throne above, sees your (amended) way of living.

GOOD DEDES.   Yet must thou led[e] with the[e]
   Thre persones of grete might.
EVERYMAN.   Who sholde they be?
660 GOOD DEDES.   Discrecion and Strength they hight,   *are called*
   And thy Beauté may not abide behinde.
KNOWLEGE.   Also ye must call to minde
   Your Five Wittes as for your counseylours.
GOOD DEDES.   You must have them redy at all houres.
EVERYMAN.   Howe shall I gette them hyder?   *hither*
KNOWLEGE.   You must call them all togyder,
   And they will here you incontinent.   *hear/immediately*
EVERYMAN.   My frendes, come hider and be present,
   Discrecion, Strengthe, my Five Wittes, and Beauté!
   [*Enter Discretion, Strength, Five Wits, and Beauty.*]

670 BEAUTE.   Here at your will we be all redy.
   What wolde ye that we sholde do?
GOOD DEDES.   That ye wolde with Everyman go
   And helpe him in his pilgrimage.
   Advise you, will ye with him or not in that vyage?   *Consider*
STRENGTH.   We will bringe him all thyder,
   To his helpe and comforte, ye may bileve me.
DISCRECION.   So will we go with him all togyder.
EVERYMAN.   Almighty God, loved may thou be!
   I give the[e] laude that I have hider brought   *praise*
680 Strength, Discrecion, Beauté and Five Wittes. Lacke I
     nought.
   And my Good Dedes, with Knowlege clere,
   All be in company at my will here.   *are together at my command*
   I desire no more to my besines.   *for my purpose*
STRENGTH.   And I, Strength, will by you stande in distres,
   Though thou wolde in bataile fight on the grounde.   *battle*
FIVE WITTES.   And though it were thrugh the worlde rounde,   *i.e., no matter where*
   We will not departe, for swete ne soure.   *i.e., in good times or bad*
BEAUTE.   No more will I, unto dethes houre,   *until*
   Whatsoever therof befall.
690 DISCRECION.   Everyman, advise you first of all;   *consider*
   Go with a good advisement and deliberacion.   *reflection*
   We all give you vertuous monicion   *i.e., assurance*
   That all shall be well.
EVERYMAN.   My frendes, harken what I will tell—
   I praye God rewarde you in his heven[ly] sp[h]ere—
   Now herken all that be here,
   For I will make my testament
   Here before you all present:
   In almes halfe my good I will give with my handes twaine

In the way of charité, with good entent,

701   And the other halfe still shall remaine

702   In queth, to be retourned there it ought to be.   *bequest/where*

This I do in despite of the fende of hell,

To go quite out of his perell   *freed from peril of him*

Ever after and this daye.   *Today and forever*

KNOWLEGE.   Everyman, herken what I saye:

Go to Presthode, I you advise,

And receive of him, in ony wise   *without fail*

The holy sacrament and ointement togyder.   *extreme unction*

710   Than shortly se ye tourne againe hyder;   *return*

We will all abide you here.

FIVE WITTES.   Ye[a], Everyman, hie you that ye redy were.   *hasten to get ready*

There is no emperour, kinge, duke, ne baron

That of God hath commicion   *authority*

As hath the leest preest in the worlde beinge;   *living*

For of the blessyd sacramentes pure and benigne

He bereth the keyes, and therof hath the cure   *care, responsibility*

For mannes redempcion—it is ever sure—

Whiche God for our soules medicine

720   Gave us out of his herte with grete paine.

Here in this transitory life, for the[e] and me,

The blessyd sacramentes seven there be:

Baptim, confirmacion, with preesthode good,   *ordination to priesthood*

And the sacrament of Goddes precious flesshe and blod,

Mariage, the holy extreme unccion, and penaunce.

These seven be good to have in remembraunce,

Gracious sacramentes of hye devinité.

EVERYMAN.   Faine wolde I receive that holy body,   *i.e., the sacrament*

And mekely to my ghostly fader I will go.   *spiritual father*

730   FIVE WITTES.   Everyman, that is the best that ye can do.

God will you to salvacion bringe,

For preesthode excedeth all other thinge.

To us holy Scripture they do teche,

And converteth man fro sinne, heven to reche.   *reach*

735   God hath to them more power given

736   Than to ony aungell that is in heven.

With five wordes he may consecrate   *i.e., "Eat, this is my body"*

Goddes body in flesshe and blode to make,

And handeleth his Maker bitwene his hande[s].

701-2(Everyman, who like every "Mankind" protagonist has gotten his wealth at others' expense, evidently provides that this wealth is to be repaid by his estate.)

735-36(For contemporaneous instances of this idea, placing priests above the angels in degree, see Thomas à Kempis, *The Imitation of Christ*, IV,v, and G. R. Owst, *Literature and Pulpit in Medieval England*, p. 530.)

740 The preest bindeth and unbindeth all bandes,
741 Bothe in erthe and in heven.
 Thou ministres all the sacramentes seven;   *administer*
 Though we kist thy fete, thou were worthy!
 Thou arte [the] surgyon that cureth sinne deedly;
 No remedy we finde under God
 But all onely preesthode.   *Except only from*
 Everyman, God gave preest[s] that dignité,
 And setteth them in his stede amonge us to be.   *place*
 Thus be they above aungelles in degree.
  [*Everyman goes to receive the sacrament and extreme unction
  from the priest, while the others await his return.*]

750 KNOWLEGE.   If preestes be good, it is so, suerly.
 But whan Jesu hanged on the crosse with grete smarte,   *pain*
 There he gave out of his blessyd herte
 The seven sacramentes in grete tourment.
 He solde them not to us, that Lorde omnipotent!
755 Therefore Saint Peter the Apostell dothe saye
 That Jesus' curse hath all they
 Whiche God their Saviour do b[u]y or sell,
758 Or they for ony money do take or tell.
 Sinfull preestes giveth the sinners example bad:
760 Their children sitteth by other mennes fires, I have harde;   *heard*
 And some haunteth womens company
 With unclene life, as lustes of lechery.
 These be with sinne made blinde.
 FIVE WITTES.   I trust to God no suche may we finde.
 Therfore let us preesthode honour,
 And folowe their doctrine for our soules socoure.
 We be their shepe, and they shepeherdes be,
 By whome we all be kepte in suerté.   *safety*
 Peas, for yonder I se Everyman come,   *Silence*
770 Whiche hath made true satisfaccion.   *Who*
 GOOD DEDES.   Methinke it is he indede.
  [*Everyman returns.*]

740–41 (As the medieval Church interpreted Christ's charge to Peter, Matthew 16:19, whatever priests bind on earth will be bound in heaven; i.e., those to whom the Church promises salvation will achieve heaven, and those the Church condemns will be damned.)

750 *it is so:* i.e., that priests are above angels in degree.

755 (Acts 8:18–23. The allusion is to the practice of simony, the buying or selling of spiritual things.)

758 Or who for (their Saviour) receive or pay out money.

760 i.e., I have heard that priests have illegitimate children.

EVERYMAN.   Now Jesu be your alder spede!   *be helper to you all*
I have received the sacrament for my redempcion,
And than mine extreme unccion.
Blessyd be all they that counseyled me to take it!
And now, frendes, let us go without longer respite;
I thanke God that ye have taried so longe.
Now set eche of you on this rodde your honde,   *rood, cross*
And shortely folowe me.   *quickly*
780   I go before there I wolde be. God be our g[u]ide!   *where I wish to be*
STRENGTH.   Everyman, we will not fro you go
Till ye have done this vyage longe.
DISCRECION.   I, Discrecion, will bide by you also.
KNOWLEGE.   And though this pilgrimage be never so stronge,   *taxing*
I will never parte you fro.   *from you*
Everyman, I will be as sure by the[e]   *steadfast at your side*
787   As ever I dide by Judas Machabee.
  [*They proceed to Everyman's grave.*]

EVERYMAN.   Alas, I am so faint I may not stande!
My limmes under me do folde.
Frendes, let us not tourne againe to this lande,
Not for all the worldes golde;
For into this cave must I crepe
And tourne to erth, and there to slepe.
BEAUTÉ.   What, into this grave? Alas!
EVERYMAN.   Ye[a], there shall ye consume, more and lesse.   *decay everyone*
BEAUTÉ.   And what, sholde I smoder here?   *smother*
EVERYMAN.   Ye[a], by my faith, and never more appere.
In this worlde live no more we shall,
But in heven before the hyest Lorde of all.
BEAUTÉ.   I crosse out all this! Adewe, by Saint Johan!   *cancel*
801   I take my tappe in my lappe and am gone.   *flax for spinning*
EVERYMAN.   What, Beauté, whider will ye?
BEAUTÉ.   Peas, I am defe! I loke not behinde me,   *Peace, silence*
Not and thou woldest give me all the golde in thy chest!   *if*
  [*Exit Beauty.*]

EVERYMAN.   Alas, wherto may I truste?
Beauté gothe fast awaye fro me.
She promised with me to live and die.
STRENGTH.   Everyman, I will the[e] also forsake and denye.

787(See the first apocryphal Book of the Maccabees, chap. 3. Judas Maccabeus was a successful warrior against the heathen dynasty of Antiochus IV, ca. 160 B.C.)

801i.e., I'll gather up my knitting or spinning and be on my way. (*Tappe* or *top* is the flax or
tow put on the spinning distaff.)

Thy game liketh me not at all.   *pleases*

810   EVERYMAN.   Why than, ye will forsake me all?
Swete Strength, tary a litell space.   *while*

STRENGTH.   Nay, sir, by the rode of grace!   *rood, cross*
I will hie me from the[e] fast,
Though thou wepe till thy herte to-brast.   *burst in pieces*

EVERYMAN.   Ye wolde ever bide by me, ye said.

STRENGTH.   Ye[a], I have you ferre inoughe conveyde!   *far*
Ye be olde inoughe, I understande,
Your pilgrimage to take on hande.
I repent me that I hider came.

820   EVERYMAN.   Strength, you to displease I am to blame,
Yet promise is dette, this ye well wot.

STRENGTH.   In faith, I care not.
Thou arte but a foole to complaine.
You spende your speche, and wast[e] your braine.   *spend (in vain)*
Go thrist the[e] into the grounde! [*Exit.*]   *thrust yourself*

EVERYMAN.   I had wende surer I sholde you have founde.   *weened, supposed*
He that trusteth in his Strength
She him deceiveth at the length.
Bothe Strength and Beauté forsaketh me,
830   Yet they promised me faire and lovingly.

DISCRECION.   Everyman, I will after Strength be gone.
As for me, I will leve you alone.

EVERYMAN.   Why, Discrecion, will ye forsake me?

DISCRECION.   Ye[a], in faith, I will go fro the[e],
For whan Strength goth before
I folowe after evermore.

EVERYMAN.   Yet, I pray the[e], for the love of the Trinité,
Loke in my grave ones piteously!   *once*

DISCRECION.   Nay, so nye will I not come.
840   Farewell, everychone! [*Exit Discretion.*]   *everyone*

EVERYMAN.   O, all thinge faileth, save God alone—
Beauté, Strength, and Discrecion;
For whan Deth bloweth his blast
They all renne fro me full fast.

FIVE WITTES.   Everyman, my leve now of the[e] I take.
I will folowe the other, for here I the[e] forsake.

EVERYMAN.   Alas, than may I waile and wepe!
For I toke you for my best frende.

FIVE WITTES.   I will no lenger the[e] kepe.   *guard*

820Strength, I am to blame for displeasing you; i.e., I apologize for reminding you of your
promise.

850   Now farewell, and there an ende. [*Exit Five Wits.*]

EVERYMAN.   O Jesu, helpe! All hath forsaken me.

GOOD DEDES.   Nay, Everyman, I will bide with the[e].
 I will not forsake the[e] indede;
 Thou shalte finde me a good frende at nede.

EVERYMAN.   Gramercy, Good Dedes! Now may I true frendes
  se.
 They have forsaken me, everychone;
 I loved them better than my Good Dedes alone.
 Knowlege, will ye forsake me also?

KNOWLEGE.   Ye[a], Everyman, whan ye to Deth shall go;
860   But not yet, for no maner of daunger.

EVERYMAN.   Gramercy, Knowlege, with all my herte!

KNOWLEGE.   Nay, yet I will not from hens departe
 Till I se where ye shall be come.

EVERYMAN.   Methinke, alas, that I must be gone
 To make my rekeninge and my dettes paye,
 For I se my time is nye spent awaye.
 Take example, all ye that this do here or se,   *hear*
 How they that I love[d] best do forsake me
 Excepte my Good Dedes, that bideth truely.

870   GOOD DEDES.   All erthly thinges is but vanité:
 Beauté, Strength, and Discrecion do man forsake,
 Folisshe frendes, and kinnesmen, that faire spake—
 All fleeth save Good Dedes, and that am I.

EVERYMAN.   Have mercy on me, God moost mighty,
 And stande by me, thou moder and maide, Holy Mary!

GOOD DEDES.   Fere not; I will speke for the[e].

EVERYMAN.   Here I crye God mercy!

GOOD DEDES.   Shorte our ende, and minisshe our paine; *Shorten/diminish*
 Let us go and never come againe.

880   EVERYMAN.   Into thy handes, Lorde, my soule I commende.
 Receive it, Lorde, that it be not lost.
 As thou me boughtest, so me defende,   *redeemed*
 And save me from the fendes boost,   *fiend's*
 That I may appere with that blessyd hoost
 That shall be saved at the day of dome.

886   *In manus tuas,* of mightes moost

887   Forever, *commendo spiritum meum!*
  [*Everyman and Good Deeds descend into the grave.*]

880(Christ's last words, Luke 23:46.)

886–87Into your hands, (you who are) the greatest of powers forever, I commend my spirit.
(Luke 23:46.)

KNOWLEGE.   Now hath he suffred that we all shall endure.   *that which*
    The Good Dedes shall make all sure.
890   Now hath he made endinge.
    Methinketh that I here aungelles singe,   *hear*
    And make grete joy and melody
    Where Everymannes soule received shall be.
THE AUNGELL [*above, or within*].   Come, excellente electe spouse   *bride*
        to Jesu!
    Here-above thou shalte go,
    Bicause of thy singuler vertue.
    Now thy soule is taken thy body fro,
    Thy rekeninge is crystall clere.
    Now shalte thou into the hevenly sp[h]ere,
900   Unto the whiche all ye shall come
    That liveth well before the daye of dome.

      [*Enter doctor as epilogue.*]   *learned cleric*

DOCTOUR.   This morall men may have in minde.
    Ye herers, take it of worth, olde and yonge,   *prize it highly*
    And forsake Pride, for he deceiveth you in the ende.
    And remembre Beauté, Five Wittes, Strength, and Di[s]cre-
        cion,
    They all at the last do every man forsake,
    Save his Good Dedes there dothe he take.   *Unless*
    But beware; [for], and they be small,   *if*
    Before God he hath no helpe at all.
910   None excuse may be there for every man.
    Alas, how shall he do than?
    For, after dethe, amendes may no man make,
    For than mercy and pité doth him forsake.
    If his rekeninge be not clere whan he doth come,
915   God will saye: "*Ite, maledicti, in ignem aeternum!*"
    And he that hath his accounte [w]hole and sounde,
    Hye in heven he shall be crounde.
    Unto whiche place God bringe us all thyder,
    That we may live body and soule togyder.
920   Therto helpe, the Trinité!
    Amen, saye ye, for saint Charité.   *holy*
      Finis.

    Thus endeth this morall playe of Everyman.
      Imprinted at London in Poules
        Chyrche yarde by me
          Johan Skot.

[915]Depart, ye cursed, into everlasting fire. (See Matthew 25:41.)

PART SIX

Humanist Drama

Humanist Drama

WHEN WE TURN from morality plays of the fifteenth century to humanist plays of the early sixteenth century, we turn from a primarily religious drama to one that is often concerned with issues of politics, social change, law, and education. Yet humanist drama was by no means as radical a departure as this statement might suggest. The morality play was also beginning to show an awareness of social and economic issues during the early Tudor period. Even in the early *Mankind,* the tempters are not simple allegorical abstractions but rowdies, highwaymen, and tavern-frequenters who pose a threat to order. The interest of humanist drama in similar issues was thus part of a developing social concern in the English drama generally. Structurally, moreover, humanist drama is much closer to the drama and literature of medieval England than to the drama and literature of classical Greece or Rome. Nowhere in humanist drama prior to the 1550's do we find classical five-act structure or the unities of time, place, and action. Henry Medwall's *Fulgens and Lucrece* (ca. 1490–1501) is set in ancient Rome, but structurally the play is a *débat* interspersed with farcical antics. John Redford's *Wit and Science* (1531–47) combines romantic narrative with a morality structure in a charming play about the perils and rewards of education. Humanist writers also borrowed such morality conventions as the comic vice-figure and the beleagured mankind hero. Lastly, the language and verse forms employed in humanistic plays are characteristically medieval. Blank-verse approximations of classical meters were not attempted until the mid-sixteenth century.

The humanists who wrote these plays were an extraordinary group of men, most of them closely associated with Thomas More and Erasmus. Henry Medwall was chaplain to Cardinal Morton, in whose household Thomas More grew up. John Rastell married Thomas More's sister Elizabeth, and John Heywood married the daughter of John and Elizabeth Rastell. John Redford, although not allied to this group by marriage, seems to have been professionally associated with Heywood. In various ways these men devoted their lives to reform of the educational system and of classical and textual study, the law, the education of women, and a host of similar concerns. They advocated church reform as well, even though most of them opposed the break with Rome.

We have space in this volume for only a few of their plays. A brief survey of some other works by them will suggest, however, the extent of their commitment to serious humanistic themes. Medwall's *Fulgens and Lucrece* presents a debate between a virtuous but humbly-born courtier and a degenerate aristocrat of inherited wealth and rank. Clearly the victory belongs to the man who practices true virtue. Just as clearly, the contest reflects an actual power struggle going on in the court of Henry VII between "new men" and the ancient aristocracy. Henry VII granted enormous power to efficient administrators of humble birth like Cardinal Morton or Edmund Dudley. He needed such loyal administrators in order to curtail baronial privilege after the long and chaotic years of civil war. The "new men" generally endorsed humanism with its teaching of "true gentilesse" based on inner virtue rather than rank. John Rastell's *Of Gentleness and Nobility* (ca. 1527–30) similarly debates the worth of inherited rank. The play features a peasant who talks back unabashedly to a knight and a merchant, offering them his radical theories of inheritance and ownership of property as mere systems by which the landed classes have exploited the poor. He regards even monarchy itself as a form of exploitation. Such a debate affords no basis for viewing society as a divinely-ordained hierarchy; even the knight and the merchant accept the theory of a social contract. Rastell's *Calisto and Melibea* (ca. 1527–30) satirizes aristocratic idleness. His earlier play on *The Nature of the Four Elements* (ca. 1517–18) waxes eloquent on proofs of the roundness of the earth and other matters of "natural philosophy." John Skelton, author of *Magnificence* (1515–18), though not close to the humanist circle of Thomas More, shared with them a serious concern for the perils of tyranny. John Heywood, although more of a professional entertainer than some other humanist writers, pleads in his *Play of the Weather* (1525–33) for social harmony. The play celebrates the ideal monarch who can adjudicate the conflicting claims of society with complete impartiality. Even Heywood's hilarious *The Four PP* (ca. 1520–22) concludes on a sober note of tolerant submission to the Catholic Church. John Redford's *Wit and Science* (1531–47), for all its high jinks, defends the ideals of a humanistic education.

Although the "new learning" of humanism does represent the sort of change we associate with the term "Renaissance," humanist drama is derived in many important ways from medieval literature and especially from traditions of courtly entertainment. Medieval romance and Chaucer's tales offered models for nonreligious love stories and fabliaux that were suitable for the stage. The fragmentary *Interludium de Clerico et Puella* (ca. 1290–1335) suggests that fabliaux were presented in dramatic form during the Middle Ages. Equally important as sources were tournaments and other chivalric ceremonials. As Glynne Wickham has shown in his *Early English Stages,* many tournaments were elaborately staged and costumed like plays on heroic themes, with verse texts derived from the tradition of the *Roman de la Rose.* Courtly "mummings" or "disguisings," forerunners of the Elizabethan masque, similarly featured semidramatic recitation and dancing with elaborate costuming and scenic effects. Still another semidramatic courtly pastime was the *débat,* often a facetious and ingenious disputation. It could be incorporated into a mumming or disguising: for example, John Lydgate's *Mumming at Hertford* (ca. 1430) features a *débat* among six husbands and six wives on the battle of the sexes, with the king as arbiter. In sum, the court had long enjoyed a tradition of extravagant indoor entertainment to which the new genre of humanist drama was heavily indebted for such features as witty disputations, appeals to the judgment of the audience, songs (evidently performed with exquisite skill), expensive costuming, and fabliau humor. To this court tradition the humanist writers added some of the conventions of popular morality drama.

The staging of humanist drama was often courtly. *Fulgens and Lucrece,* called an "interlude" in the original text, was designed for intervals in a state banquet. *Weather* must also have been performed during the evening in a patrician banqueting hall. The actors in these and similar plays were usually choir boys, who were particularly adept at witty exchange and the portrayal of feminine characters. The acting area was frequently set close to the banqueting tables. In such an environment the *débat* format, with its lack of stage movement, proved eminently suitable. For some of their plays, however, the humanists turned to experimental or popular stages like that used for *Mankind* as a means of reaching out for more general audiences. The plays designed for more general appeal were probably acted by adult itinerant actors. Humanist drama thus made use of both courtly and popular traditions, and tried to appeal to audiences on divergent social levels. By so doing, it helped to prevent the kind of irreconcilable split between elite neoclassical drama and popular entertainment that occurred in the drama of Italy and France.

A MERY PLAY BETWENE
JOHAN JOHAN THE HUSBANDE,
TIB HIS WIFE, AND SIR JOHAN THE PREEST

Johan Johan (1520–33) is usually assigned to John Heywood, although his name does not appear on the title page and no other external evidence can substantiate his claim. Whether or not by him, the play appears to be an adaptation from the French *Farce du Pasté*. Accordingly, it is close in spirit to continental traditions of the farce and the fabliau. The play lacks even a hint of moralizing, of conciliatory attitude toward the Church, or of humanist purpose, such as we generally find in Heywood's other works. Rather than inviting men to laugh at their own quarrelsomeness, this play ends, as it begins, on a note of sexual rivalry and hatred. Moral vantage point is totally absent. The author's lampooning of the cuckolded husband is as merciless as that of the sexy wife and libidinous priest. The priest is a hypocrite for cuckolding the man whom he professes to serve as spiritual father, but the husband is so stupid that he brings misfortune on himself. We applaud clever devices for the sake of their own ingenuity and thereby enter the amoral world of the fabliau which is governed solely by its own artistic rules.

Johan Johan is a brilliant satirical comedy of jealousy and vituperation. The play strips away all veneer of civilization and revels in pure sexual fantasy. In this fantasy, we are invited to share both the desire for orgiastic gratification and the aching fear of sexual inadequacy. The play is organized around sexual symbols, especially the cleft water pail and the wax candle representing the female and male organs. The act of eating also becomes a symbol of carnal appetite: the priest gorges himself on the wife's pie while Johan Johan withdraws to a corner and fiddles with his stiff wax, unable to fill the cleft in his wife's pail.

The simple staging of this play would allow it to be carried to popular audiences anywhere by a small professional troupe, although it may well have been acted at court also. The acting space must provide two "houses," with doors, for Johan Johan and the priest. Conceivably these "houses" were stage structures, or they may simply have been two stage areas in the vicinity of the doors. Johan Johan's house, where most of the action takes place, contains a fireplace, trestles and a board for a table, a stool, and the simple props mentioned in the dialogue: pie, pail, candle, cups, pots, and so on. The actors appeal directly to the audience, some of whom are close at hand.

The verse is generally in four-stress couplets. The present text is based on the edition printed by William Rastell, 1533, existing in two copies: that in the Pepys Collection, Magdalene College, Cambridge, and that in the Ashmolean Museum, Oxford. The very few typographical press corrections differentiating the two copies suggest that the Pepys copy is the corrected version, and it has been followed here.

A Mery Play Betwene Johan Johan the Husbande, Tib His Wife, and Sir Johan the Preest

[Interior of Johan Johan's home.]
Johan Johan, the Husbande.

[JOHAN.] God spede you, maysters, everychone!		

Wote ye not whither my wife is gone?
I pray God the divell take her!
For all that I do, I cannot make her   *Despite/prevent*
But she will go a gaddinge, very miche   *much*
6   Like an Anthony pig, with an olde wi[t]che
Whiche ledeth her about hither and thither.
But, by Our Lady, I wote not whither!
But, by Gogges blo[o]d, were she come home   *God's*
10   Unto this, my house, by Our Lady of Crome,
I wolde bete her or that I drinke.   *ere*
12   Bete her, quod a? yea, that she shall stinke!   *so that*
And at every stroke lay her on the grounde,
And traine her by the here about the house rounde.   *drag/hair*
I am evyn mad that I bete her not nowe.
But I shall rewarde her hardly well inowe: *vigorously*
There is never a wife betwene heven and hell
Whiche was ever beten halfe so well.
     Beten, quod a? Yea, but what and she therof die?   *what if*
Than I may chaunce to be hanged shortly.   *Then*
And whan I have beten her till she smoke,
And given her many a hundred stroke,
Thinke ye that she will amende yet?
24   Nay, by Our Lady, the devill spede whit!
Therfore I will not bete her at all.
     And shall I not bete her? No shall?
Whan she offendeth and doth amis,
And kepeth not her house, as her duetye is?
Shall I not bete her, if she do so?
30   Yes, by Cokkes blood, that shall I do!   *Christ's*

TITLE *Sir:* not indicating knighthood, but a polite form of address used before the Christian name of ordinary priests.

⁶*Anthony:* St. Anthony, the patron saint of swineherds, was often depicted accompanied by a pig.

¹⁰*Crome:* location of a shrine to the Virgin Mary.

¹²*quod a:* quotha, i.e., "said he," a contemptuous phrase meaning "forsooth!"

²⁴*the . . . whit:* i.e., the devil she'll improve any at all; or, the devil take it.

I shall bete her and thwak her, I trow,
That she shall be-shit the house for very wo.
     But yet I think what my neybour will say than.
He will say thus: "Whom chidest thou, Johan Johan?"
"Mar[r]y," will I say, "I chide my curst wife,   *shrewish*
The veriest drab that ever bare life,
Whiche doth nothing but go and come,   *Who*
And I cannot make her kepe her at home."
Than I thinke he will say by and by: *at once*
40   "Walke her cote, Johan Johan, and bete her hardely!"   *i.e., Give her a beating*
But than unto him min[e] answere shal be:
"The more I bete her, the worse is she,
And wors and wors make her I shall!"
     He will say than: "Bete her not at all."
"And why?" shall I say, "This wolde be wist: *i.e., I'd like to know this*
Is she not mine to chastice as I list?"   *wish*
     But this is another point worst of all:
The folkes will mocke me whan they he[a]re me brall.
But, for all that, shall I let therfore   *desist*
50   To chastice my wife ever the more,
And to make her at home for to tary?
Is not that well done? Yes, by Saint Mary!
That is a point of an honest man,   *a characteristic of*
For to bete his wife well nowe and than.
     Therfore I shall bete her, have ye no drede.
And I ought to bete her, till she be starke dede.
And why? By God, bicause it is my pleasure!
58   And if I shulde suffre her, I make you sure,
Nought shulde prevaile me, nother staffe nor waster;   *avail/neither/club*
Within a while she wolde be my mayster.
     Therfore I shall bete her, by Cokkes mother,
Both on the tone side and on the tother,   *one*
Before and behinde—nought shall be her bote—   *remedy*
From the top of the heed to the sole of the fote.
     But, masters, for Goddes sake, do not entrete
For her whan that she shal be bete!
But, for Goddes Passion, let me alone,
And I shall thwak her that she shall grone.
Wherfore I beseche you, and hartely you pray,
70   And I beseche you say me not nay,
But that I may beate her for this ones.
And I shall beate her, by Cokkes bones,
That she shall stinke like a pole-kat!
But yet, by Gogges body, that nede nat,   *isn't necessary*

---

[58]And if I would let her (have her way), I assure you.

For she will stinke without any beting;
For every night, ones she giveth me an heting,   *a quarrel*
From her issueth suche a stinking smoke
That the savour therof almost doth me choke.
But I shall bete her nowe, without faile.

80   I shall bete her toppe and taile,
Heed, shulders, armes, legges, and all.
I shall bete her, I trowe—that I shall!
And, by Gogges boddy, I tell you trewe,
I shall bete her till she be blacke and blewe.
    But where the divell trowe ye she is gon?
I holde a noble she is with Sir Johan.   *wager/coin worth 6s. 8d.*
I fere I am beg[u]iled alway;
But yet, in faith, I hope well nay.   *I certainly hope not*

89   Yet I almost enrage that I ne can
90   Se the behav[i]our of our gentilwoman.
And yet, I thinke, thither as she doth go,   *the places where she goes*
Many an honest wife go'th thither also
For to make some pastime and sporte.
But than my wife so ofte doth thither resorte
That I fere she will make me weare a fether.   *i.e., badge of a fool, cuckold*
But yet I nede not for to fere nether,

97   For he is her gossip, that is he.
    But abide a while—yet let me se!

99   Where the divell hath our gossipry begon?
My wife had never childe—doughter nor son.
    Nowe if I forbede her that she go no more,
Yet will she go as she did before;
Or els will she chuse some other place,
And then the matter is in as ill case.
    But, in faith, all these wordes be in wast,   *wasted*
For I thinke the matter is done and past.
And whan she cometh home she will begin to chide,

108   But she shall have her payment-sti[c]k by her side!
For I shall order her, for all her brawling,   *manage*
110   That she shall repent to go a catter-wawling.
    [*Tib has entered during this speech.*]

TIB.   Why, whom wilt thou beate, I say, thou knave?

89–90Yet I'm almost in a rage that I can't see what my wife is up to.

97For Sir Johan is the godfather of her children, truly he is.

99i.e., What the devil is the basis for any relationship based on baptism of our children?

108i.e., She'll receive a beating.

110*catter-wawling:* making lecherous expeditions, like a cat.

JOHAN.   Who, I, Tib? None, so God me save.

TIB.   Yes, I h[e]arde the[e] say thou woldest one bete.   *beat someone*

114   JOHAN.   Mar[r]y, wife, it was sto[c]kfisshe in Temmes Strete,   *Thames*

Whiche will be good meate against Lent.   *food for*

Why, Tib, what haddest thou thought that I had ment?

TIB.   Mar[r]y, me-thought I h[e]arde the[e] bawling.

Wilt thou never leve this wawling?   *leave off*

Howe the divell dost thou thyselfe behave?

120   Shall we ever have this worke, thou knave?

JOHAN.   What, wife, howe sayst thou? Was it well gues't of   *Did I guess right*
      me

That thou woldest be come home in safeté

As sone as I had kendled a fire?

Come warme the[e], swete Tib, I the[e] require.   *urge*

TIB.   O, Johan, Johan, I am afraid, by this light,

That I shal be sore si[c]k this night.

JOHAN [*aside*].   By Cokkes soule, nowe, I dare lay a swan   *bet something valuable*

That she comes nowe streyght fro Sir Johan.

For, ever whan she hath fatched of him a lyk,   *received pleasure from him*

130   Than she comes home and saith she is syk.

TIB.   What say'st thou?

JOHAN.   Mar[r]y, I say

It is mete for a woman to go play   *fitting*

Abrode in the towne for an houre or two.

TIB.   Well, gentilman, go to, go to!   *i.e., come, come*

JOHAN.   Well, let us have no more debate.

TIB [*aside*].   If he do not fight, chide, and rate,   *scold*

Brawle, and fare as one that were frantike,   *behave like*

138   There is nothing that may him like.   *please him*

JOHAN [*aside*].   If that the parisshe preest, Sir Johan,

Did not se her nowe and than

And give her absolution upon a bed,

For wo and paine she wolde sone be deed.

TIB.   For Goddes sake, Johan Johan, do the[e] not displease;   *don't be angry*

Many a time I am ill at ease.

What thinkest nowe: am not I somwhat si[c]k?

JOHAN [*aside*].   Nowe wolde to God, and swete Saint Diri[c]k,

That thou warte in the water up to the throte,

Or in a burning oven red hote,

To se and I wolde pull the[e] out!   *see if*

150   TIB.   Nowe, Johan Johan, to put the[e] out of dout,

114*sto[c]kfisshe:* dried fish, tenderized by beating.

120i.e., Will you ever get your housework done?

138i.e., He just doesn't enjoy life unless he's scolding.

Imagin thou where that I was
Before I came home.

JOHAN.   My percase   *My guess (is)*
Thou wast prayenge in the Churche of Poules
Upon thy knees for all Christen soules.

TIB.   Nay.

JOHAN.   Than if thou wast not so holy,
Shewe me where thou wast, and make no lie.

TIB.   Truely, Johan Johan, we made a pie—
I and my gossip Margery,
And our gossip the preest, Sir Johan,
And my neybours yongest doughter, An.

161   The preest paide for the stuffe and the making,
And Margery she paide for the baking.

JOHAN [*aside*].   By Kokkes lilly woundes, that same is she   *Christ's lovely*
That is the most bawde hens to Coventré.   *greatest bawd from here*

TIB.   What say you?

JOHAN.   Mar[r]y, answere me to this:
Is not Sir Johan a good man?

[TIB.]   Yes, that he is.

JOHAN.   Ha! Tib, if I shulde not greve the[e],
I have somwhat wherof I wolde meve the[e].   *exhort, request*

TIB.   Well, husbande, nowe I do conject
170   That thou hast me somwhat in suspect.
But, by my soule, I never go to Sir Johan
But I finde him like an holy man;
For either he is sayenge his devotion,
Or els he is goinge in procession.

JOHAN [*aside*].   Yea, rounde about the bed doth he go,
You two together, and no mo;
And for to finisshe the procession,
He lepeth up, and thou liest downe.

TIB.   What say'st thou?

JOHAN.   Mar[r]y, I say he doth well.
180   For so ought a shepherde to do, as I h[e]arde tell,
For the salvation of all his folde.

TIB.   Johan Johan!

[JOHAN.]   What is it that thou wolde?

TIB.   By my soule, I love the[e] too too!   *exceedingly*
And I shall tell the[e], or I further go: *ere*
The pie that was made, I have it nowe here,
    [*She reveals the pie.*]
And therwith I trust we shall make good chere.

161(This pie takes on a sexual double meaning, signifying Johan Johan's being cuckolded, with Margery acting as bawd.)

JOHAN.   By Kokkes body, that is very happy!

TIB.   But wotest who gave it?   *do you know*

JOHAN.   What the divel re[c]k I?   *do I care*

TIB.   By my faith, and I shall say trewe, than:

190   The divell take me and it were not Sir Johan.   *if*

JOHAN.   O, holde thy peas[e], wife, and swere no more!   *be quiet*

   [*Aside*].   But I beshrewe both your hartes therfore.

TIB.   Yet peradventure thou hast suspection

   Of that that was never thought nor done.   *that which*

[JOHAN.]   Tusshe, wife, let all suche matters be.   *i.e., never mind*

   I love the[e] well, though thou love not me.

   But this pie doth nowe catche harme:

   Let us set it upon the harth to warme.

   [*They set the pie on the hearth.*]

TIB.   Than let us eate it as fast as we can.

   But bicause Sir Johan is so honest a man,

201   I wolde that he shulde therof eate his part.

JOHAN.   That were reason, I the[e] ensure.   *That's sensible*

TIB.   Than, sins[e] that it is thy pleasure,

   I pray the[e] than go to him right,   *then/directly*

   And pray him come sup with us tonight.

JOHAN [*aside*].   Shall he cum hither? By Kokkes soule, I was

     a-curst

   Whan that I graunted to that worde furst!   *agreed*

   But sins[e] I have said it, I dare not say nay,

   For than my wife and I shulde make a fray.

210   But whan he is come, I swere by Goddes mother,

   I wold give the divell the tone to cary away the tother!   *one/other*

TIB.   What say'st?

JOHAN.   Mar[r]y, he is my curate, I say,

   My confessour, and my frende alway.

   Therfore go thou and seke him by and by,   *at once*

   And till thou come againe, I will kepe the pie.   *watch*

TIB.   Shall I go for him? Nay, I shrewe me than!   *Curses on me if I do*

   Go thou and seke as fast as thou can,

   And tell him it.

JOHAN.   Shall I do so?

   In faith, it is not mete for me to go.

220 TIB.   But thou shalte go tell him, for all that.

JOHAN.   Than shall I tell him—wotest what?—   *do you know what?*

   That thou desirest him to come make some chere.

TIB.   Nay, that thou desirest him to come sup here.

JOHAN.   Nay, by the rode, wife, thou shalt have the worship   *cross/honor, credit*

   And the thankes of thy g[u]est that is thy gossip.

201*eate his part:* with sexual connotation.

TIB [*aside*].   Full ofte, I se, my husbande will me rate   *scold*
    For this hether comming of our gentill curate.
JOHAN.   What say'st, Tib? Let me he[a]re that againe.
TIB.   Mar[r]y, I perceive very plaine
230   That thou hast Sir Johan somwhat in suspect.
    But, by my soule, as far as I conject,
    He is vertuouse and full of charité.
JOHAN [*aside*].   In faith, all the towne knoweth better—that he
    Is a [w]horemonger, a haunter of the stewes,   *whorehouses*
    An [h]ypocrite, a knave that all men refuse,
    A lier, a wretche, a maker of strife—
    Better than they knowe that thou art my good wife.
TIB.   What is that that thou hast saide?
JOHAN.   Mar[r]y, I wolde have the table set and laide,
    In this place or that, I care not whether.   *which*
241 TIB.   Than go to, bringe the trestels hither.
JOHAN.   Abide a while, let me put of[f] my gown.
    But yet I am afraide to lay it down,
    For I fere it shal be sone stolen.
    And yet it may lie safe inough unstolen.
    It may lie well here, and I list—   *if I wish*
        [*Starts to put his coat down.*]
    But, by Cokkes soule, here hath a dogge pis't!
    And if I shulde lay it on the harth bare,
    It might hap to be burned or I were ware.   *ere*
        [*To one of the audience.*]
250   Therfore I pray you take ye the paine
    To kepe my gowne till I come againe.
        [*Snatches it back.*]
    But yet he shall not have it, by my fay!   *faith*
    He is so nere the dore he might ron away.
        [*To another spectator.*]
    But bicause that ye be trusty and sure,
    Ye shall kepe it, and it be your pleasure.   *if*
    And bicause it is aray'de at the skirt,   *befouled*
    While ye do nothing, skrape of[f] the dirt.
        [*To Tib.*]
    Lo, nowe am I redy to go to Sir Johan,
    And bid him come as fast as he can.
TIB.   Ye[a], do so without ony taryeng.
        [*As he is leaving she calls him back.*]
    But, I say, harke! Thou hast forgot one thing:
    Set up the table, and that by and by.   *at once*

---

²⁴¹*trestels:* trestles, upon which a board was placed at mealtimes for a table.

[*Johan returns and sets the boards on the trestles.*]
Nowe go thy ways.

JOHAN.   I go shortly.

264   But se your candelstikkes be not out of the way.
[*He starts out again.*]

TIB.   Come againe, and lay the table, I say!
[*He does so.*]
What, methinkes ye have sone don.

JOHAN.   Nowe I pray God that his malediction
Light on my wife and on the baulde preest!   *bald, tonsured*

TIB.   Nowe go thy ways, and hie the[e], see'st?   *hurry up, see?*

JOHAN.   I pray to Christ, if my wishe be no sinne,
That the preest may breke his neck whan he comes in!
[*He starts out again.*]

272   TIB.   How! cum again!

JOHAN.   What a mischefe wilt thou, fole?

TIB.   Mar[r]y, I say, bringe hether yender stole.

JOHAN.   Nowe go to! A littell wolde make me
For to say thus: "A vengaunce take the[e]!"
[*He brings her the stool.*]

TIB.   Nowe go to him and tell him plain
277   That, till thou bringe him, thou wilt not come again.

278   JOHAN.   This pie doth borne here as it doth stande.   *burn*
[*He starts out again.*]

TIB.   Go, washe me these two cuppes in my hande.
[*He returns and does so.*]

JOHAN.   I go, with a mischiefe light on thy face!   *i.e., and may*

TIB.   Go, and bid him hie him apace,   *come quickly*
And the while I shall all thinges amende.   *meanwhile*

JOHAN.   This pie burneth here at this ende.
Understandest thou?

TIB.   Go thy ways, I say!

JOHAN.   I will go nowe, as fast as I may.
[*He starts out again.*]

TIB.   How! Come ones againe. I had forgot:
Loke and there be ony ale in the pot.   *See if*

JOHAN.   Nowe, a vengaunce and a very mischiefe
Light on the pil'de preest and on my wife,   *tonsured*
290   On the pot, the ale, and on the table,
The candyll, the pie, and all the rable,   *pack (of things and people)*

264i.e., But don't forget to get out the candlesticks.

272What in the name of mischief do you want, fool?

277i.e., That you won't return home unless he comes with you.

278*stande:* i.e., too near the fire.

On the tristels, and on the stole!

It is moche ado to please a curst fole.   *shrewish*

   [*He fills her ale pot.*]

TIB.   Go thy ways nowe, and tar[r]y no more,

For I am a-hungred very sore.

JOHAN.   Mar[r]y, I go.

   [*He starts out again.*]

TIB.   But come ones againe yet!

Bringe hither that breade, lest I forget it.

   [*He brings the bread.*]

JOHAN.   Iwis, it were time for to torne   *Truly/turn*

The pie, for, iwis, it doth borne.

300   TIB.   Lorde, howe my husbande nowe doth patter,

And of the pie stil doth clatter!

Go nowe, and bid him come away.

I have bid the[e] an hundred times today.

JOHAN.   I will not give a strawe, I tell you plaine,   *care a bit*

If that the pie waxe colde againe—

TIB.   What, art thou not gone yet out of this place?

307   I had went thou haddest ben come againe in the space.   *supposed*

308   But, by Cokkes soule, and I shulde do the[e] right,

I shulde breke thy knaves heed tonight!

JOHAN.   Nay, than, if my wife be set a-chiding,

It is time for me to go at her bidding.

There is a proverbe whiche trewe nowe preveth:

"He must nedes go that the divell driveth."   *whom*

   [*He arrives at the priest's house.*]

How, mayster curate, may I come in

At your chamber dore, without ony sin?   *i.e., without offense*

SIR JOHAN.   Who is there nowe that wolde have me?

What, Johan Johan! What newes with the[e]?

JOHAN.   Mar[r]y, sir, to tell you shortly,

My wife and I pray you hartely,

And eke desire you with all our might,   *also*

That ye wolde come and sup with us tonight.

SIR J.   Ye must pardon me. In faith, I ne can.

JOHAN.   Yes, I desire you, good sir Johan,

324   Take paine this ones. And yet, at the lest,

If ye will do nought at my request,

Yet do somwhat for the love of my wife.

SIR J.   I will not go, for making of strife.   *for fear of making*

307-8I had supposed you'd have returned again in that amount of time. But, by Christ's soul, if I should treat you as you deserve.

324Trouble yourself this once. At the very least.

But I shall tell the[e] what thou shalte do:
Thou shalt tar[r]y and sup with me, or thou go.   *ere*

330 JOHAN.   Will ye not go, than? Why so?
I pray you tell me, is there any disdaine
Or ony enmité betwene you twaine?

SIR J.   In faith, to tell the[e]—betwene the[e] and me—
She is as wise a woman as any may be.
I know it well, for I have had the charge

336 Of her soule, and serchyd her consciens at large.   *at length*
I never knew her but honest and wise,
Without any yvill or any vice
Save one fau[l]t—I know in her no more—
And because I rebuke her now and then therfore,
She is angré with me, and hath me in hate.
And yet that that I do, I do it for your welth.   *advantage*

JOHAN.   Now God yeld it yow, go[o]d master curate!   *reward you for it*

344 And, as ye do, so send you your helth.
345 Iwis, I am bound to you a plesure.

SIR J.   Yet thou thinkist amis, peradventure,
That of her body she shuld not be a good woman.   *she is not*
But I shall tell the[e] what I have done, Johan,
For that matter: she and I be somtime aloft,   *in my chamber*

350 And I do lie uppon her many a time and oft
351 To prove her; yet could I never espy
That ever any did wors with her than I.   *anyone else*

JOHAN.   Sir, that is the lest care I have of nine,   *i.e., my least worry*
Thankyd be God and your good doctrine.
But, if it please you, tell me the matter   *argument*
And the debate betwene you and her.   *quarrel*

SIR J.   I shall tell the[e], but thou must kepe secret.

JOHAN.   As for that, sir, I shall not let.   *fail*

SIR J.   I shall tell the[e] now the matter plain:
She is angry with me and hath me in disdain

361 Because that I do her oft intice
To do some penaunce, after mine advise,
Because she will never leve her wrawling,   *squalling*
But alway with the[e] she is chiding and brawling.
And therfore, I knowe, she hatith my presens.

336*serchyd*: with sexual double meaning.

344–45And, in return for your goodness, may God send you good health. Truly, I am indebted
to you for (your) kindness.

350*lie uppon*: importune, urge (with obvious sexual double meaning).

351*prove*: examine (spiritually or sexually).

361*intice*: (1) urge (2) tempt. (The "penaunce" sir Johan awards her is presumably sexual.)

366   JOHAN.   Nay, in good feyth, saving your reverens.

     SIR J.   I know very well she hath me in hate.

     JOHAN.   Nay, I dare swere for her, master curate.

       [*Aside.*] But, was I not a very knave!   *an utter fool*

       I thought surely, so God me save,

       That he had lovyd my wife for to dyseive me—

       And now he quitith himself. And here I se   *acquits, clears*

373   He doth as much as he may, for his life,

       To stint the debate betwene me and my wife.   *cease*

     SIR J.   If ever she did or though[t] me any ill,

       Now I forgive her with my fre will.

       Therfore, Johan Johan, now get the[e] home

       And thank thy wife, and say I will not come.

     JOHAN.   Yet let me know now, good sir Johan,

380   Where ye will go to supper than.

     SIR J.   I care not greatly and I tell the[e].   *if*

       On Saterday last, I and two or thre

       Of my frendes made an appointement,

       And against this night we did assent   *in anticipation of*

       That in a place we wolde sup together.

       And one of them said [s]he wold bringe thether

       Ale and bread, and for my parte I

       Said that I wolde give them a pie—

       And there I gave them money for the makinge.

390   And another said she wolde pay for the baking,

       And so we purpose to make good chere

       For to drive away care and thought.   *sorrow*

     JOHAN.   Than I pray you, sir, tell me here:

       Whither shulde all this geare be brought?

     SIR J.   By my faith, and I shulde not lie,   *if*

       It shulde be delivered to thy wife, the pie.

     JOHAN.   By God, it is at my house standing by the fire!

     SIR J.   Who bespake that pie, I the[e] require?   *arranged for/ask*

     JOHAN.   By my feyth, and I shall not lie,   *if*

400   It was my wife and her gossip Margerye,

       And your good mas'ship called sir Johan,   *mastership*

       And my neybours yongest doughter An.   *neighbour's*

       Your mas'ship paide for the stuffe and making,

       And Margery she paide for the baking.

     SIR J.   If thou wilte have me nowe, in faithe, I will go.

     JOHAN.   Ye[a], mar[r]y, I beseche your mas'ship do so.

       My wife taryeth for none but us twaine;

---

³⁶⁶*saving . . . reverens:* i.e., respectfully begging to differ with you.

³⁷³*for his life:* i.e., as much as his life is worth.

She thinketh longe or I come againe.   *(it) long ere*

SIR J.   Well, nowe if she chide me in thy presens
410   I wil be content, and take [it] in paciens.

JOHAN.   By Cokkes soule, and she ones chide,   *if she once*
Or frowne, or loure, or loke aside,
I shall bringe you a staffe, as myche as I may heve.   *big/lift*
Than bete her, and spare not! I give you good leve   *permission*
To chastice her for her shreude varyeng.   *ill-natured quarrelsomeness*
       [*They return to Johan's house.*]

TIB.   The devill take the[e] for thy longe taryeng!
Here is not a whit of water, by my gowne,
To washe our handes that we might sit downe.   *sit at table*
Go and hie the[e] as fast as a snaile,
And with faire water fill me this paile.

421   JOHAN.   I thanke our Lorde of his good grace
That I cannot rest longe in a place!

TIB.   Go fetche water, I say, at a worde,
For it is time the pie were on the borde.

425   And go with a vengeance, and say thou art pray'de!   *asked politely*
       [*Johan starts out with the water pail.*]
426   SIR J.   A, good gossip, is that well saide?

TIB [*aside to Sir Johan*].   Welcome, min[e] owne sweteharte!
We shall make some chere or we departe.   *ere we separate*

JOHAN [*aside*].   Cokkes soule, loke howe he approcheth nere
Unto my wife! This abateth my chere.
       [*He goes out for water.*]

SIR J.   By God, I wolde ye had h[e]arde the trifils,
The toys, the mokkes, the fables, and the nifils   *fictitious tales*
That I made thy husbande to beleve and thinke!
Thou mightest as well into the erthe sinke
As thou coudest forbeare laughing any while.

TIB.   I pray the[e], let me he[a]re parte of that wile. *stratagem*

SIR J.   Mar[r]y, I shall tell the[e] as fast as I can—
But peas, no more! Yonder cometh thy good man.
       [*Johan re-enters.*]

JOHAN.   Cokkes soule, what have we here?
440   As far as I sawe, he drewe very nere
Unto my wife.

---

[421](Said sardonically).

[425-26]i.e., Go do it, curse you! A curse is all the thanks you'll get from me. —Ah, my dear friend, is that any way to talk? (Sir Johan, speaking aloud for the husband's benefit, makes a pretence of chiding Tib's shrewish tongue.)

TIB.   What, art come so sone?

 Give us water to wasshe, nowe; have done.

 Than he bringeth the paile empty.

JOHAN.   By Kockes soule, it was even nowe full to the brink,

 But it was out againe or I coude thinke!   *ere*

 Wherof I marveled, by God almight.

 And than I loked betwene me and the light,   *examined (it)*

447 And I spied a clifte, bothe large and wide.

 Lo, wife, here it is on the tone side.   *one*

TIB.   Why dost not stop it?   *plug it up*

JOHAN.   Why, howe shall I do it?

TIB.   Take a litle wax.

JOHAN.   Howe shal I come to it?   *obtain it*

SIR J.   Mar[r]y, here be two wax candyls, I say,

452 Whiche my gossip Margery gave me yesterday.

TIB.   Tusshe, let him alone, for, by the rode,

 It is pité to helpe him or do him good.

SIR J.   What, Johan Johan, canst thou make no shifte? *expedient*

 Take this waxe and stop therwith the clifte.

JOHAN.   This waxe is as harde as any wire.

TIB.   Thou must chafe it a litle at the fire.

JOHAN.   She that broughte the[e] these waxe candelles

  twaine,

460 She is a good companion, certain!

  [Johan goes to the fire to mend the pail.]

TIB.   What, was it not my gossip Margery?

SIR J.   Yes. She is a blessed woman, surely.

TIB.   Nowe wolde God I were as good as she,

 For she is vertuous and full of charité.

JOHAN *[aside]*.   Nowe, so God helpe me, and by my holydome, *things sacred*

 She is the erran'st baud betwene this and Rome. *most arrant bawd*

TIB.   What say'st?

JOHAN.   Mar[r]y, I chafe the wax,

 And I chafe it so hard that my fingers krakkes.

 But take up this pi[e] that I here torne!

470 And it stand long, iwis, it will borne.   *If/burn*

TIB *[removing the pie]*.   Ye[a], but thou must chafe the wax,

  I say.

  [Johan tries to join the lovers at the table.]

447*clifte:* In the sexual double entendre, the bucket and its slit are Tib and her sexual appetites, which Johan is unable to keep filled or satiated. The wax represents his phallus, which his wife suggests he rub or chafe as a sexual substitute.

452(It is fitting that Margery, in her role as bawd, has procured the means of filling the cleft in the bucket.)

470*borne:* burn (signifying the burning passion of Tib's appetite, about to be consummated).

JOHAN.   Bid him sit down, I the[e] pray—
  Sit down, good sir Johan, I you require.   *urge*
TIB.   Go, I say, and chafe the wax by the fire,
  While that we sup, sir Johan and I.
JOHAN.   And how now! what will ye do with the pi[e]?
  Shall I not ete therof a morsell?

478 TIB.   Go, and chafe the wax while thou art well!
  And let us have no more prating thus.
    [*Sir Johan starts to say grace.*]
SIR J. *Benedicité*—
JOHAN [*approaching*].   *Dominus.*
TIB.   Now go chafe the wax, with a mischife!   *with a curse on you*
JOHAN.   What! I come to blisse the bord, swete wife.
  It is my custome now and than.

484 Mych good do it you, master sir Johan.
TIB.   Go chafe the wax, and here no lenger tary.
    [*John returns to the fireside.*]
JOHAN [*aside*].   And is not this a very purgatory:
  To se folkes ete, and may not ete a bit?
  By Kokkes soule, I am a very wo[o]dco[c]k.   *simpleton*
  This paile here, now a vengaunce take it!
  Now my wife giveth me a proud mo[c]k!
TIB [*eating*].   What dost?
JOHAN.   Mar[r]y, I chafe the wax here;

492 [*Aside.*] And I imagin[e], to make you good chere,
  That a vengaunce take you both as ye sit!
  For I know well I shall not ete a bit.
  But yet, in feyth, if I might ete one morsell
  I wold think the matter went very well.

497 SIR J. [*eating*].   Gossip Johan Johan, now, mych good do it
      you,
  What chere make you there by the fire?
JOHAN.   Master parson, I thank yow, now
  I fare well inow after mine own desire.   *enough according to*
SIR J.   What dost, Johan Johan, I the[e] require?   *ask*
JOHAN.   I chafe the wax here by the fire.
TIB [*to sir John*].   Here is good drink and here is a good pi[e]!
SIR J.   We fare very well, thankyd be Our Lady.
TIB.   Loke how the kokold chafith the wax that is hard,

478Go and rub the wax (i.e., your male member) before I make you ill with a beating!

484(Said sardonically; Johan Johan is expressing his resentment at having the priest usurp the role of head of the family.)

492i.e., And I picture to myself, as a way of enhancing your merriment.

497*mych . . . you:* The priest throws Johan's previous taunt, l. 484, back in his face.

And, for his life, darith not loke hetherward.

SIR J.   [*to Johan*]. What doth my gossip?

JOHAN.   I chafe the wax—

[*Aside.*]   And I chafe it so hard that my fingers krakkes!

And eke the smoke puttith out my eyes two;   *also*

510   I burne my face, and ray my clothys also,   *soil*

And yet I dare nat say one word—

And they sit laughing yender at the bord.

TIB.   Now, by my trouth, it is a prety jape   *clever jest*

For a wife to make her husband her ape.

Loke of Johan Johan, which maketh hard shift   *Look at/who struggles*

To chafe the wax to stop therwith the clift!

JOHAN [*aside*].   Ye[a], that a vengeaunce take ye both two,

Both him and the[e], and the[e] and him also!

And that ye may choke with the same mete   *food*

520   At the furst mursell that ye do ete.

TIB.   Of what thing now dost thou clatter,

Johan Johan? Or wherof dost thou patter?

JOHAN.   I chafe the wax, and make hard shift   *am hard put to it*

To stop her[e]with of the paill the rift.

525   SIR J.   So must he do, Johan Johan, by my father kin,

That is bound of wedlo[c]k in the yoke.   *in wedlock's yoke*

JOHAN [*aside*].   Loke how the pil'd preest crammith in;   *tonsured*

That wold to God he might therwith choke!

TIB.   Now, master Parson, pleasith your goodnes   *may it please*

530   To tell us some tale of mirth or sadnes   *seriousness*

For our pastime, in way of communicacion?

SIR J.   I am content to do it for our recreacion:

And of three miracles I shall to you say.

JOHAN.   What? Must I chafe the wax all day,

And stond here, rosting by the fire?

SIR J.   Thou must do somwhat at thy wives desire.

I know a man which weddyd had a wife—

As faire a woman as ever bare life—

And within a se'night after, right sone,   *sevennight, week*

540   He went beyond se[a], and left her alone,

And taried there about a seven yere.

And as he cam homeward, he had a hevy chere,   *sad countenance*

For it was told him that she was in heven.

But when that he comen home again was,

He found his wife, and with her children seven

Whiche she had had in the mene space;   *meantime*

547   Yet had she not had so many by thre

---

[525] So must any married man, Johan Johan, by my father's ancestors (an oath).

[547] Yet she wouldn't have had within three children as many (i.e., not so many by half).

If she had not had the help of me.
Is not this a miracle, if ever were any,
That this good wife shuld have children so many
Here in this town, while her husband shuld be   *was*
Beyond the se[a] in a farre contré?

JOHAN [*aside*].   Now, in good soth, this is a wonderous
        miracle.

554   But, for your labour, I wolde that your tac[k]le   *in payment for*
Were in a skalding water, well sod!   *boiled*

TIB.   Peace, I say! Thou lettest the worde of God.   *interrupt*

SIR J.   Another miracle eke I shall you say,
Of a woman whiche that many a day   *a woman who*
Had ben wedded, and in all that season   *time*

560   She had no childe, nother doughter nor son.
Wherfore to Saint Modwin she went on pilgrimage,
And offered there a live pig, as is the usage
Of the wives that in London dwell.
And, through the vertue therof, truly to tell,
Within a moneth after, right shortly,
She was delivered of a childe as moche as I.   *i.e., resembling me (?)*
How say you, is not this miracle wonderous?

JOHAN.   Yes, in good soth, sir, it is marvelous.
But surely, after min[e] opinion,   *according to*

570   That childe was nother doughter nor son.
For certainly, and I be not beg[u]il'de,   *if*
She was delivered of a knave childe.   *male (with pun)*

TIB.   Peas[e], I say, for Goddes Passion!
Thou lettest sir Johans communication.   *interrupt*

SIR J.   The thirde miracle also is this:
I knewe another woman eke, iwis,

577   Whiche was wedded, and within five monthis after
She was delivered of a faire doughter
As well formed in every membre and joint,
And as perfite in every point,
As though she had gone five monthis full to th' ende.

582   Lo, here is five monthis of advantage.

JOHAN.   A wonderous miracle, so God me mende!
I wolde eche wife that is bounde in mariage
And that is wedded, here within this place,
Might have as quicke spede in every suche case.

554*tac[k]le*: equipment, i.e., genitals.

577*five monthis*: The implication is that Sir Johan fathered the child long before the mother married.

582Lo, here is five months saved. (This is on the basis of a ten-month pregnancy.)

TIB.   Forsoth, sir Johan, yet for all that
  I have sene the day that Pus[s], my cat,
  Hath had in a yere kit[t]lins eighteene.
590 JOHAN.   Ye[a], Tib my wife, and that have I sene.
  But howe say you, sir Johan: was it good, your pie?
  The divell the morsell that therof eate I.
  By the good Lorde, this is a piteous warke!
  But nowe I se well the olde proverbe is trew:
  "The parisshe preest forgetteth that ever he was clarke."
  But, sir Johan, doth not remember you   *don't you remember*
  How I was your clerke, and holpe you masse to sing,
  And hilde the basin alway at the off'ring?
  Ye never had halfe so good a clarke as I.
600 But, notwithstanding all this, nowe our pie
  Is eaten up—there is not lefte a bit—
  And you two together there do sit
  Eatinge and drinkinge at your owne desire,
  And I am Johan Johan, which must stande by the fire *remain*
  Chafing the wax, and dare none otherwise do.
SIR J.   And shall we alway sit here still, we two?
  That were to[o] mych.
TIB.   Then rise we out of this place.
608 SIR J.   And kis me, than, in the stede of grace.
  And farewell, leman and my love so dere! *lover*
JOHAN.   Cokkes body, this waxe it wax'te colde again here.
  But what, shall I anone go to bed
  And eate nothing, nother meate nor brede?
  I have not be wont to have suche fare. *been accustomed*
TIB.   Why, were ye not served thereas ye are, *there where*
  Chafing the waxe, standing by the fire?
JOHAN.   Why, what mete gave ye me, I you require? *food/ask*
SIR J.   Wast thou not served, I pray the[e] hartely,
  Both with the brede, the ale, and the pie?
JOHAN.   No, sir, I had none of that fare.
620 TIB.   Why, were ye not served thereas ye are,
  Standing by the fire chafing the waxe?
JOHAN [*aside*].   Lo, here be many trifils and knakkes; *tricks*
  By Kokkes soule, they wene I am other dronke or mad! *either*
TIB.   And had ye no meate, Johan Johan? no had?
JOHAN.   No, Tib my wife, I had not a whit.
TIB.   What, not a morsell?
JOHAN.   No, not one bit.
  For honger, I trowe, I shall fall in a sowne. *swoon*
SIR J.   O, that were pité, I swere by my crowne.

608*in . . . grace:* instead of grace ending the meal.

TIB.   But is it trewe?

JOHAN.   Ye[a], for a sureté.

630 TIB.   Dost thou li[e]?

JOHAN.   No, so mote I the[e]!   *as I hope to prosper*

TIB.   Hast thou had nothing?

JOHAN.   No, not a bit.

TIB.   Hast thou not dronke?

JOHAN.   No, not a whit.

TIB.   Where wast thou?

JOHAN.   By the fire I did stande.

TIB.   What didist?

JOHAN.   I chafed this waxe in my hande,

Whereas I knewe of wedded men the paine   *Whereby*

That they have and yet dare not complaine;

For the smoke put out my eyes two,

I burned my face, and ray'de my clothes also,   *soiled*

Mending the paile whiche is so rotten and olde

640 That it will not skant together holde.   *scarcely*

And sith it is so, and sins[e] that ye twain

Wold give me no meate for my suffisaunce,

By Kokes soule, I will take no lenger pain!   *I'll strive no longer*

Ye shall do all yourself, with a very vengaunce,

For me. And take thou there thy paile now,   *For all I'll do it*

And if thou canst mend it, let me se how.

         [*Hurls the pail to the floor.*]

TIB.   A, [w]horson knave, hast thou brok my paill?

648 Thou shalt repent, by Kokes lilly naill.

Re[a]ch me my distaf, or my clipping-she[a]rys!   *Hand*

I shall make the blood ronne about his e[a]rys.

         [*Johan takes up a shovelful of hot coals.*]

JOHAN.   Nay, stand still, drab, I say, and come no nere;   *whore/nearer*

For, by Kokkes blood, if thou come here,

Or if thou onys stir toward this place,

I shall throw this shovyll-full of colys in thy face.

TIB.   Ye[a], [w]horson drivill, get the[e] out of my dore!   *menial, imbecile*

JOHAN.   Nay, get thee out of my house, thou prestes

         [w]hore!

657 SIR J.   Thou liest, [w]horson kokold, evyn to thy face!

JOHAN.   And thou liest, pil'd preest, with an evill grace!   *bad luck to you*

TIB.   And thou liest!

JOHAN.   And thou liest!

648*by . . . naill:* by Christ's lovely nail (of the cross, or fingernail).

657You lie, you good-for-nothing cuckold—(I say this) to your very face! (The epithet "cuckold" would seem to contradict what the priest is saying.)

SIR J.   And thou liest again!

660   JOHAN.   By Kokkes soule, [w]horson preest, thou shalt be
                slain.

         Thou hast eate our pie, and give me nought.   *given*

         By Kokkes blod, it shal be full derely bought!   *paid for*

    TIB.   At him, sir Johan, or els God give the[e] sorow!

    JOHAN.   And have at you, [w]hore and thefe, Saint George
                to borow!   *be my speed*

         Here they fight by the e[a]rys a while, and than the preest and the   *at variance*
         wife go out of the place.

    JOHAN.   A, sirs! I have paid some of them even as I list.

         They have borne many a blow with my fist.

         I thank God, I have walkyd them well,   *beaten them*

         And driven them hens. But yet, can ye tell

         Whether they be go? For, by God, I fere me   *Whither*

670   That they be gon together, he and she,

         Unto his chamber. And perhappys she will,

         Spite of my hart, tary there still.

         And, peradventure, there he and she

         Will make me cokold, evyn to anger me.

675   And then had I a pig in the woyrs[e] panier!   *basket*

         Therfore, by God, I will hie me thider

         To se if they do me any vilany.

         And thus, fare well this noble company.

         [*Exit after the other two.*]

         Finis.

    Imprintyd by William Rastell the twelfth day
       of February the yere of our Lord
             MCCCCC and XXXIII.
                Cum privilegio.

    675*in . . . panier:* in the worse basket (i.e., in a worse position than before).

THE PLAY OF THE WEATHER

BY JOHN HEYWOOD

As a professional entertainer and member of the Thomas More circle, John Heywood wrote both popular plays and more sophisticated courtly plays. *The Four PP* and *Johan Johan* seem intended on the whole for popular audiences, whereas *The Play of the Weather* (1525–33) is essentially courtly. The distinction is not entirely clear-cut, for many popular plays were also appreciated by noble audiences while courtly plays often included rollicking merriment in the fabliau vein. Nevertheless, *Weather* is manifestly more suited for a courtly environment than are some of Heywood's other entertainments.

Weather, with its procession of suitors appearing before a royal and godlike arbitrator, is a fully-developed *débat* in the courtly mode and is thus closely related to other medieval courtly genres such as the mumming and the disguising (see Introduction to Humanist Drama, above). The judge-figure, Jupiter, represents the interests of noble and royal spectators and vicariously involves them in the action, as in the courtly disguising. The setting of the play is patrician, for we are told that Jupiter has come "This night to suppe here with my lorde" (l. 1027). The banquet is not otherwise alluded to, but the action may well have taken place in a banqueting-hall. The set requires a curtained throne for Jupiter, by means of which he can retire from the audience's view. Musicians are in attendance, and the actors, ten in all, are primarily if not exclusively choir boys. No doubling of roles is possible; a company of boy choristers did not need to double up many parts as did the smaller traveling adult troupes.

Like Medwall's *Fulgens and Lucrece*, *Weather* shows some acquaintance with classical learning even though the play is thoroughly English in structure and characterization. The presence or mention of such classical gods as Jupiter, Phoebus, Saturn, Aeolus, and Phoebe invokes the machinery of ancient epic, portraying strife among the Olympian gods as the cause of divisiveness among men. This epic machinery is clearly discernible in *Weather* even if it is used with loving mockery to produce a comically absurd effect. In this lighthearted play, the quarrels of gods and men turn out to revolve about that most exquisitely banal of subjects, the weather. Despite the presence of epic machinery, however, the play is not classical in structure. It is not organized into five acts, and is instead serial and linear in its presentation. The number of suitors appealing to Jupiter could be expanded almost indefinitely. The characters are also English rather than classical for the most part. They are social types chosen to represent, as in the *Canterbury Tales*, the spectrum of English society (with the notable absence of the Church).

Weather is also a courtly play in that it contains a political fable requiring tactful presentation before a Tudor aristocratic audience. The representatives of Tudor society—aristocrat, merchant, petty official (the forest ranger), and tradesmen (the millers)—hotly debate their relative importance to the commonwealth. Such a quarrel is so vehement and politically touchy, in fact, that it requires the presence of a jester to deflate the quarrel by reducing it to comic absurdity. Merry-Report is essential to Heywood's dramatic technique of exposing political factionalism to curative laughter. More than another character, then, Merry-Report is Heywood's

990

persona. He jests at the gentleman's assertions of social superiority, the merchant's self-serving economic claims, the ranger's bureaucratic paranoia against his superiors in the chain of command, and the millers' fratricidal impulses. By mocking all pretensions impartially, Merry-Report exposes self-aggrandizement to laughter. In the case of the female suitors, he ridicules both aristocratic idleness and the self-righteous morality of the working classes. Through Merry-Report's jesting, fabliau humor and scatological joking help establish the tone of satirical laughter. The presence of the boy, asking for snow for his snowballs, completes the comic impression that each claim of exclusive importance is just about as ridiculous as any other.

Merry-Report is called the "vice" of the play, although the term (used here for the first time in English drama) does not mean that he is the tempter in a morality play. He is really more the courtly fool in the vein later used by Shakespeare in *As You Like It* and *King Lear*. Because his mind is nominally unsophisticated, Merry-Report naively perceives truths to which the nominally sane petitioners are blind. Wisdom and folly become inverted. Merry-Report realizes far sooner than the petitioners how their quarrel must end: in the establishment of the weather as it always has been. Merry-Report is, however, only the exposer of folly. It is Jupiter's task to represent the principle of order and stability. In his infinite wisdom he adjudicates among the various rivalries of society and so prevents men from destroying one another through greed. Men can be made to understand the need for impartial justice, but are incapable of providing it without authority imposed

from above. Hence the role of Jupiter becomes a forceful argument for monarchical absolutism as practiced by the early Tudors. The king must retain his prerogative of distributing royal favor among competing social groups, since only he is impartial (see especially ll. 1200–3). This medieval world view of order and degree sees an essential analogy between kingship and divine control of the four elements, earth, fire, air, and water. As in the great vision of Boethius, these elements, and the four corresponding qualities of cold, heat, wind, and rain, conspire to destroy one another until brought under the rule of God as the embodiment of harmony, dance, pattern, and Platonic being. Heywood ends his play on a note of joyful affirmation and acceptance, both in political and cosmic terms. Yet he does not let us forget the delicious irony that the petitioners are thus obtaining exactly what they began with.

Weather is chiefly composed in rhyme royal seven-line stanzas (especially for Jupiter's speeches) and in the four-stress couplets used in Heywood's other plays. There is also an occasional tail-rhyme stanza *(aaabcccb)* for Merry-Report, and some *abab cdcd* quatrains for several of the petitioners' more formal arguments. The play was printed in at least four editions in the sixteenth century, but the last three appear to have been derived directly or indirectly from the first edition printed by William Rastell in 1533. That edition (in the Pepys Collection of Magdalene College, Cambridge) is the basis of this present text; when readings from the other early editions are used, they have been noted in the textual apparatus.

The Play of the Weather

A New and a Very Mery Enterlude of all Maner Wethers
Made by John Heywood

The Players Names

JUPITER, a god

MERY-REPORTE, the vice

THE GENTILMAN

THE MARCHAUNT

THE RANGER

THE WATER MILLER

THE WINDE MILLER

THE GENTILWOMAN

THE LAUNDER

A BOY, the lest that can play

[Jupiter is enthroned in a scaffold or curtained pew by means of which he can retire from the audience's view.]

1 JUPITER.   Right farre to[o] longe, as now, were to recite
2   The auncient estate wherin ourselfe hath rei[g]ned—
      What honour, what laude given us of very right,   *praise*
      What glory we have had dewly unfai[g]ned
      Of eche creature, which dewty hath constrained.
      For above all goddes, sins[e] our fathers fale,   *since Saturn's fall*
      We, Jupiter, were ever principale.

      If we so have ben—as treuth it is indede—
      Beyond the compas of all comparison,   *limit*
10   Who coulde presume to shew, for any mede,   *reward*
11   So that it might appere to humayne reason,
12   The hye renowme we stande in at this season?
      For, sins[e] that heven and erth were firste create,   *created*
      Stode we never in suche triumphaunt estate

      As we now do. Wherof we woll reporte
      Suche parte as we se mete for time present,   *suitable*

THE PLAYERS NAMES: *Ranger:* the keeper of a forest. *Launder:* a person of either sex who washes linen; here, a washerwoman.

[1] It would take far too long at the present time to tell.

[2] *ourselfe:* the royal plural, signifying Jupiter.

[10–12] What person would dare attempt, even for a very large reward, to describe my present indescribable glory in terms that mortals could comprehend?

17 Chiefely concerninge your perpetuall conforte,
18 As the thinge selfe shall prove in experiment;
Whiche hyely shall binde you, on knees lowly bent,
Soolly to honour oure hyenes, day by day. *highness*
And now to the mater give eare, and we shall say:

Before our presens, in our hye parliament,
Both goddes and goddes[s]es of all degrees
Hath late assembled, by comen assent, *lately*
25 For the redres of certaine enormitees
26 Bred amonge them thorow extremitees
27 Abusyd in eche to other of them all;
28 Namely, to purpose, in these moste speciall:

Our foresaid father Saturne, and Phebus,
Eolus, and Phebe, these four by name—
31 Whose natures not onely so farre contrarious,
32 But also of malice eche other to defame
Have longe time abused, right farre out of frame, *predictable path*
The dew course of all their constellacions *due, proper*
To the great damage of all yerthly nacions. *earthly*

Whiche was debated in place saide before. *i.e., in parliament*
And firste—as became—our father, moste auncient, *as befitted his age*
With berde white as snow, his lockes both cold and hore, *white*
Hath ent'red such mater as served his entent, *entered on the record*
40 Laudinge his frosty mansion in the firmament
41 To aire and yerth as thinge moste precious,
42 Pourginge all humours that are contagious.

Howbeit, he alledgeth that of longe time past
44 Littell hath prevailed his great diligens.
Full oft uppon yerth his faire frost he hath cast,
All things hurtfull to banish out of presens—
But Phebus, entendinge to kepe him in silens,

17–18(I intend to tell you) chiefly about a perpetual benefit to mankind, as will become self-evident in the course of the following action.

25–28In order to correct certain hostilities arising among the gods because of their having spoken injuriously against one another; in particular, the following. (The four gods Saturn, Phoebus, Eolus, and Phoebe represent cold, heat, wind, and rain respectively.)

31–32Who, not only so inherently contradictory, but also motivated by malice to attack one another.

40–42i.e., Praising cold (his quality) as most necessary to air and earth, since it purges (cleanses) all contagious vapors.

44His great diligence has come to little avail.

48   When he hath labored all night in his pow'res,   *he (Saturn)*
         His glaringe beamys mar[r]ith all in two howres.   *His (Phoebus')*

         Phebus to this made no maner answeringe.   *no sort of answer*
         Wheruppon they both then Phebe defied.
         Eche for his parte leyd in her reprovinge   *alleged in reproof of her*
         That, by her show'res superfluous, they have tried   *found by experience*
54   In all that she may, their pow'res be denied.
         Wherunto Phebe made answere no more
         Then Phebus to Saturne hadde made before.

         Anone uppon Eolus all these did fle,   *flew in verbal attack*
         Complaininge their causes, eche one a-row,   *in turn*
59   And said, to compare none was so evill as he;
         For, when he is disposed his blastes to blow,
         He suffereth neither sone-shine, raine, nor snow.
         They eche againste other, and he againste all thre—
         Thus can these four in no maner agre.

64   Whiche sene in themselfe, and further consideringe,
65   The same to redres was cause of their assemble.
66   And also that we, evermore beinge,
67   Beside our puis[s]aunt power of deité,
68   Of wisedome and nature so noble and so fre—   *excellent*
69   From all extremitees the meane devidinge,
70   To pease and plenté eche thinge attemperinge—

         They have, in conclusion, [w]holly surrend'ryd
72   Into our handes—as mych as concerninge
73   All maner wethers by them engend'ryd—
         The full of their pow'rs for terme everlastinge,
75   To set suche order as standith with our pleasinge.
76   Whiche thing, as of our parte no parte required,
         But of all their partys right humbly desired   *by all of them*

[48]i.e., When Saturn has labored all night spreading frost and snow.

[54]That in everything she does, the effects of cold and sun are cancelled out.

[59]And said none could compare with him (Eolus) for evil.

[64-70]i.e., Which, when they saw this contentiousness in themselves, to consider it further and then to correct the same was the cause of their assembly. And also since I, Jupiter, am eternally (in addition to my great power of godhead) so noble and excellent in my wisdom and my essential being, and am always distinguishing the golden mean from extremes and harmoniously attuning all things to a condition of peace and prosperity.

[72-73]Into my hands—regarding the whole question of all the various weathers engendered by them.

[75-76](Empowering me) to establish such order as agrees with my pleasure. Which thing (the decision-making power), not on my part sought at all.

To take uppon us, wherto we did assente.
79 And so in all thinges with one voice agreable,
We have clerely finished our foresaid parleament,
To your great welth—whiche shall be firme and stable—   *well-being*
And to our honour farre inestimable.
83 For sins[e] their powers, as ours, addyd to our owne,
84 Who can, we say, know us as we shulde be knowne?

But now, for fine, the reste of our entent   *to conclude*
Wherfore, as now, we hither are discendyd,   *For which at present*
Is onely to satisfye and content
All maner people whiche have ben offendyd   *All kinds of*
By any wether mete to be amendyd;   *fit, needing*
Uppon whose complaintes, declaringe their grefe,
We shall shape remedy for their relefe.   *devise*

92 And to give knowledge for their hither resorte,
We wolde this afore proclaimed to be   *wish/ahead of time*
To all our people, by some one of this sorte,   *i.e., of this audience*
Whom we liste to choise here amongest all ye.
Wherfore eche man avaunce, and we shall se
Whiche of you is moste mete to be our crier.   *fit*
Here ent'reth Mery-Reporte [from among the audience].

98 MERY-REPORT.   Brother, holde up your torche a litell hyer!
Now, I beseche you, my lorde, loke on me furste.
I truste your lordship shall not finde me the wurste.
JUPITER.   Why, what arte thou that approchist so ny?
MERY-REPORT.   Forsothe, and please your lordshippe, it is I.   *if (it)*
JUPITER.   All that we knowe very well. But what "I"?
104 MERY-REPORT.   What "I"? Some saye I am I *per se* I.
But, what maner "I" soever be I,
I assure your good lordship, I am I.
JUPITER.   What maner man arte thou? Shewe quickely.
MERY-REPORT.   By God, a poore gentilman, dwellith here
        by.   *who dwells nearby*
JUPITER.   A gentilman? Thyselfe bringeth witnes naye,   *You prove the contrary*
110 Bothe in thy light behaviour and araye.   *frivolous*

79i.e., And so, with everyone in unanimous agreement on everything.

83–84i.e., For, since they now harmoniously add their powers over the elements to mine, what mortal can know the full power of God?

92i.e., And to let all people know they may come here to complain.

98*Brother:* one of the torch-bearers in the vicinity of the acting area.

104*per se:* i.e., "I" is a letter which by itself forms a word.

But what arte thou called where thou dost resorte?

MERY-REPORT.   Forsoth, my orde, mayster Mery-Reporte.

JUPITER.   Thou arte no mete man in our bisines,

For thine apparence is of to[o] mych lightnes.

MERY-REPORT.   Why, cannot your lordship like my maner,

Mine apparell, nor my name nother?   *neither*

117   JUPITER.   To nother of all we have devocion.

MERY-REPORT.   A proper licklihod of promocion!   *excellent*

Well, than, as wise as ye seme to be,

Yet can ye se no wisdome in me.

But sins[e] ye dispraise me for so lighte an elfe,   *for being*

I praye you give me leve to praise myselfe.   *permission*

And, for the firste parte, I will begin

In my behavour at my comminge in:

Wherin I thinke I have litell offendyd,

126   For, sewer, my curtesy coulde not be amendyd!   *surely*

And, as for my sewt your servaunt to be,   *suit, petition*

128   Mighte ill have bene mis[s]'t, for your honesté;

For, as I be saved, if I shall not lie,   *as I (hope to) be*

I saw no man sew for the office but I!

Wherfore, if ye take me not or I go,   *ere*

Ye must anone, whether ye will or no.   *soon/wish to or not*

And sins[e] your entent is but for the wethers,

134   What skils our apparell to be fri[e]se or fethers?

I thinke it wisdome, sins[e] no man forbad[e] it,

136   With this to spare a better—if I had it!

And, for my name: reporting alwaye trewly,   *as long as I'm truthful*

What hurte to reporte a sad mater mer[r]ely?   *serious*

139   As, by occasion, for the same entent:

To a serteyne wedow this daye was I sent

Whose husbande departyd without her wittinge—   *died/knowing it*

142   A speciall good lover, and she his owne swettinge.   *sweetheart*

143   To whome, at my comming, I caste such a figure,

---

[117]I'm not pleased by any of them.

[126](1) My courtesy was exemplary (2) My behavior is incorrigible.

[128]It might sorely have been missed, in the interests of your good name (i.e., you could ill afford to do without it).

[134]i.e., For such a frivolous subject, what does it matter if we be dressed in a coarse woolen cloth or in finery?

[136]i.e., To wear what I have on, and thus save a better—which I don't have in any case.

[139]As, for example, to prove the same point.

[142]i.e., This woman and her departed husband were totally fond of one another.

[143]*caste . . . figure:* created such an impression.

144   Minglinge the mater accordinge to my nature,
        That when we departyd, above all other thinges   *separated*
        She thanked me hartely for my mery tidinges!
        And if I had not handled it merily,
        Perchaunce she might have take[n] it hevely;   *sadly*
        But in suche fac[h]ion I conjured and bounde her
150   That I left her merier then I founde her.
        What man may compare to shew the like comforte
        That daily is shewed by me, Mery-Reporte?
        And, for your purpose at this time ment,   *intended*
        For all wethers I am so indifferent,   *impartial*
        Without affeccion, standinge so upright—   *having such integrity*
        Sonlight, monelight, sterlight, twilight, torchlight,
        Cold, hete, moist, drye, haile, raine, frost, snow, lightning,
            thunder,
        Cloudy, misty, windy, faire, fowle above hed or under,   *underfoot*
        Temperate or distemperate, whatever it be—
160   I promise your lordship, all is one to me.

        JUPITER.   Well, sonne, consid'ringe thine indifferency,
        And partely the rest of thy declaracion,
        We make the[e] our servaunte. And immediately
        We woll thou departe and cause proclamacion,   *We wish you to go*
        Publishinge our pleasure to every nacion.   *decree*
        Whiche thinge ons[e] done, with all diligens   *When this is done*
        Make thy returne againe to this presens,

        Here to receive all sewters of eche degre.
169   And suche as to the[e] may seme moste metely,
        We will thow bringe them before our majesté;
        And for the reste, that be not so worthy,
        Make thou reporte to us effectually,
        So that we may heare eche maner sewte at large.   *each kind of petition fully*
        Thus se thow departe, and loke uppon thy charge.   *see to your assignment*

        MERY-REPORT.   Now, good my lorde god, Our Lady be with
            ye!
            [*To the audience.*]
        Frendes, a fellyshippe, let me go by ye.   *for fellowship's sake*
        Thinke ye I may stand thrusting amonge you there?   *crowding*
        Nay, by God, I muste thrust about other gere!
        Mery-Report go'th out [*to make proclamation*].

144i.e., Offsetting the sad news with my cheerful nature.

169*metely*: i.e., of suitably high rank to be granted a royal audience.

JUPITER.   Now, sins[e] we have thus farre set forth our
                purpose,
       A while we woll withdraw our godly presens,
181   To enbold all such more plainely to disclose,
182   As here will attende, in our foresaide pretens.   *intention*
       And now, accordinge to your obediens,   *(oath of) obedience*
       Rejoice ye in us with joy most joyfully,
       And we ourselfe shall joy in our owne glory!
            [*Jupiter withdraws from the audience's view into his curtained
            recess.*]
            At th'ende of this staf, the god hath a song played in his trone or   *the previous stanza/ere*
            Mery-Report come in.

            Mery-Report cometh in [*through the audience*].

MERY-REPORT.   Now, sirs, take hede, for here cometh goddes
                servaunt!
187   Avaunte, carte[r]ly keytifs, avaunt!   *boorish*
188   Why, ye dronken [w]horesons, will it not be?
189   By your faith, have ye nother cap nor kne?
       Not one of you that will make curt'sy
       To me, that am squire for goddes precious body?
       Regarde ye nothinge mine authorité?   *not at all*
       No "Welcome home!" nor "Where have ye be?"   *been*
       Howbeit, if ye axyd, I coulde not well tell;   *even if you asked*
       But suer I thinke a thousande mile from hell,   *surely*
       And, on my faith, I thinke, in my consciens,
       I have ben from hevyn as farre as heven is hens—
       At Lovyn, at London, and in Lombardy,   *Louvain (Belgium)*
       At Baldock, at Barfolde, and in Barbary,
       At Canturbery, at Coventré, at Colchester,
       At Wansworth and Welbeck, at Westchester,
       At Fullam, at Faleborne, and at Fenlow,   *Fulham (London)*
       At Wallingford, at Wakef[i]eld, and at Waltamstow,   *Walthamstow (London)*
204   At Tawnton, at Tiptré, and at Totnam,
       At Glouce[s]ter, at Gilford, and at Gotham,
       At Hartforde, at Harwiche, at Harrow on the Hill,
       At Sudbery, S[o]uthhampton, at Shoters Hill,   *Shooter's Hill (London)*

181–82To embolden all such as will come here to disclose (their complaints) more freely (than
they would if I were present), in regard to my previously-discussed intention.

187–89Out of the way, boorish wretches! What, you drunken rascals, aren't you going to do
what I tell you? Aren't you going to take off your caps and bend your knees?

204At Taunton (Somerset), at Tiptree Heath (Essex), and at Tottenham (Middlesex, London area). (Many of the names on Merry-Report's list are in England.)

At Walsingham, at Wittam, and at Werwicke,   *Witham (Essex)*

At Boston, at Bristow, and at Berwicke,   *Bristol*

210   At Gravelyn, at Gravesend, and at Glastynbery,   *Gravelines (France)*

Ynge Gingiang Jayberd, the parishe of Butsbery—

The devill himselfe, without more leasure,

Coulde not have gone halfe thus myche, I am sure!

But, now I have warned them, let them even cho[o]se,   *given them notice*

For, in faith, I care not who winne or lose.

Here the gentilman, before he cometh in, bloweth his horne.

MERY-REPORT.   Now, by my trouth, this was a goodly
     hearing!

I went it had ben the gentilwomens blowinge;   *weened, supposed*

But it is not so, as I now suppose,

219   For womens hornes sounde more in a mannys nose.

[The gentleman enters with a retinue of followers.]

GENTILMAN.   Stande ye mery, my frendes, everychone.   *Be at ease*

MERY-REPORT.   Say that to me and let the reste alone!

Sir, ye be welcome, and all your meyny.   *retinue*

GENTILMAN.   Now, in good sooth, my frende, god-a-mercy!   *thanks*

And sins[e] that I mete the[e] here thus by chaunce,

I shall require the[e] of further acqueyntaunce.   *ask*

And brevely to shew the[e], this is the mater: *briefly*

I come to sew to the great god Jupiter   *sue, petition*

For helpe of thinges concerninge my recreacion,

Accordinge to his late proclamacion.

230   MERY-REPORT.   Mar[r]y, and I am he that this must spede.   *who must help in this*

But firste tell me, what be ye indede?

GENTILMAN.   Forsoth, good frende, I am a gentilman.

MERY-REPORT.   A goodly occupacion, by Seynt Anne!

On my faith, your ma'ship hath a mery life.   *mastership*

But who maketh al these hornes, yourself or your wife?   *i.e., cuckold's horns*

Nay, even in ernest I aske you this question.

GENTILMAN.   Now, by my trouth, thou art a mery one!

MERY-REPORT.   In faith, of us both I thinke never one sad,   *neither one serious*

For I am not so mery but ye seme as mad!   *madcap, merry*

240   But stande ye still and take a littell paine;   *suffer a brief inconvenience*

I will come to you by and by againe.

[He approaches Jupiter's throne.]

Now, gracious god, if your will so be,

I pray ye let me speke a worde with ye.

JUPITER.   My sonne, say on: let us he[a]re thy minde.

---

²¹⁹*in . . . nose:* more nasal (with a joke on cuckold's horns, implanted on a man's forehead
by his wife's infidelities).

MERY-REPORT. My lord, there standeth a sewter even here
behinde,
A gentilman, in yonder corner;
247   And, as I thinke, his name is mayster Horner.
A hunter he is, and comith to make you sporte.
249   He wolde hunte a sow or twaine out of this sorte.
Here he pointeth to the women.
JUPITER. Whatsoever his minde be, let him appere.
MERY-REPORT. Now, good mayster Horner, I pray you
come nere.
GENTILMAN. I am no horner, knave! I will thou know it.
MERY-REPORT. I thought ye had [been], for when ye did
blow it,
H[e]arde I never [w]horeson make horne so goo.
As lefe ye kis'te mine ars as blow my hole soo!   *I'd just as soon*
Come on your way before the god Jupiter,
And there for yourselfe ye shall be sewter.
[*The gentleman approaches Jupiter's throne.*]
GENTILMAN. Moste mighty prince and god of every nacion,
Pleasith your highnes to vouchsave the he[a]ringe   *May it please*
Of me, whiche, according to [y]our proclamacion,   *who*
Doth make apparaunce, in way of besechinge   *Do*
Not sole for myselfe, but generally   *solely*
For all come of noble and auncient stock,   *(who) are descended from*
264   Which sorte above all doth most thankfully
265   Daily take paine for welth of the com[m]en flocke—   *the well-being*
With diligent study alway devisinge
To kepe them in order and unité,
In peace to labour the encrees of their livinge
Wherby eche man may prosper in plenté.
270   Wherfore, good god, this is our [w]hole desiringe,
That for ease of our paines, at times vacant,   *in leisure hours*
In our recreacion—whiche chiefely is huntinge—
It may please you to sende us wether pleasaunt:
Drye and not misty, the winde calme and still,
275   That, after our houndes yourninge so merily,
Chasinge the dere over dale and hill,   *deer*
277   In he[a]ringe we may folow and to-comfort the cry.

247*Horner:* joking again on cuckoldry, as well as the idle sport of hunting.

249i.e., He'd like to chase one or two of the female spectators here.

264–65Who more than any other group earn thanks by making painstaking efforts on behalf of the commoners.

275So that, following after our hounds that are crying out eagerly.

277We may follow within hearing of the hounds and encourage them as they cry.

JUPITER.   Right well we do perceive your [w]hole request,
          Whiche shall not faile to reste in memory.   *Which I won't forget*
          Wherfore we will ye set yourselfe at rest
          Till we have he[a]rde eche man indifferently;
          And we shall take suche order, universally,   *make such provision*
          As best may stande to our honour infinite,   *may be consistent with*
          For welth in commune and ech mannys singuler profite.   *common benefit*
              [*Jupiter retires into his curtained throne.*]

GENTILMAN.   In heven and yerth honoured be the name
          Of Jupiter, who, of his godly goodnes,
          Hath set this mater in so goodly frame   *order*
          That every wight shall have his desire, doutles!
          And first for us nobles and gentilmen,
          I doute not, in his wisedome, to provide
          Suche wether as in our huntinge, now and then,
          We may both teyse and receive on every side.   *chase/bring down the game*
          Whiche thinge ones had, for our seyd recreacion,   *aforesaid*
294   Shall greatly prevaile you in preferringe our helth.
          For what thinge more nedefull then our preservacion,
          Beinge the weale and heddes of all com[m]enwelth?

MERY-REPORT.   Now I beseche your ma'ship, whose hed be
              you?
GENTILMAN.   Whose hed am I? Thy hed. What sey'st thou
              now?
MERY-REPORT.   Nay, I thinke it very trew, so God me helpe!
300   For I have ever ben, of a littell whelpe,
          So full of fansies and in so many fittes,
302   So many smale reasons, and in so many wittes,
303   That, even as I stande, I pray God I be dede
304   If ever I thought them all mete for one hede.
          But sins[e] I have one hed more then I knew,
          Blame not my rejoicinge—I love all thinges new.
307   And suer it is a treasour of heddes to have store.
          One feate can I now that I never coude before.
GENTILMAN.   What is that?
MERY-REPORT.   By God, sins[e] ye came hither,

294i.e., Will greatly profit all men by improving the well-being of gentlemen.

300*of . . . whelpe:* ever since I was a little cub.

302–4So full of little notions, and so scatterbrained, that right here and now I wish to God I
might be dead if ever I thought my fancies would all fit into one head.

307And surely it's great riches to have an extra supply of heads (said ironically).

310   I can set my hedde and my taile togither!
       This hed shall save mon[e]y, by Saint Mary:
       From hensforth I will no potycary,   *will (need)/apothecary*
       For at all timys when suche thinges shall mister   *will be needed*
       My new hed shall geve mine olde taile a glister.   *suppository*
       And, after all this, then shall my hedde waite
316   Uppon my taile, and there stande at receite.
317   Sir, for the reste I will not now move you,
318   But if we live ye shall smell how I love yow.
       And, sir, touching your sewt here, depart when it please   *regarding*
           you,
       For, be ye suer, as I can I will ease you.   *I'll aid your suit*
       GENTILMAN.   Then give me thy hande. That promise I take.
       And if for my sake any sewt thou do make,
323   I promise thy paine to be requited
       More largely then now shall be recited. [*Exit.*]

325   MERY-REPORT.   Alas, my necke! Goddes pity, where is my
           hed?
       By Saint Ive, I feare me I shall be ded!
       And if I were, methinke it were no wonder,
       Sins[e] my hed and my body is so farre asonder.
           Ent'reth the marchaunt.

329   Mayster person, now welcome, by my life!   *parson*
330   I pray you, how doth my mastres, your wife?   *mistress*
       MARCHAUNT.   Sir, for the presthod, and wife that ye alledge,
       I se ye speke more of dotage then knowledge.   *folly*
       But let pas, sir. I wolde to you be sewter   *But never mind that*
       To bringe me, if ye can, before Jupiter.
       [MERY-REPORT.]   Yes, mar[r]y, can I, and will do it indede.
       Tary, and I shall make wey for your spede.
           [*He goes to the throne of Jupiter.*]
       In faith, good lord, if it please your gracious godship,
       I muste have a worde or twaine with your lordship.
       Sir, yonder is another man in place

³¹⁰i.e., I can make your head (which you say is my second head) kiss my tail.

³¹⁶*stande at receite:* i.e., stand ready to receive excrement in the face.

³¹⁷⁻¹⁸i.e., Sir, I won't insist on your doing all these things now, but later you'll smell my tail.

³²³I promise that your efforts (in my behalf) will be rewarded monetarily.

³²⁵i.e., How can I live without my second head, the gentleman? (said mockingly).

³²⁹(Perhaps the merchant's long cloak and general sobriety give him a clerical mien.)

³³⁰(A clergyman should of course not be married.)

Who maketh great sewt to speke with your grace.
341   Your pleasure ones knowen, he commeth by and by.
    JUPITER. Bring him before our presens sone, hardely.   *certainly*
       [*Merry-Report returns to the merchant.*]
    MERY-REPORT. Why, where be you? Shall I not finde ye?
    Come away. I pray God the devill blinde ye!
       [*The merchant approaches Jupiter's throne.*]
    MARCHAUNT. Most mighty prince and lorde of lordes all,
    Right humbly besecheth your majesté
    Your marchaunt-men thorow the worlde all,
    That it may please you, of your benignité,
    In the daily daunger of our goodes and life
    Firste to consider the desert of our request—   *merit*
    What welth we bring the rest, to our great care and
       strife—
    And then to rewarde us as ye shall thinke best.
353   What were the surplisage of eche commodité
    Whiche groweth and encreaseth in every lande,
    Excepte exchaunge by suche men as we be   *Without*
    By wey of entercours, that lieth on our hande?   *trade/is in our keeping*
    We fraught from home thinges wherof there is plenté,   *convey*
    And home we bringe such thinges as there be scant.
    Who sholde afore us marchauntes accompted be?   *be reckoned as superior*
360   For were not we, the worlde shuld wishe and want   *if it weren't for us*
    In many thinges, which now shall lack rehersall.   *which needn't be named*
    And, brevely to conclude, we besche your highnes
    That of the benefite proclaimed in generall
    We may be parte-takers, for comen encres,   *for the common good*
    'Stablishinge wether thus, pleasinge your grace: *if it please*
    Stormy nor misty, the winde mesurable,   *(Neither) stormy/moderate*
    That savely we may passe from place to place,   *safely*
368   Beringe our seylys for spede moste vayleable;
    And also the winde to chaunge, and to turne
    Eest, west, north, and south, as beste may be set—
    In any one place not to[o] longe to sojourne,   *remain*
372   For the length of our vyage may lese our market.

    JUPITER. Right well have ye saide; and we accept it so,
    And so shall we rewarde you ere we go hens.

341As soon as your wish is known, he will approach at once.

353How would there be plentiful supply of each commodity.

368Setting our sails for the most advantageous speed.

372i.e., Because sailing against a steadily adverse wind will produce a long voyage and so risk the losing of a business opportunity.

But ye muste take paciens till we have h[e]arde mo,   *others*
That we may indifferently give sentens.
There may passe by us no spot of negligence,
But justely to judge eche thinge so uprighte
That ech mans parte maye shine in the selfe righte.   *may be valued impartially*
    [*Jupiter retires into his curtained throne.*]

380 MERY-REPORT.   Now, sir, by your faith: if ye shulde be
       sworne,   *on your oath*
    H[e]arde ye ever god speke so, sins[e] ye were borne?
    So wisely, so gentilly his wordes be show'd!
MARCHAUNT.   I thanke his grace. My sewte is well bestow'd.   *in good hands*
MERY-REPORT.   Sir, what vyage entende ye nexte to go?
MARCHAUNT.   I truste or mid-Lente to be to Sio.   *ere/Chios (an Aegean isle)*
MERY-REPORT.   Ha, ha! Is it your minde to saile at Sio?   *to*
    Nay, then, when ye will, by'r Lady, ye maye go,   *by Our*
    And let me alone with this. Be of good chere;   *i.e., with your petition*
    Ye maye truste me at Sio as well as here.
    For, though ye were fro me a thousande mile space,
391   I wolde do as myche as ye were here in place;   *as if*
    For, sins[e] that from hens it is so farre thither,
    I care not though ye never come againe hither.
MARCHAUNT.   Sir, if ye remember me when time shall
       come,
    Though I requite not all, I shall deserve some.   *pay you somewhat*
    Exeat Marchaunt.

MERY-REPORT.   Now, fare ye well and God thanke you, by
       Saint Anne!
    [*To the audience.*]
    I pray you marke the fasshion of this honeste manne:
    He putteth me in more truste at this metinge here   *more trust in me*
    Then he shall finde cause why this twenty yere!   *i.e., any time soon*
    Here ent'reth the ranger.

400 RANGER.   God be here! Now Crist kepe this company!
MERY-REPORT.   In faith, ye be welcome—evyn very skantely.
    Sir, for your cominge, what is the mater?
RANGER.   I wolde faine speke with the god Jupiter.
MERY-REPORT.   That will not be. But ye may do this:
    Tell me your minde. I am an officer of his.
RANGER.   Be ye so? Mar[r]y, I cry you marcy!

391(The implication is that in either case Merry-Report will do nothing.)

407	Your maystership may say I am homely.	*unmannerly*
	But sins[e] your minde is to have reportyd	*you wish to hear*
	The cause wherfore I am now resortyd,	*have now come here*
	Pleasith your maystership it is so:	*May it please*
	I come for myselfe and suche other mo,	
	Rangers and kepers of certaine places,	
413	As forestes, parkes, purlews, and chasys,	
	Where we be chargyd with all maner game.	*held responsible for*
	Smale is our profite and great is our blame.	
	Alas, for our wages, what be we the nere?	*how are we any better off?*
	What is forty shillinges, or five marke, a yere?	
418	Many times and oft, where we be flittinge,	
	We spende forty pens apece at a sittinge!	*at each location*
420	Now, for our vauntage, whiche chefely is winde-fal[l]e,	
	That is right nought—there blowith no winde at all.	
	Whiche is the thinge wherin we finde most grefe	
	And cause of my comminge to sew for relefe:	
	That the god, of pity, all this thinge knowinge,	*when he knows all this*
	Maye sende us good rage of blust'ring and blowinge.	
	And if I cannot get god to do some good,	
	I wolde hier the devill to runne thorow the wood	
	The rootes to turne up, the toppys to bringe under.	
	A mischiefe upon them, and a wilde thunder!	
430	MERY-REPORT. Very well said! I set by your charité	
431	As mych, in a maner, as by your honesté.	
	I shall set you somwhat in ease anone:	
433	Ye shall putte on your cappe when I am gone.	
	For I se ye care not who win or lese,	*lose*
	So ye maye finde meanys to win your fees.	*So long as/perquisites*
436	RANGER. Sir, as in that, ye speke as it please ye.	
	But let me speke with the god, if it maye be.	
	[*He tries to approach the throne.*]	
	I pray you, lette me passe ye.	
	MERY-REPORT. Why, nay, sir, by the masse, ye!	
	RANGER. Then will I leve you evyn as I founde ye.	

[407](The ranger cringes and flatters abjectly when he discovers Merry-Report is a court official.)

[413]*purlews*: forest borders, often game preserves. *chasys*: hunting grounds.

[418]*flittinge*: moving location, including the shifting of position of tethered animals.

[420]*winde-fal[l]e*: trees felled by wind, which rangers could sell for fuel.

[430-31](sardonically) Well said! I admire your charity as much as your honesty, as it were (i.e., you're deficient in both).

[433]i.e., You can stop bowing and scraping to impress me after I've left.

[436]i.e., Sir, from your position of privilege you can say what you please.

MERY-REPORT.   Go when ye will. No man here hath bounde
 ye.
    Here ent'reth the water miller, and the ranger go'th out.

442   WATER MILLER.   What the devill shold skil though all
        the world were dum,
      Sins[e] in all our spekinge we never be h[e]arde?
444   We crye out for raine—the devill sped drop will cum!
      We water millers be nothinge in regarde.   *are totally ignored*
      No water have we to grinde at any stint: *price*
      The winde is so stronge the raine cannot fall,
      Whiche kepeth our mil[l]-dams as drye as a flint.
      We are undone! We grinde nothinge at all—
      The greter is the pité, as thinketh me.
      For, what availeth to eche man his corne   *grain*
      Till it be grounde by such men as we be?
      There is the losse, if we be forborne.   *dispensed with*
      For, touching ourselfes, we are but drudgys   *with regard to*
      And very beggers, save onely our tole—   *were it not for our toll*
456   Whiche is right smale, and yet many grudges
457   For griste of a busshell to give a quarte bole.
      Yet, were not reparacions, we might do wele: *were it not for repairs*
459   Our mil[l]ston[e]s, our whele with her kogges, and our
        trindill,
      Our floodgate, our mil[l]pooll, our water whele,
      Our hopper, our ex-tre[e], our iren spindill—   *axletree of a wheel*
      In this, and mych more, so great is our charge   *expense*
463   That we wolde not recke though no water ware;
464   Save onely it toucheth eche man so large,
465   And ech for our neighbour Criste biddeth us care.
      Wherfore, my conscience hath pricked me hither
      In this to sewe—according to the cry—   *petition/proclamation*
      For plenté of raine, to the god Jupiter,
      To whose presence I will go evyn boldely.
        [*Mery-Report bars his way.*]
470   MERY-REPORT.   Sir, I dowt nothinge your audacité,   *not at all*

442What the devil would it matter if no one could speak (to present his petition to the un-
feeling gods).

444*the . . . cum:* i.e., the devil take it for all we get any rain.

456-57Our toll is very small, and yet many people begrudge, in return for our grinding a
bushel of grain, to pay a quart bowl's worth as toll.

459*kogges:* teeth on a gear-wheel. *trindill:* another kind of cog-wheel.

463-65That it wouldn't matter to us even if there were no water (since we can't afford repairs
in any case), except that the business concerns every man so greatly, and Christ bids each
of us love our neighbour. (A transparently hypocritical argument.)

But I feare me ye lacke capacité;　　　　　　　　　*mental ability*
For, if ye were wise, ye mighte well espye
How rudely ye erre from rewls of curtesye.
What? Ye come in revelinge and reheytinge,　　　*railing*
Evyn as a knave might go to a beare-beytinge.　　*bear-baiting*

476　WATER MILLER [*to the audience*].　All you bere recorde what
　　　　favour I have!
Herke how familierly he calleth me knave!
Dowtles the gentilman is universall.　　　　　　*widely accomplished*
But marke this lesson, sir: you shulde never call
Your felow knave, nor your brother [w]horeson,　*Your equal*
For nought can ye get by it when ye have done.

MERY-REPORT.　Thou arte nother brother nor felowe to me,　*neither*
For I am goddes servaunt—may'st thou not se?
Wolde ye presume to speke with the great god?
Nay, discrecion and you be to[o] farre od!　　*at variance*
By'r Lady, these knavys muste be tied shorter.　*restrained*
Sir, who let you in? Spake ye with the porter?

WATER MILLER.　Nay, by my trouth, nor with no nother
　　　　man;
489　Yet I saw you well when I first began.　　*first entered*
Howbeit, so helpe me God and holydam,　　　*things sacred*
I toke you but for a knave, as I am.
But mar[r]y, now, sins[e] I knowe what ye be,
I muste and will obey your authorité.
And if I maye not speke with Jupiter,
I beseche you be my soliciter.

MERY-REPORT.　As in that, I wil be your well-willer.　*well-wisher*
I perceive you be a water miller;
And your [w]hole desire, as I take the mater,
Is plenté of raine for encres of water.
500　The let wherof, ye affirme determinately,　*hindrance/emphatically*
Is onely the winde, your mortall enemy.

WATER MILLER.　Trouth it is, for it blowith so alofte
We never have raine, or, at the most, not ofte.
Wherfore, I praye you, put the god in minde
Clerely forever to banish the winde.

　　　[*Here*] ent'reth the wind miller.

WIND MILLER.　How? Is all the wether gone or I come?　*ere*
For the Passion of God, helpe me to some!
I am a wind miller, as many mo be.
No wretch in wretchidnes so wrechyd as we!

476All of you can testify how I'm treated.

489i.e., I took you for the porter.

The [w]hole sorte of my crafte be all mar[r]'d at onys.   *class, profession*

511   The winde is so weyke it sturrith not our stonys,   *weak/millstones*

Nor skantely can shatter the shittyn saile   *scarcely can shake*

That hangeth shatteringe at a womans taile.   *waving*

The raine never resteth, so longe be the show'res

From time of beginning till foure and twenty howres;

And, ende when it shall, at night or at none,   *noon*

Another beginneth as soone as that is done.

Such revell of raine, ye knowe well inough,   *riotous excess*

Destroyeth the winde, be it never so rough;

520   Wherby, sins[e] our millys be come to still standinge,   *to a standstill*

Now maye we wind millers go evyn to hanginge.

A miller? With a moryn and a mischiefe!   *murrain, plague*

Who wolde be a miller? As good be a thefe.

Yet in time past, when grindinge was plenté,

Who were so like goddys felows as we?   *good fellows*

As faste as God made corne, we millers made meale.

Whiche might be best forborne for comynweale?   *done without*

But let that gere passe, for I feare our pride   *matter*

Is cause of the care whiche God doth us provide.   *sorrow*

530   Wherfore I submit me, entendinge to se

What comforte maye come by humilité.   *remedy*

And now, at this time, they said in the crye,   *proclamation*

The god is come downe to shape remedye.   *devise*

MERY-REPORT.   No doute he is here, even in yonder trone;

But in your mater he trusteth me alone.

Wherin I do perceive, by your complainte,

Oppression of raine doth make the winde so fainte

That ye winde millers be clene caste away.   *i.e., out of luck*

WIND MILLER.   If Jupiter helpe not, it is as ye say.

540   But, in few wordes to tell you my minde rounde,   *plainly*

Uppon this condicion I wolde be bounde

Day by day to say Our Ladyes sauter: *psalter*

That in this world were no drope of water,

Nor never raine, but winde continuall.

Then shold we winde millers be lordes over all!

MERY-REPORT.   Come on, and assay how you twaine can
    agre—

A brother of yours, a miller, as ye be!

WATER MILLER.   By meane of our craft we may be brothers,

But whiles we live shall we never be lovers.

550   We be of one crafte, but not of one kinde:

I live by water and he by the winde.

    Here Mery-Reporte go'th out.

511(The millstones are connected by gears to the sails.)

And, sir, as ye desire winde continuall,
So wolde I have raine evermore to fall—
Whiche two, in experience right well ye se,
Right selde or never together can be.   *seldom*
For as longe as the winde rewleth, it is plaine,
Twenty to one ye get no drop of raine;
And when the element is to[o] farre oppres't,
Downe commeth the raine and setteth the winde at rest.
By this, ye se, we cannot both obtaine,
For ye must lacke winde or I must lacke raine.
Wherfore I thinke good, before this audiens,
563   Eche for ourselfe to say, or we go hens.   *ere*
And whom is thought weykest, when we have finish't,
Leve of[f] his sewt and content to be banish't.
WIND MILLER.   In faith, agreed. But then, by your licens,
567   Our milles for a time shall hange in suspens.
Sins[e] water and winde is chiefely our sewt,
Whiche best may be spared we woll first dispute.   *be done without*
Wherfore to the see my reason shall resorte,   *sea*
Where shippes by meane of wind try from port to port,   *sail*
From lande to lande, in distaunce many a mile—
573   Great is the passage and smale is the while.
So great is the profite, as to me doth seme,
That no mans wisdome the welth can exteme.   *estimate*
And sins[e] the winde is conveyer of all,
Who but the winde shulde have thanke above all?
578   WATER MILLER.   A[d]mitte in this place a tree here to growe,
And therat the winde in great rage to blowe;
When it hath all blowen, this is a clere case:
The tre removith no here-bred from his place.   *moves not a hair's-breadth*
582   No more wolde the shippys, blow the best it cowde;
583   Allthough it wolde blow downe both mast and shrowde,
584   Except the shippe flete uppon the water   *Unless/float*
585   The winde can right nought do—a plaine mater.
Yet maye ye on water, without any winde,
Row forth your vessell where men will have her sin'de.   *sent*
Nothinge more rejoiceth the mariner

563Each to speak on his own behalf, before we leave.

567Our mills will have to stop work while we argue.

573Long is the distance and brief the time (since wind enables ships to move swiftly and far).

578Suppose for the sake of argument we had a tree growing here.

582-85A ship wouldn't move either (on land), no matter how hard the wind blew; even if the wind should blow hard enough to knock down mast and shrouds, unless the ship floats the wind can do nothing—this is a self-evident truth.

Then meane coolys of winde and plenté of water,   *Than moderate breezes*

590   For commenly the cause of every wracke
Is excesse of winde where water doth lacke.
In rage of these stormys the perell is suche
That better were no winde then so farre to[o] muche.

WIND MILLER.   Well, if my reason in this may not stande,
I will forsake the see and lepe to lande.
In every chirche where Goddys service is,

597   The organs beare brunt of halfe the quere, iwis.   *choir*
Whiche causith the sounde, or water or winde?   *either water or*
Moreover, for winde this thinge I finde:
For the most parte, all maner minstrelsy
By winde they deliver their sound chefly.
Fill me a bagpipe of your water full,
As swetly shall it sounde as it were stuffyd with wull.   *as if*

WATER MILLER.   On my faith, I thinke the moone be at the
full!
For franti[c]ke fansies be then most plentefull,

606   Which are at the pride of their springe in your hed,   *springtime*
So farre from our mater he is now fled.
As for the winde in any instrument,
It is no percell of our argument.   *parcel, part*
We speke of winde that comith naturally,
And that is winde forcyd artificially—   *that (used in music)*
Whiche is not to purpose. But, if it were,   *even if*
And water, indede, right nought coulde do there,
Yet I thinke organs no suche commodité   *aren't all that valuable*
Wherby the water shulde banished be.
And for your bagpipes, I take them as nifuls.   *as for/trifles*
Your mater is all in fansies and trifuls.

WIND MILLER.   By God, but ye shall not trifull me of[f] so!
If these thinges serve not, I will reherse mo.   *recite, name*
And now to minde there is one olde proverbe come:

621   "One bushell of March dust is worth a kinges raunsome."
What is a hundreth thousande bushels worth, than?

WATER MILLER.   Not one mite, for the thinge selfe, to no   *in itself*
man.

WIND MILLER.   Why, shall winde everywhere thus be
objecte?   *objected to*
Nay, in the hyewayes he shall take effecte,
Whereas the raine doth never good, but hurt;

---

[597]The organ provides half the sound for the choir, certainly.

[606]i.e., Which flourish at their height in your head.

[621]i.e., Dry ground in England in March is extremely scarce and valuable.

For winde maketh but dust, and water maketh durt.
Powder or syrop, sirs, whiche lycke ye beste?
629   Who lycketh not the tone maye licke up the reste.   *one*
But, sure, whosoever hath assayed such sippes
Had lever have dusty eyes then durty lippes.   *rather*
And it is said sins[e] afore we were borne   *before*
That "drought doth never make derth of corne."
And well it is knowen to the most foole here
635   How raine hath priced corne within this seven yere.   *raised the price of*

WATER MILLER.   Sir, I pray the[e], spare me a litill season,   *give me/time*
And I shall brevely conclude the[e] with reason.   *quickly confute*
Put case on[e] som[m]ers daye without winde to be,   *Suppose for example*
And ragious winde in winter dayes two or thre:
640   Mych more shall dry that one calme daye in som[m]er
Then shall those thre windy dayes in winter.
Whom shall we thanke for this, when all is done?
The thanke to winde? Nay, thanke chiefely the sone.   *sun*
And so for drought: if corne therby encres,
The sone doth comforte and ripe all, dowtles.   *ripen*
And oft the winde so ley'th the corne, God wot,   *knocks down*
That never after can it ripe, but rot.
If drought toke place, as ye say, yet maye ye se   *Even if there was dryness*
Litell helpeth the winde in this commodité.   *benefit*
650   But now, sir, I deny your principyll.   *basic argument*
If drought ever were, it were impossibyll
To have ony graine; for, or it can grow,   *ere*
Ye must plow your lande, harrow, and sow,
Whiche will not be except ye maye have raine   *cannot happen unless*
To temper the grounde. And after, againe,
656   For springinge and plumping all maner corne
Yet muste ye have water, or all is forlorne.   *lost*
If ye take water for no commodité,   *to be no convenience*
Yet must ye take it for thinge of necessité
For washinge, for skowringe, all filth clensinge.
Where water lacketh, what bestely beinge!   *beastly existence*
In brewing, in bakinge, in dressinge of meate,
If ye lacke water what coulde ye drinke or eate?
Without water coulde live neither man nor best,
For water preservith both moste and lest.   *i.e., everyone*
For water coulde I say a thousande thinges mo,

629i.e., Whoever chooses not to prefer dust will be tasting mud (with a pun on *like* and *lick*).

635(Referring seemingly to actual periods of scarcity and high prices in the years just before this play was written, such as in 1523 and 1528; these floods were more of a hazard in England than drought.)

656For inducing all sorts of grain to germinate and grow plump.

Savinge as now the time will not serve so.   *Except that*
And as for that winde that you do sew fore,   *entreat for*
Is good for your windemill and for no more!
Sir, sith all this in experience is try'de,   *since/proven*
I say this mater standeth clere on my side.

672   WIND MILLER.   Well, sins[e] this will not serve, I will alledge
            the reste.
Sir, for our millys, I saye mine is the beste.
My windmill shall grind more corne in one [h]our
Then thy watermill shall in thre or foure—
Ye[a], more then thine shulde in a [w]hole yere,
If thou mightest have as thou hast wishyd here.   *obtain what you've asked*
For thou desirest to have excesse of raine,
Which thing to the[e] were the worst thou coudist
            obtaine.

680   For, if thou didist, it were a plaine induccion   *first step*
To make thine owne desier thine owne destruccion.
For in excesse of raine, at any flood
Your millys must stande still—they can do no good.
And whan the winde doth blow the uttermost,
Our windmilles walke amaine in every cost.   *go full speed everywhere*
For, as we se the winde in his estate,   *the wind's condition*
We moder our sailys after the same rate.   *moderate, adjust*
Sins[e] our millys grinde so farre faster then yours,
And also they may grinde all times and howrs,
I say we nede no watermilles at all,
For windmilles be sufficient to serve all.

WATER MILLER.   Thou spekest of "all" and considerest not halfe.
In boste of thy griste thou arte wise as a calfe!   *grinding*
For, though above us your milles grinde farre faster,
What helpe to those from whome ye be myche farther?
696   And, of two sortes, if the tone shold be conserved,
697   I thinke it mete the moste nomber be served.
698   In vales and we[a]ldes, where moste commodité is,
699   There is most people—ye must graunte me this.
On hilles and downes, whiche partes are moste barayne,   *barren*
There muste be few—it can no mo sustaine.
I darre well say, if it were tried even now,   *dare*
That there is ten of us to one of you.
And where shuld chiefely all necessaries be,

672i.e., Well, since I haven't convinced you yet, I'll bring forward the rest of my instances.

696–99And if, of two classes (of mills), only one is to be preserved, I think it proper that the most numerous (among the customers) be served. In valleys and wooded country or open lands, where the living is most convenient, there's where most people are to be found—as you must concede.

But there as people are moste in plenté?
More reason that you come seven mile to mill   *It's more reasonable*
Then all we of the vale sholde clime the hill.
If raine came reasonable, as I require it,
We sholde of your windemilles have nede no whit.   *no need at all*
  Ent'reth Mery-Reporte.

710 MERY-REPORT. Stop, fo[o]lish knaves! For your reasoninge
    is suche
  That ye have reasoned even inough—and to[o] much.
  I h[e]ard all the wordes that ye both have hadde.
  So helpe me God, the knaves be more then madde!
  Nother of them both that hath wit nor grace   *Neither*
  To perceive that both millys may serve in place.
  Betwene water and winde there is no suche let   *mutual antipathy*
  But eche mill may have time to use his fet.   *But that/customary action*
  Whiche thinge I can tell by experiens:
  For I have, of mine owne—not farre from hens,
  In a corner together—a couple of millys,
721 Standinge in a marres betwene two hillys—   *marsh*
722 Not of inheritaunce, but by my wife;
723 She is feofed in the taile for terme of her life—
  The one for winde, the other for water.
  And of them both, I thanke God, there standeth nother.   *neither stands idle*
726 For, in a good hour be it spoken,
  The water gate is no so[o]ner open
  But clap! say'th the windmill, even straight behinde.
729 There is good spedde the devill and all they grinde!
  But whether that the hopper be dusty,
  Or that the mil[l]stonys be sumwhat rusty,
  By the mas, the meale is mischevous musty!   *i.e., evil-smelling*
  And if ye thinke my tale be not trusty,
  I make ye trew promise: come when ye list,
  We shall finde meane ye shall taste of the grist.   *i.e., kiss*
 WATER MILLER. The corne at recei[p]t happely is not good.   *perhaps*
 MERY-REPORT. There can be no sweeter, by the sweet rood!   *cross*
  Another thinge yet, whiche shall not be cloked: *concealed*

721(In this scatological passage, the marsh represents the privy region between the two
buttocks (hills); the two "mills" are for urinating and venting air.)

722–23i.e., I'm not talking about my own bottom, but my wife's; she is put in legal possession of an entail, landed estate (with pun on "tail," bottom) for her lifetime.

726For, may this be said at a propitious time (an oath).

729i.e., Then there's a world of turmoil in grinding!

739   My watermill many times is choked.

WATER MILLER.   So will she be, though ye shuld burste
    your bones,

741   Except ye be perfit in setting your stones.   *Unless*

742   Fere not the lydger, beware your ronner.

743   Yet this for the lydger, or ye have wonne her: *ere*

744   Perchaunce your lydger doth lacke good pecking.

MERY-REPORT.   So say'th my wife, and that maketh all our
    checking.   *quarreling*

She wolde have the mill peck't, peck't, peck't every day!

But, by God, millers muste pecke when they may.

So oft have we peck't that our stones wax right thin,

And all our other gere not worth a pin;

For with peckinge and pecking I have so wrought

That I have peck't a good peckinge-iron to nought.

752   Howbeit, if I sticke no better till her,   *to*

My wife say'th she will have a new miller.

But let it passe. And now to our mater:

I say my millys lack nother winde nor water—

No more do yours, as farre as nede doth require.

But sins[e] ye cannot agree, I will desire

Jupiter to set you both in suche rest

As to your welth and his honour may stande best.

760   WATER MILLER.   I pray you hertely, remember me!

WIND MILLER.   Let not me be forgoten, I beseche ye!

Both millers go'th forth.

MERY-REPORT.   If I remember you not both alike,

I wolde ye were over the eares in the dike!   *ditch*

Now be we rid of two knaves at one chaunce.

By Saint Thomas, it is a knavishe riddaunce.

The gentilwoman ent'reth.

GENTILWOMAN.   Now, good God, what a fol[l]y is this?

What sholde I do where so mych people is?

I know not how to passe in to the god now.

769   MERY-REPORT.   No, but ye know how he may passe into you.

739i.e., My wife's private parts are often clogged (by sexual activity).

741–44Unless you adjust perfectly your millstones (i.e., your stones, testicles). Don't worry that the trouble is in your nether or fixed millstone; look to see if it isn't in the upper or moving millstone (referring to the male sexual organ). Still, bear this in mind about the ledger, until you've fixed it (or, until you've engaged sexually with your wife): maybe the ledger isn't grinding properly (i.e., maybe your pecker isn't pecking).

752*sticke*: remain with, persist (with sexual meaning).

769–71*passe, backe side, foreside*: sexual punning.

770   GENTILWOMAN.   I pray you, let me in at the backe side.
771   MERY-REPORT.   Ye[a], shall I so and your foreside so wide?
       Nay, not yet! But sins[e] ye love to be alone,
       We twaine will into a corner anone.
       But firste, I pray you, come your way hither
       And let us twaine chat a while togither.
       GENTILWOMAN.   Sir, as to you I have littell mater.
       My comminge is to speke with Jupiter.
       MERY-REPORT.   Stande ye still a while, and I will go prove   *discover*
       Whether that the god will be brought in love.   *into*
          [*He approaches Jupiter's throne.*]
780   My lorde, how now, loke uppe lustely:
       Here is a derlinge come, by Saint Antony!
       And if it be your pleasure to mar[r]y,
       Speke quickly, for she may not tar[r]y.
       In faith, I thinke ye may winne her anone,   *at once*
       For she wolde speke with your lordship alone.
       JUPITER.   Sonne, that is not the thinge at this time ment.
       If her sewt concerne no cause of our hither resorte,
       Sende her out of place. But if she be bent
       To that purpose, heare her and make us reporte.
          [*Jupiter retires; Merry-Report returns to the gentlewoman.*]
790   MERY-REPORT.   I count women lost, if we love them not well,   *account*
       For ye se god loveth them never a dele!   *not a bit*
       Maystres, ye cannot speke with the god.   *Mistress*
       GENTILWOMAN.   No? Why?
       MERY-REPORT.   By my faith, for his lordship is right besy   *because*
       With a pece of worke that nedes must be doone:
       Even now he is makinge of a new moone.
       He saith your old moones be so farre tasted   *nibbled at (i.e., waning)*
       That all the goodnes of them is wasted;
798   Whiche of the great wete hath ben moste mater,
       For olde moones be leake—they can holde no water.   *leaky*
       But for this new mo[o]ne, I durst lay my gowne,   *wager*
       Except a few droppes at her going downe,   *Other than/setting*
       Ye get no raine till her arisinge—
       Without it nede, and then no mans devisinge   *Unless rain is needed*
       Coulde wishe the fashion of raine to be so good:
       Not gushinge out like gutters of Noyes flood,   *Noah's*
       But smale droppes sprinkling softly on the grounde;
       Though they fell on a sponge they wold give no sounde.   *As though*
       This new moone shal make a thing spring more in this while   *plants grow*
       Then a old moone shal while a man may go a mile.   *walk*
810   By that time the god hath all made an ende,

798Of which the greatest consequence has been the heavy rains.

Ye shall se how the wether will amende.
By Saint Anne, he go'th to worke even boldely!
I thinke him wise inough, for he loketh oldely!
Wherfore, maystres, be ye now of good chere,
For though in his presens ye cannot appere,
Tell me your mater and let me alone—   *trust me*
Mayhappe I will thinke on you when you be gone.

GENTILWOMAN.   Forsoth, the cause of my comminge is this:
I am a woman right faire, as ye se;
820   In no creature more beauty then in me is.
And, sins[e] I am faire, faire wolde I kepe me.
But the sonne in som[m]er so sore doth burne me,
In winter the winde on every side me,
No parte of the yere wote I where to turne me,   *know*
But even in my house am I faine to hide me.   *obliged*
And so do all other that be[a]uty have.
In whose name at this time this sewt I make,
Besechinge Jupiter to graunt that I crave,   *what I ask*
Whiche is this: that it may please him, for our sake,
830   To sende us wether close and temperate,
No sonneshine, no frost, nor no winde to blow.
Then wolde we jet the stretes trim as a parate.   *strut/parrot*
Ye shold se how we wolde set ourselfe to show!

MERY-REPORT.   Jet where ye will, I swere, by Sainte Quintine,
Ye passe them all, both in your owne conceit and mine.   *opinion*

GENTILWOMAN.   If we had wether to walke at our pleasure,
Our lives wolde be mery out of measure: *immoderately merry*
One parte of the day for our apparellinge,
Another parte for eatinge and drinkinge,
And all the reste in stretes to be walkinge
Or in the house to passe time with talkinge.

842   MERY-REPORT.   When serve ye God?
GENTILWOMAN.   Who bosteth in vertue are but daws.   *fools*
843   MERY-REPORT.   Ye do the better, namely sins[e] there is no   *especially*
        cause.
How spende ye the night?
GENTILWOMAN.   In daunsinge and singinge
Till midnight, and then fall to slepinge.
MERY-REPORT.   Why, swete herte, by your false faith, can ye
        sing?
GENTILWOMAN.   Nay, nay, but I love it above all thinge.
MERY-REPORT.   Now, by my trouth, for the love that I owe
        you,

842–43Those who boast of virtue are none other than fools. —You avoid that fault, especially
since you haven't any virtue to boast of (said mockingly).

You shall he[a]re what pleasure I can shew you.

850   One songe have I for you, suche as it is,

And if it were better ye shold have it, by Gis.   *even if/Jesus*

GENTILWOMAN. Mar[r]y, sir, I thanke you even hartely.

MERY-REPORT. Come on, sirs, but now let us singe lust[e]ly.   *the musicians (?)*

    Here they singe.

GENTILWOMAN. Sir, this is well done. I hertely thanke you.

Ye have done me pleasure, I make God avowe.

Ones in a night I longe for suche a fit;   *song*

For longe time have I ben brought up in it.

MERY-REPORT. Oft time it is sene, both in court and towne;

Longe be women a bringing up, and sone brought down.   *in/seduced*

860   So fete it is, so nete it is, so nise it is,   *So becoming she is/elegant*

So tricke it is, so quicke it is, so wise it is!   *handsome*

I fere myselfe, excepte I may entreat her   *unless*

I am so farre in love I shall forget her.

Now, good maystres, I pray you, let me kis ye.

GENTILWOMAN. Kis me, quoth a! Why, nay, sir, I wis ye.   *I tell you*

MERY-REPORT. What? Yes, hardely! Kis me ons[e] and no

    more.

I never desired to kis you before.

    Here the launder cometh in.   *washerwoman*

LAUNDER. Why, have ye alway kis't her behinde?

869   In faith, good inough, if it be your minde.

And if your appetite serve you so to do,

By'r Lady, I wolde ye had kis't mine ars, to[o]!

MERY-REPORT. To whom dost thou speke, foule [w]hore,

    canst thou tell?

LAUNDER. Nay, by my trouth, sir, not very well.

But by conjecture this g[u]es[s] I have:

That I do speke to an olde baudy knave!

I saw you dally with your simper-de-cokket;   *flirt*

I rede you beware she pick not your pokket.   *advise*

Such idyll huswifes do now and than

Thinke all well wonne that they pick from a man.   *fairly won/steal*

880   Yet such of some men shall have more favour

Then we, that for them daily toile and labour.

But I trust the god will be so indifferent   *impartial*

That she shall faile some parte of her entent.

MERY-REPORT. No dout he will deale so graciously

That all folke shall be served indifferently.

Howbeit, I tell the trewth, my office is suche

869i.e., Go ahead, if that's your idea of pleasure (to kiss the "behinde," punning on Merry-Report's word "before").

        That I muste reporte eche sewt, littell or muche.
        Wherfore, with the god sins[e] thou canst not speke,
        Trust me with thy sewt. I will not faile it to breke.   *to disclose it*
890   LAUNDER.   Then leane not to[o] myche to yonder giglet,   *don't be partial/wanton*
        For her desire contrary to mine is set.
        I he[a]rde by her tale she wolde banishe the sonne,
        And then were we pore launders all undonne.
        Excepte the sonne shine that our clothes may dry,   *Unless*
        We can do right nought in our laundry—
896   Another maner losse, if we sholde mis,
897   Then of such nicebiceters as she is.
        GENTILWOMAN.   I thinke it better that thou envy me
        Then I sholde stande at rewarde of thy pitté.   *be the object of*
        It is the guise of such grose queynes as thou art,   *manner/gross whores*
901   With such as I am evermore to thwart.
        Bicause that no beauty ye can obtaine
        Therfore ye have us that be faire in disdaine.
        LAUNDER.   When I was as yonge as thou art now,
        I was within littel as faire as thou,   *nearly as beautiful*
        And so might have kept me if I hadde wolde—   *if I'd wished*
        And as derely my youth I might have solde
        As the trickest and fairest of you all.   *handsomest*
        But I feared parels that after might fall.   *(spiritual) perils*
910   Wherfore some besines I did me provide
        Lest vice might enter on every side,
        Whiche hath fre entré where idylnesse doth reyne.
        It is not thy beauty that I disdeyne,
        But thine idyll life that thou hast rehersed,   *described*
        Which any good womans hert wolde have perced.   *pierced (with sorrow)*
        For I perceive in daunsinge and singinge,
        In eating and drinkinge and thine apparellinge,
        Is all the joye wherin thy herte is set.
919   But nought of all this doth thine owne labour get.
        For haddest thou nothing but of thine owne travaile   *labor*
        Thou mightest go as naked as my naile.
        Methinke thou shuldest abhorre suche idylnes
        And passe thy time in some honest besines.
        Better to lese some parte of thy beauté   *lose*
        Then so oft to jeoberd all thine honesté.   *jeopardize/virtue*
        But I thinke, rather then thou woldest so do,

896–97(This would be) an entirely different sort of loss, if we should be deprived of our livelihood, than the loss would be for such dainty and fashionable women as she is.

901To be always at variance with such as I am.

919But your own labor earns none of these things.

Thou haddest lever have us live idylly to[o].   *rather*
And so, no doute, we shulde, if thou mightest have
The clere son[n]e banish't, as thou dost crave!
930   Then were we launders mar[r]'de. And unto the[e]
Thine owne request were smale commodité.   *would prove of small value*
For of these twaine I thinke it farre better
Thy face were son[n]eburned, and thy clothis the swetter,   *sweeter, cleaner*
Then that the sonne from shininge sholde be smitten
To kepe thy face faire and thy smocke beshitten.
Sir, how lycke ye my reason in her case?   *like*

MERY-REPORT.   Such a railinge [w]hore, by the holy mas,
I never he[a]rde in all my life till now!
Indede I love right well the ton of you;   *one*
940   But, or I wolde kepe you both, by Goddes mother,   *ere*
The devill shall have the tone to fet the tother!   *one/fetch*

LAUNDER.   Promise me to speke that the son[n]e may shine
      bright,
And I will be gone quickly for all night.

MERY-REPORT.   Get you both hens, I pray you hartely.
Your sewtes I perceive, and will reporte them trewly   *I understand your petitions*
Unto Jupiter at the next leisure,
And, in the same, desire to know his pleasure;
Whiche knowledge hadde, even as he doth show it,
Feare ye not, time inough ye shall know it.

GENTILWOMAN.   Sir, if ye medill, remember me firste.   *meddle, intercede*

LAUNDER.   Then in this med'linge my parte shal be the wurst.

MERY-REPORT.   Now, I beseche our Lorde, the devill the[e]
      burst!
953   Who med'lith with many, I hold him accurst.
Thou [w]hore, can I med[d]il with you both at ones?
      Here the gentilwoman go'th forth.

955   LAUNDER.   By the mas, knave, I wold I had both thy stones
956   In my purs, if thou med[d]il not indifferently,
957   That both our maters in issew may be lyckly.

MERY-REPORT.   Many wordes, littell mater, and to no
      purpose—
Suche is the effect that thou dost disclose.

---

[953]Anyone who deals with many (women) at once, I account him plagued with troubles.
(In the following lines, "meddling" takes on explicitly sexual meaning.)

[955]*stones*: (1) valuables, jewels (2) testicles.

[956]*purs*: (1) moneybag (2) vagina.

[957]So that both our petitions may have a happy outcome.

The more ye bib, the more ye babyll;   *chatter/babble*
The more ye babyll, the more ye fabyll;   *speak falsely*
The more ye fabyll, the more unstabyll;
The more unstabyll, the more unabyll
In any maner thinge to do any good.
No hurt though ye were hanged, by the holy rood!   *cross*
  LAUNDER.   The les your silence, the lesse your credence;   *credibility*
The les your credens, the les your honesté;
The les your honesté, the les your assistens;   *usefulness*
The les your assistens, the les abilité
In you to do ought. Wherfore, so God me save,
No hurte in hanginge suche a railinge knave!
  MERY-REPORT.   What monster is this? I never h[e]arde none
      suche!

973   For loke how myche more I have made her to[o] myche,
974   And so farre, at lest, she hath made me to[o] littell.
Wher be ye launder? I thinke in some spittell.   *leper house*
976   Ye shall washe me no gere, for feare of fret[t]inge;
I love no launders that shrinke my gere in wettinge.
I pray the[e] go hens and let me be in rest!
I will do thine erand as I thinke best.
  LAUNDER.   Now wolde I take my leve, if I wiste how.
The lenger I live, the more knave you!
  MERY-REPORT.   The lenger thou livest, the pité the gretter;   *greater the pity*
983   The so[o]ner thou be rid, the tidinges the better!
    [*Exit the launder.*]

Is not this a swete office that I have,
When every drab shall prove me a knave?
Every man knoweth not what goddes service is,   *whore*
Nor I myselfe knew it not before this.
I thinke goddes servauntes may live holily,
But the devils servauntes live more merily.
990   I know not what god geveth in standinges fees,
But the devils servauntes have casweltees   *fixed salary*
A hundred times mo then goddes servauntes have.   *perquisites*
For, though ye be never so starke a knave,
If ye lacke money the devill will do no wurse   *arrant*
But bringe you straight to another mans purse.
Then will the devill promote you here in this world,

973–74 i.e., For by as much as I have amplified her faults, by at least the same amount she has minimized my virtues.

976 *fret[t]inge:* rubbing the cloth to shreds (alluding to her abrasive manner; *gere, fret[t]inge,* and *shrinke* also take on sexual meaning in this and the following line).

983 The sooner you're gone, the better the news.

997 As unto suche riche it doth moste accord:
998 Firste *"Pater noster, qui es in caelis,"*   *"Our Father" etc.*
999 And then ye shall sens the shrife with your helys.   *cense/sheriff*
    The greatest frende ye have in felde or towne,   *tallest*
    Standinge a-tipto[e], shall not reche your crowne.   *head*
      The boy comith in, the lest that can play.   *youngest (boy actor)*

BOY.   This same is even he, by al lycklihod.
    Sir, I pray you, be not you master god?
MERY-REPORT.   No, in good faith, sonne. But I may say to
      the[e]
    I am suche a man that god may not misse me.   *do without*
    Wherfore with the god if thou woldest have ought done,   *anything*
    Tell me thy minde, and I shall shew it sone.   *soon*
BOY.   Forsothe, sir, my minde is this, at few wordes:
    All my pleasure is in catchinge of birdes,
1010 And makinge of snow-ballys and throwing the same.
    For the whiche purpose to have set in frame,   *in order*
    With my godfather god I wolde faine have spoken,
    Desiringe him to have sent me by some token
    Where I mighte have had great frost for my pitfallys
    And plenté of snow to make my snowballys.
1016 This onys had, boyes livys be such as no man leddys.
    O, to se my snowballys light on my felowes heddys,
    And to he[a]re the birdes how they flicker their winges
    In the pitfale! I say it passeth all thinges.
    Sir, if ye be goddes servaunt, or his kinsman,
    I pray you helpe me in this if ye can.
MERY-REPORT.   Alas, pore boy, who sent the[e] hether?
BOY.   A hundred boys that stode together,
    Where they he[a]rde one say in a cry   *proclamation*
    That my godfather, god almighty,
    Was come from heven, by his owne accorde,
    This night to suppe here with my lorde.   *i.e., the host for this play*
    And farther he saide, come whoso wull,
    They shall sure have their bellies full
1030 Of all wethers, who liste to crave—   *whoever wishes to ask*
    Eche sorte suche wether as they liste to have.
    And when my felowes thought this wolde be had,
    And saw me so pretty a pratelinge lad,
    Uppon agrement, with a great nois,

997–99i.e., As most befits such persons who are rich (by stealing): first you'll say the Lord's Prayer (before being executed), and then you'll hang in the air and swing your heels over the sheriff who hangs you, as though you were scattering incense on him.

1016Once this can be had, boys' lives are superior to any man's.

"Sende littell Dicke!" cried all the boys.

By whose assent I am purvey'd   *provided, prepared*

To sew for the wether aforeseyd.

Wherin I pray you to be good, as thus,

To helpe that god may give it us.

1040 MERY-REPORT.   Give boys wether, quoth a? nonny, nonny!

BOY.   If god of his wether will give nonny,   *none*

I pray you, will he sell ony?

Or lend us a bushell of snow or twaine,

And 'point us a day to pay him againe?   *appoint, set*

MERY-REPORT.   I cannot tell, for, by this light,

I che[a]p't nor borowed none of him this night.   *bargained with*

But by suche shifte as I will make   *device*

Thou shalte se soone what waye he will take.

BOY.   Sir, I thanke you. Then I may departe?

The boye go'th forth.

1050 MERY-REPORT.   Ye[a], farewell, good sonne, with all my
harte!

Now, such another sorte as here hath bene   *crowd*

In all the dayes of my life I have not sene!

No sewters now but women, knavys, and boys,

And all their sewtys are in fansies and toys.

If that there come no wiser after this cry   *proclamation*

I will to the god and make an ende quickely.

[He makes a proclamation to the audience.]

Oyes! If that any knave here

Be willinge to appere

For wether fowle or clere,

1060 Come in before this flocke,   *crowd*

And—be he [w]hole or sickly—   *in good health*

Come shew his minde quickly.

And if his tale be not lyckly   *likely, plausible*

Ye shall licke my taile in the nocke.   *notch, cleft*

[He pauses, but is not answered.]

All this time, I perceive, is spent in wast

To waite for mo sewters. I se none make hast.

Wherfore I will shew the god all this procys,   *account, argument*

And be delivered of my simple offys.   *humble duty*

[He goes to the throne of Jupiter.]

Now, lorde, according to your commaundement,

1070 Attendinge sewters I have ben diligent.

And, at beginning as your will was I sholde,

1040*nonny*: a meaningless exclamation, often used as a substitute for an indelicacy.

I come now at ende to shewe what eche man wolde.
The first sewter before yourselfe did appere:
A gentilman desiringe wether clere,
Clowdy nor misty, nor no winde to blow
For hurt in his huntinge. And then, as ye know,
The marchaunt sew'de—for all of that kinde—   *i.e., for all merchants*
For wether clere and mesurable winde,   *moderate*
As they maye best bere their sailys to make spede.
1080 And streyght after this there came to me, indede,
Another man who namyd himselfe a ranger,
And said all of his crafte be farre brought in daunger
For lacke of livinge, whiche chefely is windefall.
But he plainely saith there bloweth no winde at al.
Wherfore he desireth, for encrease of their fleesys,   *plunder*
Extreme rage of winde, trees to tere in peces.
Then came a water miller, and he cried out
For water, and saide the winde was so stout
The raine could not fale. Wherfore he made request
1090 For plenty of raine to set the winde at rest.
And then, sir, there came a winde miller in,
Who saide for the raine he could no winde win.   *because of*
The water he wish't to be banish't all,
Besechinge your grace of winde continuall.   *for*
Then came there another that wolde banish all this:
A goodly dame, an idyll thinge, iwis!
Winde, raine, nor froste, nor sonshine wold she have,
But faire close wether, her beautye to save.
Then came there another that liveth by laundry,
1100 Who muste have wether hote and clere, her clothys to dry.
Then came there a boy for froste and snow continuall,
Snow to make snowballys and frost for his pitfale—
For whiche, God wote, he seweth full gredely!
Your first man wold have wether clere and not windy;
The seconde the same, save cooles to blow meanly;   *breezes/moderately*
The third desired stormes and winde most extremely;
The fourth all in water, and wolde have no winde;
The fift[h] no water, but all winde to grinde;
The sixt[h] wold have none of all these, nor no bright
    son[ne];
The seventh extremely the hote son wold have wonne;
The eight[h] and the last, for frost and snow he pray'd.
By'r Lady, we shall take shame, I am afraid!
1113 Who marketh in what maner this sort is led
May thinke it impossible all to be sped.   *for all to be helped*

1113Anyone who considers how this crowd (of suitors) has conducted itself.

This nomber is smale—there lacketh twaine of ten—
And yet, by the masse, amonge ten thousand men
No one thinge could stand more wide from the tother!
Not one of their sewtes agree'th with another.
I promise you, here is a shrewed pece of warke!
1120   This gere will trye w[h]ether ye be a clarke.   *learned divine*
If ye trust to me, it is a great fol[l]y,
For it passeth my braines, by Goddes body!

JUPITER.   Son, thou haste ben diligent, and done so well
That thy labour is right myche thankeworthy.
But be thou suer we nede no whit thy counsell;   *not at all*
For in ourselfe we have foresene remedy,
Whiche thou shalt se. But firste, depart hens quickly
To the gentilman and all other sewters here,
And commaunde them all before us to appere.

MERY-REPORT.   That shall be no lenger in doinge
Then I am in comminge and goinge.
        Mery-Report go'th out.

JUPITER.   Suche debate as from above ye have h[e]arde,   *i.e., among the gods*
Suche debate beneth amonge yourselfes ye se.   *i.e., on earth*
1134   As longe as heddes from temperaunce be defer'd,
1135   So longe the bodies in distemperaunce be.
This perceive ye all, but none can helpe save we.
But as we there have made peace concordantly,   *i.e., among the gods*
So woll we here now give you remedy.
        Mery-Reporte and all the sewters ent'reth.

MERY-REPORT.   If I hadde caught them
1140   Or ever I raught them,   *Ere/reached*
I wolde have taught them
To be nere me.   *To stay nearby*
1143   Full dere have I bought them,
1144   Lorde, so I sought them.
Yet have I brought them—
Suche as they be.

1134-35 As long as heads are distempered, bodies will be also; i.e., while the gods quarrel men
will be at strife, and while rulers contend the commoners will be factional.

1140 i.e., Before I realized they had wandered so far.

1143-44 i.e., I expended a lot of effort finding them, lord, I sought for them so earnestly.

GENTILMAN.   Pleaseth it your majesté, lorde, so it is: *May it please*

We, as your subjectes and humble sewters all,

1149   Accordinge as we he[a]re your pleasure is,

Are pres[s]yd to your presens, beinge principall   *Hasten/to you who are chief*

Hed and governour of all in every place.

1152   Who joyeth not in your sight, no joy can have.

Wherfore we all commit us to your grace

As lorde of lordes, us to perishe or save.   *destroy*

JUPITER.   As longe as discrecion so well doth you g[u]ide

Obediently to use your dewté,

Dout ye not we shall your saveté provide.

Your grevys we have h[e]arde; wherfore we sent for ye

To receive answere, eche man in his degre.   *rank*

1160   And first, to content—most reason it is—   *as is most reasonable*

The firste man that sew'de, wherfore marke ye this:

Oft shall ye have the wether clere and still

To hunt in, for recompens of your paine.   *efforts (for the commonwealth)*

Also you merchauntes shall have myche your will:

For, oft-times when no winde on lande doth remaine,

Yet on the see plesaunt cooles you shall obtaine.

1167   And sins[e] your huntinge maye reste in the night,

Oft shall the winde then rise, and before daylight

It shall ratyll downe the wood in suche case

That all ye rangers the better live may.

And ye water millers shall obteyne this grace:

Many times the raine to fall in the valey,

When at the self times on hillys we shall purvey   *same*

Faire wether for your windmilles, with such coolys of winde

As in one instant both kindes of milles may grinde.

And for ye faire women that close wether wold have,

We shall provide that ye may sufficiently

Have time to walke in, and your beauty save.

And yet shall ye have, that liveth by laundry,

1180   The hote sonne oft inough your clothes to dry.

Also ye, praty childe, shall have both frost and snow.

Now marke this conclusion, we charge you a-row: *one by one*

1149Acting according to what we hear is your desire.

1152He who does not rejoice in seeing you cannot experience true joy.

1167And since you hunters won't hunt at night.

Myche better have we now devised for ye all
Then ye all can perceive, or coude desire.
Eche of you sew'd to have continuall
Suche wether as his crafte onely doth require.   *occupation*
1187   All wethers in all places if men all times might hire,
1188   Who could live by other? What is this negligens,
1189   Us to atempt in suche inconveniens?

Now, on the tother side, if we had graunted
The full of some one sewt, and no mo,
And from all the rest the wether had forbid,
1193   Yet whoso hadde obtained had wonne his owne wo.
1194   There is no one craft can preserve man so;
But by other craftes, of necessité,
He muste have myche parte of his commodité.

All to serve at ones, and one destroy another,
Or ellys to serve one and destroy all the rest—
Nother will we do the tone nor the tother,
1200   But serve as many, or as few, as we thinke best.
And where, or what time, to serve moste or lest,
The direccion of that doutles shall stande
Perpetually in the power of our hande.

Wherfore we will the [w]hole worlde to attende,   *we want everyone*
Eche sort, on suche wether as for them doth fall—   *Each group*
Now one, now other, as liketh us to sende.   *as it pleases me*
Who that hath it, ply it; and suer we shall   *Let him who has it use it*
So g[u]ide the wether in course to you all,   *in due course, by turns*
That eche with other ye shall [w]holé remaine   *wholly*
1210   In pleasure and plentifull welth, certaine.

GENTILMAN.   Blessyd was the time wherin we were borne!
First, for the blisfull chaunce of your godly presens,   *good fortune*
Next for our sewt. Was there never man beforne   *There was*
That ever h[e]arde so excellent a sentens
As your grace hath gevyn to us all a-row!   *one by one*
Wherin your highnes hath so bountifully
Distributed my parte, that your grace shall know

1187–89:i.e., If men everywhere could always obtain constantly the kind of weather each man desires, how could these conflicting weathers (and the men desiring them) coexist without destroying one another? What sort of thoughtlessness is this, to petition me for such a discordant solution?

1193–94Yet whoever obtained this suit (his own weather in excess) would have insured his own destruction. Mankind cannot live by one occupation alone.

1218   Yourselfe sooll possessed of hertes of all chivalry.   *solely*
    MARCHAUNT.   Likewise we marchauntes shall yeld us
        [w]hol[l]y
    Onely to laude the name of Jupiter   *To praise only*
    As god of all goddes, you to serve soolly;
    For of everythinge, I se, you are norisher.

    RANGER.   No dout it is so, for so we now finde;
    Wherin your grace us rangers so doth binde
    That we shall give you our hertes with one accorde,
    For knowledge to know you as our onely lorde.   *To acknowledge you*
    WATER MILLER.   Well, I can no more but: for our water,   *I can say only this*
    We shall geve your lordship Our Ladies sauter.   *psalter*
    WIND MILLER.   Myche have ye bounde us; for, as I be saved,   *(hope to) be saved*
1230   We have all obteyned better then we craved.
    GENTILWOMAN.   That is trew. W[h]erfore, your grace shall
        trewly
    The hertes of such as I am have, surely.
    LAUNDER.   And such as I am—who be as good as you—   *i.e., as the gentlewoman*
    His highnes shall be suer on, I make a vow.   *assured of*
    BOY.   Godfather god, I will do somwhat for you againe: *in return*
    By Criste, ye may happe to have a bird or twaine!
    And I promise you, if any snow come,
    When I make my snowballys ye shall have some.
    MERY-REPORT.   God thanke your lordship. Lo, how this is
        brought to pas!
1240   Sirs, now shall ye have the wether even as it was.

    JUPITER.   We nede no whit ourselfe any farther to bost,
    For our dedes declare us apparauntly.   *reveal me self-evidently*
    Not onely here on yerth, in every cost,   *land*
    But also above in the hevynly company,
    Our prudens hath made peace universally;
    Whiche thinge, we sey, recordeth us as principall   *shows us to be chief*
    God and governour of heven, yerth, and all.

    Now unto that heven we woll make retourne,
    Where we be glorified most triumphantly.
    Also we woll all ye that on yerth sojourne—   *I desire that all of you*
1251   Sins[e] cause giveth cause—to know us your lord onely,   *acknowledge*
    And now here to singe moste joyfully,

1218That you alone are loved by those who practice chivalry.

1251Sins[e] . . . cause: i.e., since I am glorified in heaven, it follows causally that I should
be glorified on earth.

Rejoicinge in us. And in meanetime we shall
Ascende into our trone celestiall.
   [*As they sing, Jupiter ascends and withdraws.*]

   Finis.

            Printed by W. Rastell.
                 1533.
            Cum privilegio.

The play of the wether

A new and a very
mery enterlude of
all maner we-
thers made
by Johñ Heywood.

The players names.
Jupiter a god.
Mery reporte the vyce.
The gentylman.
The marchaunt.
The ranger
The water myller.
The wynde myller.
The gentylwoman.
The launder.
I hop the lest that can play.

WIT AND SCIENCE
BY JOHN REDFORD

Because of its use of allegorical abstraction, John Redford's *Wit and Science* (ca. 1530–48) is often described as a morality play adapted to the humanistic concerns of early Tudor England. The play tells of Wit's spiritual struggle to be virtuously deserving of Lady Science (Learning), his inevitable fall into the wicked company of Idleness and Ignorance, and his eventual recovery through the mediation of Reason. Yet the plot of *Wit and Science* is less a morality plot than an allegorical romance, like Book 1 of Spenser's *The Faerie Queene* (1590). The essential metaphor is one of chivalric quest. Before Wit can win the hand of his lady fair, he must slay a monster. Unfortunately his good intentions, like those of Spenser's Redcrosse Knight, are vitiated by callow self-assurance. Wit's first encounter with evil leaves him vulnerable to the deceiving appearances of sinfulness. Just as Redcrosse confuses Una, the one truth, with Duessa, duplicity, Wit fails to grasp the vital distinction between Honest Recreation and Idleness. Moral enervation leads to apathy, ignorance, loss of self-respect, and despair, from which the fallen protagonist can be recovered only by a force greater than himself: divine Reason. Wit must confess his transgressions and beg for mercy in excess of his merit. His final successful assault on the monster Tediousness must nonetheless be his alone.

This fable operates consistently at both the romantic and allegorical levels. As a romantic protagonist, Wit is convincingly cocky, flamboyant, and easily rattled. Although his fondness for Lady Science is real, he is undeniably interested also in her money, reputation, and connections. She herself is an admirable heroine: tender, unconcerned about wealth, loyal, long-suffering in adversity, and yet visibly perturbed by Wit's folly and brilliantly caustic in rejecting her wayward lover dressed as Ignorance. (As Reason later observes, she certainly recognizes Wit beneath the guise of Ignorance and feigns misunderstanding in order to teach Wit a lesson.) At the same time, Wit and Lady Science are fully-developed abstractions in a metaphorical quest for wisdom. Wit is the young scholar who very much needs to be guided by Reason and Instruction, but is impatient of both. Setting forward jauntily on his own, armed only with his own Diligence (which is never enough), Wit misses the convenient way to wisdom that Instruction would have taught him and so loses himself in the maze of Tediousness. Faced with defeat and loss of Confidence, he turns to idle diversion not as a permissible holiday from study (Honest Recreation) but as self-indulgent escape (Idleness). Only when he accepts the sage counseling of his teachers does he realize that Tediousness must be cajoled and outwitted, not recklessly confronted.

Wit and Science derives its form not only from allegorical romance but from education drama. This genre had emerged in the late Middle Ages in the schools of Northern Europe as an instructive entertainment for schoolboys. Works of the classical drama were often adapted to the aptitudes and moral sensibilities of young scholars. Although *Wit and Science* is not classical, it shares with other school plays an interest in learning through entertainment. *Wit and Science* is quite serious in drawing an analogy between the educative quest and man's Christian journey through life; humanists fervently believed in education as a key to man's religious nature. Yet the play is festive, providing its own illustration of Honest Recreation.

Redford probably wrote the play for the choir boys of St. Paul's when he was master there. The songs are intended for expert performance. The actors' parts are designed for boys, concentrating on female roles and on witty exchange (see for example the catechizing of Ignorance in his own name by Idleness, ll. 449–549). The cast is relatively large and provides some roles for inexperienced actors. The costumes are elaborate and often illustrate an allegorical point, as in Wit's transformation into a fool by means of Ignorance's coat, ass's ears, and cockscomb and subsequent retransformation by means of the gown of knowledge. The stage, with such fixed *loca* as Mount Parnassus and the den of Tediousness, is suitable for indoor acting. The verse is generally in four-stress couplets, with the occasional variation of shorter lines and alternating rhymes. The text exists only in a single manuscript now located in the British Museum, from which a brief portion of the beginning is missing.

Wit and Science

By John Redford

[THE NAMES OF THE ACTORS

WIT, a student	TEDIOUSNES
LADY SCIENCE, whom he seeks to wed	IDLENES
	INGNORANCE
REASON, her father	SHAME
EXPERIENCE, her mother	COMFORT
INSTRUCCION	QUICKNES
STUDY	STRENGTH
DILIGENCE	FAME
HONEST RECREACION	RICHES
CONFIDENCE	FAVOR

WOORSHIP]

[*The manuscript lacks the beginning of the play. Evidently Wit has sought the hand in marriage of Lady Science from her father, Reason. Reason has consented on the condition that young Wit overcome Tediousness and make a journey to Mount Parnassus. As our scene opens, Reason is presenting Wit with the glass of Reason in which to understand himself more clearly.*]

REASON.   Then in remembrance of Reson, hold yee
　　　　A glas of Reson, wherein beholde yee　　　　　*mirror*
　　　　Youresealfe to youreselfe. Namely when ye　　*Especially*
　　　　Cum neere my dowghter Science, then see

That all thinges be cleane and tricke abowte ye,   *trim*
Least of sum sloogishnes she might dowte ye.   *Lest/suspect*
   [*Gives him a mirror.*]
This glas of Reason shall show ye all;
While ye have that, ye have me, and shall.
Get ye foorth, now! Instruccion, farewell.

10   INSTRUCCION. Sir, God keepe ye.
REASON.   And ye all, from parell.   *peril*
    Heere all go out save Resone.

If anye man now marvell that I
Woolde bestowe my dowghter thus baselye,
Of truth I, Reson, am of this minde:
Where parties together be enclin'de
By giftes of graces to love ech other,
There let them joine the tone with the toother.   *one*
This Wit such giftes of graces hath in him
That mak'th my dowghter to wish to win him:
Yoong, painefull, tractable, and capax—   *painstaking/capable*
20   Thes[e] be Wites giftes which Science doth axe.   *ask*
And as for her, as soone as Wit sees her,
For all the world he woold not then leese her.   *lose*
Wherfore, sins[e] they both be so meete matches   *suitable*
To love ech other, strawe for the patches   *have no regard for*
Of wo[r]ldly mucke! S[c]ience hath inowghe   *worldly wealth*
For them both to live. If Wit be throw[g]he   *thoroughly*
Striken in love, as he si[g]nes hath show'de,
I dowte not my dowghter welbestow'de.
Th'ende of his jornay will aprove all:
30   If Wit hold owte, no more proofe can fall.   *no better proof can befall*
And that the better hold out he may,
To refresh my soone Wit now by the way
Sum solas for him I will provide.
An honest woman dwell'th here beside   *nearby*
Whose name is cal[l]'d Honest Recreacion.
As men report, for Wites consolacion
She hath no peere; if Wit were halfe deade,
She cowld revive him—thus is it sed.
Wherfore, if monye or love can hire her,
40   To hie after Wit I will desire her. [*Exit.*]   *hasten*

    Confidence cum'th in with a picture of Wit.

[CONFIDENCE.] Ah, sir, what time of day is't, who can tell?
The day is not far past, I wot well,
For I have gone fast, and yet I see

I am far from where as I wold be.
Well, I have day inowgh yet, I spye.
Wherfore, or I pas hens[e], now must I   *ere I leave from here*
See this same token heere, a plaine case,
What Wit hath sent to my ladyes grace.   *i.e., to my gracious lady*
  [*Holds the picture up to the audience.*]
Now, will ye see a goodly picture
Of Wit himsealfe? His owne image sure—
Face, bodye, armes, legges, both lim[b] and joint—
As like him as can be in every point.   *detail*
53   It lak'th but life. Well I can him thanke,
54   This token indeede shall make sum cranke!   *merry*
For, what with this picture so well faver'de,
And what with those sweete woordes so well saver'd
Distilling from the mowth of Confidence,
Shall not this ap[p]e[a]se the hart of Science?
Yes, I thanke God, I am of that nature
60   Able to compas this matter sure,   *encompass, contrive*
As ye shall see now, who list to marke it,   *whoever wishes to heed it*
How neately and feately I shall warke it. [*Exit.*]   *adroitly*

        Wit cum'th in, without Instruccion, with Study, etc.

[WIT.]   Now sirs, cum on. Whiche is the way now,
This way or that way? Studye, how say you?
  [*Study ponders.*]
Speake, Diligence, while he hath bethowghte him.   *reflected*
66   DILIGENCE.   That way, belike; most usage hath wrow[g]ht
  him.
STUDY.   Ye[a], hold your pease. Best we here now stay
For Instruccion. I like not that waye.
WIT.   Instruccion? Studye, I weene we have lost him.
  Instruccion cum'th in.

[INSTRUCCION.]   Indeade, full gently abowte ye have tost him!   *Indeed*
What me[a]ne you, Wit, still to delighte   *always*
Runninge before thus, still owt of sighte,
And therby out of your way now quighte?
What doo ye here excepte ye woold fighte?   *unless*
Cum back againe, Wit; for I must choose ye
An esier way then this, or ells loose ye.   *or otherwise lose you*

53–54 If a picture could live, this would be Wit himself. Thanks to him, this memento will indeed make someone (i.e., Lady Science) merry!

66 (I urge) this way, in all likelihood; customary usage has taken it. (Diligence points in the direction he urges.)

WIT.   What aileth this way? Parell here is none.   *Peril*

INSTRUCCION.   But as much as your life stand'th upon!   *Only/depends upon*

 Youre en[e]mye, man, lieth heere before ye:

80 Tediousnes, to braine or to gore ye!

WIT.   Tediousnes? Doth that tyrant rest

 In my way now? Lord, how am I blest

 That occacion so nere me sturres,   *stirs, moves*

 For my dere hartes sake to winne my spurres!

 Ser, woold ye fere me with that fowle theeafe,   *frighten*

 With whome to mete my desire is cheafe?

INSTRUCCION.   And what woold ye doo, you having nowghte

 For your defence? For thowgh ye have cawghte   *acquired*

 Garmentes of Science upon your backe,

90 Yet wepons of Science ye do la[c]k.

WIT.   What wepons of Science shuld I have?

INSTRUCCION.   Such as all lovers of ther looves crave:

 A token from Ladye Science, wherbye

 Hope of her favor may spring, and therbye

 Comforte, which is the weapon dowteles

 That must serve you against Tediousnes.

WIT.   If Hope or Comfort may be my weapen,

 Then never with Tediousnes mee threten.

 For, as for hope of my deere hartes faver

100 And therby comfort, inowghe I gather.   *I have enough*

INSTRUCCION.   Wit, he[a]re me. Till I see Confidence   *(that) Confidence*

 Have browght sum token from Ladye Science   *Has*

 That I may feele that she favor'th you,   *So that*

 Ye pas not this way, I tell you trew.

WIT.   Which way, than?

INSTRUCCION.   A plainer way I told ye,

 Out of danger from youre foe to hold ye.   *to keep yourself*

WIT.   Instruccion, he[a]re me. Or my swetehart   *Ere*

 Shall he[a]re that Wit from that wreche shall start   *flinch*

 One foote, this bodye and all shall cracke!

110 Foorth I will, sure, whatever I lacke.

DILIGENCE.   If ye lacke weapon, sir, here is one.

WIT.   Well saide, Diligence; thowe art alone.   *i.e., my best supporter*

 How say ye, sir, is not here [a] weapon?

INSTRUCCION.   With that weapon your en[e]my never

  threton!

 For, withowt the returne of Confidence

 Ye may be slaine sure, for all Diligence.

DILIGENCE.   God, sir! and Diligence, I tell you plaine,

 Will play the man or my master be slaine.   *Will strive manfully ere*

INSTRUCCION.   Ye[a]; but what, saith Studye no wurde to

  this?

120   WIT.   No, sir. Ye knowe Studyes ofice is
    Meete for the chamber, not for the feeld.   *Suitable*
    But tell me, Studye, wilt thow now yeld?
STUDY.   My hed ak'th sore; I wold wee return'd.
WIT.   Thy hed ake now? I wold it were burn'd!
    Cum on, walking may hap to ese the[e].
INSTRUCCION.   And will ye be gone, then, without mee?
WIT.   Ye[a], by my faith; except ye hi[e] ye after,   *unless you hasten*
    Reson shall know yee are but an hafter.   *caviller, dodger*
       Exeat Wit, Study, and Diligenc[e].

INSTRUCCION.   Well, go your way. Whan your father Reson
    Heer'th how ye obay me at this season,
    I thinke he will thinke his dowghter now
    May ma[r]ry another man, for you.   *instead of you*
133   When wit[t]es stand so in ther owne conceite,
    Best let them go, till pride at his heighte
    Turne and cast them downe hedlong againe—
    As ye shall see provyd by this Wit plaine.
    If Reson hap not to cum the rather,   *the sooner, quickly*
    His owne distruccion he will sure gather.   *His (Wit's)*
    Wherefore to Reson will I now get me,
140   Leving that charge whereabowt he set mee.   *Abandoning*
       Exeat Instruccion.

       Tediousnes cum'th in with a viser over his hed [and a club in his
       hand].

[TEDIOUSNES.]   Oh, the bodye of me!
    What kaitives be those   *wretches*
    That will not once flee
    From Tediousnes' nose,
    But thus disese me   *disturb*
    Out of my nest,
    When I shoold ese mee   *ease myself*
    This body to rest?
    That Wit, that vilaine,
150   That wrech—A shame take him!—
    It is he, plaine,
    That thus bold doth make him,
    Withowt my licence
    To stalke by my doore
    To that drab, S[c]ience,   *whore*
    To wed that whore.

---

[133]When Wits have such exaggerated estimations of themselves.

But I defye her!
And for that drab[b]es sake,
Or Wit cum ny her,   *Ere/nigh*
160   The knaves hed shall ake.
Thes[e] bones, this mall,   *club*
Shall bete him to dust
Or that drab shall   *Ere*
Once quench that knaves lust.
But hah! mee thinkes
I am not halfe lustye;   *vigorous*
Thes[e] jo[i]ntes, thes[e] linkes,   *joints of the body*
Be ruffe and halfe rustye.   *rough*
I must go shake them,
170   Supple to make them.
        [*He swings his club*.]
Stand back, ye wrechys!
Beware the fechys   *tricks*
Of Tediousnes,
Thes[e] kaitives to bles.   *wound, thrash*
Make roome, I say,
Rownd ev'ry way!
This way! That way!
What care I what way?
Before me, behind me,
180   Rownd abowt wind me!
Now I begin
To swete in my skin.   *sweat*
Now am I nemble
To make them tremble.
Pash hed! pash braine!   *Smash*
The knaves are slaine—
All that I hit.
Where art thow, Wit?
Thow art but deade;
190   Of[f] go'th thy hed
A' the first blo[w].
Ho, ho, ho, ho! [*Sits down*.]
        Wit spekith at the doore.

[WIT.]   Studye?
STUDY.   Here, sir.
WIT.   How? doth thy hed ake?
STUDY.   Ye[a], God wot, sir, much paine I do take.
WIT.   Diligens?
DILIGENCE.   Here, sir, here!
WIT.   How dost thow?

Doth thy stoma[c]k serve the[e] to fight now?   *courage*

DILIGENCE.   Ye[a], sir, with yonder wrech—a veng[e]ans on
    him!—

That thret'neth you thus. Set evyn upon him!

STUDY.   Upon him, Diligence? Better nay.

DILIGENCE.   Better nay, Studye? Why shoold we fray?   *be afraid*

STUDY.   For I am wery; my hed ak'th sore.   *Because*

DILIGENCE.   Why, fo[o]lish Studye, thow shalt doo no more
    But aide my master with thy presens.

204 WIT.   No more shalt thow ne[i]ther, Diligence.
    Aide me with your presence, both you twaine,
    And for my love, myselfe shall take paine.

STUDY.   Sir, we be redye to aide you so.

WIT.   I axe no more, Studye. Cum then, goe!
    [*They advance.*] *Tediousnes risith up.*

[TEDIOUSNES.]   Why, art thow cum?

WIT.   Ye[a], wrech, to thy paine!

210 TEDIOUSNES.   Then have at the[e]!

WIT.   Have at the[e] againe!
    Here Wit fallith downe and dieth.

TEDIOUSNES.   Lie thow there. Now have at ye, kaitives!
    [*The others flee.*]

Do ye fle[e], i'faith? A, [w]horeson theves!

By Mahowndes bones, had the wreches tary'd,   *Mohammed's/tarried*

Ther neckes withowt hedes they showld have cary'd.   *carried*

Ye[a], by Mahowndes nose, might I have patted them,   *struck*

In twenty gobbetes I showld have squatted them,   *pieces of flesh/squashed*

To teche the knaves to cum neere the snowte

Of Tediousnes. Walke furder abowte,

I trow, now they will. And as for thee [*indicating Wit*],

220 Thow wilt no more now troble mee.

Yet, lest the knave be not safe inowghe,

The [w]horeson shall bere me another kuffe.   *receive from me*
    [*Strikes Wit again.*]

Now li[e] still, kaitiv[e], and take thy rest,

While I take mine in mine owne nest. *Exeat Tedi[ousnes].*
    *Here cum'th in Honest Recreacion, Cumfort, Quicknes, and
    Strength, and go and knele abowt Wit, [singing as
    follows]:*

When travelles grete in matters thicke   *great labors*

204i.e., You won't have to do anything more, either (than give me moral support by your
presence), Diligence. (Wit vaingloriously undertakes to do all the fighting himself.)

Have dul[l]'d your wittes and made them sicke,
What med'son than your wittes to quicke?   *medecine then/revivify*
If ye will know, the best physicke
Is to geve place to Honest Recreacion.
230   Give place, we say, now for thy consolacion.

Where is that Wit that we seeke than?
Alas, he lieth here pale and wan!
Helpe him at once, now, if we can.
O Wit, how doest thow? Looke up, man!
O Wit, geve place to Honest Recreacion.
Give place, we say, now for thy consolacion.

After place givyn, let eare obay.
Give an eare, O Wit, now we the[e] pray;
Give eare to that we sing and say;
240   Give an eare, and healp will cum straighteway.
Give an eare to Honest Recreacion.
Give an e[a]re, now, for thy consolacion.

After eare givyn, now give an eye.
Behold thy freendes abowte the[e] lie:
Recreacion, I, and Comfort, I,
Quicknes am I, and Strength herebye.
Give an eye to Honest Recreacion.
Give an eye, now, for thy consolacion.

After eye givyn, an hand give ye.
250   Give an hand, O Wit, feele that ye see:
Recreacion feele, feele Comfort fre,   *excellent*
Feele Quicknes here, feale Strength to the[e].
Give an hand to Honest Recreacion.
Give an hand, now, for thy consolacion.

Upon his feete woold God he were!
To raise him now we neede not fere.
Stay you his handes, while we him bere.
Now all at once upright him rere.
O Wit, give place to Honest Recreacion.
260   Give place, we say, now for thy consolacion.
        And at the last verce reisith him up upon his feete, and so make
        an end. And than Honest Recreacion saith as folowith:

HONEST RECREACION.   Now Wit, how do ye? Will ye be lustye?   *strong*
WIT.   The lustier for you needes be must I.

HONEST RECREACION.   Be ye all [w]hole yet after your fall?
WIT.   As ever I was, thankes to you all.
    Reson cumm'th in and saith as folowith:

[REASON.]   Ye might thanke Reson that sent them to ye;
  But sins[e] the[y] have done that the[y] shoold do ye,   *done what/do for you*
  Send them home soonne, and get ye forwarde.
WIT.   Oh, Father Reson, I have had an hard
  Chance since ye saw me!
REASON.   I wot well that.
270 The more to blame ye, when ye wold not
  Obay Instruccion as Reson wil[l]'d ye.
  What marvell thowgh Tediousnes had kil[l]'d ye?
  But let pas. Now since ye ar well againe,
  Set forward againe S[c]ience to attaine.
WIT.   Good Father Reson, be not to[o] hastye.
276 In honest cumpany no time wast I;
  I shall to youre dowghter all at leiser.
REASON.   Ye[a], Wit, is that the grete love ye raise her?   *bear her*
  I say if ye love my dowg[h]ter Science,
  Get ye foorth at once, and get ye hence.
    Here Comfort, Quiknes, and Strength go out.

WIT.   Nay, by Saint George, they go not all yet!
REASON.   No? Will ye disobey Reson, Wit?
WIT.   Father Reson, I pray ye content ye;
  For we parte not yet.   *we (Wit and Honest Recreation)*
REASON.   Well, Wit, I went ye   *I supposed*
  Had bene no such man as now I see.
  Farewell. *Exeat.*
HONEST RECREACION.   He is angry.
WIT.   Ye[a], let him be;
  I doo not passe.   *don't care*
  Cum now, a basse.   *(give me) a kiss*
HONEST RECREACION.   Nay, sir; as for bassys,
  From hence none passys
  But as in gage   *Except in pledge*
  Of mariage.
293 WIT.   Mar[r]y, evyn so;
294 A bargaine, lo.
HONEST RECREACION.   What, without lisence

276i.e., I'm not wasting time now, in this virtuous and pleasant company. (Wit is trying to prolong his recreation.)

293-94i.e., All right, that's a bargain, then; let's get married.

Of Ladye Science?

WIT.   Shall I tell you trothe?
I never lov'de her.

HONEST RECREACION.   The common voice go'th   *Rumor has it*

300   That mariage ye mov'd her.   *proposed to her*

WIT.   Promise hath she none.
If we shal be wone,   *one (i.e., husband and wife)*
Without mo wurdes grawnt!   *grant, agree*

HONEST RECREACION.   What, upon this soodaine?

305   Then mighte ye plaine   *frankly*
306   Bid me avawnt.   *get away*
Nay, let me see
In honesté
What ye can doo
To win Recreacion.
Upon that probacion
I grawnt therto.

WIT.   Small be my dooinges;
But apt to all thinges
I am, I trust.

HONEST RECREACION.   Can ye dawnce, than?

WIT.   Evyn as I can,
Prove me ye must.   *Test*

HONEST RECREACION.   Then for a while

320   Ye must excile   *rid yourself of*
This garment cumb'ring.

WIT.   Indeede, as ye say,
This cumb'rus aray
Woold make Wit slumb'ring.

HONEST RECREACION.   It is gay geere;   *apparel*
Of Science cleere,
It seem'th her aray.

WIT.   Whose-ever it were,
It li'the now there. [*Throws off his gown.*]

330   HONEST RECREACION.   Go to, my men, play!
Here they dawnce, and in the menewhile Idellnes cum'th in and
sit'th downe. And when the galiard is doone, Wit saith as
folowith, and so fal[l]ith downe in Idellnes' lap.

WIT.   Sweetehart, gramercys.   *great thanks*

HONEST RECREACION.   Why, whether now? Have ye doone   *Are you finished*
    since?

WIT.   Ye[a], in faith; with wery bones ye have posses't me.
Among thes[e] damselles now will I rest me.

305-6 i.e., Then you might think me too easily won and so get rid of me quickly.

HONEST RECREACION.   What, there?

WIT.   Ye[a], here I wil be so bold.

IDLENES.   Ye[a], and wellcum, by him that God sold!   *by Judas*

HONEST RECREACION.   It is an harlot, may ye not see?

IDLENES.   As honest a woman as ye be!

HONEST RECREACION.   Her name is Idlenes. Wit, what mene
        you?

IDLENES.   Nay, what meane you to scolde thus, you quene,   *whore*
        you?

341   WIT.   Ther[e], go to! Lo now, for the best game!

342   Whille I take my ese, youre toonges now frame.   *give expression to*

        [*Wit prepares to enjoy watching the women fight.*]

HONEST RECREACION.   Ye[a], Wit, by youre faith, is that youre
        fac[h]ion?

        Will ye leave me, Honest Recreacion,

        For that common strumpet Idellnes,

        The verye roote of all viciousnes?

WIT.   She saith she is as honest as ye.

        Declare yourselves both now as ye be.

HONEST RECREACION.   What woolde ye more for my
        declaracion

350   Then evyn my name, Honest Recreacion?

        And what wold ye more her to expres   *to describe her*

        Then evyn her name, to[o], Idlenes—

        Distruccion of all that with her tarye?   *dally, remain*

        Wherfore, cum away, Wit; she will mar ye!

IDLENES.   Will I mar him, drabb—thow calat, thow!—   *whore*

        When thow hast mar[r]'d him allredye now?

        Cawlist thow thysealfe Honest Recreacion?

        Ord'ring a poore man after this fac[h]ion,

        To lame him thus and make his limmes faile   *lame himself*

360   Evyn with the swinging there of thy taile!   *i.e., your dancing*

        The divill set fire on the[e]! For now must I,

        Idlenes, hele him againe, I spye.   *heal*

        I must now lull him, rock him, and frame him   *fashion, assist*

        To his lust againe, where thow didst lame him.   *robustness/whereas*

        Am I the roote, sayst thow, of viciousnes?

        Nay, thow art roote of all vice dowteles.

        Thow art occacion, lo, of more evill

        Then I, poore gerle—nay, more then the divill.   *Than*

        The divill and his damm cannot devise   *mother*

370   More dev'lishnes then by the[e] doth rise.

341–42i.e., There, go to it! May the best woman win! While I rest, you two go ahead and
quarrel (to entertain me).

Under the name of Honest Recreacion,
She, lo, bring'th in her abhominacion.
Mark her dawnsing, her masking, and mumming—
Where more concupiscence then ther cumming?—   *arising*
Her carding, her dicing daily and nightlye;   *card-playing*
Where find ye more falcehod then there? Not lightly!   *Not easily*
With lyeng and swering by no poppetes,   *idols*
But tering God in a thowsand gobbetes.   *tearing/pieces of flesh*
As for her singing, piping, and fid'ling;
380   What unthriftines therin is twid'ling!   *being busy about trifles*
Serche the tavernes, and ye shall he[a]re cleere   *hear clearly*
Such bawdry as bestes wold spue to heere.   *beasts/vomit to hear*
And yet this is kal[l]'d Honest Recreacion,
And I, poore Idlenes, abhominacion!   *(am called) abomination*
But which is wurst of us twaine? Now jud[ge], Wi[t].

WIT.   By'r ladye, not thow, wench, I judge yet.
    [*While Honest Recreation exhorts him, Wit falls asleep in Idle-*
    ness' lap.]

HONEST RECREACION.   No? Is youre judgment such then that
     ye
Can neither pe[r]seve that best, how she   *beast*
Go'th abowte to dyce[i]ve you, nor yet
390   Remembre how I savyd youre life, Wit?
Thinke you her meete with mee to compare,   *suitable*
By whome so manye wit[t]es curyd are?
When will she doo such an act as I did,
Savinge your life when I you revived?
And as I savyd you, so save I all
That in like jeoperdy chance to fall.   *similar*
When Tediousnes to grownd hath smitten them,
Honest Recreacion up doth qui[c]ken them   *bring them to life*
With such honest pastimes, sportes, or games
400   As unto mine honest nature frames;   *suits*
And not, as she saith, with pastimes suche
As be abusyd, litell or muche.
For where honest pastimes be abusyd,
Honest Recreacion is refused.
Honest Recreacion is present never
But where honest pastimes be well usyd ever.
But indeede Idlenes, she, is cawse
Of all such abuses. She, lo, drawes   *entices*
Her sort to abuse mine honest games,   *Those of her persuasion*
410   And therby full falsly my name defames.
Under the name of Honest Recreacion
She bring'th in all her abhominacion,
Distroy[i]ng all wit[t]es that her imbrace,

As youreselfe shall see within short space.   *time*
She will bring you to shamefull end, Wit,
Except the sooner from her ye flit.   *Unless you quickly flee*
Wherefore cum away, Wit, out of her pawse!   *paws*
Hence, drabb! Let him go out of thy clawse!   *whore*

IDLENES.   Will ye get ye hence? Or, by the mace,   *mass*
   Thes[e] clawes shall clawe you, by youre drabbes face!

HONEST RECREACION.   It shall not neade. Sins[e] Wit liethe as
       wone   *like one*
   That neither heer'th nor see'th, I am gone. *Exeat.*

423   IDLENES.   Ye[a], so? farewell! and well fare thow, toonge!
424   Of a short pe[a]le this pe[a]le was well roong—
425   To ring her hence and him fast asleepe,
   As full of sloth as the knave can kreepe!
   How, Wit, awake! How doth my babye?
   Neque vox neque sensus, by'r Ladye.   *Neither voice nor feeling*
   A meete man for Idlenes, no dowte.   *suitable*

430   Hark, my pigg! How the knave dooth rowte!   *snore*
   Well, while he sleep'th in Idlenes' lappe,
   Idlenes' marke on him shall I clappe.
   Sum say that Idlenes cannot warke;
   But those that so say, now let them marke.   *pay attention*
   I trowe they shall see that Idlenes
   Can set hersealfe abowt sum busines;
   Or at the lest, ye shall see her tri'de   *proven*
   Nother idle nor yet well oc[c]upi'de.   *Neither*
     [*She blackens his face.*]
   Lo, sir, yet ye la[c]k another toye.
440   Wher is my whistell to call my boye?
     Here she whistleth and Ingnorance cum'th in [in a fool's coat,
     with ass's ears and a coxcomb].

[INGNORANCE.]   I cum, I cum.
IDLENES.   Coomme on, ye foole.
   All this day or ye can cum to scoole?   *ere*
INGNORANCE.   Um, Mother will not let me cum.
IDLENES.   I woold thy mother had kis't thy bum!
   She will never let the[e] thrive, I trow.
   Cum on, goose. Now, lo, men shall know
   That Idlenes can do sumwhat; ye[a],
   And play the scoolemistres, to[o], if neade bee.
   Mark what doctrine by Idlenes cummes.

423–25Is it so, indeed? Farewell! and good luck to you, (my) tongue! Although you pealed—
i.e., spoke—only briefly, your speech rang out effectively: it chased her (Honest Recreation)
off and put Wit to sleep.

450   Say thy lesson, foole.

INGNORANCE.   Upon my thummes?

IDLENES.   Ye[a], upon thy thummes. Is not there thy name?

INGNORANCE.   Yeas.

IDLENES.   Go to, than; spell me that same.
Wher was thou borne?

INGNORANCE.   'Chwas ibore in Ingland, Mother sed.   *I was born*

IDLENES.   In Ingland?

INGNORANCE.   Yea.

IDLENES.   And what's half "Inglande"?
    [*Pointing to his thumb and first finger.*]
    Heere's "Ing" and heere's "land." What's t'is?

INGNORANCE.   What's t'is?

460   IDLENES.   What's t'is, [w]horeson, what's t'is?
    Heere's "Ing" and heere's "land." What's t'is?

INGNORANCE.   T'is my thum.

IDLENES.   Thy thum! "Ing," [w]horeson, "Ing," "Ing."

INGNORANCE.   Ing, ing, ing, ing.

IDLENES.   Foorth! Shal I bete thy narse now?   *your arse*

INGNORANCE.   Ummm.

IDLENES.   Shall I not bete thy narse now?

INGNORANCE.   Ummm.

IDLENES.   Say "no," foole, say "no!"

470   INGNORANCE.   No-o, no-o, no-o, no-o, no-o.

IDLENES.   Go to, put together: Ing.

INGNORANCE.   Ing.

IDLENES.   No.

INGNORANCE.   No-o.

IDLENES.   Forth now! What saith the dog?

INGNORANCE.   Dog barke.

IDLENES.   Dog barke! Dog ran, [w]horeson, dog ran.

INGNORANCE.   Dog ran, [w]horson, dog ran, dog ran.

IDLENES.   Put together: Ing.

480   INGNORANCE.   Ing.

IDLENES.   No.

INGNORANCE.   No-o.

IDLENES.   Ran.

INGNORANCE.   Ran.

IDLENES.   Foorth now! What seyth the goose?

INGNORANCE.   Lag, lag.

IDLENES.   "His," [w]horson, "his."

INGNORANCE.   His, his-s-s-s-s.

IDLENES.   Go to, put together: Ing.

490   INGNORANCE.   Ing.

IDLENES.   No.

INGNORANCE.   No-o.

IDLENES. Ran.

INGNORANCE. Ran.

IDLENES. His.

INGNORANCE. His-s-s-s-s-s.

IDLENES. No[w], who is a good boy?

INGNORANCE. I, I, I, I, I, I.

IDLENES. Go to, put together: Ing.

500 INGNORANCE. Ing.

IDLENES. No.

INGNORANCE. No-o.

IDLENES. Ran.

INGNORANCE. Ran.

IDLENES. His.

INGNORANCE. His-s-s-s-s.

IDLENES. I.

INGNORANCE. I.

IDLENES. Ing-no-ran-his, I.

510 INGNORANCE. Ing-no-ran-his-s-s-s.

IDLENES. I.

INGNORANCE. I.

IDLENES. Ing.

INGNORANCE. Ing.

IDLENES. Foorth!

INGNORANCE. His-s-s-s.

IDLENES. Ye[a]? "No," [w]horeson, "no."

INGNORANCE. No-o, no-o, no-o, no-o.

IDLENES. Ing-no.

520 INGNORANCE. Ing-no-o.

IDLENES. Forth now!

INGNORANCE. His-s-s-s-s.

IDLENES. Yet againe! "Ran," [w]horson, "ran," "ran."

INGNORANCE. Ran, [w]horson, ran, ran.

IDLENES. "Ran," say!

INGNORANCE. Ran say.

IDLENES. "Ran," [w]horson.

INGNORANCE. Ran, [w]horeson.

IDLENES. "Ran."

530 INGNORANCE. Ran.

IDLENES. Ing-no-ran.

INGNORANCE. Ing-no-ran.

IDLENES. Foorth now! What said the goose?

INGNORANCE. Dog barke.

IDLENES. Dog barke! "His," [w]horson, "his-s-s-s-s-s."

INGNORANCE. His-s-s-s-s-s-s.

IDLENES. I.

INGNORANCE. I.

IDLENES.   Ing-no-ran-his, I.

540   INGNORANCE.   Ing-no-ran-his-s-s-s.

IDLENES.   I.

INGNORANCE.   I.

IDLENES.   How sayst now, foole? Is not there thy name?

INGNORANCE.   Yea.

IDLENES.   Well than, con me that same.   *recite from memory*
What hast thow lern'd?

I[N]GNORANCE.   Ich cannot tell.

IDLENES.   "Ich cannot tell"! Thow sayst evyn very well;
For if thow cowldst tell, then had not I well
Towght the[e] thy lesson, which must be tawghte:

549   To tell all, when thow canst tell righte no[u]ght.

INGNORANCE.   Ich can my lesson.   *I know*

IDLENES.   Ye[a], and therfore
Shalt have a new cote, by God I swore.

INGNORANCE.   A new cote?

IDLENES.   Ye[a], a new cote by and by.   *at once*
Of[f] with this old cote; "a new cote," crye.

INGNORANCE.   A new cote! A new cote! A new cote!

IDLENES.   Pease, [w]horson foole!
Wilt thow wake him now? Unbuttun thy cote, foole!

556   Canst thow do nothing?

INGNORANCE.   I note how 'choold be.   *I don't know*

557   IDLENES.   "I note how 'choold be"! A foole betide the[e],
So wis[e]ly hit spekith! Cum on now. Whan!   *it (i.e., Ignorance)*
Put ba[c]k thine arme, foole.

INGNORANCE.   Put backe?
[*She removes the fool's coat from Ignorance.*]

IDLENES.   So. Lo now, let me see how this gecre   *apparel*
Will trim this jentleman that lieth heere—
Ah, God save hit, so sweetly hit doth sleepe!—
While on your back this gay cote can creepe,   *can go*
As feete as can be for this one arme.   *suitable, elegant*

INGNORANCE.   Oh, 'cham a-cold!   *I am*
[*She put Wit's gown of learning on Ignorance.*]

IDLENES.   Hold, foole; keepe the[e] warme,
And cum hither. Hold this hed here; softe now, for
waking.   *don't wake him*
Ye shall see wone here browgght in such takinge   *one/plight*

549To enumerate or recite all, when you can explain nothing.

556*I . . . be:* I don't know how I should be (without my coat). (I.e., Ignorance seems reluctant to part with his fool's garment.)

557*A . . . the[e]:* i.e., May folly be your fate.

That he shall soone scantlye knowe himsealfe.

Heere is a cote as fit for this elfe

570   As it had bene made evyn for this bodye.   *As if*

[*She puts the fool's coat on Wit. Ignorance is having trouble keeping his new coat on him.*]

So, it begin'th to looke like a noddye.   *fool*

INGNORANCE.   Ummmm.

IDLENES.   What ailest now, foole?

INGNORANCE.   New cote is gone!

IDLENES.   And why is it gone?

INGNORANCE.   'Twooll not bide on.   *It will*

IDLENES.   " 'Twool not bide on"! 'Twoold if it cowlde,

575   But marvell it were that bide it shoold,

576   Sciens' garment on Ingnorance' ba[c]k.

[*Looking at Wit.*]

But now let's se, sir; what do ye la[c]k?

Nothing but evin to bu[c]kell heere this throte,

579   So well this Wit becum'the a fooles cote.

INGNORANCE.   He is I now!

IDLENES.   Ye[a], how lik'ste him now?

Is he not a foole as well as thow?

INGNORANCE.   Yeas.

IDLENES.   Well than, won[e] foole keepe another!   *(may) one fool*

583   Geve me this, and take thow that brother.

[*She changes the caps of Ignorance and Wit.*]

INGNORANCE.   Umm.

IDLENES.   Pike the[e] home; go!   *Depart*

INGNORANCE.   'Chill go tell my moother.   *I will*

IDLENES.   Yea, doo! [*Exit Ignorance.*]

But yet to take my leve of my deere, lo,

With a skip or twaine heere, lo, and heer[e], lo,

And heere againe; and now this heele

589   To bles this weake braine! Now are ye weele,   *wound, kick/well, thoroughly*

590   By vertu of Idellnes' blessing toole,

Cunjur'd from Wit unto a starke foole. [*Exeat.*   *Conjured, transformed*

Wit remains on stage, asleep.]

575–76 i.e., It would be a marvel indeed, if Ignorance should be able to wear the garment of Science.

579 So perfectly does a fool's coat suit this Wit.

583 Give me your cap, and take you the brother to it, i.e., Wit's cap.

589–90 *bles:* (1) wound (2) bestow a blessing on. (Idleness dances around Wit in a mocking conjuration, kicking him in the head and punningly describing this kick as a blessing or spell.) *blessing toole:* wounding weapon, i.e., her heel (again, with punning sense of bestowing a blessing).

Confidence cum'th in with a swoord by his side, and saith as folowith:

[CONFIDENCE.]   I seake and seake as won[e] on no grownde   *as one who nowhere*
Can rest, but like a masterles hownde
Wand'ring all abowt, seaking his master.
Alas, jentle Wit, I feare the fasster
That my tru[e] service clev'th unto thee,   *cleaves, clings*
The slakker thy mind cleev'th unto mee.
I have doone thye message in such sorte   *in such a way*
That I, not onlye for thy comfort
600   To vanquishe thine en[e]my, have browght heere
A swoord of comfort from thy love deere,
But also, furder, I have so enclin'd her
That upon my wurdes she hath assin'd her   *taken it upon herself*
In her owne parson halfway to meete thee,   *person*
And hitherward she came for to greete thee.
And sure, except she be turned againe,   *unless/returned*
Hither will she cum or be long, plaine,   *ere*
To seake to meate the[e] heere in this cost.   *this place*
But now, alas, thyselfe thow hast lost;
610   Or, at the least, thow wilt not be fownd.
Alas, jentle Wit, how doost thow woonde
Thy trusty and tru[e] servant, Confidence,
To lease my credence to Ladye Science!   *To lose my credit with*
Thow lesist me, to[o]. For if I cannot   *You lose me*
Find the[e] shortly, lenger live I ma[y] not,
But shortly get me evyn into a corner
And die for sorowe throw[g]he such a scorner! *Exeat.*

Here the[y] cum in with violes.

FAME.   Cum sirs, let us not disdaine to do
That the World hath apointed us too.   *That which/to*
620   FAVOR.   Sins[e] to serve Science the World hath sent us,
As the World wil[l]'th us, let us content us.
RICHES.   Content us we may, since we be assin'de
To the fairest lady that liv'th, in my minde.
WOORSHIP.   Then let us not stay here muet and mum,
But tast[e] we thes[e] instrumentes till she cum.   *touch, play*
Here the[y] sing "Excedinge Mesure" [while Experience and Science enter].

Exceeding mesure with paines continewall,
Langueshing in absens, alas, what shall I doe?—
Infortunate wretch, devoide of joyes all,

Sighes upon sighes redoobling my woe,
630   And teres downe falling fro mine eyes toe.   *two*
Bewty with truth so doth me constraine
Ever to s[er]ve where I may not attaine.

Truth bindith me ever to be true,
How so that Fortune faver'th my chance.
During my life none other but you
Of my tru[e] hart shall have the governance.
637   O good swetehart, have you remembrance
638   Now of your owne, which for no smart
639   Exile shall yow fro my tru[e] hart.

EXPERIENCE.   Dowghter, what meanith that ye did not sing?
641   SCIENCE.   Oh, Mother, for heere remain'th a thinge.
Freendes, we thanke you for thes[e] your plesures,
643   Takyn on us as chance to us measures.
WOORSHIP.   Ladye, thes[e] our plesures, and parsons too,   *Honor/persons*
Ar sente to you, you service to doo.   *to do you service*
FAME.   Ladye Science, to set foorth your name,   *as you are called*
The World to waite on you hath sent me, Fame.
FAVOR.   Ladye Science, for your vertues most plentye,
The World, to cherish you, Favor hath sent ye.
650   RICHES.   Lady Science, for youre benefites knowne,
The World, to maintaine you, Riches hath throwne.
WOORSHIP.   And, as the World hath sent you thes[e] three,
So he send'th mee, Woorshipp, to avawnce your degre[e].   *enhance your dignity*
SCIENCE.   I thank the World, but cheefly God be praised
That in the World such love to Science hath raised.
But yet, to tell you plaine, ye four ar suche
As Science look'th for litell nor muche;   *i.e., desires not at all*
For being as I am a lone wooman,
Neede of your service I ne[i]ther have nor can.
But, thanking the World and you for your pain,
I send ye to the World evyn now againe.
662   WOORSHIP.   Why, ladye, set ye no more store by mee,
663   Woorshipp? Ye set nowght by yourselfe, I se[e].
FAME.   She set'th nowght by Fame, wherby I spye her: *I see this about her*

637-39O good sweetheart, remember now your own true lover (i.e., myself), who will never
drive you out of my heart, no matter what pain I may suffer.

641i.e., Because, Mother, a sorrow hangs over me.

643Received by us as fortune measures out benefits to us.

662-63Why, lady, do you value me, Honor, no more than this? In that case, I see you do not
value yourself.

She carethe not what the World saith by her.   *about her*

FAVOR.   She set'the nowght by Favor, wherby I trye her: *I prove this about her*
She carith not what the World saith or dooth by her.

RICHES.   She set'th nowght by Riches, which dooth showe
She careth not for the World. Cum, let us goe.
[*Exeunt Woorship, Fame, Favor, and Riches.*]

670   SCIENCE.   Indeede, smalle cawse gevyn to care for the
Worldes favering,
Seeing the wittes of Worlde be so wavering.

EXPERIENCE.   What is the matter, dowghter, that ye
Be so sad? Open your mind to mee.

SCIENCE.   My marvell is no les, my good moother,   *astonishment*
Then my greefe is greate: to see of all other   *of all people*
The prowde scorne of Wit, soone to Dame Nature,   *son*
Who sent me a picture of his stature   *of his bodily form*
With all the shape of himselfe there opening,   *there revealed*
His amorous love therby betokening,

680   Borne toward me in abundant fac[h]ion.
And also, furder to make right relacion
Of this his love, he put in commishion
Such a messenger as no suspicion
Cowld growe in mee of him: Confidence.

EXPERIENCE.   Um.

SCIENCE.   Who, I ensure ye, with such vehemence
And faithfull behavoure in his movinge   *urging*
Set foorth the pith of his master's lovinge,   *vigor, force*
That no living creature cowld conjecte   *conjecture*
But that pure love did that Wit direct.

690   EXPERIENCE.   So?

SCIENCE.   Now, this beinge, since the space
691   Of three times' sending from place to place
692   Betwene Wit and his man, I he[a]re no more,
Ne[i]ther of Wit nor his love so sore.
How think you by this, my nowne deere mother?   *my own*

EXPERIENCE.   Dowghter, in this I can thinke none oother
But that it is true, this proverbe old:
"Hastye love is soone hot and soone cold."
Take hede, dowghter, how you put youre trust
To light lovers to[o] hot at the furst.
For had this love of Wit bene growndyd
And on a sure fowndashion fowndyd,

690 691 *i.e.*, Now, in spite of all these protestations of love, I've heard nothing at all in the space
of time it would take to send *three* messages back and forth between me and Wit, by means
of his servant.

702   Litell voide time wold have bene betwene ye,
703   But that this Wit wolde have sent or seene ye.
    SCIENCE.   I thinke so.
    EXPERIENCE.   Ye[a], thinke ye so or no,
    Youre mother, Experience, proofe shall showe
    That Wit hath set his love—I dare say   *i.e., on another woman*
    And make ye warrantise—another way.
       Wit cum'th before [in Ignorance's clothing, with his face   *comes forward*
       blackened].

708   [WIT.]   But your warrantise warrant no trothe!
    Faire ladye, I praye you, be not wrothe
    Till you he[a]re more. For, deere Ladye Science,
    Had your lover Wit—ye[a], or Confidence
    His man—bene in helth all this time spent,   *time that has passed*
    Long or this time, Wit had cumme or sent.   *ere this*
    But the trothe is, they have bene both sicke,
    Wit and his man; ye[a], and with paines thicke   *many*
    Bothe stay'de by the way, so that your lover   *Both were held back*
    Could neither cum nor send by none other.
    Wherefore blame not him, but chance of siknes.
    SCIENCE.   Who is this?
    EXPERIENCE.   Ingnorance, or his likenes.
720   SCIENCE.   What, the common foole?
    EXPERIENCE.   It is much like him.
    SCIENCE.   By my soothe, his toong serv'th him now trim!   *trimly, smartly*
    What sayst thow, Ingnorance? Speak again.
    WIT.   Nay, ladye, I am not Ingnorance, plaine,   *plainly*
    But I am your owne deere lover, Witt,
    That hath long lov'd you and lov'th you yet.
    Wherefore I pray the[e] now, my nowne sweting,
    Let me have a kis at this our meeting.
       [*Tries to kiss her.*]
    SCIENCE.   Ye[a], so ye shall anone, but not yet.
    Ah, sir, this foole here hath got sum wit!
    Fall you to kissing, sir, nowadayes?
    Your mother shall charme you. Go your wayes.   *i.e., make you obey*
    WIT.   What ne[e]d'th all this, my love of long growne?   *of long duration*
    Will ye be so strang[e] to me, your owne?
734   Youre aquaintance to me was thow[g]ht esye;

702–3There would have been only a short time of separation between you and Wit until he
would have sent you a message or seen you in person.

708But your assertion proves no true fact. (Wit, who has been on stage since he fell asleep in
Idleness' lap, wakes up in time to hear the conversation of Science and Experience.)

734I thought we were well acquainted.

But now your woordes make my harte all quesye,
Youre dartes at me so strangely be shott.

SCIENCE.   Heere ye what termes this foole here hath got?   *vocabulary, expressions*

WIT.   Well, I perse[i]ve my foolishnes now;
Indeede, ladies no dasterdes alowe.   *don't grant favors to cowards*
I wil be bolde with my nowne darling.

741   Cum now, a bas, my nowne proper sparling!   *a kiss*
    [*Again tries to kiss her.*]

SCIENCE.   What wilt thow, arrand foole?

WIT.   Nay, by the mas,
I will have a bas or I hence pas.   *kiss ere I go*

SCIENCE.   What wilt thow, arrande foole? Hence, foole,
    I say!

WIT.   What, nothing but "foole" and "foole" all this day?

746   By the mas, madam, ye can no good.

SCIENCE.   Art a-swering, to[o]? Now, by my hood,
Youre foolishe knaves breeche six stripes shall bere.

WIT.   Ye[a]? Godes bones! "Foole" and "knave," to[o]!
    Be ye there?
By the mas, call me "foole" once againe
And thow shalt sure call a blo[w] or twaine!   *ask for*

EXPERIENCE.   Cum away, dowghter. The foole is mad.

WIT.   Nay, nor yet ne[i]ther hence ye shall gad!
We will 'gre better or ye pas hence.   *agree/ere*
I praye the[e] now, good swete Ladye Science,
All this strange maner now hide and cover,
And play the good felowe with thy lover.

SCIENCE.   What good felowshippe wold ye of me,
Whome ye knowe not, ne[i]ther yet I knowe ye?

760   WIT.   Know ye not me?

SCIENCE.   No, how shoold I know ye?

WIT.   Dooth not my picture my parson shoow ye?   *person*

SCIENCE.   Your picture?

WIT.   Ye[a], my picture, ladye,
That ye spake of. Who sent it but I?

SCIENCE.   If that be youre picture, then shall we
Soone se how you and your picture agree.
Lo, here; the picture that I named is this.
    [*She displays the picture of Wit.*]

WIT.   Ye[a], mar[r]y, mine owne likenes this is.
You having this, ladye, and so lothe   *this (i.e., the picture)*
To knowe me, which this so plaine show'the?

741*sparling*: literally, little fish (a term of endearment).

746i.e., By the mass, madam, you don't know what's good for you, you don't know what
you're saying.

770   SCIENCE.   Why, you are nothing like, in mine eye.

WIT.   No? [*To Experience.*] How say ye?

EXPERIENCE.   As she saith, so say I.

WIT.   By the mas, than are ye both starke blinde!
　　What diference betwene this and this can ye find?   *i.e., picture and face*

EXPERIENCE.   Mar[r]ye, this is fayer, plesant, and goodlye;
　　And ye are fowle, displesant, and uglye.

WIT.   Mar[r]y, avawnt, thow fowle ugly whoore!

SCIENCE.   So! Lo, now I perse[i]ve ye more and more.

WIT.   What, perse[i]ve you me as ye wold make me,

779   A naturall foole?

SCIENCE.   Nay, ye mistake me;
　　I take ye for no foole naturall,
　　But I take ye thus—shall I tell all?

WIT.   Ye[a], mar[r]ye; tell me youre mind, I pray ye,
　　Wherto I shall trust. No more delay ye.

SCIENCE.   I take ye for no naturall foole
　　Browght up among the innocentes scoole,
　　But for a nawg[h]ty, vicious foole
　　Browght up with Idellnes in her scoole.
　　Of all arrogant fooles, thow art one.

WIT.   Ye[a]? Goges bodye!   *(By) God's*

EXPERIENCE.   Cum, let us be gone.
　　　[*Exeunt Experience and Science.*]

WIT.   My swerd! Is it gone? A vengeance on them!
　　Be they gone, to[o], and ther hedes upon them?
　　But, prowde quenes, the divill go with you both!   *whores*
　　Not one point of curtesye in them go'the.   *bit*

794   A man is well at ease by sute to paine him
795   For such a drab, that so doth disdaine him!
　　So mo[c]k'te, so lowted, so made a sot—   *flouted, mocked*
　　Never was I erst since I was begot!   *before this*
　　Am I so fowle as those drab[b]es wold make me?
　　Where is my glas that Reson did take me?   *give*

800   Now shall this glas of Reson soone trye me   *prove me*
　　As faire as those drab[b]es that so doth belie me.
　　　[*He looks in his mirror.*]
　　Hah, Goges sowle! What have we here, a divill?
　　This glas, I se well, hath bene kept evill.   *poorly maintained*
　　　[*He cleans the mirror and looks again.*]

[779]*naturall foole*: mentally defective at birth (not a professional entertainer counterfeiting folly).

[794-95](said bitterly) A man is greatly comforted, when he puts himself to considerable pains to pay suit to a whore like this who disdains him so!

Goges sowle, a foole! A foole, by the mas!
What a very vengeance ail'th this glas?
Other this glas is shamefully spotted,   *Either*
Or els am I to[o] shamefully blotted.
Nay, by Goges armes, I am so, no dowte.
How looke ther facis heere rownd abowte?
        [*He holds the mirror up to the audience.*]
810   All faire and cleere, they, ev'rychone;   *everyone*
And I, by the mas, a foole alone—
Deck't, by Goges bones, like a very asse!
Ingnorance' cote, hoode, eares—ye[a], by the masse,
Kokscom[b]e and all. I la[c]k but a bable.   *bauble (a fool's baton)*
And as for this face, [it] is abhominable,
As black as the devill. God for his Passion,
Where have I bene 'ray'de affter this fassion?   *arrayed in this fashion*
This same is Idlenes'—a shame take her!—
This same is her wurke. The devill in hell rake her!
820   The whoore hath sham'd me forever, I trow.
I trow? Nay verely, I knowe
Now it is so. The stark foole I playe   *utter*
Before all people. Now se it I maye,
Ev'rye man I se law[g]he me to scorne.
Alas, alas, that ever I was borne!
It was not for nowght, now well I se,
That those t[w]oo ladies disdained me.
Alas, Ladye Science, of all oother—   *of all people*
How have I rail'd on her and her moother!
830   Alas, that lady I have now lost
Whome all the world lov'th and honorith most.
Alas, from Reson had I not vari'd,
Ladye Science or this I had mar[r]i'd.   *ere*
And those fower giftes which the World gave her
I had woon to[o], had I kept her favor.
Wher now, instede of that lady bright   *Whereas*
With all those gallantes seene in my sight—
Favor, Riches, ye[a], Worship, and Fame—
I have woone Hatred, Begg'ry, and open Shame.   *won*
        Shame cum'th in with a whippe [*accompanied by Reason*].

840   Out upon the[e], Shame! What doost thowe heere?
    REASON.   Mar[r]y, 1, Reason, bad[e] him heere appeere.
Upon him, Shame, with strippes inow smitten,   *enough*
While I reherce his fawtes herein written:
        [*He reads.*]
First, he hath broken his promise formerly

Made to me, Reson, my dowghter to mar[r]ye.
Nexte, he hath broken his promise promisyd
To obay Instruccion, and him dispised.
Thurdlye, my dowghter Science to reprove,
Upon Idlenes he hath set his love.

850   Forthlye, he hath folowed Idellnes' scoole
Till she hath made him a verye stark foole.
Lastlye, offending both God and man,
Swering grete othes as any man can,
He hath abused himselfe to the grete shame
Of all his kinred and los of his good name.
Wherfore spare him not, Shame, bete him well there!
He hath deservyd more then he can beare.   *than*
    Wit knelith downe.
[WIT.]   Oh, Father Reson, be good unto me!
Alas, thes[e] stripes of Shame will undo mee.

860   REASON.   Be still a while, Shame. Wit, what sayst thow?
WIT.   Oh, sir, forgeve me, I beseech you!
REASON.   If I forgeve the[e] thy ponishment,
Wilt thow than folow thy first entent
And promise made, my dowghter to mar[r]ye?
WIT.   Oh, sir, I am not woorthy to car[r]ye
The dust out where your dowghter shoold sit.
REASON.   I wot well that. But if I admit
The[e], unworthy, againe to her wooer,   *to (be)*
Wilt thow then fol[l]ow thy sewte unto her?

870   WIT.   Ye[a], sir, I promise you; while life endurith.
REASON.   Cum neere, masters. Heere is wone ensurith   *one who pledges himself*
In woordes to becum an honest man.
    Here cum'th Instruc[c]ion, Studye, and Diligens in.

Take him, Instruccion; do what ye can.
INSTRUCCION.   What, to the purpose he went before?
REASON.   Ye[a], to my dowghter prove him once more.
Take him and trim him in new aparell
And geve that to Shame, there, to his farewell.   *as his dismissal*
INSTRUCCION.   Cum on your way, Wit. Be of good cheere;
After stormy clowdes cum'th wether clere.
    Instruc[c]ion, Study, Wit, and Diligens go out [with Shame].

880   REASON.   Who list to marke now this chance heere doon   *Whoever may wish*
May se what Wit is without Reson.
What was this Wit better then an asse,
Being from Reson stray'de as he was?
But let pas now, since he is well poonishyd,   *never mind now*

And therby, I trust, meetely well monishyd.   *fittingly admonished*
Ye[a], and I like him never the wurs, I,
Thowgh Shame hath handled him shamefullye.
For, like as if Wit had prowdly bent him   *For if Wit/determined*
To resist Shame, to make Shame absent him,   *to make Shame vanish*
890 I wold have thowght than that Wit had bene—   *then*
As the sayeng is, and dailye seene—
"Past shame once, and past all amendment."
So, contrarye, sins[e] he did relent
To Shame when Shame ponish't him evyn ill,
I have, I say, good hope in him still;
And thinke as I thowght, if joine they can,
My dowg[h]ter wel bestow'd on this man.
But all the dowte now is to thinke how
My dowghter tak'th this. For I may tell yow
900 I think she knew this Wit, evyn as weele
As she seem'd heere to know him no deele;   *not at all*
For la[c]k of kno[w]ledge in Science there is none.
Wherfore, she knew him; and therupon
His misbehaver, perchance evyn striking   *i.e., turning*
Her hart against him, she now misliking—
As women oft times wil be hard-hartyd—
907 Wil be the stranger to be revertyd.
This must I helpe. Reson must now walke
On Wit[t]es part with my Science to talke.
A neere way to her know I, wherebye
My soonnes cumming prevent now must I.   *son's/anticipate*
Perchance I may bring my dowghter hither.
If so, I dowght not to joine them together.   *doubt*
     Exeat Reson. Confidence cum'th in.

[CONFIDENCE.]   I thanke God, yet at last I have fownd him!
I was afraide sum mischance had drown'd him—
My master, Wit—with whome I have spoken,
Ye[a], and deliver'd token for token,
And have anoother to Science againe: *for Science*
A hart of gold, singnifyeng plaine   *plainly*
920 That Science hath wun Wit[t]es hart forever.
Whereby, I trust, by my good endever
To that good ladye, so sweete and so sortly,   *suitable*
A mariage betwene them ye shall see shortlye.
     Confidens exeat.

     Instruccion cum'th in with Wit, Study, and Diligence.

907She will be all the more reluctant to go back (to Wit).

[INSTRUCCION.]   Lo, sir, now ye be ent'ryd againe
   Toward that passage where dooth remaine
   Tediousnes, your mortall en[e]my.
   Now may ye choose whether ye will trye
   Your handes againe on that tyrant stowte,   *strong*
   Or els walking a litell abowte—
930 WIT.   Nay, for Godes Pashion, sir, let me meete him!
   Ye se I am able now for to greete him.
   This sword of Cumfort, sent fro my love,
   Upon her en[e]my needes must I proove.
  INSTRUCCION.   Then foorth, there, and turne on your right
        hand
935 Up that mownt before ye shall see stand.
   But heere ye, if your en[e]mye chance to rise,
   Folowe my cowncell in anye wise:
   Let Studye and Diligence flee ther towche,   *blow*
939 The stroke of Tediousnes, and then cowche   *hide*
   Themselves as I told ye. Ye wot how.
941 WIT.   Ye[a], sir; for that "how" marke the proofe now.
    [*Wit, Study, and Diligence advance on the mount.*]

  INSTRUCCION.   To mark it indeede, heere will I abide
   To see what chance of them will betide.   *what will happen to them*
   For heere cum'th the pith, lo, of this jornaye.   *essential part*
   That mowntaine before which they must assaye   *strive*
   Is cal[l]'d in Laten *Mons Pernassus;*
   Which mowntaine, as old auctors discus,
   Who attain'th ones to sleepe on that mownt,   *Whoever/once*
   Ladye Science his owne he may cownt.
950 But, or he cum there, ye shall see fowght   *ere*
   A fight with no les policye wrowght   *clever tactics*
   Then strength, I trow—if that may be praised.
  TEDIOUSNES [*within his lair*].   Oh, ho, ho!
  INSTRUCCION.   Hark!
  TEDIOUSNES [*entering*].   Out, ye kaitives!
  INSTRUCCION.   The feend is raisyd!
  TEDIOUSNES.   Out, ye vilaines! Be ye cum againe?
   Have at ye, wretches!
  WIT.   Fle, sirs, ye twaine!
    [*Study and Diligence flee.*]

[935]Up that mountain which you will see standing before you.

[939]*cowche:* Evidently, Instruction has told Study and Diligence to retreat and lead Tediousness into an ambush.

[941]i.e., To show you just how well I've learned what you taught, watch my demonstration.

TEDIOUSNES.   They fle not far hens[e]!

[*Tediousnes pursues them, but is ambushed. They turn on him.*]

DILIGENCE.   Turne againe, Studye!

STUDY.   Now, Diligence!

INSTRUCCION.   Well saide; holde fast now.

STUDY.   He fleeth.

DILIGENCE.   Then folowe!

[*They beat Tediousness into his lair, where Wit is ready for him.*]

INSTRUCCION.   With his owne weapon now wurke him sorow!

960   Wit li'th at reseite.

TEDIOUSNES   [*within*]. Oh, ho, ho! *Dieth.*

INSTRUCCION.   Hark, he dieth!

Where strength lack'th, policye supplieth.   *cunning*

*Heere Wit cum'th in and bring'th in the hed upon his swoorde,
and saith as folowith:*

WIT.   I can ye thanke, sirs; this was well doone.

STUDY.   Nay, yours is the deede.

DILIGENCE.   To you is the thank.

INSTRUCCION.   I can ye thank all; this was well doone.

WIT.   How say ye, man? Is this feelde well woonne?

Confidence cum'th running in.

[CONFIDENCE.]   Ye[a], by my faith, so saith your deere hart.

WIT.   Why, where is she, that here now thow art?

CONFIDENCE.   Upon yonder mowntaine on hye;

She saw ye strike that hed from the bodye,

970   Wherby ye have woonne her, bodye and all.

In token whereof, rese[i]ve heere ye shall

A gowne of kno[w]ledge, wherin you must

Rese[i]ve her here straight.   *at once*

WIT.   But sayst thow just?   *are you telling the truth*

[CONFIDENCE.]   So just I say that, except ye hie ye,   *unless you hurry*

Or ye be redye, she wil be by ye.   *Ere/at your side*

WIT.   Holde; present unto her this hed heere

And give me warning when she cum'th ne[e]re.

[*Exit Confidence with the head of Tediousness.*]

Instruccion, will ye helpe to devise

To trim this geere now, in the best wise?

980   INSTRUCCION.   Geve me that gowne; and cum with me, all.

DILIGENCE.   Oh, how this gere to the purpose dooth fall!

960i.e., Wit takes up a hunting position to await driven game.

Confidens cum'th running in.

[CONFIDENCE.] How, master, master! Where be ye now?
WIT. Here, Confidence; what tidinges bring'st thow?
CONFIDENCE. My ladye at hand heere dooth abide ye;
  Bid her wellcum. What, do ye hide ye?

Here Wit, Instruccion, Studye, and Diligence sing "Wellcum,
my nowne"; and S[c]ience, Experience, Reson, and Confidence
cum in at "As" and answer ev're second verse: *every*

WIT AND HIS CUMPANYE: O ladye deere,
  Be ye so neere
  To be knowne?
  My hart yow cheere   *You cheer my heart*
990 Your voice to he[a]re.
  Welcum, mine owne.

SCIENCE AND HIR CUMPANYE: As ye rejoise
  To he[a]re my voice
  Fro me thus blowne,   *sent*
  So in my choice
  I show my voice
  To be your owne.

WIT AND HIS COMPANYE: Then drawe we neere
  To see and heere
1000 My love long growne!
  Where is my deere?
  Here I apeere
  To see mine owne.

SCIENCE AND HIR CUMPANYE: To se and try
  Your love truly
  Till deth be flowne,
  Lo, here am I
  That ye may spye
  I am your owne.

1010 WIT AND HIS CUMPANYE: Then let us meete,
  My love so sweete,
  Halfeway heere throwne!

SCIENCE AND HIR CUMPANYE: I will not fleete,   *fly away*
  My love to greete.
  Welcum, mine owne!

WIT AND HIS CUMPANYE: Welcum, mine owne!

ALL SING: Welcum, mine owne!
  And when the song is doone, Reson sendith Instruccion, Studye,
  and Diligence, and Confidens out; and then, standing in the
  middell of the place, Wit saith as folowith:

WIT.   Wellcum, mine owne, with all my [w]hole harte,

Which shal be your owne till deth us depart.   *separate*

1020   I trust, ladye, this knot evyn sins[e] knit.   *is knitted together by now*

SCIENCE.   I trust the same. For sins[e] ye have smitt

Downe my grete en[e]mye, Tediousnes,

Ye have woon me forever, dowghtles—

Allthowgh ye have woon a clogg withall.   *a hindrance*

WIT.   A clogg, sweetehart? What?

SCIENCE.   Such as doth fall

To all men that joine themselves in mariage

In keping ther wives—a carefull cariage.   *worrisome responsibility*

WIT.   Carefull? Nay, ladye, that care shall imploye   *entail*

No clogg, but a key of my most joye.

1030   To kepe you, swetehart, as shall be fit,

Shal be no care, but most joy to Wit.

SCIENCE.   Well, yet I say—mark well what I saye—

My presence bringh'th you a clogg, no naye,   *undeniably*

Not in the kepinge of me onelye,

But in the use of Science cheeflye.

For I, Science, am in this degree   *of this condition*

As all or most part of woomen bee:

If ye use me well in a good sorte,

Then shall I be youre joy and comfort;

1040   But if ye use me not well, then dowt me,   *fear me*

For sure ye were better then without me.

WIT.   Why, ladye, thinke you me such a Wit

As being avansyd by you, and yet   *advanced, favored*

Wold misuse ye? Nay, if ye dowt that,

Heere is wone lov'th thee more then sumwhat.   *one (who)*

If Wit mi[s]use ye at any season,

Correct me then your owne father Reson.   *(Let) Reason correct me*

REASON.   Lo, dowghter, can ye desire any more?

What neede thes[e] dowtes? Avoide them, therfore.

1050   EXPERIENCE.   By'r Lakyn, sir, but under your favor,

1051   This dowt our dowghter doth well to gather

1052   For a good warning now at beginninge

1053   What Wit in the end shall looke for in winning.

Which shal be this, sir: if Science here,

Which is Godes gift, will be usyd meere   *solely*

Unto Godes honor and profit, both

Of you and your neybowre—which go'th   *By/which pertains*

In her of kind, to do good to all—   *To her naturally*

1050–53By our Ladykin (a dimunitive, here a mild oath), sir, but by your leave, (let me say that) our daughter does well to bring together (and present) as a clear warning, now at the beginning (of their marriage), these factors that Wit can expect to find ultimately.

1059	This seene to, Experience, I, shall
1060	Set you forth, Wit, by her to imploye
1061	Doble encrece to your doble joye.
	But if you use her contrariwise
	To her good nature, and so devise
	To evill effectes to wrest and to wry her,	*distort, twist*
	Ye[a], and cast her of[f] and set nowght by her,
	Be sure I, Experience, shall than
	Declare you so before God and man	*Testify against you*
1068	That this talent from you shal be taken
	And you ponish't for your gaine forsaken.	*for abandoning your treasure*

WIT.   "Once warn'd, half arm'd," folk say; namely whan
    Experience shall warne a man, than
    Time to take heede. Mother Experience,
    Towching youre dowghter, my deere hart, S[c]iens, *Regarding*

1074	As I am sertaine that to abuse her	*Since*
1075	I brede mine owne sorow, and well to use her	
1076	I encrece my joy—and so to make it	
1077	Godes grace is redye, if I will take it—	

    Then, but ye cownt me no Wit at all, *unless you account*
    Let never thes[e] dowtes into your hed fall;

1080	But, as yourselfe, Experience, clering
1081	All dowtes at lenght, so, till time apering,
1082	Trust ye with me in God. And, swetehart,

    While your father Reson tak'th Wit's parte,
    To rese[i]ve Godes grace as God shall send it,
    Dowte ye not our joy till lives end end it. *i.e., till death part us*

1086	SCIENCE. Well than, for the end of all dowtes past
1087	And to that end whiche ye spake of last,
1088	Among our wedding matters heere rend'ring,
1089	Th'end of our lives wold be in rememb'ring;

    Which remembrance, Wit, shall sure defend ye
    From the misuse of Science, and send ye
    The gaine my mother to mind did call:
    Joy without end—that wish I to all.

1059-61 If this is done, I, Experience, shall put you, Wit, in a position to gain through her a twofold prosperity, yielding you twofold joy.

1068 *talent:* a sum of money (referring to the parable of the talents; see Matthew 25:14–29).

1074-77 Since I am certain that by abusing her I would cause my own sorrow, and that by using her well I will increase my joy—and that God, through his grace, is ready to make it so (i.e., increase my joy) if I will take the opportunity.

1080-82 i.e., Rather, as your name "Experience" implies, trust as I do in God, dispelling all doubts and waiting to see the outcome (of our marriage) in the fulness of time.

1086-89 Well, then, in order to end all our past doubts, and also to satisfy the other end you just mentioned (i.e., our deaths), the end of our lives must be kept in mind even in the midst of our wedding festivities.

REASON.　Well said; and as ye, dowghter, wishe it,
That joy, to all folke in generall,
So wish I, Reson, the same. But yet
First in this life wish I here to fall
To our most noble king and quene in especiall,
To ther honorable cowncell, and then to all the rest,
1100　Such joy as long may rejoise them all best!

ALL SAY.　Amen.

Heere cum'th in fowre with violes and sing "Remembreance";
and at the last quere all make cur[t]sye and so goe forth singing.　verse
Thus endith the play of Wit and Science made by Master Jhon
Redford.

Textual Notes

In the following textual notes, the italicized words are the emended readings adopted in this edition whereas the unitalicized words are the rejected original readings of the manuscript or book. In some short plays or dramatic ceremonials, no emendations have proved necessary; such works are silently omitted here. For identity and location of the copy texts used in each instance, see the headnotes to the various plays throughout this edition.

PART ONE LITURGICAL BEGINNINGS

1. Concerning Tragedies (Honorius of Autun)

(no textual notes)

2. A Palm Sunday Procession in Fourth-Century Jerusalem (The Lady Etheria)

(no textual notes)

3. The Service for the Consecration of a Church (Bishop of Metz)

(no textual notes)

4. Adoration of the Cross (*Regularis Concordia*)

4 *Quia eduxi* Quia edux   13 s.d. *competentibus decantando* compenitentibus decantato

5. The Interment of the Cross in the Sepulchre (*Regularis Concordia*)

s.d. *monumenti* monumento   1 s.d. *Dominicae* dominica

6. The Raising of the Host from the Sepulchre (St. Gall)

(no textual notes)

7. Antiphons for Easter Vespers

(no textual notes)

8. Antiphons with Responses for the Vigil of the Most Holy Easter

(no textual notes)

9. Trope for Easter (Limoges)

Title: *TROPHI* TROPm (?)

10. Of the Resurrection of the Lord (St. Gall)

(no textual notes)

11. The Visit to the Sepulchre (*Regularis Concordia*)

s.d. *alba* abba   3 s.d. *jussionis* iussimus

12. The Visit to the Sepulchre (Winchester)

s.d. *Christi* XPE   2 s.d. *vocis consolatio* uoces con-

solatus   6 s.d. *Mulieres* Mulieri

13. The Visit to the Sepulchre (Aquileia?)

(no textual notes)

14. The Visit to the Sepulchre (St. Lambrecht)

(No emendations to the copy text, ms A, are included in this edition. For textual variants in mss B and C, see Young, *Drama of the Medieval Church*, I, 363–65.)

15. [The Service] for Representing the Scene at the Lord's Sepulchre (Fleury)

8 *frendet vesania* frendens uasania   10 *nece* nace   11 *saeva* seuam   48 *liquit* liquid   58 *ego* ego ego   78 *Reseratur* Reserator   78 s.d. *is* his *dalmaticatus* dalmaticus

16. The Service [for Representing] the Pilgrim, at Vespers of the Second Holy Day of Easter (Beauvais)

19 *cucurrerunt* curcurrerunt

17. For the Mass of Our Lord (Limoges)

(no textual notes)

18. The Service for Representing Herod (Fleury)

s.d. *salutem* salus   1 *evangelizo* euuangelizo   11 s.d. *Responsio* Respond   15 s.d. *dicentem* dicens   26 s.d. *dicens* dicentes   29 *profectus* perfectus   38 *segniter* signiter   53 s.d. *symmystis* sinistris   57 *Bethleem* belleem *civitate* ciuitatate   70 *extrahet* extrabet   82 *ab* ad   87 *praebitura* prehitum   99 s.d. *per aliam* per aliam per aliam

19. [The Service for Representing] the Slaughter of the Innocents (Fleury)

1–2 (in the ms, the first two rubrics are erroneously written together as though they were one rubric, and are then followed by the two antiphons "O quam gloriosum" and "Emitte agnum")   1 *gloriosum* glosiosum   1 s.d. *improviso* inprouiso   13 s.d. *Herodi dicens* Herodes dicentes   14 *occisos* oculos   15 s.d. *quem abeuntem* qui abeuntes   16 *tollis* tollit   17 s.d. *admoneat* ut moneant   40 *ploras* plorans   41 *vultus* uultum   42 *Ceu* seu *anniculae* agnicule   43 *lippitudo* limpitudo   45 *genarum* genatum   46 *Quid* quid quid   49 *extuli* extulit *esset* essi   51 *frequenti* frequenta   54 s.d. *admoneat* ammoneat

PART TWO TWELFTH-CENTURY CHURCH DRAMA

1. The Service for Representing Adam

s.d. *humeros* humeris *serantur* seruantur *amoenissimus* amenissemus *videatur* uideatur *coram* choram *propius* proprius (and elsewhere in the ms) *instructus* instructis *aut* aud *sic* sint *manu demonstret* manum demonstre   24 *mariage* manage   57 *demeneras*

1063

demeneuras   76 *metrai* metrai met   84 erroneously assigned to Adam   100 *qu'en* que   112 s.d. *ecclesiam* ecclessiam   *Eva* euam   117 *coment* comet   139 *mal* mal mal   155 s.d. *Adae* adam   159 this line unnecessarily repeats the speech prefix for the devil   172 s.d. *faciet* ficiet   204 s.d. *colloquia* colloquiam   *laeto* letu   213 *Orras* orrras   219 *ma ta* 231 *cuple* culpe   242 *mot* molt   253 *bel* bels   275 *dutance* dutante   282 *l'asajai* jo sai oi   283 *que chalt* quen chat   292 s.d. *vetitae* vetito   *adhibebit* adhibebibit   *auscultans* ascultans   *porriget* poeriget   *eum* eam   301 this line unnecessarily repeats the speech prefix for Eve   302 s.d. *Eva* eue   314 s.d. *pomi* pomum   *incipiet* incipiens   335 *avrai irrai* (?) urai (?)   338 *d'ités* ditel (?)   357 *desvee deauee*   360 *poste* poeste   386 s.d. *circumspiciens* circumspicientes   394 assigned to Adam in the MS   404 *gaainnié* gainnie   429 *soz* sor   439 *male* mala   455 *Tes* Test   469 *pome* pomo   472 s.d. *serpenti* serpentis   484 *mult* m (rest of word erased)   514 *faidis* faudis   517 *flamboie* flamblioe   518 s.d. *demonstrabit* demonstrans   *chorus* eorum   *rastrum habebit* rostrum   *incipient* incipiet   *fatigati* fatigari   *venerint venient* (?) venerit (?)   *gestu fatentes* gestum fatencentes   522 s.d. *dicet* dicens   525 *Jetez* Jotez   534 s.d. *ab eo* alto   *dicet* dicens   556 *forfait* sorfait   558 *tarzera* tazera   *el* il   559 *m'avez* maue   573 *car me que* car me   582 *en* n   590 s.d. *impellent* inpellunt   *se facient* se faciunt   *gaudentes* gaudendes   *discurrentes* discucientes   *inferno* infernum   605 *la* a   613 *si est qu'il* q si est quil   622 *pleigne* pleingne   622 s.d. *qui* quo   624 *de* de de   657 *la disme* (corrected in a later hand to "las dismes")   665–66 *Alom . . . voldra* Alom offrir de ca/Chescons par soi quil uoldra   666 s.d. *Chaim offeret* Chaym offerret   *manipulum* maniplum   *benedicet* benedicens   674 *bon* d bon   691 *quei* qui   698 *di* di por quoi   717 *parlé* parole   722 s.d. *quam percutiet Chaim* que percusciet eam   *ipsum* ipsam   727 *ou* (the *u* is perhaps expunged in the MS)   734 *rumor* nimor   744 s.d. *ducent Chaim* ducetur Chaim   *vocentur* vocat eum   *suorum* tuorum   754 *contrediz contrediz* (?)   764 *sentence* sentente   768 s.d. *dextra* dextram   770 *nostre* uostre   780 *nature* natura   790 s.d. *quo* quod   *essetis ceteris* his qui in his que   804 *esleecié* (*i* written over the line, between *ee* and *ce*)   819 *surdra verge d'Israel* vus ducs del pople israel   821 *orguil* grouil   826 s.d. *ad quos* a quos   834 *Qui vold* Tuz cels qui   852 *fra* frai   876 s.d. *Isaias* ysaiam   882 s.d. *Isaia* ysaiam   *dicet* dicit   895, 903 JUDEUS Judei 912 *Escutera* estuterai

2. The Holy Resurrection

[C] refers to the Canterbury MS; rejected readings are from the Paris MS   29 *Pharaon* [C] Phraon   54 *l'avez* lanez   79 *nostre* vostre   88 *devié* denie   95 *avras* anras   114 [*sai*] word added from C   119 *des* [C] del   145 *out* ont   157 *Dunt* Dut   160 *Malveis* Malveil   164 *tes* tels   165 *m'ad* [C] mas (?)   175 *n'en* [C] ne   191 *l'avrat* lanrat   194 *li* [C] le   221 *Aler* [C] Alez   231 *te* le   233 NICHODEMUS Nicodemus   248 *Saches* Sachef   253 *l'oinnement* loinnemt   264 *pacient* [C] pacennt   268 *le* be

270 *as* [C] al   285 *releverait* releuerat   300 *venge* [C] ne venge   302 *n'en* [C] ne   317 *paierai* paiera   318 *l'esturnerai* lesturnera   319–40 these lines appear after line 371 in the Paris MS   340 the bracketed line added following line 340 was omitted from the Paris MS evidently as a result of the rearrangement of lines 319–40; it is supplied from C   341–53 these lines are erroneously attributed to Pilatus in the Paris MS   341 *tendrez* rendrez   345 *poisse* poissez   346 *nel* le   348 *petit u grant* grant u petit (but marked as in reverse order in the MS)   359 *nel* le   370 *lai* [C] lait (this line, imperfect in the Paris MS, has been supplemented in the edition by the reading of C)

3. The Play of Daniel (Beauvais)

280 *flamine* fla flamine   317 *numinibus* muminibus

4. The Raising of Lazarus (Hilarius)

8 *cuique* quique   19 *iussi* iuxi   30 *damnantur* dannatur   49 *efflagito* afflagito   91 *proficere* profiscere   112 *somno* sunno   114 *somnum* sumnum   115 *Non* Nun   139 *Resurgere* Rexurgere (and similarly at ll. 144, 183)   168 *mitis* mittis   187 *fetens* ferens   191 *mundo* mondo

5. [The Service] for Representing the Conversion of the Blessed Apostle Paul (Fleury)

s.d. *similitudine Sauli* similitudinem Sauli   1 *vobis* nobis   41 *principis* princeps   51 *praedicet* prodicet   60 *feres* ferres

6. [The Service] for Representing How Saint Nicholas Freed the Son of Getron (Fleury)

31 *aethere* etthere   40 s.d. *invenerit* inueniret   52 *qui* quo   *consilium* consiliu   79 *mei* mee   107 *qui* quo   128 s.d. *comedere* commedere

7. The Christmas Play (Benediktbeuern)

57 *intactae virginis* dei et hominis (an erroneous repetition of line 55)   134 *id naturae rubor* nature robur   156–57 *carnis copulam* (in the MS, this phrase is written following "ante partum")   233 s.d. *Archisynagogus* archysanagogus   263 *sol* sol quando   267 *noxius* nociuus   274 *coniicio* conitio   317 *hebent* habent   349 *notum* noturum   359 *poscimus* possumus   361 *nolumus* uolumus   389 *Nam* num   395 *disserat* differat   397 *Ego* et ego   473 *colligis* colligit   491 *Fer* fert

8. The Passion Play (Benediktbeuern)

22 s.d. *cantet* cantent   38 *omnem* omnen   49 s.d. *Item* ℞   74 *wunechliche* wnnechliche   77 s.d. *evanescat* iterum evanescat (both words crossed through by a horizontal line)   80 *exitialis* exsicialis   88 *nobis mercator* mercator nobis   122 *salvam* saluum   126 *unseleich* vnselaeich (?)   129 *gŭeten* gŭetem   136 *ligatus* ligatis   141 s.d. JUDAS Jesum   175–76 (written in right margin; the order of the speeches here is uncertain)   176 *Nescio* (corrected from "Nescis"; see Luke 22:60)   180 *nobis* uobis   188 s.d. *induitur*

inducitur 198 s.d. *blasphemando* plasphemando
200 *percussit* percussitur 238 *doloris* doloros 270
lama Lema

PART THREE THE CORPUS CHRISTI CYCLE

The Banns (N Town)

65 *Example* exawple 105 *Of* Off 115 *her* (to
avoid ambiguity, the rising flourish on the final *r* is
not expanded here into the letter *e* as it normally is in
this edition; the final *e* is similarly omitted in the
feminine personal pronoun at lines 116, 132, 155, 161,
166, 167, 174, 176, 290, 376, 398, 430, 436, 437, 456,
and 459) 119 *eighte* (in the MS, the original word
is erased and "tende" is written in) 144 *ninte* (in
the MS, the original ix^te is corrected to x^te, while similarly
the pageant numbers at 157 and 170 are corrected by
adding one number; this present edition preserves the
original numbering) 155 *maidenys* maydonys 183
twelfte (in the MS, the original xii^te is corrected to xiiij;
similarly, the pageant numbers at lines 187 and 191
are corrected by adding two numbers) 285 *they*
thay (?) 325 *befor* bo for 356–57 (line order is
reversed in the MS, with markings to indicate correct
order) 425 *thretty-third* xxiij 474 *knew* know (?)

The Creation and the Fall of the Angels (Wakefield)

48 *thryd* thyrd 59 *now ye* now y ye 174 *strength*
strenght

The Fall of Man (York)

1 DIABOLUS (in the left margin in the MS) 6–7 (here
and at several other places in the MS, as at lines 8–9 and
10–11, two lines are written as one line; this present
text follows the lineation of the edition of Lucy Toulmin
Smith, Oxford, 1885) 25 EVA (the MS has both
"Eva" and "Eve" here) SATANAS (the MS has both
"Satanas" and "Diabolus" here) 43 *matere* materere
54 (the MS has both "Satanas" and "Sathanas" here)
67 *none therin* thernone in 87 *wrothe* wrorthe 145
thee thei 147 *thertill* therto 163 *wha ne* whanne

The Killing of Abel (Wakefield)

123 *a neld* an eld 213 *I will* ffor I will 273 (at
this point the scribe mistakenly began to write on folio
6a rather than 5b, so that the order of these two pages
must be reversed) 459 *Godys* Codys

Noah (Wakefield)

33 *commaund* commaundement 42 *and* in 125
thirté thirrte 129 *chese* chefe 461 *How* Now

The Sacrifice of Isaac (Brome)

6 *of* off (and elsewhere in this text, e.g., ll. 32, 40, 150,
209, 398) 17 *well* wyll (and elsewhere, e.g., ll. 38, 59,
86, 91, 94, 113, 141, 199, 211, 220, 258, 389, 409, 432,
452, 454; also *for-well* for forwyll at ll. 219, 260, 290,
329) 23 *night* nygth (and elsewhere, because of
rhymes, as at ll. 110, 143, 171, 182, 192, 199, 337,

338, 345, 372, 404) 29 *prest* glad 40 *he* yf he
44 *lovith* lovyd (also, at l. 152, *brekyd*, and at l. 208,
begynnyd) 45 *him by* be hym 46 *fulfill* kepe 58
alon in trenyte 76 *erde* erthe (also at ll. 220, 286)
93 *dismayd* dismasyd 94 *apayd* plesyd 95 *plese*
pelsse 110 *Yevyn* yovyn 127 *twain* tewyn 130
hold bere 141–42 (these lines are transposed in the
MS) 151 *so* os 152 *on sonder* on too 157 *me* ye
162 *or* (the rising flourish on the final *r* is not represented here by the letter *e*; see also ll. 176, 185, 448)
165 *hide it* hydygth (also *find it* for fyndygth at ll. 300,
304) 206 *dwelling* dewllyng 222 *swerd* sword
(also at l. 288) 230 *fewe* feve (also *avooe* for awooe
at l. 452, and *schowyd* for schovyd at l. 461) 233
afray afrayed 298 *bite* synke 300 *smite* smygth
310 *deth* degth 317 *sent* senth 323 *fair* fayyr
328 *ram* rame 334 *ethed* yeyed 337 *now[gh]t* not
yyt 345 *tale* tall 351 *For . . . ram* For yyn same
rame he hath vs sent 354 *worchup* worpchup 363
in hie of heuyn 368 (written as two lines in MS)
370 *liffe* leve 374 *present* present 376 *sped* spyd
381 *gled* glad 399 *end* yynd 402 *wend* goo 406
grucched grutthed (?) 411 *dereworthy* dere wordy
413 *have* hath 427 *other* erthe 432 (this line
follows l. 427 in the MS) 434 *tho* thow 436 *story to
story* hath schowyd to 444 *yowre child to slayn* to
smygth of yowre chyldys hed 448 *or* or a 451
woll woll woll

Pharaoh (Wakefield)

11 *knawne* knowne 183 *thy* my 185 *skape* skake
304 *the ragyd* ragyd the 308 (a line is missing here,
to rhyme with *blowre*) 358 *Pestilence* pentilence
365 *done* doyn 404 *Go* So (? the capital is more like
the scribe's S than his G, but the case is not clear)

The Ten Commandments, Balaam and Balak, and the Prophets (Chester)

The copy text for this pageant is MS H (Brit. Museum
Harl. 2124), the only one of the five extant MSS to
include the Procession of Prophets. To this text have
been added two passages from MS D (Huntington HM 2)
as indicated in the following notes. 7 *name* not
(other MSS) myn not 24 s.d. *eum* (an error for *se*?)
25 SINAGOGAE sinagoga 28 *see* looke 90 *had I* I
had 102 *bethought* (other MSS) vnthought 116a
(the five following stanzas are supplied from MS D; the
first three stanzas are found in that MS at the bottom of
30^v, the last two stanzas at the top of 29^r) 116j *on*
one (D) 216a (this stanza is supplied from MS D,
where it appears at the top of 28^v) 268 *river* rivers
302 *forgeat* foryeat 360a *occursus* occisus 429
beleve beleven 431 *On* one 438 *strive* shryue

The Annunciation (Wakefield)

52 *said* (inserted in a later hand in the MS) 266 *ying*
yong 307 (the rest of this stanza appears to be incomplete) 352 *long* longe (?)

The Salutation of Elizabeth (Wakefield)

(no textual notes)

The Birth of Jesus (York)

47 *Of* fo   76 *belde* bilde

The Shepherds (York)

7 *a* I   12 *be* by   41–42 (written in one line in MS)
43 (assigned to 2 Pastor in MS)

The Second Shepherds' Pageant (Wakefield)

10 *husbandys* shepardes   57 *windys* weders   70 *or
to clok* (partially obscured by a large blot in the MS)
71 *is oure* is or oure   72 *shakyls* shekyls   93 *that*
it   218 *teyn* (apparently a later scribe has written
"le" over the original "n")   235 *my* thy (?)   *sho*
she (?)   244 *now* not   291 *From* ffron   359 *me*
my   370 *3* ij   372 *2* Tercius   383 *Stevyn* strevyn
407 *se* be   421 *That* A That   428 *will suppose* will
sr suppose   621 *1* iij^us   623 *3* primus   629 1
PASTOR (this speech prefix is missing in the MS)   673
to lose to s lose

The Offering of the Magi (Wakefield)

53 *to* to to   128 *it* me   201 *shewys* se shewys   241
red reede   295 *thay* (written over an "I" that is not
expunged)   312 *Who made him* who the dewill made
hym   366 *me* b me   402 *go to* go s to (?)   481
nobill noble nobyll   628 *To* Ty

The Flight into Egypt (York)

47 *that* at that   94–95 (written as one line in the MS,
with dividing mark)   137 *tharne* thrane   170 *Of*
Off of   209 JOSEPH Iosep

Herod the Great (Wakefield)

11 *sourmonting* Iourmontyng   177 *I* r (?)   263 *a
pope* (partly erased in the MS)   269 *soundys* sandys
282 *2* MILES (not marked off as a speech prefix, but
written as though part of the line of verse)   381 *say
I* I say I   426 *emange* emangys   508 *rokyn* rekyn

The Death of Herod (N Town)

138 *neither* neythey   143 *thinkith* thynkygh   246
Of Off   255–258 (written as two lines in the MS,
with dividing marks)   279 *lowte* lowth

The Woman Taken in Adultery (N Town)

55 *folwith* ffolwygh   67 *a right* ryght a   71 *her* (to
avoid ambiguity, the rising flourish on the final *r* is not
expanded into the letter *e* as it normally is in this edition; the final *e* is similarly omitted in the feminine
personal pronoun at ll. 72, 83, 84, 85, 88, 102, 197,
200, 207, 208, 223, 231)   130 *he* I   132 *him* hem
135 JUVENIS Iuuenes   137 (paragraph sign missing
in the MS)   141 *a fray* affray   183 *us* ut   285
JHESUS (cancelled and replaced by "Doctor" in a later
hand)

The Raising of Lazarus (Wakefield)

3–4 (these lines are transposed in the MS, but are marked

with the letters *a* and *b* to indicate proper order)   57
trowys trewys

The Passion Play (N Town)

Prologue   22 *to* do   46 *purpose* puurpose   69 *Of*
Off   71 *comparicon* comparycion   89 *Onto* On to the
94 *canon* canoun (?)   104 *her* (to avoid ambiguity,
the rising flourish on the final *r* is not expanded into
the letter *e* as it normally is in this edition; the final *e* is
similarly omitted in the feminine personal pronoun at
line 105, and, in Passion Play I, lines 186, 498, 500, 525,
and 1040 S.D.)   JOHN THE BAPTIST   23 *showe*
shove   39 *declaracion* declararacion   PASSION
PLAY I   61 CAIPHAS Cayfas   124 *We* Whe
124 S.D. *Pharisees mete at* pharaseus (or pharasens) mett
&   137 *this* thus   158 *werkys* werke   161 *werkys*
werke   178 (at this point, the MS copies and then
cancels several lines by Peter appearing later at ll.
222–7)   188 *man* mas   234 *denyed* deny id (?)
274 *with* whit   275 *were* where   329 *morn* morwyn
(?)   345 *wilt* wytl   374 *cald Sion* calsydon (?)
378 *Contenwing* Contewnyng   384 *at* dat   397 (in
the MS this line comes at the beginning of the stanza,
before line 394)   462 MAGDALEN (so at the top of
149^r; "Mawdelyn" at the foot of 148^v)   525 *Of* Off
607 *New* mew   673 *Egypth* egythp   702 (this line
is written in the right margin with some cropping, but
is repeated at the foot of the page)   848 S.D. *sithin*
sythym   881 *yn* thu (?)   924 *wil* vyl   940 *gret*
gret f   998 S.D. *Malchus* Malcheus (?)   1013 *lede*
ledde (?)   1032 *save* sawe   1036 *knowe* knove
1041 MAGDALENE Magdelene   *immaculate* in maculate
1052 *bete* bety   1066 *mende* meende   PASSION
PLAY II (this edition omits a passage in the MS between Passion Plays I and II, on fol. 163, in which two
"doctors" sing the praises of the apostles St. Paul, John
the Baptist, etc.; the passage appears to be an insertion,
and is not numbered among the sections of the MS)
15 *to* toke   THE TEXT   1 HERODES REX (this
speech prefix appears at the top of 165^v; on the bottom
of 165^r is the duplicatory speech prefix *herowdys*)
111 *doctrine* dottryne (?)   175 ANCILLA Ancille
191 *companye* compayne   212 *loke* lode (?)   309–
314 (these six lines are doubled up in the MS, appearing
as three lines)   287 *wole* wele (?)   356 S.D. *Herodes*
Herodys

The Buffeting (Wakefield)

82 *wiles* lyes   91 *king* prophete   337 *sitt ye and see
it* see ye and sytt   345 *Fraward* frawrard   382
thurst thrust   423 *Knokyd* knokyp   427 *trate* crate

The Scourging (Wakefield)

179 *three* iiij   254 (added in a later hand in the MS)
266–67 (written as four lines in the MS; also the last two
lines of the following five stanzas)   295 *behovys*
behowys   306 *him* me *folowe* felowe   408 *oure*
oure oure

The Crucifixion of Christ (York)

9–12 (written as two lines in the MS)   44 *on* one   91 *spede* speede   101 1 MILES ii^{us} mil   154 *you [and]* youe   155 *They* I   266 *pratis* patris   273 *Vah* Vath   *destruis* destruit

Christ's Death and Burial (York)

6 *evenly* neuenly   75 CAIPHAS (in a later hand)   126 (in a later hand)   157 *site* sigte   213–16 (written as two lines in the MS)   239 GARCIO (this speech prefix is at line 235 in the MS)   241 *spare* sware   313 CENTURIO Centerio   352 NICHODEMUS Nichomedis (and elsewhere in the speech prefixes in this pageant)   *Well* wiell (?)   373 *wene* wyne   395 *To Do*   404 JOSEPH Joshep   410 *mende* wende

The Harrowing of Hell (Wakefield)

5 *thirty* thryrty   236 *bot* ff bot   247 *minnys* mymnys   375 *tormentys* tornamentys

The Resurrection of the Lord (Wakefield)

26 *bees* beas (?)   315 *shaw* shew (?)   471 *And* had   500 *waking* walkyng   509 *pas* pes (?)   554 *ye* I

Christ Appears to the Disciples (Chester)

The copy text for this edition is MS H, Brit. Museum Harl. 2124. Also referred to in these notes are MS D (Huntington HM 2) and MS W (Brit. Mus. Add. MS. 10,305).   2 *Mone* myne owne   32 *him* (other MSS) he   45 *those* these (?)   48 *and* (other MSS) in   112 S.D. *omnes* omnies (also at ll. 168 S.D. and 240 S.D.) *eunt* erunt (also at l. 168 S.D.)   133 *mase* masse   144 S.D. *ceteros* Cateros   153 *With us* (other MSS) With   160 *thrawe* (W) thrall   175 *now can* (other MSS) he can   192 *signes* (W, D) signe   238 *leeve* loeve   249 *no more so* (other MSS) so no more

The Last Judgment (Wakefield)

27 *on oure* oure on   202 *knawen* knowen   233 *be I* I be   246 *knawen* knowen   269 (MS partly illegible)   401 S.D. *vulnera* Wlnera   504 1 MALUS (at line 505 in MS)   532 *furth go* go furth   608 *anger* angre   618 *as* os

PART FOUR SAINTS' PLAYS OR CONVERSION PLAYS

The Conversion of St. Paul (Digby)

1 (in a later hand, the MS adds the name "Myles Blomefylde" after the word "Poeta")   *gloriae* glorie   2 *thy* the   *power* pouer (and similarly *powre* for poure at 232 and 322, *alway* for aluay at 146, 224, and 316)   14 *Daunce* (in a later hand in the MS; also at ll. 154 and 345)   16 *garnement* garlement   21 *me* my   23 *menace* menaces   24 *noble and high* hye & noble   59–60 (these lines are reversed in the MS, with lettering in the margin to indicate correct order)   91 *crabbish* crabyysh   100 *wide* ("wyde" has been cancelled in the MS and replaced by "brode")   119

mare nare   141 *vyage* wyage (and similarly *vessell* for wessell at 234, *availe* for awayle at 276)   153 *like him* ("to" added after "like" in a later hand)   183 DEUS Deuus   205 *sesse* serse   217 *wise* vyse   261 S.D. *contemplacion* comtemplacion   278 *He &*   281 *this* the   293 *Discendit* Discendet   294 *his* hys hys   352 *tellys* tellyd   359 *benigne* benygne &   359 S.D. *tertia* tarcia   396 (four lines are evidently missing here in the MS at the bottom of page 44^r)   398 CAIPHAS (so at the top of 44^v; "Caypha" at the bottom of 44^r)   411 S.D. (this scene of the devils, through l. 502 S.D., is in a later hand inserted on three separate leaves in the MS)   *avaunte* avaunce   428 *soug[h]te* sowgte   470 S.D. *crye* trye   502 S.D. (the passage from l. 502 through 516, first written on 44^v, was cancelled by the scribe who wrote the devil scene and recopied by him; the text here is based on the original version)   517 *Of* Off   546 *us* ys   548 *For* ffror   579 *Subdue* subdwe   588 *Com* Con

Mary Magdalene (Digby)

1 (at the top of the page in the MS appear the initials M.B.)   3 *volunté* wolunte (and similarly *veriours* for weryouns at 36 and 92, *avansyd* for awansyd at 107, *verely* for werely at 172, *love* for lowe at 352, *avansse* for awansse at 385, *fawor* for favor at 431, 483, and 638, *Evyn* for ewyn at 543, *vois* for woys at 920, etc.)   22 *prosperité* presporyte   35 *dawnnes* davnnes   38 *grocch* grocth (?)   42 *dowte* doth   50 *barons* borons   58 *caitifys* cayftyys   90 *plesawns* plesowans   176 *splendore* spelndore   185 *veniat qui mittendus* veniet Imitendus   187 *dastardes* dastardus   193 MILES milis   205 *woth* woys   207 (speech prefix *Herowdes* unnecessarily repeated at top of page)   213 *Tiberius* tyberyuus (also at 252, *Mercuryuus* at 318, etc.)   222 *swich* swych swych   236 *ye* he   252 *here* herre   292 *life* lyfy   303 MARY Maria (also at l. 445 and occasionally elsewhere; the speech prefixes are standardized to "Mary" throughout except in scenes where Mary Magdalene appears with the other Marys)   330 WORLD mundus (the speech prefixes, which use "Mundus" and "World" interchangeably in the MS, have been standardized to "World" throughout; similarly, the interchangeable "Lechery" and "Luxuria" have been standardized in this edition to "Lechery")   *declaracion* declareracyon   338 *comfortativys* comfortatywys   379 SATAN dylfe   380 *hur* hure (also at 424, 550, 551, 556, 559, etc.)   387 *asemlauns* asemlaunvs (also *aliauns* at 440, *afiauns* at 442, etc.)   404 *of* fo   407 MESSENGER senswalite   429 *Hir* hyre (also at 499, 1365, 1593, 1600 S.D.)   431 (the speech prefix *Satan* is unnecessarily added here at the top of the page in the MS; similarly with *Corios[i]te* at 518, *Jhesus* at 643, *Jhon* at 1054, etc.)   445 *comende* comendyd   462 *plesauns* pleȝauns (also in *plese* at 659, *plesant* at 957, *pleseauns* at 1304, *plesing* at 1491 and at 1504, 1506, 1514, 1520, 1540, 1548; etc.)   464 *governauns* governons   475 *wine* wynne (also at 476, 477, 536)   480 *better* bertter   484 *finest* finnest   495 *tappysstere* tasppysstere   *rown* rownd   514 *drink* dryng   519 *peynes* peynnes

526 *my* me 542 *ye* we 554 *her* here (also at 1370) 555 SATAN diablus *these* ȝese 559 S.D. *Mary* maria 560 SATAN rex diabolus (also at 722) 584 *the* ȝe (also at 587 S.D., 664, and 1251) 593 *the[e]* ȝe (also at 601, 641, 657, 1727, 1740) 636 *dampdnyd* damdpnyd 640 S.D. *ointtment* noyttment 651 *wer* wher (also at 971, 1288, 1436) 664 *dettours* dectours 670 *intent* In entent 692 *glorius* gloryuus (also at 815, 1016, 1018, etc.) 697 *Isaye* Iȝaye 716 *we* I 717 *Spiritus* sperytus 722 SATAN Rex deabolus 725 *Belȝabub* belȝabub 727 SATAN tercius diabolus (possibly there is an omission in the text, since two devils appear and no speech is assigned to the third) 730 BAD ANGEL speritus malignus 731 SATAN primus diabolus (also at 735, 740, 744) 732 *yon* yen 733 BAD ANGEL malinus speritus 739 S.D. *serve* serva 748 MARY Mari mavgleyn (also at 768) 827 *for* fore (also at 908, 1762) 836 *done* donne 851 *childyrne* chyldyunre 863 *skornyd* skoernyd 865 *Therfor* I therfor 881 *reyne* reynne 885 *thou* the 924 *boste* bost(?) 959 *ruby* rubu 962 S.D. *wine* wynne 967 *firys* fire ys 973 *crosse* crosce 984 *or* ore 998 *Jewys* Jevys 1005 [MARYIS] M maudleyn 1046 S.D. *Here* How 1054 (speech prefix *Jhon* unnecessarily repeated) 1073 *thee* thou 1079 *Simond* symovd 1120 *et Filii* ett felii *Spiritus* speritus 1149 BOY clericus 1278 *lorde* lordes 1308 *ar* are 1311 *sentens* sentelles (also at 1315) 1345 *disipilles* dysyllpylles 1365 *Ner* nere 1394 S.D. *entyr* entyre 1395 MASTER shepman (also at 1402) 1411 MASTER the master (also at 1415) 1419 BOY the boy (also at 1445) 1442 *a-lond* a-land (?) 1456 *yow* yow yow 1476 *And* & and 1481 (this line is at the bottom of the page in the lower margin) 1494 *sonne* sonn 1529 *so[o]n* sonn 1533 *what* with (also at 1545) 1542 *Christeyn* christetyn 1554 *trepidabo* trepedabo 1582 *mesure* mesuer 1618 *quen* qwen 1627 *God* good 1642 S.D. *Tunc transit* thunc transiunt 1692 *nor* nore (also at 1815, 2059) 1702 *wild* wylld 1704 *And yow* yow & 1738 *shall* xall xall 1748 *wommanhed* wommanned 1809 *Nauta* nawta 1818 *Itt* att 1825 *pilgrimmage* pylgramage 1826 *ye* the (?) 1830 *Satanas* saternas 1839 *bond* lond 1846 *labor* lobor 1882 *thether* ȝether 1892 *pure* puer 1906 *Maryis* maryvus 1908 *s[a]we* sye 1933 *blissit[h]* blyssyd 1939 S.D. *queene* quvene 1972 *sine* sene 1992 *abide* abyte 2012 *sprong* sporng 2031 S.D. *filium felium* 2045 *graunt* grvant 2051 *sawe* save 2072 PREST pryst (also at 2090, 2124) 2113 *recummend* recumdmend 2127 *game* name

The Play of the Sacrament (Croxton)

6 *Of* off (also at ll. 7, 8, etc.) 17 *him* hyn 21 *freyned* freynend 23 *pound* li (and elsewhere in this play) 25 *merchaunte* merarchaunte 30 *bey* bye 31 *wolde* woldr 38 *new* nell 42 *boile* boylde 46 *ovyn* ob ouyn 50 *shewyd* sheuyd 55 *con[v]ertyd* counteryd 58 *our* your 59 *woth* with 61 *showyd* shovyd 63 *gan* gayn 77 *save* sawe *from*

fron trey treyn 79 *us* ys 80 "*The Namys*" etc. (found at the end of the MS) *namys* nanys *numbere* nmbere 82 *He* be 84 *his* thys 96 *Surrey* surgery 99 *ringe* ryngys 100 *cliffys* chyffys 118 *it that* (?) 120 *waiteth* waytheth 122 *will* well 127 *conning* comnyng 147 *onkowth* onknowth 148 S.D. *bost* best 150 *Whose* whoses 158 *Gold* godd 167 *achatys* machatys 173 *have* hawe (also at 519, *Clovys* for Clowys at 181, *valew* for walew at 290, *avoid* for awoyd at 500, *ovyn* for owyn at 712 S.D., and *avance* for awance at 737) 179 *reys* rys (with *y* written over an *e*?) 181 *greynis* grenyis 187 *iwis* I wyse 188 *of* of eyer 194 *Eraclea* graclea 196 *merchaunte* merchauntys 197 *wolld* wolldys (also *wolde* for "woldys" at 203) 208 *preve* praye 211 *swer* seuer 217 MALCUS malcyus 220 *consent* counsent 228 S.D. *Aristory* acrystori 232 *come* coume 234 *done* doune 235 *com* coum 236 S.D. *man* men 238 *thy* they 245 JONATHAS Jhonattas *bargenes* bargened 253 *told* toll 265 S.D. *merchaunte* merchauntys 269 *am* an 273 *bargeyn* bargeny 275 *yow* yoll 276 *bartre* vartre 280 *distre[n]* dystrre 291 JONATHAS Jonathaus (also at 303) 297 *dere* bere 302 *[h]eresye* tresye (?) 313 *here* hir 325 *is* hys 335 *done* doun 339 *wine* wynne 350 *gone* gonne (also at 353) 352 *night* rest 375 *commith* commytht 396 *crucified* crwcyfyed 402 *togethere all* all togethere 414 *hir* hyre 428 *pymente* pymentys 440 *Judicare* Judecare 441 *their* or 452 *if* ys 461 *owr* yowr 475 *augur* augus 493 *galous* galouns thre iiij 496 *might* mygthe 497 JONATHAS Janathas (also at 520) 504 *renne* reme 507 *him* hyme 512 MASPHAT Malspas 515 S.D. *hang* sang 517 *iwis* I wyse 531 *sittith* sytthyt 539 *judgement* Judyyment 550 *wot* wotr 557 *But* By *aileth* dyleth 562 *can him* cam I 564 *do[o]n* doun 568 *mede* mdn (or "men") 569 *cut* tut 582 *medicament* medycamentys 583 *annoyment* anoyntment 587 *Letuce* letwyce *sauge* sawge 590 *Between* betuynn 595 *wife* wyse 597 *drink* drynkys 599 *shrugg* shruggys 617 *colt-evill* Coltugll 623 *phesiscian* phesyscion 627 *master* mastere (?) 631 *here* hyre 636 *can* cane 637 *hermes* hermet 638 *[un]henly* honnly (?) 640 *Voideth* voydoth 655 *witte* wittys 675 *rin* run 682 *That* ys that 683 *Is* to to 688 *done* donne (?) 708 *for* fore (also at 861, 972) 716 S.D. *Jewys* Juys 718 *sicut* similis 749 *nostram* nostraȝ 758 *wise* vyse 770 *Ser* No 771 *this* ys 791 *hast* haste 820 *gertt* grett 840 *sacrum scacrum* 865 *amendys* a menyn 865 S.D. *[h]ost u[p]on* of non 866 *cum* co 868 *be ye* ye be 877 *mischeves* myschevos 886 *From* fform 912 *done* donne 921 *on* in (?) 930 S.D. *Jewys* Juys 934 *wo[u]nde* wondys 940 *might* mygth not 967 *Never* Neuerer *before* befere 982 *Him* & hym 985 *stedfastly* stodfastly

PART FIVE THE MORALITY PLAY
The Castle of Perseverance

1 1 VEXILLATOR Primus vexil (speech prefixes are standardized throughout) 25 *govyn* govym 64 *strivith*

strywyth (also *ravin* for rawyn at 168, *drive* for drywe at 262, *devilys* for dewylys at 308, *evil* for ewyl at 312, 1373, 1374, and 1440, *servaunt* for serwaunt at 532, 576, 586, and 614, *thrive* for thrywe at 544, *live* for lywe at 545, *schrive* for schrywe at 546, *knave* for knawe at 548, *service* for serwyce at 844, *love* for lowe at 2104, *drevyn* for drewyn at 2824, *grucchyn* for grwcchyn at 2833, *grevaunse* for grewaunse at 3172, etc.)   92 2 VEXILLATOR Primus Vexillator (this and the next four stanzas are misassigned in the MS) 156 *Haec sunt* etc. (the names of the players are found at the end of the MS) 165 *World* (or "werld")   198 *chafe* chase   308 *To* do   340 MALUS Maluus   356 *sittith* syt-tyht   499 *To* do   513 *nowt* nout   570 *broun* bron   585 *welcum* welcun   631–46 (written as four lines with dividing marks; similarly at 785–88, 1084–87, 1114–17, 1144–47, 1174–77, 1204–7, 1234–37, 1286–97, 1746–53, 1767–68, 1791–98, 1812–13, 1836–43, 1853–54, 3127–28, 3229–48, and 3574–97)   676 *thridde* thyrde   713 *al his* al hys al hys   856 *purs* purus   903 *comme* comne   920 *Wrethe* wreche (?)   934 *steriste or stariste* sterystys or starystys   945 *childryn* chyrdryn   970 *kloy* kloyet   984 *What* waht   1005 *of* off   1043 *crust* curst   1092 *spil[l]e* spidle (*with* d *blotted*)   1145 ("Mankinde" is followed by a diamond-shaped mark in the MS)   1150 *thou* the   1236 *Com* con   1298 *trewe* trowe   1324 CONFESSIO Confescio (also at 1355, 1429, 1455, 1494, 1546)   1340 *name* mane   1374 *But* that   1404 *syhe* shye   1422 *my* I   1460 *kepe* h kepe   1551 *werldly* werldyly   1554 *sende* seende   1602 (a leaf is missing here in the MS, and the following leaves are out of order; line 1602 appears at the top of fol. 173, line 1697 at the top of fol. 172)   1631a *placere* plcere   1633 *hir* hyre (also at 1891)   1634 *her* here   1638 *brimme* brymmne   1699 *cumme* cunne   1766 S.D. *vocabit Superbiam, Invidiam, et Iram* vocauit sperbia inuida & Ira   1822 S.D. *verberabit* uerberauit   1855 *Lewde* lowde   1863 S.D. *verberabit* verberauit   1940 *Whanne* wahanne   1960 *whow* whov (also at 2077, 2244, and 3262; similarly *Jewys* for Jevys at 3136, *whou-so* for whovso at 3320, *Jewes* for Jeves at 3353, *dewnesse* for devnesse at 3434, etc.)   1969 *herawd* heyward   2000 *they* ben 2007a *incideritis* insideritis   2109 *fro thy* fro thi fro thi   2112 (in the misordering of pages, the text jumps here from 175ᵛ to 177, while fol. 176 begins at line 2217; the speech prefix "Ira" has been added in another hand at the top of 177)   2177 *had he* (MS blotted and unclear)   2240 *winne* with   2255 *vow* wou   2300 CASTITAS Castias   2322 (here the text jumps from fol. 176ᵛ to 179; fol. 178 begins at line 2431)   2336 *for* fror   2364a *ora* hora   2452 *an* an h   2482 *olde* colde   2521 *frende* fremde   2550 *chace* chach (*with final* h *erased*)   2579 *endowyd* endewyd   2598 *like* kyke   2612a *relinquent* relinquam   2739 (here the text jumps from 181ᵛ to 184, followed in turn by fols. 183 and 182)   2759 *doun* dounn   2836 *broche* broche   2878 *Werldys* werldlys   2969 *welaway* welesay   3029 (a leaf missing from the MS at this point)   3047 *founde* I founnde he   3110 *schalt* f

schalt   3113 *peynnys* peymys   3152 *misdede* mys-dode   3163 *mede* mode (?)   3187 *goode* goodys   3200 *put* pud   3228 S.D. *dicet* dixit   3260 *trewthe* threwthe   3339a *gravidata* grauidada   3352 *Sitio* scitio   3383 *fro* ffre   3392 *born* bornn   3397 *pompe* ponpe   3404 *Domini* dcum   3467 *endinge* begynnynge   3549 *Pascioun* pasciounn   3626 *ryth* ryde

Mankind

2 *us* ws (also at lines 77, 98, 108, 193, 323, 334, etc.; similarly *avise* for awyse at 25, *uppe* for wppe at 29, 31, 218, 361, 549, 620, and 661, *verse* for werse at 56, *lewde undyrstondinge* for leude wndyrstondynge at 58, *revelinge* for rewelynge at 85, *hevyn* for hewyn at 175, 558, 660, 752, and 869, *livinge* for lywynge at 214, *evyn* for ewyn at 261 and 275, *very* for wery at 275, *unkinde* for wnkynde at 280, etc.)   22 *mediacion* medytacyon   27 *avaunte* a vaunte   33 *certifye* crertyfye   40 *venimousse* vemynousse   42 *strait* strerat   49 *Misse-masche, driff-draff* dryff draff mysse masche   88 *play* pray   100 *cuppe* cuppe redy   110 *brether* brethern   125–28 (written in right margin in MS)   128 NOWA[DAYS] (in left margin at line 129)   157 *Felowse* ffelouse (also at lines 256, 348, 401, 517, and 703; similarly *schrowde* for schroude at 369, *schrewde* for schreude at 437 and 446, *schewde* for scheude at 591, *galows* for galous at 598 and 608, etc.)   201–2 (in right margin in MS)   216 *sinfull* sympull   228 *militia* nnilicia   238 (line added in right margin in MS)   252 *gesunne* gesumme   261 *sooner* sonner   276 *to-morn* to morow   286 *in* &   287 *fiere* feere   292 *ita factum est* (added in right margin at line 290 in a different hand)   296 *yowr* ther   303 *ey* eyn   336 (the bracketed completions of this and the following lines are indicated in the MS by a mark for *cetera*)   358 *alone* alonne   385 *shuld* xull   397 *hasta* hastu   422 *New-G[u]ise* Neugyse (also at 429, 441, 457, 518, 602, 625, 628, 635, 662, 694, 790, 804, and 808)   *to-betyn* to beton   442 *Cristys* crastys   453 *flowte* flewte   457 *Ye* Yo   468 *us* as   477 *hem* hym   482 *velan* felow   483 *qwitt* qwyll   509 *Walton* Waltom   516–17 (lines transposed in MS)   518 *ware* ware e   520 *con* com   543 *dylve* dylew   555 (in a different hand, this speech of Titivillus is assigned to New Guise; also at lines 565 and 589)   564 *ellys* cumme (but *ellys* is written in a cancelled version of this line at 562)   581 *wh[i]le* wyll   584–86 (added at foot of the page)   597 *as* ab   618 *her* (the flourish on the final *r* is not expanded to *e*; also at 852)   671 *solde* tolde   678 *mow* may   687 *Curia* Carici   736 *solace* solalace   746 *thin[e]* this   *mutabilité* imutabylyte   748 *on-curtess* ouer curtess   750 *thy* this   751 *Thy* Thys   752 *God and* go on   754 *et omnia* sit omnia   764 *caityfs* cayftys   776 *ny* my   780 *cape* cepe   805 *thye* pye   812 *is* ys ys   825 *pirssid* pirssic   833 *precho* precyse   834 *here* 844 *Incline yowyr capacité; my doctrine is convenient* My doctrine ys conuenient Inclyne yowyr capacite   848 *The* They   854 *I* he   863 *his* yys   870 *prove*

prewe   879 *monitorye* manyterge   894 *libere nolle* liebere nolle   895 *envi[o]us* (unclear in MS; prob. reads "enmys")   906 *condicions* condocions   908 *Serche* Serge

Everyman

Copy text is the "Britwell" copy of an edition printed by John Skot, now located in the Huntington Library (A). Other readings are occasionally adopted, as indicated in the following notes, from three other early editions: the "Huth" copy of an edition printed by Skot, now located in the British Museum (B); a fragment of an edition printed by Richard Pynson, now located in the Bodleian Museum (C); and another fragment of an edition printed by Pynson, in the British Museum (D).   28 *rod* (B) rood   29 *love* lawe   111 *ado that* (B) I do   168 *mad* (B) made   260 *againe come* come agayne   286 *remembre* (B) remenbre   303 *thus* (B) this   317 *them* them go   325 *holde* (BD) bolde   326 *bolde* (BD) holde   471 *forsoke* (D) forsake (AB)   504 *Beholde* (B) Ase   508 *Here* (D) There (AB)   525 *[w]holy* hole (A) holy (BD)   526 *be* (BD) by   558 *voider* (BD) voyce voyder   594 *of thy benignitye* (B) vnworthy in this heuy lyfe   643 *the* (BD) a   647 *It* (B) He   654 *Than* (B) Thau   656 KNOWLEGE Kynrede (also at 666)   671 *wolde* (BD) wyll   678 *may* (BD) myght   682 *in* (BD) in my   684 STRENGTH Strengthe (also at l. 812; speech prefixes standardized throughout)   725 *extreme* (B) excreme   743 *kist* (D) kysse   753 *seven sacramentes* same sacrament   780 *our* (BCD) your   814 *till* (BCD) to   821 *Yet . . . wot* (D) Wyll ye breke promyse that is dette (ABC)   897 *thy . . . thy* (BD) the . . . the

PART SIX   HUMANIST DRAMA

A Mery Play Betwene Johan Johan the Husbande, Tib His Wife, and Sir Johan the Preest (John Heywood?)

Text based on William Rastell's edition of 1533 in the Pepys Collection, Magdalene College, Cambridge (R). References below to MS A are to the edition preserved in the Ashmolean Museum, Oxford   32 *be-shit* beshyte   99 *gossipry* gyssypry   111 TIB (this and the following three speech prefixes are printed one line above their correct positions in R and A; they are corrected in ink in A)   137 *Brawle* Braule   153 *Churche* churthe   191 *thy* the   195 [JOHAN] (the speech prefix is added in R in a later hand)   202 JOHAN Tyb   203 TIB Johan   252 (speech prefix JOHAN repeated unnecessarily)   258 (speech prefix TYB erroneously provided in R and A)   260 TIB Johan   314 (a paragraph sign here)   316 SIR JOHAN Sir Johan, the preest   365 *my* me   374 *stint* stynk   376 *my* me   521 *clatter* clatier   523 *chafe* thafe   567 *wonderous* monderous   594 *trew* treu   600 *notwithstanding* notwithstankyng   656 *thee* thy   659 SIR J. syr   661 *nought* nonght   664 *you* your

The Play of the Weather (John Heywood)

Text based on the edition printed by John Rastell, 1533, in the Pepys Collection, Madgalene College, Cambridge (R). MS A is the edition printed by J. Awdeley, now located in the British Museum. The other two known early editions are that of Anthonie Kytson in the Bodleian, and an imperfect text in University Library, Cambridge. R appears to be the ultimate source for the other three editions.   13 *heven* heueu   82 *honour* houour   164 *We* (A) Well   185 S.D. (in left margin in R; also at ll. 249, 328, 395, 551, and 954)   286 *who* whome (R and other early editions)   331 *Marchaunt* Marchaunte (speech prefixes standardized throughout)   354 *encreaseth* euereaseth   396 *fare* farre   410 *Pleasith* Pleasyth it   461 *our ex-tre[e]*, our onr extre onr   598 *or water* of water   610 *speke* spake   832 *jet* get   873 *sir* I syr   980 *if* yt   1002 BOY ("Mery report," cancelled, in the MS)   1028 *whoso* whose   1100 *her* here   1106 *extremely* extermely   1109 *sixt[h]* syxst   1115 *lacketh* lackelh   1133 *debate* bebate   1171 *obteyne* abteyne   1187 *hire* hyer   1241 *whit* whyte

Wit and Science (John Redford)

Copy text is British Museum Additional MS 15233.   10 REASON Reson (speech prefixes standardized throughout, as in STUDY for *Studye* at 67, IDLENES for *Idelnes* at 355, WOORSHIP for *Woorshyppe* at 644 and 662, and SCIENCE for *syence* at 685)   25 *Of* as (or "af")   31 *he* ye   58 *ap[p]e[a]se* apose   66 DILIGENCE dylygenge   96 *you* your (*changed to* youe?)   157 *her* here   193 *sir* of   199–201 (heavily lined through in the MS)   208 S.D. *Tediousnes* Tedyiousnes   224 S.D. *Strength* strenght   225–60 (The song is added from the end of the MS, fol. [3] y^r. It is labeled "The first song in the play of sience," and clearly belongs here. It begins with two lines of refrain, evidently intended as a title for the song; hence they are omitted here.)   257 *him* here   269 REASON Reson cumth in (in margin)   278 (in the left margin here, MS has "al go out save honest recre"; and, below that, squeezed in between the speech prefix "Wyt" and line 281, "here comfort quiknes & strength go out")   364 *on* one   405 *present* prsesent (?)   457 *what's* whates (and elsewhere)   544 *con* cum   555–56 (in the MS these lines are incorrectly lineated, ending with "now" and "nothing")   572 *New* now (?)   577 *let's* letes   626 (this song is from the end of the MS, following the song at 225–60, and is labeled "The ii song")   653 *your* y^ou   712 *spent* spenn   713 *cumme* cumne   714 *sicke* sykke   840 (speech prefix "Wit" is unnecessarily repeated)   874 INSTRUCCION Insturucion   884 *well* welll   931 *for* (lined through in the MS)   953 *kaitives* kaytyvss   985 S.D. *Diligence* digigence (the song, labeled "The third song," is at the end of the MS)   1017 S.D. *and Confidens* (the & is cancelled in the MS, probably in error; the scribe may have meant to cancel the & before "Diligence")   1051 *dowt* dowgt   1083 *Wit's* wyth   1085 *end* end (the second "end" is crossed through in the MS, seemingly by mistake)   1091 *ye* you

Suggestions for Further Reading

Adams, Joseph Quincy, ed. *Chief Pre-Shakespearean Dramas*. Boston: Houghton Mifflin, 1924.

Anderson, M. D. *Drama and Imagery in English Medieval Churches*. London: Cambridge University Press, 1963.

Axton, Richard. *European Drama of the Early Middle Ages*. London: Hutchinson's University Library, 1974.

Block, K. S., ed. *Ludus Coventriae, or The Plaie Called Corpus Christi*. Early English Text Society. London: Oxford University Press, 1922, reprinted 1960.

Brody, Alan. *The English Mummers and Their Plays: Traces of Ancient Mystery*. Philadelphia: University of Pennsylvania Press, 1969.

Cameron, Kenneth, and Stanley J. Kahrl. "Staging the N-Town Cycle," *Theatre Notebook*, xxi (1967), 122–38, and subsequent issue.

Cawley, A. C., ed. *Everyman and Medieval Miracle Plays*, 2nd ed. New York: E. P. Dutton, 1959.

———, ed. *The Wakefield Pageants in the Towneley Cycle*. Manchester: Manchester University Press, 1958.

Chambers, E. K. *The Mediaeval Stage*. 2 vols. London: Oxford University Press, 1903.

Collins, Fletcher, Jr. *The Production of Medieval Church Music-Drama*. Charlottesville: University of Virginia Press, 1972.

Craig, Hardin. *English Religious Drama of the Middle Ages*. London: Oxford University Press, 1955.

———, ed. *Two Coventry Corpus Christi Plays*. Early English Text Society. London: Oxford University Press, 1902, 2nd ed. 1957.

Creeth, Edmund, ed. *Tudor Plays*. Garden City, N.Y.: Doubleday, 1966.

Davis, Norman, ed. *Non-Cycle Plays and Fragments*. Early English Text Society. London: Oxford University Press, 1970.

Deimling, Hermann, ed. *The Chester Plays*. 2 vols. Early English Text Society. London: Oxford University Press, 1892, reprinted 1926, 1959.

Denny, Neville, ed. *Medieval Drama*. Stratford-upon-Avon Studies 16, gen. eds. Malcolm Bradbury and David Palmer. London: Edward Arnold, 1973.

Eccles, Mark, ed. *The Macro Plays*. Early English Text Society. London: Oxford University Press, 1969.

England, George, and Alfred W. Pollard, eds. *The Towneley Plays*. Early English Text Society. London: Kegan, Paul, Trench, Trübner, 1897.

Frank, Grace. *The Medieval French Drama*. London: Oxford University Press, 1954.

Furnivall, F. J., ed. *The Digby Plays*. Early English Text Society. London: Oxford University Press, 1896, reprinted 1930, 1967.

Gardiner, Harold C., S.J. *Mysteries' End: An Investigation of the Last Days of the Medieval Religious Stage*. New Haven: Yale University Press, 1946.

Harbage, Alfred, ed., rev. S. Schoenbaum. *Annals of English Drama 975–1700*. Philadelphia: University of Pennsylvania Press, 1940, rev. ed. 1964.

Hardison, O. B., Jr. *Christian Rite and Christian Drama in the Middle Ages*. Baltimore: Johns Hopkins Press, 1965.

Harris, Markham, trans. *The Cornish Ordinalia*. Washington, D.C.: Catholic University of America Press, 1969.

Hosley, Richard. "Three Kinds of Outdoor Theatre before Shakespeare," *American Journal of Theatre History*, XII (1971), 1–33.

James, Montague Rhodes, ed. *The Apocryphal New Testament*. London: Oxford University Press, 1924.

Johnston, Alexandra F., and Margaret Dorrell. "The Doomsday Pageant of the York Mercers, 1433," *Leeds Studies in English*, New Series, V (1971), 29–34.

———. "The York Mercers and Their Pageant of Doomsday, 1433–1526," *Leeds Studies in English*, New Series, VI (1973), 10–35.

Kahrl, Stanley J. *Traditions of Medieval English Drama*. London: Hutchinson's University Library, 1974.

Kolve, V. A. *The Play Called Corpus Christi*. London: Edward Arnold, 1966.

Longsworth, Robert. *The Cornish Ordinalia: Religion and Dramaturgy*. Cambridge, Mass.: Harvard University Press, 1967.

Manly, John Matthews, ed. *Specimens of the Pre-Shakesperean Drama*. 2 vols. Boston: Ginn, 1897, reprinted 1925; New York: Dover, 1967.

Nelson, Alan. *The Medieval English Stage: Corpus Christi Pageants and Plays*. Chicago: University of Chicago Press, 1974.

Nicoll, Allardyce. *Masks, Mimes, and Miracles: Studies in the Popular Theatre*. London: Harrap, 1931.

Owst, G. R. *Literature and Pulpit in Medieval England*. Cambridge, Eng.: Cambridge University Press, 1933. 2nd rev. ed. Oxford: B. Blackwell, 1961.

Potter, Robert. *The English Morality Play: Origins, History, and Influence of a Dramatic Tradition*. London: Routledge and Kegan Paul, 1975.

Prosser, Eleanor. *Drama and Religion in the English Mystery Plays*. Stanford, Calif.: Stanford University Press, 1961.

Reed, A. W. *Early Tudor Drama*. London: Methuen, 1926.

Rose, Martial, ed. *The Wakefield Mystery Plays*. Garden City, N.Y.: Doubleday, 1962.

Rossiter, A. P. *English Drama from Early Times to the Elizabethans*. London: Hutchinson's University Library, 1950. New York: Barnes and Noble, 1967.

Salter, F. M. *Mediaeval Drama in Chester*. Toronto: University of Toronto Press, 1955.

Schell, Edgar T., and J. D. Shuchter, eds. *English Morality Plays and Moral Interludes*. New York: Holt, Rinehart and Winston, 1969.

Smith, Lucy Toulmin, ed. *York Plays*. Oxford: Clarendon Press, 1885.

Smoldon, William L. "The Melodies of the Medieval Church Dramas and Their Significance," in *Medieval English Drama*, ed. Jerome Taylor and Alan Nelson. Chicago: University of Chicago Press, 1972.

———. "The Origins of the *Quem Quaeritis* Trope and the Easter Sepulchre Music-Dramas, as Demonstrated by their Musical Settings," in *The Medieval Drama*, ed. Sandro Sticca. Albany: State University of New York Press, 1972.

Southern, Richard. *The Medieval Theatre in the Round*. London: Faber and Faber, 1957.

Spivack, Bernard. *Shakespeare and the Allegory of Evil*. New York: Columbia University Press, 1958.

Sticca, Sandro, ed. *The Medieval Drama*. Albany: State University of New York Press, 1972.

Symons, Thomas D., trans. and ed. *The Monastic Agreement of the Monks and Nuns of the English Nation*. London: Nelson, 1953.

Taylor, Jerome, and Alan H. Nelson, eds. *Medieval English Drama: Essays Critical and Contextual*. Chicago: University of Chicago Press, 1972.

Thomas, R. G., ed. *Ten Miracle Plays*. Evanston, Ill.: Northwestern University Press, 1966.

Wickham, Glynne. *Early English Stages: 1300 to 1660*. 2 vols. London: Routledge and Kegan Paul, 1959–1972.

Williams, Arnold. *The Characterization of Pilate in the Towneley Plays*. East Lansing: Michigan State College Press, 1950.

———. *The Drama of Medieval England*. East Lansing: Michigan State University Press, 1961.

Woolf, Rosemary. *The English Mystery Plays*. Berkeley and Los Angeles: University of California Press, 1972.

Young, Karl. *The Drama of the Medieval Church*. 2 vols. London: Oxford University Press, 1933.

Credits

Iron Age Communities
in Britain

Iron Age Communities in Britain

An account of England, Scotland and Wales
from the Seventh Century BC until the Roman Conquest

Barry Cunliffe

London and New York

First published 1991
by Routledge
11 New Fetter Lane, London EC4P 4EE

Simultaneously published in the USA and Canada
by Routledge
a division of Routledge, Chapman and Hall, Inc.
29 West 35th Street, New York, NY 10001

Typeset by Touchpaper (Oxford) Ltd
Printed and bound at the University Press, Cambridge

British Library Cataloguing in Publication Data
Cunliffe, Barry
 Iron age communities in Britain : an account of England,
 Scotland and Wales from the seventh century BC until the
 Roman conquest. 3rd. edn (Archaeology of Britain).
 1. British Iron Age civilization
 I. Title   II. Series
 936.1

Library of Congress Cataloging in Publication Data
Cunliffe, Barry W.
 Iron age communities in Britain : an account of England, Scotland,
 and Wales from the seventh century BC until the Roman conquest /
 Barry Cunliffe. – 3rd ed.
    p.   cm.
 Includes bibliographical references and index.
 1. Iron age – Great Britain.   2. Great Britain – History – To 55 B.C.
 3. Great Britain – Antiquities, Celtic.   4. Britons.   I. Title
 GN780.22.G7086   1991
 936.1–dc20   90–24328

ISBN 0–415–05416–8

Who the first inhabitants of Britain were,
whether natives or immigrants, remains obscure;
one must remember we are dealing with barbarians.

Tacitus, *Agricola*, 2

Contents

Preface to the first edition

When, in 1969, I mentioned to my colleague Leo Rivet that I was thinking of writing a book on the British Iron Age, he said that it could not be done. Now that I have finished the work, I am inclined to agree with him. To write a complete account of the period *is* impossible. Thought on the subject is changing rapidly; established dictums which have found worldwide support for decades are being overthrown; and new ways are developing for looking at familiar material. While the actual body of data increases only gradually, the new questions now being asked of it are enlarging our understanding dramatically. Indeed, some might consider it to be too early to write a book such as this, but since it will *always* be too early a beginning must be made sometime.

The most difficult problem to be faced in producing a work of this kind lies in selecting and balancing the material. Three types of selection have been made here. First, Ireland has been omitted, partly through problems of space and partly because I have no first-hand familiarity of the sites and material. Second, I have attempted to limit comment on the vast mass of interpretive writing which befogs the actual data and much of which is now redundant, always preferring to begin with the factual material and build up to a synthesis. It is surprisingly difficult to distinguish fact from interpretation in many examples of the earlier publication of primary material. The third type of selection is liable to be more open to criticism – that is the actual choice of which evidence to include and which to leave out. Any such choice is likely to be biased by personal interests. I can only hope that I have given a balanced review of the material and have done justice to most of the major issues and problems.

The arrangement of the book falls into two parts. [The chapters have been rearranged in the third edition.] Chapters 2 to 9 deal with Britain from a chronological and regional standpoint, underlining minor points of difference from one area or period to another, while chapters 10 to 16 are concerned with the broader mechanisms at work which tend to slur over the minor differences. The problems of constructing theoretical models are referred to in the historical chapter 1 and again finally in chapter 17. Such an approach, while necessitating some repetition, has the advantage of allowing the threads to be more loosely spread out for examination. The fabric of which they form a part is, and should remain, loosely knit. To be of any lasting value, a work of this kind should be thoroughly illustrated and referenced and periodically revised. The publishers have encouraged the first and will, I hope, subsequently request the second. One slightly novel procedure has been adopted with regard to the referencing of sites. To include references in the text would be unnecessarily cumbersome, particularly when several locations are mentioned in a single line. Instead, a list of principal sites is provided in appendix C, in which the major published sources are given. Similarly, with radiocarbon dates, the nature of the sample, the laboratory number and other details are all given in a separate appendix (B). The illustration of a large quantity of pottery referred to in the main text has also been relegated to an appendix (A).

Finally, I would like to thank the large number of individuals and institutions who have helped during the preparation of this work and in particular those museum staffs who have allowed me to work through their reserve collections, making the occasion as comfortable as possible. Several bodies have been kind enough to supply photographs from which the plates have been reproduced, and one need hardly emphasize the enormous debt of gratitude to those authors whose illustrations have been redrawn for the text figures, an undertaking in which I was considerably aided by the Cartographic Unit of the Department of Geography, University of Southampton, who undertook to add the lettering and scales. Lastly, I would like to thank Frances Cunliffe and Denise Brenchley for translating the manuscript of this book into a typescript, and Jane Holdsworth for her help and advice in all aspects of the work during the last stages of preparation.

Barry Cunliffe
Southampton,
31 December 1971

Preface to the second edition

The first edition of this book was sold out rather more rapidly than was anticipated. The publishers accordingly invited me to choose between having the original work reprinted or revising it for a second edition. I gladly chose the latter course, partly because it gave me the opportunity to correct a number of minor errors which had escaped notice at proof stage, but largely because it allowed me to incorporate a selection of the impressive mass of new material which has been published during the last five years. In all, some 300 new books and papers directly relevant to our theme have had to be considered.

All sections of the book have been revised and updated, but some aspects of the subject are developing more rapidly than others and have called for more extensive revision. The problems posed by the significance and development of hillforts are now more clearly appreciated, and results from excavations in various parts of the country are beginning to throw a completely new light upon the social dynamics of the period, while fieldwork and excavations in Essex and the Midlands are together showing that these areas, previously blank on the distribution map, were originally densely settled with expanding populations. In the later periods, conventional interpretations of the coin evidence are currently being challenged, requiring us to rethink previously-held views about both the events and the economic and social development of the last century and a half of British prehistory. These are a few of the areas where current work has required extensive revision.

Another aspect about which a great deal has been written is Iron Age art. It may be felt that the comparatively few pages that have been devoted here to the subject do not do it justice. This may be so, but in a book such as this, which deals principally with communities and their social dynamics, it could be argued that the vagaries of art-historical argument deserve little place. We can, however, look forward to a time when the artistic achievements of our Iron Age communities are at last presented, by those who specialize in the field, in their proper context as part of the culture-process which as archaeologists we are attempting to understand.

Since the first edition of this book was rewritten, local government reorganization, involving the redrawing of the county boundaries, has taken place. Since it will be some time before we become familiar with the names and extents of the new counties, and since old publications relate to pre-reorganization boundaries, the pre-1974 counties are retained in the body of the text, but in the list of principal sites, which constitutes appendix C, new county names are given as well as the old.

The distribution maps have for the most part been updated from published sources, but in the case of coins I have made use of the Index of Celtic Coins maintained by Professor Sheppard Frere in the Institute of Archaeology, Oxford.

The revision of this book was undertaken during the autumn of 1976 and takes into account all work available to me up to the end of that year. In producing it I have been greatly encouraged by the publishers, in particular by Norman Franklin. I would also like to record my gratitude to all friends and colleagues who have helped by offering new material and by discussion and criticism. I owe a particular debt of gratitude to Angela Ambrose for undertaking the not inconsiderable secretarial work involved, Mike Rouillard for helping to revise and correct the line illustrations, and to Tim Ambrose, who has been a constant help and thoughtful critic throughout.

Barry Cunliffe
Oxford,
31 December 1976

Preface to the third edition

The second edition of this book was published ten years ago as an updated version of a volume originally completed in 1971 and first published in 1974. The old introductions, renamed here prefaces, have been left for the sake of idle curiosity. The volume which follows is substantially revised – it has had to be for in the last decade about 700 new papers and books have been published, all directly relevant to our theme, adding a wealth of new information. Some reflection of all this can be gauged by comparing the length of the bibliographies of the second and third editions, remembering that they are highly selective!

The mass of new evidence and the quite radical change of emphasis which has occurred in prehistoric studies has required major changes to be made in the text. While for the most part the chapter headings have been retained the chapters have been grouped and two new introductory sections inserted: chapter 2 Time and space and chapter 11 Themes. New chapters have also been added dealing with Food producing strategies (chapter 15) and Warfare (chapter 18) and there have been readjustments between the contents of chapters 7 and 8 reflecting a new approach to our understanding of the Late Iron Age in the south-east. Two chapters, chapter 6 Protohistory to history and chapter 20 Iron Age society and social change, have been completely rewritten. All other chapters have enjoyed some modification and additional material has been added liberally where relevant.

All line drawings for this edition have been prepared anew by Alison Wilkins and the half-tone illustrations have been augmented. I am most grateful to colleagues and institutions who have provided photographs and to Ms Wilkins for her skill and hard work in preparing the artwork. I also owe an enormous debt of gratitude to Lynda Smithson for typing the entire text on word processor with great efficiency and minute attention to detail. Without her dedication and very high standards this work would have taken very much longer to produce and would have been the poorer.

The revision of the text took place between September 1988 and September 1989 and has incorporated all published works available to me up to that date. The task has been an arduous one, far more demanding than I had anticipated, but it has been immensely enjoyable. The pace at which new information is appearing and our conceptual frameworks are changing leaves little doubt that Iron Age studies are vigorous in Britain today: we have advanced significantly in our understanding of our Iron Age ancestors in the last ten years. Let us hope that the next decade of work will be equally as invigorating.

Barry Cunliffe
Oxford,
September 1989

Part I
Introduction

1
The development of Iron Age studies

It is not proposed in this chapter to indulge in an extensive and somewhat incestuous examination of the growth of Iron Age studies in Britain simply for the sake of conventional completeness, nor for the specious exercise of holding up to ridicule the views of previous generations who have written on the subject. But some idea of how patterns of thought have developed to their present state is essential, not only because the models of the past have necessarily influenced the interpretations, and indeed the gathering, of the facts, but also because current views may tend to overreact against established dogma.

That an 'Iron Age' existed at all was suggested by the Danish archaeologist, C.J. Thomsen in a book published in 1836, but it was not until G. Ramsauer's excavation at Hallstatt, between 1846 and 1862, and the discoveries made at La Tène in 1858, that any permanent chronological divisions could be made. Then followed several schemes: C. Schumacher divided the Hallstatt material into four groups: A (1000–800 BC), B (800-700), C (700–600) and D (600–500); while G.O.A. Montelius, working on French discoveries, propounded three periods for the La Tène epoch: I (400–250 BC), II (250–150 BC) and III (150–1 BC). Subsequently P. Reinecke, J. Déchelette, R. Viollier and others evolved finer and differing classifications influenced by new material and by regional considerations. It was against this background that the British finds came to be interpreted.

The first half of the nineteenth century saw the gradual amassing in museums and private collections of quantities of Iron Age finds, usually tools, weapons and art objects, brought together by casual discovery and by the pilferings of the early barrow diggers like the Rev. E.W. Stillingfleet, who managed to excavate between 100 and 200 barrows of the Arras culture between 1815 and 1817. Barrow-sacking in high Victorian style continued to produce Iron Age finds from east Yorkshire throughout the century, but ended with the carefully observed researches of J.R. Mortimer, published between 1895 and 1911. Outside Yorkshire the British Iron Age was not susceptible to this type of acquisitive excavation, and the bulk of the finds continued to be made by accident. The emphasis of the early collectors was naturally enough upon works of art. In 1857, the year before the discovery at La Tène, J. Thurnham listed objects of 'Late British Art' and even six years later, when Sir Wollaston Franks illustrated a series of La Tène objects at the British Museum, he was forced to refer to them as 'Late Keltic' for want of a more precise terminology. With the development of the Continental Hallstatt and La Tène classifications after 1872, however, British archaeologists were provided with a simple system with which to compare their own material; thus gradually the European nomenclature gained acceptance.

In the second half of the nineteenth century, excavations began to be mounted on occupation sites and hillforts in an attempt to understand the people and their way of life. This was a marked advance on the somewhat sterile art-historical approach. Between 1857 and 1858 the first large-scale excavation of a settlement site was undertaken at Standlake in Oxfordshire by Stephen Stone, in advance of gravel-working. Altogether 134 pits were exposed, and were duly reported to the Society of Antiquaries. Ten years after the Standlake excavation, a similar area of Iron Age settlement was cleared at Highfield, Fisherton, near Salisbury. At both sites it was naturally the more obvious features such as pits and gullies that were examined, but quantities of occupation rubbish were recovered and gradually the nature of Iron Age peasant settlement began to force itself on the attention of an archaeological world hitherto blinded by the quality of a few art objects.

The next major advances were made by General A.H.L.F. Pitt Rivers. Following a meticulously recorded but relatively small-scale excavation at the Caburn, Sussex, in 1877–8, during which he had sectioned the ramparts as well as clearing out pits (Figure 1.1), he finally turned his attention to his Cranborne Chase estates, where between 1880 and 1890 he totally excavated the two settlements of Woodcuts and Rotherley Down, and sampled the hillfort at Winklebury, Wilts. (Pitt Rivers 1887, 1888). His work was of an exceptionally high standard and was published in a detailed manner never before achieved. It emphasized two things above all: the value of considering the commonly occurring debris of occupation as the principal means by which people and their lives could be reconstructed, and the importance of large-scale regional studies.

The last decade of the nineteenth century saw the unremitting development of these two principles. In Devon the Dartmoor Exploration Committee was set up in 1894, and within the first ten years of its existence had examined twenty sites and excavated nearly 150 hut circles, under the direction of S. Baring-Gould. At the turn of the century Baring-Gould extended his interests into south-west Wales with the excavations of the hillforts of St David's Head and Moel Trigarn. Other hillforts were now receiving attention: excavations at Worlebury in Somerset were finally published in 1902 at the same time as the first adequate consideration of Bigbury in Kent.

Pitt Rivers's dictum of large-scale excavation was extended into Somerset by his assistant H.St George Gray who, in conjunction with A. Bulleid, began the famous excavations at the so-called Glastonbury Lake Village in 1892, work which was to continue until 1907 and was finally published in 1911 and 1917 (Figure 1.2). Nor were regional studies neglected: in Wiltshire Benjamin Cunnington and his wife Maud undertook annually an impressive series of excavations: Oliver's Camp (published 1908), Oare (1909), Knap Hill (1911), Casterley Camp (1913) and Lidbury (1917), but the most famous of all was their work at All Cannings Cross between 1911 and 1922, finally published in 1923. A two-year programme at Hengistbury Head started in 1911 (Bushe-Fox 1915); excavations began on the Somerset village of Meare under the direction of Bulleid and Gray in 1910, and between 1908 and 1912 the cave of Wookey Hole was carefully examined (Balch 1914) (Figure 1.3).

After the First World War, discoveries continued to be made and reported in increasing numbers: Hallstatt style pottery from Eastbourne, excavations at Abington Pigotts in

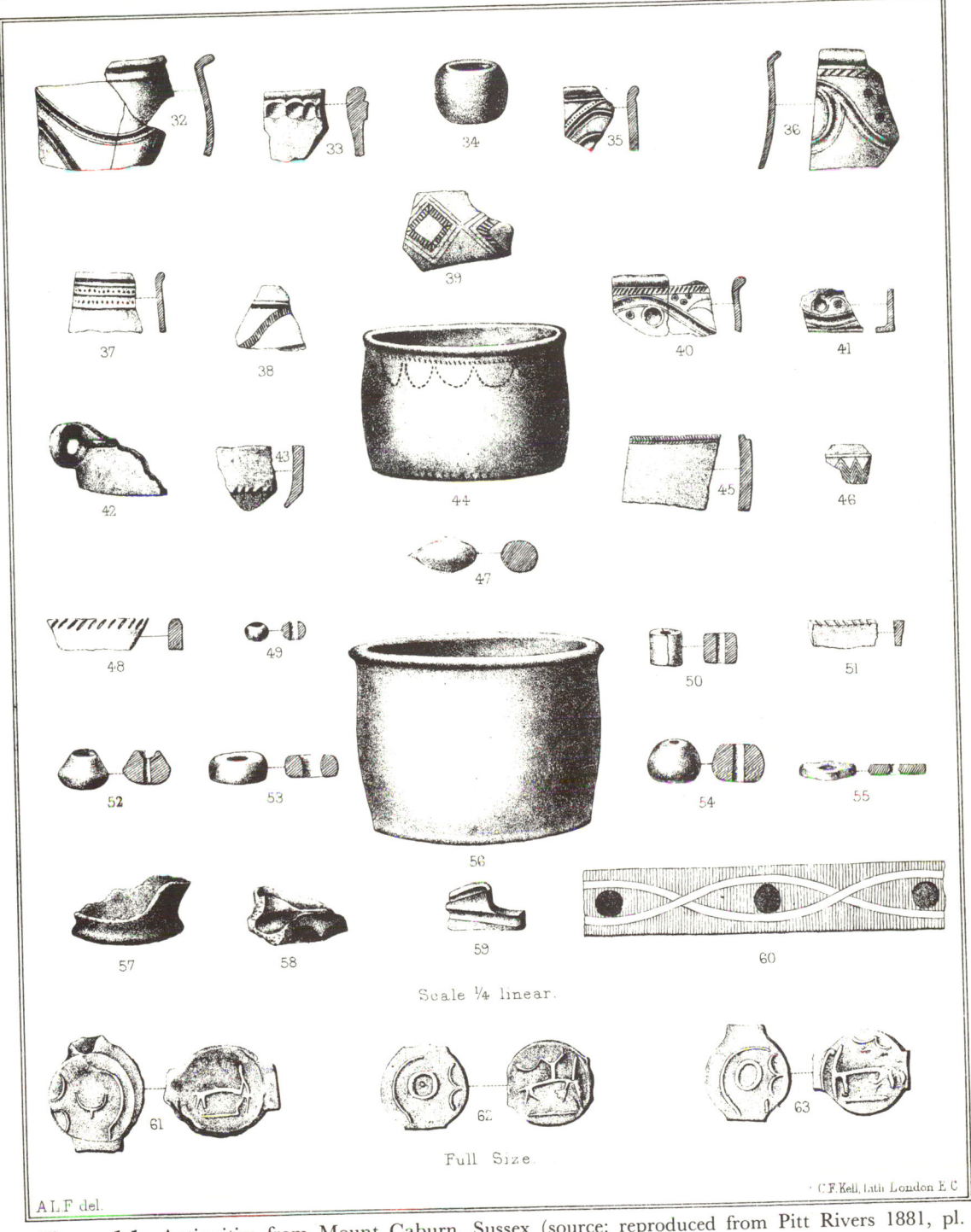

Figure 1.1 Antiquities from Mount Caburn, Sussex (source: reproduced from Pitt Rivers 1881, pl. XXV).

Figure 1.2 Excavations at Meare Village East, August 1935. St George Gray stands on the left (photo: Somerset County Museum Service and Somerset Archaeological and Natural History Society).

Cambridgeshire, Park Brow in Sussex and Fifield Bavant in Wiltshire, all in 1924, and excavations at Swallowcliffe Down and Figsbury in Wiltshire in 1925. Thus by the year of publication of the second edition of the British Museum's *Guide to the Antiquities of the Early Iron Age* (R.A. Smith 1925), a vast mass of material – common artefacts – had been amassed to redress the balance of the collectors' pieces, and it is much to the credit of Reginald Smith, the *Guide*'s compiler and a Deputy Keeper of the Museum, that so much was said of these common things. Iron Age communities were at last being considered in all their aspects.

With the rapid increase in the bulk of the potential evidence, classifications and interpretation developed in parallel. The turning point was undoubtedly the discovery in 1886 of the Belgic cemetery at Aylesford and its publication four years later by A.J. (later Sir Arthur) Evans (Figure 1.4). The report was an outstanding contribution to Iron Age studies: in it Evans characterized the Aylesford people, showing their differences from the inhabitants of the rest of Britain, and tracing their immediate origins to northern France and ultimately back through the Marnian culture to the Illyro-Italic cultures of the fifth century. After a masterly consideration of the metalwork, he concluded that the Aylesford cemetery dated to after 150 BC and went on to link the Aylesford culture to the statement by Caesar that the coastal parts of Britain had been

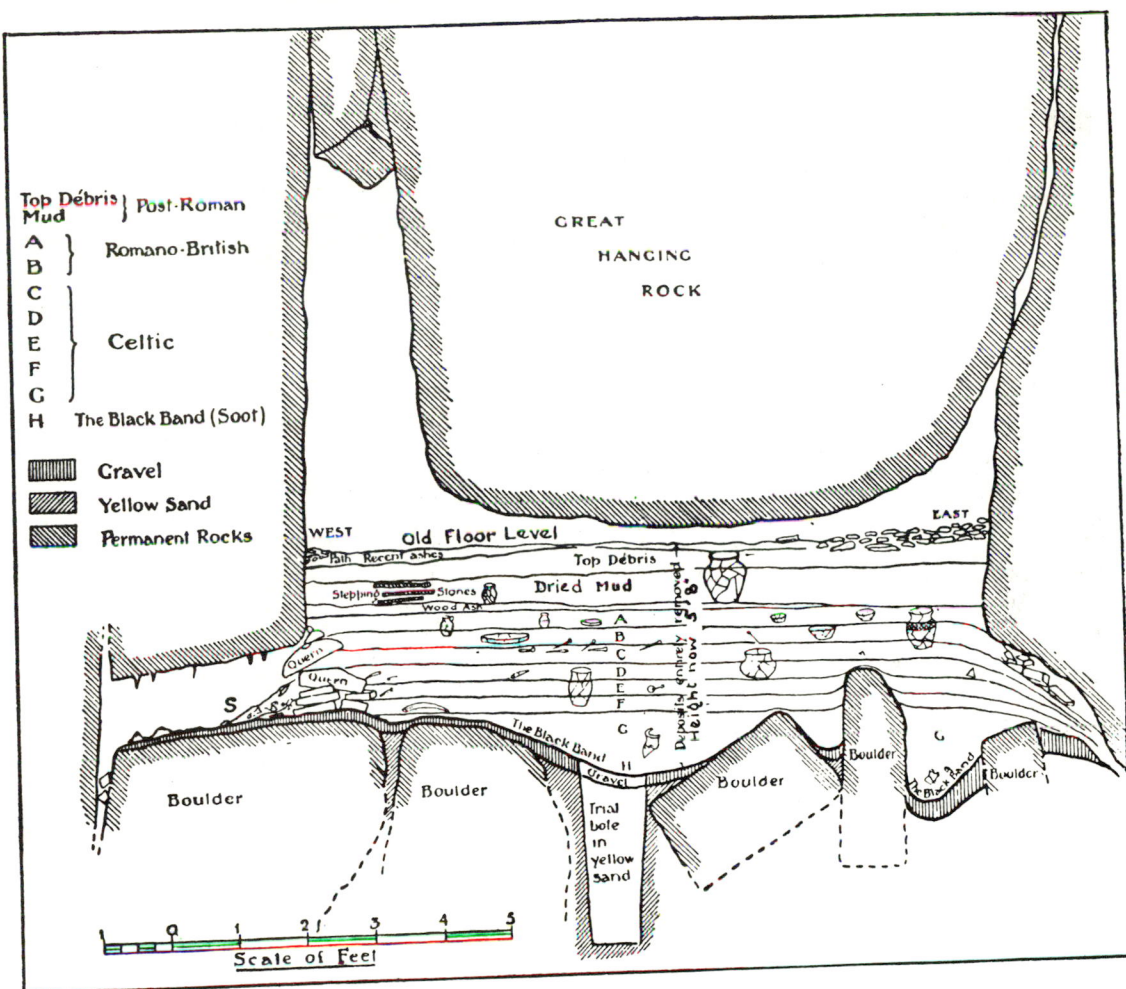

Figure 1.3 Stratified Iron Age deposits at Wookey Hole, Somerset (source: reproduced from Balch 1914, pl. IX).

settled by Belgic invaders. In spite of a somewhat cursory treatment of the archaeological evidence by T. Rice Holmes in his famous work *Ancient Britain and the Invasions of Julius Caesar* (1907), Evans's conclusions were widely accepted and further consolidated by Reginald Smith's publication of the rich Belgic grave groups from Welwyn in 1912. Some geographical precision was given to the distribution of the Aylesford culture by Sir Cyril Fox in his *Archaeology of the Cambridge Region* (1923), but he retained reservations about its exact identity. New discoveries of a major cemetery at Swarling, Kent, in 1921 and its subsequent publication by J.P. Bushe-Fox in 1925, however, firmly established the Aylesford–Swarling culture as an intrusive element but refined Evans's dating, showing that there was nothing with the burials earlier than 75 BC.

With the demonstrable reality of a Belgic invasion and the growing awareness of the intrusive nature of the Arras culture represented in the La Tène style barrow cemeteries of Yorkshire, a

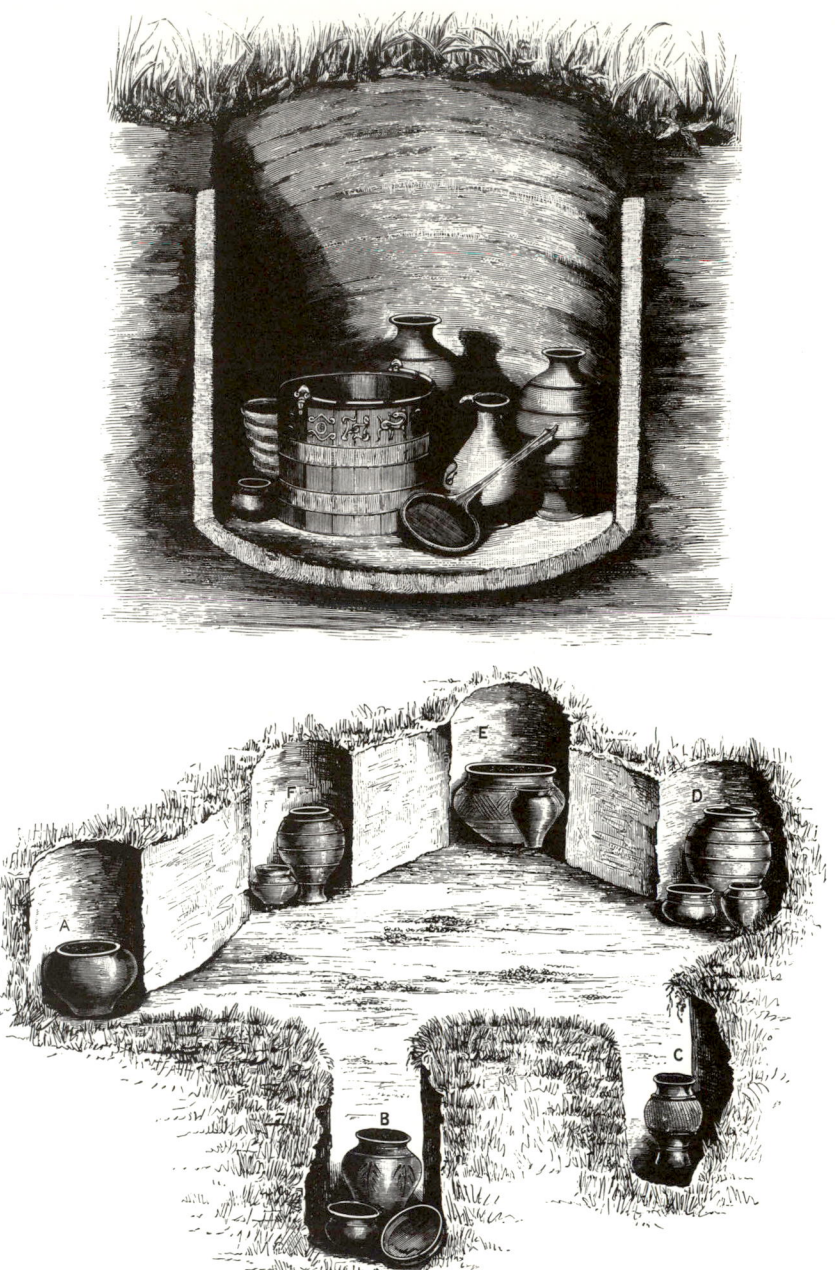

Figure 1.4 The Aylesford cemetery, Kent (source: reproduced from A.J. Evans 1890, Figs 1 and 4).

climate of opinion arose in the first two decades of the twentieth century which considered invasion to be the principal, and sometimes the sole, cause of change. Such views were well rooted in the ideology of Victorian imperialism: after all, nineteenth-century colonial history could produce many striking parallels. In 1912, J. Abercromby suggested that the so-called Deverel–Rimbury urns were introduced into Britain from the Lausitz culture area of central Europe between 700 and 650 BC, and ten years later O.G.S. Crawford developed the invasion theory further by suggesting that the immigrants were Goidelic Celts, but arriving a century or so earlier, bringing with them weapon-types which characterized the Late Bronze Age. H. Peake elaborated the idea still further in *The Bronze Age and the Celtic World* (1922) in which, arguing principally from the evidence of the swords, he proposed three invasions: the first about 1200; the second about 900, bringing much of the Deverel–Rimbury assemblage; and the third about 300 BC, representing the intrusion of the Brythonic Celts, after iron and elements of the La Tène culture had already arrived as the result of trade.

While the Abercromby–Crawford–Peake invasion hypothesis was evolving, discoveries were made at Hengistbury Head and All Cannings Cross of assemblages containing furrowed haematite-coated bowls and coarse finger-impressed wares. The Continental Hallstatt analogies were at once evident. Moreover, the association at All Cannings Cross of haematite pottery, finger-impressed wares like Deverel–Rimbury types and bronze implements suggested to some that the All Cannings Cross community represented an intrusive population, which Peake readily ascribed to his second invasion. Maud Cunnington summed up the situation in the following words:

> A big movement of people northwards on the continent, whether the incentive was search for better farming land, or mere love of adventure, was bound sooner or later to make itself felt in Britain. This invasion is not likely to have come about as a single incursion but . . . by a long continued series of small incursions and colonisation.
>
> (1923, 22)

So by 1925 linguistics, implement typology, settlement archaeology and historical parallels were in broad agreement: a complex of Late Bronze to Early Iron Age invasions led to the All Cannings Cross style of culture before the middle of the first millennium; an incursion from the Marne gave rise to the Yorkshire barrow culture in the third century; and the Belgae colonized the south-east of Britain in the first century.

The discoveries of the next five years were, however, to complicate the issue. Several new hillforts were being excavated, including Ham Hill, Somerset (1925–7); Chun, Cornwall (published 1927); the Caburn, Sussex (published 1927); Bury Hill, Glos. (published 1929); the Trundle, Sussex (published 1929 and 1931); and St Catharine's Hill, Hants. (excavated 1925–8 and published 1930). New groups of finds from occupation sites at Findon Park, Sussex, and Scarborough, Yorks., were published in 1928, while in the previous year Fox's paper on La Tène I fibulae had appeared. In this atmosphere of rapid new discovery Christopher Hawkes produced three important papers: the first, entitled 'The earliest Iron Age culture of Britain', appeared in the St Catharine's Hill report (Hawkes, Myres and Stevens 1930); the second, 'Hill forts', was published in *Antiquity* for March 1931; while the third, written with Gerald Dunning and called 'The Belgae of Gaul and Britain', appeared in the *Archaeological Journal* in the same year. These three papers totally altered the direction of thought on the Iron Age and paved the way for the next three decades of constructive study. Taking account of all the evidence at the time available, a new scheme was proposed as a logical development of the invasion hypothesis bandied about somewhat loosely in the previous twenty years. Hawkes visualized a massive series of migratory movements among the Celts in central and northern Europe, beginning in the

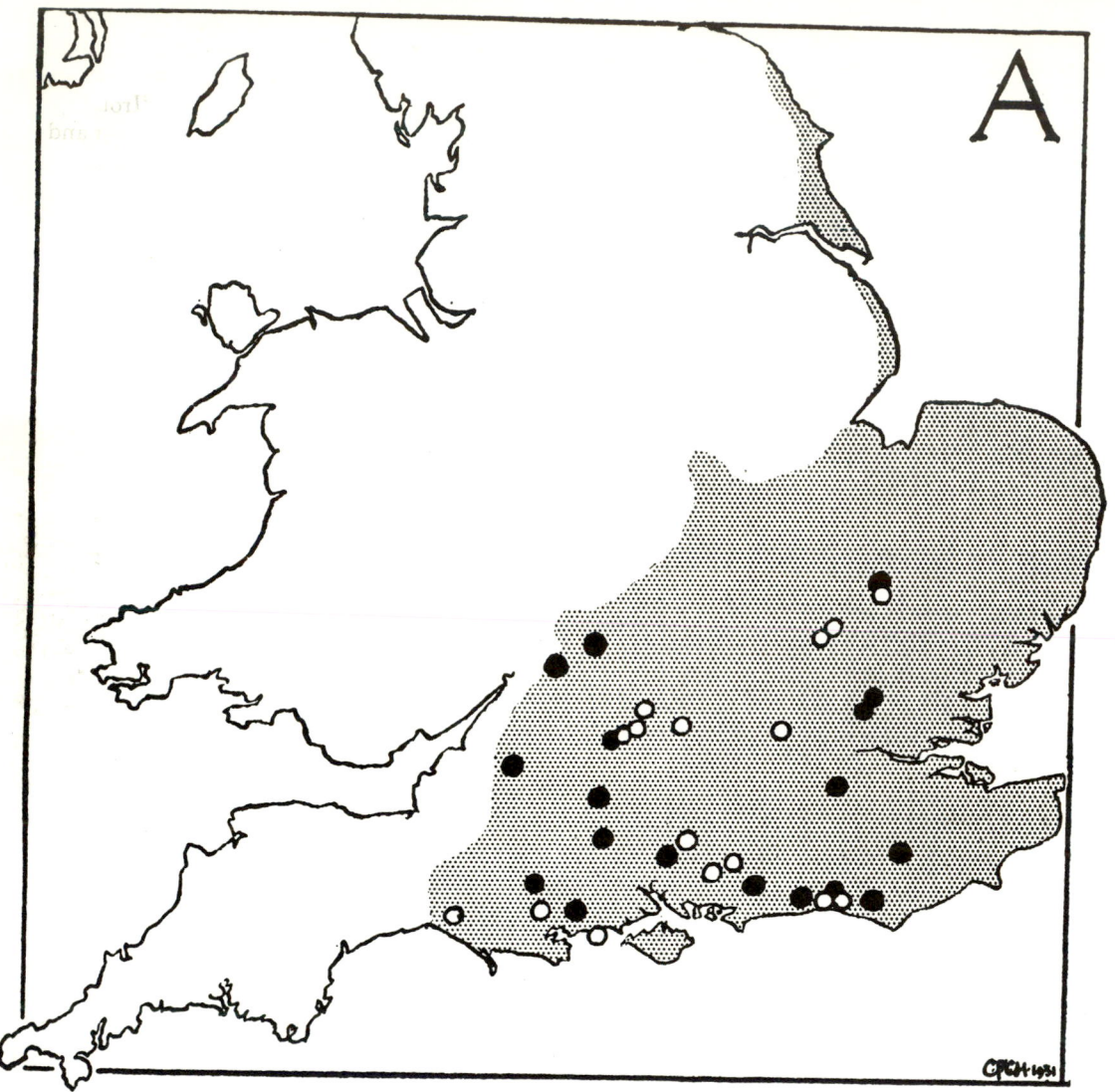

Figure 1.5 Distribution of Iron Age hillforts, period A (source: reproduced from C.F.C. Hawkes 1931, Fig. 1).

seventh century or before (Figure 1.5). 'It reached its height in the sixth century, when those groups who crossed over to Britain became our principal Early Iron Age immigrants.' Other Celts in the Late Hallstatt stage of culture who were displaced from France also migrated to Britain.

Thus was completed our widespread agglomeration of Late Hallstatt immigrant groups, predominantly Celtic in blood, but inevitably including other racial elements out of the melting pot of contemporary Europe. Fusing here and there with the Late Bronze Age peoples, they established

Iron Age civilisation all over the south and south east of Britain . . . The main block of their area remained in their undisturbed tenure till the first century B.C., and their civilisation, though essentially of Hallstatt character, soon began to absorb influence from the La Tène culture across the Channel. Thus it really requires a name of its own: here we shall be content to call it 'Iron Age A', and the succeeding immigrant cultures 'Iron Age B' and 'C'. The former, in the south west and north east, merely bit into its fringes; it was only the latter, brought by the Belgae, that superseded it in its real home, and in some districts, notably east Sussex, it was never superseded at all till the Roman conquest.

(C.F.C. Hawkes 1931, 64)

Hawkes, then, visualized a complex folk movement impinging in stages on south-east Britain in the sixth century, giving rise to his Iron Age A culture. Life was at times troubled and great hillforts had to be built, 'for as there was no doubt constant tribal bickering, warfare must always have been liable to spring from the background into the foreground of existence' (ibid., 76). Early in the fourth century a new invasion took place: La Tène peoples from Spain, the Atlantic seaboard and Brittany thrust their way into Cornwall (an idea put forward by E.T. Leeds in 1927, following his excavation at Chun Castle) and spread into Devon, Somerset, Dorset and the Cotswolds, 'absorbing or driving out such Iron Age A people as they found, and superseding their settlements' (ibid., 77). These were the Iron Age B people: Spanish La Tène I fibulae, distinctive decorated pottery and historical contacts connected with the tin trade could be quoted in support of this view. In this country the south-western Iron Age B immigrants built great multivallate earthworks and lived in the Somerset lake villages, making highly ornamented pottery. The northern counterpart to the south-western B invasions came in the third century with the incursion of a band of immigrants from Gaul, spreading from Yorkshire to the Cambridge region. These northern Iron Age B peoples eventually linked up with the south-western invaders by means of the Jurassic zone, encircling the A people of the south-east.

The third major series of invasions, giving rise to Iron Age C, began in about 75 BC with an influx of Belgic tribesmen from northern Gaul initially into Kent and the Thames valley (A.J. Evans 1890), spreading subsequently into Essex, the Fens and the Cherwell valley (Figure 1.6). Later, soon after Caesar's expedition, a second Belgic invasion – refugees from the Roman advance – took place further west (Bushe-Fox 1925) and spread from the Hampshire harbours into Berkshire and Wiltshire, and probably west Wessex, with subsequent extensions into Dorset and some parts of Somerset.

This précis of the original ABC system has been laid out in some detail because the scheme was to serve as the basis of Iron Age studies in Britain for more than thirty years. The scheme was not revolutionary; it took over the main elements of the earlier historical model with a few additions. Its importance lay in its break from the stranglehold of Continental terminology and in its elegant simplicity. British Iron Age studies had at last come of age.

The restatement did not pass unchallenged: in 1932 Maud Cunnington (1932c) threw doubt upon the whole concept of a second Belgic invasion. She considered that the change to bead-rimmed wheel-made pottery did not herald an incursion of new people, but merely a technological advance brought about by the introduction of the potter's wheel. Hawkes replied to her criticisms (Hawkes and Dunning 1932) and the second Belgic invasion stayed.

The theorizing and consolidation of 1930 and 1931 focused British archaeological activity firmly upon the problems of the Iron Age. Many relationships were hazy and some parts of the country were virtually unstudied. It was natural in such a climate that many excavators should decide to concentrate their energies upon Iron Age sites. In the next decade the results were impressive. The publication of hillfort excavations came thick and fast. Hawkes writing in 1931 could list only thirty-seven hillforts where the defences had been sectioned; in less than ten years the number had more than doubled.[1]

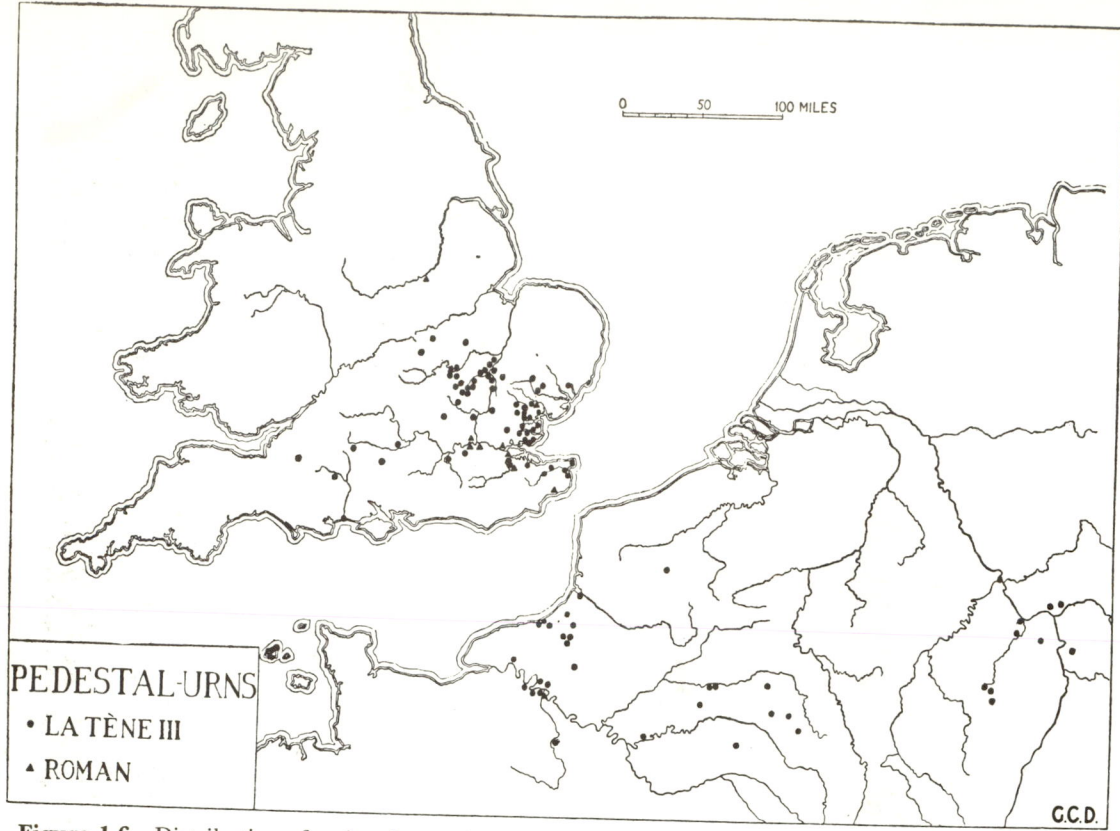

Figure 1.6 Distribution of pedestal urns (source: reproduced from Hawkes and Dunning 1931, Fig. 7).

Not all the activity centred upon defended sites. Meon Hill, Kimmeridge, Twyford Down, Chysauster, Horsted Keynes and Little Woodbury – all open settlements – were excavated; old collections of material from Hunsbury and Spettisbury were published, a number of specific articles were written about metal objects, including the Llyn Fawr hoard and groups of swan's-neck and ring-headed pins from various parts of the country (Dunning 1934) and in 1933 Leeds published his book *Celtic Ornament*, summarizing the main elements of British Iron Age art. Attempts were also made to collate the new material on a regional basis in articles like E.C. Curwen's 'The Iron Age in Sussex' (1939) and R.R. Clarke's 'The Iron Age in Norfolk and Suffolk' (1939). Finally, attention was being paid to Belgic settlement sites and their relationship to Roman urbanization in the large and important excavations at Camulodunum and Verulamium, both of which began in 1930.

It is hardly surprising that such phenomenal activity and the vast increase in material available for study should demand the modification of the ABC system, put forward when relatively little data were to hand. The large-scale excavations at Maiden Castle forced the issue (Figure 1.7). In the first interim report (1935) R.E.M. (later Sir Mortimer) Wheeler proposed a threefold division of Iron Age A: A1 (600–400 BC) was typified by the classic All Cannings Cross haematite-coated assemblage; A2 (400–200) was marked by derivatives of the sharp-shouldered situla types; while AB (200–early first century AD) showed a hybridization of A2 and B ceramic forms. The next year the date of 200 was modified to 100, with the hint that the incoming cultural elements constituting the B assemblage may have been dislodged from Gaul by the invasions of the Cimbri and Teutones. The new subdivisions

Figure 1.7 Excavations in progress at Maiden Castle, Dorset 1935 (photo: Royal Commission on Historical Monuments (England)).

were widely accepted in southern Britain although Myres (1937, 26–7), writing of the pottery from Mount Farm, Dorchester, Oxon, found the system difficult to apply in the Oxford region. Curwen, in his *Archaeology of Sussex* (1937, 2nd ed 1954), using the improved nomenclature to describe the finds from the South Downs and the Weald, proposed a further category, called ABC, which ran broadly parallel to La Tène III and showed an overlap in styles between the AB wares and Belgic C elements.

Iron Age B was similarly subdivided, but on a regional rather than a chronological basis. In the third interim report on Maiden Castle, Wheeler referred to 'that composite culture which, in Britain, has been named Early Iron Age B' (1937, 274). In the south-west, he suggested, there were in fact three groups: a *Cornish group* extending up the Bristol Channel to the Cotswolds at Bredon Hill, a *Glastonbury group* originating from refugee landings in the Lyme Bay and Exe valley region, and a *Wessex hillfort group* founded by a relatively few newcomers, 'since their culture . . . only slowly and incompletely modified the established A2 culture. But they were determined and masterful, and their influence upon the military aspect of Maiden Castle was immediate and drastic' (ibid., 275). He was referring to the remodelling of the defences in glacis style. In the definitive publication (Wheeler 1943, 56), it was finally suggested that the immigrants were Venetic refugees ousted by Caesar's Gaulish campaigns.

The excavations at Bredon Hill, Worcs., in 1935–7 refocused attention on the stamped wares of the south-west. Leeds (1927) had put forward the view that stamped ware was introduced by way of the Atlantic sea-ways, probably from Iberia, while in 1936 Donovan and Dunning had drawn attention to the rather different group of this general type found in the Cotswolds. Petrological examination implied contact with Cornwall. (More recent work (Peacock 1968) has, however, disproved the Cornish connections.) At Bredon, Mrs T.C. Hencken was able to define two pottery styles: linear-tooled wares, which she called Iron Age A (more strictly, the parallels were with the AB wares only then being defined in the south), and duck-stamped wares. The former she considered to be the product of the native population, the latter an importation by immigrants coming from the Breton area *c.* 100–50 BC by way of the Bristol Channel. It was on the basis of this evidence that Wheeler proposed his 'Cornish group'.

The complexities of Iron Age B were further developed by the work of J.B. Ward Perkins (1938, 1939) and C.F.C. Hawkes (1939a) in their discussion of material from south-eastern Britain. Describing pottery from Crayford, Ward Perkins drew together a group of similar highly decorated vessels distributed principally in Sussex, Kent and Essex, calling them *South-eastern B* in contrast to the decorated pottery of the Glastonbury group. As to its origins, he concluded: 'it does seem more probable that . . . the pottery of the Crayford type represents an intrusive element, than that it was evolved spontaneously from the preceding culture. The source of this intrusive element can hardly as yet be defined' (1938, 156). A year later C.F.C. Hawkes published his considerations of the Caburn pottery (1939a) and in it stated firmly his belief that the south-eastern B wares were introduced by intrusive people, who were probably displaced from Armorica by Caesar in the middle of the first century. Following the excavations at Oldbury, Ward Perkins defined another group – the *Wealden culture* – typified by plain vessels with foot-rings, which he concluded was earlier than south-eastern B and had spread to the Weald from Sussex (1938, 152–5; 1944, 146).

At the same time C.F.C. Hawkes's work on the pottery and finds from various of the Sussex sites (1939a) and from Worth in Kent (1940b) led him to the view that:

About 250 B.C. an incursion of Iron Age B Celtic peoples from the continent, after first forcing all the South Downs peoples to defend themselves by building hillforts, was successful in establishing a new domination in the Cissbury region of central Sussex, depopulating the Brighton region and leaving the Caburn I folk as an isolated group of Iron Age A culture in East Sussex.

(1939a, 241)

The invasion was by 'Marnians' from northern Gaul and for the resulting hybrid he adopted Curwen's term 'AB' (after Wheeler 1935). 'But', he warns,

> the A–B–C terminology is no more than a set of symbols for use while we are feeling our way towards the correct identification of culture-groups defined in factual terms of time and space. Now that such culture-groups are beginning to acquire definition of that order, we ought not to hesitate to give them regional names to which, according to established archaeological usage, they are thereby entitled.
>
> (C.F.C. Hawkes 1939a, 238–9)

He goes on to suggest that 'Iron Age AB' in Sussex includes the *Wealden culture* in the north-west and the *Cissbury culture* in the central area.

By 1940, then, the southern British Iron Age was still thought of in terms of the three basic cultural groups suggested ten years earlier; Iron Age A, approximately equivalent to the Continental Hallstatt culture, Iron Age B, running parallel to La Tène I and II, and Iron Age C, reflecting La Tène III. But an unprecedented spate of excavation had so complicated the picture that each of the three broad divisions was now thought to be the result of multiple incursions of invaders, who could be recognized and defined by their pottery types.

In northern Britain the pace of Iron Age research was more leisurely. After the pioneer work of John Williams on vitrified forts (1777), D. Christison's survey of hillforts (1898) and R. Munro's publication of his work on crannogs (1882), little advance was made until V. Gordon Childe began a series of hillfort excavations: Earn's Heugh (Childe and Forde 1932), Castle Law Fort (1933) and Finavon (1935b) followed by Rahoy (Childe and Thorneycroft 1938), where he carried out experiments into the nature of vitrification, and Kaimes hillfort (1941). It was in 1935 that he published his celebrated *Prehistory of Scotland*, in which for the first time he arranged the Scottish Iron Age against the general background of British and European development, defining a native continuum represented by the continued occupation of the hilltop towns and crannogs, upon which two major intrusive elements impinged. In the east he recognized an *Abernethy complex* consisting of the vitrified forts and a scatter of La Tène artefacts, while in the west and north lay the *castle complex* of brochs, duns and wheelhouses with their associations of bone artefacts similar in form to those from south-west Britain. To Childe, then, the more distinctive characteristics of the Scottish Iron Age were introduced from the south of Britain during the latter part of the first millennium.

The next decade in the south saw little change in established views and the publication of comparatively little new material. Regional surveys were being undertaken in Oxfordshire (Bradford 1942b) and the Isle of Purbeck (Calkin 1949), and W.J. Varley (1950b) produced a lengthy consideration of the hillforts of the Welsh Marches, in which he suggested the diffusion of hillfort architecture from a 'primary area of contour hillforts' in Hampshire, Wiltshire and Sussex into Dorset, Surrey, the Welsh borderland, north Wales and the Midlands, taking place some time before 100 BC. About 100 BC or soon after he proposed a second diffusion, this time from the south-west peninsula into the Bristol Channel area and west Wales. Other notable contributions of the period concentrated on non-ceramic material. D.F. Allen published his definitive account of 'The Belgic dynasties of Britain and their coins' in 1944; C.F. Fox described the metalwork of the Llyn Cerrig hoard in a monograph published in 1946; and A.S. Henshall examined the problems of textiles and weaving in an article which appeared in 1950.

Although it is true that there was more diversification of interest, hillfort excavation continued, at Blewburton Hill (sporadically), Highdown, High Rocks, Breedon-on-the-Hill and elsewhere. In her publication of the last-named site, Dr K.M. Kenyon appended an analysis of the pottery of the area, defining a *Trent valley* regional group which was culturally Iron Age A but so dissimilar to that from sites further to the south that she suggested an invasion 'at a late date from a backward area of the Low Countries' in the first century BC into the central Midlands, 'an area apparently hitherto unoccupied by Iron Age people. Here they developed a fairly widespread, but crude and unprogressive culture, which may have lasted until the Roman conquest' (1950, 67). In 1952 she extended her study of the earliest Iron Age material in an important article, 'The chronology of Iron Age A', setting out broad ideas on a number of regional 'A' groups and calling for a complete redating. In Sussex she discussed the idea of a Marnian invasion, concluding: 'It is therefore suggested that in the South Downs area, as in Wessex, Iron Age A lasted down, without any supervening AB or Cissbury culture, until the first century BC' (Kenyon 1952, 58). The article was essentially an attempt to bring the existing ABC framework into line with new discoveries. The essentials of the invasion hypotheses remained unchallenged.

The 1950s saw increased interest in hillfort excavation. Sutton Walls and several neighbouring sites were examined between 1948 and 1951, Hod Hill between 1951 and 1958. Excavations at Blewburton Hill continued to be published in 1947, 1953 and 1959, and Little Solisbury in 1957 and 1962; more limited programmes were undertaken at Blackbury, Devon (published 1955), Torberry, Sussex (1956–8), St Mawgan, Cornwall (1957), Wandlebury, Cambs. (1957), Poston, Herefordshire (1958), etc. Several papers on the regional groupings of hillforts were now published. Dr M.A. Cotton discussed Cornish cliff castles (1959), Gloucestershire hillforts (1961b), Wealden forts (1961a) and Berkshire forts (1962), while Lady A. Fox considered the south-western multiple-enclosure forts (1953 and 1961b). Regional variations in style and function were now being emphasized.

Large-scale examination of settlement sites was becoming more widespread, no doubt encouraged by the impressive results of G. Bersu's excavation of Little Woodbury (1940). The work at Kestor on Dartmoor (1955), Bodrifty, Cornwall (1957), Itford Hill, Sussex (1957) and Staple Howe, Yorks. (1963) marked an important advance in our understanding of social structures and economy. There was an increase too in the number of articles on Iron Age metalwork, culminating in a detailed study of art and technology in Sir Cyril Fox's *Pattern and Purpose* (1958).

The reviving interest in the problems of subsistence economy and class structure, which these developments encouraged, was reflected in more studies biased towards understanding the economic basis, an approach which received an added stimulus from J.G.D. Clark's *Prehistoric Europe, the Economic Basis* (1952). Since before the war, many of the better excavation reports had contained brief summaries of the faunal and floral remains, and sometimes of the mollusca which served as an indication of environmental conditions, but no attempts were made to synthesize or assess the data statistically until H. Helbaek produced a valuable account of the early crops in southern Britain (1953): adequate studies of animal bones were still lacking. The nature of arable farming in the south, however, received attention from E.S. Applebaum in his studies of field systems near Sidbury (1955), from Lady A. Fox, writing of farms and fields on Dartmoor (1955), and from H.C. Bowen in several important papers including *Ancient Fields* (1961) and 'The Celtic background' (1969).

Tribal organization and political structure were also examined in several articles, beginning with a general survey of the tribes of southern Britain (Radford 1955). D.F. Allen's work on coinage subsequently extended the picture still further with 'The origins of coinage in Britain: a reappraisal' (1961a), 'A study of the Dobunnic coinage' (1961b), an article and maps issued with the Ordnance Survey's *Map of Southern Britain in the Iron Age* (1962), *The Coins of the Coritani* (1963), 'The chronology of Durotrigian coinage' (1968a), 'The coins of the Iceni' (1970) and 'British potin coins: a review' (1971); together these papers provided an essential historical basis for the first centuries BC and AD.

The post-war period in northern Britain was highly productive for Iron Age studies. In the east of Scotland, extending down to Northumberland and Durham, extensive fieldwork was undertaken leading to the publication of important regional surveys (Jobey 1962a, 1965, 1966a, 1966b, 1971a, 1971c and RCHM(S) *Stirlingshire* 1963, *Roxburghshire* 1956, *Selkirkshire* 1957, *Peeblesshire* 1967), while in parallel a programme of excavation was carried out to examine the range and development of the smaller fortified settlements. Between 1950 and 1975 more than twenty settlements were excavated.[2] As a result, it was now realized that homesteads and hamlets, defended first by palisades and later by earthworks, were densely distributed over much of the area and that they must have had a considerable ancestry. Paucity of material culture, however, prevented firm dating until the first radiocarbon dates became available (MacKie 1969a), showing that their origins lay in the sixth century or earlier.

The west and north of Scotland, the area of brochs, wheelhouses and duns, was also intensively studied, beginning with two papers by Sir Lindsey Scott (1947, 1948) in which he put forward the view of colonization from the south-west. New evidence from the excavations at Jarlshof (1956) and Clickhimin (1968) led to a more extensive reassessment. In 1964 A. Young published her survey of brochs and duns, and in the following year E. MacKie's important and detailed consideration entitled 'The origin and development of the broch and wheelhouse building cultures of the Scottish Iron Age' appeared (1965c). He rejected the idea of late colonists bringing broch architecture with them, and instead suggested a local development arising from hillfort traditions. The material culture, he felt, was however derived from the south. Regional differences brought out by these two areas of study were formalized by Stuart Piggott (1956) when he proposed four major regions in Scotland: Atlantic, Solway–Clyde, Tyne–Forth and North-eastern.

In southern Britain the advances made to general Iron Age theory in the immediate post-war period were considerable. Some modifications had been made to the ABC classifications like those proposed by Kenyon and noted above (p. 14). Kenyon (1954) had also introduced the term *Bristol Channel B* for both the linear pottery and the duck-stamped wares, which she regarded as co-intrusive into the Severn region, while J.W. Brailsford (1958b) distinguished the Iron Age C *Durotrigian culture* of Dorset from the Iron Age C Belgic cultures further east. In addition to the cultural–historical ABC scheme of description and classification, archaeologists were now developing other broader approaches based on the classic definitions of 'culture' and upon systems of trading, subsistence economy and political organization.

In this atmosphere of change, the Council for British Archaeology held a conference entitled 'The Problems of the Iron Age in Southern Britain' in December 1958, which was subsequently published in 1961 (ed. S.S. Frere). The central paper at the conference, 'The ABC of the British Iron Age', was given by Hawkes. In this he restated the ABC model in a more advanced form, enlarging upon ideas which he had previously placed in outline form before the International Congress at Madrid in 1954 (C.F.C. Hawkes 1956). Taking note of the increasing desire for regional definition, he divided Britain south of the Tyne into five provinces, subdivided into thirty regions. This formed the horizontal structure of a grid, the vertical element being provided by a fixed series of periods further divided into phases and sub-phases. Within the three-dimensional framework thus formed, the cultural material, still described in ABC terms, could be supported (Figure 1.8). To avoid confusion with the regional and chronological numbering schemes, Hawkes proposed that the cultural letters should be prefixed with an ordinal number; thus 'A1' now became 'First A'. Regional differences could be brought out by adding a geographical prefix such as 'eastern First A' or 'southern First A'. 'The whole array of determinable cultures, lastly, like the hanks of an embroiderer's coloured wools or silks, has to be stitched on to the net of absolute time, which our frame of Periods and Phases holds stretched between its bars' (C.F.C. Hawkes 1959). He followed his summary of the new method of classification with a short historical outline demonstrating the way in which the existing material could neatly be fitted into the classificatory structure.

The newly formulated scheme, first published in *Antiquity* in 1959, was generally adopted: T.C.M. Brewster (1963) used it to describe the Yorkshire material published in his report on Staple Howe; Cotton (1961b) based her consideration of the Cotswold finds and sites firmly on the new scheme, and

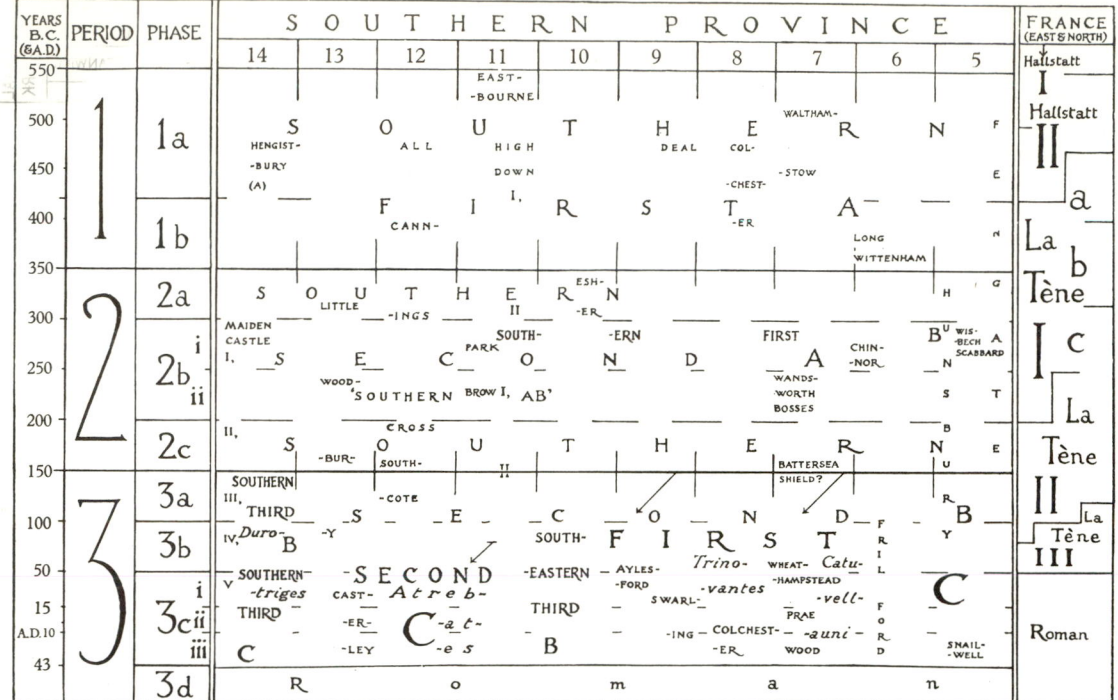

Figure 1.8 Hawkes's scheme for the southern British Iron Age (source: reproduced from C.F.C. Hawkes 1961, Fig. 4).

when in October 1961 a second CBA conference was held on the problems of the Iron Age in northern Britain, Piggott projected the classification to Scotland (S. Piggott 1966). The most extended treatment of the Iron Age in terms of the restated ABC was provided by Frere in the introductory chapters of the first edition of *Britannia* (1967).

But in other circles some disquiet was becoming manifest. In 1960 F.R. Hodson offered a number of theoretical criticisms based upon the fear that the rigidity of the framework would obscure the true pattern of Iron Age cultures. 'Might it not, after all, be both simpler and more objective', he asked, 'to define cultural groups in the accepted way, by starting with type-sites and type-fossils. . . . Cultural boundaries could then be defined by the distribution of type-fossils and not by fixed "provinces" or "regions", and a different pattern for the British Iron Age might emerge' (1960, 140). Hodson was in fact making a plea, much as Hawkes had done in 1939 (p. 13 above), for the introduction of a classic 'cultural' model of the type formalized by Childe. A few years later he provided an outline for testing this approach (1964), in which he proposed an indigenous *Woodbury culture* developing in the seventh century out of native traditions divisible only in terms of regional pottery styles (Figure 1.9). Upon this was imposed a possible group of Hallstatt adventurers, the La Tène I and II *Arras culture* of Yorkshire and the La Tène III *Aylesford–Swarling culture* centred upon Kent, Hertfordshire and Essex. Both the Arras culture and the Aylesford–Swarling culture were at this time receiving detailed study as the subjects of doctoral theses subsequently published as *The La Tène Cultures of Eastern Yorkshire* (Stead 1965) and 'The Aylesford–Swarling culture: the problem of the Belgae reconsidered' (Birchall 1965). Later MacKie extended the general concept of broadly defined cultures to Scotland by

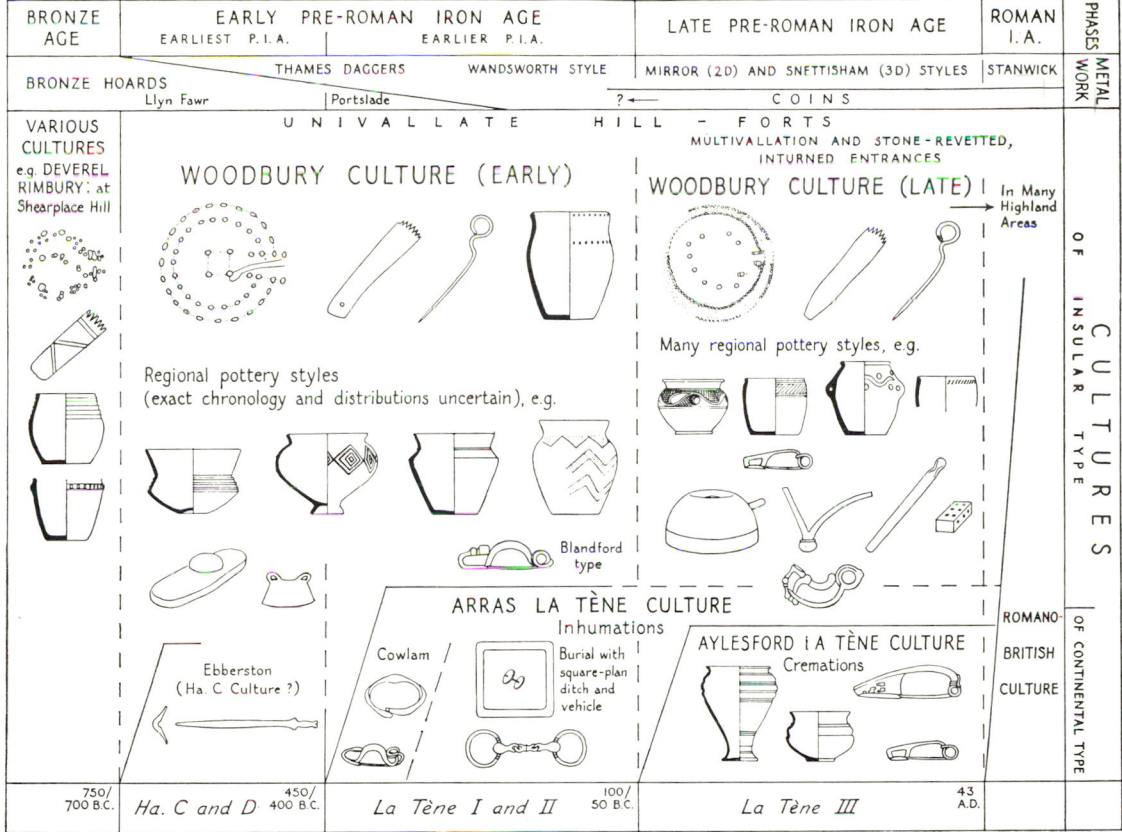

| BRONZE AGE | EARLY PRE-ROMAN IRON AGE | | LATE PRE-ROMAN IRON AGE | ROMAN I.A. | PHASES | METAL WORK |
| | EARLIEST P.I.A. | EARLIER P.I.A. | | | | |

Figure 1.9 Hodson's scheme for the Woodbury Culture (source: reproduced from Hodson 1964, Fig. 1).

proposing three substantially indigenous groups: the *Broch culture*, the *Abernethy culture* and the *Hownam culture* (1969a).

Chronological divisions were more difficult to define but Hodson recognized three horizons indicated by the presence of imported metalwork, which could be used to distinguish three periods. The first, or *earliest pre-Roman Iron Age* phase, began with the appearance of Hallstatt C types; the second, or *earlier pre-Roman Iron Age*, was marked by the introduction of La Tène I types; the third, or *late pre-Roman Iron Age*, began only after La Tène III contacts were underway. A little later the production of radiocarbon dates offered an independent method of calibration which proved particularly important in placing the early northern British material in perspective (MacKie 1969a).

The cultural model emphasized two things: the indigenous nature of much of the material and the completely false emphasis which had been placed on changes of pottery styles. Much of the earlier writing reads as though the Iron Age consisted only of animated ceramics endowed with all the qualities of living creatures, with evolutionary properties appropriate to the theories of Lysenko. Hodson showed the weaknesses of such a syndrome by systematically demolishing the basis of the 'Marnian invasion' theory (Hodson 1962) while the later work of D.P.S. Peacock (1968, 1969) demonstrated with some clarity that the differing pottery styles of the south-west and the west Midlands were as much the result of commercial production centres as of cultural determinates. As a consequence of his work, much of the complex reasoning surrounding Bristol Channel B (or western

Second and Third B) can be swept away and many thousands of words of intricate discussion rendered obsolete.

By 1970 when the first edition of this book was in preparation the study of the British Iron Age was at a point of change: there was great dissatisfaction with the old explanatory models and a realization that without large-scale projects of fieldwork and excavation there could be little significant advance. If the intellectual climate was right for a new move forward so too was the rapidly developing infrastructure for dealing with the escalating destruction of sites by road building, urban expansion, afforestation and ploughing. The result was a renewed interest in settlement archaeology but with the emphasis now on large-scale excavation and the study of sites in their landscapes. Whereas before 1970 the total number of large-scale excavations was no more than five, in the last two decades the list has increased more than tenfold. In the Upper Thames region the Oxford Archaeological Unit has undertaken a systematic programme of Iron Age settlement excavation at Ashville, Barton Court Farm, Mount Farm, Appleford, Claydon Pike, Mingies Ditch, Gravelly Guy and Farmoor, adding enormously to our understanding of settlement variety and the economic basis of agricultural production. Further north in Northamptonshire complete settlement plans are now available from Twywell, Wakerley, Blackthorn, Aldwincle, Fengate and Brigstock. Other Midland sites include Beckford (Heref. and Worcs.) and Fisherwick (Staffs.). On the chalklands of the south and neighbouring regions major excavations have been completed at Gussage All Saints, Dorset, Winnall Down, Micheldever Wood, Old Down Farm, Ructstalls Hill, Hants., Potterne and Groundwell Farm, Wilts., and Bishopstone and Slonk Hill, Sussex. And in Somerset new programmes of excavation and assessment are underway at Glastonbury and Meare. For Wales a number of totally excavated settlements are now available. In the south-west of the Principality in particular a concerted programme of settlement excavations has revolutionized our understanding of the socio-economic system (G. Williams 1988). Here, in addition to Walesland Rath, there have been total excavations at Woodside camp, Dan y Coed, Drim Camp and Castel Henllys, while in Snowdonia important work is in progress at Bryn y Castell.

In the north-east of Britain the list of large-scale settlement excavations is impressive: Burradon, Hartburn, Belling Law, Kennel Hall Knowe, Thorpe Thewles and Great Ayrton Moor are among the more important. Further north in Scotland excavations at Leckie Broch, Crosskirk Broch, The Dod, Dryburn Bridge, Douglasmuir and Broxmouth and on the brochs of Orkney at the Howe and Bu Broch are changing our perception quite dramatically.

Hillforts and oppida too are now being tackled on a scale in keeping with the problems they pose. Large-scale excavations (sadly not all of them published in full) have been completed at Moel y Gaer and Breiddin in Wales, Crickley, Glos., Midsummer Hill, Heref. and Worcs., Balksbury, Winklebury and Danebury, Hants., Hengistbury Head, Dorset and South Cadbury, Somerset, and a new programme is underway at Stanwick, Yorks.

Simply listing the more important settlement excavations in this way, though rather tedious for the reader, gives some idea of the enormous expansion of data there has been in recent years, particularly when it is remembered that the list has of necessity been highly selective. The site list given in appendix C, itself a selection of the total, has increased by 30 per cent between the first and third editions of this book while the bibliography has more than doubled.

Alongside this exponential growth in settlement data there has been a fast-developing interest in the environmental context of sites and the exploration of their economic systems through the detailed assessments of plant and animal remains. This work is particularly well advanced in the south of England, especially in the Upper Thames valley where environmental concerns have been written into research designs from the beginning (Robinson 1984). More wide-ranging reviews have been provided by Martin Jones (1981, 1984) and Annie Grant (1984b). The detail now emerging is such that general overviews can at last be attempted. The environmental context has been explored by J.G. Evans

(1975), Jones and Dimbleby (1981) and Simmons and Tooley (1981) while aspects of the farming regimes were considered by P.J. Fowler (1983) and in Mercer (1981). The emphasis on environmental data has generated a renewed interest in wetland settlement. The study is at its most advanced in the Somerset Levels (recorded in the various volumes of the *Somerset Levels Papers*) and the current state throughout the country has been usefully reviewed by Murphy and French (1988).

In parallel with these approaches a number of regional studies have been carried out in an attempt to reconstruct historic landscapes. Among the more impressive are the Dartmoor survey (Fleming 1988), the Bodmin Moor survey carried out for RCHM(E) and the survey of the chalk downlands around Danebury (R. Palmer 1984). The work of the three Royal Commissions is continuing to improve the record county by county.

The study of ritual and religion has fared less well, largely because of the paucity of evidence, but two major surveys of burial rite (Whimster 1977; C. E. Wilson 1981) have created a degree of order in the otherwise rather chaotic data base, while major fieldwork and excavation projects in eastern Yorkshire have yielded a range of new evidence of high quality (Dent 1978, 1982, 1985; Stead 1976b, 1986). The nature of Iron Age religious beliefs has been further explored by Wait (1985) and M. Green (1986): evidence for religious structures is gradually accumulating through excavations at Danebury, Hayling Island, Lancing Down and Ivy Chimneys, Witham.

The technical abilities of Iron Age craftsmen are coming under increasing scrutiny. Tylecote has produced a useful overview of Iron Age metallurgy within a more general framework (Tylecote 1986). Specific aspects of iron-working have been considered in several papers (Salter 1983, 1987; Salter and Ehrenreich 1984; Ehrenreich 1985) while the art of the bronze caster has received thorough consideration in the light of the discovery of foundry waste at Gussage All Saints (Foster 1980). The nature of the copper alloys used is at last being given the attention it deserves (Northover 1984, 1987, 1988). Recent work on glass is also beginning to show something of the skill and proficiency of local craftsmen (Henderson and Warren 1981; Henderson 1985, 1987a and b).

Questions of trade and exchange have continued to fascinate. Two subjects dominate the literature: the export of Cornish tin (S. Piggott 1978; Maxwell 1972; Mitchell 1983; Cunliffe 1983; C.F.C. Hawkes 1984; Penhallurick 1986) and importation of wine in amphorae (D.F. Williams 1981; Peacock 1984; Galliou 1984; Sealey 1985). The nature of the trading systems in operation have been considered by Cunliffe (1984d, 1987) for the Atlantic systems and Partridge (1981), Nash (1984), Haselgrove (1984b) and Cunliffe (1988a) for the systems linking northern Gaul to south-eastern Britain. Our understanding of the means of transport used has been much enlivened by Sean McGrail's discussion of navigation techniques (McGrail 1983) and by the discovery of a well preserved log boat at Hasholme (Millett and McGrail 1988). A Greco-Roman anchor stock of the first century BC from off the Welsh coast provides direct evidence of actual trading ships (Boon 1976).

The study of objects of insular British art has recently intensified. In addition to the publication of a number of new items, and reassessments of old, there have been several regional surveys – northern Britain by MacGregor (1976) and Wales by Savory (1968) – together with overviews of the British material seen against the Continental background (Frey 1976; Stead 1985b; Megaw and Megaw 1986, 1989).

British coinage has undergone several reassessments (D.F. Allen 1961a; Rodwell 1976; Kent 1978, 1981) while questions of the economic interpretation of coinage have been actively debated (Collis 1975; Cunliffe 1976b, 1981a). Meanwhile the original list published by Allen has twice been updated (Haselgrove 1978, 1983). These lists, together with Haselgrove's wide-ranging discussion of coin finds from archaeological sites (1987), form the essential background. But all previous work, including that of Mack and Allen has been overshadowed by Bob Van Arsdell's magisterial and thought-provoking survey of British Celtic coins which must serve as a basis for all future work both numismatic and historical (Van Arsdell 1989).

Skimming in this rather breathless way through some of the highlights of the past two decades can do no more than underline the immense amount of new thought and data being published almost every week. The 1970s and early 1980s have been a time of almost exponential growth in accumulated knowledge, though there are now signs that the graph is beginning to level out. Where does this torrent of new material leave us, other than in a state of bewildered exhaustion? First and foremost it is with the realization that the pattern of Iron Age communities in Britain was infinitely more complex than we could have conceived of a few years ago. Simple models are worse than useless nor is it of much value to impose complex models, derived from theoretical considerations, on the data in the hope that understanding will dawn. There is no place in Iron Age studies for the *Deus ex Machina*. Instead we must order the material and recognize recurring patterns within it and use these patterns, against the trajectory of time, to help us to understand some of the systems at work in society. Only then will it be possible to relate these systems and to assess their interaction. In this way we may hope to begin to understand something of the dynamic which gave life to society and helped it to reproduce itself.

Part II
Space and time

2
Space and time

As a preliminary to any archaeological study it is necessary to consider two parameters: the spacial context within which societies under consideration developed and the time span covered. In the context of this book, space is restricted to the islands of Britain, excluding Ireland: the time span begins in the eighth century BC and ends in the first century AD. In the seven chapters to follow (chapters 3–10) various aspects of these themes will be discussed. Here, by way of introduction, we will consider the two parameters in the broadest of terms.

Landscape

Britain is a large island, 1,200 km in length from north to south, stretching from latitudes 50° N to 61° N. Its landforms are varied: in the west the land rises to 1,000 m OD while in the east much of it is below 100 m. These simple facts create a varied biome. Along the entire western seaboard and for some considerable distance inland rainfall today exceeds 100 mm per year while in the east it is less than 60 mm. In the north-west there are less than 4½ hours of sunshine a day in July compared with over 6½ hours along the south coast (Figure 2.1). Figures of this kind serve to illustrate the stark climatic contrasts between different regions and it hardly needs emphasizing that variations of this magnitude constrain arable regimes. The picture is, however, more complex than this: climate can alter, sometimes quite dramatically, while the extensive exploitation of an environment by man may set in motion a series of irreversible changes.

Much has been written on the question of climatic change in Britain during the first millennium BC (J. Turner 1981; H.H. Lamb 1981; Mercer 1981; Robinson 1984). The consensus view is that there were significant changes during this period but that given the varied structure of Britain the effects in some regions will have been far more noticeable than in others.

H.H. Lamb (1981) has argued that between 1000 and 750 bc there was a 2°C fall in overall mean temperature. Conditions improved about 400 bc but there was a return to colder conditions c. 200 bc. Such a drop could have shortened the growing season by up to five weeks. In

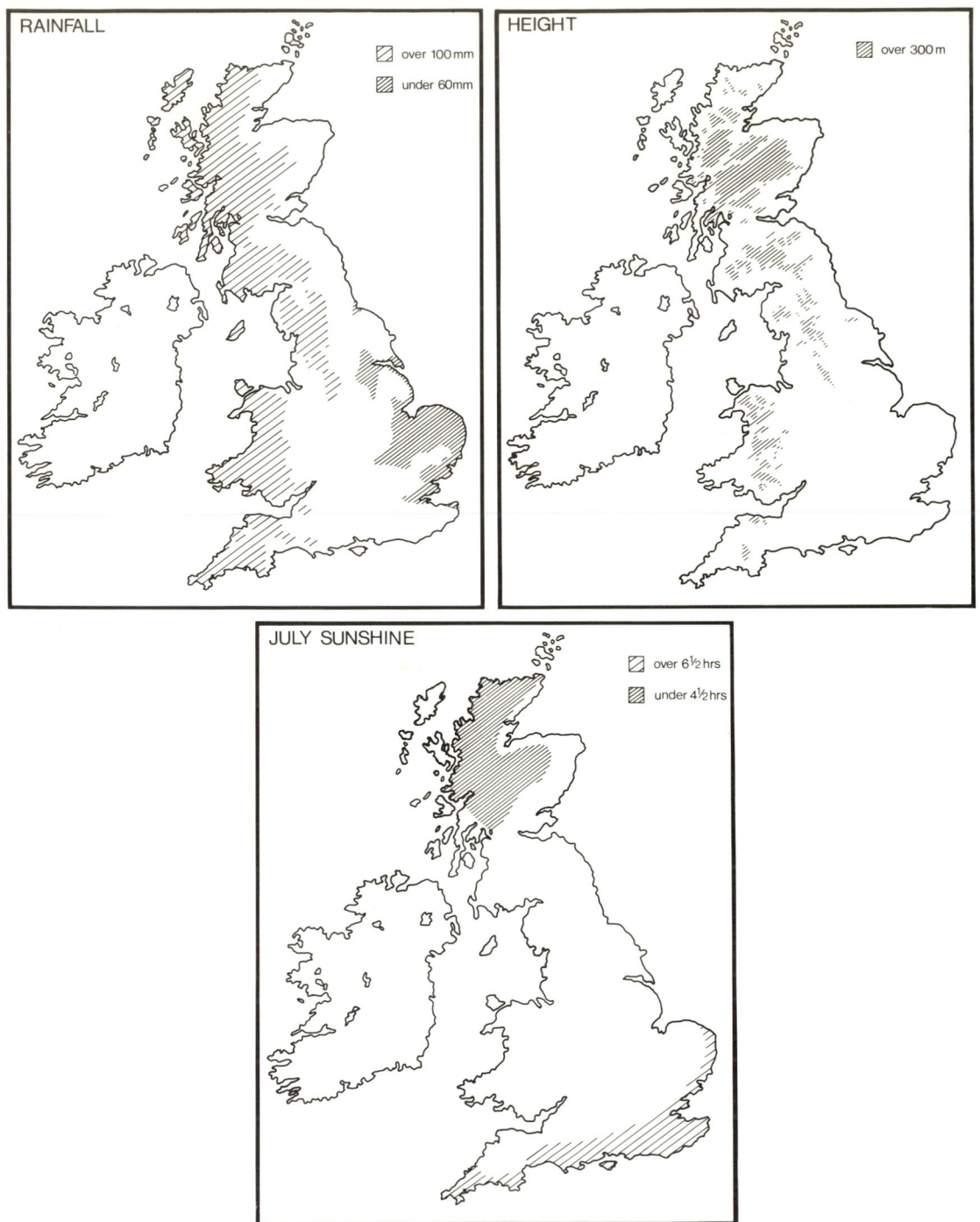

Figure 2.1   The physical characteristics of the British Isles (sources: various).

the north, with its limited number of hours of sunshine a day during the ripening period, a change of this magnitude could have been disastrous particularly on the uplands. Crops would no longer have ripened and thus the economic base of the upland communities would have been dislocated. There is, indeed, convincing evidence that upland fields and settlements were abandoned at this time. In contrast, in the south, with many hours of sunshine a day, the shortened growing season would have had much less effect.

It is widely accepted that during this period the climate also became noticeably wetter. Deterioration began just before 1250 bc, accelerating after 850 bc and reaching its wettest about 650 bc. After *c.* 450 bc there was a return to somewhat drier conditions. Dramatic evidence for this is seen in a series of peat bog sequences where a rapid rise in peat growth can be detected (J. Turner 1981, 251–61) and on upland massifs like Dartmoor, blanket bog becomes far more extensive (I.G. Simmons 1970). The effects of this increase in precipitation will have varied across the country. In the highland region of the west annual rainfall rose rapidly and was accompanied by vegetational changes of considerable magnitude sufficient to dislocate subsistence strategies and settlement. In the east, on the other hand, in the rain shadow of the highland ranges, increases in rainfall would have been much less and such increases as there were may not have had any significant effect on agriculture.

From what has been said it follows that some parts of Britain, in particular the north and the west, were more susceptible to climatic change than others. Here quite minor fluctuations in rainfall or temperature would have caused widespread environmental change and this in turn would have affected settlement and society. The relationship between man and landscape in these regions was one of unstable equilibrium whereas in the south-east the equilibrium was less easily upset. Given these differences it is hardly surprising that social systems developed along diverging lines.

The disruptive effects of man on his environment will undoubtedly have provided another dynamic factor. That changes occurred is not in doubt but their magnitude is more difficult to define. On the light soils of the south-east constant cropping since the neolithic period must have depleted soil nutrients and affected soil structure. Erosion was also a serious reality. Work on the colluvial deposits in the valleys of the South Downs has shown that considerable volumes of soil moved from the hill slopes to the valley bottoms during the later prehistoric period (Bell 1981, 1982). Alluviation in the Midland river valleys also reflects large-scale aerial erosion of arable land at this time (Robinson and Lambrick 1984). While the processes which led to this may have been accentuated by increased rainfall, the primary cause was man's tilling of the land.

Even the formation of peat bogs could have been triggered by human activity where the environmental conditions were nicely balanced (Moore 1975). A twentyfold increase in the growth of peat at Leach Fen, an upland bog in Derbyshire, after 340 bc coincided with large-scale clearance for pasture. The clearance created a wetter environment which tipped the ecosystem to peat formation. On fragile soils such as the sands of the New Forest and the North York Moors human activity had brought about podsol formation by the middle of the second millennium (Dimbleby and Gill 1955; Dimbleby 1965).

These examples are sufficient to show that human subsistence strategies were having a continual effect on the environment. On fragile soils the effects could be very rapid. Elsewhere they were usually gradual but cumulative. Change could, however, be greatly accelerated where climatic deterioration and human activity interacted to tip the balance.

Social space

Each individual exists in a landscape and requires space. Normally groups of individuals live and work together within a corporate space. By the first millennium BC the typical unit was the family or extended family who were sufficiently sedentary to require permanent settlements. These homesteads will have existed within a zone of exploitation within which the community's basic needs for food and raw materials could be met. Some parts of these zones may have been shared between more than one community. Pasture land, for example, may well have been held in common and apportioned between a group of farming communities. As population increased the need to create boundaries intensified and in some areas larger social groupings represented by hillforts emerged. By the first century BC even larger settlements with urban characteristics (oppida) can be identified in the south-east developing as a response to changing economic pressures.

The structures representing social space – settlements, boundaries, defences – can be recognized archaeologically and the distinctive spacial patterns which they make can be used to define broader groupings. If, for example, one accepts that settlement type reflects socio-economic structure, then zones of like settlement contrasting with other zones allow broad patterns representing aspects of social organization to be defined. The data for the Iron Age are particularly susceptible to this kind of approach.

Other types of pattern recognition may also be used to enhance our understanding of the material evidence. Over much of southern Britain pottery is plentiful and is often elaborately decorated. The definition of style-zones reflects an aspect of social patterning. In some instances it could well be that a decorative range was deliberately chosen by a society as a means of defining its ethnic identity. In such cases, if they can be identified, the distribution pattern will represent the territory of a clan or a tribe. Even greater interest attaches to those situations where distribution patterns of this kind remain the same throughout successive style changes, implying continuity of boundary over a considerable period of time. There are some examples in southern Britain where a territory thus defined in the Middle Iron Age can be recognized again in the Late Iron Age through coin distributions identifiable to particular tribes. In such cases it becomes possible to consider the ethnogenesis of tribes.

Time and chronologies

The establishment of a firm chronology is essential to enable data to be ordered and compared and to allow rate of change to be assessed. To provide a suitable framework for a subject as complex as the British Iron Age many methods have to be adopted.

The creation of relative chronologies is comparatively straightforward. There now exist for most parts of the country reliable stratified sequences established by excavation. Where these excavations have been undertaken on a large scale the artefact assemblages recovered are often adequate in size to allow typological changes to be detected within certain artefact classes. These typologies can be greatly enhanced by considering a wider corpus of items, whether stratified or not. Typological sequences of fine metalwork, particularly brooches, are among the most useful for the country as a whole but on a local or regional basis pottery – a plastic medium susceptible to rapid style change – is by far the most valuable. As we will see in chapter 4, quite detailed sequences can be constructed for much of southern Britain.

Typology and stratigraphy enable sequential changes to be defined but they do not provide absolute chronologies. For this other methods are required.

Of limited use is association with datable artefacts. For Britain this is only relevant for the Late Iron Age when local coinage develops and datable imports from the Mediterranean world begin to appear in any quantity. Even so the date brackets are not always particularly helpful. The dating of Celtic coinage is still a matter of debate though the limits of each of the major types are fixed within certain comparatively narrow limits. Roman imports also take with them wide brackets of dating tolerance. A Dressel 1A wine amphora, for example, could have arrived in the country any time beween *c.* 140 and 40 BC and a few may have come in even later. Nor is there any assurance that an amphora, or amphora sherd, need have been buried or discarded within this bracket: some may well not have reached their archaeological context until two or three decades after their importation.

Radiocarbon dating offers a rather different method of assessing age. In the early years after the technique was first introduced many archaeologists tended to quote even individual dates with a high degree of confidence. As the method has been further tested, and its limitations have become better understood, a more cautious attitude has prevailed, some archaeologists going so far as to doubt the usefulness of radiocarbon at all for the Iron Age. They argue that when all the calibrations and statistical deviations have been taken into account the brackets attached to each date are so wide as to be of little value. This may be true of individual dates but where sequences exist or large numbers of dates are available for a single horizon or type some broad indication of date may be gained. The example of Danebury is informative. More than seventy dates were obtained in accordance with a rigorous programme of sampling but after careful analysis the actual date brackets arrived at for the major ceramic phases were uncomfortably wide (Cunliffe and Orton 1984). These reservations apart, radiocarbon dates have a value even if it is more limited than had first been hoped. A list of dates from Iron Age contexts will be found in appendix B together with an explanation of the procedures adopted.

A far more promising method of absolute dating is dendrochronology (dating by counting tree rings). In recent years it has been possible to construct a continuous tree ring sequence back to 5200 BC based on Irish oak (Pilcher, Baillie, Schmidt and Becker 1984). A suitable sample of undated wood from an archaeological deposit can be compared to the master sequence and approximately dated. If sapwood and bark are present then the date of felling of the piece can be ascertained within fairly narrow limits. This has been used to good effect in dating substantial artefacts like the Hasholme log boat (Millett and McGrail 1988), and in the case of a bridge found at Fiskerton, although absolute dates have not yet been determined, dendrochronology has been of considerable value in distinguishing phases of repair (Field 1986). The technique promises to be of very considerable value in dating waterlogged sites but the average dry site is unlikely to produce suitable material.

Establishing a chronology is far from a straightforward matter but if all available methods are used, together with a little common sense, and attempts at spurious accuracy are avoided, then it is possible to provide a broad usable chronology for the Iron Age.

Dates BC/AD	Europe	Britain		
1300				
	Bronze D			
1200				
	Hallstatt A1	Penard I	LBA A1	
1100				
	Hallstatt A2	Penard II	LBA A2	
1000				
	Hallstatt B1	Wilburton	LBA B1	
900				
	Hallstatt B2	Ewart Park/ Blackmoor	LBA B2	
800				
	Hallstatt B3	Ewart Park/ Carp's Tongue	LBA B3	
700				
	Hallstatt C	Llyn Fawr	LBA C	Earliest IA
600				
	Hallstatt D			
500				Early IA
	La Tène Ia			
400				
	La Tène Ib			Middle IA
300				
	La Tène Ic			
200				
	La Tène II			
100				
	La Tène III			Late IA
0				
100				Latest IA
200				Roman

A simple system

To contain the complex mass of data from the first millennium BC, so that it may be ordered and compared, it is necessary to create a simple chronological system of the kind offered here. For the Late Bronze Age systems are usually based on bronze implement assemblages and the phases are named after hoards. The system most widely used was formalized by Burgess (1979, 1980). This was modified by Gerloff (1981) and is presented here with further small modifications. In terms of the Continental chronology the Iron Age proper is considered to begin with Hallstatt C, that is roughly 700 BC or a little before. Thus there is a period of overlap between the last of the well-developed bronze industries and the early use of iron.

The scheme for the Iron Age in Britain is based on a range of data but relies heavily on the ceramic sequence established in the south of the country. It is, at best, a simplification which has a general usefulness rather than a specific detailed applicability. For much of the north and west of the country even these simple divisions cannot be used and we must revert to best-guess absolute dates based on the few radiocarbon assessments that are available. In the text to follow the chronological terminology used will be a mixture of this simple Early/Middle/Late scheme with rough absolute dates given where possible.

3
The background

A detailed assessment of the period conventionally called the 'Late Bronze Age' – broadly from the beginning of the first millennium until the seventh century BC – is a subject more appropriate to another volume in this series. But before we can begin to define the social, economic and technical changes which began in the eighth century, and became intensified during the seventh, it is necessary to sketch in something of the indigenous background, if only to emphasize the strong element of continuity which underlies the social and economic history of the country throughout the first millennium.

Settlement and economy in south-eastern Britain

Settlements belonging to the period 1300–700 BC are tolerably well known on the chalklands of southern Britain, where more than three dozen individual sites have been recorded and at least half of them subjected to excavations of differing thoroughness (Figure 3.1). Taken together, the evidence allows certain generalizations to be made. The basic structural unit appears to be an enclosure, frequently of sub-rectangular form, defined in various ways by combinations of banks, ditches and palisades. At Shearplace Hill, Dorset (Figure 3.2), the settlement area is enclosed by a U-shaped ditch *c.* 3 m wide, with an internal bank in which may once have been bedded a palisade or perhaps a thorn hedge. At Cock Hill, Sussex, on the other hand, the bank and palisade are external to a 2 m wide ditch. Another variant appears at New Barn Down, Sussex (Figure 3.2), and at Thorny Down, Wilts., where one side only is ditched, the other three being defined by banks, which at New Barn Down supported a close-set palisade. In all these examples, internal settings of posts show that the earthworks enclosed circular huts, usually 6.0–7.5 m in diameter. There were at least two at New Barn Down, two or three at Shearplace Hill, five or more at Cock Hill and probably as many as nine at Thorny Down. Not all, of course, need have been in use at one time, since replacement and rebuilding were probably carried out periodically. The plan is clear at Shearplace Hill, however, where two definite houses and a possible third, enclosing a working area, seem to constitute a single contemporary unit, which

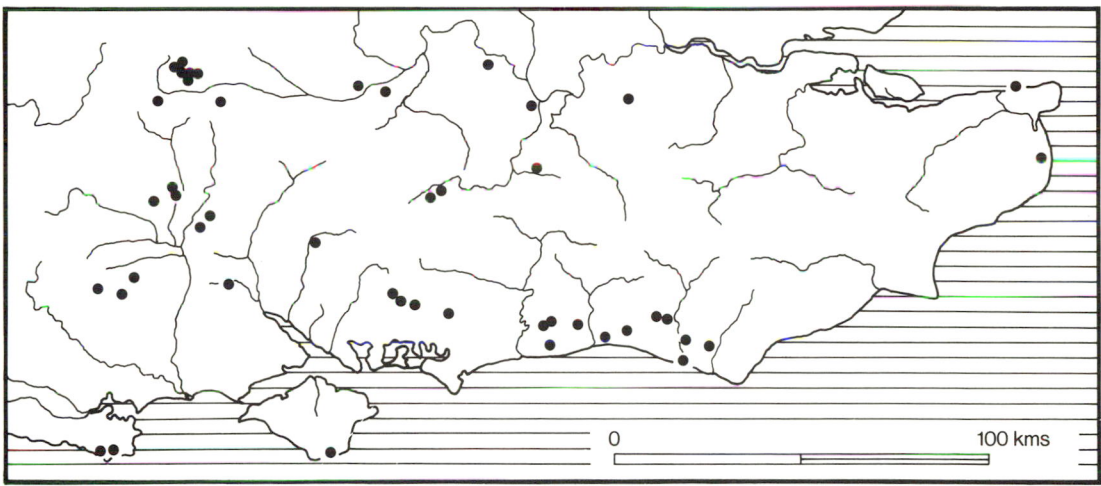

Figure 3.1 Major settlements in southern Britain: Middle Bronze Age to Early Iron Age (sources: various).

would have been ideally suited to a social group of family or extended family size. The unenclosed settlement at Chalton, Hants., was of similar size, with one large hut, a smaller hut with a central hearth for cooking and two unroofed working areas. Here a tentative assessment of grain-production, based on the capacities of the storage pits, supported the idea of a single family unit and indicated a total arable in the order of 6.5 ha.

While single enclosure habitations of the types mentioned above are relatively common on the chalklands a few sites present the appearance of nucleation, but here we face the problem of how many of the individual structural elements were strictly contemporary. The possibility remains that the overall pattern was caused by the gradual shift in location of a single enclosure representing a family unit within a defined and limited territory. Three Sussex sites, Plumpton Plain A, Itford Hill and Black Patch exemplify the problem. Plumpton Plain A (Figure 3.3) consists of four sub-rectangular enclosures defined by banks, spread out along a street over a distance of about 213 m. Three of them have been partially excavated and each has proved to contain at least one hut. While the plan could represent a contemporary situation, the agglomeration thus forming a hamlet or small village, it is equally possible that the enclosures are successive.

At Black Patch on the other hand a series of hut terraces were found scattered among contemporary fields over a distance of about a kilometre. One of these (hut platform 4) selected for total excavation, revealed five individual circular houses set in fenced enclosures containing two ponds (Figure 3.2). The plan suggests broad contemporaneity with an occupation span not exceeding thirty to fifty years. A detailed analysis of the artefacts found on the floors of the individual buildings led the excavators to believe that hut 1 was used largely for food production, hut 3 for craftwork and storage while hut 4 combined elements of both. In huts 2 and 4 little evidence of function survived. Taking the evidence of plan and activity together it is tempting to see the community as an interdependent unit, quite possibly an extended family. The question still remains how did this hut complex relate to the other three within the immediate vicinity?

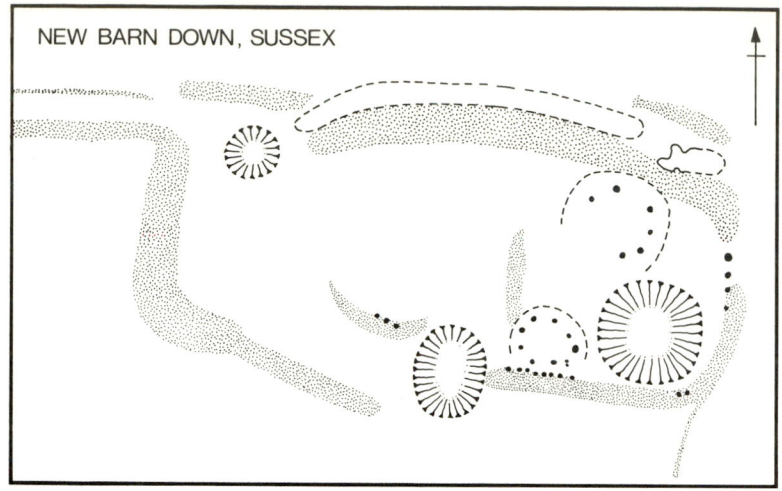

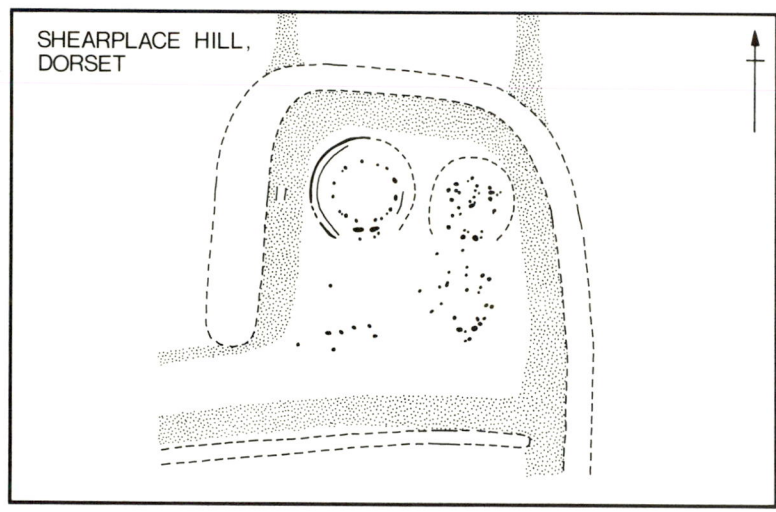

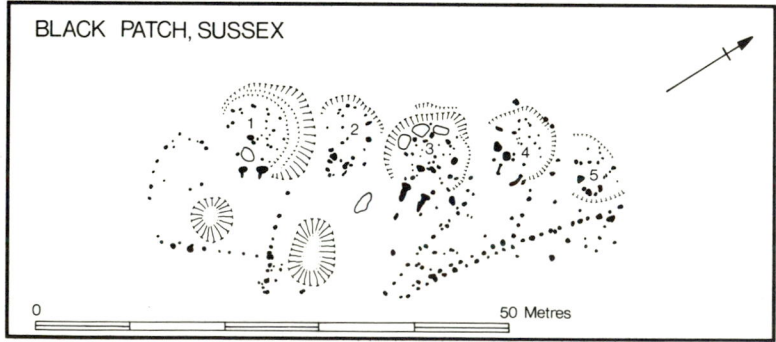

Figure 3.2 Settlements in southern Britain, second to first millennium (sources: *New Barn Down*, E.C. Curwen 1934a; *Shearplace Hill*, Rahtz and ApSimon 1962; *Black Patch*, Drewett 1982).

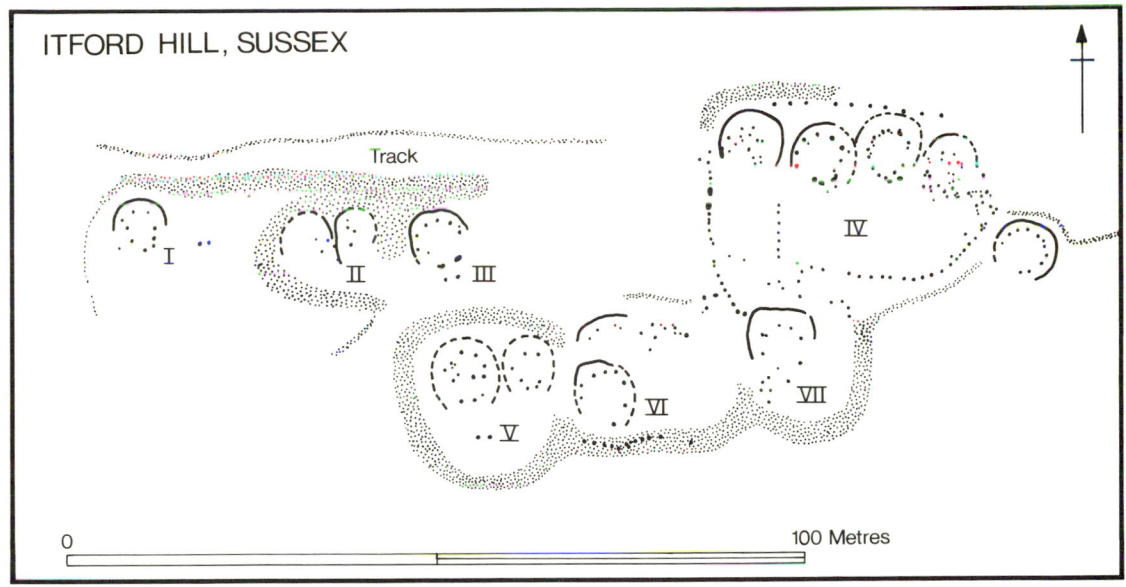

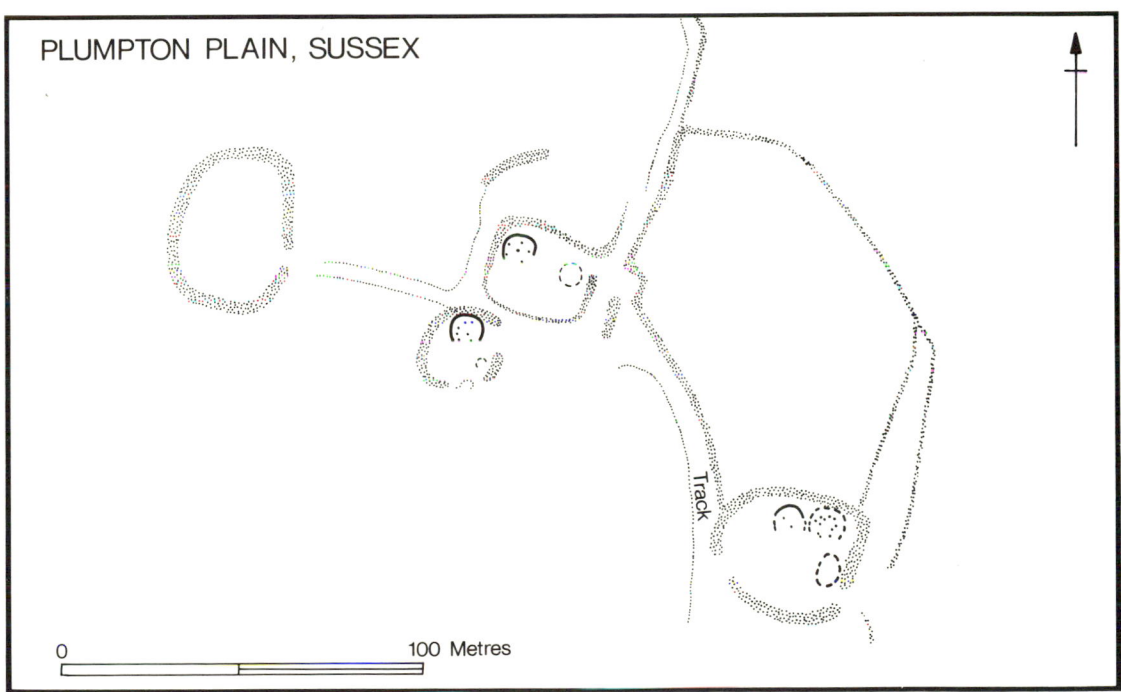

Figure 3.3 Settlements in southern Britain, second to first millennium (sources: *Itford Hill*, Burstow and Holleyman 1957; *Plumpton Plain*, Holleyman and Curwen 1935).

Are we dealing with a single extended family moving every generation or two or several such groups? The resolution of the problem is beyond the present scope of the evidence.

The third Sussex example, Itford Hill, superficially presents a dense form of nucleation (Figure 3.3). Here a complex of six enclosures lay adjacent to each other in an elongated area some 128 by 46 m. Extensive excavation, under modern conditions, has allowed much of the plan to be recovered, displaying distinctions in both size of house-type and function. A reassessment of the published evidence (Ellison 1978, 36) has suggested that the complex is divisible into four distinct structural phases, the first comprising enclosures I, II and III, the second enclosures IV and VIII, the third enclosures V, VI and VII, and the fourth enclosure IX. The successive units were broadly similar in size and function and comparable to Black Patch hut platform 4 which, we have suggested, probably represented the homestead of an extended family. Additional support for this view comes from the cremation cemetery close to Itford which can be shown, by joining potsherds, to have been closely related to the settlement. The age and sex pattern of those buried here is similar to that which would be expected of a single family unit using the burial ground over several generations. Thus the Itford evidence shows that even on apparently nucleated sites the basic settlement unit need be no larger than the extended family. Nowhere on the chalklands of southern Britain is there convincing evidence of any larger settlement agglomeration.

A second type of enclosure exists in the same general area as the enclosed settlements, and belongs to a broadly similar period. These enclosures (Figure 3.4), invariably ditched with a bank on the inner side, differ from the settlements in that they yield little evidence of intensive habitation. The two well-known examples, South Lodge Camp and Martin Down Camp, excavated by Pitt Rivers in Cranborne Chase, are both strongly rectilinear in form; South Lodge Camp possesses a single entrance while Martin Down has two entrances and an apparently undefended length along the north side which may originally have been closed with hurdles or some temporary structure leaving no archaeological trace. Pitt Rivers's excavations suggested that the interiors were largely devoid of internal features, apart from a few undated pits but the re-excavation of South Lodge Camp presents a more complex picture and, incidentally, highlights how much Pitt Rivers missed. It is now clear that the enclosure was constructed within an existing field system. Inside were two circular houses, the larger measuring 8 m in diameter, together with several small pits and isolated post-holes. In view of this new evidence the pits found in the Martin Down enclosure may be seen as the only element Pitt Rivers recognized of a more extensive settlement. Less certainty attaches to the contemporary Wiltshire enclosures on Boscombe Down East, Preshute Down and Ogbourne Down. At Boscombe Down East only limited excavation was undertaken, but sufficient to show that the enclosed 0.1 ha was largely without occupation, although a scatter of pottery was found outside. The ditch clearly related to a linear 'ranch boundary' of the type to be described later (p. 383), which formed its southern side. The northern entrance was provided with a pair of double (recut?) post-holes, presumably defining the position of a gate, a little over 1 m wide, set back to be on line with the inner bank. This suggests that the bank may have formed a bedding for a continuous palisade, the holes for which did not penetrate the solid chalk. The same may well have been the case with the South Lodge Camp and Martin Down Camp enclosures, but the possibility is not susceptible of proof. The enclosures on Preshute Down and Ogbourne Down in north Wiltshire are even less well known, but they do not differ significantly from those just described.

The exact status of the rectangular ditched enclosures of Wessex is difficult to define with so little reliable evidence available. While they could represent simply a variant of the extended

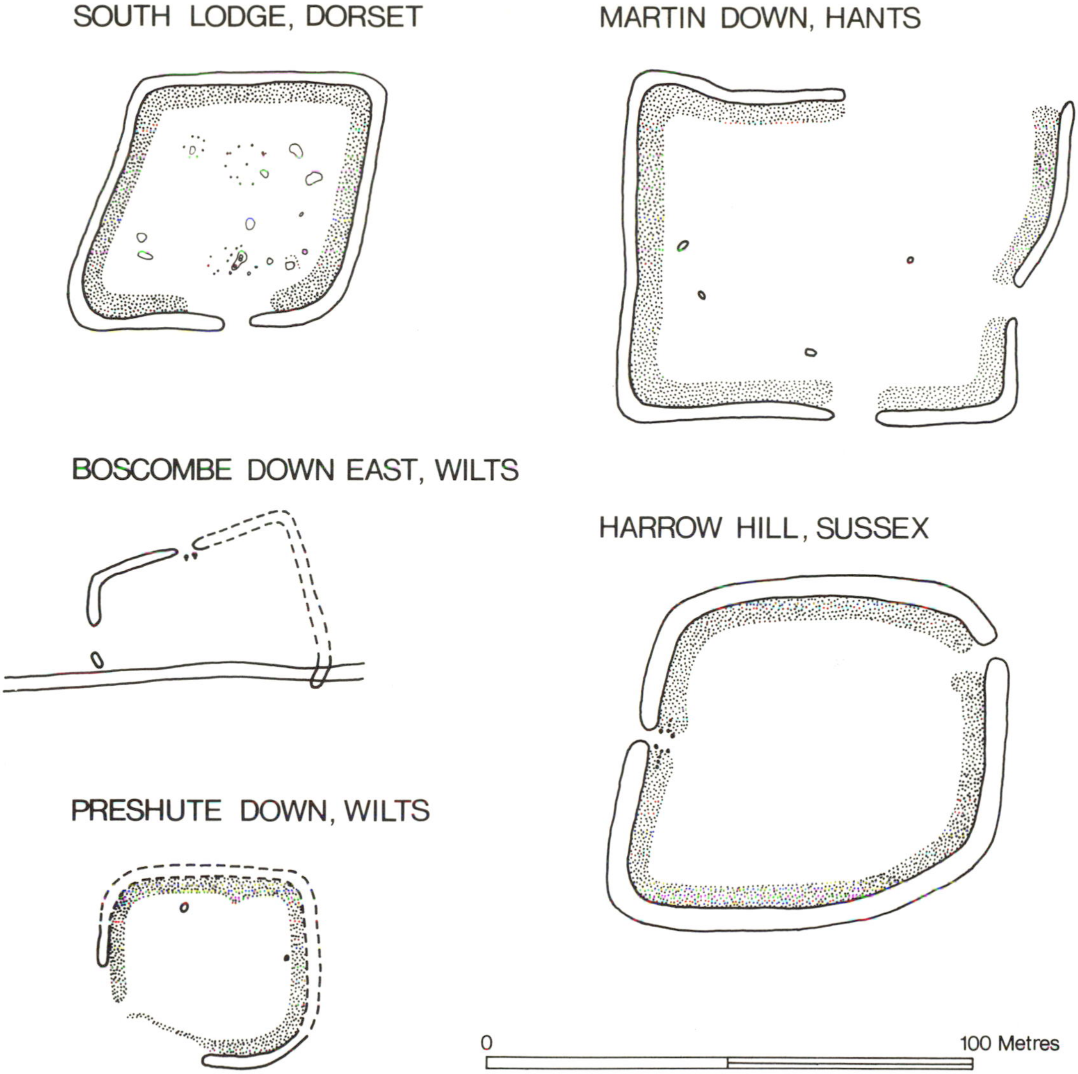

SOUTH LODGE, DORSET

MARTIN DOWN, HANTS

BOSCOMBE DOWN EAST, WILTS

HARROW HILL, SUSSEX

PRESHUTE DOWN, WILTS

0 ——————————————————— 100 Metres

Figure 3.4 Ditched enclosures in southern Britain, second to first millennium (sources: *South Lodge*, Pitt Rivers 1898, Barrett, Bradley, Bowden and Mead 1983; *Martin Down*, Pitt Rivers 1898; *Boscombe Down East*, Stone 1936; *Preshute Down*, C.M. Piggott 1942; *Harrow Hill*, Holleyman 1937).

family unit discussed above, the act of deliberate enclosure by labour-intensive ditch digging, the comparatively large house at South Lodge and the number of storage pits at South Lodge and Martin Down and Preshute, may be indicative of settlements of higher status.

Before considering the economic pattern to which these settlements and enclosures belong, something must be said of their date. Radiocarbon dates are available for Shearplace Hill, 1180 ± 180 bc; Chalton 1243 ± 69 bc, Itford Hill 1000 ± 35 bc; Black Patch, four dates between 1070 and 830 bc and South Lodge 1160 ± 110 bc, 1200 ± 120 bc and 950 ± 110 bc.[1] Although too much reliance should not be placed on such a disparate collection of dates, amassed in a somewhat *ad hoc* manner, the overall impression given is that the majority of these sites lay within the period 1400–1000 BC and were therefore traditionally Middle Bronze Age passing into the beginning of the Late Bronze Age. This is entirely consistent with the few bronzes which have been found stratified in settlement contexts. The dearth of dates in the ninth and eighth centuries is not particularly significant given so small a sample. At Plumpton Plain an analysis of the surfaces of the whetstones suggested the sharpening of iron tools which, if true, can hardly allow the site to be dated much before the eighth century. Similarly, at Boscombe Down East what was claimed to be iron slag was found in the primary silt of the ditch.[2]

Besides pottery, the surviving material culture of these Middle to Late Bronze Age settlements is sparse. Awls and needles of bone and scrapers of flint point to leather-working on a large scale. Cylindrical loom weights of clay, clay spindle whorls and a single example of a bone weaving comb from Shearplace Hill together with a set of loom weights from Black Patch show that wool was being spun and woven, and numbers of fragmentary querns of saddle type underline the significance of grain production to the economy. Bronze tools and weapons are relatively rare, no doubt because of their value, but awls were found at Black Patch, Chalton, Martin Down and South Lodge Camp; socketed spears occur at Thorny Down, South Lodge and New Barn Down; knives of various kinds are known from Chalton, New Barn Down, Black Patch and Plumpton Plain, where a ferrule and a fragment of winged axe were also found. The early settlement at Chalton produced a palstave. Razors from Black Patch, South Lodge Camp and Martin Down Camp, ribbed bracelets from Thorny Down and South Lodge Camp and a conical bronze mounting from Chalton show that bronze was also used for less utilitarian purposes. While it is fair to suppose that many of the above types could have been current after 1000 BC, the palstave, conical mounting and ribbed bracelets all derive ultimately from the 'ornament horizon' of the thirteenth to twelfth centuries BC and must indicate a second-millennium origin for the sites on which they occur. In contrast, the winged axe and socketed knife from Plumpton Plain and the collection of objects from Highdown Hill, near Worthing, are firmly in the Late Bronze Age tradition of metalwork, dating perhaps to as late as the eighth or seventh century.

The presence of saddle querns and grain storage pits on many of the settlement sites (both cultural traits can be traced back into the Neolithic period) emphasizes the fact that the basis of the subsistence economy was corn-growing. Analysis of carbonized grains and grain impressions on pottery provides a general picture of Late Bronze Age grain production, with barley predominating – amounting to about 80 per cent of the total output compared to emmer wheat.[3] Of the total barley crop some 70 per cent was of the hulled variety – a type suitable for winter sowing. A large quantity of carbonized grain found in one of the pits at Itford Hill proved to be almost entirely of hulled barley of both the nodding bere variety (*Hordeum tetrastichum*) and the erect form (*Hordeum hexastichum*); only five grains of emmer wheat were recorded in the entire sample, but careful analysis allowed the seeds of fourteen different weeds of cultivation to be isolated, including false cleavers, barren broom, black bindweed, opium poppy and many others.

Systematic sampling at Black Patch has produced a detailed picture of crop growing on the downs of eastern Sussex. Of the contexts sampled hulled barley occurred in 88 per cent, emmer in 47 per cent and spelt in 18 per cent. The total absence of naked barley is surprising. In addition 6 per cent of the contexts also produced bean (*vicia faba*) which was to become of far greater importance to the later Iron Age economy. These figures for the Mid–Late Bronze Age must be seen against a gradually increasing amount of hulled barley at the expense of naked, and of wheat gaining in importance over both types of barley, as improved farming methods, including a greater reliance on winter-sown crops, gradually came into use towards the beginning of the first millennium (Burgess 1985, 203–4).

Several of the settlements referred to in the foregoing pages are intimately connected with field systems defined by banks – known as lynchets – created largely as the result of ploughing on a slope, a process which allows soil to accumulate at the lower boundaries of the ploughed area. These banks were often increased in height by flints and rubble picked off the fields during cultivation. Since the light ard available at the time would only have broken the soil and not turned a furrow, as in the case of a plough provided with a mould-board, it is generally assumed that each field was ploughed in two directions to break the soil sufficiently for sowing. Archaeological traces of cross-ploughing are well attested in Bronze Age contexts in this country and abroad. Such a treatment would result in a patchwork of small, squarish fields, many hundreds of hectares of which are known. It is often very difficult to distinguish between fields of Bronze Age, Iron Age or Roman date, but one of the Ogbourne Down enclosures evidently post-dates the initial use of a group of fields and the same is true at South Lodge, while at Itford Hill, New Barn Down, Martin Down Camp and Plumpton Plain A, the trackways leading to the settlements are closely related to field systems, which may therefore be contemporary.

While the preparation of crops must have accounted for much of the communities' efforts, the tending of flocks and herds can have been of no less importance. Each of the excavated occupation sites has produced evidence of oxen, sheep and goats, with lesser numbers of pigs, horses, dogs and deer usually present. Where samples are large enough, and adequate quantitative records have been kept, as at Black Patch, Martin Down Camp and South Lodge Camp, oxen are found to predominate.

In the relatively simple type of subsistence economy in operation during the Mid–Late Bronze Age in south-east Britain, there would have been a close interreliance between the arable and pastoral sides of farming, particularly the use of cattle to manure fields while gleaning from the stubble after the harvest. During the growing seasons the flocks and herds would no doubt have been turned loose on the open downland to forage for themselves. All the time that settlements were few, the system would have worked well, but with increased pressure on land consequent upon a rapidly growing population more formal methods of land-division would have been required, leading eventually to the construction of ditched boundaries – the so-called 'ranch boundaries', cross-ridge dykes and spur dykes – many of which originated in the Late Bronze Age and continued to be constructed throughout the early part of the first millennium BC. These structures will be discussed in more detail in a later chapter (p. 383).

Elsewhere in south-eastern Britain evidence of Bronze Age economy is slight, but on the edge of the Cambridgeshire fens at Fengate, area excavation has recently brought to light clear evidence of regularly laid out fields bounded by ditches and associated with ditched trackways, for which radiocarbon assessment suggests a date in the Mid–Late Bronze Age. One explanation for the system, favoured by the excavator (Pryor 1975, 336–7), is that the fields represent the winter pasture for flocks and herds, which would have spent the summers roaming free on the rich grass of the fen islands. The regularity of the layout of the fields certainly implies a strict order of the kind one would expect if the scarce resources of winter pasture were to have been fairly apportioned between the rival claims of a large and well-established community. Whatever the true explanation, the evidence from Fengate is a salutary reminder that not all the economic regimes of the south-east need be similar to those observed on the chalkland.

Settlement in the Thames valley

Several recent excavations in the Middle and Upper Thames valley have focused attention on the region, hitherto known largely only for its wealth of metal finds. Most remarkable of the sites is the riverside settlement found at Runnymede Bridge, Egham, close to the confluence of the Thames and the Colne Brook. Here the complex piling of the river bank over a distance of more than 35 m implies a considerable expenditure of effort in the interests of providing landing facilities. The associated assemblage is particularly rich including a range of bronze tools, implements and ornaments of Late Bronze Age type, together with ample evidence of metalworking. In addition there was a range of bone and antler tools, clay spindle whorls and loom weights and exotic imports including shale armlets and amber beads. The richness of the assemblage may, at least in part, be due to the high status and (or) trading nature of the settlement. Its extent is at present undefined but traces of contemporary occupation have been found at various points up to 400 m from the river suggesting a complex of considerable size. The discovery of the Runnymede settlement is a reminder of the importance of the Thames as a route of communication. Similar riverside settlements may well exist along its length as for example at Syon Reach, Brentford where a suggestive range of bronzes and timber piles were recorded earlier this century.

In addition to these high status riverside settlements others of a more normal agricultural kind have been excavated on the terraces of the Middle and Upper Thames valley and its tributary the Kennet. At Aldermaston an extensive spread of pits and post-holes were uncovered representing part of a settlement of unknown extent. Radiocarbon dates of 1290 ± 140 bc, 1050 ± 40 bc and 840 ± 35 bc are rather unhelpful for a site thought to be of short duration but might indicate occupation centring on the twelfth century BC. Eight kilometres away, at Knights Farm, another scatter of pits and post-holes was partly explored. Radiocarbon dates range from 1245 ± 100 bc, associated with typologically early pottery, to a group of dates for the latest phase (870 ± 110 bc, 740 ± 80 bc, 600 ± 80 bc, 565 ± 250 bc and 290 ± 120 bc). Together they suggest occupation spanning the period from the fourteenth to the seventh centuries BC.

These two Kennet valley sites are of interest both in providing useful ceramic assemblages and in offering some hint of the complexities of the economic system. At Aldermaston large quantities of cereal grain were found presumably reflecting the production of the surrounding land, while at Knights Farm, around which was a high percentage of seasonally waterlogged land, there appears to have been a greater emphasis on livestock. Loom weights, however, were common on both sites. The actual percentages of the cereals recovered from Aldermaston were similar to those from the southern chalkland sites with the wheat/barley ratio varying from 7.7 per cent/92.3 per cent to 18 per cent/82 per cent depending on context. Of the barley between 63 and 92 per cent was hulled compared with the naked variety. Although the evidence is not sufficient to support a detailed economic model it does point to variety between sites while suggesting that the economy of the valley sites was not noticeably different from that of the chalkland settlements.

Hill-top enclosures in south-eastern Britain

It will be shown in chapter 15 that the construction of hillforts had begun by or soon after 800 BC, but the tradition of building enclosures on hill-tops and of partially enclosing large areas of upland by means of lengths of earthworks can be traced back well into the second millennium. Here we must briefly examine selected sites belonging to these two early categories.

Hill-top enclosures are best exemplified by two sites: Harrow Hill, Sussex, and Ram's Hill, Berks. At Harrow Hill a sub-rectangular enclosure was defined by a ditch and a shallow bank into which had been set a close spaced palisade of timbers, the holes for which had penetrated the natural chalk (Figure 3.4, p. 33). Of the two entrance gaps evident, one was excavated, exposing an entrance passage flanked by two pairs of timbers 2 m apart. Excavation was limited and finds were few, but pottery evidence would hint at an early first-millennium date. More remarkable was the collection of animal bones which included the remains of between fifty and 100 cows' skulls with hardly a trace of a limb bone. If this density proved to be even throughout the enclosure it is estimated that more than 1,000 animals would be represented. Interpretation is difficult: it may be that some form of ritual deposit is indicated; alternatively, the enclosure could have been used for slaughtering surplus stock at certain times of the year, the worthless parts of the carcasses, including the heads, being discarded before the rest was carried off. The two explanations are not mutually exclusive. The Harrow Hill enclosure has much in common with the enclosures of Dorset and Wiltshire described above (p. 32), but its more substantial earthworks and prominent hill-top location serve to distinguish it.

The second enclosure, Ram's Hill, is situated in a similar position on the crest of the Berkshire Downs. Although virtually flattened by ploughing, a recent campaign of excavation has brought to light many structural details and has allowed the excavators to propose a three-phase sequence. In the first phase an area of about 1 ha was enclosed by a flat-bottomed ditch 2 m deep, backed by a bank faced with chalk blocks. Pottery from the ditch silt indicated a possible Early Bronze Age date. It appears that at a later stage, about the twelfth century (based on radiocarbon assessments) the bank was faced with a palisade of timbers tied back to an inner row of verticals, to create a box-structured rampart. Finally, a little later, a double palisade was erected in front of the rampart set largely within the filling of the ditch. One principal entrance and a small subsidiary gate were excavated, but two others are apparent on the air photographs. Internally a few post-holes were recovered, some possibly belonging to circular huts, others to regular settings of four posts of a kind thought to represent granaries. Finds were sparse, but one notable observation was that the pottery displayed a very wide range of fabrics, suggesting perhaps use by communities coming from far afield. It is possible, therefore, that at some stage Ram's Hill was used for a communal, perhaps socio-religious, purpose.

Ram's Hill, Harrow Hill and two similar enclosures at Highdown Hill, Sussex, and Norton Fitzwarren, Somerset, are sufficiently comparable in size, structure and date to suggest that they may have performed similar economic, social or religious functions in their respective regions, but more than this it is difficult to state. They do however seem to differ significantly from the 'pastoral enclosures' and the farms described above, and it is not unreasonable to suppose that they may have served a community larger than the extended family group. The distribution of Bronze Age farms on the hill-slopes around Harrow Hill gives the impression that the hill-top enclosure was a central point of a territory containing a number of scattered farming communities.

If the hill-top enclosures represent a degree of social cohesion, it is reasonable to ask whether a higher level of selected location can be defined, reflecting perhaps tribal gatherings. One type of site, which can be called the *plateau enclosure*, seems to be relevant here. A number of high hill-top locations can be shown to have been partially enclosed by lengths of bank and ditch thrown across spurs in such a way as to define relatively large flat areas of hill-top. Characteristically the

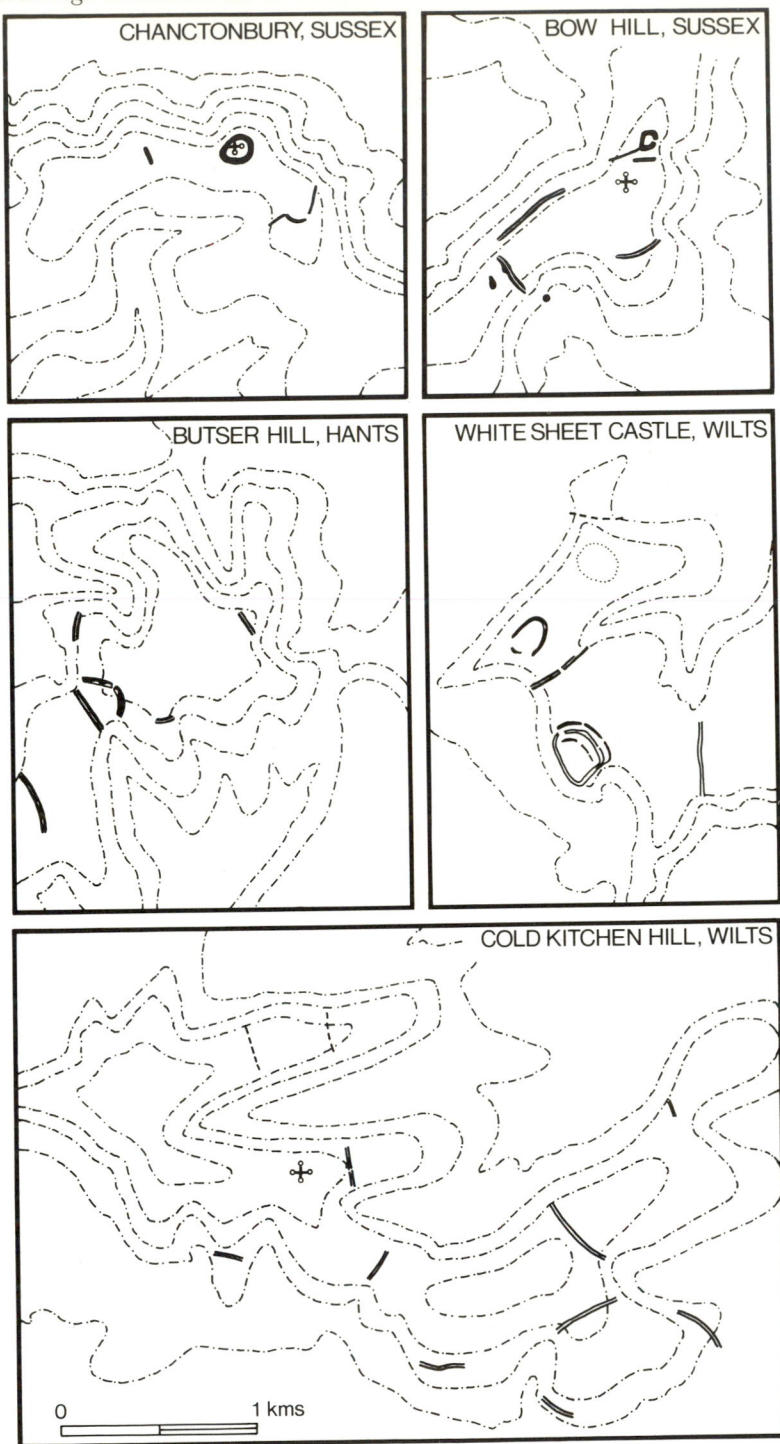

Figure 3.5 Plateau enclosures on the chalk downs. All plans are orientated with north at the top; contours at 100 ft. intervals. The cross-symbols represent the positions of Romano-Celtic temples (source: author).

banks are on the outside of the ditches (Cunliffe 1972b, 1976b). A selection of sites of this type are illustrated here (Figure 3.5). Others possibly include the spur dykes on Hambledon Hill, Dorset, the earthworks on Minchinhampton Common, Glos., and, further afield, the earthwork on Ratlinghope/Stitt Hill, Shropshire. Sites of this type have been very little studied and are virtually undated, but the Hambledon Hill spur dykes, if they belong to this category, have a third-millennium date indicated by radiocarbon assessments. In our present state of ignorance it is safer to recognize the existence of plateau enclosures without attempting to assign a date range or function to them.

The defended enclosures of eastern England

Excavations at Mucking, Springfield Lyons (Essex) and Thwing (Yorks.) have produced striking evidence of a kind of defensive enclosure which appears to be restricted to eastern Britain. At Mucking (Figure 3.6) two ditched enclosures of broadly similar date were discovered and largely excavated. They had been superimposed on a second-millennium field system. The South Ring consisted of a double ditched enclosure of circular plan, with opposed entrances, measuring 83 m in diameter overall, with a circular building 13 m in diameter placed in the centre of the inner enclosure. The North Ring was smaller, some 48 m in diameter and contained three circular post-built houses and a substantial fence shielding them from one of the entrances. The ditch had been recut on one occasion. Radiocarbon dates were obtained from both sites: for the South Ring: 820 ± 110 bc, 860 ± 70 bc, 840 ± 90 bc; and from the North Ring: 680 ± 110 bc, 750 ± 80 bc. Since the samples for the North Ring were taken from the recut ditch the initial dates of both sites are likely to have been much the same, somewhere in the tenth–ninth century BC.

The enclosure at Thwing, though similar in many respects to Mucking South Ring, was conceived on a grander scale (Figure 3.6). It comprised two concentric ditches with opposed entrances, the outer ditch enclosing an area of 105 m diameter. Immediately inside the outer ditch was a rampart of chalk rubble fronted by a palisade of timbers set in a continuous bedding trench. The rear face of the bank was given stability by two rows of timber presumably laced together to form a box-like structure. The inner ditch had no rampart. Inside was a circular timber building 25 m in diameter with an inner setting of posts on a 16 m diameter. A radiocarbon date of 950 ± 70 bc was obtained for an unweathered occupation layer immediately beneath the rampart.

Springfield Lyons was more complex (Figure 3.6). The ditch, roughly circular in plan and 54 m in diameter internally, was discontinuous with the main entrance lying to the east. Immediately inside the ditch was a 6 m gap where the rampart may have stood. This was backed by a double circle of post-holes interpreted as an inner revetment and walkway. Within these enclosing structures the remains of three circular post-built houses were discovered one of which was centrally placed and faced the entrance. Radiocarbon dates of 1140 ± 150 bc and 720 ± 140 bc for charcoal from the enclosure ditch and 880 ± 70 for charcoal from a post of the central house suggest a possible date range in the tenth or ninth centuries.

The Mucking, Springfield Lyons and Thwing enclosures were built on a monumental scale. At Thwing the associated assemblage included spindle whorls, loom weights, querns and a range of pottery appropriate to a domestic site but some objects of status were recovered including beads, pendants and bracelets of jet together with a range of decorated bronze pins, rings and a

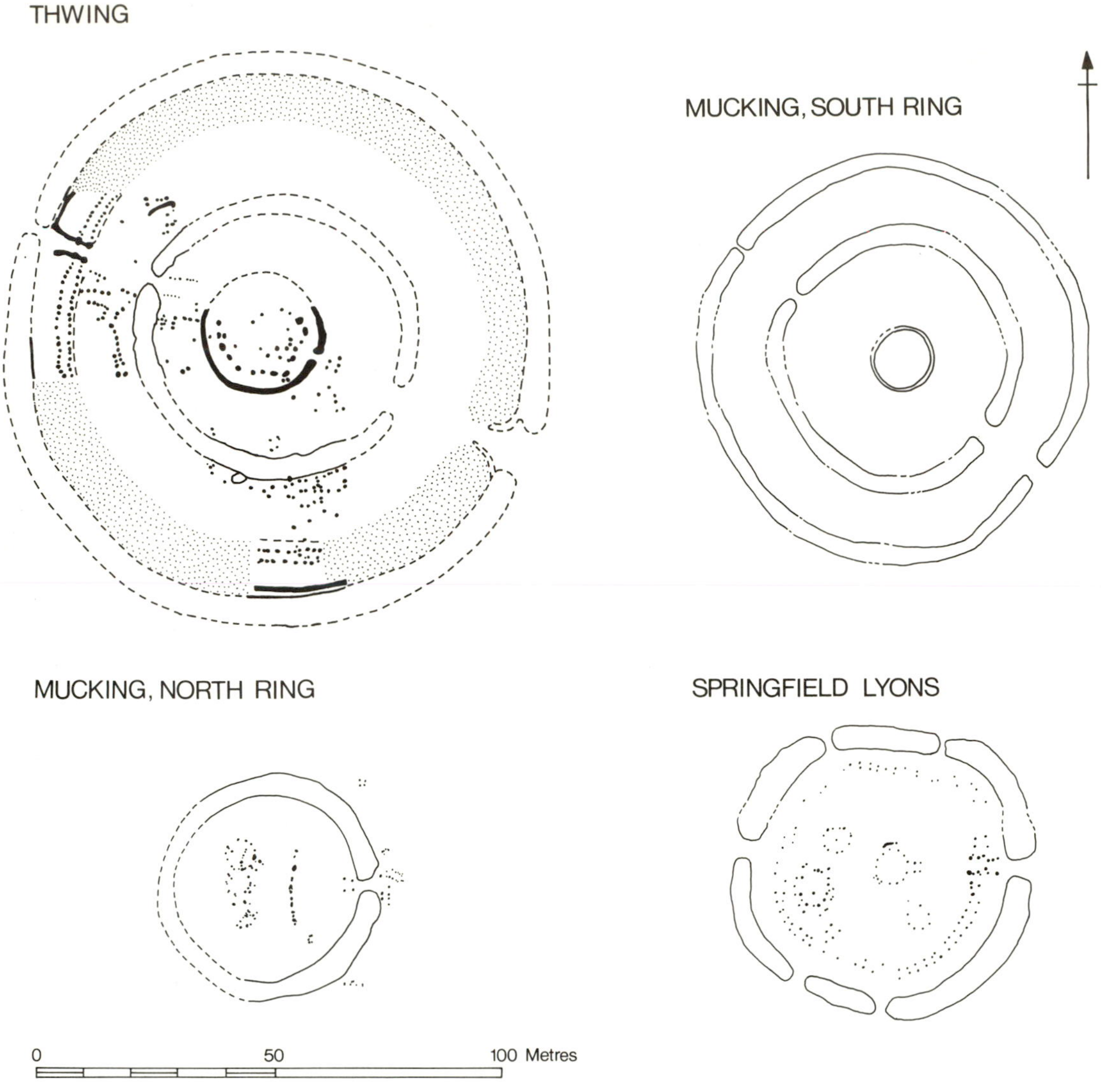

THWING

MUCKING, SOUTH RING

MUCKING, NORTH RING

SPRINGFIELD LYONS

```
0              50              100 Metres
```

Figure 3.6 Circular defended enclosures of the early first millennium (sources: *Thwing*, Manby 1980; *Mucking*, Jones and Bond 1980; *Springfield Lyons*, Buckley and Hedges 1987).

fragment of a spearhead. The Mucking Rings also produced normal domestic assemblages, the South Ring yielding in addition a bronze pin and a fragment of a copper ingot, while the North Ring produced a fragment of a socketed axe. The assemblage from Springfield Lyons was more limited but included spindle whorls and loom weights together with debris from bronze casting. The available evidence would suggest therefore that the enclosures were domestic sites but the monumentality of the architecture and exotic artefacts imply an unusually high status.

Several other sites, less extensively excavated, appear to belong to the same general type. At Mill Hill, near Deal in Kent, a circular enclosure 50 m in diameter was discovered, producing among other things, a range of bronze and shale items. A similar, but somewhat larger site was located at Queen Mary's Hospital, Carshalton, Surrey: others are also known (Figure 3.7). The predominantly easterly distribution may be fortuitous but the circular ditched enclosures are unknown in the well-studied area of Wessex and they may therefore reflect a particular social manifestation restricted to the east coast region in the first two or three centuries of the first millennium.

The south-west peninsula

Another area to have received detailed study is the south-west peninsula, particularly Dartmoor, Exmoor and Penwith. Of these regions, the settlement history of Dartmoor is the most informative, not least because of the attention which it has received from soil scientists and palaeobiologists, enabling regional ecological variations to be mapped in relation to the contemporary settlement patterns (Figure 3.8) (I.G. Simmons 1970). It is now clear that in the Middle to Late Bronze Age the high moorland areas above the 427 m contour were already covered with a blanket bog in excess of 0.6 m in depth. Below this and down to approximately the 243 m contour, the limit of the thick forest, lay a densely settled area of open grassland or heathland interspersed with relict woodland. The open areas originated in the coalescence of clearings which began at the beginning of the third millennium or even a few centuries earlier. Once the forest cover had been removed, continuous grazing and the leaching effect of heavy rainfall prevented forest regeneration.

Three types of settlement have been defined, each showing some preference for different climatic environments. The first, the pastoral enclosures, are concentrated on the south side of the moor, usually on south-facing slopes above river valleys close to a water supply (Figure 3.9). These enclosures have substantial walls inside which lie scattered stone-built huts usually in sufficient numbers for the settlements to be considered as villages. While it is not impossible that small-scale cultivation was carried out within the enclosed area – and indeed at Rider's Rings there are several small, walled garden plots – evidence of agricultural activity on a large scale is lacking. Some of these settlements show signs of growth. At Legis Tor a sequence of walls can be traced, demonstrating that the enclosed area was greatly increased in three successive stages, but whether this was related to a growth in the size of the population is impossible to say.

Only one site in this general category, Shaugh Moor, in the valley of the river Plym, has been extensively examined by modern methods (Figure 3.10). Here a complex of linear boundaries, burial cairns and walled enclosures litter the moor. One of the enclosures, selected for total excavation, was oval in shape, some 75 m across the large axis and was surrounded by a stone-built wall without gates. Within lay five stone walled huts, with internal timber supports, arranged around the periphery, together with a scatter of post-holes in the central area. The range of radiocarbon dates suggests continuous use throughout the second millennium until c. 850 bc (Otlet and Walker 1982, 237). Finds were sparse but included quernstones, flint scrapers and a little pottery. The virtual absence of grain (in spite of an extensive programme of sieving) and the comparatively few querns covering the 1,000 years or so of use tends to support the view that the enclosure reflected a pastoral aspect of the economy. One scenario would be to see enclosures of this sort used by a segment of the population who spent the summers on the move tending the livestock and possibly collecting metal ore as a major ancillary activity.

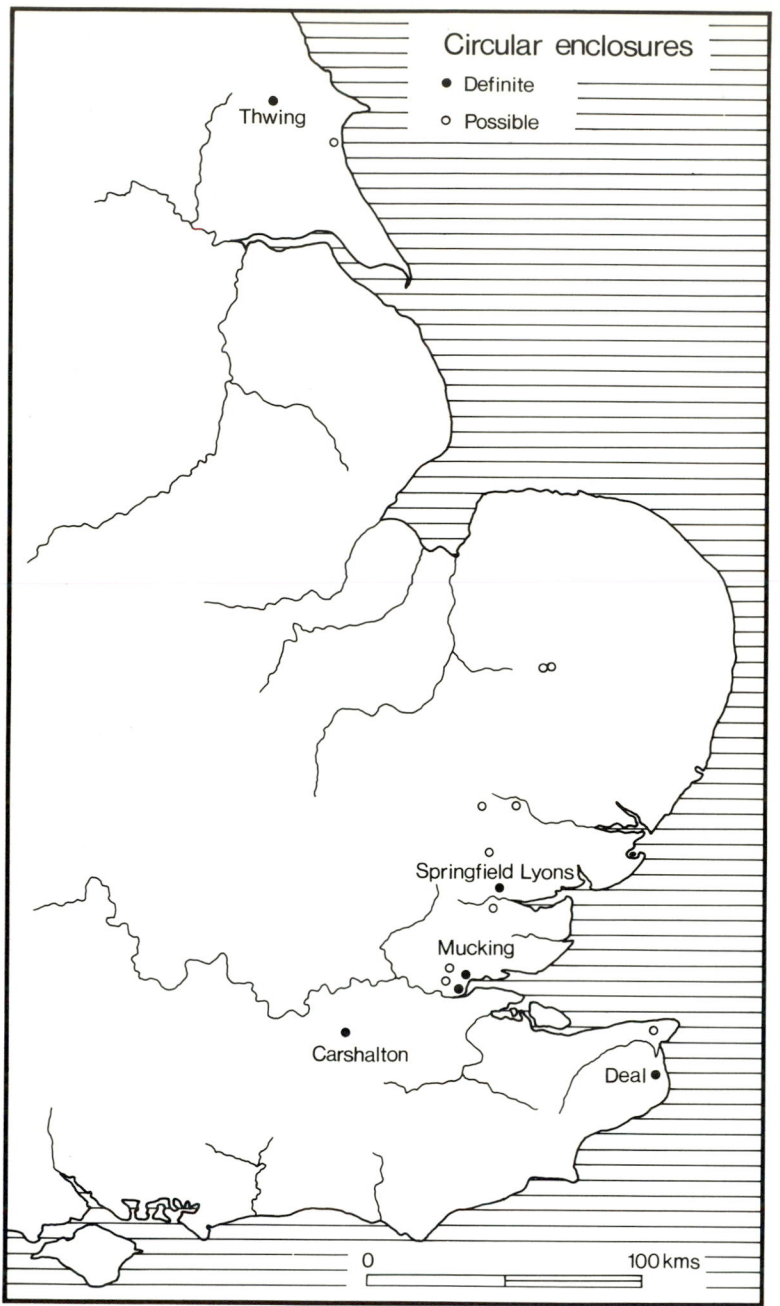

Figure 3.7   Distribution of circular defended enclosures of the early first millennium BC (sources: various).

The second type of Dartmoor settlement is the unenclosed village, where clusters of circular huts are linked together by low stone walls, creating multi-angular enclosures which could well have served as both cultivation plots and paddocks for stock at different times of the year.

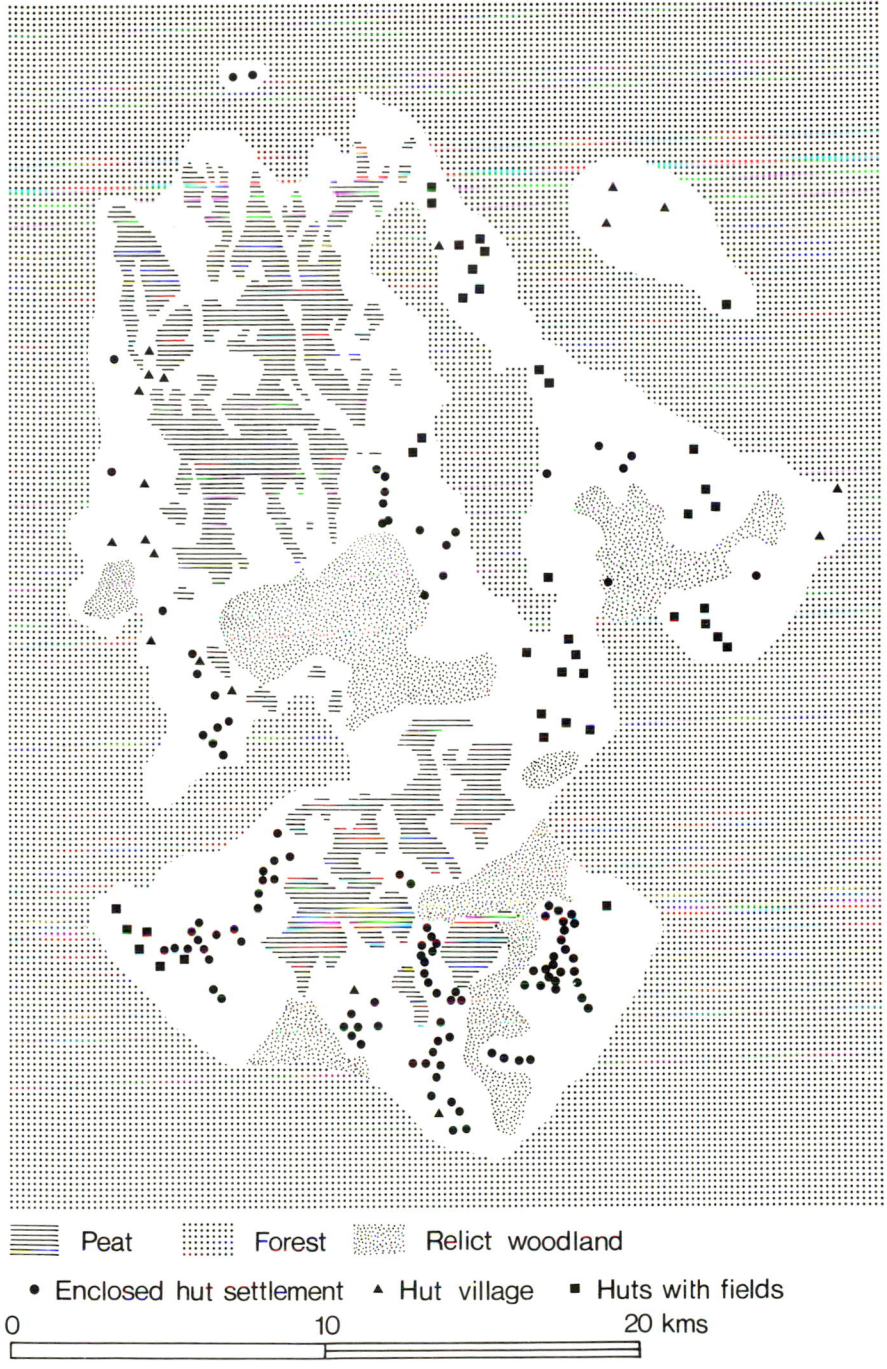

Figure 3.8 The ecology and settlement pattern on Dartmoor, late second to early first millennium (source: I.G. Simmons 1970).

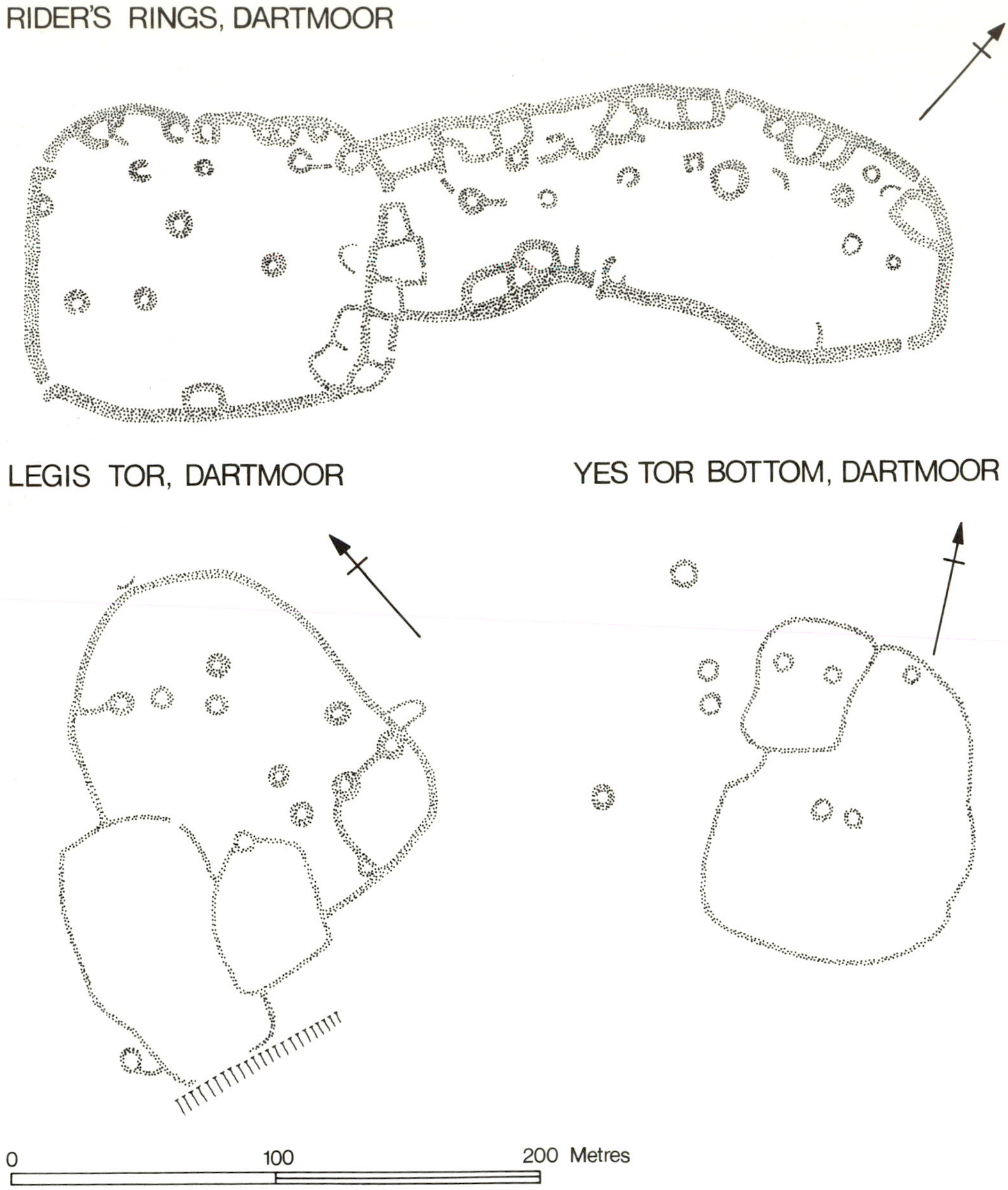

RIDER'S RINGS, DARTMOOR

LEGIS TOR, DARTMOOR   YES TOR BOTTOM, DARTMOOR

0   100   200 Metres

Figure 3.9 Nucleated settlements on Dartmoor, late second to early first millennium (sources: *Rider's Rings*, Worth 1935; *Legis Tor*, Worth 1943; *Yes Tor Bottom*, Worth 1943).

Sometimes these villages reach considerable proportions – sixty-eight huts are recorded at Stanton Down (Figure 3.11) but not all are so strictly nucleated: at Rough Tor on Bodmin Moor, for example, huts and their attached enclosures spread for about 0.8 km along a track, but here we may well be dealing with a linear development representing settlement shift over a considerable period of time. Unenclosed villages are not particularly numerous; with rare

Figure 3.10 Shaugh Moor, Dartmoor showing the enclosure fully excavated (photo: Geoffrey Wainwright).

exceptions, they concentrate on the climatically wetter western fringes of Dartmoor, usually within easy reach of streams.

The third type of settlement is the isolated farm or group of farms found in intimate association with rectangular stone-walled fields (Figure 3.12). Several such settlements are known in their entirety, showing that the arable area is hardly likely to have produced sufficient food for the occupants – only 0.4 ha for the single-hut farm at Rippon Tor and 0.8 ha for the three huts at Blissmoor. The implication must be that additional food supplies were available, presumably in the form of flocks and herds reared on the upland pastures. The arable farms cluster to the east of Dartmoor on the fertile 'brown soils' sheltered from extremes of climate by the mass of the moor itself. The dating of these sites presents some difficulties since material finds are sparse. Comparisons of the pottery from the Dartmoor settlements with the better dated Cornish sequence, however, suggests a Middle Bronze Age date (Read 1970). This gains some support from the discovery of a 'Bohemian style' palstave dated approximately to the fourteenth to twelfth century, found in relation to a field system on Horridge Common (Fox and Britton 1970, 225).

It would appear that the large pastoral villages and the small arable farms are different responses to different environments, and it may well be that they represent two divergent subsistence economies, but the possibility remains that this is the archaeological evidence of a transhumant society – the population leaving the scattered farmsteads of the east during the

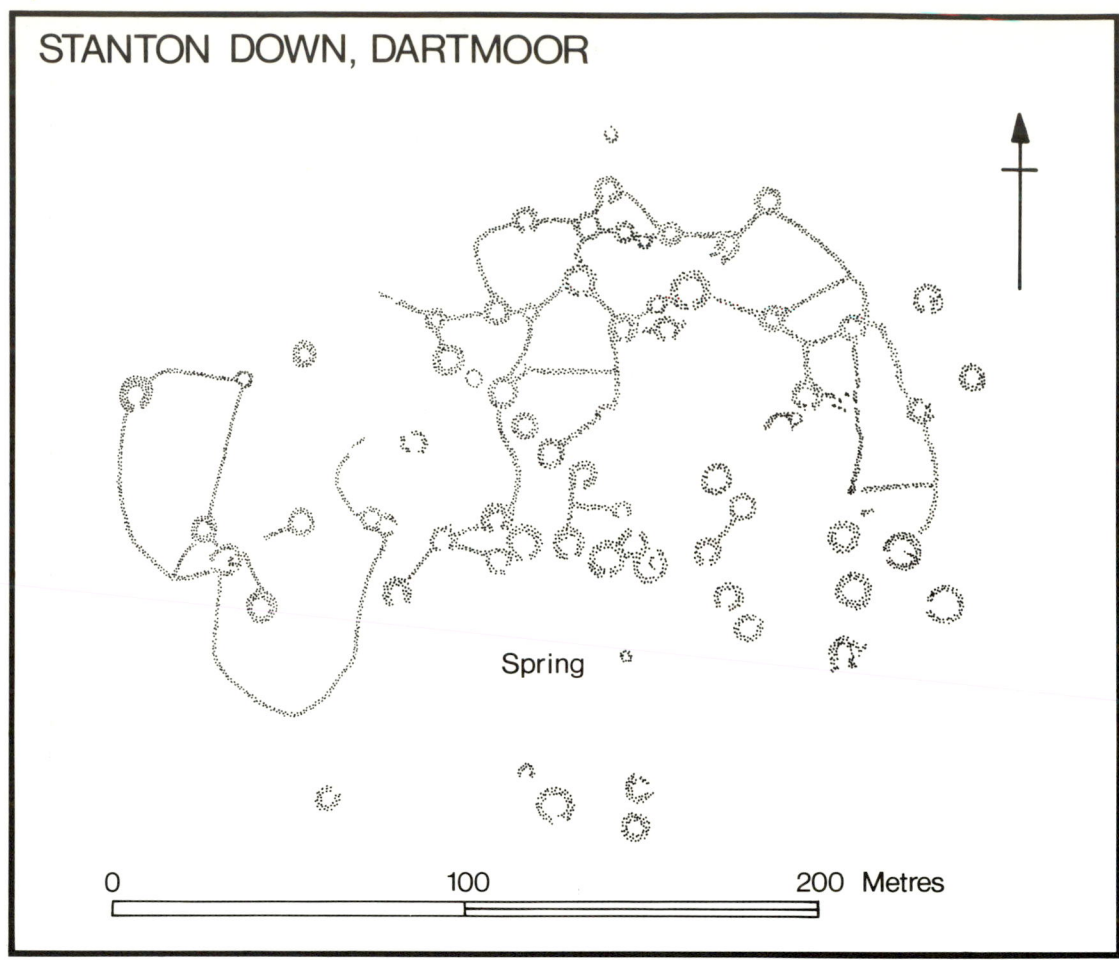

Figure 3.11   A Dartmoor village of the late second to early first millennium (source: Baring-Gould 1902).

spring and summer, taking their herds and flocks to the wetter western pastures, to return again in time for harvest. Some form of transhumance is certainly implied by the small hectareage of the eastern group of farms. It has been argued, however, that in addition to an important pastoral component an infield–outfield system of farming was being practised, the small areas of enclosed fields representing only the infields (Denford 1975).

In recent years, as a result of intensive field survey on the south edge of Dartmoor in the Cholwich Town region, it has been possible to demonstrate that large areas of moorland were enclosed at this time by linear banks of stone known as reaves (Figure 3.13) to which enclosed settlements were attached (Fleming 1978, 1984, 1988). Whether the boundaries divided territories in different ownership or land subject to different usage is unclear, but the extent of the reave system and the associated huts and settlements leave little doubt that the population was large and the available land well organized.

Further west, in Cornwall, structural evidence for Middle–Late Bronze Age settlement is less

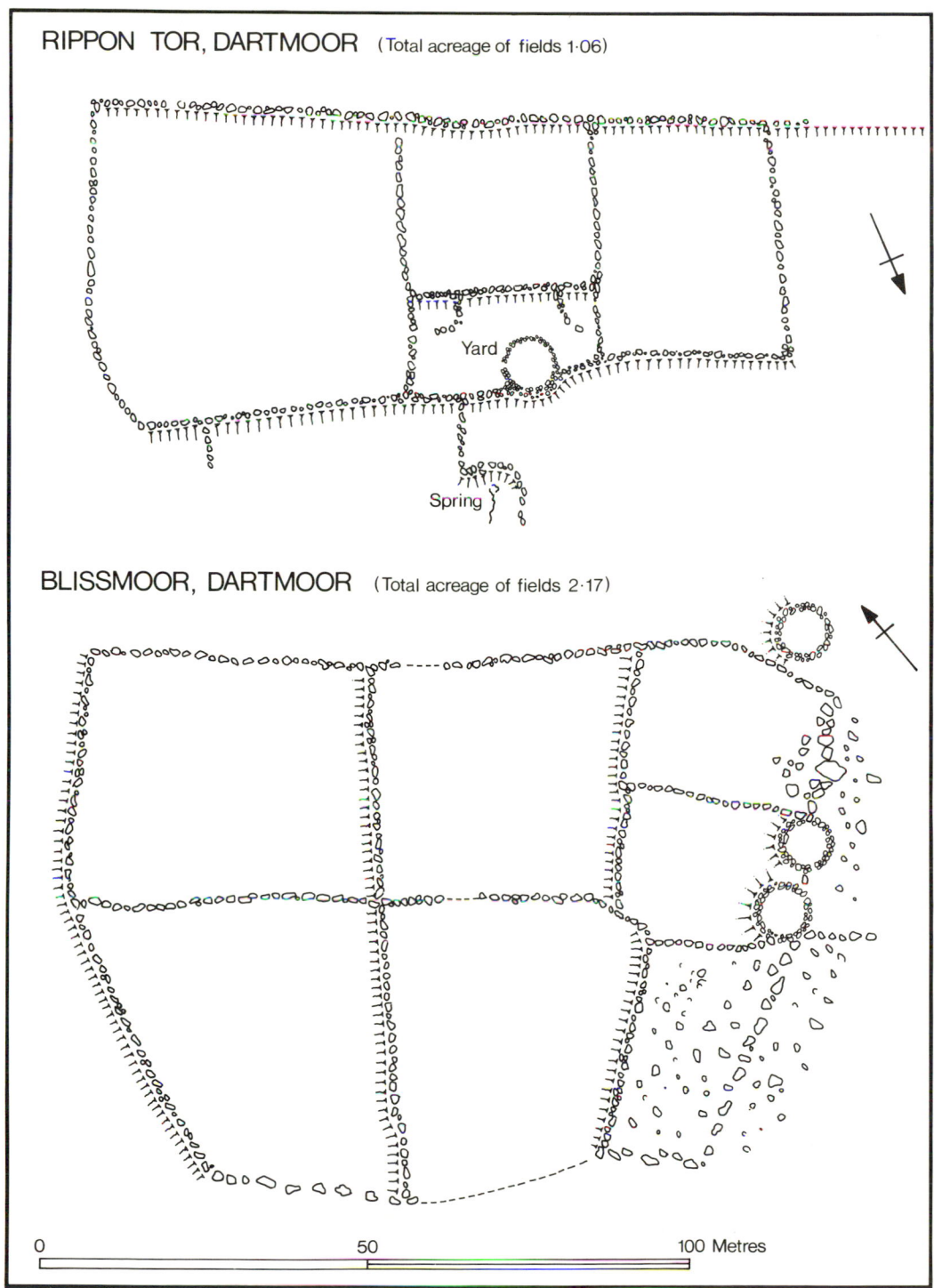

RIPPON TOR, DARTMOOR (Total acreage of fields 1·06)

Yard

Spring

BLISSMOOR, DARTMOOR (Total acreage of fields 2·17)

0   50   100 Metres

Figure 3.12 Dartmoor farmsteads of the late second to early first millennium (source: A. Fox 1955).

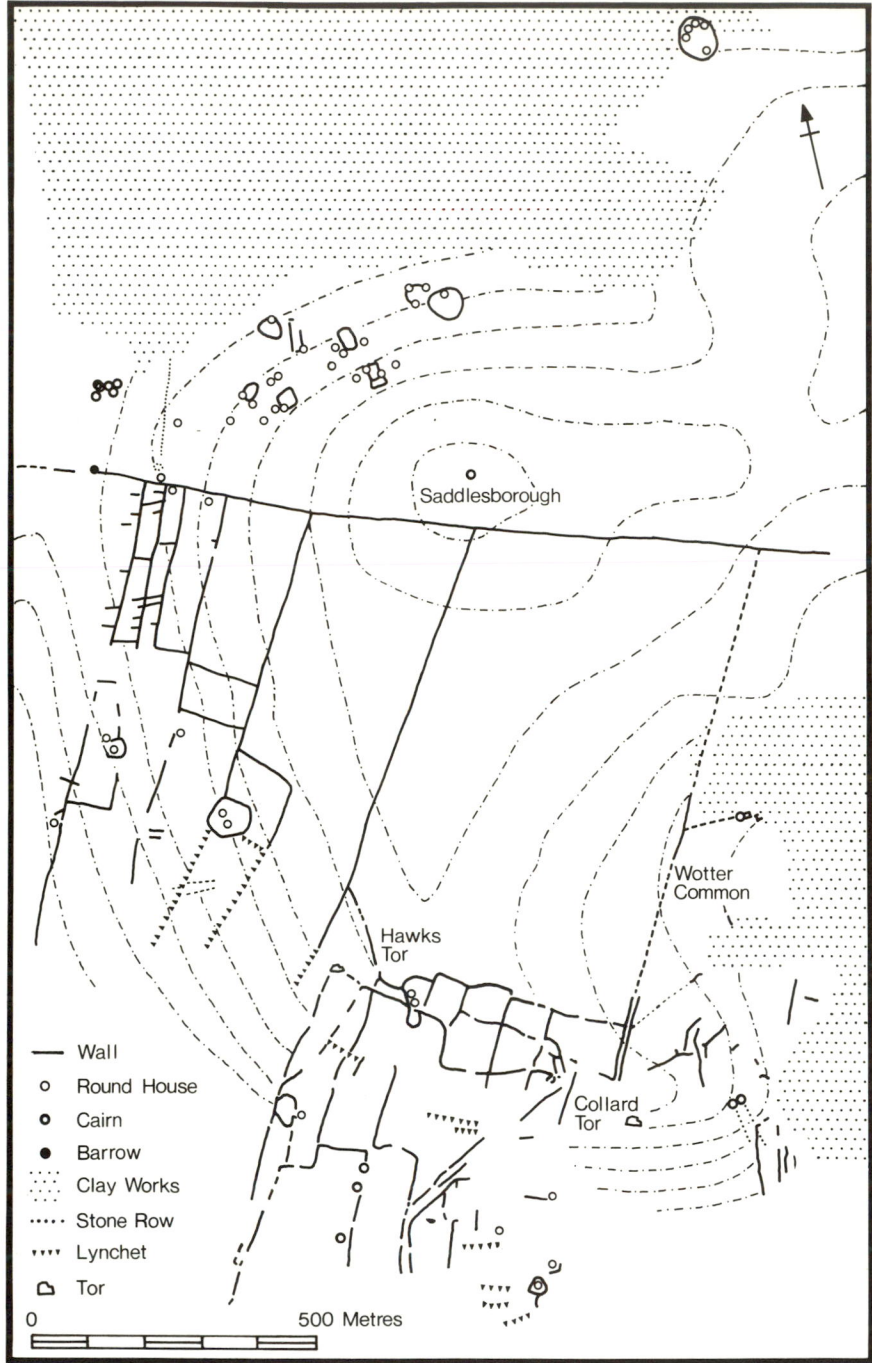

Figure 3.13 Reaves on Dartmoor. The system on Shaugh Moor and Wotter Common (source: Smith, Coppen, Wainwright and Beckett 1981).

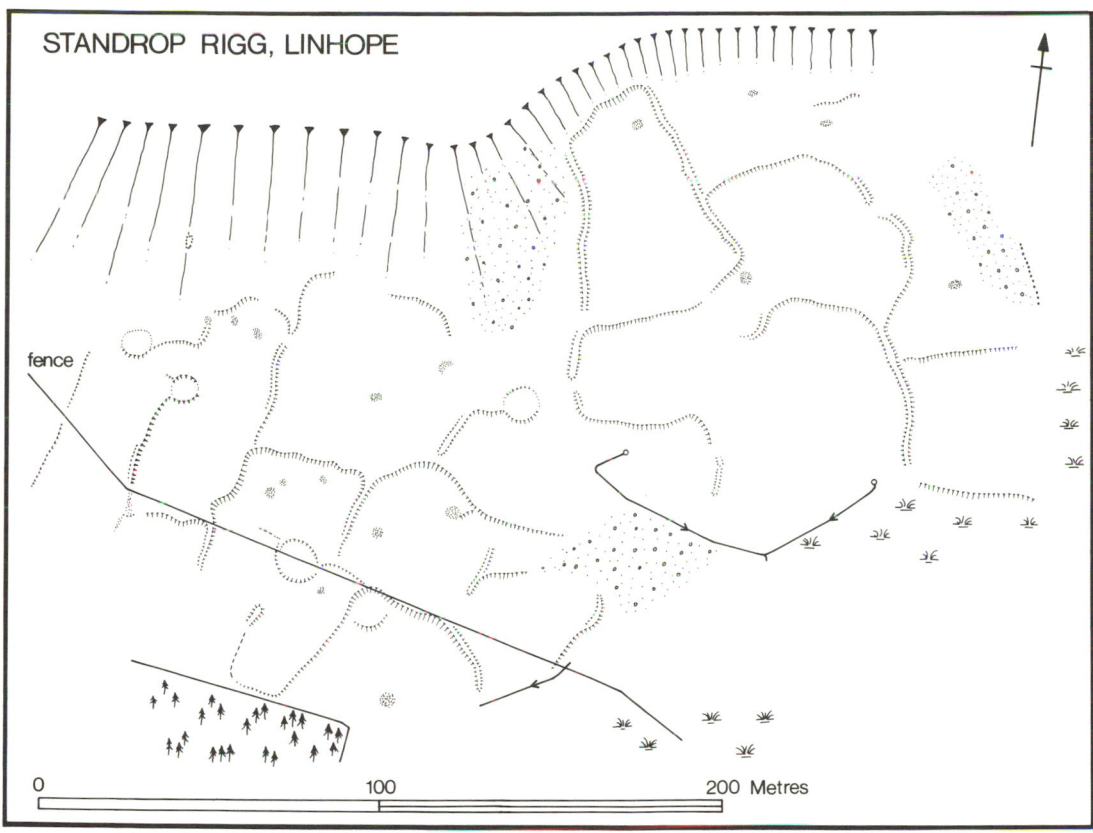

STANDROP RIGG, LINHOPE

fence

0   100   200 Metres

Figure 3.14   Standrop Rigg, Northumberland. Settlement of the late second to early first millennium (source: Jobey 1983).

prolific, although the settlement stratified beneath the Iron Age round at Trevisker is a reminder that many of the locations chosen for later settlement may well have been occupied on one or more previous occasions. The single radiocarbon date from the site (1110 ± 95 bc) suggests a real date in the thirteenth century BC. The wide distribution of Trevisker style pottery implies the existence in Cornwall of an extensive and settled population, utilizing the best farming land. On the more marginal lands, on the fringes of the granite moors, clusters of circular stone-built huts, like those of Dartmoor, are well known, but few have been extensively examined. At Stannon Down, on the western edge of Bodmin Moor, however, a group of eighteen houses apparently associated with corrals and strip fields have been planned and partially excavated. Estimates of population and crop yield suggest that here, as on Dartmoor, an infield–outfield system and a significant pastoral element would have been necessary to supply the needs of the community.

The Midlands, Wales and the north

Much of what has been said of the settlement pattern and economy of southern Britain must apply to the rest of the country but at present the evidence is, to say the least, sparse. In Wales several inhabited cave sites of the period have been defined, e.g. Lesser Garth Cave, Radyr, and Culver Hole Cave, Llangenydd (Gower), but open settlements are rarer. The ring-work on Marros Mountain, Pendine, may have been occupied at this time, but the evidence is not conclusive and it may possibly belong to the later first millennium. The above-mentioned sites all produced pottery in the Late Bronze Age tradition but little is known of other aspects of the material culture and economy – except, of course, for the numerous bronze hoards.

The Midlands and north are no better known. Work at Mam Tor, Derbyshire, has however demonstrated the existence of a cluster of Bronze Age huts producing radiocarbon dates of 1130 ± 115 and 1180 ± 132 bc, sited on the top of a hill later enclosed by the bank and ditch of an Iron Age hillfort. At the neighbouring hillfort of Portfield, Lancs., the discovery of a Late Bronze Age hoard lends some support to the idea that many of the hill-tops later fortified in the Iron Age may have originated as settlements even as early as the late second millennium. The same conclusions may be true of certain of the Scottish sites. At Traprain Law, for example, traces of an extensive Late Bronze Age settlement were discovered to underlie the subsequent Iron Age occupation.

In northern Britain it is now clear that many, if not all, of the unenclosed hut sites found in upland areas belong to the later Bronze Age (Jobey 1980). The most extensively excavated are the clusters at Green Knowe, Peeblesshire, and Standrop Rigg, Northumberland (Figure 3.14) for which radiocarbon dates focusing on the last three centuries of the second millennium BC have been obtained. Sites of this kind lie at the upper limit of prehistoric land exploitation and owe their survival to the fact that they have escaped the ravages of later agricultural activities. Other classes of settlement are less well known. Clusters of hut circles in the Yorkshire Dales, e.g. at Grassington, occasional cave deposits as at Covesea (Moray) and Heathery Burn, Co. Durham, the so-called crannogs of eastern Yorkshire and parts of Scotland and the cellular stone houses of Jarlshof (Figures 3.15 and 3.16), are all part of an extensive and varied settlement pattern about which few details are known. The general impression which these fragments provide is of well-established communities not unlike those of the south-east, which had adapted themselves closely to the more varied environments of the west and north. In the absence of positive evidence to the contrary, it would seem likely that the economy was heavily dependent upon pastoralism, cereal-production playing a lesser but still significant part. In this respect it is worth noting that the upland settlement of Green Knowe lay within a landscape that was being cleared of boulders either to improve pasture or to provide scope for cultivation. Views on this matter are, however, liable to modification in the light of current work.

Pottery

The dating of pottery belonging to the period 1500–500 BC is fraught with difficulties, and detailed discussion is not directly relevant to this volume (but see Barrett 1976, 1980). Nevertheless, some generalizations must be made, if only to prepare the way for the more lengthy consideration of the later period in subsequent chapters. The south-east of Britain, south of the Severn–Wash axis, has produced a large amount of pottery of Middle to Late Bronze Age date which, until recently, was conventionally classed together under the general title of the Deverel–Rimbury culture (Preston and Hawkes 1933), a name derived from two Dorset cemeteries excavated in the nineteenth century. Pottery of Deverel–Rimbury type has been recovered from two main contexts: cremation cemeteries and settlement sites of the types already

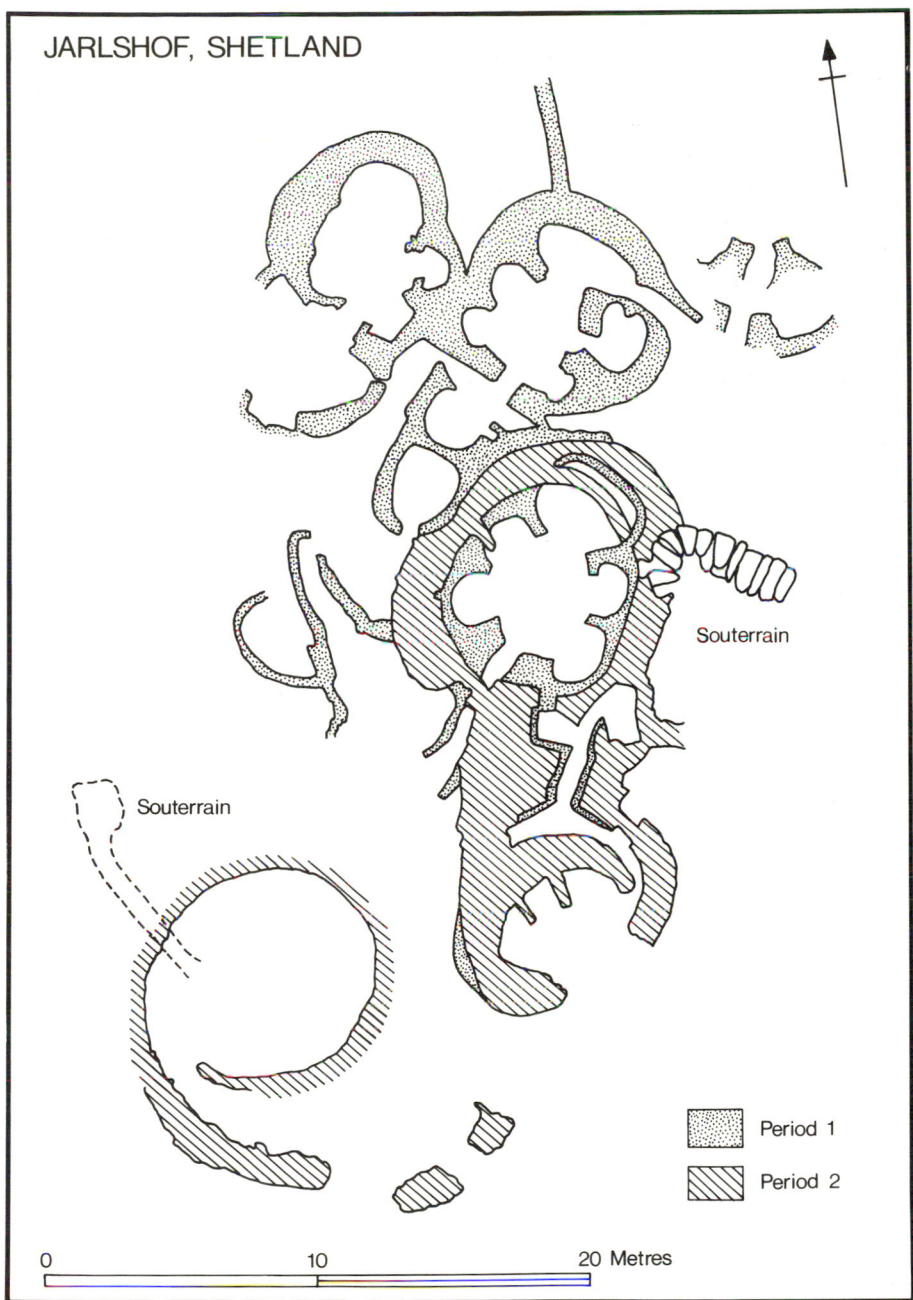

JARLSHOF, SHETLAND

Souterrain

Souterrain

Period 1

Period 2

0   10   20 Metres

Figure 3.15 Late Bronze Age homestead at Jarlshof, Shetland (source: J.R.C. Hamilton 1956).

described. In the cemeteries it is seldom found in any form of association with datable metalwork, but at the settlements bronze implements are occasionally found and can be used to provide broad date-brackets for the pottery.

Figure 3.16   Jarlshof, Shetland. The houses of the Bronze and Iron Age settlement (Crown Copyright reserved).

An assessment of the associated bronzes (M.A. Smith 1959) has shown that they ran broadly contemporary with the Montelius III phase of the north European Bronze Age, currently dated to 1300–1100 BC. This dating for an early stage of the Deverel–Rimbury culture gains further support from a typological study of the individual ceramic forms, which suggests internal development from indigenous types independently dated to the middle of the second millennium. Further confirmation is offered by an increasing number of radiocarbon dates. Thus the date-bracket 1400–1000 may reasonably be proposed to contain the 'classic' Deverel–Rimbury culture.

Within the ceramic assemblages of this 'classic' phase it is possible to recognize a number of regional variations evident in the fine wares which partly reflect the basic folk tradition of the region and partly local inventiveness (Figure 3.17). These differences may be used to define regional groups. Thus in Devon and Cornwall lies the *Trevisker group* (ApSimon and Greenfield 1972), in Dorset, south and west of the Stour, is the *South Dorset group*, on the Dorset coast at the confluence of the Stour and Avon is the *Stour valley group* and in Wiltshire and south-east Hampshire is the *Cranborne Chase group* (Calkin 1964; Ellison 1981). The contemporary pottery of

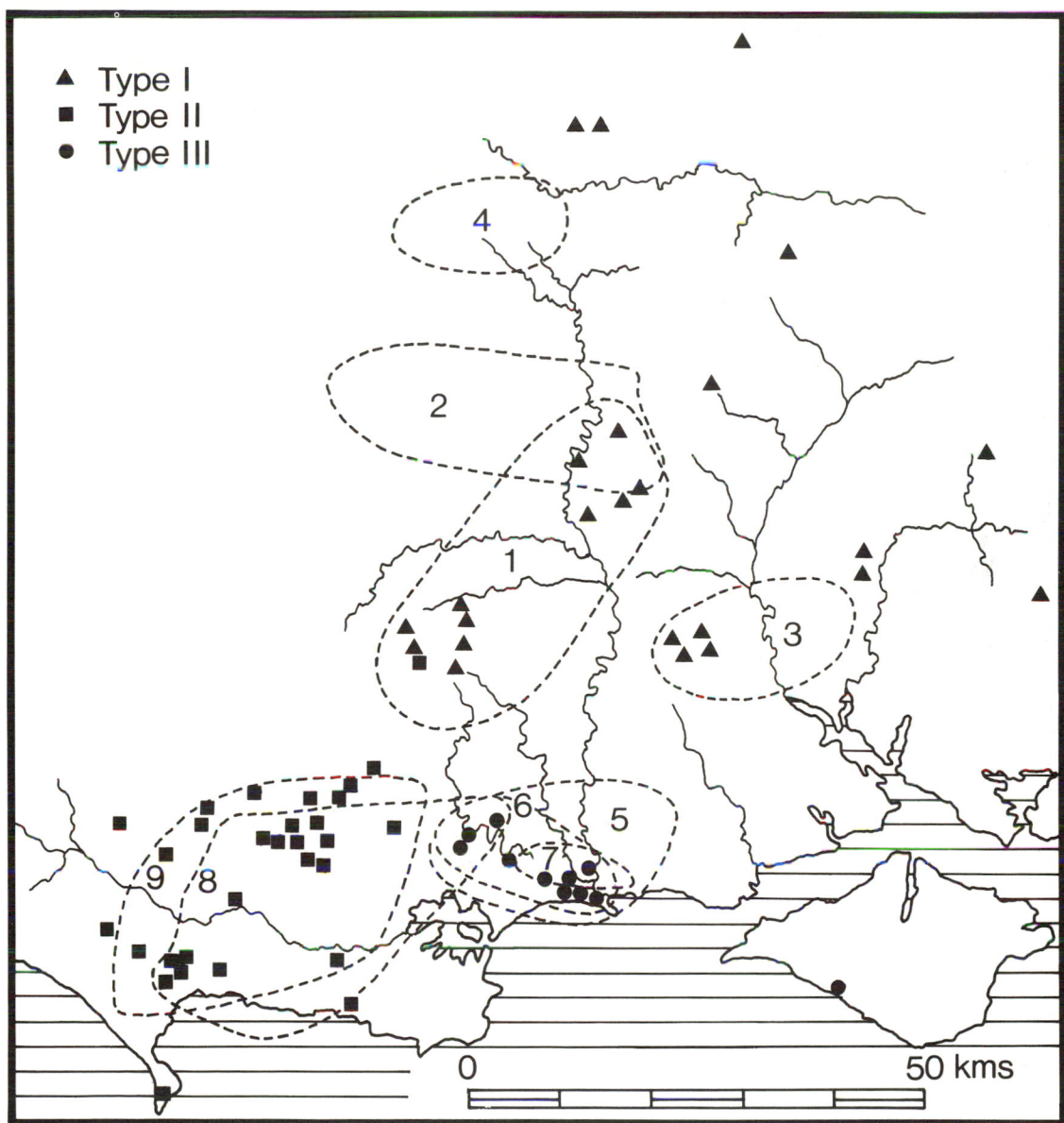

Figure 3.17 Distribution of Deverel–Rimbury pottery styles (source: Ellison 1981).

Sussex differs significantly enough from the western groups to be considered as a separate *South Downs group*, and in Essex and Suffolk the *Ardleigh group* has been distinguished (Erith and Longworth 1960). Other regional groups can be isolated in the *Thames valley*, the *west Midlands* and the *east Midlands* (Burgess 1974, 214–15).

The characteristic fine wares which enable the regional groups to be defined do not seem to have lasted long after 1000 BC though in parts of northern Wessex the tradition may have lingered (Gingell 1980). For much of the country the period from *c.* 1000–800 is marked by an intense conservatism in pottery technology, during which time the barrel and bucket forms continued to be made but in a simplified range of types. This phase may reasonably be called Late Deverel–Rimbury. Eventually, during the eighth century, or perhaps a little earlier in some precocious regions, innovations appeared alongside traditional forms: large angular jars were manufactured probably in imitation of bronze situlae, a range of bowls appeared and a few vessels in peripheral Urnfield style are to be found in the south-east. This phase of innovation has been called Ultimate Deverel–Rimbury (Cunliffe 1978a, 27) or Post Deverel–Rimbury (Barrett 1980). Neither term is satisfactory: here it is proposed to refer to it with the less emotive term *LBA transitional* phase. These ninth–eighth century innovations heralded the development of an inventive and dynamic ceramic industry in the south and east of the country which can properly be considered to be Iron Age.

In the Midlands, Wales and much of the north, pottery gradually ceased to be a significant element of material culture and many areas became virtually aceramic. Several urnfields have, however, been recorded in central England, including a large cemetery at Bromfield, Salop, where a series of cremations has been dated to 1560 ± 180, 850 ± 71 and 762 ± 75 bc, that is roughly seventeenth to ninth centuries BC.

In the extreme north of Scotland, in the Hebrides, Orkneys and Shetlands, a well-established ceramic tradition, rooted ultimately in the third millennium but with French Urnfield influences, flourished throughout this period and well into the Iron Age.

The bronze industry[4]

In the foregoing pages emphasis has been placed on the indigenous development of the British Late Bronze Age communities and the relative self-sufficiency of their subsistence economies. Superimposed upon this pattern of intense regionalism is a complicated and wide-flung trading system best exemplified by the distribution of bronze weapons and implements. Trading was on two levels: overseas trade, which brought in exotic types – often copied locally – and local trade, distributing the products of British smiths over more limited territories. This kind of specialist activity had a long ancestry in Britain; the Late Bronze Age was to see its ultimate development and the beginning of its decline.

The general assemblage of twelfth- to eleventh-century date contains a wide range of implements, including flange-hilted, leaf-shaped swords based on imported Erbenheim and Hemigkofen weapons; leaf-shaped Ballintober swords; dirks; looped palstaves; experimental types of socketed axe; basal-looped spearheads; razors and ring-socketed sickles. Distribution of these types is broad but centres upon south-eastern England. In the south it is generally known as the *Penard phase*, after a Glamorganshire hoard; in Scotland it is represented in the *Glentrool tradition*. Trading connections were wide, linking England and Scotland to Wales, Ireland and the northern and western areas of France.

From the beginning of the tenth century until the middle or end of the eighth,[5] Britain south of the Humber was served by bronze smiths casting a range of new implements in bronze with a high lead content, a technical practice which was to last in the south for some centuries. These new types constitute what is known as the *Wilburton complex*: they include leaf-shaped swords with splayed V-shaped shoulders, long tongue-shaped chapes, simple socketed spearheads pegged into position on the shaft, late types of palstaves and socketed axes. Again trading connections were maintained between southern Britain and north-west France, but the new types do not appear to have penetrated far into northern England, Scotland, Wales and Ireland. In these regions, traditions and technology harking back to the preceding phases remained dominant. In northern Britain, for example, where the contemporary assemblage is known as the *Wallington complex*, some of the implements such as the side-looped spearhead and low-flanged palstave are close to types developed before the eleventh century. In Wales, too, early types continued in use to the eighth century, although late hoards in the Wilburton tradition are found in the Upper Severn valley. A similarly retarded industry, called the *Poldar phase* (Coles 1962b), has been defined for Scotland, where a number of Wilburton and Wallington types have turned up, but only in small quantities. Most of the elements of ninth- to eighth-century metallurgy belonging to the Wilburton complex are represented in a remarkable founder's hoard discovered in 1959 at Isleham, Cambs., where some 6,500 fragments of bronze were found buried in a small pit cut into the chalk. In addition to weapons of Wilburton Complex type, the hoard contained fragments of bronze cauldrons and a series of harness fittings which included cheek-pieces, annular strap-crossings and cruciform strap-crossings. Thus this single hoard exemplifies most aspects of the developed bronze technology and trading systems of the period, while the presence of the bronze harness trappings and the cauldron fragments reflects new elements, which we shall find recurring more frequently in hoards of the later eighth, seventh and sixth centuries.

In the middle or end of the eighth century south and east Britain developed a series of new types in parallel with the western areas of France, with which close contacts were maintained, but now on a more intensive scale. The new assemblage, known after the site of *Ewart Park* incorporates Continental material of the *Carp's-Tongue Sword Complex* (Savory 1948; Briard 1965), including the long sword with a narrowed point (after which the industry is named), characteristic bag-shaped chapes, knives of hog's back and triangular form, various types of socketed axe, socketed knives, pegged and socketed spearheads, various chisels and gouges, and several decorative attachments of which the so-called 'bugle-shaped' objects are the most characteristic (Figure 5.2, p. 97). In Britain the locally produced leaf-shaped sword of Ewart Park type occurs in considerable numbers throughout the whole of the country and serves as a linking feature between the Carp's-Tongue Sword Complex of the south-east and the regional industries of the north and west, which can be defined largely by typological variations in their socketed axes.

In addition to the cast bronze implements just described, vessels and shields of beaten bronze make their appearance in the British Isles from the early eighth century, or perhaps a little earlier, as a result of far-flung contacts with central Europe. One group of vessels to arrive, the high-shouldered situlae known as Kurd buckets, find their way into Wales and Ireland, where some were modified by Irish smiths and later copied, giving rise to a distinctive Irish–British type which appeared in small numbers in the north and west in the first half of the seventh century (Figures 16.1, p. 406 and 16.6, p. 413). Broadly contemporary was the manufacture of bronze cauldrons the earliest of which, from Colchester and Shipton are thought to have originated at the end of the second millennium in the wake of contacts with central Europe and were probably manufactured in southern Britain. Early in the first millennium Ireland seems to have taken over as the main production centre (Gerloff 1987) whence cauldrons were exported along the Atlantic sea-ways.

The duality of the trading contacts between Britain and the Continent implied by the importation of bronze vessels – a central European Rhine route and possibly a Mediterranean Atlantic route – is also reflected in the origins of the beaten bronze shields, which give rise to local types widely distributed over most of the British Isles by the eighth century (Coles 1962a). Recent work has indicated a possible Hungarian origin for the type a century or two earlier and the transmission of the idea may have come via Denmark (Burgess 1974, 205; Thrane 1975, 79–81). Other exotic types found their way in at this time, principally from central and northern Europe. Among these must be mentioned the first appearance of bronze fittings appropriate to horse harness, which surely implies the introduction of more sophisticated methods of harnessing and possibly the greatly increased practice of horse-riding. Such developments are largely in parallel with those discernible in Europe during the Hallstatt B phase of the Urnfield culture.

Behind the complexity and the detail of the early first millennium bronze industry, it is possible to discern several general trends, not the least of which is the development of numerous local schools of craftsmen specializing in the production of the more sophisticated objects such as the buckets, cauldrons and shields, all in beaten metal. The swords too, with their rapid and subtle evolution, were clearly made by specialists; many of these, to judge by the distribution pattern, were centred upon the Lower Thames, where new foreign imports were evidently carefully studied and improved upon. Less skill would have been required for the production of the smaller cast implements and, as might be expected, intensive regionalization is recognizable, representing the distribution of the products of single smiths or, at the most, small schools; craftsmen in the remoter parts sometimes worked in alloys and made types long outdated by advances in the more forward areas. In the south-east innovations kept appearing, partly because of native inventiveness and partly because of widespread trading contacts, particularly with northern and western France, which were maintained over several centuries. Thus by the end of the eighth century a wide range of weapons, tools, ornaments and other utensils was being manufactured and traded on an unprecedented scale, vigorous local production centres maintained high standards of inventiveness, and a common market existed between Britain and Atlantic Europe. Superimposed upon this was a well-defined pattern of smaller-scale trading with northern Europe across the North Sea. It was with this area that the first contacts with the Hallstatt C communities of the seventh century developed.

Burials

The best-known aspect of the culture of the thirteenth to eighth century is the burial rite (Ellison 1980a; Bradley 1981). The dead were cremated and frequently, but by no means invariably, placed in urns, sometimes buried in urnfields of considerable size: more than 100 burials at Ardleigh, Essex; 104 at Moordown, Bournemouth and 100+ at Kimpton, Hants. In many cases it can be shown that urnfields grew up around earlier barrows, as at Steyning, Sussex, for example, where at least thirty-two urned and four un-urned cremations were inserted into an existing Middle Bronze Age barrow; at Latch Farm, Hants., more than ninety cremations, mostly urned, were found in a similar relationship. A further example is provided by the small barrow just north of the Itford Hill settlement. Here the central cremation was contained in a Middle Bronze Age urn to one side of which was a group of cremations representing between fourteen and nineteen individuals, some contained in vessels closely similar to those found on the settlement site. Presumably this cemetery, together perhaps with others, served the settlement. It is tempting to see the burials as those of a single kinship group.

Another impressive example of continuity is provided by the cemetery at Kimpton, Hants. The cemetery began in the Late Neolithic/Early Bronze Age focused on one or more large sarsen stones and developed as an urn cemetery associated with a complex platform of flints the latest burials dating to the end of the seventh century BC. Thus it remained in use as a burial place for a period of some 1,500 years.

The Latch Farm excavation gives a clear indication of the range of burial ritual employed: frequently cremations were in upended urns placed in shallow pits; sometimes, however, the pots were set upright in the ground and in several cases subsidiary vessels, presumably containing offerings of food and drinks, were included. Some examples, usually those placed upright, were covered with stone slabs set flush with the surface of the ground and were therefore possibly intended to be visible. Two post-holes were also recognized, which might have belonged to wooden markers. The burials are usually clustered together without apparent order, but sometimes, as at Ardleigh and at Pokesdown, Hants., groups and isolated burials were strung out in a linear arrangement which suggests the directional growth of the cemetery. At Barnes, Isle of Wight, between ten and fifteen urns were laid in a circle, 3–4 m in diameter, implying a considerable degree of forward planning, unless it is assumed that all the cremations were interred at the same time.

Burial beneath barrows continued alongside the urnfield rite. In Wessex it is estimated that 12 per cent of the excavated barrows contained primary Deverel–Rimbury cremations but the barrows are generally only about half the size of the earlier barrows. A typical example was excavated at Plaitford, Hants., where two urns were found set in a shallow pit beneath a small cairn of clay, sand and pebbles, in which had been set a vertical marker post. Over the cairn had been heaped a circular mound 1.5 m high and 10.7 m in diameter. The use of a vertical marker post has also been noted at several urnfield sites.

In other parts of the country the urnfield rite was also practised. At Bromfield, Salop, an arc-shaped urnfield of urned and un-urned cremations has been totally excavated, producing three radiocarbon dates (p. 54). Another urnfield at Ryton-on-Dunsmoor, Warwickshire, yielded a series of dates from the tenth to ninth century. In Wales and Scotland urnfields are rare, but urned burials are often found as secondary interments in earlier barrows and cairns, and less frequently as primary burials beneath small cairns.

Climatic change

The first half of the first millennium BC was a period of climatic deterioration, during which the comparatively warm dry conditions of the Sub-Boreal period gave way to a cooler, wetter phase, conventionally known as the Sub-Atlantic period. In sequences constructed from bog profiles, this phase of relatively rapid change can usually be recognized from a study of the pollen content and the macro plant remains. So clear was this change in many exposures in Europe that it became known as the *Grenzhorizont*, or 'boundary horizon'. In terms of the British pollen sequence it marks the boundary between Zone VIIb and Zone VIII (Pennington 1974, 79–88).

There has been much discussion about the date and duration of the *Grenzhorizont* (summarized in S. Piggott 1973), but Godwin's work on the prehistoric trackways in the Somerset Levels has clarified the situation (Godwin 1960; Coles 1972). Here, as the raised sphagnum bog of the preceding period began to be flooded with calcareous ground water, presumably caused by increased rainfall, the local communities responded by building trackways of timber and brushwood across the surface of the bog to maintain easy contact between the higher, settled areas. A number of these trackways have now been subjected to radiocarbon dating (appendix B, p. 591), providing a consistent range of assessments between 1000 and 500 BC, representing the maximum duration of the Zone VIIb–VIII transition. Confirmatory dates in the eighth century have been obtained from Tregaron in Wales and Flanders Moss in Scotland.

It is difficult at this stage to assess the significance of a relatively rapid period of climatic deterioration on settlement pattern and economy, but it is evident that upland areas in the north and west would have become unsuitable for permanent habitation as areas of blanket bog began to form, while increased rainfall particularly in the west would have rendered certain kinds of cereal growing more hazardous. In the period of climatic optimum, roughly 1250–1000 BC, cultivation of the northern uplands reached 400 m but as conditions deteriorated in the next few centuries, giving rise to a cold and stormy period, the mean temperature fell by nearly 2°C reducing the growing season by about five weeks (H.H. Lamb 1981, 55). For the upland settlements this would have spelt disaster, drastically reducing the maximum altitude at which successful cultivation was feasible to about 250 m. Such a rapid change cannot have failed to have had a dislocating effect on society. It is perhaps in causes of this kind that explanations for the apparent retardation of cultural development in parts of the west and north of Britain should be sought.

Regional and interregional systems

In recent years much effort has been expended in an attempt to formulate the social and economic systems which allowed the later Bronze Age communities to articulate, and to discover the trajectories of development apparent in the period as a whole. This work is, of necessity, based on a grossly inadequate database and is highly speculative even though the individual theories appear to have a degree of coherence within the available data. Yet, putting these reservations aside, a number of valuable generalizing statements have been made.

Perhaps the most striking observation to emerge is the massive cultural continuity which spans the period from about 2000–700 BC. Traditional burial sites continue to be used throughout (Ellison 1980a) and there is an increasing body of evidence to suggest a degree of continuity in the choice of settlement locations (e.g. Gingell 1980). Against this background may be placed the dynamics of climatic change. Current work suggests a climatic optimum in the period 1300–1000 BC and a rapid decline in the next three centuries. The magnitude of these changes cannot have failed to have affected marginal areas such as the moors of the south-west, the Welsh hills and the northern uplands where considerable fluctuations would have occurred in the maximum altitude of effective cultivation: whether or not the communities of the south-east noticed the change is debatable. Burgess (1985) has hypothesized a period of disease and rapid population decline concurrent with the climatic deterioration beginning about 1000 BC. The model he uses, based on Roman and medieval evidence, may not, however, be entirely applicable in a non-urban situation.

Against the British developments must be seen the broader European scene usefully reviewed by Rowlands (1980). The demand for raw materials such as tin and to a lesser extent copper, by the developing Mediterranean states, created a complex network of trade and exchange which bound the coastal communities of southern Britain closely to the Continent thus ensuring a constant interchange of ideas and technology. Various regions of Britain, favoured by virtue of their geographical location, such as the Thames valley and the Solent coast, remained significant interfaces between Britain and the Continent throughout much of the period and were, not surprisingly, zones of innovation.

On a more regional scale the Middle and Late Bronze Age of southern Britain, where the dataset is now considerable, has been subjected to detailed consideration (Ellison 1980b, 1981). Sites like Norton Fitzwarren, Martin Down, Rams Hill and Highdown are seen as foci where regional exchange was articulated, while the study of artefact distribution demonstrates a complex system of small-scale interlinking exchange networks the origin of which is thought to lie in the development of an established mixed farming regime after the middle of the second millennium. This development paves the way for what is to follow in the Iron Age.

Attempts have also been made to consider the relationship of the chalklands of southern Britain and their peripheral interfaces with the Continent – the Thames valley and the Solent coast (Bradley 1980, 1981; Barrett and Bradley 1980b and c). The early Deverel–Rimbury cemeteries of the Solent are seen by them as broadly contemporary with the rich Wessex burials of inland Wessex, the coastal zone growing in strength as the wealth of the inland communities declined in the thirteenth and twelfth centuries. By the end of the Bronze Age the Wessex communities are thought to be in a state of stress with large areas, previously arable, being abandoned and perhaps given over to cattle ranching while the centre of innovation now focuses on the Thames corridor. Views such as these, while inherently plausible, depend on close chronological arguments based on radiocarbon dates and may well prove to be over-simple generalizations. None the less the exercise has considerable value in focusing for the first time on the social dynamics which must lie behind the patterning evident in the archaeological material.

The Middle to Late Bronze Age was a period of transition from the simple agricultural regimes of Neolithic–Early Bronze Age, to the settled and intensive exploitation which typified the Iron Age and Roman period. The economic strategies, settlement patterns and much of the technology developed in the period 1400–700 BC paved the way for the Iron Age, and in the emergence of a hierarchic social system, evident in the diversity of settlement type from about 1000 BC, we can discern one of the principal motive forces which was to dominate the later first millennium.

4
Regional groupings: south and east

In this chapter and the next an attempt is made to offer a geographical and chronological framework which will allow the regional differences between the Iron Age communities of Britain to be described in a manner as objective as possible. There are several potential approaches which could have been adopted – pseudo-historical, chronological or cultural. All present difficulties. A pseudo-historical model couched in terms of invasion and folk movement would have imposed a prejudged structure upon the evidence; a purely chronological system lacks sufficient absolute dates for calibration and would, in any event, take no account of spheres of contact or different rates of development; while a cultural model, in the style laid down by Childe, is extremely difficult to apply to the British material and is of very doubtful value in characterizing a territory in which the communities are in close contact and share many systems in common. Accordingly, these conventional schemes have been rejected.

The framework given below relies very largely upon the characterization of pottery styles and the definition of the areas in which the types constituting the style were commonly in use. The *style-zones*, resulting from such a definition, need represent little more than areas of contact. There are many potential explanations for the resulting pattern; at one extreme a style-zone could represent the marketing pattern of a single pottery production centre; at the other it might indicate an area with such a free interchange of personnel from one community to another that technology and fashion developed in common over an extensive region. The reality, at least for the earlier periods, is likely to lie between these extremes, with a number of locations in each style-zone manufacturing like products, those towards the periphery adopting traits from neighbouring zones.

One advantage in using pottery as the basis for classification in this way is that it is relatively common over most of the south-east; moreover, it is a plastic medium highly sensitive to change. A further advantage lies in the fact that regional sequences can be built up by means of stratigraphy and these can be linked to developments in neighbouring areas. In this way an interrelated pattern of style-zones emerges, the individual components of which can be seen to develop at different rates in different areas.

The actual definition of a style-zone must necessarily be based on a detailed assessment of stylistic traits. While the intricacies cannot be enlarged upon here, the broad results are given

60

below. Wherever possible, the style-zones have been named after two of the classic sites where the types are found. This kind of nomenclature has the advantage of being easy to remember while at the same time reflecting something of the geographical range of the zone. The use of two site-names also goes some way towards overcoming the objection that no single site can be typical.

In the last two decades or so a series of comparatively large-scale excavations have produced useful stratified assemblages demonstrating local sequences, while an increasing number of radiocarbon dates are permitting a greater confidence in assigning broad date ranges to at least some of the styles. It is also becoming apparent that regionalization in pottery styles, once established in the sixth and fifth centuries, persisted, in some areas, until the Roman Conquest. For these reasons a rather more structured approach has been taken in presenting the ceramic material in this chapter than was thought advisable in earlier editions of this book. Three broad chronological groupings have been adopted: Earliest Iron Age (*c.* 800–600); Early Iron Age (*c.* 600–400/300); and Middle Iron Age (*c.* 400/300–100). These are at best 'best-fit' approximations based on a range of available evidence far too extensive and various to discuss fully here. When using this shorthand we should always remember that there may well be regional variation requiring the boundary dates to be modified by up to a century. Continuity in the spacial patterning of the individual style-zones presents fascinating possibilities for considering such questions as ethnicity and the genesis of tribal groupings. At the end of this chapter we will summarize the salient points but further discussion of possible socio-political interpretations will be reserved for a later chapter (pp. 531–6).

The Earliest Iron Age (*c.* 800–600 BC) (Figure 4.1)

The eighth and seventh centuries represent a transition period spanning the end of the Bronze Age and the beginning of iron-using technology. It was a time of rapid change and innovation when many of the old socio-economic systems were dislocated and new systems emerged to replace them. Developments in ceramics tend to reflect this. At the beginning assemblages have much in common with indigenous Deverel–Rimbury traditions and, except for Wessex, there is little regional variation. But by the end of the period a number of distinctive regional styles have emerged and ceramic technology has greatly improved. The quantity of pottery recovered, together with the considerable variation shown in form, suggests that ceramic containers were now widely in use at all social levels.

Although dating is still far from secure there are some grounds for arguing that a chronological distinction can be made between the assemblages here called *LBA transitional* and the broadly contemporary *Early All Cannings Cross* and the four other style-zones discussed in this section: the *Later All Cannings Cross*, *Kimmeridge–Caburn*, *West Harling–Staple Howe* and *Ivinghoe–Sandy* groups. As a very rough approximation the first group could be eighth century though possibly beginning earlier, the second group belonging largely to the seventh century.

The LBA transitional phase (Figure A:1, p. 554)

Over much of south-eastern England, classic Deverel–Rimbury was followed by a period typified by assemblages of largely plain vessels. Many of the shapes were direct developments of earlier

Figure 4.1 Distribution of eighth-century pottery styles in south-east Britain (source: author).

'buckets' and 'barrels' but a new and consistent element, in the form of jars with high angled shoulders and smaller carinated bowls, now made an appearance. These angular forms may well have been inspired by metal vessels circulating in Britain at this time. 'Plain ware' assemblages of this kind have been discussed in detail by Barrett (1980) who prefers to refer to them as Post Deverel–Rimbury. His careful assessment of the available dating evidence suggests a period of currency spanning the ninth and eighth centuries. A few examples will suffice to indicate the nature of the surviving material.

The characteristic pottery types represented at Eldon's Seat (Encombe), on the Isle of Purbeck, include bucket-and barrel-shaped urns, often with applied finger-tipped cordons, plain cordons or bosses, which derive from local Bronze Age forms. In addition, however, there were several examples of the angular bowl type, some of which are large enough to be considered to be copies of metal situlae. The same range of forms is known from several other Dorset sites. At Eldon's Seat, Chalbury and Kimmeridge the material is stratified beneath later assemblages which themselves date to an early stage in the Iron Age, probably the seventh to sixth centuries, a fact which tends to support an eighth- to seventh-century date for what has been called the Eldon's Seat I assemblage.

Along the Sussex Downs a number of settlements belonging to this period are known, but in the absence of closed groups of stratified material it is necessary to distinguish them largely by typological considerations. Whetstones were recovered from the two settlements on Plumpton Plain, Sussex, which are claimed to show signs of having been used for sharpening iron objects. If this evidence can be accepted, it would imply that they must date to not much earlier than 700. The pottery from the sites was discussed in some detail by C.F.C. Hawkes (1935), who put forward the view that site A preceded site B, A dating from 1000 to 750 and B from 750 to 500. The principal differences in the two assemblages lay in the presence on site A of globular vessels with strap handles and incised decoration, related to the globular urns of the Deverel–Rimbury tradition, and their absence from site B. At site B, on the other hand, jars with high shoulders together with the characteristic carinated bowls appear, both of which look forward to later Iron Age forms. In spite of the recent trend to date sites of this kind considerably earlier, Hawkes's original arguments still seem to hold good, and if the dating were slightly adjusted to allow the change-over to centre upon 700 and not 750 the evidence of the iron-stained whetstones could be neatly accommodated.

The significance of the Plumpton Plain sites is considerable, for not only do their ceramic assemblages demonstrate chronological differences, they also emphasize a marked continuity. Thus the large bucket- or barrel-shaped urns with applied bosses or finger-printed cordons occur in quantity on both sites and remain a constituent of local assemblages which can be more firmly dated to the sixth and fifth centuries. The suggestion that the Plumpton Plain settlements should be updated brings with it further implications for other Sussex sites. The pottery from Itford Hill, for example, is best paralleled at Plumpton Plain A, but that from New Barn Down is much closer to Plumpton Plain B. A detailed reassessment of the Sussex Bronze Age settlements, therefore, might well allow them to be arranged in a sequence stretching from before 1000 and continuing into the seventh or even the sixth century (Ellison 1978).

Large skeuomorphic carinated bowls, of the types considered here to belong to the eighth to seventh centuries, occur on a number of other coastal sites amid collections of pottery of various dates: at Kingston Buci, Highdown Hill and Castle Hill (Newhaven) in Sussex, and Mill Plain (Deal) and Minnis Bay in Kent. Related types are also known from the east coast at West Harling and Castle Hill, Scarborough. Coarse wares in Deverel–Rimbury tradition invariably occur alongside them, and from many of the sites items of bronze equipment of Late Bronze Age type are known.

Recent work in the Thames valley has produced a number of comparable assemblages for which a series of radiocarbon dates are available. Of particular significance are the settlements at Knights Farm and Aldermaston Wharf in Berkshire, Runnymede Bridge, Surrey, and Mucking, Essex. Taken together the data would suggest that the plain ware tradition of the region could have begun before 1000 BC and continued into the seventh century, the majority of the dates favouring the latter part of the period (Barrett 1980, 306–9). At Knights Farm a 'plain ware' assemblage can be shown to have been succeeded by a typical Early All Cannings Cross decorated assemblage for which dates of 740 ± 80 bc and 600 ± 80 bc were obtained. The implication of this is that by the eighth century BC the plain ware tradition was already being superseded by Wessex styles on the western fringes of the distribution. Further east plain ware traditions are likely to have continued at least into the seventh century.

The distribution of the LBA transitional plain wares is predominantly south-eastern with a strong emphasis on the coastal zone and the river valleys, particularly the Thames valley. It is in precisely this region that the contemporary metalwork of the Carp's Tongue and Ewart Park complexes concentrates. Drawing simple conclusions from pottery, which may represent very complex processes, is dangerous but taking the two distributions together, it is tempting to see them as the reflection of a zone of vigorous industrial activity involving the intensive local production of a range of bronzes and widespread contact with the Continent. In such a context it is hardly surprising that the new ceramic forms which developed alongside traditional types in this region should show an angularity strongly suggestive of the copying of Continental metal prototypes. Broad similarities in pottery styles over a large area, matched by the wide distribution of a limited range of metal types, implies extensive and persistent interactions throughout the region leading to a degree of cultural uniformity. We will see below that a similar uniformity can be suggested for the seventh century.

The Early All Cannings Cross group (Figure A:2, p. 555)

In parallel with the coastal developments, a totally different ceramic style arose around the western fringes of the Wessex chalkland – a style which was to remain dominant in the area for several centuries. Since most of the sites continued in use throughout this period, it is very difficult to distinguish the earliest groups except upon typological grounds, but among the earliest types must be listed the large jars with evenly out-curved rims and a rounded shoulder and body which in most cases is decorated with incised and stamped motifs, often in the form of stab-filled geometric shapes. The second distinctive type is the bipartite bowl with beaded rim and sharp shoulder angles, between which are bands of decoration, either stamped or incised. Sometimes these vessels are decorated with a coating of haematite burnished and fired to a shiny copper colour. Other types include large tripartite jars with sharp shoulders and flared necks, as well as a variety of coarse jars.

The classic site for the occurrence of these forms is All Cannings Cross in Wiltshire, where unfortunately the earliest assemblages were not distinguished from the later material. Nevertheless, we may reasonably call the range of selected types the *Early All Cannings Cross group*. The discovery here of a tanged bifid razor and a fragment of Breton axe suggests an origin in the eighth or seventh century, but the bronzes could also have been residual material. Firmer dating evidence comes from the broadly contemporary site of Cow Down (Longbridge Deverill), Wilts., where a radiocarbon date of 630 ± 155 bc was obtained for wood charcoal collected from the post-holes of the main timbers of the earliest house. At Knights Farm, Berks., on the north-west fringe of the distribution a typical assemblage produced two dates, 740 ± 80 bc and 600 ± 80 bc, confirming a broad ninth–seventh-century date bracket. Potterne, Wilts., has recently yielded a comprehensive and well-stratified sequence, and, when fully published, will undoubtedly become a classic type site.

While some of the ceramic forms can be explained away as indigenous copies of exotic metal types, the weak profiled jars with stabbed decoration stand out as something very new that cannot be easily paralleled except among Late Urnfield assemblages in eastern France and western Germany (Sandars 1957, 225, Figure 54; Hatt 1960, Figure 68). Thus it is probable that an Urnfield element lies behind the origins of the Early All Cannings Cross group, but it is impossible at present to define the nature of the link more precisely. There is no firm evidence for a folk movement of any magnitude into the area, but limited immigration cannot be ruled out.

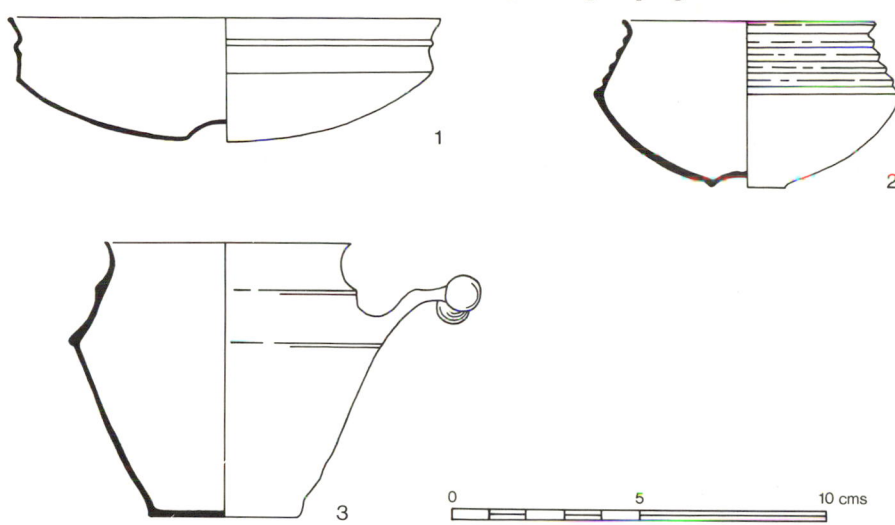

Figure 4.2 Bronze vessels serving as possible prototypes for angular pottery (sources: 1 *Mindelheim*, Kossack 1954; 2 *Welby, Leics., Inv. Arch. GB*, 24; 3 *Glentanar, Aberdeenshire*, Pearce 1974).

The continuation of intensive trading contacts during the seventh and sixth centuries introduced new types of metalwork into the country, among which were a series of fine carinated bowls (Figure 4.2), like the elegant vessel with a sharp shoulder and furrowed neck found in a hoard at Welby in Leicestershire and dated to the eighth or seventh century. These vessels were immediately copied in pottery, giving rise to an extensive series of haematite-coated bowls centred on Wessex. Similarly, the tripartite jars with sharp shoulders and flaring necks may be seen to be copies of bronze containers, like the two from a seventh-century hoard found at Glentanar, Aberdeenshire. The presence in Britain of other metal vessels, similar to the bipartite bowl with median neck cordon from the Mindelheim cemetery (Kossack 1954), can also be postulated on the basis of their widely distributed ceramic copies. Thus it seems that the tendency to imitate bronze vessels, which began among the LBA transitional communities of the south and east coastal regions continued throughout the seventh century in parallel with a general improvement of ceramic technology and the gradual disappearance of traditional forms like the bucket- and barrel-shaped urns. Beneath the broad similarities of parallel development lie well-defined regional differences which must be described in detail.

The Later All Cannings Cross group

Many of the ceramic elements of the early group continued into the later period, but in general the tendency was for the large decorated jars to become less common and the smaller carinated bowls with furrowed shoulders to increase in number. Similarly, the technique of coating the vessels with haematite came into wider use. The general impression, then, is of a strong continuing local tradition, but one in which the relative proportions of the various types changed with time. There is as yet no good evidence for a stratigraphical distinction between the early and later phases of the group, but several sites would appear, on typological grounds, to have been first occupied only during the later period.

The Kimmeridge–Caburn group (Figure A:3, p. 556)

Along the south coast of Britain a number of occupation sites can be recognized as producing a distinctive assemblage of material (Figure 4.3). The most characteristic vessels are the bipartite bowls, almost all of which have beaded rims and sharp shoulder angles, proclaiming their skeuomorphic origins. Median shoulder cordons occur widely, but furrowed and stamped decoration is restricted more to the western end of the distribution. Tripartite jars with flared rims, constricted necks and sharply angled shoulders are also a feature of this group, as are coarser shouldered jars often with finger-tip or finger-nail impressions along the rim-tops and shoulders.

At Kimmeridge a well-stratified assemblage was recovered from an occupation site on the edge of a cliff, where Kimmeridge shale had been worked into armlets. Stratigraphically the group could be shown to succeed a layer containing pottery of Eldon's Seat I type (LBA transitional) and at Eldon's Seat it could be argued that the Kimmeridge assemblage was probably current during the hiatus between phases I and II (Cunliffe 1968b). In Dorset and Wiltshire there is a considerable degree of overlap between the All Cannings Cross and Kimmeridge traditions, but the Sussex sites show far less evidence of contact with the Wessex developments. Indeed, the traditions of the LBA transitional style remain apparent throughout the seventh century. At sites like the Caburn and Stoke Clump the angular types occur alongside coarse vessels of devolved bucket- and barrel-type. Traditional types likewise predominate among the assemblages from the farmstead at Weston Wood, Albury, Surrey, and from Minnis Bay, Kent, but at both of these sites occupation probably began in the late eighth or early seventh century and continued to the end of the sixth.

Dating depends largely upon typological considerations, but there is some additional independent evidence. Occupation at Weston Wood, Surrey, for example, produced a radiocarbon determination of 510 ± 110 bc, an assessment totally in keeping with the typological dating of the pottery. Furthermore the semi-submerged settlement site of Minnis Bay, off the Kentish coast, has yielded a bronze hoard of the Carp's-Tongue Sword Complex, but not in direct association with the occupation levels. Among the many items represented in the hoard is a fragment of a bronze cauldron which, taken together with a consideration of the other objects, would suggest a deposition date centring upon 750 bc, a date within the range to which some of the pottery could be assigned on typological grounds. It is not unreasonable, therefore, to suggest that the hoard was deposited during the main phase of occupation. While it must be admitted that the dating evidence for the individual sites is a little weak, taken together it consistently points to the bracket *c.* 750–550 for the developments categorized here as belonging to the Kimmeridge–Caburn group.

There is no reason to suppose that the ceramic innovation arose in response to an intrusion of people; the strong native undercurrent and the evidence of skeuomorphism together suggest an indigenous population absorbing new ideas. Burial rites also continued in native style: at the Caburn, immediately outside the palisaded settlement, a cremation was found placed in a large jar and buried in a pit covered by a low barrow. Similar cremations are recorded from East Anglia.

The West Harling–Staple Howe group (Figure A:4, p. 557)

The angular bipartite bowl form occurs on a number of sites in eastern England, invariably mixed up with quantities of pottery made in local traditions. At Staple Howe the native forms are

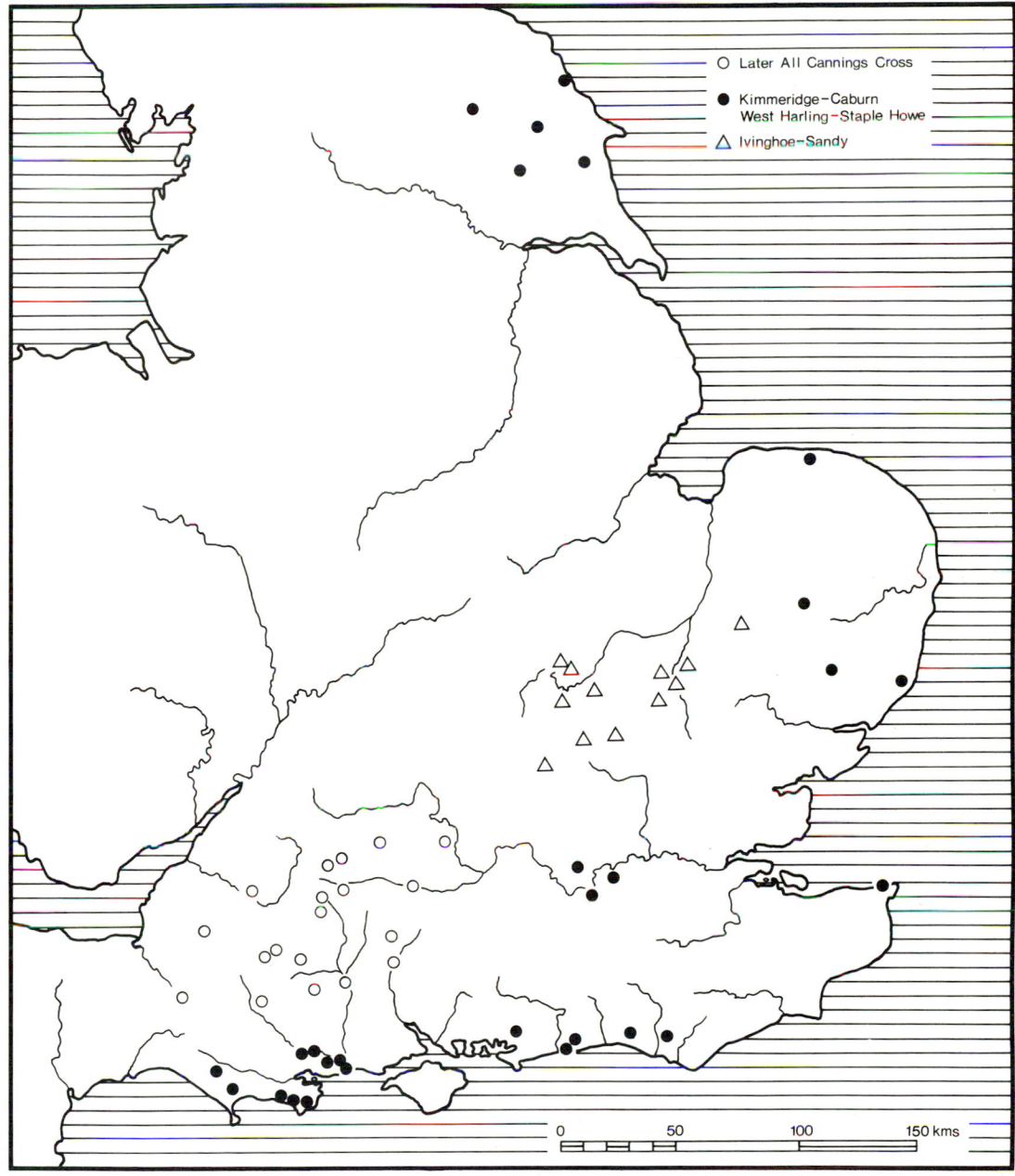

Figure 4.3 Distribution of seventh-century pottery styles (source: author).

usually jars with finger-impressed shoulders; at Scarborough, Yorks., which began a little earlier, finger-impressed neck cordons in Late Bronze Age tradition predominate; while at West Harling, Norfolk, both types occur in approximately equal quantities.

Dating evidence is provided at Staple Howe by a group of loosely associated bronze objects, including three Hallstatt C razors, a tanged chisel, part of a socketed axe and a small fragment of harness mount like those found at Llyn Fawr and Court-St-Etienne in seventh-century contexts. A single radiocarbon date of 450 ± 150 bc from the site, suggesting a sixth-century BC date, is in keeping with the character of the metalwork and pottery. The metal finds from Scarborough are not closely associated with the pottery but it seems reasonable to suppose them to be broadly contemporary. They include a tanged chisel like that from Staple Howe, a socketed axe, a flat-headed pin and two harness-rings– all paralleled in the Heathery Burn deposit, Co. Durham – which together suggest a date early in the sixth century or late in the seventh.

It now seems probable that the vessels found at the hillfort of Grimthorpe, which include jars with flared rims, shouldered jars and bowls, and simple hemispherical bowls, should be regarded as belonging to an early phase in the West Harling–Staple Howe tradition. The two radiocarbon dates for bones found in the ditch, 690 ± 130 and 970 ± 130 bc, were surprisingly early to the excavator, but when the similarities between the Grimthorpe pottery and the vessels of the LBA transitional tradition are considered, a date in the eighth or seventh century would seem acceptable. Some further support is provided by a group of similar pottery from within and below a group of nine barrows on Ampleforth Moor, Yorks., which is also comparable to the sherds from the Heathery Burn Cave. Two radiocarbon dates were obtained: 582 ± 90 and 537 ± 90 bc, indicating a date probably in the seventh century.

At Ampleforth Moor the burial rite was cremation, the ashes being placed below small barrows, barely 1.5 m high and 7.3–9.8 m in diameter; each was surrounded by a ditch. The native tradition of cremation was also continued at Creeting St Mary, Suffolk, where a typical tripartite vessel decorated with plain cordons containing a cremation was found buried apparently without a covering barrow; while at Warborough Hill, Norfolk, what appears to have been a cremation beneath a barrow was recorded.

While it is too early to be definite, it might eventually be necessary to divide the West Harling–Staple Howe group into an early and later phase: the early phase of LBA transitional origin dating to the eighth century or earlier, including Ampleforth Moor, early Scarborough and Grimthorpe, the later phase of seventh- to sixth-century date being represented by the angular bipartite wares of the two type-sites. The large assemblage of pottery recovered from the open settlement at Hesterton on the north edge of the Yorkshire Wolds, and broadly similar to the Staple Howe and Scarborough material, will eventually allow a far finer definition of the ceramic traditions of the period from the ninth to fifth centuries in Yorkshire.

It will be apparent that significant similarities existed between communities living in southern and eastern Britain in the seventh century. All areas showed a strong indigenous element overlaid by a parallel development in fine ceramics – a development which implies contacts with the Continent – further emphasized by the presence of the Hallstatt C metal types at Staple Howe. Interregional exchange, perhaps by sea, is also suggested by the presence of large decorated jars of All Cannings Cross type at Minnis Bay, Kent, and Darmsden, Suffolk. While there can be little doubt, therefore, that the coastal regions were in close contact with each other – a contact which acted as a spur to innovation – inland areas like the Chilterns received little stimulus and appear to have developed along more isolated lines.

The Ivinghoe–Sandy group (Figure A:5, p. 558)

The excavation of the hillfort on Ivinghoe Beacon has brought to light a distinctive assemblage of pottery found in loose association both with the structure of the fort and with a group of bronze implements. A number of isolated groups of broadly contemporary material are known from sites such as Sandy, Harrold, Kempston, Puddlehill and Totternhoe – all in Bedfordshire – Hawthorn Hill, Herts., and several others, many of them unpublished; but apart from the material from Sandy, the finds were unassociated and mainly recovered under non-archaeological conditions.[1]

The Ivinghoe pottery is generally coarsely made. The principal types include the shouldered bowl or jar with the rim-top out-curved and the shoulder sometimes ornamented with finger-impressions, jars with applied neck cordons impressed with finger-printing, round-shouldered jars with flared rims, open hemispherical bowls and occasionally bipartite bowls and jars, one of which has incised decoration on the shoulder. The same range of types recurs on the other sites mentioned but the bipartite bowl with rounded shoulder tends to be rather more common. There are obvious similarities between this group and the pottery from Scarborough, Minnis Bay, the Caburn, etc., the only significant difference lying in the general lack of the tightly moulded and cordoned vessels imitating bronze types. The impression which the pottery gives, therefore, is of a contemporary native tradition largely untouched by external influences.

Exactly the same conclusions can be reached from a study of the associated bronze work, which at Ivinghoe includes a tanged bifid razor, fragments of two swords probably of Ewart Park type, a ring, various mounts and studs, tweezers and several pins. To these may be added the winged axe found unassociated in 1929. All the bronze work falls within native Late Bronze Age tradition of the late eighth and seventh centuries, uninfluenced by obvious Hallstatt C techniques. On a conservative estimate, a date of about 650 BC might be suggested for the initial occupation of the site.[2] Within this same general range of pottery can be placed the vessels recovered from the Totternhoe quarry, Beds., found together with a bronze vase-headed pin of Late Urnfield type. A similar pin was recovered from All Cannings Cross and an iron copy is known from Fifield Bavant, Wilts. The bronze examples cannot be dated too closely, since individual pins might have survived in use for some time, but an eighth- to sixth-century range would seem most likely.

Thus the evidence at present available suggests the existence of a regional group centred upon the Chilterns and the gravel terraces to the west, defined by pottery made in the traditional manner and by the continued use of Late Bronze Age metalwork. Exact dating is impossible, but the range 700–500 probably covers the main developments which the pottery style characterizes.

The Early Iron Age (c. 600–400/300 BC) (Figure 4.4)

During the sixth century it is possible to recognize a number of distinctive local ceramic assemblages crystallizing from the more widely distributed groups of the earlier period. The distinction between fine and coarse wares is now more clear cut and the fine wares show a high technical competence which in some cases suggests the emergence of specialist production centres. In both form and decoration the fine wares of one style-zone are clearly distinguishable from those of the next.

Some time, probably towards the end of the fifth century, well-made angular bowls and jars appeared with pedestals copying the *vases carenées* and *vases piriformes* of the Continental La Tène cultures. The influence of these ceramic innovations was felt most strongly in the Thames valley and eastern England, contributing to the regional assemblages called here the Long Wittenham–Allen's Pit group, the Chinnor–Wandlebury group and the Darmsden–Linton

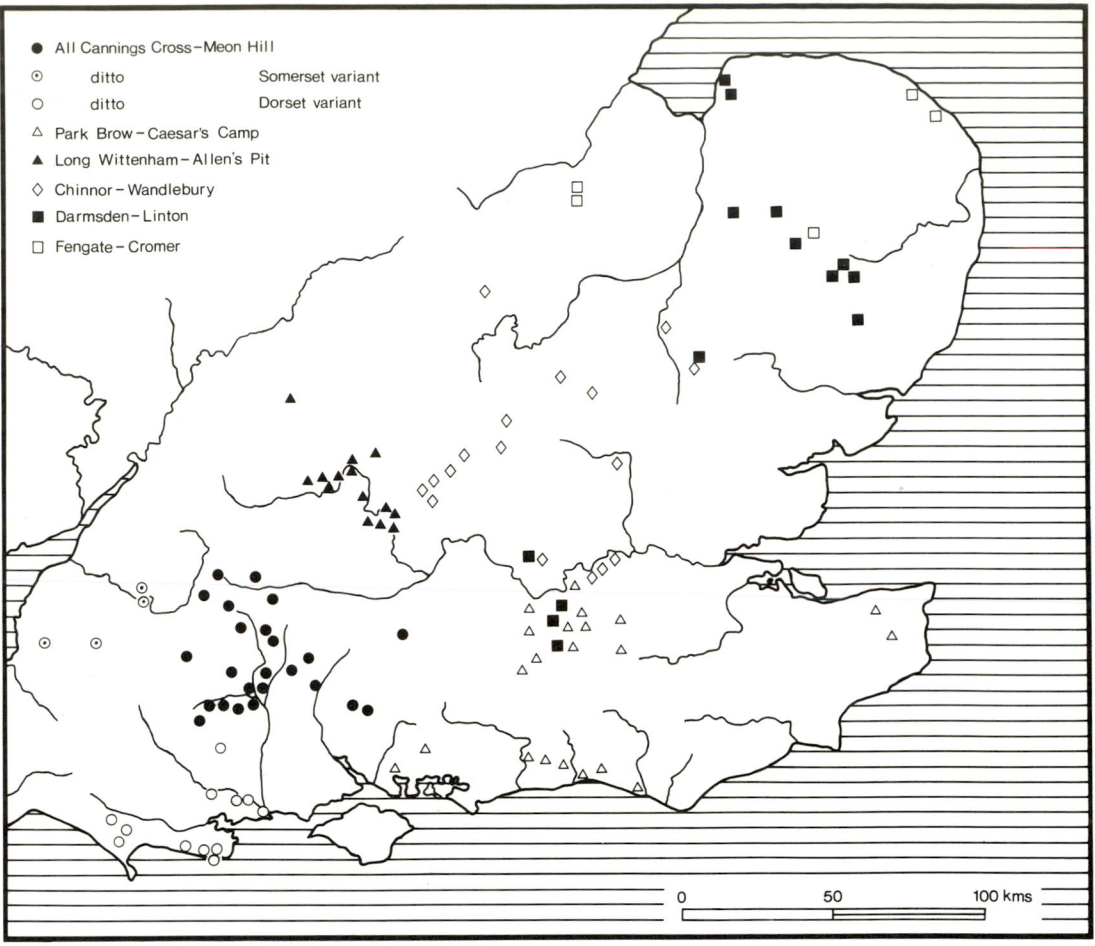

Figure 4.4   Distribution of sixth- and fifth-century pottery styles (source: author).

group. Further south in Sussex and west in Hampshire and Wiltshire, elements of the new types, though apparent, are more dimly reflected in the contemporary ceramic development. The mechanism by which these La Tène I types were introduced into Britain remains unclear. While it is possible that an actual folk movement took place, penetrating Britain by means of the Thames to introduce an alien population, it is no less likely that the new types emerged as the result of close trading relations between the two sides of the Channel. Since the nature of the evidence does not allow the problem to be resolved, it is preferable simply to characterize the regional groups as objectively as possible.

The centre south

In central southern Britain, from Somerset to Sussex, a series of distinctive styles developed. The most technically advanced forms are found in the central Wessex area with related variants in Somerset and Dorset. In Sussex and Surrey the assemblage contains a rather more generalized range.

The All Cannings Cross–Meon Hill group (Figure A:6, p. 559)

The All Cannings Cross settlement continued in use for several hundred years following the initial occupation of the site in the eighth century. No stratigraphical distinction was made by the excavator between the early and late phases, but the later pottery can be distinguished on typological grounds and can be shown to be the same as that found at the Hampshire site of Meon Hill, where occupation did not begin until the late phase. At the more recently excavated settlement of Cow Down (Longbridge Deverill), Wilts., a stratigraphical distinction has been recognized between early All Cannings Cross pottery and later All Cannings Cross–Meon Hill group. The latter assemblage can therefore be regarded as distinct from and succeeding the earlier group.

There is a wide area of continuity between the two assemblages. In particular, the haematite coating of bowls continued on an extensive scale, but the bipartite form gave way to shouldered bowls with widely flaring rims. The commonest of these was still ornamented with furrowed shoulders, as in the earlier tradition, but other forms of shoulder decoration were now adopted, including groups or areas of diagonal lines and stroke-filled triangles, the decoration now being applied by shallow tooling with a blunt point before firing and not by incision or stamping. At a later stage a highly characteristic form of haematite-coated bowl was produced in central Wessex, with the angles of the body accentuated by cordons, between which various forms of geometric decoration were scratched on to the surface after firing: these were filled with white paste. Unlike the other bowl types, these scratched cordoned bowls were provided with a carefully moulded foot-ring to enable them to stand firmly. There can be little doubt that vessels of this type were made in a single, or a limited number of production centres and distributed locally from there. Fabric analysis has shown that the prime (and possibly sole) source was a brickearth deposit found in the vicinity of Salisbury. Radiocarbon dates from Danebury suggest that assemblages containing scratched cordoned bowls without other types of haematite-coated bowls were current in the middle of the sixth century. In addition to the decorated bowls, several plain types with variously moulded profiles commonly occur but always with a haematite-coated surface.

The coarse ware types are restricted to plain shouldered jars, seldom with any form of decoration on the shoulder or rim. Occasionally jars with horizontally or vertically perforated handles are found, and at a late stage plain bucket-shaped types come into more common use. A more exotic type, found twice at Swallowcliffe Down, Wilts., consisted of a high-shouldered jar with flaring rim and a narrow squat pedestal foot, made in a black fabric with a well-burnished surface. Since parallels with Continental La Tène types are fairly close, it is possible that the Swallowcliffe vessels are local copies of imported types.

The distribution of the principal types centres upon the Wessex chalkland extending from the Marlborough Downs in the north to the river Itchen in the east. The same assemblage also recurs as far south as Hengistbury Head.

In south Dorset, south of the Stour, a more restricted range of types occurs, typified by the flared bowl and bipartite bowls with near-vertical concave sides (Figure A:7, p. 560). The assemblage is clearly within the broad tradition of the Wessex haematite-coated bowls but, distributionally lies outside the range of the centres producing the more characteristic decorated types.[3] A westerly extension of the generalized assemblage can also be recognized at the Somerset sites of Bathampton Down, Pagan's Hill, Banwell and South Cadbury (Figure A:7, p. 560). Like the south Dorset ceramics, there is some divergence from the typical central Wessex groups, but similarities in form and the use of haematite coating serve to link the two traditions closely.

Some indication of the date range covered by the assemblage is provided by a few stratified metal objects. From Maiden Castle comes a Viollier type Ia fibula dating to the second half of the fifth century, which may have arrived just before 400 BC. The latest datable metal objects from All Cannings Cross are two local versions of the La Tène II fibulae of a type in use in the fourth or third century, and the Meon Hill settlement has produced an iron La Tène II fibula of fourth-century origin but these associations are not reliable and both sites have produced some pottery of later type. The mid-sixth-century date indicated by the radiocarbon assessments from Danebury provides a fixed point for the scratched cordoned bowls. This admittedly sparse evidence, taken in conjunction with typological considerations and sequence, suggests that the All Cannings Cross–Meon Hill group, together with its south Dorset and Somerset outliers, developed out of the late All Cannings Cross and Kimmeridge–Caburn groups in the sixth century, and may have continued in use into the fourth century. Throughout this time there was, of course, internal development: the flared furrowed bowls were gradually replaced by the scratched cordoned bowls in the central areas and the coarse ware vessels lost their sharp-shouldered profiles, developing towards simpler barrel-shaped containers by the end of the period when there was also a noticeable preference for darker fired fabrics.

Other aspects of material culture, economy and settlement pattern are shared with the rest of south-eastern Britain, emphasizing the cultural unity of the area. The only other distinctive Wessex artefacts are the local copies of the La Tène I fibulae with their bows decorated by a simple row of punched dots. More than twenty have now been found, all from the central Wessex area (Figures 17.13, p. 459 and 17.14, p. 459). Clearly this was a local product made for a market of restricted size. Like the pottery, the fibulae serve to emphasize a sphere of contact, implying that the Wessex sites were linked by well-developed exchange mechanisms.

The Park Brow–Caesar's Camp group (Figure A:8 p. 561)

The south-east of Britain, particularly the chalk areas of the North and South Downs, is scattered with settlement sites, most of them ill-recorded but producing similar assemblages of pottery.[4] The range of types is not wide but consistently includes bowls with well-defined shoulders and flaring rims, usually made in dark well-burnished fabrics. The coarse ware vessels consist of jars with rounded shoulders, upright or flaring necks and flattened rim-tops. Finger-impressions on the rims and shoulders sometimes occur, and occasionally jars and bowls are provided with squat pedestal bases. Well-stratified groups have been found at Chalton (site 50), Hants.

The type-sites chosen to define the group were not extensively excavated but at the open settlement at Park Brow, Sussex, a bent silver ring of Viollier type Ic was discovered, which is hardly likely to have reached Britain before 270; while at Caesar's Camp (Wimbledon), Surrey, an assemblage of pottery was found associated with the rampart of a timber-laced hillfort. Dating and internal development are difficult to assess in any detail, but on typological grounds it is probable that the finger-impressed coarse ware, which occurs in quantity at Caesar's Camp, is earlier than the plainer forms from Park Brow. The development would appear to be largely parallel with that of the All Cannings Cross–Meon Hill group in Wessex and probably covers the same time span, from the sixth to the fourth century.

The south-west

The early pottery of the south-west is at present sparse and ill-known and is without reliable dating evidence. Pottery generally similar to the type in use in southern and eastern Britain from the eighth–fifth centuries has been found in small quantities at several sites including Norton Fitzwarren and Worlebury, Somerset, Dainton and Mount Batten, Devon, and Bodrifty, Cornwall. The settlement at Keston, Devon, may also belong to this early group but the assemblage is not sufficiently distinctive. No internal dating evidence is forthcoming from these sites but comparison with the pottery of the Kimmeridge–Caburn group suggests a broad contemporaneity. What the scarcity of early pottery implies – a sparse population, a largely aceramic culture or a continuation of Bronze Age forms – it is at present impossible to say.

The Midlands

The pottery of the Midlands, from the Trent to the Thames, can best be considered at two levels: as a widespread tradition of coarse wares, called here the Breedon–Ancaster group, and as two localized style-zones typified by distinctive decorated fine wares, the Long Wittenham–Allens Pit group and Chinnor–Wandlebury group, which emerged on the southern and eastern fringes of the region.

The Breedon–Ancaster group (Figures 4.5 and A:9, p. 562)

The ceramic and cultural development of the east Midlands between the Trent, the Welland and the Nene is at present far from clear but it has long been possible to recognize a group of weak-shouldered jars, frequently scored on the outside with irregularly arranged lines. This general category has been referred to in the past as Trent valley A ware, following definition of the type at Breedon-on-the-Hill, Leics. At the time scored coarse ware jars were thought to be predominantly of the first century BC and later, but later work has extended both the distribution and the time range.

The original Breedon excavations provided no close dating evidence for the pottery, but Wacher (1964) has demonstrated a stratigraphical sequence suggesting occupation over a considerable period. Moreover, at Ancaster, Lincs., the excavation of a substantial open settlement, occupied by a community using scored jars, has yielded an iron involuted brooch and a bronze wire fibula with a four-coiled spring, high bow and a recurved foot – characteristics which proclaim a La Tène I ancestry. While the brooches do not prove an early date, they are more likely to have been in use in the third or second century than much later. Typologically the pottery would not be out of place in a fifth- or fourth-century context. Two radiocarbon determinations are now available: Twywell, Northants., has produced a date of 280 ± 90 bc while Fengate (Padholm Road site) was dated 350 ± 46 bc. Both fall within the range anticipated on typological grounds.

The Long Wittenham–Allen's Pit group (Figures 4.4, p. 70 and A:10, p. 563)

In the Upper Thames valley and extending into the Cotswolds are a number of sites which have produced varied but distinctive assemblages of pottery (illustrated in detail in D.W. Harding

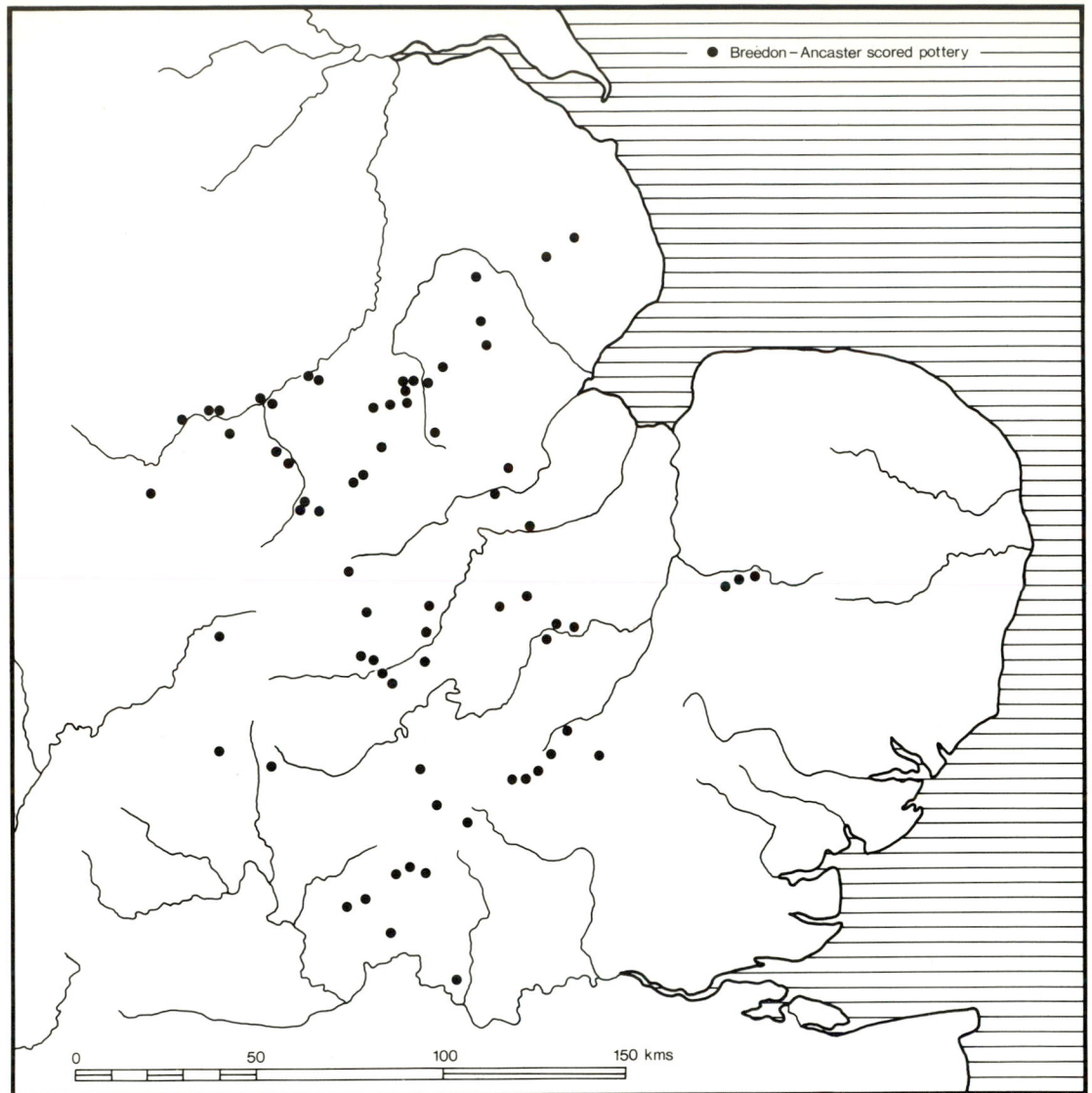

● Breedon–Ancaster scored pottery

0   50   100   150 kms

Figure 4.5 Distribution of scored vessels of the fifth to second centuries in the east Midlands (source: author).

1972). The principal types include bowls with well-defined shoulders and flaring rims, fired usually to dark tones and well finished by smoothing or burnishing. The shoulders of these vessels were frequently decorated with shallow-tooled decoration in a variety of patterns resembling the contemporary Wessex examples; but, with the exception of occasional haematite-coated sherds which may be imported into the region, the decorated bowls are distinctive enough to be regarded as locally made. There are three major coarse ware types: weak-shouldered jars sometimes with finger-impressions on the shoulders, open bowls with heavy T-shaped rims, finger-impressed on the outside, and large-shouldered jars with sharply flaring rims closely related to the tripartite jars of the Early All Cannings Cross group. These are usually plain but occasionally the shoulders are tooled with simple geometric decoration.

Although good stratigraphical evidence is lacking from practically every site, it seems that the tripartite jars and some of the plainer, less flared bowls belonging to the beginning of the sequence overlap with the Early All Cannings Cross and Kimmeridge–Caburn groups; then follows the development of the highly decorated bowls in parallel with the Wessex, All Cannings Cross–Meon Hill group. Towards the end of the period the bowl form becomes simpler in profile and less frequently decorated, while the coarser vessels take on a slacker and more barrel-shaped form. The picture is to some extent confused by regionalization and by the differential distribution of the more elaborate types. Thus further from the Thames, in the eastern flanks of the Cotswolds, very few of the bowls are found and the coarse wares are of a very generalized form.

Internal dating evidence is lacking apart from a La Tène I fibula from Radley, Oxon., but analogies with Wessex might suggest a beginning in the late sixth or fifth century and a development continuing as late as the third century. Well-stratified groups are required before subdivision or more precise dating is possible.

The Chinnor–Wandlebury group (Figures 4.4, p. 70 and A:11, p. 564)

The area occupied by this group approximates to that of the Chilterns,[5] but extends in the north up to the Fen margins and in the south to the Thames valley and the Berkshire Downs. The pottery by which the group is characterized consists of bowls with flaring rims and shoulders frequently decorated with simple geometric patterns, often dot-filled triangles. At Blewburton Hill, Oxon., and Chinnor, Oxon., rosette lamps were sometimes employed, the rosettes being arranged between pendent swags at Blewburton Hill; this mode of decoration is strictly limited in distribution. More common and more widely spread were the flared bowls, the lip splaying beyond the maximum diameter of the shoulder. These were invariably made in a black burnished fabric and were sometimes ornamented with a zigzag pattern scratched after firing. This type of bowl was often provided with a simple foot-ring base, a technique apparently learnt from the East Anglian group to be described below (pp. 76–7). The coarse ware jars were of normal shouldered type, sometimes with finger-impressions on the rim-tops and shoulders. Several stratified groups have been recovered from Puddlehill, Beds., where the excavator distinguishes two chronological groups (Matthews 1976, Figures 96–8).

Both of the type-sites also provide evidence of internal development. At Chinnor two phases of occupation were recognized. The first yielded a large number of bowls, mostly decorated with simple linear zigzag motifs or groups of lines, although some were ornamented with pendent stab-filled triangles frequently in association with stab-filled arcs, possibly imitating handles. The second phase, stratigraphically distinct from the first, included bowls in a brownish ware stamped with rosettes. In all probability, different production centres are indicated. At the hillfort of Wandlebury, Cambs., it was possible to relate a pottery sequence to two separate phases of the fort construction. The earlier group contained the basic forms defined above but the later assemblage was more generalized, exhibiting few distinctive features but sufficiently similar to the first group to suggest a logical development from it. Clearly over such a large area, factors such as local development in isolation, as well as specialized production offering geographically limited distribution, tend to complicate the apparent unity of the region. A further possibility that cannot be ruled out is that some sites like Wandlebury may have continued to be inhabited as late as the first century, while the communities further south came under the influence of more advanced pottery traditions.

Dating with precision is impossible. Similarities to Wessex, the Upper Thames and East Anglia suggest a broad contemporaneity which may have spanned the two or three centuries following 600, but no internal evidence is yet available.

Eastern England

The ceramic development of eastern England is surprisingly ill-understood and anything said at this stage must be regarded as highly provisional, but two style-zones can tentatively be defined.

The Darmsden–Linton group (Figures 4.4, p. 70 and A:12, p. 565)

The east of England from the Wash as far south as the Thames supported a group of settlements linked by a common ceramic tradition typified by a large assemblage of pottery found at Darmsden in Suffolk. The most characteristic type of vessel is the bowl in a fine black burnished ware with a sharp narrow shoulder and a short upright or slightly flared rim. The shoulders are usually ornamented with deeply impressed horizontal grooves, while the bases may be rounded or provided with simple foot-rings. Similar bowls with more rounded shoulders also occur, together with larger bowls with widely flared rims. The jar forms are usually shouldered and frequently, but not invariably, decorated.

The little bowl form has certain similarities to La Tène I types on the Continent, suggesting a fifth-century date for their first appearance in this country. The similarity does not necessarily imply a folk movement into Britain at this time since trading contact would be quite sufficient to explain the likeness. Links with adjacent groups are demonstrated at several sites. At Sandown Park (Esher), Surrey, Darmsden–Linton pottery is found with types of Park Brow–Caesar's Camp forms and at Linton, Cambs., associations with Chinnor–Wandlebury wares are recorded. A general contemporaneity is therefore implied.

The Fengate–Cromer group (Figures 4.4, p. 70 and A:13, p. 566)

In Norfolk and the Fen margins a few sites have been discovered yielding a group of well-made and highly decorated pottery typified by a large collection recovered from the habitation site at Fengate, and by a much smaller group discovered during a cliff fall at Cromer, Norfolk. At Fengate a typological sequence was proposed (Hawkes and Fell 1945) starting with bowls with flaring rims and somewhat globular bodies, usually decorated with shallow tooling above and below the shoulder or girth. Associated with this early group were jars with sharp shoulders and finger-nail or finger-tip decoration on the rims and shoulders, and sometimes cordons at the junction of the neck and rim. But since the pottery of the middle group included bipartite bowls and the use of slashed cordons, presumably derived from earlier local traditions such as those evident at West Harling, it is possible that the typological arguments originally put forward should be reversed: the 'middle' group becoming the earliest, thus allowing for an indigenous development diverging from the forms of the local West Harling–Staple Howe group. An assemblage recently found in a controlled excavation at Fengate (Vicarage Farm) included the bowl and decorated jar types together with flared bowls and a vessel with a foot-ring base similar to Darmsden–Linton types.

Typologically the Fengate–Cromer group probably began in the sixth century or earlier, before the development of the Darmsden–Linton group, and continued perhaps as late as the third century. Some support for this view was provided by the discovery of a pin of sunflower swan's-neck type in one of the Fengate pits. These pins, once regarded as being fifth-century imports, must now be dated more generally to the sixth–third centuries (Spratling 1974).

Pryor has argued (1974, 35–6) that the differentiation of a separate Fengate–Cromer style-zone is unnecessary on the basis that the material can be divided typologically into two groups, one equating with West Harling, the other with Darmsden. This may well prove to be so. The style-zone has, however, been retained here, perhaps temporarily, pending the discovery and publication of more material from Norfolk.

The north-east

The Arras group

The early La Tène contacts between the Continent and most of southern Britain were on the basis of casual trading and exchange, but in eastern Yorkshire it is possible to distinguish a group of burials which have very close connections with France, implying some form of intrusive folk movement bringing with it burial traditions alien to those of the indigenous culture (pp. 499–504). These new burials are conventionally referred to as the Arras culture, after the Yorkshire barrow cemetery partially examined for the first time in 1815. The Arras cemetery provides evidence of most of the rites characteristic of the Yorkshire burials: there were several inhumations buried with the remains of carts; some were covered by barrows constructed within rectangular ditched enclosures; the barrow mounds were invariably small; and the cemetery was large, containing between 100 and 200 graves. These elements are repeated on a number of sites, the more important of which include Dane's Graves, Driffield, Eastburn, Cowlam, Pexton Moor, Hunmanby, Huntow, Sawdon, Burton Fleming, Garton Slack and Wetwang Slack.

A distributional analysis of the rite of cart burial shows that two distinct methods were employed: either the carts were placed upright in the graves, sometimes with recesses cut for the wheels so that the body of the cart could rest on the ground surface; or the carts were dismantled, the wheels being placed flat. That burials of the first type were found on the limestone hills, while the second were restricted to the Wolds, suggests the possibility of some form of cultural distinction between the two areas – a suggestion further supported by the apparent absence of large cemeteries, as opposed to isolated barrows, on the limestone hills in reverse of the situation on the Wolds.

The surviving grave-goods can be divided into two groups: the cart-and harness-fittings, and personal ornaments and offerings. The first category covers a wide range of types including iron cart-tyres, nave hoops and miscellaneous wheel-fittings, linchpins to prevent the wheels from coming loose, bronze pole sheaths, three-link horse-bits and various terret-rings from the leather harnesses. Detailed comparisons with Continental types (Stead 1965, 28–45, 1979, 7–39) show that while the British versions were closely related to them, they are nevertheless sufficiently distinctive to be considered the result of several generations of local development. Not one of the cart- or harness-fittings at present known can be regarded as a direct import from France.

Among the ornaments, on the other hand, there is an assemblage from Cowlam which is clearly of direct Continental inspiration. It includes a fibula of Münsingen Ia type, a bracelet with 'tongue-in-glove' terminals, expanded at five points around the circumference, which can be paralleled in Alsace and Burgundy in early La Tène contexts, and a necklace composed of seventy blue and white beads. Again, parallels can be found for such necklaces in the phase Ia graves at Münsingen although they do occur later. The Cowlam burial is the earliest assemblage that can be defined within the Arras culture, probably dating to the early part of the fourth century: it might reasonably be thought to represent the burial of first-generation imported trinkets. The Cowlam bracelet and necklace are similar to finds from the Arras cemetery, where knobbed and ribbed bracelets of early La Tène type provide a further link with Burgundy and Switzerland. The remainder of the ornaments – the inlaid and involuted brooches, the incised bronze mirror, the ring-headed pins, finger-rings, pendants, toilet sets and toggles – all belong to a decidedly British tradition and must be later developments influenced more by internal British traditions than by Continental ideas.

It is widely believed that the Arras culture arose as the result of a folk movement into eastern Yorkshire late in the fifth or early in the fourth century. Thereafter local development modified the culture, but as late as the first century BC its alien origins were still apparent. A careful consideration of the niceties of burial rite and the typology of the earliest group of artefacts has led Stead (1965) to propose a complex origin for the invaders, coming from the Burgundian area (where dismantled carts and the absence of weapons and pottery are similar to the British burials) via the Seine. In the Nanterre–Paris region part of the band remained to give rise to the Parisii while those destined for Britain moved on, to found another community in Yorkshire, known to Ptolemy as the Parisi: the coincidence is noteworthy. The cultural affinities of the Pexton Moor burial, with its rectangular enclosure ditches and wheel pits, may however indicate that some part of the immigrant force had connections with the La Tène group in the Champagne. The alternative view, that the Arras phenomenon was a local development, the aristocracy adopting 'foreign' burial rites as a means of expressing status, has been persuasively argued by Higham (1987).

A close study of the Arras culture emphasizes some of the problems involved in recognizing immigrant communities by means of the archaeological record. Seldom is it possible to discover material of the first generation; what survives is more likely to belong to subsequent developments, which invariably diverge from the traditions of the homeland. Nevertheless, the Yorkshire evidence is impressive. It suggests small bands arriving, with little more than their personal equipment, and settling down among the natives in whose pottery traditions they shared. When time came for burial they maintained their own rituals, using a mortuary cart to bring the body to the grave and sometimes burying it with the dead. So strong were these religious practices that they remained dominant for several hundred years.

At present it is difficult to link the burial tradition of the Arras folk to other aspects of the material culture of the region, since so few occupation sites have been excavated. The pottery tradition, which must run broadly parallel to the burials, should post-date the Staple Howe assemblage but pre-date the simple coarse wares of the Dane's Graves/Staxton style (p. 90) which are predominantly second to first century BC in date. The class of large jars with upright or everted rims, like those from Kendal, Kilham and Atwick, might be considered to be of fifth- to third-century date on typological grounds, but sequential or absolute dating is at present lacking. A full survey of the sparse cultural material, particularly the pottery, from Yorkshire has been given by Challis (Challis and Harding 1975), but until the important excavations at Garton and Wetwang Slack are published little further advance can be made.

The Middle Iron Age (c. 400/300–100 BC)

During the Middle Iron Age most regions of southern Britain developed their own distinctive styles of decorated pottery. These may be divided into four broad regional continuua: a central southern group dominated by the saucepan pot form; a south-western group of highly decorated necked jars; a Midlands group of decorated bowls; and an eastern group in which the decorated bulbous jar form predominates. To some extent these broad regional divides reflect patterns already present in the Early Iron Age or even earlier. It will be argued later (chapter 20) that the four regions now represent real cultural (and tribal?) divisions which are also distinguishable in terms of settlement pattern and economy.

Petrographical studies of Middle Iron Age pottery (Peacock 1969, 1979; Morris 1981) have demonstrated clearly that in some regions, especially the south-west and the Welsh borderlands, a very limited range of clays were used and that the products were distributed over considerable distances suggesting a degree of specialist activity. In the west Midlands and Welsh borderlands the distributions lie within a discrete territory but some of the products of the south-western production centres spread far into adjacent territories implying a system of long-distance exchange. It should be possible in the not too distant future to examine the nature of the boundaries between regions or style-zones in order to test the degree of intercourse between adjacent territories, but this will depend upon the availability of large and adequately published ceramic assemblages.

The centre south

The saucepan pot continuum (Figure 4.6)

During the fourth to second centuries BC, the pottery over a large area of southern Britain developed a remarkable degree of uniformity characterized by vertical-sided 'saucepan pots' and jars with rounded shoulders and beaded rims. Broadly speaking this continuum covers Sussex, Hampshire, Wiltshire, Surrey, Berkshire, Somerset, Gloucestershire, the Welsh borderlands and parts of south Wales (Cunliffe 1984a, 254–8; Morris 1981). The only differences which can be

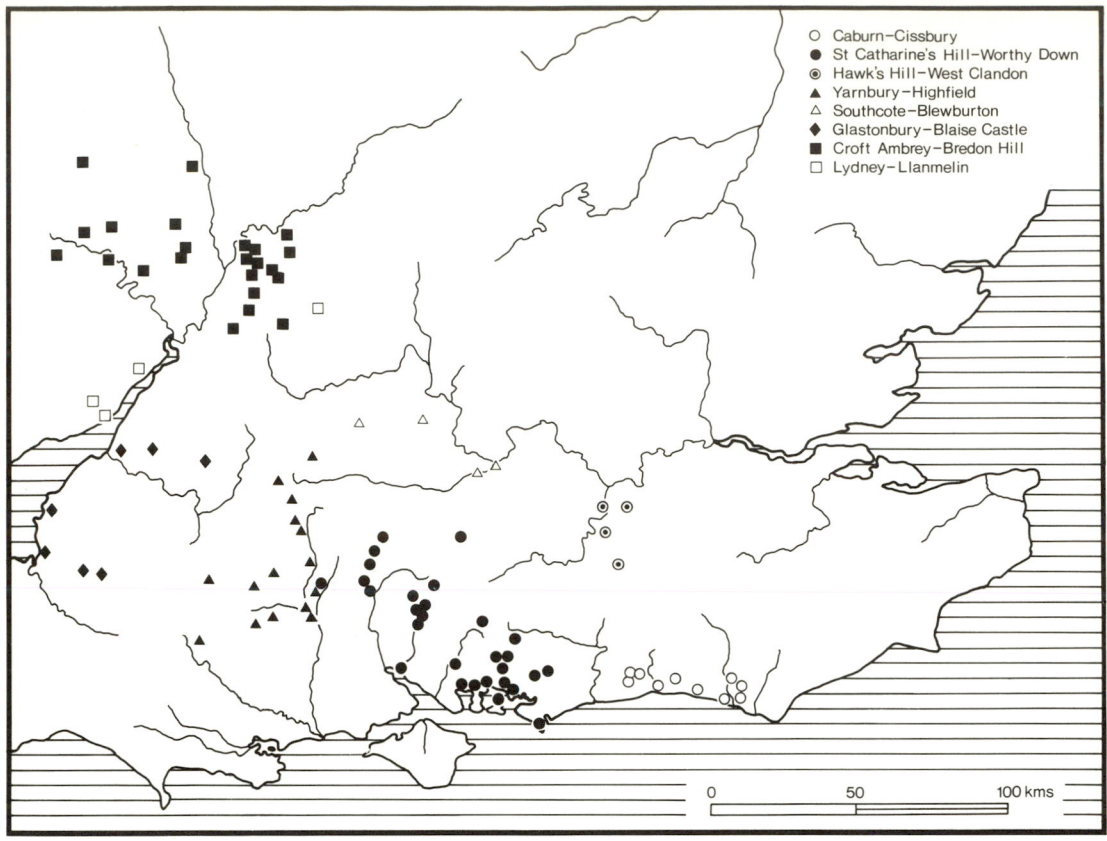

Figure 4.6 Simplified distribution of fourth- to second-century pottery styles in southern Britain (source: author).

recognized in the ceramic assemblages of these regions are minor variations of profile, regional decorative preferences and fabric variation. The Dorset group, however, presents more significant differences and is something of an anomaly.

To describe in any detail the range of pottery from each of the regional styles constituting the saucepan pot continuum is unnecessary here, since the illustrations of selected vessels (Figures A:14–A:18, pp. 567–71) together with the distribution map summarize in a simple visual form the major points. Nevertheless, a few generalizations must be offered.

The Caburn–Cissbury style (Figure A:14, p. 567)   has been so called after two partially excavated hillforts in Sussex. The main characteristic of the pottery is that it tends to be decorated with simple regular and asymmetrical curvilinear designs. The rims and bases of the 'saucepans' are frequently thickened, perhaps to imitate the strengthening of leather prototypes of which the vessels may be copies. A few sites in Surrey producing a broadly similar range of types are best included in this grouping though they are separated on Figure 4.6.

The St Catharine's Hill–Worthy Down style (Figure A:15, p. 568),   centred upon Hampshire, also shows signs of skeuomorphism in the frequent use of a decorative zone, incorporating oblique lines between rows of dots, presumably meant to imitate stitching. The group is also characterized by a greater predominance of jars, often similarly decorated, some of which are large while others have about the same capacity as the saucepan pots. A study of stratified groups from Torberry, Sussex, and Chalton, Hants., has suggested that chronological differences may be recognized, the later groups containing a greater number of small jars (Cunliffe 1976a). At Danebury, Hants., where a considerable assemblage of pottery has been recovered, it was possible to show that a phase in which decoration was popular was preceded by an undecorated phase.

The Yarnbury–Highfield style (Figure A:16, p. 569)   of Wiltshire differs from the Hampshire group in that narrow-necked jars frequently occur and the decorative motifs often incorporate simple tooled arcs springing from shallow depressions. For the most part the vessels of this style were made in a distinctive sandy fabric containing the mineral glauconite derived from clays found to the west of Salisbury.

The Southcote–Blewburton Hill style (Figure A:17, p. 570)   is distributed in the Berkshire Downs–Reading area. The basic pottery forms show considerable variation, reflecting influences both from the decorated hemispherical bowl types of the Upper Thames and from Hampshire. The general preference in decoration is for rectilinear areas filled with shallow tooled lines or dots.

The Croft Ambrey–Bredon Hill style (Figure A:18, p. 571)   is represented in the Herefordshire–Cotswold region by occupation sites and hillforts producing pottery in the saucepan pot tradition which is decorated either with bands of stamped impressions below the rim or with a similarly placed zone of linear tooling. It was originally thought that the two styles represented different cultural groups of complementary dates, but the excavation at Croft Ambrey, together with a petrological examination of the fabrics (Peacock 1968), has demonstrated that both types were contemporary and were the output of three production centres in the Malvern area, which developed to serve the needs of a region hitherto largely aceramic. The complexities of production and distribution which the study underlines are probably typical of those which existed over much of southern Britain at this time and have recently been examined in detail by Morris (1981).

The Lydney–Llanmelin style (Figure A:18, p. 571)   is centred upon the south Welsh coastal plain east of the Usk, where a group of sites producing a distinctive saucepan pot assemblage have been excavated. Salmonsbury, Glos., has yielded pottery of a broadly similar kind. The range of decorative motifs is limited but includes chevron patterns and large oval-shaped stab marks which tend not to occur in other groups. The few sites and lack of good stratigraphical sequences, however, prevent an adequate definition of this style at present (Spencer 1983).

The Glastonbury–Blaise Castle Hill style   It is a moot point whether the Middle Iron Age assemblages of Somerset and Avon should be included with the saucepan pot continuum or one of the south-western groups characterized by the presence of necked jars and of distinctive curvilinear decoration. That many of the assemblages show a distinct resemblance to the saucepan pot styles further to the east is evident. At Little Solisbury excavation has yielded a unique assemblage of decorated vessels which may lie towards the beginning of a sequence and another group of material was found at Blaise Castle Hill, Glos., in a pit together with a La Tène I fibula allowing the possibility of an early date. Other saucepan pot assemblages, from Camerton and Worlebury, Somerset, and from Bury Wood Camp, Wilts., are limited in quantity and without useful associations.

From the Mendips and to the south the quantity of decorated south-western pottery ('Glastonbury wares') increases and certainly dominates the publications, though we should remember that at the two villages of Meare only 5–10 per cent of the total assemblage showed any form of decoration. Radiocarbon dates now becoming available from Meare villages East and West suggest occupation starting as early as the third century BC (Coles 1987, 246–9) by which date decorated wares were well in evidence. What is not yet clear is the chronology of the decoration forms. If the simpler forms, jars and saucepan pots with geometric and simple curvilinear designs, come early in the sequence and the more elaborate forms – the neck bowls and jars and the open hemispherical bowls – with complex stamped and curvilinear motifs are later, then it could be argued that a traditional saucepan pot style-zone of the Middle Iron Age preceded but developed into a more complex and artistically evolved assemblage of Late Iron Age date under influences emanating from the south-west. That the villages of Meare and Glastonbury continued to be occupied into the first century AD is well established and adds some support to this view. It is, however, equally possible that the 'south-western' influences appeared early and dominated the assemblage throughout the Middle and Late Iron Age. These problems will only be resolved after a series of well-stratified assemblages have been studied.

Dating evidence for the Middle Iron Age saucepan pot assemblages rests largely with the Danebury sequence where a large body of well-stratified material has been studied and subjected to a programme of radiocarbon dating (Cunliffe and Orton 1984). The earliest groups of undecorated saucepan pots date to the early fourth century BC, the decorated forms becoming common in the third and second centuries. At Hengistbury Head the latest saucepans are found in association with Dressel 1A amphorae suggesting an end c. 100 BC date or soon after. Other scraps of dating evidence include the La Tène I fibula from Blaise Castle Hill and a coin of Ptolemy V (204–180) from Winchester: neither provides close dating in its own right but both are consistent with the range suggested by the radiocarbon dates at Danebury.

The end of the saucepan pot styles is likely to have varied from region to region. Over much of central southern Britain the change will have come with the introduction of the potter's wheel some time around 100 BC. In Somerset the essentially Middle Iron Age traditions appear to have continued little changed until the Roman Conquest, while in Gloucestershire, Herefordshire, Shropshire and south Wales the local styles may have continued in use even later until these areas were gradually subdued by the Roman army between 47 and c. 60.

The Maiden Castle–Marnhull style (Figures 4.7 and A:19, p. 572)

From the lower reaches of the Wiltshire Avon west approximately to the valley of the river Brit and from the Channel coast to the river Ebble, a range of pottery is found typified by the large and well-stratified collection from the hillfort of Maiden Castle and from the open settlement at Marnhull. The forms and decoration readily distinguish the style from the adjacent saucepan pot

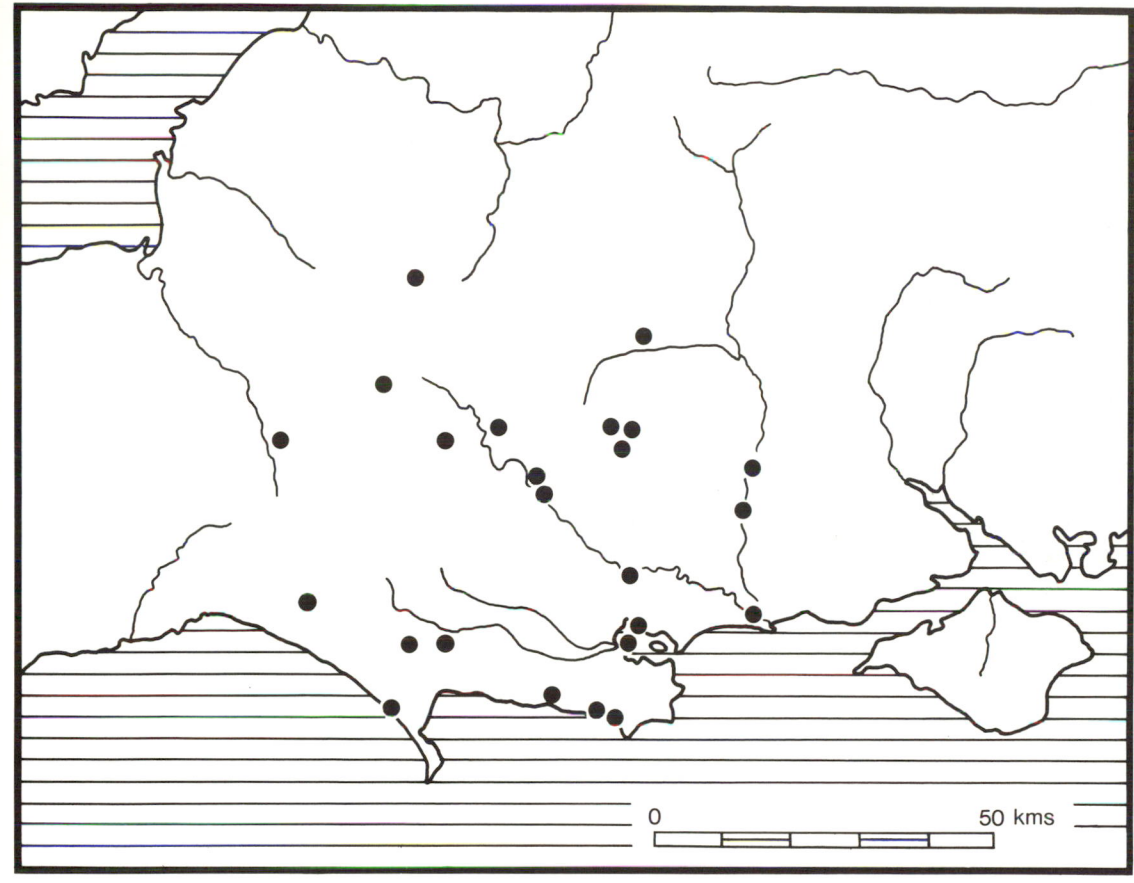

Figure 4.7   Distribution of Maiden Castle–Marnhull style pottery (source: author).

groups. The commonest types are large ovoid jars with beaded rims and smaller bowls of similar shape. Some jars were provided with countersunk lugs, and occasionally open bowls with flat-topped rims occur. Decoration often takes the form of grooved scrolls, arcs or wavy lines. Sometimes single or grouped dimples are employed, either associated with other patterns or in isolation; less often shallow-tooled arcs occur. A consideration of the sequences and associations from the two type-sites leaves little doubt that the entire assemblage could easily have developed out of preceding traditions. Even the countersunk lugs, which were once thought to have derived from Brittany, are now best regarded as a local feature.

At what stage pottery of the Maiden Castle–Marnhull type began to develop its distinctive characteristics is difficult to say, but a beginning in the fourth or third century would allow a sufficient time span for the associated structural developments at Maiden Castle to take place. The end of the sequence was marked by the rapid evolution of better-made and more sophisticated pottery of Durotrigan type which resulted from the introduction of the potter's wheel and resumed contacts with the Continent towards the beginning of the first century BC.

The south-west

South-Western Decorated Wares (Figures 4.8, A:20, p. 573 and A:21, p. 574)

It has long been recognized that in the later pre-Roman Iron Age the communities of south-west England used a range of ceramics among which were distinctive and highly decorated necked-bowl and jar forms. These were called *Glastonbury ware* after the Somerset lake village – a term which is no longer favoured because of the potential misunderstanding which it can cause. Instead, the less specific term *South-Western Decorated Wares* is preferred and until more work is undertaken on regional stylistic variations it will serve usefully as a portmanteau category.

A petrological study of the fabrics of selected types (Peacock 1969 and below p. 462) has distinguished six regional groups, each of which was based on a different parent rock ranging from the Gabbro of the Lizard Peninsula to the Carboniferous Limestone of the Mendips (Figure 17.17, p. 464). Clearly a number of different production centres must have been in operation, but not all were necessarily contemporary.

The origins and development of the style are extremely difficult to untangle in the absence of

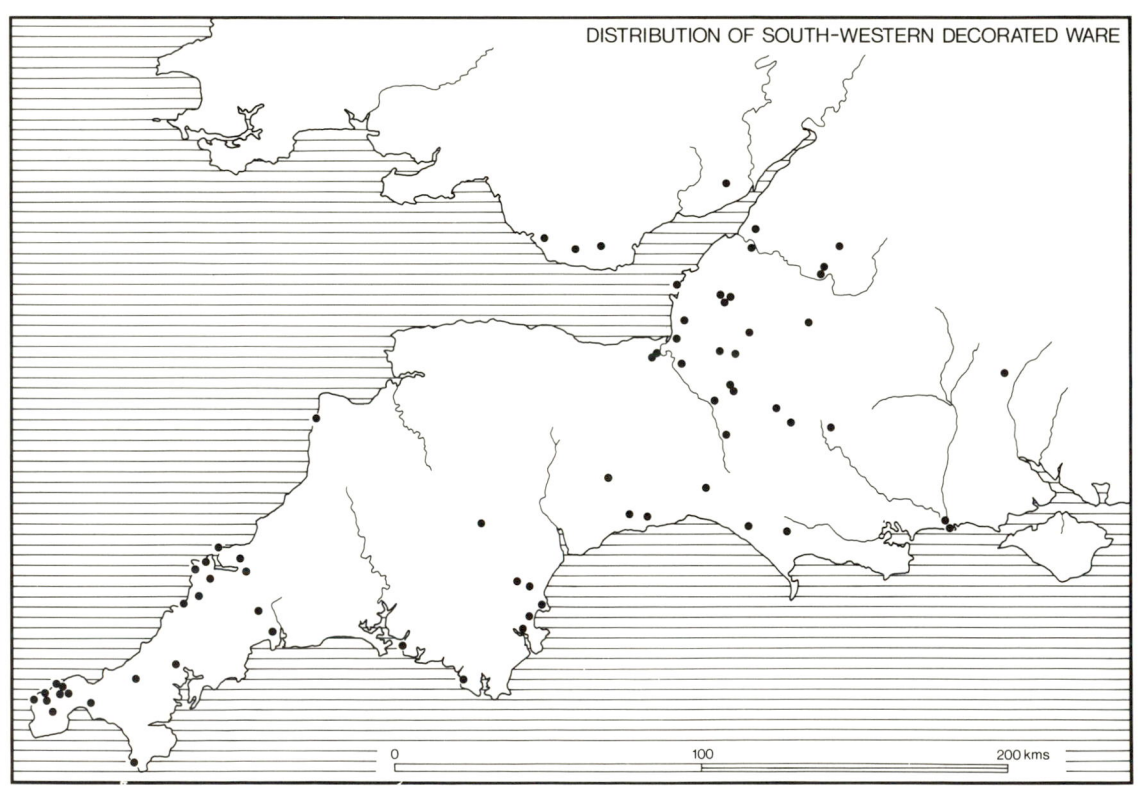

Figure 4.8 Distribution of South-Western Decorated Wares (source: author).

well-stratified sequences, but the publication of the pottery from Carn Euny provides a useful yardstick (Elsdon 1978). The earliest decorated sherds were ornamented with stamped designs highly reminiscent of Breton motifs considered on stylistic grounds to be of fifth-century date (Schwappach 1969, 272). A single radiocarbon date of 420 ± 70 bc for the Carn Euny sherds would be consistent with this dating. Later, probably in the third century BC, rouletted decoration becomes evident to be followed by a range of curvilinear and geometric designs incised with a shallow tool on the leather-hard fabric. These types, comparatively common and widespread, may have begun as early as the third century but were certainly in use in the second and possibly, in some areas, even later. The stratified assemblages from Castle Dore, Cornwall, add support to the Carn Euny sequence. On present, albeit tenuous, evidence therefore it would appear that the earliest South-Western Decorated Wares were probably inspired from Brittany at the end of the fifth century BC and thereafter developed throughout the Middle Iron Age as the result of local inventiveness. It was some time during this period that the potters of Devon began local production but little can yet be said of the chronology of these more easterly developments.

Developments in Somerset need not have followed the same course as Cornwall. Although vessels from Cornwall and Devon were imported into Somerset it may well be that local production of the typical decorated jars and necked-bowls began somewhat later, perhaps after a local version of the saucepan pot continuum had already developed. If so it ought to be possible eventually to identify a saucepan pot phase belonging to an early part of the Middle Iron Age as has tentatively been anticipated above (pp. 81–2).

Whereas in Cornwall, decorated wares eventually gave way to plain cordoned wares some time in the first century BC it would appear, on present evidence, that in Devon and Somerset decorated wares continued in use for some decades longer and may even have lasted until the time of the Roman invasion. Much work remains to be done on the pottery of the south-west and until the results of more large-scale excavations are available little significant advance is likely. In the meantime it may be convenient to divide the South-Western Decorated Wares in three regional groupings based on the principal production centres in Cornwall, Devon and Somerset.

The Midlands (Figure 4.9)

In the south and east Midlands, broadly the area between the Chilterns and the Jurassic Ridge, the ceramic assemblage is dominated by the open hemispherical bowl, usually with a simple beaded lip, made in a dark well-burnished fabric. In the early (undecorated) phase little regional distinction can be made among the bowl forms, but the coarse ware traditions show a twofold division between the Oxfordshire region, where the coarse vessels are usually plain, and the Northamptonshire region, where scored wares, continuing the techniques of the Breedon–Ancaster style, predominate. This twofold division becomes strikingly apparent in the later (decorated) period when the decorative motifs of the bowls are considered. For these reasons, two separate style-zones are recognized.

The Stanton Harcourt–Cassington style (Figure A:22, p. 575)

In the Upper Thames valley a change to dark, well-burnished bowls becomes noticeable towards the end of the Long Wittenham–Allen's Pit style, and thereafter development continued until finely decorated vessels marked the culmination of the native tradition. Since many of the sites

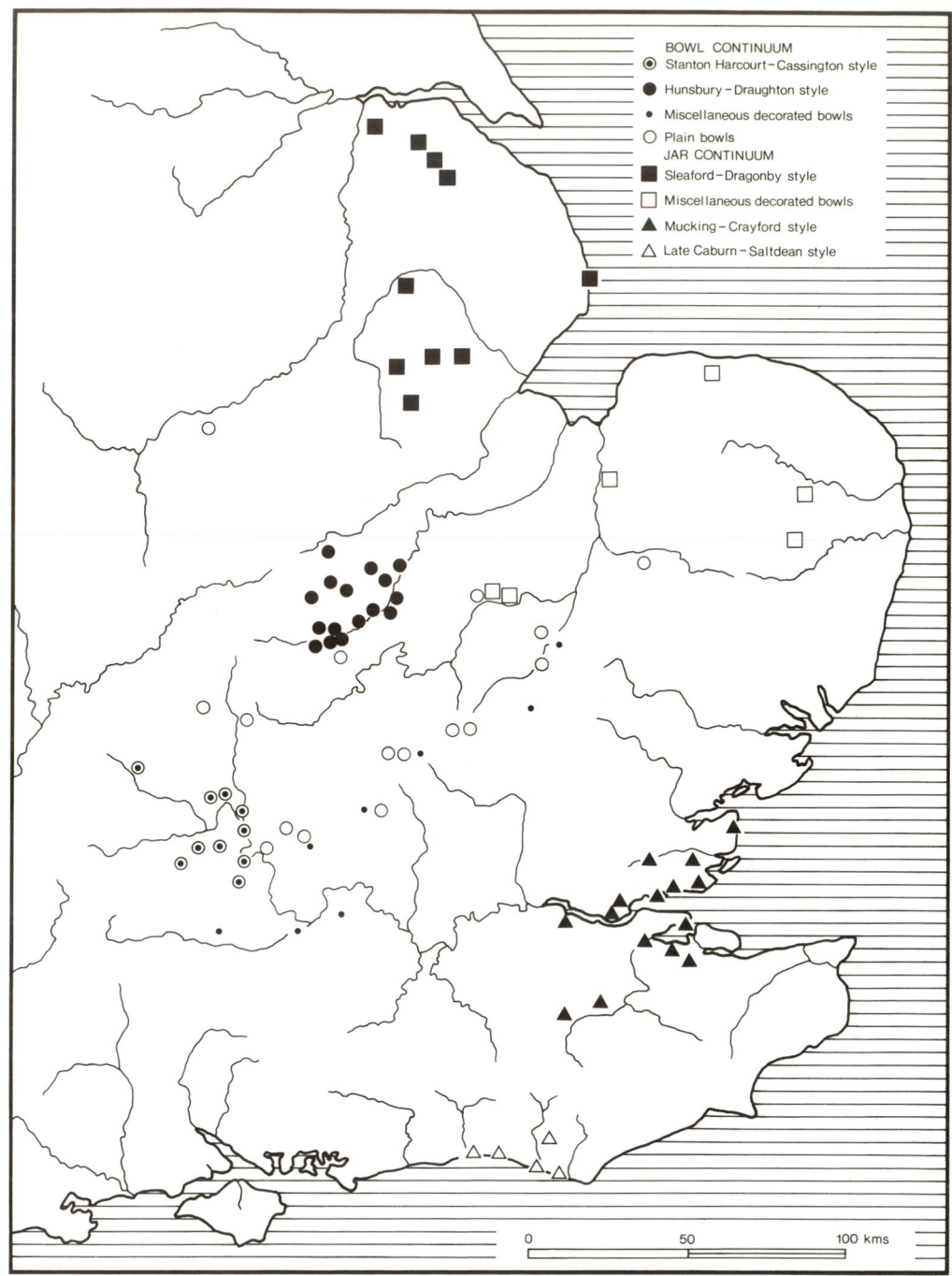

Figure 4.9 Distribution of decorated pottery styles in eastern England (source: author).

continued in use throughout this period, and few well-stratified groups have yet been recorded, it is difficult to isolate groups of the early undecorated phase from the later decorated phase. Nevertheless, the type-sites of Stanton Harcourt and Cassington have produced loosely associated assemblages containing only the ultimate simplification of the coarse ware shouldered jar together with plain bowl forms. Similar groups have recently been discovered at Ashville (Abingdon) and Farmoor, Oxon.

Decorated bowls probably began to be manufactured some time in the second century. In the Oxford region common motifs, particularly well displayed by the material from Frilford, include pendent swags and arcs drawn in a variety of ways, often incorporating impressed circlets. Less frequently, zones of diagonally shaded lozenges were used. Decorated bowls of this type cluster in the Middle Thames valley, with outliers as far west as Salmonsbury. The form also occurs sporadically on the chalk to the south, as for example at Blewburton Hill. Some of the complexities of the data arising from a detailed regional study, and taking cognizance of site status, have recently been reviewed by Lambrick (1984).

Several sequences show that assemblages of bowl types were superseded by wheel-turned vessels of Aylesford–Swarling type, but the precise date of this change is at present undefined. In all probability it took place in the second half of the first century BC, but a later date is possible.

The Hunsbury–Draughton style[6] (Figure A:23, p. 576)

A number of sites in Northamptonshire have now produced assemblages containing coarse jars, often of scored-type, in association with plain well-made bowls. At Twywell, Northants., several well-stratified groups of this kind have been recovered, for one of which a single radiocarbon determination of 280 ± 90 bc indicates a possible beginning for the style in the fourth century BC. At Draughton, a stratigraphical sequence was recognized, demonstrating that decorated forms developed later than assemblages containing only plain bowls. In all probability the hillfort at Hunsbury underwent a similar development, but all of the material recovered in the nineteenth century is unstratified. The fibulae, however – three La Tène I types and two of La Tène III – no doubt reflect the chronological range of the occupation. On typological grounds it is likely that the coarse shouldered jars, simple bead-rimmed bowls and large jars with perforated lug handles, belong to the earlier period, while the elaborately decorated bowls developed later. The decoration of these vessels tends to be freer and more lively than those of Oxfordshire, relying on the Yin-Yang, or flowing scroll, for its effect. The influence of metalwork can be discerned (Elsdon 1976). Within Northamptonshire two separate local groups can be distinguished on the basis of decorative preferences: a southern group, close to Hunsbury, typified by the running scroll and berried cluster motif, and a northern group between Draughton and Stanwick where the running scroll is enlivened with a single dimple. These local groups are likely to reflect the output of specific production centres (Jackson and Dix 1989).

Several sites occupied in the decorated bowl phase continued in use during the period when Aylesford–Swarling types were common, but the change in ceramic style remains undated. At Moulton Park, however, a date in the first half of the first century AD has been suggested.

The Chilterns (Figures 4.9, p. 86 and A:24, p. 577)

Ceramic material of the fourth to first centuries from the Ouse valley, the Chilterns and adjacent areas of East Anglia, is at present sparse, and, with the exception of a few notable sites, poorly stratified. For this reason no attempt has yet been made to define individual style-zones.

The most distinctive pottery types, apart from a few imported saucepan pots, include wide-mouthed bowls with beaded lips, usually made in dark highly-burnished wares, and coarse ware jars frequently decorated with deeply scored lines. Decoration of the bowls is rare but includes shallow tooling, the use of impressed dots and rouletted lines. The only unifying factor between the various sites is the existence of heavily scored jars which recur frequently over the whole area, and derive from the coarse ware tradition of the Breedon–Ancaster style.

Some sites have produced decorated bowls. At Puddlehill, Beds., a number of stratified groups have been found associating the coarse ware and bowl types. Decoration is rare, but shallow tooled curvilinear lines were used on one vessel to give a flowing scroll effect. Shallow tooling of this kind is also recorded at Barley, Herts., and at Cambridge (Addenbrooke's), where the decoration resembles that of the Hunsbury style. Further north at St Ives, Hunts., Arminghall and Wareham, Norfolk, rouletting and dot impression occur, but the quantity of material is small.

The style must have begun after the decline of the Chinnor–Wandlebury and Darmsden–Linton styles, but it is difficult to demonstrate the exact relationship between them. In all probability one developed imperceptibly into the other some time during the fourth or third century. During the latter part of the first century BC or early first century AD, the area gradually came under the influence of Aylesford–Swarling ceramic technology, which brought native traditions to an end.

Although it would be possible to group the Chiltern material together as a single style-zone named after one or more of the sites producing decorated wares, e.g. Puddlehill, it is felt advisable at present to leave the group unnamed and only loosely defined until more well-stratified assemblages become available for study.

The Trent valley

Few sites are known in the Trent valley, but in the pages above (p. 73) it has been possible to define in general terms a Breedon–Ancaster group dating broadly from the fourth or third centuries. It would seem that this tradition continued to develop throughout the second and first centuries, during which time regional styles became recognizable among the finer decorated wares. Some of these have now been described.

In the Trent valley itself, few groups of the second or first century are available, with the exception of a small collection from Breedon-on-the-Hill, which includes bowl and open jar forms decorated with shallow tooled designs of curvilinear form incorporating impressed dots. It may well be possible in the future to recognize a distinctive style-zone in this region.

Eastern England

It has long been recognized that a number of sites in the east of England, in Essex, Kent and Sussex, have produced a stylistically similar range of decorated jars. These were at one time classified together as 'South-Eastern B' (Ward Perkins 1938), later renamed 'Southern Third B' (C.F.C. Hawkes 1959). More recently the decorative motifs of these vessels have been discussed

(Elsdon 1975). The discovery of well-stratified groups of similar material from Lincolnshire, in particular at Dragonby and Old Sleaford, and from Essex, at Gun Hill and Mucking, has enabled the chronological position of these loosely related types to be considered afresh.

There would appear to be some value in regarding the widely distributed groups as sharing in a common tradition, for not only do the forms of the vessels closely resemble each other, but so also do the motifs of decoration and the techniques by which they were applied.

The Sleaford–Dragonby style (Figure A:25, p. 578)

Between the rivers Welland and Humber a number of sites have recently been identified, producing a range of ceramics which typologically follow the Breedon–Ancaster group and are succeeded by wheel-turned types, similar to Aylesford–Swarling ceramics, which characterize the pottery of the Corieltauvi. The predominant type is the bowl or jar form with slightly everted rim, usually fired black and frequently burnished on the surface. Alongside the fine wares are found coarse shouldered jars made in gritty ware. Some of the finer bowls and jars are decorated with stamped circlets linked with arcs and swags impressed with a fine-toothed roulette wheel. At both of the type-sites these assemblages lie at the beginning of a sequence which develops uninterruptedly into the first century AD. The high technical quality and the uniformity of the fine wares suggest the probability of commercial production, but it is too early to speculate on the number of production centres involved. That many of the decorative techniques continued to be practised after the introduction of Aylesford-Swarling types is an indication of the strength of the local traditions.

The date range of the Sleaford–Dragonby style is difficult to define, but it is possible that the decorated types began to develop in the second century BC or even earlier, and that Aylesford–Swarling influence interrupted the development towards the middle of the first century BC.

East Anglia

East Anglia is at present virtually a blank largely because surprisingly few Iron Age sites have been recorded, but a few decorated sherds from Arminghall and Wareham hint at the existence of a fine ware tradition that has yet to be adequately examined.

The Mucking–Crayford style (Figure A:26, p. 579)

A number of sites clustering around the Thames estuary have produced assemblages containing well-made burnished jars, usually with everted rims and high shoulders, and with bases which may be of the omphalos or foot-ring type. A number of the vessels are decorated, the favourite motifs including arcs, often interlacing and sometimes in relation to stamped circlets. In the past the decorated vessels have been selected for comment with little notice being taken of the associated plain wares. This unfortunate tendency has resulted, in part, from the lack of good stratified groups, a lack which the excavations at Mucking and Little Waltham, Essex, are fast making good. At Gun Hill, Essex, coarse wares and fine plain wares have been discovered in loose association with decorated vessels, indicating a considerable range of broadly contemporary types including plain bead-rimmed jars and everted-rimmed bowls in burnished fabrics, the ancestors of both of which can be traced back to the Darmsden–Linton group. At Little Waltham, however, the entire Middle Iron Age sequence consists of plain wares.

Across the Thames in Kent no associated groups have yet been recovered, but the unstratified collections from Crayford include plain vessels of bead-rimmed and everted-rim type together with decorated forms. Elsewhere in Kent and the Weald the once-named 'Wealden Culture' (Ward Perkins 1944) is best seen as a part of the same style-group, possibly representing an early phase before decoration became common. Among the more important sites producing this limited range of undecorated types is the hillfort at Oldbury.

Little dating evidence has yet been published, but at Gun Hill pottery of the Mucking–Crayford style can be shown to pre-date the appearance of wheel-turned vessels of the Aylesford–Swarling group. More precision will be possible when the assemblage from Mucking has been published. That the style fits between the Darmsden–Linton group and the Aylesford–Swarling group is, however, clear.

The Late Caburn–Saltdean style (Figure A:26, p. 579)

A considerable range of decorated ceramics has been recovered from Sussex, but seldom from reliably stratified contexts. A number of groups have, however, been found in which saucepan pots predominate: these have been referred to above (p. 80) as the Cissbury–Caburn style of the saucepan pot continuum. At the Caburn several pits, presumably late in the occupation sequence, have produced vessels unlike those of the saucepan pot phase but comparable to those of the Mucking–Crayford style. They may be characterized as large jars with bulbous bodies, constricted mouths and out-rolled rims. Frequently they are decorated with curvilinear designs, sometimes in the form of arcs and occasionally stamped circlets are employed. The simplest explanation is that these types, which we here characterize as the Late Caburn–Saltdean style, developed out of the preceding saucepan pot tradition. Vessels of this type have been found on a number of sites in East Sussex, but almost invariably in unstratified contexts. One of the best preserved examples is the single vessel from Saltdean.

At what stage the style developed is at present undefined, but sometime late in the second century would seem probable. Thereafter elements of the style continued in use until the Roman Conquest, apparently little influenced by Aylesford–Swarling types. The only readily distinguishable changes include the appearance of cordons, the development of simple zoned decoration and a change in fabrics as the technique of wheel-turning became widespread. These later developments, which can tentatively be dated to the late first century BC and early first century AD, are considered again below, where they are referred to as Eastern Atrebatic pottery (p. 151).

Northern England

The Dane's Graves–Staxton style (Figure A:27, p. 580)

In a detailed discussion of the metalwork of the La Tène cultures of Yorkshire, Stead (1965) has suggested a division into two phases. The first, characterized by the burial at Cowlam, is considered to have begun in the fifth century; the second phase, represented by the burials at

Arras and Dane's Graves, is not earlier than the third to second century. The excavations of Dane's Graves and of the Driffield and Rigg's Farm burials have produced a collection of pottery belonging to a single stylistic group in which bucket-shaped vessels with thick bases and frequently with internally bevelled rims predominate. These types probably derive from vessels in the earlier Grimthorpe style, but some influence from the saucepan pot style of the south, or indeed from contemporary and similar types in France, might possibly be represented. A settlement site producing pottery of this kind is known at Staxton, where a palisade trench was found together with pits and a quantity of occupation debris. How long the style continued in use is impossible to say, but it is unlikely to have outlived the end of the first century BC.

Summary

This brief survey of the ceramic development of south-eastern Britain, imperfect though it must of necessity be, provides a valuable insight into many aspects of Iron Age society. It not only informs our understanding of the technological and artistic achievements of the different groups but provides a sound basis for the establishment of a chronology and allows something of the spacial organization of society to be appreciated.

By the ninth century BC south-eastern Britain was occupied by stable sedentary communities whose agrarian systems had developed in the second millennium. The pottery in use at the time showed a notable degree of similarity in part due to several centuries of conservatism. In the eighth and seventh centuries much of the south-east, particularly the coastal and riverine regions, was caught up in a complex exchange network which linked Britain to the Continent and is best exemplified in the archaeological record by the bronze metalwork of the Ewart Park and Carp's-Tongue Sword Complexes. The pottery of this considerable region was similar throughout. It owed much to traditional Bronze Age technology and stylistic preferences but new types in the form of sharp-shouldered jars and angled bowls were appearing. It is tempting to suggest that these types reflected bronze vessels, particularly the high shouldered buckets which were now reaching the country. While the coastal zone was showing a broadly common material culture, in the heart of Wessex a quite different ceramic assemblage was developing characterized by a highly distinctive series of decorated bowls and jars. The contrast between the pottery of the two zones is striking and may, in part, be a statement of socio-political differences. This dichotomy was maintained throughout the seventh century: the Wessex group continued to evolve while the southern and eastern coastal group maintained a broad ceramic similarity throughout all parts of the zone, developing a similar range of small angular bowls and jars strongly reminiscent of contemporary bronze forms.

In the period which followed (Early Iron Age, 600–400 BC), radical changes took place the most significant of which was the emergence of a number of highly distinctive regional styles each characterized by a limited range of forms and an exclusive repertory of decorative techniques. It is tempting to see in this development a growing awareness of ethnic identity.

During the latter part of the fifth century Continental influences become apparent in three disparate regions: in Cornwall the earliest decorated pottery so far discovered, though produced in local fabrics, was similar to contemporary Breton styles; La Tène pottery forms turned up in the region of the Thames, and adjacent areas to the north; while in Yorkshire the appearance of a distinctive style of burial rite involving the use of the mortuary cart reflects contemporary rites in northern France. Clearly the interchange of ideas between the coastal regions of Britain and the

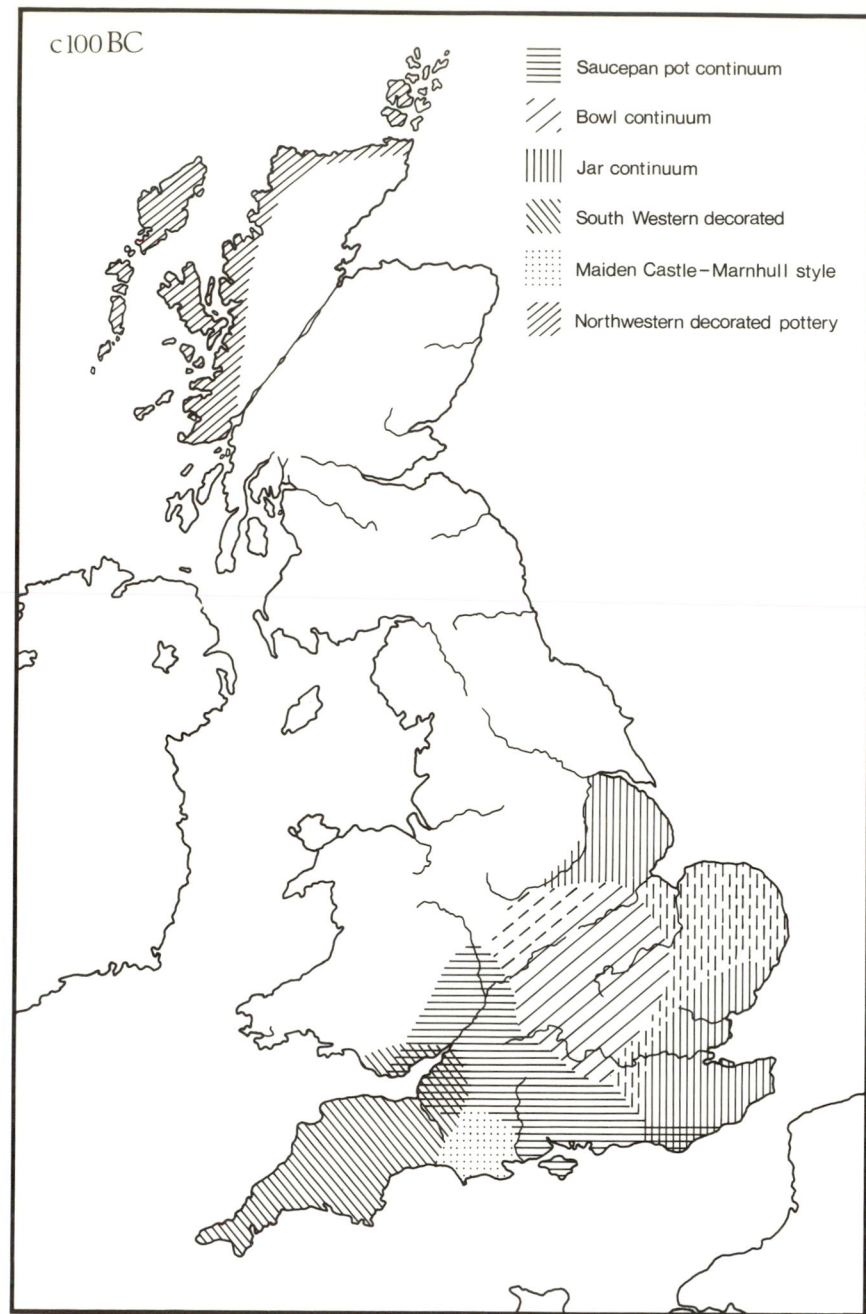

c 100 BC

Saucepan pot continuum
Bowl continuum
Jar continuum
South Western decorated
Maiden Castle – Marnhull style
Northwestern decorated pottery

Figure 4.10   Distribution of the major groupings of decorated pottery of the second to first century BC (source: author).

adjacent Continent was widespread if only for a brief period in the decades before 400 BC. The evidence of imported metalwork tells the same story (p. 424). The nature of these contacts is difficult to assess. The introduction of a mortuary rite, together with the associated range of Continental-inspired artefacts, strongly suggests the immigration of a small population including an elite, but the ceramic innovations in the Thames region and Cornwall need imply little more than active systems of cross-Channel exchange.

After *c*. 400 BC Britain appears to become more cut off from Continental development. During this Middle Iron Age period (400/300–100 BC) regional styles of pottery continued to evolve, reflecting much the same territorial divides which had become established in the sixth century. Standing back from the palimpsest of localized style-zones, it is possible to distinguish four broad divisions (Figure 4.10): a *south-west region*, extending into Somerset and south Wales and characterized by a free curvilinear style of ceramic ornament which has much in common with Armorica; a *central southern region* stretching from Sussex west across Wessex into the Cotswolds and Welsh Marches, typified by straight-sided saucepan pots; a *Midland region*, extending from the Thames valley to the Trent, characterized by hemispherical bowls; and an *eastern region* essentially coastal in distribution from East Sussex to Lincolnshire where the predominant form was the highly decorated jar. Three broad regional divisions are also reflected in the type of settlement pattern which had emerged, a fact which suggests that the pottery styles provide an insight into real socio-economic groupings. It will be argued later (chapter 20) that in the distinctive style-zones which begin to crystallize in the sixth century BC we may be seeing incipient tribal groupings. Once established these entities are maintained throughout the Middle Iron Age with little change. The broader regional groupings which it is possible to discern by the third century may indicate tribal confederacies: at the very least they present a generalized picture of regional contact and contrast.

By about 100 BC the Middle Iron Age system was at its most developed. In some areas ceramic styles continued to evolve little changed well into the first century BC and even the first century AD but in others – the coastal region of central southern Britain and the Lower Thames valley – new influences from the Continent initiated widespread socio-political and economic change. These Late Iron Age developments will be considered more fully in chapters 6–8.

5
Regional groupings: north and West

The communities of the highland areas of Britain differed in many ways from those of the south-east: settlement appears to have been generally sparser, the material culture was poor, and pottery was very little used over most of the area except in the extreme north-west of Scotland. For these reasons, definition of regional groupings is more difficult, and in some places impossible, and even where there is some material basis for chronological or regional division, precise definitions comparable with those obtainable in the south-east can rarely be achieved.

For most of the north and west, bronze implement typology offers the only method at present available for assessing regional groupings in the seventh and sixth centuries BC. The groups thus defined do little more than reflect spheres of contact but since these must imply some degree of cultural cohesion, or even uniformity, they may be thought to offer an initial, albeit tenuous, basis for regional definition (Figure 5.1). By the fifth century the organization of specialist bronze industries had virtually disappeared. The development of hillfort architecture in many parts of the west and north provides some basis for regional grouping (Hogg 1965, for Wales; Feachem 1966, for east Scotland), but so few forts have been adequately excavated (in some areas even surveys are wanting) that stylistic groupings based on them are at best uneven and at worst misleading. Some of these problems will, however, be returned to later.

The rest of the material culture is, to say the least, sparse: pottery occurs but rarely and is seldom distinctive; other artefacts, such as spindle whorls and bone and iron implements, lack sufficient form or specialization for typological assessment. Thus we are at present without the means of defining regional groups or chronological phases for much of the north and west.

Wales

In the seventh and sixth centuries BC three distinctive bronze industries can be defined.

The Llantwit–Stogursey tradition

In south Wales, principally Monmouthshire and Glamorganshire and spreading into Somerset, Devon and Cornwall, a group of related domestic bronze implements has been defined and

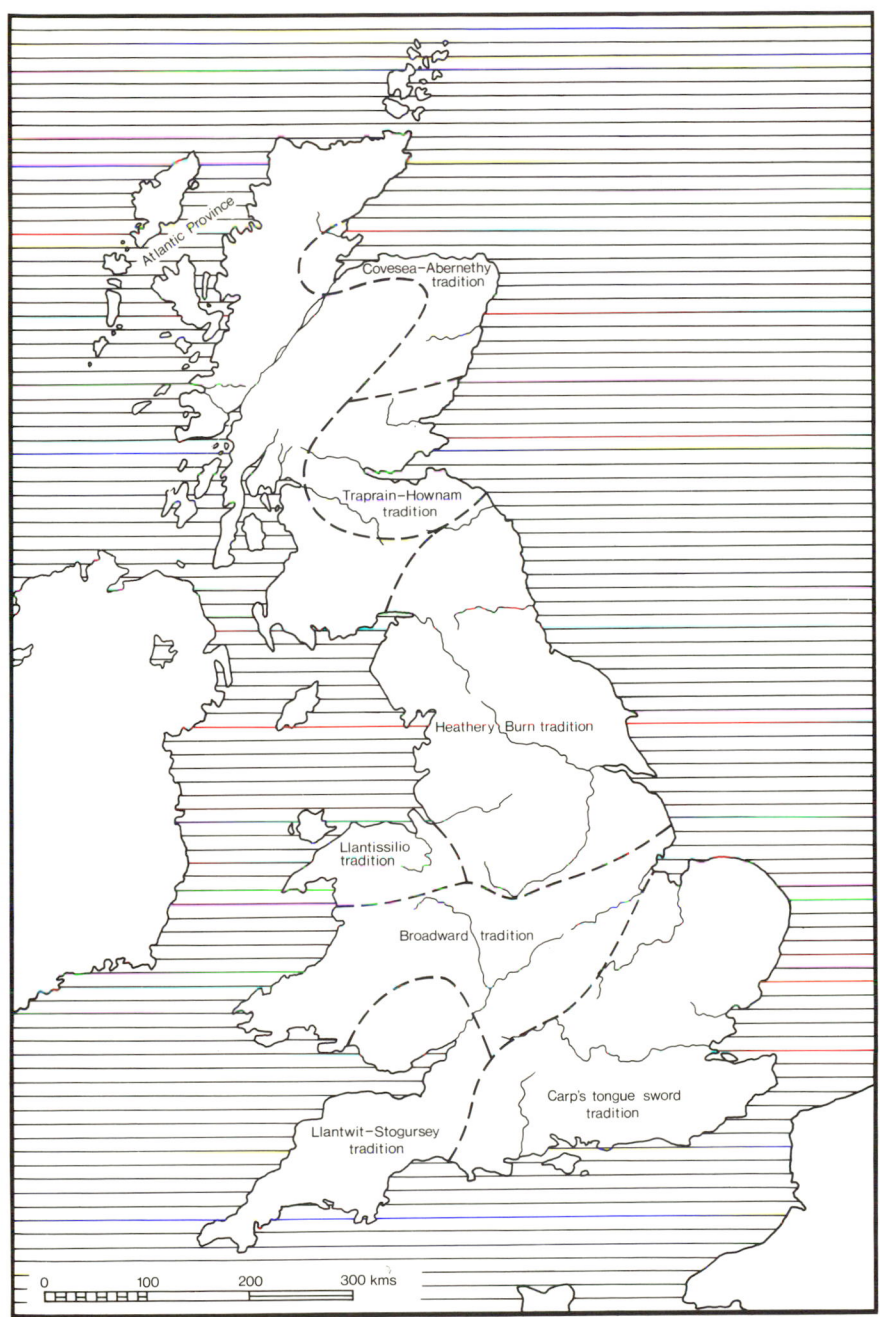

Figure 5.1   Distribution of the major bronze traditions in the eighth to fifth centuries (source: author).

named after two of the important hoards (Burgess 1969a, 19–21; also Fox and Hyde 1939, 390; Savory 1958, 37 and McNeil 1973). Distinctive among the tools represented is the socketed axe with a heavily moulded lip, decorated with parallel ribbing on the two faces. The type is frequently found in association with a range of tools including socketed gouges and tanged chisels. Varieties of the axe also occur in the Llyn Fawr and Cardiff hoards together with horse harness-fittings indicating a seventh- to sixth-century date which is further supported by occasional associations with material of the Carp's-Tongue Sword Complex. Scattered finds, a few hoards and occasional moulds for axes have turned up in south-west Britain, implying the use of the Severn estuary and western sea approaches for trading – no doubt in connection with the exploitation of Cornish tin – but the main distribution of hoards is centred upon south Wales.

No settlement sites of the period have yet been discovered, but the relatively fertile south Welsh plain in all probability supported a well-established agricultural economy which would have allowed a settled way of life comparable with that practised in the south and east. Whether or not pottery was in common use is a problem to which no answer can yet be given.

The Broadward tradition

The Broadward group, named after a Herefordshire hoard, can be defined in terms of an assemblage of weapons which includes swords of Ewart Park type, chapes and spearheads, among which a barbed variety is characteristic (Burgess, Coombs and Davies 1972). The contrast between the predominantly domestic character of south-east Welsh hoards and the military nature of the Broadward hoards may possibly reflect a difference in social structure, but the lack of occupation sites which can definitely be assigned to the period prevents any consideration of settlement pattern or economy. The area covered by the group extends from Pembrokeshire through central Wales into Cheshire and from there into the Welsh borderland, while some of the diagnostic weapons are found even further afield. The territory is well suited to a basically pastoral economy which would be consistent with a warlike society. The absence of pottery is another feature suggestive of pastoralism, since under such living conditions pottery would tend to break easily and would be better replaced by leather, wooden or metal containers. Indeed, there is clear evidence from the later forts in the Welsh borderland that the communities remained largely aceramic into the fourth or third centuries BC.

Northern Wales – the Llantissilio tradition

The northern corner of Wales appears to have been a technological backwater in the seventh and sixth centuries, receiving exotic types from Ireland and other parts of England and Wales rather than developing its own. A degree of conservatism is shown by the retention of the late type of palstave, which had been replaced by socketed axes elsewhere.

The famous Parc y Meirch hoard (Figure 16.7, p. 414 and p. 411), containing horse harness-fittings of eighth–seventh-century date, belongs geographically to this group. Its presence clearly demonstrates the extensive trading systems which, whether directly or indirectly via Ireland, allowed exotic north European objects to be transported to this relatively isolated territory.

Recent excavations on a number of north Welsh hillforts, in particular Moel y Gaer, Breiddin and Dinorben, have indicated a long tradition of occupation, extending back in some cases to c. 1000 BC and continuing largely uninterrupted throughout the first millennium, during which time defences were modified and internal structures were rearranged and rebuilt. The Breiddin

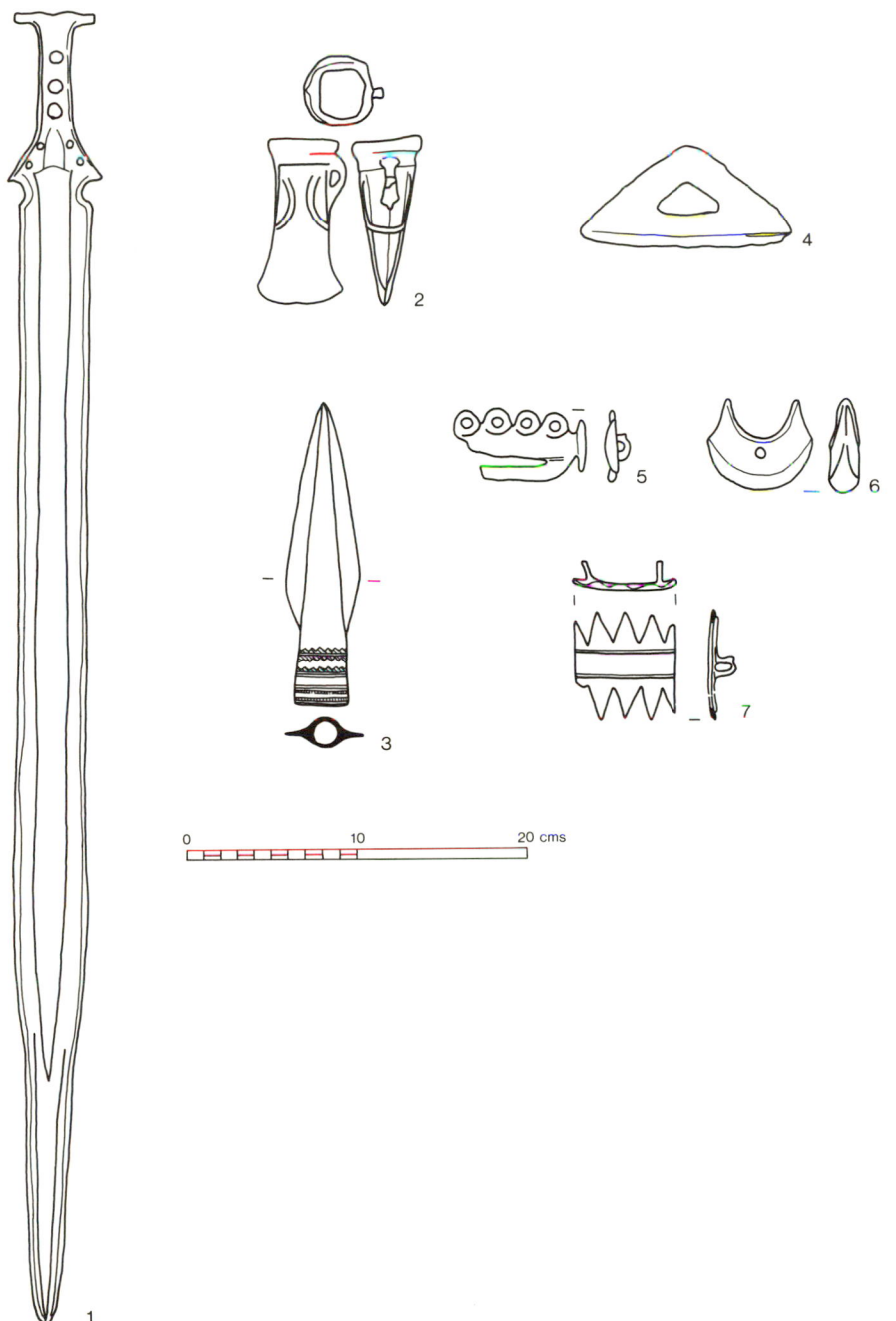

Figure 5.2 Implements and weapons of the Carp's-Tongue Sword Complex. 1 Sword from the river Thames; 2 socketed axe from the Thames at Brentford, Middx.; 3 socketed spear from Chingford, Essex; 4 knife from Eaton, Norwich; 5 'belt attachment' from the Thames at Sion Reach; 6 chape from Levington, Suffolk; 7 leather attachment from Watford, Herts. (source: Burgess 1969b).

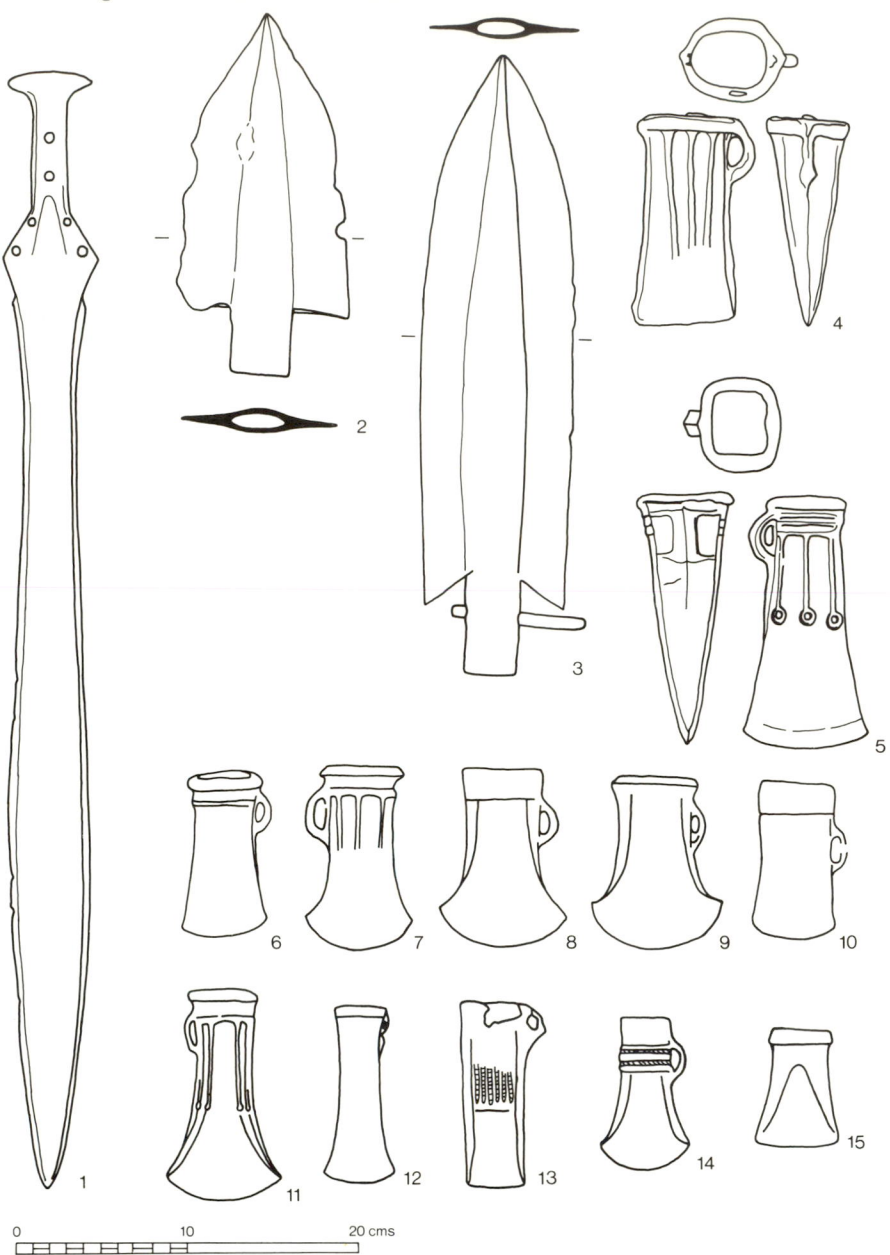

Figure 5.3 Implements and weapons of various bronze traditions of the seventh to fifth centuries. 1 Sword from Ewart Park, Northumberland; 2 spear from Broadward, Herefordshire; 3 spear from Plaistow Marshes, Essex; 4–15 socketed axes: 4 Llantwit Major, Glam.; 5 Leeds(?); 6 Dalduff, Ayr.; 7 Shetland; 8 Tomintoul, Banff.; 9 Culloden, Inverness; 10 Mawcarse, Kinross; 11 Delvine, Perth; 12 Annan, Dumfries; 13 Carse Loch, Kirkcudbright.; 14 Birse, Aberdeen; 15 Angus(?) (sources: 1–5 Burgess 1969b; 6–15 Coles 1962b).

has produced a particularly impressive range of plain coarse pottery, together with a number of items of Late Bronze Age metalwork representing occupation in the period 1000–700; but thereafter pottery and metalwork are sparse even though the radiocarbon dates indicate continued use. The hillfort of Moel y Gaer, which appears to have been constructed in the seventh or sixth century, is almost devoid of finds. Moel Hiraddug in the Vale of Clwyd produced several radiocarbon dates suggestive of occupation going back to the sixth and fifth centuries while the presence of a fine La Tène I fibula indicates occupation continuing into the fourth or third century.

Evidence from smaller settlements is slight, but at Castell Odo, Caerns., where an area excavation was undertaken, it was possible to define an early phase in the sequence consisting of a palisaded enclosure containing circular huts which were associated with large jars decorated with finger-tip impressions on the rims. These vessels bear a general resemblance to southern British pottery of the sixth century but there is no need to assume that the settlement originated as the result of an alien intrusion from the south.

A study of regional groupings and cultural change in the early first millennium in Wales must therefore depend almost entirely upon an assessment of metalwork and the definition of structural sequences calibrated by radiocarbon dates.

Wales from the fifth century

In the period lasting from the fifth to the first century BC, the south Welsh coastal plain west of the Usk and the hills of Carmarthenshire and Pembrokeshire were densely settled. In Glamorganshire the settlement on Merthyr Mawr Warren, with its two La Tène I brooches, offers an insight into an occupation site of the third or second century where, in addition to the normal domestic rubbish, debris from bronze-and iron-working was recovered. Pottery, however, was far from plentiful and the few surviving vessels are hardly distinctive. A typologically earlier vessel recovered from Bacon Hole, Glam., hints at a well-established ceramic tradition. The pot, an elegant flared bowl with a carinated shoulder and decoration above, would not be out of place among the fifth- to third-century assemblages of southern Britain, but at present it stands alone in south Wales. The settlement sites of the south-west are better known, as the result of several large-scale excavations. At Coygan Camp, situated on a limestone promontory overlooking Carmarthen Bay, an open settlement producing LBA transitional pottery was overlain by the construction of a small enclosure defended by two banks and ditches. To this phase probably belong two La Tène bracelets and a selection of plain bucket-shaped vessels, two of which were decorated with simple incisions forming pendent arcs. This type of decoration has similarities to the Lydney–Llanmelin style. The excavation of defended settlements on Pembrey Mountain, Dyfed, has produced a sequence similar to that of Coygan suggesting continuity between an open settlement dated by radiocarbon to c. fifth century BC and the later defended enclosure. Other Pembrokeshire excavations, at the cliff fort on St David's Head and at the hillfort of Moel Trigarn, produced little distinctive pottery, but a number of spindle whorls, decorated shale discs, hammer stones, glass beads and jet rings give some indication of the contemporary material culture.

Of the smaller farmsteads, which from recent work appear to be scattered densely over much of the south-west, the ditched enclosure of Penycoed, Llangynog, Dyfed, provides an interesting insight into a single family unit beginning some time in the late second or early first century BC and continuing into the Roman period. A more substantial farmstead at Whitton, Glam., which began life *c.* AD 30 shows a similar continuity but developed into a small villa during the latter part of the Roman period.

In central and northern Wales the material culture is even more sparse than in the south of the principality. The communities seem to have been aceramic; moreover, since they were not in close contact with the materially richer areas of southern England, few imported artefacts are found. But that some contact was maintained is demonstrated by the duck-stamped pot imported to Pen Dinas, near Aberystwyth from the Malvern region. This paucity alone serves to distinguish north Wales from much of the rest of the country.

The lack of pottery is to some extent compensated for by the occurrence of salt containers, often referred to in the literature as Very Coarse Pottery (VCP). Two sources of production have been defined, one based on Droitwich in Worcestershire, the other in Cheshire possibly situated near Nantwich. Salt production began possibly as early as 500 BC and thereafter distinctive salt containers are found on a number of the central and northern Welsh settlements (Morris 1985). The differential distributions from the two production centres seem to reflect the divide between the Llantissilio and Broadward bronze distributions. While this need reflect little more than ease of access from the nearest source the pattern could imply the maintenance of distinct socio-economic territories from the sixth century until as late as the Roman period.

The structural evidence and radiocarbon dates from a number of settlements and hillforts in the region are beginning to show that many sites, once settled, continued in use for centuries. A series of assessments from Bryn y Castell, a small but strongly defended settlement in Snowdonia, suggests continuous occupation spanning the first centuries BC and AD though possibly beginning much earlier. It is probable that many of the hillforts established in the early first millennium BC were also in continuous use up to the Roman Conquest.

Northern England

Throughout the seventh and sixth centuries a well-defined bronze-working tradition, called here the *Heathery Burn tradition*, served northern England, overlapping with the northern part of the West Harling–Staple Howe pottery style-zone.

The extensive collection of material from the Heathery Burn Cave, Co. Durham, may be regarded as representative of the range of artefacts in use. The maximum distribution of this range, typified by the Yorkshire type of three-ribbed socketed axe, was centred upon Yorkshire, Northumberland and County Durham with outliers in adjacent counties. The Heathery Burn deposit is particularly valuable, not only for its cart- and harness-fittings and bucket referred to below (p. 411), but also for the associated metal types, including a Covesea bracelet, a Ewart Park sword, spearheads of northern type, socketed knives and chisels and a group of Yorkshire socketed axes. A fragment of copper ingot, a casting jet and half a bronze mould for a Yorkshire axe suggest the probability of local metalworking. Non-metallic finds from the cave include jet armlets, stone spindle whorls, a range of bone tools and fittings, and five sherds of pottery belonging to coarse shouldered vessels with internally flattened rims.

There is a substantial overlap between the southern extension of the Yorkshire axe distribution, pushing down through Lincolnshire to East Anglia, and the northern part of the West Harling–Staple Howe group of occupation sites defined above (pp. 66–8) on the basis of their distinctive pottery. At Staple Howe a Yorkshire axe, jet armlets and other items of the non-metallic material culture are shared with the Heathery Burn Cave, and again at Scarborough a Yorkshire axe was found on the settlement site. Such associations are a salutary reminder of the fact that groupings defined on ceramic grounds may have little relationship to those depending upon the distribution of bronze types. The two classes of evidence are seldom mutually compatible. Nevertheless, the dense distribution of the Yorkshire axes emphasizes a zone of contact from the eighth to the sixth century which deserves recognition (Burgess and Miket 1976). At present, however, it is impossible to compare the distribution of metal types to other cultural traits in the same region.

The Pennines show remarkably little evidence of occupation before the first century BC. Apart from the impressive hillforts at Almondbury, Yorks., and Mam Tor, Derbyshire, where the sequences supported by radiocarbon dates imply a lengthy occupation, there is little to show. At Grafton, in the West Riding of Yorkshire, an open settlement was partly excavated, producing shouldered jars with finger-impressed rims and finger-tip decoration on the shoulder. Finer wares were few in number but several sherds appear to belong to slightly flaring bowls. No internal dating evidence was available, but on analogy with the styles of southern Britain, a date in the fifth to third century would be reasonable. Further west at Roomer Common a small barrow was found over a grave of broadly the same period.

Excluding the area of eastern Yorkshire, which has already been described (pp. 77–9), the general impression given by the sparse material culture and the apparent paucity of settlements is that the population of northern England was small compared with the south. The evidence for the economy in the latter part of the Iron Age suggests that animal husbandry may have featured large, though not to the exclusion of cereal cultivation. Presumably in the preceding centuries we are dealing with much the same pattern which in many areas may have involved a degree of transhumance between summer and winter pastures. In such a system material culture and settlement archaeology are seldom well represented: regional and chronological distinctions are accordingly difficult to define.

Scotland: south and east

In the seventh and sixth centuries the area was covered by two overlapping bronze-working traditions.

The Traprain-Hownam tradition

The eastern coast of northern England and Scotland, from the Tyne north to the Esk in the county of Angus, exhibits some degree of cultural unity which can be defined principally through the distribution of locally manufactured bronze implements such as the Traprain Law type of socketed axe (Coles 1962b) and British varieties of Hallstatt swords. To these should be added imported Hallstatt types, including a Hallstatt sword (Cowen's class b) from Cambuskenneth, Stirling, the Horshope cart- and harness-fittings, the Adabrock bronze bowl (Figure 5.4), razors from Traprain Law and Kinleith, Midlothian, and a group of sunflower swan's-neck pins (Figure

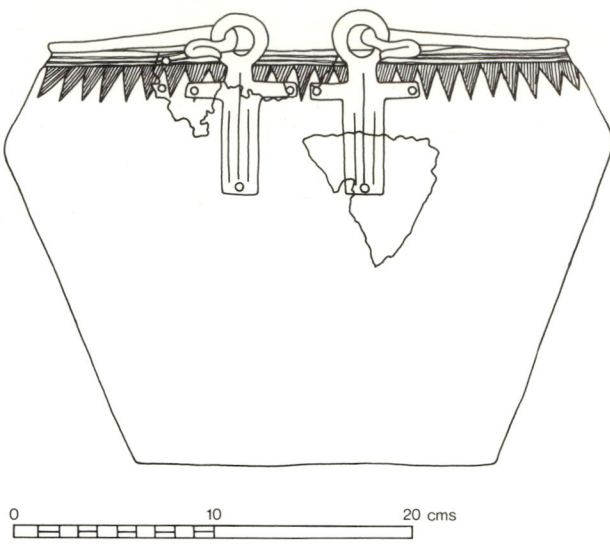

0   10   20 cms

Figure 5.4   The Adabrock bronze bowl, Lewis (source: Coles 1962b).

16.16, p. 424). Evidently close contact was maintained with mainland Europe throughout the period, allowing a wide range of exotic material to reach this part of Britain.

Within this region a number of settlement sites have been discovered and a few excavated. Mostly they are palisaded enclosures containing one or more circular timber huts, similar in many ways to the early settlements of southern Britain. Several radiocarbon dates are available: 510 ± 40 bc for charcoal from the palisade trench at Huckhoe, Northumberland, and 590 ± 40 bc for an occupation layer associated with the palisaded enclosure at Craigmarloch Wood, Renfrewshire, both dates indicating occupation in the seventh–sixth centuries. Together they leave little doubt that the metal objects, both imported and local, were contemporary with the early settlements, even though direct associations are not yet recorded. Many of the excavated settlements in the region suggest a long and complex structural development, as exemplified by the multi-phase defended settlement at Broxmouth. Sites of this kind must have been in use over a considerable period of time. These early settlements and their sparse and virtually aceramic material culture have been called the Hownam culture (MacKie 1969a, 21).

The Covesea–Abernethy group

Between the Firth of Forth and the Moray Firth, and overlapping with the northern distribution of the Traprain–Hownam sites, lies the Covesea–Abernethy group, which can be defined by both metal implements and distinctive techniques of hillfort construction. The metal types include the Covesea armlet with unevenly expanded terminals, a type thought to have been imported into Britain from northern Europe in the eighth to seventh century together with the pendant necklets of Braes of Gight and Wester Ord (Coles 1962b, 39–44). Locally made products are also represented, including the short socketed axes with heavy multiple

Figure 5.5   The hillfort of Finavon, Angus (source: Dr J.K.S. St Joseph. Crown Copyright reserved).

neck-mouldings, named after the Meldrum hoard, which are found in eastern Scotland mainly, but not invariably, north of the Forth.

From the Sculptor's Cave at Covesea, Moray, and Balmashanner, Angus, metalwork has been found in association with a widely distributed group of pottery belonging to the rather generalized flat-rimmed class. The north-east Scottish group of pottery belongs to the rather generalized type named Covesea ware, and is thought to have ultimately originated in northern Europe (Coles 1962b, 44). If this derivation is correct, it would suggest some form of folk movement into north-east Scotland in or about the seventh century, introducing both pottery and the new metal objects. Such a view is difficult to substantiate but may be thought to gain some support from a radiocarbon date of 590 ± 70 bc (seventh century BC) for beams and planks belonging to the initial occupation of the timber-laced hillfort at Finavon, Angus (Figure 5.5). The style of timber-lacing of this fort and of others from eastern Scotland is comparable in many details to structures found in Late Urnfield contexts in central and northern Europe. Thus the seventh-century date proposed for Finavon is consistent with the view of an incursion from Europe during the seventh century or perhaps a little earlier, but by no means proves it.

While the bronze-working traditions were eventually replaced by iron-working, other aspects of the material culture together with the timber-lacing of forts continued in use over many centuries, giving rise to a broad continuum known as the Abernethy culture (MacKie 1969a, 16–21).

It will be evident from the foregoing paragraphs that the Traprain–Hownam tradition and the Covesea–Abernethy group have much in common. Hallstatt and Hallstatt-derived artefacts extend far into the Covesea–Abernethy region and the characteristic palisaded settlements are now being discovered north of the Firth of Forth. Similarly, Covesea-style flat-rimmed pottery has been found at an occupation site at Green Knowe in Peeblesshire, well within the distribution pattern of the Traprain–Hownam group, and indeed a variety of flat-rimmed pottery is also known from Traprain Law itself. The distribution pattern of the Meldrum and Traprain Law axes also overlaps, the Meldrum type extending across most of eastern Scotland from the border to the Moray Firth. In view of such a widespread similarity, it might be thought to be more reasonable eventually to treat the entire area as a single east Scottish group, abandoning the conventional terminology of a Tyne–Forth Hownam culture and a north-eastern Abernethy culture (MacKie 1969a, 20). At present, however, some semblance of the accepted system is retained here.[1]

From the fifth to the first century the area stretching from Northumberland to the southern edge of the Highlands was covered with small settlements, usually groups of huts enclosed within palisades or earthworks. The radiocarbon dates show that many of the sites must have been first inhabited in the sixth or even the seventh century but a high percentage remained in use throughout the pre-Roman Iron Age, the huts being rebuilt and the palisades replaced by banks and ditches. At Huckhoe the replacement must have come soon after the burning of the palisade, for which there is a radiocarbon date of 510 ± 40 bc, but at Ingram Hill the bank, ditch and palisade are three centuries later, as indicated by a radiocarbon date of 220 ± 90 bc.

Apart from the structural evidence of development, calibrated by radiocarbon dates, there is little to be said of material culture or of cultural change. Pottery, when it occurs, is generally simple in form and of little diagnostic value. A few trinkets like La Tène fibulae and spiral finger- and toe-rings occur sporadically but generally the sites are poor and produce little. Since there is no evidence of any cultural change during the entire period from the seventh century BC until the Roman Conquest, it is simpler to regard the occupation as a continuum divisible into stages only by radiocarbon dating or by stratigraphical sequence.

Scotland: north and west

Unlike the rest of northern Britain, the extreme north and west – including the coastal area north of the Firth of Clyde, Caithness and Sutherland and the Western Isles, Orkney and Shetland – were occupied by communities capable of producing distinctive pottery often of high quality. The ceramic traditions, rooted in third- and second-millennium types, developed throughout the first millennium, occasionally influenced by outside traits, well into the Roman era. Excavations at Dun Mor Vaul on Tiree and at Jarlshof and Clickhimin on Shetland provide firm stratigraphical sequences against which the ceramic and cultural development can be traced, while radiocarbon dates from Dun Mor Vaul allow part of the sequence to be calibrated.

At Clickhimin continuous occupation from the seventh century BC until the sixth or seventh century AD enables the ceramic tradition to be seen in relation to the structural development of the site. In the pre-broch phase, which concerns us here, three periods have been isolated, of which the first two can be collated with the early occupation at Jarlshof.

Clickhimin I: seventh to sixth century

The first period of occupation is represented at the type-site by the establishment of an oval stone-built house constructed in a technique dating back to the Neolithic period. Similar buildings were in use at Jarlshof at this time. Throughout the period the material culture was simple, consisting largely of heavy stone tools and a limited range of bone implements, but at Jarlshof a bronzesmith established himself, his presence being indicated by fragments of clay moulds for swords, socketed axes and sunflower pins.

The range of pottery was restricted to barrel- and bucket-shaped jars, sometimes with flat-topped rims (Figure A:36, p. 589). At Jarlshof they were occasionally decorated with one or two plain cordons. These simple forms are closely related to the indigenous tradition of the Bronze Age.

Clickhimin II: sixth to fifth century

The second phase was marked at Clickhimin by the establishment of a round house within the earlier enclosure and at Jarlshof by the construction of clusters of circular stone-built huts over the ruins of the earlier houses. The discovery of iron slag at Jarlshof shows that the new metal was not only in use but was being worked locally. There was now a marked change in the quality of the pottery, with the introduction of shouldered jars alongside the simple bucket and barrel shapes (Figure A:36, p. 589). Some differences, possibly chronological, exist between the vessels from the two sites: those from Clickhimin are finer and slacker in profile compared with the Jarlshof assemblage. Since many similarities exist between these Shetland types and contemporary pottery from the south and east of Britain, it has been suggested that a colonizing movement from the south was the cause, introducing the round house tradition as well as knowledge of iron-working and improved ceramic technology. The evidence is inconclusive, however, since it may equally well be argued that the change was brought about by casual maritime trading rather than folk movement.

Clickhimin III: fifth to first century

The third period at Clickhimin, not represented at Jarlshof, was initiated by the construction of a stone ring-wall to defend the farmstead. The associated pottery was more varied in form than in the previous periods, the commonest types being ovoid jars with short everted or beaded rims (Figures A:36, p. 589 and A:37, p. 590). Four decorative techniques were employed: the internal fluting of the rims, the application of a plastic moulded strip in the neck angle, the deliberate curvilinear grooving of the inside of the base, and various forms of impressed or stabbed decoration – usually stab-filled pendent triangles, isolated impressed circlets and impressed arcs of circles. There is a strong regional character about the assemblage, but general similarities with peripheral Urnfield wares in France may hint at the possibility of some kind of maritime contact dating back to the fifth century.

Elsewhere in north-western Britain, well-stratified deposits of the seventh to first century are few, but beneath the broch at Dun Mor Vaul on Tiree an early midden deposit was recovered, sealing a living floor. The occupation rubbish included a quantity of pottery representing two main types: bucket and barrel urns, sometimes with simple geometric decoration stamped and scored beneath the rim, and smaller S-profiled vessels similarly decorated (Figure A:35, p. 588). Just above the midden a more angular vessel was found, its sharply everted rim and reddish slip-coated surface possibly echoing traditions current in southern Britain. Another settlement on Tiree, Balevullin, produced evidence of occupation during this period. The site of what appears to be a circular timber-built hut was associated with a range of pottery which bears vague, and not necessarily significant, similarities to pottery from eastern England dating to the sixth to fifth century. A few fragments of iron show that iron was used, even if not extracted locally.

The ceramic assemblages from the two sites on Tiree have a number of types in common with Clickhimin phases II and III which might be thought, on the internal evidence of sequence, to lie within the sixth to third centuries. The radiocarbon dates from Dun Mor Vaul are entirely consistent with this, ranging from 400 ± 110 bc for roots from the old ground surface and 445 ± 90 bc for charred grain to 280 ± 100 bc for animal bones belonging to a late phase in the midden occupation. Few other ceramic sequences are available for study. At the broch of Crosskirk, Caithness, several small groups of pottery were isolated from layers pre-dating and contemporary with the broch but apart from generalized similarities with the Shetland sequence the wares seem to be very local in style. Much the same can be said of the assemblages from Bu Broch and the broch of Gurness on Orkney.

Summary

This brief survey of the evidence relevant to regional and chronological definitions in northern and western Britain gives some idea of the scarcity of reliable data. Distinctive bronze types enable broad groupings to be recognized at the end of the Bronze Age but thereafter, apart from in the extreme north-west, where ceramic sequences can be built up, there is little to be said: settlements are ill-known, pottery is very scarce and indistinctive and all that can be done at present is to define localized sequences based on structural changes observed in the few hillforts and settlements which have been adequately excavated. Apart from these changes the impression given by the evidence at present available is that cultural development in the region was virtually static for a 1,000 years. It is not until the first century AD that distinctive groups can begin to be recognized and then only because they, and their behaviour, came within the notice of Roman writers.

6

Protohistory to history, *c.* 150 BC to AD 43

Until the middle of the second century BC the history of the British Isles cannot be written in terms of identifiable individuals and their actions. At best we have to be content to define groups of people through their artefacts, the structures they built and the effects they had on their environment. But the two centuries preceding the Roman invasion of AD 43 lie in the shadows of history – the literate world was encroaching. Broadly, this period, which is conventionally referred to as the Late Iron Age, can be divided into two: *c.* 150–55 BC and 55 BC–AD 43. In the first part, movements of people and spheres of tribal influence can be dimly distinguished, largely through the evidence of coin typology and distribution; by the second, following the invasions of Julius Caesar, we can write of the actual people, the kings and demi-kings of the British aristocracy, and begin to assess their relationship to each other and the Roman world, reflected in contemporary historical writings as well as in the numismatic evidence.

Historical sources and coins introduce a new dimension to our understanding of Late Iron Age society but they also pose new problems of interpretation. The brief historical references which survive for this period have come down to us through a series of filters: at best they are anecdotal and incomplete; at worst they may be deliberately misleading. Clearly considerable care must be taken before using them too literally and we must accept that the scraps that do survive are quite inadequate to allow an historical narrative to be created for the period.

The interpretation of Celtic coinage presents a rather more complex array of problems and not surprisingly views have changed quite radically over the years. It has long been recognized that the coins found in Britain can be divided into two broad groups: those minted in Gaul and transported across the Channel by undefined mechanisms and those made in Britain, the types being based in the first instance on imported examples. The most prolific group of imports came from Belgic Gaul, roughly the area between the Seine and the Rhine, and were found concentrated in south-eastern Britain. These were called Gallo-Belgic and were divided by D.F. Allen into six types, A–F which, he believed, reached Britain in a series of waves between *c.* 120 and 50 BC (D.F. Allen 1961a). The belief that these waves represented successive bands of invaders was further elaborated by C.F.C. Hawkes (1968). Both writers accepted that Gallo-Belgic A–D coins were brought to Britain at different periods before Caesar's invasions, Gallo-Belgic E roughly dated to the time of the Gallic War and Gallo-Belgic F reflected a later incursion led by Commius about 50 BC. An alternative view was put forward by Kent (1978) who saw the first wave as Gallo-Belgic B reaching Britain in the early first century BC, followed by A and C arriving at the same time as Gallo-Belgic E which is now widely believed to be the coinage used by the Belgic confederacy to wage war against the Romans in and after 58 BC (Scheers 1972).

In recent years there has been much debate about the validity of using coin evidence to reconstruct a protohistory. Collis (1971a and b) preferred to interpret coinage according to an economic rather than a political model while Hogg (1971) went so far as to question whether coin distributions represented significant tribal or political entities, or were the result of 'random flight'. A detailed reconsideration of the Gallo-Belgic coinage and that conventionally ascribed to the Catuvellauni and Trinovantes, however, encouraged Rodwell (1976) to conclude that, with care, coins can legitimately be used to reconstruct the outlines of political history and to define tribal territories. His interpretations, however, differed in a number of significant respects from the older and more conventional views.

The most recent development in British Celtic numismatics has been a thorough reassessment of the entire series by R. Van Arsdell (1989) based on a detailed study of the coins themselves. This has provided a number of totally new perspectives reflecting on the social, economic and political development of the Late Iron Age. Van Arsdell's assessments of the coins and his nomenclatures are for the most part accepted and integrated into the discussion which follows.

External influences: Belgae and Romans 150–55 BC

We have seen in the preceding chapters that by the end of the Middle Iron Age the communities of south-eastern Britain had established an equilibrium with their landscape. Many settlements had been in use for centuries, farmsteads were densely scattered, and there is some evidence to suggest that population was increasing. Against this background it is possible to detect in the ceramic evidence a degree of territoriality which may well reflect the emergence of distinct tribal units. The picture is essentially one of indigenous development with little evidence of external contact from Continental Europe.

The Late Iron Age presents many significant contrasts; above all it was a time when the British Isles was brought once more into direct contact with the Continent by the interchange of peoples: mercenaries, invading armies, embassies and traders. All are directly attested in the historical sources and may sometimes, with the eye of faith, be seen dimly reflected in the archaeological evidence.

One question which has occupied commentators for over a century has been the problem of the Belgic invasion. Julius Caesar was quite explicit: he records that people from Belgic Gaul raided the maritime areas of Britain and eventually settled. Assuming this to be correct the problem has been to locate the area settled by the immigrants and to assess their impact. Most writers since A.J. Evans (1890) have preferred to equate the Belgae with the Aylesford–Swarling culture of Kent, Essex and Hertfordshire basing part of the argument on the distribution of imported Gallo-Belgic coins. This would take with it the assumption that the numbers were large enough to inspire widespread and lasting cultural change. One problem, however, is that no element of the Aylesford–Swarling culture can be shown to pre-date the Caesarian invasion. This does not pose an insuperable problem for the traditional view but it calls for caution. An alternative approach is to ask where the Romans themselves believed the Belgae to be located. The answer is in Hampshire

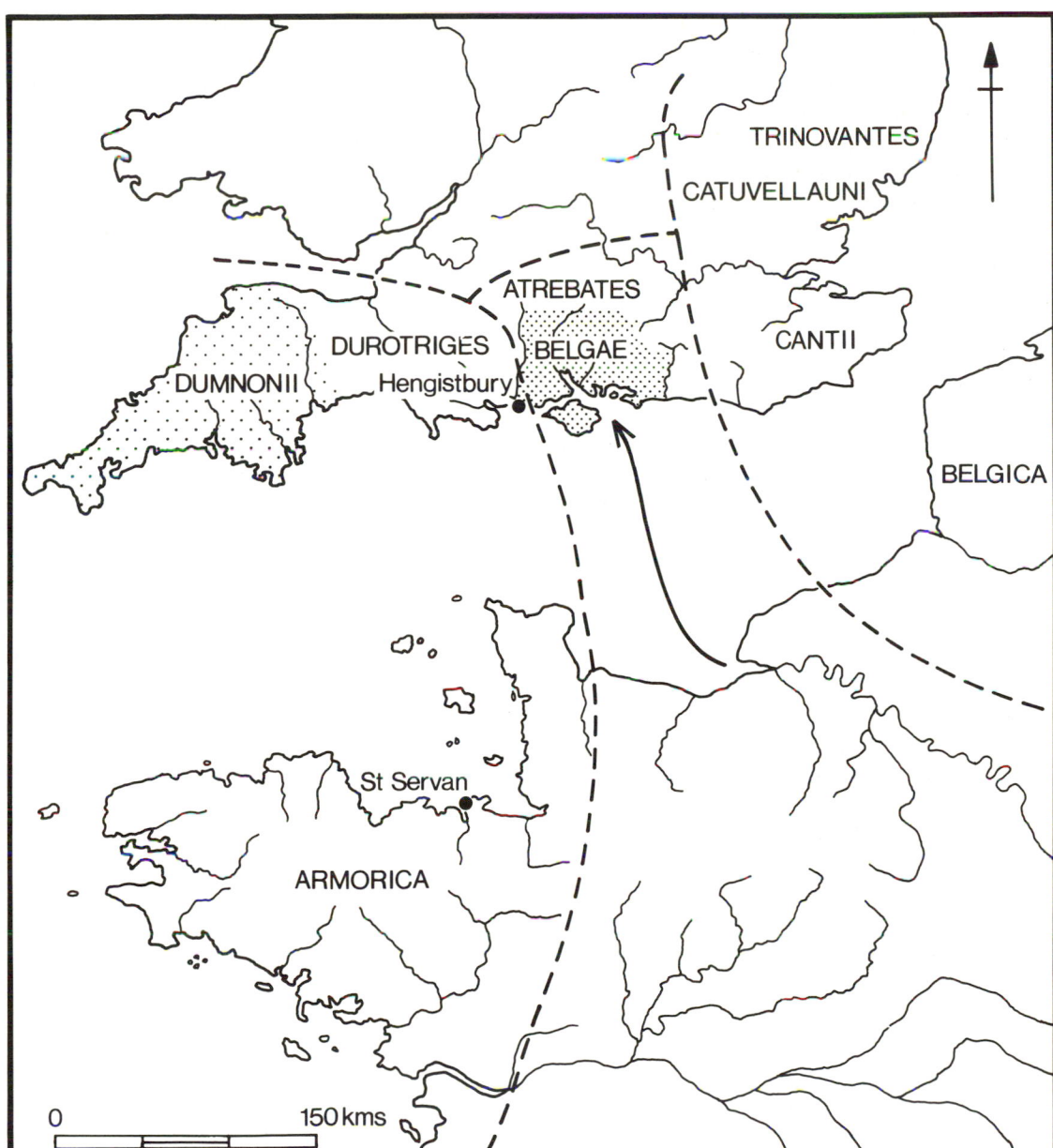

Figure 6.1 The location of the Belgae (source: Cunliffe 1988a).

where the Roman name of Winchester, *Venta Belgarum*, refers to the market of the Belgae (Figure 6.1). If these were the descendants of the Belgae to whom Caesar referred then the 'maritime' region where they initially settled would have been the shores of the Solent (Cunliffe 1984d). Additional support for this view comes in part from the settlement evidence, which suggests a dislocation some time towards the beginning of the first century BC, and from the fact that about 50 BC another group of Belgae, led by Commius, fleeing from the Romans to Britain to 'join his own people', must have made a similar landfall before establishing their new territory to the north of the first Belgae, with its capital at Calleva (Silchester) (p. 154). If it is accepted that Caesar's Belgae settled in Hampshire the numbers may have been comparatively small since they seem to have made comparatively little impact on the material culture of the area.

The second cultural influence to impinge upon the coast of southern Britain came, albeit indirectly, from the Roman world. At the end of the second century BC Rome annexed the Mediterranean coastal region of Gaul and created the province of Transalpina. The ramifications for free Gaul and for southern Britain were considerable for the annexation was quickly followed by the economic exploitation of the neighbouring barbarian lands. In return for wine and other Mediterranean luxuries the natives provided slaves and a range of raw materials particularly metals (Cunliffe 1987).

One of the trade routes used at this time was the Atlantic route linking the Gaulish river systems of the Garonne and Loire to Brittany and Britain. The details of this commerce will be considered below (chapter 12). Suffice it to say here that a major port-of-trade developed at Hengistbury Head, Dorset through which the exploitation of the resources of southern Britain was articulated. The impact which the sudden proximity of the Roman consumer market had on the communities of central southern and south-western Britain is difficult to assess, but its demands for raw materials and slaves in return for luxury goods cannot have failed to have had a disrupting effect on the traditional embedded economy of the Middle Iron Age. It may have been one of the causes for the wide-scale abandonment of hillforts over much of the south at about this time.

The reformation of British society 130–55 BC

While central southern Britain was experiencing the effects of long-distance trade and (if we are correct) a limited immigration of Belgic settlers, the south-east was locked in contact of a different kind with the adjacent parts of Belgic Gaul. The nature of these contacts is obscure but the classical sources provide some hints. Caesar offers two relevant comments: that the Britons had served in most of the Gallic Wars (*BG* IV 20,1) and that Diviciacus, King of the Suessiones had dominions in Britain (*BG* II 4,7). Both statements are open to a wide variety of interpretations but at the very least they imply close diplomatic ties across the Channel. In Celtic society at this time it would not have been at all unusual for tribes in Britain to have offered allegiance to Belgic high kings. The obligations thus entailed would have been met by providing warriors in time of need and in gift exchange involving, among other things, high value coins (Nash 1984).

It is in this context of social intercourse that we might best explain the earliest imported Gallo-Belgic coins (Figures 6.2–6.5). The two earliest issues, the *Large Flan type* of the Ambiani and the *Defaced Die type* of the Caletes (i.e. Gallo-Belgic A and B in Allen's nomenclature) were minted in Gaul in the last thirty years of the second century BC and could have reached Britain at this time or later. These were followed by four later types: the *Abstract Design type* (Gallo-Belgic C) which may have been minted by the Suessiones; the *Gallic War types* (Gallo-Belgic E) which began minting about 65 BC and circulated in vast numbers on both sides of the Channel presumably to finance the war against Caesar; the *Triple Tailed Horse type* (Gallo-Belgic F) minted by the Suessiones about 60 BC and appearing in Britain in only small numbers; and a quarter stater, the *Geometric type* (Gallo-Belgic D) which was probably current in Britain from about 65 BC.

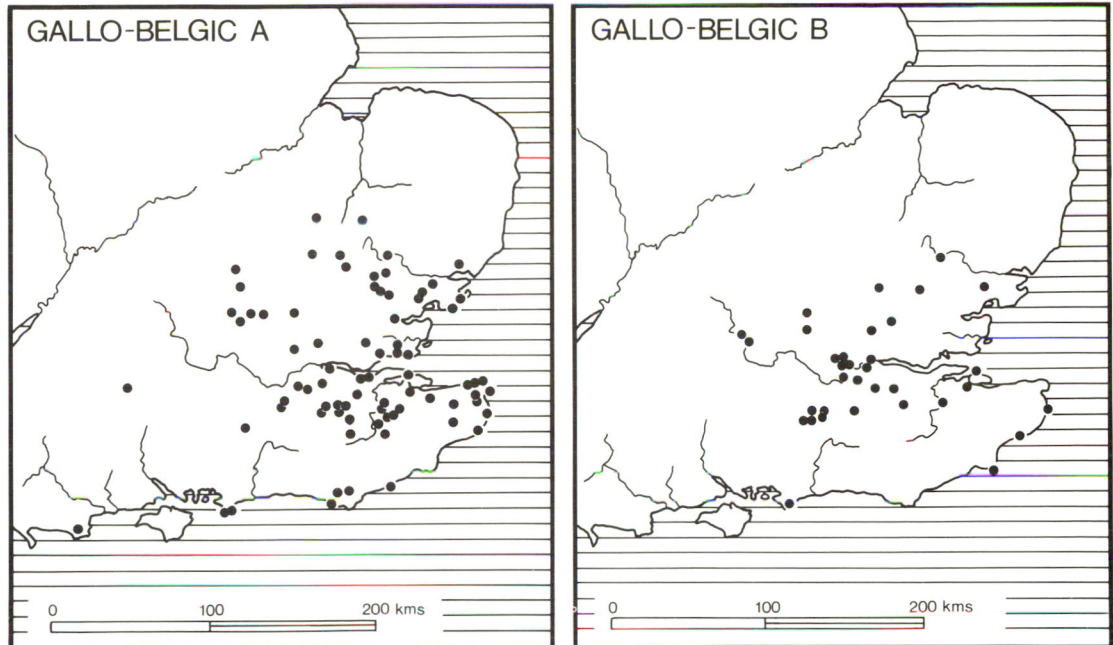

Figure 6.2   Distribution of Gallo-Belgic A and B coins (source: Cunliffe 1981b).

The distribution maps will give some idea of the spacial extent and density of the individual issues in Britain. What stands out in particular is the concentration in the Thames region and in Kent with a scatter along the Sussex coast and northwards into Essex and Hertfordshire. Bearing in mind the complex histories of each coin, from the time it reached Britain until the moment it was archaeologically recorded, it would be unwise to base too detailed an argument on distribution particularly since many of the issues may have been in circulation for decades before being finally lost or buried. In other words the patterns recorded archaeologically reflect deposition after a long and no doubt complex history. Even so the Thames valley/Kent/Essex distribution is so dominant throughout as to suggest a distinct zone of early coin circulation.

To what extent it is legitimate to construct a 'protohistory' on the basis of these early Gallo-Belgic imports is debatable. The 'successive waves' theory (as exemplified by C.F.C. Hawkes (1968) and in a modified form by Rodwell (1976)) is no longer acceptable, but it would be legitimate to see in the distributions of the *Large Flan* and *Defaced Die* types (i.e. Gallo-Belgic A and B), emanating from the Ambiani and Caletes in the Somme valley and Belgic coastal zone, a vestige of a folk movement. Such a view could be reconciled with the theory propounded above, of a Belgic incursion into the Solent region, by supposing that in the decades around 100 BC many bands of settlers arrived on the British shores but only the Solent group remained ethnically identifiable in the eyes of the later Roman geographers. The alternative view, that the early Gallo-Belgic coins simply reflect diplomatic links, is equally plausible. The evidence is such that there can be no certainty.

Two of the later Gallo-Belgic imports, the *Abstract Design type* (Gallo-Belgic C) and the *Triple Tailed Horse type* (Gallo-Belgic F), which are both thought to have been issued by the Suessiones, present the interesting possibility that they reflect the overlordship of Diviciacus, King of the Suessiones, over the British tribes. The fact that the *Triple Tailed Horse type*, though excessively

Figure 6.3 Gallo-Belgic coins. 1 Gallo-Belgic A; 2 Gallo-Belgic B; 3 Gallo-Belgic C; 4 Gallo-Belgic D; 5 Gallo-Belgic E; 6 Gallo-Belgic F. Twice actual size (photos: Institute of Archaeology, Oxford).

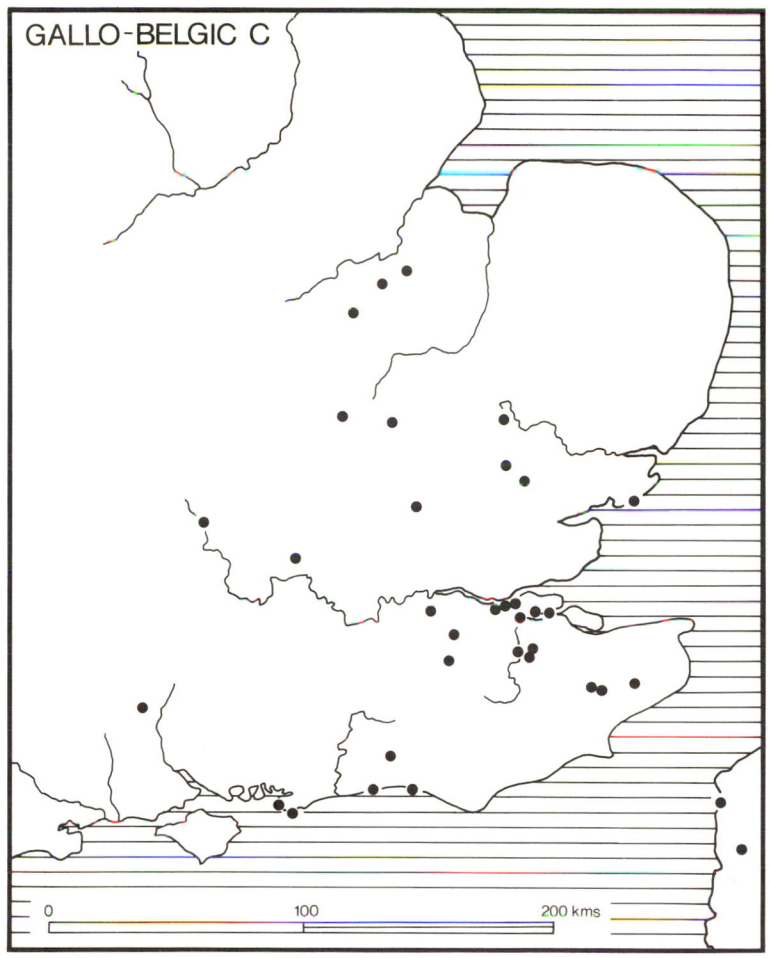

Figure 6.4 Distribution of Gallo-Belgic C coins (source: Cunliffe 1981b).

rare in Britain, was chosen as the prototype for several of the native British coinages strongly suggests its symbolic importance in the political developments of the time.

The earliest of the British-minted coinages was a cast high-tin bronze issue found in great numbers in Kent and the Lower Thames valley. These coins, originally called 'potin' and now known as *Kentish Cast Bronzes*, were copied from Masilliote prototypes a few of which arrived in east Kent possibly as the result of long distance trade along the Atlantic route. Dating cannot be precise but the series is now thought to have begun soon after 100 BC and to have continued to develop until a decade or two after the Gallic War. These coins constitute the Cantian A–E series. The early appearance of low denomination coinage in just the region where the high-value Gallo-Belgic imports are distributed is of considerable interest for there can be little doubt that they were minted to facilitate exchange within the early monetary system. Whether or not this implies the emergence of a fully-formed market economy is a moot point but when seen against the background of the development of oppida in the same region (pp. 146–7) it is difficult to resist the view that major developments in trade and exchange were now underway.

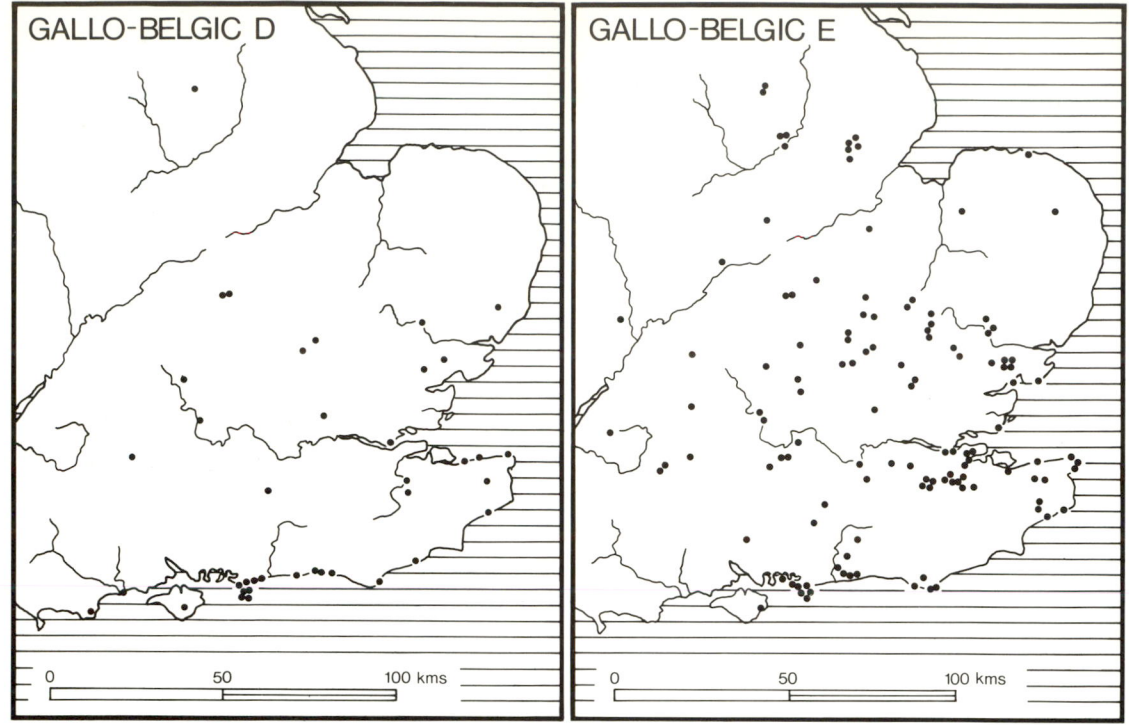

Figure 6.5   Distribution of Gallo-Belgic D and E coins (source: Cunliffe 1981b).

In the two decades before the outbreak of the Gallic War several of the British tribes began to strike their own coinages. The earliest to appear, in or soon after 75 BC, were gold staters struck by the Atrebates/Regni based on Gallo-Belgic C prototypes (Atrebatic A) and this was soon followed by the first staters of the Durotriges (Durotrigan A and B). By *c.* 60 BC the Iceni, Trinovantes/Catuvellauni and Corieltauvi were issuing their own coinages (Icenian A, Trinovantian A and B and Corieltauvian A) while the Cantii seem to have been content to use the large quantities of Gallo-Belgic staters already circulating within their territory. The early British staters were all minted to match the weight standard of the pre-war Gallo-Belgic issues no doubt to facilitate exchange one with another. The appearance of quarter staters in the territory of the Atrebates, Cantii and Durotriges would have further eased exchanges across tribal boundaries.

The use of tribal designations at this early stage needs a word of explanation. Tribal names do not begin to appear on coins until much later and it is not until the Roman period, in the writings of the classical historians and geographers, that any precision can be given to tribal boundaries. However in the early British, pre-Gallic War, coinage we can recognize the precursors of the later dynastic and tribal coinages and, albeit dimly, perceive geographical distributions which presage the more clear-cut patterns of the post-war decades. For this reason the use of tribal names in the pre-war period is justified. Indeed it will be argued later (chapter 20) that territorial boundaries and tribal identities can be recognized in a much earlier period.

Caesar's campaigns in Gaul, beginning in 59 BC, caused widespread social and economic

Figure 6.6 Early British coins. 1 Cantii 'potin'; 2 Atrebates; 3 Trinovantes/Catuvellauni; 4 Iceni; 5 Corieltauvi; 6 Durotriges. Twice actual size (photos: Institute of Archaeology, Oxford).

disruption not only among the Gaulish tribes but in Britain as well. His campaign against the Armorican tribes in 57 BC dislocated the Atlantic trading systems and brought the flow of Mediterranean imports into the Hengistbury region almost to an end, while his attempted subjugation of Belgica must have created turmoil in south-eastern Britain requiring the intervention of British mercenaries on the side of their Belgic allies. These events are reflected in the British coinage of the early war years.

The most dramatic effect was the flow of large quantities of gold into Britain in the form of Gallo-Belgic E staters which are thought to have been minted to finance the Gallic War and may therefore have been payment for mercenary services. It seems likely that this was the source of the gold used by the Atrebates to mint their own very considerable gold series (Atrebatic B and C). The neighbouring Durotriges, however, seem to have run out of gold and their stater series became increasingly debased (Durotrigan C and D) and after the war gold disappeared from the area altogether.

This contrast between the Atrebates and Durotriges is particularly interesting. In part at least it must be due to the breakdown of the Atlantic trade network but there may be other factors at work. Caesar records that before his invasion of Britain in 55 BC he sent over a Gaulish chieftain, Commius, to encourage certain of the British tribes to ally themselves with Rome (*BG* IV 21). It would not be unreasonable for these efforts to be concentrated in central southern Britain where the tribes could provide a buffer between the hostile Durotriges, whose long established Armorican allies had been decimated, and the tribes of the south-east where Caesar was proposing to land. That five years or so later Commius fled to this area adds some support to this view. It may be, then, in this context of Roman diplomacy that gold reached the Atrebates.

The period from *c.* 120–60 BC was one of rapid change for the tribes of the south-eastern part of Britain. Undreamed of trading possibilities were opening up with distant Mediterranean systems, migrating bands were arriving, and the proximity of Caesar in Gaul was creating a turmoil of diplomatic activity and mercenary movements. These various stimuli were spread unevenly in time and space but their cumulative effect was to cause such disruption that the socio-economic systems established in the third and second centuries BC became destabilized and collapsed. Signs of this dislocation can be most clearly seen in the last stages of hillfort development. At Danebury, Hants., in the heart of Wessex the east entrance was massively defended some time towards 100 BC. Previously a simple timber gate had existed in the univallate defence. This was now replaced with a more massive construction set further back in the entrance gap, while in front two curved inner hornworks were built, creating a flint-walled approaching corridor 46 m long and 6 m wide along which any attacker would have had to run the gauntlet while defenders on the north inner hornwork could have rained down volleys of slingstones (Figure 6.7). The inner hornworks were further defended by two claw-like outer hornworks fronted by V-shaped ditches, which returned to join the main ditches of the fort. In the centre of these outer works was a dual-portal outer gate. The entire complex was brilliantly designed so that every part was clearly visible from the sling platform on the end of the north inner hornwork and all lay within the slingers' range of 60 m. There can be little doubt that the concept was purely military. Some indication of the date is given by the discovery of a gold-plated Gallo-Belgic C coin from the top of the primary silt of the outer hornwork ditch. The coin was in a fresh condition and is hardly likely to have been dropped much after 70 BC. Judging by the degree of silting beneath it, a construction date of *c.* 100 BC would seem reasonable.

The eastern entrance of Maiden Castle was treated in an even more impressive way (see Figure. 14.13, p. 336). After the initial phase of multivallation (phase III), the entire approach

Figure 6.7 The east entrance of the hillfort at Danebury, Hants., taken from position of the final burnt gate looking outwards along the approach corridor (Danebury Trust).

was remodelled (phase IV) with a complex of overlapping earthworks designed to create a circuitous approach protected by carefully sited platforms for slingers. The gates themselves (two separate gates) were set in long stone-walled corridors, close to one of which was a hoard of 22,000 slingstones. Dating is not direct but depends upon the total absence of coins. Since Durotrigan coins began to be minted in c. 65 BC, phase IV is likely to pre-date this period and may well have begun about 100 BC.

There are a number of other, unexcavated, forts with similar complex outworks, e.g. Beacon Hill (Burghclere), Badbury and Hambledon Hill (Dorset), Yarnbury (Wilts.), etc., but their dating and sequence cannot easily be determined. Other forts in the area, where more limited excavation has taken place, frequently show late entrance modifications, invariably giving rise to a long corridor approach. St Catharine's Hill, Winchester, can be interpreted in this way. So can the Caburn, Trundle, Torberry, Bredon and, further afield, the forts of the Welsh borderland and north Wales. Moreover, in these areas, even where excavation has not taken place, the present physical form of the earthworks frequently suggests the existence of similar long corridors.

We have evidence, then, that over much of the south and west of Britain the defences of hillforts were improved by the construction of either long corridor entrances or complex outworks or both. Wherever dating evidence is available, these refurbishings can be seen to belong late in the period of the saucepan pot continuum, broadly second to first century, and there are indications from some sites that the construction date lies at about 100 BC or a little before. It must be stressed that the techniques involved in the rebuildings were not alien to the local traditions. Multivallation and simple forms of hornworks already existed in the south-west, and the earlier gate developments were moving towards the inturned or corridor form. Far more significant is the fact that it was always long-established sites that were brought into defensive order. While the nature of the evidence so far stated does not allow us to say that all the rebuildings were local responses to the same stimulus, it does point to intense defensive activity spread over a few decades at the most.

Evidence of defence prompts us to look for evidence of attack. It can indeed be found. At Worlebury and Bredon war cemeteries of mutilated bodies have been discovered close to the entrances; at Danebury the gate was destroyed by fire; while at Torberry the dry-stone walls flanking the entrances were thrown down deliberately, filling the hollowed roadway. These acts took place while saucepan pots were in use and must therefore reflect intertribal warfare or raiding, probably within the late second or the first half of the first century BC. It can be argued, then, that certain parts of Britain offer evidence of stress in the period before Caesar's invasions. Distributions are informative. The new defensive activities spread along the South Downs, the Wessex chalklands, the Upper Thames, the Cotswolds and into the south-west and the Welsh border areas – a distribution almost exactly complementary to the contemporary coinage distributions of Gallo-Belgic A, B and C, which cover the North Downs and North Weald, the Lower Thames, Essex and parts of Suffolk, spreading up to the Chilterns. While this may be a coincidence, it could be that we are seeing here a Thames-centred core territory undergoing rapid socio-economic development in the early years of the first century BC with the emergence of a money economy, surrounded by a periphery where the old social system was coming under excessive stress. By the 70s and 60s, however, substantial parts of that periphery had begun to adapt to the new economic reality by adopting their own coinages compatible with that of the core. In the centre south the effects of the Atlantic trading system are likely to have exacerbated the collapse of the old order.

The campaigns of Julius Caesar, 55 and 54 BC

In 55 BC Britain was still very much of an unknown quantity to the Roman world, and even after interviewing traders Caesar could find out relatively little about it. To provide the necessary intelligence he sent a warship commanded by Volusenus on a reconnaissance mission with orders to find out as much as possible and return quickly. Meanwhile he set about preparing a fleet based upon the warships used the previous summer against the Veneti. Inevitably the Britons got wind of the preparations and sent envoys to offer hostages and thereby allegiance. Caesar's reaction was to extract promises of good behaviour and send them home, accompanied by Commius, a king of the Gaulish Atrebates who, Caesar tells us, was greatly respected in Britain. As we have seen, his task was to warn the British leaders of the impending invasion and to persuade as many as possible to seek allegiance with Rome. The move was ill-judged, however, and Commius was soon taken prisoner, only to be returned with suitable contrite regrets after Caesar had landed.

Eventually the expedition set sail for Britain in eighty transports carrying the two legions and another eighteen for the cavalry, accompanied by a large number of warships (C.F.C. Hawkes 1977). The landing was opposed and difficult, not least because the Roman cavalry failed to arrive, but eventually a foothold was obtained and the army moved forward. Envoys were sent by the British chieftains and a temporary peace ensued, but was soon broken by the Britons when the Romans appeared to be in difficulty. Only after several indecisive engagements was Caesar able to extricate himself and sail back to the relative safety of Gaul taking with him a large number of British hostages.

The campaign of 54 BC was more massively staged: over 800 ships were involved, transporting an army of five legions and 2,000 cavalry. The campaign was more extended than in the previous year and Caesar's account is more informative. In addition to details of the actual fighting, Caesar has much to say about the politico-military situation in Britain. Before the invasions a powerful local king, Cassivellaunus, whose territory appears to have lain to the north of the Thames,[1] had been warring with neighbouring tribes. He had killed the King of the Trinovantes and had driven out his son Mandubracius, who fled to Caesar in Gaul. Yet as soon as the Roman threat appeared, personal animosities were forgotten and Cassivellaunus was elected the overall war leader of the resistance, commanding a vast confederate army. Even so, through sheer force of arms, Caesar managed to cut his way through Kent, crossed the Thames and took the battle into Cassivellaunus's kingdom. Gradually the British resistance crumbled and Cassivellaunus was reduced to guerrilla tactics and a scorched-earth policy. With the growing inevitability of Roman success, the unstable British alliance gradually broke up, the Trinovantes sending envoys to Caesar and promising to surrender if Mandubracius was returned and the tribe protected against Cassivellaunus. The immediate success of these negotiations brought over other tribes, including the Cenimagni, Segontiaci, Aucalites, Bibroci and Cassi (whose whereabouts and subsequent history are unknown); Caesar also obtained information leading to the location of Cassivellaunus's stronghold.

The last stages could now be fought out. As Caesar was attacking the oppidum, Cassivellaunus rushed orders to Kent ordering the four kings of the region, Cingetorix, Carvilius, Taximagulus and Segovax, to launch a surprise swoop on Caesar's naval base. The plan was sound but the attack failed and with it the British resistance. Cassivellaunus, using Commius as an intermediary, was forced to sue for peace, which Caesar granted (no doubt gladly) in return for hostages, the assurance of an annual tribute to Rome and on the understanding that

Cassivellaunus should not molest Mandubracius or the Trinovantes. The arrangements having been settled, Caesar departed.

The episode is invaluable for the light it throws on the British scene. The country was split into innumerable tribal groups in conflict with each other and while in matters of national emergency a single war leader would be elected, old rivalries could lead to eventual betrayal. This is precisely the kind of picture one would expect after reviewing the coin evidence of the previous half-century; Caesar, however, provides us with names, motives and a story-line. The proximity of Rome introduces a new factor into British protohistory: tribes in conflict could now ally themselves with Rome, as the Trinovantes had done, using the threat of Roman protection as a significant bargaining counter. Moreover, Roman life and luxury offered a new outlet for those who desired to enhance their own prestige. Thus political and economic ties with the Continent increased and British history takes on a new clarity.

It is surprising that after so many years of archaeological research no direct trace of Caesar's campaigns have been found. It has, however, been suggested that the invasion scare may have caused the sudden deposition of a number of hoards (Rodwell 1976, 198–203). In all, twelve can be shown to be roughly contemporary with Caesar's landing, many of them lying in Kent and Essex – the territory through which Caesar campaigned (Figure 6.8). Others, from further afield, such as coin hoards from Carn Brea and Grimsby and the metalwork hoards from Ulceby and Snettisham, could be explained as 'flight hoards' deposited by those escaping to safety from Caesar's advance. The hypothesis is both plausible and attractive.

From first-hand accounts of Caesar's battles we learn much of Belgic fighting tactics. They possessed three forces: infantry, cavalry and charioteers, who seldom fought in close formation but usually attacked in open order interspersed with groups of reserves to cover the retreat or to relieve the fighters when they began to tire. Caesar found that fighting such a foe was difficult. Even greater problems were posed by the natives' use of chariots, of which Cassivellaunus is said to have had 4,000 under his control. Evidently this kind of warfare was new to Caesar. He describes how the Britons drove about wildly to create a din and to inspire fear while throwing their javelins at the enemy. They would then drive out through their own cavalry and jump down to engage the enemy on foot while the charioteers retired a short way, positioning themselves so as to be able to swoop in and rescue their masters if required. 'They combine', said Caesar, 'the mobility of cavalry with the staying power of infantry.' He goes on to describe how by daily training they became highly skilled – able to drive up steep inclines with horses at full gallop, checking and turning with ease. They could also run out along the chariot pole, stand on the yoke and get back into the vehicle with great speed. Altogether Caesar was impressed. But even so, the British defence could not stand up to Roman attack. Like the Celtic personality, it was daring, fierce and brave but lacked staying power. It was impetuous and instinctive rather than considered. When faced with the grinding solidarity of the Roman military machine, the British resistance melted into the forests to engage in guerrilla warfare. Even the two hillforts which Caesar mentions, possibly Bigbury in Kent and Wheathampstead in Hertfordshire,[2] were overrun by the army without much difficulty. British fighting techniques were geared far more closely to the rapid raids of intertribal fighting (as indeed were the defences of the hillforts) than to the relentless force of organized military imperialism.

The emergence of tribal kingdoms 54–10 BC

The Caesarian invasion was a traumatic time for the British tribes of the south-east. Suddenly the might of Rome had become a reality. Not only were the tribal leaders made all too aware of

Figure 6.8 Hoards of the Caesarian period (source: Rodwell 1976).

the political significance of friendship with Rome as a totally new factor in their intratribal dealings but now that Gaul was notionally a Roman preserve the basis of cross-Channel trading had to be restructured. In the Roman mind the tribes of the south-east who had submitted to Caesar and had entered into treaty relationships with Rome would have been regarded as part of the Roman sphere in much the same way as the tribes of Gaul. This much is implied by Horace in his poem *Epode* (VII,7–8). The Channel was merely a tiresome irrelevance. It is not surprising therefore that in the immediate post-Caesarian period south-eastern Britain and northern Gaul came to share a broadly similar culture, reflected in styles of pottery and modes of burial, bound together by trading networks consumer-led by the demands of Rome. The native aristocracies in both areas demonstrated status by manipulating Roman luxury goods – frequently the accoutrements of the wine-drinking ritual – which were buried with the nobility. In Britain the resulting manifestation is referred to as the Aylesford–Swarling culture and will be considered in more detail in chapter 7.

Figure 6.9 Coins of the early British dynasties. 1 Commius (Atrebates); 2 Addedomaros (Trinovantes/Catuvellauni); 3 Dubnovellaunus (Cantii); 4 Bodvoc (Dobunni); 5 Anted (Iceni); 6 AVN AST (Corieltauvi). Twice actual size (photos: Institute of Archaeology, Oxford).

All the time that Rome was prepared to accept the rather tenuous Caesarian political settlement a degree of stability could be maintained, though the fact that Octavian (later Augustus) visited Gaul in 34 BC with the idea of continuing Caesar's conquest of Britain implies that the central authorities were keeping the situation under review (Dio Cassius XLIX,38,2). Nothing came of this but a few years later, in 27 BC, Augustus set out to lead an expedition to Britain but was once again detained in Gaul. In any event we are told 'the Britons seemed likely to make terms with him' (LIII,22,5). However, by the next year, negotiations had broken down – the Britons 'would not come to terms'. These passages are not without their problems but the implication would seem to be that the treaties negotiated by Caesar with the British tribes had fallen into abeyance after twenty years and Augustus at first thought to reconstitute them by force of arms or diplomacy but failed to do so and lost interest when other more pressing commitments demanded his attention (C.E. Stevens 1951). Thereafter, as we shall see, a desultory interest was maintained in British affairs from a distance.

The political development of south-eastern Britain between the campaigns of Caesar and the conquest of Claudius, beginning in AD 43, can to some extent be reconstructed from the study of British coinage. The coins themselves are tangible symbols of authority and suitably interpreted can provide valuable insights into dynastic developments, spheres of influence and aspirations of ethnicity. Moreover, changes of weight and of metal content have direct chronological and economic implications allowing roughly-dated sequences to be constructed and questions of economic power to be approached.

Standing back from the confusing detail of coin types and distributions it is possible to order the material into several broad groupings which remain relevant for the ninety years or so before the Claudian conquest. At the highest remove we can distinguish between the *core region* of south-eastern Britain and the *peripheral tribes* – the Durotriges, Dobunni and Corieltauvi. The core region can be seen to fall into four broad tribal regions: the Atrebates and the Cantii south of the Thames and the Trinovantes/Catuvellauni and Iceni to the north. These groupings have their origins in the pre-Caesarian reformations and remain a significant factor in the subsequent administrative structure of the Roman province.

The effects of the Gallic War on the coinage of Britain were twofold: a progressive reduction in the weight of staters and the introduction of silver coinages. The weight reduction ran in parallel with the decline in weight of Gallo-Belgic E coins from 6.35 to 5.80 grams during the course of the war. As new and progressively lighter coins flooded into Britain so the British mints followed, the latest and most dramatic weight reductions being accompanied by changes of style signifying lower value. The new stater issued by the Trinovantes/Catuvellauni (Trinovantian C), while basing its design on the traditional Triple-tailed horse type, adopted a series of design elements copied from contemporary Roman denarii. This striking innovation might well have been to symbolize their treaty relationship with Caesar. The adoption of silver, some of the designs of which were also taken from denarii, is likely to have had more complex causes. The most significant of these was probably the desire to match, for reasons of easy exchange, the new silver issues being struck by the neighbouring Gallic tribes. By the end of the war the Trinovantes/Catuvellauni, Atrebates, Iceni and Corieltauvi were all striking silver alongside their gold.

One significant political event at the end of the war was the flight to Britain of Commius and his followers. Commius, a member of the Gallo-Belgic Atrebatic aristocracy, had been a trusted supporter of Caesar's and had mediated on behalf of Rome during the British campaigns. He had returned to Gaul in the late summer of 54 BC but two years later made a volte-face by supporting Vercingetorix, the leader of the Gallic rebellion. When this failed he was hunted down and almost murdered by the Roman authorities. Eventually, in about 50 BC, he escaped to Britain to join his people already settled here. He probably landed somewhere in the Solent and eventually set up a kingdom in northern Hampshire and Berkshire based on *Calleva* (Silchester). Once established he modified the local Atrebatic Abstract type staters (Atrebatic C) by adding his name on the reverse (Atrebatic D) thereby initiating the first of Britain's dynastic coinages. Three subsequent rulers, Tincommius, Eppillus and Verica, all claimed a filial relationship though this may have had more to do with attempts to legitimize their overlordship than a record of direct genetic descent.

In the period between Caesar's campaigns and the interest shown in Britain by Augustus (54–30 BC) the rapidly developing coinage allows us to trace the emergence of several dynasties while the distribution patterns created by coin finds provide both an indication of territorial boundaries and some insight into the power struggles of the time.

North of the Thames two new coin types appeared about 45 BC (Trinovantian F and G); both were light-weight versions of the earlier Wadden Chase series (Trinovantian C) and were in circulation around the periphery of the Trinovantian core territory where a late version of the Wadden Chase type (Trinovantian E) continued in use. These light-weight peripheral coinages may have been deliberately minted for exchange purposes beyond the tribal boundaries. Significantly, however, they formed the prototypes from which the first dynastic coinages of the Trinovantes/Catuvellauni were derived. The first was of Addedomaros who issued coins from about 40 BC for about ten years (Trinovantian H, I and J) and these were replaced by those of Dubnovellaunus (E)[3] in the period from roughly 30–25 BC (Trinovantian K).

The Iceni whose territory lay in East Anglia to the north seem to have experienced economic or political uncertainty. Their main gold issue (Icenian A) had become very debased in the decade after the war. About 45 BC standards were restored with a new issue (Icenian B) but it appears to have been short-lived and by about 40 BC local production ceased, its place being taken by the Trinovantian staters, first of Addedomaros and later Dubnovellaunus. While this could suggest political dominance by the Trinovantes, it need imply little more than the acceptance, by the Iceni, of one element of their neighbour's value systems. The fact that the Iceni now issued their own silver modelled on that of their northern neighbours the Corieltauvi hints at their continued political independence.

To the south the coins of Commius continued to circulate in Atrebatic territory but the situation in Kent was altogether more complex. After about 50 BC a series of staters and their quarter staters were issued (Cantian E and F) leading to the first dynastic issue, *c.* 35 BC inscribed with the letters -IVII- but within five years that had been replaced with issues of the Kentish Dubnovellaunus (Cantian H, I and J) which continued until about 10 BC. The Kentish cast bronze series ('potins') which had begun about 100 BC came to an end at about the time that the first inscribed coins began.

In the peripheral zone the three coinages developed individually in a manner suggestive of a considerable variation in tribal fortunes. The Durotriges, who had run out of gold during the war struck only silver coins which became gradually debased over the next twenty years (Durotrigan E, F and G) until, about 30 BC, the issues were so low in silver that they are best considered to be bronze. The Dobunni seem to have made a hesitating start to issuing coins. Throughout the war and for sometime after they were content to use Atrebatic coins not issuing their own until *c.* 35 (Dobunnic A) and then only in small quantities perhaps as a special one-off minting. The first inscribed issue, bearing the name of Corio (Dobunnic B), did not appear until about 30 BC. Silver, issued in parallel with Dobunnic A, was more plentiful and it may be that, like the neighbouring Durotriges, the Dobunni were content at this stage with a silver-based system for inter- and intratribal exchange. The Corieltauvi continued issuing gold in a complex and highly original series (Corieltauvi B–H) until the first dynastic issue appeared about 10 BC. Their silver series began about 45 with a copy of a Roman denarius.

The two decades from 30–10 BC were, for Gaul, a period of consolidation during which time Augustus had taken the shattered country and had moulded it into an integrated part of the Roman empire. New towns were being built and major road systems were laid out, and a census had been taken allowing the new provincials to be taxed in accordance with Roman practice. The culmination of this process of integration was the dedication in 10 BC of the great altar at Lyon to Rome and Augustus. From now on, symbolically at least, Gaul was pacified and the armies in the west could be fully deployed advancing into Germany.

For Britain this meant a period of increasing isolation from their Gaulish kinsmen as the old systems of exchange, articulated between the native elites on both sides of the Channel, were replaced by direct contact with Roman traders making use of the newly installed road system. No doubt diplomatic exchanges between Rome and the native British chieftains continued, consolidating old allegiances and creating new ones. In about 15 BC Horace could list the Britons among those who 'admired' or 'heard' Augustus (Ode IV 14,41–52) implying at the very least a stable treaty relationship. Judging from the distribution of Italian luxury goods in Britain the principal focus of Roman goodwill continued to be the Trinovantes/Catuvellauni (p. 134–41).

The Trinovantian ruler Dubnovellaunus (E) was succeeded in about 25 BC by Tasciovanus who issued an elaborate series of coins until about 10 BC. His gold staters were conservative in style the only significant innovation being the addition of the title RIGNON – 'high king' to his name – the first time in Britain that a claim to kingship is made. The parallel bronze and silver coinages were far more varied and frequently copied images from Roman coinage. Tasciovanus was also the first ruler to record the names of towns on his coins – presumably the places where the mints were located. VER (Verulamium) appeared first to be followed by CAM (Camulodunum).

We have seen that from the time of Addedomaros (c. 40–30 BC) the Iceni were content to use the gold of their southern neighbours while issuing their own silver based on that of the Corieltauvi. This situation continued throughout the reign of Tasciovanus the only difference being that the Icenian silver gradually became more original and some time about 25 BC an issue inscribed CAN DVRO appeared the significance of which is not immediately apparent.

To the south of the Thames the issues of Commius ceased about 30 BC to be replaced with those of Tincommius who claimed to be a son of Commius. The distribution of his output, both gold and silver, seems to have remained restricted to Atrebatic territory centred on Hampshire and Sussex implying a degree of continued isolation following the war. Much the same can be said of the Cantii who minted their own distinctive coinage in gold, silver and bronze struck under the name of Dubnovellaunus. Since these issues are stylistically very different from those of the Dubnovellaunus who was minting in Essex from c. 30–25 BC there is no need to regard them as the products of one person. The possibility remains, however, that there was only one Dubnovellaunus who at first had overlordship of both Essex and Kent and later, after about 25 BC, lost control of Essex. The fact that the two series were stylistically different is not a positive argument against such an interpretation since overlordship need require little more than the explicit statement of the fact that Dubnovellaunus was legitimizing coin production. The problem is one without positive solution.

The coinage of the peripheral tribes continued to follow tendencies established in the immediate post-war period: the Durotriges issued only an impoverished bronze series; the Dobunni maintained a silver series with sporadic gold issues inscribed first with the name Corio and, later, Bodvoc; while the Corieltauvi continued their traditional 'South Ferriby type'.

The Interregnum *c.* 10 BC–*c.* AD 10

The individual British coin series established in the post-war years developed with little disruption in each of the seven tribal areas until about 10 BC but then followed a period of disruption and discontinuity which Van Arsdell (1989) refers to as the interregnum. It was during this time that two of the British leaders, Tincommius and Dubnovellaunus fled to Rome to put themselves under the protection of Augustus. Their names appear on the *Monumentum Ancyranum* which is thought not to be later than AD 7. The coin evidence suggests that this flight might have been as early as 10 BC. It was at approximately this time that Strabo could write that 'certain of the British dynasts have obtained the friendship of Caesar Augustus by embassies and courtesies and set up offerings in the Capitol' (IV, 5,3). Whilst this may reflect a slightly earlier situation, it could represent a flurry of diplomatic activity on the part of aspiring British overlords vying with each other to win the support of Rome in their attempts to legitimize their territorial claims at the outset of the interregnum. The chronology is too imprecise for certainty.

The causes of the disruption remain unknown. One contributory factor could have been the effects of the Roman advance into Germany which coincided with this period but why this should have affected the British tribes is difficult to understand unless destabilization was a deliberate part of Roman policy to keep a potentially troublesome flank occupied with its own problems. Such a suggestion may seem a trifle over-complex. A more likely reason is internal strife consequent upon the death of Tasciovanus who had ruled north of the Thames for about fifteen years. This would appear to be the implication of the Trinovantian/Catuvellaunian coinage of the period. Four new names appear: SEGO, RUIIS, DIAS and ANDOCO the first three coupled with the name of Tasciovanus possibly in an attempt to claim legitimacy.[4] The Sego and Andoco coinage was issued in gold, silver and bronze though there was a considerable weight reduction of the stater from 5.60–5.40 grams. Dias, who followed, issued no gold at all while the last of the names, Rues, appears only on bronze. If the sequence has been correctly interpreted the implication would seem to be of a progressive economic crisis. The Iceni now took a more independent line issuing their own silver and a little gold inscribed with the name Anted.

The tribes south of the Thames seem also to have faced disruption at about this time not least since both of their rulers, Tincommius and Dubnovellaunus, are known to have fled to Rome. The Atrebates were taken over by Eppillus who claimed a filial relationship with Commius and at the same time styled himself REX. The mint mark CALLE shows that at least one of the centres of power at this time was Calleva (Silchester). The situation of the Cantii is particularly interesting. For a few years after the departure of Dubnovellaunus coins were issued by Vosenos but these were soon replaced by a new series issued under the authority of Eppillus. The fact that one of the designs chosen depicted a winged Victory goes some way to support the view that the Cantii had now been brought firmly under Atrebatic overlordship.

The last decades of freedom *c.* AD 10–43

In the early years of the first century AD a degree of stability was re-established in the Trinovantian/Catuvellaunian area with the emergence of Cunobelin as high king. He ruled for more than thirty years issuing throughout that time a prodigious amount of gold reflecting the evident prosperity of his kingdom. These two facts – his long reign and the ability of his aristocracy to accumulate wealth, made evident in their burials – together with the increasing Romanization of his coinage, leave little doubt that the basis of his power rested on official Roman support. Cunobelin, in adopting the legend *Tasc Fil* was claiming descent from Tasciovanus, and therefore the legitimate right to rule. Whether he was actually a son of Tasciovanus it is impossible to say. From the beginning of his reign his coins were adopted in Cantian territory ousting those of the Atrebates. This suggests that Cunobelin had immediately extended his authority south of the Thames thus controlling not only the river routes of Essex but the Thames as well. It is easy to see why, from a Roman viewpoint, Suetonius could refer to him as *Britannorum rex*.

Whether or not Cunobelin re-established a degree of authority over the Iceni is less clear. It seems unlikely that he did for his coinage occurs infrequently in their territory. Moreover the Iceni continued to strike their distinctive silver throughout this period bearing a series of inscriptions: ANTED, ECEN, SAENU and AESU.

The situation among the Atrebates was complex. About AD 10 Eppillus was replaced by Verica, who also claimed to be a son of Commius though this is unlikely since Commius died about forty years before Verica's accession. But already Atrebatic influence seems to have been waning. Their short-lived dominance of the Cantii was rapidly terminated by Cunobelin from the beginning of Verica's reign and about AD 35 the coins of a new ruler, Epaticcus, appear in Atrebatic territory. They are not numerous and tend to concentrate in the north, in Berkshire and northern Hampshire. Epaticcus poses entertaining problems. He calls himself a son of Tasciovanus and indeed copies the obverses of Cunobelin's staters but the reverses are derived from Atrebatic issues. The simplest explanation is that he was a rival of Verica's, descended from the Trinovantian/Catuvellaunian dynasty, who was carving out a territory for himself on the north-western frontier between the two tribes. It may have been under pressure from this northern enclave that Verica finally fled to the emperor seeking help in AD 42.

While these events were being played out in the core territories the peripheral tribes continued much as before. The Durotriges continued with a bronze issue changing from striking to casting. The Dobunni maintained their gold and silver inscribed with a succession of names: ANTEDRIG, COMUX, EISV, CATTI and INAM. The Corieltauvian series of gold and silver were also continued with complex inscriptions grouping two or three names together. Whether these are kings in the traditional sense, or joint magistrates is not altogether clear.

The emergence of Epaticcus, on the northern frontier of the Atrebates about AD 35, seems to herald another period of instability. It was at about this time that the coins of a new ruler Adminius appeared in Kent. Adminius was a son of Cunobelin who had argued with his father in AD 39 and had fled the country to seek the help of the Emperor Gaius, who at this time was involved in problems in Germany. The short-lived Kentish issue suggests a brief attempt to establish a power base among the Cantii.

Gaius was encouraged by the appearance of Adminius to contemplate invading Britain in AD 40 but faced with the Channel and the fear of what lay beyond the troop rebelled and the planned attack was shelved. Cunobelin died in or soon after AD 40 and was succeeded by two young men Togodumnus and Caratacus possibly his sons. After so long a reign the change of leadership must have had a further destabilizing effect. At about this time the coins of Epaticcus were replaced by identical types bearing the legend CARA which it is tempting to see as the coinage of Caratacus replacing, perhaps by force, his kinsman hitherto firmly established in the northern part of Atrebatic territory. It may have been as a result of these events that Trinovantian/ Catuvellaunian authority was extended to embrace the Dobunni lying to the west for Dio, writing of the situation at the time of the invasion, tells us that the 'Bodunni [presumably the Dobunni] were subject to Catuvellaunian kings' (LX, 6). Another casualty of these troubled times was Verica who fled to the emperor, now Claudius, in AD 42 precipitating the invasion of AD 43.

The coin evidence, aided by occasional literary references, clearly demonstrates that in the century between Caesar's comings and goings and the Claudian invasion of AD 43 the distinct tribal entities, already apparent before the war, had crystallized out. The indications are that the volume of internal warfare, if not of dynastic bickering, had substantially decreased in the south-east and with the exception of the 'interregnum' of c. 10 BC–c. AD 10 and the last years of Cunobelin's reign there may have been long periods of stability. In the core area of the south-east there is little evidence of major hillfort refortification or occupation, and even in the peripheral areas, while many hillforts continued to be inhabited, none show signs of large-scale rebuilding. New types of defences were, however, erected to defend the urban nucleations based around the royal courts and mints. At Camulodunum massive linear dykes were thrown across the tongue of land between the river Colne and the Roman river, enclosing an area of 30 square kilometres while similar earthworks straddle the coastal plain around Selsey, near Chichester, in the territory of the Atrebates – their most extended form defines an area of 150 square kilometres. Fragments of similar systems are found around the urban settlements of Verulamium and at Bagendon, Glos., and in North Oxfordshire where, however, no settlement area has yet been discovered. Evidently the new defences involved new strategic concepts. Territories were now being defended – territories which included not only the main urban nucleus but also scattered satellites, individual farms, cultivation plots and pastures. It has sometimes been assumed that the earthworks were designed against threat of chariot warfare; in any event, they are massive enough to be considered as defensive rather than merely as territorial boundaries.

The troubled times following the death of Cunobelin and the growing threat of Roman invasion must have had some effect and there may well have been a wave of refortification at some of the old defended sites. This is certainly apparent in the West Country.

At Maiden Castle and at South Cadbury the earlier ramparts were refurbished, while at Hod Hill a hasty attempt at multivallation was being undertaken but was halted by the Roman advance of 43. A totally new bivallate earthwork appears to have been constructed about this time at Boscombe Down West, Wilts., and there is some evidence of similar activity in many of the other hillforts of the south and west. The well-known reference to the Roman attack of the western forts (Suetonius, *Vesp.* 4), more than twenty of which Vespasian had to subdue in the campaign of 43–4, is supported by the evidence of slaughter at Maiden Castle and Spettisbury and by the ballista attack on Hod Hill. There can be little doubt that in the early 40s feverish attempts were made to bring the old forts of the area into a defensive readiness, using traditional techniques of fortification.

Basic fighting techniques seem to have remained much the same between the invasions of Caesar and the Claudian conquest. Chariots were still in use at the Medway battle in 43, during the Boudican rebellion in 60 and at the routing of the Caledonians under Calgacus in 84. Indeed, Tacitus, while stating that the strength of the British armies lay in their infantry, admitted that 'some tribes also fought from chariots driven by noblemen and defended by their dependants' (*Agricola*, 12). The contemporary battle accounts still bear out the fierce but uncontrolled nature of the Briton at war but, as Tacitus remarks, 'they eventually failed because they are distracted between the jarring factions of rival chiefs. Indeed, nothing has helped us more in war with their strongest nations than their inability to co-operate. It is but seldom that two or three states unite to repel a common danger: fighting in detail they are conquered wholesale.' Evidently little had changed in a hundred years.

7

The tribes of the south-eastern core: Catuvellauni/Trinovantes, Iceni, Cantii and Atrebates

In the late Iron Age Britain can be divided into three broad zones: a *core* comprising the south-east which shared many cultural characteristics with the Continent; a *periphery* comprising an arc of coin-issuing tribes stretching from Dorset to Lincolnshire; and a *beyond*, that is the rest of Britain west and north of the periphery where coinage had not been introduced into the economy. This threefold division provides a convenient way of considering the late Iron Age and will form the basis for the next three chapters. In this chapter we will be concerned with the tribes of the core: the Trinovantes/Catuvellauni, who cannot be distinguished from each other numismatically, the Iceni, the Atrebates and the Cantii.

Much of this region, from Kent to the Wash and from the east coast inland to the Ouse valley and the Upper Thames, shared a number of cultural aspects with the Belgic areas of northern Gaul (Figure 7.1). Ceramic technology, burial rites, economy and socio-political structure showed only slight variation from one end of the region to the other. Nevertheless, behind this apparent unity lay three major tribal groupings – the Trinovantes/Catuvellauni, Iceni and Cantii – all recognizable through their distinctive coinages and all following discrete political policies in relation to each other and to the threat of Roman invasion. Given only the material and structural evidence it would have been very difficult to distinguish between them yet the coin evidence and subsequent history leaves no doubt that very different political entities were involved.

Until comparatively recent times it has been conventional to refer to this cultural continuum as 'Belgic'. The term was convenient in that it reflected the similarity of culture between this region and the Belgic area of northern Gaul, but it took with it the underlying assumption that the region had been settled by the immigrant Belgae referred to by Caesar. Since, however, serious doubt has been cast on this latter view, and a good case can now be made out for the undoubted similarities resulting from regular and intensive social and economic intercourse between the tribes on either side of the Channel, the word Belgic is best avoided. Instead the term *Aylesford–Swarling* culture will be used, which is defined on purely archaeological criteria without historical preconception.

The southern part of the core zone, which eventually became the territory of the Atrebates, shares a range of cultural similarities which are sufficiently different to the Aylesford–Swarling

130

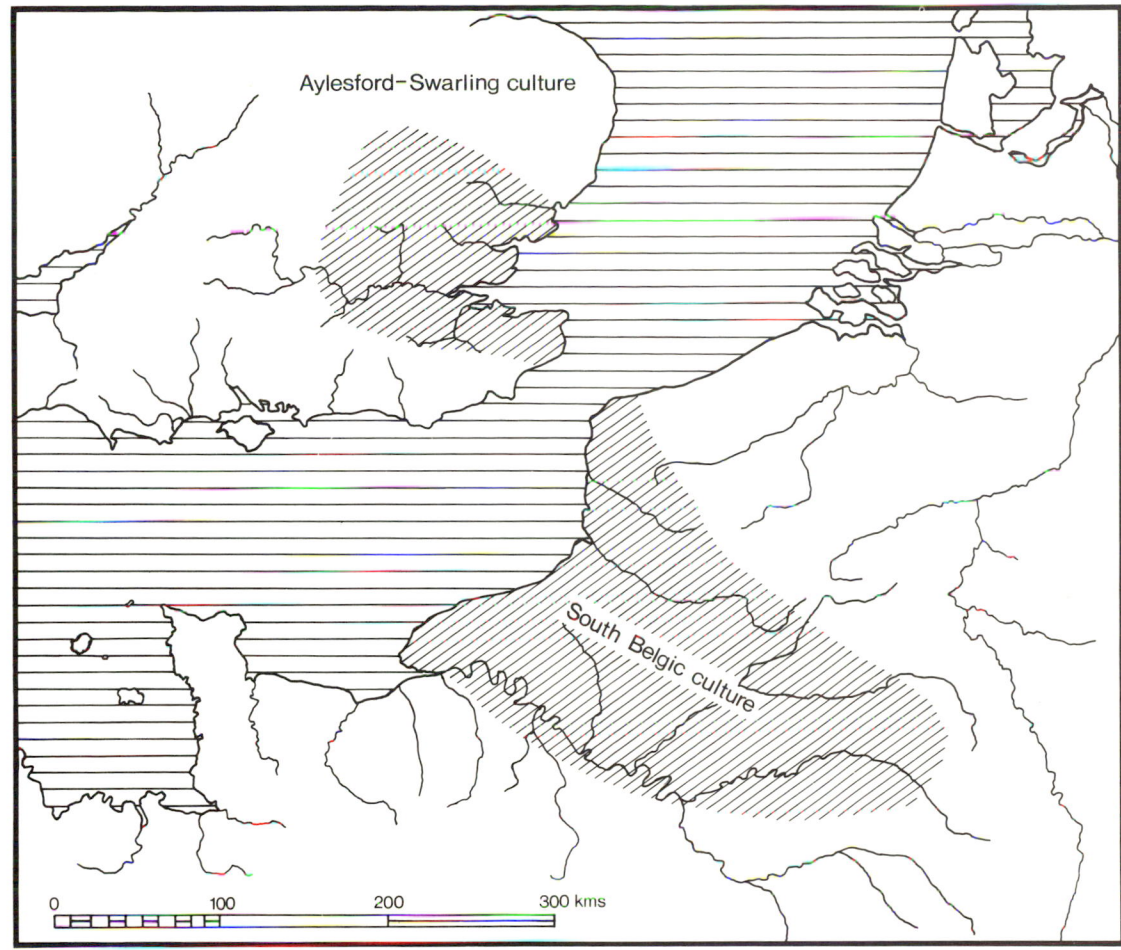

Figure 7.1 Distribution of the Aylesford–Swarling and south Belgic cultures (source: author).

culture to require a separate name: here we will use the phrase *Atrebatic culture* since it is the culture of the historically attested Atrebates and does not extend beyond their normal boundaries.[1]

The Atrebatic and Aylesford–Swarling terminology reflects broad cultural groupings defined archaeologically while the tribal entities based on coinage are essentially political constructs. Moving down the scale, a more detailed appraisal of the coin evidence allows the possibility of discerning, albeit dimly, smaller *socio-economic units*. The method used to define them is to attempt to recognize recurring patterns in successive coin distributions (Cunliffe 1981b). Though a rather inexact tool, and to a degree subjective, it does allow a number of zones to be postulated and the fact that most of these contain a major settlement site or oppidum in a roughly central position, lends credibility to their reality (Figure 7.2). These socio-economic zones provide a convenient framework for discussing the political geography of the individual tribes.

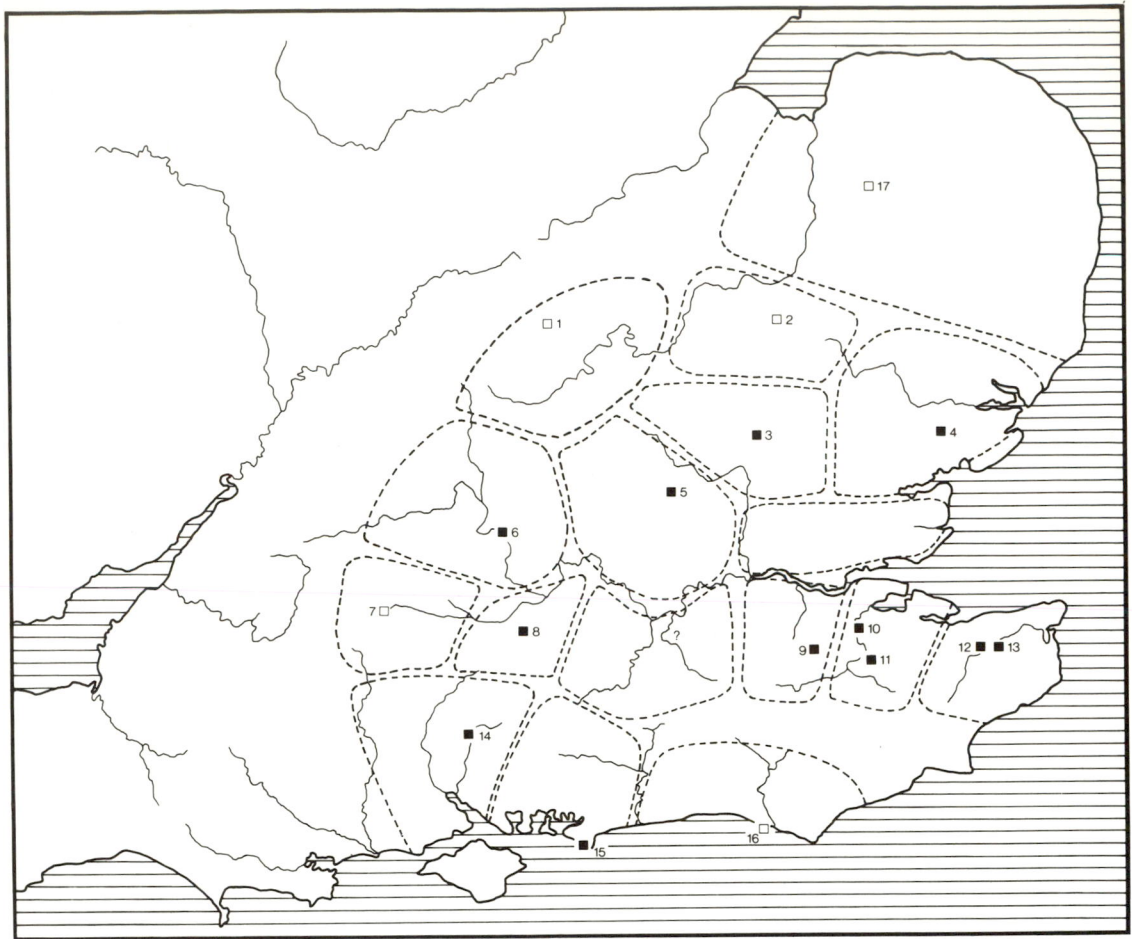

Figure 7.2 Socio-economic zones in the core region in the period 50 BC–AD 10. Black squares denote nucleated settlements with some evidence of urban functions; open squares are possible nucleated settlements. 1 Duston, 2 Cambridge, 3 Braughing, 4 Colchester, 5 Verulamium, 6 Dyke Hills, 7 Marlborough, 8 Silchester, 9 Oldbury, 10 Rochester, 11 Loose, 12 Bigbury, 13 Canterbury, 14 Winchester, 15 Selsey, 16 Castle Hill, Newhaven, 17 Woodcock Hill, Saham Toney (source: Cunliffe 1981b with modifications).

The Aylesford–Swarling culture: pottery and burials

The Aylesford–Swarling culture is named after two Kentish cremation cemeteries of La Tène III date excavated in 1886 and 1921 respectively. The relevant material was first brought together with a full discussion in a paper by Hawkes and Dunning published in 1931. The subject was reconsidered in the light of new finds, both British and Continental, by Birchall (1965) and received a further reassessment by Rodwell in 1976. The Continental background has been discussed by Hachmann (1976) since when there have been further considerations of aspects of the cultural complex (Stead 1976a; Tyers 1980; F.H. Thompson 1983).

The culture is characterized by a distinctive range of pottery, usually wheel-made, together with the rite of cremation in flat graves. The associated metalwork is invariably La Tène III. The classic statement of the distribution of the Aylesford–Swarling culture was provided by the distribution map of pedestal urns published by Hawkes and Dunning (1931, Figure 7) and reproduced here as Figure 1.6 (p. 10) which shows the vessels concentrating in Kent, Essex, Hertfordshire, Bedfordshire and the London area with a few outliers further north and west. In the last sixty years many more sites have been discovered but the pattern has not changed significantly. Thus, in terms of the known tribes the Aylesford–Swarling culture is the folk culture of the Catuvellauni, Trinovantes and Cantii.

D.F. Allen's reassessment of Celtic coinage in Britain (1961a) showed that a number of Gallo-Belgic issues were reaching Britain from the end of the second century BC and for a while it seemed reasonable to interpret this as evidence of a series of migratory movements from the Continent into eastern Britain bringing an array of new cultural elements with them (C.F.C. Hawkes 1968). Several detailed studies, however, have failed to trace any substantial body of 'Belgic' material pre-dating Caesar's invasion, though Birchall tentatively recognized a potentially early group of pottery. It is clear, therefore, that the developed culture (in the form defined here) is unlikely to have been introduced by Caesar's invaders from Belgium along with Gallo-Belgic coinage. The interpretation which best fits all the evidence is that a long period of social and economic intercourse existed between Britain and Belgic Gaul, allowing the possibility of limited movements of people, but that the Aylesford–Swarling culture proper developed after Caesar's conquest of Gaul as the result of an intensification of trade between the eastern British tribes and their increasingly Romanized Belgic neighbours.

Before proceeding to a discussion of the individual tribal areas some of the general characteristics of the Aylesford–Swarling culture must be considered.

Pottery is the most characteristic artefact (Figures A:28, p. 581 and A:29, p. 582). It is usually of exceptionally high quality, most of it being wheel-made with an assurance and similarity of design which suggests commercial production on a large scale by specialists who, in the first instance, may well have been immigrants. Tall, elegantly-shaped urns with pedestal bases, conical urns, corrugated vessels and a wide range of elaborately cordoned and grooved bowls make up the bulk of the types, with butt-beakers, tazze, platters and lids occurring less frequently. Also relatively common are the coarser narrow-mouthed jars with their outer surfaces wiped or scored to create crude patterns. This type probably originated in an earlier period but takes on a new formality with the introduction of the techniques of wheel-turning.

After 15–10 BC the locally produced vessels were supplemented by imported fine wares from Gaul, Germany and the Mediterranean, including terra rubra and terra nigra platters, Gallo-Belgic butt-beakers, Arretine wares and eventually samian pottery, while from the middle of the first century BC wine was being imported in some quantity in large amphorae. Some local copying of the imports occurred, particularly of the Gallo-Belgic beakers and platters, and it is probable that the production of the pale fabric butt-beakers of Gaulish type had begun at Camulodunum before the invasion of AD 43.

The culture is best known through its cemeteries and isolated burials, which form a significant part of the archaeological record. A few examples will suffice to demonstrate the range of burial rites. At Verulamium a typical cemetery has been excavated in its entirety close to the nucleus of the Prae Wood Belgic settlement (Figure 7.3). Here no less than 463 individual cremations were discovered, usually placed inside an urn buried in a small pit, and often accompanied by one or more accessory vessels and by bronze brooches. Less frequently other grave-goods were buried,

Figure 7.3   The cremation cemetery at Prae Wood, Verulamium, Herts. (source: Stead 1969).

including mirrors, bracelets, keys, knives, shears, gaming pieces, spoons and toilet sets – in fact, a range of personal belongings appropriate to both males and females. Some of the burials, richer than others, were heaped up on the floor of larger grave-pits, and several of these were placed in the centres of rectangular ditched enclosures containing poorer satellite burials arranged in a circle around the principal grave. The cemetery also produced eighteen inhumations, of which sixteen were unaccompanied. Judging by the quantity of imported Gallo-Belgic wares, which are unlikely to have arrived in Britain much before 10 BC, the cemetery must have been in use throughout the half-century before the invasion of AD 43.

The large-scale excavation of the Verulamium cemetery allows the site to serve as a type example for La Tène III cremation cemeteries in general. To this category belong the two type-sites of Aylesford and Swarling, both of which are somewhat earlier than Verulamium. Neither site was excavated under modern conditions, and apart from the groups of grave-goods little is known of the general arrangement or plan of the cemeteries. At Swarling, however, two groups of cremations were found: an eastern group of nine and a western group of ten burials. Class distinctions were evident in the care with which some of the graves were dug, as well as from the number of accessory vessels provided and the occasional presence of fibulae. Grave 13 was outstanding in that the main burial was placed in an iron-bound wooden bucket together with two elaborate bronze fibulae, while standing around were six pottery vessels, no doubt once containing offerings of food and drink. Such elaboration suggests the burial of a person of wealth and status.

Elaborate bucket burials were also a feature of the Aylesford cemetery, where three such groups can be reconstructed (Birchall 1965, 243 ff.). Burial X contained a large wooden bucket bound with iron, together with six pots; burial Y was richer (Figure 7.4), consisting of a circular chalk-lined pit within which lay a bronze-plated bucket (Figure 7.5) containing the cremation

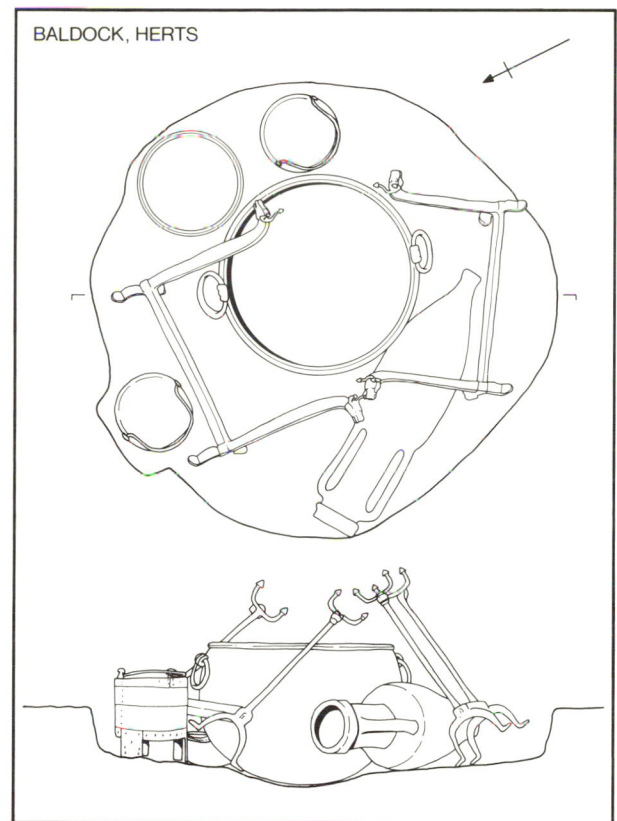

Figure 7.4 Bucket burials from Baldock, Herts., and Aylesford, Kent (source: *Baldock*, Stead and Rigby 1986; *Aylesford*, A.J. Evans 1890).

and a fibula, a bronze oenochoe (jug) and patella (pan), both of Italian manufacture, together with a number of pots. The third burial, Z, produced a bronze-mounted wooden tankard with bronze handles surrounded, apparently, by five or six pots. Since the Italian bronze vessels and the brooch from grave Y are types well known on the Continent in contexts dating to 50–30 BC, it may be assumed that the Aylesford burial dates to somewhere within the second half of the first century BC. The exact relationship of the three rich burials to the poorer cremations is unrecorded but the existence of circular settings of burials hints at the possibility of satellite arrangements comparable to those at Verulamium.

An even richer bucket burial was found at Baldock, Herts., in 1967 during construction work (Figure 7.4): a subsequent excavation enabled details of the grave to be reconstructed. It comprised a roughly circular pit 1.6 m in diameter dug down into the solid chalk to a depth of 0.3 m in which had been placed a large bronze cauldron, two bronze dishes, two bronze mounted wooden buckets, two iron firedogs, an Italian Dressel 1A amphora and part of a pig. The cremated body, much of which was recovered from the cauldron, had been wrapped in the skin of a brown bear since phalange bones of the beast were found mixed with those of the human occupant. The Dressel 1A amphora might suggest that the burial belonged to the first half of the first century BC but the type does go on in use and a post-Caesarian date seems more likely.

Bucket burials, though few in number, occur widely in the south-east of Britain at Old Warden, Harpenden and Great Chesterford (Figure 7.5) as well as at Aylesford, Swarling and Baldock. Further afield they also occur at Hurstbourne Tarrant and Silkstead in Hampshire and Marlborough in Wiltshire (Stead 1971a). These peripheral burials presumably represent the adoption of Aylesford–Swarling traditions by the local Atrebatic aristocracy.

North of the Thames a group of exceptionally rich cremation burials (Figure 7.6) has been defined and named after the type-site of Welwyn, Herts. (Stead 1967). Six examples definitely belong to this group – Hertford Heath, Mount Bures, Snailwell, Stanfordbury, Welwyn and Welwyn Garden City – and a further eight sites in the same general area are possibly also of this kind. The Welwyn type burials may be characterized as cremations placed in large grave-pits with no covering mound (Figure 7.7). The pits contained a wide range of grave-goods including at least one wine amphora (usually more, six being the maximum) and quantities of tableware, much of it imported. Some were provided with imported bronze vases, strainers and patellae, others with silver cups, while one produced imported glass dishes and containers. Clearly the dead person was being provided with sufficient food and wine to see him on his journey to the next world. Surprisingly, however, meat (or at least meat on the bone) is seldom found. Most burials contained a few other personal belongings such as buckles, bracelets, beads and gaming

Figure 7.5   Reconstruction of bronze-bound buckets from Aylesford, Kent (left) and Great Chesterford, Essex (above) (scales: approx. ½). (*Aylesford*, photo: British Museum, *Great Chesterford*, photo: University Museum of Archaeology and Ethnology, Cambridge).

pieces, but weapons are conspicuously absent. Iron firedogs (e.g. Figure 7.8), spits and in one case a tripod represent the dead man's hearth furniture in several of the graves. The imported material, particularly the Italian bronzes in the earlier graves and the Gallo-Belgic and samian vessels in the later, allow the burials to be arranged in a chronological sequence spanning the century between the invasions of Caesar and Claudius. Welwyn type cremations represent a tradition of aristocratic burial deeply rooted in the formative period of the Aylesford–Swarling culture north of the Thames.

The most impressive of the rich La Tène III graves in the Aylesford–Swarling region is the burial found at Lexden, Essex, close to Camulodunum in 1924. It comprised an enormous oval

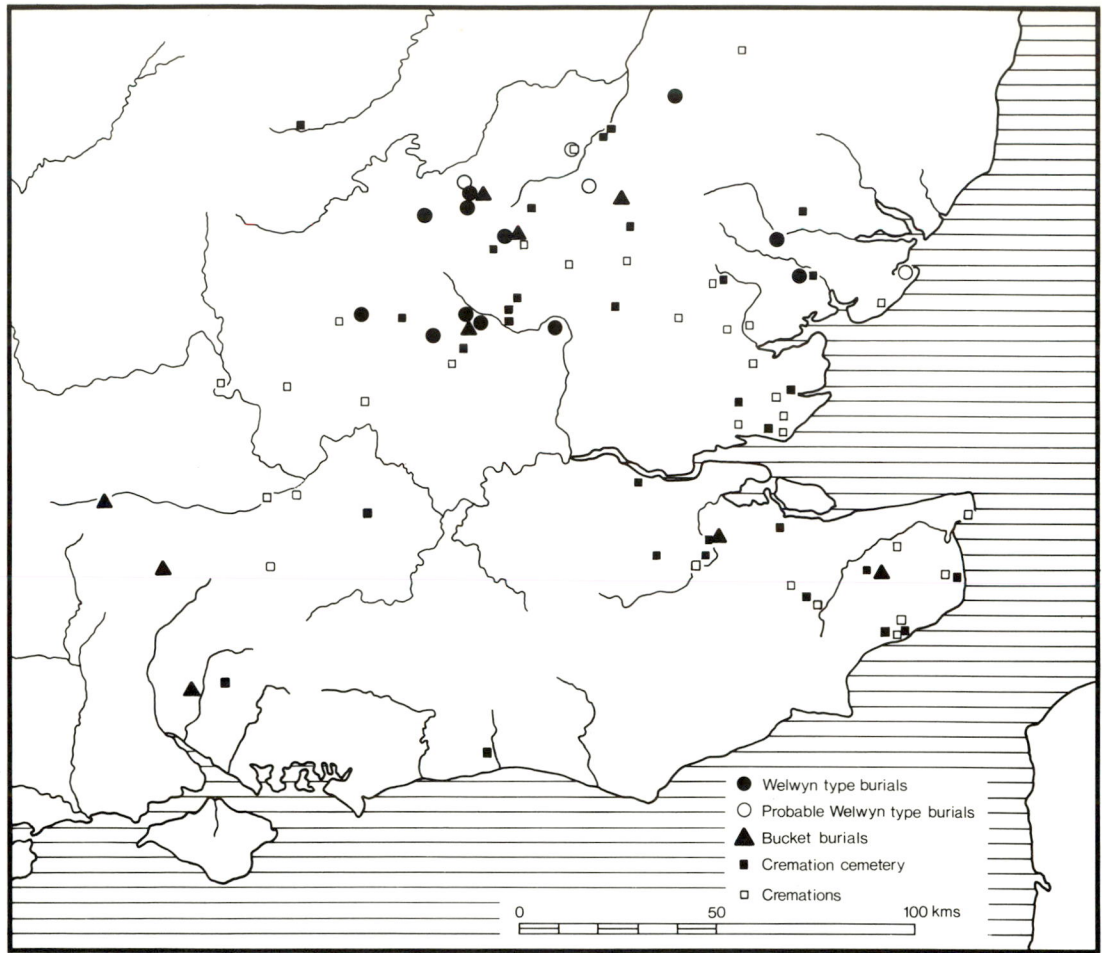

Figure 7.6 Cremation cemeteries of the Aylesford–Swarling culture (source: Whimster 1977 with modifications).

burial pit 8.2 m long placed beneath a barrow 30 m in diameter. The excavation was only summarily published (Laver 1927) but has been recently reassessed, providing a far fuller picture of the grave and its contents (Foster 1986). The body had been cremated and placed in the pit together with an astonishing collection of grave-goods including a bronze cupid, a boar, a bull, a griffin attachment, a pedestal for a statuette and a number of other copper alloy fittings and attachments. A suit of iron-chain mail, possibly once complete, and fitted with bronze buckles and hinges and silver studs, had been cut up and spread about the grave-pit. There were also silver mounts in the form of corn stems, a quantity of small silver trefoil attachments and a cast silver medallion displaying the head of Augustus moulded from a coin type minted between 19–15 BC. A large piece of gold fabric was found in close proximity to the cremation. Among the numerous iron fittings recovered were the bars of a folding stool. The grave was also furnished with a set of local pottery and a number of Italian wine amphorae – at least six of the Dressel 1B type and twice as many of Dressel 2–4.

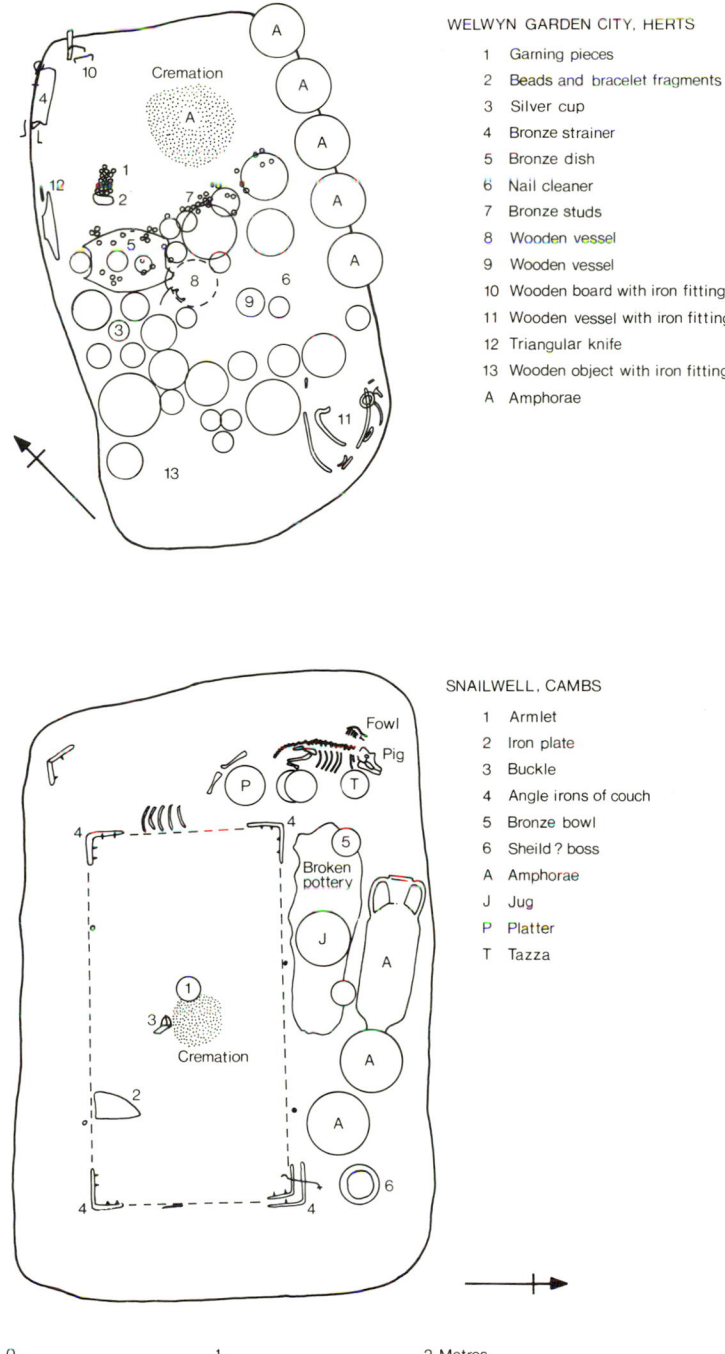

WELWYN GARDEN CITY, HERTS

1   Gaming pieces
2   Beads and bracelet fragments
3   Silver cup
4   Bronze strainer
5   Bronze dish
6   Nail cleaner
7   Bronze studs
8   Wooden vessel
9   Wooden vessel
10 Wooden board with iron fittings
11 Wooden vessel with iron fittings
12 Triangular knife
13 Wooden object with iron fittings
A   Amphorae

SNAILWELL, CAMBS

1   Armlet
2   Iron plate
3   Buckle
4   Angle irons of couch
5   Bronze bowl
6   Sheild ? boss
A   Amphorae
J   Jug
P   Platter
T   Tazza

Figure 7.7   La Tène III chieftains' burials (sources: *Welwyn Garden City*, Stead 1967; *Snailwell*, Lethbridge 1953).

Figure 7.8   Iron firedog from Chapel Garmon, Denbigh. Hearth furniture of the type sometimes buried with the dead (photo: National Museum of Wales).

The grave-goods, taken together, would suggest a date of about 15–10 BC though burial may have occurred some little time later. The occupant of the grave was evidently a man of enormous wealth and status who chose a form of burial, under a barrow, more usual in Gaul than in Britain. His taste in Roman luxury objects and his ability to acquire them implies that he was a member of the Catuvellaunian/Trinovantian aristocracy thoroughly conversant with Roman taste. We will never know the identity of this British king but it is tempting to point out that, on the coin evidence, Tasciovanus died about 10 BC.

From the foregoing summary it will be seen that the burial rite of the Aylesford–Swarling culture, while varied, was relatively consistent. It reflects a strong belief in the afterlife and it mirrors very clearly the rigid social stratification which must have existed. Simple cremations, bucket burials, Welwyn burials and Lexden represent four distinct levels in the social hierarchy from peasant through two tiers of 'lordship' to king.

It is not surprising that the 'kingly' burial of Lexden should be situated at Camulodunum which was probably the paramount tribal capital at this time. What is more noteworthy is the cluster of rich chiefly burials on either side of the Chilterns in the valleys of the Lea, Ouse and Cam. What these may reflect are the centres of power of those able to command the trade routes between the periphery and the core (Cunliffe 1988b, 150–3). If so then the Welwyn burials represent the vassal chieftains upon whom the paramounts – the dynastic rulers – built their power.

Within the territory of the Aylesford–Swarling culture there developed a series of large nucleated settlements which justify the use of the term urban or proto-urban. Their form and size vary considerably but for ease of discussion we shall divide them into three categories *enclosed oppida*, *territorial oppida* and *nucleated oppida*. Figure 7.2 shows the distribution of the major sites of this kind for which the evidence is convincing. Individual sites will be considered in the following sections.

The Trinovantes/Catuvellauni

The Trinovantes and Catuvellauni were the two principal tribes occupying a wide swathe of territory north of the Thames including the modern counties of Essex, Hertfordshire and parts of Oxfordshire, Buckinghamshire, Northamptonshire, Cambridgeshire and Suffolk. Some indication of the extent of their territory and influence is indicated by the distribution of the coins of Tasciovanus and Cunobelin (Figure 7.9). Since it is impossible at present to distinguish the coinages of the two tribes they are here considered together.

North of the Thames the extent of the Aylesford–Swarling culture is roughly coterminous with Trinovantian/Catuvellaunian coinage but the coin evidence allows the tentative recognition of a series of discrete socio-economic regions (Figure 7.2) in several of which large nucleated settlements, or *oppida* have been identified. While it must be admitted that little is yet known of these oppida in Britain the work at Verulamium has defined the main characteristics of this type of site (Figure 7.10). The earliest nuclear settlement is thought to lie on a gravel plateau above the river Lea at Wheathampstead, Herts., where massive earthworks flank at least three sides of an enclosure of some 36–40 hectares – the size of the average Romano-British town. Limited excavation within has demonstrated the presence of occupation spanning the latter part of the first century BC but apparently ending before 15–10 BC (if the absence of Gallo-Belgic vessels, which began to be imported at about this time, is regarded as significant and reliable). It has been suggested that Wheathampstead was the oppidum where Cassivellaunus made his last stand against Caesar. Caesar tells us that British strongholds in general were densely wooded spots fortified with ramparts and ditches and that Cassivellaunus's stronghold was protected by forests and marshes and had been filled with a large number of men and cattle for their own protection. Wheathampstead would indeed fulfil these conditions, but the identification is unlikely ever to be proven and some doubt has been cast on the exact status of the site (Dyer 1976b).

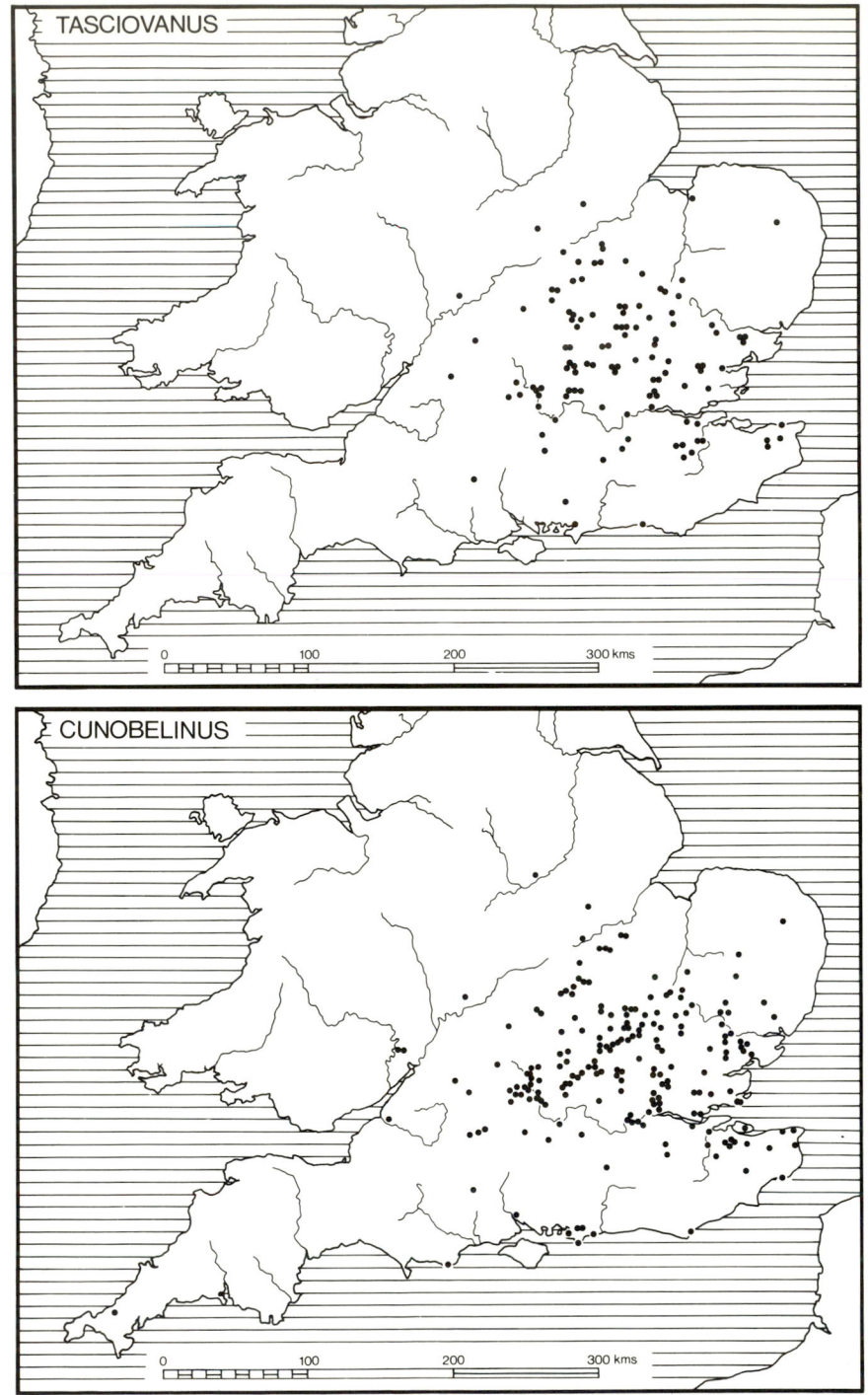

Figure 7.9   Distribution of the coins of Tasciovanus and Cunobelinus indicating extent of Catuvellaunian/Trinovantian territory and influence (source: Cunliffe 1981b).

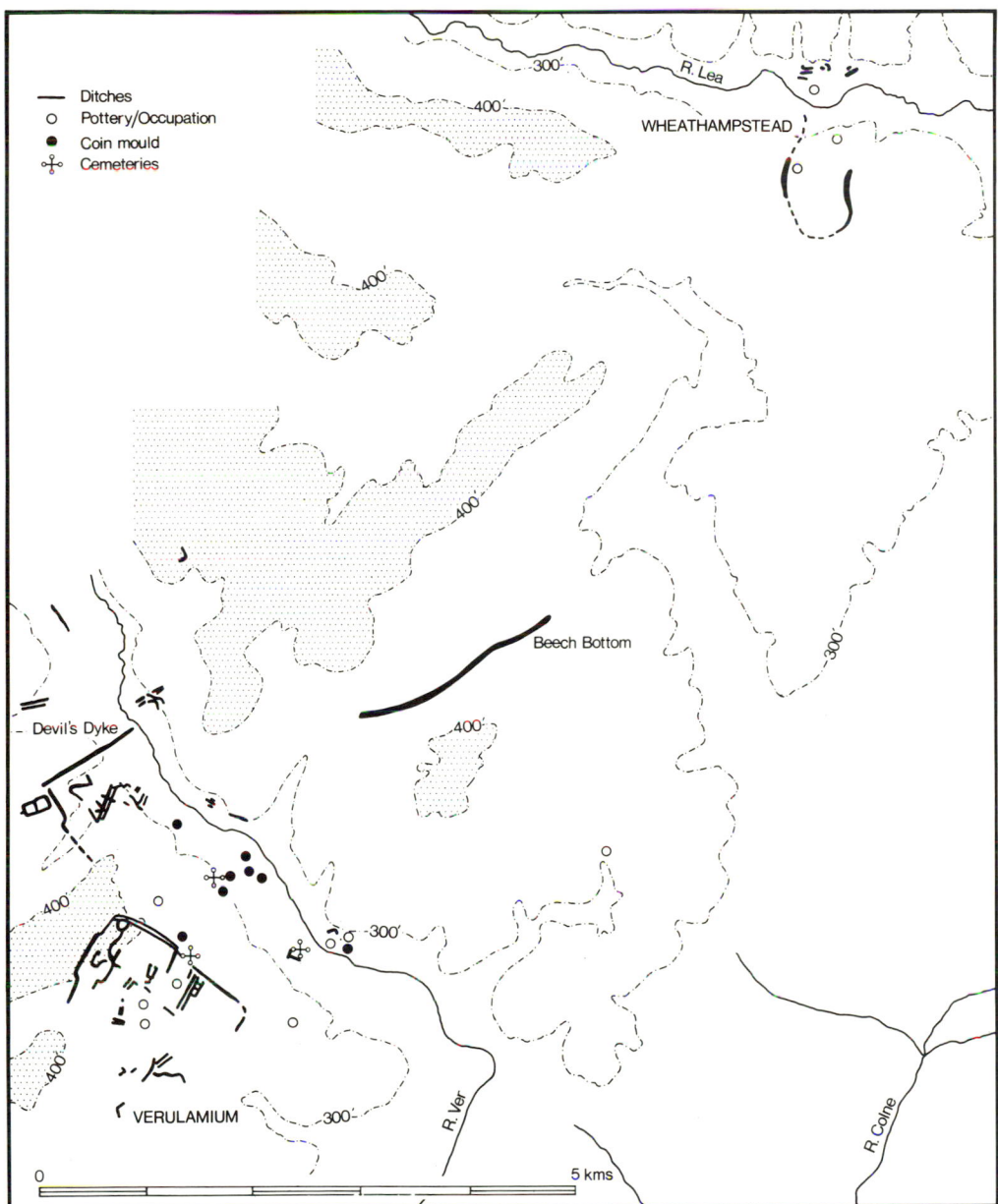

Figure 7.10 Late Iron Age occupation in the Verulamium–Wheathampstead region (source: Saunders and Havercroft 1982).

The abandonment of Wheathampstead is apparently matched by the growth of Verulamium, 8 km to the south-west and occupying a similar plateau position above the river Ver in the area of what is now Prae Wood. Plentiful imports were found showing that the site reached its maximum period of occupation in the first half of the first century AD. Instead of massive earthworks, the main inhabited area of the oppidum was enclosed by relatively slight ditches and palisades, altered on several occasions, within which lay the huts, drainage ditches and ovens of the settlement. Outside the boundary ditch flanking this nucleus was the cemetery referred to above. Other settlement areas must have existed nearby; one, found closer to the river beneath the Roman town, produced the debris of a Late Iron Age mint, another has been identified at Gorhambury to the north just within the Devil's Dyke. Indeed it is possible that the Gorhambury and Prae Wood settlement areas are simply the outlying parts of the oppidum the core of which lies beneath the later Roman town. Another possibility is that settlement was dispersed rather than concentrated at a single nucleus.

One further aspect of the local settlement pattern deserves consideration. From a point close to Wheathampstead to as far as the river Ver opposite the settlement at Prae Wood runs a massive defensive bank and ditch known as Beech Bottom Dyke, the staggered line of which is continued by a lesser earthwork, Devil's Dyke, to the west of the river a little way north of the settlement. It seems probable that these banks and ditches form part of a series of dykes designed to defend and define the territory of the oppidum and its satellite settlements. As we shall see, systems of linear earthworks reach complex proportions at Camulodunum and in the Chichester region. The lack of such a development at Verulamium might be explained by the fact that the seat of centralized government had moved to Camulodunum early in the first century AD, relieving Verulamium of its political importance. If so, the Beech Bottom Dyke–Devil's Dyke complex could be seen as an early stage in the development of territorial defences, arrested before the system could achieve its ultimate form.

Linear earthworks must be regarded as a new concept in defensive architecture arising late in the British Iron Age. Similar systems are recorded on the Continent. Tacitus (*Annals* ii, 19), describing the assembly of a Germanic tribe called the Cherusci, specifically mentions their choice of a location hemmed in by a river and forests which were surrounded by deep bogs. On the one side without natural defences the neighbouring tribe, the Angrivarii, had constructed a 'broad earthwork as a boundary'. Here, surely, is a direct reference to large-scale linear defences erected to supplement natural obstacles in much the same way as the Beech Bottom complex makes careful use of the landscape.

If Verulamium represents the beginnings of linear defensive systems, Camulodunum must demonstrate the ultimate development (Figure 7.11), for here a series of dykes, usually laid out in straight lines running between the Roman river and the river Colne, carve out a territory of some 31 square kilometres. The system is so complex that more than one phase of construction must be involved. It is, in fact, possible to postulate an early nucleus in the Gosbecks Farm area, where a Roman (and presumably pre-Roman) temple complex lies within a curved line of earthworks of early appearance. Rodwell (1976, 339–59) has put forward a sequence of development involving six major phases. His assessment is based largely upon topographical considerations and while plausible it is only by an extensive programme of excavation that the true complexity of the system will finally be demonstrated. How many separate nuclear settlements lay within the territory is not known, but the Sheepen site, which has been examined by excavation (Hawkes and Hull 1947), has yielded ample evidence of scattered huts of apparently circular and sub-rectangular form together with pits, ditches, the debris from a mint and masses of imported pottery. Here, evidently, lay a centre of some importance. The enormous quantity of imported wares found in one area has even suggested to the excavator the possibility of it being the actual residence of Cunobelin. Such an attribution, while possible, can never be proved.

While Verulamium and Camulodunum are undoubtedly the two principal urban centres in

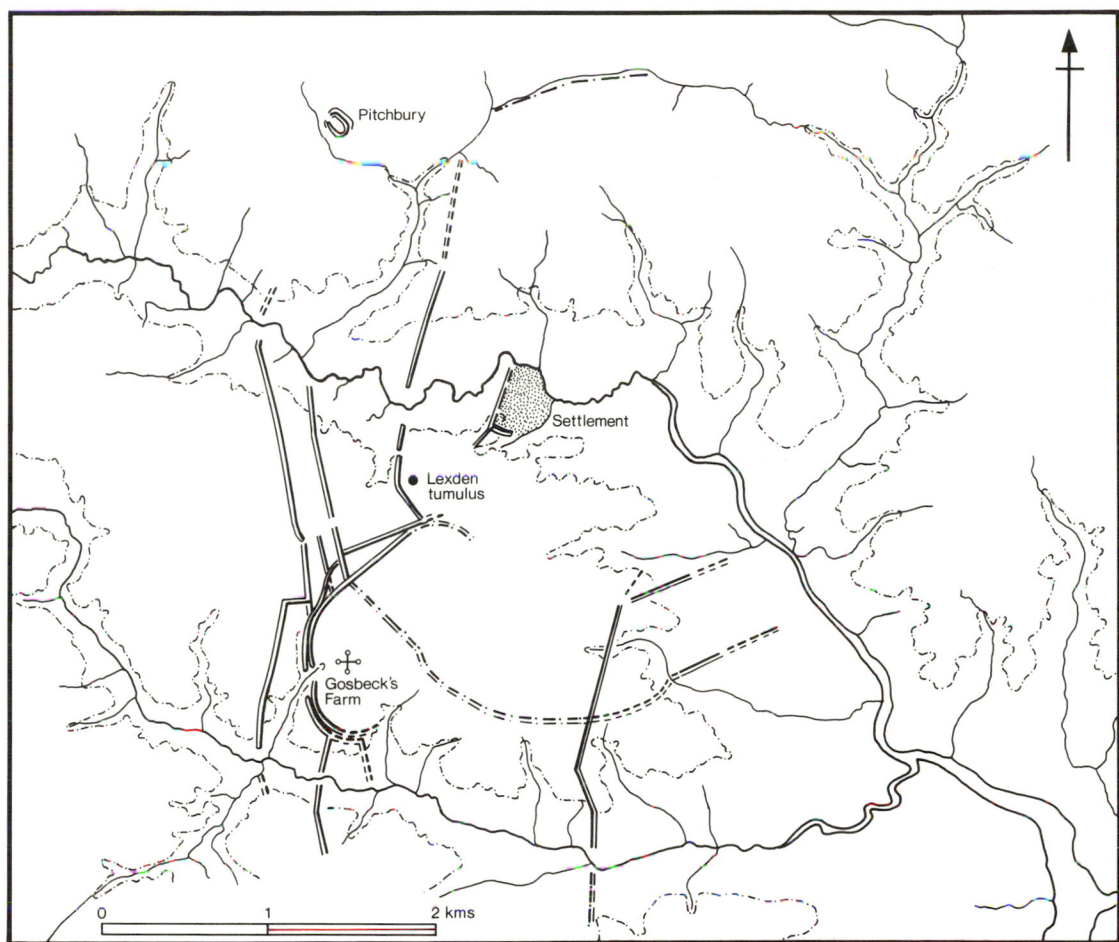

Figure 7.11   Late Iron Age settlement in the vicinity of Camulodunum (source: Rodwell 1976).

the territory of the Trinovantes/Catuvellauni, several other sites may be claimed to have urban status. Of these the best known lies in the vicinity of Braughing, Herts. Early occupation, beginning in the Middle Iron Age, was probably focused on the hillfort at Gatesbury Wood overlooking the river Rib but by the last decades of the first century BC occupation had spread to cover an area of *c.* 100 ha. No enclosing dyke systems have yet been traced so at present Braughing must be classed as an unenclosed oppidum. Excavation, most extensively at Skeleton Green, has exposed evidence of rectangular timber buildings associated with chalk floors and gravel spreads spanning the period from *c.* 15 BC to the Roman conquest.

A potentially similar site lies beneath the Roman settlement at Baldock, Herts.: occupation here began *c.* 50 BC. Since the extent of the pre-Roman settlement is not known it cannot yet be claimed to be of urban status though its subsequent Roman development is suggestive of its economic potential. Two other possible minor oppida have been claimed at Norsey Wood, Billericay and Mount House, Bramtree but firm evidence is wanting.

Turning now to the outer fringes of the territory, extensive pre-Roman occupation existed beneath nucleated Roman settlements at Cambridge and Duston near Northampton; both are potential locations for oppida but in the absence of adequate publication the question must remain open. In the Upper Thames valley, at Dorchester, the evidence is somewhat more convincing. Here the massive earthworks of an enclosed oppidum known as Dyke Hills defend an area in the bend of the river Thames close to a major crossing point overlooked by the Early and Middle Iron Age hillfort of Wittenham Clumps. In the post-conquest period a small Roman town developed just north of the oppidum. Further west, on the slopes of the Cotswolds the North Oxfordshire Grim's Ditch complex has the appearance of a territorial oppidum rather like Camulodunum but no concentrations of pre-conquest occupational activity have yet been identified.

Within the territory of the Trinovantes/Catuvellauni the reoccupation of hillforts does not seem to have been particularly common but several sites on the Chilterns, like Wilbury, Ravensburgh Castle and Cholesbury, produced finds of Aylesford–Swarling type. The same is true of the multivallate fort of Wallbury, Essex, the massive size of which, 12.4 ha, and its location suggest that it has more the characteristics of an enclosed oppidum than a hillfort.

The history of the Trinovantes and Catuvellauni cannot yet be disentangled though a number of general statements, based on an interpretation of the coinage, can be made (and have been summarized in the previous chapter). What all this means in terms of the relative fortunes of the different urban centres and their socio-economic territories is impossible to say except to stress the rise in power of Camulodunum. The vast size of the site, the richness of the Lexden burial and the considerable bulk of imported pottery found there leaves little doubt that Camulodunum had gained pre-eminence by the last decades of the first century BC and maintained its status until the conquest when it was chosen by the Roman administrators to be the first of the coloniae of Britannia. Eventually, with better evidence from the other oppida and a more detailed consideration of the chronology of the rich burials, it may be possible to chart the changing fortunes of the smaller units that made up the larger territory over which Cunobelin became the 'great king'.

The Cantii

The Cantii evidently had a complex history. They were the first of the British tribes to issue their own coinage to serve as small change alongside Gallo-Belgic staters imported before the Caesarian campaigns. After the war they continued to issue their own coins until the turn of the millennium when, for a brief period, they came under the influence of the Atrebates before passing into the Trinovantian/Catuvellaunian sphere at about the time when Cunobelin took over leadership. At the time of Caesar's invasions the Cantii had four kings (*BG* V 22) suggesting, but not proving, that they may have been divided into four self-contained kingdoms. Three distinct socio-economic units can be postulated on the basis of the coin distribution, centred respectively on the rivers Stour, Medway and Darent and it is possible that the Weald constituted a fourth. The separate nature of the three coastal units is further emphasized by the distribution patterns of different pottery fabrics: in addition to the ubiquitous grog-tempered wares, the Darent zone used shell tempering, the Medway greensand tempering and the Stour flint tempering (I. Thompson 1982, 7). These regions, determined largely by

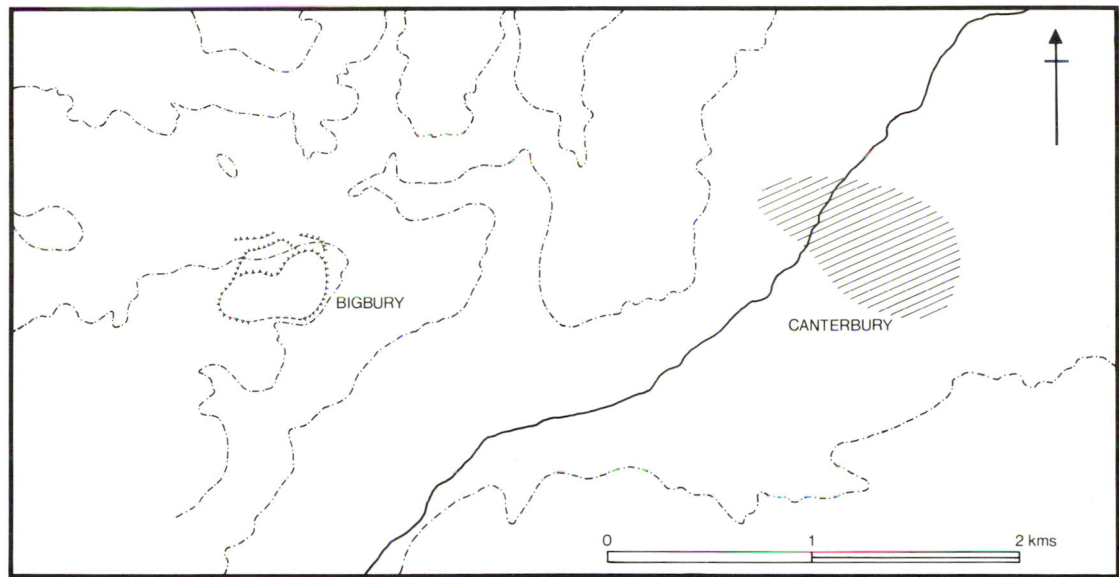

Figure 7.12   Late Iron Age settlement in the vicinity of Canterbury (source: author).

geographical considerations, could approximate to the kingdoms which Caesar noted.

The principal 'urban' centres of the Cantii have been located though excavation has been minimal. In the Stour valley the urban nucleus became focused on the site later to be occupied by Roman Canterbury where occupation, in the form of rectangular huts and drainage gullies, has been found in the valley bottom on both sides of the river (Fig. 7.12). Two kilometres to the west is the large hill-top fortification of Bigbury which conforms to the characteristics of an enclosed oppidum. It has produced an impressive range of metalwork including a series of tools, horse- and vehicle-fittings, a slave chain and hearth fittings in the form of a firedog and a cauldron chain – objects which tend to emphasize the essentially aristocratic nature of the latest occupation. It is quite possible that Bigbury was the first native fort attacked by Caesar and that sometime in the post-war period the focus of occupation gravitated to the river crossing at Canterbury. The dating evidence from the two sites is at present insufficient to demonstrate the point with any degree of precision.

In the Medway valley two sites show urban attributions: an enclosed oppidum with associated linear earthworks at Loose and the site of the Roman town at Rochester where coin flan moulds have come to light. Here again the possibility of a move from one focus to the other is possible but unproven. Further west the high hill-top enclosure of Oldbury has produced some evidence of refortification and occupation in the Late Iron Age but excavation has been on too small a scale to gauge its nature.

The Aylesford–Swarling culture of Kent contrasts with that of the Trinovantes/Catuvellauni in that there is little evidence of wealth accumulation in the post-war period. Apart from Aylesford and Swarling rich burials are lacking and neither is of the status of the Welwyn graves. Moreover the Dressel type 1 amphorae, so prolific north of the Thames, are hardly known in Kent. The implication must surely be that in the period following Caesar's campaigns the tribes

Figure 7.13 Distribution of coins of the Iceni (source: Cunliffe 1981b).

of Kent were peripheral to the economic expansion enjoyed by those north of the Thames. It may be that they were deliberately excluded from trading contracts with the Roman province of Gaul because of their violent opposition to Caesar in 55 and 54 BC.

The Iceni (Fig. 7.13)

The territory of the Iceni, as defined by the distribution of their coins, centred upon Norfolk stretching west towards the valley of the Nene. The development of Icenian coinage, outlined in the previous chapter, shows a consistent reliance for inspiration and supply on the Trinovantes/Catuvellauni to the south to the extent that for long periods southern gold was used exclusively, though the tribe continued to mint its own silver, sometimes inspired by styles current among their western neighbours the Corieltauvi. The strong southern influence could be interpreted as political dominance or at the very least, strong social ties with the Trinovantes/ Catuvellauni. Practically nothing is yet known of the settlements of the period, although it appears probable that many of the earlier sites continued to be occupied. Defended enclosures are few and many originate before the first century BC, but at the multivallate fort of Wareham Camp pottery of the immediate pre-Roman period has been found in limited quantity. Other than this, and possibly the continued use of others of the camps, no major defended centre or oppidum is yet known in Icenian territory. However, at Woodcock Hill, Saham Toney, Norfolk a collection of metalwork together with four gold coins and sixty silver issues of the Iceni indicates unusual activity possibly indicative of a large nucleated settlement. The site lies at the junction of the Breckland and the Boulder clay plateau of central East Anglia where a major north–south track crosses a tributary of the river Wissey – a location well suited to a central urban function. However, without excavation the status of the site must remain in doubt.

The material culture of the territory differs little from that of the south-east. The ceramic sequence, as it is at present known, suggests strong influence from the Aylesford–Swarling culture, and in the first century AD Gallo-Belgic imported wares were adopted in limited quantities. The most dramatic aspect of Icenian culture lies, however, in the wealth and display of the ruling classes. The famous hoards from Snettisham, Bawsey and North Creake together contain no less than fifty torcs and arm-rings of gold and electrum (Sealey 1979), while at Santon Downham, Ringstead and Westhall large collections of horse-trappings, including bits, terret-rings, harness mounts, linchpins and other chariot fittings, have come to light. No other tribal area has yet yielded such vivid evidence of opulent aristocratic display. This was the society which, less than twenty years after the Roman invasion, produced the energetic and almost successful war-leader Queen Boudicca.

The Atrebates

The territory of the Atrebates lay, for the most part, south of the Thames covering the modern counties of East and West Sussex, Surrey, Hampshire, Wiltshire and Berkshire. The tribe came first into historical perspective when Commius arrived in Britain to join his people already here, after fleeing from Caesar. Commius was a king of the Gallo-Belgic Atrebates and it was probably from this time onwards that his British followers were known by the tribal name. At the time of the Roman Conquest in AD 43 their chief oppidum was formally named *Calleva Atrebatum* (Silchester). The name of the tribe or tribes over whom Commius established his authority is unrecorded but their identity and approximate location are recorded by the distribution of coin types minted in the period 75–50 BC on which Commius modelled his own issues. These have been called Atrebatic A and B (Van Arsdell 1989) though strictly pre- or proto-Atrebatic would

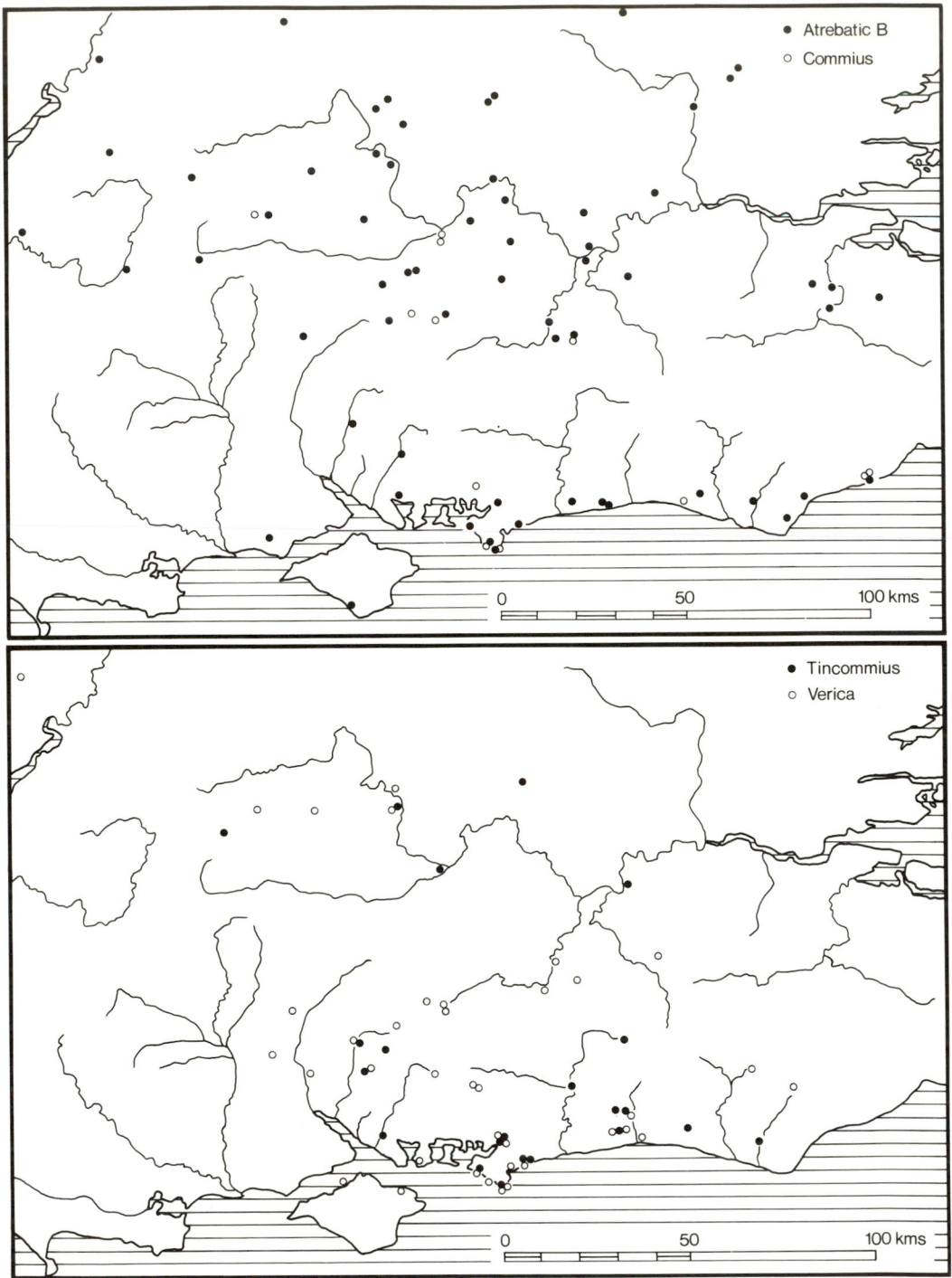

Figure 7.14 Distribution of coins of the Atrebates (source: Cunliffe 1981b).

be a more appropriate term. The distribution of these pre-war types (Figure 7.14) concentrated in the Middle Thames valley, Wiltshire, Berkshire and Hampshire with a scatter along the Sussex coast, whereas the coins of Commius and his successors are found more commonly in the southern part of this region suggesting the possibility that this northern zone – the socio-economic territory based on Dyke Hills, Dorchester-on-Thames – may have been absorbed into the Trinovantian/Catuvellaunian sphere during the Gallic War. Some further incursion into the northern part of Atrebatic territory came in *c*. AD 35 when Epaticcus began minting coins at Calleva. His exact origins are uncertain. Though claiming a legitimate relationship to the Trinovantian/Catuvellaunian royal house, he continued to use an Atrebatic reverse type. However his allegiance is interpreted, the fact remains that the northern marches of Atrebatic territory were unstable. The fluidity of boundaries between the two main power blocks is further shown by the brief ascendancy which the Atrebatic king Eppillus enjoyed over the Cantii between *c*. 5 BC and AD 10 after when he was replaced by the northern king Cunobelin.

The area of the original territory under Commius corresponds closely to the distribution of the saucepan pot wares belonging to the Sussex, Hampshire, Surrey and Wiltshire groups, hinting that some degree of cultural unity may well have existed in the pre-Caesarian period, stretching back into the second or third century BC. It was from this background that the new ceramic traditions of the Atrebates developed. Three new style-zones can be recognized, gradually emerging from indigenous traditions (Figure 7.15). These may be defined as an Eastern group, extending along the Sussex coastal plain and downs approximately to the Arun; a Southern group, covering the rest of Sussex and Hampshire west to the Test; and a Northern group, centring on Salisbury Plain and spreading north to the edge of the Thames valley.

The Eastern group (Figure A:32, p. 585), is characterized by globular jars with a narrow mouth and out-bent rim, some with flat bases and others with foot-rings. Another common type was the jar with a high shoulder, upright or slightly everted rim and a foot-ring base. Decoration was carried out variously with shallow tooling, rouletting, stamping, painting and the addition of applied cordons, to create horizontal zones of swags and arcs, or sometimes simpler rectilinear zones. It is possible to trace many of the forms and decorative elements back to the preceding Late Caburn–Saltdean tradition, but some influence from the Aylesford–Swarling areas of Kent may be thought to be apparent in the foot-ring and cordoned types.

The Southern Atrebatic ceramic style (Figure A:31, p. 584), centred upon Hampshire and west Sussex, is typified by bead-rimmed jars with high shoulders and wide mouths, found together with high-shouldered bowls with simple upright rims, and necked jars often with a cordon at the junction of the neck and body. Less frequent (and occurring only in the first century AD) are local copies of Gallo-Belgic platters and butt-beakers. The Northern assemblage (Figure A:31, p. 584) is similar in many ways, but the bead-rimmed jars are frequently tightly grooved, and ovoid jars which hark back to the saucepan pot phase of the area occur together with rather larger quantities of Gallo-Belgic imports. There is nothing in either the Southern or Northern assemblages to suggest an intrusive element (except, of course, the imported Gallo-Belgic wares, which were presumably the result of trade). All the basic forms and decorative styles were already in existence in the preceding saucepan pot phase, the only difference being that the Atrebatic wares were for the most part wheel-turned. The apparent differences, then, are best explained in terms of the introduction of the technological innovation of the potter's wheel rather than a significant folk movement although it is possible that some 'Belgic' elements may have been introduced by the supposed immigrants arriving before the Caesarian wars.

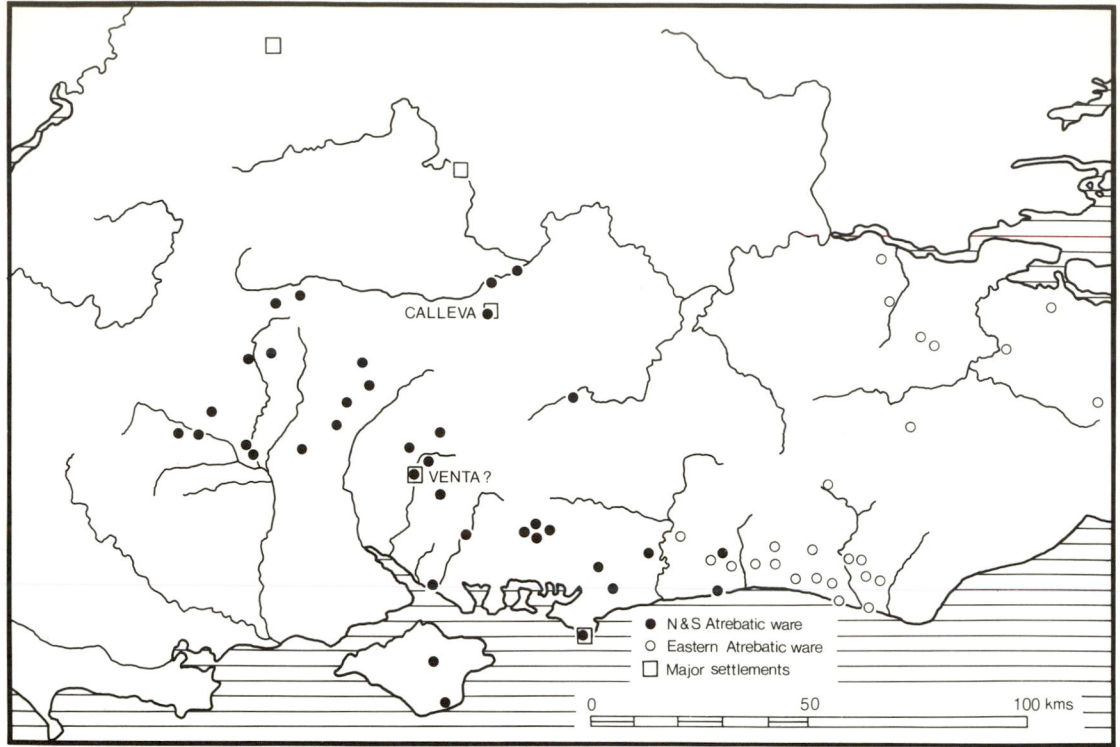

Figure 7.15   Distribution of Atrebatic pottery (source: author).

The three broadly defined ceramic zones probably owe their identity partly to the indigenous folk tradition and partly to the distributional ranges of the production centres, but it is conceivable that the regionalization in the later period also reflects a political fragmentation and realignment. On coin evidence it is possible to postulate the spread of Trinovantian/ Catuvellaunian control over much of the north-west zone, centred particularly upon the valley of the river Kennet. It is in this region that the two south-eastern style burials were discovered, the bucket burial from Marlborough and the barrow cremation at Hurstbourne Tarrant. Furthermore, coins of Tasciovanus and Cunobelin are far more common here than those of the later Atrebatic rulers.

The evidence from East Sussex is less dramatic, but we have already seen that links with the Aylesford–Swarling culture of Kent developed, and to this can be added the fact that a number of Aylesford–Swarling pots are found on the South Downs sites. More impressive, however, is the fate of the hillforts in the first century AD. Several of the East Sussex and Wealden sites, like those of Kent, show evidence of continuous occupation. The impression of unrest, and very probably an anti-Roman outlook, in the east contrasts noticeably with the south-western Atrebatic zone of West Sussex and Hampshire, where not only were the old hillforts abandoned but there is ample historical evidence of a pro-Roman alliance. Some support for the significance of this class of evidence is provided by the parallel situation in the north-west zone, where again many of the hillforts were occupied and some refortified. In summary, it is not unreasonable to suppose that by the time of Verica the northern part of the original kingdom was under the domination of

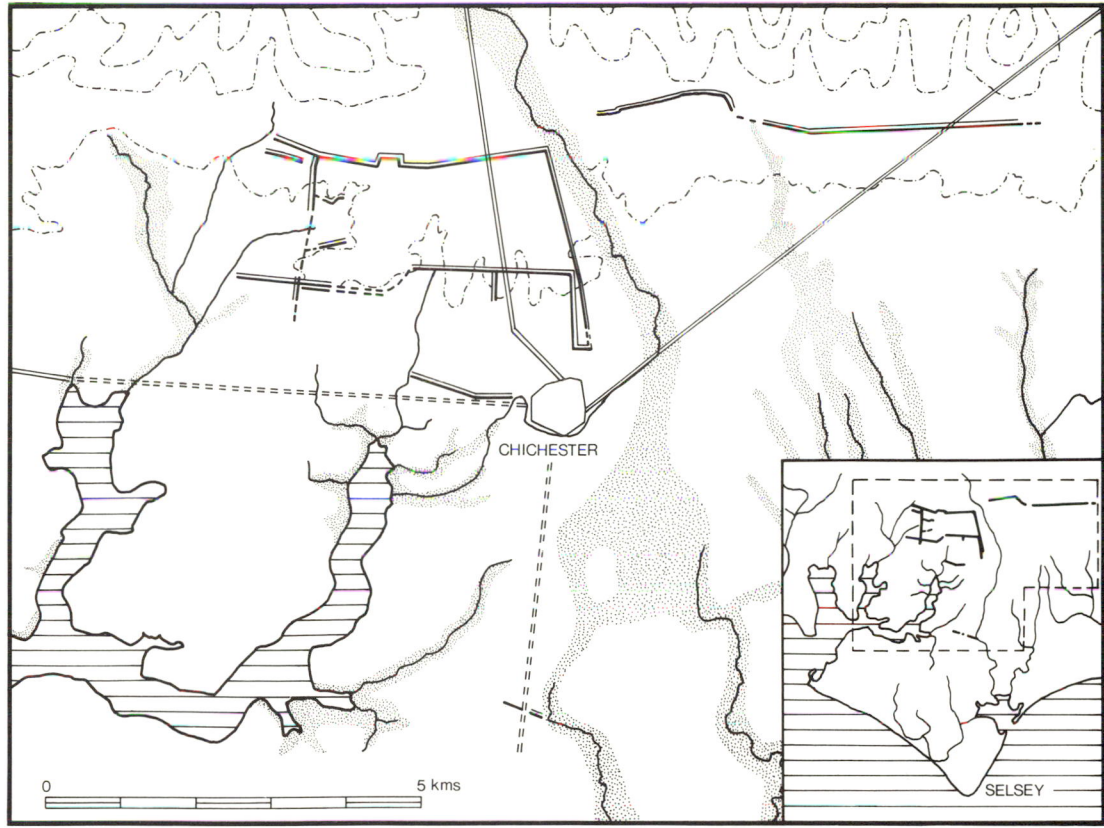

Figure 7.16   The entrenchments in the vicinity of Chichester (source: Bradley 1971a).

dynasts from north of the Thames while the eastern part had realigned itself politically with the Kentish kingdoms, leaving only the central area in the hands of the original dynasty.

The coin evidence suggests that the greater Atrebatic region can be divided into six socio-economic zones in three of which urban settlements are known: *Calleva*, *Venta* and Selsey. In the easternmost zone no convincing centre has yet been identified, unless Castle Hill, Newhaven or the Devil's Dyke once served some central-place function. The Surrey-based zone, centred on the rivers Mole and Wey, is also without a known focus, but in the western zone in Wiltshire there is some evidence to suggest a major centre in the Marlborough district close to the location of the Roman town of *Cunetio*. The nature of the Selsey centre is a matter for some speculation, but in general terms there are marked similarities between this region and the site of Camulodunum. The nucleus of the settlement probably lay in the region of Selsey Bill, where extensive coastal erosion has removed most of the evidence apart from large quantities of coins and fragments of gold washed up on the shore. The entire peninsula is protected by a series of dykes running across the gravel terrace between the valleys of the south-flowing streams, while the lines of the valleys themselves are further strengthened by north–south earthworks (Figure 7.16). The most recent survey (Bradley 1971a) has postulated three major phases of defence protecting progressively smaller territories, but nevertheless the intention throughout was clearly to defend the whole peninsula between the Lavant and the streams flowing into Bosham harbour – that is, to protect the farmland belonging to the oppidum as well as the main nucleated settlement and its satellite farms. It was within the northern part of this territory that the Roman town of Chichester (*Noviomagus Regnensium*) was subsequently built, together with the large palatial building 1.6 km away at Fishbourne, which has tentatively been ascribed to the client king Cogidubnus.

The nucleus of the northern centre, Calleva, was subsequently buried beneath the Roman town of *Calleva Atrebatum* (Silchester) but its existence has long been attested by the discovery of large numbers of Celtic coins together with quantities of pre-Roman pottery, including imported amphorae, Gallo-Belgic wares and Arretine vessels (Boon 1969) and a campaign of excavations beneath the Roman basilica has exposed evidence of the settlement layout (Fulford 1987). The site lies on a tongue of gravel projecting between West End Brook and the Silchester Brook (Figure 7.17). Numerous earthworks exist in the area but all are undated except for the polygonal enclosure for which a construction date in mid-first century BC is argued. If future work supports this then it could reasonably be suggested that the enclosure belongs to the period when Commius was establishing his kingdom in the region. The lengths of massive earthwork which command the approach to the promontory are likely to belong to a subsequent, but pre-Roman, phase. They are similar to the dykes comprising the territorial oppida at Selsey and Camulodunum.

The basilica excavation has defined two major phases of occupation, the first dating to the mid-first century BC, represented by a number of gullies and pits, and the second beginning *c.* 20 BC when a road grid was laid out to serve rectangular timber buildings. This was presumably the capital of Tincommius and Eppillus and it was from here that Eppillus minted his coins with the mint marks *Callev* and *Calle*. The finds recovered show that *Calleva* was a high-status site enjoying quantities of coins and metalwork together with an impressive range of imported pottery.

A preliminary analysis of the pottery has suggested that in the later period *Calleva* shared in the economic systems of eastern Britain, a fact further emphasized by the density of coins of Tasciovanus and Cunobelin in the region. It is tempting to see this as an economic reorientation coming about in the last decades of the first century BC which eventually, *c.* AD 35, led the Trinovantian leader to establish his authority over the region and mint his coins from the capital.

The third oppidum, at *Venta Belgarum* (Winchester), lies largely beneath the Roman town (Figure 14.37, p. 367). Intensive occupation of the valley side began in the second to first century BC during the currency of saucepan pots. At this time a bank and ditch were constructed to enclose on the north, west and south sides an area in excess of 14 hectares. The eastern limit is not known, but it is conceivable that the earthworks simply ran down the hill and terminated on the edge of the marshy river valley. Occupation within the enclosure was probably continuous but by the first half of the first century AD the nucleus had moved further towards the river, where fragments of coin moulds and quantities of Gallo-Belgic pottery suggest a settlement of some importance.

The three Atrebatic oppida so far considered may all have begun to be occupied in the pre-Caesarian period, but their siting and subsequent development show that they were not hillforts in the strict sense of the word. Some earlier hillforts did, however, continue to be maintained (Figure 7.18). At Bury Hill, Hants., the original enclosure was remodelled in bivallate form, while at Boscombe Down West, Wilts., a bivallate enclosure of similar type was constructed towards the middle of the first century AD on a hitherto open settlement site. Chisbury, Wilts., may also belong to this class. Elsewhere in Wiltshire at Yarnbury, Ebsbury,

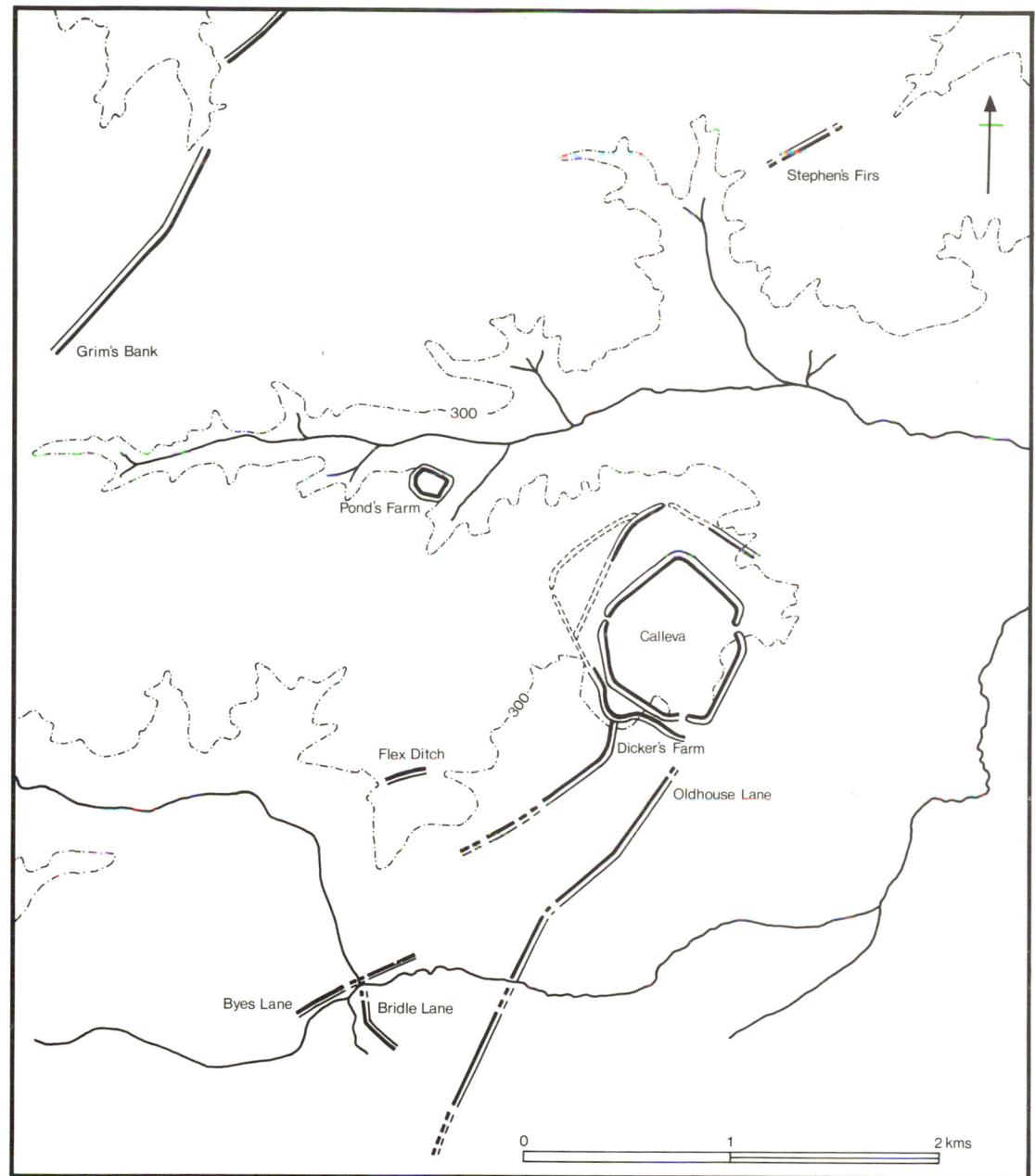

Figure 7.17   The site of Calleva, Hants. (sources: Boon 1969; Fulford 1986).

Oldbury, etc., the earlier defensive circuits continued in use, but nothing is known of the refortification, if any, to which the sites were subjected. In all probability the occupation within these old enclosures was of a domestic kind and need have been little more than peasant farms

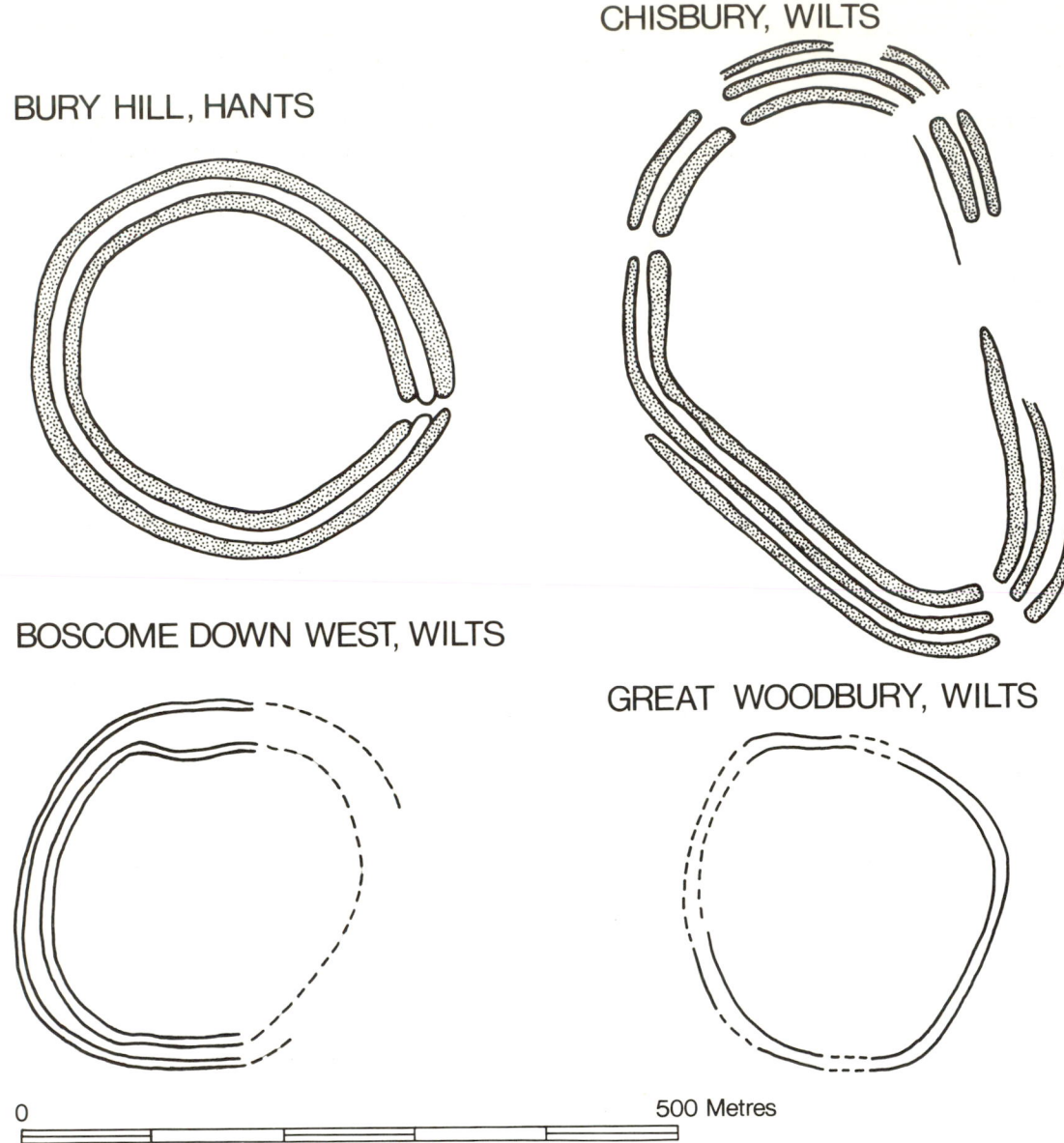

Figure 7.18   Atrebatic enclosures (sources: various).

making use of the old earthworks as convenient boundaries. This was clearly the case at Danebury and Balksbury. The large double ditched enclosures of Boscombe Down West type are altogether different and may represent the residences of the tribal elite: excavation is needed to test this hypothesis.

Rather less is known of the settlement sites of this period, largely because excavations have seldom been on a large enough scale to uncover a reasonable sample of the ground plan, but at Worthy Down and Owslebury in Hampshire and at Casterley in Wiltshire, substantial areas have been exposed, together with sufficient evidence to demonstrate a continuity of occupation from the time of the saucepan pot tradition. These sites are complexes of ditched enclosures designed to create corral space as well as habitation areas (pp. 223–6).

Burial rites within the Atrebatic area varied considerably. At Owslebury and St Lawrence, Isle of Wight, inhumation burials of warriors with their swords and shields were recorded in La Tène III contexts. In the northern part of the region, however, the Trinovantian/Catuvellaunian style of cremation was practised, for example at Marlborough and Hurstbourne Tarrant, and over most of the rest of the area cremation was the general rule. To what extent this represents the gradual spread of the cremation idea from the Aylesford–Swarling cultural area it is difficult at the moment to say.

Summary

In the Late Iron Age the core zone of south-eastern Britain was dominated by two dynastic kingdoms, the Trinovantes/Catuvellauni north of the Thames and the Atrebates (and their immediate predecessors) to the south. Two lesser tribes, the Iceni of Norfolk and the Cantii of Kent, came under the influence of their neighbours. The north–south divide was an unstable one: the numismatic evidence suggests that the northern dynasty established authority over the Middle Thames region and eventually dominated Berkshire and northern Hampshire, and the entire territory of the Cantii. To what extent this expansion of influence was purely economic or involved political dominance it is difficult to say. At any event the classical writers believed that the British tribes were in a state of perpetual warfare and refugees from the various royal households fleeing to the emperor must have encouraged this view.

The cultural development over much of the core area followed similar lines: the skills of the metalworkers increased and there was a marked technical improvement in pottery manufacture with the introduction of the potter's wheel. There is also evidence for the intensification of production not only in pottery-making but in salt extraction on coastal sites and iron-working in the Weald. This increase must, to some extent, have been encouraged by the development of trade with the Continent through the east coast ports. In return luxury goods from the Roman empire poured in and were used in complex patterns of exchange to maintain, and enhance, the status of the aristocracy. The concentration of luxury goods in Essex and Hertfordshire, now preserved mainly in elite burials, provides a clear indication of where the centres of power lay. The Iceni of Norfolk seem to have used a different means of demonstrating status by converting their wealth into gold torcs, though the social mechanisms through which these were consigned to the soil remain obscure.

In the southern zone the Atrebates and the Cantii benefited little from the wealth-generating trade: amphora burials of Welwyn type are unknown and even lower status bucket burials are rare. One possible explanation for this is that in the political settlement which followed Caesar's campaign in Britain, the southern tribes were regarded as hostile and trading monopolies were established to reward Roman allies in eastern Britain. Some such explanation is needed to account for the decline in the wine trade focused at Hengistbury on the Solent coast, and its rapid development, in post-war times, with the Essex coastal ports.

In spite of the apparent disparity in trading opportunities large nucleated settlements (oppida) developed in all parts of the south-east, usually on route nodes where the movement of goods could be more easily controlled. At many of these sites coins were minted and there is evidence of such a range and intensity of activity that we can fairly regard them as serving urban functions. Proto-urban or urban centres and complex systems of coinage involving a set of denominations show that the south-east was fast acquiring a market economy at the moment when Rome struck.

8

The tribes of the periphery: Durotriges, Dobunni and Corieltauvi

In the Late Iron Age the core zone of south-eastern Britain was fringed by three coin-issuing tribes, the Durotriges, the Dobunni and the Corieltauvi, the numismatic history of each of which was quite distinct from that of its neighbours. The gross distribution of coins of these peripheral tribes (Figure 8.2) is interesting. Not only are tribal boundaries quite closely adhered to but remarkably few peripheral coins are found in the core territory. While this could be thought to imply little intercourse between the core and periphery it is far more likely to mean that peripheral coinage was unacceptable in the core territories and was melted down for re-minting. The reverse is less evident and in the territory of the Dobunni and Corieltauvi, Atrebatic and Trinovantian/Catuvellaunian coins are by no means rare. Such issues no doubt had value in intertribal exchanges. The western fringes of the peripheral tribes are far less easy to define since their boundaries are with non-coin-using neighbours. Even so the distribution maps suggest a fairly rapid fall off.

The Durotriges (Figure 8.3)

The Durotriges were a close-knit confederacy of smaller units centred upon modern Dorset. To the east and north their boundaries with the Atrebates seem to have been marked by the Avon and its tributary the Wylye. The New Forest may have formed something of a buffer zone between the two tribes. Further west Durotrigan coins and pottery extend along the valley of the Yeo and Parrett giving the tribe a narrow outlet to the Bristol Channel. The river Brue would approximate to a northern boundary with the Dobunni and it may be that the marsh-edge settlement of Meare served as a market centre on the interface between the two. The western boundary with the Dumnonii lies roughly on the line from the Parrett estuary to the river Axe. The territory thus defined exhibits a considerable degree of cultural unity with marked dissimilarities to the cultures of the neighbouring Dumnonii, Dobunni and Atrebates.

The history of the Durotriges can be divided into two broad phases, an *early phase*, roughly 100–60 BC and a *late phase* from 60 BC until the Roman Conquest. The early phase was a time of

Figure 8.1   The tribes of southern Britain (sources: various).

rapid development brought about by overseas trade while the late phase was a time of retraction, isolation and economic impoverishment.

The background to the development of overseas trade *c.* 100 BC or a little before will be discussed in more detail below (p. 434). Suffice it to say that a major trading axis was established linking the Solent ports of Hengistbury and Poole Harbour to the north Breton trading stations and, through them, to the Atlantic trading network. The most important of the British ports lay on the northern shore of Hengistbury Head overlooking the tranquil waters of Christchurch Harbour (Figures 8.5 and 8.6). Here, within the protection of the double dykes which cut off the neck of the promontory there developed a complex entrepôt with a spacious anchorage, improved by the construction of hards for beaching ships, admirably sited to control the two main river routes into the heart of Wessex. Excavation has shown a concentration of Late Iron Age activity

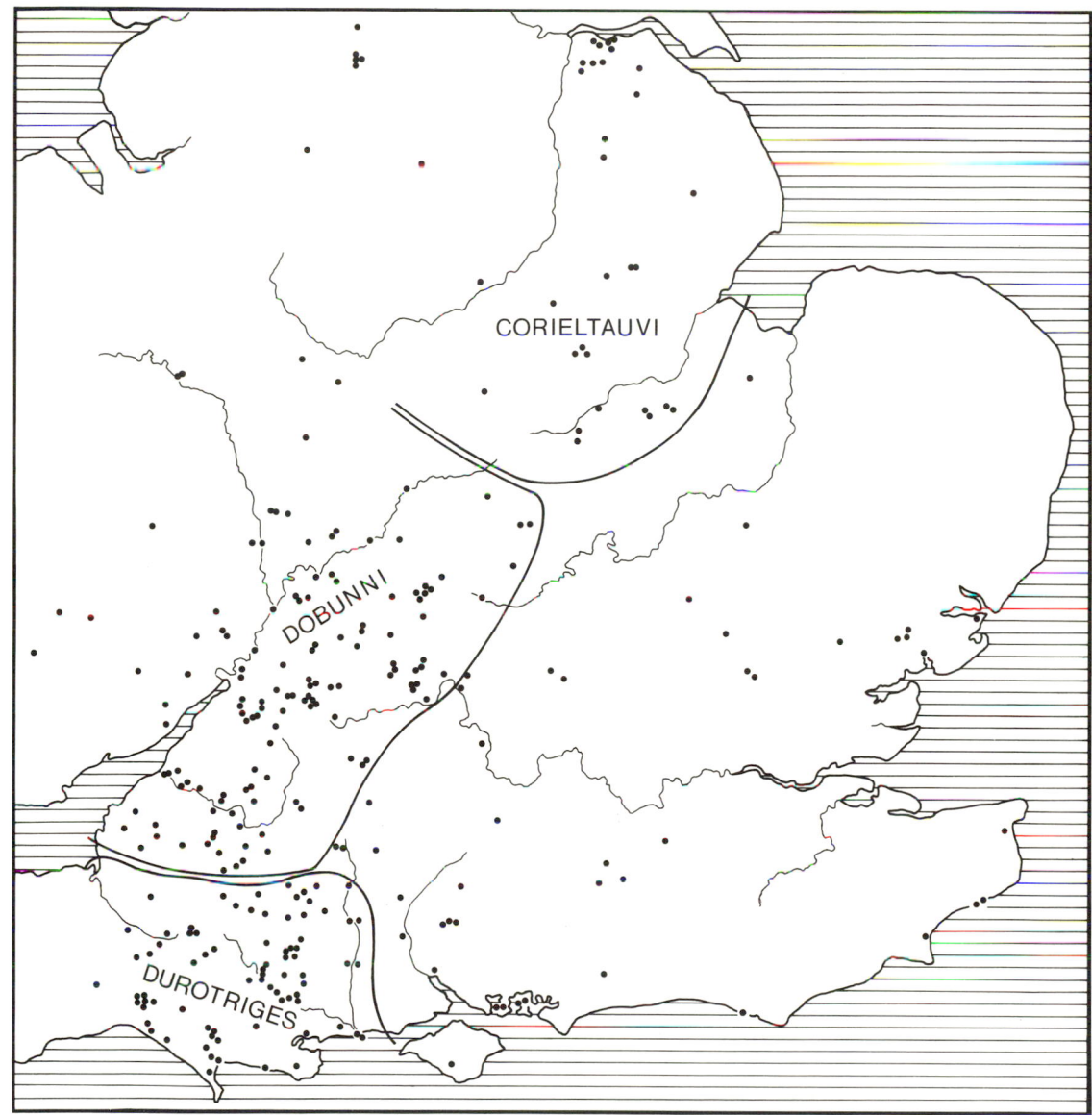

Figure 8.2 Distribution of the coins of the peripheral tribes (source: Cunliffe 1981b).

stretching for a kilometre along the shore. Evidence for long-distance trade comes in the form of large quantities of Dressel 1 amphorae, mostly of the 1A type, in which north Italian wine was imported in the first half of the first century BC. Among the other commodities brought in at this time were raw purple and yellow glass and dried figs: no doubt there were many other luxury goods of a kind which would show no trace in the archaeological record.

The range of commodities amassed for export was considerable. Metals are attested by evidence of smelting and refining. Iron ore was avilable locally from the headland itself. Copper

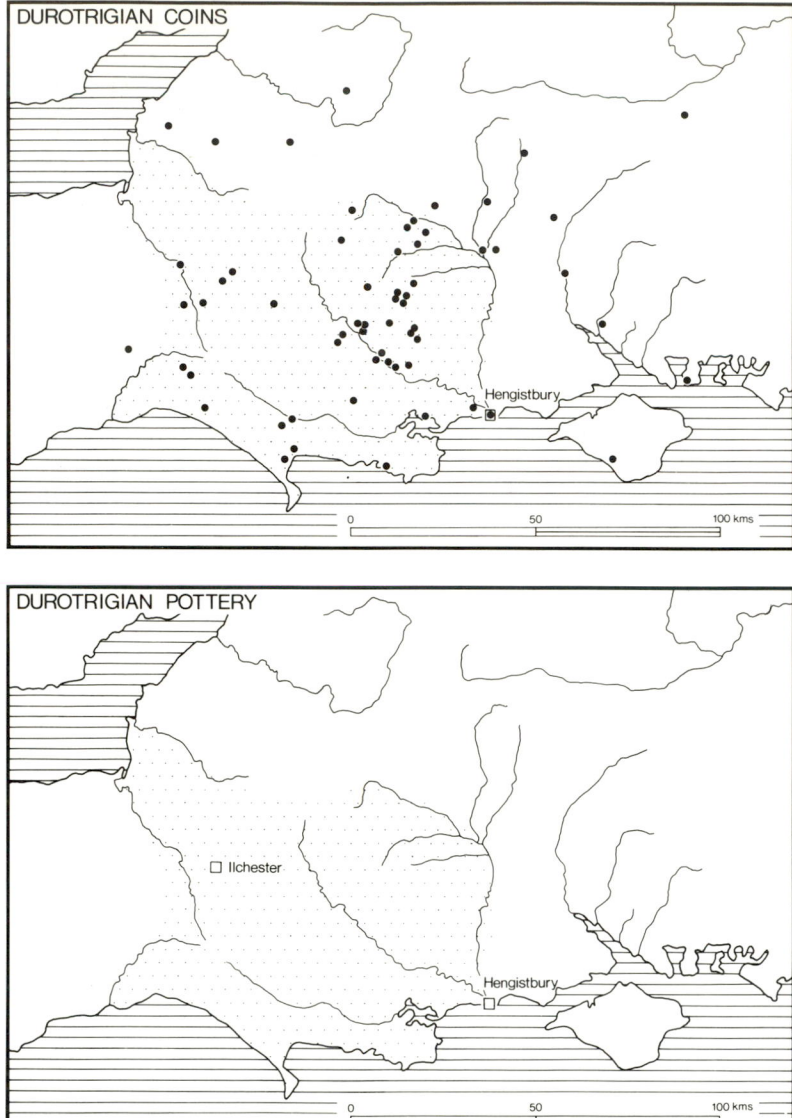

Figure 8.3 The territory of the Durotriges (source: author).

and tin ore were imported from the West Country and were smelted in the same crucibles to make bronze: a massive block of high-silver copper ore from the borders of Dartmoor was recorded weighing 4 kg. High-silver lead from the Mendips was also imported and was refined by cupellation to produce silver, while gold, in the form of scrap, was stockpiled. In addition to the metalworking activity there is evidence to suggest the manufacture of shale armlets, the extraction of salt and the amassing of quantities of grain brought in from the Wessex hinterland. An unexpectedly high percentage of cows' teeth (bones are poorly preserved at the site) could hint at the value of hides and salt meat for export.

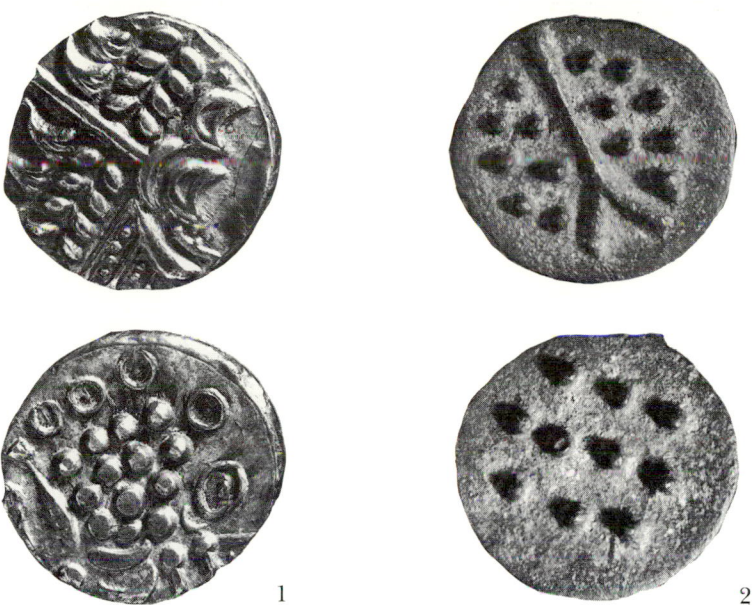

1   2

Figure 8.4   Coins of the Durotriges. 1 Silver stater; 2 cast bronze unit. Twice actual size (photo: Institute of Archaeology, Oxford).

The acquisition of such a range of commodities by those controlling the Hengistbury entrepôt implies well developed trade networks not only with the hinterland of Wessex but further afield to the metal-rich areas of the south-west. The river Stour provided access both to the Mendips and, via the Parrett, to the Bristol Channel and the metal resources of south Wales, while the south coast route conveniently linked the south-west peninsula with its supplies of copper, tin and cattle to the Solent ports. Hengistbury served various functions: it was not only a place where raw materials could easily be collected together for export but it also supported a range of specialists who could add value to the materials by refining them and manufacturing consumer durables.

The southern orientation of Hengistbury's overseas links is amply demonstrated by a range of imported Armorican coins and pottery. Most prolific were coins of the Coriosolites, whose territory lay in the Côte du Nord focused on the estuary of the river Rance. Others came from several north-western French tribes: the Osismii, Namnetes, Aulerci Diablintes, Abricatui and Baiocasses. Large quantities of Armorican pottery were also recovered, principally the black cordoned wares made in the territory of the Coriosolites (Figure A:30, p. 583) but with high percentages of graphite-coated wares and rilled micaceous wares coming from other parts of Brittany. Together this evidence leaves little doubt that the long-distance trade, emanating from the Roman-controlled Mediterranean coast of France, was effected by middle men providing short-haul links between a network of ports along the Atlantic route. Hengistbury's immediate trading partner was evidently the Coriosolites whose principal port lay at St Servin close to St Malo in the Rance estuary.

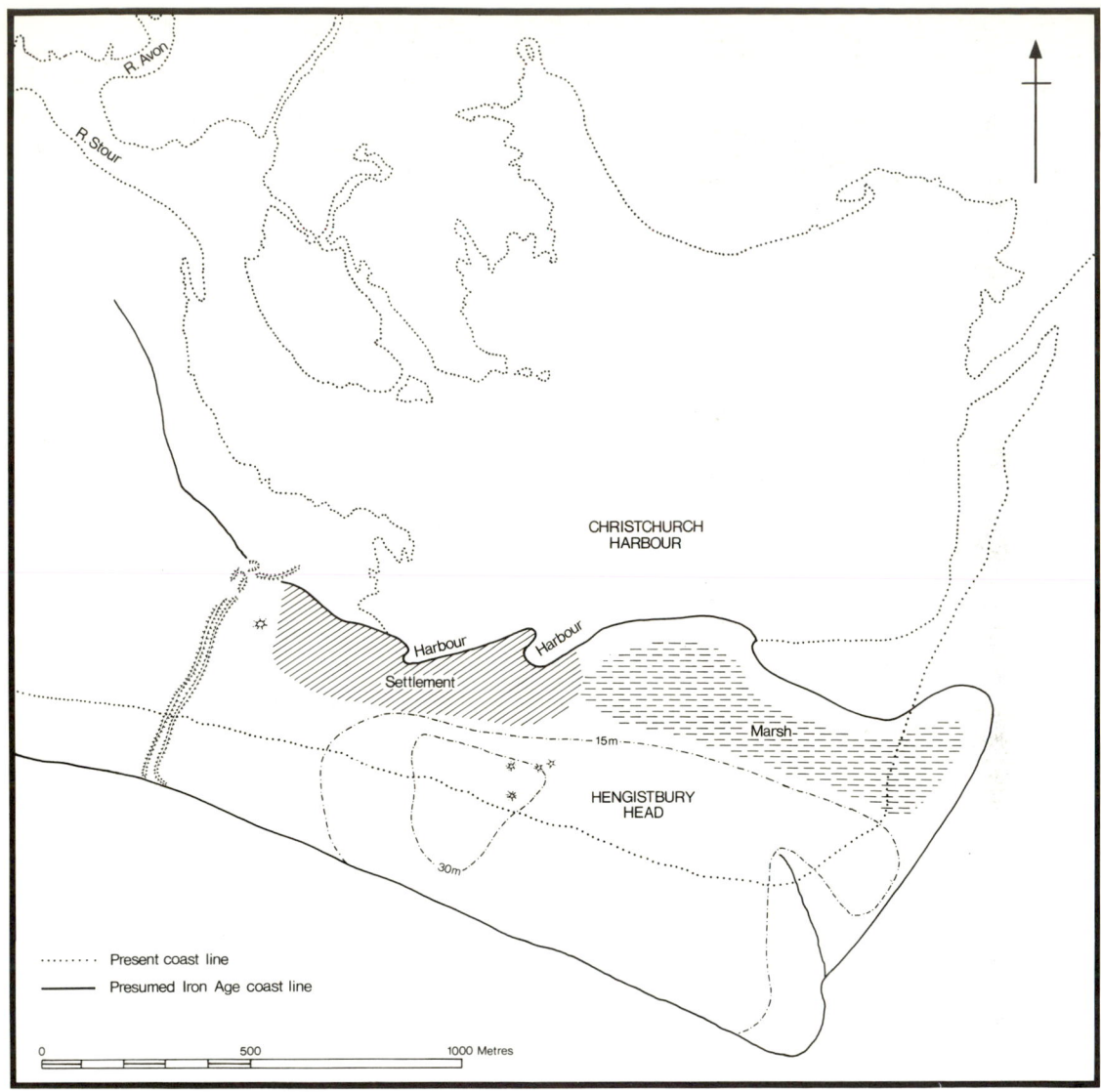

Figure 8.5   Hengistbury Head, Dorset (source: Cunliffe 1987).

The archaeological evidence from Hengistbury suggests that after the middle of the first century BC trade along the Atlantic route dwindled dramatically and all but dried up. The immediate reason was probably Caesar's harsh treatment of the Armorican tribes in 56 BC following their rebellion but in the long term the virtual monopoly of overseas trade which the tribes of eastern Britain seem to have captured provides a plausible explanation. The Gallic War therefore marks the end of the period of Durotrigan prosperity and heralds nearly a century of economic and cultural isolation. This is well demonstrated by the history of Durotrigan coinage. In the decades immediately before the Caesarian campaigns a gold standard had been adopted

Figure 8.6 Aerial view of Hengistbury Head, Dorset (photo: K. Hoskins).

and was maintained during the early stages of the war for external trade, but already, for local use, a debased coinage of white gold was being produced. Immediately after the war the coinage was further debased: the gold content soon disappeared altogether and then the percentage of silver began to be reduced until about 30 BC, by which time the issues were entirely of bronze. Along with this economic collapse came growing cultural isolation.

One effect of the brief period of overseas trade was to introduce into Durotrigan territory an improved ceramic technology involving the potter's wheel. At first copies of imported north-west French black cordoned wares were made for internal trading purposes but soon a wide range of types was being produced. The local assemblage is distinctive and shows little regional differentiation (Figure A:33, p. 586). The commonly occurring forms include shallow bowls with straight or slightly convex sides, a bead lip and a foot-ring base; high-shouldered bead-rimmed bowls; necked bowls; large jars with or without countersunk handles; handled tankards; and occasionally tazze. Decoration is usually restricted to simple wavy lines, cross-hatched zones and sometimes the use of dots or rouletting. With very few exceptions, the forms can all be traced back to traditions current in the area in the preceding period, the main difference being that much of the material was now wheel-finished. A few of the vessels, like the tankards, probably developed as copies of metal or wood-and-metal containers while others, such as the necked bowls and tazze, may well have been inspired by imported north-western French types. The general impression given by Durotrigan ceramics is that production was now largely centralized: fabric analysis has suggested that the main centre lay in the vicinity of Poole Harbour.

Unlike the Atrebatic and the Aylesford–Swarling regions, where large newly built oppida surrounded by defensive dykes played an increasingly important part in centralizing political power, in the Durotrigan territory trends towards urbanization remained focused on the old hillforts. At Maiden Castle, the 18 hectare enclosure was tidied up, streets were metalled and defences maintained in good order, while the close-packed houses continued to be inhabited and rebuilt. An even more impressive demonstration of a Late Iron Age nucleated settlement is the fort on Hod Hill (Figure 8.7). Within its 21 ha fortified area, the one wedge-shaped quadrant which has escaped modern ploughing is covered with traces of small circular huts, some of them with annexed enclosed yards and many associated with storage pits. Spacing tends to be haphazard but several well-defined street lines can be traced. While it is evident even from the ground survey that not all the huts were in use at the same time, selective excavation has shown that many were occupied during the last decades before the Roman invasion. The excavated sample is not large enough to permit firm conclusions but it indicates a rapid increase in resident population after c. 50 BC, developing into what can only be described as a town by the time of the invasion.

The individual houses were each built within a penannular drainage ditch c. 9–10.5 m in diameter (Figure 8.8). The superstructure consisted simply of a circular setting of upright posts set into the natural chalk and packed around with a low wall of chalk rubble, giving a living area of up to 6 m in diameter unimpeded by central supports. Many of the huts seem to have been provided with a cupboard immediately inside the door on the left-hand side, where weapons could be placed. In two of the huts this space was occupied by a bag of slingstones, and presumably the sling; in another it contained a group of harness-fittings; while in the fourth a spear was placed in the same position. Several of the huts were set within an attached yard, defined by an arc-shaped ditch and low bank. In the case of hut 56 the enclosure housed a rectangular stable suitable for two or three horses, with a space beside it adequate for parking a cart.

Hut 36 was unusual in that it lay in the corner of a sub-rectangular palisaded enclosure some 21 m across, the rest of the enclosed area containing timber structures of undefined form. Since it was this hut that appears to have been singled out for bombardment by Roman ballistae at the time of the invasion, the excavator may well be correct in his assumption that it was a chieftain's residence (Richmond 1968). Its siting, in a prominent position close to the main street which ran towards the principal gate of the fort, is indicative of its importance.

Maiden Castle and Hod Hill are not unique among the Dorset forts. Hambledon Hill, for example, appears from a ground survey to have been equally as densely occupied as Hod, and the recent work at South Cadbury, Somerset, has demonstrated a similar urban aspect in the immediate pre-Roman period when the old Middle Iron Age defences were refurbished. The evidence is now sufficiently strong to leave little doubt that many, if not most, of the Durotrigan forts were in active use in AD 43; it was, after all, across this territory that Vespasian had to force his way, destroying one hillfort after another.

Localized defence based on the forts does not necessarily mean that all the forts were permanently occupied on a large scale. It could be argued that the countryside population fled to the protection of the defences only when the threat of Roman attack occurred; indeed, it would be

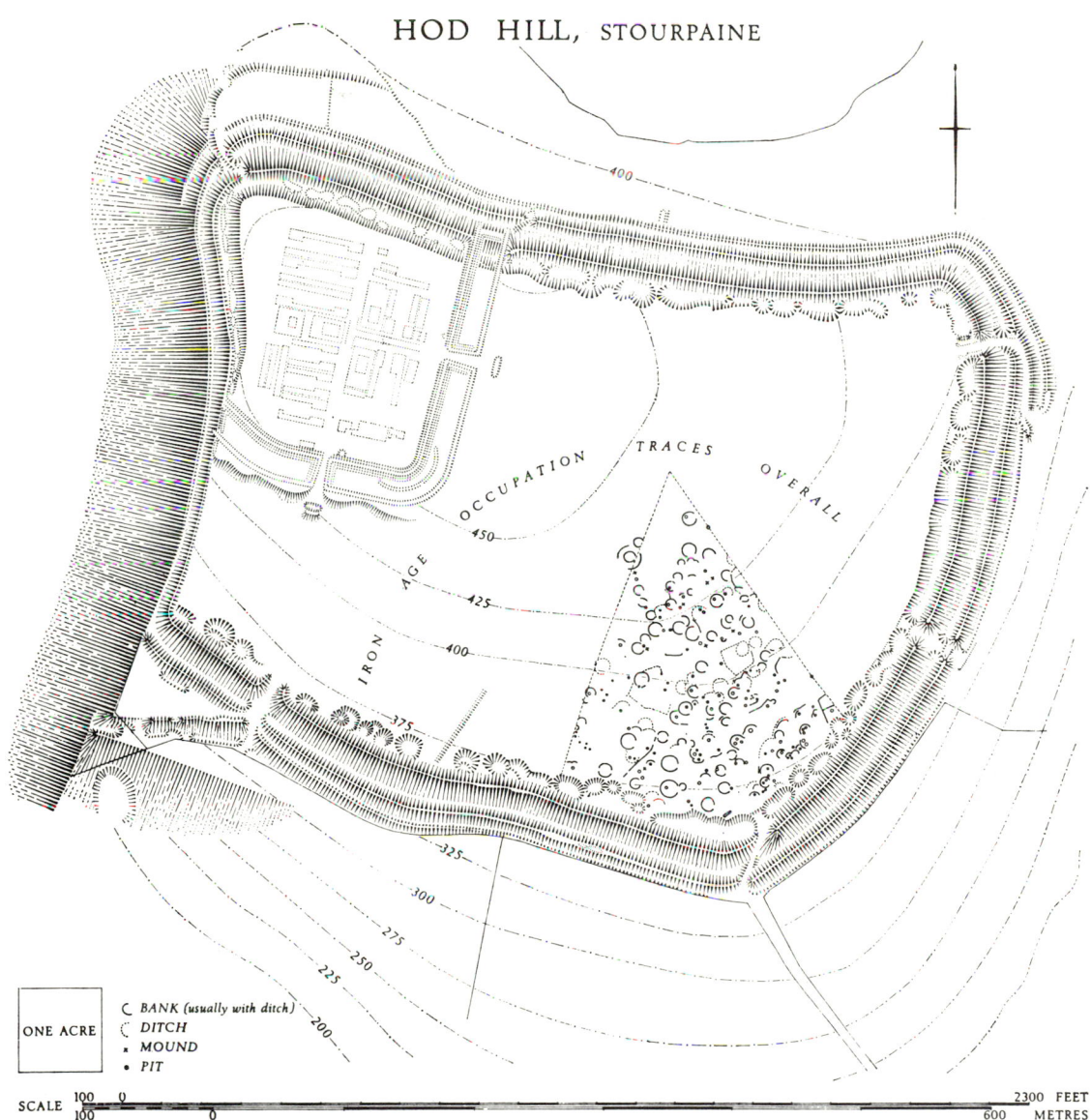

Figure 8.7 Hod Hill, Dorset (source: reproduced from *RCHM Dorset* vol. iii).

surprising if some such movement did not take place, swelling the population within. Just to the north of Maiden Castle air photography and limited excavation has demonstrated a very considerable undefined settlement of Late Iron Age date. It could well be that this was now the centre of nucleated population leaving the old hillfort only sparsely occupied but conveniently close to be used and refortified in times of danger.

The possibility of a general movement from hillforts to valley locations is further suggested by the recognition of what may be an enclosed oppidum at Wincepool Meadow in the vicinity of

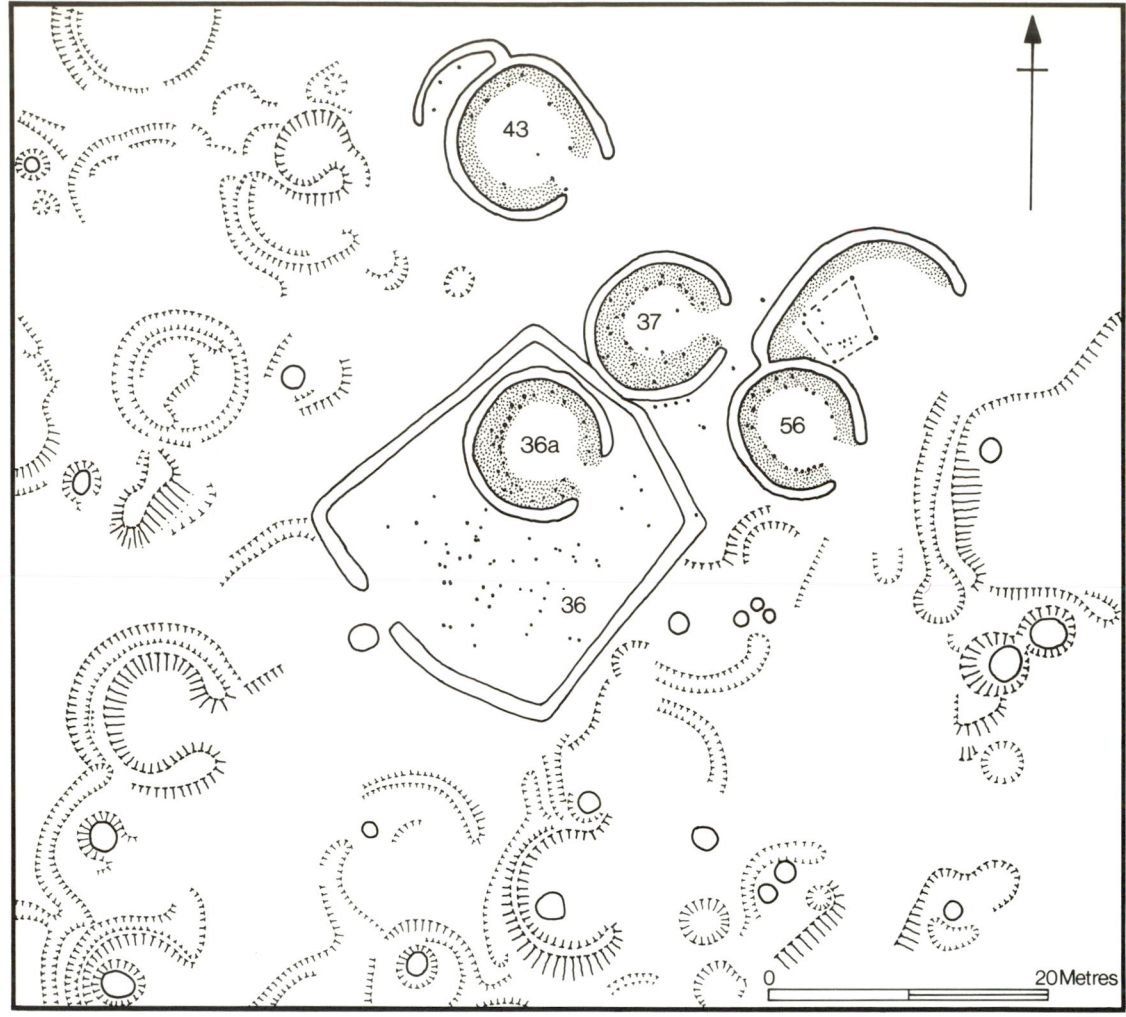

Figure 8.8 Interior settlement at Hod Hill, partly excavated (source: Richmond 1968).

Ilchester 6 km north of the hillfort of Ham Hill (Figure 8.9). Without excavation however it is difficult to say more of the potential relationship of the two sites.

The nature of Durotrigan settlement in the countryside is best demonstrated by four sites, all in Cranborne Chase: Tollard Royal, Rotherley, Woodcuts and Gussage All Saints (Figure 12.7, p. 224). Of these Tollard Royal provides the clearest picture, partly because it has been totally excavated and partly because it was not encumbered by a Roman phase of occupation. The economy of the farm lies well within the tradition of downland and mixed farming stretching back to the second millennium and must represent a typical homestead farm worked by a single family. The adjacent farms of Rotherley and Woodcuts are in much the same tradition, but would appear to represent somewhat larger establishments, perhaps holdings belonging to extended families (C.F.C. Hawkes 1948). The early date of these excavations and the subsequent

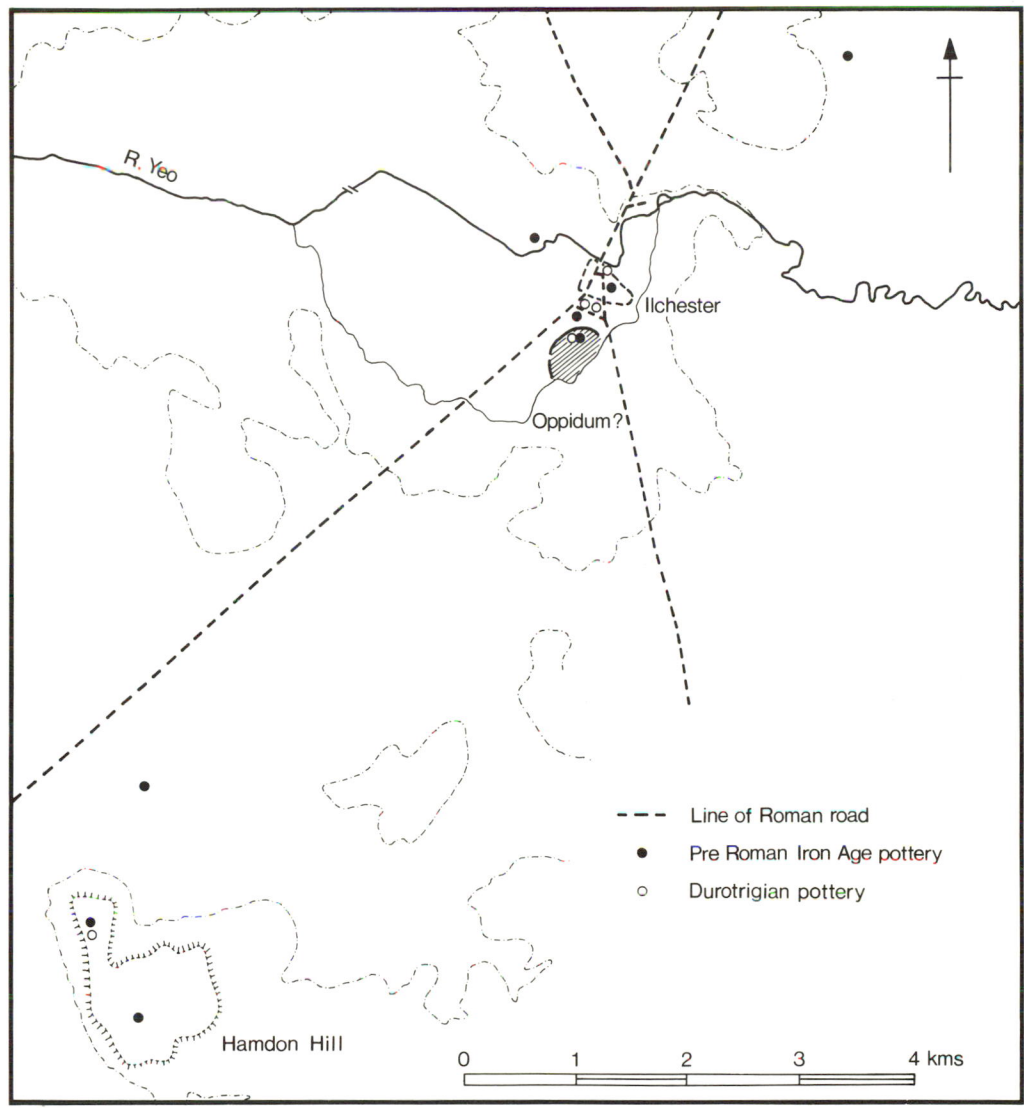

Figure 8.9 Late Iron Age settlement in the vicinity of Ilchester, Somerset (source: Leach and Thew 1985).

Roman occupation prevents a more detailed assessment of the Iron Age phase of settlement. However, at Gussage All Saints, the near total excavation of an Iron Age enclosure has provided an impressive example of a farmstead beginning life in the Early Iron Age and continuing in use until the Roman period. There is a marked contrast between the large ditched enclosure of the Early–Middle Iron Age and the cluster of small enclosures, so typical of Late Iron Age farms, which replaced it. The change must imply some shift in the socio-economic systems underlying settlement pattern but these are at present difficult to discern.

The aspects of Durotrigan culture so far considered owe practically nothing to influences derived from the Aylesford–Swarling culture of the south-east. This regionalism is further demonstrated by the continuance of the rite of inhumation, not only until the invasion but for sometime afterwards. The famous war cemetery at Maiden Castle provides dramatic evidence for burial ritual in the hours following the Roman attack. The dead, thirty-eight of them, were all interred, somewhat hurriedly to judge by the positions of the bodies, but many of them were provided with a ritual meal contained in a pottery vessel placed beside the body in the grave. Rather less ceremony attended the mass burial at Spettisbury, where more than eighty bodies were thrown into a single pit, but this may conceivably have been a Roman tidying-up operation after a battle rather than an example of native burial practice.

The only two rich burials from the Durotrigan area were also inhumations. One, from Whitcombe near Dorchester, was the burial of a male warrior complete with sword, spear, La Tène II fibula, strap-rings, a spindle whorl and a hammer; the other, from West Bay near Bridport, was probably a female burial but all that remained were a few human bones, a pot and the handle of a mirror, exposed in a cliff-fall. Both lie within the traditions practised over much of southern Britain and appear to owe little to any particular regional culture or to intrusive elements.

While it is true to say that Durotrigan culture developed in its own characteristic way, little influenced by its eastern neighbours, trading contacts were nevertheless maintained. The production of armlets and vessels of Kimmeridge shale became a not inconsiderable cottage industry on the Isle of Purbeck (Calkin 1949). Both finished products and raw shale were exported over some distance, to the Trinovantian/Catuvellaunian area, for example – where it was turned into the elegant pedestal urns and tazze found in several of the rich burials. Salt-extraction too, which had already begun in the early part of the pre-Roman Iron Age, continued along much of the Dorset coast (Farrar 1963; 1975) no doubt as a specialized commercial enterprise. Yet in spite of this the Durotriges remained an isolated body, with an impoverished coinage, showing no signs of wealth accumulation or the emergence of an elite. When the Romans arrived in AD 43 they were unified in their hostility but fought piecemeal and were easily overcome.

The Dobunni (Figure 8.10)

The distribution of Dobunnic coinage places the nucleus of the tribal territory in Gloucestershire, extending into north Somerset, down to the river Brue, north and west Wiltshire, Oxfordshire, west of the Cherwell, and most of Worcestershire. The full extent of this area is defined by the earliest uninscribed gold coinage (Dobunnic A) and continued to be the Dobunnic nucleus until the Roman Conquest (D.F. Allen 1961b).

The Dobunni introduced their own coinage in about 35 BC adopting stylistic motifs from the Atrebates whose issues they had previously been content to use (Figure 8.11). Gold was not plentiful at first but silver was comparatively abundant. In about 30 BC the first of the inscribed staters appeared, bearing the name of CORIO. Then followed a succession of rulers: BODVOC (c. 15–10 BC), ANTED (c. 10 BC–AD 10), COMUX (c. AD 10–15), EISU (AD 15–30) and CATTI (AD 15–43). This sequence, proposed by Van Arsdell (1989) on the basis of a recent detailed study, is at variance with that put forward by D.F. Allen (1961b) (upon which Hawkes based a complex

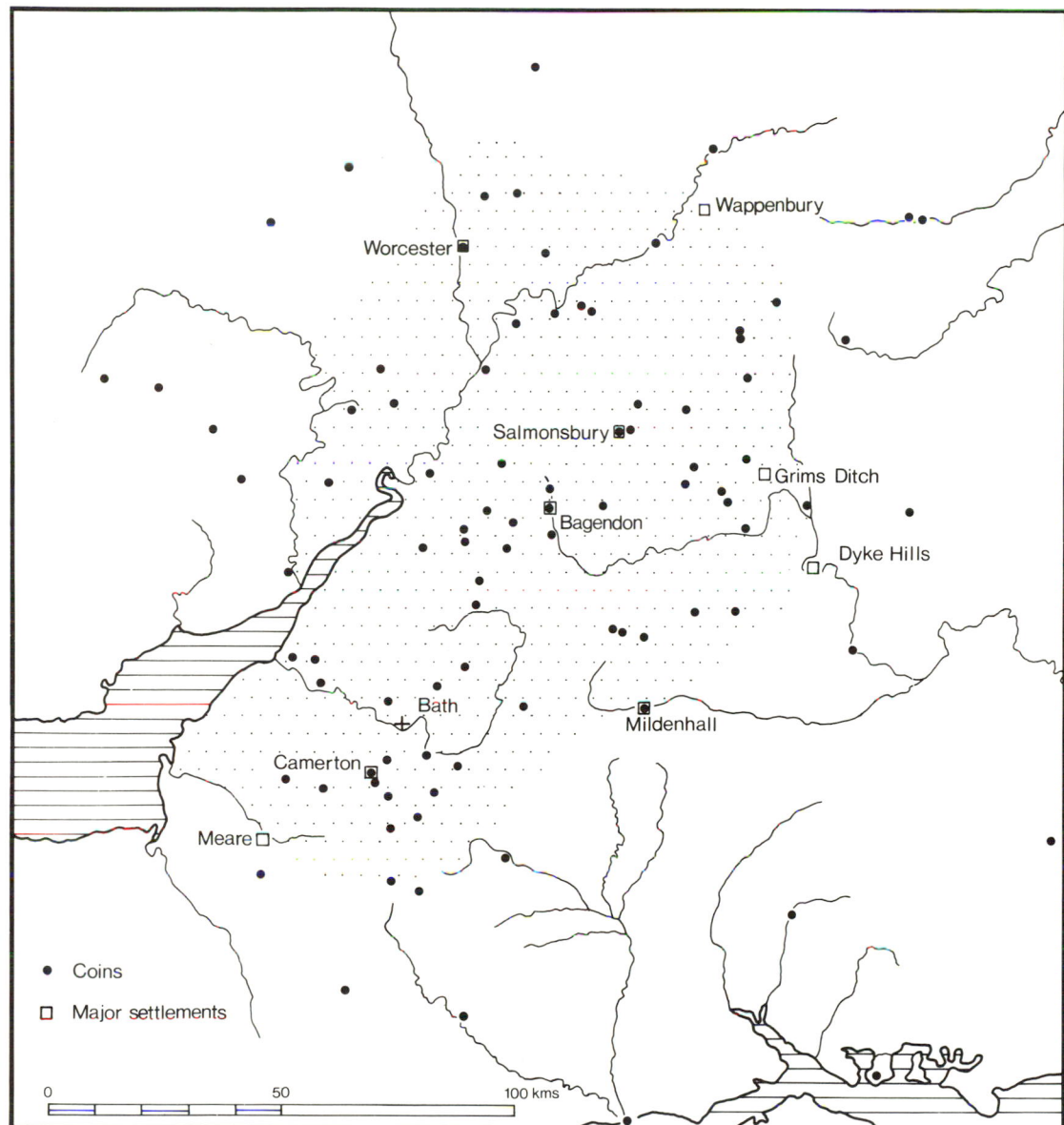

Figure 8.10   The territory of the Dobunni (source: author).

historical interpretation (C.F.C. Hawkes 1961), now best abandoned). Allen originally argued that the Dobunni were split in their last decades of independence into two kingdoms one based on Gloucestershire and the other on north Somerset. While the details of the argument are no longer valid, it is true that the coin distribution in general falls into two clusters, roughly separated by the Bristol Avon, and may therefore reflect two power centres within the single tribal territory.

Figure 8.11   Coins of the Dobunni. 1 Uninscribed silver unit; 2 Bodvoc, silver unit. Twice actual size (photo: Institute of Archaeology, Oxford).

A similar twofold division can be traced in the native pottery and its distribution in the first century BC (Figures 4.6, p. 80 and 4.8, p. 84). North of the Bristol Avon the principal types included jars and saucepan pot shapes decorated with a zone of either linear tooling or stamping below the rim, types which petrological examination (Peacock 1968) has shown were manufactured in the Malvern area and exported widely, not only to the communities of the Cotswolds but also to the basically aceramic communities further west in the Welsh borderland (Figure 4.6, p. 80). The form and style of decoration places these stamped and linear-tooled wares firmly within the saucepan pot tradition of the south. Indeed, it is possible to see over this entire area a convergence of development which could only have occurred had the Severn region been in close contact with the south. It is therefore surely no coincidence that it was over precisely this area that gold staters, based on the triple-tailed horse types of the Atrebates, rapidly spread following Caesar's campaigns.

The north Somerset region, on the other hand, was developing a totally different style of ceramics, growing ultimately out of a linear-tooled saucepan pot tradition and influenced partly by technological developments in the Durotrigan area, but involving a new and vigorous art style which derived some inspiration at least from the ceramics of Cornwall (Figure 4.8, p. 84). This Somerset version of South-Western Decorated Ware is characterized by necked bowls, saucepan pots and simple bead-rimmed jars, the best of which are decorated with elaborate curvilinear or geometric designs carried out in shallow tooling, frequently incorporating areas of cross-hatching. Most of the Somerset South-Western Decorated Wares were made from clays incorporating grit fillers derived from the Old Red Sandstone, Mendip limestone or Jurassic limestone, all of north Somerset origin (Peacock 1969, 43; 1979).

To what extent the two ceramic styles represent cultural differences is difficult to say. At the very least, however, they must reflect discrete spheres of social or commercial contact. Taken

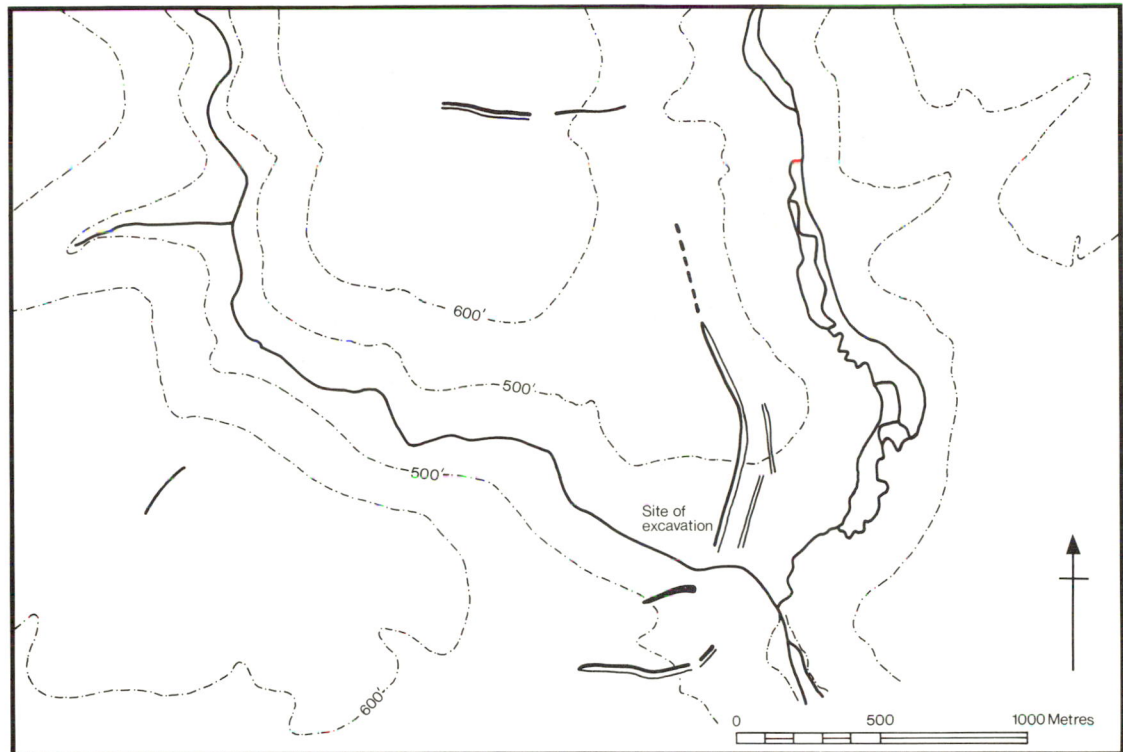

Figure 8.12   The siting of Bagendon, Glos. (source: Clifford 1961).

together with the numismatic evidence mentioned above, it could be argued that both areas retained a degree of identity throughout.

It is impossible at present to say how long the indigenous traditions of pottery manufacture remained dominant. Wheel-turned south-eastern types occurred to the exclusion of earlier types at Bagendon, Glos., in the first century AD, while at several sites (including Meare, Camerton and Kingsdown Camp in Somerset, and Salmonsbury in Gloucestershire) these south-eastern varieties replace the local types within the decades immediately before the invasion. The overall impression given by the present state of our knowledge is that acculturation was slow and patchy, particularly in Somerset, but that ceramics of south-eastern type were being introduced into the east Cotswolds soon after the beginning of the first century AD. Even so, in many areas of the Dobunnic territory native traditions may have continued until the region was eventually subdued in the years following AD 43.

The apparent dual focus reflected in the distribution of pottery and coins strongly suggests the presence of two 'urban' centres. The northern centre was at Bagendon, a promontory of about 80 ha partly encircled by linear ditches (Figure 8.12). At one location excavations have defined evidence of occupation commencing at the beginning of the first century AD and continuing until the 60s, by which time the civilian settlement at the Roman town of Cirencester, 5 km to the south-east, was under way. Although the exact nature and extent of the occupation remains to be defined, evidence for metalworking and the minting of coins, together with the relatively large quantity of Gallo-Belgic imported pottery, strongly suggests an important settlement, perhaps a tribal oppidum in south-eastern style.[1]

The location of the southern centre is less certain but there is some evidence to suggest Camerton where an impressive array of coins, metalwork and Late Iron Age pottery has come to light over the years. Nor should the possibility of secondary markets within the territory or close to the borders be overlooked. We have already suggested that Meare may have served such a function on the southern border with the Durotriges (see below, p. 242) while at Worcester a massive defensive ditch was found beneath the town and Iron Age coins cluster in the vicinity. An enclosed oppidum, here on the river Severn, could have served as a focus for articulating exchange between the Dobunni and the neighbouring Cornovii. Other possible border markets include Wappenbury in the Avon valley, Dyke Hills on the Thames and Mildenhall on the Kennet. Another centre, well within the territory, is Salmonsbury on the river Windrush. Here a substantial defended enclosure was constructed conforming to the type defined as an enclosed oppidum. It was admirably sited to control movement from the Thames valley, through the Cotswolds, to the Severn valley. Finally there is the massive system of linear earthworks known as the North Oxfordshire Grim's Ditch lying on the edge of the Cotswolds between the rivers Glyme and Evenlode. While a Late Iron Age date seems probable the function of the system remains unknown but its location, close to the supposed boundary between the Dobunni and the Trinovantes/Catuvellauni (at least in their latest stage of political expansion), is suggestive of a border function.

One further site might be considered here – the sacred spring at Bath. The hot water gushing out of the ground close to the valley bottom cannot have failed to have attracted attention. The recent excavation has shown that the spring was slightly modified in the pre-Roman period so that people could approach the centre to throw offerings, including coins, into the water. The sacred location was given added significance by virtue of its position commanding an excellent crossing point on the river Avon dividing the northern Dobunni from the southern group.

In the remoter areas, hillforts probably continued in use for some time – actively defended, if the evidence for massacres at Bredon Hill, Worcs., and Worlebury, Somerset, is considered to be of this period; but outside the Cotswolds there is little trace of late refortification in the first century AD. This may, however, be due more to the lack of excavation than to lack of continued occupation.

A number of smaller settlements are known but very few have been extensively excavated. Langford Downs., Oxon, however, offers a fairly complete plan of a small farmstead of the first century AD lying on the extreme eastern fringes of the territory. Here two adjacent ditched enclosures both appear to have protected broadly contemporary circular huts, but the full extent of the enclosures could not be traced. Similarities lie with the complex ditched enclosures of the Atrebatic area. Claydon Pike in the Upper Thames valley conforms to the same general type though is more extensive (Figure 12.12, p. 232). At Butcombe in Somerset, on the north flank of the Mendips, a farm of about this date has been excavated, yielding evidence of circular huts and associated pits of the late pre-Roman Iron Age. These belong to the first phase of a farming settlement which continued in occupation well into the Roman period.

The burial practices of the Dobunni are known from relatively few sites. At Barnwood, Glos., a cemetery containing a single inhumation together with a small cremation group suggests a mixture of traditions not necessarily contemporary. The survival of inhumation is further demonstrated by the Birdlip cemetery, Glos., where at least four inhumations were found in stone-lined graves covered by slabs of limestone and buried beneath cairns of stone 1.2–1.5 m high. The principal burial was of a female who was provided with an impressive array of grave-goods, including two bronze bowls, a silver brooch plated with gold, a bronze mirror, a necklace of amber, jet and stone, an animal-headed knife, a tubular bronze bracelet and four bronze rings.

With so little evidence to go on it would be unwise to speculate too far, but the survival of the inhumation rite, here as among the Durotriges, points to a strong indigenous tradition largely unaffected by the Aylesford–Swarling culture of the south-east. The whole question of the relationship of the Dobunni to the Catuvellauni is a difficult one to untangle. While the intricate political history based on Allen's interpretations of the coinage (C.F.C. Hawkes 1961) can no longer be sustained in detail, the coin evidence does suggest close relations with the Atrebates at first but with an increasing Catuvellaunian involvement beginning in the early years of the first century AD. The changes in the ceramic technology in the northern Dobunnic area, and the appearance of increasing quantities of Gallo-Belgic imports, again point to direct contact with the east of Britain in the last few decades before the invasion. The evidence could be interpreted as little more than an intensification of trading contacts but the possibility of some form of political domination cannot be ruled out. After all Dio Cassius was of the view that the Dobunni were subservient to the Catuvellauni at the time of the conquest.

The Corieltauvi (Fig. 8.13)

The territory of the Corieltauvi, as defined by the distribution of their coinage, lay between the rivers Trent and Nene, with a southern border with the Dobunni somewhere to the south of Leicester. The tribe used to be known as the Coritani but the name has been corrected in the light of new epigraphic evidence (Tomlin 1983).

The coinage of the Corieltauvi shows vigorous and continuous development throughout the period from about 70 BC to the time of the conquest, with the first dynastic name, VEP, appearing about 10 BC. Thereafter two or three names were commonly inscribed representing joint rulers or magistrates or else a combination of personal names and mint name. The standard of the gold issue was carefully maintained throughout the Gallic War but was eventually reduced to bring it into line with the issues of the southern tribes and by the end of the war the tribe, like those of the core area, had begun to strike silver to complement the gold, the first issue being based on the style of a contemporary Roman denarius. This would have facilitated trade not only between the tribes of eastern Britain but also with the Continent.

The ceramic sequence in the region is comparatively well understood from three excavated assemblages, from Ancaster Gap, Old Sleaford and Dragonby (Elsdon 1975; Elsdon and May 1987). Three phases can be distinguished. In the earliest the fine ware vessels were hand-made or wheel-finished with highly burnished surfaces. Many were decorated with horizontal zones, usually on the shoulders, infilled with geometric or lightly curvilinear designs executed with a roulette wheel and with shallow tooling enhanced with triple impressed dimples. There is considerable variety and the earliest of the pottery from Dragonby differs in detail from the other two sites but can be regarded as belonging to the same broad tradition. The dating of this early assemblage cannot be defined precisely but it probably began in the second century BC and continued until about the time of the Gallic War. The second phase, which develops from the first, is characterized by a greater use of the potter's wheel and an increasing uniformity in fabric

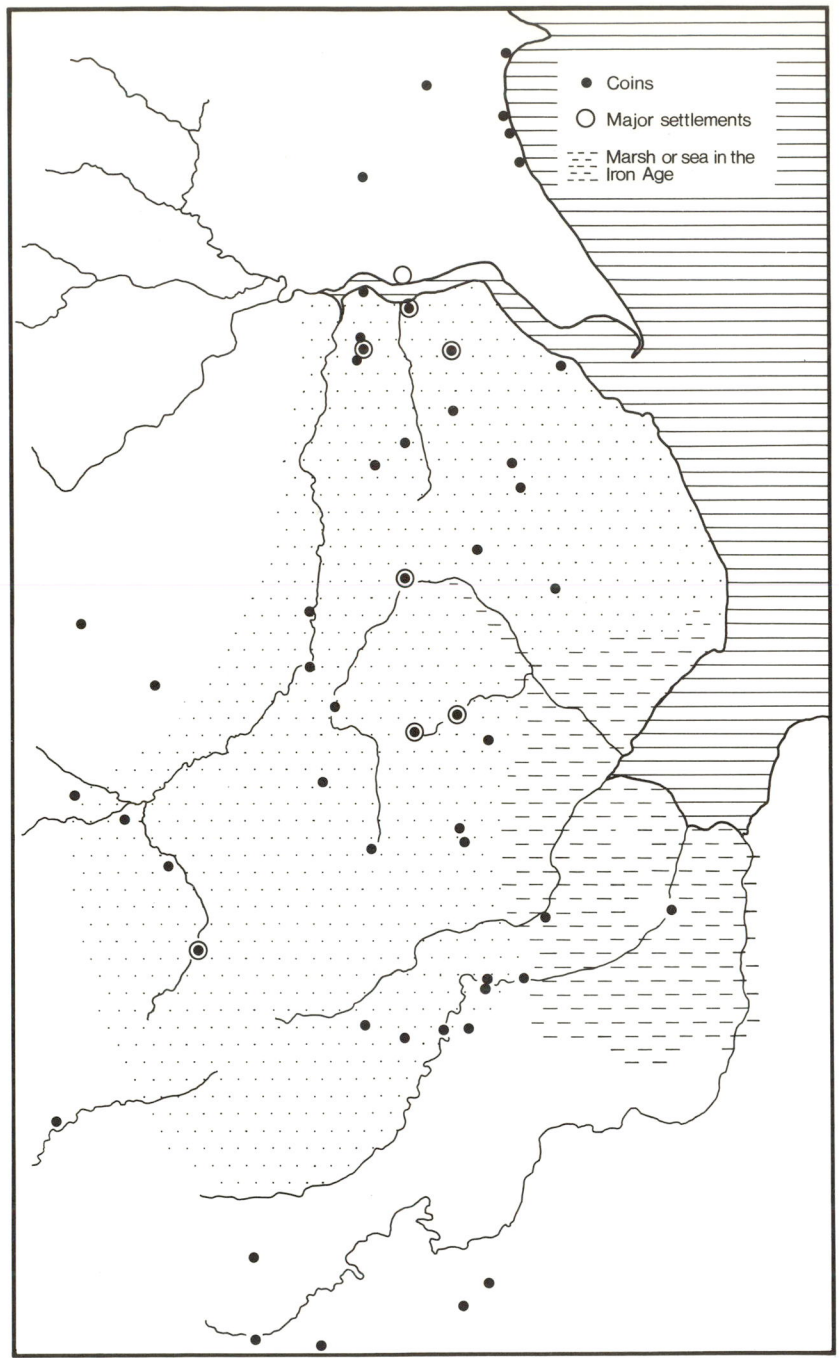

Figure 8.13   The territory of the Corieltauvi (source: Cunliffe 1981b, May 1984).

Figure 8.14 Coins of the Corieltauvi. 1 Uninscribed silver unit; 2 Volisios Dumnocoveros, gold stater. Twice actual size (photo: Institute of Archaeology, Oxford).

suggesting the emergence of centralized production. Decoration is now usually restricted to horizontal zoning defined by grooving and cordons occasionally infilled by simple linear shading. Some forms develop beaded rims and pedestal bases. These types are very similar to the Aylesford–Swarling assemblages of the south-east and imply a close contact between the two areas in the post-war period. This need be little more than a parallel development brought about by increased trading connections as the pace of exchange between Britain and the Continent grew. The third ceramic phase reflects a further intensification of this trend. Alongside developed forms of traditional coarse wares, Gallo-Belgic imports, such as butt-beakers, *terra rubra* and *terra nigra*, appear together with imported amphorae. The locally produced wares now tended to copy imported forms. This phase probably began in the last decade of the first century BC and continued until the invasion.

A number of large nucleated settlements have been discovered within the tribal territory (May 1976a, 1984). At Dragonby, 11 km south of the Humber estuary, a substantial settlement consisting of ditched enclosures and circular houses and covering some 8 ha, has been partly excavated. Considerable quantities of pottery together with La Tène III metalwork and thirty-three Iron Age coins represent intensive occupation beginning about 100 BC and continuing until after the conquest. A similar long sequence was discovered at Old Sleaford, a site of unknown extent which produced 3,000 fragments of clay moulds probably used for making coin blanks.

Two other sites which have some claim to urban status are Leicester (*Ratae*) and Lincoln (*Lindum*), both important Roman towns. At Leicester small quantities of Late Iron Age pottery and metalworking debris have come to light from beneath the Roman settlement, while at

Lincoln Late Iron Age occupation has been found just to the south of the Roman town near Brayford Pool. Although the evidence from both sites is sparse the importance which the two locations attained in the Roman period hints at their potential significance in the pre-Roman period.

Among the other Lincolnshire sites which have yielded unusual quantities of Late Iron Age material are Kirmington, Ancaster, Ludford, Old Winteringham, Owmby, South Ferriby, Spilsby and Thistleton (May 1984) but in the absence of extensive excavation their status must remain uncertain. Some may be little more than rich farms, others are perhaps religious centres, but some at least are likely to be major markets possibly with urban functions. Of these, South Ferriby, on the southern shore of the Humber estuary, is admirably sited to command the Humber crossing. The discovery of nearly 200 Iron Age coins and an impressive collection of La Tène III brooches and other metalwork hints at a site of considerable significance.

Two other sites of lesser status have been excavated. At Colsterworth, Lincs., a substantial ditched enclosure containing a number of circular houses was uncovered. The associated pottery shows that the site was occupied during the middle of the first century AD, beginning in the pre-Roman period. Since the number of huts occupied at any one time cannot be accurately assessed, the size of the social group is impossible to define but in all probability the settlement was a small hamlet or a large farm the status of which was indicated by the massiveness of its enclosing ditch. A rather different kind of settlement was excavated at Tallington, near Stamford. Here a number of roughly rectangular ditched enclosures were laid out along the north bank of the river Welland in the largest of which was a circular house. The general arrangement is that of a typical farmstead.

No survey of the Corieltauvi would be complete without a brief consideration of the coastline. An extensive survey of the Lincolnshire Fens (B.B. Simmons 1980) has shown that in the Iron Age the high-tide line was far inland of its present position (Figure 8.13) but at low tide extensive mud flats would have been exposed with islands of higher ground in between. While such a shore line would have inhibited communication by sea it provided a valuable range of resources. The marsh edge would have made ideal pasture land for cattle or horses while along the coastal strip there developed a vigorous salt-extraction industry. Sea-birds and the fish would not have been overlooked as a resource. This range of products, together with the fertility of the Lincolnshire soils and the ready supplies of high quality iron ore, provided the Corieltauvi with a considerable resource potential which could be maximized in order to provide surplus for exchange. The quantities of imported Gallo-Belgic ceramics found on the major settlements and the vigorous, high quality coinage maintained throughout is an indication of their economic stability.

Summary

The three coin-issuing tribes of the peripheral zone separated the southern core zone from the less developed areas of western and northern Britain and it was through their territories that raw materials and other commodities had to pass in the period of intensified trade that characterized the Late Iron Age. Thus they formed a buffer zone between the developed and underdeveloped parts of the island. Their socio-economic systems must, therefore, have evolved to provide the enabling mechanisms necessary for the through flow of products. The emergence of a peripheral zone, along the Jurassic ridge, is no accident since this broad geomorphological region, providing ease of communication along its length, effectively divides Britain into two parts each with different resource potentials, microclimates and degrees of access to Continental trading networks. The communities occupying the ridge would thus become subjected to economic forces once cross-Channel trade intensified. This may have led to the emergence of large tribal entities by the coalescence of smaller ethnic groups and would, in any event, have necessitated the development of a coinage to facilitate exchange.

The different 'histories' of the three tribes reflect changes in orientation and intensity of trade. The earliest trading axis favoured the Solent harbours and thereby the Durotriges but by the time the Gallic War was over a new eastern axis had been created leaving the Durotriges to become isolated and impoverished. The resources of west Britain could now be reached via the Upper Thames valley and across the northern part of Dobunnic territory while those of the north called for a route across the Chilterns and through Bedfordshire, skirting the fen margin, to the southern part of the Corieltauvian territory. These two routes were in all probability broad corridors along which exchange goods passed in both directions making use of a complex system of social relationships. One might anticipate that such enhanced activity created conditions for exceptional change. Some evidence for this can be found in the archaeological record. In the Middle Thames region, for example, a bewildering variety of coins are found making it difficult to decide in which tribal territory the region lay: such a mixture could have come about as the result of constant traffic between the eastern communities and the northern Dobunni. The northern 'corridor' through the Chilterns and across Bedfordshire is probably reflected in the dense scatter of elite burials belonging to those able to benefit from controlling the passage of goods. While it must be admitted that this picture is both incomplete and oversimplified it has some value in helping to focus on the complex processes at work at the time.

9

The late pre-Roman Iron Age in western and northern Britain

Beyond the peripheral zone of coin-issuing tribes – the Durotriges, Dobunni and Corieltauvi – lay vast expanses of Britain: the south-western peninsula, Wales and the north. The south-west differed from the rest in that it remained in contact by sea with both the south-eastern tribes and with Armorica and thus absorbed cultural influences from both. Wales and the north on the other hand were far removed from the rapidly expanding economies of the south-east and were largely isolated from Continental influences until the second half of the first century AD by which time Roman rule, or the bow-wave effects of the Roman presence, had penetrated all but the extreme north-west. For these reasons there is a considerable degree of cultural unity over large stretches of country and it is sometimes difficult to isolate material of the Late Iron Age from that of earlier periods. Nevertheless the writings of several Roman authors provide a valuable descriptive horizon from which to assess the social and economic changes of the preceding decades.

The south-west peninsula: The Dumnonii (Figure 9.1)

The Dumnonii occupied the south-west peninsula probably as far east as the Parrett–Axe line. In this position of relative isolation, cultural contact with the communities of the south-east was limited and it is therefore hardly surprising that the disparate peoples who occupied the broken and varied landscape of the peninsula failed to develop a coinage of their own: exchange remained embedded in traditional social systems. Apart from coin hoards at Mount Batten, Carn Brae, Penzance and Paul, coins are virtually unknown.

The ceramic development of the region can be divided into two distinct traditions, one following the other and in parts replacing it. The earliest is characterized by the South-Western Decorated Wares which used to be called 'Glastonbury wares'. These decorated vessels were produced at several centres including the Lizard peninsula and on the Permian outcrops of the Exe region. As we have seen (above, pp. 84–5) the tradition probably originated in the fourth century BC, inspired by Breton developments, and decorated wares continued to be made well

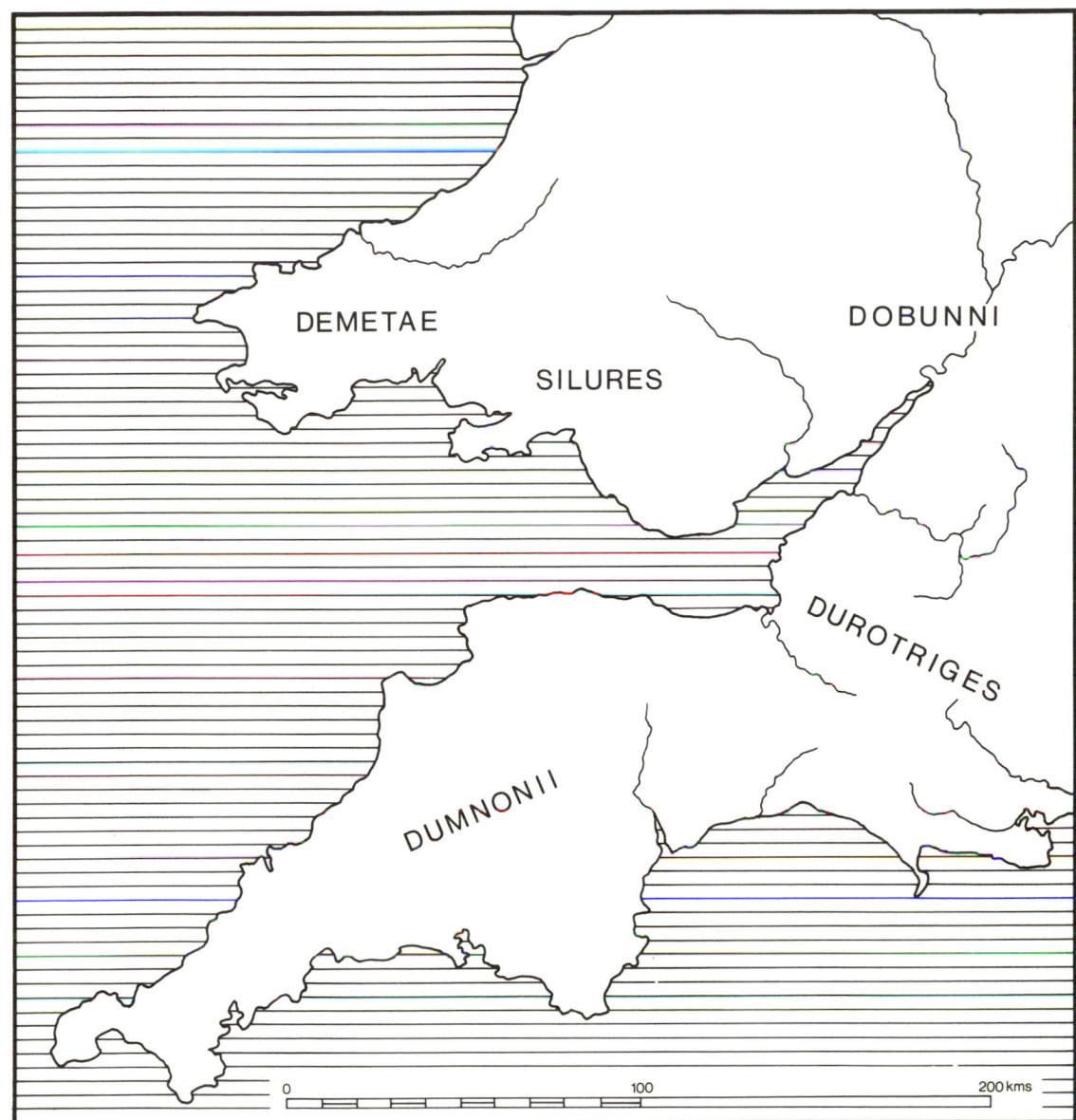

Figure 9.1   The tribes of western Britain (sources: various).

into the first century BC. The classic forms were necked-bowls and jars decorated with elaborated curvilinear motifs executed by shallow tooling, stamping and, less frequently, with the roulette wheel.

The second, later, tradition is generally known as *cordoned ware*. The repertoire includes necked-jars, tazza-like bowls and large everted-rimmed jars all undecorated except for prominent horizontal cordons sometimes used in combination with grooves (Figure A:34, p. 587). The vessels were well made and turned on a wheel. At several sites, including Castle Dore, cordoned ware could be shown to be generally later than South-Western Decorated Wares and there is ample evidence from Cornwall to show that the cordoned ware tradition continued into the Roman period.

It used to be thought that cordoned wares were brought to the south-west by refugees from Armorica fleeing in the wake of the Roman advance of 56 BC and that fogous and cliff castles, both of which had close parallels to similar structures in Brittany, were introduced at the same time (C.F.C. Hawkes 1966). This view can no longer be sustained since the Cornish fogous (Christie 1979) and cliff castles can be shown to date back to the beginning of the Middle Iron Age if not earlier and are part of a shared cultural tradition which linked the two peninsulas for centuries before the Caesarian episode (Figure 9.2). The appearance of cordoned ware could be better explained in the general context of continuing social intercourse rather than as the result of a single event.

The dating of the Cornish cordoned wares is difficult to establish but stylistically they have little in common with Armorican ceramics of the Caesarian period. They do, however, share a general resemblance to developments in north-western France and central southern Britain dating to the second half of the first century BC. They are best explained therefore as the result of local trading contacts between these areas in the post-Caesarian period. That the distribution is restricted largely to Cornwall, extending as far east as the port of Mount Batten, suggests that most of Devon was excluded from the system: here the traditional decorated wares probably continued until the Roman Conquest.

Dumnonian settlement of the period c. 100 BC–AD 50 forms part of a continuous pattern well rooted in the preceding centuries and continuing in some areas throughout the Roman period (Johnson and Rose 1982). In Devon the multiple-ditched enclosures of the third or second century remain the dominant form of defended homestead or hamlet into the first century AD, with little apparent change in either size of community or the predominantly pastoral economy. Thus Milber Down Camp, one of the few excavated sites in this category, remained in use well into the first century BC, while later occupation into the Roman period continued outside the main enclosure. Similarly, at Castle Dore first-century AD occupation is attested by cordoned ware. Further west, in Cornwall, rounds (i.e. small defended homesteads seldom exceeding 2 ha in extent) which form a dominant element in the Roman settlement pattern, originate in the Late Iron Age. At Crane Godrevy, Castle Gotha and Gwithian cordoned ware has been found; and at the somewhat larger site of Carloggas, St Mawgan-in-Pydar, occupation began during the late second or early first century BC, while South-Western Decorated Wares were in use and continued into the Roman period. Another large settlement, the bivallate site of Killibury, began equally early but was abandoned before Roman pottery reached the area. The settlement at Trevisker, close to Carloggas, spanned the period from the Middle Bronze Age into Roman times. It is estimated (A.C. Thomas 1966b, 88–90) that in Cornwall and south and west Devon between 750 and 1,000 rounds existed, with a density averaging one per 2.6 square kilometres. Clearly they must represent the homesteads or small hamlets of an essentially non-nucleated population.

Another type of settlement which appears later, representing the same-sized social group, is the courtyard house – a central courtyard surrounded by rooms, all enclosed within a massive stone wall. Sometimes courtyard houses were built within rounds (e.g. Goldherring) or were otherwise enclosed, but open villages like Chysauster and Carn Euny are also known. The origin of the courtyard house is still a matter of uncertainty but the evidence from the long-lived

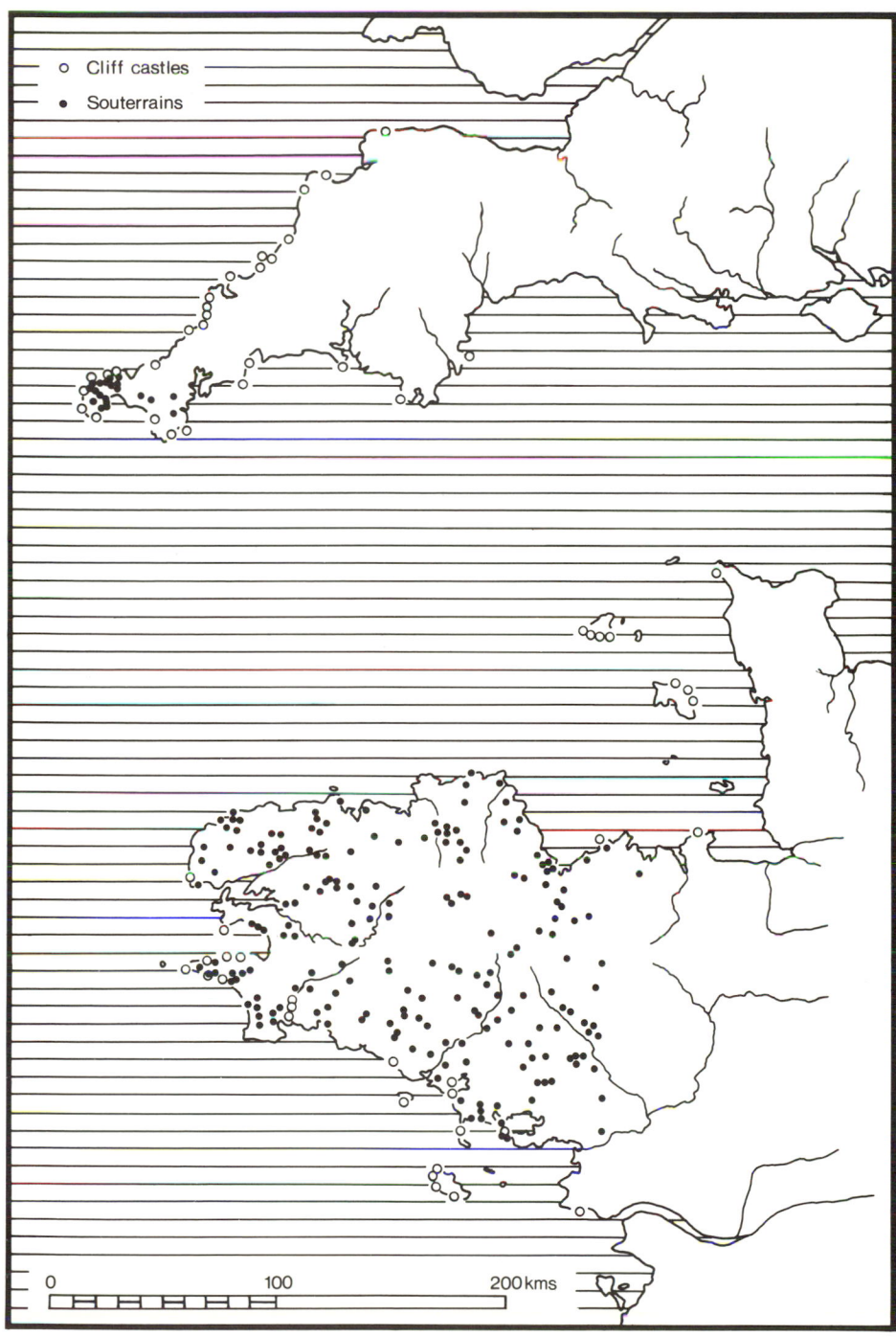

Figure 9.2 Settlement similarities between Cornwall and Brittany (source: Cunliffe 1982a).

settlement at Carn Euny suggests local evolution though perhaps not until after the beginning of the Roman occupation.

The best defined category of hillforts in the south-west are the cliff castles, which densely ring the coasts of Cornwall and north Devon. Essentially, a cliff castle is a promontory projecting into the sea, the neck of which is defended by one or more series of banks and ditches. The obvious similarities between the cliff castles of south-west Britain and those of Brittany (Wheeler and Richardson 1957) has frequently been used as an argument in favour of a Venetic invasion of Cornwall, but of the sites excavated, Maen Castle seems to have originated at least as early as the second century BC, while Gurnard's Head has produced a range of pottery beginning not very much later. At the Rumps occupation began in the second century BC and lasted until the early first century AD. Thus, from the available evidence it would appear that cliff castles formed an essential part of the settlement pattern for at least three centuries and are therefore unlikely to be the result of the arrival of refugees in the mid-first century BC.

The enclosed areas of the cliff castles vary according to the shape and size of the promontory selected, but since in every case the actual length of the defences was kept to a minimum, the amount of labour involved in construction was relatively slight. Massive hillfort-building on the scale practised in the south-east is almost unknown, and even when an inland site was chosen, like Tregear or Chun Castle, size was restricted. At Chun, for example, while the two defensive walls were substantial, the area enclosed was only about 52 m across.

The relationship between the homesteads (rounds and courtyard houses) and the fortified sites is not easy to determine, but it may well be that the forts served as the strongholds of the local leaders. They were not suited to serve as foci for larger social groups as were the hillforts in Wessex.

The port-of-trade established at Mount Batten, Plymouth in the Late Bronze Age and serving throughout much of the Iron Age as a link with the Atlantic trading system, remained in use during the Late Iron Age but the intensity of occupation does not appear to have been great though there is evidence of contact with the Solent harbours. The cemetery on Stamford Hill nearby did, however, produce a group of well-furnished burials dating to the middle decade of the first century AD suggesting the possibility of an upturn in fortunes at about the time of the Roman Conquest.

The rite of inhumation in small cists, which was practised in the area in the preceding periods (e.g. at Harlyn Bay and Trevone), continued unhindered into the Roman period. It is represented at several sites, including the large cemetery at Stamford Hill, Mount Batten and the smaller group of burials at Trelan Bahow near St Keverne, where one of the graves was of a rich female who had been provided with a bronze mirror, two bracelets, rings, brooches and a necklace of blue glass beads, all dating to the first century AD. The similarities between this burial and female inhumations in the territory of the Durotriges and Dobunni may suggest an element of unity underlying the burial rites of the south-west.

In summary, it may be said that many of the elements which together constitute the culture of the Dumnonii owe much to social intercourse with their Armorican neighbours, but it would appear that Dumnonian culture developed slowly in parallel with the Continent and was not suddenly altered by incursions of refugees.

The proximity of the two peninsulas facilitated social interaction but it was probably the tin trade, stretching back into the Bronze Age, which acted as the main stimulus for contact. In this way the communities of Armorica and the south-west were brought together. This process and the striking geomorphological similarities of the two territories led to a degree of parallel cultural development. The ceramic sequences, though distinct, shared much in common, while settlement morphology, with its cliff castles, rounds and fogous or souterrains was remarkably similar on both sides of the Channel. The development of a major trading axis between Brittany and the Solent harbours in the first half of the first century BC may have temporarily deflected contact but in the aftermath of the Caesarian campaign relations were reaffirmed. It was probably in this context that the Cornish cordoned wares developed and a few Italian amphorae reached sites like Carloggas and the Rumps. The contrast between the culture and economy of the Dumnonii and that of the other tribes of southern Britain is very marked. The Dumnonii were in every way closer to the tribes of Armorica than they were to their neighbours in Britain.

Wales

Any consideration of the cultural groupings and developments in Wales during the first centuries BC and AD is likely to be fraught with difficulty, largely because of the lack of large-scale excavation and the almost total absence of datable cultural material. Moreover, the inhospitable nature of much of the countryside has ensured that considerable areas remained uninhabited while in others pastoralism probably played a significant part. Together these factors militate against an adequate description of the material culture on a regional basis.

Knowledge of tribal groupings rests largely upon the writings of the geographer Ptolemy whose lists, taken together with descriptive accounts by Tacitus and other fragments of epigraphic evidence, show that Wales was divided into a minimum of five tribal areas roughly approximating to broad geographical divisions. In the extreme south-west were the Demetae. Next to them, from the Gower peninsula stretching along the coastal plain to the Wye and extending into the Black Mountains, were the Silures, whom Tacitus describes as ruddy-faced and curly-haired, reminding him of Iberians. In the north-west, centred on the Lleyn peninsula, lay the Gangani, who were presumably related to a tribe of the same name living in north-west Ireland, while along the north coast lived the Deceangli. Lastly, between these four tribes were the Ordovices, occupying the mountainous area in the centre of the principality.

The Silures

The exact limits of Silurian territory cannot be precisely drawn but it is clear that the bulk of the tribe occupied the lowland coastal areas of Glamorganshire and Monmouthshire and the valleys of the Black Mountains with the river Wye forming the approximate boundary with the Dobunni. In all probability, the cluster of small defended settlements centred on the upper reaches of the Usk, in the heart of the Brecon Beacons, can also be regarded as belonging to a geographically isolated community of the Silures.

Material culture and settlement type have many similarities with those of adjacent territories. Some of the hillforts in the eastern part of the territory, such as Sudbrook and Llanmelin in Monmouthshire, are closely similar to Wessex sites; others are best paralleled by the multiple-ditched enclosures of the south-west peninsula; while the cliff castles of the coastal group have much in common with those of Cornwall. Environment, economy and commercial communications must have encouraged this parallelism. At Llanmelin a 2.2 hectare multivallate enclosure with a semi-inturned entrance was shown to have been in use during the local phase of the saucepan pot continuum, roughly second to first century BC, and there is some evidence of modification after south-eastern style pottery had arrived on the site, probably during the first century AD. Occupation continued into the Roman period. A similar continuity into Roman times was demonstrated by the multivallate enclosure at Sudbrook, where the defences came late in the sequence, post-dating occupation containing first-century BC saucepan pots. The levels contemporary with the defences contained a mixture of first-century AD pottery continuing until early Flavian times.

Both of the sites so far considered lie at the east side of the territory where influence from Dobunnic and Roman culture might be expected. Further west, however, along the Glamorganshire coast, the material culture is far less well represented. The forts which have been excavated, The Knave, The Bulwarks, the West Fort on Harding's Down, Bishopston Valley Fort and High Penard, have produced very little apart from a few imported sherds of South-Western Decorated Ware, odd scraps of Roman pottery and a few indeterminate sherds. Nevertheless, there can be little doubt that the forts were inhabited during the last century of Silurian independence.

Only two settlements have been excavated on any scale. At Mynydd Bychan, a walled enclosure was examined containing a group of circular huts. In the first period the buildings were of timber but later they were rebuilt in stone within walled courtyards. Occupation began in the latter part of the first century BC and continued probably as late as Flavian times, the later decades being characterized by the appearance of wheel-turned vessels manufactured in the south-eastern manner but in an orange-buff fabric.

The farmstead at Whitton presented a rather different sequence. Here a rectangular ditched enclosure was built c. AD 30 to defend a series of circular timber-built houses. Occupation continued until the end of the century when rectangular timber buildings replaced them. These in turn were succeeded by simple masonry-based buildings in the second century. The evidence suggests a largely unbroken sequence spanning the period of transition from freedom to incorporation with little trace of a change in status.

From the inception of the Fosse frontier in AD 47, Silurian territory would have been in close contact with the Roman world, and the foundation of the fortress at Usk in c. 55–60, followed by several decades of campaigning before the final annexation in c. AD 74, would soon have brought the natives of the coastal plain into an intimate relationship with the Roman army. It may well have been under these conditions that the south-eastern style ceramics were introduced from Dobunnic territory (Spencer 1983).

The Demetae

The Demetae occupied the extreme south-west corner of Wales, probably extending along the valleys of the Tywi and Teifi into the foothills of the Cambrian mountains. Much of the more hospitable parts of this territory was densely scattered with small enclosed settlements, usually 0.4–1.2 hectares in extent, comparable in many ways to the rounds of Cornwall (Figure 9.3). Excavations at Walesland Rath, Pembs., have demonstrated the existence of a moderate sized community living in a cluster of circular huts from the first century BC into the first century AD. In the second century, after a period of abandonment, the site was reoccupied by a community existing in much the same way as before but now living in a simple rectangular stone building

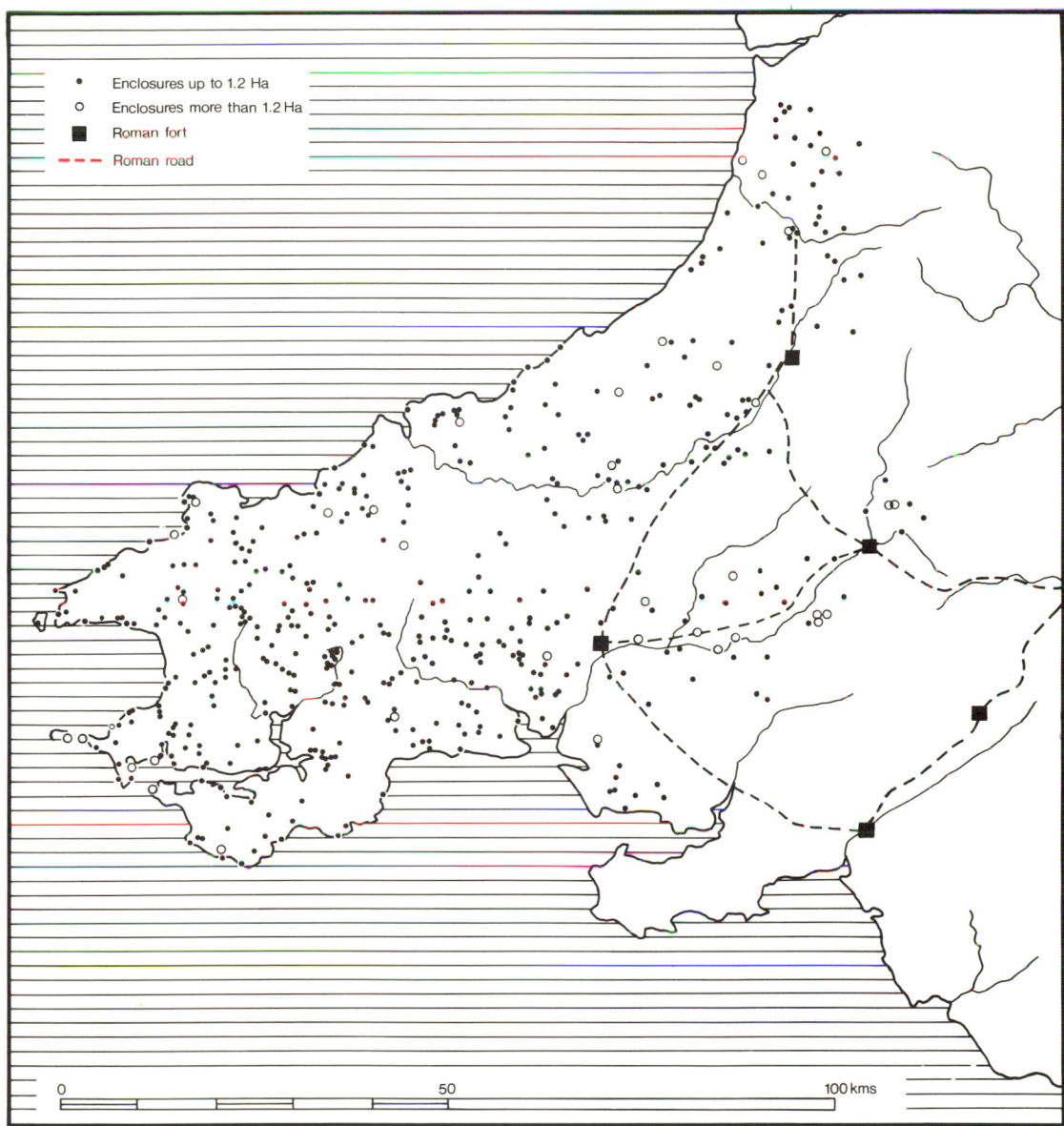

Figure 9.3   Settlements in south-west Wales (source: G. Williams 1988 with additions).

and using Romanized pottery. Continuity of this kind may also be suspected at two nearby sites, Cwmbrwyn and Trelissey, where Romanized buildings have been excavated inside apparently earlier earthworks. Not all of the native sites which continued in use into the Roman period and beyond showed evidence of Romanized improvements as a series of comprehensive excavations in the Llawhaden region have amply demonstrated (G. Williams 1988). This pattern of unhampered indigenous development spanning many centuries may well have been even more deeply rooted. Indeed, the discovery of La Tène I bracelets at Coygan Camp tends to emphasize the antiquity of settlement in the area, but the extreme paucity of artefacts makes any assessment of material development and chronology a matter of difficulty for the pre-Roman phases.

Several observers have pointed out the relative lack of Roman military activity in the south-west of Wales, suggesting that the Demetae offered no resistance to the advance and therefore required no substantial holding force save a garrison based at Carmarthen. If this were so, it would explain the peaceful uninterrupted occupation of the peasant villages and hamlets – a process which, on present evidence, offers some contrasts to the settlement of the hostile Silurian territory.

The Ordovices, Gangani and Deceangli

The settlement pattern of north Wales appears to have been little affected by the events of the late pre-Roman Iron Age in the south-east of the country. The material culture remained as sparse as ever and many of the sites continued to be occupied well into the Roman period with little evidence of significant change. The Roman campaigns of AD 47–51 and indeed the Roman presence in Britain from AD 43 tend, however, to be reflected in the structural development of some of the defended sites. At Dinorben, Denbigh., it has been suggested that the final reconstruction of the ramparts on the south side of the fort (period V) could have resulted from Roman threats in the neighbourhood, while at Castell Odo, Caerns., the slighting of the defences may have been carried out by the Romans in the last quarter of the first century AD.

Perhaps the most impressive feature of the settlement pattern of the area is the continued use of the hillforts like Tre'r Ceiri, Caerns., with their densely occupied interiors, and the development of large numbers of enclosed farmsteads usually working on average 6 hectares or so of associated terraced fields (C.A. Smith 1978b). While the exact origin of this system is still in some doubt (Hogg 1966), it is clear that the social grouping and some aspects of the architecture must relate to pre-Roman tradition and it would indeed be surprising if many of the farms in use in the Roman period did not originate in the first century BC or even earlier. The problem is one of establishing calibrated sequences in a virtually aceramic region.

The Cornovii

According to Ptolemy, the territory of the Cornovii included both the cantonal capital at Viroconium and the legionary base at Deva (Chester), which in terms of modern counties would have meant that the tribe occupied Cheshire and Shropshire and probably parts of surrounding areas. To the south, their boundary with the Dobunni probably approximated with the river Teme, an east-flowing tributary of the Severn; in the east they would have met the Corieltauvi in the Trent valley; and to the north the boundary with the Brigantes may have lain along the Mersey. The western limit of the tribal territory is far more difficult to define. The great number of defended enclosures in the hills and mountains of the Welsh borderland could equally well have been under Ordovician domination, but the structural peculiarities of some of the larger forts (e.g. Old Oswestry, the Breiddin, Ffridd Faldwyn and Titterstone Clee) tend to link them more with the forts of the south and east, suggesting a zone of contact, although this does not necessarily imply that the borderland forts belonged to Cornovian territory. The absence of coins and the relative lack of cultural material makes the definition of the tribal boundary hereabouts uncertain.

In the century or so before the Roman Conquest, the area seems to have continued to develop along earlier lines uninfluenced by the social and economic systems of the south-east. Many of the hillforts were kept in defensive order and a little pottery and fine metalwork was imported from outside the area but, like the other territories outside the aggressive range of the south-eastern chieftains and of their trading patterns, there was little discernible change until the entire territory was annexed by the Roman army led by Ostorius Scapula, in and soon after AD 48.

Northern England (Figure 9.4)

The Greek geographer Ptolemy writing in the second century AD tells us of a northern tribe, the Brigantes, whose territory stretched from 'sea to sea' (*Geog.* II, 3, 10). This vision of a northern people 'the most populous in the whole province' was also conjured up by Tacitus writing of the conquest of Britain (*Agricola* XVII, 2). From these descriptions has sprung the modern construct of *Brigantia*, conceived of as a vast territory extending from the Peak District to Hadrian's Wall and from the Irish Sea to the North Sea, a political and cultural monolith. The vision is given enhanced respectability by the story of the Brigantian queen, Cartimandua and her husband Venutius recorded in part by Tacitus. Much has been written on the subject especially by Sir Mortimer Wheeler in his report on the excavations at Stanwick (Wheeler 1954) and until recently Wheeler's interpretation of the Brigantes and their history has been widely accepted; but new work at Stanwick and several reviews of the northern evidence (Braund 1984; Haselgrove 1984a; and Higham 1987) have refocused attention on the varied and complex nature of the evidence and have amply demonstrated that many old preconceptions must now be abandoned.

The Brigantes were not the only tribe to be recorded in northern England. The Parisi were noted by Ptolemy and may be equated with the archaeologically-defined Arras culture occupying the Yorkshire Wolds north of the Humber. Several other tribes mentioned by Ptolemy in the west and north of the territory can also be approximately located, though their cultural attributes are less well known.

While there can be little doubt that the dominant force at the time of the Roman invasion was the Brigantes, the other tribal groups should not be overlooked nor should the whole north be written off as a 'Brigantian confederacy'. A far more likely model would be to see the Brigantes (whose name means 'high ones') as having hegemony over their neighbours whose position was that of clients. The Brigantes themselves probably occupied the Pennines and their flanks thus commanding not only a central position controlling the principal routes north to south and east to west but also having access to a range of varied and well-drained soils (Higham 1987). In this probably lay the basis of their power.

The Brigantes and their neighbours

Relatively little is known of the settlement pattern and economy of the north at this time but the varied geology and altitude, and the considerable differences in rainfall on either side of the

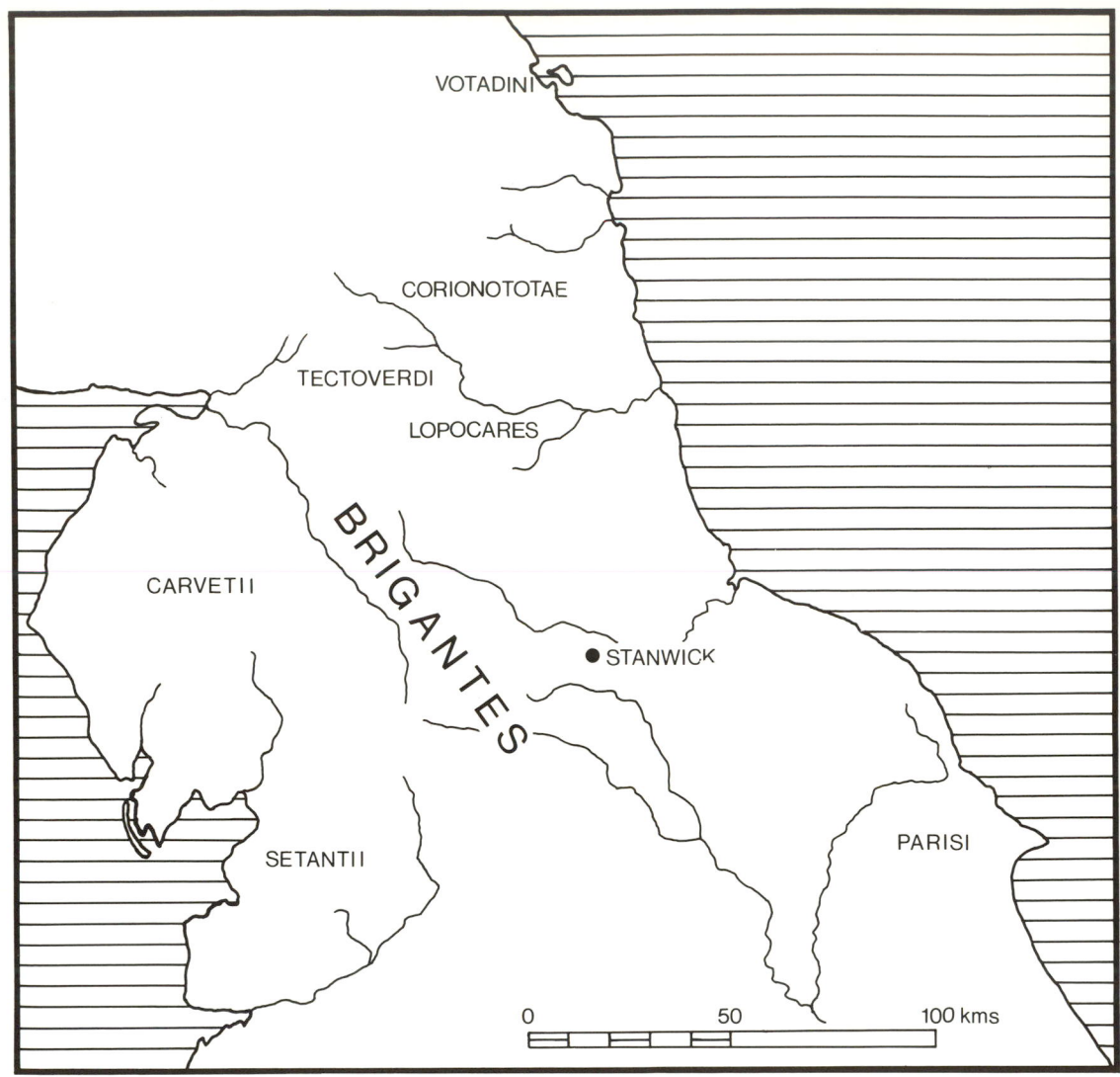

Figure 9.4 The tribes of northern England (sources: various).

Pennine ridge have created numerous micro-environments demanding different economic strategies. The traditional generalization – that the Brigantes were largely pastoralists (Wheeler 1954; S. Piggott 1958) – must now be abandoned in the face of growing evidence of agriculture in the north-east both from the results of pollen analysis (J. Turner 1979, 1981) and from actual crop remains recovered from sites such as Coxhae, Co. Durham, Thorpe Thewles, Cleveland, and Stanwick, Yorks. The large numbers of beehive querns found in north-eastern Yorkshire, closely associated with good arable land, is a further indication of widespread agricultural activity, though the type is not exclusively of Late Iron Age date (Hayes, Hemingway and Spratt 1980). Animals, however, played a significant part in the economy, cattle being the most numerous. Clearly a mixed economy must have been practised over much of north-eastern Britain at this time though the specific regimes will have varied from area to area (Haselgrove 1984a).

In the Pennine valleys early field systems, such as the well-preserved groups in Wharfedale and adjacent valleys, are a further indication of agricultural activity, but flocks and herds may well have been tended in upland pastures for much of the year. The use, well into the Roman era, of caves and isolated huts on the Pennine moors is an indication that a transhumant economy continued to be practised for many centuries. There is little evidence yet available for settlement and economy in the north-west at this time but high rainfall would have made the arable strategies of the drier north-east less appropriate and there may well have been a greater reliance on animal husbandry.

Apart from dimly-conceived differences between economic systems there is little evidence on which to distinguish regional or tribal variation. Ceramic technology was ill-developed. Northern pottery consists almost entirely of coarsely-made cooking and storage vessels, generally without decoration and of simple form lacking distinctive characteristics. No doubt most of the containers were made of wood, basketry and leather – materials more appropriate to the needs of a society practising a degree of mobility. An example of an elegant wooden dish was found in a waterlogged deposit at Stanwick. That the population was not entirely unappreciative of fine pottery is vividly demonstrated by the high percentage of imported wares found at Stanwick: of all the pottery recovered some 60 per cent consisted of samian ware, butt-beakers and other Roman imports from the south.

With the exception of Stanwick there is little evidence of centralized settlement in the north. Of those hillforts which have been excavated, Almondbury, Yorks., Mam Tor, Derbyshire, Castercliff, Lincs., and Skelmore Head, Lancs., none appear to have been occupied after the fourth century BC and the normal unit of settlement remained the isolated farm of family or extended family size. Against this background the earthworks of Stanwick stand out in stark contrast (Figure 9.5). Stanwick lies at the junction of two major routes, one running along the east side of the Pennines joining the south to Scotland and the other branching west across the mountains through the Stainmore Pass. The site now consists of over 300 ha of pasture and arable land enclosed and traversed by 10 km of massive earthworks surviving in places to a height of 5 m. The choice of location and the vast investment of energy in its fortification fairly reflect the great economic and political importance of the place sited as it is in the heart of Brigantian territory.

The potential interest of the site was fully appreciated by Sir Mortimer Wheeler who chose it as a research project in 1951 and 1952. Wheeler's excavations were limited but his conclusions were far-reaching (Wheeler 1954). He saw Stanwick as a military stronghold of the Brigantes – a rallying place for anti-Roman resistance beginning with a 7 ha enclosure, the Tofts, constructed in c. AD 47–8, which was then enlarged in two stages. In its final form Stanwick provided protection for the tribe in its last stand against the Ninth Legion led by Petillius Cerialis in a victorious sweep through the north in 71–2.

A more recent programme of fieldwork and excavation has shown that the structural sequence proposed by Wheeler is wrong and that his military interpretation of the earthworks is likely to be incorrect (Chadburn 1983; Turnbull 1984). While excavation is still in progress views are likely to change but it now seems quite possible that most of the system was laid out as part of a single plan. More important is the function of the site. The straggling earthworks and vast enclosed area are highly reminiscent of the territorial oppida of the south. This, together with the

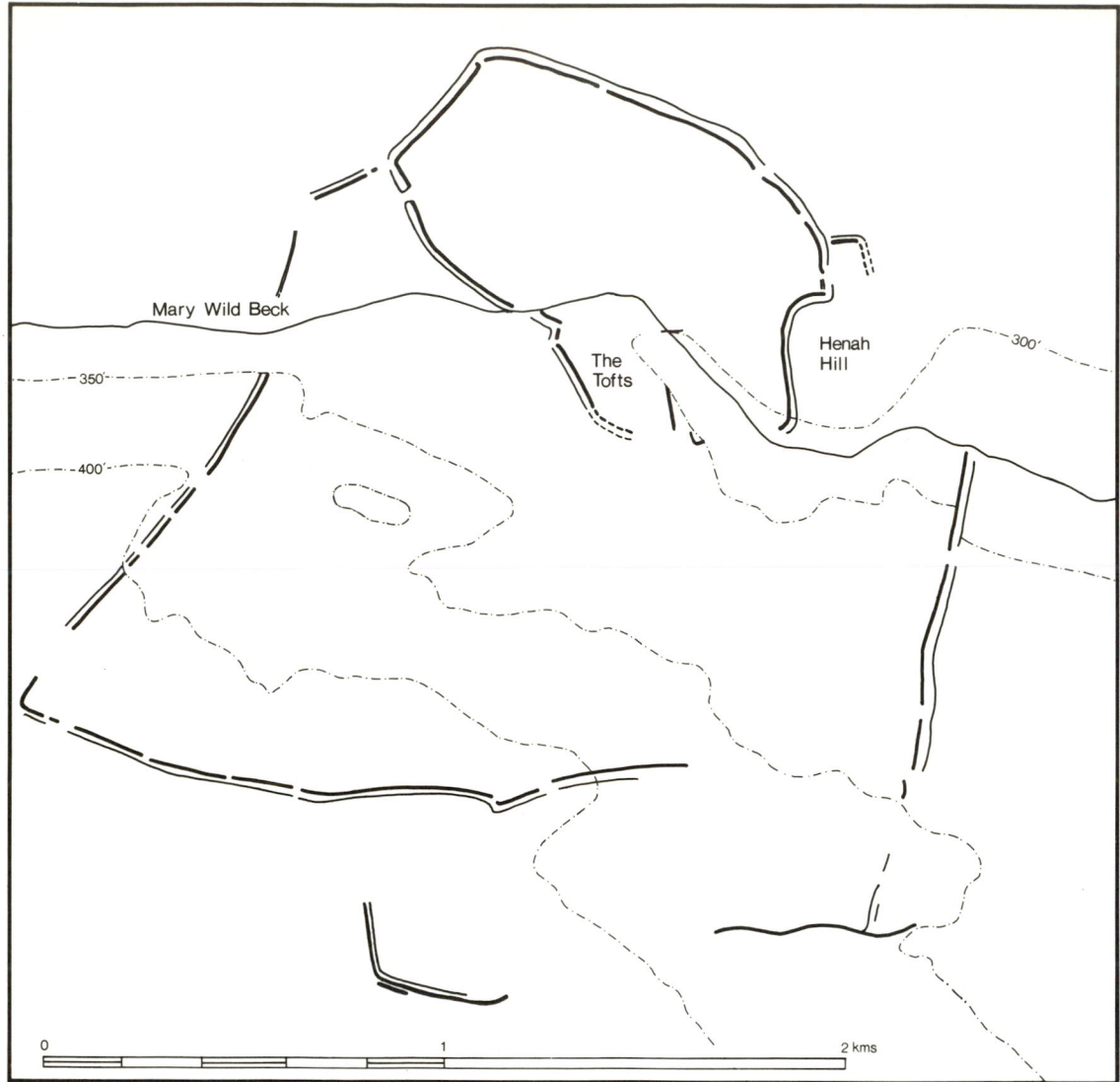

Figure 9.5 The Stanwick fortifications (sources: Wheeler 1954, Chadburn 1983, Turnbull 1984).

surprisingly high proportion of luxury pottery imported from the south suggests that Stanwick may have served, in much the same way as the southern oppida, as a centre of tribal power where long-distance trade was articulated with local distribution networks. The evidence for metalworking which has now been identified (Spratling 1981) is entirely consistent with this view for at such centres raw materials would be given added value through refinement and manufacture.

The dating evidence suggests that occupation began at about the time of the conquest and declined in the later decades of the first century AD. This is explicable against the background of the early military history of the province (chapter 10). The initial intention was to secure only the south-east and to this end a frontier zone was established from Lincoln to Exeter. Though campaigning, followed by expansion, took place in the Midlands and Wales, the north was left as a friendly buffer state ruled by Queen Cartimandua until the early 70s. In such a context the development of vigorous trade between the province and its northern neighbours would be expected. Stanwick, deep in Brigantian territory and commanding the major routes was admirably sited to serve as the principal entrepôt where the Brigantian monopoly, established through treaty with the Roman authorities, could be exercised, further strengthening their hegemony over their lesser neighbours.

The situation in the north was politically unstable. Literary evidence relating to the first century AD provides several glimpses of the factions and rivalries within upper echelons of society, and it may fairly be supposed that these reflect the deep divisions that might be expected within the structure of a people divided by tribal loyalties and whose territory and resources were so diverse. The flamboyant and aggressive aspects of this northern society are manifest in a group of distinctive swords (Piggott's class IV) made, no doubt, by a single school of craftsmen for the northern elite, and by the scattered discoveries of horse-trappings including the remarkable hoard found at Stanwick in 1845 (MacGregor 1962) which contained a sword, a wide range of chariot-and horse-trappings and a number of fragments of personal equipment. While the exact nature of the Stanwick hoard must remain in doubt, it provides a vivid impression of the degree of wealth and display attained by the upper classes of Brigantian society at the end of their period of freedom.

The Parisi

On the east flank of the Brigantes lay the Parisi, occupying the territory stretching from the Humber estuary to the north Yorkshire moors. The region was in close contact with northern France in the late fifth century, giving rise to the Arras culture (pp. 77–9 and Stead 1979), which developed possibly after a small-scale folk movement brought new people into the area from the Seine valley. Stead has demonstrated a degree of continuity from the fifth- or fourth-century beginning until the Roman Conquest, unhindered by any further Continental contact – a fact which has led him to support the idea that the tribal name of Parisi, recorded by Ptolemy in describing the situation in the first century AD, must date back to the fifth to fourth century. He further points out that the closest parallels for the Yorkshire burials occur in the territory of the Gallic Parisii.

The cemeteries of the Arras culture at Dane's Graves and Eastburn continued in use throughout the first century BC and well into the first century AD. There was little change, except that metal associations were rare in the later periods and, where objects occurred at all, they related more directly to the developing styles of southern Britain. Pottery buried with the dead, however, became more common. At Wetwang Slack the only discernible difference in a long established cemetery, laid out along a track, was that in the Late Iron Age a ditch had been dug through many of the old burials to delimit a more restricted cemetery zone. By the Late Iron Age, however, the rite of vehicle burial had been totally abandoned throughout the region of the Arras culture.

One new element to appear in the area during the first century BC was the rite of single warrior inhumation – known from North Grimston, Bugthorpe and Grimthorpe, all sited along the western side of the Wolds. The presence of weapons and lack of indigenous features – such as the cart buried with the body, rectangular enclosures and barrows – suggest a different tradition and ritual. It is, however, quite unnecessary to define a separate culture (as Stead 1965, 84, where he calls it the North Grimston culture). It is simpler to regard the burials, which are similar to others found in various parts of Britain, as representing a general and widespread change. What exactly the new style of burial means is less clear; in all probability, it is little more than a change of fashion but the possibility that it signifies the presence of extra-tribal mercenary warriors or simply a more warlike tendency in society, should not be overlooked. In this connection, the discovery at Garton Slack of small chalk-cut figures carrying swords might be taken as evidence of a new militarism (Stead 1988, 32–4).

Settlement morphology and economy among the Parisi is becoming much better understood as the result of the large-scale excavation of extensive, but scattered settlements in the valley of Garton and Wetwang Slack (Dent 1982) where there is some evidence to suggest that, by the Late Iron Age, hitherto open settlements were being enclosed. Elsewhere, for example at Rillington, near Malton, complex patterns of enclosure had already been established a century or two earlier. Continuity of occupation into the Roman period is demonstrated at the ditched enclosures at Langton and Staxton: at Langton and again at Rudston Late Iron Age settlements were eventually replaced by Roman villas. The overall impression given by the settlement evidence is of continuity and gradual change.

The quality of ceramic production improved throughout the first centuries BC and AD, probably under the influence of traditions emanating from the territory of the Corieltauvi across the Humber. Such an improvement would be consistent with the gradual introduction of a more settled economy. The development can perhaps best be seen by comparing the coarse plain vessels from Dane's Graves with the later collection from an occupation site at Emmotland in Holderness (Brewster 1963). The Emmotland vessels are not only better made and finished but are constructed in more positive forms, mostly jars with everted rims but occasionally bead-rimmed jars and small bowls reminiscent of the styles from the south. A scatter of Claudio-Neronian brooches from Parisian territory, together with the large quantity of imported Gallo-Belgic wares from North Ferriby on the north bank of the Humber, leaves little doubt that trading relations had been established with the south by the Claudian period, if not earlier. North Ferriby may well have been the principal 'gateway community' through which products from the Roman province south of the Humber were introduced into the territory of the Parisi. A settlement, producing a similar range of material, lay on the opposite bank at South Ferriby and must have been part of the transshipment system. It is possible that this was the way by which commodities entered barbarian territory en route to Stanwick though some must have been deflected into the hands of the Parisian elite. An awareness of the material advantages of Romanization may have been instrumental in encouraging the tribe to offer no resistance to the eventual penetration by the Roman army in 71–2.

Southern Scotland: Votadini, Novantae, Selgovae and Damnonii

(Figure 9.6)

Between the Tyne–Solway and the Clyde–Forth lines, which later approximated to the frontiers constructed under Hadrian and Antoninus Pius, four major tribal groups can be distinguished.

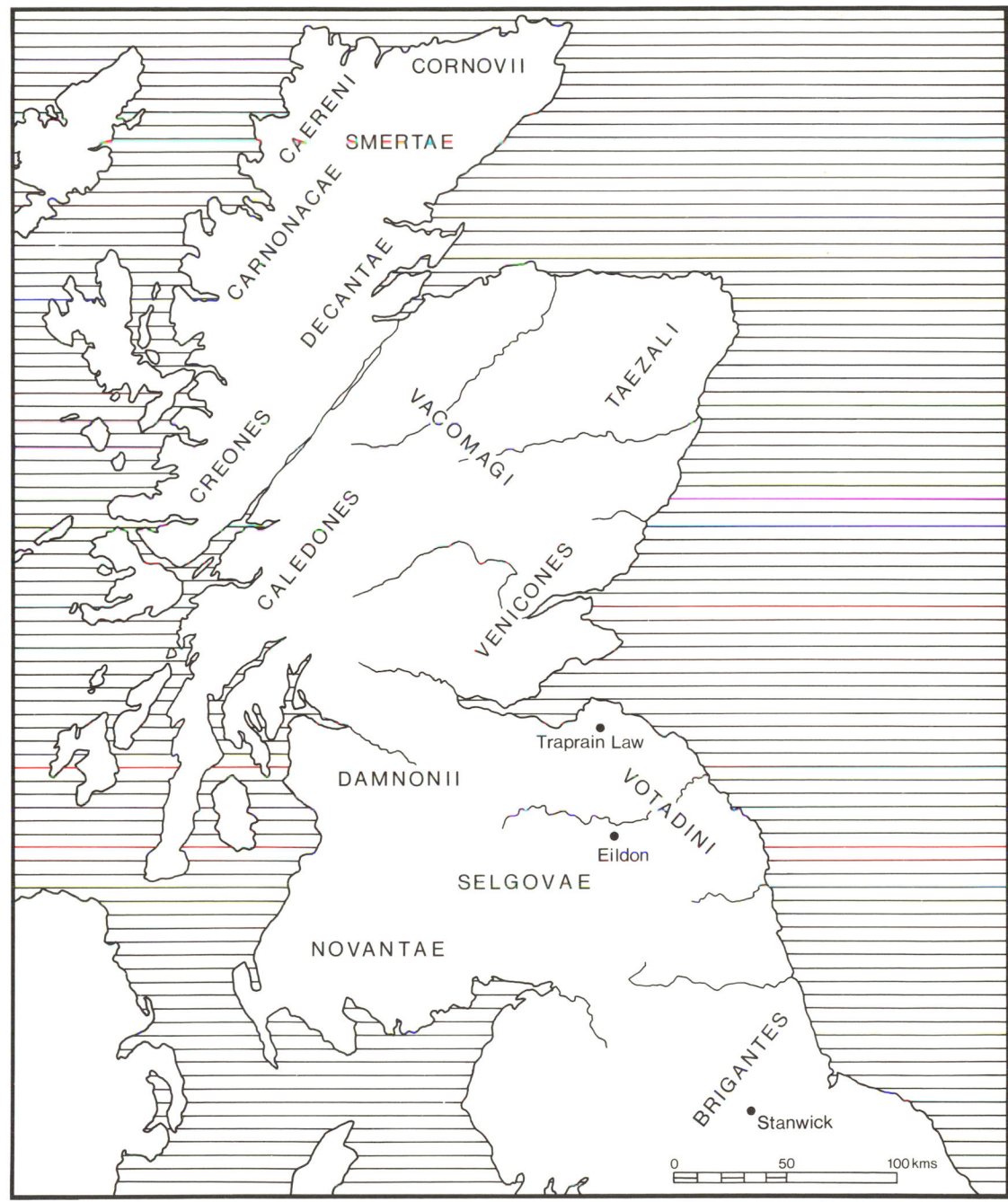

Figure 9.6 The tribes of northern Britain (sources: various).

The Votadini occupied the eastern coastal region and the lowlands between the Tyne and the Clyde, the Novantae covered the area of Galloway and Dumfriesshire, while the Selgovae lay between the two. North of the Novantae and stretching along the west coast to the Clyde was the territory of the Damnonii. How significant were the social and political differences between the groups at the time when they were distinguished by Roman writers in the first and second centuries AD it is impossible to say, except that the Votadini appear to have been more generously treated by the Romans than their neighbours the Selgovae, an observation which, if substantiated, might hint at a distinction between tribal policies. Nor is it possible to define how far back in time tribal distinctions can be traced, since there is no historical or numismatic evidence upon which to base conclusions. Any description of the area must, therefore, rely substantially on the form and distribution of settlement sites and upon the somewhat sparse material culture recovered by excavation.

While a very large number of settlement sites are known in the area, as a result of extensive field surveys carried out by the staff of the Royal Commission on Historical Monuments and by G. Jobey, it is extremely difficult to assign dates to them except for the earlier sites (pp. 49–50) for which a number of radiocarbon determinations are available. On typological grounds, however, two major classes of settlements and homesteads can be defined as belonging to the period stretching from the end of the pre-Roman Iron Age into the Roman era: 'scooped enclosures', consisting of walled enclosures containing huts and yards terraced into the natural slope of the hill, and settlements of stone-built huts. The latter are relatively common, particularly in the territory of the Votadini, but any apparent differential distribution may be due largely to different intensities in the archaeological fieldwork. The dating evidence obtained for some of these settlements suggests an initial occupation in the second century AD but this does not preclude an earlier beginning for others. The abandonment of many of the small hillforts and defended enclosures probably occurred throughout the first century AD, but no indisputable dating evidence survives and it may well be that some at least continued in use. By the end of their life, many of them had developed into multivallate structures, some with close-set defences, others with their ramparts more widely spaced in a manner similar to that of the multiple-ditched enclosures of south-west Britain.

Many of the larger hillforts evidently continued to be occupied. The principal fort of the Votadini, the long-established Traprain Law in East Lothian, remained the tribal centre throughout the Roman occupation, but the Selgovian centre on Eildon Hill North, Roxburgh, seems to have been abandoned by the time of the Flavian advance. A general consideration of the forts of both the Selgovae and the Votadini tends to suggest a gradual amalgamation of nucleated communities at an increasingly restricted number of sites in a manner paralleled in southern Britain. This might well represent a growing political cohesion which eventually manifested itself in organized tribal attitudes to Rome. Herein might lie the reason why Agricola subdued the eastern areas of Scotland first before turning his attention to the more fragmented Novantae and Damnonii, where there are only four hillforts in excess of 2.5 ha compared with thirteen in the territory of the Selgovae and Votadini.

A few brochs are known in Votadinian territory, with rather more spreading down the west coast into the lands of the Damnonii and Novantae. One can be shown to be secondary to the multivallate hillfort at Torwoodlee, Selkirk, while at Edin's Hall, Berwick, a broch follows a hillfort but is replaced by a stone-built settlement. Dates ranging from the first into the second century AD are indicated for the occupation of the southern brochs where there is sufficient material to be sure. Various suggestions have been made to explain the occurrence of brochs in the area, including the importation of broch-building mercenaries by the Votadini, following the first Roman withdrawal from Scotland, but the matter must remain beyond proof.

Northern Scotland (Figure 9.6)

North of the Forth–Clyde line the names of some twelve tribes are recorded, but since they are not easy to differentiate historically or archaeologically it is simpler to describe the area and its settlements in general terms.

The Highland Massif, the homeland of the Caledonians, divides the area into two: the eastern coastal region occupied by the Venicones, the Vacomagi and the Taezali; and the north and west coasts and islands (the Atlantic province) settled by the Epidii, Creones, Carnonacae, Caereni, Cornovii, Smertae, Lugi and Decantae. In the north-eastern region the basic folk culture of the Abernethy complex continued largely unchanged. Defended settlement sites, duns, hillforts and occasional brochs occur but are relatively little-known in archaeological terms. It was through this area that the last campaigns of Agricola were fought, and it was somewhere here that the great army of the Caledonians under their leader Calgacus met its defeat, leaving the countryside depleted for a generation or two. Events of this magnitude must have left their mark on the settlement pattern but it still remains to be defined.

The Atlantic province, largely untouched by Rome, continued to develop in relative isolation, giving rise to a range of highly distinctive structures and a material culture well adapted to the needs of the environment. Reassessing the evidence in 1934, Childe referred to the structures of the area as the *castle complex*, in order to emphasize the basic unity of the hundreds of small forts, duns and brochs which characterized the densely fortified landscape. Broadly speaking, these 'castles' can be divided into duns and brochs, both of which can be further subdivided on the basis of their form, siting and regional distribution (MacKie 1965c, figure 2). The details of these structures are considered below (chapter 14) and need not concern us now.

The material culture belonging to the settlements of the Atlantic province presents much the same variety as that of the contemporary sites in the south, with the one exception that iron was never plentiful. Bone was made into needles, awls, gouges, bobbins, long-handled combs, spindle whorls and dice; bronze was used for ring-headed pins and spiral finger-rings; while stone of various kinds continued in use for tool-making, for the production of armlets out of jet and for the manufacture of small vessels. Another similarity to southern Britain is that pottery was well made and relatively plentiful; moreover, it is susceptible to regional and chronological division. In the west several distinct styles have been defined; these include *Clettraval ware*, characterized by globular jars with everted rims, decorated by a finger-pinched girth cordon with concentric channelled semi-circles in a zone above (Figure A:36, p. 589). Alongside the later stages of the development, *Vaul ware* appears in two basic forms: large barrel-shaped urns and smaller jars with an S-shaped profile and slightly everted rim; both types are often decorated with incised geometric patterns. Broadly contemporary with the Vaul wares are the barrel-shaped *Balevullin* vessels with finger-printed girth cordons, sometimes ornamented with simple incised patterns.

In the northern area of Orkney, Shetland, Caithness and Sutherland incised and cordoned wares are almost entirely lacking. Instead, the commonest types are tall jars with small beaded or everted rims, sometimes with well-burnished surfaces, which developed out of the pre-broch wares at Clickhimin and can therefore be referred to as the *Clickhimin IV* style. The type is widespread in the north and occasionally penetrates into the west. The main feature is the shouldered jar with internally-fluted everted rim (Figures A:36, p. 589 and A:37, p. 590). Sometimes cordons are applied at the junction of rim and body and a few examples have bases internally impressed with patterns of finger-marks.

Very few well-stratified sites have yet been adequately examined in the Atlantic province but the range of material now available from Clickhimin, Jarlshof, Dun Mor Vaul, Crosskirk, Bu Broch, etc., is at last allowing the copious material culture to be arranged in a sequence related to structural development. A first assessment of this was offered by MacKie (1965c, figure 6) but until more excavation has been undertaken, details of sequential development and regionalism will remain obscure.

Childe believed that the broch culture arose as the result of intrusive elements emanating from south-west Britain (1935b, 237–9; 1946, 94). This view was expanded by Sir Lindsey Scott (1948), who attempted to show that the pottery, as well as the architecture and the rest of the material culture, could be derived directly from the south-west and that in his view the entire culture was introduced by 'colonists'. MacKie (1965c) has argued convincingly for the indigenous development of the broch and the wheelhouse together with much of the ceramic tradition, but still retains the belief (1969a) in an immigration from the south some time in the first century BC. As D.V. Clarke (1970) has shown, however, the supposed evidence for immigration is far from satisfactory and can all be explained in terms of trade and other forms of peaceful contact not requiring folk movement.

By the time of the Roman invasion, the Northern and Western Isles were very strongly defended by more than 500 local chieftains living in their broch towers. The fact that in AD 43 a treaty was concluded between the Roman fleet and the Orcadian chieftains is perhaps indicative of their significance in the eyes of the Roman commanders. The treaty probably continued to be honoured, for when Agricola destroyed the mainland resistance in the battle of Mons Graupius in AD 84, he was able to claim that the conquest of Britain had been completed, though not before the islands had been visited by the Roman fleet.

In the ensuing peace the fortifications were gradually dismantled and were replaced by wheelhouses representing a resurgence of the native traditions of domestic architecture. Local economy flourished at first and trading relations were maintained with the Roman world, during which time luxury goods like glass and pottery together with a few coins trickled in, but with the collapse of the Roman administration in the south a decline set in and the material culture became much simpler until it was once more reduced to a level not unlike that of the Late Bronze Age.

10
The establishment of Roman control

The military history of Britain in the first century AD has received considerable attention from archaeologists and historians and need not be enlarged upon here, but it is necessary, for the sake of our theme, to examine the reaction of the native tribes of Britain to the threat and actuality of Roman rule.

In the early decades of the first century AD the presence of Rome just across the Channel was a political reality to which the British tribes had to relate. The Trinovantes/Catuvellauni seem to have been on friendly terms with Rome and the quantity of trade goods and diplomatic gifts which poured into their territory is a measure of this relationship. Using the same yardstick it could be argued that the other coastal tribes – the Cantii, Atrebates and Durotriges were far less favoured and may even have been hostile. Such a situation would not be at all surprising: the Cantii had opposed and attacked Caesar, the Atrebatic household was founded by Commius – a sworn enemy of Rome – while the Durotriges may have been punished and thereby impoverished for supporting the Armoricans in their revolt against Rome in 56 BC. But attitudes and allegiances established in the wake of the Gallic Wars are likely to have changed in the ninety years or so leading up to the conquest, especially if the growing strength of the Trinovantes/Catuvellauni was seen as a threat by neighbouring tribes and perhaps also by the Roman authorities. Pressures of this kind would have created new hegemonies and new rivalries while the immediacy of the Roman invasion threat might have encouraged the more opportunist leaders to alter their allegiances in the interests of expediency. Certainly the flight of the Atrebatic king, Verica, to Rome just before the invasion, could suggest that the tribe was beginning to look to Rome as a patron in time of stress.

Tension was further heightened by the accession of the two Trinovantian or Catuvellaunian leaders Togodumnus and Caratacus in or very soon after AD 40, following the death of Cunobelin. The instability which must have been created by a change of leadership after so many years of unified rule may well have led to internal divisions within the tribe, in addition to a feeling of unease in the surrounding areas. In about 42 Verica fled to Rome to ask for the help of the Emperor Claudius. No doubt Verica would have provided the emperor and his advisers with an up-to-date assessment of the political situation in Britain. Moreover, his flight could have been interpreted by the Roman propaganda machine as the expulsion of a friend and ally in whose interests military intervention in Britain was the only honourable course.

The invasion began towards the end of April AD 43 with the landing of the Roman army in Kent. After several unsuccessful skirmishes in east Kent, Caratacus and Togodumnus withdrew their army behind the river Medway and there pitted the whole weight of the British resistance against the Romans. For two days the river line was held but Roman superiority of arms eventually triumphed. The battle was decisive. British opposition melted away; Togodumnus subsequently died in battle while Caratacus moved to the west to continue the fight, eventually ending up as a resistance leader in south Wales among the Silures. The dramatic collapse of centralized opposition in the south-east was rapidly followed up by the Roman advance across the Thames and the drive on the native capital at Camulodunum, led by the emperor himself. By the end of July the opposition of the south-eastern tribes had been totally smashed and all that remained was to mop up pockets of resistance and establish military control.

The relative ease of the initial stages of the advance had depended to a large extent upon a stable left flank, a stability which was provided by the buffering effect of the Atrebatic enclave in Sussex and east Hampshire. Had it not been for the presence of this friendly tribe, the hostile elements of the south-west could have created a serious threat to the extended Roman supply lines across Kent. It was, then, very much in the Roman interest to ensure the political stability of the area. The flight of Verica to Rome implies unrest, but whether as the result of external threats or of internal differences is unknown. The Roman attitude was clear enough, for almost immediately there appears in the area a client king, Tiberius Claudius Cogidubnus, who was later to style himself 'great king in Britain' (Bogaers 1979). While it is possible that he was left by Verica to hold on to the reins of government in his absence and was therefore already in power when the Romans landed, it could be argued either that he was a Roman nominee selected at the time of the invasion from among the ruling household or, more likely, that he was a member of the Atrebatic aristocracy living in exile who was brought in by the army. An explanation in these terms would account for the rapid and dramatic Romanization of the kingdom in the thirty years following the invasion. Whatever the precise explanation, there is a good case for suggesting the landing of a military detachment in the Chichester region in parallel with the main advance through Kent to stabilize the area and keep an eye on dissident elements. Such a force could have brought the king with it and established his right to rule by its very presence. A strongly pro-Roman client king could have been used as a diplomatic tool to persuade neighbouring rulers, uncertain of their allegiance, to support the Roman cause. Indeed it may have been through the good offices of Cogidubnus that a king of the Dobunni capitulated while the Roman army was still fighting its way across Kent.

Cogidubnus was a success as a client king, for Tacitus records his faithful support of Rome into the 70s or 80s. Two inscriptions from Chichester serve to emphasize the extent of Romanization. One records the erection of a statue, probably equestrian, to Nero in AD 58, while the second, a dedicatory slab from a temple to Neptune and Minerva erected to the honour of the Divine House of the Emperor, probably in the early 80s, gives Cogidubnus the title of great king, which he may have been granted as a supporter of Vespasian following the upheavals of AD 69. It has also been suggested that the great palatial building at Fishbourne, Sussex, may have been the residence of the king in his later years (Cunliffe 1971b). In total, the evidence for rapid and thorough Romanization is impressive but that Cogidubnus may at first have had difficulty with his subjects is hinted at by the growing evidence of military remains at Chichester, the possibility being that the king may have required a supporting garrison to establish and maintain his

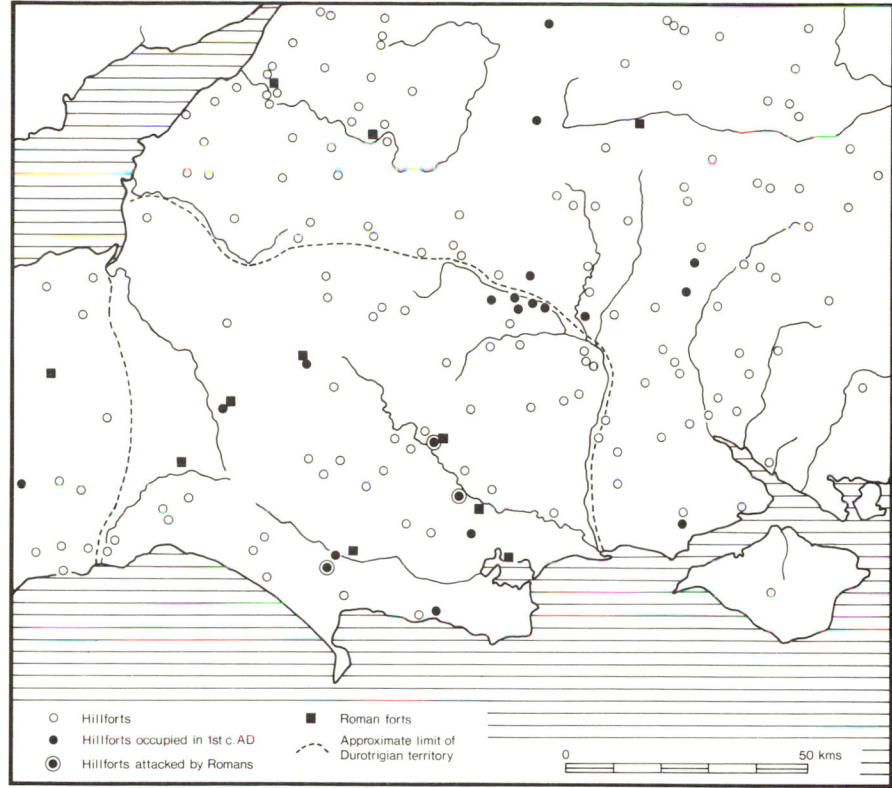

Figure 10.1 Native and Roman forts among the Durotriges (source: Ordnance Survey, Map of Southern Britain in the Iron Age, with additions).

control at least in the early years of his reign. Nevertheless, from the Roman point of view the arrangement was a resounding success, as Tacitus puts it (*Agricola*, 14), 'an example of the long-established Roman custom of employing even kings to make others slaves'.

The Durotriges offered a more intractable problem. They remained culturally isolated from the tribes of the south-east and in place of unified government it may well be that the tribe was split into smaller units owing allegiance to local chieftains. At any event it fell to Vespasian, leading the *Legio II Augusta*, to hack his way, one hillfort at a time, across Durotrigan territory late in 43 or early in 44. After taking the Isle of Wight, fighting thirty battles and destroying more than twenty hillforts, he could claim to have conquered two powerful tribes. Archaeological traces of the campaign are vivid (Figure 10.1). At the time, native forts like Hod Hill, Maiden Castle and South Cadbury were being actively strengthened in archaic defensive styles, and it is probable that many of the other Dorset sites were being brought into defensive order to meet the threat. Actual attack can be demonstrated at several forts. At Hod Hill the chieftain's hut was softened up by ballista fire from a tower sited close to the defences, as is shown by the concentration and distribution of iron ballista bolts around the hut. How the inhabitants responded is unknown, but shortly afterwards the fort was cleared and a Roman garrison housed in one corner. Maiden Castle succumbed to a violent attack in which a number of its defenders were cut down in close fighting or killed by ballista fire, their bodies later to be buried hurriedly, but in native style, in a cemetery at the east entrance (but see p. 208). At Spettisbury, on the other hand, a number of bodies together with fragments of their equipment were bundled unceremoniously in a large pit, possibly at the hands of the Roman army tidying up after an attack. As more of the Dorset hillforts are excavated similar evidence will no doubt come to light, although not necessarily all were assaulted at this time. Tiresome though this method of warfare must have been to the Romans, it posed little real difficulty, for the hillforts of the south-west were designed to withstand local raids rather than Roman siege methods. Nevertheless, the strength of the resistance demanded the garrisoning of a number of separate contingents at strategic points throughout the territory, simply to remind the Durotriges of the military presence.

The reference in Suetonius's account of the conquest of *two* tribes in the south-west raises problems to which there are at present no clear answers. It is generally assumed that the second tribe were the Dumnonii but the early military dispositions hardly support this. On balance, it would seem more reasonable to suppose that the area referred to was Salisbury Plain north of the Nadder and west of the Test, which had originally been under Atrebatic domination but may, by the time of the conquest, have split with the pro-Roman rulers and become allied with one of the anti-Roman tribes – either the Dobunni or the Durotriges. Possibly it was under some form of Catuvellaunian control. At any event, many of the hillforts of the region appear to have been maintained in defensive order, although firm archaeological evidence of attack is at present wanting. That the region was regarded as administratively, and presumably culturally, separate from the surrounding tribes is shown in its classification by the Roman authorities as part of the administrative region of the Belgae.

The political situation among the Dobunni at the time of the invasion is difficult to ascertain but Dio records that a king of the Dobunni offered his submission to Rome. This could imply that the entire tribe went over to the Roman side but it need only have been a faction. Culturally the tribal area was divided into two separate entities, roughly by the Bristol Avon (p. 172) and in the Roman administrative reorganization of the province the southern territory was incorporated into an artificial creation, *civitas Belgarum*. One possible explanation for these facts is that the northern core of the Dobunni, based on Bagendon, threw in their lot with Rome, perhaps as a reaction to the Catuvellaunian dominance which they appear to have suffered, while the loosely attached southern group went their own way opposing Rome and paying the price for their opposition by losing their identity. Both regions were, however, garrisoned as part of the military frontier zone, anchored to the line of the Fosse Way running parallel to the Severn–Trent axis.

The northern neighbours of the Trinovantes, the Iceni of East Anglia, submitted to Rome immediately after the initial stage of the invasion, their leader being among the eleven kings who offered their support to Claudius. The identity of the king is unknown but it may well have been Prasutagus who remained faithful to Rome until his death. As a Roman client king he continued to issue silver coins bearing a Roman bust and the legend SUBRI PRASTO on the obverse and a horse with the words ESICO FECIT on the reverse. The client kingdom came to a dramatic end with the king's death in AD 60, and the revolt, led by his wife Boudica, consequent upon it.

The political attitudes of the two remaining tribes in the Midlands, the Corieltauvi and the Cornovii, are not recorded but the apparent ease with which the Roman frontier was constructed across the land belonging to the former and close to the territory of the latter would suggest some kind of treaty relationship. Quite possibly the Corieltauvi, along with the Iceni and Dobunni, were suffering from the expansionist policies of their south-eastern neighbours and regarded the Romans as the lesser of the two evils.

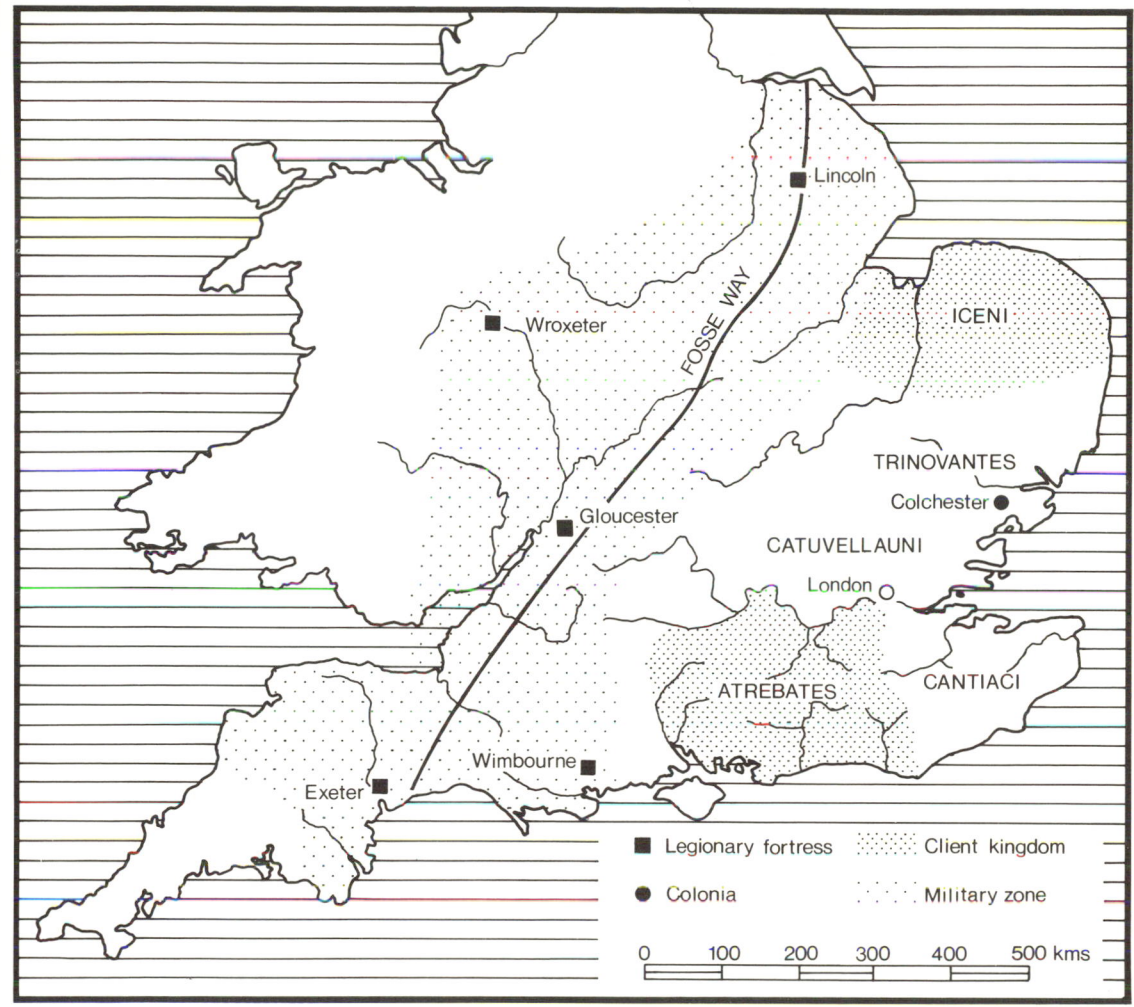

Figure 10.2   Southern Britain in the decades following the invasion of AD 43 (source: Cunliffe 1988a).

Thus by AD 47 the most civilized part of Britain – the area south and east of the Fosse frontier – had been thoroughly subdued by the army and, apart from the client kingdoms of the Iceni and the Regni (as the southern Atrebates were called), the region was now under direct military control (Figure 10.2). The positioning of the first frontier zone along the Jurassic ridge is interesting. In adopting this line the Roman strategists were choosing a natural line of communication fronted by an almost continuous river line – the Severn–Trent axis – but they were also using the three peripheral tribes – the Durotriges, Dobunni and Corieltauvi as their military zone leaving the south-eastern core tribes to develop into the province while excluding the underdeveloped tribes of the west and north. The use of the peripheral zone as a frontier shows a keen understanding of the political geography of the country.

To the west and north of the Fosse frontier were less congenial regions, difficult to conquer and of uncertain productive capacity. These evidently lay beyond Roman territorial desires, but those

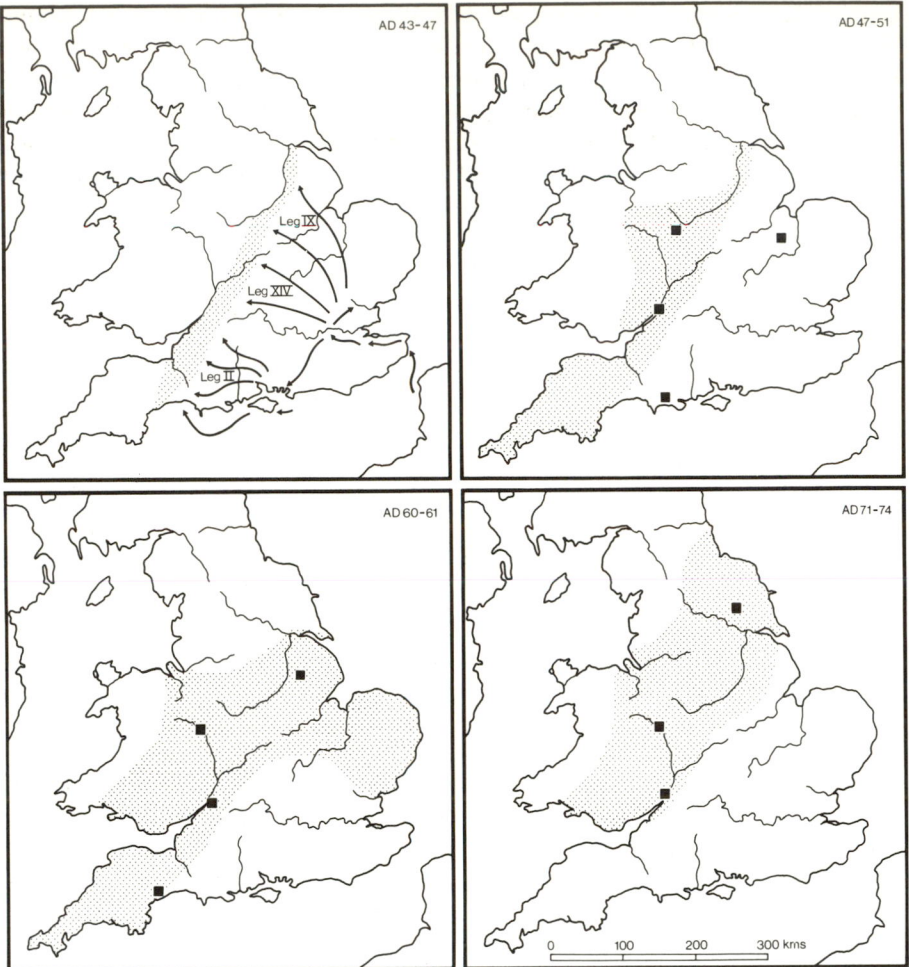

Figure 10.3 The Roman conquest of southern Britain. The military zone is stippled; black squares indicate legionary bases (sources: various).

tribes immediately adjacent to the frontier had to be brought into some form of relationship with the new government. The Dumnonii in the south-west peninsula were probably quite friendly: they had, after all, been trading freely with foreigners for years. Moreover, the frontier and the military presence at Exeter successfully isolated the peninsula and rendered the tribe of little potential danger. In the Midlands were the Dobunni, part of whose territory lay inside the military zone and who were therefore forced to behave, and the Cornovii, with whom a treaty had probably been negotiated. Finally, across the north of Britain 'from sea to sea' lay a complex of tribes dominated by the Brigantes, whose loyalty to Rome was at most times evident but precarious. Thus the Dobunni and Cornovii were employed as buffer states against Wales, while the Brigantes served to absorb pressures from the northern tribes.

Native resistance had been virtually wiped out in the south-east but, with the powerful war-leader Caratacus, the focus of the anti-Roman movement passed to south Wales, to the territory of the Silures whence, in the winter of 47–8, he launched a fierce attack against a tribe allied to Rome – presumably the Dobunni in the Severn valley. This event, and the growing strength of the British resistance which it represented, forced the new Roman governor Ostorius Scapula to adopt a more aggressive military policy which entailed occupying the west Midlands and thus isolating the tribes of Wales from the Brigantes. To gain the necessary mastery of the Bristol Channel, Dumnonia had to be occupied as well. The preparations did not go unnoticed by the free Britons: the advance into the territory of the Deceangli in north Wales was greeted by a minor uprising among the Brigantes or one of their clients, some of whom may have considered their independence further threatened by this move, while the disarming of the south-eastern tribes, a necessary precaution to protect the Roman rear, was met by a revolt in Icenian territory which had to be put down by an auxiliary detachment.

After these preparations had been consolidated and the consequent unrest dealt with, the army moved against Caratacus, first in Silurian territory and then into the Ordovician lands of north Wales where Caratacus had moved, presumably to be closer to his escape route to the north. After a while Caratacus finally abandoned his guerrilla tactics and chose to make a stand at a strongly fortified hill-top. The battle was lost and he was forced to flee to the Brigantes, whose Queen Cartimandua handed him over to the Roman authorities in AD 51. The capture of the war-leader did not, however, mean the end of Welsh resistance, which was to last for nearly thirty years more. In 51 or 52 the Silures defeated a legion, inflicting very considerable casualties, but during the later 50s they were gradually worn down by the continuous campaigning of Didius Gallus and kept under some form of control by the establishment of forts. But at this time the Roman intention was not to conquer: it was merely to destroy resistance and thus remove the threat to the frontier.

Imperial policy changed dramatically in AD 58 with the arrival of Q. Veranius, whose orders were evidently to conquer the rest of Britain. A single season's campaigning among the Silures was sufficient to smash their resistance once and for all. When the next season's campaign began in 59 (under the command of Suetonius Paullinus) the army was able to concentrate on the north, presumably weakening the resistance of the Ordovices before marching against the Druid stronghold on Anglesey, described by Tacitus as a 'source of strength to the rebels' (*Agricola* xiv) – a reference, no doubt, to the widespread respect and power which the Druids still held as well as to the island's function as a haven for refugees. Tacitus's description of the storming of the island is vivid: 'The enemy lined the shore in a dense armed mass. Among them were black-robed women with dishevelled hair like Furies, brandishing torches. Nearby stood the Druids raising their hands to heaven and screaming dreadful curses.' Overcoming their fear, the Roman soldiers pushed on to victory and destroyed 'the groves devoted to Mona's barbarous superstitions' (*Annals* xiv, 30).

The annexing of Anglesey meant the end to organized resistance in Wales, but before consolidation could be undertaken, the Boudican rebellion broke out, requiring the full attention of the army in the south-east. Fourteen years passed before the Welsh problem was faced again, by which time old wounds had healed and a new generation of fighters had emerged. From 74 to 77 Julius Frontinus campaigned to and fro across the principality, suffering some serious setbacks, but by the end of his term of office most of the area had been subdued and it only remained for the next governor, Julius Agricola, to complete the work in a single campaign in AD 78. Thereafter the Ordovices and Silures were kept in the firm grip of a complex of permanent forts and roads. Other tribes like the Demetae of the south-west, who are never recorded as having opposed Rome, were left to develop in peaceful isolation.

While the Welsh tribes on the western border of the province were gradually being beaten into submission, trouble broke out among the northern confederacy of the Brigantes. The first hint of unrest (*discordiae*) occurred in 47–8 as a result of the Roman thrust into Flintshire. It was serious enough to compel the Roman general to return, but 'after a few who began the hostilities had been slain and the rest pardoned, the Brigantes settled down quietly' (Tacitus, *Annals* xii, 32). The use of the word 'discord' to describe the uprising tends to suggest internal troubles, which were probably put down by the ruling house without the need for Roman help. It was probably a minor incident but it heralded the split between the pro-Roman and anti-Roman factions which was eventually to destroy the confederacy.

Caratacus must have been relying on the strength of the anti-Roman feeling when in 51 he fled into Brigantia 'seeking the protection of Queen Cartimandua', but he had misjudged the situation and was immediately turned over to the Roman authorities. Such an act is best seen as an attempt by the queen to demonstrate a loyalty to Rome and to underline her own position of power in the eyes of the army of occupation. She had, after all, just witnessed the overwhelming successes of the Roman forces in Wales; some token of loyalty may have been deemed necessary to prevent Roman intervention in her kingdom.

Within the next seven years, however, the unified rule of the confederacy began to split up. A quarrel broke out between Cartimandua and her husband Venutius, both of whom had previously been loyal to Rome. Civil war followed, Venutius immediately assuming an anti-Roman position and, by doing so, taking upon himself the mantle of resistance leader of the free Britons. Cartimandua 'by cunning stratagems, captured the brothers and kinsfolk of Venutius' (Tacitus, *Annals* xii, 40), which understandably annoyed him and led him to invade her part of the kingdom. The position became so serious that it was eventually necessary for a Roman legion to be sent some time about 57–8, with the purpose of keeping the two sides apart.

Matters finally came to a head during the confusion in the year 69.

> Inspired by the differences between the Roman forces, and by the many rumours of civil war that reached them, the Britons plucked up courage under the leadership of Venutius who, in addition to his natural spirit and hatred of the Roman name, was fired by personal resentment towards Queen Cartimandua.
>
> (Tacitus, *Hist.* iii, 45)

One of the reasons for Venutius's evident distaste for his wife was that she had married his armour-bearer Vellocatus. 'So Venutius, calling in aid from outside, and at the same time assisted by a revolt among the Brigantes themselves, put Cartimandua into an extremely dangerous position.' Cartimandua was forced to ask the Roman administration for military assistance but even the intervention of a substantial contingent of cavalry and infantry could do little more than snatch the queen from danger. Thus by *c.* 70 'the throne was left to Venutius, the war to us'.

The narrative of Tacitus leaves very little doubt that the north was now in a state of widespread open rebellion led by the Brigantes, backed up by tribes extending far north into the interior. For the Roman province to the south the situation was serious. Immediately Vespasian had gained the throne and the civil disturbances were at an end, the new governor of Britain, Petillius Cerialis, began a three-year campaign in the north from 71–4. 'After a series of battles, some not uncostly, Cerialis had operated, if not actually triumphed, over the major part of the [Brigantian] territory' (Tacitus, *Agricola* xvii). During this time Brigantian resistance must have been smashed and Venutius defeated, for in spite of a lull of five years or so while Wales was being subdued, there was little further trouble in the area when Agricola began his thrust to the far north. By the early 80s the whole of Brigantia was enmeshed in a close-knit network of forts and roads, which divided the old confederacy into a multiplicity of easily patrolled fragments.

In the three decades during which the Roman armies were forced to subdue the warlike peoples of Wales and the Pennines, the Romanization of the south-east was being completed, but in spite of a deliberate and well-used programme employing client kings, making substantial monetary loans to noble families, founding *coloniae* and undertaking elaborate schemes of urban building, progress was by no means smooth. The first hints that all was not well occurred in AD 47, when some of the Icenian tribesmen, objecting to being disarmed, organized a resistance movement and constructed fortifications. The revolt was easily put down but it must have shown the authorities that a certain instability existed in the client kingdom of the Iceni.

Trouble came to a head in 59–60 with the death of Prasutagus. In his will he had adopted the wise procedure of making the emperor joint heir with his two daughters, but it is evident from what followed that the Roman administration intended to absorb the client kingdom into the province, quite probably because it was regarded as a point of instability. The Icenian nobles, led by Boudica, resisted with the result that a military detachment was sent in;

> the first outrage was the flogging of his wife Boudica and the rape of his daughters: then the Icenian nobles were deprived of their ancestral estates. . . these outrages, and the fear of worse now that they had been reduced to the status of a province, moved the Iceni to arms.
>
> (Tacitus, *Annals* xiv, 32)

The time was ripe for rebellion, for a new generation of fighters had grown up, the Roman army was heavily occupied in Anglesey and there was a widespread dissatisfaction with Roman fiscal measures.

The Iceni were not alone: their neighbours to the south, the Trinovantes, joined in together with 'other tribes who were unsubdued by slavery' (ibid., 32), implying help from beyond the Fosse frontier, perhaps from the Brigantes. The Trinovantes had a particular reason for dissatisfaction, for it was at the site of their tribal capital, Camulodunum, that the Romans had established a *colonia* which had entailed the appropriation of thousands of hectares of the surrounding farmland for the veterans now settled there. To make the situation even worse, the government had built a temple to the Emperor Claudius in the *colonia* – no doubt in an attempt to refocus the religious feeling of the natives on the empire and away from Druidic nationalism. The policy misfired.

The revolt which followed was violent: London, Camulodunum and Verulamium were destroyed, the Ninth Legion was driven back and the procurator fled to Gaul.

> The Britons had no thought of taking prisoners or selling them as slaves, nor for any of the usual commerce of war, but only of slaughter, the gibbet, fire and the cross. They knew they would have to pay the penalty: meantime they hurried on to extract vengeance in advance.
>
> (ibid., 33)

It is evident that in the initial stages, the rebellion succeeded more by its fury than by its planning. Gradually, as the impetus was dissipated, the power of the rebels waned and eventually Boudica was forced to accept a set battle at a site chosen by the Roman commander,

Suetonius Paullinus, probably because winter was approaching and food supplies were running short. British fighting tactics had changed little since the invasions of Caesar: cavalry and infantry were mixed up, chariots were still used, and women and children came along as spectators to watch the fight. It was a classic contest with British enthusiasm pitted against Roman order. Inevitably British resistance broke:

> The Romans did not spare the women, and the bodies of the baggage-animals, pierced with spears, were added to the piles of corpses. It was a glorious victory equal to those of the good old days: some estimate as many as 80,000 British dead . . . Boudica ended her life with poison.
>
> (ibid., 37).

The situation among the Durotriges seems to have been tense throughout the revolt and indeed the military commander thought it expedient to remain there rather than join the army of Paullinus as he was commanded. Some hint of the trouble comes from the hillfort of South Cadbury, Somerset, where a war cemetery dating to the Boudican period has been found. This raises the possibility that the famous Maiden Castle war cemetery may also be of this date rather than belonging to the initial advance in AD 43 but the dating evidence is too imprecise to be sure.

The situation did not ease with the British defeat. 'The territory of all tribes that had been hostile or neutral was laid waste with fire and sword. But famine was the worst of the hardships, for they had omitted to sow crops . . . .' The events of 60–1 must have reduced eastern England to a virtual desert, and not until Paullinus was replaced could the process of reconstruction begin. Indeed, it was to take ten years before the province was stable enough for renewed military activity in the north.

As we have seen, much of Brigantia was explored by Cerialis in 71–4 and some part of the area must have been thoroughly garrisoned, sufficient at least to prevent further trouble from recalcitrant tribesmen. With the arrival of the new governor, Julius Agricola, in the summer of AD 78, a new forward policy was initiated. After tidying up the occupation of north Wales, Agricola could concentrate on the conquest of the north (Figure 10.4). He spent the campaigning season of 79 consolidating the somewhat tentative occupation of Brigantia, probably as far north as the Tyne–Solway line. By a series of minor plundering raids followed up by bribes, he was able to take control of the entire region, including some tribes which had previously been outside the Roman sphere of interest. The ease with which Brigantia was thus absorbed is a clear reflection of the success of the Cerialian campaigns and presumably of the spread of the enervating luxuries of Romanization from the south. The spirit of resistance and the unity of the area had been smashed.

To the north of the Brigantes lay three tribes: the Novantae of the south-west lowlands, the Selgovae in the centre and the Votadini occupying the east coast. Since it was probably from these tribes that Venutius had received help ten years earlier, they were clearly regarded as a potential threat to the security of the Roman province and had to be brought under Roman control. Accordingly, in 80 Agricola marched north, forcing his way to the river Tay. After wintering in Scotland, he spent the next year building forts and roads with the evident intention of consolidating the Clyde–Forth line as a frontier. 'This neck was now secured by garrisons, and the whole sweep of country to the south was safe in our hands. The enemy had been pushed into what was virtually another island' (Tacitus, *Agricola* xxiii). Much of the military activity in the lowlands was concentrated in Selgovian territory, where presumably the main resistance lay.

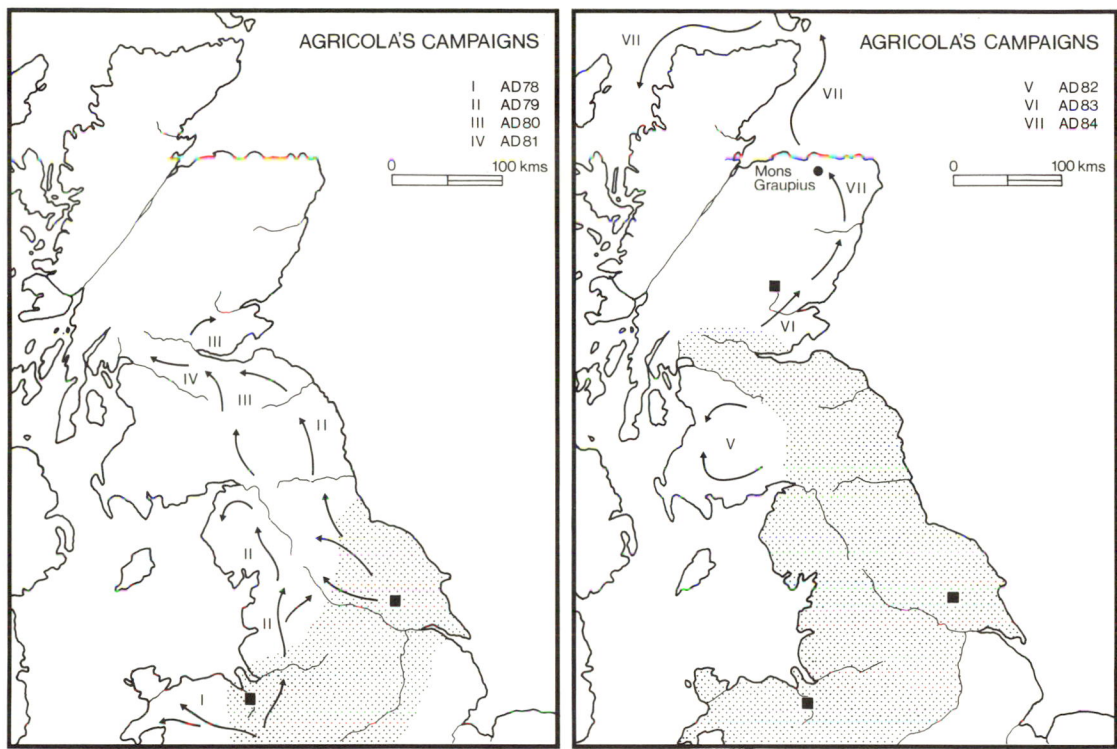

Figure 10.4   The Roman conquest of northern Britain. The military zone is stippled; black squares indicate legionary bases (sources: various).

The tribal oppidum on Eildon Hill may have been slighted at this time, and the principal Roman fort of the whole northern system was built close by at Newstead. The Votadini, on the other hand, were less harshly treated: fewer forts were established in their territory and their tribal capital on Traprain Law was allowed to remain in occupation. The Novantae of south-western Scotland, together with other more remote tribes, were the subject of a separate campaign in 82, at the end of which Agricola stood on the shore and looked across to Ireland, estimating that it could be conquered and held with a single legion and a few auxiliaries.

So far the army had met with little organized opposition, but when in the next spring they moved north again along the eastern coastal plain beyond the Tay, Caledonian resistance began to harden. Even with the support of sea-borne supplies and reinforcements, Roman communications were seriously stretched, but gradually forts were established at the mouths of the glens to bottle up the tribesmen in the mountains, and the Roman hold strengthened. Once they had overcome their initial surprise at the speed of the Roman advance, the Caledonians began to organize a more aggressive resistance, culminating in the attack on a Roman fort which only narrowly escaped destruction. 'With unbroken spirit', says Tacitus, 'they persisted in arming their whole fighting force, putting their wives and children in places of safety and ratifying their league by conference and sacrifice' (*Agricola*, 27).

Thus by the beginning of the summer of AD 84 the scene was set for the final confrontation between the two armies at Mons Graupius. 'The Britons, undaunted by the loss of the previous battle, welcomed the choice between revenge and enslavement . . . . Already more than 30,000 of them made a gallant show, and still they came flocking to the colours' (Tacitus, *Agricola* xxix). To the Caledonians, pushed literally to the edge of Britain, this was clearly the last stand. As their war-leader Calgacus is reported to have said in his pre-battle oration:

> We, the last men on earth, the last of the free, have been shielded till today by the very remoteness of the seclusion for which we are famed . . . but today the boundary of Britain is exposed; beyond us lies no nation, nothing but waves and rocks.

Even if the actual words are those of Tacitus (*Agricola* xxxii), it is tempting to believe that the sentiments are accurately reported.

The battle was fought, the Britons lost: the final organized resistance of free Britain had fallen and with it 10,000 British casualties. The last words must be left with Tacitus:

> The Britons wandered all over the countryside, men and women together, wailing, carrying off their wounded and calling out to the survivors. They would leave their homes and in fury set fire to them . . . sometimes they would try to organize plans . . . sometimes the sight of their dear ones broke their hearts . . . . The next day revealed the quality of the victory more clearly. A grim silence reigned on every hand; the hills were deserted, only here and there was smoke seen rising from chimneys in the distance and our scouts found no one to encounter them.

(ibid., 38)

Part III
Themes

11
Themes

The mass of data recovered from the soil of Britain, which reflects upon the life of Iron Age communities, is very considerable but it is at best a partial statement of the reality of Iron Age being. Everything that has been recovered comes to us through a series of filters. Objects have had to be discarded or selected for deposition rather than being destroyed or recycled. The burial conditions have had to be suitable to encourage preservation and the object has had to be discovered, by accident or design, and been considered worthy of retention. Only a minute percentage of Iron Age material culture has come down to us, and what survives is by no means a random sample of what once existed.

Much the same can be said of the settlement or burial context in which the material remains are found. The majority of the settlements are little more than negative traces – pits and post-holes – interspersed with rubbish. Except in waterlogged conditions the organic component seldom survives. Only in areas where stone is plentiful do the superstructure and internal fittings of settlements sometimes remain. The ravages of time, and more recently accelerated destruction by ploughing and reafforestation, are fast destroying what little structural evidence has survived.

Given this partial and fragmentary database it is difficult to know where to begin to reconstruct the life of the Iron Age communities who inhabited Britain.

The best preserved body of data is undoubtedly the physical evidence of Iron Age settlements. Many thousands are known and of these hundreds have been examined by excavation, some of them on a comparatively large scale. The settlement evidence from Britain is fuller than that from any other country in Europe. In the section to follow, though three chapters are devoted to settlement, the treatment barely does justice to the richness and variety of the record. Considerable regional variation is apparent and hints of social differentiation can be seen. The emergence of hillforts in the centre south is indicative of a more complex level of social organization while the oppida of the first century BC and early first century AD, though still ill-known, must imply a degree of socio-economic complexity never before seen in the country. Through the settlement evidence therefore glimpses of social order and social change can be had.

Evidence for food producing strategies is fast growing as the systematic retrieval of animal bones and flotation techniques become normal practice on excavations. Integrated environmental studies are now underway and in combination with regional sampling strategies are just beginning to reveal the rich complexity of the potential data. The chapter dealing with Food producing strategies (chapter 15) is at best a preliminary statement of one of the fastest growing fields in Iron Age studies.

The artefacts themselves allow several themes to be developed. The productive capacity of the communities is considered in chapter 17 focusing on craft, industry and art. Here again current work on characterizing materials and examining waste products such as slag are opening up new fields reflecting both on the technological capacity of the population and the networks of exchange which supplied them with raw materials.

The recognition of imported goods and their local copies touches upon the complex question of exchange with the Continent (chapter 16). To what extent these exchanges were the result of normal social intercourse or were driven by external forces such as folk movement and the aggressive marketing practices of Mediterranean states are difficult questions to approach. The data set is not yet susceptible to the statistical treatment necessary if the study is to advance from the purely descriptive. But for the last century or so before the Roman invasion classical sources throw some light on the question.

Finally we come to altogether more difficult questions of behaviour. Warfare, death and religion are three convenient headings under which to begin to consider these matters. But here the archaeological data is poor and the subject obscure not least because of the difficulty which modern observers face in attempting to explain prehistoric behaviour patterns. The dangers inherent in over-interpretation are many.

In the section to follow therefore the different strands of evidence are teased out and displayed as simply as possible to expose their quality. What we are doing is to recognize the elements of social reconstruction and arrange some of them into simple systems. The interrelationships of those systems and their complex feedback mechanisms we will consider in the final section.

12
Settlement and settlement pattern in the south and east

When Aulus Plautius founded the Fosse frontier in the years AD 44–7 he was simply emphasizing a geographical and political truth. Britain could be divided into two parts about a line drawn along the Jurassic ridge from Lincoln to Lyme Bay. To the south and east lay a densely settled region with authority centralized about oppida and with a subsistence economy depending to a large extent on the production of grain. To the north and west settlement was more scattered and in places sparse, there was little centralization of power and, while cereals were widely grown, there appears to have been a greater reliance on stock rearing. To the Roman military mind the south-east was clearly the part to become a province, for grain was an immensely valuable commodity and arable farmers, because of their dependence upon the seasons, were sedentary and thus easier to control. Admittedly, Plautius was seeing Iron Age Britain at its most developed, after a 150 years or more of close contact with the Continent, but this basic geographical divide was equally relevant in the earlier period and played a considerable part in influencing the form, density and the distribution of settlements.

Settlement is a complex subject since settlements interact with landscape in a continuum of time. To parcel up the subject tidily for the purposes of discussion certain arbitrary divisions must be made. Settlements vary in size from single houses providing shelter for families to vast oppida encompassing a range of functions. In this chapter and the next we will consider the lower end of this range – the homestead, hamlet and village – leaving larger agglomerations like hillforts and oppida, which represent coercive powers commanding a greater input of social effort, for separate treatment. Even so there will be some overlap especially in the discussion of house form. There is a similar problem with subsistence economy which is intimately bound up with settlement morphology and location, but to discuss it along with the settlements themselves would be cumbersome. For this reason a separate chapter is devoted to food production where there will be some discussion of the socio-economic systems which linked production strategies to settlement form.

The ridge of Jurassic limestone provides a convenient notional western limit for the south-eastern zone but it is convenient to stray beyond it on occasion to include such areas as the Somerset wetlands, and the valleys of the Worcestershire Avon and the Trent. The south-eastern zone itself is geologically varied but the lighter soils of the limestone hills, the chalk uplands and the river gravels were particularly conducive to Iron Age agricultural techniques and were accordingly more densely settled than the less hospitable sands and the more densely wooded clay lands. These factors to a large extent influence the availability of archaeological data. It is on the chalklands of Wessex and the Sussex Downs and on the gravel terraces of the Midland rivers that most of the excavated sites lie and these regions must, of necessity, bulk large in the discussion, but other smaller and more varied regions have also been included to show something of the range of sites available for study.

The settlements of the chalklands

The chalklands of Wessex and Sussex were densely occupied in the Iron Age and the number of known settlements runs into thousands but of these less than twenty have been excavated on a scale sufficient to allow worthwhile generalizations to be made. In areas where systematic plotting from air photographs has been attempted, as for example between the Test and the Bourne (R. Palmer 1984), something of the complexity of the landscape and the great variety of settlement components can begin to be appreciated, emphasizing the problems inherent in any form of classification. Nevertheless certain recurring patterns emerge which allow 'types' to be defined, albeit tentatively.

Mid–Late Bronze Age settlements

The characteristics of the settlements belonging to the thirteenth to sixth centuries have already been referred to in some detail above (pp. 28–39). Normally the inhabited area was enclosed by a bank in which the timbers of a palisade or a thickset hedge were based (although traces do not always survive), and each enclosure was provided with a gate of simple construction. Within the enclosed area, which averaged 0.4–0.8 ha, was a simple circular hut, or sometimes more than one, arranged so as to leave sufficient space around for the more domestic activities of the farm to be carried out. Sometimes, as at New Barn Down, Sussex, the total settlement consisted of only two enclosures, but at Plumpton Plain A, Sussex, there were found to be at least three broadly contemporary huts arranged along a trackway, while at Itford Hill, Sussex, seven or eight conjoined enclosures, not all contemporary, were found with at least three more isolated huts scattered further away. Evidently, while some settlements were individual farmsteads, others may have taken on the aspect of hamlets or even small villages.

  The settlement at Shearplace Hill, Dorset, which belongs to the late second millennium, was enclosed by a substantial and well-cut ditch backed by a bank with no signs of a palisade but possibly capped by a thorn hedge. Ditches are also present at Boscombe Down East, Wilts., and various sites on the Marlborough Downs; but at the Sussex sites, most of which are early first millennium in date, ditches (if they occur at all) are insignificant features, the emphasis being placed more upon the palisade embedded in a bank. This may, of course, be a regional peculiarity rather than a chronological development, but the universal emphasis on palisades from the seventh century until the fourth or third century suggests that the period c. 1000–800 may have seen a change of fashion, the fenced enclosures gaining favour over enclosing ditches.

Palisaded enclosures

Palisaded enclosures containing settlements of various sizes are a common feature of Iron Age settlement pattern in eastern Scotland (pp. 281–5), but a widespread, if sporadic occurrence over the rest of Britain is sufficient to show that enclosures of this kind were a normal element in the mid-first-millennium settlement pattern over many parts of the country. The most extensively excavated of the southern British palisaded settlements is Little Woodbury, Wilts., where two phases in the continuous occupation of the site can tentatively be recognized (see Figures 12.2 and 12.3). In the first phase the farm was enclosed by a palisade traced only on the east side, where a four-post gate – the principal entry to the compound – was uncovered. Within lay a large circular hut 13.7 m in diameter, with its entrance porch aligned exactly upon the gate.

The extent of the palisaded enclosure is unknown, but the ditched enclosure which replaced it defended about 1.6 ha, which may well approximate to the area of the original. Within the enclosure many domestic activities have left their mark. Behind the house lay a large irregular working hollow where grain-parching and cooking were probably carried out. Corn was stored in rectangular four-post granaries, usually placed around the periphery of the enclosure, while hay, and possibly seed corn in the ear, was hung up on two-post racks to dry. At a later stage, in the fourth to second century, grain storage in large underground silos became widespread; these pits, later used for rubbish disposal, were found in large numbers. A high proportion of those from Little Woodbury relate to the later phase of the site's occupation. Other aspects of the day-to-day routine were carried out within the enclosure – processes such as the grinding of corn, spinning, weaving, leather-working, basketry, etc., and on occasion animals in need of special attention may have been temporarily tethered inside.

The date of the early phase occupation cannot be given with precision, but the earliest assemblage of pottery belongs to the All Cannings Cross–Meon Hill style, of the sixth to fifth centuries, while a few scraps of Kimmeridge–Caburn wares might suggest a beginning within the sixth century or a little earlier, but these fragments may be nothing more than the survival of archaic types.

The second Wiltshire site to have begun life as a palisaded enclosure is Swallowcliffe, where the initial occupation is approximately contemporary with that of Little Woodbury. The excavation, however, was carried out before the development of modern techniques and apart from pits little else of structural significance was found. In Hampshire the excavations at Meon Hill near Stockbridge (Figure 12.1) provided further evidence of a palisaded settlement, again related to the All Cannings–Meon Hill style of pottery. As at Little Woodbury, the old palisaded enclosure was replaced by a bank and a ditch of hillfort proportions. A further example of just such a replacement occurred at the Caburn, Sussex, in the phase pre-dating the hillfort. Here little of the early plan can now be recovered, but a length of palisade trench outside the entrance to the later fort and two huts just inside, together with several pits, represent the initial phase producing pottery of the Kimmeridge–Caburn style of seventh- or sixth-century date.

Excavations at other southern British hillforts have occasionally suggested the pre-existence of palisaded settlements. Quarley Hill, Hants., Blewburton Hill, Oxon., and Wilbury, Herts., have produced some evidence of early palisades but work has never been on a sufficient scale to show whether or not the later defences exactly followed the lines of the earlier enclosures. If they did, it would have to be supposed that fenced enclosures exceeding 6 ha in extent were being built in the first half of the first millennium.

Two other sites deserve mention: at Hollingbury and Park Brow, both in Sussex, trenches

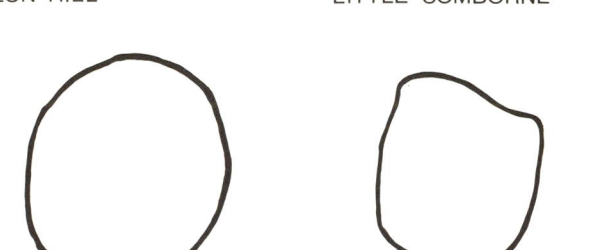

LITTLE WOODBURY   OLD DOWN FARM   FARLEY MOUNT

PEWSEY HILL   GUSSAGE ALL SAINTS   WINNALL DOWN

MEON HILL   LITTLE SOMBORNE

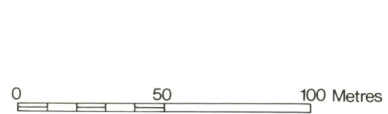

0   50   100 Metres

Figure 12.1 Settlements on the Wessex chalklands (source: Cunliffe 1984c based on various sources).

belonging to palisaded enclosures of rectangular plan have been partly excavated. Three sides of the Park Brow enclosure – some 30–7 m – were examined, while at Hollingbury only one side 46 m long with a central entrance came to light. Since the plans are therefore incomplete and the enclosed areas have not been extensively excavated, speculation as to function is difficult, but these may have been specialized structures, perhaps even religious enclosures, and not settlement sites at all.

Sufficient has been said to show that in the period from the seventh to the fifth century a number of settlements in southern Britain were surrounded by fences bedded in palisade trenches. Since the emphasis of the earlier first-millennium enclosures was also upon a vertical timber barrier rather than ditches or banks, it is not unreasonable to suppose that the later palisades were an indigenous development from these earlier beginnings. Details of the

WOODBURY, WILTS

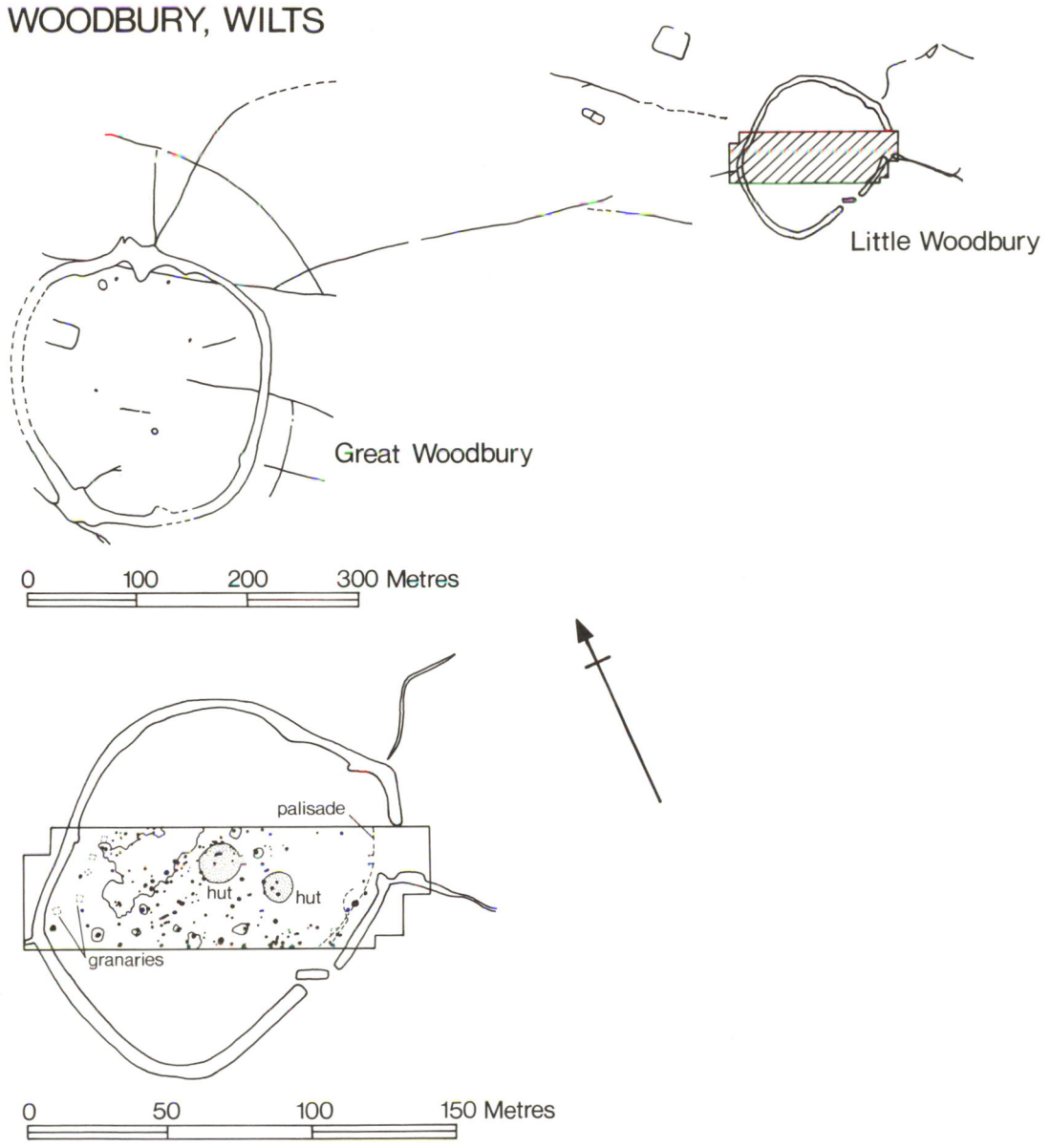

Figure 12.2   Little Woodbury, Wilts. (source: Bersu 1940).

settlements themselves are few, but most of the recorded palisades enclosed individual farms and it may well be that most of the farms of the period were palisaded, but the point is difficult to demonstrate. That some of the hillforts were preceded by palisaded enclosures of comparable size shows that the palisade idea was not restricted to small settlements alone.

Earthwork-enclosed settlements (Figure 12.1)

At Little Woodbury, Meon Hill and the Caburn, palisades had been replaced by ditched enclosures by the time that saucepan pots were in use, that is, the fourth to early first century on current reckoning. The class of earthwork-enclosed settlement which they typify can usually, but not invariably, be shown to belong to this later period.

Little Woodbury in its later phase can be taken as a type-site for the class (Figures 12.2 and 12.3). Excavation has shown that the palisade was replaced by a ditch some 3.4 m wide by 2 m deep, which must once have been backed by a bank of chalk dug from it. The ditch enclosed a roughly circular area some 1.6 ha in extent, provided with a single wide entrance, apparently without a gate, from which two linear ditches radiated out like antennae.

Even more informative has been the excavation at Gussage All Saints, Wilts., where two pre-Durotrigan phases have been recognized (Figures 12.1 and 12.4). In the first, which can be dated on the basis of radiocarbon assessment and artefacts to about the fifth century, a 1.2 ha enclosure was surrounded by a ditch 1.2 m wide and 0.8 m deep, apparently with an external bank. The enclosure was provided with a complex entrance flanked by antennae ditches. Within were found an area of pits and, towards the centre, a group of four-post structures of 'granary' type. No houses were recognized, but had there been stake-built structures all trace would have

Figure 12.3　Little Woodbury from the air (Crown Copyright reserved).

Figure 12.4   Gussage All Saints from the air (photo: Geoffrey Wainwright).

been destroyed by subsequent ploughing. In the second phase a more substantial ditch was dug, 2.2 m wide and 1.4 m deep, approximately on the line of the original ditch, and the entrance antennae ditches were remodelled on either side of an elaborate timber gateway. Within, pits continued to be dug and circular gullies indicate the locations of huts. Radiocarbon dates suggest that occupation lasted from the third to second centuries, during which time undecorated saucepan pots were in use. Late in this sequence evidence of extensive bronze foundry activity was discovered (p. 456).

At Old Down Farm, near Andover in Hampshire, a large-scale excavation of a 1.2 hectare enclosure revealed a long-lived settlement (Figure 12.1). The earliest occupation began in the eighth century and *may* have been enclosed, but if so the ditch was almost entirely recut in the next phase dating to the seventh–sixth centuries, when a substantial ditch up to 2 m deep was dug around a settlement nucleus leaving only one entrance (without any trace of a gate). Inside was a single substantial house, comparable to the early house at Little Woodbury, together with a scatter of storage pits. By the fifth century the ditch had largely silted but houses and pits still occupied the central area and occupation continued into the Middle Iron Age (fourth to early first century) though no houses have been identified. This absence of recognizable houses in the Middle Iron Age need occasion no surprise for it is now clear that in central southern England the normal house type in this period was built of wattlework most traces of which would have been removed by ploughing, apart from the paired door-posts. Old Down Farm is of particular interest in that it shows that enclosure ditches, and presumably the banks and hedges going with them, were a feature of the Early Iron Age dating back possibly to as early as the seventh century. These early ditched enclosures must therefore have been contemporary with the early palisaded enclosures.

Another site of outstanding interest is the settlement on Winnall Down near Winchester, Hants. (Figure 12.1). Here in the sixth to fifth century a ditched enclosure comparable in size and shape to Old Down Farm was established on a site which had already been occupied in the Mid–Late Bronze Age. The single entrance was provided with an impressive gate and inside were a number of circular houses, storage pits and two-and four-post structures. Clearly not all were contemporary but several of the houses could have been in use at the same time. By the Middle Iron Age, not only had the ditch become silted but the settlement completely overrode the earlier boundary and was now divided into two distinct zones: a group of circular houses (and one rectangular structure), the majority of which could have been contemporary; and a zone of pits and four-post granaries. Some intercutting between the pits suggests a considerable duration of occupation.

Closely similar enclosures are known at an increasing number of sites recognized on air photographs and from partial excavations, but the few chosen for brief description above present the principal characteristics. Sizes range from about 0.6 ha at Mancombe Down, Wilts., to about 2.5 ha at Farley Mount, Hants., a range which may reflect the status of the individual owner and the size of his holding. This type of settlement was widespread not only on the chalkland of Wessex but over much of southern Britain and can therefore be regarded as a type-site representing a particular kind of socio-economic structure.

The recent series of large-scale excavations have, however, shown something of the complexities of the picture. The actual enclosure, so dominant in the archaeological record, may have been a feature of transitory significance, dug to define a settlement area at one moment and maintained or abandoned as the settlement developed. What does stand out is the fact that once a location was chosen for settlement, sometimes as early as the eighth–sixth centuries BC, occupation usually continued throughout the Iron Age with no recognizable break, implying a remarkable degree of social stability.

'Banjo' enclosures (Figures 12.5 and 12.6)

A second type of earthwork-enclosed site, usually about 0.2–0.4 ha in extent, occurs in Wessex and sporadically elsewhere (Perry 1966, 1970). Characteristically these sites are provided with a single entrance, to which runs a roadway defined on either side by V-shaped ditches *c*. 1 m deep. Frequently the roadway joins a linear ditch at right angles at a distance of between 45 m and 90 m from the enclosure. At Blagden Copse, Hants., a limited excavation undertaken at the junction of the road ditches and the linear ditch showed that both had been planned in relation to each other and were therefore broadly contemporary.

The planning and construction of the 'banjo' enclosures and the so-called 'spectacle' sites, which are essentially two conjoined banjos, strongly imply that they were designed, at least in part, to aid the collection, selection and temporary corralling of cattle. The three Hampshire examples which have been excavated, Bramdean, Micheldever Wood and Owslebury, have, however, all produced evidence of occupation although in no case does it appear to have been as intensive as in the ditched enclosures of Little Woodbury type.

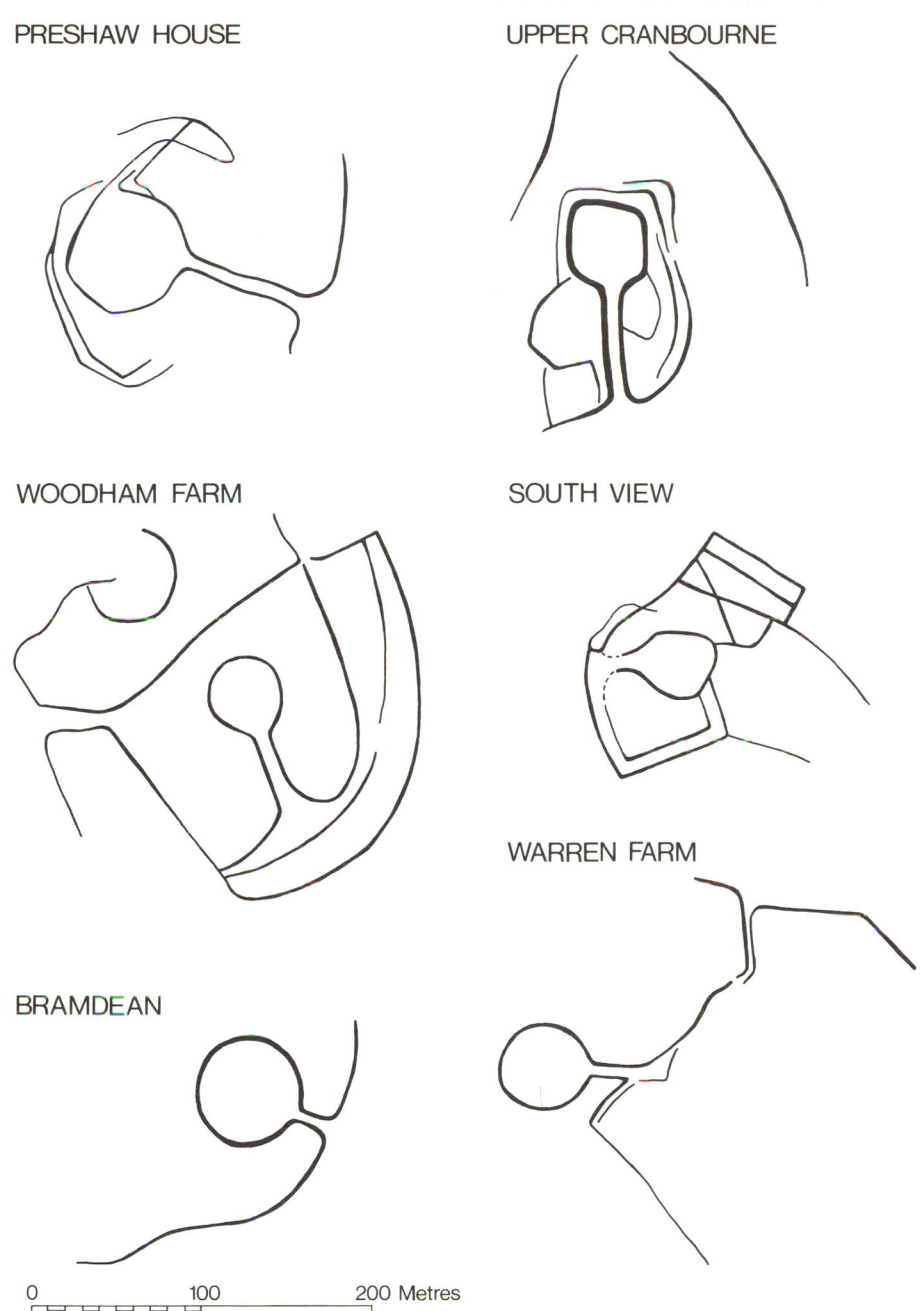

PRESHAW HOUSE

UPPER CRANBOURNE

WOODHAM FARM

SOUTH VIEW

WARREN FARM

BRAMDEAN

0   100   200 Metres

Figure 12.5 'Banjo' enclosures in Hampshire, drawn from air photography (source: Perry 1966, 1970).

No banjo site has yet been totally excavated though the example at Micheldever Wood, Hants., has been two-thirds cleared. No buildings have been identified but the central area seems to have been kept clear with the storage pits arranged around the periphery: much the same

BRAMDEAN

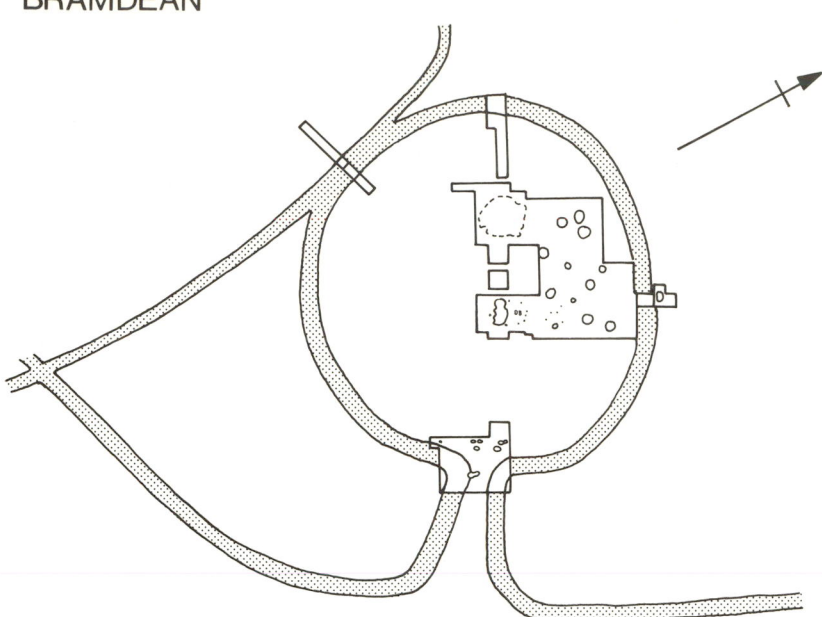

MICHELDEVER WOOD

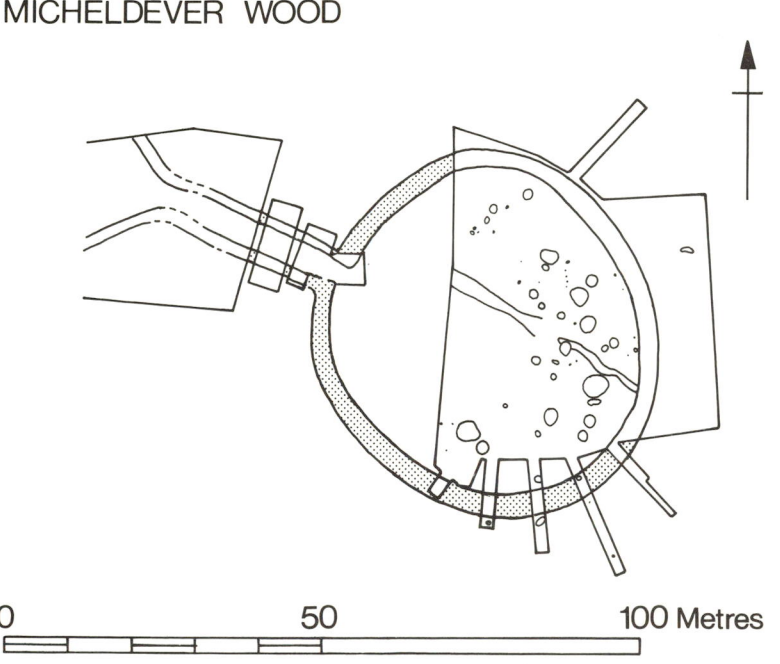

0   50   100 Metres

Figure 12.6   Excavated 'banjo' enclosures in Hampshire (source: *Bramdean*, Perry 1982, 1986; *Micheldever Wood*, Fasham 1987).

pattern is indicated at Bramdean. The domestic rubbish which found its way into the pits does not differ significantly from that from the contemporary phases of larger enclosures.

In each of the excavated examples the primary phase of construction is associated with saucepan pots of the Middle Iron Age suggesting that as a class banjos are late in date. It is possible that they developed out of the ideas inherent in the 'antennae' ditches associated with the entrances of some of the Little Woodbury type of enclosures.

The relationship of the banjo enclosures to the larger enclosed settlements of Little Woodbury type is not easy to define except to say that chronologically banjos appeared after the enclosures and related settlements had become well established. Moreover, they appear to occupy higher and potentially more marginal land. If this is borne out by further fieldwork it could be argued that they reflect agrarian expansion around the fringes of established Early to Mid Iron Age farming units. How banjos, with their evidence of settlement and mixed agricultural economies functioned is less clear (Fasham 1987, 61–5). It is simplest at present to regard them as a specialized form of settlement component fitting into a complex system which, in the absence of further large-scale excavation, will remain obscure.

Open settlements

Enclosed settlements of Little Woodbury and banjo type have received considerable attention from archaeologists largely because they are evident from the air as major landscape features though they may be largely invisible from the ground. Two excavations of enclosures have, however, accidentally focused on a different problem – that of the unenclosed settlement. One of these, Winnall Down, has already been referred to (p. 220). Here a considerable Middle Iron Age settlement developed with little reference to an earlier enclosed settlement. The second site is Boscombe Down West, Wilts., where occupation of Early and Middle Iron Age date extended over 6.5 ha: the site was only recognized because a double ditched enclosure had been constructed in the first century AD. In fact unenclosed settlements of considerable size are not at all uncommon. In the eighth and seventh centuries All Cannings Cross and Potterne, Wilts., are two well-known examples while in the sixth and fifth centuries we may cite Boscombe Down West, Wilts., Slonk Hill, Sussex, and the unenclosed phase of Bishopstone, Sussex. Boscombe Down West continued in use into the Middle Iron Age at which time, as we have seen, the Winnall settlement outgrew its enclosure. These seven sites spanning the Iron Age are probably only the tip of the iceberg and provide a salutary reminder of the potential complexity of the settlement pattern.

Ditched enclosures of the first century BC and first century AD (Figure 12.7)

The tradition of surrounding farmsteads with a simple enclosing ditch was maintained in some areas of the south, notably Dorset, into the first century AD. The classic example of such a settlement is Tollard Royal in Cranborne Chase, Wilts., where total excavation has exposed the complete ground plan of the farm (Figures 12.8 and 12.9), consisting of a kite-shaped ditched enclosure of about 0.5 ha in extent, provided with a single entrance. Inside were found a single hut, thirty-five storage pits of varying capacity and three or four granaries. One of the most impressive features of the plan is the large open area within the enclosure, where presumably

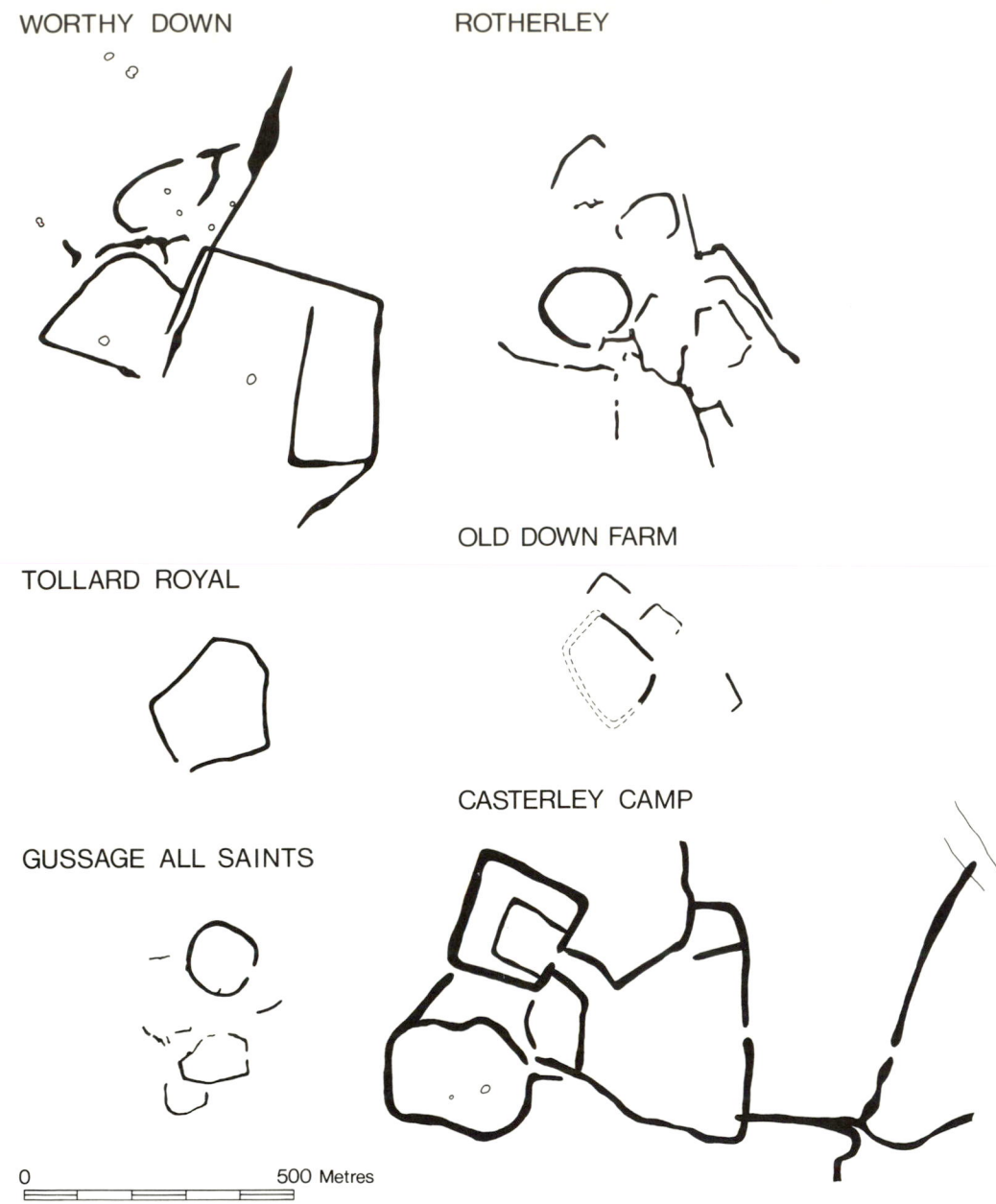

Figure 12.7 Ditched enclosures of the Late Iron Age (source: Cunliffe 1984c based on various sources).

flocks and herds could have been temporarily corralled. The basic plan, clearly a direct
continuation of the traditional Little Woodbury type, is further reflected in the neighbouring
settlements of Rotherley and Woodcuts, which continued in use little changed well into the
Roman period, and in the latest phase at Gussage All Saints and Old Down Farm (Figure 12.7).

TOLLARD ROYAL, DORSET

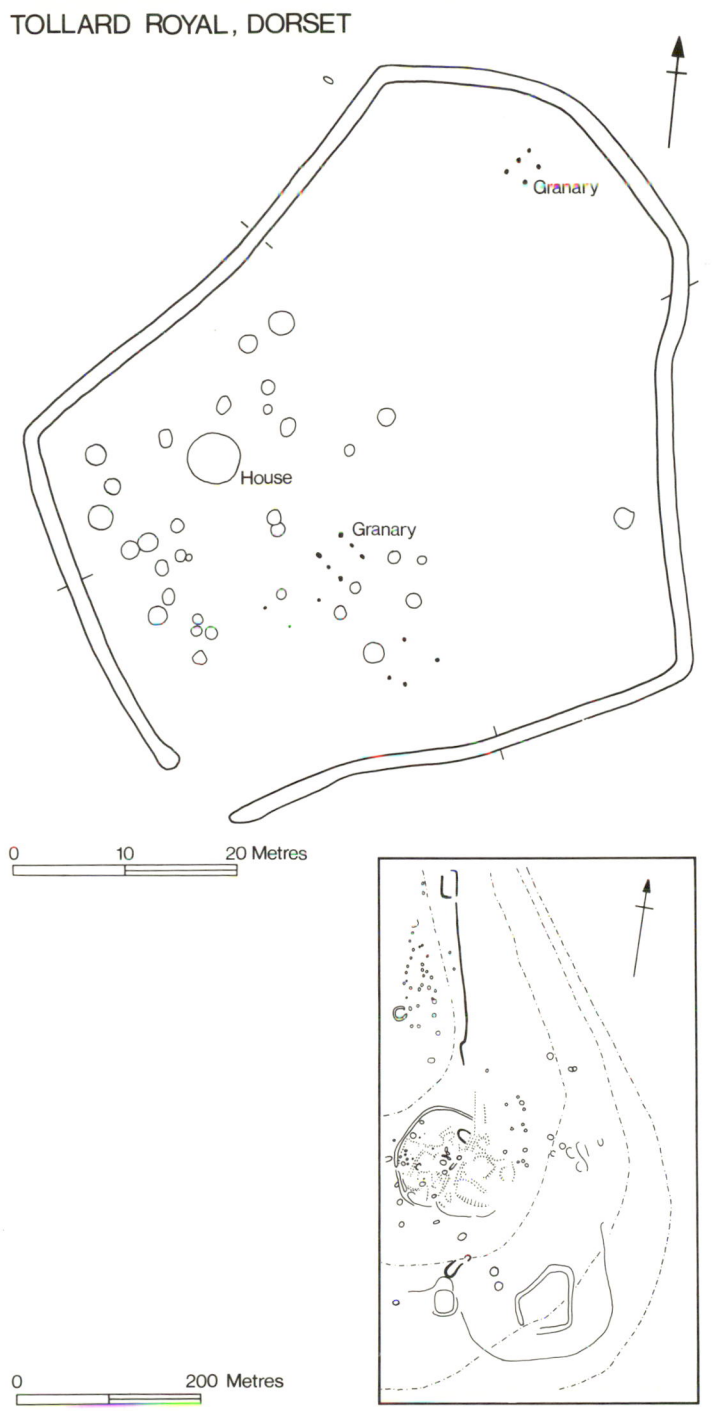

Figure 12.8   Tollard Royal, Dorset (source: Wainwright 1968).

Figure 12.9 Tollard Royal enclosure from the air (photo: Dr J.K.S. St Joseph. Crown Copyright reserved).

A rather more extensive type of settlement, found sporadically in the south, is represented by the Wessex examples of Worthy Down and Owslebury, Hants., and Casterley Camp, Wilts. (Figure 12.7). All three sites are characterized by a complex series of ditches which define enclosures of varying sizes and shapes, some used for habitation, some (e.g. at Owslebury) for burial, others presumably for livestock. The plan of Casterley Camp is particularly informative for here it is possible to recognize the careful placing of entrances so as to allow maximum inter-use of enclosures. Such an arrangement would have been of value at those times during the year when flocks and herds needed to be brought together and sorted for culling, castrating or redistribution. The development of these complex ditched enclosures as an adjunct to settlements suggests the increased importance of stock-rearing – a matter which will be returned to again later (pp. 338–9).

Settlement size, status and siting

Many of the sites described above were single farming units. Little Woodbury, whatever its social implications, probably had only one centrally placed house in use at any one time (although the possibility remains that other contemporary huts may have been placed around the periphery of the enclosure). With its fine early house, 1.6 ha farmyard and considerable grain-storing capacity, it must have been the homestead of a wealthy man and his family. A short distance from the excavated site lay a far more substantial ditched enclosure, known as Great Woodbury (Figure 12.2), covering an area of about 4 ha and enclosed by a massive ditch of hillfort proportions some 6 m wide and 3.6 m deep. A single section through the ditch revealed pottery of saucepan pot type in the primary silting. While it would clearly be wrong to base too much on this limited evidence, it could well be argued that Great Woodbury replaced Little Woodbury. Certainly the relatively small percentage of saucepan pot wares from Little Woodbury would suggest that it ceased to be occupied fairly early in the period during which these types were commonly in use; moreover, it is hardly likely that the two sites were occupied at the same time.

By virtue of its non-defensive siting, Great Woodbury can hardly be regarded as a hillfort, but it may well represent a stage in the social development of the owning family, moving from the old site to the new when wealth had increased sufficiently to allow a new building programme to be undertaken. If these speculations are correct, there is no need to suppose that the actual size of the homestead community had increased; a larger area enclosed and a more massive ditch need be nothing more than status symbols. Massive enclosures for apparently single homesteads are known elsewhere, as at Pimperne Down, where the large house was retained within a 4.7 ha enclosure. Thus size of enclosure does not necessarily reflect size of community: in many cases it may reflect the status of the occupants.

A further indication of status is provided by artefacts which can be associated with aristocratic behaviour. At Gussage a bronzesmith was at work making a large number of horse harness and chariot-fittings presumably under the auspices of the owner. The product of this one craftsman would have been sufficient to deck out a considerable number of chariot teams, surely in excess of the needs of the particular community. It is possible, of course, that they were produced under the patronage of the owner who could then have used them as gifts to dependants thus establishing or maintaining his superior status. The question is an intriguing but insoluble one. Articles of horse/chariot equipment occur sporadically on other enclosure sites, like the pair of linchpins from Old Down Farm, suggesting that enclosed settlements of this kind may have been of 'aristocratic' status. The relationship of these to the open settlements and banjos is impossible to define and the whole question is bound up with the function of the contemporary hillforts.

The principal difference between the settlements discussed here and hillforts is one of siting. Hillforts were always placed in defensive positions, usually on hill-tops or ridge-ends with good visibility and control of the main approaches, while settlement sites were chosen to be close to the arable land. Even the massive ditch of Great Woodbury cannot disguise the fact that the site has little tactical significance. The close relationship between settlement and arable land is demonstrated on a number of sites, but the Farley Mount enclosure in Hampshire is perhaps one of the more dramatic, showing hectares of rectangular 'Celtic' fields spreading out regularly from the boundaries of the settlement. It is tempting here to think of both fields and settlement being laid out at the same time to colonize a piece of virgin downland.

It is difficult to generalize about the overall pattern of rural settlement, largely because adequate area surveys are practically unknown. On the South Downs, however, in the area of Chalton, Hants., a detailed field study has shown a remarkable density of occupation sites, many of them sited by choice on the shoulders of east-facing slopes, linked to each other and to their fields by a network of trackways. In an area of 5 km² eleven settlements are known, some less than 0.5 km from their neighbours (Cunliffe 1974, Figure 4). Such a density is not universal even on the chalk, for in a comparable survey of the Marlborough Downs based on the parishes of West Overton and Fyfield, only three settlements were found in a block 12.9 km^2, the average distance between them being 1.6 km.

An exhaustive survey of the evidence gleaned from aerial photography covering the area from the rivers Test to the Bourne has provided a glimpse of the real complexity of the settlement evidence (R. Palmer 1984) but two well-defined patterns stand out (Cunliffe 1984a, Figure 10.2). Around the hillfort of Quarley Hill the settlements cluster on a circumference about 1.5 km from the fort and at intervals of 1 km from each other, while to the south of Danebury strings of settlements line the flanks of the river Test and the Wallop Brook spaced at intervals of about 1 km and sited at about the same distance from the valley bottoms. This latter group looks very much like a total pattern with the landscape filled with farming units optimally sited to exploit the range of available resources. The Quarley grouping on the other hand, while packed at the same density, controlled a more limited range of resources in their immediate neighbourhoods. Most significantly they lacked easy access to well-watered meadow. Thus, either their subsistence regimes differed radically from those of the Danebury group or else the meadow environment was available to them through some mechanism which involved limited transhumance. Whether or not this difference is manifest in the settlement form as preserved in the archaeological record it is impossible to say since only one of the sites, Meon Hill, has been partially excavated.

None of the figures given above can be regarded as of statistical value since the recognition of a site is conditioned by a number of chance factors and however much the chances of discovery are increased by intensive fieldwork, as in the case of the examples quoted, there can be no assurance that all the sites were in use at the same time, nor is it possible to compare the sizes of individual settlements. Even so it is now tolerably clear that on favoured land, like the chalk downs, substantial farms were closely spaced.

The Cotswolds and the Thames and Avon valleys

The Upper Thames valley is one of the most systematically explored Iron Age landscapes in Britain thanks almost entirely to the work of the Oxford Archaeological Unit initiated in 1973 (Hingley and Miles 1984). The complexity of the landscape was first demonstrated as the result of a systematic survey of the air photographic cover (Benson and Miles 1974) since when a carefully controlled programme of large-scale excavation has been in operation. It is now possible to stand back from the detail to see a clear pattern emerge (Figure 12.10).

Three distinct geographical zones can be defined: the Cotswold flanks; the gravel terraces; and the river flood plain, and each has its own type of settlement. On the Cotswold dip slope, cut by the tributaries of the Thames, small enclosed settlements prevail. In plan at least, these have much in common with the banjo enclosures of the Wessex chalk (Darvill and Hingley 1982) but excavation has been minimal and there is little yet to say of them. Hingley (1984b) has, however, suggested that they represent individual farms each with their own distinct territories. The excavation of part of a ditched enclosure of Mid Iron Age date at Guiting Power, Glos., in the heart of the Cotswolds gives some idea of what can be expected: the dense scatter of pits and post-holes is not unlike a typical Wessex enclosed settlement. To the south of the Thames, 5 km north of Swindon, at Groundwell Farm, a ditched enclosure, superficially of banjo form was

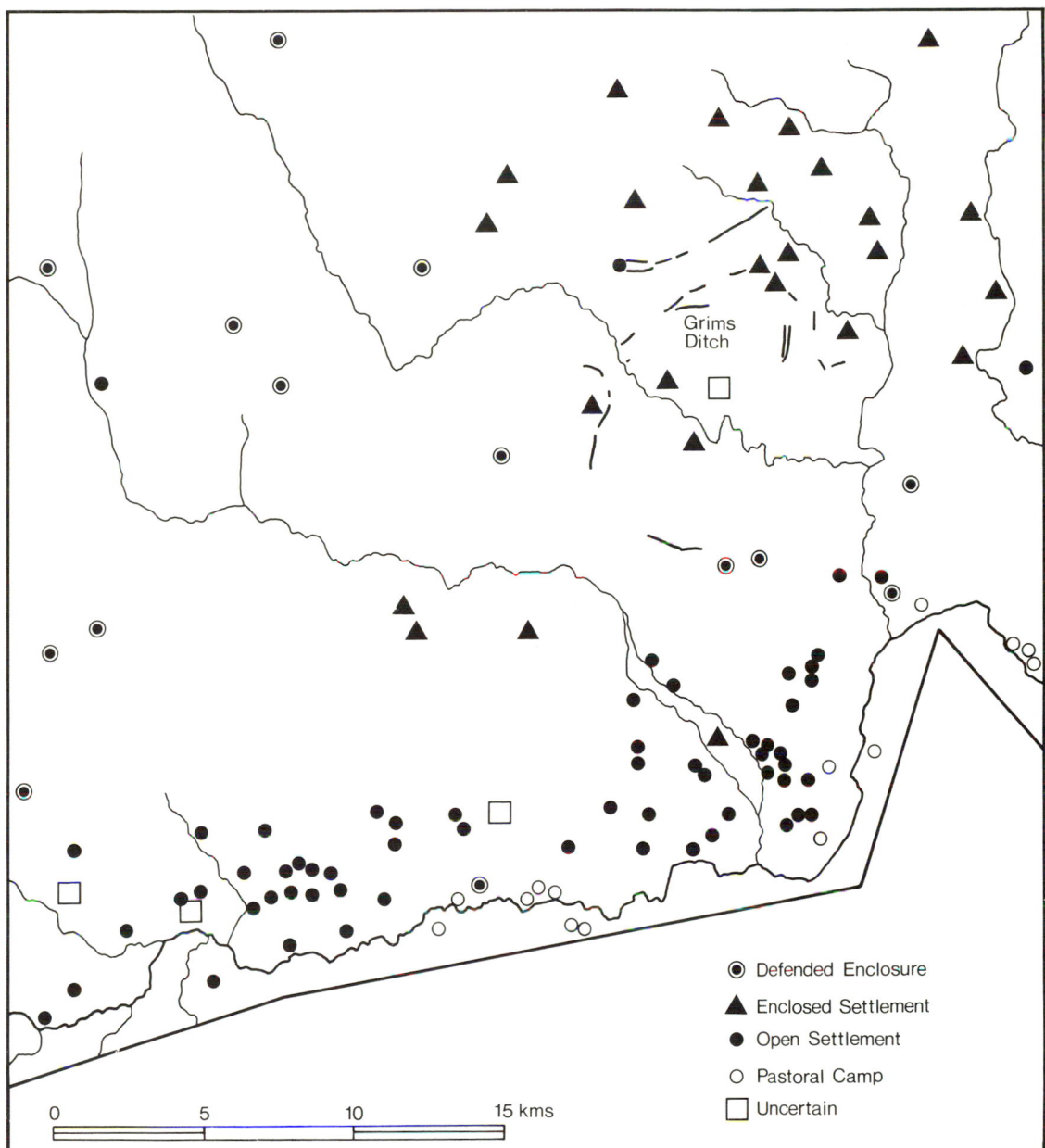

Figure 12.10   Settlement distribution in the Upper Thames valley (source: Hingley and Miles 1984).

examined (Figure 12.11). The pottery, which is closely similar to that of the Upper Thames basin, suggests that occupation began in the fifth century and continued to the third century or later during which time a succession of houses were built together with post-built storage structures. We are clearly dealing here with a single family unit, practising mixed agriculture,

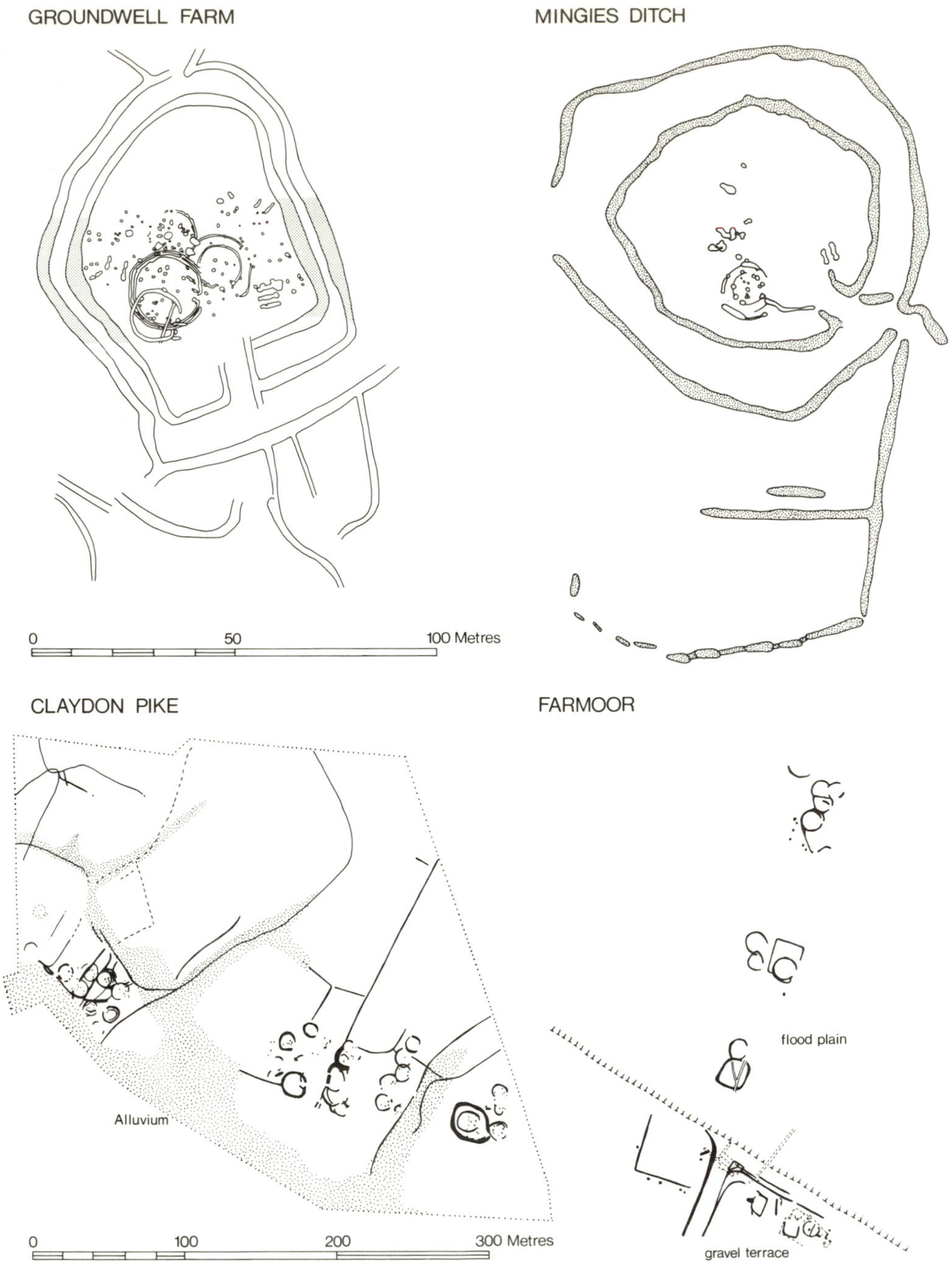

Figure 12.11 Settlements in the Upper Thames valley (sources: *Groundwell Farm*, Gingell 1982; *Mingies Ditch*, Allen and Robinson 1979; *Claydon Pike*, Miles and Palmer 1982; *Farmoor*, Lambrick and Robinson 1979).

occupying the same site for many generations. Groundwell Farm may well be typical of the enclosed settlements of the Cotswolds and provides a salutary warning that the superficial resemblance in plan to the banjo enclosures of Wessex should not be taken to imply a similarity of socio-economic function.

In contrast to the hill sites the settlements of the gravel terraces are far better known from a series of large-scale excavations. On present evidence it seems that two different social units can be recognized. On the first gravel terrace the settlements are of extended family or hamlet type. An example of the first is Mingies Ditch (Figure 12.11). Here a settlement was established on a dry hillock of gravel some time in the Middle Iron Age. It consisted of no more than two contemporary houses and ancillary storage structures, which were rebuilt on at least five occasions, enclosed within a double-ditched system with external antennae ditches. The two enclosing ditches were probably designed to provide corral space between for animals. Environmental studies have suggested that the settlement was set in a landscape predominantly of grassland. Mingies Ditch is clearly a settlement of family or extended family size though whether the enclosure formed the sole residence of the family or was only occupied seasonally is unclear.

A more complicated pattern is presented by the Middle Iron Age settlement at Claydon Pike, near Lechlade (Figures 12.11 and 12.12). Here three distinct gravel rises, separated by wetland, were in occupation, each producing evidence of a complex sequence of houses. In the case of the western 'island', where the sequence could be worked out in detail, it is clear that only two or three houses were in contemporary use. Thus each 'island' was probably the homestead of a single family. If all three were in occupation at one time then the settlement is best regarded as a hamlet.

The second gravel terrace is dominated by a different type of settlement typified by those excavated at Ashville and Gravelly Guy (Figure 12.13). Both cover many hectares and within a distinct zoning is apparent with the settlement and pit storage areas kept quite separate throughout much of the life of the settlement. This type of arrangement is well known at a number of second terrace sites (Hingley and Miles 1984, 62–3) and the very considerable grain storage capacity which they exhibit may suggest that sites of this kind performed centralized storage and redistribution functions for the larger community.

Finally, a number of sites are known on the flood plain itself: of these Farmoor provides a well-excavated example (Figure 12.11). Here three separate groups of houses and attached enclosures were discovered spaced at intervals of about 50 m across the meadow. Each was sufficient to house a single family, but since all flood plain sites would have been under water for much of the winter they presumably represent summer steadings providing shelter for the family, or that part of it, who came to the meadows with the flocks and herds. During the winter months they and their stock would have rejoined the rest of the community at the larger settlements on the first or second terrace.

From what has been said above it is tempting to see the complex of valley settlements on the gravel terraces and flood plain as part of a single socio-economic system operating a subsistence strategy based on the exploitation of a number of discrete ecological zones. Such a system would have required co-operation which would have encouraged the growth of larger settlement agglomerations. The limestone hill sites, on the other hand, could well have been self-contained units exploiting the range of rich soils in their hinterlands. Thus two entirely different social systems may have emerged in the region by the Middle Iron Age (Hingley 1984b).

Viewed against the perspective of time the Middle Iron Age seems to have been a period of

Figure 12.12   Claydon Pike, Lechlade, Glos. View of Middle Iron Age roundhouse sites on an 'island' of gravel bounded by drainage ditches (photo: Oxford Archaeological Unit).

population expansion, colonization and consolidation. From the beginning of the first century BC onwards further changes can be detected: a more organized landscape now develops with trackways and rectangular paddocks laid out, sometimes impinging upon earlier, more scattered, settlements (Hingley and Miles 1984, 65). This is particularly apparent at Claydon Pike where a large new settlement complex replaced the Middle Iron Age homesteads. As part of this pattern of change a new type of settlement appears, typified by Barton Court Farm where a farm, enclosed in a rectangular ditched enclosure, was established at the beginning of a sequence which led eventually to the development of a small Roman villa. The details of these changes are still rather ill-focused but the evidence is consistent with a continuing population rise and the emergence of a more integrated trading network, occasioned by the increased demands of the Roman world, in the century or so before the conquest.

Figure 12.13 Gravelly Guy, Stanton Harcourt, Oxon. Middle Iron Age farm with over 600 storage pits. The rectilinear enclosures are Roman (photo: Oxford Archaeological Unit).

Our detailed knowledge of the settlements of the Upper Thames valley is based on a tradition of intensive fieldwork and excavation. Had equivalent effort been put into the archaeology of the Avon valley, to the west of the scarp slope of the Cotswolds, it is not at all unlikely that a similar pattern would have emerged. As it is we have only glimpses of the richness of the data through surveys (Webster and Hobley 1965; Oswald 1969; Hingley 1989) and through the excavations at Barford and Beckford, Warks. At Beckford, close to Bredon Hill Camp, a sufficient area has been examined to show that the settlement was extensive and consisted of a series of large ditched enclosures which had been refurbished on a number of occasions. Within each enclosure settlement structures consisting of smaller ditched enclosures, circular huts with drip gullies around them, four-post 'granaries', cobbled yards and storage pits were found in abundance, together with artefacts representing all the normal farmyard activities, as well as bronze casting. The extensive nature of the remains would suggest that the Beckford settlement was a village of some size: it is possible that each of the large enclosures represented the holding of a single family unit. The complex has similarities to those found on the second terrace of the Upper Thames but how it fitted into the regional system of the Avon is at present ill-defined and will remain so until more sites are excavated in the general vicinity.

Hingley's detailed survey of the evidence from central and southern Warwickshire (1989) provides the first serious attempt to consider the evidence available in terms of regional systems. Its potential is considerable but without a concerted input of carefully designed excavations, of the kind mounted in the Upper Thames valley, few significant advances in understanding will be possible.

The east Midlands

Until the mid-1960s the Midland river valleys and the Jurassic limestones and clays were largely devoid of recorded Iron Age settlements, with the exception of the regions in the immediate vicinity of Oxford (OS 1962). Intensified aerial survey combined with a number of excavations in advance of gravel and ironstone extraction and a tradition of high quality field-work has, however, totally altered the picture. Far from being sparsely occupied the Midlands can now be shown to have been exceptionally densely populated (Hall and Hutchings 1972; Knight 1984; Pryor 1984, 230–40). Moreover it has become clear that, during the Iron Age, communities had begun to spread from the lighter soils of the limestone and gravel on to clay land which had previously been thought to be totally unsuitable for prehistoric settlement.

Many settlements have now been partially or extensively excavated. Of these Twywell, situated on the limestone uplands of Northamptonshire, provides an example of a complex habitation site dating to the period from approximately the fourth to the second century (Figure 12.14). The site consisted of a number of ditched enclosures of which one, only 0.1 ha in area, was totally excavated. Its development was complex, the ditch, averaging 3.7 m wide and 1.22 m deep, having been recut on several occasions. Evidence of structures, in the form of pits, post-holes and drainage gullies, was not restricted to the enclosed area, but spread densely outside; indeed it would appear that the huts had been sited so as to line the approach road leading to the enclosure entrance, but contemporaneity was difficult to prove. The evidence of Twywell therefore shows that ditched enclosures form only one element in otherwise more extensive settlement complexes. It may be compared to the contemporary sites of Abingdon and Beckford.

A number of discrete enclosures, unencumbered by neighbouring structures, are known. At Blackthorn, Northants., a double-ditched enclosure of about 0.1 ha, dating to the second or first century BC, was found to contain a single house together with twenty-eight pits, some of which could well have been for grain storage. Three kilometres away at Moulton Park a contemporary, but larger, enclosure was found to protect several houses. Here, however, occupation continued into the first century AD as the settlement spread away from its original nucleus. A rather different settlement type is presented by the excavations at Draughton and Brigstock, Northants. (Figure 12.14). At Draughton, a ditched enclosure 30 m across was found enclosing three houses, not necessarily contemporary, ranging in diameter from 5.8 to 10.4 m, the largest presumably being the principal house. A similar settlement was excavated at Brigstock where the enclosure was 22 m in internal diameter and protected a single house 7.8 m in diameter set in a penannular drainage ditch and with a stone-built pathway leading from its door to the enclosure entrance. The enclosure excavated at Brigstock is only one element of a complex settlement pattern revealed by air photography. The selection of single houses (or homesteads) for enclosure in this monumental way can only reasonably be explained in terms of the exceptional status of the owners.

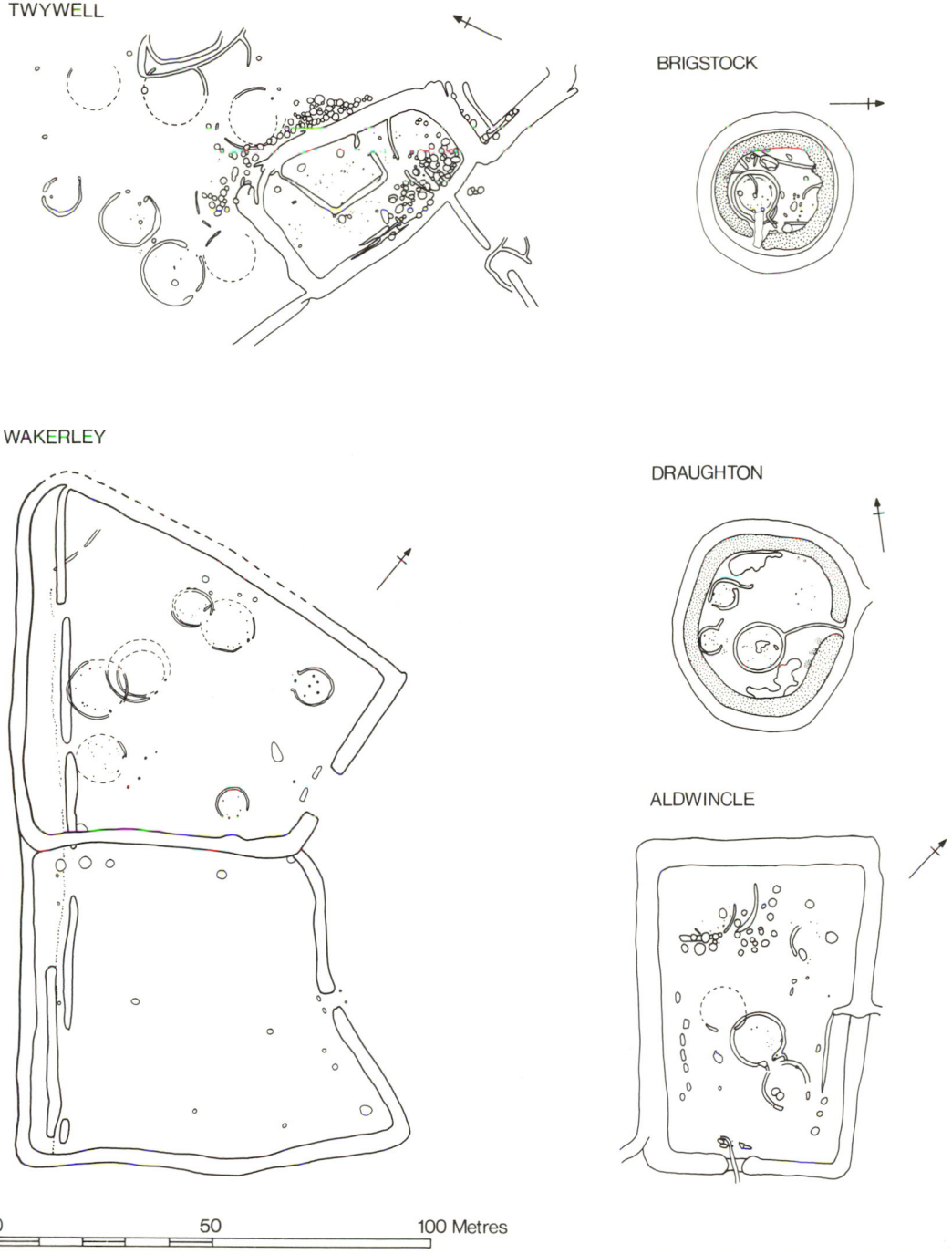

Figure 12.14 Settlements in the east Midlands (sources: *Twywell*, Jackson 1975; *Brigstock*, Jackson 1983; *Wakerley*, Jackson 1970; *Draughton*, Grimes 1961, *Aldwincle*, Jackson 1977).

Elsewhere in the east Midlands details of Early and Middle Iron Age settlement, though plentiful, are rather more scattered. Regional surveys exist for Leicestershire (Liddell 1982) and Bedfordshire (Dyer 1976a) and a number of partial excavations have exposed elements of sites but the evidence is not yet adequate for systematic survey.

The tradition of enclosing the principal settlement area with a ditch and presumably a bank continued into the late first century BC and early first century AD. An example of this later type of settlement is provided by Colsterworth, Lincs. (Figure 12.15), which consisted of a ditched enclosure measuring 73 by 64 m, containing two clusters of huts of varying dates, the largest being some 13.4 m in diameter. At the broadly contemporary site at Tallington, in the Welland valley, a rectangular ditched enclosure 65.5 by 48.8 m lying alongside a trackway was totally excavated, revealing most of the structures of the Little Woodbury type of enclosure with the exception of the house (quarried away?) and grain storage pits which would have been impossible to construct in the wet gravelly soil; grain must therefore have been stored in above-ground containers. An enclosure of the same date and closely similar size, excavated at Orton Longueville, Northants., provides interesting evidence for the continuity of socio-economic units of this size well into the Roman period.

Not all of the Late Iron Age settlements in the east Midlands were simple ditched enclosures: as in Wessex more complex forms developed and many can now be recognized as the result of aerial photography. The later stages of the settlement at Moulton Park, Northants., and the partially excavated site at Hardingstone, Northants., clearly belong to this category. The evidence at present available would therefore suggest that here, as in the south, simple and complex ditched enclosures continued to be constructed side by side up to the time of the Roman Conquest.

In general terms, it can be said that in the east Midlands enclosures, usually, but not invariably, representing single family units, formed a recurring element in the settlement pattern from at least as early as the fourth century BC to the Roman Conquest and later. Where the subsoil was suitable storage pits were dug but, elsewhere, on the gravels and on the clay land, grain must have been stored above ground. On present evidence it would seem that the enclosed settlements of the Midlands were significantly smaller than the broadly contemporary Wessex sites of Little Woodbury type. This might suggest that the Little Woodbury type of settlement reflects a particular socio-economic system restricted to central southern Britain in the Early and Middle Iron Age. How the systems varied is a matter for further detailed investigation.

We have already seen that on the Wessex chalkland and in the Upper Thames valley large unenclosed settlements were not infrequent. These, it has been suggested, may represent large agglomerations of people living together in hamlets or villages. Evidence from Northamptonshire suggests that here too substantial unenclosed settlements are to be found. The spread of occupation at Twywell has already been mentioned and at Wakerley, Northants., ironstone quarrying has exposed a settlement in excess of 500 m in length, but given the absence of total excavation and bearing in mind the difficulties of assessing what is contemporary in such palimpsests (Knight 1984, 227–38) it would be rash to talk of villages rather than groupings of two or three family units.

Within the east Midlands lies a rather specialized environment – the long sinuous fen edge where the dry land of Lincolnshire, Cambridgeshire and Norfolk met the vast expanse of waterlogged fen that fringed what is now the Wash into which the rivers Ouse, Nene, Welland and Witham drain. The fens have recently been subjected to campaigns of systematic fieldwork with the result that much has been learnt of the environmental changes to which the area has

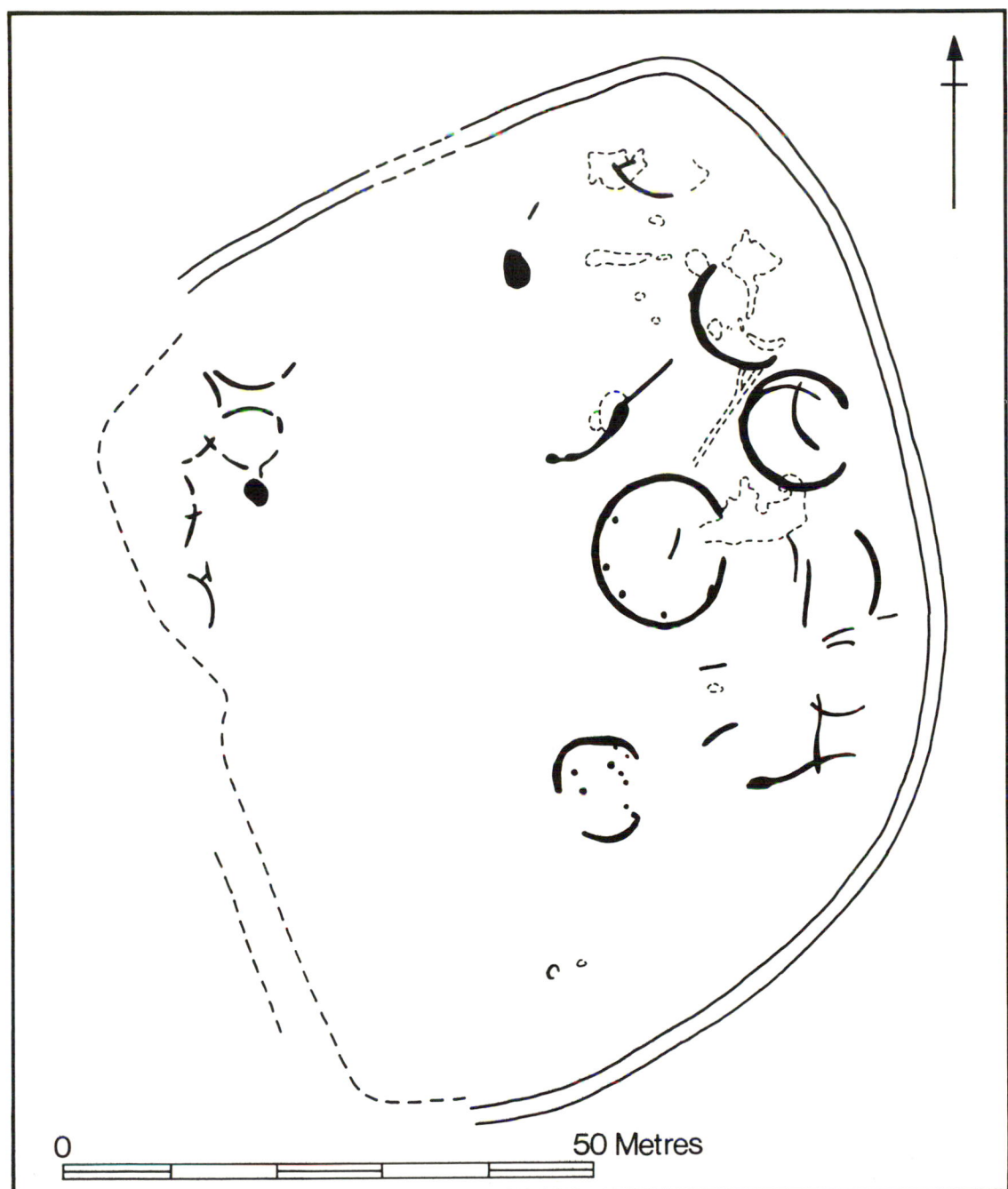

0   50 Metres

Figure 12.15   Colsterworth, Lincs. (source: Grimes 1961).

been subjected (Waller 1988) and the settlement patterns of successive periods including the Iron Age are now becoming much more clearly focused (B.B. Simmons 1980; Hall 1981, 1987; Lane 1988). Large-scale excavations of fen-edge settlements of Iron Age date are at present few but three sites of outstanding interest show something of the complexity of the problem: Fengate, Northants., Upper Delphs (Haddenham), Cambs., and Tattershall Thorpe, Lincs.

Fengate is a complex open settlement of considerable extent comprising a series of ditched enclosures or paddocks associated with at least eighteen circular houses, a few pits and isolated post-holes (Figure 12.16). The size and longevity of the settlement, which was occupied throughout much of the Iron Age, suggests a stable economic system based, presumably, upon the exploitation of the clay and limestones of the dry land to the west and the varied resources of the fen to the east.

Much the same resource potential attracted a small community to colonize a gravel spread on the edge of the fen at Upper Delphs, Haddenham, where boundary ditches and enclosures have been traced over about 5 ha. One element in this complex, on excavation, showed a succession from open settlement to enclosure (Figure 12.16). In the open phase, at least two contemporary houses were associated with fields (or cross-ploughed plots). This was succeeded by a ditched enclosure containing a substantial circular house which was later replaced by two houses, the enclosure ditch continuing to function. The sequence suggests a well-established community, possibly of single family size, while the environmental evidence would support the view that occupation was year round.

Tattershall Thorpe, Lincs., is altogether different in form and presumably function. It consists of a substantial double-ditched enclosure, roughly oval in shape, situated on a gravel rise 5 km from the fen edge. The nature of the internal occupation is unknown but the ditches have been sampled providing valuable environmental evidence pointing to intensive stock-raising. The site would be well suited as a corral for controlling flocks and herds at certain times during the year while the wetlands to the south would have provided admirable summer grazing. It is tempting to see some such system in operation but until the interior of the enclosure is sampled the complexities of the subsistence regime will remain obscure.

The fen edge is clearly an environment of some considerable interest for Iron Age studies not least because the survival of organic material holds out the possibility of examining the subtleties of the subsistence economy. Settlements occupying the interface between wetland and dry-land resources are the key to an understanding of how regional systems work since they controlled the production of a range of marshland resources some of which may have been desired by the dry-land communities of the interior. By studying the processes of exploitation and transmission significant advances in understanding Iron Age society are within reach.

Finally, to questions of population: extensive field surveys carried out in recent years, especially in Northamptonshire, are revolutionizing our ideas of settlement pattern and necessarily reflect on estimates of population. Until a quantitative assessment is made firm conclusions cannot be attempted, but it is clear even now that by the third century BC much, if not most, of the river gravel area was settled to capacity and in eastern Northamptonshire, at least, settlement was already spreading on to heavy clay land. Whether or not this phenomenon represents the result of a rapid increase in population in the fourth or third century is a problem which can only be resolved in the light of future fieldwork and excavation, but even on present showing the population of the east Midlands must have been similar to that of the more densely occupied chalkland of the south.

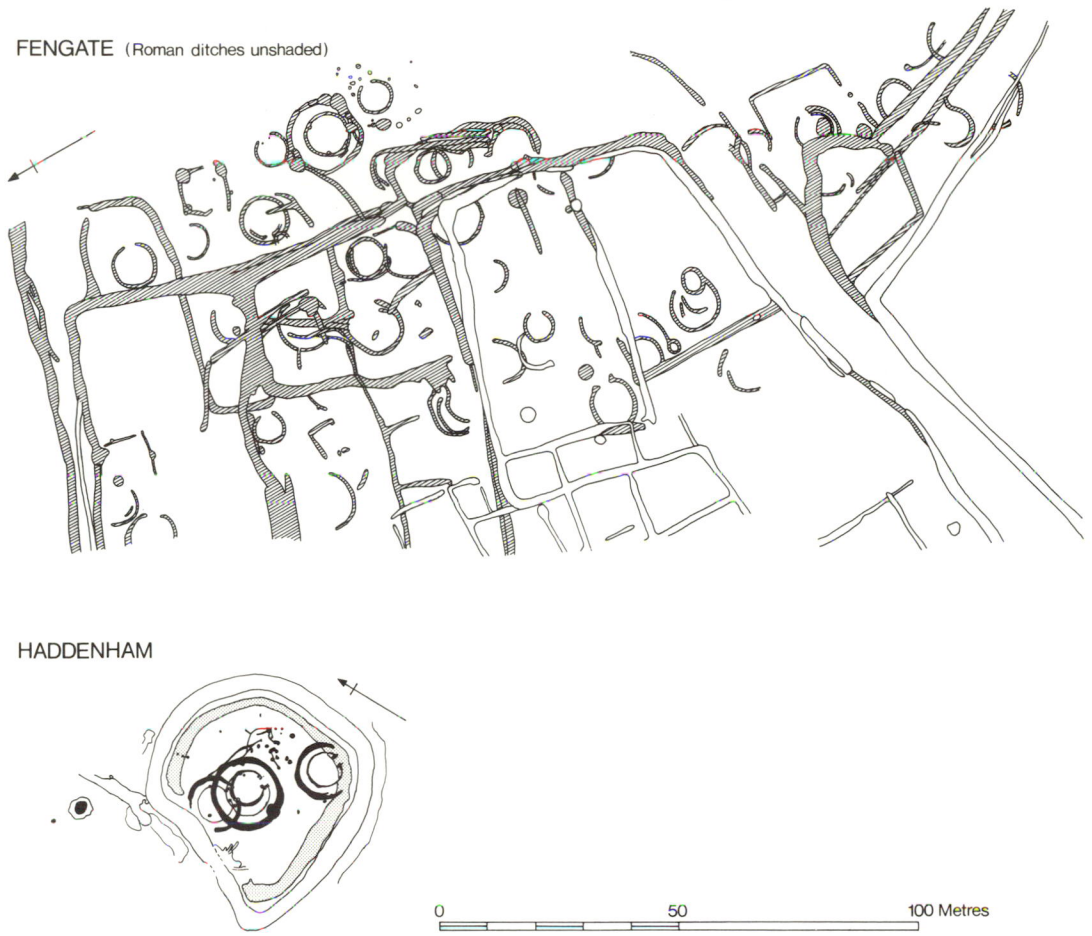

Figure 12.16 Contrasting Fen edge settlements (sources: *Fengate*, Pryor 1978; *Haddenham*, Evans and Serjeantson 1988).

The Thames basin

The triangle of land fringed by the Chilterns and the North Downs and dominated by the river Thames has produced comparatively little good evidence of settlement apart from a number of casual observations and the results of limited excavation. But the few large-scale excavations that are available for assessment are of considerable interest and show the potential richness of the record. At Little Waltham, Essex, a straggling settlement of circular houses, extending for 200 m along the terrace flanking the flood plain of the river Chelmer, is hardly likely to represent less than a hamlet or small village of the Early–Middle Iron Age (Figure 12.17). This is in marked contrast to the strongly defended homestead of Late Iron Age date found at Orsett commanding the lower reaches of the Thames (Figure 12.17) or the small farm at Farningham Hill in the

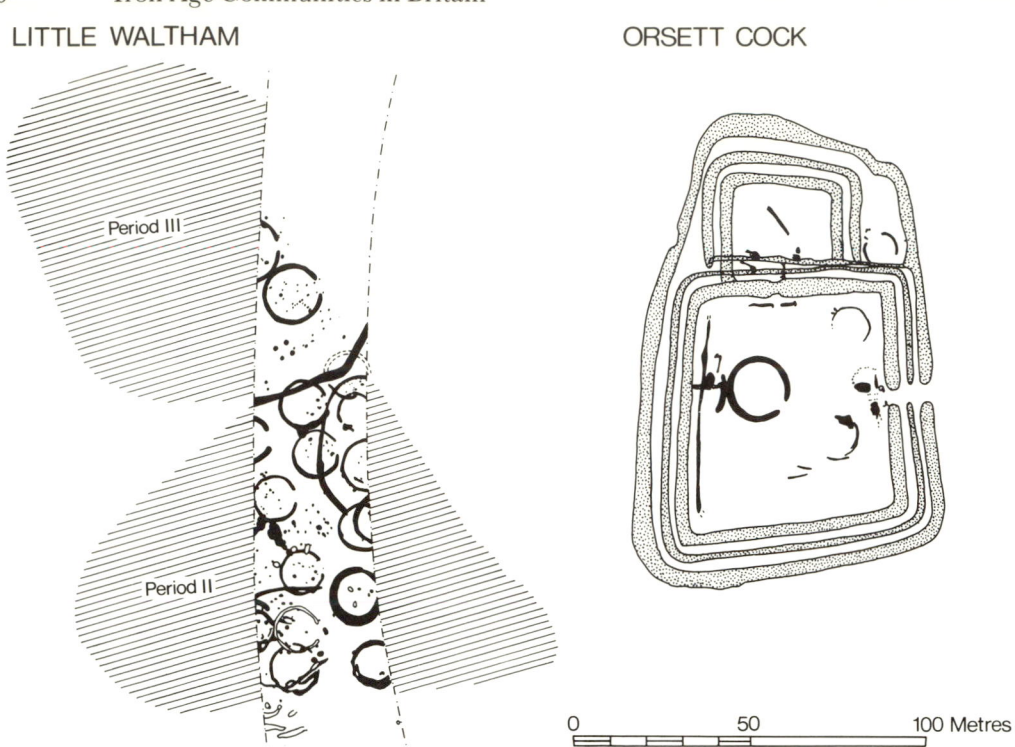

Figure 12.17   Settlements of the Lower Thames basin (sources: *Little Waltham*, Drury 1978; *Orsett Cock*, Toller 1980).

Darenth valley in Kent, 12 km upstream from the Thames, where a modest house together with a few storage pits, was set within a comparatively slight ditched enclosure. These three examples, together with a few other large-scale excavations (e.g. Gun Hill and Mucking), suggest that the settlement types of the Thames basin conform to the general range found elsewhere in the south-east but are yet too few to warrant a more detailed regional assessment.

The Somerset Levels

The expanse of wetland between the Mendips and the Quantock hills is of considerable archaeological potential but it is only since about 1960 that it has been systematically explored in advance of intensified peat cutting and the lowering of the water table (B. and J. Coles 1986). The best-known area lies between the Polden hills and the Wedmore ridge and includes the two famous Iron Age settlements of Glastonbury and Meare: Glastonbury was almost entirely excavated between 1892 and 1907 by Bulleid and Gray while Meare, consisting of two separate sites, was partially excavated by the same team from 1908 to 1956 and by Michael Avery from 1966–9. In 1978 the Somerset Levels project began a systematic re-examination of both villages.

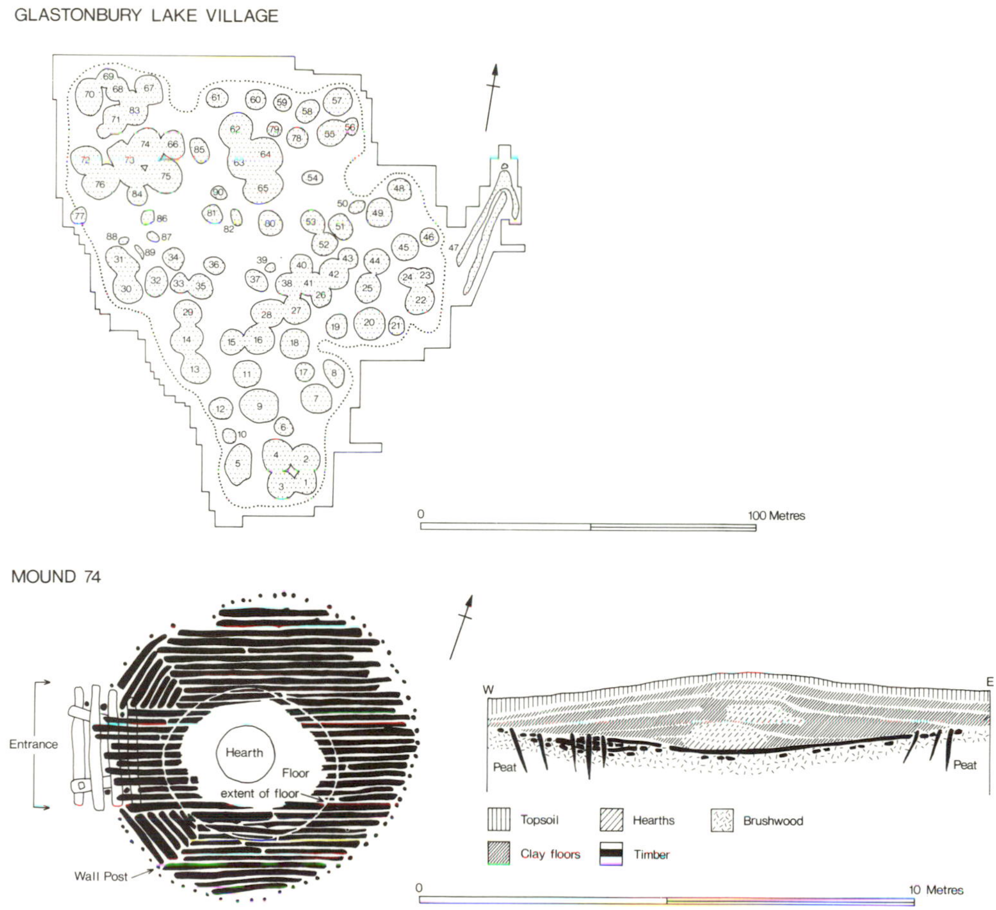

GLASTONBURY LAKE VILLAGE

MOUND 74

Figure 12.18   Glastonbury, Somerset (source: Coles and Coles 1986).

The literature is extensive (site list pp. 616, 619) but the clearest and most authoritative overview of the problem is provided by Bryony and John Coles (1986, 153–83).

Glastonbury can fairly be regarded as a 'lake village' in that it was built on a morass, in an area of the Levels where water was prevalent, on an artificial foundation of brushwood and larger timber packed with bracken, rubble and clay. Upon this foundation up to eighty circular buildings had been constructed during the Middle and Late Iron Age (Figure 12.18). The settlement, roughly triangular in shape, was surrounded by a timber palisade, more to retain the artificial island than to provide a defensive enclosure. The circular buildings varied in size and construction. The larger and more elaborate had walls of vertical timbers supporting wattle and daub and successive floors of clay usually with a hearth in the centre. The door frames were frequently carefully constructed, often with a porch. By no means all of the circular structures conformed to this type: some were without recognizable walls and others without hearths. The particular interest of the site focuses upon the possibility it offers of reconstructing social groupings within the settlement. Assuming that different types of circular building performed different functions, for example for living and sleeping, cooking, storage, weaving, etc., it ought in theory to be possible to define the grouping of structures which a single extended family might inhabit. An attempt to do this by D.L. Clarke (1972) raised expectations but under critical analysis has been found wanting (B. and J. Coles 1986, 164–71; Barrett 1987). This does not mean, however, that the general approach is invalid and a detailed reassessment by the staff of the Somerset Levels project is now underway. One thing is clear – the eighty or so circular buildings do not mean eighty families. In all probability the village of Glastonbury was never larger than a cluster of four or five families at the most.

The two 'villages' of Meare were altogether different. They comprise two separate elongated clusters of mounds, 60 m apart, built on the edge of a raised bog without any form of brushwood foundation. The individual mounds, like those of Glastonbury, were built of superimposed clay floors usually with central hearths replaced more often than the floors. Very little evidence was found of superstructures, a fact which has led to the conclusion that the buildings were flimsy and perhaps little more than tents. This does not, however, mean that the settlement was impoverished. The artefacts recovered are impressive in both quality and quantity and there is ample evidence for a range of activities being undertaken including the manufacture of glass beads. J. Coles has put forward the interesting hypothesis that the Meare 'villages' were a very specialized kind of site – the meeting-place of an annual 'trade fair' where people from considerable distances could assemble in peace to trade and exchange goods and to take part in a range of social, and perhaps religious, interactions. Such meetings form an essential component of European folk history and are still evident today in fairs, usually held on saints' days on common land. The Meare site is well situated for intertribal meetings since it lies on the border between the Dobunni and the Durotriges.

Glastonbury and Meare represent two very different kinds of settlement but they are only a part of a far more complex socio-economic system which includes the extensive use of the Mendip caves and of an arc of hillforts which fringe the Levels. The details of the interrelationship of these various settlement elements have still to be worked out.

Houses (Figure 12.19)

Having considered the variety of settlement sites in the south and east of Britain something must now be said of the houses, or more accurately the circular buildings, within which the community lived and worked. Since more than 1,000 house plans are now known the brief discussion which follows can be little more than a broad overview.

Houses of the late second and early first millennia are now well known, principally from the excavation of the Sussex settlements. Characteristically they are simple circular structures averaging 6 m or so in diameter, constructed of a series of upright timbers placed somewhat irregularly in a circular or oval setting; central supports were seldom employed and indeed were not necessary for structures of such small span. Where huts have been terraced slightly into a sloping hillside, it is evident that the upright timbers did not form the outer wall of the hut but were simply supports for the sloping rafters, the lower ends of which probably rested on the outer edge of the terrace, which in some cases was up to 1.5 m away from the ring of vertical timbers. Thus two areas were created: a central area with a high roof-line where the principal activities of the house were carried out, and a surrounding area between the posts and the wall of the hut

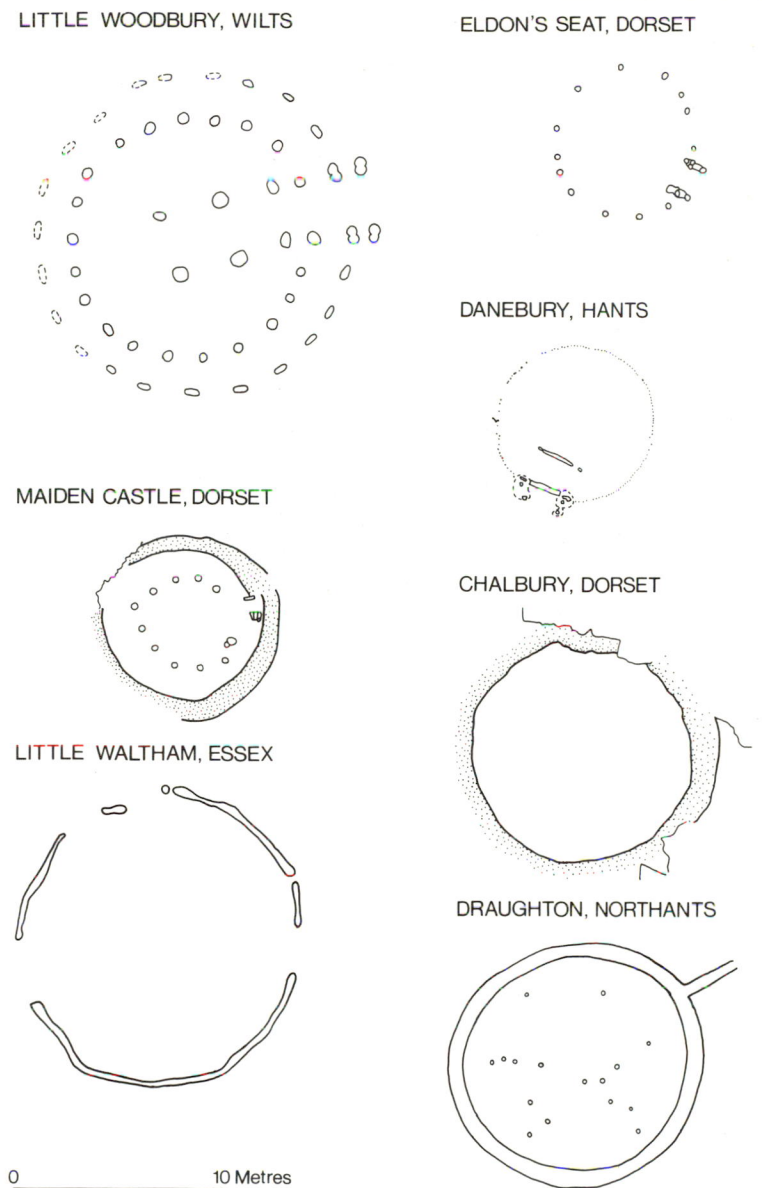

LITTLE WOODBURY, WILTS

ELDON'S SEAT, DORSET

DANEBURY, HANTS

MAIDEN CASTLE, DORSET

CHALBURY, DORSET

LITTLE WALTHAM, ESSEX

DRAUGHTON, NORTHANTS

0   10 Metres

Figure 12.19 Plans of southern British houses (sources: *Little Woodbury*, Bersu 1940; *Maiden Castle*, Wheeler 1943; *Eldon's Seat*, Cunliffe 1968b; *Danebury*, Cunliffe 1984a; *Little Waltham*, Drury 1978; *Chalbury*, Whitley 1943; *Draughton*, Grimes 1961).

which could have served as storage or sleeping space. Approximate calculations for the small hut N from Itford Hill, Sussex, show that 14 m^2 were available for 'living' and 19 m^2 for sleeping and storage (see Figure 3.3, p. 31). Few of the early huts show any great refinement in structure but substantial door-posts and short porches are known.

This basic house type continued in use throughout the Iron Age (Guilbert 1981). The sequence at Eldon's Seat (Encombe), Dorset, spanning the period from the eighth to the sixth century, shows a gradual increase in diameter from 6 m up to 9 m for the latest house. There was also a trend towards a more regular spacing of timbers and one hut was provided with an entrance porch. The latest house was very regularly constructed, and the spacing of the vertical posts in relation to the edge of its platform implies that they served not only as rafter supports but also as the wall timbers. A series of structures of comparable date were found within the hillfort of Winklebury, Hants., ranging in size from 8–12 m: most of them had short porches. Simple houses of this kind continued into the third or second century BC, for example at Little Woodbury, house 2, which can be shown to belong to the Middle Iron Age (see Figure 12.2, p. 217).

In parallel to the tradition of simple ring-post houses, more complex structures developed. House 1 at Little Woodbury, Wilts., offers one of the clearest examples. Here two concentric circles of posts were erected, the inner circle being more massive and taking most of the weight of the roof timbers, the outer circle taking the slighter posts. The house is further complicated by the central setting of four timbers which served to support the centre of the roof and probably, at the same time, stood above the roof-level to create a louvre for smoke to escape. The Little Woodbury plan is essentially only a modification of the early houses mentioned above, in which the total enclosed area was divided into a central region and peripheral space. Little Woodbury shows the additional modification of a substantial porch or entrance passage 4.6 m long. Provided with an inner and outer door, it would have created a trap to prevent cold air from sweeping in.[1] The overall diameter of the house, 14 m, compares with three other large houses of the same general type, one from Cow Down (Longbridge Deverill), Wilts., and one from Pimperne Down, Dorset, both 15 m in diameter, and a third from Old Down Farm, Hants., measuring 11 m in diameter. All four houses belong to the period from the eighth to the fifth century: at present no house of comparable size or complexity has been found in the latter part of the Iron Age.

A structure of rather different type was found at West Harling, Norfolk. In plan it consisted of a circular ditch broken by two wide causeways, with an internal bank with corresponding openings. Within lay a mass of post-holes which probably belonged to a house-like structure. One interpretation suggests that the roofed area was annular about a central open yard (R.R. Clarke 1960, 95), but it would be simpler to reconstruct it as a conventional circular house standing within a ditched enclosure, the ends of the rafters resting on the bank. The possibility that it was a religious building is unlikely in view of the presence of hearths and drainage gullies, which would argue for domestic use. Another West Harling house was of a more conventional structure: a circular setting of posts about 11.5 m in diameter. This too was built in the centre of a circular ditched enclosure about 34 m across.

While houses built of individual posts occur widely, and are likely to survive in most archaeological contexts, it is now clear that less substantial forms of house building were not infrequently employed. At Danebury, Hants., for example, the majority of the houses belonging to the Middle Iron Age were constructed of wattle based on vertical stakes some 2 cm in diameter driven into the ground at intervals of 10–15 cm. It was only at the doorway that substantial timbers were employed to strengthen the entrance gap and give support to the door. The buildings varied in diameter from 6–9 m. How the roof was constructed is a matter of debate: one possibility is that the vertical wall was bound at the top with withies to form a ring beam upon which the lower ends of rafters were based, but it is equally possible that some of the vertical poles were carried up and bound together at the apex to create the framework for a beehive-like structure entirely of wattle which could then have been weather-proofed with thatch. The door frames of the Danebury houses frequently had two vertical timbers on each side of the door with a space of 20–30 cm between. This would have provided a suitable framework to support a movable door of wattle which could have been slotted into place or removed at will. Similar kinds of stake-built structures have been found at the hillforts of Moel y Gaer, Flints., and South Cadbury, Somerset, and at Hengistbury Head, Dorset. Clearly, the survival and recognition of such buildings is dependent on a number of factors and the strong probability remains that while many may have passed unnoticed most will have been destroyed by subsequent agricultural activities. The very simplicity of stake-built houses suggests that the type may once have been widespread.

A second type of less substantial house has been noted at Little Waltham, Essex. Here a number of round houses were discovered which were represented archaeologically by foundation trenches 10–14 m in diameter. Two types can be recognized: the first, in which the walls consisted of vertical posts placed in an evenly curving trench, and a second of a more polygonal plan which hints that horizontal wall plates may have been adopted. In both types a ring beam at eaves level would have been all that was required to provide the strength necessary to carry the roof. Ring-groove houses of this type are quite common in southern Britain but the simplicity of the plan may well obscure variation in structure. At Danebury, for example, the walls of one such house were composed of vertical planks placed side by side. Elsewhere vertical timbers appear to have been more widely spaced and were presumably infilled with wattle.

Penannular or completely circular drainage ditches surrounding huts are known on a number of sites, and the type, though uncommon on the chalk, is evidently widespread throughout much of southern Britain. The gully or ditch would serve to collect rain-water running off the roof, either to conserve it or prevent it from flooding the house in times of heavy rain. Such an arrangement would have been a necessity on less permeable soils as at Draughton, Northants., where a circular enclosing gully was found to be linked by a drainage gutter to the main ditch of the enclosure but elsewhere gullies would have served to keep the soil, in which the vertical timbers of the walls were bedded, sufficiently drained to slow down their disintegration through rot.

In the western part of the region, particularly in Dorset where stone was readily available, many of the houses were provided with dwarf walls of dry-stone work. In the case of one building at Maiden Castle, the stone outer wall would have been used to bed the ends of the rafters, the main weight of which must have been taken on the concentric setting of large posts. The hut circle from Chalbury, Dorset, on the other hand, while possessing an outer dry-stone wall, was apparently without central timbers, but while it could easily have been spanned by rafters supported only upon the wall itself, verticals without post-holes may once have existed. Thus there is little structural difference between the huts built wholly of timber and those in which some dry-stone work has been incorporated.

The internal arrangements of the individual houses vary considerably. Frequently, but not invariably, there were hearths either centrally placed, as at Maiden Castle and Glastonbury, or more usually to one side, as they are in the houses at Eldon's Seat and West Overton Down; less frequently bread ovens occur. Some of the huts were also provided with drainage gullies leading from the centre of the hut out of the entrance, either to remove rain-water which may have seeped in through any central gap left in the roof structure or to provide a draught to allow the fire to burn more efficiently. Beneath the floors of some houses, for example at Danebury, grain storage pits had been dug: in other cases smaller holes or even partially buried ceramic containers were found in which food or liquids may have been stored.

It should be stressed, again, that circular buildings would have served a variety of uses: some undoubtedly provided living space for the social group while others may have been ancillary structures such as cook houses or weaving sheds. In addition many settlements have produced evidence of other structures such as four- or six-post 'granaries' and two-post 'racks' (p. 375) and arcs of slots or post settings which may represent screens or shelters. The average Iron Age homestead must have presented a complex and cluttered appearance which the archaeological evidence allows us only to glimpse.

Summary

In this chapter we have restricted ourselves to a discussion of the homesteads and hamlets of the south and east of Britain. No attempt has been made to consider the larger defended sites, which are usually classed together and referred to as hillforts, nor has much been said of the economic system of which the settlements formed one element. Divisions of this kind are to some extent arbitrary but a line has to be drawn somewhere. Hillforts are more conveniently dealt with together (chapter 14) since they differ from the homesteads in being a communal undertaking reflecting the exercise of some kind of coercive power and therefore represent a higher order of social organization than the homestead or hamlet, while the question of the subsistence economy is best considered after the full range of the settlement archaeology has been presented (chapter 15).

So rich is the settlement evidence from the south and east of Britain that much has had to be omitted, but the main characteristics of the settlements have been summarized and something of their variety made evident. It would be no exaggeration to say that the settlement data from this region are far more prolific than for any other part of Iron Age Europe, with the possible exception of the Netherlands, and yet it is only in a few regions – the Wessex chalklands, the Upper Thames valley and Northamptonshire – that sufficient sites have been excavated on a large enough scale to allow patterns to be recognized and socio-economic systems to be discerned, albeit incompletely.

13

Settlement and the settlement pattern in the west and north

Beyond the Jurassic ridge the landscape of Britain becomes more varied. Considerable expanses of old hard rock have created barren mountainous areas like the core of Wales and the Highlands of Scotland while the predominantly westerly air currents ensure that the Atlantic coasts have a higher precipitation rate than much of the rest of the country. Since height above sea-level (which affects temperature) and mean annual rainfall are crucial factors in controlling crop growth, considerable areas of the north and west lie at or beyond the limit of viable agriculture. Thus, slight fluctuations in climate can cause major dislocations in settlement pattern (pp. 57–8). This factor, and the harsh nature of some of the environments, has tended to create an intense regionalism in settlement form and a high degree of specialization in economy. In the discussion to follow each major region is treated separately.

The south-west peninsula

The south-west peninsula has a distinctive character unlike any other area of Britain. Bounded on three sides by the sea and separated from Wessex by the marshlands of Somerset, its communities have developed along individual lines influenced more by the structure and food producing potential of the land than by external stimulus. The peninsula is dominated by six areas of moorland: the sandstone uplands of Exmoor in the north-east and the granite masses of Dartmoor, Bodmin, Hensbarrow, Carnmenelis and Penwith – all providing some areas of light, if not particularly fertile, soil more suitable for pasture than for arable farming. Between these upland masses lie the Culm measures of the middle Devonian and the Permian rocks yielding an intractable clay soil far less congenial to prehistoric settlement.

The literature concerning the Iron Age settlement pattern in the south-west has grown considerably in recent years. For the environmental background the reader is referred to two important papers summarizing the evidence from Cornwall (Caseldine 1980) and Devon (Caseldine and Maguire 1981). Cornish defended settlements are discussed in detail by Nicholas

Johnson and Peter Rose (1982) and the background to the Cornish Iron Age is assessed by Henrietta Quinnell (1986). The first-millennium BC settlements of Devon are fully treated by Bob Silvester (1979).

Moorland settlements

In chapter 3 the principal types of settlement centring upon the Dartmoor massif and dating to the late second and early first millennia were discussed. Briefly summarized, they included large enclosed villages, sometimes with attached stockpens, sited around the south and west limits of the moor; open villages with huts linked by stone walls found in much the same area; and small farmsteads of one or two huts associated with a few embanked fields. This last type is concentrated on the more protected and correspondingly drier eastern edges of the moor. The dating of these Mid–Late Bronze Age settlements is notoriously difficult, for while there can be little doubt that many of them began to be occupied in what is conventionally the Bronze Age, the upper limit of dating is difficult to define. In some cases they may have continued in use as late as the latter half of the first millennium. Two Dartmoor settlements have produced artefacts suggesting an Iron Age date – Kestor, near Chagford (Figure 13.1), and Foale's Arrishes. Both settlements comprise a group of huts scattered among small rectangular fields with a single larger hut protected by an enclosing wall. Strictly, this type of site is little more than an agglomeration of small farmsteads but their close spacing and the provision of a single more impressive house might suggest that we are dealing with hamlets or even villages, in which some form of class structure prevailed. A tighter nucleation can be recognized at other undated sites such as Broadall Lake in the Upper Yealm valley, Devon, where ten circular huts were grouped along the side of two fields.

The excavation at Kestor has provided a valuable insight into a type of settlement which may tentatively be dated to the fifth or fourth century BC. One of the isolated huts, lying at the junction of three field walls, was totally excavated. It was a simple structure, some 8.2 m across internally, enclosed by an outer wall to take the lower ends of the rafters, which were further supported by a circular setting of posts and a central post to hold up the crown of the roof. Internal fittings were restricted to a hearth and an area of cobbling close to the entrance. The larger hut, built towards the centre of the enclosure known as the Round Pound, was 11.3 m across internally and of a more complex structure, but here too internal posts acted as roof supports – the difference being that a central opening seems to have been provided with a drip-pit beneath to collect and drain away rain-water (Figure 13.3). The reason for the opening is thought to be that the hut was used for iron-smelting and fumes therefore had to be removed. Inside were found a small bowl furnace filled with iron slag and nearby a forging pit, presumably for reheating the bloom prior to the hammering necessary to remove impurities. However, some doubt has been expressed as to the date of the iron-working, one possibility being that it was a medieval intrusion (Silvester 1979, 178–9). The hut was enclosed within an oval stone-walled pound 30–3 m across, provided with a single narrow doorway opening on to a terraced drove road which ran between the surrounding fields. A second, much smaller hut lay close to the pound wall but was completely undated and may indeed belong to the medieval period. While it would be wrong to argue from the evidence of one site alone, and one where there is some doubt about the stratigraphy, the fact that the largest hut may have belonged to the iron-smith could be taken to be an indication of the high status in which the community held such a man.

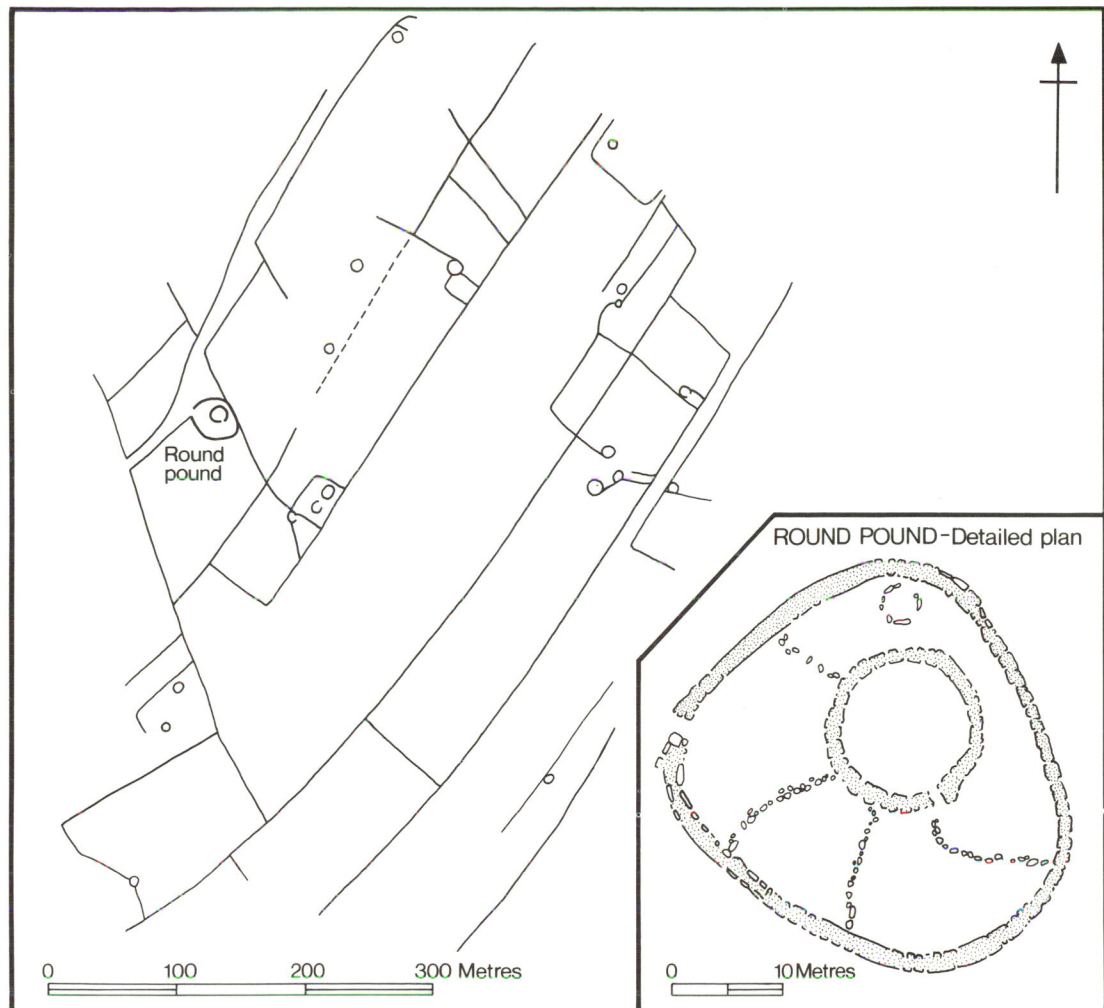

Figure 13.1   The settlement at Kestor, Devon (source: A. Fox 1955).

The close relationship between the pound, the trackway, the other huts and the fields leaves little doubt that all functioned together. Indeed, it was possible for the excavator to show that the ancient ploughsoil stopped 1.8 m clear of one of the huts and that a slight negative lynchet had been formed, demonstrating clearly that the field had been ploughed after the hut had been constructed. Nearby, the ploughsoil was found to overlie a layer of peat, which was shown by pollen analysis to belong to the sub-Atlantic period – a time when the climatic conditions were becoming much wetter. The Kestor settlement and its fields therefore belonged to a community which colonized an area of virgin moorland after the middle of the first millennium, at a time when climatic deterioration had already set in. In all probability it was one of the last inroads to be made on the moor before wetter weather drove the long-established population from the uplands.

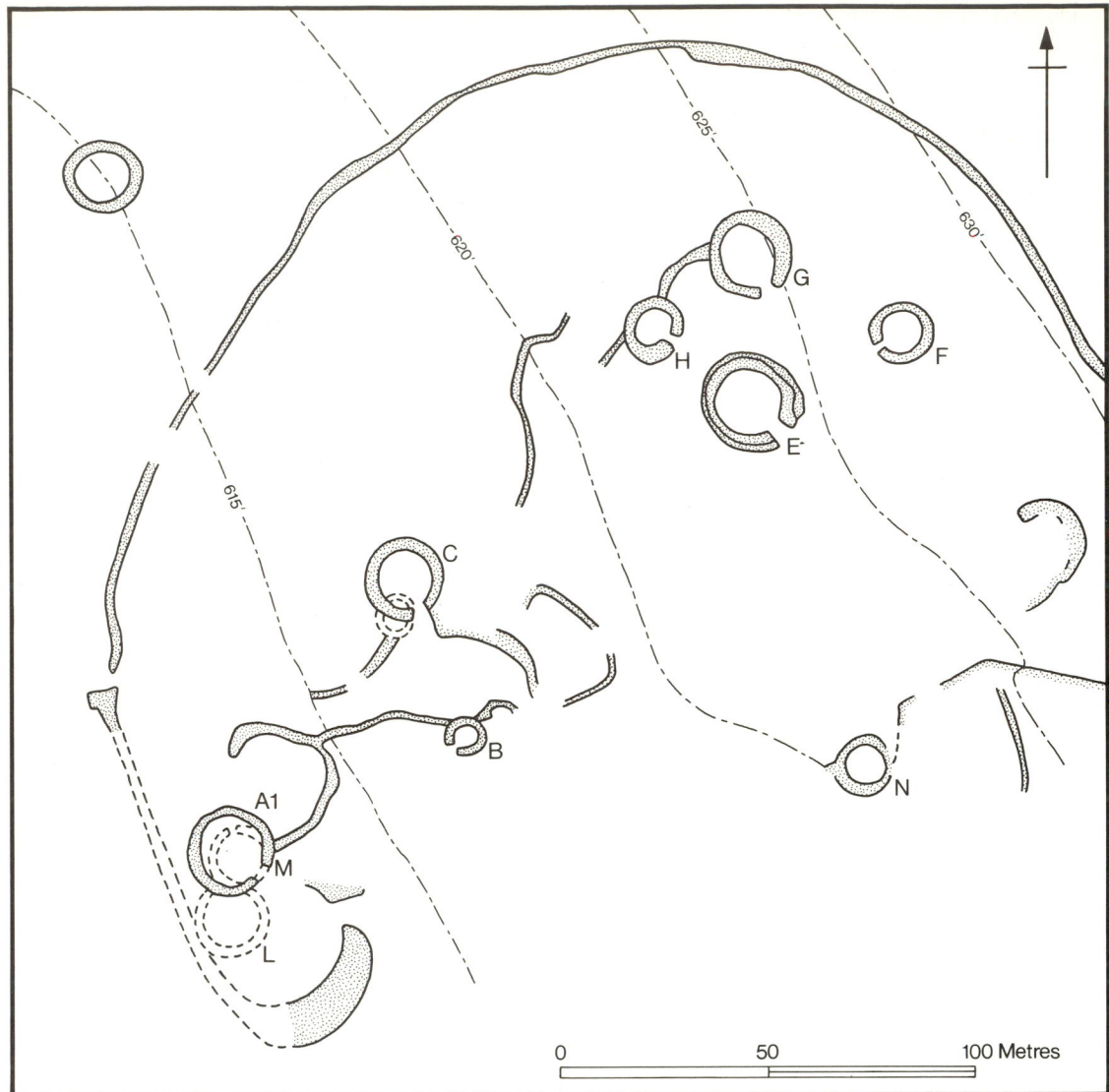

Figure 13.2 The settlement at Bodrifty, Cornwall. Letters refer to the identifications in the excavator's report (source: Dudley 1957).

The presence of fields and the discovery of a saddle quern are sufficient to show that arable farming was practised, but the field systems tend to be far more limited in extent than those of the south-east, implying – but by no means proving – that corn production was of subsidiary significance. Of the pastoral aspects of the economy little can be said: animal bones are destroyed by the acid moorland soils and relevant artefacts, apart from a spindle whorl from Kestor, are exceedingly rare. Flocks and herds must, however, have been a dominant feature of the early first-millennium economy, to judge by the large pounds of Mid–Late Bronze Age date, and in all probability pastoral activities continued to be of first-rate importance throughout the latter part

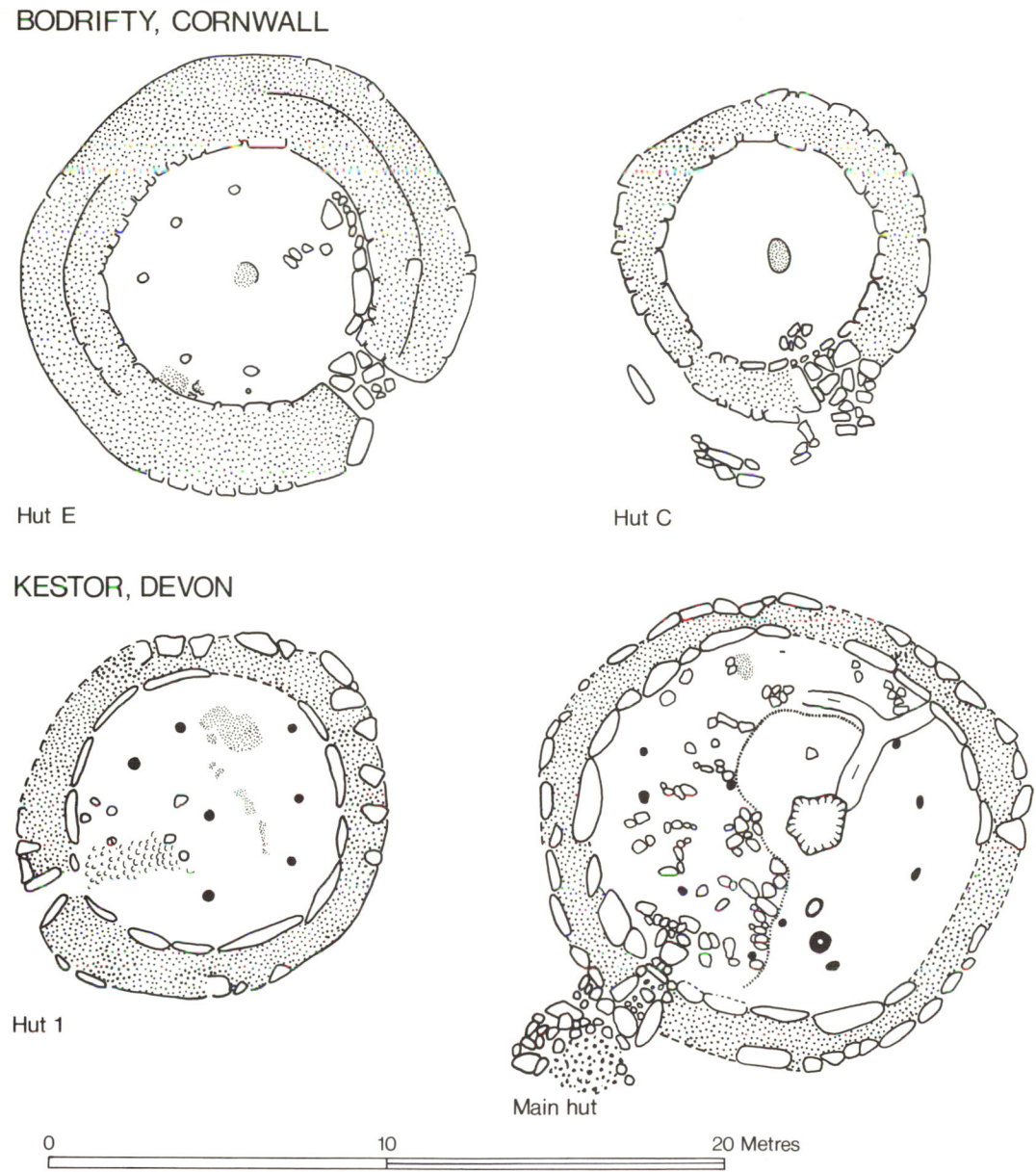

Figure 13.3 House plans from south-west Britain (sources: *Bodrifty*, Dudley 1957; *Kestor*, A. Fox 1955).

of the period – as, indeed, the multiple-enclosure forts to be described below imply.

Scattered huts among small rectangular fields is a pattern of settlement reflected over most of the south-west peninsula from Dartmoor to Land's End, but while many such sites are known, few have been excavated outside Dartmoor itself. One site, Bodrifty on Mulfra Hill near Penzance, Cornwall (Figure 13.2), has however provided some details in response to limited excavation. Here more than twenty simple circular huts were spread over a tract of land 0.4 km across, but at least nine are clustered together and were later enclosed by a pound wall built probably in the second or first century BC at about the time when some of the huts show signs of rebuilding. In the original pre-pound settlement, beginning perhaps as early as the sixth or fifth century, the individual huts were joined by lengths of walling rather like the technique employed on some of the Dartmoor villages such as Stanton Down. The huts themselves (Figure 13.3) are closely similar in structure to the Dartmoor examples, with wide stone walls, central hearths and sometimes internal settings of posts to help support the rafters in the case of the larger buildings. The excavation produced few finds, but spindle whorls and saddle querns give some hint of the agricultural and pastoral activities of the community. The significance of Bodrifty lies in the relatively large quantities of pottery recovered, ranging from types which would not be out of place in sixth- to fifth-century contexts in Wessex to jars of the second to first centuries decorated in the South-Western Decorated style. The ceramic evidence allows the possibility that occupation continued well into the first century BC.

Thus the Dartmoor and Cornish settlements are very close in details of planning, structure and economy, but on Dartmoor there is no evidence to suggest that occupation continued after the third or second centuries, since no trace of South-Western Decorated pottery has ever been found nor do any of the sites show signs of Roman use. The contrast with Cornwall is striking but can be explained if it is assumed that the onset of sub-Atlantic conditions forced the inhabitants of the high moors to abandon their traditional farmlands, while those living around the fringes of the less elevated and more hospitable Cornish moors were able to continue and even expand their territories. If this is correct, it would mean that a considerable shift of population took place away from Dartmoor and Bodmin Moor over a period of a century or two. It is necessary, therefore, to consider where these dislocated pastoralists might have settled.

Multiple-enclosure forts

The lowland areas of Devon and eastern Cornwall are densely scattered with settlements commonly referred to as multiple-enclosure forts (Figures 13.4–13.6), evidently designed for pastoral communities and (where evidence is available) not built until the fourth or third century BC. It is tempting to see these structures as the successors of the moorland settlements, colonizing the richer low-lying soils of the Devon and Cornish hills, but until the dating of a sufficient sample has been established it would be unwise to be too dogmatic as to their origins and relationships.

Characteristically, the multiple-enclosure settlements are often sited, more for pastoral convenience than for strength, on hill-slopes or the ends of ridges overlooking springs or river valleys. Normally the inner enclosure, between 0.2 and 1.6 ha in extent, is defended by a fairly massive bank and ditch laid out in a circular or sub-rectangular plan with a single entrance in one side. The additional enclosures were created in several ways (Figure 13.4). At Milber Down Camp, Devon, two outer banks and ditches were arranged concentrically with the inner earthwork, both enclosing a considerable additional hectareage. An even more impressive example of this type is Clovelly Dykes, where two enclosures are concentric with the main camp and two additional areas are attached to one side of the outermost, thus providing four separate enclosed areas in addition to the central element. All were interlinked with entrances, the main entrance being so sited as to give easy access to nearby springs. A variation on this type can be seen at Castle Dore, Cornwall, Denbury, south Devon, and at several other sites where the outer

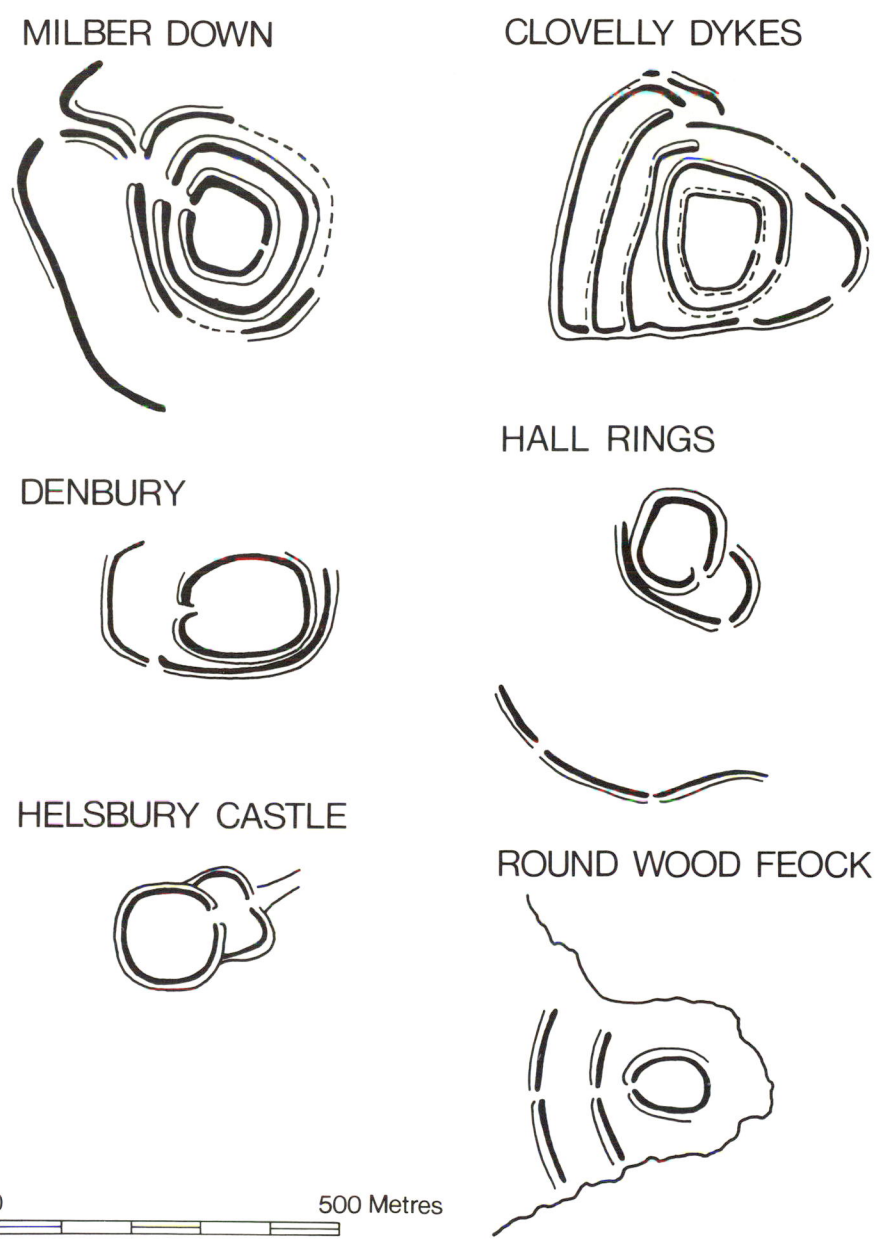

Figure 13.4   Multiple-enclosure forts in Devon and Cornwall (sources: A. Fox 1953, 1961b).

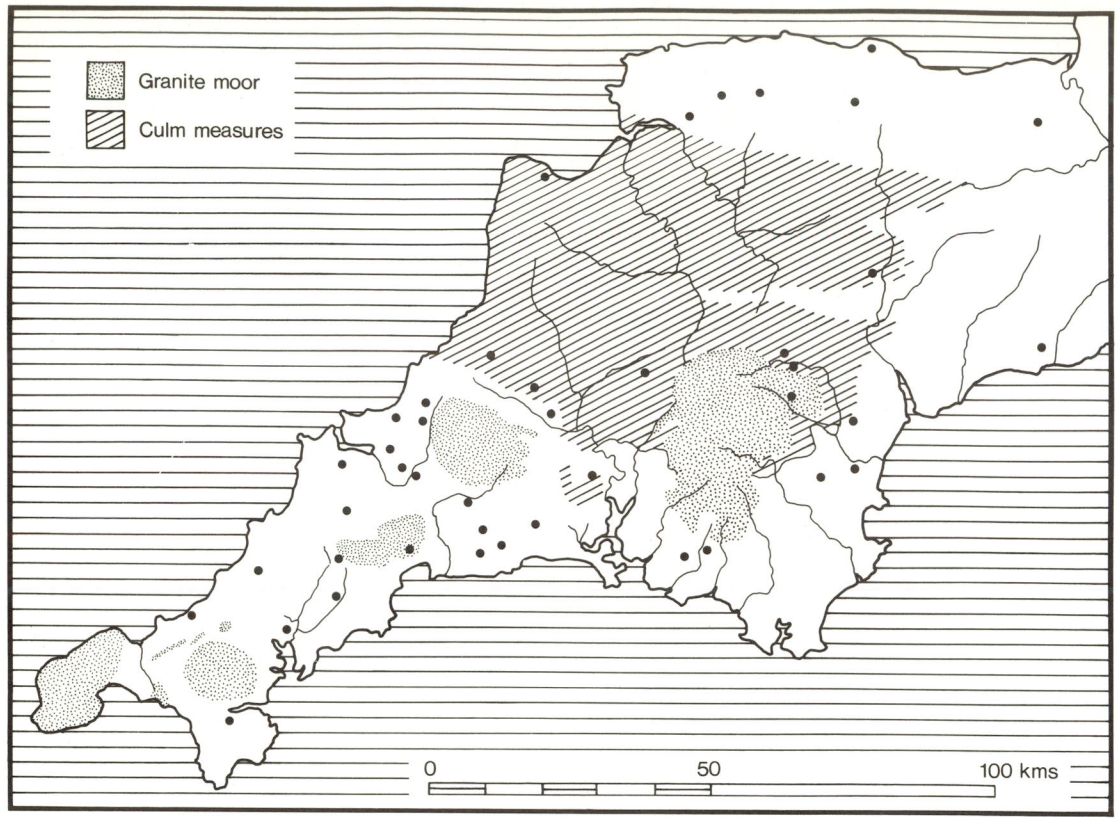

Figure 13.5 Distribution of multiple-enclosure forts in south-west Britain (source: A. Fox 1961b).

enclosure is pendent upon the inner, the two ramparts being close-spaced for part of their length but diverging widely towards the entrance to form an outer enclosure. A third type occurs in which the main camp is provided with a separate annex attached to the side with the entrance. Strictly, the little fort at Blackbury Castle, Devon, belongs to this class, but here the passage between the two entrances was flanked by banks and ditches, giving rise to the so-called barbican approach. More distant cross-banks were also extensively used, usually to cut off the neck of the promontory or spur upon which the main enclosure was situated. This type of arrangement frequently enclosed a substantial hectareage, which almost invariably included springs or streams.

The intention behind the siting and planning of these settlements is clear enough: the inner enclosures, some of which were comparable in size to enclosures of Little Woodbury type though others were smaller, presumably formed the inhabited area where the owner and family lived while the outer enclosures were designed to protect the homestead pastures and their watering-places.

The most extensively examined example of a multiple-enclosure fort is the double-ditched enclosure at Killibury, Cornwall. Excavation within the inner enclosure has produced ample evidence of long-lived occupation in the form of a dense scatter of post-holes associated with a depth of stratified occupation levels. This contrasts markedly with the space between the two

Figure 13.6 The multiple-enclosure fort of Castle-an-Dinas, Cornwall (photo: Dr J.K.S. St Joseph. Crown Copyright reserved).

defensive enclosures where a single trial trench exposed only a series of shallow gullies showing that activity in the outer enclosure had been slight. Much the same picture is provided by Castle Dore, Cornwall. In a reassessment of the 1936–7 excavation, it has been argued (Quinnell and Harris 1985) that the densely occupied interior was in use from the fourth to first centuries BC during which time there were a series of circular timber buildings sited mainly against the rampart in the southern half of the enclosure. The outer enclosure was not extensively examined but in the late phase a single hut was identified close to the outer gate.

Apart from pottery, artefacts are not particularly prolific from the few multiple-ditched enclosures that have been excavated but signs of moderate wealth have come from Milber Down Camp, in the form of an iron dagger handle, and from Castle Dore where armlets of bronze, shale and glass have been found as well as glass beads (Fitzpatrick 1985b; Henderson 1985). Items of this kind, together with the effort required to construct the impressive earthworks of these sites, suggest that multiple-enclosure settlements were the homesteads of an elite. It is hardly surprising therefore that Castle Dore should have produced sherds of imported wine amphorae of first-century BC and first-century AD date.

The form of the enclosures and their general orientation towards rivers or streams has long suggested that the economy depended heavily on livestock. The nature of the husbandry is difficult to assess since animal bones seldom survive in the acid soils of the area. The consistent occurrence of spindle whorls does, however, point to the significance of sheep and one can hardly doubt that cattle too were important. Field systems were notably absent from the vicinity of the enclosures but that some cereal cultivation was carried out seems certain in the light of the evidence from Killibury where emmer wheat, spelt wheat and oats were identified. The relative balance between husbandry and cultivation necessarily remains unclear but the overall impression must be that the economic wealth of the elite was founded on their control of flocks and herds.

Rounds (Figure 13.7)

Another type of habitation site occurs widely in Cornwall and north-west Devon, usually in hilly country 60–120 m above sea-level. These settlements, called rounds in Cornwall, consist of a simple banked and ditched enclosure, seldom exceeding a hectare in extent and sited invariably on good arable land. Inside a few huts were usually built close against the bank. In size and form, however, rounds display a considerable variety (Johnson and Rose 1982). Several have been excavated: the round at Trevisker, Cornwall, produced evidence of two successive Iron Age phases, the later comprising a 1.2 ha enclosure. The settlement, which dated to the second or early first century BC, superseded an earlier unenclosed settlement dating back to the second millennium. At Castle Gotha, Cornwall, a 0.6 ha enclosure and its two huts, built late in the second century BC, continued in occupation for about 500 years.

Detailed fieldwork in Cornwall (A.C. Thomas 1966b; Johnson and Rose 1982) has shown that rounds were densely distributed, varying from one per 2.1 km^2 to one per 4.5 km^2, but since only a few have been excavated, it is impossible to say that all were in use at the same time; many of them may not have been built until the Roman period. Nevertheless, as a settlement type rounds were probably widespread before the first century BC. The nature of the economy is difficult to assess but rotary querns and a possible iron sickle from Trevisker indicate that cereal growing played a significant part.

Courtyard houses (Figures 13.8–13.10)

A different type of settlement, the so-called courtyard house, is found on the high ground in west Cornwall. This is essentially a central paved courtyard surrounded by rooms and byres, the whole complex being enclosed with a massive stone wall, usually with a single entrance leading into the yard. Houses of this kind are normally associated with adjacent fields or cultivation plots. When courtyard houses occur in clusters, as they do at Chysauster (Figures 13.8 and 13.9), the appearance is not at all unlike a deserted medieval village.

At Carn Euny, where excavation of a cluster of courtyard houses has been thorough, the complex growth of the settlement can be appreciated by observing the relationship of the various walls. Here the courtyard houses represented the last phase in a settlement which began probably as early as the sixth or fifth century with circular timber buildings. It was early in this sequence that a fogou (an underground chamber) was built.

Whether single or in groups, courtyard houses are usually unenclosed but several sites are known where houses are contained within a round (Figure 13.10). At Porthmeor at least three

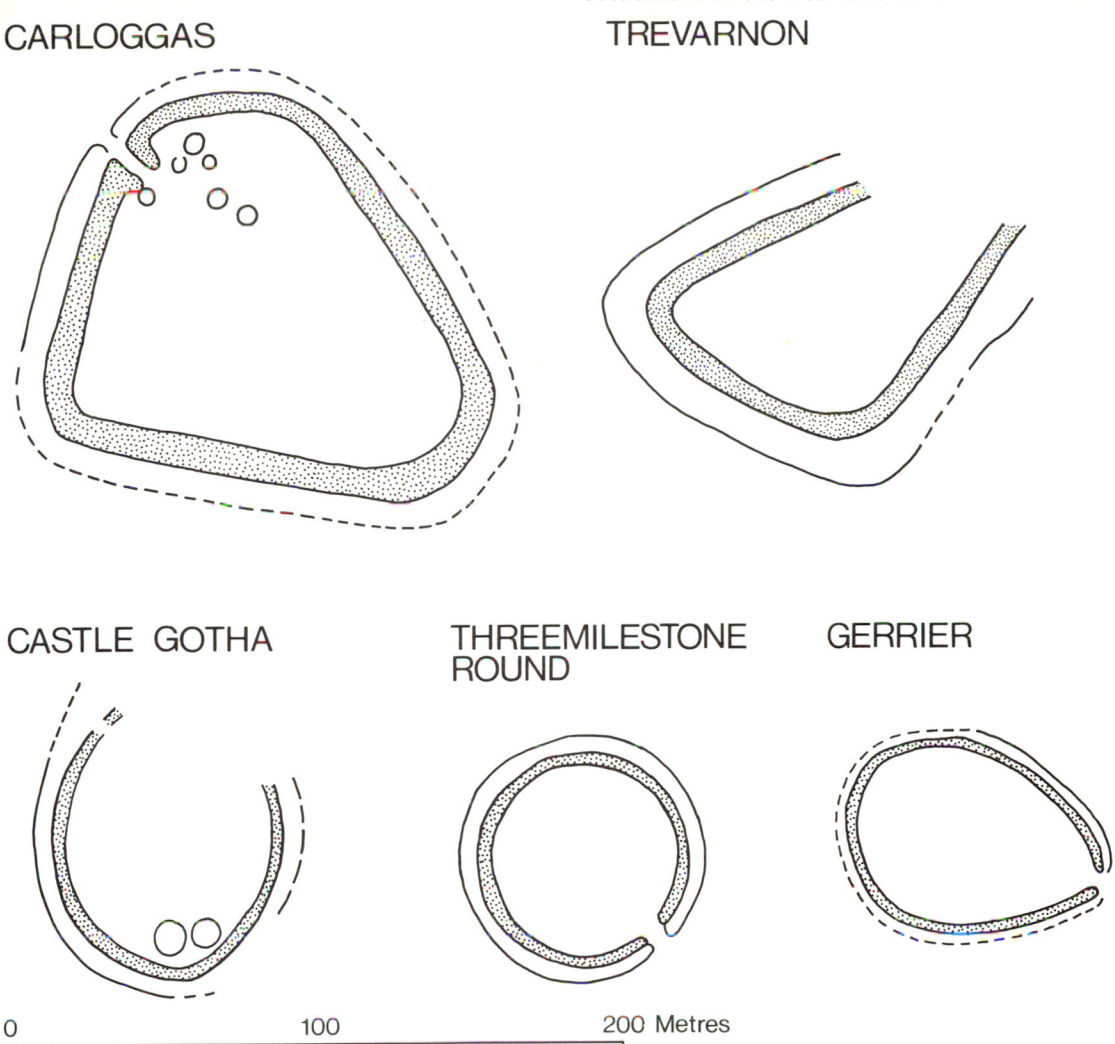

Figure 13.7   Plans of Cornish rounds (source: A.C. Thomas 1966b).

houses and their gardens were enclosed in this way at a date subsequent to their erection, while at Goldherring the round contained a single house with its cultivation plots outside. Where evidence of date is available, it is generally found that courtyard houses could not have begun before the first century BC and the majority of them continued in use throughout the Roman era. In a thorough review of the dating evidence Henrietta Quinnell has argued that courtyard houses are best regarded as a Roman phenomenon (1986, 120).

Cliff castles (Figure 13.11)

Cliff castles, situated as their popular name suggests, on rugged headlands jutting into the sea and protected from landward approach by complex lines of banks and ditches, feature

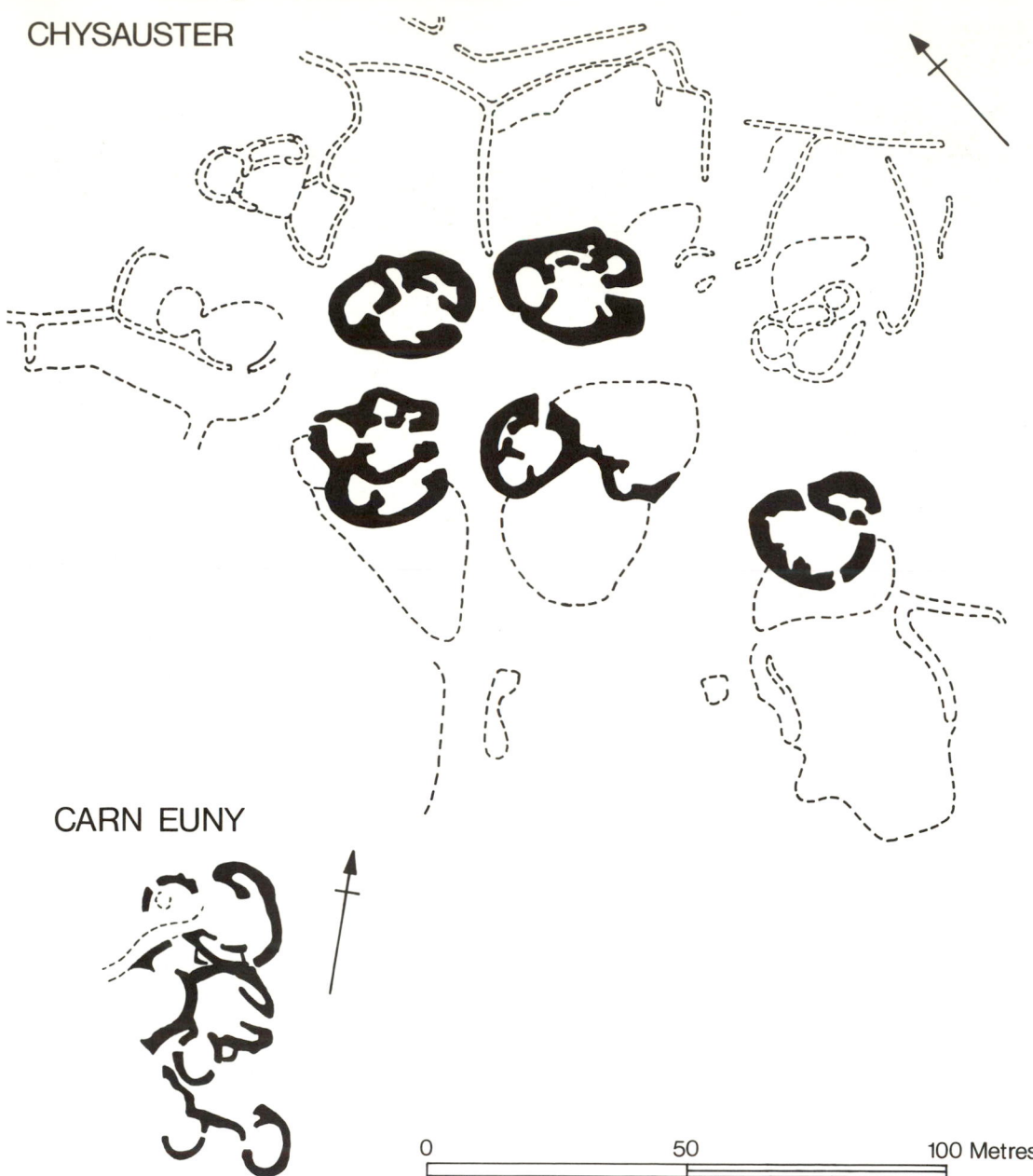

Figure 13.8 Courtyard houses at Chysauster and Carn Euny (sources: *Chysauster*, H.O'N. Hencken 1933; *Carn Euny*, Christie 1978).

prominently in the archaeological literature. Their similarity to comparable structures in Brittany has been used to argue for an immigration of Breton Veneti into the south-west in the first century BC. Such a view must now be discarded since several of the cliff castles have

Figure 13.9   Chysauster, Cornwall (photo: English Heritage).

produced pottery of considerably earlier date and it is simplest to see the Cornish and Breton
sites as the obvious response, of communities requiring defence, to closely similar landscape
potentials. This is not, however, to deny contact between the two peninsulas over many
centuries.

The choice of dramatic location and the investment of energy in creating massive defences was
meant to impress. But the purpose of these enclosures, whether for large communities or simply
the household of an aristocrat, is impossible to judge. It is tempting to see them as equivalent, in
social terms, to the multiple-enclosure forts – the homes of the elite – but deriving their power
from a different resource base. Until at least one has been adequately excavated and published
the matter will remain obscure.

Summary (Figure 13.12)

The landscape and settlement pattern of the south-west peninsula is diverse but the majority of
the settlements can be divided into two broad categories: minor enclosures, i.e. the rounds; and
major enclosures, the multiple-enclosure forts and the cliff castles. In addition there is a scatter of
unenclosed farmsteads about which very little is known. What is noticeably absent are the large
hillforts of Wessex type which, we suggest, represent the power centres of large territorial
groupings. In other words this level of social organization, so evident in the centre south, is not

CORNWALL

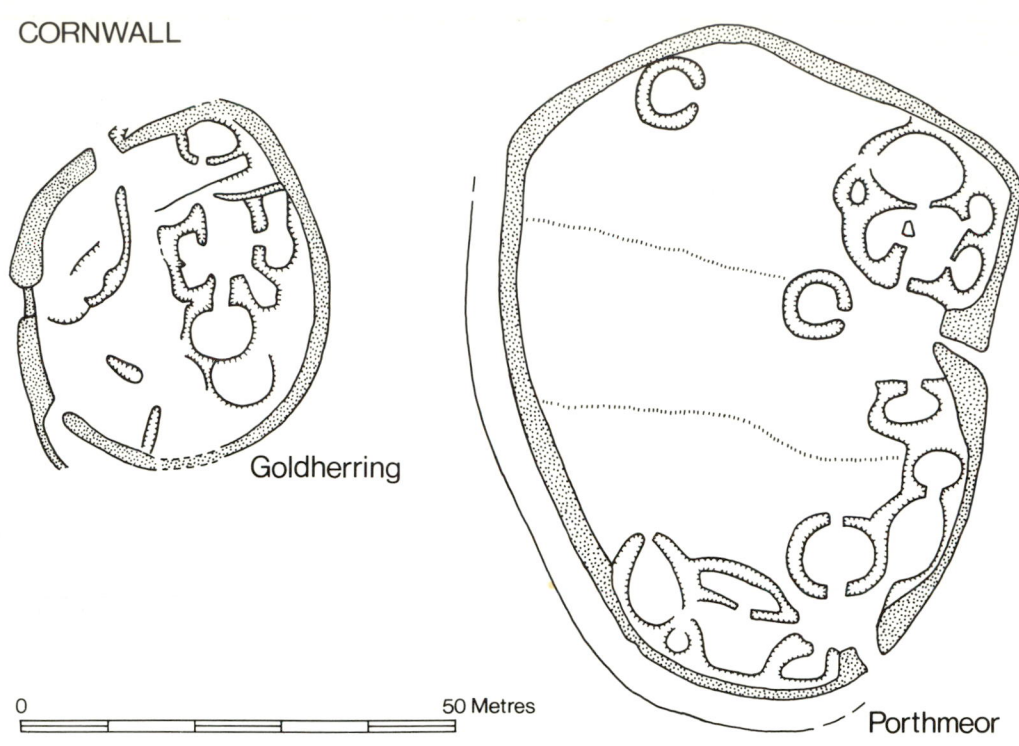

Goldherring

0   50 Metres

Porthmeor

Figure 13.10 Courtyard houses built into rounds (sources: *Goldherring*, Guthrie 1969; *Porthmeor*, Hirst 1936).

present in the south-west. Instead the most appropriate model would seem to be a simple three-tier structure with the major enclosures representing the residences of the elite while the minor enclosures were the homesteads of their vassals. Below these would have come the unfree living in the unenclosed settlements. In such a system one might expect the elite to be more concerned with wealth in the form of livestock leaving the vassals to till the land and to provide them with grain on a tithe basis in return for protection and patronage. The archaeological evidence would not contradict such a model but is hardly yet sufficient to support or modify it.

The large hillforts of Wessex type are rare west of the Exe. The south-east of Britain is a hillfort-dominated landscape, each fort being surrounded by farms relying heavily on arable production, while in the south-west isolated settlements of pastoral type (the multiple-enclosure forts) and mixed farming types (the rounds) replace open settlements and villages which show the same range of specialization. Clearly the social structure and political organization of the two areas must have been different, a difference further emphasized later by the total absence of coinage in the south-west. It is tempting to suggest that the pastoral-dominated economy of the south-west prevented the growth of political centralization to the extent to which it developed in the south-east. Instead, there arose a society composed of individual lordships of approximately equivalent status, covering much of the area. In the extreme west, however, where arable farming was practised to a greater extent, individual farmsteads were as closely spaced as in the south-east. Here the larger cliff castles possibly served as the centres upon which the farming community were in some way dependent.

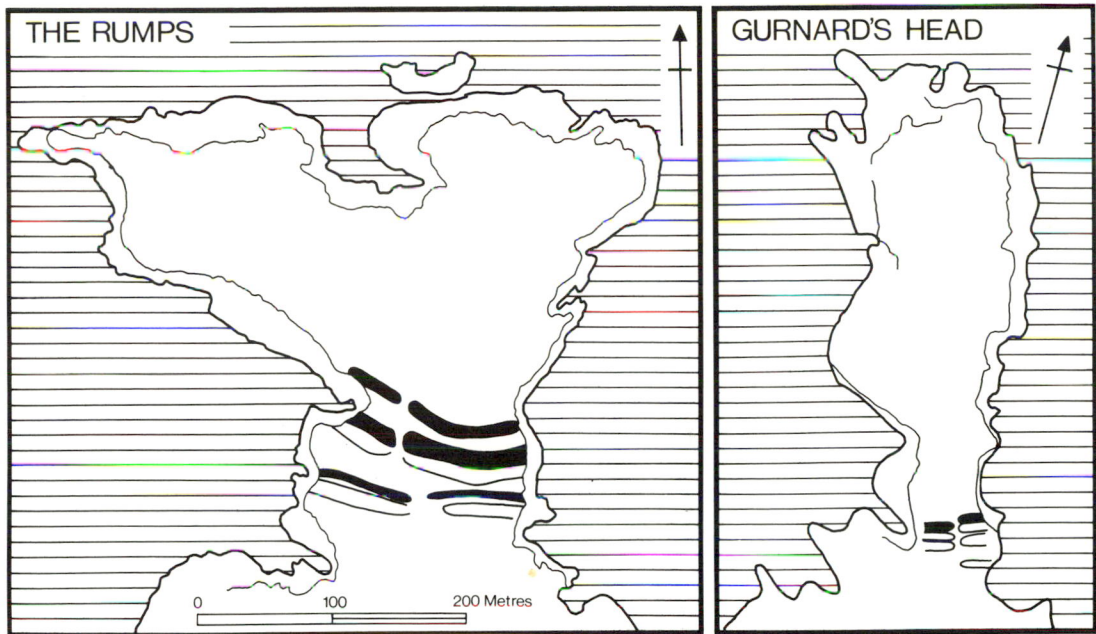

THE RUMPS

GURNARD'S HEAD

0   100   200 Metres

Figure 13.11   Cornish cliff castles (sources: *The Rumps*, Brooks 1964; *Gurnard's Head*, A.S.R. Gordon 1941).

South and west Wales

The southern coastal area of Wales stretching from the Usk valley to Pembrokeshire was in many ways similar in its settlement pattern to the south-west peninsula of England, a similarity which can be explained, in part at least, by the geomorphological likeness of the two areas. The Carboniferous and Triassic rocks of Glamorganshire and Monmouthshire and the Ordovician rocks of the western counties give rise to soils comparable to those of Devon and eastern Cornwall, while the craggy coastline west of Swansea Bay could easily be mistaken for Cornwall. Similarly, the predominantly north–south flowing rivers tend to cut the territory, lying between the mountains and the sea, into strips and blocks, making communication by land difficult.

Two very useful surveys of settlement in the region have been published in recent years: the Royal Commission has surveyed all the Iron Age settlements in Glamorganshire (RCHM(W) Glamorganshire 1, 1976) while the settlements of Carmarthenshire have been considered in an environmental and historical framework by G. Williams (1978, 1979, 1988).

Unenclosed hut groups, generally undated, occur in Carmarthenshire and Pembrokeshire but they are ill-known compared with the Dartmoor sites. One group, partly excavated in 1899, lay on the top of Moel Trigarn in the Prescelly Mountains. Aerial photography has shown that some of the huts pre-date the multiple walls of the later hillfort and must therefore belong to an open settlement of some size.

Multiple-enclosure settlements of the types defined in the south-west occur in some number in all four of the south Welsh counties. Site location again indicates a preference for valley-sides dominating springs or streams, suggesting that here, as in the south-west, the enclosures were

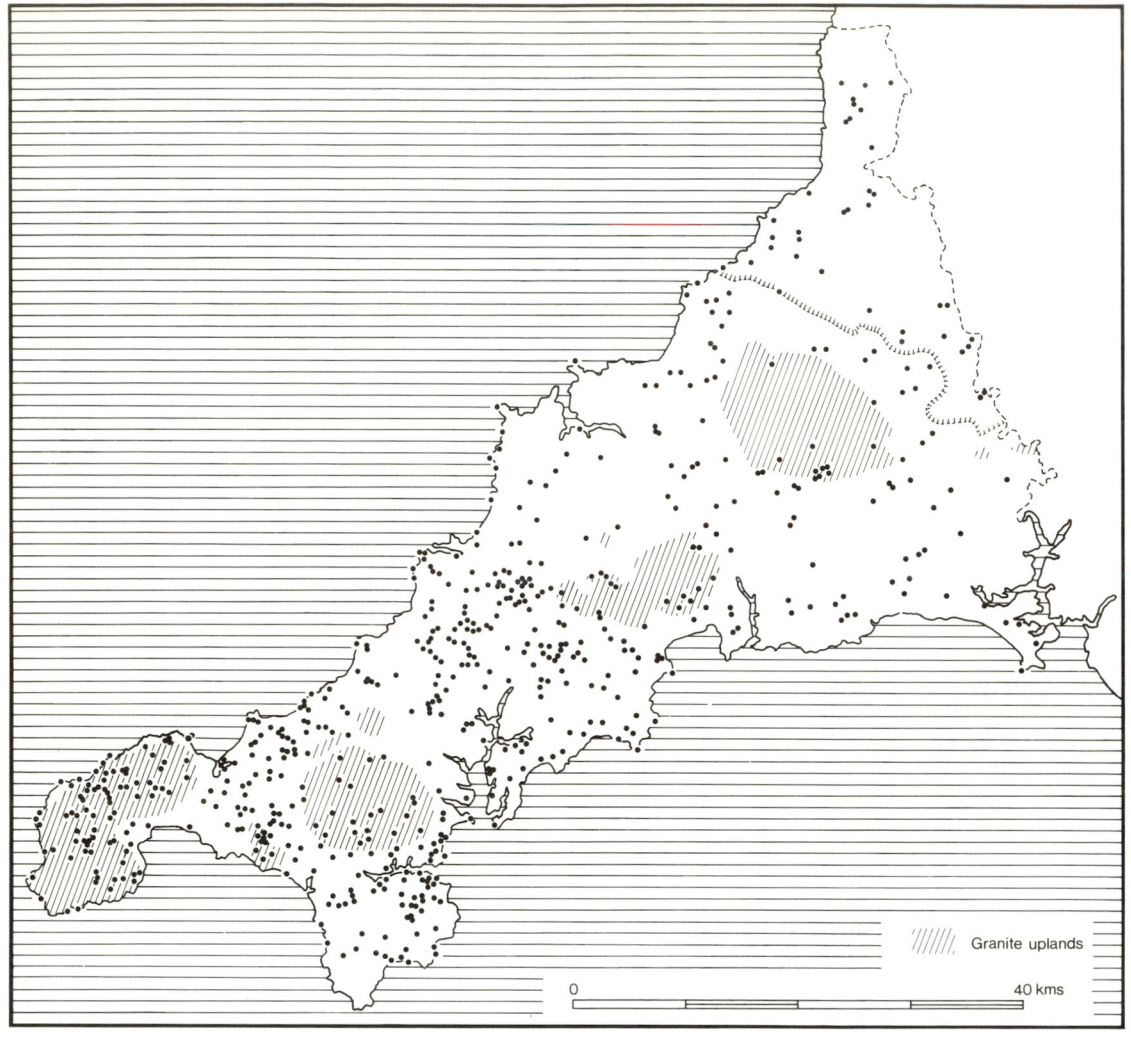

Figure 13.12   Distribution of enclosed settlements, including rounds and cliff castles, in Cornwall (source: Johnson and Rose 1982).

constructed by predominantly pastoral communities more concerned with watering their flocks and herds than with purely military considerations.

The West Country round also has its counterparts in the raths of south-west Wales. It is estimated that of the 580 hillforts in Wales about 230 enclose less than 0.4 ha, and of these three-quarters lie in the south-west. While it is true that many were occupied in the Roman period, and some may even have been constructed then, a high percentage probably dates back to the Iron Age. Total excavation of Walesland Rath near Haverfordwest, Pembs., provides a rare insight into the structure and development of this type of establishment (Figure 13.13). Here an oval-shaped area, 64 by 49 m internally, was enclosed by a bank and ditch pierced by two entrances. The south-west gate was massively constructed with three pairs of timbers which must

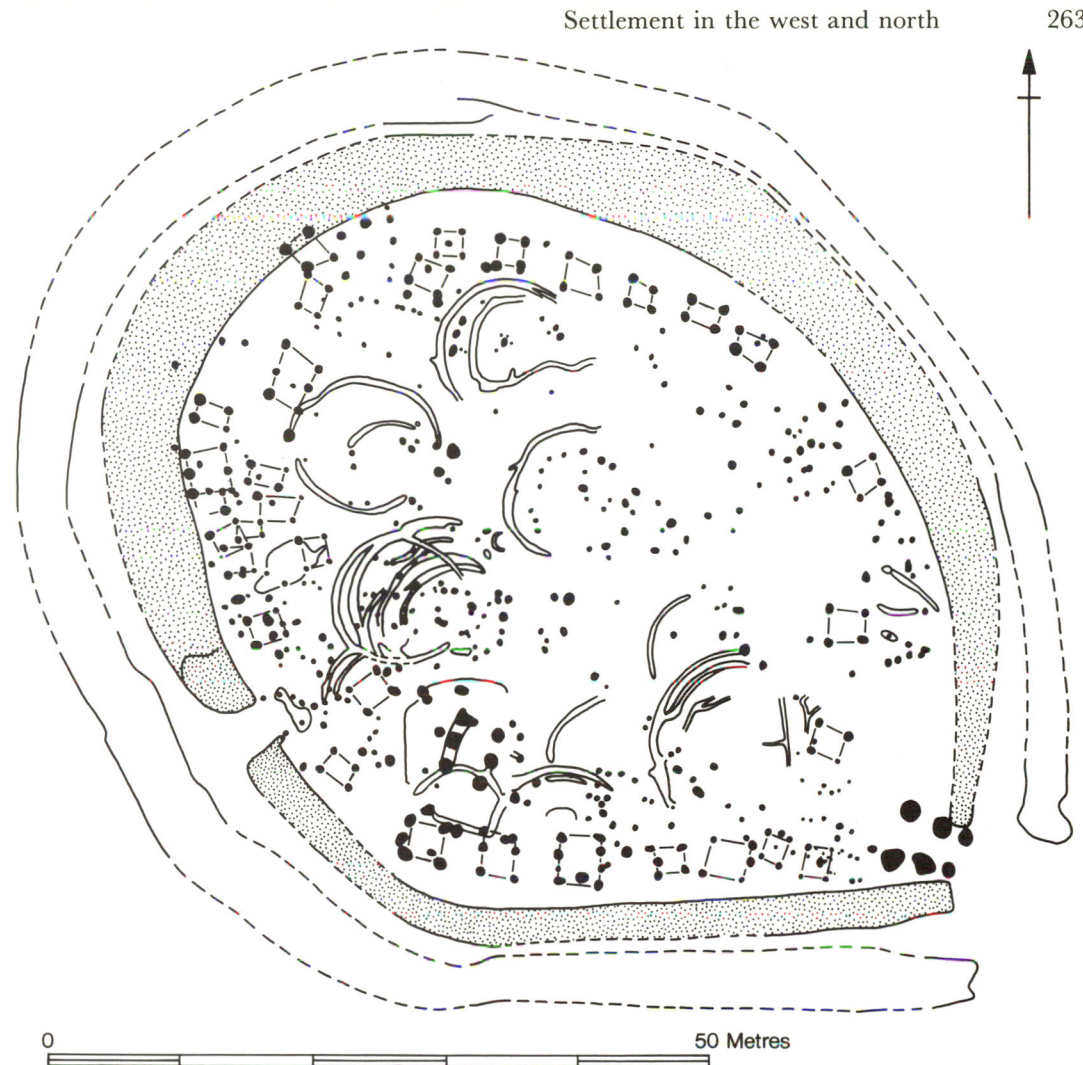

0   50 Metres

Figure 13.13   Walesland Rath, Dyfed (sources: Wainwright 1971a, G. Williams 1988).

have once supported a tower, while the western entrance was flanked by dry-stone walling, with its gate set back within the line of the ramparts. Internally the enclosure was packed with timber structures, including at least six circular timber huts, several of which show signs of rebuilding on a number of occasions. A more unusual type of building was constructed from three pairs of large timbers; this resembles the structures found in the Wessex and Welsh borderland hillforts. The provision of an eaves-drip trench around it shows that it was roofed and may possibly have been a house but does not necessarily preclude the possibility of its serving as a granary in this context. A maze of post-holes arranged in alignments around the periphery of the enclosure close to the rampart are best interpreted as a zone of four- and six-post storage buildings, reconstructed on numerous occasions. Dating evidence at Walesland Rath was sparse but radiocarbon determinations allow the first phase to be assigned to the third century BC or a little earlier, while the second phase, defined by the rebuilding of the rampart on a more massive scale and the blocking of the west gate, began in the early part of the first century BC. Occupation continued into the third century AD.

A second excavated site in the same category is Coygan Camp, sited on a promontory of Carboniferous limestone overlooking Carmarthen Bay. An initial occupation, tentatively assigned to the eighth to second century, was followed by the construction of the enclosure bank and ditch. Two entrances were provided: a north-west gate, the approach to which was further protected by a length of additional rampart built across the neck of the promontory, and a south-west entrance leading down to the marshy pasture at the base of the hill. Contemporary internal structures were not found, nor was the material culture particularly rich, apart from producing a pair of bronze early La Tène bracelets, but a large quantity of animal bones was well preserved in the alkaline soil. The collection from the enclosure phase shows that numerically cattle predominated, amounting to 64 per cent of the total, with sheep/goats a mere 16 per cent, closely followed by pigs at 15 per cent. Allowing for the fact that a single cow produced about seven times the meat yield of a sheep, it will be evident that the basic diet was beef, the intake of mutton and pork being negligible by comparison. The relative importance of meat to grain cannot be assessed, but quernstones were very rare and storage facilities unrecorded. In all probability, the inhabitants were pastoralists, using the fertile pastures of the neighbouring Devonian soils and the marshland fringes at the foot of the hill for rearing and maintaining herds of cattle. The proximity of the sea provided an additional food source: fish bones were not preserved but shellfish were collected in quantity from the estuary of the Taf and from the rocky pools at the base of the Pendine Cliffs. Like Walesland Rath, Coygan Camp continued to be occupied well into the Roman period. The neighbouring sites of Trelissey and Cwmbrwyn, both earthwork enclosures, also contained substantial Roman-style masonry buildings. It is not unreasonable to suggest that here too we are dealing with Iron Age settlements which remained in use for some centuries after the Roman Conquest.

Several other settlements which could be classed either as raths or as multiple enclosures have recently been examined. At Parc Cynnog not far from Coygan Camp in Carmarthenshire, the earthworks of a partially multivallate enclosure, about 0.4 ha in area, were sectioned, but little evidence of internal occupation was discovered. However, the excavation of Castell Coyan, Carm., produced clear indications of circular buildings of timber within a small enclosure, but dating evidence was lacking. At Pen y Coed, Llangynog, Carm., the almost total excavation of a small embanked and ditched enclosure yielded a complete plan of an Iron Age farmstead (Figure 13.15) with one large round house, a yard divided by fences and a four-post granary set against the bank. The entrance to the enclosure was approached by a road flanked by ditches similar to the banjo enclosures of Wessex. A similar arrangement is evident at Woodside Camp, one of a pair of presumably contemporary enclosures barely 50 m apart (Figure 13.14). The enclosure at Castell Henllys, Pembs., contained a similar range of structures. Excavations at Woodbarn Rath, Caer Cadwgan and Pembry Mountain, though on a less extensive scale, have all shown occupation to have been quite intensive, the last two yielding significant samples of cereals (see below p. 394).

Few of the rath-like enclosures in Glamorganshire or Monmouthshire have been adequately excavated, with the notable exception of Mynydd Bychan, Glam., overlooking the Ewenny valley, where a small enclosure was found to contain a group of timber-framed circular huts, probably dating to the first century BC. Rebuilding in stone took place in the middle of the first century AD (Figure 13.15). At Whitton, South Glam., a roughly rectangular ditched enclosure

WOODSIDE

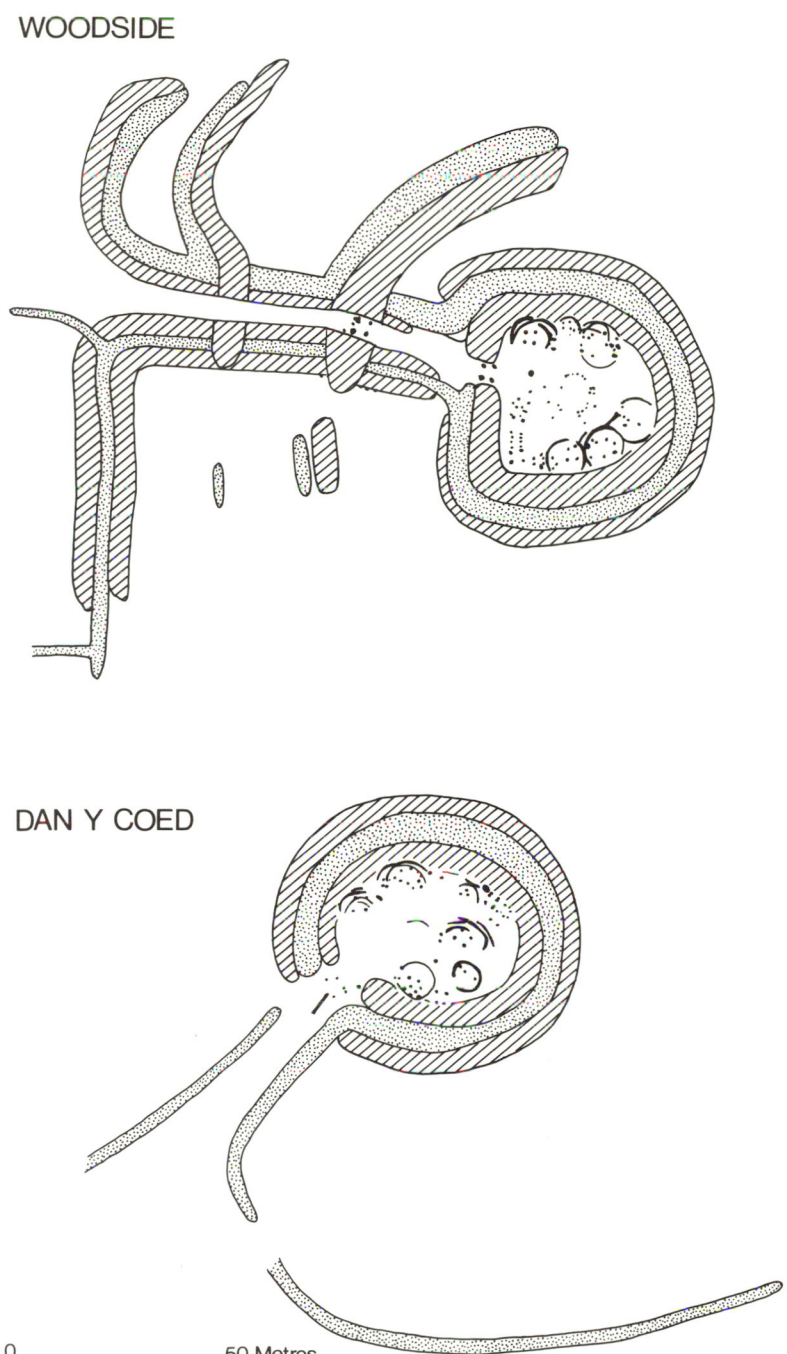

DAN Y COED

0   50 Metres

Figure 13.14   Woodside Camp and Dan y Coed enclosure, Dyfed (source: G. Williams 1988).

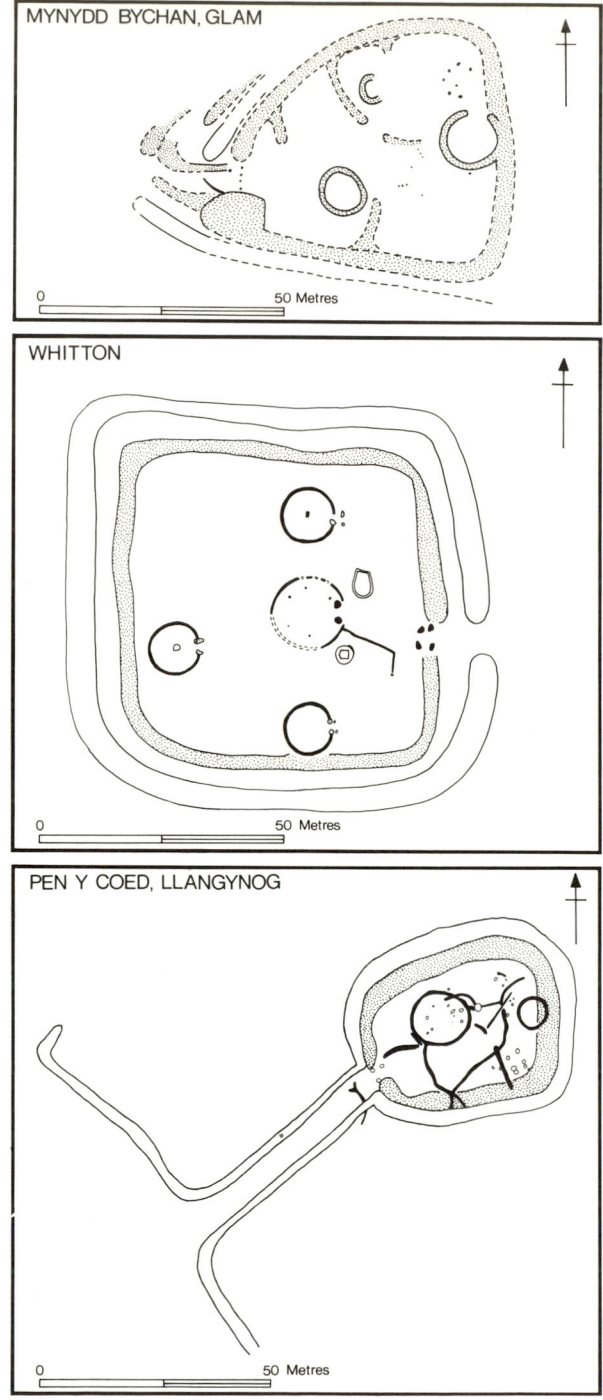

Figure 13.15 Welsh settlements (sources: *Mynydd Bychan*, Savory 1954, 1956; *Whitton*, Jarrett and Wrathmell 1981; *Pen y Coed*, Murphy 1985).

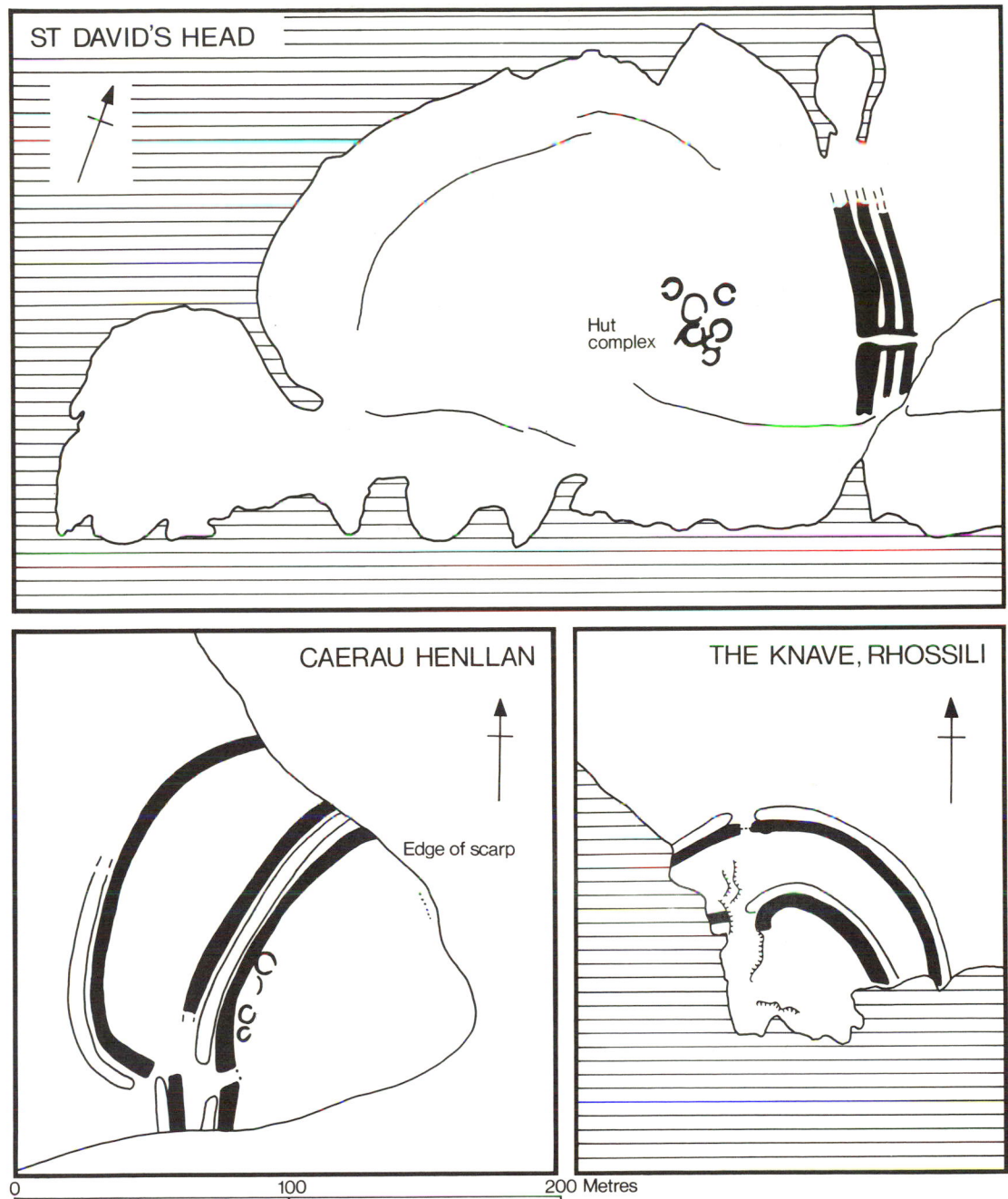

Figure 13.16 Welsh promontory forts (sources: *St David's Head*, Baring-Gould, Burnard and Enys 1899; *Caerau Henllan*, Ordnance Survey; *The Knave*, A. Williams 1939b).

established in the early decades of the first century AD was provided with seven timber roundhouses of different dates. Romanization, in the form of rectangular timber buildings, becomes apparent at the end of the first century AD (Figure 13.15). Both sites are best regarded as single family farmsteads.

Many of the promontories of south-west Wales were defended by banks and ditches, turning them into the equivalent of the Cornish cliff castles (Figure 13.16). Several have been partially examined by excavation. On St David's Head, Pembs., a complex rampart protected a small group of six conjoined stone-walled huts 4.5–6.0 m in diameter, excavated in 1900. The material culture was sparse but whetstones, spindle whorls, hammer stones and fragments of iron were found together with a few glass beads and decorated shale pendants. No precise evidence of the date range of the settlement has come to light. An excavation on a closely similar promontory fort at Tower Point, St Brides, Pembs., has demonstrated a two-phase construction for the inner stone-faced rampart and has shown that here, too, huts were built within the protection of the rampart, but little cultural material was found and there was no direct evidence of date. Limited work at Llanstephan Castle, Carm., an inland promontory enclosure beneath the later medieval castle, has however produced a group of radiocarbon assessments indicating a date in the sixth century BC for an early phase in the occupation sequence.

Further east several enclosed sites have now been partially examined by excavation. At The Knave, a promontory fort near Rhossili in Glamorganshire, two widely spread ramparts protected a cliff-top, the inner area of which was barely 46 m across. Pottery akin to South-Western Decorated Wares suggests a date in the second or first century BC but occupation could well have begun much earlier. The 0.1 ha promontory fort at Bishopston valley, Glam., produced pottery of similar date together with samian ware, showing that occupation continued into the Roman period, and at High Penard, Glam., a 0.8 ha promontory fort with widely spaced ramparts was examined, but yielded only Roman objects. Limited excavation at the Bulwarks, Porthkerry, Glam., a major promontory fort of some 4.1 ha, showed that here too occupation which began in the Iron Age continued into the Roman period.

Of the inland multiple-enclosure forts, Harding's Down West Fort on the Gower peninsula, Glam., is the most extensively excavated. The main enclosure was small, only 0.6 ha, and strongly defended, but the outer compound, presumably for stock, more than doubled the size of the protected area. The approach to the main enclosure was made along a trackway which flanked the side of the annexe earthworks. The gate itself consisted of two pairs of posts 1.4 m apart which gave direct access to the enclosure, in which three house terraces could be recognized. Excavation of two of these has shown them to have been occupied by substantial timber-built houses. Artefacts were few, but pottery of Late Iron Age burnished type was found, together with an iron bloom. The evidence is therefore sufficient to suggest that the enclosure was probably occupied by a single family unit during the latter part of the Iron Age.

Finally, the excavation at Castle Ditches, Llancarfan, a small univallate hillfort, 5 km inland from the coast of the Vale of Glamorgan, revealed a complex structural history beginning with a small stone-walled enclosure which was later extended with an earth rampart and ditch to enclose about 2 ha. Internal occupation, when sampled against the rampart, was intensive and produced a few sherds of South-Western Decorated Wares. Evidence of iron-working was apparent throughout the sequence.

From the above descriptions it is clear that the distinction between raths, promontory forts, univallate forts and multiple enclosures is blurred. The small promontory forts like The Knave and High Penard could strictly be classed as multiple-enclosure settlements modified to suit a promontory position, while the areas enclosed by many of them correspond to the areas of raths on inland sites. It is doubtful, therefore, whether the promontory forts should be regarded as economically or socially distinct from the other types of enclosure. It is simpler to suppose that most of them were merely variants of the multiple-enclosure and rath types.

In summary, it may be said that the settlement pattern and economy of south and west Wales had much in common with Devon and Cornwall, the reason being chiefly that the climate and geomorphology of both areas encouraged the development of basically pastoral economies, which in turn directly influenced the nature of the social structure. The emphasis appears to have been on individually defended homesteads, sometimes large enough to house not only the owner and family but also a considerable entourage. The absence of large hillforts strongly suggests a lack of centralized government. Cattle-rearing played an important part in the economy, the animals no doubt serving as a manifestation of wealth which could be treated as currency. In the more mountainous regions sheep may have been more significant but positive evidence is at present lacking. The relative importance of cereal-growing is uncertain: querns are not uncommon but no extensive traces of Celtic field patterns have been recognized in the area although cereal grains have been recovered from Caer Cadwgan and Pembry Mountain. At present, all that can be said is that limited corn-growing was practised but in many areas may have been subservient to animal husbandry.

North Wales

The study of the settlement pattern of north Wales is made difficult by the almost total absence of dating evidence from the many excavated sites, but the high quality of the field-work carried out, particularly in Caernarvonshire, makes it possible to describe in some detail the basic settlement forms belonging to the pre-Roman Iron Age.

Discussion must begin with the small multivallate enclosure of Castell Odo near Aberdaron, Caerns. (Figure 13.17), where as a result of extensive excavation a development sequence can be recognized, beginning with an open settlement composed of several circular timber houses associated with a small quantity of pottery similar in some forms to southern British assemblages dating to the fifth or fourth century. At some stage, while the huts were in use, work began on the construction of a timber palisade, but it appears never to have been completed – a fact which might be linked to the destruction of one of the houses by fire. In the third phase the settlement was enclosed by a bank of earth surrounding an area approximately 76 m across, in which were built several circular huts of stone. Later still the bank was revetted back and front with dry-stone walling and a new, similarly constructed bank was erected inside it, leaving a space of about 12 m between the two. Finally, possibly as the result of the Roman invasion, the defences were slighted and circular stone houses were built over them.

In terms of size and social structure, Castell Odo compares closely with the raths of south-west Wales. In all probability, it developed as the homestead of the local chieftain's family, providing perhaps some protected accommodation for dependants within the enclosure. The intervallum space created later could well have served as a safe corral for stock, functioning in much the same way as the multiple-enclosure forts of the south-west. Elsewhere in north Wales this type of small defended settlement is by no means uncommon; several are found in the Aberdaron peninsula and along the coastal strip. Further inland at Dinas Emrys, Caerns., traces of a fenced

CASTELL ODO, CAERNS

LLWYN DU BACH, CAERNS

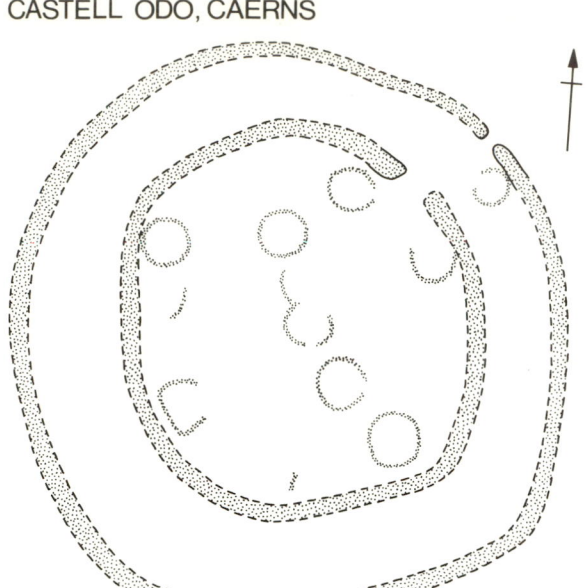

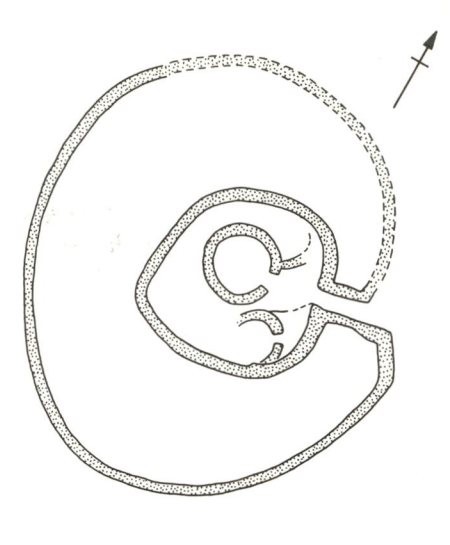

BRYN Y CASTELL

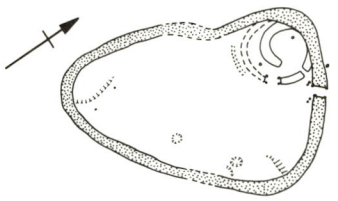

0   50 Metres

Figure 13.17   Settlements from north Wales (sources: *Castell Odo*, Alcock 1961; *Llwyn du Bach*, Bersu and Griffith 1949; *Bryn y Castell*, Crew 1985).

settlement, possibly of similar type, have been recognized. It has been suggested that the palisade idea and the use of timber were alien traditions introduced by Hallstatt warriors. Admittedly timber-work of this kind is not known in earlier contexts in the region, but this may be due more to absence of evidence than evidence of absence. The palisade tradition could equally well have developed in Britain; it is not necessary to invoke Hallstatt invaders to explain it.

A second class of enclosed homesteads, generally known as concentric circle sites, has been recognized in Caernarvonshire. A typical example, Llwyn du Bach, consists of a circular stone-built hut 9 m across, with two concentric enclosing walls 26 and 60 m in diameter (Figure 13.17). Suitable corral space was provided between the outer and inner walls while the inner enclosure contained the domestic features. No indication of dating was found but it has been suggested (Hogg 1966) that concentric circle sites belong to the pre-Roman Iron Age and may have formed the prototype from which some at least of the native Roman Iron Age enclosures developed.

A third type of settlement are simple stone-walled enclosures of varying forms, well typified by the large-scale excavation of Bryn y Castell in Snowdonia (Figure 13.17). Here the roughly pear-shaped enclosed area measured only 40 by 25 m and consisted of a cobbled yard with a single circular house in one corner. The economic basis of the community who used this exposed site is unclear but it is evident from a considerable mass of debris and several structures that the smelting and forging of iron was an important activity. Dating evidence would suggest occupation beginning in the first century BC and continuing to the first century AD.

A fourth type of settlement has been called the *enclosed group* (Gresham 1973). These can be defined as consisting of two or more separate huts situated close enough to each other to be considered as part of the same social unit. The individual huts are often linked by walls and are usually associated with a small field system composed of separate cultivation plots edged with boulders cleared from their surfaces. In general appearance they closely resemble the Dartmoor settlements described above (p. 248). A detailed field survey in the Cwm Ystradllyn district of southern Caernarvonshire has brought to light a large number of such settlements which tend to cluster on the gentle mountain slopes around the 300 m contour. The one excavated site, Braich y Cornel, has produced no dating evidence, but it may well pre-date the Roman occupation.

Many other types of enclosed settlement are known in north Wales and have been discussed from time to time (Gresham 1973; Hogg 1966; C.A. Smith 1974, 1978b), but many if not most of these are likely to be of Roman date, at least in their final form.

One of the most dramatic aspects of the north Welsh settlement pattern is the development of large hill-top settlements defended by stone walls. The evidence from the Caernarvonshire forts of Garn Boduan, Tre'r Ceiri and Conway Mountain (Figures 13.18 and 13.19) shows that many of them were occupied by sizeable communities of between 100 and 400 people living in circular, but largely undated, stone-walled huts, there being some twenty to eighty huts in each settlement. Normally the huts were totally enclosed by dry-stone ramparts, but occasionally, as at Garn Fadrun, Caerns., a considerable part of the settlement lay on the surrounding slopes. Further east at Dinorben, Denbigh., a settlement of comparable size was recognized, but in this case the huts were of timber and some at least pre-dated the construction of the hillfort.

The Welsh borderland

The wide strip of countryside west of the Dee–Severn axis, extending into the foothills of the Welsh mountains, has produced abundant evidence of pre-Roman Iron Age occupation, but mostly from the excavation of large hillforts which have tended to attract the attention of archaeologists at the expense of smaller settlements. Settlements are, however, becoming increasingly well known particularly in the upper reaches of the Severn and the foothills of the Berwyn Mountains where enclosures of less than 1.2 ha abound as they do between the Wye and Usk in the south (Spurgeon 1972).

In the Upper Severn valley between Montgomery and Oswestry many settlements have been discovered almost entirely as the result of systematic aerial survey. That the great majority of them have been ploughed out reflects their siting on good agricultural land. One of these sites at Collfryn, 10 km north of Welshpool, has been totally excavated (Figure 13.20). The settlement

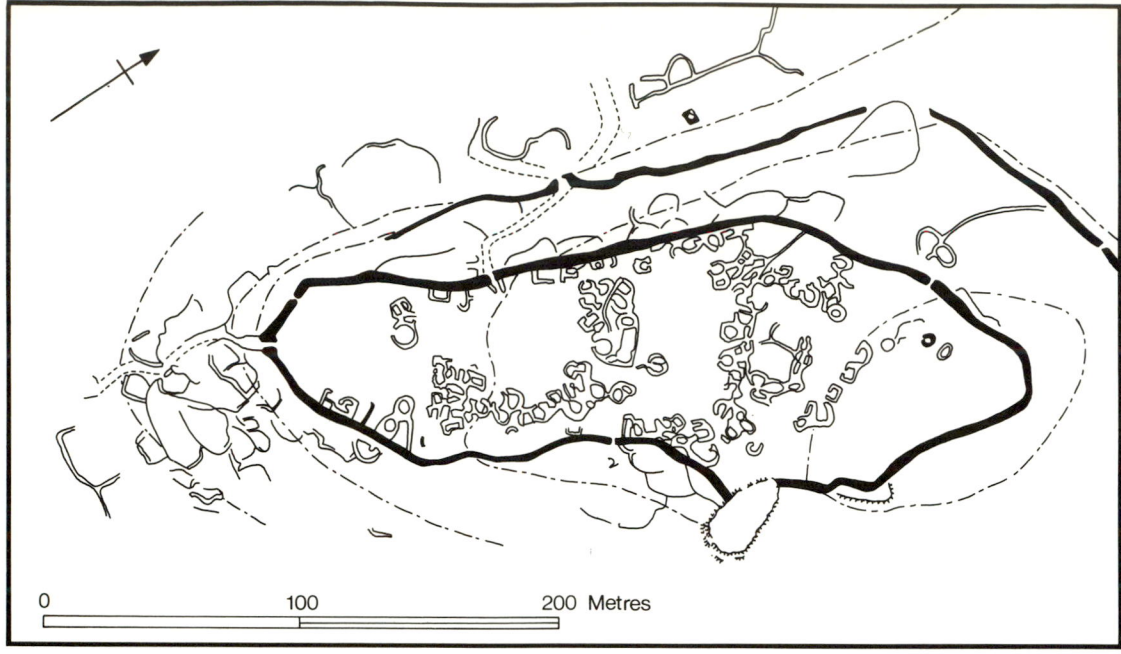

Figure 13.18   Plan of Tre'r Ceiri, Gwynedd (source: Hogg 1962).

began life as an unenclosed settlement but some time around 300 BC a triple-ditched enclosure was created with widely spaced ditches. The innermost ditch enclosed a roughly square area about 80 m across and it was here that the settlement concentrated. In the western part of the enclosure evidence of a series of superimposed roundhouses was discovered, while around the fringes of the eastern part, on either side of the entrance, four-post granaries were situated. The numerous rebuildings of both houses and granaries suggest a long-lived occupation: the enclosure continued in use into the Roman period. Until the site is published in full there is little to be said of its economy, but the widely spaced ditches are suggestive of cattle corrals while the granaries imply the storage of cereal. Indeed the rich and varied soils of the Severn valley would be ideal for mixed farming regimes.

Of the excavated hillforts, several show signs of rebuilding and extensive occupation over a considerable period of time, and in the southern part of the area at least, many of the basic elements of the south-eastern economy are found.

The west Midlands

The triangle of country west of the Avon–Soar–Trent, east of the Severn–Dee and south of the Pennines is composed of vast tracts of Keuper marl, Triassic sandstones and coal-measure shales, highly unconducive to pre-Roman Iron Age settlement. Apart from the river gravels and the more fertile sandstone and limestone hills, much of the area appears, on present evidence, to have been largely unsettled.

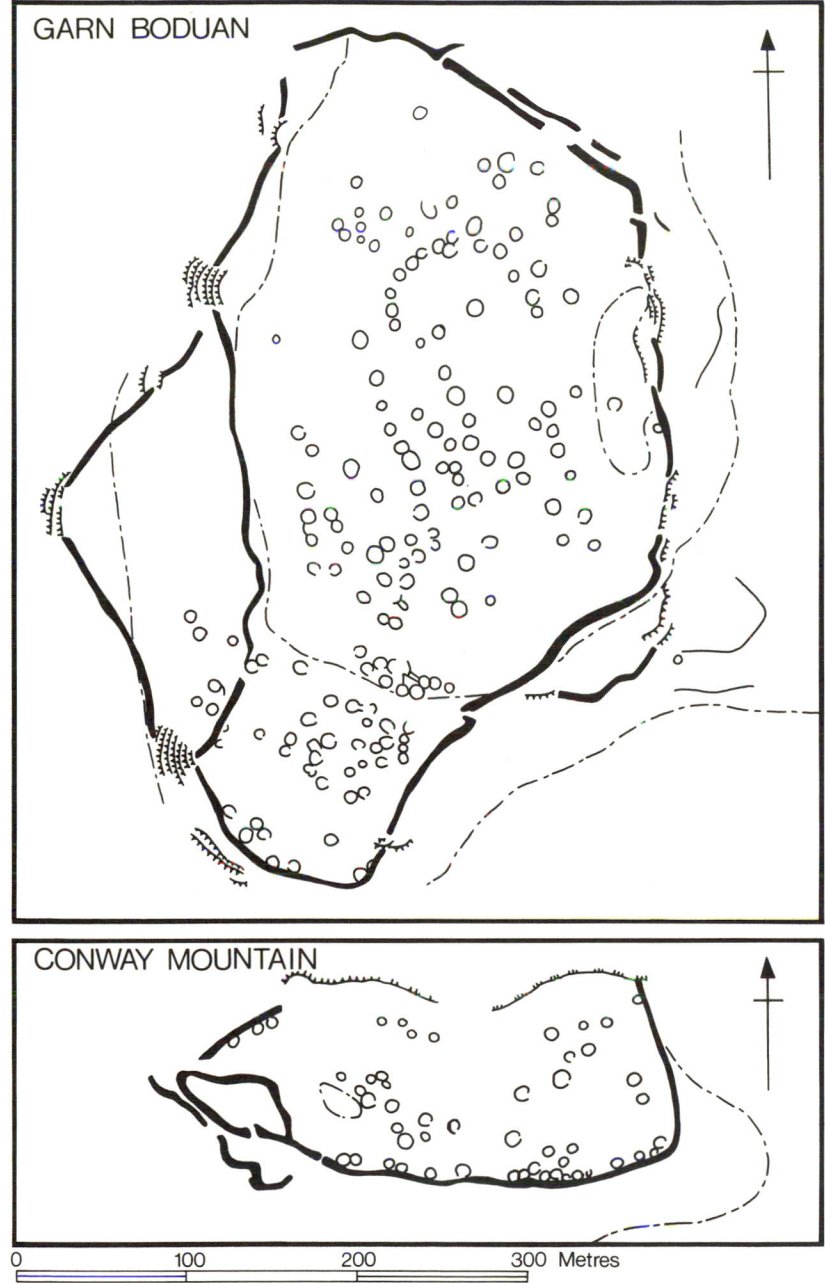

Figure 13.19 Plans of two north Welsh hillforts (sources: *Garn Boduan*, Hogg 1962; *Conway Mountain*, Griffiths and Hogg 1957).

Of the few hillforts known in the area the only site to have been excavated in any detail is Breedon-on-the-Hill, Leics., sited on a hill of Magnesian limestone overlooking the valleys of the Soar and Trent. No internal buildings were recognized, but occupation appears to have been

COLLFRYN, POWYS

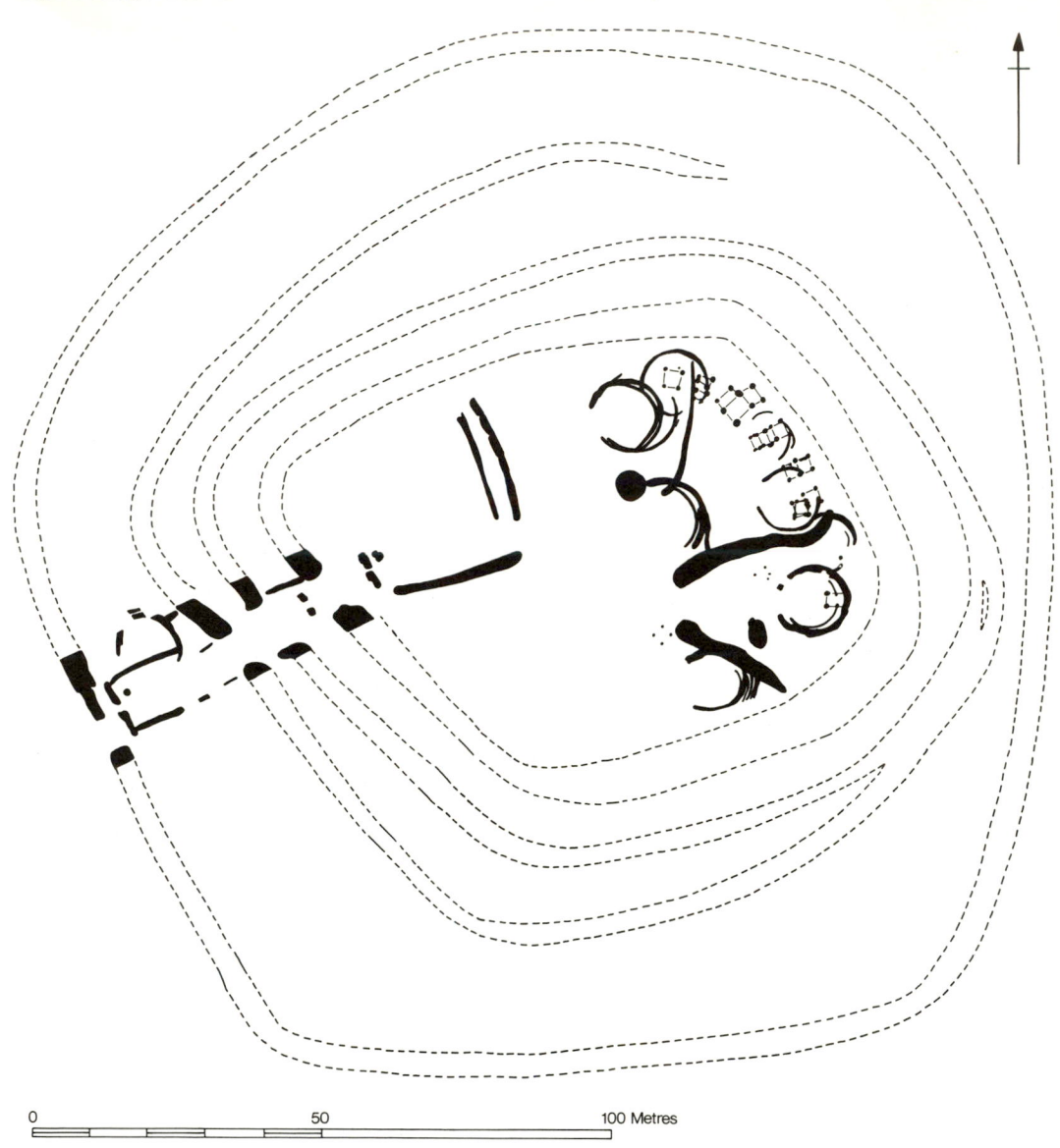

Figure 13.20   Collfryn, Powys (source: Britnell forthcoming).

extensive. Pits, possibly for storage, and a number of quernstones suggest that grain production was widely practised. The quantity of animal bones recovered was not large but cattle were numerically more common than sheep (50 per cent compared with 36 per cent), underlining the importance of the pastures along the Soar valley. The use of sheep as wool producers is, however, reflected in the discovery of a weaving comb.

Largely as the result of extensive programmes of aerial photography it is now known that the river gravels of the west Midlands were as densely occupied as those of the south and east Midlands. One of the most comprehensively studied regions is the valley of the Tame (C. Smith 1977, 1978a) but only at Fisherwick has a detailed excavation been carried out and published. Here a Middle Iron Age enclosure of some 0.25 ha, containing evidence of at least two circular houses was partially examined. The enclosure was part of an organized landscape, divided by drainage ditches, which included several other enclosures. Environmental evidence suggests that the fields in the immediate neighbourhood may have served largely for stock-rearing but there is ample evidence of cereal production from occupation levels associated with the settlement.

The Pennines and the north of England

The north of England is geomorphologically varied and is best considered as a number of distinct sub-regions. Through the centre runs the backbone of the Pennines, composed largely of Carboniferous limestone capped with large tracts of moorland, even today creating a real barrier between the two faces of northern England. East of the divide the landscape divides naturally into three sub-zones. To the south are the chalk Wolds and the limestone Moors divided from each other by the Vale of Pickering which is itself part of an extensive tract of lowlands drained by the river system of the Ouse and Swale serving to separate the calcareous massifs of the east from the Pennine ridge. West of the Pennines the Lake District massif forms a major barrier between the coastal plain of Cheshire and Lancashire and the lowlands drained by the rivers flowing to the Solway Firth. Variation in climate, geology and altitude serve to create a palimpsest of micro-environments while mountain ridges and wide river flood plains present barriers to easy communication. It is hardly surprising therefore that the settlement potential of each region has imposed its stamp on settlement pattern.

For a long while knowledge of Iron Age settlement was confined to evidence from a few well-excavated sites. More recently, however, not only has the number of excavations increased but a series of regional and general surveys has been prepared. Among the more important may be listed two overviews of the available pollen sequences which allow the framework of localized environmental change to be sketched out (J. Turner 1981; D. Wilson 1983), and a series of regional surveys including the Wolds (Ramm 1980), the North York Moors (Spratt 1982) and the Pennine Dales and the Aire–Wharfe drainage system (West Yorks CC 1981). The whole of the north-east region has been thoroughly reviewed by Haselgrove (1984a). No comparable surveys are yet available for the far less well-known zone west of the Pennines. In the pages to follow the better recorded settlements will be briefly discussed.

The Yorkshire Wolds

The best known of the Yorkshire Wold settlements is the site of Staple Howe, situated on a chalk hillock overlooking the Vale of Pickering (Figure 13.21). Here a farmstead dating to the sixth and fifth centuries has been substantially excavated, revealing an oval palisaded enclosure, subsequently remodelled, containing several huts and a massively constructed five-post rectangular granary. The excavator has suggested that in the first phase the only hut in use was

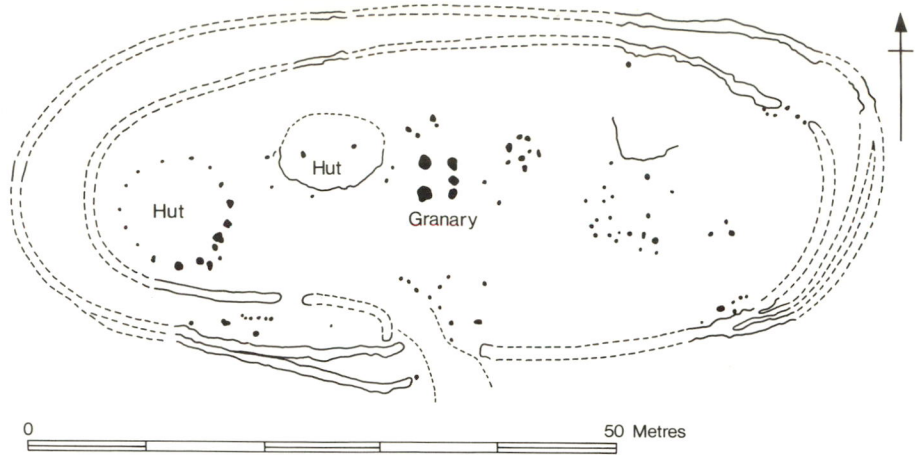

Figure 13.21   Staple Howe, Yorks. (source: Brewster 1963).

an oval structure which was subsequently replaced by two circular huts. While the circular huts are of generalized type similar to those found over most of southern Britain, the oval hut is more unusual: its roof appears to have been constructed around a horizontal ridge-post supported on two verticals, while the lower ends of the rafters would have rested on the ground or upon dwarf walls constructed of turf or chalk. In addition to large quantities of pottery and a range of imported bronze objects referred to below (p. 415), the surviving material remains included masses of animal bones, principally of cattle, sheep and swine, together with an amount of carbonized grain, all of which proved to be club wheat (*Triticum compactum*).

The same general pattern of economy is reflected in the evidence from the hillfort of Grimthorpe, which occupies a somewhat similar position on the west edge of the Yorkshire Wolds overlooking a low-lying area of densely-wooded Keuper marl. Within the defences of the fort were found eight four-post granaries, emphasizing the importance of cereal-growing. The animal bones showed a preponderance of cattle – 55 per cent compared with 25 per cent sheep; pigs (7.8 per cent) were only a little more plentiful than horses (7.3 per cent). If these figures are corrected for actual meat yield, beef consumption would be seen to amount to about 82.4 per cent of the total meat intake. A more detailed examination of the cattle bones shows that more than 70 per cent of the herd was maintained over two winters before eventual slaughter. Sheep, on the other hand, were killed off at a constant rate. The implications are clear enough: the economy was sufficiently stable for extensive over-wintering, a fact which in itself adds support to the view that corn-growing, producing straw fodder, played a significant part in balancing the complex processes of food production. Clearly, then, mixed farming was practised – indeed, there is very little difference between the socio-economic basis of Staple Howe and Grimthorpe and that of a typical Wessex farm, except for the absence of querns and storage pits. Since, however, storage pits were rare or unknown among the southern sites before the fifth century BC, their absence from the early Yorkshire sites is hardly surprising. The lack of querns is a little puzzling, but this may be nothing more than an accident of survival.

Staple Howe, Grimthorpe and Thwing belong to the first half of the first millennium BC and it was probably in this period that the linear ditch systems which traverse the Wolds were constructed (Ramm 1978; Manby 1980). These boundaries are similar in form and date to those found in Wessex and on the North York Moors and presumably reflect a need to demarcate social territories possibly associated with grazing rights.

Some indication of the developing settlement pattern in the valleys is provided by an extensive and straggling settlement excavated at Garton and Wetwang Slack. The settlement consisted of a number of circular houses 9–12 m in diameter built of timbers placed in bedding trenches. The discovery of carbonized grain, grain storage pits, often within the houses, and four- and six-post granaries, is a fair indication that cereal-growing played an important part in the economy. A date in the fifth/fourth century is indicated by a single radiocarbon date. By the third and second centuries changes were taking place. The straggling settlement was now replaced by a nucleated settlement with associated fields while an extensive cemetery was allowed to develop along the valley road. The cemetery was carefully defined by a linear earthwork. A little later, in the first century, ditched enclosures, possibly for animals, were added. Ditched enclosures representing individual farmsteads continued in use into the first century AD and at several sites, e.g. Rudston and Wharram Percy, preceded Roman occupation.

The North York Moors

The Moors are essentially an upland zone fringed with lower lying areas of better quality soil. The upland areas were divided into great tracts of pasture land by natural features enhanced by a series of linear earthworks and by pit alignments (Spratt 1982) suggesting a predominantly pastoral use formalized in the early first millennium BC and presumably continuing throughout the Iron Age. However, the distribution of beehive querns, an artefact of the first century BC and first century AD, which corresponds precisely to the distribution of good arable land, suggests that by the first century BC the agrarian base of the economy was becoming well established (Hayes, Hemingway and Spratt 1980). Settlements are not well known but sub-rectangular or D-shaped enclosures containing circular houses have been recorded at Great Ayton Moor, Levisham Moor and Roxby.

The Pennines and the west Pennine fringes

West of the Vale of York lie the Pennines, offering three basic environments to potential settlers: the upland limestone areas of Derbyshire and the Yorkshire Dales, the acid ill-drained moors of the coal-measures and millstone grit, and the wide valleys floored with glacial drift which dissect the range. Little is known of the area in the pre-Roman Iron Age, but several large hillforts are recorded. At Castle Hill (Almondbury), Yorks. (Figure 13.22), overlooking the valley of the Holme, substantial annexes were added close to the main entrance of the fort, and later an outer series of banks and ditches were constructed to enclose the annexes and the original fort together with a considerable hectareage of protected pasture. Such an arrangement, which has parallels in the Welsh borderland and Wessex, strongly suggests the increasing importance of livestock, which needed protection.

The limestone hills and valleys between the rivers Wharfe and Greta, where intensive field-work has been carried out, were densely settled (Raistrick 1939; R.F. White 1988) and there is no reason to suppose that other limestone areas were any less thickly inhabited (Figure 13.23). Three types of settlement have been defined, the most common being the isolated hut, or

CASTLE HILL, ALMONDBURY, YORKS

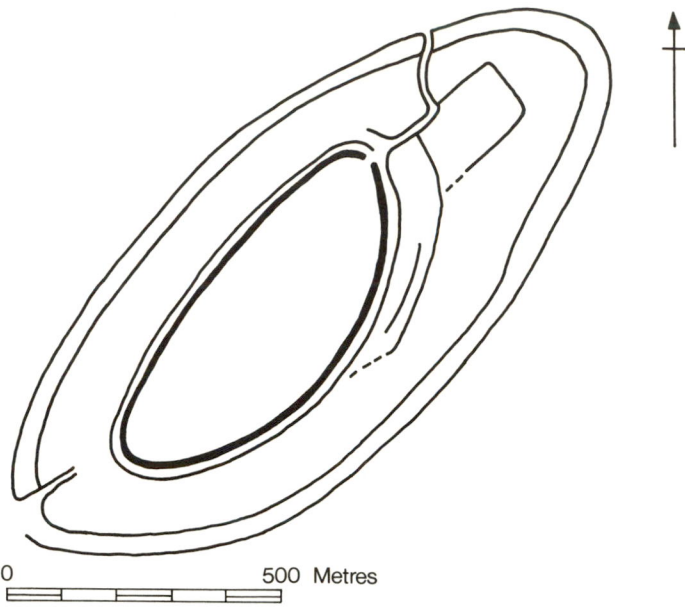

Figure 13.22   Castle Hill, Almondbury (source: Varley 1976).

sometimes a pair, set in a small embanked enclosure with a field or two nearby. This type is found mainly on the limestone plateau. The second type of settlement is the larger nucleation of huts which might reasonably be referred to as a village. One of the best-known examples, at Grassington in Wharfedale, consists of about 0.8 ha of huts and enclosures associated with about 33 ha of rectangular fields. The third type of site is the inhabited cave, quite often with a group of small fields laid out close by. The nature of the economy seen through the material culture is clear enough: grain was grown but in relatively small quantities, the principal food-sources being meat and milk from the flocks and herds. The relative percentages of cattle and sheep are uncertain, but the equipment of spinning and weaving occurs in quantity and the limestone pastures would have been far better suited to sheep than to cows.

Although most of the sites in the area are difficult to date and many were occupied throughout the Roman period, it is highly likely that many of them began earlier. Indeed, in all probability the Roman settlement pattern closely reflected that of the preceding period. It cannot, however, be demonstrated that there were no substantial changes in the economic system consequent upon the conquest. All that can be safely said at present is that the land supported a considerable population who, by the Roman period at least, were cultivating fields as well as maintaining flocks and herds. Until the large-scale excavation of some of the settlements has been undertaken, further conclusions are impossible.

The general absence of hillforts in the northern Pennines, with the exception of Ingleborough, Yorks., is notable. Presumably the pastoral nature of the economy prevented the development of politically cohesive tribes requiring defended foci. The dissected nature of the landscape would also encourage the isolation of smaller groups.

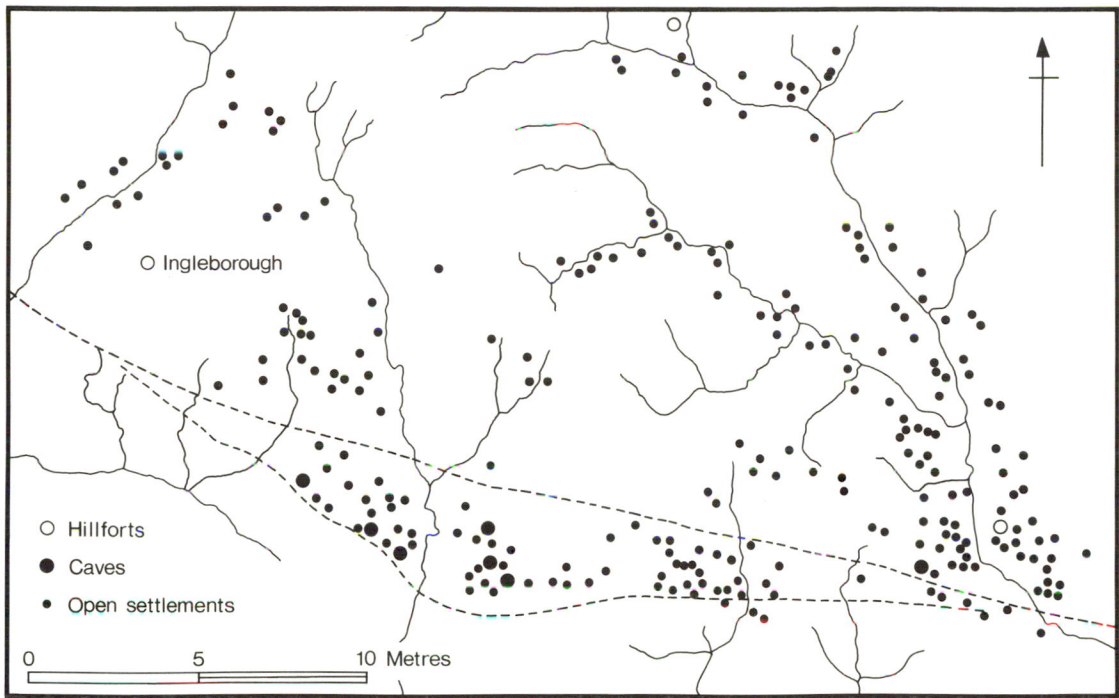

O Ingleborough

O Hillforts

● Caves

· Open settlements

0   5   10 Metres

Figure 13.23   Distribution of settlements in the Wharfedale area of Yorkshire. The broken lines represent geological fault lines with limestone to the north (source: Raistrick 1939).

The Magnesian limestone hills provide an environment more congenial to an agrarian-based economy and aerial photography is beginning to show something of the complexity of the ancient landscape with its trackways and extensive field systems (D. Riley 1976, 1977, 1978). Two settlement sites of considerable significance have been examined. At Ledston, Yorks., the part of the site excavated produced concentrations of rectangular storage pits, four-post 'storage' structures and circular buildings associated with beehive querns and weaving combs, while at Dalton Parlours, Yorks. (Figure 13.24), an agglomeration of ditched enclosures was found, several of them containing circular houses, four-post structures and rectangular storage pits. The radiocarbon dates suggest that the occupation spanned the period from the fourth to second centuries but pottery hints at a continuity of use until the late first century AD. A considerable number of querns and the animal bones recovered reflect on a balanced mixed economy. Both Ledston and Dalton Parlours share most of the characteristics of the farming settlements of the south.

The Tees–Forth region

The settlement pattern of the eastern part of northern Britain, centred upon the Tees–Forth region but extending to the north and south of it, is well known as the result of intensive fieldwork (Jobey 1962b, 1965, 1966a, 1966b, 1971a, 1971b; RCHM(S) *Peeblesshire, Argyll and Roxburghshire,*

DALTON PARLOURS, W. YORKS

Figure 13.24   Dalton Parlours, West Yorkshire (source: Sumpter 1988).

Haselgrove 1982; MacInnes 1982; Ralston, Sabine and Watt 1983), backed up by limited but carefully planned excavation. Most of the known sites now lie in the foothills of the main mountain ranges, on marginal land which has escaped recent ploughing, but aerial photography is now showing that occupation extended on to the richer boulder clays of the lowlands, where all surface indications have long since disappeared (Haselgrove 1982).

The earliest first-millennium BC settlements to be identified are the unenclosed groups of circular houses which now survive in upland areas beyond the limits of present-day agriculture and up to *c.* 380 m OD (Gates 1983; Jobey 1985) of which the best known is the settlement at Green Knowe, Peeblesshire. Such radiocarbon dating evidence as there is for unenclosed settlements suggests a span from the mid-second to mid-first millennium, one of the latest being Dryburn Bridge, East Lothian where the settlement can be shown to post-date a palisaded enclosure, of the type described below, for which a date of *c.* 750 BC is suggested.

Surveys in the immediate environment of many of the Northumberland sites (Gates 1983) show them to be associated with clearance cairns and field walls, the latter occasionally lapped by minor lynchets caused by ploughing. The pollen evidence provides further support for the view that even the settlements at the highest altitudes were engaged in some agricultural

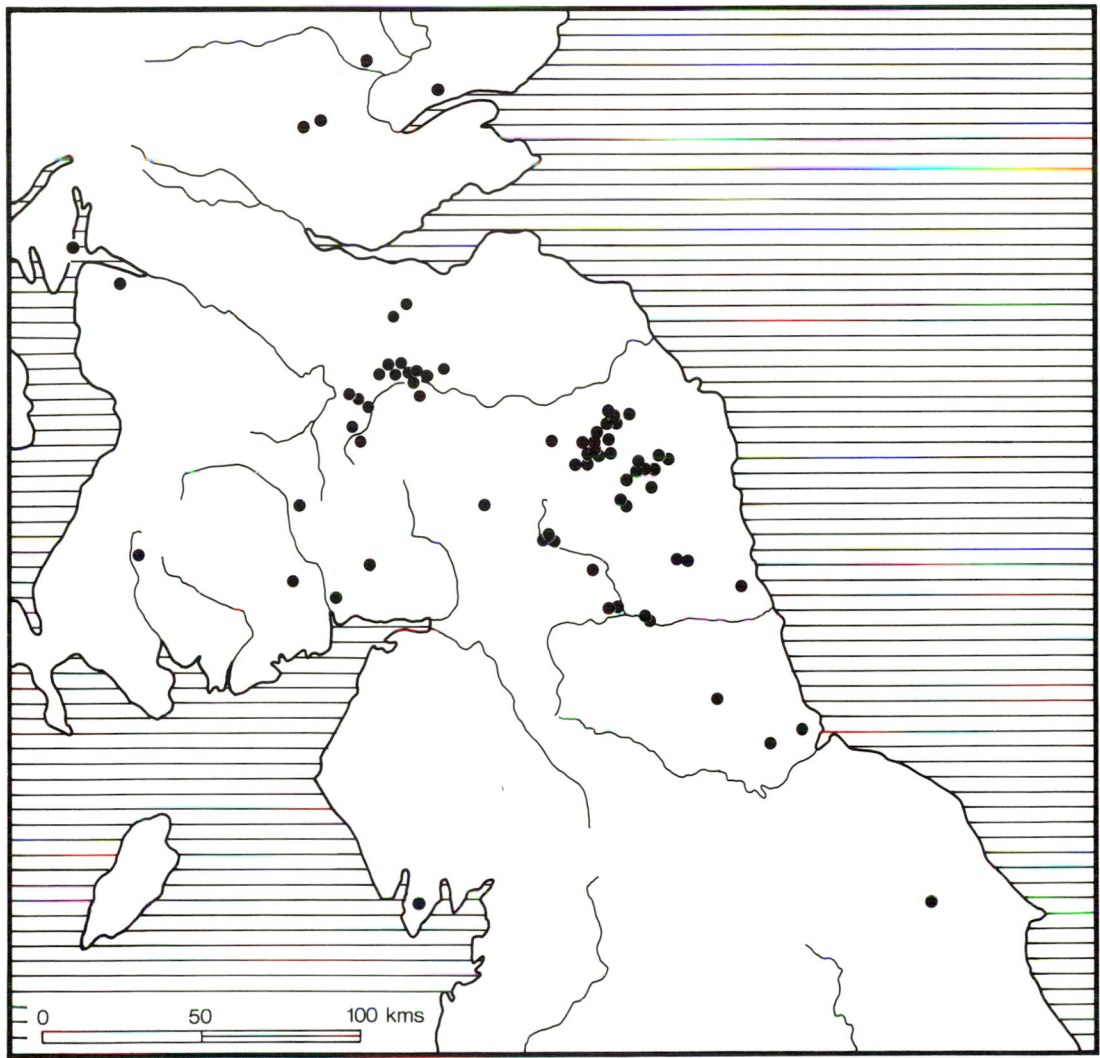

Figure 13.25   Distribution of settlements defended by palisades (source: Ritchie 1970 with additions).

activities albeit on a limited scale. These questions will be returned to in chapter 15.

From the eighth century BC onwards, one of the commonest forms of settlement, numerous examples of which are now recorded, is the palisaded enclosure (Figure 13.25): a circular, oval or sub-rectangular area surrounded by a continuous palisade trench in which close-spaced vertical timbers were wedged. A variety of plans are known (Figures 13.26–13.28). At one of the largest of the sites, White Hill, Peebles, two concentric palisades were erected 6.1–15.2 m apart, the inner enclosing an area of 0.7 ha. Hayhope Knowe, Roxburgh (Figure 13.27), follows much the same arrangement, the only difference being that here the inner palisade was double, while at Castle Hill (Horsburgh), Peebles., both inner and outer palisades were double. These examples were all provided with simple opposed entrances, but others are known with only one entrance.

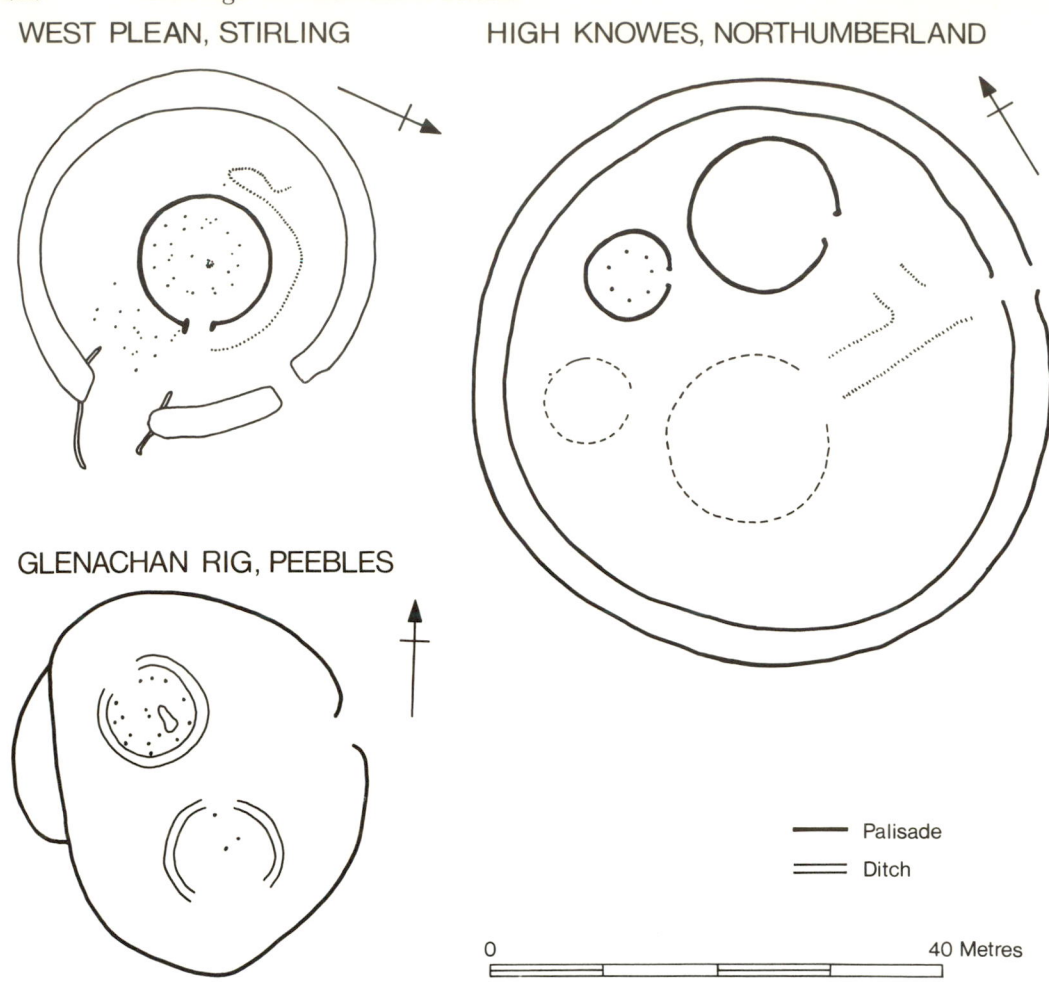

WEST PLEAN, STIRLING

HIGH KNOWES, NORTHUMBERLAND

GLENACHAN RIG, PEEBLES

——— Palisade

=== Ditch

0   40 Metres

Figure 13.26 Comparative plans of palisaded enclosures (sources: *West Plean*, Steer 1958; *High Knowes*, Jobey and Tate 1966; *Glenachan Rig*, Feachem 1961).

At the thoroughly excavated site of West Brandon, Co. Durham (Figure 13.28), the simple double palisade ended in four large gate-posts in the centre of one side, and at Harehope, Peebles. (Figure 13.27), a single central gate was provided in each of the two periods represented; in the second, however, it was flanked with substantial timber-built towers. Harehope is atypical in another way since the palisades, instead of being set in a rock-cut trench, were bedded in a shallow bank of soil and rubble. While it may be true that this was a modification developed with time, the method of construction is not unlike that practised in Late Bronze Age contexts in southern Britain.

Stylistically the palisaded settlements have parallels among early sites further south which belong to the eighth to fifth centuries. At Dryburn Bridge, E. Lothian, a series of radiocarbon dates suggests a construction date for the palisaded enclosure in the eighth century or even earlier. A radiocarbon date for charcoal from one of the palisade trenches at Huckhoe,

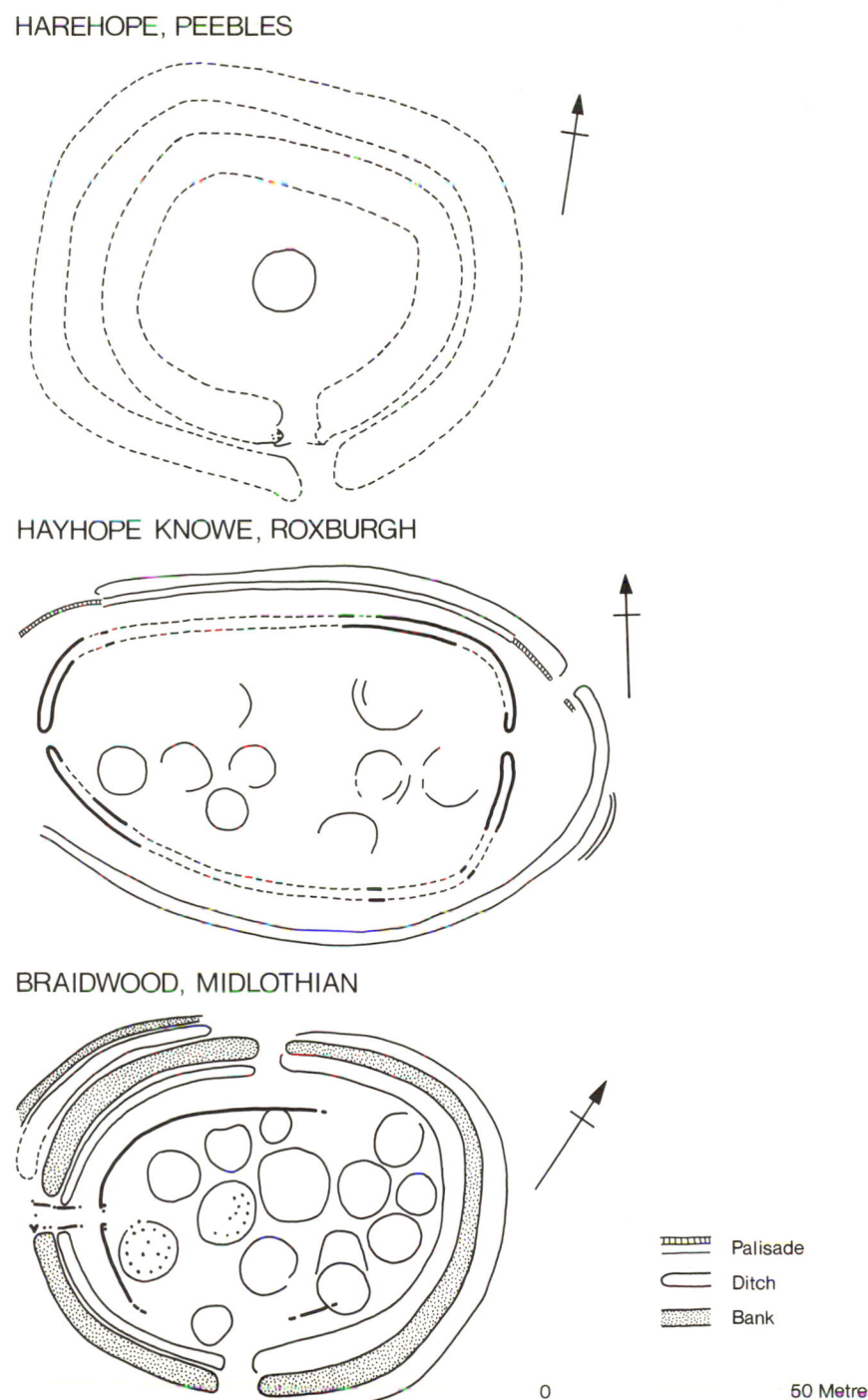

HAREHOPE, PEEBLES

HAYHOPE KNOWE, ROXBURGH

BRAIDWOOD, MIDLOTHIAN

Palisade
Ditch
Bank

0   50 Metres

Figure 13.27 Comparative plans of palisaded settlements (sources: *Harehope*, Feachem 1962; *Hayhope Knowe*, C.M. Piggott 1951; *Braidwood*, S. Piggott 1960).

WEST BRANDON, CO. DURHAM

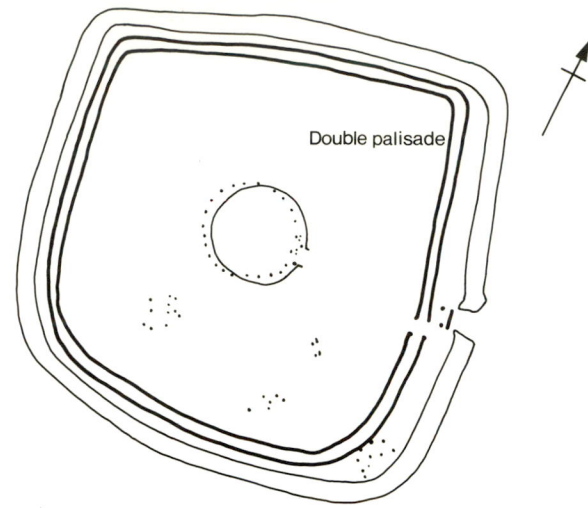

BURRADON, NORTHUMBERLAND

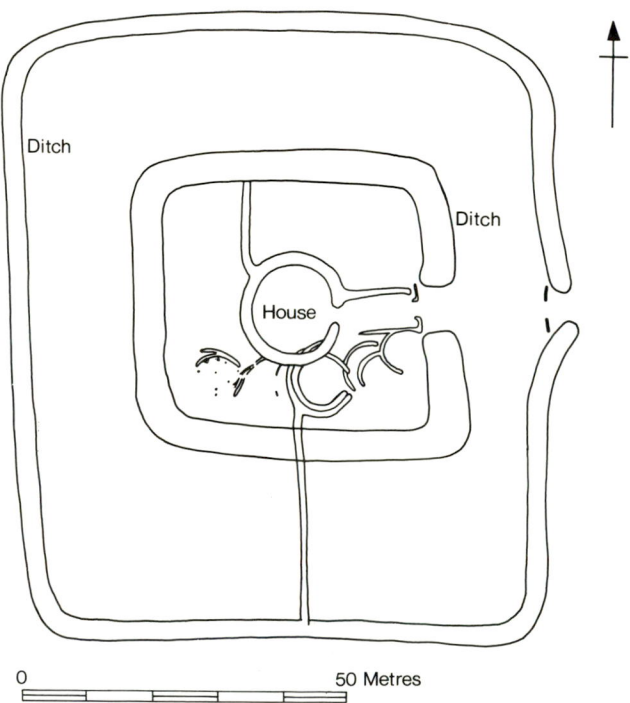

Figure 13.28   Comparative plans of rectangular enclosures (sources: *West Brandon*, Jobey 1962a; *Burradon*, Jobey 1970).

Northumberland, provided a reading of 510 ± 40 bc while the palisade at Burnswark has been dated to 500 ± 100 bc. Clearly, then, the northern palisades are of the same broad date as those in the south. Excavation at Tower Knowe, Northumberland, has, however, suggested that palisaded enclosures could have continued to have been built as late as the first century AD. A further point of similarity to the south is that some of the palisades were later rebuilt as earthwork-enclosed sites. A good example of such a refurbishing can be seen at West Brandon, where a ditch was dug outside the palisades, the rampart without revetment being piled up behind, sealing the original palisade trenches. At Huckhoe both the inner and outer lines of palisade, 15 m apart, were replaced by stone-faced ramparts, while at Castle Hill (Horsburgh) the two palisades were again echoed in later earthworks but enclosed a more restricted area. At Kennel Hall Knowe, the later earthwork enclosed a more considerable area than the earlier palisades.

The sequence, from palisade to earthwork can be shown to be *generally* secure though in detail the situation is more complex (Hill 1982b) and the change can no longer be assumed to represent a narrow chronological horizon. At Huckhoe the earthworks must have been built immediately after the destruction of the palisade by fire in the sixth century, but radiocarbon dates of 245 ± 90 bc for Brough Law and 220 ± 90 bc for Ingram Hill, both in Northumberland, show that not all the earthworks were as early, while at Kennel Hall Knowe, Northumberland, radiocarbon dates for houses associated with the early palisades centre on the first century BC and first century AD. Here the earthwork phase is therefore probably Roman.

A point worthy of emphasis is that many of the sites, both palisaded or earthwork-enclosed, were provided with multiple lines of defence, commonly though not invariably 15 m or so apart. While there can be no certainty on the matter, it is very tempting to see such an arrangement as the deliberate provision of protected corralling space for livestock, on analogy with the multiple-enclosure forts of the south-west. Pastoral activities must have played a significant part in the economy but the general lack of faunal material renders any detailed assessment of the composition of flocks and herds difficult. Some quantification for sites in the Tees–Tyne region, however, showed cattle to predominate (Haselgrove 1982, 80). This is borne out by the assemblage from Thorpe Thewles, Cleveland.

Cultivation was by no means neglected, as the four saddle querns from West Brandon and the rotary quern from Harehope show. Huckhoe has also provided evidence of what could be interpreted as a four-post granary, but the storage pits and corn-drying hollows of the south are entirely lacking and no field systems of definitely pre-Roman date have yet been defined. However, recent environmental sampling at Coxhoe and Thorpe Thewles has produced carbonized remains of spelt, six-row hulled barley and probably emmer wheat, establishing the presence of a clear, but unquantifiable, arable component in the subsistence economy.

The size of the settlements varies considerably from homesteads of one house like West Brandon to hamlets or even villages like the sixteen houses of Hayhope Knowe. Unless the house plans actually overlap, however, it is difficult to be sure how many phases of replacement were involved. This problem is clearly demonstrated by the excavation of the native settlement at Hartburn, Northumberland, where no less than thirty-six houses were discovered representing a minimum of twelve replacement phases. Quite possibly occupation was continuous from the middle of the first millennium to the second century AD.

While the majority of settlements conform to homestead or hamlet type it is evident that the complex defences of some quite small sites distinguish them as settlements of high status. An example of such a site is Broxmouth hillfort, E. Lothian, substantially excavated in 1977–8. The enclosed area was small, less than 80 m across, but, after an open phase, there followed five successive phases of enclosure each incorporating at least one aggrandized entrance. The contrast with the neighbouring settlement at Dryburn Bridge, only 3 km away, where a simple palisaded settlement was replaced by an open settlement, can only be explained as a difference of status. Status may also be reflected in a society's access to rare commodities. This is to some extent exemplified by the settlement at Thorpe Thewles, Cleveland. In the Middle Iron Age the settlement appears to have conformed to the local norm with a roundhouse set within a rectangular ditched enclosure. In the later phase (first century BC–first century AD) the enclosure was replaced by a large open settlement of undefined extent which was in receipt of a range of luxury items including gold and silver, imported through the southern trade networks. The potential exists, therefore, to allow settlements in the Tees–Forth region to be ranked, but without large-scale excavation and a firm chronological framework it is unlikely to be realized.

Houses were invariably circular, ranging from about 6 to 15 m in diameter (Figure 13.29). The simplest were merely circular settings of posts like Harehope house 1 and the house which pre-dates the palisades at West Brandon. A slightly more complex arrangement occurs at Glenachan Rig where a central post was provided to support the roof and the lower ends of the rafters were bedded in a shallow trench, thus providing some storage space behind the verticals. The earliest house in the palisaded enclosure at West Brandon is even more elaborate, with a roof taken on three concentric circles of posts, the outermost being 15 m in diameter. Beyond this is a further set of stake-holes, perhaps to tie down the roof-timbers, while the entrance passage seems to have been provided with double doors. In size and sophistication, the house rivals Little Woodbury, Wilts., and Pimperne Down, Dorset.

The earliest house at West Brandon was replaced by a structure of similar size, the outer wall of which was bedded in a continuous trench. Inside, a multiple setting of individual posts would have supported the main weight of the roof, while again an outer setting of stakes was provided, presumably as anchors for the rafters. A closely similar house was found at West Plean in period 2 – similar even to the extent of having the same type of short porch. The period 3 house at Harehope belonged to this general category but in this case it would appear that the outer wall was made of split timbers erected as a continuous wall rather than wattle infilling between individual posts.

A variety of the circular house, commonly known as the 'ring ditch' house, is found only in Scotland. It is characterized by a central area separated usually by a timber ring or partition from a sunken peripheral area which is sometimes paved. Examples have been excavated at Glenachan Rig, Harehope, Broxmouth, Dryburn Bridge and Douglasmuir and the type has been widely discussed (Hill 1982a, 12–21; 1984; D.M. Reynolds 1982; Reid 1989). No convincing reason has been put forward for the separation of the two zones but the possibility that the type may in some way be associated with the over-wintering of cattle has much to commend it.

Turning now to the end of the Iron Age, one development, well-represented among settlements discovered in Northumberland, is the appearance of stone-walled huts set in enclosures sometimes overlying the defences of hillforts (Figure 13.30, p. 288). Such settlements are normally so sited as to make use of sheltered slopes, comfort being more important than defensive potential. Some regional differences are evident. In the Cheviot foothills the usual type of enclosure is circular, containing a number of huts fronting on to a sunken yard which is sometimes paved. Further south in Northumberland rectilinear plans prevail, the enclosures containing four or five round huts opening on to a pair of cobbled yards divided by a central

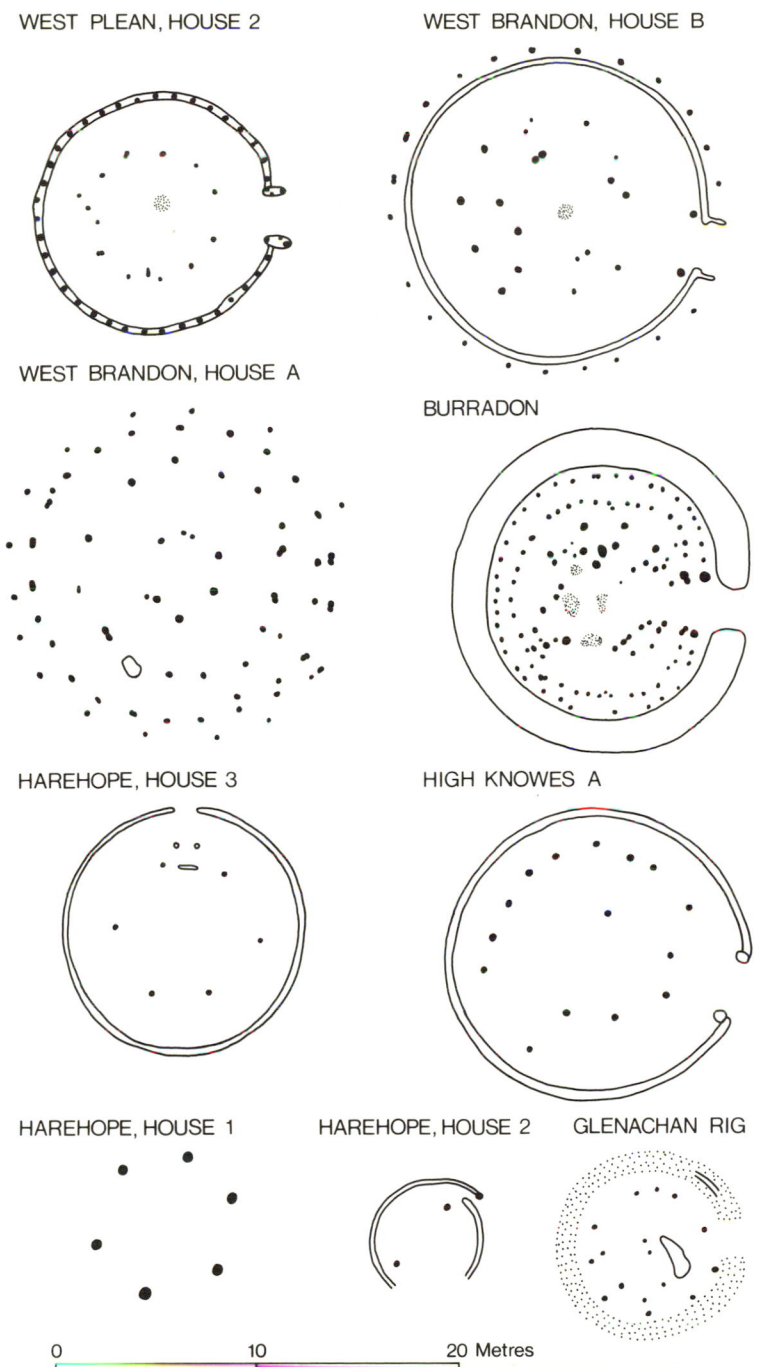

Figure 13.29 Types of north British house plans (sources: *West Plean*, Steer 1958; *West Brandon*, Jobey 1962a; *Burradon*, Jobey 1970; *Harehope*, Feachem 1962; *High Knowes*, Jobey and Tait 1966; *Glenachan Rig*, Feachem 1961).

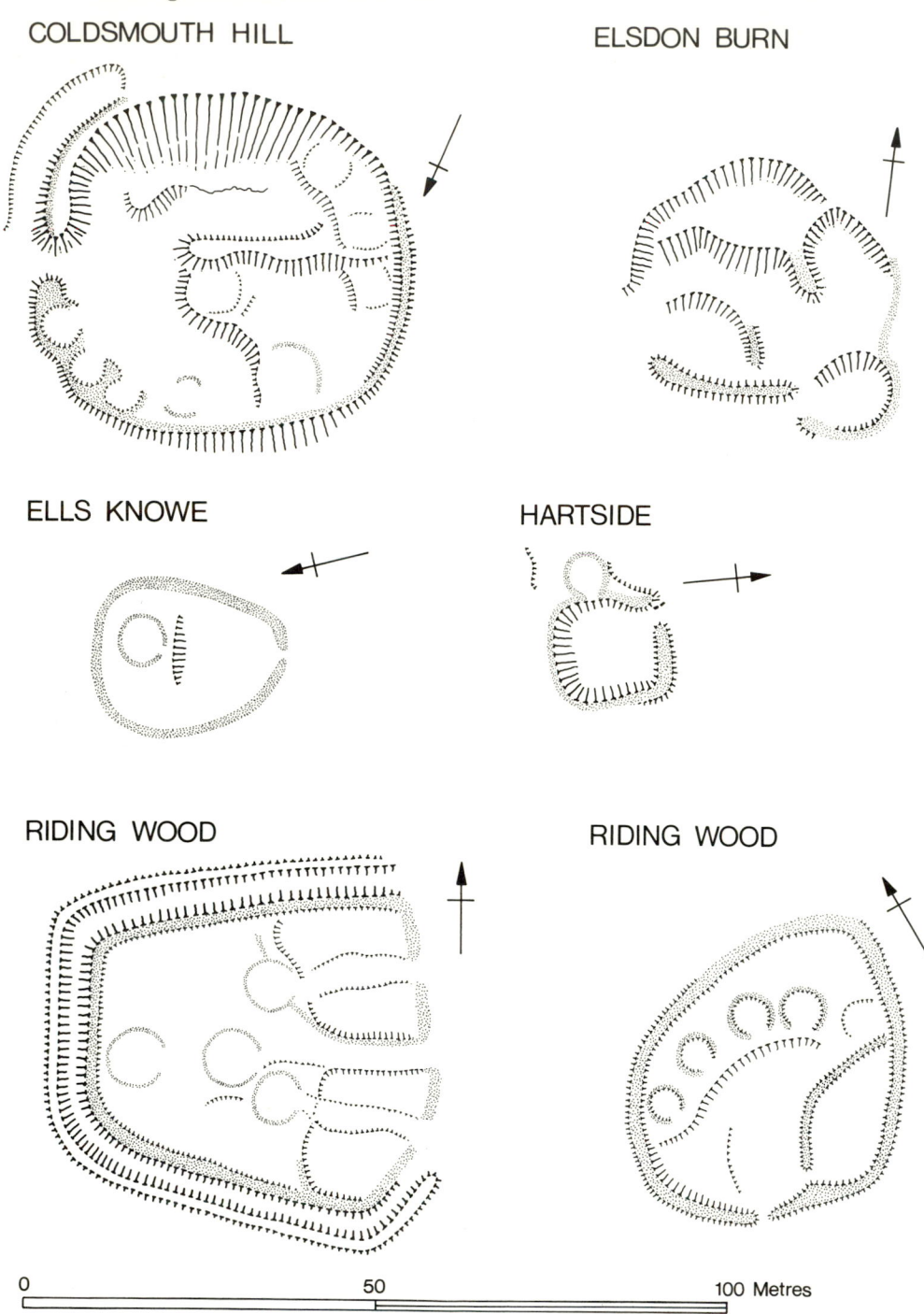

Figure 13.30 Settlement sites from Northumberland (source: Jobey 1966a).

pathway leading to the rear of the enclosure. The huts show no significant variation in size or complexity; suggesting little social differentiation, but in some areas larger settlements arise as the result of gradual growth and addition to a basic nucleus. Nucleation of this kind is not, however, common and the normal settlement unit remained throughout more appropriate to the family and the extended family than to more complex social groupings.

Dating evidence, where it exists, shows that many of the sites were occupied during the second century AD – a fact which, together with the rectangularity of the plans, has suggested direct Roman inspiration – but the discovery of a rectangular enclosed homestead at Burradon, Northumberland (Figure 13.28), dating to the middle of the first millennium BC shows that little can be based on plan alone. In all probability, enclosures with stone-walled huts developed out of the strong local tradition and may even have come into use before Roman interference in the area. There is often an element of continuity in choice of site between the small defended hillforts and the settlements: on some occasions the settlements actually overlie lengths of the disused defences. In such a case it is possible that a direct continuity of occupation took place. Elsewhere, the proximity of settlements to hillforts could be interpreted as a community moving to a more hospitable site nearby when need for defence was removed.

Another type of settlement, less well known, is the so-called 'scooped enclosure': a group of hut platforms terraced into the hillside and enclosed by a bank or wall (Figure 13.30). Dating is at present uncertain but typologically a Late Iron Age or early Roman context would seem to be most likely.

The replacement of palisades with earthworks has given many of the early homesteads and settlements the appearance of hillforts, but not only do most of them not exceed 1.2 ha in overall extent, the siting of many is clearly not defensive. For this reason, there is frequently considerable uncertainty in the use of the term 'hillfort' in Scotland: many of the 1,500 or so recorded (at least three-quarters of them in the Tyne–Forth region) are no more than rampart-enclosed homesteads and settlements. To avoid confusion Feachem (1966) has used the term 'minor oppidum' to describe fortifications of a more massive size, 2.4–16.2 ha in extent, sited with an eye to the defensive possibilities of the land. These are far less numerous – some fourteen within the region under discussion. Many of them enclosed massive settlements: more than 500 houses within the 16.2 ha of Eildon Hill North, Roxburgh, and at least 130 within the 5.3 ha of Yeavering Bell, Northumberland.

These North British sites with their ten to twelve huts per half hectare were three times more densely settled than those of north-west Wales. Excavation of Traprain Law, East Lothian, which at one time reached 16 ha, has shown that here at least occupation began in the Late Bronze Age and continued throughout the Iron Age and Roman period; the same complexity of occupation may well be true of the other large 'oppida' of the region. It is therefore impossible to know without excavation how many of the huts were in use at any one time or what the density of occupation was in the Iron Age compared with the Roman period. It is not unreasonable, however, to suppose that by the later part of the Iron Age these oppida had developed into large nucleated settlements which in some way commanded the allegiance of the inhabitants of the surrounding countryside.

A more specialized type of settlement, known as the crannog, has been identified in many parts of Scotland (T.N. Dixon 1982; Morrison 1985). Crannogs were usually built at the edge of lochs and consisted of artificial islands composed of layers of brushwood and rubble revetted around the edges by vertical piles and surfaced with oak logs. Upon these platforms a single hut usually

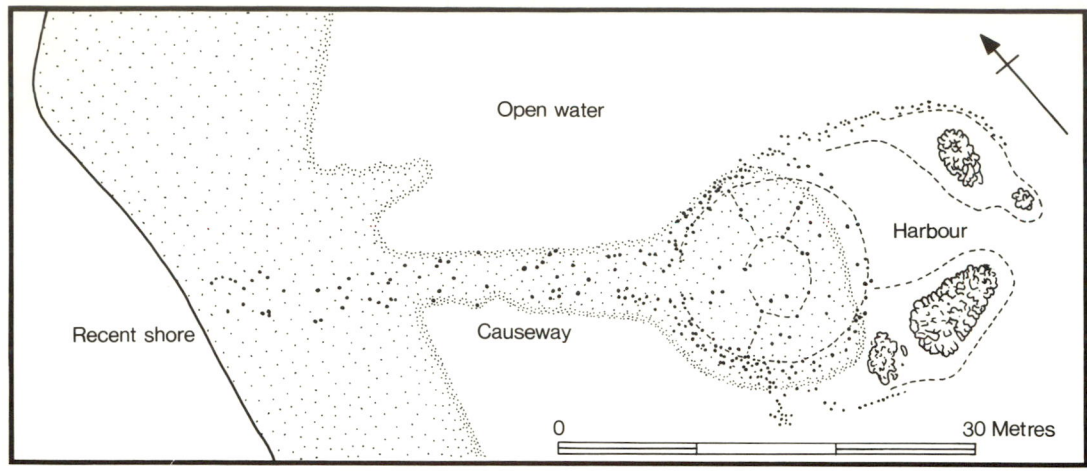

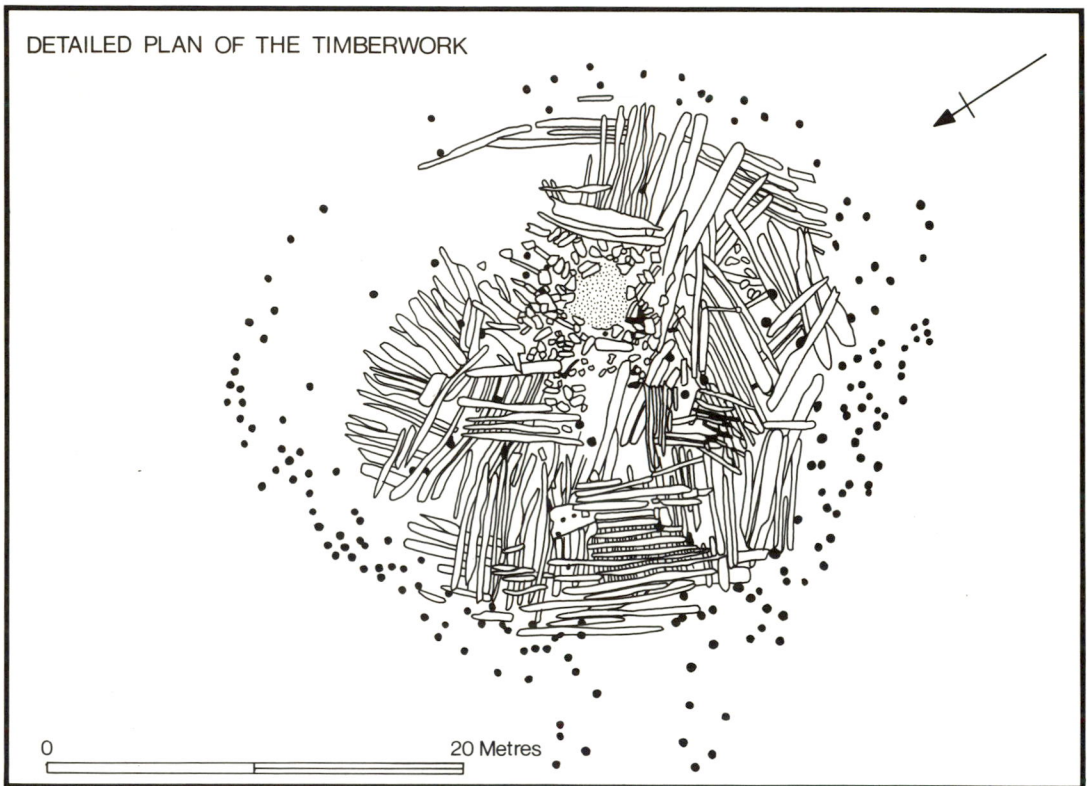

Figure 13.31 Milton Loch Crannog (source: C.M. Piggott 1955).

stood, the whole structure being joined by a causeway to the shore. Many of the known sites in Scotland were occupied during the Roman period but there is no reason to suppose that all were built after the Roman Conquest. Indeed a number have recently been dated to the Late Bronze

Age by radiocarbon. The best known of the crannogs is on Milton Loch, Kirkcudbright., where the artificial island and its associated jetty and small harbour were totally excavated (Figure 13.31). The platform was largely occupied by a large circular hut 12.8 m in diameter, divided internally into a series of rooms. The hut was surrounded by a narrow platform to provide access from the causeway to the harbour facing on to deep water behind the hut. Radiocarbon assessments for an ard found during excavation and for one of the piles of the crannog indicate a date in the fifth century BC.

Crannogs are probably best seen as a specialized type of homestead built, for defensive purposes, offshore from a lake edge. In size they are comparable to their land-based equivalent, the dun, as Morrison was able to demonstrate by comparing the crannogs and duns on Loch Aire (Morrison 1985, fig. 4.6).

Duns occur widely particularly in the west of Scotland. They are characterized as a stone-walled structure enclosing up to 370 m^2 and usually of sub-circular or sub-oval plan (M. Gordon 1969). Duns normally possess rebated entrance passages, as well as various combinations of mural galleries, cells and stairs. This type of fortified homestead probably has a considerable antiquity but some are known to have continued in use during the Roman Iron Age. Very few duns occur in the territory of the Votadini and Selgovae but they are common along the western coast and islands, and concentrations occur east of the Highlands in the valleys of the Forth and Tay (Figure 13.32).

The basic economy of southern Scotland in the late pre-Roman and Roman Iron Age is not clearly understood but the not infrequent occurrence of rotary querns and the appearance of field systems suggests that cereal cultivation was extensively practised (Halliday 1982). Discoveries of carbonized grain such as bread wheat and hulled barley from Rispain Camp, Whithorn, Galloway, are beginning to fill in the detail. Flocks and herds would have been maintained in large numbers and hunting and fishing evidently played a significant part. The development of a stable economy allowed the growth of the same range of settlement type-homesteads, hamlets and 'oppida' (hillforts) – as appeared in the south. Even constructional details of the palisades and houses can be closely paralleled in Wessex. Where differences occur, they result from the different physical provisions required for pastoral-based rather than cereal-based subsistence. Little evidence of change can be recognized before the Roman Conquest in the late first century AD, but thereafter, in the eastern part of the area, there seems to have been a gradual abandonment of fortified sites for the greater comfort of more congenially situated farms. In the west, however, Roman occupation seems to have had even less effect on the native culture.

North-west Scotland and the islands

The north-western part of Scotland, together with the Hebrides, Orkney and Shetland, still retains one of the best preserved Iron Age settlement patterns of any part of the British Isles (Barrett 1982). The most evident structures are the stone-built brochs and duns, many hundreds of which survive in recognizable form (Figure 13.32). So dramatic are they that they have inspired a considerable literature and many attempts at classification have been offered. Against this background it is surprising how little systematic excavation has been carried out. A number of sites were examined in the late nineteenth and early twentieth centuries but techniques of recovery were ill-developed and the record is, on the whole, poor. In the post-war period a new

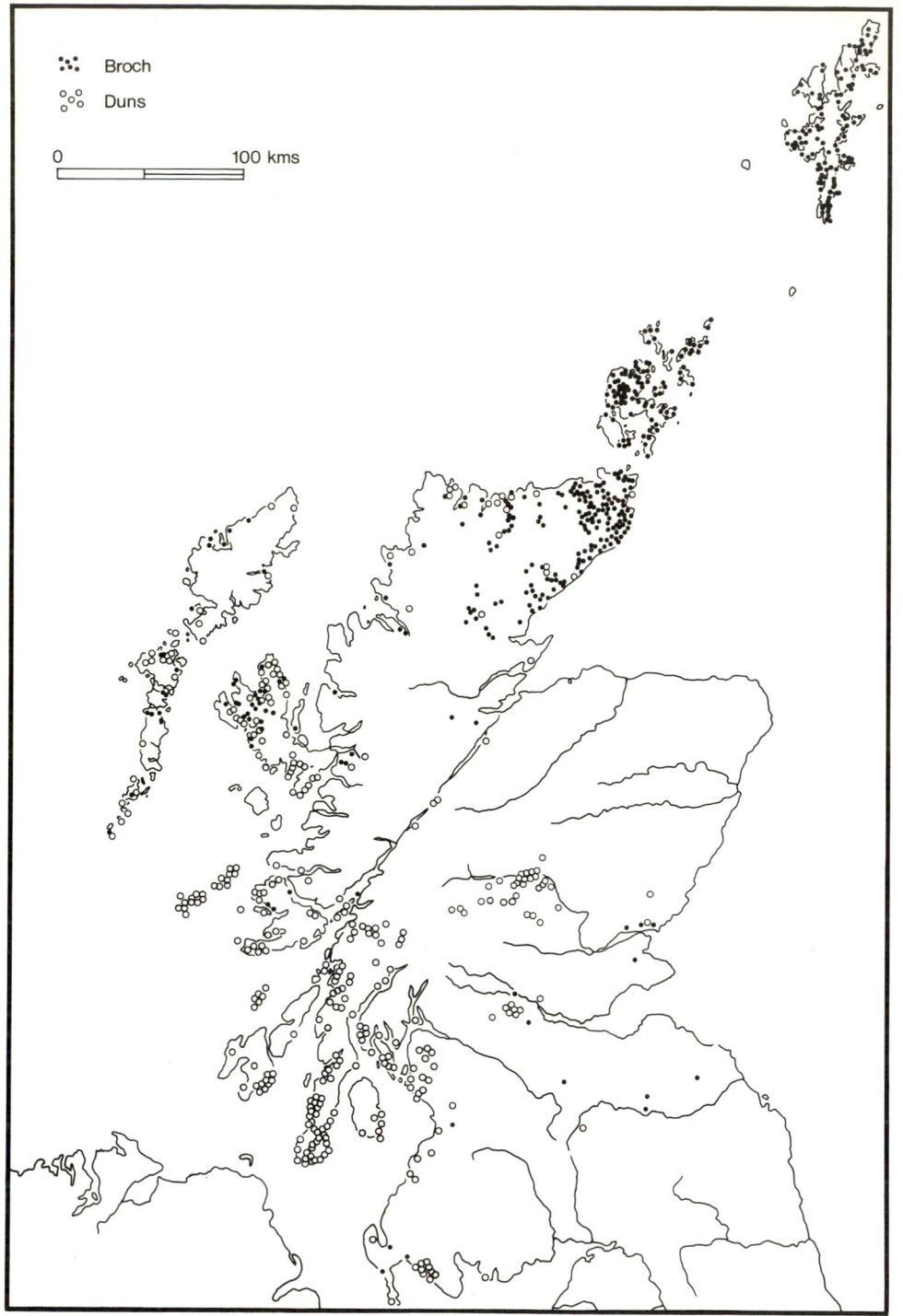

Figure 13.32   Distribution of brochs and duns (source: Rivet (ed.) 1966).

phase of study began with the excavation of Jarlshof, Shetland, and there are now a dozen or so well-excavated sites providing sequences useful for assessing settlement development. These will be considered in the paragraphs to follow.

Recent work has shown how complex the sequence probably is. Ten years ago it was possible to define three broad stages in settlement evolution beginning with open settlements and small enclosed farmsteads dating from the seventh to the second century BC. This was followed by a phase of strongly defended farmsteads, the brochs and duns which were dated from the second century BC to the first century AD after which wheelhouses made their appearance. While, as a very broad generalization, this simple threefold sequence still holds true there is now much blurring at the edges. Radiocarbon dates from Bu Broch, Orkney, indicate a construction date about 600 BC and while it could be argued that Bu does not display all the characteristics of a 'true' broch (MacKie 1983; Swanson 1984) it is difficult to deny that it was a close ancestor. If the date is accepted it takes with it the assumption that brochs and broch-like structures began much earlier than had hitherto been thought possible. Similarly the round house found at Quanterness, Orkney, constructed, on radiocarbon evidence, about 700 BC, already shows many of the characteristics of wheelhouses of the first and second centuries AD. It is inconceivable that there were no structures of intermediate date and form to link the two extremities.

The evidence, at present available, suggests, therefore, that in the Late Bronze Age and Early Iron Age a wide variety of settlement types were in use. This does not, however, deny the generally accepted view that the floruit of the brochs came later with the wheelhouses coming into their own later still in the early centuries of the first millennium AD. Several excavations, notably Jarlshof and Clickhimin on Shetland, Dun Mor Vaul on Tiree and Dun Lagaidh near Ullapool, Wester Ross, provide sequences which allow pre-broch settlements to be defined.

Pre-broch settlements

The excavations at Jarlshof have provided a sequence of pre-broch settlement spanning about a 1,000 years (Figure 3.15, p. 51). The first settlement consisted of several stone-built oval houses (Figure 3.16, p. 52). Each house was internally divided into a number of cells by projecting partition walls, leaving the centre clear for a general living space around the hearth. While there are obvious similarities between this type of construction and the courtyard houses of Cornwall, it is probably more accurate to think of the Jarlshof houses as stone versions of circular timber huts, the cells being equivalent to the space between the main roof supports and the outer walls of the more sophisticated types of timber structure.

Rebuilding was carried out on several occasions, and at an early stage a souterrain (or underground storage cellar) was constructed beneath the courtyard of one of the houses. Later the house was totally rebuilt as a circular structure averaging 7.3 m across, with cubicles set into the wall and a large souterrain opening out of one side. At about the time that the first souterrain was built, angular pottery with flat rims came into fashion and iron began to be used. Whether or not these innovations represent a single significant cultural change, or are simply the result of gradual development under some external influence, is debatable.

A similar sequence has been recognized beneath the broch of Clickhimin 35 km north of Jarlshof (Figure 13.33). The earliest settlement (period I) consisted of an oval cubicled house built entirely of stone, belonging to the Late Bronze Age. This was replaced by a large roundhouse (period II) associated with carinated pottery like that from Jarlshof. Eventually

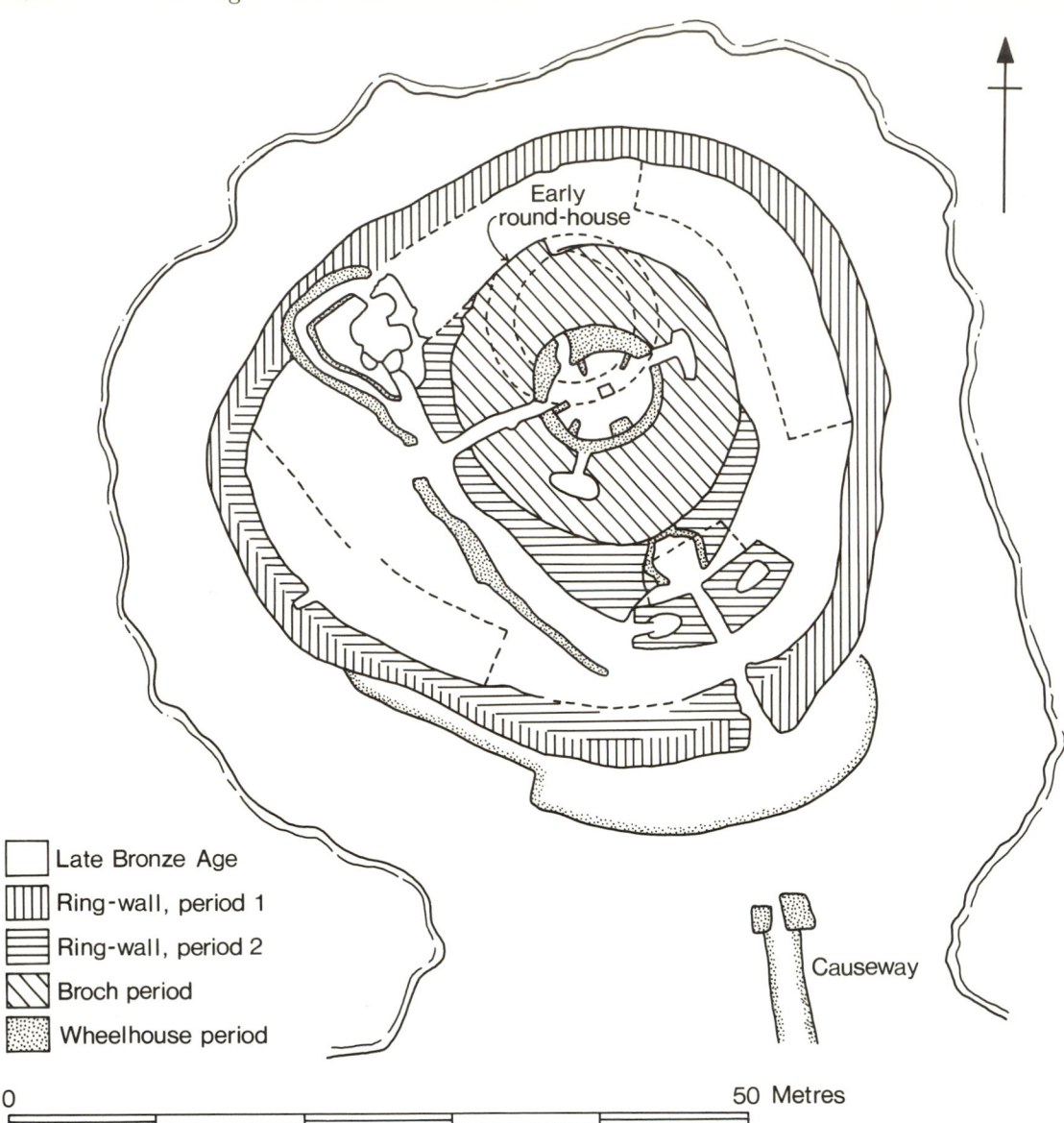

Late Bronze Age
Ring-wall, period 1
Ring-wall, period 2
Broch period
Wheelhouse period

0   50 Metres

Figure 13.33   Plan of the settlement at Clickhimin, Shetland (source: J.R.C. Hamilton 1968).

(period III) the house was encircled with a defensive fort wall, inside which lay a blockhouse, to protect the entrance. At this time the accommodation was greatly increased by the construction of timber ranges around the inside of the fort wall, probably standing to a height of two storeys with stalls below and living space above. The blockhouse is a remarkable structure (Figure 13.34). Originally it would have been three storeys high with an attached timber-built range behind. At ground-floor level a central passage was provided in the masonry leading to the dwelling space behind, while at first-floor level a door gave access between the rooms of the

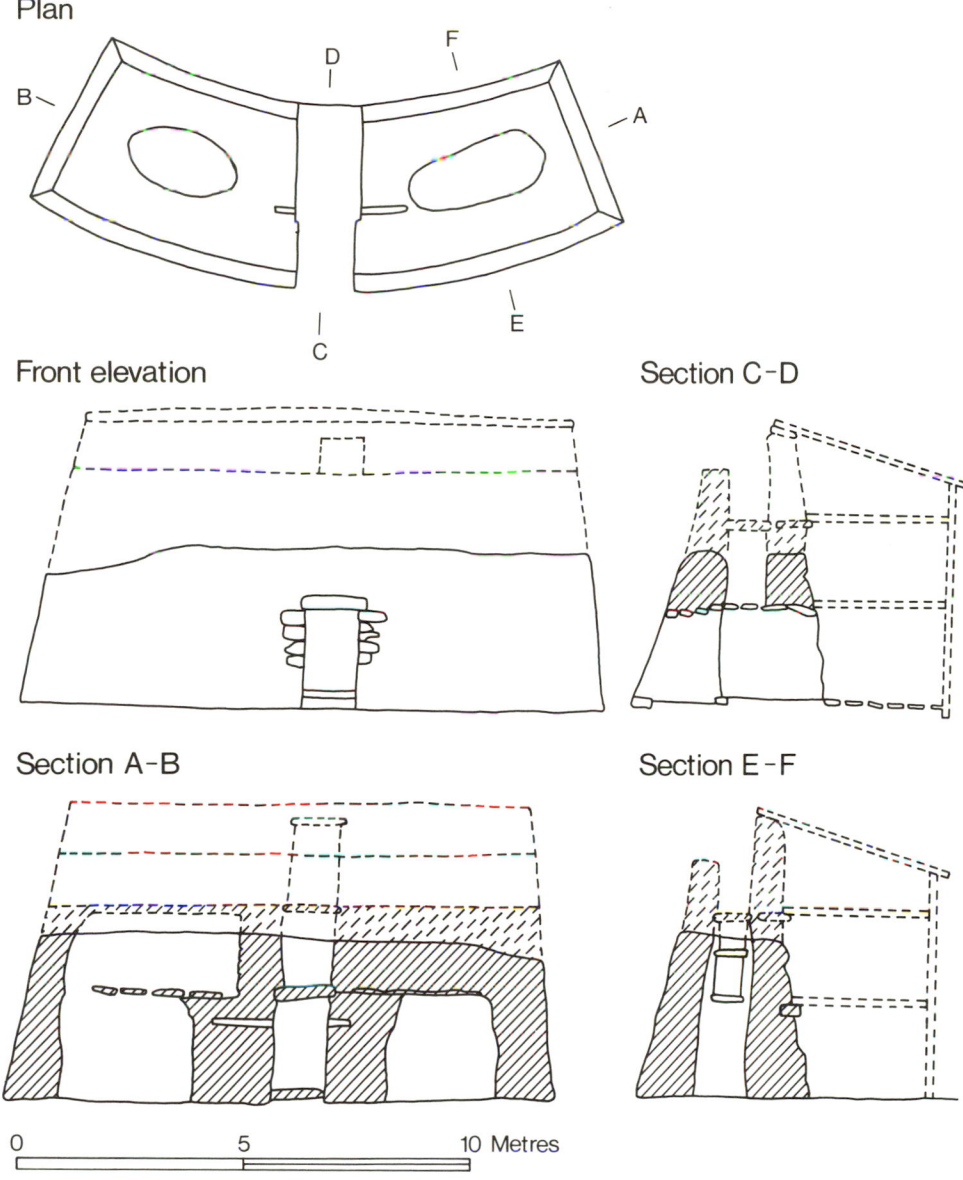

Figure 13.34   The blockhouse at Clickhimin, Shetland (source: J.R.C. Hamilton 1968).

timber range and mural cells constructed within the thickness of the blockhouse masonry; the second floor was probably a wall-walk to provide a vantage point. Blockhouses of this kind are known at two other Shetland sites (Figure 13.35), at Ness of Burgi, Sumburgh, and on an islet in the Loch of Huxter, Whalsay. At both sites the structures appear to have been integral with the main defensive wall, a situation which may have been intended at Clickhimin but never achieved. In the final pre-broch phase at Clickhimin (period IV), after repair of the outer fort

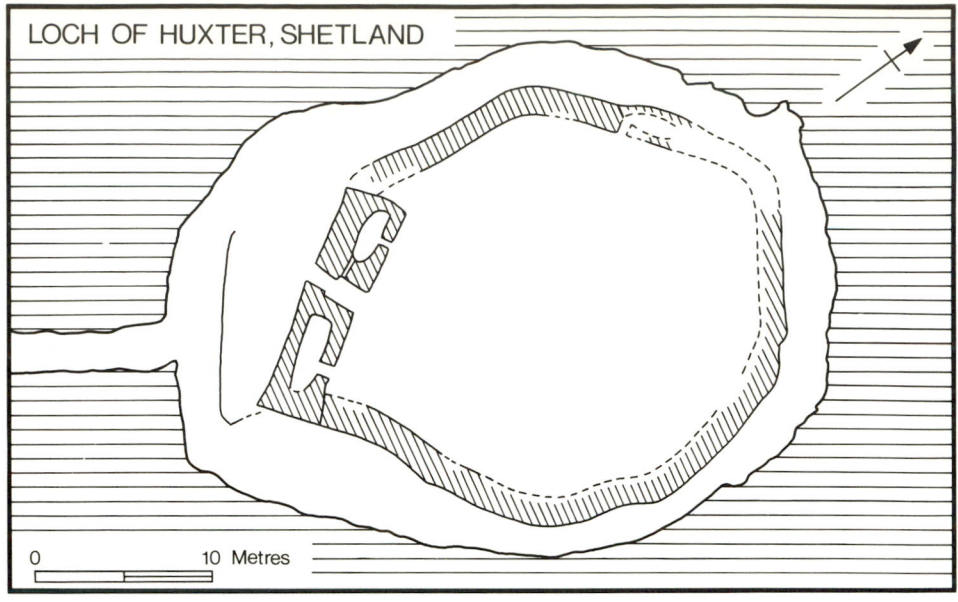

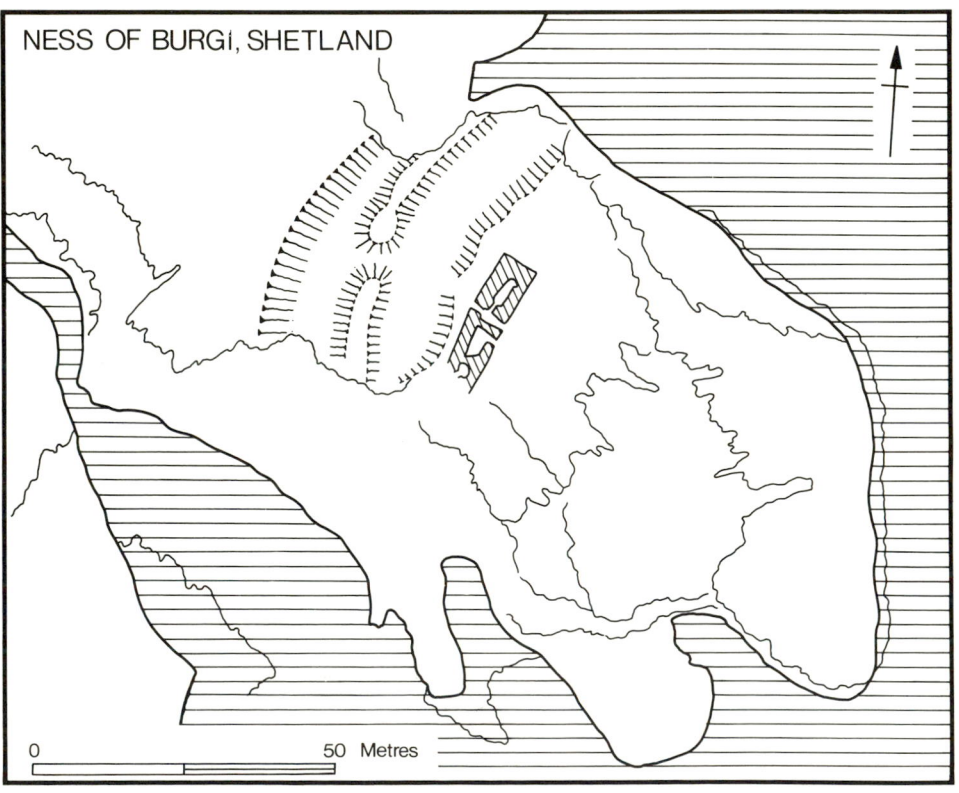

Figure 13.35 Comparative blockhouses on Shetland (source: J.R.C. Hamilton 1968).

wall and the demolition of the timber ranges, work began on the construction of an inner ring-wall around the island, butting up to the original Iron Age circular hut, which remained in use. The work was, however, unfinished by the time that the broch was constructed.

The Clickhimin sequence is of immense value in that it presents a complete and unbroken development spanning the period from the seventh to the first century before the broch was built. It has been suggested (J.R.C. Hamilton 1968) that the blockhouse architecture should be considered to be immediately ancestral to the development of the brochs, implying that brochs originated somewhere in the Northern Isles – perhaps on Orkney, where the building stone is eminently suitable. The problem, however, is a difficult one and will be considered again below (pp. 305–5).

Elsewhere in north and west Scotland positive evidence of early occupation is scarce, but survey work has shown that hut circles are not uncommon and in Sutherland alone there are estimated to be some 2,000 still surviving. One group, at Kilphedir, has been thoroughly examined. Here, two phases of occupation are represented, the first, dated by a single radiocarbon assessment to the fifth century BC, consisted of five circular huts with stone outer walls and with roofs supported on settings of internal vertical timbers. Around them it would seem that the land had been cleared for limited agricultural use leaving a scatter of clearance cairns. The second phase of occupation was represented by a single, more massively built, hut, the walls of which had been extended on either side of the entrance to create a narrow entrance passage 3 m long. In plan the structure was not unlike a primitive form of broch. This phase was dated by radiocarbon to the second century BC and it was probably in this period that a group of irregular fields lined with boulders were laid out.

A survey of similar settlements in the vicinity has shown that most are found between the 60 and 120 m contours. It is probable that the land below this, in the river valleys, was densely wooded, while above, the exposed position and poor soils would have been too inhospitable for settlement. The Kilphedir evidence is interesting in that it suggests the sporadic rather than continuous occupation of marginal land.

The settlements of the west coast and Western Isles are less well known, but at Dun Mor Vaul on Tiree (Argyll.) a pre-broch midden of the fifth to third century has been examined, and at Dun Lagaidh near Ullapool a vitrified fort with radiocarbon dates of 490 ± 90 bc and 460 ± 100 bc has been shown to pre-date a broch. Some evidence for economy was recovered from Dun Mor Vaul, indicating mixed farming with sheep predominating in number over cattle. The hunting of deer, both red and roe, appears to have played a highly significant part and quantities of limpets, winkles and whelks were collected from the nearby sea-shore. Cereal growing seems to have been largely restricted to the production of barley, mostly of the hulled variety (*Hordeum vulgare*).

Brochs and duns (Figure 13.32)

The principal feature of the Late Iron Age landscape in north and west Scotland is the density of small fortified sites which Childe (1935b) referred to as the 'castle complex'. These fortified sites can be divided into two main types: duns and brochs.

Duns are essentially dry-stone walled enclosures seldom exceeding 370 m² in internal area (Figure 13.36). The walls, originally about 3 m high, were normally solid but some were provided with mural galleries or simple mural cells. Brochs, on the other hand, were generally taller, with a few rising to 9 m or more in height, and are characterized by the cellular nature of

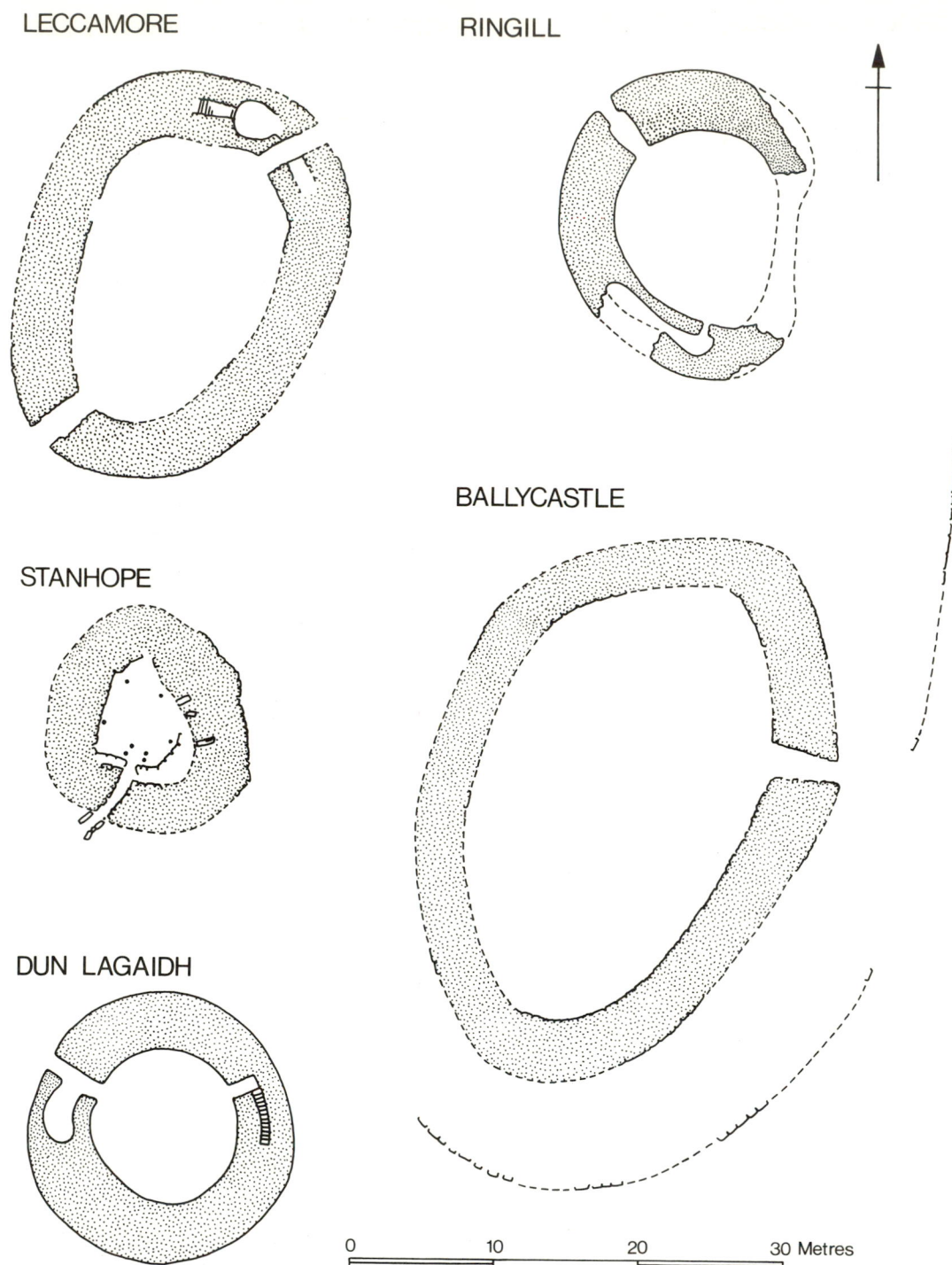

LECCAMORE

RINGILL

STANHOPE

BALLYCASTLE

DUN LAGAIDH

0   10   20   30 Metres

Figure 13.36   Plans of Scottish duns (sources: *Stanhope, Peebles.*, MacLaren 1962; *Ringill, Skye*, Young 1964; *Dun Lagaidh, Ross and Cromarty*, MacKie 1968; *Leccamore and Ballycastle, Argyll, RCHM(S)* Argyll).

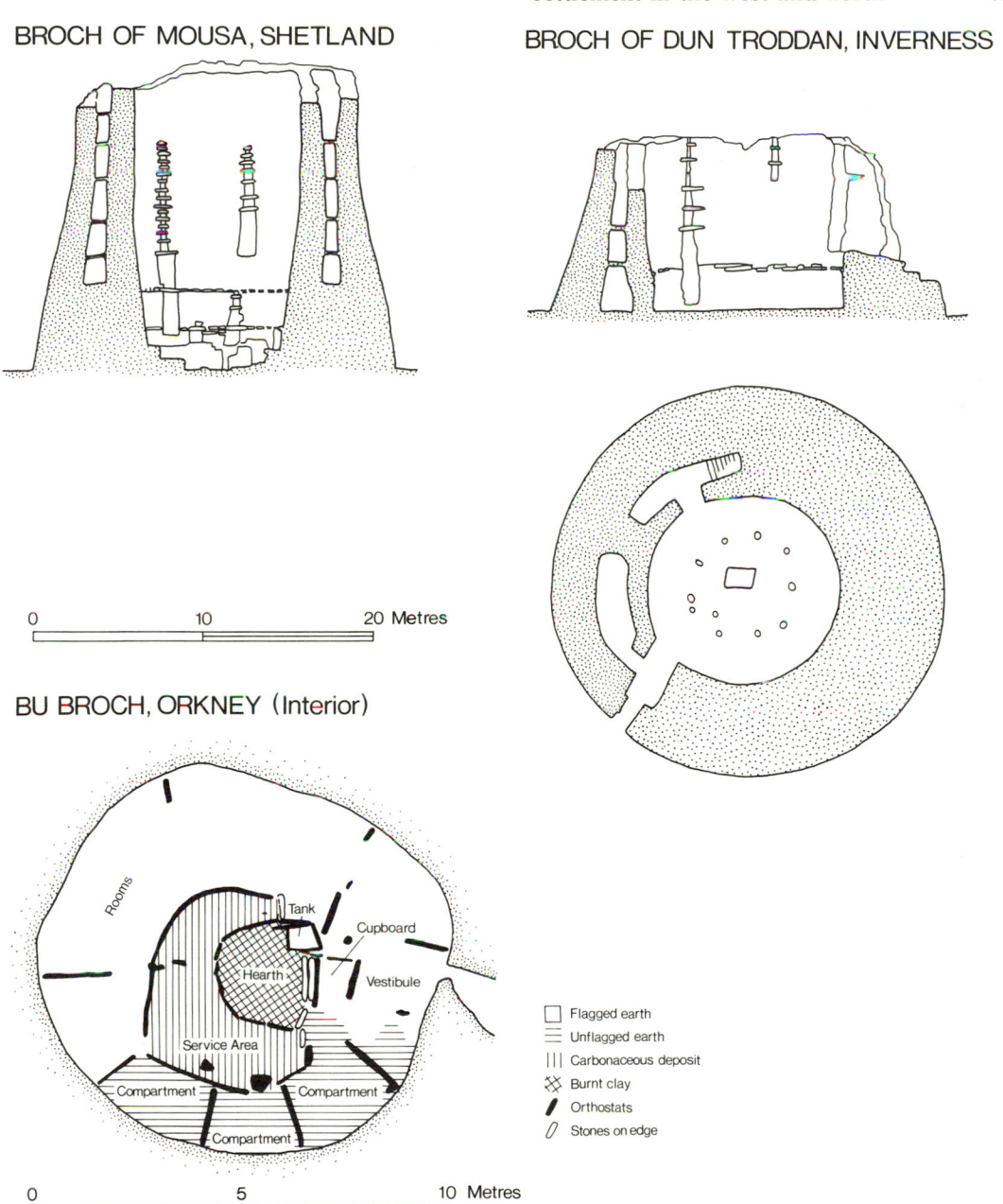

BROCH OF MOUSA, SHETLAND

BROCH OF DUN TRODDAN, INVERNESS

0   10   20 Metres

BU BROCH, ORKNEY (Interior)

Rooms

Tank

Cupboard

Hearth

Vestibule

Service Area

Compartment   Compartment

Compartment

☐ Flagged earth
≡ Unflagged earth
||| Carbonaceous deposit
⧓ Burnt clay
⟋ Orthostats
⟐ Stones on edge

0   5   10 Metres

Figure 13.37 Brochs (sources: *Mousa* and *Dun Troddan*, Curle 1927; *Bu*, Hedges 1987).

their wall structure, which consisted of two concentric skins about 1 m apart, held together by rows of stone lintels inserted every 1.5 or 1.8 m in vertical intervals and bonded into both walls (Figure 13.37). The result of this structure was the creation of superimposed mural galleries interlinked by stone staircases. The outer walls are always built solid, with no openings save the single ground floor entrance, but in some examples the inner wall-face is broken by vertical openings divided by horizontal lintels placed at intervals. The main entrance is always a long narrow passage passing through both walls, frequently with a cell or guard-chamber opening off one side of the passage (Martlew 1983).

The inner wall-face is usually provided with at least one ledge or scarcement 1.5 m or so above the floor level, apparently to support a gallery, the inner edge of which was taken on a setting of posts (MacKie 1965c, 104–5). The alternative view, that the scarcement took the gable-ends of a high pitched conical roof supported by the vertical posts should not be completely rejected, particularly when it is remembered that some brochs contain internal features like hearths which would benefit from roofing.

The excavation of the brochs of Bu and Howe and the reconsideration of Gurness, all on Orkney, leave little doubt that in their original forms the structures were designed to house single family units. The common arrangement was to divide the interior into a central communal space, surrounded by a peripheral zone subdivided into a series of small cells (Figure 13.37). The central zone contained the hearth and boiling tank. The peripheral zone was probably used for storage and as sleeping compartments. Such an internal arrangement is closely comparable to that of the wheelhouses and to certain of the crannogs (e.g. Milton Loch). The concept of the central living area with peripheral sleeping and storage space can also be postulated for the larger timber houses of the Forth–Tees region and of parts of southern England. In a few examples, e.g. Gurness and Burrian, the interiors were later rearranged in a manner which suggests occupation by more than one family group (Hedges 1985; Reid 1989, 14–15). This may be a reflection of social changes consequent upon contact with the Roman world.

Some brochs form the central element of considerable settlements. The best known of these is Gurness on Orkney (Figures 13.38 and 13.39) where fourteen conjoined buildings cluster around the broch, all lying within the protection of a double walled enclosure. Similar settlements are found at Howe, Midhouse and Lingro. In the case of Gurness and Howe there is evidence that the external settlements were broadly contemporary with the main occupation of their broch. In these instances we are clearly dealing with large social groupings, the extra broch settlement presumably housing the dependants of the broch owner.

Mention of the defences around the brochs raises the difficult question of the promontory fortifications which occur around the coasts of Orkney, Shetland and Caithness (R.G. Lamb 1980). While a number are evidently associated with brochs others are not. Only in one case, Crosskirk, Caithness, is it possible to show that the promontory fort pre-dates a broch. In the general absence of dating evidence elsewhere all that can be said is that some of these structures may be of Iron Age date.

Regional varieties of brochs have been defined (MacKie 1965c, 105–10), but the details cannot be examined here except to say that those of Caithness, Sutherland and Orkney tend to be more sophisticated in structure. Another difference is one of siting: while those in the Western Isles are usually built in isolation, the northern group more often stand in fortified enclosures of masonry or earth-and-rubble construction. One variety, which may prove to have a significance when considering the origin of brochs, is the broch-like structure sited on the edge of a promontory or precipice so that one side of the building can be omitted or represented by a low parapet. This has been called a semi-broch.

The earliest broch so far identified is the structure excavated at Bu, Orkney, for which a date of *c*. 600 BC is suggested by radiocarbon assessments. At Crosskirk, Caithness, another thoroughly excavated site, radiocarbon dates suggest a construction date of about 200 BC but the broch

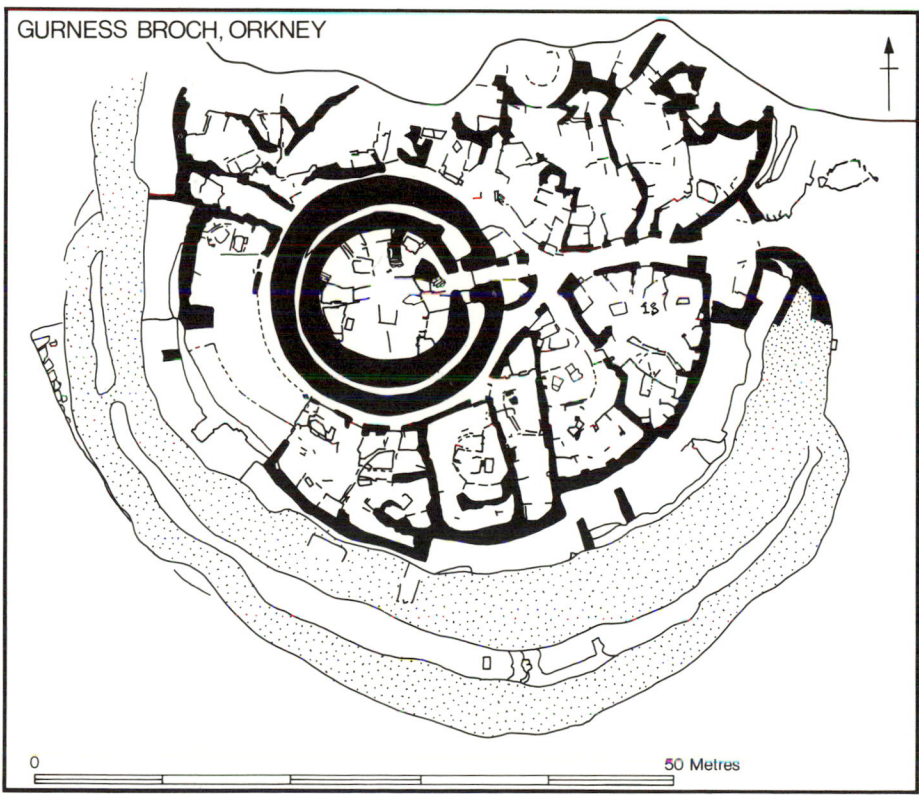

Figure 13.38 Brochs with adjacent settlements (sources: *Gurness*, Hedges 1987; *Howe*, Carter, Haigh, Neil and Smith 1984).

Figure 13.39   The broch of Gurness (photo: Crown Copyright reserved).

continued in use well into the second century AD. Dun Ardtreck, a semi-broch on Skye, produced a second-century BC assessment for charcoal from the rubble foundations while from Dun Mor Vaul on Tiree, dates of AD 60 ± 90 for a primary floor level and AD 160 ± 90 for rubble which accumulated in the first wall gallery imply that construction and use spanned the late first century AD. A number of brochs have also produced artefact assemblages showing that occupation continued throughout the first and second centuries AD. Further south, at Leckie, Stirlingshire, the broch was not built until the late first century AD.

The available evidence therefore suggests that the main period of use of the brochs was from the second century BC to the second century AD but the Bu radiocarbon dates, if they can be accepted as reliably dating the construction of the broch, would require that the tradition of broch building began much earlier, on Orkney at least (Hedges and Bell 1980b).

The origin of the brochs has been a matter of some dispute but it is now generally agreed that they developed somewhere in the Atlantic province. One suggestion is that they originated in the Caithness–Orkney region, in the area of their greatest concentration (Childe 1935b, 204; J.R.C. Hamilton 1962, 82); another is that they arose in the west, possibly on Skye, where there is a considerable variety of stone structures including a concentration of semi-brochs which might be thought to be ancestral to the true brochs (MacKie 1965c, 124–6). In support of this latter view, it has been argued that the broch was more appropriate to the defence of the small pockets of farmland typical of the western Highlands and Islands and is strictly alien to the more open countryside of Caithness and Sutherland. The early dated examples at Bu and Crosskirk would favour an origin in the Caithness–Orkney region but further radiocarbon dates may call for some revision. However, added support for a northern origin is also provided by Caufield's study of querns (Caufield 1980) which shows that a significant number of northern brochs had the early type of saddle querns in primary layers whereas the western brochs have produced only the later rotary type.

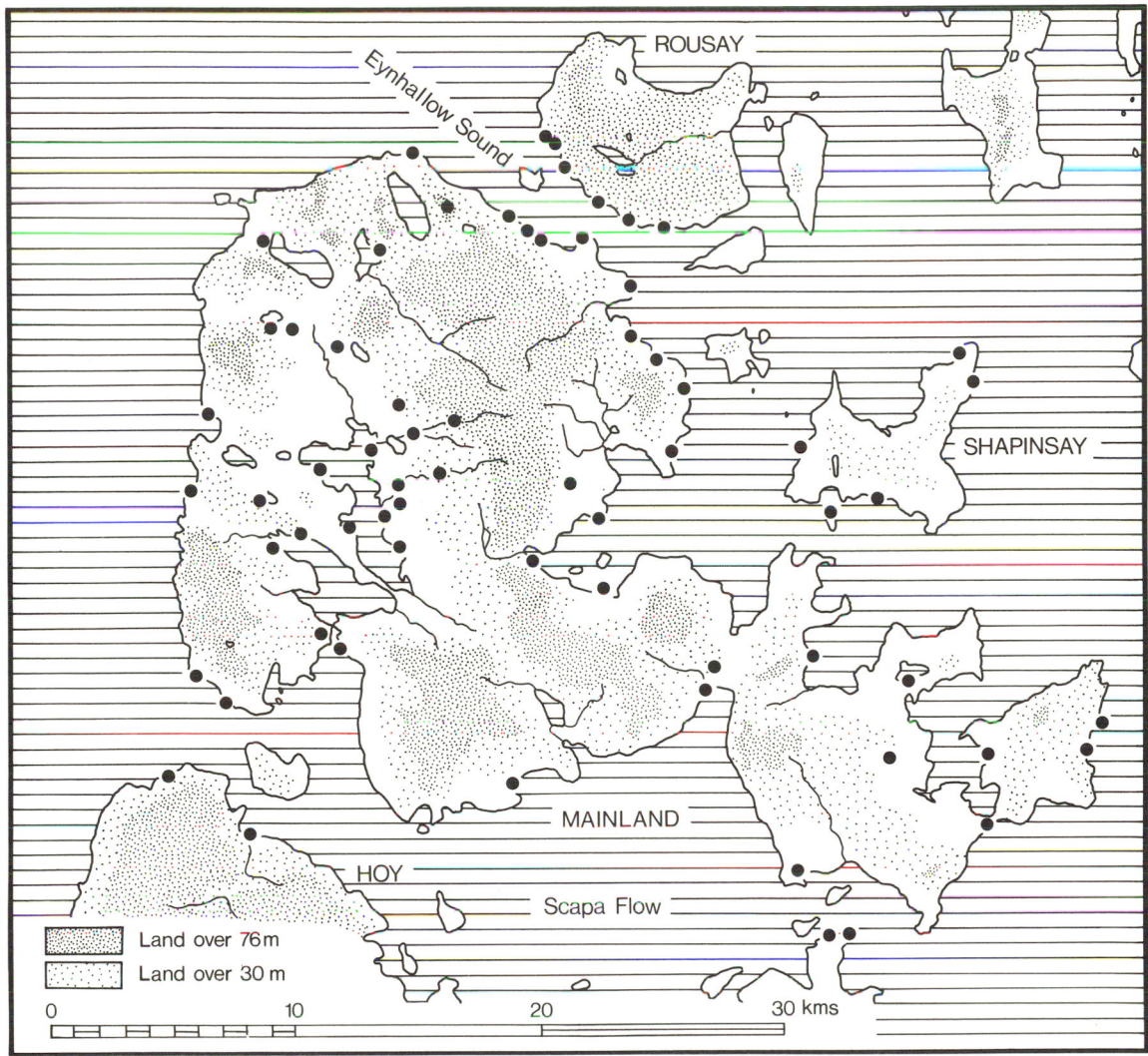

Figure 13.40   The siting of brochs on Orkney (source: *RCHM(S)*, Orkney and Shetland).

Several excavations should be mentioned because of the light they throw on the relative position of brochs in the structural development of the individual sites. In each case there is clear proof of a degree of continuity. At Dun Mor Vaul the broch was shown to have been built on a site already occupied for several hundred years, but at Dun Lagaidh, Wester Ross, the later structure was built over part of a vitrified fort for which a sixth-century radiocarbon date is available, suggesting a period of abandonment between periods of occupation. At Crosskirk, Caithness, the broch was built inside an already existing promontory fort while at Howe, on Orkney, a long sequence of houses existed before the broch was built to replace them. Clickhimin, Shetland, provides the most complete sequence of fortification at present available;

Figure 13.41   The brochs of Shetland indicating their possible economic territories (source: Fojut 1982b).

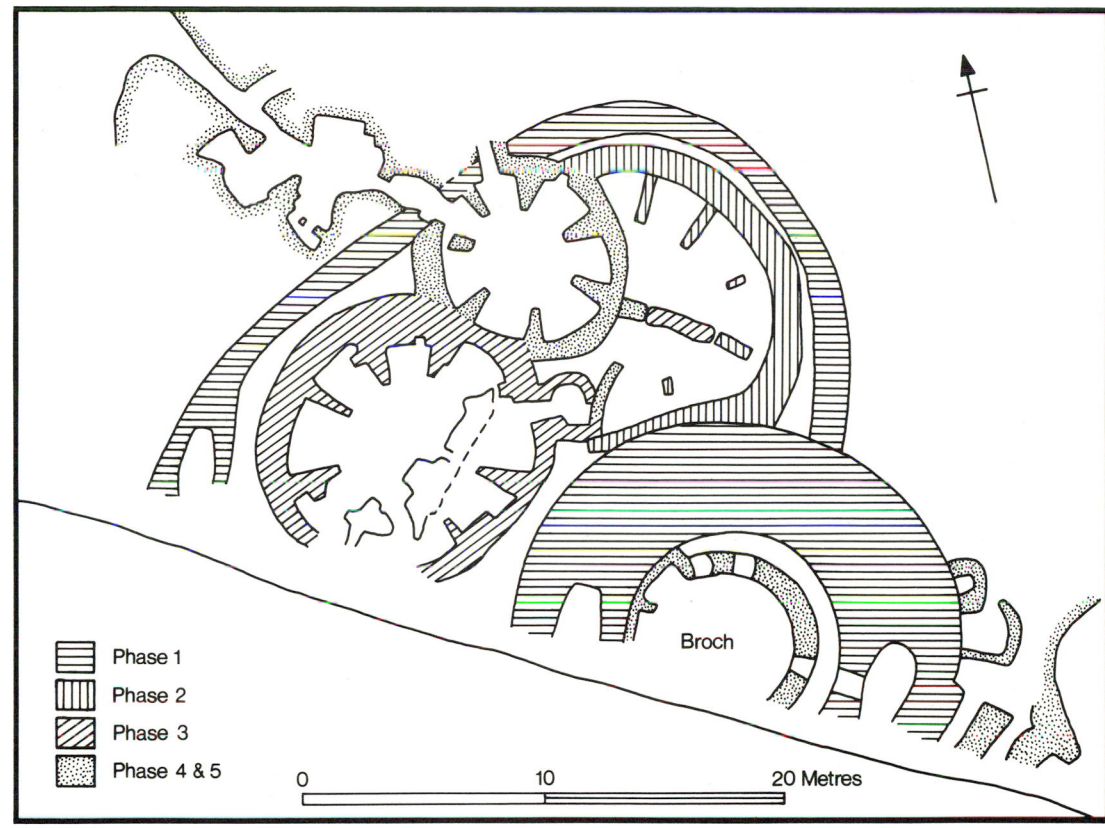

Phase 1
Phase 2
Phase 3
Phase 4 & 5

0   10   20 Metres

Broch

Figure 13.42   The settlement at Jarlshof, Shetland beginning with the construction of the broch (source: J.R.C. Hamilton 1956).

the broch was built late in the history of the site but the presence of the earlier blockhouse, which embodies several of the constructional techniques of the broch-builders, evidently represents a stage of construction towards the beginning of the complex sequence which must lie behind the eventual emergence of the fully-fledged broch.

Many brochs are sited close to the sea, and evidently depended to a considerable extent on seafood. On Orkney, for example, brochs are found regularly spaced along the shores, particularly of the more sheltered waters, like Eynhallow Sound between Mainland and Rousay (Figure 13.40). Each was sited so that its resource potential would have included upland sheep grazing, a length of coastal shelf suitable for crop growing, the shore zone itself for shellfish collecting, and the sea, providing a range of possible food sources. Even the inland brochs on Orkney show a distinct preference for siting near lochs. Evidently fish must have played a significant part in the economy. On Skye, too, the brochs and duns favoured a coastal location but clustered on areas of good arable and pasture land (MacSween 1985). A detailed survey of the brochs on Shetland (Fojut 1982b) has shown a similar preference for siting brochs close to the sea but within easy reach of good quality farming land. The survey has further suggested that the majority of the broch territories were self-sufficient but there may have been some localized

Figure 13.43 Jarlshof, Shetland. The aisled roundhouse and wheelhouse (photo: Crown Copyright reserved).

redistribution of consumer goods between neighbours. An even more interesting conclusion was that, in spite of the considerable density of settlements, the population was far below the holding capacity of their island territory. The desire for fortification was not therefore occasioned by stress brought about by uncomfortably high population levels.

Wheelhouses

The wheelhouse represents a somewhat different type of structure, which occupies the same area as the brochs and is broadly contemporary with them. A wheelhouse is a circular stone-built structure, the interior of which is divided by short radial stone piers projecting from the wall but leaving the interior clear. The piers presumably supported the roof of wood and turf in much the same way as internal settings of vertical posts would have done in the timber-built houses of the south. In some examples, known as aisled wheelhouses, the piers are free-standing but are joined to the outer wall by lintels.

Some wheelhouses, like Tigh Talamhanta (Allasdale) and Clettraval in the Hebrides (Figures

Figure 13.44   Jarlshof, Shetland. The interior of the wheelhouse (photo: Crown Copyright reserved).

13.45 and 13.46), were built as free-standing houses surrounded by a farmyard enclosure containing working areas as well as subsidiary structures like byres or barns. At Jarlshof, Shetland, on the other hand, the first aisled wheelhouse was built into the yard attached to the broch with a byre close by (Figures 13.42–13.44). This building is of particular interest because in its original stage the roof was supported on vertical timbers which were only later replaced by free-standing stone piers. Later still the original aisled wheelhouse was dismantled and replaced by a conjoined pair of wheelhouses, superbly built with radial piers corbelled out at the top to roof the individual bays. Jarlshof, then, appears to demonstrate the entire sequence of wheelhouse development. Elsewhere on Shetland, as for example at Clickhimin, most of the wheelhouses were found to be inserted into brochs.

While there is some evidence to suggest that elements of wheelhouse architecture were developing on Shetland before the brochs, possibly in the third and second centuries BC, and may well derive from the type of simple circular house of the seventh century found at Quanterness, Orkney, the major occurrence of the type dates to after the brochs had begun to go out of use as defended structures. The range of stratified Roman imports suggests a second- to third-century AD date and in the Outer Hebrides houses of this type can be shown to span the period from the first to fourth centuries AD.

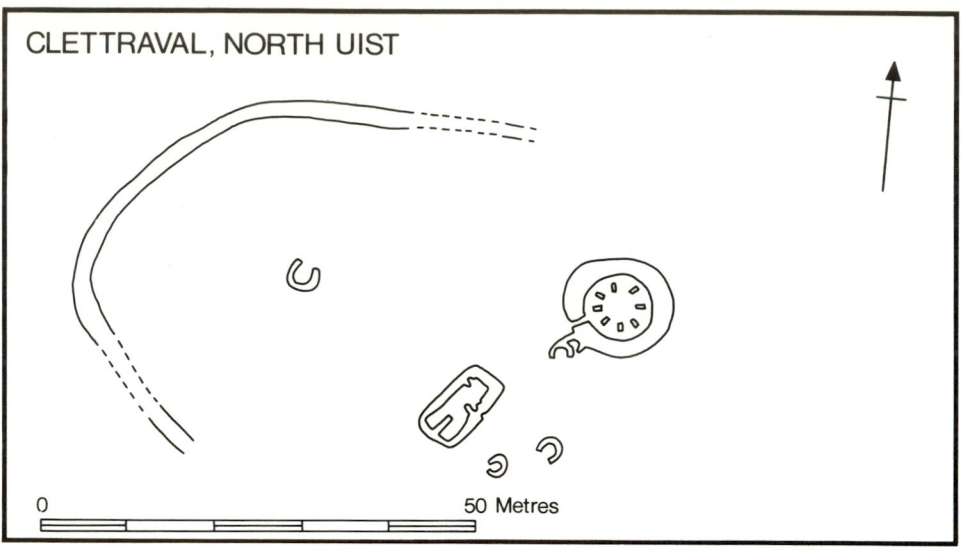

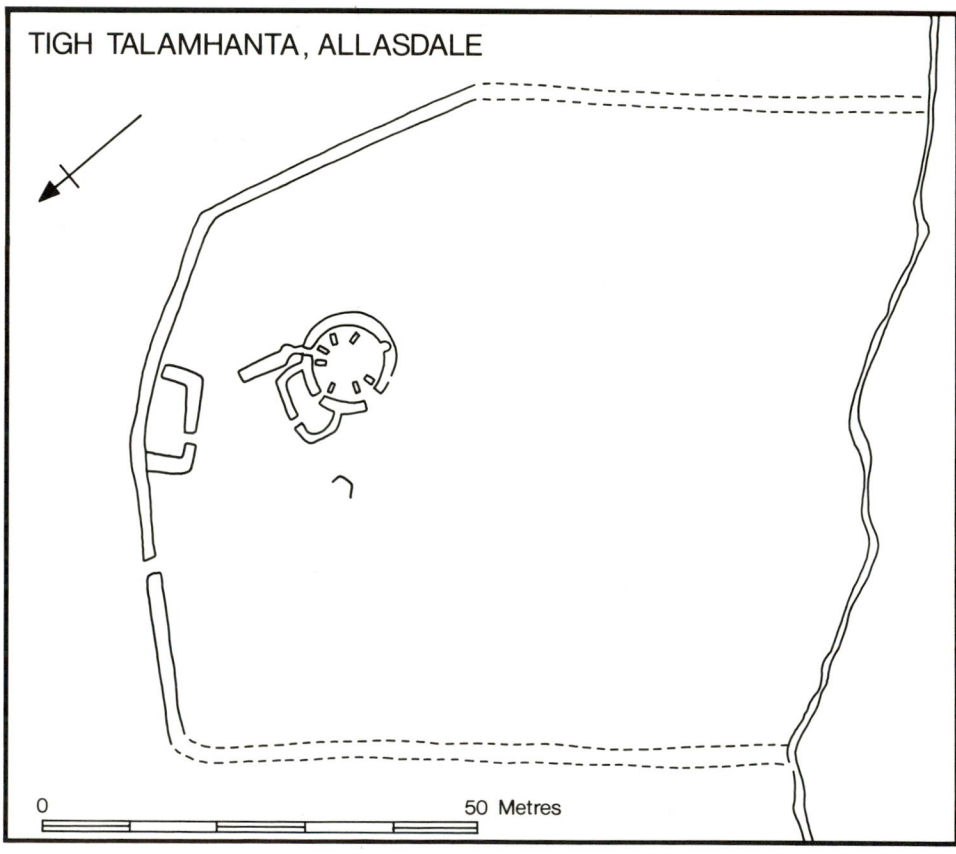

Figure 13.45 Farmsteads in north-west Britain (sources: *Clettraval*, Scott 1948; *Tigh Talamhanta*, Young 1955).

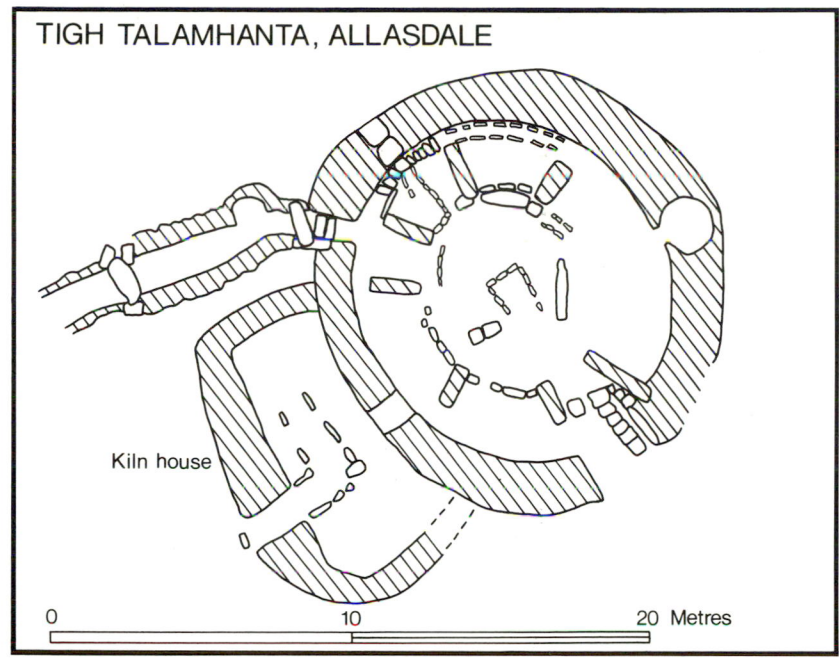

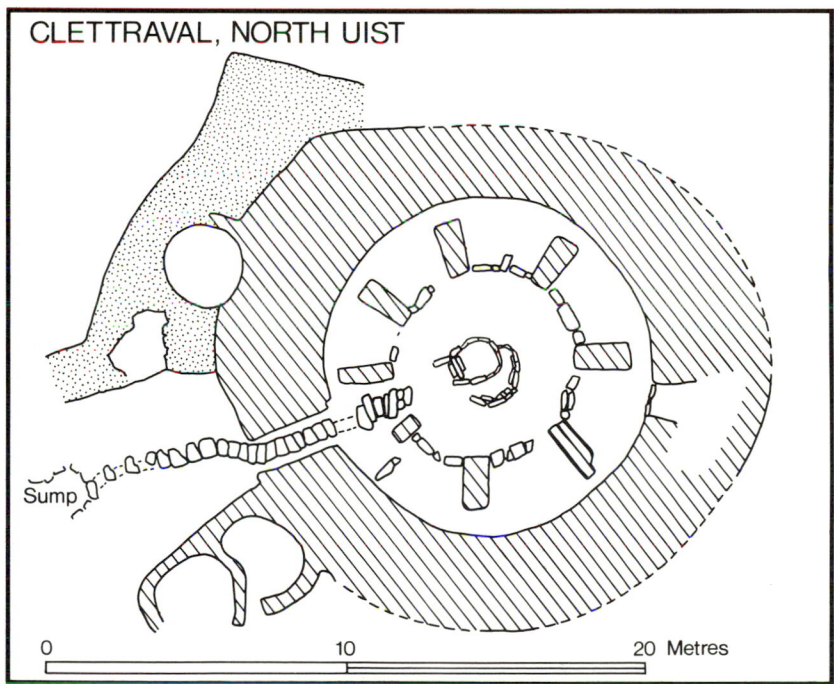

Figure 13.46 Wheelhouses (sources: *Clettraval*, Scott 1948; *Tigh Talamhanta*, Young 1955).

The economy of the north and west was largely self-sufficient: sheep and cattle were kept, deer were hunted, cereals were grown, while the sea provided seals, whales, fish, limpets and sea-birds. Throughout the period, tools tended to be made in local materials like bone, slate and quartz, while utensils were manufactured in pottery, steatite and presumably leather. Apart from a restricted range of bronze and iron tools and ornaments, metal was never common.

It seems, therefore, that for much of the early part of the Iron Age, communities lived peacefully in open settlements but gradually defences multiplied, giving rise to a densely fortified landscape in which almost every homestead was defended. Such a process may well have developed in parallel with the increased emphasis on defence apparent in most other parts of the country. There is no need to introduce the idea of an alien breed of 'castle-builders' to explain a process which in all probability was the result of widespread pressures created by internal social development. Over much of the western area the land was broken into isolated fertile pockets by natural barriers such as mountains and deep inlets. Inevitably, in such conditions, communities tended to remain isolated and settlements failed to nucleate.

Some time in the second century BC or a little earlier a specialized type of fortified house – the broch – perfectly adapted to the requirements of society and its environment became the dominant type. It is hardly surprising that it spread (possibly at the instigation of expert builders) over the whole of the Atlantic province, even into areas like Caithness and Sutherland, where the more gentle undulating land might be thought to be less suitable for such a specialized form of fortification. Brochs continued to dominate the landscape into at least the second century AD, but in the more peaceful conditions which then arose they ceased to be built and were superseded (and sometimes physically replaced) by wheelhouses, which represented the resurgence of the indigenous house type, deeply rooted in the native building traditions of the area.

Throughout the period under discussion the communities of the Atlantic province remained dependent on the sea as a means of communication as well as for food gathering and protection. While the sea linked the far-flung parts of the province together, it seems to have isolated it from the rest of the country.

Summary

From the above survey it will be apparent that the communities living in the north and west of Britain were far more diverse in their life-style than those of the south-east, but the coarseness of the archaeological evidence allows only the more obvious differences to be appreciated. There does, however, appear to be a correspondence between basic economy, settlement pattern and social structure. In those areas which were predominantly pastoral, like Devon and south and west Wales, strongly defended homesteads emerged packed into a densely populated landscape, suggesting a fragmented society based on small kin groups having little overall centralized control. In other areas, like the Tyne–Forth regions and the Welsh borderland, a more mixed economy involving corn production created communities rooted for centuries to their homesteads. Stability led to the formation of larger political groupings and the emergence of coercive power, which is reflected in the construction of large tribal hillforts. In Yorkshire, there was a mixed economy of south-eastern type from the sixth century which developed unaffected by the arrival of new communities or social customs from France. Elsewhere there are hints of well-established transhumant economies which would require seasonal gatherings and an element of nucleation, discernible perhaps in the settlement patterns of north Wales and the Pennines.

Against this regional variation there was change. In Devon climatic deterioration appears to have caused the depopulation of the moors, forcing the people to exploit the lusher pastures of lower-lying areas, breaking down the transhumant way of life and allowing the development of a more stable pastoralism reflected in the numerous defended homesteads.

The true picture must have been one of infinite variety, ever-changing at different rates in different regions. At present we can only dimly comprehend its complexity, but each new discovery will allow some aspect of the finer texture to emerge more clearly into focus.

14
The development of hillforts and oppida

England, Scotland and Wales together can boast about 3,300 structures classed loosely under the heading of hillforts and other defended enclosures (Hogg 1979). Many more than half are small sites of 1.2 ha or less which need be little more than defended homesteads: these include the rounds of the south-west peninsula, the raths of south Wales and the numerous homesteads and small settlements of eastern Scotland. As a broad generalization it may be said that the bulk of the hillforts proper are concentrated in central southern England (Figure 14.1) in a broad band running from the south coast to north Wales. To the west the settlement pattern is dominated by the strongly defended homesteads while to the east single-family farmsteads and undefended hamlets are the norm. Hillforts are essentially a specialized form of settlement: their size, complexity and siting suggests that they represent the communal effort of a large sector of the social group working under the coercive power of the leadership. If this is so then they represent a level of social organization above that of the farmstead and hamlet and may legitimately be considered as a separate phenomenon.

This said, some words of caution are necessary. The word 'hillfort' is a portmanteau term covering a variety of fortifications of differing sizes spanning 800 or 900 years. Given such broad parameters it is only to be expected that there will be, hidden within their structures, evidence of a range of functions varying with time and geographical location. Such variety can only dimly be appreciated because of the paucity of well-excavated data. While a large number of hillforts have suffered some form of excavation, very few have been examined on a large enough scale to enable their developing functions to be properly identified. In consequence, while theories and generalizations abound, hard evidence is difficult to come by.

The vast majority of those hillforts which have been 'excavated' have had their ramparts sectioned and sometimes their gates uncovered, but little else. In consequence there is a fair body of evidence reflecting upon hillfort defence which, with the advent of radiocarbon dating, can be presented in a broad chronological perspective. A summary of the present state of knowledge will be given below. Using this evidence in conjunction with topographical and locational studies it is possible to offer, for some regions, a general assessment of hillfort development throughout the first millennium BC. This can be further enhanced with much rarer evidence derived from the sampling of hillfort interiors to throw some light on questions of function and social organization. Such an approach, focused on central southern Britain, will also be attempted.

The next level of abstraction – an assessment of the changing social and economic functions of hillforts – depends upon evidence derived from very few large-scale excavations. Some general comments will be offered in this chapter but the question will be returned to later in a rather broader context in chapter 20.

Finally we will consider the end of the hillfort phenomenon and the emergence of larger oppida.

The structure of hillfort defences

Between 100 and 200 hillforts have had their defences sectioned exposing the structure of their ramparts. Unfortunately, many sites were dug before the subtleties of internal timber-work were understood and frequently the trenches were too narrow and too few to provide decisive evidence bearing on the presence or absence of internal structure. However, a number of sites have yielded useful results and this evidence can be synthesized into a general pattern of development relevant to most areas of the country.

Earth and timber structures in England and Wales

Palisades

One of the earliest kinds of defensive barrier employed on sites of hillfort size was the palisade of close-set timbers embedded in a continuous foundation trench without ditches or the banking up of spoil behind. This is clearly the same technique as that used on the smaller settlements (discussed above, pp. 215–17), which developed out of a tradition of fencing going back to the beginning of the first millennium or earlier. Wherever excavation has been adequate, palisades, if they occur, can be shown to precede earthwork defences. At the Breiddin, Montgomery, a double palisade bedded in a shallow bank lies at the beginning of a complex development and the evidence of associated finds and radiocarbon determinations suggest that a ninth- or even tenth-century date might not be out of place. At Moel y Gaer, Flints., one or more palisades are thought to pre-date a long development sequence and are probably related to a phase of settlement for which a date in the eighth or seventh century is indicated by radiocarbon determinations. A similar succession of palisades also preceded the construction of a rampart at Dinorben. The palisade at Blewburton Hill, Oxon., antedates by some time the construction of a timber-box rampart, and the same interpretation is possible for the foremost palisade at Bindon Hill, Dorset. At Woodbury Castle, Devon, Skelmore Heads, Lancs., Wilbury, Herts., and Eddisbury, Cheshire, short lengths of early palisades have been found, again in early contexts pre-dating the subsequent developments on these sites.

Although in the examples noted above the later defences generally follow the earlier palisades at the points excavated, there is no positive proof that the lines were coincident throughout. The rather more extensive excavations at Hembury, Devon, have however demonstrated that here the defences of the later fort follow what appears to be an earlier palisade more or less exactly on

Figure 14.1   Distribution of hillforts in southern Britain (source: Ordnance Survey, Map of Southern Britain in the Iron Age).

at least two sides of the circuit (Figure 14.2). Admittedly, the interpretation of the sequence is not straightforward but the outer palisade would appear to be the earliest feature, since at the position occupied by the later east entrance it was refilled at the point where the new roadway crossed it. The inner 'palisade' may, however, be the fronting timbers of the earliest box rampart (Todd 1984). The implication here, then, is that the construction of the earthwork defences followed hard upon the abandonment of the palisade. Both the later entrances were placed close to the sites of the palisade entrances, but the digging of the later ditches has obscured some of the details. Even so, the outer palisades can be seen to curve back inwards and at the east entrance there is some evidence to suggest a timber structure within the incurve not at all unlike the towers of the second period gates at Harehope in Peeblesshire.

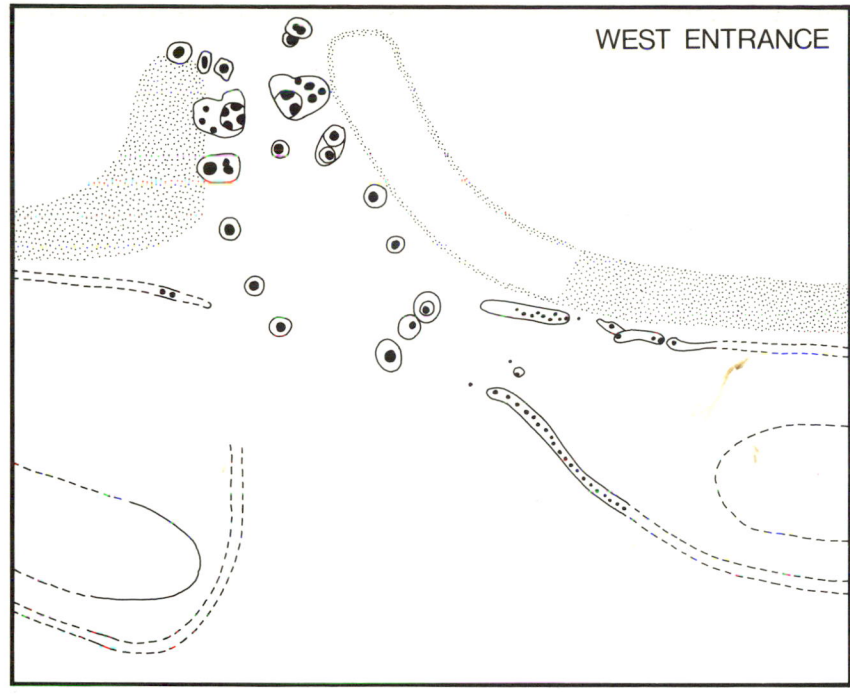

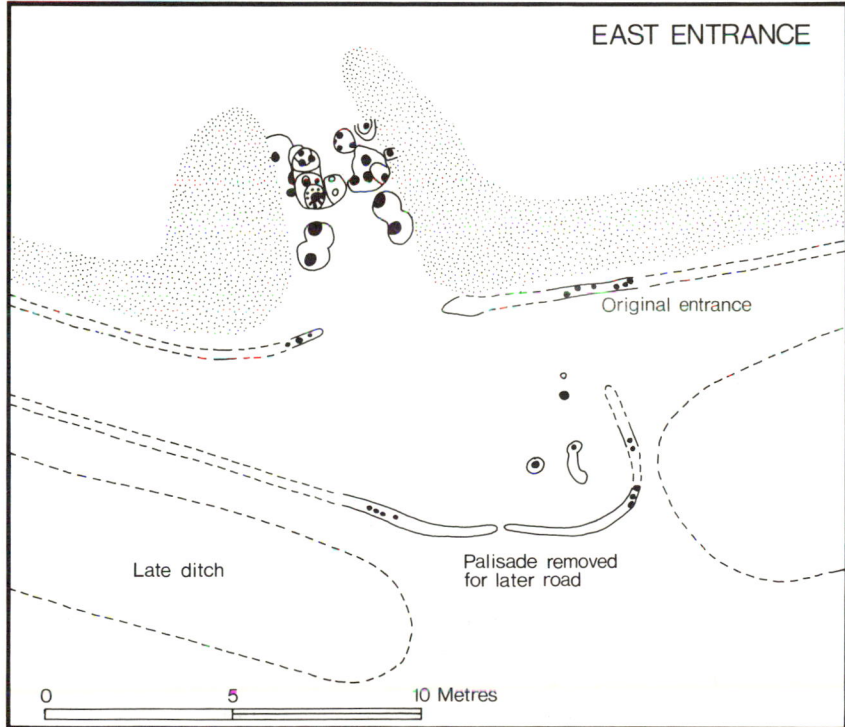

Figure 14.2   The palisaded enclosure at Hembury, Devon (source: Liddell 1935a)

Large palisaded enclosures can therefore be seen generally to precede hillforts, sometimes by a considerable period of time. Few absolute dates can yet be given but it is known from the smaller palisaded homesteads of the north that the method of defence was being practised in the eighth century (pp. 281–5) and the finds from the Breiddin point to an origin here going back a century or two earlier, an indication supported by the evidence from Moel y Gaer.

The Ivinghoe Beacon style of timber strengthening (Figure 14.3)
In parallel with the palisaded enclosures a second type of defence developed known at present from Ffridd Faldwyn, Montgomery, Ivinghoe Beacon, Bucks., Grimthorpe, Yorks., Castercliff, Lancs., and Dinorben, Denbigh. At Grimthorpe rubble and soil from a relatively shallow U-shaped ditch was retained between two rows of timber about 2.4 m apart, the timbers in each row being placed at about the same spacing, thus forming a rough grid which would have allowed cross-bracing to keep the structure rigid. Between the verticals of both the back and front rows one must imagine a close boarding of planks or halved timbers to prevent the rubble fill from spilling out. Although dating evidence is by no means decisive, it is now becoming clear that simple box ramparts probably pre-date the conventional beginning of the Iron Age. At Rams Hill, Berks., a radiocarbon series suggests that this type of construction should be dated to the twelfth century BC. The box ramparts at both Ffridd Faldwyn and Dinorben lie at the beginning of long development sequences: at Dinorben a series of radiocarbon dates from the most recent excavation (Guilbert 1979a, 1980) range from 500 ± 60 bc to 440 ± 45 bc suggesting a construction date in the sixth century. Grimthorpe provided two early dates for bone samples recovered from the partially silted ditch: 690 ± 130 bc and 970 ± 130 bc. The dates from Ivinghoe Beacon span the eighth to fifth centuries but the metalwork from the fort lies within the eighth to seventh centuries. Finally the box rampart from Castercliff produced radiocarbon dates suggestive of a seventh- or sixth-century construction. Taking this evidence together, there is a degree of consistency about the overall pattern, suggesting initial occupation in the twelfth to sixth centuries. Thus the earliest hillforts in Britain must have developed in parallel with those of the European Urnfield cultures. Strictly, the box rampart could be thought of as a double palisade, of the type well represented in northern Britain (pp. 281–2), filled with earth and rubble. The nature of this relationship both structurally and chronologically remains to be further examined.

The Hollingbury Camp style of timber strengthening (Figure 14.3)
A simple development following the rubble-filled timber wall of Ivinghoe Beacon type was the addition of a sloping rampart behind the inner face of the inner row of timbers. This would have provided two additional advantages: ease of access at all points and an added strength and rigidity. While at Hollingbury Camp, Sussex, the bank was slight – barely 2.7 m wide – backing a timber wall of the same width, in the first phase of Danebury, Hants., the 2.1 m wide timbering was backed by a far more substantial structure almost 9 m wide. At Maiden Castle, Dorset, the timber structure of period I was 3.6 m wide, with a bank of equivalent width behind, standing to a maximum height of 1.4 m, while at South Cadbury, Somerset, the earliest rampart measured in total width 4.4 m, the distance between the two faces of the timber structure being only 2.2 m. At Blewburton, Oxon., the total width of the rampart was 6.4 m, the distance between the two timber rows being 4.0 m. Finally at Winklebury, Hants., the overall width of the rampart was about 3 m while the two timber faces were only 2 m apart. Clearly, there were considerable variations in proportion.

TIMBER FACED RAMPARTS

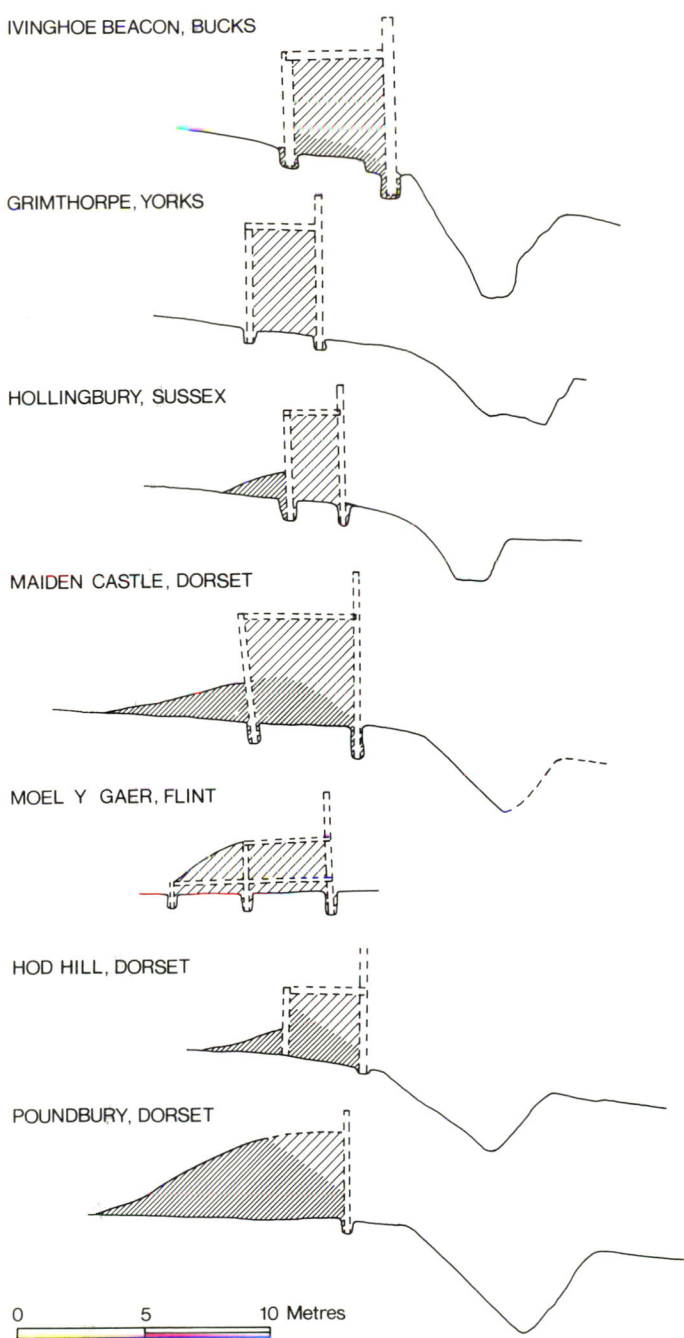

Figure 14.3 Comparative sections of box ramparts and their derivatives (sources: *Ivinghoe Beacon*, Cotton and Frere 1968; *Grimthorpe*, Stead 1968; *Hollingbury Camp*, E.C. Curwen 1932; *Maiden Castle*, Wheeler 1943; *Moel y Gaer*, Guilbert 1975a; *Hod Hill*, Richmond 1968; *Poundbury*, Richardson 1940).

THE STRUCTURAL DEVELOPMENT
OF WANDLEBURY, CAMBRIDGESHIRE

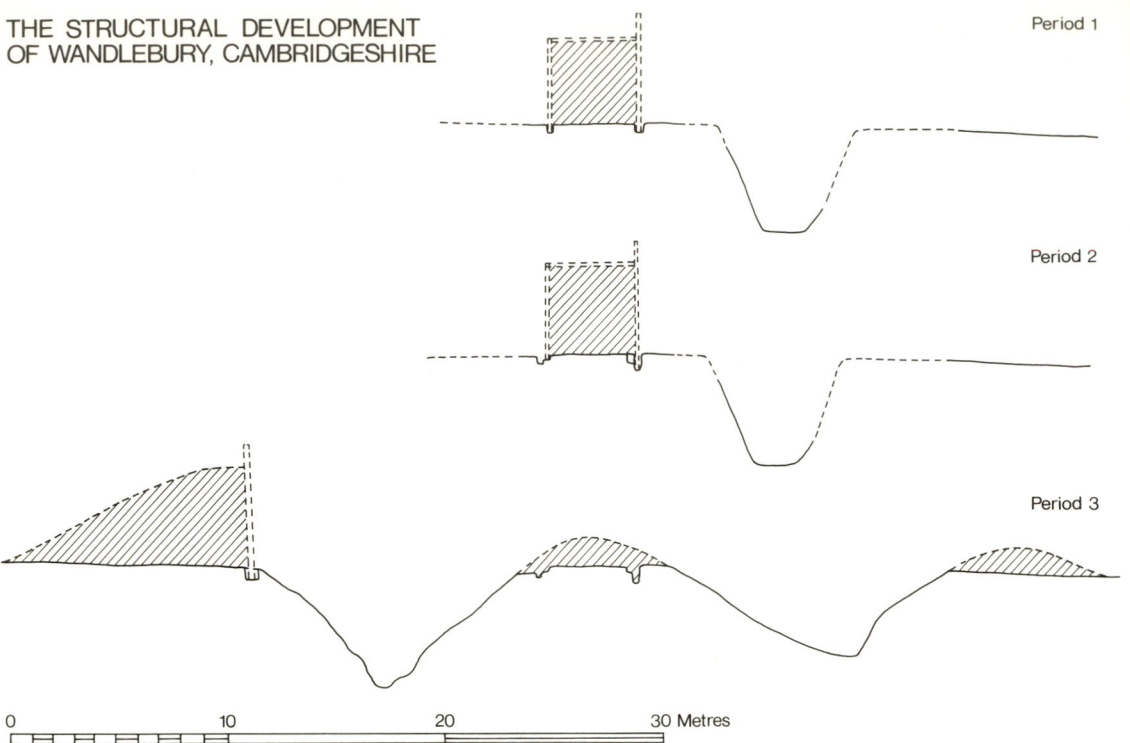

Period 1

Period 2

Period 3

0   10   20   30 Metres

Figure 14.4   The development of the defences at Wandlebury, Cambs. (source: Hartley 1957).

Wandlebury, Cambs., is a particularly important example demonstrating a sequence of development (Figure 14.4). In the first period a box-type rampart was constructed with timber faces 4.0 m apart, the front timbers being placed at 0.76 m intervals, and those of the bank face even closer. Whether or not a backing ramp was built will never be known, since a later ditch would have dug it away. In the second phase the rampart was rebuilt 4.3 m wide, with the timbers in both rows set at 2.7 m centres, again possibly with a backing rampart. In the third major phase a totally new rampart was thrown up *behind* the original work, and was fronted by a ditch. This third period work was constructed in a style to be described below as the Poundbury style. Thus, what was presumably a Hollingbury type of rampart had an extended use at Wandlebury. Its replacement is, however, a reminder that timber had a relatively short life and major rebuilding would have had to be carried out perhaps as often as every decade or two if the defences were to be kept in good order.

The dating of this type of construction technique is tolerably well known. At Hollingbury Camp pottery of the sixth to fifth centuries has been found within the fort, but not in direct relationship to the rampart, while at most of the other sites the associated material lies consistently within the sixth to third-century range.

The Moel y Gaer style of timber strengthening (Figure 14.3)
Area stripping of a length of the rampart of Moel y Gaer has produced startling results. Here the

earliest rampart was faced with upright timbers 0.6–0.9 m apart, the gaps between being infilled with dry-stone walling, usually incorporating large orthostats. The inner row of timbers, which the excavator considers was merely a curb and an anchor for horizontal lacing timbers, was 6 m from the outer row, but a more widely spaced middle row was found, probably representing the main vertical supports to which the front revetting was tied. The rampart was sufficiently well preserved to suggest that it stood originally to a height of 1.7 m above which there would probably have been a breastwork. Careful excavation of the rampart body showed that it had originally been divided, front to back, probably by hurdles, to create a series of compartments which were filled with different tips of rubble. A cellular structure of this kind would have been particularly valuable in containing the rampart when repairs to the front face became necessary.

The Moel y Gaer style of rampart construction differs from the typical Hollingbury style in that the main anchor timbers for the front face were widely spaced and the tail of the rampart was revetted with close spaced verticals which may also have served to give a rigidity to the timber structure. Had a substantial length of rampart not been excavated, it is unlikely that the middle row of structural timbers would have been found. With this in mind it is possible that the rampart of Buckland Rings, Hants., should be placed in this category. Here limited excavation suggested two rows of timbers 5.8 m apart set within an earthwork of 9 m width overall. The distance between the timber rows is excessive for simple cross-bracing, but if a middle row of more widely spaced timbers had occurred, as at Moel y Gaer, the problem would not have existed. In this context, Breedon-on-the-Hill, Leics., should also be considered. In the first phase, the fronting fence was of closely spaced timbers, with the tail of the rampart 7.6 m away revetted by individually bedded posts. The trenches were too narrow to have been sure to have picked up a middle row of widely spaced timbers, if this had existed, and no cross-bracing was noted, but superficial similarities to Moel y Gaer suggest that Breedon-on-the-Hill may well have been of the same type. Caesar's Camp (Wimbledon), Surrey, poses a similar problem. Two narrow sections observed under rescue conditions brought to light evidence of front and rear timbers 8.2 m apart, but no middle row was noted. Once more the distance apart is probably too great for simple cross-bracing and a more complex structure of Moel y Gaer type might be anticipated.

The construction of the Moel y Gaer rampart post-dates two samples dated by radiocarbon to 580 ± 90 bc and 620 ± 70 bc. This would be consistent with a construction date in the sixth century or later.

The Hod Hill type of timber strengthening (Figure 14.3)
The first phase of the defences of Hod Hill, Dorset, possessed an internal structure at present unique. A rampart some 9.7 m wide was fronted by a continuous palisade trench in which were placed vertical timbers, no doubt backed by horizontal timber cladding. Within the body of the mound was found a second row of individual timbers, the bases of which did not penetrate the natural subsoil; to these the front fence would presumably have been anchored. The defences differ from the more normal Hollingbury Camp type in that the inner timbers were supported only by the spoil of the rampart itself. In an excavation less skilfully observed, they may well have passed unnoticed.

It is tempting to see the constructors of Hod Hill adapting time-honoured building methods in the realization that the inner timbers were needed only to anchor the fronting fence, post-holes specially cut into the bedrock being no longer required. Strictly the Hod Hill structure is only a variant of the Moel y Gaer style.

The Poundbury type of timber strengthening (Figure 14.3)

The logical development following the breakthrough at Hod Hill was to further modify the nature of the inner timbering. At Poundbury, Dorset, controlled excavations demonstrated a 9 m wide rampart fronted by a palisade of closely spaced timbers 1 m apart. No trace of internal timbering, either vertical or horizontal, was seen. It may, of course, be that the trenches were so sited as to miss inner verticals, but this is unlikely. A more reasonable explanation is that the front face was attached only to horizontal beams embedded within the body of the rampart: these would have been extremely difficult to trace and would have appeared only under ideal conditions. It is inconceivable that the fence could have withstood the thrust without some such back-pinning. As with the Hod Hill type of construction, it could be that the Poundbury type was simply a variant of the Moel y Gaer style.

The third phase of Wandlebury, Cambs., which demonstrably replaces the rampart of Hollingbury type, was of a similar construction. The same technique appears to have been adopted at Yarnbury, Wilts., Titterstone Clee, Salop, and Cissbury, Sussex.

The dating of the Poundbury technique is difficult to ascertain with precision: at Wandlebury it is later than the Hollingbury style and associated with pottery which could centre upon the fifth to fourth centuries. The evidence from the other sites, such as it is, does not conflict with this broad generalization.

The glacis style

In the constructional variations described, the overriding consideration was to provide a vertical wall of timber confronting the outside world, usually protected by a ditch dug some metres in front of it. Yet, however the backing structure was modified, the basic flaws in design remained: the timber would soon rot and would have to be replaced (a difficult task in such circumstances); it could easily be fired by an enemy; and the gradually crumbling lip of the ditch would eventually loosen the fronting timbers.

All these problems were overcome by a new method which appears to have been widely adopted in the south and east some time in the fourth century or soon after. Ditches were dug deeper and the rampart face was sheered back at an angle following the ditch side, thus creating a continuous slope from the bottom of the ditch to the crest of the rampart at an angle of 30–45°. At Hod Hill, Dorset, the overall distance from top to bottom was 17.4 m and at Danebury, Hants. (Figure 14.5), 16.1 m, while at Maiden Castle, Dorset, it reached 25.2 m. Covered with a loose scree and capped by a breastwork of timber or flint, the approach would have been daunting to the attacker. The only maintenance problem was to keep the ditch clear of silt. This would have been undertaken periodically, the scree being thrown out on the downhill side creating a spoil bank sometimes referred to as a counterscarp. In one section at Danebury, it was possible to trace evidence of eleven different periods of addition to the counterscarp bank each representing a periodic clearing-out operation.

Glacis style defences can be shown to replace timber structures at a number of sites from the Dorset forts of Poundbury, Maiden Castle and Hod Hill and the Somerset site of South Cadbury to as far north as Breedon-on-the-Hill in Leicestershire, and it will be shown below (p. 324) that some early stone-built forts were also remodelled in this way. Dating evidence, where it survives, shows that glacis defences were in use in the south during the time when saucepan style pots were being manufactured, centring therefore on the Middle Iron Age (fourth to second centuries); but at Croft Ambrey, Herefordshire and Midsummer Hill, Worcestershire, in the Welsh borderland, dump-constructed ramparts were constructed at the beginning of the occupation sequence,

Figure 14.5 The defensive ditch at Danebury (photo: David Leigh. Danebury Trust).

which probably started in the fifth or even the sixth century. There is evidence from the south that here too dump ramparts without revetting were established by the sixth century. Such a rampart was found at Balksbury, Hants., in an eighth- to sixth-century context, at Quarley Hill, Hants., dating to the fifth to fourth centuries and at St Catharine's Hill, Hants., a little later. On present evidence, therefore, it is simpler to assume that the technique of defending a site with a bank of spoil and a ditch was long established, dating back into the second millennium, and that after a brief period when timber- and stone-faced ramparts predominated, the older technique came back once more into common use and persisted in some areas until the Roman Conquest.

At Maiden Castle six subsequent extensions and modifications all adopted the basic glacis style, and at Hod Hill there were three phases. Evidently the glacis was regarded as the ultimate in defensive tactics until the wide flat-bottomed ditches of Fecamp style were introduced in the first century AD (p. 366).

Multivallation

Superficial surface examination of the British hillforts shows that many of them were provided with more than one rampart and ditch; such forts are listed on the Ordnance Survey *Map of Southern Britain in the Iron Age* as multivallate. The term is confusing, however, for it covers several different situations. The multiple-enclosure forts of the south-west, while strictly multivallate, were so because extra lines of banks and ditches were required to enclose space for livestock. Danebury, Hants., is termed multivallate for much the same reason. Other forts like Wandlebury, Cambs., Bredon Hill, Glos., the Caburn, Sussex, and Croft Ambrey, Heref., give the appearance of multivallation because of their growth or shrinkage and not necessarily from a general policy of extending the line of fire. Thus, surface assessment alone can seldom be decisive. Nevertheless, deliberate multivallation for the purpose of defence can be demonstrated on sites like Maiden Castle, Dorset, beginning in phase III and reaching its ultimate development in phase IV (Figure 14.6). At Hod Hill, Dorset, it is possible to trace the development of multivallation, starting in stage IIa (the first glacis remodelling) with the construction of a palisade in front of the ditch. Subsequently a second ditch was begun but not finished, the spoil being thrown up over the line of the palisade, which was now isolated between the two ditches. Whether or not the palisade belongs to stage IIa, the fact remains that multivallation came late in the development of the fort and, as the excavator has suggested, may have been initiated and subsequently abandoned at the time of the Roman advance in AD 43.

A somewhat similar situation occurred at Buckland Rings, Hants., where, in spite of large-scale levelling, it was possible to trace a fence outside the line of the inner ditch and in front of an outer ditch. No evidence of a rampart behind or sealing the fence-posts survived. At what stage the outer features were constructed it is impossible to say, but in all probability they were added to the original construction, and it is possible that the Buckland Rings sequence is a direct parallel to Hod Hill. The occurrence, at Moel y Gaer, of a palisade of timbers set in a shallow bank outside the ditch, which may be contemporary with the rampart, is a reminder that outer palisades may well prove to be more widespread than has hitherto been appreciated.

Generally it may be assumed that multivallation was a late development in most areas, sometimes – as at Hod Hill – not appearing until the first century AD but certainly at least a century earlier at Maiden Castle. At Rainsborough Camp, Northants., it has been argued that the second rampart and ditch date to as early as the fifth century, but the evidence can be variously interpreted and is best regarded as unproven.

In all probability, development varied in different areas of the country and in different

Figure 14.6 Maiden Castle, Dorset (photo: Major G.W. Allen. Copyright, Ashmolean Museum, Oxford).

geographical situations. Two or three banks and ditches thrown across a neck of land to protect a promontory do not necessarily have to be related to the same time or philosophy of warfare as the multiple girding of Maiden Castle. Thus, while most true multivallation was late, one may expect considerable variation between one part of the country and another. One final point is clear: there is now no need to suggest that intrusive ideas were the cause – local inventiveness is quite sufficient.

Chevaux-de-Frise

A few forts in Wales and northern Britain were provided with an additional form of defence commonly known as *chevaux-de-frise*, a term used to describe zones of obstacles, usually stones, set upright in the ground to make access to the fort by men and horses more difficult. The stones vary in height, but average 0.60–1.0 m and were sited either in discrete areas, where the approach was easiest, or in continuous zones, in front of the defences. In all, only five examples of *chevaux-de-frise* have been identified in Scotland and three in Wales, but it is possible, as Harbison has pointed out (1971), that many more may have existed in wood. No firm dating evidence exists, but the example at Kaimes Hill, Midlothian, is unlikely to be far removed in date from the date of the second rampart, for which there is a radiocarbon assessment in the fifth or fourth century.

Stone and stone and timber defences in England and Wales (Figures 14.7 and 14.8)

Although palisaded structures were constructed in areas where good building stone occurs naturally, later developments in these regions usually adopted the technique of dry-stone walling, with or without internal timber binding. Unfortunately, horizontal timbers are far less easy to trace archaeologically than verticals, and it is therefore a distinct possibility that a higher proportion of the stone-faced ramparts were timber-laced than is at present apparent. Nevertheless, for the purpose of this discussion a distinction will be made between those where no timbering was observed and those known to have been timber-laced.

One of the earliest of the simple forts possessing a rubble rampart encased at the front and back with dry-stone walling is Chalbury, Dorset (Figure 14.7), where the total thickness of the rampart was 6 m. Since associated pottery leaves little doubt that the defences belong to the sixth to fifth centuries, Chalbury is presumably the stone-built equivalent of the timber box rampart of Maiden Castle I, only 5 km away. An earlier date in the sixth century can now be proposed for the first fort at Rainsborough Camp, Northants. (Figure 14.7), where the stone-faced rampart, 5.2 m wide at the base, was reduced in width by two steps at the back. The excavator's suggestion that a similar stepping was adopted at the front carries less conviction. The thickness of the ramparts between the wall faces varies from fort to fort but is usually between 5.9 and 7.4 m. The enclosure at Bathampton Down, Somerset, was however protected by a wall only 2.9 m wide, divided by a 3.6 m berm from a wide flat-bottomed ditch. At Mam Tor, Derbyshire the wall faces were 3.6 m apart, while at Worlebury, Somerset (Figure 14.7), the overall thickness of the main stone wall was 11.5 m; but this was apparently created by several additions or rebuildings at the back and front of a wall of normal width.

At several sites in the south, stone-structured ramparts were replaced by glacis style defences. This is particularly well demonstrated at Llanmelin, Mon., and at Rainsborough Camp; in both cases, excavation has shown that the major remodelling in glacis style came late in the occupation of the site. One apparent exception to the rule is the much-quoted Bredon Hill, Glos.; here the usual interpretation is that the inner rampart, built in a dump-constructed or glacis style, was followed by the outer rampart, stone-faced and fronted by a berm and U-shaped ditch. There are difficulties with this interpretation, not the least being that the two entrances through the outer rampart were almost blocked by the inner defences. If, however, the supposed constructional sequence is reversed, this problem would be overcome and the development of the rampart styles – first stone-faced then glacis – would be in accordance with the general pattern elsewhere, Bredon Hill being no longer the exception. The fact that the outer rampart and ditch were sited opposite the entrance in the inner rampart might be thought to provide further support for the reinterpretation.

Outside the south and east of Britain, the stone facing of the rampart seems to have survived to the time of the Roman invasion. In north-west Wales, Tre'r Ceiri, Garn Boduan, Carn Fadrun and Conway Mountain in Caernarvonshire all maintained their stone wall defences until the last, but the glacis style was adopted at some of the Welsh borderland sites like the Wrekin, Salop, and Croft Ambrey, Heref., and even penetrated as far north as Dinorben, Denbigh.

A combination of timbering and stone facing has been recorded on several southern British sites close to stone outcrops. In the outworks of the phase II east entrance at Maiden Castle, Dorset, dry-stone facing was employed instead of split timber or planks as a revetting material between vertical timbers erected in the general tradition of the timber box rampart of the first period; while at South Cadbury, Somerset, exactly the same technique was employed. It should

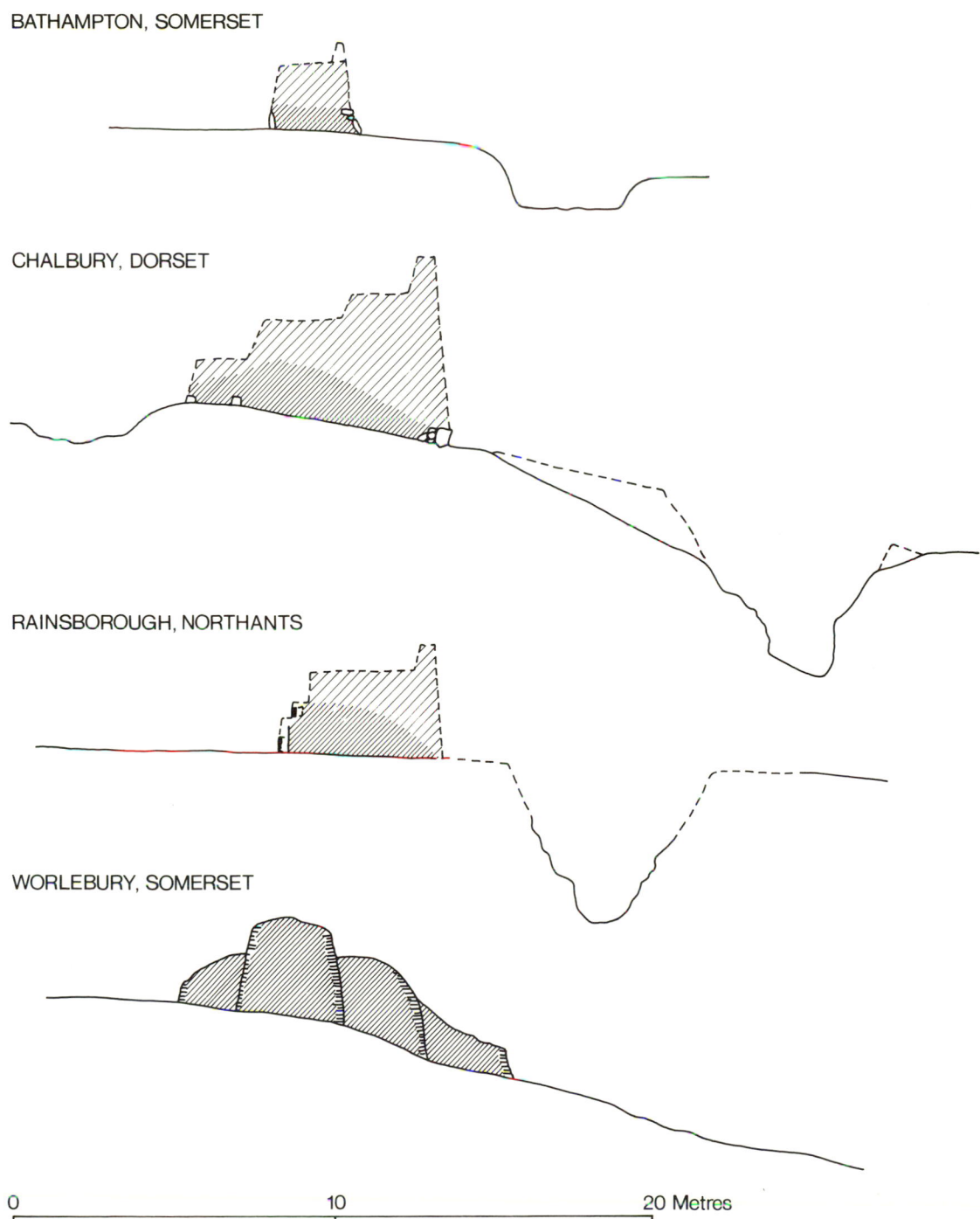

BATHAMPTON, SOMERSET

CHALBURY, DORSET

RAINSBOROUGH, NORTHANTS

WORLEBURY, SOMERSET

0   10   20 Metres

Figure 14.7 Stone-faced ramparts (sources: *Bathampton*, Wainwright 1967b; *Chalbury*, Whitley 1943; *Rainsborough*, Avery, Sutton and Banks 1967; *Worlebury*, Dymond 1902).

CASTLE HILL
ALMONDBURY, YORKSHIRE

CASTLE LAW
ABERNETHY, PERTHSHIRE

MAIDEN CASTLE
BICKERTON, CHESHIRE

CASTLE DITCH
EDDISBURY, CHESHIRE

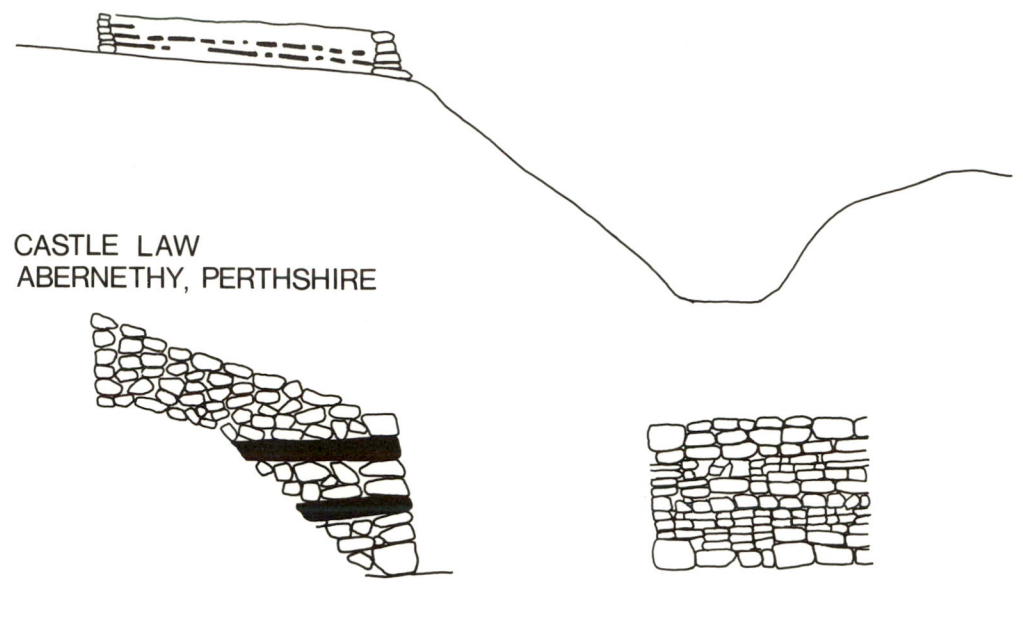

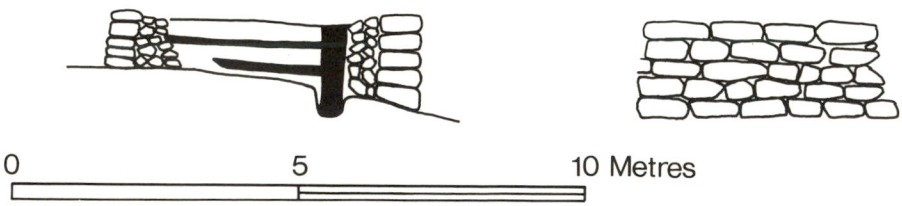

0   5   10 Metres

Figure 14.8 Sections and elevations of stone- and timber-laced ramparts (sources: Varley 1936, 1950b).

be emphasized that in both cases stone walling was being used only as a filling material in place of timber and not as an integral part of the rigid structure. This is essentially a local variation of the timber box-constructed rampart, in areas where stone was readily available.

Further west and north, in an arc spreading from the Cotswolds through the Welsh borderland and Cheshire into Yorkshire, a series of partially excavated forts provides clear evidence of the use of timber-and stone-structured ramparts. Some of the forts like Castle Ditch (Eddisbury), Cheshire (Figure 14.8), Dinorben, Moel y Gaer, Flints., and Ffridd Faldwyn, Montgomery, began as simple palisaded enclosures which were replaced by box-constructed timber ramparts employing vertical and horizontal timbering. Between the front verticals infilling was usually by dry-stone walling in the manner of South Cadbury and Maiden Castle. The same technique was used in the first and second phases of the rampart at Castle Hill (Almondbury), Yorkshire (Figure 14.8). All, except for Dinorben, were later rebuilt using a rubble rampart laced with horizontal timbers which in the case of Castle Ditches, Ffridd Faldwyn and Castle Hill was fronted, both inside and out, by dry-stone walling unbroken by timber verticals: the second phase of the rampart at Moel y Gaer does not however appear to have been stone-faced. The rebuilding of the Moel y Gaer rampart in this style post-dates a radiocarbon assessment of 260 ± 70 bc.

Some of the forts in the west and north, such as Leckhampton Hill and Crickley Hill in Gloucestershire, Maiden Castle (Bickerton) in Cheshire (Figure 14.8), and Corley Camp in Warwickshire, began with horizontally timber-laced ramparts fronted by continuous dry-stone facings and many underwent subsequent modification.

The sequence at Crickley Hill, Glos., is particularly interesting. In the first defensive phase (the excavator's period 2) the rampart appears to have been constructed in a composite form, with two rows of vertical timbers 2.1 m apart, giving rigidity to a rubble core which was laced with horizontal timbers and faced back and front with dry-stone walling, the timber ends projecting into the outer stone face. The overall width between the stone facing was 5.8 m. It is very tempting to interpret Crickley as a transitional type representing a stage between box-structured ramparts and timber-laced types. In theory all the builders have done here is to move the stone infilling of a conventional box-structured rampart outwards away from the vertical timbers, perhaps to give more protection to the otherwise exposed woodwork. It would soon have been realized that the internal verticals were of little significance to the rigidity of the structure and could in future be omitted. This theory, while attractive, is difficult to substantiate. In a subsequent phase of rebuilding at Crickley (period 3b), when the wall was in part thickened and a hornwork constructed in front of the gate, only horizontal timbering appears to have been used.

From the above description, it will be seen that the use of stone and timber followed a series of complex patterns which are only now being gradually sorted out. Tentatively, however, we may define a phase in which stone was used as an infilling material in box-constructed ramparts of Ivinghoe Beacon and Hollingbury Camp type, spanning the period from the seventh to the fourth century. In the west and north of England, the technique of lacing the ramparts with horizontal timbers and facing them back and front with stone walls soon emerged locally, probably as a development from the earlier style. The dating evidence, such as it is, shows that the technique was being practised from the sixth to the third centuries. Eventually the use of horizontal timbers was abandoned and ramparts were built with stone facings only, in a simple style which probably originated earlier and continued in use in some parts throughout the Iron Age. Finally, in southern England and occasionally elsewhere, stone-constructed ramparts were eventually replaced by the glacis style. At present this generalized scheme fits all available evidence but regional and chronological differences may be expected to complicate the issue.

The stone and timber forts of Scotland

The Scottish hillfort development is in some respects different from that of the rest of Britain. Like the south, some forts began as palisaded enclosures, but after these had gone out of use, vertical timbering is virtually unknown again except in the gate at Cullykhan, where a date in the fifth century is indicated by a radiocarbon assessment. In the north the characteristic rampart structure consists of a rubble-and-earth core faced inside and out with dry-stone walling, the whole bonded by rows of horizontal timbers which project through the outer, and sometimes the inner, wall-face. At Abernethy, Perth (Figure 14.8), two rows of rectangular beam-holes 0.24–0.30 m square appeared through the outer wall-facing of the innermost rampart: the lower row was 0.60–0.90 m above the ground, the second row 0.60 m above the first. The outer rampart proved to be of the same construction, but in neither the inner nor the outer rampart did the timbers penetrate the inner wall-facing. It is impossible to say how extensive the use of longitudinal timbering was, since only at Abernethy are the timbers recorded. Ditches do not seem to have been an integral part of this kind of defensive scheme.

Half a dozen or so forts have produced direct evidence of timber-lacing but more than sixty of the Scottish sites belong to what is called the vitrified class, all examples showing signs of widespread burning of the timber-lacing causing the core material of the rampart to become discoloured and to fuse. The exact nature of the timber structure of most of these forts has not been recorded, but at Finavon and Monifieth in Angus, and Castle Law (Forgondenny), Perth – all forts timber-laced in the Abernethy style – vitrified material was found in the rampart cores. In all probability, therefore, we are dealing with a single class of horizontally timber-laced ramparts, some of which were fired. Whether the firing was deliberately carried out by the builders to consolidate the rampart, or by attackers, is a matter of some debate (summarized in Cotton 1955, 94–101, and more recently by MacKie 1976), but the potentially destructive nature of a fire, the unevenness of the firing within individual sites, and the relatively slight firing of many of them would suggest accident or attack rather than design. These vitrified forts should be compared with the burnt timber-laced ramparts of the west, e.g. Dinorben, Denbigh., Crickley Hill and Leckhampton Hill, Glos., and Bower Walls Camp, Somerset, where the limestone rubble cores have been turned to lime by the intensive heat.

There has been much discussion as to the date and origin of the Scottish forts (Cotton 1955) but most of it is now rendered obsolete by the production of a group of radiocarbon dates (MacKie 1969a). For charred beams or planks from behind the wall at Finavon an estimate of 590 ± 90 bc was obtained, with supporting dates of 410 ± 80 bc and 320 ± 90 bc for subsequent levels. At the vitrified fort of Dun Lagaidh, Wester Ross, a carbonized branch under the fort wall gave an estimate of 490 ± 90 bc but at Craigmarloch Wood in Renfrewshire a date of 35 ± 40 bc was obtained apparently for a timber-laced rampart which replaced a palisaded enclosure. The sample does not, however, seem to have been securely linked to the construction period and charcoal from beneath the wall provided a date of 590 ± 40 bc. Finally at Craig Phadrig, Inverness, dates of 330 ± 100 bc, 270 ± 100 bc, 180 ± 110 bc were obtained for charcoal associated with the vitrified rampart of the fort. Together the evidence is impressive: there can now be little doubt that many of the forts must originate in the seventh or even the eighth century, while the discovery of La Tène artefacts from some of the excavated examples, together with the Craig Phadrig dates, shows that occupation continued for several centuries during which time new forts were being built.

The Abernethy style forts originate, therefore, at the time when contacts between Scotland and the Hallstatt cultures of Europe were at their height. Similarities have been noted (S. Piggott 1966, 7) between the Scottish style of timber-lacing and the method employed on the Swiss site of Wittnauer Horn in both its Hallstatt B3 (Late Urnfield) and its Hallstatt C/D phases, and at Montlingerberg, another Late Urnfield fort in Switzerland. It is indeed tempting to suggest that the concept of using only horizontal timbers together with dry-stone walling was introduced into northern Britain from Continental Europe at the time of these maximum cultural contacts, but positive evidence is lacking.

Not all the Scottish forts were provided with timber-laced ramparts. Several of the fortified enclosures examined in the Cheviots, including Hownam Rings, Hayhope Knowe and Bonchester Hill in Roxburghshire, were enclosed by simple stone-faced ramparts without internal timbering. At Kaimes Hill, Midlothian, the excavations have demonstrated the replacement of a timber-laced rampart with a simple stone-faced structure; twigs from its core were radiocarbon dated to *c.* 298 ± 90 bc, thus suggesting a fourth-century date for the change in style at this site.

Summary of hillfort defences

Controlled excavation, together with a substantial series of radiocarbon dates, is beginning to provide a sequence for the development of defensive structures which is consistent over the whole country. The tradition of building defensive palisades appeared in most parts of Britain by the ninth century and continued to be employed probably into the seventh. In the south of Britain, including Wales, the use of palisades runs parallel with the construction of box-framed earth and timber ramparts of Ivinghoe type, which developed a backing rampart (Hollingbury and Moel y Gaer styles) by or soon after the sixth century. At present these types, incorporating vertical timbers, are unknown in the north. The seventh century saw the appearance in Scotland of the timber-laced rampart with external stone faces, a style of construction which was also adopted in western Britain as far south as the Bristol Avon. Which area, if any, can claim priority in the use of timber-lacing is uncertain. On one hand, it could be argued that the technique was introduced into Scotland from abroad, spreading to the south later, but an equally plausible explanation is that it was a British invention originating somewhere in the Cotswold–Welsh border area out of the box rampart idea. At present this latter hypothesis seems the more reasonable but the matter will only be solved when more radiocarbon dates become available.

By the fourth century timber-lacing had ceased to be practised, and over most of the stone-producing areas of northern and western Britain, ramparts were constructed simply of stone-faced rubble. In the south, however, the vertical revetment of ramparts with close-spaced timbers persisted (Hod Hill and Poundbury types) probably throughout the fifth and even into the fourth century. During the fourth or third century old-established methods of building ramparts from dumped earth with a sloping face became widespread over much of the south and parts of the south-west. Eventually, by the first century AD, a new type of flat-bottomed ditch (Fécamp type) was introduced into the south-east, possibly from northern Gaul.

Entrances

Hillforts were provided with one or, less usually, two entrances which were necessarily the weak links of the defensive circuit. It is hardly surprising, therefore, that much care and attention were lavished on these points, the entrances frequently being remodelled and rebuilt on more occasions than the main lines of the defences. A substantial number of entrances have been excavated on a reasonable scale. These, together with an examination of the earthworks of unexcavated examples, allow some general inferences to be drawn, and collated sequences can now be built up for the chalk downs of the south and the Welsh borderland.

In the south two sites, Torberry in Sussex and Danebury in Hampshire, offer continuous sequences spanning the period from the sixth to the first century BC. These can be used in conjunction with the results from other excavations to produce a consistent picture of entrance development relevant for most of the south-east of the country.

One of the earliest known gates, that belonging to the hillfort of Ivinghoe Beacon, Bucks., is a relatively simple structure consisting of a short timber-lined passageway 3.4 m long and of equivalent width, set back slightly at the end of a courtyard formed by turning the ends of the ditch inwards (Figure 14.9). The exact arrangement is not altogether clear but in all probability the rampart abutted on the timbers flanking the passage, although the possibility of additional side passages cannot be ruled out. An even simpler timber structure was provided at the east gate of Hollingbury Camp, Sussex (Figure 14.9). Two vertical timbers 3.7 m apart were set at the inner side of a gap in the box-constructed rampart; on them the gates would have been hung. This arrangement is exactly comparable to the first gate of Danebury, which probably dates to the sixth century (Figure 14.9).

The second phase at Danebury represents the development of a more complex gate (Figure 14.10), embodying the idea of the dual-portal carriageway, which was maintained in use throughout several phases of rebuilding. Gates of almost exactly similar plan were in use in the first phases of St Catharine's Hill, Hants., and at the Trundle, Sussex. A simpler form of the same basic concept, but with only a single passageway, was found in the first period at Torberry in the rampart which cut off the neck of the promontory defining the original defended area. The entrance, which lay on the north side of the ridge below the crest, consisted of a simple gap in the rampart, the ends being revetted with a continuous palisade of posts, with the large post-holes for the gate set a little in front, about 1.5 m apart. The ditch-ends were askew to each other so that the approach would have to be oblique. From the gate-posts shallow palisade trenches ran forward to the ditch-ends. This same type of arrangement can be traced, with modifications, at Quarley Hill, Hants., and at Yarnbury, Wilts. The main feature of both the dual- and single-portal entrances is that the gates themselves were set halfway along the entrance passage on line with the rest of the ramparts. Dating is fairly consistent: on the basis of sequence and associated pottery they should fall within the fifth century, possibly lasting into the fourth.

In the second period at Torberry the earthwork was carried around the summit of the hill, enclosing about 2.2 ha. The first entrance continued to be used at this time but in the third period the cross-defence and entrance were abandoned and partly dismantled while the fort was extended eastwards, continuing the contour works of the second period along the sides of the ridge and enclosing a further 1.2 ha. The entrance through the new circuit lay on the axis of the ridge. In its original form the ditch-ends were placed askew to each other to form an oblique approach, but other details were obscured except for a row of posts which would have revetted one of the rampart-ends, creating a passageway 15–18 m long. The exact siting of the gate at this

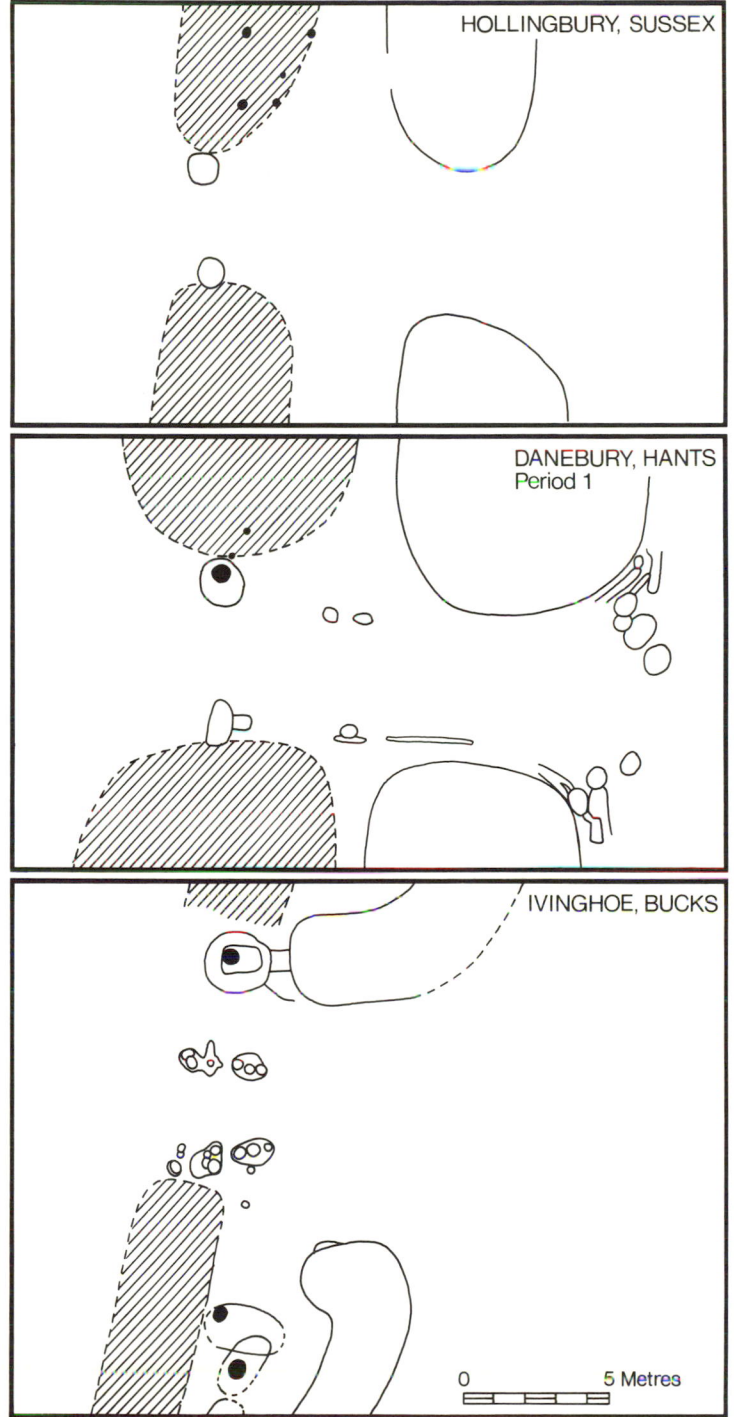

Figure 14.9 Single-portal entrances (sources: *Hollingbury Camp*, E.C. Curwen 1932; *Danebury*, Cunliffe 1972a; *Ivinghoe Beacon*, Cotton and Frere 1968).

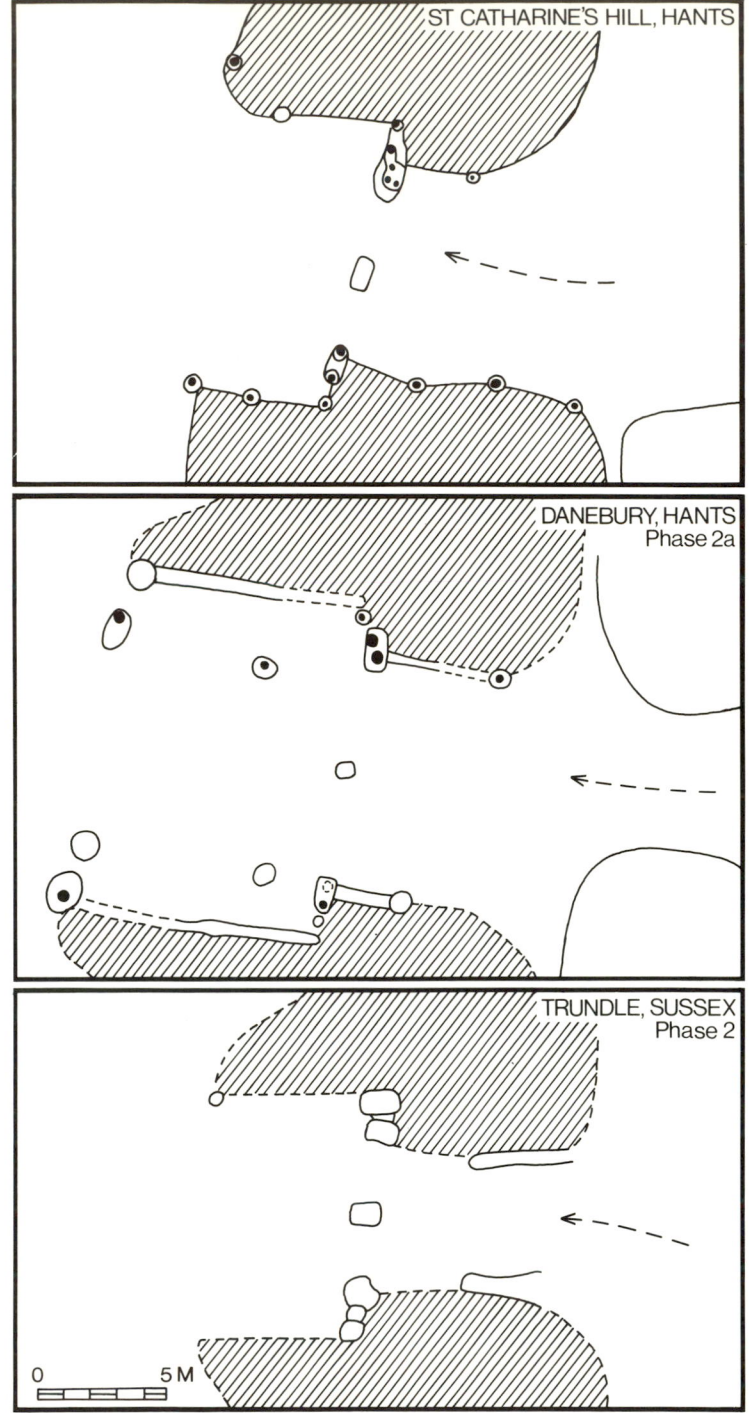

Figure 14.10 Dual-portal entrances (sources: *St Catharine's Hill*, Hawkes, Myres and Stevens 1930; *Danebury*, Cunliffe 1972a; *Trundle*, E.C. Curwen 1931 (author's interpretation)).

stage has been lost. The intention of the new entrance is, however, clear enough: the creation of a defended corridor extending into the fort between the rampart ends.

The same appears to be true of other entrances. At Danebury, the third period entrance was provided with a simple dual gate set back at the end of a revetted corridor 13 m long, while at the Trundle the gate of the second phase lay at the end of a corridor 15 m long. Much the same arrangement seems to have been constructed at the inner entrance at Yarnbury and at Blewburton Hill, Oxon. Little dating evidence is available but in terms of the individual sequences a fourth-century date is probable.

In the final stage at Torberry (phase IV) the entrance was remodelled on a massive scale (Figure 14.11): the ditch-ends were walled across and filled in and the corridor was flanked on either side by substantial dry-stone walls 3.0–3.6 m wide extending into the camp for 27 m. At the inner end of the gradually narrowing passage lay the gate, represented by two post-pits. Both phases III and IV were associated with saucepan pots, showing that the creation of the corridor entrances lay within the Middle Iron Age. Much the same development was found at Danebury (Figure 6.7, p. 117), where in the fifth period a long corridor approach to the gate was created by turning the ends of the rampart outwards to form a passage 45 m long, and building around them, as protection, a pair of claw-like hornworks containing an outer gate (Figure 14.12). From a platform created on the crest of the out-turned rampart it would have been possible for the defenders to control both gates and the entire compass of the entrance earthworks, as well as the approach to the fort.

Corridor entrances were common throughout the hillfort areas of southern Britain (Figure 14.12). At the neighbouring sites of the Trundle and St Catharine's Hill, long in-turned corridors were now created out of the earlier gate structures, while at Bury Wood Camp, Wilts., the north-east entrance seems to have been first built in this style. Normally the corridor was constructed by turning the ends of the rampart into the camp as at Torberry, but in some cases, for example Buckland Rings, Hants., the Caburn, Sussex, and Llanmelin, Mon., partial or full multivallation contributed to the length of the defended approach, while at other sites like Danebury the corridor effect was created by out-turning the earthworks and protecting them with outer hornworks. A prime example of such an arrangement is the east entrance of Maiden Castle, Dorset (Figures 14.6 and 14.13), in phases II and III. Here any would-be attacker would have been confronted by a long tortuous corridor approach of more than 73 m, winding in and out between earthworks which shielded strategically placed artillery platforms designed, no doubt, to be manned by defenders with slings.

A somewhat simpler method, with the same overall advantages, entailed the construction of a single flanking earthwork attached to one side of the entrance and running parallel to it (Figure 14.13). This type can be most clearly seen at the Steepleton Gate of Hod Hill, Dorset, where a hornwork, unfinished presumably because of Roman attack, was added in front of an already in-turned gate, creating a corridor of 90 m overall length. The same technique was employed at the neighbouring Hambledon Hill and, in a modified form, at Rawlsbury and Badbury Castle, all in Dorset; the outworks of Yarnbury, Wilts. (Figures 14.13 and 14.14), in their latest form would have created a similar general effect.

Wherever dating evidence is available, simple in-turned corridor entrances of the Torberry type seem to date to the end of the Middle Iron Age and even the more complex earthworks of Danebury belong to the same period, but the addition of flanking outworks is generally a later development, quite possibly not appearing in the south-west until the first century AD. Flanking works designed to deflect frontal attack are a far more sophisticated reaction to defence than the

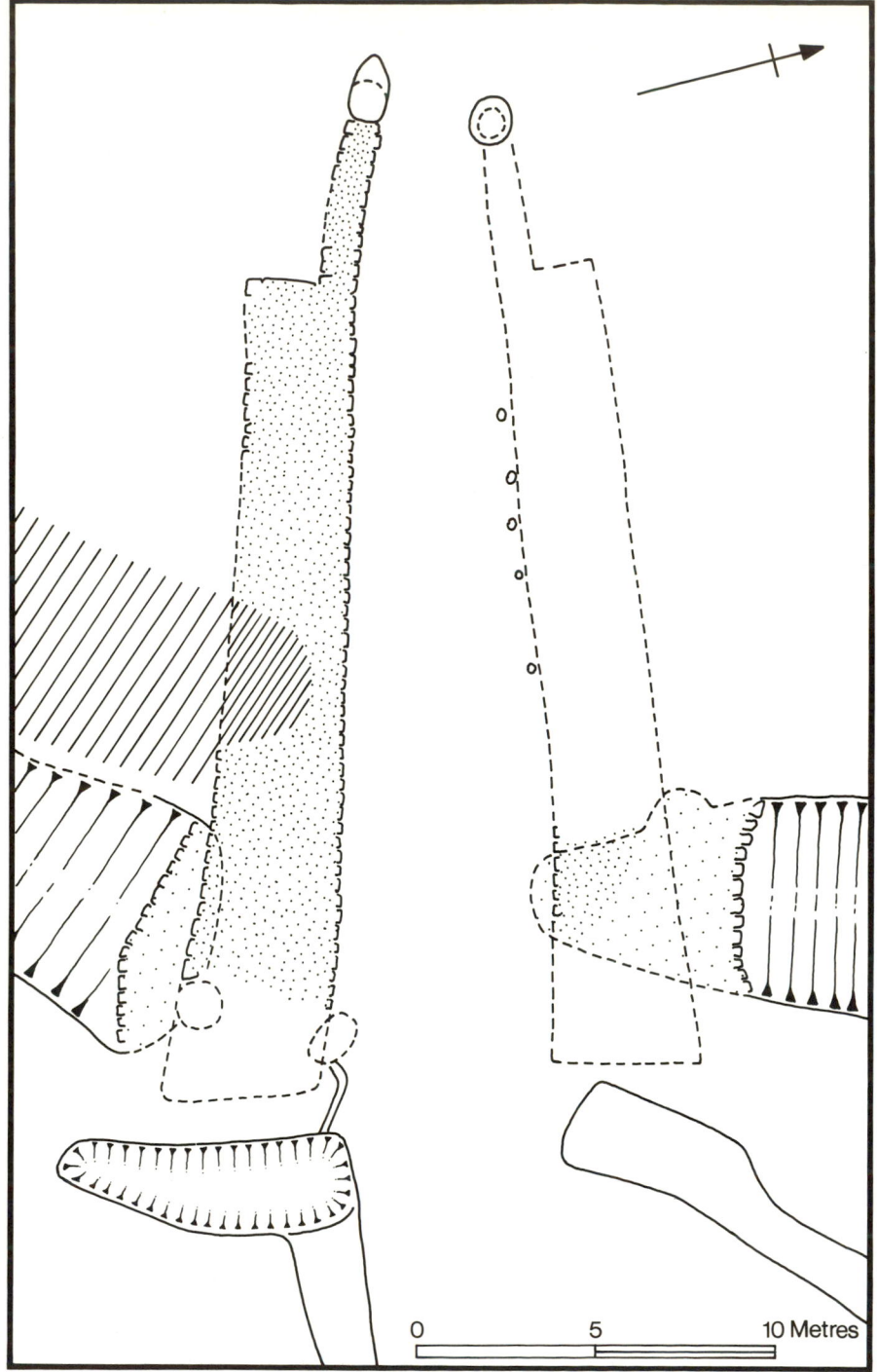

Figure 14.11   The last phase of the main entrance of Torberry, Sussex (source: Cunliffe 1976a).

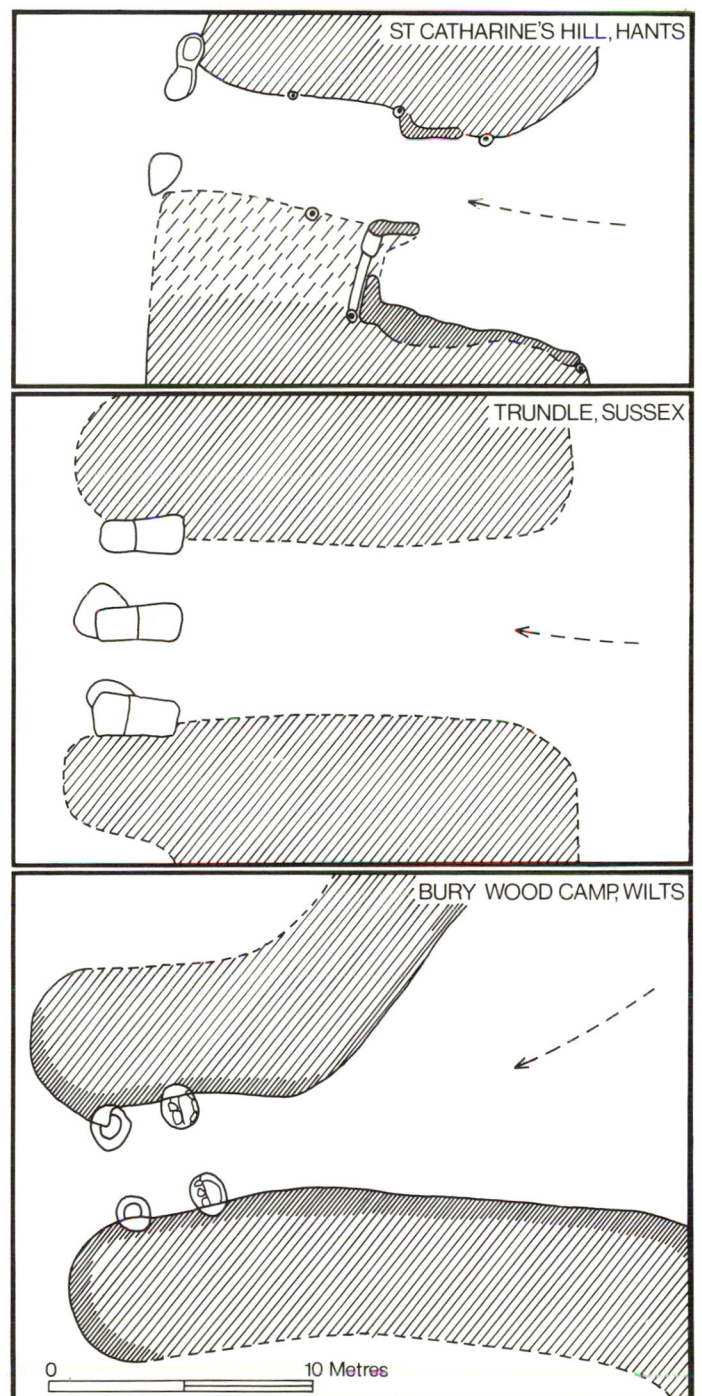

Figure 14.12 Inturned entrances (sources: *St Catharine's Hill*, Hawkes, Myres and Stevens 1930 (authors' interpretation); *Trundle*, E.C. Curwen 1931; *Bury Wood Camp*, King 1967).

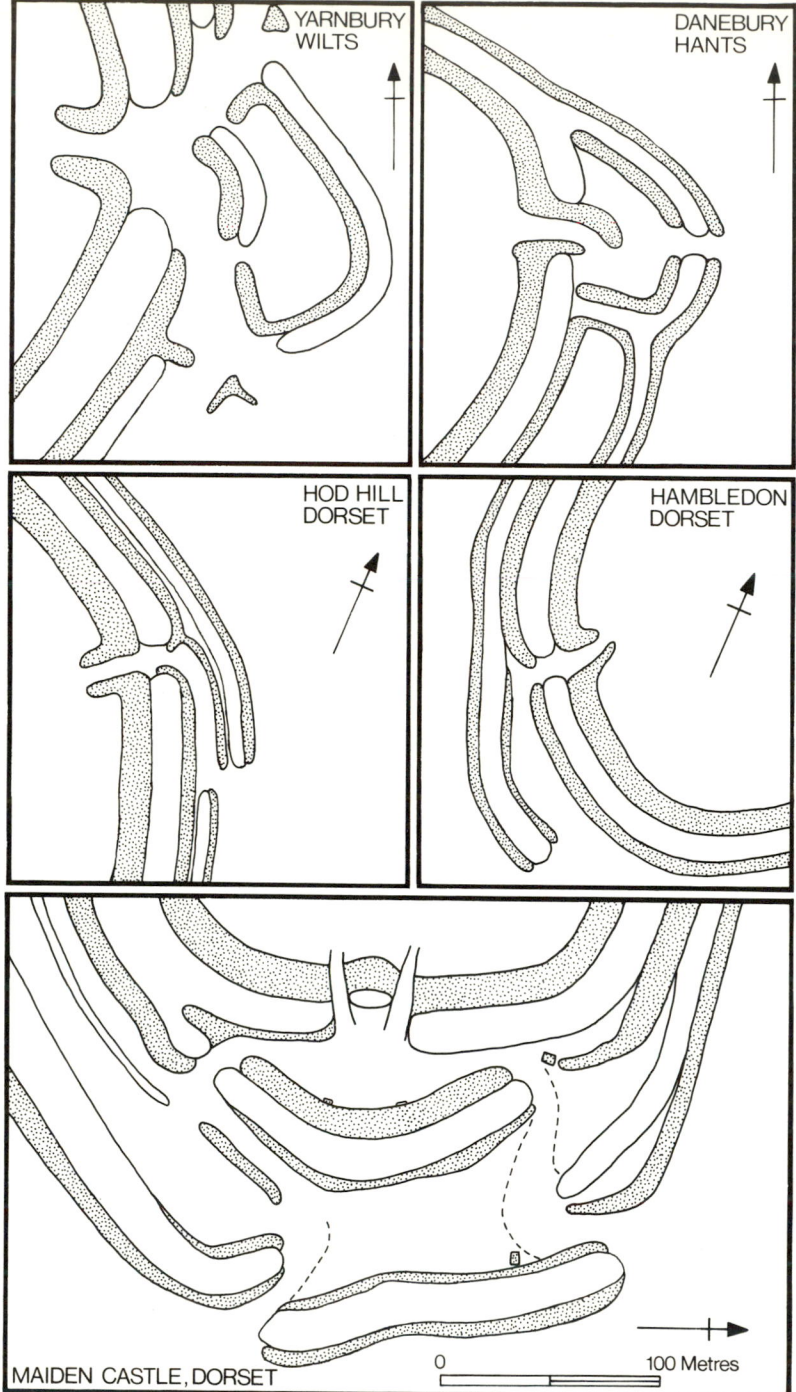

Figure 14.13   Comparative plans of complex outworks protecting hillfort entrances (sources: *Yarnbury*, M.E. Cunnington 1933; *Hod Hill* and *Hambledon Hill*, Richmond 1968; *Maiden Castle*, Wheeler 1943; *Danebury*, Cunliffe 1972a).

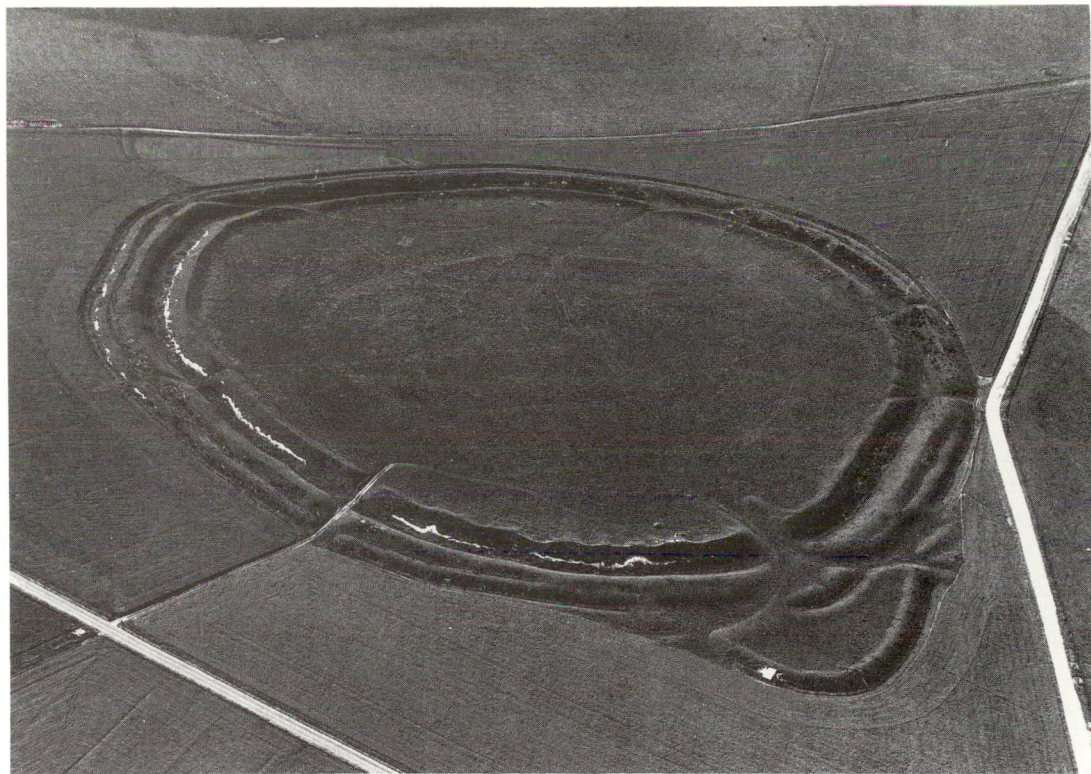

Figure 14.14   Yarnbury, Wilts. (photo: Dr J.K.S. St Joseph. Crown Copyright reserved).

building of long corridors. It remains to be seen whether it was threat of Roman attack in AD 43 or earlier intertribal fighting which sparked off the development.

Turning now to the sequence in the Welsh borderland hillforts, the work at Croft Ambrey, Midsummer Hill and Credenhill Camp in Herefordshire and Ffridd Faldwyn, Montgomery, when collated allows the main development trends to be isolated (Stanford 1971b). The earliest gate is a simple single-portal type found at Ffridd Faldwyn in association with a box rampart and tentatively dated to the eighth and seventh centuries. This was replaced by a series of twin-portal gates spanning the sixth to fourth centuries. Croft Ambrey, where occupation began towards the end of the sixth century, was also provided with a succession of twin-portal gates of broadly similar type.

It was probably during the fifth century or earlier that timber guardrooms came into common use, appearing at Midsummer Hill and probably Credenhill Camp, but soon to be replaced by stone-built guard-chambers of a kind which were also added to the Croft Ambrey gate for which a radiocarbon date of 460 ± 135 bc has been obtained. Guard-chambers are well represented among the hillforts built in the stone areas of north Wales and the Welsh Marches, and extend south into Northamptonshire (Figure 14.15). Strictly, two different types can be recognized: chambers added immediately behind the ramparts – as at Rainsborough, Northants., Castle Ditch (Eddisbury), Cheshire, Leckhampton Hill, Glos., Moel Hiraddug and Dinorben, Denbigh. – and those built at the ends of long corridor entrances like Titterstone Clee and the Wrekin,

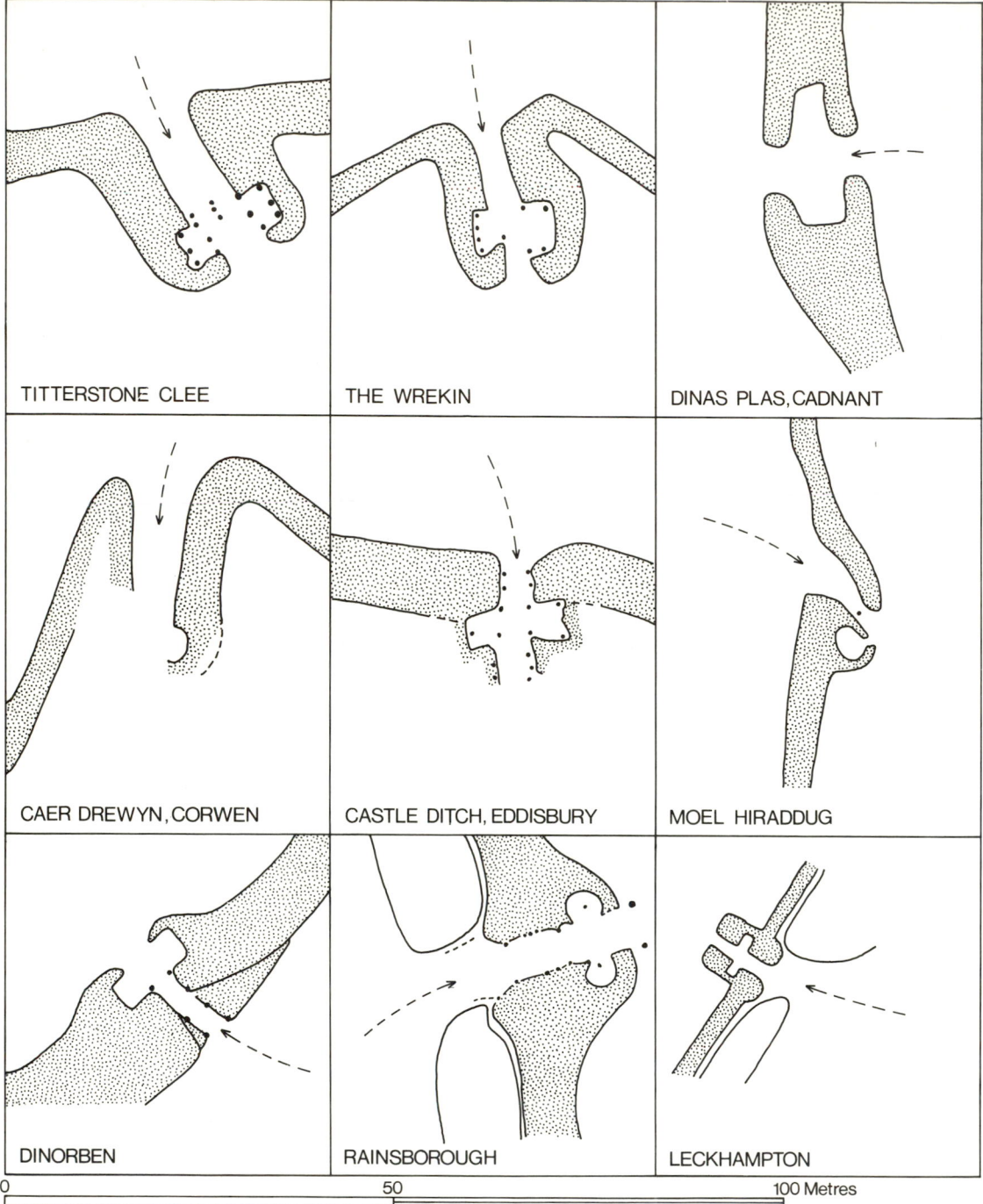

Figure 14.15 Comparative plans of hillfort entrance guard-chambers (source: Gardner and Savory 1964 with amendments and additions).

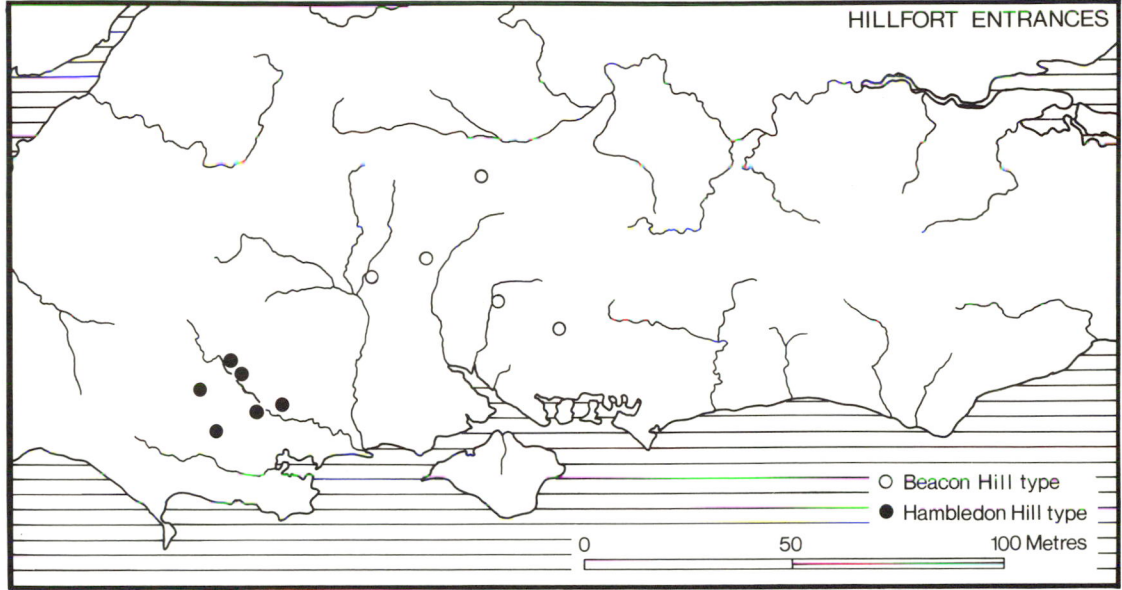

Figure 14.16   Distribution of hillfort entrance types (source: author).

Salop, and Pen y Corddyn Mawr, Denbigh. No positive evidence is yet available to suggest whether or not there is a chronological difference between the two types. If we accept the sixth- or fifth-century dating suggested by the single radiocarbon date for the appearance of guard-chambers at Croft Ambrey, which gains support from the two radiocarbon dates now available from Rainsborough, and if the long corridor type of entrance plan was adopted in this area in parallel with its fourth- to third-century appearance in the south, then guard-chambers must have been in use for several centuries. The problem is one which may eventually be solved by further excavation and radiocarbon dating. The possibility that the guard-chambers may, in some regions, have been constructed at the same time is suggested by the very close similarities of those at the south-east gate of Dinorben and the main entrance of Moel Hiraddug (Guilbert 1979b).

One characteristic of the corridor entrances of the south, which recurs in the Welsh border sites, is the construction of a bridge over the gate linking one side of the entrance passage with the other, providing obvious defensive advantages. In the south bridges are found with long corridor entrances dating to the third and second centuries. In the west similar features appear, also at a late stage in the local sequence – for example at Midsummer Hill and Croft Ambrey – associated at the former site with a radiocarbon date of 50 ± 100 bc. The consistency in dating is impressive.

In summary, it may be said that in the two areas where hillforts have been studied in some detail, a well-defined parallel development can be recognized, although there are some apparent differences in dating in the early stages. Divergence in structural detail begins in the sixth or fifth century with the development of guard-chambers in the western group, while at the southern sites the gates tend to be set further and further back. Some time during the Middle Iron Age, many of the gates in the south were remodelled as long corridor types in which the gates, combined with bridges, were constructed at the inner ends of corridors sometimes as much as 45 m long. At about this time bridges appear in the western group, possibly together with the limited adoption of the corridor type of entrance plan. It was probably during the first century BC or early first century AD that several forts in the south were provided with complex outworks, perhaps as a defence against threat of Roman attack, but outworks are not a common characteristic of the forts of the western group.

When more radiocarbon dates become available, particularly from forts in the south, greater refinements will be possible, and with further excavation regional variations will no doubt appear. Nevertheless, the general similarity of development over a large area tends to suggest a degree of parallelism, reflected also in basic hillfort structure, which can best be explained by supposing a community of common culture and persistent contact over a considerable period of time.

Regional differences in the planning and siting of hillforts

In the same way that the vernacular architecture of medieval Britain differs from region to region, so too it is possible to recognize peculiarities in the planning and siting of hillforts (Forde-Johnston 1976). The problem cannot be discussed in any detail here but attention must be drawn to the larger and more generalized groupings.

The normal hillfort of southern Britain – the so-called contour type – is in its initial stages usually a univallate structure with ramparts enclosing the crest of a hill (Figures 14.17 and 14.18). With exceptions like Cissbury and the Trundle in Sussex and St Catharine's Hill, Hants., where the original circuits were not subsequently enlarged, many were increased in size. At some, like Yarnbury, Wilts., the early fort was completely replaced by an entirely new rampart roughly concentric with the first (Figures 14.14 and 14.19), while others were enlarged with a single addition as in the case of Maiden Castle, Dorset, and Torberry, Sussex (Figure 14.19), or more than one addition like Hambledon Hill, Dorset (Figure 14.20). Multivallation, where it occurs, can usually be shown to be late.

Contour forts are to a large extent the natural result of fortifying a gentle downland landscape, but even within the area of the chalk downs there are steeper ridges and promontories demanding different treatment. Torberry is a good example of this: here in its first period (Figure 14.19), a cross-defence was constructed across the ridge, cutting off and protecting the end of a promontory; only later was the fort converted into a conventional contour work.

In the Weald, where much of the countryside is more sharply dissected by streams, promontories were usually chosen for the siting of forts. In the case of High Rocks and Hammer Wood (Iping) in Sussex (Figure 14.21), multiple defences were constructed across the neck of the ridge with much slighter earthworks around the other slopes where the land falls steeply away. The Wealden forts were simply making the optimum use of the defensive possibilities of the landscape.

The same general principles can surely be applied to the cliff castles of Cornwall and south-west Wales (Figures 13.11, p. 261 and 13.16, p. 267). Headlands projecting into the sea needed only short lengths of artificial defences cut across the neck to render them virtually impregnable. Admittedly, the structural similarities of the Cornish cliff castles as well as certain aspects of the material culture show strong links with the Armorican peninsula – an area of similar geomorphological structure. But the absence of cliff castles in Cornwall would have been more

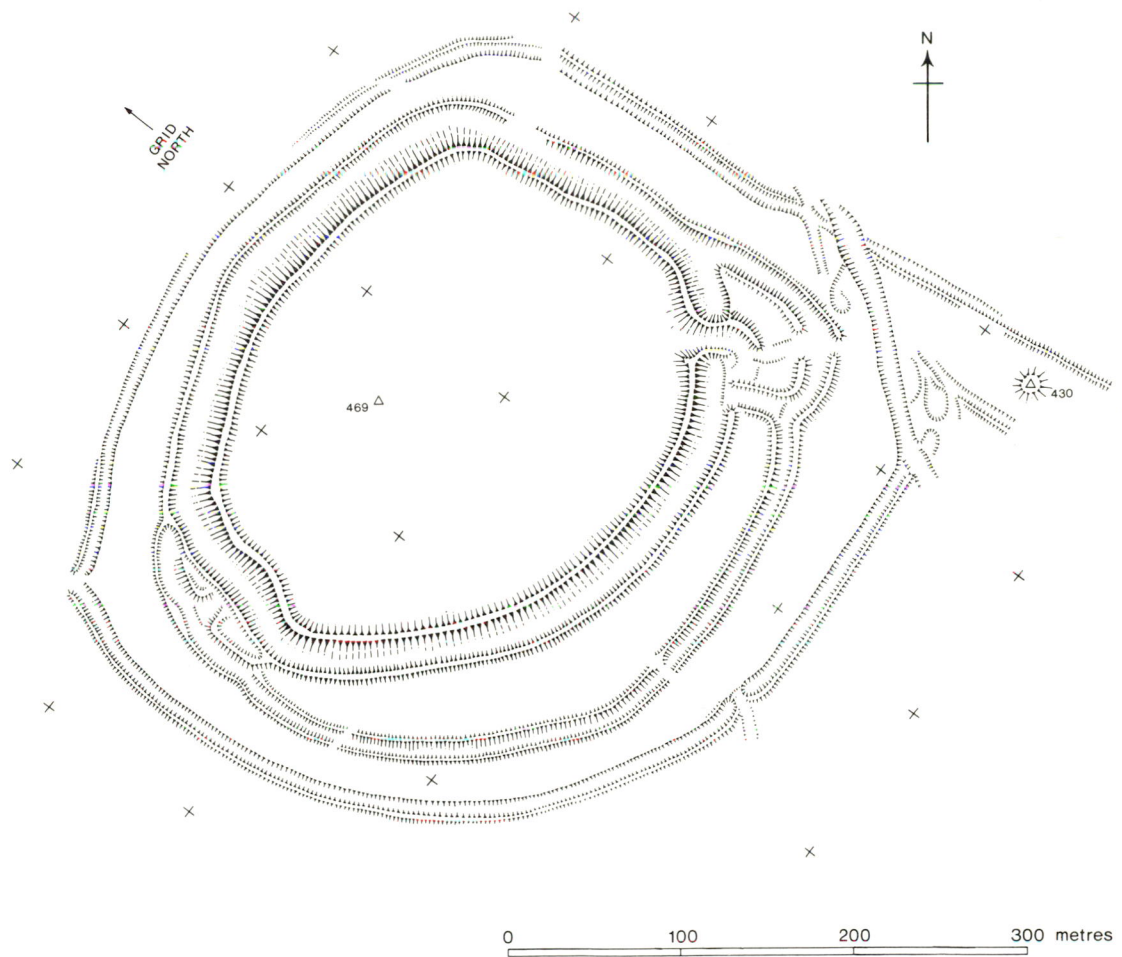

Figure 14.17 Danebury, Hants. (source: Cunliffe 1972a with amendments).

culturally significant than their presence, for the structure of the countryside demands this type of fortification.

While geomorphology is a significant factor in the siting and form of hillforts, geological considerations, particularly the availability of good building stone, can sometimes have a direct effect on actual structure and perhaps on form. In the Cotswolds it is possible to trace a group of relatively small univallate forts of almost circular plan – including Lyneham, Ilbury, Idbury Camp and Chastleton in Oxfordshire and Windrush Camp, Glos. – which contrast with the vast enclosures of more than 22 ha, usually sited on ridges, like Norbury Camp (Northleach) and Nottingham Hill, Glos. (Rivet 1961, 33). Exactly what factors were involved in the evolution of these two classes is not clear but economic and social considerations may well have been important, while the circular form of the smaller category may have been encouraged by the availability of building stone.

Economic factors were of considerable significance in influencing fort type. It has already been

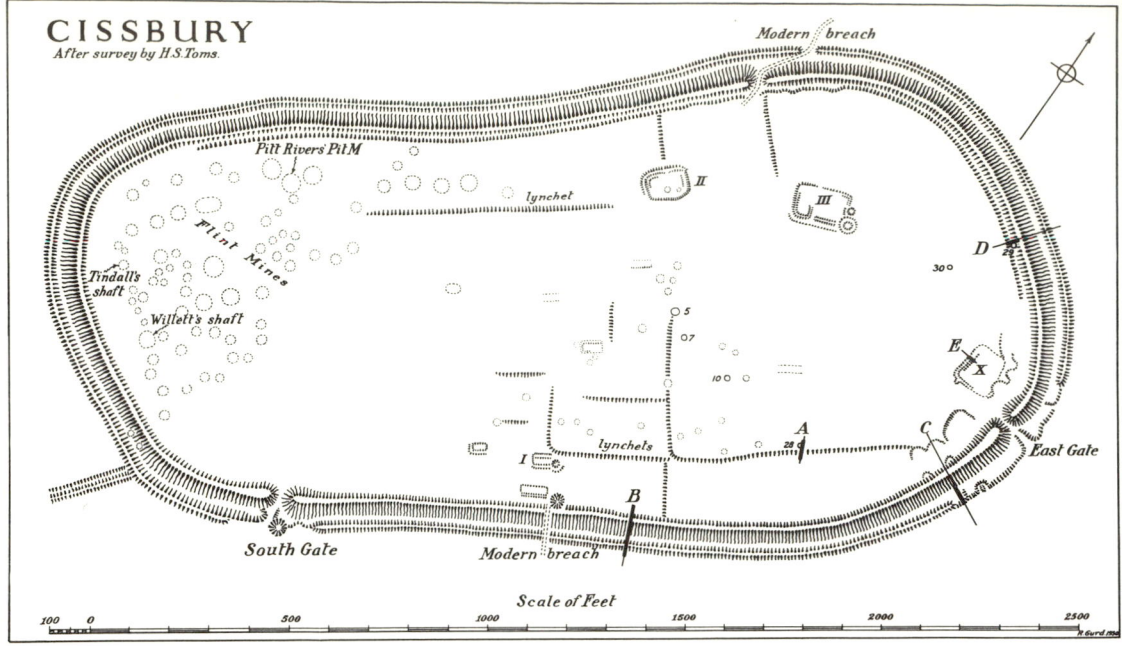

Figure 14.18   Cissbury, Sussex (source: reproduced from Curwen and Williamson 1931).

emphasized (chapter 13) that the multiple-enclosure forts of the south-west peninsula and south-west Wales were a response to the predominantly pastoral economy of these regions, but it would be more accurate to regard them as fortified homesteads. The adding of annexes to the large forts, however (a response to the same economic pressures), gives several of the forts in the Welsh borderland an overall similarity to them but a similarity brought about by the demands of the farming economy rather than by culture, chronology or geology.

To some extent, isolation can give rise to regional variations. The hillforts of Caernarvonshire (Hogg 1962) demonstrate this particularly well. Their large size, hill-top siting, simple dry-stone walled structure and dense internal occupation serve to unite the group and to distinguish them from the structures in the north-east of the Principality, which relate more closely to those in the Welsh borderland. An even more impressive demonstration of regionalization is provided by a consideration of forts in Scotland (Feachem 1966) where by ground survey alone several distinctive types of plan, clustering significantly together, have been recognized.

This brief survey may have erred too much on the side of geographical determinism, but in the past too much emphasis has been placed on cultural/historical explanations when discussing hillfort form. Regional isolation, geology, geomorphology, economy and social structure are of far greater significance in determining siting and planning. In those areas between which cultural contacts were strong, a degree of uniformity and parallel development prevailed. Where, however, areas of countryside were isolated by natural features, a greater regionalization is apparent.

YARNBURY

TORBERRY

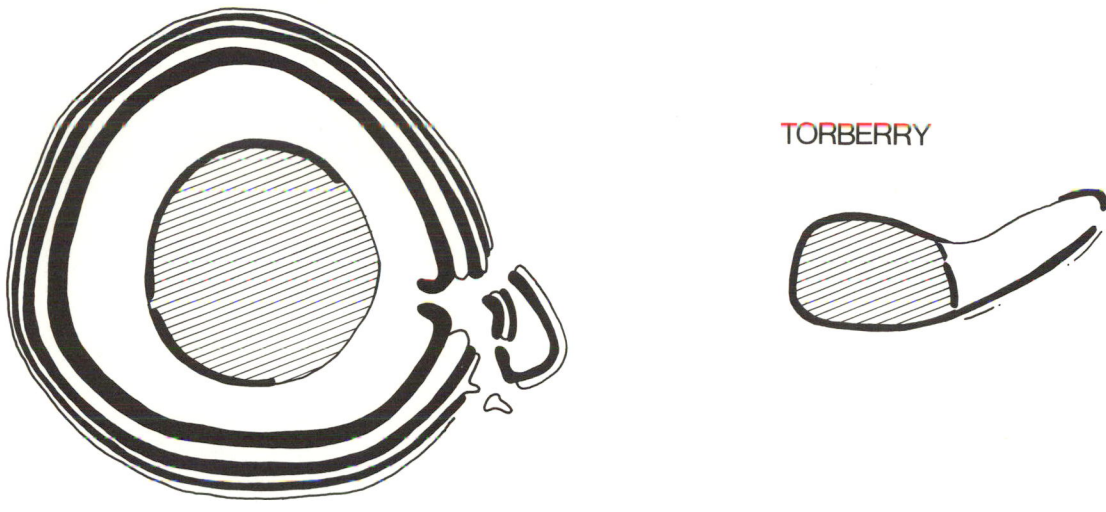

MAIDEN CASTLE

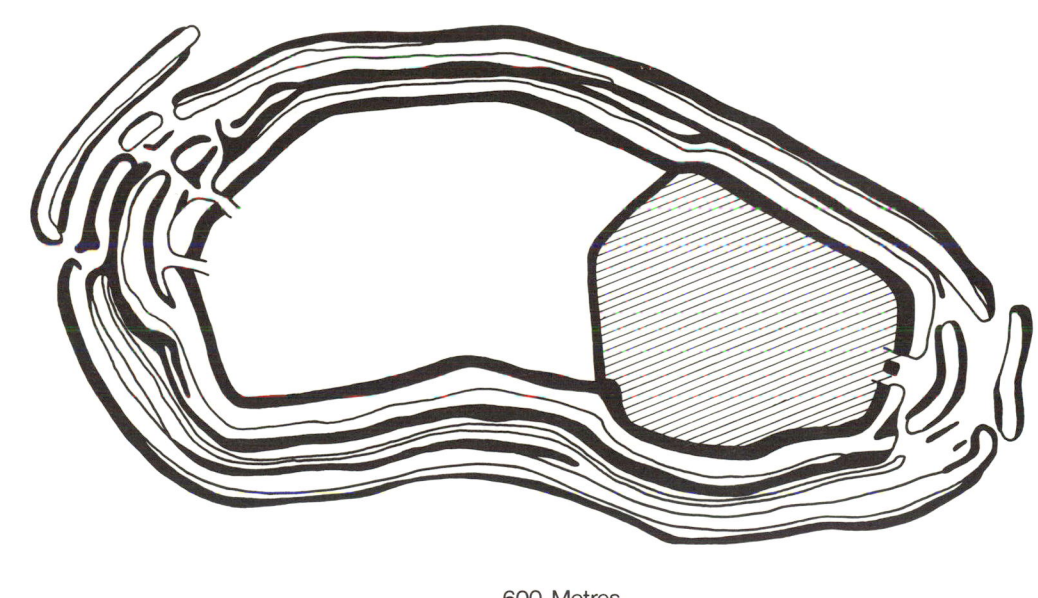

0   600 Metres

Figure 14.19 Hillforts which have been extended. The shaded areas represent the initial enclosures (source: Cunliffe 1984c).

Figure 14.20 Hambledon Hill, Dorset. Successive extensions can be discerned (photo: Dr J.K.S. St Joseph. Crown Copyright reserved).

The development of hillforts

Wessex and adjacent areas

Leaving aside considerations of chronology, the distribution of hillforts in Britain is far from even. As Figure 14.1 (p. 314) so clearly shows there is a marked concentration in a zone beginning in Wessex and the South Downs and continuing through the Cotswolds and the Welsh borderland to the coast of north Wales. It is within this *central southern* zone that the majority of the hillfort excavations have been carried out and all the large-scale excavations of recent years have been focused. Thus the database for the region, though leaving much to be desired, is far better than for any other part of Britain or the adjacent Continent. Sufficient is now known to allow a general development model to be put forward (Cunliffe 1984c). For ease of discussion the simple chronological framework outlined in chapter 2 will be adopted: *earliest* refers to the period from *c*. 800–600/550, *early* to 600/550–*c*. 400 and *middle* to the period from 400 to 100 BC.

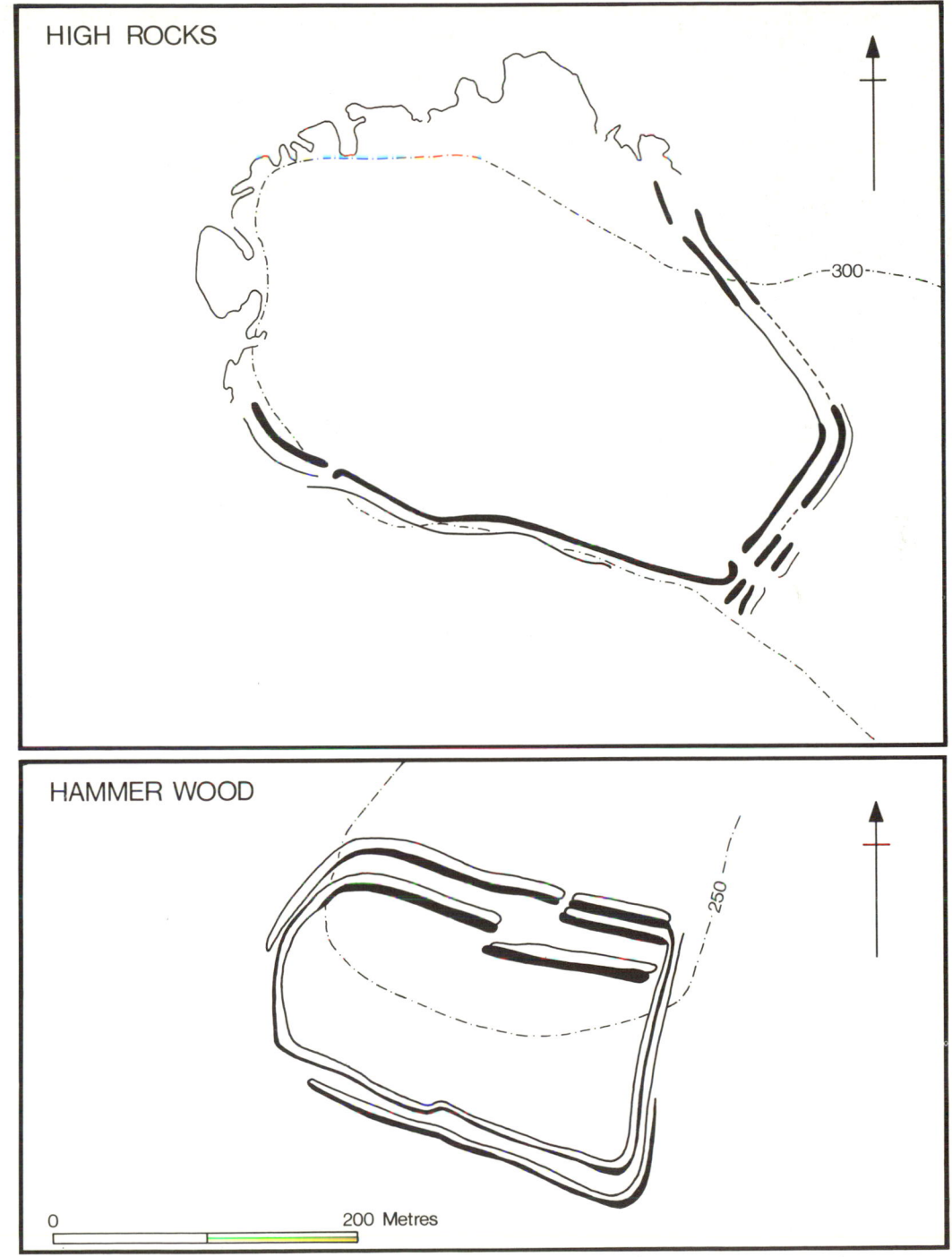

Figure 14.21   Wealden promontory forts (sources: *High Rocks*, Money 1968; *Hammer Wood*, Boyden 1957).

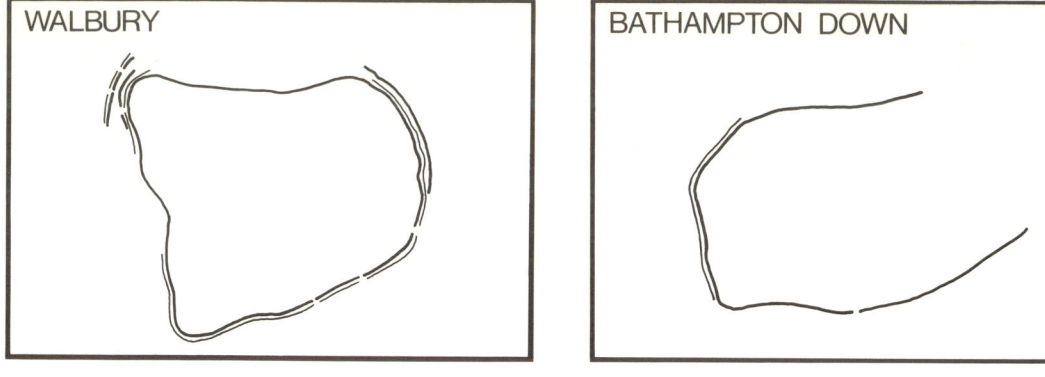

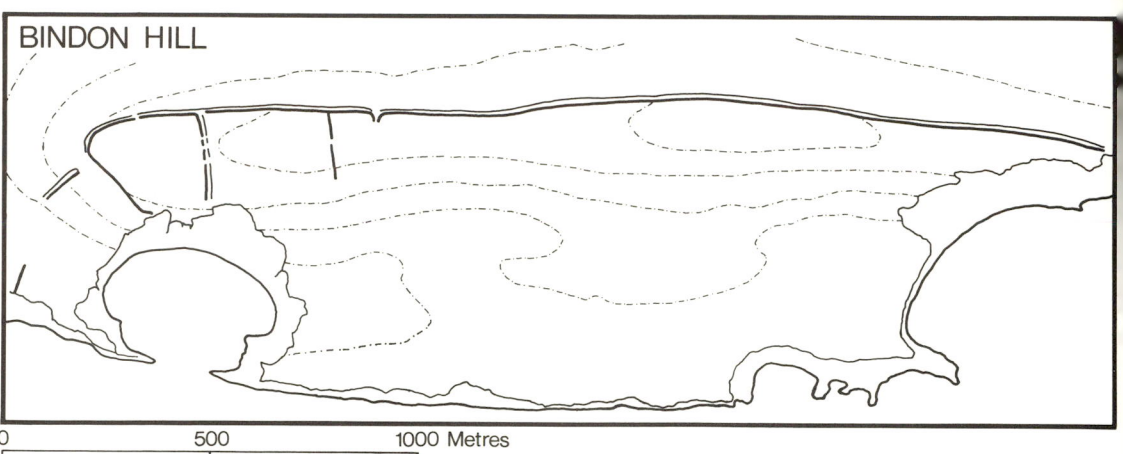

Figure 14.22   Early hill-top enclosures (source: author).

The earliest hillforts (Figures 14.22 and 14.23)
Hillforts of the earliest period fall into two distinct categories: vast straggling structures with
slight defences usually over 10 ha in extent; and small strongly defended enclosures usually
multivallate and occupying ridge-ends.

The larger group are better referred to as *hill-top enclosures* since their enclosing earthworks are
hardly of defensive quality. Size varies from the small enclosure of Winklebury I (6.8 ha) to
gigantic sites like Ogbury, Wilts. (25 ha), Norbury, Glos. (32 ha), Bathampton Down, Avon
(32.5 ha), and Walbury, Berks. (35.2 ha); Bindon Hill, Dorset, is considerably larger if all the
land to the present sea coast is included. Altogether there are ten to fifteen sites of this kind
centring on Wessex but stretching from Sussex to Gloucestershire (Wainwright 1967b). Others
can be identified further afield at Nadbury Camp and Borough Hill, both in Northamptonshire,
and at Ivinghoe Beacon, Herts. The interiors of four have been sampled on a reasonable scale:
Harting Beacon, Sussex, Balksbury I, Hants., Winklebury I, Hants., and Norbury, Glos. All
share similar characteristics: the defences were comparatively slight, there was a dearth of
occupation debris and internal structures were sparse. In Harting Beacon and Norbury only a
few small four-post structures were discovered, but at the more extensive excavations of

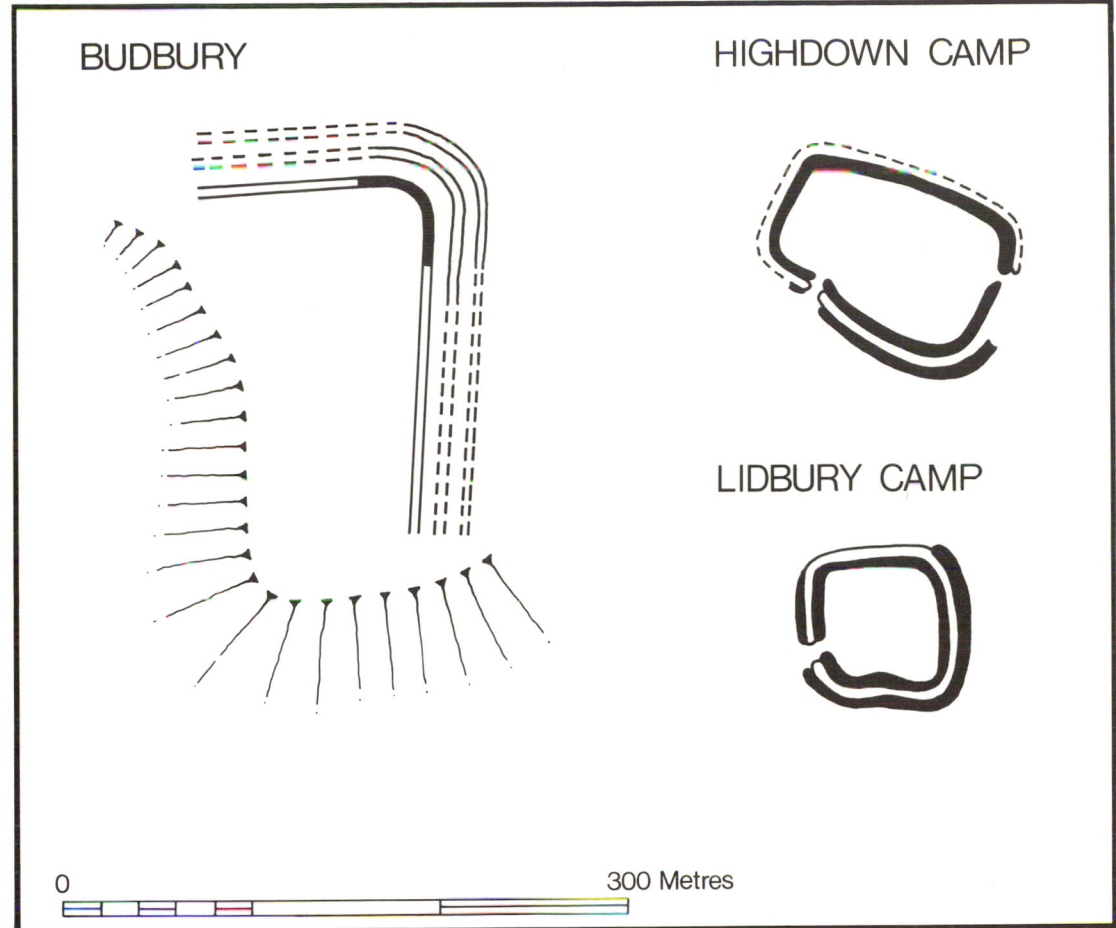

Figure 14.23 Defended ridge-end forts (source: Cunliffe 1984c).

Balksbury and Winklebury a few contemporary circular structures, possibly houses or shelters, were found. The enclosure at Hog Cliff Hill, Dorset, belongs to this same general category. Here, following a Late Bronze Age settlement, a slight ditched enclosure of some 5.6 ha was constructed within which were a series of circular buildings. The enclosure was subsequently enlarged to 10.5 ha and the buildings were replaced by penannular mounds of flints built apparently as shelters.

While the function of these early hill-top enclosures is obscure, the lack of evidence for intensive occupation is consistent and points to the possibility that they may have been used only sporadically, but the replacement of circular structures at Winklebury I is sufficient to show that occupation was more than a single brief event. The four-post structures, which characterize the internal occupation, are conventionally called 'granaries'. This however is an observer-imposed terminology and such simple post settings could equally well have served as racks or platforms for any kind of storage. While no firm conclusion can yet be offered as to the function of these enclosures one possibility is that they represented communally-built structures related to a seasonal activity within the farming year. If the small four-post structures are interpreted as hay racks or fodder stores of some kind, then the enclosures could well have served for autumn corralling. Flocks and herds would need to be rounded up for sorting, castrating and culling and this is most likely to have been a communally organized activity. It is possible that over-wintering of stock may also have been focused on enclosures of this kind in which case some accommodation for the guardians of the livestock would have been necessary. These are, of course, only hypotheses – firm evidence is not yet available – but some such use would fit well with our general concepts of socio-economic development which will be considered in more detail below (chapter 20).

The second category of 'hillfort' in the earliest phase of the Iron Age can be characterized as small enclosures of 1–3 ha in extent, strongly defended often with multiple earthworks, the interior producing rich occupation deposits (Figure 14.23). Sites of this kind are not particularly well known but at Budbury, Avon, excavation has defined a 3 ha enclosure with a complex of ramparts and ditches occupying the end of a steep promontory. Limited excavation within the interior produced a considerable range of debris pointing to intensive occupation. Lidbury Camp, Wilts., is also of this period. Here a small strongly-defended rectangular enclosure produced eleven storage pits in a comparatively limited area excavation. Oliver's Camp, Wilts., and Highdown, Sussex, are among others that have been examined on a sufficient scale to show that they belong to the same general category. It is tempting to see these defended settlements as the permanent bases of a sector of society, perhaps an aristocracy if the defences are thought to reflect status. Once more, however, the excavated data are too sparse to allow firm conclusions to be drawn.

Hill-top enclosures and defended settlements are two features of the contemporary settlement pattern of Wessex. Others include the large, and apparently, open settlements typified by All Cannings Cross and Potterne, Wilts., while the ditch-enclosed farmstead of Old Down Farm, Hants., represents another type. Our so-called earliest 'hillforts' must then be seen as only one element in a varied pattern representing a complex social hierarchy.

Early hillforts (Figures 14.24 and 14.25)
The Early Iron Age in central southern Britain, which covers the period roughly of the sixth and fifth centuries, was a time of developing cultural uniformity. Though distinctive regional pottery styles serve to distinguish what might be regarded as emerging ethnic entities, throughout the broadest region a new type of *early hillfort* appeared. These were usually contour works, averaging 5 ha in extent. They were defended by a single ditch, backed by a rampart usually faced inside and out with stonework or timber or a combination of the two. There were normally two entrances on opposite sides of the enclosure (Figure 14.25). From what is known of their distribution in Wessex, forts of this kind would seem to have been densely and quite evenly scattered across the landscape and many of the typologically later hillforts may, on excavation, prove to have originated in this period (Cunliffe 1984c, 19–23). Few, if any, developed from fortified enclosures of the earliest period but at Danebury there is some evidence to suggest that the early hillfort was constructed within a larger and slighter enclosure which contained four-post structures. This may prove to be a more widespread phenomenon than was originally appreciated but such relationships are impossible to discern from surface characteristics alone.

The area of downland between the rivers Test and Bourne has been thoroughly investigated and can provide a fair indication of the density of early hillforts in the landscape (Figure 14.26). In all, five hillforts are known. Of these one, Balksbury, originated as an early hill-top enclosure but was not fortified or occupied in the early period. The other four, Bury Hill, Figsbury, Danebury and Quarley all provide some evidence to suggest that they were built and used within

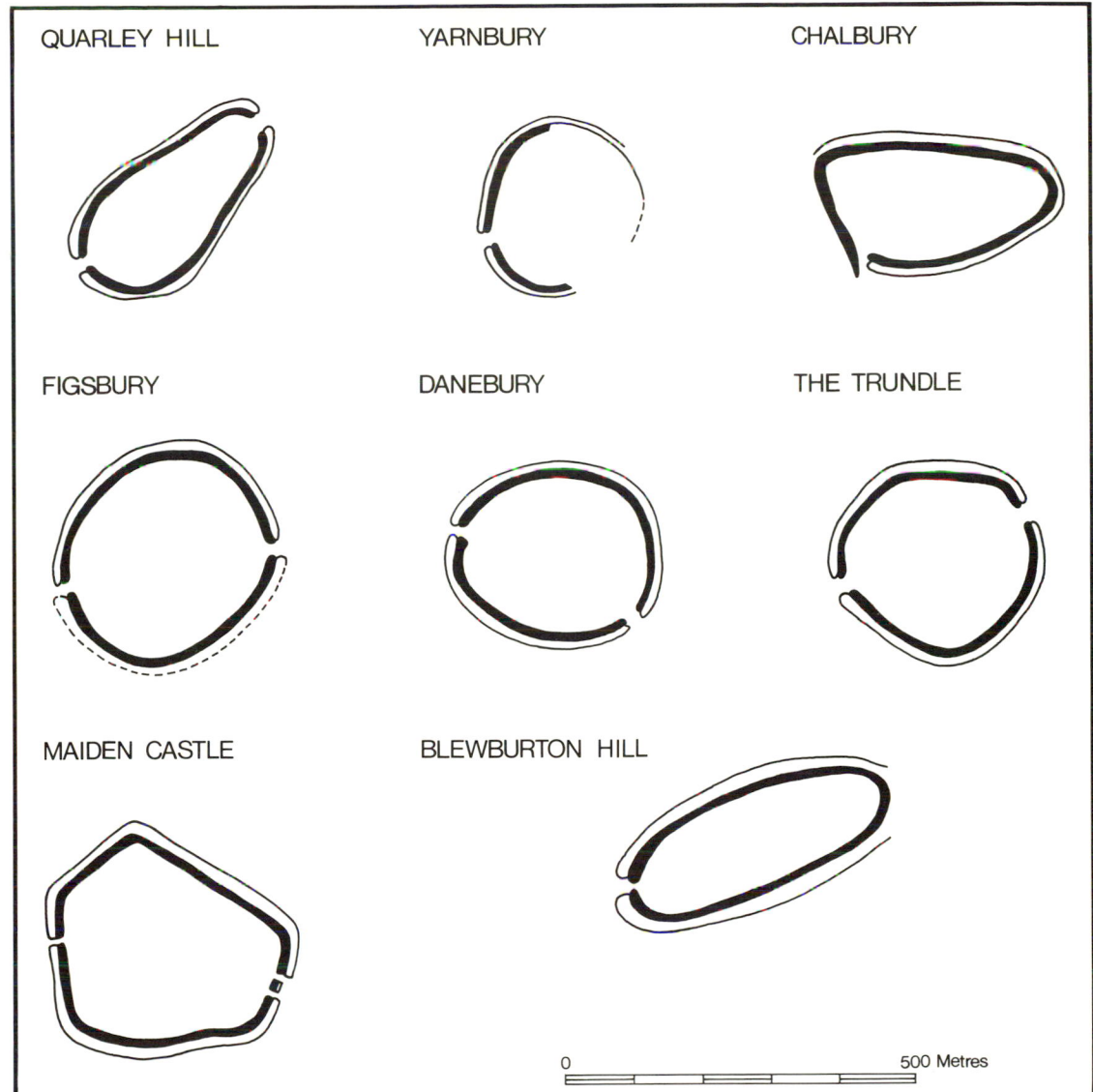

Figure 14.24   Comparative plans of early hillforts (source: Cunliffe 1984c).

the early period. These sites were closely located between 8 and 11 km apart but there is no reason to suppose that this density was unusual for Wessex in the early period.

Four *early hillforts* have been the subject of programmes of area excavation but on varying scales: South Cadbury, Somerset, Chalbury and Maiden Castle, Dorset, and Danebury, Hampshire (Figure 14.25). Only at Chalbury was the site found to be uncluttered with later occupation. Here surface evidence of thirty or so large circular depressions was recognizable and the three of these that were excavated proved to be houses. The many smaller depressions

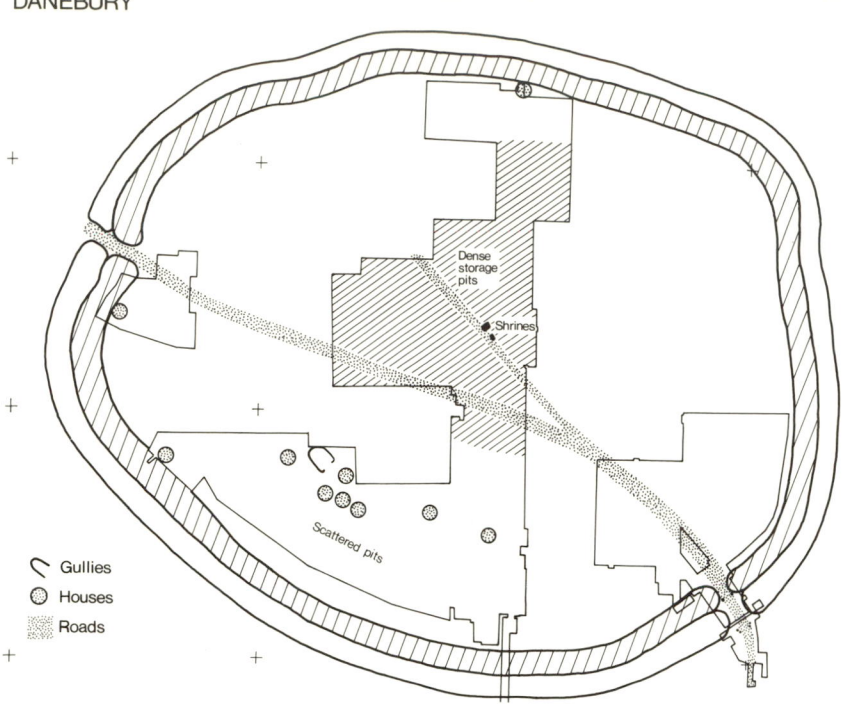

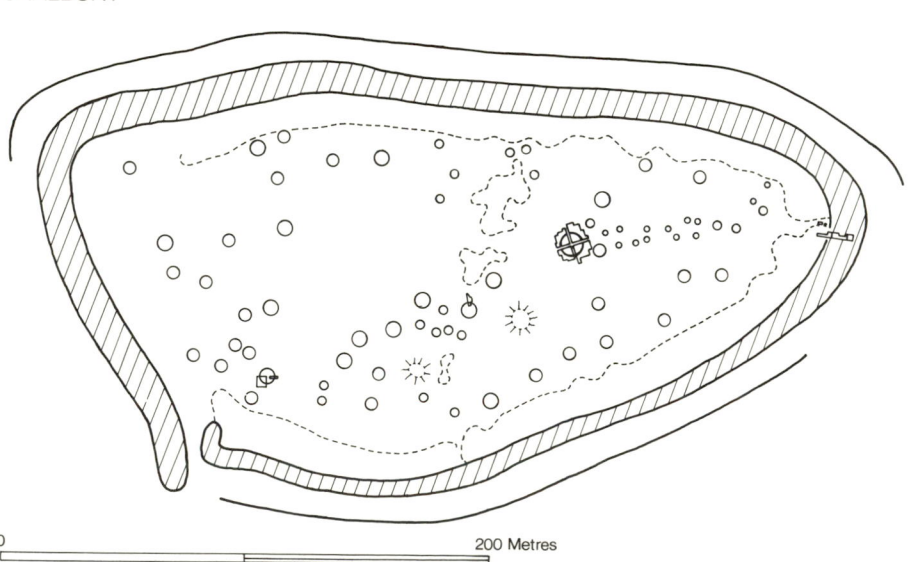

Figure 14.25 The interiors of early hillforts (source: Cunliffe 1984c).

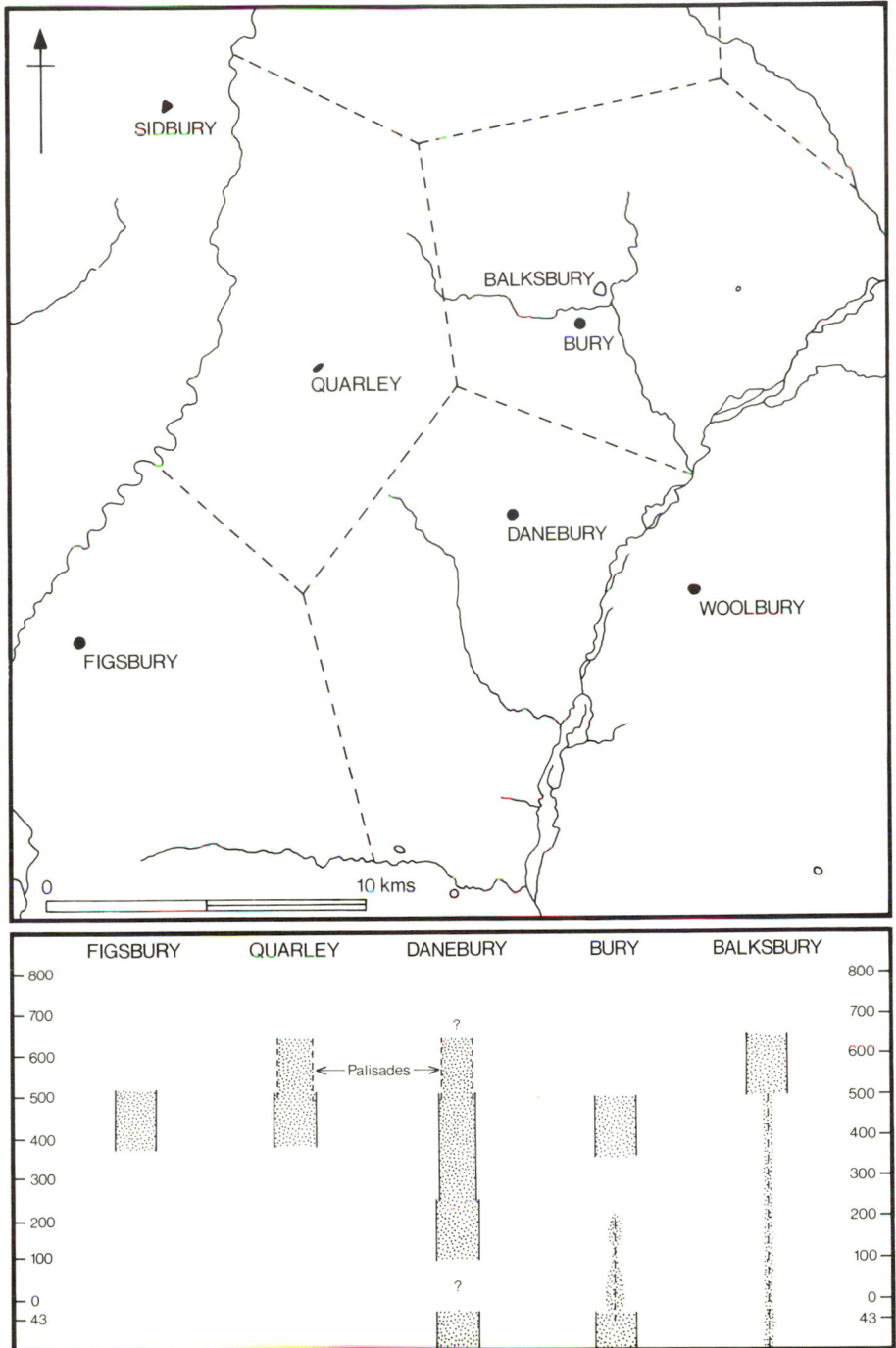

Figure 14.26   The hillforts of the Danebury region, showing their theoretical territories constructed on the basis of Thiessen polygons. The lower diagram indicates duration of occupation of the forts (source: Cunliffe 1976b).

probably represented pits only one of which was uncovered. The surface features suggest that some zoning may have existed but without intensive excavation it is impossible to say. A rather clearer picture emerges from the large-scale area excavation at Danebury where, in spite of much later occupation, the early plan can be clearly discerned. Much of the central area, around two buildings which may have served as shrines, was used solely for the siting of pits, probably for grain storage, while in the peripheral zone behind the ramparts, wider on the south than the north, circular houses, storage pits and post-structures concentrated: it was here that occupation debris was at its densest. The more limited evidence from Maiden Castle and South Cadbury suggests that all four sites were broadly comparable in this early period.

Early hillforts differ noticeably from early hill-top enclosures in that they were smaller and better defended and internal occupation was dense and probably continuous, the debris showing that a wide range of normal domestic activities were undertaken. The enclosing earthworks were clearly regarded as defensive. Their siting was carefully chosen to make the most of the natural contours and the gates were strongly fortified. At Danebury and Maiden Castle forward projecting hornworks were added during the early period. There is also ample evidence at both sites and elsewhere, e.g. Figsbury, South Cadbury, Chalbury and St Catharine's Hill, that the defensive circuits were refurbished from time to time. Copious collections of slingstones from Danebury and Maiden Castle provide added evidence of defence while traces of burning at Danebury and St Catharine's Hill may have resulted from an attack. For all these reasons we may fairly regard these sites as fortifications designed to protect the community from raids. The social implications which follow from this are best left for later discussion in chapter 20.

Middle Iron Age hillforts

After about 400 BC a widespread change can be detected in Wessex: a number of the early hillforts were abandoned while those that remained in use were refortified, frequently on a massive scale: these we refer to as *developed hillforts*. Danebury provides a good example of what this entailed. Here the early rampart was greatly increased in volume with material largely derived from a wide quarry trench dug just behind the rampart tail. The ditch was also recut as a deep V, the inner side of which was continuous with the front slope of the rampart. One of the entrances was now blocked while the remaining one underwent a series of changes culminating in a long corridor type protected by a complex of outworks.

A number of early forts, including South Cadbury and Blewburton, were modified in this way but elsewhere enclosed areas were increased. At Maiden Castle and Torberry the new defences, while following part of the earlier circuit, incorporated new areas, while at Yarnbury the old defences were entirely abandoned, the new enclosure taking a much wider circuit (Figure 14.19). Clearly within the general pattern of Middle Iron Age re-defence a range of strategies were adopted. Moreover, one has only to compare the three plans illustrated on Figure 14.19 to appreciate the considerable variation in size, and presumably therefore status, among the developed hillforts.

Although a majority of the developed hillforts emerged as modifications of functioning early forts there are a few possible examples of early hill-top enclosures being brought back into use after a century or two of abandonment. Winklebury (if accepted as an early hill-top enclosure) may be one such and it is possible that Hod Hill, Dorset, is another though the available evidence is ambiguous. Sometimes virgin sites seem to have been chosen for developed hillforts. This would appear to be true of a number of the hillforts of Kent and Surrey where radiocarbon evidence suggests that occupation began in the fourth or third centuries (Cunliffe 1982b).

As a broad generalization it can be said that over most of central southern Britain there were fewer developed hillforts than there were early hillforts. This is particularly clearly demonstrated in the Test–Bourne region (Figure 14.16) where of the four early forts occupying the territory in the early period only one, Danebury, continued as a developed hillfort in the Middle Iron Age. In other words Danebury became the single dominant focus in a landscape which previously may have functioned as four separate territories.

Reflections of a similar process can be discerned on the Sussex Downs, an elongated chalk ridge divided into distinct blocks by rivers. The total number of hillforts is quite large (Figure 14.27) but when the few forts producing evidence of Middle Iron Age occupation are plotted they can be seen to be spaced evenly with each fort occupying a discrete block of downland giving the impression of distinct territoriality (Bedwin 1978b).

Much the same pattern emerges on the downs of northern Hampshire and Berkshire (Figure 14.28). The twelve sites displaying characteristics of Middle Iron Age developed hillforts are evenly spaced within the landscape and all occupy similar positions in relation to the two principal resource potentials: the unwatered downland and land within easy reach of permanent water supply. These fortified locations have emerged from a complex of earlier fortifications to be the focal points of discrete territories, their survival, no doubt, aided by their favourable locations.

The date of the appearance of developed hillforts would seem to lie in the fourth or third century BC based partly upon a series of radiocarbon dates and partly upon an assessment of the associated ceramic assemblages. Even so dating cannot be precise and while it is possible that the forts sprang into existence in their developed form at more or less the same time in the early fourth century BC, the possibility must be allowed that they emerged over a far more extended period.

Consideration of the function of developed hillforts must begin with Danebury where half of the interior has been excavated and the general arrangement of features is now clear (Figures 14.29 and 14.32). A dendritic pattern of roads and paths branched out from the entrance providing easy access to every part of the interior. The principal settlement area lay around the periphery of the fort and consisted of a series of closely spaced circular houses with associated storage buildings, storage pits and working areas. In some parts, especially around the north side, there is some evidence for larger houses set a little further into the fort away from the ramparts. The interior was divided into two by a main road. The southern half was given over almost entirely to rows of massively built storage buildings aligned along paths and replaced frequently on the same spot. To the north of the main road these buildings were much rarer but storage pits, which occurred widely within the fort, were much in evidence. It was here, too, that a group of shrines was located (pp. 512–14).

Standing back from the detail of the excavation two things emerge: the ordered regularity of the plan and the intensity of the occupation, an intensity manifesting itself in the repeated replacement of buildings and the sheer bulk of the occupation debris.

Danebury is by no means unusual. Maiden Castle and South Cadbury have produced a comparable range of evidence, though the areas excavated were more limited (Figure 14.33), and even the small-scale trial holes dug at Yarnbury yielded a surprising density of pits. Winklebury II, on the other hand, produced a rather different pattern (Figure 14.32). Pits and post-holes and a range of domestic debris were found but the density of use was evidently much lighter. The differences are quantitative rather than qualitative and are best explained by suggesting that Winklebury was used for only a short time whereas Danebury remained in occupation

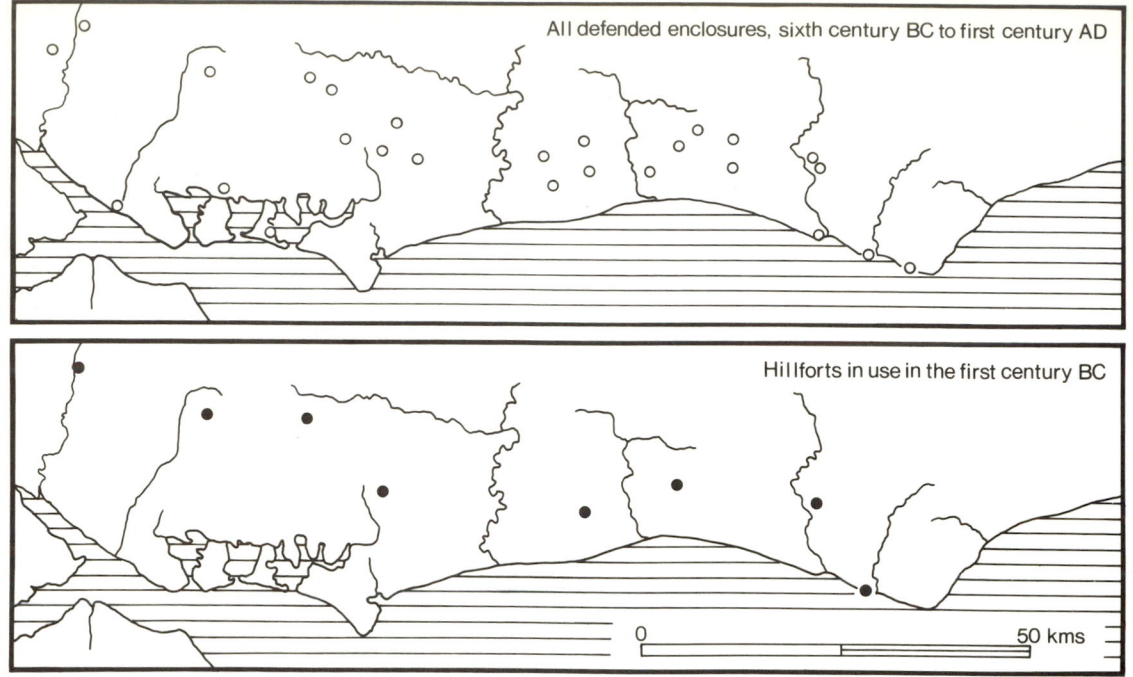

All defended enclosures, sixth century BC to first century AD

Hillforts in use in the first century BC

0   50 kms

Figure 14.27   Hillforts on the South Downs (source: author).

throughout the Middle Iron Age. The differences, however, serve as a reminder that site history probably varies considerably from fort to fort and not all developed hillforts commanded territories throughout the entire duration of the Middle Iron Age.

How the developed forts functioned within the socio-economic system is a matter of speculation but a strong case can be made for suggesting that some of them served central-place functions. They generally occupied dominant positions in large territories and commanded a series of resources. There is ample evidence of massive storage facilities (well in excess of contemporary farmsteads when assessed area by area) to enable local products like corn and wool to be stockpiled. Rarer raw materials, derived from outside the immediate territories, such as iron, bronze, shale and salt, were also being brought in for manufacture into products of enhanced value. Taken together the evidence is strongly suggestive of a complex of redistribution functions being articulated within the protection of the ramparts. This possibility gains considerable support from the discovery, at Danebury, of a number of regularly cut stone weights. Clearly, if redistribution was a function of developed hillforts some mode of accurate measurement would have been required (Cunliffe 1984a, 556–9). How these activities were enacted within the broader socio-economic system is a question to which we must return in chapter 20.

One further function which developed hillforts may have performed was that of providing a religious focus of the community. Buildings which might be regarded as temples have now been found, occupying prominent positions, in three forts. At Maiden Castle the main street entering the east gate ran through the fort directly to a circular stone-walled structure 9 m in diameter

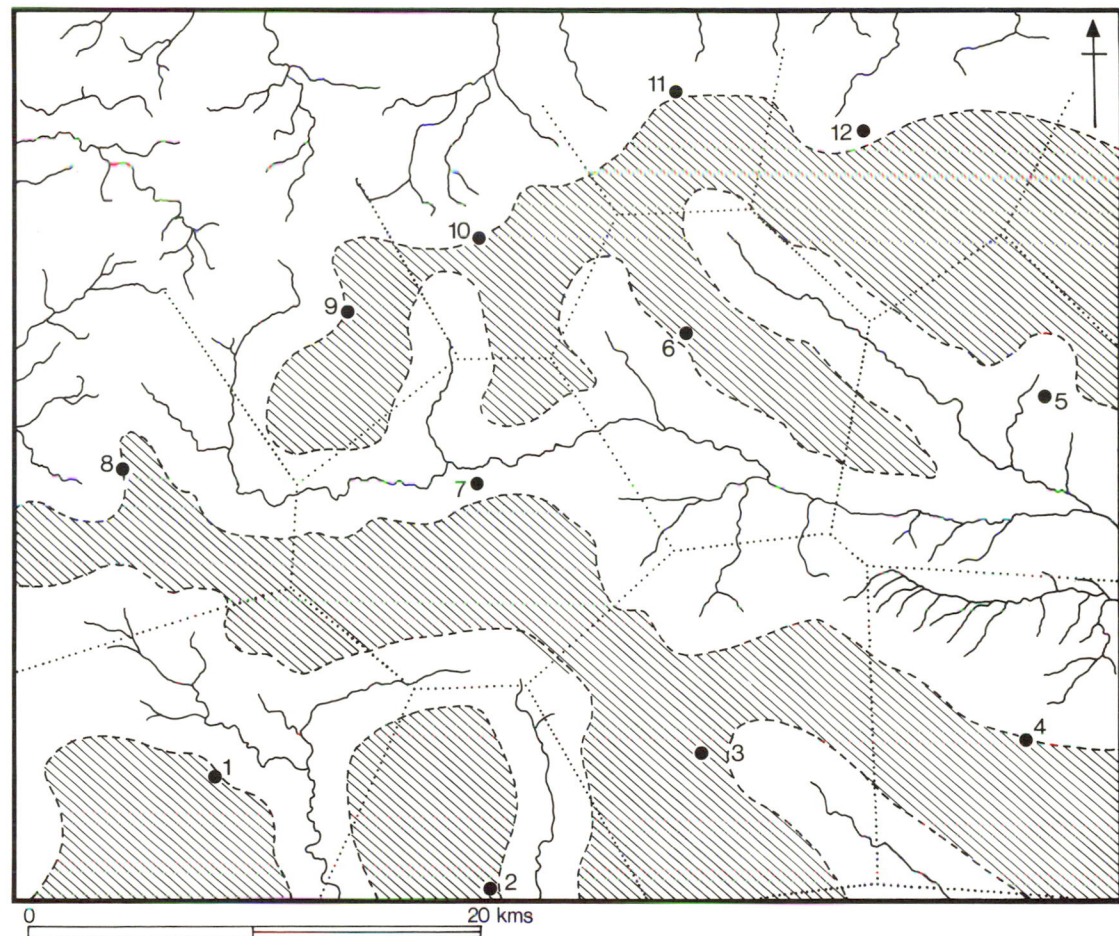

Figure 14.28   Hillforts on the north Wessex Downs *c.* 200 BC. The shaded area indicates land more than 1 mile from the nearest permanent water supply. 1 Broadway Banks; 2 Sidbury; 3 Fosbury; 4 Beacon Hill; 5 Bussocks; 6 Membury; 7 Forest Hill; 8 Oldbury; 9 Barbury; 10 Liddington Castle; 11 Uffington Castle; 12 Segsbury. (Source: Cunliffe 1976a with amendments).

(Figure 14.33). The fact that this building was replaced in the Roman period by a similar circular building that lay immediately adjacent to a Romano-Celtic temple hints at the possibility that the pre-Roman building served a religious function: its imposing approach certainly singles it out as a structure of some significance. This arrangement is also reflected at South Cadbury, where a processional way led to what was undoubtedly a shrine or a temple. Work at Danebury has also brought to light a group of rectangular buildings, all facing the fort entrance and aligned close to the main road (p. 512 and Figure 19.10, p. 513). These three sites provide a reminder that sanctuaries are to be expected as an integral part of hillfort occupation. The presence of late Romano-Celtic temples within a number of forts surely implies a continuity of religious practice from the pre-invasion period.

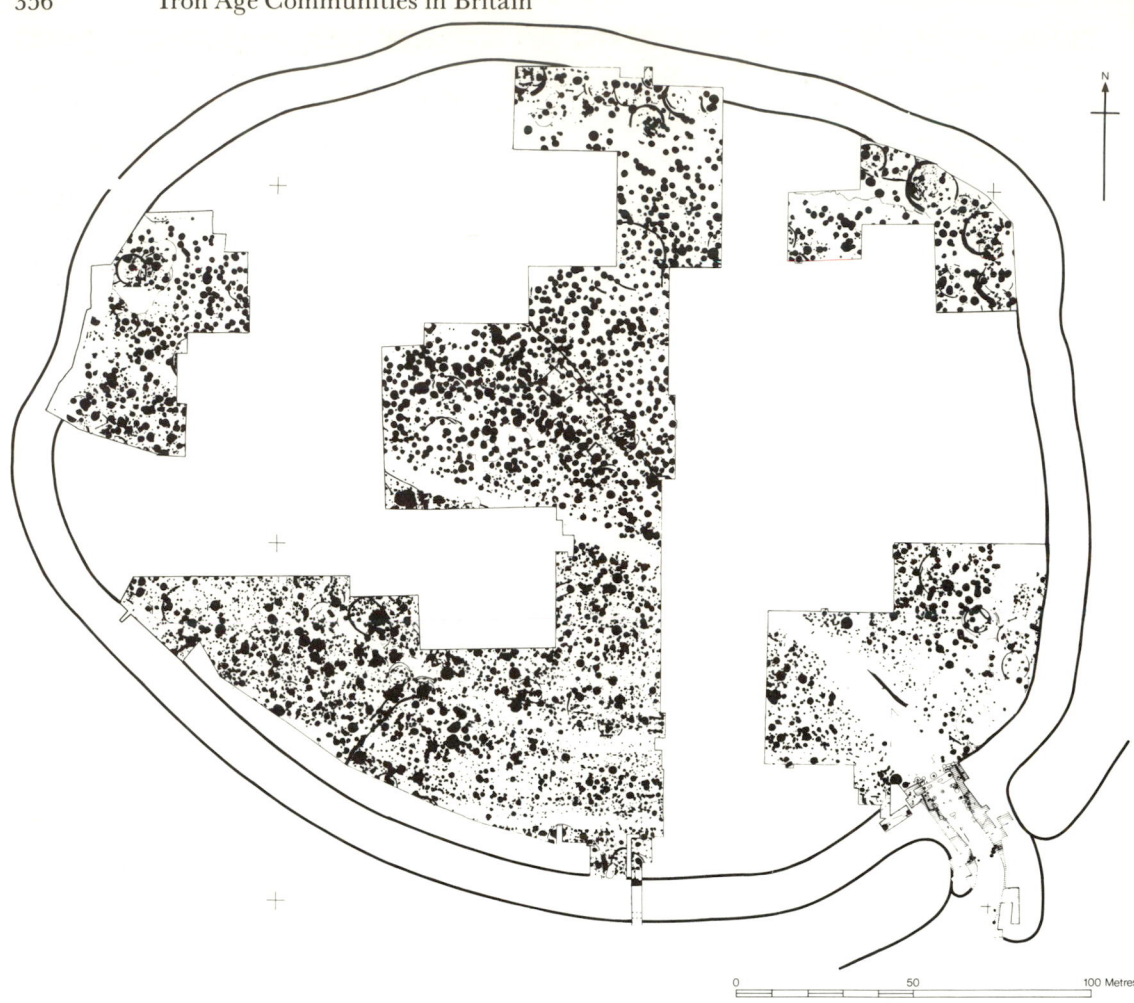

Figure 14.29   The interior of Danebury. The features represent occupation over the period *c.* 550–100 BC (source: author).

In summary, it may be said that of the hillforts of Wessex a broad three-phase development can be recognized between 800 and 100 BC. In the earliest phase (800–600) large communal hill-top enclosures were built probably to serve as bases for the autumn and winter management of stock. At the same time 'aristocratic' settlements were strongly defended but probably more to display status than to provide protection. Some time during the sixth century the system underwent a significant change when the first early hillforts were built in considerable numbers across the face of the countryside. These were occupied by substantial communities and some bear evidence of defence and attack. Finally, in the fourth century a few forts rose to positions of dominance. They were massively re-defended and formed focal points in well-defined territories. Internal occupation was intense and continuous and there is good reason to suppose that they served as central places in complex redistribution networks. They were also religious foci and may well have been centres of coercive power for their region. The further implications of these developments will be explored in chapter 20.

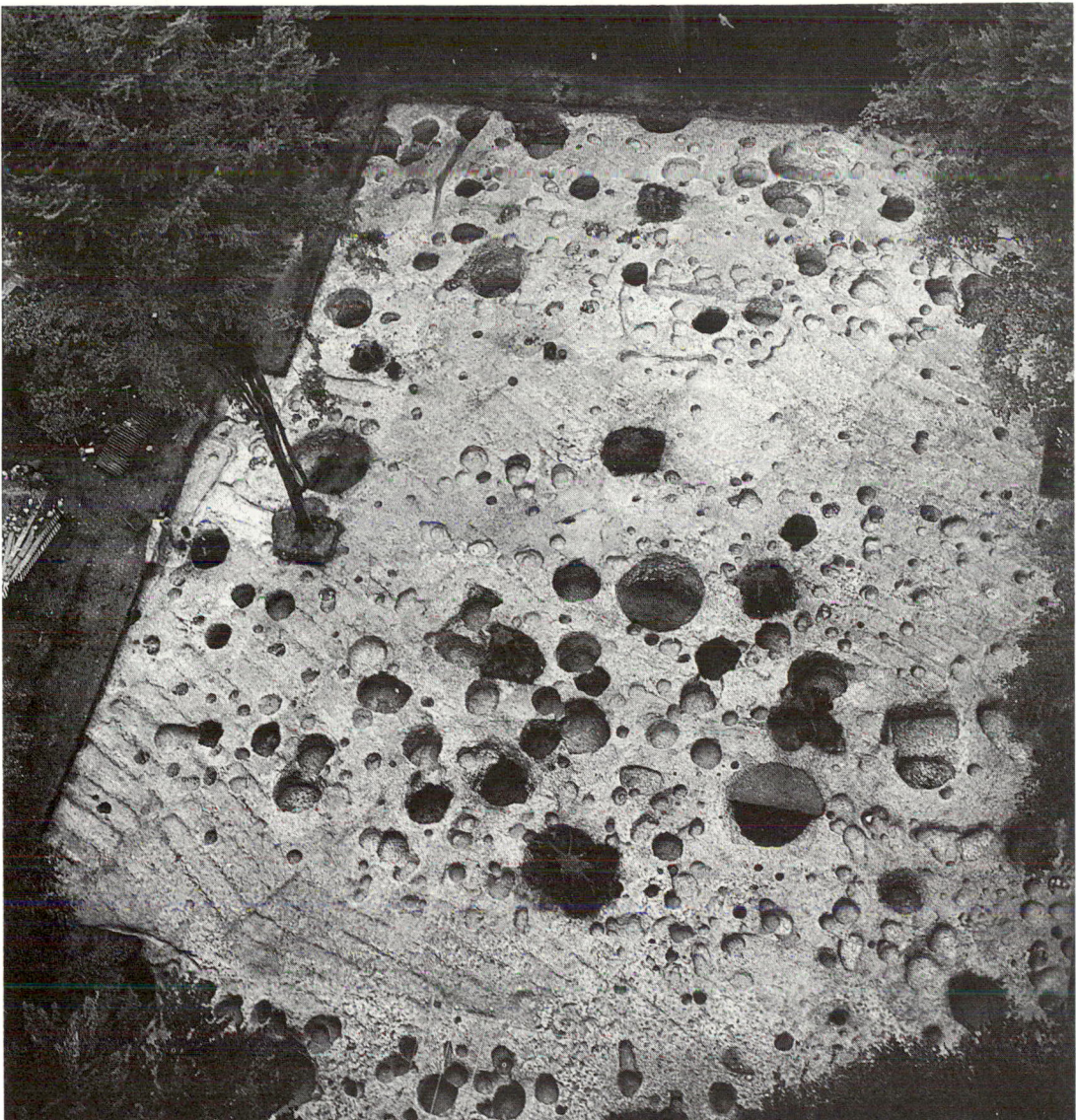

Figure 14.30   Excavation inside the hillfort of Danebury, Hants., showing streets, the post-holes of timber buildings and storage pits (photo: David Leigh. Danebury Trust).

The Cotswolds and the Northamptonshire uplands

The general pattern of development outlined for Wessex seems to hold true for the hillforts of the Jurassic ridge (Cunliffe 1984b). Norbury Camp, Glos., clearly belongs in the early hill-top enclosure category while others, including Nottingham Hill and Borough Hill, conform to the general characteristics of the class.

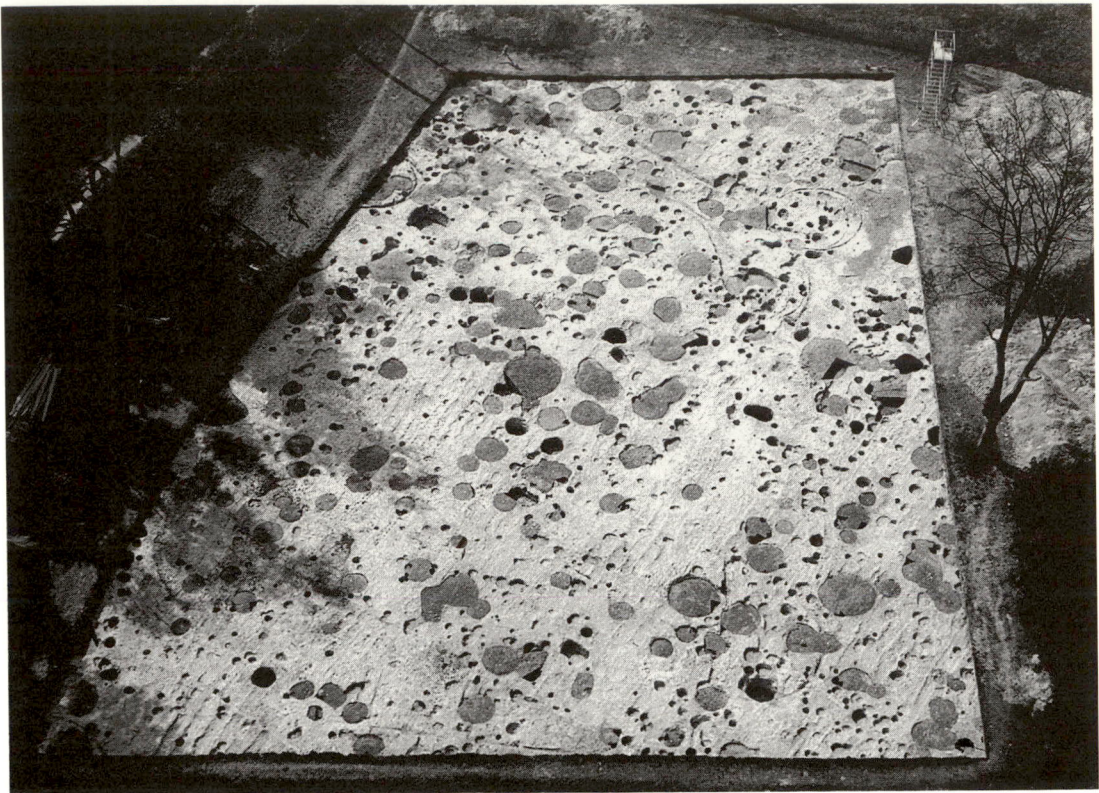

Figure 14.31 Excavations inside the hillfort of Danebury, Hants. General view showing the density of occupation behind the southern defences (photo: Danebury Trust).

Early hillforts are well represented. The best known is Crickley Hill, Glos., where an extensive programme of excavation is in progress. The earliest defence (Crickley period 2) consisted of a massive timber-laced rampart with a well-built external stone face: the radiocarbon dates suggest a construction date in the seventh or sixth century BC. Inside, the principal features to be recovered are four-post structures and several large rectangular structures which are either houses (as the excavator prefers) or rows of four-, five- and six-post storage buildings, some of them in fenced enclosures. In the late sixth or early fifth century the defences were reconstructed and an outer hornwork was added to protect the gate. The settlement continued to develop with several circular houses now added, dominated by a massive round house built just inside the gate.

Other forts of the early period, defined by more limited excavation, include Leckhampton, Shenberrow, Glos., Little Solisbury, Avon, Chastleton and Lyneham, Oxon., Bredon, Heref. and Worcs., and Hunsbury, Northants. As in Wessex, early hillforts seem to be prolific.

Much less is known of the developed hillforts of the Middle Iron Age but Kimsbury and Sodbury are likely, on typological grounds, to belong to this group while excavation at Bury Wood Camp, Wilts., Hunsbury, Northants., and Madmarsden, Oxon., have produced evidence of intensive occupation in this period.

WINKLEBURY

DANEBURY (1983)

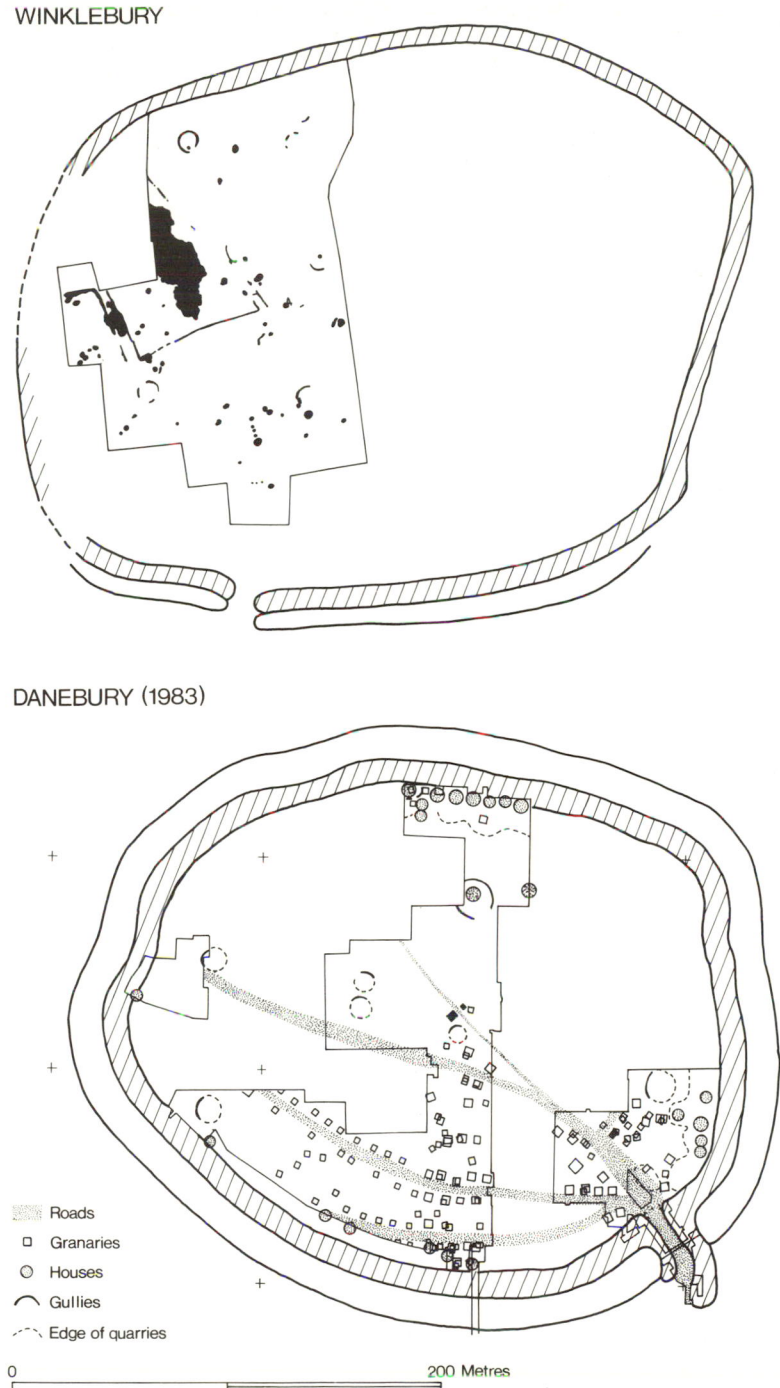

Roads
□ Granaries
○ Houses
⌒ Gullies
⌒ Edge of quarries

0   200 Metres

Figure 14.32 The interiors of the hillforts of Winklebury and Danebury in the Middle Iron Age (source: Cunliffe 1984c).

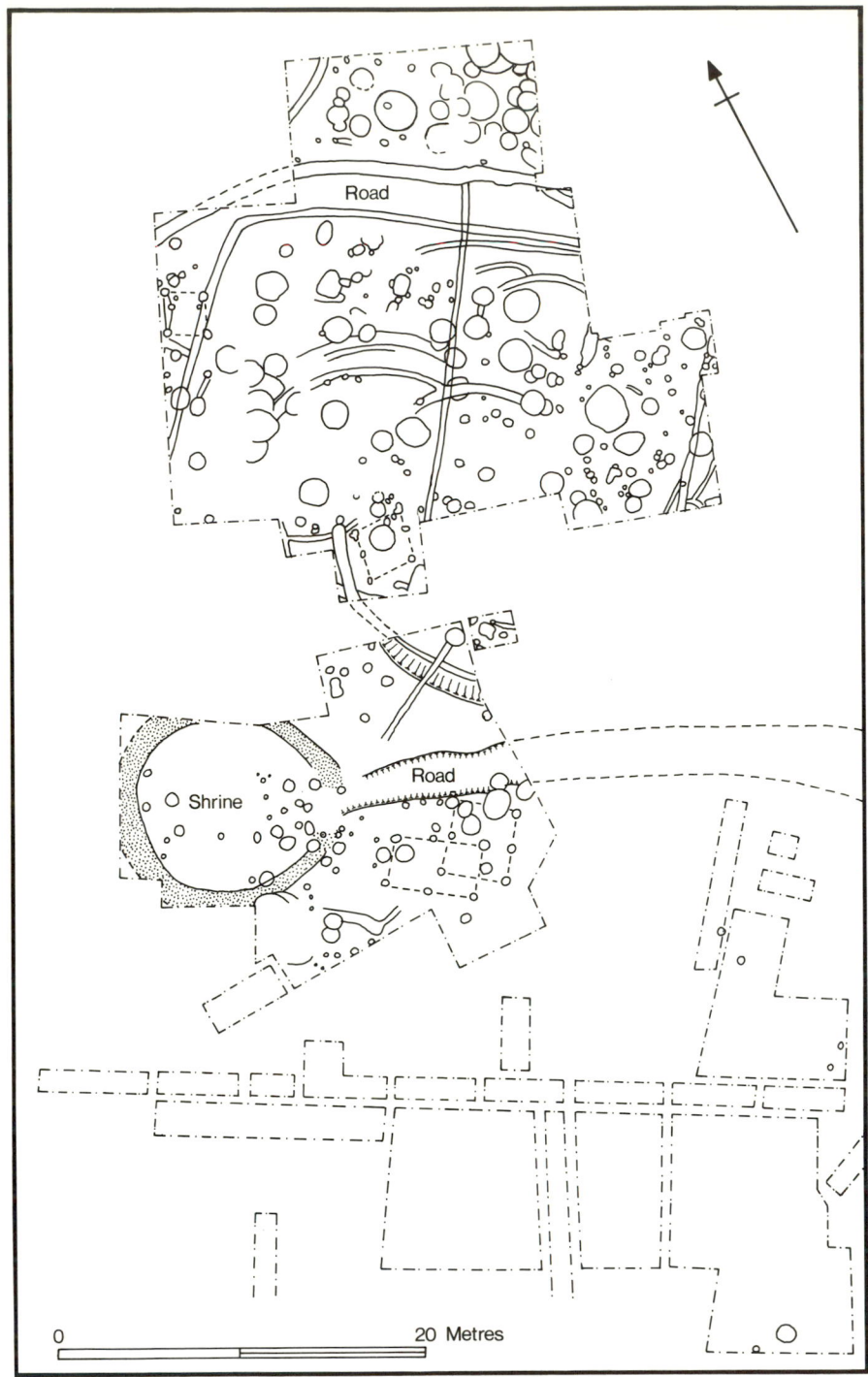

Figure 14.33   The settlement plan within Maiden Castle, Dorset (source: Wheeler 1943).

The Chilterns

The hillforts of the Chilterns have not been extensively examined but from what little is known of them they appear to follow the broad trends outlined for Wessex and the Cotswolds. The Chiltern ridge is much like the chalk downs of Sussex and presents some evidence to suggest that it too was divided into distinct territories (Figure 14.34), but the situation is complicated by the fact that the chalk ridge is seldom dissected by rivers except in the case of the Cam and the Lea. Nevertheless, the scarp slope rivers created partial natural barriers, which were projected across the ridge by artificial boundaries composed of lines of banks and ditches; Dray's Ditches, Beds., the only boundary of this kind to be examined, has proved to be a complex structure composed of multiple ditches and timber stockades originating probably as early as the late second millennium. Within all but one of the six territories thus defined lies a single major hillfort (Dyer 1961). Subsidiary forts are known in three of the regions, but the absence of adequate excavations prevents any firm conclusion as to their date or development. The general impression given by this pattern, however, is that the eastern Chilterns were subjected to the same social and economic pressures as the South Downs, leading eventually to the domination of each territory by a single fort.

The Welsh borderland

Between the valley of the river Severn and the mountains of Wales is a zone of broken land some 50 km wide, densely studded with hillforts (e.g. Hogg 1976). Many of them have been subjected to limited campaigns of excavation but six have been excavated on a scale sufficient to enable their structural sequences and interior occupation to be assessed: Moel y Gaer, Breiddin, Dinorben, Croft Ambrey, Credenhill and Midsummer Hill.

Among the earliest is the Breiddin, a massive enclosure of some 30 ha. The enclosing feature at this stage consisted of a comparatively slight bank less than a metre high into the front of which had been set two rows of posts about a metre apart with the individual posts in each row spaced at the same interval. Radiocarbon dates suggest that construction took place some time in the tenth to eighth century BC – a date borne out by a collection of Late Bronze Age finds from the interior. Several other sites have produced evidence of enclosure in the first half of the first millennium BC. At Moel y Gaer the later hillfort is preceded by a palisaded enclosure of which two (possibly three) lines, not necessarily contemporary, have been traced. The outermost of these, which consists of posts set at 1 m intervals in a low bank, is not at all unlike the defensive structure at Breiddin. The Moel y Gaer palisades are undated but within them, pre-dating the first rampart, was a settlement of post-ring round houses with radiocarbon dates indicating occupation in the seventh century or possibly a little earlier (Figure 14.35). At Dinorben five lines of palisade trench were traced (Guilbert 1980) but they are undated and it is difficult to distinguish what of the internal occupation was contemporary with them.

At all three sites the early palisaded enclosures were later replaced with ramparts. At Breiddin the rampart of stone-faced soil and rubble was built over the earlier bank and appears to have been associated with a number of roundhouses some of which produced radiocarbon dates implying occupation centring on the fifth century. At Moel y Gaer the timber-laced stone-faced rampart was built within the palisade lines and inside the new enclosure an orderly settlement of stake-built roundhouses interspersed with regular rows of four-post structures was laid out

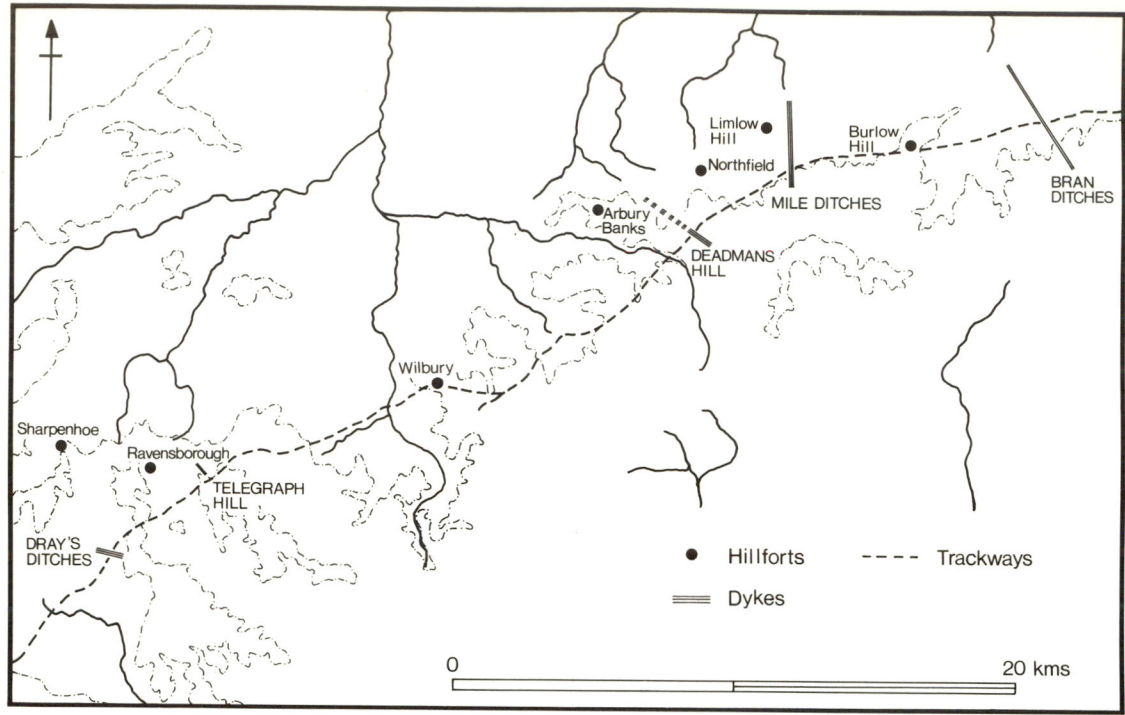

Figure 14.34 Territorial boundaries in the eastern Chilterns (source: Dyer 1961).

(Figure 14.35). Radiocarbon dates indicate a sixth- to fourth-century span but the ordered plan of the settlement and the fact that no structures were rebuilt might suggest a single phase occupation of a brief duration. At Dinorben the earliest rampart – a timber-framed structure with stone facing (Guilbert 1979a) – was built in the sixth century. Internal occupation was dense but it is difficult to say which features belonged to this period.

The evidence, so far discussed, presents a tolerably consistent picture. The earliest enclosures were palisaded and these seem to have enclosed substantial settlements dating to within the first half of the first millennium BC. Thereafter, ramparts were built, either with box structures faced with stone walls or with stone facing alone, some time in the period of the sixth to fifth century. The evidence from Moel y Gaer shows that the contemporary settlements were carefully laid out though some may have been short lived.

The situation during the Middle and Late Iron Age is rather less clear but all three forts appear to have continued in use. At Breiddin a number of large four-post structures apparently followed the phase dominated by circular buildings, producing a range of radiocarbon dates between 294 ± 40 bc and 170 ± 40 bc suggesting occupation within the fourth to third century (Musson 1976, 302), while at Dinorben dates for interior occupation range from 475 ± 60 bc to 345 ± 60 bc (Guilbert 1980). At Moel y Gaer, the rebuilding of the rampart was preceded by a single date of 240 ± 80 bc and seems to have been associated with rectangular structures represented now only by rubble platforms.

The hillfort of Wrekin, Salop, provided some additional evidence. Here two separate defensive circuits presumably represented at least two major phases in the history of the site. A limited area

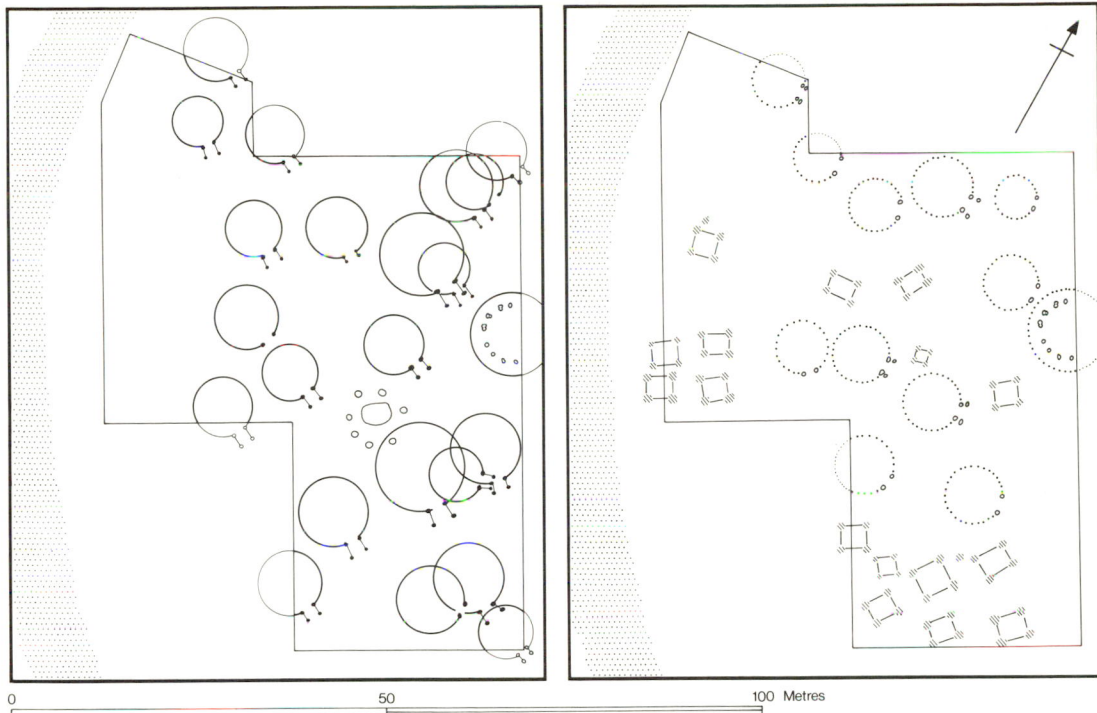

0   50   100 Metres

Figure 14.35   The interior of the hillfort of Moel y Gaer. The early phase of ring-groove houses is replaced in the later phase by ring-post houses and four-post 'granaries' (source: Guilbert 1976).

excavation between the two circuits provided clear evidence of a number of large four-post structures, rebuilt many times on the same sites for which radiocarbon dates ranging from 520 ± 180 bc to 340 ± 100 bc were obtained suggesting construction somewhere within the period from the seventh to the fifth centuries. These buildings were presumably contemporary with the outer (earliest) rampart. The inner circuit probably represents a new phase of activity dating to the fifth–fourth century or perhaps a little later. After this the outer area seems to have come back into use.

So far the discussion has focused on the hillforts of the northern borderland. Turning now to the south, three well-excavated sites are of considerable importance: Croft Ambrey, Salop, and Midsummer Hill and Credenhill, Heref. and Worcs. At Croft Ambrey two major phases of defence were recognized, the 'Plateau Camp' of some 2.2 ha defended by a small dump-constructed rampart and the extended or 'Main Camp', comprising an enclosure of 3.6 ha defended by a massive dump-constructed rampart. At Midsummer Hill the defences appear to be of only one phase closely similar in form to the Main Camp fortifications at Croft Ambrey. A single radiocarbon date of 420 ± 185 bc is available for an early phase in the gate development. No firm conclusions can safely be based on such slight evidence but taken on face value it might suggest a phase of hillfort building (and rebuilding) some time in the sixth to fourth centuries. The associated pottery is typologically Middle Iron Age.

The area excavations in the interiors of Croft Ambrey, Midsummer Hill and Credenhill showed that considerable areas close to the ramparts were occupied by rows of large four-post structures which had been reconstructed many times on the same sites. The size of the structures, the ordered layout and the continuity of building are closely comparable to the pattern of structures found in the southern sector of Danebury during the Middle Iron Age.

While it would be wrong to interpret the evidence from the Welsh borderland in too precise a manner, the broad sequence of development has much in common with the Wessex pattern. In the earliest period (ninth to seventh centuries) lightly defended hill-top enclosures were comparatively widespread; these were replaced frequently on the same sites, with box-structured ramparts in the seventh or sixth century. The interior features of these early hillforts leave little doubt that some at least were occupied by ordered settlements of considerable size. Later, at some time centring on the sixth or fifth century there was a phase of massive hillfort building, or rebuilding, creating fortified sites showing all the characteristics of the developed hillforts of the south. It is possible that this development was restricted to the southern zone of the borderland leaving the forts of the north to evolve as local pressures dictated. This apparent north–south divide is also dramatically reflected in the material culture of the Middle Iron Age and hints at a real ethnic divide. The question is one to which we shall return in chapter 20.

The latest hillfort development in the west and north

Throughout much of southern Britain there is clear evidence to show that a number of developed hillforts were abandoned towards the beginning of the first century BC. In the west of Britain, however, some were in occupation at the time of the Roman Conquest when, we are told, in the south-west alone, Vespasian had to destroy twenty fortified sites. Impressive evidence of ultimate pre-Roman occupation is provided by Hod Hill, Dorset, where the fort was packed with circular huts, some of them provided with annexes, some set in enclosures (Figures 8.8, p. 168 and 14.36). Whether or not occupation was continuous from the end of the Middle Iron Age (c. 100 BC) to the time of the conquest in AD 43 it is impossible to say on the available evidence. At any event it is likely that the densely settled appearance at the time of the invasion was accentuated by refugees seeking the protection of the old fortifications. The remarkable plan of the south-east sector of the enclosure, which survives because the area has never been ploughed (Figure 8.7, p. 167), gives the impression of a heavily built-up complex as it would have been at the time of the Roman attack in AD 43. More than forty-five circular houses can be recognized, which, if the same density is applied to the entire enclosure, would have meant a total of about 270 houses. Allowing for some to represent abandoned or replaced structures, and a unit of three persons to a house, the potential population can hardly have been less than 500 and may have approached 1,000.

Only one small area has been examined by excavation (Figure 8.8, p. 168) close to the road leading from the Steepleton Gate. Several circular huts were uncovered, two of them with annexes. One of the huts, set in a rectangular ditched enclosure, was thought by the excavator to be a chieftain's hut at the time of the Roman Conquest since it provided a focus for the ballista attack which the fort suffered under the Romans.

To what extent Hod Hill is a special case it is impossible to say. Other forts in the south-west were evidently in use at about the time of the invasion. At South Cadbury and probably at Maiden Castle the rampart was strengthened in the first century AD and at both forts there is evidence of internal occupation though the extent and intensity is difficult to define. While there

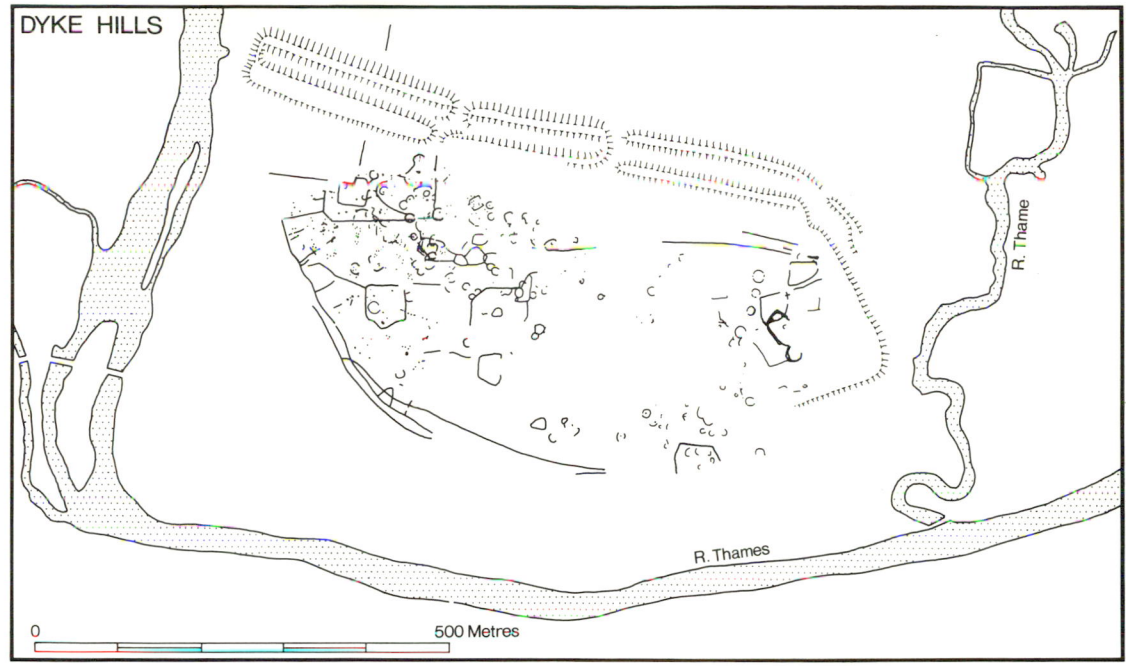

Figure 14.36   The enclosed oppidum of Dyke Hills, Oxon. (source: Hingley and Miles 1984).

is no reason to reject the idea of continuous occupation from the Middle Iron Age the possibility that the late occupation was a short-lived response to the imminence of Rome seems more likely.

In other parts of Britain, a number of hillforts show signs of a dense internal settlement. North Wales has several such sites, including Dinorben, Denbigh., and Garn Boduan, Carn Fadrun, Conway Mountain and Tre'r Ceiri in Caernarvonshire, each with numbers of huts ranging from nineteen to over 100 (Figures 13.18, p. 272 and 13.19, p. 273). Hogg's assessment of their significance has led him to propose a population density averaging about fifteen persons per acre (Hogg 1962, 22–3), which in terms of actual numbers gives a maximum of about 400 people living in Garn Boduan at any one time. Alcock (1965, 194), reconsidering the same evidence, offers the suggestion that the population approximated more closely to 700, a density averaging twenty-five per acre. Clearly, figures of this kind are open to many sources of error, but the order of magnitude is interesting since it approximates to the rough figures suggested above for Hod Hill. Hogg and Alcock differ again over the problem of permanent residence, Alcock preferring to suppose transhumance between forts and the lowland settlements rather than permanent occupation. Certainly, the extreme climate of the region might weigh in favour of this. The matter is highly complex and cannot easily be solved in the absence of extensive excavation, and without good dating evidence there is little chance of assessing the chronological development of any of these sites.

Most of the large Scottish oppida show similar signs of intensive occupation rising to more than 300 houses within the 16.2 ha of Eildon Hill North, Roxburgh., the capital of the Selgovae. Allowing for undiscovered huts in the area beneath a plantation, Feachem (1966, 79) estimates the population to be between 2,000 and 3,000. Further south, at Yeavering Bell,

Northumberland, a 5.3 ha enclosure contains about 130 huts which, if they were all occupied at the same time, might point to a community of at least 500 souls. The same functional problems arise in Scotland as in Wales: were the forts permanently occupied or not and over what time span were the houses built? The answers are not as yet forthcoming.

The late use or re-use of hillforts is a question still thwart with difficulties. The simplest generalization which can be offered is that in the centre south and south-east, developed hillforts were abandoned on a large scale after the beginning of the first century BC as the result of fundamental socio-economic changes which had gripped the area following the establishment of extensive contacts with the Continent. In the west and north, however, many forts appear to have continued in use to the time of conquest and in some cases well into the Roman period, though whether or not occupation was continuous it is impossible to say. In intermediate regions, like the territory of the Durotriges and Dobunni the picture is complex. While the old forts may have remained in occupation the balance of the evidence would suggest that intensity of use had dramatically declined after the beginning of the first century BC. It is, however, abundantly clear that many of them had been refurbished by the time that the Roman threat had appeared. Vespasian, faced with more than twenty to subdue, would have been all too aware of the problem.

Fécamp style defences

Sir Mortimer Wheeler's campaign of excavation and survey in northern France (Wheeler and Richardson 1957) focused attention on a distinctive form of defensive system dating to the time of the Caesarian campaigns in the middle of the first century BC. The characteristics were a massive dump rampart fronted by a wide, shallow, flat-bottomed ditch. This type he named after the hillfort of Fécamp. The possibility that defensive systems of this kind were adopted in south-eastern Britain has been widely considered (Ward Perkins 1944; Cotton 1961a, 66). But several of the sites previously canvassed are now regarded as doubtful (T.K. Green 1979; F.H. Thompson 1985). Two, however, still remain as distinct possibilities: Calleva, Hants., and Loose, Kent.

The fortifications of Calleva enclose an area of about 35 ha and belong to the category of *enclosed oppida* defined below. They were originally thought to date to the post-conquest period (Boon 1969) but subsequent excavations suggest redating to *c.* 20 BC (Fulford 1987, 275–7). The enclosure at Quarry Wood, Loose, can also be classified as an enclosed oppidum. Its date is less certain but would appear to lie within the late-first-century BC–early-first-century AD bracket.

Both were built afresh at previously undefended locations. That the style of the defences was similar to that adopted in northern Gaul need occasion no surprise since the two regions were in close contact throughout the first century BC and early first century AD.

The development of oppida in the south-east

Over much of south-east Britain during the first century BC hill-top fortifications went out of general use, and there appears to have been a corresponding shift of concentrations of population to valley-side sites, often to locations which controlled major river crossings. From what little evidence is at present available, it would seem that while some of these settlements were wholly

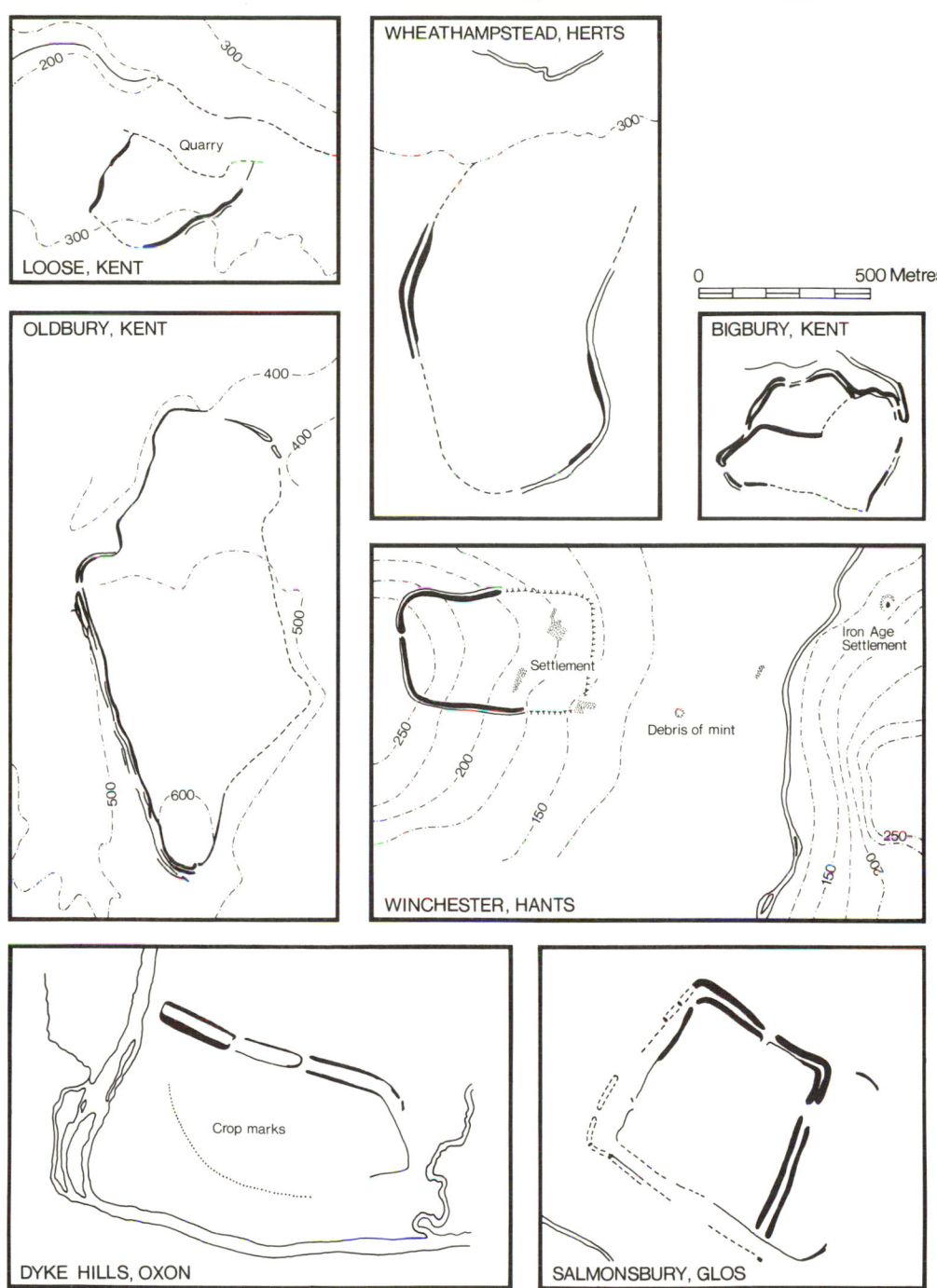

Figure 14.37 Comparative plans of enclosed oppida (source: Cunliffe 1976b).

or partially enclosed by earthworks, others may have been open and undefended (Cunliffe 1976b, 145–53). Those sites with defences have been called *enclosed oppida* (Figure 14.37).

A clear example of the type is provided by the settlement at Winchester, of which the Oram's Arbour earthwork forms a part. The settlement occupies a valley-side location and is defended on at least three sides by a V-shaped ditch and dump-constructed rampart. Pottery from the ditch points to a construction phase in the first half of the first century BC and there is now evidence of extensive internal occupation (Biddle 1975a, 98–100). In Kent, Quarry Wood Camp, Loose, provides a comparable, though less well-dated, example. Here an enclosure of more than 12 ha was sited on sloping ground overlooking a stream. The rampart was of dump construction, but unlike Winchester the ditch, at least in its latest phase, suggests a flat-bottomed profile; it may however have been preceded by a ditch of V-section. To this same category would appear to belong the earthwork of Wheathampstead, Herts., but some doubt has been cast on the nature of the site (Dyer 1976b).

Closely related types of settlement are found sited in low-lying situations near to rivers. Dyke Hills (Dorchester), Oxon., is perhaps the best surviving example (Figure 14.36). Its multiple defences now enclose an area of approximately 46 ha at the confluence of the Thame and the Thames. A shift in the river course in the last 2000 years has probably increased the apparently defended area, but aerial photography shows dense occupation covering about 25 ha. No excavation has been undertaken in the enclosure and the site must therefore remain undated. At the comparable site of Salmonsbury, Glos., however, a multiple-ditched enclosure lying close to the river Windrush, excavation has produced ample evidence of first-century occupation.

To this same category the defended enclosure at Silchester belongs. The Inner Earthwork (Boon 1969) defines a polygonal enclosure of about 35 ha which is now thought to be of pre-Roman date. Within there is evidence of intensive and regularly planned occupation (Fulford 1987).

Comparatively few *enclosed oppida* have yet been recognized in valley-side and valley-bottom locations, but the strong possibility exists that more will be found now that the category has been defined. In each of the examples noted above the settlements would appear to have developed during the first century BC in positions chosen specifically for their economic importance in relation to trade routes. The further implications of this will be considered below (pp. 543–5).

Although it is true that the majority of hillforts had gone out of use in the south-east by the early first century BC, a few hill-top locations continued to develop. In Kent two such sites are known: Oldbury, in west Kent between the Medway and the Darent; and Bigbury, near Canterbury, both of which have produced finds suggesting first-century BC and early first-century AD use. These sites, and others of similar type, can best be regarded as varieties of the generalized *enclosed oppida* category and should be distinguished from hillforts of the kind which may have continued to have been used as convenient sites for farms or small rural settlements. Only where extensive excavations have been carried out will the distinction be possible to make.

The enclosed oppida represent the last stage of 'hillfort' development in south-eastern Britain. Thereafter open settlements of urban character continued to develop. Some, e.g. Verulamium, Braughing, Canterbury and Old Sleaford, were apparently without significant boundaries, while other locations were delimited, often at a considerable distance from the settled nucleus, by massive linear dykes. Sites like Camulodunum, Selsey and Bagendon, together with Silchester and the North Oxfordshire Grim's Ditch, fall into this category of *territorial oppida* (Cunliffe 1976b, 135–6), and have been discussed individually in detail above (chapters 7 and 8).

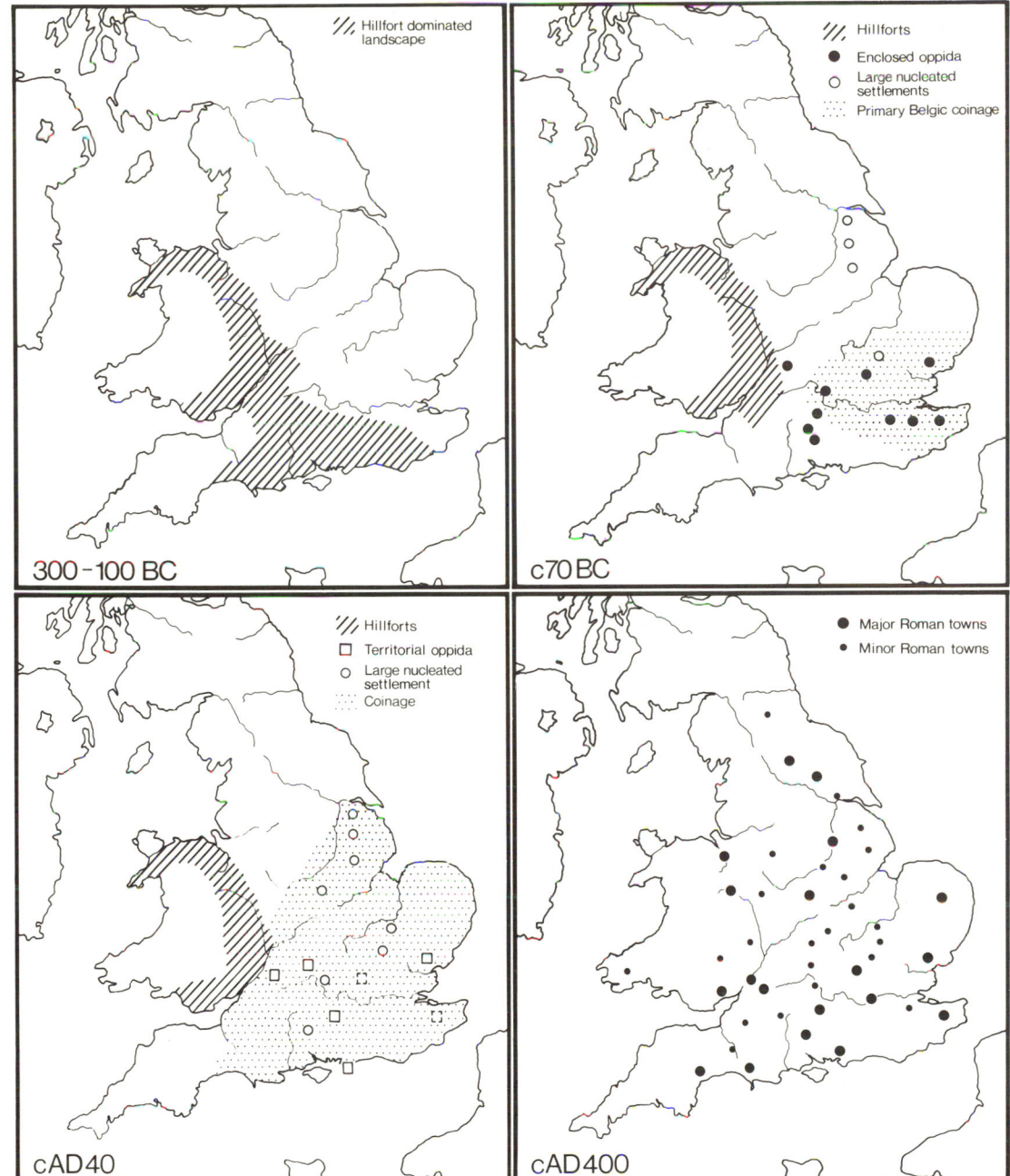

Figure 14.38   Summary maps showing spread of urban sites in Britain (source: Cunliffe 1976b with amendments).

The nature and development of enclosed oppida, territorial oppida and open urban settlements is at present ill-understood, largely because excavation on such sites has been minimal. It is therefore highly likely that, when more work has been carried out, the classification offered above will be shown to be over simple. In the meantime, however, the sequence – from developed hillforts to enclosed oppida and from enclosed oppida to open urban settlements and territorial oppida – fairly contains the available evidence. In all probability it represents the change from a pre-urban to a fully urban system.

15
Food producing strategies

The processes by which a community produces its basic food supply are conditioned by climate, soil and the technological capability of society at the time. All three are variable. Climate, as we have seen (pp. 57–8) can change even over comparatively short periods, soil can degenerate and lose its nutrients through over-use, while better tools or new varieties of cereal can be introduced at any time. There is a dynamic relationship between these three constraining variables. Together they control the food producing strategy, but since the variables are constantly, if often only imperceptibly, changing, so the food producing regime is never entirely static. Another factor adds to the variety. A country such as Britain, with an immensely varied geomorphology and microclimate, is a palimpsest of different bioclimatic regions. Each provides a framework within which society has to adapt its systems. Thus, in attempting to study the way in which Iron Age communities raised their food we are dealing not with a single system but with many, each with its own trajectory of change.

The evidence at our disposal is of differing types and qualities. The analysis of pollen from peat deposits provides an invaluable yardstick. In the west and north the data is tolerably good (J. Turner 1981; D. Wilson 1983; Caseldine 1980; Caseldine and Maguire 1981) but from the chalklands of central southern Britain sequences are few (Waton 1982). Against this background the cereals themselves can be assessed. Palaeobotany has come a long way since Helbaek's pioneering study of 1952 based entirely upon seed impressions found in pottery. Techniques of flotation, whereby carbonized grains are separated from soil, were not developed on any systematic scale until the late 1960s and then it was only Martin Jones's seminal study of the plant remains from Ashville, Oxon., published in 1978, that showed how much could be gained from a thorough integrated study of a single site. The debate was further advanced by Gordon Hillman's critical discussion of our techniques for reconstructing crop husbandry practices from charred remains (1981) in which he stressed the importance of studying the entire process of crop treatment from surviving residues.

The study of animal bones has a longer pedigree but even by as late as 1980 very few large assemblages had been published and those which had were usually simply treated. The work of Annie Grant (1984a) on the bone assemblages from Danebury, Hants., shows what can be gained from the thorough numerical study of a large and well-stratified assemblage. Not all soils, however, preserve bone, and there are large tracts of the country, where acid soil conditions prevail, from which no useful bone assemblages can be expected. Differential survival will always unbalance the picture.

A further source of useful data is provided by a study of insect remains from waterlogged situations. The species present are a ready indicator of local conditions and may also reflect on the activities being undertaken in the immediate environment. The impact which such a study could have on the understanding of an Iron Age settlement was demonstrated for the first time by Mark Robinson for the flood plain settlement at Farmoor in Oxfordshire (Lambrick and Robinson 1979). Finally, the study of terrestrial molluscs in ancient soils provides an invaluable tool in reconstructing the vegetational setting of sites and showing how landscape use has changed with time (J. G. Evans 1972).

While the study of the faunal and floral remains themselves are central to an understanding of food producing strategies, an assessment of the technical competence of the communities and the field monuments which they created, has much to offer. Tools are well represented in the archaeological record by those iron parts which remain, and from these it is possible to deduce much of the general technological level at which society functioned (Rees 1979). In addition we have the physical marks of man on the landscape – the clearance cairns, lynchetted fields, ditched fields, linear boundaries, corrals, etc. – which resulted from society imposing its agricultural and stock management schemes on the land. Taken together the evidence is rich and varied.

In the pages to follow we will first consider the range and potential of the plants and animals so essential to society's well being, before proceeding to outline the evidence for a series of regional strategies.

Plant cultivates and agrarian technology

Over most of the inhabited parts of south-east Britain, grain production formed the basis of the economy. Throughout the second millennium emmer wheat (*Triticum dicoccum*) and barley, in particular the naked variety (*Hordeum tetrasticum*), constituted the main crops though not to the exclusion of other varieties, but late in the second and early in the first millennium two changes became apparent: first naked barley was replaced by the hulled variety (*Hordeum hexasticum*) so that by the middle of the first millennium the percentage of the naked type had been reduced to less than a third, and second, the popularity of emmer wheat began to give way to spelt (*Triticum spelta*). This change is part of a broader pattern of diversification which becomes noticeable at this time (M. Jones 1984, 121–2).

The implications of the change in staples can best be appreciated by considering the characteristics of the various cereals. Emmer, while growing well on most soils is particularly well suited to light, comparatively dry soils like those of the chalk and limestone uplands but since it is susceptible to frost it is not well adapted to winter sowing. Spelt, however, grows well on heavy soils and is a hardy variety able to withstand cold, wind and disease (M. Jones 1981, 106). Barley, on the other hand, whether naked or hulled, may be grown practically anywhere in Britain except in areas of poor drainage or high acidity (ibid., 105).

The growth in popularity in spelt could, then, be taken to imply the colonization of heavier soils and a greater reliance on winter sowing. The spread of cultivation to a wider range of ecological niches is supported by the settlement evidence in the south-east of the country, which shows that farmsteads were now spreading to heavy clay soils, and by a study of weeds of cultivation associated with carbonized plant remains. From two Hampshire chalkland sites, Micheldever Wood and Danebury, seeds of the acid-loving weed *Chrysanthemum segetum* have been discovered implying that the clay-with-flints capping to the chalk downs was being exploited by the Middle Iron Age. Weeds from damp locations, found at Danebury, show that crops were being brought into the site from nearby river flood plains. A similar study of the weeds of cultivation found with the crops at Ashville, Oxon., leaves little doubt but that all the easy exploitable soil in the region was being farmed.

The advantages of winter sowing are considerable: some fields could be sown in the otherwise dull autumn season after the main harvest, thus spreading the work-load, while the harvest season was thus extended yielding a fresh supply of corn at just the time when the winter's stores would have been running low. The introduction of spelt on a large scale would, therefore, have had considerable advantages particularly if, as other evidence suggests, parts of Britain were experiencing an increase in population. New land could be brought under cultivation and the seasonal work-load better apportioned.

There may, however, be another factor influencing diversification – the decline in fertility of free-draining light soils which had, by this time, been under cultivation for more than 2,000 years. Evidence in support of this is varied. At Ashville it was possible to chart a gradual increase of leguminous weeds commonly associated with decreasing levels of soil nitrogen, and similar data are becoming widely available from central southern Britain (M. Jones 1984, 121–2). It may also be that the increase in periodontal disease in sheep at Danebury is related to the declining quality of the pasture (A. Grant 1984a). The dynamics of soil fertility could provide an important constraining variable in the study of Iron Age society: it is a subject well deserving of further concerted research.

Towards the end of the Iron Age there is evidence of the growing popularity of bread wheat (*Triticum aestivocompactum*) – a variety which grows well on heavy silt or clay and is responsive to high nitrogen levels. Thus its increase may be the direct result of the earlier colonization of heavy clay land. Significantly it has so far been found in quantity only in the south Midlands, at Bierton, Bucks., and Barton Court Farm, Oxon. – sites close to easily exploitable clay deposits. Its rise in popularity may be more a factor of regional specialization than of general change (M. Jones 1984, 123–4).

Other cereals were grown but on a much smaller scale. Rye (*Secale cereale*), another first-millennium introduction, occurs sporadically in Wessex, and oats (*Avena* spp.), of both the wild and cultivated varieties, are recorded from various sites but only in small proportions. Rye is a particularly hardy crop with a wide tolerance of soil types and is suitable for both autumn and spring sowing. Oats is less adaptable, preferring a milder and moister growing season. Since it is less hardy to frost it thrives better when spring sown. It was at the beginning of the first millennium that the Celtic bean (*Vicia faba*) made its first appearance in Britain and became widespread later in central southern Britain. Since it has nitrogen fixing qualities it is a useful break-crop to improve soil fertility, as well as being an acceptable food. Finally chess (*Bromus* spp.) occurs consistently in relatively small quantities, but this does not necessarily mean that it was sown as a crop in its own right.

The processes involved in reaping and storing the grain are open to debate, but it is probable that the corn was cut with reaping hooks (Figure 15.1) and was carried back to the farmstead for further treatment. While the traditional way of gripping below the ear and cutting below the

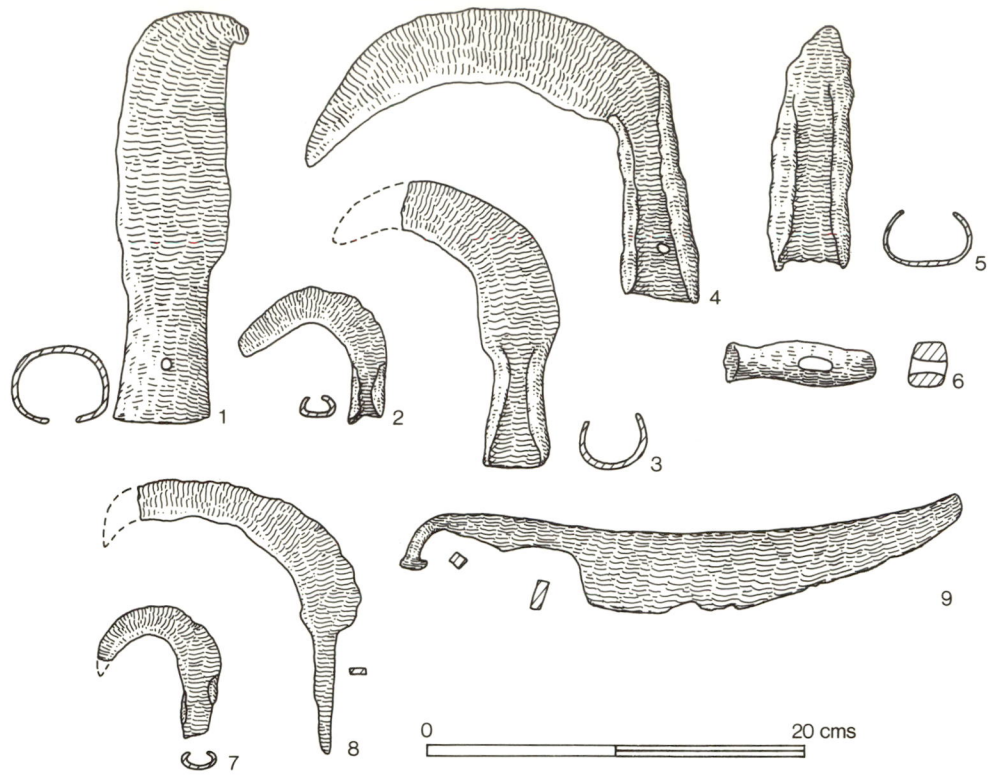

Figure 15.1   Iron tools. 1 Bill-hook from the Caburn, Sussex; 2,3,4,7,8 reaping hooks from Barbury Castle, Wilts.; 5 ploughshare from the Caburn, Sussex; 6 hammer from the Caburn, Sussex; 9 knife from Barbury Castle, Wilts. (sources: *Barbury Castle*, MacGregor and Simpson 1963; *The Caburn*, Curwen and Curwen 1927).

hand may have been generally employed, the occurrence of seeds from short-growing weeds of cultivation suggests that in some cases the stalks were cut low down. If the crop had been reaped when ripe the next process would have been threshing, but if a damp or slightly unripe crop had been cut some form of drying process would have been necessary, perhaps the artificial parching of the ears in order to drive off excess moisture and to loosen the grain from the husk to facilitate threshing. There is no direct archaeological evidence for this, but the discovery of quantities of charred grain on archaeological sites and the fact that grain was dried in specially constructed ovens in the Roman period has led to the belief that corn drying was widely practised in the Iron Age. It is generally assumed that temporary ovens built of cob were constructed for this process, but another possibility is that drying may have been carried out on a larger scale on skins spread over pre-heated flint nodules. The indirect heat which the flints would have imparted would have been quite sufficient to dry the ears to the necessary degree, with the added advantage of keeping the grain away from the direct source of heat, thus cutting down risk of combustion. That accidents did happen, however, is shown by quantities of charred grain from various sites, including deposits from pits at Itford Hill, Sussex, Fifield Bavant, Wilts., Totternhoe, Beds., Danebury, Hants., and Little Solisbury, Somerset. This type of process would explain the vast quantities of fire-crackled flints ('pot-boilers') which are found on most of the settlement sites,

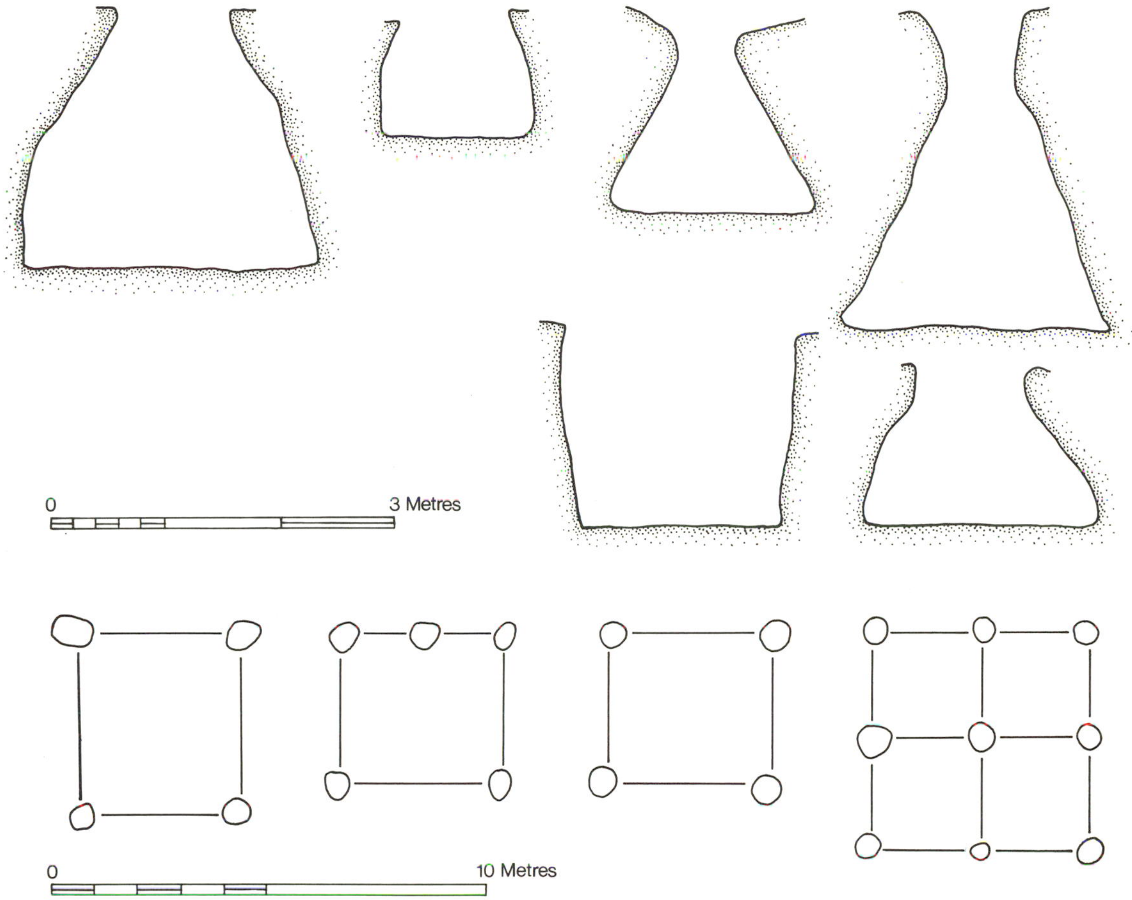

0   3 Metres

0   10 Metres

Figure 15.2   Storage pit profiles and granary plans from Danebury, Hants. (source: Cunliffe 1984a).

usually lying in thick layers mixed up with charcoal in the so-called 'irregular working hollows'. Indeed the working hollows may well have been the sites where parching, among other activities, was carried out.

As soon as the ears were dried, they would in all probability have been threshed before storage, but it is not inconceivable that some of the corn may have been stored in the ear. Such a deposit is claimed to have been found in the hillfort of Little Solisbury, but details are obscure. Two different modes of storage are implied by the archaeological evidence: below ground storage in pits and above ground storage in timber-built 'granaries'. Both types of structure constantly occur together, particularly on the chalkland of south-eastern Britain.

Pits were normally of beehive, barrel or cylindrical shape (Figure 15.2). In the early period they tended to be small, but by the third and second centuries BC they usually averaged about 2 m deep. Pits dug into the solid chalk were not necessarily lined. Although some form of wicker lining tends to cut down wastage through mould growth by keeping the grain away from the damp sides of the pit, the degree of caking together of the outer crust of grain would not have differed greatly between lined and unlined pits so long as an airtight seal of clay or marl was placed over the pit mouth. The effort involved in providing each of the grain storage pits with a wicker lining may well have been considered unnecessary – at least in the chalk areas, where the sides were firm and tolerably dry. Wicker linings have, however, been recorded at Dane's Camp, Worcs., Poxwell, Dorset, and Worlebury, Somerset, but there is nothing to show that these pits were used for storing grain rather than other commodities. Some pits were lined with dry-stone work, but these are restricted to areas where stone commonly occurs. On the Isle of Portland about seventy stone-lined pits of beehive shape were discovered, narrowed at the top so that they could be easily closed by a single slab. One of them contained a mass of carbonized grain. Various types of flooring have also been recorded, ranging from stone and wood to clay and sand.

A variety of pit forms is known, no doubt reflecting an equally wide range of function in addition to grain storage. Some, lined with clay, may have served for water storage, being linked by gullies to the eaves-drips of roofs; some were perhaps vats for such processes as tanning; while others may have been used as larders where dried or smoked meat may have been stored.

The second type of storage structure is the so-called 'granary' represented now by settings of four, five, six, or more rarely nine posts (Figure 15.2). These are usually supposed to have consisted of square or rectangular timber buildings, averaging 2.5–3.0 m in overall length, the floors of which were raised above ground level to allow the free circulation of air beneath and to prevent rodents from eating the stored supplies. Granaries occur widely over most of south-east Britain and into the Welsh borderland. Frequently, as at Little Woodbury and Walesland Rath, they were built on the periphery of the settlement, often against the boundary, to keep them as far removed as possible from the domestic activities of the settlement and the potential threat of fire, but at Gussage All Saints they cluster in the centre. Granaries have also now been found in a number of hillforts (Gent 1983): at Danebury, Hants., for example, several rows of regularly spaced buildings separated by streets were restricted to one part of the fort, implying that a special area had been reserved for this type of storage activity and a similar pattern is apparent in some of the forts of the Welsh borderland. Not all of the four- or six-post buildings were necessarily granaries; some may have been sheds for storing a range of equipment or products, others may have served as accommodation or cooking shelters. But in all probability they were built as grain stores, whatever secondary uses they were later put to.

The problem now arises as to how pits and granaries related to the storage needs of the community. It used to be thought that the seed grain, which would have amounted to probably about one-third of the crop, was stored in the granaries, while the corn for consumption was parched and tipped into pits. A series of experiments have shown, however, that there is no preservative advantage to be gained in parching grain before pit storage; moreover, the germination rate of grain stored below ground was found to be in excess of 90 per cent (P.J. Reynolds 1974). In other words, there is now no reason to suppose that all seed corn was kept through the winter in granaries since it could equally as well have been stored in pits. Further experiments showed that for pit storage to be satisfactory it was essential to keep the seal airtight. This might argue against the use of large pits as silos for consumption grain, for once they had been opened it would have been necessary for the contents to have been emptied quickly in order to prevent degeneration. Rapid use is, however, possible if the contents of each pit was common property to be shared out between all members of the community, or was used for exchange for other goods. Clearly the problem of grain storage is fraught with imponderables, but on balance it is simplest to accept the granaries as stores for the consumption cereal while the pits were used for the seed grain.

With the approach of spring the flocks and herds which throughout the winter would probably have been allowed free access to the fields, except those winter sown, would have been driven off to the fallow and to the upland pastures, while fields were further manured with household refuse brought out of the homestead.

If the fields had been heavily grazed or trampled by animals, ploughing may have been unnecessary. In most cases, however, ploughing was undertaken using the simple iron-shod crook or bow ard (without a mould-board to turn the sod), the effect of which would have been simply to scratch a furrow in the soil (Figures 15.1 and 15.4). The excavation of Celtic field surfaces is now bringing to light evidence of actual ploughing in the form of the bottoms of the individual furrows scored into the bedrock. At Overton Down, Wilts. (Figure 15.3), the remnants of furrows belonging to at least five ploughings have been examined. Although the pattern is necessarily incomplete, because the ard did not always bite deep enough to scratch the chalk, sufficient survives to show that the individual furrows were about 30 cm apart, and that in all probability the field was ploughed in two directions at right angles, to break up the soil sufficiently for sowing. Very approximate estimates for the work involved in each ploughing can be arrived at by considering an average-sized Celtic field about 64 m square, ploughed by an ard drawn by two oxen travelling at about 3 km an hour. It would take between six and eight hours to complete the area: in other words, a field could be ploughed in a day. The Overton Down field is not necessarily of Iron Age date (it could belong to the Roman period) but there is little doubt that the practices recognized there are exactly comparable to the pre-Roman situation. Indeed, evidence is now accumulating from various parts of the country to show that this basic system of arable production dates back to the second and third millennia BC, and probably remained little changed until the end of the Roman period.

In addition to using the ard for cultivation, hand-digging with a wooden spade was undertaken. At the second millennium site at Gwithian, Cornwall, individual spade-marks were found in the headland of the ploughed fields.

Iron Age fields, where they can be defined on hill-slopes, are usually squarish in shape and bounded by lynchet banks created largely by the process of ploughing, which encouraged particles of soil to move down the slope to form a positive lynchet, at the lower edge of ploughing, leaving a negative lynchet at the upper edge. That the lynchets formed at all implies the continuous ploughing of defined areas over a period of many years. Little is yet known about the mechanism of primary land division, but fences, hedges, marking stones or posts, and gullies or setting-out banks were all used to define the original limits of the fields. After the first ploughing or two the land was probably cleared of large stones and flints, which would have been thrown to the edges of the fields thus adding to the permanence of the boundaries. As ploughing continued, lynchets increased in size until gradually the stage was reached when the uncultivated slopes of the banks themselves would have been extensive enough to be used as strips of pasture between arable plots. As a general rule, therefore, it may be said that as arable farming developed within a given area of hill slopes, the actual arable hectareage must have decreased with the growth of lynchet slopes. If the thick soil of the lynchets was allowed to support the scrub and woodland which would tend to grow naturally, the areas of potential pannage and forage for pigs and cattle would have gradually increased. Such swathes of scrub would also have served as valuable wind-breaks and, if properly coppiced, would have provided a continuous supply of timber for wattlework and other purposes much as the bocage of north-western France still does today.

On the low-lying gravel soils fields were bounded by ditches and presumably hedges. In areas such as this constant ploughing would not have led to the formation of lynchets: in consequence

Figure 15.3 Plan of plough ruts discovered beneath a lynchet on Overton Down, Wilts. (source: P.J. Fowler 1967).

the only archaeological traces to survive are buried ditches, which are frequently recorded on aerial photographs. In upland areas stones cleared off the arable plots were frequently piled into mounds or low ridges known as clearance cairns.

The colonization of wasteland was systematic in many areas. The fields around the Farley Mount settlement have a distinctly well-planned regularity about them, and around the hillfort of Sidbury, Wilts., hundreds of hectares of ordered field systems are known, pre-dating linear earthworks linked to the fort. It is difficult to resist the assumption that at times during the first millennium massive and concentrated programmes of land clearance and distribution were undertaken.

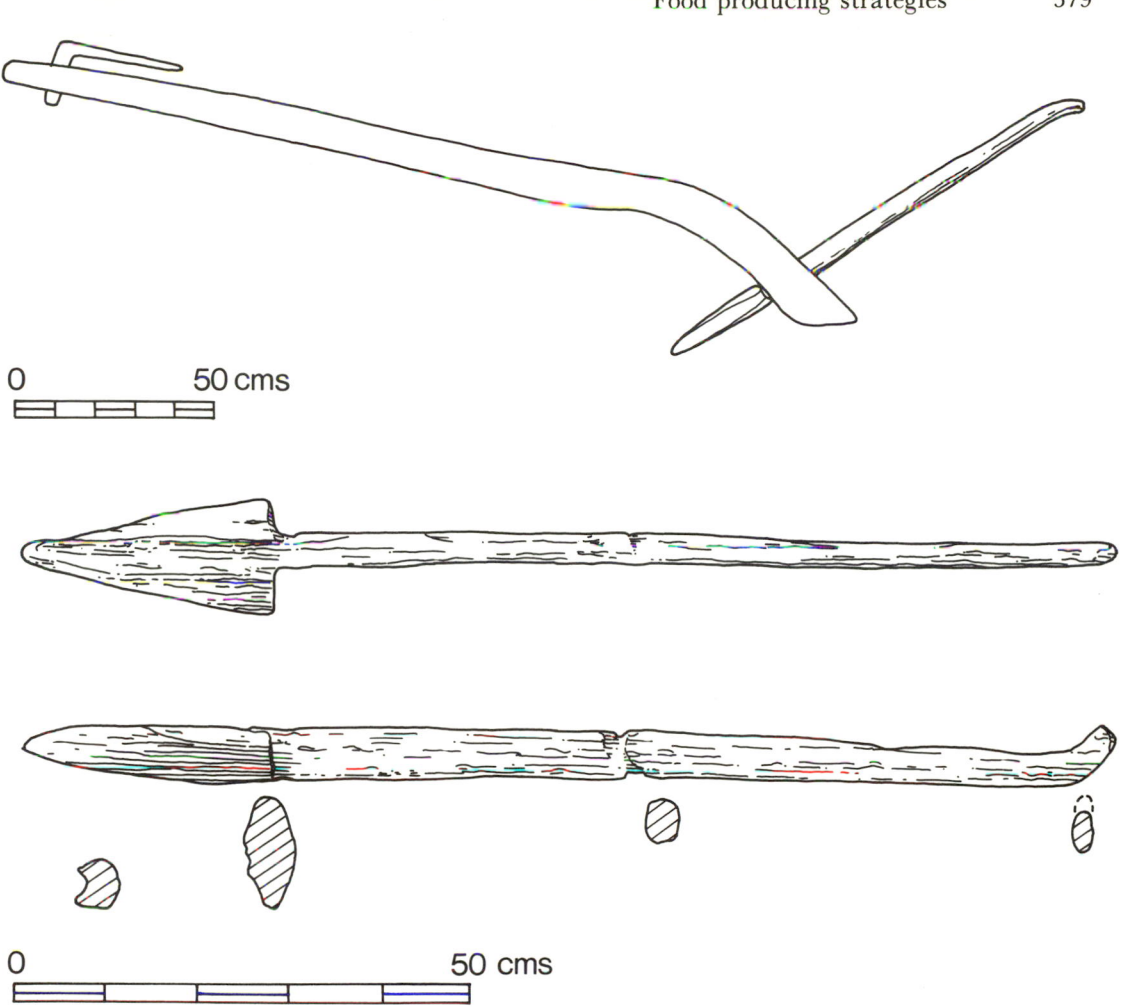

0   50 cms

0   50 cms

Figure 15.4   Plough head and stilt from Milton Loch Crannog (source: C.M. Piggott 1955).

Animal domesticates and their management

Arable farming on the scale outlined above could not have been maintained without considerable flocks and herds to provide manure for the fields. Cattle and sheep were reared in large numbers while pigs played a subsidiary role. The cattle were the small Celtic shorthorns (*Bos longifrons*), about the size of modern Dexter cows; the sheep were a small straggly variety, not unlike the modern Soay type. Goats were also kept but it is difficult to distinguish them from sheep on the basis of their skeletal remains. In addition to the three basic farmyard animals, dogs were kept, probably as pets and work-animals, and small horses or, more correctly, ponies about 12 hands (120 cm) high, rather like an Exmoor pony, were reared mainly for traction.

Statistics based on the quantities of animal bones found on occupation sites give some idea of the relative importance of the different species, but it must always be remembered that the bones can do no more than represent animals butchered at the homestead and possibly joints of meat brought in from elsewhere. If, for example, sheep were kept solely for wool, their bones would tend to be scarce in such deposits. In broad terms, however, there appears to have been a gradual increase in the numbers of sheep relative to cattle during the first millennium. At the Cranborne Chase sites of South Lodge Camp, Martin Down Camp and the Angle Ditch, the percentage of cattle in the total faunal assemblage varied between 48 and 67 per cent (the lower figure being abnormally depressed by exceptionally large numbers of deer and dogs) while in the first-century BC settlement at Glastonbury sheep outnumber oxen by almost seventeen to one. It is of course possible that the assemblages are affected to some extent by the different functions of the sites or by environment, but the general trend towards sheep-rearing is clear enough. The same story is told by the collection of bones from Eldon's Seat (Encombe), Dorset, where between the seventh and fifth centuries the proportion of sheep increased from 40.7 to 61.7 per cent and cattle correspondingly declined from 50.6 to 28.3 per cent. Figures for the south Midlands are less reliable but at Twywell and Ravenstone, where statistics are available, sheep outnumbered cattle by nearly three to one. In the north-east however cattle remained dominant in number well into the Late Iron Age.

The relative increase in the numbers of sheep, in the south, throughout the first millennium is probably linked to the spread of downland arable. To maintain the enormous hectareages of fields farmed during the Iron Age, flocks and herds would have been essential in providing manure for the land. Sheep would have been the obvious choice, for not only could they survive for long periods on the downs without water, but they were also relatively easy to maintain over the autumn and winter. From September until December they could be turned loose on the stubble without the need for special feeding and from December until March or April, when the pastures began to grow again, straw fodder carted to the fields would have been sufficient to keep them alive. For the remainder of the year, from April to August, there would have been ample pasture for the flocks to grow fat on in the fields left fallow and on the open downland. The symbiosis between sheep and fertile arable land cannot be over-stressed: it is no exaggeration to say that without large flocks, grain production on the level attained in the south would have been impossible to maintain.

Sheep also had other uses: at various times they could provide wool and milk, and eventually meat, bone, sinew and skin. Relatively few were slaughtered in the first year – only 9.2 per cent at Encombe and about the same percentage from Hawk's Hill, Surrey – and over 40 per cent of the flock lived to more than 2 years of age at both sites. These figures were not universal, however, for at Barley, Herts., 39 per cent were killed in each of the first two years. One possible explanation is that at Barley the slaughter of yearlings reflects a reliance on sheep as a meat source, the carcasses being salted down for winter, while in the south sheep were kept more for their wool and manure, mutton being of secondary importance. Clearly, there were regional variations in farming practice which need to be worked out in detail when further data become available. In spite of the numerical advantage of sheep, mutton was not consumed in very large quantities compared with beef. The average weight of a sheep was only about 57 kg, while that of a cow might be as much as 410 kg. Thus at Hawk's Hill the 57 per cent of sheep produced only 23 per cent of the meat supply while the 17 per cent of cattle yielded 53 per cent. The figures are of course approximate, but they emphasize the fact that for the most part the Iron Age farmers of the south were beef-eaters.

Cattle were far more difficult to maintain than sheep. They needed constant watering and from December until March they would have required protection from the weather in corrals, enclosures and in byres in more extreme climates, and provision of regular feeds of straw, hay or leaf fodder or silage. It would seem unlikely that the beasts were brought into the actual farmstead enclosures unless special provision was made to keep them well clear of the domestic fittings and houses, as may have been the case at Farley Mount, where the corner of the 2.4 ha enclosure was divided off by another length of ditch, presumably to protect the house. At Little Woodbury, Wilts., no internal divisions are known, but the antennae ditches in front of the main entrance could well have enclosed a stockyard. The advantages in having the stock close by during the winter months are obvious: not only could they be protected from raiders and wild animals, but the constant foddering and watering which would have been necessary could more easily have been carried out from the home farm. Foodstuffs for the cattle would have proved no problem; hay would have been important, so too would leaf fodder cut in the spring and stored throughout the summer. Nor must the significance of straw be overlooked. If, as we have assumed, the harvest was undertaken before the cereals had ripened, the straw would have retained a far greater nutritional value. Indeed, this may be one of the reasons for the early harvesting which necessitated drying and roasting before threshing. In some upland areas, where the ripening season was short, barley could have been cut green and stored in the ear with the stalk attached to provide animal feed. Straw and hay may have been stacked on the two-post racks or small four-post standings which occur so frequently. Leaf fodder was probably stored in a similar way or in underground silos. Some of the grass crop may also have been turned into silage, perhaps in pits.

In addition to their value as meat- and milk-producers, cattle were used for many kinds of tractions, in particular ploughing. For these reasons, the tendency was to keep the herd to maturity. Of the thirty-nine individual animals recognized at Hawk's Hill, only three were killed in the range of 0–6 months and sixteen were older than 3 years when they died or were slaughtered. At Eldon's Seat the figures were comparable: of the twenty-eight represented, seventeen had reached maturity. Apart from the plough teams and the bulls kept for breeding, the main herd was probably composed of cows kept in milk during the spring and summer months, when they would have been allowed out to browse in the forest fringes, the pastures and the steep faces of the lynchets. Their very presence implies the provision of water in reasonable quantities, possibly collected and conserved in dew-ponds. No certain traces of Iron Age dew-ponds have been recognized, but their existence on the downs can hardly be doubted. At the settlement on Park Brow, Sussex, a structure suggestive of an ancient dew-pond was found in close relationship to the trackway which joined the various sites and another possibility has been noted in Micheldever Wood, Hants., close to a settlement. If they are indeed Iron Age in date, their siting would have suited them admirably to the pastoral needs of the community.

Pigs of a domesticated variety played a significant part in the economy. Normally numbers were low: 3.5 and 4.0 per cent in the two periods at Eldon's Seat, 1, 0 and 9 per cent on the Cranborne Chase sites, but rising to 22 per cent at Hawk's Hill and 33 per cent at Highfield, near Salisbury, Wilts. The range is interesting, since it must indicate a considerable variation of practice in the reliance placed on the animal. Settlements close to tracts of woodland on nearby clay soils, in river valleys or on steep hangers, would have been able to maintain large herds of swine without much trouble, but where pannage was sparse, on the more open downs, pig-rearing would have been difficult and consequently numbers were much lower.

Hunting appears to have been of little economic significance. Red deer, roe deer and fallow deer are all recorded on settlement sites, but since shed antlers were collected for tool-making, percentages are unreliable. Various birds are known, including duck, swan, raven, quail, wood pigeon, teal, goose, blackcock and red grouse(?), and occasionally small mammals like water voles and hedgehogs turn up in reliable archaeological contexts; fish are very rarely found. On the coasts, however, shellfish were collected in great quantity.

Dogs were general purpose animals used for hunting, herding and probably as pets. They occur widely but little reliable work has yet been carried out on the various breeds represented. At Highfield about twenty dogs were found (22 per cent of the total animal bones), of which five were of foxhound type, one like a retriever and one rather smaller than a fox terrier. Evidently selective breeding was by this time well under way. The large number of dogs from Highfield is puzzling. The site does not appear to have religious connections, which could have accounted for ritual killings, but some of the bones showed knife-cuts possibly resulting from the collection of sinews, which may be thought to indicate some form of industrial activity.

The importance of animal husbandry to the economy was considerable. It is therefore not surprising that specialized structures were designed and built to cope with the problems of looking after the flocks and herds. These will be more appropriately considered in the regional reviews to follow.

Some regional regimes

Sufficient will have been said in the preceding survey to show that there was considerable regional variation. This may be due to a number of factors: chronological differences, variation in regional strategies and specialization between contemporary sites within a given region. Not all regions are equally well known but evidence is fast accumulating and some indication of the different subsistence patterns may be sketched out.

Central southern Britain

Central southern Britain is dominated by the chalklands of Wessex which tend to impose a broadly similar set of environmental constraints over much of the region. Standing back from the detail various general trends emerge. In terms of the agricultural regime it is possible to recognize an increase in the scale of arable production accompanied by a diversification of crops and a movement into more marginal areas. This may have been occasioned in part by an overall increase in population and by a degree of soil exhaustion on the lighter soils which had been cropped for 2,000 years. Alongside this there is evidence to suggest a dramatic rise in the numbers of sheep in the first half of the first millennium reaching a high by the fifth century which was maintained for the rest of the millennium. The relative increase in the percentage of sheep does not imply a decline in the actual numbers of cattle: it may simply be that large flocks of sheep were run to maintain the fertility of the thin upland soil which by this time was degenerating.

That a careful balance was kept between cereal-growing and stock-rearing is axiomatic. The two halves of the regime were entirely interdependent. A field of stubble turned over first to cattle, then to sheep and finally to pigs, in the late summer or early autumn, would have provided nutrients to all three while the land benefited from their manure. Threshing waste was a useful additive to animal feed during the winter, and in the spring, when the majority of the storage pits were opened for seed, the caked crusts of partially fermented grain from around the pit edges would have provided a rich food source for penned beasts at the crucial time in the run up to lambing and calving.

Each animal would have had its particular uses but none was more valuable than the pig as a living store of readily accessible fat and protein. The pig could turn virtually any waste into calories: inedible acorns, bracken, grubbed-up roots and all the offal, still births and excess milk generated by husbanding the flocks of sheep and herds of cattle.

It seems highly probable that the basic diet comprised cereals and milk products with meat as a luxury. Herds of cattle were too valuable to slaughter: they were probably a sign of status and wealth and thus numbers were important. The function of the herds was therefore to provide milk and to reproduce. Sheep on the other hand were more expendable. Large numbers were needed to maintain the fertility of the fields, though wool and milk would have been useful by-products. When the herds and flocks needed culling there was meat to be had, otherwise the only readily available source, having little bearing on other social and economic systems, was the pig. All swine surplus to the needs of the breeding herd could be culled at will. The model proposed is not unlike that prevalent among many peasant societies throughout much of Europe before the Industrial Revolution. For the Iron Age it is plausible but, since the faunal and floral data are impossible to quantify in a way that allows direct comparison, the model cannot be tested.

The close interrelationship between man, domesticates and crops has left a clear mark on the landscape. Fields, linear boundaries and corrals abound and their occasional juxtaposition permits local sequences to be constructed. Among the most striking of the Wessex field monuments are the linear boundaries which run for many kilometres across the landscape marking out blocks of territory, some of which extend from the high downland down into the river valleys. Where sectioned these ranch boundaries, as they are sometimes called, usually consist of a V-shaped ditch with a bank on one or both sides. Sometimes, as in the case of the Danebury linear, there were two ditches 3 or 4 m apart with the upcast in the middle forming the basis of a wide hedgerow. Other boundaries are less recognizable. At Portsdown Hill, near Portsmouth the boundary was a gully flanked by timber palisades. A comparable example was found at Winterbourne Dauntsey, Wilts. Slight features of this kind leave little mark on the present landscape and may well pass unnoticed except when exposed in excavation.

The Wessex linears are particularly well represented in the vicinity of the hillforts of Sidbury, Quarley and Danebury. At Quarley Hill, Hants. (Figure 15.5), excavation has demonstrated the superimposition of the hillfort, dating to the fifth century, on part of a system of ditches which appears to converge upon the hill-top, while other sections of ditch appear to be contemporary with the fort. Similarly at Ladle Hill, Hants. a 'ranch boundary' seems to precede the construction phase of the unfinished fort. At Danebury, Hants., a major linear earthwork approaching the hill-top becomes one with a slight ditched enclosure which encircles the hill: it was within this enclosure that the hillfort was eventually built in the sixth century. Thus, where relationships have been established, the Wessex linears can be shown to pre-date the sixth/fifth century but were still significant features in the landscape at this time. Where the actual relationships of hillforts to linears have not been tested by excavation, as for example at Sidbury, Wilts., and Woolbury, Hants., the superficial dependence of the linears on the fort may be illusory. However, the occurrence of a number of hillforts at nodes in systems of linear

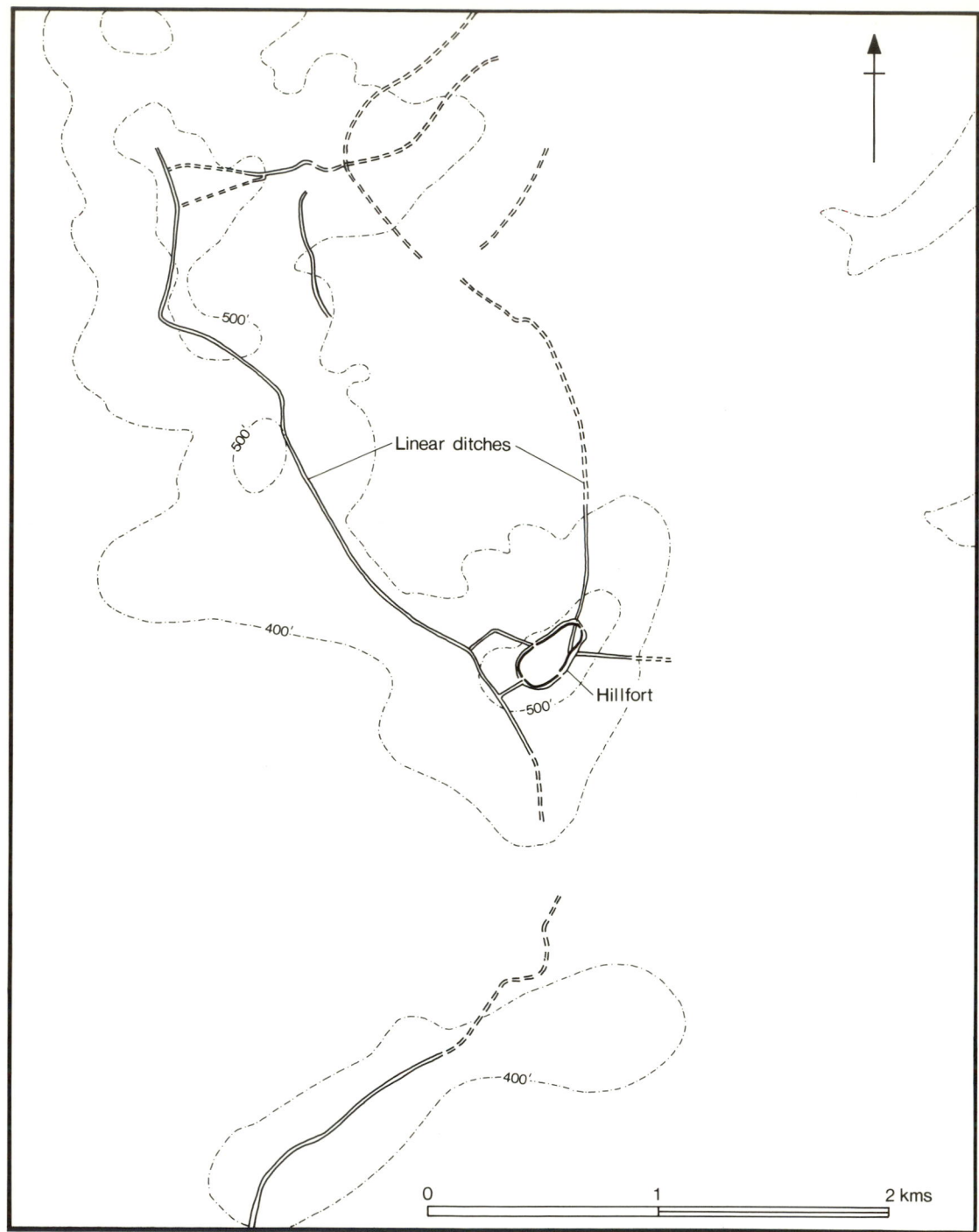

Figure 15.5   Quarley Hill, Hants. and its 'ranch boundaries' (source: C.F.C. Hawkes 1939b).

earthworks is sufficient to suggest that these focal points continued to be of significance: there is no reason to suppose that the original purpose of the linears had been abandoned by the time the forts were built.

One further relationship is worth stressing: many of the Wessex linears can be shown to cut indiscriminately through field systems: the implication must be that the fields had been abandoned at or by this time and this in turn suggests a major act of territorial reorganization.

In this complex of relationships three distinct stages are recognizable. In the first, probably dating to the late second millennium, the landscape was scattered with discrete blocks of small square 'Celtic' fields. Then, in the early first millennium, territory was reapportioned on a massive scale and divided into new units by systems of ditched boundaries which put at least some old arable out of commission. This was the period during which the early hill-top enclosures were in use. Finally, in about the sixth century, early hillforts were built on several of the nodes within the linear ditch system.

These massive changes in landscape organization must represent a major reorientation of the socio-economic system from that of the Neolithic to Mid-Bronze Age cycle to that of the Early Iron Age to Roman cycle. The considerable social implications of this will be returned to below in chapter 20 but here we must briefly consider what all this could mean in terms of changes in the subsistence strategy. At its very simplest we are witnessing a change from a comparatively scattered farming system based on the individual homestead to one which involves greater central control. The laying out of the linear earthworks and the construction of the hill-top enclosures were labour-intensive acts requiring centralized coercive power, and their very nature suggests a dominant pastoral element in the economy. Later on the building of early hillforts, within the framework of the earlier system, implies a degree of social consolidation and the beginnings of an even more rigorous territoriality. This may well have taken with it a greater emphasis on arable production which soon becomes manifest in the very considerable storage capacity provided in the forts as they developed. In this scenario the period *c.* 1000–500 BC was one of major economic transformation. Significantly it is at precisely this time that the botanical evidence points to a phase of intensification and agrarian expansion (M. Jones 1981, 1984).

Beyond these generalizations and suppositions it is difficult to go at present. Few sites of the transition period have been systematically examined. A notable exception is the small undefended settlement at Black Patch, Sussex, dating to the Late Bronze Age. From a thorough analysis of the settlement detritus a detailed economic model has been produced (Drewett 1982, 392–9). Barley occurred in quantity but there were significant quantities of both emmer and spelt wheat while beans were also present. Bone preservation was poor but even so the dominance of cattle was impressive, outnumbering sheep by almost two to one. Taken together the evidence is typical of that which might be expected of a site on the transition between the second millennium system and that of the later first millennium.

The economic model proposed by the excavator suggests that settlements of the Black Patch kind were largely self-contained but were able to produce a small surplus for redistribution. To what extent these Sussex farmers collaborated is unclear but a small rectangular earthwork at Harrow Hill, Sussex, implies communal activity. The enclosure comprised a palisade set in a shallow bank with opposed gated entrances. Finds were sparse but some pottery of the seventh–sixth century was recovered together with an unusual quantity of ox skulls. The excavators estimated that if the density of bones found in their limited excavation was typical of the enclosure as a whole, there must have been at least 1,000 oxen present. That the bones were almost entirely skulls hints at a ritual significance, but an alternative suggestion, not necessarily exclusive of the first, is that beasts were collected here for slaughter, perhaps in animal round ups, the carcasses being carried off and the useless heads left. A structure of this kind is most likely to have served more than one farmstead.

Similar rectangular earthworks occur widely throughout Wessex but most are undated. One, Portsdown Hill, Hants., is associated with a linear boundary while another, on Bow Hill, Sussex, is attached to a linear ditch system defining a large area of upland pasture (Figure 15.6). Two enclosures just south of Ladle Hill, Hants., occupy a vast area of pasture roughly defined by linear ditches. Two are known to the east of Danebury alongside a linear boundary, which originated in the period before the sixth century BC, running from the fort to the valley of the Test. While not all of the examples quoted, and the many more known, need be stock enclosures, their siting, always in association with linear boundaries and pasture land, is suggestive. The few for which there are dates appear to belong to the transitional period but this does not preclude others from being later.

The rash of hillfort building in the sixth century and the subsequent emergence of developed hillforts in the Middle Iron Age suggests that the reordered economic system, once established, remained little altered until the first century BC. This is borne out by the detailed studies of the animal bones and seed residues from Danebury, economic indicators which both show little detectable change over nearly half a millennium. Between sites however there were differences due, presumably, to differences in status and function and variations in local resource potential. The hillfort of Danebury produced a very varied assemblage of seeds and threshing debris showing that a full range of processing had been carried out in the fort and that the crops had been brought in from several different ecological zones. Together the evidence points to the hillfort as a territorial focus for processing and storage. The storage capacity of Danebury was considerable. Leaving aside the numerous 'granaries' the number of pits per unit area was about four times greater than at the average contemporary farmstead. The implication is that the hillfort provided storage capacity for the surplus grain of the larger community.

The crop debris from the smaller chalkland farmsteads like Old Down Farm, Winnall Down and Micheldever Wood, all in Hampshire, was more coherent as would befit the product from the immediate hinterlands processed for the use of the community (Monk and Fasham 1980). Even so variations between sites in the percentages of the different cereals, represented in the residues, is an indication of the different potentials of the soils local to the settlements.

The animal bone assemblage from Danebury in general mirrors that of the neighbouring farmsteads as far as general percentages are concerned. By simply counting bones sheep were the most common, 60 per cent, followed by cattle at 20 per cent, pig at 15 per cent with smaller numbers of dog and horse, but in terms of meat yield beef came first, 67 per cent, with mutton and pork being respectively 23 per cent and 10 per cent. However, that meat production was not the prime aim of husbandry is shown by the fact that animals were not killed when at the optimum ages to provide the best meat. Instead the culling of cattle and sheep was geared to the maintenance of large and vigorous herds and flocks. The detailed analysis of the faunal assemblage from Danebury has yielded a mass of information about Iron Age husbandry (A. Grant 1984a), the most significant points, for the present discussion, being those which reflect upon the special use to which the hillfort was put. The high percentage of neonatal deaths among sheep and cattle strongly suggests that lambing and calving were carried out in close proximity to the fort, quite probably in the corrals created by the outer earthworks immediately outside the defences. There would have been much sense in driving the pregnant beasts into the protection of these enclosures at the beginning of the spring breeding season. Labour needed to provide special

BOW HILL, SUSSEX

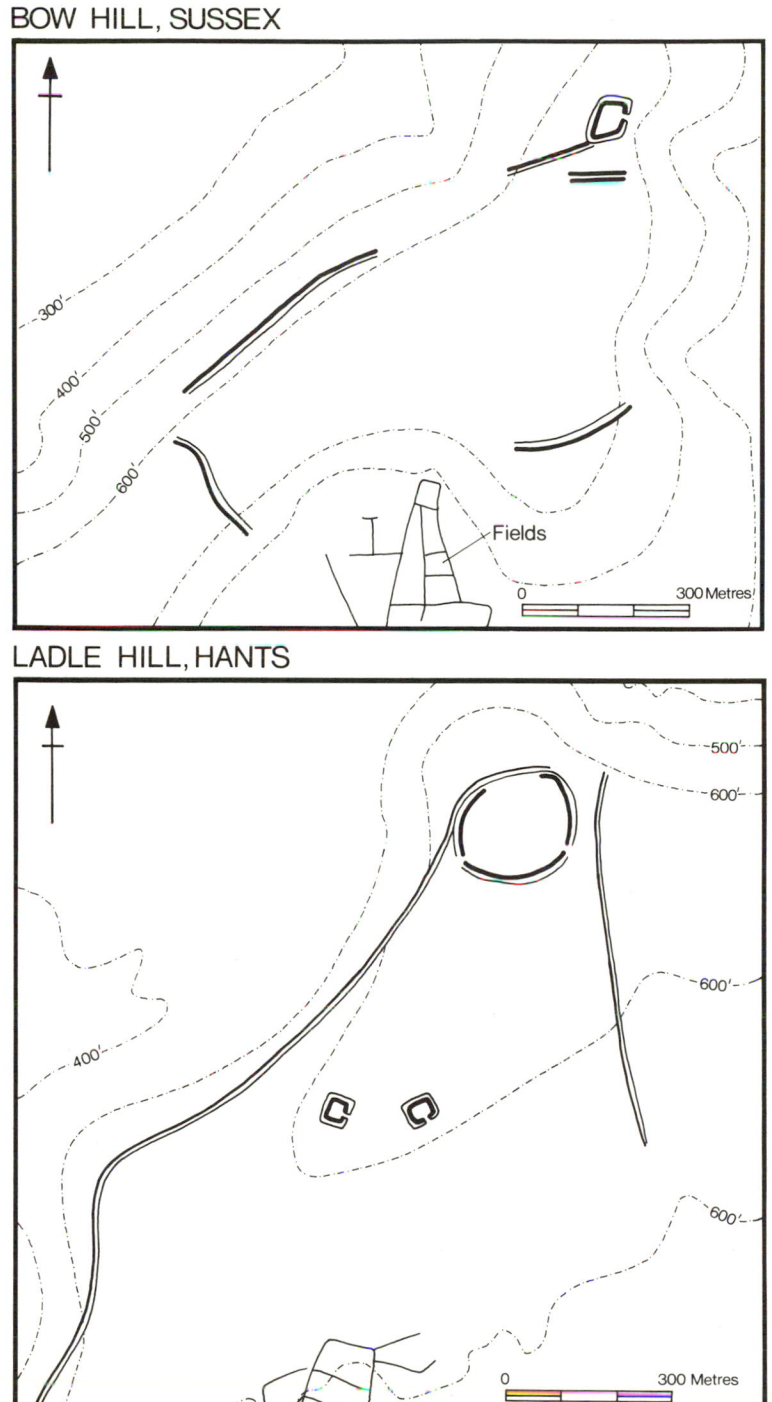

LADLE HILL, HANTS

Figure 15.6   Rectangular enclosures and associated pasture land (sources: *Bow Hill*, author; *Ladle Hill*, S. Piggott 1931).

feed would have been minimized and predators more easily kept at bay. Comparison with chalkland farmsteads is not easy because samples are so much smaller and detailed statistics not always readily available, but in general there were proportionately fewer deaths within the first weeks after birth. If this impression is sustained by further work then it might indicate that hillforts like Danebury served as foci for lambing and calving.

Taken together the evidence from the crop debris and the animal bones shows that hillforts differed significantly in function from farmsteads in that they seem to have performed a more communal role at certain crucial stages in the farming year. In other words the individual farms were no longer the centres of self-sufficient economic systems but were now, with the hillforts, part of more complex systems which involved a degree of specialization at different levels in the settlement hierarchy. The increased storage capacity of the hillforts shows that the stockpiling of surplus for redistribution was now an important element in the economy.

Such a system would allow a degree of specialization to develop. There are hints of this at various sites. At Gussage All Saints, Dorset, horse remains were comparatively high, between 5 and 10 per cent, and the age profile differed from that of the normal farmyard animals in that new born and young individuals were conspicuously absent. One interpretation of this is to suppose that horses were allowed to breed in the wild on the wastelands and were annually rounded up for selection and subsequent training. The proximity of Gussage to the heathlands of what is now the New Forest is suggestive; so too is the workshop debris representing the mass production of horse gear. Another specialization is also implied by the abnormally large number of dogs found at Highfield, Wilts.

Until recently much effort has been spent on the study of typical downland economies to establish a chalkland norm. What is now needed is a concerted study of sites fringing the downs where variant economies may have been in operation. After all there was little point in the downland systems producing surpluses if there was little chance of exchanging that surplus for a different range of commodities.

The interrelationship of animal husbandry and crop production is well represented in the field archaeology of the Middle Iron Age. We have already mentioned the linear boundaries of the Later Bronze Age, which seem to have continued as significant landscape features throughout much of the period and the animal pens attached to hillforts. Many of the forts were, in addition, provided with large areas of pasture land nearby to provide feed for livestock during the summer months. At the Trundle, Sussex, the pasture lay all around the fort, and was separated from arable land by a series of earthwork boundaries crossing the spurs and so sited that the browsing beasts would always have been within sight, and therefore the protection, of the fort. At Danebury (Figure 15.7) a large hectareage of pasture visible from the fort lay between a linear earthwork and a block of arable through which a droveway led to inner corrals which themselves provided 11 ha of well-protected pasture. A variation of this arrangement can be seen on Stockbridge Down, near Woolbury (Figure 15.8), where two linear boundaries run up to the fort from the south defining an area of pasture and dividing it from neighbouring arable fields.

Stock management systems are also well in evidence around farmsteads. The settlement enclosures at Gussage All Saints are intimately bound up with trackways and boundaries running for many kilometres (Wainwright 1979, fig. 111) and much the same complex system can be found around many of the settlements on the downlands between the rivers Test and Bourne (R. Palmer 1984). It was during the Middle Iron Age that a new type of settlement configuration, the banjo enclosure, appeared in central southern Britain (pp. 220–3). The characteristics of the banjo, the long ditched causeway leading from a linear boundary to the

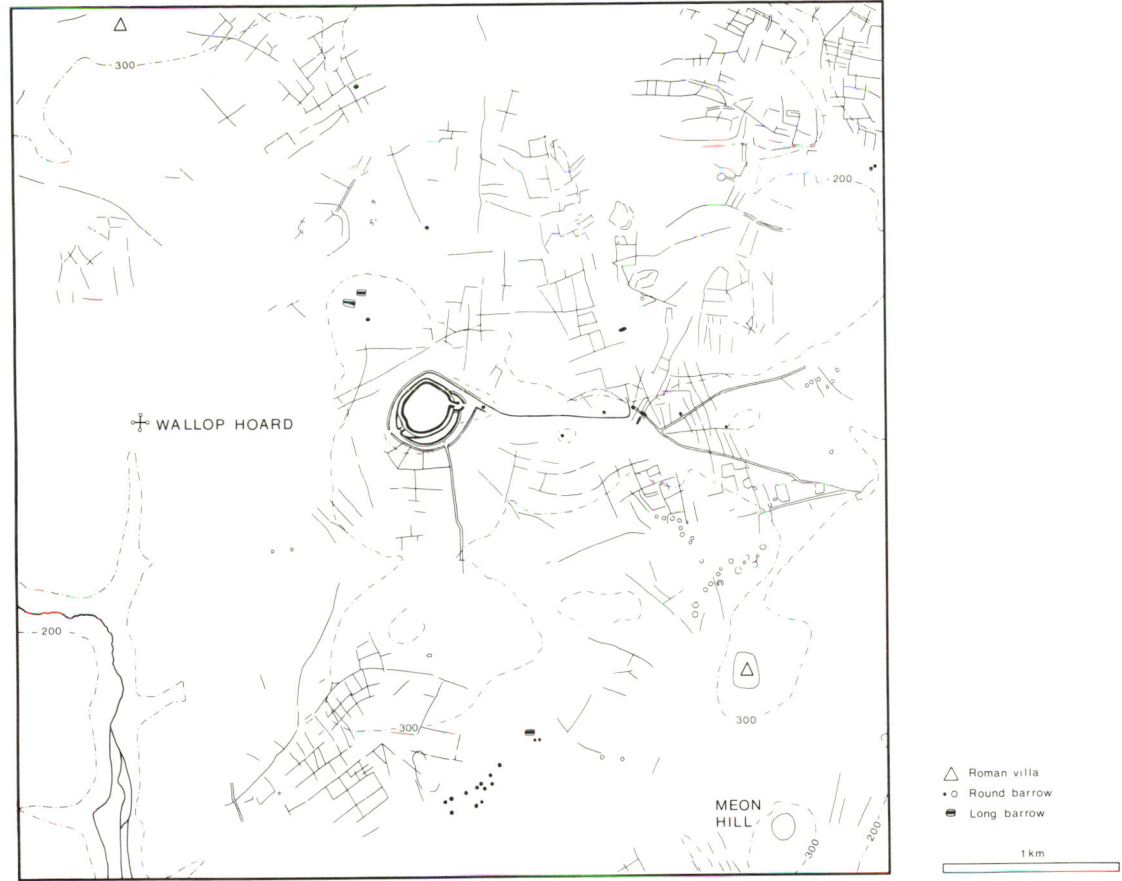

Figure 15.7   Arable and pasture land around Danebury (source: Cunliffe 1984a).

enclosure, if divided by temporary fences and hurdles, would have been of considerable value in sorting out stock. The very numbers of these enclosures scattered over Wessex might suggest a reorientation of the economy to more pastoral pursuits. It is difficult to prove on present evidence but if it were so, such a change could be seen as a response to the progressive impoverishment of the thin downland soil for which there is firm botanical evidence (M. Jones 1984).

The economy of the first century BC and early first century AD in Wessex is not at all well known largely because of the lack of well-published excavations of this period. But there is a marked change in settlement configuration: hillforts generally go out of regular use and the enclosed farmstead gives way to a more extensive pattern of associated ditched enclosures (pp. 223–6) though the banjo type, once established in the Middle Iron Age, continues. Two causative factors may be relevant: the reorientation of the economy as the result of the proximity of the Roman market; and the progressive degeneration of traditional farmland.

The first is reflected in the export of raw materials to the Roman world through ports such as Hengistbury Head, Dorset, where there is evidence for the collection of grain from a variety of inland environments and an unusually high percentage of cattle which might suggest the

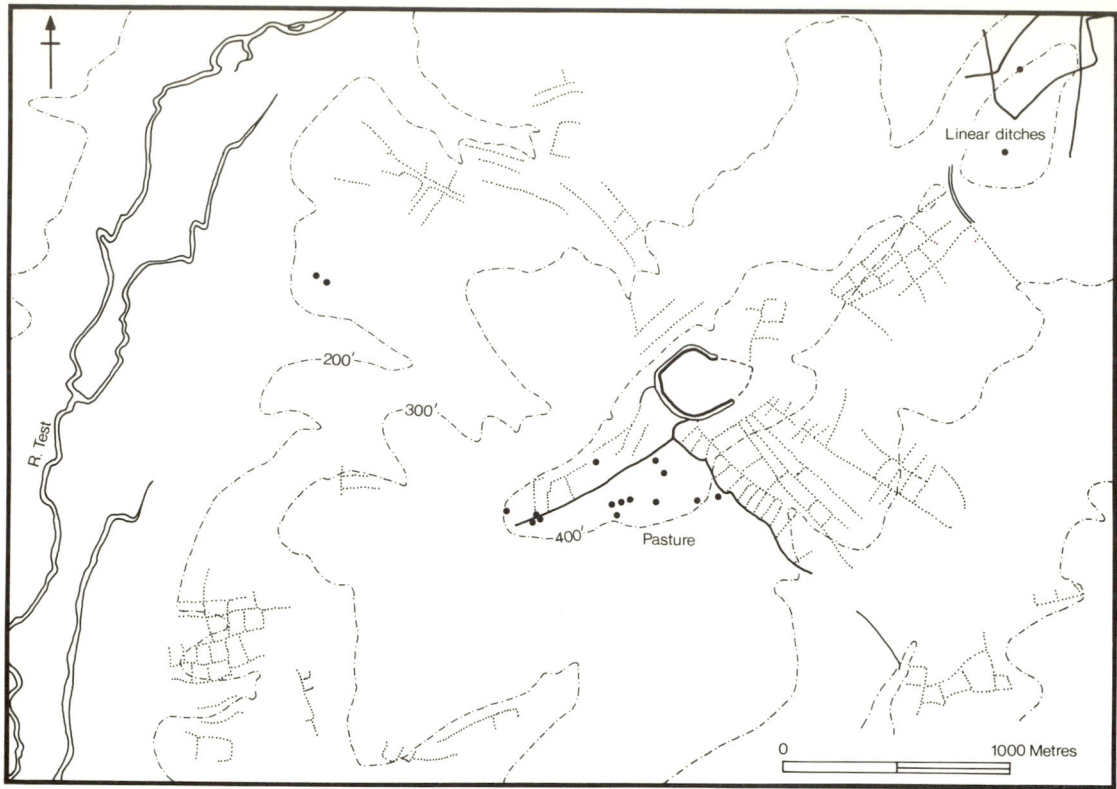

Figure 15.8 The landscape around Woolbury, Hants. (source: author).

amassing of stock on the hoof for the local production of leather – a desirable commodity in the Roman market. The very existence of an export market if served on a sufficiently intensive scale would have caused a significant change in local systems.

The supposed degeneration of traditional arable is more difficult to document but the increasingly weedy nature of the crops, the opening up of new ecological zones and the introduction of new varieties like bread wheat are all indicators of significant change (M. Jones 1984).

Standing back from the mass of data so briefly reviewed here it is possible to suggest three broad stages in the evolution of Wessex economy (cf. M. Jones 1981, 119):

Tenth to sixth century: Transition from the second-millennium system. Diversification and innovation in crop regimes accompanied by a rise in the numerical importance of sheep. Massive redivision of land by linear earthworks and the emergence of hill-top enclosures for communal stock management.

Sixth to first century: Stable system of mixed farming geared to produce cereals and milk products for consumption. Early and developed hillforts provide services for storage and at lambing and calving times. The production of surpluses for redistribution. Soil exhaustion becomes evident.

First century BC to first century AD: Rapid change occasioned by the development of overseas trade and increasing soil depletion. Settlement spreads to damper and heavier soils accompanied by the introduction of new cereal varieties and changes in balance. Possibility of an increase in the importance of husbandry as traditional soils further degenerate.

The Midlands

Our understanding of the Iron Age economy of the Midlands has been revolutionized by a series of large-scale excavations accompanied by detailed environmental investigation in the Upper Thames valley. Of these Ashville, Barton Court Farm, Appleford, Mount Farm and Farmoor have been fully published while Mingies Ditch, Claydon Pike, Hardwick and Gravelly Guy are reported in more summary form. Several general overviews considering the economic implications of these sites have been presented (especially Robinson 1984; Hingley and Miles 1984; M. Jones 1984).

A summary of the major settlement types has been given above in chapter 12. Suffice it to say that three broad ecozones can be defined: the upland areas of the Cotswold dip slope; the well-drained gravel terraces of the Thames and its tributaries; and the river flood plain. Each supported its own range of settlement types and each offered a different resource potential for exploitation. Little is yet known of the economy of the dip slope settlements but in general form they resembled the banjo enclosures of Wessex and are most likely to have been single family farmsteads. The valley sites are more diverse and there is clear evidence of a degree of transhumance from the gravel terrace settlements to temporary summer establishments on the flood plain so that livestock could crop the hay meadows (Lambrick and Robinson 1979).

A detailed assessment of the crop waste suggests that a distinction can be made between sites on the well-drained second terrace, such as Ashville and Mount Farm, Oxon., and first terrace sites like Claydon Pike and Hardwick. The second terrace assemblages were rich in cereal grain while those of the first terrace were dominated by weeds and chaff. This may suggest that the latter were the production sites where the crops were cleaned and threshed, while the former received the processed grain. If this distinction proves to be consistent then the differences are either purely functional or are status-led. In either case it suggests a high degree of specialization within a narrow environmental zone and implies a mechanism for redistribution. It may be that special redistribution centres developed within the system: a site like Gravelly Guy, which is characterized by an exceptionally large number of storage pits, has some claim to be such a centre.

Sheep, cattle and pigs were reared. The percentages of sheep were low compared to the chalkland zone but this is only to be expected. Sheep do not fare well in damp situations: they are prone to foot-rot and liver fluke as the discovery of the molluscan host to liver fluke at Appleford reminds us. Small flocks were however kept. They seem to have been composed largely of mature females and the scarcity of bones of young animals suggests that the flocks were probably raised on the upland calcareous soils and brought to the drier pastures of the valleys during the summer months. Cattle were better suited to the valley environment and invariably occur in the highest numbers. However at sites like Ashville and Barton Court Farm bones of very young animals are rare. This would seem to imply that, as with sheep, breeding took place elsewhere. The terrace settlements were well located to provide rich pasture throughout the year, the hay meadows of the flood plain being a particularly valuable asset.

The observation that both sheep and cattle were bred elsewhere than at the valley sites takes with it a number of interesting implications. It could well be that stock was raised on the calcareous uplands and brought to the valley settlements for exchange, possibly for surplus grain or other less tangible commodities. Such a system, comprising two specialized but interdependent subsystems would be consistent with the constraints of the geomorphology and would help to explain the different types of settlement pattern evident between the uplands and the valley.

Whatever the overall system, there are likely to have been a number of settlements specializing in the exploitation of their local environments. One such site, dating to the Early Iron Age, has been excavated at Groundwell Farm, Wilts., located on the richer clayey soils south of the Thames valley. Of the bone assemblage recovered, between 30–40 per cent was of pig. It is tempting to see this as an isolated community relying heavily upon the products of its own immediate territory which would have been dominated by tracts of woodland providing admirable pannage for swine.

It is not yet possible to provide a detailed view of economic development throughout the first millennium but several generalizations may tentatively be offered. At present few sites of the Mid–Late Bronze Age are known within the region but from about the eighth century settlements begin to be established on the gravels. By the Middle Iron Age settlement has become prolific and it is to this period that the developed system, outlined above, belongs. The gravel tracts are now fully utilized and farms have been established on the Cotswold slopes though these are more widely spaced. The picture is consistent with the view that considerable population expansion was taking place and all ecological niches were being exploited but there is no evidence of settlement hierarchy at this time.

In the Late Iron Age changes can be discerned. New crops such as bread wheat were being introduced, and it seems that the increased alluviation of the river valleys, probably caused by intensive cultivation of the valley sides, was forcing the abandonment of the flood plains. The emergence of long distance trade networks may well have been responsible for the creation of large enclosed oppida at Salmonsbury and Dyke Hills, commanding major route nodes.

While the Thames valley has so far produced the fullest evidence for Iron Age economic systems in the Midlands much detail has been added by settlement excavation in Northamptonshire and Bedfordshire. Along the valleys of the Ouse and Nene settlements appear to be densely scattered much as they are in the Thames valley but few have been examined. Elsewhere, on the varied soils of the Northamptonshire uplands and the flanking clay lands, a number of large-scale excavations have been carried out. The overall picture is one of settlement expansion in the Middle Iron Age filling up the lighter soils and spreading into the heavy clay land (Knight 1984, 266–83).

Evidence for animal husbandry and cereal growing does not differ significantly from that of the Wessex region. There is support for the view that a greater diversity of crops came into use as the Iron Age proceeded. The animal bone assemblages from several sites, e.g. Twywell, Brigstock and Weekley, show that sheep were the most numerous animal, the percentage rising to 76 per cent at Weekley. The prominence of sheep reflects the potential of the calcareous soils of the uplands. Elsewhere, however, at Moulton Park, Bradwell and Bierton where the resource potentials differ, cattle are the more numerous. Differences of this kind are only to be expected in a region where the geology is so varied.

Field systems are not well represented in the region but droveways and linear ditches divide the landscape. Another boundary feature known as 'pit alignments' is frequently recorded. In the Nene and Ouse valleys 114 have been noted principally as a result of aerial photography

(Jackson 1974; Knight 1984, 259–65) and several of these have now been subjected to limited excavation. At Briar Hill Farm the alignment, which was traced for 152 m, consisted of closely spaced sub-rectangular pits averaging 2 m by 1 m and dug to a depth of about 1 m. The pit row had evidently replaced an earlier linear arrangement of small pits or post-holes. The only indication of date consisted of a few sherds of Early Iron Age pottery from the pit fillings. Better dating evidence was obtained at Gretton, Northants., where 114 m of an alignment was carefully examined. Early Iron Age pottery was found in the pits and the filling of one was overlapped by a hoard of currency bars probably dating to the first century BC. There can therefore be no doubt that the pits were of Iron Age date.

While it is clear that pit alignments in some way served to divide land, the physical form of the boundary remains in doubt. It is possible that the spoil was piled between the pits or in a continuous bank along one side, but if this is what was intended it would surely have been more efficient to dig a linear ditch. A more likely explanation, therefore, is that pit alignments were designed to mark the limit of a territory but not to inhibit movement across the line. The phenomenon is particularly interesting and deserves careful attention, not least in the relationship of alignments to other boundary features and to occupation sites.

The south-west of Britain

While the settlement pattern of south-western Britain is comparatively well understood and the broad outlines of the environmental changes experienced by the moorland massifs can be charted from pollen sequences, very little direct evidence can be brought to bear on the basic questions of crops and herds. The reasons are twofold – flotation has seldom been used to extract crop processing debris and the soils are, for the most part, too acid for bones to be preserved.

It is clear, however, that the majority of the settlements relied on a mixed farming regime. Querns and spindle whorls attest to the grinding of grain and to spinning, while stone-walled field systems, largely undated, abound. The provision of outer corrals to a number of the more massively defended settlements (the hill-slope forts or multiple-ditched enclosures) are indications of the importance of animal husbandry at sites which might be regarded as high status.

At the Cornish multiple-enclosure fort of Killibury, where flotation was carried out, emmer, spelt and oats were identified, while from Goldherring, barley, oats and rye were recovered. In both cases the samples were too small to allow the relative importance of the cereal types to be demonstrated.

A systematically collected assemblage of animal bones from the coastal site of Mount Batten presents a somewhat unusual picture. In the earliest, Late Bronze Age, phase sheep were the most numerous followed by cattle and then pigs, but the much larger Iron Age group showed that cattle were by now the most important followed by pig and then sheep. The age at death of the various species implied that while cattle and pig were reared primarily for meat (they were killed as juveniles or young adults), sheep lived until they were mature and were therefore presumably kept to provide wool (A. Grant 1988). This pattern is in marked contrast to the normal husbandry pattern of the south where meat production was a secondary consideration. It is difficult to assess the Mount Batten evidence since there is nothing with which to compare it locally. While it could be typical of a south-western regime it is more likely that the site was either of high status or that meat was being processed for export.

From such sparse evidence it is difficult to generalize. The great variety within the south-western landscape will have created a patchwork of different subsistence strategies but we are far from beginning to understand them.

Wales

Our knowledge of the food producing economy of Wales in the Iron Age is patchy but as a broad generalization the principality can be divided into two zones: a mountainous central zone most suited to pastoral activities and a northern and southern periphery where climate and soils combine to create conditions conducive to mixed farming. The map of farming regions in Wales in the Tudor period (Figure 15.9) encapsulates the dichotomy.

As we have seen in the discussion in chapter 13 concerted programmes of fieldwork and excavation in the southern peripheral zone, most particularly in Dyfed, have greatly advanced our understanding of settlement type and social interactions (most conveniently summarized in G. Williams 1988). Three distinct socio-economic regions have been proposed: a Coastal South-West area, an Inland South-West area and an Upland North and East area (Figure 15.10). This zoning neatly contains the settlement variations and is supported by what little direct evidence there is for food producing systems.

The Inland South-West zone is characterized by small defended enclosures less than 1.2 ha in extent. The economy was probably mixed. Arable activities are attested by iron plough tips from Walesland Rath and querns from several settlements. Traces of pre-rampart ploughing are recorded at Woodborn Rath and Drim and cereal pollen has been identified from below the rampart at Merryborough. Charred grain has also been recovered from Woodside. It may also be that some of the four-post storage structures found at a number of sites served as grain stores. However at Pen y Coed, where querns and four-post structes were found, the well-preserved environmental evidence showed that the homestead was surrounded by an essentially pastoral landscape. The implication, therefore, is that while some of the settlements may have been directly involved in cereal production, others may have been receivers of processed cereals redistributed through a regional or interregional socio-economic system (G. Williams 1988). The nature of animal husbandry within the zone depends upon the analysis of very few bone assemblages. At Coygan Camp cattle predominated (64 per cent) with sheep and pig coming a poor second at 16 per cent and 15 per cent respectively. This emphasis on cattle is not surprising given the extent of the lush pastures of south-west Wales.

The Coastal South-West zone includes six major defended sites in excess of 1.2 ha in area: most are multivallate coastal promontory forts of the type which might be thought to represent centres for the storage and redistribution of surpluses. Within this zone there is clear evidence of arable production. Field systems have been identified on Stackpole Warren, the earliest phase, defined by banks and ditches, producing a radiocarbon date of 405 ± 70 bc. Terraced fields were also found close to the defended enclosure of Pembry Mountain from the excavation of which grain was recovered. Emmer and spelt were found in a pre-rampart soil associated with a radiocarbon date of 335 ± 45 bc, while grain from the vicinity of a four-post structure was largely spelt. The absence of weed seeds and chaff from the deposits implies that both were processed crops. This raises the possibility that the cleaning and threshing occurred elsewhere and the processed grain was brought to the settlement for storage.

The Upland North and East zone is characterized by defended sites ranging from farmsteads

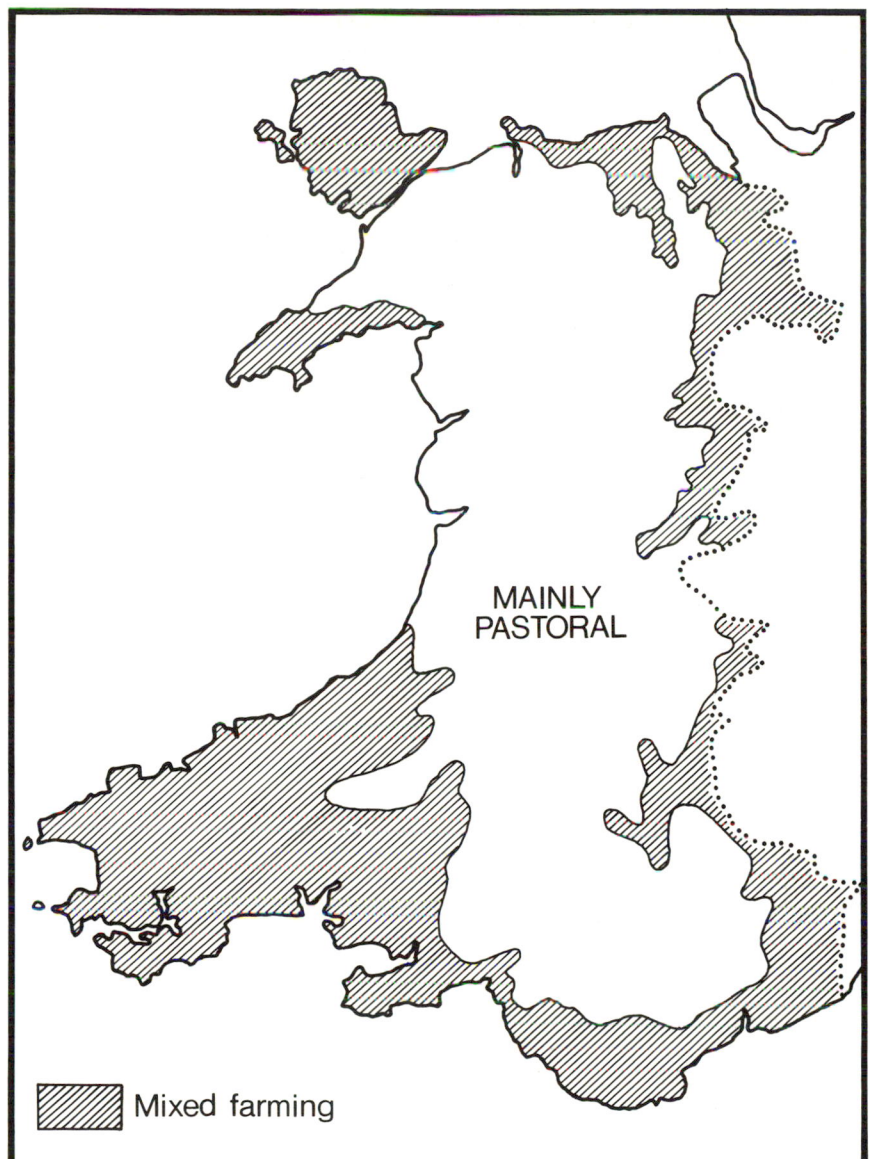

MAINLY PASTORAL

Mixed farming

Figure 15.9   The farming potential of Wales in the Tudor period (source: Thirsk 1967).

to substantial enclosures though rarely over 5 ha in extent. An important pollen sequence from Tregaron Bog demonstrates the rapid development of pastoral clearances following the onset of sub-Atlantic conditions in the early first millennium BC (J. Turner 1964). While the sequence provides a general indication of regional conditions and supports the idea of a predominantly pastoral economy in which sheep probably played a major role, this does not preclude cereal growing in more favoured micro-environments. The excavation at the defended enclosure of Caer

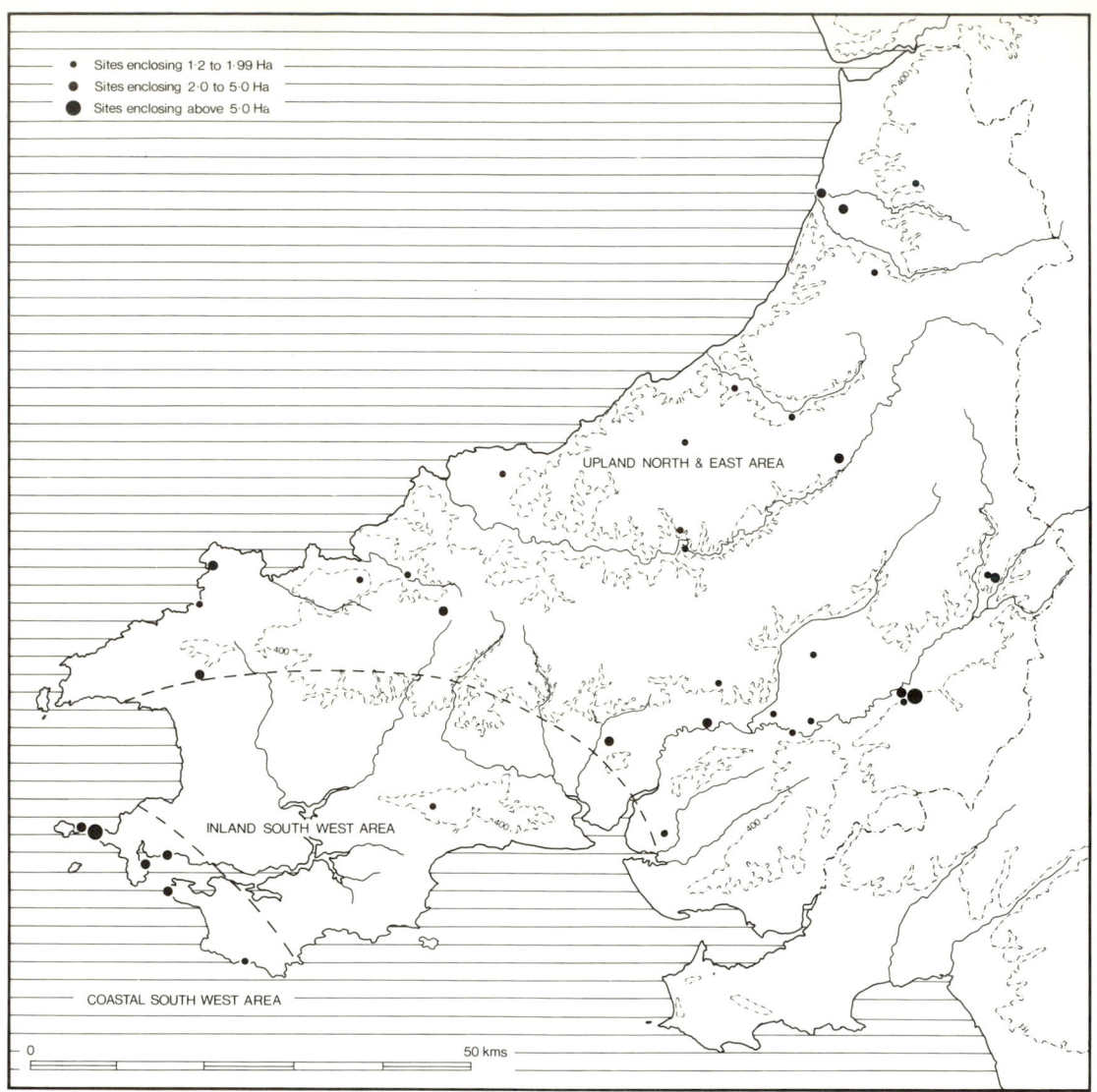

Figure 15.10   Economic zones in south-west Wales in the Iron Age (source: G. Williams 1988).

Cadwgan has produced a small quantity of grain including spelt, barley and possibly emmer and rye. From the same site the small animal bone assemblage suggests that sheep were twice as numerous as cattle.

Over and above the variation in regional economy some general chronological trends emerge of which the most significant is an apparent increase in population during the Middle Iron Age leading perhaps to an increase in competition. In the South-West Coastal zone there is some evidence for the increase in size of hillforts which could be taken to imply a greater degree of centralization in production and redistribution (G. Williams 1988, 42–3).

The detailed model which is beginning to emerge as the result of carefully thought out research programmes in south-west Wales provides an indication of what might be achieved in other parts of the Principality where the evidence is at present too sparse.

In the south-east periphery, from the Gower to the river Wye, the settlement pattern has more in common with central southern Britain than with south-west Wales. Large hillforts dominate a landscape scattered with small enclosed farmsteads several of which can be shown to continue in use well into the Roman period. The environment is one conducive to mixed farming and it may well be that here, as in Wessex, the hillforts provided central services including mechanisms for storage and distribution. Quantifiable economic data is at present lacking.

In north Wales the Lleyn peninsula, the fertile Vale of Clwyd and the comparatively narrow coastal plain between were densely settled. There is yet little evidence bearing on the economy of the region. At Dinorben sheep were numerically more common than cattle but exact percentages are not recorded. The implication is that at first the sheep-runs of the mountains were more widely used than the pastures of the Clwyd valley. By the Roman era the emphasis had been reversed. Sheep may have been of importance in the pre-Roman period in other parts of the region, for the mountainous landscape would have been conducive to their rearing. Herein may lie one of the reasons why the multiple-enclosure forts of the south-west are rare in the north, for sheep would not have required the same corralling facilities as cattle. It may also be relevant that spindle whorls, reflecting the importance of wool, are more commonly found on the occupation sites of the north.

The significance of grain production to the economy is difficult to assess, but saddle querns were surprisingly common at Dinorben, Castell Odo and Conway Mountain, although at other sites they are absent. That the region possessed a fine grain-growing potential was shown by extensive development of arable farming under Roman domination. It may well be that large-scale cultivation began a few centuries earlier.

The occurrence of large hillforts in some parts of the region suggests a centralization uncommon in the predominantly pastoral areas of the south-west. It is possible, however, that they represent the kind of complex social organization which was potentially possible in a community practising mixed farming based on grain-growing and sheep-rearing – an economy closely similar to that of south-eastern Britain. If so, the occurrence of hillforts is not surprising. Hogg (1966) put forward the suggestion that the hillforts were permanently occupied on the grounds that the houses within were substantially built and no houses have been found in the surrounding lowlands. Nevertheless, the possibility remains that they were used only as the summer refuge of people following a transhumant way of life, their winter farms being sited on the rather more hospitable lowlands (Alcock 1965). The virtual absence of lowland farms may be more apparent than real, for many of the Roman period homesteads might well have been in use before the conquest; the fact that no distinctive pre-Roman artefacts have been found may only reflect the widespread dearth of the surviving elements of the pre-Roman material culture. That transhumance was practised to some degree seems likely, but there are difficulties in accepting the hillforts as positive evidence for it. Migration to upland summer pastures might tend to disperse rather than nucleate population, although it could of course be argued that raiding was more prevalent in the summer months, making communal defence necessary. At present, it must be admitted that the problems are rather too many to allow firm conclusions to be reached: more statistical evidence is required of the composition and age range of the flocks and herds from various sites. Sadly, this kind of data has seldom been published in the past.

Finally we must consider the Welsh borderland, the wide strip of hilly country lying between the plain of the river Severn and the mountainous interior of Wales. The settlement pattern of this zone is tolerably well known and many of the hillforts which dominate it have been excavated, some of them on a considerable scale. Smaller settlements, however, are ill known except where they survive as earthworks in the upper reaches of the Severn valley and the foothills of the Berwyn Mountains. The available environmental evidence is therefore biased heavily towards hillforts and gives a somewhat one-sided picture.

There can be little doubt that over much of the region mixed farming was practised. Many of the excavated hillforts, e.g. Credenhill, Midsummer Hill, Croft Ambrey, the Wrekin and Breiddin, have produced ample evidence of concentrations of large four-and six-post storage structures, querns are not at all uncommon, and cereal grain has been found in most of the forts excavated under modern conditions. Wheat, of unspecified type, comes from Croft Ambrey, Caynham Camp, Midsummer Hill and Wrekin while Breiddin has produced emmer wheat. Midsummer Hill and Wrekin have also yielded barley and *bromus* sp. Good arable land is to be found in the general proximity of all the forts.

Direct evidence for husbandry has to rely largely on the assemblage from Croft Ambrey. The animal bones show that sheep were the most numerous but cattle and pig occurred in quantity. There is also some evidence that horse meat was eaten and freshwater mussels were collected. That many of the animals were mature when killed suggests that flocks and herds were kept more for their meat and wool, and no doubt as a measure of status, than for their meat. The production of woollen fabric is further emphasized by the discovery of spindle whorls and loom weights. A similar picture can be reconstructed for the hillfort of Sutton Walls, Heref., but here there seems to have been a slight numerical predominance of cattle over sheep. A weaving comb and several loom weights are added evidence of wool production.

The significance of stock-rearing to the economy is shown by the provision of annexes to several of the forts. Croft Ambrey offers an example of a simple annex attached to one side of the fort enclosing about 2.8 ha – an area equivalent to that of the main camp. A more complex pattern occurs at Old Oswestry, Salop (Figure 15.11), where in a late period subdivided enclosures were added on either side of the main entrance; these were later contained within a bank and ditch which enclosed the entire fort and protected a considerable hectareage well suited to the control of livestock. The divided enclosures are more difficult to explain in their present form but had suitable provision been made for an entrance they might have served as stock-pens. Further north at Earls Hill, Salop, and Breiddin multiple enclosures are also found.

Apart from the extreme rarity of storage pits in the borderland forts there is little to distinguish them in terms of their structure and economy from the hillforts of Wessex. It seems reasonable, therefore, to suppose that the socio-economic systems of the two regions were not significantly dissimilar. If so the hillforts should be seen as central places providing storage and redistribution facilities for the larger community, the majority of whom lived in small enclosed farmsteads in the vicinity.

The evidence is too coarse-grained at present to allow chronological or regional variation to be recognized but the considerable variation in environment within the borderland would strongly suggest that many local economic strategies differed from the norm. The differences in the animal bone assemblages between Croft Ambrey and Sutton Walls could reflect the upland nature of the former, well suited to sheep, and the location of the latter on the edge of the valley of the river Lugg where well-watered meadow was to be had in plenty. Many of the settlements on the western extremity of the borderland, fringing the Welsh mountains, might well have utilized the mountainous pastures in a transhumant system. Evidence of these subtleties at present eludes us.

OLD OSWESTRY, SALOP

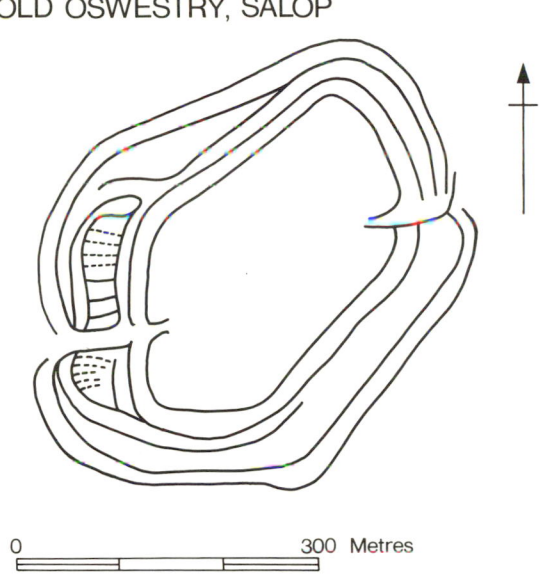

0   300 Metres

Figure 15.11 Old Oswestry, Salop. A hillfort with outer corrals (source: Varley 1950b).

Northern Britain

Our knowledge of the economy of northern Britain has changed dramatically in recent years. The simple 'pastoral' model put forward by S. Piggott (1958) can be shown to be no longer valid, but we are still far from appreciating, even at a very simple level, the range of subsistence strategies which the varied bioclimatic sub-zones of the north called for. At a level of gross simplification, the pollen evidence suggests a progressive opening up of the forest cover during the first millennium (J. Turner 1979; D. Wilson 1983) while the distribution of artefacts such as quernstones and spindle whorls is a reflection of a mixed economy. Settlement location and morphology, with rare examples of fields and paddocks, add a further dimension, but direct evidence of crops and herds from which valid assessments can be made is at present all too rare. Against this we must constantly bear in mind the variables created by soil type and altitude.

For the purpose of this brief overview we may consider two well-studied regions: the north-east from the Humber to the Tyne; and the north-east from the Tyne to the Forth.

The Humber–Tyne region has produced an impressive range of new data since Piggott wrote in 1958, much of which has been brought together in a valuable reassessment by Haselgrove (1984a). The area is dominated by upland regions such as the Wolds and North York Moors and the Pennines, interspersed with wide clay vales and areas of undulating boulder clay: the potential for varied economic strategies is considerable.

Early first-millennium land divisions on the Wolds (Ramm 1978) and the North York Moors (Spratt 1982) have been interpreted, not unreasonably, as evidence of large-scale reorganization of upland pastures by communities occupying the valleys or the interface between the upland zone and the more productive heavier soils of the lowlands. The arrangement is not at all unlike that created by the linear earthworks of Wessex which are thought to have been laid out at about the same time. Upland pastures of this kind and those of the Pennines would have provided ideal runs for flocks of sheep, the relative importance of which are reflected in the quantity of spinning and weaving equipment found on the Pennine sites and by comparatively high percentages of sheep identified at sites like Garton, Rudston and Staple Howe. Elsewhere, however, where well-watered pastures were near at hand, cattle predominated as at Stanwick, Thorpe Thewles, Levisham, Burradon, Coxhoe and Catcote (Haselgrove 1984a, 18).

The most complete evidence for a food producing system comes from Thorpe Thewles, Cleveland. Cereal-growing is well represented by crop and processing residues. The main crops were spelt and six-row hulled barley with only very small quantities of emmer. Oats were also present but may have been of the wild variety. Analysis of the seeds and processing waste suggested that the crops came from the well-drained fertile soils close to the settlement: the site was self-sufficient but probably did not produce a surplus. Pollen analysis from three separate locations within the vicinity was entirely consistent with the excavated evidence. It showed that large-scale deforestation began in the middle of the second millennium BC when arable farming begins, arable production intensifying in the Late Iron Age to early Roman period.

Animal bones were tolerably well preserved though the sample was not large. Cattle were most numerous followed by sheep, pig and horse, horse being more common than pig in the Middle Iron Age phase. Geese and chicken were also recorded. In the earlier period stock management was concerned more with secondary products than with meat but by the later period a change can be recognized in herding practices with greater emphasis being placed on the production of beef and hides while there was an accompanying increase in the number of sheep and pigs being kept. The cause of this change is uncertain. It could be that the economy changed from being one geared to exporting prime stock for exchange to one of higher status where quality surplus was consumed. An alternative would be to see socio-economic structure changing from one in which status was defined by the number of cattle owned to one in which surplus stock were slaughtered to provide meat and hides for local consumption and export. In this context it should be remembered that hides were much in demand by the Roman army and from the first century BC were exported from Britain in bulk. The enhanced value which this would have given the product might well have been sufficient to cause readjustments in local economic strategies.

Thorpe Thewles provides a valuable and detailed insight into one food producing system but we should remember that, while it may be typical of the farmsteads of the Cleveland boulder clays, other ecological zones will have imposed different constraints. Nor should we forget the effect that factors such as climatic change and population growth would have had on local strategies.

Turning now to the vast tract of densely settled land stretching from the Tyne northwards to the Forth we find that direct evidence for systems of food production is seldom available, in spite of the exceptionally high quality of the fieldwork and excavation which has taken place largely on what is now marginal land. An assessment of the unenclosed sites of Northumberland (Gates 1983) has, however, raised many intriguing issues. Settlements of this kind are frequently found at high altitudes, above 230 m. A number of them can be shown to be associated with clearance cairns and small fields, and at one site, Snear Hill, Northumberland, there is field evidence which could be interpreted as lazy bed cultivation at an altitude of 330 m. The evidence provided by pollen diagrams from Northumberland is somewhat ambiguous (Davies and Turner 1979). Persistent small-scale clearances are indicated but cereal pollen is rare. This however may be explained by the fact that few of the samples have come from close to settlements and since cereal pollen is not easily wind-borne over large distances, the pollen sequences may not be truly representative of the actual situation. However pollen of barley has been recorded at over 380 m at Broad Moss in the north Cheviots, and at Hartshill, Northumberland, a settlement dating to between the twelfth to sixth centuries BC, carbonized remains of emmer, barley, oats and flax have been recovered together with a range of weeds typical of cultivated grain. Adjacent to the settlement 0.6 ha of fields have been identified. Taken together the evidence is sufficient to suggest arable farming at high altitudes in the first half of the first millennium BC.

This is of particular interest in the light of the evidence for climatic deterioration thought to have taken place between 1200 and 500 BC (see above, pp. 57–8). At first sight a plausible scenario would be to suppose that these high altitude settlements were progressively abandoned as the climate worsened forcing settlers down to lower altitudes but this was not invariably the case. In the vicinity of Alnham, in the Cheviots, six unenclosed settlements were recorded between 270 and 380 m, but in the same area there were six palisaded settlements and two hillforts. Although no direct dating evidence exists for this group of settlements, palisaded enclosures were generally (but not invariably) later than open settlements though there is a considerable degree of overlap in dates, while hillforts usually succeeded palisaded settlements. The implication of the Alnham settlement pattern is, therefore, that occupation continued at high altitude throughout the height of the climatic deterioration. However, the emergence of palisaded enclosures, located with an eye to defence rather than choosing the best agricultural land, might hint at a change to a more pastoral economy in what must have been, by then, marginal areas (Gates 1983, 118–19).

The evidence for the whole of this north-east region is biased towards settlement in marginal regions. This does not mean that the richer lowland soils were sparsely occupied but simply that more recent land-use has obscured most of the detail.

Further north, across the border in Scotland a variety of earthwork features, many very ephemeral, point to the possibility of settled agriculture (Halliday 1982), but the supposed cultivation plots are not widespread and the occurrence of linear ditches and enclosures are a reminder of the importance of herding. Evidence of cereal-growing may be deduced from large numbers of quernstones found on sites like Dryburn Bridge, E. Lothian, but crop processing waste has not yet been recovered from the region. The discovery of hulled barley and bread wheat at Rispain Camp, Whithorn, Galloway, is, however, an indication of what might be expected. Evidence for animal husbandry is equally ill-defined but bones have been recovered and the comparatively large assemblage from Broxmouth offers hope of elucidating the economic strategy of the site (Barnetson 1982). The care of animals throughout the winter in these northern latitudes would almost certainly have required undercover shelter. The possibility that ring-ditch houses, frequently found in the region, served as animal byres has much to commend it (D.M. Reynolds 1982, 53–4).

North-western Scotland and the Islands

The exposed north-western part of Scotland together with the Western and Northern Isles presented a largely treeless landscape subject to extremes of climate, but the indented rocky coastlines offered an environment rich in fish and shellfish as well as the products of stranding, which more than compensated for the uncertainties of husbandry and cereal-growing. Three sites provide a range of relevant data: Dun Mor Vaul on Tiree (Argyll), Crosskirk Broch, Caithness, and Bu Broch, Orkney.

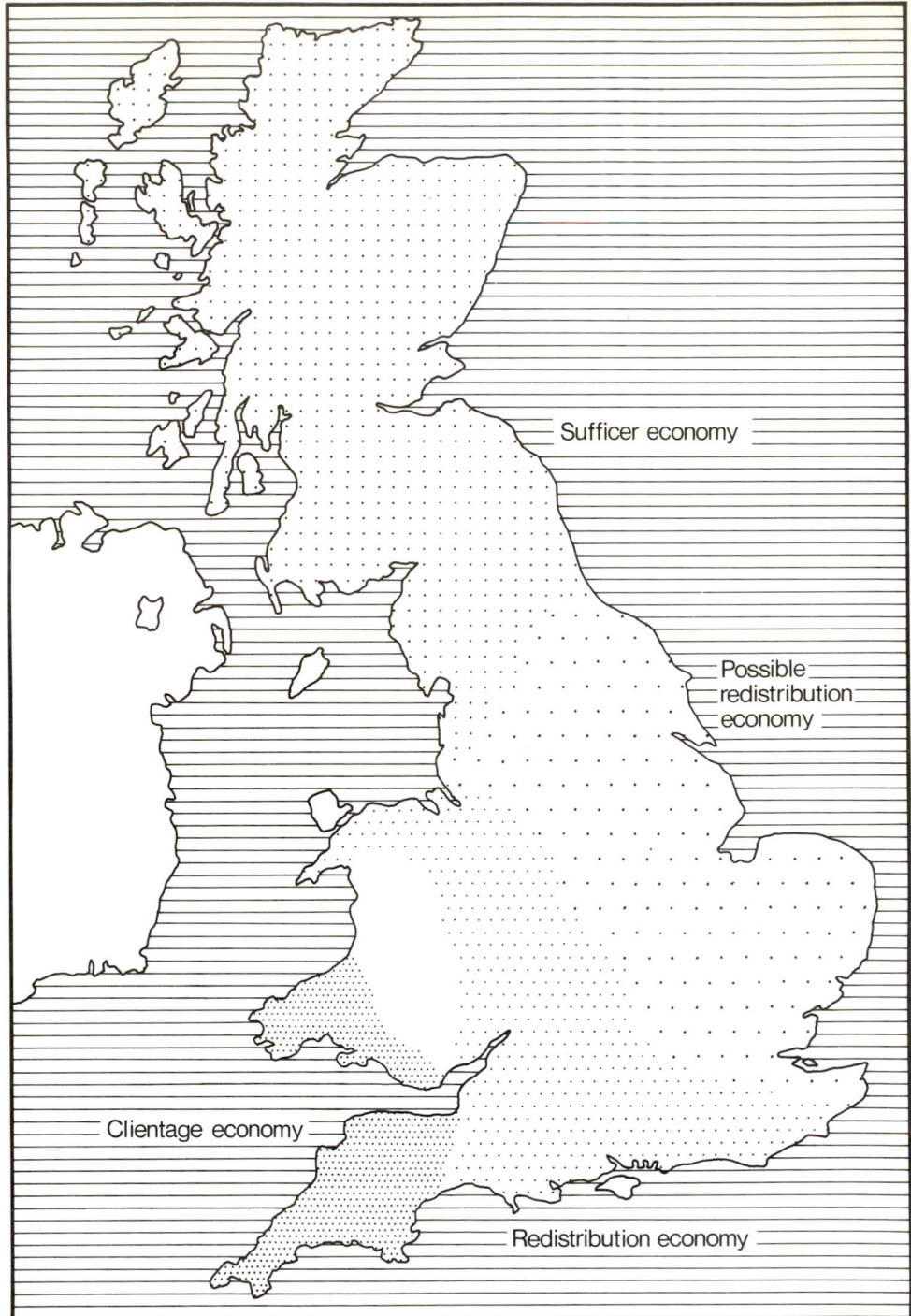

Figure 15.12   Economic systems in Iron Age Britain (source: author).

Crop production seems to have been based almost entirely on barley, either the hulled variety, which dominated the Dun Mor Vaul assemblage, or the naked variety identified at Bu and Crosskirk. Emmer wheat was found at Bu and at Balloch Hill, Argyll, but in very small quantity. The samples from both Crosskirk and Bu were rich in weed seeds including fat hen, sorrel and chick weed all of which had nutritional and medical qualities and presumably reflect a deliberate collecting policy designed to enhance the basic cereal diet.

The three farmyard animals, cattle, sheep and pigs, were husbanded. At Crosskirk and Bu cattle were the most numerous but at Dun Mor Vaul sheep predominated. Problems of over-wintering were evidently overcome since a significant proportion of the livestock survived to maturity. To maintain even quite small flocks and herds it would have been necessary to make good use of gleanings from the shore line and from areas of inland rough grazing during the summer months. The importance of seaweed as feed for sheep is evident in the area even today. Collecting and gathering contributed to the economy. Shellfish, especially limpets, winkles and whelks, were well-represented as were the bones of sea-birds. Fish bones survived less well but plaice and cod were identified at Bu, the latter implying deep-sea fishing. Deer bones were sufficiently numerous at Dun Mor Vaul to suggest that venison contributed to the diet.

Thus the varied ecological niches provided by the region yielded food in plenty so long as a range of micro-environments could be exploited. This is reflected in the settlement pattern, the great majority of the sites choosing locations within easy reach of the full range of resources. The most favoured type of location was one on good agricultural land optimally sited to allow easy exploitation of the littoral zone and the sea while at the same time being within reach of inland rough grazing. All the available evidence points to self-contained communities needing little recourse to communally organized redistributive networks.

Conclusion

The foregoing survey has given some idea of the range of economic strategies adopted by the Iron Age communities of Britain. Knowledge has advanced rapidly within the last decade and methods of study are now in operation which will allow a dramatic improvement of our understanding as more sites are excavated. There is, however, still a long way to go before we can begin fully to appreciate food producing strategies as dynamic systems.

Standing back from the detail certain general points are worth emphasizing. First and foremost is the fact that for much of the country there is sufficient evidence to suggest a significant increase in population throughout the first millennium BC. In parallel with this there are clear indications, in some areas, of soil impoverishment while in other more marginal zones climatic deterioration cannot have failed to have driven agriculture from the higher altitudes. The result of all this is that in favoured areas settlement density increased, heavier soils were opened up to permit occupation and a greater diversification occurred in agriculture, and probably in husbandry.

In some parts of the country, in particular in the north and west, it seems probable that homestead settlements were self-contained, able to satisfy their own food requirements but unable (or unwilling) to produce a surplus for organized exchange. This kind of system can be styled a *sufficer economy*. In other areas, however, in Devon and Cornwall and south-west Wales in particular, there are clear indications of a dichotomy between producer settlements with an agricultural base and consumer settlements of higher status. This type of system we might call a *clientage economy*. At a more complex level is the economy of the hillfort-dominated zone stretching from Wessex to the Welsh borderland. Here there is evidence for the production of surpluses which were stored in specially designated settlements (the hillforts) where a range of services including the articulation of exchange mechanisms were provided. The system was complex and must have involved intraregional exchange on a considerable scale. We might call this a *redistribution economy*.

Clearly this simple threefold division is a gross oversimplification of an immensely complex pattern but it serves to provide some kind of preliminary ordering to the data and contains all the more evident variables. The map (Figure 15.12) is an attempt to show the geographical extent of these economies in the Middle Iron Age.

That there was change, and in some areas quite rapid change, has been emphasized in the more detailed discussions but, with the exception of Wessex, the evidence is too coarse-grained for the trajectories to be defined or for the causative factors to be teased out. None the less these matters are of profound importance in allowing us to understand social dynamics and we will need to return to them again later in chapter 20.

16
Continental trade and contact

The title of this chapter to some extent prejudges the processes by which a wide range of artefacts, manufactured on the Continent, arrived in Britain. Clearly there was organized trade, with well-defined mechanisms and, no doubt, recognized exchange rates; this much is evident for the later period from the surviving documentary references. But there were many other means by which exotic material could be imported, ranging from folk movement to gift exchange and bride-price. Archaeological methods can seldom distinguish precisely between the various possible systems. In the discussion to follow the scope of the evidence is laid out in chronological order and, where it is thought to be appropriate, some of the wider implications of the material are discussed.

Britain, by virtue of its geographical position, has always been receptive of influences from two directions: from central and northern Europe across the North Sea (though with little direct Scandinavian influence (Thrane 1975, 233–5)); and from the Mediterranean and Iberia along the Atlantic coastal routes to south-west Britain and the Irish Sea province. Both spheres of contact were maintained throughout the Iron Age but superimposed on these broad patterns were a variety of processes which influenced the intensity of contact and thus the volume of material which passed through the exchange systems. The reasons for these variations are difficult to isolate: they may have involved political policies which deliberately encouraged or hindered relationships, or social factors such as the development of conserving or inward-looking attitudes in society resulting in a lack of motivation to engage in commerce or social intercourse. Changing economic pressures among Continental communities would also have contributed to the complex situation. Occasionally these separate factors can be isolated with some degree of certainty but frequently they remain ill-defined and confused.

European contacts: seventh and sixth centuries (Figure 16.1)

The beginning of what can reasonably be called the Iron Age in Europe is linked to the development of the Hallstatt culture, characterized by the appearance of a horse-riding

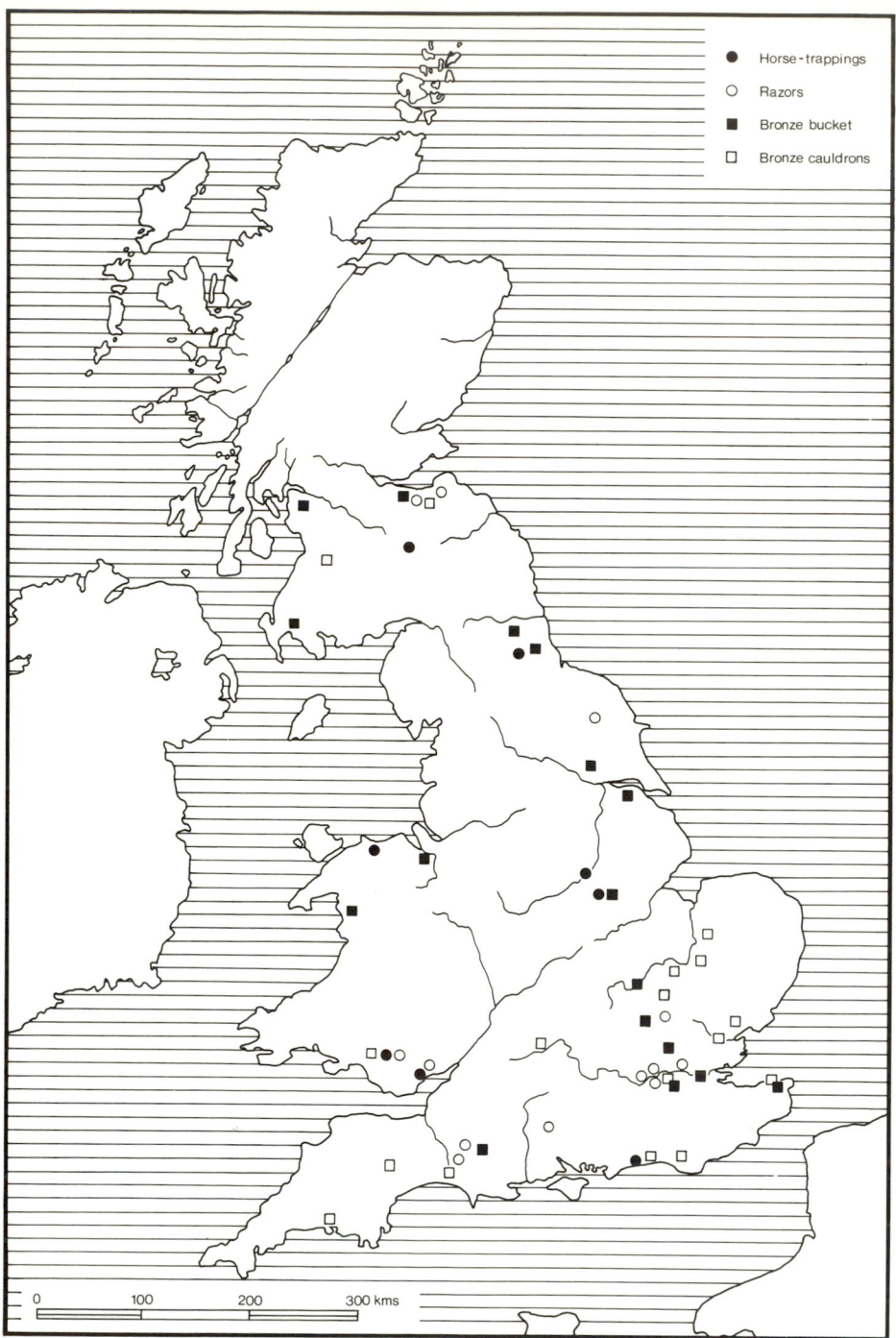

Figure 16.1 Distribution of selected types of Hallstatt metalwork, Ireland omitted (sources: various including Hawkes and Smith 1957 with additions).

aristocracy using a long slashing sword and frequently burying their dead in timber-built tombs beneath barrows. Some of the burials were very rich, containing trappings belonging to the chieftain's horses as well as a cart upon which the body may have been transported to the grave, along with weapons and selected items of personal equipment. Rich burials of this type cluster in Czechoslovakia and southern Germany but are known sporadically across most of central Europe, spreading into central and southern Belgium. What their sudden appearance means is not immediately clear. Some writers have proposed an invasion of an eastern aristocracy, ultimately from the Steppes, spreading west and gaining overlordship of the Late Urnfield communities. In support of such a view, close parallels are drawn between the harness-fittings and burial rites in the two areas; moreover, the rapid spread of the burials over Europe would be consistent with the concept of a mobile warrior aristocracy. Against this view, however, it can be argued that the characteristic long sword of the Hallstatt warriors owes nothing to eastern Cimmerian influence (Cowen 1967) and is best seen as the invention of the Late Urnfield bronzesmiths in response to cavalry warfare. Similarly, there is nothing new about rich burial rites involving the use of vehicles. Earlier examples are known in central and northern Europe but only incompletely, since the cremation ritual has destroyed much of the evidence. Extending these arguments, another model can be constructed which supposes that the Hallstatt aristocracy is simply an indigenous upper class adopting the rite of inhumation and making an increased use of the horse as a cavalry animal. The arguments for and against these two views cannot be paraded in full here, but the majority of scholars now favour the latter view.

In Europe the chronology of the period is now tolerably well known. In the central area of southern Bavaria, Hallstatt C began about 720 BC and reached its full development by about 700 (Kossack 1954; Dehn and Frey 1962; Peroni 1973). The period lasted for about 100 years and by c. 580 it was superseded by the Hallstatt D phase. To what extent there was a time-lag in the spreading of artefacts into western Europe and Britain, it is impossible to say. Mariën (1958), writing of the Belgian burials at Court-St-Etienne, considered the first intrusive Hallstatt C types to have arrived about 675, but it should be emphasized that the artefacts concerned are closely similar to those found at the beginning of the period in Bavaria, and there is no reason why they should not have reached Belgium nearer 700 – the two areas are, after all, only 480 km apart. Similarly, there *need* be no recognizable time-lag between technological developments in central Europe and their appearance in the British Isles. Unless other evidence is forthcoming, it is simpler to assume that Hallstatt C artefacts reached Britain during the time of their currency in Europe, that is, roughly between 700 and 600 BC.

The most characteristic weapon of the Hallstatt period is the long slashing sword of bronze, of which two varieties have been identified: the Mindelheim type, found exclusively in central and northern Europe, and the Gündlingen type, a far more common weapon spread over the whole of Europe. In a detailed study (1967), Cowen has distinguished four broad classes of Gündlingen sword on the basis of their hilt form (Figure 16.2). Of his classes a and b, both Continental products, twelve are known from Britain – eight of them from the Thames area; but with the possible exception of the sword from Ebberston, Yorks., none are from closed archaeological contexts. Once established in Britain, the new weapon-type was closely copied by the local swordsmiths, giving rise to Cowen's type c and d, of which twenty-seven recognizable examples are known in Britain and two from the Continent. Cowen has argued that in parallel with this development, various composite and hybrid forms were manufactured locally as native inventiveness took over, culminating in the evolution of the *Thames type* of sword, which represents the eventual dominance of the native traditions over the foreign. The type proved to

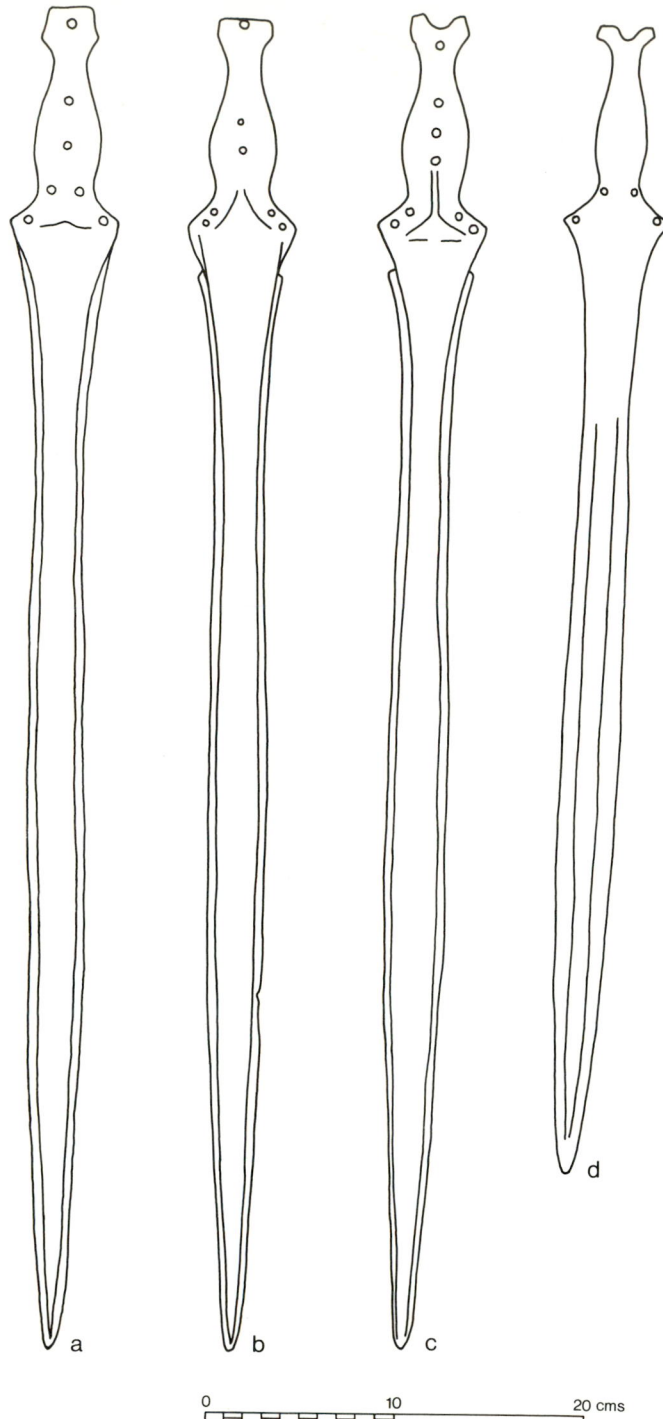

Figure 16.2 Hallstatt swords. 1 Brentford, Middx. (type a); 2 Henley, Oxon. (type b); 3 Newcastle upon Tyne (type c); 4 Cambridge (type d). (Source: Cowen 1967).

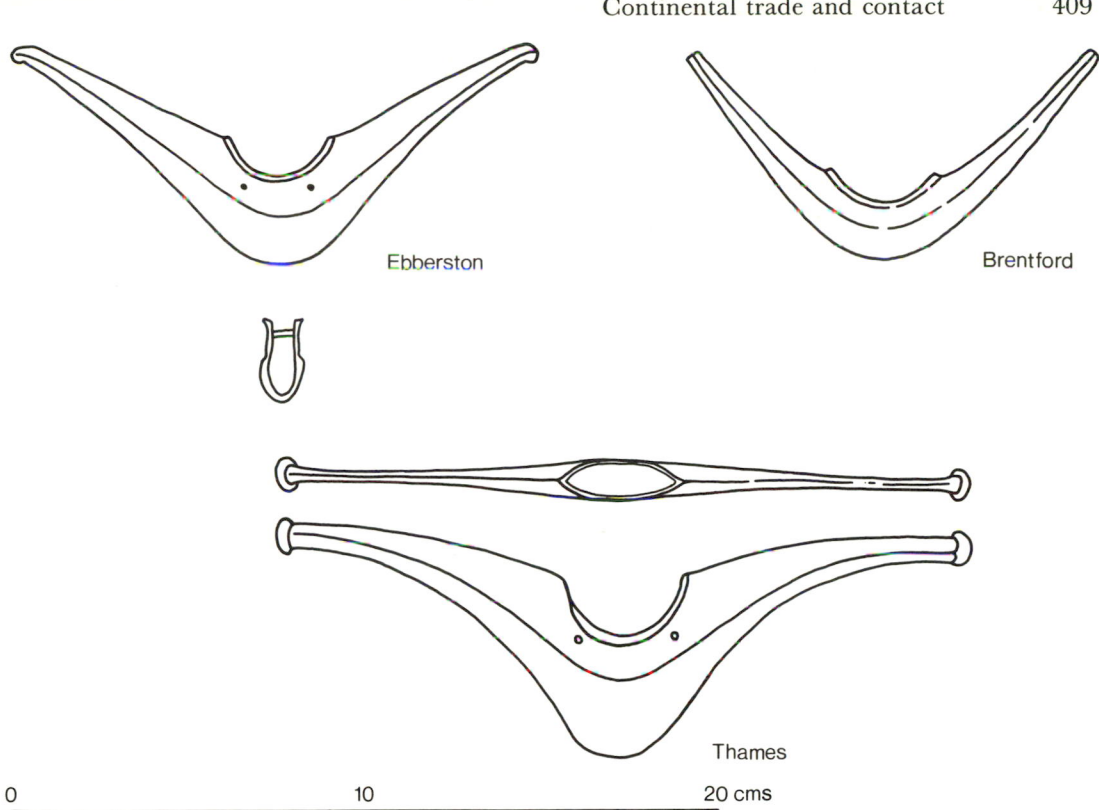

Figure 16.3   Hallstatt C chapes (sources: *Ebberston*, Burgess 1969b; *Brentford*, Wheeler 1929; *Thames* R.A. Smith 1925).

be popular not only in southern Britain but also in north-western Europe, where some fifteen exported examples have been recognized. Although it has been suggested that the *Thames type*, rather than being derived from the Gündlingen prototype, was in fact its predecessor (Schauer 1972) the British evidence argues in favour of Cohen's view.

The long sword was kept in a sheath of wood or leather terminating in a metal chape, the sides of which were splayed out into wings so formed, it is suggested, to enable a mounted warrior to keep the end of the sheath steady with his left foot while drawing the sword with his right hand. The chapes, like the swords, are characteristic of Continental burials and occur sporadically in Britain; there are eight known from England and ten from Ireland (Figure 16.3).

The occurrence of the swords and chapes in Britain (Figure 16.4) requires explanation. Clearly a number of weapons must have been brought in from the Continent, but conversely, once British manufacturing centres had developed, home-produced varieties were exported. Without special pleading, simple exchange mechanisms could explain the entire pattern. If, as has been argued by some, the swords had accompanied an immigrant warrior elite one would have expected them to be buried with the dead in the Continental manner, but this is not so; the majority were found in rivers where, like their Late Bronze Age predecessors, they had been deliberately deposited. No certain burial find is known in Britain – with the possible exception of

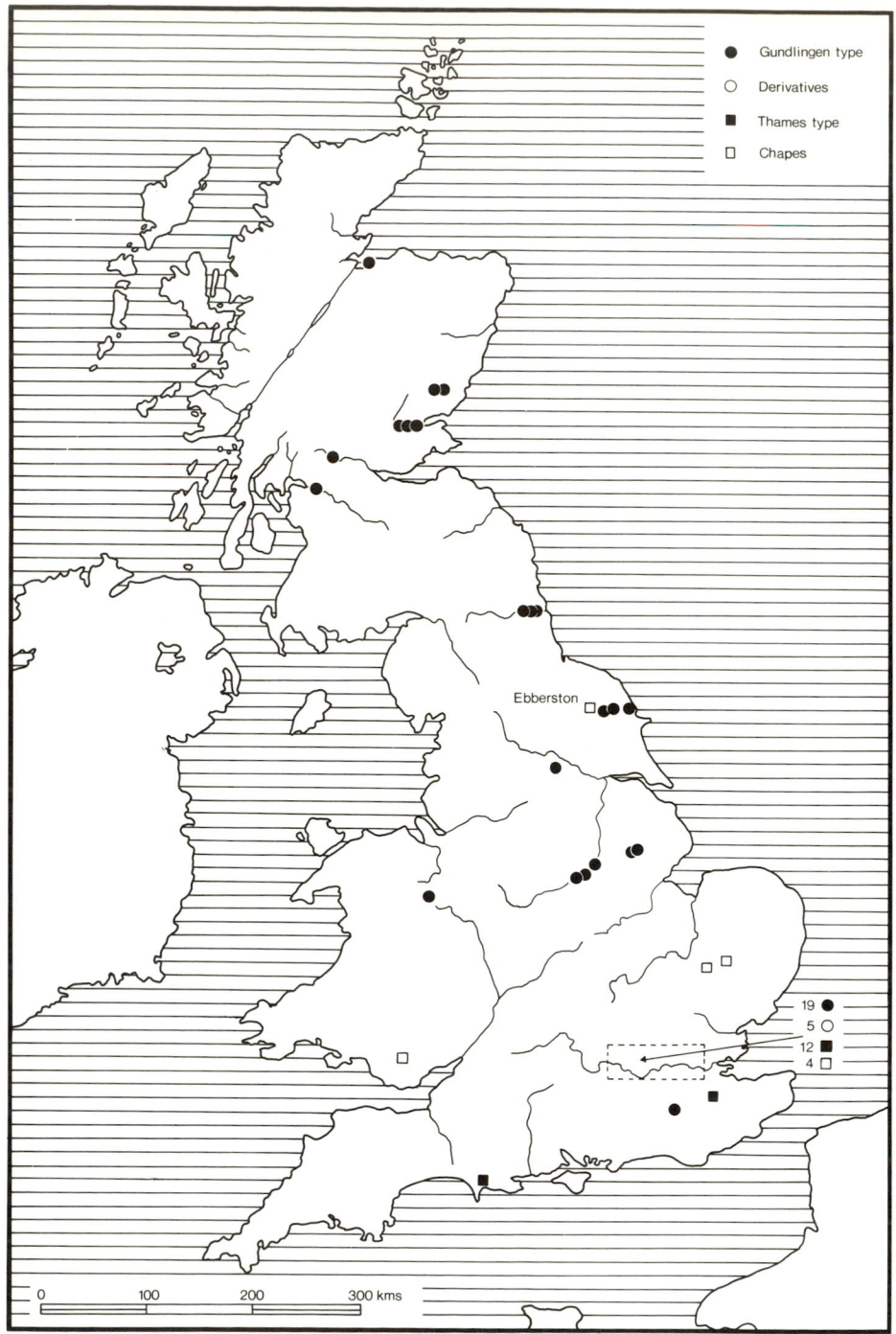

Figure 16.4 Distribution of Hallstatt swords and chapes, Ireland omitted (source: Cowen 1967).

the ill-recorded discovery at Ebberston in Yorkshire, where two swords and a chape were found together with a quantity of human bones. Even if this is accepted as a typical Hallstatt C burial in Continental style, it need not necessarily represent a foreign warrior aristocrat. Hallstatt swords are therefore most likely to have been worn by British warriors and disposed of in a manner consistent with traditions which had been in operation in Britain for centuries. The appearance of these swords is best explained in terms of a continuation of the existing exchange systems, linking Britain to northern Europe, which had been in operation for centuries.

The seventh century saw the importation of a wide range of harness-and cart-fittings from northern and central Europe and their eventual deposition here in hoards, together with locally produced tools and weapons and sometimes imports from western Europe (Figure 16.5). Hoards of this kind are therefore of considerable significance in establishing synchronisms between local industry and datable foreign products. While it must be admitted that close dating is extremely difficult, the hoards can be divided into a loose sequence stretching throughout the eighth and seventh centuries. At the beginning of the sequence must be placed the famous collection of material found beneath a layer of stalagmite on the floor of the cave at Heathery Burn, Co. Durham. In addition to socketed spears, socketed axes, knives, gouges, awls, a bifid razor and a range of bone and stone artefacts, there was recovered a group of bronze cart- and harness-fittings (Figure 16.5). The cart-fittings consisted of eight bronze bands, presumably for binding the ends of the axles of a wheeled vehicle. Similar objects are recorded in Late Urnfield contexts in central Europe dating to the eighth century or a little later. The harnesses are now represented by a bronze strap-distributor (i.e. a disc with perforated vertical sides to allow leather straps to cross at right angles), a ribbed disc with attachment loops, two large disc-shaped mountings and a group of bronze rings of various diameters. In addition, two cheek-pieces of bone were found. Dating evidence is provided by a bronze bucket (Figure 16.6) of a type in use in the first half of the seventh century – a date which corresponds well with the Ultimate Urnfield character of the material.

The strap-distributor and the looped disc can be closely paralleled at two other hoards from Welby, Leics. (Figure 16.5), and Parc y Meirch, Denbigh. (Figure 16.7), which together with the Horsehope hoard from Peeblesshire (Figure 16.5) constitute a closely similar group of horse equipment hoards broadly datable to the middle of the seventh century. At Welby five strap-distributors were found, together with a perforated looped disc and double-looped harness-fitting identical to those from the other two hoards. Other central European types at Welby include two T-shaped handle attachments for a bowl and possibly the small carinated bronze cup with furrowed decoration on the shoulder (Figure 4.2, p. 65), of a type which is frequently reproduced in pottery in southern England. The local bronze industry was represented by socketed axes, a spear and a sword.

The Parc y Meirch hoard is altogether more substantial, containing some ninety individual pieces among which is a group of harness-trappings including double-looped fittings and strap-distributors as well as rattle-pendants composed of plaques of bronze joined loosely together with bronze rings (Figure 16.7). This type of bridle decoration is represented in Scandinavia in the eighth and seventh centuries, and a slightly different form of the same idea appears in one of the south Belgian burials at Court-St-Etienne in the early part of the seventh century. In origin the type is probably French (Savory 1976a, 44). In the Horsehope hoard a range of harness-rings occurs, including the characteristic double-looped ring, but in addition C.M. Piggott (1955) has recognized several cart-fittings which include a dish-shaped mounting and ribbed discs, the latter possibly serving as decorative attachments for the axle caps of a small

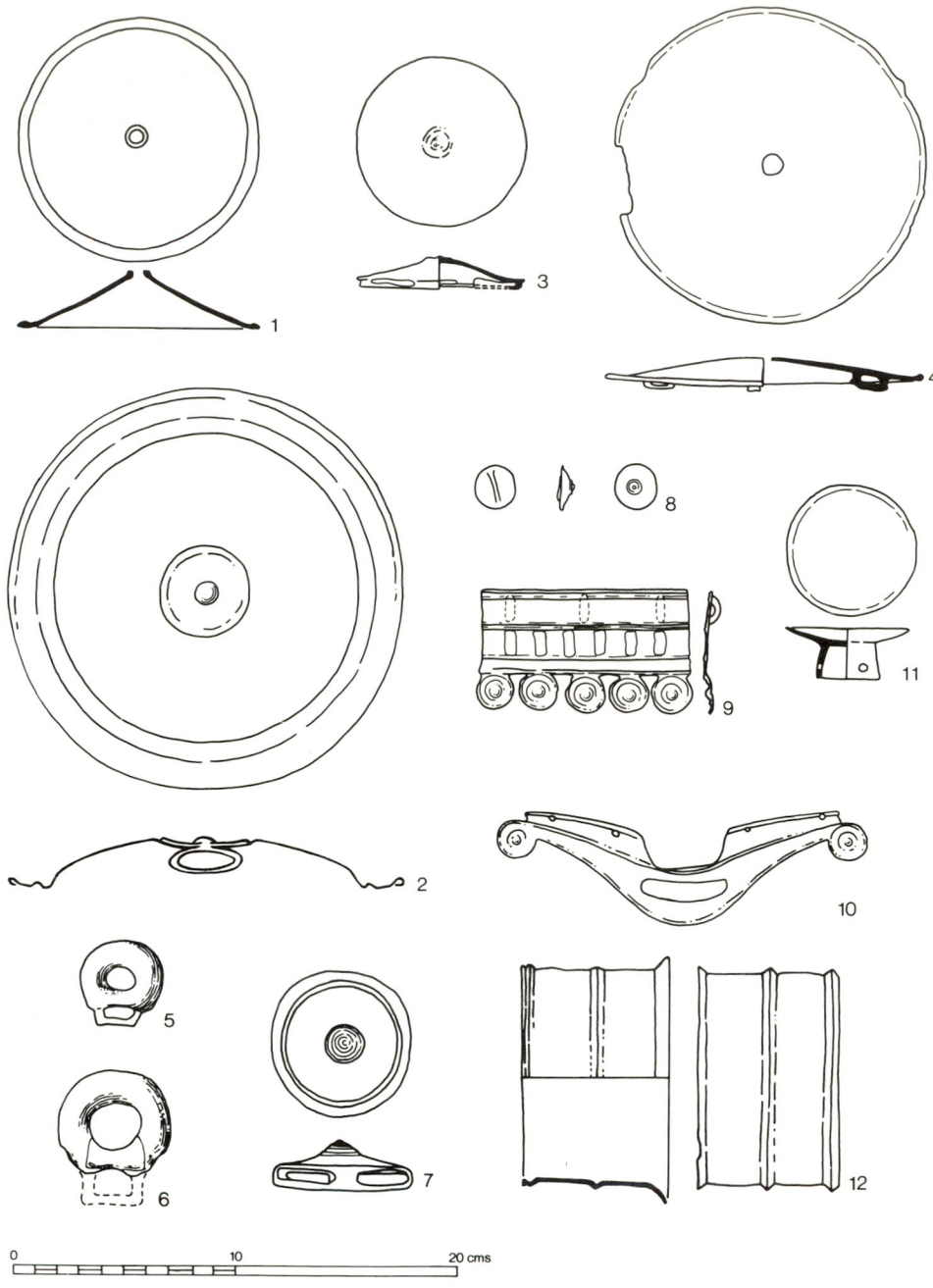

Figure 16.5 Selection of Hallstatt horse-trappings and cart fittings. 1 Newark-on-Trent, Notts.; 2,9,10 Llyn Fawr, Glam.; 3,4,8,12 Heathery Burn, Co. Durham; 5,7 Welby, Leics.; 6,11 Horsehope, Peebles (sources: 1,3,4,8,12 *Inv. Arch. GB*; 2,9,10 Grimes 1951; 5,7 Powell 1950; 6,11 S. Piggott 1955).

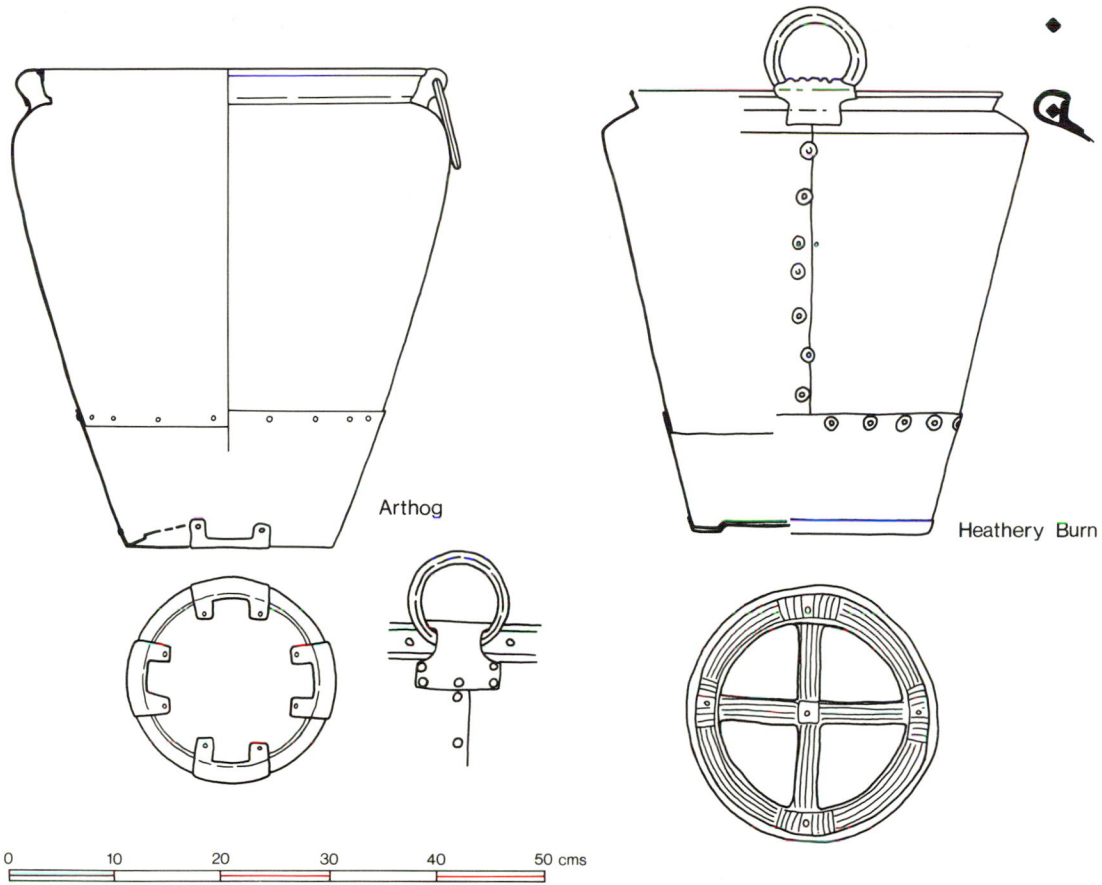

Figure 16.6 Bronze buckets (source: Hawkes and Smith 1957).

(or model) vehicle. The closest parallels for these pieces are among the Hallstatt cart burials of Czechoslovakia, dating to the seventh century.

Of the later seventh-century hoards, by far the most significant is the collection of material recovered from the bottom of an ancient lake at Llyn Fawr in Glamorganshire. Local products are well represented by seven socketed bronze axes, four of them of a distinctive Welsh type, three socketed sickles, two of bronze and one of iron, and three socketed chisels. It is possible that the socketed iron spearhead recovered was also of local manufacture, but the type is simple and could equally well have been imported from the Continent, where identical forms were in use. Clearly, the presence of a local type of sickle made in iron implies that iron extraction was by now under way, if only on a small scale. Atlantic trade is represented by two bronze cauldrons of class B1 (Figure 16.9) – a type which first came into use in the first half of the seventh century or a little before. North European Hallstatt C types (Figures 16.5 and 16.10) include an iron sword with hilt plates of bone, two bronze cheek-pieces, three bronze discs or phalerae from harness decorations, an openwork harness mount, a belt hook and a crescentic razor. All the types can be

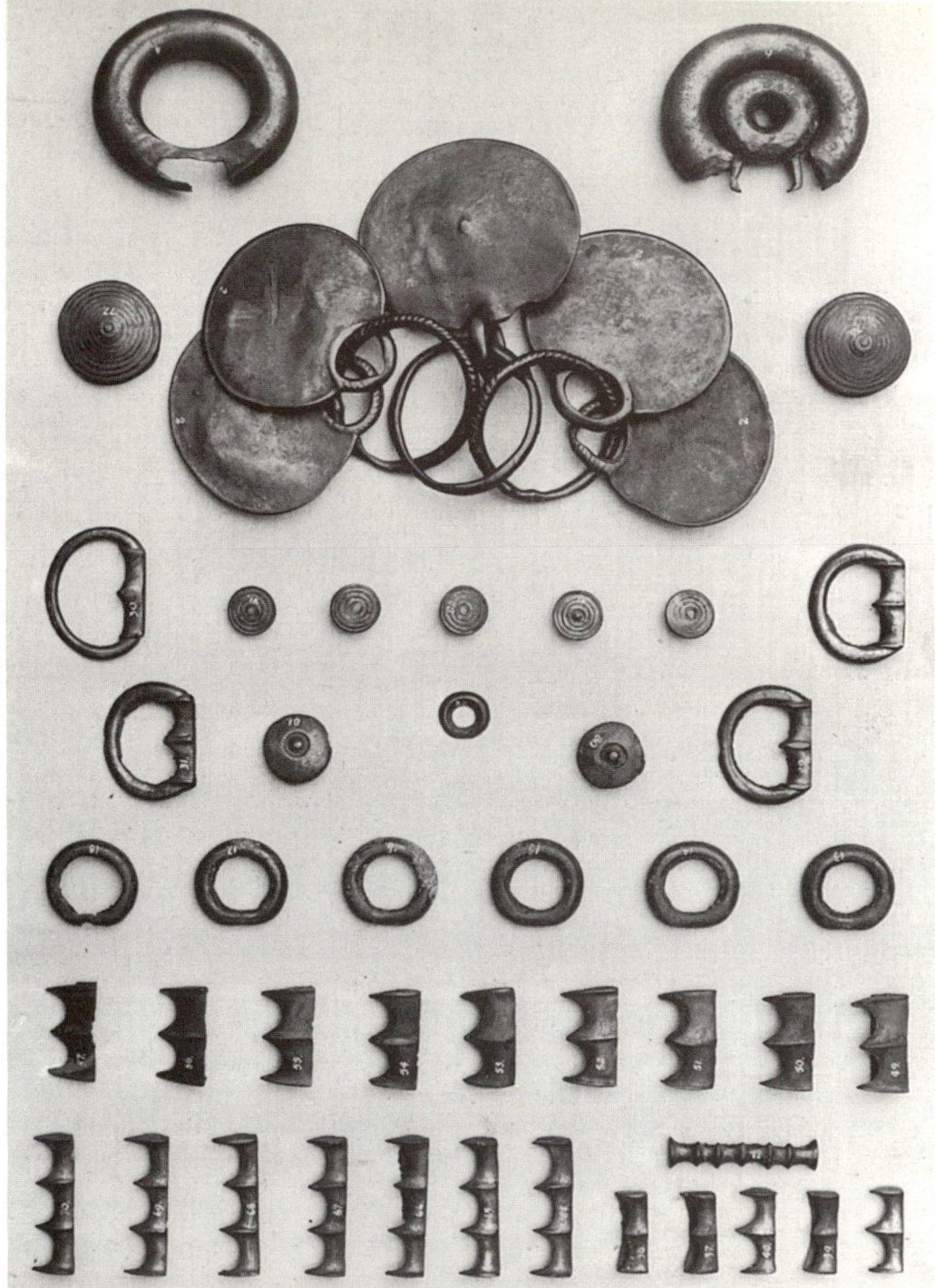

Figure 16.7   Part of the hoard from Parc y Meirch, Denbigh. (photo: National Museum of Wales).

very closely paralleled in early Hallstatt C burials in southern Germany and Belgium, particularly at Court-St-Etienne. So close are the parallels that direct importation from the Continent is the only reasonable explanation for the presence of these objects in western Britain. Precise dating for the deposition of the hoard is, of course, difficult since there is no way of assessing how long the individual items had been hoarded nor indeed is there any certainty that all were deposited together, but the fact that all appear to be broadly contemporary and identical to Continental types hints at a date not far removed from the middle of the seventh century. By this time, then, iron production was established.

A second hoard to show an association between Late Bronze Age types and iron comes from Sompting, Sussex, where the remains of a class B2 cauldron (Figure 16.8) were recovered, together with seventeen axes and a Hallstatt phalera of hollow conical form. To one of the axes adhered a mass of corroded iron. On the basis of the cauldron, a date of 650–600 would seem to be most likely, but a later date in the sixth century cannot be completely ruled out.

Finally, from the river Avon at Melksham, Wilts. two iron socketed spears were found in a probable hoard together with three bronze socketed spearheads and the blade of a dirk (Gingell 1979) suggesting a date in the late seventh or early sixth century.

Several other but less closely datable discoveries of harness- and cart-fittings have come to light. Phalerae of Hallstatt type have been recovered from the Thames at Brentford, Middx., with masses of bronze work of Late Bronze Age type (O'Connor 1975). A phalera of similar date with a central perforation came from a hoard at Newark-on-Trent, Notts. (Figure 16.5), together with socketed axes and spears, and a hoard at Cardiff, Glam., produced an axle cap and two Hallstatt C razors as well as various implements in the local Bronze Age tradition.

This brief survey of the more significant hoards leaves very little doubt that throughout the seventh century, harness- and cart-fittings of Continental type were finding their way into this country in some quantity and not infrequently ending up in hoards along with local types. The mechanisms by which this material arrived are impossible now to recover. Conceivably horses and their tack were being traded together, perhaps with carts, but we cannot completely rule out the possibility that a few people were now making their way into the country, bringing with them the outward and visible signs of their aristocracy.

Superimposed upon this trade in aristocratic military equipment, was the importation of minor objects such as razors (Figure 16.10) (C.M. Piggott 1946), swan's-neck pins (Figure 16.11) (Dunning 1934), and brooches (Figure 16.12) (Harden 1950). Razors from the Llyn Fawr and Cardiff hoards have already been mentioned; others have come from the settlement at Staple Howe, Yorks., from a hoard at Danebury, Hants., unstratified from early occupation sites on Ham Hill and South Cadbury and as isolated finds from half a dozen or more sites. Razors are frequently found in Hallstatt burials on the Continent, where they must represent a standard piece of a warrior's equipment. The British finds do not, however, come from burials and many of them may have been manufactured locally.

Swan's-neck pins occur sporadically in Britain. In all about ten are known, mainly from the south but, apart from the examples at the settlement site of All Cannings Cross, Wilts., they are not generally found in closely stratified contexts, and since the type is likely to have continued in use for some time, it is not a very useful chronological indicator. Even less certainty attaches to the large number of Hallstatt fibulae from Britain. Not one has been recovered in an Iron Age context, but the number is so great that some at least must have found their way into Britain in the seventh or sixth century, on the dresses of visiting womenfolk or as traded trinkets.

In north-eastern Scotland a more substantial group of intrusive metal types has been found,

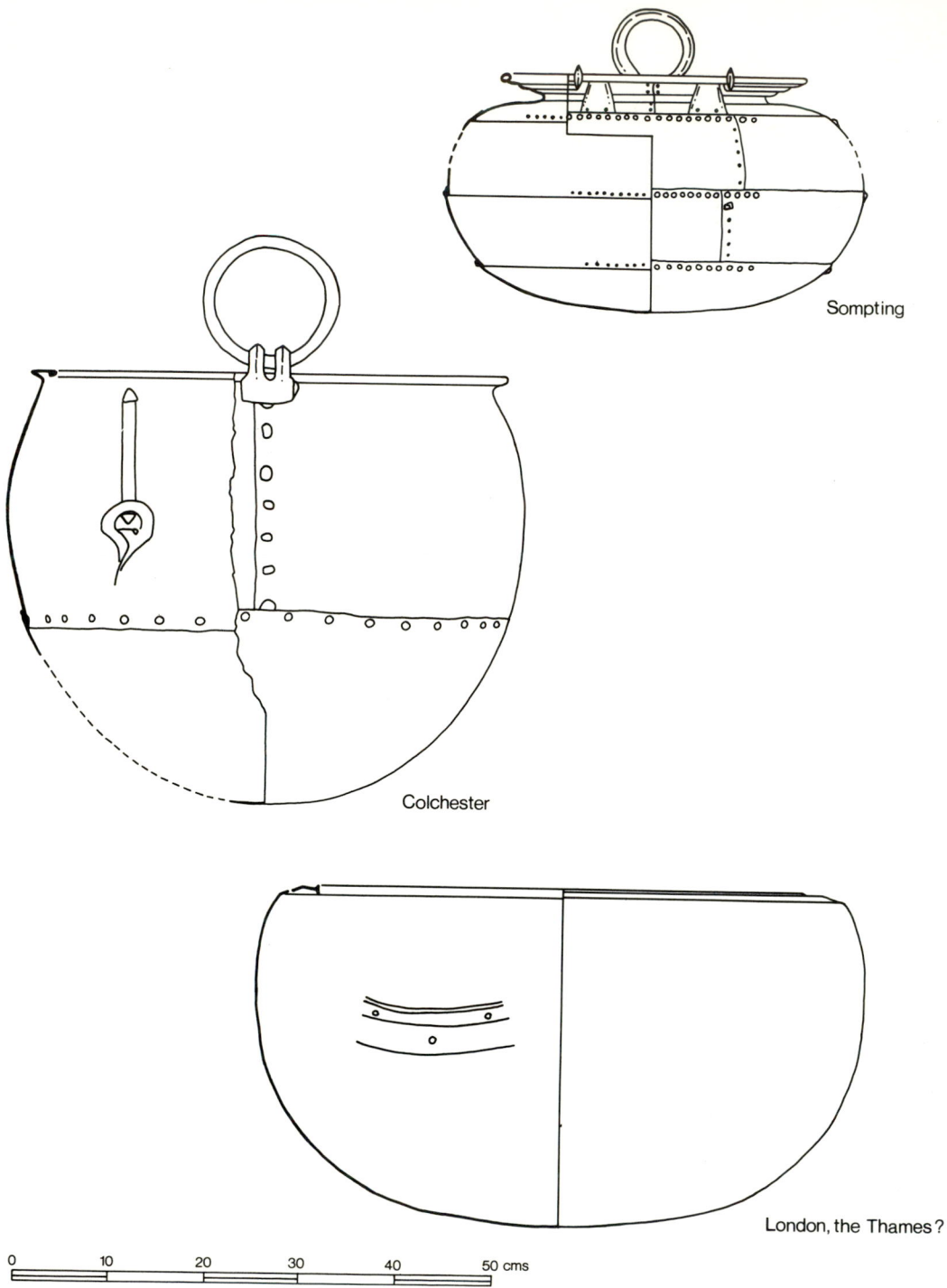

Figure 16.8 Bronze cauldrons (sources: *Sompting*, E.C. Curwen 1948; *Colchester and London*, Hawkes and Smith 1957).

Figure 16.9   Bronze cauldron from Llyn Fawr, Glam. (photo: National Museum of Wales).

constituting what is called the Covesea phase of the local metal industry (Coles 1962b). Dominant among the types which define the phase are simple penannular armlets with their terminals expanded outwards, related to a type found in Late Urnfield contexts in north-western Europe, whence it is suggested they were imported to Scotland. In two important hoards, Wester Ord, Ross, and Braes of Gight, Aberdeen, Covesea armlets were found associated with penannular necklets with free-swinging loops and pendants. These too have close north European parallels dated to *c.* 700 BC. In a third hoard of some significance, from Balmashanner, Angus, three Covesea armlets were found with a bronze bowl and an iron ring, demonstrating beyond doubt the overlap between the Covesea phase and the use of iron. Other associations showed that Covesea types were used in parallel to an already vigorous indigenous bronze industry, the various phases of which are named after the hoards at Adabrock, Ballimore and Tarves (Coles 1962b).

    While a north European origin can be demonstrated for the Covesea types, the nature of the contact is far less clear. It has been suggested that the distinctive flat-rimmed pottery found at Covesea itself, Balmashanner and a number of other sites is of Late Urnfield derivation (Coles 1962b, 11), hinting at the possibility of a limited folk movement, but the pottery is so generalized

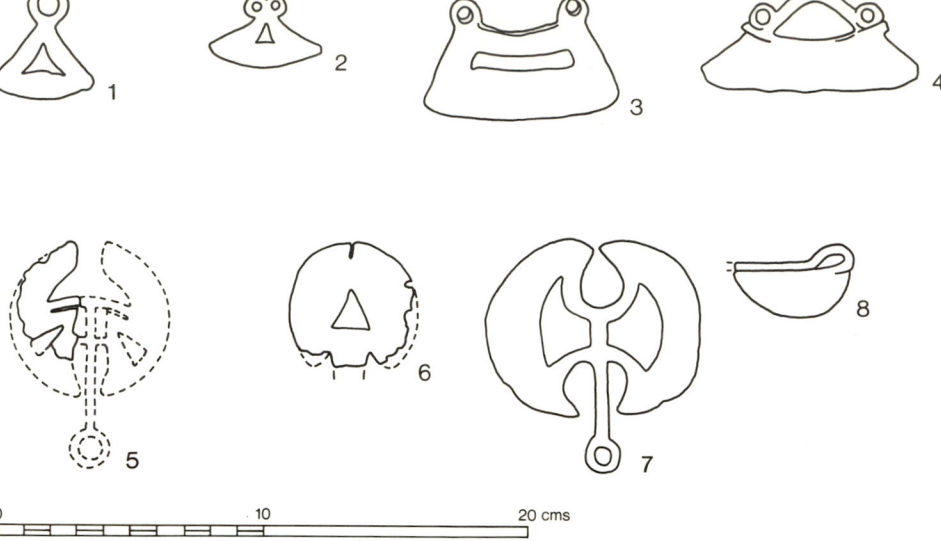

Figure 16.10   Hallstatt razors. 1,6 Cardiff, Glam.; 2 Llyn Fawr, Glam.; 3 river Thames at Richmond, Surrey; 4,5,8 Staple Howe, Yorks.; 7 Midlothian. (Sources: 1,6 Nash-Williams 1933b; 2 Grimes 1951; 3,7 C.M. Piggott 1946; 4,5,8 Brewster 1963).

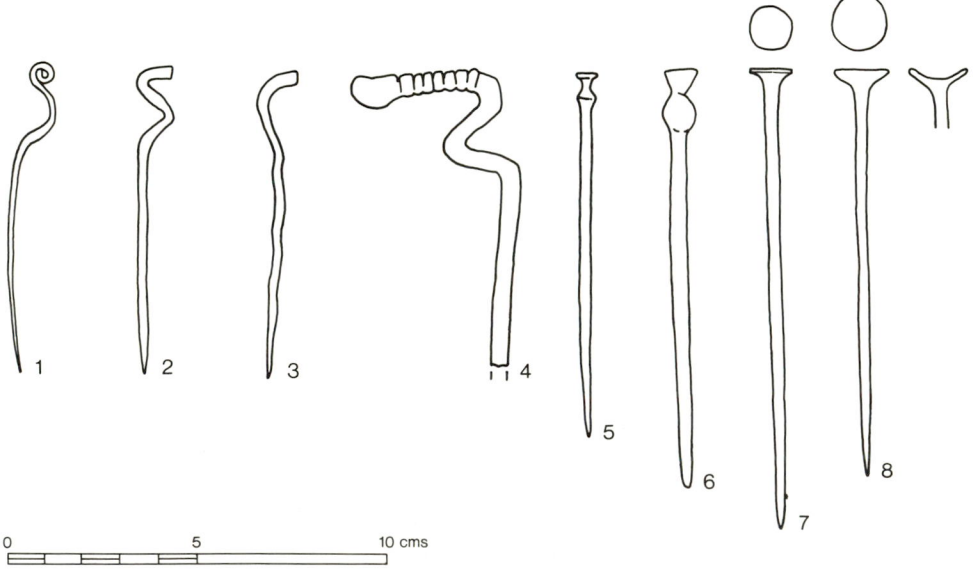

Figure 16.11   Bronze pins. 1 Hammersmith, London; 2 Brighton, Sussex; 3 Portslade, Sussex; 4,6 All Cannings Cross, Wilts.; 5 Totternhoe, Beds.; 7,8 Heathery Burn, Co. Durham. (Sources: various).

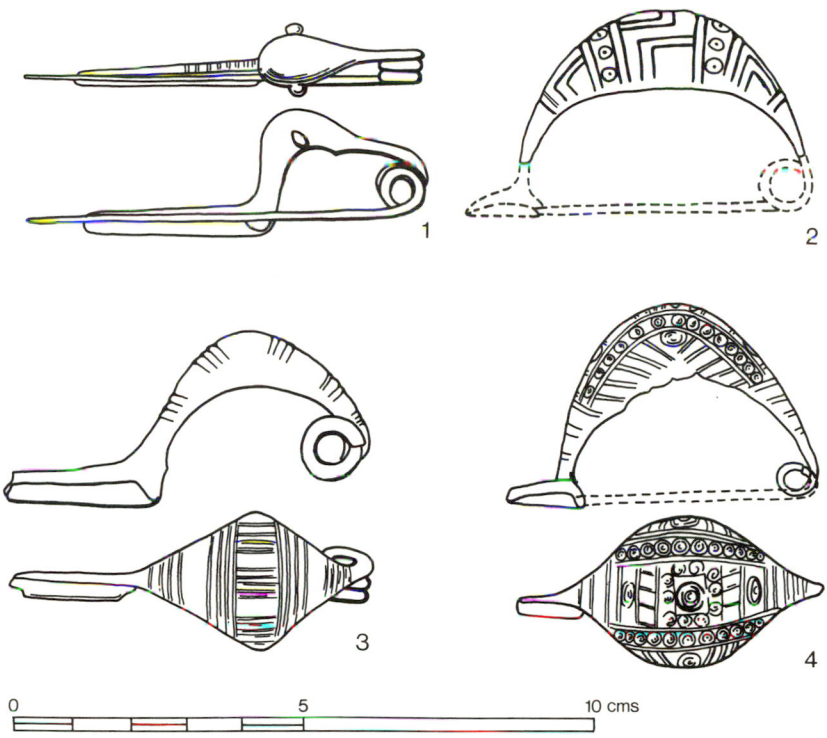

Figure 16.12 Hallstatt fibulae. 1 Hod Hill, Dorset; 2 York; 3 North Wraxall, Wilts.; 4 Box, Wilts (Sources: 1,4 R.A. Smith 1925; 2 *Antiq. Journ.* 12 (1932), 454; 3 Cunnington and Goddard 1934).

that firm assumptions cannot be based on it. Seventh-century radiocarbon dates for the timber-laced forts of north-east Scotland have also been quoted to add support to the idea of an immigration from northern Europe (MacKie 1969a, 1976) but none of these observations are compelling arguments for folk movement: at best it shows a period of contact and innovation.

Atlantic trade: eighth to sixth centuries

Trading contacts along the Atlantic coasts of Iberia and France to Britain had by the eighth century developed a new intensity, manifesting itself in the south-east of the country in the hoards of the Carp's-Tongue Sword Complex. It is now clear that this trade was maintained throughout the seventh and well into the sixth century, running therefore in parallel with the Hallstatt C incomings. It was once thought that cauldrons of type A were distributed along the Atlantic sea-ways originating from an eighth-century Mediterranean prototype (Hawkes and Smith 1957), but further research has shown the situation to be more complicated. That the idea of the cauldron was introduced from northern Europe was suggested by Eogan (1974b, 322 n. 18). Further work has confirmed this view and has dated the earliest British examples (Colchester and Shipton) back to the later years of the second millennium. But thereafter cauldron production seems to have passed to Ireland whence examples were traded to England, Scotland, western France and Denmark (Gerloff 1987) along the Irish Sea/Atlantic routes. The tradition, once established, continued with the somewhat later class B cauldrons which originated before 650 BC in Ireland and continued to be distributed for a century or so after. Associations between the cauldrons and Hallstatt C types have been referred to above (pp. 413–15) in the consideration of the Llyn Fawr and Sompting hoards.

Some at least of the Carp's-Tongue Sword Complex hoards occur later than the eighth century though close dating in Britain is impossible. The Continental material offers support for this later dating of the end of the Carp's-Tongue Complex. A Hallstatt C razor in the Ile Guenoc hoard, Finistère (Briard 1957, Figure 28), and a radiocarbon date of 559 ± 130 bc for Saint-Guganen Loudéac, Côte du Nord, are suggestive evidence for the continuation of trade into the seventh century.

On both sides of the Channel there appeared at this time large numbers of small non-functional axes with rectangular sockets and unprepared cutting edges, known as Breton or Armorican axes. Altogether in north-western France, it is estimated that 315 hoards contained this type exclusively, producing some 25,000 individual specimens (Briard 1979, 164), and the type is found widely in south-east Britain. The opinion now is that they formed some kind of currency and continued to be used as such into the fifth century or even later. At Saint-Martin-des-Champs, Finistère, Breton axes were found in association with an iron ingot, demonstrating a late survival. The axes, then, are the last manifestation of the Atlantic bronze trade, out of which grew the sophisticated trading contacts first mentioned by classical writers in the fourth century, and to which Caesar refers in some detail a few centuries later.

European contacts: sixth to fifth century

In central Europe the change to the Hallstatt D stage of culture took place a little before 600 BC. By this time the central areas of development, typified by the rich chieftains' burials, had shifted west into the middle Rhine and Moselle region and into Burgundy – areas which now benefited from the new trade routes along the Rhône that had opened up following the foundation of the trading port of Massilia (Marseilles). Trading systems were by this time well established between central Europe and the Mediterranean world, and luxury goods belonging to wine-drinking and feasting rituals were being imported from Greek and Italian workshops, eventually finding their way into the tombs of the aristocracy (Cunliffe 1988a, 24–35). Trading contacts between Britain and the Continent appear to have been less intensive in the sixth and early fifth centuries than they had been in the preceding 100 years, but nevertheless a number of imported metal objects of Hallstatt D type are known.

The Thames was evidently an important point of entry, to judge by the number of new types found in the London area. From the Thames came a short iron sword with an antennae-shaped hilt (Figure 16.13) (R.A. Smith 1925; Stead 1984b) characteristic of sixth-century Continental types, and from the same general provenance was recovered a simple hemispherical bronze cauldron of Hallstatt D type (Hawkes and Smith 1957) which can be paralleled on many west central European sites, more commonly in the second half of the century (Figure 16.8).

The long-established school of swordsmiths in the Thames region, who by now were manufacturing their own varieties of the Hallstatt C imports, soon absorbed the idea of the

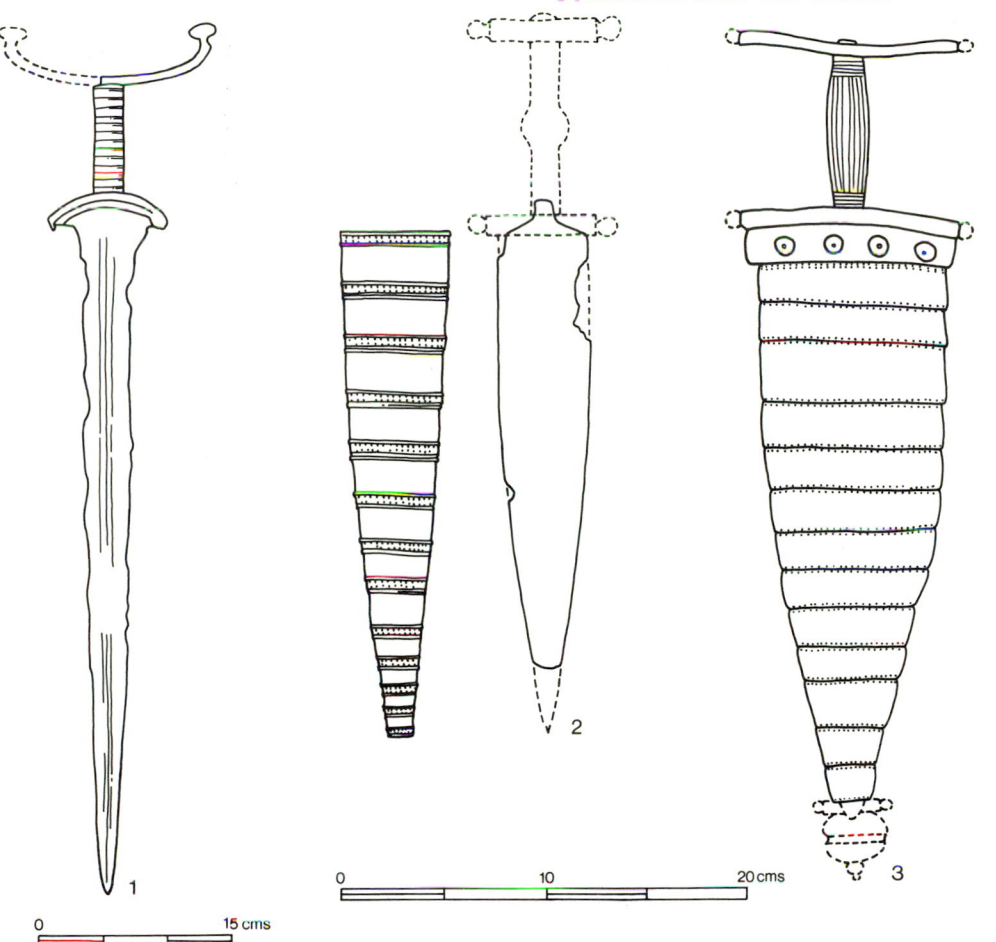

Figure 16.13 Hallstatt D weapons. 1 river Thames; 2 Battersea, London; 3 Mortlake, Surrey. (Sources: 1 R.A. Smith 1925; 2,3 Jope 1961a).

Hallstatt D short dagger – a type in use in the early sixth century in southern Germany – and began to manufacture their own elegant versions with an improved method of suspension using twin loops at the back of the sheath to strengthen the attachment to the belt (Figures 16.13 and 16.14). Only one certain import is known, found in the bed of the Thames at Mortlake (Figure 16.13, no. 3) and its sheath was probably repaired in Britain (Jope 1983). Diplomatic gifts of this kind inspired a vigorous British tradition. The industry continued to flourish until about 300 BC, influenced in its later stages by new La Tène ideas coming in after about 450 (Jope 1961a).

A comparable example, showing the same process of adoption and rapid modification of Hallstatt D ideas, is exhibited by the representative of a class of fibulae found in the Thames near Hammersmith (Hodson 1971). Evidently there must have been schools of craftsmen working in the area, always receptive of new Continental ideas.

More widely flung contacts with northern Italy are emphasized by the ribbed pail, dug up at Weybridge, Surrey, made of strips of corrugated bronze riveted together along a single vertical

Figure 16.14   Hallstatt D dagger and sheath from the river Thames at Hammersmith, London (photo: Museum of London).

seam and provided with two movable handles (Stead 1984a, 43–4). The type is well known in western Europe and was probably made in a European workshop some time in the sixth century whence, directly or indirectly, it reached Britain (Stjernquist 1967, 70–4).

Several other Italian Mediterranean bronzes have been found in Britain, but all in dubious circumstances (Harbison and Laing 1974). Among the more significant should be mentioned a fragment of 'Rhodian' flagon of late seventh- to early sixth-century date found at Minster in Kent, an Etruscan bronze oenochoe of the late sixth to early fifth century from Northampton, a trefoil-mouthed flagon of the early fifth century from the river Crouch, Essex, and two bronze jugs of fourth-century date, one from Tewkesbury, the other from Bath. In no case is it possible to be sure that the vessel was a contemporary Iron Age import, and the possibility must therefore be allowed of the more recent importation.

Other west European or Mediterranean objects found in Britain include about eighty examples of Continental fibulae dating to the period of the eighth to fourth centuries (Harden

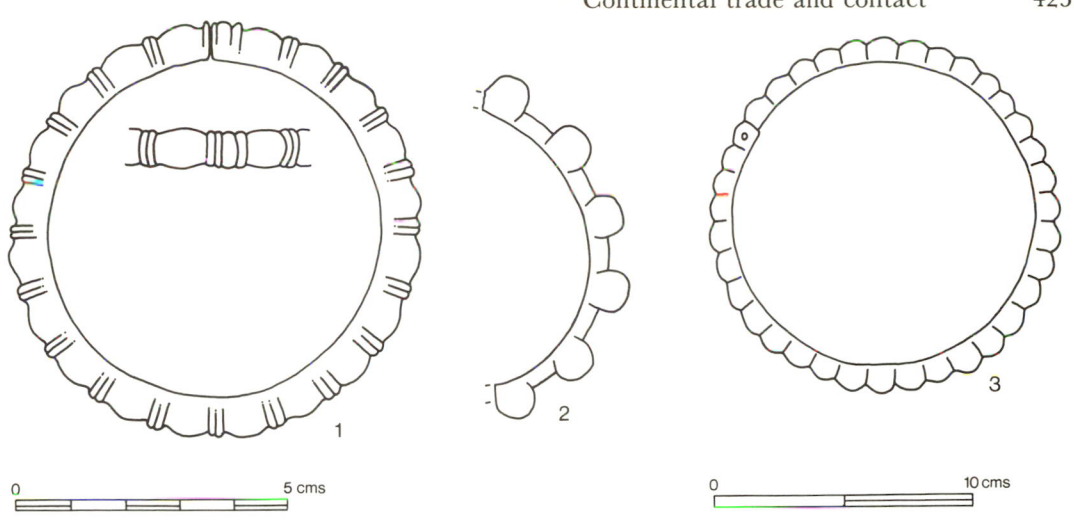

Figure 16.15   Hallstatt bracelets and neck-rings. 1 Scarborough, Yorks.; 2 Cold Kitchen Hill, Wilts.; 3 Clynnog, Caerns. (sources: 1 R.A. Smith 1934; 2 *DMC*; 3 Grimes 1951).

1950). It is, of course, impossible to be sure when they were imported. Some of them may have arrived during the Roman period or even later in the collections of travellers, but many must have been imported into Britain during the time when they were current on the Continent. Other personal ornaments of Hallstatt type, including neck- and arm-rings of bronze with 'nut' moulded decoration, occur less frequently. One was found close to an early occupation site at Scarborough, Yorks., several came from the Iron Age port site at Mount Batten (Cunliffe 1988b), and another unassociated example is recorded from Clynnog, Caerns. (Figure 16.15). The general type does not seem to have been widely copied by local craftsmen.

Another class of imported material is pottery. Several finds of Mediterranean vessels have been made in Britain, but again the date of their importation is, without exception, unknown since no examples have yet been found on stratified occupation sites. Several vessels have been dredged from rivers, including a Greek Black Figure kylix from the Thames near Reading, which is reliably dated on stylistic grounds to the late sixth century (Boon 1954, 178). From the same river, at Barnes, an Italic handled cup of the seventh century was dug out of the river bank, and from Barking Creek came a Greek hydriskos of the sixth century (Harden 1950, 321–2). A squat lekythos of fourth-century date was also recovered from Billingsgate. Finally, mention should be made of a group of three Greek vessels, one of them an Attic drinking cup of the late fourth century, which were found together in an artificial cave at Teignmouth, Devon, during the last century. It must be stressed that none of these finds need represent Iron Age importation, but there is nothing inherently difficult in supposing that some Mediterranean vessels found their way into southern Britain during the course of normal trading expeditions.

Scotland appears to have maintained direct contact with northern Europe at this time as shown by the distribution of distinctive sunflower swan's-neck pins (Figure 16.16): eight from Scotland, one from Ireland and one from Fengate, Northants. Coles (1959) has shown that the genesis of the type – the fusing of the Hallstatt swan's-neck pins and the Irish-Scandinavian sunflower pins – probably took place in north Germany in the sixth and fifth centuries, though an

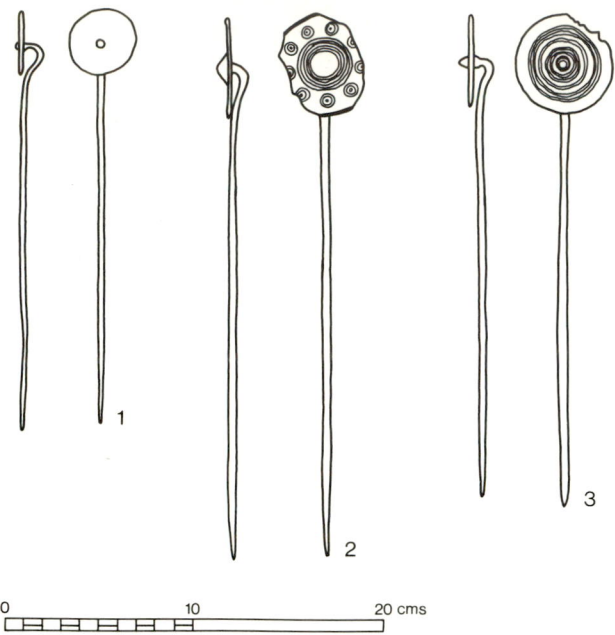

Figure 16.16   Sunflower swan's-neck pins. 1 Taves, Aberdeen; 2 Loch Broom, Ross; 3 Campbeltown, Argyll. (source: Coles 1959).

earlier origin is possible (Eogan 1974a, 58). From there the idea penetrated to Scotland. Two associated finds, the hoards from Grosvenor Crescent, Edinburgh, and Tarves, Aberdeen, show that the pins were in use at the same time as bronze swords of Ewart Park type, still manufactured in the Late Bronze Age tradition.

It can be seen from the above paragraphs that imported material of Hallstatt D date is sparse in Britain, but sufficient survives to imply continuous contact with the Continent throughout the sixth and early fifth centuries. Nothing in the surviving archaeological record needs, however, to be explained in terms other than of casual trade.

Contacts between Britain and the Continent: fifth to second century

From the fifth to the second century, contacts between Britain and adjacent parts of the Continent were maintained. Metalwork in the new La Tène style, which developed in Europe towards the beginning of the fifth century, found its way into the country largely as the result of trade. Many of the incoming types were copied by local craftsmen, giving rise to specifically British varieties. In Yorkshire, however, a more extensive cultural assemblage appears to have been introduced, including not only metal types but alien burial customs best paralleled among the La Tène cultures of northern France. This group – referred to as the Arras culture – has been considered in some detail above (pp. 77–9). Elsewhere in Britain northern French decorative metalwork is rare, but a fine openwork disc, probably a horse-harness decoration, was found at

Figure 16.17 Openwork disc of early La Tène date from Danebury, Hants. Actual size (photo: Institute of Archaeology, Oxford. Danebury Trust).

the hillfort of Danebury, Hants. (Figure 16.17). It is closely comparable to ornaments from the late fifth-century chieftains' burials of the Marne region and is either an import or an assured local copy of one. A broadly similar type from the Thames at Hammersmith (R.A. Smith 1905, fig. 122) is almost certainly a British-made version.

The sixth-century production of a distinctive series of daggers and dagger sheaths in the Thames region, noted above, was evidently carried out by local craftsmen influenced at first by Hallstatt D prototypes but soon evolving their own improved techniques and style. Production continued throughout the fifth and fourth centuries absorbing, after about 450, La Tène improvements, which were being developed in parallel on the Continent. The earliest of these La Tène-inspired sheaths, one discovered at Chelsea, is so close to northern French types of the mid-fifth century, while evidently itself of British manufacture, that the British craftsmen must have responded directly to new Continental ideas. Close contact appears only at this time; thereafter the British and French traditions diverged, hinting at the beginning of some degree of cultural isolation. The eighteen daggers of La Tène I type found in Britain, mainly in the Thames area, can be arranged in a typological sequence lasting until the late fourth century. Among the latest to be made was the scabbard from Wisbech, decorated in a free-hand curvilinear style with S-shaped scrolls arranged in lyre and palmette patterns about a central ridge. This must be regarded as a provincial version of an art style current in Europe during the fourth century, from which the early beginnings British Celtic art eventually developed.

While the later British daggers continued to evolve throughout the beginning of the La Tène period a range of swords of La Tène I type was being manufactured. At least seventeen have been identified from the rivers Thames and Witham but of these only two or three have any claim to being actual imports (Figure 16.18). One came from Wandsworth and had a blade engraved or chased with close-set parallel lines in a style known as laddering best represented on Swiss examples; another, from the Thames at Battersea was found in a scabbard decorated at the hilt end with facing dragons in a style more common in Hungary (Stead 1984a, 47–50). A third, possible, import was a finely decorated version from the river Trent at Sutton, Notts., which is closely similar to examples belonging to the Swiss sword style. Even the scabbard from Standlake, Oxon. (Figure 17.24, p. 473), which has close connections with Continental

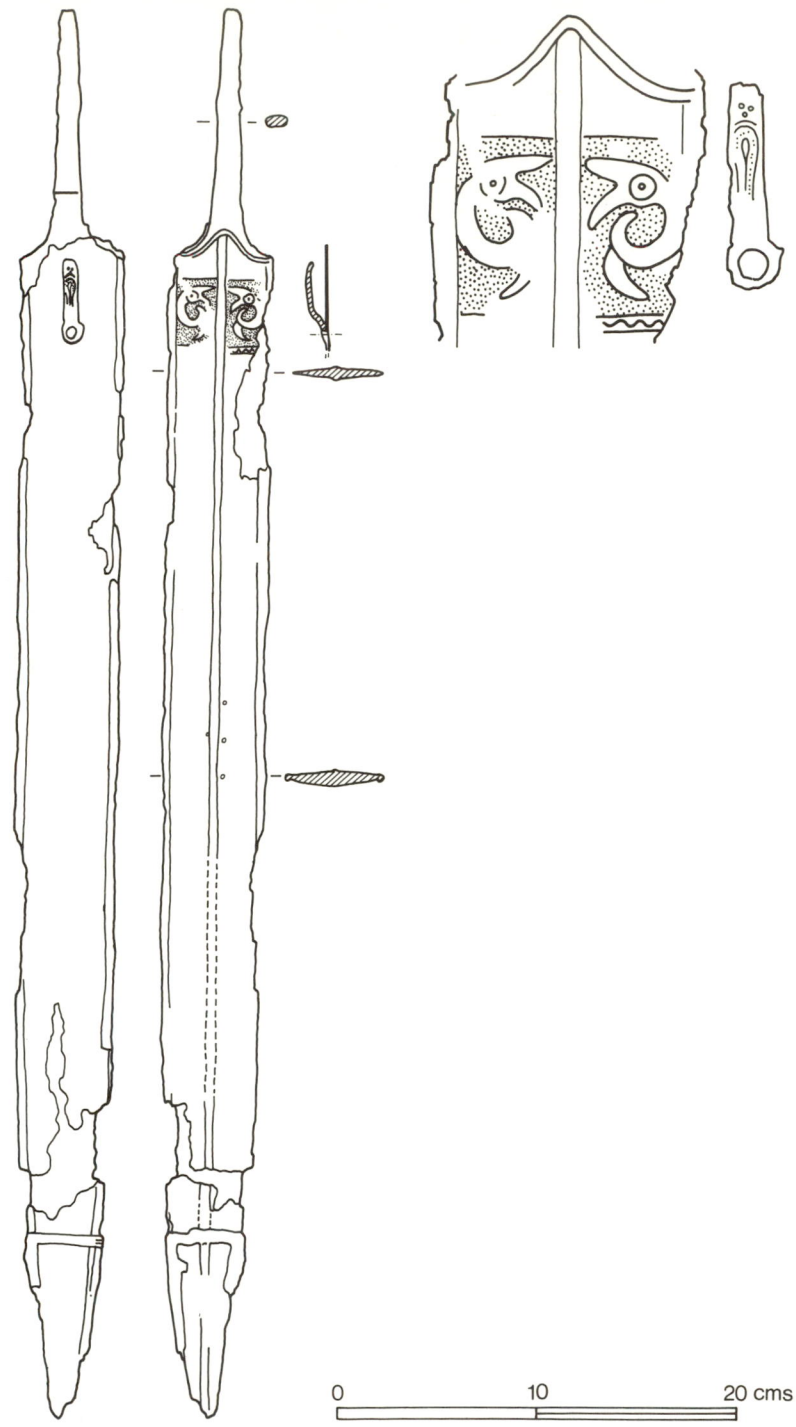

Figure 16.18   Imported La Tène sword from the Thames at Hammersmith (source: Stead 1984a).

technological tradition, is best regarded as a British product standing at the head of a long development series lasting throughout the rest of the pre-Roman period. What is perhaps most impressive about the British swords is their relative isolation from Continental development. This fact, together with the general lack of imported varieties, might suggest that Britain now lacked the close contacts with the Continent which it had previously maintained during the seventh and sixth centuries.

Personal ornaments are found scattered over much of southern Britain and of these the commonest category are brooches. The earliest of the La Tène brooches found in Britain – those of La Tene I type (*c.* 450–300 BC) – are the most numerous: over 100 have come to light mostly from the south-east. Characteristically they have an arching bow, bilateral spring and a catch plate made by bending the foot back to touch the bow (Figures 16.19 and 16.20). The bow is often decorated with simple grooved, curvilinear or stamped decoration and the foot is usually expanded into a disc shape decorated with stamped or incised motifs, or very occasionally inlaid with coral. The first serious attempt to classify these brooches was put forward by C.F. Fox (1927). There have been several subsequent additions to the debate but the publication of a full corpus (Hull and Hawkes 1987) puts the subject on a firm basis. From the point of view of the present discussion it is sufficient to note that of the large number of La Tène I brooches known from Britain very few can be identified as actual imports. However the number alone, and the Continental style and technology which they adopt, shows that Britain remained in contact with Continental developments. The earliest brooches are of the Marzabotto type found commonly in Europe north of the Alps and in smaller numbers in northern Italy (Stead 1984b, 50–2). They were in use from the late fifth to early fourth century. At the Swiss cemetery of Münsingen, where a comprehensive sequence has been established, they are known as type Ia (Hodson 1968, 35). Of the British examples less than a dozen are possible imports. The type was particularly popular in Wessex where a distinctive local version was produced (p. 459). Of the next group, the Dux fibulae (Münsingen Ib, *c.* 350–280 BC) no contemporary imports have been recorded, if the Wallingford examples are now accepted as recent imports (Stead 1984b, 53–4), but there are a few native copies. Thereafter imported La Tène types and their copies become far less common. There is a bent silver ring characteristic of the Münsingen Ic phase (*c.* 280–200 BC) from Park Brow, Sussex (Figure 16.19, no. 8) and a few British brooches of Ic type, but the paucity of material is in marked contrast to the number of earlier La Tène types found. The same may be said of the succeeding La Tène II period (*c.* 200–100 BC). Thus, if the number of brooches found in Britain can be taken to be a reflection of the intensity of importation, then the period from 450–350 was a time of much interaction after which, until about 100 BC, the intensity of contact had dramatically declined. The figures cannot, however, be taken too literally since a high percentage of the locally manufactured Ia types were probably being made and used in the third and even the second century. Even so the relative lack of inspiration from Continental types of the period 350 and 100 is best explained by a sharp diminution in imports.

Bracelets of La Tène types are not common in Britain outside the territory of the Yorkshire Arras culture, where two basic types are found: the relatively plain version with a 'tongue-in-glove' fastening and the more elaborate knobbed and ribbed type with a thick and often heavy body formed into adjacent bosses or ribs (Figure 16.21). The plain types occur once at Cowlam and four times at Arras, both Yorkshire graves. The only other examples to be found are the pair of bracelets with circular bezels from Coygan Camp, Carm.; but here the fastening is simple and not specially tongued. The knobbed and ribbed varieties are rather more widely

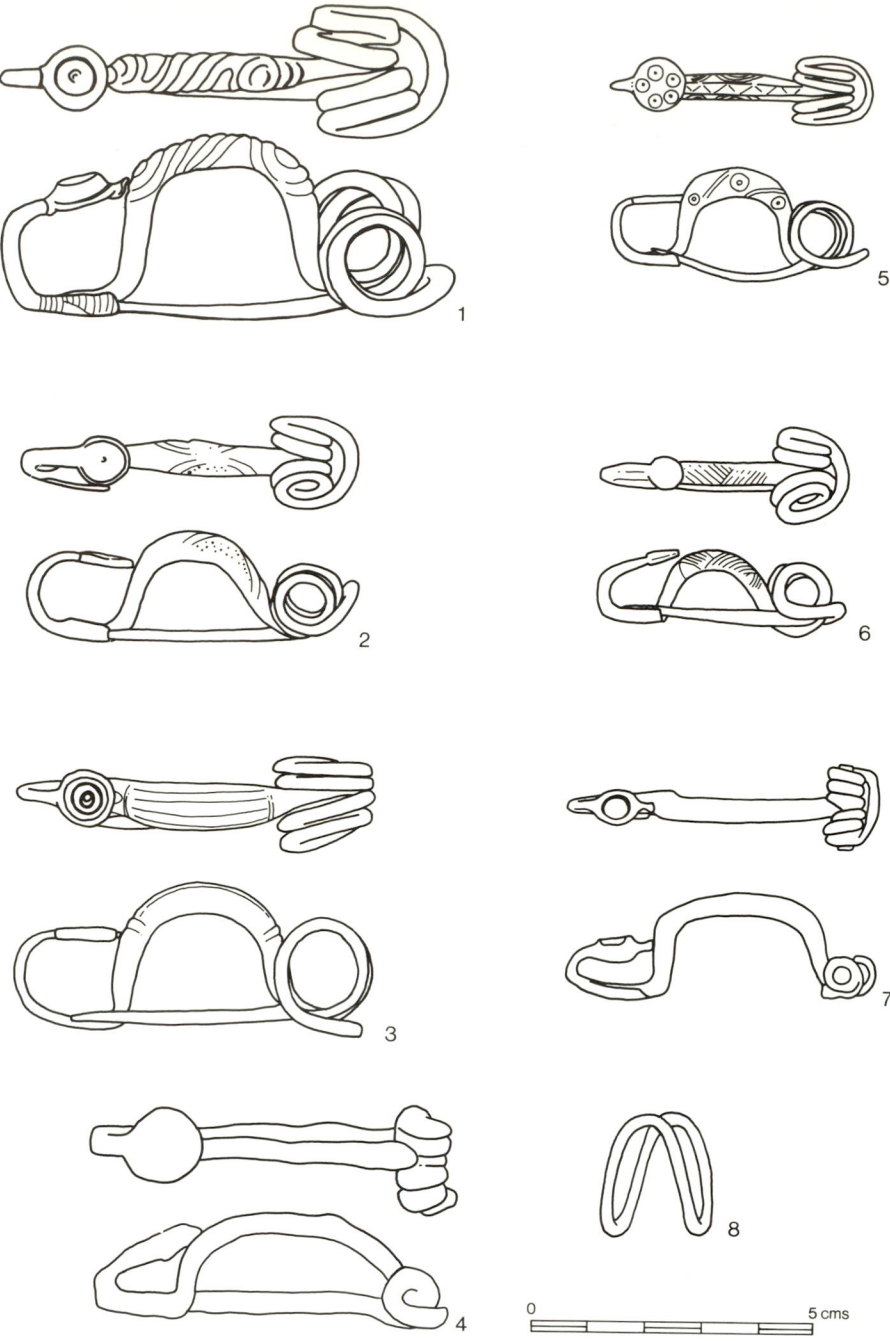

Figure 16.19 La Tène style fibulae and a bent silver ring. 1 Box, Wilts.; 2,6 Blaise Castle Hill, Avon; Merthyr Mawr Warren, Glam.; 4 Findon Park, Sussex; 5 Water Eaton, Oxon.; 8 Park Brow, Sussex. (Sources: 1,5 R.A. Smith 1925; 2,6 Rahtz and Brown 1959; 3,7 Grimes 1951; 4 Wolseley, Smith and Hawley 1927; 8 R.A. Smith 1927).

Figure 16.20 La Tène I style fibula from Danebury, Hants. (actual length: 46 mm) (photo: Nick Bradford. Danebury Trust).

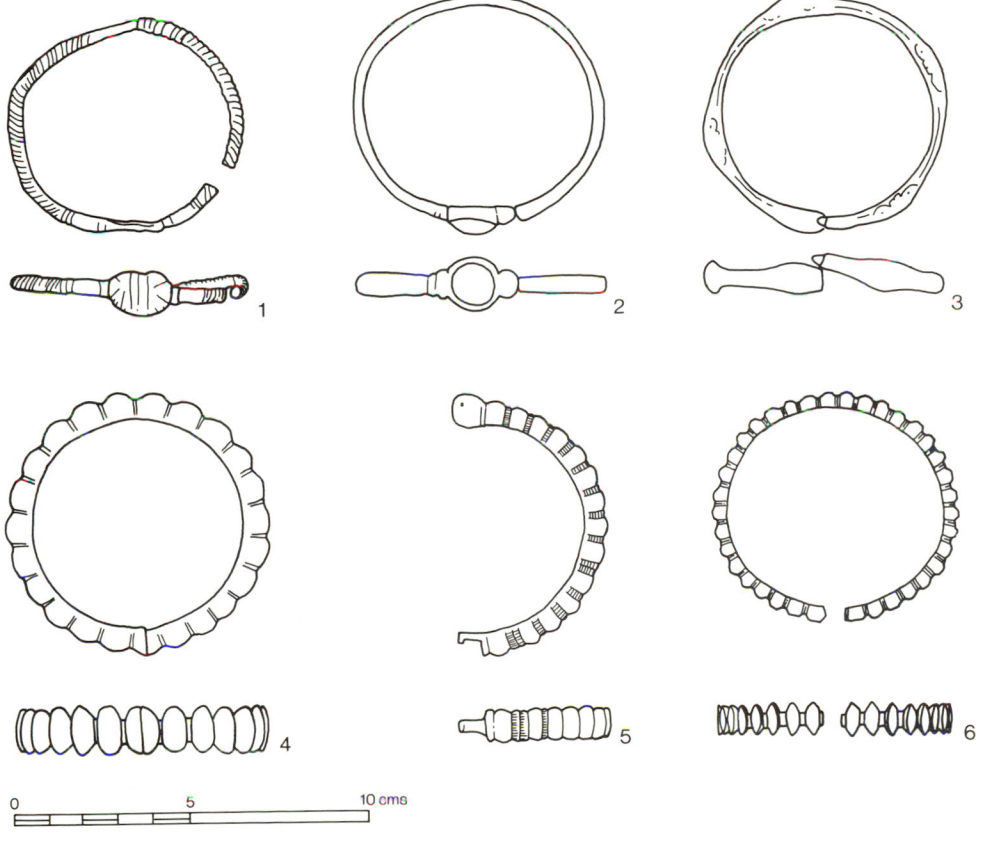

Figure 16.21 La Tène bracelets. 1 Coygan Camp, Carm.; 2,4 Arras, Yorks.; 3,6 Cowlam, Yorks.; 5 South Ferriby, Lincs. (sources: 1 Wainwright 1967a; 2–6 Stead 1965).

spread but are difficult to distinguish from Hallstatt types. It is impossible to be certain how many of these bracelets are direct imports and how many are locally made, but most of the specimens can be paralleled among La Tène I and early La Tène II contexts in eastern France and Switzerland, whence it is likely they or the types which inspired them were derived.

Trading contact between the west of Britain and the Atlantic coasts of Gaul and Iberia is well attested both in the classical literature and in the archaeological record. The fourth-century Roman poet Avienus, in his poem *Ora Maritima*, uses scraps of information taken from a very early account of the Atlantic sea-ways known as the Massaliote Periplus, which describes the journeyings of the Tartessians and the Carthaginians from southern Iberia to Brittany, Ireland and Britain (Albion) for purposes of trade. After Tartessos had become a Phoenician monopoly in the early fifth century, the Greek city-states which had previously been supplied with tin via Iberia began to look further afield for their vital supplies. One Greek merchant, Pitheas, sailed to Brittany along the Atlantic route between 330 and 325 and recorded his experiences, which survive only in the writings of later classical authors such as Strabo (C.F.C. Hawkes 1978). Nevertheless, sufficient appears in these secondary sources to show that the tin-producing areas of the south-west were in constant contact with the Iberian and Mediterranean world from the fifth century onwards, no doubt following upon trading traditions already established in ancient times.

The texts relating to the later period are somewhat obscure and have led to extensive debate (Maxwell 1972; Cunliffe 1983; Mitchell 1983; C.F.C. Hawkes 1984). The question hinges upon the location of Ictis mentioned by Diodorus Siculus, in a famous descriptive passage based upon earlier sources. He describes the peninsula of Belerium where tin is to be had. After mentioning the process of extraction, leading to the preparation of knuckle-bone-sized ingots of metal, he goes on to say that they are carried

> to an island which lies off Britain and is called Ictis, for at the time of ebb-tide the space between this island and the mainland becomes dry and they can take the tin in large quantities over to the island on their wagons . . . . On the island of Ictis the merchants purchase the tin of the natives . . . whence it is taken to Gaul and overland to the Mediterranean.

The question is complicated however by a text of Pliny, quoting Timaeus (*Nat. Hist.* IV, 16, 104) in which he tells us that 'there is an island named Mictis lying inwards, six days' sail from Britain where tin is found and to which the Britons cross in boats of osier covered with stitched hides'. The two texts taken together provide a fertile ground for imaginative speculation! The simplest interpretation would be that Ictis and Mictis, despite similar sounding names, were two entirely different places, Ictis being just off the shore of south-western Britain with Mictis being considerably nearer, along the trade route, to Rome. Six days' sail 'inwards' could place it anywhere off the Armorican coast as far south as the mouth of the Loire.

The location of the British trading port, Ictis, has been hotly debated, the most favoured contender being St Michael's Mount, Cornwall, for which no shred of archaeological evidence has been presented. A better claim can be made for Mount Batten, a promontory jutting into Plymouth Sound (Cunliffe 1983). Before the construction of the Plymouth breakwater it frequently became an island at high tide. Moreover, it is admirably sited to provide a well-protected haven and to command the rivers Tamar, Tavy and Plym which lead to the metal-rich fringes of Dartmoor. There is ample archaeological evidence to show that it was

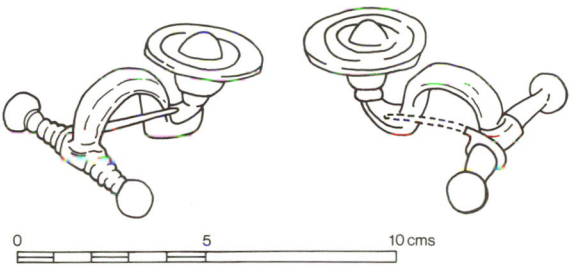

Figure 16.22   Fibulae of 'Iberian' type from Mount Batten, Devon (source: H.O'N. Hencken 1932).

actually used from the Late Bronze Age and throughout the period described by the classical writers (Cunliffe 1988b), but whether or not Mount Batten was Ictis will remain a matter of personal opinion.

Archaeological evidence for trade along the Atlantic sea-ways is not plentiful but contact with the south-west of Europe is demonstrated by a group of distinctive fibulae, two of bronze found at the port of Mount Batten (Figure 16.22) and two bronze and one iron from the cemetery at Harlyn Bay on the north coast of Cornwall. The brooches are characterized by a knob-ended cross piece for the pin to pivot on, a high bow and an upturned foot ornamented with a large disc head. They belong to a well-recognized class of fifth-century brooches found in Spain and Aquitania (south-western France) and while it has been argued that the British finds were locally made (Boudet 1988), the essentially Atlantic distribution of the type is a clear indication of maritime activity which presumably brought to Britain the prototypes which inspired them.

A more enigmatic object, frequently quoted as evidence of Atlantic trade, is a small bronze statuette found on the shore of Aust close to the site of the Severn Bridge (Dawson 1980) (Figure 16.23). The figure, a female, is provided with a crescentic head-dress and has eyes enlivened with inset glass beads. Traditionally it has been referred to as an Iberian import but Stead has cast doubt on this attribution preferring a British origin (Stead 1984b, 60). However, not only can no British parallels be quoted, but the head-dress and, more significantly, the stance and simplification of the figure have distinct analogies among first-millennium BC Iberian figurines. The example well illustrates the problems posed in attempting to identify imports.

The documentary and archaeological evidence together emphasize the continuance of well-established patterns of trade along the Atlantic sea routes from the fifth to the second century. It may have been by these means that some, at least, of the large number of Greek and Carthaginian coins arrived in Britain. The distribution pattern now extends across much of southern and eastern Britain, but rarely have the coins come from undoubted Iron Age contexts (Laing 1968). While it remains a possibility that some of them may have come in during the Roman period or as later collectors' items, many must have arrived during the pre-Roman period in the wake of Atlantic trade. Only one, a coin of Ptolemy V (204–181 BC) from Winchester, has so far been found stratified in an Iron Age level (Cunliffe 1964, 75; Collis 1975; Biddle 1975b).

One final item remains to be considered – the famous 'hanging bowl' found in a stone cist at Cerrig y Drudion, Clwyd, in 1924 (Figure 16.24). A reinterpretation of the surviving fragments has suggested that more than one item may be represented and that the major pieces are probably part of an ornamented lid rather than a bowl (Stead 1982), the chains being for attachment not for suspension as originally thought. The domed surface and the underside of the

Figure 16.23   Bronze figurine from Aust, Avon (actual height: 146 mm) (photo: British Museum).

flange are decorated with an elaborate scheme of incised palmettes and acanthus half-palmettes thrown into greater prominence by a cross-hatched 'basketry background'. The style of decoration has much in common with Celtic art styles in western France and in particular with the finely decorated pottery of Brittany but the 'basketry' technique is generally considered to be a British development. Thus, one of the finest pieces of Celtic art found in Britain must remain of uncertain origin. Its importance, however, is that it demonstrates a lively exchange in artistic concepts in the western sphere of contact in the early fourth century at a time when the British schools of craftsmen were beginning to develop their own distinct styles in the service of their artistic patrons.

The archaeological evidence for contact along the Atlantic sea routes in the period from the fifth to the second century, though not extensive, usefully augments the tantalizing accounts

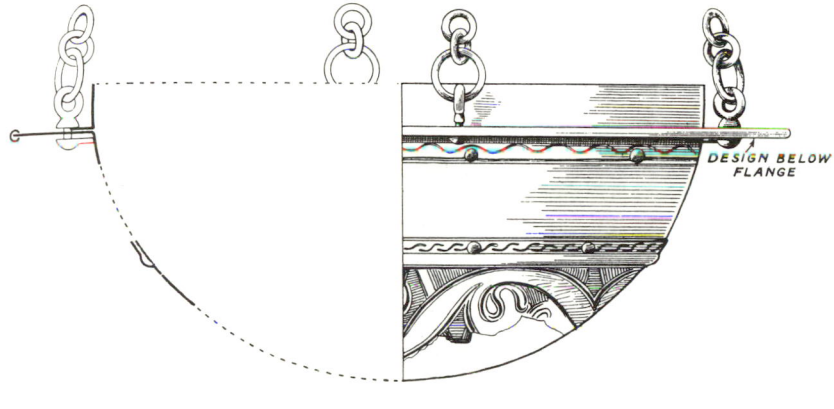

DESIGN BELOW
FLANGE

Figure 16.24 Bronze vessel from Cerrig y Drudion. The original drawing (reproduced here from Smith 1926) shows the find reconstructed as a hanging bowl. It is now thought to be parts of one or more lids. Actual maximum diameter of flange 26 cm.

provided by the classical texts. The impression given is that trade was organized and that certain locations had emerged as ports-of-trade where commodities could be exchanged in safety. Ictis is the only named place but in all probability a number of coastal locations in the south-west had by now developed trading connections. Mount Batten is the best attested archaeologically but others suggest themselves. At Exeter, for example, a surprisingly large number of Mediterranean coins have been found which *may* reflect pre-Roman trade. More certainty attaches to Methyr Mawr Warren, at the mouth of the rivers Ogmore and Ewenny, in South Wales where a range of material including La Tène brooches and evidence for metalworking indicates a settlement of some importance. The site is well located to be a port articulating with the metal-producing areas of south Wales. Sites such as these may well have taken on a more than local significance at times when the Atlantic route was being actively exploited.

Trade in the first century BC and early first century AD

After the beginning of the first century BC evidence for trade and exchange with the Continent increases dramatically. This is amply demonstrated by a wide range of imports including Gallo-Belgic and Armorican coins, north-western French pottery, Italian and Spanish amphorae, bronze and silver tableware from Italy and a number of other luxury commodities. In addition to actual imports rapid style change in the pottery of the south-east and the appearance of large numbers of fibulae modelled on La Tène III types in circulation on the Continent show that Britain and the adjacent parts of Europe were now in close and continuous contact. What we are seeing is essentially the bow-wave effect in advance of the increasing Romanization of Gaul, and to understand it something must be said of events on the Continent.

In the latter part of the second century BC Rome was increasingly drawn into the affairs of southern France in response to pleas from the Greek cities of the Mediterranean coast for military support against the aggressive attentions of neighbouring hill tribes. By the 120s events had become so serious that the Roman authorities decided that the only solution was to station a legion at *Aquae Sextiae* (Aix-en-Provence). In this way the Romanization of Gaul formally began and Roman entrepreneurs poured in bent on exploiting the new commercial opportunities which occupation provided. In 118 BC a colony was founded at *Narbo Martius* (Narbonne) greatly facilitating access to the new markets. For the next sixty years or so the province of Transalpina, as it was known, was thronged with merchants trading with the barbarian Gauls beyond the frontier. Enormous quantities of Italian wine and no doubt other consumer goods, were exchanged for slaves and raw materials, particularly metals (Tchernia 1983; Cunliffe 1988a, 80–92). The sudden development of this market invigorated the traditional trading routes, particularly the Atlantic route along the western coast of France to southern Britain.

In 59 BC Roman involvement in Gaul entered a new phase when Julius Caesar began a war of conquest against the Gauls which was to last for almost a decade. By the time it was over the political geography of Europe had changed out of all recognition. Rome had now established a somewhat shaky control over a vast territory of what is now France, Belgium and parts of Holland up to the river Rhine. This new reality, and the fact that Caesar had campaigned in Britain in 55 and 54 BC, where he had negotiated treaties with the tribes of eastern Britain, brought about a reorientation of trade with the island. While the old Atlantic route still continued to function, trade was on a drastically reduced scale: it was the coastal tribes of eastern Britain who were now in the forefront of commerce.

By about 10 BC Gaul had become thoroughly stabilized. From this time onwards the Rhine frontier, and the route via the Rhône leading to it, became a 'commercial corridor' – a zone of production, consumption and transshipment linking the Thames estuary to the Mediterranean. The effects of all this on the tribes of south-eastern Britain can be clearly recognized as quantities of comparatively low value goods, such as pottery, manufactured in the commercial corridor, began to pour in.

It is against this broader background that the pattern of imports enjoyed by Britain from about 100 BC until the Roman Conquest must be assessed.

The effects of the reinvigoration of the Atlantic route, following the foundation of the Roman province of Transalpina, can best be seen at Hengistbury Head, Dorset. The headland, a dominant feature of the Solent coast, protects the sheltered expanse of Christchurch harbour from the predominant south-west winds and currents, thus providing an attractive anchorage for shipping (Figures 8.5, p. 164 and 16.25). Not only this, the site was also admirably located at the hub of a natural route network which linked the productive hinterland of Wessex (via the rivers Stour and Avon), to the land-hugging south coast routes and the favoured cross-Channel passage, via the Channel Islands, to the ports of the Côte du Nord and beyond (McGrail 1983). Excavation has shown the existence of a substantial settlement along the protected northern shore producing a wide range of imported goods including quantities of Italian Dressel 1A amphorae, lumps of raw purple and yellow glass, figs and masses of pottery from Brittany including elegant black cordoned wares, graphite-coated wares and rilled vessels made in a micaceous fabric (Figure 16.26). There can be little doubt that in the first half of the first century BC Hengistbury was receiving cargoes of merchandise made up of goods amassed at various points along the 1600 km route which led from northern Italy, via Narbonne, through the Carcassonne Gap and the Garonne/Gironde, along the Atlantic coast of France and around Brittany to the Solent shore. In return the merchants at Hengistbury were collecting together an impressive range of exports. Local products included iron, Kimmeridge shale and salt, grain came from the Wessex chalkland, while metals including gold, silver, copper, tin and lead were gathered as ore, ingots and scrap from the Mendips and the south-western peninsula for refinement, and perhaps manufacture, before export. All these commodities are attested in the archaeological record but many more were probably involved. When, a few decades later, Strabo listed the principal exports from Britain, he included 'grain, cattle, gold, silver and iron . . . also hides, and slaves and dogs that are by nature suited to the purposes of the chase' (*Geog.* 4.5.2). His list gives some idea of significant local products which are archaeologically invisible.

Although Hengistbury was clearly a major focus of trade, it may not have been the only one in the area. Poole Harbour, nearby, has produced a comparable range of imports especially from Green Island and Hamworthy, from both of which have come Italian Dressel 1A amphorae and north-western French pottery. An impressive array of Mediterranean coinage has also been found in the vicinity (Cunliffe 1982a, Figure 3). With ease of access to salt and Kimmeridge shale and with a convenient route, via the river Frome, deep into Durotrigan territory, Poole Harbour has obvious attractions as a trading focus. We might therefore regard the two harbours as integral elements in a single contact zone.

From this zone imports were distributed to the hinterland. French pottery (and its contents?) barely got as far as 10 km from the ports, amphorae were found further inland up to 50–60 km, while coins of the Armorican tribes, particularly the Coriosolites but also the Baiocasses,

Figure 16.25   Hengistbury Head, Dorset. The excavation of the Late Iron Age port on the shore of the harbour (photo: author).

Redones, Unelli and Osismii, reached much further (and may anyway have arrived by a variety of routes). Of the British commodities needed for export, metals from the south-west would have come by sea while the lead/silver alloy from the Mendips was probably brought via the Stour valley route (Figure 16.27).

The dense distribution of Dressel 1A amphorae in Armorica (Figure 16.28), the presence of Armorican pottery and coins in the British contact zone and the occurrence of Kimmeridge shale

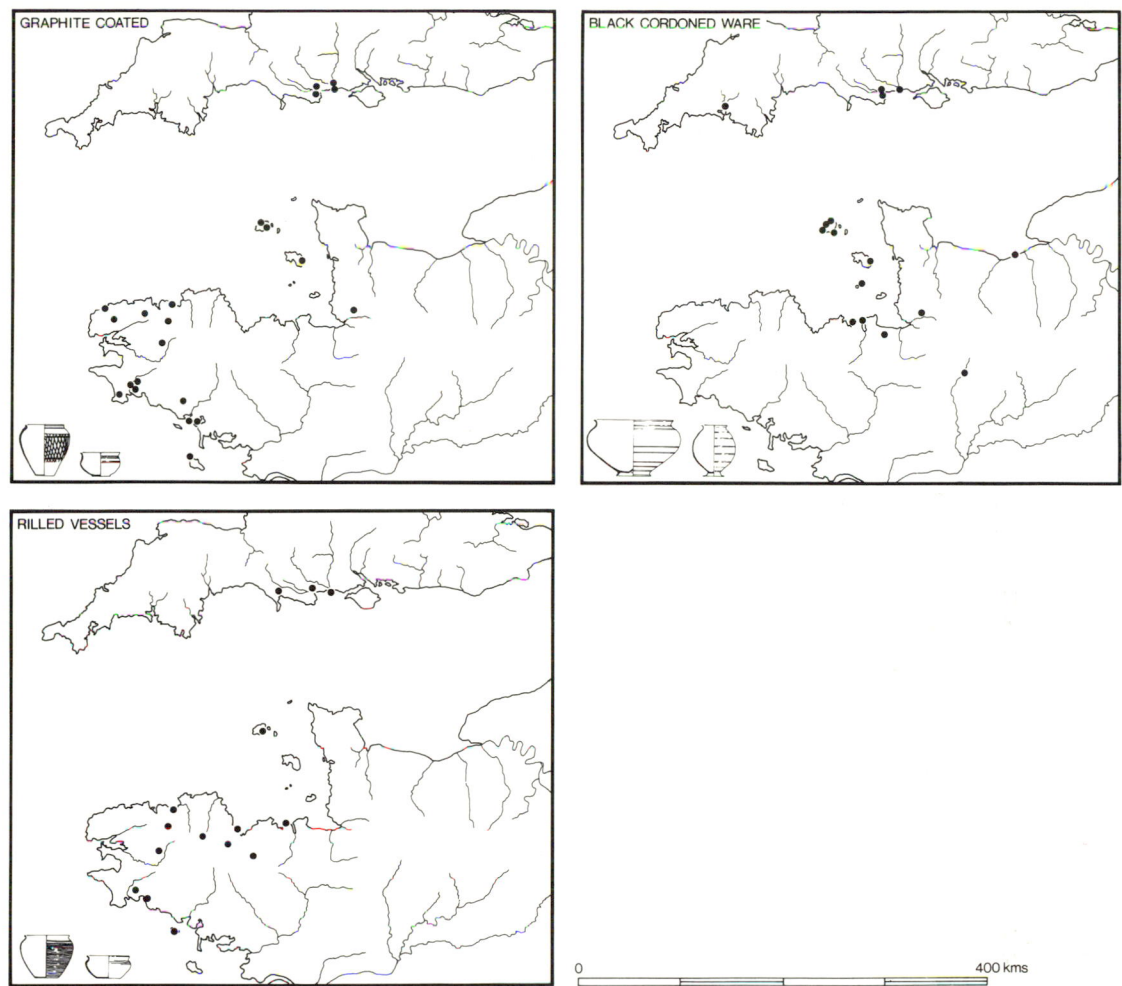

Figure 16.26   Distribution of Late Iron Age pottery made in Brittany (source: Cunliffe 1987).

bracelets in Brittany is sufficient to show that the tribes of Armorica were intimately bound up in the trading system. Caesar discovered this and writing of them says

> the Veneti are by far the strongest. They have a great many ships and regularly sail to and from Britain. When it comes to knowledge and experience of navigation, they leave all the other tribes standing . . . . They are able to extract tolls from almost all who regularly use those waters.
>
> (*BG* III, 8)

It is curious that in Britain Venetic coins are extremely rare while those of the Coriosolites, from the Côte du Nord, are far more common. One possible explanation for this is that the Veneti were the receivers of the Atlantic cargoes coming from the south, and were thus well known to

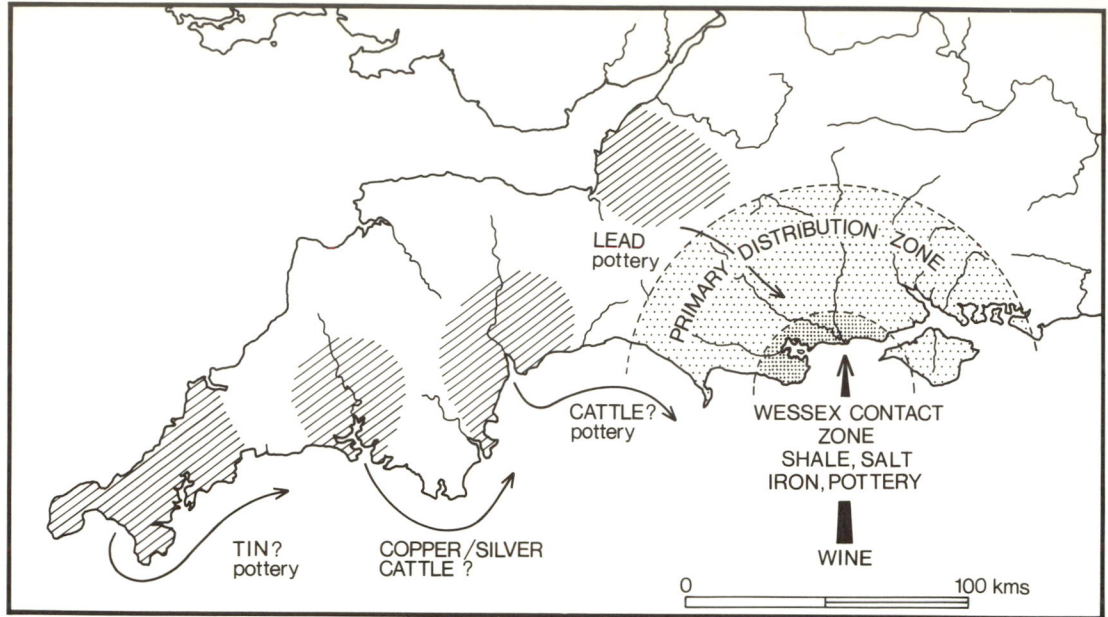

Figure 16.27   Model for trade with Hengistbury (source: Cunliffe 1982a).

Roman traders, while the final leg of the journey from Brittany to Britain was under the control of the Coriosolites.

A trading network as complex as this could not have survived Caesar's devastating attack on the Armorican tribes in 56 BC and the evidence from Hengistbury bears witness to this. The importation of French pottery virtually ceases and amphorae which can be dated with some certainty to the second half of the first century BC occur in negligible quantities. A few Dressel IB types show that a little Italian wine was arriving and occasional examples of Dressel 1/Pascual 1 reflect the growing importance of the Tarragona region of Spain as a supplier, but even together the quantity represents only a fraction of that which had previously arrived in Dressel IA amphorae. While the chronology of these vessels is not precise the evidence from Hengistbury clearly shows a marked decline in wine importation after the mid-first century BC (Cunliffe 1987).

Direct archaeological evidence of Iron Age shipping around the shores of Britain is slight, but a complete iron anchor together with a length of chain was discovered in a hoard at Bulbury, Dorset, together with other material suggesting a date in the first half of the first century AD (Figure 16.29). Although the anchor may have come from a Venetic ship (Cunliffe 1972b) its form suggests that it is more likely to have been of Roman origin. More recently a lead anchor stock of Graeco-Roman type was found by divers off the coast of north-west Wales, near Porth Felen (Figure 16.29). Typological considerations indicate a date in the second or first century BC (Boon 1976). These two anchors provide an interesting hint of the type of Mediterranean shipping with which the inhabitants of pre-Roman Britain may well have been familiar.

In the last hundred years before the Claudian conquest, the tribes of south-eastern Britain seem to have developed a lively trade with Roman Gaul. Throughout the second half of the first century BC, Italian wine was imported in large quantities (as the widespread occurrence of

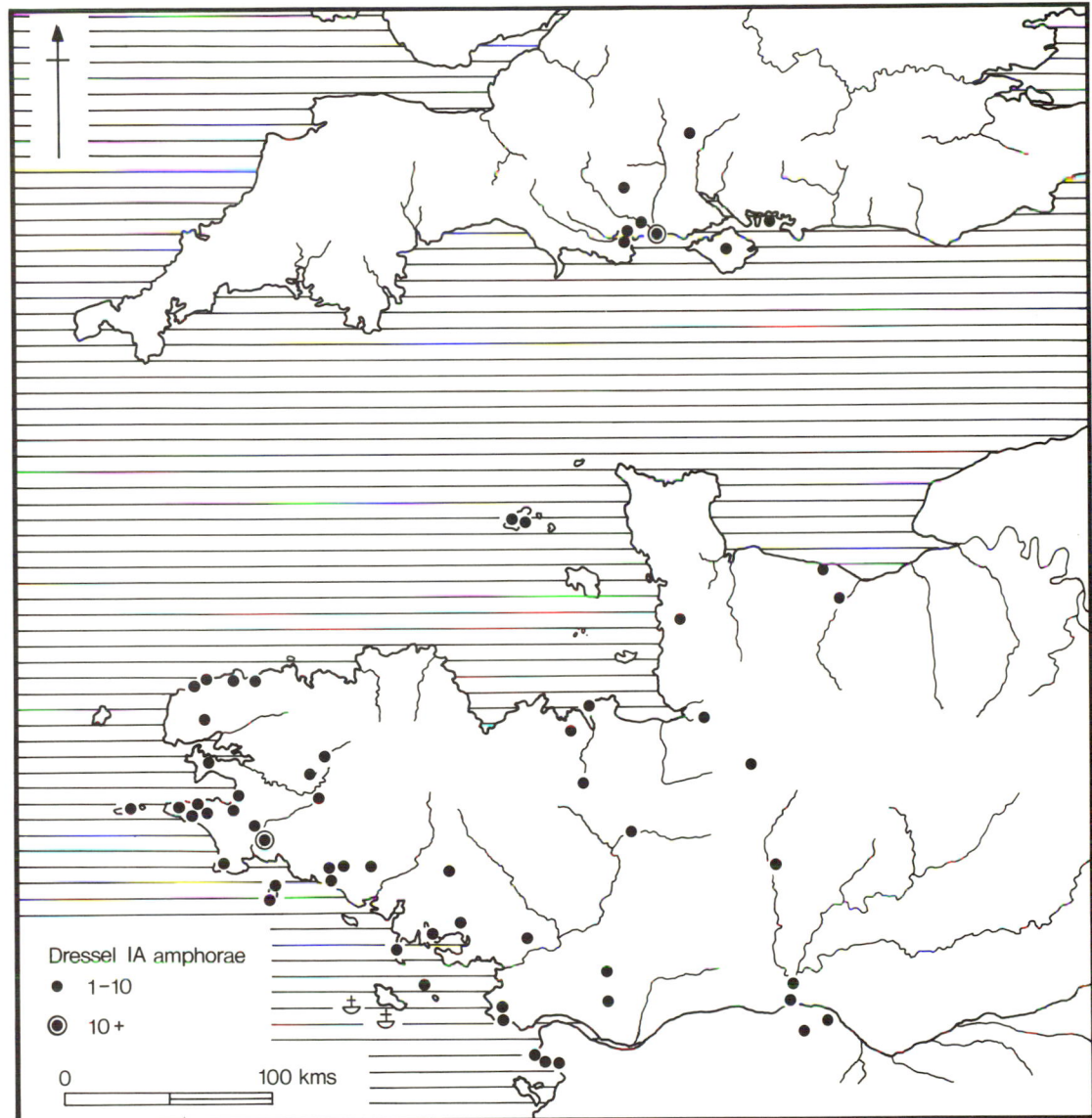

Figure 16.28 Distribution of Dressel 1A amphorae in Brittany and southern Britain (source: Cunliffe 1987 after Galliou 1982).

Dressel type 1B amphorae shows) (Figure 16.30), and along with the wine came the tableware appropriate to its consumption. Bronze jugs (oenochoe) and bronze patellae, found in the burials at Aylesford and Welwyn, were imported from the Ornavasso region of northern Italy some time between 50 and 10 BC, while silver cups of Augustan date were brought in eventually to be buried with dead chieftains at Welwyn and Welwyn Garden City. Bronze bowls and wine-strainers, probably of Gaulish or Italian manufacture, were also introduced. The forty years or so following

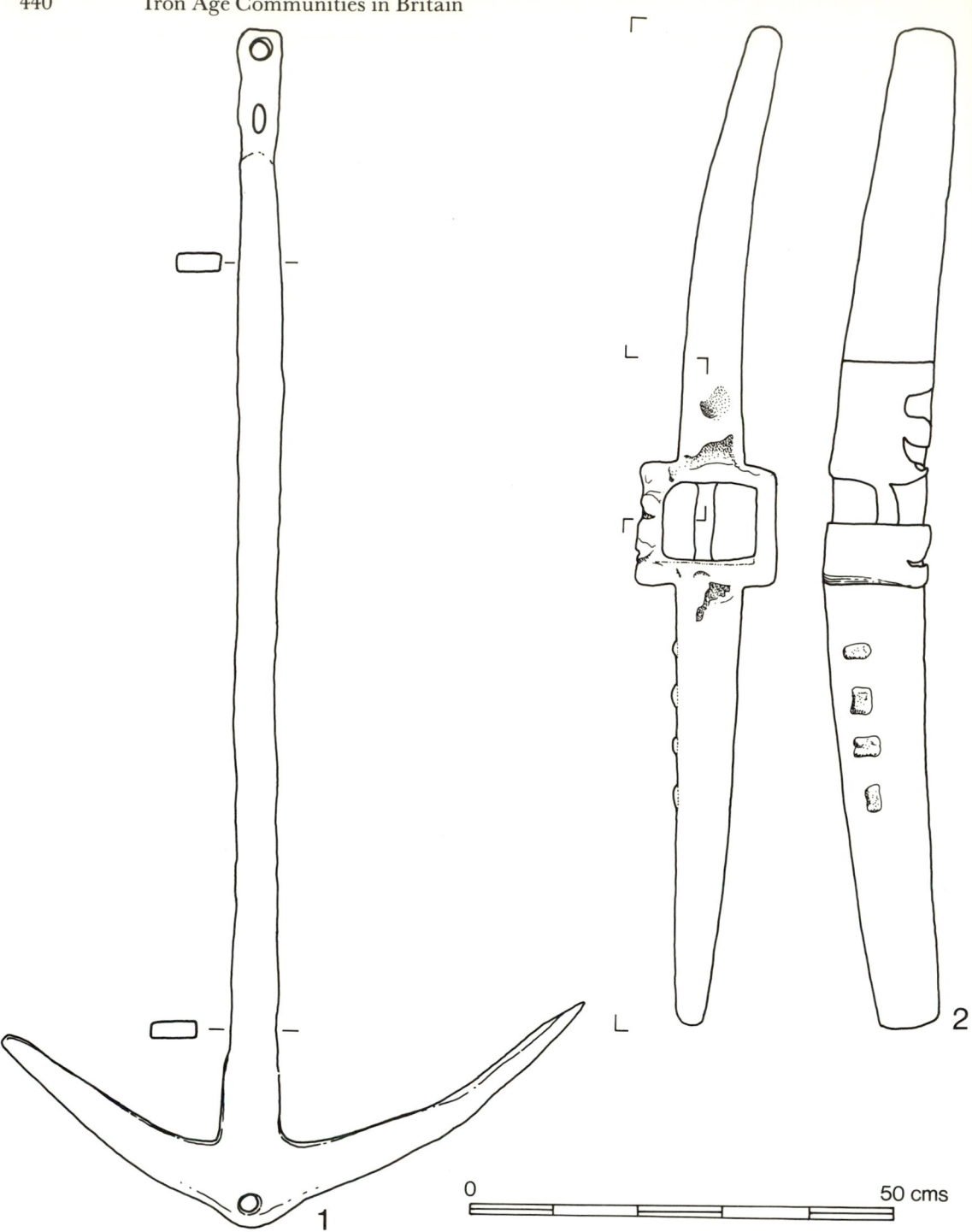

Figure 16.29 Anchors from Britain. 1 Iron anchor from Bulbury, Dorset; 2 lead anchor stock dredged up from near Porth Felen, Aberdaron (sources: 1 Cunliffe 1972b; 2 Boon 1977).

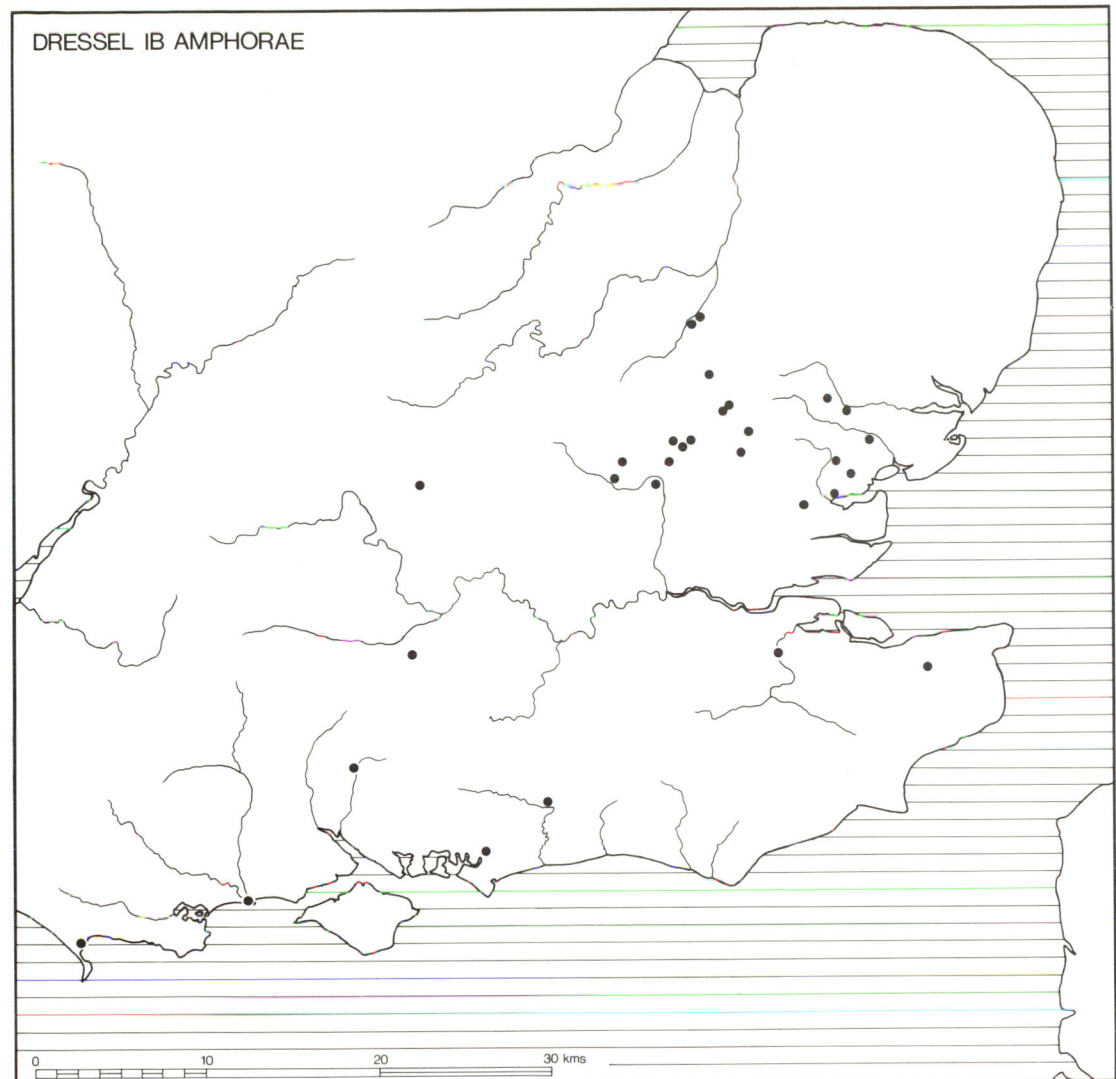

DRESSEL IB AMPHORAE

Figure 16.30   Distribution of Dressel 1B amphorae in eastern Britain (source: Fitzpatrick 1985a).

Caesar's conquest of Gaul saw the tribes of south-eastern Britain develop in parallel with their neighbours in Belgic Gaul who were now under Roman authority. Exchange was probably still manipulated through traditional mechanisms embedded in the social systems of the two areas (Cunliffe 1988a, 137–44) but with the more rigid control of Gaul and the development of the Rhine 'corridor' the old order gave way to a new commercialism.

From about 10 BC until the conquest of AD 43 the volume of trade seems to have increased. Fine Gallo-Belgic tablewares were being imported in quantity, together with smaller consignments of Arretine vessels made in northern Italy: later, samian ware from southern Gaul reached Britain. A limited number of glass vessels also made an appearance at this time. Wine too continued to be imported in bulk, as well as increasing quantities of fish sauce and olive oil from the Spanish province of Baetica, the two delicacies arriving in characteristic amphorae (Peacock 1971, 1984). In addition to food, wine and tableware, other luxury goods appeared, like the pairs of silver fibulae from Great Chesterford and elsewhere (Stead 1976a), the set of glass gaming pieces from the burial at Welwyn Garden City and the small medallion of the Emperor Augustus found in the tumulus burial at Lexden – the latter surely a diplomatic gift of some kind. In fact, in the few generations before the conquest, the wealthy members of south-eastern British society must have been able to enjoy much the same range of Roman consumer luxuries as their distant relations now living across the Channel in Roman Gaul.

Some insight into this flow of commodities is provided by a telling passage written by Strabo at the turn of the millennium, 'Some of the chieftains', he writes,

after procuring the friendship of Caesar Augustus . . . have managed to make the whole of the island virtually Roman property. Further, they submit so easily to heavy duties, both on the exports from there to Celtica and on the imports from Celtica (these latter are ivory chains and necklaces, and amber-gems and glass vessels and other pretty wares of that sort) that there is no need of garrisoning the island.

(*Geog.* 4.5.3)

A few decades after these words were written the Roman legions landed in Kent.

Summary of Continental contacts from the seventh century BC to the first century AD

Standing back from the mass of evidence briefly surveyed in the foregoing pages, it is possible to make a number of broad generalizations. From the middle of the eighth century until the middle of the fourth it would seem that the British Isles maintained vigorous trading contacts with the Continent, demonstrated by the appearance in these islands of a large number of metal types ranging from personal ornaments like pins and bracelets to swords and horse-harness fittings. Much of this exotic material is of central and north European origin, but the long-established trade routes along the Atlantic coasts of France and Iberia (leading ultimately to the Mediterranean) continued to be used, particularly by the traders distributing bronze weapons and tools manufactured in the local Atlantic Bronze Age styles. Imported types did not, however, materially alter the traditional range of weapon-and tool-types although many of the new ideas were adopted and rapidly modified by the British craftsmen.

The appearance in the seventh century of imported Hallstatt C swords together with harness- and cart-fittings was once thought to imply an incursion of a mobile, horse-riding aristocracy from Continental Europe, but no positive trace of a large-scale folk movement into Britain survives, and the virtual absence of the characteristic Hallstatt burial rite in Britain argues that no such movement took place. Indeed swords and horse-trappings were already being imported in the preceding period. The general picture to emerge is therefore of a broadly parallel development between Britain and the Continent, the two areas retaining a close contact, which encouraged a free flow of ideas and an exchange of goods, while indigenous traditions remained dominant.

This pattern was maintained throughout the fifth and fourth centuries, allowing the importation of luxury objects such as daggers and swords, by means of which elements of the contemporary Continental art styles first appeared in Britain. Along with the more valuable types came a scattering of trinkets including fibulae, bracelets and occasionally rings. Throughout this period the Atlantic trade routes to and from south-western Britain were maintained, the principal export being Cornish tin for the Mediterranean world. Occasional references to the tin trade in classical literature suggest that the system was well established and flourishing. No doubt equally complex trading patterns linked the south-east of the country to mainland Europe.

Some time just before 400 BC it seems probable that a group of people migrated from France to eastern Yorkshire, establishing a community which maintained its identity until, and even after, the Roman invasion. Apart from this one possible instance, there is no evidence to support the idea of a widespread invasion.

The material culture and settlement pattern of the third and second centuries suggest that Continental contact decreased during this period, allowing the British communities to assume an intensely regional aspect reflecting little of contemporary European developments. Contact was reintensified about 100 BC when the activities of the Roman entrepreneurs in southern Gaul impinged upon the Solent harbours and the south-west and bound these areas closely once more in an Atlantic trading network. But after Caesar's conquest of Gaul this trade rapidly declined, to be replaced by even more intensive contacts between the Roman world and the pro-Roman tribes of eastern Britain. This system was subsumed when Rome invaded Britain in AD 43.

17
Craft, industry and art

The manufacture and distribution of consumer goods in Iron Age Britain was a complex process involving trade and production on several different levels. Beneath the all-embracing pattern imposed by overseas trade, which remained a significant factor throughout, there lay two systems of no lesser importance: specialist localized production, with its own limited spheres of distribution, and home production geared to the needs of the immediate kin group. The latter satisfied the bulk of the population's needs.

Home industries: wool, leather, carpentry and basketry (Figures 17.1 and 17.2)

One of the most widely practised of the home crafts was the manufacture of woollen fabrics, which seems to have been carried out in most parts of the British Isles, presumably on a part-time basis within each household. Exactly how the fleece was removed from the sheep is a matter of some debate, in view of the absence of shears in all but the very latest Iron Age deposits. If shearing was necessary a sharp iron knife would have been adequate but it is more likely that sheep were plucked either by hand or with the aid of objects commonly known as weaving combs. After cleaning, the wool would have been combed, probably with bone and antler combs, and then spun into yarn on a simple hand-spindle weighted with a whorl of stone or baked clay. It was probably at this stage that dyeing was undertaken, using vegetable dyes.

The nature of the loom used in Britain is still a matter of uncertainty but in all probability it was of the upright warp-weighted type. No archaeological trace of such a structure survives in this country, with the exception of the loom weights of clay and stone used for keeping bunches of warp threads taut and of even tension. Some simple machinery would have been used for shedding, i.e. parting the warp threads to allow the weft to be woven through – a process probably carried out with a shuttle of wood which may have been provided with a tip made from a pointed metapodial or tibia bone. The tamping down of the weft could most efficiently have

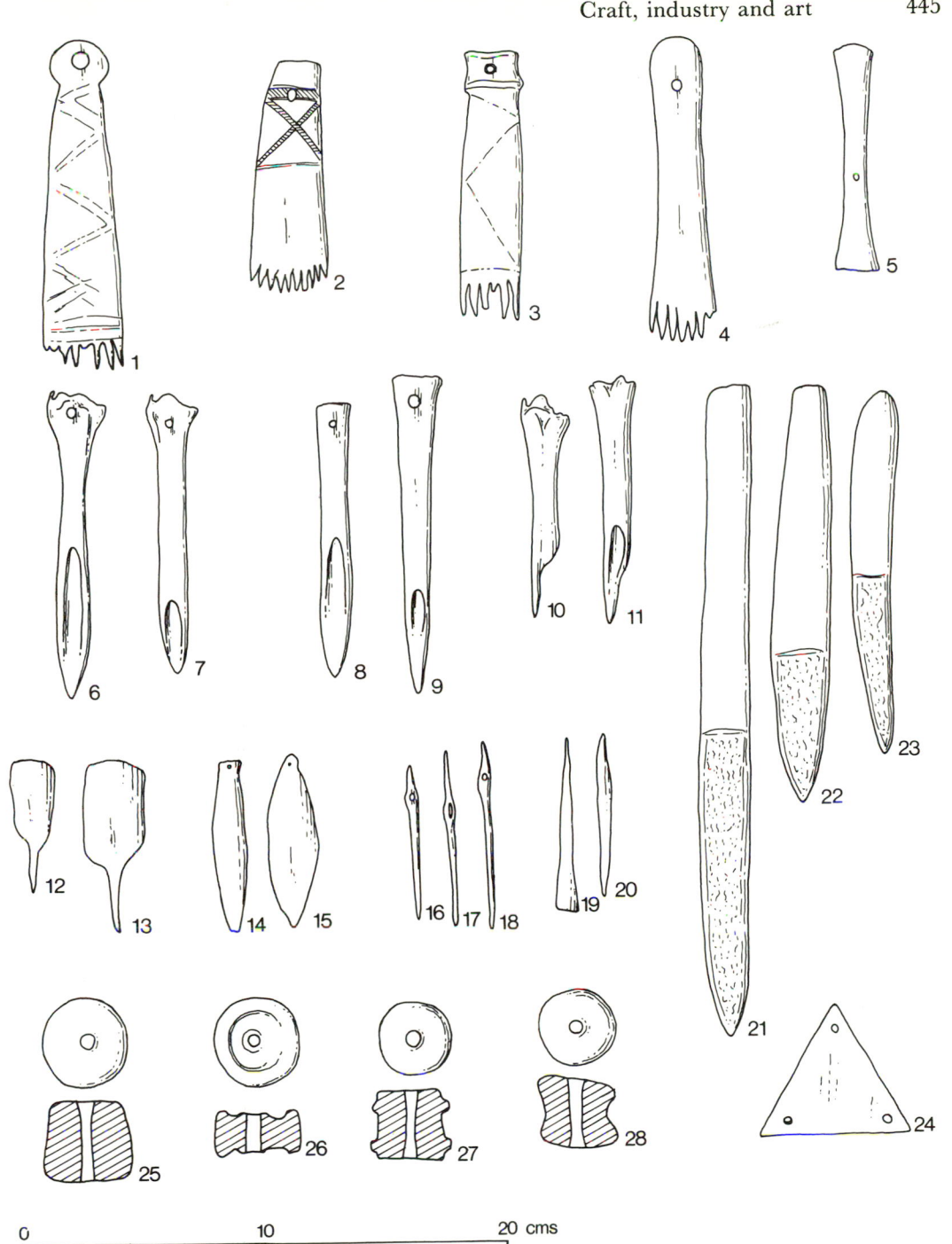

Figure 17.1 Bone and ceramic equipment connected with spinning, weaving and the preparation of skins. 1–23, 25–8 All Cannings Cross, Wilts.; 24 Wookey Hole, Somerset (sources: *All Cannings Cross*, M.E. Cunnington 1923; *Wookey Hole*, Balch 1914).

Figure 17.2   Antler weaving combs from Danebury, Hants. (photo: Institute of Archaeology, Oxford. *Danebury Trust*).

been carried out with a wooden sword, although comb beaters (i.e. weaving combs) or pin beaters, in the form of hafted bone points, may sometimes have been used.

For the manufacture of braids, tablet weaving may have been practised. This is a method which requires the use of bone or wood plates perforated with two or more holes close to the edge to control the positioning and spacing of the warp. The technique was widely used in Scandinavia during the pre-Roman Iron Age and also during the Roman period in Britain, but the only indisputable evidence of earlier use in this country is a group of triangular weaving tablets found in Iron Age contexts at Wookey Hole, Somerset. In spite of the lack of direct archaeological evidence the process was probably common.

The more durable artefacts connected with spinning and weaving are found over much of the country throughout the pre-Roman Iron Age, and many of the basic types can be traced back into the second millennium. A weaving comb (or a plucking comb) is known in a Middle to Late Bronze Age context at Shearplace Hill, Dorset, and functionally similar objects made of antler are found in Neolithic contexts. Similarly, loom weights of cylindrical form made from baked clay are a recurring component of Middle to Late Bronze Age assemblages, and the type continues into the Iron Age, eventually to be replaced by the more characteristic triangular variety. Even the bone threading points are sporadically found in pre-Iron Age contexts. There can therefore be little doubt that the manufacture of woollen cloth was an old-established craft in Britain and, to judge by the dense distribution of artefacts concerned with spinning and weaving, most households were geared to supplying their own requirements.

The weaving of organic materials other than wool would have been equally widely practised, although little evidence survives today. Basketry is implied by the impressions of basket-work on a pot from Dun Croc a Comhdhalach, on North Uist, and some kind of matting made from rushes was found in a pit at Worlebury, Somerset. These few survivals do scant justice to the fact that basket-making and matting must have been common occupations during the prehistoric period, particularly in those areas in which pottery was scarce. Another occupation, the production of fishing-nets, would presumably have been carried out on a large scale, but apart from a few netting needles and lead and stone net weights no trace survives.

Leather-working was of no less importance to the community than the production of woollen fabrics. The manufacture of a serviceable leather garment or container would have involved three separate stages: first the removal and cleaning of the skin, then tanning, and finally the making up of the finished article. These processes can be expected to leave little archaeological trace but general purpose iron knives would have been quite sufficient for skinning and cutting, while the stretching out of the pelt would probably have involved the use of wooden or bone pegs. Fatty substances rising gradually to the surface were scraped off, possibly with the use of the rib-knives (ribs thinned down to give a good scraping edge) frequently found on occupation sites or with metal knives, while the removal of the hair was probably undertaken using a comb or scraper. The actual process of tanning could have been carried out in vats or in specially lined pits, using preparations containing oak bark and oak galls as the principal sources of tannin. The elder Pliny mentions the importance of the trade in oak galls for this purpose in the first century BC, and indeed a small quantity of galls were found in a pit of the second century BC at Chalton, Hants., suggesting their deliberate collection. At present this is the only evidence for what can hardly be doubted to have been a process commonly practised throughout the period. Finally, the manufacture of the finished articles would have required only iron knives and bone needles, both of which are commonly found in domestic contexts.

While clothing and harness would have been the principal leather goods to be manufactured, containers must have been made for use alongside, or instead of, ceramics. At times when livestock had to be driven to distant pastures leather vessels would have been far more practical than pottery. Indeed, it is possible to see in the decoration of some of the Middle Iron Age pottery in Hampshire what might well be a skeuomorphic representation of stitching, the diagonal lines representing the thread, the shallow dots being the needle holes (Figure A:15, p. 568). Moreover, the form of the saucepan pot is more naturally produced in wood, leather-work or bark-work than in a ceramic medium. The use of leather containers is likely to have been more widespread than we can ever demonstrate.

Other home crafts would have included hurdle-making and carpentry. Little is known of hurdle-work, although it must have been widespread, but there is now growing evidence for the use of wattle as a common walling material for houses. Some storage pits may also have been wicker lined, but only at Dane's Camp, Poxwell, and Worlebury has such a lining been recognized. The tools required by the hurdle-maker would have been limited to the saw, bill hook and knife. It is possible that the small curved 'reaping hook' may also have been used to trim leaves off branches and to split withies. Some indication of the finished product is provided by the hurdles found preserved at Glastonbury in a second- or first-century context. The demand for suitable timber for this work could only have been met by the proper management of woodland, which would have entailed the pollarding of willows and coppicing of hazel.

There can be little doubt that skilled carpentry was widespread. Carpenters' tools including saws, axes, adzes, chisels and gouges are fairly common, and detailed knowledge of the properties of timber is implied by the complex nature of some of the earliest houses like West Brandon, Co. Durham, Little Woodbury, Wilts., and Pimperne Down, Dorset.

The collection of well-preserved wood from Glastonbury gives an idea of the wide range of domestic objects manufactured, including small wooden vessels, often with incised decoration, ladles, handles for iron tools, mallets, ladders and frameworks for furniture or looms (Figure

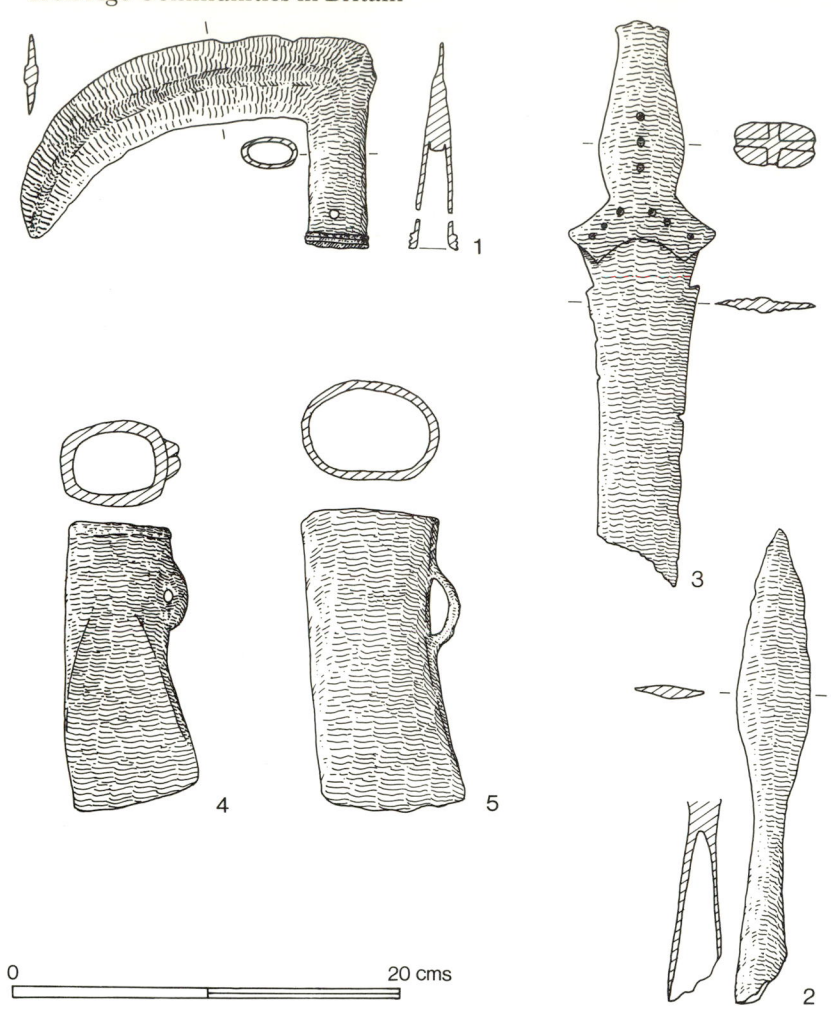

0 _____ 20 cms

Figure 17.3   Early types of iron weapons and implements. 1–3 Sickle, spear and sword from Llyn Fawr, Glam.; 4 axe from Walthamstow, Essex; 5 axe from Cold Kitchen Hill, Wilts. (Sources: *Llyn Fawr*, Grimes 1951; *Walthamstow*, R.A. Smith 1925; *Cold Kitchen Hill*, author).

17.4) (Earwood 1988). Among the more specialized products were found parts of several axle boxes from spoked wheels of the kind represented by soil marks in the Yorkshire vehicle burials, and by the well-preserved wheels found at Holme Pierrepont, Notts., in a second-century BC context (Musty and MacCormick 1973), and at the Roman fort of Newstead, Scotland, dating to the first century AD. The Holme Pierrepont wheel demonstrates a high level of technical accomplishment. The felloe (outer rim) was made of six segments in ash joined together with dowels of oak and to each two oak spokes were attached. The hub was made of birch. The iron tire, which held the structure rigid was shrunk on; that is it was heated and dropped over the wooden structure. On cooling the iron hoop would contract drawing the component parts tightly together. There can be little doubt but that skilled wheel-wrights were present in many communities.

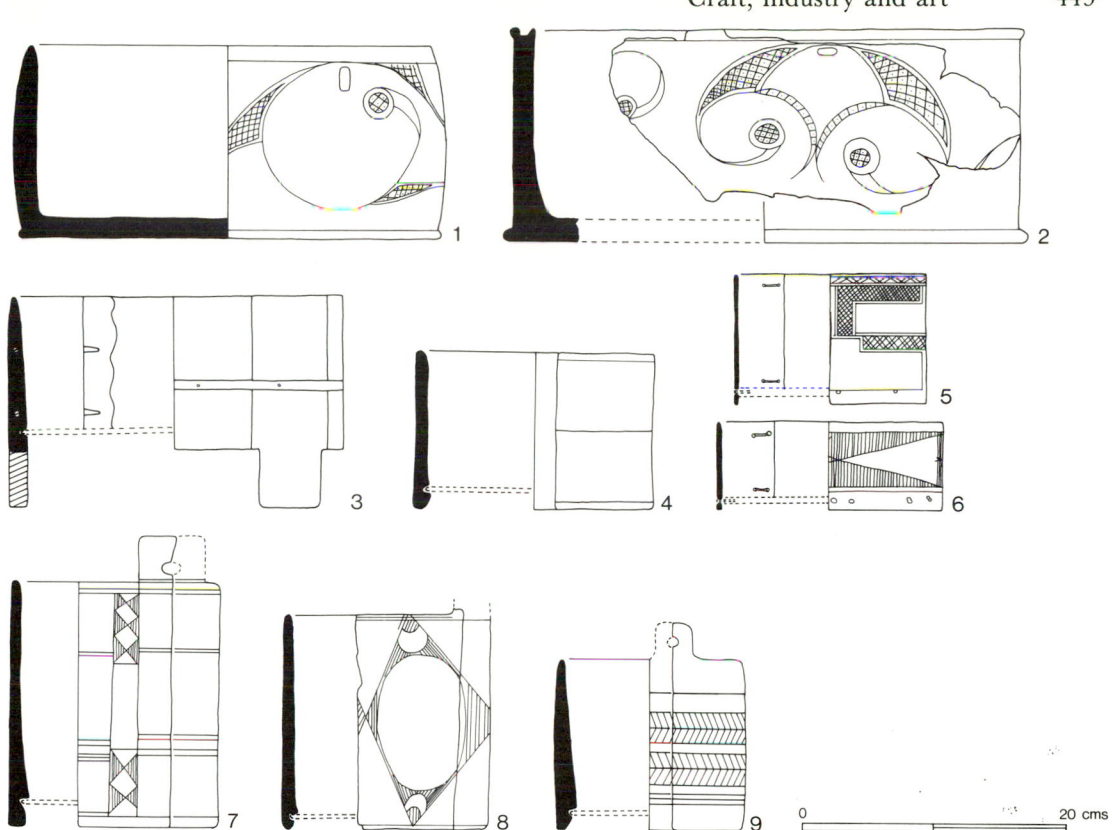

Figure 17.4 Wooden containers from the Glastonbury Lake Village, Somerset (source: Earwood 1988).

Boat building, too, must have been widely practised. Caesar's accounts of the sturdy Venetic ships built to contend with the rough seas of the Bay of Biscay and the English Channel provide an invaluable insight into the kind of craft that might be expected to have been constructed by the coastal communities. Archaeological evidence for sea-going ships is at present wanting except for the iron anchor found with a hoard of metalwork at Bulbury, Dorset. The classical sources also refer to skin boats plying the Channel (Pliny, *NH* vii.57). These would have been constructed of hides stretched over a wicker framework but nothing survives in the archaeological record.

Evidence for the navigation of inland waterways is more plentiful. A number of log boats have been found close to rivers. Most are without context, but those from Shapwick, Somerset, Poole, Dorset, and Holme Pierrepont, Notts., can, with some assurance, be dated to the Iron Age (McGrail and Switzur 1975). In 1984 a finely preserved log boat was discovered at Hasholme on Holme-on-Spalding Moor in East Yorkshire and subsequently excavated and studied with care (Millett and McGrail 1988). The boat (Figures 17.5 and 17.6) was constructed from an oak trunk more than 12 m in length which was cut in 323 BC (according to the dendrochronological study). It was a sophisticated structure with a fitted transom, extended bow, wash strake, beam ties and transverse timbers. Estimates of performance suggest that it would have been able to carry a load of over 5.5 tonnes in as little as 75 cm of water but was neither fast nor sufficiently stable to put

Figure 17.5 The Hasholme boat during excavation (photo: Sean McGrail).

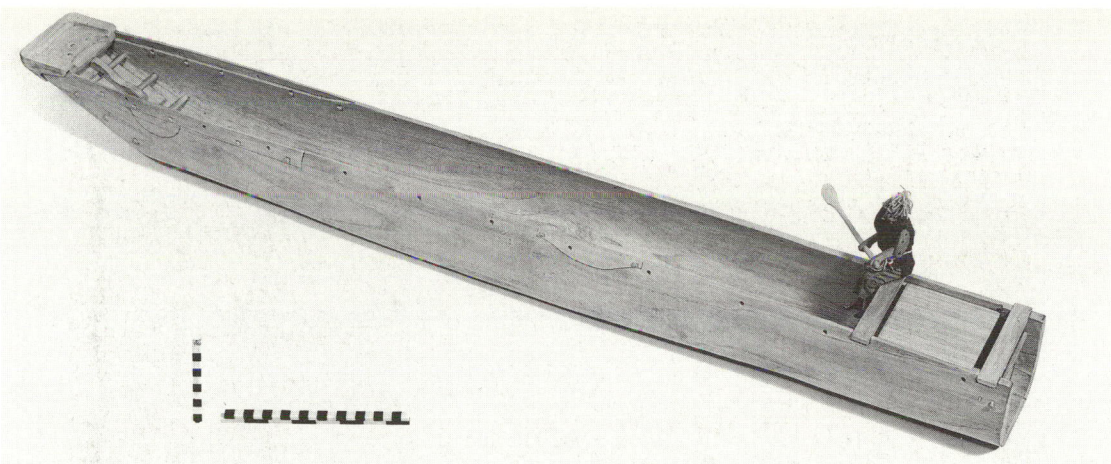

Figure 17.6   Model of the Hasholme boat (photo: Sean McGrail).

out to sea. It would, however, have been ideally suited to the transport of men or cargo in the local rivers as far as the middle reaches of the estuary (McGrail 1988). An even more complex structure was found at Brigg in north Lincolnshire (Figure 17.7). When originally exposed it was considered to be a raft, but its system of luting, with complicated cleats and transverse timbers, are now thought to be consistent with it being the remains of a flat-bottomed boat. Radiocarbon estimates suggest a date in the second quarter of the first millennium BC (McGrail 1975).

Though fragmentary, the remains of boats from Iron Age Britain and their remarkable precursors at Ferriby on the Humber estuary, leave little doubt that boat building was a long-established craft.

Metalworking: iron, copper, tin, lead, silver and gold

The home crafts referred to so far could have all been practised using material locally available, the collection of which would have been a simple matter. Iron smithing, on the other hand, involved more complex mechanisms, for while most areas of Britain lay within relatively easy reach of iron deposits, some element of specialist knowledge would necessarily have been involved in its extraction.

The discovery at Llyn Fawr, Glam., of an iron sickle made in close imitation of a native bronze prototype establishes beyond reasonable doubt that iron products were being manufactured in Britain probably as early as the middle of the seventh century (Figure 17.3, no. 1). This is not the only evidence: at Sheepen Hill (Colchester), Essex, a cauldron of the early seventh century was found, together with a small iron stud (Hawkes and Smith 1957, 161), and the Sompting hoard from Sussex, of the later seventh century, also contained a mass of corroded iron of undistinguishable form. Iron, then, was a component of some seventh-century hoards and the Llyn Fawr sickle shows that competent blacksmiths were at work. The change-over from the common use of one metal to another must have been gradual, and it is only to be expected that to

Figure 17.7   The Brigg 'raft' during excavation (photo: Sean McGrail).

begin with old bronze types were copied in the new metal. The single-looped socketed axe made in iron appears on a number of sites as far apart as Scotland, the Berwyn Mountains, Cold Kitchen Hill, Wilts., and Walthamstow, Essex (Figure 17.3, nos 4 and 5), but in no case has such an implement been found in a stratified context (Manning and Saunders 1972). It might, however, be relevant that the Cold Kitchen Hill axe came from a site producing quantities of pottery of sixth- or even seventh-century date.

How extensively iron was used in the seventh, sixth or even fifth century is impossible to say. The survival of Late Bronze Age types on several Iron Age sites suggests that its introduction was gradual and that old traditions lingered for centuries. Indeed, it was not until the fourth to third centuries that the metal began to come into use on any scale (Manning 1972). Smelting and forging seem generally to have been carried out at the homestead. Three examples serve to emphasize the point.

Within the small defended enclosure of Bryn y Castell, Ffestiniog, north Wales, two bowl furnaces were found associated with extensive slag deposits and other smithing debris concentrated at the southern end of the enclosure. One, F208, was built in a shallow pit cut into the bedrock. The surviving walls show that it would have been little more than 20 cm high and thus of limited capacity. The other, F200, was more complex, having been rebuilt on at least two occasions. The first was oval in shape, 20 cm by 30 cm with walls of stony clay. The associated debris suggested that the furnace had probably been used to reheat raw blooms during the early stage of the smithing process. Similar deposits were found in the subsequent rebuildings. The dates associated with this activity belong in the first half of the first century AD. Another more extensive iron-working area was located and excavated outside the fort to the north-east. Taken together the evidence from Bryn y Castell singles it out as one of the most important sites for the study of pre-Roman iron-working to be excavated in the Highland zone.

WEST BRANDON, CO. DURHAM

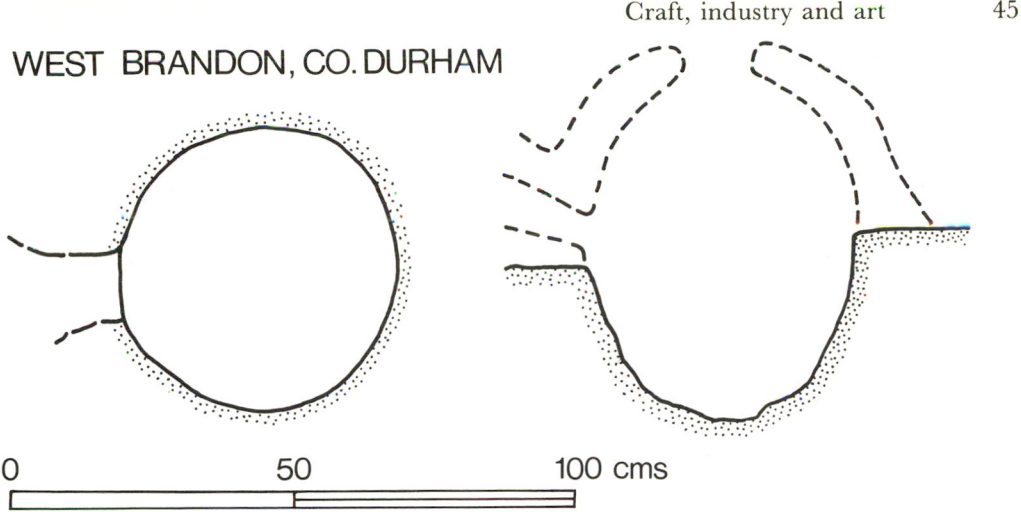

0   50   100 cms

Figure 17.8   Iron-smelting furnace at West Brandon, Co. Durham (source: Jobey 1962a).

The second example comes from the open settlement at Brooklands, Weybridge, Surrey. Two separate iron-working areas were identified, a western area where smelting was carried out and an eastern area dedicated to forging. In the smelting area the bases of seven bowl furnaces were found. The forging area was characterized by an absence of bowl furnaces but quantities of slag of the type generally associated with the initial stages of forging were found. In spite of the comparatively large extent of the iron-working area Henry Cleere (in Hanworth and Tomlin 1977, 22) estimated that no more than 5–10 kg was produced at each smelt, the total output of the works during its lifetime being in the order of 200 kg which would be more than adequate to meet the demands of a small community. The third example comes from the early palisaded homestead of West Brandon, Co. Durham, where two simple bowl furnaces were discovered, each about 30 cm in diameter and 20 cm deep (Figure 17.8). One of them was provided with a groove, in which the tuyère would have been placed, and contained the broken-up remains of a clay dome, showing that it had been at least partially enclosed.

While only about twenty furnaces have been found (Tylecote 1986, 138–9; Gibson-Hill 1980), other evidence of iron-smelting – such as slag, cinder or iron ore – is more commonly found and leaves little doubt that iron extraction and forging was a widespread home craft and not solely a skill in the hands of specialists. The processes involved in extraction were simple enough: the crushed ore, mixed with charcoal, would have been placed in a bowl furnace which may then have been partially covered with clay. Gradually, with the aid of bellows, the temperature would have been raised to above 800°C, at which point the reduction of the oxide would have taken place, the metal itself remaining as a spongy mass while the molten slag drained to the bottom of the furnace. On cooling, the reduced iron bloom would have been removed and continually heated and beaten until the remaining slag was forced out. The bloom was then ready for forging into implements or weapons. There seems to have been no deliberate attempt to strengthen the iron by the addition of carbon or phosphorus, but where stronger phosphorus-containing or carburised iron was produced by the normal extraction process, it may well have been selected for manufacture into weapons or tools requiring strong cutting edges (Ehrenreich 1985). Few blacksmith's tools have been identified but the Bulbury 'hoard' contains a heavy sledge hammer (Figure 17.9, no. 1) and a pair of tongs dating to the first century BC have been discovered at Garton Slack (Figure 17.9, no. 4).

The extraction processes were sufficiently simple for the production of iron to have been carried out on a part-time home basis, and over a large part of the country it would have been possible for many communities to extract enough ore for themselves from nearby deposits. Moreover, iron was not consumed in large quantities, since broken implements could be reforged into replacements with little difficulty. Thus a complex system of trade and specialization would not have been necessary except in those areas far away from ore deposits. Nevertheless, by the second and first centuries BC ingots of iron appear, and frequently turn up in hoards. There are two types of ingot: rhomboidal ingots of Continental type, of which only two have been found in Britain, on Portland Bill, Dorset, and currency bars, widespread in the south of the country (Figures 17.10 and 17.11). Currency bars can be divided into four different types. Sword-shaped bars, with a short pinched-up hilt and a flat blade usually between 78 and 90 cm long, are found in an area stretching from Hampshire and Dorset in the south along the Jurassic Way to the Humber. Spit-shaped bars, usually much narrower than the sword-shaped versions and with a shorter pinched end are concentrated in the Cotswolds and Somerset, with an outlier in Anglesey. The third variety, plough-shaped bars, are usually 4–6 cm wide and about 1 cm thick, roughly pointed at one end and with short raised wings or flanges at the blunt end. Distributionally they cluster in the Thames valley, spreading into Kent and the Midlands. The last type are bay leaf-shaped, with a long semi-circular sectioned hilt: only a few are known, principally from the Cambridgeshire region.

Much has been written on the subject of currency bars (e.g. more recently Tylecote 1962, 206–11; D.F. Allen 1968b), leading to the conclusion that there were many regional variations and that, since many of them were carefully hoarded, they were likely to have been of value. The simplest explanation is therefore that the bars represented a medium of exchange or barter, the iron content providing an actual as well as a perceived value. Further implications might be that they were manufactured by specialist iron-smelters and were traded to the neighbouring communities within restricted regions, the bars being then either hoarded as a form of wealth or manufactured into implements.

Analysis of the slag inclusions in bars from three hoards, Beckford, Danebury and Gretton, showed that it was possible to distinguish three different sources but the task of tracking down the actual location of the ore would be very much more difficult (Hedges and Salter 1979).

The very existence of the bars, and the fact that each hoard was probably produced from a single source (at least in the three cases examined) is sufficient to show that iron extraction had become a specialist skill in south-east Britain by the second century BC. Although exact dating of furnaces is difficult and the number known is not large the majority seem to belong to the period before the second century. It is tempting therefore to suggest that there may have been a move away from small-scale local production to more centralized production in the south-east as the Iron Age progressed. Such a change would have required the development of more organized redistribution mechanisms. In this context it is interesting to note the concentration of currency bar hoards in hillforts and the evidence from Danebury that bars were being cut up there for manufacture into tools and weapons. The appearance of the bars, implying specialist production, may have taken with it the development of specialist smiths working from selected locations. Eventually there may be enough analytical data to test this hypothesis. In any event the production of prestige goods like swords and daggers would certainly have been the prerogative

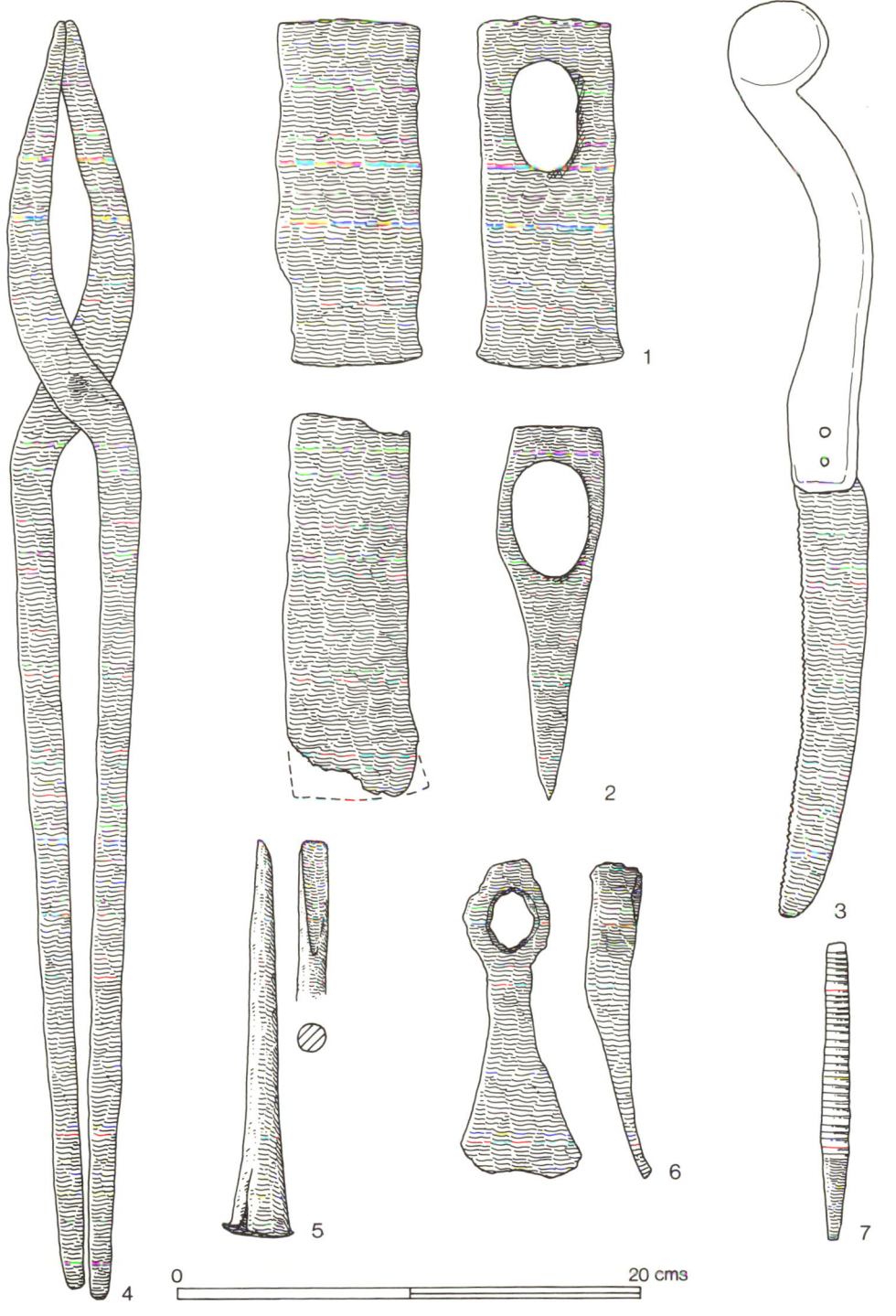

Figure 17.9   Iron tools. 1 Hammer from Bulbury, Dorset; 2 axe-hammer from Bulbury, Dorset; 3 saw from Glastonbury, Somerset; 4 tongs from Garton Slack; 5 gouge from Danebury; 6 adze from Danebury; 7 file from Danebury. (Sources: *Bulbury*, Cunliffe 1972b; *Glastonbury*, Bulleid and Gray 1917; *Danebury*, Cunliffe 1984a; *Garton Slack*, Brewster 1976).

of highly skilled craftsmen, perhaps organized in distinct schools (pp. 468–86).

Itinerant trading was a well-established pattern in the preceding Late Bronze Age for the production and distribution of bronze tools and weapons. No doubt these long-established traditions were maintained until as late as the fifth century, by which time iron was beginning to replace bronze as the common everyday metal. Bronze, however, continued to be used for the manufacture of vessels and for trinkets such as brooches, rings, bracelets, harness-trappings and other decorative fittings, but on a much more limited scale than before. No longer do we find founders' hoards scattered over the country, but instead small-scale production, probably in the hands of specialists resident in the larger centres.

It is only with the development of the urban and semi-urban centres like Hengistbury Head, Dorset, and Camulodunum, Essex, that large-scale metallurgical activities can be recognized. Archaeological evidence for bronze-working in the Early and Middle Iron Age is not common but crucibles and other waste are recorded from various sites (Figure 17.12) including Danebury, Hants., in both the Early and Middle Iron Age, Glastonbury and Meare in Somerset, probably within the first century BC, and bronze-workers' areas have been defined at South Cadbury, Somerset, Stanwick, Yorks. (Spratling 1981), Beckford, Heref. and Worcs. (Hurst and Wills 1987), and elsewhere.

But the most dramatic evidence of bronze-working has come from the excavation of the settlement at Gussage All Saints, Dorset. Here in a pit of the late second or early first century extensive remains of a bronze foundry were recovered including slag, crucibles, tuyères, a small copper ingot, bone modelling tools for wax proformas, and 8,000 fragments of clay investment moulds (Spratling 1979; Foster 1980). The moulds are of particular importance, for since they had been part of the lost-wax method of casting, each mould could have been used only once, thus allowing the total number of objects manufactured to be calculated. The range of products was restricted to horse gear and included three-link bridle bits, terret rings, linchpin terminals and strap-unions of figure-of-eight type. In all, it is thought that about fifty sets of fittings had been manufactured. The discovery is important not only for the technical information it gives about bronze casting, but for the questions it raises about the position of the craftsman in society. While it is possible that he (or they) was a resident member of the Gussage community, it would seem equally likely that skilled metalworkers of this kind were itinerant. Another possibility is that such men served under particular leaders but were seconded to the establishments of clients as a form of patronage. The various possible options are difficult to distinguish by archaeological means. A consideration of the distribution of Gussage products could help. No detailed study has yet been made but items from Hagbourne Hill, Berks., and Polden, Somerset, are closely similar.

The products of individual craftsmen can occasionally be traced distributed over a restricted territory. In Wessex, for example, there appears to have been a workshop producing a distinctive local version of the La Tène I fibula, with incised lines and impressed dots on the bow (Figure 17.13). More than twenty have been found, all within a 50 km radius of Salisbury in Wiltshire (Figure 17.14) (Hull and Hawkes 1987, 98–101). Although the actual production centre of the type is unknown, it is tempting to think in terms of a single bronze-worker based somewhere in the area supplying local needs in the fourth or third century. Small-scale manufacturing of this kind is likely to have been the normal pattern for much of the country wherever communities were sufficiently large to have supported a non-food producing specialist.

Our understanding of the bronze-working in the Iron Age is being improved dramatically by metal analyses which are now becoming available (Northover 1988). Although it is too early to make detailed generalizations, Northover has suggested that special alloys were being used for

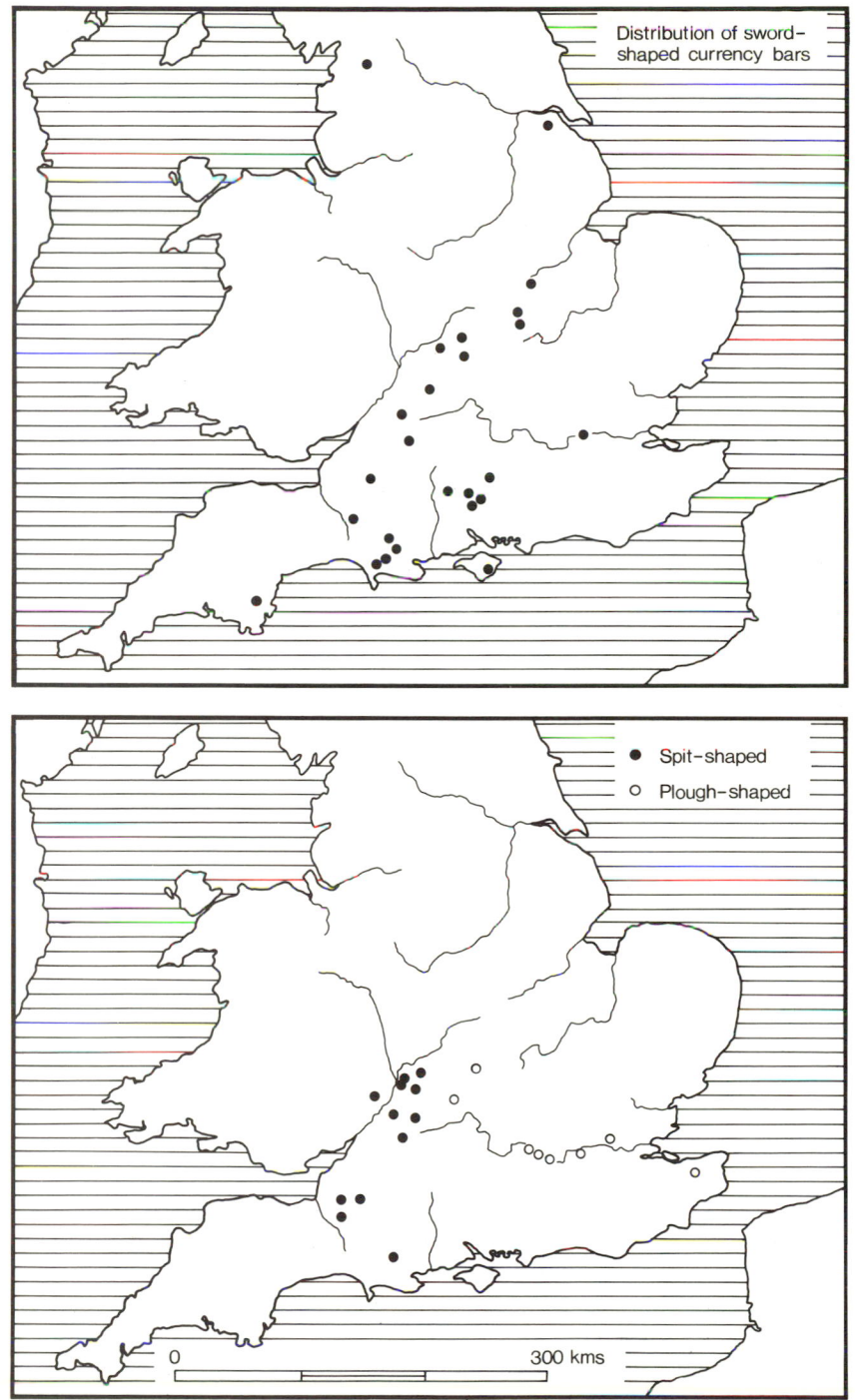

Figure 17.10   Distribution of iron currency bars (source: D.F. Allen 1968b with additions).

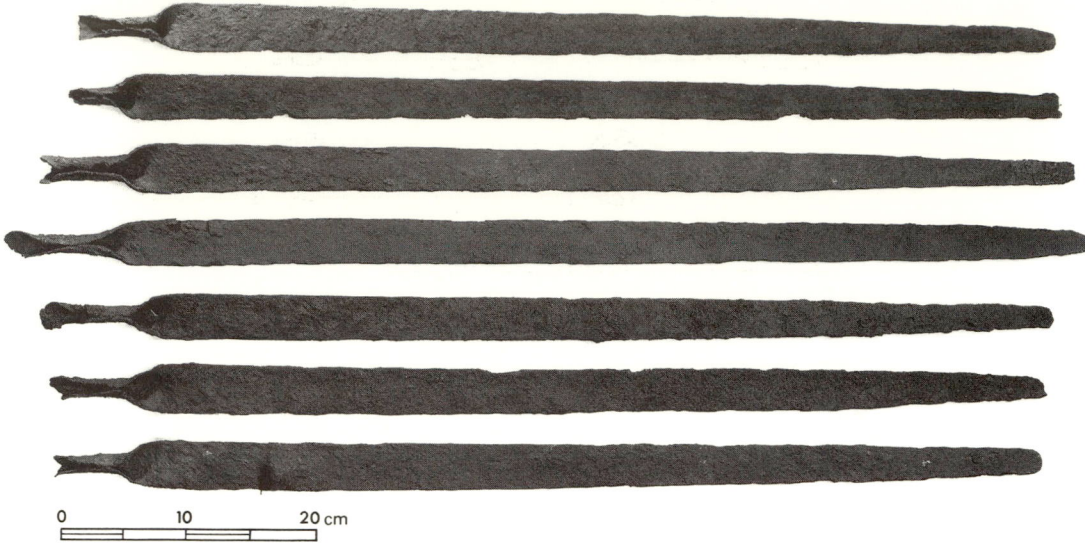

Figure 17.11   Part of a hoard of iron sword-shaped currency bars from Danebury, Hants. (photo: David Leigh. Danebury Trust).

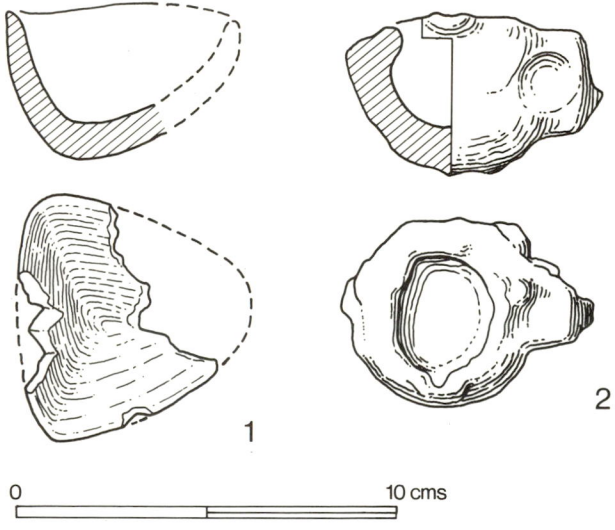

Figure 17.12   Bronze-working crucibles. 1 Breedon-on-the-Hill, Leics.; 2 Danebury, Hants (sources: *Breedon-on-the-Hill*, Kenyon 1950; *Danebury*, author).

prestige sheet bronze-work and that production may have been centred on the hillforts, contrasting with the manufacture of cast horse gear the evidence for which tends to concentrate on homestead sites. If trends such as this are substantiated and amplified by further work major advances in our understanding of the place of craft production in Iron Age social systems will be possible.

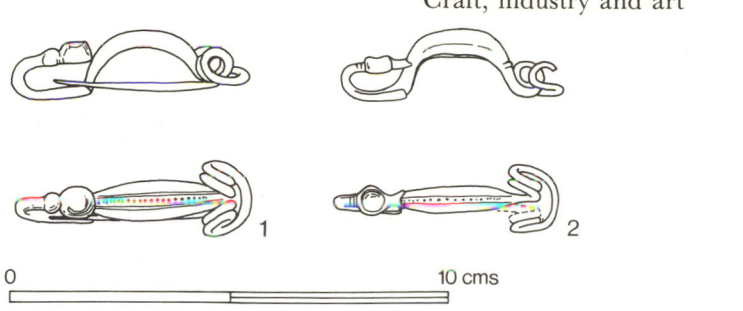

Figure 17.13   Wessex La Tène fibulae. 1 Blandford, Dorset; 2 Avebury, Wilts. (Source: R.A. Smith 1925).

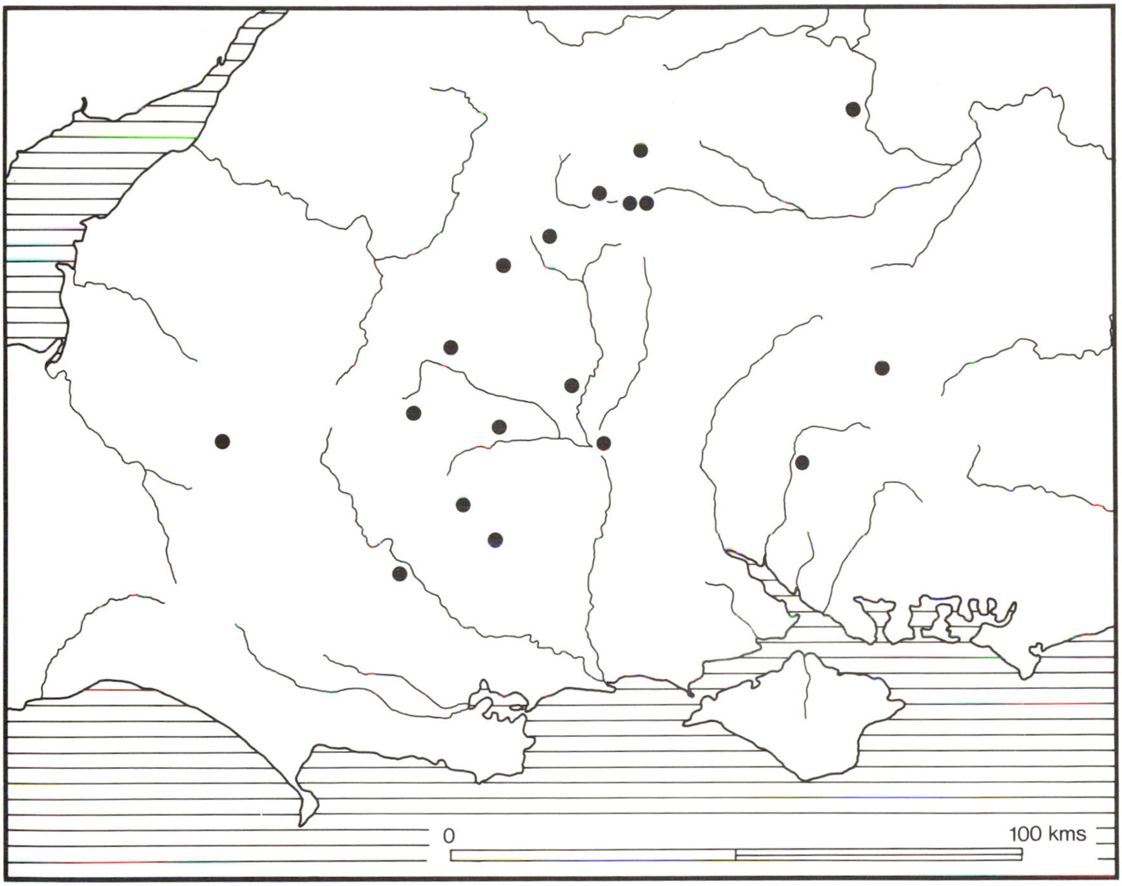

Figure 17.14   Distribution of Wessex fibulae (source: M.J. Fowler 1954 with additions).

Until the fifth century or a little later, bronze scrap hoards were common in most parts of the country, particularly the south-east, but thereafter they ceased to be deposited. The extraction of copper would however have been maintained in Cornwall and Devon, north Wales and the Welsh borderland, Scotland and Ireland, and tin continued to be extracted from the Cornish deposits – in both cases by traditional techniques now more than 1,000 years old. Details of the extraction sites and processes are at present unknown, but ingots of the refined metals must have been widely traded, particularly to the populous south-east.

Tin was also exported to the Continent. The elder Pliny (*Nat. Hist.* iv, 30, 104) tells us that the fourth-century historian Timaeus reported that 'the island of Mictus, where tin is to be got, is six days' sailing from Britain further inwards'. Similarly, Diodorus Siculus, referring to the voyaging of the explorer Pytheas in the late fourth century states:

> In Britain the inhabitants of the promontory called Belerion are particularly friendly to strangers and have become civilized through contacts with merchants from foreign parts . . . . They prepare the tin, working the ground in which it is produced very carefully . . . they beat the metal into masses shaped like an ox hide and carry it to a certain island lying off Britain called Ictis.
>
> (v, 22).

Although there is still some doubt as to the exact identification of Ictis (Cunliffe 1983; C.F.C. Hawkes 1984), the impression of a well-developed tin trade between Cornwall and the civilized world is evident – tin was being produced for the export market as well as home consumption. To what extent copper continued to be exported in the first millennium cannot yet be ascertained.

Lead was not of great significance in the pre-Roman period. Admittedly, in the Late Bronze Age it was added to the bronze used for implements distributed in the south-east and lead objects are found sporadically on occupation sites of the Iron Age, but it was never extensively used. Only in the first-century BC contexts at Glastonbury are any number of lead objects found, and here the metal was usually restricted to double perforated net-sinkers and spindle whorls. Lead is unlikely to have been extracted for its own properties, but as an additive to bronze to improve its casting properties it would have been of some value. Later, when silver was being extracted from argentiferous galena by the process of cupellation, lead would have been a by-product which could have been put to use locally. The finds from Glastonbury imply the working, albeit limited, of the Mendip lead deposits, but of the exploitation of ore deposits elsewhere – in Shropshire, Flintshire, Derbyshire and Yorkshire – little is known before the Roman period.

Silver was extracted in limited quantities, but intensive production did not develop until the first century BC, when the demand for coinage increased in the south-east and the metal was also used alloyed with gold to make torcs. Gold too is rare before the first century. Objects of Irish gold made in the Late Bronze Age tradition were still finding their way into Britain in the seventh and sixth centuries, but it was the social and economic development of the first century BC that encouraged more widespread exploitation. D.F. Allen (1975) has estimated that during the thirty-year reign of Cunobelin more than 1 million gold coins were issued requiring over 5,000 kg of gold.

Glass

Comparatively few glass objects have been found in Britain (Guido 1978), but many of them have been subjected to a systematic analysis (Henderson 1981, 1985, 1987a and b; Henderson and Warren 1981). As a result it is now becoming clear that the production of beads and bracelets was a complex matter. Manufacture seems to have been restricted to very few sites. At Hengistbury Head, Dorset, raw glass, in the form of blocks of purple and yellow glass, was being imported, presumably from Gaul or the Mediterranean, and although direct evidence of manufacture was not found, the number of fragments of finished beads and bracelets recovered from the site strongly suggests that Hengistbury was a production centre converting imported raw materials into finished items (Henderson 1987a). Another glass works has been located at Meare, Somerset, where the unusually large number of glass items from the old excavations has hinted at local production for some time. The discovery of a partially finished bead now provides direct evidence that this was the case (Henderson 1981). The rarity of glass beads and bracelets in Britain and the very slight evidence of production so far discovered is an indication of the prestige in which glass was probably held and the high status of glass-workers.

Pottery production

In south-east Britain the production of pottery was on a considerable scale. As the discussion in chapters 4, 7 and 8 will have shown, well-defined regional styles can be recognized from an early date – a fact which might be thought to imply some degree of commercial production, at least of the finer wares.

Types like the scratched cordoned bowls of Wessex, made in very fine black ware with an evenly applied haematite-coated surface, fired red and scratched after firing in simple geometric patterns, are so similar to each other and so restricted in their distribution that it is highly likely that they were manufactured in a single centre: petrological examination of the fabrics suggests that the production may have concentrated on the brickearth deposits close to Salisbury. Later, in the Middle Iron Age, much the same region used a saucepan pot assemblage decorated in a distinctive manner and made from a fabric incorporating the mineral glauconite found in the Jurassic and cretaceous clays to the west of Salisbury. The combination of specially chosen clay and the restricted decorative repertoire in both of these examples suggests specialist production (Figure 17.15). The same may be said with less certainty of much of the early fine ware in the south, but until a detailed programme of petrological examination has been undertaken on this early material, it would be unwise to speculate further.

The pottery of two other regions – the stamped and linear tooled ware of the Welsh borderland and Gloucestershire, and the highly decorated 'Glastonbury' ware of the south-west – has been examined in detail with these problems in mind (Peacock 1968, 1969, 1979; Morris 1981). Both groups date largely to the fourth to first century BC but manufacture probably began in the preceding century. On the basis of the filling material added to the clay, the linear tooled and stamped ware of the west can be divided into four groups (Peacock 1968): group A contains igneous and metamorphic rock derived from the Malvern Hills; group B1 is gritted with a Palaeozoic limestone; group B2 with a Mesozoic limestone, probably from the Jurassic outcrop; and group C contains a crushed sandstone from the Llandovery beds west of the Malverns. The types belonging to all four groups, while generally similar, can be shown to have distinctive features and some degree of differential distribution can be observed. The implication, however, seems to be that within one culturally related area, specialist potters were at work in at least four centres supplying the ceramic needs of the communities living within a broad territory 80–130 km from the production centres.

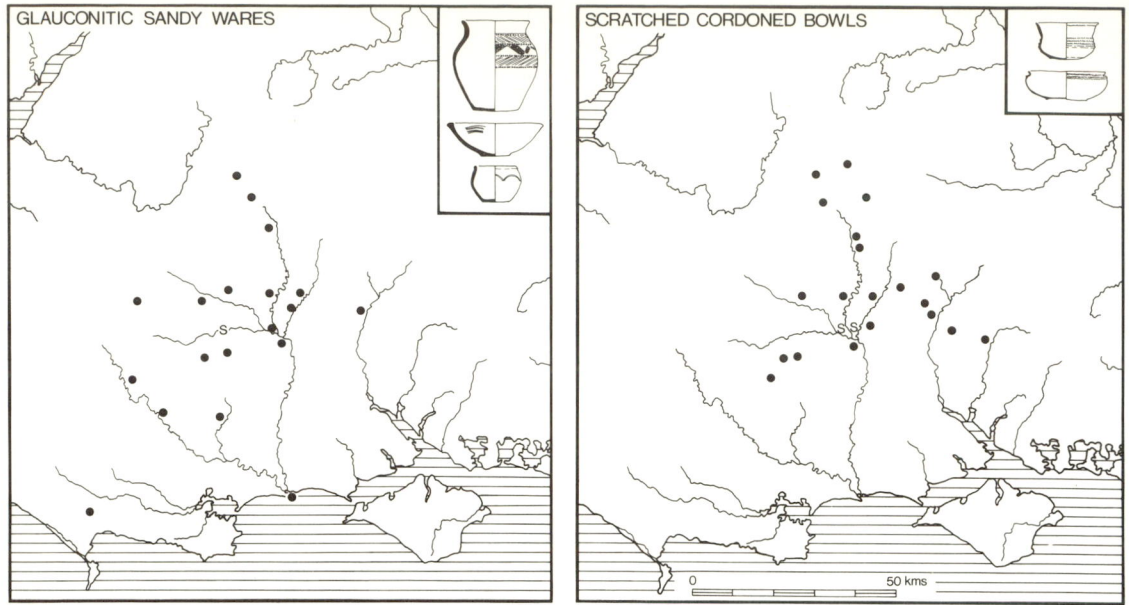

Figure 17.15   Specialist pottery production in Wessex. S indicates source of the clay used (source: author after Cunliffe 1984a).

If, however, the distribution of these decorated wares is compared with that of a simple coarse ware made from clay gritted with diorite from the Clee Hills an interesting contrast is apparent, with the coarse ware covering a much smaller territory, no more than 40 km from the source (Figure 17.16). The contrast is between the local distribution of a low quality product and the regional distribution of one of high quality (Morris 1981).

Much the same pattern has emerged from a petrological study of the South-Western Decorated Wares (Figure 17.17). Six different groups have been recognized, each with distinctive typological characteristics and a restricted distribution pattern. Only in the case of group 1, which contains gabbro inclusions and must therefore have been made in Cornwall, is there any evidence of widespread trade, some of the vessels of this category reaching Devon, Somerset, Hampshire and Northamptonshire.

If this kind of analysis is extended, the stylistic considerations which serve to distinguish the regional groups of the saucepan pot continuum may prove to result from the work of separate manufacturing centres in much the same way.

It is, then, becoming increasingly clear that the manufacture of fine pottery was a specialist craft by the first century BC and the probability remains that specialization in some regions dates back to the fifth century or even earlier. Nothing is yet known of the production centres themselves, but it is unlikely that elaborate kilns existed since simple bonfire firings would have been quite sufficient to produce the wares: little archaeological evidence of manufacture can therefore be expected to survive. Some degree of commercial production does not, of course, exclude home production, and indeed it is probable that a reasonably high percentage of the local coarse wares were home-made in the earlier periods, but by the second and first centuries even the plainer and simpler vessels take on a mass-produced appearance, suggesting that commercial enterprise was now dominant.

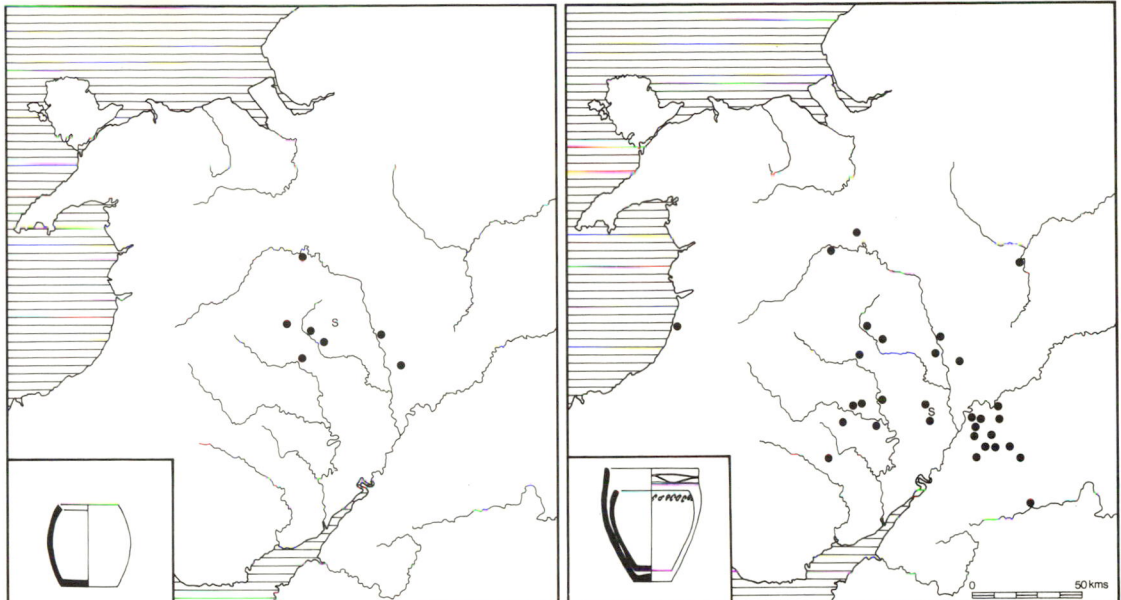

Figure 17.16 Specialist pottery production in the Welsh borderland. S indicates source of clay used (source: Morris 1981).

Shale, jet, lignite and other stone

Certain areas of the country developed specializations because of their mineral wealth. In Cornwall some communities were geared to the extraction of tin at an early date and later the Wealden population specialized in iron production. In other areas stone was exploited for the manufacture of trinkets such as rings and bracelets. The best-known centre of this kind is the Isle of Purbeck in Dorset, where the black or dark brown oily shale, known as Kimmeridge shale, was quarried from the cliffs and taken to neighbouring occupation sites for manufacture into armlets. Judging by the number of sites producing evidence of shale-working in the vicinity, the industry was well established and must have had a sizeable output. Excavations at Eldon's Seat (Encombe), Dorset, have allowed the various stages in the manufacturing process to be worked out (Figure 17.18). First, it seems that large slabs of shale were brought to the site, possibly threaded on poles for ease of carrying. Then, with the aid of simply-struck knives of flint, flat discs, some 13 cm across, were carved out. The next stage involved either boring a central hole or cutting out a core, thus creating a ring which could gradually be whittled down and finally ground to form finished bracelets, armlets, anklets or, occasionally, pendants.

The Kimmeridge shale industry flourished throughout the Iron Age and Roman period, but from the sixth to the second century, techniques of manufacture changed little. It was only after the introduction of lathe-turning in the first century that the nature of production began to take on a more commercial aspect and the range of products was increased to include quite large vessels. The distribution of Kimmeridge shale artefacts spread over much of central southern Britain but does not seem to have been particularly extensive outside an 80 km radius of Purbeck. The exact nature of the processes of exchange and distribution are unclear. The intense activity

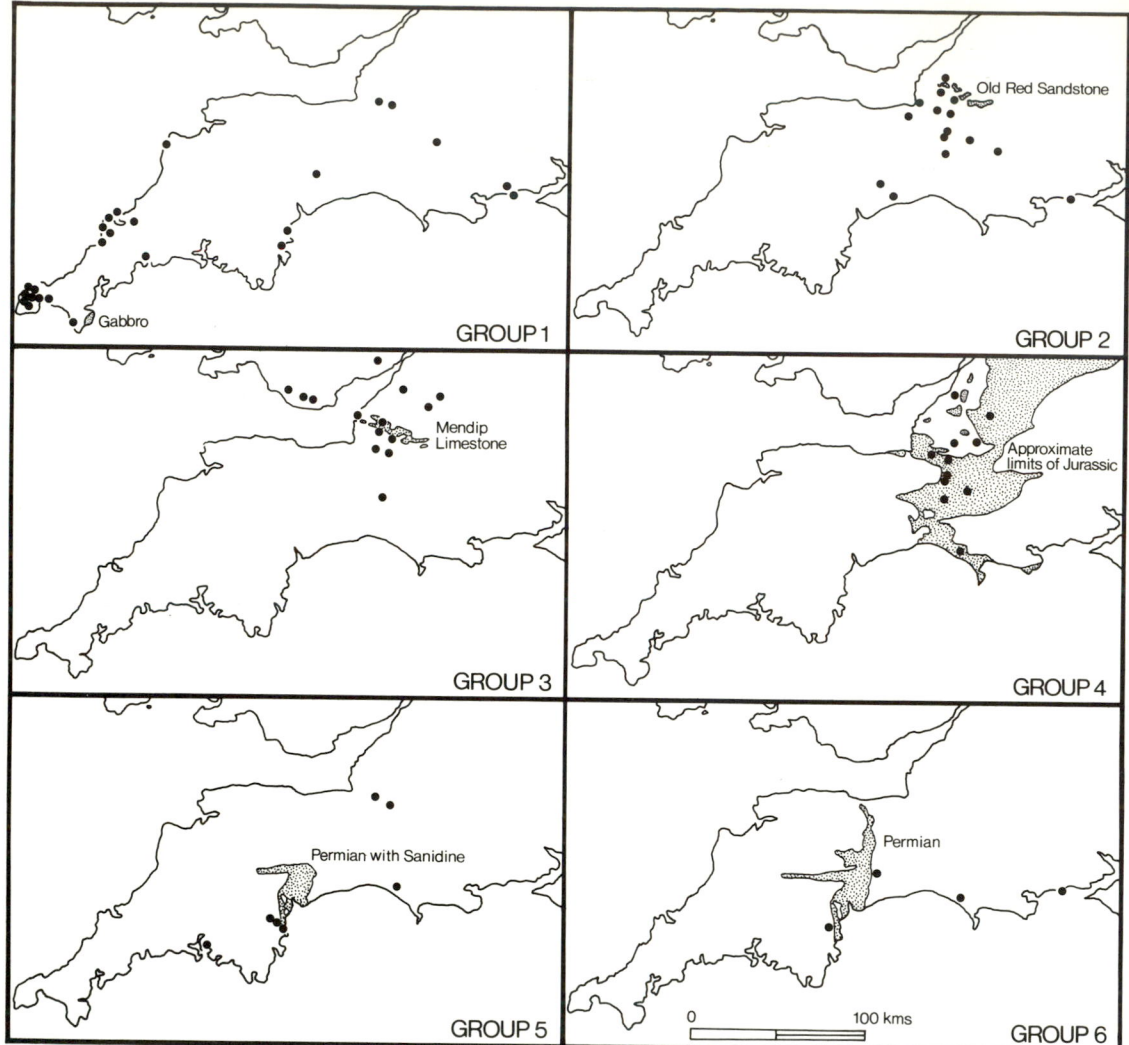

Figure 17.17   Specialist pottery production in the south-west (source: Peacock 1969).

recognized at the production sites on Purbeck leaves little doubt that finished objects were being manufactured, but the occurrence of rough-out armlets at various sites, including Hengistbury, Glastonbury, Danebury, etc., means that trade in raw materials also formed part of the system.

In northern Britain the place of shale was taken by jet, a black shiny rock found in the upper lias exposed on the Yorkshire coast between Ravenscar and Port Mulgrave. The crude jet seems to have been taken to occupation sites and worked, in much the same way as shale, into bracelets, finger-rings and pendants, a number of which were found at Staple Howe in sixth-century contexts. The discovery of jet or lignite bracelets at the Heathery Burn Cave in County Durham implies that production was underway as early as the seventh century. Jet trinkets are also found in later contexts, among the Arras culture burials of eastern Yorkshire, and it is well known that

Figure 17.18 Kimmeridge shale-working debris from Eldon's Seat, Encombe, Dorset (photo: George Keene).

production continued into the Roman period. Jet was also popular in Scotland as far north as the Orkneys. It is, however, possible that more than one source of material was exploited and that the more northerly finds were derived from deposits in Scotland. Until a programme of chemical analysis is undertaken, the problem will remain unresolved.

Finally some mention must be made of quernstones – the most important stone artefact in the Iron Age repertoire since it was required to process the staple food. Petrological studies show that selected quarries were preferred. The 120 or so beehive querns of Yorkshire have been identified to five rock types all comparatively local (Hayes, Hemingway and Spratt 1980), while one of the most widespread quernstone types in use in Wessex has been traced to a quarry near Midhurst, Sussex (Peacock 1987). The control of good stone supplies and the manufacture and distribution of the finished querns, often over considerable distances, would have required complex systems of control embedded within the social system.

Salt

One of the more important of the consumer products of Iron Age Britain was salt, the principal sources of which were seawater and the brine springs of the west Midlands. Salt would have been

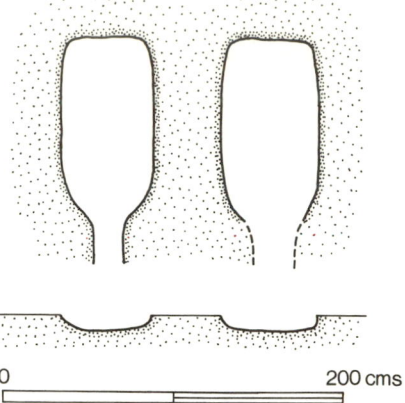

Figure 17.19   Salt-boiling hearths at Ingoldmells, Lincs. (source: Baker 1960).

required not only as an essential part of the diet but also as a preservative for meat stored during the winter.

Evidence for salt extraction is now well known around much of the south-east coast of Britain, particularly the low-lying areas of Lincolnshire, Norfolk, Essex, Hampshire and Dorset (Bradley 1975; Baker 1975; Riehm 1961; Nenquin 1961; Farrar 1963, 1975; May 1976b, 143–55; De Brisay 1978; Kirkham 1975), and as a result of the abundant but somewhat fragmentary evidence now available, the main stages in the extraction processes are reasonably clear, though not everywhere represented (Figures 17.19 and 17.20).

Seawater was first encouraged to flow into large evaporation pans, probably at the beginning of the summer, and allowed to stand to evaporate, suitably covered from the rain, until autumn. The crust of crude salt and the underlying salt-impregnated clay were then broken up and roasted in an open fire to facilitate the next stage, which involved dissolving the salt from the resulting granular mass using a strong brine solution and then decanting off the salt-rich liquor which was evaporated in large boiling pans, supported on clay bars. More often, however, the damp crystalline salt seems to have been scooped out and packed into porous clay moulds, which were probably warmed to 60–70°C to complete the drying operation. At Halle in Germany, where a number of complete moulds have been found, it is evident that standard sizes were aimed at so that the resultant salt-cakes would have been of equal value. It follows that the simplest way to market the salt would have been in the moulds. Insufficient data are available from the British sites to show whether or not the same standardization applied here, but in all probability it did.

The division between the initial extraction of the salt and its packaging and drying is emphasized by two sites in the Isle of Purbeck, Dorset – Hobarrow Bay and Kimmeridge (Calkin 1949, 56–7; Farrar 1975) – both of which occur on the tops of cliffs overlooking shelving beaches. Since it would have been impracticable to carry seawater to them for evaporation, it is more reasonable to suppose that pans and evaporation tanks lay on the beach, the damp salt being carted to the cliff-top site for drying and packing in clay moulds ready for distribution. Hobarrow Bay produced a range of briquetage including parts of rectangular trays and cylindrical tray supports associated with masses of burnt shale, while at Kimmeridge in a similar context hemispherical bowls were recovered together with cylindrical vessels cut in halves partially or

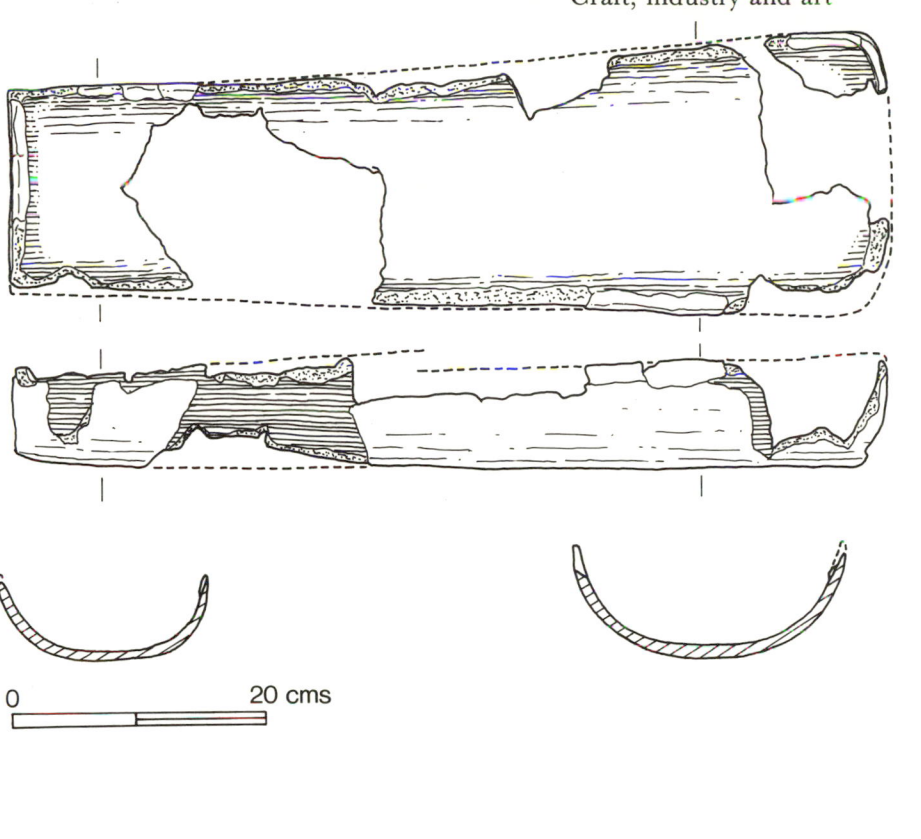

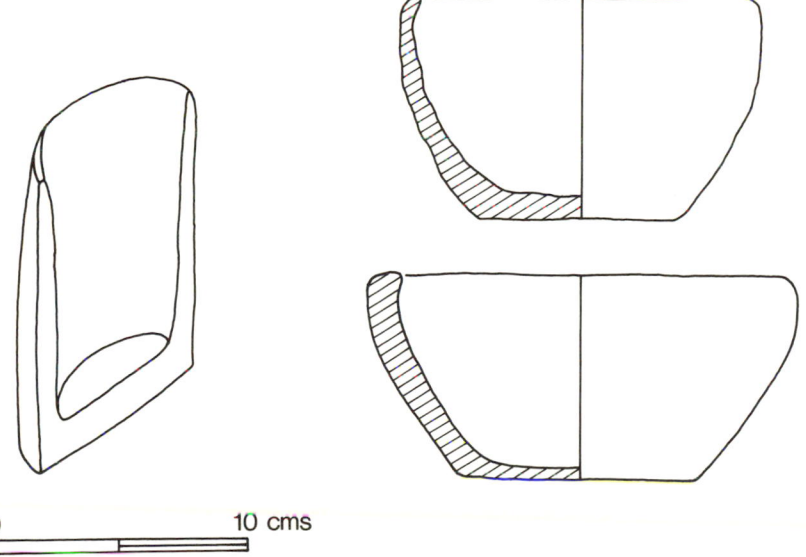

Figure 17.20   Salt containers. Top, from Ingoldmells, Lincs. (source: May 1976b); bottom, from the Isle of Purbeck (source: Calkin 1949).

totally before firing (Figure 17.20). The former belong to a well-known type of drying mould found on many of the salt-works but the half-cylinders are more puzzling. Some, which were completely cut through before firing, could conceivably have been bound together during the drying process, to be then sliced in two, together with their salt-cake, to produce two half-measures; while those cylinders which were only incompletely separated could easily have been cracked apart after the contents had dried. Admittedly, both explanations seem to be over-complicated but it is difficult to suggest a simpler process. Whatever the final outcome of the problem, the fact remains that the cliff-top sites were concerned predominantly with drying the salt and not with its primary extraction, which must have been carried out on the beaches.

Both Hobarrow Bay and Kimmeridge belong to the early part of the Iron Age, dating to as early as the fifth century. At Paulsgrove, in Portsmouth harbour, Hants., a production centre of the fourth or third century has been found. Sites of the second to first centuries are more common, occurring at Wyke Regis (Dorset), Hayling Island and at many locations around the fringes of Langstone and Chichester harbours. The Lincolnshire industry seems to have begun in the early part of the period – perhaps the third or second century to judge by the few sherds of associated pottery (Baker 1960, Figures 1 and 2) – and to have continued into the Roman period (May 1976b, 143–55), while the even more extensive centres on the Essex coast span the first century BC to first century AD, possibly beginning earlier (Rodwell 1976, 298–301). A similar date range can be assigned to the group in Poole Harbour, Hants. The extent and duration of most of the production centres speaks of an intensive industry becoming more important as time proceeded. While it is likely that in the earlier period salt extraction was practised on a part-time basis (Bradley 1975), there can be little doubt that in the later centuries it was carried out by specialists working full time and supplying the needs of a considerable inland market.

The salt springs of Droitwich, Worcs., and Nantwich, Cheshire, producing high quality salt, were both extensively utilized in the Iron Age. The salt was packed in briquetage containers for drying and transport and, since the fabrics of these can be distinguished and related to source, it is possible to trace the distribution of the different production centres across the Midlands. A detailed assessment of this data (Morris 1985) has thrown important new light on patterns of trade and exchange. The Droitwich spring was in use as early as the sixth–fifth century and its characteristic briquetage containers though not common in this period were found up to 60 km to the north and 48 km to the south of the source. From the fourth century onwards there is abundant evidence of production but the distribution is concentrated to the south-west and south-east of the spring with very little reaching the north (Figure 17.21). The reason for this may well be that salt from the Nantwich area, identified by its own distinctive containers, was now being traded far more extensively and was beginning to 'capture' some of the market once supplied by the Droitwich spring. The social implications of these patterns are especially interesting. As Morris has shown (1981) the distribution of the fine Malvernian A pottery is closely similar to that of the Droitwich salt containers: together they define a socio-economic territory occupying the southern Marches. The appearance of 'northern' salt within this southern territory after the fifth century might suggest a degree of social reorientation which may reflect on changing concepts of ethnic identity or simply herald an intensification of production and exchange.

Specialist schools of metalworkers

The crafts and industries discussed so far were designed to serve the immediate needs of the community, providing clothing, tools, utensils, salt and a few trinkets such as brooches and

CHESHIRE SALT CONTAINERS   DROITWICH SALT CONTAINERS

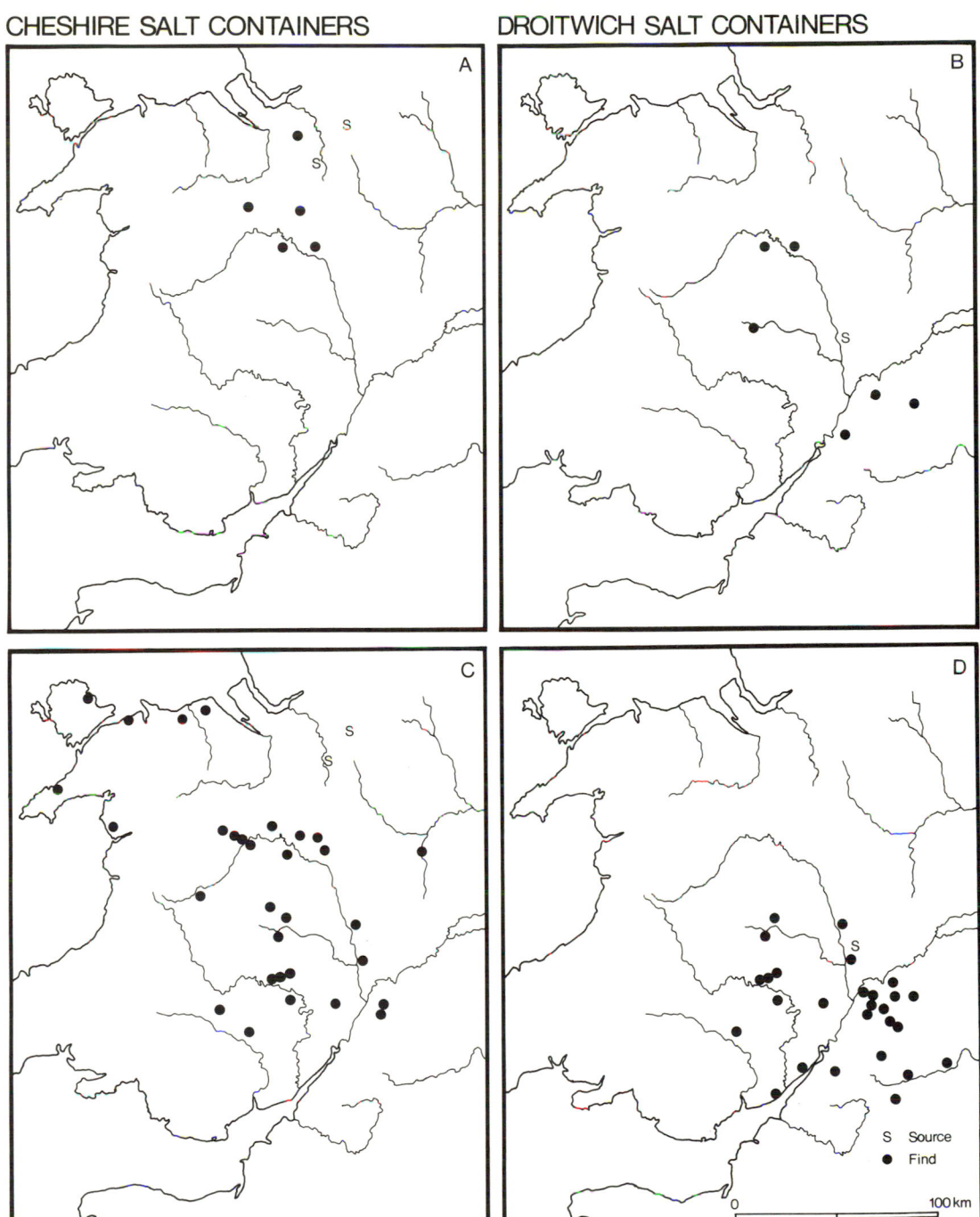

Figure 17.21   Salt containers in western Britain showing competing spheres of distribution: A and B, sixth and fifth century; C and D, fourth century and later (source. Morris 1985).

bracelets made of metal and stone. Luxury products were scarce before the second century BC, perhaps implying that the development of a class society requiring expensive forms of display had not proceeded far. Without surplus wealth and the desire for display there could be little patronage, and without patronage schools of artist–craftsmen are unlikely to have flourished. That some specialists were at work, however, is evident. The production of cauldrons and buckets in the west, probably Ireland (Hawkes and Smith 1957; Gerloff 1987), in the late second and early first millennium is a reflection of the feasting aspects of a heroic society, and the elaborate harness-fittings and cart-trappings (pp. 411–13) show that some members of society were sufficiently wealthy to indulge in such luxuries, all of which were the products of craftsmen working in the old Bronze Age traditions.

The most impressive evidence of a continuous tradition of inventive craftsmanship is provided by the swords and daggers from the river Thames, so densely distributed that there can be little doubt of their local origin. Production began in the late second or early first millennium with the manufacture of local bronze types copied from Continental imports. Later in the seventh century the Hallstatt C Gündlingen sword developed in Continental Europe and was immediately taken up locally, leading to the production of a series of distinctively British types (Cowen 1967). In the sixth and fifth centuries new Continental trends, particularly the appearance of iron daggers of Hallstatt D1 date, were quickly absorbed and there arose a British dagger series which spanned the period until the end of the third century (Jope 1961b, 1983). Thereafter swords, influenced by Continental La Tène I types, became common again.

The evidence of the Thames daggers argues convincingly for a highly skilled workshop geared to the aristocratic market of the fifth and fourth centuries, turning out exquisitely made iron daggers in elaborate bronze sheaths. This British development runs parallel to Continental sword and dagger production which, from the fourth century, provided a medium for the practice of the decorative techniques belonging to the general repertoire of the La Tène artist. In Britain no well-established schools are known to have existed at this time but a few of the dagger sheaths bear simple decoration. Those from the Thames at Windsor and at Wandsworth have openwork chapes while the entire scabbard from the Thames at Hammersmith is formed in an openwork technique (Figure 16.14, p. 422). These pieces show a high degree of skill but are hardly comparable to the decorative art style appearing at this time on the European mainland.

Much has been written on the problem of British La Tène art and its relationship to Continental styles. De Navarro, basing his work on the scheme created by Paul Jacobsthal, divided the British finds into four styles which he numbered I–IV. This terminology has been revised by Stead (1985b) who has extended it by adding a Style V. Stead's scheme provides a simple classification which helps to place individual pieces in a broad chronological context.

Style I is characterized by motifs of recognizable Greek ancestry incorporating palmettes flanked by lotus flowers. Few objects decorated in this style are known in Britain. The scabbard from Minster Ditch, near Oxford, with its somewhat halting attempts at a flowing pattern (Figure 17.22), is close to the early Continental style though evidently of local manufacture, but by far the most impressive of the early British pieces is the scabbard of a dagger found in the Wisbech area, Cambs. (Figure 17.23). It is decorated in the rocked tracer technique with a palmette flanked by lotus petals or lyres. The same motifs, though in more elaborate combinations, decorate the flange of a bronze lid from a cist grave at Cerrig y Drudion, Clwyd (Stead 1982). This last item is particularly interesting in that it may be an import; such pieces would have inspired native craftsmen, like those who made the Minster Ditch and Wisbech scabbards, in their experiments which created the first insular La Tène art style in Britain.

Figure 17.22 Bronze dagger sheath from Minster Ditch, Oxford (actual length of sheath: 350 mm) (photo: Ashmolean Museum, Oxford).

Figure 17.23 Top of the bronze dagger sheath from Wisbech, Cambs. (actual length: 127 mm) (photo: Wisbech Museum).

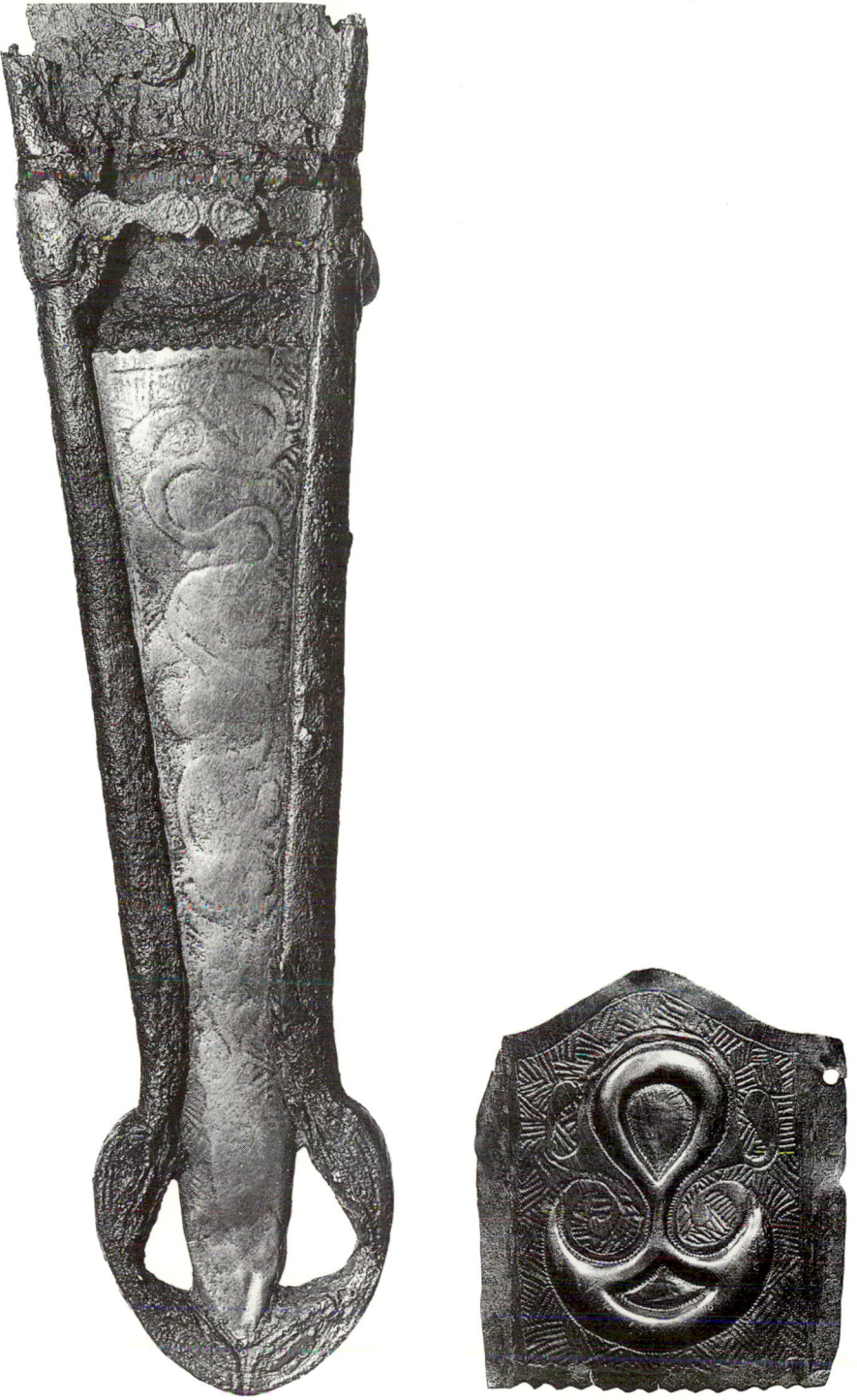

Figure 17.24   Top and bottom plates of bronze from a sword sheath from Standlake, Oxon. (actual width of top plate: 50 mm; actual length of bottom plate illustrated: 150 mm) (photo: Ashmolean Museum).

Style II derives its inspiration from the Continental 'Waldalgesheim Style' and is characterized by running scrolls of linked fleshy triangles in vogue on the Continent in the fourth and early third century BC. The best example from Britain is the more assured and elegantly worked sword scabbard from Standlake, Oxon. (Figure 17.24) (Case 1949). Although probably of British manufacture, several structural details – such as the iron chape-binding – are comparable to Continental examples of the middle La Tène period, suggesting a close relationship with European developments. The tip-plate too, worked in a pelta with end scrolls, dimly reflects the split palmette motif of mature Waldalgesheim work but is infinitely superior in quality to the first falterings of the Minster Ditch example. Other British examples include the heavy cast bronze bracelet from a burial at Newnham Croft, Cambs., and the bronze pommel fitting (or 'horn cap') from Brentford.

British Style III, which corresponds to Jacobstahl's 'plastic style' and 'sword style', is not well represented in Britain. Two brooches, from Danes Graves, Yorks., and Newnham Croft, Cambs., both with high relief carving on their bows can, however, be regarded as a pale British reflection of this otherwise vigorous Continental tradition, while from the Thames at Hammersmith were recovered two swords the sheaths of which were decorated with 'dragon pairs' (Stead 1984b). This motif is found throughout Europe and may ultimately have developed in Hungary influenced by patterns in vogue among the Thracian artists in what is now Bulgaria.

By the second century BC schools of native craftsmen were producing highly accomplished works of art which can be classed as Style IV. Of these the famous parade shield dredged up from the river Witham in Lincolnshire in about 1826 (Figure 17.25) is perhaps the most remarkable for the bringing together in one harmonious work of a number of isolated themes, some of them archaic, which ultimately derive from southern Gaul and Italy (Jope 1971). There can be little doubt of its local British production, for several peculiarities of the decoration can be found on earlier works in the area and continue to appear on later products.

The same river has yielded another superb example of decorative art of much the same period in the form of a bronze mounting from the mouth of a scabbard. Like the shield, the Witham scabbard involves the same combination of gentle three-dimensional moulding and delicate incised curvilinear designs carefully planned with a great love of the asymmetric. These themes recur on two shield bosses recovered from the Thames at Wandsworth (Figures 17.26 and 17.27) which, though of the same date range or a little later, are evidently the work of different craftsmen. Of the two mountings the circular boss (Figure 17.26) is the most dramatic, its surface decorated with a pair of great birds, wings outstretched and tail feathers trailing behind, each so arranged and selectively illustrated as to be a mirror image of the other. With its careful use of repoussé and incised ornament, this must be considered among the masterpieces of British Celtic art.

To this same tradition of second-century aristocratic art must be added the so-called Torrs chamfrein from Kirkcudbrightshire (Figure 17.28) which now, as the result of detailed study, can be seen to be a pony cap to which two horns have subsequently been attached (Atkinson and Piggott 1955). The cap itself is decorated in repoussé with bilaterally similar patterns based on the open-looped pelta motif, each ending in a superbly executed bird's head with evident similarities to the Wandsworth shield boss. The two bronze horns found with the pony cap may well originally have served as terminals for drinking horns. Both end in recurved birds' heads moulded in relief, originally with inset eyes of glass or coral, not at all unlike the repoussé birds' heads depicted on the cap. The sides of the horns were decorated with finely incised symmetric curvilinear designs, many details of which – particularly the use of tightly coiled spirals to fill in

Figure 17.25   Bronze shield from the river Witham in Lincolnshire (actual length: 1.12 m) (photo: British Museum).

Figure 17.26   Bronze shield boss from the river Thames at Wandsworth (actual length: 360 mm) (photo: British Museum).

Figure 17.27 Detail of incised and repoussé decoration on a circular bronze shield boss from the river Thames at Wandsworth (overall diameter of boss: 325 mm) (photo: British Museum).

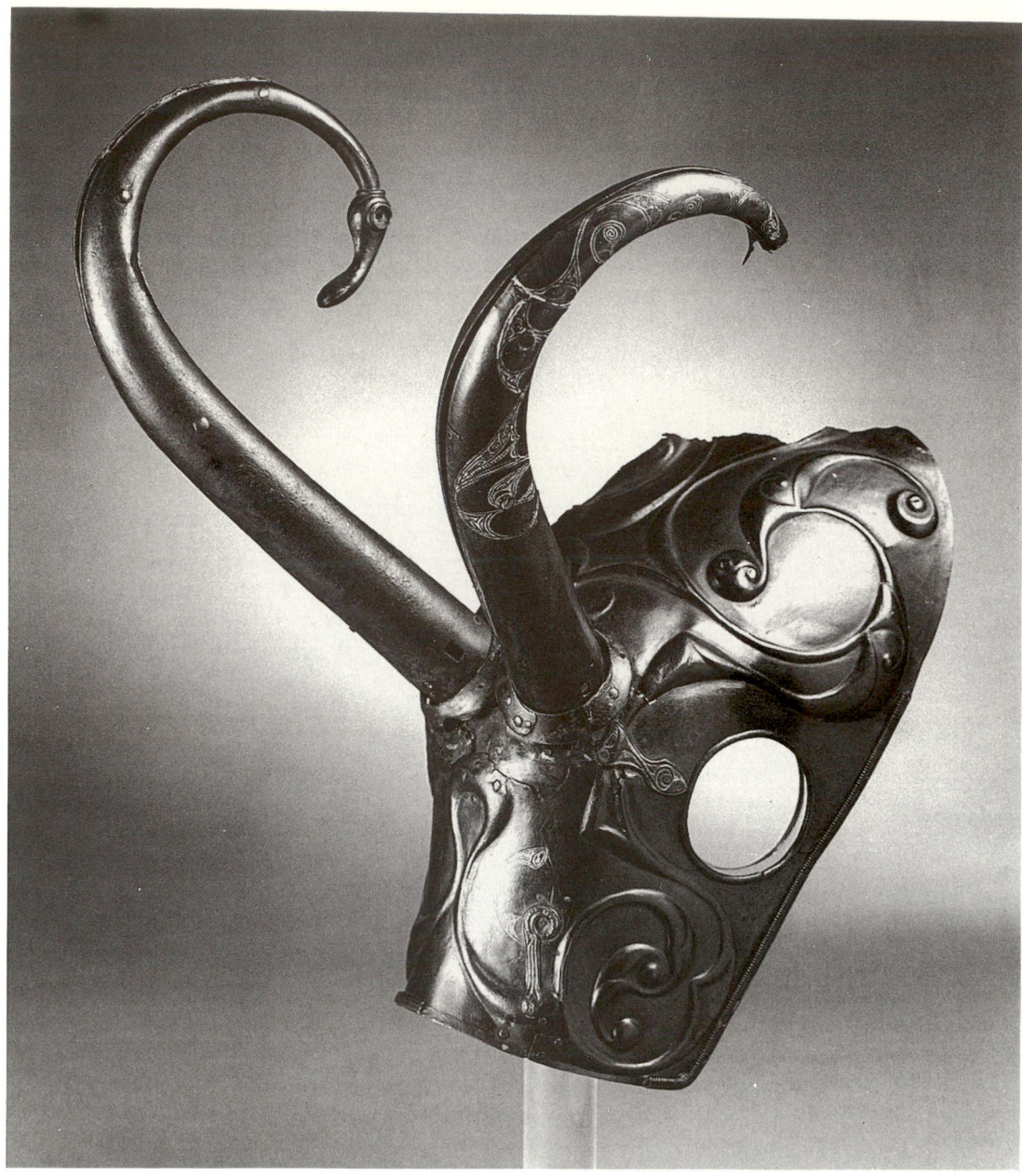

Figure 17.28   The Torrs pony cap, Kirkcudbrightshire, Scotland. The cap is shown here with horns, once terminals of drinking horns, attached. The horns do not belong to the cap as it was originally designed for use (photo: National Museums of Scotland, Edinburgh).

the leaves – can be paralleled on the other objects decorated in the Witham–Wandsworth tradition.

The pieces belonging to the Witham–Wandsworth–Torrs group described here are the major items of an artistic tradition, centred in the east of England, which was providing articles of display for the aristocratic market in the second century BC. The fineness of the craftsmanship and delicacy of the material leaves little doubt that these objects were created for parade purposes under the patronage of very wealthy clients. That all of them ended up in rivers or bogs suggest that after their earthly uses they were eventually dedicated to the gods.

From the beginning of the first century BC the volume of insular art increases dramatically and is sufficiently different to what has gone before to warrant a separate stylistic designation – Style V – characterized by tendrils and shapes which are more curvilinear. Tendrils often terminate in trumpet shapes reminiscent of birds' heads and there is now a careful play made between the shape of the motif and the enclosed spaces of the background (Stead 1985b, 22). Many different classes of objects were ornamented in this style: scabbards, shield bosses, mirrors, torcs and a variety of horse gear. Style V was truly *the* style of the British Late Iron Age.

The production of parade gear continued throughout the first centuries BC and AD. Two famous pieces, the helmet from Waterloo Bridge and the shield from Battersea, both dredged up from the Thames, serve as a demonstration. The Waterloo Bridge helmet (Figure 17.29), found in 1868, consists of a cap made from sheets of repoussé-decorated bronze to which are attached two horns also of sheet bronze, each terminated by a separately cast button. The decoration, of slack asymmetric tendril motifs partially filled in with areas of hatching carried out with a rocked tracer tool, was constructed around six discs scored to take roundels of red enamel or cupric glass. Stylistic similarities between the helmet decoration and a group of gold torcs found in eastern England would suggest a date in the first century BC.

The Battersea shield came to light in 1857 and has been subject to an exhaustive analysis (Stead 1985a) which leaves entirely open the question of date. However, while it shows a certain overall similarity to the Witham shield, the waisted form of the body and the rigid symmetrical design suggest Roman influence. Similarly, the technique of pressing semi-molten red glass into the openwork roundels, which are then attached by means of pitch and rivets, is more appropriate to the immediate pre-Roman period. If this late dating is accepted then the Battersea shield can be seen to be one of the last of the great parade artworks to be made before the conquest; it would stand at the end of a tradition lasting at least three centuries which must have provided a livelihood for generations of master-craftsmen, as well as inspiration for many lesser men.

The works which have been mentioned so far were essentially the masterpieces of the east British workshops but it would be wrong to give the impression that all art was the preserve of the very wealthy. Throughout the first centuries BC and AD there developed a large number of centres producing specialized artefacts, sometimes enlivened with decorative motifs, which would have been within the aspirations of a much larger percentage of the population. Swords provide a good illustration of the point. From the fourth century swords came back into fashion once more, replacing daggers as the general purpose weapon (Figure 17.30). Stylistic and structural consideration of the later Iron Age sword types has allowed a number of groups to be recognized, each occupying a fairly distinct geographical region (S. Piggott 1950). Some types had a much wider distribution than others and many styles, once developed, remained in use up to the time of the Roman Conquest, but there can be little doubt that several well-defined regional schools were at work serving the needs of their local communities. Some swordsmiths

Figure 17.29   Bronze helmet from the river Thames at Waterloo Bridge (actual size 205 mm in diameter at base) (photo: British Museum).

were sufficiently proud of their work to stamp their blades with identifying marks like the boar figures on the swords from Isleham, Cambs., and West Row, Suffolk (Stead 1985b, 49–50).

Much the same pattern is suggested by the study of other luxury goods. Brooches, mirrors, tankards, bowls and a wide range of harness-trappings must all have been produced by specialist craftsmen skilled in the art of bronze-work and enamelling, and capable of practising, and sometimes developing, the elements of the insular British art style. Where and how these men worked is at present uncertain but the discovery of bronze-worker's tools at South Cadbury, Somerset, points to the existence of a workshop inside the hillfort and a survey of sheet bronze-working has suggested a distinct concentration on hillforts including Danebury and Maiden Castle (Northover 1988). In all probability, each of the large nucleated centres was capable of supporting one or more full-time specialists, but this need not imply that all craftsmen were attached to sedentary communities. The occasional discovery of hoards of scrap metal like that from Ringstead in Norfolk and the foundry waste discovered at Gussage All Saints, Dorset, and Beckford, Heref. and Worcs., is a reminder that the itinerant craftsman may well have continued to play a part in late pre-Roman Iron Age society.

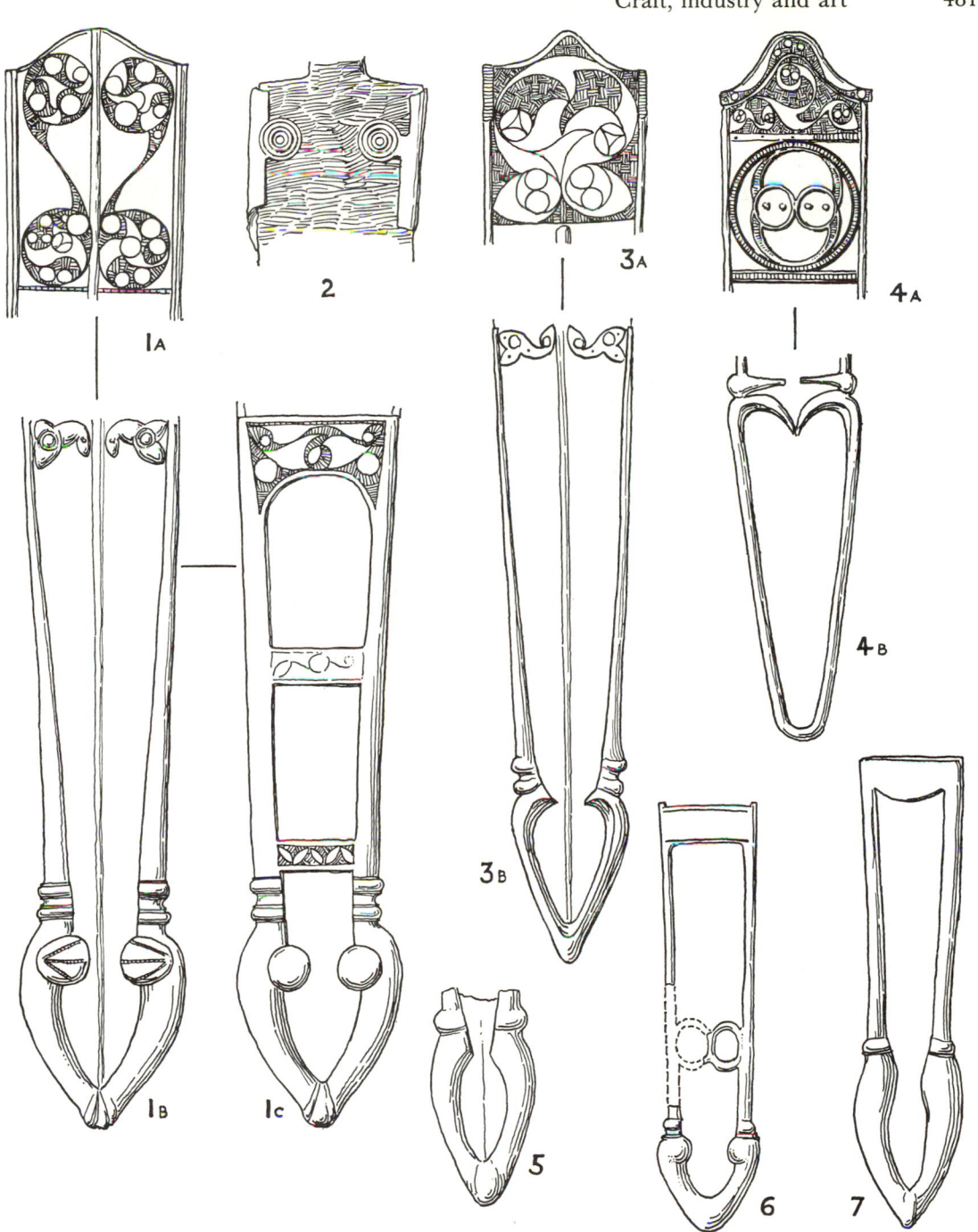

Figure 17.30   British La Tène swords. 1,2 Hunsbury, Northants.; 3 Meare, Somerset; 4 Amerden, Bucks.;
5 Woodeaton, Oxon.; 6,7 Spettisbury Rings, Dorset (source: reproduced from S. Piggott 1950).

Among certain classes of metalwork it is at last becoming possible to distinguish the products of specific workshops, if not of individual craftsmen. A dramatic illustration of this is provided by the torcs of gold and electrum found mainly in eastern England in three famous hoards at

Figure 17.31 Gold torcs from the Ipswich hoard (various scales but approx. 185 mm in maximum diameter) (photos: British Museum).

Snettisham, Norfolk, Ipswich, Suffolk (Figure 17.31), and Ulceby, Lincs., and as isolated finds at Bawsey, Sedgeford (Figure 17.32) and North Creake, also in Norfolk (Sealey 1979). Others have come from further afield, from Clevedon, Somerset, Needwood and Glascote (Tamworth), Staffs., and Netherurd, Peebles. (Figure 17.33). The actual form of the torcs varies: they may be tubular, of twisted rods, plaited rods or braided strands, while the terminals are either of plain loops or decorated with cast curvilinear ornament.

A range of structural and stylistic peculiarities serves to interrelate the group so closely that it is difficult not to consider them as the work of one school. On those with decorated terminals, for example, there are three distinctive elements: curved ridges, filling in the style of 'matting' and small spherical bosses sometimes decorated with finely executed punch-marks, while notched ridges occur less frequently. These stylistic tricks are found on all except the examples from Bawsey and Ulceby. But the Bawsey torc, with its simple two-strand twisted body and plain loop terminals, is of a kind found in the Ipswich hoard, while of the two torcs from Ulceby one, with

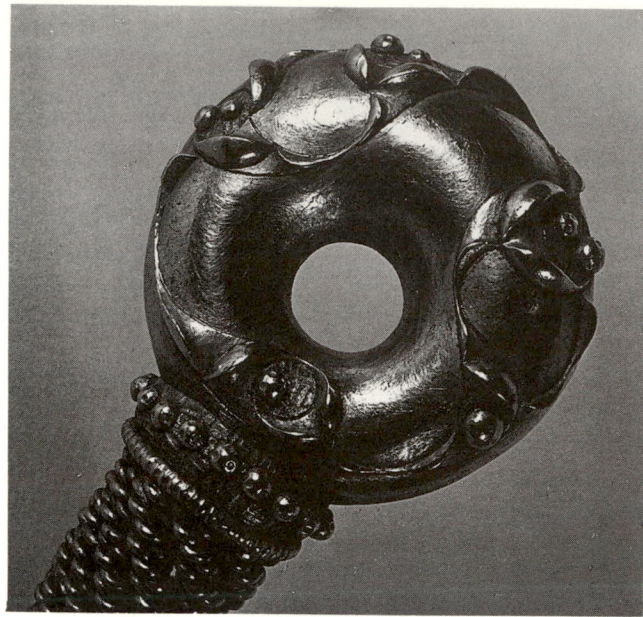

Figure 17.32   Terminal of gold torc from Sedgeford, Norfolk (photo: British Museum).

double-loop terminals, is paralleled at Snettisham, the other of plaited rods is similar to one found in the Ipswich hoard. Admittedly, the structural similarities are less decisive than the decorative links but the overall impression to be gained from these comparisons is of a single production centre in the first century BC specializing in the manufacture of gold-work for the immensely rich aristocratic market of East Anglia. The fact that the Waterloo Bridge helmet shares many decorative techniques in common with the torcs might hint at some diversification of output.

A rather less exotic class of neck-rings, somewhat later in date than the Snettisham–Ipswich types, can be defined in the south-west (Megaw 1971): these have been called the Wraxall class, after the best example of the group. Their main characteristic is that the neck-rings were cast in two separate halves which were then hinged together at one end and provided with a simple clasp at the other. The cast decoration was further enhanced with incisions to bring out the main theme of elongated S-curves set against dot-filled backgrounds. In all, some seven examples are known, all single finds and all coming from south-west Britain: one from Somerset, one from Wales, one from Cornwall and four from Dorset. Together they must represent the output of a somewhat second-rate workshop producing for a local market probably in the first century AD.

These two examples, the East Anglian gold torcs and the south-western bronze neck-rings, show that the regional distributions of some of the craft schools or workshops are capable of definition by stylistic analysis where sufficient distinctive material is available. By the first century AD, however, the workshops had proliferated to such an extent that copying between one craftsman and another had become widespread and it is doubtful if the work of many more of the individual schools will ever be isolated with any degree of certainty.

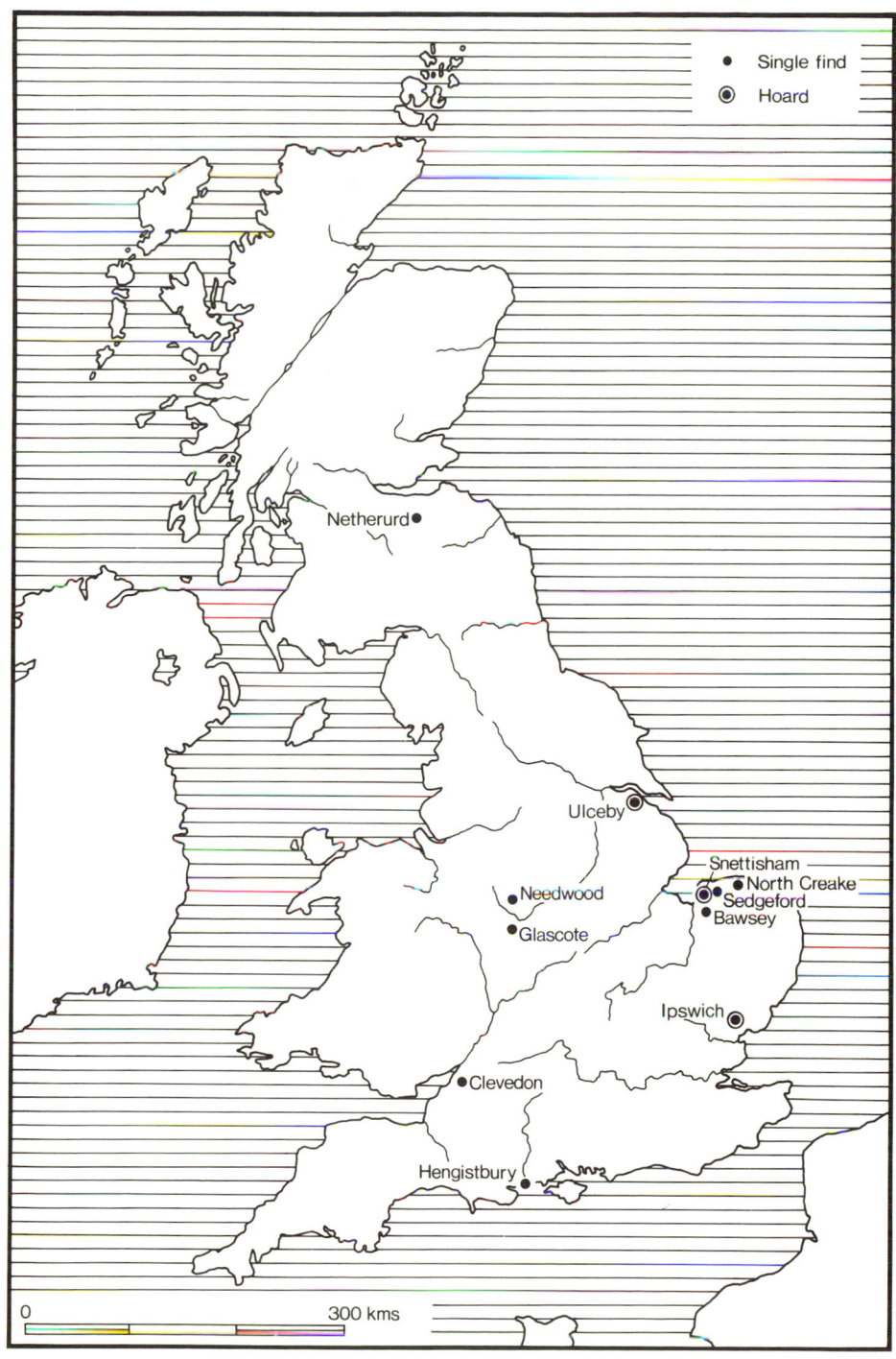

Figure 17.33   Distribution of gold and electrum torcs (source: author).

Figure 17.34 The craftsmanship of the die cutter as exemplified by British coins. 1 Atrebatic uninscribed gold stater; 2 Cunobelin bronze unit; 3 Cunobelin gold stater; 4 Caratacus silver unit. Twice actual size (photos: Institute of Archaeology, Oxford).

Coinage

The production of coinage, which became increasingly common after the beginning of the first century BC, must have involved the work of specialists. Whether or not metal was extracted by them is a matter for debate but the cupellation hearths and block of copper-silver alloy found at

Hengistbury Head, Dorset, might have resulted from the activities of moneyers. Their principal task would have been the measuring of the correct amounts of raw metal and the production of blanks by melting down the mixture in the clay 'coin moulds', examples of which have appeared on a number of sites. The blanks would then have been struck individually between dies. The basic production method required relatively little technical skill but analytical work has shown that great care was taken to control the actual metal content, the relative proportions of gold, silver and copper being adjusted to obtain the desired colour (Van Arsdell 1989). Weights were also very finely controlled, the progressive diminutions being so slight as to be unnoticeable. Die cutting was also in the hands of men of great skill and while it was once thought that the classical motifs, favoured by Tincommius and Verica, implied Roman or Gaulish die-cutters it can now be shown that the design and creation of the dies used in Britain was almost certainly the work of British craftsmen (Van Arsdell 1989).

Not all coins were struck; some were cast in clay moulds none of which survive, but a study of the Potin coins of Kent (D.F. Allen 1971; Van Arsdell 1983, 1984) has suggested the use of relatively simple multiple moulds, which would allow a strip of coins to be cast in one process. For the conventional types of cast coins, however, more complex techniques must have been adopted.

The production of coins was the last of the craft skills to be developed in Britain before the Roman Conquest. It embodied old techniques such as the extraction, alloying and casting of metal, but in addition it required much that was new: careful measurement, the development of engraving – often of high artistic merit – and an awareness of literacy. The sophistication of techniques fossilized in the production of a coin symbolized the complexity of the social and economic system for which the artist–craftsman of the first century AD was now working.

18
Warfare

'The whole race', wrote Strabo, 'is war mad, high-spirited and quick to battle.' This generalized picture of the Celt is one repeated many times by other classical writers and there is no reason to suppose that the British tribes were in any way different: weapons are not infrequently found, massive fortifications abound and bodies with battle wounds are by no means uncommon (Dent 1984). Here we will review some of the evidence for the aggressive nature of British Iron Age communities.

Weapons

The principal weapons were swords and daggers, spears and slings. In Britain swords have a long ancestry: fine examples were being manufactured in bronze in many parts of Britain, particularly the south-east, throughout the Late Bronze Age and as we have seen above (pp. 407–11) the introduction of the Hallstatt C Gündlingen type in the seventh century was widely accepted by British swordsmiths who soon responded by developing variants of their own. How long these Hallstatt long swords continued in use it is impossible to say on the evidence from Britain alone. There is no reason to suppose that they were short-lived, but on the Continent, in late Hallstatt and early La Tène times (c. 600–450 BC), daggers and short swords were more frequently found accompanying warrior burials. Short swords are rare in Britain but daggers seem to have become popular among the aristocracy as the remarkable collection of high quality weapons recovered from various parts of the Thames amply demonstrates (pp. 470–3). It is possible, therefore, that fashions in Britain followed those of the Continent.

By the end of the fifth or beginning of the fourth century, long swords, now of iron, became common again and from this time forward the sword was once more the principal weapon. The early swords of La Tène I type were comparatively short, measuring between 50 and 65 cm long but by La Tène III times the norm was from 70–90 cm. There was also a change in shape. The earlier varieties had tapering blades with long sharp points designed for both thrusting and slashing, while the later swords, with their longer parallel sided blades, were better adapted for slashing. Clearly a change in fighting methods is indicated. One possibility is that the La Tène III slashing sword was designed for fighting from horseback. The mounted warrior is depicted on several British coins and Gaulish cavalry were a great nuisance to Caesar during his campaigns in France in the mid-first century BC.

In Britain most of the known swords have been recovered from rivers where they were ritually deposited, but a few warrior burials have been discovered (pp. 508–9). These provide some indication of the normal equipment of the warrior. At Grimthorpe, Yorks., and Owslebury, Hants., each dead man was accompanied by his sword, spear and shield; at North Grimston, Yorks., the burial contained two swords and a shield; at Whitcombe, Dorset, and five graves from Burton Flemming (North Humberside) a sword and a spear, but no shield, were interred; another of the Burton Flemming graves, however, was accompanied by a sword and seven spears (Stead 1985b, 44). Of the two male burials with vehicles from Wetwang Slack, Yorks., one was equipped with a sword, seven spears and a shield, the other with a sword and possibly a shield. The sample is too small to allow patterns of grave sets to be recognized but the norm of sword, shield and one or more spears is clear enough.

Spears, javelins and lances feature prominently in the archaeological record and are illustrated on some British coins. Caesar also makes specific reference to them in his conquest of Britain (*BG* IV, 24). The spear thrown in volleys at the beginning of an engagement was an effective weapon for it could not only maim and kill but, by piercing the shields of the defenders and remaining lodged there, it could greatly encumber the opponent and might cause him to throw away his shield. Thus the prime function of the spear was for use as an artillery weapon in the opening stages of an engagement. The lance, used for thrusting, was essentially a cavalry weapon and as such is sometimes depicted on coins.

The other weapon of considerable importance in southern Britain was the sling. Slings could easily and cheaply be made from a strip of leather while ammunition, usually rounded pebbles from rivers or beaches, was readily available. The prime purpose of the sling seems to have been as a defensive weapon, frequently associated with hillforts. Huge hoards of slingstones have been found in pits close to the main entrances of Maiden Castle and Danebury while the defence of the gates of both forts, and no doubt others, was greatly enhanced by carefully placed platforms from which bands of slingers could command the approaches. The sling could be used in two modes, swung in a vertical plane it could send volleys of stones into the air to rain down on attackers at some distance, while used in a horizontal swing stones could be sent at considerable velocity into a body of troops accurately at head height with devastating effect.

It seems quite probable that the sling came into its own in Britain in the Middle Iron Age in parallel with the emergence of strongly defended hillforts and it has long been argued that multivallation was a local response to the increasingly sophisticated use of the sling. The earliest evidence for the widespread use of slings in relation to hillforts, however, comes from Danebury where large quantities of slingstones have been recovered from just behind the ramparts in a fifth-century BC context. Slingstones, sometimes of baked clay, occur at earlier dates on settlement sites but these could have been used in more domestic pursuits such as hunting or driving off predators from flocks and herds.

The popular image of the Celt in battle is of a naked warrior protected only by his shield, helmet and neck torc, a vision based on certain classical references and also upon depictions on Celtic coins and Greco-Roman sculpture. To what extent this practice was adopted in Britain we will never know, but the existence of shields and helmets is well attested. The Iron Age shield was made of leather or wood or a resilient combination of the two and in rare occasions was faced with bronze as for example in the case of the shields from Witham, Battersea and Chertsey. In shape they were invariably sub-rectangular or oval. They were held in the left hand by means of a centrally placed grip fixed across a circular opening which was covered by an umbo of wood, leather or metal to protect the knuckles. In British contexts the only surviving parts are the metal fittings, edge binding of bronze, umbos of bronze or iron and, rarely, the facing sheets of bronze. Strictly speaking we should distinguish two types of shield – the functional shield of wood and leather with plain metal fittings like those found in the warrior burials and the parade shield faced with bronze and with elaborately tooled bronze embellishments. The famous Battersea shield is the prime example of this type, so too are the elaborate shield bosses found in the river Thames at Wandsworth (Figures 17.26, p. 476 and 17.27, p. 477). Heavily adorned examples of this kind would have been too cumbersome for use in battle.

Of helmets we know comparatively little. Two have been found in Britain: the horned helmet from Waterloo Bridge and the helmet from the Meyrick Collection the provenance of which is unrecorded. Diodorus Siculus gives a vivid description of Celtic head gear.

On their heads they wear bronze helmets which possess large projecting figures lending the appearance of enormous stature to the wearer. In some cases horns form one piece with the helmet while in other cases it is relief figures of the fore parts of birds and quadrupeds.

Representations of helmets of this kind are clearly to be seen on a number of coins and, most dramatically, on the famous Gunderstrup cauldron from Denmark. The Waterloo Bridge helmet clearly fits with this general description and it is quite probable that many of the little bronze boar figures from Britain once adorned helmets to afford the wearers some symbolic protection (Foster 1977). As with the shields it is possible that we should distinguish between aristocratic parade helmets of bronze and more normal, functional, head protection of leather. A well-padded helmet of thick hide would have been far more effective in deflecting a blow than a thin sheet of bronze.

Diodorus Siculus also mentions that some of the Continental Celts wore chain mail for protection. A few examples have been found in Britain at the Lexden burial (pp. 137–40) and Kirkburn, near Garton Slack in Yorkshire.

One other weapon of warfare which should not be overlooked is noise. In his description of the battle of Telamon fought in Italy in 225 BC Polybius gives a frightening description of a pitched battle: The Roman forces, he tells us

were terrified by the fine order of the Celtic host, and the dreadful din, for there were innumerable hornblowers and trumpeters and, as the whole army were shouting their war-cries at the same time, there was such a tumult of sound that it seemed that not only the trumpeters and the soldiers but all the country round had got a voice caught up in the cry.

Diodorus Siculus provides a little more information about the war trumpets. 'They are of·a peculiar barbaric kind; they blow into them and produce a harsh sound which suits the tumult of war.' Clearly both writers are referring to the carnyxes so vividly illustrated on the Gunderstrup cauldron and less clearly on the coins of Tasciovanus, Cunobelin, Eppillus and Dubnovellaunus (D.F. Allen 1958, 44–5). Two actual examples are known from the British Isles, from the river Witham at Tattershall Ferry and from Deskford, Banff. (Figure 18.1) (S. Piggott 1959).

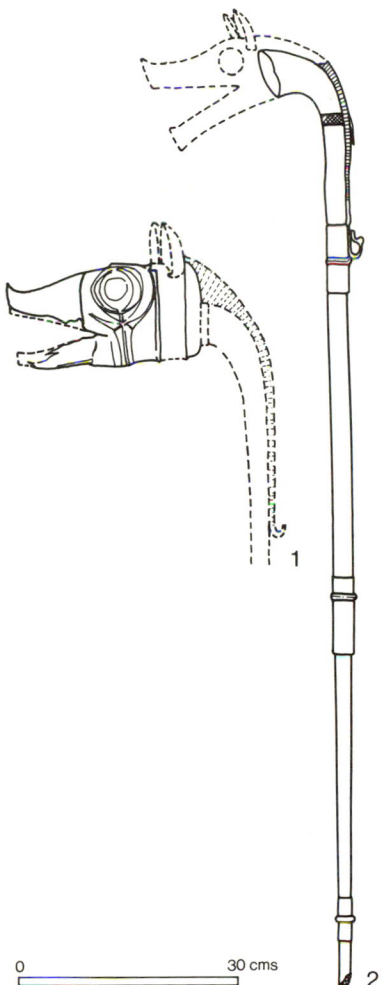

0 _____ 30 cms

Figure 18.1 War trumpets. 1 The head from Deskford, Banff restored as a carnyx-mouth; 2 the carnyx from Tattershall Ferry, Lincs. restored (source: S. Piggott 1959).

Chariots

The earliest first-hand account of Britons as a fighting force is provided by Julius Caesar describing his opening encounter in the summer of 55 BC.

> We ran the ships ashore on a flat and open beach. But the natives had discovered our intention. They had sent on ahead their cavalry and the chariots which they regularly use in battle. The rest of their troops came on behind and were stopping our men landing.
>
> (*BG* IV, 23–4).

From this succinct introduction, and from subsequent accounts, we can build up a clear impression of the tactics used by the inhabitants of south-east Britain in the mid-first century BC.

They possessed three forces: infantry, cavalry and charioteers, who seldom fought in close formation but usually attacked in open order interspersed with groups of reserves to cover the retreat or to relieve the fighters when they began to tire. Caesar found that fighting such a foe was difficult not least because he seems to have been unused to dealing with chariots which were deployed in large numbers: Cassivellaunus was said to have had 4,000 under his control. Admiration for the flexibility of the British chariot caused Caesar to pause in his narrative to give a detailed description of them which deserves quotation in full.

> These are the tactics of chariot warfare. First they drive in all directions hurling spears. Generally they succeed in throwing the ranks of their opponents into confusion just with the terror caused by their galloping horses and the din of the wheels. They make their way through the squadrons of their own cavalry, then jump down from their chariots and fight on foot. Meanwhile the chariot drivers withdraw a little way from the fighting and position the chariots in such a way that if their masters are hard pressed by the enemy's numbers, they have an easy means of retreat to their own lines. Thus when they fight they have the mobility of cavalry and the staying power of infantry: and with daily training and practice they have become so efficient that even on steep slopes they can control their horses at full gallop, check and turn them in a moment, run along the pole, stand on the yoke and get back into the chariot with incredible speed.
>
> (*BG* IV, 33).

British tribes were evidently wedded to this kind of warfare. Queen Boudicca relied on chariots to strengthen her rebellious army in AD 60, and in Scotland, twenty-five years later, Calgacus employed them in his final attempt to stop the army of conquest commanded by Agricola.

Archaeological evidence for chariots is widespread throughout the British Isles. Actual two-wheeled vehicles, possibly of the war chariot kind, have been recorded in a number of Yorkshire burials, most notably at Wetwang Slack and Garton Slack (below pp. 501–4), while metal fittings from the vehicles or their harnesses have been found in most regions (Figure 18.2). These include items such as linchpins, yoke mounts like the decorative bulls from Bulbury and the 'yoke terminals' from Brentford (Middx.), High Cross (Leicester) and Llyn Cerrig Bach. Several examples of nave bindings, also possibly from chariots, are known. Horse-trappings, including bridle-bits (Palk 1984), strap buckles, rings and the unique pony cap from Torrs (Kirkcudbright.) are even more widespread.

A fascinating insight into the social and technical background of chariots comes from the settlement site of Gussage All Saints, Dorset, where a dump of founders waste was found representing the manufacture of about fifty sets of vehicle and harness-fittings. This, combined with the evidence suggesting that young horses may have been rounded up for training, points to the possibility that the settlement was producing trained chariot teams and their vehicles, presumably as an input into the system of gift-exchange and patronage.

At what stage war chariots were introduced into Britain is unclear. Horse-riding and vehicles are well attested in the Hallstatt period (pp. 411–15) but there is no evidence to suggest that chariots were in use this early. It is more likely that the light two-wheeled vehicle was introduced during the La Tène I period in the late fifth or early fourth century. Thereafter, as we have seen, it remained in use into the first century AD in Scotland. In Ireland it survived for several centuries more.

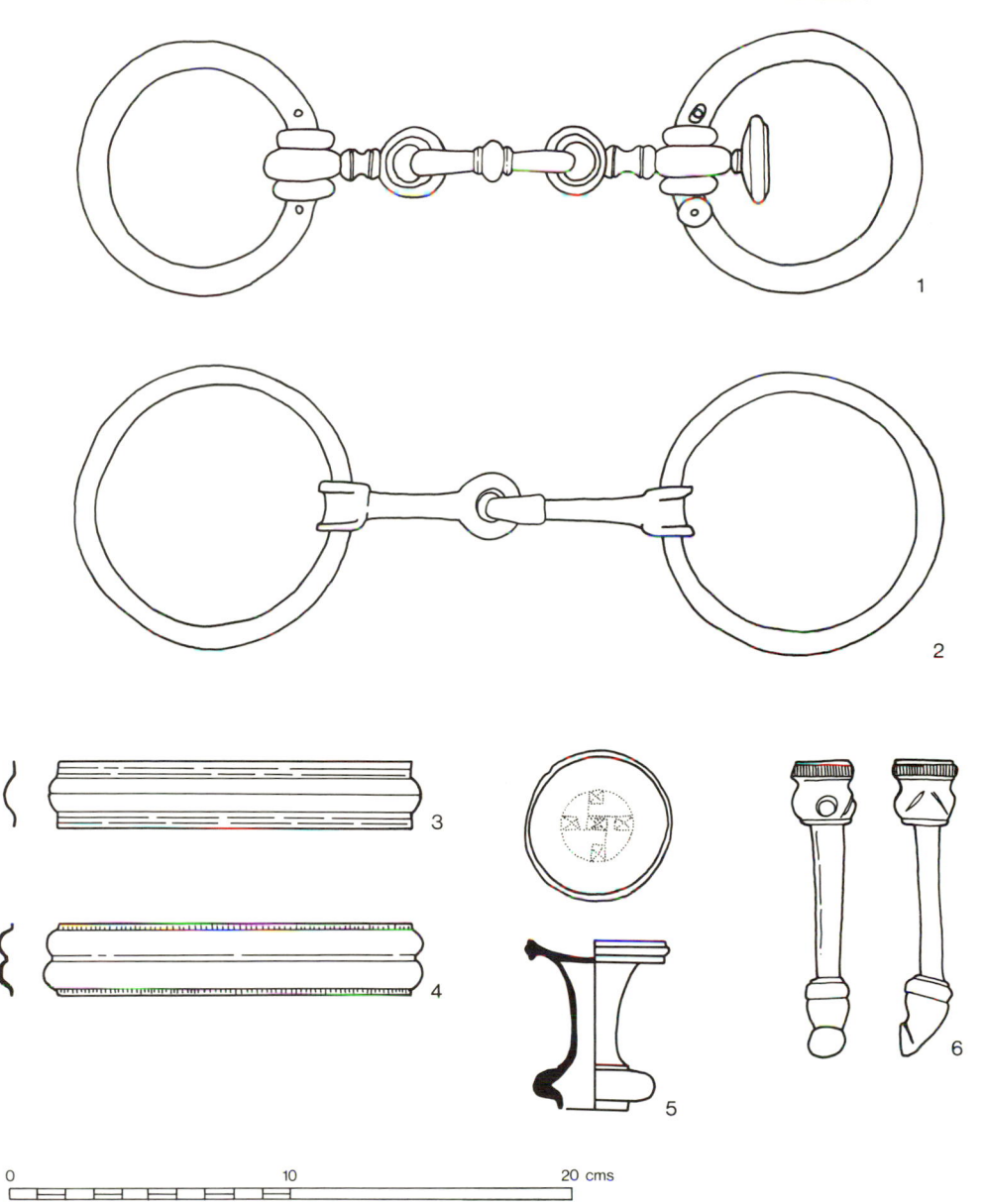

Figure 18.2 Chariot and harness fittings from Llyn Cerrig Bach, Anglesey. 1,2 Bridle-bits; 3,4 nave bindings; 5 yoke mount; 6 linchpin (source: C.F. Fox 1946).

Defensive architecture

In previous chapters we have considered in some detail the wide range of settlement enclosures found in various parts of Britain. These range from comparatively slight ditches defining settlement areas to the massive fortifications of hillforts like Maiden Castle. Enclosure itself does

Figure 18.3 Set of harness fittings found together in a house at Danebury, Hants. (photo: Institute of Archaeology, Oxford. Danebury Trust).

not necessarily imply the need for defence. Ditches and fences would have been erected for a variety of reasons ranging from the desire to keep domestic animals away from the settlement area to the social need to define status. The fact that 'defensive' enclosures tend to increase in number in most parts of the country through the Middle and Late Iron Age has frequently been ascribed to an increase in aggression: while this is most likely to be so, we must allow that other social explanations may have played a part.

This said, the hillforts do seem to be in a different category: choice of position, massiveness of defences and the sheer defensive ingenuity lavished on the entrances is sufficient to suggest that their enclosure works were designed to withstand attack. To this may be added the evidence for sling defence mentioned above. Caesar, writing of the Gauls and Belgae, provides a direct insight into the methods used by Celts to reduce a native hillfort.

> They begin by surrounding its entire wall with a large number of men and hurling stones at it from all sides. When this has stripped the wall of its defenders, they hold up their shields to provide a protective shell, set fire to the gates, and begin to undermine the wall.
>
> (*BG* II, 6)

The vulnerability of the gate, implied in this passage, explains why so much attention was paid to providing complex foreworks at many hillfort entrances in central southern Britain (Avery 1986).

That some of the forts actually came under attack is more difficult to prove but layers of burning associated with entrances and defences at several sites are suggestive. At Danebury, for example, both entrances showed signs of burning in the fifth century and at the end of the Middle Iron Age, *c.* 100 BC, the main east entrance was burnt again: thereafter the site was largely

Figure 18.4   Warriors on British coins. 1 Horseman with a carnyx, Tasciovanus gold stater; 2 horseman with sword and rectangular shield, Tasciovanus gold stater; 3 horseman with sword and round shield, Cunobelin bronze unit; 4 horseman, Epaticcus gold stater. Four times actual size (photos: Institute of Archaeology, Oxford).

abandoned. The burning of massive gate timbers 70 cm across could hardly have been accidental. But while the most likely explanation is enemy action we cannot completely rule out a symbolic act on the part of the community.

The nature of warfare

That the natives of Britain engaged in warfare before the arrival of Caesar is certain. The evidence of the hillforts alone is sufficient to show this and to this may be added several war cemeteries associated with hillforts (Whimster 1981, appendix L). In addition a number of isolated burials show evidence of wounding, sometimes fatal. Most dramatic are the burials from Burton Flemming and Wetwang Slack found with spearheads embedded in their body cavities (Dent 1984). Elsewhere, at Danebury, Rotherley, Gussage All Saints, Harlyn Bay, etc., wounds, usually to the head, are all too evident.

In what social context these injuries took place it is impossible to say with certainty, but something of the nature of Continental Celtic warfare can be deduced from the classical sources and this may have relevance to Britain. Warfare was endemic and could flare up at any time, but it was not the all-out, long-term affair we read of in Gaul at the time of Caesar's conquest: the presence of Roman armies of conquest created an unnatural situation.

Classic Celtic warfare was a means of establishing status. At an individual level it was the status of the war leader who could encourage an entourage to follow him in a successful raid; at the group level, it was a demonstration of the prowess of the tribe or clan in maintaining or extending the territorial boundaries in a manner considered to be appropriate to their standing. An example is provided by the Helvetii, who occupied modern Switzerland. They were hemmed in by natural barriers which 'meant that they could not range over a wide area and had great difficulty in making war on neighbouring tribes. Since the Helvetii enjoyed fighting they bitterly resented the restriction' (*BG* I, 2). Tacitus makes the same point about the Germans when he says that they regarded it as essential to their well-being that they maintained a zone of devastation around their borders.

Warfare, therefore, was in the form of a raid. Raids could be on an individual level against a specific settlement or group of settlements, they could be intertribal or they could range wider as did the Celtic war bands who left their homes in the Po valley and attacked the Roman sphere south of the Apeninnes in the fourth and third centuries. Whatever the scale, the aim was the same – the gaining of plunder and prowess.

The conduct of battle must have varied considerably with time and place. Raids against property would have led to attacks on farmsteads and hillforts, the circumstances dictating the progress. In more general conflict involving opposing forces in the open, a certain standard procedure can be discerned. The two hordes would face each other across a field of battle with the women and children behind the men, on baggage carts to get a good view of the proceedings. The conflict was opened with the warrior heroes from each side driving in their chariots along the enemy's front ranks hurling abuse and challenges. Then the field would clear so that individual contests between champions could begin. Once this stage was completed, either the result would be clear in which case the proceedings were at an end, or a general mêlée might break out. At any event hostilities would cease at nightfall.

Although there would have been frequent deviations from this norm, the model of the archaic Celtic battle, constructed from various classical sources, is likely to have held good in many regions distant from the distorting influences of the Mediterranean world. To what extent it was relevant to Britain it is impossible to say except to point out that the model is not dissimilar to the picture provided by the vernacular Irish literature of the first millennium AD.

It is difficult to bring the generalized Continental Celtic pattern of warfare into direct and useful juxtaposition with the archaeological evidence from Britain except possibly in relation to hillforts. Their development as defensive structures can strictly be divided into two phases, an early phase, roughly 600–400 BC when early hillforts were numerous and widespread, and a late phase c. 400–100 BC when a more restricted zone of strongly developed hillforts emerged. Since both types were (among other things) a response to warfare it could be argued that they bear witness to a phase of widespread but intermittent raiding covering much of the country, followed by a crystallizing out of socio-economic zones in one of which, the centre south, raiding persisted and even intensified, while in parallel there was a greater nucleation of power and population at fewer strongly defended locations. In such a scenario we might imagine allegiances between certain groups of hillforts, but a flexible pattern changing with time.

This is not to imply that the other socio-economic zones of Middle–Late Iron Age Britain were free from stress. The sword burials of Yorkshire and the speared bodies at Burton Flemming and Wetwang Slack indicate a level of aggression but this is impossible to quantify. Similarly the strongly defended homesteads stretching along the western seaboard of Britain and much of the north-east imply that defences were desirable but this may be more for social reasons than for military necessity. All we can safely say, therefore, is that while the inhabitants of Britain were in a perpetual state of endemic warfare the communities of the central southern zone enjoyed it to an aggravated degree.

The widespread abandonment of hillforts in the south-east in the first century BC presents an interesting phenomenon. It coincides both geographically and chronologically with the development of organized long-distance trade with the Continent. The most satisfactory way to explain this change is to suppose that the acquisition of rare prestige goods imported from the Continent provided a new and acceptable method of status display rendering obsolete traditional means based on warrior prowess. As the raiding party gave way to the trader's caravan so hillforts were abandoned in favour of markets at route nodes.

Beyond the coin-issuing zone of the south-east lay a vast tract of land untouched by the direct effects of the Late Iron Age trading systems. From this zone raw materials and manpower, in the form of slaves, would have been procured to feed the demands of the new south-eastern economic system. Thus raiding, now to provide slaves, would not only have continued but would probably have intensified. It is possible that the warrior burials of Yorkshire and the carved chalk figurines of warriors (Stead 1988) are a reflection of increasing aggression caused by these changes.

By the time that the Claudian armies sailed to Britain the communities of the south-east had lost much of their socially motivated aggression and were easily overrun within a year. Those to the north and west were made of sterner stuff: it was forty years before Rome could regard them as conquered.

19
Death and the gods

The evidence available for studying the religious beliefs and burial rituals of the Iron Age communities varies considerably both in volume and quality, and in its geographical spread over the country. There are three basic categories which can be called upon: direct archaeological data in the form of structures, cemeteries and ritual deposits; literary references concerned largely with the Druids; and less tangible assumptions which can be drawn from the limited place-name evidence and from the situation in the early years of the Roman occupation. Together this material offers the impression of a highly complex religious pattern pervading the everyday life of the people and ever present in the landscape.

Burial customs

It has frequently been said that little trace survives of the burials of the Iron Age period in Britain, and by comparison with the large cemeteries of Continental Europe, this might at first sight appear to be so, but when the material evidence is amassed, a well-defined series of ritual practices can be distinguished which can be seen to change with time and to show variation reflecting both long-established regional traditions and the external influences to which an area has been subjected (Whimster 1977; 1981).

The principal recognizable method of disposing of the dead in the first part of the first millennium BC was cremation, the ashes being buried, either urned or un-urned, in cemeteries which sometimes originated at the sites of older barrows. Occasionally ashes were buried under individual barrows, usually much smaller than those of the second millennium. These practices continued throughout the seventh, sixth and probably fifth centuries. Many urnfields show signs of continued use and, in all probability, most of the old-established burial grounds were maintained well into the fifth century. Since, however, many of the later cremations were buried without grave-goods or pottery containers, there is nothing with which they can be dated unless by a series of radiocarbon assessments.

The disposal of the dead in urns placed under small individual barrows is well attested in the seventh to fifth centuries. Sometimes cemeteries of barrows are found, like the small group of round barrows on Ampleforth Moor, Yorkshire (Figure 19.1), which have produced pottery characteristic of the seventh century together with two confirmatory radiocarbon dates. The barrows were simple, ranging from 7.3 to 9.7 m in diameter and less than 1.5 m high; each was surrounded by a shallow ditch. Burial was by means of cremation: each was placed in a small pit or scattered on the original ground-surface. Other apparently isolated barrow burials are known scattered over southern Britain. Beneath slight mounds at the Caburn, Sussex, Buntley and Creeting St Mary, Suffolk, and Warborough Hill, Norfolk, ashes have been found in pottery urns of the Kimmeridge–Caburn type, indicating a date in the seventh or sixth century. Burials of this kind are direct descendants from preceding Bronze Age traditions.

Inhumations of this early period are much rarer. One possible example has been found under a barrow at Beaulieu Heath in the New Forest, Hants. The barrow, barely 4.6 m in diameter and surrounded by an irregularly cut ditch, was built of turf and survived to a maximum height of 0.6 m. On the original ground-surface beneath the mound lay the remains of several wooden planks, a bronze ring, smaller fragments of bronze, two small pieces of iron and a sherd of a coarse shouldered jar of Early Iron Age type. While no interpretation can be offered with assurance, it is *possible* that the remains represent a cart burial of Hallstatt type, the bones of the inhumation having been totally destroyed by the acidity of the soil.

A second, though ill-recorded, inhumation burial was discovered at Ebberston in Yorkshire in 1861 and briefly reported to a meeting of the British Archaeological Association held in that year. The account describes a bronze sword (of Hallstatt C type) and its chape, found 'together with another sword and a quantity of human bones'. Both swords were broken into four pieces. It is impossible to be sure now of the nature of the find, but the apparent ritual breaking of the swords is a feature which can be paralleled among Continental burials and might be thought to support the idea that the Ebberston deposit was a genuine inhumation in Hallstatt C style. If so, it is the only example yet known in Britain.

A surprising difference exists between Britain and the Continent in the seventh and sixth centuries. On the Continent most of the Hallstatt swords known come from burials, whereas in Britain all except for Ebberston come from rivers. One possible explanation of this phenomenon is that in Britain the dead were cremated and disposed of, with their equipment, in rivers. This would account both for the riverine distribution of swords and chapes and the relative lack of burial grounds. Such a hypothesis is impossible to prove but the ritual is well attested among more recent primitive societies and need occasion no surprise.

By the fifth century it seems that cremation was being replaced by inhumation in some areas. In Yorkshire a new pattern of burial ritual is thought to have been introduced from France, presumably by a group of settlers, resulting in what has been called the Arras culture (pp. 77–9), which until recently was represented almost entirely by its burials (Stead 1979; Dent 1982, 1985). Three separate ritual practices are represented: the grouping together of small barrows in large cemeteries; the occasional rite of cart burial; and the practice of surrounding individual barrows with a rectangular ditched enclosure. Many barrow cemeteries are known (Figure 19.2), ranging from small clusters to larger groups such as Eastburn (75), Scorborough Park (170), Dane's Graves (up to 500), and Burton Fleming (500+). The individual barrows were usually small, up to 9 m in diameter, and normally covered crouched inhumations, although very occasionally extended inhumations and even cremations have been found. In many cases the barrows were surrounded by circular ditches but cemeteries of rectangular ditched barrows are becoming increasingly common as aerial surveys proliferate (Ramm 1978; Stead 1979, 29–35).[1]

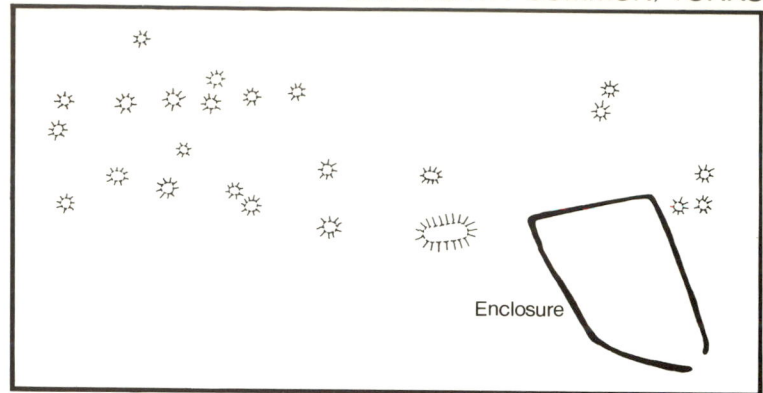

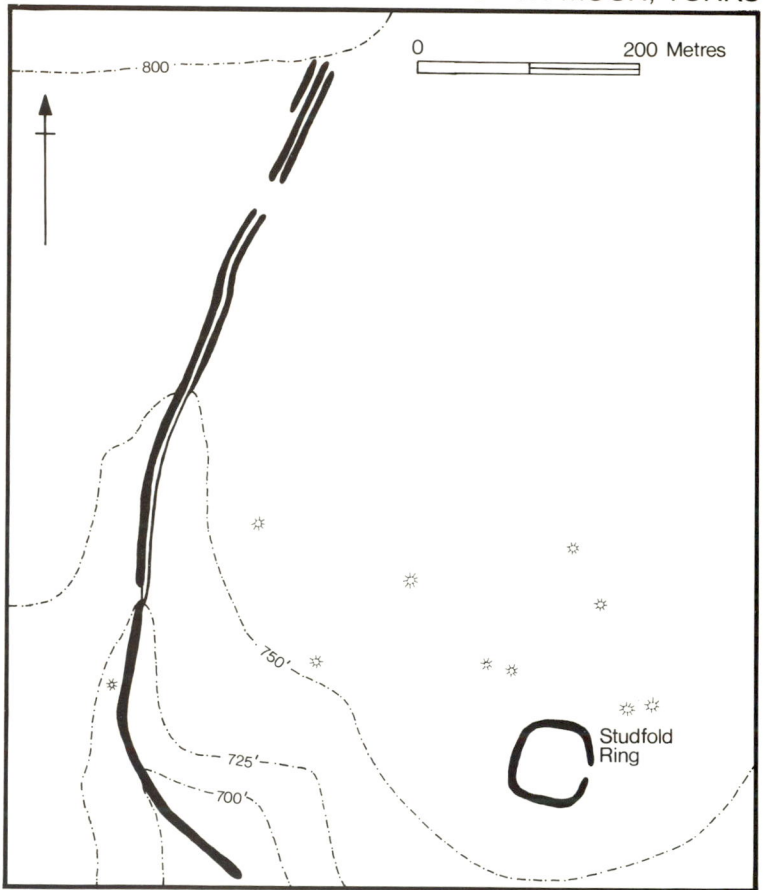

Figure 19.1 Yorkshire cemeteries (sources: *Skipworth Common*, Stead 1961; *Ampleforth Moor*, Wainwright and Longworth 1969).

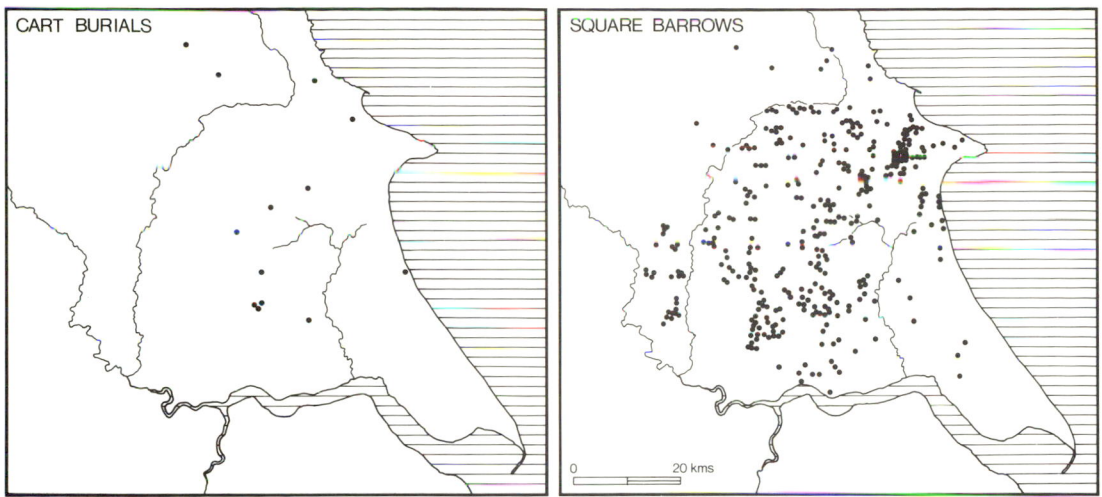

Figure 19.2   The Arras burials in Yorkshire (source: Ramm 1978 with amendments).

Generally the burials were without elaborate grave-goods but some were provided with brooches and joints of pork. Richer graves occur sporadically, and more rarely mortuary carts were buried with the dead.[2] The cart burial at Dane's Graves (Figure 19.3) lay beneath a barrow some 8.2 m in diameter in a rectangular grave-pit about 0.8 m deep and measuring 2.6 by 2.3 m. The deposits consisted of two crouched inhumations laid on the bottom of the pit together with the remains of a dismantled cart and several items of harness-fittings. The 'king's barrow' at Arras was a little larger, covering a circular grave-pit c. 3–3.5 m in diameter, in which had been placed a single extended inhumation with the bodies of two horses, one laid on either side. The wheels from the cart had been removed and propped against each of the horses while the harness-trappings, including two harness-loops, five terret-rings and two horse-bits, were placed together with the two linchpins in the western half of the grave. Close to the head of the burial had been placed two pigs' heads, presumably as an offering to the spirit of the deceased.

Another example of a cart burial, one of the few to be excavated under modern conditions, was found at Garton Slack, near Driffield, in 1971. Here the inhumed body had been placed on the bottom of the grave-pit and covered with the funerary cart. The two twelve-spoked wheels had been removed and laid on either side of the body. The grave-goods included the harness-trappings, consisting of two bits, five terret-rings and four buckles, a whip and a pig's head as an offering.

In 1984 three remarkable cart burials were discovered in close proximity to each other at Wetwang Slack (Figures 19.3 and 19.4). All three were buried in pits set beneath rectangular ditched barrows. In each case the body was flexed and was placed together with grave-goods in a box structure, presumably the body of the vehicle, above the two wheels of the cart which had been dismantled and laid side by side on the ground beneath. Burial 1, that of a young male, was accompanied by chariot- and harness-fittings, a long sword, seven spears, iron coverings for the spine of a wooden shield and the forequarters of a pig. In Burial 2, in addition to the vehicle and harness parts, there were personal possessions, including a mirror, a decorated bronze box of cylindrical form with a chain for suspension and a gold and iron pin decorated with coral. Two

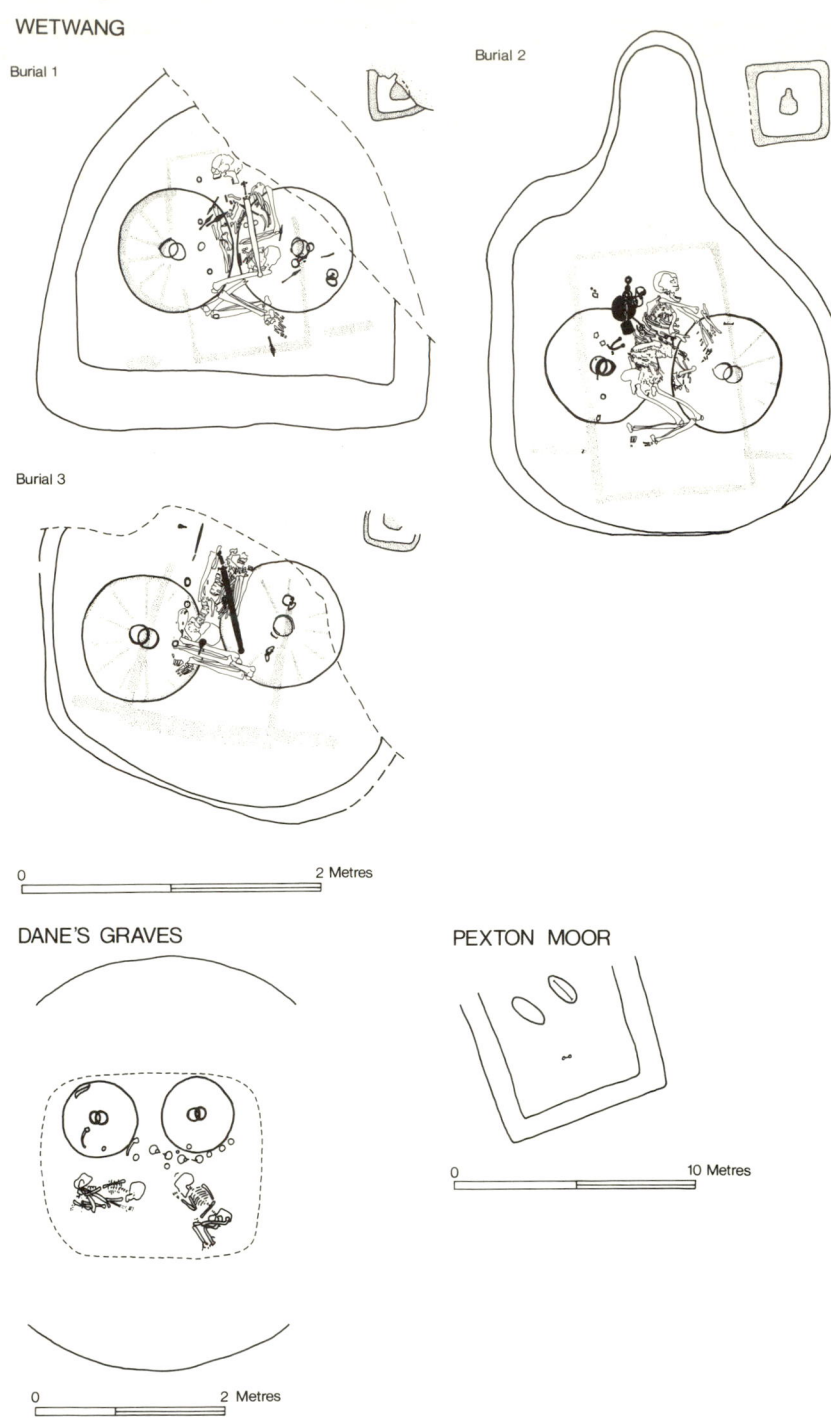

Figure 19.3 Vehicle burials from the Arras culture (sources: *Dane's Graves* and *Pexton Moor*, Stead 1965; *Wetwang Slack*, Dent 1985).

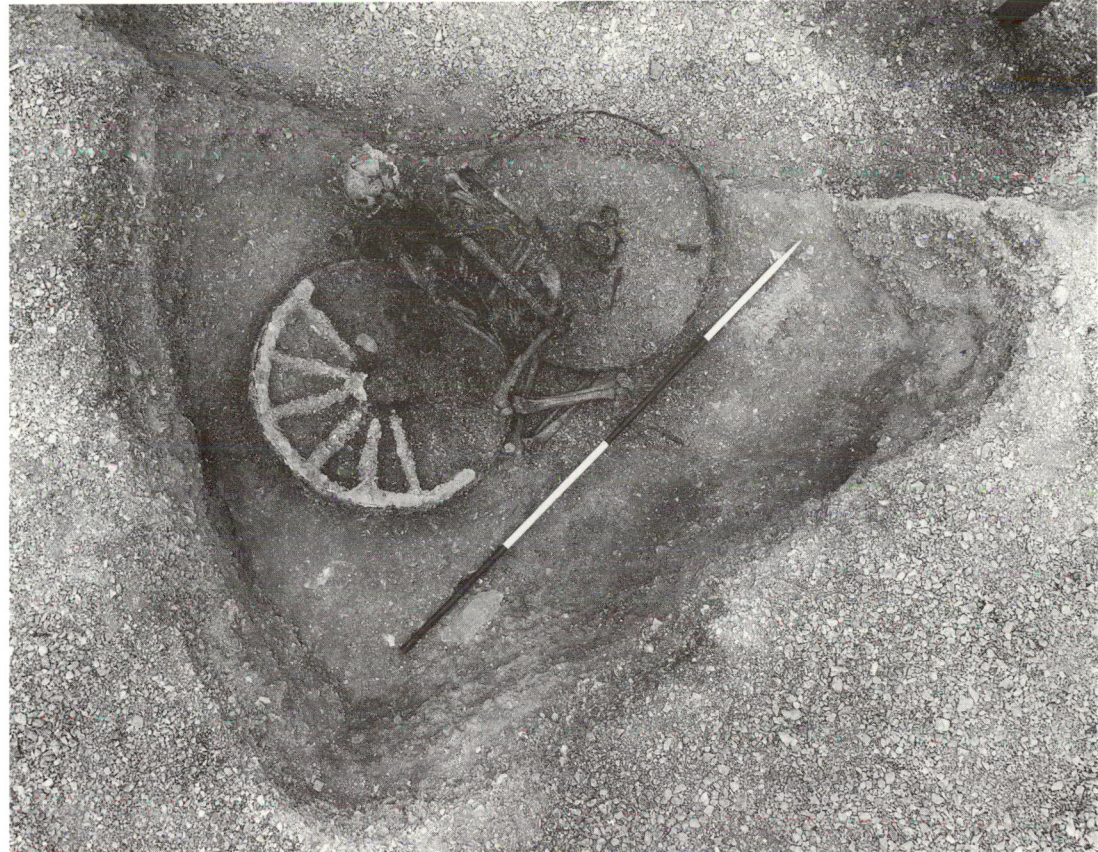

Figure 19.4 Burial from Wetwang Slack (photo: Bill Marsden).

forequarters of pig were placed over the stomach of the dead person. The third burial, like the first, was accompanied by weaponry – a large iron sword, together with its suspension rings and iron fittings for the shield. With such a comparatively small sample available for study generalizations are difficult, but it is tempting to contrast the warrior equipment of Burials 1 and 3 with the essentially female equipment of Burial 2. This might suggest that the vehicle rite was associated with status rather than gender.

Yet another vehicle burial was discovered in the same area at Garton Station in 1985. Here the ritual differed from the others mentioned in that the wheels were placed together upright against the side of the grave-pit. Most of the carts found in the Arras graves had been dismantled at the time of burial, but at Pexton Moor the cart was buried intact, with its wheels set into two oval pits dug into the bedrock (Figure 19.3). The barrow in this example was also surrounded with a rectangular ditched enclosure.

The principal elements of the Yorkshire cart burials can therefore be seen to be inhumation – either extended or contracted, the burial of the mortuary cart itself, the deposition of some or all of the harness-fittings, the occasional ritual sacrifice and burial of the horses and the provision of some personal ornaments and food offerings. These features can all be paralleled among

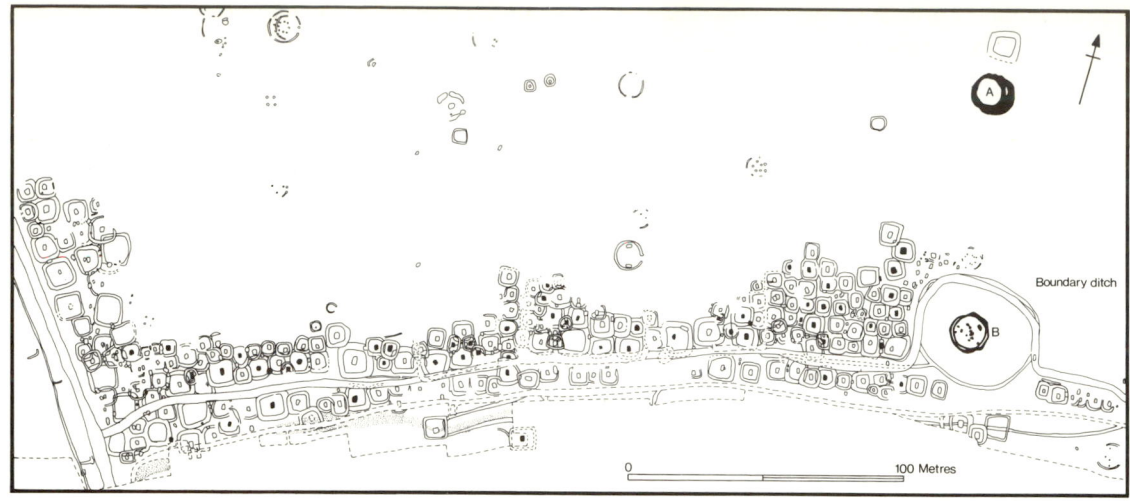

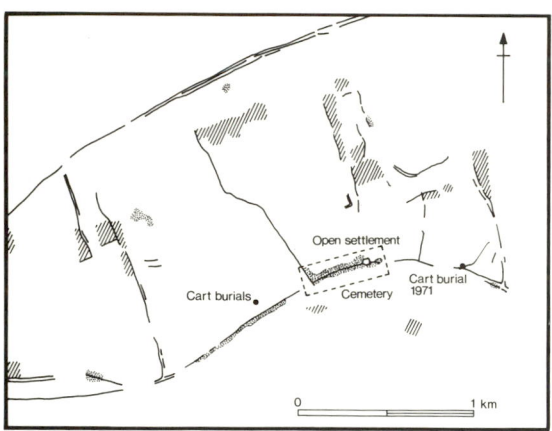

Figure 19.5   The cemetery and settlement at Wetwang and Garton Slack (source: Dent 1982).

contemporary Continental burials, but the rarity of pottery and weapons in the Yorkshire group serves to distinguish the area. It should, however, be stressed that the Wetwang Slack and Garton Slack cart burials were simply the elite element in a straggling cemetery running for more than a kilometre along the valley bottom (Figure 19.5), the 'normal' burial rite being simple inhumation in a small pit surrounded by a rectangular ditch. Grave-goods, if they occurred, were restricted to small items of personal equipment such as brooches.

Apart from the Arras group in Yorkshire, evidence for cart burial elsewhere in Britain is rare, though not entirely absent. At Mildenhall, Suffolk, an extended inhumation was found, possibly under a barrow, accompanied by a long iron sword, an axe and a gold torc and flanked by the skeletons of two horses. No fittings of a cart appear to have been found, but the discovery was made some years ago and is ill-recorded; the likelihood that significant details passed unnoticed is extremely high. An even more interesting burial was found at Newnham Croft, Cambs., where a contracted inhumation was recovered accompanied by three brooches, one of which was penannular, a bracelet, part of what may be the head-harness for a pony and four simple bronze rings. Dating cannot be precise but on stylistic grounds the decorated bracelet is thought to belong to the fourth or third century. Again, there is no positive evidence for a cart. A third example comes from Fordington, just outside Dorchester in Dorset, where the bones of a man and a horse were found in 1840 together with a bronze bit of Iron Age type. The fact that only three possible cart burials have been found outside Yorkshire is a fair indication that the rite was not widely adopted in Britain.

In western and northern Britain, inhumation burial was often in stone cists which were sometimes arranged in large cemeteries. In the south-west four substantial cemeteries have been found, at Mount Batten in Devon, and Harlyn Bay, Trelan Bahow and Trevone in Cornwall, but apart from a single cist excavated at Trevone in 1955, and the re-excavation of part of the Harlyn Bay cemetery (Whimster 1978), details of general cemetery layout and of the individual graves are inadequately recorded. Nevertheless, certain details emerge: the bodies were usually, though not invariably, buried in contracted positions in their stone-lined graves, and it would appear that the cists were sometimes arranged in rows. Grave-goods frequently accompanied the dead, but were usually restricted to personal equipment such as pins, bracelets and fibulae, though occasionally more expensive items such as mirrors, necklaces and bronze vessels were included. The surviving material from these sites in Devon and Cornwall would suggest a date range spanning the fourth century BC to mid-first century AD.

Cist burials are recorded sporadically from other parts of Britain. In Wales, for example, the famous bronze 'hanging bowl' (now thought to be the lid of a vessel) from Cerrig y Drudion, Clwyd, was found in a cist which may have been constructed originally for burial, while in Scotland many of the burials which can, on the basis of their grave-goods, be assigned to the Iron Age have been found in cists, either isolated or arranged in cemeteries as at Cairnconan, Angus. Inhumations of this kind continued in use into the second and third centuries AD.

Over much of south-east Britain, careful burial was by no means common before the first century BC. Indeed, evidence is now rapidly accumulating to suggest that some bodies were commonly disposed of with little recognizable ceremony. On a number of settlement sites, both open farms and hillforts, complete articulated bodies have often been found tucked away in disused storage pits (Figure 19.7). In most examples the body lies flexed, often quite tightly, on the pit bottom close against one side of the pit and in a number of the better excavated examples heavy stones have been recorded over the body. Occasionally these pit burials have been found to pre-date rampart extensions, as at Hod Hill and Maiden Castle in Dorset, in situations suggestive of foundation burial, but more normally pit burials are found scattered at random throughout the settlement areas. This rite was widespread throughout central southern Britain and appears to be represented in all areas where storage pits were dug.

A number of settlement sites in the south-east have produced evidence of what might superficially appear to be more casual treatment of dead bodies. Isolated human bones are frequently found in rubbish deposits and in some cases articulated parts of human carcasses have been found in pits along with other occupation debris. At Wandlebury, Cambs., for example, a child's body less the legs was apparently wrapped in a cloth or sack and thrown into a pit, while at Danebury odd limbs and pieces of human trunk occur sporadically. In one case at Danebury, a deliberate deposit was created in a specially dug elongated pit in which had been placed three legs, part of a trunk and a lower jaw. Unlike the other pits, this one had been left open for some time, the fragments of body remaining exposed to view. It is difficult to resist the conclusion that the deposit had some kind of ritual overtones.

OWSLEBURY, HANTS

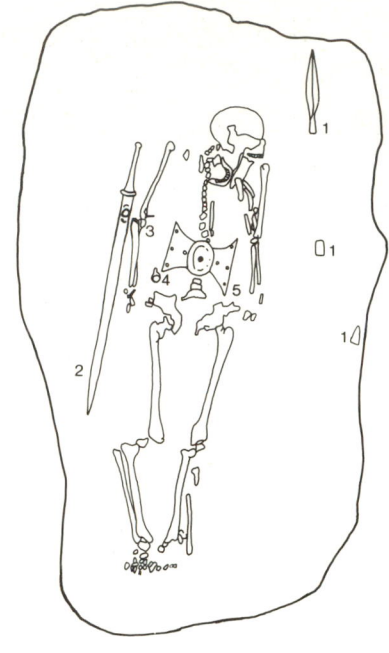

1 Iron spearhead, ferrule and
  bronze strip
2 Iron sword
3 Bronze rings from sword belt
4 Silvered bronze belthook
5 Bronze shield boss

WHITCOMBE, DORSET

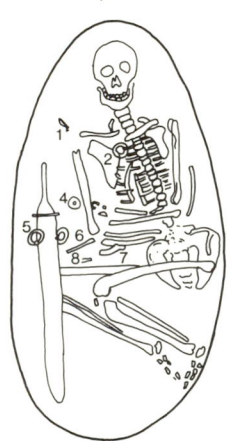

1 Bronze fibula
2 Circular belthook
3 Iron spearhead
4 Circular lump of chalk
5 Iron sword
6 Iron tool
7 Iron hammer
8 Broken bronze object

0   100 cms

Figure 19.6   Warrior burials from Owslebury, Hants., and Whitcombe, Dorset (source: Collis 1973).

Another factor of some significance is the apparent interest shown in the human head (Figure 19.8) (a matter which will be returned to below, p. 519). On several occupation sites skull fragments are noticeably more common than other human bones. Thirty-two fragments of human skulls were found at All Cannings Cross, Wilts., four of which had been deliberately cut to shape, one perforated for suspension, the others polished by use. Similarly, at Lidbury, Wilts.,

Figure 19.7   Pit burial from Danebury, Hants. (photo: Danebury Trust).

a piece of cranium had been carefully shaped and perforated. It must be assumed that skulls were selected for some kind of special treatment, which eventually resulted in token pieces being retained by individuals, perhaps as good-luck charms.

Clearly what we are observing in the evidence of the disposal of human remains from central southern Britain is a pale reflection of a complex of rites and beliefs. The complete or partial pit burials could be interpreted as the deliberate burial of a sector of the population for ritual purposes, perhaps in propitiatory rites (see below p. 517), while the skulls and cureated fragments could have served quite a different socio-religious purpose. How all this reflects on the 'normal' disposal of the dead in this region is more difficult to say, but in the absence of cemeteries the most satisfactory explanation of the observed facts is that excarnation was the normal rite. Such systems are well known in recent ethnographic literature, the essential features being the exposure of the body for a set period, while the spirit was considered to be hovering around in a liminal state. This was usually followed by a later rite during which part of the remains might be brought back into the domestic situation, sometimes to be used in propitiatory rites. A belief system of this kind could accommodate the evidence of the scattered bones found in settlements, while at the same time explaining the lack of cemeteries in south-east Britain throughout much of the period from the sixth to first century. It is possible to speculate that this practice might have been a revival of the mortuary rites carried out in the Neolithic period in the same area. The problem is one of considerable interest but requires more evidence than is at present available to elucidate it further.

Figure 19.8   Skull burial from Danebury, Hants. (photo: Danebury Trust).

While it is true that few cemeteries are known outside the Arras culture of Yorkshire and the cist graves of the south-west, isolated examples of individual burials have been found from time to time. Towards the end of the period from the second century BC until the first century AD, a class of richer burials can be defined (Collis 1973). Of these, warrior burials form a distinctive group, characterized by the rite of male inhumation, accompanied by weapons, the bodies being disposed of in shallow graves without barrows (Figure 19.6). The grave found at North Grimston, Yorks., in 1902 was one of the richest: besides the body it contained an iron sword, a short sword with anthropomorphic hilt, bronze and iron rings, fragments of a jet ring, part of a bronze tube and a skeleton of a pig. The warrior at Owslebury, Hants., was similarly provided with his long iron sword in a wooden sheath together with rings and a scabbard hook for attaching it. By his side was a spear, broken so as to fit into the grave, while the body appears to have been covered with a wooden or leather shield of which the central bronze boss now survives. These two examples demonstrate most of the characteristics of the group as a whole, the others being summarized in the table on p. 522. There is no need to assume that warrior burials have any particular cultural or geographical significance: it is simpler to regard them as representatives of a social class that existed during the second century BC in south-east Britain. In Yorkshire these warrior burials are essentially a continuation of the tradition which begins earlier with the warrior burials of the Wetwang Slack type, the only difference being that they were not of a status to warrant being buried with carts. When the chronologies of these Yorkshire burials have been refined we may find that both rites were being conducted in parallel for some period.

Parallel with the warrior burials there appear a number of rich female burials, usually characterized by the presence of mirrors, beads, bronze bowls and other trinkets appropriate to female attire.[3] One of the best recorded of the group was discovered at Birdlip in Gloucestershire in 1879. Three cist graves were found, the centre one containing the burial of a rich female, with a male on either side. Her body was extended and over her face a large bronze bowl had been placed; a smaller bowl lay near-by. The other grave-goods included a gilded silver fibula, four bronze (?) dress-rings, a bronze armlet, a superb knife with a bronze animal-head terminal, a necklace of amber, jet and marble, and an engraved bronze mirror. The rich female burials at Trelan Bahow, Cornwall, and Mount Batten, Devon, were also interred in cists, placed in larger cemeteries. A variation occurs at Colchester, Essex, where the body had been cremated and the ashes buried in a pedestal urn alongside a range of accessory pottery vessels. The metalwork, including an engraved mirror, a bronze bowl and a bronze pin, serves to link the grave to the general category of rich female burials. Another variant of a mirror burial was found at Dorton, Bucks. Here the body was cremated and accompanied by a mirror contained in a wooden box, together with three amphorae, two flagons and a cup.

The tradition of including mirrors with the departed can be traced back to the fourth century at Arras in Yorkshire, where two graves contained mirrors. The graves at Mount Batten, Birdlip and Colchester date to the first century AD. Like the warrior burials, there is no need to attach any cultural significance to the type; they merely represent the standard practices involved in burying moderately wealthy women.

There is a third type of inhumation which might be considered sufficiently distinctive to be regarded as involving a separate ritual practice. At Burnmouth in Berwickshire and Deal in Kent extended inhumations have been found, each provided with a pair of bronze spoons. In each pair one spoon was marked with a cross, the other had a small hole punched to one side. Spoons of this kind have been found in various parts of Britain.[4] Some occur in contexts which might suggest ritual deposits. At Crosby Ravensworth in Westmorland a pair was discovered by a spring in a bog; at Penbryn in Cardiganshire another pair had been buried under a pile of stones; the river Thames produced a single spoon and some of those from Ireland were probably from bogs. It is difficult to resist the conclusion that these spoons were in some way connected with ritual procedures. If so, it may be that those with whom they were buried were involved in the practice of religion. This is, of course, pure speculation but it is not too much to expect that the graves of the religious leaders of the community may have been distinguished in some way, as were those of the aristocratic class.

Over much of the British Isles inhumation remained the basic rite up to the time of the Roman Conquest. In the territory of the Durotriges, for example, a group of victims of the Roman advance was hastily buried in a cemetery at Maiden Castle. Even though the military situation was tense, trouble was taken to inhume the bodies in specially dug graves and to provide them with ritual meals buried alongside in pottery containers. Inhumation rites were very deeply rooted in Durotrigan territory, and even after the Roman Conquest, when cremation became the norm, the bulk of the population continued to be buried in the old inhumation manner (Whimster 1981).

In the south-east, cremation became increasingly common from the beginning of the first century BC. The normal practice was to bury the ashes of the deceased in an urn in a well-defined cemetery area. A wealth differential is clearly reflected in the nature of the ancillary equipment buried with the ashes. The simpler graves were without grave-goods but a reasonable percentage was provided with small articles such as brooches and other personal trinkets. The richer individuals were buried either in or with bronze-plated buckets[5] and occasionally, as in the case of the rich graves at Aylesford and Swarling in Kent, other bronze vessels were included (p. 134–6). In Essex and Hertfordshire, a group of extremely rich burials have been defined, characterized by a deep grave-pit containing considerable volumes of wine stored in amphorae together with the vessels and other equipment appropriate to its consumption. The ritual belief behind such aristocratic burials was evidently to provide the dead man (or woman in the case of Dorton) with the means of feasting and amusement in the afterlife to which he had been accustomed on earth. Burials of this kind were being undertaken in eastern England from the middle of the first century BC until the Roman Conquest (p. 136–40).

In summary, it may be said that the burial patterns recognizable in the British Isles were complex. Cremation rites in the old Bronze Age style continued over much of the country into the sixth century but thereafter three distinctive burial zones can be distinguished: in the west cemeteries of inhumations in cists were the norm; in Yorkshire inhumation in barrow cemeteries was common, while in the centre south excarnation seems to have been widely practised. From the beginning of the first century BC the rite of cremation became established once again in the south-east of the country where cremation cemeteries, sometimes of considerable size, developed: beyond this zone however the traditional rites of the Middle Iron Age continued.

Superimposed upon this regional pattern and chronological development was a separate pattern reflecting the social status of the dead person. Status variations are first apparent among the Middle Iron Age burials of Yorkshire where a certain sector of society was afforded burial rite involving the deposition of a two-wheeled vehicle in the grave. Discrete sets of grave-goods were also used to indicate status and gender. By the beginning of the Late Iron Age these grave-sets (female burials with mirrors and male burials with weapons) are found sporadically in other parts of the country indicating a change of practice. This was contemporary with, and may in part have been occasioned by, a change in burial rite in the south-east of Britain as social and economic contact with Belgic Gaul intensified. In this area the considerable variations in wealth that could occur in society were closely reflected in grave-goods ranging from the simplest unaccompanied cremation to the conspicuous display of wealth represented at the Lexden tumulus.

Religious and ritual locations

The ritual centres of the Iron Age can be divided into two major types: shrines incorporating some kind of man-made structure, and natural locations such as springs, streams or clumps of trees.

The clearest example of the few shrines at present known was found inside a ditched enclosure at Heathrow, Middx., along with a number of domestic buildings (Figure 19.9). The temple consisted of a central *cella*, defined by trenches in which timber uprights had been set, surrounded by an 'ambulatory' constructed of individual close-set posts, the whole building

HEATHROW, MIDDX

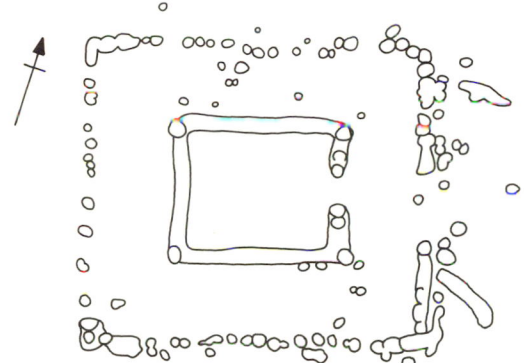

SOUTH CADBURY, SOMERSET

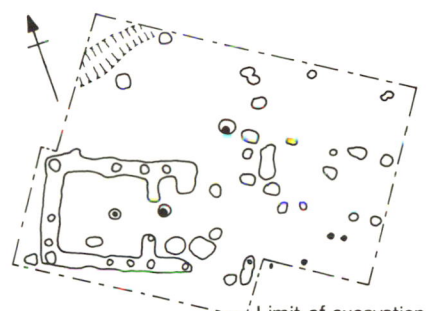

Limit of excavation

LANCING DOWN, SUSSEX

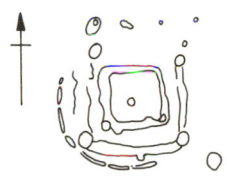

FRILFORD, BERKS

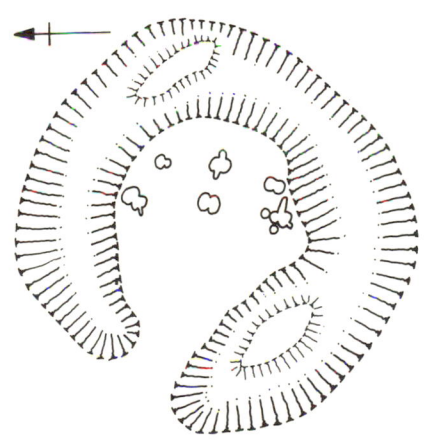

MAIDEN CASTLE, DORSET

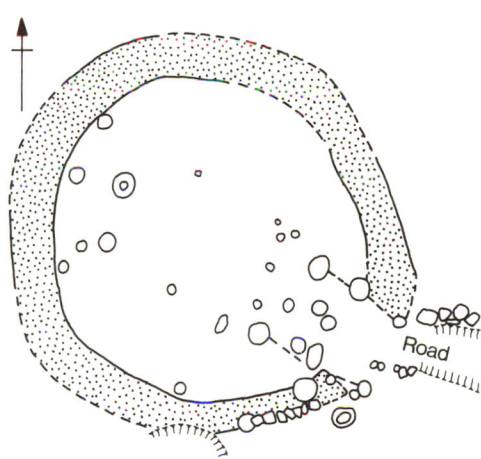

Road

0   20 Metres

Figure 19.9 Temples and shrines (sources: *Maiden Castle*, Wheeler 1943; *South Cadbury*, Alcock 1970; *Lancing Down*, Bedwin 1981; *Heathrow*, Grimes 1961; *Frilford*, Bradford and Goodchild 1939).

being little more than 10 m square. The similarity between this structure and the later Romano-Celtic temples is so striking that there can be little doubt of the Roman form being modelled upon pre-conquest styles. Another rectangular shrine, similar in many respects to the Heathrow temple, has been uncovered towards the centre of the hillfort of South Cadbury, Somerset (Figure 19.9). The surviving part of the South Cadbury shrine is a small *cella* with an attached porch, comparable in size to Heathrow but apparently without the surrounding ambulatory. Its ritual connotations were further emphasized by the discovery of a number of animal burials in shallow pits lining the approach.

A group of buildings which may have served a religious function have been discovered within the hillfort of Danebury, Hants. (Figures 19.10 and 19.11). One structure was closely similar to the *cella* of the Heathrow temple. Of the three other buildings which appear to have been associated with it, two were smaller, while the third consisted of a large square fenced enclosure: all were oriented in the same direction towards the entrance of the fort and were sited close to the main road, but no evidence of ritual activity was recognized.

The discovery of three examples of shrines within fortified enclosures raises the possibility that many of the hillforts may have contained religious centres, though the religious association of the buildings may not always be apparent. In Maiden Castle, Dorset, the building which is evidently the shrine is a simple circular stone-walled structure lying at the end of one of the streets leading into the fort from the east gate (Figure 19.9). The only hint of ritual activity is an infant burial just outside the door, but the fact that the building was reconstructed in the Roman period alongside a rectangular Romano-Celtic temple is a strong indication of the religious continuity of the particular location. It raises the possibility that many of the Roman temples sited in hillforts may have been constructed on the sites of pre-Roman shrines.

Continuity of this kind is not restricted to hillforts. A sequence of structures almost identical to the Maiden Castle arrangement has been exposed at Frilford, Oxon., where a rectangular and a circular Roman temple were found to succeed an earlier religious centre, the circular Roman building lying above a penannular ditched enclosure of Iron Age date which contained a setting of six post-sockets (Figure 19.9). Evidently Frilford served as a ritual centre for some decades before the Roman invasion.

The same is probably true of the religious site on Lancing Down, Sussex (Figure 19.9), where a small rectangular building comparable to the smaller structures at Danebury was found close to a typical Romano-Celtic temple of later date. Direct structural continuity is unproven, but that the site was revered for its religious associations over centuries spanning the Iron Age and Roman period seems likely.

One of the most remarkable examples of religious continuity to be discovered in recent years is the temple on Hayling Island, West Sussex (Figure 19.12). The Iron Age complex, built in the second half of the first century BC consisted of a circular structure set towards the centre of a rectangular courtyard enclosed by a palisade: both elements were closely reflected in the masonry rebuilding which took place in the second half of the first century AD. So close in plan and location were the two structures that there can be little doubt that the Iron Age building was still standing in some form at the time when the Roman builders moved in. The layer associated with the pre-Roman shrine produced a rich range of votive items including horse gear, spears, fragments of sword scabbards, brooches, tankards, currency bar fragments and almost 100 coins mainly of the Atrebates, Durotriges, Dobunni and from Continental Gaul. The collection provides a unique insight into the range of votive items thought to be appropriate to the unknown deity who was worshipped there.

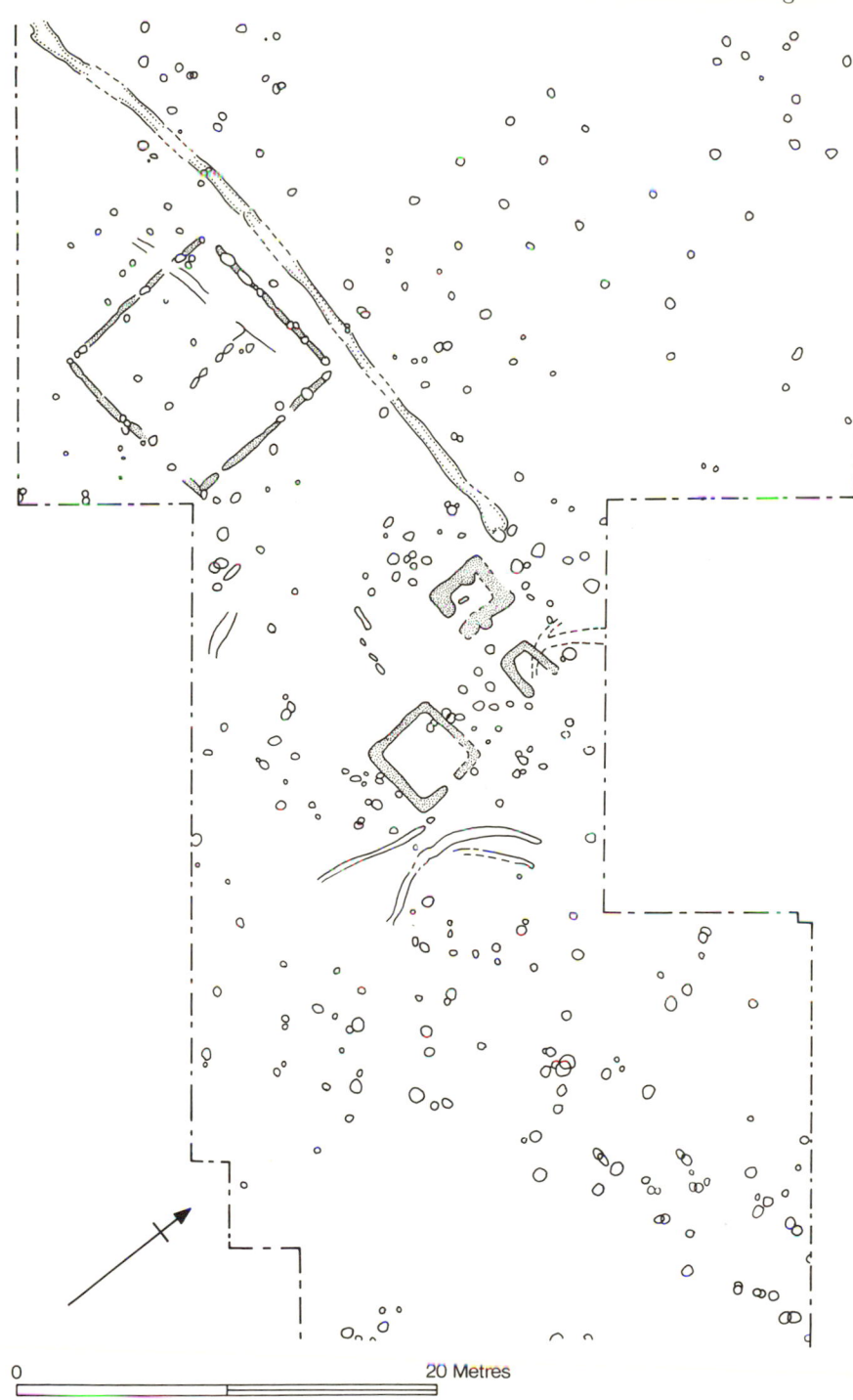

Figure 19.10 Rectangular buildings, probably of a religious nature in the hillfort of Danebury, Hants. (source: Cunliffe 1984a).

Figure 19.11   The principal 'shrine', Danebury, Hants. (photo: Danebury Trust).

Continuity is also probable at Harlow, Essex, where an Iron Age deposit associated with pits and post-holes was found beneath a Romano-Celtic temple. More than 230 Iron Age coins were found, many of which are likely to have been deposited in the pre-Roman phase. The numbers are sufficiently large to suggest the presence of a pre-conquest religious sanctuary dating back to the first century BC. Similar evidence suggestive of continuity comes from a number of Romano-Celtic temples. For example at Worth in Kent a small group of model shields (Figure 19.13) must be indicative of Iron Age ritual activity but there is little else to indicate the form of the buildings, if any, which constituted the sanctuary. In all probability, the continuity of temple locations between the Iron Age and Roman periods will prove to be widespread when the early levels beneath Roman structures are more fully explored.

Sacred locations unmarked by shrines must have abounded in Britain, as in the rest of the Celtic world. Springs, bogs and rivers would have been the obvious foci for ritual practices, as well as other striking natural features such as large rocks, very old trees or groves of trees. In all of these places the gods were thought to live and there they had to be served or placated.

Direct archaeological evidence for such locations is seldom forthcoming but many of the items of metalwork recovered from bogs and rivers may well have been offerings deliberately dedicated to the spirits of the place (Fitzpatrick 1984; Wait 1985). The enormous numbers of exotic objects from the Thames and the smaller, but no less impressive, collections from other rivers like the Witham and the Tyne probably originated in this way. Bog deposits are also relatively common

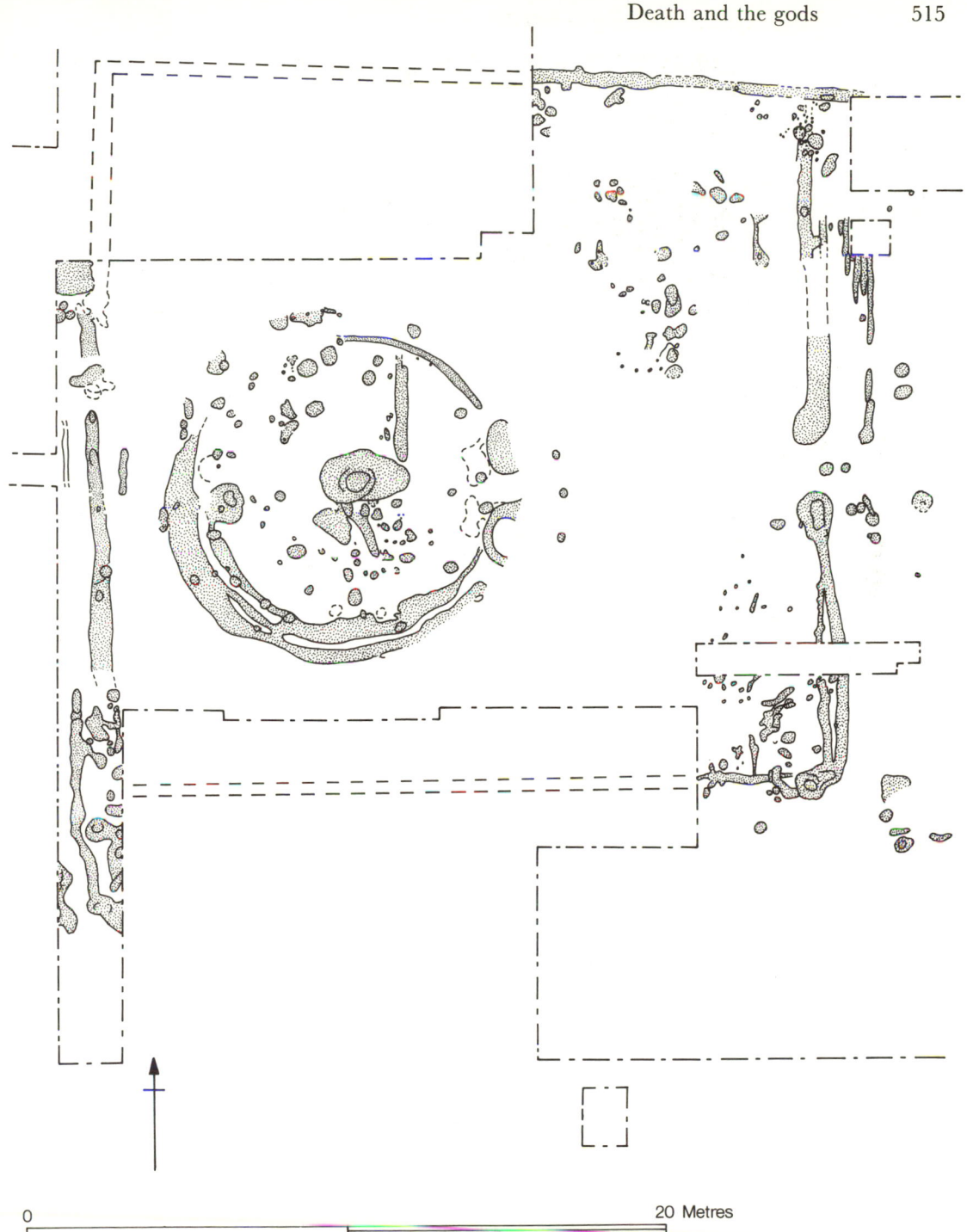

0   20 Metres

Figure 19.12   The temple at Hayling Island, Hants. (source: Downey, King and Soffe 1979).

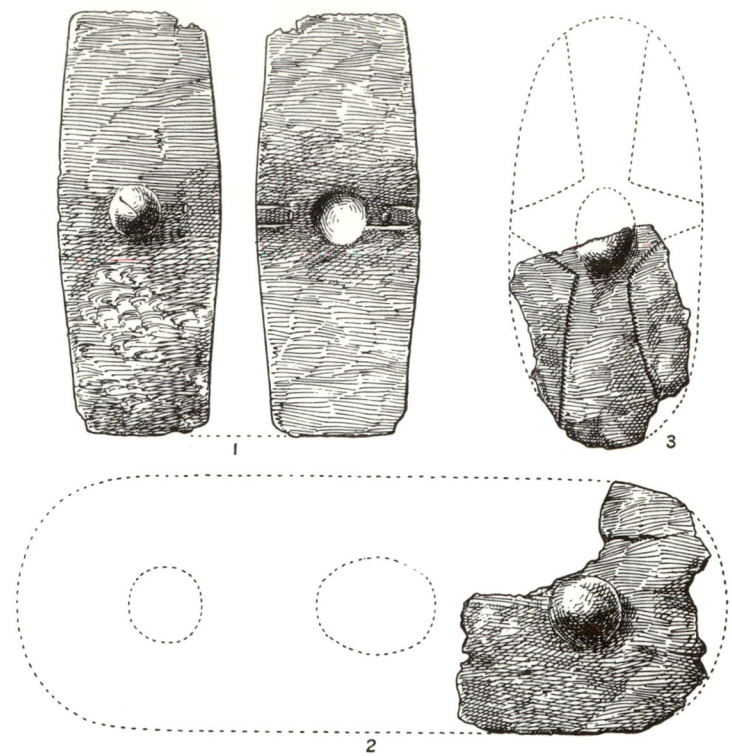

Figure 19.13   Votive model shields from Worth, Kent (scale 1:3) (source: reproduced from Klein 1928).

in some parts of Britain; among these must be included the large collection of metalwork thrown into the lake at Llyn Cerrig-Bach on Anglesey, and the hoard of material, including two cauldrons, from Llyn Fawr in Glamorganshire. The pair of bronze ritual spoons from Crosby Ravensworth, Westmorland, and the pony cap and horns from Torrs in Kirkcudbrightshire, were also bog deposits. Besides the Llyn Fawr find, several other cauldrons from Britain, including an example from Feltwell in Norfolk, and others from Ireland had been thrown into bogs. Tankards too were sometimes found in rivers and bogs, like the famous Trawsfynydd tankard from Merionethshire and the vessel from Shapwick Heath, Somerset. The metalwork from these locations is impressive not only in quantity but also for its very high quality. One must suppose that a surprisingly high percentage of society's wealth was dedicated to the gods in this manner.

While the discovery of fine metalwork tends to pinpoint sacred places besides bogs or rivers, the sacred groves mentioned by the classical writers are more difficult to locate. Some help is, however, provided by the distribution of the Gallo-Britannic word *nemeton*, which means a sanctuary in a woodland clearing. The word occurs in several Romano-British place-names in different parts of Britain, such as *Vernemeton* near Leicester, *Medionemeton* in southern Scotland, and *Nemetostatio* near North Tawton in Devon (Griffith 1985). The Roman name for the thermal spring at Buxton, *Aquae Arnemetiae*, also includes the element *nemet-*, suggesting that the spring was in use as a religious centre long before the invasion. That so many *nemeton* elements are

Figure 19.14   Propitiatory offering of a dog and a horse leg in a pit at Danebury, Hants. (photo: Danebury Trust).

incorporated in Roman place-names in Britain is an indication of the large numbers of sacred woodland clearings of pre-conquest date, the memory of which lingered on.

The deposition of valuable goods in rivers, bogs and springs would have been undertaken within the context of a complex pattern of religious beliefs now entirely beyond reconstruction. All we can safely surmise is that the rites would have involved some element of propitiation – the thanking of the deity for support in some enterprise or in anticipation of divine intervention in the future. Similar acts probably pervaded Iron Age life. A further example is worth considering. At Danebury, Hants., a study of the contents of nearly 2,000 storage pits has demonstrated recurring patterns of deposition involving animal carcasses, whole or in joints (Figure 19.14), human bodies, groups of pots and sets of artefacts. These are the archaeologically recognizable component of a behaviour pattern which might well have required a range of products, including perhaps cheese, hides, bales of wool, etc., to be placed on the bottom of storage pits when they were no longer to be used. Reflections of this pattern can be recognized quite widely in central southern Britain. Explanations must necessarily lie in the realms of guesswork, but the context of these deposits – in storage pits – is suggestive of a rite to ensure the maintenance of crop fertility. If we are correct in supposing that these pits were used for storing seed-corn then, to ensure a good harvest or in retrospect to give thanks for one, an offering would have been appropriate. In these special pit deposits we are perhaps seeing, albeit dimly, the propitiation of the deities who controlled fertility. This would have been a counterpart to the deposits of weaponry in watery places, thrown into the depths to thank the gods of war.

One further deposit requires brief consideration – the deposition of a human body in a bog at Lindow, Cheshire. The man had been hit violently on the head, garrotted and had his throat cut before being consigned to the bog. It is tempting to see this as a ritual act and to remember, in this context, the tightly flexed skeletons found on the bottoms of the pits in Danebury and elsewhere in central southern Britain. Lindow man may differ from them only in that local burial conditions preserved his skin and hair allowing the manner of death to be determined. In other words it is a distinct possibility that the sacrifice of human beings was widespread in pre-Roman Britain.

Druids and the Gods[6]

The practitioners of religious ritual in Britain, as in Gaul, were the Druids. Caesar believed that Druidic religion originated in Britain, whence it was introduced to the Continent: 'Even today', he says, 'anyone who wants to make a study of it goes to Britain to do so' (*Gallic Wars* vi, 14).

The Druids served Celtic society in various ways: they were responsible for administering and guiding the religious life of the people, supervising ceremonies and sacrifices and divining the future from such omens as the death struggles of a sacrificial victim. They also maintained the theory and practice of the law and were the teachers of the old oral traditions of the people, holding schools where the novices learnt verses off by heart. Caesar reports:

> They seem to have established this custom for two reasons: because they do not want their knowledge to become widespread and because they do not want their pupils to rely on the written word instead of their memories; for once this happens, they tend to reduce the effort they put into their learning.

(ibid., 15)

The literary evidence relating to the Druids can frequently be used to enhance and explain the archaeological material. Belief in the afterlife, which is demonstrated by the provision of grave-goods with the dead, is referred to several times. Caesar says that the one idea that the Druids wanted to emphasize above all others was that souls do not die but pass from one body to another as each body dies. Pomponius Mela, writing in the first century AD, elaborates on this belief: because of their very strongly held views on the afterlife, he says :

they burn and bury with their dead the things they had owned while they were alive. In the past they even used to put off the completion of business and the payment of debts until they had arrived in the next world. Some even went so far as to throw themselves willingly on to their friends' funeral pyres in order to share the new life with them.

(*Place of the World* iii, 19)

A firm conviction about immortality was of particular encouragement to those required to act bravely in battle, as several classical writers were quick to point out.

Pomponius Mela writes of Druids teaching in caves or inaccessible woods, while Tacitus mentions 'groves devoted to Mona's [Anglesey's] barbarous superstitions', implying that at these places human sacrifice was carried out. An altogether more gentle ritual is, however, described in some detail by Pliny the Elder. The passage is worth quoting at length because of the insight it gives into ritual beliefs and practices which would otherwise be unrepresented in the archaeological record.

They choose groves of oak for the sake of the tree alone and they never perform any sacred rite unless they have a branch of it. They think that everything that grows on it has been sent from heaven by the god himself. Mistletoe, however, is very rarely found on the oak and, when it is, it is gathered with a great deal of ceremony, if possible on the sixth day of the moon . . . . They choose this day because, although the moon has not yet reached half-size, it already has considerable influence. They call the mistletoe by the name that means all-healing.

He goes on to describe the cutting of the mistletoe with a golden sickle by a white-robed Druid, followed by the ritual sacrifice of two white bulls, and concludes: 'They believe that if the mistletoe is taken in a drink, it makes barren animals fertile, and is a remedy against all poison' (*Nat. Hist.* xvi, 249). Later Pliny mentions other herbs which, if collected under certain conditions, possessed curative properties: selago (or sabine) warded off evil and could cure eye diseases, while a marsh plant, samolus, was regarded as a charm against cattle disease. Mistletoe, selago and samolus are just three which Pliny happens to note but hundreds of other herbs must have been endowed with medicinal properties about which the Druids would have known and taught.

Many of the classical accounts refer to the Druids carrying out human sacrifice, and that ritual killing may well have an archaeological reality has been suggested above (p. 518). Ritual killing for the purpose of augury is mentioned by Diodorus Siculus and Strabo, while the mass sacrifices of men and beasts, burnt to death in cages made of branches, are described in some detail by Caesar and Strabo. Strabo also records ritual deaths by archery and crucifixion, and Tacitus, describing the destruction of the Druid centre on Anglesey in AD 59, justifies the Roman attack by saying of the Druids that 'it was their religion to drench their altars in blood of prisoners and consult their gods by means of human entrails' – words calculated to conjure up a sense of horrified distaste among his sophisticated Roman audience. One wonders whether the partly dismembered child from Wandlebury, the human limbs and torso from the 'ritual pit' at Danebury or the man buried in the bog at Lindow were in any way connected with Druidic practices. The only other archaeological evidence for ritual is the decapitation of bodies, like those found at Bredon Hill, Worcs., and the setting up of heads on gates as witnessed by the skull found near the entrance to the Stanwick fort in Yorkshire. Decapitation is, however, more likely to have been a normal part of the battle scene than the preserve of the priestly cult.

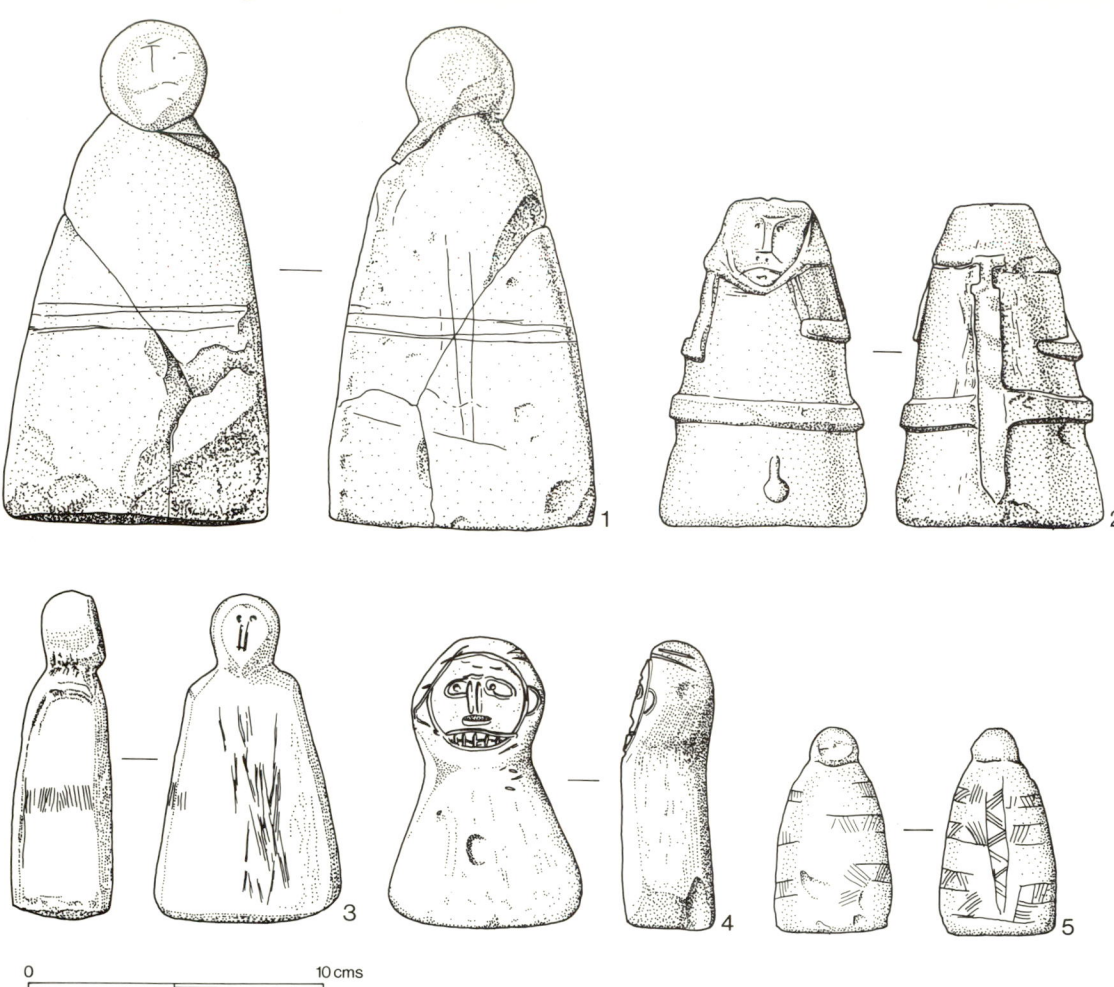

0 _____ 10 cms

Figure 19.15   Stone figurines from North Humberside. 1 Wetwang Slack, 2 Withernsea, 3 Garton Slack, 4 uncertain, 5 Malton (North Yorks.) (source: Stead 1988).

The Druids mediated between men and their gods, of whom there were many. Caesar gives the clearest picture of the Celtic pantheon by equating the native deities with their nearest Roman counterpart (*Gallic Wars* vi, 17–18): 'Their main god', he says, 'is Mercury; they have many images of him. They consider him the inventor of all arts, the god of travellers and of journeys and the greatest god when it comes to obtaining money and goods.' He then goes on to describe the lesser gods: Apollo who wards off disease, Minerva presiding over work and art, Jupiter the ruler of the heavens, and Mars the god of war. 'When they have decided to go to battle, they generally promise the captured goods to Mars. When they are victorious, they sacrifice the captured animals and make a pile of everything else.' As we have suggested above (p. 518), perhaps some of the ritual deposits from rivers and bogs were votive dedications made to the god in thanks for victory.

Iconography

There are few indisputable representations of gods or men from pre-Roman Iron Age contexts in Britain, but wooden figurines from Roos Carr, Holderness, Dagenham, Essex, and Ballachulish, Argyllshire, are all likely to be of first-millennium BC date and provide a valuable reminder of a facet of religious behaviour which was in all probability widespread in Britain, and may perhaps be compared with the votive offerings found in considerable numbers at sacred locations in Gaul, usually associated with water.

Stone carvings are equally rare in Britain, but the work at Garton Slack, and elsewhere in Yorkshire, has produced a group of remarkable chalk figurines (Stead 1971b, 1988; Brewster 1976). The figures (Figure 19.15), averaging about 13 cm high, were usually wedge-shaped, with simply moulded heads which in most cases had been broken off. No attempt had been made to show legs, but arms were indicated by incisions and shallow carving, and several of the figures were shown to be wearing belts and swords. In addition to the human figures a model of an oval-shaped shield was recovered. While most of the objects were without a clearly defined context, one was found under archaeological conditions stratified in the ditch of a rectangular 'ritual enclosure' which formed part of a religious and burial complex. There can therefore be little doubt that the figurines should be regarded as some kind of votive offering.

The iconography of Britain before the conquest, reflected largely in the Roman formalization of the situation, shows that an immense number of local or tribal gods existed, each known by a regional name and each endowed with specific qualities. Caesar's broad summing up, linking the Celtic deities to their nearest Roman counterpart, was little more than rationalization of an exceptionally complex and bewildering pattern. After the Roman Conquest the gods were frequently depicted in various guises, sometimes as a disembodied head, which must have represented a generalized portrait of divinity, and sometimes with specific characteristics. One of the more common types is the horned god which, depending upon his attributes, might variously represent the war-god Cernunnos (as Mars), Mercury, who Caesar says was the most commonly illustrated, or sometimes the hunting god Silvanus. Among the female deities the old triad of mother goddesses frequently occurs, particularly in the north and west, representing a deep-seated traditional belief in the power of three, a belief further emphasized by the occasional discovery of triple-faced heads.

Besides sculptural representations, the old gods are often named on dedicatory altars and other inscriptions. The names might include tribal deities like Brigantia or more widely respected gods like Camulos, the powerful war-god, whose shrine probably lay in the defended area at Camulodunum – perhaps at the site of Gosbecks Farm, an important cult centre in the Roman period. Other gods were more specific to certain localities, like Sulis who, later paired with Minerva, presided over the sacred spring at Bath, whereas others possessed more prescribed skills: Taranis the thunder-god or Nodens the cloud-maker. Some deities were rather more generalized in their stated powers: Nemetona and Mars Rigonemeta were respectively the goddess and god of the sacred grove, while Leucetius was simply 'the shining one'.

The list of gods is very long: each tribe must have had its own pantheon of favourite deities and every one of the many thousands of sacred locations would have been the special preserve of a local god whose name and presence would have been part of the natural awareness of the local community. It would have been difficult to travel far in Iron Age Britain before coming into contact with some sign of the gods, for religion and superstition pervaded all aspects of pre-Roman life.

	Sword	Metal chape or binding	Attachment rings or hooks	Spear	Metal shield fittings	Food offering	Other grave-goods
North Grimston, Yorks.	XX		X			X	Jet ring, bronze tube
Bugthorpe, Yorks.	X	X					2 bronze discs and 2 bronze studs
Grimthorpe, Yorks.	X	X		X	X		Bronze disc and 16 bone 'shroud' pins
Thorpe, Yorks.	X	X					
Clotherholme, Yorks.	X X						
Shouldham, Yorks.	X						
St Lawrence, I.O.W.	X	X			X		
Owslebury, Hants.	X		X	X	X		
Whitcombe, Dorset	X	X	X	X			Brooch, chalk pommel

Table 19.1 *Grave-goods found with warrior burials*

Part IV
Systems

20
Iron Age society and social change

The dynamics of change

All societies exist in a state of dynamic equilibrium with their environments: this relationship constitutes a system. Systems are infinitely complex and can be approached at any level. Thus, at a very simple level, a climatic change affecting the environment could lead a community to change its agricultural regime over a period of years but that change would probably lead to some readjustment in social organization and this might, in turn, create new demands which could only be met by making further changes to the agricultural practices. In this example a *prime mover*, climatic change, initiates a modification in the man:landscape system which sets up further reverberations around the system. In other words each change *feeds back* into the system causing further change.

These feedback mechanisms are an essential feature of all systems and it is through them that directional change is initiated. Once underway a feedback cycle may gain momentum and change within a system may be forced along a particular trajectory. Sometimes rate of change escalates to such a point that the old systems collapse and a new set of systems emerges.

This somewhat bland and oversimple statement belies the real complexity of the situation but is sufficient to give some sense of the dynamic nature of society. Yet not all societies are in a state of rapid change: some seem to have established a state of near-stable equilibrium and little change is evident. These have been referred to as *conserving societies*. Others, in which rapid change can be seen, have been called *innovating societies*. While these terms are helpful characterizations they tend to overlook another feature of society – its innate desire to remain unchanged. Change is seen as a threat, a move from what is known and safe to what is unknown and potentially dangerous. Thus there is usually a strong force, inherent in every society, to resist change: this has been called *dynamic conservatism*. The forces of dynamic conservatism serve as a brake to hold the trajectory of change, caused by feedback within the system. The two forces are in constant tension.

Tensions between opposing forces are evident throughout social systems. At a very basic level, within the average individual, there is the conflict between the aggressive desire to achieve and the need for gregariousness. This conflict is resolved by systems of social behaviour which provide a framework within which the individual can operate, safeguarding on the one hand the structure of the community, and thus its power to reproduce itself, while providing the individual with carefully circumscribed opportunities to engage in competitive display.

Another tension inherent in humanity is that between an individual's conception of the known, tangible, world and the world which he senses lies outside it – the unknown – above and below our world, inhabited by spirits and the gods. To control and constrain the uncertainties belief systems with their attendant rituals are developed and by these means the natural and supernatural are kept in equilibrium.

Sufficient has been said to give some idea of the complexities inherent in the study of societies. We have seen that all social systems are bound together by mechanisms which have developed to control inner tensions and that the resulting systems exist in a dynamic relationship with their environments. Left to themselves and given the power of dynamic conservatism, there would tend to be comparatively little change over time, but a number of motive forces, often originating from outside the system, may interpose themselves to upset the equilibrium or alter the trajectory. Of these the most significant are climatic change, external intervention, disease and population growth.

The question of climatic change has been addressed in earlier chapters (pp. 22–3, 57–8). In summary climatic deterioration throughout the first half of the first millennium BC encouraged the growth of blanket bog over many tracts of uplands in western parts of the British Isles, which had previously been incorporated in farming systems, creating a dislocation of settlement. Added to this a fall in mean temperature caused many upland areas in the north to be abandoned as arable land because the conditions were such that crops would no longer ripen. There can be little doubt that in these areas climatic deterioration had a significant effect on the resident communities. The land would no longer provide for them and in consequence there must have been a degree of readjustment ranging from a reordering of cropping and pastoral regimes where this was possible to abandonment and migration where it was not.

The upland areas of the north and west of Britain suffered most from the climatic changes of the first millennium but it is doubtful whether the effects over the rest of the country were significant enough to cause rapid readjustment.

External intervention as a prime causative factor for change was at one time a popular belief among scholars studying the Iron Age (chapter 1). Invasions of people from the Continent, bringing with them alien material cultures and social systems, were called up as an explanation whenever cultural change was identified. Simple models of this kind are now no longer in favour except possibly in the case of the Arras culture of Yorkshire where the archaeological evidence seems quite strong, and the Belgae of southern Britain about whose coming Caesar was explicit. But if 'invasions' in the traditional sense are no longer accepted it is abundantly clear that much of south and east Britain was in contact with the Continent throughout the Iron Age and that sometimes contact was intense. In the Early and Middle Iron Age the systems of interaction are difficult to determine but exchange of commodities as trade goods, or in cycles of gift exchange, probably bulked large. Movements of people, however, except as gifts or brides, are unlikely to have been on a significant scale.

By the beginning of the first century BC, when the economic systems of the Roman world began to make themselves felt in Gaul and beyond, the tribes of south-east Britain began to experience entirely new and unfamiliar pressures. A wide range of luxury goods became available and could be acquired by the wealthy to enhance their prestige, while an external demand now existed for British goods which had previously not been produced in surplus. The Roman desire for slaves alone would have caused a widespread disruption to existing social systems. While slavery probably existed in British society the consumption of slaves would have been slight. But once Roman entrepreneurs had moved in on the trade routes to Britain their demands would have been such that slaves became a cash crop practically overnight. One has only to look at the effects of the American slave trade on the tribes of west Africa to appreciate the disruptive potential which was unleashed.

The effects of disease can be devastating on population. The Black Death of the fourteenth century AD totally altered the face of Europe but there is no evidence at all that epidemics raged in Iron Age Britain. Indeed, given the dispersed nature of the population and the lack of extensive communication networks, it is unlikely that plagues played a significant part in British prehistory. Local epidemics no doubt occurred and many communities may well have been decimated but this can hardly have been on a scale large enough to have disrupted social systems.

Finally, we come to the question of population pressure. An understanding of the dynamics of population is crucial to any archaeological study, but that so little attention has been paid to the problem is largely due to the lack of tangible evidence which can be quantified (Cunliffe 1978b). This should not however be taken to mean that population is unimportant – quite the contrary it is probably the most important single factor bearing on social change.

The theory of demographic change has been extensively studied and a few generalizations are relevant here. At its simplest we may say that a closed population would normally increase until such time that the *holding capacity* of its environment imposed a constraint at which point it would level out below that holding capacity (Figure 20.1). Holding capacity is an arbitrary level created by the interactions of environment, climate, technological ability and social taboos. Any one of these factors may change or be changed raising or lowering the productive threshold. For example, climatic deterioration could significantly reduce holding capacity, so too could soil degeneration resulting from overcropping. Alternatively pressure of population, nearing the holding capacity, could cause stress conditions in which innovations were adopted to improve agricultural practices or social taboos were lifted to allow a more effective redistribution and utilization of resources. The theme of population pressure is one which will recur throughout the rest of this chapter.

From the above discussion it will be evident that the dynamics of change present a complex pattern of tightly interwoven factors. Social systems were delicately balanced: most aimed for a state of equilibrium but that equilibrium was never stable. Change could be imperceptibly slow or catastrophic. While we may not be able to discern much of these dynamics we can at least be sure that in the Iron Age world they were an ever-present reality.

Space and territory

Many of the discussions in previous chapters have made explicit the spacial patterning which occurs within the archaeological data. It is not proposed to recapitulate the evidence presented there but simply to offer a few basic generalizations which will be relevant to the rest of this

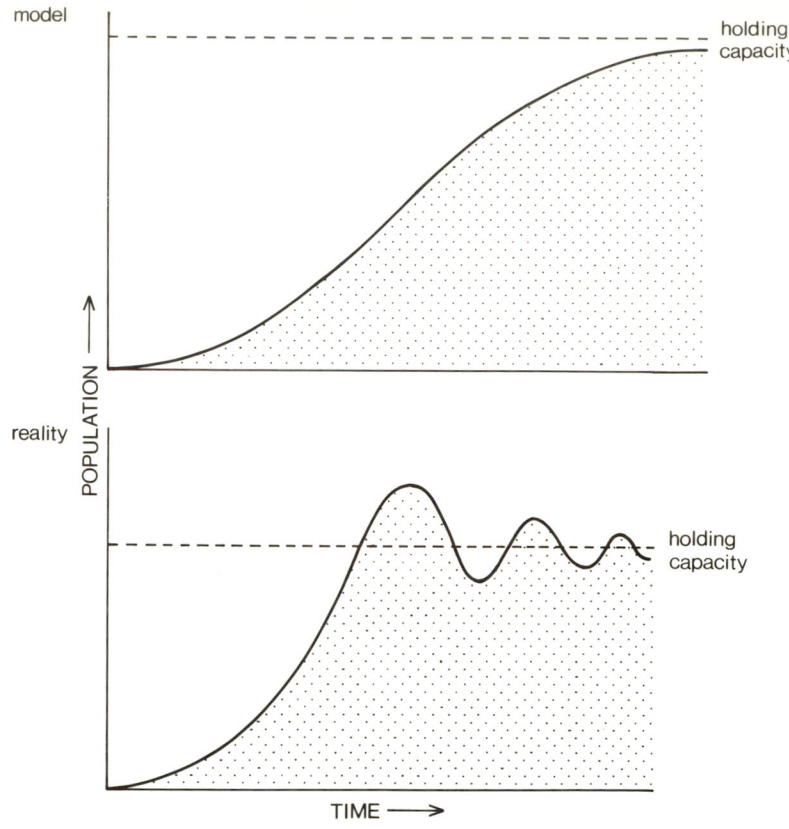

Figure 20.1   Diagram to illustrate holding capacity (source: author).

chapter. Standing back from the detail it becomes evident that Britain divides into five basic zones (Figure 20.2):

a *South-western zone* stretching from Cornwall to north Wales
a *North-western zone* including west coasts of Scotland and and the Western and Northern Isles
an *Eastern zone* extending from Kent to Yorkshire
a *North-eastern zone* from Yorkshire to Highland fringes
and a *Central southern zone* occupying the area from the southern Channel coast, through the Welsh borderland to north Wales.

While there is of course a considerable blurring of the boundaries this broad fivefold division seems to hold good for much of the Iron Age, each zone developing its own range of distinctive socio-economic systems. The reason for the zoning is largely geographical, landscape potential, microclimate and communication imposing constraints within which a limited range of strategies emerge as the most appropriate. Another factor of some significance is ease of contact with the Continent. The South-western, Central southern and Eastern zones all have coast lines facing Europe and inevitably contact existed across the intervening seas. Indeed it could be argued that

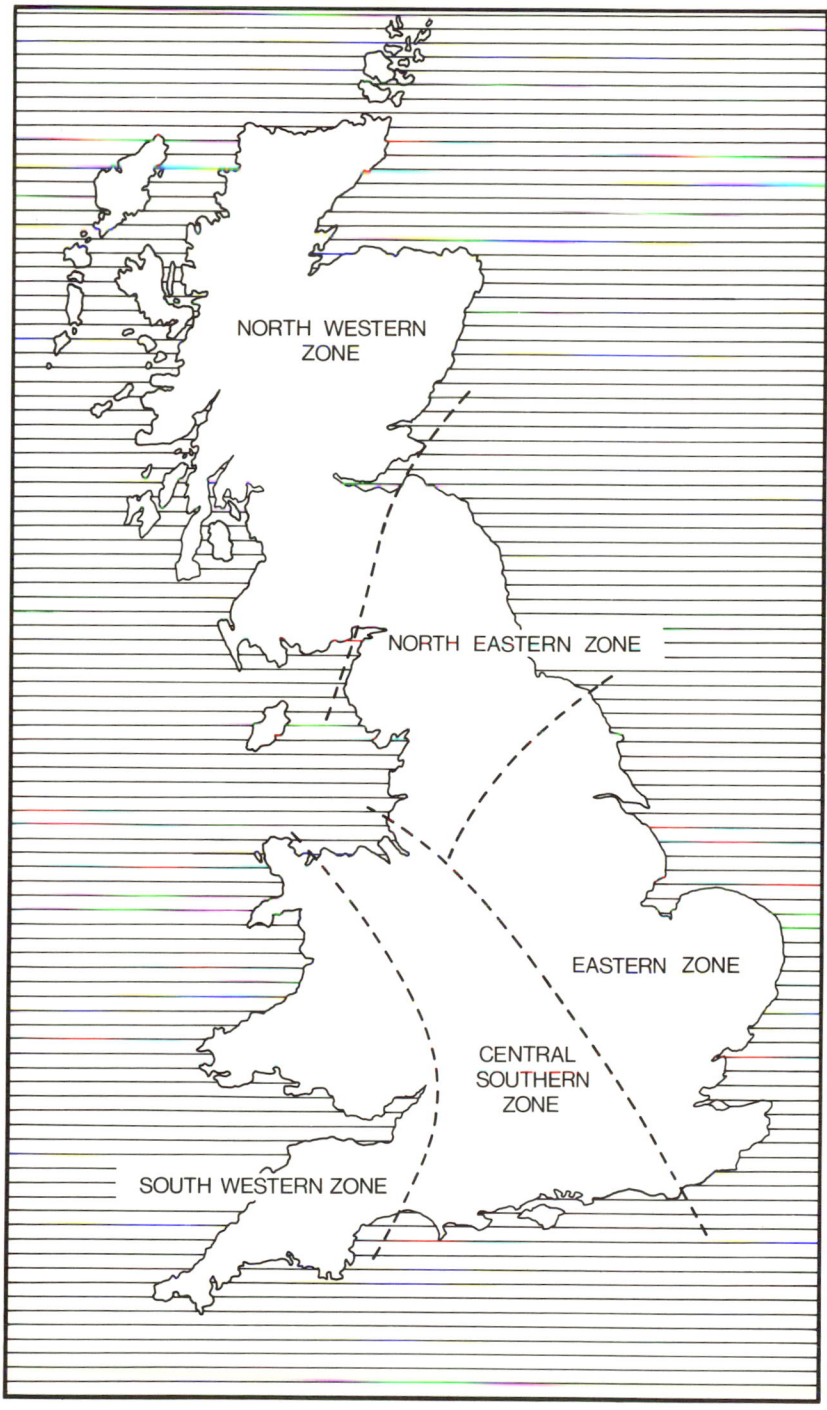

Figure 20.2 The zones of Iron Age Britain (source: author).

contact between these zones and their Continental interfaces was easier than between one British zone and the next.

Within each of the broadly defined zones regional variations can be distinguished. In some cases, especially in the Central southern zone, it is possible to show that these variations were maintained over a considerable period of time and may reasonably be identified with some of the tribal groupings recorded at the end of the Iron Age.

The five zones defined here provide a convenient framework within which to discuss the developing societies of Iron Age Britain so long as the boundaries are not regarded as too rigid either geographically or culturally.

The Earliest, Early and Middle Iron Age: *c.* 800–100 BC

The Eastern zone

The Eastern zone of Britain may loosely be characterized as that territory drained by the rivers flowing into the Humber, Wash and Thames. It looks east to the North Sea and across the sea to the coasts of Belgium and Holland.

At the beginning of the eighth century the Eastern zone was experiencing an intensification of the belief systems which led to the deposition of bronze. Bronze was taken out of circulation and either buried in hoards or thrown into rivers. The distribution of finds of the Carp's-Tongue Complex, which are typical of the later part of the Ewart Park phase and date roughly to the eighth century (pp. 55–6), shows a massive concentration in the Thames valley and in East Anglia (Burgess 1969a, Figure 14). What social pressures lay behind this spate of deposition is more difficult to discern. The deposition of weapons, particularly swords, in rivers had been a feature of the region since the beginning of the Late Bronze Age and was to continue, though in a somewhat abated form, throughout the rest of the Iron Age. Clearly, the act of consigning weapons to rivers had a deep-rooted religious meaning and is one of the characteristics which serves to distinguish the culture of the Eastern zone from that of other parts of Britain. It is a question to which we shall return.

The burying of large quantities of bronze in the ground is, in all probability, a reflection of a totally different behaviour pattern. 'Hoarding' in this manner had been going on throughout much of the Bronze Age but the quantity of material consigned to the earth had greatly increased. One plausible explanation, favoured by several scholars, is that the practice arose from the necessity of removing surplus bronze from circulation so that the metal would retain a high value in society. Its supply and distribution could then be controlled by paramount chiefs and in doing so they would maintain their status. This kind of socio-economic system, called a prestige goods economy, was widespread in the ancient world. The intensification of hoarding in the later part of the Ewart Park phase (*c.* 800–700 BC) marked the end of the process in the Thames valley and adjacent regions, but in East Anglia the deposition of hoards continued into the subsequent Llyn Fawr phase (*c.* 700–600 BC). This suggests that the prestige goods economy collapsed in the Thames valley during the eighth century but still lingered in East Anglia for possibly as much as a century before there, too, the old systems finally came to an end.

What caused the collapse of this long established traditional system it is difficult to say. It has been suggested that the appearance of iron so destabilized the system in introducing a new and widely available metal that a power structure based on the control of the supply of bronze could no longer maintain itself. R. Thomas (1989) has rejected this view, arguing instead that the reason may be that the control of land now began to take over as the means by which the elite maintained their power. With the collapse of bronze as a prestige material the way was now open for iron to emerge from obscurity. This still leaves open the question of why land began to take on a new importance, but population pressure, if it could be demonstrated archaeologically, would provide a suitable moving force.

The settlement pattern of the Eastern zone in the Earliest and Early Iron Age is not yet well known but it is now clear that the entire zone from Yorkshire to Kent shared a common settlement form which we may call *ring-forts*. These circular ditched enclosures, protected by ramparts and enclosing a single homestead usually consisting only of a large circular house, occur sporadically throughout the area. There is every reason to regard them as high status sites: the massiveness of the defences, the size of the central houses and evidence of bronze working is sufficient to distinguish them (pp. 39–41). Within the broad category of ring-forts may be included the somewhat larger enclosure at Grimthorpe in Yorkshire, measuring some 200 m across, and possibly also the much smaller structures on Micklemoor Hill, West Harling, Norfolk, only 30 and 36 m in diameter. The considerable variation in the size of these sites implies a significant difference in the social status of the communities which they housed.

The chronology of the ring-forts is still imprecise but a combination of evidence, including radiocarbon assessments and ceramic dating, suggest that they were all probably in use throughout at least the early part of the Earliest Iron Age. Some may have begun earlier. What is clear is that none continued in use into the Early Iron Age. They are therefore a phenomenon of the transitional phase and should be interpreted in the light of the social changes occurring at that time. At the very least they must represent the emergence of an elite able to use its coercive power to create 'monumental structures'. The massiveness of the enclosing earthworks is more likely to be for display than purely for defence. It is possible that in the ring-forts we are witnessing the rise of a landholding elite rooted in their own territories at the time when the bronze-based prestige goods economy was breaking down. A greater chronological precision is needed before detailed models can be constructed directly relating the two.

Contact with the Continent was maintained throughout this period as is shown by the quantity of Hallstatt C metalwork arriving in the Eastern zone and being copied locally during the seventh century. That most of the swords known come from rivers is a clear indication that traditional belief systems continued unimpeded.

The ceramic evidence for the Earliest Iron Age is not plentiful. The earliest pottery (LBA transitional) shows a distinct technological improvement over earlier types with a sharpening of forms leading to a greater angularity which develops, probably in the seventh century, into a more distinctive range of angular forms apparently copying metal prototypes (Kimmeridge–Caburn, West Harling–Staple Howe types). What stands out is a considerable similarity of form in all parts of the zone. There was no attempt at this stage to use pottery as a means of displaying ethnic identity.

The situation in the Early and Middle Iron Age (c. 550–100) is more difficult to determine. Settlement evidence suggests a variety of settlement form ranging from small enclosed homesteads like Brigstock and Draughton, not unlike the earlier ring-forts, to large straggly agglomerations like Fengate and Little Waltham which are best considered to be villages.

Strongly defended hill-top enclosures, while they occur, for example in Essex and the Chilterns, are by no means common, and where excavation has taken place occupation can usually be shown to be restricted to the early period. The best that can be said from the disparate and rather scrappy evidence available is that settlement systems probably differed from region to region but there is little to suggest the centralization of power or any well-developed sense of territoriality except along the Chiltern ridge.

The ceramic evidence gives some insight into regionalization. Although throughout the area and over much of the time, a basic coarse ware tradition of scored jars was in evidence, regional groupings of decorated ceramics appear from the Early Iron Age. East Anglia, the Chilterns and the Upper Thames valley all have their own very distinctive styles, but these seem to be comparatively short lived and throughout much of the Middle Iron Age ceramics revert to plain and largely undifferentiated styles. By the end of the Middle Iron Age and the beginning of the Late Iron Age elaborately decorated pottery is once more the norm particularly around what may be regarded as the fringes of the Eastern zone from Lincolnshire, through Northamptonshire to the Upper Thames region and then to the Lower Thames.

While there are considerable dangers inherent in overinterpreting evidence of this kind it could be argued that the late decorated styles were developed to distinguish the ethnicity of those communities who occupied what might be regarded as frontier positions around the fringes of the Eastern zone in those areas where confrontation with differently ordered social groups might have occurred. The suggestion is at least plausible. If it is accepted then the brief appearance of distinct styles in the Early Iron Age might suggest another period of tension.

The situation in Yorkshire, on the northern fringes of the Eastern zone, was altogether different. Some time in the late fifth century a highly distinctive burial rite was adopted involving inhumation in cemeteries, the individual burials usually being enclosed within a rectangular ditched enclosure. The richer burials were accompanied by grave-goods reflecting both gender and status. In a few cases two-wheeled vehicles accompanied the body to the grave. The burial rite, which characterizes the Arras culture, is virtually unknown elsewhere in the British Isles but has striking similarities to traditions well established in northern Gaul and beyond. The simplest explanation, and the one most frequently adopted, is that the Arras culture emerged as the result of an incursion of population from the Continent. An interesting alternative view has, however, been put forward by Higham (1987) who argues that we may be seeing little more than a powerful local elite, emulated to a lesser extent by their followers, adopting the burial ritual of outsiders to heighten their own status. This would imply that the Arras nobility were in some form of social contact with communities on the opposite side of the North Sea. That such a contact existed can hardly be doubted since the range of artefacts found in the Arras burials, and indeed elsewhere in the Eastern zone, demonstrate exchange with the Continent. Both explanations are equally plausible and it is difficult to see how archaeological evidence alone will further elucidate the problem.

The long established exchange systems which linked the Eastern zone with the Continent were maintained throughout the Early and Middle Iron Age as the range of imported goods reviewed in chapter 16 will show: the distribution patterns suggest that the Thames was a major point of entry. Types of weapon, horse gear and personal ornaments, once adopted in Britain, were soon modified by highly competent local craftsmen. Nowhere is this better shown than with the Hallstatt D daggers found in profusion in the Thames.

Thus the Eastern zone emerges as a distinct but varied territory facing the North Sea from across which it absorbed a consistent flow of cultural influences. The settlement pattern, apart from suggesting the emergence of an elite in the eighth century BC, offers little clear hint of development but the burial rite, adopted exclusively in the region immediately north of the Humber, is indicative of another elite-dominated society lasting for a century or two from the fifth century. Regional variation is well-expressed in the ceramic data but the ritual, involving the deposition of weapons in rivers, established in the second millennium, remains vigorous throughout the Iron Age and serves as a link between the disparate regions of the zone.

The Central southern zone

The social development of the Central southern zone differs in many ways from that of the Eastern zone. At the very beginning of the period the spate of bronze 'hoarding' overtakes the region at different times. Along the South Downs, for example, the last major phase of hoarding takes place in the late Ewart Park phase (eighth century) while in Wessex hoarding is concentrated in the subsequent Llyn Fawr phase (seventh century). The rest of the region appears to escape the phenomenon altogether (R. Thomas 1989). At a simple level of explanation this might suggest two things: that the social changes reflected in hoarding reached Wessex significantly later than they did the east of Britain, and that the prestige goods economy, of which 'hoarding' is thought to represent the final stages, extended to only part of the Central southern zone.

In the late second and early first millennium the settlement evidence suggests the existence of a hierarchy, the upper echelons being represented by sub-rectangular ditched enclosures like Norton Fitzwarren, Highdown Hill, Rams Hill, etc., which appear to occupy central positions in complex exchange networks (Ellison 1981). The distribution of distinctive styles of Deverel–Rimbury pottery add to the evidence for a degree of regionalism. How late into the Late Bronze Age this essentially Middle Bronze Age system extended it is difficult to say but at Highdown ceramic evidence and other finds suggest occupation as late as the eighth or even seventh century, while at Rams Hill a larger enclosure associated with pottery of the earliest Iron Age replaced the earlier centre. The hints are therefore that this system may have persisted in some places at least into the eighth century.

At some stage within the early first millennium BC a major reorganization of the landscape took place. The most far-reaching change was the reapportionment of land by means of linear earthworks. In some places these cut across old field systems and in others form the axes from which new systems are laid out. The change focuses on the chalkland of Wessex. Exact dating is difficult to obtain but there are various indications suggesting that the system of linears may have been laid out comparatively late in the eighth or perhaps even the seventh centuries.

The second change dating to about this time was the construction of a number of large hill-top enclosures, extensive in area, slightly defended and often occupying high exposed hill-tops. Where excavation has taken place internal occupation has proved to be slight and was generally restricted to groups of four-post storage structures. We have suggested (pp. 346–8) that these early enclosures may be communal structures built to contain and control flocks and herds at certain times during the year. Dating evidence suggests that they lie within the Earliest Iron Age (eighth and seventh centuries).

Direct relationships between linear boundaries and early hill-top enclosures are difficult to demonstrate but at Danebury a very considerable linear is integrated with a ditched enclosure which encircled the hill before the hillfort was constructed in the Early Iron Age. The only structures associated with this early stage are four-post storage units. A similar relationship between a linear and an early enclosure can be seen at Ladle Hill before the construction of the early hillfort began.

It is tempting to see the linear boundaries and the early hill-top enclosures as being part of a single system emerging from the reorganization consequent upon the collapse of the bronze-based prestige goods economy. The very nature of the earthworks imply a far greater control of land and livestock which now may have begun to take precedence as a symbol of status.

The linear earthworks and hill-top enclosures represent the stock-rearing/land management aspects of the new system. Contemporary occupation sites are not particularly well known but a variety of different types can be identified. At one end of the spectrum are strongly defended settlements usually occupying ridge-end sites such as Budbury and Lidbury in Wiltshire. Enclosures of this kind have usually produced quantities of occupation debris including a wealth of elaborately made ceramics. Other contemporary settlements like All Cannings Cross and Potterne, equally rich in pottery, appear to be undefended and occupy less dominant positions. A third category, typified by Little Woodbury and Old Down Farm, consists of ditched enclosures containing the structures of homesteads but have produced comparatively little occupation debris. The evidence is not yet sufficient to allow a detailed social model to be constructed but it is tempting to see in the defensive works of the ridge-end settlements a display of strength appropriate to the homesteads of the elite.

The settlement pattern of the Earliest Iron Age represents a marked break with what had gone before. Everything points to an intensified interest in land and territory. The linear boundaries and hill-top enclosures are massive communal undertakings requiring a significant sector of the community to work together under some kind of coercive leadership, while many of the settlements, especially the ditched homesteads, once established continued to be occupied, or were frequently reoccupied, over a period of hundreds of years. In other words a degree of permanence was now developing for the first time.

Throughout the Earliest Iron Age the south coast of Hampshire and Dorset served as a contact zone linking Britain with Armorica and Normandy. It was through the Solent ports that Armorican axes were imported and it may have been via the same routes that the inspirations for the elaborately decorated pottery of Early All Cannings Cross type came. These distinctive and highly accomplished wares were widely distributed in Wessex from the Dorset coast to the Berkshire Downs with little evidence of regional variation. Such uniformity must surely imply a degree of ethnic unity binding much of Wessex together as a single social region.

Further to the north, in the Cotswolds and the Welsh borderland, evidence for the earliest occupation is still very sparse but large hill-top enclosures can be identified in the Cotswolds and the earliest slight defence around the exposed hill-top of the Breiddin is best dated to this period. The indications are therefore that similarities with Wessex exist and may be more widespread than at first appears.

The Early Iron Age (c. 550–400) saw a significant change in settlement pattern. The hill-top enclosures and ridge-end settlements were widely abandoned and there emerged a large number of *early hillforts* (pp. 348–52) all of which were sited in well-chosen naturally defensive positions. This fact, together with the strength of their defensive works and occasional evidence of attack is sufficient to suggest that a more aggressive situation was now developing. The exact chronology of these early hillforts cannot yet be worked out, but there are hints that the earliest are to be found in the Cotswolds. Their spread throughout Wessex and into the Welsh borderland seems to have occurred a little later in the Early Iron Age during which time a considerable number were erected.

The sudden spread of hillforts over most of the Central southern zone in a comparatively short time in the late sixth and fifth centuries must indicate a significant change in the social system. The simplest explanation would be to see this in terms of intensifying pressure on land leading to a situation of stress in which it was necessary to demonstrate proprietorship of territory, the symbol of control being a communal defensive structure. But these early hillforts were more than just symbols. Internal excavation has shown that at least some of them were intensively occupied with zones of houses, storage buildings and storage pits leaving little doubt that the forts were in constant, if not necessarily continuous, use throughout the period.

The Middle Iron Age saw a further development which is best characterized as a crystallizing out of the hillfort system: many of the early forts went out of use but a number were maintained, strengthened and sometimes enlarged. There is also some evidence to suggest that hillforts spread further to the east into Surrey and west into eastern Devon during this period. This thinning out of numbers is best seen as the result of a coalescence of power at certain sites – in other words the emergence of larger territories after the initial period of hillfort building.

Whatever their symbolic significance, these *developed hillforts* were intensively occupied and performed a range of central-place functions for their territories. Their massive storage capacities imply the stockpiling of goods for redistribution, while the occurrence in some quantities of bulk raw materials such as shale, querns, salt and iron, produced outside their immediate territories, indicates that it was probably to the forts that these materials were transported before being redistributed to the settlements in the hinterland (Figure 20.3).

What segment of the community was resident in the forts it is impossible to say. Various models have been offered (Cunliffe 1984a, 559–62) but firm evidence is lacking. At best we should see them as centres of power dominating and serving territories, but the precise social mechanisms by which these relationships were enacted are elusive.

By the end of the Middle Iron Age it is clear that much of the Central southern zone was divided into distinct territories each dominated by a hillfort. The sense of territoriality is further heightened by a consideration of ceramic styles which serve to delineate larger groups perhaps of ethnic significance (Figure 20.4). The pattern is clearest towards the end of the Middle Iron Age but many of these zones had already defined themselves in the Early Iron Age (pp. 70–2). Together the evidence strongly suggests that we are witnessing the emergence of the tribal structure which comes increasingly into focus as the Late Iron Age advances. Since it is difficult to trace these 'tribal' regions back before the Early Iron Age it is possible that ethnogenesis did not begin in the Central southern zone until the end of the sixth century. The comparatively sudden appearance of hillforts at just this time is surely no coincidence.

The simplest model to contain all the salient facts is one of population growth giving rise to increasing pressure on land. This would lead to territoriality on a local scale manifesting itself in appearance of a rash of early hillforts and the gradual rationalization of the system as many went out of use while a few rose to dominance. Allegiances on a larger scale created a sense of regional identity visible in the archaeological record as discrete style-zones. Population increase is easy to propose but more difficult to prove. It is significant however that a number of writers viewing different aspects of the settlement data have all suggested an increase of population throughout the Early and Middle Iron Age. Population pressure can lead to stress situations which manifest themselves in different ways one of which is in heightened aggression. This could explain the very existence of the hillforts and in particular the growth of more massive defences during the Middle

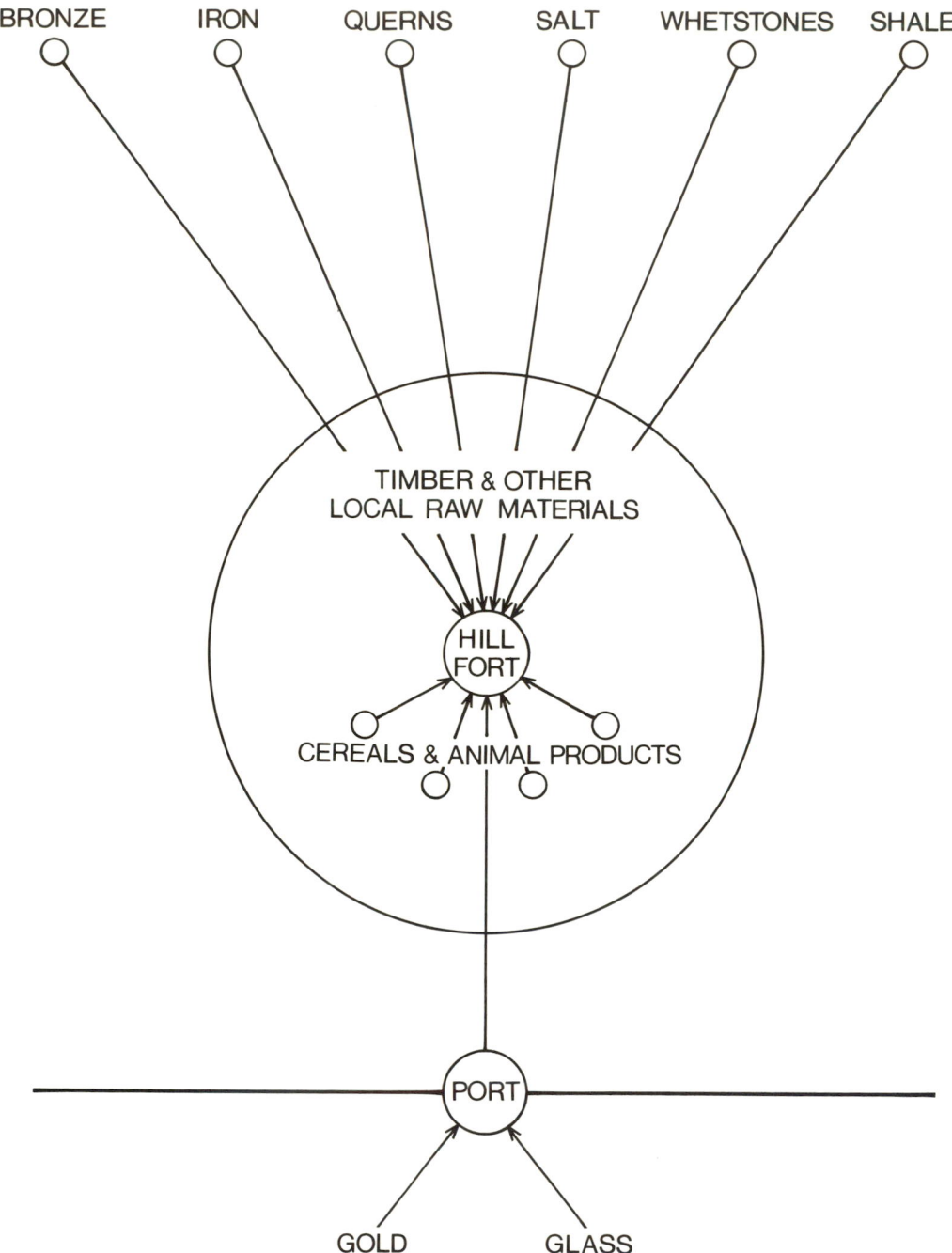

Figure 20.3   Diagram to show the relationship of a developed hillfort like Danebury, to its economic environment (source: author).

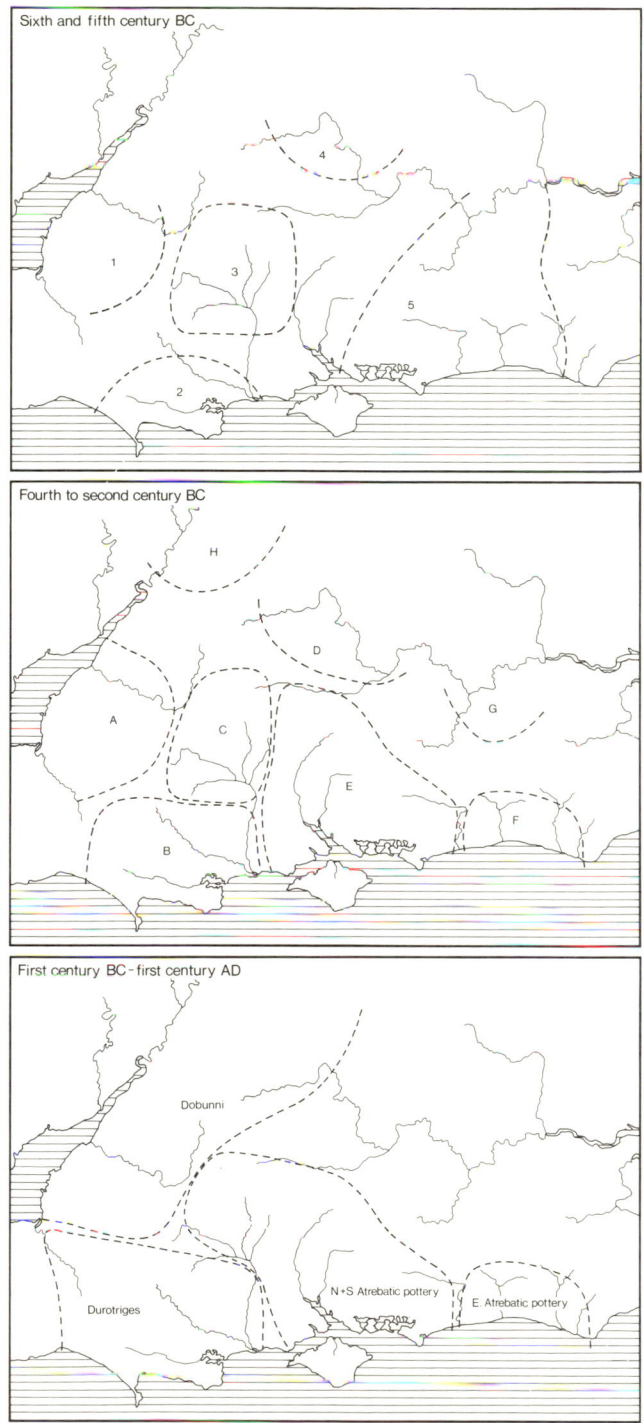

Figure 20.4   Ethnogenesis in central southern Britain. Distribution of distinctive pottery styles reflecting possible ethnic divisions. (source: author).

Iron Age. Occasional evidence for attack and defence shows that there was a need for defence while mutilated bodies from a number of sites are a reminder of the reality of Iron Age warfare.

It would be wrong to give the impression of constant warfare. No doubt there were long periods of peace. Alliances would be made, held and broken. It is possible that some hillforts were abandoned for periods and reoccupied later. The situation would have been one of constant change but the archaeological evidence is generally too coarse-grained to allow subtleties of this kind to be distinguished.

The ritual systems in operation in the Central southern zone are at last becoming clearer. We can now be tolerably sure that the burial of the dead, either cremated or inhumed, in cemeteries was not a normal rite: all the evidence that survives points to complex rituals involving excarnation and possibly the later curation of selected bones. But the number of bodies found in abandoned storage pits shows that the behaviour patterns associated with the dead were complicated. Indeed it is worth considering the pits themselves. The consignment of grain, probably seed grain, to a pit is an over-complex way of solving the storage problem especially when perfectly serviceable storage buildings were in use at the same time alongside the pits. If, however, the pit itself was a structure dug for ritual purposes it would be easier to understand. The pit could be seen as a means of placing the seed-corn in the realm of the deities so that it would be divinely protected and its powers of regeneration assured. If such a system were in operation then propitiatory offerings of humans, animals or sets of artefacts placed on the pit bottoms when the pits were no longer used would be entirely understandable. Thus the pits themselves, and the propitiatory offerings in them, would represent a distinct belief system and the distribution of storage pits would demonstrate the extent of that belief. The concentration of storage pits in the Central southern zone is another characteristic which serves to distinguish it from neighbouring zones but pits are absent from the Welsh borderland which is part of the Central southern zone.

Grain storage pits of Iron Age type have a comparatively limited chronological span. They occur but are uncommon in the Earliest Iron Age: by the Early Iron Age they are extremely numerous and continue throughout the Middle Iron Age but they are virtually unknown in the Late Iron Age. Thus the *storage pit belief system* developed in the period of stress in which the hillforts began to develop but was over by the beginning of the Late Iron Age: we will consider the end below (pp. 543–5).

While, clearly, there were regional differences in the Central southern zone and a variety of local systems must have been at work, a considerable cultural and developmental similarity can be seen throughout: an increasingly rigorous territoriality emerges associated with evidence of stress and aggression and for part of the zone at least a belief system concerned with the fertility of the crops is much in evidence. We have suggested that population growth was a significant factor in cultural development. In view of the belief system it may be that soil deterioration, particularly on the light calcareous soils, created another pressure enhancing stress.

The South-western zone

The South-western zone includes much of Devon, Cornwall and the south and west of Wales. It is a geographically disparate zone but basic geology and climate and the importance of the sea serve to create a broadly similar environment within which the settlement systems have developed. By virtue of its west-facing location and the high altitude of some parts of the region the climatic deterioration of the early first millennium has had a significant effect rendering uninhabitable some of the upland areas and presumably, in consequence, putting pressure on the more congenial lowlands.

It is not easy at present to recognize a regular pattern of change in the settlement evidence but certain generalizations appear to hold good for much of the zone. First, hillforts of the type which characterize the Central southern zone are virtually unknown, but a few large hill-top enclosures are to be found in upland areas of Wales. These are largely undated but may in some way be associated with the seasonal use of upland pastures throughout all or part of the period. Second, the normal settlement type – the defended homestead – occurs widely throughout the zone and there is now reasonable evidence to suggest that settlements of this kind increased in number throughout the Middle and Late Iron Age, strongly hinting at a significant increase in population.

Defended settlements vary considerably in form and size and it is best to consider them as a continuum rather than a series of discrete types (Johnson and Rose 1982). The smallest, the rounds and raths, are less than a hectare in size while the larger sites – the multiple-enclosure forts and cliff castles – may extend to many hectares. Presumably in this gradation we are seeing a social range at the head of which are the elite. The simple model which we have offered above is that the multiple-enclosure forts, cliff castles and small 'hillforts' represent the homesteads of the aristocrats who expressed their status in terms of the massiveness of their defences. That many of these sites are planned with stock management in mind and lie in areas apparently devoid of field systems suggests that wealth and status may have been measured in terms of cattle. This raises a further interesting question – were there two subsystems at work in the west, the low status freeholders managing the land while the elite maintained herds? This would be consistent with the archaeological evidence but is difficult to test. The corollary of such a divide is that the two subsystems would have had to be linked into a single system by ties of obligation and clientage. If so the social system of the South-western zone would have been very similar to that in operation in early Christian Ireland. The model does not necessarily require the two subsystems to have been co-located within a single region: different environmental potentials may have created regional differentiations as has been suggested for south-west Wales (G. Williams 1988).

It is not yet possible to give a convincing account of change through time apart from the point already made that settlement density increases noticeably. Multiple-enclosure forts, however, appear to date to the Middle and Late Iron Age, thus implying that the complex social pattern which they characterize develops comparatively late some time after c. 400 BC.

One further characteristic of the settlement pattern deserves consideration: the close spaced nature of some of the settlements. The two landscapes depicted in Figure 20.5 from Cornwall and south Wales, serve to illustrate the point. Not all of the settlements need be contemporary but many of them are likely to have been at various stages throughout the Iron Age. The pairing of settlements in particular stands out and it may be that here we are seeing the archaeological manifestation of the Celtic system of partable inheritance which survived in Wales into the late first millennium AD.

The belief systems of the south-west are at present ill-defined, but where burial evidence survives the rite was invariably inhumation in stone-built cists usually arranged in cemeteries, and spans the Middle and Late Iron Age. It therefore differs significantly from that of the Central southern zone. Another difference is the absence of storage pits but this is hardly surprising if the subsistence system was differently structured. Evidence for ritual behaviour, while limited, also shows distinct regional characteristics with a preference for depositing luxury goods in bogs.

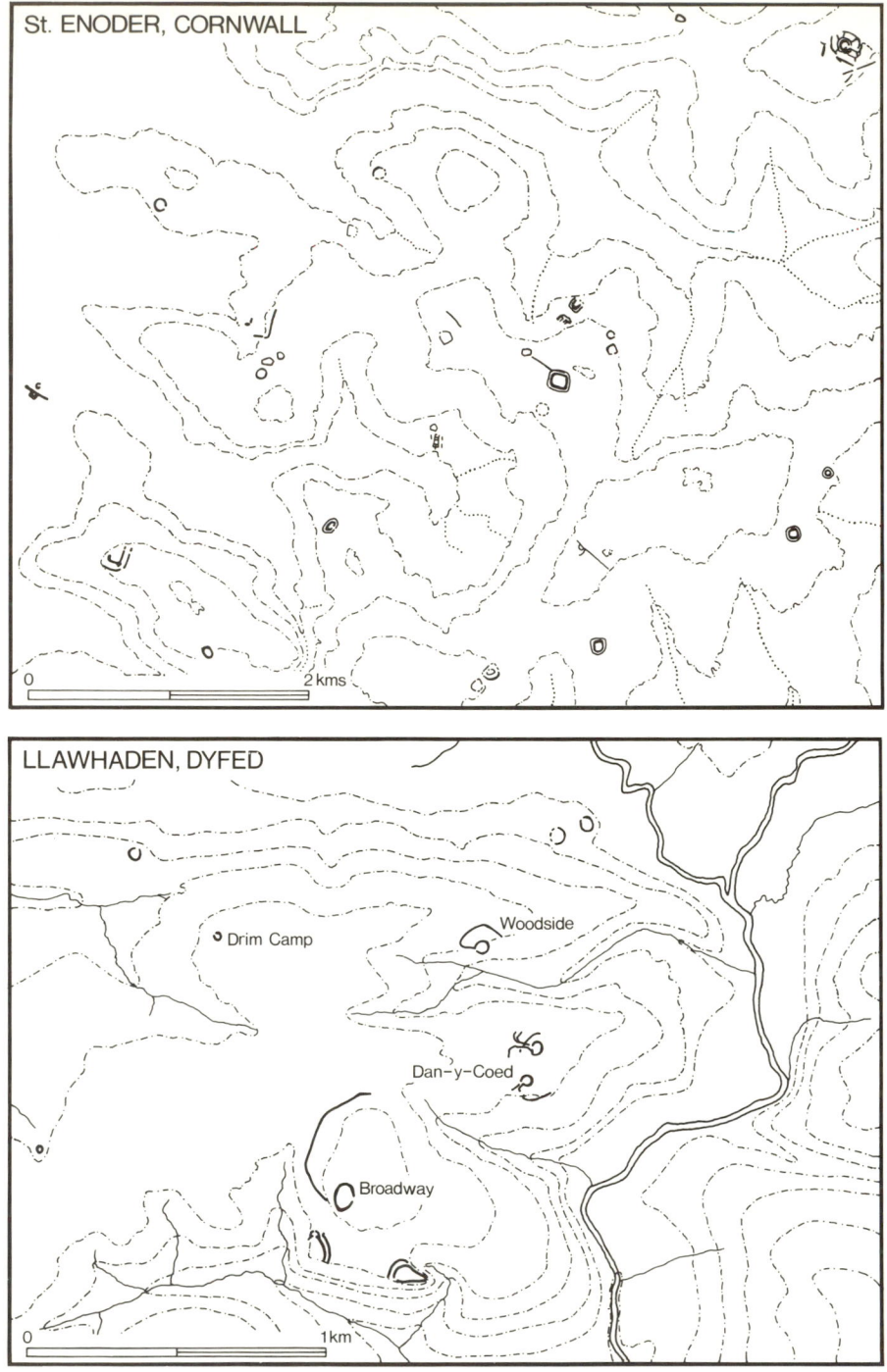

Figure 20.5 Iron Age landscapes in the south-west of Britain. St Enoder, Cornwall (source: Johnson and Rose 1982) and Llawhaden, Dyfed (source: G. Williams 1988).

While it could be argued that this is more a reflection of the prevalence of bogs in the south-west the fact that so many bog finds have been made, and virtually none from rivers, must surely indicate a specific set of distinctive beliefs associated with the sanctity of this type of watery location. If the apparent contrast to the belief system of the Central southern zone is valid then it could be explained in terms of the differences between a cattle-dominated economy in which water was vital and a corn-dominated economy depending on the fertility of the earth – though the antithesis may seem a little far-fetched.

There is little evidence from the South-western zone of rigorous territoriality of the kind which can be recognized in the Central southern zone and this might be thought to support the social model which we have suggested for the region with centralization of power and services not extending beyond the level of a minor dispersed aristocracy. High quality ceramics were being produced in the south-west but they were widely distributed and not restricted to distinct territories. Thus there is no hint of the tribal or sub-tribal grouping, which we can recognize in the Central southern zone. By the beginning of the historic period tribal names like the Dumnonii, Silures, Demetae and Ordovices are recorded but they tend to occupy geographically distinct territories divided from each other by mountains or the sea. In such circumstances tribal conflict is unlikely to have broken out and thus the need to define ethnicity would have been slight.

Contact with the adjacent Continent was maintained throughout the Iron Age and is most evident in the parallel development of material culture and settlement pattern which occurred between Cornwall and Brittany. No doubt trade in tin and other commodities contributed but other forms of social intercourse are likely. The exchange systems extended into the Severn estuary and seem to have involved the communities of Silurian territory, but beyond this south Welsh fringe, to the west and north, there is little evidence of contact.

The social, economic and religious systems, once established, were maintained little changed throughout the Late Iron Age into the Roman period.

The North-western zone

The North-western zone, stretching from Galloway to Shetland constitutes a well-defined physical region – an Atlantic province of indented coasts and uplands with a distinctive settlement pattern characterized by strongly defended homesteads – the duns of the southern part of the zone and the brochs of the north. Comparatively little variety can be recognized among the settlements that might suggest significant social differentiations except that in Orkney a number of the brochs became central elements in small defended villages.

Several important excavations have allowed some threads of chronological development to be distinguished. Simply stated the first half of the first millennium BC seems to have been a time of open settlements sometimes large enough to be classed as hamlets. Defensive architecture was more a feature of the later first millennium with the brochs beginning to emerge as a frequent element in the north from the second century BC onwards (though originating some time earlier). Brochs were sometimes built within existing duns and a few, as we have said, went on to become centres of small villages. The most obvious facet of this development sequence is the increasing emphasis placed on defence. There is no direct evidence to suggest that this was brought about by pressure on land and indeed a survey of settlement pattern and resource potential in Shetland shows that the holding capacity had by no means been reached (Fojut 1982b). The simplest explanation, therefore, is that defensive strength was more a matter of social display than of military need.

The economic systems of the North-western zone seem to have been small-scale and based on the self-sufficiency of the individual settlement: no extensive trade networks are known to have existed.

Our knowledge of belief systems is negligible. Burials are rare as indeed are ritual deposits or evidence of behaviour which might be interpreted as ritual. While this does not imply that belief systems were impoverished it strongly suggests that they differed significantly from those of the south.

The North-eastern zone

The North-eastern zone stretching from the Yorkshire Moors to the foothills of the Grampians is an extremely varied zone made up of a number of regions displaying cultural and economic variation. This variation together with a general lack of good evidence for sequential development makes it difficult to offer general statements about social and economic change except at a very simple level.

What stands out from the settlement pattern evidence, which has been extensively explored, is that the basic unit was the enclosed homestead, the method of enclosure changing over time from timber palisades to banks and ditches. Variation in size of these enclosures seems to reflect different social configurations but only in rare instances do these seem to exceed two or three extended families living together.

Hillforts occur in small numbers but their chronology and function remain obscure. What little evidence there is suggests a general scattering of Early Iron Age forts, like the early hillforts of southern England, the majority of which have ceased to be occupied by the beginning of the Middle Iron Age. This holds good for the region south of the Tyne–Firth line but to the north, especially in the valley of the Tweed and on either side of the Firth of Forth, a number of comparatively large and well defended hillforts are known, some of which can be shown to have been in use during the Middle Iron Age and perhaps later. Thus we can recognize two distinctive regimes within the North-eastern zone, in the northern of which some kind of social hierarchy, not unlike that of the Central southern zone can be distinguished. Something of the potential complexities of this hierarchization are beginning to emerge as the result of the excavation of the defended settlement of Broxmouth and other sites in the region.

It is difficult at this stage to offer an assessment of change through time. The abandonment of some of the upland regions as a result of climatic change early in the first millennium is now fairly well established and in many areas continuity of settlement over several centuries can be demonstrated. There are also indications that the landscape was beginning to fill up and it may be that the increase in strength of defensive works over time reflects periods of stress, but it could equally be argued that style of enclosure was used as a demonstration of status in a society which was becoming increasingly stratified.

There is little that can be said of ritual and religious systems in the North-eastern zone. Inhumation burials in small cemeteries are known but are not particularly common. The rite of depositing weapons and other valuable items of metalwork in rivers is reasonably well attested. Thus the North-eastern zone shares certain cultural characteristics with the Eastern zone.

Summary of the Earliest, Early and Middle Iron Age, *c.* 800–100 BC

The comments offered so far in this chapter are in themselves a summary of the preceding nineteen chapters and here we step back still further to attempt an even broader perspective (Figure 20.6). Perhaps the simplest generalization is that culturally Britain in the Iron Age divides east–west and north–south. The north–south divide separates the southern part with its more moderate climate and ease of contact with the adjacent Continent from the harsher more isolated north, while the east–west divide allows us to distinguish a western, Atlantic, zone with its damper climate and fragmented landscape from the eastern, North Sea, zone, drier and more open. These various constraints have helped to mould the Iron Age communities of Britain.

A quite separate theme has contributed to the variety – that of population increase. Throughout the whole island there is evidence of a constant growth in the density of settlement and in some regions, particularly the Central southern zone, the population appears to have been under stress exacerbated perhaps by falling crop yields. Growth of population was one of the factors which led to the crystallizing out of well-defined social hierarchies accompanied, especially in the centre south, by a degree of territoriality.

To what extent we can generalize about social and ritual systems is debatable but the east–west divide seems to be valid. In the west the social system was based on a simple hierarchical divide with a numerous elite – rather like petty lords. In the east social agglomerations were often larger and there appear to have been a number of sites which can reasonably be called villages, extending over quite considerable territories, in use for generations. This kind of settlement pattern, and the social system which it implies, is very similar to that of the adjacent Continent. Between the two lies the hillfort-dominated zone of central southern Britain with an outlier in the north-east. The very existence of these large forts maintained over centuries and intensively used shows that a totally different system was in operation, the forts presumably performing a range of central functions for the territories they dominated.

This simple threefold social divide is also borne out by what little we know of ritual systems: the west with its inhumation cemeteries and votive offerings in bogs, the east with its emphasis on the deposition of weapons in rivers and the centre with excarnation being the normal rite associated with a developed system of propitiation to ensure fertility.

The interaction of these three broad socio-religious systems is a matter of great potential interest but one which we cannot yet begin to approach. Indeed until far more is known about the workings of the individual system at a local and regional level it is doubtful if any significant advance can be made in understanding the broader issues. One idea which might, however, be worth exploring is to see the eastern and western systems as essentially stable (as indeed the archaeological evidence seems to suggest) with the central southern system being unstable, its instability caused or enhanced by virtue of its intermediate location. This idea has some attraction in that it emphasizes the dynamic relationships between zonal systems, a theme from which considerable illumination may eventually come.

The Late Iron Age reorganization *c.* 100 BC–AD 43

Until the end of the second century BC it can fairly be said that Britain lay beyond the periphery of the Mediterranean world. Admittedly certain commodities such as Cornish tin found their way into the Mediterranean system, but only by means which distanced totally the tin-producing

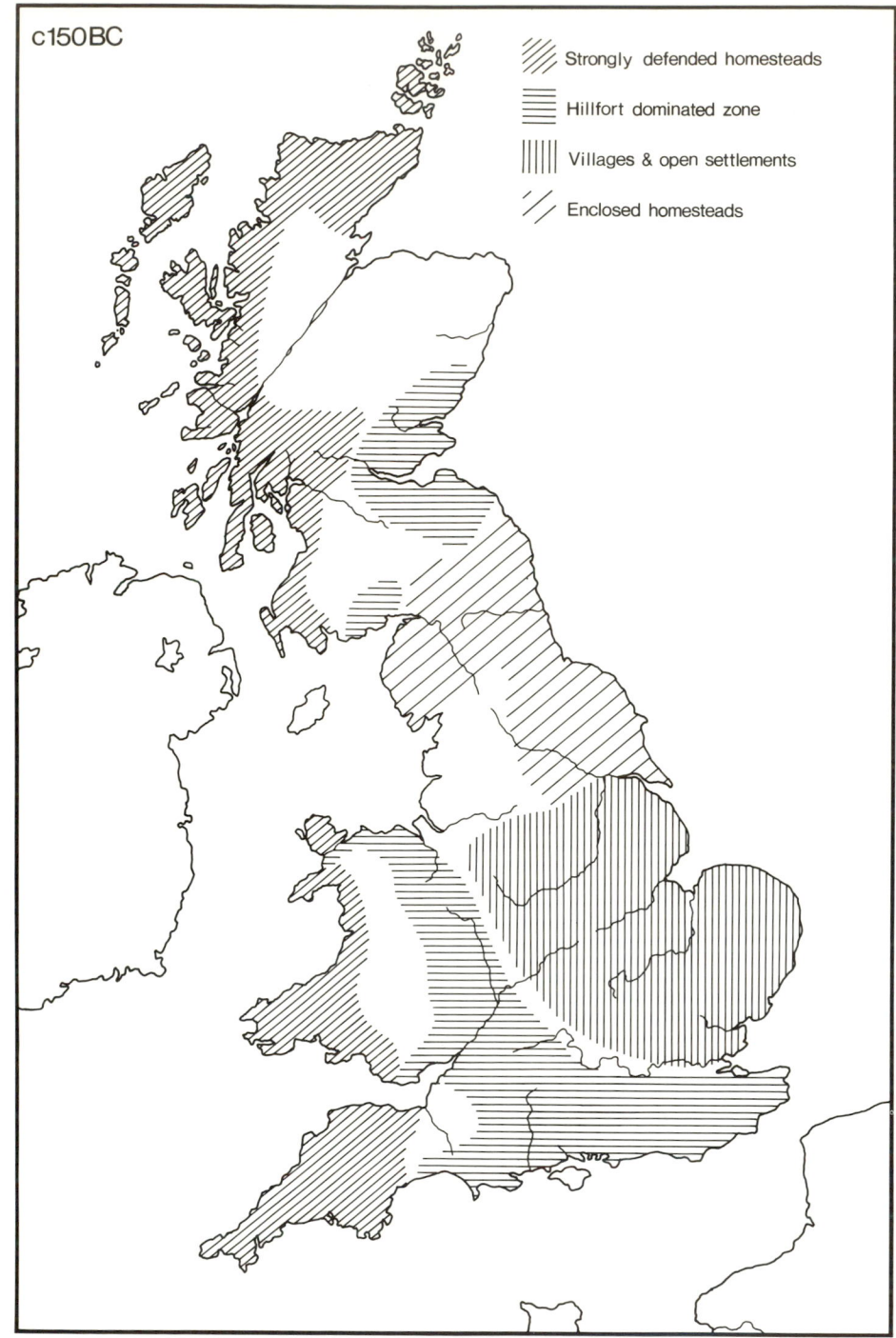

Figure 20.6   Settlement types in Britain *c.* 150 BC (source: author).

communities from the consumers. But all this was to be changed in the closing decades of the second century BC when the Romans began to colonize the southern shores of Gaul. The period, roughly 120–60 BC, saw the establishment of a stable Roman system in the south. During this time the rest of Gaul and southern Britain beyond became a periphery to that system and Britain began to experience the bow-wave effect of Romanization. Then in the decade 60–50 BC Julius Caesar extended Rome's direct influence over the whole of Gaul changing Britain's position from being on the distant edge of that periphery to one of immediate proximity.

We can use this simple historical model to structure our discussion of the changes which came about in Britain. The first period, c. 120–60 BC, can be called the *contact period*, the second c. 60–50 BC is the *Caesarean episode*, while the third period, c. 50 BC to AD 43 is the *impact period*.

The contact period c. 120–60 BC

There is no need to suppose that developing Roman interests in the barbarian west created entirely new modes of exchange. In all probability the movement of commodities took place largely within existing social systems, the only significant difference being the intensity and volume of the materials passing along the traditional axes of contact. This appears to have been how it was with Britain. The first evidence of Roman contact came along the Atlantic sea-ways which had functioned as a route of communication for 2,000 years or more. The ports of entry were on the Dorset coast at Hengistbury and Poole Harbour. These were linked directly, via the Channel Islands, to ports on the north coast of Brittany and from these, by transshipment and short-haul trade, commodities passed to the mouths of the Loire and Gironde and via the great rivers and short overland hauls to the ports on the Mediterranean coasts of Gaul.

The Roman demand for raw materials such as metals and hides, corn and slaves created an entirely new situation in Britain. These products were suddenly endowed with a greatly increased value and could be used to procure luxury items such as Italian wine, coloured glass trinkets and no doubt a good deal more besides. External demand would have provided the impetus for production. Metals extracted in various parts of western Britain were now transported in bulk to the Dorset ports for refinement and transshipment – lead/silver from the Mendips, copper/silver from the Dartmoor fringes and tin from Cornwall. Long-established exchange mechanisms between the South-western zone and the Central southern zone would no doubt have provided the systems by which these products were moved to the ports and stockpiled for export. Grain and hides were probably acquired in a similar way. None of this need have greatly disrupted existing systems of production and exchange, but the demand for slaves was an entirely new factor. While slavery no doubt existed in Iron Age Britain the production of slaves for export cannot have failed to have had a dramatic effect on social systems and may have been as disruptive in Britain in the first century BC as it was in west Africa in the sixteenth and seventeenth centuries AD.

The range of items traded and the routes used can be distinguished reasonably accurately from the archaeological evidence but the volume and consistency of the traffic cannot. All that can safely be said from the very limited excavation at Hengistbury is that considerable quantities of Italian wine were being brought in over a period of time.

Italian wine and other luxury goods provided the aristocracy of central southern Britain with an entirely new means of displaying prestige. It may be no accident that it was at this time that the hillforts of the region go out of regular use. If we were correct in interpreting them as central

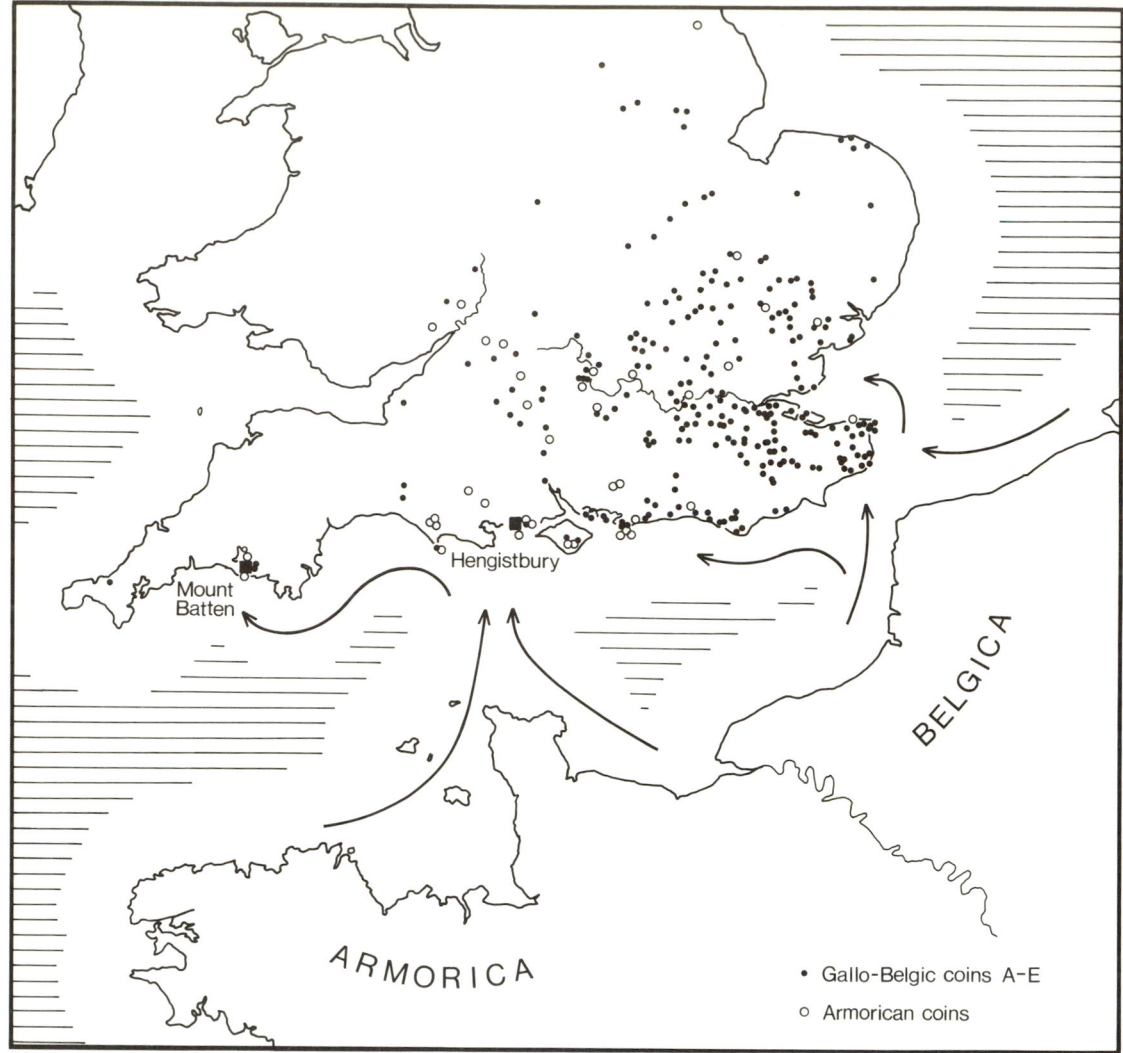

Figure 20.7 Britain and the Continent *c.* 100–50 BC. The unshaded area of sea represents area within easy reach of land, i.e. no more than 30 miles from land (source: author).

places controlling redistribution in a society in which raiding was prevalent, then their demise can most easily be explained in terms of the breakdown of the old system and its replacement by something new. It may be that access to a new range of prestige goods provided the elite with a mode of display which replaced raiding as a means of establishing and maintaining prowess. The symbols of that system – the hillforts – could then be abandoned and the function of redistribution could be transferred to more convenient locations on route nodes where major land routes crossed rivers. The enclosed oppida which developed in these valley sites are thus explained. In any event the abandonment of hillforts by the middle of the first century BC appears to have been restricted to the chalklands of the south – the region most directly affected by the Roman-inspired trade of the contact period.

The Eastern zone was not immediately influenced by the bow-wave effect. Close social contact did however exist between the communities of the south-east, bordering the Thames estuary, and those of the neighbouring ports of Belgic Gaul. This is most clearly demonstrated by the distribution of Gallo-Belgic coinage in south-eastern Britain (Figure 20.7). At a superficial level this looks like a sudden new development but there is no need to interpret it in this way. Contact between the two areas was long established and the exchange of items and ideas had been part of the social scene for centuries. The appearance of Gallo-Belgic coins in the south-east was merely another manifestation of the social interactions linking the communities on either side of the Channel.

There was, however, one significant development – the appearance of low denomination coinage in Kent before the Caesarean episode. While the gold staters of Gallo-Belgic type no doubt changed hands in gift exchange systems, low denomination coinage – the so-called 'potins' – implies the beginning of a market economy. It could therefore be that the distribution of Gallo-Belgic coinage in Britain represents an intensification of traditional social links brought about by enhanced trade between the two regions. The development of local markets in Britain would be a natural follow-on. What motivated the intensification is difficult to say but the simplest explanation is that it was one of the bow-wave effects of Romanization working, in this instance, through Belgic middlemen in northern Gaul.

One further factor must briefly be mentioned – the possible migration of a Continental Belgic community to southern Britain. The question has been considered in detail above (pp. 108–10). Here all that need be said is that an incursion probably took place in the Solent region some time during this period adding another destabilizing factor to the already fluid situation.

The impact period

Caesar's invasion and the political settlement which followed deflected the trajectory of change already under way. Whether by deliberate political design or by the natural reordering of axes of contact, the impact of Roman trading pressures swung from the Atlantic–Solent route to the Belgic-Thames route. Hengistbury and the Dorset ports declined while the ports of Kent and Essex rose dramatically in importance. Within a few decades of Caesar's invasion the Solent and its hinterland had become a backwater, a fact vividly demonstrated by the rapid impoverishment of Durotrigan coinage. Meanwhile the volume of trade goods reaching the communities of eastern Britain had begun to increase very substantially.

While this could be explained entirely in political terms, by Caesar offering trading monopolies to the eastern tribes who had concluded peace treaties with him, it is more likely to be the result of the simple fact that the Thames estuary was conveniently placed to link to the newly-established Roman road systems in Gaul and to the Rhine corridor which was fast becoming a major trade route. Thus in the period following the Caesarean episode the Essex coast became the main interface with the Roman world.

For a while it seems that the exchange processes were articulated through traditional systems allowing the Belgic tribes of Gaul to act as middlemen, but gradually by about 10 BC more direct trade with the Rhine mouth seems to have taken over.

The effects of all this on the tribes of south-eastern Britain were far-reaching. While the old divide between the Eastern and Central southern zones was to some extent maintained a new zonal configuration emerged. The south-east, roughly up to a line joining the Wash to the Hampshire Avon, became a *core zone* beyond which lay a *periphery* extending up to the Humber–Trent–Severn–Exe line. Beyond that old configurations remained largely untouched to continue much as they had in the Early and Middle Iron Age.

The core zone divided politically into two power blocks roughly separated by the Thames though with Kent floating between them. This reflects the traditional divide between the Eastern and Central southern zones. Real power lay with the north of Thames group – the Catuvellauni/Trinovantes and their allies or dependants, the Iceni. The group to the south – the Atrebates – were largely excluded from the benefits of direct trade with the Roman world but the productivity of the territory and their long interface with the peripheral tribes allowed a degree of socio-political development similar to the tribes of the northern configuration. It was in this core zone that oppida developed and a market economy began to emerge. Phases of dynastic instability and a jockeying for control over the border regions between the two power blocks created tension but there is little evidence of extensive aggression.

But changes went deeper than the socio-political system. New belief systems were adopted and cremation, in small cemeteries, became the normal burial rite. The deposition of weapons in rivers declined dramatically and so too did the storage of grain in pits with the accompanying propitiatory rites. It is changes of this kind, bringing to an end traditions centuries old, which show just how fast society was evolving and how deep were the upheavals.

Around the core was a peripheral zone comprising three tribal configurations: the Durotriges, Dobunni and Corieltauvi. All three issued coins and in each territory there are signs of the centralization of market activities at convenient route nodes. Thus the peripheral tribes shared some of the characteristics of the core but were culturally separate from it.

The dynamic relationships between core, periphery and the territories beyond was a complicated one. At its simplest the periphery facilitated the movement of raw materials and manpower from the territories beyond to the core where they were consumed or traded on to the Roman world. Products from the periphery would have joined this drift. In reverse some luxury goods, particularly imported pottery, and gold passed back to the periphery and some part of that, together with local products, were traded out to the tribes beyond. The elements of this system can be traced in the archaeological record. The elite, who by virtue of their status and their control over trade routes, were able to acquire added wealth leading to the emergence of a prestige goods economy manifest in the rich burials of Essex, Hertfordshire and Bedfordshire.

On the eve of the Roman invasion of AD 43 the system had been in full operation for several decades and appears to have reached a degree of equilibrium maintained by the authority of Cunobelin – the 'great king of Britain'. It was his death about AD 40 and the destabilization which followed which gave the Emperor Claudius his opportunity to gain military honours through conquest.

The Roman authorities clearly understood the political geography of Britain: the core was totally annexed, the periphery became a military buffer zone linked from one end to the other by the military road known as the Fosse Way, while the tribes beyond were left to their own devices until because of their hostile actions Rome reluctantly had to begin its advance to the west and north.

The beginning of the Roman interlude

The ease with which the south-east was overrun by the army of Aulus Plautius between AD 43 and 47 was in some part a measure of incipient Romanization — after all, 'eleven kings' were prepared to throw in their lot with Rome immediately. The economy and social structure of the area had developed so far towards a fully urbanized state that effective resistance was no longer possible or, in the minds of many, desirable. The abortive attempt by the resistance army, led by Togodumnus and Caratacus, failed. Togodumnus was killed while Caratacus was forced to beat a retreat to the west, where the pleasures of the Roman life-style were largely unknown. There, among the mountain tribes of Wales, he stirred up such trouble that Ostorius Scapula was forced to take action by occupying a considerable area of the Midlands before routing out the ringleader, who was finally captured as the result of native treachery.

Other war-leaders followed: Boudica in 60 spearheading the rebellion in eastern England, Venutius about ten years later leading the Brigantes against the advance of Cerialis, and ultimately Calgacus opposing the final thrust of Agricola into Scotland. On each occasion the British tribes showed an ability to unite under one leader, but resistance was seldom sustained for long and inevitably collapsed without lasting effect. The furious impetus of the Boudiccan rebellion and the total lack of forward planning is perfectly in keeping with what is known of the Celtic character.

As the areas of conflict moved away from the south-east, Roman civilization rapidly took root. Old tribal boundaries, many of them going back for centuries, were adopted as administrative boundaries while many native oppida became Roman towns. In a vivid and cynical piece of prose Tacitus explains, with obvious relish, the processes of social change:

> To induce a people, hitherto scattered and uncivilized, and therefore prone to fight, to grow pleasurably inured to peace and ease, Agricola gave private encouragement and official assistance to the building of the temples, public squares and private mansions. He praised the keen and scolded the slack, and competition for honour proved as effective as compulsion. Furthermore, he trained the sons of the chiefs in the liberal arts and expressed a preference for British natural ability over the trained skill of the Gauls. The result was that in place of distaste for the Latin language came a passion to command it. In the same way, our national dress came into favour and the toga was everywhere to be seen. And so the Britons were gradually led on to the amenities that make vice agreeable — arcades, baths and sumptuous banquets. They spoke of such novelties as 'civilization' when really they were only a feature of their enslavement.
>
> (*Agricola* 21).

Much of this would have been true of the lowland areas of the province. The Roman money economy, and the ease of trading which the *pax Romana* made so possible, would have allowed the easy accumulation of wealth. In the Roman hierarchical system social and administrative status was totally dependent on money qualifications. Moreover, land could now be bought. These new factors brought about a total revolution in society: the old clan system, with its dynastic leadership based on prestige and birth, gave way to capitalism. But in the Highland areas much of the old order would have prevailed. The survival of the Gaelic and Welsh law and literature with its echo of the Celtic past is sufficient to demonstrate the fact, but in many ways an even more dramatic reminder is found in the seventh-century document, the Ravenna Cosmography, which lists for Scotland a number of *loca* – the meeting places for the northern tribes in the third century AD. These tribal foci are part of a social tradition which we have been able to trace back to the beginning of the first millennium, and which must have been distantly rooted among the Neolithic communities of the third millennium. They symbolize above all the strong undercurrent of tradition which characterizes so much of British prehistory.

21
Models, systems and beyond

The Iron Age, like all prehistoric periods, has been subject to changing fashions in explanation. Each generation of scholars has imposed its own views and prejudices on the evidence in an attempt to explain the inanimate scraps, which are so carefully rescued from the soil, in terms of human activity and the dynamics of society. This is, after all, what archaeology is about. Inevitably, as the database increases, new generations of archaeologists improve upon, and sometimes reject, the views of their elders. In this way all sciences advance. But for the general reader, unused to following detailed debates in obscure journals, all this can be confusing. With this in mind, in the first chapter we have traced the development of the discipline over the last century or so. In this concluding chapter we must attempt to put our current prejudices in perspective and consider possible future directions.

Until 1960 it was usual to explain the British archaeological record in terms of invasion from the Continent. This kind of model was frequently used to give structure to the British Iron Age (pp. 4–13). It was, after all, merely an extension backwards of the historic situation: the Roman invasion of AD 43 was a well-attested fact, as were Caesar's invasions of 55 and 54 BC. Before that, we are told by Caesar of an influx of Belgae, peoples from Gaul, settling in the coastal areas of Britain. It was not an illogical step, therefore, to suppose that a series of such incursions extended back deep into British prehistory, each marked by a recognizable change in the archaeological record. Moreover, such a view could be supported where necessary by reference to the great upheavals and folk movements which affected the contemporary European mainland and were reported by classical writers.

In the 1920s and 1930s 'invasion' became almost synonymous with changes in pottery styles. Thus it was thought that the south-east received the major part of the Continental expansion largely because, one suspects, little pottery was then known from the rest of Britain. Invasion hypotheses became so inherent in archaeological thinking that it was unusual at this time for an excavation report to be written without considerable reliance on a pseudo-historical model. The model not only supported the data, it encased it.

Whenever the material has been studied objectively, as in the case of Hodson's examination of the 'Marnian invasion' (Hodson 1962), conventional invasion models have seldom stood up, with the probable exception of the supposed incursion into Yorkshire which initiated the Arras culture. The problem, nevertheless, is more complex: it may reasonably be asked whether the archaeological record *need* reflect invasion, even if invasion occurred; Caesar's Belgic immigration is notoriously difficult to define in conventional terms. Without the explicit statement of incursion, one might be tempted to explain the changes in the archaeological record entirely in terms of increased trading relations had Caesar not specifically said, 'People came to raid and stayed to till.' Since there is no reason to suppose him wrong, the archaeological evidence must be scanned to look for suggestive traces (pp. 108–10). Even the more widely accepted Arras 'invasion' is not so strongly founded as one might think partly because the equipment of the first-generation settlers has seldom been found and the intrusive culture can be seen only through its subsequent diluted developments, and partly because, as some now think, the change in burial rite should be explained in terms of social emulation rather than actual immigration.

Thus we are forced to ask whether it is permissible to use an invasion hypothesis at all where there is no direct supporting historical evidence. Strictly, I think the answer is 'yes', but only in exceptional cases where all other models seem inferior; even then, invasion should be presented as only one of a series of possible explanations. We must not allow prehistory to become dominated by pseudo-history again.

This is not to say that we should not attempt to recognize 'events' (I use the word 'event' to refer to a series of linked happenings occurring closely together in time). It used to be thought that the appearance of hillforts in southern Britain constituted an event – a response to the stimulus of invasion. This has since been rejected. Might it not be, however, that the late second- or early first-century abandonment, sometimes associated with the destruction, of many of the southern hillforts, occurred at approximately the same time as a result of a related series of socio-political happenings? If so, this would be an event, requiring a political, social or economic model as an explanation in the manner we have attempted in the previous chapter. The settlement pattern evidence, notably that obtained from the detailed excavations of hillforts, is particularly susceptible to analysis and to explanations of this kind, and presents a far more fruitful field for studying political change than the propounding of generalized invasion theories which can seldom be substantiated.

It has long been recognized that the Iron Age communities of Britain formed regional groups, which used to be thought to result from the settlement of different bands of invaders. Now it is accepted that regionalization is caused by a variety of factors, not the least of which is simply the ease or otherwise of geographical communication between one area and another. A simple scheme for defining the principal groups has been given in chapters 4–8 and need not be repeated here. What does need emphasizing, however, is that it owes little to conventional methods of defining 'culture' as laid down by Childe. In 1939a, Christopher Hawkes called for 'cultural' definition within the Iron Age, while in 1964 Hodson went some way towards defining basic folk cultures for southern Britain, to be followed by MacKie for the north in 1969a. However, apart from underlining the basic unity of Iron Age culture over the country as a whole there seems to be little value in pursuing the concept further. The communities of Britain were in such close contact and shared so many systems in common that their similarity far outweighs the significance of their differences. The value to be gained from defining regional groups in this way is that when considered together and seen in perspective it is possible to recognize broad zones within which systems were shared. These zones are however made up of a palimpsest of smaller units characterized by different manifestations in different systems. At neither level are we observing cultures in Childe's sense of the word. The situation, as we now perceive it, was far more complex.

By the end of the 1960s the two basic models commonly used in British archaeology, namely invasion hypotheses and the concept of culture, were failing to satisfy the critical attention of scholars working on the Iron Age, but attention was beginning to turn to a range of analytical techniques then current in geography and the social sciences. These offered some hope of discovering new structures inherent in the data. The settlement pattern of the south-western peninsula was subjected to nearest neighbour analysis (Newcomb 1968, 1970) while the hillforts of southern Britain were seen as fair game for various species of locational analysis (Hogg 1971; Cunliffe 1976b; Groube 1981; E. Grant 1986). But the limitations of these approaches soon became apparent. It was little use employing sophisticated techniques when the database was so crude. Comparing sites which cannot be shown to have been contemporary may provide patterns but hardly patterns of archaeological significance. Similarly the value of propounding general laws about the settlement pattern of a region while the bulk of sites remains to be discovered, has limited relevance.

In parallel with the early attempts to use the techniques of 'new geography' simple economic theory was explored using the evidence of Celtic coins (Collis 1971a and b; Hogg 1971). Contemporary criticism (Rodwell 1976) and more mature reflection (Van Arsdell 1989) have suggested that while stimulating at the time the very limited nature of the database prevents significant generalizations at this level.

The general dissatisfaction and disappointment felt in the aftermath of these pioneering attempts to break the mould has had a depressing and somewhat negative effect on the development of the discipline. On the theoretical level criticism has taken over where once there had been creative thought.

Meanwhile the database has dramatically improved. Large-scale excavation and programmes of fieldwork have been undertaken (and many of them have even been published) while analyses of classes of data, especially ceramics, metals, fauna and flora, have revolutionized our understanding of the quality and complexity of the evidence with which we have to deal. On the one hand we may feel intimidated by the sheer volume and intricacy of what is now available but on the other there is the exuberance borne of knowing that we are on a new threshold of understanding.

In the last ten years anthropological models have been increasingly perfected in attempts to understand the patterning apparent in archaeological data (Hodder 1977; Blackmore, Braithwaite and Hodder 1979) and in more fully worked out examples this has led to stimulating contributions (Hingley 1984a and b). Clearly this is a field which has much to offer but if we are to move away from purely theoretical considerations a much improved dataset is required. Gradually we are moving towards this. But there are real dangers in calling for more evidence. This can lead to excavation for the sake of excavation and analysis *ad absurdum* – a simple accretion of knowledge in the belief that more means better. This is not the way forward – it is wasteful of rare resources. A more creative approach is to adopt a twofold attack. First and foremost we need to define broad-based research strategies which ask questions of the existing database, devise methods of enhancing it and use these results for improved model building which in turn generates new questions. Already high quality results have come from studies of food producing economies mounted in this way and a preliminary examination of belief systems has pointed the way for further potentially revealing work. These are just two examples from many. The second approach is to respond to opportunity: the unexpected can appear at any time and to exclude it by over-rigorous planning would be undesirable.

Standing back from the great mass of evidence now available to us and viewing it against the perspective of how it was acquired we can see two periods of data gathering: the first, up to the 1960s, which was personally motivated and generally small-scale, and the second from the 1960s to the end of the 1980s characterized by site-focused teamwork undertaken on a comparatively large scale. There are indications that this period is coming to an end. What is fast taking over is problem-orientated research geared towards solving some of the more significant questions of which so many still remain. It requires more thought, more careful planning and the pooling of the ideas and aspirations of a large number of specialists. And what are these questions? The reader will by now have formed his or her own ideas, but among them must surely be a better understanding of the motive forces which formed society – climate, population and productivity. It was these, after all, which were, in different part, responsible for giving Iron Age society its infinite variety.

Appendix A   Pottery

In several chapters, particularly 4, 7 and 8 it has been necessary to refer extensively to assemblages of pottery. Pottery is vitally important for the establishment of sequences, the definition of regional groupings and for throwing some light on the complexities of commercial production and trade. It has therefore been decided to illustrate a representative selection of the major groups. Where vessels have been drawn from the original material by the author, the source is given as 'author'; when they are drawn from published sources, the publication is cited. Reference to the site list (Appendix C) will, in the case of unpublished material, give the present location of the collections. All drawings are at 1/4 the original size.

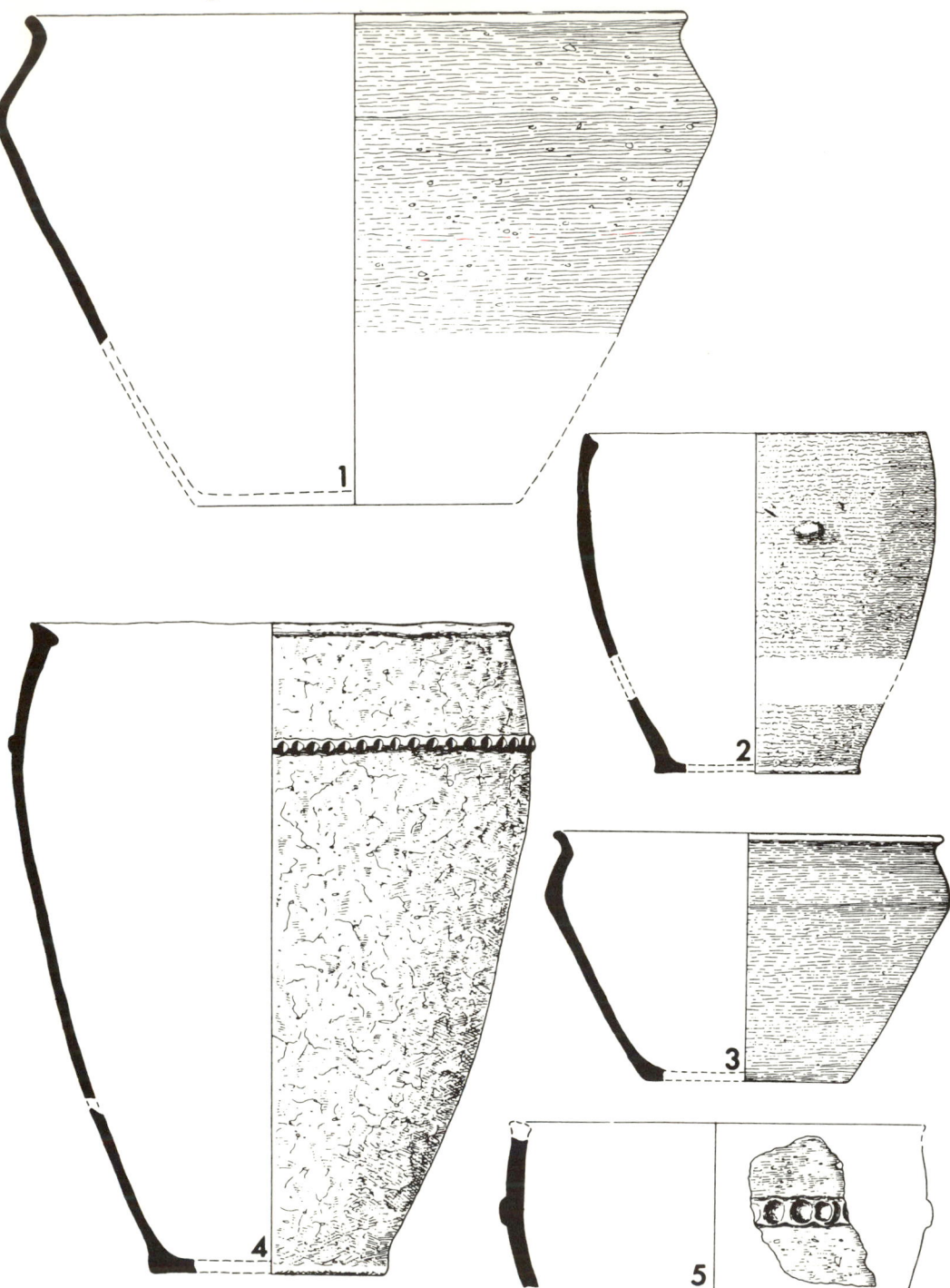

Figure A:1 The Ultimate Deverel–Rimbury tradition: eighth to seventh centuries. 1–5 Eldon's Seat (Encombe), Dorset. (Source: Cunliffe 1968b).

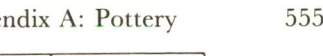

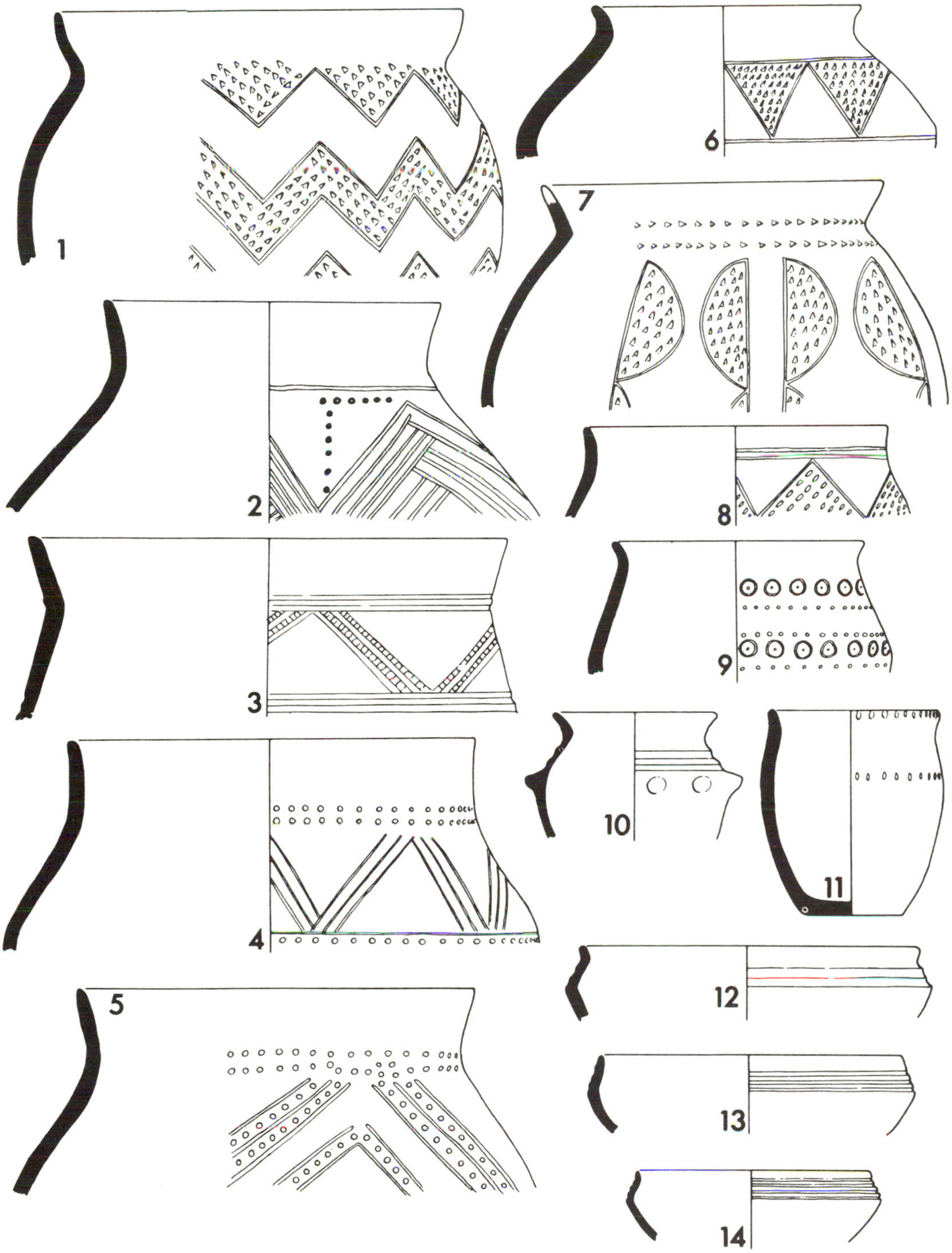

Figure A:2 The Early All Cannings Cross group: eighth to seventh centuries. 1–11 All Cannings Cross, Wilts.; 12–14 Cold Kitchen Hill, Wilts. (Source: author).

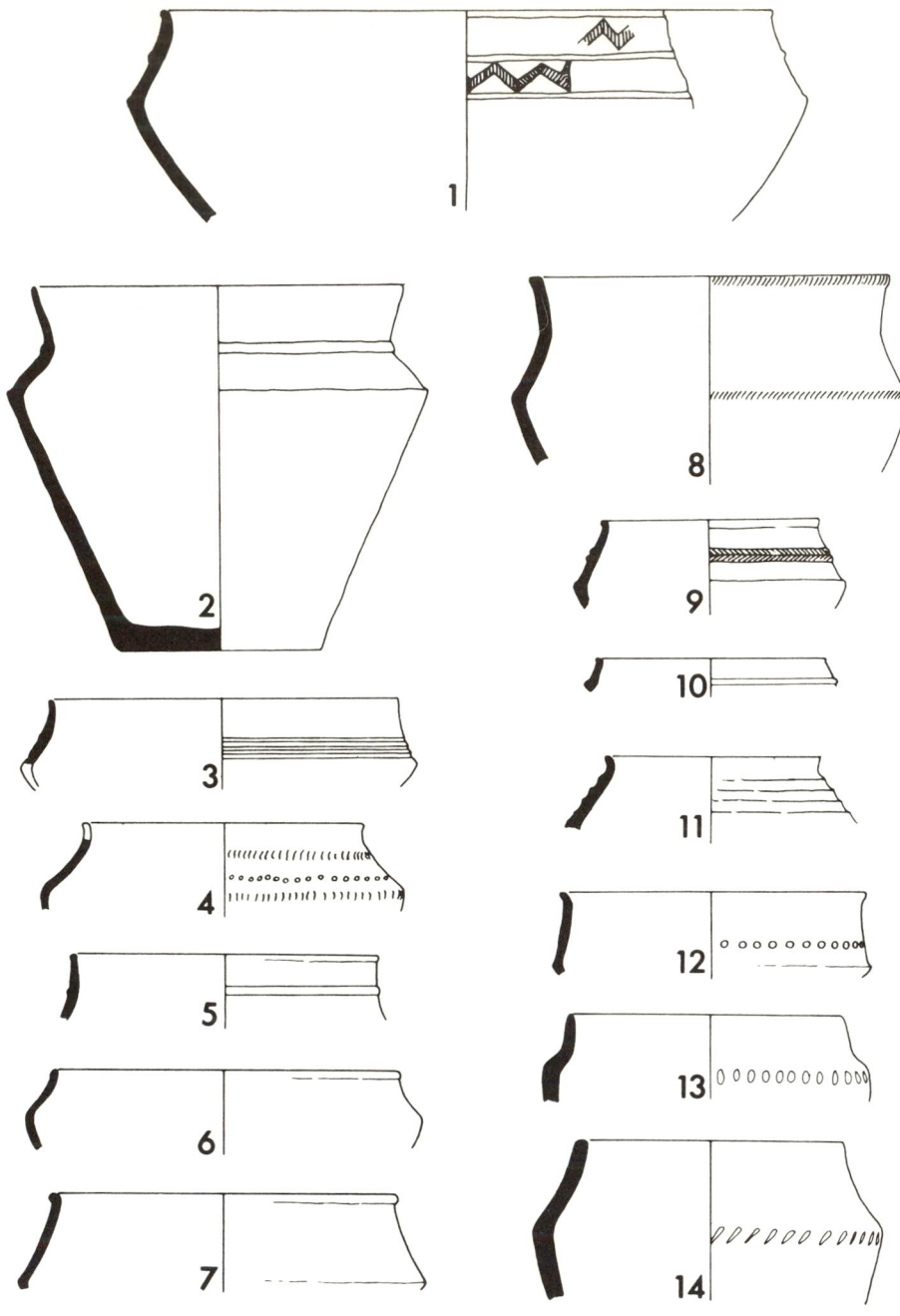

Figure A:3   The Kimmeridge–Caburn group: sixth century. 1–2 the Caburn, Sussex; 3–7 Kimmeridge, Dorset; 8–9 the Caburn, Sussex; 10 Hollingbury Camp, Sussex; 11 Kingston Buci, Sussex; 12–14 Kimmeridge, Dorset. (Source: author).

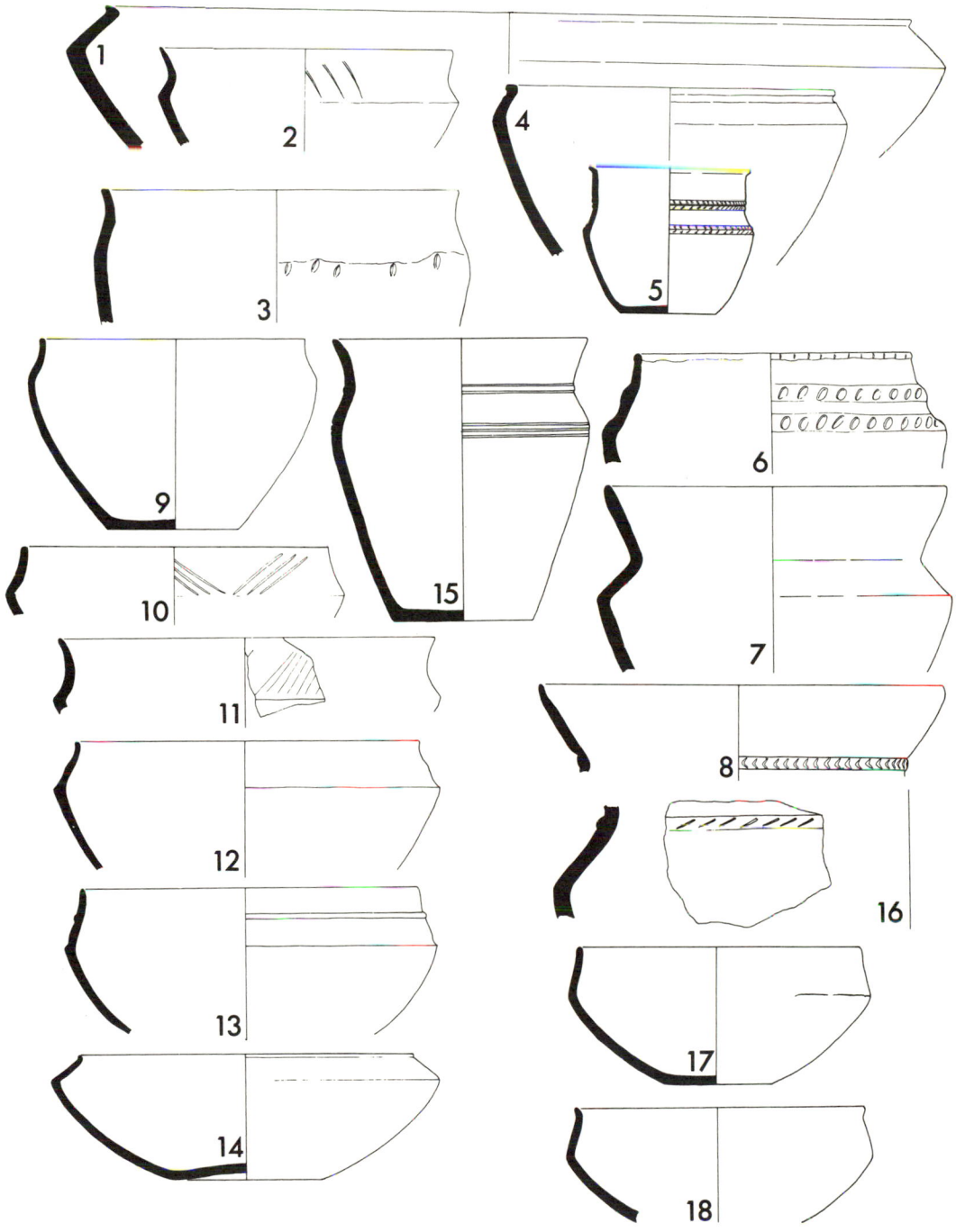

Figure A:4 The West Harling–Staple Howe group: sixth century. 1–4 Staple Howe, Yorks.; 5 Buntley, Suffolk; 6–14 West Harling, Norfolk; 15 Creeting St Mary, Suffolk; 16–18 Minnis Bay, Kent. (Sources: 1–4 Brewster 1963; 5–18 author).

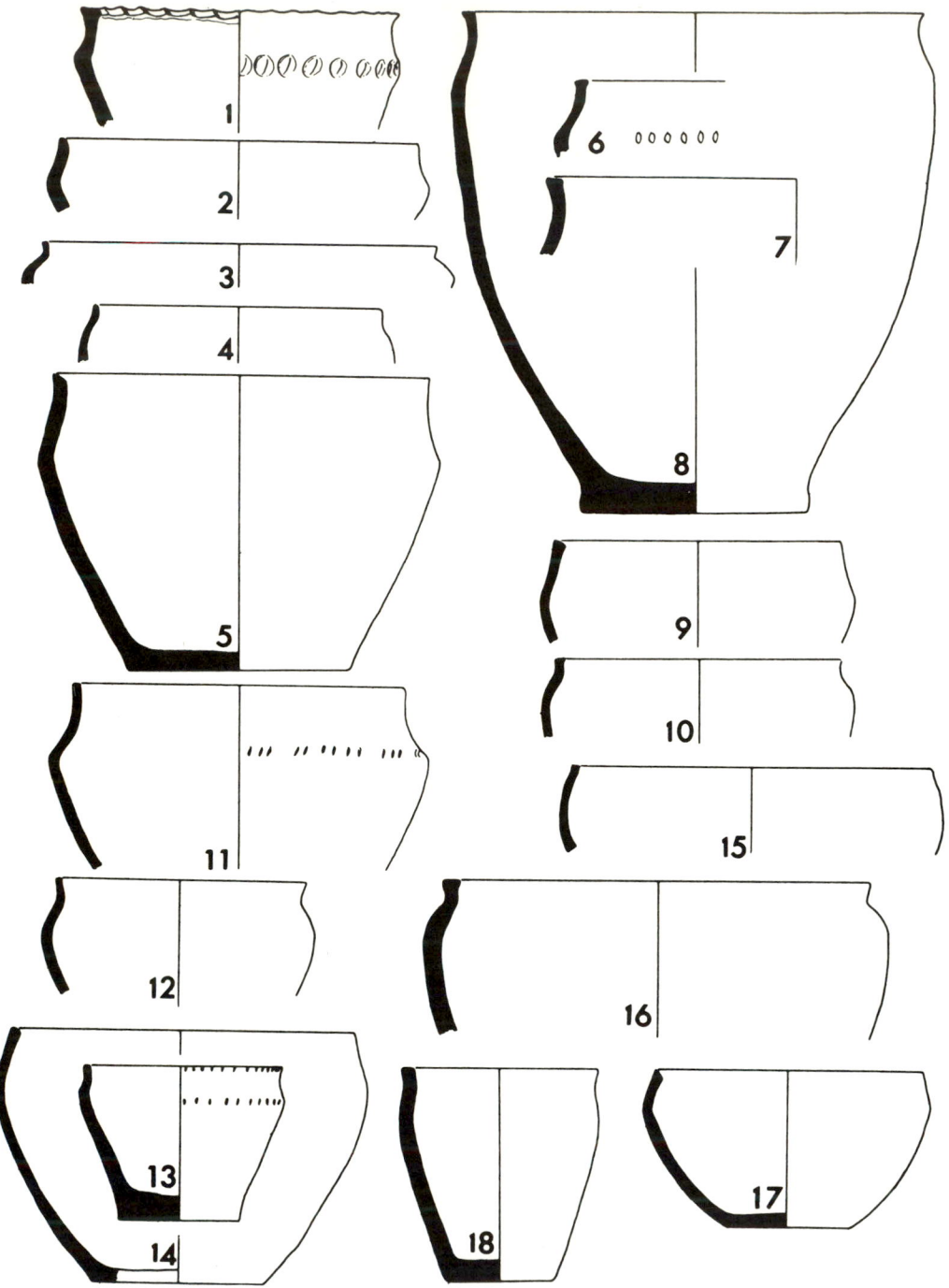

Figure A:5   The Ivinghoe–Sandy group: sixth century. 1–4 Sandy, Beds.; 5 Chippenham, Cambs.; 6–8 Sandy, Beds.; 9–10 Green End Road, Cambs.; 11 Grantchester, Cambs.; 12 Kempston, Foster's Pit, Beds.; 15 Totternhoe, Beds.; 16–18 Harrold, Beds. (Source: author).

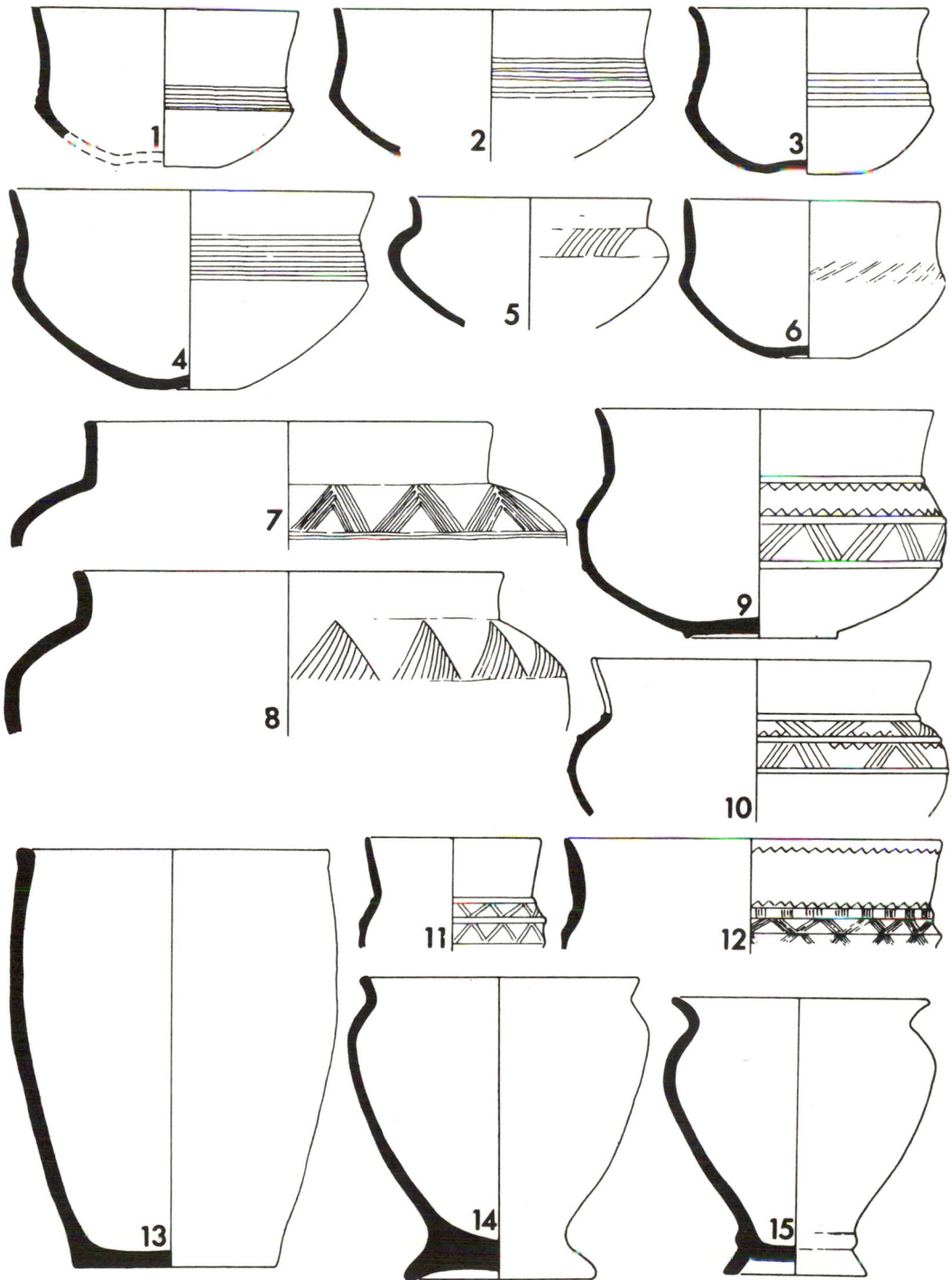

Figure A16   The All Cannings Cross–Meon Hill group: fifth to third centuries. 1 Winchester, Hants.; 2 Boscombe Down West, Wilts.; 3–4 All Cannings Cross, Wilts.; 5 Boscombe Down West, Wilts.; 6 All Cannings Cross, Wilts.; 7–8 Boscombe Down West, Wilts.; 9 All Cannings Cross, Wilts.; 10 Meon Hill, Hants.; 11 Yarnbury, Wilts.; 12 Quarley Hill, Hants.; 13 Boscombe Down West, Wilts.; 14–15 Swallowcliffe, Wilts. (Source: author).

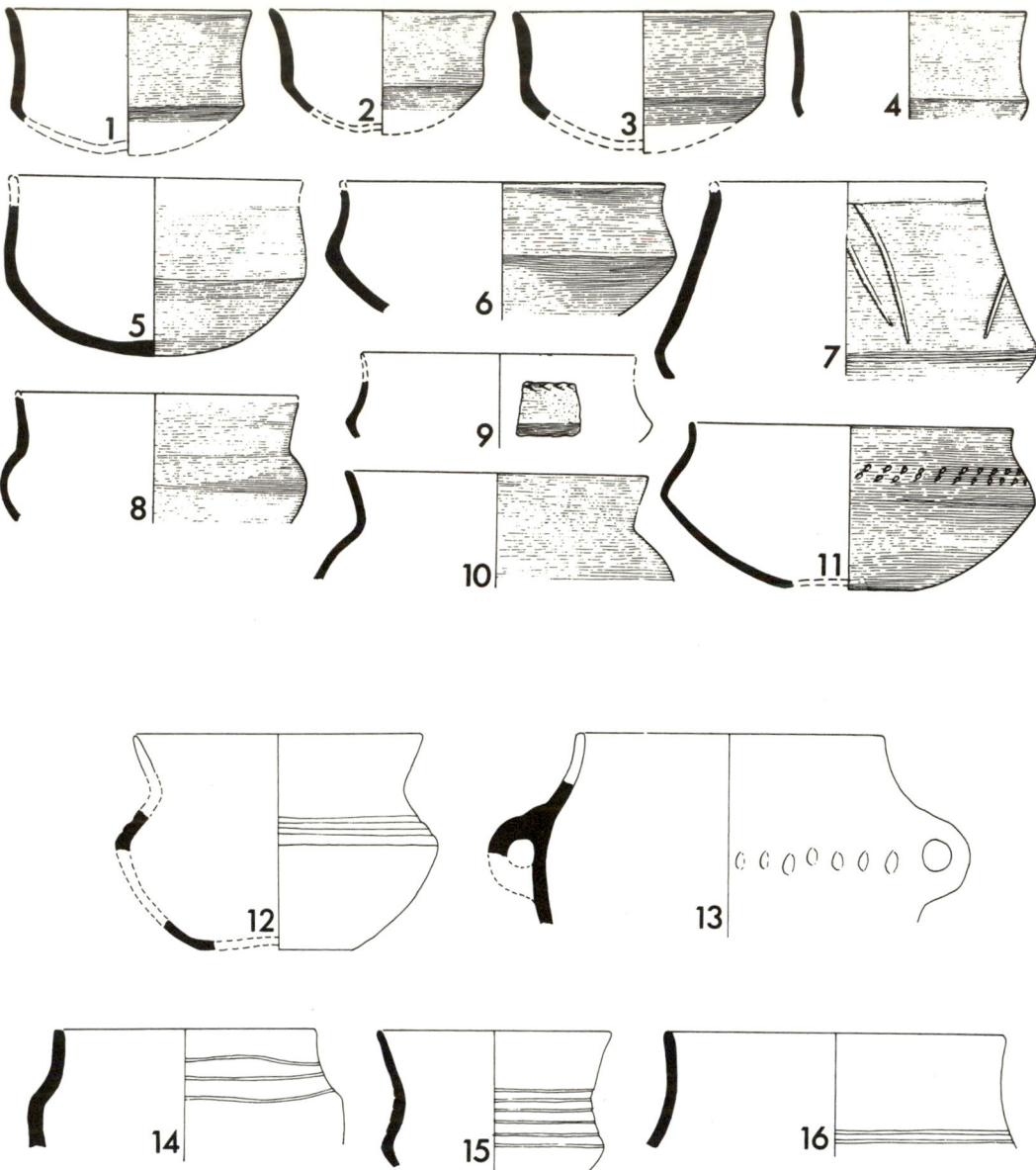

Figure A:7 Dorset and Somerset variants of the All Cannings Cross–Meon Hill group: fifth to third centuries. 1–11 Eldon's Seat, Dorset; 12–13 Pagan's Hill, Somerset; 14–16 Bathampton Down, Somerset. (Sources: 1–11 Cunliffe 1968b; 12–16 author).

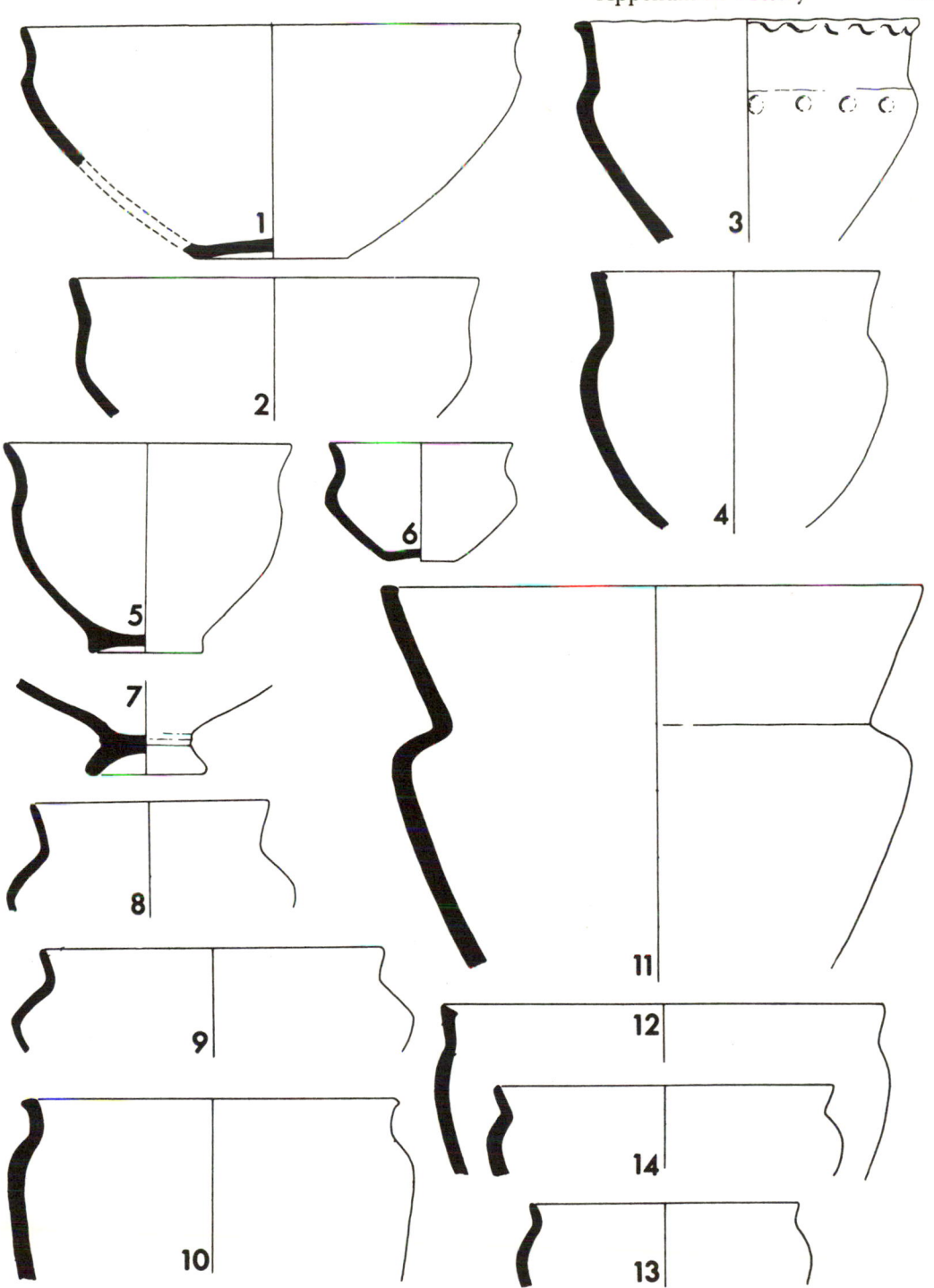

Figure A:8 The Park Brow–Caesar's Camp group: fifth to third centuries. 1 St Catharine's Hill, Guildford, Surrey; 2–3 Caesar's Camp (Wimbledon), Surrey; 4 St Martha's Hill, Surrey; 5 Chertsey, Surrey; 6 St George's Hill (Weybridge), Surrey; 7–13 Park Brow, Sussex; 14 Muntham Court, Sussex. (Source: author).

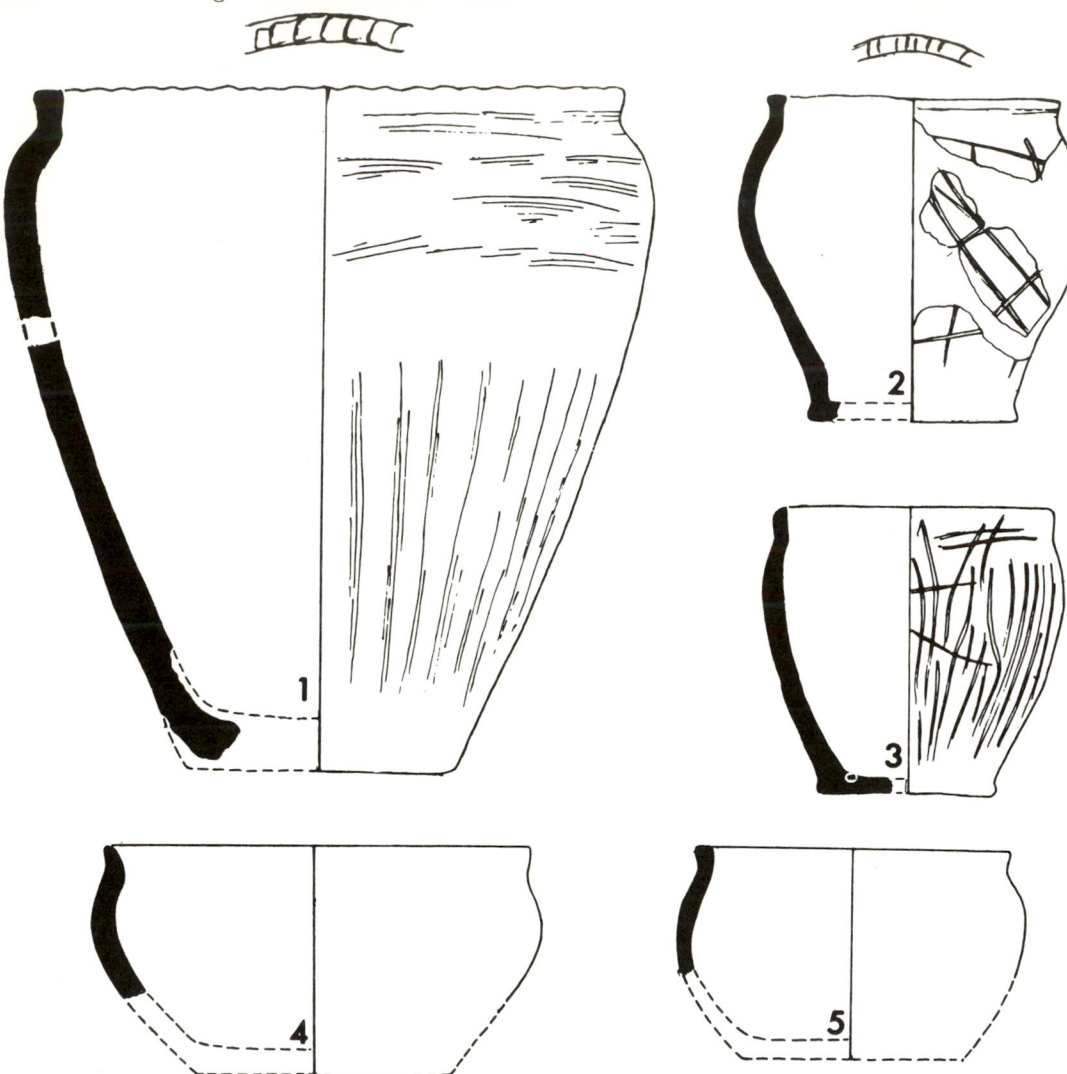

Figure A:9   The Breedon–Ancaster group: ?fifth to second/first centuries. 1–5 Breedon-on-the-Hill, Leics. (Source: Kenyon 1950).

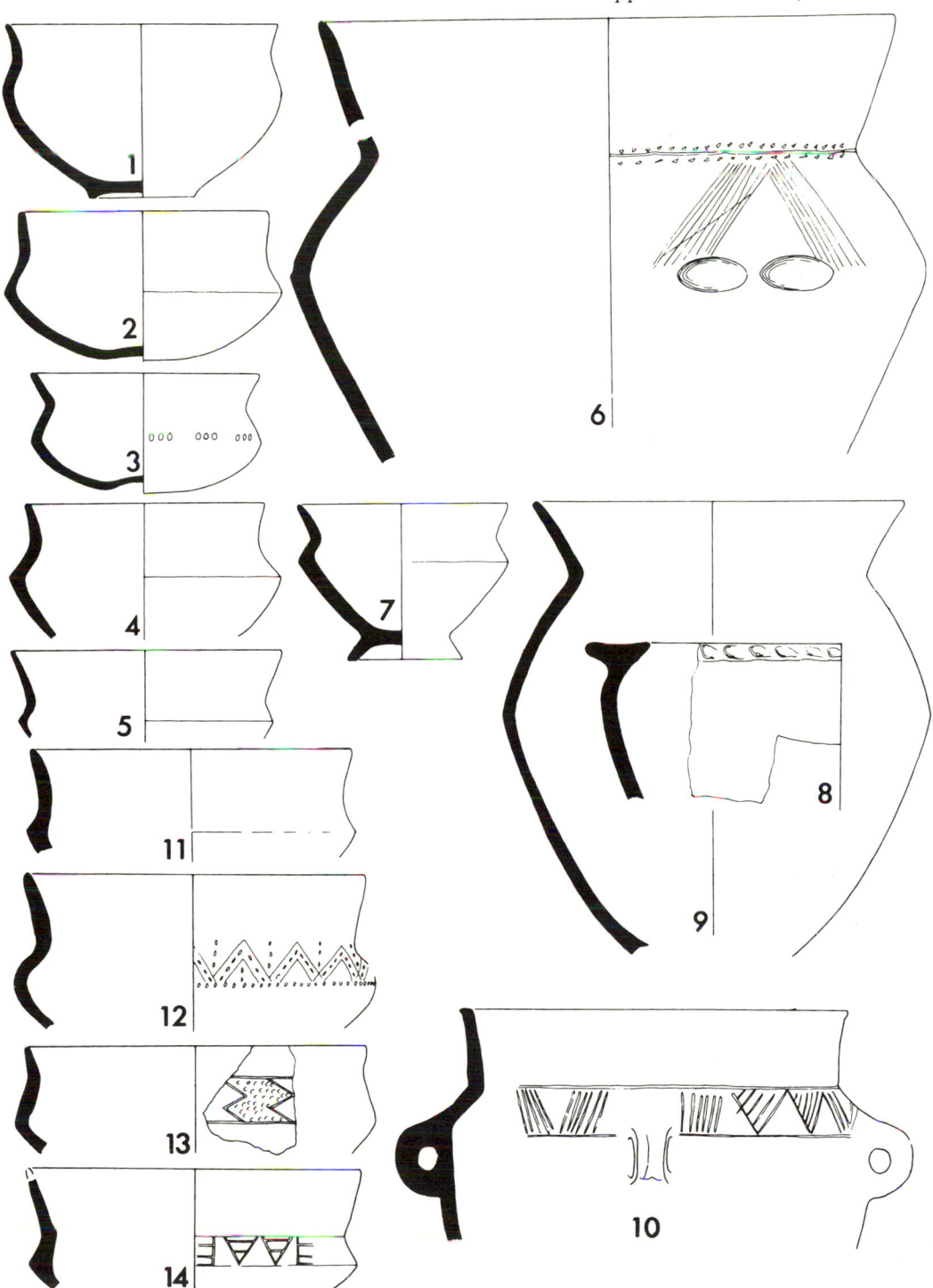

Figure A:10 The Long Wittenham–Allen's Pit group: fifth to third centuries. 1 Chinnor, Oxon.; 2–5 Long Wittenham, Oxon.; 6 Allen's Pit, Oxon.; 7 Chinnor, Oxon.; 8 Mount Farm, Oxon.; 9 Long Wittenham, Oxon.; 10 Allen's Pit, Oxon.; 11 Mount Farm, Oxon.; 12 Dennis Pit, Old Marden, Oxon.; 13 Bampton, Oxon.; 14 Witham, Berks. (Source: author).

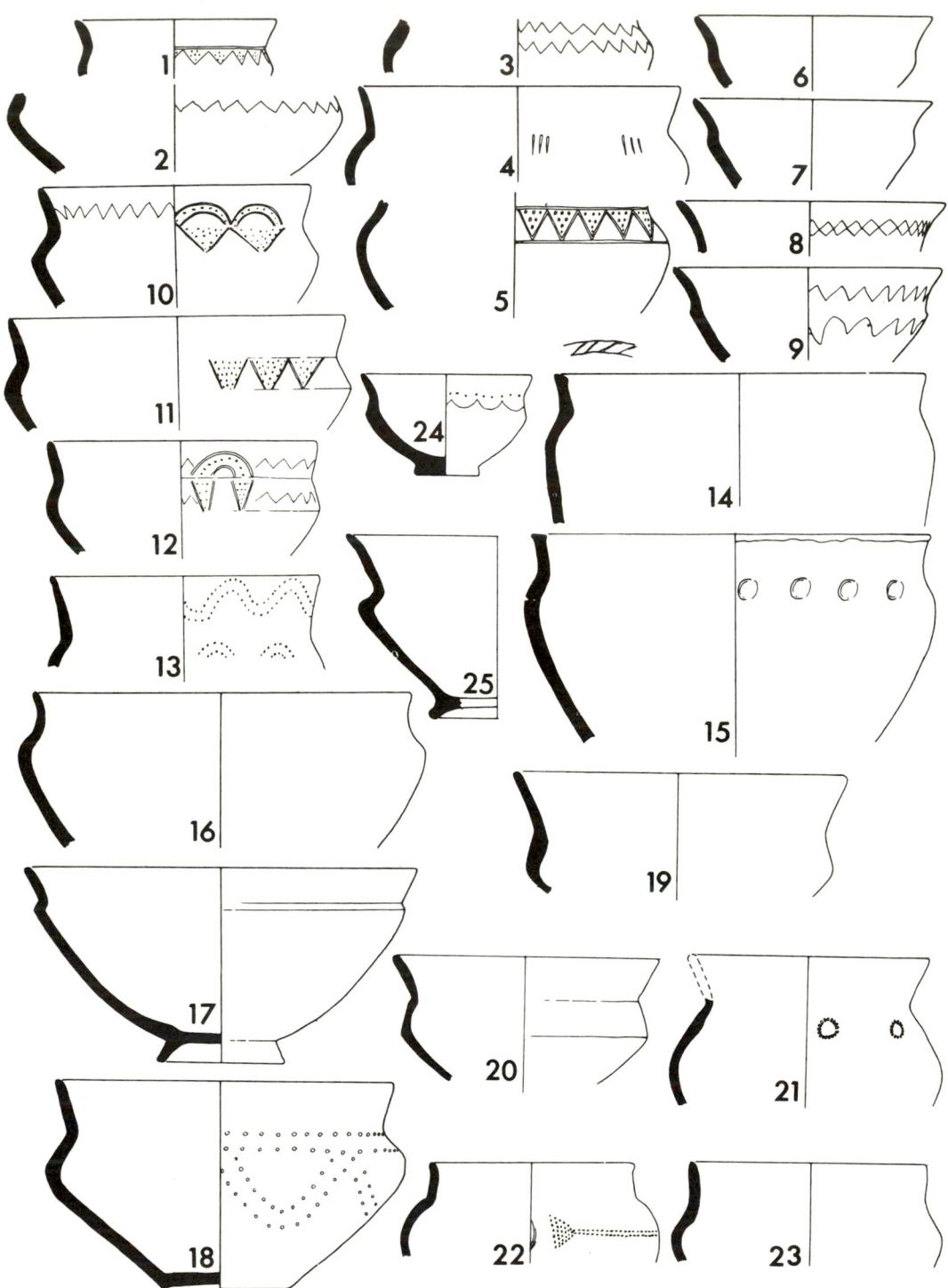

Figure A:11 The Chinnor–Wandlebury group: fifth to third centuries. 1–2 Bledlow, Bucks.; 3–5 Ellesborough, Bucks.; 6–9 Great Wymondley, Herts.; 10–13 Chinnor, Oxon.; 14 Great Wymondley, Herts.; 15 Chinnor, Oxon.; 16–17 Wandlebury, Cambs.; 18 Abington Pigotts, Cambs.; 19–23 Blewburton, Berks.; 24 Chinnor, Oxon.; 25 Mortlake, Middlesex. (Source: author).

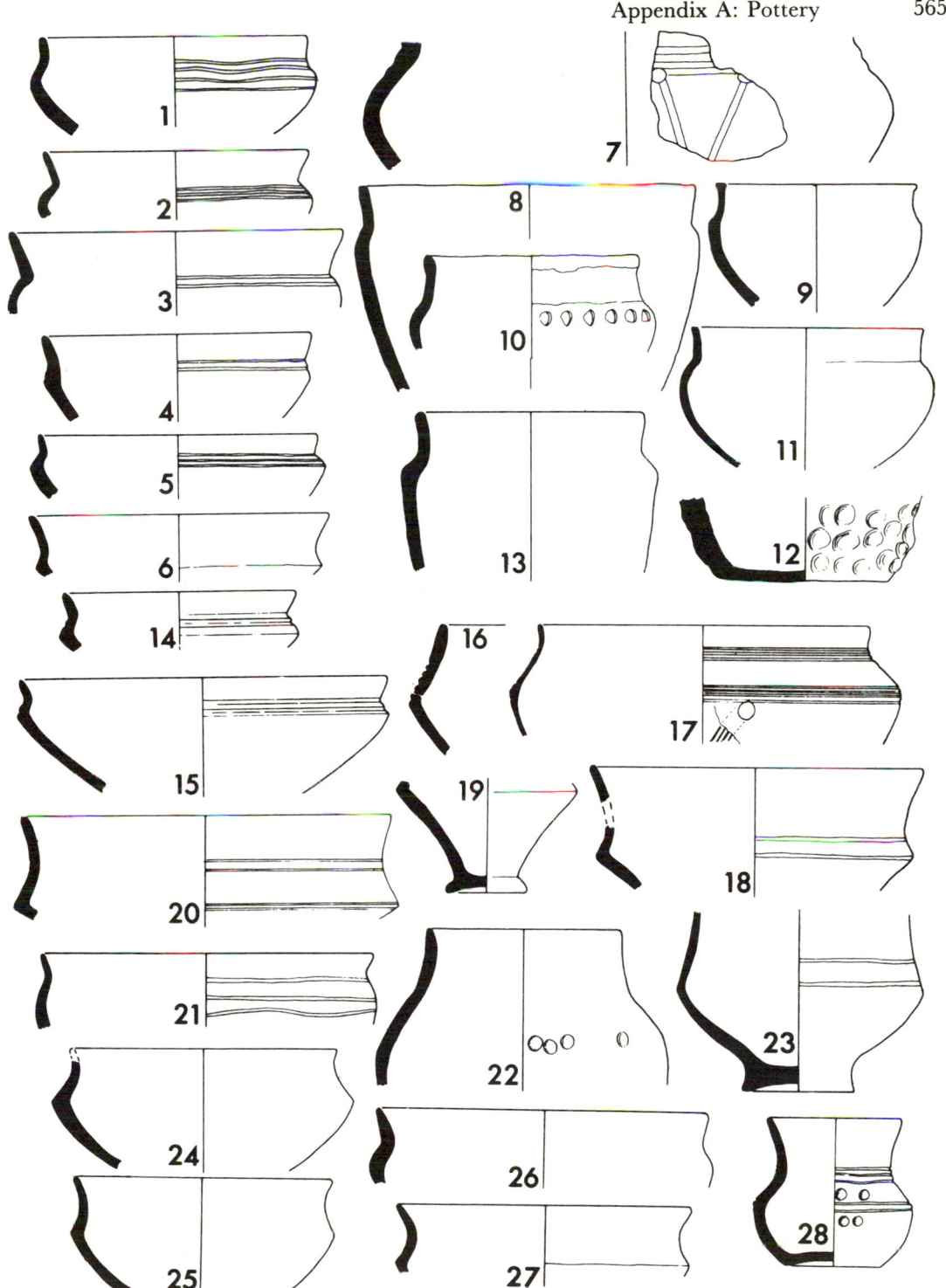

Figure A:12   The Darmsden–Linton group: fifth to third centuries. 1–9 Darmsden, Suffolk; 10 Hawk's Hill, Surrey; 11–15 Linton, Cambs.; 16–18 Hinderclay, Suffolk; 19 Linton, Cambs.; 20 Leigh Hill, Cobham, Surrey; 21–2 Linton, Cambs.; 23–4 Feltwell, Norfolk; 25 Leigh Hill, Cobham, Surrey; 26–7 Hawk's Hill, Surrey; 28 Esher, Surrey. (Source: author).

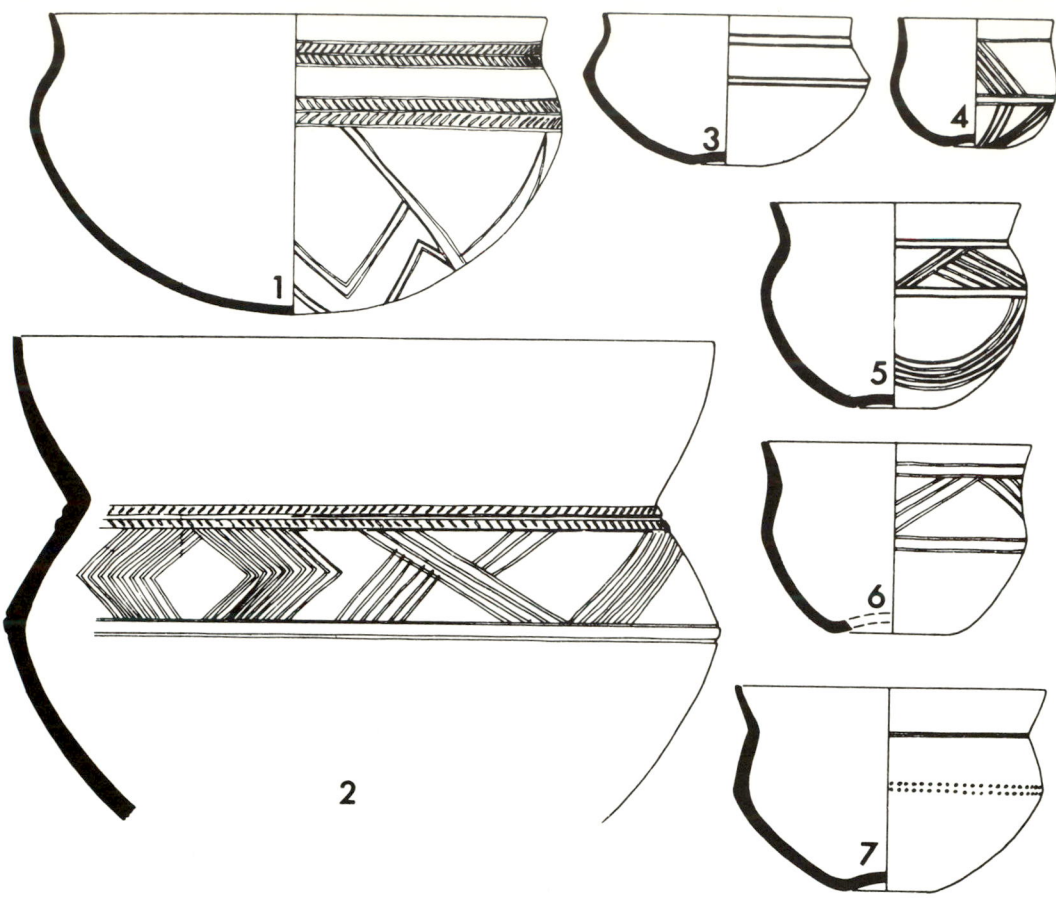

Figure A:13   The Fengate–Cromer group: fifth to third centuries. 1 Cromer, Norfolk; 2–7 Fengate, Northants. (Source: author).

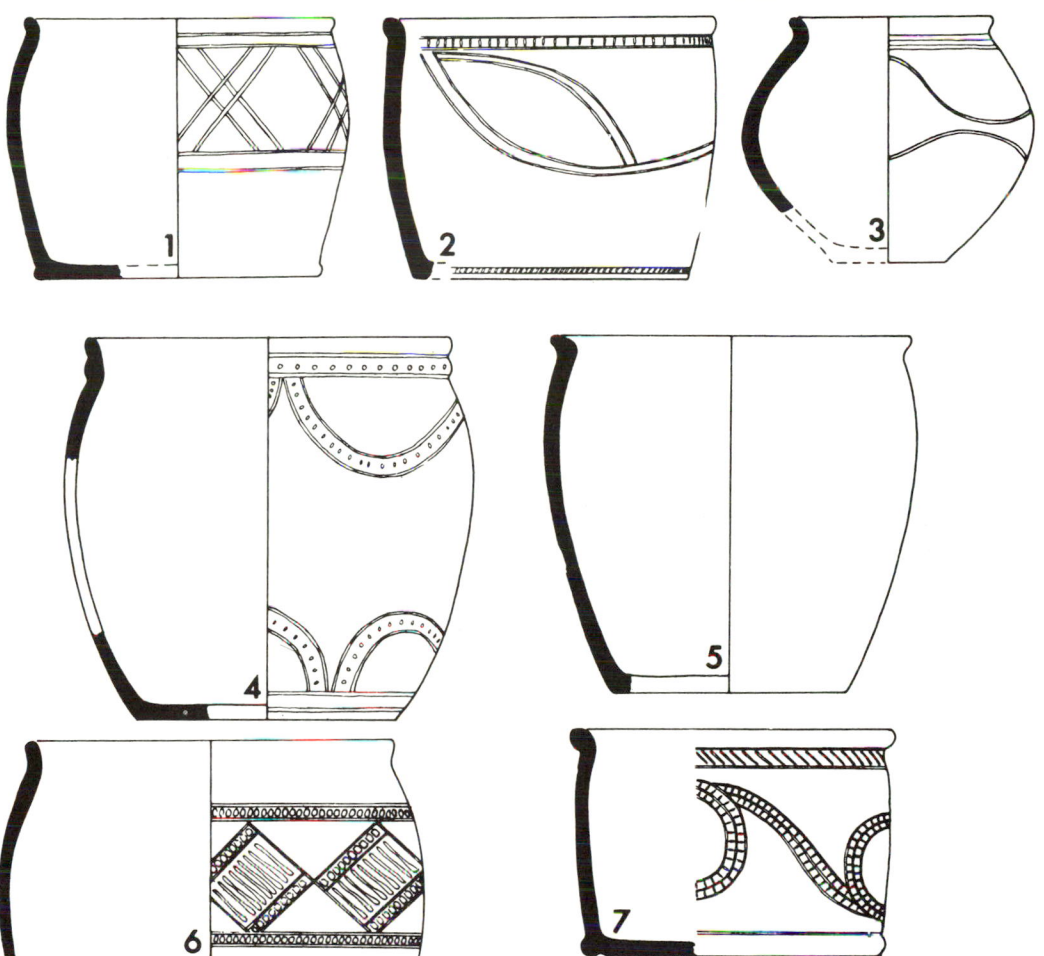

Figure A:14   The Caburn–Cissbury style: third to first centuries. 1 Cissbury, Sussex; 2 Elm Grove, Brighton, Sussex; 3 Cissbury, Sussex; 4–5 Park Brow, Sussex; 6 Newhaven, Sussex; 7 the Caburn, Sussex. (Source: author).

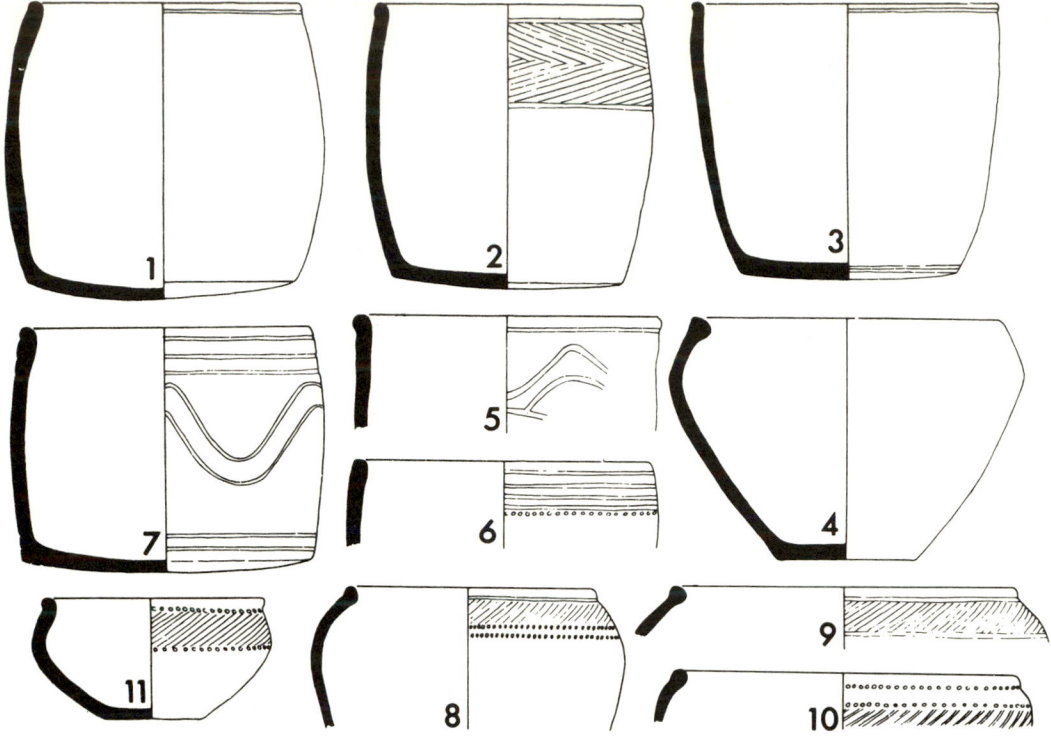

Figure A:15   The St Catharine's Hill–Worthy Down style: second to first centuries. 1 Twyford Down, Hants.; 2–4 St Catharine's Hill, Hants.; 5–6 Twyford Down, Hants.; 7 Trundle, Sussex; 8–11 Worthy Down, Hants. (Source: author).

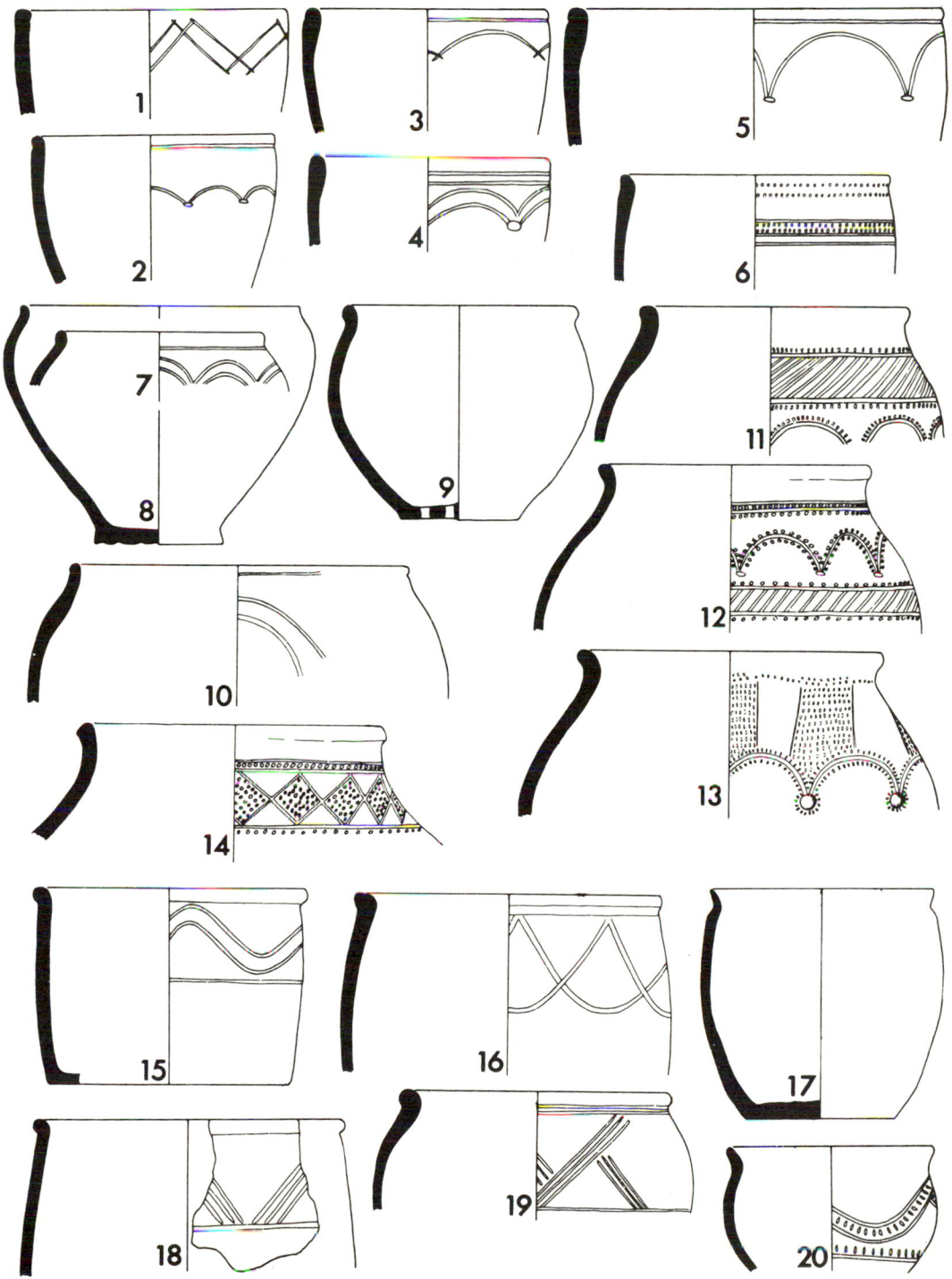

Figure A:16 The Yarnbury–Highfield style (nos 1–13) and the Hawk's Hill-West Clandon style (nos 15–20): both third to first centuries. 1 Yarnbury, Wilts.; 2 Highfield, Wilts.; 3–4 Yarnbury, Wilts.; 5 Fifield Bavant, Wilts.; 6 Yarnbury, Wilts.; 7 Highfield, Wilts.; 8–10 Fifield Bavant, Wilts.; 11 Yarnbury, Wilts.; 12 Highfield, Wilts.; 13–14 Yarnbury, Wilts.; 15 Hawk's Hill, Surrey; 16–17 West Clandon, Surrey; 18 Hawk's Hill, Surrey; 19 West Clandon, Surrey; 20 Hawk's Hill, Surrey. (Source: author).

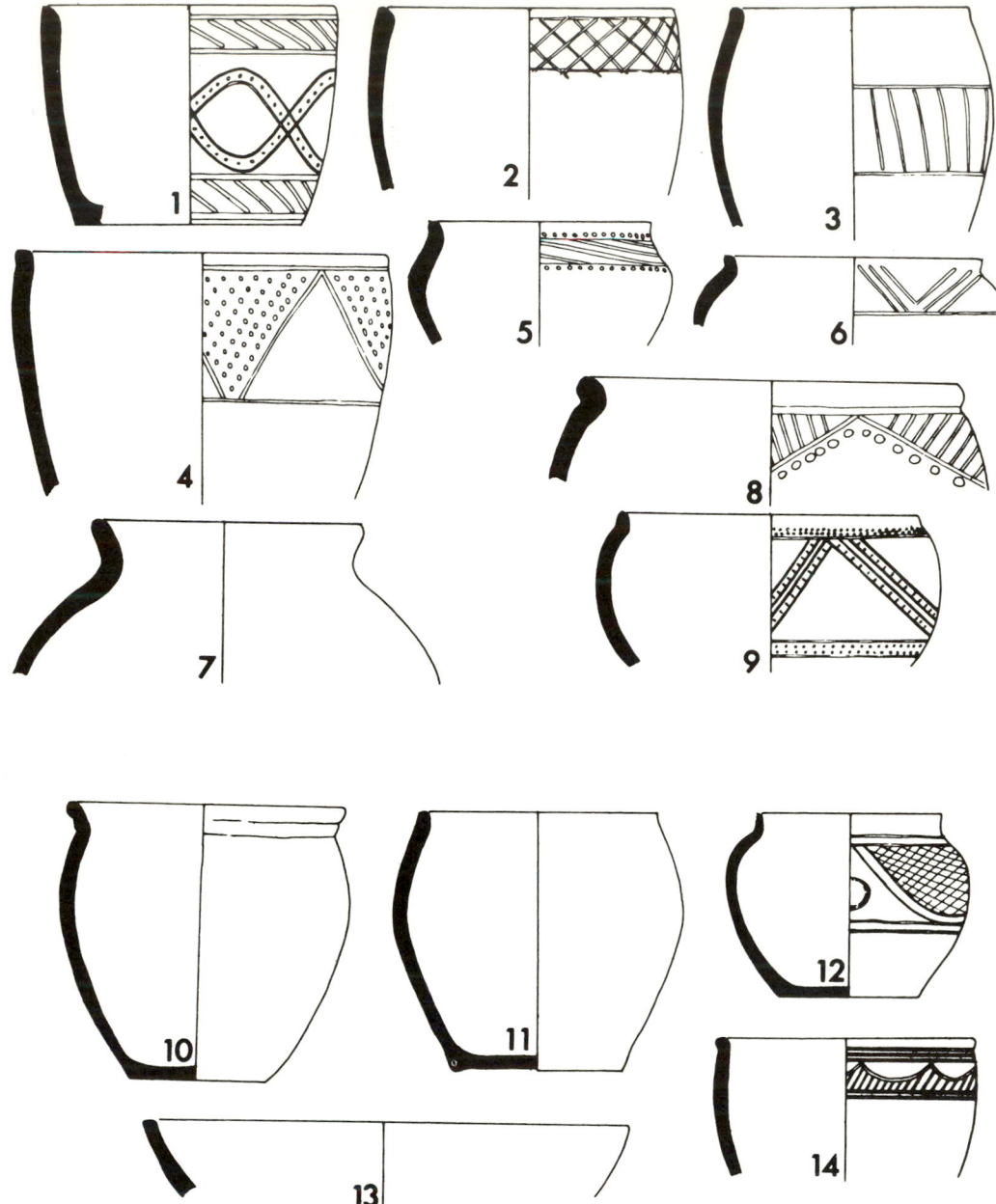

Figure A:17 The Southcote–Blewburton Hill style (nos 1–9) and the Glastonbury–Blaise Castle Hill style (nos 10–14): both third to first centuries. 1–3 Blewburton Hill, Oxon.; 4 Knighton Hill, Berks.; 5–6 Theale, Berks.; 7–8 Southcote, Berks.; 9 Blewburton Hill, Oxon.; 10–11 Worlebury, Somerset; 12 Read's Cavern, Somerset; 13 Blaise Castle, Glos.; 14 Read's Cavern, Somerset. (Source: author).

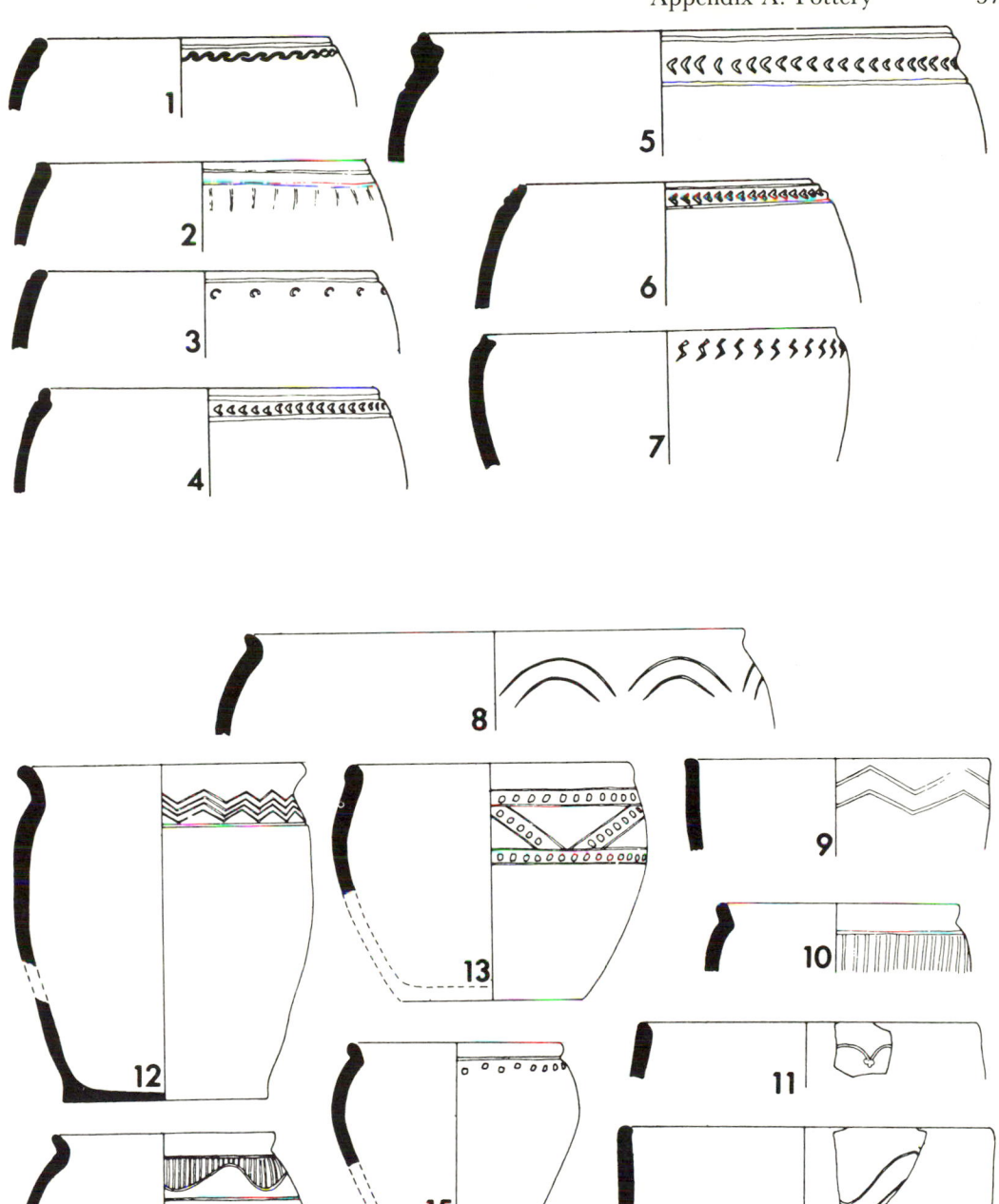

Figure A:18 The Croft Ambrey–Bredon Hill style (nos 1–7): fifth/fourth to first centuries; the Lydney–Llanmelin style (nos 8–16): third to first centuries. 1–6 Sutton Walls, Hereford; 7 Cleeve Hill, Glos.; 8 Lydney, Glos.; 9 Llanmelin, Mon.; 10 Lydney, Glos.; 11–12 Llanmelin, Mon.; 13–15 Lydney, Glos.; 16 Llanmelin, Mon. (Source: author).

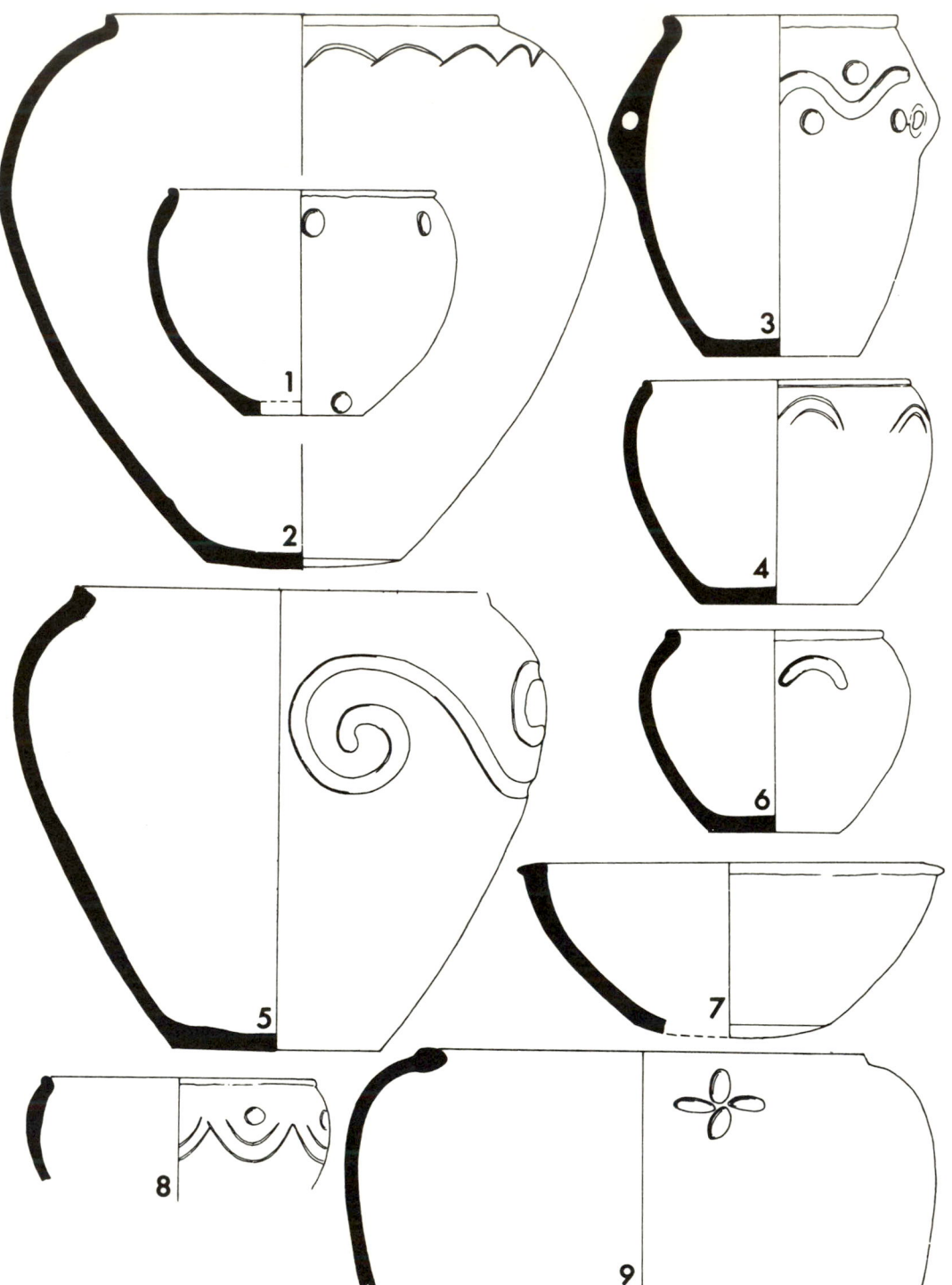

Figure A:19   The Maiden Castle–Marnhull style: third to first centuries. 1–9 Maiden Castle, Dorset. (Source: author).

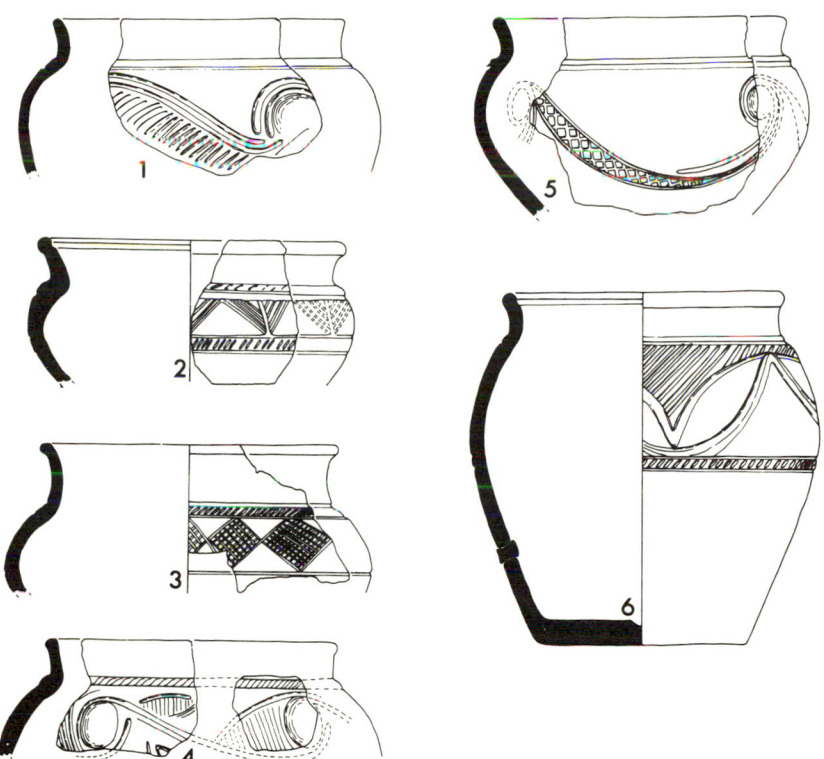

Figure A:20 Glastonbury ware types (group 1): ?second century BC. 1 Castle Dore, Cornwall; 2–3 Carloggas Camp, St Mawgan-in-Pydar, Cornwall; 4–5 Castle Dore, Cornwall; 6 Carloggas Camp, St Mawgan-in-Pydar, Cornwall. (Sources: *Castle Dore*, Radford 1951; *Carloggas Camp*, Threipland 1957).

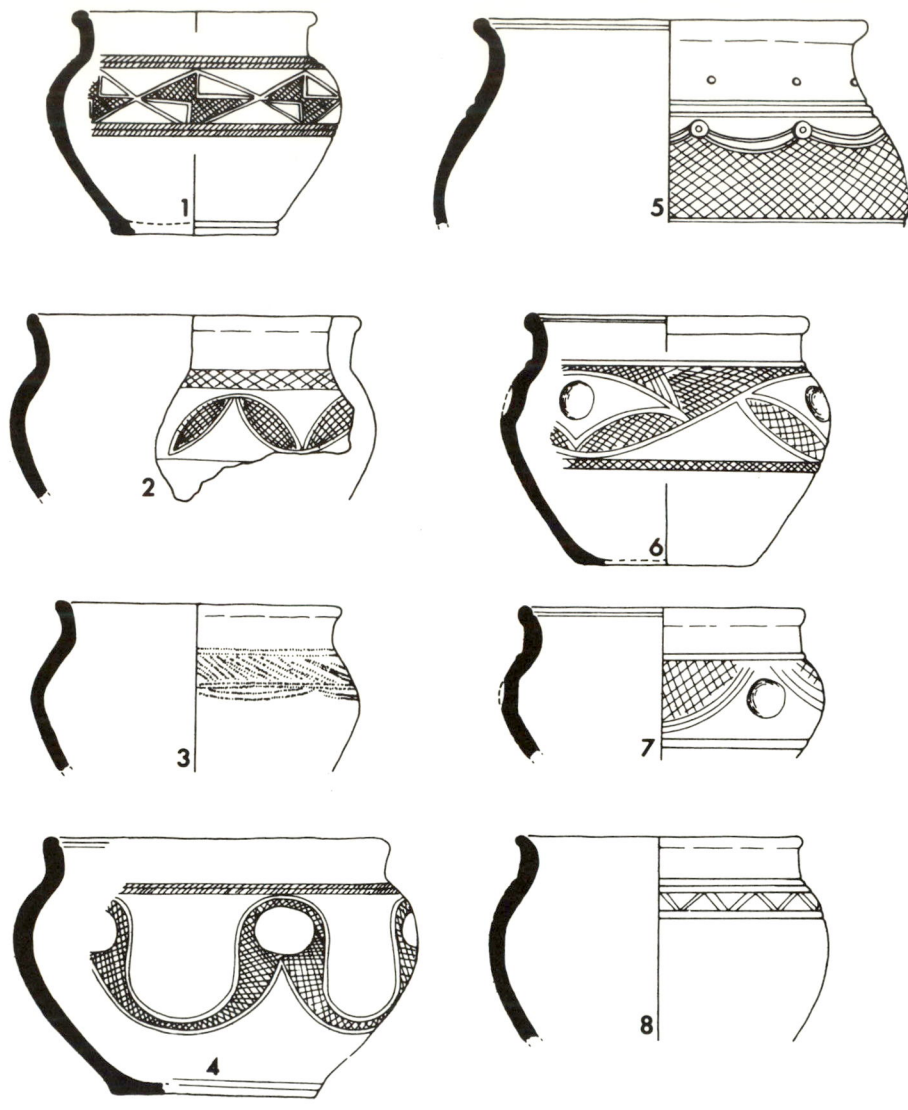

Figure A:21   Glastonbury ware types (group 2): first century BC to first century AD. 1–2 Glastonbury, Somerset; 3 Wookey Hole, Somerset; 4 Meare, Somerset; 5–8 Glastonbury, Somerset (Sources: *Glastonbury*, Bulleid and Gray 1917; *Meare*, Bulleid and Gray 1948; *Wookey Hole*, Peacock 1969).

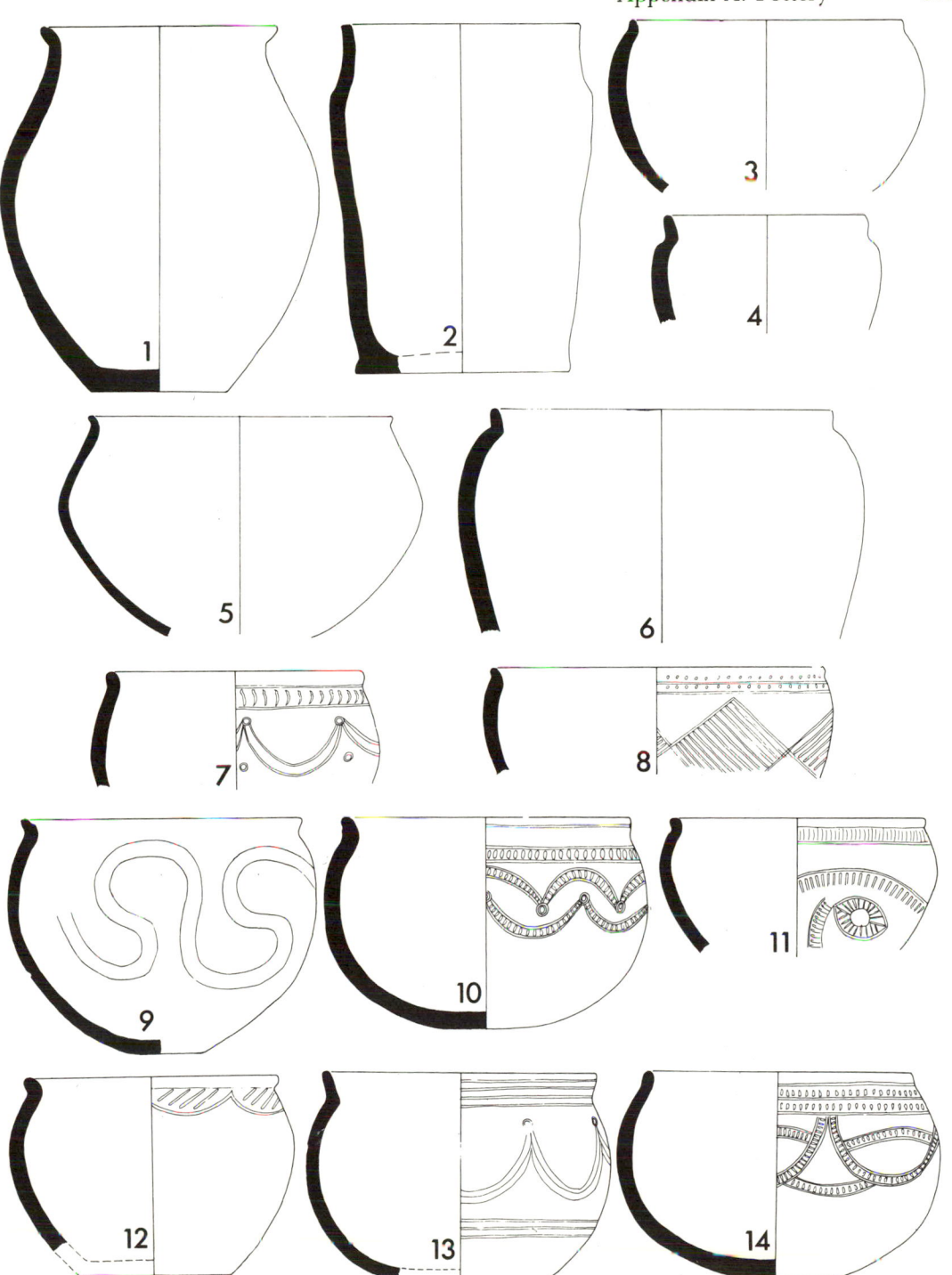

Figure A:22 The Stanton Harcourt–Cassington style: third to first centuries. 1 Frilford, Oxon.; 2 Chastleton, Oxon.; 3–4 Cassington, Oxon.; 5 Yarnton, Oxon.; 6 Mount Farm, Oxon.; 7 Hatford, Berks.; 8 Cassington, Oxon.; 9 Boxford Common, Berks.; 10 Frilford, Oxon.; 11 Iffley, Oxon.; 12 Wokingham, Berks.; 13 Cassington, Oxon.; 14 Frilford, Oxon. (Source: author).

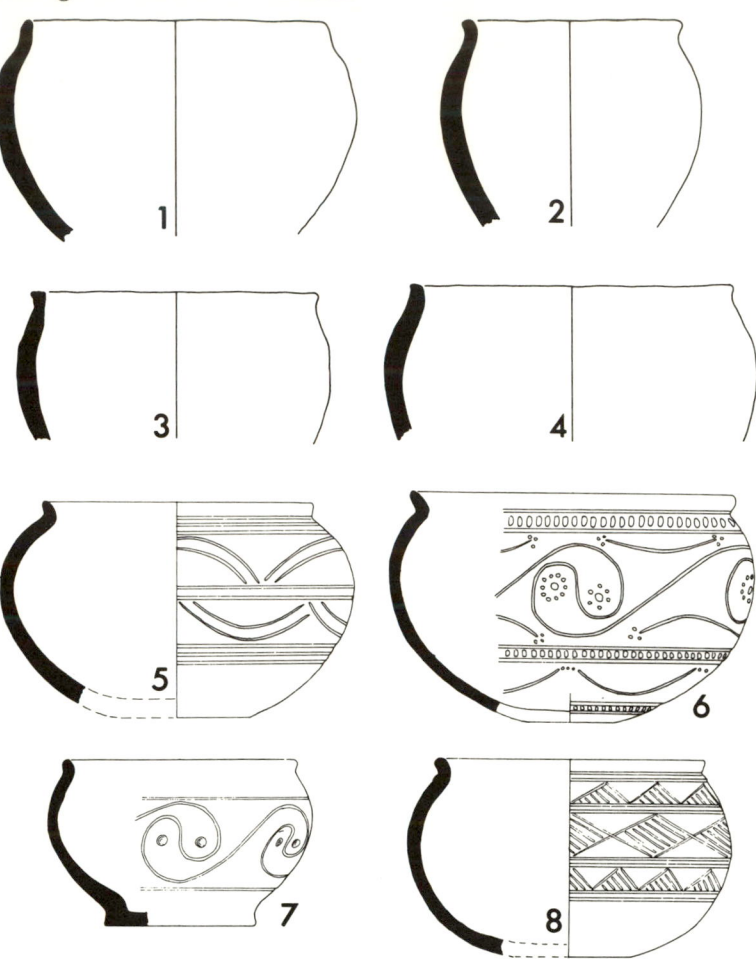

Figure A:23   The Hunsbury–Draughton style: second century BC to first century AD. 1–4 Moulton Park, Northants.; 5–6 Hunsbury, Northants.; 7 Draughton, Northants.; 8 Hunsbury, Northants. (Sources: 1–4 J.H. Williams 1974; 5–8 author).

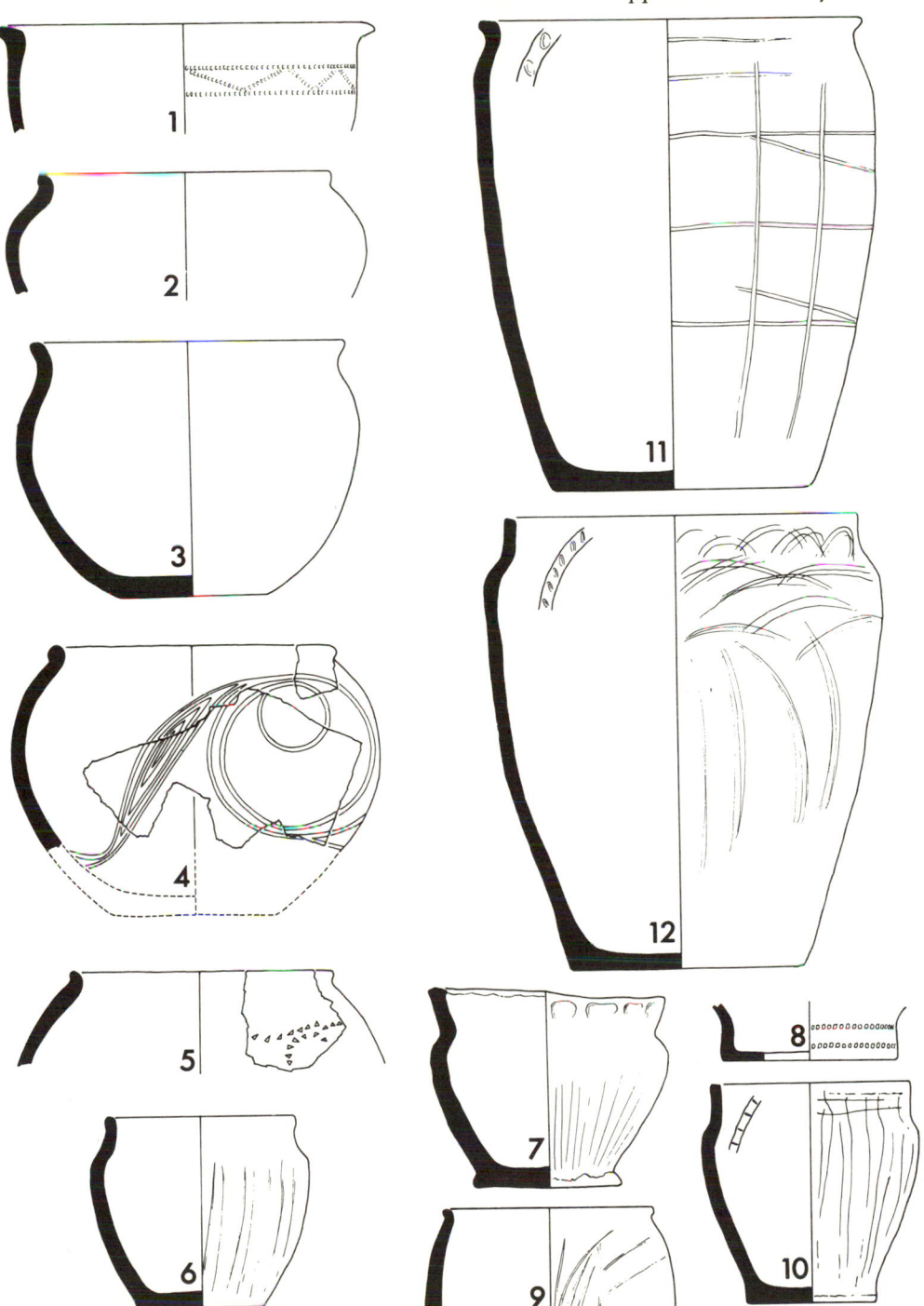

Figure A:24   Bowls and coarse ware from eastern England: third to first centuries. 1 Abington Pigotts, Cambs.; 2 St Ives, Hunts.; 3 South Wilson, Bucks.; 4–5 Puddlehill, Beds.; 6 Slough, Bucks.; 7 Abington Pigotts, Cambs.; 8 St Ives, Hunts.; 9 Houghton, Hunts.; 10–12 Barley, Herts. (Sources: 4–5 Matthews 1976; rest author).

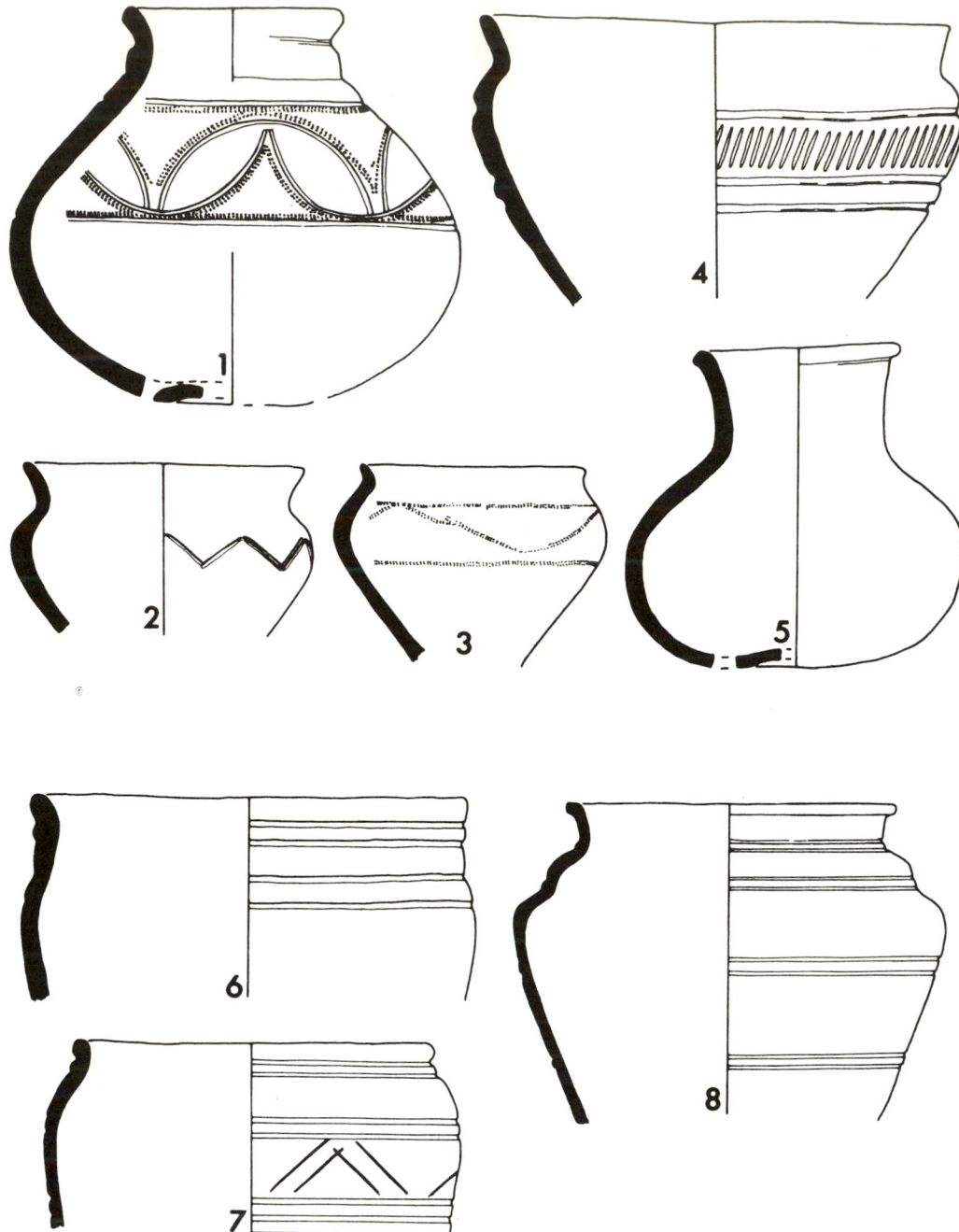

Figure A:25   The Sleaford–Dragonby style: first century BC. All from Dragonby, Lincs.: 1–5 early, ?pre *c.* 50 BC; 6–8 later, *c.* 50–10 BC   (Source: May 1970).

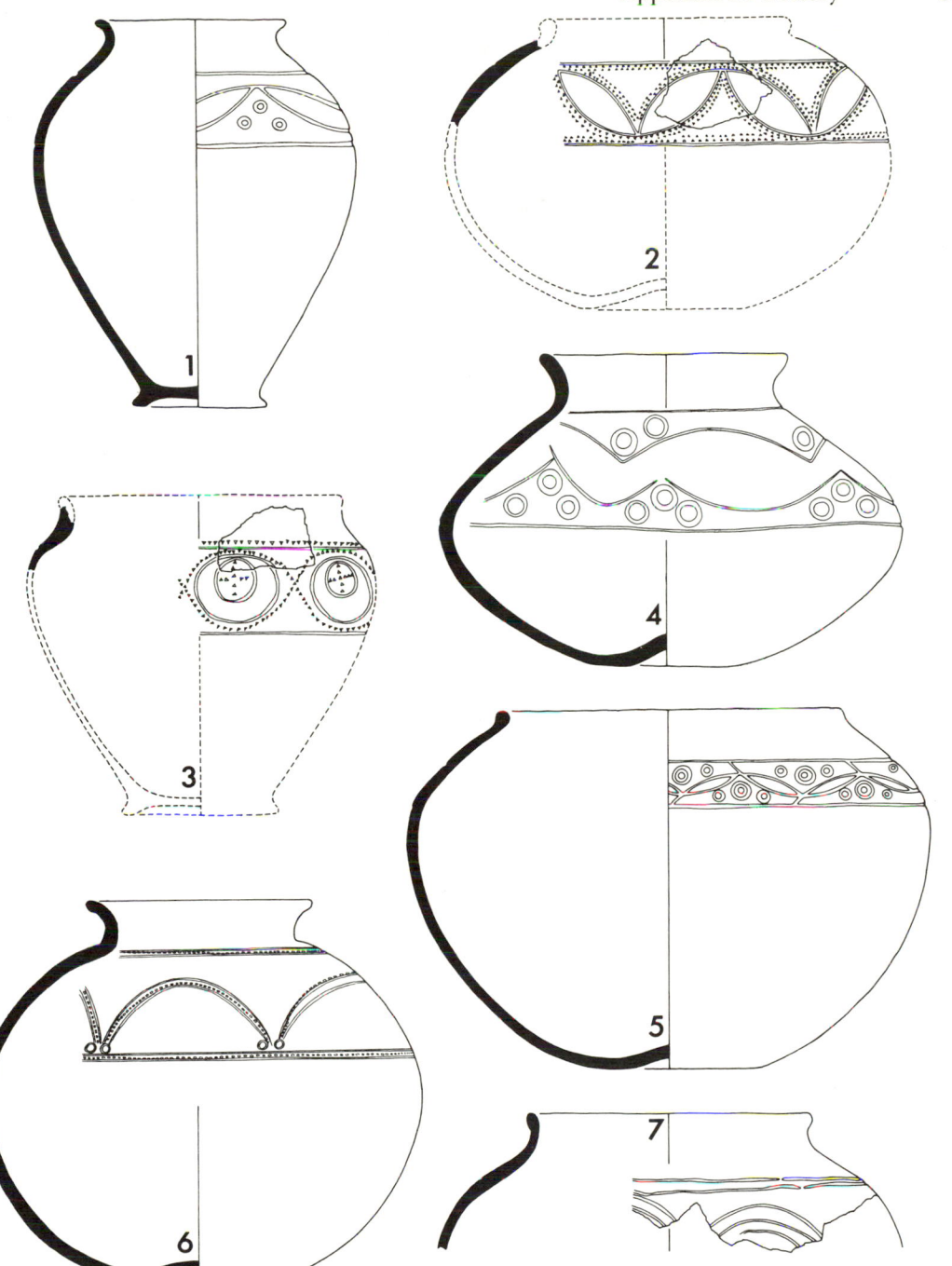

Figure A:26   The Mucking–Crayford style (nos 1–5) and the Late Caburn–Saltdean style (nos 6–7). 1 Canewdon, Essex; 2 Gun Hill; 3 Canvey Island; 4 Mucking, Essex; 5 Canewdon, Essex; 6 Saltdean, Sussex; 7 Caburn, Sussex (Sources. 1,4,5 Elsdon 1975; 2,3 Drury and Rodwell 1973; 6,7 author).

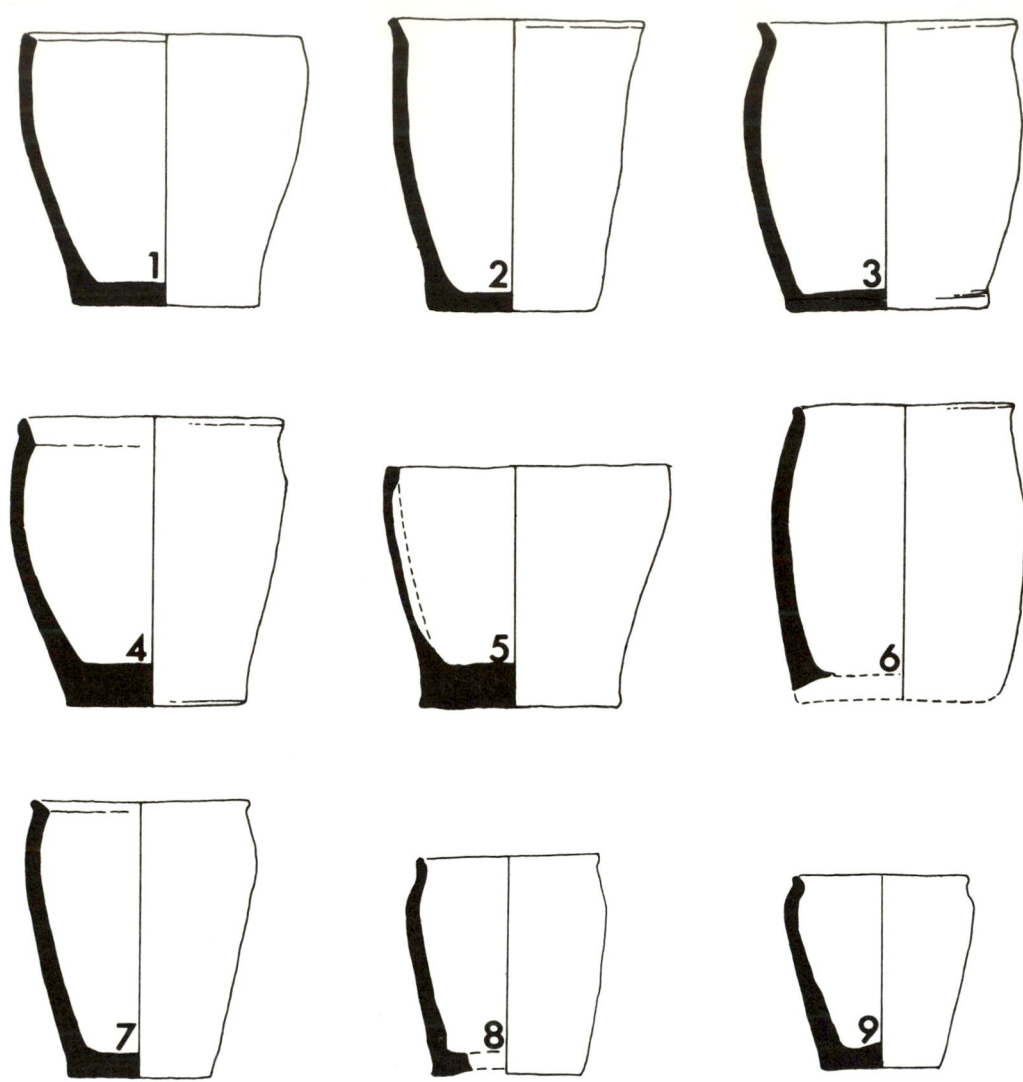

Figure A:27   The Dane's Graves–Staxton style: third to first centuries. 1–6 Dane's Graves, Yorks.; 7–9 Driffield, Yorks. (Source: Brewster 1963).

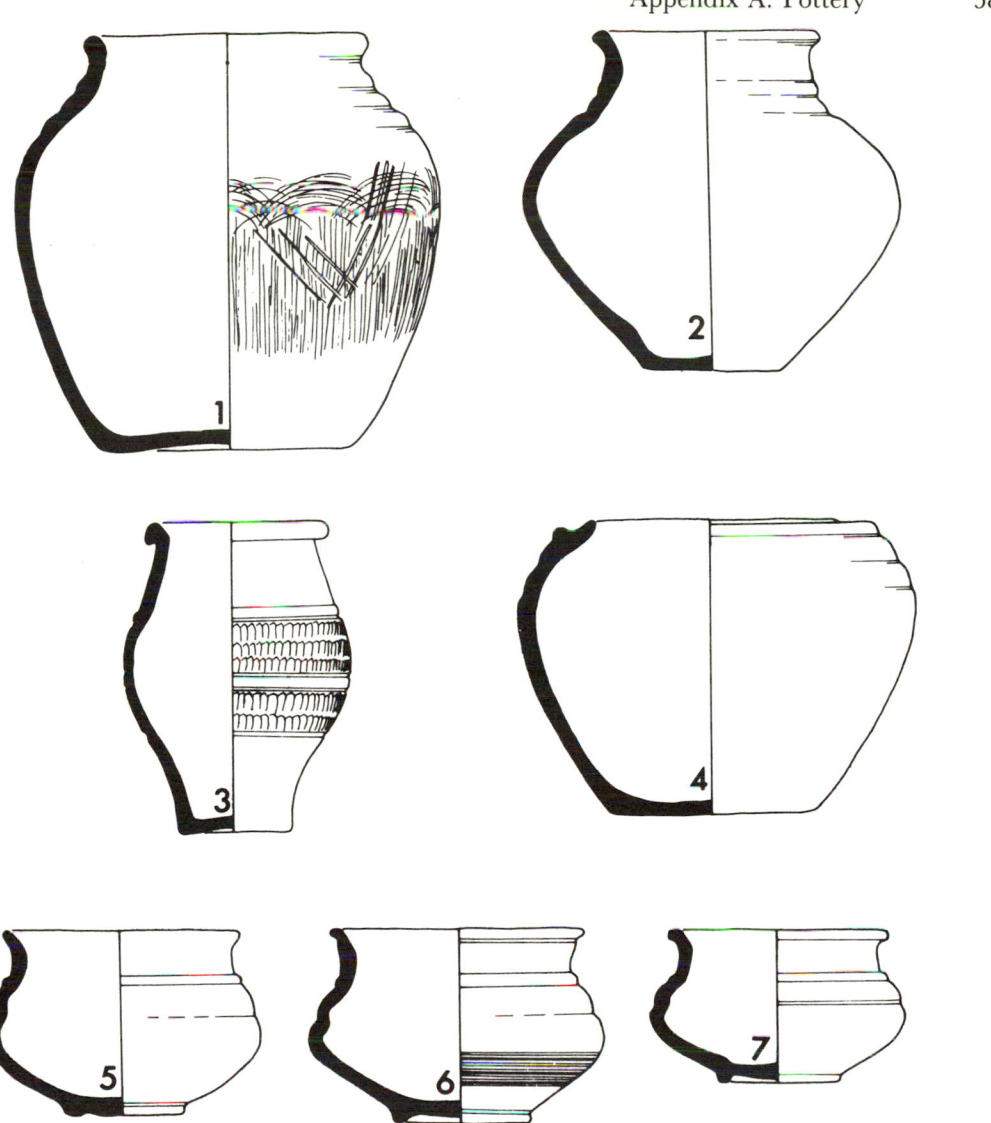

Figure A:28   The Aylesford–Swarling style: *c.* 50 BC–AD 43. 1–7 Swarling, Kent (Source: Birchall 1965).

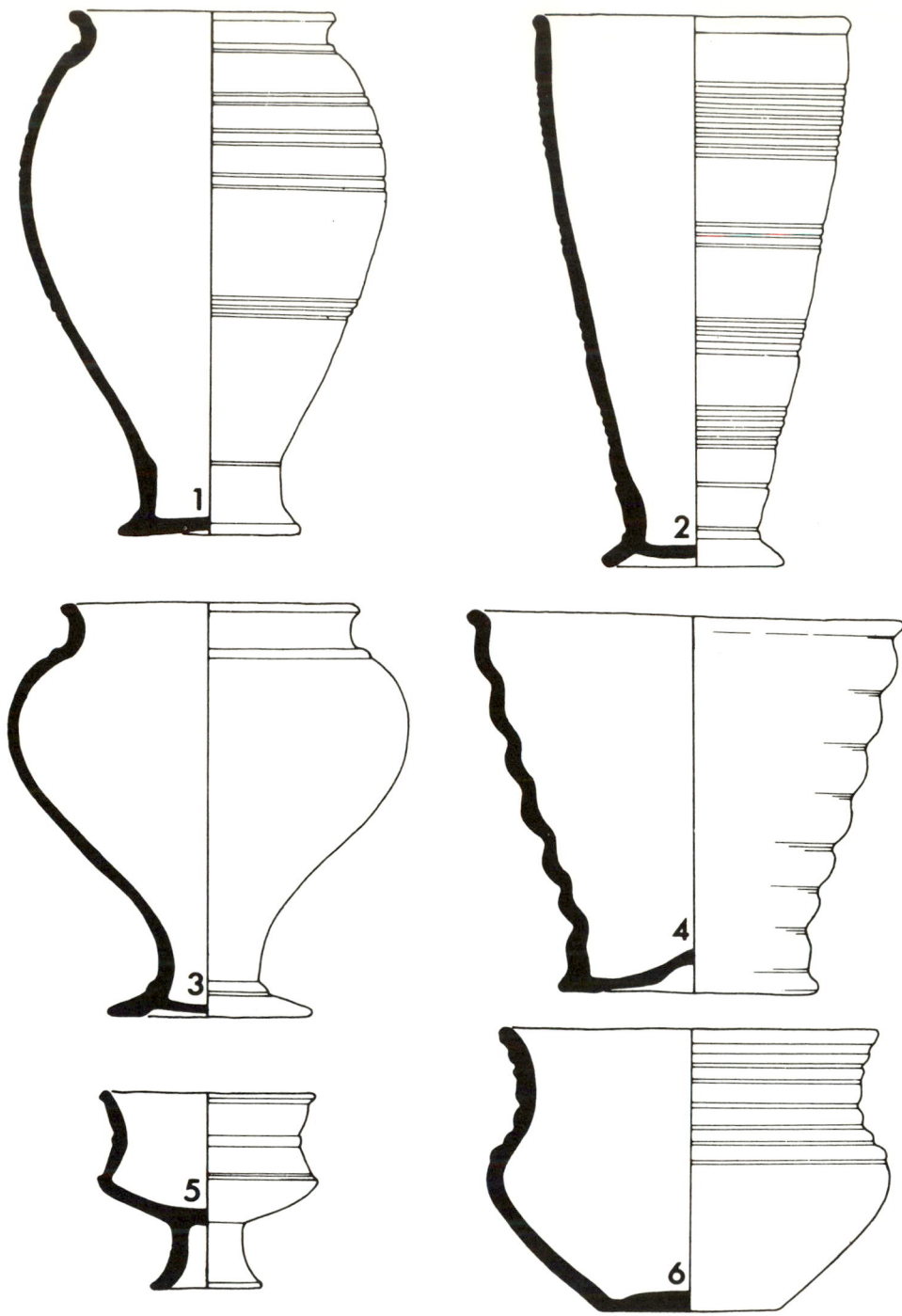

Figure A:29 The Aylesford–Swarling style: *c.* 50 BC–AD 43. 1–4 Swarling, Kent; 5 Welwyn, Herts.; 6 Aylesford, Kent (Source: Birchall 1965).

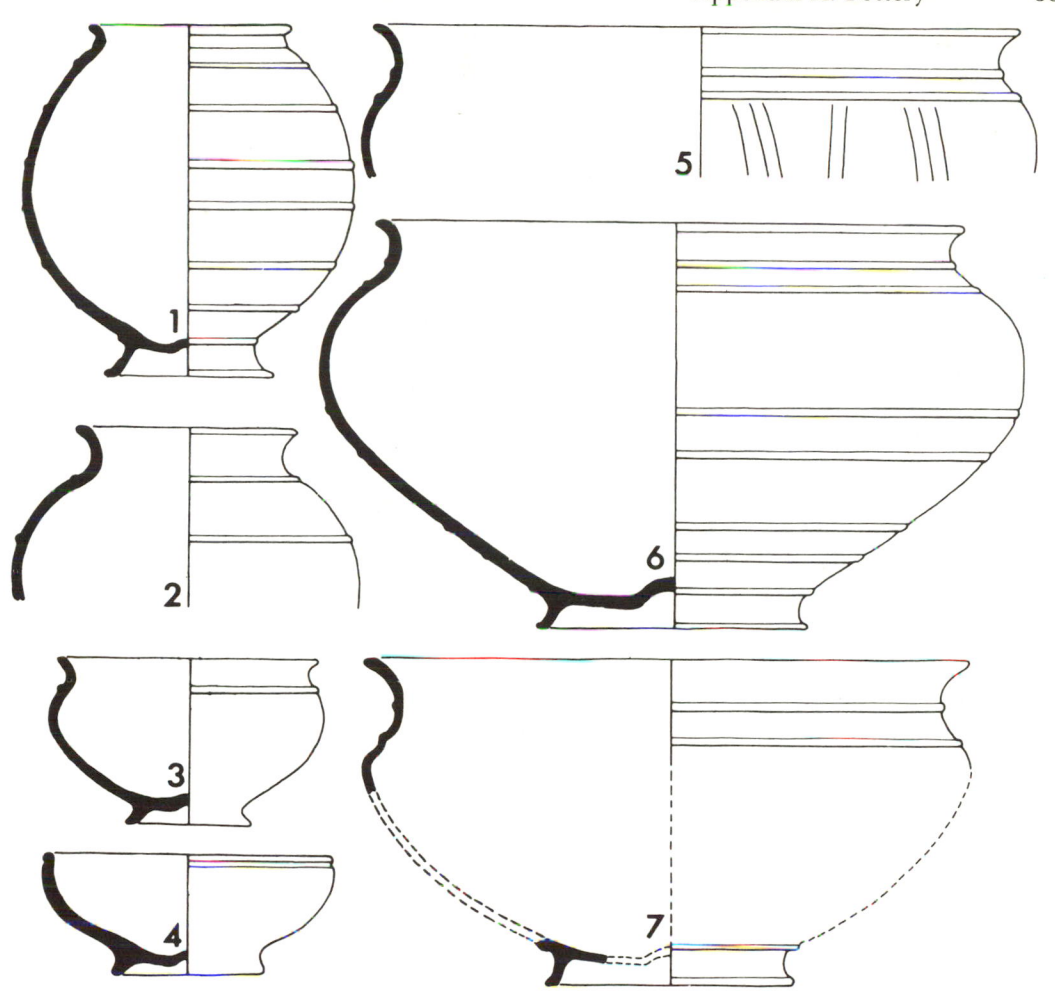

Figure A:30 Imported Hengistbury class B ware: first century BC. 1–7 Hengistbury Head, Hants. (Source: Bushe-Fox 1915).

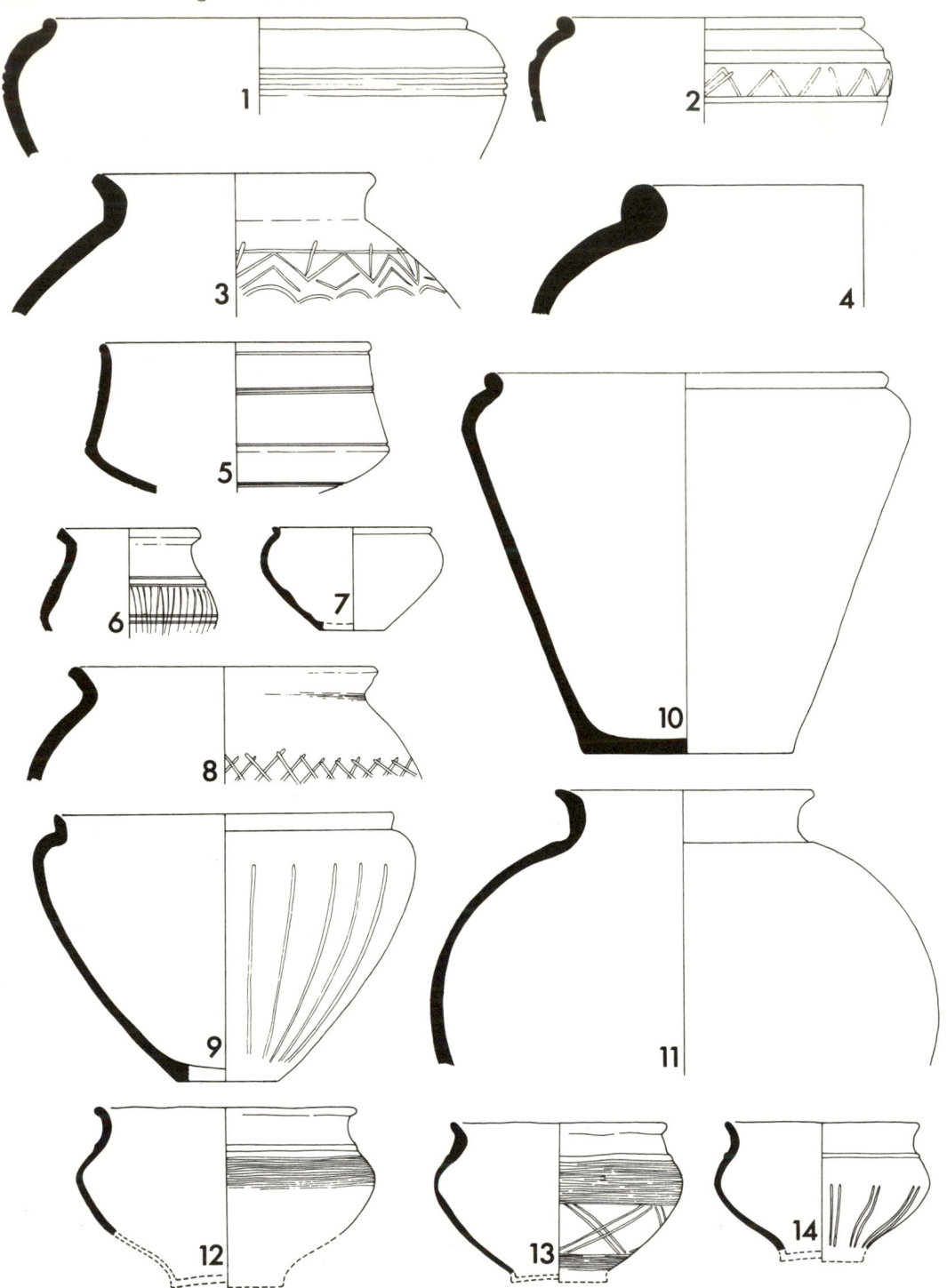

Figure A:31   Northern and Southern Atrebatic types: *c.* 50 BC–AD 43. 1 Oare, Wilts.; 2 Boscombe Down West, Wilts.; 3–7 Oare, Wilts.; 8 Winchester, Hants.; 9–11 Horndean, Hants.; 12–14 Chalton, Hants. (Source: author).

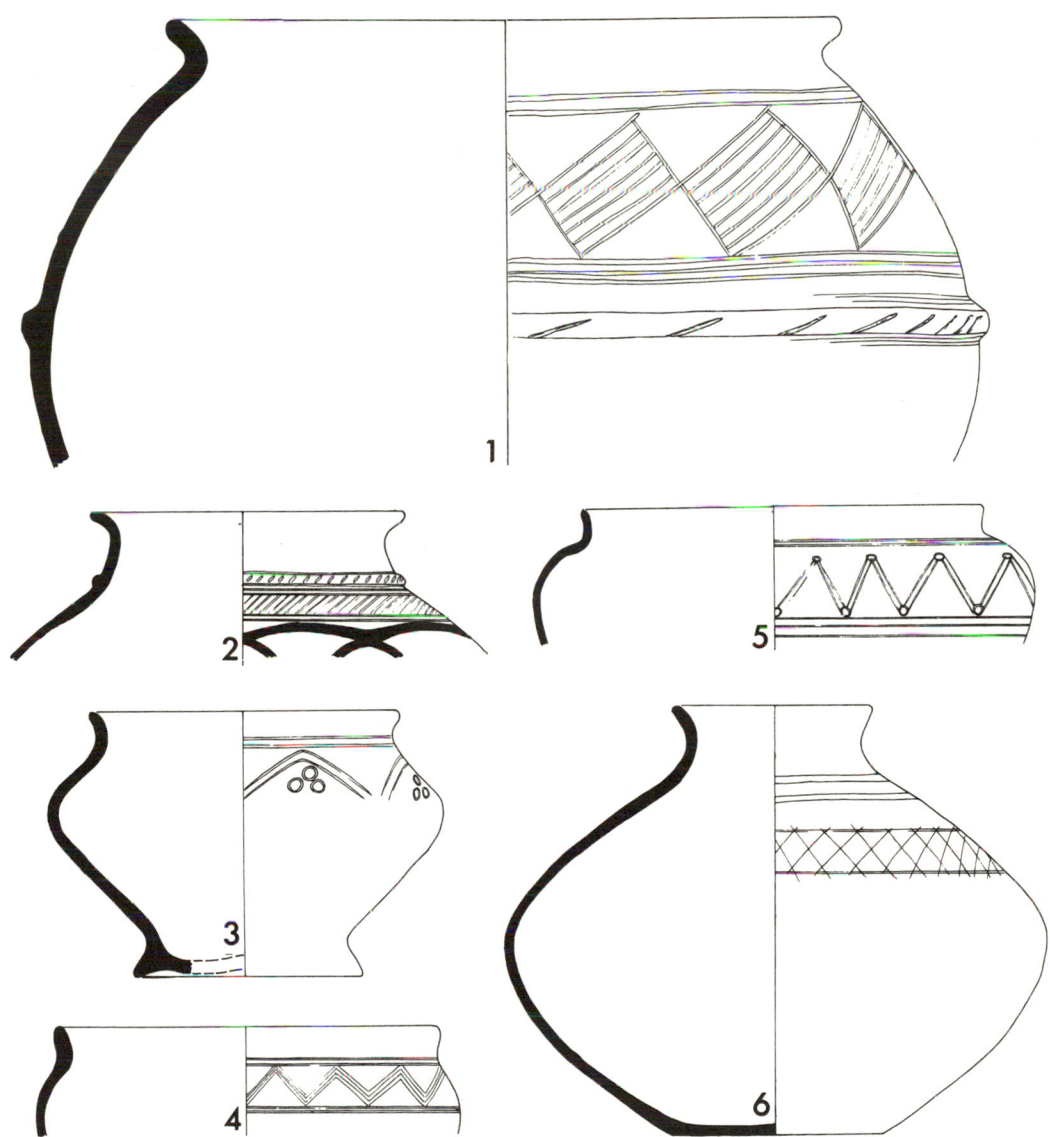

Figure A:32 Eastern Atrebatic types: *c.* 50 BC–AD 43. 1 Broadwater, Sussex; 2 Horsted Keynes, Sussex; 3 Little Horstead Lane, Sussex; 4 Glyne, Sussex; 5 Charleston Brow, Sussex; 6 Ashman, Sussex (Source: author).

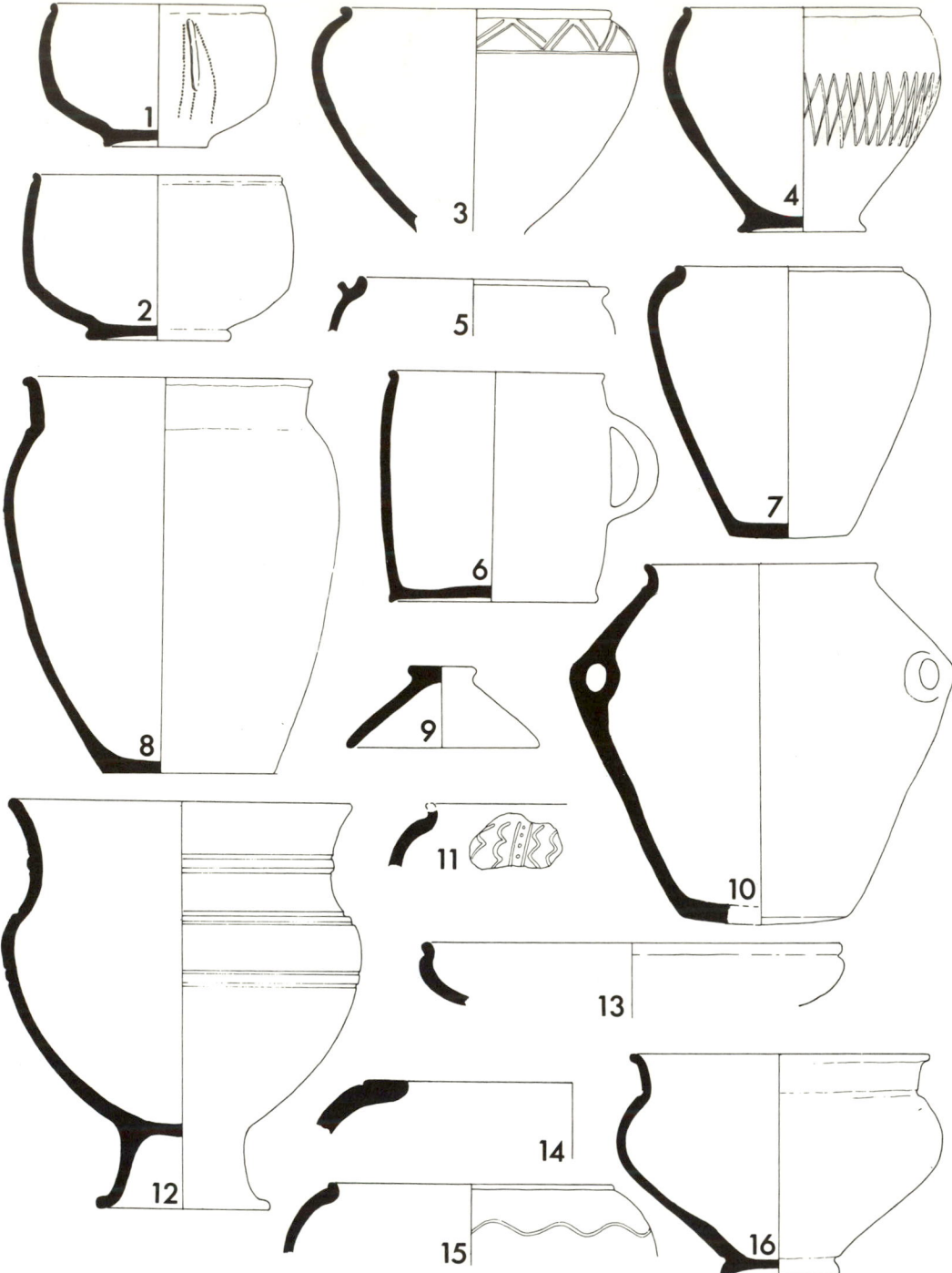

Figure A:33 Durotrigan types: *c.* 50 BC–AD 43. 1–10 Maiden Castle, Dorset; 11 Fitzworth, Dorset; 12–16 Maiden Castle, Dorset (Source: author).

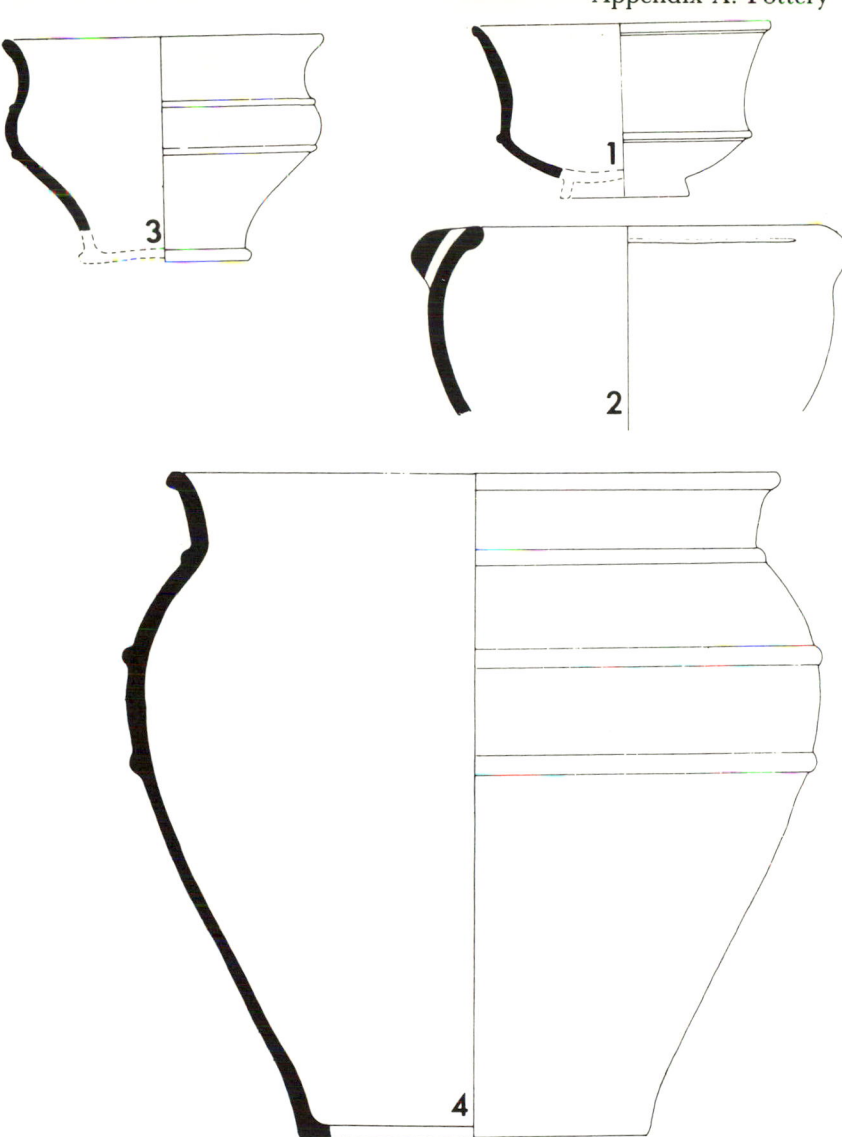

Figure A:34 Cordoned ware types: *c.* 50 BC–AD 43. 1–4 Carloggas Camp, St Mawgan-in-Pydar, Cornwall (Source: Threipland 1957).

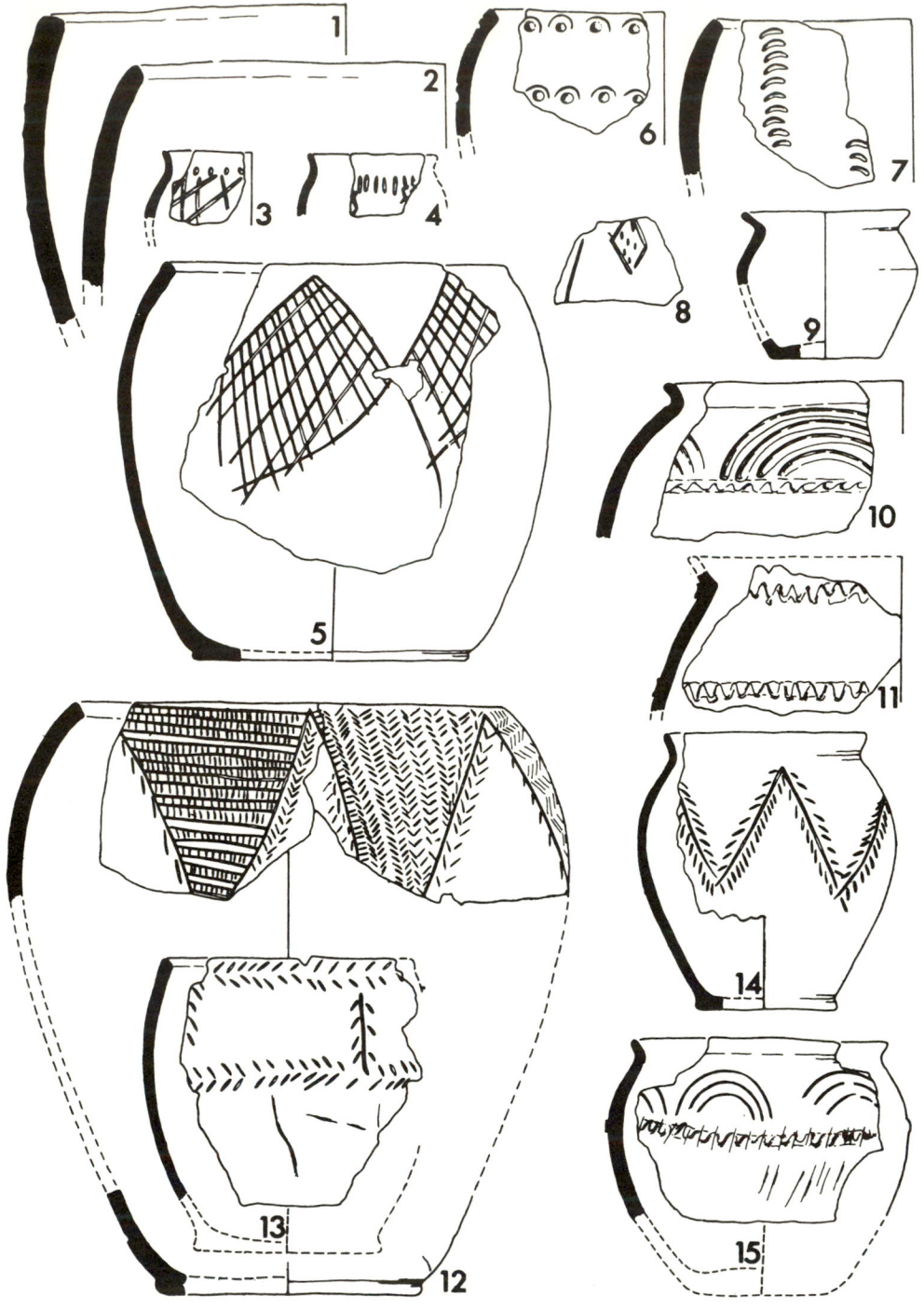

Figure A:35   Pre-broch pottery: sixth to first centuries. Dun Mor Vaul, Tiree (Source: MacKie 1965b).

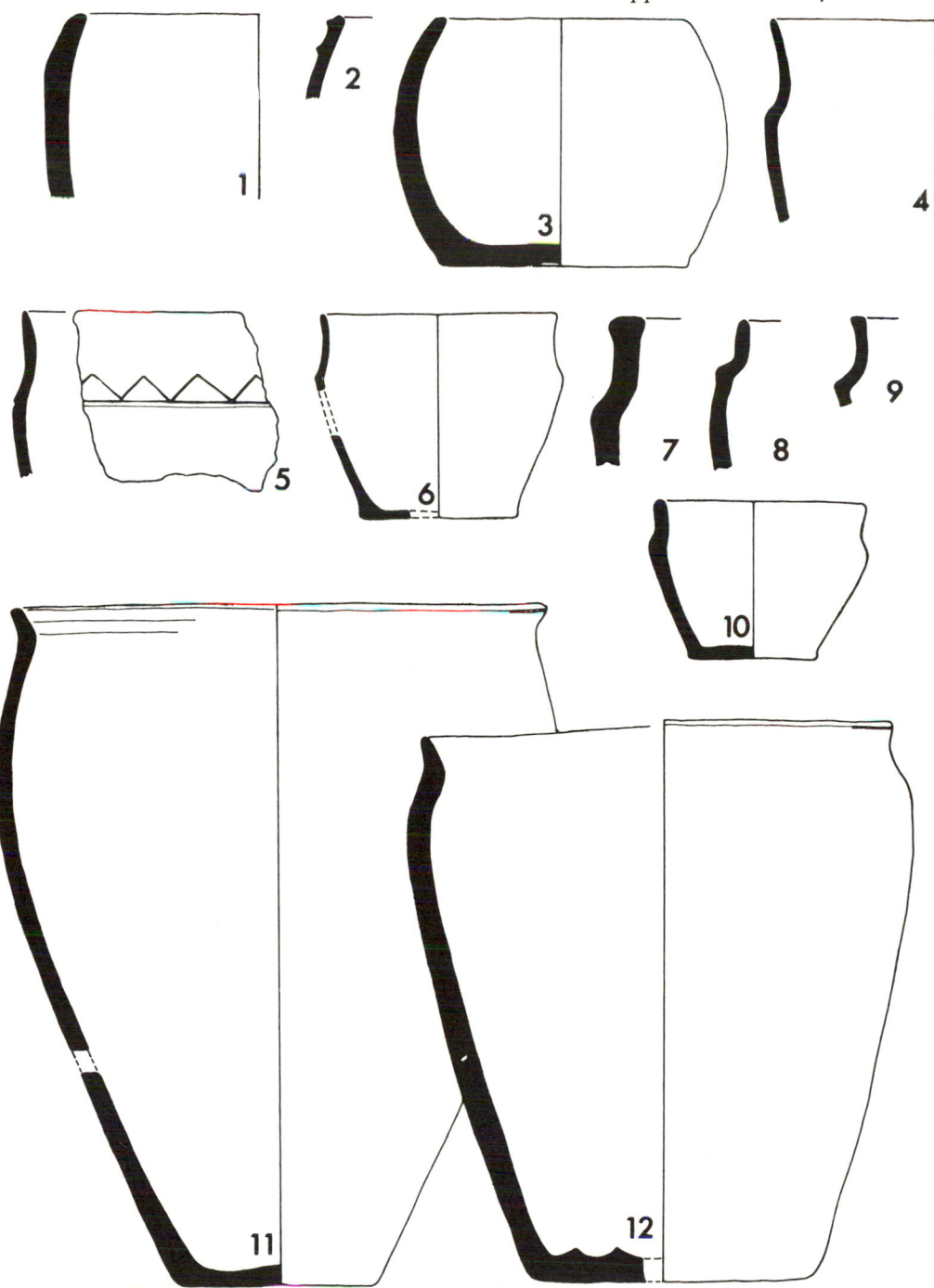

Figure A:36   Pottery from Shetland. 1 Clickhimin (Late Bronze Age); 2–3 Jarlshof (Late Bronze Age); 4–6 Clickhimin (first Iron Age farm); 7–10 Jarlshof (village II) (first Iron Age farm); 11–12 Clickhimin (fort period) (sources: J.R.C. Hamilton 1956, 1968).

Figure A:37 Pottery from Orkney and Shetland. 1–4 Clickhimin (fort period); 5–6 Orkney (broch pottery); 7 Clickhimin (broch pottery); 8 Jarlshof (wheelhouse pottery) (Sources: J.R.C. Hamilton 1956, 1968).

Appendix B   Selected radiocarbon dates

A large number of radiocarbon dates are now available for the first millennium BC and many are referred to in the text. For ease of reference a selection of dates is given below together with their laboratory numbers. Since radiocarbon years are not real years it has become a widely used convention to quote them as bc/ad. This convention is not accepted by radiocarbon scientists but since it is deeply rooted in the archaeological literature it has been adopted throughout the present work. Dates are quoted with their standard deviation (σ) e.g. 200 bc ± 60. In theory this means that there is a 68 per cent probability that the actual date (bc) lies anywhere within the range 140–260 bc. To increase the probability to 95 per cent the 2 σ band width is used. Thus for a radiocarbon assessment of 200 bc ± 60 there is a 95 per cent chance of the date (bc) lying between 80 and 320 bc. (There is an added complication that the standard deviation quoted is not a realistic assessment of the overall error and it should be multiplied by a factor.)

In recent years much effort has been expended on the problem of calibrating radiocarbon years to calendar years. Several calibration curves have been produced. The most reliable, and those now universally accepted, have been published by Stuiver and Pearson (1986) and Pearson and Stuiver (1986) for the years from 2500 BC to the present. These curves have been based on the high precision dating of tree rings from known age samples. The resulting curves for the period which concerns us are reproduced (Figure B:1) here incorporating 1 σ error bands. The wiggles in the curve introduce an additional uncertainty. For example a single radiocarbon date of 250 bc could be produced by samples with calendar ages of 353, 306 or 236 BC. If one standard deviation is ± 60 then there is a 68 per cent probability of the date lying within the range 379–186 BC and a 95 per cent probability of it falling between 400 and 100 BC. These calculations can be made on the basis of the published curve, a set of tables or, more simply, a computer programme listed and described by Stuiver and Reimer (1986) using the curve discussed in Stuiver and Becker 1986.

The date 250 bc falls on part of the curve where the wiggles are at their most complex. If we take another example, 370 bc, from a simpler part of the curve the correlation (cal BC) is 395. With a standard deviation of ± 60, the range is 405–378 but at 2 σ it becomes 520–350 or 307 to 235 because the increased probability brings the date within the range of one of the wiggles.

Standing back from all these complexities one is bound to conclude that radiocarbon

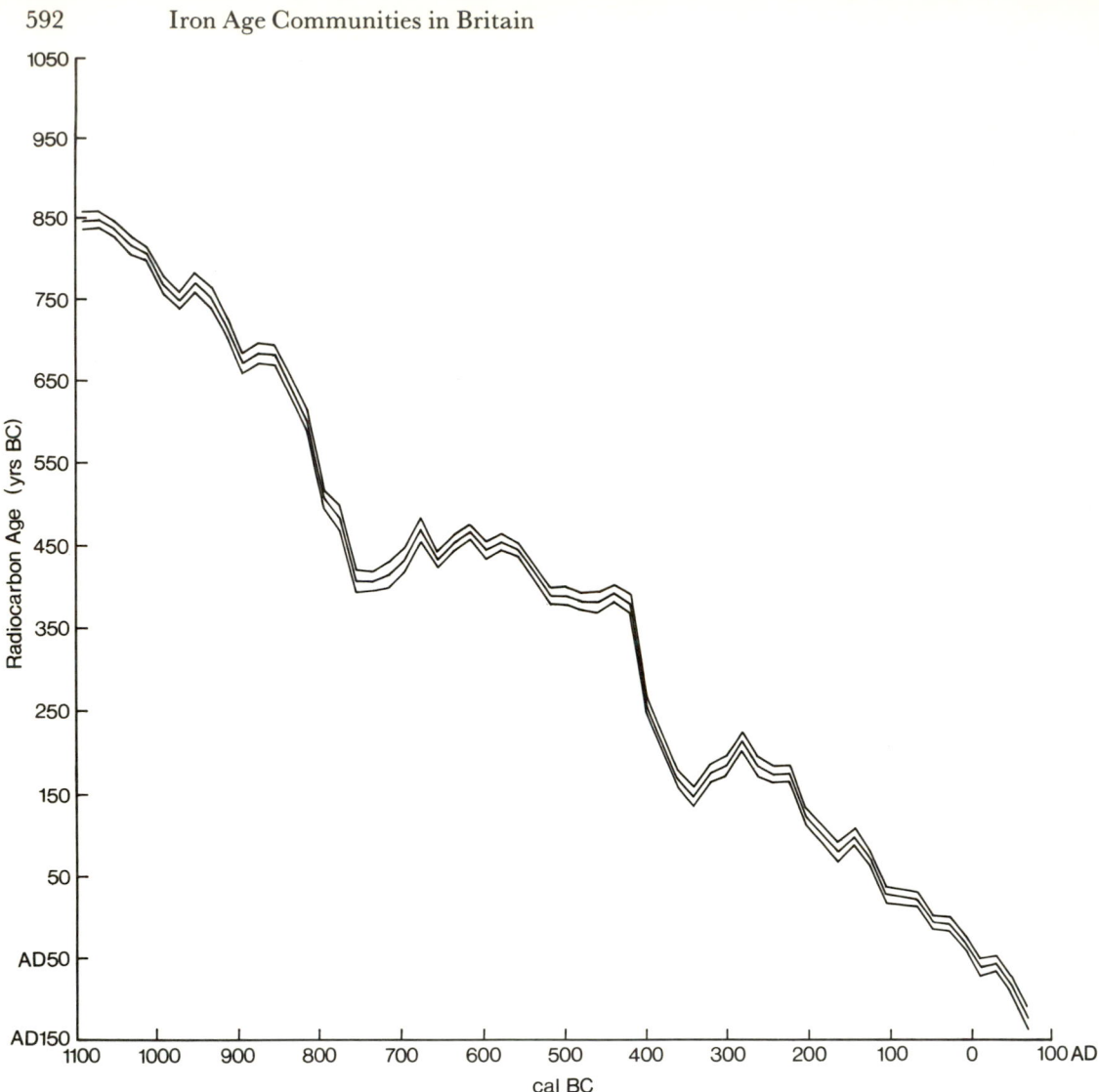

Figure B:1   Radiocarbon calibration curves (sources: Stuiver and Pearson 1986 and Pearson and Stuiver 1986).

assessments for the first millennium BC are not particularly helpful in creating reliable chronologies. If 95 per cent probability is used the range of possibilities for the average date becomes so wide as to be worthless. At 68 per cent probability parts of the curve are able to give greater precision but even so individual dates between 570 and 430 bc and 310–190 bc are best disregarded. This being said techniques of high precision dating or of 'wiggle-matching' using a series of samples from the growth rings of timber hold out exciting possibilities for more precise chronologies (Pearson 1986).

The literature on calibration is vast and fast growing but an invaluable introduction is provided by Pearson (1987) to which the curious or the puzzled are confidently referred.

Note: Problems were experienced by the British Museum radiocarbon laboratory between 1980 and 1984 but only became evident after the dates had been published and had begun to appear in the general literature. To avoid unnecessary confusion each of the sites relevant to this book for which incorrect dates have been published, is listed and the numbers of the erroneous dates are given. In some cases part of the sample remained and new dates were run, these are suffixed N. In other cases it has been possible to recalculate the dates: these are identified with the suffix R.

	radiocarbon years bc	most likely cal bc age range, one sigma using Stuiver and Reimer (1986) programme
Aldermaston Wharf, Surrey		
a. Grain from pit 68	1050±40 (BM−1590)	1319–1214
b. Repeat date of above	840±35 (BM−1591)	977–899
c. Charcoal from lower fill of pit 3	1290±140 (BM−1592)	1690–1390
Ampleforth Moor, Yorks.		
a. Charcoal from ground-surface beneath barrow 3	582±90 (BM−369)	696–538
b. Charcoal from ground-surface beneath barrow 7	537±90 (BM−368)	664–518
Anstiebury, Surrey		
Charcoal from post-hole at entrance of fort	430±120 (BIRM−468)	590–390
Beckford, Worcs.		
Bulked sample from pit with 'duck-stamped' pottery	160±120 (BIRM−432)	230–90
Bigbury, Kent		
(BM date 1768 in error)		
a. Charcoal from pit with LIA pottery	130±45 (BM−1530)	174–89
b. As above	110±50 (BM−1768N)	128–87
Bishops Cannings, Wilts.		
(BM dates 1713–17 in error, not repeatable)		
Blackpatch, Sussex		
(BM date 1643 in error, not repeatable)		
a. Grain from hut platform 4, pit 5	830±80 (HAR−2939)	1016–888
b. Grain from hut platform 4, pit 3	1070±70 (HAR−2940)	1393–1213
c. Grain from hut platform 4, pit 4	840±70 (HAR−2941)	1017–892

d.	Grain from hut platform 1, pit	1020±80 (HAR–3735)	1318–1188
e.	As above	1130±70 (HAR–3736)	1438–1290
f.	As above	900±70 (HAR–3737)	1111–969

Breiddin, Montgomery.

a.	Charcoal from rampart timber of first defence: phase 2	828±71 (BM–879)	1012–890
b.	Similar to a: phase 2	800±41 (BM–878)	881–834
c.	Charcoal from early pit: phase 2	710±80 (HAR–1223)	928–787
d.	Charcoal from 'furnace': phase 2	610±90 (HAR–1224)	694–587
e.	Charcoal from wall of roundhouse: phase 3	479±55 (BM–881)	544–458
f.	Charcoal from roundhouse post-holes: phase 3	460±100 (HAR–467)	560–400
g.	Charcoal from pit in roundhouse: phase 3	375±63 (BM–963)	443–355
h.	Charcoal from roundhouse floor: phase 3	320±80 (HAR–842)	324–206
i.	Charcoal from four-post structure: phase 4	294±40 (BM–964)	388–354 or 292–256
j.	As above	238±70 (BM–884)	361–269
k.	As above	240±80 (HAR–468)	364–266
l.	As above	170±70 (HAR–469)	211–91
m.	As above	172±45 (BM–969)	205–96
n.	Charcoal from occupation behind rampart	201±31 (BM–1158)	210–169
o.	As above	192±31 (BM–1159)	209–166
p.	As above	158±31 (BM–1160)	174–95
q.	Charcoal from floor of house	191±31 (BM–1161)	209–166

Brigg, Lincs.

a.	'Raft'; planking from oak cleat	680±100 (Q–1199)	930–760
b.	'Raft'; timber from raft	593±100 (Q–1200)	720–540
c.	Dug-out canoe	834±100 (Q–78)	1050–830

Broadway Enclosure, Dyfed

a.	Charcoal from pre-rampart occupation	500±65 (CAR–493)	759–685 or 560–484
b.	As above	470±60 (CAR–465)	543–458
c.	As above	460±65 (CAR–401)	756–689 or 525–459

Bromfield, Salop
Bronze Age cremation cemetery:

charcoal from three separate cremations	1560±180 (BIRM–64)	sigma too large
	850±71 (BIRM–63)	1025–895
	762±75 (BIRM–62)	930–805

Brough Law, Northumberland
Charcoal from beneath rampart   245±90   (I–5315)   381–197

Broxmouth
a. Charcoal from below hearth of house 4   95±105 (GU–1206)   200–ad30
b. Animal bone from infill of house 4   ad230±65 (GU–1069)   AD235–AD393
c. Charcoal from entrance revetment of
   Period III   520±65   (GU–1201)   599–517
d. Charcoal from primary midden in ditch
   of Period VI   370±60   (GU–1197)   434–354
e. Charcoal from core of vitrified wall of
   Period VI   340±50   (GU–1205)   404–356
f. Charcoal from vitrified rampart of
   Period VI   300±5   (GU–1225)   294–231
g. Charcoal from beam: Period VI/VII
   ?old timber   570±55   (GU–1202)   693–588
h. Charcoal from midden: Period VI/VII   265±55   (GU–1226)   320–227
i. Animal bone, upper fill of outer ditch:
   Period VI/VII   230±55   (GU–1070)   320–227
j. Bone from burial: Period VI/VII   250±65   (GU–1144)   334–202
k. Charcoal from gate-post   155±50   (GU–1199)   205–92

Bu Broch, Orkney
a. Charcoal from floor inside broch   520±95   (GU–1228)   661–515
b. Animal bones from floor deposit inside
   broch   510±80   (GU–1154)   595–509 or
                                                                         762–681
c. Animal bone from bottom of rubble fill
   of broch   490±65   (GU–1152)   758–687 or
                                                                         550–477
d. Animal bones from floor deposit inside
   earth house   595±65   (GU–1153)   654–588

Burnswark, Northumberland
a. Charcoal from palisade   500±100 (GaK–2203)   590–480
b. Charcoal from gateway timber of
   ?hillfort   525±90   (I–5314)   661–517

Burton Fleming, Humberside
a. Human bone from cemetery   650±70   (HAR–1057)   835–758
b. As above   570±70   (HAR–1058)   695–587
c. As above   100±80   (HAR–1129)   172–ad26
d. As above   200±150 (HAR–1130)   390–90

Caer Cadwgan, Dyfed
a. Charcoal from entrance passage   630±70   (CAR–969)   830–757
b. As above   410±70   (CAR–968)   452–381

Carn Euny, Cornwall
a. Charcoal under entrance of house 1   420±70   (HAR–238)   452–388 or
524–459
b. Charcoal from E entrance of fogou   130±80   (HAR–334)   205–86
c. Charcoal from storage pit in house IV   ad 90±100   (HAR–335)   AD50–260
d. Charcoal from pit 1 in house II   ad 210±70   (HAR–237)   AD224–364

Castercliff, Lancs.
a. Wood charcoal from timber of box
   rampart   510±60   (HAR–287)   594–511 or
762–681
b. Charcoal from beam under vitrified
   inner rampart   510±70   (HAR–286)   595–510 or
762–681

Castle Hill (Almondbury), Yorks.
a. Wood charcoal from rampart   555±100 (I–4542)   720–520
b. Charcoal behind inner rampart, sealed
   by destruction   460±110 (HAR–83)   560–400
c. Charred log base of inner rampart of
   bivallate fort. Penultimate stage of
   defence   520±130 (HAR–84)   660–510
d. Charcoal from same location as b   450±110 (HAR–135)   560–400

Castle Hill (Tonbridge), Kent
a. Charcoal from old ground surface below
   the rampart   228±61   (BM–809)   359–287
b. As above   315±50   (BM–810)   396–354

Caynham Camp, Salop
Charcoal dating timber-laced rampart   360±300 (BIRM–553)   sigma too large

Chalton, Hants.
Charcoal from a Middle Bronze Age hut
site   1243±69   (BM–583)   1531–1411

Combe Hay, Somerset
Charcoal from Bronze Age occupation level   700±120 (BIRM–445)   970–760

Craigmarloch Wood, Renfrew.
a. Charcoal from palisaded enclosure   590±40   (GaK–1995)   796–758
b. Core of vitrified wall   35±40   (GaK–996)   3–AD32

Craig Phadrig, Inverness.
a. Charcoal from timber lacing 330±100 (N–1122) 430–200
b. Outer rampart, charred timber 300±100 (N–1120) 410–200
c. Charcoal below inner face of rampart 270±100 (N–1123) 390–200
d. Charcoal below rampart 180±100 (GX–2441) 230–90

Crickley Hill, Glos.
a. Charcoal from gate-post of Period 3b
   Entrance 570±90 (HAR–391) 722–538
b. Charcoal from thin branches in the
   period 2 rampart 640±60 (HAR–392) 831–759
c. As above 360±70 (HAR–393) 433–351
d. As above 400±80 (HAR–394) 453–361

Croft Ambrey, Herefordshire
a. Charcoal from guardroom destruction 460±135 (BIRM–185a) 600–400
b. Second determination 427±136 (BIRM–185b) 600–380

Cullykhan, Banffshire
a. Outer wood of trunk in entrance post-hole 397±59 (BM–639) 448–376
b. Charcoal from top of first occupation
   level 387±65 (BM–446) 448–359

Dalton Parlours, W. Yorks.
a. Inhumation 120±90 (HAR–6715) 204–AD4
b. Animal bone, lower fill of enclosure ditch 140±80 (HAR–6716) 208–87
c. As above 370±120 (HAR–6727) 450–350
d. Animal bone from roundhouse 6 370±90 (HAR–6725) 448–351

Danebury, Hants.
A sequence of some seventy dates obtained
from the hillfort has been listed and
discussed in detail in Cunliffe and Orton
1984

Dan y Coed, Dyfed
a. Charcoal from pre-rampart house ad 50±65 (CAR–734) AD46–175
b. Charcoal from mound probably pre-
   rampart 130±65 (CAR–705) 202–87
c. Charcoal immediately pre-dating
   defences 120±65 (CAR–706) 174–86
d. Charcoal from hearth of house VI 100±60 (CAR–676) 124–AD2
e. Charcoal from hearth above building V ad 30±60 (CAR–674) AD1–133
f. Charcoal associated with building IX ad 105±65 (CAR–665) AD77–231

Dinorben, Denbigh.
A. Dates published by Savory 1971a
a. Charcoal from occupation layer below
    period 1 rampart   945±95   (V–123)   1135–998
b. Charcoal from collapsed beam north-
    east of period 1 rampart   895±95   (V–122)   1113–902
c. Charcoal, ?derived from period 1
    rampart   765±85   (V–125)   941–801
d. Charcoal, ?from destruction of period 2
    rampart   535±85   (V–124)   663–518
e. Charcoal from timber-lacing of period 2   420±70   (V–176)   452–388 or
    rampart   524–549

B. Dates published by Guilbert 1980
f. Wood charcoal, platform 38   475±60   (CAR–123)   544–458
g. Twig charcoal, platform 38   405±55   (CAR–124)   448–385
h. Charcoal, platform 39   345±60   (CAR–125)   410–351
i. Charcoal from pit   360±60   (CAR–126)   415–352
j. Bone fill of ditch 1   545±60   (CAR–128)   664–586
k. Bone, pre-rampart occupation   520±60   (CAR–167)   598–517
l. Branches from rampart bank 1   440±45   (CAR–119)   596–518
m. As above   455±55   (CAR–120)   523–460
n. As above   460±60   (CAR–121)   525–459
o. As above   500±60   (CAR–122)   759–685 or
                                                                             559–484
p. Bone fill of ditch 2   ad 145±50   (CAR–133)   AD132–254
q. Bone from quarry below bank 2   215±60   (CAR–131)   357–288
r. As above   100±60   (CAR–132)   124–AD2
s. Bone from lower fill of ditch 3   ad 30±60   (CAR–129)   AD1–133
t. Bone from mid fill of ditch 3   ad 475±55   (CAR–130)   AD536–642

Down Farm, Dorset
(BM dates 1850–4 in error)
a. Charcoal from ditch 1   950±160   (BM–1850R)   1320–970
b. Charcoal from burnt layer   1000±110 (BM–1851R)   1320–1070
c. Charcoal from burnt flint dump   1170±50   (BM–1852N1)   1456–1372
    Repeat   1320±50   (BM–1852N2)   1607–1497
    Repeat   1150±50   (BM–1852N3)   1439–1368
    Repeat   1200±60   (BM–1852N4)   1500–1378
d. Charcoal from burnt flint dump   1030±50   (BM–1853N)   1317–1210
e. As above   1080±100 (BM–1854R)   1410–1210

Drim Camp, Dyfed
a. Charcoal from four-post structure late
    in primary phase   ad 25±65   (CAR–560)   BC1–AD133
b. As above   ad 95±60   (CAR–557)   AD75–182
c. Charcoal probably associated with later
    stage of primary occupation   ad 55±65   (CAR–474)   AD48–175

Dryburn Bridge, East Lothian

a. Charcoal from house 2	665±55	835–765
b. As above	600±55	803–756
c. As above	500±50	759–686
d. As above	330±55	402–354
e. Cemetery, individual burials associated with later phase of settlement	715±165	1020–750
	465±80	548–457
	450±100	560–400
	350±125	521–462

Dun Ardtreck, Skye

Charcoal from rubble foundations of semi-broch	55±105 (GX–1120)	130–AD80

Dun Lagaidh, Wester Ross

a. Carbonized branch under vitrified fort wall	490±90 (GX–1121)	558–411
b. Burnt grain associated with burning of timber fort	460±100 (GaK–2492)	560–400

Dun Mor Vaul, Tiree, Argyll.

a. Roots from old ground-surface below broch	400±110 (GaK–1092)	455–357
b. Charred grain from pre-broch level	445±90 (GaK–1098)	551–457
c. Bones from midden under outer wall	280±100 (GaK–1225)	400–200
d. Primary floor in broch wall gallery	ad 60±90 (GaK–1097)	AD19–231
e. Rubble in wall gallery	ad 160±90 (GaK–1099)	AD127–264

Fengate, Northants.

a. Padholm Road site: charcoal from field ditch 3	1280±70 (UB–676)	1543–1442
b. Padholm Road site: charcoal dating field ditch 1	935±135 (UB–677)	1260–970
c. Padholm Road site: wood charcoal from small pit	350±46 (GaK–4198)	407–357
d. Vicarage Farm: charcoal from pit with early pottery	340±125 (UB–822)	450–200

Finavon, Angus

a. Charcoal from low in fallen rubble	410±80 (GaK–1222)	544–458 or 453–377
b. Occupation layer of fort	320±90 (GaK–1223)	410–201
c. Beams and planks along inner wall face	590±90 (GaK–1224)	695–586

Fiskerton, Lincs.
Short Ferry dug-out canoe   846±100 (Q–79)   1050–890

Flag Fen, Northants.
(BM date 2123 in error)
Timber from platform   880±120 (BM–2123R)   1110–890

Glastonbury, Somerset
a. Peat below causeway   25±70   (Q–2618)   72–AD78
b. As above   ad 30±70   (Q–2619)   AD1–134

Green Knowe, Borders Region
a. Charcoal, platform 2, later house   984±45   1195–1138
b. As above   1205±105   1530–1310
c. Charcoal, platform 2, earlier house   1025±36   1265–1210
d. As above   1095±130   1450–1210
e. Charcoal, platform 2, midden and initial
     field clearance   972±87   1262–1011
f. As above   1048±124   1410–1190
g. Charcoal, platform 8   781±75   (   )   940–813

Grimthorpe, Yorks.
a. Bones from ditch   690±130 (NPL–136)   940–760
b. Bones from ditch   970±130 (NPL–137)   1320–1000

Gussage All Saints, Dorset
a. Charcoal from pit of phase 1   514±80   (Q–1204)   764–679 or
                                                                                 597–511
b. Animal bone from phase 1 ditch   452±75   (Q–1209)   544–458
c. Charcoal from pit of phase 1 with La
     Tène 1a brooch   418±90   (Q–1203)   552–456
d. Charcoal from phase 2 ditch   229±75   (Q–1201)   361–270 or
                                                                                 262–171
e. Charcoal from pit of phase 2   212±75   (Q–1205)   359–287
f. Charcoal from top of foundry pit   147±65   (Q–1207)   207–89
g. Charcoal from foundry pit   68±70   (Q–1206)   110–AD32
h. Charcoal from ditch of late phase   ad 20±75   (Q–1202)   BC3–AD133

Hambledon Hill, Dorset
Charcoal from bottom of 'plateau
enclosure' ditch   2790±90   (NPL–76)   3634–3494

Hascombe, Surrey
a. Charcoal ground surface beneath
     rampart   290±70   (HAR–1698)   305–227
b. Charcoal core of entrance earthwork   170±70   (HAR–1699)   211–91

c. Charcoal fill of pit in trench 8	0±100	(HAR–1701)	70–AD130
d. Pit 1, grain deposit: grain only	110±50	(BM–1244a)	128–87
e. As above	120±70	(HAR–2076)	175–86
f. As above	170±70	(HAR–2809)	211–91
g. As above	230±80	(HAR–2817)	362–268
h. As above	80±70	(HAR–2818)	117–AD28
i. Pit 1, grain deposit: grain and charcoal	10±70	(HAR–1289)	5–AD82
j. As above	150±70	(HAR–1290)	209–89
k. As above	230±120	(BIRM–705)	390–160
l. Pit 1, grain deposit: charcoal only	110±60	(HAR–1700)	84–18
m. As above	70±80	(HAR–2803)	119–AD33
n. As above	ad 80±80	(BM–1244b)	AD52–233
o. Charcoal – lowest fill of pit 2 in trench 6	100±50	(BM–1485)	84–36
p. Charcoal – hearth in trench 2	210±50	(BM–1487)	355–291
q. Charcoal – lowest fill of pit in trench 13	20±50	(BM–1490)	3–AD70
r. Charcoal – lowest fill of pit 1 in trench 6	10±50	(BM–1491)	2–AD77
s. Charcoal – upper fill of pit 2 in trench 6	ad 130±50	(BM–1489)	AD128–251
t. Grain – fill of pit in trench 12	ad 50±45	(BM–1486)	AD 50–133

Hod Hill, Dorset
Charcoal associated with main rampart	460±150	(BM–47)	660–390

Holgan Camp, Dyfed
a. Charcoal from early occupation within defences	335±65	(CAR–787)	407–350 or 300–229
b. As above	280±60	(CAR–762)	303–228
c. As above	205±65	(CAR–786)	233–161
d. Charcoal from later occupation horizon	525±65	(CAR–761)	604–518
e. As above	290±65	(CAR–785a)	303–228
f. As above	190±65	(CAR–785b)	212–96

Holmbury Hill, Surrey
Charcoal from small pit within fort	310±100	(BIRM–591)	410–170

Holme Pierrepont, Notts.
Dug-out canoe I	230±110	(BIRM–132)	390–160

Huckhoe, Northumberland
Charcoal from palisade trench	510±40	(GaK–1388)	760–683 or 593–516

Ingram Hill, Northumberland
Charcoal from settlement site with palisade: beneath bank	220±90	(I-5316)	363–268 or 264–166

Itford Hill, Sussex
Charred grain   1000±35   (GrU-6167)   1182–1128

Ivinghoe Beacon, Bucks.
a. Animal bone sealed by chalk rubble
   behind rampart   720±100 (BIRM–804)   950–770
b. As above   520±100 (BIRM–893)   660–510
c. As above   350±100 (BIRM–803)   330–200

Killibury, Cornwall
a. Soil – early level in hillfort interior   260±70   (HAR–745)   326–204
b. Charcoal from pit   230±70   (HAR–1950)   360–270
c. Charcoal from early level in hillfort   230±70   (HAR–1951)   360–270
d. Charcoal from pit preceding rampart   930±70   (HAR–1952)   1115–999
e. Charcoal in late hillfort occupation   160±70   (HAR–1953)   210–90

Kilphedir, Sutherland
a. Charcoal from hut 3   420±40   (GU–299)   446–394
b. Charcoal from hut 5   150±80   (L–1061)   210–88
c. Charcoal from hut 5   114±55   (GU–11)   133–87

Knights Farm, Berks.
a. Charcoal from oven fill   1680±50   (BM–1593)   2002–1924
b. Charcoal from pit with
   Deverel–Rimbury pots   1250±100 (BM–1594)   1610–1390
c. Charcoal from pit with angular pots   290±120 (BM–1595)   410–160
d. Charcoal from post-hole of house   870±110 (BM–1596)   1110–890

Ledston, W. Yorks.
a. Bone from burial in storage pit   130±100 (HAR–2805)   210–AD1
b. Charcoal from post-hole   320±70   (HAR–2825)   302–228

Little Waltham, Essex
a. Burnt debris from the wall trench of a
   house   610±80   (HAR–1081)   693–588
b. As above   1390±90   (HAR–1082)   1737–1524
c. As above   210±80   (HAR–1088)   235–160 or
                                                                                       359–286

Longbridge Deverill (Cow Down), Wilts.
a. Wood charcoal from post-hole of house
   1 in enclosure 2   630±155 (NPL–105)   840–510
b. Wood charcoal from post-hole of house
   2 in enclosure 2   500±90   (NPL–106)   563–482 or
                                                                                       760–684

c. Wood charcoal from loom post-hole of
    house 2 in enclosure 2   420±95 (NPL–107)   557–384
d. Wood charcoal from pit 7   460±140 (NPL–108)   600–400
e. Wood charcoal from pit 37   490±90 (NPL–109)   558–411
f. Carbonized grain from base of pit 37   440±70 (HAR–253)   525–459
g. Wood charcoal from post of smallest
    house (house 4)   470±60 (HAR–254)   543–458
h. Wood charcoal from post of porch of
    house 4   490±90 (HAR–256)   558–411
i. Wood charcoal from post of largest
    house (house 3)   380±60 (HAR–255)   446–358

MacNaughton's Fort, Kirkcudbright.
Charcoal in palisade trench enclosing
wooden roundhouse   280±100 (GaK–808)   400–200

Mam Tor, Derby
a. Interior occupation   1130±115 (BIRM–192)   1470–1210
b. Interior occupation   1180±132 (BIRM–202)   1530–1260

Meare Village West, Somerset.
a. Plank from pool between hearth and
    central floor   250±70 (HAR–3489)   365–201
b. Brushwood from lowest structural level   250±70 (HAR–2654)   365–201
c. Wood on west edge of central floor   240±70 (HAR–3719)   362–268
d. Elm plank from north-west area   220±70 (HAR–3693)   359–286
e. Oak stake from construction   180±90 (HAR–2668)   233–91
f. Plank from lower hearth of north mound   180±60 (HAR–3492)   210–94
g. Peat and wood associated with
    occupation floor   330±80 (HAR–3744)   326–204
h. Raised bog immediately below
    occupation at east end of site   390±80 (HAR–2620)   450–357
Other dates from peat monoliths associated
with the village are published in Orme
1982

Midsummer Hill Camp, Heref.
a. Charcoal from quarry ditch
    associated with first gate   420±190 (BIRM–142)   sigma too large
b. Carbonized grain associated with
    destruction of eighth gate   50±100 (BIRM–143)   120–AD80

Milton Loch Crannog, Kirkcudbright.
Oakwood from Ard   400±100 (K–1394)   454–358

Moel Hiraddug, Clwyd
a. Charcoal from main gate   430±60   (CAR–374)   522–461
b. As above   410±65   (CAR–373)   451–384
c. As above   350±65   (CAR–372)   413–350

Moel y Gaer
a. Planks from foundation trench for front
    of rampart A   580±90   (HAR–604)   696–538
b. Burnt twigs beneath tail of rampart B   240±80   (HAR–603)   364–266
    Replica date   160±70   (HAR–1562)   210–90
c. Charcoal from soil sealed by post ring
    roundhouse beneath rampart A   620±70   (HAR–606)   828–756
d. Charcoal from core of rampart A   260±70   (HAR–1122)   326–204
e. Charcoal beneath bank of palisade slot   1660±40   (SRR–495)   2033–1920
f. Charcoal, silt fill of palisade quarry ditch   ad 72±45   (SRR–496)   AD65–135
g. Charcoal, post ring roundhouse (P21)   470±80   (HAR 1196)   550–457
h. Charcoal, post ring roundhouse (P22)   610±90   (HAR–1197)   694–587
i. Charcoal, post ring roundhouse (P16)   400±90   (HAR–1293)   453–359
j. Charcoal, post ring roundhouse (P21)   440±80   (HAR–1353)   544–458
k. Charcoal, post ring roundhouse (P30)   560±100   (HAR–1126)   720–520
l. Charcoal – small 4 poster (F77)   1015±35   (SRR–498)   1264–1209
m. Charcoal – 4 poster (F54)   430±70   (HAR–1249)   524–459
n. Charcoal – 4 poster (F52)   270±80   (HAR–1295)   329–203
o. Charcoal – stake wall roundhouse (S39)   480±140   (HAR–1125)   600–400

Mucking, North Ring, Essex
a. Charcoal over primary fill of ditch   680±110   (HAR–2893)   930–760
b. Charcoal from primary fill   750±80   (HAR–2911)   932–799

Mucking, South Ring, Essex
a. Charcoal from outer ditch   820±110   (HAR–1634)   1050–820
b. As above   860±70   (HAR–1708)   1052–896
c. Charcoal from inner ditch   840±90   (HAR–1630)   1051–889

Oldbury, Kent
(BM dates 2290–2 in error)
a. Charcoal from hearth near main rampart   660±130   (BM–2290R)   920–750
b. Charcoal from hearth S end of fort   120±50   (BM–2291N)   172–88
c. Charcoal from hearth in trench 9   260±140   (BM–2292R)   410–90

Pembry Mountain, Dyfed
Charcoal from pre-rampart occupation   335±45   (CAR–105)   402–357

Pen y Coed, Dyfed
a. Charcoal from drain around large house   160±60   (CAR–768)   209–91
b. Charcoal from palisade trench   75±60   (CAR–769)   108–AD28

c. Charcoal from post-hole   55±70   (CAR–711)   99—AD66
d. Charcoal from base of ditch   25±60   (CAR–712)   45—AD71

Petters Field, Egham, Surrey
(BM dates 1620–5 in error)
Charcoal from fill of enclosure ditch   680±70   (BM–1624N)   901–765

Poole, Dorset
Dug-out canoe   295±50   (Q–821)   295–230

Quanterness, Orkney
a. Soil rich in organic material.
    Primary occupation of roundhouse   620±85   (Q–1465)   693–588
b. As above   490±85   (Q–1464)   557–456
c. Soil rich in organic material within
    roundhouse   180±60   (Q–1463)   210–94

Rainsborough, Northants.
a. Charcoal from pit K   510±70   (UB–736)   595–510
b. Wood charcoal from N guardroom   540±35   (UB–737)   662–587
c. Wood charcoal from S guardroom   480±75   (UB–853)   550–457
d. Carbonized grain from post-hole of
    4-post structure   500±75   (UB–855)   561–483 or
                                                                  759–685

Rams Hill, Berks.
a. Charcoal from post-hole of double
    palisade   1070±90   (HAR–228)   1409–1211
b. Ash, etc. related to double palisade   1010±80   (HAR–229)   1317–1080
c. Charcoal from feature cutting primary
    levels at south entrance   740±70   (HAR–230)   907–800
d. Charcoal from similar location to c   1050±90   (HAR–231)   1325–1208
e. Charcoal from packing of palisade   1060±70   (HAR–232)   1325–1211

Roxby, Yorks.
(BM date 2207A in error)
Charcoal from post-hole of house 3   230±180 (BM–2207AR)   sigma too large

Ryton-on-Dunsmoor, Warwicks.
a. Charcoal from a cremation   751±41   (BIRM–26)   899–821
b. Charcoal from a cremation   920±106 (BIRM–228)   1130–970
c. Charcoal from low in ditch   835±120 (BIRM–227)   1060–830

St Eval, Cornwall
Wood charcoal from hut 2 associated with
Glastonbury style pottery   185±90   (NPL–135)   233–92

Shapwick Station, Somerset
Dug-out canoe   345±120 (Q–357)   450–200

Shearplace Hill, Dorset
Miscellaneous charcoal and animal bone
from Middle Bronze Age hut   1180±180 (NPL–19)   sigma too large

Somerset Levels
Dates for timber from trackways across the
levels
a. Meare Heath track: stake   890±110 (Q–52)   1110–900
                                                900±110 (Q–52)   1120–900
b. Westhay track: wood   850±110 (Q–308)   1060–830
c. Toll Gate track: wood   650±110 (Q–306)   860–750
d. Skinner's Wood track, peg   680±70   (HAR–650)   901–765
e. Vipers track: wood   680±110 (Q–312)   930–760
f. Vipers track: post   570±110 (Q–7)   730–520
g. Nidon's track: timber   635±100 (Q–313)   690–590 or
                                                                                  835–753
h. Nidon's track: peat around   640±120 (Q–316)   720–540
i. Nidon's track: peat over   678±120 (Q–317)   930–760
j. Shapwick Heath track: timber   520±110 (Q–39)   660–510
k. Platform track: timber   460±100 (Q–311)   560–400

South Cadbury, Somerset.
a. Wood charcoal from pre-rampart soil   870±110 (SRR–443)   1110–890
b. As above   955±140 (SRR–451)   1270–970
c. Antler from sub rampart level   985±90   (I–5970)   1265–1048
In addition seven dates were obtained for
the rampart sequence and a further ten for
a massacre level thought to date to *c.* AD
60. Both sets showed considerable
anomalies. See Alcock 1980 and Campbell,
Baxter and Alcock 1979 for discussion

South Lodge Camp, Dorset
(BM dates 1917–24 in error)
a. Charcoal with cremation, barrow 3   1060±120 (BM–1917R)   1410–1190
b. As above   950±150 (BM–1918R)   1270–970
c. Charcoal with unurned cremation near
    barrow 3   1190±120 (BM–1919R)   1530–1290
d. Charcoal with cremation in ditch of
    barrow 2   940±120 (BM–1920R)   1200–970
e. Charcoal from post-hole of house   1290±120 (BM–1921R)   1640–1410
f. As e above   1160±110 (BM–1922R)   1520–1260
g. As d above   950±110 (BM–1923R)   1200–970
h. Charcoal with cremation outside
    barrow 3   1010±120 (BM–1924R)   1320–1070

Springfield Lyons, Essex
(BM dates 2313–4 in error)
a. Charcoal from enclosure ditch   1140±150 (BM–2313R)   1520–1210
b. Charcoal from secondary fill of
    enclosure ditch   720±140 (BM–2314R)   1020–760
c. Charcoal from post-hole of the central
    roundhouse   880±70 (HAR–6622)   1055–902

Stackpole Warren, Dyfed
a. Charcoal from burnt mound   820±60 (CAR–854)   975–892
b. As above   760±60 (CAR–843)   919–814
c. Bone from occupation horizon   285±60 (CAR–103)   302–228
d. Bone from crouched burial   160±55 (CAR–104)   208–91
e. Bone from occupation horizon   105±60 (CAR–102)   129–16
f. Charcoal from lower fill of ditch of early
    field system   405±70 (CAR–145)   451–377
g. Charcoal from below wall of later field
    system   95±70 (CAR–144)   126–AD5

Staple Howe, Yorks.
Charred grain   450±150 (BM–63)   660–390

Thwing, Humberside
Charcoal from below the rampart   950±70 (HAR–1398)   1134–1006

Trevisker, Cornwall
Oak charcoal from floor of house A   1110±95 (NPL–134)   1440–1210

Twyn y Gaer, Gwent
Charcoal from the late phase of the hillfort
annex   286±38 (BM–1118)   294–231

Twywell, Northants.
Carbonized grain from pit 132   280±90 (NPL–225)   395–201

Walesland Rath, Pembs.
a. Charcoal from between phase 1 and 2
    banks   210±90 (NPL–245)   360–271
b. Charcoal on top of primary ditch silt   85±90 (NPL–244)   134–AD33

Weston Wood (Albury), Surrey
Carbonized cereal from a pit   510±110 (Q–760)   600–480

Winklebury, Hants.
a. Charcoal from house   250±60 (HAR–1764)   333–266
b. Charcoal from top of pit   30±90 (HAR–1778)   95–AD84

c. As above	70±80	(HAR–1794)	119–AD33
d. Charcoal from pit bottom	ad 20±70	(HAR–1765)	BC2–AD132

Woodbarn Rath, Dyfed

a. Charcoal from revetment of late phase of defences	150±60	(CAR–825)	207–90
b. Charcoal underlying late phase of defences	110±60	(CAR–826)	84–18

Woodside Camp, Dyfed

a. Charcoal from layer contemporary with rampart construction	250±60	(CAR–760)	333–266
b. Charcoal from turf pre-dating first outwork bank	50±65	(CAR–735)	74–AD60
c. Charcoal from pit early in sequence	ad 50±65	(CAR–678)	AD46–175
d. Charcoal from late occupation layer	60±30	(CAR–462)	45–AD3
e. As above	ad 75±60	(CAR–457)	AD62–178
f. Charcoal from ditch fill post-dating second phase outwork	5±65	(CAR–733)	BC3–AD82

Wrekin Hillfort, Salop

a. Wood charcoal from final socket hut 2	520±180	(BIRM–531)	800–400
b. Wood charcoal from final socket hut 2	410±80	(HAR–4454)	544–458 or 453–377
c. Wood charcoal from penultimate socket, hut 3	390±70	(HAR–4452)	449–359
d. Wood charcoal from final socket, hut 3	340±100	(BIRM–530)	430–200
e. Wood charcoal on terrace	210±70	(HAR–4451)	358–288 or 234–164
f. Carbonized grain on terrace	120±90	(HAR–4450)	204–AD4
g. Carbonized grain from final socket	10±90	(BIRM–532)	72–AD129
h. Wood charcoal from final socket, hut 6	ad 280±100	(HAR–4453)	AD240–430

The author is indebted to Dr Gary Lock for calculating the cal BC dates.

APPENDIX C   List of principal sites

The major sites mentioned in the text above are listed here in alphabetical order, together with their more significant bibliographical references or, if unpublished, the source of the information or location of the finds. No attempt has been made to list all of the references for each site, nor have sites of only passing significance been included. Where county boundaries have changed as a result of local government reorganization old county names are given in brackets before the new.

Abernethy, *see* Castle Law, Perths.
Abington Pigotts, Cambs.   *C.F. Fox 1924*
Adabrock (Lewis), Western Isles Islands Area   *Coles 1962b, 48–50*
Aldermaston, Berks.   *Bradley, Lobb, Richards and Robinson 1980*
Aldwincle, Northants.   *Jackson 1977*
Allasdale, Isle of Barra (Inverness.), Western Isles Islands Area   *Young 1955*
All Cannings Cross, Wilts.   *M.E. Cunnington 1923*
Allen's Pit (Dorchester), Oxon.   *Bradford 1942b*
Almondbury, *see* Castle Hill, Yorks.
Alnham, *see* High Knowes, Northumberland
Ampleforth Moor (Yorks.), North Yorkshire   *Wainwright and Longworth 1969*
Ancaster, Lincs.   *May 1965–9, 1976b*
Angle Ditch, *see* Handley Down, Dorset
Anstiebury, Surrey   *F.H. Thompson 1979*
Appleford (Berks.), Oxon.   *Hinchcliffe and Thomas 1980*
Ardleigh, Essex   *Erith and Longworth 1960*
Arminghall, Norfolk   *Clark 1936*
Arras (Yorks.), Humberside   *Stead 1965; Greenwell 1906*
Asham (Sussex), East Sussex   *E. Curwen 1930*
Ashville, Oxon.   *Parrington 1978*
Atwick (Yorks.), Humberside   *Greenwell and Gatty 1910; Brewster 1963, 143*
Aust (Glos.), Avon   *Ellis 1900; R.A. Smith 1925, 148; Dawson 1980*

609

Aylesford, Kent   *A.J. Evans 1890; Birchall 1963, 1965; Stead 1971a*
Bacon Hole (Glam.), West Glamorgan   *A. Williams 1939b*
Badbury, Dorset   *Crawford and Keiller 1928*
Bagendon, Glos.   *Clifford 1961; Courtney and Hall 1984*
Baldock, Herts.   *Stead 1971a; Stead and Rigby 1986*
Balevullin, Tiree (Argyll.), Strathclyde Region   *MacKie 1965b*
Balksbury, Hants.   *J. Hawkes 1940; Wainwright 1970a*
Balloch Hill, Argyll   *Peltenburg 1982*
Balmashanner (Angus), Tayside Region   *Coles 1962b, 98–9*
Bampton, Oxon.   *Savory 1939*
Banwell (Som.), Avon   *Unpublished: Taunton Museum*
Barbury Castle, Wilts.   *MacGregor and Simpson 1963*
Barford, Warwicks.   *Oswald 1969*
Barley, Herts.   *Cra'ster 1961*
Barn Down West, Wilts.   *Fowler, Musty and Taylor 1965*
Barnes, Isle of Wight, Hants.   *Preston and Hawkes 1933*
Barnwood, Glos.   *Clifford 1934*
Barton Court Farm, Oxon.   *Miles 1984*
Bath (Som.), Avon   *Cunliffe 1988c*
Bathampton Down (Som.), Avon   *Wainwright 1967b*
Battersea, London   *C.F. Fox 1958, pls. 14, 16*
Battlesbury, Wilts.   *Chadwick and Thompson 1956*
Bawsey, Norfolk   *Maryon 1944*
Beacon Hill (Burghclere), Hants.   *Williams-Freeman 1915*
Beaulieu Heath, Hants.   *C.M. Piggott 1953*
Beckford (Worcs.), Hereford and Worcester   *Oswald 1974; Britnell 1974, 1975*
Belle Tout (Sussex), East Sussex   *Bradley 1971b*
Belling Law, Northumberland   *Jobey 1977*
Bexley Heath (Kent), Greater London   *Inv. Arch. GB 8th Set (1960), 53*
Bigbury, Kent   *Jessup and Cook 1936; F.H. Thompson 1983*
Billericay, Essex   *C.F. Fox 1958, 96*
Bindon, Dorset   *Wheeler 1953*
Birdlip, Glos.   *Bellows 1881; C. Green 1949; Staelens 1983*
Bishopston (Glam.), West Glamorgan   *A. Williams 1940*
Bishopstone (Sussex), East Sussex   *Bell 1977*
Blackbury Castle, Devon   *Young and Richardson 1955*
Blackpatch (Sussex), East Sussex   *Drewett 1980, 1982*
Blackthorn, Northants.   *J.H. Williams 1974*
Blagden Copse, Hants.   *Stead 1970*
Blaise Castle Hill (Glos.), Avon   *Rahtz and Brown 1959*
Bledlow, Bucks.   *Head and C.M. Piggott 1944*
Blewburton Hill (Berks.), Oxon.   *Collins 1947, 1953; A.E.P. and F.J. Collins 1959; Bradford 1942c;*
   D.W. Harding 1976a
Blissmoor, Dartmoor, Devon   *A. Fox 1955*
Bodrifty, Cornwall   *Dudley 1957*

Bonchester Hill (Roxburgh.), Borders Region   *Curle 1910; C.M. Piggott 1952*

Boscombe Down East, Wilts.   *Stone 1936*

Boscombe Down West, Wilts.   *Richardson 1951*

Bower Walls Camp (Som.), Avon   *Cotton 1955, 85–6*

Boxford Common, Berks.   *Peake, Coghlan and Hawkes 1932, 1933*

Braes of Gight (Aberdeen.), Grampian Region   *Coles 1962b, 94–5*

Braich y Cornel (Caerns.) Gwynedd   *Gresham 1973*

Braidwood Fort (Midlothian), Lothian Region   *Stevenson 1949; S. Piggott 1960*

Braintree (Mount House), Essex   *Eddy 1983*

Bramdean, Hants.   *Perry 1974, 1982, 1986*

Brampton (Hunts.), Cambs.   *D.A. White 1969*

Bredon Hill (Worcs.), Hereford and Worcester   *T.C. Hencken 1938*

Breedon-on-the-Hill, Leics.   *Kenyon 1950; Wacher 1964, 1979*

Breiddin (Mont.), Powys   *B.H. St J. O'Neil 1937; Musson 1970, 1972, 1976*

Brentford (Middx), Greater London   *C.F. Fox 1958, pl. 3; O'Connor 1978*

Brentford, Old England (Middx), Greater London   *Wheeler 1929*

Briar Hill, Northants.   *Jackson 1974*

Bridport (West Bay), Dorset   *Farrar 1954*

Brigstock, Northants.   *Jackson 1983*

Broadall Lake, Devon   *A. Fox 1955*

Broadwater (Sussex), West Sussex   *E.C. Curwen 1954*

Bromfield, Salop   *Stanford 1982*

Brooklands *see* Weybridge

Broughing, Herts. (incl. Skeleton Green and Puckeridge) *Partridge 1979, 1981, 1982b; Potter and Trow 1988*

Brough Law, Northumberland   *Jobey 1971c*

Broxmouth (East Lothian), Lothian Region   *Hill 1982a*

Bryn y Castell, (Caerns.), Gwynedd   *Crew 1984, 1985*

Bu Broch (Orkney), Orkney Islands Area   *Hedges 1987*

Buckland Rings, Hants.   *C.F.C. Hawkes 1936a*

Budbury, Wilts.   *Wainwright 1970b*

Bugthorpe (Yorks.), Humberside   *Greenwell 1877; Stead 1965, 104*

Bulbury, Dorset   *E. Cunnington 1884; Cunliffe 1972b*

Bulwarks, the (Glam.), West Glamorgan   *J.L. Davies 1974*

Buntley, Suffolk   *Unpublished: pottery in Ipswich Museum*

Burnmouth (Berwick.), Borders Region   *Craw 1924*

Burradon, Northumberland   *Jobey 1970*

Burton Fleming (Yorks.), Humberside   *Stead 1971b, 1976b*

Bury Hill, Hants.   *C.F.C. Hawkes 1940a*

Bury Hill (Glos.), Avon   *Davies and Phillips 1929*

Bury Wood Camp, Wilts.   *King 1961, 1962, 1967*

Butcombe (Som.), Avon   *P.J. Fowler 1970*

Caburn (Sussex), East Sussex   *Curwen and Curwen 1927; A.E. Wilson 1938, 1939; C.F.C. Hawkes 1939a*

Caer Cadwgan (Cards.), Dyfed   *Austin 1984, 1985*

Caesars Camp, Wimbledon (Surrey), Greater London   *Lowther 1947*

Cairnconan (Angus), Tayside Region   *Jervise 1863*

Calf of Eday (Orkney), Orkney Islands Area   *Calder 1939*

Calleva (Silchester), Hants.   *Boon 1969; Fulford 1986. 1987*

Cambridge, Cambs.   *Cra'ster 1969*

Camerton (Som.), Avon   *Wedlake 1958*

Camulodunum (Colchester), Essex   *Hawkes and Hull 1947; Crummy 1980a, 1980b*

Canterbury, Kent   *Frere 1954*

Cardiff (Glam.), South Glamorgan   *Nash-Williams 1933b*

Carloggas (St Mawgan-in-Pydar), Cornwall   *Threipland 1957*

Carn Euny, Cornwall   *Christie 1978*

Carn Fadrun (Caerns.), Gwynedd   RCHM *Caernarvonshire III, no. 1650*

Carshalton, Surrey   *Lowther 1945; Adkins and Needham 1985*

Cassington, Oxon.   *Leeds 1935; Harden 1942*

Castel Henllys (Pembs.), Dyfed   *Mytum 1986, 1987*

Castell Coyan (Carm.), Dyfed   *Grealey, Jones and Little 1972*

Castell Odo (Caerns.), Gwynedd   *Alcock 1961*

Castercliff, Lancs.   *Coombs 1982*

Casterley Camp, Wilts.   *M.E. and B.H. Cunnington 1913*

Castle Ditch (Eddisbury), Cheshire   *Varley 1950a*

Castle Ditches, Llacarfan (Glam.), West Glamorgan   *Hogg 1977*

Castle Dore, Cornwall   *Radford 1951*

Castle Gotha, Cornwall   *A. Saunders 1961; Saunders and Harris 1982*

Castle Hill, Almondbury (Yorks.), West Yorkshire   *Varley 1939, 1976*

Castle Hill, Horsburgh (Peebles.), Borders Region   *Feachem 1966*

Castle Hill, Newhaven (Sussex), East Sussex   *C.F.C. Hawkes 1939c*

Castle Hill, Scarborough (Yorks.), North Yorkshire   *R.A. Smith 1928, 1934*

Castle Hill, Tonbridge, Kent   *Money 1973*

Castle Law (Midlothian), Lothian Region   *Childe 1933; S. and C.M. Piggott 1954*

Castle Law (Perths.), Tayside Region (*see also* Forgandenny)   *Christison and Anderson 1899*

Cerrig y Drudion (Denbigh.), Clwyd   *C.F. Fox 1958; R.A. Smith 1926; Stead 1982*

Chalbury, Dorset   *Whitley 1943*

Chalton, Hants.   *Cunliffe 1970, 1976a*

Charleston Brow (Sussex), East Sussex   *Parson and Curwen 1933*

Chastleton, Oxon   *Leeds 1931a*

Cherbury (Berks.), Oxon   *Bradford 1940*

Chertsey, Surrey   *Unpublished: Guildford Museum*

Chinnor, Oxon   *Richardson and Young 1951*

Chippenham, Cambs.   *Leaf 1936*

Chisbury, Wilts.   *M.E. Cunnington 1932a*

Chisenbury Trendle, Wilts.   *M.E. Cunnington 1932b*

Cholesbury Camp, Bucks.   *Kimball 1933*

Cholwich Town, Devon   *Fleming and Collis 1973*

Chun, Cornwall   *Leeds 1927*

Chysauster, Cornwall   *H.O'N. Hencken 1933*

Cissbury (Sussex), West Sussex   *Curwen and Williamson 1931*

Claydon Pike, Lechlade, Glos.   *Miles and Palmer 1982*
Cleeve Hill, Glos.   *Gray and Brewer 1904*
Clettraval (N. Uist), Western Isles Islands Area   *Scott 1948*
Clickhimin (Shetland), Shetland Islands Area   *J.R.C. Hamilton 1966, 1968*
Clotherholme (Yorks.), North Yorkshire   *Manby 1963*
Clovelly Dykes, Devon   *A. Fox 1953*
Clynnog (Caerns.), Gwynedd   *Grimes 1951*
Cock Hill (Sussex), West Sussex   *H.B.A. and M.M. Ratcliffe-Densham 1961*
Colchester, Essex   *Fox and Hull 1948*
Cold Kitchen Hill, Wilts.   *Cunnington and Goddard 1934*
Collfryn (Mont.), Powys   *Britnell (forthcoming)*
Colsterworth, Lincs.   *Grimes 1961*
Conway Mountain (Caerns.), Gwynedd   *Griffiths and Hogg 1957*
Corley Camp, Warwicks.   *Chatwin 1930*
Covesea, Sculpture Cave (Moray.), Grampian Region   *Benton 1931*
Cowlam, Yorks.   *Stead 1965, 105; Greenwell 1877*
Coxhoe, Co. Durham   *Van der Veen and Haselgrove 1983; Haselgrove and Allon 1982*
Coygan Camp (Carm.), Dyfed   *Wainwright 1967a*
Craig Phadrig (Inverness.), Highland Region   *Small and Cottam 1972*
Crane Godrevy (Gwithian), Cornwall   *A.C. Thomas 1964*
Crayford, Kent   *Ward Perkins 1938*
Credenhill Camp (Heref.) Hereford and Worcester   *Stanford 1971a*
Creeting St Mary, Suffolk   *R.R. Clarke 1939*
Crickley Hill, Glos.   *P. Dixon 1972a, 1972b, 1973, 1976; Dixon and Borne 1977*
Croft Ambrey (Heref.), Hereford and Worcester   *Stanford 1967, 1974a*
Cromer, Norfolk   *R.R. Clarke 1960, pl. 20*
Crosby Ravensworth (Westmorland), Cumbria   *Way 1869*
Crosskirk, Caithness   *Fairhurst 1984*
Cullykhan (Buchan), Grampian Region   *Greig 1972*
Culver Hole Cave *see* Llangenydd, Gower
Cwmbrwyn (Carm.), Dyfed   *Ward 1907*
Cwm Ystradllyn (Caerns.), Gwynedd   *Gresham 1973*
Dainton, Devon   *Willis and Rogers 1951*
Dalton Parlours (Yorks.), West Yorkshire   *Sumpter 1988*
Danebury, Hants.   *Cunliffe 1972a*
Dane's Camp (Worcs.), Hereford and Worcester   *Unpublished excavation*
Dane's Graves (Yorks.), Humberside   *Stead 1965, 105; Greenwell 1906; Mortimer 1911*
Dan y Coed (Pembs.), Dyfed   *G. Williams 1988*
Darmsden, Suffolk   *Cunliffe 1968a; Balkwill 1979*
Deal, Kent   *Woodruff 1904*
Denbury, Devon   *A. Fox 1961b*
Dennis Pit (Old Marden), Oxon   *Unpublished: Ashmolean Museum*
Desborough, Northants.   *C.F. Fox 1958*
Deskford (Banff.), Grampian Region   *S. Piggott 1959*
Dinas Emrys (Caerns.), Gwynedd   *Savory 1961*
Dinorben (Denbigh.), Clwyd   *Gardner and Savory 1964; Savory 1971a, 1971b; Guilbert 1979a, 1980*

Dod (Roxburghshire), Borders Region   *I.M. Smith 1980, 1982*

Dorton, Bucks.   *Farley 1983*

Douglasmuir (Angus), Tayside Region   *Kendrick 1982*

Down Barn West (Winterbourne Gunner), Wilts.   *Fowler, Musty and Taylor 1965*

Dragonby (Lincs.), Humberside   *May 1970, 1976a; Elsdon and May 1987*

Draughton, Northants.   *Grimes 1961*

Driffield (Yorks.), Humberside   *Brewster 1963, 147*

Drim Camp (Pembs.), Dyfed   *G. Williams 1988*

Dryburn Bridge (East Lothian), Lothian Region   *Triscott 1982*

Dun an Ruigh, Loch Broom (Ross and Cromarty), Highlands Region   *MacKie 1980*

Dun Ardtreck (Skye), Highlands Region   *Current Arch. 2 (1967), 27–30*

Dun Lagaidh (Wester Ross), Highlands Region   *Current Arch. 12 (1969), 8–13*

Dun Mor Vaul, Tiree (Argyll.), Strathclyde Region   *MacKie 1974*

Earl's Hill, Salop   *Forde-Johnston 1964*

Earn's Heugh (Berwick.), Borders Region   *Childe and Ford 1932*

Eastbourne (Sussex), East Sussex   *Bugden 1922; Hodson 1962*

Eastburn (Yorks.), Humberside   *Sheppard 1938; Stead 1965, 110*

Ebberston (Yorks.), North Yorkshire   *Cowen 1967*

Ebsbury, Wilts.   *Crawford and Keiller 1928*

Eddisbury *see* Castle Ditch, Cheshire

Edin's Hall (Berwick.), Borders Region   *Stuart 1869*

Eildon Hill North (Roxburgh.), Borders Region   *Feachem 1966, 79; Owen 1987*

Eldon's Seat (Encombe), Dorset   *Cunliffe 1968b*

Ellesborough, Bucks.   *Cocks 1909*

Elm Grove, Brighton (Sussex), East Sussex   *E.C. Curwen 1954*

Emmotland (Yorks.), Humberside   *Brewster 1963*

Esher, Surrey *see* Sandown Park

Farley Mount, Hants.   *Bowen and Fowler 1966*

Farmoor, Oxon.   *Lambrick and Robinson 1979*

Farningham Hill, Kent   *Philp 1984*

Feltwell, Norfolk   *Unpublished: Norwich Museum*

Fengate (Northants.), Cambs. *Hawkes and Fell 1945; Spratling 1974; Pryor 1974, 1975, 1978, 1984; Pryor and Cranstone 1978*

Ffridd Faldwyn (Mont.), Powys   *B.H. St J. O'Neil 1942*

Fifield Bavant, Wilts.   *R.C.C. Clay 1924*

Figsbury, Wilts.   *M.E. Cunnington 1925*

Finavon (Angus), Tayside Region   *Childe 1935a; MacKie 1969b*

Findon Park (Sussex), West Sussex   *Fox and Wolseley 1928*

Fishbourne (Sussex), West Sussex   *Cunliffe 1971b*

Fisherwick, Staffs.   *C. Smith 1979*

Fiskerton, Lincs.   *Field 1986*

Fitzworth, Dorset   *Calkin 1949*

Foale's Arrishes, Devon   *Radford 1952, 71–3*

Fordington (Dorchester), Dorset   RCHM, *Dorset II, pt 3*

Forgandenny, Castle Law (Perths.), Tayside Region   *Christison 1900*

Frilford, (Berks.) Oxon. *Bradford and Goodchild 1939*

Garn Boduan (Caerns.), Gwynedd   *Hogg 1962*

Garton Slack (Yorks.), Humberside   *Brewster 1971, 1976, 1981*

Glascote (Tamworth), Staffs.   *Painter 1971*

Glastonbury, Somerset.   *Bulleid and Gray 1911, 1917; Tratman 1970; D.L. Clarke 1972*

Glenachan Rig (Peebles.), Borders Region   *Feachem 1961*

Glentanar (Aberdeens.), Grampian Region   *Pearce 1974*

Glyne (Sussex), East Sussex   *A.E. Wilson 1954*

Goldherring, Cornwall   *Guthrie 1969*

Grafton (West Riding of Yorks.), North Yorkshire   *Waterman, Kent and Strickland 1954*

Grantchester, Cambs.   *C.F. Fox 1923*

Grassington (Yorks.), North Yorkshire   *Raistrick 1938*

Great Chesterford, Essex   *Stead 1971a, 278*

Great Woodbury, Wilts. *see* Little Woodbury

Great Wymondley, Herts.   *Tebbutt 1932*

Green End Road, Cambs.   *Unpublished: Cambridge Museum*

Green Island, Poole, Dorset   *Calkin 1953*

Green Knowe (Peebles.), Borders Region   *Feachem 1963; Jobey 1981*

Gretton, Northants.   *Jackson   1974*

Grimthorpe (Yorks.), Humberside   *Mortimer 1869, 1905; Stead 1965, 110; 1968*

Grosvenor Crescent, Edinburgh (Midlothian), Lothian Region   *Coles 1962b, 118*

Groundwell Farm, Wilts.   *Gingell 1982*

Guiting Power, Glos.   *Saville 1979*

Gun Hill, Essex   *Drury and Rodwell 1973*

Gurnard's Head, Cornwall   *A.S.R. Gordon 1941*

Gurness (Orkney), Orkney Islands Area   *Hedges 1987*

Gussage All Saints, Dorset   *Wainwright and Spratling 1973; Wainwright and Switzur 1976; Wainwright 1979*

Gwithian, Cornwall (*see also* Crane Godrevy)   *Megaw, Thomas and Wailes 1961*

Haddenham, Cambs.   *Evans and Serjeantson 1988*

Hambledon, Dorset   RCHM, *Dorset III*

Ham Hill, Somerset. *Gray 1925, 1926, 1927; Morris 1987*

Hammer Wood, Iping (Sussex), West Sussex   *Boyden 1957*

Handley Down, Dorset   *Pitt Rivers 1898*

Harding's Down West (Glam.), West Glamorgan   *Hogg 1974*

Hardingstone, Northants.   *Woods 1969*

Harehope (Peebles.), Borders Region   *Feachem 1962*

Harlow, Essex   *France and Gobel 1985; Haselgrove 1989*

Harlyn Bay, Cornwall   *Crawford 1921; Whimster 1978*

Harpenden, Herts.   *Bagshawe 1928; Stead 1971a*

Harrold, Beds.   *Eagles and Evison 1970*

Harrow Hill (Sussex), West Sussex   *Holleyman 1937*

Hartburn, Northumberland   *Jobey 1973a*

Harting Beacon (Sussex), West Sussex   *Bedwin 1978a, 1979, 1983*

Hascombe, Surrey   *F.H. Thompson 1979*

Hawk's Hill, Surrey   *Hastings and Cunliffe 1966*

Hawthorn Hill, Herts.   *Unpublished: Letchworth Museum*

Hayhope Knowe (Roxburgh.), Borders Region   *C.M. Piggott 1951*
Hayling Island, Hants.   *Downey, King and Soffe 1979*
Heathery Burn Cave, Co. Durham   *Inv. Arch. GB 55 (1968); Britton 1971*
Heathrow (Middx), Greater London   *Grimes 1961*
Hembury, Devon   *Liddell 1930, 1931, 1932, 1935a; Todd 1984*
Hengistbury Head (Hants.), Dorset   *Bushe-Fox 1915; Cunliffe 1987*
Hertford Heath, Herts.   *Holmes and Frend 1959; Hüssen 1983*
Hesterton (Yorks.), North Yorkshire   *Powlesland, Haughton and Hanson 1986*
High Cross, Leics.   *C.F. Fox 1958, pl. 3*
Highdown (Sussex), West Sussex   *A.E. Wilson 1940, 1950*
Highfield, Wilts.   *F. Stevens 1934*
High Knowes (Alnham), Northumberland   *Jobey and Tait 1966*
High Penard (Glam.), West Glamorgan   *A. Williams 1941*
High Rocks (Sussex), East Sussex   *Money 1941, 1960, 1968*
Hinderclay, Suffolk   *Balkwill 1979*
Hobarrow Bay, Dorset   *Calkin 1949*
Hod Hill, Dorset   *Richmond 1968*
Hog Cliff Hill, Dorset   *Bowen and Fowler 1966; Ellison and Rahtz 1987*
Hogsthorpe, Lincs.   *Kirkham 1981*
Holcombe, Devon   *A. Fox 1972; A. Fox and Pollard 1973; Pollard 1974*
Hollingbury (Sussex), East Sussex   *Toms 1914; E.C. Curwen 1932; S. Hamilton 1984; J. Holmes 1984*
Holmbury, Surrey   *F.H. Thompson 1979*
Holme Pierrepont, Notts.   *Musty and MacCormick 1973*
Horndean, Hants.   *Cunliffe 1961*
Horsehope (Peebles.), Borders Region   *S. Piggott 1955*
Horsted Keynes (Sussex), West Sussex   *Hardy and Curwen 1937*
Howe (Orkney), Orkney Islands Area   *Hedges and Bell 1980a; Carter, Haigh, Neil and Smith 1984*
Hownam Rings (Roxburgh.), Borders Region   *C.M. Piggott 1950*
Huckhoe, Northumberland   *Jobey 1959*
Hunmanby (Yorks.), North Yorkshire   *Sheppard 1907; Stead 1965*
Hunsbury, Northants.   *Fell 1937*
Huntow (Yorks.), Humberside   *Stead 1965, 111*
Hurstbourne Tarrant, Hants.   *Hawkes and Dunning 1931*
Iffley, Oxon.   *Savory 1939*
Ilchester, Somerset. *Leach and Thew 1985*
Ingoldmells, Lincs.   *Swinnerton 1932; Baker 1960*
Ingram Hill, Northumberland   *Hogg 1942, 1956; Jobey 1971c*
Ipswich, Suffolk   *Owles 1969, 1971; Brailsford and Stapley 1972*
Isleham, Cambs.   *Britton 1960*
Itford Hill (Sussex), East Sussex   *Burstow and Holleyman 1957; Holden 1972; Ellison 1978*
Ivinghoe Beacon, Bucks.   *Cotton and Frere 1968*
Ivy Chimneys, Witham, Essex   *R. Turner 1982*
Ixworth, Suffolk   *R.R. Clarke 1939*
Jarlshof (Shetland), Shetland Islands Area   *J.R.C. Hamilton 1956*
Kaimes Hill (Midlothian), Lothian Region   *Childe 1941; D.D.A. Simpson 1969*
Kempston, Fosters Pit, Beds.   *Simco 1973*

Kendall (Yorks.), Humberside *Brewster 1963*

Kennel Hall Knowe, Northumberland *Jobey 1978*

Kestor (Chagford), Devon *A. Fox 1955*

Kilham (Yorks.), Humberside *Brewster 1963*

Killibury, Cornwall *Miles* et al. *1978*

Kilphedir (Sutherland), Highland Region *Fairhurst and Taylor 1974*

Kimmeridge, Dorset *H. Davies 1936; Calkin 1949; Cunliffe 1968b*

Kimpton, Hants. *Dacre and Ellison 1981*

Kingsdown Camp, Somerset. *Gray 1930*

Kingston Brill (Sussex), West Sussex *E. and E.C. Curwen and Hawkes 1931*

Kirkburn (Yorks.), Humberside *Current Arch.* 111, 115–17

Knap Hill, Wilts. *Cunnington and Goddard 1934*

Knave, the (Glam.), W. Glamorgan *A. Williams 1939a*

Knighton Hill (Berks.), Oxon. *S. Piggott 1927*

Knights Farm, Berks. *Bradley, Lobb, Richards and Robinson 1980*

Ladle Hill, Hants. *S. Piggott 1931*

Lancing Down (Sussex), West Sussex *Bedwin 1981*

Langenhoe, Essex *Ward Perkins 1938*

Langford Downs, Oxon. *A. Williams 1947*

Langton (Yorks.), North Yorkshire *Corder and Kirk 1932*

Latch Farm (Hants.), Dorset *C.M. Piggott 1938b*

Leckhampton, Glos. *Burrow, Paine, Knowles and Gray 1925; Champion 1972, 1976*

Leckie Broch (Stirlingshire) Central Region *MacKie 1982*

Ledston (Yorks.), West Yorkshire *West Yorks. CC 1981*

Legis Tor, Devon *Baring-Gould 1896; Worth 1943*

Leicester, Leicestershire *Clay 1977*

Leigh Hill (Cobham), Surrey *R.A. Smith 1908, 1909b*

Lesser Garth Cave (Glam.), South Glamorgan *Grimes 1951*

Levisham Moor (Yorks.), North Yorkshire *Spratt 1982*

Lexden, Essex *Laver 1927; Foster 1986*

Lidbury, Wilts. *M.E. and B.H. Cunnington 1917*

Lindow, Cheshire *Stead and Turner 1985; Stead, Bourke and Brothwell 1986*

Linton, Cambs. *Fell 1953*

Little Horstead Lane (Sussex), West Sussex *A.E. Wilson 1954*

Little Solisbury (Som.), Avon *Dowden 1957, 1962; Falconer and Adams 1935*

Little Waltham, Essex *Drury 1973, 1978*

Little Woodbury, Wilts. *Bersu 1940; Brailsford 1948, 1949*

Llanfair (Denbigh.), Clwyd *E.L.B. 1862*

Llangenydd, Culver Hole Cave (Glam.), West Glamorgan *Grimes 1951, 110*

Llanmelin (Mon.), Gwent *Nash-Williams 1933b*

Llanstephan Castle (Carm.), Dyfed *Guilbert 1974*

Llwyn du Bach (Caerns.), Gwynedd *Bersu and Griffiths 1949*

Llyn Cerrig Bach (Anglesey), Gwynedd *C.F. Fox 1946*

Llyn Fawr (Glam.), West Glamorgan *Fox and Hyde 1939; Crawford and Wheeler 1921; H.S. Green 1985*

Loch Broom (Dun an Ruigh Ruaidh), (Ross and Cromarty), Highlands Region *MacKie 1980*

Loch of Hunter, Whalsey (Shetland), Shetland Islands Area   *J.R.C. Hamilton 1968*

Longbridge Deverill (Cow Down), Wilts.   *S.C. Hawkes 1961*

Long Wittenham (Berks.), Oxon.   *Savory 1937*

Lydney, Glos. *R.E.M. and T.V. Wheeler 1932*

Lyneham Camp, Oxon.   *Bayne 1957*

Maen Castle, Cornwall   *Cotton 1959*

Maiden Castle (Bickerton), Cheshire   *Varley 1935, 1936; Taylor 1981*

Maiden Castle, Dorset   *Wheeler 1943*

Mam Tor, Derby   *Coombs and Thompson 1980*

Mancombe Down, Wilts.   *Fowler, Musty and Taylor 1965*

Marlborough, Wilts. *C.F. Fox 1958, 69; Stead 1971a, 279*

Marnhull, Dorset   *A. Williams 1951a*

Marros Mountain, Pendine (Carm.), Dyfed   *Grimes 1951*

Martin Down Camp, Dorset   *Pitt Rivers 1898*

Meare, Somerset.   *Bulleid and Gray 1948, 1953; Avery 1968; Coles 1987; Orme, Coles and Silvester 1983; Orme, Coles and Sturdy 1979; Orme, Coles, Caseldine and Bailey 1981*

Melksham, Wilts.   *Gingell 1979*

Meon Hill, Hants.   *Liddell 1933, 1935b*

Merthyr Mawr Warren (Glam.), Mid Glamorgan   *Grimes 1951, 126–8*

Micheldever Wood, Hants.   *Fasham 1976, 1987*

Midsummer Hill (Heref.), Hereford and Worcester   *Stanford 1981*

Milber Down Camp, Devon   *Fox, Radford, Rogers and Shorter 1952*

Mildenhall, Suffolk   *R.R. Clarke 1939, 43*

Mill Hill, Deal, Kent   *Stebbing 1934*

Milton Loch (Kirkcudbright.), Dumfries and Galloway Region   *C.M. Piggott 1955; Guido 1974*

Minchinhampton, Glos.   *Clifford 1961, 157*

Mingies Ditch, Oxon.   *Allen and Robinson 1979*

Minnis Bay, Kent   *Worsfold 1943*

Minster Ditch, Oxford   *Jope 1961b*

Moel Hiraddug (Flint.), Clwyd   *Hemp 1928; Brassil, Gilbert et al. 1982*

Moel Trigarn (Pembs.), Dyfed   *Baring-Gould, Burnard and Anderson 1900*

Moel y Gaer (Flint.), Clwyd   *Guilbert 1973, 1975b, 1976*

Monifieth, the Laws of (Angus), Tayside Region   *Neish and Stuart 1860*

Mortlake (Middx), Greater London   *Unpublished: London Museum*

Moulton Park, Northants.   *J.H. Williams 1974*

Mount Batten, Devon   *Bates 1871; P.J. Clarke 1971; Cunliffe 1988b*

Mount Bures (Essex), Suffolk   *C.R. Smith 1852*

Mount Farm, Oxon.   *Myres 1937; Lambrick 1979, 1981*

Mousa (Shetland), Shetland Islands Area   *Fojut 1982a*

Mucking, Essex   *M.U. Jones 1974; Jones and Bond 1980*

Muntham Court (Sussex), West Sussex   *Unpublished excavation*

Mynydd Bychan (Glam.), West Glamorgan   *Savory 1954, 1956*

Needwood, Staffs.   *Leeds 1933b*

Ness of Burgi, Samburgh (Shetland), Shetland Islands Area   *J.R.C. Hamilton 1968*

Newark-on-Trent, Notts.   *Inv. Arch. GB 36 (1958)*

New Barn Down (Sussex), West Sussex   *E.C. Curwen 1934a*

Newhaven (Sussex), East Sussex *see* Castle Hill, Newhaven
Newnham Croft, Cambs. *C.F. Fox 1923, 81*
Norbury, Glos. *Saville 1983*
North Creake, Norfolk *R.R. Clarke 1951a*
North Ferriby (Yorks.), Humberside *Corder and Pryce 1938*
North Grimston (Yorks.), North Yorkshire *Mortimer 1905; Stead 1965, 111*
Norton Fitzwarren, Somerset. *Langmaid 1971*
Oare, Wilts. *M.E. Cunnington 1909*
Ogbourne Down, Wilts. *C.M. Piggott 1942*
Ogbury, Wilts. *Crawford and Keiller 1928*
Oldbury, Kent *Ward Perkins 1944; F.H. Thompson 1978, 1984, 1985*
Oldbury, Wilts. *H. Cunnington 1871*
Old Down Farm, Hants. *S.M. Davies 1981*
Old Oswestry, Salop *Varley 1950b*
Old Sleaford, Lincs. *Unpublished excavation*
Old Warden, Beds. *Dryden 1845; Spratling 1970*
Oliver's Camp, Wilts. *M.E. Cunnington 1908*
Orsett, Essex *Toller 1980; Hedges and Buckley 1978*
Orton Longueville, Northants. *Dallas 1975*
Overton Down, Wilts. *P.J. Fowler 1967*
Owslebury, Hants. *Collis 1968, 1970*
Pagan's Hill (Som.), Avon *ApSimon, Rahtz and Harris 1958*
Parc Cynnog (Carm.), Dyfed *Quincey 1970*
Parc y Meirch (Denbigh.), Clwyd *Sheppard 1941*
Park Brow (Sussex), West Sussex *R.A. Smith 1927; Hawley 1927*
Parkle Lane, Somersham, Cambs. *Unpublished: Cambridge Museum*
Paulsgrove, Portsmouth, Hants. *Unpublished excavation*
Pembrey Mountain (Carms.), Dyfed *G. Williams 1981*
Penbryn (Cardigan.), Dyfed *E.L.B. 1862*
Pen Dinas, Aberystwyth (Cardigan.), Dyfed *Forde, Griffiths, Hogg and Houlder 1963*
Penigent Gill (Yorks.), North Yorkshire *W.B. 1938*
Pen y Coed, Llangynog (Carms.), Dyfed *Murphy 1985*
Pen y Corddyn (Denbigh.), Clwyd *Gardner 1910*
Percy Rigg (Yorks.), North Yorkshire *Close 1972*
Pexton Moor (Yorks.), North Yorkshire *Stead 1965, 95*
Pilsdon Pen, Dorset *Gelling 1970, 1971, 1972 and 1977; Thackray 1983*
Pimperne Down, Dorset *Harding and Blake 1963*
Plaitford, Hants. *Preston and Hawkes 1933*
Plumpton Plain (Sussex), East Sussex *Holleyman and Curwen 1935*
Pokesdown (Hants.), Dorset *R.C.C. Clay 1927a*
Portfield, Lancs. *Longworth 1968*
Porthmeor, Cornwall *Hirst 1936*
Portland, Dorset RCHM, *Dorset II, part 3, 605–6*
Portsdown Hill, Hants. *Bradley 1969a*
Poston (Heref.), Hereford and Worcester *Anthony 1958*
Potterne, Wilts. *Gingell and Lawson 1984*

Poundbury, Dorset   *Richardson 1940*
Poxwell, Dorset   *Wacher 1968*
Prae Wood Cemetery (Verulamium), Herts.   *Stead 1969*
Preshute Down, Wilts.   *C.M. Piggott 1942*
Puckeridge, Herts. *see* Broughing
Puddlehill, Beds.   *Matthews 1976*
Quanterness (Orkney), Orkney Islands Area   *Renfrew 1979*
Quarley Hill, Hants.   *C.F.C. Hawkes 1939b*
Quarry Wood Camp, Kent   *Kelly 1971*
Radley (Berks.), Oxon.   *Leeds 1931b, 1935*
Rahoy, Morvern (Argyll.), Strathclyde Region   *Childe and Thorneycroft 1938*
Rainsborough Camp, Northants.   *Avery, Sutton and Banks 1968*
Rams Hill (Berks.), Oxon.   *S. and C.M. Piggott 1940; Bradley and Ellison 1975*
Ratlinghope/Stitt Hill, Salop   *Guilbert 1975c*
Ravensburgh Castle, Herts.   *Dyer 1970, 1976b*
Ravenstone, Bucks.   *Mynard 1970*
Read's Cavern, Somerset   *L.S. Palmer 1922, 1923; Langford 1924, 1925*
Rider's Rings, Devon   *Worth 1935*
Rigg's Farm (Yorks.), Humberside   *Brewster 1963, fig. 81*
Rillington (Yorks.), North Yorkshire   *Turnbull 1983*
Ringstead, Norfolk   *R.R. Clarke 1951b*
Rippon Tor, Dartmoor, Devon   *A. Fox 1955*
Rispain Camp, Whithorn (Galloway), Dumfries and Galloway Region   *A. and G. Haggarty 1983*
Roomer Common (Yorks.), North Yorkshire   *Waterman, Kent and Stickland 1954*
Rotherley Down, Wilts.   *Pitt Rivers 1888*
Roxby (Yorks.), North Yorkshire   *Spratt 1982; Inman, Brown, Goddard and Spratt 1985*
Ructstalls Hill, Hants.   *Oliver and Apflin 1978*
Rudston (Yorks.), Humberside   *Stead 1971b*
Rumps, the (St Minver), Cornwall   *Brooks 1964, 1966, 1968, 1974*
Runnymede Bridge, Surrey   *Needham and Longley 1980*
Ryton-on-Dunsmore, Warks.   *Bateman 1978*
Saham Toney (Woodcock Hill), Norfolk   *Brown 1986*
St Catharine's Hill, Hants.   *Hawkes, Myres and Stevens 1930; C.F.C. Hawkes 1976*
St David's Head (Pembs.), Dyfed   *Baring-Gould, Burnard and Enys 1899*
St George's Hill (Weybridge), Surrey   *Lowther 1949*
St Ives (Hunts.), Cambs.   *Unpublished: St Ives Museum*
St Lawrence, Isle of Wight, Hants.   *Stead 1968, fig. 19*
St Martha's Hill, Surrey   *Lowther 1935*
St Mawgan *see* Carloggas, Cornwall
Salmonsbury, Glos.   *Dunning 1931, 1976; H.E. O'Neil 1978; Rawes 1984*
Saltdean (Sussex), East Sussex   *E.C. Curwen 1954*
Sandown Park (Esher), Surrey   *Burchell and Frere 1947*
Sandy, Beds.   *Unpublished: Bedford Museum*
Santon Downham, Suffolk   *R.A. Smith 1909a*
Sawdon (Yorks.), North Yorkshire   *Stead 1965*
Scarborough *see* Castle Hill, Yorks.

Scorborough Park (Yorks.), Humberside   *Mortimer 1895; Stead 1975*

Sedgford, Norfolk   *Brailsford 1971*

Selsey (Sussex), West Sussex   *G.H. White 1934; E.C. Curwen 1954, 257–8*

Shapwick Heath, Somerset   *Gray 1940*

Shaugh Moor, Devon   *Wainwright, Fleming and Smith 1979; Smith, Coppen, Wainwright and Beckett 1981; Wainwright and Smith 1980; Balaam, Smith and Wainwright 1982*

Shearplace Hill, Dorset   *Rahtz and ApSimon 1962*

Sheepen Hill (Colchester), Essex   *Hawkes and Smith 1957, 161; Sealey 1985*

Sheepsleights, Dorset   *Calkin 1949*

Shenbarrow, Glos.   *Fell 1962*

Shouldham, Norfolk   *Clarke and Hawkes 1955*

Sidbury, Wilts.   *Applebaum 1955*

Silchester, Hants. *see* Calleva

Silkstead, Hants.   *Note, JRS xxviii (1938), 196*

Skelmore Heads (Lancs.), Cumbria   *Powell 1963*

Sleaford, Lincs. *see* Old Sleaford

Slonk Hill, East Sussex   *Hartridge 1978*

Snailwell, Cambs.   *Lethbridge 1953*

Snettisham, Norfolk   *R.R. Clarke 1955; Burns 1971*

Sompting (Sussex), West Sussex   *E.C. Curwen 1948*

South Cadbury, Somerset   *Alcock 1968, 1969, 1970, 1980*

Southcote, Berks   *Piggott and Seaby 1937*

South Ferriby (Lincs.), Humberside   *S.C. Hawkes 1964*

South Lodge Camp, Dorset   *Pitt Rivers 1898; Barrett, Bradley, Bowden and Mead 1983*

South Wilson, Bucks.   *Unpublished: Aylesbury Museum*

Spettisbury, Dorset   *Gresham 1939*

Standlake, Oxon.   *Akerman and Stone 1857; Bradford 1942a; D.N. Riley 1947*

Standrop Rigg, Northumberland   *Jobey 1983*

Stanfordbury, Beds.   *Dryden 1845*

Stannon Down, St Breward, Cornwall   *Mercer 1970*

Stanton Down, Devon   *Baring-Gould 1902*

Stanton Harcourt, Oxon.   *Grimes 1944; A. Williams 1951b*

Stanwick (Yorks.), North Yorkshire   *Wheeler 1954; Chadburn 1983; Turnbull 1984; Haselgrove and Turnbull 1983, 1985, 1987*

Staple Howe (Yorks.), North Yorkshire   *Brewster 1963*

Staxton (Yorks.), North Yorkshire   *Brewster 1963, fig. 91*

Steyning (Sussex), West Sussex   *Burstow 1958*

Stoke Clump (Sussex), West Sussex   *Cunliffe 1966*

Strixton, Northants.   *Hall 1971*

Sudbrook (Mon.), Gwent   *Nash-Williams 1939*

Sutton, Notts.   *C.F. Fox 1958*

Sutton Walls (Heref.), Hereford and Worcester   *Kenyon 1954*

Swallowcliffe Down, Wilts.   *Clay 1925, 1927b*

Swarling, Kent   *Bushe-Fox 1925*

Syon Reach (Middx), Greater London   *Wheeler 1929*

Tallington, Lincs.   *W.G. Simpson 1966*

Tal y Llyn (Merioneth.), Gwynedd   *Savory 1964; Spratling 1966*
Tattershall Bridge, Lincs.   *S. Piggott 1959*
Tattershall Thorpe, Lincs.   *Chowne, Girling and Greig 1986*
Teignmouth, Devon   *A. Fox 1956*
Theale, Berks.   *C.M. Piggott 1938a*
Thorny Down, Wilts.   *Stone 1941; Ellison 1987*
Thorpe (Yorks.), Humberside   *Stead 1965, 68*
Thorpe Thewles, Cleveland   *Heslop 1987*
Thundersbarrow (Sussex), West Sussex   *E.C. Curwen 1933*
Thwing (Yorks.), North Yorkshire   *Manby 1980*
Tigh Talamhanta *see* Allasdale
Titterstone Clee, Salop   *B.H. St J. O'Neil 1934*
Tollard Royal, Wilts.   *Wainwright 1968*
Torberry (Sussex), West Sussex   *Cunliffe 1976a*
Torrs (Kirkcudbright.), Dumfries and Galloway Region   *Atkinson and Piggott 1955*
Torwoodlee (Selkirk.), Borders Region   *S. Piggott 1951*
Totternhoe, Beds.   *C.F.C. Hawkes 1940c*
Tower Knowe, Northumberland   *Jobey 1973b*
Tower Point (Pembs.), Dyfed   *Wainwright 1971b*
Traprain Law (East Lothian), Lothian Region   *Feachem 1958; Jobey 1976*
Trawsfynydd (Merioneth.), Gwynedd   *J.R. Allen 1896*
Trelan Bahow, Cornwall   *H.O'N. Hencken 1932, 120*
Trelissey (Pembs.), Dyfed   *Thomas and Walker 1959*
Tre'r Ceiri (Caerns.), Gwynedd   *Hogg 1962*
Trevisker, Cornwall   *ApSimon and Greenfield 1972*
Trevone, Cornwall   *Dudley and Jope 1965*
Trundle (Sussex), West Sussex   *E.C. Curwen 1929, 1931*
Twyford Down, Hants.   *Stuart and Birbeck 1936; C.F.C. Hawkes 1936b*
Twywell, Northants.   *Jackson 1975*
Ulceby (Lincs.), Humberside   *Leeds 1933b*
Upper Delphs, Haddenham, Cambs.   *Evans and Serjeantson 1988*
Ventnor (Gills Cliff), Isle of Wight   *Benson 1953*
Verulamium, Herts. (*see also* Prae Wood)   *R.E.M. and T.V. Wheeler 1936; Hunn 1980; Saunders and Havercroft 1982*
Wakerley, Northants.   *Jackson 1978*
Walesland Rath (Pembs.), Dyfed   *Wainwright 1969, 1971a*
Wandlebury, Cambs.   *Hartley 1957*
Warborough Hill, Norfolk   *Clarke and Apling 1935*
Wareham, Norfolk   *Gray 1933*
Welby, Leics.   *Powell 1950*
Welwyn, Herts.   *R.A. Smith 1912; Brailsford 1958a; C. Saunders 1977*
Welwyn Garden City, Herts.   *Stead 1967*
West Bay *see* Bridport, Dorset
West Brandon, Co. Durham   *Jobey 1962a*
West Clandon, Surrey   *Frere 1946*
Wester Ord (Wester Ross), Highlands Region   *Coles 1962b, 129–30*

Westhall, Suffolk   *R.R. Clarke 1939*

West Harling, Norfolk   *Clark and Fell 1953; R.R. Clarke 1960*

Weston (Som.), Avon   *Craw 1924, 147–9*

Weston Wood (Albury), Surrey   *J.M. Harding 1964*

West Plean (Stirling.), Central Region   *Steer 1958*

Wetwang Slack (Yorks.), Humberside   *Dent 1978, 1982, 1985*

Weybridge (Brooklands), Surrey   *Hanworth and Tomalin 1977*

Wharram Percy (Yorks.), North Yorkshire   *Britannia (1983), 249*

Wheathampstead, Herts.   *R.E.M. and T.V. Wheeler 1936; I. Thompson 1979; Saunders and Havercroft 1982*

Whitcombe, Dorset   *Unpublished: Dorset County Museum*

White Hill (Peebles.) Borders Region   *Feachem 1966*

Whitton (Glam.), West Glamorgan   *Jarrett and Wrathmell 1981*

Wilbury, Herts.   *Applebaum 1951; Moss-Ecgardt 1964*

Winchester, Hants.   *Cunliffe 1964; Biddle 1966, 1967, 1968, 1975a, 1975b*

Winklebury, Hants.   *C.M. Piggott 1940; K. Smith 1977, 1979; Robertson-Mackay 1977; Fisher 1985*

Winnall Down, Hants.   *Fasham 1985; Fasham, Farwell and Whinney 1989*

Winterbourne Dauntsey, Wilts.   *Stone 1935*

Wisbech, Cambs.   *Jope 1961b*

Witham, Lincs.   *Jope 1971*

Wokingham, Berks.   *Unpublished: Ashmolean Museum*

Woodbarn Rath (Pembs.), Dyfed   *Vyner 1983, 1986*

Woodbury Castle, Devon   *H. Miles 1975*

Woodcutts, Dorset   *Pitt Rivers 1887*

Wookey Hole, Somerset   *Balch 1914, 1928*

Woolbury, Hants.   *Crawford and Keiller 1928*

Worlebury (Som.), Avon   *Dymond 1902*

Worth, Kent   *Klein 1928; C.F.C. Hawkes 1940b*

Worthy Down, Hants.   *Dunning, Hooley and Tildesley 1929*

Wrekin, Salop *Kenyon 1943; Stanford et al 1985*

Wyke Regis, Dorset   *Bailey 1963*

Wytham (Berks.), Oxon.   *Bradford 1942b*

Yarnbury, Wilts.   *M.E. Cunnington 1933*

Yarton, Oxon.   *Bradford 1942b*

Yeavering Bell, Northumberland   *Jobey 1966a*

Notes

1   The development of Iron Age studies

1 Hembury (published 1930–5), Cissbury, Salmonsbury and Chestleton (1931), Hollingbury Camp, Lydney and Chisbury (1932), Llanmelin, Thundersbarrow, Yarnbury and Chisenbury Trendle (1933), Little Solisbury (1935), Maiden Castle, Bickerton (1934 and 1935), Bigbury and Buckland Rings (1936), Harrow Hill and the Breiddin (1937), Bredon Hill (1938), Quarley, Castle Hill (Newhaven), the Caburn, the Knave, Castle Hill (Almondbury) and Sudbrook (1939), Balksbury, Poundbury, Bury Hill, Highdown and Cherbury (1940), Gurnard's Head (1941). Several other important excavations carried out during the decade were published later: Chalbury, excavated 1939 (1943); Oldbury, excavated 1939 (1944); Pen Dinas, excavated 1933–7 (1963); Castle Ditch (Eddisbury), excavated 1935–8 (1950); Ffridd Faldwyn, excavated 1937–9 (1942). Other equally important excavations have never been fully published.
2 Including Hownam Rings (1950), Bonchester Hill (1952), Castle Law (1954), Huckhoe (1959), Harehope (1962), West Brandon (1962), Alnham (1966), Burradon (1970), Brough Law (1971), Hartburn (1973) and Tower Knowe (1973).

3   The background

1 For an explanation of the citation and for further details see appendix B.
2 The sample, however, cannot now be traced and should be viewed with some reserve.
3 Dennell (1976) has suggested that the apparant prominence of barley may reflect conditions specific to chalkland only.
4 For general surveys of Late Bronze Age metalwork see Burgess 1969a, 1969b, 1979; Gerloff 1981.
5 Here I follow the chronology proposed by Gerloff (1981, 197).

4 Regional groupings: south and east

1 C. Saunders (1972) has described some of the Chiltern pottery of this type calling it phase 1. Some of the Bedfordshire groups have been published by Simco (1973).
2 For a discussion of the radiocarbon dates see H.S. Green 1981.
3 The largest groups of finds of this type occur at the hillforts of Chalbury and Maiden Castle (where it is called Maiden Castle A) and at Eldon's Seat, Encombe (where it has been referred to as the Eldon's Seat II assemblage).
4 Pottery of this style from Surrey has been discussed by Bishop (1971): it constitutes his group 2.
5 This group has been described by C. Saunders (1972). It corresponds to his phase 2.
6 A detailed assessment of the pottery from the Nene and Ouse Basins is given by Knight (1984).

5 Regional groupings: north and west

1 The validity of the concept of a Hownam culture has been debated by Ritchie (1970) and MacKie (1970).

6 Protohistory to history, c. BC to AD 43

1 There is no reason to identify Cassivellaunus with the Catuvellauni. This was an unwarranted assumption sometimes made in the past.
2 Though doubts have been expressed as to the nature of Wheathampstead, it was evidently a defended enclosure of this period.
3 The E distinguishes the Dubnovellaunus who issued coins in Essex from the ruler of the same name whose coins circulated mainly in Kent.
4 The possibility that these names are those of mints rather than rulers cannot be totally dismissed.

7 The tribes of the south-eastern core

1 Strictly the area only became 'Atrebatic' after the arrival of Commius and to use the term for the situation before Caesar's campaigns is anachronistic but so long as this is borne in mind it provides a convenient shorthand.

8 The tribes of the periphery

1 Swan (1975, 59–61) has attempted to show that the earliest occupation at Bagendon post-dated the Roman Conquest but as Rodwell has pointed out (1976, 308–9) her arguments are without significant foundations.

12 Settlement and settlement pattern in the south and east

1 It has been suggested (Tratman 1970) that the ground plan of the main house at Little Woodbury was produced in more than one phase, the internal setting of four posts and the entrance passage representing rectangular structures differing in date from the circular building. On balance, the original interpretation of the excavator, given above, seems preferable.

19 Death and the gods

1 The best known are: Arras, Cawthorn Camps, Hutton Buschel Moor, Pexton Moor, Seamer Moor, Skipworth Common, Thorganby, Cowlam, Garton Slack, Garton Station, Wetwang Slack and Burton Fleming.

2 The best-attested cart burials occur at Arras (three), Dane's Graves, Beverley, Hummanby, Middleton-on-the-Wold, Huggate, Cawthorn Camps, Pexton Moor, Garton Slack, Garton Station and Wetwang Slack. Possible examples are recorded at Seamer Moor and Hornsea (Stead 1965).

3 These occur at Arras and Garton Slack, Yorks., Birdlip, Glos., Bridport, Dorset, Trelan Bahow, Cornwall, Mount Batten, Devon, Dorton, Bucks., and Colchester, Essex. The mirrors from Bulbury, Dorset, Billericay, Essex, and Desborough, Northants., may also have come from burials.

4 The sites producing pairs of spoons are Burnmouth and Deal, Llanfair, Denbigh., Penbryn, Cardigan., Crosby Ravensworth, Westermorland, Weston, Somerset, and two sites in Ireland. Single spoons come from Ireland, the river Thames and Upper Thames Street, London. A female grave with a pair of spoons is known in France at Pogny, Marne.

5 Bucket burials include: Aylesford and Swarling, Kent, Chesterford, Essex, Hurstbourne Tarrant and Silkstead, Hants., Marlborough, Wilts., Old Warden, Beds., Harpenden, Welwyn Garden City and Baldock, Herts.

6 For general discussions see Ross 1967, S. Piggott 1968 and M. Green 1986.

Abbreviations

AAL	*Acta Archaeologica Lundensia*
Aerial Arch.	*Aerial Archaeology*
Antiq. Journ.	*Antiquaries Journal*
Arch. Ael.[4]	*Archaeologia Aeliana* (fourth series)
Arch. Ael.[5]	*Archaeologia Aeliana* (fifth series)
Arch. Atlant.	*Archaeologia Atlantica*
Arch. Camb.	*Archaeologia Cambrensis*
Arch. Cant.	*Archaeologia Cantiana*
Arch. Journ.	*Archaeological Journal*
Arch. Korrespondenzbl.	*Archäologisches Korrespondenzblatt*
Ark.-Hist. raekke	*Arkaeologisk-Historisk raekke*
BAJ	*Berkshire Archaeological Journal*
BAR	British Archaeological Reports
BAR Brit. Ser.	British Archaeological Reports, British Series
BARG Rev.	*Bristol Archaeological Research Group Review*
BAR Supp. Series	British Archaeological Reports, Supplementary Series (now called International Series)
BBCS	*Bulletin of the Board of Celtic Studies*
Beds. AJ	*Bedfordshire Archaeological Journal*
B and H Arch.	*Brighton and Hove Archaeologist*
BLIA	*Bulletin of the London Institute of Archaeology*
BMQ	*British Museum Quarterly*
BNJ	*British Numismatic Journal*
Carm. Ant.	*Carmarthenshire Antiquary*
Carm. Antiq. Soc.	*Transactions of the Carmarthenshire Antiquarian Society*
CBA Res. Rep.	Council for British Archaeology Research Report
Cheshire Arch. Bull.	*Cheshire Archaeological Bulletin*
Cornish Arch.	*Cornish Archaeology*

CRAAGS	Committee for Rescue Archaeology in Avon, Gloucestershire and Avon
Current Arch.	*Current Archaeology*
CW²	*Cumberland and Westmorland Transactions* (second series)
DAJ	*Derbyshire Archaeological Journal*
DES	*Discovery and Excavation in Scotland*
DMC	*Devizes Museum Catalogue* (*see* Cunnington and Goddard 1934)
Durham Arch. Journ.	*Durham Archaeological Journal*
East Anglian Arch.	*East Anglian Archaeology*
E. Herts. Arch. Soc. Trans.	*East Hertfordshire Archaeological Society's Transactions*
ERA	*East Riding Archaeology*
Essex Arch. Hist.	*Essex Archaeology and History News*
Flints. Hist. Soc. Journ.	*Flintshire Historical Society Journal*
Glasgow Arch. Journ.	*Glasgow Archaeological Journal*
Herts. Arch.	*Hertfordshire Archaeology*
HFC Monog.	Hampshire Field Club and Archaeological Society's Monograph
IJNAUE	*International Journal of Nautical Archaeology and Underwater Exploration*
Inv. Arch. GB	*Inventaria Archaeologica* (Great Britain)
Jahrb. Numismatik und Geldgeschichte	*Jahrbuch für Numismatik und Geldgeschichte*
Jahrb. Röm.-Germ. Zentralmus. Mainz	*Jahrbuch des Römisch-Germanischen Zentralmuseums Mainz*
J. Arch. Sci.	*Journal of Archaeological Science*
JBAA	*Journal of the British Archaeological Association*
J. Hist. Metall.	*Journal of Historical Metallurgy*
JHS	*Journal of Hellenic Studies*
JRIC	*Journal of the Royal Institution of Cornwall*
JRS	*Journal of Roman Studies*
JRSAI	*Journal of the Royal Society of Antiquaries of Ireland*
KAR	*Kent Archaeological Review*
LAAA	*Annals of Archaeology and Anthropology*, Liverpool
Lincs. AAS	*Lincolshire Architectural and Archaeological Society*
Lincs. HA	*Lincolnshire History and Archaeology*
Nat. Mus. Wales	National Museum of Wales
NA	*Norfolk Archaeology*
Northants. Arch.	*Northamptonshire Archaeology*
Numis. Circ.	*Spinks Numismatic Circular*
OJA	*Oxford Journal of Archaeology*
OUCA Monog.	Oxford University Committee for Archaeology Monograph
Oxon.	*Oxoniensia*
PBUSS	*Proceedings of the Bristol University Spelaeological Society*
PCAS	*Proceedings of the Cambridge Antiquarian Society*
P. Cott. NHFC	*Proceedings of the Cotteswold Natural History and Field Club*
PDAES	*Proceedings of the Devonshire Archaeological Exploration Society*

PDNHAS	*Proceedings of the Dorset Natural History Archaeological Society*
PHFC	*Proceedings of the Hampshire Field Club and Archaeological Society*
Phil. Trans. Royal Soc.	*Philological Transactions of the Royal Society*
PIOWNHAS	*Proceedings of the Isle of Wight Natural History and Archaeological Society*
PPS	*Proceedings of the Prehistoric Society*
PPSEA	*Proceedings of the Prehistoric Society of East Anglia*
Proc. Brit. Acad.	*Proceedings of the British Academy*
Proc. Royal Soc. London	*Proceedings of the Royal Society of London*
PSANHS	*Proceedings of the Somerset Archaeological and Natural History Society*
PSAS	*Proceedings of the Society of Antiquaries of Scotland*
PSIAH	*Proceedings of the Suffolk Institute of Archaeology and History*
Pubs. Cambs. Arch. Soc.	*Publications of the Cambridge Archaeological Society*
PWCFC	*Proceedings of the West Cornwall Field Club*
RCHM	Royal Commission on Historical Monuments
RCHM(S)	Royal Commission on Historical Monuments (Scotland)
Rec. of Bucks.	*Records of Buckinghamshire*
Rep. Oxon. Arch. Soc.	*Reports of the Oxfordshire Archaeological Society*
Res. Vol. Surrey Arch. Soc.	*Research Volume of the Surrey Archaeological Society*
Royal Ontario Mus., mon. series	*Royal Ontario Museum, monograph series*
SAC	*Sussex Archaeological Collections*
Scottish Arch. Forum	*Scottish Archaeological Forum*
Scottish Arch. Rev.	*Scottish Archaeological Review*
Soc. Ant. Res. Rep.	Society of Antiquaries Research Report
Soc. Ant. Scot. Monog.	Society of Antiquaries of Scotland Monograph
Sy. AC	*Surrey Archaeological Collections*
TBAS	*Transactions of the Birmingham Archaeological Society*
TBGAS	*Transactions of the Bristol and Gloucestershire Archaeological Society*
TDA	*Transactions of the Devon Association*
TDGNHAS	*Transactions of the Dumfriesshire and Galloway Natural History and Archaeological Society*
TEAS	*Transactions of the Essex Archaeological Society*
TERAS	*Transactions of the East Riding Archaeological Society*
THSLC	*Transactions of the Historical Society of Lancashire and Cheshire*
TLAS	*Transactions of the Leicestershire Archaeological Society*
TLCAS	*Transactions of the Lancashire and Cheshire Antiquarian Society*
TLMAS	*Transactions of the London and Middlesex Archaeological Society*
TNDFC	*Transactions of the Newbury and District Field Club*
Trans. Hawick Arch. Soc.	*Transactions of the Hawick Archaeological Society*
Trans. Leics. Arch. Hist. Soc.	*Transactions of the Leicester Archaeological and Historical Society*

Trans. S. Staffs. AHS	*Transactions of the South Staffordshire Archaeological and Historical Society*
TWAS	*Transactions of the Worcestershire Archaeological Society*
TWNFC	*Transactions of the Woolhope Naturalists' Field Club*
VCH	*Victoria County Histories*
VEHSRP	*Vale of Evesham Historical Society Research Papers*
WAM	*Wiltshire Archaeological Magazine*
World Arch.	*World Archaeology*
YAJ	*Yorkshire Archaeological Journal*

Bibliography

The date quoted after the author's name is the year in which the paper was published. In some cases this does not correspond to the year for which the journal was issued. Volume numbers are all quoted in arabic figures.

Abercromby, J. 1912: *The Bronze Age Pottery of Great Britain and Ireland*, 2 vols. (Oxford).

Adkins, L. and Needham, S. 1985: New research on a Late Bronze Age enclosure at Queen Mary's Hospital, Carshalton. *Sy. AC* 76, 11–50.

Akerman, J.V. and Stone, S. 1857: An account of the investigation of some remarkable circular trenches and the discovery of an Ancient British cemetery at Standlake, Oxon. *Archaeologia* 37, 363–70.

Alcock, L. 1961: Castell Odo: an embanked settlement on Mynydd Ystum, near Aberdaron, Caernarvonshire. *Arch. Camb.* 109 (1960), 78–135.

Alcock, L. 1965: Hillforts in Wales and the Marches. *Antiquity* 39, 184–95.

Alcock, L. 1968: Excavations at South Cadbury Castle, 1967. *Antiq. Journ.* 48, 6–17.

Alcock, L. 1969: Excavations at South Cadbury Castle, 1968. *Antiq. Journ.* 49, 30–40.

Alcock, L. 1970: Excavations at South Cadbury Castle, 1969. *Antiq. Journ.* 50, 14–25.

Alcock, L. 1980: The Cadbury Castle Sequence in the First Millennium bc. *BBCS* 28, 656–718.

Allen, D.F. 1944: The Belgic dynasties of Britain and their coins. *Archaeologia* 90, 1–46.

Allen, D.F. 1958: Belgic coins as illustrations of life in the Late Pre-Roman Iron Age of Britain. *PPS* 24, 43–63.

Allen, D.F. 1961a: The origins of coinage in Britain: a reappraisal. In Frere, S.S. (ed.) 1961, 97–308.

Allen, D.F. 1961b: A study of the Dobunnic coinage. In Clifford, E.M. 1961, 75–149.

Allen, D.F. 1962: Celtic coins. Ordnance Survey *Map of Southern Britain in the Iron Age*, 19–32.

Allen, D.F. 1963: *Sylloge of Coins of the British Isles: the Coins of the Coritani* (Oxford).

Allen, D.F. 1968a: The chronology of Durotrigian coinage. In Richmond, I.A. 1968, 45–55.

Allen, D.F. 1968b: Iron currency bars in Britain. *PPS* 33 (1967), 307–35.

Allen, D.F. 1970: The coins of the Iceni. *Britannia* 1, 1–33.

Allen, D.F. 1971: British potin coins: a review. In Jesson, M. and Hill, D. (eds) 1971, 127–54.

Allen, D.F. 1975: Cunobelin's Gold. *Britannia* 6, 1–19.

Allen, J.R. 1896: The Trawsfynydd tankard. *Arch. Camb.* 13, 212–32.

Allen, T., Miles, D. and Palmer, S. 1984: Iron Age buildings in the Upper Thames Region. In Cunliffe, B. and Miles, D. (eds) 1984, 89–101.

Allen, T. and Robinson, M. 1979: Mingies Ditch, Hardwick. *CBA Group 9 Newsletter* 9, 24–35.

Anthony, I. 1958: *The Iron Age Camp at Poston, Herefordshire* (the Woolhope Club).

Applebaum, E.S. 1951: Excavations at Wilbury Hill, an Iron Age hillfort near Letchworth, Hertfordshire 1933. *Arch. Journ.* 106 (1949), 12–45.

Applebaum, E.S. 1955: The agriculture of the British Early Iron Age as exemplified at Figheldean Down, Wiltshire. *PPS* 20 (1954), 103–14.

ApSimon, A.M. 1958: Notes on the Hammersmith type of La Tène I brooch. *PBUSS* 8, 164–8.

ApSimon, A.M. and Greenfield, E. 1972: The excavation of Bronze Age and Iron Age settlements at Trevisker, St Eval, Cornwall. *PPS* 38, 302–81.

ApSimon, A.M., Rahtz, P.A. and Harris, L.G. 1958: The Iron Age A ditch and pottery at Pagan's Hill, Chew Stoke. *PBUSS* 8, 97–105.

Atkinson, R.J.C. and Piggott, S. 1955: The Torrs chamfrein. *Archaeologia* 96, 197–235.

Austin, D. 1984: *The Caer Cadwgan Project: interim report 1984* (Lampeter).

Austin, D. 1985: *The Caer Cadwgan Project: interim report 1985* (Lampeter).

Avery, M. 1968: Excavations at Meare East 1966. *PSANHS* 112, 21–39.

Avery, M. 1973: Caesar and Cassivellaunus (typescript: May 1973).

Avery, M. 1986: 'Stoning and Fire' at hillfort entrances of southern Britain. *World Arch.* 18(2), 216–30.

Avery, M., Sutton, J.E.G. and Banks, J.W. 1967: Rainsborough, Northants, England: Excavations 1961–5. *PPS* 33, 207–306.

Bagshawe, T.W. 1928: Early Iron Age objects from Harpenden. *Antiq. Journ.* 8, 520–2.

Bailey, C.J. 1963: An Early Iron Age B hearth site indicating salt working on the north shore of the Fleet at Wyke Regis. *PDNHAS* 84 (1962), 132–6.

Baker, F.T. 1960: The Iron Age salt industry in Lincolnshire. *Lincs. AAS* 8 (1959–60), 26–34.

Baker, F.T. 1975: Salt making sites on the Lincolnshire Coast before the Romans. In De Brisay, K.W. and Evans, K.A. (eds) 1975, 31–2.

Balaam, N.D., Smith, K. and Wainwright, G.J. 1982: The Shaugh Moor project: fourth report – environment, context and conclusions. *PPS* 48, 203–78.

Balch, H.E. 1914: *Wookey Hole, its Caves and Cave Dwellers* (Oxford).

Balch, H.E. 1928: Excavations at Wookey Hole and other Mendip caves 1926–7. *Antiq. Journ.* 8, 193–209.

Balkwill, C.J. 1979: The Iron Age Assemblages from Darmsden, Hinderclay and Kettleburgh. *PSIAH* 34, 207–10.

Baring-Gould, S. 1896: Third report of the Dartmoor Exploration Committee. *TDA* 28, 174–99.

Baring-Gould, S. (ed.) 1902: Eighth report of the Dartmoor Exploration Committee. *TDA* 34, 160–5.

Baring-Gould, S., Burnard, R. and Anderson, I.K. 1900: Exploration of Moel Trigarn. *Arch. Camb.* 17, 189–211.

Baring-Gould, S., Burnard, R. and Enys, J.D. 1899: Exploration of the stone camp on St David's Head. *Arch. Camb.* 16, 105–31.

Barnetson, L.P.D. 1982: Animal husbandry: clues from Broxmouth. In Harding D.W. (ed.) 1982, 101–5.

Barrett, J. 1976: Deverel–Rimbury: problems of chronology and interpretation. In Burgess, C. and Miket, R. (eds), *Settlement and Economy in the Third and Second Millennia* BC (BAR Brit. Ser. 33: Oxford), 289–307.

Barrett, J. 1980: The pottery of the later Bronze Age in lowland England. *PPS* 46, 297–320.

Barrett, J.C. 1982: Aspects of the Iron Age in Atlantic Scotland. A case study in the problems of archaeological interpretation. *PSAS* 111, 205–9.

Barrett, J. 1987: The Glastonbury Lake Village: Models and Source Criticism. *Arch. Journ.* 144, 409–23.

Barrett, J. and Bradley, R. 1980a: Later Bronze Age settlements in South Wessex and Cranborne Chase. In Barrett, J. and Bradley, R. (eds) 1980c, 181–208.

Barrett, J. and Bradley, R. 1980b: The Later Bronze Age in the Thames Valley. In Barrett, J. and Bradley, R. (eds) 1980c, 247–70.

Barrett, J. and Bradley, R. (eds) 1980c: *Settlement and Society in the British Later Bronze Age* (BAR Brit. Ser. 83).

Barrett, J., Bradley, R., Bowden, M. and Mead, B. 1983: South Lodge after Pitt Rivers. *Antiquity* 57, 193–204.

Bateman, J. 1978: A Late Bronze Age cremation cemetery and Iron Age to Romano-British enclosures, Ryton-on-Dunsmore, Warwickshire. *TBAS* 88 (1976–7), 9–47.

Bates, C.S. 1871: A British cemetery near Plymouth. *Archaeologia* 40, 500.

Bayne, N. 1957: Excavations at Lyneham Camp, Lyneham, Oxon. *Oxon.* 22, 1–10.

Bedwin, O. 1978a: Excavations inside Harting Beacon Hill-fort 1976. *SAC* 116, 225–40.

Bedwin, O. 1978b: Iron Age Sussex – The Downs and the Coastal Plain. In Drewett, P.L. (ed.) 1978, 41–51.

Bedwin, O. 1979: Excavations at Harting Beacon, West Sussex; Second Season 1977. *SAC* 117, 21–36.

Bedwin, O. 1981: Excavations at Lancing Down, West Sussex 1980. *SAC* 119, 37–55.

Bedwin, O. 1983: Miss P.A.M. Keef's excavations at Harting Beacon 1948–52. *SAC* 121, 199–202.

Bell, M. 1977: Excavations at Bishopstone. *SAC* 115.

Bell, M. 1981: Valley sediments and environmental change. In Jones, M. and Dimbleby, G.W. (eds) 1981, 75–91.

Bell, M. 1982: The effects of land-use and climate on valley sedimentation. In Harding, A.F. (ed.) 1982, 127–42.

Bellows, J. 1881: On some bronze and other articles found near Birdlip. *TBGAS* 5 (1880–1), 137–41.

Benson, D. and Miles, D. 1974: *The Upper Thames Valley: An Archaeological Survey of the River Gravels* (Oxford).

Benson, G.C. 1953: Belgic occupation site at Gill's Cliff, Ventnor. *PIOWNHAS* 4, 303–11.

Benton, S. 1931: The excavation of the Sculptor's Cave, Covesea, Morayshire. *PSAS* 65 (1930–1), 177–216.

Bersu, G. 1940: Excavations at Little Woodbury, Wiltshire, part I. *PPS* 6, 30–111.

Bersu, G. and Griffiths, W.E. 1949: Concentric circles at Llwyn-du-Bach, Pen-y-Groes, Caernarvonshire. *Arch. Camb.* 100, 173–206.

Biddle, M. 1966: Excavations at Winchester, 1965. *Antiq. Journ.* 46, 308–32.

Biddle, M. 1967: Excavations at Winchester, 1966. *Antiq. Journ.* 47, 251–79.

Biddle, M. 1968: Excavations at Winchester, 1967. *Antiq. Journ.* 48, 250–84.

Biddle, M. 1975a: Excavations at Winchester, 1971. *Antiq. Journ.* 55, 96–126.

Biddle, M. 1975b: Ptolemaic coins from Winchester. *Antiquity* 49, 213–15.

Birchall, A. 1963: The Belgic problem: Aylesford revisited. *BMQ* 28, 21–9.

Birchall, A. 1965: The Aylesford–Swarling culture: the problem of the Belgae reconsidered. *PPS* 31, 241–367.

Bishop, M.W. 1971: The Non-Belgic Iron Age in Surrey. *Sy. AC* 68, 1–30.

Blackmore, C., Braithwaite, M. and Hodder, I.R. 1979: Social and Cultural patterning in Late Iron Age in Southern Britain. In Burnham, B.C. and Kingsbury, J. (eds) 1979, 93–112.

Bogaers, J.E. 1979: King Cogidubnus: another reading of *RIB* 91. *Britannia* 10, 243–54.

Boon, G.C. 1954: A Greek vase from the Thames. *JHS* 74, 198.

Boon, G.C. 1969: Belgic and Roman Silchester: the excavations of 1954–8 with an excursus on the early history of Calleva. *Archaeologia* 102, 1–82.

Boon, G.C. 1976: A Graeco-Roman Anchor-stock from North Wales. *Arch. Atlant.* 1(2) (1975), 195–9.

Boon, G.C. 1977: A Graeco-Roman Anchor-stock from North Wales. *Antiq. Journ.* 57, 10–30.

Boudet, R. 1988. Iberian type brooches [from Mount Batten, Plymouth]. In Cunliffe, B. 1988b, 64.

Bowen, H.C. 1961: *Ancient Fields* (British Association for the Advancement of Science: undated).

Bowen, H.C. 1969: The Celtic background. In Rivet, A.L.F. (ed.), *The Roman Villa in Britain* (London), 1–48.

Bowen, H.C. and Fowler, P.J. 1966: Romano-British rural settlements in Dorset and Wiltshire. In Thomas, A.C. (ed.) 1966b, 43–67.

Boyd, W.E. 1985: Environmental change and Iron Age land management in the area of the Antonine Wall, Central Scotland: a summary. *Glasgow Arch. Journ.* 11 (1984), 75–81.

Boyden, J.R. 1957: Excavations at Hammer Wood, Iping, 1957. *SAC* 96, 149–63.

Bradford, J.S.P. 1940: The excavation of Cherbury Camp, 1939. *Oxon.* 5, 13–20.

Bradford, J.S.P. 1942a: An Early Iron Age settlement at Standlake, Oxon. *Antiq. Journ.* 22, 202–14.

Bradford, J.S.P. 1942b: An Early Iron Age site at Allen's Pit, Dorchester. *Oxon.* 7, 36–60.

Bradford, J.S.P. 1942c: An Early Iron Age site on Blewburton Hill, Berks. *BAJ* 46, 97–104.

Bradford, J.S.P. and Goodchild, R.G. 1939: Excavations at Frilford, Berks., 1937–8. *Oxon.* 4, 1–70.

Bradley, R. 1969a: Excavations on Portsdown Hill, 1963–5. *PHFC* 24 (1967), 42–58.

Bradley, R. 1969b: The South Oxfordshire Grim's Ditch and its significance. *Oxon.* 33, 1–13.

Bradley, R. 1971a: A field survey of the Chichester entrenchments. In Cunliffe, B. 1971b, 17–36.

Bradley, R. 1971b: An Iron Age promontory fort at Belle Tout. *SAC* 109, 8–19.

Bradley, R. 1975: Salt and settlement in the Hampshire Sussex Borderland. In De Brisay, K.W. and Evans, K.A. (eds) 1975, 20–5.

Bradley, R. 1980: Subsistence, exchange and technology – a social framework for the Bronze Age in Southern England. In Barrett, J. and Bradley, R. (eds) 1980c, 57–76.

Bradley, R. 1981: 'Various styles of urn': Cemeteries and settlement in Southern England *c.* 1400–1000 bc. In Chapman, R., Kinnes, I. and Randsborg, K. (eds), *The Archaeology of Death* (Cambridge), 93–104.

Bradley, R. and Ellison, A. 1975: *Rams Hill* (BAR Brit. Ser. 19: Oxford).

Bradley, R., Lobb, S., Richards, J. and Robinson, M. 1980: Two Late Bronze Age settlements on the Kennet gravels: excavations at Aldermaston Wharf and Knight's Farm, Burghfield, Berkshire. *PPS* 46, 217–96.

Brailsford, J.W. 1948: Excavations at Little Woodbury, part II. *PPS* 14, 1–23.

Brailsford, J.W. 1949: Excavations at Little Woodbury, parts IV and V. *PPS* 15, 156–68.

Brailsford, J.W. 1958a: A corrected restoration of the Belgic iron frame from Welwyn. *Antiq. Journ.* 38, 89–90.

Brailsford, J.W. 1958b: Early Iron Age 'C' in Wessex. *PPS* 24, 101–19.

Brailsford, J.W. 1971: The Sedgeford torc. In Sieveking, G. de G. (ed.) 1971, 16–19.

Brailsford, J.W. 1975a: *Early Celtic Masterpieces from Britain in the British Museum* (London).

Brailsford, J.W. 1975b: The Polden Hill hoard, Somerset. *PPS* 41, 222–34.

Brailsford, J.W. and Stapley, J.E. 1972: The Ipswich torcs. *PPS* 38, 219–34.

Brassil, K.S., Guilbert, G.C., Livens, R.G., Stead, W.H. and Bevan-Evans, M. 1982: Rescue excavations at Moel Hiraddug between 1960 and 1980. *Flints. Hist. Soc. Journ.* 30, 13–88.

Braund, D. 1984: Observations on Cartimandua. *Britannia* 15, 1–6.

Brewster, T.C.M. 1963: *The Excavation of Staple Howe* (Scarborough).

Brewster, T.C.M. 1971: The Garton Slack chariot burial, east Yorkshire. *Antiquity* 45, 289–2.

Brewster, T.C.M. 1976: Garton Slack. *Current Arch.* 51 (1975), 104–16.

Brewster, T.C.M. 1981: *The Excavation of Garton and Wetwang Slacks* (Microfiche, National Monuments Record: London).

Briard, J. 1957: Le bronze de facies Atlantique en Armorique. *Congrès Préhistorique de France* 15 (1956), 313–27.

Briard, J. 1965: *Les Dépôts bretons et l'âge du bronze atlantique* (Rennes).

Briard, J. 1979: L'Age du Bronze. In Giot, P-R., Briard, J. and Pape, L., *Protohistoire de la Bretagne* (Rennes), 29–213.

De Brisay, K. 1978: The excavation of a Red Hill at Peldon, Essex, with notes on some other sites. *Antiq. Journ.* 58, 31–60.

De Brisay, K.W. and Evans, K.A. (eds) 1975: *Salt: The study of an ancient industry* (Colchester).

Britnell, W. 1974: Beckford. *Current Arch.* 45, 293–7.

Britnell, W.J. 1975: An interim report upon excavations at Beckford, 1972–4. *VEHSRP* 5, 1–12.

Britnell, W. forthcoming: The Collfryn hillslope enclosure Llansantffraid Denddwr, Powys: excavations 1980–1982. *PPS* (forthcoming).

Britton, D. 1960: The Isleham hoard, Cambridgeshire. *Antiquity* 34, 279–82.

Britton, D. 1971: The Heathery Burn cave revisited. In Sieveking, G. de G. (ed.) 1971, 20–37.

Brooks, R.T. 1964: The Rumps, St Minver: interim report on the 1963 excavations. *Cornish Arch.* 3, 26–34.

Brooks, R.T. 1966: The Rumps: second interim report on the 1965 season. *Cornish Arch.* 5, 4–10.

Brooks, R.T. 1968: The Rumps, St Minver: third interim report, 1967 season. *Cornish Arch.* 7, 38–9.

Brooks, R.T. 1974: The Excavation of the Rumps Cliff Castle, St. Minver, Cornwall. *Cornish Arch.* 13, 5–50.

Brown, R.A. 1986: The Iron Age and Romano–British Settlement at Woodcock Hall, Saham Toney, Norfolk. *Britannia* 17, 1–58.

Buckley, D.G. and Hedges, J.D. 1987: *The Bronze Age and Saxon Settlement at Springfield Lyons, Essex* (Norwich).

Budgen, W. 1922: Hallstatt pottery from Eastbourne. *Antiq. Journ.* 2, 354–60.

Bulleid, A. and Gray, H.StG. 1911: *The Glastonbury Lake Village* Vol. 1 (Glastonbury Antiquarian Society).

Bulleid, A. and Gray, H.StG. 1917: *The Glastonbury Lake Village* Vol. 2 (Glastonbury Antiquarian Society).

Bulleid, A. and Gray, H.StG. 1948: *The Meare Lake Village* Vol. 1 (Taunton).

Bulleid, A. and Gray, H.StG. 1953: *The Meare Lake Village* Vol. 2 (Taunton).

Burchell, J.P.T. and Frere, S.S. 1947: The occupation at Sandown Park, Esher, during the Stone Age, the Early Iron Age and the Anglo-Saxon period. *Antiq. Journ.* 27, 24–46.

Burgess, C.B. 1969a: Chronology and terminology in the British Bronze Age. *Antiq. Journ.* 49, 22–9.

Burgess, C.B. 1969b: The Later Bronze Age in the British Isles and north-western France. *Arch. Journ.* 125 (1968), 1–45.

Burgess, C.B. 1974: The Bronze Age. In Renfrew, C. (ed.), *British Prehistory* (London), 163–232.

Burgess, C.B. 1976: The Gwithian Mould and the forerunner of South Welsh axes. In Burgess, C. and Miket, R. (eds), *Settlement and Economy in the Third and Second Millennium BC* (BAR Brit. Ser. 33: Oxford), 289–307.

Burgess, C. 1979: A find from Boyton, Suffolk and the end of the Bronze Age in Britain and Ireland. In Burgess C. and Coombs, D. (eds) 1979, 269–82.

Burgess, C.B. 1980: The Bronze Age in Wales. In Taylor, J.A. (ed.), *Culture and Environment in Prehistoric Wales* (BAR Brit. Ser. 76: Oxford), 243–86.

Burgess, C.B. 1985: Population, climate and upland settlement. In Spratt, D. and Burgess, C. (eds) 1985, 195–230.

Burgess, C. and Coombs, D. (eds) 1979: *Bronze Age Hoards: some finds old and new* (BAR Brit. Ser. 67: Oxford).

Burgess, C., Coombs, D. and Davies, D.G. 1972: The Broadward Complex and Barbed Spearheads. In Lynch, F. and Burgess, C. (eds), *Prehistoric Man in Wales and the West* (Bath), 211–83.

Burgess, C. and Miket, R. 1976: Three socketed axes from north-east England, with notes on faceted and ribbed socketed axes. *Arch. Ael.*[5] 4, 1–9.

Burnham, B.C. and Kingsbury, J. (eds) 1979: *Space, Hierarchy and Society* (BAR Int. Ser. 59: Oxford).

Burns, J.E. 1971: Additional torcs from Snettisham, Norfolk. *PPS* 37, 228–9.

Burrow, E.J., Paine, A.E.W., Knowles, W.H. and Gray, J.W. 1925: Excavations on Leckhampton Hill, Cheltenham, during the summer of 1925. *TBGAS* 47, 81–112.

Burstow, G.P. 1958: A Late Bronze Age urnfield on Steyning Round Hill, Sussex. *PPS* 24, 158–64.

Burstow, G.P. and Holleyman, G.A. 1957: Late Bronze Age settlement on Itford Hill, Sussex. *PPS* 23, 167–212.

Bushe-Fox, J.P. 1915: *Excavations at Hengistbury Head, Hampshire, in 1911–12* (Soc. Ant. Res. Rep. 3: Oxford).

Bushe-Fox, J.P. 1925: *Excavation of the Late-Celtic Urn-Field at Swarling, Kent* (Soc. Ant. Res. Rep. 8: Oxford).

Calder, C.T. 1939: Excavations of Iron Age dwellings on the Calf of Eday in Orkney. *PSAS* 73 (1938–9), 167–85.

Calkin, J.B. 1949: The Isle of Purbeck in the Iron Age. *PDNHAS* 70, 29–59.

Calkin, J.B. 1953: Kimmeridge coal-money. *PDNHAS* 75, 45–71.

Calkin, J.B. 1964: The Bournemouth area in the Middle and Late Bronze Age, with the 'Deverel–Rimbury' problem reconsidered. *Arch. Journ.* 119 (1962), 1–65.

Campbell, J.A., Baxter, M.S. and Alcock, L. 1979: Radiocarbon dates for the Cadbury massacre. *Antiquity* 53, 31–8.

Carter, S.P., Haigh, D., Neil, N.R.J. and Smith, B. 1984: Interim report on the structures at Howe, Stromness, Orkney. *Glasgow Arch. Journ.* 11, 61–73.

Case, H.J. 1949: The Standlake Iron Age sword. *Rep. Oxon. Arch. Soc.* 87, 7–8.

Case, H.J., Bayne, N., Steele, S., Avery, G. and Sutermeister, H. 1966: Excavations at City Farm, Hanborough, Oxon. *Oxon.* 29–30 (1964/5), 1–98.

Caseldine, C.J. 1980: Environmental change in Cornwall during the last 13,000 years. *Cornish Arch.* 19, 3–16.

Caseldine, C.J. and Maguire, D.J. 1981: A Review of the Prehistoric and Historic Environment on Dartmoor. *PDAES* 39, 1–16.

Caufield, S. 1980: Quern replacement and the origin of the brochs. *PSAS* 109 (1977–8), 129–39.

Chadburn, A. 1983: The Stanwick fortifications reconsidered. *Northern Archaeology* 4(1), 1–20.

Chadwick, S. and Thompson, M.W. 1956: Note on an Iron Age habitation site near Battlesbury Camp, Warminster. *WAM* 56, 262–4.

Challis, A.J. and Harding, D.W. 1975: *Later Prehistory from the Trent to the Tyne* 2 vols (BAR Brit. Ser. 20: Oxford).

Champion, S.T. 1972: Excavations on Leckhampton Hill. *TBGAS* 90 (1971), 5–21.

Champion, S.T. 1976: Leckhampton Hill, Gloucestershire, 1925 and 1970. In Harding, D.W. (ed.) 1976b, 177–91.

Chapman, J.C. and Mytum, H. (eds) 1983: *Settlement in North Britain 1000 BC–AD 1000* (BAR Brit. Ser. 118: Oxford).

Chatwin, P.B. 1930: Excavations on Corley Camp, near Coventry. *TBAS* 52, 282–7.

Childe, V.G. 1933: Excavations at Castle Law Fort, Midlothian. *PSAS* 67 (1932–3), 362–89.

Childe, V.G. 1935a: Excavation of the vitrified fort of Finavon, Angus. *PSAS* 69 (1934–5), 49–80.

Childe, V.G. 1935b: *The Prehistory of Scotland* (London).

Childe, V.G. 1941: The defences of Kaimes hillfort, Midlothian. *PSAS* 75 (1940–1), 43–54.

Childe, V.G. 1946: *Scotland Before the Scots* (London).

Childe, V.G. and Forde, C.D. 1932: Excavations in two Iron Age forts at Earn's Heugh, near Coldingham. *PSAS* 66 (1931–2), 152–83.

Childe, V.G. and Thorneycroft, W. 1938: The vitrified fort at Rahoy, Morvern, Argyll. *PSAS* 72 (1937–8), 23–43.

Chowne, P., Girling, M. and Greig, J. 1986: The excavation of an Iron Age defended enclosure at Tattershall Thorpe, Lincolnshire. *PPS* 52, 159–88.

Christie, P.M.L. 1978: The Excavation of an Iron Age souterrain and settlement at Carn Euny, Sancreed, Cornwall. *PPS* 44, 309–434.

Christie, P.M.L. 1979: Cornish souterrains in the light of recent research. *BLIA* 16, 187–213.

Christison, D. 1898: *Early Fortifications in Scotland* (Edinburgh).

Christison, D. 1900: The forts, camps and other fieldworks of Perth, Forfar and Kincardine. *PSAS* 34 (1899–1900), 74–6.

Christison, D. and Anderson, J. 1899: On the recently excavated fort on Castle Law, Abernethy, Perthshire. *PSAS* 33 (1898–9), 13–33.

Clark, J.G.D. 1936: The timber monument at Arminghall and its affinities. *PPS* 2, 16–51.

Clark, J.G.D. 1952: *Prehistoric Europe, the Economic Basis* (Cambridge).

Clark, J.G.D. and Fell, C.I. 1953: An Early Iron Age site at Micklemoor Hill, West Harling, Norfolk, and its pottery. *PPS* 19, 1–40.

Clarke, D.L. 1972: A provisional model of an Iron Age society and its settlement. In Clarke, D.L. (ed.), *Models in Archaeology* (London), 801–70.

Clarke, D.V. 1970: Bone dice and the Scottish Iron Age. *PPS* 36, 214–32.

Clarke, P.J. 1971: The Neolithic, Bronze and Iron Age and Romano-British finds from Mount Batten, Plymouth, 1832–1939. *PDAES* 29, 137–61.

Clarke, R.R. 1939: The Iron Age in Norfolk and Suffolk. *Arch. Journ.* 96, 1–113.

Clarke, R.R. 1951a: A Celtic torc-terminal from North Creake, Norfolk. *Arch. Journ.* 106 (1949), 59–61.

Clarke, R.R. 1951b: A hoard of metalwork of the Early Iron Age from Ringstead, Norfolk. *PPS* 17, 214–25.

Clarke, R.R. 1955: The Early Iron Age treasure from Snettisham, Norfolk. *PPS* 20 (1954), 27–86.

Clarke, R.R. 1960: *East Anglia* (London).

Clarke, R.R. and Apling, H. 1935: An Iron Age tumulus on Warborough Hill, Stiffkey, Norfolk. *NA* 25, 408–28.

Clarke, R.R. and Hawkes, C.F.C. 1955: An iron anthropoid sword from Shouldham, Norfolk, with related continental and British weapons. *PPS* 21, 198–227.

Clay, P.N. 1977: Excavations in Blackfriars St., Leicester. In McWhirr, A.D., Archaeology in Leicestershire and Rutland. *Trans. Leics. Arch. Hist. Soc.* 52, 82–102.

Clay, R.C.C. 1924: An Early Iron Age site on Fifield Bavant Down. *WAM* 42, 457–96.

Clay, R.C.C. 1925: An inhabited site of La Tène I date on Swallowcliffe Down. *WAM* 43, 59–93.

Clay, R.C.C. 1927a: A Late Bronze Age urnfield at Pokesdown, Hants. *Antiq. Journ.* 7, 465–84.

Clay, R.C.C. 1927b: Supplementary report on the Early Iron Age village on Swallowcliffe Down. *WAM* 46, 540–7.

Clifford, E.M. 1934: An Early Iron Age site at Barnwood, Glos. *TBGAS* 56, 227–30.

Clifford, E.M. 1961: *Bagendon – a Belgic Oppidum* (Cambridge).

Close, R.S. 1972: Excavation of Iron Age hut circles at Percy Rigg, Kildale. *YAJ* 44, 23–31.

Cocks, A.H. 1909: Prehistoric pit-dwellings at Ellesborough. *Rec. of Bucks.* 9, 349–61.

Cocoran, J.X.W.P. 1965: A bronze bucket in the Hunterian Museum, University of Glasgow. *Antiq. Journ.* 45, 12–17.

Coles, B. and J. 1986: *Sweet Track to Glastonbury* (London).

Coles, J.M. 1959: Scottish swan's-neck sunflower pins. *PSAS* 92 (1958–9), 1–9.

Coles, J.M. 1962a: European Bronze Age shields. *PPS* 28, 156–90.

Coles, J.M. 1962b: Scottish Late Bronze Age metalwork: typology, distributions and chronology. *PSAS* 93 (1959–60), 16–134.

Coles, J.M. 1972: Later Bronze Age activity in the Somerset Levels. *Antiq. Journ.* 52, 269–75.

Coles, J.M. 1987: *Meare Village East. The excavation of A. Bulleid and H. St. George Gray 1932–1956* (Somerset Levels Papers 13).

Collins, A.E.P. 1947: Excavations on Blewburton Hill, 1947. *BAJ* 50, 4–29.

Collins, A.E.P. 1953: Excavations on Blewburton Hill, 1948 and 1949. *BAJ* 53, 21–64.

Collins, A.E.P. and F.J. 1959: Excavations on Blewburton Hill, 1953. *BAJ* 57, 52–73.

Collis, J.R. 1968: Excavations at Owslebury, Hants. *Antiq. Journ.* 48, 18–31.

Collis, J.R. 1970: Excavations at Owslebury, Hants.: a second interim report. *Antiq. Journ.* 50, 246–61.

Collis, J.R. 1971a: Functional and theoretical interpretations of British coinage. *World Arch.* 3(1), 71–84.

Collis, J.R. 1971b: Markets and money. In Jesson, M. and Hill, D. (eds) 1971, 97–104.

Collis, J.R. 1973: Burials with weapons in Iron Age Britain. *Germania* 51, 121–33.

Collis, J.R. 1974: A functionalist approach to pre-Roman coinage. In Casey, J. and Reece, R. (eds), *Coins and the Archaeologist* (BAR Int. Ser. 4: Oxford), 1–11.

Collis, J.R. 1975: The coin of Ptolemy V from Winchester. *Antiquity* 49, 47–8.

Collis, J. (ed.) 1977: *The Iron Age in Britain – a review* (Sheffield).

Coombs, D.G. 1982: Excavations at the hillfort of Castercliff, Nelson, Lancashire 1970–71. *TLCAS* 81, 111–30.

Coombs, D.G. and Thompson, F.H. 1980: Excavation of the Hill Fort of Mam Tor, Derbyshire 1965–69. *DAJ* 99 (1979), 7–51.

Corder, P. and Kirk, J.L. 1932: A Roman villa at Langton, near Malton, E. Yorkshire. *Roman Malton and District*, report no. 4.

Corder, P. and Pryce, T.D. 1938: Belgic and other early pottery found at North Ferriby, Yorkshire. *Antiq. Journ.* 18, 262–77.

Cotton, M.A. 1955: British camps with timber-laced ramparts. *Arch. Journ.* 111 (1954), 26–105.

Cotton, M.A. 1959: Cornish cliff castles. *PWCFC* 2, 113–21.

Cotton, M.A. 1961a: Observations on the classification of hillforts in southern England. In Frere, S.S. (ed.) 1961, 61–8.

Cotton, M.A. 1961b: The pre-Belgic Iron Age cultures of Gloucestershire. In Clifford, E.M. 1961, 22–42.

Cotton, M.A. 1962: Berkshire hillforts. *BAJ* 60, 30–52.

Cotton, M.A. and Frere, S.S. 1968: Ivinghoe Beacon, excavations 1963–5. *Rec. of Bucks.* 18, 187–260.

Courtney, T. and Hall, M. 1984: Excavation at the Perrott's Brook Dyke, Bagendon, 1983. *TBGAS* 102, 197–200.

Cowen, J.D. 1967: The Hallstatt sword of bronze: on the continent and in Britain. *PPS* 33, 377–454.

Cra'ster, M.D. 1961: The Aldwick Iron Age settlement, Barley, Hertfordshire. *PCAS* 54, 22–46.

Cra'ster, M.D. 1969: New Addenbrooke's Iron Age site, Long Road, Cambridge. *PCAS* 62, 21–8.

Craw, J.H. 1924: On two bronze spoons from an Early Iron Age grave near Burnmouth, Berwickshire. *PSAS* 63 (1923–4), 143–60.

Crawford, O.G.S. 1921: The ancient settlements at Harlyn Bay. *Antiq. Journ.* 1, 283–99.

Crawford, O.G.S. 1922: A prehistoric invasion of England. *Antiq. Journ.* 2, 27–35.

Crawford, O.G.S. and Keiller, A. 1928: *Wessex from the Air* (Oxford).

Crawford, O.G.S. and Wheeler, R.E.M. 1921: The Llynfawr and other hoards of the Bronze Age. *Archaeologia* 71, 133–40.

Crew, P. 1984: *Bryn y Castell 1979–1984: interim reports* (Maentwrog).

Crew, P. 1985: *Bryn y Castell 1985: interim report* (Maentwrog).

Crummy, P. 1980a: Camulodunum. *Current Arch.* 7, 6–10.

Crummy, P. 1980b: Crop marks at Gosbecks, Colchester. *Aerial Arch.* 4 (1979), 77–82.

Cunliffe, B. 1961: Report on a Belgic and Roman site at the Causeway, Horndean, 1959. *PHFC* 22, 25–9.

Cunliffe, B. 1964: *Winchester Excavations, 1949–1960* Vol. 1 (Winchester).

Cunliffe, B. 1966: Stoke Clump, Hollingbury, and the Early pre-Roman Iron Age in Sussex. *SAC* 104, 109–20.

Cunliffe, B. 1968a: Early pre-Roman Iron Age communities in eastern England. *Antiq. Journ.* 48, 175–91.

Cunliffe, B. 1968b: Excavations at Eldon's Seat, Encombe, Dorset. *PPS* 34, 191–237.

Cunliffe, B. 1970: A Bronze Age settlement at Chalton, Hants. (site 78). *Antiq. Journ.* 50, 1–13.

Cunliffe, B. 1971a: Aspects of hill-forts and their cultural environments. In Jesson, M. and Hill, D. (eds) 1971, 53–70.

Cunliffe, B. 1971b: *Excavations at Fishbourne: Vol. 1, The Site* (Soc. Ant. Res. Rep. 26: London).

Cunliffe, B. 1972a: Danebury, Hampshire: first interim report on the excavation 1969–70. *Antiq. Journ.* 51 (1971), 240–52.

Cunliffe, B. 1972b: The Late Iron Age metalwork from Bulbury, Dorset. *Antiq. Journ.* 52, 293–308.

Cunliffe, B. 1974: Chalton, Hants: the evolution of a landscape. *Antiq. Journ.* 53 (1973), 173–90.

Cunliffe, B. 1976a: *Iron Age Sites in Central Southern England* (CBA Res. Rep. 16: London).

Cunliffe, B. 1976b: The origins of urbanization in Britain. In Cunliffe, B.W. and Rowley, T. (eds) 1976, 135–62.

Cunliffe, B. 1978a: *Iron Age Communities in Britain* (2nd edition) (London).

Cunliffe, B. 1978b: Settlement and population in the British Iron Age: some facts, figures and fantasies. In Cunliffe, B. and Rowley, T. (eds) 1978, 3–24.

Cunliffe, B. (ed.) 1981a: *Coinage and Society in Britain and Gaul* (CBA Res. Rep. 38: London).

Cunliffe, B. 1981b: Money and society in pre-Roman Britain. In Cunliffe, B. (ed.) 1981a, 29–39.

Cunliffe, B. 1982a: Britain, the Veneti and beyond. *OJA* 1(1), 39–68.

Cunliffe, B. 1982b: Social and economic development in Kent in the pre-Roman Iron Age. In Leach, P.E. (ed.), *Archaeology in Kent to AD 1500* (CBA Res. Rep. 48: London).

Cunliffe, B. 1983: Ictis: is it here? *OJA* 2(1), 123–6.

Cunliffe, B. 1984a: *Danebury: an Iron Age Hillfort in Hampshire. Volume 1, The Excavations, 1969–1978: the site. Volume 2, The Excavations, 1969–1978: the finds* (CBA Res. Rep. 52: London).

Cunliffe, B. 1984b: Gloucestershire and the Iron Age of Southern Britain. *TBGAS* 102, 5–16.

Cunliffe, B. 1984c: Iron Age Wessex: continuity and change. In Cunliffe, B. and Miles, D. (eds) 1984, 12–45.

Cunliffe, B. 1984d: Relations between Britain and Gaul in the First Century BC and Early First Century AD. In Macready, S. and Thompson, F.H. (eds) 1984, 3–23.

Cunliffe, B. 1987: *Hengistbury Head, Dorset. Vol. 1: prehistoric and Roman settlement, 3500 BC–AD 500* (OUCA Monog. 13: Oxford).

Cunliffe, B. 1988a: *Greeks, Romans and Barbarians: spheres of interaction* (London).

Cunliffe, B. 1988b: *Mount Batten, Plymouth. A prehistoric and Roman Port* (OUCA Monog. 26: Oxford).

Cunliffe, B. 1988c: *The Temple of Sulis Minerva at Bath. Vol. 2: The Finds from the Sacred Spring* (OUCA Monog. 16: Oxford).

Cunliffe, B. and Miles, D. (eds) 1984: *Aspects of the Iron Age in Central Southern Britain* (OUCA Monog. 2: Oxford).

Cunliffe, B. and Orton, C. 1984: Radiocarbon age assessment [at Danebury, Hants.]. In Cunliffe, B. 1984a, 190–8.

Cunliffe, B.W. and Rowley, T. (eds) 1976: *Oppida: the beginnings of urbanism in barbarian Europe* (BAR Supp. Series. 11: Oxford).

Cunliffe, B. and Rowley, T. (eds) 1978: *Lowland Iron Age Communities in Europe: papers presented to a conference of the Department for External Studies held at Oxford, October 1977* (BAR Supp. Series 48: Oxford).

Cunnington, E. 1884: On a hoard of bronze, iron and other objects found in Bulbury Camp, Dorset. *Archaeologia* 48, 115–20.

Cunnington, H. 1871: Oldbury Camp, Wilts. *WAM* 28, 277.

Cunnington, M.E. 1908: Oliver's Camp, Devizes. *WAM* 35, 408–44.

Cunnington, M.E. 1909: Notes on a Late Celtic rubbish heap near Oare. *WAM* 36, 125–39.

Cunnington, M.E. 1911: Knap Hill Camp. *WAM* 37, 42–65.

Cunnington, M.E. 1923: *The Early Iron Age Inhabited Site at All Cannings Cross* (Devizes).

Cunnington, M.E. 1925: Figsbury Rings: an account of excavations in 1924. *WAM* 43, 48–58.

Cunnington, M.E. 1932a: Chisbury Camp. *WAM* 46, 4–7.

Cunnington, M.E. 1932b: The demolition of Chisenbury Trendle. *WAM* 46, 1–3.

Cunnington, M.E. 1932c: Was there a second Belgic invasion represented by bead-rim pottery? *Antiq. Journ.* 12, 27–34.

Cunnington, M.E. 1933: Excavations in Yarnbury Castle Camp, 1932. *WAM* 46, 198–213.

Cunnington, M.E. and B.H. 1913: Casterley Camp excavations. *WAM* 38, 53–105.

Cunnington, M.E. and B.H. 1917: Lidbury Camp. *WAM* 40, 12–36.

Cunnington, M.E. and Goddard, E.H. 1934: *The Devizes Museum Catalogue*, Part II (Devizes).

Curle, A.O. 1910: Notice of some excavation on the fort occupying the summit of Bonchester Hill, parish of Hobkirk, Roxburghshire. *PSAS* 44 (1909–10), 225–36.

Curle, A.O. 1927: The development and antiquity of the Scottish brochs. *Antiquity* 1, 290–8.

Curwen, E. 1930: Lynchet burials near Lewes. *SAC* 71, 254–7.

Curwen, E.C. 1929: Excavations in the Trundle, Goodwood, 1928. *SAC* 70, 33–85.

Curwen, E.C. 1931: Excavations in the Trundle. *SAC* 72, 100–50.

Curwen, E.C. 1932: Excavations at Hollingbury Camp, Sussex. *Antiq. Journ.* 12, 1–16.

Curwen, E.C. 1933: Excavations on Thundersbarrow Hill, Sussex. *Antiq. Journ.* 13, 109–33.

Curwen, E.C. 1934a: A Late Bronze Age farm and a Neolithic pit-dwelling on New Barn Down, Clampham, nr. Worthing. *SAC* 75, 137–70.

Curwen, E.C. 1934b: A prehistoric site in Kingley Vale, near Chichester. *SAC* 75, 209–16.

Curwen, E.C. 1939: The Iron Age in Sussex. *SAC* 80, 214–16.

Curwen, E.C. 1948: A bronze cauldron from Sompting, Sussex. *Antiq. Journ.* 28, 157–63.

Curwen, E.C. 1954: *The Archaeology of Sussex*, 2nd edition (London).

Curwen, E.C. and Williamson, R.P.R. 1931: The date of Cissbury Camp. *Antiq. Journ.* 11, 14–36.

Curwen, E. and E.C. 1927: Excavations in the Caburn, near Lewes. *SAC* 68, 1–56.

Curwen, E. and E.C. and Hawkes, C.F.C. 1931: Prehistoric remains from Kingston Buci. *SAC* 72, 185–217.

Dacre, M. and Ellison, A. 1981: A Bronze Age Urn Cemetery at Kimpton, Hampshire. *PPS* 47, 147–203.

Dallas, C. 1975: A Belgic farmstead at Orton Longueville. *Durobrivae* 3, 26–7.

Darvill, T.C. and Hingley, R.C. 1982: A 'banjo' type enclosure at Northleach. *TBGAS* 100, 249–51.

Davies, G. and Turner, J. 1979: Pollen diagrams from Northumberland. *New Phytologist* 82, 783–804.

Davies, H. 1936: The shale industries at Kimmeridge, Dorset. *Arch. Journ.* 93, 200–19.

Davies, J.A. and Phillips, C.W. 1929: The Percy Sladen Memorial Fund excavation at Bury Hill

Camp, Winterbourne Down, Gloucestershire, 1926. *PBUSS* 3, 8–24.

Davies, J.L. 1974: An excavation at the Bulwarks, Porth Kerry, Glamorgan, 1968. *Arch. Camb.* 122 (1973), 85–98.

Davies, S.M. 1981: Excavations at Old Down Farm, Andover. Part II: prehistoric and Roman. *PHFC* 37, 81–163.

Dawson, D. 1980: The Mystery of the Aust Bronze Figures from Aust Cliff. *BARG Rev.* 1, 40–1.

Dehn, W. 1961: Zangentore an Spätkeltischen Oppida. *Pamatky Archaeologicke* 52(2), 390.

Dehn, W. and Frey, O.H. 1962: Die absolute Chronologie der Hallstatt- und Frühlatenezeit Mitteleuropas auf Grund des Südimports. *Atti VI° Cong. Int. Scienze Preist. e Protoist, 1 (Relazioni generali)*, 197–208.

Denford, G.T. 1975: Economy and location of Bronze Age 'arable' settlements on Dartmoor. *BLIA* 12, 175–96.

Dennell, R.W. 1976: Prehistoric crop cultivation in Southern England: a reconsideration. *Antiq. Journ.* 56, 11–23.

Dent, J.S. 1978. Wetwang Slack. *Current Arch.* 6, 46–50.

Dent, J.S. 1982: Cemeteries and settlement patterns of the Iron Age on the Yorkshire Wolds. *PPS* 48, 437–57.

Dent, J.S. 1984: Weapons, wounds and war in the Iron Age. *Arch. Journ.* 140 (1983), 120–8.

Dent, J.S. 1985: Three cart burials from Wetwang, Yorkshire. *Antiquity* 59, 85–92.

Dimbleby, G.W. 1965: Post-glacial changes in soil profiles. *Proc. Royal Soc. London* 161, 355–62.

Dimbleby, G.W. and Gill, J.M. 1955: The occurrence of podzols under deciduous woodland in the New Forest. *Forestry* 28, 95–106.

Dixon, P. 1972a: Crickley Hill, 1969–71. *Antiquity* 46, 49–52.

Dixon, P. 1972b: *Crickley Hill, fourth report, 1972* (duplicated).

Dixon, P. 1973: *Crickley Hill, fifth report, 1973* (duplicated).

Dixon, P. 1976: Crickley Hill, 1969–72. In Harding, D.W. (ed.) 1976b, 162–76.

Dixon, P. and Borne, P. 1977: *Crickley Hill and Gloucestershire Prehistory* (Gloucester).

Dixon, T.N. 1982: A survey of crannogs in Loch Tay. *PSAS* 112, 17–38.

Donovan, H.E. and Dunning, G.C. 1936: The Iron Age pottery and Saxon burials at Foxcote Manor, Andoversford, Gloucestershire. *TBGAS* 58, 157–70.

Dowden, W.A. 1957: Little Solisbury Hill Camp. *PBUSS* 8, 18–29.

Dowden, W.A. 1962: Little Solisbury Hill Camp. *PBUSS* 9, 177–82.

Downey, R., King, A. and Soffe, G. 1979: *The Hayling Island temple: third interim report on the excavation of the Iron Age and Roman Temple 1976–9* (duplicated).

Drew, C.D. 1935: A Late Bronze Age hoard from Lulworth, Dorset. *Antiq. Journ.* 15, 449–51.

Drewett, P.L. (ed.) 1978: *Archaeology in Sussex to AD 1500* (CBA Res. Rep. 29: London).

Drewett, P. 1980: Black Patch and the Later Bronze Age in Sussex. In Barrett J. and Bradley, R. (eds) 1980c, 377–96.

Drewett, P. 1982: Later Bronze Age downland economy and excavation at Black Patch, East Sussex. *PPS* 48, 321–400.

Drury, P.J. 1973: Little Waltham. *Current Arch.* 36, 10–13.

Drury, P. 1978: *Excavations at Little Waltham 1970–71* (CBA Res. Rep. 26: London).

Drury, P.J. and Rodwell, W.J. 1973: Excavations at Gun Hill, West Tilbury. *TEAS* 5, 48–112.

Dryden, H. 1845: Roman and Romano-British remains at and near Shefford, Co. Beds. *Pubs. Cambs. Arch. Soc.* 1 (1840–6), no. 8, 184.

Dudley, D. 1957: An excavation at Bodrifty, Mulfa Hill, near Penzance, Cornwall. *Arch. Journ.* 113 (1956), 1–32.

Dudley, D. and Jope, E.M. 1965: An Iron Age cist-burial with two brooches from Trevone, north Cornwall. *Cornish Arch.* 4, 18–23.

Dunning, G.C. 1931: Salmonsbury Camp, Gloucestershire. *Antiquity* 5, 489–91.

Dunning, G.C. 1934: The swan's-neck and ring-headed pin of the Early Iron Age in Britain. *Arch. Journ.* 91, 269–95.

Dunning, G.C. 1976: Salmonsbury, Burton-on-the-Water, Gloucestershire. In Harding, D.W. (ed.) 1976b, 76–118.

Dunning, G.C., Hooley, W. and Tildesley, M.L. 1929: Excavation of an Early Iron Age village on Worthy Down, Winchester. *PHFC* 10, 178–92.

Dyer, J.F. 1961: Dray's Ditches, Bedfordshire, and Early Iron Age territorial boundaries in the eastern Chilterns. *Antiq. Journ.* 41, 32–43.

Dyer, J.F. 1970: *Ravensburgh Castle excavations 1970* (duplicated: Putteridge Bury College of Education, Luton).

Dyer, J.F. 1976a: The Bedfordshire region in the first millennium BC. *Beds. AJ* 11, 7–18.

Dyer, J.F. 1976b: Ravensburgh Castle, Hertfordshire. In Harding, D.W. (ed.) 1976b, 153–61.

Dymond, C.W. 1902: *Worlebury, an Ancient Stronghold in the County of Somerset* (Bristol).

Eagles, B.N. and Evison, V.I. 1970: Excavations at Harrold, Bedfordshire, 1951–53. *Beds. AJ* 5, 17–55.

Earwood, C. 1988: Wooden containers and other wooden artefacts from the Glastonbury Lake Village. *Somerset Levels Paper* 14, 83–94.

Eddy, M.R. 1983: Excavations on the Braintree Earthworks, 1976 and 1979. *Essex Arch. Hist.* 15, 36–53.

Ehrenreich, R. 1985: *Trade, technology and the ironworking community in the Iron Age of Southern Britain* (BAR Brit. Ser. 144: Oxford).

E.L.B. 1862: Bronze articles supposed to be spoons. *Arch. Camb.* 8, 208–19.

Ellis, F. 1900: An ancient bronze figure from Aust Cliff, Gloucestershire. *TBGAS* 23, 323–5.

Ellison, A. 1978: The Bronze Age of Sussex. In Drewett, P. (ed.) 1978, 30–7.

Ellison, A. 1980a: Deverel-Rimbury urn cemeteries: the evidence for social organization. In Barrett, J. and Bradley, R. (eds) 1980c, 115–26.

Ellison, A. 1980b: Settlements and Regional exchange: a case study. In Barrett, J. and Bradley, R. (eds) 1980c, 127–40.

Ellison, A. 1981: Towards a socio-economic model for the Middle Bronze Age in southern England. In Hodder, I., Isaac, G. and Hammond, N. (eds), *Pattern of the Past: studies in honour of David Clarke* (Cambridge), 413–38.

Ellison, A. 1987: The Bronze Age Settlement at Thorny Down: pots, post-holes and patterning. *PPS* 53, 385–92.

Ellison, A. and Drewett, P. 1971: Pits and post-holes in the British Early Iron Age: some alternative explanations. *PPS* 37, 183–94.

Ellison, A. and Rahtz, P. 1987: Excavations at Hog Cliff Hill, Maiden Newton, Dorset. *PPS* 53, 223–70.

Elsdon, S.M. 1975: *Stamped Iron Age Pottery* (BAR Brit. Ser. 10: Oxford).

Elsdon, S.M. 1976: The Influence of Iron Age Metalworking Techniques as seen on the Decoration of a Pottery Bowl from Hunsbury, Northants. *Northants. Arch.* 11, 163–5.

Elsdon, S.M. 1978: The pottery [from Carn Euny, Sancreed, Cornwall]. In Christie, P.M.L. 1978, 396–424.

Elsdon, S. and May, J. 1987: *The Iron Age pottery from Dragonby. A draft report* (Nottingham).

Eogan, G. 1974a: Pins of the Irish Late Bronze Age. *JRSAI* 104, 74–119.

Eogan, G. 1974b: Regionale Gruppierungen in der spätbronzezeit Irlands. *Arch. Korrespondenzbl.* 4, 319–27.

Erith, F.H. and Longworth, I. 1960: A Bronze Age urnfield on Vinces Farm, Ardleigh, Essex. *PPS* 26, 178–92.

Evans, A.J. 1890: On a Late-Celtic Urn-Field at Aylesford, Kent. *Archaeologia* 52, 315–88.

Evans, C. and Serjeantson, D. 1988: The backwater economy of a fen-edge community in the Iron Age: the Upper Delphs, Haddenham. *Antiquity* 62, 360–70.

Evans, J.G. 1972: *Land Snails in Archaeology* (London).

Evans, J.G. 1975: *The Environment of Early Man in the British Isles* (London).

Fairhurst, H. 1984: *Excavations at Crosskirk Broch, Caithness* (Soc. Ant. Scot. Monog. 3: Edinburgh).

Fairhurst, H. and Taylor, D.B. 1974: A Hut-Circle Settlement at Kilphedir, Sutherland. *PSAS* 103 (1970–1), 65–99.

Falconer, J.P.E. and Adams, S.B. 1935: Recent finds at Solisbury Hill Camp, near Bath. *PBUSS* 4, 133–222.

Farley, M. 1983: A mirror burial at Dorton, Bucks. *PPS* 49, 269–302.

Farrar, R.A.H. 1954: A Celtic burial with mirror-handle at West Bay near Bridport. *PDNHAS* 76, 90–4.

Farrar, R.A.H. 1963: Note on prehistoric and Roman salt industry. *PDNHAS* 84 (1962), 137–44.

Farrar, R.A.H. 1975: Prehistoric and Roman saltworks in Dorset. In De Brisay, K.W. and Evans, K.A. (eds.) 1975, 14–20.

Fasham, P.J. 1976: An Iron Age site in Micheldever Wood, R27. In Fasham, P.J. (ed.), *M3 Archaeology 1975* (Winchester), 10–15.

Fasham, P.J. 1985: *The Prehistoric settlement at Winnall Down, Winchester* (HFC Monog. 2: Winchester).

Fasham, P.J. 1987: *A Banjo enclosure in Micheldever Wood, Hampshire* (HFC Monog. 5: Winchester).

Fasham, P.J., Farwell, D.E. and Whinney, R.J.B. 1989: *The Archaeological site at Easton Lane, Winchester* (HFC Monog. 6: Winchester).

Feachem, R.W. 1958: The fortifications on Traprain Law. *PSAS* 89 (1955–6), 284–9.

Feachem, R.W. 1961: Glenachan Rig Homestead, Cardon, Peeblesshire. *PSAS* 92 (1958–9), 15–24.

Feachem, R.W. 1962: The palisaded settlements at Harehope, Peeblesshire: excavations 1960. *PSAS* 93 (1959–60), 174–91.

Feachem, R.W. 1963: Unenclosed platform settlements. *PSAS* 94 (1960–1), 79–85.

Feachem, R.W. 1966: The hill-forts of northern Britain. In Rivet, A.L.F. (ed.), 1966, 59–88.

Feachem, R.W. 1973: Ancient agriculture in the Highland of Britain. *PPS* 39, 332–53.

Fell, C.I. 1937: The Hunsbury hill-fort, Northants: a new survey of the material. *Arch. Journ.* 93, 57–100.

Fell, C.I. 1953: An Early Iron Age settlement at Linton, Cambridgeshire. *PCAS* 46 (1952), 31–42.

Fell, C.I. 1962: Shenbarrow Hill Camp, Stanton, Gloucestershire. *TBGAS* 80, 16–41.

Field, N. 1986: An Iron Age timber causeway at Fiskerton, Lincolnshire. *Fenland Research* 3 (1985–6), 49–53.

Fisher, A.R. 1985: Winklebury Hillfort: a study of artefact distributions from subsoil features. *PPS* 51, 167–80.

Fitzpatrick, A. 1984: The deposition of La Tène Iron Age metalwork in watery contexts in Southern England. In Cunliffe, B. and Miles, D. (eds) 1984, 178–90.

Fitzpatrick, A. 1985a: The distribution of Dressel 1 Amphorae in North-West Europe. *OJA* 4(3), 305–40.

Fitzpatrick, A. 1985b: The Iron Age Glass Bracelets from Castle Dore. *Cornish Arch.* 24, 133–40.

Fleming, A. 1978: The prehistoric landscape of Dartmoor: Part 1 South Dartmoor. *PPS* 44, 97–123.

Fleming, A. 1984: The prehistoric landscape of Dartmoor: wider implications. *Landscape History* 6, 5–19.

Fleming, A. 1988: *The Dartmoor Reaves* (London).

Fleming, A. and Collis, J. 1973: A late prehistoric reave system near Cholwich Town, Dartmoor. *PDAES* 31, 1–21.

Fletcher, M. and Lock, G. 1984: Post-built structures at Danebury Hillfort. An analytical search method with statistical discussion. *OJA* 3(2), 175–96.

Fojut, N. 1982a: Is Mousa a broch? *PSAS* 111, 220–8.

Fojut, N. 1982b: Towards a Geography of Shetland Brochs. *Glasgow Arch. Journ.* 9, 37–59.

Forde, Daryll C., Griffiths, W.E., Hogg, A.H.A. and Houlder, C.H. 1963: Excavations at Pen Dinas, Aberystwyth. *Arch. Camb.* 112, 125–53.

Forde-Johnston, J. 1964: Earl's Hill, Pontesbury, and related hill forts in England and Wales. *Arch. Journ.* 119 (1962), 66–91.

Forde-Johnston, J. 1976: *Hillforts of the Iron Age in England and Wales* (Liverpool).

Foster, J. 1977: *Bronze Boar Figurines in Iron Age and Roman Britain* (BAR Brit. Ser. 39: Oxford).

Foster, J. 1980: *The Iron Age Moulds from Gussage All Saints* (Brit. Mus. Occ. Paper 12: London).

Foster, J. 1986: *The Lexden Tumulus. A re-appraisal of an Iron Age burial from Colchester, Essex* (BAR Brit. Ser. 156: Oxford).

Fowler, M.J. 1954: The typology of the brooches of the Iron Age in Wessex. *Arch. Journ.* 110, 88–105.

Fowler, P.J. 1967: The archaeology of Fyfield and Overton Downs, Wiltshire. *WAM* 62, 16–33.

Fowler, P.J. 1970: Fieldwork and excavation in the Butcombe area, north Somerset. *PBUSS* 12(2), 169–94.

Fowler, P.J. 1983: *The Farming of prehistoric Britain* (Cambridge).

Fowler, P.J., Musty, J.W.G. and Taylor, C.C. 1965: Some earthwork enclosures in Wiltshire. *WAM* 60, 52–74.

Fox, A. 1953: Hill-slope forts and *Arch. Journ.* 109 (1952), 1–22.

Fox, A. 1955: Celtic fields and farms on Dartmoor, in the light of recent excavations at Kestor. *PPS* 20 (1954), 87–102.

Fox, A. 1956: Teignmouth. *TDA* 88, 216–7.

Fox, A. 1961a: An Iron Age bowl from Rose Ash, north Devon. *Antiq. Journ.* 41, 186–98.

Fox, A. 1961b: South western hillforts. In Frere, S.S. (ed.) 1961, 35–60.

Fox, A. 1964: *South West England* (London).

Fox, A. 1972: The Holcombe mirror. *Antiquity* 46, 293–6.

Fox, A. and Britton, D. 1970: A Continental Palstave from the Ancient Field System on Horridge Common, Dartmoor, England. *PPS* 35 (1969), 220–8.

Fox, A. and Pollard, S. 1973: A decorated bronze mirror from an Iron Age settlement at Holcombe, near Uplyme, Devon. *Antiq. Journ.* 53, 16–41.

Fox, A., Radford, R., Rogers, E.H. and Shorter, A.H. 1952: Report on the excavations at Milber Down, 1937–8. *PDAES* 4, 27–78.

Fox, C.F. 1923: *The Archaeology of the Cambridge Region* (Cambridge).

Fox, C.F. 1924: A settlement of the Early Iron Age at Abington Pigotts, Cambs, and its subsequent history as evidenced by objects preserved in the Pigott Collection. *PPSEA* 4, 211–33.

Fox, C.F. 1927: A la Tène I brooch from Wales: with notes on the typology and distribution of these brooches in Britain. *Arch. Camb.* 82, 67–112.

Fox, C.F. 1946: *A Find of the Early Iron Age from Llyn Cerrig Bach, Anglesey* (Cardiff).

Fox, C.F. 1958: *Pattern and Purpose: a Survey of Early Celtic Art in Britain* (Cardiff).

Fox, C.F. and Hull, M.R. 1948: The incised ornament on the Celtic mirror from Colchester, Essex. *Antiq. Journ.* 28, 123–37.

Fox, C.F. and Hyde, H.A. 1939: A second cauldron and an iron sword from the Llyn Fawr hoard, Rhigos, Glamorganshire. *Antiq. Journ.* 19, 369–404.

Fox, C.F. and Wolseley, G.R. 1928: The Early Iron Age site at Findon Park, Findon, Sussex. *Antiq. Journ.* 8, 449–60.

France, N.E. and Gobel, B.M. 1985: *The Romano-British Temple at Harlow* (Gloucester).

Frere, S.S. 1946: An Iron Age site at West Clandon, Surrey, and some aspects of Iron Age and Romano-British culture in the Wealden area. *Arch. Journ.* 101, 50–67.

Frere, S.S. 1954: Canterbury excavations, summer 1946, the Rose Lane sites. *Arch. Cant.* 68, 101–43.

Frere, S.S. (ed.) 1961: *The Problems of the Iron Age in Southern Britain* (London).

Frere, S.S. 1974: *Britannia* (London).

Frey, O.-H. 1976: Palmette and Circle: early Celtic art in Britain and its continental background. *PPS* 42, 47–66.

Fulford, M. 1986: *Silchester Excavations 1986* (Reading).

Fulford, M. 1987: *Calleva Atrebatum*: an interim report on the excavations of the oppidum, 1980–86. *PPS* 53, 271–8.

Galliou, P. 1982: *Corpus des amphores découvertes dans l'ouest de la France. Vol. 1, Les amphores tardo-républicaines* (Brest).

Galliou, P. 1984: Days of Wine and Roses? Early Armorica and the Atlantic Wine Trade. In Macready, S. and Thompson, F.H. (eds) 1984, 24–36.

Gardner, W. 1910: Pen-y-Corddyn, near Abergele. *Arch. Camb.* 10, 79–156.

Gardner, W. and Savory, H.N. 1964: *Dinorben: a Hillfort Occupied in Early Iron Age and Roman Times* (Cardiff).

Gates, T. 1983: Unenclosed settlements in Northumberland. In Chapman, R. and Mytum, H. (eds) 1983, 103–48.

Gelling, P.S. 1970: Excavations at Pilsdon Pen, 1969. *PDNHAS* 91 (1969), 177–8.

Gelling, P.S. 1971: Excavation at Pilsdon Pen, 1970. *PDNHAS* 92 (1970), 126–7.

Gelling, P.S. 1972: Excavations at Pilsdon Pen hillfort, 1971. *PDNHAS* 93 (1971), 133–4.

Gelling, P.S. 1977: Excavations at Pilsdon Pen, Dorset, 1964–71. *PPS* 43, 263–86.

Gent, H. 1983: Centralized storage in later prehistoric Britain. *PPS* 49, 243–67.

Gerloff, S. 1981: Westeuropäische Griffzungenschwerter in Berlin. *Acta praehistorica et archaeologica* 11/12, 183–217.

Gerloff, S. 1987: Bronze Age Class A Cauldrons: typology, origins and chronology. *JRSAI* 116 (1986), 84–115.

Gibson-Hill, J. 1980: Cylindrical shaft furnaces of the early Wealden Iron industry: *c.* 100 BC–AD 300. *J. Hist. Metall.* 14, 21–7.

Gingell, C. 1979: The Bronze and Iron Hoard from Melksham and another Wiltshire find. In Burgess, C. and Coombs, D. (eds) 1979, 245–52.

Gingell, C. 1980: The Marlborough Downs in the Bronze Age: The first results of current research. In Barrett, J. and Bradley, R. (eds) 1980c, 209–22.

Gingell, C. 1982: Excavation of an Iron Age Enclosure at Groundwell Farm, Blunsdon St Andrew, 1976–7. *WAM* 76, 33–75.

Gingell, C. and Lawson, A.J. 1984: The Potterne Project: Excavation and Research at a Major Settlement of the Late Bronze Age. *WAM* 78, 31–4.

Giot, P.R. 1960: *Brittany* (London).

Godwin, H. 1941: Studies of the post-glacial history of British vegetation. VI. Correlations in the Somerset levels. *New Phytologist* 40, 108–32.

Godwin, H. 1955: Studies of the post-glacial history of British vegetation. XIII. The Meare Pool region of the Somerset levels. *Phil. Trans. Royal Soc.* 239, B662, 161–90.

Godwin, H. 1960: Prehistoric wooden trackways of the Somerset levels: their construction, age and relation to climatic change. *PPS* 26, 1–36.

Gordon, A.S.R. 1941: The excavation of Gurnard's Head, an Iron Age cliff castle in western Cornwall. *Arch. Journ.* 97, 96–111.

Gordon, M. 1969: Duns and forts – a note on some Iron Age monuments of the Atlantic province. *Scottish Arch. Forum 1969*, 41–52.

Grant, A. 1984a: Animal husbandry [at Danebury, Hants.]. In Cunliffe, B. 1984a, 496–548.

Grant, A. 1984b: Animal husbandry in Wessex and the Thames Valley. In Cunliffe, B. and Miles, D. (eds) 1984, 102–19.

Grant, A. 1988: Bone deposition and animal husbandry: The animal bone remains [from Mount Batten, Plymouth, Devon]. In Cunliffe, B. 1988b, 28–35.

Grant, E. 1986: Hill-forts, central places and territories. In Grant, E. (ed.), *Central places, archaeology and history* (Sheffield), 13–26.

Gray, H.StG. 1925: Excavations at Ham Hill, south Somerset (part 1). *PSANHS* 70, 104–16.

Gray, H.StG. 1926: Excavations at Ham Hill, south Somerset (part 2). *PSANHS* 71, 57–76.

Gray, H.StG. 1927: Excavations at Ham Hill, south Somerset (part 3). *PSANHS* 72, 55–68.

Gray, H.StG. 1930: Excavations at Kingsdown Camp, near Mells, Somerset. *Archaeologia* 80, 59–96.

Gray, H.StG. 1933: Trial-excavations in the so-called 'Danish camp' at Wareham, near Wells, Norfolk. *Antiq. Journ.* 13, 399–413.

Gray, H.StG. 1940: Metal vessels found on Shapwick Heath, Somerset. *PSANHS* 85 (1939), 191–202.

Gray, J.W. and Brewer, G.W.S. 1904: Evidence of ancient occupation on Cleeve Hill, near Cheltenham. *P. Cott. NHFC* 15, 49–57.

Grealey, S., Jones, G.D.B. and Little, J.H. 1972: Excavations at Castell Coyan 1971, an interim report. *Carm. Ant.* 8, 17–22.

Green, C. 1949: The Birdlip Early Iron Age burials: a review. *PPS* 15, 188–90.

Green, H.S. 1981: The dating of Ivinghoe Beacon. *Rec. of Bucks.* 23, 1–3.

Green, H.S. 1985: The Llyn Fawr hoard: two new finds. *BBCS* 32, 288–9.

Green, M. 1986: *The Gods of the Celts* (London).

Green, T.K. 1979: The Fécamp-style refortification of High Rocks. *SAC* 117, 37–46.

Greenwell, W. 1877: *British Barrows* (Oxford).

Greenwell, W. 1906: Early Iron Age burials in Yorkshire. *Archaeologia* 60, 251–324.

Greenwell, W. and Gatty, R.A. 1910: The pit dwelling at Holderness. *Man* 10 (48).

Greig, C. 1972: Cullykhan. *Current Arch.* 32, 227–31.

Gresham, C.A. 1939: Spettisbury Rings, Dorset. *Arch. Journ.* 96, 114–31.

Gresham, C.A. 1973: Dr Gerhard Bersu's Excavations in Cwm Ystradllyn. *Arch. Camb.* 121 (1972), 51–60.

Griffith, F.M. 1985: A *nemeton* in Devon. *Antiquity* 59, 121–4.

Griffiths, W.E. and Hogg, A.H.A. 1957: The hill-fort on Conway Mountain, Caernarvonshire. *Arch. Camb.* 105 (1956), 49–80.

Grimes, W.F. 1944: Excavations at Stanton Harcourt, Oxon., 1940. *Oxon.* 8–9 (1943–4), 19–63.

Grimes, W.F. 1951: *The Prehistory of Wales* (Cardiff).

Grimes, W.F. 1953: Art on British Iron Age pottery. *PPS* 18, 160–75.

Grimes, W.F. 1961: Draughton, Colsterworth and Heathrow. In Frere, S.S. (ed.) 1961, 21–8.

Groube, L. 1981: Black holes in British Prehistory: The analysis of settlement distributions. In Hodder, I., Isaac, G. and Hammond, N. (eds), *Pattern of the Past: Studies in honour of David Clarke* (Cambridge), 185–209.

Guido, M. 1974: A Scottish Crannog redated. *Antiquity* 48, 54–5.

Guido, M. 1978: *The glass beads of the prehistoric and Roman periods in Britain and Ireland* (Soc. Ant. Res. Rep. 35: London).

Guilbert, G. 1973: Moel y Gaer, Rhose Mor. *Current Arch.* 37, 38–44.

Guilbert, G. 1974: Llanstephan Castle: 1973 Interim Report. *Carm. Ant.* 10, 37–48.

Guilbert, G. 1975a: Moel y Gaer, 1973: an area excavation on the defences. *Antiquity* 49, 109–17.

Guilbert, G. 1975b: Planned Hill-fort Interiors. *PPS* 41, 203–21.

Guilbert, G. 1975c: Ratlinghope/Stitt Hill, Shropshire: earthwork enclosures and cross-dykes. *BBCS* 26, 363–73.

Guilbert, G. 1976: Moel y Gaer (Rhosemor) 1972–1973: an area excavation in the interior. In Harding, D.W. (ed.) 1976b, 303–17.

Guilbert, G. 1979a: Dinorben 1977–8. *Current Arch.* 6, 182–8.

Guilbert, G. 1979b: The Guard-chamber Gateways at Dinorben and Moel Hiraddug Hill-forts, and the Problem of Dating the Type in North Wales. *BBCS* 28, 516–20.

Guilbert, G. 1980: Dinorben C14 dates. *Current Arch.* 6, 336–8.

Guilbert, G. 1981: Double-ring roundhouses, probable and possible in prehistoric Britain. *PPS* 47, 299–311.

Guthrie, A. 1969: Excavation of a settlement at Goldherring, Sancreed, 1958–61. *Cornish Arch.* 8, 5–39.

Hachmann, R. 1976: The problem of the Belgae seen from the continent. *BLIA* 13, 117–38.

Haggarty, A. and G. 1983: Excavations at Rispain Camp, Whithorn, 1978–81. *TDGNHAS* 58, 21–51.

Hall, D.N. 1971: Pre-Roman Iron Age sites at Bozeat and Strixton, Northamptonshire. *Beds. AJ* 6, 17–22.

Hall, D.N. 1981: The changing landscape of the Cambridgeshire silt fens. *Landscape History* 3, 37–49.

Hall, D.N. 1987: *Fenland landscapes and settlement between Peterborough and March. East Anglian Arch.* 35.

Hall, D.N. and Hutchings, J.B. 1972: The distribution of archaeological sites between the Nene and the Ouse valleys. *Beds. AJ* 7, 1–16.

Hall, D.N. and Nickerson, N. 1969: Iron Age pottery from North Bedfordshire and South Northamptonshire. *Beds. AJ* 6, 1–12.

Halliday, S.P. 1982: Later prehistoric farming in south-east Scotland. In Harding, D.W. (ed.) 1982, 75–91.

Hamilton, J.R.C. 1956: *Excavations at Jarlshof, Shetland* (Edinburgh).

Hamilton, J.R.C. 1962: Brochs and broch builders. In Wainwright, F.T. (ed.), *The Northern Isles* (London), 53–90.

Hamilton, J.R.C. 1966: Forts, brochs and wheel-houses in northern Scotland. In Rivet, A.L.F. (ed.) 1966, 111–30.

Hamilton, J.R.C. 1968: *Excavations at Clickhimin, Shetland* (London).

Hamilton, S. 1984: Earlier first millennium pottery from the excavations at Hollingbury Camp, Sussex, 1967–9. *SAC* 122, 55–61.

Hamlin, A. 1968: Early Iron Age sites at Stanton Harcourt. *Oxon.* 31 (1966), 1–27.

Hanworth, R. and Tomlin, D.J. 1977: *Brooklands, Weybridge: The excavation of an Iron Age and Medieval site, 1964–5 and 1970–71* (Res. Vol. Surrey Arch. Soc. 4: Guildford).

Harbison, P. 1971: Wooden and stone chevaux-de-frise in Central and Western Europe. *PPS* 37, 195–225.

Harbison, P. and Laing, L. 1974: *Some Iron Age Mediterranean Imports in England* (BAR Brit. Ser. 5: Oxford).

Harden, D.B. 1942: Excavations in Smith's Pit II, Cassington, Oxon. *Oxon.* 7, 104–7.

Harden, D.B. 1950: Italic and Etruscan finds from Britain. *Atti I Congr. Preist. e Protoist. Mediterr.* (Florence), 315–24.

Harding, A.F. (ed.) 1982: *Climatic change in later prehistory* (Edinburgh).

Harding, D.W. 1968: The pottery from Kirtlington, and its implications for the chronology of the earliest Iron Age in the Upper Thames region. *Oxon.* 31 (1966), 158–61.

Harding, D.W. 1972: *The Iron Age in the Upper Thames Basin* (Oxford).

Harding, D.W. 1974: *The Iron Age in Lowland Britain* (London).

Harding, D.W. 1976a: Blewburton Hill, Berkshire: Re-excavation and reappraisal. In Harding, D.W. (ed.) 1976b, 133–46.

Harding, D.W. (ed.) 1976b: *Hillforts. Later Prehistoric Earthworks in Britain and Ireland* (London).

Harding, D.W. (ed.) 1982: *Later prehistoric settlement in south-east Scotland* (Edinburgh University: Occ. Paper 8).

Harding, D.W. and Blake, I.M. 1963: An Early Iron Age settlement in Dorset. *Antiquity* 37, 63–4.

Harding, J.M. 1964: Interim report on the excavation of a Late Bronze Age homestead in Weston Wood, Albury, Surrey. *Sy. AC* 61, 29–38.

Hardy, H.R. and Curwen, E.C. 1937: An Iron Age pottery site near Horsted Keynes. *SAC* 78, 252–65.

Hartley, B.R. 1957: The Wandlebury Iron Age hill fort, excavations of 1955–6. *PCAS* 50, 1–28.

Hartridge, R. 1978: Excavations at the Prehistoric and Romano-British Site on Slonk Hill, Shoreham. *SAC* 116, 69–142.

Haselgrove, C. 1978: *Supplementary gazetteer of find-spots of Celtic coins in Britain 1977* (London).

Haselgrove, C. 1982: Indigenous settlement patterns in the Tyne-Tees Lowlands. In Clack, P. and Haselgrove, S. (eds), *Rural Settlement in the Roman North* (Durham), 57–104.

Haselgrove, C. 1983: Celtic Coins found in Britain 1977–82. *BLIA* 20, 107–54.

Haselgrove, C. 1984a: The Later pre-Roman Iron Age between the Humber and the Tyne. In Wilson, P.R., Jones, R.F. and Evans, D.M. (eds), *Settlement and Society in the Roman North* (Bradford), 9–26.

Haselgrove, C. 1984b: 'Romanization' before the Conquest: Gaulish Precedents and British Consequences. In Blagg, T.F.C. and King, A.C. (eds), *Military and Civilian in Roman Britain* (BAR Brit. Ser. 136: Oxford), 5–63.

Haselgrove, C. 1987: *Iron Age coinage in South-East England: the archaeological context* (BAR Brit. Ser. 174: Oxford).

Haselgrove, C. 1989: Iron Age coin deposition at Harlow Temple, Essex. *OJA* 8(1), 73–88.

Haselgrove, C.C. and Allon, V.L. 1982: An Iron Age settlement at West House, Coxhoe, County Durham. *Arch. Ael.*[5] 10, 25–51.

Haselgrove, C.C. and Turnbull, P. 1983: *Stanwick excavations and fieldwork. Interim report 1981–3* (Univ. Durham Dept. Arch. Occ. Paper 4).

Haselgrove, C. and Turnbull, P. 1985: *Stanwick: excavation and fieldwork. Second Interim Report 1984* (Durham: Occ. Paper 5).

Haselgrove, C. and Turnbull, P. 1987: *Stanwick: Excavation and Research. Interim Report 1985–86* (Durham: Occ. Paper 8).

Hastings, F. and Cunliffe, B. 1966: Excavation of an Iron Age farmstead at Hawk's Hill, Leatherhead. *Sy. AC* 62, 1–43.

Hatt, J-J. 1960: Note in *Gallia* 18, 245–6, fig. 68.

Hawkes, C.F.C. 1931: Hill forts. *Antiquity* 5, 60–97.

Hawkes, C.F.C. 1935: The pottery from the sites on Plumpton Plain. *PPS* 1, 39–59.

Hawkes, C.F.C. 1936a: The excavations at Buckland Rings, Lymington, 1935. *PHFC* 13, 124–64.

Hawkes, C.F.C. 1936b: The Twyford Down village, the abandonment of St. Catharine's Hill and the first settlement of Winchester. *PHFC* 13, 208–12.

Hawkes, C.F.C. 1939a: The Caburn pottery and its implications. *SAC* 80, 217–62.

Hawkes, C.F.C. 1939b: The excavations at Quarley Hill, 1938. *PHFC* 14, 136–94.

Hawkes, C.F.C. 1939c: The pottery from Castle Hill, Newhaven. *SAC* 80, 269–92.

Hawkes, C.F.C. 1940a: The excavations at Bury Hill, 1939. *PHFC* 14, 291–337.

Hawkes, C.F.C. 1940b: The Marnian pottery and La Tène I brooch from Worth, Kent. *Antiq. Journ.* 20, 115–21.

Hawkes, C.F.C. 1940c: A site of the Late Bronze–Early Iron Age transition at Totternhoe, Beds. *Antiq. Journ.* 20, 487–91.

Hawkes, C.F.C. 1948: Britons, Romans and Saxons round Salisbury and in Cranborne Chase. *Arch. Journ.* 104 (1947), 27–81.

Hawkes, C.F.C. 1956: The British Iron Age: cultures, chronology and peoples. *Cong. Int. Sciences Pré- et Protohistoriques, Actes de la IV Session* (Madrid 1954), 729–37.

Hawkes, C.F.C. 1959: The ABC of the British Iron Age. *Antiquity* 33, 170–82.

Hawkes, C.F.C. 1961: The western Third C culture and the Belgic Dobunni. In Clifford, E.M. 1961, 43–74.

Hawkes, C.F.C. 1966: Appendix to Brooks, R.T., The Rumps, St. Minver: second interim report on the 1965 season. *Cornish Arch.* 5, 9–10.

Hawkes, C.F.C. 1968: New thoughts on the Belgae. *Antiquity* 42, 6–16.

Hawkes, C.F.C. 1976: St. Catharine's Hill, Winchester: the Report of 1930 re-assessed. In Harding, D.W. (ed.) 1976b, 59–75.

Hawkes, C.F.C. 1977: Britain and Julius Caesar. *Proc. Brit. Acad.* 63, 125–92.

Hawkes, C.F.C. 1978: *Pytheas: Europe and the Greek Explorers* (London).

Hawkes, C.F.C. 1984: Ictis disentangled, and the British tin trade. *OJA* 3(2), 211–33.

Hawkes, C.F.C. and Dunning, G.C. 1931: The Belgae of Gaul and Britain. *Arch. Journ.* 87, 150–335.

Hawkes, C.F.C. and Dunning, G.C. 1932: The second Belgic invasion. *Antiq. Journ.* 12, 411–30.

Hawkes, C.F.C. and Fell, C.I. 1945: The Early Iron Age settlement at Fengate, Peterborough. *Arch. Journ.* 100, 188–223.

Hawkes, C.F.C. and Hull, M.R. 1947: *Camulodunum* (Soc. Ant. Res. Rep. 14: Oxford).

Hawkes, C.F.C., Myres, J.N.L. and Stevens, C.G. 1930: *St. Catharine's Hill, Winchester* (Winchester: reprinted from *PHFC* 11 (1930)).

Hawkes, C.F.C. and Smith, M.A. 1957: On some buckets and cauldrons of the Bronze and Early Iron Ages. *Antiq. Journ.* 37, 131–98.

Hawkes, J. 1940: The excavations at Balksbury, 1939. *PHFC* 14, 338–45.

Hawkes, S.C. 1961: Longbridge Deverill, Cow Down, Wilts. *PPS* 27, 346–7.

Hawkes, S.C. 1964: *Some Belgic Brooches from South Ferriby* (Hull Museum's Publications, no. 214).

Hawkes, S.C. 1970: Finds from two Middle Bronze Age pits at Winnall, Winchester, Hampshire. *PHFC* 26 (1969), 5–18.

Hawkes, S.C. 1975: A Rare Bronze Escutcheon from Canterbury. *KAR* 41, 5–8.

Hawley, W. 1927: Further excavations on Park Brow. *Archaeologia* 76, 30–40.

Hayes, R.H., Hemingway, J.E. and Spratt, D.A. 1980: The distribution and lithology of beehive querns in N.E. Yorkshire. *J. Arch. Sci.* 7, 297–334.

Head, J.F. and Piggott, C.M. 1944: An Iron Age site at Bledlow, Bucks. *Rec. of Bucks.* 14, 189–209.

Hedges, J. and Buckley, D. 1978: Excavations at a Neolithic causewayed enclosure, Orsett, Essex 1975. *PPS* 44, 219–308.

Hedges, J.W. 1985: The Broch period. In Renfrew, C. (ed.), *The Prehistory of Orkney* (Edinburgh), 150–75.

Hedges, J.W. 1987: *Bu, Gurness and the Brochs of Orkney* (BAR Brit. Ser. 163: Oxford).

Hedges, J.W. and Bell, B. 1980a: The Howe. *Current Arch.* 73, 48–51.

Hedges, J.W. and Bell, B. 1980b: That tower of Scottish prehistory – the broch. *Antiquity* 54, 87–94.

Hedges, R.E.M. and Salter, C.J. 1979: Source determination of iron currency bars through analysis of the slag inclusions. *Archaeometry* 21(2), 161–76.

Helbaek, H. 1953: Early crops in southern England. *PPS* 18 (1952), 194–233.

Hemp, W.J. 1928: A La Tène shield from Moel Hiraddug, Flintshire. *Arch. Camb.* 83, 253–84.

Hencken, H. O'Neill 1932: *The Archaeology of Cornwall and Scilly* (London).

Hencken, H. O'Neill 1933: An excavation by H.M. Office of Works at Chysauster, Cornwall, 1931. *Archaeologia* 83, 237–84.

Hencken, T.C. 1938: The excavation of the Iron Age camp on Bredon Hill, Worcestershire, 1935–37. *Arch. Journ.* 95, 1–111.

Henderson, J. 1981: A report on the glass excavated from Meare Village West 1979. In Orme, B.J., Coles, J.M., Caseldine, A.E. and Bailey, G.N. 1981, 55–60.

Henderson, J. 1985: The Glass from Castle Dore: archaeological and chemical significance. *Cornish Arch.* 24, 141–8.

Henderson, J. 1987a: Glass [from Hengistbury Head, Dorset]. In Cunliffe, B. 1987, 160–3.

Henderson, J. 1987b: The Iron Age of 'Loughey' and Meare: some inferences from glass analysis. *Antiq. Journ.* 67, 29–42.

Henderson, J. and Warren, S.E. 1981: X-ray fluorescence analysis of Iron Age glass: beads from Meare and Glastonbury lake villages. *Archaeometry* 23, 83–94.

Henshall, A.S. 1950: Textiles and weaving appliances in prehistoric Britain. *PPS* 16, 130–62.

Heslop, D.H. 1983: The excavation of an Iron Age settlement at Thorpe Thewles. In *Recent Excavations in Cleveland* (Cleveland), 16–26.

Heslop, D.H. 1987: *The Excavation of an Iron Age Settlement at Thorpe Thewles, Cleveland 1980–1982* (CBA Res. Rep. 65: London).

Higham, N. 1987: Brigantia Revisited. *Northern History* 23, 1–19.

Hill, P.H. 1982a: Broxmouth Hill-fort excavations, 1977–78: an interim report. In Harding, D.W. (ed.) 1982, 141–88.

Hill, P.H. 1982b: Settlement and chronology. In Harding, D.W. (ed.) 1982, 4–43.

Hill, P.H. 1984: A sense of proportion: a contribution to the study of double-ring round houses. *Scottish Arch. Rev.* 3, 80–6.

Hillman, G. 1981: Reconstructing crop husbandry practices from charred remains of crops. In Mercer, R. (ed.) 1981, 123–62.

Hinchliffe, J. and Thomas, R. 1980: Archaeological Investigations at Appleford. *Oxon.* 45, 9–111.

Hingley, R. 1984a: The archaeology of settlement and the social significance of space. *Scottish Arch. Rev.* 3, 22–7.

Hingley, R. 1984b: Towards social analysis in archaeology: Celtic society in the Iron Age of the Upper Thames Valley. In Cunliffe, B. and Miles, D. (eds) 1984, 72–88.

Hingley, R. 1989: Iron Age Settlement and Society in Central and Southern Warwickshire. In Gibson, A. (ed.), *Midlands Prehistory* (BAR Brit. Ser. 204: Oxford), 122–57.

Hingley, R. and Miles, D. 1984: Aspects of Iron Age settlement in the Upper Thames Valley. In Cunliffe, B. and Miles, D. (eds) 1984, 52–71.

Hirst, F.C. 1936: Excavations at Porthmeor, Cornwall. *JRIC* 24, 1 ff.

Hodder, I. 1977: How are we to study distributions of Iron Age material. In Collis, J. (ed.) 1977, 8–16.

Hodson, F.R. 1960: Reflections on the 'ABC' of the British Iron Age. *Antiquity* 34, 138–40.

Hodson, F.R. 1962: Some pottery from Eastbourne, the 'Marnians' and the pre-Roman Iron Age in southern England. *PPS* 28, 140–55.

Hodson, F.R. 1964: Cultural groupings within the British pre-Roman Iron Age. *PPS* 30, 99–110.

Hodson, F.R. 1968: The La Tène cemetery at Münsingen-am-Rain. *Acta Bernensia* 5.

Hodson, F.R. 1971: Three Iron Age brooches from Hammersmith. In Sieveking, G. de G. (ed.), 1971, (London), 50–6.

Hogg, A.H.A. 1942: Excavations in a native settlement at Ingram Hill, Northumberland. *Arch. Ael.*[4] 20, 110–33.

Hogg, A.H.A. 1956: Further excavations at Ingram Hill. *Arch. Ael.*[4] 34, 150–60.

Hogg, A.H.A. 1962: Garn Boduan and Tre'r Ceiri, excavations at two Caernarvonshire hill forts. *Arch. Journ.* 117 (1960), 1–39.

Hogg, A.H.A. 1965: Early Iron Age Wales. In Foster, I.Ll. and Daniel, G. (eds), *Prehistoric and Early Wales* (London), chapter V.

Hogg, A.H.A. 1966: Native settlements in Wales. In Thomas, A.C. (ed.) 1966b, 28–38.

Hogg, A.H.A. 1971: Some applications of surface fieldwork. In Jesson, M. and Hill, D. (eds) 1971, 105–26.

Hogg, A.H.A. 1974: Excavations at Harding's Down West Fort, Gower. *Arch. Camb.* 122 (1973), 55–68.

Hogg, A.H.A. 1975: *Hill-forts of Britain* (London).

Hogg, A.H.A. 1976: Hillforts in Herefordshire. *TWNFC* 41 (1973), 14–21.

Hogg, A.H.A. 1977: Castle Ditches, Llancarfan, Glamorgan. *Arch. Camb.* 125 (1976), 13–39.

Hogg, A.H.A. 1979: *British Hill-forts: An Index* (BAR Brit. Ser. 62: Oxford).

Holden, E.W. 1972: A Bronze Age Cemetery-Barrow on Itford Hill, Beddingham. *SAC* 110, 70–117.

Holleyman, G.A. 1937: Harrow Hill excavations, 1936. *SAC* 78, 230–52.

Holleyman, G.A. and Curwen, E.C. 1935: Late Bronze Age lynchet-settlements on Plumpton Plain, Sussex. *PPS* 1, 16–38.

Holmes, J. 1984: Excavations at Hollingsbury Camp, Sussex 1967–9. *SAC* 122, 29–53.

Holmes, J. and Frend, W.H.C. 1959: A Belgic chieftain's grave on Hertford Heath. *E. Herts. Arch. Soc. Trans.* 14, part 1, 1–19.

Holmes, T.Rice. 1907: *Ancient Britain and the Invasions of Julius Caesar* (Oxford).

Hughes, M.J. 1972: A technical study of opaque red glass of the Iron Age in Britain. *PPS* 38, 98–107.

Hull, M.R. and Hawkes, C.F.C. 1987: *Corpus of Ancient Brooches in Britain. Pre-Roman bow brooches* (BAR Brit. Ser. 168: Oxford).

Hunn, J.R. 1980: The Earthworks of Prae Wood. *Britannia* 11, 21–30.

Hurst, J.D. and Wills, J. 1987: A 'horn-cap' mould from Beckford, Worcestershire. *PPS* 53, 492–3.

Hüssen, C-M. 1983: *A rich late La Tène burial at Hertford Heath, Hertfordshire* (Brit. Mus. Occ. Paper 44: London).

Inman, R., Brown, D.R., Goddard, R.E. and Spratt, D.A. 1985: Roxby Iron Age settlement and the Iron Age in north-east Yorkshire. *PPS* 51, 181–213.

Jackson, D.A. 1974: Two new pit alignments and a hoard of currency bars from Northampton-shire. *Northants. Arch.* 9, 13–45.

Jackson, D.A 1975: An Iron Age Site at Twywell, Northamptonshire. *Northants. Arch.* 10, 31–93.

Jackson, D.A. 1977: Further excavations at Aldwincle, Northamptonshire, 1969–71. *Northants. Arch.* 12, 9–54.

Jackson, D.A. 1978: Excavation at Wakerley, Northants., 1972–5. *Britannia* 9, 115–242.

Jackson, D.A. 1983: The excavation of an Iron Age site at Brigstock, Northants. *Northants. Arch.* 18, 7–32.

Jackson, D. and Dix, B. 1989: Late Iron Age and Roman settlement at Weekley, Northants. *Northants. Arch.* 21 (1986–7), 41–58.

Jarrett, M.G. and Wrathmell, S. 1981: *An Iron Age and Roman Farmstead in South Glamorgan* (Cardiff).

Jervise, A. 1863: An account of the excavation of the round or 'bee-hive' shaped house and other underground chambers at West Grange of Conan, Forfarshire. *PSAS* 4 (1860–2), 492–9.

Jesson, M. and Hill, D. (eds) 1971: *The Iron Age and its Hill-forts* (Southampton).

Jessup, R.F. and Cook, N.C. 1936: Excavations at Bigberry Camp, Harbledown. *Arch. Cant.* 48, 151–68.

Jobey, G. 1959: Excavation at a native settlement at Huckhoe, Northumberland. *Arch. Ael.*[4] 37, 217–78.

Jobey, G. 1962a: An Iron Age homestead at West Brandon, Durham. *Arch. Ael.*[4] 40, 1–34.

Jobey, G. 1962b: A note on scooped enclosures in Northumberland. *Arch. Ael.*[4] 40, 47–58.

Jobey, G. 1965: Hillforts and settlements in Northumberland. *Arch. Ael.*[4] 43, 21–64.

Jobey, G. 1966a: A field survey in Northumberland. In Rivet, A.L.F. (ed.) 1966, 89–110.

Jobey, G. 1966b: Homesteads and settlements of the frontier area. In Thomas, A.C. (ed.) 1966b, 1–14.

Jobey, G. 1970: An Iron Age settlement and homestead at Burradon, Northumberland. *Arch. Ael.*[4] 48, 51–95.

Jobey, G. 1971a: Early settlement and topography in the Border counties. *Scottish Arch. Forum 1970* (Edinburgh), 73–84.

Jobey, G. 1971b: Early settlements in Eastern Dumfriesshire. *TDGNHAS* 48, 78–105.

Jobey, G. 1971c: Excavations at Brough Law and Ingram Hill. *Arch. Ael.*[4] 49, 71–93.

Jobey, G. 1972: Notes on additional early settlements in Northumberland. *Arch. Ael.*[4] 50, 71–80.

Jobey, G. 1973a: A native settlement at Hartburn and the Devils Causeway, Northumberland. *Arch. Ael.*[5] 1, 11–53.

Jobey, G. 1973b: A Romano-British settlement at Tower Knowe, Wellhaugh, Northumberland. *Arch. Ael.*[5] 1, 55–79.

Jobey, G. 1976: Traprain Law: a summary. In Harding, D.W. (ed.) 1976b, 192–204.

Jobey, G. 1977: Iron Age and later farmsteads on Belling Law, Northumberland. *Arch. Ael.*[5] 5, 1–38.

Jobey, G. 1978: Iron Age and Romano-British Settlements on Kennel Hall Knowe, North Tynedale, Northumberland 1976. *Arch. Ael.*[5] 6, 1–28.

Jobey, G. 1980: Settlement potential in Northern Britain in the later second millennium BC. In Barrett, J. and Bradley, R. (eds) 1980c, 371–6.

Jobey, G. 1981: Green Knowe unenclosed platform settlement and Harehope cairn, Peeblesshire. *PSAS* 110, 72–113.

Jobey, G. 1983: Excavations of an unenclosed settlement on Standrop Rigg, Northumberland, and some problems related to similar settlements between Tyne and Forth. *Arch. Ael.*[5] 11, 1–21.

Jobey, G. 1985: Unenclosed Settlements of Tyne-Forth: a summary. In Spratt, D. and Burgess, C. (eds) 1985, 177–94.

Jobey, G. and Tait, J. 1966: Excavations on palisaded settlements and cairnfields at Alnham, Northumberland. *Arch. Ael.*[4] 44, 5–48.

Johnson, N. and Rose, P. 1982: Defended Settlement in Cornwall – an illustrated discussion. In Miles, D. (ed.), *The Romano-British Countryside* (BAR Brit. Ser. 103: Oxford), 151–207.

Jones, M. 1978: The plant remains [from Ashville, Oxon.]. In Parrington, M. 1978, 93–110.

Jones, M. 1981: The development of crop husbandry. In Jones, M. and Dimbleby, G.W. (eds) 1981, 95–127.

Jones, M. 1984: Regional patterns in crop production. In Cunliffe, B. and Miles, D. (eds) 1984, 120–5.

Jones, M. and Dimbleby, G.W. (eds) 1981: *The environment of man: The Iron Age to the Anglo-Saxon period* (BAR Brit. Ser. 87: Oxford).

Jones, M.U. 1974: Excavations at Mucking, Essex: a second interim report. *Antiq. Journ.* 54, 183–99.

Jones, M.U. and Bond, D. 1980: Late Bronze Age settlement at Mucking, Essex. In Barrett, J. and Bradley, R. 1980a, 471–82.

Jope, E.M. 1961a: The beginnings of La Tène ornamental style in the British Isles. In Frere, S.S. (ed.) 1961, 69–83.

Jope, E.M. 1961b: Daggers of the Early Iron Age in Britain. *PPS* 27, 307–43.

Jope, E.M. 1971: The Witham shield. In Sieveking, G. de G. (ed.) 1971, 61–8.

Jope, E.M. 1983: Hallstatt D daggers: Britain and Europe. *BLIA* 19, 83–9.

Kelly, D.B. 1971: Quarry Wood Camp, Loose: a Belgic oppidum. *Arch. Cant.* 86, 55–84.

Kendrick, J. 1982: Excavations at Douglasmuir, 1979–80. In Harding, D.W. (ed.) 1982, 136–40.

Kent, J.P.C. 1978. The origin and development of Celtic Gold Coinage in Britain. *Actes du Colloque International d'Archaeologie* (Rouen).

Kent, J.P.C. 1981: The origins of coinage in Britain. In Cunliffe, B. (ed.) 1981a, 40–2.

Kenyon, K.M. 1943: Excavations on the Wrekin, Shropshire, 1939. *Arch. Journ.* 99 (1942), 99–109.

Kenyon, K.M. 1950: Excavations at Breedon-on-the-Hill, 1946. *TLAS* 26, 17–82.

Kenyon, K.M. 1952: A survey of the evidence concerning the chronology and origins of Iron Age A in southern and Midland Britain. *London Institute of Archaeology report* 8, 29–78.

Kenyon, K.M. 1954: Excavations at Sutton Walls, Herefordshire, 1948–51. *Arch. Journ.* 110 (1953), 1–87.

Kimball, D. 1933: Cholesbury Camp. *JBAA* 34, 187.

King, D.G. 1961: Bury Wood Camp. Report on excavations, 1959. *WAM* 58, 40–7.

King, D.G. 1962: Bury Wood Camp. Report on excavations, 1960. *WAM* 58, 185–208.

King, D.G. 1967: Bury Wood Camp. *WAM* 62, 1–15.

Kirkham, B. 1975: Salt making sites found in North-East Lincolnshire since 1960. In De Brisay, K.W. and Evans, K.A. (eds) 1975, 41–2.

Kirkham, B. 1981: The excavation of a prehistoric saltern at Hogsthorpe, Lincolnshire. *Lincs. HA* 16, 5–10.

Klein, W.G. 1928: Roman temple at Worth, Kent. *Antiq. Journ.* 8, 76–86.

Knight, D. 1984: *Late Bronze Age and Iron Age settlement in the Nene and Great Ouse Basins* (BAR Brit. Ser. 130: Oxford).

Kossack, G. 1954: Pferdegeschirr aus Gräbern der älteren Hallstatt zeit Bayerns. *Jahrb. Röm.-Germ. Zentralmus. Mainz* 1, 111–78.

Laing, L.R. 1968: A Greek tin trade with Cornwall. *Cornish Arch.* 7, 15–23.

Lamb, H.H. 1981: Climate from 1000 BC-AD 100. In Jones, M. and Dimbleby, G.W. (eds) 1981, 53–65.

Lamb, R.G. 1980: *Iron Age Promontory Forts in the Northern Isles* (BAR Brit. Ser. 79: Oxford).

Lambrick, G. 1979: Mount Farm, Berinsfield. *CBA Group 9 Newsletter* 9, 113–5.

Lambrick, G. 1981: Mount Farm, Berinsfield. *CBA Group 9 Newsletter* 11, 148.

Lambrick, G. 1984: Pitfalls and possibilities in Iron Age pottery studies – experiences in the Upper Thames Valley. In Cunliffe, B. and Miles, D. (eds) 1984, 162–77.

Lambrick, G. and Robinson, M. 1979: *Iron Age and Roman riverside settlements at Farmoor, Oxfordshire* (CBA Res. Rep. 32: London).

Lane, T. 1988: Pre-Roman origins for settlement on the Fens of south Lincolnshire. *Antiquity* 62, 314–21.

Lang, J. and Williams, A.R. 1975: The hardening of iron swords. *J. Arch. Sci.*, 199–207.

Langford, F. 1924: Third report on Read's Cavern. *PBUSS* 1, 135–43.

Langford, F. 1925: Fourth report on Read's Cavern. *PBUSS* 2, 51–5.

Langmaid, N. 1971: Norton Fitzwarren. *Current Arch.* 28, 116–20.

Laver, P.G. 1927: The excavation of a tumulus at Lexden, Colchester. *Archaeologia* 76 (1926–7), 241–54.

Leach, P. and Thew, N. 1985: *A Late Iron Age 'Oppidum' at Ilchester, Somerset* (Western Arch. Trust).

Leaf, C.S. 1936: Two Bronze Age barrows at Chippenham, Cambridgeshire. *PCAS* 36, 134–55.

Leeds, E.T. 1927: Excavations at Chun Castle in Penwith, Cornwall. *Archaeologia* 76, 205–40.

Leeds, E.T. 1931a: Chastleton Camp, Oxfordshire, a hill fort of the Early Iron Age. *Antiq. Journ.* 11, 382–98.

Leeds, E.T. 1931b: An Iron Age site near Radley, Berks. *Antiq. Journ.* 11, 399–404.

Leeds, E.T. 1933a: *Celtic Ornament* (Oxford).

Leeds, E.T. 1933b: Torcs of the Early Iron Age in Britain. *Antiq. Journ.* 13, 466–7.

Leeds, E.T. 1935: Recent Iron Age discoveries in Oxfordshire and north Berkshire. *Antiq. Journ.* 15, 30–41.

Lethbridge, T.C. 1953: Burial of an Iron Age warrior at Snailwell. *PCAS* 47, 25–37.

Liddell, D.M. 1930: Report on the excavations at Hembury Fort, Devon, 1930. *PDAES* 1, 40–63.

Liddell, D.M. 1931: Report on the excavations at Hembury Fort, Devon. Second season 1931. *PDAES* 1, 90–120.

Liddell, D.M. 1932: Report on the excavations at Hembury Fort. Third season 1932. *PDAES* 1, 162–90.

Liddell, D.M. 1933: Excavations at Meon Hill. *PHFC* 12, 127–62.

Liddell, D.M. 1935a: Report on the excavations at Hembury Fort, 1934–5. *PDAES*, 135–70.

Liddell, D.M. 1935b: Report on the Hampshire Field Club's excavation at Meon Hill. *PHFC* 13, 7–54.

Liddell, P. 1982: *Leicestershire Archaeology – the present state of knowledge Vol. 1, to the end of the Roman period* (Leicester).

Longworth, I.H. 1968: A Bronze Age hoard from Portfield Farm, Whalley, Lancashire. *BMQ* 32, 1–2, 8–14.

Lowery, P.R., Savage, R.D.A. and Wilkins, R.L. 1971: Scriber, Graver, Scorper, Tracer: notes on experiments in bronze working. *PPS* 37, 167–82.

Lowther, A.W.G. 1935: An Early Iron Age oven at St. Martha's Hill, near Guildford. *Sy. AC* 43, 113–14.

Lowther, A.W.G. 1945: Report on Excavations at the Site of the Early Iron Age camp in the Grounds of Queen Mary's Hospital, Carshalton, Surrey. *Sy. AC* 49, 56–74.

Lowther, A.W.G. 1947: Caesar's Camp, Wimbledon, Surrey, the excavation of 1937. *Arch. Journ.* 102, 15–20.

Lowther, A.W.G. 1949: Iron Age pottery from St. George's Hill Camp, Weybridge. *Sy. AC* 41, 144–6.

McGrail, S. 1975: The Brigg Raft re-excavated. *Lincs. HA* 10, 5–13.

McGrail, S. 1983: Cross-channel seamanship and navigation in the late 1st millennium BC. *OJA* 2(3), 299–337.

McGrail, S. 1988: Assessing the performance of an ancient boat – the Hasholme Logboat. *OJA* 7(1), 35–46.

McGrail, S. and Switzur, R. 1975: Early British boats and their chronology. *IJNAUE* 4(2), 191–200.

MacGregor, M. 1962: The Early Iron Age metalwork from Stanwick, N.R. Yorks, England. *PPS* 28, 17–57.

MacGregor, M. 1976: *Early Celtic Art in Northern Britain* 2 vols. (Leicester).

MacGregor, M. and Simpson, D.D.A. 1963: A group of iron objects from Barbury Castle, Wilts. *WAM* 58, 394–402.

MacInnes, L. 1982: Pattern and purpose: the settlement evidence. In Harding, D.W. (ed.) 1982, 57–74.

MacKensen, M. 1974: Die älteste Keltische Goldung Silberprägung in England. *Jahrb. Numismatik und Geldgeschichte* 24, 7–63.

MacKie, E.W. 1965a: Brochs and the Hebridean Iron Age. *Antiquity* 39, 266–78.

MacKie, E.W. 1965b: A dwelling site of the Earlier Iron Age at Balevullin, Tiree, excavated in 1912 by A. Henderson Bishop. *PSAS* 96 (1962–3), 155–83.

MacKie, E.W. 1965c: The origin and development of the broch and wheelhouse building cultures of the Scottish Iron Age. *PPS* 31, 93–146.

MacKie, E.W. 1968: *Excavations on Loch Broom, Ross and Cromarty: second interim report 1968* (Glasgow: duplicated).

MacKie, E.W. 1969a: Radiocarbon dates and the Scottish Iron Age. *Antiquity* 43, 15–26.

MacKie, E.W. 1969b: Timber-laced and vitrified walls in Iron Age forts: causes of vitrification. *Glasgow Arch. Journ.* 1, 69–71.

MacKie, E.W. 1970: The Hownam culture: a rejoinder to Ritchie. *Scottish Arch. Forum 2* (Glasgow), 68–72.

MacKie, E.W. 1971a: English migrants and Scottish brochs. *Glasgow Arch. Journ.* 2, 39–71.

MacKie, E.W. 1971b: Some aspects of the transition from the Bronze- to Iron-using periods in Scotland. *Scottish Arch. Forum 3* (Glasgow), 55–72.

MacKie, E.W. 1974: *Dun Mor Vaul: an Iron Age Broch on Tiree* (Glasgow).

MacKie, E.W. 1976: The vitrified forts of Scotland. In Harding, D.W. (ed.) 1976b, 205–35.

MacKie, E.W. 1980: Dun an Ruigh Ruaidh, Loch Broom, Ross and Cromarty: excavations in 1968 and 1978. *Glasgow Arch. Journ.* 7, 32–79.

MacKie, E.W. 1982: The Leckie broch, Stirlingshire: an interim report. *Glasgow Arch. Journ.* 9, 60–72.

MacKie, E.W. 1983: Testing hypotheses about brochs. *Scottish Arch. Rev.* 2, 117–28.

MacLaren, A. 1962: Stanhope Dun, Peeblesshire. *PSAS* 93 (1959–60), 192–201.

McNeil, R. 1973: A report on the Bronze Age hoard from Wick Park, Stogursey, Somerset. *PSANHS* 117, 47–64.

MaCready, S. and Thompson, F.H. (eds) 1984: *Cross-channel trade between Gaul and Britain in the pre-Roman Iron Age* (Soc. of Antiq. Occ. Paper 4: London).

MacSween, A. 1985: The brochs, duns and enclosures of Skye. *Northern Archaeology* 5–6 (1984–5), 1–57.

Manby, T.G. 1963: (Note on Clotherholme sword). *YAJ* 41, 15–17.

Manby, T.G. 1980: Bronze Age settlement in Eastern Yorkshire. In Barrett, J. and Bradley, R. (eds) 1980c, 307–70.

Manning, W.H. 1972: Ironwork hoards in Iron Age and Roman Britain. *Britannia* 3, 224–50.

Manning, W.H. and Saunders, C. 1972: A socketed iron axe from Maids Moreton, Buckinghamshire, with a note on the type. *Antiq. Journ.* 52, 276–92.

Mariën, M.-E. 1958: *Trouvailles du Champ d'Urnes et des tombelles hallstattiennes de Court-Saint Etienne* (Brussels).

Markotic, V. (ed.) 1978: *Ancient people and the Mediterranean* (London).

Martlew, R. 1983: The typological study of the structure of the Scottish brochs. *PSAS* 112, 254–76.

Maryon, H. 1944: The Bawsey torc. *Antiq. Journ.* 24, 149–51.

Matthews, C.L. 1976: *Occupation Sites on a Chiltern Ridge* (BAR Brit. Ser. 29: Oxford).

Maxwell, I.S. 1972: The Location of Ictis. *JRIC* 6(4), 293–319.

May, J. 1964–5: *Dragonby* (duplicated annual interim reports: University of Nottingham).

May, J. 1965–9: *Ancaster* (duplicated interim reports on each season's digging: University of Nottingham, Dept. of Classics).

May, J. 1970: Dragonby – an interim report on excavations on an Iron Age and Romano-British site near Scunthorpe, Lincolnshire, 1964–9. *Antiq. Journ.* 50, 222–45.

May, J. 1976a: The growth of settlements in the Later Iron Age in Lincolnshire. In Cunliffe, B. and Rowley, T. (eds) 1976, 163–80.

May, J. 1976b: *Prehistoric Lincolnshire* (Lincoln).

May, J. 1984: The major settlements of the Later Iron Age in Lincolnshire. In Field, N. and White, A. (eds), *A Prospect of Lincolnshire* (Lincoln), 18–22.

Megaw, J.V.S. 1971: A group of Later Iron Age collars or neck rings from western Britain. In Sieveking, G. de G. (ed.) 1971, 145–55.

Megaw, J.V.S., Thomas, A.D. and Wailes, B. 1961: The Bronze Age settlement at Gwithian, Cornwall, preliminary report. *PWCFC* 2(5), 200.

Megaw, R. and V. 1986: *Early Celtic Art in Britain and Ireland* (London).

Megaw, R. and V. 1989: *Celtic Art from its beginnings to the Book of Kells* (London).

Mercer, R.J. 1970: The excavation of a Bronze Age hut-circle settlement Stannon Down, St. Breward, Cornwall, 1968. *Cornish Arch.* 9, 17–46.

Mercer, R. (ed.) 1981: *Farming practice in British prehistory* (Edinburgh).

Miles, D. (ed.) 1984: *Archaeology at Barton Court Farm, Abingdon, Oxon* (CBA Res. Rep. 50: London).

Miles, D. and Palmer, S. 1982: *Figures in a Landscape: archaeological investigations at Claydon Pike, Fairford/Lechlade. An interim report 1979–82* (Oxford).

Miles, H. 1975: Excavations at Woodbury Castle, East Devon, 1971. *PDAES* 33, 183–208.

Miles, H. and T.J. 1969: Settlement sites of the Late pre-Roman Iron Age in the Somerset levels. *PSANHS* 113 (1968–9), 17–55.

Miles, H. *et al.* 1978: Excavations at Killibury Hillfort, Egloshayle 1975–6. *Cornish Arch.* 16 (1977), 89–121.

Millett, M. and McGrail, S. 1988: The Archaeology of the Hasholme Logboat. *Arch. Journ.* 144 (1987), 69–155.

Mitchell, S. 1983: Cornish Tin, Julius Caesar and the Invasion of Britain. *Latomas* 180, 80–99.

Money, J.H. 1941: An interim report on excavations at High Rocks, Tunbridge Wells, 1940. *SAC* 82, 104–9.

Money, J.H. 1960: Excavations at High Rocks, Tunbridge Wells, 1954–56. *SAC* 98, 173–222.

Money, J.H. 1968: Excavations in the Iron Age hill-fort at High Rocks, near Tunbridge Wells, 1957–61. *SAC* 106, 158–205.

Money, J.H. 1973: Iron Age hill-forts on Castle Hill, Tonbridge. *Arch. Cant.* 87 (1972), 219.

Monk, M.A. and Fasham, P.J. 1980: Carbonized plant remains from two Iron Age sites in central Hampshire. *PPS* 46, 321–44.

Moore, P.D. 1975: The origin of blanket mires. *Nature* 256, 267–9.

Morris, E.L. 1981: Ceramic Exchange in Western Britain: A preliminary review. In Howard, H. and Morris, E.L. (eds), *Production and Distribution: a Ceramic Viewpoint* (BAR Int. Ser. 120: Oxford), 67–81.

Morris, E.L. 1985: Prehistoric salt distributions: two case studies from Western Britain. *BBCS* 32, 336–79.

Morris, E.L. 1987: Later prehistoric pottery from Ham Hill. *PSNHAS* 131, 27–47.

Morrison, I. 1985: *Landscape with Lake Dwellings. The Crannogs of Scotland* (Edinburgh).

Mortimer, J.R. 1869: Notice of the opening of an Anglo-Saxon grave, at Grimthorpe, Yorkshire. *Reliquary* 9, 180–2.

Mortimer, J.R. 1895: The opening of six mounds at Scarborough, near Beverley. *TERAS* 3, 21–3.

Mortimer, J.R. 1905: *Forty Years' Researches in British and Saxon Burial Mounds of East Yorkshire* (London).

Mortimer, J.R. 1911: Dane's Graves. *TERAS* 18, 30–52.

Moss-Ecgardt, J. 1964: Excavations at Wilbury Hill, an Iron Age hill-fort near Letchworth, Herts., 1959. *Beds. AJ* 2, 34–46.

Munro, R. 1882: *Ancient Scottish Lake Dwellings* (Edinburgh).

Murphy, K. 1985: Excavations at Penycoed, Llangynog, Dyfed 1983. *Carm. Ant.* 21, 75–112.

Murphy, P. and French, C. 1988: *The Exploration of Wetlands* (BAR Brit. Ser. 186: Oxford).

Musson, C. 1970: *Breiddin 1969* (duplicated: University of South Wales and Monmouthshire, Dept of Archaeology, Cardiff).

Musson, C. 1972: Two winters at the Breiddin. *Current Arch.* 33, 263–7.

Musson, C. 1976: Excavations at the Breiddin 1969–1973. In Harding, D.W. (ed.) 1976b, 293–302.

Musty, J. and MacCormick, A.G. 1973: An early Iron Age wheel from Holme Pierrepont, Notts. *Antiq. Journ.* 53, 275–7.

Mynard, D.C. 1970: An Iron Age enclosure at Ravenstone, Buckinghamshire. *Rec. of Bucks.* 18, 393–413.

Myres, J.N.L. 1937: A prehistoric and Roman site on Mount Farm, Dorchester. *Oxon.* 2, 12–40.

Mytum, H. 1986: Excavation and Experiment at Castell Henllys. *Popular Archaeology* 7(5), 8–14.

Mytum, H. 1987: *Excavations at the Iron Age fort of Castell Henllys in North Pembrokeshire. An Interim Report 1980–86* (York).

Nash, D. 1976: Reconstructing Poseidonios' Celtic ethnography: some considerations. *Britannia* 7, 111–26.

Nash, D. 1984: The Basis of Contact between Britain and Gaul in the Late Pre-Roman Iron Age. In Macready, S. and Thompson, F.H. (eds) 1984, 92–107.

Nash-Williams, V.E. 1933a: An Early Iron Age hill fort at Llanmelin, near Caerwent, Monmouthshire. *Arch. Camb.* 88, 237–315.

Nash-Williams, V.E. 1933b: A Late bronze hoard from Cardiff. *Antiq. Journ.* 13, 299–300.

Nash-Williams, V.E. 1939: An Early Iron Age coastal camp at Sudbrook, near the Severn Tunnel, Monmouthshire. *Arch. Camb.* 94, 42–79.

Needham, S. and Longley, D. 1980: Runnymede Bridge, Egham: a late Bronze Age riverside settlement. In Barrett, J. and Bradley, R. (eds) 1980c, 397–436.

Neish, J. and Stuart, J. 1860: Reference notes to plan and views of ancient remains on the summit of the Laws, Forfarshire. *PSAS* 3 (1857–60), 440–54.

Nenquin, J. 1961: *Salt, a Study in Economic Prehistory* (Brugge).

Newcomb, R.M. 1968: Geographical location analysis and Iron Age settlement in West Penwith. *Cornish Arch.* 7, 5–13.

Newcomb, R.M. 1970: The spatial distribution of hill-forts in West Penwith. *Cornish Arch.* 9, 47–52.

Northover, P. 1984: Analysis of the bronze metalwork [from Danebury, Hants.]. In Cunliffe, B. 1984a, 430–3.

Northover, P. 1987: Non-ferrous metallurgy [from Hengistbury Head, Dorset]. In Cunliffe, B. 1987, 186–90.

Northover, P. 1988: Copper, tin, silver and gold in the Iron Age. In Slater, E.A. and Tate, J.O. (eds), *Science and Archaeology Glasgow 1987* (BAR Brit. Ser. 196: Oxford), 223–34.

O'Connor, B. 1975: Six prehistoric phalerae in the London Museum and a discussion of other phalerae from the British Isles. *Antiq. Journ.* 55, 215–26.

O'Connor, B. 1978: A Late Urnfield pendant from the Thames at Old England. *TLMAS* 29, 146–7.

Oliver, M. and Applin, B. 1978: Excavation of an Iron Age and Romano-British settlement at Ructstalls Hill, Basingstoke, Hampshire 1972–5. *PHFC* 35, 41–92.

O'Neil, B.H.StJ. 1934: Excavation at Titterstone Clee Hill Camp, Shropshire, 1932. *Antiq. Journ.* 14, 13–32.

O'Neil, B.H.StJ. 1937: Excavations at Breiddin Hill Camp, Montgomeryshire, 1933–35. *Arch. Camb.* 92, 86–128.

O'Neil, B.H.StJ. 1942: Excavations at Ffridd Faldwyn Camp, Montgomeryshire, 1937–39. *Arch. Camb.* 97, 1–57.

O'Neil, H.E. 1978: Salmonsbury, Bourton-on-the-Water. *TBGAS* 95 (1977), 11–23.

Orme, B.J. 1982: The use of radiocarbon dates from the Somerset levels. *Somerset Levels Papers* 8, 9–25.

Orme, B.J., Coles, J.M., Caseldine, A.E. and Bailey, G.N. 1981: Meare Village West 1979. *Somerset Levels Papers* 7, 12–69.

Orme, B.J., Coles, J.M. and Silvester, R.J. 1983: Meare Village East 1982. *Somerset Levels Papers* 9, 49–74.

Orme, B.J., Coles, J.M. and Sturdy, C.R. 1979: Meare Lake Village West: a report on recent work. *Somerset Levels Papers* 5, 6–24.

OS 1962: *Ordnance Survey Map of Southern Britain in the Iron Age* (Chessington).

Oswald, A. 1969: Excavations at Barford, Warwickshire. *TBAS* 83 (1966 and 1967), 1–64.

Oswald, A. 1974: Excavations at Beckford. *TWAS* 3 (1970–72), 7–47.

Otlet, R.L. and Walker, A.J. 1982: Radiocarbon Dating. In Balaam, N.D., Smith, K. and Wainwright, G.J. 1982, 237–40.

Owen, O. 1987: *An interim report on trial excavations on the fort on Eildon Hill North, Roxburghshire 1986* (duplicated).

Owles, E.J. 1969: The Ipswich gold torcs. *Antiquity* 43, 208–11.

Owles, E.J. 1971: The sixth Ipswich torc. *Antiquity* 45, 294–6.

Painter, K.S. 1971: An Iron Age gold-alloy torc from Glascote, Tamworth, Staffordshire. *Trans. S. Staffs. AHS* 11 (1970), 1–6.

Palk, N.A. 1984: *Iron Age bridle-bits from Britain* (Edinburgh University: Occ. Paper 10).

Palmer, L.S. 1922: The Keltic cavern. *PBUSS* 1, 9–20.

Palmer, L.S. 1923: Second report on the Keltic cavern. *PBUSS* 1, 87–91.

Palmer, R. 1984: *Danebury: an Iron Age hillfort in Hampshire. An aerial photographic interpretation of its environs* (RCHM(E): London).

Parrington, M. 1978: *The excavation of an Iron Age settlement, Bronze Age ring ditches and Roman feature at Ashville Trading Estate, Abingdon (Oxfordshire) 1974–6* (CBA Res. Rep. 28: London).

Parson, W.J. and Curwen, E.C. 1933: An agricultural settlement on Charleston Brow, near Firle Beacon. *SAC* 74, 164–80.

Partridge, C. 1979: Excavations at Puckeridge and Braughing 1975–9. *Herts. Arch.* 7, 28–132.

Partridge, C. 1981: *Skeleton Green. A Late Iron Age and Romano-British site* (Britannia Monog. Series no. 2: London).

Partridge, C. 1982a: Braughing, Wickham Kennels 1982. *Herts. Arch.* 8, 40–59.

Partridge, C. 1982b: Graffiti from Skeleton Green. *Britannia* 13, 325–6.

Peacock, D.P.S. 1968: A petrological study of certain Iron Age pottery from western England. *PPS* 34, 414–27.

Peacock, D.P.S. 1969: A contribution to the study of Glastonbury ware from south-western Britain. *Antiq. Journ.* 49, 41–61.

Peacock, D.P.S. 1971: Roman amphorae in pre-Roman Britain. In Jesson, M. and Hill, D. (eds) 1971, 161–88.

Peacock, D.P.S. 1979: Glastonbury Ware: An Alternative View. In Burnham, B.C. and Kingsbury, J. (eds) 1979, 113–18.

Peacock, D.P.S. 1984: Amphorae in Iron Age Britain: a Reassessment. In Macready, S. and Thompson, F.H. (eds) 1984, 37–42.

Peacock, D.P.S. 1987: Iron Age and Roman quern production at Lodsworth, West Sussex. *Antiq. Journ.* 67, 61–85.

Peake, H. 1922: *The Bronze Age and the Celtic World* (London).

Peake, H., Coghlan, H. and Hawkes, C.F.C. 1932: Early Iron Age remains on Boxford Common, Berks. *TNDFC* 6 (1931), 136–50.

Peake, H., Coghlan, H. and Hawkes, C.F.C. 1933: Further excavations on Boxford Common. *TNDFC* 6, 211–17.

Pearce, S.M. 1974: A late Bronze Age hoard from Glentanar, Aberdeenshire. *PSAS* 103 (1970–1), 57–64.

Pearson, G.W. 1986: Precise calendrical dating of known growth-period samples using a 'curve fitting' technique. *Radiocarbon* 28(2A), 292–9.

Pearson, G.W. 1987. How to cope with calibration. *Antiquity* 61, 98–103.

Pearson, G.W. and Stuiver, M. 1986: High-precision calibration of the radiocarbon time scale 500–2500 BC. In Stuiver, M. and Kra, R.S. (eds) 1986a, 839–62.

Peltenburg, E.J. 1982: Excavations at Balloch Hill, Argyll. *PSAS* 112, 142–214.

Penhalluric, R.D. 1986: *Tin in Antiquity* (London).

Pennington, W. 1974: *The History of British Vegetation* (London).

Peroni, R.L. 1973: *Studi di cronologia Hallstattiana* (Rome).

Perry, B.T. 1966: Some recent discoveries in Hampshire. In Thomas, A.C. (ed.) 1966b, 39–42.

Perry, B.T. 1970: Iron Age enclosures and settlements on the Hampshire chalklands. *Arch. Journ.* 126 (1969), 29–43.

Perry, B.T. 1974: Excavations at Bramdean, Hampshire, 1965 and 1966, and a discussion of similar sites in southern England. *PHFC* 29 (1972), 41–77.

Perry, B.T. 1982: Excavations at Bramdean, Hampshire, 1973–1977. *PHFC* 38, 57–74.

Perry, B.T. 1986: Excavations at Bramdean, Hampshire, 1983 and 1984, with some further discussion of the 'Banjo' syndrome. *PHFC* 42, 35–42.

Philips, J.T. 1960: An Iron Age site at Driffield, East Riding, Yorks. *YAJ* 40 (1959–62), 183–91.

Philp, B. 1984: The Iron Age farmstead on Farningham Hill. In Philp, B., *Excavations in the Darent Valley, Kent* (Dover), 8–71.

Piggott, C.M. 1938a: The Iron Age pottery from Theale. *TNDFC* 8, 52–62.

Piggott, C.M. 1938b: A Middle Bronze Age barrow and Deverel–Rimbury urnfield, at Latch Farm, Christchurch, Hampshire. *PPS* 4, 169–87.

Piggott, C.M. 1940: Report on the pottery from Winklebury Camp, Hants. *PHFC* 15, 56–7.

Piggott, C.M. 1942: Five Late Bronze Age enclosures in north Wiltshire. *PPS* 8, 48–61.

Piggott, C.M. 1946: Late Bronze Age razors of the British Isles. *PPS* 12, 121–41.

Piggott, C.M. 1950: The excavations at Hownam Rings, Roxburghshire 1948. *PSAS* 82 (1947–8), 193–224.

Piggott, C.M. 1951: The Iron Age settlement at Hayhope Knowe, Roxburghshire: excavations, 1949. *PSAS* 83 (1948–9), 45–67.

Piggott, C.M. 1952: The excavations at Bonchester Hill, 1950. *PSAS* 82 (1949–50), 113–37.

Piggott, C.M. 1953: An Iron Age barrow in the New Forest. *Antiq. Journ.* 33, 14–21.

Piggott, C.M. 1955: Milton Loch Crannog I: a native house of the second century A.D. in Kirkcudbrightshire. *PSAS* 87 (1952–3), 134–52.

Piggott, C.M. and Seaby, W.A. 1937: Early Iron Age site at Southcote, Reading. *PPS* 3, 43–57.

Piggott, S. 1927: Early Iron Age rubbish pits at Knighton Hill, Berks. *Antiq. Journ.* 7, 517.

Piggott, S. 1931: Ladle Hill – an unfinished hill-fort. *Antiquity* 5, 474–85.

Piggott, S. 1950: Swords and scabbards of the British Early Iron Age. *PPS* 16, 1–28.

Piggott, S. 1951: Excavations in the broch and hillfort of Torwoodlee, Selkirkshire, 1950. *PSAS* 85 (1950–1), 92–117.

Piggott, S. 1955: A Late Bronze Age hoard from Peeblesshire. *PSAS* 87 (1952–3), 175–86.

Piggott, S. 1956: Introduction in RCHM(S), *Roxburghshire* I, 15.

Piggott, S. 1958: Native Economies and the Roman Occupation of North Britain. In Richmond, I.A. (ed.), *Roman and Native in North Britain* (London), 1–27.

Piggott, S. 1959: The carnyx in Early Iron Age Britain. *Antiq. Journ.* 39, 19–32.

Piggott, S. 1960: Excavations at Braidwood fort, Midlothian. *PSAS* 91 (1957–8), 61–77.

Piggott, S. 1966: A scheme for the Scottish Iron Age. In Rivet, A.L.F. (ed.) 1966, 1–16.

Piggott, S. 1968: *The Druids* (London).

Piggott, S. 1973: A note on climatic deterioration in the first millennium B.C. in Britain. *Scottish Arch. Forum 4* (Glasgow), 109–13.

Piggott, S. 1978. A glance at Cornish tin. In Markotic, V. (ed.) 1978, 141–5.

Piggott, S. and C.M. 1940: Excavations at Ram's Hill, Uffington, Berks. *Antiq. Journ.* 20, 465–80.

Piggott, S. and C.M. 1954: Excavations at Castle Law, Glencorse, and at Craig's Quarry, Dirleton, 1948–9. *PSAS* 86 (1951–2), 191–5.

Pilcher, J.R., Baillie, M.G.L., Schmidt, B. and Becker, R. 1984: A 7,272-year tree-ring chronology for Western Europe. *Nature* 312, 150–2.

Pitt Rivers, A.H.L.F. 1881: Excavations at Mount Caburn Camp, near Lewes. *Archaeologia* 46, 423–95.

Pitt Rivers, A.H.L.F. 1887: *Excavations in Cranborne Chase* Vol. 1 (London).

Pitt Rivers, A.H.L.F. 1888: *Excavations in Cranborne Chase* Vol. 2 (London).

Pitt Rivers, A.H.L.F. 1892: *Excavations in Cranborne Chase* Vol. 3 (London).

Pitt Rivers, A.H.L.F. 1898: *Excavations in Cranborne Chase* Vol. 4 (London).

Pollard, S. 1974: A Late Iron Age settlement and Romano-British villa at Holcombe, near Uplyme, Devon. *PDAES* 32, 60–162.

Potter, T.W. and Trow, S.D. 1988: Puckeridge-Broughing, Herts.: The Ermine Street excavation, 1971–72. *Herts. Arch.* 10.

Powell, T.G.E. 1950: The Late Bronze Age hoard from Welby, Leicestershire. *Arch. Journ.* 105 (1948), 27–40.

Powell, T.G.E. 1963: Excavations at Skelmore Heads near Ulverston. *CW*² 63, 1–30.

Powlesland, D., Haughton, C. and Hanson, J. 1986: Excavations at Hesterton, North Yorkshire, 1978–82. *Arch. Journ.* 143, 53–173.

Preston, J.P. and Hawkes, C.F.C. 1933: Three Late Bronze Age barrows on the Cloven Way. *Antiq. Journ.* 13, 414–54.

Pryor, F. 1974: *Excavations at Fengate, Peterborough, England: the First Report* (Royal Ontario Mus. mon. series no. 3: Ontario).

Pryor, F. 1975: Fengate. *Current Arch.* 46, 19, 332–9.

Pryor, F. 1978: *Excavations at Fengate, Peterborough, England. The Second Report* (Royal Ontario Mus. mon. series no. 5: Ontario).

Pryor, F. 1984: *Excavations at Fengate, Peterborough, England. The Fourth Report* (Royal Ontario Mus. mon. series no. 7: Northampton).

Pryor, F. and Cranstone, D. 1978: An Interim Report on Excavations at Fengate, Peterborough 1975–77. *Northants. Arch.* 13, 9–27.

Quincey, A.B. de 1970: A promontory fort at Parc Cynog, Carmarthenshire. *Arch. Camb.* 118 (1969), 73–85.

Quinnell, H. 1986: Cornwall during the Iron Age and the Roman period. *Cornish Arch.* 25, 111–34.

Quinnell, H. and Harris, D. 1985: Castle Dore: The Chronology Reconsidered. *Cornish Arch.* 24, 123–32.

Radford, C.A.R. 1951: Report on the excavations at Castle Dore. *JRIC* (NS) 1, 1–119.

Radford, C.A.R. 1952: Prehistoric settlements on Dartmoor and the Cornish Moors. *PPS* 18, 55–84.

Radford, C.A.R. 1955: The tribes of southern Britain. *PPS* 20 (1954), 1–26.

Rahtz, P.A. 1969: Cannington hillfort 1963. *PSANHS* 113 (1968–9), 56–68.

Rahtz, P.A. and ApSimon, A.M. 1962: Excavations at Shearplace Hill, Sydling St. Nicholas, Dorset, England. *PPS* 28, 289–328.

Rahtz, P.A. and Brown, J.C. 1959: Blaise Castle Hill, Bristol, 1957. *PBUSS* 8, 147–71.

Raistrick, A. 1938: Prehistoric cultivations at Grassington, West Yorkshire. *YAJ* 33 (1936–8), 166–74.

Raistrick, A. 1939: Iron Age settlements in West Yorkshire. *YAJ* 34, 115–50.

Ralston, I., Sabine, K. and Watt, W. 1983: Later prehistoric settlements in North East Scotland: a preliminary assessment. In Chapman, R. and Mytum, H. (eds) 1983, 149–73.

Ramm, H. 1978: *The Parisi* (London).

Ramm, H. 1980: Native settlements East of the Pennines. In Branigan, K. (ed.), *Rome and the Brigantes* (Sheffield), 28–40.

Ratcliffe-Densham, H.B.A. and M.M. 1953: A Celtic farm on Blackpatch. *SAC* 91, 69–83.

Ratcliffe-Densham, H.B.A. and M.M. 1961: An anomalous earthwork of the Late Bronze Age, on Cock Hill. *SAC* 99, 78–101.

Rawes, B. 1984: Observations at Salmonsbury Camp 1983. *TBGAS* 102, 215–19.

Read, R.C. 1970: Cornish Middle Bronze Age Pottery (unpublished Ph.D. thesis: University of London).

Rees, S.E. 1979: *Agricultural implements in prehistoric and Roman Britain* (BAR Brit. Ser. 69: Oxford).

Reid, H.L. 1989: A room with a view: an examination of round-houses, with particular reference to northern Britain. *OJA* 8, 1–40.

Renfrew, C. 1979: *Investigations in Orkney* (Soc. of Ant. Res. Rep. 38: London).

Reynolds, D.M. 1982: Aspects of later prehistoric timber construction in south-east Scotland. In Harding, D.W. (ed.) 1982, 44–56.

Reynolds, P.J. 1974: Experimental Iron Age storage pits: an interim report. *PPS* 40, 118–31.

Richardson, K.M. 1940: Excavations at Poundbury, Dorchester, Dorset, 1939. *Antiq. Journ.* 20, 429–48.

Richardson, K.M. 1951: The excavation of Iron Age villages on Boscombe Down West. *WAM* 54, 123–68.

Richardson, K.M. and Young, A. 1951: An Iron Age A site on the Chilterns. *Antiq. Journ.* 31, 132–48.

Richmond, I.A. 1968: *Hod Hill* Vol. 2: *Excavations carried out between 1951 and 1958* (London).

Riehm, K. 1961: Prehistoric salt boiling. *Antiquity* 35, 181–91.

Riley, D. 1976: Aerial Reconnaissance of West and South Yorkshire in 1975. *YAJ* 48, 13–17.

Riley, D. 1977: Air Reconnaissance in Central and Southern Yorkshire, 1976. *YAJ* 49, 19–33.

Riley, D. 1978: Air reconnaissance in 1977. *YAJ* 50, 21–4.

Riley, D.N. 1947: A Late Bronze Age and Iron Age site on Standlake Downs, Oxon. *Oxon.* 11–12 (1946–7), 27–43.

Ritchie, A. 1970: Palisaded sites in northern Britain: their context and affinities. *Scottish Arch. Forum 2* (Glasgow), 48–67.

Rivet, A.L.F. 1961: Some of the problems of hill-forts. In Frere, S.S. (ed.) 1961, 29–34.

Rivet, A.L.F. (ed.) 1966: *The Iron Age in Northern Britain* (Edinburgh).

Robertson-MacKay, R. 1977: The defences of the Iron Age hillfort at Winklebury, Basingstoke, Hampshire. *PPS* 43, 131–54.

Robinson, M. 1984: Landscape and Environment of Central Southern Britain in the Iron Age. In Cunliffe, B. and Miles, D. (eds) 1984, 1–11.

Robinson, M.A. and Lambrick, G.A. 1984: Holocene alluviation and hydrology in the upper Thames basin. *Nature* 308(5962) April 1984, 809–14.

Rodwell, W.J. 1976: Coinage, Oppida and the rise of Belgic Power in South-Eastern Britain. In Cunliffe, B. and Rowley, T. (eds) 1976, 181–367.

Ross, A. 1967: *Pagan Celtic Britain* (London).

Rowlands, M.J. 1980: Kinship, alliance and exchange in the European Bronze Age. In Barrett, J. and Bradley, R. (eds) 1980c, 15–56.

Rutter, J.G. and Duke, G. 1958: *Excavations at Crossgates near Scarborough, 1947–56* (Scarborough).

Salter, C.J. 1983: The Relevance of Chemical Provenance Studies to Celtic Ironwork in Britain. *BLIA* 19, 73–81.

Salter, C.J. 1987: Ferrous metallurgy and other slags [from Hengistbury Head, Dorset]. In Cunliffe, B. 1987, 197–205.

Salter, C. and Ehrenreich, R. 1984: Iron Age iron metallurgy in Central Southern Britain. In Cunliffe, B. and Miles, D. (eds) 1984, 146–61.

Sandars, N.K. 1957: *Bronze Age Cultures in France* (Cambridge).

Saunders, A. 1961: Excavations at Castle Gotha, St. Austell, Cornwall. *PWCFC* 2, 5, 216–20.

Saunders, A. and Harris, D. 1982: Excavations at Castle Gotha, St. Austell. *Cornish Arch.* 21, 109–53.

Saunders, C. 1972: The Pre-Belgic Iron Age in the Central and Western Chilterns. *Arch. Journ.* 128, 1–30.

Saunders, C. 1977: The Iron firedog from Welwyn, Hertfordshire reconsidered. *Herts. Arch.* 5, 13–21.

Saunders, C. and Havercroft, A.B. 1982: Excavations on the line of the Wheathampstead bypass 1974 and 1977; with some thoughts on the oppida at Wheathampstead and Verulamium. *Herts. Arch.* 8, 11–39.

Saville, A. 1979: *Excavations at Guiting Power Iron Age Site, Gloucestershire 1974* (CRAAGS Occ. Papers No. 7: Bristol).

Saville, A. 1983: *Uley Bury and Norbury Hillforts* (Western Arch. Trust Monog. 5: Bristol).

Savory, H.N. 1937: An Early Iron Age site at Long Wittenham, Berks. *Oxon.* 2, 1–11.

Savory, H.N. 1939: The Early Iron Age. *VCH Oxon.* 1, 251–61.

Savory, H.N. 1948: The sword-bearers. *PPS* 14, 155–76.

Savory, H.N. 1954: The excavation of an Early Iron Age fortified settlement on Mynydd Bychan, Llysworney (Glam.), 1949–50, part I. *Arch. Camb.* 103, 85–108.

Savory, H.N. 1956: The excavation of an Early Iron Age fortified settlement on Mynydd Bychan, Llysworney, Glam., 1949–50, part II. *Arch. Camb.* 104 (1955), 14–51.

Savory, H.N. 1958: The Late Bronze Age in Wales: some new discoveries and new interpretations. *Arch. Camb.* 107, 3–63.

Savory, H.N. 1961: Excavations at Dinas Emrys, Beddglent, Caernarvonshire, 1954–56. *Arch. Camb.* 109 (1960), 13–77.

Savory, H.N. 1964: The Tal-y-Llyn hoard. *Antiquity* 38, 18–31.

Savory, H.N. 1968: *Early Iron Age Art in Wales* (Cardiff).

Savory, H.N. 1971a: *Excavations at Dinorben, 1965–9* (Cardiff).

Savory, H.N. 1971b: A Welsh Bronze Age hillfort. *Antiquity* 45, 251–61.

Savory, H.N. 1976a: *Guide Catalogue of the Early Iron Age Collections* (Cardiff).

Savory, H.N. 1976b: Welsh Hillforts: a reappraisal of recent research. In Harding, D.W. (ed.) 1976b, 237–92.

Schauer, P. 1972: Zur Herkunft der bronzenen Hallstatt-schwerter. *Arch. Korrespondenzbl.* 2, 261–70.

Scheers, S. 1972: Coinage and currency of the Belgic tribes during the Gallic War. *BNJ*, 1–6.

Schwappach, F. 1969: Stempelverzierte Keramik von Armorica. *Fundberichte aus Hessen* 1, 213–87.

Scott, L. 1947: The problem of the brochs. *PPS* (1944), 1–36.

Scott, L. 1948: Gallo-British colonies: the aisled round-house culture in the north. *PPS* 14, 46–125.

Sealey, P.R. 1979: The Later History of Icenian Electrum Torcs. *PPS* 45, 165–78.

Sealey, P.R. 1985: *Amphoras from the 1970 excavations at Colchester Sheepen* (BAR Brit. Ser. 142: Oxford).

Sheppard, T. 1907: Note on a British chariot-burial at Hunmanby in East Yorkshire. *YAJ* 19, 482 8.

Sheppard, T. 1938: Excavations at Eastburn, East Yorkshire. *YAJ* 34, 35–47.

Sheppard, T. 1941: The Parc-y-Meirch hoard, St. George Parish Denbighshire. *Arch. Camb.* 96, 1–10.

Sieveking, G. de G. (ed.) 1971: *Prehistoric and Roman Studies* (London).

Silvester, R.J. 1979: The Relationship of First Millennium Settlement to the Upland Areas of the South-West. *PDAES* 37, 176–90.

Simco, A. 1973: The Iron Age in the Bedford Region. *Beds. AJ* 8, 5–22.

Simmons, B.B. 1975: Salt making in the silt fens of Lincolnshire in the Iron Age and Roman periods. In De Brisay, K.W. and Evans, K.A. (eds) 1975, 33–6.

Simmons, B.B. 1980: Iron Age and Roman Coasts around the Wash. In Thompson, F.H. (ed.), *Archaeology and Coastal Change* (Soc. Ant. Occ. Paper 1: London), 56–73.

Simmons, I.G. 1970: Environment and early Man on Dartmoor. *PPS* 35 (1969), 203–19.

Simmons, I.G. and Tooley, M. (eds) 1981: *The environment in British prehistory* (London).

Simpson, D.D.A. 1969: Excavations at Kaimes hillfort, Midlothian, 1964–8. *Glasgow Arch. Journ.* NS 1, 7–28.

Simpson, W.G. 1966: Romano-British settlement on the Welland Gravels. In Thomas, A.C. (ed.) 1966b, 15–25.

Small, A. and Cottam, M.B. 1972: *Craig Phadrig* (Dundee).

Smith, C.A. 1974: A morphological analysis of Late Prehistoric and Romano-British settlements in North-West Wales. *PPS* 40, 157–69.

Smith, C. 1977: The valleys of the Tame and middle Trent – their population and ecology during the late first millennium BC. In Collis, J. (ed.) 1977, 51–61.

Smith, C.A. 1978a: The landscape and natural history of Iron Age settlement on the Trent gravels. In Cunliffe, B. and Rowley, T. (eds) 1978, 91–102.

Smith, C.A. 1978b: Late Prehistoric and Romano-British enclosed homesteads in north west Wales: an interpretation of their morphology. *Arch. Camb.* 126 (1977), 38–52.

Smith, C.A. 1979: *Fisherwick: The reconstruction of an Iron Age landscape* (BAR Brit. Ser. 61: Oxford).

Smith, C.R. 1852: *Collectanea Antiqua* Vol. 2. (London)

Smith, I.M. 1980: Excavations at The Dod, Roxburghshire, 1980: an interim report. *Trans. Hawick Arch. Soc.* for 1980, 9–20.

Smith, I.M. 1982: The Excavations at The Dod, 1979–81. In Harding, D.W. (ed.) 1982, 129–35.

Smith, K. 1977: The excavation of Winklebury Camp, Basingstoke, Hampshire. *PPS* 43, 31–129.

Smith, K. 1979: Winklebury Camp, Basingstoke – a note. *PPS* 45, 321–2.

Smith, K., Coppen, J., Wainwright, G.J. and Beckett, S. 1981: The Shaugh Moor Project: Third Report – settlement and environmental investigation. *PPS* 47, 205–73.

Smith, M.A. 1959: Some Somerset hoards and their place in the Bronze Age of southern Britain. *PPS* 25, 144–87.

Smith, R.A. 1905: *A Guide to the Antiquities of the Early Iron Age* (London).

Smith, R.A. 1908: Romano-British remains at Cobham. *Sy. AC* 21, 192–203.

Smith, R.A. 1909a: A hoard of metal found at Santon Downham, Suffolk. *PCAS* 13, 146–63.

Smith, R.A. 1909b: Romano-British remains at Cobham. *Sy. AC* 22, 137–55.

Smith, R.A. 1912: On Late-Celtic antiquities discovered at Welwyn, Herts. *Archaeologia* 63 (1911–12), 1–30.

Smith, R.A. 1925: *A Guide to the Antiquities of the Early Iron Age of Central and Western Europe* (London).

Smith, R.A. 1926: Two early British bronze bowls. *Antiq. Journ.* 6, 276–83.

Smith, R.A. 1927: Park Brow, the finds and foreign parallels. *Archaeologia* 76, 14–29.

Smith, R.A. 1928: Pre-Roman remains at Scarborough. *Archaeologia* 77, 179–200.

Smith, R.A. 1934: Scarborough and Hallstatt. *Antiq. Journ.* 14, 301–2.

Spencer, B. 1983: Limestone-tempered pottery from South Wales in the late Iron Age and early Roman period. *BBCS* 30, 405–19.

Spratling, M. 1966: The date of the Tal-y-Llyn hoard. *Antiquity* 40, 229–30.

Spratling, M. 1970: The Late Pre-Roman Iron Age bronze mirror from Old Warden. *Beds. AJ* 5, 9–16.

Spratling, M. 1974: The dating of the Iron Age swan's-neck sunflower pin from Fengate, Peterborough, Cambridgeshire. *Antiq. Journ.* 54, 268–9.

Spratling, M. 1979: The debris of metalworking [from Gussage All Saints, Dorset]. In Wainwright, G.J. 1979, 125–53.

Spratling, M. 1981: Metalworking at the Stanwick Oppidum: some new evidence. *YAJ* 53, 13–16.

Spratt, D.A. 1982: *Prehistoric and Roman Archaeology of North-East Yorkshire* (BAR Brit. Ser. 104: Oxford).

Spratt, D. and Burgess, C. (eds) 1985: *Upland Settlement in Britain. The Second Millennium BC and after* (BAR Brit. Ser 143: Oxford).

Spurgeon, C.J. 1972: Enclosures of Iron Age type in the Upper Severn Basin. In Lynch, F. and Burgess, C. (eds), *Prehistoric Man in Wales and the West* (Bath), 321–44.

Staelens, Y.J.E. 1983: Th Birdlip cemetery. *TBGAS* 100, 19–31.

Stanford, S.C. 1967: Croft Ambrey hillfort. *TWNFC* 39, 31–9.

Stanford, S.C. 1971a: Credenhill Camp, Herefordshire: an Iron Age hill-fort capital. *Arch. Journ.* 127 (1970), 82–129.

Stanford, S.C. 1971b: Invention, adoption and imposition – the evidence of the hill-forts. In Jesson, M. and Hill, D. (eds) 1971, 41–52.

Stanford, S.C. 1972: Welsh Border Hill-forts. In Thomas, C. (ed.), *The Iron Age in the Irish Sea Province* (CBA Res. Rep. 9: London), 25–35.

Stanford, S.C. 1974a: *Croft Ambrey* (Hereford).

Stanford, S.C. 1974b: Native and Roman in the Central Welsh Borderland. In Birley, E., Dobson, B. and Jarrett, M. (eds), *Roman Frontier Studies* (Cardiff), 44–61.

Stanford, S.C. 1981: *Midsummer Hill; an Iron Age hillfort on the Malverns* (Leominster).

Stanford, S.C. 1982: Bromfield, Shropshire – Neolithic, Beaker and Bronze Age Sites 1966–79. *PPS* 48, 279–302.

Stanford, S.C. *et al.* 1985: The Wrekin hillfort: excavations 1973. *Arch. Journ.* 141, 61–90.

Stead, I.M. 1961: A distinctive form of La Tène barrow in Eastern Yorkshire and on the continent. *Antiq. Journ.* 41, 44–62.

Stead, I.M. 1965: *The La Tène Cultures of Eastern Yorkshire* (York).

Stead, I.M. 1967: A La Tène III burial at Welwyn Garden City. *Archaeologia* 101, 1–62.

Stead, I.M. 1968: An Iron Age hill-fort at Grimthorpe, Yorkshire, England. *PPS* 34, 148–90.

Stead, I.M. 1969: Verulamium, 1966–8. *Antiquity* 43, 45–52.

Stead, I.M. 1970: Excavations in Blagden Copse, Hurstbourne Tarrant, Hampshire, 1961. *PHFC* 23 (1968), 81–9.

Stead, I.M. 1971a: The reconstruction of Iron Age buckets from Aylesford and Baldock. In Sieveking, G. de G. (ed.) 1971, 250–82.

Stead, I.M. 1971b: Yorkshire before the Romans: some recent discoveries. In Butler, R.M. (ed.), *Soldier and Civilian in Roman Yorkshire* (Leicester), 21–43.

Stead, I.M. 1975: The La Tène cemetery at Scarborough, East Riding. *ERA* 2, 1–11.

Stead, I.M. 1976a: The earliest burials of the Aylesford culture. In Sieveking, G. de G. *et al.* (eds), *Problems in economic and social archaeology* (London), 401–16.

Stead, I.M. 1976b: La Tène burials between Burton Fleming and Rudston, North Humberside. *Antiq. Journ.* 56, 217–26.

Stead, I.M. 1979: *The Arras Culture* (York).

Stead, I.M. 1982: The Cerrig-y-Drudion 'hanging bowl'. *Antiq. Journ.* 62, 221–34.

Stead, I.M. 1984a: Celtic dragons from the River Thames. *Antiq. Journ.* 64, 269–79.

Stead, I.M. 1984b: Some Notes on Imported Metalwork in Iron Age Britain. In Macready, S. and Thompson, F.H. (eds) 1984, 43–66.

Stead, I.M. 1985a: *The Battersea shield* (London).

Stead, I.M. 1985b: *Celtic art in Britain before the Roman Conquest* (London).

Stead, I.M. 1986: Iron Age chariot burials. *Illustrated London News* 274 (July 1986), 60–1.

Stead, I.M. 1988: Chalk figurines of the Parisi. *Antiq. Journ.* 68, 9–29.

Stead, I.M., Bourke, J.B. and Brothwell, D. 1986: *Lindow Man. The body in the bog* (London).

Stead, I.M. and Rigby, V. 1986: *Baldock: The excavation of a Roman and pre-Roman settlement 1968–72* (Britannia Monog. 7: London).

Stead, I.M. and Turner, R.C. 1985: Lindow Man. *Antiquity* 59, 25–9.

Stebbing, W.P.D. 1934: An early Iron Age site at Deal. *Arch. Cant.* 46, 207–9.

Steer, K.A. 1958: The Early Iron Age homestead at West Plean. *PSAS* 89 (1955–6), 227–51.

Stevens, C.E. 1951: Britain between the Invasions (B.C. 54–A.D. 43): a study in ancient diplomacy. In Grimes, W.F. (ed.), *Aspects of archaeology in Britain and beyond* (London), 332–44.

Stevens, F. 1934: The Highfield pit dwellings, Fisherton, Salisbury. *WAM* 46, 579–624.

Stevenson, R.B.K. 1949: Braidwood fort, Midlothian: the exploration of two huts. *PSAS* 83 (1948–9), 1–11.

Stjernquist, B. 1967: Ciste a cordoni (Rippenzisten) Produktion, Funktion, Diffusion. *AAL* series in 4°, 6 (Bonn/Lund).

Stone, J.F.S. 1935: Three 'Peterborough' dwelling pits and a doubly-stockaded Early Iron Age ditch at Winterbourne Dauntsey. *WAM* 46, 445–53.

Stone, J.F.S. 1936: An enclosure on Boscombe Down East. *WAM* 47, 466–89.

Stone, J.F.S. 1941: The Deverel–Rimbury settlement on Thorny Down, Winterbourne Gunner, South Wiltshire. *PPS* 7, 114–33.

Stuart, J. 1869: Notes on wooden structures in the Moss of Whiteburn, on the estate of Spottiswoode, Berwickshire. *PSAS* 8 (1868–9), 16–20.

Stuart, J.D.M. and Birbeck, J.M. 1936: A Celtic village on Twyford Down. *PHFC* 13, 118–207.

Stuiver, M. and Becker, B. 1986: High-Precision Decadal Calibration of the Radiocarbon time scale, AD 1950–2500 BC. *Radiocarbon* 28, 863–5.

Stuiver, M. and Kra, R.S. (eds) 1986: *Radiocarbon* calibration issue: proceedings of the Twelfth International Radiocarbon Conference, June 24–28 1985, Trondheim, Norway. *Radiocarbon* 28(2B).

Stuiver, M. and Pearson, G.W. 1986: High precision calibration of the radiocarbon time scale AD 1950–500 BC. In Stuiver, M. and Kra, R.S. (eds) 1986, 805–38.

Stuiver, M. and Reimer, T. 1986: A Computer Programme for Radiocarbon Age Calibration. *Radiocarbon* 28, 1022–30.

Sumpter, A. 1988: Iron Age and Roman at Dalton Parlours. In Price, J. and Wilson, P.R. (eds), *Recent research in Roman Yorkshire* (BAR Brit. Ser. 193: Oxford), 171–96.

Sutton, J.E.G. 1966: Iron Age hill-forts and some other earthenworks in Oxfordshire. *Oxon.* 31, 28–42.

Swan, V.G. 1975: Oare reconsidered and the origins of Savernake ware in Wiltshire. *Britannia* 6, 37–61.

Swanson, C.B. 1984: The problem of the Problem of the Brochs. *Scottish Arch. Rev.* 3, 19–21.

Swinnerton, H.H. 1932: The prehistoric pottery sites of the Lincolnshire coast. *Antiq. Journ.* 12, 239–53.

Taylor, J.J. 1981: Maiden Castle, Bickerton Hill. *Cheshire Arch. Bull.* 7, 34–6.

Tchernia, A. 1983. Italian wine in Gaul at the end of the Republic. In Garnsey, P., Hopkins, K. and Whittaker, C.R. (eds), *Trade in the Ancient Economy* (London), 87–104.

Tebbutt, C.F. 1932: Early Iron Age settlement on Jack's Hill, Great Wymondley, Herts. *PPSEA* 6, 371–4.

Thackray, D.W.R. 1983: Excavations at Pilsdon Pen hillfort, 1982. *PDNHAS* 104, 178–9.

Thirsk, J. 1967: *The Agrarian History of England and Wales. Vol. IV, 1500–1640* (Cambridge).

Thomas, A.C. 1964: Minor sites in the Gwithian area (Iron Age to recent times). *Cornish Arch.* 3, 37–62.

Thomas, A.C. 1966a: The character and origins of Roman Dumnonia. In Thomas, A.C. (ed.) 1966b, 74–98.

Thomas, A.C. (ed.) 1966b: *Rural Settlement in Roman Britain* (CBA Res. Rep. 7: London).

Thomas, R. 1989: The Bronze–Iron transition in southern England. In Sørensen, M.L.S. and Thomas, R. (eds), *The Bronze Age–Iron Age Transition in Europe* (BAR Int. Ser. 483: Oxford), 263–86.

Thomas, W.G. and Walker, R.F. 1959: Excavations at Trelissey. *BBCS* 18(3), 295–303.

Thompson, F.H. 1978: Kentish Hill-forts. *KAR* 51, 2–6.

Thompson, F.H. 1979: Three Surrey Hillforts: Anstiebury, Holmbury and Hascombe 1972–7. *Antiq. Journ.* 59, 245–318.

Thompson, F.H. 1983: Excavations at Bigberry, near Canterbury 1978–80. *Antiq. Journ.* 63, 237–78.

Thompson, F.H. 1984: Oldbury 1983. *KAR* 76, 140–4.

Thompson, F.H. 1985: Excavations at Oldbury, 1984. *KAR* 80, 239–41.

Thompson, I. 1979: Wheathampstead revisited. *BLIA* 16, 159–85.

Thompson, I. 1982: *Grog tempered 'Belgic Pottery' of South-eastern England* (BAR Brit. Ser. 108: Oxford).

Thrane, M. 1975: Europaeiske forbindelser Nationalmuseets Skrifter. *Ark.-Hist. raekke* 16 (Copenhagen). English summary, 254–63.

Threipland, L.M. 1957: An excavation at St. Mawgan-in-Pydar, north Cornwall. *Arch. Journ.* 113 (1956), 33–81.

Tinkler, B.M. and Spratt, D.A. 1978: An Iron Age Enclosure on Great Ayton Moor, North Yorkshire. *YAJ* 50, 49–56.

Todd, M. 1984: Excavations at Hembury (Devon), 1980–83: a summary report. *Antiq. Journ.* 64, 251–68.

Toller, H.S. 1980: An interim report on the excavation of the Orsett 'Cock' enclosure, Essex: 1976–9. *Britannia* 11, 35–42.

Tomlin, R. 1983: Non Coritani sed Corieltauvi. *Antiq. Journ.* 63, 353–5.

Toms, H.S. 1914: Notes on a survey of Hollingbury Camp. *B and H Arch.* 1, 12.

Tratman, E.K. 1931: Final report on the excavation at Read's Cavern. *PBUSS* 4, 8–10.

Tratman, E.K. 1970: The Glastonbury Lake Village: a reconsideration. *PBUSS* 12, 143–67.

Triscott, J. 1982: Excavations at Dryburn Bridge, East Lothian. In Harding, D.W. (ed.) 1982, 117–24.

Turnbull, P. 1983: Excavations at Rillington, 1980. *YAJ* 55, 1–9.

Turnbull, P. 1984: Stanwick in the Northern Iron Age. *Durham Arch. Journ.* 1, 41–9.

Turner, J. 1964: The anthropogenic factor in vegetational history I, Tregaron on Whixall Mosses. *New Phytologist* 63, 73–90.

Turner, J. 1979: The environment of North-east England during Roman times as shown by pollen analysis. *J. Arch. Sci.* 6, 285–90.

Turner, J. 1981: The Iron age. In Simmons, I.G. and Tooley, M. (eds) 1981, 250–81.

Turner, R. 1982: *Ivy Chimneys, Witham: an Interim Report* (Chelmsford).

Tyers, P.A. 1980: Correspondances entre la ceramique commune La Tène III du Sud-est de l'Angleterre et du Nord de la France. *Septentrion* 10, 61–70.

Tylecote, R.F. 1962: *Metallurgy in Archaeology* (London).

Tylecote, R.F. 1986: *The Prehistory of Metallurgy in the British Isles* (London).

Van Arsdell, R.D. 1983: A note on the earliest types of British potin coins. *Numis. Circ.* 91, 8–9.

Van Arsdell, R.D. 1984: A note on the date of the British potin coinage. *Numis. Circ.* 92, 257–8.

Van Arsdell, R.D. 1986: An industrial engineer (but no papyrus) in Celtic Britain. *OJA* 5(2), 205–22.

Van Arsdell, R.D. 1989: *Celtic Coinage of Britain* (London).

Van Der Veen, M. and Haselgrove, C.C. 1983: Evidence for pre-Roman crops from Coxhoe, Co. Durham. *Arch. Ael.*[5] 11, 23–5.

Varley, W.J. 1935: Maiden Castle, Bickerton. Preliminary excavations, 1935. *LAAA* 22(1–2), 97–110.

Varley, W.J. 1936: Further excavations at Maiden Castle, Bickerton, 1935. *LAAA* 23(3–4), 110–12.

Varley, W.J. 1939: *Report of the first year's excavations, 1939. Castle Hill, Almondbury* (Excavation Committee's pamphlet).

Varley, W.J. 1950a: Excavations of the castle ditch, Eddisbury, 1935–1938. *THSLC* 102, 1–68.

Varley, W.J. 1950b: The hillforts of the Welsh Marches. *Arch. Journ.* 105 (1948), 41–66.

Varley, W.J. 1976: A summary of the excavations at Castle Hill, Almondbury, 1939–72. In Harding, D.W. (ed.) 1976b, 119–32.

Vyner, B.E. 1983: Excavations at Woodbarn Rath, Wiston, 1969. *Arch. Camb.* 131, 49–57.

Vyner, B.E. 1986: Woodbarn, Wiston: a Pembrokeshire rath. *Arch. Camb.* 135, 121–33.

Wacher, J.S. 1964: Excavations at Breedon-on-the-hill, Leicestershire, 1957. *Antiq. Journ.* 44, 122–42.

Wacher, J.S. 1968: *Poxwell 1968, Interim Report* (duplicated).

Wacher, J.S. 1979: Excavations at Breedon-on-the-Hill. *Trans. Leics. Arch. Hist. Soc.* 52 (1976–7), 1–35.

Wainwright, G.J. 1967a: *Coygan Camp* (Cardiff).

Wainwright, G.J. 1967b: The excavation of an Iron Age hillfort on Bathampton Down, Somerset. *TBGAS* 86, 42–59.

Wainwright, G.J. 1968: The excavation of a Durotrigian farmstead near Tollard Royal in Cranborne Chase, southern England. *PPS* 34, 102–47.

Wainwright, G.J. 1969: Walesland Rath. *Current Arch.* 12, 4–7.

Wainwright, G.J. 1970a: The excavations of Balksbury Camp, Andover, Hants. *PHFC* 26 (1969), 21–55.

Wainwright, G. 1970b: An Iron Age promontory fort at Budbury, Bradford-on-Avon, Wiltshire. *WAM* 65, 108–66.

Wainwright, G.J. 1971a: The excavation of a fortified settlement at Walesland Rath, Pembrokeshire. *Britannia* 2, 48–108.

Wainwright, G.J. 1971b: Excavations at Tower Point, St. Brides, Pembrokeshire. *Arch. Camb.* 120, 84–90.

Wainwright, G.J. 1979: *Gussage All Saints: An Iron Age Settlement in Dorset* (London).

Wainwright, G.J., Fleming, A. and Smith, K. 1979: The Shaugh Moor Project: First Report. *PPS* 45, 1–33.

Wainwright, G.J. and Longworth, I.H. 1969: The excavation of a group of round barrows on Ampleforth Moor, Yorkshire. *YAJ* 42, 283–94.

Wainwright, G.J. and Smith, K. 1980: The Shaugh Moor project: Second Report – the Enclosure. *PPS* 46, 65–122.

Wainwright, G. and Spratling, M. 1973: The Iron Age settlement of Gussage All Saints. *Antiquity* 47, 109–30.

Wainwright, G.J. and Switzur, V.R. 1976: Gussage All Saints – chronology. *Antiquity* 50, 32–9.

Wait, G.A. 1985: *Ritual and Religion in Iron Age Britain* (BAR Brit. Ser. 149: Oxford).

Waller, M. 1988: The Fenland project's environmental programme. *Antiquity* 62, 336–43.

Ward, T. 1907: Roman remains at Cwmbrwyn, Carmarthenshire. *Arch. Camb.* 24, 175–212.

Ward Perkins, J.B. 1938: An Early Iron Age site at Crayford, Kent. *PPS* 4, 151–68.

Ward Perkins, J.B. 1939: Iron Age metal horse bits of the British Isles. *PPS* 5, 173–92.

Ward Perkins, J.B. 1940: Two early linch-pins from Kings Langley, Herts., and from Teddington, Stratford on Avon. *Antiq. Journ.* 20, 358–67.

Ward Perkins, J.B. 1944: Excavations on the Iron Age hill fort of Oldbury, near Ightham, Kent. *Archaeologia* 90, 127–76.

Waterman, D.M., Kent, B.W. and Stickland, H.J. 1954: Two inland sites with Iron Age A pottery in the West Riding of Yorkshire. *YAJ* 38 (1952–5), 383–97.

Waton, P.V. 1982: Man's impact on the chalklands: some new pollen evidence. In Bell, M. and Limbrey, S. (eds), *Archaeological aspects of woodland ecology* (BAR Supp. Series 146: Oxford), 75–91.

Waugh, H., Mynard, D.C. and Cain, R. 1974: Some Iron Age pottery from mid and north Bucks with a gazetteer of associated sites and finds. *Rec. of Bucks.* 19, 373–421.

Way, A. 1869: Notices of certain bronze relics of a peculiar type assigned to the Late Celtic period. *Arch. Journ.* 26, 52–83.

W.B. 1938: Iron Age settlements in Penigent Gill. *YAJ* 34, 413–19.

Webster, G. and Hobley, B. 1965: Aerial Reconnaissance over the Warwickshire Avon. *Arch. Journ.* (1964), 1–22.

Wedlake, W.J. 1958: *Excavations at Camerton, Somerset* (Camerton).

West Yorks. CC 1981: *West Yorkshire: an archaeological survey to AD 1500* (Wakefield).

Wheeler, R.E.M. 1929: Old England, Brentford. *Antiquity* 3, 20–32.

Wheeler, R.E.M. 1935: The excavation of Maiden Castle, Dorset. First interim report. *Antiq. Journ.* 15, 265–75.

Wheeler, R.E.M. 1936: The excavation of Maiden Castle, Dorset. Second interim report. *Antiq. Journ.* 16, 265–83.

Wheeler, R.E.M. 1937: The excavation of Maiden Castle, Dorset. Third interim report. *Antiq. Journ.* 17, 261–82.

Wheeler, R.E.M. 1943: *Maiden Castle, Dorset* (Soc. Ant. Res. Rep. 12: Oxford).

Wheeler, R.E.M. 1953: An Early Iron Age 'beach-head' at Lulworth, Dorset. *Antiq. Journ.* 33, 1–13.

Wheeler, R.E.M. 1954: *The Stanwick Fortifications* (Soc. Ant. Res. Rep. 17: Oxford).

Wheeler, R.E.M. and T.V. 1932: *Report on the Excavation of Prehistoric, Roman and post-Roman Site in Lydney Park, Gloucestershire* (Soc. Ant. Res. Rep. 9: Oxford).

Wheeler, R.E.M. and T.V. 1936: *Verulamium: a Belgic and Two Roman Cities* (Soc. Ant. Res. Rep. 11: Oxford).

Wheeler, R.E.M. and Richardson, K.M. 1957: *Hillforts of Northern France* (Soc. Ant. Res. Rep. 19: Oxford).

Whimster, R. 1977: Iron Age burial in southern Britain. *PPS* 43, 317–27.

Whimster, R. 1978: Harlyn Bay Reconsidered: The Excavations of 1900–1905 in the Light of Recent Work. *Cornish Arch.* 16 (1977), 61–88.

Whimster, R. 1981: *Burial practices in Iron Age Britain* (BAR Brit. Ser. 90: Oxford).

White, D.A. 1969: Excavations at Brampton, Huntingdonshire, 1966. *PCAS* 62, 1–20.

White, G.M. 1934: Prehistoric remains from Selsey Bill. *Antiq. Journ.* 14, 40–52.

White, R.F. 1988: A Pennine gap. The Roman period in the North Yorkshire Dales. In Price, J. and Wilson, P.R. (eds), *Recent work in Roman Yorkshire* (BAR Brit. Ser. 193: Oxford), 197–218.

Whitley, M. 1943: Excavations at Chalbury Camp, Dorset, 1939. *Antiq. Journ.* 23, 98–121.

Williams, A. 1939a: Excavations at the Knave promontory fort Rhossili, Glamorgan. *Arch. Camb.* 94, 210–19.

Williams, A. 1939b: Prehistoric and Roman pottery in the Museum of the Royal Institution of South Wales, Swansea. *Arch. Camb.* 94, 21–9.

Williams, A. 1940: The excavation of Bishopston Valley promontory fort, Glamorgan. *Arch. Camb.* 95, 9–19.

Williams, A. 1941: The excavation of the High Penard promontory fort, Glamorgan. *Arch. Camb.* 96, 23–30.

Williams, A. 1947: Excavations at Langford Downs, Oxon. (near Lechlade) in 1943. *Oxon.* 11–12 (1946–7), 44–64.

Williams, A. 1951a: Excavations at Allard's Quarry, Marnhull, Dorset. *PDNHAS* 72, 20–75.

Williams, A. 1951b: Excavations at Beard Mill, Stanton Harcourt, Oxon., 1944. *Oxon.* 16, 5–22.

Williams, D.F. 1981: The Roman amphorae trade with Late Iron Age Britain. In Howard, H. and Morris, E.L. (eds), *Production and Distribution: A Ceramic Viewpoint* (Oxford), 123–32.

Williams, G. 1978: Aspects of Later prehistoric and native Roman Carmarthenshire Part 1. *Carm. Antiq. Soc.* 14, 3–19.

Williams, G. 1979: Aspects of Later prehistoric and native Roman Carmarthenshire Part 2. *Carm. Antiq. Soc.* 15, 15–37.

Williams, G. 1981: Survey and excavation on Pembrey Mountain. *Carm. Antiq. Soc.* 17, 3–33.

Williams, G. 1988: Recent work on rural settlement in Later prehistoric and early Historic Dyfed. *Antiq. Journ.* 68, 30–54.

Williams, J. 1777: *An Account of Some Remarkable Ancient Ruins, Lately Discovered in the Highlands and Northern parts of Scotland* (Edinburgh).

Williams, J.H. 1974: *Two Iron Age Sites in Northamptonshire* (Northampton).

Williams-Freeman, J.P. 1915: *An Introduction to Field Archaeology as Illustrated by Hampshire* (London).

Willis, L. and Rogers, E.H. 1951: Dainton earth works. *PDAES* 4(4), 79–101.

Wilson, A.E. 1938: Excavations in the ramparts and gateway of the Caburn, August–October 1937. *SAC* 79, 169–94.

Wilson, A.E. 1939: Excavations at the Caburn, 1938. *SAC* 80, 193–213.

Wilson, A.E. 1940: Report on the excavations at Highdown Hill, Sussex, August 1939. *SAC* 81, 173–204.

Wilson, A.E. 1950: Excavations on Highdown Hill, 1947. *SAC* 89, 163–78.

Wilson, A.E. 1954: Sussex on the eve of the Roman Conquest. *SAC* 93, 59–77.

Wilson, B. 1978: The animal bones [from Ashville, Oxon]. In Parrington, M. 1978, 110–39.

Wilson, C.E. 1981: Burials within settlements in southern Britain during the pre Roman IA. *BLIA* 18, 127–69.

Wilson, D. 1983: Pollen analysis and settlement archaeology of the first millennium BC from North-east England. In Chapman, R. and Mytum, H. (eds) 1983, 29–54.

Wolseley, G.R., Smith, R.A. and Hawley W. 1927: Prehistoric and Roman Settlements on Park Brow. *Archaeologia* 76, 1–40.

Woodruff, C.H. 1904: Further discoveries of Late Celtic and Romano-British interments at Walmer. *Arch. Cant.* 26, 9–23.

Woods, P.J. 1969: *Excavations at Hardingstone, Northants., 1967–8* (Northampton).

Worsfold, F.H. 1943: A report on the Late Bronze Age site excavated at Minnis Bay, Birchington, Kent, 1938–1940. *PPS* 9, 28–47.

Worth, R.H. 1935: Dartmoor Exploration Committee, twelfth report. *TDA* 67, 115–30.

Worth, R.H. 1943: The prehistoric rounds of Dartmoor. *TDA* 75, 273–302.

Young, A. 1955: An aisled farmhouse at Allasdale, Isle of Barra. *PSAS* 87 (1952–3), 80–105.

Young, A. 1964: Brochs and duns. *PSAS* 95 (1961–2), 171–98.

Young, A. and Richardson, K.M. 1955: Report on the excavations at Blackbury Castle. *PDAES* 5, 43–67.

Index

Page references in bold are to line drawings and illustrations